A DICTIONARY OF SELECTED
SYNONYMS IN THE PRINCIPAL
INDO-EUROPEAN LANGUAGES

A DICTIONARY OF SELECTED SYNONYMS IN THE PRINCIPAL INDO-EUROPEAN LANGUAGES

A CONTRIBUTION TO THE HISTORY OF IDEAS

By

CARL DARLING BUCK

WITH THE CO-OPERATION OF COLLEAGUES
AND ASSISTANTS

THE UNIVERSITY OF CHICAGO PRESS

CHICAGO & LONDON

This paperback edition reproduces every page
of the original, larger-format volume.

The University of Chicago Press, Chicago 60637

The University of Chicago Press, Ltd., London

Copyright 1949 by The University of Chicago
All rights reserved. Published 1949
Paperback edition 1988
Printed in the United States of America

97 96 95 94 93 92   5 4

Library of Congress Catalog Card Number 49-11769

International Standard Book Number 0-226-07937

PREFACE

How do we get our ideas?

The kind of thinking that distinguishes man from brute has been built up by and is dependent upon the use of symbols. Since vocal utterance attained a higher development than gesture as a means of communication, these symbols are, in fact, the words. Animals, to be sure, have cries which in some cases cover a very considerable range of emotions and to a certain extent serve to communicate. But these are limited to the immediate experience: they are not detachable symbols capable of expressing past or future experience or any abstract concept. Yet such cries, which comprise all that primitive man inherited from his ancestry, must perforce be the starting-point of human speech. Primitive man, with his more highly developed brain, gained an awareness of a connection between the sound and something expressed by it. With this step taken, a nucleus provided, and doubtless aided by gesture, human speech progressed and in turn became the dominant factor in man's further mental growth. That is, we have the spiral development: superior brain (there is, of course, a "why?" to this too) > primitive human speech > organized conceptual thought. Any more detailed picture of the process, of the much discussed "origin of language", we shall never have. The relatively brief period of recorded speech is separated by a vast interval from the beginnings of human speech—far beyond the reach of the historical-comparative method. Nor are we further concerned here with this remote problem.

The history of ideas is embodied in the history of the words used to express them. Whether the 'idea', 'notion', 'concept', or 'mental image' (I shall commonly use the innocuous 'notion') is, as many believe, only an abstraction (the concrete object or the uttered and heard sound of the word being the only realities), or whether it corresponds to some reality in the brain (as an eminent neurologist has assured me he thinks quite tenable), need not concern us. For its close dependence upon its verbal expression is beyond dispute. It is a pattern of reaction answering to a given stimulus, which (apart from the actual perception of an individual concrete object, which also suggests the general notion) is normally the word or group of words. It is this pattern of reaction which constitutes the meaning of a word. A word means what it refers to, in a given context or situation. The meaning of a word as a whole may be a composite of various allied applications.

In a limited number of words for certain concrete notions the meaning has remained virtually constant for thousands of years, as, for example, those for the numerals and for close family relationship like 'father', 'mother', etc. But such cases are the exception. Change is the rule—sometimes so radical that, without the connecting links, one would be at a loss to see any relation between the earliest known and the latest use. The meaning of most words is not a fixed point, but an area of variable dimensions. It is subject to complex associations, some of them inevitable associations of universal scope, others originating in some particular verbal context, external situation, or among a special social or occupational class.

Any such association leads to the so-called "occasional" special meanings, like *stone* as used by a jeweler = *precious stone*, or the diverse uses of *play*. But such an occasional use may spread until it becomes the dominant one, as in the case of *deer*, originally an 'animal' (like NHG *tier*, etc.), and doubtless first used in its present sense by hunters, as the favorite animal of the hunt.

The associations underlying semantic changes are so complex that no rigid classification of the latter is possible. Many changes may be variously viewed. In a sense, each word has its individual semantic history. Nevertheless, there are certain types which it is convenient to recognize.

The two most general types are generalization or extension vs. specialization or restriction. Generalization, as in *barn* etymologically 'barley-place' whence storehouse for any grain or farm produce (now even *carbarn*), *mill* originally 'machine for grinding' (corn, etc.), and all words of such broad application as *do, get, go, thing*. Specialization, as in *deer* (see above), *hound*, originally any 'dog' (like NHG *hund*), *sermon* from Lat. *sermō* 'discourse' specialized in church writings. The history of a given word may show successively a specialization and generalization from a new center, as *starve* from 'die' (as NHG *sterben*) to 'die of hunger' to 'suffer from hunger'. But this classification is from one point of view only, that of scope. There are many other more specific types of shift within certain associated groups.

Commonplace is the figurative use of words like *head, foot, mouth*, without reference to parts of the body. Such use is, of course, not a rhetorical or poetical device, except in unfamiliar and hence striking figures, but a feature of ordinary speech everywhere.

Widespread is the interchange of application between space and time, as in *long, short;* between size and quantity, as in *small, little;* between quantity and number, as in *all* (*all day* vs. *all men*) and the frequent expression by forms of the same word of 'whole' and 'all', of 'much' and 'many', of 'little' and 'few'. In such groups one or the other application may become dominant, as in *brief* normally used with reference to time vs. its source Lat. *brevis* 'short' in both senses. Or there may be extensions or shifts. Thus Lat. *paucus*, usually pl. *paucī* 'few', was in Vulgar Latin extended to cover 'little' in quantity (hence It. *poco*, Fr. *peu*, etc.) at the expense of *parvus*, which itself had covered 'small' in size and 'little' in quantity.

Material and product. The name of a material is applied to some special product and persists in that sense. The name of the papyrus plant is the source of the most widespread words for 'paper', unaffected by the successive changes in the material used. Most of the words for 'pen' reflect the old quill pen, being derived from Lat. *penna* or other words for 'feather'. Similarly, in many other cases. The converse is much less common, but is seen in *rubber* as material named after its early and now insignificant use in rubbing out pencil marks, in *graphite* (from Grk. γράφω 'write') after its use for pencils. In general, in studying the history of words for material objects like implements, mechanical devices, etc. one must always take into consideration the evolution of the things themselves. Thus many of the words for 'lock' and 'key' reflect the primitive devices of bar and peg.

Words for thought processes or emotions are, all theoretically and a great many demonstrably, based upon indicative physical acts or conditions. Thus 'understand' from 'seize, grasp', or 'stand on or under'; 'forget' from 'lose'; 'fear' from 'trembling'; 'anger' and some other emotions from physical 'agitation'.

Extension or transfer from one to another sense perception—linguistic "synasthesia". The widespread group of cognate words to which *sweet* belongs was doubtless applied primarily to taste but also commonly to smell and hearing (*sweet voice*, *sweet sound*), while the Greek and Latin cognates were still further extended to 'pleasant' and mostly replaced by others for the sense perception. Obvious extensions are seen in *warm colors, loud colors, sharp taste*, etc. Lat. *clārus*, connected with verbs for 'call, cry out', must have been first used with reference to hearing ('clear voice') but was applied equally to sight ('clear night'). A nearly complete transfer is seen in OHG *hel* used only of sound 'clear, loud' vs. NHG *hell* usually of sight 'clear, bright'.

Interchange between subjective and objective or personal and impersonal. This is seen in words for sense perception, as *I taste, smell* vs. *it tastes, smells* (in some languages differentiated), or emotion, as *sad* of persons but also *sad news*, and many others. Several words for 'safe, sure', or 'difficult' were first used only of persons ('without care, anxiety'; 'hard to please') and only secondarily of things. The old form of *fear* denoted the objective 'danger', hence the emotion which it excited.

Various miscellaneous extensions or transfers are due to a similarity of condition or result or some natural sequence. 'Green' and 'unripe' usually coincide, though, to repeat a phrase often quoted, *blackberries are red when they are green*. This use of *green* is felt as secondary; yet in origin the color word itself, derived from the root of *grow*, was based on the color of growing vegetation. What 'seems good, is pleasing' implies approval and may give rise to legal terms for voting approval. The lack of anything may lead to the more urgent 'need, necessity', or 'distress', or sometimes to the resulting 'wish' for something, as shown in the history of *want* as noun and as verb (*it wants = it lacks*, then *he wants it, he wants to do it*).

An important factor in the history of many words is their emotional value, which may vary according to time and circumstance and may show itself in the tone of utterance. Words may be used in a "good sense" or a "bad sense". Or one or the other sense may become dominant. Words for 'old' have a highly emotional value, sometimes friendly, affectionate, sometimes derogatory, abusive. Our *old man* is generally friendly; but in modern Greek the compound meaning literally 'old man' denotes a 'scoundrel', and that for 'old woman' a 'common woman, prostitute'. Words for 'woman', also highly emotional, may rise to 'wife' or even 'king's wife, queen', or may sink to 'hussy' (*hussy* also originally 'housewife') and 'prostitute' (cf. *queen* and *quean*). A Polish word, related to one for 'mare' and first used as a derogatory epithet, is now the regular word for 'woman' without trace of derogatory feeling. A certain group of cognates contains words for the opposites 'reward' and 'penalty', based on a neutral 'requital'. The movement in one or the other direction, up or down, is known technically as "(a)meliorative" vs. "pejorative" development, the former as in *knight* originally 'servant' (like NHG *knecht*), *nice* once 'foolish, stupid' (from Lat. *nescius* 'ignorant'), etc.; the latter in *knave* originally 'boy, servant' (like NHG *knabe*), *stink* originally 'have a smell' good or bad, etc.

Further examples of semantic change, of the types just mentioned, will be found in great numbers in the body of this work—and many others characteristic of particular groups. For example, in the history of words for domestic animals the conspicuous feature is the frequent interchange between classes of the same species, as when words of the same cognate group denote in different languages 'bull', 'ox', or 'cow', and in another species 'ram, wether', or 'lamb', or show a shift from 'wether', through an intermediate generic use, to 'ewe'.

"Semantic borrowing" refers to the borrowing not of the formal word but of some special meaning. There are, of course, great numbers of actual loanwords, some in Greek from pre-Greek sources, many in Latin from Greek, still more in most of the European languages from Latin or in many cases more specifically from French; again from early Germanic and later from German in Balto-Slavic and from Slavic in Rumanian. But besides these there are "translation words". A special use of a familiar foreign word was adopted for the usually corresponding native word. Thus Lat. *nāvis* 'ship' came to be used in Christian times for the 'nave' of a church; and, while we have borrowed the word itself in this special sense, the Germans borrowed this sense for their native *schiff*. In Rumanian the inherited word for 'light' (from Lat. *lūmen*) is also the regular word for 'world', owing to the fact that in Slavic the same word covers both notions. Grk. πτῶσις 'fall' became, through the notion of 'modification', the grammatical term for 'case' and was faithfully rendered by Lat. *cāsus* 'fall'. Nearly all our grammatical terminology rests on such Latin translations of Greek terms. This semantic borrowing is widespread, obvious in many cases. But where a given secondary use is so natural that it might easily arise independently, there is room for doubt; and some of the examples generally cited are, in fact, doubtful or even definitely to be rejected on chronological grounds.

Words not only change in meaning, they may be lost outright, displaced by others. Why? There is no one answer. Of the various alleged causes, each has some validity as a factor but is likely to be exaggerated by one whose attention is riveted on it in a hunt for examples. The existence of homonyms may favor the loss of one of them, as the verb *let* 'hinder' (cf. the noun in the old phrase *let or hindrance* and *let* in tennis) vs. *let* 'permit'. Phonetic changes which have left little body to the word no doubt favored the partial displacement of Lat. *dare, diēs, apis, avis* by *dōnāre, diurnum, apicula, avicellus* in the evolution of the Romance words. But the great number of homonyms in English, and monosyllabic at that, shows that neither of these factors is a compelling cause.

"Taboo", now used in linguistics to denote the avoidance of words believed to be of ill omen or improper (but many of the latter have proved notably persistent in actual speech), is another factor, the importance of which in our group of languages it is difficult to estimate. It has been frequently invoked, for example, as the cause of the loss in some languages of the old words for 'bear' and some other animal names but never for the much more widespread loss of the old word for 'horse' (3.41).

Somewhat allied to taboo is the dualism of vocabulary in the Avesta, where, for example, there are two words for 'son', both with equally respectable cognates in Sanskrit, one used with reference to good beings (the Ahurian world), the other only of evil beings (the Daevic world).

Loss of words due to the substitution of those of another language is illustrated on the largest scale (except for the extreme case where the whole language is replaced, like Gallic by Vulgar Latin) by the history of English. A considerable part of the Old English vocabulary was permanently lost in favor of French words in the centuries following the Norman Conquest. In Rumanian too, owing to the historical conditions, much of the inherited Latin vocabulary was replaced by Slavic words, though partially restored by literary neologisms.

Very often the loss of words is due to the simple fact that what were at first colloquial or even slang words gained increasing currency until they superseded the old standard words. Thus Lat. *loquī* 'speak' disappeared without trace in the Romance languages, being replaced at first by a colloquial word which is attested from the time of Plautus on. Lat. *caput* 'head' was in many regions replaced (in the literal sense) by *testa* 'potsherd', whence first 'skull' and then 'head' (Fr. *tête*, etc.). Old words for 'eat' have often been replaced by others meaning originally 'chew, chaw', 'gnaw, nibble', or the like.

Semantic word study may proceed from two opposite points of view, form or meaning. For example, one may study the history of Lat. *dīcere* 'say' and its cognates in Latin, or, with enlarged scope, its cognates in all the Indo-European languages; in other words the diverse uses of derivatives of the Indo-European root *deik̑- and its probable primary sense. Such is the material brought together in the etymological dictionaries of the usual type. Conversely, one may start from the notion 'say' and study the history of words used to express it in different languages. Even for those who regard the notion as an abstraction (see above), there can, of course, be no objection to taking it as a convenient center. By the study of synonyms, their etymology and semantic history, one seeks to show the various sources of a given notion, the trails of its evolution. With some notable exceptions (as numerals, 'father', 'mother', etc. and some others), a group of synonyms has little resemblance to a group of formal cognates such as we find in the etymological dictionaries. The disparity, though less, is considerable within the Romance languages, or the Germanic, or even the Celtic and Slavic. Hence this type of investigation, besides its mainly semantic character and the purpose of revealing the linguistic sources of a given notion, also presents an interesting picture of word distribution.

A constantly increasing number of journal articles, dissertations, and other monographs have dealt with particular groups of synonyms in special fields —a few of them in a non-Indo-European family like Semitic or Finno-Ugrian, most of them in Indo-European or some branch of it, like the Romance or the Germanic languages. Such monographs furnish some of the stones for building a more comprehensive structure. But they are scattered, they cover only a small number of even the commonest notions, and some are written on such a grand scale (running to hundreds of pages; e.g. on words for 'child', 'boy', 'girl' in the Romance languages 426 pages, in Old English 271 pages) as to be unwieldy for use without the most severe trimming. A "Dictionary of Ideas" (a title that would suggest to laymen the point of such study) in a truly comprehensive sense (history of words for all ideas in all known languages) is, of course, an idle dream. Even for the Indo-European field anything like a complete semantic dictionary is beyond probable realization at present.

Yet some more modest form of synthesis has seemed to me, even now, possible and worth while. In announcing the project many years ago, in Language 5(1929).215 ff., it was proposed to collect and study about a thousand groups of synonyms. Actually the number in the present work goes somewhat beyond this.

The principal Indo-European languages are covered. Some of the minor Indo-European languages, as Albanian, Armenian, and all modern forms of Indic and Iranian, are excluded from the survey, except for incidental mention, since to include them systematically would increase the labor out of all proportion to the results added. Danish, with which Norwegian agrees in large measure, and Swedish are taken as representative of the modern Scandinavian languages, though thus one may miss certain interesting divergences in word preference between Danish and Norwegian and the more frequent persistence of the Old Norse words in Modern Icelandic. Of the Romance languages, Portuguese is omitted as generally going with Spanish in vocabulary, though here, too, occasional differences are missed or only incidentally noted. There is no room to follow out the chronological and geographical distribution of Romance words on the elaborate scale which is customary and fitting in monographs in that field. Of the important Slavic languages, the (modern) Bulgarian is omitted, the words generally going with those quoted under either Church Slavic or Serbo-Croatian. Under Church Slavic are given preference the genuine Old Church Slavic (Old Bulgarian) words, especially from the Gospels, where such are quotable, but not to the exclusion of others which are (in part accidentally) quotable only from later times. The latter are sometimes marked "late", but probably without consistency. As is well known, Miklosich's Lexicon is full of late forms that are merely Serbian, etc. in Church Slavic dress, and conversely fails sometimes to give early quotations for words occurring in the best records. In this regard, Jagić's Entstehungsgeschichte der kirchenslavischen Sprache, with its indexes, is of inestimable value, though even this at times fails to answer the questions that arise. Since the quotable Old Irish vocabulary is too limited to serve, Old and Middle Irish forms are generally given without distinction and both marked as Ir. (as in Pedersen's Vergleichende Grammatik der keltischen Sprachen and elsewhere), while the modern forms are marked NIr. But under Welsh and Breton are given the modern forms, with special designation of the Old or Middle. Cornish words, which generally go with the Breton or Welsh or both, are not included in the list but often in the discussion, especially those quotable from the old Latin-Cornish vocabulary.

The difficulties involved in a project of this kind are perhaps less apparent to the layman than to the specialist. In gathering the raw material, preparing the lists, the matter is rarely so simple as turning up the pages of dictionaries or asking a native speaker "What is your word for so-and-so?"

The familiar difficulties which assail the author of a two-language dictionary are here vastly multiplied. For if it is true even of word comparisons between two languages, how much more so of those between twenty-odd, that the words are only roughly synonymous. They do not often coincide in all their applications; they rarely cover quite the same ground. Wholly valid are only the equations of words in a particular application, attested by specific fully equivalent phrases. Such tests must be made, and at least lie beneath the surface in all our work. But to insist on this as a principle of arrangement would be a counsel of perfection that would so complicate matters as to wreck any comprehensive project. Furthermore, the combination of applications may be so nearly the same for different languages that they are best united under one head, with indication, where required, of differentiation. Only from a study of the material in a given case can one decide, and then often doubtfully, whether it is better to combine it in one group or break it up into several. The difficulties and complications of this kind are illustrated in the discussion of words for 'world' and for 'earth and land'.

The words given in the lists are intended to be the most usual expressions of the given notion in the accepted written and spoken language. To try to include all obsolete and dialectal forms would be folly, though such as come to one's attention and offer interesting parallels in semantic development may be mentioned. The specialist in any given language will always find facts of pertinent interest to supply. We have used the best available dictionaries, but only those with extensive citation of phrases are satisfactory, and for some of the languages covered there are no such. For nearly all the modern languages quoted the words have been supplied or reviewed by native speakers. But even so, owing partly to local and social differences, informants may differ as to what is the best current term. A good old word may be familiar to one but quite unknown to another. Shall it be entered in the list or omitted as obsolete? The choice is particularly difficult in the case of languages that are just now undergoing a new standardization, like Lithuanian and Modern Greek. Many of the Lithuanian words given by Kurschat, representing the Prussian Lithuanian of his time, are not those preferred in the present standard, which was more nearly anticipated by Lalis. I have relied chiefly on the Niedermann, Senn, and Brender, so far as it has appeared, Senn's Kleine Litauische Sprachlehre, and Hermann's Litauisch-Deutsches Gesprächsbüchlein; also, in many cases, on direct information from Professor Senn.

For Modern Greek the words of most interest are those of the spoken language (δημοτική) and the new literary type based thereon. But many ancient or medieval words that have come down in the literary tradition to the καθαρεύουσα and are still considerably used, beside others more colloquial, are also cited. No native Greek, much less myself, though I have considerable first-hand familiarity with the present spoken and written language, can draw any hard and fast rule.

Classification. The arrangement of word lists by subjects is an old story. Not to mention the "determinatives" or "classifiers" of Sumerian, Chinese, etc., there were in the Indo-European field many such Greek glossaries culminating in the Ὀνομαστικά of Pollux, likewise in Latin (for the Greek and Latin works of this type, cf. Pauly-Wissowa, s.v. Onomastikon), the Sanskrit Amarakoça (all the native glossaries were more or less of this type), similarly Latin–Old English (as Aelfric's Vocabulary), Latin–Old High German (as Heinrici Summarium), Latin-Cornish (the Cottonian Vocabulary), German–Old Prussian, etc. In modern times there have been numerous dictionaries of the leading European languages known variously as 'analogical', 'analytical', 'ideological', 'methodical', 'synthetic', 'topical'; and, the best known and imitated, Roget's Thesaurus. Of all these, no two, apart from direct imitations, will agree in the order or classification. For example, Pollux thought proper to begin with the gods (so in many other lists), passing to man (with the parts of the body), relationship, science and art, hunting, meals, trades, law, town organization, utensils. Aelfric began with agricultural tools, passing to men (by office or craft), diseases, law, insects, vessels, drinks, birds, plants, trees, arms, winds, cereals, clothes, physical world, parts of the body, colors. But actually all sorts of miscellaneous items are mixed in. In Roget's Thesaurus the parallelism of opposites and some of the minor subdivisions may be convenient. But the main groups and larger subdivisions are so comprehensive as to have no obvious coherence. What may one not find under Motion (e.g. *eat, food*) or Volition (e.g. *clean*)! The fact is, of course, that relations are too complex to admit any truly scientific and complete classification (cf. the remark of Jespersen, Philosophy of Grammar 34); and, even if such were possible, it would have little relation to our instinctive associations.

Yet, because the ideal is hopeless, to abandon all such classification would be to sacrifice the obvious advantages of a semantic grouping (cf. e.g. Jost Trier, Der deutsche Wortschatz im Zinnbezirk des Verstandes. Die Geschichte eines sprachlichen Feldes; also Wartburg, Z. rom. Ph. 57.297 ff.) in the many cases where this is feasible. Accordingly, the arrangement will be by semantically congeneric groups, like Parts of the Body, Food and Drink, Clothing, Dwelling, Sense Perceptions, Emotions, Quantity and Number, etc.—but with some recourse to Miscellaneous. The particular order and classification adopted is not copied from others, but no remarkable merit is claimed for it. Like any other, it will be an easy mark for criticism. There will be much that is frankly arbitrary, both in the classification and in the selection of synonyms to be included. A notion which, taken by itself, looks absurd under a given chapter heading may be included because of its relations to another that does clearly belong there, e.g. under Emotion, 'danger' because of its relation to 'fear', or 'good fortune' which leads to 'happiness'. Many a heading in a given chapter might equally well be put in another, e.g. 'swift' under Time or Motion. Any infelicities of grouping will not be a serious drawback to use, for an alphabetical index according to the English words will be a necessary complement.

The uneven size of the chapters is mostly what might be expected but is partly somewhat arbitrary. For example, if chapter 4 is disproportionately long, it may be for no better reason than that the Parts of the Body form such a neat distinctive class that one is constantly tempted to further inclusions. Yet most of these words have developed such a wealth of secondary uses that their importance is multiplied.

Etymologies. Only those that are reasonably obvious and certain give genuine satisfaction. The specialist can recognize these, and at the same time is aware of how large a proportion of the current etymologies, even in most of the best etymological dictionaries, are uncertain, with varying degrees of probability or plausibility. The layman, unacquainted with matters of phonetic correspondence and other refinements, cannot distinguish the gold from the dross. To him the certain etymologies may look uncannily difficult, and the doubtful or even untenable the easiest. I have considered giving only the more certain etymologies, using "etym. unknown", "origin obscure", or the like, even more freely than I have, which would have resulted in the saving of much labor and space. Yet, on the whole, it has seemed best not to be ultra-conservative but to record, with reservations, many of the less certain etymologies. The notations "perhaps", "probably", "possibly", etc. reflect my subjective reaction at the time of writing, and not any rigid system of gradation.

The standard etymological dictionaries and the journals are of course consulted; but to save space the references are, in large measure, concentrated on the Walde-Pokorny, Vergleichendes Wörterbuch der indogermanischen Sprachen (cited as Walde-P.), where earlier discussions (up to about 1927) are cited. In many cases my tacit agreement applies only to the immediate grouping on the page cited, and not necessarily to the much wider and more doubtful grouping under the whole heading. The uncertainty and speculation which are often involved in the grouping under roots and root extensions (which, as the layman should understand, are only convenient abstractions of elements common to groups of actual words) are well known. The other etymological dictionaries are cited mainly for words characteristic of particular branches, as Falk-Torp, Norwegisch-dänisches etymologisches Wörterbuch, for Germanic, REW (Meyer-Lübke) for Romance, Berneker, Slavisches etymologisches Wörterbuch, for Slavic, etc. But Ernout-Meillet, Dictionnaire étymologique de la langue latine (Ernout-

M.), is cited with greater frequency. For, apart from its notable excellence for the interrelations of Latin words and their semantic development, it represents an independent attitude, with notable differences from the views favored in the Walde-Pokorny. It is conservative in regard to many current etymologies—indeed, in my judgment, ultra-conservative at times, rejecting some connections that appear to me beyond reasonable doubt (as of Grk. θῡμός with Lat. *fūmus*, etc., where the semantic relation, from a common physical notion of 'agitation', is as easy as that between Grk. ἄνεμος and Lat. *animus, anima*)—and conversely even daring in some new proposals. Walde-Hofmann, Lateinisches etymologisches Wörterbuch (Walde-H.), is also often cited for matters other than Latin, since its references are the most recent.

The criticism may be anticipated that I have held too closely to the factual and said little of the causes of semantic change and the loss of words. And it is true that, apart from the remarks above, I have, in fact, generally preferred to leave it to others to add, if they like, a given case to their collections in support of their favorite theses.

Similarly in regard to areal word distribution. No doubt, there are several significant instances of agreement in peripheral areas, e.g. in the Romance field between Spanish-Portuguese and Rumanian, or in the Indo-European field between Italic, Celtic, and Indo-Iranian. Some of these are clearly inherited words, preserved in contrast to innovations spreading in the central area. But the exponents of "areal linguistics" (an expansion of the more factual "linguistic geography") appear to me to overrate the validity of their "norms" ("marginal, central, isolated") and to indulge in rash inferences therefrom as to what constitutes an archaism and what an innovation. Thus for 'fire' (1.81) the group represented by Lat. *ignis*, etc. (Lat., Balto-Slavic, Skt.) is claimed as older than that of the more widespread group, Grk. πῦρ, NE *fire*, etc. (Grk., Osc.-Umbr., Gmc., Arm., Toch., Hitt.) because the former is in the marginal group. Both are inherited, doubtless with some original but lost difference of aspect. It is still more perverse to say that for 'water' (1.31) Lat. *aqua* (which has Germanic cognates in the sense of running water, esp. 'river', and perhaps in some Tocharian and Hittite verbs, but only in Latin is the regular word for 'water') is older than the group represented by Grk. ὕδωρ, NE *water*, etc. (Grk., Umbr., Ir., Gmc., Balto-Slavic, Skt., Hitt.) with its typical archaic r/n type. Actually, instances of agreement in vocabulary (as in phonology and morphology) may be found between any two and almost any combination of the main Indo-European branches, and it is best to let the facts speak for themselves in each case.

The work has been carried on with the kindly co-operation of colleagues and with the help of paid assistance, provided for out of the research grant of the General Education Board to the University of Chicago. Sir William

Craigie, while in Chicago, was always generous in opening his store of knowledge of the Old Norse and English vocabulary. For the Romance languages I have pestered with queries virtually all my colleagues, past and present, in that field—Altrocchi, Borgese, Bullock, Castillo, David, Jenkins, Keniston, Korominas, Merrill, Norman, Parmenter, Rowland, Treviño, Vigneron, and Wartburg; also Professor Siever (a Rumanian, formerly a graduate student in our Romance department) for Rumanian. For Sanskrit, Professor Clark (in the first chapter) and later Professor Bobrinskoy have assisted. Father J. G. O'Neil, now of Maynooth College, Ireland, formerly a graduate student here in the Department of Classics, originally supplied the Modern Irish words, which were further revised by his colleague Professor O'Nolan; and through Father O'Neil's interest in the matter arrangements were made for the listing of the Old Irish words by Miss E. Knott under the supervision of her teacher, Professor O. Bergin. These Irish lists have been of great service in a difficult field, but it is only fair to say that (partly owing to changes or refinements in the headings themselves) many changes have been made and that much of the critical work on Irish, as for Celtic in general, has been done by Professor G. S. Lane. Professors T. P. Cross and Myles Dillon have also been consulted on some questions of Irish usage. For Slavic, beside other informants, my past or present colleagues, Bobrinskoy, Nykl, Spinka, and Gelb, have been consulted for Russian, Bohemian, and Polish respectively. Professor Senn has answered many special inquiries on Lithuanian, often giving the precise history of neologisms in more detail than could be repeated here. That I have also, on occasion, consulted my colleagues in the departments of Greek, Latin, and the Germanic languages goes without saying.

For most of the other modern languages covered, various students or citizens of foreign birth have supplied or been consulted on the words of their respective mother-tongues.

Of the research assistants who supplied a first draft of etymological notes and references, either for particular linguistic fields or for particular chapters, G. S. Lane served for four years, working first on chapter 6, a part of which was published as a dissertation (Words for Clothing [1931]), and later on other chapters, with especial responsibility for Celtic and Germanic. Others who served for one year or more are J. J. Lund (chap. 9, part of which furnishes his dissertation [1932]), F. R. Preveden (especially for Balto-Slavic; also dissertation, The Vocabulary of Navigation in the Balto-Slavic Languages [1927, unpublished]), and F. T. Wood (for chaps. 4, 5, 7). It is impossible to separate their work from my revision, and I can give them credit only in this general way.

While I am thus indebted to all the above mentioned, there have been so many changes, even in the headings (relative to the precise notion intended), and so much has been re-written and re-written, that I must assume the responsibility for such errors as may be found in the word lists, as well as for the etymological judgments.

I am further indebted to Professors Bobrinskoy and Lane and Dr. Georgiacas for assistance in proofreading, in the course of which they have supplied several additions, and to the editor and readers of the University of Chicago Press for numerous helpful suggestions.

It is hoped that, with all its inevitable limitations, the omissions intentional or otherwise, and the errors of detail which may be pointed out by scholars in the special fields, the book may be found useful and worth while as a tentative and skeleton dictionary of synonyms.

CARL DARLING BUCK

CHICAGO
1949

TABLE OF CONTENTS

EXPLANATIONS

ABBREVIATIONS FOR LANGUAGES AND DIALECTS

Afgh.	Afghan	Goth.	Gothic
Akkad.	Akkadian (-Babylonian-Assyrian)	Grk.	Greek (ancient)
Alb.	Albanian	Hebr.	Hebrew
AmSp.	American Spanish	Hitt.	Hittite
Anglo-Fr.	Anglo-French	Hung.	Hungarian (= Magyar)
Arab.	Arabic	Icel.	Icelandic
Aram.	Aramaic	IE	Indo-European
Arc.	Arcadian	Illyr.	Illyrian
Arg.	Argolic	Ion.	Ionic
Arm.	Armenian	Ir.	Irish (Old and/or Middle, only
Att.	Attic		occasionally distinguished as
Av.	Avestan		OIr, MIr)
Boeot.	Boeotian	Iran.	Iranian
Boh.	Bohemian (= Czech, a better	It.	Italian
	term, but Boh. more convenient	Lac.	Laconian
	abbreviation)	Lat.	Latin
Br.	Breton (modern)	Lesb.	Lesbian
Bulg.	Bulgarian	Lett.	Lettic
Byz.	Byzantine (= Middle Greek)	LG	Low German
Cat.	Catalan	Lith.	Lithuanian
ChSl.	Church Slavic	Liv.	Livonian
Cor.	Corinthian	Maced.	Macedonian
Corn.	Cornish	Mars.	Marsian
Cret.	Cretan	MBr	Middle Breton
Cypr.	Cyprian	MDu.	Middle Dutch
Dan.	Danish	ME	Middle English
Dor.	Doric	MHG	Middle High German
Du.	Dutch	MLat.	Medieval Latin
El.	Elean	MLG	Middle Low German
Elam.	Elamite	MW	Middle Welsh
Esth.	Esthonian	N	New (in following) = Modern
Eub.	Euboean		(preferred to latter for con-
Eur.	European		venience in abbreviations, be-
Fal.	Faliscan		side M = Middle)
Fr.	French	NE	New English
Frank.	Frankish	NG	New Greek
Fris.	Frisian	NHG	New High German
Gael.	Gaelic (of Scotland)	NIcel.	New Icelandic
Gall.	Gallic	NIr.	New Irish
Gmc.	Germanic (for general Germanic,	NPers.	New Persian
	or with reconstructed forms =	Norw.	Norwegian
	Proto-Germanic)	O	Old (in following and others)

1

OE	Old English		Scand.	Scandinavian
OFris.	Old Frisian		SCr.	Serbo-Croatian
OHG	Old High German		Skt.	Sanskrit
ON	Old Norse (Old Icelandic)		Slov.	Slovenian (not Slovak which is spelled out).
OPers.	Old Persian			
OPruss.	Old Prussian		Sogd.	Sogdian
OS	Old Saxon		Sorb.	Sorbian
Osc.	Oscan		Sp.	Spanish
Osset.	Ossetan		Sumer.	Sumerian
Pael.	Paelignian		Sw.	Swedish
Pahl.	Pahlavi		Thess.	Thessalian
Phoen.	Phoenician		Toch.	Tocharian
Pol.	Polish		Turk.	Turkish
Port.	Portuguese		Ukr.	Ukrainian (= Little Russian)
Praen.	Praenestine		Umbr.	Umbrian
Prov.	Provençal		VLat.	Vulgar (= Popular) Latin
Rhaet.	Rhaetian		W.	Welsh
Rum.	Rumanian		WGmc.	West Germanic
Russ.	Russian		WSax.	West Saxon
Sc.	Scotch (as NE dial.)		WhRuss.	White Russian

ABBREVIATIONS FOR WORKS OF REFERENCE

References are regularly to pages; but to numbers in the case of collections of inscriptions and works with numbered entries, such as REW, Puşcariu, and Lokotsch.

Abbreviation of names of literary authors, works, codices, etc., familiar enough in the respective fields, are not listed.

Abh. Preuss. Akad. Abhandlungen der preussischen Akademie der Wissenschaften.

Abh. Sächs. Ges. Abhandlungen der sächsischen Gesellschaft der Wissenschaften.

Ahd. Gloss. Steinmeyer und Sievers, Die althochdeutschen Glossen.

AJA American Journal of Archaeology.

AJPh. American Journal of Philology.

Alminauskis. K. Alminauskis, Die deutschen Lehnwörter im Litauischen.

Arch. glott. it. Archivio glottologico italiano.

Arch. lat. Lex. Archiv für lateinische Lexikographie und Grammatik.

Arch. sl. Ph. Archiv für slavische Philologie.

Barth. Bartholomae, Altiranisches Wörterbuch.

BB (Bezzenberger's) Beiträge zur Kunde der indogermanischen Sprachen.

BBCS Bulletin of Board of Celtic Studies.

Ber. Preuss. Akad. Sitzungsberichte der preussischen Akademie der Wissenschaften.

Ber. Sächs. Ges. Berichte über die Verhandlungen der sächsischen Gesellschaft der Wissenschaften zu Leipzig.

Ber. Wien. Akad. Sitzungsberichte der Akademie der Wissenschaften in Wien.

Berneker E. Berneker, Slavisches etymologisches Wörterbuch. References are to the pages of vol. 1 unless otherwise noted, since vol. 2 was suspended after one fascicle.

Bloch O. Bloch, Dictionnaire étymologique de la langue française.

Böhtlingk, Wtb. Böhtlingk, Sanskrit-Wörterbuch in kürzerer Fassung.

Boisacq E. Boisacq, Dictionnaire étymologique de la langue grecque.

Bosworth-Toller   J. Bosworth, An Anglo-Saxon Dictionary, etc., with Supplement by T. N. Toller.

BR   Böhtlingk und Roth, Sanskrit-Wörterbuch.

Brückner   A. Brückner, Słownik etymologiczny języka polskiego.

Brückner, Sl. Fremdwörter   A. Brückner, Die slavischen Fremdwörter im Litauischen.

Brugmann, Grd.   K. Brugmann, Grundriss der vergleichenden Grammatik der indogermanischen Sprachen, 2te Aufl.

BSL   Bulletin de la société de linguistique de Paris.

Buck, Grk. Dial.   C. D. Buck, Introduction to the Study of the Greek Dialects, 2d ed.

Buck, Osc.-Umbr. Gram.   C. D. Buck, A Grammar of Oscan and Umbrian.

Busch-Chomskas   A. Busch und T. Chomskas, Litauisch-deutsches Wörterbuch.

Byz. Z.   Byzantinische Zeitschrift.

CGL.   Corpus glossariorum Latinorum.

Cl. Ph.   Classical Philology.

Cl. Q.   Classical Quarterly.

Cl. R.   Classical Review.

Dahlerup   Ordbog over det danske Sprog, grundlagt af V. Dahlerup.

Dal'   Vladimir Dal', Tolkovyj slovar' živogo velikorusskago jazka.

Denk. Wien. Akad.   Denkschriften der Akademie der Wissenschaften in Wien.

Densusianu   O. Densusianu, Histoire de la langue roumaine.

Dicţ. enc.   Dicţionarul enciclopedic ilustrat (Rumanian).

Dict. gén.   Hatzfeld et Darmesteter, Dictionnaire général de la langue française.

Diez   F. Diez, Etymologisches Wörterbuch der romanischen Sprachen, 5te Ausgabe.

Dinneen   P. S. Dinneen, Irish-English Dictionary, new ed.

Drawneek   J. Drawneek, Deutsch-lettisches Wörterbuch.

Du Cange   Du Cange, Glossarium mediae et infimae latinitatis; id., Glossarium ad scriptores mediae et infimae graecitatis.

Ebert, Reallex.   Reallexikon der Vorgeschichte unter mitwirkung zahlreicher Fachgelehrter herausgegeben von M. Ebert.

Endz., Gram.   J. Endzelin, Lettische Grammatik.

Ἐπετηρίς   Ἐπετηρὶς Ἐπιστημονικὴ Ἐπετηρὶς τοῦ Πανεπιστημίου (Athens).

Ernault, Dict. étym.   E. Ernault, Dictionnaire étymologique du breton moyen.

Ernault, Glossaire   E. Ernault, Glossaire moyen-breton.

Ernout-M.   A. Ernout et A. Meillet, Dictionnaire étymologique de la langue latine, 2e éd.

Falk-Torp   H. Falk und A. Torp, Norwegisch-dänisches etymologisches Wörterbuch.

Feist   S. Feist, Vergleichendes (formerly Etymologisches) Wörterbuch der gotischen Sprache, 3te Aufl.

Franck-v. W.   J. Franck, Etymologisch Woordenboek der nederlandsche Taal, 2de Druk, door N. van Wijk.

Fritzner   J. Fritzner, Ordbog over det gamle norske Sprog.

Gailius-Šlaža   Vk. Gailius ir M. Šlaža, Deutsch-litauisches Wörterbuch.

Gamillscheg   E. Gamillscheg, Etymologisches Wörterbuch der französischen Sprache.

Gebauer   J. Gebauer, Historicka mluvnice jazyka českého.

Gerof   Naĭdenŭ Gerovŭ, Rečnikŭ na blŭgarskyj jazykŭ.

Glotta   Glotta, Zeitschrift für griechische und lateinische Sprache.

Godefroy   F. Godefroy, Dictionnaire de l'ancienne langue française.

Godin   Marie Amelie Freiin von Godin, Wörterbuch der albanischen und deutschen Sprache.

Gött. gel. Anz.   Göttingische gelehrte Anzeigen.

Gött. Nachr.   Nachrichten von der Gesellschaft der Wissenschaften zu Göttingen.

Graff   E. G. Graff, Althochdeutscher Sprachschatz.

Grimm   J. und W. Grimm, Deutsches Wörterbuch.

GRM   Germanisch-romanische Monatschrift.

Harper   Harper's Latin Dictionary.

Hatzidakis, Einl.   G. Hatzidakis, Einleitung in die neugriechische Grammatik.

Hatzidakis, Μεσ.   Γ. Χατζιδάκις, Μεσαιωνικὰ καὶ νέα Ἑλληνικά.

Hellquist   E. Hellquist, Svensk etymologisk Ordbog, 2d ed.

Henry   V. Henry, Lexique étymologique du breton moderne.

Hermann, Lit.-deutsches Gesprächsb.   E. Hermann, Litauisch-deutsches Gesprächsbüchlein.

Hessen   Hessen's Irish Lexicon, a Concise Dictionary of Early Irish.

Hesych.   Hesychii Alexandrini Lexicon.

Hirt, Idg. Gram.   H. Hirt, Indogermanische Grammatik.

Holthausen   F. Holthausen, Altenglisches etymologisches Wörterbuch.

Horn   P. Horn, Grundriss der neupersischen Etymologie.

Hübschmann, Arm. Gram.   H. Hübschmann, Armenische Grammatik, I. Theil.

Idg. Anz.   Anzeiger für indogermanische Sprach- und Altertumskunde.

Idg. Jhrb.   Indogermanisches Jahrbuch.

IF   Indogermanische Forschungen.

IG   Inscriptiones Graecae.

Ἱστ. Λεξ.   Ἱστορικὸν Λεξικὸν τῆς νέας Ἑλληνικῆς.

Jagić, Entstehungsgesch.   V. Jagić, Entstehungsgeschichte der kirchenslavischen Sprache.

JAOS   Journal of the American Oriental Society.

JEGPh.   Journal of English and Germanic Philology.

JHS   Journal of Hellenic Studies.

Kluge-G.   F. Kluge, Etymologisches Wörterbuch der deutschen Sprache, 11. Aufl., bearbeitet von Alfred Götze.

Kretschmer, Einl.   P. Kretschmer, Einleitung in die Geschichte der griechischen Sprache.

Kretschmer, Wortgeogr.   P. Kretschmer, Wortgeographie der hochdeutschen Umgangssprache.

Kurschat   F. Kurschat, Litauisch-deutsches und Deutsch-litauisches Wörterbuch.

KZ   Kuhn's Zeitschrift (Zeitschrift für vergleichende Sprachforschung).

Lalis   A. Lalis, A Dictionary of the English and Lithuanian Languages.

Language   Language (Journal of the Linguistic Society of America).

Laws, Gloss.   Ancient Laws of Ireland, vol. VI, Glossary, comp. R. Atkinson.

Le Gonidec   Le Gonidec, Dictionnaire français-breton et breton-français.

Leskien, Ablaut   A. Leskien, Der Ablaut der Wurzelsilben im Litauischen.

Leskien, Bildung d. Nom.   A. Leskien, Die Bildung der Nomina im Litauischen.

Leskien, Gram.   A. Leskien, Grammatik der altbulgarischen Sprache.

Lewis-Pedersen   H. Lewis and H. Pedersen, A Concise Comparative Celtic Grammar.

Lidén, Arm. Stud.   E. Lidén, Armenische Studien.

Lidén, Stud.   E. Lidén, Studien zur altindischen und vergleichenden Sprachgeschichte.

Linde   M. S. B. Linde, Słownik języka polskiego.

Littré   E. Littré, Dictionnaire de la langue française.

Lokotsch   K. Lokotsch, Etymologisches Wörterbuch der europäischen Wörter orientalischen Ursprungs.

Loth, Mots lat.   J. Loth, Les mots latins dans les langues brittaniques.

LS   Liddell and Scott, Greek-English Lexicon, 9th ed.

Lunds Univ. Årssk.   Lunds Universitets årsskrift.

Macbain   A. Macbain, An Etymological Dictionary of the Gaelic Language.

Macdonell-Keith   A. Macdonell and A. Keith, Vedic Index of Names and Subjects.

McKenna   L. McKenna, English-Irish Dictionary.

Marstrander, Bidrag   C. Marstrander, Bidrag til det norske sprogs historie i Irland. (Videnskapselskapets skrifter, hist.-filos. klasse, 1915, No. 5.)

Meillet; *see* Ernout-M.

Meillet, Études   A. Meillet, Études sur l'étymologie et le vocabulaire du vieux slave.

Meillet, Introd.   A. Meillet, Introduction à l'étude comparative des langues indo-européennes.

Meillet, Ling. hist.   A. Meillet, Linguistique historique et linguistique générale.

G. Meyer, Alb. Etym. Wtb.   G. Meyer, Etymologisches Wörterbuch der albanesischen Sprache.

G. Meyer, Alb. Stud.   G. Meyer, Albanesische Studien I–IV.

G. Meyer, Neugr. Stud.   G. Meyer, Neugriechische Studien I–IV.

K. Meyer, Contrib.   K. Meyer, Contributions to Irish Lexicography.

Meyer-Lübke; *see* REW.

Miklosich   F. Miklosich, Etymologisches Wörterbuch der slavischen Sprachen.

Miklosich, Lex. Palaeoslov.   F. Miklosich, Lexicon palaeoslovenico-graeco-latinum.

Miklosich, Turk. Elem.   F. Miklosich, Die türkischen Elementen in den südost- und osteuropäischen Sprachen (Denk. Wien. Akad. 34, 35, 37, 38).

MLN   Modern Language Notes.

Mnemos.   Mnemosyne.

Mod. Ph.   Modern Philology.

Monde Or.   Le monde oriental.

Morris Jones   J. Morris Jones, A Welsh Grammar, Historical and Comparative.

Moulton-Milligan   J. H. Moulton and G. Milligan, Vocabulary of the Greek Testament.

MSL   Mémoires de la société de linguistique de Paris.

Mühl.-Endz.   K. Mühlenbacha Latviešu volodas vārdnīca, redigējis, papildinājis, nobeidzis J. Endzelīns.

NED   A New English Dictionary on Historical Principles.

Nord. Tidsskrift   Nordisk tidsskrift for filologi.

Norsk Tidskrift   Norsk tidskrift for sprogvidenskap.

NSB   Niedermann, Senn, und Brender, Wörterbuch der litauischen Schriftsprache.

O'Curry   E. O'Curry, On the Manners and Customs of the Ancient Irish.

O'Reilly   E. O'Reilly, An Irish-English Dictionary, new ed. with Supplement by J. O'Donovan.

Osthoff, Parerga   H. Osthoff, Etymologische Parerga.

Parry-Williams   T. H. Parry-Williams, The English Element in Welsh.

Paul, Deutsches Wtb.   H. Paul, Deutsches Wörterbuch.

Pauly-Wissowa   Pauly's Real-Encyclopädie der klassischen Altertumswissenschaft, herausgegeben von Georg Wissowa.

PBB   Paul und Braune, Beiträge zur Geschichte der deutschen Sprache und Litteratur.

Pedersen   H. Pedersen, Vergleichende Grammatik der keltischen Sprachen.

Pernot, Recueil   H. Pernot, Recueil de textes en grec usuel.

Persson, Beiträge   P. Persson, Beiträge zur indogermanischen Wortforschung.

Ph. W.   Philologische Wochenschrift.

Preisigke   F. Preisigke, Wörterbuch der griechischen Papyrusurkunden.

Prellwitz   W. Prellwitz, Etymologisches Wörterbuch der griechischen Sprache, 2. Aufl.

Pușcariu   S. Pușcariu, Etymologisches Wörterbuch der rumänischen Sprache. I. Lateinisches Element.

RC   Revue celtique.

Rev. ét. anc.   Revue des études anciennes.

Rev. ét. indo-eur.   Revue des études indo-européennes.

Rev. ét. sl.   Revue des études slaves.

Rev. sl. Revue slavistique.

REW W. Meyer-Lübke, Romanisches etymologisches Wörterbuch, 3te Aufl.

Rh. M. Rheinisches Museum für Philologie.

RIA Contrib. Contributions to a Dictionary of the Irish Language.

RIA Dict. Dictionary of the Irish Language, published by the Irish Academy.

Riv. fil. Rivista di filologia e di istruzione classica.

Riv. IGI Rivista Indo-Greco-Italica.

Rječnik Akad. Rječnik hrvatskoga ili srpskoga jezika na svijet izdaje jugoslavenska Akademija.

Rom. Romania.

Rom. Forsch. Romanische Forschungen.

Romance Ph. Romance Philology.

Şaineanu Şaineanu, Dictionar universal al limbei romāne; or Dictionnaire français-roumain.

Sandfeld, Ling. balk. Kr. Sandfeld, Linguistique balkanique.

Schrader, Reallex. O. Schrader, Reallexikon der indogermanischen Altertumskunde, 2te Aufl. von Nehring.

Schwers J. Schwers, Die deutschen Lehnwörter im Lettischen.

Schwyzer, Dial. Graec. Ex. E. Schwyzer, Dialectorum Graecarum exempla epigraphica potiora.

Schwyzer, Gr. Gram. E. Schwyzer, Griechische Grammatik.

Senn, Lit. Sprachl. A. Senn, Kleine litauische Sprachlehre.

Skardžius Pr. Skardžius, Die slavischen Lehnwörter im Altlitauischen, Tauta ir Žodis 7.1 ff.

Solmsen, Beiträge F. Solmsen, Beiträge zur griechischen Wortforschung.

Solmsen, Unters. F. Solmsen, Untersuchungen zur griech. Laut-und Verslehre.

Sommer, Gr. Lautstud. F. Sommer, Griechische Lautstudien.

Sophocles E. A. Sophocles, Greek-English Lexicon of the Roman and Byzantine Periods.

Sperber, Einleitung Hans Sperber, Einleitung in die Bedeutungslehre.

Spurrell Spurrell's English-Welsh Dictionary, by J. Anwyl, 9th ed.

SSS E. Sieg, W. Siegling, und W. Schulze, Tocharische Grammatik.

Stender-Petersen A. Stender-Petersen, Slavisch-germanische Lehnwortkunde.

Stokes W. Stokes, Urkeltischer Sprachschatz = Fick, Vergleichendes Wörterbuch der indogermanischen Sprachen II.

Sturtevant, Hitt. Gloss. E. H. Sturtevant, Hittite Glossary, 2d ed.

Sturtevant, Hitt. Gram. E. H. Sturtevant, A Comparative Grammar of the Hittite Language.

Sv. Akad. Ordb. Ordbok över svenska språket utgiven av svenska Akademien.

TAPA Transactions of the American Philological Association.

Thes. (for Celtic) W. Stokes and J. Strachan, Thesaurus Palaeohibernicus.

Thes. (for Greek) Stephanus, Thesaurus Graecae linguae.

Thes. (for Latin) Thesaurus linguae Latinae.

Thomsen, Beröringer W. Thomsen, Beröringer mellem de finske og de baltiske Sprog.

Thurneysen, Gram. R. Thurneysen, A Grammar of Old Irish.

Thurneysen, Heldensage R. Thurneysen, Die irische Helden- und Königsage bis zum siebzehnten Jahrhundert.

Thurneysen, Irisches Recht Abh. Preuss. Akad., phil.-hist. Kl., 1931, No. 2.

Thurneysen, Keltorom. R. Thurneysen, Keltoromanisches.

Tiktin H. Tiktin, Rumänisch-deutsches Wörterbuch.

Tobler-Lommatzsch A. Tobler, Altfranzösisches Wörterbuch herausgegeben von E. Lommatzsch.

Torp, Nynorsk A. Torp, Nynorsk etymologisk ordbog.

Trautmann R. Trautmann, Baltisch-slavisches Wörterbuch.

Trautmann, Altpreuss. R. Trautmann, Die altpreussischen Sprachdenkmäler.

Uhlenbeck   C. Uhlenbeck, Kurzgefasstes etymologisches Wörterbuch der altindischen Sprache.

Ulmann   C. Ulmann (und Brasche), Lettisches Wörterbuch.

Uppsala Univ. Årssk.   Uppsala Universitets årsskrift.

Vallée   F. Vallée, Grand dictionnaire français-breton.

Vendryes, De hib. voc.   J. Vendryes, De hibernicis vocabulis quae a latina lingua originem duxerunt.

Vetensk. Skr.   Skrifter utgivna av kungl. humanistiska vetenskapssamfundet i Uppsala.

Vidensk. Med.   Meddelelser udgivne af det kgl. danske videnskabernes Selskab.

Vidensk. Skr.   Skrifter utgit av Videnskapsselskapet i Kristiania; since 1925 Skrifter utgitt av det norske Videnskaps-Akademi i Oslo.

Vigfusson   G. Vigfusson, An Icelandic-English Dictionary Based on the MS. Collections of the Late Richard Cleasby.

Vondrák   W. Vondrák, Vergleichende slavische Grammatik, 2te Aufl.

Wackernagel, Altind. Gram.   J. Wackernagel, Altindische Grammatik.

Walde-H.   A. Walde, Lateinisches etymologisches Wörterbuch, 3te Aufl. , von J. B. Hofmann.

Walde-P.   A. Walde, Vergleichendes Wörterbuch der indogermanischen Sprachen, herausgegeben und bearbeitet von J. Pokorny.

Wartburg   W. von Wartburg, Französisches etymologisches Wörterbuch.

Weekley   E. Weekley, An Etymological Dictionary of Modern English.

Weigand-H.   F. Weigand, Deutsches Wörterbuch, 5te Aufl., von H. Hirt.

Williams   R. Williams, Lexicon Cornu-Brittanicum.

Windisch   E. Windisch, Irische Texte mit Wörterbuch I.

Wört. u. Sach.   Wörter und Sachen.

Z. celt. Ph.   Zeitschrift für celtische Philologie.

Z. deutsch. Alt.   Zeitschrift für deutsches Altertum.

Z. deutsch. Ph.   Zeitschrift für deutsche Philologie.

Z. deutsch. Wortf.   Zeitschrift für deutsche Wortforschung.

ZDMG   Zeitschrift der deutschen morgenländischen Gesellschaft.

Z. frz. Spr.   Zeitschrift für französische Sprache und Literatur.

Z. Ind. Iran.   Zeitschrift für Indologie und Iranistik.

Z. rom. Ph.   Zeitschrift für romanische Philologie.

Z. sl. Ph.   Zeitschrift für slavische Philologie.

Zeuss   Zeuss, Grammatica Celtica, editio altera, curavit H. Ebel.

Zupitza, Gutt.   Zupitza, Die germanischen Gutturale.

OTHER ABBREVIATIONS

abl.	ablative	comp.	comparative
acc.	accusative	cons.	consonant
act.	active	cop.	copulative (e.g. ά- cop. in Greek)
adj.	adjective	cpd.	compound
adv.	adverb(ial)	dat.	dative
arch.	archaic	denom.	denominative
assim.	assimilation, assimilated	deriv.	derivative
caus.	causative	desid.	desiderative
class.	classical	dial.	dialect(s), dialectal(ly)
coll.	collective	dim.	diminutive
colloq.	colloquial(ly)	dissim.	dissimilation, dissimilative

du.	dual	obj.	objective
dub.	dubious, doubtful, uncertain	obs.	obsolete
eccl.	ecclesiastical	op. cit.	opere citato, in work cited
esp.	especially	opp.	opposite
etym.	etymology	opt.	optative
fem.	feminine	orig.	origin, original(ly)
fig.	figurative(ly)	pap.	papyri
fr.	from (either from an earlier actual or reconstructed form; or often, for the sake of brevity = derivative of)	pass.	passive
		perf.	perfect
		perfect.	perfective
		perh.	perhaps
freq.	frequent(ly)	pl.	plural
frequent.	frequentative	pop.	popular (= colloquial)
gen.	genitive	poss.	possessive
gl.	gloss, gloss to, glosses	pple.	participle
gramm.	grammarians	prec.	preceding
ib.	ibidem, in the same work	prep.	preposition
id.	idem (used to indicate the same form, or the same meaning)	pres.	present
		pret.	preterite
i.e.	id est, that is	priv.	privative
imperat.	imperative	prob.	probably
imperf.	imperfect	pron.	pronoun, pronominal
impers.	impersonal	redupl.	reduplication, reduplicated
ind.	indicative	refl.	reflexive
indef.	indefinite	refs.	references
infin.	infinitive	reg.	regular(ly)
init.	initial	rhet.	rhetorical
instr.	instrumental	sb.	substantive (= noun, also used)
intr.	intransitive	sc.	scilicet, understand, supply
iter.	iterative	sg.	singular; with reference to Welsh, Cornish, Breton, sg. or new sg. = the so-called singulative
l.c.	loco citato, in passage cited		
lit.	literary; also literally (context obviating confusion)		
		spec.	specifically
masc.	masculine	subj.	subjunctive; also subjective
mid.	middle	superl.	superlative
misc.	miscellaneous	trans.	transitive
neg.	negative	vb.	verb
neolog.	neologism	vbl. n.	verbal noun (for Celtic)
neut.	neuter	v.l.	varia lectio
nom.	nominative	vs	versus, in contrast to, against
nom. pr.	proper name	:	related to, cognate with

ORTHOGRAPHY AND TRANSCRIPTION

The macron is used as the sign of vowel length, not only for Latin, etc., but likewise for Old English, Old Norse, Irish (instead of ′), and Lettic. But the customary ′ in Bohemian and Lith. ė = ē, y = ī are retained.

The sign of vowel length is employed in the case of the older languages (including Goth. ē, ō to conform to practice in other Germanic languages;

but omitted for Sanskrit *e, o;* likewise usually omitted in Greek nouns of the first declension like χώρα, καρδία, the short *a* of the smaller class like μοῖρα, θάλασσα being shown by the accent) and some of the modern, as Irish (but omitted in Welsh and Breton), Lithuanian, and Lettic.

Word accentuation is generally indicated only where this is customary in the normal orthography, as in Greek and in particular Spanish words (Polish ´ in *ó* is not a sign of accent but of vowel quality as in the case of the French accent signs; likewise in the transcription of Oscan). Thus, for Sanskrit, Lithuanian, Lettic, and Serbo-Croatian the accent marks are omitted, as not essential for the purposes of this work.

The signs *š* (= NE *sh*) and *ž* (= NE *z* in *azure*, Fr. *j.*) are used for Lithuanian (formerly *sz, ż*), Lettic, Slavic, Iranian, Arabic, etc.

In reconstructed IE forms involving the different guttural series, k^w, g^w, $g^w h$ are used for the labiovelars; $\hat{k}$, $\hat{g}$, $\hat{g}h$ for the palatals; and plain k, g, gh both for the so-called "plain velars" (Grk. κρέας, Skt. *kravis*) and for others of indeterminate value.

The peculiar modification of the gutturals resulting in forms like Grk. τέκτων = Skt. *takṣan-*, since it is clearly not an independent phoneme (cf. esp. Benveniste, BSL 38.139 ff.), should properly be represented by a superior letter, e.g. $k^{\flat}$, or $\hat{k}^{\cdot}$ (Benveniste). Those who believe that the IE "voiced aspirates" are wrongly so called will nevertheless recognize *bh, dh,* etc. as the best-understood symbols for this third order of stops. Similarly, $\bar{\imath}$, $\bar{r}$, etc. are still employed as the most convenient symbols for those phonemes which, whatever their precise phonetic value, correspond to $\bar{\imath}$, $\bar{u}$ in other series.

The laryngeals, so much discussed in recent years, are left out of account in the reconstructed IE forms. They concern, as even those who operate with them and at the same time reject the Indo-Hittite hypothesis should admit, a stage preceding that to which the comparison of the main IE languages, those formerly known, points. They belong to what might be called a Proto-IE stage, the forms of which deserve a double asterisk. For example, if the familiar IE **dhē-* 'put' goes back to an earlier ***dhe* + a laryngeal, the contraction must have taken place before the separation of the main IE languages. That it took place independently in all the languages which show the simple long vowel (Grk., Lat., Gmc., Balto-Slavic, Indo-Iranian) is too much to believe.

But all such phonetic matters as the preceding are unimportant for the purpose of this work, where the reconstructed forms merely serve as convenient symbols for certain groupings. It should be further stated here that such reconstructed forms do not necessarily imply the actual existence of such a form in the IE period. In some cases they are merely the proper theoretical bases for certain limited sets of correspondence. Similarly, a reconstructed VLat. form need not imply its existence over the whole VLat.-speaking territory.

Albanian.—The new standardized orthography is followed.

Armenian.—Transcribed as in Hübschmann, Armenische Grammatik.

Avestan and Old Persian.—Transcribed as in Bartholomae, Altiran. Wörterbuch (including OPers. θ^r, although ς is preferable). Thus $č, ǰ$ (not c, j as in Sanskrit) and x, γ for the guttural fricatives, and likewise for Modern Persian, etc.

Church Slavic.—Transcribed mostly as in Leskien, Altbulgarische Grammatik. But ѣ, ѥ, ю, etc. are transcribed in the older fashion ja, je, ju (and so Russ. я, ю as ja, ju), instead of $'a, 'e, 'u$, indicating the palatalization of the preceding consonant and strictly more correct (Leskien, op. cit. 37 ff.). The ъ and ь are transcribed $ŭ$ and $ĭ$.

Danish.—The orthography of the Dansk Retskrivningsordbog (3d ed.) by J. Glahder (published by the Committee on Orthography of the Danish Ministry of Education) is followed.

Gothic.—The transcription hw, in accord with the OE, OHG, is preferred to the ligature $ƕ$; e, o marked long, $ē, ō$; diphthongal and monophthongal ai, au not distinguished.

Greek.—Forms quoted from inscriptions in the archaic alphabet are generally given in the familiar spelling with $\eta, \omega, ^ϲ$.

Modern Greek (NG).—As between the historical spelling of the καθαρεύουσα and the phonetic spelling of writers in the δημοτική, I have generally used the latter in truly popular words, e.g. φτωχός 'poor', χτένι 'comb', with the normal development of $\pi\tau > \phi\tau, \kappa\tau > \chi\tau, \sigma\theta > \sigma\tau$, etc. (vs. e.g. λεπτόν 'minute' or 'centime', with pronounced $\pi\tau$), or νύφη 'bride' vs. νύμφη 'nymph', or νερό 'water', vs. lit. words with the old ν of the neuter retained. But I can see no need of changing αὐτός to ἀφτός or αὐγά to ἀβγά, since the pronunciation of v in αυ, ευ as f before voiceless or v before voiced sounds is uniform. It is immaterial whether one writes ποτήρι (from ποτήριον) or ποτῆρι; presents in -ωνω or -ονω (from -οω with new present formed to aor. -ωσα). In several of these matters there is no consistency, in individual cases, even among writers in the δημοτική. Initial ρ, not ῥ, is now preferred.

Irish.—Genuine Old Irish diphthongs are marked with the macron on the first element (as Pedersen) without attempt to distinguish them from the long vowels with glide (as Thurneysen).

Lettic.—New orthography as in Mühl.-Endz., except k', etc. (not $ķ$) for palatalized consonant, and $ł$ not used ($ł$ in Mühl.-Endz. only in headings).

Lithuanian.—Present standardized orthography, as in NSB.

Old Norse.—For the mutated vowels it is intended to follow the now generally adopted spelling, as e.g. in Heggstad, Gamalnorsk Ordbok.

Oscan-Umbrian.—The usual practice of distinguishing by different type the forms written in the native or Roman alphabets, respectively, is abandoned here as unimportant for the purposes of this work.

Rumanian.—Not *â*, but *î* in *cîmp*, etc. as in REW, Pușcariu, and Tiktin after vol. 1; and now accepted as standard, cf. Grai și Suflet 5.207 ff.

Russian.—Transcription after the new official spelling. Thus стол 'table' (not столъ) in transcription *stol*, but путь 'way' transcribed *put'*; ѣ discarded and so *ĕ* in transcription, *e* being used for former *e* and *ĕ*, and *ë* (for *e* pronounced as *o*) not used.

Sanskrit.—Transcription as in Whitney's Sanskrit Grammar.

Swedish.—The reformed spelling is used (i.e. *v* instead of *fv*, etc.).

Turkish.—The new official orthography in the Latin alphabet is followed, with the new and annoying conflicts of values thus introduced. Thus *c* = NE *j*, where *j* is used in transcription of Persian, Turkish dialects, etc.; *ç* = NE *ch* in *church*, in contrast to *c* used elsewhere.

FORM OF CITATION

In general, words are cited in the form customary in the grammars and dictionaries of the respective languages, except for Latin verbs (see below).

Thus nouns are given in the nominative singular and adjectives in the nominative singular masculine, except in Indo-Iranian, where they are given in the stem form but with an added hyphen to make this clear. Occasionally Sanskrit forms are quoted in the nominative singular, the absence of the hyphen showing this.

The Latin sources of Romance nouns and adjectives are likewise given in the nominative form, since the constant substitution of the accusative form would be a cumbersome and superfluous concession to strict accuracy.

Verbs are cited in the first person singular for Greek and Irish (OIr. sometimes in the third singular, but so marked); otherwise for the European languages in the infinitive (so even for Latin, to conform to the practice for the Romance languages; in Balto-Slavic first person singular present occasionally given also). For Indo-Iranian they are usually given in the root form, as is customary, the Sanskrit mostly as in Whitney's Roots, and the Iranian conforming, e.g. Av. *vid-*, like Skt. *vid-*, not *vaēd-* as in Bartholomae. Similarly in cases like *hṛ-*, preferred by most Sanskritists, vs. *har-* in BR, the former is generally adopted. But here the strong form is generally better for Iranian; and it is a harmless inconsistency to use it also for Indic in quoting Indo-Iranian roots, e.g. Skt., Av. *tar-*.

For Slavic verbs it seems futile to cite the forms of the different aspects. The shorter form is generally given.

In the lists the inclusion of certain words in parentheses indicates some reservation, such as obsolete, archaic, poetic, dialectal, in special sense, uncommon, or the like.

CHAPTER 1

THE PHYSICAL WORLD IN ITS LARGER ASPECTS

1.1 WORLD

Grk.	κόσμος (οἰκουμένη, b)	Goth.	fairhwus (midjun-	Lith.	pasaulis
NG	κόσμος		gards, manasēþs, b)	Lett.	pasaule
Lat.	mundus	ON	heimr, verǫld	ChSl.	světŭ
It.	mondo	Dan.	verden	SCr.	svijet
Fr.	monde	Sw.	verld	Boh.	svět
Sp.	mundo	OE	middangeard, weorold	Pol.	swiat
Rum.	lume	ME	werld, world	Russ.	mir, svet
Ir.	domun (bith, b, c)	NE	world	Skt.	loka-, jagat-, bhū-,
NIr.	domhan (saoghal, b,	Du.	wereld		bhuvana-, etc.
	c, bith, b, c)	OHG	mittilgart, werald	Av.	(gaēþā-, aᵑhu-, b, c)
W.	byd	MHG	werlt		
Br.	bed	NHG	welt		

'World' is considered here primarily as the common comprehensive term for the physical world, so far as it lies within the knowledge of the unsophisticated man, namely 'the heavens above and earth beneath'. But other applications are inextricably bound up with its history. From the manifold uses of the NE

12

world (which fill some thirteen columns in the NED), we may note three main types as of especial importance in the discussion, namely:

a. The physical world in the broadest sense, the universe[1]

b. The known world ('the highest mountain in the world'), the earth with all that belongs to it, especially the inhabited earth, mankind ('the world knows')

c. Life on earth, worldly life, this world, in contrast to the next

Most of the words listed above are used in all these senses. Where it is necessary to differentiate them for a given language or period, this will be indicated by a, b, c respectively. The etymology and in some cases the known history of these words show that the semantic development may have proceeded from any of these spheres of usage.

More specifically their semantic sources may be summarized as follows: orderly arrangement; open space; foundation; under the sun; mid-inclosure; abode, home; existence; life; light; age, generation; peace.

1. Grk. κόσμος (etym. dub.; Walde-P. 1.403, Boisacq 500 f.) means properly 'order', 'orderly arrangement' as commonly in Homer (whence also κοσμέω used in Homer of marshaling troops, and from this again κοσμήτωρ λαῶν 'leader of the people'). A frequent secondary meaning is 'ornament, decoration, dress'. In Crete κόσμος designated an official ruling body (collective) and later a single official.

[1] To distinguish more specifically the broadest sense, the common words for 'world' have been partly replaced in technical language by other terms, as e.g. Lat. universum, Fr. univers, NHG weltall, Russ. vselennaja (both lit. 'allness'), Boh. ves-mir, SCr. svemir (both lit. 'all-world'). These will not be included in the discussion.

The early philosophers (Pythagoras first, according to the frequently repeated tradition) applied this term to the universe as an 'orderly arrangement' in contrast to primeval chaos. Either it was used of the universe as observed from the earth, the starry firmament, the heavens (e.g. ὁ περὶ τὴν γῆν ὅλος κόσμος Aristotle), and this was probably its earliest application, or it was used of the universe including the earth, the whole world, and this became its normal meaning.

But for the world of people, the inhabited earth, the classical phrase was ἡ οἰκουμένη (γῆ), 'the inhabited (earth)'. Not until Hellenistic times is κόσμος used in this sense. In the NT it is common, beside occasional οἰκουμένη. Cf. Mt. 4.8 πάσας τὰς βασιλείας τοῦ κόσμου = Lk. 4.5 .... τῆς οἰκουμένης. It is also used for this world, worldly life, for which, however, the more frequent expression is αἰών. So κόσμος finally comes to cover all the main senses of 'world', noted above as a, b, c. So NG κόσμος, with rich idiomatic use like that of NE world or Fr. monde.

Grk. αἰών 'lifetime, age' (:Lat. aevum, aetās, etc., 14.12) is used in the NT for 'worldly life, this world' in sense c, e.g. Mt. 13.22, Mk. 4.19 ἡ μέριμνα (αἱ μέριμναι) τοῦ αἰῶνος τούτου 'the care(s) of this world'. Although this use itself was not extended to 'world' in other senses in Greek, it is important for the history of other words used to translate it.

2. Lat. mundus is the result of semantic borrowing, starting as a literary imitation of Grk. κόσμος. It is the same word as mundus used of a woman's 'ornaments, dress', this being related to the adj. mundus 'clean, elegant' (15.87). This was a synonym of Grk. κόσμος in one of its frequent uses (see above), one that was probably more familiar to the

---

Romans than that of 'order'. Hence the Roman writers used mundus also as the equivalent of κόσμος in both its applications to the physical world as noted above, namely the 'firmament, vault of the heavens' (mundus caeli, Ennius, mundi lumina, Verg., etc.; hence also the underground mundus in the forum), and 'universe, world'.[1] Hence also for 'mankind', mostly poetical and ecclesiastic for this 'world' (beside saeculum). It has furnished the common words for 'world' in all the Romance languages (Fr. monde, etc.), except Rumanian, where lume orig. 'light' (Lat. lūmen) is used for 'world', by semantic borrowing from the Slavic světŭ, which is both 'light' and 'world' (below, 6).

Lat. saeculum 'age, generation' is used in ecclesiastic writings, like Grk. αἰών, of 'this world', in sense c. The Romance derivatives, Ital. secolo, Fr. siècle, Sp. siglo, are still used in this special sense; and examples occur of their use for 'world' in the wider sense, as Ital. il Creatore dell' universo secolo (quoted in Tomaseo-Bellini). But they have never become serious rivals of the descendants of mundus. Lat. saeculum is the source of Ir. sáigul 'age', NIr. saoghal (saol), which is the normal word for 'world' in sense c, and is freely used for 'world' in sense b beside domhan. "Domhan and saoghal are interchangeable in general references to the world we live in" (Dinneen).

Lat. saeculum is also probably the in-

[1] This view of Lat. mundus is, I think, beyond any reasonable doubt, but it is not universally accepted. It has been objected that in the earlier quotable occurrences the meaning is 'heavens', while that of 'universe' is later. Even if this is not accidental, it is no valid objection, in view of the use of κόσμος stated above. Pliny's words, nam quem κόσμος Graeci nomine ornamenti apellavere, eum nos a perfecta absolutaque elegantia, mundum, show just that understanding of κόσμος which accounts for the Roman use of mundus.

direct source of the present Gmc. words for 'world', of which NE world is representative. See below.

3. Ir. domun, NIr. domhan, 'world' in sense a and b, fr. *dub-no- (cf. Gall. Dubnoreix on coins, Dumnorix in Caesar, lit. 'world-king') : ChSl. dŭno (n from bn) 'bottom, foundation', Ir. domain, NIr. domhain 'deep', NE deep, etc. The development was from 'bottom, foundation' to 'earth' (as in Rum. pamint 'earth' fr. Lat. pavimentum), then extended to 'world'. Walde-P. 2.847 ff. Pedersen 1.35.

W. byd, Br. bed, OCorn. bit, MCorn. bys used for world in all senses, Ir. bith 'age', also 'world' in senses b and c, fr. a Celtic *bi-tu- (cf. Gall. Bitu-rīges) : Grk. βίος 'life', Lat. vīvus, Skt. jīva- 'living', etc. (4.74). Pedersen 1.41.

4. Goth. fairhwus (the commonest rendering of κόσμος) : ON fjǫr, OE feorh, OHG ferah 'life', ON firar, OE firas 'men' root connection? Walde-P. 2.45. Feist 139.

Goth. manasēþs (renders κόσμος 'world of people, mankind'), lit. 'seed of man', -sēþs : OE sǣd, Lat. sēmen, etc. 'seed'. Walde-P. 2.459 ff. Feist 344.

ON heimr 'abode' and the usual word for 'world' in the broadest sense : OE hām 'home', etc. (7.122).

Goth. midjun-gards (renders οἰκουμένη when this is used instead of the usual κόσμος), ON miδ-garδr, OE middan-geard, OHG mittin-gart, mittil-gart (lit. 'mid-yard, mid-inclosure'), represent a term of Gmc. mythology denoting the earth as the abode of man, as pictured in the Edda (cf. Vigfusson and Fritzner, s.v. miδ-garδr). OE middan-(g)eard is used likewise for the inhabited earth, but also for 'world' in the broadest sense. In the OE gospels it is the common word for world, e.g. Mt. 25.34 'from the foundation of the world', Jn. 17.5 'be-

---

fore the world was'), and Aelfric gives it as the equivalent of Lat. mundus. OHG mittilgart and werall are both freq. for mundus (e.g. Tat.; Otfr. only worolt).

ON verǫld, OE weorold, OHG werall, etc. general Gmc. except Gothic, a cpd. of wer 'man' (2.21) and a noun form of adjs. for 'old' (14.15), hence 'age of man'. Thus it was equivalent to and followed Lat. saeculum in its ecclesiastical use (above, 2). For the early period this is the prevailing use, e.g. in the OE gospels, Mt. 12.32, 13.22 (Grk. αἰών, Vulgate saeculum). The further development was from this sense c to sense b and eventually to sense a, until the words in question became the common expressions for 'world' in all senses as in all the Gmc. languages. NED s.v. world. Falk-Torp 1368.

5. Lith. pasaulis, Lett. pasaule, a cpd. of pa- 'under' and saule 'sun' (1.52), is 'world' in all senses. Lith. pasaulis is now preferred to the formerly current svietas, a Slavic loanword.

6. In Slavic there are two rival words for 'world', both still in common use in Russian, and both so used in dialects or older records of other Slavic languages.

ChSl. mirŭ (also vĭsĭ mirŭ with vĭsĭ 'all'), the regular translation of Grk. κόσμος, is the same word as mirŭ 'peace',

used in Christian terminology as a collective 'community of peace' (cf. Russ. mir, also 'village community'), hence 'world' first in sense b. Berneker 2.60 f.

ChSl. světŭ 'light' (1.61) is used once in the gospels (Mt. 13.22) to translate Grk. αἰών (above, 2). The semantic development was from 'light' to the 'realm of light, life' (cf. the association between 'light' and 'life', e.g. Grk. ὅστις φῶς ὁρᾷ 'whoever sees the light' = 'lives', hence 'world' in sense c, later 'world' in all senses, as in the present Slavic languages.

7. Skt. loka- 'open space, earth, world' : Lat. lūcus 'grove', Lith. laukas 'field', Skt. roca- 'shining', Grk. λευκός 'bright', etc. Walde-P. 2.408 ff.

Skt. jagat- 'that which moves, lives, all creation, world', fr. gam- 'go'.

Skt. bhū-, bhuvana- 'existence, creation, earth, world', fr. bhū- 'be'.

Av. gaēþā- 'life, mankind, world', fr. the root of gaya- 'life', jīva-, Skt. jīva-, Lat. vīvus, etc. 'living' (4.74). Cf. Ir. bith, etc., above, 3.

Av. aᵑhu- 'life, mankind, world', fr. ah- 'be' : Skt. as-, etc., IE *es-.

Neither of these Av. words, of which gaēþā- has the wider scope (Barth. 477 ff.), is actually quotable for 'world' in sense a, but only in senses b or c.

1.21 EARTH, LAND

Grk.	γῆ, χθών	Goth.	airþa, land	Lith.	žeme
NG	γῆ	ON	jǫrδ, land	Lett.	zeme
Lat.	terra, tellus, humus	Dan.	jord, land	ChSl.	zemlja
It.	terra	Sw.	jord, land	SCr.	zemlja
Fr.	terre	OE	eorþe, land	Boh.	země
Sp.	tierra	ME	erthe, land	Pol.	ziemia, ląd
Rum.	pamint, ţară	NE	earth, land	Russ.	zemlja
Ir.	talan, tír	Du.	aarde, land	Skt.	bhū-, bhūmi-, kṣam-
NIr.	talamh, tír	OHG	erda, lant		pṛthivī-, mahī, etc.
W.	daear, tir	MHG	erde, lant	Av.	zam-, būmi, OPers.
Br.	douar	NHG	erde, land		būmi-

The various ideas expressed by NE *earth* and *land* are frequently covered by the same word, and where different words are employed their uses overlap. We may distinguish here:

a. The whole earth, as distinguished from sun, moon, etc. Commonly expressed by the same words that are used in the following senses, and representing a relatively later conception. Special terms may be introduced to distinguish this sense, as (from the present state of knowledge) words meaning 'globe, sphere', or compounds like NHG *erdkreis, erdreich.* But these do not displace the common words and are not considered further here.

Since the earth is felt as the known world, words for 'earth' in this sense and 'world' may overlap in use (*the highest mountain in the world = on earth*), and some of the words discussed under 'world' belong here not only in origin but also in actual use. So regularly ON *miðgarðr*, OS *middilgard*, and frequently OE *middangeard*, OHG *mittilgart*.

b. The solid surface of the earth, viewed either simply as a surface (one lies *on the earth* or more commonly *on the ground*), or as the source of vegetation, (good) *earth, land, soil,* or *ground.* For other words used in these senses, see 1.212.

c. The solid surface of the earth in contrast with that which is covered with water, now regularly *land.* This sense is in some languages commonly expressed more specifically as 'dry (land)', as Byz., NG ξηρά, Rum. *uscat* (fr. adj. *uscat* 'dry'), Lith. *sausžemis* (*sausas* 'dry' and *žemė*).

d. The earth as material in general. This may be expressed by the common words for 'earth' (cf. NE *earthenware*), but more often by special words for a particular kind of earth, like NE *clay,* NHG *ton,* Fr. *argile,* etc. (9.73).

e. A definite portion of the earth's surface, from the land of an individual to a whole country (19.11).

The association between these various senses is such that any one of them may be the starting-point of an extension to some or all of the others.

Of the two Gmc. words represented by NE *earth* and *land,* the latter started with sense e, as indicated by the etymology and the use in Gothic, but was at an early period extended to sense c, eventually displacing *earth,* etc., which were once freely used in this sense. In English, on the other hand, *land* in a part of its earlier uses is mostly displaced by *country.*

1. IE *ĝhem- and *ĝhᵊem-, representing the most widespread cognate group, though the precise character of the IE variant form involves a difficult problem. Walde-P. 1.662 f. Ernout-M. 464. Walde-H. 1.664 f. The inclusion in this group of Hitt. *tekan,* Toch. A *tkaṃ* 'earth', and the resulting assumption of IE *dheghom-, *dhghom- (Kretschmer, Glotta 20.66 f.), is rejected by Benveniste, Mélanges Ginneken 193 ff. But some ultimate connection is probable.

Grk. χθών (mostly poet. and in sense b), beside χαμαί 'on the ground', χθαμαλός, χαμηλός 'on the ground, low lying'; Lat. *humus* (mostly in sense b) beside *humī* 'on the ground', *humilis* 'low'; Ir. *dū,* gen., acc. *don* 'place', early 'earth' (Pedersen 1.89, Vendryes, RC 40.437 ff.); Lith. *žemė,* Lett. *zeme,* OPruss. *semmin* (acc. sg.), ChSl. *zemlja,* etc., general Balto-Slavic for 'earth' and 'land'; Skt. *kṣam-* (gen. usually *jmas*), Vedic and in sense b, esp. 'earth' vs. 'sky'; Av. *zam-* (gen. *zemō* = Skt. *jmas*) 'earth' in all senses (Barth. 1662 ff.); Alb. *dhe* 'earth'.

While there is no clear root connection for this group, its primary sense seems to have been that of 'earth's surface, ground'.

2. Grk. γῆ, Hom. γαῖα, etym. unknown, perh. of pre-Greek origin. The poetical αἶα is also of dub. etym., but possibly 'the mother (earth)'. Brugmann, IF 15.93 ff.

3. Lat. *terra* (Osc. *teerúm, terúm* 'territory'), prob. fr. *tersā- : *torrēre* 'dry up, parch', Grk. τέρσομαι 'dry up', Skt. *tṛṣ-* 'be thirsty', Goth. *ga-þairsan* 'dry up, wither', NE *thirst,* etc., in which case its orig. meaning was 'dry land' vs. 'sea' as in the frequent *terrā marīque.* Here belong also, though of somewhat different formation, Ir. *tīr* ('land' mainly in sense e), W. *tir,* and the now obs. Br. *tir.* Walde-P. 1.737 ff. Ernout-M. 1034 f.

The descendants of Lat. *terra* remain the usual words in all the Romance languages except Rumanian, where *ţara* is now mostly 'land' = 'country' (also 'country' vs. 'city'), otherwise displaced by the following.

Rum. *pamînt,* fr. Lat. *pavīmentum* 'floor, pavement'. Used first of the 'ground' (sense b), it became the common word for 'earth, land' in most of the other senses. REW 6312.

4. Ir. *talam,* NIr. *talamh,* Lat. *tellus* (mostly poet.) : Skt. *tala-* 'surface, bottom, plain', ChSl. *tĭlo,* SCr. *tlo* 'ground', etc. Here also the starting-point was sense b. Walde-P. 1.740. Pedersen 1.132.

W. *daear,* Br. *douar,* Corn. *doar,* etym.? Pedersen 1.66. Henry 104.

5. Goth. *airþa,* ON *jǫrð,* OE *eorþe,* OHG *erda,* etc., general Gmc. : Ir. *ert* 'land' occurring only in cpds., OHG *ero* 'earth', Grk. ἔρā attested by ἔρας· γῆς Hesych. and ἔραζε 'to the ground'. Any further root connection is uncertain, so that the semantic starting-point remains obscure, though prob. b. Walde-P. 1.142. Feist 25 f.

Goth. *land,* etc., general Gmc. : Ir. *ith-land* 'threshing floor' (cpd. of *ith* 'grain'), W. *llan* 'inclosure, yard', etc. Its earliest use was sense e, and in Gothic it is only so used, namely for 'piece of land' or 'country', *airþa* being used in all other senses, including 'land' in contrast to sea. Walde-P. 2.438. Feist 321 f.

6. Balto-Slavic words, above, 1.

Pol. *ląd* fr. NHG *land.*

7. Skt. *kṣam-* (Vedic), Av. *zam-,* above, 1.

Skt. *bhū-, bhūmi-,* OPers. *būmi-,* Av. *būmi-* (less common than *zam-*), fr. *bhū-* 'be', hence first used of the earth as the known world.

Other common Skt. words for 'earth' are *pṛthivī-* fem. of *pṛthu-* 'wide', *mahī-* fem. of *mah-* 'great', *kṣiti-* properly 'abode', *vasu-dhā-* lit. 'yielding good', etc.

1.212 EARTH = GROUND, SOIL

As already remarked, the words for 'earth', among their various applications, are used for the earth's solid surface ('falls to earth, the ground') or its soft surface for cultivation ('good earth, land, ground, soil'). They are, in fact, the usual expressions of these senses, so that a list would be mainly a repetition of that in 1.21. But there are also other words, some less common, others (like NE *ground, soil,* NHG *boden*) now more common in these senses.

1. Grk. οὖδας (poet.) and ἔδαφος (also 'bottom, base'), prob. fr. the same root (also Hom. οὐδός, Att. ὀδός 'threshold'), perh. *wed- in Arm. *getin* 'ground'. Walde-P. 1.254.

Grk. πέδον : Umbr. *peřum, perso* 'solum', Skt. *pada-* 'step, foot', Lith. *padas* 'sole' and ultimately the words for 'foot', Skt. *pad-* Grk. πούς, ποδός, Lat. *pēs, pedis,* etc. Walde-P. 2.24.

Grk. χῶμα 'earth heaped up, bank, mound' (: χόω 'heap up', χέω 'pour', etc., Walde-P. 1.563), in LXX once 'dust', in NG the usual word for 'ground, soil'.

2. Lat. *solum* 'bottom, base, sole (of the foot or shoe)', and esp. 'ground, soil' (> It. *suolo,* Fr. *sol,* etc.; ME *soyle,* NE *soil,* fr. OFr. *soil,* this by confusion with *soil, souil* 'sill', fr. Lat. *solium* 'seat'), root connection doubtful. Walde-P. 2.532. Ernout-M. 953. REW 8079. NED s.v. *soil,* sb.

3. OE *grund,* NE *ground,* OHG *grunt* (also esp. *erdgrunt* Otfr.), NHG *grund* (less common in this sense than *boden* or NE *ground*), Dan., Sw. *grund,* etc., all orig. 'bottom' (12.34). NED s.v. These words, when applied to earth, denote mostly the solid surface rather than that for cultivation, but in NT Lk. 8.8, etc. (Goth. *ana airthai godai,* OE *on gōde eorthan,* Wycliff *to good erthe*), *on good ground* fr. Tyndale on, for which we should now say *soil.*

OE *molde* 'loose earth, soil' (NE *mold*) = Goth. *mulda* 'dust', Skt. *mṛd-* 'earth, clay', fr. root *mel- in Lat. *molere,* Goth. *malan,* etc. 'grind' (5.56). Walde-P. 2.288. Feist 366.

NHG *boden,* Du. *bodem,* etc. 'bottom' (12.34) and 'ground, soil'.

4. Boh. *půda* 'bottom, ground, soil' (Russ. *pod* 'bottom of a haycock, hearth') : Grk. πέδον etc. (above, 1). Here also prob. Russ. *počva* (the reg. technical term for 'soil'), fr. *pod(ŭ)šva beside *podošva* 'sole'?

1.213 DUST

Grk.	κόνις	Goth.	*mulda, stubjus*	Lith.	*dulkės* (pl.)
NG	σκόνη	ON	*dupt, dust*	Lett.	*pīsli* (pl.), *putekli* (pl.)
Lat.	*pulvis*	Dan.	*støv*	ChSl.	*prachŭ*
It.	*polvere*	Sw.	*stoft*	SCr.	*prah*
Fr.	*poussière*	OE	*dūst*	Boh.	*prach*
Sp.	*polvo*	ME	*dust*	Pol.	*proch*
Rum.	*praf, pulbere*	NE	*dust*	Russ.	*pyl*
Ir.	*luaithred*	Du.	*stof*	Skt.	*reṇu-, pāṅsu-, dhūli-*
NIr.	*luaithreadh*	OHG	*stuppi, stoub* (*melm*)	Av.	*pąsnu-*
W.	*llwch, pylor*	MHG	*stoup*		
Br.	*poultr*	NHG	*staub*		

Many of the words for 'dust' are from a widespread root (*dheu-), seen in words for 'agitate, shake', 'vapor, smoke', etc., or from others having the notion of 'stir', 'scatter', or 'blow'. All such were obviously applied first to the flying 'dust' in the air. Others are cognate with words for 'loose earth, soil', 'fine meal', 'ashes', with the common notion of 'small particles'. But it is only a secondary association of this kind that is shown in the Ir. derivative of the word for 'ashes' used for 'dust' and in the use of OE *asce* 'ashes' for 'dust' in the Lindisf. gospels (Lk. 9.5, 10.11, etc. *asca* vs. *dust* in the WSax. versions), since these words for 'ashes' were not based in origin on the notion of small particles.

Words of this group either cover also 'powder', or, especially Lat. *pulvis,* are the source of those now used for 'powder' (so far as this notion, as for a prepared product—medicinal, toilet, etc.,

is differentiated), e.g. Fr. *poudre* vs. *poussière,* NG ποῦδρα, NE *powder,* Dan. *pudder,* Sw. *puder,* NHG *pulver, puder,* Boh. *pudr,* etc. Cf. also 'gunpowder' (20.29).

1. Grk. κόνις (also κονι-ορτός 'dust stirred up', but simply 'dust' in NT), NG pop. σκόνη (σ fr. forms of the article, τῆς, etc.; cf. Hatzidakis, Μεσ. 2.412) : Lat. *cinis* 'ashes', perh. fr. the root seen in Grk. κνάω 'scrape'. Walde-P. 1.392. Boisacq 490.

2. Lat. *pulvis, -eris* (> It. *polvere,* OFr. *pouldre,* Fr. *poudre,* Rum. *pulbere;* Sp. *pólvora* now 'gunpowder'; VLat. *pulvus > OSp. *polvos,* Sp. *polvo,* Cat. *pols,* OFr. *pous, whence F. *poussière*) : Lat. *pollen,* Grk. πάλη, παιπάλη 'fine meal, fine dust', Lat. *puls,* Grk. πόλτος 'porridge', etc. Walde-P. 2.60. Ernout-M. 785, 824. REW 6842. Gamillscheg 714.

Rum. *praf,* fr. Slavic, ChSl. *prachŭ,* etc. (below, 6).

3. Ir. *luaithred,* NIr. *luaithreadh* (also *-reān,* etc.) 'ashes' and 'dust', fr. *luaith* 'ashes' (1.85).

NIr. *ceo* 'mist' (1.74), also 'dust', esp. *ceo bōthair* 'dust of the road'.

W. *llwch,* beside *lluwch* 'snowdrift', *lluchio* 'throw, hurl,' root connection?

W. *pylor,* fr. Lat. *pulvis, -eris* (above, 2). Loth, Mots lat. 196.

Br. *poultr,* fr. OFr. *pouldre* (above, 2). Henry 227.

4. Goth. *mulda* = OE *molde* 'loose earth, soil', etc. (1.212).

Goth. *stubjus,* OHG *stuppi, stoub,* MHG *stoup,* NHG *staub,* MLG, Du. *stof* (MLG > ODan. *stov,* now *støv* with *ø* fr. vb., Sw. *stoft*), root connection? Falk-Torp 1201. Feist 457.

ON *dupt* (ODan., Norw. *duft* 'fine meal', MHG *tuft* 'vapor, dew', NHG *duft* 'fragrance'), ON, Norw. *dust* (Dan. *dyst* 'fine meal'), OE *dūst* (if *ū* correct = NHG *dunst* 'vapor'), ME, NE *dust,* all fr. extensions of the root *dheu- seen in Skt. *dhū-, dhu-* 'shake', Grk. θύω 'rage, seethe', Skt. *dhūma-,* Lat. *fūmus,* etc. 'smoke'. Walde-P. 1.840, 846. Falk-Torp 163, 168. NED s.v. *dust.* Prob. fr. the same root Toch. A *tor,* B *taur* 'dust' (G. S. Lane, Language 14.27).

OHG *melm* (Tat. 49.9 = Mk. 10.14) : Goth. *malma* 'sand', etc., fr. the same root as Goth. *mulda* 'dust' (above).

5. Lith. *dulkės* (pl.) : Skt. *dhūli-* 'dust', Lat. *fūlīgō* 'rust', fr. the same root as Skt. *dhūma-* 'smoke', ON *dupt* 'dust', etc. (above, 4). Walde-P. 1.836. Ernout-M. 398.

Lett. *putekli* (pl.), fr. *putēt* 'fly like dust, disappear', this prob. : *pūst,* Lith. *pūsti* 'blow'. Mühl.-Endz. 3.440.

Lett. *pīsli* (pl.), fr. *pīst* 'unravel', this : Lat. *pīnsere* 'crush', etc. (Walde-P. 2.1)? Mühl.-Endz. 3.35, 2.34. Leskien, Ablaut 280.

6. ChSl. *prachŭ* (> Russ. *prach* now used only in some phrases), SCr. *prah,* Boh. *prach,* Pol. *proch* (Russ. *poroch* now 'gunpowder') : Boh. *pršeti* 'emit sparks, rain', Pol. *pierszyć* 'scatter sparks, rain, or snow', prob. Skt. *pṛṣata-* 'speckled, a drop of water', fr. a common notion of 'scatter' or the like. Walde-P. 2.50.

Russ. *pyl* (Pol. *pyl, pyłek* less common), fr. the root seen in Lith. *pūsti* 'blow'. Brückner 449.

7. Skt. *reṇu-* (RV +), fr. the root seen in Skt. *ri-* 'let go', mid. 'flow, dissolve', Grk. ὀρίνω 'stir, move', etc. Walde-P. 1.140.

Skt. *dhūli-,* fr. the same root as Lith. *dulkės,* ON *dupt,* etc. (above, 4, 5).

Skt. *pāṅsu-, pāṅsuka-,* Av. *pąsnu-* : ChSl. *pěsŭkŭ* 'sand', prob. fr. a root *pēs- 'blow' in ChSl. *pachati* 'toss, fan', Russ. *pachnút'* 'blow', etc. Walde-P. 2.68. Barth. 903.

1.214 MUD

Grk.	*πηλός*	Goth.	*fani*	Lith.	*purvas*
NG	*λάσπη*	ON	*leir*	Lett.	*dubl'i* (pl.)
Lat.	*lutum, līmus*	Dan.	*mudder, dynd* (*smuds*)	ChSl.	*brĭnĭje*
It.	*fango*	Sw.	*gyttja, dy, mudder* (*smuts*)	SCr.	*blato*
Fr.	*boue* (*fange*)	OE	*fen*	Boh.	*bláto*
Sp.	*lodo, fango, barro, cieno*	ME	*mudde, fen*	Pol.	*błoto*
Rum.	*noroiu*	NE	*mud*	Russ.	*grjaz'*
Ir.	*lathach*	Du.	*modder, slijk*	Skt.	*pañka-, kardama-*
NIr.	*laitheach, draoib*	OHG	*leimo*	Av.	. . . .
W.	*llaid, mwd*	MHG	*quāt, kāt*		
Br.	*fank*	NHG	*schlamm, kot, dreck*		

Although 'mud' is wet earth, none of the common words for 'mud' are connected with those for 'earth'. Several come from the more generic 'dirt, filth', these in part originally 'excrement'. Some are used also for, or are cognate with, others for 'marsh, swamp'. Others are connected with words for 'liquid', 'pour, flow' (through 'flood, inundation' to the resulting 'mud'), 'sink' (what one sinks into), etc. Some are perhaps based on certain color notions. A few are used for both 'mud' and 'clay'.

Where several words are entered for the same language, they may be in part somewhat differentiated in application ('deep mud, mire', 'mud' such as dredged from the bottom of a river, 'mud' in the roads, etc.) or in local preference (cf. NHG *kot, dreck,* etc.).

1. Grk. πηλός, Dor. πᾱλός most commonly potters' and masons' 'clay' (9.73), strictly moistened earth (γῆ ὑγρῷ φυραθεῖσα Plat. Tht. 147c), but also 'mud' (Hdt., Aristoph., etc., and so clearly in NT Jn. 9.6, though rendered as 'clay' in our versions since Wycliff), etym. dub.; perh. (if 'clay' is the earlier sense) : Grk. πολιός 'gray', Lat. *pallēre* 'be pale', etc. Walde-P. 2.53 (1.441). Boisacq 779.

NG λάσπη, orig.? There is no tenable Grk. etymology, and no apparent source for it as a loanword. G. Meyer, Alb. Stud. 4.77 ("unbekannter Herkunft").

2. Lat. *lutum* ('mud', also sometimes 'clay'; > Sp. *lodo* 'mud', It. *loto*, Rum. *lut* 'clay') : Lat. *pol-luere* 'pollute', Grk. λύθρον 'defilement from blood, gore', λῦμα 'dirt', Ir. *loth* 'dirt', etc., root connection dub. Walde-P. 2.406. Ernout-M. 570. Walde-H. 1.840. REW 5189.

Lat. *līmus* (esp. 'river mud') prob. : OHG *leim*, OE *lām* 'clay', and fr. the root seen in Grk. ἀλῑ́νω, Lat. *linere* 'smear'; perh. also (with init. *sl-* beside *l-*) OE *slīm* 'soft mud, slime', etc. Walde-P. 2.389 f. Ernout-M. 552. Walde-H. 1.804 f.

It., Sp. *fango*, OFr. *fanc* (> Br. *fank*), Fr. *fange*, loanword fr. a Gmc. deriv. of the word seen in Goth. *fani*, OE *fen* 'mud' (below, 4). REW 3184a. Wartburg 3.410 ff. Gamillscheg 405.

Fr. *boue*, loanword fr. a Celtic form like W. *baw* 'dirt, filth'. REW 1000. Wartburg 1.302. Gamillscheg 126.

Sp. *barro* 'clay' (9.73), used also for 'mud'.

Sp. *cieno*, fr. Lat. *caenum* 'dirt, filth'. REW 1468.

Rum. *noroiu*, loanword fr. Slavic, cf. late ChSl. *norojĭ* 'onrushing', deriv. of *ri-* in *rijati* 'push, press', *rěka* 'river', etc. Development fr. the 'onrushing stream' to the 'mud' carried along with it. Tiktin 1062.

3. Ir. *lathach*, NIr. *laitheach*, W. *llaid*, beside Corn. *lad* 'liquid', Ir. *laith* 'beer' :

Grk. λάταγες 'drops of wine in the bottom of the cup', Lat. *latex* 'liquid', OHG *letto* 'clay' (NHG *letten*), etc. Walde-P. 2.381. Walde-H 1.770.

NIr. *draoib*, apparently : *drab* 'stain, spot of mud' (fr. NE *drab* or conversely? NED s.v. *drab*, sb.[1]).

W. *mwd*, fr. NE *mud*.

Br. *fank*, fr. OFr. *fanc* (above, 2).

4. Goth. *fani* (renders πηλός Jn. 9.6), OE, ME *fen* ('marsh' and 'mud', latter in Gospels Jn. 9.6, as gloss to Lat. *līmus, lutum,* etc.; cf. NED s.v. 2) = ON *fen*, OHG *fenni*, etc. 'bog, marsh, swamp' : OPruss. *pannean* 'swampland', Skt. *pañka-* 'mud', etc. Walde-P. 2.5. Feist 142.

ON *leir* 'clay' (9.73) also sometimes 'mud' (esp. of riverbank or seashore). So OHG *leimo* (Tat. 132.4 = *lutum* Jn. 9.6), beside *leim* 'clay'.

Dan. *dynd*, Sw. *dy* (ON *dȳ* 'bog', rare), fr. Gmc. **dunja-*, fr. the root seen in ME *damp*, OHG-NHG *dampf* 'vapor, steam', with development through notion of 'wetness' (cf. the current use of NE *damp* as adj.). Walde-P. 1.851. Falk-Torp 170. Hellquist 165.

Sw. *gyttja* (esp. 'deep mud, mire'), fr. the root of *gjuta*, Dan. *gyde*, Goth. *giutan*, etc. 'pour', like OE *gyte* 'pouring, flood'. Hellquist 315.

Dan. *søle* (more common in Norw.) : OE, OHG *sol* 'mud puddle', Goth. *bisauljan*, OE *sylian* 'defile'. Falk-Torp 1233 f.

ME *mudde*, NE *mud*, MLG *mudde*, MLG, Du. *modder* (MLG > Dan., Sw. *mudder*), fr. a root **meu-*, **mu-* and extensions, seen in many words with a common notion of 'wet' or 'dirty', as Grk. μύδος 'damp', μυδάω 'be damp', μύσος (*μυδσος) 'defilement', Pol. *muł* 'slime', Skt. *mūtra-* 'urine', Av. *mūθra-* 'excrement, filth', etc. Here also, fr. a parallel **smu-*, NHG *schmutz* (> Dan. *smuds*, Sw. *smuts*) 'dirt', but also used for 'mud' in the roads. Walde-P. 2.249 ff. Falk-Torp 734.

ME *myre* ('boggy place' and 'mire'), NE *mire*, fr. ON *mȳrr* 'bog'. NED s.v.

Du. *slijk*, MLG *slik* (> NHG *schlick*, used in some regions for 'mud', Kretschmer, Wortgeogr. 614) : OHG-NHG *slich* (now esp. 'crushed ore'), OE *slīcian* 'make smooth', etc. Franck–v. W. 616 f.

MHG *quāt, kāt, kōt*, NHG *kot*, orig. 'excrement' (4.66) and now most familiar in this sense in northern Germany, but 'mud' in southern Germany (so used by Luther Jn. 9.6).

NHG *dreck*, orig. and still in part 'excrement' (4.66), but also the usual word for 'mud' in many regions. On the local distribution of *dreck* vs. *kot* in this sense, cf. Kretschmer, Wortgeogr. 178. In avoidance of these common but ambiguous words there may be preferred either the innocuous *schmutz* 'dirt' or *schlamm* 'mud, slime' (orig.?), this latter being the most frequent dictionary translation of words like NE *mud*, Fr. *boue*, and now the standard term in official use.

5. Lith. *purvas* (used in NT, Jn. 9.6, and still the reg. word for 'mud' in the roads; Lett. *purvs* 'swamp'), etym. dub. Walde-P. 2.14. Mühl-Endz. 3.421.

Lett. *dubl'i* (pl.), beside Lith. *dumblas* 'slime' in river bottom, etc., prob. (cf. Russ. *grjaz'* below) : Lith. *dubus* 'deep', 'hollow', *dubti* 'sink in', Lett. *dubra* 'swamp', etc. Walde-P. 1.848. Mühl.-Endz. 1.509.

6. ChSl. *brĭnĭje* (reg. in older texts for πηλός 'mud'), etym.? Berneker 95.

ChSl. *kalŭ* (Supr. once beside *brĭnĭje*, in general later; cf. Jagić, Entstehungsgesch. 328), Boh. *kal* 'slime, muddy water', etc., prob. : Skt. *kāla-* 'dark blue', Grk. κηλίς 'spot, stain', etc. Walde-P. 1.441. Berneker 476. Trautmann 113 f.

SCr. *blato*, Boh. *bláto*, Pol. *błoto*, these also or in earlier use 'marsh, swamp', like late ChSl. *blato*, Russ. *boloto*, prob. : Lith. *bala* 'marsh, swamp', OE *pōl* 'pool', etc. Berneker 70. Otherwise (: Lith. *baltas* 'white') Walde-P. 2.176, Brückner 31.

Russ. *grjaz'* (cf. Pol. *grąz* 'deep mud, bog') : ChSl. *po-gręznąti, -grązití* 'sink' (10.33). Berneker 350.

7. Skt. *pañka-* : Goth. *fani*, etc. (above, 4).

Skt. *kardama-*, etym. dub. Walde-P. 1.428.

1.215 SAND

Grk.	*ψάμμος, ἄμμος*	Goth.	*malma*	Lith.	*smėlis, smiltis*
NG	*ἄμμος*	ON	*sandr*	Lett.	*smēlis, smilts*
Lat.	*(h)arēna, sabulum*	Dan.	*sand*	ChSl.	*pěsŭkŭ*
It.	*sabbia, rena*	Sw.	*sand*	SCr.	*pijesak*
Fr.	*sable, arène*	OE	*sand*	Boh.	*písek*
Sp.	*arena*	ME	*sand*	Pol.	*piasek*
Rum.	*nisip*	NE	*sand*	Russ.	*pesok*
Ir.	*ganem*	Du.	*zand*	Skt.	*vālukā-, sikatā-*
NIr.	*gaineamh*	OHG	*sant*	Av.	. . . .
W.	*tywod*	MHG	*sant*		
Br.	*traez*	NHG	*sand*		

Words for 'sand', apart from one widespread but difficult group (Grk., Lat., Gmc., Arm.) and some of doubftul origin, come from verbs for 'grind', 'scatter', 'blow', 'whirl', with reference to the small particles of sand or their action in the air (hence some overlapping in cognate groups with words for 'dust'). In a few the (sandy) 'shore' becomes 'sand'.

1. Group of words belonging together, but of partly obscure phonetic relations, prob. (init. doublets *ps-, s-*) fr. the root seen in Grk. ψάω 'rub, crumble', ψῆφος 'pebble', etc. (Skt. *bhas-, psā-* 'chew, devour', fr. 'crush'). Kretschmer, KZ 31.420. Ernout-M. 881.

Grk. ψάμμος, ἄμμος (orig. ἅμμος, cf. ὕφαμμος), Hom. ψάμαθος, ἄμαθος (ἀ- for ἁ- by dissim., hence also ἄμμος); Lat. *sabulum* (> It. *sabbia*, Fr. *sable*); ON *sandr*, OE *sand*, etc. (**samdho-*, nearest to Grk. ἄμαθος), general Gmc. except Goth.; Arm. *awaz*.

2. Lat. *arēna* (> It. *rena*, Fr. *arène*, Sp. *arena*), beside the correct spelling *harēna*, fr. *hasēna* (gl.; cf. also Sabine *fasēna* (Varro), etym.? Ernout-M. 444. Walde-H. 1.634. REW 630.

Rum. *nisip*, fr. Slavic, late ChSl. *nasŭpŭ* 'powder', Slov. *nasip* 'what is scattered' : ChSl. *(na-)sypati* 'strew, scatter' (9.34). Tiktin 1058. Miklosich 334.

3. Ir. *ganem*, NIr. *gainemh*, etym.? Connected by some with Lat. *harēna*, but dub. (cf. Walde-H. 1.634).

W. *tywod* : *tywyn*, Corn. *towan* 'sandy shore, strand' (cf. W. *tywynnog* 'sandy') root connection?

Br. *traez, treaz*, fr. MBr. *traez* 'shore, strand' = W. *traeth*, Ir. *tracht* id. (1.27). Cf. also Corn. *trait* 'harena' (Corn. Voc.) and *traeth* in local names like Pentraeth 'head of the sands'. Loth, Mots lat. 212.

4. Goth. *malma* = ON *mālmr* 'ore, metal', OE *mealm* in *mealmstān* 'malmstone', OHG *melm* 'dust', all fr. the root of Goth. *malan*, Lat. *molere*, etc. 'grind'. Walde-P. 2.285. Feist 343.

5. Lith. *smėlis, smiltis*, Lett. *smēlis*,

smilts, fr. **smel-* beside **mel-* in Lith. *malti*, Goth. *malan*, etc. 'grind'. Walde-P. 2.286.

6. ChSl. *pěsŭkŭ*, etc., general Slavic : Skt. *pāṅsu-, pāṅsuka-*, 'dust' (1.213).

7. Skt. *vālukā-* (mostly in pl.), prob. fr. *val-* 'turn' (: Lat. *volvere* 'turn around', etc.), with reference to the whirling sand. Uhlenbeck 283.

Skt. *sikatā-* (mostly in pl.), prob. fr. *sic-* 'pour out', or perh. more nearly (but not necessarily) : Av. *haēčaya-* 'make dry', *haēčah-* 'dryness, drought'. Walde-P. 2.467.

1.22 MOUNTAIN; HILL

Grk.	*ὄρος; λόφος, κολωνός, βουνός*	Goth.	*fairguni; hlains*	Lith.	*kalnas; kalnelis*
NG	*βουνό; βουνάκι*	ON	*fjall*	Lett.	*kalns; pakalne*
Lat.	*mōns; collis, clīvus*	Dan.	*bjerg, fjeld; bakke*	ChSl.	*gora; chlŭmŭ*
It.	*montagna, monte; collina, colle*	Sw.	*berg* (*fjäll*); *backe*	SCr.	*gora; brijeg, brežuljak* (*hum*)
Fr.	*montagne, mont; colline*	OE	*beorg, dūn, munt; hyll*	Boh.	*hora* (*vrch*); *pahorek, kopec* (*cklum*)
Sp.	*montaña; colina, cerro*	ME	*mount, mountain; hill*	Pol.	*góra; pagórek, wzgórek*
Rum.	*munte; deal, colina*	NE	*mountain* (*mount*); *hill*	Russ.	*gora; cholm*
Ir.	*sliab; telach, cnoc, brī*	Du.	*berg; heuvel*	Skt.	*giri-, parvata-, acala-,* etc.
NIr.	*sliabh; cnoc* (*tulach*)	OHG	*berg; buhil, houc*	Av.	*gairi-, paurvatā, barəzah-,* OPers. *kaufa.*
W.	*mynydd; bryn* (*bre*)	MHG	*berg; bühel, hübel, houc*		
Br.	*menez; krec'h, bre*	NHG	*berg; hügel*		

Words for 'mountain' and 'hill' are taken together because of their frequent relations and the fluctuating discriminations. The application of NE *hill* may range from a height of several thousand feet (cf. NED) to a *hill of beans*, or in some regions a height of only a few hundred feet may be called a *mountain*. The same word may vary in its application as between languages or even in different periods of the same language. Thus Lat. *collis* 'hill', but Lith. *kalnas* 'mountain', dim. *kalnelis* 'hill'; Grk. βουνός 'hill', but NG βουνό 'mountain', dim. βουνάκι 'hill'. Some languages have a great variety of terms for 'hill', from which it is difficult to choose the most important.

The most frequent source, as to be expected, lies in the notion of 'high, rising, projecting', or 'incline, slope' viewed as rising. Other underlying meanings are 'hump, heap, swelling', 'back of the neck, crest', 'knot' (through 'knotty, rugged'), 'heavy, solid, immovable', even 'plain' (through 'high plateau').

The association between a (bare, rugged) 'mountain' and 'rock' shows itself in the frequent relationship between words for 'mountain' and 'rock, stone' (1.44) in which now one, now the other, meaning is the earlier. Again, association between the (wooded) 'mountain' and 'woods, forest' (1.41) shows itself in a similar relationship, a word for 'mountain' coming to mean 'woods' or sometimes conversely.

1. Grk. ὄρος, Ion. οὖρος, Dor. ὦρος, fr. *ὀρσϝος(?) : Skt. *ṛṣva-* 'high', fr. IE **er-* 'move, raise, rise', seen in Skt. *ṛ-*, Grk. ὄρνῡμι, Lat. *orīrī*, etc. Walde-P. 1.137.

Grk. κολωνός : Lat. *collis* (fr. **colnis*), Lith. *kalnas* 'mountain', *kalnelis* 'hill', Lett. *kalns* 'mountain', *pakalne* 'hill', OE *hyll*, ME, NE *hill*. Here also OS, LG *holm* 'hill' (ON *holmr* 'islet in the bay, etc.', OE *holm* 'sea', NE *holm*).

All fr. IE *kel- in Lith. *kelti* 'raise', Lat. *-cellere* 'rise', *celsus* 'high', etc. Walde-P. 1.434. Ernout-M. 204. Walde-H. 1.197, 245.

Grk. λόφος 'nape of the neck, crest' and 'ridge, hill', etym.? Walde-P. 1.93. Boisacq 588 f. For 'hill' from 'neck, crest', cf. also Sp. *cerro*, Ir. *cnoc*, below.

Grk. βουνός 'hill', quoted as Cyrenaic (Hdt. 4.199) and Syracusan (Phryn. 333), but prob. a widespread colloq. word, emerging in Hellenistic writings (Polyb., LXX, NT, etc.). Hence NG τὸ βουνό 'mountain', dim. βουνάκι 'hill'. Prob. to be analyzed as βου-νός : βουβών 'groin', fr. the notion of 'swelling'. Walde 2.114. Boisacq 128 f.

2. Lat. *mōns, montis* (> It. *monte*, etc.), W. *mynydd*, Corn. *meneth*, Br. *menez* 'mountain', Av. *mati-* 'mountain top', fr. the root seen in Lat. *ē-*, *prō-minēre* 'stand out, project' (cf. NE *eminence, prominence* in physical sense), *minae* 'projecting points, threats'. Walde-P. 2.263. Ernout-M. 628 f.

Lat. adj. *montānus*, VLat. **montāneus* (cf. *subterrāneus*, etc.), neut. pl. **montānea* 'mountainous regions, mountain chain', whence It. *montagna*, OFr. *montai(g)ne* (> ME *mountain*), Fr. *montagne*, Sp. *montaña*, which have encroached on the shorter form or even displaced it. Sp. *monte* now 'woods'. REW 5664, 5666.

Lat. *collis*, : Grk. κολωνός, etc., above, 2. Hence It. *colle, collina*, Fr. *colline*, Sp. *colina, collado*, Rum. *colina* (neolog.).

Lat. *clīvus* 'slope, hill' : Goth. *hlains* 'hill', Grk. κλῖτύς 'slope, hillside', fr. IE *klei- 'bend, incline', in Lat. *clīnāre*, Grk. κλῖνω, Skt. *çri-*, NE *lean*, etc. Walde-P. 1.490 ff. Ernout-M. 197 f. Walde-H. 1. 236.

Sp. *cerro* 'hill', also 'back of the neck, spine', fr. Lat. *cirrus* 'tuft of feathers, crest (of birds)'. REW 1949. Other Sp. words for 'hill' are *otero* fr. Lat. *altārium* 'high altar', *poyo* (cf. It. *poggio* 'hill', Fr. *pui* in place names) fr. Lat. *podium* 'balcony'. Cf. Menéndez-Pidal, Orig. del español 425 ff.

Rum. *deal* 'hill', loanword fr. Bulg., SCr.-ChSl. *dělŭ* 'part', through 'boundary'. Tiktin 515. Berneker 195.

3. Ir. *sliab*, NIr. *sliabh* 'mountain' : W. *llyfr* 'heel of a drag', OHG *slīfan* 'slip, glide', etc. (**sleib-* beside **sleidh-* and **sleub-*, Walde-P. 2.391, 707, 710), the development being through 'slope' (cf. NE *slope* fr. pple. of OE *slūpan* 'slip'), hence 'hill' (cf. Lat. *clīvus*, Goth. *hlains*, above), 'mountain'. Thurneysen, Gram. 117. Stokes 319. Pedersen 1.84.

W. *mynydd*, Br. *menez* 'mountain' : Lat. *mōns*, etc., above, 2.

Ir. *telach, tulach* 'hill' (also NIr. in phrases) : Grk. τύλη 'swelling', Lat. *tumulus* 'mound', etc. Walde-P. 1.710.

Ir. *cnoc* 'hill', Br. *krec'h*, OBr. *cnoch* (W. *cnwch* 'boss, knuckle') : ON *hnakki* 'nape of the neck', NE *neck*, etc. Walde-P. 1.390 ff. Pedersen 1.160.

Ir. *brī*, W., Br., Corn. *bre* 'hill' : OE *beorg*, etc. below, 4.

W. *bryn* 'hill' : Ir. *bruinne*, W. *bronn* 'breast', Ir. *brū*, W. *bru* 'belly, womb', NE *breast*, etc. Walde-P. 2.197. Pedersen 1.86, 376.

4. Goth. *fairguni* 'mountain' : OE *firgen* in cpds., as *firgen-gāt* 'mountain goat', and prob. a loanword fr. Celtic **perkunia*, represented by *Hercynia silva* (with regular Celtic loss of initial *p*), this further connected with Lat. *quercus* 'oak'. Relation between 'woods' and '(wooded) mountain', as elsewhere. Walde-P. 2.48. Feist 137 ff.

Goth. *hlains* 'hill' : Lat. *clīvus*, etc., above, 2.

ON *fjall (-fell)*, Dan. *fjeld* 'mountain', Sw. *fjäll* 'high mountain' (ME, NE *fell* fr. ON) : OHG *felis*, NHG *fels* 'rock', Skt. *pāṣāṇa-* 'stone', etc. (1.44). Although the root connection is uncertain, the sense 'rock, stone' is more widely distributed and prob. earlier.' Walde-P. 2.66 f. Falk-Torp 223.

Dan. *bjerg*, Sw. *berg*, OE *beorg* ('mountain, hill' and 'burial mound', in former sense replaced by the Fr. forms, in the latter sense NE *barrow*), OHG, NHG *berg*, etc., the most widespread Gmc. word for 'mountain' (but ON *bjarg* 'rock, precipice'; in Goth. only *bairgahei* = ὀρεινή 'hill country') : Skt. *bṛhant-* 'high, great', Av. *bərəzant-* 'high', *barəzah-* 'height, mountain', Arm. *berj* 'height', Ir. *brī*, acc. *brig*, W., Br. *bre* 'hill'. Walde-P. 2.172 ff. Falk-Torp 77.

OE *dūn* 'mountain, hill' (NE *down*), ODu. *dūna* (> Du. *duin* 'sandhill', Fr., NE *dune*), formerly believed to be a loanword fr. Celtic (Ir. *dūn* 'fortified place'), but this is now generally doubted; perh. fr. the root seen in Skt. *dhū-* 'shake', etc., with development similar to that in Grk. θῖς, θῖνός 'sandbank' (*θϝ-ῑν-). Walde-P. 1.837. Falk-Torp 171. Franck-v. W. 141. NED s.v. *down*, sb.

OE *munt* fr. Lat. *mōns, montis;* ME *mount, mountain* fr. OFr. *mont, montai(g)ne* (above, 2).

OE *hyll*, ME, NE *hill* : Grk. κολωνός, Lat. *collis*, etc. (above, 1).

Dan. *bakke*, Sw. *backe* 'hill' : ON *bakki* 'bank', NE *bank*, etc. (1.33). Walde-P. 2.148.

Du. *heuvel*, MHG *hübel* 'hill' : OHG *hovar*, OE *hofer* 'hump', Lith. *kupra* 'hump'. Here also Av. *kaofa-* 'mountain peak, camel's hump', OPers. *kaufa* 'mountain' (NPers. *kūh* 'mountain') : Lith. *kaupas*, ChSl. *kupŭ*, NE *heap*, NHG *haufe* 'heap', Grk. κῦφός 'bent', all fr. IE **keup-*, **keub-*, **keubh-* in words for 'bend, curve'. Walde-P. 1.372 ff.

OHG, MHG *houc* (gen. *houges*) 'hill' : ON *haugr* 'mound', fr. the adj. seen in Goth. *hauhs*, OHG *hōh*, etc. 'high' (12.31), ultimately connected with the preceding group **keubh-*, etc., above. Walde-P. 1.371. Hence also NHG *hügel* 'hill', by blend with MHG *hübel*. In the same group Dan. *hoj* 'hill' : *hoj* 'high', like NHG *höhe*, NE *height* fr. the respective adj. forms.

OHG *buhil*, MHG *bühel* 'hill' : ON *bōla* 'blister, boss', prob. fr. an extension of IE **bhu-* beside **bu-* in words for 'swell' (cf. Grk. βουνός, above, 1). Walde-P. 2.114, 146.

5. Lith. *kalnas*, etc. : Lat. *collis*, etc., above, 1.

6. ChSl. *gora*, etc., general Slavic for 'mountain' (in some regions 'forest', as always Lith. *gire*, 1.41) : Skt. *giri-*, Av. *gairi-* 'mountain', and prob. Alb. *gur* 'stone'. Walde-P. 1.682. Berneker 329. Further connection with Skt. *guru-*, Grk. βαρύς 'heavy', through the notion of 'heavy, solid mass' (Thumb, IF 9.299) is plausible. Cf. Skt. *acala-* 'mountain' fr. adj. *acala-* 'immovable'.

ChSl. *chlŭmŭ*, SCr. *hum*, Boh. *chlum*, Russ. *cholm*, the most widespread Slavic word for 'hill', is prob. a Gmc. loanword (LG *holm* 'hill', etc., above, 2). So Berneker 410 f., Stender-Petersen 263 ff.; otherwise Brückner, KZ 48.194.

The usual Boh. and Pol. words for 'hill' are dims. of *gora*, as Boh. *pahorek*, Pol. *pagórek, wzgórek*.

SCr. *brdo* 'height' ('mountain' or 'hill'), late ChSl. *brŭdo*, etc., either cognate with or loanword fr. the Gmc. group OHG *bort* 'edge', etc. Walde-P. 2.163. Berneker 118 f. Stender-Petersen 267 f.

SCr. *brijeg* 'height, hill' (dim. *brežuljak*), also 'shore, bank' as general Slavic, ChSl. *brěgŭ*, etc. See 1.27. The meaning 'hill' or 'mountain' also in Bulg., Slov., Slovak. Berneker 49.

Bulg. *planina* 'mountain' (the usual word, *gora* being 'forest'), SCr. *planina*

'high mountain range' : Boh. *planina* 'plain', *planý* 'wild (country)', Lat. *plānus* 'flat', etc. Walde-P. 2.61. Development through 'high plateau'.

Boh. *vrch* 'top, summit' (as ChSl. *vrŭchŭ*, etc. 12.33), used also for 'mountain'.

Boh. *kopec* 'hill', fr. *kopa* 'heap'. Berneker 562.

7. Skt. *giri-*, Av. *gairi-* : ChSl. *gora*, etc., above, 5.

Av. *barəzah-* : OE *beorg*, etc., above, 4.

OPers. *kaufa-* : Du. *heuvel*, etc., above, 4.

Skt. *parvata-* 'mountain, mountain range, rock', Av. *paurvatā-* 'mountain range', fr. adj. Skt. *parvata-* 'knotty, rugged', fr. *parvan-* 'knot'.

Skt. *acala-* 'mountain' fr. adj. *acala-* 'immovable'.

Skt. *çāila-* 'mountain', fr. *çilā-* 'stone, rock'.

1.23 PLAIN, FIELD

Grk.	*πεδίον*	Goth.	*staþs ibns*	Lith.	*lyguma, laukas*
NG	*πεδίον, πεδιάδα, κάμπος*	ON	*slētta*	Lett.	*līdzenums, lauks*
Lat.	*plānum, campus*	Dan.	*slette, mark*	ChSl.	*město ravĭno, polje*
It.	*pianura, campo*	Sw.	*slätt, mark*	SCr.	*ravan, ravnica, polje*
Fr.	*plaine, champ*	OE	*emnet, feld*	Boh.	*ravina, pláň, pole*
Sp.	*llanura, campo*	ME	*plaine, feld*	Pol.	*równina, płaszczyzna, pole*
Rum.	*cîmp*	NE	*plain, field*		
Ir.	*mag, rōi*	Du.	*vlakte, veld*	Russ.	*ravnina, pole*
NIr.	*magh*	OHG	*ebanōti, feld*	Skt.	*sama-, ajra-*
W.	*gwastad, maes*	MHG	*ebene, velt*	Av.	. . . .
Br.	*maez*	NHG	*ebene, fläche, feld*		

Distinctive words for a 'plain' in the strict sense of 'expanse of level ground' are substantive forms of adjectives for 'even, level, flat'. But 'plain' is also included in the scope of, and in some languages more commonly expressed by, words for 'field' in the broad sense of 'open country' (vs. 'field' for cultivation, 8.12; Lat. *campus* vs. *ager*).

1. Grk. πεδίον, NG pop. πεδιάδα (fr. class. πεδιάς, -άδος, adj.), fr. πέδον 'ground' (1.212).

Byz., NG κάμπος, fr. Lat. *campus*.

2. Lat. *plānum* (much less common than *campus;* > Fr. *plaine* > ME *plaine*, NE *plain*), fr. *plānus* 'even, level, flat' (12.71), whence also, with suffix, It. *pianura*, Sp. *llanura*.

Lat *campus* (> Romance words), prob. : Grk. κάμπτω 'bend' (9.14) and first used of a hollow between hills like the Campus Martius, which may be the specific starting-point of its wide use. Cf. Lith. *lanka* 'valley' fr. *lenkti* 'bend' (1.24). Walde-P. 1.350. Walde-H. 1.148 f. Ernout-M. 140 (without etym.).

3. Gall. *-magus* in *Arganto-magus*, etc., Ir. *mag*, NIr. *magh*, W. *maes*, Br. *maez*, prob. as orig. 'expanse' : Lat. *magnus*, Skt. *mah-*, etc. 'large, great' (12.55), Skt. *mahī-* 'earth'. Pedersen 1.96. Stokes 198 f. Walde-P. 2.258 (adversely).

Ir. *rōi*, perh. : Av. *ravah-* 'free room', ChSl. *ravĭnŭ* 'even, level' (see below, 6). Pedersen 1.251. Stokes 235. Walde-P. 2.356 (adversely).

W. *gwastad*, fr. adj. *gwastad* 'even, level, flat' (12.71).

4. Goth. *staþs ibns* (rendering exactly the Grk. τόπος πεδινός 'level place'), OE *emnet* (rare), OHG *ebanōte* (Otfr., where *ebeni* is 'likeness'), MHG, NHG *ebene*, fr. adj. seen in Goth. *ibns*, OE *efen* (*emn*, etc.), OHG *eban*, etc. 'level, even', root connection? Walde-P. 1.102. Feist 287.

ON *slētta*, Dan. *slette*, Sw. *slätt*, fr. adj. seen in ON *slēttr* 'level, even, smooth' = Goth. *slaihts* 'smooth' (15.77). Falk-Torp 1061.

Dan., Sw. *mark* 'field, ground, land' : Goth. *marka* 'boundary', OE *mearc* 'boundary, territory', etc. Falk-Torp 699 f.

OE, OHG *feld*, etc., WGmc. word for 'field' with a wide range of applications (cf. e.g. NED s.v. *field*) : ChSl. *polje*, etc., general Slavic for 'field, plain', both groups fr. a root seen in many other words with the common notion of 'flat, spread out' or the like, including Lat. *plānus* (above, 2). Walde-P. 2.61 ff. Falk-Torp 212.

Du. *vlakte*, NHG *fläche*, fr. adjs. *vlak*, *flach* 'flat' (12.71).

5. Lith. *lyguma*, Lett. *līdzenums*, fr. adjs. Lith. *lygus*, Lett. *līdzens* 'equal' (12.91) and 'even, level'.

Lith. *laukas*, Lett. *lauks*, OPruss. *laucks* 'field' : Skt. *loka-* 'open space', Lat. *lūcus* 'grove', orig. 'clearing' : Lat. *lūx* 'light', etc. Walde-P. 2.408. Ernout-M. 564 f. Mühl.-Endz. 2.426 f.

6. ChSl. *město ravĭno* (rendering τόπος πεδινός 'level place'), SCr. *ravan, ravnica*, Boh. *rovina*, etc., fr. adj. ChSl. *ravĭnŭ*, etc., general Slavic for 'level, even' and 'equal' (12.91).

ChSl. *polje*, etc., general Slavic for 'field', fr. the same root as OE *feld*, etc. (above, 4).

Boh. *pláň* (beside *planý* 'wild, uncultivated') : Lat. *plānus* 'level, flat', etc. Walde-P. 2.61. Miklosich 248.

Pol. *płaszczyzna*, fr. *płaski* 'flat' (12.71).

7. Skt. *sama-*, neut. sb. of adj. *sama-* 'equal' (12.91) also 'even, level'. Also (rarely) *sama-bhūmi-*, *sama-sthalī-*, cpds. with words for 'earth, ground' or 'place'.

Skt. *ajra-* (RV, 'field, plain') : Grk. ἀγρός, Lat. *ager* 'cultivated field' (8.12).

1.24 VALLEY

Grk.	*νάπη, κοιλάς*	Goth.	*dals*	Lith.	*klonis, slėnis (lanka)*
NG	*κοιλάδα*	ON	*dalr*	Lett.	*leja*
Lat.	*vallēs, vallis*	Dan.	*dal*	ChSl.	*(dĭbrĭ)*
It.	*valle*	Sw.	*dal*	SCr.	*dolina, dol*
Fr.	*vallée*	OE	*dæl, denu*	Boh.	*údolí, dolina*
Sp.	*valle*	ME	*dale, dene, valley, vale*	Pol.	*dolina, padół*
Rum.	*vale*	NE	*valley (vale, dale, dell)*	Russ.	*dolina*
Ir.	*glenn*	Du.	*dal*	Skt.	*upatyakā-*
NIr.	*gleann*	OHG	*tal*	Av.	*ją fnu-* (?)
W.	*dyffryn, glyn, cwm*	MHG	*tal*		
Br.	*traonienn, saonenn*	NHG	*tal*		

Words for 'valley' are mostly connected with words applied to curved, hollow shapes, from a common notion of 'bend, curve'. Other sources are 'flat surface', 'low lying', 'slope', 'waterway', 'beneath the mountain'.

1. Group comprising the Gmc. and Slavic words, namely Goth. *dals* (also 'ditch'), ON *dalr*, OE *dæl*, etc., general Gmc. (but NE *dale* now poet. or dial.) and SCr. *dolina*, etc. (ChSl. only advs. *dolě, dolu* 'below, downward'; Boh. *údolí* fr. older *dol* with *u* 'near, at') : Grk. θόλος 'round vaulted building', θάλαμος 'chamber', ON *dalr* 'bow', etc., fr. a common notion of 'bend, curve'.

Walde-P. 1.864 f. Feist 115. Berneker 208 f.

2. Grk. νάπη (also νάπος, τό), etym.? Boisacq 656 f.

Grk. ἄγκος 'mountain glen' : ἀγκύλος 'crooked, curved', Lat. *uncus* 'hook', Skt. *añc-* 'bend', etc. Walde-P. 1.60.

Grk. κοιλάς 'hollow' and 'valley,' NG κοιλάδα : κοῖλος 'hollow' (12.72), which is also used in agreement with place names to denote a valley.

Grk. φάραγξ generally 'ravine' is the usual word for 'valley' in the LXX, and so in NT Lk 3.5 (= Isaiah 40.4), where it is so rendered in the Vulgate and other versions.

3. Lat. *vallēs, vallis* (> Romance forms; deriv. Fr. *vallée* displacing *val*), perh. fr. the root in Lat. *volvere* 'turn, roll', etc. Walde-P. 1.301. Ernout-M. 1071. REW 9134.

4. Ir. *glend, glenn*, NIr. *gleann* (NE *glen* fr. Gael.), W. *glyn* : W. *glan* 'brink, shore', Br. *glann* 'riverbank' (1.27). Pedersen 1.38. Development fr. 'steep slope' through 'ravine' to 'valley'?

W. *dyffryn*, cpd. of *dwfr* 'water' and *hynt* 'way'. Pedersen 1.281.

W. *cwm* (Br. *komb, komm* in place names) : Ir. *cum* 'vessel', Grk. κύμβη 'drinking vessel, boat', Skt. *kumbha-* 'pot', NE *hump*, etc., all with notion of curved shape. Walde-P. 1.376.

Br. *traonienn*, MBr. *tnaou, tnou* 'valley', OW *tnou*, W. *tyno* 'dale, meadow', etym. dub., possibly : Grk. στενός 'narrow', or fr. IE **ten-* 'stretch'. Walde-P. 2.627. Stokes 128. Henry 269. Morris Jones 108.

Br. *saonenn*, etym.? Henry 239.

5. Goth. *dals*, etc., above, 1.

OE *denu*, ME *dene* (NE *dean, dene, -den*, dial. or in local names; NED s.v. *dean*[2].) : OE *denn* 'den, lair', OHG *tenni* 'threshing floor', Lith. *denis* 'deck', Grk. θέναρ 'palm of the hand', 'sole of the foot', all having in common the notion of flat surface. Walde-P. 1.853.

ME, NE *vale, valley*, fr. Fr. *val, vallée* (above, 3).

6. Lith. *klonis* : Lith. *at-si-kalti* 'lean on', ChSl. *kloniti* 'bend, bow', etc. Walde-P. 1.431, 2.599.

Lith. *slėnis* : Lith. *slėnas*, Lett. *slēns* 'low lying', root connection? Leskien, Bildung. d. Nom. 356. Mühl.-Endz. 3.928.

Lith. *lanka* (Kurschat's main word for 'valley', now less common in this sense than the two preceding) : Lith. *lenkti* 'bend', ChSl. *lęką, lęšti* 'bend', *ląka* 'bay, marsh', etc. Walde-P. 2.435. Berneker 739.

Lett. *leja* : Lett. *lejš* 'low lying', Grk. λειμών 'meadow', λίμνη 'lake', Lat. *līmus* 'sidelong, askew', etc. Walde-P. 1.158. Mühl.-Endz. 2.447.

7. SCr. *dolina*, etc., above, 1.

ChSl. *dĭbrĭ* rendering φάραγξ Lk. 3.5, OBoh. *debř* 'valley', etc. : Lith. *dubus* 'deep, hollow' (12.67), *dauba* 'ravine', OPruss. *padaubis* 'valley'. Walde-P. 1.148. Berneker 242 f.

8. Skt. *upatyakā-*, fr. *upa-tya-* 'beneath', hence 'land at the foot of a mountain'.

Av. *jąfnu-* : Av. *jafra-* 'deep'. Only in phrase *jąfnavō raonąm*, 'valleys of the rivers' according to Barth. 608, 1512, while Darmesteter translates 'depths of the vale', taking *ravan-* as the word for 'valley'.

1.25 ISLAND

Grk.	νῆσος	Goth.	. . . .	Lith.	*sala*
NG	νῆσος, νησί	ON	*ey, eyland*	Lett.	*sala*
Lat.	*īnsula*	Dan.	*ø*	ChSl.	*otokŭ, ostrovŭ*
It.	*isola*	Sw.	*ö*	SCr.	*otok, ostrvo*
Fr.	*île*	OE	*īg, īgland, ēaland*	Boh.	*ostrov*
Sp.	*isla*	ME	*iland, isle*	Pol.	*wyspa*
Rum.	*insulă* (*ostrov*)	NE	*island* (*isle*)	Russ.	*ostrov*
Ir.	*inis*	Du.	*eiland*	Skt.	*dvīpa-*
NIr.	*oileān* (*inis*)	OHG	*īsila*	Av.	*dvaēpa-*
W.	*ynys*	MHG	*insel*		
Br.	*enez*	NHG	*insel*		

Words for 'island' reflect its relation to the water, as 'floating', 'water-land', 'flowed around', etc.

1. Grk. νῆσος, Dor. νᾶσος, prob. : νήχω 'swim', Lat. *nāre* 'swim', Skt. *snā-* 'bathe', etc. Walde-P. 2.692. Brugmann, Grd. 2.1.541. Solmsen, Beiträge 244.

2. Lat. *īnsula* (> Romance words, but Rum. *insulă* neolog.), etym. disputed, but perh. best taken as fem. of an adj. **en-salos* 'in the sea' (like Grk. ἐν-άλιος) : *salum* 'sea' (or : *sāl, salis* 'salt', but its use for 'sea' seems to be only poet.). Walde-P. 2.452. Walde-H. 1.707. The view that *īnsula* and Grk. νῆσος belong together, reflecting some Aegean word (Ernout-M. 491; Skok, Glotta 25.217 ff.), has no substantial support.

Rum. *ostrov* (formerly the usual word, but now displaced by *insulă*, except locally), fr. Slavic, ChSl. *ostrovŭ*, etc. (below, 6).

3. Ir. *inis* (NIr. mostly in place names), Gael. *innis*, W. *ynys*, Br. *enez*, fr. a Celtic **inissi*, this perh. (Strachan, quoted by Macbain s.v. *innis*) fr. **eni-sti-* 'standing in' (the water), fr. **stā-* 'stand', like other cpds. in *-sto-* and *-sti-* (Walde-P. 2.604).

NIr. *oileān*, Gael. *eilean*, loanword fr. ON *eyland*. (Disputed by Marstrander, Bidrag 120).

4. ON *ey, eyland*, Dan. *ø*, Sw. *ö*, OE *īg, īgland*, ME *iland*, NE *island* (with spelling influenced by *isle*), Du. *eiland*, also MHG *ouwe* 'water, island' (NHG *aue* 'meadow'), fr. a fem. deriv. (in part + *land*) of the word seen in Goth. *ahwa* 'river', OE *ēa* 'water, river', Lat. *aqua* 'water', etc. Walde-P. 1.34. Similarly OE *ēaland* directly fr. *ēa*.

ME, NE *isle*, fr. OFr. *isle*; OHG *īsila* fr. Lat. *īnsula* in its spoken form, MHG, NHG *insel* with restored *n*.

5. Lith., Lett. *sala* : Lith. *salti* 'flow', *atsala* 'pool of stagnant water', etc. Perh. for **api-sala*, like Lett. *saule* for *pasaule* 'world' in certain phrases, and so 'flowed around' like ChSl. *ostrovŭ*. So Mühl.-Endz. 3.664.

6. ChSl. *otokŭ* (cf. Jagić, Entstehungsgesch. 374), SCr. *otok*, fr. **obu-tokŭ*, cpd. of *obŭ* 'around' and the root of *tešti, teką*, Lith. *tekti* 'flow, run', etc. Walde-P. 1.715 ff. Miklosich 347 f.

ChSl. *ostrovŭ*, etc., general Slavic, fr. **obŭ-strovŭ*, cpd. of *obŭ* 'around' and the root of *struja* 'stream', Grk. ῥέω 'flow', etc. Walde-P. 2.703. Miklosich 318. Brückner 385.

Pol. *wyspa* (which has displaced the older *ostrów* except in place names) = Boh. *výspa* 'sandbank, small island', fr. *vy-* 'out' and the root of ChSl. *sŭpą, suti*, iter. *sypati* 'pour, scatter', hence something 'poured out, shaken out'. Cf. Pol., Russ. *nasyp* 'bank of earth, dam' fr. the same root. Miklosich 334. Brückner 639.

7. Skt. *dvīpa-*, Av. *dvaēpa-*, cpd. of Skt. *dvi-* (Grk. δι-, Lat. *bi-*), Av. *dvaē-* and the weak grade of Skt. *āp-* 'water', hence 'having water on both sides'. Barth. 763.

1.26 MAINLAND

Grk.	ἤπειρος	Goth.	. . . .	Lith.	*sausžemis*
NG	στερεά, στεριά	ON	*meginland*	Lett.	*cietzeme*
Lat.	*continēns*	Dan.	*fastland*	Ch. Sl.	. . . .
It.	*continente* (*terra ferma*)	Sw.	*fastland*	SCr.	*kopno*
Fr.	*continent*	OE	. . . .	Boh.	*pevnina*
Sp.	*continente* (*tierra firme*)	ME	*mayn land*	Pol.	*stały ląd*
Rum.	*continent*	NE	*mainland*	Russ.	*materik*
Ir.	*tīr*	Du.	*vasteland*	Skt.	(*dvīpa-*)
NIr.	*mōirthīr, tīr mōr*	OHG	. . . .	Av.	(*karšvar-*)
W.	*tir mawr*	MHG	. . . .		
Br.	*douar braz*	NHG	*festland*		

Words for 'mainland', as contrasted with 'island', are mostly from the notion of 'great', 'continuous', or 'firm' land, being such adjectives combined with 'land' in phrases or compounds, or used substantively with 'land' understood. Some are simply words for 'land' or 'dry land' used par excellence for the 'mainland'. Several, even of the former group, may also be used in the wider sense of 'land' vs. 'sea'.

Most words for 'continent' are the same as or cognate with those for 'mainland', with much literal or semantic borrowing. Exceptions are NHG *erdteil* (beside *kontinent*) 'part of the earth'. Du. *werelddeel* 'part of the world', W. *cyfandir*, cpd. of *cyfan* 'whole' and *tir* 'land'.

1. Grk. ἤπειρος, Dor. ἄπειρος, Lesb. ἄπερρος, fr. *ἄπερ-ιος, perh. : OE *ōfer* 'shore', NHG *ufer*, etc. Walde-P. 1.47. From the point of view of the islander, the use of 'shore' for 'mainland' would be natural enough. But the chronology of Greek usage makes it probable that this was not the course of development and that the meaning 'shore' of the Gmc. words, if they are cognate, is secondary (cf. 1.27). In Homer ἤπειρος means 'land' vs. 'sea', even applied to an island, though also 'mainland', as prevailingly later. (Hence Ἤπειρος, the 'mainland' from Corcyra.) The word was also used for the 'continents' of Asia and Europe, and (Aristot. de Mundo 392[b]) in general.

NG στερεά, στεριά : στερεός 'firm, solid'.

2. Lat. *continēns, -entis*, pres. pple. of *continēre* 'hold together' in sb. use, lit. the 'continuous' (land). Hence the Romance words, and NE *continent*, which was also formerly used in the sense 'mainland' (NED s.v., 4), and hence specifically for the European mainland as distinguished from the British Isles. Its present application to the grand divisions of the earth's surface is shared by the Romance words, though not to the similar exclusion of the meaning 'mainland'; and it is mainly in this sense that the word has become international.

The Romance words of this group are of lit. origin. The more colloq. expression was orig. the following:

MLat. *terra firma* 'firm land' was also used for 'mainland', and so It. *terra ferma*, Fr. *terre ferme* (now obs. in this sense), Sp. *tierra firme*. This is prob. also the model of NHG *festland*, and the latter again of Lett. *cietzeme*, Boh. *pevnina*, Pol. *stały ląd* (below, 5, 6).

3. Ir. *tīr* '(main)land' (1.21), NIr. *mōirthīr, tīr mōr*, W. *tir mawr*, with Ir. *mōr*, W. *mawr* 'great'. So Br. *douar braz*, fr. *douar* 'land' and *braz* 'great'. (W. *cyfandir*, fr. *cyfan* 'whole' and *tir* 'land', is now rather 'continent').

4. ON *meginland*, cpd. of *megin* 'might', in cpds. 'main'. Similarly and perh. of Norse origin ME *mayn land*, NE *mainland* (NED s.v. *main*, a).

NHG *festland* (earlier NHG always *festes land*, Kluge, Seemannssprache 247 f.), fr. *fest* 'firm' and *land* after the ML. *terra firma* (above, 2). Similarly Du. *vasteland*, Dan., Sw. *fastland*.

5. Lith. *sausžemis*, cpd. of *sausas* 'dry' and *žemė* 'land'.

Lett. *cietzeme*, cpd. of *ciet* 'hard, firm' (: Lith. *kietas* 'hard') and *zeme* 'land', modeled on NHG *festland*.

6. SCr. *kopno*, in earliest use 'bare, dry land' : *kopan* 'without snow', Boh. *kopno* 'unfrozen ground', etc. Berneker 566. Rječnik Akad. s.v.

Boh. *pevnina*, fr. *pevný* 'firm, solid'.

Pol. *stały ląd*, fr. *stały* 'firm, solid' and *ląd* 'land'.

Russ. *materik*, fr. *materoj* 'firm, strong'.

7. Skt. *dvīpa-* 'island' (above, 1.25) is also used for the grand divisions of the earth's surface, pictured as islands surrounded by oceans. It is 'continent' rather than 'mainland' vs. 'island', but other words for 'mainland' (such as given by Apte) seem not to be quotable.

Av. *karšvar-* (: Av. *karša-*, Skt. *karṣū-* 'furrow') is used in the same way as Skt. *dvīpa-*, that is, 'continent'. Barth. 459.

1.27 SHORE

(Shore, Strand, Beach, Coast; Bank)

Grk.	αἰγιαλός, ἀκτή, παραλία; ὄχθη	Goth.	*staþs*	Lith.	*krantas, kraštas, pamaris*
NG	(αἰ)γιαλός, ἀκρογιαλιά, etc.	ON	*strǫnd; bakki*	Lett.	*krasts*
Lat.	*lītus, ōra; rīpa*	Dan.	*strand, bred, kyst*	ChSl.	*brěgŭ, krajĭ*
It.	*lido, spiaggia, riviera, costa, sponda; riva*	Sw.	*strand, kust*	SCr.	*obala, žal, primorje*
Fr.	*rivage, bord, plage, côte; rive*	OE	*strand, waroþ, ōfer*	Boh.	*břeh, pobřeží, pomoří*
Sp.	*ribera, playa, orilla, costa*	ME	*strand, schore, coste; banke*	Pol.	*brzeg, wybrzeże*
Rum.	*mal, țărm, coastă*	NE	*shore, strand, beach, coast; bank*	Russ.	*bereg, vzmor'e*
Ir.	*trāig, tracht, brū, bruach*	Du.	*oever, strand, kust*	Skt.	*tīra-, kūla-, velā-, pāra-*
NIr.	*trāig, bruach*	OHG	*stad*	Av.	(*pāra-*)
W.	*glan, tywyn, traeth, arfordir*	MHG	*stade, gestat, uover*		
Br.	*aod, arvor; glann*	NHG	*ufer, gestade, strand, küste*		

A single general term for land bordering on the water, as comprehensive as NE *shore*, is often lacking; and it is necessary to include in the survey a variety of words that are used with some differentiation, like NE *coast, beach, bank*. Besides more generic terms, some of those listed apply only to the 'coast' of the sea, or to a sandy 'beach', or to the 'bank' of a river. But their applications in the several languages are too diverse and overlapping to be indicated in the list, except that those used distinctively for 'riverbank' are separated by a semicolon.

Only a few of the words are etymologically descriptive, as (land) 'by the sea', 'edge of the sea'. Most of them are words for 'edge', 'end', 'side', 'bank', etc., many of them still used in the general sense as well as specifically for 'edge of the sea', 'bank of the river', etc., others completely specialized in this direction. 'Land' or 'standing place' is the 'shore' from the point of view of those on the water. In a few cases 'stretch of land, tract' has been specialized to 'shore'.

1. Grk. *αἰγιαλός*, the regular Homeric word for 'seashore, beach', distinguished from *ἀκτή* the (precipitous) 'coast', but eventually the commonest word for 'shore' down to the present day (NG pop. *γιαλός*). First part : *αἶγες* 'waves, surf' (Artem., Hesych.), *αἰγίς* 'hurricane', *ἐπαιγίζω* 'rush upon', Skt. *ej-*, *iñg-* 'shake', etc.; further analysis disputed, but perh. second part : *ἅλλομαι* 'spring, leap', hence orig. 'place upon which the waves dash'. Walde-P. 1.11. Bechtel, Lexilogus 16. Kretschmer, Glotta 27.28 f.

Grk. *ἀκτή*, in Homer 'headland' or 'rugged coast', and so generally 'coast', fr. the root of *ἄκρος* 'highest, outermost', *ἀκμή* 'point', Lat. *ācer* 'sharp', etc. Walde-P. 2.28.

Grk. *παραλία* (*γῆ* expressed or understood) 'seacoast, seaboard', fr. *παράλιος* 'by the sea'.

Grk. *ὄχθη* 'bank, dyke', esp. 'riverbank', also *ὄχθος*, NG pop. *ὄχτος*, etym.? Boisacq 735.

NG, beside (*αἰ*)*γιαλός*, also *ἀκρογιαλιά*, *ἀκροθαλασσιά* lit. 'having the shore (or the sea) at the edge'; also *παραγιάλι*, *περιγιάλι*, cpds. of dim. of *γιαλός*, and *παραθαλασσία* fr. adj. *παραθαλάσσιος* 'by the sea'.

2. Lat. *lītus* (> It. *lido*), the most generic term for 'shore', vs. *ōra* 'coast' of the sea, *rīpa* 'bank' of a river, etym. dub., perh.: OHG *līsta*, OE *līste* 'edge, hem'. Rejected by Walde-P. 2.392, 405 and Walde-H. 1.815, but derivation fr. **lei-* 'flow' is without semantic parallel in words for 'shore', and improbable.

Lat. *ōra* 'edge' and 'coast' : OE *ōr* 'beginning', *ōra* 'edge, bank' (esp. in place names, cf. NE *Windsor*, etc.) also Lat. *ōs*, Skt. *ās-*, etc. 'mouth'. Hence deriv. Sp. *orilla* 'edge' and 'shore' (of sea or river). Walde-P. 1.168. Ernout-M. 709, 714. REW 6080.

Lat. *rīpa* 'riverbank' : Grk. *ἐρείπω*, 'throw down', *ἐρείπια* 'ruins', *ἐρίπναι* 'abrupt cliffs', ON *rīfa* 'tear to pieces' (NE *rive*), etc. Development fr. 'thrown down' to 'abrupt, steep' as in Lat. *abruptus* and Grk. *ἐρίπναι*, then specialized to the (steep) 'riverbank'. Hence It. *ripa*, *riva*, Fr. *rive* 'bank' (but Sp. *riba*, Rum. *rîpa* 'slope, embankment', not 'riverbank'), and the derivs., which are used in wider sense of ('bank-territory', hence) 'shore', Fr. *rivage*, *rivière*, It. *riviera*, Sp. *ribera*, etc. Walde-P. 2.345. Ernout-M. 866. REW 7328.

Lat. *costa* 'rib' and 'side' (12.36) > It. *costa*, Fr. *côte* (OFr. *coste*) 'side' and 'coast', Sp. *cuesta* 'slope' but *costa* 'coast', Rum. *coastă* 'rib, side, coast'. OFr. *coste* > ME *coste* 'side' and 'coast', NE *coast;* > Du. *kust*, MLG *kost* > Sw. *kust;* > NHG *küste* > Dan. *kyst.* The Gmc. loanwords, in contrast to the Romance words, are fully specialized to 'coast'. REW 2279. Falk-Torp 612.

Grk. *πλάγια* 'sides' (neut. pl. of *πλάγιος* 'slanting') > MLat. *plagia* 'shore' (fem. sg.), It. *spiaggia*, Fr. *plage*, Sp. *playa.* REW 6564.

It. *sponda* 'side' (of a bed, cart, etc.; fr. Lat. *sponda* 'bedframe, parapet'), hence also 'bank' of a river and even 'shore' of the sea. REW 8170.

Fr. *bord* 'edge, side' and 'bank, shore', loanword fr. Gmc. *bord* 'edge' (12.353), REW 1215.

Rum. *mal*, fr. Alb. *mal* 'mountain' (or its older source), and first applied to a

precipitous bank or coast. Cf. ChSl. *brěgŭ*, below, 6. The meaning 'mountain, hill' appears in Rum. and Hung. place names. Densusianu 1.317, 349 f.

Rum. *ţărm*, fr. Lat. *termen* 'boundary, end'. REW 8665. Titkin 1565.

3. Ir. *trāg*, *trāig* 'shore' as the place where the sea ebbs : Ir. *trāigim*, W. *treio* 'ebb', Lat. *trahere* 'draw', etc. Walde-P. 1.752. Pedersen 1.101.

Ir. *tracht*, W. *traeth*, loanword fr. Lat. *tractus* 'stretch of land, tract'. Vendryes, De hib. voc. 183. Loth, Mots lat. 212.

Ir. *brū*, *bruach* (also and orig. 'edge') : Lith. *briauna* 'edge', prob. also OE *brū* 'brow', etc. Walde-P. 2.196, 207. Pedersen 1.62.

W. *glan* 'side, shore, bank', Br. *glann* 'bank' belong with MBr. *glenn* 'country', Ir. *glenn*, W. *glyn* 'valley' (1.24), but outside connection dub. Possibly : LG, Dan. *klint* 'cliff' (Pedersen 1.38; Celtic forms not included in Walde-P. 1.614), with development fr. 'steep slope' to 'bank' (as in Lat. *rīpa*, above), and through 'ravine, gorge' to 'valley'?

W. *tywyn:* Br. *tevenn* 'cliff', Corn. *towan* 'sandy shore', orig. 'dune, cliff', fr. IE **teu-* 'swell' in Lat. *tumulus* 'mound', etc. (Walde-P. 1.706 ff.). Loth. RC 41.406 ff.

Br. *aod*, OCorn. *als* : Ir. *alt*, W. *allt* 'cliff', all : (or loanwords fr.?) Lat. *altus* 'high'. Pedersen 1.137. Loth, Mots lat. 131.

W. *arfordir*, Br. *arvor* 'coast', fr. *ar* 'on' and *mor* 'sea', like Grk. *παραλία*, Boh. *po-moři* 'coast'.

4. Goth. *staþs* (or *staþ* neut.) OHG *stad*, *stado*, MHG *stade*, *gestat*, NHG *gestade*, beside Goth. *staþs*, OE *stæþ*, OHG *stat*, etc. 'place', two parallel groups of derivs. : Lat. *status*, *statiō*, etc., fr. **stā-* 'stand'. The specialization in the first group is from the point of view of those on the water, 'standing place' to 'shore'. Cf. Goth. (Lk. 5.3) *aftiuhan fairra staþa* = *ἀπὸ τῆς γῆς ἐπαναγαγεῖν* 'put out from land'. Walde-P. 2.605. Weigand-H. 1.707, 2.942.

ON *strǫnd* 'edge' and 'coast', Dan., Sw., OE-NE, Du. *strand* (NHG *strand* fr. LG) : Lat. *sternere*, etc. 'spread out'. Walde-P. 2.638 ff. Franck-v. W. 674. Otherwise Falk-Torp 1177.

ON *bakki* 'riverbank', but also 'bank' in general, as ME *banke* (fr. ON), NE *bank* : OHG *banch*, OE *benc* 'bench,' etc. perh. Skt. *bhañj-* 'break.' NED s.v. *bank*, sb.[1]. Falk-Torp 43. Walde-P. 2.148.

Dan. *bred* 'border, edge' and also 'shore, bank' : OE *brerd* 'brim, margin', OHG *brart* 'edge', etc. Walde-P. 2.133. Falk-Torp 100.

OE *ōfer*, Du. *oever*, MHG *uover* (fr. LG), NHG *ufer*, perh. : Grk. *ἤπειρος* 'land' (vs. sea), then 'mainland', with specialization, again from the point of view of one on the water, of 'land' to 'shore'. See 1.26.

OE *waroþ* : OHG *werid* 'island' (used of land rising above the water in rivers and swamps), OE *wer* 'dam, weir' (NE *weir*), etc. fr. root of OE *werian* 'keep off', NHG *wehren*, etc. Walde-P. 1.282.

ME *schore*, NE *shore*, MLG *schore* (Du. *schor*, esp. 'marshy shore'), fr. the root of OE *sceran* 'cut, shear' (NE *shear*), with semantic development prob. through 'division' (between land and sea). NED s.v. *shore*, sb.[1]. Franck-v. W. 593.

NE *coast*, NHG *küste*, etc., see above, 2.

NE *beach*, of unknown orig., first used of pebbles on the seashore, then, of a pebbly sandy beach, and still so restricted in pop. use though not in geology. NED s.v.

5. Lith. *kraštas*, Lett. *krasts*, 'shore,

bank' but in Lith. also 'edge' and 'country, region', etym.? Mühl.-Endz. 2.260.

Lith. *krantas* (> Lett. dial. *krants*), orig. 'steep bank' (Kurschat), but now the usual word for 'shore' (Lalis, NSB, etc.) : ChSl. **krątŭ*, Russ. *krut* 'steep', Ukr. *kruča* 'steep bank'. Trautmann, KZ 46.265 (against Berneker 628).

Lith. *pamaris*, *pajuris* 'seacoast' lit. 'by the sea', cpds. of words for 'sea', like SCr. *primorje*, etc., Grk. *παραλία*.

6. ChSl. *brěgŭ*, Boh. *břeh* (and *pobřeži*), Pol. *brzeg* (and *wybrzeże*), Russ. *bereg*, etc., the general Slavic word for 'shore, bank', in part also used for 'hill' or 'mountain' (1.22; esp. SCr. *brijeg*, now less common than others for 'shore'). Prob. an early loanword fr. (but some take as cognate with) the Gmc. word for 'mountain' (NHG *berg*, etc.). In either case the development is fr. 'height' to 'riverbank', then 'shore' in general. Stender-Petersen 266 (for loanword, as Berneker 50). Walde-P. 2.173 (for cognate, as Brückner).

ChSl. *krajĭ* (beside *brěgŭ* for *αἰγιαλός*; Jagić, Entstehungsgesch. 328), SCr. *kraj* (also sometimes 'shore', cf. Rječnik Akad. s.v.), generally 'edge, border' (12.353). Berneker 605 f.

SCr. *obala*, fr. *obaliti* 'throw down', cpd. of *ob* and *-valiti*, *valjati* 'turn around' : Lat. *volvere*, etc. The semantic development is fr. 'overturn, throw down', through 'abrupt, steep', as in Lat. *rīpa* (above, 2) and others. Rječnik Akad. s.v.

SCr. *žal*, loanword fr. Alb. *zal* 'gravel, sand', dial. 'shore', this fr. Lat. *sabulum* 'gravel'. So G. Meyer, Alb. Etym. Wtb. 480, comparing for the variation in the sibilant Alb. *šūr*, dial. *žūr*, fr. Lat. *saburra.* Possibly also some influence of Grk. (*αἰ*)-*γιαλός*, which is represented in SCr. by *igalo* and *jalija.*

SCr. *primorje*, Boh. *pomoři*, Russ. *vzmor'e*, etc. 'seacoast', cpds. of word for 'sea', like Lith. *pamaris*, Grk. *παραλία*, etc.

7. Skt. *tīra-*, fr. *tṛ-* 'cross over' (3 sg. *tirati*), IE **ter-* in Lat. *termen* 'boundary', etc. (Walde-P. 1.732 ff.) with development through 'boundary'. Uhlenbeck 113.

Skt. *kūla-* ('slope' in Regveda), etym.? Uhlenbeck 62. Walde-H. 1.305.

Skt. *velā-* 'end, boundary', and esp. 'shore, coast', etym.? Uhlenbeck 297.

Skt. *pāra-* 'end' and 'shore', Av. *pāra-* in cpds., NP *-bār* (*Daryā-bār*, etc.) : Skt. *para-* 'opposite, extreme, etc.', *paras* 'beyond', Grk. *πέρᾱ* 'beyond', etc. Walde-P. 2.32. Barth. 889. Horn 158.

1.31 WATER

Grk.	*ὕδωρ*	Goth.	*watō*	Lith.	*vanduo*
NG	*νερό*	ON	*vatn*	Lett.	*ūdens*
Lat.	*aqua*	Dan.	*vand*	ChSl.	*voda*
It.	*acqua*	Sw.	*vatten*	SCr.	*voda*
Fr.	*eau*	OE	*wæter*	Boh.	*voda*
Sp.	*agua*	ME	*water*	Pol.	*voda*
Rum.	*apă*	NE	*water*	Russ.	*voda*
Ir.	*usce*	Du.	*water*	Skt.	*jala-*, *āp-*, *udan-*, *ambhas-*, etc.
NIr.	*uisce*	OHG	*wazzar*	Av.	*āp-*, OPers. *āpi-*
W.	*dwfr*	MHG	*wazzer*		
Br.	*dour*	NHG	*wasser*		

The words for 'water', with few exceptions, belong to certain widespread groups of cognates, one of these reflecting what was clearly the general IE word for 'water', and three others also reflecting IE words for 'water', but perhaps in some more special application, such as 'running water' or 'rain water'. Many words belonging to these groups appear in other lists, as under 'sea', 'wave', 'river', 'rain'.

1. IE **wedōr*, **wodōr*, **uden-*, a typical *r/n* stem neuter, with gradation of the root syllable, fr. root **wed-* in Skt. *ud-* 'wet, flow'. Some forms with nasal in root syllable (intrusion from verb forms with nasal infix, or anticipation of *n* of stem). Walde-P. 1.252 ff. Ernout-M. 1124.

Grk. *ὕδωρ*; Umbr. *utur* (Lat. *unda* 'wave'); Ir. *usce*, NIr. *uisce* (Gael. *uisgebeatha* 'water of life' > NE *whiskey*); the Gmc. group, Goth. *watō*, OE *wæter*, etc.; Lith. *vanduo*, Lett. *ūdens*, OPruss. *wundan*, *unds;* ChSl. *voda*, etc. general Slavic; Skt. *udan-*; Hitt. *watar*, gen. *wetenas;* Alb. *ujë*.

2. IE **akʷā-* or **ak̂wā-*. Walde-P. 1.34 f. Ernout-M. 64. Walde-H. 1.60. Feist 18 f. Lat. *aqua* with its Romance derivatives. Elsewhere mostly of 'running water' in words for 'river', as Goth. *ahwa*, OE *ēa*, etc. (1.46). Here Hitt. *eku-*, *aku-*, Toch. *yok-* 'drink'?

3. IE **āp-*. Walde-P. 1.46. Skt. *āp-*, *ap-* mostly pl. *āpas*, used esp. of the personified 'Waters', Av. *āp-*, *ap-* the reg. word for 'water', also freq. personified, OPers. *āpi-*, NPers. *āb* 'water'. Elsewhere only of 'running water' in words for 'river', as Lith. *upė*, Lat. *amnis*, Ir. *abann*, etc. (1.46).

4. IE **wer-*. Walde-P. 1.268 f. Skt. *vār-*, *vāri*, 'water' (of all kinds), Toch. A *wär*, B *war* 'water'. Elsewhere in words for 'rain water, rain', as Av. *vār-*, ON *ūr* (1.75), or for 'sea' or 'lake', as Av. *vairi-*, Lith. *jurēs*, etc. (1.32, 1.33). Also Grk. *οὖρον*, Lat. *ūrina* 'urine' (cf. NE *make water*).

5. Miscellaneous:

NG *νερό* fr. *νεαρὸν* (*ὕδωρ*) 'fresh water', through *νηρόν* (cf. Phrynichus *νηρὸν ὕδωρ μὴ εἴπῃς*), with regular change of *ir* to *er* (Hatzidakis, Μεσ. 2.598).

Ir. *dobur* (rare, but cf. *dobur-chū* 'otter', lit. 'water dog'), W. *dwfr*, Br. *dour* (Celt. **dubro-*) : *δύβρις· θάλασσα* Schol. Theocr. (prob. Illyr.), Alb. *det* 'sea', and these : W. *dwfn*, Goth. *diups*, etc. 'deep' (12.67), ChSl. *dŭno* 'bottom', *dĭbrĭ* 'valley', etc. Pedersen 1.35 f. Kretschmer, Glotta 22.216. Pokorny, Z. celt. Ph. 20.513. Otherwise (: Ir. *dub* 'black') Walde-P. 1.840.

Skt. *jala-*, the commonest word for 'water' : *gal-* 'drip', NHG *quelle* 'spring', etc. Walde-P. 1.690 ff.

Skt. *ambhas-* and *ambu-* : Grk. *ὄμβρος*, Lat. *imber* 'rainstorm', Skt. *abhra-* 'cloud, rainy weather', *nabhas-* 'cloud, sky', etc. Walde-P. 1.131.

1.32 SEA

Grk.	*θάλασσα* (*ἅλς, πόντος, πέλαγος*)	Goth.	*marei*	Lith.	*jūra* (*marės*)
NG	*θάλασσα, πέλαγος*	ON	*haf, sær* (*marr*)	Lett.	*jūra*
Lat.	*mare* (*aequor*, etc.)	Dan.	*hav* (*sø*)	ChSl.	*morje*
It.	*mare*	Sw.	*hav* (*sjö*)	SCr.	*more*
Fr.	*mer*	OE	*sǣ* (*mere, hæf*)	Boh.	*moře*
Sp.	*mar*	ME	*see*	Pol.	*morze*
Rum.	*mare*	NE	*sea*	Russ.	*more*
Ir.	*muir, fairrge, ler*	Du.	*zee*	Skt.	*sāgara-, samudra-*, etc.
NIr.	*fairrge, muir, lear*	OHG	*mari, sēo*	Av.	*zrayah-*, OPers. *drayah-*
W.	*mor*	MHG	*mer, sē*		
Br.	*mor*	NHG	*meer, see* (fem.)		

'Sea' is understood here as covering the most general terms applied to large bodies of water and used in such a phrase as 'by land and sea'. But between 'sea' and 'lake' there is no rigid demarcation (either by size, or as salt vs. fresh water), and the same word or related group may serve for either or both, or shift its prevailing application with changed physical conditions. This is notably the case in the Gmc. languages, with the divergent distribution of the groups represented by NE *sea* and NHG *meer*.

Special words for 'ocean' are mostly derived from Grk. *ὠκεανός* and are not considered here.

The words for 'sea' reflect such notions as 'deep', 'level', 'way', 'glistening'(?), 'salt', or simply 'water'.

1. IE **mari* (or **mori*). Walde-P. 2.234. Ernout-M. 592. Walde-H. 2.39 f. Root connection uncertain, but that with Grk. *μαρμαίρω* 'glisten' the most likely. The wide distribution shows the existence of the word in the IE period, but cannot in itself determine whether what was denoted by it in that period was an ocean, or an inland sea like the Euxine or the Caspian, or even a fresh-water lake.

Lat. *mare* (> Romance words); Ir. *muir*, W., Br. *mor;* Goth. *marei*, ON *marr* (poet.), OHG *mari*, MHG *mer*, NHG *meer* (OE *mere* rarely 'sea', surviving in NE *mer-maid*, but mostly 'lake', as also Du. *meer*); Lith. *marės* (now mostly in names of special seas, as the Black Sea, etc.; NSB s.v.), ChSl. *morje*, etc., general Slavic.

2. Grk. *θάλασσα*, the main word at all periods, fr. **θάλα-χ-ι̯α* (cf. *δαλάγχαν· θάλασσαν* Hesych., presumably a Maced. form) or the like : *θάλαμος* 'inner room', *θόλος* 'vaulted room', ChSl. *dolŭ* 'pit', Goth. *dals* 'valley', etc. Transition from 'hollow, deep', to 'sea'. Cf. Lk. 5.4 *εἰς τὸ βάθος*, OE *on dypan* 'into the deep', NE *cross the deep*, and the gloss *δύβρις· θάλασσα* (prob. Illyr.), with Alb. *det* 'sea' : Goth. *diups*, etc. 'deep' (Kretschmer, Glotta 22.216). There is no need to assume, as is generally done, that *θάλασσα* is of pre-Greek origin. Buck, Class. Studies Presented to E. Capps 42 ff.

Grk. *πόντος*, poet. or of a special sea (*πόντος Εὔξεινος, Πόντος*) : Skt. *path-*, nom. *panthās* 'road, way', etc. (10.71). Specialization of 'way' to 'seaway', like *κέλευθος* 'way' in Hom. *ὑγρὰ κέλευθα, ἰχθυόεντα κέλευθα*, etc. Walde-P. 2.26.

Other poetical expressions are *ἅλς* 'salt' used for 'sea'; *πέλαγος* : Lat. *plānus* 'level, flat', etc. (12.71) for the (flat surface of the) open sea.

3. Lat. (beside usual *mare*) poet. *aequor* : *aequus* 'level, flat', and *pontus, pelagus*, loanwords fr. Greek.

4. Ir. *foirrce, fairrge* 'ocean, sea' (rare), NIr. *fairrge* (Gael. *fairge* 'sea', esp. 'stormy sea, surge', Manx *faarkey*), now the common generic word (*muir* prevailing in the name of special seas, as the Irish Sea, etc.) etym. disputed the old comparison with Ir. *ferg* 'anger' and the *ὠκεανὸς Οὐεργιούιος* of Ptolemy is phonetically difficult. Stokes 273. Bergin, Eriu 3.86. Pedersen 2.669 f. Walde-P. 1.289. Perh. best taken as fr. **foirsge* : *fairsiung* 'wide' (12.61). So Thurneysen, Z. celt. Ph. 11.312, Gram. 95.

Ir. *ler* (gen. *lir*), NIr. *lear* also 'flood, surge (of the sea)', W. *llyr* 'flood, sea' (arch.), beside *lliant* 'flood, stream', fr. the root in ChSl. *lĭjati* 'pour', etc. (9.35). Loth, RC 50.70 ff.

5. The Gmc. group, Goth. *saiws* 'lake', ON *sær* (*sjār, sjōr*) 'sea' (Dan. *sø*, Sw. *sjö*, usually 'lake', but also 'sea' in phrases), OE *sǣ*, ME *see*, NE *sea*, Du. *zee* 'sea'. OHG *sēo*, MHG *sē* 'sea' or 'lake', NHG *see* fem. 'sea', masc. 'lake', all fr. a Gmc. **saiwi-*, outside connections wholly doubtful. Walde-P. 2.464. Feist 406 f. Falk-Torp 1232.

ON *haf*, Sw., Dan. *hav*, OE *hæf* (poet. and rare), MLG *haf* (> NHG *haff* in specialized application), is the same word as ON *haf* 'lifting' : Goth. *hafjan*, ON *hefja* 'lift', NE *heave*, etc. Walde-P. 1.343. Falk-Torp 385. Development through the notion of the convex surface of the high sea, or, more likely, that of the lifting, surging, of the waves.

6. Lith. *jūra* or pl. *jūrės*, Lett. *jūra*, OPruss. *jūrin* (acc. sg.) : Skt. *vār-, vāri-* 'water', Av. *vār-* 'rain', *vairi-* 'lake', ON *ver* 'sea' (poet.), OE *wær* 'sea' (rare), ON *ūr* 'fine rain', etc. (1.31). Walde-P. 1.268.

7. Skt. *sāgara-*, with secondary vṛddhi fr. *sa-gara-*, with cop. *sa-* and *gara-* 'drink, swallowing', fr. *gṛ-* 'swallow'. Conception of the sea as swallowing rivers. Walde-P. 1.682.

Skt. *sam-udra-* and *uda-dhi* : *udan-* 'water'.

Skt. *arṇava-* (freq. late term for 'sea', cf. BR s.v.), sb. of *arṇava-* 'flowing, rising', fr. *arṇas-* 'wave, flood, stream', this fr. *ṛ-* 'move'. Uhlenbeck 13.

Av. *zrayah-*, OPers. *drayah-* (NPers. *daryā* 'sea' or 'large river') : Skt. (Vedic) *jrayas-* 'flat surface' (so BR), in which case one would compare the Iranian use with that of Grk. *πέλαγος*, Lat. *aequor* (above), but according to Geldner, Ved. Stud. 2.248 ff., 'onset, onrush, course', fr. *jri-* 'rush upon'. Walde-P. 1.660.

1.33 LAKE

Grk.	*λίμνη*	Goth.	*saiws, mari-saiws*	Lith.	*ežeras*
NG	*λίμνη*	ON	*vatn*	Lett.	*ezers*
Lat.	*lacus*	Dan.	*sø, indsø*	ChSl.	*jezero*
It.	*lago*	Sw	*sjö, insjö*	SCr.	*jezero*
Fr.	*lac*	OE	*mere, sǣ*	Boh.	*jezero*
Sp.	*lago*	ME	*lac*	Pol.	*jezioro*
Rum.	*lac*	NE	*lake*	Russ.	*ozero*
Ir.	*loch* (*lind*)	Du.	*meer*	Skt.	*saras-, hrada-*
NIr.	*loch* (*linn*)	OHG	*sēo, wāc*	Av.	*vairi-*
W.	*llyn*	MHG	*sē*		
Br.	*lenn, loc'h, lagenn*	NHG	*see* (masc.)		

The interchange between 'lake' and 'sea', notably in Germanic, has been discussed under 'sea'. On the other hand, there is no rigid line between 'lake' and 'pond' or 'pool'. Several of the words listed here cover all these, and started from modest beginnings like 'hole, depression', so that 'lake' may be a glorified 'water hole' or 'pond'. NE *pond* (the same word as *pound* for stray animals) was formerly in New England the usual word for 'lake' (the familiar *ponds* of my boyhood are now mostly *lakes*, but still *Toddy Pond*, nine miles long).

A few of the words for 'lake', like some for 'sea', are from 'water', or 'wetness'.

1. Grk. *λίμνη* 'pool' (so in Homer, where also 'sea'), 'marshy lake' (cf. also *Λίμναι* orig. the 'marshlands' in Athens), 'lake' : *λειμών* 'meadow', *λιμήν* 'harbor' or (dial.) 'market place', Lett. *leja* 'valley', all with a common notion of 'depression, lowland', fr. **lei-* 'bend'. Walde-P. 1.158. This is much more probable than derivation fr. **lei-* 'pour, flow' (Walde-P. 2.392), favored by some.

2. Lat. *lacus* 'basin, tank', and 'lake' (> It., Sp. *lago*, Fr., Rum. *lac;* Fr. *lac* > ME *lac*, NE *lake*), Ir. *loch* 'lake, pool', Br. *loc'h, lagenn* 'lake, pool' (OE *lagu*, ON *lǫgr* 'sea, water') : Lat. *lacūna* 'hole, pit', Grk. *λάκκος* 'pit, tank, pond', all prob. fr. a common notion of 'hole, basin'. Walde-P. 2.380. Ernout-M. 517. Walde-H. 1.748. Pedersen 1.361.

3. Ir. *lind*, NIr. *linn*, W. *llyn*, Br. *lenn*, all meaning 'lake, pool, pond' (in Irish mostly 'pool, pond'), fr. **plend* : Grk. *πλαδαρός* 'wet', or fr. **plē-ndh-* : Goth. *flōdus* 'flood', etc. Walde-P. 2.438. Pedersen 1.37.

4. The Gmc. words are mostly those discussed under 'sea'. But ON *vatn*, same as *vatn* 'water'. Dan., Sw., beside *sø, sjö*, also *indsø, insjö*, with prefix *ind-, in-* 'in'. Cf. NHG *binnensee*.

OHG *wāc* 'wave, sea, lake' (usual gl. to Lat. *lacus;* also locally NHG *wog* 'lake', Paul, Deutsches Wtb. s.v. *woge*) : ON *vāgr*, OE *wǣg* 'wave, sea', etc. (1.35).

5. The Balto-Slavic word, Lith *ežeras* (or *ažeras*), OPruss. *assaran*, Lett. *ezers*, ChSl. *jezero*, etc. etym.? Connected with the Greek river name *Ἀχέρων* by Prellwitz, BB 24.106 (cf. also Kretschmer, Glotta 14.98); with ChSl. *jazŭ* 'canal, fishweir', etc. (Berneker 277), Lith. *ežė* 'pool', by Meillet, BSL 29. 1.38 ff.

6. Skt. *saras-* 'lake, pond, pool, tank' (whence Skt. *Sarasvatī-*, name of a river, Av. *Haraxᵛaitī-*, OPers. *Harauvatī-* 'Arachosia') : Grk. *ἕλος* 'marsh', root connection? Walde-P. 2.507.

Skt. *hrada-* 'lake, pool, deep water' (*Gāṅgahrada-* 'water of the Ganges') : *hlād-* 'refresh'. Uhlenbeck 362.

Av. *vairi-* : Skt. *vāri-* 'water', Lith. *jūrės* 'sea', etc. (1.31).

1.34 GULF, BAY

Grk.	*κόλπος*	Goth.	. . . .	Lith.	*įlanka*
NG	*κόλπος*	ON	*fjǫrðr*	Lett.	*jūras līcis*
Lat.	*sinus*	Dan.	*bugt*	ChSl.	. . . .
It.	*golfo, seno, baia*	Sw.	*bukt, vik*	SCr.	*zaliv*
Fr.	*golfe, baie*	OE	*sǣ-earm*	Boh.	*záliv, zátoka*
Sp.	*golfo, seno, bahia*	ME	*goulf, baye*	Pol.	*zatoka*
Rum.	*golf*	NE	*gulf, bay*	Russ.	*zaliv*
Ir.	*cūan*	Du.	*golf*	Skt.	. . . .
NIr.	*cuan*	OHG	*ocrinch*	Av.	. . . .
W.	*morgainc*	MHG	?		
Br.	*plegmor*	NHG	*meerbusen, golf, bai*		

The distinction between the (more inclosed) *gulf* and the (more open) *bay* is a secondary one, which must be ignored here.

The commonest source is that of 'curved shape'. Others are 'harbor', 'branch', 'inlet', or 'inflow' (of the sea).

1. Grk. *κόλπος* 'bosom', 'fold of a garment', and 'gulf, bay' : ON *hvalf*, OE *hwealf* 'vault', NHG *wölben* 'form an arch', etc. Walde-P. 1.474.

Hence, with peculiar change in form, the international word, NE *gulf*, etc., the history of which is as follows (cf. Kretschmer, Byz. Z. 10.581 ff.). Late Lat. *colphus* with spelling *ph*, then pronounced and spelled *colfus* (cf. *τρόπαιον* > Lat. *tropaeum*, late *trophaeum* > Fr. *trophée*, NE *trophy*). This *colfus* > late Grk. *κόλφος*, whence NG pop. *κόρφος* (with *ρ* as in *ἦρθα* = *ἦλθα*; but this form now usual only for 'bosom', not for 'gulf', which is *κόλπος*); also (with *g* for *c* as in late *gummi* for *cummi* = Grk. *κόμμι* 'gum') It. *golfo* (> Fr. *golfe* > ME *goulf*, NE *golf*, NHG *golf*, Rum. *golf*, etc.), Sp. *golfo*.

2. Lat. *sinus* 'curve, fold, bosom' and 'gulf, bay', etym.? Ernout-M. 946.

Hence It., Sp. *seno*, generally 'bosom', etc. (as Fr. *sein*), but also used for a (small) 'gulf, bay', though mostly replaced by *golfo*, etc. (above 1).

MLat. *baia*, Sp. *bahia*, It. *baia*, Fr. *baie* (> ME *baye*, NE *bay*, Du. *baai*, NHG *bai*), orig. dub., perh. loanword fr. some Mediterranean (Iberian?) source. Walde-H. 1.93. REW 882. Wartburg 1.205.

3. Ir. *cūan*, NIr. *cuan* 'harbor' and 'bay' (in Gael. 'ocean') : ON *hǫfn*, 'harbor', NE *haven*, etc., ON *haf* 'sea', etc. (1.32). Walde-P. 1.342 ff.

W. *morgainc*, cpd. of *mor* 'sea' and *cainc* 'branch'.

Br. *plegmor*, cpd. of *plek* 'fold' and *mor* 'sea'.

4. ON *fjǫrðr* (whence NE *firth, frith*), Dan. *fjord*, Sw. *fjärd*, used of the long, narrow arms of the sea characteristic of the Scandinavian coast : OE *ford* 'ford', Lat. *portus* 'harbor', etc. Walde-P. 2.40. Falk-Torp 226.

ON *vīk*, Dan. *vig* 'small inlet', but Sw. *vik* also of a large 'bay' : ON *vīkja*, OE *wīcan*, NHG *weichen* 'fall back, recede', fr. the notion of 'recession, bend'. Falk-Torp 1376.

Dan. *bugt*, Sw. *bukt* (also 'bend') fr. LG *bucht* (whence also Du. *bocht*, ME *boght*, NHG *bucht*) : OE *byht* 'bend', NE *bight*, all fr. the root of Goth. *biugan* 'bend', etc. Falk-Torp 114. Only the Dan., Sw. word is common for 'bay', the others being used in narrower sense, like NE *bight* (cf. *bight of a bay*).

OHG *ocrinch* lit. 'eye-ring' once glosses Lat. *sinus*. Other OHG or MHG words?

NHG *meerbusen*, in 16th cent. also *meerschoss*, both lit. 'sea-bosom'. Cf. Grk. *κόλπος* and Lat. *sinus*.

5. Lith. *įlanka* (NSB s.v.) : *lenkti* 'bend'.

Lett. *jūras līcis*, lit. 'curve of the sea' fr. *līcis* 'curve' : *likt*, Lith. *linkti* 'bend'

6. SCr., Boh., Russ. *zaliv* : *za-liti, za-livati* 'overflow', ChSl. *liti* 'pour'.

Boh., Pol. *zatoka* : *za-teci, za-ciec* 'flow in', ChSl. *tešti, teką* 'flow'. Hence an 'inflow' (of the sea).

1.35 WAVE

Grk.	κῦμα	Goth.	wēgōs (pl.)	Lith.	vilnis, banga
NG	κῦμα	ON	bāra, alda, bylgja,	Lett.	vilnis, banga
Lat.	unda, fluctus		vāgr	ChSl.	vlŭna, valŭ
It.	onda	Dan.	bølge (vove)	SCr.	val, talas
Fr.	rague (flot, onde)	Sw.	våg, bölja	Boh.	vlna
Sp.	ola, onda	OE	wǣg	Pol.	fala (wal)
Rum.	val, talaz (undă)	ME	wawe	Russ.	volna (val)
Ir.	tonn	NE	wave	Skt.	ūrmi-
NIr.	tonn	Du.	baar, golf	Av.	varəmi-
W.	ton, gwaneg	OHG	wella, wāc		
Br.	gwagenn, koumm,	MHG	welle, wāc		
	houlenn	NHG	welle, woge		

Words for 'wave' are from such notions as 'move', 'roll', 'swell', 'flow', 'break', 'roar', rarely from 'water'. They readily develop secondary applications ('waves' of invaders, of light, sound, etc.), which in some cases (Fr. onde, etc.) have almost smothered the original use.

1. Derivs. of IE *wel- 'turn, roll' in Goth. -walwjan, Lat. volvere, etc. (10.15). Walde-P. 1.298 ff.

OHG wella, MHG, NHG welle; Lith., Lett. vilnis; ChSl. vlŭna, valŭ, etc., general Slavic (but Pol. fala, now the usual word, fr. NHG welle); Skt. ūrmi-, Av. varəmi-.

2. Grk. κῦμα, lit. 'swelling' : κυέω 'be pregnant', Skt. çvā- 'swell', etc. Walde-P. 1.365.

3. Lat. unda : Grk. ὕδωρ, Skt. udan-, etc. 'water' (1.31).

Hence, It., Sp. onda, Fr. onde, Rum. unda, of which only It. onda is still the common word for 'wave' of the sea.

Lat. fluctus 'flow, flood', and 'wave' : fluere 'flow'.

Fr. vague, loanword fr. Gmc., ON vāgr, OHG wāc (pl. wāgi), etc. (below, 5).

Fr. flot, OFr. fluet, loanword fr. Gmc., OHG fluot, etc. 'flood, stream' (1.36). Gamillscheg 426.

Sp. ola, fr. Fr. houle 'surge of the sea', this fr. Br. houl 'waves'(?). REW 9673 (p. 808). Celtic orig. doubted by Thurneysen, Keltorom. 69 f.

Rum. val, loanword fr. Slavic, ChSl. valŭ, etc., above, 1.

Rum. talaz 'heavy wave, surge', through Turk. fr. NG θάλασσα 'sea'. See below, 7.

4. Ir., Br. tonn, W. ton : early NHG tünne 'wave', LG dünen 'swell', Lat. tumēre 'swell', Grk. τύλος 'swelling, lump', etc., fr. *teu- 'swell'. Walde-P. 1.708.

W. gwaneg 'wave', formerly more general 'course' (of a wave, wind, snow, also 'gait' or 'aspect' of a person), etym.? (: gwan 'thrust, stab'?).

Br. gwagenn, coll. pl. gwag, fr. Fr. vague. Henry 146.

Br. koumm, variant form of komm 'trough'. Henry 78.

Br. houlenn, coll. pl. houl, orig.?

5. Goth. wēgōs (pl.; sg. wēgs 'tempest, surge'), ON vāgr, Sw. våg (Dan. vove poet.), OE wǣg, OHG wāc (pl. wāgi), NHG woge : Goth. ga-wigan 'move', OE wegan 'carry, move', NHG bewegen 'move', Lat. vehere 'carry', etc. Walde-P. 1.250. Falk-Torp 1338.

NE wave has displaced waw, ME wawe, under the influence of the vb. wave, of different origin but also meaning originally 'move'. NED s.v.

ON bylgja, Dan. bølge, Sw. bölja (NE billow fr. ON), MLG bulge : OHG belgan 'swell', OE belgan 'get angry', belg 'bag, belly, bellows', Ir. bolgaim 'swell', etc. Walde-P. 2.183.

ON alda : OE ealdoþ, aldaht 'trough', etc. Walde-P. 1.82. Falk-Torp 789. Otherwise (: Lat. altus 'high, deep') Persson, Beiträge 15.

ON bāra, MLG bāre, Du. baar, prob. : ON bera, OE, OHG beran 'carry', fr. 'carrying', either through an intermediate 'rising' (cf. OHG burjan, Du. beuren 'raise'), or 'moving' (cf. Goth. wēgōs, etc., above); or : ON berja 'strike'. Walde-P. 2.156. Persson, Beiträge 15. Franck-v. W. 25.

Du. golf, form influenced by golf 'gulf, bay', but fr. MDu. ghelve (also golve), MLG gelve 'wave' : ON gjalfr 'noise of the sea' and 'sea', OE gielpan 'boast' (NE yelp), etc., fr. extension of *ghel- in

OE giellan 'cry out' (NE yell), etc. Walde-P. 1.628. Franck-v. W. 206 f. Specialization of 'noise, roar' to 'noise of the waves', then 'wave'.

OHG wella, etc. above, 1.

6. Lith., Lett. vilnis, above, 1.

Lith., Lett. banga : Skt. bhanga- 'breaking' and sometimes 'wave', bhañj- 'break'. From the 'breaking' (of the waves). Walde-P. 2.149.

7. ChSl. vlŭna, etc., above, 1.

SCr. talas (also Bulg., Alb.; Rum. talaz) fr. Turk. talas 'surge, wave', this fr. NG θάλασσα 'sea' (cf. πολλὴ θάλασσα 'heavy sea').

8. Skt. ūrmi-, Av. varəmi-, above, 1.

1.36 RIVER; STREAM; BROOK

Grk.	ποταμός; ῥεῦμα; χεί-	Goth.	ahwa, flōdus; rinnō	Lith.	upė; sriovė; upelis
	μαρρος	ON	ā; lœkr (bekkr)	Lett.	upe; strāva, upele
NG	ποταμός, ποτάμι; ρεμα;	Dan.	flod; strøm; bæk	ChSl.	rěka; tokŭ, potokŭ
	ρυάκι	Sw.	flod; ström; bäck	SCr.	rijeka; tok, struja;
Lat.	fluvius, flūmen (am-	OE	ēa; strēam; rīþ, brōc		potok
	nis); rīvus	ME	river; stream; broke	Boh.	řeka; potok
It.	fiume; rivo, ruscello,	NE	river; stream; brook	Pol.	rzeka; potok; ruczaj,
	etc.	Du.	rivier; stroom; beek		strumyk
Fr.	fleuve; rivière; ruis-	OHG	fluz, aha; strōm; bah	Russ.	reka; potok; ručej
	seau	MHG	vluz; ström; bach	Skt.	nadī-; sarit-, srotas-;
Sp.	río; arroyo	NHG	fluss; strom; bach		kulyā-
Rum.	fluviu, rîŭ; pîrîŭ			Av.	θraotah-, ravan-, etc.,
Ir.	ab(a); sruth; glais				OPers. rauta-
NIr.	abha; sruth; sruthān				
W.	afon; ffrwd; nant,				
	afonig				
Br.	ster (aven); gouer				

Between the large 'river' emptying into the sea and the tiny 'brook' there are infinite gradations, and often a wealth of words for these, which must be mostly ignored here. But generally there are distinctive words for 'river' and 'brook', and also one for 'stream', used generally for all forms of running water or mainly for those intermediate between the extremes of 'river' and 'brook'.

Words for 'brook' may be diminutives of those for 'river'. Conversely, a word

for 'brook' may be displaced by a diminutive form of it (or otherwise) and itself serve for 'river'.

Most of the words are derived from roots meaning 'flow, run'. Some are cognate with words for 'water', perhaps originally 'flowing water' (cf. 1.31). Some are from verbs for 'rush, plunge', or 'roar', applied first to a rushing, roaring stream.

1. Derivs. of IE *sreu- 'flow' in Grk. ῥέω, Skt. sru-, etc. Walde-P. 2.702 f.

Grk. ῥεῦμα, ῥόος, ῥοή 'stream, current',

ῥύαξ, 'swollen brook' (Thuc. 4.96), NG dim. ρυάκι 'brook', also ρεματιά 'watercourse' (with or without water); Ir. sruaim, sruth 'stream, river' (NIr. 'river' in river names), NIr. srutān 'brook', W. ffrwd 'stream', Br. froud 'torrent' (so Pedersen 1.35; fr. *spru-tu- : OE sprūtan 'sprout', etc. Walde-P. l.c.); ON straumr, OE strēam, OHG strōm, etc. 'stream'; Lith. sr(i)ovė, Lett. strāva, etc., 'stream', Pol. strumień, strumyk 'brook'; Skt. srotas-, sravat-, Av. θraotah- (in cpds.), ravan-, raoδah-, 'stream, river', OPers. rauta 'river' (used of the Nile), NPers. rūd 'river'.

2. Derivs. of IE *rei- in Skt. ri- 'let go', mid. 'flow', Goth. rinnan 'run, flow', etc. Walde-P. 1.139 ff., Ernout-M. 866 f.

Lat. rīvus 'brook'; OE rīþ 'brook' (gl. Lat. rīvus), MLG ride 'brook'; Goth. rinnō 'brook'; ChSl. rěka, etc., general Slavic for 'river'.

From Lat. rīvus (through rīus) come Sp. río 'river' (Olt. rio 'brook' and 'river', OFr. ri 'brook'), Rum. rîŭ 'river' (now fluviu for large rivers like the Danube). Dim. forms for 'rivulet, brook', Lat. rīvolus, It. rivolo, Rum. rîŭleţ, It. ruscello, Fr. ruisseau. REW 7341, 7338a. Gamillscheg 777.

3. From IE *āp (and ab-) 'water', Skt. āpas, etc. (1.31). Walde-P. 1.46. Ernout-M. 45. Walde-H. 1.40.

Lat. amnis 'river' (poet.); Ir. ab (aba, oub, etc.), NIr. abha 'river', W. afon 'river', afonig 'brook', Br. aven 'river' (mostly obs.), Lith. upė, Lett. upe, OPruss. ape 'river', Lith. upelis, Lett. upele 'brook' (but Lett. upe 'river'.

4. Grk. ποταμός (NG pop. ποτάμι), fr. root of πίπτω 'fall', πέτομαι 'fly', Skt. pat- 'fly, fall', etc. That is, ποταμός was at first the 'falling, plunging, rushing' stream. Walde-P. 2.19. Persson, Beiträge 654. Kretschmer, Glotta 27.248 f.

'Brook' would be covered by ῥεῦμα, etc. (above, 1), otherwise by words that commonly denote 'mountain-torrent'. So χαράδρα : χαράσσω 'cut into'; χείμαρρος (but once 'river' in LXX, and 'brook' in NT), Hom. χειμάρρους, χειμάρροος, cpd. of χεῖμα 'cold, winter' and ῥέω 'flow'.

5. Lat. fluvius (> Fr. fleuve; Rum. fluviu neolog.), and flūmen (> It. fiume), both common words for 'river' (fluvius preferred in earlier writers, flūmen in Caesar; Arch. lat. Lex. 7.588), fr. fluere 'flow'. Walde-P. 2.213. Ernout-M. 371. Walde-H. 1.519.

OFr. river, riviere, fr. Lat. rīpāria, deriv. of rīpa 'riverbank' (1.27), was used for 'shore' (like It. riviera, etc.), then also for the stream flowing between the banks. Hence ME, NE river, Du. rivier 'river', while Fr. rivière is used of the smaller river tributary to the fleuve. REW 605.

Sp. arroyo, Port. arroio 'brook', fr. a pre-IE word attested by arrugia 'mine gallery' in Spain (Pliny HN 33.70), Basque arroila 'canal', etc., appropriate to the deep-gullied arroyo of the dry season. REW 678. Bertoldi, BSL 32.122. Wartburg, Entstehung d. rom. Völker 22 f.

Rum. pîrîŭ 'brook', prob. : rîŭ 'river', influenced by Alb. pёrrue 'brook'. G. Meyer, Alb. Etym. Wtb. 335. Spitzer, Mitt. d. rum. Inst. 1.296. Jokl, IF 37.91.

6. Ir. ab, W. afon, etc., above, 3.

Ir. sruth, etc., above, 1.

Br. ster 'river', MBr. staer, fr. *stagro- : Grk. στάζω 'drip', σταγών 'drop', Lat. stagnum 'pool'. Walde-P. 2.612. Pedersen 1.103.

Ir. glais 'brook', perh. : Ir. glass 'green'. Macbain 196 s.v. glaiseach.

Br. gouer, Corn. gover (OCorn. guuer, gl. rivus) 'brook', W. gofer 'overflow, rill', Ir. fobar in place names, cpd. of

go- (= Ir. fo, Grk. ὑπό, etc.) and IE *bher- 'bear' (so Henry s.v.), or better IE *bher- 'gush' in Ir. topur 'spring', etc. (Walde-P. 2.157 ff., but without mention of Br. gouer, etc.). Vendryes, RC 37.306 f.

W. nant 'brook' also 'valley, gorge', OBr. nant 'gorge, brook', Gall. nanto 'valley', fr. IE *nem- 'bend', Skt. nam-, etc. Walde-P. 2.302. Stokes 192. Otherwise (: Grk. νομή 'pasturage', etc.) Benveniste, BSL 32.85. In either case, 'brook' fr. 'valley'.

7. Goth. ahwa, ON ā, OE ēa, OHG aha : Lat. aqua 'water' (1.31).

Goth. flōdus (once for ποταμός) = OE flōd, OHG fluot 'flood' (sometimes also 'river') fr. root of OE flōwan 'flow', etc. (10.32). The use of the corresponding Dan., Sw. flod as 'river' is after that of MLG vlōt (Falk-Torp 239). OHG fluz, MHG vluz, NHG fluss, fr. (extension of the same root in) OHG fliozan 'flow'.

Norw. elf (usual word for 'river'), Sw. älf = ON elfr 'Elbe', prob. : Lat. albus 'white', etc. (cf. Grk. ἀλφός and the river 'Αλφειός). Falk-Torp 188 f. Hellquist 1434.

ON lœkr 'brook' : ON leka 'drip, leak', Du. leken 'leak' (NE leak, loanword), OE (caus.) leccan 'moisten', OE lace, NE dial. lake 'small stream' (cf. NED s.v. lake, sb.³), Ir. legaim 'melt away'. Walde-P. 2.423. Falk-Torp 619.

The most widespread Gmc. word for 'brook', ON bekkr (poet.), Dan. bœk, Sw. bäck, OE bece (rare), ME becc (fr. ON), NE dial. beck, Du. beek, OHG bah, MHG, NHG bach, prob. : Lith. bėgti

'run', etc. Falk-Torp 123. Weigand-H 1.134. Kluge-G. 32. Otherwise Walde-P. 2.187.

OE brōc 'torrent' (gl. Lat. torrens), brook', ME broke, NE brook, in form = OHG bruoh, NHG bruch, Du. broek 'marsh', root connection? Deriv. fr. the root of OE brecan 'break' is most attractive for English (as orig. 'breaking torrent'), but difficult for the other words. NED s.v. brook.

NE dial. burn for 'brook', fr. OE burna 'spring' (1.37).

NE, creek, orig. a 'narrow inlet of the sea', is common for 'small stream, brook' in parts of U.S. and elsewhere. NED s.v. creek, sb.¹ 2 b. (In driving, one notices the change of signs from Creek to Brook.)

8. Baltic words, above, 1 and 3.

9. ChSl. rěka, etc., above, 2.

ChSl. tokŭ 'stream', potokŭ 'brook', SCr. potok 'brook', Pol., Russ. potok 'stream' : tekǫ, tešti 'flow, run' (10.32).

Pol. ruczaj, Russ. ručej 'brook' (Boh. ručej 'torrent') : SCr. ruknuti, ChSl. rykati 'roar', etc., (fr. *reuk-, beside *reug- in Lat. rugīre 'roar', both extensions of *reu- in Skt. ru- 'roar', etc. (Walde-P. 2.349 ff.). Brückner 467.

10. Skt. srotas, Av. θraotah- etc., above, 1.

Skt. nadī- 'river' : nad- 'sound, roar'. Uhlenbeck 142.

Skt. sarit- 'stream, river' : sṛ- 'flow' (10.32).

Skt. kulyā- 'brook, canal,' beside kulya- 'bone', both from the notion of 'hollow' : OE hol, etc. 'hollow' (12.72). Walde-P. 1.332.

1.37 SPRING; WELL

Grk.	*κρήνη, πηγή; φρέαρ*	Goth.	*brunna*	Lith.	*šaltinis, versmė; šulinys*
NG	*βρύση; πηγάδι*	ON	*kelda, brunnr*	Lett.	*avuots; aka, acina*
Lat.	*fōns; puteus*	Dan.	*kilde; brønd*	ChSl.	*istočĭnikŭ; studenĭcĭ, kladęzi*
It.	*fonte, sorgente; pozzo*	Sw.	*källa; brunn*	SCr.	*izvor, vrelo; studenac*
Fr.	*source; puits*	OE	*wella, spryng; pytt*	Boh.	*pramen, zřídlo, zdroj; studně*
Sp.	*fuente; pozo*	ME	*welle, spring*	Pol.	*źródło, zdrój; studnia*
Rum.	*izvor; puţ, fîntînă*	NE	*spring; well*	Russ.	*ključ, rodnik, istočnik; kolodec*
Ir.	*topur*	Du.	*wel, bron; put*	Skt.	*utsa-; avata-, kūpa-*
NIr.	*tobar*	OHG	*brunno, ursprinc; pfuzzi*	Av.	*xān-; čāt-*
W.	*ffynnon, pydew*	MHG	*brunne, sprinc; pfutze*		
Br.	*eienenn, mammenn; puñs*	NHG	*quelle; brunnen*		

The natural 'spring' and the constructed 'well' are taken together because of their close relations. The distinction may be a secondary one, or the application of the same word may shift from one to the other. From 'spring' develops also 'fountain', the artificial jet of water or the structure for it. But words for 'fountain', if different from those for 'spring' or 'well', are not included in the list.

Words for 'spring' are most commonly from verbs for 'flow, gush, boil up, spring', etc. Several are from adjectives for 'cold'. Words for 'spring' readily come to be used for 'source, origin', or even cease to be the usual words for 'spring' (cf. NE *source* vs. Fr. *source*, NHG *ursprung*). Conversely, 'source, origin' is the earlier sense of a few words that are used also for 'spring'.

Words for 'well' are mainly words for 'spring' with extension or shift to 'well', but some are of independent origin, reflecting 'hole, pit' or some feature of the construction.

1. Grk. *φρέαρ* 'well' (**φρῆϝαρ*), Arm. *albiur*, Ir. *topur* (**to-od-bhoro-*), NIr. *tobar* 'spring, well', Goth. *brunna* 'flow, spring', ON *brunnr* 'well', Dan. *brønd* 'well', Sw. *brunn* 'well', OE *burna* 'spring' (renders Lat. *fons* of the Vulgate; but usually 'brook' as NE dial. *burn*), Du. *bron* 'spring, well', OHG *brunno* 'spring', NHG *brunnen* mostly 'well' or 'fountain' : Lat. *fervēre* 'boil', Grk. *φῡ́ρω* 'mix', Skt. *bhur-* 'quiver, stir', etc. (IE **bher-*, **bheru-*, **bhreu-*, etc.). Walde-P. 2.157 ff., 167 ff. Ernout-M. 353.

2. Grk. *κρήνη* 'spring', Dor. *κρᾱ́νᾱ*, Lesb. *κράννᾱ*, fr. **κράσνᾱ* (also *κρουνός*, fr. **κροσνός*); etym.? Walde-P. 1.488 f. Boisacq 515.

Grk. *πηγή*, Dor. *πᾱγά*, Hom. pl. *πηγαί* 'streams', later 'spring, source', etym.? Boisacq 777. In NT also 'well' (Jn. 4.6 = *φρέαρ*, Jn. 4.11, 12). Hence NG *πηγάδι* 'well'.

NG *βρύση* 'spring', fr. late *βρύσις* 'bubbling up' (Suid., Eust.) : *βρύω* 'be full, swell, gush forth'.

3. Lat. *fōns, fontis* 'spring' : Skt. *dhan-, dhanv-* 'run, flow'. Walde-P. 1.852. Ernout-M. 375. Walde-H. 1.525.

Hence It. *fonte*, Sp. *fuente*. Deriv. *fontāna*, whence It. *fontana*, Fr. *fontaine* (> ME, NE *fountain*, formerly used for 'spring'), OSp. *hontana*, Rum. *fîntînă* 'well, fountain'; also W. *ffynon* 'spring, well, fountain', MW *fynhawn*, OCorn. *funten*, Br. *feunteun*. REW 3425, 3426. Pedersen 1.195. Loth, Mots lat. 171 f.

Lat. *puteus* 'well, pit', prob. : *putāre* 'cut, prune', *pavīre* 'strike', etc., that is, a 'cut' in the ground, but thought by some to be a loanword from Etruscan. Walde-P. 2.12. Ernout-M. 827.

Hence It. *pozzo*, Fr. *puits* (> Br. *puñs*), Sp. *pozo*, Rum. *puţ;* also OE *pytt* 'pit, well' ('well' e.g. in gospels Jn. 11.12), Du. *put* 'pit, well', OHG *pfuzzi*, MHG *pfutze* 'well' (NHG *pfütze* 'puddle'); also W. *pydew* 'pit, well, spring'. REW 6877. Weigand-H. 419. Loth, Mots lat. 200.

It. *sorgente*, Fr. *source*, fr. pple. of Lat. *surgere* 'rise', It. *sorgere*, Fr. *sourdre*. REW 8475.

Rum. *izvor* 'spring', loanword fr. Bulg., SCr. *izvor* (below, 7).

4. Ir. and W. words, above, 1, 3.

Br. *eienenn* 'spring', MBr. *eyen* : *eon* 'foam'? Henry 6.

Br. *mammenn* 'source, spring' : MBr. *mamm* 'mother'. Henry, s.v.

5. ON *kelda*, Dan. *kilde*, Sw. *källa* 'spring' : ON *kaldr* 'cold', etc. Falk-Torp 507.

OE *wella* (*wylle*, etc.) 'spring' and 'well', so ME *welle*, but NE *well* normally only in second sense (for 'spring' arch. or dial.), Du. *wel* 'spring' : OE *weallan* 'bubble up', OHG *wella* 'wave', Lat. *volvere* 'turn, roll', etc. Walde-P. 1.302. NED s.v. *well*, sb.

OE *spryng* (rare), ME, NE *spring* (OHG *ursprinc*, MHG *sprinc*, also used for 'spring') : OE *springan* 'move suddenly, spring', etc. NED s.v. *spring*, sb.

NHG *quelle* 'spring' : *quellen* 'flow, gush', Skt. *gal-* 'drip', etc. Walde-P. 1.691.

6. Lith. *šaltinis* 'spring' : *šaltas*, Lett. *salts* 'cold'. Leskien, Bildung d. Nom. 402.

Lith. *versme* 'spring' (Lett. *versme* 'glow, blast of heat') : *virti* 'boil', etc. Walde-P. 1.269.

Lith. *šulinys* 'well' : *šulas* 'post, stave'. Descriptive of the most primitive type of well, that is, a spring dug out and its sides supported by wooden staves. Leskien, Bildung d. Nom. 403.

Lett. *avuots* 'spring' : Skt. *avata-* 'well', *avaṭa-* 'pit', *avani-* 'river, river bed', perh. Grk. *ἄναυρος* 'mountain torrent', Lat. *Avernus*, etc. Walde-P. 1.254. Mühl.-Endz. 1.233. Walde-H. 1.31 f.

Lett. *aka*, dim. *acina* 'well' : Lith. *akas* 'hole cut in the ice', ChSl. *oko* 'eye', Grk. *ὀπή* 'hole', Arm. *akn* 'eye, hole, spring'. Development from 'eye' to 'hole', then 'well'. Cf. NPers. *čašm* 'eye', *čašma* 'spring'. Walde-P. 1.170 ff.

7. ChSl. *istočĭnikŭ* (reg. for *πηγή* in Gospels, Supr. etc.), Russ. *istočnik* 'spring' (now mostly as 'source'), lit. 'outflow', fr. *is-* 'out' and root of ChSl. *teką, tešti* 'flow'.

ChSl. *studenĭcĭ* 'well', so SCr. *studenac*, Boh. *studně*, Pol. *studnia* : ChSl. *studenŭ* 'cold' (15.86). Miklosich 327. Brückner 523.

ChSl. *kladęzi* (v.l. of *studenĭcĭ* in Gospels), Russ. *kolodec* 'well', loanword fr. a Gmc. **kaldinga*, deriv. of *kalds* 'cold', like ON *kelda* 'spring' (above, 5). Berneker 543. Stender-Petersen 277 f.

SCr., Bulg. *izvor* 'spring' (> Rum. *izvor*) : ChSl. *iz-* 'out' and *vĭrěti* 'boil' (10.31). Fr. the same root also SCr. *vrelo* 'spring'. Miklosich 381.

Boh. *pramen* 'spring', also 'jet, stream, strand' : ChSl. *pramenĭ* 'thread', SCr. *pramen* 'tuft of hair', Pol. *promień* 'ray', fr. **por-men-*, deriv. of IE **per-* 'pass through' (Grk. *περάω*, etc.). Development in Bohemian through 'thin stream' to 'spring'. Brückner 438.

Pol. *źródło*, Boh. *zřídlo* 'spring' : Russ. *žerlo* 'opening, crater', Pol. *gardło* 'throat, gullet' (**gor-dlo-*), Lith. *gurklys* 'crop' (of a bird), Lat. *gurges* 'abyss, whirlpool', Grk. *βάραθρον* 'pit', etc. fr. IE **gʷer-* in Skt. *gṛ-* 'swallow', Grk. *βιβρώσκω* 'devour', etc. Development through 'opening' (as in Russ.) to 'spring'. Walde-P. 1.682. Brückner 667.

Pol. *zdrój*, Boh. *zdroj* 'spring', ChSl. *izrojĭ* 'emission of semen', fr. *iz-* 'out' and the root of *rijati* 'flow', *rěka* 'river', etc. (1.36). Miklosich 278. Brückner 650.

Russ. *rodnik* 'spring' : *rod* 'race, birth, origin'. Specialization of 'source' to 'source of water, spring', the opposite of the development in NE *source*.

Russ. *ključ* 'spring' : SCr. *ključ* 'gushing of water', *kljukati* 'stuff, cram', *ključati* 'well up, boil', Pol. *klukać* 'coo, kluck', etc., all of imitative orig., like NE *cluck*. Berneker 529.

8. Skt. *utsa-* 'spring' : *udan-* 'water'. Walde-P. 1.252.

Skt. *avata-* 'well' : Lett. *avuots* 'spring', etc. (above, 6).

Skt. *kūpa-* 'hole, pit, well' (cf. *kūpa-jala-* 'well-water') : Grk. *κύπη* 'hut', *κύπελλον* 'goblet', Lat. *cūpa* 'tub, vat', etc., all fr. the notion of 'bent, hollow'. Walde-P. 1.373.

Av. *xan-* (nom. pl. *xå*) 'spring' : Skt. *khan-* 'dig', *kha-* 'hole, opening', *khā-* or *khan-* (acc. sg. *khām*) 'spring, source'. Walde-P. 1.399. Barth. 531.

Av. *čāt-* 'well', NPers. *čāh* 'well' : Av. *kan-* 'dig', parallel form to Skt. *khan-*, Barth. 583.

1.41 WOODS, FOREST

Grk.	*υλη*	Goth.	....	Lith.	*girė*
NG	*δάσος*	ON	*viðr, mǫrk, skōgr*	Lett.	*mežs, dzir'a*
Lat.	*silva*	Dan.	*skov*	ChSl.	*lěsŭ*
It.	*selva, bosco, foresta*	Sw.	*skog*	SCr.	*šuma*
Fr.	*bois, forêt*	OE	*weald, wudu*	Boh.	*les*
Sp.	*selva, bosque, monte*	ME	*wode, forest*	Pol.	*las*
Rum.	*pădure*	NE	*woods, forest*	Russ.	*les*
Ir.	*caill, fid, fidbad, ross*	Du.	*woud*	Skt.	*vana-, araṇya-, aṭavī-*
NIr.	*coill*	OHG	*wald, holz*	Av.	*razura-*
W.	*coedwig, coed, gwydd*	MHG	*wald, holz*		
Br.	*koad*	NHG	*wald*		

The difference between NE *woods*, the more generic and popular term, and *forest*, applied only to the larger tracts, will be ignored here. To avoid ambiguity, 'woods' (not 'wood' as in *a wood*) will be used in this sense, and 'wood' only in the sense of material.

Where the same word or cognate group covers 'woods' and 'wood' (or sometimes 'tree'), 'woods' is historically the earlier sense.

Words for 'woods' are mostly from notions that were adventitiously associated, such as (wooded) 'mountain', (woodland) 'pasture', 'promontory', 'wild land', once even 'swamp'; often 'boundary' (as formed by woods); rarely 'remote', or 'noisy' (as in a storm).

1. Grk. *ὕλη* 'woods', also 'timber' and 'material', etym. dub. Walde-P. 2.504. Boisacq 1000. Wackernagel, Sprachliche Unters. zu Homer 185.

NG *δάσος* 'woods' (*ὕλη* now 'material'), in class. Grk. 'thicket' : *δασύς*, Lat. *dēnsus* 'thick'. Walde-P. 1.793.

2. Lat. *silva* (> It., Sp *selva*, O.Fr. *seuve*), etym.? Possibly (with *l* fr. *d*, as in *lingua*) : Grk. *ἴδη* 'timber, forest', and as 'wooded hill' the mountains known as *Ἴδη* or *Ἴδᾱ*, all prob. of pre-Greek origin. Solmsen, IF 28.109 ff.

MLat. *boscus* (> It. *bosco*, Fr. *bois*, Sp. *bosque*) was used esp., like Lat. *saltus*, for 'woodland pasture' (cf. *unusquisque liber homo agistet boscum suum in foresta* 'every free man may let out his pasture

land in the forest', etc.; cf. Du Cange s.v. *agistare*). It is now taken by many as a loanword fr. Gmc. (OHG *busc*, NE *bush*, etc.), instead of conversely as formerly. Of other views, the derivation fr. Grk. *βοσκή* 'fodder' with transfer to 'pasture' (cf. CGL 2.258 *βοσκή pastio, pabula, pascua*) is semantically most attractive (so Baist, Z. rom. Ph. 32.426 ff.). REW 1419b. Wartburg 1.453. Kaufmann, Die gallo-romanischen Bezeichungen für den Begriff 'Wald' 44 ff. Rohlfs, Etym. Wtb. der unteritalienischen Gräzitat 350.

MLat. *forestis, foresta*, OFr. *forest* (> It. *foresta*, Sp. *floresta*, ME, NE *forest*, Fr. *forêt;* also OHG *forst*) denoted at first esp. 'forest preserve, game preserve', and so is best derived fr. Lat. *forum* in its legal sense 'court, judgment', that is, as land subject to a ban. Otherwise, as formerly preferred, fr. Lat. *forās, foris* 'outside'. In either case the formation is on the analogy of *agrestis* fr. *ager*, etc. REW 3459. Wartburg 3.708 ff. Kaufmann, op. cit. 26 ff.

Sp. *monte*, orig. 'mountain' (1.22) with development through 'upland woods' to 'woods'. Cf. Lith. *girė*, below, 5.

Rum. *pădure*, fr. Lat. (*palūs*) *palūdem* 'swamp', VLat. *padūlem* (with metathesis; cf. It. *padule*). Cf. Alb. *pyll* 'woods' fr. the same source. REW 6183. G. Meyer. Alb. Etym. Wtb. 360.

3. Ir. *caill*, NIr. *coill* 'woods', W. *celli* 'grove', ON, OE *holt* 'woods, copse', OHG, MHG *holz* 'woods' and 'wood', NHG *holz* 'wood' (as 'woods' arch.), Du. *hout* 'wood' : Grk. *κλάδος* 'branch', ChSl. *klada* 'beam, block', Skt. *kāṣṭha-* 'stick, piece of wood, wood' (Gypsy *karšt, kašt* 'wood'), fr. **keld-d-* 'break off, split'. Walde-P. 1.438 f. Falk-Torp 417. NED s.v. *holt*. According to this connection, the meaning 'piece of wood' would seem to be ultimately the earlier, but in Celtic and Germanic the collective 'woods' is clearly the earlier sense.

Ir. *fid*, (also cpd. *fidbad*, Pedersen 1.14), W. *gwydd* : OE *widu* 'woods, wood', etc. (below, 4).

Ir. *ross* 'promontory' and 'woods' (W. *rhos* 'moor'), fr. **pro-sto-* 'that which stands forth'. Walde-P. 2.604. Stokes 312.

W. *coed* 'woods, wood, trees' (*coeden* 'a tree'), Corn. *cuit, cos* 'woods', Br. *koad* 'woods' and 'wood' : Goth. *haiþi* 'field', OE *hǣþ* 'uncultivated, wasteland', NE *heath*, NHG *heide*, etc., root connection? Walde-P. 1.328. Feist 237.

Hence W. *coedwig* 'woods', a cpd. with *gwig* 'lodge, grove' (fr. Lat. *vīcus* 'village', Pedersen 1.210).

4. ON *viðr* 'woods, wood', Dan., Sw. *ved* 'wood' (mostly 'firewood'), OE *widu, wudu* 'woods, wood', so ME *wode*, NE *wood(s)* OHG *witu* 'wood', Ir. *fid* 'woods, tree, wood' (NIr. *fiodh* esp. in cpds. 'wooded' or 'wooden'), W. *gwydd* 'woods, trees', Br. *gwez* 'trees' prob. : Lat. *dīvidere* 'separate', Skt. *vidhu-* 'solitary', Lith. *vidus* 'inside', etc., with development of 'woods' through 'borderland' (as in ON *mǫrk*, see foll.). Walde-P. 1.314. Falk-Torp 1357.

ON *mǫrk* 'forest', orig. 'borderland' : Goth. *marka*, OHG *marca*, OE *mearc* 'boundary, borderland' (NE *march*), Lat. *margō* 'edge, border'. Walde-P. 2.284. Falk-Torp 700.

ON *skōgr*, Dan. *skov*, Sw. *skog* 'woods' : ON *skaga* 'project', *skagi* 'promontory', OE *sceaga* thicket' (NE *shaw*), ChSl. *skočiti*, iter. *skakati* 'jump', etc., with development fr. 'project, jut out', (wooded) 'promontory'. Walde-P. 2.557. Falk-Torp 1017. Hellquist 940.

OE *weald* 'woods', also 'hill, upland plain' (NE *wold*), Du. *woud*, OHG-NHG *wald* 'woods', ON *vǫllr* 'untilled field',

Sw. *vall* 'pasture', etym. much disputed, but best taken as orig. 'wildland' : Goth. *wilþeis*, OE *wilde* 'wild'. Walde-P. 1.297. Falk-Torp 1391. Kluge-G. 668.

OHG-NHG *holz*, see under Ir. *caill*, above, 3.

5. Lith. *girė*, Lett. *dzir'a* 'woods', OPruss. *garian* 'tree' : ChSl. *gora*, Skt. *giri-*, etc. 'mountain' (1.22).

The development from 'mountain' to 'woods' (whence 'tree' in OPruss.) is complete in Baltic, and also known in Slavic in some regions, as regularly Bulg. *gora*, and frequently SCr. *gora* (Rječnik Akad. 3.271). Cf. Sp. *monte* 'woods', and the dial. use of LG *berg* for 'woods' (Osthoff, Parerga 48), etc.

Lett. *mežs* 'woods', OPruss. *median* 'woods', Lith. *medis* 'tree, wood' : ChSl. *mežda*, Russ. *meža* 'boundary', Lat. *medius*, Skt. *madhya-*, Goth. *midjis* 'mid', with development through 'borderland' as in ON *mǫrk*, etc. Walde-P. 2.261. Mühl.-Endz. 2.611.

6. ChSl. *lěsŭ*, Boh. *les*, Pol. *las*, Russ. *les*, the general Slavic word for 'woods' (but SCr. *lijes* 'timber', etc.), etym.? Berneker 713.

SCr. *šuma*, the usual word for 'woods', back formation fr. *šumiti* 'make a noise', denom. of *šum* 'noise'. Similarly the Transylvanian Saxons are said to use *geräusch* of the 'woods' (Miklosich, Lex. Palaeoslov. s.v. *šumŭ*).

7. Skt. *vana-* 'woods, tree, wood', Av. *vanā-* 'tree', etym.? Walde-P. 1.259.

Skt. *araṇya-* 'wilderness, forest', also 'distant land' : *araṇa-* 'distant'.

Skt. *aṭavī-* 'forest', prob : *aṭ-* 'wander about, roam'. BR s.v. Uhlenbeck 5.

Av. *razura-* 'woods' and 'pit to catch animals' : Av. *razah-*, Skt. *rahas-* 'remoteness, loneliness'. The development assumed by Barth., s.v., namely 'woods' from the trees used to cover the pit, is less likely than 'woods' from 'remoteness', as in Skt. *araṇya-*.

1.42 TREE

Grk.	δένδρον	Goth.	*bagms*	Lith.	*medis*
NG	δένδρον	ON	*trē, baðmr* (poet.)	Lett.	*kuoks*
Lat.	*arbor*	Dan.	*træ*	ChSl.	*drěvo, dąbŭ*
It.	*albero*	Sw.	*träd*	SCr.	*drvo*
Fr.	*arbre*	OE	*trēow, bēam*	Boh.	*strom*
Sp.	*árbol*	ME	*tre*	Pol.	*drzewo*
Rum.	*arbore, copac*	NE	*tree*	Russ.	*derevo*
Ir.	*crann, fid*	Du.	*boom*	Skt.	*vṛkṣa-, vana-, druma-*, etc.
NIr.	*crann*	OHG	*boum*	Av.	*vanā- (varəša-?)*
W.	*coeden, pren*	MHG	*boum*		
Br.	*gwezenn*	NHG	*baum*		

A widespread group of words for 'tree', many of them meaning also 'wood', go back to an IE word which probably denoted a particular kind of tree, namely the oak. Others are from those for 'woods' (1.41); some perhaps from the notion of 'growth'; while several are of obscure origin.

1. IE *dor*u-*, **derwo-*, etc. Walde-P. 1.804 ff. Osthoff, Parerga 169 ff.

Grk. δόρυ 'tree' (rare), 'beam, shaft, spear', δρῦς 'oak'; Ir. *daur* 'oak'; Goth. *triu* 'stick of wood, stave', *weinatriu* 'vine', ON *trē* 'tree, wood', Dan. *træ* 'tree, wood', Sw. *trä* 'wood', *träd* 'tree' (fr. *træ-et*, with def. article; cf. W. *coeden*), OE *trēow*, ME *treo, tre* 'tree, wood', NE *tree* (no longer used for 'wood'); ChSl. *drěvo* 'tree', *druva* (pl.) 'wood', SCr. *drvo* 'tree, wood' (distinguished in pl.), Boh. *dřevo* 'wood', *drevno* 'piece of wood', Pol. *drzewo*, Russ. *derevo* 'tree, wood'; Skt. *dāru-, dru-* 'wood', *druma-* 'tree', Av. *dāuru-* 'piece of wood, club'.

2. Grk. δένδρεον (Hom.), δένδρον (also δένδρος, -εος), perh. fr. *δεν-δρεϝο- (with dissimilated reduplication?) : δόρυ etc. (above, 1). Walde-P. 1.804. For other views, cf. Boisacq 176.

3. Lat. *arbor*, etym. dub., perh. (through a by-form with *dh* beside *d*) : Lat. *arduus* 'high, steep', Ir. *ard* 'high, tall', etc. with development through 'growth' or 'tall' (cf. Boh. *strom*, below, 7). Walde-P. 1.148 ff. Walde-H. 1.62.

Hence It. *albero*, Fr. *arbre*, Sp. *árbol*, Rum. *arbore* (neolog.; early *arbure*; Tiktin 88).

Rum. *copac* (the pop. word) is thought to be a loanword fr. Alb. *kopaç* 'tree trunk', but the ultimate origin is obscure. Tiktin 410. Densusianu 1.356.

4. Ir. *crann* 'tree', W. *pren* 'tree, log', Br. *prenn* 'wood' : Grk. πρῖνος 'holm oak'? Pedersen 1.44. Walde-P. 1.524.

W. *coeden*, sg. of coll. *coed* 'woods, wood, trees' (1.41).

Br. *gwezenn*, sg. of coll. *gwez* 'trees' = Ir. *fid*, W. *gwydd* 'woods' (1.41).

5. Goth. *bagms*, ON *baðmr* (poet.), OE *bēam* ('tree' and 'beam', NE *beam*), Du. *boom*, OHG, MHG *boum*, NHG *baum*, etym. dub. (: Grk. φῦμα 'growth', etc.?). Walde-P. 2.143. Feist 73. Falk-Torp 92.

ON *trē*, OE *trēow*, etc., above, 1.

6. Lith. *medis* 'tree' and 'wood' : Lett. *mežs*, OPruss. *median* 'woods' (1.41).

Lett. *kuoks* 'tree' and 'wood' : Lith. *kuoka* 'stick, cudgel', further connection? Mühl-Endz. 2.343.

7. ChSl. *drěvo*, etc., above, 1.

ChSl. *dąbŭ* (Supr., etc.; in gospels only *drěvo*, cf. Jagić, Entstehungsgesch. 342), orig. 'oak' as general Slavic (8.61). Berneker 216.

Boh. *strom* : *strměti* 'project, tower up', *strmý* 'precipitous', ChSl. *strŭmŭ*, SCr. *strm* 'precipitous'. Miklosich 325, 326. Gebauer 1.60.

8. Skt. *vṛkṣa-* 'tree', Av. *varəša-* 'tree' or 'woods' (? cf. Barth. IF 9.27?, ftn.), etym.? Walde-P. 1.286, 289.

Skt. *taru-*, late and possibly a dial. form belonging with *dāru*. BR s.v. Uhlenbeck 109.

Skt. *pādapa-* 'tree, plant', a poet. expression, lit. 'drinking with the foot, root' (*pāda-* and *pā-* 'drink').

Av. *vanā-* : Skt. *vana-* 'woods, tree, wood' (1.41).

1.43 WOOD

Grk.	ξύλον	Goth.	*triu*	Lith.	*medis*
NG	ξύλον	ON	*trē, viðr*	Lett.	*kuoks*
Lat.	*lignum*	Dan.	*træ, ved*	ChSl.	*drŭva* (pl.)
It.	*legno*	Sw.	*trä, ved*	SCr.	*drvo*
Fr.	*bois*	OE	*trēow, wudu*	Boh.	*dřevo*
Sp.	*madera*	ME	*tre, wode*	Pol.	*drzewo*
Rum.	*lemn*	NE	*wood*	Russ.	*derevo*
Ir.	*fid*	Du.	*hout*	Skt.	*dāru-, kāṣṭha-*
NIr.	*adhmad, fiodh-*	OHG	*holz, witu*	Av.	*dāuru-*
W.	*coed*	MHG	*holz*		
Br.	*koad, prenn*	NHG	*holz*		

Most of the words for 'wood' as material are the same as, or connected with, those for 'woods' or 'tree' (from the standing tree through the felled tree, 'timber, log' to 'wood'), and have been included in the discussion of these (1.41, 1.42).

There remain for notice here.

1. Grk. ξύλον, perh. : Lith. *šulas* 'post', Goth. *sauls*, OE *sȳl* 'pillar', etc., with initial doublets (*k̂s, s*). Walde-P. 2.503 f. Boisacq 679.

2. Lat. *lignum* : *legere* 'collect', hence first used of the collected 'firewood' (cf. NHG *leseholz* 'firewood'), and in actual use most commonly pl. *ligna* 'firewood'. Ernout-M. 549. Walde-H. 1.799.

Hence It. *legno*, OFr. *leigne* (replaced by *bois*), Rum. *lemn*. But Sp. *leño* is 'timber, log' and *leña* 'firewood' (fr. Lat. pl. *ligna*), being replaced in sense of 'wood' as material by *madera* fr. Lat. *māteria* 'material' and especially 'building material, timber'. Cf. the opposite development in Grk. ὕλη 'woods, timber, material', and NE *timber* in the more general sense of 'stuff, material'.

3. NIr. *adhmad* 'timber, wood' (including firewood), also 'matter, stuff', MIr. *admat* 'timber, material' : NIr. *maide* 'stick', Lat. *mālus* 'mast', OE *mæst* 'mast', etc. Walde-P. 2.235. NIr. *fiodh* (Ir. *fid*, 1.41) still used for 'wood' in cpds. and derivs.

1.44 STONE; ROCK

Grk.	λίθος; πέτρα	Goth.	*stains; hallus*	Lith.	*akmuo; uola*
NG	πέτρα, λιθάρι	ON	*steinn*	Lett.	*akmens; klints*
Lat.	*lapis; saxum, petra*	Dan.	*sten; klippe*	ChSl.	*kamy (skala)*
It.	*pietra, sasso; roccia*	Sw.	*sten; klippa*	SCr.	*kamen; strijena*
Fr.	*pierre; roche, rocher*	OE	*stān*	Boh.	*kámen; skála*
Sp.	*piedra; roca*	ME	*stone; rokke*	Pol.	*kamień; skała, opoka*
Rum.	*piatră; stîncă, rocă*	NE	*stone; rock*	Russ.	*kamen'; skala*
Ir.	*cloch, līa; carric, all, craic*	Du.	*steen; rots*	Skt.	*açman-, açan-, çilā-pāṣāṇa*, etc.
NIr.	*cloch; carraig, craig*	OHG	*stein; felis, feliso*	Av.	*asan-, zarštva-*
W.	*carreg, maen; craig*	MHG	*stein; vels, velse*		
Br.	*maen; karreg*	MHG	*stein; fels, felsen*		

Words for 'stone' and 'rock' are given together because of the overlapping usage (the separation by a semicolon in the list is not to be taken too rigidly) and the frequent shift from 'rock' to 'stone'.

While in normal English usage *stone* is the generic term and *rock* applied only to a large mass of stone, *rock* tends to encroach on *stone*, and in U.S. colloquial speech may be used for a stone of any size (as a boy, I picked up a handful of *rocks;* cf. also NED s.v.). So Grk. πέτρα 'rock' became the colloquial word for 'stone' and has displaced the old λίθος, as the borrowed Lat. *petra* likewise displaced the old *lapis*. 'Rock' is always a possible intermediate stage in the development of 'stone', and 'rock' may rest on adventitious association with 'cliff', 'hill', 'mountain' (but in one group conversely 'rock' > 'mountain').

The inherited word, common to Balto-Slavic and Indo-Iranian, is from the root of words for 'sharp, pointed'; and this seems to reflect what was one of the most conspicuous uses of stone in early times, namely as material for tools and weapons. Several of the words are based on the notion of 'solid' (connected with words for 'stiff' or 'stand') or 'hard, rough, rugged'. A few words for 'rock' are from verbs for 'cut' or 'split', with probable development through a steep 'cliff'. But several of the important words are of quite uncertain origin.

1. Grk. λίθος 'stone', NG (λίθος lit.) pop. λιθάρι 'a (large) stone', etym.? Walde-P. 2.379. Boisacq 581.

Grk. πέτρα 'rock', πέτρος 'a stone', NG πέτρα 'stone, rock', etym.? Boisacq 776.

Grk. λᾶας 'stone', also λᾶος, ὁ (mostly poet., but in dial. inscriptions), fr. *λᾶϝος, etc. (cf. λεύω 'to stone'), perh. fr. the root seen in Grk. λύω 'loose', Skt. *lu-* 'cut' (cf. Lat. *saxum*, below). Walde-P. 2.405 f. Boisacq 546 f.

2. Lat. *lapis* 'stone' : Grk. λέπας 'bare rock' (this apparently fr. λέπω 'peel')? Walde-P. 2.431. Ernout-M. 523. Walde-H. 1.761.

Lat. *saxum* 'large stone, rock' (> It. *sasso* 'stone, rock') : *secāre* 'cut', and prob. used first of a sharp cliff. Cf. *rūpēs* 'cliff' : *rumpere* 'break'. Walde-P. 2.474. Ernout-M. 899.

Lat. *petra*, an early loanword fr. Grk. πέτρα 'rock', becoming the pop. word for 'stone', whence the usual Romance words. Ernout-M. 765. REW 6445.

MLat., It. *rocca* 'citadel, lofty fortress', It. *roccia* 'rock', OFr. *roke, rocque* 'castle on a rock' (> ME *rocke* 'rocky cliff', NE *rock*, MDu. *rotse*, Du. *rots*), Fr. *roche* (whence also *roc*), *rocher*, Sp. *roca*, Rum. *rocă*, of unknown origin. REW 7357. NED s.v. *rock*, sb.[1].

Rum. *stîncă* 'rock', loanword fr. Slavic. Cf. SCr. *stanac* 'rock', fr. *stati* 'stand'. Densusianu 1.268.

3. Ir. *cloch* 'stone', W. *clog* 'rock, cliff' (mostly in place names), etym.? Stokes 73 (**klukā-*, fr. same root as Goth. *hallus* 'rock', etc., but ??).

Ir. *līa*, gen. *līach* (Br. *liac'h* 'stone monument'), fr. **lipenk-* or the like, and so perh. : Lat. *lapis* (above, 2). Pedersen 2.100. Loth, RC 44.293 (but doubtful of outside connection).

Ir. *carric*, NIr. *carraig* 'rock', W. *carreg* 'stone', Br. *karreg* 'rock' (cf. also Ir. *carrach* 'scabbed, mangy'), and with this the group Ir. *craic, crec*, NIr. *craig* and *creag*, W. *craig* 'rock' (NE *crag* fr. Gael.), prob. with primary Celtic sense of 'rough, rugged', fr. different extensions of **kar-* in Ir. *crach* 'harsh, rough', Skt. *karkara-*, Goth. *hardus* 'hard', etc. (15.74). Loth, RC 43.401 ff. Walde-H. 1.151.

W. *maen*, Corn. *men*, Br. *maen* 'stone' : NIr. *magen* 'place', Ir. *mag* 'plain, field' (1.23). Pedersen 1.96. Walde-P. 2.258. Development fr. (stony) 'field' to 'stone'?

Ir. *all* 'rock, cliff' : OHG *felis*, below, 4.

4. Goth. *stains*, ON *steinn*, OE *stān*, OHG *stein*, etc., the general Gmc. word for 'stone' and in the earlier periods also 'rock' : Grk. στία 'pebble', στέαρ 'stiff, fat', Skt. *styā-* 'stiffen', ChSl. *stěna* 'wall', SCr. *stijena* 'rock', etc. 'Stone' fr. 'stiff, solid'. Walde-P. 2.610 ff. Feist 447. Falk-Torp 1157.

Goth. *hallus* 'rock' (so only once for πέτρα, which is otherwise rendered, like λίθος, by *stains*), ON *hallr* 'large stone', also 'slope, hill' (cf. adj. *hallr* 'sloping'), OE *heall* 'stone, rock' (rare except in proper names), prob. : Lat. *collis* 'hill', Lith. *kalnas* 'mountain', etc. (1.22), with development through 'cliff'. Feist 241. Otherwise Walde-P. 1.434, 454, Falk-Torp 395, 1480.

Dan. *klippe*, Sw. *klippa* 'rock', fr. NHG *klippe* 'cliff' : ON *klif*, OE *clif*, NE *cliff*, fr. the same root as ON *klifa* 'climb', NHG *kleben* 'stick to', NE *cleave*, etc. Walde-P. 1.620. Falk-Torp 533, 531.

OHG *felis, feliso*, MHG *vels, velse*, NHG *fels, felsen* : ON *fjall* 'mountain', Grk. πέλλα 'stone' (Ulp. ad Dem., Hesych.), Ir. *all* 'rock, cliff', Skt. *pāṣya-, pāṣāṇa-* 'stone', root connection? Walde-P. 2.66 ff. Falk-Torp 223.

5. Lith. *akmuo*, Lett. *akmens* 'stone', ChSl. *kamy* 'stone, rock' (renders both λίθος and πέτρα), SCr. *kamen*, etc. 'stone', Skt. *açman-, açan-*, Av. *asan-* (*asman-* 'sky') 'stone', adj. Av. *asmana-*, OPers. *aθa(n)gaina-* 'of stone', NPers. *sang* 'stone', the general Balto-Slavic and Indo-Iranian word for 'stone', Grk. ἄκμων 'anvil' ('meteoric stone' in Hesiod) : Grk. ἀκμή 'point, edge', ἄκρος 'topmost', Skt. *açri-* 'edge', Lat. *ācer* 'sharp', etc. Walde-P. 1.28 ff.

Lith. *uola* 'rock' (also 'whetstone'), Lett. *uola* 'pebble, egg, rock' : Lett. *velt, velvere* 'roll', Lith. *apvalus*, ON *valr* 'round', etc. (Walde-P. 1.298 ff., without *uola*). Mühl.-Endz. 4.416.

Lett. *klints* 'rock', loanword fr. LG *klint* 'rock, cliff' : ON *klettr* 'rock, cliff',

etc., fr. IE **gel-* in words denoting spherical shape, whence 'protuberance', then 'cliff', 'rock'. Walde-P. 1.614. Mühl.-Endz. 2.229.

SCr. *stijena* 'rock' : ChSl. *stěna* 'wall', Goth. *stains* 'stone', etc., above, 4.

Boh., Russ. *skala*, Pol. *skała* 'rock' (ChSl. *skala* rare) : Lith. *skelti* 'split', ON *skilja* 'separate', etc. Walde-P. 2.594. Brückner 493.

Pol. *opoka* 'rock' = Boh. *opoka, opuka* 'tufa, marl', Russ. *opoka* 'marl', beside SCr. *upeka* 'brick', fr. root of ChSl. *opeka, peští* 'bake'. Miklosich 234. Brückner 380.

6. Skt. *açman-, açan-*, Av. *asan-*, above, 5.

Skt. *çilā-* 'stone, rock' : *çita-* 'sharp', *çā-, çi-* 'sharpen', Lat. *cōs* 'whetstone', ON *hein* 'whetstone', OE *hān* 'stone', ME *honne*, NE *hone* 'whetstone'. Walde-P. 1.454.

Av. *zarštva-* 'stone' : Skt. *hṛṣ-*, Lat. *horrēre* 'be stiff, stick up, bristle'. Cf. Mars. *herna* 'saxa'. Walde-P. 1.610. Development presumably through stones that 'stick up' out of the ground. Walde-P. 1.610. Barth. 1684.

1.51 SKY, HEAVENS

Grk.	οὐρανός	Goth.	himins	Lith.	dangus
NG	οὐρανός	ON	himinn	Lett.	debess
Lat.	caelum	Dan.	himmel	ChSl.	nebo
It.	cielo	Sw.	himmel, sky	SCr.	nebo
Fr.	ciel	OE	heofon	Boh.	nebe, obloha
Sp.	cielo	ME	heven, sky	Pol.	niebo
Rum.	cer	NE	sky, heavens	Russ.	nebo
Ir.	nem	Du.	hemel	Skt.	div-, nabhas-
NIr.	spēir (neamh)	OHG	himil	Av.	asman-, asan- (div-,
W.	wybr, wybren (nef)	MHG	himel		nabah-)
Br.	nenv, oabl	NHG	himmel		

Words for 'sky' often reflect the unsophisticated notion of the sky as a 'covering' or 'vault', the latter in part conceived as a vault of 'stone'. Another frequent source is 'cloud'. There was an IE word for the bright daytime sky, but

only in Sanskrit does this remain a common word for 'sky', elsewhere personified or in the sense of 'god' or 'day'.

For the use of these words as 'heaven', see 22.31.

1. Grk. οὐρανός, Dor. ὡρανός, Lesb.

ὠρανός and ὄρανος. Much disputed, but in spite of some difficulties the derivation fr. IE **wer-* 'cover' is the most probable view. Walde-P. 1.281. Otherwise Wackernagel, Glotta 7.296 (: Skt. *varṣa-* 'rain'), and Schulze-Specht, KZ 66.200 (: Skt. *varṣīyas-* 'higher').

2. Lat. *caelum* (> the Romance words), etym. dub., perh. fr. **kaid-slo-* : ON *heið* 'bright sky', *heiðr*, OHG *heitar*, etc. 'bright'. Walde-P. 2.537. Ernout-M. 430. Walde-H. 1.130.

3. Ir. *nem*, NIr. *neamh* (now mostly 'heaven'), W. *nef* (now 'heaven'), Br. *nenv* (also *env*) : ChSl. *nebo* 'sky', Grk. νέφος 'cloud', etc. (below, 5 and 1.73)? So Rhys, Duvau, RC 22.82, Pedersen 1.255, 387, Walde-P. 1.131, 2.332. But Ir. *nem* with so early *m* for *b* is at variance with the other evidence (*nōib* 'holy', etc., Pedersen 1.387), and the old derivation fr. IE **nem-* 'bend', hence 'vault', is not to be disregarded.

NIr. *spēir*, now the usual word for 'sky', also 'sphere, atmosphere', fr. Lat. *sphaera*, Grk. σφαῖρα 'ball'. 'Sky' conceived as a hollow sphere. Cf. the similar, though now unfamiliar, use of NE *sphere* (NED s.v. 1.1).

W. *wybr, wybren* 'sky', formerly also 'cloud', Br. *oabl* 'sky' (dial. also *ebr*), both orig. 'cloud', like OCorn. *huibren*, Br. *koabrenn*. See 1.73.

4. Goth. *himins*, OE *heofon*, OHG *himil*, etc., the general Gmc. word for 'sky', Gmc. **hemina-, *hemila-* with suffix variation, etym. dub., perh. : Grk. καμάρα 'vault', or as orig. 'covering' : OE *hemeþe* 'shirt', etc. Walde-P. 1.349 ff., 386 ff. Falk-Torp 404 f. Feist 256.

ME, NE *sky*, orig. 'cloud' (both senses in ME), fr. Norse, ON *skȳ*, Dan. *sky* 'cloud', Sw. *sky* 'cloud' and 'sky' (1.73).

Similarly ME *wolke, welken* 'sky', NE *welkin* (in *make the welkin ring*, etc.), orig. 'clouds' : NHG *wolken* 'clouds', etc. (1.73).

5. ChSl. *nebo* (gen. *nebese*), SCr. *nebo*, etc., the general Slavic word, also, with initial *d* fr. the influence of some other word, Lett. *debess* 'sky' sometimes 'cloud', Lith. *debesis* 'cloud' : Skt. *nabhas-* 'moisture, cloud, mist' in Rigveda, later also 'sky', Av. *nabah-* 'sky' (rare), Grk. νέφος 'cloud', Hitt. *nepis* 'sky'. Walde-P. 1.131.

Lith. *dangus*, fr. *dengti* 'cover' (12.26).

Boh. *obloha* : *obložiti* 'cover' (ChSl. *obložiti* 'put around', cpd. of *ob* 'about' and caus. of *legq, ležti* 'lie').

6. Av., OPers. *asman-* 'sky', beside Av. *asan-* 'stone' and 'sky', Skt. *açan-, açman-* 'stone' (Skt. *açman-* also 'cloud'; as 'sky' rare and disputed), all orig. 'stone' (1.44), whence 'sky' as a vault of 'stone'. Cf. Reichelt, IF 32.23 ff. For obscure traces of Grk. ἄκμων = οὐρανός, cf. Bergk, Poet. lyr. graeci 3⁴.68.

Skt. *div-*, nom. *dyāus* 'sky', also personified, also 'day' : Grk. Ζεύς, Lat. *Iuppiter, Iovis, diēs* 'day', *deus* 'god', OE *Tīg*, gen. *Tīwes*, etc. fr. IE **dyeu-*, **deiw-*, extension of **dei-* 'shine'. Walde-P. 1.772 ff. So orig. the 'bright' daytime sky, but except in Skt. (and the rare Av. *div-*) only personified or 'day' or 'god'.

1.52 SUN

Grk.	ἥλιος (dial. ἀϝέλιος, etc.)	Goth.	sauil, sunnō	Lith.	saulė
NG	ἥλιος	ON	sol, sunna	Lett.	saule
Lat.	sōl	Dan.	sol	ChSl.	slŭnĭce
It.	sole	Sw.	sol	SCr.	sunce
Fr.	soleil	OE	sunne, sunna	Boh.	slunce
Sp.	sol	ME	sonne	Pol.	słonice
Rum.	soare	NE	sun	Russ.	solnce
Ir.	grían	Du.	zon	Skt.	suar (Ved.), sūrya-, ravi-, etc.
NIr.	grian	OHG	sunna		
W.	haul	MHG	sunne	Av.	hvara, gen. hūrō and xᵛēng
Br.	heol	NHG	sonne		

Nearly all the usual words for 'sun' belong to a single inherited group.

1. IE **sāwel-*, etc., a group with vowel gradation, parallel *l-* and *n-* forms (the Slavic fr. **sulno-* with added dim. suffix), and variation in gender. Walde-P. 2.446. Ernout-M. 950 f. Falk-Torp 1105. Feist 412, 460. Here belong all the words listed except the following.

2. Ir. *grían*, NIr. *grian*, fr. **greinā*, prob. formed fr. the weak grade of IE **gʷher-* seen in words for 'hot, heat', as NIr. *gor*, NE *warm*, Grk. θερμός, Skt. *gharma-*, etc. This connection is ques-

tioned by Pedersen, KZ 38.197 (Walde-P. 1.688). But cf. esp. Skt. *ghṛṇa-* 'heat' and 'sunshine', and (fr. Skt. *gharma-*) Hind. *ghām* 'sunshine', Gypsy *gam, kʼam* 'sun' (Sampson, Dial. of Gypsies of Wales, 166).

3. Skt. *ravi-*, perh. the commonest class. word for 'sun', Arm. *arev* 'sun' : Skt. *aruṇa-, aruṣa-* 'reddish' (both often applied to the sun), Av. *auruṣa-* 'white'. Walde-P. 2.359. Uhlenbeck 246.

Among other Skt. words for 'sun' are : *bhāna-* fr. *bhā-* 'shine', *bhās-kara*, lit. 'light-making', *dina-kāra-* lit. 'day-making', *arka-* fr. *arc-* 'shine'.

1.53 MOON

Grk.	σελήνη	Goth.	mēna	Lith.	mėnuo, mėnulis
NG	φεγγάρι (σελήνη lit.)	ON	māni (poet.), tungl	Lett.	mēnesis
Lat.	lūna	Dan.	maane	ChSl.	luna, mĕsęcĭ
It.	luna	Sw.	måne	SCr.	mjesic
Fr.	lune	OE	mōna	Boh.	měsíc
Sp.	luna	ME	mone	Pol.	księżyc
Rum.	lună	NE	moon	Russ.	luna
Ir.	ésce (luan)	Du.	maan	Skt.	(mās-), candra-, çaçin-, etc.
NIr.	gealach, rē (ēasca)	OHG	māno		
W.	lleuad, lloer	MHG	māne	Av.	māh-
Br.	loar	NHG	mond		

1. IE **mēnes-, **mēn(n)s-* 'moon' and 'month', presumably fr. **mē-* 'measure'. Walde-P. 2.271 f. Ernout-M. 607 f. Walde-H. 2.71. Berneker 2.51.

Here belong: (1) with the same form in both senses, Lith. *mėnuo*, etc. (but here also with differentiation *mėnulis*

'moon', *mėnesis* 'month', Lett. *mēnesis*, ChSl. *mĕsęcĭ* (but mostly 'month'; *luna* more common for 'moon'), SCr. *mjesic*, Boh. *měsíc*, Skt. *mās-* (as in Rigveda, later mostly 'month', rarely 'moon'), Av. *māh-* (OPers. *māh-* 'month'), NPers. *māh-*, Toch. A *mañ*, or for 'moon' *mañ*

nkāt (*nkāt* 'god, goddess' used as a determinative); (2) with differentiation, all the Gmc. forms, as Goth. *mēna* 'moon', *mēnōþs* 'month', NE *moon, month*, etc.; Toch B *meṃ* 'moon' *meñe* 'month' (so Benveniste, Festschrift Hirt. 2.234, but S. Levi, Fragments Koutsch. 1.121 gives 'lune' for both forms).

Elsewhere, namely in Greek, Italic, Celtic, Albanian, Armenian, and in some of the Slavic languages, the words of this group have persisted only in the sense of 'month' (Grk. μήν, Lat. *mēnsis*, Ir. *mī*, etc.; 14.61) and have been displaced in the sense of 'moon' by other words, most of them from the notion of 'brightness' as follows.

2. Grk. σελήνη, Dor. σελάνα, Lesb. σελάννα : σέλας 'light, brightness' (of fire or the heavenly bodies). Walde-P. 2.531. Boisacq 858.

NG φεγγάρι, dim. of Grk. φέγγος 'light, splendor' (of daylight or moonlight).

3. Lat. *lūna*, fr. **leuksnā-* (cf. Praen. *losna*) : Lat. *lūx, lūmen* 'light', Grk. λευκός 'bright', Av. *raoxšnā-* 'light', OPruss. *lauxnos* 'stars', etc. Here also as 'moon', ChSl., Russ. *luna*, Arm. *lusin*, Ir. *luan*, (poet.; Thurneysen, Z. deutsch. Wortf. 1.189) and, fr. a parallel form of

the root, W. *lleuad, lloer*, Br. *loar*? Walde-P. 2.408 ff. Ernout-M. 570 ff.

From Lat. *lūna* come It., Sp. *luna*, Fr. *lune*, and Rum. *lună*, the last both 'moon' and 'month', because of the double sense of Slavic *mĕsęcĭ*.

4. Ir. *ésce*, NIr. *ēasca* : Osc. *eiduis*, Lat. *īdus* 'ides'? Walde-P. 1.103.

NIr. *gealach* 'moon' also 'light, brightness', fr. *geal* 'bright, white' (15.57).

Ir. *rē* 'period of time', NIr. also esp. 'moon' : Av. *ravah-* 'space, room', etc.(?). Vendryes, RC 28.141.

5. ON *tungl*, replacing *māni* in prose, beside *himun-tungl* 'heavenly body' : Goth. *tuggl*, OE *tungol* 'heavenly body', root connection? Walde-P. 1.792. Feist 481 f.

6. Pol. *księżyc*, displacing *miesiąc* in the sense of 'moon', dim. of *ksiądz* in its older meaning 'prince' (19.35). As the sun was the lord of the day, the moon of the night, the latter was the lesser 'prince'. Brückner 277.

7. Skt. *candra-*, also (combined with *mās-*) *candramas-* 'bright', (*ç*)*candra-* 'shine', Lat. *candēre* 'shine', Alb. *hānë* 'moon', etc. Walde-P. 1.352.

Skt. *çaçin-*, fr. *çaça-* 'hare', after the supposed resemblance of the markings on the moon.

1.54 STAR

Grk.	ἀστήρ, ἄστρον	Goth.	stairnō	Lith.	žvaigždė
NG	ἄστρο, ἀστέρι	ON	stjarna	Lett.	zvaigzne
Lat.	stēlla, astrum	Dan.	stjerne	ChSl.	zvězda
It.	stella	Sw.	stjärna	SCr.	zvijesda
Fr.	étoile	OE	steorra	Boh.	hvězda
Sp.	estrella	ME	sterre	Pol.	gwiazda
Rum.	stea	NE	star	Russ.	zvezda
Ir.	rétglu, rind	Du.	ster	Skt.	star-, tā ā-
NIr.	réalt	OHG	sterro, sterno	Av.	star-
W.	seren	MHG	stërne		
Br.	steredenn	NHG	stern		

1. IE *ster-, orig. disputed. The old deriv. fr. IE *ster- 'spread out', as first in pl. 'the scattered ones' = 'stars', may seem colorless, but no more so than, e.g. that of several words for 'moon' fr. 'light, brightness' (1.53). Walde-P. 2.635 f. (with refs.). Or (to me less likely) old IE (!) loanword fr. Akkad. *istar* 'Venus'. Ipsen, IF 41.179 ff. Feist 448 (with refs.; add Wackernagel-Debrunner, KZ 67.161 fr.).

Grk. ἀστήρ, ἄστρον, NG ἀστέρι fr. dim. form; Lat. *stēlla* (fr. **stēr-lā;* otherwise Ernout-M.) and *astrum* (fr. Grk. ἄστρον), It. *stella*, Fr. *étoile*, Rum. *stea*, fr. *stēlla*, but Sp. *estrella* by mixture with *astrum;* W. *seren*, Br. *sterenn, steredenn;* Goth. *stairnō*, OE *steorra*, etc., all the Gmc. forms; Skt. *star-* (Vedic) and *tārā-*, Av. *star-;* Arm. *astł;* Hitt. *astiras;* Toch. A *śreñ*, nom. pl. (SSS 3, ftn.; Lane, Language 21.23).

2. Ir. *rētglu*, MIr. *rētla*, NIr. *rēalt*, cpds. of *rēt* 'thing' (prob.) and *glan* 'pure, bright' (cf. dat. pl. *rētglannaib*). Otherwise Pedersen 1.485 (cpd. of *rēt* 'star', but where is this quotable?), 2.47.

Ir. *rind* (neut.) 'star', same word as *rind* (masc.) 'point, top', perh. : Grk. πείρω 'pierce', etc. Pedersen 1.37.

3. Lith. *žvaigždė*, ChSl. *zvězda*, etc. (all the Balto-Slavic forms; also OPruss. *swaigstan* rendering NHG *schein*), clearly belong together, though the Baltic forms point to an initial palatal, the Slavic to an initial velar (explained by Meillet as dissimilation). Brückner 165 assumes forms with voiced consonants parallel to IE **kweit-* 'bright' in ChSl *světŭ* 'light', etc. (Walde-P. 1.470). But the words have all the appearance of imitative orig., like Lith. *žvigti* 'squeal', ChSl. *zvizdati*, Pol. *gwizdać* 'whistle', etc. (Berneker 365), in which the consonant relations are precisely the same. A shift of application from sound to light is entirely possible. Cf. NE *flash*, of imitative orig. and once used only of the rushing or splashing of the sea, now only with reference to fire or light (NED s.v.).

4. Other Skt. words besides *star-*, *tāra-*, are mostly such as are applied to any heavenly body, as *bhā-* fr. *bhā-* 'shine', *jyotis-* fr. *jyut-* 'shine', *nakṣatra-* of obscure orig.

1.55 LIGHTNING

Grk.	ἀστραπή	Goth.	*lauhmuni*	Lith.	*žaibas*
NG	ἀστραπή	ON	*elding*	Lett.	*zibens*
Lat.	*fulgur, fulgor*	Dan.	*lyn*	ChSl.	*mlŭnĭjĭ, bliscanije*
It.	*lampo, baleno, folgore*	Sw.	*blixt*	SCr.	*munja, blijesak*
Fr.	*éclair*	OE	*lēget(u), līget(u)*	Boh.	*blesk*
Sp.	*relámpago*	ME	*leit, liȝtnynge*	Pol.	*błyskawica*
Rum.	*fulger*	NE	*lightning*	Russ.	*molnija*
Ir.	*lōchet*	Du.	*bliksem*	Skt.	*vidyut-*
NIr.	*teintreach*	OHG	*blic*	Av.	. . . .
W.	*mellt, lluched*	MHG	*blick(e)ze, blitze*		
Br.	*luc'hedenn, daredenn*	NHG	*blitz*		

Words for 'lightning' are mostly from 'light, fire, shine, blaze, flash, dance'.

1. Grk. ἀστραπή, poet. also ἀστεροπή, στεροπή, Arc. στορπά : ἀστήρ, ἄστρον 'star', and prob. formed fr. this with -π-, -οπ-, etc. (IE **ok^{w}-* in words for 'eye', 'see'), like the numerous words in -οψ, -ωψs, -οπος, etc., hence lit. 'starlike'. Walde-P. 2.635.

2. Lat. *fulgur* n. (gen. *-uris*) and *fulgor* m. (gen. *-ōris*) : *fulgēre* 'flash', *flagrāre* 'blaze', Grk. φλέγω 'blaze', etc. Hence It. *folgore*, Rum. *fulger* (OFr. *fuildre, fouldre, foudre* rarely of visual

lightning; see 1.57). Walde-P. 2.214 ff. Ernout-M. 397 f. REW 3555.

It., Sp. *lampo*, now Sp. *relámpago*, fr. Lat. *lampas* 'torch, lamp' through a late deriv. *lampāre* 'shine'. REW 4870.

It. *baleno*, fr. *ballare* 'dance'. REW 909.

Fr. *éclair*, fr. *éclairer* 'shine'. REW 2973.

3. Ir. *lōchet*, W. *lluched*, Br. *luc'hedenn*, Goth. *lauhmuni*, Dan. *lyn*, OE *lēget(u), līget(u)*, ME *leit* (NE *layth* obs.), *liȝtnynge*, NE *lightning* : Lat. *lūx*, Goth. *liuhaþ* 'light', etc. (1.61). Walde-P. 2.408 ff. Pedersen 1.54. Feist 324 f.

NIr. *teintreach* : adj. *teintreach* 'fiery', fr. *teine* 'fire' (1.81).

W. *mellt*, prob. : OPruss. *mealde*, ChSl. *mlŭnĭjĭ*, etc., below, 6. Walde-P. 2.300.

Br. *daredenn* 'heat lightning', fr. *dared* 'a dart' (fr. Fr. *dard*).

4. Goth. *lauhmuni*, OE *liget*, NE *lightning*, etc., above, 3.

ON *elding* 'lightning', also 'firing, smelting', fr. *eldr* 'fire' (1.81).

OHG *blic*, MHG *blick(e)ze, blitze*, NHG *blitz*, Du. *bliksen*, Sw. *blixt* (formed fr. *blixa*, after NHG *blitz* : *blitzen*, Hellquist 79), ChSl. *bliscanije*, SCr. *blijesak*, Boh. *blesk*, Pol. (*błysk* 'flash') *błyskawica* : OE *blīcan* 'shine', Russ. *blesk* 'luster', ChSl. *blištati* 'shine', iter. *bliscati* (whence *bliscanije*), etc., fr. **bhleig-*, **bhleig-sk-*, ultimately connected with **bhleg-* in Grk. φλέγω, Lat. *fulgor* etc. (above, 2). Walde-P. 2.211 ff. Berneker 63.

5. Lith. *žaibas*, Lett. *zibens* : Lith. *žibėti*, Lett. *zibti* 'shine, glitter' (15.56).

6. ChSl. *mlŭnĭjĭ*, SCr. *munja*, Russ. *molnija*, OPruss. *mealde* : ON *mjǫllnir* 'Thor's hammer', *myln* 'fire', Lett. *milna* 'Perkun's hammer', fr. **meld-*, further root connection dub. Walde-P. 2.300. Mikkola, IF 23.122 f.

7. Skt. *vidyut-*, i.e. *vi-dyut-* fr. *dyut-* 'shine' (15.56).

1.56 THUNDER

Grk.	βροντή	Goth.	*þeihwō*	Lith.	*perkūnas, griausmas*
NG	βροντή	ON	*reiðar, þruma*	Lett.	*pērkuons*
Lat.	*tonitrus*	Dan.	*torden*	ChSl.	*gromŭ*
It.	*tuono*	Sw.	*åska (tordön)*	SCr.	*grom, grmljavina*
Fr.	*tonnerre*	OE	*þunor*	Boh.	*hrom*
Sp.	*trueno, tronido*	ME	*thunder*	Pol.	*grzmot, grom, piorun*
Rum.	*tunet*	NE	*thunder*	Russ.	*grom*
Ir.	*torainn*	Du.	*donder*	Skt.	*stanita-*
NIr.	*tōirneach*	OHG	*donar*	Av.	. . . .
W.	*taran*	MHG	*doner*		
Br.	*kurun, kudurun, taran*	NHG	*donner*		

Words for 'thunder' are mostly from various roots denoting noise, of which one is especially widespread in its application to thunder. But in one group the development is probably through 'thunderbolt' from a root meaning 'strike', in another word through 'thick cloud'; and there are some mythological terms.

1. From IE **(s)ten-*, in Grk. στένω, OE *stenan* (cf. NHG *stöhnen*), Lith. *stenėti*, ChSl. *stenati*, all meaning 'groan', Skt. *stan-* 'roar, thunder', Lat. *tonāre* 'roar, thunder'. Walde-P. 2.626 ff. Ernout-M. 1045 f. REW 8778, 8780. Falk-Torp 1273.

Lat. *tonitrus*, whence Fr. *tonnerre*, OSp. *tonidro*, later *tronido* with transposition, while It. *tuono*, ORum. *tun* (now

'cannon'; as 'thunder' replaced by *tunet* formed after *sonet* 'sound'), Sp. *trueno* (with *r* from *tronido*) are back-formations fr. the vb. Lat. *tonāre;* OE *þunor*, gen. *þunres*, ME, NE *thunder*, Du. *donder*, OHG *donar*, NHG *donner* (ON *þōrr*, the god of thunder), Norw. dial. *tōr*, Dan. *torden*, Sw. (arch.) *tordön*, these last compounded with *døn, dön* 'rumbling' (NE *din*); Skt. *stanita-*.

2. Grk. βροντή : βρέμω 'roar', of imitative orig., parallel to **bhrem-* in Lat. *bremere*, OHG *breman*, etc. 'roar, growl'.

3. Ir. *torainn*, NIr. (*torann* 'noise'), *tōirneach*, W., Br. *taran* : Ir. *tairm* 'noise', OPruss. *tārin* 'voice', Lith. *tarti* 'say', Grk. τορός 'piercing' (sound, etc.). Walde-P. 1.744.

Br. *kurun, kudurun:* W. *gorun* 'tumult'. Loth, RC 38.164.

4. Goth. *þeihwō*, prob. fr. **tenkwā-* : ChSl. *tąča* 'shower', Russ. *tuča* 'dark cloud', SCr. *tuča* 'hail', Lith. *tankus* 'thick'. Development through 'thick cloud', 'thundercloud' to 'thunder'. Walde-P. 1.726 (with doubt). Feist 495.

ON *reiðar* (cf. *reiðar ok eldingar* 'thunder claps and lightning flashes'), pl. of *reið* 'riding, wagon', hence (Thor's) 'driving'. Also cpds. *reiðarþruma* (cf. below) and *reiðarduna* (with *duna* 'a crash').

ON *þruma* (alone and in *reiðarþruma*) : *þruma* 'to rattle', *þrymr* 'alarm, noise', etc. (Walde-P. 1.749).

Sw. *åska*, older *åsekja*, lit. 'god's (= Thor's) driving' : ON *āss* 'god' and *ekja* 'carrying', *aka* 'drive'. Hellquist 1425.

OE *þunor*, etc., above, 1.

5. Lith. *perkūnas*, Lett. *pērkuons*, OPruss. *percunis*, Pol. *piorun* (Boh., Russ. obs. *perun*), used for both 'thunder' and 'thunderbolt', beside Lith. *Perkunas*, Slav. *Perun* the Balto-Slavic thunder-god, prob. as orig. 'thunderbolt' : ChSl. *pĭrati, perą* 'strike', etc. Walde-P. 2.43. Mühl.-Endz. 3.209.

Lith. *griausmas* (also *griaustinė, -tinis*) : *griausti* 'thunder', beside *griauti* 'thunder', this ultimately the same as *griauti* 'overthrow, destroy', beside *griūti* 'fall in ruins', all with the common notion of 'crash'. Walde-P. 1.647 ff.

6. ChSl. *gromŭ*, SCr. *grom, grmljavina*, Boh. *hrom*, Pol. *grom, grzmot*, Russ. *grom*, with vb., ChSl. *grĭměti* 'thunder', etc. : Lith. *grumėti* 'thunder', Grk. χρεμίζω 'neigh', ON *grimmr*, OE *grim* 'fierce, grim', OE *grimman* 'rage, roar', Av. *granta-* 'enraged', etc. Walde-P. 1.655 ff. Berneker 353 f., 360.

7. Skt. *stanita-*, above, 1.

1.57 LIGHTNING (AS STRIKING), THUNDERBOLT

Grk.	κεραυνός	Goth.	. . . .	Lith.	*perkūnas*
NG	κεραυνός, ἀστροπελέκι	ON	*þōrs hamarr*	Lett.	*pērkuons, zibens*
Lat.	*fulmen*	Dan.	*lyn(-slag), tordenkile*	ChSl.	. . . .
It.	*fulmine*	Sw.	*blixt (åskslag, -vigg)*	SCr.	*grom*
Fr.	*foudre*	OE	*þunor, līȝet*	Boh.	*hrom*
Sp.	*rayo*	ME	*thunder, liȝtnynge, foudre*	Pol.	*grom, piorun*
Rum.	*trăsnet*	NE	*lightning, thunderbolt*	Russ.	*molnija*
Ir.	*saignēn*	Du.	*blixem(-straal), donderkeil*, etc.	Skt.	*vajra-, taḍit-*
NIr.	*caor*	OHG	*donarstrāla*	Av.	. . . .
W.	*mellten, taranfollt*	MHG	*donerstrāle, donerstein*, etc.		
Br.	*(tan-)foeltr, (tan-)kurun*	NHG	*blitz, donnerkeil*		

Words for lightning in its destructive aspect, the supposed bolt of lightning or 'thunderbolt', are partly identical with, or connected with, the usual words for 'lightning'; partly with those for the accompanying 'thunder'; while some are independent of either but are cognate with verbs for 'strike' or 'destroy' or with nouns for 'arrow, ray, ball, club', etc. (such words also in compounds with those for 'thunder' or 'lightning').

1. Grk. κεραυνός : κεραΐζω (*κεραϝίζω) 'despoil, plunder', κήρ 'death, ruin', Skt. *çr-* 'crush, break', etc. Walde-P. 1.410. Boisacq 440.

Grk. βροντή 'thunder' is never used in this sense. But there is a curious approach to it, with distinction, in πίπτει κεραυνὸς εἰς τὸ στρατόπεδον· καὶ οἱ μέν τινες πληγέντες, οἱ δὲ καὶ ἐμβροντηθέντες ἀπέθανον Xen., Hell. 47.7. Cf. also τὸ ἐμβρονταῖον 'place struck by lightning' rendering Lat. *bidental*.

NG ἀστροπελέκι, by haplology fr. *ἀστραπο-πελέκι, lit. a 'lightning-ax'. Hatzidakis, Μεσ. 2.193.

2. Lat. *fulmen* (> It. *fulmine*), fr. **fulgmen* : *fulgur* 'lightning' (1.55), whence Fr. *foudre* (OFr. also *fuildre, fouldre*) with (extension to and then) shift to the striking lightning, being replaced by *éclair* in the sense of visual lightning. Wartburg 3.841.

Sp. *rayo* (also 'ray'), fr. Lat. *radius* 'ray'. REW 6999.

Rum. *trăsnet* ('thunderbolt' and 'thunderclap'), fr. *trasni* 'strike with lightning', also 'crash', loanword fr. Slavic, ChSl. *trěsnati* 'strike, crash', etc. Tiktin 1637.

3. Ir. *saignēn* (gl. Lat. *fulmen*), deriv. of *saigit* 'arrow' fr. Lat. *sagitta*. Vendryes, De hib. voc. 173. Cf. Br. dial. *seah* 'thunderbolt' fr. same source. Loth, Mots lat. 204.

NIr. *caor* 'berry, ball' and 'thunderbolt' as 'ball of fire', like Ir. *cāer thened* 'ball of fire, thunderbolt, meteor' (K. Meyer, Contrib. 298).

Gael. *beithir* 'monster, huge snake', used also for 'thunderbolt'.

W. *taranfollt*, cpd. of *taran* 'thunder' and *bollt* fr. NE *bolt*. But commonly *mellten* 'a lightning' (1.55) in this sense.

Br. *foeltr*, fr. OFr. *fuildre, fouldre* (above, 2). Also *kurun* 'thunder' so used. But esp. *tan-foeltr, tan-kurun, tan-taran*, cpds. with *tan* 'fire' (cf. Vallée s.v. *foudre*).

4. The Gmc. words are those for 'lightning' or 'thunder' or compounds of either with words meaning 'hammer', 'wedge', 'bolt', 'stone', 'ray', 'stroke'.

ON *þōrs hamarr* 'Thor's hammer' was the thunderbolt, but it seems to be quotable only as a term of mythology.

The compounds are of obvious make-up, and too numerous to be cited in full (cf. NE *thunder-stone*, now obs.). Most of them are now poetical or figurative. The tendency is also to use the words for 'lightning' instead of those for 'thunder', which were more common in the earlier periods. Cf. NE *struck by lightning* (or NHG *von blitz getroffen*), though NE *thunder* was used in this sense down through the eighteenth century and poetically in the nineteenth (cf. NED s.v.).

ME also *fouldre, foudre*, fr. Fr. (above, 2).

5. Lith. *perkūnas*, Lett. *pērkuons* 'thunder' are used with verbs of striking for the striking lightning (and this prob. the orig. sense, cf. 1.56), but also Lett. *zibens* 'lightning'.

Most of the Slavic languages use the words for 'thunder', SCr. *grom*, Boh. *hrom*, Pol. *grom* and also *piorun*, as formerly Russ. *grom*. But Russ. *molnija* 'lightning' in both senses. In ChSl. prob. both *mlŭnĭjĭ* and *gromŭ* so used, but no early evidence.

6. Skt. *vajra-*, a term of mythology, Indra's 'thunderbolt' : Av. *vazra-* 'club', NPers. *gurz* 'club'.

Skt. *taḍit-*, fr. *taḍ-* 'strike'.

1.61 LIGHT (sb.)

Grk.	φῶς	Goth.	*liuhaþ*	Lith.	*šviesa*
NG	φῶς	ON	*ljōs*	Lett.	*gaisma*
Lat.	*lūx, lūmen*	Dan.	*lys*	ChSl.	*světŭ*
It.	*luce, lume*	Sw.	*ljus*	SCr.	*svijetlo*
Fr.	*lumière*	OE	*lēoht*	Boh.	*světlo*
Sp.	*luz*	ME	*liȝt(e), light*	Pol.	*światło*
Rum.	*lumină*	NE	*light*	Russ.	*svet*
Ir.	*soilse*	Du.	*licht*	Skt.	*jyotis-, bhās-,* etc.
NIr.	*solus, soillse*	OHG	*liocht*	Av.	*raočah-*
W.	*golen*	MHG	*liecht*		
Br.	*goulou*	NHG	*licht*		

Words for 'light' (sb.) are cognate with others meaning 'bright' or 'shine', and the majority of them belong to one inherited group.

1. Fr. IE **leuk-* in Skt. *ruc-* 'shine', Grk. λευκός 'bright, white', etc. Walde-P. 2.408 ff. Ernout-M. 570 f. REW 5161, 5162. Pedersen 1.98, 351. Falk-Torp 670.

Lat. *lūx, lūcis* (> It. *luce*, Sp. *luz*), *lūmen* (> It. *lume*, Rum. *lumină;* deriv. *lūmināre* > Fr. *lumière*); Goth. *liuhaþ*, ON *ljōs*, OE *lēoht*, etc., general Gmc.; Skt. *ruci-, rocis-* (but not the usual words), Av. *raočah-* (OPers. *rauča* 'day'); Arm. *lois;* Ir. *soilse* (*solus* 'bright'), NIr. *soillse, solus*, fr. a cpd. **su-luks-*; OW *louber*, W. *lleufer* (obs.) fr. a parallel **leug-*, and W. *goleu*, Br. *goulou*, cpd. of same.

2. Grk. φῶς, Ion. φάος, fr. *φάϝος (cf. Aeol. φαυοφόρος) : Skt. *bhā-* 'shine', *bhās-, bhāsas-* 'light', etc. Walde-P. 2.122 ff.

3. Lith. *šviesa*, ChSl. *světŭ* with the other Slavic forms : Lith. *šviesti*, ChSl. *světiti* 'shine', Skt. *çveta-* 'white', Goth. *hweits* 'white', etc. Walde-P. 1.469 f. Brückner 535.

Lett. *gaisma* : *gaišs* 'bright', Lith. *gaisas, gaisras* 'distant brightness', *gaidrus* 'clear' (of the sky), Grk. φαιδρός 'bright'. Walde-P. 1.665. Mühl.-Endz. 1.687 ff.

4. Skt. *jyotis-*, fr. *dyut-* 'shine' (*jy* fr. *dy*, Wackernagel, Altind. Gram. 1.163), extension of *dyu-* beside *div-* in words for bright 'sky', etc. (1.51). Walde-P. 1.772 ff.

Skt. *ruci-*, Av. *raočah-*, above, 1.

Skt. *bhās-*, etc., above, 2.

1.62 DARKNESS

Grk.	σκότος	Goth.	*riqis*	Lith.	*tamsa*
NG	σκότος, σκοτάδι	ON	*myrkr*	Lett.	*tumsa*
Lat.	*tenebrae*	Dan.	*mørke*	ChSl.	*tĭma, mrakŭ*
It.	*tenebre, buio, oscurita*	Sw.	*mörker*	SCr.	*tmina, tama, mrak*
Fr.	*ténèbres, obscurité*	OE	*þēostru, mirce, deorcnes*	Boh.	*temnota, tma*
Sp.	*tinieblas*			Pol.	*ćiemność, ćma*
Rum.	*întuneric*	ME	*mirk, derk(nes)*	Russ.	*temnota, t'ma, mrak*
Ir.	*temel, dorche*	NE	*dark(ness)*	Skt.	*tamas-, timira-, andhakāra-*
NIr.	*dorchadas, doircheacht*	Du.	*duistermis, donker*		
W.	*tywyllwch*	OHG	*finstarnissi, tunchali*	Av.	*təmah-, tąθra-*
Br.	*teñvalienn, amc'houlou*	MHG	*vinsternisse, tunkel (-heit)*		
		NHG	*finsterniss, dunkel (-heit)*		

For 'darkness' there is one widespread inherited group, common to Italic, Celtic, Germanic (in part), Balto-Slavic, and Indo-Iranian (unknown in Greek). The other words are in part cognate with others meaning 'shade', 'cloud', 'twilight', or from adjectives for 'dark' of diverse origin.

1. IE **tem-*, **temes-*, etc. in sbs. for 'darkness' and adjs. for 'dark'. Walde-P. 1.720 ff. Ernout-M. 1027 f. REW 8643, 4484. Weigand-H. 1.535. Brückner 65.

Skt. *tamas-, tamisra-, timira-*, Av. *təmah-, tąθra-*; Lat. *tenebrae* (fr. **temesrā-*, cf. Skt. *tamisra-*), It. *tenebre*, Fr. *ténèbres*, Sp. *tinieblas*, Rum. *întuneric* (fr. **in-tenebricus*); Ir. *temel* (here also perh. ultimately Br. *teñvalienn*, fr. adj. *teñval* 'dark', and even W. *tywyllwch*, fr. adj. *tywyll* 'dark', the latter by a blend with *gwyll* 'gloom, darkness'; cf. Loth, RC 18.95 f.); OHG *finstarnissi* (*dinstar, finstar* 'dark'), NHG *finsterniss* (cf. also OHG *demar*, NHG *dämmerung* 'twilight'); Lith. *tamsa*, Lett. *tumsa;* ChSl. *tĭma*, SCr. *tama, tmina*, Boh. *tma, temnota*, Pol. *ćma, ciemność*, Russ. *t'ma, temnota*.

2. ON *myrkr*, Dan. *mørke*, Sw. *mörker*, OE *mirce*, ME *mirk*, NE *mirk* (still common in Scottish for 'darkness'), ChSl. *mrakŭ*, SCr. *mrak* (Boh. *mrak* 'cloud', Pol. *mrok* mostly 'dusk, twilight'), Russ. *mrak* (fr. ChSl.) : Lith. *merkti* 'shut the eyes, blink', *mirgėti* 'twinkle, glisten', Grk. μαρμαίρω 'glisten', etc., IE **mer-*, **mer-k-*, **mer-g-*. Walde-P. 2.273 ff. Falk-Torp 750. Berneker 2.78. The development seems to be from 'flickering' light through 'twilight' to 'darkness'.

3. Grk. σκότος : Ir. *scāth* 'shade', Goth. *skadus* 'shade', etc. (1.63). Walde-P. 2.600. NG pop. σκοτάδι.

4. It. *lo scuro, oscurita*, Fr. *obscurité*, fr. Lat. *obscūrus* 'dark' : OE *scuwa* 'shade', *scēo* 'cloud', etc. (1.63, 1.73), Skt. *sku-* 'cover'. Walde-P. 2.546 ff. Ernout-M. 694.

It. *il buio* 'the dark', *buio* 'dark' : OFr. *buire*, Sp. *buriel* 'dark red', fr. Lat. **būrius, burrus* 'rufus' (Festus), this fr. Grk. πυρρός 'yellowish red'. Ernout-M. 122. REW 1410.

5. Ir. *dorche* (also adj.), NIr. *dorchadas, doircheacht*, a cpd. *do-rche* (*do-* 'ill' : Grk. δυσ-, etc.), opp. of *so-rche* 'bright' (*so-* 'well' : Skt. *su-*, etc.), second part perh., as suggested by M. Dillon, fr. a cpd. of *cī-* 'see' (cf. *ad-cīu*, 15.54). Otherwise Stokes 229 (but *rīched* 'heaven' is prob. cpd. **rīgo-sedon* 'seat of kings'; K. Meyer, Ber. Preuss. Akad. 1913, 955).

Br. *amc'houlou*, cpd. of neg. *am-* and *goulou* 'light' (1.61).

6. Goth. *riqis* : ON *røkkr* 'twilight',

Grk. Ἔρεβος 'place of nether darkness' (myth.), Skt. *rajas-* 'dim space, cloud, etc'. Walde-P. 2.367. Feist 399.

OE *þēostru, þȳstru*, Du. *duisternis* : adj. OE *þēostre*, OS *thiustri*, MLG *duster*, Du. *duister*, NHG *düster* 'dark', etym.? Falk-Torp 173 : ON *þoka*, Dan. *taage* 'mist', and so 'dark' fr. 'misty', 1452. Franck–v. W. 141 (: Russ. *tusklyj* 'dim', as also Kluge-G. 119).

OE *deorcnes* (rare), ME *derknes*, NE *darkness*, also ME *derke*, NE *dark* used substantively : OE adj. *deorc* 'dark', OHG *tarchanjan* 'conceal, hide', MHG *terken* 'soil', MLG *dork* 'place where dirt collects', Lith. *dargus* 'dirty, filthy', etc. Walde-P. 1.855. NED s.v. *dark*, adj.

OHG *tunchali*, MHG *tunkel, tunkelheit*, NHG *dunkel, dunkelheit* (less grim than *finsterniss* and more often fig.), Du. *donker*, fr. adj. OHG *tuncha*, Du. *donker* 'dark' (ON *døkkr*), prob. through 'misty, hazy' : Norw., Sw. dial. *dunken* 'damp, sultry', NE *dank* 'wet, damp', OHG *dampf* 'steam, smoke', also ON *dimmr*, OE *dim* 'dim, somewhat dark', Skt. *dham-* 'blow', that is, IE **dhem-* with various extensions and complicated semantic development. Walde-P. 1.851 f. Falk-Torp 165, 166.

7. Skt. *andha-, andhas-, andhakāra-*, fr. adj. *andha-* 'blind' (4.94), perh. : Lat. *umbra* 'shade' (1.63).

1.63 SHADE

Grk.	σκιά	Goth.	*skadus*	Lith.	*šešėlis, pavėsis, paunksnė*
NG	σκιά, ἤσκιος	ON	*skuggi*		
Lat.	*umbra*	Dan.	*skygge*	Lett.	*pavēnis, ēna, pačna*
It.	*ombra*	Sw.	*skugga*	ChSl.	*sěnĭ, štěnĭ*
Fr.	*ombre*	OE	*scead, sceadu, scū(w)a*	SCr.	*sjena, hladovina*
Sp.	*sombra*	ME	*shade, shadow*	Boh.	*stín*
Rum.	*umbră*	NE	*shade (shadow)*	Pol.	*cień*
Ir.	*scāth, foscad*	Du.	*schaduw*	Russ.	*ten'* (*sen'*)
NIr.	*scāth*	OHG	*scato, scūwo, scû*	Skt.	*chāyā-*
W.	*cysgod*	MHG	*schate*	Av.	**saya-*
Br.	*skeud*	NHG	*schatten*		

Most of the words for 'shade' are used also, without differentiation, for the image cast, the 'shadow'. The figurative use for 'disembodied spirit' is also widespread from Homer on.

1. Grk. σκιά, ChSl. *sěnĭ*, SCr. *sjena*, Russ. *sen'* (Boh. *siň*, Pol. *sień*, Russ. *seni* 'entrance room', etc., as room without light), Skt. *chāyā-*, Av. **saya-* (*a-saya-* 'without shadow'), NPers. *sāya-*, Alb. *hē*, fr. IE **skāi-*, **ski-*, prob. the same root as in Goth. *skeinan*, OE *scīnan*, ChSl. *sijati* 'shine' (15.56). Connection through a notion of 'faint light' (as in NE *shimmer*, NHG *schimmer*) or 'reflection'. Cf. OE *scima* 'shadow, gloom' beside *scīma* 'light, brightness'. Walde-P. 2.535 ff. Boisacq 875 f. Brückner 489. NG pop. ἤσκιος (freq. spelled ἴσκιος), fr. ἠσκιά with influence of the opp. ἥλιος 'sun, sunshine,' Hatzidakis, Einl. 328.

2. Lat. *umbra* (> It. *ombra*, Fr. *ombre*, Rum. *umbră;* Sp. *sombra* 'shade', like Fr. adj. *sombre* 'dark, gloomy', back-formation fr. deriv. vb. VLat. *subumbrāre*), etym. dub., perh. : Skt. *andha-* 'blind'. Walde-P. 1.182. Ernout-M. 1122 f. REW 9046, 8405.

3. Ir., NIr. *scāth* (also *fo-scad*, but NIr. *foscadh* chiefly 'shelter'), W. *cysgod* (i.e. *cy-sgod*), Br. *skeud*, Goth. *skadus*, OE *scead, sceadu*, ME, NE *shade, shadow* (latter now mostly for the image cast), Du. *schaduw*, OHG *scato*, MHG *schate*,

NHG *schatten* : Grk. σκότος 'darkness', but without any clear root connection. Walde-P. 2.600. Feist 427.

4. ON *skuggi*, Dan. *skygge*, Sw. *skugga* (Goth. *skuggwa* 'mirror'), OE *scū(w)a*, OHG *scūwo, scū* : Lat. *obscūrus* 'dark', Skt. *sku-* 'cover', also ON *skȳ* 'cloud', etc. (1.73). Walde-P. 2.546 ff. Falk-Torp 1045. Hellquist 959.

5. Lith. *šešėlis*, a reduplicated formation (with suffix *-lio-*) fr. *šė-* : ChSl. *sěnĭ*, etc. (above, 1). Senn (privately).

Lith. *pavėsis*, Lett. *pavēnis* : Lith. *vėsus* 'cool, airy', *vėjas* 'wind', Lett. *vējš* 'wind', Lat. *vēntus* 'wind', with development fr. 'windy, airy place' through 'cool place' to 'shady place, shade'. Walde-P. 1.222. Mühl.-Endz. 3.136.

Lith. *paunksnė* (Senn), *paūksnis* (Gailius-Šlaža), beside *pauksmė* (used until recently, now avoided, Senn) and obs. or dial. *unksmė, ūksmė, unksna* : *ūkas* 'fog, mist', *ūkanas* 'cloudy, overcast', etc., outside connections dub.

Lett. *ēna, paēna*, abstracted fr. forms like *pavēnis*(?). (Nothing in Mühl.-Endz. s.vv.).

6. ChSl. *šěnĭ*, etc., above, 1.

ChSl. *štěnĭ*, Boh. *stín*, Pol. *cień*, Russ. *ten'*, history obscure. Perh. **těnĭ* fr. **tem-ni-* : ChSl. *tĭma* 'darkness', etc. (1.62), and *štěnĭ* a blend of this and *sěnĭ* (above, 1). Vondrák, Verg. Gram. 1. 431. Otherwise (double development of init. *sk*) Brückner 62.

SCr. *hladovina* 'coolness' (fr. *hladan* 'cool', 15.86), also 'shade'.

1.71 AIR

Grk.	ἀήρ	Goth.	*luftus*	Lith.	*oras*
NG	ἀέρας	ON	*lopt*	Lett.	*gaiss*
Lat.	*āēr*	Dan.	*luft*	ChSl.	*vŭzduchŭ*
It.	*aria*	Sw.	*luft*	SCr.	*uzduh, vazduh, zrak*
Fr.	*air*	OE	*lyft*	Boh.	*vzduch*
Sp.	*aire*	ME	*lift, air*	Pol.	*powietrze*
Rum.	*aer, vazduh*	NE	*air*	Russ.	*vozduch*
Ir.	*āer*	Du.	*lucht*	Skt.	*vāta-, vāyu-*
NIr.	*aer*	OHG	*luft*	Av.	*vayu-, vayah-*
W.	*awyr*	MHG	*luft*		
Br.	*aer*	NHG	*luft*		

Words for 'air' are connected with those for 'wind', 'blow'; 'brightness'; 'ceiling' through 'sky'; 'open field' through 'outdoors, in the open air'; 'breath'. The last source is uncommon. That 'air' is what we breathe was recognized by the Greeks, but is a sophisticated notion which plays a small part in the derivation.

1. Grk. ἀήρ, in Homer mostly 'thick air, haze' (ἀέρα ἔχευεν, ἐσκέδασεν, ἀήρ ἐρεβεννή, etc.), later simply 'air' as one of the four elements : ἄημι, Skt. *vā-* 'blow', *vāta-, vāyu-* 'wind, air', Av. *vayu-, vayah-* 'air' (personified), Lat. *vēntus* 'wind', OE *wind*, etc. (1.72). Walde-P. 1.221.

Hence Lat. *āēr*, OIt. *aire*, It. *aria*, Fr. *air* (> ME, NE *air*), Sp. *aire*, Rum. *aer*, Ir. *āēr*, NIr. *aer*, W. *awyr*, Br. *aer*. REW 240. Pedersen 1.203.

(Grk. αἰθήρ, in Homer 'sky, heavens, the upper air, ether', above the ἀήρ : αἴθω 'burn', αἴθριος 'clear, bright', etc. Hence Lat. *aether*, NE *ether*, etc.).

2. The Gmc. group, Goth. *luftus*, ON *lopt*, OE *lyft*, ME *lift* (NE *lift* rare and only for 'sky', but the vb. *lift* 'raise' is fr.

same source), OHG-NHG *luft* (> Dan., Sw. *luft*), is in origin the same as ON *lopt* 'loft, attic, etc.' (> ME, NE *loft*; OE *loft* 'sky'). Development from 'ceiling, loft' to 'sky, air'. Further connection prob. (but less certain and immaterial for the immediate source of 'air') with OHG *louft* 'bark', *louba* 'roof, attic, etc.', *loub*, Goth. *laufs*, OE *lēaf* 'leaf', Lith. *lupti* 'peal', etc., with development from 'bark' to '(bark) roof, ceiling'. Walde-P. 2.418. Falk-Torp 652.

3. Lith. *oras* : Lett. *ãra* 'open field, the outdoors, the outside', prob. fr. the the root of Lith. *arti*, Lett. *art* 'plow', with development indicated by the Lett. uses. Walde-P. 1.79. Mühl.-Endz. 1.240.

1.72 WIND

Grk.	ἄνεμος	Goth.	winds	Lith.	vėjas
NG	ἄνεμος	ON	vindr	Lett.	vėjš
Lat	ventus	Dan.	vind	ChSl.	větrŭ
It.	vento	Sw.	vind	SCr.	vjetar
Fr.	vent	OE	wind	Boh.	vitr
Sp.	viento	ME	wind	Pol.	wiatr
Rum.	vint	NE	wind	Russ.	veter
Ir.	gāith	Du.	wind	Skt.	vāta-, vāyu-, anila-
NIr.	gaoth	OHG	wint	Av.	vāta-
W.	gwynt, awel	MHG	wint		
Br.	awel, gwent	NHG	wind		

Most of the words for 'wind' belong to an inherited group connected with (less widespread) verbs for 'blow'.

1. From IE *wē- 'blow' in Skt. *vā-*, Grk. ἄημι, etc. Walde-P. 1.220 ff. Ernout-M. 1086. Pedersen 1.37, 60.

Lat. *ventus* (> Romance words); W. *gwynt*, Br. *gwent*, W. *awel*, Br. *avel* (cf. Grk. ἄελλα 'whirlwind'); Goth. *winds*, etc.; general Gmc.; Lith. *vėjas*, ChSl. *vėtrŭ*, etc., general Balto-Slavic; Skt., Av. *vāta-*, Skt. *vāyu-*; Toch. A *want*, B *yante*.

Lett. *gaiss* : *gaišs* 'bright', *gaisma* 'light', etc. (1.61).

4. ChSl. *vŭzduchŭ*, SCr. *uzduh, vazduh*, Boh. *vzduch*, Russ. *vozduch*, cpd. of *vŭzŭ* 'up' and *duchŭ* 'breath'. Berneker 234 f.

SCr. *zrak* : ChSl. *zrakŭ* 'sight, look', *zĭrěti* 'look at, see', Lith. *žerėti* 'shine', etc., with development through 'brightness'. Cf. SCr. *zraka* 'ray'. Miklosich 402.

Pol. *powietrze* : *wiatr* 'wind', with perfect. prefix and coll. suffix. Cf. Boh. *povětří* 'air, weather, storm'. Brückner 433, 611.

5. Indo-Iranian words, above, 1.

2. Grk. ἄνεμος : Lat. *anima* 'breath', *animus* 'soul', Skt. *ana-* 'breath', *anila-* 'breath, wind', vb. *an-* 'breathe', etc. (4.51). Walde-P. 1.56 ff. Boisacq 61. Ernout-M. 53 f.

3. Ir. *gāith*, NIr. *gaoth*, etym.? Stokes 104.

4. Skt. (beside *vāta-, anila-*, above, 1, 2) *pavana-*, fr. *pū-* 'cleanse, purify'; *samīraṇa-*, fr. *sam-ṛ-* 'come together'; *ṛ-* 'move'.

1.73 CLOUD

Grk.	νέφος, νεφέλη	Goth.	milhma	Lith.	debesis
NG	νέφος, σύννεφο	ON	skȳ	Lett.	mākuona, padebesis
Lat.	nūbēs, nūbila (pl.)	Dan.	sky	ChSl.	oblakŭ
It.	nuvola, nube	Sw.	moln, sky	SCr.	obluk
Fr.	nuage	OE	wolcen	Boh.	oblak, mrak
Sp.	nube	ME	sky, cloud	Pol.	chmura, oblok
Rum.	nor	NE	cloud	Russ.	oblako
Ir.	nél	Du.	wolk	Skt.	megha-, abhra-,
NIr.	néal	OHG	wolkan		nabhas-, etc.
W.	cwmwl	MHG	wolken	Av.	maēγa-, awra-, snaoδa-, dvqnman-
Br.	koabrenn, koumoulen	NHG	wolke		

The relation of 'cloud' and 'mist' is such that cognate words may mean 'cloud' in some languages, 'mist' in others. For the frequent relationship between 'cloud' and 'sky', see 1.51.

Words for 'cloud' are connected with words for 'moisture', 'covering', and 'mass'.

1. IE *nebh-, *embh-, *ṃbh-, in words for 'cloud' (> 'sky'), 'mist', 'shower'. Walde-P. 1.131. Ernout-M. 660 f.

Grk. νέφος, νεφέλη, NG νέφι, σύννεφο 'cloud', Skt. *nabhas-* 'mist, vapor' (also 'sky'); Lat. *nebula* 'mist', OHG *nebul*, etc. 'mist' (1.74); Lith. *debesis* 'cloud', Lett. *debess* 'cloud' but mostly 'sky', *padebesis* 'cloud' (all with init. *d* for *n* under the influence of some other word), ChSl. *nebo* 'sky', etc. Further, fr. *embh-, *ṃbh-, etc., Skt. *abhra-*, Av. *awra-* 'cloud', Grk. ὄμβρος, Lat. *imber* 'shower', etc.

Here also(?) W. *wybren* once 'cloud', now 'sky', OCorn. *huibren* 'cloud', Br. *oabl* 'sky', and the cpd. Br. *koabrenn* 'cloud', MBr. *couffabren*. Morris Jones 154 f. But the assumed phonetic development is very doubtful.

2. Lat. *nūbēs* (> It., Sp. *nube*, Fr. *nue, nuage*, Rum. *nor*) : W. *nudd* 'mist', Av. *snaoδa-* 'cloud', fr. *sneudh-*, extension of *sneu-* beside *snā-* 'be wet, bathe', in Skt. *snuta-* 'dripping' beside *snā-* 'bathe', Lat. *nāre* 'swim', etc. Walde-P. 2.697,

692 ff. Ernout-M. 682 f. REW 5974, 5975.

From late Lat. *nibulus* for *nūbilus* (REW 5975.2) also W. *niwl, nifwl* 'mist', Ir. *nél*, NIr. *néal* 'cloud'. Walde-P. 1.131. Loth, Mots lat. 190. Pokorny, KZ 50.45 f. Vendryes, RC 42.235.

3. W. *cwmwl*, Br. *koumoulenn* 'cloud', fr. Lat. *cumulus* 'mass, pile' (like NE *cloud* fr. ME *clūd* 'mass of rocks, pile')? Morris Jones 88 (rejected by Loth, Mots lat. 155 as phonetically impossible; but cf. *swmwl* ib. 209). Connection with Br. *koum* 'wave' preferred by Loth, l. c., and Henry 74.

Br. *koabrenn*, the more usual word, above, 1, end.

4. Goth. *milhma* 'cloud', etym. much disputed and dub. Walde-P. 2.297, 299. Feist 359. Falk-Torp 738.

Sw. *moln* 'cloud', Dan. *mulm* (ODan. *moln*) 'darkness', connected by some with preceding (with loss of guttural). Falk-Torp 738. Hellquist 658.

ON *skȳ*, Dan. *sky* 'cloud', Sw. *sky* 'cloud' or 'sky', ME *sky* 'cloud' or 'sky' (NE *sky* only in latter sense), OS *scio* 'cloud' : Skt. *sku-* 'cover', Lat. *obscūrus* 'dark', ON *skuggi* 'shade', etc. Walde-P. 2.547. Falk-Torp 1044. Hellquist 963.

OE *wolcen* (NE *welkin* 'sky'), Du. *wolk*, OHG *wolkan*, MHG *wolken*, NHG *wolke* 'cloud' : OHG *welc* 'with-

ered, weak' (secondary sense, cf. foll.), Lith. *vilgyti* 'moisten', Lett. *valgs*, ChSl. *vlaga* 'moisture', etc. Walde-P. 1.306. Weigand-H. 2.1283.

ME, NE *cloud*, fr. OE *clūd* 'mass of rocks, hill' (cf. NE *clod*, fr. same root), fr. IE *gleu-, *gel- in words for round-shaped objects. Walde-P. 1.612 ff., 618. NED s.v. *cloud*.

5. Lith. *debesis*, Lett. *padebesis*, above, 1.

Lett. *mākuona* 'cloud' : *makna* 'swamp', Lith. *miklus* 'damp', ChSl. *mokrŭ* 'wet', Russ. *moknut* 'get wet', etc., with common notion of 'moisture'. Walde-P. 2.224. Mühl.-Endz. 2.580.

6. ChSl. *oblakŭ*, etc., general Slavic for 'cloud', lit. 'covering', fr. *obŭ-volkŭ*, cpd. of *obŭ* 'about' and root of *vlěšti, vlěkǫ* 'draw' (: Lith. *vilkti* 'clothe', etc.; Walde-P. 1.306). Miklosich 379. Brückner 371.

Boh. *mrak* 'cloud' (cf Russ. *morok* 'dark cloud') : ChSl. *mrakŭ*, SCr. *mrak*, OE *mirce*, etc. 'darkness' (1.62).

Pol. *chmura* 'cloud' : Boh. *chmoura*, Russ. *chmura* 'dark cloud', beside Russ. *smuryj* 'dark gray', etc. Root connection dub., but notion of 'dark' the immediate source. Miklosich 311. Brückner 180.

7 Skt. *megha-*, Av. *maēγa-* : Grk. ὀμίχλη 'mist', etc. (1.74).

Skt. *abhra-*, Av. *awra-*, above, 1.

Skt. *ghana-* 'solid mass' (fr. *han-* 'strike') cloud'.

In Sanskrit many poet. expressions like *su-dāman-* lit. 'well-giving', *jala-da-* 'water-giving', etc.

Av. *dvqnman-, dunman-* 'cloud, mist' : Skt. *dhvan-* 'cover', *dhvānta-* 'darkness'. Barth. 749, 766.

Av. *snaoδa-*, above, 2.

1.74 MIST (FOG, HAZE)

Grk.	ὀμίχλη	Goth.	. . . .	Lith.	migla
NG	ὀμίχλη (lit.), καταχνιά	ON	poka	Lett.	migla
Lat.	nebula	Dan.	taage	ChSl.	migla
It.	nebbia	Sw.	dimma, töcken	SCr.	màgla
Fr.	brouillard, brume	OE	mist	Boh.	mha
Sp.	niebla, neblina, bruma	ME	mist	Pol.	mgła
Rum.	ceaţă, negură	NE	mist	Russ.	tuman, mgla
Ir.	cēo	Du.	nevel, mist	Skt.	mih-
NIr.	ceo	OHG	nebul	Av.	dunman-
W.	niwl, nudd	MHG	nebel		
Br.	latar, lusenn	NHG	nebel		

The present differentiation of NE *mist, fog*, and *haze* cannot be matched in the other languages, where with some exceptions the same word answers roughly to all three. Many of the words are cognate with some of those for 'cloud'. Others are from such diverse notions as 'vapor', 'dim', 'gray', 'wet', 'winter', etc.

1. Grk. ὀμίχλη, Lith., Lett. *migla*, ChSl. *mĭgla*, etc., general Slavic (but Russ. *mgla* less common than *tuman*)

also OE-NE, Du. *mist*, Skt. *mih-*, all 'mist' beside Skt. *megha-*, Av. *maēγa-* 'cloud', fr. a root *meigh-* perh. the same as in ChSl. *mĭgnǫti* 'blink', Lith. *mìgti* 'fall asleep', etc., with development of 'mist, cloud' through the notion of 'dim'. Walde-P. 2.247. Boisacq 701.

NG καταχνιά : ἀχνίζω 'evaporate, reek', ἄχνη 'breath, reek', in class. Grk. 'froth, dew, chaff, etc.' (light substance).

2 Lat. *nebula* (> It. *nebbia*, OFr.

nieble, Sp. *niebla, neblina*; Rum. *negură*, blend with *negru* 'black'), OHG *nebul*, MHG, NHG *nebel*, Du. *nevel* (ON *nifl-* in cpds.) : Grk. νέφος 'cloud', etc. (1.73).

Fr. *brouillard* : *brouiller* 'mix up', It. *imbroglio* 'confusion', of dub. orig. REW 1325.

Fr. *brume*, Sp. *bruma*, fr. Lat. *brūma* 'winter', by association of 'mist' with the winter season. Cf. Rum. *brumat* 'gray'. REW 1335.

Rum. *ceaţă*, fr. late Lat. *caecia* 'dimsightedness', fr. *caecus* 'blind'. REW 1457. Puşcariu 359.

3. Ir. *cēo* (gen. *cíach*), NIr. *ceo*, perh. : Ir. *ciar* 'dark brown', OE *hār* 'gray' (NE *hoar*), etc. Walde-P. 1.360.

W. *nudd* and *niwl*, see 1.73 under Lat. *nūbēs*.

Br. *latar* : Corn. *lad* 'liquid', W. *llaid*, Ir. *lathach* 'mud', Grk. λάταγες 'drops of wine in the bottom of the cup', all fr. the notion of 'wet, liquid'. Walde-P. 2.381. Henry 181.

Br. *lusenn* and *lugenn* ('brouillard chaud') : *lug* 'heavy, stifling' (of temperature), this prob. : W. *llwg* 'livid', Ir. *loch* 'black'. Henry 192. Ernault, Glossaire 180.

4. ON *poka*, Dan. *taage*, Sw. *töcken*, MLG *dake*, fr. *tug-, *teug-, perh. extension of IE *teu-* 'swell, be thick' (Lat. *tumēre* 'swell', etc.). Falk-Torp 1238. Hellquist 1268.

Sw. *dimma* : Sw. dial. *dimba* 'vapor', Norw. dial. *demba* 'mist', *dumba* 'dust', Dan. *dum* 'dim, dull', OE *dumb* 'dumb'; also ON *dimmr*, OE *dimm* 'dim'; also, fr. a parallel form of the root, OHG-NHG *dampf* 'vapor, steam', used also for 'mist', as sometimes Du. *damp*, and formerly NE *damp* (cf. NED); all fr. *dhembh-, *dhemb-, extensions of *dhem-* in Skt. *dham-* 'blow', etc. Walde-P. 1.851 ff. Falk-Torp 165, 135. Hellquist 143.

NE *fog*, prob. a back-formation fr. *foggy*, this fr. ME *fogg* 'coarse grass', with development through 'boggy, flabby, thick, murky'. NED s.v.

NE *haze*, prob. a back-formation fr. *hazy*, earlier *hawsey*, this fr. OE *hasu, haswe* 'gray' : Lat. *cānus* 'gray', etc. Walde-P. 1.357. Falk-Torp 380.

5. Russ. *tuman*, now the usual word for 'mist, fog', Pol. *tuman* 'cloud' (of dust, smoke, etc.) fr. Turk. *dumān* 'smoke'. Lokotsch 545, 2105. Brückner 584.

1.75 RAIN (sb.)

Grk.	ὑετός, βροχή	Goth.	rign	Lith.	lytus
NG	βροχή	ON	regn	Lett.	lietus
Lat.	pluvia	Dan.	regn	ChSl.	dŭždĭ
It.	pioggia	Sw.	regn	SCr.	kiša, dažd
Fr.	pluie	OE	regn	Boh.	dešt
Sp.	lluvia	ME	rein	Pol.	deszcz
Rum.	ploaie	NE	rain	Russ.	dožd
Ir.	flechud, brōen	Du.	regen	Skt.	varṣa-
NIr.	fearthainn, bāisteach	OHG	regen	Av.	vār-
W.	glaw	MHG	regen		
Br.	glao	NHG	regen		

Some of the words for 'rain' are connected with one special group of words for 'water'; others with words for 'flow', 'pour', 'wet', etc.

Words for 'shower, storm', though often used for 'rain', as Grk. ὄμβρος, Lat. imber, are not included.

1. Grk. ὑετός, with vb. ὕει 'it rains' : Toch. A swase, B swese 'rain', Skt. su- 'press out, extract', soma- 'juice', Lat. sūcus 'juice', sūgere 'suck', OE sūcan 'suck', etc. Walde-P. 2.468 ff. Boisacq 399.

Grk. βροχή, quotable as 'rain' once from 5th cent. B.C. and regular word from Hellenistic times on, fr. βρέχω 'wet' (vb. trans., mid. 'get wet'), 3 sg. βρέχει 'it rains' (quotable once from 5th cent. B.C., as regularly NG) : Lett. merga 'light rain', etc., ultimate root connection? Walde-P. 2.280. Boisacq 133.

2. Lat. pluvia (> Romance words), with vb. pluit 'it rains' : Grk. πλέω 'sail', Skt. plu- 'float, swim, sail', ChSl. pluti 'sail', OE flōwan 'flow', etc., IE *pleu- 'flow, float', etc. Walde-P. 2.94 ff. Ernout-M. 781 f. REW 6620.

3. Ir. flechud : Ir. fliuch 'wet' (15.83). Ir. brōen 'drop, rain, shower' (K. Meyer, Contrib. 266), etym.? Walde-P. 1.268.

Ir. bāistech (rare), NIr. bāisteach, same word as Ir. baitsech 'shower' (orig.

'baptism'), fr. Ir. baitsim, NIr. baistim 'baptize' (22.25). K. Meyer, Contrib. 169.

NIr. fearthainn : Ir. feraim 'pour', Skt. vāri- 'water', etc. Walde-P. 1.268.

W., Corn. glaw, Br. glao, etym.? Henry 133 (: Lat. lavāre 'wash', rejected by Walde-P. 2.441). Morris Jones 214.

4. Goth. rign, OE regn, etc., general Gmc., etym. dub., perh. (rek- beside reg-?) : ON rakr 'wet', Lat. rigāre 'moisten, water' (with i fr. cpds.), etc. Walde-P. 2.365. Falk-Torp 887. Feist 397.

5. Lith. lytus, Lett. lietus, with vb. Lith. lyti, Lett. līt 'rain' : Lith. lieti, Lett. liet, ChSl. liti, lějǫ 'pour' etc. (9.35). Walde-P. 2.392.

ChSl. dŭždĭ, etc., general Slavic, etym. dub. Berneker 248. Troubetskoj, Z.sl.Ph. 4.62, Vaillant, Rev. ét. sl. 7.112 f. (both as *duz-dju- 'bad sky'). Endzelin Z. sl. Ph. 13.79.

SCr. kiša, back-formation fr. kišnuti 'get wet, soaked' : ChSl. kysnǫti 'get sour, fermented'. Berneker 678.

6. Skt. varṣa-, vṛṣṭi-, with vb. vṛṣ- 'rain' : Grk. ἐέρση, ἔρση 'dew', fr. *wers-, extension of *wer- in Skt. vāri- 'water', etc. Here prob. also Ir. frass, NIr. fras 'shower'. Walde-P. 1.268 f.

Av. vār- : Skt. vāri- 'water', ON ūr 'fine rain', etc. (1.31). Walde-P. 1.268 f.

1.76 SNOW (sb.)

Grk.	χιών (νίφα poet.)	Goth.	snaiws	Lith.	sniegas
NG	χιόνι	ON	snær (snjōr, snjār)	Lett.	sniegs
Lat.	nix	Dan.	sne	ChSl.	sněgŭ
It.	neve	Sw.	snö	SCr.	snijeg
Fr.	neige	OE	snāw	Boh.	snih
Sp.	nieve	ME	snow	Pol.	śnieg
Rum.	zăpadă	NE	snow	Russ.	sneg
Ir.	snechte	Du.	sneeuw	Skt.	hima-
NIr.	sneachta	OHG	snēo	Av.	vafra-
W.	eira (nyf)	MHG	snē		
Br.	erc'h	NHG	schnee		

Words for 'snow' are mostly inherited from an IE noun and verb meaning 'snow', any further analysis of which is futile. For the meaning of Skt. snih- 'be sticky', if this is the same word, is probably secondary rather than the primary notion. Of the others, some are connected with words for 'winter, cold', and some rest on specialization of 'fall', etc. to 'snowfall, snow'.

1. IE. snigʷh-, *snoigʷho-, with vb. *sneigʷh-. Walde-P. 2.695. Ernout-M. 673.

Grk. νίφα acc. sg. (poet.), with vb. νείφει; Lat. nix, nivis, with vb. ninguit, It. neve, OFr. noif, Fr. neige (fr. neiger, *niviāre. REW 5934), Sp. nieve, Rum. nea (dial.); Ir. snechte (but snigid 'it rains'), NIr. sneachta, W. nyf (obs.); Goth. snaiws, OE snāw, etc. general Gmc.; Lith. sniegas, ChSl. sněgŭ, etc., general Balto-Slavic; Av. snaēg- only in vb., pres. snaēža- (but Pahl. sb. snēhr 'snow', Horn 292); here prob., but with

no trace of meaning 'snow', Skt. snih- 'be sticky', sneha- 'stickiness'.

2. Grk. χιών, NG χιόνι : χειμών 'winter', Arm. jiun 'snow', Skt. hima- 'snow, ice, winter', Av. zyąm, Lat. hiems, Lith. žiema, ChSl. zima 'winter' (1.76). Walde-P. 1.546 ff.

3. Rum. zăpadă, loanword fr. Slavic, cf. ChSl. za-pasti 'fall', ChSl. zapadŭ specialized to 'going down of the sun, sunset, west', while a parallel *zapada was specialized in Rumanian to 'fall of snow', then 'snow' in general. Tiktin 1792.

Cf. Rum. dial. omăt, nămete, fr. Slavic o-(na-)metati 'heap up', hence 'heap of snow, snow'. Tiktin 1032, 1088.

4. W. eira, Corn. er, Br. erc'h : Ir. arg 'drop', Lat. spargere 'strew, sprinkle', etc. Walde-P. 2.674. Pedersen 1.104.

5. Av. vafra, rare but confirmed by Pahl. vafr, NPers. barf 'snow', etym.? Barth. 1347.

1.77 ICE

Grk.	κρύσταλλος (πάγος)	Goth.	. . . .	Lith.	ledas
NG	πάγος	ON	īss	Lett.	ledus
Lat.	glaciēs	Dan.	is	ChSl.	ledŭ
It.	ghiaccio	Sw.	is	SCr.	led
Fr.	glace	OE	īs	Boh.	led
Sp.	hielo	ME	ise	Pol.	lód
Rum.	ghiață	NE	ice	Russ.	led
Ir.	aig, aigred	Du.	ijs	Skt.	hima-
NIr.	oighreadh	OHG	īs	Av.	aēxa-
W.	rhew, ia	MHG	īs		
Br.	sko(u)rn	NHG	eis		

Words for 'ice' are mostly of obscure root connection; but in some it is clear that the underlying notion was that of hard or solid surface and that the meaning 'cold' in cognates is secondary, from 'icy'.

1. Grk. κρύσταλλος : κρύος 'icy cold, frost', Lat. crusta 'hard surface, shell, crust', Skt. krūd- 'make hard, thicken',

Av. xruždra-, xraoždva- 'hard', all fr. *krus-, *krus-t, *kruz-d, with the common notion of 'hard, hard surface', whence 'ice' in κρύσταλλος and secondarily 'icy cold' in κρύος. Further connection with the group denoting 'bloody, raw, raw flesh' (Skt. kravis, Grk. κρέας, Lat. cruor, etc.), if actual, is more remote. Walde-P. 1.479.

Grk. πάγος 'frost' (also 'rocky hill'), sometimes 'ice', as NG πάγος 'ice' (also παγωτό 'ice cream') : πήγνῡμι 'fix, make solid, freeze'.

2. Lat. glaciēs (VLat. glacia > It. ghiaccia, now ghiaccio, Fr. glace, Rum. ghiață) : gelu 'icy cold' (> Sp. hielo 'ice'), adj. gelidus, Goth. kalds 'cold', etc. (15.86). Walde-P. 1.622, 612. Ernout-M. 412, 423. REW 3718, 3771.

3. Ir. aig, aigred, NIr. oighreadh, W. ia : ON jaki 'piece of ice', dim. jǫkull 'icicle, glazier', OE gicel 'icicle' (īses gicel > NE icicle). Walde-P. 1.206. Pedersen 1.65.

W. rhew (now more usual for 'ice' than ia), rewi 'freeze', Br. reo 'frost', riou 'cold', riel 'thin ice' : Ir. reod 'frost',

perh. : Lat. pruīna 'frost', OE frēosan 'freeze', etc. Henry 232 with query. Morris Jones 103 f. (Not included in Walde-P. 2.88). Otherwise Stokes 231. Br. sko(u)rn, etym.? Henry 243.

4. ON īss, OE īs, etc., general Gmc., prob. : Av. aēxa- 'frost, ice', isu- 'frosty, icy', NPers. yak 'ice', Afghan asaī 'frost', root connection? Walde-P. 1.108. Falk-Torp 468, 1490. Barth. 372.

5. Lith. ledas, OPruss. ladis, Lett. ledus, ChSl. ledŭ, etc., general Balto-Slavic, outside connections? Walde-P. 2.428. Berneker 699.

6. Skt. hima- 'ice, snow, winter' : Grk. χιών 'snow', Lat. hiems 'winter', etc. (1.76).

Av. aēxa-, above, 4.

1.78 WEATHER

Grk.	. . . .	Goth.	. . . .	Lith.	oras
NG	καιρός	ON	veðr	Lett.	laiks
Lat.	tempestās, caelum	Dan.	vejr	ChSl.	. . . .
It.	tempo	Sw.	väder	SCr.	vrijeme
Fr.	temps	OE	weder	Boh.	počasí
Sp.	tiempo	ME	weder	Pol.	czas, pogoda
Rum.	timp, vreme	NE	weather	Russ.	pogoda
Ir.	sín	Du.	weder, weer	Skt.	kāla-(?)
NIr.	sion, aimsir	OHG	wetar	Av.	. . . .
W.	tywydd, hin	MHG	weter		
Br.	amzer	NHG	wetter		

The 'weather' is most commonly expressed by words for 'time', in a few cases by those for 'air' or 'sky', while the Gmc. group is cognate with words for 'wind'.

1. Words for 'time' (14.11), or derivs., either used also for, or in some cases specialized to, 'weather'. NG καιρός, Lat. tempestās (deriv. of tempus 'time', but used mainly for 'weather', then esp. 'bad weather, tempest', hence for 'weather' replaced in VLat. by tempus > Romance words), It. tempo, Fr. temps, amzer; Lett. laiks; SCr. vrijeme, Boh. počasí (beside čas 'time'), Pol. czas,

Russ. (also Pol. in phrases) pogoda (: ChSl. godŭ 'point of time', Russ. god 'year'); Skt. kāla- (quotable for weather?).

2. In classical Greek there were words for 'good weather', as αἰθρία (: αἴθριος 'clear, bright', αἰθήρ 'sky, ether') and εὐδία (: εὔδιος 'fine, clear', cpd. of εὐ- 'good' and *διρος-. : Ζεύς, Διός orig. 'sky' like Skt. dyāus, gen. divas, 1.51); and 'bad weather' might be expressed by 'winter' or 'storm', but there was no generic term for 'weather' until καιρός 'time' came to be so used (Byz. and NG).

3. Lat. caelum 'sky' (1.51), used also for 'weather'.

4. Ir. sín, NIr. sion, W. hin, etym.? Macbain 321. Stokes 299.

W. tywydd, perh. : Ir. tōid 'shine' and fr. cpd. of root in Lat. vidēre 'see', etc. Pedersen 2.651.

5. ON veðr, OE weder, OHG wetar,

etc., general Gmc. (though not quotable in Goth.) : ChSl. vedro 'εὐδία, good weather', fr. the root seen in words for 'blow' as Skt. vā-, Grk. ἄημι, and 'wind' (Lat. ventus, Goth. winds, Skt. vāta-, etc., 1.72). Walde-P. 1.222. Falk-Torp 1363. NED s.v. weather.

6. Lith. oras 'air' (1.71) and 'weather'.

1.81 FIRE

Grk.	πῦρ	Goth.	fōn	Lith.	ugnis
NG	φωτιά	ON	eldr (fūrr, funi poet.)	Lett.	uguns
Lat.	ignis	Dan.	ild	ChSl.	ogni
It.	fuoco	Sw.	eld	SCr.	vatra, oganj
Fr.	feu	OE	fȳr (œled poet.)	Boh.	oheň
Sp.	fuego	ME	fyre	Pol.	ogień
Rum.	foc	NE	fire	Russ.	ogon'
Ir.	tene, daig (āed)	Du.	vuur	Skt.	agni- (vahni-, anala-)
NIr.	teine	OHG	fiur, fuir	Av.	ātar-
W.	tan	MHG	viur		
Br.	tan	NHG	feuer		

Most of the words for 'fire' belong to one of two inherited groups, represented respectively by Grk. πῦρ, NE fire, and Lat. ignis. The root connections are unknown. It has been suggested (Meillet, MSL 21.249 ff.) that originally the first group, regularly neuter, denoted fire as a lifeless element, while the second group, regularly masculine, denoted the active personified fire of religious cult, so prominent in the use of Skt. agni-. This seems likely, but in actual use the two groups are synonymous. Thus Umbr. pir, of the first group, is used of the ritual fire no less than Lat. ignis, as also Osc. aasaí purasiaí 'in ara igniaria'.

The others are connected with words for 'burn', 'heat', 'light', etc.

1. IE *pewōr(?), *pūr, *pun-, etc., r/n stem neut. (like that for 'water'), with complicated and partly dub. phonetic relations and of unknown root connection. Walde-P. 2.14. Feist 158 f. Sturtevant, Laryngeals 36 f. Ben-

veniste, Origines 169. Pedersen, Hittitisch 187.

Grk. πῦρ; Umbr. pir (fr. *pūr, cf. acc. purom-e, Osc. adj. purasiaí); Goth. fōn, gen. funins, ON fūrr, funi (poet.), OE fȳr, NE fire, Du. vuur, OHG fiur, fuir, NHG feuer; (Boh. pýr 'embers'); Arm. hur; Toch. A por, B puwar; Hitt. paḫḫur, paḫḫwar, dat. paḫḫuni, etc.

2. IE *egni-, *ogni-(?). Walde-P. 1.323. Ernout-M. 473. Walde-H. 1.676. Lat. ignis; Lith. ugnis, Lett. uguns, ChSl. ognĭ, etc., general Balto-Slavic; Skt. agni-.

3. NG φωτιά : Grk. φῶς, gen. φωτός 'light' (1.61), used also for the household fire, as Xen. πρὸς φῶς πίνειν 'drink by the fire', NT καθήμενον πρὸς τὸ φῶς 'sitting by the fire'. Cf. following.

4. It. fuoco, Fr. feu, Sp. fuego, Rum. foc, fr. Lat. focus 'fireplace, hearth', hence 'household fire' and 'fire' in general, replacing ignis in VLat.

5. Ir. tene, NIr. teine, W., Br. tan, fr. *tep-n- : Skt. tapas-, Av. tafnah- 'heat',

Lat. *tepor* 'warmth', etc. Walde-P. 1.718 f. Pedersen 1.93 f.

Ir. *daig* (MW *goddaith* 'great fire, conflagration', Loth, RC 38.169) : Skt. *dah-* 'burn', etc. (1.84). Pedersen 1.108.

Ir. *āed* (rare) : Grk. αἴθω 'kindle', αἴθομαι 'burn, blaze', Skt. *idh-* 'kindle', etc. Walde-P. 1.4 f. Pedersen 1.57.

6. ON *eldr*, Dan. *ild*, Sw. *eld*, OE *æled*, gen. *ældes* (poet.) : OE *ǣlan* 'burn', Grk. αἴθω 'kindle', αἴθομαι 'burn, blaze', Skt. *idh-* 'kindle', etc. Walde-P. 1.4 ff.

7. SCr. *vatra* (now more usual than *oganj*) : Ukr., Boh. dial. *vatra*, Pol. dial. *watra*, Rum. *vatră*, Alb. *vátrë*, all meaning 'fireplace' or in part 'fire'. Possibly (with prefixed *w-*) a loanword fr. Iranian or cognate with Av. *ātar-* 'fire'. Walde-P. 1.42. Brückner 604.

8. Av. *ātar-*, NPers. *ādar* 'fire', Av. *āθravan-*, *aθaurvan-*, Skt. *atharvan-* 'fire-priest', root connection? Walde-P. 1.42.

Skt. *vahni-* 'draught animal, bearer' (fr. *vah-* 'carry'), freq. epithet of Agni, later alone for 'fire'.

Skt. *anala-*, fr. *an-* 'breathe'(?), or perh. of Dravidian orig. Schrader, KZ 56.125.

1.82 FLAME (sb.)

Grk.	φλόξ	Goth.	....	Lith.	*liepsna*
NG	φλόγα	ON	*logi, leygr* (poet.)	Lett.	*liesma*
Lat.	*flamma*	Dan.	*flamme, lue*	ChSl.	*plamy*
It.	*fiamma*	Sw.	*flamma, låga*	SCr.	*plamen*
Fr.	*flamme*	OE	*līeg*	Boh.	*plamen*
Sp.	*llama*	ME	*leye, lowe, flamme*	Pol.	*płomień*
Rum.	*flacără*	NE	*flame*	Russ.	*plamja*
Ir.	*lassar, breo*	Du.	*vlam*	Skt.	*jvala-, çocis-*, etc.
NIr.	*lasair*	OHG	*loug*	Av.	**saočah-*
W.	*fflam, ffagl*	MHG	*flamme, lohe*		
Br.	*flamm*	NHG	*flamme* (*lohe*)		

1. From the root of Grk. φλέγω, Lat. *flagrāre* 'burn, blaze', etc. Walde-P. 2.214. Ernout-M. 666 f. Walde-H. 1.513.

Grk. φλόξ, gen. φλογός, NG φλόγα; Lat. *flamma*, whence It. *fiamma*, Fr. *flamme*, Sp. *llama*, also, through Fr., ME *flamme*, NE *flame*, Br. *flamm*, or direct fr. Lat.(?) W. *fflam*, Du. *vlam*, MHG, NHG *flamme* (> Dan. *flamme*, Sw. *flamma*).

2. Rum. *flacără*, fr. **flacula* (It. *fiaccola* 'torch'), this fr. Lat. *facula* 'torch' (dim. of *fax* id.) with *l* fr. *flamma*, *flagrāre*. Cf. W. *ffagl* 'blaze, flame, torch' fr. Lat. *facula*. REW 3137.

3. Ir. *lassar*, NIr. *lasair* (fr. **lap-s-*) : W. *llachar* 'bright', Grk. λάμπω 'shine', OPruss. *lopis* 'flame'. Lith. *liepsna*, Lett. *liesma*, fr. a parallel root **leip-*. Walde-P. 2.383. Pedersen 1.75.

Ir. *breo*, perh. fr. **bhrī-wo-* : OE *brīw* 'porridge', *brīwan* 'coquere', ON *brimi* 'fire', etc. (Walde-P. 2.158 f.) G. S. Lane, Language 13.22.

4. ON *logi*, poet. *leygr*, Dan. *lue*, Sw. *låga*, OE *lieg* (*lēg, lig*), ME *leye* and *lowe* (latter fr. ON), MLG *log*, OHG *loug*, MHG *lohe* (NHG *lohe*) : Goth. *liuhaþ*, NE *light*, etc. (1.61). Walde-P. 2.410. Falk-Torp 659. NED s.vv. *leye*, *low*, sb.

5. Lith. *liepsna*, Lett. *liesma*, above, 3.

6. ChSl. *plamy*, etc., general Slavic : ChSl. *polěti*, *paliti* 'blaze, burn' (1.84). Walde-P. 2.59. Miklosich 235. Brückner 421 f.

7. Skt. *jvala-* : *jval-* 'blaze, glow', *jvara-* 'fever', *jvar-* 'be feverish', Lett. *zvērs* 'flashing', etc. Walde-P. 1.643 (rejecting connection with OE *col* 'live coal', NE *coal*, etc.).

Skt. *çocis-*, *çoka-*, Av. **saočah-* (*saočahin-*, *saočinavant-* 'flaming') : Skt. *çuc-* 'glow, flame', etc. Walde-P. 1.378.

1.83 SMOKE (sb.)

Grk.	καπνός	Goth.	....	Lith.	*dūmai* (pl.)
NG	καπνός	ON	*reykr*	Lett.	*dūmi* (pl.)
Lat.	*fūmus*	Dan.	*røg*	ChSl.	*dymŭ*
It.	*fumo*	Sw.	*rök*	SCr.	*dim*
Fr.	*fumée*	OE	*rēc, smoca*	Boh.	*dým*
Sp.	*humo*	ME	*reke, smoke*	Pol.	*dym*
Rum.	*fum*	NE	*smoke*	Russ.	*dym*
Ir.	*dē, dethach*	Du.	*rook*	Skt.	*dhūma-*
NIr.	*deatach*	OHG	*rouh*	Av.	....
W.	*mwg*	MHG	*rouch*		
Br.	*moged*	NHG	*rauch*		

1. IE **dhūmo-*, fr. the root seen in Skt. *dhū-* 'shake, agitate', Grk. θύω 'rush, rage', θύελλα 'storm', etc. Most of the words belonging here are used for 'vapor, steam' as well as 'smoke', while Grk. θυμός is used only in the figurative sense (mental agitation) 'spirit, passion', etc. Walde-P. 1.835 f. Ernout-M. 399. Walde-H. 1.561 f.

Lat. *fūmus*, whence It. *fumo*, OFr. *fum* (> ME, NE *fume*), Fr. *fumée* (fr. *fūmāta*, cf. *fūmāre*, Fr. *fumer*), Sp. *humo*, Rum. *fum;* Lith. *dūmai* (pl.), ChSl. *dymŭ*, etc., general Balto-Slavic; Skt. *dhūma-* (Av. form lacking, but NPers. *dūd* fr. the same root).

2. Grk. καπνός : Lith. *kvapas* 'breath, odor', Lat. *vapor* 'vapor, steam' (prob., but disputed), Goth. *af-hwapjan* 'choke', etc. Walde-P. 1.379 f.

3. Ir. *dē* (gen. *diad*), *dethach*, NIr. *deatach* : W. *dew* 'fog, gloom, dusk', fr. the same root as Lat. *fūmus*, etc. (above, 1). Loth, RC 42.85 f., 43.398 f.

W. *mwg*, Br. *moged* (NIr. *mūch* now mostly fig. 'gloom'), OE *smoca*, ME, NE *smoke* (Du. *smook*, NHG *schmauch*, now esp. 'thick smoke') : OE *smēocan* 'smoke', Lith. *smaugti* 'choke', Grk. σμύχω 'make smoulder', etc. Here also Arm. *mux* 'smoke'. Walde-P. 2.689. Pedersen 1.122.

4. ON *reykr*, OE *rēc*, ME *reke* (NE *reek* still the usual word for 'smoke' in Scotland), OHG *rouh*, etc., general Gmc., beside vb. ON *rjūka*, OE *rēocan*, etc., prob. : Grk. ἐρεύγομαι, Lat. *ructāre* 'spew out, belch', with specialization to the belching-out of smoke. Walde-P. 2.357. Falk-Torp 934.

1.84 ASHES

Grk.	τέφρα, σποδός	Goth.	*azgō*	Lith.	*pelenai*
NG	στάχτη	ON	*aska*	Lett.	*pelni*
Lat.	*cinis, favilla*	Dan.	*aske*	ChSl.	*popelŭ* (*pepelŭ*)
It.	*cenere*	Sw.	*aska*	SCr.	*pepeo*
Fr.	*cendre*	OE	*asce*	Boh.	*popel*
Sp.	*ceniza*	ME	*ashe*	Pol.	*popiól*
Rum.	*cenușe*	NE	*ashes*	Russ.	*pepel*
Ir.	*luaith*	Du.	*asch*	Skt.	*bhasman-, āsa-*
NIr.	*luaith*	OHG	*asca*	Av.	*ātrya-*
W.	*lludw*	MHG	*asche*		
Br.	*ludu*	NHG	*asche*		

Words for 'ash, ashes' (NE now usual-pl. *ashes*, though also the *ash* of a cigar) are mostly either derived from words for 'burn', 'fire', 'be dry', 'warm', 'devour' (by fire), or are cognate with words for 'dust'. A few come from or through 'washing fluid, lye', with shifted application to the 'ashes' which produce it.

1. Grk. τέφρα, fr. the root seen in Skt. *dah-*, Lith. *degti*, etc. 'burn' (1.85). Walde-P. 1.849. Boisacq 963 f.

Grk. σποδός, etym.? Walde-P. 2.680. Boisacq 899.

NG στάχτη (pop. vs. lit. τέφρα, σποδός), Byz. στακτή (Const. Porph. as 'ashes'), fr. στακτὴ κονία lit. 'trickling dust' (στακτός fr. στάζω 'drop, drip') used first for 'lye' made from ashes and then for the 'ashes'.

2. Lat. *cinis*, *cineris* (> It. *cenere*, Fr. *cendre;* derivs. > It. *cinigia*, Sp. *ceniza*, Rum. *cenușe*) : Grk. κόνις 'dust'. Walde-P. 1.392. Ernout-M. 187 f. Walde-H. 1.217 f. REW 1929, 1930.

Lat. *favilla*, esp. 'glowing ashes', fr. the root of *fovēre* 'warm', Skt. *dah-* 'burn', etc. (1.84). Ernout-M. 339. Walde-H. 1.466.

3. Ir. *luaith*, W. *lludw*, Br. *ludu* : Grk. λούω, Lat. *lavere* 'wash', OE *lēag*, NE *lye*, OHG *louga*, NHG *lauge* 'lye', with Celtic development through 'washing fluid, lye' to the 'ashes' from which it was made. Walde-P. 2.441. Pedersen 1.63.

4. Goth. *azgō*, ON *aska*, OE *asce*, OHG *asca*, etc., general Gmc., fr. a root **as-* seen in Lat. *ārēre* 'be dry', *āridus* 'dry', *ardēre* 'burn', Grk. ἄζω 'be dry', Skt. *āsa-* 'ashes, dust', Toch. A *āsar* 'dry', Arm. *ačium* 'ashes'. Falk-Torp 35. Feist 72. Walde-H. 1.65.

5. Lith. *pelenai* (pl.), Lett. *pelni* (pl.), OPruss. *pelanne*, ChSl. *popelŭ* (later *pepelŭ*), SCr. *pepeo*, etc., general Balto-Slavic word, prob. (like Lat. *cinis* : Grk. κόνις 'dust') : Lat. *pulvis* 'dust, powder', *pollen* 'fine flour or dust', Grk. πάλη 'fine flour or dust', etc.; less prob. : ChSl. *polěti*, *paliti* 'blaze, burn' (1.84). Walde-P. 2.60: Ernout-M. 785.

6. Skt. *bhasman-*, fr. *bhas-* 'devour', here through (attested) 'devour by fire, reduce to ashes'.

Skt. *āsa-* : Goth. *azgō* 'ashes', etc. (above, 4).

Av. *ātrya-*, fr. *ātar-* 'fire' (1.81).

1.85 BURN (vb.)

(Transitive and intransitive, when distinguished, are marked "a" and "b")

Grk.	καίω (a), καίομαι (b), πίμπρημι (a)	Goth.	*brinnan* (b), *brannjan* (a)	Lith.	*degti*
NG	καίω	ON	*brinna* (b), *brenna* (a)	Lett.	*degt*
Lat.	*ūrere* (a), *ardēre* (b), *cremāre* (a)	Dan.	*brænde*	ChSl.	*žešti* (a), *gorěti* (b)
It.	*bruciare*	Sw.	*bränna*	SCr.	*žeći* (a), *gorjeti* (b)
Fr.	*brûler*	OE	*beornan* (b), *bærnan* (a)	Boh.	*spaliti* (a, refl. b), *horeti* (b)
Sp.	*quemar* (a), *quemarse* (b)	ME	*birne*, etc.	Pol.	*palić* (a, refl. b), *gorsec'* (b)
Rum.	*arde*	NE	*burn*	Russ.	*žeč'* (a), *goret'* (b)
Ir.	*loscim* (a), *breoaim*(a)	Du.	*branden*	Skt.	*dah-*, *uș-* (act. a, pass. b)
NIr.	*dōighim* (*loiscim*)	OHG	*brinnan* (b), *brennan* (a)	Av.	*dag-*
W.	*llosgi*	MHG	*brinnen* (b), *brennen* (a)		
Br.	*devi, leski*	NHG	*brennen*		

The transitive and intransitive 'burn', namely a) 'consume with fire', b) 'be on fire', may be expressed by 1) the same form, as NE *burn* (*he burns it, it burns*); 2) different voices or otherwise differentiated forms of the same root, as Grk. καίω, Skt. *dah-*, *uș-*, a in active, b in middle or passive, Goth. *brinnan* b, but caus. *brannjan* a; 3) unrelated words, as ChSl. *žešti* a, but *gorěti* b.

Words for 'burn' may be also used transitively not in the sense of 'consume

by fire' but for 'burn slightly, scorch, singe' (NE *burn one's hand*). Words that are used primarily in this latter sense are not included in the table, e.g. Grk. εὕω in contrast to the cognate Lat. *ūrere*, Skt. *uș-*.

In some groups the intransitive meaning is either the prevailing one or demonstrably the earlier; in others the transitive meaning appears to be the earlier. The former are connected with words meaning 'hot', 'shine, be bright', 'spurt'(?), etc. The latter either are of obscure etymology (Grk. καίω) or are inherited from IE roots in which the meaning 'burn' was already developed, so that the ultimate source is unknown. It is noticeable that there is no etymological connection between the words for 'burn' and the common words for 'fire'.

1. IE **dhegʷh-*. Walde-P. 1.849. Ernout-M. 384. Walde-H. 1.466 f.

Skt. *dah-*, Av. *dag-* (3 sg. *dažaiti* = Skt. *dahati*); Lith. *degti*, Lett. *degt;* here also the Slavic forms, with assimilatory change of **deg-* to **geg-* (cf. Russ. *izgaga* 'heartburn'), whence *žeg-*, ChSl. *žešti*, *žegą*, SCr. *žeći* (Boh. *žeci*, Pol. *żec* formerly the usual words for 'burn', now mostly 'scorch, singe'), Russ. *žeč'*; NIr. *dōigim* (denom., cf. MIr. *daig* 'fire', NIr. *doigh* 'pain'); Alb. *djégë* 'burn'; Toch. *tsäk-* 'burn'; cf. Lat. *fovēre* 'warm'.

2. IE **eus-*. Walde-P. 1.111. Ernout-M. 1137 f.

Skt. *uș-*, Lat. *ūrere* 'burn', Grk. εὕω 'singe'.

3. Grk. καίω, Att. κάω, fr. *κάϝ-ιω, aor. Hom. ἔκηα (*ἐκηϝα), Att. ἔκαυσα, the principal Greek word for 'burn' at all periods, with numerous derivatives. Without any clear outside connections. Walde-P. 1.376. Καίω a, καίομαι b (or in Homer also 'light for themselves'). NG καίω a, b (cf. καίει 'it burns'), distinguished in aor. ἔκαψα (ἔκαυσα) a, ἐκάηκα b.

Grk. πίμπρημι : πρήθω 'blow up, inflate', Russ. *pret'* 'stew, sweat', ChSl. *para* 'steam, vapor', etc. Walde-P. 2.27. Prob. first intrans. 'burn' from the notion of 'spurting out'.

Grk. αἴθω (poet.) 'light up, kindle', αἴθομαι 'burn' b, 'blaze' : Skt. *idh-* 'kindle', *edhas-* 'fuel', *iddha-* 'blazing, bright' (cf. Grk. αἴθων 'blazing', αἴθριος 'bright, clear'), Lat. *aestus* 'heat', etc. Walde-P. 1.4 ff. Walde-H. 1.15 f. In this group the underlying notion is 'blaze' rather than 'burn' in the sense of consume by fire.

Grk. φλέγω, φλέγομαι 'blaze, burn' b, φλέγω also 'kindle', or 'burn' a : φλόξ 'flame', Lat. *flamma* 'flame', *flagrāre* 'blaze', etc. (1.82). Walde-P. 2.214.

4. Lat. *ardēre* : *āridus* 'dry', *ārēre* 'be dry', Grk. ἄζω 'be dry', Skt. *āsa-* 'ashes, dust', Goth *azgō*, OE *asce* 'ashes', etc. Ernout-M. 75. Walde-H. 1.65.

Hence Rum. *arde*, the common word for 'burn', both a and b, while It. *ardere* and Sp. *arder* are mostly used in figurative sense.

Lat. *cremāre*, fr. **krem-* prob. : **ker-* in Lat. *carbo*, Goth. *hauri* 'coal', Lith. *kurti* 'light a fire', etc. Walde-P. 1.418 ff. Ernout-M. 229. Walde-H. 1.287.

Lat. *adolēre* ('burn', a sacrificial term), Umbr. *uřetu* 'adoleto', root connection dub. Ernout-M. 14. Walde-H. 1.13.

It. *bruciare* (cf. *abbrustiare* 'singe'), Fr. *brûler* (OFr. *brusler*), of much disputed orig. Perh. fr. Lat. *ustulāre* 'singe', with init. *br* by a blend with Gmc. words like OHG *brennan, brunst.* REW 9097.

Sp. *quemar*, Port. *quiemar*, prob. fr. a late Grk. κάημα 'burning, heat' (*caima* gl.) formed fr. ἐκάην aor. of καίω, like NG καημός 'sharp pain, grief'. REW 2309.

5. Ir. *loscim*, NIr. *loiscim*, W. *llosgi*, Br. *leski*, etym. dub. (fr. **lop-sk-* : OPruss. *lopis* 'flame', Grk. λάμπω 'shine', etc.?). Stokes 256. Walde-P. 2.383. Pedersen 1.76 (fr. **luks-* : Lat. *lūx* 'light').

Ir. *breoaim*, deriv. of *breo* 'flame' (1.82).

Br. *devi* : W. *deifio* 'singe', Ir. 3 sg. *attai* 'kindles' (cpd. with *ad-*), Skt. *du-* 'burn', Grk. δαίω (**δαϝ-ω*) 'kindle', etc. Walde-P. 1.768. Thurneysen, Z. celt. Ph. 8.64 f. Pedersen 2.507 f. (but here and 1.108 preferring to derive the Br. and W. words fr. **degʷh-*, above, 1).

6. Goth. *brinnan*, caus. *brannjan*, etc., all the Gmc. words, with uses b and a expressed by simple verb or causative respectively in the earlier periods, but later merged in a single form. Here the intransitive meaning of the simple verb is, of course, the more original (in contrast to the opposite relation in Grk. καίω,

καίομαι, and others), and this, analyzed as **bhre-n-wo-*, may be combined with **bher-*, **bhreu-* in words used for the gushing and seething of liquids, as Lat. *fervēre* 'boil', Goth. *brunna* 'spring', etc. Walde-P. 2.168. Feist 106. Falk-Torp 111.

7. Lith. *degti*, ChSl. *žešti*, etc., above, 1.

ChSl. *gorěti*, etc., general Slavic for 'burn' b, : Skt. *gharma-* 'heat', Grk. θερμός 'hot', etc. (15.85), Ir. vb. *gorim* 'heat, warm'. Walde-P. 1.688. Berneker 333 f.

Boh. *spaliti*, Pol. *palić* (now the usual words for 'burn' a and used with reflexive for 'burn' b) = ChSl. *paliti* (also *polěti*) 'blaze, burn' (e.g. Supr. = φλέγομαι), SCr. *paliti* 'set on fire, burn' a, Russ. *palit'* 'blaze, burn, singe', all with primary notion of 'blaze' fr. **pel-* in ChSl. *plamy* 'flame', etc. (1.82). Walde-P. 2.59 f. Miklosich 235. Brückner 392.

1.86 LIGHT (vb.), KINDLE

Grk.	(ἀν)άπτω (δαίω, αἴθω)	Goth.	*tandjan*	Lith.	*uždegti*	
NG	ἀνάφτω, ἀνάβω	ON	*tendra, kynda*	Lett.	*aiz-* (or *ie-*)*dedzināt*	
Lat.	*incendere* (also *ac-, suc-*)	Dan.	*(an)tænde*	ChSl.	*vžešti*	
		Sw.	*(upp)tända*	SCr.	*zapaliti*	
It.	*accendere*	OE	*onǣlan, (on)tendan*	Boh.	*zapáliti*	
Fr.	*allumer*	ME	*lihte, kindle*	Pol.	*zapalić*	
Sp.	*encender*	NE	*light, kindle*	Russ.	*zažeč'*	
Rum.	*aprinde, încinge*	Du.	*aansteken*	Skt.	*idh-*	
Ir.	*attai* (3 sg. pres.)	OHG	*zunten*	Av.	. . . .	
NIr.	*lasaim*	MHG	*zünden*			
W.	*ennyn, cynneu*	NHG	*anzünden (anstecken)*			
Br.	*enaoui*					

Words for 'light' (a fire, etc.), 'kindle' are mostly connected with words for 'burn', 'blaze', 'flame', but some are based on the notion of 'make light' or on that of 'grasp, seize' (cf. NE *catch fire*).

1. Grk. ἄπτω 'fasten, grasp, touch, (15.71), also 'light, kindle', esp. ἀνάπτω, NG pop. ἀνάφτω or ἀνάβω (new pres. to aor. ἄναψα).

Grk. δαίω (poet.): Skt. *du-* 'burn, torment', etc. Walde-P. 1.767 f.

Grk. αἴθω (poet.), see 1.85.

2. Lat. *accendere* (> It. *accendere*), *incendere* (> It. *incendere*, Sp. *encender*, Rum. *încinge*), *succendere*, cpds. of **candere*: *candēre* 'shine, glow' (15.56).

Fr. *allumer*, fr. VLat. **allūmināre*: *lūmen* 'light' (1.61). REW 372. Wartburg 1.73.

Rum. *aprinde*, fr. Lat. *apprehendere* 'seize'. Cf. *prinde* for 'catch fire', Fr.

(obs.) *eprendre* 'kindle', refl. 'catch fire'. REW 554, 6736. Tiktin 80 f.

3. Ir. *attai* (3 sg. pres.), vbl. n. *atud*, etc., cpd. : Grk. δαίω 'kindle', etc. Here also W. *cynneu* and perh. W. *ennyn*, Pedersen 2.507 f.

NIr. *lasaim* : *lasair* 'flame' (1.82).

Br. *enaoui*, also and orig. 'animate, give life to', fr. *ene* 'soul' (16.11). Henry 113.

4. Goth. *tandjan*, ON *tenda, tendra*, Dan. *(an)tænde*, Sw. *(upp)tända*, OE *ontendan* (also *a-*, but *for-tendan* 'burn off'), ME *tenden*, NE dial. *tind*, OHG *zunten*, MHG *zünden*, NHG *anzünden*, outside root connection wholly dub. Feist 474. Falk-Torp 1311. NED s.v. *tind*, vb.

ON *kynda*, whence ME, NE *kindle*, etym.? Falk-Torp 610. NED s.v. *kindle*, vb.

ME *lihte*, NE *light* (much more common than *kindle* even with fire, and only *light*, not *kindle*, with candle, lamp, pipe, etc.), orig. 'give light'. NED s.v. *light*, vb.[2]2.

So locally NHG *anstecken*, Kretschmer, Wortgeogr. 79 f.

5. Lith. *uždegti*, Lett. *aiz-* (or *ie-*)*degt*, more commonly *dedzināt*, cpds. of Lith. *degti*, Lett. *degt* 'burn' (1.85).

6. ChSl. *vžešti*, Russ. *zažeč'*, cpds. of ChSl.. *žešti*, Russ. *žeč'* 'burn' (1.85).

Scr. *zapaliti*, Boh. *zapáliti*, Pol. *zapalić*, cpds. of ChSl. *paliti* 'blaze, burn', etc. (1.85).

Boh. *rozsvititi* ('light' a candle, etc.), cpd. of *svititi* 'make light, light the way' : ChSl. *světŭ* 'light', etc. (1.61).

7. Skt. *idh-*: Grk. αἴθω 'kindle' etc. (see 1.85).

1.87 MATCH (sb.)

NG	σπίρτο (πυρεῖον)	Dan.	*tændstik*	Lith.	*degtukas*	
It.	*fiammifero*	Sw.	*tändsticka*	Lett.	*sērkuocin'š*	
Fr.	*allumette*	NIcel.	*eldspýta*	SCr.	*žigica, šibica*	
Sp.	*fósforo*	NE	*match*	Boh.	*sirka*	
Rum.	*chibrit*	Du.	*lucifer*	Pol.	*zapałka*	
NIr.	*maiste*	NHG	*streichholz, zündholz*	Russ.	*spička*	
W.	*matsen*					
Br.	*enaoui*					

Although the inclusion in this chapter of the humble and strictly modern 'match' for lighting seems the acme of incongruity, its present importance in connection with the preceding groups is obvious; and the great diversity of the terms that are in common use for this invention is of some interest. Several are derived from the verbs for 'light, kindle', or 'burn', or more literally 'flame-bringing' or 'light-bringing'. The old sulphur matches (the offensive brimstone matches of my boyhood) were often denoted by a compound or deriva-

tive of the word for 'sulphur'; and some of these remained, either generally or locally, in common use for the 'match', regardless of the change in materials used. Less common was the use of 'phosphorus' for 'match'. Terms which apply to the wax tapers but not to matches in general, as It. *cerino* (vs. *flammifero*), Sp. *cerilla* (Am. Sp. *cerillo*) are not included in the list. The wooden 'stick' appears in some of the words, either in combination (NHG *streichholz*, etc.) or alone (SCr. *šibica*, Russ. *spička*). The important notion of friction has

furnished only one of the words listed (NHG *streichholz*). A few of the words (NE *match*, Fr. *allumette*) were originally names of an antecedent implement used as a help in lighting.

1. Grk. πυρεῖον, a kind of fire stick, fr. πῦρ 'fire', was adopted as the NG official term, but σπίρτο is the only popular word. One asks for σπίρτα and gets a box labeled πυρεῖα. This σπίρτο is the same word as σπίρτο 'alcohol, spirits', fr. Lat. *spiritus*, its application to a match being apparently based on the notion of something inflammable.

2. It. *fiammifero*, an obvious cpd., lit. 'flame-bringing', created to denote the 'match'.

Fr. *allumette*, fr. *allumer* 'light' (1.86), but quotable from the 14th cent. as applied to a bit of shaving for lighting. Gamillscheg 29. Wartburg 1.74.

Sp. *fósforo* 'phosphorus' and the usual word for 'match', except the wax taper (*cerilla, cerillo*). Similar words elsewhere are quotable for 'match', as NG φωσφόρον, but are not common in this sense.

Rum. *chibrit*, fr. Turk. *kibrit* 'match', this fr. an Arab. word for 'sulphur'. Tiktin 337. Lokotsch 93.

3. Ir. *maiste*, W. *matsen*, fr. NE *match*.

Br. *enaouidenn*, fr. *enaoui* 'light' (1.86), evidently after the analogy of Fr. *allumette*.

4. Dan. *tændstik*, Sw. *tändsticka*, cpds. of Dan. *tænde*, Sw. *tända* 'light' (1.86) with Dan. *stik*, Sw. *sticka* 'stab' here as 'stick'.

NIcel. *eldspýta*, cpd. of *eld* 'fire' and *spýta* 'stick'.

NE *match*, fr. ME *macche, matche*, this fr. *mesche* (= Fr. *mèche*) 'wick'. First used for 'wick', then for a piece of wick or cord prepared for burning in firing a gun (cf. the old *matchlock*) and finally applied to the modern 'match'. NED s.v. *match*, sb.[2]2.

Du. *lucifer*, fr. NE *lucifer, lucifer match* (fr. Lat. *lūcifer* 'light-bringing'), once used more consistently than now. NED s.v. *Lucifer*, 3.

NHG *streichholz*, fr. *streichen* 'rub, strike' and *holz* 'wood'. Less commonly *zündholz* fr. *zünden* 'light' (1.86), also *schwefelholz*, fr. *schwefel* 'sulphur', the old word for the sulphur match (like Dan. *svovelstikke*, Du. *zwavelstok*, etc.) still used in some places for the current match, Kretschmer, Wortgeogr. 503 f.

5. Lith. *degtukas*, fr. *degti* 'burn' (1.85) and formed on the analogy of words like *peštukas* fr. *pešti*, etc., for which see Leskien, Bildung d. Nom. 516 f.

Lett. *sērkuocin'š* (still the usual word?), cpd. of *sērs* 'sulphur' and *kuocin'š: kuoks* 'tree, stick'. Mühl.-Endz. 3.829.

6. Scr. *žigica* : *žeči* 'burn' (1.85), *žig* 'burning'.

Scr. *šibica* : *šiba* 'rod, twig'.

Boh. *sirka*, fr. *sira* 'sulphur'.

Pol. *zapałka*, fr. *zapalić* 'light' (1.86).

Russ. *spička*, dim. of *spica* 'pointed stick,' this fr. NHG *spitze* 'point'.

CHAPTER 2

MANKIND: SEX, AGE, FAMILY RELATIONSHIP

2.1 MAN[1]

(Human Being)

Grk.	ἄνθρωπος	Goth.	*manna*	Lith.	*žmogus*, pl. *žmonės*
NG	ἄνθρωπος	ON	*maðr, gumi*	Lett.	*cilvēks*
Lat.	*homō*	Dan.	*menneske*	ChSl.	*člověkŭ*
It.	*uomo*	Sw.	*menniska*	SCr.	*čovjek*
Fr.	*homme*	OE	*man(n), guma*	Boh.	*člověk*
Sp.	*hombre*	ME	*man*	Pol.	*człowiek*
Rum.	*om*	NE	*man*	Russ.	*čelovek*
Ir.	*duine*	Du.	*mensch*	Skt.	*manu-, puruṣa-*
NIr.	*duine*	OHG	*man, mannisco, gomo*	Av.	*mašya-, mašyāka-*
W.	*dyn*	MHG	*mensch*		OPers. *martiya-*
Br.	*den*	NHG	*mensch*		

The more general notion of 'man' as a human being ('man'[1]) and the more specific notion of 'man' as an adult male human being ('man'[2]) may be combined in the same word, as in NE *man*, Fr.

homme, etc.; or they may be differentiated (1) by related forms, as NHG *mensch* vs. *mann*, (2) by unrelated words, as Lat. *homō* vs. *vir*, etc. An old differentiation may be lost, as in VLatin, where the use of *homō* was extended at the expense of *vir;* or it may be resumed, as in Rumanian, where *bărbat* is frequently preferred to *om* when the meaning is 'man'[2]. There is not only extension but sometimes complete shift of application from '*man*'[1] to '*man*'[2], and of the latter again to 'husband'.

The principal source of words for '*man*'[1], so far as their etymology is clear, is the notion of 'earthly' or 'mortal', thus distinguishing men from the gods. But a few are derivatives of words for 'man'[2], and the ultimate semantic source of one important group (NE *man*, etc.) is uncertain.

1. Lat. *homō* (> It. *uomo*, Fr. *homme*, etc.), OLat. *hemo*, Osc. *humuns* 'homines'; Ir. *duine*, W. *dyn*, Br. *den;* OLith. *žmuo*, OPruss. *smoy*, Lith. *žmogus*, pl. *žmonės;* Goth. *guma* (but translates ἀνήρ), ON *gumi*, OE *guma*, OHG *gomo* (old Gmc. word, now surviving only in cpds., as NHG *bräutigam*, NE *bridegroom* fr. OE *brydguma*); Toch. B *śaumo*, pl. *śāmna* : Lat. *humus*, Grk. χθών, Lith. *žemė*, etc. 'earth' (1.21). Cf. Hom. ἐπιχθόνιοι ἄνθρωποι, in contrast to ἐπουράνιοι θεοί, and even ἐπιχθόνιοι alone (Il. 24.220). Walde-P. 1.663. Ernout-M. 457 f. Walde-H. 1.654 f. Pedersen 1.89. Vendryes, RC 40.437 ff.

2. Goth. *manna*, ON *maðr*, OE *man(n)*, *mon*, NE *man*, OHG *man*, NHG *mann*, etc. (the most widespread Gmc. word, with extension fr. 'man'[1] to 'man'[2]); ChSl. *mąžĭ* (fr. *mągjo- with a guttural suffix, as in Lith. *žmogus*), SCr., Boh., Russ. *muž*, Pol. *mąż* (general Slavic word, with shift from 'man'[1] to 'man'[2]); Skt. *manu-*, *manuṣ-*, *manuṣa-*, *mānuṣa-*. These point to an IE word for 'man'[1], but its root connection and so its ultimate semantic source are wholly uncertain. It has been derived from IE *men- 'think', or, since the designation 'thinker' seems too sophisticated, from *men- in an assumed earlier meaning 'breath' or the like; or by some connected with Lat. *manus* 'hand' (cf. NE *all hands*). Walde-P. 2.266. Falk-Torp 693. Feist 344 f.

In Germanic the prevailing meaning in the earlier period is 'man'[1] (so Goth. *manna* reg. = ἄνθρωπος, only a few times = ἀνήρ). After the extension of use to include 'man'[2], its place in the sense of 'man'[1] was taken, except in English, by forms going back to a deriv. adj. like Goth. *mannisks* = ἀνθρώπινος. Hence OHG *mannisco*, *mennisco*, MHG, NHG, Du. *mensch*, Dan. *menneske*, Sw. *menniska*. Falk-Torp 714. Weigand-H. 2.168.

In Slavic there was a complete shift from 'man'[1] to 'man'[2] and 'husband', and in part a later restriction to 'husband' with new derivatives in the sense of 'man'[2], as SCr. *muškarac*, Russ. *mužčina*, etc.

3. Grk. ἄνθρωπος, etym. much disputed. But the old analysis ἄνθρ-ωπος 'man-faced, man-like', fr. the stem of ἀνήρ, ἀνδρός remains the most probable. Cf. Hesych. δρώψ· ἄνθρωπος, and for the semantic relation cf. OHG *mannisco* fr. *man* (above, 2). The change of ἀνδρ- to ἀνθρ- is due to a ʽ in the second element (cf. τέθριππον fr. *τετρ-ιππον), which does not belong properly to the root ὀπ- but may be due to the influence of ὁράω. Kretschmer, Glotta 9.231 f., 27.246.

4. Ir. *duine*, W. *dyn*, Br. *den*, above, 1.

5. ChSl. *člověkŭ*, etc., the general Slavic word for 'man'[1] (SCr. *čovjek* also 'man'[2]), whence Lett. *cilveks* (fr. Russ.), much disputed but best explained as cpd. of a *čelo- (whence ChSl. *čeljadĭ* 'household') and *věkŭ : Lith. *vaikas* 'child', hence orig. 'member of the household', with later extension to 'man'[1]. Cf.

SCr. *čeljad* coll. for 'household' but also 'men, people.' Berneker 141. Brugmann, Festgabe Kaegi 33. Brückner 79 (differently for second part of cpd.)

6. Skt. (beside *manu-*, etc., above, 2) *puruṣa-* etym.? Uhlenbeck s.v.

Av. *mašya-* mostly 'man'[1], OPers. *martiya-* 'man'[1] and 'man'[2], NPers. *mard* 'man'[2], Arm. *mard* 'man'[1], orig. 'mortal' : Skt. *mṛta-* 'dead', *martya-* 'mortal, man', Lat. *mortuus* 'dead', Grk. βροτός 'a mortal', fr. IE *mer- 'die' in Skt. *mṛ-*, Lat. *morī*, etc. Walde-P. 2.276. Barth. 1148 ff.

2.21 MAN[2]

(vs. Woman)

Grk.	ἀνήρ	Goth.	*wair (guma, manna)*	Lith.	*vyras*
NG	ἄντρας	ON	*karl, karlmaðr*	Lett.	*vīrs*
Lat.	*vir*	Dan.	*mand*	ChSl.	*mąžĭ*
It.	*uomo*	Sw.	*man*	SCr.	*čovjek, muškarac*
Fr.	*homme*	OE	*wer (wǣpnedman, ceorl, man)*	Boh.	*muž*
Sp.	*hombre, varón*	ME	*man (were)*	Pol.	*mąž, mężczyzna*
Rum.	*bărbat, om*	NE	*man*	Russ.	*mužčina*
Ir.	*fer*	Du.	*man*	Skt.	*nar-, nara-, vīra-, pumaṅs-*
NIr.	*fear*	OHG	*man, gomman (wer, karl)*	Av.	*nar-, vīra-,* OPers. *martiya-*
W.	*gwr*	MHG	*man*		
Br.	*gwaz*	NHG	*mann*		

Many of the words for 'man'[2], namely most of the Romance and Germanic and all the Slavic, were originally words for 'man'[1], or derivatives of these and have been included in the discussion 2.1.

Many of the words for 'man'[2] were also used for 'husband', and some of them are quotable only in the latter sense, so that they do not appear in this list (so ON *verr*).

1. IE *wīro-, that is, *wī-ro- : Lat. *vīs*, Skt. *vayas*, etc. 'strength'. Walde-P. 1.314 ff. Ernout-M. 1112 f.

Lat. *vir*, Umbr. *uiro* (acc. pl.); Ir. *fer*, NIr. *fear*, W. *gwr*, MBr. *gour* (now used with neg. for 'no one'); Goth. *wair* (ON *verr* 'husband'), OE *wer*, etc. (old Gmc. word, but now obs. except in cpds., as NE *werewolf*, NHG *wergeld;* also NE *world*, etc. 1.1); Lith. *vyras*, Lett. *vīrs;* Skt., Av. *vīra-*.

2. IE *ner-. Various cognates, as Ir. *nert* 'strength, might', show that the notion of 'strength' is dominant, as in IE *wīro-, but the ultimate root connection is uncertain. Walde-P. 2.332 f. Ernout-M. 667 f.

Grk. ἀνήρ, gen. ἀνδρός, NG ἄντρας; Osc.-Umbr. *ner-* used of men of rank, officials (here also Lat. *Nerō* and *Neriō;* cf. also MW *ner* 'chief, master', Loth, RC 41.207); Skt. *nar-*, *nara-*, Av. *nar-;* Alb. *njeri;* Arm. *air*.

3. Sp. *varón* = late Lat. *barō*, *-ōnis* 'man'[2] (Lex Salica, etc.), OFr. *baron*, 'husband' fr. a Gmc. word meaning orig. 'fighting man' (: ON *berjask* 'fight'), whence 'man', 'retainer', etc. Wartburg 1.254 f. (best account of the complicated history). REW 962. Gamillscheg 83. NED s.v. *baron*.

Rum. *bărbat*, fr. Lat. *barbātus* 'bearded' through Byz. βαρβᾶτος used for one who was not a eunuch. Cf. NG βαρβᾶτος used of an animal that is not castrated, as ἄλογο βαρβᾶτο 'stallion'.

4. Br. *gwaz*, fr. OBr. *guas*, MBr. *goas*

'servant' = W. *gwas*, Ir. *foss* 'servant', etc. (19.43).

5. ON *karl* and *karlmaðr*, OE *ceorl*, OHG *karl*, all meaning 'man'[2], esp. the 'man without rank, freeman', in the earlier period a term of esteem (as in the proper name *Karl*), later one of disparagement or contempt, as in NE *churl*, NHG *kerl*. Perh. as 'full-grown man' : Grk. γέρων, Skt. *jarant-* 'old man'. Walde-P. 1.600. Falk-Torp 497. Kluge-G. 296.

OE *wǣp(en)-man*, *wǣpned-man* 'man, male', cpds. of *wǣpen* 'weapon, penis' (4.492), *wǣpned* 'male'.

OHG *gomman*, cpd. of *gomo* (2.1) and *man*.

6. Skt., Av. *vīra-*, *nar-*, above 1, 2.

Skt. *pumaṅs-*, *puṁs-* 'man, male' (vs. *strī-* 'woman, female') : Lat. *pūbēs* 'adult'. Walde-P. 2.83. Ernout-M. 819 f.

2.22 WOMAN

Grk.	γυνή	Goth.	*qinō*	Lith.	*moteris, moteriškė, žmona*
NG	γυναῖκα	ON	*kona*	Lett.	*sieva*
Lat.	*mulier, fēmina*	Dan.	*kvinde*	ChSl.	*žena*
It.	*donna*	Sw.	*kvinna*	SCr.	*žena*
Fr.	*femme*	OE	*cwene, wīf, wīfman*	Boh.	*žena*
Sp.	*mujer*	ME	*quene, wife, woman*	Pol.	*kobieta*
Rum.	*femeie*	NE	*woman*	Russ.	*ženščina*
Ir.	*ben, fracc*	Du.	*vrouw*	Skt.	*jani-, nārī-, strī-*
NIr.	*bean*	OHG	*wīb, quena*	Av.	*jani-, nāiri-, strī-*
W.	*gwraig, benyw, dynes*	MHG	*wīp*		
Br.	*maouez*	NHG	*frau, weib*		

Many of the words for 'woman' were also the usual words for 'wife', and some became restricted to the latter use, with replacement in the sense of 'woman', as NE *wife*, Pol. *żona*, Russ. *žena*.

Words for 'woman' carry an emotional value which is liable to wide fluctuation, either at the same period, according to circumstances, or as between different periods, social classes, or languages. They may suggest the nobility of woman or her frailties. They may move up or down the social scale. Of OE *cwēn*, *cwene* both orig. 'woman', the former was from early times a 'king's wife, queen', while the latter became a 'quean, harlot'. Dan. *kone* is 'wife', but Sw. *kona*, formerly 'woman, wife', is now used only of a woman of loose character. NHG *weib* was for a time mostly derogatory and was displaced by *frau*, permanently for 'wife', while for 'woman' it has regained respectability.

Conversely, a derogatory epithet may come to be used as a whimsical term of endearment and eventually as the standard word for 'woman'. So notably Pol. *kobieta* (below, 5).

1. IE *gʷenā-, *gʷeni-, etc., with gradation of the root syllable. Without known root connection, unless at some remote period, before differentiation of the gutturals (?), with IE *ĝen- 'beget' and 'bear' of Lat. *gignere*, etc. Walde-P. 1.681.

Grk. γυνή (Boeot. βανά), gen. γυναικός, NG γυναῖκα (γυνή lit.); Ir. *ben*, NIr. *bean*, W. *benyw;* Goth. *qinō* (and *qēns* 'wife'); ON *kona* (gen. pl. *kvinna*); Dan. *kvinde* (and *kone* 'wife'), Sw. *kvinna*, OE *cwene* (and *cwēn* 'wife'), OHG *quena;* OPruss. *genna*, ChSl. *žena*, etc.; Skt. *jani-*, *janī-*, *-jāni-*, Av. *jani-* (NPers. *zan*), *gənā-*, etc.; Arm. *kin;* Toch. *śäṃ*.

2. Lat. *mulier* (> It. *moglie* 'wife', OFr. *moillier* 'wife', Sp. *mujer* 'woman,

wife', Rum. *muiere* formerly 'woman, wife', now derogatory), etym. dub., possibly formed with a comp. suffix from the root of Lat. *mollis* 'soft, delicate', and so used of the weaker sex, or from the same root in an obscene sense? Walde-P. 2.285. Ernout-M. 637 f.

Lat. *fēmina* 'a female' in general and 'woman' (> It. *femmina* formerly 'woman', now only 'female', Fr. *femme* 'woman, wife', Sp. *hembra* 'female'), orig. mid. pple. fr. the root of Lat. *fēlāre* 'suck', Grk. θῆσθαι 'suck', θῆλυς 'female', Skt. *dhayati* 'sucks', etc., (5.16), hence 'one who gives suck'. Walde-P. 1.829 ff. Ernout-M. 341, 343.

It. *donna*, now 'woman', formerly 'mistress, lady', like Fr. *dame*, etc., fr. Lat. *domina* 'mistress'.

Rum. *femeie* 'woman, wife', dial. 'children, family', fr. Lat. *familia* 'household'. REW 3180. Pușcariu 595.

3. Ir. *fracc* 'woman', W. *gwrach* 'old woman, witch', *gwraig* 'woman, wife', Br. *gwreg* 'wife', prob. fem. derivs. of Ir. *fer*, W. *gwr*, etc. 'man'[2] (Pedersen, 1.159 dub.). Cf. Lat. *virāgō* 'manlike female', *virgō* 'maiden', fr. *vir*, W. *dynes* 'woman' (cf. Morris Jones 223) fr. *dyn* 'man'[1], and Skt. *nārī-* 'woman' fr. *nar-* 'man'[2].

Br. *maouez* : Corn. *mowes* 'girl', Goth. *mawi* 'girl', fem. of Ir. *magu* 'servant', Goth. *magus* 'boy', etc. (2.25–26). Walde-P. 2.228. Pedersen 1.98.

4. ON *vīf* (poet.), OE *wīf*, ME *wife* 'woman, wife', cpd. *wīfman* 'woman' > ME, NE *woman*, finally displacing *wife* in its wider sense (except dial. or in cpds.), OHG *wīb*, MHG *wīp*, NHG *weib* 'woman' and 'wife', now mostly (but not always) derogatory and replaced by *frau*, as likewise Du. *wijf* by *vrouw*. Etym. much discussed and wholly dub. Falk-Torp 1390. Weigand-H. 2.1224. Paul, Deutsches Wtb. s.v. *Weib* (on its use).

NHG *frau*, Du. *vrouw*, orig. 'mistress' as OHG *frouwa*, fem. of OHG *frō*, Goth. *frauja* 'master' : Skt. *pūrva-* 'in front, former', Grk. πρῶτος 'first', etc. Walde-P. 2.37. Falk-Torp 278.

NHG *frauenzimmer*, orig. a room for the women at court, then coll. for 'women', finally 'a woman, female', now mostly with derogatory feeling. Weigand-H. 1.577.

5. Lith. *motė*, gen. *moters* (now usually *moteris* or *moteriškė*), orig. 'mother' = Lett. *māte*, ChSl. *mati*, Lat. *māter*, etc. (2.42).

Lith. *žmona* (but now mostly 'wife'), fem. of *žmogus* 'man' (2.1).

Lett. *sieva* 'wife' (2.32), also 'woman'.

6. Pol. *niewiasta*, formerly the common word for 'woman' (*żona* being 'wife'), orig. 'bride' : ChSl. *nevěsta* 'bride', this a cpd. of neg. prefix *ne* and fem. of *věstŭ* 'known', hence the 'unknown', that is, the newcomer in the husband's family. Zubatý, Arch. sl. Ph. 16.406. Brückner 362.

Pol. *kobieta*, first appearing as a derogatory epithet and plausibly explained as a blend of *kobyla* 'mare' (this also epithet of a 'clumsy, stupid woman', as is also Russ. *kobyla*) with names like *Bieta* 'Betty'. Since 18th. cent. without derogatory sense and displacing *niewiasta*. Brückner 241.

7. Skt. *nārī-*, Av. *nāiri-*, fem. deriv. of *nar-* 'man'[2] (2.21).

Skt., Av. *strī-* 'female, woman', etym.? Walde-P. 2.457, 460. P. Trost, IF 56.197.

2.23 MALE / 2.24 FEMALE

	2.23 MALE	2.24 FEMALE
Grk.	ἄρσην, ἄρρην	θῆλυς
NG	ἀρσενικός	θηλυκός
Lat.	mās (masculus, masculīnus)	fēmina
It.	maschio	femmina
Fr.	mâle	femelle
Sp.	macho	hembra
Rum.	bărbătesc	femeiesc
Ir.	fer-, firend	ban-
NIr.	fireann	baineann
W.	gwryw	benyw
Br.	gwaz	maouez
Goth.	gumeins, gumakunds	qineins
ON	karl- (karlligr)	kvenn-
Dan.	mandlig	kvindelig
Sw.	manlig	kvinlig
OE	wǣpned, wǣpman	wīf, wīfman
ME	male	female
NE	male	female
Du.	mannelijk	vrouwelijk
OHG	gomman	wīb
MHG	man	wīp
NHG	männlich	weiblich
Lith.	vyriškas	moteriškas
Lett.	vīrišks	sieveškīgs, sievietisks
ChSl.	mǫžiskŭ	ženskŭ
SCr.	muški	ženski
Boh.	mužký	ženský
Pol.	męski	żeński
Russ.	mužkoj, mužeskij	ženskij
Skt.	vṛṣan-, pumṣ-, nara-	strī-
Av.	aršan-, nairya-	strī-, hāirišī-, xšaθrī-

2.23, 2.24. Most of the words listed are the adjective forms; some of these are also used substantively. But in some cases it is the substantive form that is commonly used, either prefixed or added in apposition to another noun and so with virtually adjectival force. So Lat. fēmina, It. femmina, Fr. femelle, Sp. hembra, etc.

Many of them, but not all, are applied to animals as well as to human beings. See 3.12, 3.13.

The majority are obvious derivatives or compounds of the words for 'man' or 'woman' (2.21, 2.22) and need no further discussion.

Those of different origin are as follows:

1. Grk. ἄρσην 'male', ἔρσην, ἄρρην (without ϝ; alleged El. gen. sg. ϝάρρενορ now rejected), late also ἀρσενικός, ἀρρενικός (cf. θηλυκός, below, 2), NG ἀρσενικός, Skt. vṛṣan- (cf. vṛṣabha-, and ṛṣabha- 'bull'), Av. aršan- (also varəšna-, cf. NPers. gušan 'male'), parallel forms with and without init. w, the former : Skt. vṛṣ- 'to rain', varṣa- 'rain', Grk. ἔρση 'dew', the latter : Skt. ṛṣ- 'flow'. Whether or not these two roots belong together formally, the semantic development is the same, 'male' from the notion of emitting semen. Walde-P. 1.149 ff., 269.

2. Grk. θῆλυς 'female', whence θηλυκός 'woman-like', 'like the female' (Aristot.), later (pap., LXX, etc.) simply 'female', as in NG; Lat. fēmina (> It. femmina, Sp. hembra), dim. fēmella (> Fr. femelle > ME; NE female), also fēmineus, fēmīnus, It. femineo, feminino, feminile, etc. (but these mostly 'feminine' rather than 'female'), all orig. 'giving suck' : Grk. θῆσθαι 'suck', Skt. dhayati 'sucks', etc. Walde-P. 1.829 ff. Ernout-M. 341, 343. Walde-H. 1.476.

3. Lat. mās 'male', also māsculus (> It. maschio, maschile, Fr. mâle, ME, NE male, Sp. macho), māsculinus (> It. mascolino, Fr. masculin, NE masculine, now mostly of gender, attributes, etc.), etym.? Ernout-M. 594. Walde-H. 2.46 f.

4. OE wǣpned 'male', also cpd. wǣpedman, wǣpman fr. wǣpen 'weapon, penis' (4.492, 20.21).

OE werlīc, wīflīc are used for 'masculine, feminine' gender (so Aelfric) but rarely, if at all, for 'male, female'.

5. Skt. (beside adj. vṛṣan-) prefixed pumṣ- or nara- (2.21) for 'male' human beings or animals. Similarly strī- (2.22) prefixed or added for 'female' human beings or animals.

Av. (beside adj. aršan-) also adj. nairya- fr. nara- 'man' (2.21), for 'male' human beings or animals.

Av. hāirišī- noun for 'female', applied to human beings and animals, perh. *hār- : second part of IE *swe-sor- 'sister' (2.45). Benveniste, BSL 35.1.104 f.

Av. xšaθrī- likewise noun for 'female', etym.? Barth. 547.

2.242 SEX

Grk.	γένος, φῦλον	Goth.	....	Lith.	gimtis, lytis
NG	φῦλον	ON	kyn	Lett.	dzimums
Lat.	sexus	Dan.	køn	ChSl.	polŭ
It.	sesso	Sw.	kön	SCr.	spol
Fr.	sexe	OE	cyn(n)	Boh.	pohlaví
Sp.	sexo	ME	kynde, sexe	Pol.	płeć
Rum.	sex	NE	sex	Russ.	pol
Ir.	gnē(?)	Du.	geslacht, kunne, sekse	Skt.	(liṅga-, jāti-)
NIr.	gnē, cenēal, saghas	OHG	....	Av.	....
W.	rhyw, ystlen	MHG	gesleht(e)		
Br.	reiz	NHG	geschlecht		

The abstract notion of 'sex' is in many languages expressed only by words of broader scope, the special reference to sex being shown by the context (as 'man kind' = 'male sex'). But there are some distinctive words in which the specialization to 'sex' is complete (so Lat. sexus, with derivs.) or nearly so. The semantic source is most commonly 'sort, kind' (this often from 'birth, kin, race'), but in part 'section', 'side', 'half', or 'flesh, complexion'.

Natural 'sex' and grammatical 'gender' are most commonly expressed by the same word, as in the case of Grk. γένος, OE cynn, gecynde, NHG geschlecht. But they may be differentiated, as in Lat. sexus vs. genus (with their Romance and English derivs.), NG φῦλον vs. γένος, Russ. pol vs. rod ('race, clan' 19.23, 'kind', and 'gender').

1. Grk. γένος 'race, kin, clan' (19.23), hence 'class, kind' and 'sex'.

Grk. φῦλον 'race, tribe' (beside φυλή, 19.23) and 'sex' (Aristoph., Xen.), later reg. NG.

2. Lat. sexus (> It. sesso, Fr. sexe, Sp. sexo; Rum. sex neolog. fr. Fr.), beside secus prob. : secāre 'cut' (9.22), hence orig. 'section', but with prehistoric specialization to 'sex' (old etym. questioned by Ernout-M. 935, but still prob.).

3. Ir. gnē 'countenance, appearance,

form, kind' (: W. gne 'color, hue, complexion'), also, at least in NIr., 'sex' in phrases with 'male', etc.

Ir. cenēl 'race, kin, kind' (: cinim 'spring from'), NIr. cenēal also 'sex' in phrases.

NIr. saghas 'sort, kind' (etym.?), also for 'sex' in phrases 'what kind is your child, boy or girl?' (Dinneen, McKenna).

W. rhyw 'sort, kind' (etym.? Pedersen 1.67) and 'sex'.

W. ystlwn 'connection, kind' (beside cystlwn 'kindred', Pedersen 1.84), now ystlen 'kind, sex'.

Br. reiz 'order, law' (21.11), also 'sex'.

4. ON kyn, Dan. køn, Sw. kön, OE cyn(n), Du. kunne, all orig. 'race, kin' (like Goth. kuni), hence 'kind' and 'sex', with same semantic history as the cognate Grk. γένος.

OE gecynde, ME kynde (NE kind) 'birth, (inborn) character, nature' (fr. the same root as preceding group) and sometimes 'sex'. NED s.v. kind, sb. 7.

ME sexe (rare), NE sex, Du. sekse fr. Lat. sexus or Fr. sexe (above, 2).

Du. geschlacht, MHG geslehte, NHG geschlecht 'kin, family, clan' (19.23), orig., like OHG slahta, 'sort, kind', whence 'sex'. Weigand-H. 2.698.

5. Lith. gimtis, Lett. dzimums 'birth, family', etc. and 'sex', fr. Lith. gimti, Lett. dzimt 'be born' (4.71). Mühl-Endz. 1.551.

Lith. lytis 'form' and 'sex' (NSB s.v.) : lieti 'pour'. Trautmann 156.

6. ChSl. polŭ, SCr. spol, Russ. pol, same word as ChSl. polŭ, Pol. pol, etc. 'half' (13.24).

Boh. pohlaví, fr. a phrase containing po 'after, according to' and hlava 'head' (4.20).

Pol. płeć : ChSl. plŭtĭ, Russ. plot' 'flesh, body', Boh. plet 'complexion' (also ženska plet 'female sex'). Brückner 420 f.

7. Skt. liṅga- 'mark, phallus', also 'gender' (BR s.v.), quotable also for 'sex'?

Skt. jāti- 'birth' (: jan- 'be born', etc.), 'class, kind', prob. used also for 'sex', but quotable?

	2.25 BOY	2.26 GIRL	2.27 CHILD	2.28 INFANT
Grk.	παῖς ὁ, κόρος	παῖς ἡ, κόρη, παρθένος	παῖς	νήπιος, παιδίον, βρέφος
NG	ἀγόρι	κόρη, κορίτσι, κοπέλλα	παιδί	βρέφος, μωρό
Lat.	puer	puella	puerī	infāns
It.	ragazzo	ragazza	fanciullo, bimbo	bambino
Fr.	garçon	jeune fille	enfant	petit enfant, bébé
Sp.	muchacho	muchacha	niño	criatura
Rum.	băiat (făt)	fată	copil	copilaș, prunc
Ir.	macc	ingen	lelap, lenab	nóidiu
NIr.	buachail	cailín	leanbh, páiste	naoidhe
W.	bachgen, hogyn	geneth, hogen	plentyn	maban
Br.	paotr	plac'h	bugel, krouadur	bugelig, krouadurig
Goth.	magus	mawi	barn	barn
ON	sveinn	mær, stúlka	barn	ungbarn
Dan.	dreng, Norw. gut	pige, Norw. jente	barn	spæd barn
Sw.	gosse, pojke	flicka	barn	spädt barn
OE	cnapa, cniht	mæʒden	bearn, cild	cild
ME	knave, lad, boy	maid(en), girle, lasce	child (barne)	enfaunt, babe, babi
NE	boy (lad)	girl (maid, lass)	child	infant, baby (babe)
Du.	knaap	meisje	kind	kind
OHG	knabo, kneht	magad	kind, barn	kind
MHG	knabe, kneht	maget	kind	kind
NHG	knabe	mädchen	kind	säugling, kleines kind
Lith.	vaikas	mergaitė, mergelė	vaikai	kūdikis
Lett.	puisis, puika	meita	bērns	pupa bērns
ChSl.	otrokŭ	děvica, otrokovica	děti	otročę, mladiněcĭ
SCr.	djećak	djevojke	dijete	djetešce
Boh.	chlapec, pachole, hoch	holka, dívka	dítě	dět'atko, nemluvně
Pol.	chłopiec	dziewczyna	dziecko, dziecię	dziecię, niemowlę
Russ.	mal'čik	devica	rebenok (d. ti. pl.)	mladenec
Skt.	bāla, kumāra-	bālī-, kumārī-, kanyā-	bāla-, kumāra-, etc.	bāla-, çiçu-, etc.
Av.	....	kainyā		aparənāyuka-

2.25, 2.26, 2.27. Several of the words for 'boy' and 'girl' are correlative masculine and feminine forms, as Grk. ὁ παῖς, ἡ παῖς, Lat. puer, puella, It. ragazzo, ragazza, Sp. muchacho, muchacha, Goth. magus, mawi, Skt. bāla-, bālī-. In such cases the discussion will be under 'boy'.

The same words often apply to 'boy' or 'girl' and to a young male or female 'servant, attendant'. Either the former or the latter may be the earlier meaning, as indicated by the etymology.

Since 'boy' and 'girl' are, with reference to the parents, the 'son' and 'daughter', the words for the former may also be used, and in part are the usual ones for the latter. See 2.43, 2.44. The extension in the opposite direction also occurs, but less frequently.

A noticeable number of the modern words for 'boy', 'girl', and 'child' were originally colloquial nicknames, derogatory or whimsical, in part endearing, and finally commonplace. These, as is natural, are of the most diverse, and in part obscure, origin. The enumeration of the colloquial expressions that are in occasional or dialectic use would fill a volume. They are based on names of animals and all sorts of inanimate objects, like NE kid, brat (orig. 'cloth, rag'), flapper (in U.S.), NHG bengel ('cudgel'), etc.

Many such are collected in v. Friesen, De germ. mediageminatorna; Brugmann, Sächs. Ges. d. Wiss. 1906.173; Johanssen, KZ 36.373 ff.; Björkman, IF 30.257 ff.; Much, Wört. u. Sach.

1.45; Ivan Pauli, 'Enfant', 'garçon', 'fille' dans les langues romanes (426 pp.!); Taylor, Mod. Lang. Notes 1929. 309 ff.; Hilding Bäck, The Synonyms for 'Child', 'Boy', 'Girl' in Old English (271 pp.).

Here only those that have become the usual words are considered, unless incidentally.

2.25. 'Boy. 1. Grk. παῖς, gen. παιδός (fr. *παϝιδ-) 'boy, girl, child', NG παιδί 'child' (fr. dim. παιδίον), Lat. *puer* 'boy', whence *puella* 'girl' : Skt. *putra-*, Av. *puθra-* 'son', Osc. *puklum* 'filium', Pael. *puclois* 'pueris', Skt. *pota-* 'young of an animal', Grk. παῦρος 'little', Lat. *putus* 'boy' (rare), *pusillus* 'very small', Goth. *fawai* 'few', etc., all fr. the notion of 'small'. Walde-P. 2.75 ff. Ernout-M. 782, 790.

Grk. κόρος (mostly poet.), Ion. κοῦρος, fr. *κόρϝος, with fem. κόρη 'girl', Ion. κούρη, Dor. κώρα, Arc. κόρϝα : κορέννυμι 'satisfy' orig. 'nourish', Lat. *crēscere* 'grow', etc. Walde-P. 1.408. Hence NG κόρη 'girl, daughter' or κορίτσι with dim. suffix.

NG ἀγώρι 'boy' (of school age), dim. of Grk. ἄωρος 'untimely, immature'. Cf. ἄγωρος in a late Theban epitaph of a youth of 23 years (Glotta 15.174).

2. It. *ragazzo* (whence *ragazza* 'girl'), in earliest use 'stableboy, servant', orig. dub. REW 7019.3. Pauli, op. cit. 143.

Fr. *garçon*, OFr. *gars* (nom.), *garçon* 'servant, young man', of Gmc. orig., perh. fr. a Frank. **wrakjo* = OFris. *wrekkio* = OHG *reccheo* 'exile, adventurer' (NHG *recke*), OE *wrecca* 'exile, wretched person' (NE *wretch*). Gamillscheg 457 f. Bloch 1.327. Otherwise (fr. a Frank. **wurkjo* 'worker') REW 9578a.

Sp. *muchacho*, with fem. *muchacha* 'girl', perh. through *mocho* fr. Lat. *mutilus* 'maimed'. REW 5791.

Rum. *băiat*, generally taken as pple. of *băia* 'bathe' (mostly *îmbaia*). So Tiktin, Şaineanu, s.v. Otherwise REW 887, fr. a *băia* 'streicheln', easier semantically, if *băia* in this sense exists (not in Tiktin and unknown to informant).

Rum. *făt* (now used only in certain phrases), fr. Lat. *fētus* 'offspring'. REW 3273. Hence fem. *fată* 'girl' (so with Diez, Densusianu, and Pauli, op. cit. 71, more probably than as directly fr. Lat. *fēta* 'pregnant, newly delivered', with shift of application to 'one capable of childbearing', as REW 3269, Puşcariu 588, Tiktin s.v.).

3. Ir. *macc* 'boy' and 'son' (NIr. *mac*, W., Br. *mab* 'son'), see under 'son' (2.41).

NIr. *buachaill* 'boy, servant, cowherd', fr. MIr. *buachaill* 'cowherd', like W. *bugail* 'cowherd', Corn. *bugel* 'herdsman, shepherd', Br. *bugel* 'child' : Grk. βουκόλος 'cowherd'. Walde-P. 1.696. Pedersen 1.54. Henry 47.

W. *bachgen*, cpd. of *bach* 'little' and *cen* of *cenau* 'offspring' : Ir. *cinim* 'spring from', *cenēl* 'race', etc. Pedersen 2.33.

W. *hogyn*, prob. new masc. to *hogen* 'girl' (2.26).

Br. *paotr* 'boy, valet', MBr. *pautr*, loanword through OFr. fr. Gmc. Cf. OFr. *pautraille* 'canaille', orig. 'pack of ragamuffins', LG *paltrig* 'ragged', NE *paltry*, dial. *palt* 'rubbish', Dan. *pjalt* 'rag', etc. Henry 217. Falk-Torp 831.

4. Goth. *magus* 'boy', ON *mǫgr* 'boy, son, man', OE *magu* 'son, servant, young man', with derivs. for 'girl', Goth. *mawi* (*magaþs* 'virgin'), ON *mǣr*, OE *mægeþ*, *mægden*, ME, NE *maiden*, *maid*, Du. *meisje* (dim. of *meid*, dial. form of *maagd*, Franck–v. W. s.v. *meid*), OHG *magad*, MHG *maget*, NHG *magt*, *mädchen* : Ir. *magu* (Ogam), *mug* 'servant', Br. *maouez* 'woman', Av. *maγava-* 'unmarried', etc., all with a common notion of 'young person', and perh. fr. the same root as Goth. *mag* 'can', *mahts* 'strength, might', NE *might*, etc. Walde-P. 2.228. Falk-Torp 748. Feist 339.

ON *piltr* 'boy', Dan., Sw. *pilt* 'small boy', orig. dub., but perh. (cf. Br. *paotr*, above, 3) : Sw. *palt*, Dan. *pjalt* 'rag', Sw. dial. *pult* 'bit of wood', orig. something broken off. Johansson, KZ 36.377. Cf. NE *runt*, orig. 'stump' now applied to a small person, *a little runt*.

Dan. *dreng* : Sw. *dräng* 'servant', ON *drengr* 'youth, brave man', *drangr* 'rock pillar', ChSl. *drągŭ* 'beam'. Cf. NHG *bengel* 'cudgel' applied to a child, *der kleine bengel*. Falk-Torp 154. Johansson, KZ 36.374.

Norw. *gut* (vs. Dan. *dreng*) = Du. *guit* 'rogue' : Norw. dial. *gauta* 'prate, chatter', MDu. *guiten* 'make fun of', etc. Falk-Torp 362. Torp, Nynorsk 191.

Sw. *gosse* : Norw. *gosse* 'strong fellow' and 'boar', NE dial. *gussie* 'swine, pig', etc., a colloq. word of the most diverse applications. Björkman, IF 30.252 ff. Hellquist 294.

Sw. *pojke*, fr. Finn. *poika* 'boy', Hellquist 774.

OE *cnapa*, *cnafa*, ME *knave* 'boy, servant' (NE *knave* 'rascal'), Du. *knaap*, OHG *knabo*, MHG, NHG *knabe* (also OHG *knappe* 'boy, youth', NHG *knappe* 'page') : ON *knappr* 'knob', OE *cnæp* 'top', Sw. dial. *knabb* 'peg, knob, small thick-set person or animal'. Falk-Torp 543, 544. Johansson, KZ 36.374. Walde-P. 1.585 f. Bäck, op. cit. 139.

OE *cniht* 'boy, servant, attendant' (NE *knight*), OHG, MHG *kneht* 'boy, servant' (NHG *knecht*) : ME, LG *knagge* 'peg', etc. Wood, Mod. Ph. 2.474. Holthausen, KZ 47.307. Falk-Torp 1498 f. Walde-P. 1.580.

ME, NE *boy*, E. Fris. *boi* 'boy', prob. : ON *bōfi*, Du. *boef* 'knave, rogue', NHG *bube* 'knave, servant', dial. 'boy', orig. a nursery word like NE *baby*, etc. NED s.v. Weigand-H. 1.298.

ME *ladde*, NE *lad*, etym. dub., but perh., as orig. 'attendant', fr. the pass. pple. of ME *leden* 'lead'. NED s.v.

5. Lith. *vaikas*, OPruss. *waix* : Lith. *viekas* 'strength', *veikti* 'do, work' (these : Lat. *vincere* 'conquer', Goth. *weihan* 'fight', etc. Walde-P. 1.232 ff.). Brugmann, IF 38.141.

Lett. *puisis*, fr. Liv. *pois* 'young man'. Mühl.-Endz. 3.403.

Lett. *puika*, fr. Finn. *poika* 'boy' (or the Esth. *poeg*), same as the source of Sw. *pojke*. Mühl.-Endz. 3.403.

6. ChSl. *otrokŭ* 'boy, servant' (Boh., Pol., Russ. *otrok*, but not the usual words for 'boy'), with fem. *otrokovica* 'girl', cpd. of *otŭ* 'out of' and the root of *reką*, *rešti* 'say, speak', hence orig. 'one who cannot speak, infant', like Lat. *infāns*, but with extension to one older (as in Fr. *enfant*) and use of dim. *otročę* for 'infant'. Miklosich 274. Brückner 387.

SCr. *dječak*, deriv. of *dijete* 'child', ChSl. *děti* (2.27).

Boh. *chlapec*, Pol. *chłopiec* : ChSl. *chlapŭ* 'servant', Russ. *cholop* 'serf', etc., outside connection dub. Berneker 394. Brückner 180 (: Goth. *skalks* 'servant').

Boh. *hoch*, short form of *holec* 'bald head', *holek* '(beardless) young man' : *holý* 'bald', ChSl. *golŭ* 'bare', etc. Hence also fem. *holka* 'girl'. Similarly Sorb. *holc* 'boy', *holca* 'girl'. Berneker 325.

Boh. *pachole* : Pol. *pachołek* 'servant, bootblack', etc., cpd. fr. root seen in Russ. *cholit'* 'clean, take care of'. Berneker 395.

Russ. *mal'čik*, fr. *malyj* 'small', ChSl. *malŭ* 'small', etc. Berneker 2.13.

7. Skt. *bāla-* 'boy', with fem. *bālī-* 'girl', adj. *bāla-* 'young', prob. fr. *bala-*

'strength'. Brugmann, IF 38.140 ff. Walde-P. 2.110 ff.

Skt. *kumāra-* 'boy', with fem. *kumārī-* 'girl', etym.? Perh. prefix *ku-*, here in dim. sense) : Skt. *marya-* 'young man', Grk. μεῖραξ 'young girl', μειράκιον 'boy', etc. (Walde-P. 2.281, but without mention of Skt. *kumāra-*). Against connection with Lith. *kumelys* 'foal' (Charpentier, Monde oriental 1.22), cf. Pokorny, KZ 56.131.

2.26. Several of the words for 'girl' are feminine forms of words for 'boy', and so already discussed in 2.25.

1. Grk. παρθένος 'maiden', esp. 'young unmarried woman', perh. a cpd. παρθένος : εὐ-θενής 'vigorous', εὐθηνία 'abundance', etc. applied to the young woman as of exuberant physique. Walde-P. 1.679. Boisacq 747.

NG κοπέλλα 'girl' (used without derogatory sense; also κοπέλι 'boy, servant') : Rum. *copil* 'child', *copila* 'young girl', Alb. *kopil* 'servant, young man', SCr. *kopile* 'bastard', etc., a general Balkan word the ultimate source of which is unknown. Berneker 564. Sandfeld, Ling. balk. 94.

2. Fr. *fille* 'girl' and 'daughter', fr. Lat. *fīlia* 'daughter' (2.44).

3. Ir. *ingen* 'girl' and 'daughter', orig. the latter (2.44).

NIr. *cailīn* (*caile* mostly derogatory), Gael. *caile*, *caileag*, Br. *plac'h*, prob. loanword fr. Lat. *pellex* 'concubine'. Vendryes, De hib. voc. 119. Henry 224.

W. *geneth*, fr. *geni* 'bear' (4.72).

W. *hogen*, perh. fr. **sukā* : Ir. *sūgim*, OE *sūcan*, etc. 'suck', and so orig. 'suckling'. G. S. Lane, Language 13.25 f.

4. ON *stūlka* (also the common NIcel. word for 'girl'), Sw. dial. *stulka* : Sw. dial. *stulk* 'stump, piece', etc. Björkman, IF 30.273.

Dan. *pige* 'girl', Sw. *piga* now 'servant girl' : Dan. *pig* 'spike', OE *pīc* 'point, spike', NE *pike*, *pick*, etc. Falk-Torp 824. Johansson, KZ 36.331. Björkman, IF 30.266.

Norw. *jente* (*gjente*), fem. to Dan. *gante*, Sw. dial. *gant* 'fool'. Falk-Torp 316.

Sw. *flicka* : ON *flīk* 'patch, rag', Sw. *flik* 'flap', Norw. dial. *flicka* 'go about with flapping clothes'. Hellquist 220. Flom, J. Eng. and Germ. Ph. 12.85 ff. Cf. the current slang use (U.S.) of NE *flapper*.

ME *gurle*, *girle*, etc., NE *girl*, orig. 'child, boy or girl' (cf. *knave-gerlys* 'boys' 1450), later only 'girl' : LG *göre* 'child' ("Pomerani in contemptum pro infante" 1593, quoted in Weigand-H. 1.750), perh. also the group MLG *gorre*, *gurre* 'mare', Norw. dial. *gurre* 'lamb', etc., all colloquial epithets of obscure orig. Björkman, IF 30.260, 278.

ME *lasce*, NE *lass* (esp. Sc.), prob. fr. an ON form meaning 'unmarried'. NED s.v.

5. Lith. *merga* now mostly 'maidservant', *mergaitė*, *mergelė*, 'girl', OPruss. *mergu* 'girl' : W. *merch*, Br. *merc'h* (both 'girl' only as 'daughter'), Skt. *marya-* 'young man', Grk. μεῖραξ 'young girl', μειράκιον 'child', etc. Walde-P. 2.281.

Lett. *meita*, fr. MLG *meid* 'girl' (see 2.25). Mühl.-Endz. 2.593.

6. ChSl. *děva*, *děvica*, SCr. *djevojka*, Boh. *dívka*, etc. (the general Slavic word, with a variety of suffix forms), fr. the root of ChSl. *dojiti* 'give suck', Skt. *dhayati* 'sucks', etc. Berneker 197. Walde-P. 1.830. Semantic development prob. fr. 'one who gives suck, female' (like Grk. θῆλυς, Lat. *fēmina*), only here, beside the existing *žena* 'woman, female', applied to the physically matured marriageable young woman, whence dim. forms for 'young girl'. So Berneker (after J. Schmidt), Walde-P., and favored by the actual use of ChSl. *děva* = παρθένος, *děvisto* = παρθενία. Otherwise, as orig. 'suckling', like ChSl. *děti* 'child' (2.27), Miklosich and recently Pedersen, Gram. Misc. Jespersen 67, in connection with a similar question regarding OE *fǣmne* 'young woman'.

7. Skt. *kanyā-*, Av. *kainyā-*, *kainī-* : Skt. *kanīna-* 'young', Grk. καινός 'new', etc. Walde-P. 1.397 ff.

2.27. 'Child' is understood here as 'boy or girl'. Most of the words serve also for 'child' with reference to the parents, 'son or daughter', and in several cases this was the original application as shown by the etymology. But there are also some words that are normally used only in the second sense, as Grk. τέκνον, Lat. *līberī* vs. *puerī*, etc. See 2.43.

Some of the words for 'child' belong with those for 'boy', already discussed (2.25). So Grk. παῖς, NG παιδί, Skt. *bala-*, *kumāra-*, and in plural for 'children' Lat. *puerī*, Lith. *vaikai*. Colloquially and in dialects many of the other words for 'boy' are used in the plural for 'children'.

1. Lat. *infāns* 'infant' (2.28) extended its scope to include older children. Hence Fr. *enfant* and with suffix It. *fanciullo* ('child' and 'little boy' beside *fanciulla* 'little girl'). REW 4393.

It. *bimbo*, nursery word. REW 921.

Sp. *niño*, nursery word belonging with a large group of affectionate terms for 'father, mother, grandfather', etc. (below, p. 94). REW 5817. Walde-P. 1.55.

Rum. *copil* : Grk. κοπέλλα 'girl', etc., Balkan word (2.26).

2. Ir. *lelap*, later *lenab*, NIr. *leanbh* prob. an old nursery word of reduplicated type. (This more likely than connection with the root of Lat. *labāre* 'totter, waver', Pedersen 1.491).

NIr. *pāiste*, fr. NE *page* (in earlier sense 'boy'). Pedersen 1.230.

W. *plentyn*, new sg. to *plant* 'children', orig. a coll. 'offspring' fr. Lat. *planta* 'sprout, shoot'.

Br. *bugel* 'child' also 'cowherd' : W. *bugail* 'cowherd', Ir. *buacchail* 'cowherd, boy' (2.25).

Br. *krouadur*, *kroeadur*, orig. 'creature', fr. Lat. *creātūra*. Loth, Mots lat. 153 f. Cf. Sp. *criatura* 'infant' (2.28).

Corn. *floch* (OCorn. *flogh* gl. *puer*), pl. *fleches* 'children' = Br. *floc'h* 'page' (cf. NIr. *pāiste* 'child' fr. NE *page*, above), etym.? Henry 123.

3. Goth., ON, OHG *barn*, OE *bearn* (NE *bairn* in Sc.), etc., once general Gmc., fr. **barna-* 'born', pple. of Goth. *bairan*, OE *beran*, etc. 'bear'. Cf. Lith. *bernas* 'servant' and Lett. *bērns* 'child', fr. the same root. Walde-P. 1.56. Falk-Torp 51. Feist 82.

OE *cild*, ME, NE *child* : Goth. *kilþei* 'womb', Skt. *jaṭhara-* 'belly, womb' (4.46). Shift from 'womb' to 'child in the womb' (so sometimes in OE), hence 'infant' (cf. Grk. βρέφος 'foetus' and 'newborn babe'), then with extension of scope as in Fr. *enfant* fr. Lat. *infāns*. Walde-P. 1.614. NED s.v. child.

Du., OHG–NHG *kind*, fr. **gen-to-m* 'born' fr. the root of Skt. *jan-*, Lat. *gignere* 'bear, beget', Grk. γίγνομαι 'be born', etc. Walde-P. 1.576. Weigand-H. 1.1035.

4. Lett. *bērns* : Goth. *barn*, etc. (above, 3).

ChSl. *dětĭ* (pl. *děti* renders Grk. παιδία and τέκνα), SCr. *dijete*, etc., the general Slavic word (Russ. sg. *ditja* no longer in common use, but pl. *deti* more common than pl. of *rebenok*), orig. 'suckling' : ChSl. *dojiti* 'give suck', Skt. *dhayati* 'sucks', etc. Berneker 197. Walde-P. 1.831 ff.

Russ. *rebenok*, deriv. of *rob*, ChSl. *rabŭ* 'servant' (19.43).

5. Av. *apərənāyu-*, *apərənāyūka-*, cpd. of *apərəna-* 'unfilled' and *āyu-* 'age', hence 'one of unfilled age, child'.

2.28. 'Infant' may be covered by words for 'child', some of which had this sense originally. More commonly it is expressed by derivatives of words for 'child' (or 'boy'), either with dim. suffix, or cpds. or phrases with words for 'little' or 'young'. But there are also many words of different origin. The numerous nursery words are not included, except where they have become the normal terms of reference, like It. *bambino*, or at least common as such, like NE *baby* beside *infant*.

1. Grk. νήπιος (adj. and noun) in Homer 'child, infant' (so also νηπύτιος) and 'childish, silly', prob. fr. *νή-πϝιος with neg. νη- and the root of πινυτός 'wise', etc. Walde-P. 2.13. Otherwise F. Specht, KZ 56.122 ff.

Grk. παιδίον, dim. of παῖς 'child', is 'young child', in NT frequently 'infant' (Mt. 2.11, 13, etc. of the infant Jesus, in our version 'the young child').

Grk. βρέφος 'foetus' and 'newborn babe' (Simon. +, so in LXX, pap., NT, Lk. 2.12, 16, etc.), in NG the usual lit. word for infant : ChSl. *žrěbę*, 'foal'. Walde-P. 1.689.

NG μωρὸ παιδί or simply μωρό, the usual pop. word, fr. Grk. μωρός 'stupid, foolish'.

2. Lat. *infāns*, lit. 'not speaking', fr. neg. *in-* and pple. of *fārī* 'speak'. Hence OFr. *enfant* (> ME *enfaunt*, NE *infant*), Fr. *enfant* now 'child', *petit enfant* 'infant'.

It. *bambino*, nursery word beside *bimbo* 'child' (2.45).

Fr. *bébé*, nursery word like NE *baby* (below), and if not an actual loanword its present common use in this sense is doubtless due to the latter. Gamillscheg 93. Wartburg 1.304.

Sp. *criatura*, fr. late Lat. *creātūra* 'creation, creature', hence as coll. for 'offspring', then 'infant'. The same use in It. dial. and elsewhere (Pauli, op. cit. 76).

Rum. *copilaş*, dim. of *copil* 'child' (2.27).

Rum. *prunc*, fr. Hung. *poronty* 'brood, little fellow, kid'. Tiktin 1274.

3. Ir. *nōidiu*, NIr. *naoidhe*, prob. fr. **no-widiōn-* or the like 'unknowing'. Stokes, BB 25.257.

W. *maban* fr. *mab* 'boy'.

Br. *bugelig*, *krouadurig*, dims. of *bugel*, *krouadur* 'chlld' (2.27), which may also be used for 'infant'.

4. Goth. *barn*, etc., OE *cild*, OHG *kind*, all words for 'child' (2.27), are used freely (as properly by origin) for 'infant'. But for the latter also cpds., dims., or phrases, like ON *ungbarn* (*ungr* 'young'), NE *young child* (often in NT versions), Dan. *spæd barn*, Sw. *spädt barn* (*spæd*, *späd* 'tender'), NHG *kindchen*, *kindlein*, *kleines kind*, *das kleine*, etc.

ME *baban*, *babe*, *babi*, NE (*babe*) *baby* nursery word, but now in more general use than corresponding forms in other languages.

NHG *säugling*, lit. 'suckling', fr. *säugen* 'suck', now the standard literary term, but not much used in the family.

5. Lith. *kūdikis*, loanword fr. Slavic, ChSl. *chudŭ* 'small, poor', etc. Berneker 405.

Lett. *pupa bērns*, lit. 'child of the breast' (*pupa* gen. sg. of *pups* 'mother's breast').

6. ChSl. *otroče*, dim. of *otrokŭ* 'boy' (2.25).

ChSl. *mladĭnĭcĭ* (translates Grk. νή-

πιος, but *otroče* for the commoner παιδίον or βρέφος), deriv. of *mladŭ* 'tender, young'. So Russ. *mladenec*.

SCr. *djetešce*, Boh. *dětatko*, Pol. *dzieciątko*, etc. dims. of *dijete*, etc. 'child' (2.27).

Boh. *nemluvně*, Pol. *niemowlę*, cpds. of neg. *ne-*, *nie-* and Boh. *mluviti*, Pol. *mowić* 'speak', prob. lit. formations in imitation of Lat. *infāns*.

7. Skt. (beside *bāla*, etc., 2.25) *çiçu-* 'child, infant, fetus, young of an animal', orig. prob. 'fetus' : Skt. *çvā-* 'swell'.

2.31 ff. WORDS FOR FAMILY RELATIONSHIP

Delbrück, Die indogermanischen Verwandschaftswörter. Schrader, IF 17.11 ff. and Reallex., s.v. Familie. Tappolet, Die romanischen Verwandtschaftswörter. Wiedermann, BB 27.205 ff. Hermann, Gött. Nachr. 1918.204 ff.

Many of the words of relationship belong to well-known groups of cognates pointing to specific words for these relations existing in the parent speech. The most widespread are those which are represented by NE *father*, *mother*, *son*, *daughter*, *brother*, *sister*. Others for which there is sufficient agreement to indicate IE origin are words for 'grandson' or 'nephew', for 'paternal uncle', and, in relationship by marriage, those for the 'daughter-in-law' and for her husband's father, mother, brother, or sister, or even her husband's brother's wife. That is, the IE family was obviously not matriarchal. The wife became one of her husband's family, and it was the relations between her and her husband's family that were important. The relations between the husband and his wife's relatives were remoter; and special terms for the 'wife's father', etc. arose only later, either by extension of the inherited group or otherwise.

For 'husband' and 'wife' there is great divergence in the actual words, but considerable agreement in employing words for 'man' and 'woman', or, to some extent, words for 'master' and 'mistress'. Probably this was the situation in the parent speech. Words for 'marry' and 'marriage' are from the most diverse sources, and there is no group of cognates that can be certainly taken as reflecting an IE word for 'marry'. Yet, of course, even from the other linguistic evidence, the existence of the institution in the IE period is apparent.

In the inherited group the suffix *-ter-* or in some cases *-er-*, *-or-*, is conspicuous (cf. Skt. *pitar-*, *mātar-*, *bhrātar-*, *duhitar-*, *jāmātar-*, *yātar-*; *devar-*, *svasar-*). Owing to the well-known use of this suffix in agent-nouns, these words of relationship were also formerly interpreted as agent-nouns from certain roots, e.g. 'father' as 'protector', 'mother' as 'measurer, thoughtful one', or the like, 'brother' as 'supporter', 'daughter' as 'milker', either the 'suckling' or the 'milkmaid', etc. Most of these derivations now seem fanciful and pointless and are generally given up. The use of the suffix is not to be connected directly with its use in agent-nouns, but rather with the use of *-tero-* (*-ero*) in words of contrasted relationship, like Lat. *dexter* vs. *sinister*, *noster* vs. *vester*, etc., that is, it was used in words for 'father' and 'mother', etc. as contrasted terms. Cf. Streitberg, IF 35.196.

The actual root connection and ultimate meaning of these inherited words of relationship is mostly obscure. But those represented by Lat. *pater*, *māter* are probably based upon the intrinsical-

ly meaningless infantile syllables *pā* and *mā*, with suffix added after the analogy of other pairs of contrasted relations, while the simpler forms with or without reduplication, like NE *pa*, *ma*, *papa*, *mama*, continued in use as pet names. Such infantile syllables or nursery words play a considerable role in the words of relationship. They give rise to pet names of loose application which may become specialized in various directions. A similar use of infantile syllables, especially for 'father' and 'mother', is observed in languages from all over the world. Cf. Kretschmer, Einleitung 353 ff., and, for Latin, Heraeus, Die Sprache der römischen Kinderstube, Arch. lat. Lex. 13.149 ff.

The principal groups of this kind may be cited here for future reference. In general, the forms characterized by a labial or dental stop are applied to male relatives 'father', 'grandfather', etc., and those with *n* or *m* to female relatives, 'mother', 'grandmother', 'aunt', 'niece', etc. But there are many exceptions, as new forms for the opposite sex may arise from either type.

1. *papa*, *appa*, *baba*, etc. Walde-P. 1.47; 2.4, 105. For 'father' or 'old man', Grk. πάππα (voc. in Hom.), ἄππα, ἄπφα, etc., late Lat. *pāpa*, Fr. *papa*, NE *papa*, etc.; It. *babbo*.

Goth. *aba* 'husband', ON *afi* 'grandfather, etc.', Grk. πάππος 'grandfather'. Slav. *baba* 'grandmother, old woman', whence Lith. *boba* 'old woman', and fr. this *bobutė* 'grandmother'. Cf. also MHG *bōbe* 'old woman', *buobe* 'boy', NE *baby*, etc.

2. *tata*, *atta*, *dada*, etc. Walde-P. 1.44, 704. For 'father' or 'old man', Skt. *tata-* (in Rigveda), Grk. τάτα, τέττα, ἄττα (but Skt. *attā-* 'mother'), Lat. *tata* (frequent in inscriptions), Rum. *tată*, W., Br. *tad*, NE *dad*, Lith. *tėtis* (OPruss. *thetis* 'grandfather'), *tėvas*, Lett. *tēvs*, *teta*, Goth. *atta*, ON *atte*, OHG *atto*, Alb. *at*, ChSl. *otĭcĭ*, etc., Hitt. *attas*, etc. Here also Slav. and Lith. *teta* 'aunt', etc.

A related group is Grk. τήθη 'grandmother', τηθίς 'aunt', θεῖος, θεία 'uncle, aunt', Lith. *dėdė* 'uncle', ChSl. *dědŭ* 'grandfather', NHG dial. *deite* 'father, old man', etc.

3. *mama*, *amma*, etc. Walde-P. 1.53, 2.221. For 'mother', Grk. μάμμη (also 'grandmother'), Lat. *mamma* (also 'grandmother' and 'nurse'), It. *mamma*, Fr. *mama*, NE *mamma*, etc., familiar in nearly all the European languages, in some as reg. word for 'mother'. Cf. also Lett. *māsa* 'sister', Lith. *moša* 'husband's sister', OHG *muoma* 'aunt', later 'niece' or 'cousin' (NHG *muhme*).

Grk. ἀμμά, ἀμμάς, ἀμμία 'mother' or 'nurse', ON *amma* 'grandmother', OHG *amma* 'mother, nurse' (NHG *amme*), Lat. *amita* 'aunt', Alb. *amë* 'mother'.

4. *nana*, *anna*, etc. Walde-P. 1.55; 2.317. Skt. *nanā-* 'mother', Grk. νάννα 'aunt', νέννος 'uncle', It. *nonna* 'grandmother', etc., Grk. ἀννίς 'grandmother', Lat. *anus* 'old woman', OHG *ano* 'grandfather', *ana* 'grandmother', OPruss. *ane* 'grandmother', Lith. *anyta* 'husband's mother'. NG μάννα 'mother', blend with forms like those in 3, above.

Forms of the above groups are not repeated in the following lists when they are only pet names on a par with NE *papa*, *mamma* beside *father*, *mother*. They are listed where they have become the normal words, like W. *tad*, *mam*, or where they are serious rivals of the old words, as in the case of It. *babbo*, *mamma*.

The use of similar forms for different relationships is mainly observed among groups like the above and is due to the originally loose application of these pet names. But there are also other factors.

The speaker may take the point of view of another, as when a man calls his wife 'mother', from the point of view of the children. Such use of Lith. *motė* as 'woman' or 'wife' replaced the original sense of 'mother'. One's father's 'nephew' is one's own 'cousin', and there are several examples of shift from 'nephew' to 'cousin'. Furthermore, there is a close association between words for reciprocal relations, as between 'grandfather' and 'grandson' (NE *grandson* formed on the model of *grandfather*, etc.; OHG *ano* 'grandfather', but dim. *eninchil*, NHG *enkel* 'grandson'), or between 'uncle' and 'nephew' (OHG *fetiro* 'uncle', MHG *vetere* also 'nephew', NHG *vetter* now 'cousin').

	2.31 HUSBAND	2.32 WIFE
Grk.	ἀνήρ (πόσις)	γυνή (ἄλοχος, ἄκοιτις)
NG	ἄντρας, σύζυγος	γυναῖκα, σύζυγος
Lat.	*vir, marītus (coniux)*	*uxor, coniux (marīta)*
It.	*marito, sposo*	*moglie, sposa*
Fr.	*mari, époux*	*femme, épouse*
Sp.	*marido (esposo)*	*mujer, esposa*
Rum.	*soţ*	*soţie, nevastă*
Ir.	*fer, cēle*	*ben, sētig*
NIr.	*fear, cēile, nuachar*	*bean, cēile, nuachar*
W.	*gwr, priod*	*gwraig, priod*
Br.	*ozac'h, pried*	*gwreg, pried*
Goth.	*aba*	*qēns*
ON	*verr, maðr (hūs-)bōndi*	*kona (kvān)*
Dan.	*mand, ægtemand*	*kone (hustru)*
Sw.	*man, äkta man (make)*	*hustru (maka)*
OE	*wer*	*wīf, cwēn*
ME	*husbonde*	*wife*
NE	*husband*	*wife*
Du.	*man (gade)*	*vrouw, gade*
OHG	*man, hīwo, gimahalo*	*quena, wīb, hīwa, gimahala*
MHG	*man, gemahele*	*kone, wīp, gemahele*
NHG	*mann, ehemann, gatte, gemahl*	*frau, ehefrau, gattin, gemahlin*
Lith.	*vyras (pats)*	*žmona, pati*
Lett.	*vīrs*	*sieva*
ChSl.	*mąžĭ, sąprągŭ*	*žena (sąprągŭ)*
SCr.	*muž suprug*	*žena, supsuga*
Boh.	*muž, manžel, chot'*	*žena, manželka, chot'*
Pol.	*mąz małżonek*	*żona, małżonka*
Russ.	*muž, suprug*	*žena, supruga*
Skt.	*pati-, bhartar-*	*patnī-, jāya-, janī-, bhāryā-*, etc.
Av.	*paiti-*	*nāirī-, nāirīkā-*

2.31, 2.32. Words for 'husband' and 'wife' are most commonly from those for 'man'[2] and 'woman'. Some are from the notion of 'master' or 'mistress' of the household. Many words meaning originally 'united, married, promised, companion', or the like are used for 'husband', and 'wife', mostly in pairs of corresponding masculine and feminine forms. These have not become the common, everyday terms but are often felt as the more refined. Some are in much more general use than others, and it is difficult to know where to draw the line in including them. But at least most of those listed are in more common use than the corresponding NE *spouse*, which is now virtually confined to poetic, humorous, or legal expression (but will be used in the following as the most convenient translation of forms used for either husband or wife).

1. From words for 'man'[2] and 'woman', which have already been discussed in 2.21, 2.22. Probably in every IE language the words for 'man'[2] and 'woman' may be used for 'husband' and 'wife', at least in colloquial or vulgar speech, as is true even in NE *my man, my woman.* Here are listed only those that are the usual terms. (So NG γυναίκα for 'wife' is not vulgar, like NE *woman* in this sense, but is used in the best circles, where σύζυγος would be felt as super-refined, almost like NE *spouse;* Dan. *kone* is now in the best usage, more usual than *hustru;* NHG *weib* for 'wife', vulgar in the north, is usual in southern Germany). While many of these retain also their earlier use, as Grk. ἀνήρ, γυνή, Lat. *vir*, Fr. *femme*, NHG *mann*, ChSl. *mąžĭ, žena*, etc., others have come to be used prevailingly or exclusively for 'husband', 'wife', as ON *verr* 'husband', Goth. *qēns* 'wife', NE *wife*, Br. *gwreg* 'wife', Lith. *žmona*, Pol. *żona* 'wife', Russ. *muž, žena* 'husband, wife'. All such relations are shown by a comparison of the lists 2.21, 2.22 and 2.31, 2.32.

In some cases where the same words serve for 'man, woman' and 'husband, wife', they may be made unambiguous in the latter sense by prefixing a word for 'marriage'. So Dan. *ægte-mand*, Sw. *äkta man*, MLG *echte man* (cf. Du. *echtgenoot*), MHG *ē-man*, NHG *ehe-mann, ehe-frau*, the first part of which belongs with OHG *ēwa* 'law, marriage state' (2.34).

2. Grk. (poet.) πόσις 'husband', πότνια 'mistress', Skt. *pati-*, Av. *paiti-* 'master, husband', Skt. *patnī-* 'mistress, wife', Lith. *pats* 'self, husband', *pati* 'self, wife' (*pati* 'wife' more common than *pats* 'husband', which is mostly obs.), Toch. A *pats* 'husband' : Lat. *potis* 'able', Goth. *bruþfaþs* 'bridegroom', Hitt. *-pat* 'self'. Walde-P. 2.77 f. For similar development of 'master, mistress' (of the house) to 'husband, wife', cf. Dan., Sw. *hustru* 'wife' (below, 6), and NHG *frau* (2.22).

3. Grk. (poet.) ἀκοίτης 'husband', ἄκοιτις 'wife', both lit. 'bedfellow, fr. ἀ- cop. and κοίτη 'bed'.

Grk. (poet.) ἄλοχος 'wife', lit. 'bedfellow', fr. ἀ cop. and λέχος 'bed'.

Grk. σύζυγος 'yoked together, united' (: ζυγόν 'yoke'), 'comrade', rarely 'wife', later (eccl.) as in NG 'consort, spouse', either 'husband' (ὁ) or 'wife' (ἡ). Cf. Lat. *coniux* (below, 4).

4. Lat. *uxor* 'wife' : Arm. *am-usin* 'spouse', and to be analyzed as **uk-sor-*, first part : Skt. *uc-* 'be accustomed to, take pleasure in', Lith. *junkti* 'be accustomed', etc. (Walde-P. 1.111), second part as in **swesor* 'sister', etc. (2.45). Ernout-M. 1143.

Hence OFr. *oissor*, OSp. *uxor*, and the verbal deriv. Rum. *însura* 'marry', etc. (REW 9106–7), but generally replaced.

Lat. *marītus* 'husband' (> It. *marito*, Fr. *mari*, Sp. *marido*), perh. as lit. one provided with a 'young woman, bride', fr. a **marī-* : Skt. *marya-* 'young man', Lith. *marti* 'bride', etc. Hence the later and much less common *marīta* 'wife'. Walde-P. 2.281. Ernout-M. 593. Walde-H. 2.40 f.

Lat. *coniu(n)x* freq. 'wife', less commonly 'husband', fr. *coniungere* 'unite'.

Lat. *spōnsus* (pple. of *spondēre* 'promise') 'betrothed, bridegroom', fem. *spōnsa* 'betrothed, bride'. Hence with extension or with complete shift to 'husband, wife', It. *sposo, sposa*, Fr. *époux, épouse* (OFr. *spus, spuse* > ME, NE *spouse*), Sp. *esposo, esposa.*

Rum. *soț* 'husband', fr. Lat. *socius* 'companion'. Hence also *soție* 'wife'. Pușcariu 1610. Cf. fr. the same source, Alb. *shoq* 'husband', *shoqe* 'wife'.

Rum. *nevastă* 'wife', loanword fr. Slav., ChSl. *nevěsta* 'bride' (cf. 2.22 on OPol. *niewasta* 'woman'). Tiktin 1054.

5. Ir. *cēle* 'companion, husband', NIr. *cēile* 'companion, spouse', prob. : OHG *hīwo, hīwa* 'husband, wife', etc. (below, 5). Walde-P. 1.359, 446.

Ir. *sētig* 'wife', orig. 'companion', deriv. of *sēt* 'way'. Pedersen 2.89.

NIr. *nuachar*, 'lover, spouse' (also *snuachar*, fr. *so-nuachar* 'good spouse'), cpd. of *nua-* 'new'; second part disputed, perh. a vbl. n. to *cuirim* 'place, put', the whole orig. 'newly settled, newcomer (in the home)'. G. S. Lane, Language 8.297 f.

W. *priod*, Br. *pried* 'spouse', fr. Lat. *privātus* 'one's own, private'. Pedersen 1.214.

Br. *ozac'h* 'master of the house, husband', etym.? Loth, RC 41.234 f.

6. Goth. *aba* 'husband' : ON *afi* 'grandfather', etc., orig. nursery word (above, p. 94). Walde-P. 1.47.

ON *hūsbōndi* 'man of the house, husband', cpd. of *hūs* 'house' and *bōndi* 'yeoman', the latter also used alone for 'husband'. Hence ME *husbonde*, NE *husband.*

Dan., Sw. *hustru*, fr. *hus-fru*, cpd. of *hus* 'house' and *fru* 'mistress', like NHG *hausfrau*, Du. *huisvrouw.*

Sw. *make*, fem. *maka*, ME *make* properly 'mate' : OE *gemæcca* 'mate' *gemaec* 'equal, well matched', etc., these : OE *macian* 'make', etc. Falk-Torp 689. Hellquist 621.

Du. (lit.) *echtgenoot* 'spouse', with new fem. *echtgenoote* for 'wife', cpd. of *echt* 'marriage' (2.35) and *genoot* 'companion' : NHG *genosse*, etc.

OHG *hīwo* 'husband', *hīwa* 'wife', OE *hīwa* 'wife' (Goth. *heiwa-frauja* 'master of the house') : Lett. *sieva* 'wife', Lat. *cīvis* 'citizen', Lith. *šeimyna* 'family', OE *hām* 'home', etc., all fr. IE **kei-* 'lie' in Grk. κεῖμαι, etc., whence the notion of 'home, household' and also its master or mistress. Walde-P. 1.359. Walde-H. 1.224. Feist 253 f.

NHG *gatte*, whence fem. *gattin*, fr. MHG *gate* 'companion', here also Du. *gade* now used mostly for 'wife' : MLG *gaden* 'be suitable', OE *gegada* 'companion', *tō gædere* 'together', Goth. *gadiligs* 'cousin', etc. Walde-P. 1.531 ff. Weigand-H. 1.628. Franck-v. W. 172.

OHG *gimahalo* 'bridegroom, husband', *gimahala, gimāla* 'bride, wife', MHG *gemahele* masc. and fem., NHG *gemahl*, fem. *gemahlin*, fr. OHG *mahal* 'contract', esp. 'marriage contract' : Goth. *maþl* 'place of assembly, market', OE *mæþel* 'assembly, speech', etc. Walde-P. 2.304. Weigand-H. 1.671.

7. ChSl. *sąprągŭ*, fem. *sąpręga* (in Gospels 'yoke, pair', late 'spouse') with SCr., Russ. *suprug, supruga*, fr. cpd. of *pręgą, pręšti* 'yoke, harness'. Miklosich 262.

ChSl. *mal(ŭ)žena*, dual 'husband and wife', cpd. of *žena* 'wife', first part Gmc. (: OHG *mahal*, etc., above, 6) or *malŭ* 'little', as prefix of affection? Hence Boh. *manžel, manželka*, Pol. *małżonek, małżonka*, etc. Berneker 2.13.

Boh. *chot'* 'spouse', used for either 'husband' or 'wife' : ChSl. *chotĭ* 'lover, beloved', fr. *chotěti* 'wish'. Berneker 398 f.

8. Skt. *bhartar-* 'husband', *bharyā-* 'wife', lit. 'the sustainer' and 'the one sustained', fr. *bhṛ-* 'bear, carry' : Grk. φέρω 'bear', etc.

Skt. *dāra-* 'wife', etym. dub. Uhlenbeck 124.

2.33 MARRY

(Partly distinguished as a) take a Wife; b) take a Husband)

Grk.	*γαμέω* (a); *γαμέομαι* (b)	Goth.	*liugan* (act. a; pass. b)	Lith.	*vesti, apsivesti; (iš)-tekėti* (b)
NG	*παντρεύομαι, νυμφεύομαι, στεφαν-ώνομαι, παίρνω*	ON	*kvāngask* (a); *giptask* (b)	Lett.	*precēt; iet pie vīra* (b)
		Dan.	*gifte sig*	ChSl.	*(o)ženiti sę* (a); *posagati* (b)
Lat.	*dūcere uxōrem* (a), *nūbere* (b)	Sw.	*gifta sig*	SCr.	*oženiti se* (a); *udati se* (b)
It.	*sposare; maritarsi* (b)	OE	*weddian; wīfian* (a)	Boh.	*(o)ženiti se* (a); *vdáti se* (b)
Fr.	*se marier, épouser*	ME	*wed, mary*		
Sp.	*casarse*	NE	*marry* (*wed*)	Pol.	*(o)żenić sie* (a); *iść za mąż* (b)
Rum.	*se căsători; se însura* (a); *se mărita* (b)	Du.	*trouwen, huwen*	Russ.	*ženit'sja* (a); *vyiti za muž* (b)
Ir.	*dobiur sēitchi* (a); *inbothigur* (b)	OHG	*hīwan*	Skt.	*vah-; pari-nī-* (a)
NIr.	*pōsaim*	MHG	*hīwen, hīrāten*	Av.	*vaz-, upa-vad-*
W.	*priodi*	NHG	*heiraten*		
Br.	*dimezi, eureuji*				

Among words for 'marry' there is in part a distinction between 'take a wife' and 'take a husband'. This is indicated by the use of a and b, it being understood that where there is no such notation the words are used of either party. In several cases words that were originally used only of the one party have lost this restriction. The forms listed are those used of the parties themselves, not those (if distinguished) that are used for 'give in marriage' of the father or the one who performs the ceremony—hence Fr. *se marier* (*avec*), not *marier*, and similarly the reflexive forms in the other Romance languages and in Slavic.

Words for 'marry' (and 'marriage') are from such diverse sources as the following: 'husband', 'wife' (the verbs, at first at least, used only in sense a or b respectively), 'spouse'; 'union', 'pairing'; 'house', 'household', through the notion of establishing a family; various practices preceding or accompanying the marriage ceremony, as 'contract', 'oath', 'bargain', 'betrothal'; 'giving' (orig. of the father giving his daughter in marriage, hence mostly in sense b); 'leading' (the husband leading the bride, so orig. in sense a); 'following' (the bride following the husband, hence in sense b); 'taking the hand' (either husband taking the hand of the bride, hence sense a, or conversely, hence sense b); 'veiling' (of the bride, hence orig. in sense b); 'crowning' (orig. used of the one performing the ceremony, then in mid. or refl. 'get crowned', of either party).

1. Grk. γαμέω (a), γαμέομαι (b, but γαμέω also for either party, NT; in pop. NG 'coire'), beside γάμος 'marriage, wedding' : Grk. γαμβρός, Skt. *jāmātar-* 'son-in-law', etc. (2.63). Walde-P. 1.574.

NG παντρεύομαι (of either party; act. παντρεύω is 'give in marriage'), fr. Hellenistic Grk. ὕπανδρος γυνή 'woman under a man, married woman'.

NG νυμφεύομαι (formerly only a, now also b, as τὸν ἐνυμφεύθη), lit. 'take a bride', fr. νύμφη 'bride'.

NG στεφαν-ώνομαι, used with special reference to the ceremony, lit. 'be crowned' fr. στέφανος 'crown' (wreaths are placed on the head of the bride and groom). Hence the similar use of Rum. *cununa* (fr. sb. *cunună*, Lat. *corōna* 'crown') and other Balkan words. Pușcariu 448. Sandfeld, Ling. balk. 35.

NG παίρνω 'take' (11.13) is a common pop. expression for 'take in marriage, marry'.

2. Lat. *dūcere uxōrem* (a), lit. 'lead a wife', fr. *dūcere* 'lead' and *uxor* 'wife'.

Lat. *nūbere* (b; late also a) prob. orig. 'veil' : *obnūbere* 'veil', ChSl. *snubiti* 'woo', fr. **sneubh-* beside **sneudh-* in Av. *snaoθa-*, Lat. *nūbēs* 'cloud'. Hence *cōnubium* 'marriage', *nupta* 'bride', and *nuptiae* 'wedding' (> It. *nozze*, Fr. *noces*, Rum. *nuntă;* REW 5999). Meringer, Wört. u. Sach. 5.167 ff. Wackernagel, Kretschmer Festschrift 289 ff. Ernout-M. 683 f. Otherwise Walde-P. 2.697.

It. *sposare*, Fr. *épouser*, derivs. of the words for 'spouse', It. *sposa*, etc. (2.31).

It. *maritarsi* (mostly b), Fr. *se marier* (OFr. *marier* > ME *mary*, NE *marry;* sb. *mariage* > ME *mariage*, NE *marriage*), Sp. *maridar* (not common), Rum. *se mărita* (b), fr. Lat. *marītāre* 'give in marriage', deriv. of *marītus* 'husband' (2.31).

Sp. *casarse*, Rum. *se căsători*, derivs. (Rum. through *căsător* 'head of the house, husband') of *casă* 'house'. REW 1728. Pușcariu 305. Hence Rum. *căsătorie* 'marriage'.

Rum. *se însura* (a, dial. also b), with some forms in It. dialects, deriv. of Lat. *uxor* 'wife'. REW 9107. Pușcariu 874.

3. Ir. *dobiur sēitchi* (a), lit. 'bring a wife' (*sētig*, 2.32).

Ir. *inbothigur* (only OIr. 3 pl. subj. dep. *inbothigetar*, referring to women), cpd. of *ind-, in-* 'in' and *both* 'hut'. Cf. Sp. *casarse*, etc., above, 2. Pedersen 1.238.

NIr. *pōsaim*, like It. *sposare*, etc., deriv. of Lat. *spōnsus* 'betrothed, bridegroom', *spōnsa* 'bride' (2.31). Pedersen 1.208.

W. *priodi*, fr. *priod* 'spouse' (2.31).

Br. *dimezi*, that is, *d-im-ezi* (Corn. *d-om-ethy*) : W. *dy-weddi* 'betrothal', Ir. *fedim* 'lead', Lith. *vedu, vesti* 'lead, marry', Skt. *vādhū-* 'bride', etc. Walde-P. 1.255. Pedersen 2.301.

Br. *eureuji*, deriv. of *eured* 'wedding' (2.34).

4. Goth. *liugan* (a in act., b in pass), also *liuga* 'marriage : Ir. *luge* 'oath', etc. Walde-P. 2.415. Feist 333.

ON *kvāngask* (a), reflex. of *kvānga* 'make a man take a wife', fr. *kvān* 'wife' (2.32).

ON *giptask* (b), reflex. of *gipta* 'give a woman in marriage', hence orig. only of the woman 'given in marriage', later of either party, as Dan. *gifte sig*, Sw. *gifta sig.* For this specialization of 'give' cf. also Goth. *fragifts* in pl. 'betrothal, espousal', ON *giptung* 'marriage' (woman's), ON *giptamāl*, Dan. *giftermaal*, Sw. *giftermål* 'marriage' (of either party), cpd. with *māl*, etc. 'speech, agreement' (: OHG *mahal* 'contract' as in *gimahalo* 'spouse'), OE *giftian* in pass. 'be given in marriage' of the woman, *gift* 'marriage gift' (purchase of the bride), pl. *gifta* 'wedding', *gifte* 'dowry', NHG *mitgift* 'dowry', etc.

OE *weddian* (> ME, NE *wed*) 'engage, undertake', usually 'marry', orig. 'make a woman one's wife by giving a pledge or earnest money', then used of either party : OE *wedd*, Goth. *wadi*, Lat. *vas, vadis* 'pledge, surety', NHG *wetten* 'wager', etc. Walde-P. 1.216. NED s.v. *wed.*

OE *wīfian* (a) fr. *wīf* 'wife'.

ME *mary*, NE *marry*, fr. OFr. *marier* (above, 2), first used for 'give in marriage' or pass. 'be married', later also for 'take in marriage' and superseding *wed*, the latter being now only lit. or dial. NED s.v. *marry.*

Du. *trouwen* 'marry' fr. earlier 'betroth', this from 'trust' : NE *trow, troth, trust, true*, NHG *trauen*, Goth.

trauan 'trust', etc. Falk-Torp 1285. Walde-P. 1.805.

OE *hīwian* (rare), Du. *huwen* (whence *huwelijk* 'marriage'), OHG *hīwan*, MHG *hīwen*, deriv. of old words for 'husband, wife', OHG *hīwo, hīwa*, etc. (2.31).

MHG *hīrāten*, NHG *heiraten, sich* (*ver*)*heiraten*, new vb. fr. OHG, MHG *hīrāt* 'marriage', a cpd. of the preceding *hīwan* with *rāt* 'arrangement', etc., like OE *hīrēd* 'household, family'.

5. Lith. *vedu, vesti* 'lead' and 'marry' (orig. and still mostly a, but also b), also *apsivesti* (cf. Tauta ir Žodis 5.656) : ChSl. *vedǫ vesti* 'lead', Ir. *fedim* 'lead', Skt. *vādhū-* 'bride', etc. Walde-P. 1.255. Hence sbs. (*ap-si-*)*vedimas* 'marriage', *vestuvės* 'wedding'.

Lith. (*iš*)*tekėti už vyro* (b), lit. 'run after a man', similarly Lett. *iet pie vīra*, are modeled on the Pol. and Russ. phrase, below, 6. Hence Lith. sb. *ištekėjimas* 'marriage' (woman's).

Lett. *precēt*, orig. 'bargain', deriv. of *prece* 'wares'. Hence *precēšanās* 'marriage'. Mühl.-Endz. 3.384.

6. ChSl. (*o*)*ženiti sę* (a), etc., general Slavic form fr. *žena* 'wife' (2.32). Hence sb. SCr. *ženidba*, Boh. *ženitba*, Russ. *ženitba* 'marriage' (man's).

ChSl. *posagati* (b), also *posagŭ* 'wedding', ORuss. *posjagat'* : ChSl. *sęgnǫti*

'stretch out' (the hand). Refers to the bride's reaching out for the hand of the bridegroom at the wedding ceremony. Cf. Skt. *pāṇi-graha-* 'marriage', lit. 'grasping the hand' (of the bride in this case). Brückner, KZ 45.318 ff. Walde-P. 2.482 ff.

SCr. *udati se*, Boh. *vdáti se* (both b) : ChSl. *vŭ-dati*, etc. 'give', hence 'give a woman in marriage' and reflex. 'be given in marriage', like ON *giftask*, above, 4. Hence sb. SCr. *udaja*, Boh. *vdaj, vdavky* (pl.) 'marriage' (woman's).

Pol. *išč za mąž*, Russ. *vyiti* (or *vydti*) *za muž* (both b), lit. 'go after a man (husband)', that is, follow him. Brückner, KZ 45.319. Hence sb. Russ. *zamužestvo* 'marriage' (woman's).

7. Skt. *vah-* 'lead, bring' and 'marry' (orig. a, like Lat. *dūcere uxōrem*, Lith. *vedu*, but also b already in Rigveda), *vivāha-* 'marriage', Av. *vaz-* (once as 'marry' a) : Lat. *vehere* 'carry', etc. Walde-P. 1.249.

Av. *upa-vad-* (in caus. form) 'give in marriage' : Skt. *vādhū-* 'bride', Lith. *vedu*, etc. (above, 5). Barth. 1343.

Skt. *pari-ṇī-*, lit. 'lead (the bride) around (the fire)', hence 'take a wife', fr. *nī-* 'lead'.

Skt. *pari-grah-* 'seize, take a wife', fr. *grah-* 'seize.'

2.34 MARRIAGE; WEDDING

Grk.	γάμος	Goth.	*liuga*	Lith.	(*apsi-*)*vedimas, ištek-*
NG	γάμος	ON	*giptung, giptamāl;*		*ėjimas* (b); *vestu-*
Lat.	*coniugium, cōnubium,*		*brūðkaup, brullaup*		*vės*
	mātrimonium; nup-	Dan.	*giftermaal, ægte; bryl-*	Lett.	*precēšanās, laulība;*
	tiae		*lop*		*kāzas*
It.	*matrimonio; nozze*	Sw.	*giftermål, äkta; bröl-*	ChSl.	*brakŭ (malŭženĭstvo)*
Fr.	*mariage; noces*		*lop*	SCr.	*brak, ženidba* (a),
Sp.	*matrimonio; bodas*	OE	*weddung, sinscipe;*		*udaja* (b); *svadba*
Rum.	*căsatorie; nuntă*		*gifta, brȳdhlōp*	Boh.	*manželstvi, sňatek,*
It.	*lānamnas*	ME	*weddyng, wedlok,*		*ženitba* (a), *vdavky*
NIr.	*pōsadh*		*mariage*		(b); *svatba*
W.	*priodas; neithior*	NE	*marriage (wedlock);*	Pol.	*małżenstwo, ślub; we-*
Br.	*dimezi; eured*		*wedding*		*sele*
		Du.	*huwelijk, echt; brui-*	Russ.	*brak, supružestvo, že-*
			loft		*nit'ba* (a), *zamu-*
		OHG	*hīrāt, ēwa; brūtlouft*		*žestvo* (b); *svad'ba*
		MHG	*hīrāt, ē(we); brūtlouft,*	Skt.	*vivāha-, patitva-*, etc.
			hōhzīt	Av.	*nāiriθwana-*
		NHG	*heirat, ehe; hochzeit*		

Of the words entered, the majority, like NE *marriage*, cover both the state and the act of marriage (*marriage as an institution*, or *the marriage took place*). A few are used only for the married state, as Lat. *mātrimōnium*, NHG *ehe*. Many words are used only for the ceremony, as NE *wedding* in its present usage. Such words are added, but separated by a semicolon.

In some cases there are distinct words for 'taking a wife' and 'taking a husband', corresponding to the distinctive verbs (2.33). These are similarly indicated by a and b.

Most of the words for 'marriage' are obvious cognates (derivs. or in some cases the source) of the verbs for 'marry' and have been noted in the discussion of the latter (2.33). But a few, and many of the special words for the wedding ceremony, are of different origin.

1. Lat. *coniugium*, lit. 'union', fr. *coniungere* 'join'. Cf. *coniu(n)x* 'spouse' (2.31).

Lat. *cōnubium*, the usual legal term for 'marriage', and *nuptial* 'wedding' (> It. *nozze*, etc.), see under *nūbere* (2.33).

Lat. *mātrimōnium* (> It., Sp. *matri-*

monio), fr. *māter* 'mother', and orig. referring to the woman's lawful motherhood, married status, as opposed to concubinage.

Sp. *boda(s)*, 'wedding', fr. Lat. *vōta* 'vows'. REW 9458.

2. Ir. *lānamnas*, deriv. of *lānamain* 'married couple', deriv. of *lān* 'full'. Pedersen 2.62. Stokes 293 (as cpd.).

W. *neithior* 'wedding', fr. Lat. *nuptiālia*. Pedersen 1.236. Loth, Mots lat. 190.

Br. *eured* 'wedding', fr. Lat. *ōrātio* 'prayer'. Pedersen 1.203. Cf. Sp. *bodas*, above.

3. ON *brūðkaup* 'wedding', cpd. of *brūð* 'bride' and *kaupa* 'buy', referring to the gifts made to the bride, and reflecting the older custom of purchasing a wife. Schrader, Reallex. s.v. Brautkauf.

ON *brūðlaup, brullaup*, Dan. *bryllop*, Sw. *bröllop*, OE *brȳdhlōp*, OHG, MHG *brūtlouft*, Du. *bruiloft* 'wedding', cpd. of *brūð*, 'bride' and *laupa*, etc. 'run', referring to the ceremonial fetching of the bride, this ultimately reflecting a primitive chase or robbery of the bride.

Schrader, Reallex. s.v. Raubehe. Falk-Torp 109.

OE, beside usual *weddung*, rarely *wedlāc* 'pledge' and 'espousals', whence ME *wedlok*, NE *wedlock*, fr. *wedd* 'pledge' with suffix *-lāc*, orig. same as *lāc* 'gift, etc.'. NED s.v. wedlock.

OE *sinscipe*, cpd. of *sin-* 'everlasting' and *scipe* 'condition', hence lit. 'permanent state'. Cf. *sinhīwan* 'married couple'.

OE *ǣw*, OHG *ēwa* (21.12) and 'lawful married state', MHG *ē(we)*, NHG *ehe*, Du. *echt* (MLG *echt* > Dan. *ægte*, Sw. *äkta*). Falk-Torp 183. Weigand-H. 1.405 f.

MHG *hōhzīt*, lit. the 'high time', used of festivals like Christmas, Easter, also of the 'marriage festival', as NHG *hochzeit*. Weigand-H. 1.875. Sperber, Einleitung 42.

4. Lith. *svodba* (formerly usual word for 'wedding'), fr. Russ. *svad'ba* (below, 5).

Lett. *laulība* 'betrothal, marriage', fr. *laulāt* 'betroth', this from Esth. (or Liv.) *loul* 'song, betrothal song' (Finn. *laulaa* 'sing'). Mühl.-Endz. 2.428.

Lett. *kāzas* 'wedding', fr. Esth. *kāza* 'husband'. Mühl.-Endz. 2.206.

5. ChSl. *brakŭ* (in the Gospels always of the marriage at Cana, the 'wedding', but there is no opportunity for any other use), SCr., Russ. *brak*, prob. fr. *berq, brati* 'take', IE *bher-* 'bear'), orig.

'taking the bride', like 'lead the bride, marry' in Lith. *vesti*, etc. Berneker 81.

ChSl. *malŭženĭstvo* (late), Boh. *manželstvi*, Pol. *małżenstvo* : ChSl. *malŭžena* 'married couple', Boh. *manžel* 'husband', etc. (2.31).

Boh. *sňatek*, orig. 'union' : *sníti* OBoh. *snieti*, pple. *sňat*, ChSl. *sŭnęti* 'take down, take together', cpd. of *sŭ* 'with' and *jęti* 'take'. Gebauer 1.381. Berneker 429.

Pol. *ślub* 'vow' (= Boh. *slib* 'vow'), hence also 'betrothal' and 'marriage' : *poślubić* 'betroth', cpd. of *lubić* 'like, love'. Hence OLith. *salubas*, OPruss. acc. sg. *salūban* 'marriage'. Berneker 757 f. Brückner 531.

Russ. *supružestvo*, fr. *suprug* 'spouse' (2.31).

SCr. *svadba*, Boh. *svatba*, Russ. *svad'ba* 'wedding', deriv. of ChSl. *svatŭ* 'kinsman' (: possessive *svojĭ*), then 'one who promotes the marriage, matchmaker', as Russ. *svat*, Pol. *swat*, etc. Miklosich 332.

Pol. *wesele* 'wedding', formerly 'merriment' : ChSl. *veselĭje* 'merriment' *veselŭ* 'merry' (16.22). Brückner 607.

6. Skt., beside *vivāha-*, etc. fr. *vah-* 'marry', also *patitva-* 'husbandhood', *janitva-* 'wifehood', also *pāṇi-graha-* lit. 'grasping the hand' (of the bride), *pari-ṇaya-* (cf. *pari-ṇī-* 2.33), etc.

Av. *nāiriθwana-*, lit. 'wifehood', fr. *nāiri-* 'wife'.

	2.35 FATHER	2.36 MOTHER	2.37 PARENTS
Grk.	πατήρ	μήτηρ	τοκεῖς, τεκόντες, γονεῖς
NG	πατέρας	μητέρα	γονεῖς
Lat.	*pater*	*māter*	*parentēs*
It.	*padre, babbo*	*madre, mamma*	*genitori*
Fr.	*père*	*mère*	*père et mère*
Sp.	*padre*	*madre*	*padres*
Rum.	*tată*	*mamă*	*părinţĭ*
Ir.	*athir*	*māthir*	*tuistidi*
NIr.	*athair*	*māthair*	*tuismhightheoiri*
W.	*tad*	*mam*	*rhieni*
Br.	*tad*	*mam*	*tad ha mam*
Goth.	*atta (fadar)*	*aipei*	*bērusjōs, fadrein*
ON	*faðir*	*mōðir*	*feðgin*
Dan.	*fader*	*moder*	*forældre*
Sw.	*fader*	*moder*	*föräldrar*
OE	*fæder*	*mōdor*	*ealdras*
ME	*fader, fadir*	*moder, mother*	*eldren, parentes*
NE	*father*	*mother*	*parents*
Du.	*vader*	*moeder*	*ouders*
OHG	*fater*	*muotar*	*altiron*
MHG	*vater*	*muoter*	*altern, eltern*
NHG	*vater*	*mutter*	*eltern*
Lith.	*tėvas*	*motyna*	*tėvai, gimdytojai*
Lett.	*tēvs*	*māte*	*vecaki*
ChSl.	*otĭcĭ*	*mati*	*rod teli*
SCr.	*otac*	*mati*	*roditelji*
Boh.	*otec*	*matka, máti*	*rodiče*
Pol.	*ojciec*	*matka (mać)*	*rodzice*
Russ.	*otec*	*mat'*	*roditeli*
Skt.	*pitar-*	*mātar-*	*pitarāu, mātarāu*
Av.	*pitar-*	*mātar-*	*pitarə*

2.35. 'Father'. 1. IE *ptér-*, prob. starting fr. a nursery word of the *pa* type (above, p. 94) orig. *pā*, reduced to *pa* before the accent. Walde-P. 2.4. Here belong the Grk., Lat., Ir., Gmc., and Indo-Iranian words, also Arm. *hair*, and Toch. A *pācar*, B *pācer*. In Balto-Slavic it is completely replaced.

2. Nursery words that have become the usual terms. Type *baba* (above, p. 94) in It. *babbo*, now a serious rival of *padre*.

Type *atta, tata* (above, p. 94) in Rum. *tată*, W., Br. *tad*, Goth. *atta* (so reg., vs. *fadar* and here not of earthly father), Lith. *tėvas*, Lett. *tēvs*, OPruss. *taws*, ChSl. *otĭcĭ*, etc. (all the Balto-Slavic forms), Hitt. *attas*.

2.36. 'Mother'. 1. IE *māter-*, prob. starting fr. a nursery word of the *ma* type. Walde-P. 2.229. Here belong the Grk., Lat., Ir., Gmc. (except Goth *aipei*), Balto-Slavic, and Indo-Iranian forms, also Arm. *mair*, and Toch. A *mācar*, B *mācer*. But Lith. *motė* became 'woman', and as 'mother' was replaced by the deriv. *motyna*.

2. Nursery words that have become the usual terms. Type *mama* (above, p. 94, Walde-P. 2.221) in It. *mamma* a serious rival of *madre*, and W., Br. *mam*.

Goth. *aipei*, prob. new fem. formed fr. some nursery word similar to, though not identical with, *atta* 'father'. Feist 28.

2.37. Words for 'parents' are fr. verbs for 'beget' or 'bear' (4.71, 72); fr. words for 'old'; or are pl. or du. forms (the latter, of course, more orig.), or derivs., of words for 'father', or rarely 'mother'.

1. Grk. τοκεῖς (so reg. Hom.), or aor. pple. τεκόντες : τίκτω 'beget, bear' (4.71).

Grk., NG γονεῖς : γίγνομαι 'be born', γεννάω 'beget, bear' (4.71).

2. Lat. parentēs (also 'ancestors', late also 'relatives'), pres. pple. of par- in parere 'bear, beget' (4.72). Hence Rum. părinţĭ 'parents', Fr. parents formerly 'parents' and 'relatives' (> ME parentes, NE parents), now 'relatives' (as 'parents' replaced by père et mère), as also It. parenti, Sp. parientes. REW 6233.

Lat. patrēs (as also Grk. πατέρες) was commonly used for 'forefathers' and occasionally in late times for 'parents'. Hence Sp. padres.

Lat. genitor 'begetter, father' : gignere 'beget', etc. Hence It. genitori.

3. Ir. tuistidi, NIr. tuismhightheoiri : Ir. do-fuismim 'beget, bear' (4.71).

W. rhieni (formerly also 'ancestors'), cpd. rhi-eni : geni 'be born', Lat. gig-nere, etc., formed like Grk. πρόγονοι 'ancestors'. Pedersen 2.533.

Br. tad ha mam, after Fr. père et mère.

4. Goth. bērusjōs, orig. a nom. pl. fem. perf. act. pple. of bairan 'bear'. For the fem., cf. Skt. matārāu, below.

Goth. fadrein 'family' and 'parents', sg. coll. (also pl. fadreina), deriv. of fadar 'father'.

ON feðgin, deriv. of faðir 'father'.

Dan. forældre, Sw. föräldrar (in the older language 'forefathers'), OE ealdras, Du. ouders, OHG altiron, NHG eltern, all fr. the Gmc. forms for 'older'.

5. Lith. tėvai, pl. of tėvas 'father'. Lith. gimdytojai : gimdyti 'bear, beget' (4.71).

Lett. vecaki, fr. vecs 'old' (influence of NHG eltern prob.).

ChSl. roditeli, etc. (all the Slavic words) : roditi 'beget, bear' (4.71).

6. Skt. pitarāu, Av. pitarə (once, Barth. 905), Skt. mātarāu, both elliptical duals of pitar- 'father' or mātar- 'mother', also copulative dual Skt. mātarāpitarā.

	2.41 SON	2.42 DAUGHTER
Grk.	ἑιος, ὑιός	θυγάτηρ
NG	υἱός (γυιός)	θυγατέρα, κόρη
Lat.	filius, nātus	filia
It.	figlio, figliolo	figlia, figliola
Fr.	fils	fille
Sp.	hijo	hija
Rum.	fiu	filcă
Ir.	macc	ingen
NIr.	mac	ingheann
W.	mab	merch
Br.	mab	merc'h
Goth.	sunus	dauhtar
ON	sunr, sonr	dóttir
Dan.	søn	datter
Sw.	son	dotter
OE	sunu	dohtor
ME	sune, sone	daughter
NE	son	doughter
Du.	zoon	dochter
OHG	sun(u)	tohter
MHG	sun	tohter
NHG	sohn	tochter
Lith.	sūnus	duktė
Lett.	dēls	meita
ChSl.	synŭ	dŭšti
SCr.	sin	kći
Boh.	syn	dcera
Pol.	syn	córka
Russ.	synŭ	doč'
Skt.	sūnu-, putra-	duhitar-
Av.	puɵra-, hunu-	dugədar-, duɣðar-

2.41, 2.42. Most of the words for 'son' and 'daughter' are inherited from the parent speech. But in part these have been replaced. The words for 'boy' and 'girl' (2.25, 2.26) are also naturally used from the parents' point of view for 'son' and 'daughter'. In a few of these cases the latter is the original sense indicated by the etymology. Even in languages where the old distinctive terms remain, the words for 'boy' and 'girl' may be common in colloquial use. In some Greek dialects we find even in legal terminology παῖς and κόρη in place of υἱός and θυγάτηρ. NG κόρη is more commonly used than θυγατέρα.

2.41. 'Son'. 1. IE *sŭnu- and *suyu-(?), fr. the root of Skt. sū- 'bear',

and orig. an abstract 'birth, offspring', then specialized to 'son'. Walde-P. 2.469. Feist 460 f. Here belong Goth. sunus, etc., all the Gmc. forms; Lith. sūnus, OPruss. souns, ChSl. synŭ, etc., all the Slavic forms; Skt. sūnu-, Av. hunu (but the latter only of evil beings, in contrast to puɵra-); Grk. υἱύς, υἱός; Toch. A se gen. sg. seyo, nom. pl. sewañ (SSS 159), B soy, gen. sg. seyi.

2. Lat. filius (> It. figlio, figliolo, Fr. fils, Sp. hijo, Rum. fiu), together with fem. filia 'daughter' (> It. figlia, figliola, Fr. fille, Sp. hija; Rum. fie arch., now dim. filcă), orig. 'suckling', fr. the root of Lat. fēlāre 'suck' (cf. Umbr. sif filiu 'suckling pigs'), Skt. dhayati 'sucks', etc., IE *dhēi-. Cf. ChSl. děti 'child'

(2.27), Lett. dēls 'son'. Walde-P. 1.829 ff. Ernout-M. 359. Walde-H. 1.496.

Lat. nātus, pple. cf. nāsci 'be born', freq. for filius.

3. Ir. macc (also 'boy'), NIr. mac, W., Br. mab, etym. dub., perh. as orig. 'boy' : Ir. magu, mug 'slave', Goth. magus 'boy', etc. (2.25). Pokorny, KZ 45.363.

4. Lett. dēls, fr. the same root as Lat. filius, above, 2.

5. Skt. putra-, very common beside sūnu-, Av. puɵra-, OPers. puɵra-, the reg. Iran. word : Osc. puklum 'filium' Pael. puclois 'pueris', Lat. puer 'boy', Grk. παῖς, etc. (2.25). Walde-P. 2.75 ff.

2.42. 'Daughter'. 1. IE *dhugh(ə)ter, root connection obscure. The root agrees in form with that of Skt. duh-'milk' and with that of Grk. τεύχω 'fashion, make'. But in neither case is there a convincing semantic explanation. Walde-P. 1.868. Here belong Grk. θυγάτηρ; Goth. dauhtar, etc., all the Gmc. words; Lith. duktė, OPruss. duckti, ChSl. dŭšti, etc., all the Slavic words (partly with added suffixes and phonetic changes that disguise the orig.); Skt. duhitar-, Av. dugədar-, duɣðar- (OPers. form not yet quotable, but represented by Elam. dukšiš, Cameron, J. Near Eastern* Stud. 1.217; NPers. duxtar; Arm. dustr; Toch. A ckācar, B tkācer (SSS 65).

2. Lat. filia (> It. figlia, etc), fem. of filius. See 2.41.

3. Ir. inigena (Ogam), ingen (also 'girl'), NIr. inghean, cpd. like Lat. indigena 'born in, native', Grk. ἐγ-γόνη 'granddaughter'. Pedersen 1.101. Walde-P. 1.577.   Walde-H. 1.599.

W. merch, Br. merc'h, orig. 'girl' : Lith. merga 'girl', etc. (2.26). Walde-P. 2.281.

4. Lett. meita, same word as for 'girl', fr. MLG meid 'girl' (2.26).

2.43. 'Child' with reference to the parents, that is = 'son' or 'daughter', is generally expressed by the same words that are used for 'child' = 'boy or girl'; and in several of these the application to 'child' as offspring is the more original, as indicated by the etymology. See 2.27.

But there are also a few words which remain restricted in normal usage to 'child' in this sense, or to 'children', being used mainly in the plural.

1. Grk. τέκνον : τίκτω 'beget, bear'. As τοκεῖς, τεκόντες 'parents', so τέκνα 'children'. This is the usual legal term in laws of inheritance, though παῖδες may also be so used.

2. Lat. liberī : liber 'free', but semantically through an earlier sense 'belonging to the nation, native' (cf. 19.44), hence specifically 'legitimate' children (= Grk. γνήσιοι παῖδες). Ernout-M. 545. Walde-H. 1.792 f. Benveniste, Rev. Et. Lat. 14.51 ff.

Lat. nāti, pl. of nātus 'born, son', also used for 'children'.

It. figlioli (in contrast to fanciulli), pl. of figliolo 'son'.

3. Goth. (beside usual barn for τέκνον) frasts, doubtless fr. fra = Grk. πρό and frasts, but precise formation (cpd. or with suffix) dub. Feist 165 (with refs.; add F. Mezger, Language 19.262 f.).

4. ChSl. cędo, the reg. translation of Grk. τέκνον, SCr. cedo, etc. (in modern Slavic mostly a pet name 'darling', or only in cpds.), prob. not a loanword fr. Gmc. (OHG kind, etc.), but fr. the root of ChSl. -čĭną, -čęti 'begin', Grk. καινός 'new', Skt. kanīna- 'young', kanyā- 'girl' (2.26), etc. Berneker 154. Brückner 542.

	2.44 BROTHER	2.45 SISTER
Grk.	ἀδελφός	ἀδελφή
NG	ἀδελφός, pop. ἀδερφός	ἀδελφή, pop. ἀδερφή
Lat.	frāter	soror
It.	fratello	sorella
Fr.	frère	sœur
Sp.	hermano	hermana
Rum.	frate	soră
Ir.	brāthir	siur
NIr.	dearbhráthair	deirbhshiur
W.	brawd	chwaer
Br.	breur	c'hoar
Goth.	brōþar	swistar
ON	brōðir	systir
Dan.	broder	søster
Sw.	broder	syster
OE	brōðor	sweostor
ME	brother	sister, suster
NE	brother	sister
Du.	broeder	zuster
OHG	bruodar	swestar
MHG	bruoder	swester
NHG	bruder	schwester
Lith.	brōlis	sesuo
Lett.	brālis	māsa
ChSl.	bratrŭ, bratŭ	sestra
SCr.	brat	sestra
Boh.	bratr	sestra
Pol.	brat	siostra
Russ.	brat	sestra
Skt.	bhrātar-	svasar-
Av.	brātar-	x̌aŋhar-

2.44. 'Brother'. 1. IE *bhrāter-, possibly fr. *bher- 'bear', as 'protector, sustainer of the sisters(?). Walde-P. 2.193. Ernout-M. 386. Walde-H. 1.542. Here belong all the words listed except the Greek and the Spanish; also Arm. elbair, Toch. A pracar, B procer. Grk. φράτηρ only as 'member of the φράτρία 'brotherhood'. So Sp. fraire, fraile only for brother in religious sense, 'friar, monk'. NIr. bráthair 'friar' or in extended sense 'relative, kinsman', as 'brother' replaced by dear-bhráthair lit. 'real brother', cpd. of dearbh 'real, true' (Ir. derb 'certain'). Similarly NIr. siur 'sister' in religious sense vs. deirbhshiur 'real sister'. Lith. brolis, Lett. brālis represent pet-name forms derived from

the first syllable of the inherited word (preserved in OPruss. brāti) with an l-suffix.

2. Grk. ἀδελφός 'brother', ἀδελφή 'sister', dial. also ἀδελφεός, ἀδελφεά, fr. *ἀ-δελφος (-εος) : Skt. sa-garbhya- 'of the same womb', cpd. of cop. sa- (Grk. ἁ-) and garbha- 'womb' (: Grk. δελφύς 'womb'). Walde-P. 1.692. This was doubtless first used as an adj. defining φράτηρ, either more specifically as 'frater uterinus' (in contrast to brother by the same father only), or simply as 'brother by blood' after φράτηρ had come to be applied to the member of a phratry.

Grk. κασίγνητος in Homer (where also κασιγνήτη 'sister'), and the reg. prose word for 'brother' in Cyprian, a cpd. of γνητός 'born' (: γίγνομαι, etc. cf. γνήσιος 'lawfully begotten, genuine') and κασι- of obscure orig.

3. Sp. *hermano* 'brother', *hermana* 'sister', fr. Lat. *germānus, germāna* (: *germen* 'sprout, germ') used with *frater, soror* and also alone for 'own, full brother, sister', more common than *frater, soror* in MLat. documents of Italy before A.D. 1000. Ernout-M. 417. Walde-H. 1.594. REW 3742. P. Aebischer, Z. rom. Ph. 57.211 f.

2.45. 'Sister'. 1. IE *swesor-, prob. *swe-sor-, cpd. of the refl. *swe-, the second part related to the rare Grk. ὄαρ 'wife', Av. *hairišī-* 'female', Lat. *uxor* 'wife' (2.32), and the fem. numeral forms like Skt. *tisras* 'three'. Walde-P. 2.533 f. Ernout-M. 958 f. Wackernagel, Altind. Gram. 3.349. Benveniste, BSL 35.1.104 f.

Here belong all the forms listed, except the Greek, Spanish, and Lettic;

also Arm. *k'oir*, Toch. A *șar*, B *șer*; Grk. (only Hesych.) ἔορ 'daughter, cousin', ἔορες 'relatives'.

2. For the Grk., Sp., and NIr. words, see 2.44.

3. Lett. *māsa* : Lith. *moša* 'husband's sister', OPruss. *moazo* 'aunt' fr. *mā-* in pet names (above, p. 94).

2.452. Special expressions for 'brother(s) and sister(s)' are uncommon.

Grk. ἀδελφοί, Lat. *frātrēs* are sometimes so used, likewise Skt. du. *bhrātarāu* (according to Pāṇini), NG ἀδέλφια (pop. ἀδέρφια).

ON *systkin*, Dan. *søskende*, Sw. *syskon*, coll. deriv. of *systir* 'sister'. Falk-Torp 1236 (where are noted similar ON derivs. for other combinations, as 'father and son', 'mother and daughter', etc.). Hellquist 1139 f.

NHG *geschwister*, orig. pl. 'sisters', in present sense since 16th cent. Weigand-H. 1.702.

	2.46 GRANDFATHER	2.47 GRANDMOTHER
Grk.	πάππος (Hom. πατρὸς πατήρ, etc.)	τήθη, μάμμη, ἀννίς (Hom. μητρὸς μήτηρ)
NG	πάππος, παπποῦς	γιαγιά
Lat.	avus	avia
It.	nonno (avo, avolo)	nonna
Fr.	grand-père (aïeul)	grand'mère (aïeule)
Sp.	abuelo	abuela
Rum.	tată mare, bunic	mamă mare, bunica
Ir.	senathir	senmáthir
NIr.	seanathair	seanmháthair
W.	taid	nain
Br.	tadkoz	mammgoz
Goth.	. . . .	awō
ON	foður-(mōður-)faðir; afi	foður-(mōður-)mōðir; amma
Dan.	bedstefar	bedstemor
Sw.	farfar, morfar	farmor, mormor
OE	ealdfæder	ealdmōdor
ME	grauntsire, grandfather	grandame, grandmother
NE	grandfather (grandsire)	grandmother
Du.	grootvader	grootmoeder
OHG	ano	ana
MHG	ane	ane
NHG	grossvater	grossmutter
Lith.	senelis (tévukas)	bobutė, močiutė
Lett.	vectēvs	vecmate
ChSl.	dĕdŭ	baba
SCr.	djed	baba, baka
Boh.	dĕd	babička
Pol.	dziad(ek)	babka
Russ.	deduška	babuška
Skt.	pitā-(mātā-)maha-	pitā-(mātā-)mahī
Av.	nyāka-	nyākā-

2.46, 2.47. 'Grandfather' and 'grandmother' may always be expressed more specifically as 'father's father' or 'mother's father', and 'father's mother' or 'mother's mother'; in some cases these are the usual expressions, as in Homer and in Old Norse and still in Swedish. Other terms are the words for 'father' and 'mother' with adjectives meaning 'great', 'old', or 'best', or in diminutive forms used as terms of endearment. Still others are pet names of the nursery type.

1. Hom. πατρὸς (μητρὸς) πατήρ, μητρὸς μήτηρ, also μητροπάτωρ, 'father's (mother's) father (mother).

Grk. πάππος (not in Hom.), NG pop. παπποῦς, pet name of the *papa* type (above, p. 94). Walde-P. 2.4.

Grk. τήθη, μάμμη ('mother', later 'grandmother'), also ἀννίς (Hesych. and inscr.), all pet names (above, p. 94).

NG γιαγιά, new pet name fr. infantile reduplicated για.

2. Lat. *avus*, fem. *avia*, late *ava* : ON *afi* 'grandfather' (late), Goth. *awō* 'grandmother' etc. Hence, mostly in dim. forms, It. *avo, avolo*, Fr. *aïeul, aïeule*, Sp. *abuelo, abuela*, of which only the Spanish are now the usual words. Walde-P. 1.20. Ernout-M. 96 f. REW 830, 839.

It. *nonno, nonna*, pet names of the *nana* type (above, p. 94). Walde-P. 2.317.

Fr. *grand-père, grand'mère*, cpds. with *grand* 'great', perh., but not necessarily, modeled on Lat. *avunculus magnus*

'great uncle', etc. Gamillscheg 482. This French type was the model of the Rum., ME, Du., and NHG forms.

Rum. *tată (mamă) mare*, with *mare* 'great', clearly after the French.

Rum. *bunic, bunica*, pet names fr. *bun* 'good'. Cf. NE *goodwife, goody*, Dan. *bedstefar*, etc. (below, 4).

3. Ir. *senathir, senmáthir*, NIr. *seanathair, seanmháthair*, cpds. with *sen* 'old'.

W. *taid, nain*, pet names of the *tata* and *nana* types (above, p. 94).

Br. *tadkoz, mammgoz*, cpds. with *koz* 'old'.

4. Goth. *awō* 'grandmother', ON *afi* 'grandfather' : Lat. *avus*, etc., above, 2.

ON *amma* 'grandmother', pet name of the *amma* type (above, p. 94). Walde-P. 1.53.

ON *foður-(mōður-)faðir(mōðir)* 'father's (mother's) father (mother). Hence Sw. *farfar, morfar, farmor, mormor*.

Dan. *bedstefar (-mor)*, cpds. with *bedst* 'best'. Cf. Du. *bestevaar* 'old man', *bestemoer* 'granny', Fr. *beau-père* 'father-in-law, stepfather', NE *goodman, goodwife, goody*, etc., all originating as polite or endearing terms.

OE *ealdfæder (-mōdor)*, cpds. with *eald* 'old'.

ME *grauntsire, grandame*, fr. OFr. *graunt sire*, etc. are much earlier than

the partly anglicized *grandfather, grandmother*. Cf. NED s.vv.

Du. *grootvader (-moeder)* and NHG *grossvater (-mutter)*, modeled on the French.

OHG *ano, ana*, MHG *ane* (NHG *ahne* 'ancestor') : Lat. *anus* 'old woman', etc., pet names of the *anna* type (above, p. 94). Walde-P. 1.55.

5. Lith. *senelis* 'grandfather', fr. *senas* 'old', *bobutė* 'grandmother', dim. of *boba* 'old woman'. Also *tévukas* dim. of *tévas* 'father', and *močiutė* dim. of *motė* 'woman', orig. 'mother'.

Lett. *vectēvs, vecmate*, cpds. of *vecs* 'old' with words for 'father' and 'mother'.

6. ChSl. *dĕdŭ* 'grandfather', etc., all the Slavic forms, pet name of the *dada* type (above, p. 94).

ChSl. *baba* 'grandmother', etc., all the Slavic forms, pet name of the *baba* type (above, p. 94). Walde-P. 2.105.

7. Skt. *pitāmaha-* 'paternal grandfather', cpd. with *mah-* 'great', but of unusual formation. Hence *pitāmahī-* 'paternal grandmother', also *mātāmaha-* 'maternal grandfather', *mātāmahī-* 'maternal grandmother'. Delbrück, op. cit. 474.

Av. *nyāka-, nyākā-* 'grandfather, grandmother' (OPers. *nyāka-* 'grandfather', *apa-nyāka-* 'ancestor', etym.? Delbrück, op. cit. 474.

	2.48 GRANDSON	2.49 GRANDDAUGHTER
Grk.	παιδὸς παῖς, υἱωνός, υἱδοῦς, θυγατριδοῦς, ἔγγονος	παιδὸς παῖς, υἱωνή
NG	ἔγγονος	ἐγγόνη
Lat.	nepōs	neptis
It.	nipote	nipote
Fr.	petit-fils	petite-fille
Sp.	nieto	nieta
Rum.	nepot	nepoată
Ir.	aue, óa, ua	aue
NIr.	mac mic, mac inghine, garmhac	inghean mic, inghean inghine, gairinghean
W.	wyr	wyres
Br.	douaren	douarenez
Goth.		łarnē barna 'grandchildren'
ON	sonar-(dōttur-)sonr	sonar-(dōttur-)dōttir
Dan.	sønnesøn, dattersøn	sønnedatter, datterdatter
Sw.	sonson, dotterson	sondotter, dotterdotter
OE	suna sunu, dohtor sunu (nefa)	(suna dohtor, dohtor dohtor?)
ME	sonys sone, neveu	(sonys doughter, etc.?) nece
NE	grandson	granddaughter
Du.	kleinzoon	kleindochter
OHG	nevo, eninchil	nift
MHG	enenkel (neve)	niftel
NHG	enkel	enkelin
Lith.	anukas, sūnaus (dukters) vaikas	anuké, sūnaus (dukters) dukté
Lett.	dēla(meitas)dēls	dēla (meitas) meita
ChSl.	vŭnukŭ	vŭnuka
SCr.	unuk	unuka
Boh.	vnuk	vnučka
Pol.	wnuk	wnuczka
Russ.	vnuk	vnučka
Skt.	nápāt-; pâutra-, dáuhitra-	pâutrī-, dáuhitrī-
Av.	napāt-	napāt-

2.48, 2.49. 'Grandson' and 'granddaughter' may always be expressed more specifically as 'son's (daughter's) son (daughter)'. Such are the usual ON, Dan., Sw., OE, Lith. (in part), and Lett. terms. Or simply 'child's child', as most commonly in Greek and so in Gothic. Some of the terms reflect an inherited IE word. Others are derivatives or phrases containing the words for 'son' or 'daughter'. A few are of the pet-name type.

1. IE *nepōt-*, fem. *neptī-*, prob. *ne-pōt-*, cpd. of neg. *ne* and a form of the stem seen in Skt. *pati-* 'master', Lat. *potis* 'able', etc., that is lit. 'powerless'.

Walde-P. 2.329 ff. Ernout-M. 666. Hermann, Gött. Nachr. 1918, 215.

Hence words for 'grandson, granddaughter', and also for 'nephew, niece' (2.53, 2.54). Lat. *nepōs, neptis* (in late Lat. also 'nephew, niece'; VLat. fem. *nepta, neptia*), It. *nipote* 'grandson, -daughter' and 'nephew, niece', Fr. *neveu, nièce* once used in both senses, now only 'nephew, niece' (> ME *neveu, nece*, NE *nephew, niece*, once used in both senses, cf. NED), Sp. *nieto, nieta* 'grandson, -daughter' (*nieto* new masc. formed to *nieta* fr. *nepot*), Rum. *nepot, nepoată* in both senses (*nepoată* new fem. formed to *nepot*); Ir. *nia, necht* 'nephew, niece', W. nai, nith 'nephew, niece', OBr. nith 'niece', Br. niz, nizez 'nephew, niece'; ON nefi, nift 'nephew, niece', OE nefa, ME neve 'nephew', rarely 'grandson', OE nift, ME nyfte 'niece', Du. neef, nicht 'nephew, niece' (and 'cousin'), OHG nevo, nift, MHG neve, niftel mostly 'nephew, niece' but sometimes 'grandson, -daughter' (OHG nevo also 'uncle, cousin'), NHG neffe, nichte 'nephew, niece'; OLith. nepotis, nepté 'grandson, -daughter'; Skt. napāt- (also naptar- after pitar-, etc.) 'descendant' and 'grandson', Av. napāt-, OPers. napā 'grandson', Skt. naptī 'female descendant', Av. naptī 'granddaughter'. Also (fr. *neptio-) Av. naptya- 'descendant', Grk. ἀνεψιός 'cousin', late 'nephew'; ChSl. (late) netĭjĭ 'nephew', nestera 'niece', SCr. nećak 'sister's son', Boh. neť 'niece'.

2. Grk. παιδὸς παῖς 'child's child, grandson (ὁ) or granddaughter (ἡ)', most often in pl. παίδων παῖδες, Hom. and in inscriptions (cf. Cypr. τῶ(ν) παίδων οἱ παῖδες 'grandsons').

Grk. υἱωνός (Hom. +), deriv. of υἱός 'son'. Hence late υἱωνή 'granddaughter'.

Grk. υἱδοῦς 'son's son' (Plato +), θυγατριδοῦς 'daughter's son' (Hdt. +), dim. formations from υἱός 'son', θυγάτηρ 'daughter'. Hence υἱδῆ (late), θυγατριδῆ for 'son's daughter', 'daughter's daughter'.

Grk. ἔκγονος, ἔγγονος 'descendant' (: γίγνομαι 'be born', etc.), later ἔγγονος 'grandson', ἐγγόνη 'granddaughter', as reg. in NG.

3. Fr. petit-fils (13th cent.), lit. 'little son', whence the much later attested petite-fille, and, by imitation of these, Du. kleinzoon, kleindochter.

4. OIr. aue, MIr. ōa, ua 'grandson', also 'granddaughter' : Lat. avus 'grandfather', Goth. awō 'grandmother', etc. Walde-P. 1.20. Here also(?) W. wyr, fem. wyres, and Br. douaren (d-ouaren), fem. douarenez. Cf. Pedersen 1.56.

NIr. mac mic, inghean mic, lit. 'son's son, son's daughter' (mic gen. of mac).

NIr. mac inghine 'daughter's son', inghean inghine 'daughter's daughter'.

NIr. garmhac 'grandson', fr. MIr. gormac 'foster-son,' cpd. with prefix gor- (fr. Brittanic = Ir. for- : Grk. ὑπέρ, etc.), and mac 'son', as also in NIr. garathair 'great grandfather', etc. Hence also NIr. gairinghean 'granddaughter'. Pedersen 1.23.

5. Goth. (only attested form) barnē barna 'children's children'.

ON sonar-(dōttur-)sonr (dōttir) 'son's (daughter's) son (daughter)', likewise the still current Dan. and Sw. words.

OE suna(dohtor)sunu 'son's (daughter's) son', but the corresponding suna (dohtor)dohtor seem not to be quotable.

NE grandson, granddaughter, formed after the opposites grandfather, grandmother, as also grandniece after grandaunt, etc., grand- being thus extended to denote corresponding relations of descent as well as ascent, as likewise great- in great-grandson after great-grandfather, etc.

OHG eninchil, MHG enenkel, NHG enkel, dim. of OHG ano 'grandfather' (2.46). Hence new fem. enkelin. Walde-P. 1.55.

6. Lith. anukas 'grandson' (hence anukė 'granddaughter') fr. Ukr. onuk = ChSl. vŭnukŭ, etc. (below, 7). Brückner, Sl. Fremdwörter 68. Skardžius 29.

Lith. sūnaus (dukters) vaikas (duktė), Lett. dēla (meitas) dēls (meita) 'son's (daughter's) son (daughter)'.

7. ChSl. vŭnukŭ 'grandson', vŭnuka 'granddaughter', etc., all the Slavic forms, prob. (with vŭn fr. on) of the

same pet-name type as OHG ano 'grandfather', etc. (above, p. 94). Brückner 628.

8. Skt. (beside nāpāt-) pāutra-, pāutrī, 'son's son', son's daughter', and dāuhitra-, dāuhitrī- 'daughter's son, daughter's daughter', derivs. of putra- 'son', duhitar- 'daughter'.

	2.51 UNCLE (a, Paternal; b, Maternal)	2.52 AUNT (a, Paternal; b, Maternal)
Grk.	πάτρως (a); μήτρως (b); θεῖος	τηθίς, θεία (late)
NG	θεῖος, θειός	θεία, θειά
Lat.	patruus (a); avunculus (b)	amita (a); mātertera (b)
It.	zio	zia
Fr.	oncle	tante
Sp.	tio	tia
Rum.	unchiu	mătușă,
Ir.	brāthir athar (a); brāthir māthar (b)	siur athar (a), siur māthar (b)
NIr.	dearbrāthair athar (a); dearbhrāthair māthar (b)	deirbhshiūr athar (a), deirbhsiur māthir (b); athaireog (a), māithreān (b)
W.	ewythr	modryb
Br.	eontr	moereb
Goth.	. . . .	. . . .
ON	fǫður-brōðir (a); mōður-brōðir (b)	fǫður-systir (a); mōðir-systir (b)
Dan.	farbror (a); morbror (b); onkel	faster (a), moster (b); tante
Sw.	fasbror (a); morbror (b); onkel	faster (a); moster (b)
OE	fœdera (a); ēam (b)	faðu (a); mōdrige (b)
ME	uncle, eme	aunt
NE	uncle	aunt
Du.	oom	tante
OHG	fetiro (a); ōheim (b)	basa (a); mustera (b), muoma (b)
MHG	vetere (a); ōheim (b)	base (a); muome (b)
NHG	onkel, oheim	tante (base, muhme)
Lith.	dėdė; avynas (b)	teta
Lett.	tēva brālis (a); mātes brālis (b)	tēva māsa (a); mātes māsa (b)
ChSl.	stryjĭ (a); ujĭ (b)	teta
SCr.	stric (a); ujak (b)	tetka
Boh.	strýc (a); ujec (b)	teta
Pol.	stryj (a); wuj (b)	ciotka
Russ.	djadja	tetka
Skt.	pitṛvya- (a); mātula (b)	pitṛṣvasar- (a); mātṛṣvasar- (b)
Av.	tūirya- (a)	tūiryā- (a)

2.51, 2.52. There were originally separate expressions for the paternal and maternal uncle or aunt, distinguished in the table by a and b respectively. This situation still prevails in Irish, Danish, and Swedish (except for the encroachment of the borrowed NHG onkel and tante), Lettish, and partly in Slavic for 'uncle'. But the general tendency has been to give up the differentiation and use the same term for 'uncle', or 'aunt', on either side. These words are commonly used also to include 'uncle' or 'aunt' by marriage, that is 'uncle-in-law', etc. Specific expressions for such relation, as for 'father's brother's wife' in Slavic, are not included in the table.

Apart from such phrases as 'father's (mother's) brother (sister)', some of the terms are derivatives of words for 'father' or 'mother', while others are from various types of pet names.

1. Grk. πάτρως, Lat. patruus, OE fœdera, OHG fetiro, MHG vetere (also

'nephew', NHG vetter 'cousin'), Skt. pitṛvya-, Av. tūirya- all meaning 'father's brother' and derivs. of the words for 'father'. Walde-P. 2.4.

2. Lat. mātertera, OE mōdrige, OHG muotera 'mother's sister', W. modryb, Br. moereb 'aunt' (Pedersen 1.48, 2.33), formed with various suffixes fr. the words for 'mother'. Walde-P. 2.229.

3. Lat. avunculus 'mother's brother', in VLat. extended at the expense of patruus, hence Fr. oncle (> ME, NE uncle, NHG onkel > Dan., Sw. onkel), Rum. unchiu; W. ewythr, Br. eontr (both with suffix as in Lat. māter-tera); OE ēam, ME, NE dial. eme, Du. oom, OHG ōheim, NHG oheim (the Gmc. forms in older period only for 'mother's brother'; cpds. with *haima- 'home'?); Lith. avynas (obs.), OPruss. awis, ChSl. ujĭ, etc. 'mother's brother'; all : Lat. avus 'grandfather', Goth. awō 'grandmother', etc. Walde-P. 1.20. Walde-H. 1.88.

4. Grk. μήτρως 'mother's brother', parallel formation to πάτρως (above, 1).

Grk. τηθίς 'aunt' : τήθη 'grandmother', Lith. dėdė 'uncle', etc., all of pet-name type (above, p. 94).

Grk. θεῖος 'uncle' (on either side), whence late θεία 'aunt', of the same pet-name type as the preceding. Hence NG θεῖος, θεία, or It. zio, zia, Sp. tio, tia. REW 8709.

5. Lat. amita 'father's sister', deriv. of pet name of the amma type (above, p. 94). Hence, with extension at the expense of mātertera, OFr. ante (> ME, NE aunt), Fr. tante (> Du., NHG., Dan. tante) with t variously explained, and with dim. suffix Rum. mătușă. Walde-P. 1.53. REW 424. Wartburg 1.89.

6. Ir. brāthir athar 'brother of the father', etc., with the corresponding NIr. phrases, all of obvious origin.

NIr. also athaireog 'father's sister', māithreān 'mother's sister', derivs. of athair 'father', māthair 'mother'.

W. ewythr, Br. eontr 'uncle', above, 3.

W. modryb, Br. moereb 'aunt', above, 2.

7. ON fǫðurbrōðir 'father's brother', etc. all phrases of obvious orig., whence the Dan., Sw. farbror, morbror, faster, moster.

OE fœdera, OHG fetiro, etc., above, 1.

OE ēam, OHG ōheim, etc., above, 3.

OE faðu, OFris. fethe, MLG vade 'father's sister', fr. a shortened pet-name form of fœder 'father'. Walde-P. 2.4.

OE mōdrige, OHG muotera, above, 2.

OHG basa, MHG base 'father's sister' (NHG base 'aunt, cousin'), prob. of the nursery-word type. Weigand-H. 1.162 f.

OHG muoma, MHG muome 'mother's sister' (NHG muhme 'aunt, cousin'), pet name, blend of the first syllable of muotera (above, 2) with the mama type.

8. Lith. dėdė, Russ. djadja 'uncle' : ChSl. dědŭ 'grandfather', etc., pet-name type (above, p. 94).

Lith. teta, ChSl. teta, etc., general Slavic for 'aunt', pet-name type (above, p. 94). Walde-P. 1.704.

Lett. tēva brālis 'father's brother', etc., phrases of obvious orig., not replaced by simple words.

ChSl. stryjĭ, etc., general Slavic (except Russ.) for 'father's brother'; perh. (with a peculiar development of ptr-) : Skt. pitṛvya-, etc., above, 1. Mikkola, IF 23.124. M. Vey, BSL 32.65.

ChSl. ujĭ, etc. general Slavic (except Russ.) for 'mother's brother', above, 3.

From both the preceding words are formed feminines applied to the wife of the father's (mother's) brother, e.g. SCr. strina, ujna.

But of the two groups, Russ. stryj and vuj are obsolete, and, according to informants, Boh. strýc is often used for 'uncle' on either side (to the exclusion of ujec, unknown to some), and Pol. stryj,

wuj are used in urban speech without the old distinction, which still prevails in the country.

9. Skt. pitṛvya-, Av. tūirya- (hence tūiryā- 'father's sister'), above, 1. Barth. 657.

Skt. mātur-bhrātar- is attested for 'mother's brother', for which the usual word is mātula, a dim. formation from mātar- 'mother'.

Skt. pitṛ-ṣvasar- 'father's sister', mātṛ-ṣvasar- 'mother's sister', both rare.

	2.53 NEPHEW (a, Brother's Son; b, Sister's Son)	2.54 NIECE (a, Brother's Daughter; b, Sister's Daughter)
Grk.	ἀδελφιδοῦς	ἀδελφιδῆ
NG	ἀνεψιός, ἀνιψιός	ἀνεψιά, ἀνιψιά
Lat.	frātris fīlius (a); sorōris fīlius (b)	frātris fīlia (a); sorōris fīlia (b)
It.	nipote	nipote
Fr.	neveu	nièce
Sp.	sobrino	sobrina
Rum.	nepot	nepoată
Ir.	niae (b)	necht
NIr.	garmhac	neacht
W.	nai	nith
Br.	niz	nizez
Goth.	. . . .	. . . .
ON	nefi	nipt
Dan.	brodersøn (a); søstersøn (b); nevø	broderdatter (a); søsterdatter (b)
Sw.	brorson (a); systernson (b); nevö	brorsdotter (a); systerdotter (b)
OE	nefa; suhterga (a)	nift
ME	neve, neveu	nyfte, nece
NE	nephew	niece
Du.	neef	nicht
OHG	nevo	nift, niftila
MHG	neve; vetere (a); brūderson (a); swestersun (b)	niftel; brūdertochter (a)
NHG	neffe; bruderssohn (a); schwestersohn (b)	nichte; bruderstochter (a); schwestertochter (b)
Lith.	brolėnas (a); seserėnas (b); broliavaiks (a), etc.	broliadukté (a); seseryčia (b)
Lett.	brāla dēls (a); māsas dēls (b)	brāla meita (a); māsas meita (b)
ChSl.	synovĭ, synovĭcĭ, netĭjĭ	synovica, nestera
SCr.	sinovac (a); nećak (b)	sinovica (a); nećaka (b)
Boh.	synovec; bratrovec (a); sestřenec (b)	neť; bratrovna (a)
Pol.	synowiec (a); bratanek (a); siostrzeniec (b)	synowica (a); siostrzenica (b)
Russ.	plemjannik	plemjannica
Skt.	bhrātrīya-, bhrātṛya-, bhrātuḥ putra- (a); svasrīya- (b)	svasrīyā- (b)
Av.	brātruya- (a)	brātruyā- (a)

2.53, 2.54. 'Nephew' and 'niece' may be differentiated as the brother's or the sister's son or daughter. So regularly in the Lat., Dan., Sw., Lith., Lett., and Skt. phrases or compounds, and by separate derivatives partly in Lithuanian and Slavic.

Apart from the phrases or compounds meaning 'brother's son', etc., which are of obvious origin and need not be discussed further, the words either belong to the group IE *nepōt-, with interchange between 'grandson' and 'nephew', 'granddaughter' and 'niece', or are derivatives of words for 'brother' or 'sister' (or rarely from 'son'), or in a few cases are specialized from 'cousin, relative'.

1. IE *nepōt-, fem. *neptī-. The forms meaning 'nephew' and 'niece'

have been included in the discussion under 2.48, 2.49. They cover most of the Romance, Celtic, and Gmc. forms and a few of the Slavic.

2. Grk. ἀδελφιδοῦς, dim. of ἀδελφός 'brother', but not restricted to 'brother's son'. Hence fem. ἀδελφιδῆ.

Byz., NG ἀνεψιός, ἀνεψιά (NG also ἀνίψιός, -ά), with shift from earlier 'cousin' (2.55).

3. Sp. sobrino, sobrina, fr. Lat. sobrīnus, -a 'cousin' (2.55).

4. NIr. garmhac 'grandson' and 'nephew'. Cf. 2.48.

5. OE suhterga, suhtriga 'brother's son', etym.? Walde-P. 2.470.

6. Lith. brolėnas 'brother's son' (also 'cousin'), deriv. of brolis 'brother'.

Lith. seserėnas 'sister's son', deriv. of sesuo 'sister'.

Lith. seserýčia 'sister's daughter', deriv. of sesuo 'sister'.

ChSl. (late) synovĭ, synovĭcĭ, fem. synovica, dim. of synŭ 'son', and orig. used for 'nephew' on either side, as still Boh. synovec. But SCr. sinovac, fem. sinovica, Pol. synowiec, fem. synowica used only for brother's son or daughter.

SCr. bratanec, Pol. bratanek, Russ. (obs.) bratanič, Boh. bratranec (also 'cousin'), bratrovec 'brother's son', with fem. SCr., Pol. bratanica, Boh. bratovna, etc. 'brother's daughter' (most of these not in common use), derivs. of brat(r)ŭ 'brother'. Berneker 82.

Pol. siostrzeniec 'sister's son', siostrzenica 'sister's daughter', derivs. of siostra 'sister'. Similar Boh. sestřenec, fem. sestřenice used also for 'cousin'.

Russ. plemjannik 'nephew', plemjannica 'niece', derivs. of plemja 'clan, family' (19.23), hence orig. 'relative'.

7. Skt. bhrātrīya- 'brother's son' (Pāṇini), svasrīya- 'sister's son', svasrīyā- 'sister's daughter', derivs. of bhrātar 'brother', svasar- 'sister'.

Skt. bhrātrvya- 'brother's son' (but also 'cousin'), Av. brātruya-, brātruyā- 'brother's son, brother's daughter', derivs. of words for 'brother', with suffix as in Skt. pitrvya-'father's brother', etc. (2.51). Wackernagel, Andreas Festschrift 1 f.

2.55 COUSIN

a, Male b, Female c, Father's Brother's Son (Daughter) d, Father's Sister's Son (Daughter) e, Mother's Brother's Son (Daughter) f, Mother's Sister's Son (Daughter)

Lang	Forms
Grk.	ἀνεψιός (a); ἀνεψιά (b)
NG	ἐξάδελφος (a); ἐξαδέλφη (b)
Lat.	consobrīnus (a); consobrīna (b); patruēlis (ac, bc); mātruēlis (ae)
It.	cugino (a); cugina (b)
Fr.	cousin (a); cousine (b)
Sp.	primo (a); prima (b)
Rum.	văr (a); vară (b); verișor (a); verișoară (b)
Ir.	macc bráthar athar (ac); macc bráthar máthar (ae), etc.
NIr.	col ceathar
W.	cefnder (a); cyfnither (b)
Br.	kenderv (a); keniterv (b)

Lang	Forms
Goth.	gadilligs
ON	brœðrunga (ac); brœðrunga (bc); systrungr (af); systrunga (bf)
Dan.	søskendebarn/fætter (a); kusine (b)
Sw.	syskonbarn, kusin
OE	fœderan sunu (ac); mōðrigan sunu (af); mōðrige (bf)
ME	cosyn
NE	cousin
Du.	neef (a); nicht (b)
OHG	fetirunsun (ac); ôheimessun (ae); muomunsun (af); feterin tohter (bc), etc.
MHG	veter(n)sun (ac), etc.
NHG	vetter (a); cousine (b); (base, muhme b)

Lang	Forms
Lith.	pusbrolis (a); pusseserė (b); brolėnas (b)
Lett.	brālēns (a); māsica (b)
ChSl.	bratu-čędŭ (a); sestričišti (a)
SCr.	bratučed (ab); bratuceda (b); brat (sestra) od strica (od ujaka, etc.)
Boh.	bratranec (a); sestřenice (b)
Pol.	kuzyn (a); kuzyna (b) brat stryjeczny (wujeczny, etc.), siostra stryjeczna, etc.
Russ.	dvojurodnyj brat (a); dvojurodnaja sestra (b)
Skt.	bhrātrvya- (ac); pitrsvasrīya- (ad); mātrsvaseya- (af); mātrsvaseyī- (bf)
Av.	tuiryō.puθra- (ac); tuirya.duγðar- (bc)

'Cousin' is understood here in the stricter and usual current sense of NE cousin, namely as 'first cousin, cousin-german'. Even so, it covers eight more specific varieties of relationship, there being three pairs of variable factors, that is, 'father's (or mother's) brother's (or sister's) son (or daughter)'.

Many of the expressions listed are specific terms for just one of these relations, as OE fœderan sunu 'father's brother's son', mōðrigan sunu 'mother's sister's son', etc. So the Ir., ON, OE, OHG, Skt., and most of the Slavic terms. These are phrases, compounds, or derivatives containing words for 'son, daughter' (2.41, 2.42), 'brother, sister' (2.44, 2.45), and the more specific terms for 'uncle, aunt' (2.51, 2.52); and their literal meaning and application are mostly too obvious to require further comment.

But those containing words for 'brother' or 'sister' have arisen in two ways. Some denote the relationship through the brother or sister of one's parent. Others reflect an early direct association between 'brother, sister', and 'cousin' as a 'kind of brother or sister'. So Lat. patruēlis started as frāter patruēlis (frater tuus erat frater patruelis meus, Plautus), Lith. pusbrolis is literally 'half-brother', SCr. brat od strica, not like OE fœderan sunu 'son of father's brother', but literally 'brother from father's brother', Russ. dvojurodnyj brat lit. 'second line brother', etc. This extension of 'brother' and 'sister' is conspicuous in Balto-

Slavic, but may also be observed elsewhere.

Some of the other terms, as Lat. consobrīnus, must, according to their etymology, once have had only a specific application, but came to be used without such restriction.

The cousin relationship is one of the fourth degree, reckoned through the common ancestor. Cf. Gaius, Dig. 38.10.1.6 quarto gradu [cognationis sunt] consobrini, consobrinaeque. This is reflected in NIr. col ceathar (lit. 'relationship four').

A few of the words represent an extension or shift from 'nephew', one's father's 'nephew' being one's own 'cousin'.

1. Grk. ἀνεψιός, ἀνεψιά 'cousin', later 'nephew, niece' (2.53, 2.54), cpd. (with cop. ά- fr. ά-) : Lat. nepōs, Skt. napāt- 'grandson', etc. (2.47). Walde-P. 2.329 ff.

Grk. (Hellenistic) ἐξάδελφος 'nephew' (LXX, Josephus) and 'cousin' (pop.; reproved by Phrynicus), also fem. ἐξαδέλφη (inscr.), hence the NG forms. A phrase-compound fr. ἐξ ἀδελφοῦ, hence orig. 'nephew', then with shift to 'cousin', as in NHG vetter, etc.

2. Lat. patruēlis, deriv. of patruus 'father's brother' (2.51), hence reg. 'father's brother's son or daughter' (rarely also 'father's sister's son').

Lat. mātruēlis formed as a pendant to patruēlis, and amitinus, fr. amita 'father's sister' (2.52), are late and rare.

Lat. consobrīnus, fem. consobrīna (also sobrīnus, sobrīna), fr. *con-swesrīno-, deriv. of soror 'sister', and prob. first used in pl. consobrīnī 'fellow descendants of sisters'. In legal language applied to cousin on the mother's side, as contrasted with patruēlis, but in common usage extended to cousin on either side. Hence It. cugino, cugina, Fr. cousin, cousine (>ME cosyn, NE cousin, Dan. kusine, Sw. kusin, NHG cousine, Pol. kuzyn, kuzyna). REW 2165.

Sp. primo, prima 'first' (Lat. prīmus) and 'cousin', latter prob. fr. phrase with sobrino, sobrina when these were still 'cousin' (above, 2). But cf. Tappolet, op. cit. 119.

Rum. văr, vară, fr. Lat. vērus 'true', orig. cusurin văr 'true cousin' (still dial. cusurin ver). Hence also, in more familiar use, dim. verișor, verișoară. Pușcariu 1856.

3. NIr. col ceathar, lit. 'relationship four', that is, reckoned from a common ancestor, 'first cousin', as col seisear lit. 'relationship six' is 'second cousin'.

W. cefnder, fem. cyfnither, Br. kenderf, fem. keniterv, OBr. comnidder, prob. fr. *com-nepter-, similar to Grk. ἀνεψιός but with suffix after other words of relationship. Henry 61. Loth, Vocab. vieux-breton 80. But last part at least influenced by *derw- 'true' (= Ir. dearbh- in dearbhbhráthair, etc.) and so derived by Morris Jones 224.

4. Goth. gadilligs : OE gædeling 'companion', tō gædere 'together', MHG gate 'companion' (NHG gatte 'husband'), etc. Walde-P. 1.531 ff. Feist 178 f.

ON brœðrunga, systrunga, with fems., cpds. of brōðir 'brother' and systir 'sister' with ungr 'young', hence '(father's) brother's son', '(mother's) sister's son'.

Dan. søskende barn, Sw. syskon barn, cpds. of the words for 'brothers and sisters' (2.452) and 'child'.

NHG vetter (>Dan. fætter), fr. OHG fetiro 'uncle' (2.51), MHG vetere 'uncle, nephew'.

Du. neef, nicht, same words for 'nephew, niece', earlier also 'grandson, granddaughter' (2.48, 2.49).

NHG base, muhme 'aunt' (2.52), sometimes used also for 'female cousin', but usually cousine fr. French (above, 2).

5. Lith. pusbrolis, pusseserė lit. 'half-brother, half-sister' and also used in that sense, cpds. of pus- 'half' and the words for 'brother' and 'sister'.

Lith. brolėnas, Lett. brālēns 'nephew' and 'cousin', derivs. of word for 'brother'. Mühl-Endz. 1.328.

Lett. māsica 'sister-in-law' and 'cousin', deriv. of māsa 'sister' (2.45).

ChSl. bratu-čędŭ, in Supr. 'nephew' and 'cousin', SCr. bratučed, fem. bratučeda 'cousin', cpd. of bratŭ 'brother' (bratu gen.-loc. dual, Vondrák 1.675) and čędo 'child'.

ChSl. sestričišti (late), deriv. of sestra 'sister'.

SCr. brat (sestra) od strica (od ujaka), etc., lit. 'brother (sister) from the father's brother (mother's brother)', etc., similarly Pol. brat stryjeczny (wujeczny), etc., with the various words for 'uncle' and 'aunt' (2.51, 2.52), seen also in the obs. Boh. strycovec, ujcovec, etc.

Boh. bratranec, also and orig. 'brother's son' like Pol. bratanek, etc. (2.53).

Boh. sestřenice, also and orig. 'sister's daughter' like Pol. siostrzenie (2.53). The masc. sestřenec is less common use.

Russ. dvojurodnyj brat, dvojurodnaja sestra, the adj. being a cpd. of coll. dvoje 'two' with rodnyj 'own' fr. rod 'family', so a sort of 'second-line brother'.

6. Skt. bhrātrvya-, orig. 'brother's son' (2.53).

Skt. pitrsvasrīya-, etc. patronymics fr. cpds. meaning 'father's sister', etc.

Av. tuiryō.puθra, tuirya.duγðar, cpds. of tuirya- 'father's brother' (2.51) and words for 'son and daughter'.

2.56 ANCESTORS

Grk.	πρόγονοι, προπάτορες
NG	πρόγονοι, προπάτορες
Lat.	maiōrēs
It.	avi, antenati
Fr.	ancêtres, aïeux
Sp.	antecesores, antepasados, abuelos
Rum.	stramoși, strabuni
Ir.	senaithir, sruithi
NIr.	sinnsir
W.	cyndadau
Br.	gourdadou

Lang	Forms
Goth.	fadreina
ON	forfeðr
Dan.	forfædre
Sw.	förfäder
OE	ealdfæderas
ME	eldren, forfadres, ancestres
NE	ancestors, forefathers
Du.	voorouderen, voorvaderen
OHG	aftfordoron, altmâgâ
MHG	altvordoren
NHG	ahnen, vorfahren, voreltern

Lang	Forms
Lith.	sentėviai, pratėviai
Lett.	senči, tēvu tēvi
ChSl.	. . . .
SCr.	predci
Boh.	předkové
Pol.	przedkowie
Russ.	predki
Skt.	pitaras
OPers.	apanyāka- (sg.)

Words for 'ancestors' are from such obvious sources as 'born before', 'going before, predecessors', 'elders', 'fathers', 'grandfathers', 'fore-fathers', 'fore-parents', 'old-fathers'.

1. Grk. πρόγονοι lit. 'of previous birth'. Also προπάτορες 'forefathers'. Also sometimes simply πατέρες 'fathers', as likewise Lat. patrēs, Fr. pères, NE fathers, etc.

2. Lat. maiōrēs lit. 'elders', comp. of magnus 'great', but in the secondary sense of maior (nātū) 'greater by birth, older'.

It. antenati lit. 'born before', fr. Lat. ante 'before' and nātus 'born'.

It. avi, pl. of avo, Lat. avus 'grandfather' (2.49).

OFr. ancestres (>ME ancestres, NE ancestors), Sp. antecesores, fr. Lat. antecessōrēs 'those going before' (fr. antecēdere 'go before'), 'predecessors' (as in office, not 'ancestors').

Fr. aïeux, Sp. abuelos, orig. 'grandparents', fr. dim. of Lat. *avus* 'grand-father' (2.46).

Sp. *antepasados*, lit. 'those who have passed before'.

Rum. *stramoși*, cpd. of strengthening prefix *stra-* (fr. Lat. *extra* 'beyond') and *moș* 'grandfather' or 'ancestor', fr. Alb. *moṣě* 'age, old man'. Tiktin 1010, 1508. G. Meyer, Alb. Etym. Wtb. 263. Also *strabuni*, with *bun* 'good' as in *bunic* 'grandfather' (2.46).

3. Ir. *senaithir*, pl. of *senathair* 'grandfather' (2.46).

Ir. *sruithi* sometimes 'ancestors' (Thes. 1.51.27, 2.97.31), pl. of *sruith* 'old, venerable, wise', prob. : ChSl. *starŭ* 'old' (14.15). Pedersen 1.81.

NIr. *sinnsir*, fr. MIr. *sinser* 'older, eldest', fr. *sen* 'old' (14.15) with suffix *-is-tero-*, as in Lat. *magister*. Pedersen 2.44.

W. *cyndadau*, cpd. of *cyn* 'before' and *dad* 'father'.

Br. *gourdadou*, cpd. of prefix *gour-* denoting superiority, etc. and *dad* 'father'.

4. Goth. *fadreina* 'parents' (2.37) also used for 'ancestors'.

ON *forfeðr*, Dan. *forfædre*, Sw. *förfäder*, ME *forfadres*, NE *forefathers*, Du. *voorvaderen*, all lit. 'fore-fathers'.

OE *ealdfæderas*, pl. of *ealdfæder* 'grandfather', lit. 'old-father' (2.46).

Du. *voorouderen*, MHG *voraltern*, NHG *vorältern*, lit. 'fore-elders, fore-parents', cpds. of the words used for parents (2.37).

OHG *altmāgā*, cpd. of *alt* 'old' and *māgā* 'relatives' (2.58).

OHG *(alt)fordoron*, MHG *(alt)vorderen*, fr. OHG *fordoro*, MHG *vorder* 'former', formed like Grk. πρότερος 'former'.

NHG *ahnen*, fr. OHG *ano*, MHG *ane* 'grandfather' (2.46).

NHG *vorfahren* lit. 'fore-goers' and formerly only 'predecessors' (as MHG *vorvaren*), with late specialization to 'ancestors', parallel to that of Lat. *antecessōres* to OFr. *ancestres*, etc. (above, 2).

5. Lith. *sentéviai*, lit. 'old-fathers' and *pratéviai* lit. 'fore-fathers', cpds. of *tévas* 'father' with *senas* 'old' and *pra-* 'fore'. Also simple *tévai* formerly so used, Lett. *tēvi*. Also Lith. *tévu tévai* (Kurschat), Lett. *tēvu tēvi* 'fathers of fathers' (Mühl.-Endz. 4.178).

Lett. *senči*, fr. *sens* 'old'.

6. SCr. *predci*, Boh. *předkové*, Pol. *przodkowie*, Russ. *predki*, all derivs. of the word for 'before', ChSl. *prědŭ*, etc.

7. Skt. *pitaras* 'fathers' regularly used for 'ancestors'.

OPers. *apa-nyāka-* (sg.) cpd. of *apa* 'from' and *nyāka-* 'grandfather' (2.46), like Lat. *ab-avus* 'grandfather'.

2.57 DESCENDANTS
(Or sg. coll. Offspring, Progeny)

Grk.	ἔκγονοι, ἀπόγονοι	Goth.	....	Lith.	ainiai
NG	ἀπόγονοι	ON	afspringr	Lett.	pēcnācēji, pēcnākami
Lat.	prōgeniēs (sg.), posteri	Dan.	efterkommere	ChSl.	....
It.	descendenti, posteri	Sw.	avkomlingar, ättlingar	SCr.	potomci
Fr.	descendants	OE	ofspring	Boh.	potomci
Sp.	descendientes	ME	ofspring	Pol.	potomkowie
Rum.	descendenți, coborîtori	NE	descendants, offspring	Russ.	potomki
Ir.	iartaige, aue	Du.	na-(af-)komelingen, afstammlingen	Skt.	prajā-, tana-
NIr.	sliocht	OHG	afterkumft	Av.	frazainti-, naptyaēšū (loc. pl.)
W.	disgynnyddion	MHG	after-(nach-)kunft-(komen)		
Br.	diskennidi	NHG	abkömmlinge, nachkommen		

Words for 'descendants' are from such obvious sources as 'born from', 'coming from', 'coming after', 'those after'.

1. Grk. ἔκγονοι, ἀπόγονοι lit 'having birth from'.

2. Lat. *prōgeniēs* lit. 'a bringing forth' (cf. *prōgignere* 'bring forth'), hence 'off-spring, progeny', used as coll. for 'descendants'.

Lat. *posterī* (> It. *posteri*), pl. of *posterus* 'coming after', deriv. of *post* 'after'. Hence sb. *posteritās* > Fr. *postérité* > ME *posterite*, NE *posterity*.

It. *descendenti*, Fr. *descendants* (> NE *descendants*), Sp. *descendientes*, Rum. *descendenți*, fr. pple. of Lat. *dēscendere* 'come down, descend'.

Rum. *coborîtori*, fr. *cobori* 'descend' (this of Slavic orig., Tiktin 379).

3. Ir. *iartaige*, sg. coll., ·cpd. of *iar* 'after' and *taig-* 'come', this fr. *to-tiag-*, cpd. of *tiagu* 'go' (Pedersen 2.645). Hence like NHG *nachkommen*.

Ir. *aui*, pl. of *aue* 'grandfather' (2.46) also used for 'descendants'.

NIr. *sliocht* 'race, family', also 'off-spring, descendants', same word as MIr. *slicht, sliocht* 'trace, track'. Walde-P. 2.706.

W. *disgynnyddion*, Br. *diskennidi*, fr. *disgyn, diskenn* 'descend' (fr. Lat. *dēscendere*).

4. ON *afspringr*, OE *ofspring*, ME, NE *offspring*, sg. coll. cpds. of *af-, of-* 'from' and 'spring', hence 'that which springs from'.

Sw. *ättlingar*, fr. *ätt* 'family' in wide sense (19.23).

Dan. *efterkommere*, Sw. *avkomlingar*, Du. *nakomelingen* (also *af-*), OHG *afterkumft* (sg. coll.), MHG *afterkunft, after-komen* and *nachkunft, nachkomen*, NHG *abkömmlinge, nachkommen*, all cpds. of words for 'after' or 'from', and 'come'.

5. Lith. *ainiai* (NSB, Lalis; not in Kurschat, who has *vaikų vaikai* 'children of children'), also coll. *ainybė* (NSB), neologisms based on *eiti*, pres. *einu* (dial. *ainu*) 'go, come' (Senn in private letter; *ainei* coined in 1885).

Lett. *pēcnācēji, pēcnākami*, fr. adv. *pēc* 'later'. Mühl.-Endz. 3.205.

6. SCr., Boh. *potomci*, Pol. *potomkowie*, Russ. *potomki*, all fr. adv. *potom* 'afterward' (ChSl. *po tomi* 'after this').

7. Skt. *prajā-*, Av. *frazainti-*, both sg. coll., fr. Skt. *pra-jan-* 'bring forth, be born', Av. *fra-zan-*, like Lat. *prōgeniēs*. Skt. *tana-, tanas-* (RV), fr. *tan-* 'stretch', as 'what stretches on, continuation'.

Av. *naptyaēšū* (loc. pl.) : *napāt-* 'grandson' (2.46). Barth. 1040.

2.61 FATHER-IN-LAW   2.62 MOTHER-IN-LAW
(a, Husband's Father; b, Wife's Father)   (a, Husband's Mother; b, Wife's Mother)

	2.61 FATHER-IN-LAW	2.62 MOTHER-IN-LAW
Grk.	ἑκυρός (a), πενθερός	ἑκυρά (a), πενθερά
NG	πεθερός	πεθερά
Lat.	socer	socrus
It.	suocero	suocera
Fr.	beau-père	belle-mère
Sp.	suegro	suegra, madre politica
Rum.	socru	socra
Ir.	cliamain	....
NIr.	athair céile	mathair céile
W.	tad yng nghyfraith (chwegrwn)	mam yng nghyfraith (chwegr)
Br.	tad-kaer	mamm-gaer
Goth.	swaihra	swaihrō
ON	māgr, verfaðir (a)	sværa, māgkona, vermōðir (a)
Dan.	svigerfar	svigermor
Sw.	svärfar	svärmor
OE	swēor	sweger
ME	fadyr in lawe	mody in lawe
NE	father-in-law	mother-in-law
Du.	schoonvader	schoonmoeder
OHG	swehur	swigar
MHG	sweher	swiger
NHG	schwiegervater (schwäher)	schwiegermutter (schwieger)
Lith.	uošvis (šešuras obs.)	uosvė, anyta (a)
Lett.	tēvuocis	mātice
ChSl.	svekrŭ (a), ttstĭ (b)	svekry (a), ttsta (b)
SCr.	svekar (a), tast (b), punac (b)	svekrva (a), tašta (b), punica (b)
Boh.	tschán	tschyně
Pol.	świekier (a), teść (b)	świekra (a), teściowa (b)
Russ.	svekor (a), test' (b)	svekrov (a), tešča (b)
Skt.	çvaçura-	çvaçrū-
Av.	xᵛasura-	....

2.63 SON-IN-LAW   2.64 DAUGHTER-IN-LAW

	2.63 SON-IN-LAW	2.64 DAUGHTER-IN-LAW
Grk.	γαμβρός	νυός, νύμφη
NG	γαμπρός	νύφη
Lat.	gener	nurus
It.	genero	nuora
Fr.	beau-fils, gendre	belle-fille, bru
Sp.	yerno	nuera
Rum.	ginere	nora
Ir.	cliamain	....
NIr.	cliamhain	baincliamhain
W.	mab yng nghyfraith, daw	merch yng nghyfraith, gwaudd
Br.	mab-kaer, deun	merc'h-kaer
Goth.	mēgs	brūþs
ON	māgr	snor, māgkona
Dan.	svigersøn	svigerdatter
Sw.	svärson	svärdotter
OE	āðum	snoru
ME	sone in lawe	doużter in lawe
NE	son-in-law	daughter-in-law
Du.	schoonzoon	schoondochter
OHG	eidum	snura
MHG	eidem	snur
NHG	schwiegersohn (eidam)	schwiegertochter (schnur)
Lith.	žentas	marti
Lett.	znuots	vedekle, jaunava
ChSl.	zętĭ	snucha
SCr.	zet	snaha
Boh.	zeť	snacha
Pol.	zięć	synowa
Russ.	zjať	snocha, nevestka
Skt.	jāmātar-	snuṣā-
Av.	zāmātar-	....

2.65 BROTHER-IN-LAW   2.66 SISTER-IN-LAW
(a, Husband's Brother; b, Wife's Brother; c, Sister's Husband; d, Husband's Sister's Husband; e, Husbands of Sisters)   (a, Husband's Sister; b, Wife's Sister; c, Brother's Wife; d, Husband's Brother's Wife; e, Wives of Brothers)

	2.65 BROTHER-IN-LAW	2.66 SISTER-IN-LAW
Grk.	δαήρ (a), γαμβρός (b, c), ἀέλιοι (e), ἀνδρός ἀδελφοί, etc.	γάλως (a); ἀνδρὸς ἀδελφή, etc.; ἐνάτηρ (d, pl. e), σύννυμφοι (d)
NG	κουνιάδος (a, b); γαμπρός (c)	κουνιάδα (a, b); νύφη (c); συννυφάδα (d, pl. e)
Lat.	levir (a); uxōris frāter (b), etc.	glōs (a); virī soror, etc.; ianitrīcēs (e)
It.	cognato	cognata
Fr.	beau-frère	belle-sœur
Sp.	cuñado	cuñada
Rum.	cumnat	cumnată
Ir.	cliamain	....
NIr.	dearbhrāthair céile	deirbhshiúir céile
W.	brawd yng nghyfraith	chwaer yng nghyfraith
Br.	breur-kaer	c'hoar-gaer
Goth.	....	....
ON	māgr; svilar (e)	māgkona; brōðurkona (c)
Dan.	svoger	svigerinde
Sw.	svåger	svägerska
OE	tācor (a); āðum (c)	weres swuster (a), etc.
ME	brother in lawe	syster in lawe
NE	brother-in-law	sister-in-law
Du.	zwager	schoonzuster
OHG	zeihhur, swāgur	geswige
MHG	swāger	swāgerinne
NHG	schwager	schwägerin
Lith.	švogeris, svainis	svainė; moša (a)
Lett.	svainis; svaini (pl., e)	māsica (a); svaine (b)
ChSl.	dēverĭ (a); šurĭ, šurinŭ (b)	zlŭva (a); svĭstĭ (b); jętry (d)
SCr.	šogor; djever (a); šurjak (b)	jęgorica; zaova (a); svast (b); jetrva (d)
Boh.	švagr	švakrova
Pol.	szwagier	szwagrowa; bratowa (c)
Russ.	dever- (a); šurin (b); svojak (d)	zolovka (a); svojačenica (b); nevestka (c)
Skt.	devar- (a); syāla- (b)	nanāndar- (a); yātar- (d)
Av.	....	....

2.61–2.66. As stated above (p. 93), there is a group of inherited IE words originally denoting only the relations between the wife and her husband's family, while terms for the relations between the husband and his wife's relatives are of later origin. All these will be discussed under the several heads. But to a considerable extent these have been replaced by a word denoting simply 'relative by marriage' or, mostly, by a series of phrases or compounds with a common element, analogous in effect to NE *-in-law*. These it is more convenient to discuss here.

1. Fr. *beau-père, belle-mère*, etc., with *beau* 'beautiful', are simply polite phrases, like *beau-sire, bel-ami*, etc., that were specialized (in 16th cent.) to 'father-in-law', etc. or 'stepfather', etc. In the former sense they are imitated in

Br. *tad-kaer, mamm-gaer*, etc. (*kaer* 'beau'), and Du. *schoonvader*, etc. (*schoon* = NHG *schön*). Cf. also Sc. *good-father*, etc. (NED s.v. *good* D 2.b).

2. ME *fadyr in lawe*, etc. (from 14th cent.) quotable from c. 1300; cf. also *frere en loi* in parliamentary records of 1386, Rot. Parl. III.216b) but Wyclif's Bible has *hosebondis modir*, etc.), NE *father-in-law*, etc. (formerly used also for 'stepfather', etc.), that is, a father in the Canon Law as contrasted to father by blood. Cf. NED s.v. *brother-in-law*. Imitated in W. *tad yng nghyfraith*, etc. (*cyfraith* 'law'), which have replaced the old words *chwegrwn, chwegr*, etc. in common use.

3. NHG *schwiegervater*, etc. started from *schwiegermutter*, an expansion of MHG *swiger* 'mother-in-law', an inherited form (2.62). Hence the first part of

Dan. *svigerfar*, etc., and by imitation Sw. *svärfar*, etc., in which, however, *svär* represents the old masc. form = Goth. *svaihra*, etc. (2.61). Falk-Torp 1216. Hellquist 1132.

4. Ir. *cliamain* 'relation by marriage', quotable for 'father-, son-, and brother-in-law' : *clemnas* 'alliance by marriage' (root connection?). Hence NIr. *cliam-hain* 'son-in-law' (dial. also 'father- or mother-in-law'), and *bainchliamhain* 'daughter-in-law' (*ban-* 'female').

NIr. *athair* (*máthair*, etc.) *céile*, 'father (mother, brother, sister) of spouse'.

5. Goth. *mēgs* 'son-in-law', ON *māgr* 'father-, son-, or brother-in-law', *māg-kona* 'mother-, daughter-, or sister-in-law', Sw. *måg* (obs.), ODan., Norw. *maag* 'son-in-law' : OE *mǣg*, OHG *māg* 'relative', all perh. (cf. Fr. *beau-père*, etc.) : Lith. *mėgti* 'be pleasing'. Walde-P. 2.256. Feist 352.

6. ON *sifjar* 'relationship by marriage' (: Goth. *sibja*, OE *sibb*, etc. 'kinship'), hence *sifjungr* for male, *sifkona* for female relative by marriage. Cf. also NIcel. *tengda-faðir*, etc. (whole series) : ON *tengdir* 'relationship' (esp. by marriage) fr. *tengja* 'fasten'.

7. Lat. *adfīnis*, lit. 'bordering, near', was used as a general term for any relative by marriage, but without displacing the specific terms.

2.61, 2.62. 'Father-in-law' and 'mother-in-law'. 1. IE *swekuro-, fem. *swe-krū-, doubtless a cpd. of refl. *swe-, but the second part dub. Walde-P. 2.521 ff. Ernout-M. 948 f. Orig. used only by the wife of her husband's father or mother, as in Vedic Sanskrit, Homeric Greek, and still in Slavic; elsewhere the differentiation is lost.

Hence (with some new stem formations, fem. fr. masc. or conversely) Grk.

ἑκυρός, with new fem. *ἑκυρά*; Lat. *socer*, *socrus* (> It. *suocero*, OFr. *suevre*, Sp. *suegro*, Rum. *socru*, with new fem. It. *suocera*, Sp. *suegra*, Rum. *socra*); W. *chwegr* fem., with new masc. *chwegrwn* (both in Bible, but mostly obs.); Goth. *swaihra*, *swaihrō* (*n*-stems), ON *svǣra* fem., OSw. *svǣr* masc., Sw. *svär(far)*, OE *swēor*, *sweger*, MLG *zweer* masc., OHG *swehur*, *swigar*, NHG *schwäher*, *schwieger*(*mutter*), whence by analogy *schwiegervater* (*-sohn*, *-tochter*); Lith. *šešuras* (obs.); ChSl. *svekrŭ*, *svekry*, SCr. *svekar*, *svekrva* (Boh. *svekr*, *svekrva* now obs.), Pol. *świekier*, *świekra*, Russ. *sve-kor*, *svekrov'*; Skt. *çvaçura-*, *çvaçrū-*, Av. *x'asura-*; Arm. *skesur* fem., with new masc. *skesrair*; Alb. *vjehër*, *vjehërë*.

From a secondary deriv. with strengthened grade of the first syllable (cf. Skt. *çvāçura-* 'belonging to a father-in-law') comes OHG *swāgur*, MHG *swāger*, NHG *schwager* 'brother-in-law', that is, by derivation 'son of one's father-in-law'.

2. Grk. *πενθερός*, in Homer only 'wife's father', later generalized at the expense of *ἑκυρός* (and sometimes used also for 'son-in-law, brother-in-law'), fem. *πενθερά* : Skt. *bandhu-* 'relative', *bandh-* 'bind', IE *bhendh-*. Walde-P. 2.152.

3. Sp. beside *suegra* 'mother-in-law', also *madra politica* 'mother by courtesy'.

4. Lith. *uošvis*, *uošvė*, formerly only 'wife's father, mother', now 'father-in-law', 'mother-in-law' without restriction, etym.?

Lith. *anyta* 'husband's mother', pet-name type : Lat. *anus* 'old woman', etc. (above, p. 94). Walde-P. 1.55.

Lett. *tēvuocis*, *mātice* derivs. of *tēvs* 'father', *māte* 'mother'. But usually *vira* (*sievas*) *tēvs* (*māte*) 'husband's (wife's) father (mother)'.

5. ChSl. *tĭstĭ*, *tĭšta*, etc., general Slavic

word for 'wife's father, mother' (but Boh. *tschán*, *tschyně* with added suffix, and extension to 'husband's father, mother' at the expense of the old *svekr*, *svekra*), pet-name type : Lat. *tata*, Lith *tétis* 'father', etc. (above, p. 94). Brückner 569.

SCr. *punac*, *punica*, etym.?

2.63. 'Son-in-law'. 1. Grk. *γαμβρός* mostly 'son-in-law', but also 'brother-in-law', 'father-in-law', 'relative by marriage', NG 'bridegroom', 'son-in-law' or 'sister's husband' : *γάμος* 'marriage'. From the same root also Skt. *jāmātar-*, Av. *zāmātar-*, with suffix as in *pitar-mātar-*, etc. Walde-P. 1.574.

2. Lat. *gener* (> It. *genero*, Fr. *gendre*, Sp. *yerno*, Rum. *ginere*), Lith. *žentas*, Lett. *znuots* (also 'brother-in-law'), ChSl. *zętĭ*, etc., the general Slavic word, all apparently fr. IE *ǵen-* in Lat. *gignere* 'beget, bear', etc. Ernout-M. 414 f. Or Lat. *gener* for *gemer* (with *n* by influence of *genitor*, etc.) and so belonging orig. to preceding group? So Walde-P. 1.574, Walde-H. 1.590 f.

3. W. *daw*, Br. *deun*, MBr. *deuff*, OCorn. *dof* : Ir. *dám* 'a following, band', NIr. *damh* 'tribe, family', with specialization of 'relative' to 'son-in-law'. Walde-P. 1.764. Pederson 1.48.

4. OE *āþum* (also 'sister's husband'), OHG *eidum*, MHG *eidem*, NHG *eidam*, perh. (Gmc. *'aiþuma-*) : Osc. *aeteis*, Grk. *αἶσα* 'portion' and orig. applied to the one who marries a man's heiress-daughter and has a share in the inheritance. Hermann, Gött. Nachr. 1918.216 ff. Kluge-G.123.

NHG now *schwiegersohn*, dial. *toch-termann*. Kretschmer, Wortgeogr. 454.

2.64. 'Daughter-in-law' 1. IE *snuso-, prob. orig. 'bride', like the various later substitutes for it, and plausibly explained as fr. *sneu-* 'bind' in Skt.

snāvan- 'sinew', etc. Walde-P. 2.701. Ernout-M. 689.

Grk. *νυός*; Lat. *nurus*, late *nura*, **nora* (> It. *nuora*, OFr. *nuere*, Sp. *nuera*, Rum. *norā*); ON *snor*, OE *snoru*, ME *snore*, OHG *snura*, MHG *snur*, NHG *schnur*; ChSl. *snŭcha*, SCr. *snaha*, Boh. *snacha*, Russ. *snocha*; Skt. *snuṣā-*; Arm. *nu*.

2. Grk. *νύμφη* 'bride' (: Lat. *nūbere* 'marry', etc., 2.33) replaced *νυός* in Hellenistic times (LXX, NT; cf. Mt. 10.35), and prob. earlier (for *νυός* is quotable only from poetry).

3. Fr. *bru*, fr. OFr. *brut* 'bride' loanword fr. Gmc. (OHG *brūt*, etc.). REW 1345. Gamillscheg 154.

4. W. *gwaudd*, Br. *gouhez*, etym.? (Pedersen 1.514, fr. **upo-siyu-*, meaning connection with Skt. *si-* 'bind', etc.?).

5. Goth. *brūþs* properly 'bride' (as in *brūþfaþs* 'bridegroom', cf. OE *brȳd*, OHG *brūt*, etc.) is used for 'daughter-in-law', prob. influenced by the similar use of Grk. *νύμφη*, which it translates (Mt. 10.35). Hence also VLat. *bruta*, *brutis* 'daughter-in-law'. Cf. Fr. *bru*, above, 3.

6. Lith. *marti* 'bride' and (now mostly) 'daughter-in-law', prob. : Skt. *mar-ya-* 'young man', Grk. *μεῖραξ* 'young girl', etc. Walde-P. 2.281.

Lett. *vedekle* orig. 'bride', fr. *vedu*, *vest* 'marry'.

Lett. *jaunava* 'young woman, bride, daughter-in-law', fr. *jauns* 'young' : Lat. *iuvenis* 'young', etc.

7. ChSl. *nevěsta* 'bride' (see 2.22 under Pol. *niewiasta*), used also for *νύμφη* as 'daughter-in-law' (Mt. 10.35). So Russ. *nevestka* beside *nevesta* 'bride'.

Pol. *synowa*, fr. *syn* 'son', hence lit. 'son's wife'.

2.65. 'Brother-in-law' covers 'husband's brother', 'wife's brother', 'sister's husband', and sometimes even

---

'wife's or husband's sister's husband', and 'husbands of sisters'; and these may be expressed by different terms. The inherited group is used only of 'husband's brother'.

1. IE *daiwer-, root connection dub. Walde-P. 1.767. Ernout-M. 541. Walde-H. 1.787 f.

Grk. *δᾱήρ* (rare; Hom., Men. and a late inscr.); Lat. *lēvir* (rare; Festus, etc.; with dial. *l* for *d*, late *ē* for *ae*, and last syllable influenced by *vir*); OE *tācor*, OHG *zeihhur*; Lith. (obs.), Lett. (obs.) *dieveris*, ChSl. *děverĭ*, SCr. *djever* (Boh. *deveř*, Pol. *dziewierz* obs. or dial.), Russ. *dever'*; Skt. *devar-*; Arm. *taigr*; all meaning 'husband's brother'.

2. Grk. *γαμβρός* 'son-in-law' (2.63), also 'husband's or wife's brother', NG also 'sister's husband'.

Grk. *ἀνδρὸς* (*γυναικὸς*) *ἀδελφός*, late *ἀνδράδελφος*, *γυναικάδελφος*.

NG *κουνιάδος*, see below, 3.

3. Lat. *cognātus* 'relative' in late inscrr. 'brother-in-law'. Hence It. *cog-nato* (> NG *κουνιάδος* 'husband's or wife's brother'), Sp. *cuñado*, Rum. *cum-nat*, with the corresponding fem. forms. REW 2029.

4. OHG *swāger*, MHG, MLG *swāger* (> Dan. *svoger*, Sw. *svåger*), Du. *zwager*, NHG *schwager* (> Boh. *švagr*, Pol. *szwagier*, Lith. *švogeris* and, through Hung., SCr. *šogor*), fr. a deriv. of the word for 'father-in-law'. See 2.61, above, p. 124.

OE *āþum* 'son-in-law' (2.63) also 'sister's husband'.

5. Lith. (obs.) *laiguonas* 'wife's brother', etym.?

6. ChSl. (late) *šuri*, *šurinŭ*, SCr. *šura*, *šurjak*, Russ. *šurin*, Skt. *syāla-*, all 'wife's brother', perh. from **siū-* 'sew' (Lat. *suere*, etc.), through 'bind'. Walde-P. 2.514.

7. Grk. *αἔλιοι* (Hesych.), *εἰλίονες* (Pollux), ON *svilar*, 'husbands of sis-

ters'; Lith. *svainis*, Lett. *svainis* (cf. Mühl.-Endz. s.v.), pl. *svaini* 'husbands of sisters'; ChSl. *svatŭ*, *svojakŭ* 'relative', SCr., Russ. *svojak* 'wife's sister's husband', Boh. *svat*, *svak* for various 'in-laws'; all fr. refl. **swo-* 'one's own', applied to these secondary relationships mainly because the primary relationships already had their fixed terms. Walde-P. 2.457, 533.

2.66. 'Sister-in-law', like 'brother-in-law', covers a variety of specific relations, which may be expressed by different terms. One inherited group applies to the 'husband's sister', another to the 'husband's brother's wife' or in the plural 'wives of brothers'.

1. IE *ǵlōu-, etc., root connection dub. Walde-P. 1.631. Ernout-M. 426.

Grk. **γάλωϝος*, Hom. *γάλοως*, Att. *γάλως* 'husband's sister'; Lat. *glōs* (attested only in glosses) 'husband's sister' (also 'brother's wife'). Cf. Arch. lat. Lex. 12.413 ff.); ChSl. *zlŭva*, SCr. *zaova*, OBoh. *zelva*, Russ. *zolovka* 'husband's sister'.

2. IE *yenǝter-, etc., root connection dub. Walde-P. 1.207 f. Ernout-M. 469.

Grk. *ἐνάτηρ*, Hom. pl. *εἰνάτερες* (cf. Il. 6.378 *γαλόων ἦ εἰνατέρων* of Andromache's 'husband's sisters or her husband's brothers' wives'); Lat. pl. *ianitrīcēs* (rare) 'wives of brothers'; OLith. *jentė*, Lett. *ietere* (obs.), ChSl. *jętry*, SCr. *jetrva*, OBoh. *jatrev*, *jatruše*, OPol. *jqtrew*, Russ. *jatrov* (obs.); Skt. *yātar-*; all used of one's 'husband's brother's wife', or in plural for 'wives of brothers'.

3. Grk. usually *ἀνδρὸς* (*γυναικὸς*) *ἀδελ-φή*, late *ἀνδραδέλφη*.

NG *κουνιάδα* 'husband's or wife's sister', fem. of *κουνιάδος* 'husband's or wife's brother' (2.65).

Grk. *νύμφη* 'bride', 'daughter-in-law' (2.64), NG *νύφη* also 'brother's wife'.

Grk. *σύννυμφος* 'husband's brother's wife' (LXX+). Hence NG *συννυφάδα* id., pl. *συννυφάδες* 'wives of brothers.'

4. Lat. usually *virī* (*uxōris*) *soror*, *frātris uxor*, for the last also *frātria* (only in glosses), deriv. of *frāter* 'brother'.

It. *cognata*, Sp. *cuñada*, Rum. *cum-natǎ*, fem. of It. *cognato*, etc. (2.65).

5. ON *māgkona* (above, p. 124) or cpds. like *brōðurkona* 'brother's wife'.

Dan. *svigerinde*, fr. NHG *schwiege-rin* = *schwieger*, but used also = *schwä-gerin*; Sw. *svägerske*, fr. MLG *swegersche*. Falk-Torp 1216. Hellquist 1131.

OHG *geswige* (gl. Lat. *glōs*) : *swigar* 'mother-in-law', etc., above, p. 124.

MHG *swāgerinne*, fem. of *swāger*, hence NHG *schwägerin*.

6. Lith. *moša* 'husband's sister' : Lett. *māsa* 'sister' (2.45).

Lett. *māsnica* 'husband's sister', deriv. of *māsa* 'sister' (2.45).

Lith. *svainė*, Lett. *svaine*, fem. of *svainis* (2.65).

SCr. *šogorica*, Boh. *švakrova* (*k* fr. old *svekra*, etc.), Pol. *szwagrowa*, fems. of *šogor*, *švagr*, *szwagier* respectively.

ChSl. *svĭstĭ*, SCr. *svast*, OBoh. *svěst* 'wife's sister' : *svat*, *svojak*, etc. (2.65).

Pol. *bratowa* 'brother's wife' fr. *brat* 'brother'.

Russ. *svojačenica*, fem. deriv. of *svojak* (2.65).

Russ. *nevestka* 'daughter-in-law' (2.64), also 'brother's wife'.

7. Skt. *nanāndar-* 'husband's sister', fr. a pet name of the *nana* type (above, p. 94), influenced by the suffix of the other words of relationship. Uhlenbeck s.v.

	2.71 STEPFATHER	2.72 STEPMOTHER	2.73 STEPSON	2.74 STEP-DAUGHTER
Grk.	(μητρυιός, πατρυιός)	μητρυιά	πρόγονος	πρόγονος, προγόνη
NG	μητρυιός	μητρυιά	πρόγονος, προγόνι	προγόνή, προγόνι
Lat.	vitricus, patrāster	noverca, mātrāster	prīvignus, fīliaster	prīvigna, fīliastra
It.	patrigno	matrigno	figliastro	figliastra
Fr.	beau-père	belle-mère (marâtre)	beau-fils	belle-fille
Sp.	padrastro	madrastra	hijastro	hijastra
Rum.	tatā vitreg	mamă vitregă	fiu vitreg	fată vitregă
Ir.	lessathair	lesmáthair	lesmac	lessingen
NIr.	leasathair	leasmháthair	leasmhac	leasinghean
W.	llysdad	llysfam	llysfab	llysferch
Br.	lez-tad	lez-vamm	lez-vab	lez-verc'h
Goth.	....	....	....	....
ON	stjūpfaðir	stjūpmōðir	stiūpson, stjūpr	stjūpdottir
Dan.	stiffader	stifmoder	stifson	stifdatter
Sw.	styffar	styfmoder	styfson	styfdotter
OE	stēopfæder	stēopmōdor	stēopsunu	stēopdohtor
ME	stepfader	stepmoder	stepsone	stepdou3ter
NE	stepfather	stepmother	stepson	stepdaughter
Du.	stiefvader	stiefmoeder	stiefzoon	stiefdochter
OHG	stiuffater	stiufmuotar	stiufsun	stiuftohter
MHG	stiefvater	stiefmuoter	stiefson	stieftohter
NHG	stiefvater	stiefmutter	stiefsohn	stieftochter
Lith.	patévis	pamoté	posūnis	poduka
Lett.	patēvs	pamāte	padēls	pameita
ChSl.	otĭčimŭ, otĭčuchŭ	maštecha	pastorŭku	pastorŭka (padŭšti)
SCr.	očuh	maćeha	pastorak	pastorka
Boh.	nevlastní otec, otčim	nevlastní matka, macecha	nevlastní syn, pastorek	nevlastní dcera, pastorkyně
Pol.	ojczym	macocha	pasierb	pasierbica
Russ.	otčim, votčim	mačicha	pasynok	padčerica
Skt.	(tāta- yavīyan-)	....	....	....
Av.	....	....	....	....

2.71-2.74. Words for 'stepfather', etc. are, with some exceptions, derivatives or compounds of the words for 'father', etc.

1. Grk. μητρυιά, Ion. μητρυιή (Hom. +) 'stepmother', deriv. of μήτηρ with suffix related to that of πάτρως, μήτρως, Lat. patruus, Skt. pitṛvya- 'uncle' (2.51). From this was formed masc. μητρυιός or πατρυιός 'stepfather' (both late and rare), NG μητρυιός.

Grk. πρόγονος, lit. 'of previous birth', hence 'ancestor' 2.56), but also, as one born of a previous marriage, 'stepson' or 'stepdaughter', for latter also προγόνη. But NG προγονός 'stepson' (thus differentiated from πρόγονος 'ancestor'), προ-γονή 'stepdaughter', or dim. form προγόνι for young 'stepchild' of either sex.

2. Lat. vitricus 'stepfather', etym. dub., but perh. an extension of IE *witero- in Skt. vitaram 'farther, more distant', etc., from *wi- 'apart', and orig. pater vitricus 'remoter father'. Walde-P. 1.313. Hence Rum. vitreg (fr. lit. Latin, prob. through Hung. official Latin, cf. Tiktin s.v.), in tatā vitreg, and by extension mamă vitregă, fiu vitreg, fată vitregă.

Lat. noverca 'stepmother', deriv. of novus 'new', as one's 'new mother'. Ernout-M. 680.

Lat. prīvignus 'stepson', prīvigna 'stepdaughter', deriv. (orig. cpd. with -gno- : gignere, genus) of prīvus 'single', hence

'one of separate birth' (i.e. of a previous marriage). Ernout-M. 811.

It. patrigno 'stepfather', matrigna 'stepmother', formed fr. the words for 'father' and 'mother', with the suffix -igno- used as in rossigno 'reddish', etc., hence 'a sort of father (mother)'. Perhaps also first based on the obs. privigno.

The above words are those used in Latin literature. Inscriptions and glosses show the series patrāster, etc., derivatives of the words for 'father', mother', etc., and meaning 'a kind of father', etc. Hence It. figliastro, figliastra, OFr. parastre, marastre, fillastre, Fr. parâtre (obs.), marâtre, Sp. padrastro, madrastra, hijastro, hijastra, Rum. (obs.) fiastru, fiastrā.

In French the words came to be used in a derogatory sense, and became obsolete, except marâtre and this now mostly the typical cruel 'stepmother'. They were replaced by the polite phrases beau-père, etc., the same as for 'father-in-law', etc. (2.61-2.64).

3. The Celtic series, Ir. lessathair, etc., NIr. leasathair, etc., W. llysdad, etc., Br. leztad, etc., cpds. of the words for 'father' etc., the first part, as in Ir. less-ainm, W. llys-enu 'nickname' (cf. cognate with Ir. leth, W. lled 'side, half'. Pedersen 2.8.

OBr. eltroguen, OCorn. altruan 'noverca', fr. al- 'nourish', perh. also associated with all- 'other'. Pedersen 1.137.

4. The Gmc. series, ON stjūpfaðir, etc. (also stjūpr alone for 'stepson'), OE stēopfæder, etc., OHG stiuffater, etc., started in words for 'stepchild, stepson' as orig. 'orphan', like OE stēopcild, stēopbarn 'orphan', the first part : OE ā-stīpan, OHG bi-stiufan 'bereave', ON stūfr 'stump', etc. Walde-P. 2.619. Falk-Torp 1161. NED s.v. step-.

5. The Baltic series, Lith. patévis, etc., Lett. patēvs, etc. (so also OPruss. patowelis, pomatre, passons, poducre; also late ChSl. padŭšti, padŭšterica, Russ. padčerica, pasynok), cpds. of words for 'father', etc. (Lith. dukra pet form of duktē 'daughter') with prefix pa-, po- 'after, under' used also like Lat. sub-, hence here 'a sort of father', etc.

6. The Slavic words for 'stepfather', stepmother', late ChSl. otĭčimŭ, otĭčuchŭ, maštecha, SCr. očuh, maćeha, Boh. otčim, macecha, etc., all derivs. of the words for 'father', mother'.

Late ChSl. pastorŭku 'stepson', pastorŭka 'stepdaughter', SCr. pastorak, pastorka, Boh. pastorek, pastorkyně, etym. disputed, but best explained as starting in a *pa-dŭktorŭka (cf. pa-dŭšti, etc., above), whence an abbreviated *padtorŭka > pastorŭka, with new masc. formed from this. Miklosich 55. Meillet, MSL 13.28. Otherwise Zubatý, Arch. sl. Ph. 13.315 f. Still otherwise M. Vey, BSL 32.66.

Pol. pasierb 'stepson', pasierbica 'stepdaughter' (also Russ. dial. paserb), cpd. of pa- (as in Lith. pa-dukra, etc., above), the second part being much disputed; taken as *serbŭ by transposition from *sebrŭ (*sębrŭ in OSerb. sebrŭ 'free peasant', Russ. sjabr 'neighbor, friend') : Goth. sibja 'kinship', by Solmsen, KZ 37.592 ff., Walde-P. 2.456; as 'one who does not suck the same milk' fr. the root of sorbać, Lat. sorbēre 'suck in' by Brückner 389.

Boh. new series nevlastní otec, etc., lit. 'not own father', etc., from neg. ne and vlastní 'own'.

7. Skt. only late and rare words tātayavīyan- 'stepfather' lit. 'younger (later) father', dvaimātura-bhrātar- 'stepbrother', lit. 'having two mothers'.

2.75 ORPHAN

Grk.	ὀρφανός	Goth.	widuwairna	Lith.	našlaitis, -é	
NG	ὀρφανός	ON	foður-(mōður-)lauss	Lett.	bāris	
Lat.	orbus, pūpillus	Dan.	forældreløs	ChSl.	sirŭ, sirota	
It.	orfano, -a	Sw.	föräldralöst	SCr.	siroče	
Fr.	orphelin, -e	OE	stēopcild, stēopbarn	Boh.	sirotek, sirota	
Sp.	huerfano, -a	ME	orphan	Pol.	sierota	
Rum.	orfan, -ă	NE	orphan	Russ.	sirota	
Ir.	dílecta	Du.	wees	Skt.	(anātha-)	
NIr.	dílleacht	OHG	weiso	Av.	saē	
W.	amddifad	MHG	weise			
Br.	emzivad	NHG	waise			

1. Grk. ὀρφανός (also ὀρφο- in ὀρφοβότης), Lat. orbus, both also adj. 'bereft' (either of parents or of children), Arm. orb 'orphan' : Goth. arbi, OE ierfe, OHG arbi (NHG erbe) 'inheritance', Ir. orbe, orpe 'inheritance', Skt. arbha- 'small, child', etc., IE *orbho-, root connection dub. Walde-P. 1.183 ff. Ernout-M. 710.

Grk. ὀρφανός > late Lat. orphanus, whence It. orfano, Sp. huerfano, Rum. orfan, all with fem. forms in -a; OFr. orfene (> ME, NE orphan with old spelling restored), dim. orfenin, Fr. orphelin, fem. -e. REW 6105.

2. Lat. pūpillus 'orphan, ward', dim. of pūpus 'boy, child' : Lat. puer 'boy', etc. (2.25).

3. Ir. dílecta, NIr. dílleacht, cpd. of neg. di- and slicht, NIr. sliocht 'race, family', hence lit. 'without family'. Pedersen 1.84.

W. amddifad, Br. emzivad (MBr. emdyvat 'abandoned'), fr. *am-di-mat-, cpd. of am- 'about', neg. di-, the last part : Ir. maith 'good', hence 'on both sides in (or simply in) mis-fortune', 'unfortunate'. Pedersen 1.487. Henry 113.

4. Goth. widuwairna, deriv. of widuwō 'widow' (2.76), so 'widow's child'.

ON foður-(or mōður-)lauss, lit. 'father-(mother-)less'.

Dan. forældreløs, Sw. föräldralöst, lit. 'parent-less' (cf. 2.37).

OE stēopcild, stēopbarn, same as for 'stepchild' (2.71-2.74).

OHG weiso, MHG weise, NHG waise, Du. wees, from an s-extension of IE *weidh- 'separate', the same root as in the inherited word for 'widow' (2.76). Walde-P. 1.239 ff. Kluge-G. 667 f.

5. Lith. našlaitis, fem. -é, deriv. of našlé 'widow' (2.76), hence like Goth. widuwairna 'widow's child'.

Lett. bāris, perh. : bārt 'scold' and orig. a term of commiseration for the orphan. Mühl.-Endz. 1.274 (with ?).

6. ChSl. sirŭ (adj.), sirota, etc. (all the Slavic forms), Av. saē (Barth. IF 11.138) : Lith. šeirė 'widow', with common notion of 'bereft', but root connection dub. Walde-P. 1.543. Brückner 489.

Skt. anātha- 'widowed, fatherless', etc., cpd. of neg. a- and nātha- 'protector'.

Av. saē, above, 6.

2.76 WIDOW

Grk.	χήρα	Goth.	widuwō	Lith.	našlé (šeirė)	
NG	χήρα	ON	ekkja	Lett.	atraitne	
Lat.	vidua	Dan.	enke	ChSl.	vĭdova	
It.	vedova	Sw.	änka	SCr.	udova	
Fr.	veuve	OE	widuwe	Boh.	vdova	
Sp.	viuda	ME	widowe	Pol.	wdowa	
Rum.	văduvă	NE	widow	Russ.	vdova	
Ir.	fedb, bantrebthach	Du.	weduwe	Skt.	vidhavā-	
NIr.	baintreabhach (feadhbh)	OHG	wituwa	Av.	viðavā-	
W.	gweddr	MHG	witeve			
Br.	intañvez	NHG	wittwe			

1. IE *widhewā-, fem. of an adj. deriv. of *weidh- 'separate' in Lat. dīvidere 'separate', Skt. vidhu- 'solitary', etc. Walde-P. 1.239 ff. Ernout-M. 1106.

Lat. vidua (> Romance words); Ir. fedb (NIr. feadhbh mostly obs. or 'nun'), W. gweddr; Goth. widuwō, OE widuwe, OHG wituwa, etc. (all the Gmc. words, except the Scand.); OPruss. widdewu, ChSl. vĭdova, etc., general Slavic; Skt. vidhavā-, Av. viðavā-. From the same root Gkr. ἤιθεος (*ἠ-ϝιθεος) 'bachelor'.

2. Grk. χήρα, fem. of χῆρος 'bereft, empty' : χῆτος 'want', χωρίς 'apart', χῶρος '(empty) place', Skt. hā- 'leave', pass. hīyate 'is left, deserted', etc. Walde-P. 1.542 ff.

3. Ir. bantrebthach, NIr. baintreabhach, lit. 'woman-householder', cpd. of ban- 'female' (2.24) and trebthach, deriv. of trebad 'dwelling, husbandry'. A 'woman-householder' was usually such by force of circumstance, the one left to carry on after her husband's death, hence a 'widow'.

Br. intañvez, fem. of intañv, MBr. eintaff 'widower' : Ir. ointam 'single person, unmarried', deriv. of oen 'one'. Pedersen 1.163. Henry 174.

4. ON ekkja, Dan. enke, Sw. änka, fem. of an adj. meaning 'alone', ODan. enke, etc., this a deriv. of the numeral for 'one', Dan. en, etc. Falk-Torp 194.

5. Lith. našlé, etym.? F. Preveden, Language 5.148 suggests a deriv. of IE *nek- in Skt. naç- 'perish', Grk. νεκρός 'corpse', etc.

Lith. šeirė : ChSl. sirŭ 'orphan' (2.75).

Lett. atraitne : (at)riest 'separate, be separated'. Mühl.-Endz. 1.184.

2.81 RELATIVES

Grk.	συγγενεῖς	Goth.	(ga)nipjōs	Lith.	giminaičiai
NG	συγγενεῖς	ON	niðjar	Lett.	radi
Lat.	cognātī, propinquī	Dan.	slægtninge	ChSl.	roždenĭje (sg. coll.)
It.	parenti	Sw.	släktingar	SCr.	rodjaci
Fr.	parents	OE	māgas, cynn, siblin-	Pol.	krewni
Sp.	parientes		gas	Russ.	rodnyje
Rum.	rude	ME	kinnesmen, kin	Skt.	bandhavas, jñātayas
Ir.	coibnestaib (dat. pl.),	NE	relatives, relations,	Av.	nāfya-
	coibdelaig		kin(smen)		
NIr.	gaolta	Du.	verwanten		
W.	ceraint, perthynau	OHG	māgā, (gi)sibbon		
Br.	kerent	MHG	māgen		
		NHG	verwandten		

Words for 'relatives' are from such notions as 'of common birth or blood', 'belonging to the family', 'near', 'related', etc.

1. Grk. συγγενεῖς, lit. 'of common kin', cpd. of συν- 'together' and γένος 'race, family' (19.23).

2. Lat. cognātī, lit. 'of common birth', cpd. of con- 'together' and (g)nātus 'born'.

Lat. propinquī, lit. 'those near', deriv. of prope 'near'.

Lat. consanguineī, lit. 'of common blood', cpd. of con- and sanguen 'blood'.

Lat. adfīnēs, used for 'relatives by marriage', lit. 'bordering on', cpd. of ad 'at' and fīnis 'boundary'.

It. parenti, Fr. parents, Sp. parientes, fr. Lat. parentēs 'parents' (2.37).

Rum. rude, pl. of ruda 'family, relative', loanword from Slavic, ChSl. rodŭ 'race, family', etc. (19.23).

3. OIr. coibnestaib 'consanguineis' (Thes. 1.88), deriv. of *coibnes (MIr. coibnius) 'relationship', this a cpd. of com- 'together' and fine 'clan' (19.23). Pedersen 1.64, 2.20.

MIr. coibdelaig : coibdeiligim 'distribute, divide' (*com-fo-deiligim, cf. deiligim 'separate, distinguish'), so presumably first used as a legal term for the 'relatives' who divide the inheritance. Laws, Gloss. 147,221.

NIr. gaolta, pl. of gaol 'relationship, kindred, family', MIr. gāel 'relationship': Gael. gaol 'love' (Goth. gailjan 'make glad', etc.?). Walde-P. 1.634.

W. ceraint, Br. kerent, pl. of car, kar : Ir. care 'friend'. Pedersen 1.249.

W. perthynau, fr. perthyn 'belong to, be related', this fr. Lat. pertinēre 'belong to, pertain to'. Loth, Mots lat. 195.

4. Goth. (ga)nipjōs, ON niðjar (OE nippas 'men'), prob. : Skt. nitya- 'innate, one's own', deriv. of an IE *ni- beside *eni- 'in'. Formerly derived fr. *neptio- in Av. naptya- 'descendant', Grk. ἀνεψιός 'cousin' beside Skt. napāt- 'grandson', etc. (2.48). Walde-P. 1.126. Feist 376 f.

Dan. slægtninge, Sw. släktingar, derivs. of slægt, släkt 'race, family' (19.23).

OE māgas, OHG māgā : Goth. mēgs 'son-in-law', ON māgr 'father-, son-, or brother-in-law', etc. (2.61-2.66).

OE siblingas (Aelfric gives siblinge = Lat. affinis or consanguineus, and māg = Lat. propinquus), OHG (gi)sibbon (ON sifjungar is restricted to 'relatives by marriage', as sifjar to 'relationship by marriage', 2.61-2.66), fr. OE sib(b), OHG sibba 'kinship' = Goth. sibja id., fr. *se-bho-, deriv. of reflex. stem *so- (Lat. sē, sibi, etc.) beside *swo-. Walde-P. 2.456. Feist 417.

OE cynn, ME, NE kin 'family' in

wide sense (19.23) and coll. 'relatives'. Hence also OE cynnes men, ME kinnes- men, NE kinsmen, also kinsfolk, both now mostly literary.

NE relations, relatives, with specialized application of relation 'connection', adj. relative, these through Fr. fr. Lat. relātiō 'report', relātīvus 'pertaining to'. In the specialized sense relations is attested earlier and was formerly in more common use than relatives. NED s.v.

NHG verwandten, Du. verwanten, fr. adj. verwan(d)t 'related', orig. pple. of MHG, MLG verwenden 'turn to'.

5. Lith. giminaičiai, deriv. of giminė 'family' in wide sense (19.23).

Lett. radi, either loanword fr. or cognate with Slavic rodŭ (see foll.). Mühl.-Endz. 3.462 f.

6. ChSl. roždenĭje, sg. coll. (Lk. 1.58, etc.), SCr. rodjaci, Russ. rodnyje, derivs. of rodŭ 'birth, race, family' (19.23).

Boh. příbuzní, fr. privuzní (v > b, Gebauer 1.430), lit. 'bound to' : ChSl. privązŭ 'bond', privęzati 'bind to', cpd. of vęzati 'bind'.

Pol. krewni, fr. krew 'blood'. Cf. Boh. krevní příbuzní 'blood relations' and Lat. consanguineī.

7. Skt. bandhavas (stem bandhu-), fr. bandh- 'bind'.

Skt. jñātayas (stem jñāti-) : jāta- 'born', Lat. nātus 'son', cognātī 'relatives', etc.

Av. nāfya-, adj. (rare, Barth. 1062), deriv. of nāfa- 'relationship, family' (2.82).

2.82 FAMILY

Grk.	οἶκος, οἰκία	Goth.	gards	Lith.	šeima, šeimyna
NG	οἰκογένεια	ON	hjū, hjūn	Lett.	saime, familija
Lat.	domus, familia	Dan.	familie	ChSl.	domŭ
It.	famiglia	Sw.	familj	SCr.	obitelj, porodica
Fr.	famille	OE	hīwan, hīrēd	Boh.	rodina
Sp.	familia	ME	familie	Pol.	rodzina
Rum.	familie	NE	family	Russ.	sem'ja
Ir.	teglach	Du.	familie	Skt.	kula-
NIr.	teaglach	OHG	hīwiski	Av.	nāfa-
W.	teulu	MHG	hīwische		
Br.	tiegez, tiad	NHG	familie		

'Family' is intended here in the narrower sense, the immediate family (even so, not precisely defined), though many of the words listed here are also used, like NE family, to cover remoter kinship, 'family' in the wide sense. But in general for the latter, see 19.23.

Many of the words are those for 'house' or derivatives of them. Lat. familia, orig. 'body of servants, household', furnished the most widespread European word.

1. Grk. οἶκος, οἰκία 'house' (7.12), also 'family', in the earliest quotations in

wider sense ('royal house', 'house of Atreus', etc.) later also of the immediate 'family'.

Late Grk. οἰκογένεια (in pap.), status of an οἰκογενής born in the house, hence NG family.

2. Lat. domus 'house' (7.12), also immediate 'family'.

Lat. familia, orig. the 'body of servants, household', then also 'family', deriv. of famulus 'servant' (19.43). Hence the Romance words, those of the modern Gmc. languages, also Lett. familija and similar forms more or less

used in the modern Slavic languages (not included in the list). Ernout-M. 329. Walde-H. 1.452.

3. Ir. teglach, NIr. teaglach, W. teulu, cpds. of Ir. tech, W. ty 'house' (7.12), and Ir. sluag, W. llu 'throng, army', hence the 'people of the house, household'. Pedersen 1.84. Walde-P. 2.716.

Br. tiegez, tiad, derivs. of ti 'house'.

4. Goth. gards 'house' (7.12) renders Grk. οἶκος also in the sense of 'family'.

ON hjū, hjūn, OE hīwan, hīwisc, hīwrǣden, hīrēd, OHG hīwiski, MHG hīwische: OHG hīwo 'husband', hīwa 'wife', OE hīwa 'wife' (2.31, 2.32), Goth. heiwa- frauja 'master of the house', Lith. šeimyna 'family', Goth. haims 'village', OE hām 'village, home', etc. Walde-P. 1.359. Walde-H. 1.224. Feist 253 f.

5. Lith. šeima, šeimyna, OPruss. seimīns, Lett. saime, Russ. sem'ja : Goth. heiwa-frauja 'master of the house', etc. (above, 4).

6. ChSl. domŭ 'house' (7.12) renders οἶκος also in sense of 'family'.

SCr. porodica, Boh. rodina, Pol. rodzina, derivs. of ChSl. rodŭ, etc. 'birth, race' and 'family' in wide sense (19.23).

SCr. obitelj: ChSl. obitělĭ 'dwelling' (of monks), 'monastery', fr. obitati 'dwell' (7.11).

7. Skt. kula- 'family' in narrow and broad senses, also 'herd, crowd', etc. : ChSl. čeljadĭ 'household, body of servants'. Walde-P. 1.517. Berneker 141 f.

Av. nāfa- 'navel' and 'family, kindred': Skt. nābhi- 'navel' and 'relationship', Grk. ὀμφαλός 'navel', etc. Walde-P. 1.130. Barth. 1062.

CHAPTER 3

ANIMALS

3.11	ANIMAL	3.45	FOAL, COLT
3.12	MALE (adj.)	3.46	ASS, DONKEY
3.13	FEMALE	3.47	MULE
3.14	CASTRATE	3.51	HEN, CHICKEN (Generic)
3.15	LIVESTOCK	3.52	COCK
3.16	PASTURE (vb.)	3.53	CAPON
3.17	PASTURE (sb.)	3.54	HEN
3.18	HERDSMAN	3.55	CHICKEN
3.19	STABLE, STALL	3.56	GOOSE
3.20	CATTLE (Bovine Species)	3.57	DUCK
3.21	BULL	3.61	DOG
3.22	OX	3.612	PUPPY
3.23	COW	3.62	CAT
3.24	CALF	3.63	MOUSE
3.25	SHEEP	3.64	BIRD
3.26	RAM	3.65	FISH
3.27	WETHER	3.66	FISHERMAN
3.28	EWE	3.71	WOLF
3.29	LAMB	3.72	LION
3.31	SWINE	3.73	BEAR
3.32	BOAR	3.74	FOX
3.33	BARROW	3.75	DEER
3.34	SOW	3.76	MONKEY
3.35	PIG	3.77	ELEPHANT
3.36	GOAT	3.78	CAMEL
3.37	HE-GOAT	3.79	HUNT (vb.)
3.38	KID	3.81	INSECT
3.41	HORSE (Generic)	3.82	BEE
3.42	STALLION	3.83	FLY
3.43	GELDING	3.84	WORM
3.44	MARE	3.85	SNAKE

In the inherited names of animals there is little to be said about their semantic source. For in most of them the root connection is wholly obscure. The interest in this chapter lies rather in the losses, substitutions, and shifts of application.

The loss of certain inherited animal names, like that of the 'bear' in Slavic and Germanic and those for 'wolf', 'ser-

pent', 'hare', and 'mouse' here and there, is attributed to taboo (cf. esp. Meillet, Ling. hist. 281 ff.). This has doubtless played a part in individual cases. But one hesitates to make too much of this factor when one observes that virtually every inherited animal name (and for that matter nearly every inherited word in other classes, as in the words of relationship, etc.) has been displaced in one or another of the IE languages. The IE word for 'horse' attested in most IE languages in the early period (Grk. ἵππος, Lat. *equus*, etc., 3.41), has been displaced in every modern European language (only the fem. Sp. *yegua*, Rum. *iapă* 'mare' surviving), and no one will ascribe this to taboo.

On the sources of animal names the following general observations may be made here.

Some are of imitative origin. Besides those derived from the animal's cry, as several words for 'cock', 'hen' (3.51 ff.), etc., there are others derived from cries used in calling the animal, the call-words, as NE *puss* for 'cat' (3.62). For the latter type, cf. Rohlfs, Z. frz. Spr. 49.109 ff. But in several cases it is doubtful which type is involved.

Color words underlie some, as 'brown' in the Gmc. words for 'bear' (3.73) and an IE word for 'beaver' (NE *beaver*, etc.); 'gray' in Lith. *pelė* 'mouse' (3.63) and prob. a widespread word for 'hare' (OE *hara*, OHG *haso*, etc.; OE *hasu* 'gray'), possibly ON *grīss* 'pig' (3.35); 'red' in several words for 'fox' (3.74), etc.

The notion of swift motion underlies several animal names, as clearly Lith. *tekis* 'ram', Ir. *reithe* 'ram' (3.26), prob. Lat. *ariēs* 'ram' (3.26), Grk. ὄρνις 'bird' (3.64), ON *hross*, OE *hors* 'horse' (3.41), ON *hestr* 'horse' (3.41).

A proper name applied to an animal, as so often in fables, may become the usual word, as Fr. *renard* 'fox' (3.74), SCr. *mačka* 'cat' (3.62).

A few were first applied to the meat of an animal as food and then to the living animal (the opposite of the usual relation, cf. 5.62), as NG ψάρι 'fish' (3.65), ON *sauðr* 'sheep' (3.25).

Specialization is frequent. Words for 'animal' may be specialized to denote such diverse creatures as 'ox', 'swine', 'small beast of prey' (cf. REW 476 on the derivs. of Lat. *animal*), 'horse' (NG ἄλογο fr. 'unreasoning' through 'animal', 3.41), 'deer' (NE *deer*, 3.75), 'louse' (NIr. *mīol*, 3.11). 'Cattle' in the wide sense ('livestock') may be partly or wholly specialized to 'cattle' in the narrow sense, the bovine species (many examples in 3.15, 3.20), or to 'sheep' (Att. πρόβατον, It. *pecora*, 3.15, 3.25).

A 'horned animal' may be an 'ox' or 'cow' (NHG *rind*, Lith. *karvė*, 3.20 ff.), a 'ram' (Grk. κριός, ON *hrūtr*, 3.26), a 'stag' (Lat. *cervus*, NE *hart*, etc., 3.75). A 'tamed animal' may be an 'ox' (Ir. *dam*, 3.22) or a 'sheep' (W. *dafad*, 3.25).

The young of an animal may be a 'calf' (NE *calf*, etc., 3.24), 'chicken' (Lat. *pullus*, 3.55), or 'foal' (Grk. πῶλος, Lat. *pullus*, NE *foal*, etc., 3.45). Similarly, a 'yearling' may be a 'calf' (Lat. *vitulus*, 3.24), a 'lamb', 'wether', 'ram' (Goth. *wiþrus*, etc., 3.27, 3.29), 'sow' (Br. *gwiz*, 3.34), 'goat' (Grk. χίμαρος, 3.36), or 'kid' (SCr. *jare*, 3.38).

Of the names of wild animals, only a small selection is considered here. The chief attention is given to domestic animals. For those of most concern in the farmer's daily life, there is a wealth of distinctions within the species (or genus; but with reference to domestic animals 'species' is generally the correct term; for our purposes the technical distinction is of no consequence), of which it is important to note, beside the generic terms, those for the breeding male, the castrated male, the female, and the young, as for the bovine species the 'bull', 'ox', 'cow', 'calf' (still other specific terms like NE *steer* for 'young ox', *heifer* for 'young cow' being ignored). There are many shifts of application and local differences even in the same language. Within the same cognate group there may be interchange, as between 'bull', 'ox', and

'young ox' (NHG *stier*, NE *steer;* Skt. *ukṣan-*, NE *ox;* 3.20 ff.); or between 'lamb', 'ram', 'wether', 'ewe' (Goth. *wiþrus*, NHG *widder*, NE *wether*, etc.; Lat. *vervex*, Rum. *berbec*, Fr. *brebis;* 3.25 ff.).

The old generic terms for bovine animals, sheep, and swine have become specialized in Germanic to denote the female, as NE *cow*, *ewe*, *sow*.

Conversely, words for a special class, especially the young or the female, may be used generically, as Lat. *porcus*, NE *pig* for swine, NE *hen* or *chicken* for domestic fowl (3.31, 3.51).

Besides such interchange within the species, words for corresponding classes of different species may show specialization to one species or shift from one species to another. Thus for the breeding male, Skt. *vṛṣabha-* 'bull', but Lat. *verrēs* 'boar'; Grk. κάπρος 'boar', but Lat. *caper* 'he-goat'; OE *bucca* 'he-goat' (as NHG *bock*), but NE *buck* 'male deer'. Similarly for the 'young' or 'yearling', as noted above.

The dissertation of E. Gottlieb, A Systematic Tabulation of Indo-European Animal Names, received after this chapter was virtually completed, includes a great many of the less common words not discussed here.

3.11 ANIMAL

(Also Wild Beast)

Grk.	*ζῷον; θήρ, θηρίον*	Goth.	*dius*	Lith.	*gyvolis; žvėris*
NG	*ζῶον; ἀγρίμι*	ON	*dȳr*	Lett.	*dzīvnieks; zvērs*
Lat.	*animal, bēstia; ferus*	Dan.	*dyr*	ChSl.	*životŭ; zvěrĭ*
It.	*animale, bestia, bruto*	Sw.	*djur*	SCr.	*životinja; zvijer*
Fr.	*animal, bête*	OE	*dēor*	Boh.	*zvíře*
Sp.	*animal, bestia*	ME	*dere, beste, animal*	Pol.	*zwierzę*
Rum.	*animal, bestie*	NE	*animal, beast*	Russ.	*zivotnoe; zver'*
Ir.	*anmanda, rop, mīl*	Du.	*dier*	Skt.	*paçu-; mṛga-*
NIr.	*ainmhidhe, beathaidheach*	OHG	*tior*	Av.	—; *daitika-, xrafstra-*
W.	*anifail, mil*	MHG	*tier*		
Br.	*aneval, loen, mil*	NHG	*tier*		

Several of the words listed, like Lat. *animal*, mean properly any 'living creature', man included, but in common usage are applied mostly to animals other than man. Others are used only in the latter sense. But the difference is not always absolute and is indicated in the list only by the order, e.g. Lat. *animal, bēstia*. Some others are added (separated by a semicolon) that are used only of a 'wild beast'. Old words for 'animal' are often specialized to 'domestic animal' (3.14) or further to particular species of the latter, especially the bovine (3.20), as well as to other animals (above, p. 136). The source of most of the words for 'animal' is the notion of 'breathing, living'.

1. Grk. θήρ, θηρίον, Lat. *ferus, fera* (also adj. *ferus* 'wild'), Lith. *žvėris*, Lett. *zvērs*, OPruss. *swirins* (acc. pl.), ChSl. *zvěrĭ*, SCr. *zvijer*, Russ. *zver'*, etc., all meaning 'wild animal', but Boh. *zvíře*, Pol. *zwierzę* now 'animal' in general, IE **ǵhwer-*, without known root connection. Walde-P. 1.642 ff. Ernout-M. 353.

2. Grk. ζῷον : ζωός 'living', ζῶ 'live', etc. (4.74). Walde-P. 1.668 ff. From the same IE root come also NIr. *beathaidheach* (4) and the Balto-Slavic words (6).

NG ἀγρίμι 'wild beast', deriv. of ἄγριος, late ἀγριμαῖος 'wild'.

3. Lat. *animal*, deriv. of *anima* 'air, breath of life, life', this : Grk. ἄνεμος 'wind', etc., IE **an-* 'breathe' (4.51). Walde-P. 1.56 ff. Ernout-M. 53. Hence It. *animale*, Fr. (>ME, NE), Sp., Rum. *animal*, also W. *anifail*, Br. *aneval* (Loth, Mots lat. 133).

Lat. *bēstia*, used of all animals exclusive of man (also *bellua* 'large wild beast'), etym. dub., but perh. fr. the same root (IE **dhwes-*) as the Gmc. words, Goth. *dius*, etc. (below, 5). Walde-H. 1.102.

Hence It., Sp. *bestia*, OFr. *beste* (>ME *beste*, NE *beast*), Fr. *bête*, Rum. *bestie*.

Lat. *brūtus* 'heavy, dull, irrational' (a dialect form related to *gravis* 'heavy'), in late Lat. used esp. of dumb animals. So It. *bruto*, NE *brute* in *brute creation*, etc. Ernout-M. 119. Walde-H. 1.117.

4. Ir. *anmanda*, NIr. *ainmhidhe*, deriv. of Ir. *anim* 'soul, breath of life' : Lat. *anima*, etc. (above, 3).

Ir. *rop*, *rob*, perh. as orig. 'fierce beast' (but for actual comprehensive use see Laws, Gloss. 618) fr. **rup-no-s* : Lat. *rumpere* 'break', OE *rēofan* 'break', *rēafian* 'plunder', or fr. **rub-no-s* : Goth. *raupjan*, OHG *roufen* 'pluck', etc. Walde-P. 2.354, 355.

Ir. *mīl* (used mostly of small animals, or as second member of cpds. in animal names; NIr. *mīol* 'louse'), W., Br. *mil* : Grk. μῆλον mostly 'sheep' or 'goat' (3.15). Walde-P. 2.296. Pedersen 1.50.

NIr. *beathaidheach* (*beathach*), deriv. of *beatha* (gen. *beathadh*) 'life' : *bēo* 'live', etc. (4.74).

Br. *loen*, MBr. *lozn* : W. *llwdn* 'young of animals', Gael. *loth* 'colt', root connection obscure. Pedersen 1.135.

5. Goth. *dius* (renders Grk. θηρίον), ON *dȳr*, OE *dēor*, OHG *tior*, etc., the general Gmc. word for 'animal' vs. 'man', but in part restricted to 'wild animal' (or even further specialized, as in NE *deer*) : Lith. *dusti* 'gasp', *dvėsti* 'gasp, perish', ChSl. *dychati* 'breathe', etc., parallel to Lat. *animal* fr. *anima*. Walde-P. 1.846. Feist 121 b. Falk-Torp 172.

6. Lith. *gyvolis*, Lett. *dzīvnieks*, ChSl. *životŭ* ('life' and 'animal'), SCr. *životinja*, Russ. *životnoe*, Boh. *živočich* (mostly replaced by *zvíře*), fr. Lith. *gyvas*, Lett. *dzīvs*, Slavic *živŭ* 'living' (4.74).

7. Skt. *prāṇin-* ('living creature', man or beast, but not common for latter), deriv. of *prāṇa-* 'breath', this fr. *pra-* and *an-* 'breathe'.

Skt. *paçu-* mostly 'domestic animal' (3.14), but also 'animal' in general (so RV 10.90.8 *paçūn vāyavyān āraṇyān grāmyāñça* 'animals of the air, the forest, and the village', and elsewhere, cf. BR).

Skt. *mṛga-* 'wild animal', esp. 'deer' : Av. *mərəγa-* 'large bird', root connection dub. Walde-P. 1.275, 284.

Av. *xrafstra-* 'beast of prey', etym.? Walde-P. 1.486. Barth. 538.

Av. *daitika-* 'wild animal', deriv. of **dant-* 'tooth'. Barth. 678.

3.12 MALE / 3.13 FEMALE

	3.12 MALE	3.13 FEMALE
Grk.	*ἄρσην, ἄρρην*	*θῆλυς*
NG	*ἀρσενικός*	*θηλυκός*
Lat.	*mās* (*māsculus*, etc.)	*fēmina*
It.	*maschio*	*femmina*
Fr.	*mâle*	*femelle*
Sp.	*macho*	*hembra*
Rum.	*bărbatesc*	*femeiesc*
Ir.	*fer-, firend*	*ban-*
NIr.	*fireann*	*baineann*
W.	*gwryw, gwr-*	*benyw*
Br.	*par, taro-*	*parez*
Goth.	. . . .	. . . .
ON	*karl-*	*kvenn-*
Dan.	*han-*	*hun-*
Sw.	*han-*; sb. *hane*	*hon-;* sb. *hona*
OE	*hē*	*hēo*
ME	*he-, male*	*female*
NE	*male, he-*	*female*
Du.	*mannelijk;* sb. *mannetje*	*vrouwelijk, wijf-*; sb. *vrouwtje*
OHG	?	?
MHG	?	?
NHG	*männlich;* sb. *männchen*	*weiblich;* sb. *weibchen*
Lith.	*vyriškas* (*patinas* sb., of birds)	*moteriškas* (*patelė* sb., of birds)
Lett.	*vīrišks* (*tēvinš* sb., of birds)	*mātē, mātite*
ChSl.	?	?
SCr.	*muški*	*ženski;* sb. *samica*
Boh.	*samec*	*samice*
Pol.	*samiec*	*samica*
Russ.	*samec*	*samka*
Skt.	*vṛṣan-, puṁs-, nara-*	*-dhenu-, strī-*
Av.	*arṣan-, nairya-*	*daēnu-, strī-, hāirišī-, xšaθrī-*

3.12, 3.13. 1. 'Male' and 'female' as applied to animals are in part expressed by the same words as those applied to human beings (2.23, 2.24). Some of those, like Grk. ἄρσην, Skt. *vṛṣan-* from the notion of emitting semen, or Grk. θῆλυς, Lat. *fēmina* from the notion of giving suck, were from the beginning equally applicable to animals. Of those derived from 'man' and 'woman', many were extended to apply to animals, but others were not. Thus NHG *männlich*, *weiblich* are used of animals (OHG, MHG words so used?), while Dan. *mandlig, kvindelig*, Sw. *manlig, kvinlig* are still restricted to human beings. Here, and in Breton, different words are applied to animals. So also generally in Slavic. But SCr. *muški*, *ženski* are applied to animals; Russ. *mužeski*, *ženskij* sometimes to unfamiliar animals, but not ordinarily.

As in 2.23, 2.24, adjective forms are given, if such are in use; otherwise noun forms which may be used in apposition to another noun (cf. Lat. *fēmina bōs*, etc.). In some cases even where adjective forms are in use, some distinctive noun forms are added, as NHG *männlich; männchen*.

2. The sex of many domestic animals is shown by the use of different words, as NE *ox—cow*, *horse—mare*, etc. More generally it is shown by distinct gender forms either of the article or adjective (Grk. ὁ ἵππος—ἡ ἵππος), or of the word itself (Lat. *equus—equa*), the latter in some languages so consistently (even for 'cat', 'dog', 'elephant', etc.) that there is only rarely occasion to use special words

for 'male' or 'female'. Cf. also the use of prefixed nicknames, as in NE *tomcat, jackass, billy-goat, nanny-goat,* etc.

3. Sex expressed by the pronoun, either alone, as OE *hē, hēo* (Aelfric, Gram. 18, 17), or prefixed, as in NE *he-goat, she-goat.* So, as the regular method, Dan., Sw. *han-* for 'male', Dan. *hun-,* Sw. *hon-* for 'female' animals, with sbs. Sw. *hane, hona.*

4. Sex expressed by the addition of 'father' or 'mother', as NE *father-bird, mother-bird.* So especially Sp. *padre, madre* of animals.

5. Words denoting the male or female of a particular animal may be prefixed to names of other animals, as NE *bull-elephant, bull-whale, cow-elephant,* and *hen* applied to the female of birds in general and sometimes even to the female fish (NED s.v.), Br. *taro-* 'bull-' in *maout-taro* 'ram', *targaz* (fr. *taro-kaz*) 'tomcat', etc.

6. Br. *par* 'the male', whence *parez* 'the female', same word as *par* 'equal', fr. Lat. *pār,* but in this sense influenced by the vb.MBr. *paraff* 'couple, make pair'. Henry 218. Ernault, Glossaire 459.

7. Lith. *patinas, patinėlis* 'the male', *patelė* 'the female' (both used mostly of birds), fr. *pats* 'husband', *pati* 'wife'.

Lett. *tēviņš* 'the male', *māte, mātīte* 'the female' (both used mostly of birds), fr. *tēvs* 'father', *māte* 'mother'.

Boh., Russ. *samec,* Pol. *samiec* 'the male', Boh. *samice,* Pol. *samica,* Russ. *samka* 'the female' (SCr. *samica* of birds), with adjs. (archaic or uncommon) Boh. *samčí,* Pol. *samczy, samczowy* 'male', Boh. *samičí,* Pol. *samiczy* 'female', all fr. *sam,* ChSl. *samŭ* 'self, alone'. Presumably the first application was to the breeding male, the 'one' who serves many, as the bull, cock, etc., then 'male' in general with new feminine forms for 'female'.

8. Skt. *dhenu-* 'cow', in cpds. 'female', as *khaḍga-dhenu-* 'female rhinoceros' (in Indic linguistic feeling prob. like NE *cow-elephant,* etc., above, 5, but here the general meaning is the more original), Av. *daēnu-* used in apposition with names of 'mule', 'elephant', etc. : Skt. *dhayati* 'sucks', Grk. θῆλυς, Lat. *fēmina,* etc. (2.24). Walde-P. 1.829 ff. Barth. 662.

Other Skt. and Av. words same as in 2.23, 2.24.

3.14 CASTRATE

Grk.	*ἐκτέμνω*	Goth.	. . . .	Lith.	*romyti*
NG	*μουνουχίζω*	ON	*gelda*	Lett.	*rūnīt, rāmīt*
Lat.	*castrāre*	Dan.	*kastrere, skære, gilde*	ChSl.	*skopiti*
It.	*castrare*	Sw.	*kastrera, snöpa, gälla*	SCr.	*škopiti, štrojiti*
Fr.	*châtrer*	OE	*belistnian, (ā)fȳran*	Boh.	*vyklestiti, vyřezati*
Sp.	*castrar, capar*	ME	*gelde*	Pol.	*mniszyć, wałaszyć, trzebić*
Rum.	*castra, scopi, jugăni*	NE	*castrate, geld, cut, alter*		
Ir.	. . . .	Du.	*lubben, ontmannen*	Russ.	*skopit', cholostit'*
NIr.	*coillim*	OHG	*arfūrian*	Skt.	*vadh-, bhid-*
W.	*disbaddu*	MHG	*versnīden*	Av.	. . . .
Br.	*spaza*	NHG	*verschneiden*		

The castration of domestic animals is a practice that goes back to the earliest times among cattle-raising peoples and so presumably to IE times (otherwise Specht, KZ 66.6 f.), although the only evidence of any common term is the limited group Skt. *vadhri-* and the rare Grk. ἴθρις 'castrated'. It was effected by cutting or crushing the testicles, also by burning, cauterizing. Aristot. HA

510b3 refers to the crushing (in case of young animals) and cutting, and elsewhere to cauterizing (see below, 4 under OE *āfȳran*). For crushing see also below, 7 under Skt. *bhid-.* Schrader, Reallex. s.v. Verschneidung.

Most of the words reflect the action involved, esp. 'cut', 'cut off', also (for the crushing process) 'strike, break, split', and rarely 'burn'. Others reflect the result, as 'make gentle', 'make imperfect', 'unman', 'make celibate', 'make a monk', 'deprive of desire'. A few are denominatives of words for a castrated man, eunuch, or a specific castrated animal.

Cf. also the words for particular castrated animals, as 'wether' (3.27), 'barrow' (3.33), 'gelding' (3.43), 'capon' (3.53).

The sterilization of the female may be expressed by the same words (so *castrantur feminae,* Pliny, NH 8.208), or by different words, not discussed here, as NE *spay.*

The uncastrated male, apart from the special terms like *bull, boar,* etc., may be expressed by words meaning 'whole', as Fr. *entier,* NE *entire.*

1. Grk. ἐκτέμνω lit. 'cut out', cpd. of τέμνω 'cut' (9.22). Hence ἐκτομή 'castration', ἐκτομίας or τομίας 'castrated man or animal', the latter the regular term in Aristot. HA for the castrated ox, swine, sheep.

NG (lit. ἐκτέμνω or εὐνουχίζω) pop. μουνουχίζω, fr. μουνοῦχος 'castrated', this fr. εὐνοῦχος 'eunuch' (> μνοῦχος > μουνοῦχος, Hatzidakis, Μεσ. 1.294), orig. the (castrated) 'chamberlain', cpd. of εὐνή 'bed' and root of ἔχω 'hold'.

2. Lat. *castrāre,* deriv. of a **kastrom* : Skt. *çastra-m* 'knife, sword, weapon', *ças-* 'cut to pieces, slaughter', Grk. κεάζω 'split'. Ernout-M. 160. Walde-H. 1.179. Hence the Romance words, also loanwords in the modern Gmc. and Slavic languages beside the native terms, as Dan. *kastrere,* Sw. *kastrera,* NE *castrate,* Du. *castreeren,* NHG *kastrieren,* Pol. *kastrować,* Russ. *kastrirovat'.*

Lat. *ūrere* 'burn' and *excīdere, exsecāre* 'cut out' are sometimes used for the usual *castrāre.*

Lat. *sanāre* 'heal', in MLat. also 'castrate', reflected in many Romance dial. words (REW 7566) and imitated (or paralleled) in OE *hǣlan* (Bosworth-Toller, Suppl. 496), MHG *heilen* (also MHG locally), MLG *bōten* (: OE *bētan* 'make better, improve'). Development prob. through 'make tame, docile', appropriate with reference to the larger animals. M. Leumann, KZ 67.215 ff.

Fr. *couper* 'cut' (9.41) also used for *châtrer;* likewise rarely *hongrer* (cf. Dict. gén. s.v.) fr. *hongre* 'castrated horse', lit. 'Hungarian' (3.43).

Sp. *capar,* deriv. of Lat. *capō* 'capon' (3.53). REW 1641.

Rum. *scopi,* loanword fr. Slavic, ChSl. *skopiti,* etc. (below, 6).

Rum. *jugăni,* also *jugan* 'gelding', fr. *jug* 'yoke', here with reference to the wooden clamps used to crush the testicles. Tiktin s.v.

3. NIr. *coillim,* lit. 'ruin, destroy', as MIr. *coillim,* deriv. of *coll* 'damage, loss' : Goth. *halts,* OE *healt* 'lame', etc. (4.94). Pedersen 1.114.

W. *disbaddu,* cpd. of older *ysbaddu, yspaddu,* this and Br. *spaza* fr. MLat. *spadāre,* deriv. of Lat. *spadō* 'impotent person or animal, eunuch', a word which is also involved in the history of NE *spade* now used mostly of females (but see NED s.v.).

4. ON *gelda,* Dan. *gilde,* Sw. *gälla,* ME *gelde* (from ON), NE *geld* (formerly sometimes also used of females), lit. 'make imperfect' : ON *geldr,* Sw. *gall,* OHG *galt* 'barren, giving no milk', out-

side root connection dub. Walde-P. 1.629. Falk-Torp 310, 337. Hellquist 319.

Dan. *skære* 'cut' (9.41), also the commonest word for 'castrate'.

Sw. *snöpa* : ON *sneypa* 'violate', *snubba* 'chide' (> NE *snub*), Dan. *snubbe* 'cut off', Sw. *snoppa* 'snuff' (a light), etc., all orig. 'cut off'. Falk-Torp 1099. Hellquist 1022.

OE *belistnian,* cpd. of *be-* priv. (as in *behead,* etc.) and *lystan* 'be pleasing to', hence lit. 'deprive of desire'.

OE *(ā)fȳran,* OHG *arfūrian* (and *urfūr* 'castrated'), derivs. of OE *fȳr,* OHG *fuir* 'fire'. The castration (of fowl) by cauterizing with a hot iron is attested by Aristot., HA 631b25, Varro, RR 3.9.3, etc. Hence there is no need to reject the more obvious etymology in favor of derivation from the root seen in Lat. *putāre* 'cut', etc., otherwise unknown in Gmc., as Holthausen, IF 32.336, followed by Walde-P. 1.12.

NE *cut* and *alter* are both common terms for 'castrate' among farmers, at least in U.S. (this use of *alter* not mentioned in NED).

Du. *lubben,* NE (obs. or dial.) *lib,* fr. the root of Goth. *laufs* 'leaf', etc., Skt. *lup-* 'break, injure', Lith. *lupti,* Russ. *lupit'* 'peel'. Franck-v. W. 400.

Du. *ontmannen* lit. 'unman', but regularly 'castrate', as in part NHG *entmannen.*

MHG *versnīden,* NHG *verschneiden,* cpds. of *snīden* 'cut' (9.41), now 'cut off, cut up', and the usual native word for 'castrate'.

MHG *heilen* and MLG *bōten,* see under VLat, *sanāre,* above, 2.

5. Lith. *romyti,* Lett. *rāmīt,* lit. 'make gentle, tame' : Lith. *romus,* Lett. *rāms* 'gentle, tame', Lith. *rimti* 'be quiet', Goth. *rimis* 'quiet', etc. (Walde-P. 1.371 ff.).

Lett. *rūnīt,* fr. or cognate with MLG *rūne* 'gelding' (Du. *ruin,* NHG dial. *raun* 'gelding'), prob. from the root of Skt. *ru-* 'break in pieces', Lith. *rauti* 'tear out', etc. Walde-P. 1.352.

6. ChSl. *skopiti* (also *skopĭcĭ* 'eunuch'), SCr. *škopiti* (Boh. *skopiti,* Pol. *skopić* esp. of sheep, cf. *skop* 'wether'), Russ. *skopit',* fr. the root of Russ. *ščepat'* 'split', Grk. σκέπαρνον 'adze', σκάπτω 'dig', Lat. *cāpō* 'capon', etc. Walde-P. 2.559 f. Walde-H. 1.161. Brückner 494.

SCr. *štrojiti,* pop. form, with specialization of meaning, of SCr., ChSl. *strojiti* 'prepare'.

Boh. *vyklestiti,* cpd. of *klestiti* 'prune' (also castrate'), fr. *klest* 'branch, twig'.

Boh. *vyřezati,* cpd. of *řezati* 'cut', hence lit. 'cut out'.

Pol. *mniszyć,* deriv. of *mnich* 'monk', hence lit. 'make a monk' of one, like NHG *mönchen* 'castrate'. Brückner 341.

Pol. *wałaszyć,* deriv. of *wałach* fr. NHG *wallach* 'gelding' (3.43). Brückner 600.

Pol. *trzebić* 'clean, weed out', and 'castrate' : SCr. *trijebati* 'peel, shell', Russ. *terebit'* 'tear out', etc. Brückner 579.

Russ. *cholostit',* deriv. of *cholostoj* 'unmarried, celibate'.

7. Skt. *vadhri-* 'castrated' (cf. Grk. ἐθρίς · τομίας κριός and ἴθρις · σπάδων, τομίας, εὐνοῦχος, Hesych.) fr. *vadh-* 'strike, slay' : Grk. ὠθέω 'thrust', etc., IE **wedh-.* Walde-P. 1.254 f.

Skt. *bhid-* 'split' is used in describing castration, AV 6.138.2 ("let Indra with the two pressing stones split his testicles"). For further evidence of castration, cf. Zimmer, Altind. Leben 226.

In the Avesta there seems to be no reference to castration, but this is doubtless accidental. The practice was familiar in Iran as elsewhere (cf. Xen., Cyrop. 7.5.62).

3.15 LIVESTOCK

(Cattle in Wide Sense)

Grk.	*κτήνη, βοσκήματα (πρόβατα)*	Goth.	. . . .	Lith.	*gyvoliai, banda*
NG	*κτήνη, σφαχτά*	ON	*fē, kvikfē, būfē*	Lett.	*luopi*
Lat.	*pecus*	Dan.	*kreaturer*	ChSl.	*skotŭ*
It.	*bestie, bestiame*	Sw.	*kreatur*	SCr.	*stoka, marva*
Fr.	*bétail*	OE	*fēoh*	Boh.	*dobytek*
Sp.	*ganado*	ME	*fe, cattell*	Pol.	*bydło*
Rum.	*vite (dobitoc)*	NE	*livestock (cattle)*	Russ.	*skot*
Ir.	*indile, crod, cethra*	Du.	*vee*	Skt.	*paçu-*
NIr.	*airnēis, eallaeh*	OHG	*fihu*	Av.	*pasu-; staora-*
W.	*anifeiliaid, da (byw)*	MHG	*vihe*		
Br.	*chatal, loened*	NHG	*vieh*		

Here are grouped the most important terms for 'livestock, cattle' (in the old wide sense of NE *cattle,* NED s.v. 4; throughout this section 'cattle' will have this sense) or for certain classes of livestock, wider than a particular species. There is a wide variation in the range of application, as between some of the words listed, and even for the same word according to period and locality. They may cover all domestic animals kept for service or useful products, but mostly domestic quadrupeds, while some are used distinctively either for 'large cattle' or for 'small cattle'. Such differences in range are ignored in the list and can be only roughly indicated in the notes below.

For the classification of 'large' and 'small cattle', cf. that of Grk. πρόβατα (below, 2; in the Arc. inscription 'swine' are mentioned separately as if not falling clearly in either division), Lat. (Varro, RR 2.1.10, 12) *pecus maius (boves, asini, equi), pecus minus (oves, caprae, sues),* It. *bestie grosse, minute,* Fr. *gros, petit bétail,* Sp. *ganado mayor, minor,* Rum. *vite mari, mici,* NHG *gross-, kleinvieh,* etc.; also Av. *pasu-* mostly 'small cattle' (sheep and goats), *staora-* 'large cattle' (ox, horse, camel).

The identity of 'cattle' and 'property' in early times is reflected in the history of many of the words. 'Cattle' may become 'property', or conversely, and both meanings may be found in the same word or in the same group of cognates.

In general, the words for 'cattle' show specialization from either 'animals' or 'property'.

1. IE **peḱu-,* fr. the same root as Grk. πέκω 'comb, shear', πόκος 'fleece', Lat. *pectere* 'comb', and so orig. 'sheep'(?). Walde-P. 2.16 f. Ernout-M. 746 ff.

Lat. (early) *pecu,* pl. *pecua,* Umbr. *pequo,* Lat. *pecus,* gen. *pecoris,* coll. 'cattle' in wide sense, also esp. 'sheep' (hence It. *pecora* 'sheep'), *pecus,* gen. *pecudis* 'a head of cattle', pl. *pecudēs* 'cattle'; (Goth. *faihu* only 'property'), ON *fē* 'cattle' esp. 'sheep', and 'property', for 'cattle' also *kvikfē* (with *kvikr* 'living') and *būfē* (with *bū* 'household'), Dan. *fæ,* Sw. *fä* 'beast, brute', OE *feoh,* ME *fie, fee* 'cattle' and 'property' (but for NE *fee,* see NED *fee,* sb.[2]), Du. *vee,* OHG *fihu, fehu,* MHG *vihe,* NHG *vieh* 'cattle'; OPruss. *pecku* 'cattle', OLith. *pekus* 'cattle' in wide sense, but also 'small cattle', esp. 'sheep' (Hermann, Arch. sl. Ph. 40.161); Skt. *paçu-* 'domestic creature' (in AV 11.2.9 covers cows, horses, men, sheep, and goats; sometimes also asses, mules, camels, dogs; sometimes 'animal'), Av. *pasu-* mostly 'small cattle'.

2. Grk. κτήνη fr. the root of κέκτημαι 'own, possess' (11.12), κτάομαι 'get' (11.16), hence lit. 'possessions', but used only for property in cattle.

Grk. βοσκήματα, fr. βόσκω 'graze' (3.15).

Grk. πρόβατα, 'cattle' in general (Hom., Hdt., etc.), classified as large or small (cf. τὰ λεπτὰ τῶν προβάτων Hdt.; τὸ πρόβατον ϝέκαστον τὸ μέζον, τῶν δὲ μειόνων προβάτων, Arc. inscription), also 'small cattle' (Cret. τὰ πρόβατα καὶ καρταίποδα 'the small and large cattle'; καρταίποδα lit. 'strong-footed', cf. καρταίπους 'bull' in Pindar), in Att. 'small cattle' (Thuc.), usually 'sheep' (so in NG); fr. προβαίνω 'step forward', which is applicable to all grazing cattle. But Lommel, KZ 46.50 ff., assumes that 'small cattle' is the earlier meaning and comes from the notion of 'go in front'.

Grk. μῆλα (Hom., only poet.) 'small cattle, sheep and goats' : Ir. mīl 'animal' (3.11), Du. maal 'heifer', further connection with Goth. smals 'small', etc. dub. Walde-P. 1.296.

NG σφαχτά, lit. 'for slaughter' (: σφάζω 'slaughter'), used mainly for sheep and goats.

3. It. bestie, pl. of bestia 'beast' (3.11). Also bestiame, coll., mostly 'large cattle'.

Fr. bétail, coll. fr. OFr. bestial, late Lat. bēstiālis, deriv. of bēstia 'beast' (3.11).

Sp. ganado, coll. fr. ganar 'gain, earn, acquire' (Fr. gagner, etc. REW 9483), through 'acquired property', hence 'cattle' as often. Cf. Boh. dobytek fr. dobyti 'acquire' (below, 7).

Rum. vite, pl. of vita 'domestic animal', ORum. 'animal', fr. Lat. vīta 'life', Semantic borrowing fr. Slavic, cf. ChSl. živòtŭ 'life' and 'animal'. Tiktin 1759. Sandfeld, Ling. balk. 86.

Rum. dobitoc 'domestic animal', fr. Slavic, Bulg. dobitŭk, etc. (below, 7).

4. Ir. indile (also 'goods, property') :

OBr. endlin 'property', W. ennil, ynnill 'gain, profit', cpd. of ind- 'in', second part obscure, orig. meaning 'income'. Pedersen 1.148.

Ir. crod (also 'wealth'), perh. : W. cordd 'group, tribe', Goth. hairda 'herd', etc., or else to W. cerdded, OBr. credam 'walk'. Walde-P. 1.424. Pedersen 1.173; 2.381. By either connection the meaning 'cattle' is earlier than 'wealth'.

Ir. cethra 'cattle' in both wide and narrow sense, pl. of cethir 'quadruped', deriv. of cethir 'four' (cpd. like Lat. quadrupēs? So Pedersen 1.94).

MIr., NIr. airnēis (also 'goods, possessions, furniture'), prob. fr. ME harneis 'equipment'. K. Meyer, Contrib. 64.

NIr. eallach (also 'poultry', and 'household goods'; same word as eallach, MIr. ellach 'union, communion') : MIr. inloing 'claims', fr., 'puts in (a claim)', OIr. ellachtae gl. (terra) conferta (pecoribus), etc., cpd. of in- 'in' and -long-, IE *legh- 'lie, lay'. Pedersen 2.570. Walde-P. 2.424. Development fr. 'what lies in, belongs to' to 'union' and to 'belongings, equipment, goods', whence also 'cattle' as a further specialization.

NIr. beathaidhigh 'animals' (3.11) also used commonly for 'domestic animals'.

W. anifeiliaid 'animals' (3.11) also used commonly for 'domestic animals'.

W. da 'goods' (sb. form of da 'good'), also 'cattle', or da byw lit. 'live goods'.

Br. chatal, fr. OFr. chatel 'property, chattels'.

Br. loened, pl. of loen 'animal' (3.11), used commonly for domestic animals.

5. ON fé, OE féoh, etc., above, 1.

ON smali 'small cattle', esp. 'sheep' : Goth. smals 'small', etc. Falk-Torp 1077.

Dan. kreaturer pl., Sw. kreatur coll., through 'animal' fr. Lat. creātūra 'creature'. Cf. the once very common use

in New England of creature, critter for cattle (NED s.v. 2b). Falk-Torp 578. Hellquist 507 f.

ME ca(t)te(l)l, NE cattle, fr. OFr. catel (northern dial., beside chatel), Lat. capitāle neut. of capitālis deriv. of caput 'head'. Used in MLat. for 'principal sum of money, capital', hence 'movable property' in OFr. and sometimes in ME (in this sense now replaced by chattels fr. OFr. chatel); but soon specialized to 'livestock' and in present use still further specialized to the bovine animals. Cf. NED s.v.

NE stock 'fund, property' also used for 'farm animals' since 16th cent., hence livestock since end of 18th cent. NED stock, sb. 54, and livestock.

6. Lith. gyvoliai, pl. of gyvolis 'animal' (3.11), commonly used for 'domestic animals'.

Lith. banda, coll., properly a 'herd of cattle' : Goth. bindan 'bind', NE bind, band, etc., IE *bhend-. Walde-P. 2.152. Lett. luopi (pl of luops 'domestic animal'; also mājas luopi with gen. sg. of māja 'house'), without clear connection, perh. : Alb. lópë 'cow'. Walde-P. 2.383. Mühl.-Endz. 2.527 ff.

7. ChSl. skotŭ, Russ. skot (SCr., Pol. skot no longer the usual word, Boh. skot

now of bovine species), loanword fr. Gmc., Goth. skatts 'money', OHG skaz 'money, riches' (NHG schatz 'treasure'), OFris. sket 'money' and 'cattle'. Root connection dub., but 'property' prob. the earlier meaning. Brückner 495. Stender-Petersen 311 ff. Feist 429.

SCr. stoka : steći 'acquire', ChSl. sŭtesti 'flow together'. Cf. Bulg. stoka 'goods, wares', živa stoka 'livestock'. Miklosich 347. Brückner 516.

SCr. marva, earlier marha, in this sense through Hung. marha 'cattle', this fr. OHG mer(c)ha 'mare'. Berneker 2.19.

Boh. dobytek, fr. dobyti 'acquire', cpd. of byti 'be'. So also Pol. dobytek (now mostly replaced by bydlo), Bulg. dobytŭk.

Pol. bydło : Boh. bydlo 'dwelling' fr. the root of ChSl. byti 'be, exist', whence various derivations meaning 'dwell' (7.11). Development in Polish fr. 'dwelling' to 'property', then 'cattle' in wide and narrow sense. Berneker 112. Brückner 52.

8. Skt. paçu-, Av. pasu-, above, 2.

Av. staora- 'large cattle' (ox, horse, camel) : Skt. sthavira- 'thick, sturdy', Goth. stiur 'male calf', OE stéor 'young ox', etc. (3.20-3.24). Walde-P. 2.609.

3.16 PASTURE, GRAZE

(vb., a, trans.; b, intr.)

Grk.	νέμω, ποιμαίνω, βόσκω (all a, mid. b)	Goth.	haldan (a)
NG	βόσκω (a, b)	ON	beita (a), bíta (b)
Lat.	pāscere (act. a, b; dep. b)	Dan.	græsse (a, b)
It.	pascere (a, b), pascolare (b)	Sw.	beta (a, b)
Fr.	paître (a, b)	OE	læswian (a, b), healdan (a)
Sp.	apacentar (a), pastar (a, b), pacer (b)	ME	leswe, pasture (a, b), grase (b)
Rum.	paște (a, b)	NE	pasture (a, b), graze (a, b)
Ir.	ingairim (a); gelim (b)	Du.	weiden (a, b)
NIr.	buachaillighim (a); ingheilim (b)	OHG	weidenōn (a, b), weidōn (b)
W.	bugeilio (a); pori, porfelu (b)	MHG	weiden, weidenen (a, b)
Br.	peuri (a, b)	NHG	weiden (a, b)
		Lith.	ganyti(a); ganytis (b)
		Lett.	ganīt (a); ganīties (b)
		ChSl.	pasti (a); pasomŭ (pple. b)
		SCr.	pasti (a, b)
		Boh.	pásti (a); pásti se (b)
		Pol.	paść (a); paść się (b)
		Russ.	pasti (a); pastisja (b)
		Skt.	car- (caus. a, act., mid. b)
		Av.	vāstrya-

Verbs for 'pasture' are partly from 'feed', partly from 'drive, guard, tend', etc.

1. Grk. νέμω, same word as νέμω 'distribute, dispense' (in Hom. esp. of food and drink), this prob. : Goth., OE niman, etc. 'take' (see 11.13). Walde-P. 2.330 f. Development in Greek either fr. 'dispense (food)' to 'ration, feed (cattle)', or more prob. through the sbs. νομός, νομή '(allotment' >) 'pasture', with reflex action on the use of the vb.

Grk. ποιμαίνω, fr. ποιμήν 'herdsman' (3.18).

Grk. βόσκω (cf. also βοτόν 'head of cattle', perh. : Lith. gauja 'pack' (of wolves, dogs), guiti 'chase, hunt', and ultimately connected with Grk. βοῦς 'ox', etc. Walde-P. 1.697.

Grk. βουκολέω, deriv. of βουκόλος 'cowherd, herdsman' (3.18), and orig. used only of bovine cattle, then also of horses, etc.

2. Lat. pāscere : ChSl. pasti 'pasture', Goth. fōdjan 'feed', OE fōda 'food', etc. (5.12). Walde-P. 2.72 ff. Ernout-M. 737 f. Hence It. pascere, pascolare, Fr. paître, Sp. pacer, apacentar (also pastar

new deriv. of the sb. pasio 'pasture', Lat. pastus), Rum. paște. REW 6263.

3. Ir. ingairim, usual word for 'herding' (cattle, etc.) in Laws; cpd. of gairim 'call' (18.41).

Ir. gelim (intr. 'graze'; also 'devour'), NIr. in-gheilim : W. gel, Ir. gelit 'leech', OHG kela, NHG kehle 'throat', etc., IE *gel- 'devour'. Walde-P. 1.621.

NIr. buchaillighim, W. bugeilio, fr. NIr. buachaill, W. bugail 'herdsman' (3.18), like Grk. ποιμαίνω fr. ποιμήν.

W. pori (also porfelu fr. porfel 'a pasture', this beside porfa lit. 'pasture-place', cpd. with ma 'place'), Br. peuri, with the sbs. W. pawr, Br. peur, fr. MLat. *pāburum, pāburāre (latter in Du Cange), Lat. pābulum 'fodder', pābulāri 'graze'(?). Henry 222. Ernault, Glossaire 353. (Not in Loth, Mots lat.).

4. Goth. haldan (renders Grk. βόσκω, ποιμαίνω), OE healdan 'keep, guard, hold' also 'tend cattle' (e.g. in Gospels, Mk. 5.14), OHG haltan 'keep, guard' also 'tend cattle' (Otfr. 1.12.1, etc.), OS haldan 'guard, preserve' perh. :

Grk. κέλλω 'drive' (a ship), Skt. kal- in caus. kālaya- 'drive', in which case the Gmc. development is fr. 'drive' to 'tend cattle' (cf. Lith. ganyti, below, 5), then generalized to 'guard, keep, hold'. Walde-P. 1.442 ff. Feist 239 f.

ON bíta 'bite' and 'graze', caus. beita (with dat.) 'let graze, pasture', Sw. beta : Goth. beitan, OE bítan 'bite', Skt. bhid-, Lat. findere 'split', etc. Walde-P. 2.138. Hellquist 67.

Dan. græsse (a and b, but for a usually sætte paa græs), OE grasian (rare), ME grase, NE graze (mostly intr.), derivs. of Dan., OE græs 'grass'.

OE læswian, ME leswe, deriv. of OE læs 'pasture', this fr. OE lætan 'let, leave', as land that was 'let alone, untilled'. Cf. NED s.v. lease, sb.[1].

ME, NE pasture, fr. OFr. pasturer, deriv. of OFr. pasture 'pasture' (Fr. pâture 'fodder', fr. late Lat. pāstūra).

OHG weidenōn, weidōn, MHG weidenen, weiden, NHG, Du. weiden, fr. OHG weida 'pasture, fodder, hunting, fishing' : ON veiðr 'hunting, fishing', OE wáþ 'hunting, wandering', fr. an extension of IE *wei- in Skt. veti, vayati 'seeks, follows', Av. vayeiti 'pursues', Lith. výti 'pursue, hunt', etc. Walde-P. 1.230. Falk-Torp 1361. Development of 'pas-

ture' fr. 'hunting ground' or 'place for seeking fodder' or both.

5. Lith. ganyti (a), refl. ganytis (b), Lett. ganīt (a), refl. ganīties (b), deriv. of Lith. genu, ginti, Lett. dzīt 'drive' : ChSl. ženą, gŭnati, goną, goniti 'drive', Skt. han-, Grk. θείνω 'strike', etc., IE *gʷhen-. Walde-P. 1.679 ff. Development from 'strike' to 'drive', then 'drive cattle', 'tend cattle'. Cf. VLat. mināre 'drive cattle' fr. minārī 'threaten', and the specialization in NE drover.

6. ChSl. pasą, pasti (a), pres. pass. pple. pasomŭ 'grazing' (b) : Lat. pāscere, above, 2. SCr. pasti (a, b), Boh. pásti (a), pásti se (b) and similarly in the other Slavic languages.

7. Skt. car- 'move about, wander', also 'graze' (b, caus. a) : Grk. πέλω 'be in motion', Lat. colere 'cultivate', etc. IE *kʷel-. Cf. NPers. čarīdan 'pasture'. Walde-P. 1.514 ff.

Av. vāstrya-, deriv. of vāstra- 'fodder' and 'pasture' (cf. also vāstar- 'herdsman'), this prob. : Skt. vas- 'consume' (rare), OE wist 'food', etc. (5.12). Walde-P. 1.306 ff. Connection with OHG weida (Barth. 1413) is to be rejected on both formal and semantic grounds, since it takes no account of the history of weida (above, 4).

3.17 PASTURE (sb.)

Grk.	νομός	Goth.	winja
NG	νομή, βοσκή	ON	hagi
Lat.	pāscuum	Dan.	græsningsland, græs-
It.	pascolo		gang
Fr.	pâture	Sw.	bete, betesmark
Sp.	apacentedero	OE	læswe
Rum.	pāşune	ME	pasture, leswe
Ir.	geliboth	NE	pasture
NIr.	ingheilt, inghealtas	Du.	weide
W.	porfel, porfa	OHG	weida, winne
Br.	peur	MHG	weide
		NHG	weide
Lith.	ganykla		
Lett.	ganība, ganīkla		
ChSl.	pažitĭ		
SCr.	paša		
Boh.	pastvišké		
Pol.	pastwisko		
Russ.	pastbišče		
Skt.	gavyūti-, etc.		
Av.	vāstra-, gaoyaoti-		

Nearly all the nouns for 'pasture' are derived from, or in a few cases are the source of, the verbs for 'pasture', discussed in 3.16. Many of these cover both 'pasture' as the place and 'pasturage' (as formerly both NE words).

The few others are:

1. Goth. *winja* : ON *vin* 'meadow', OE *wynn* 'delight', rarely 'pasture', OHG *winne* 'pasture', *wunnia* 'meadow, pasture' and 'delight' (NHG *wonne* 'bliss'), Lat. *Venus, venus* 'love', Skt. *van-* 'wish, love, win', etc. Development fr. 'delight' through 'place of comfort' or the like to 'meadow' or 'pasture'. Walde-P. 1.258 ff. Feist 565.

2. ON *hagi* : OE *haga* 'hedge, inclosure, yard', OHG *hag* 'hedge, inclosed land', Du. *haag* 'hedge', Sw. *hage* 'inclosure, inclosed pasture', Dan. *have* 'garden', Skt. *kakṣā-* 'girdle, surrounding wall', etc. Walde-P. 1.337. Falk-Torp 386.

3. ChSl. *pažitĭ* (=νομή in Gospels, etc., Jagić, Entstehungsgesch. 377; λειμών in Supr.), fr. *žiti* 'live'. Miklosich 411.

4. Skt. *gavyūti-*, Av. *gaoyaoti-*, cpd. of *gav-, gao-* 'ox, cow', second part related to Skt. *yoni-*, Av. *yaona-* 'place, home', hence 'place for cattle'. Barth. 484.

3.18 HERDSMAN
(Or Cowherd, Shepherd, Etc.)

Grk.	ποιμήν, βουκόλος,	Goth.	hairdeis
	αἰπόλος	ON	hirðir
NG	τσοπάνης	Dan.	hyrde, kvægvogter
Lat.	pāstor	Sw.	herde, boskapsherde
It.	pastore	OE	hirde
Fr.	pâtre, berger, etc.	ME	herde
Sp.	pastor, vaquero, ma-	NE	herdsman; -herd
	nadero	Du.	herder, veehoeder
Rum.	cioban (pāstor)	OHG	hirti
Ir.	buachaill, ūgaire	MHG	hirt(e), herter
NIr.	buachaill, aodhaire	NHG	hirt
W.	bugail		
Br.	bugel		
Lith.	kerdžius, ganytojas,		
	piemuo		
Lett.	gans		
ChSl.	pastyrĭ, pastuchŭ		
SCr.	pastir, čoban, kravar,		
	etc.		
Boh.	pastýř, pastucha, kra-		
	vák, etc.		
Pol.	pastuch, pasterz		
Russ.	pastuch		
Skt.	gopa-, paçupā-, etc.		
Av.	vāstar-		

Several words originally covering 'herdsman' in general have become specialized to 'shepherd', and conversely others that were originally specific, as for 'cowherd' or 'shepherd', have become generalized in use.

In general the specific terms are more common, sometimes the only ones in popular use.

1. Grk. *ποιμήν*, in Hom. 'herdsman' (of sheep or oxen), later only 'shepherd' : Lith. *piemuo* 'shepherd', Grk. *πῶυ* 'flock' (of sheep), Skt. *pā-* 'protect', *go-pa-* 'cowherd', etc., IE *pō̆(i)-*. Walde-P. 2.72.

Grk. *βου-κόλος* 'cowherd', sometimes 'herdsman' (cf. *βουκόλος ἵππων*), beside *αἰ-πόλος* 'goat-herd', *οἰο-πόλος* 'shepherd' (rare in this sense, replaced by *ποιμήν*), cpds. of *βοῦς* 'ox, cow', *αἴξ* 'goat', *οἶς* 'sheep', second part : Grk. *πέλω* 'be in motion', Lat. *colere* 'cultivate', Skt. *car-* 'move about, graze' (3.16), etc., IE *kʷel-*. Walde-P. 1.514 ff.

NG *τσοπάνης* 'shepherd' (*ποιμήν* lit. and mostly fig.), like Rum. *cioban*, SCr. *čoban*, loanword fr. Turk. *çoban* 'shepherd' (orig. Pers., Lokotsch 1921).

2. Lat. *pāstor*, fr. *pāscere* 'pasture' (3.15). Hence It. *pastore* 'herdsman', Fr. *pâtre, pasteur* (both lit.), Sp. *pastor* 'shepherd', Rum. *pāstor* 'shepherd'.

In French usually only specific terms as *berger* 'shepherd', *bouvier* 'oxherd', *vacher* 'cowherd', *chevrier* 'goatherd', derivs. of the words for 'sheep' (Lat. *vervex* 'wether', later 'sheep', 3.27), 'ox', 'cow', 'goat'.

Sp. *vaquero* fr. *vaca* 'cow'.

3. Ir. *buachaill*, W. *bugail*, Br. *bugel*, all orig. 'cowherd', but not so restricted (cf. NIr. *buachaill bō* 'cowherd'), cpds. of words for 'ox, cow', and prob. the same root as in Grk. *βουκόλος*, etc. (above, 1). Pedersen 1.127.

Ir. *ūgaire* 'shepherd', NIr. *aodhaire* 'shepherd' and 'herdsman' (cf. *aodhaire bō* 'cowherd'), cpd. of *uī* 'sheep' (3.25), and the root of *gairim* 'call' (18.41).

4. Goth. *hairdeis*, ON *hirðir*, OE *hirde*, NE *-herd* in shepherd, cowherd, etc., dial. *herd* 'shepherd', OHG *hirti*, NHG *hirt*, etc., general Gmc. word, now partly specialized to 'shepherd' (so mostly in Dan., Sw., Du., NHG), deriv. of noun Goth. *hairda*, OE *heord* 'herd', etc. : Skt. *çardha-, çardhas-* 'troop, multitude', Av. *sarǝda-* 'kind, species', etc. Walde-P. 1.424. Feist 234.

Where the word is specialized to 'shepherd', it may be replaced in other senses, as Dan. *kvægvogter*, cpd. of *kvæg*

'cattle' (3.20) and *vogte* 'watch, tend', Sw. *boskapsherde*, cpd. of *boskap* 'cattle' (3.20), Sw. *vallare* fr. *valla* 'tend' (cattle), Du. *veehoeder*, cpd. of *vee* 'cattle' (3.15) and *hoede* 'guard', like NHG *viehhüter*.

ME *herdman*, NE *herdsman*, replacing *herd* in general sense except in the cpds. *shepherd*, *cowherd*, etc., but less used than the specific terms.

5. Lith. *kerdžius* : Goth. *hairdeis*, etc., above, 4. Walde-P. 1.424.

Lith. *ganytojas*, deriv. of *ganyti* 'pasture (3.16), fr. the same root also Lett. *gans* (Lith. *ganas* '(Pferde)hirt', in NSB).

Lith. *piemuo* 'shepherd' : Grk. *ποιμήν*, above, 1.

3.19 STABLE, STALL

Grk.	σταθμός	Goth.	(avistr)
NG	στάβλοι	ON	fjōs, stallr, stallhūs
Lat.	stabulum	Dan.	stald
It.	stalla, scuderia	Sw.	stall
Fr.	étable, écurie	OE	steall
Sp.	establo	ME	stal, stable
Rum.	staul, grajd	NE	stall, stable
Ir.	lías	Du.	stal
NIr.	stábla	OHG	stal
W.	ystabl	MHG	stal
Br.	kraou, staol	NHG	stall
Lith.	tvartas, kūtē		
Lett.	kūts, stallis		
ChSl.	chlévŭ		
SCr.	staja, štala		
Boh.	stáj, chlév		
Pol.	stajnia (chlew)		
Russ.	stojlo, chlev		
Skt.	goṣṭha-, goṣṭha-		
Av.	gavŏ-stāna-, aspŏ-		
	stāna-, etc.		

The heading is intended to cover words denoting the place where the domestic animals are kept, without regard to the present distinction between NE *stall* and *stable* and the usual restriction of the latter to a place for horses. Several of the words entered are used only or mostly for 'stable' in this restricted sense, as It. *scuderia*, Fr. *écurie*.

But specific terms derived from the names of the animals, like Lat. *bovīle*, *ovīle*, W. *marchdy*, *beudy* (lit. 'horse-house', 'cow-house'), Russ. *konjušnja* (fr. *kon'* 'horse'), etc., are not included, except where generic terms are lacking (as in Avestan).

6. ChSl. *pastyrĭ*, *pastuchŭ*, fr. *pasti* 'pasture' (3.16), and so the other Slavic words. Beside these and in more common use in some of the Slavic languages is a series of specific terms derived from the names of the animals, as SCr. *govedar*, *kravar*, *ovčar*, *svinjar*, *kozar* 'cattle-, cow-, shep-, swine-, goat-herd', Boh. *kravák*, *ovčák*, etc., like Fr. *bouvier*, *vacher*, *berger*, etc.

7. Skt. *gopa-* 'cowherd' also 'protector', cpd. of *go-* 'ox, cow' and *pā-* 'protect' also *gorakṣaka-* with *rakṣ-* 'protect'. With *pā-* likewise *paçu-pā-*, *paçu-pāla-* fr. *paçu* 'cattle' (3.15), and specific *avi-pāla-* 'shepherd' fr. *avi-* 'sheep', etc.

Av. *vāstar-*, fr. the same root as *vāstra-*, vb. *vāstrya-* 'pasture' (3.16).

Also not included are the numerous words denoting an outer inclosure for domestic animals, like OE, ME *fald* (fr. vb. *fealdan* 'bend, fold'), NE *fold* (esp. *sheepfold*), Grk. *μάνδρα*, Skt. *vraja-* etc.

The majority of the words are from the notion of 'standing place', a few from 'hut', 'pen', or the like.

For occasional confusion between the notions of 'stable' and 'barn' (as in U.S. usage of *barn*), see 8.14.

1. Derivs. of IE *stā-* 'stand'. Walde-P. 2.604 ff. Ernout-M. 984.

Grk. *σταθμός*; Lat. *stabulum*, whence OFr. *estable* (> ME, NE *stable* > NIr. *stābla*, W. *ystabl*), Fr. *étable*, Sp. *establo*,

Rum. *staul*, Byz., NG *στάβλος*, Br. *staol*; (Goth. *awistr*, OE *ēowestre*, etc. 'sheepfold'); SCr. *staja*, Boh. *stáj*, Pol. *stajnia*, Russ. *stojlo*; Skt. *go-ṣṭha-* 'cow-stall', but also more general, hence even *go-goṣṭha-*), *go-sthāna-*, *uṣtra-sthāna-*, Av. *gavŏ-stāna-*, *aspŏ-stāna-*, *uštrŏ-stāna-* (cpds. with words for 'ox', 'horse', 'camel').

Here also (fr. IE *stǝ-dhlo-*, as Lat. *stabulum*, or more prob. a parallel IE *stel-*) the Gmc. group, ON *stallr* (also *stallhūs*), OE *steall*, NE *stall*, OHG *stal*, etc., whence also It. *stalla*, Lett. *stallis* (fr. MLG *stal*) and SCr. *štala*. Walde-P. 2.644. Falk-Torp 1147.

ME *stall* and *stable* were both used for the building in which domestic animals were kept, but *stall* came to be used mostly for the standing place for a single animal, and *stable* of the building for horses.

2. It. *scuderia*, Fr. *écurie* 'stable' for horses, derivs. of *scudiero*, *écuyer* orig. 'shield-bearer' fr. Lat. *scutārius*, then also 'page, groom', hence 'place where the grooms stayed, stable'. But in French prob. blended with a loanword fr. OHG *scūr* 'covered place, shed', *scūra* 'barn' (so *scuria* in Lex. Sal.). REW 7759. Gamillscheg 343.

Rum. *grajd*, loanword fr. Slavic (below, 6).

3. Ir. *lías*, etym.?

Br. *kraou* : W. (obs.) *crau* 'pigsty',

craw 'sty, hovel', Ir. *crō* 'inclosure, pen', etc. (these : OE *hrōf* 'roof', etc. Pedersen 1.92; rejected by Walde-P. 1.477).

4. ON *fjōs*, contraction of **fē-hūs* 'cattle-house', cpd. of *fē* 'cattle' (3.15).

5. Lith. *kūtē*, Lett. *kūts*, fr. MLG *kot*, *kote* 'hut, shed' (cf. OE *cot* 'hut', etc. 7.13). Mühl.-Endz. 2.338.

Lith. *tvartas*, fr. *tverti* 'comprise, inclose', like *tvora* 'fence', etc., hence orig. 'inclosure'. Walde-P. 1.750.

6. ChSl. *chlévŭ* (also 'hut'), Boh. *chlév*, Pol. *chlew* (now esp. 'pigsty'), Russ. *chlev*, loanword fr. Gmc. **χlaiwa-* 'hut' (Goth. *hlaiw* 'grave' beside *hleipra*, *hlija* 'tent', etc. fr. IE **klei-* 'incline'; Walde-P. 1.490 f f.). Berneker 389. Stender-Petersen 239 ff.

ChSl. *graždĭ* (late), Bulg. *grazd* (> Rum. *grajd*), deriv. of ChSl. *gradŭ* 'city' and 'garden', orig. 'inclosed place'. Berneker 330.

7. Skt. (beside *go-ṣṭha-*, above, 1) *go-tra-* fr. *go-* 'ox, cow' and suffix- *-tra-* denoting place, but not restricted to bovine species.

Av. *gavŏ-stāna-*, *aspŏ-stāna-*, etc. (above, 1) for the large animals, also (*nmānǝm*) *gāvayǝm*, lit. '(house) for oxen'. For small animals, as sheep, *paṣuš-hasta-*, cpd. of *paṣu-* 'small cattle' (3.15) and **hasta-* 'sit' = Skt. *sad-*. Cf. Vd. 15.23 ff., where the whole series occurs.

	3.20 CATTLE (Collective or plural forms)	3.21 BULL	3.22 OX	3.23 COW	3.24 CALF
Grk.	βόες	ταῦρος	βοῦς ὁ	βοῦς ἡ	μόσχος
NG	βόδια	ταῦρος, ταυρί	βόδι	ἀγελάδα	μοσχάρι
Lat.	bovēs	taurus	bōs	bōs, vacca	vitulus
It.	(buoi)	toro	bove, bue	vacca	vitello
Fr.	(bétail, etc.)	taureau	bœuf	vache	veau
Sp.	ganado	toro	buey	vaca	ternero, becerro
Rum.	vite	taur	bou	vacă	vițel
Ir.	buar	tarb	dam	bō, ag, ferb	lāeg
NIr.	buar	tarbh	damh	bō, fearb	laogh
W.	gwartheg	tarw	ych, eidion	buwch	llo
Br.	saout, biou	taro	ejen, oc'hen (pl.)	buoc'h	leue
Goth.	....				stiur, kalbō
ON	naut, nautfē	þjōrr, graðungr, boli	oxi (uxi)	kȳr (kū)	kālfr
Dan.	kvæg	tyr	okse	ko	kalv
Sw.	boskap	tjur	oxe	ko	kalv
OE	hrīðeru, nēat	fearr	oxa (stēor)	cū	cealf
ME	nete, rotheren	bule (bole)	oxe (steere)	cow	calf
NE	cattle	bull	ox (steer)	cow	calf
Du.	runderen, rundvee	stier, bul	os	koe	kalf
OHG	(h)rindir	far, ohso	ohso (stior)	kuo (chuo)	kalb
MHG	rinder	var(re), stier	ohse (stier)	kuo	kalp
NHG	rinder, rindvieh	stier, bulle	ochs (stier)	kuh	kalb
Lith.	galvijai	bulius	jautis	karvė	veršis, telias
Lett.	guov(s)luopi, lielluopi	bullis	vērsis	guovs	tel'š
ChSl.	*govędo, nuta	bykŭ	volŭ	krava	telę
SCr.	goveda	bik	vol, vo	krava	tele
Boh.	skot	byk	vůl	kráva	tele
Pol.	bydło	byk	wół	krowa	cielę
Russ.	skot	byk	vol	korova	telenok
Skt.	gāvas	ukṣan-, ṛṣabha-, vṛṣabha-	go-	go-, vaçā-	vatsa-
Av.	gāwō	uxšan-	gao-	gao-	....

3.20–3.24. Groups of cognates which appear under several of these headings.

1. IE *gʷou-, nom. sg. *gʷōus, the old generic word for the bovine species, 'ox' or 'cow'. Restricted to 'ox' in the Romance languages, to 'cow' in Celtic, Gmc., Lett., Arm. Walde-P. 1.696 f. Ernout-M. 115. Pedersen 2.26, 51, 93.

Grk. βοῦς 'ox, cow', pl. βόες 'cattle', dim. βοίδιον, whence NG βόδι 'ox', pl. βόδια 'cattle'; Lat. bōs 'ox', vacca (loanword fr. a rural dial., cf. Umbr. bum, bue, etc.), whence It. bue, bove, Fr. bœuf, Sp. buey, Rum. bou, all 'ox' (but also 'bull' in dialects, REW 1225); Ir. bo, W. buwch, Br. buoc'h, all 'cow', Br. pl. biou 'cattle', Ir. buar coll. 'cattle'; ON kȳr,

OE cū, etc., all the Gmc. words for 'cow' (NE kine old pl., now coll. and sometimes used generically = cattle); Lett. guovs 'cow', ChSl. *govędo, SCr. govędo 'head of cattle', SCr. pl. goveda 'cattle' (Boh. hovado 'beast', Russ. govjadina 'beef'); Skt. go-, Av. gao- 'ox, cow'; Arm. kov 'cow'.

2. Goth. stiur 'male calf' (renders τὸν μόσχον), ON stjōrr (rare), OE stēor, OHG stior, all mostly 'young ox', MHG, NHG stier 'bull' (but dial. 'ox'), NE steer '(young) ox' (in U.S., where oxen are used for hauling, steer is still 'young ox', but otherwise regularly in the packing industry steer is the grown castrated animal raised for beef, and ox is

not in use) : Av. staora- 'large cattle', Skt. sthūra- 'strong, thick', sthavira- 'thick, sturdy', OHG stūri 'strong', etc. Further inclusion in this group of Grk. ταῦρος 'bull', etc., disputed but probable (see 3.21). Walde-P. 2.609. Feist 454.

3. Goth. auhsus, auhsa, ON oxi (uxi), OE oxa, etc., the general Gmc. word for 'ox', W. ych 'ox', Br. oc'hen 'oxen', Ir. oss 'stag', Skt. ukṣan-, Av. uxšan- 'bull', prob. : Skt. ukṣ-'sprinkle, emit seed',Grk. ὑγρός 'moist', etc. Cf. Skt. vṛṣan- 'male, bull, stallion', Lat. verrēs 'boar' : Skt. vṛṣ- 'rain', etc. Walde-P. 1.248. Orig. 'bull', then kept for the castrated 'ox' in Gmc., etc. Cf. NE bullock orig. 'young bull', later 'ox' (cf. NED), likewise Lett. vērsis 'ox' (3.22). Walde-P. 1.248. Feist 66.

3.20. 'Cattle', understood here as a generic term for the bovine species, may be expressed by plural forms or by singular collectives belonging to the inherited group, Grk. βοῦς, etc. just discussed. Others have come through 'cattle' in the wider sense, mostly from 'property', several of these already discussed in 3.15. A few reflect 'living creature', 'horned', 'head'.

1. In the Romance languages there are no fully established popular and distinctive generic terms for the bovine species. It. buoi, pl. of bue 'ox', may be so used. The French peasant, according to various informants, will use le bétail (3.15), les bestiaux 'the animals' (pl. of bête, 3.11), les vaches 'the cows', etc. Sp. ganado (3.15) and Rum. vite (3.15) are also commonly used for 'cattle' in the narrower sense.

2. Ir. buar, Br. biou : Ir. bō 'cow', etc.

W. gwartheg : gwerth 'worth, value', with development through 'property' to 'cattle', as often. Loth, RC 36.159.

Br. saout, fr. Lat. soldus, solidus in its late use as the name of a gold coin, hence through 'money, property' to 'cattle' in wide sense, then in narrow sense, like NE cattle. MBr. Solt-, Soult in place-names seems to have meant a small landed property. Loth, Mots lat. 209.

3. ON naut, naut-fē (Dan. nød, Sw. nöt), OE nēat, ME nete (NE neat in neat cattle, but mostly obs.), OHG nōz, etc. : Goth. niutan, OE nēotan 'enjoy, make use of, obtain', Lith. nauda 'use, profit', Lett. nauda 'property, money'. Hence orig. 'useful property'. Walde-P. 2.325 ff. Falk-Torp 757.

Dan. kvæg, fr. MLG quek 'cattle' sb. use of quek 'living', hence orig. 'living creature, animal', then 'livestock' like ON kvikfē (3.15), now mostly 'cattle' in narrow sense. Falk-Torp 609.

Sw. boskap, in OSw. 'household, household goods, property', deriv. of bo 'house'. Hellquist 85.

OE hrīðer, ME rother, Du. rund, OHG (h)rind, MHG, NHG rind, all used in sg. for 'bovine animal, head of cattle', pl. 'cattle' (for which also coll. NHG rindvieh, Du. rundvee), prob. orig. 'horned animal' : OE horn, Lat. cornū, Grk. κέρας 'horn'. Walde-P. 1.407. NED s.v. rother.

NE cattle, see 3.15.

4. Lith. galvijas 'head of cattle', deriv. of galva 'head'.

Lett. guov(s)luops, lielluops (pl. -i in list), cpds. of luops 'domestic animal' (3.15) with guovs 'cow' or liels 'large'.

5. ChSl. *govędo (adj. govęždĭ Supr.), SCr. govędo 'bovine animal', pl. goveda 'cattle' (Russ. govjado obs., but govjadina 'beef'), etc. : Grk. βοῦς, etc. (above, p. 152). Berneker 338.

ChSl. (late) nuta, loanword fr. Gmc., ON naut, etc., above, 3. Stender-Petersen 307 ff.

Boh., Russ. skot, Pol. bydło, see 3.15.

3.21. 'Bull'. 1. Grk. ταῦρος; Lat. taurus (>It., Sp. toro, Rum. taur, OFr. tor, Fr. taureau), Osc. ταυρομ, Umbr. toru; Gall. tarvos, Ir. tarb, NIr. tarbh, W. tarw, Br. taro (Celtic forms with cons. transposition); ON þjōrr, Dan. tyr, Sw. tjur (these influenced by the group ON stjōrr, etc.) : OPruss. tauris, Lith. tauras 'wild ox', ChSl. turŭ 'wild ox'(?). Perh. IE *təu-ro- fr. *tēu- 'swell, be strong' in Skt. tāuti, tavīti 'is strong', etc. (so Walde-P. 1.711, Brugmann, Grd. 2.1.353), but more prob. to be combined with OE stēor, etc. Ernout-M. 1018. Falk-Torp 1309. Feist 454.

2. ON boli, ME bule, bole, NE bull, MLG bulle (> NHG bulle, much used in the north in place of stier; also the source of Lith. bulius, Lett. bullis), Du. bul, prob. : ON bǫllr 'ball, testicle', OHG ballo 'ball', OE beallucas 'testicles' (so NE balls in vulgar use), Grk. φαλλός 'penis', Lat. follis 'leather bag', etc. Walde-P. 2.178.

ON grað-ungr, also grað-uxi, cpds. of graðr 'entire', as in grað-hestr 'stallion', grað-hafr 'he-goat'.

ON tarfr (rare), loanword fr. Celtic, Ir. tarb, etc. (above.)

ON farri (rare), OE fearr, OHG far, farro, MHG varre, NHG farre (now dial.; Du. var 'young bull'; also Du. vaars, NHG färse 'heifer') : Grk. πόρις (Hom. πόρις, πόρταξ) 'calf, young cow', Lat. parere 'bear, beget'. Orig. 'young of an animal', variously specialized . Walde-P. 2.41. Franck-v. W. 720, 723.)

3. ChSl. (late) bykŭ, SCr. bik, etc., all the Slavic words for 'bull' : SCr. bukati 'roar', Skt. bukkati 'roars', buk-kāra- 'lion's roar', fr. an imitative bu. Walde-P. 2.112 ff. Berneker 112.

4. Skt. ukṣan-, Av. uxšan- : Goth. auhsa 'ox', etc. (above, p. 153).

Skt. ṛṣabha- and vṛṣabha-, fr. vṛṣan-, etc. 'male' (2.23).

3.22. Most of the words for 'ox' have been discussed above (pp. 152, 153). The others are:

1. Ir. dam, NIr. damh : Skt. damya- 'to be tamed', 'young bull', Grk. δαμάλης 'young ox, steer', δάμαλις 'young cow, heifer', Skt. dam-, Grk. δάμνημι, Goth. gatamjan, etc. 'tame'. Walde-P. 1.789. W. eidion, Br. ejen, OCorn. odion, etym.? Pedersen 1.370. Henry 111.

2. Lith. jautis : Lett. jūtis 'joint', Skt. go-yūti- 'yoke of cattle', yu- 'bind, yoke, harness', yuga- 'yoke', Grk. ζυγόν, Lat. iugum 'yoke', Lat. iūmentum 'draught-animal', etc., hence orig. 'yoke animal'. Walde-P. 1.201.

Lett. vērsis orig. 'bull', now 'ox' (Lith. veršis 'calf') : Skt. vṛṣan- 'male, bull, stallion', Lat. verrēs 'boar', etc. Walde-P. 1.269. Mühl.-Endz. 4.565.

3. ChSl. volŭ, etc., all the Slavic words, etym.?

3.23. The majority of the words for 'cow' represent the IE word for 'ox, cow', Grk. βοῦς, etc., with specialization to 'cow' in Gmc. and Celtic. See above, p. 152. The others are:

1. NG ἀγελάδα, through ἀγελάς, -άδος, fr. Grk. ἀγέλη 'herd'.

2. Lat. vacca (> Romance words), prob. : Skt. vaçā- 'cow' (for use cf. BR s.v., Macdowell-Keith 2.273). Walde-P. 1.214 (adversely). Ernout-M. 1068.

3. Ir. ferb, NIr. fearbh : Lat. vervex 'wether'? Walde-P. 1.270. Pokorny, Z. celt. Ph. 17.304 ff.

Ir. ag : Skt. ahī- 'cow' (rare), Av. azī- adj. 'with young' (of cows or mares), Arm. ezn 'ox'. Walde-P. 1.38.

4. Lith. karvė, ChSl. krava, etc., all the Slavic words for 'cow' (also OPruss. curvis, Pol. karw 'ox') : Lat. cervus, W. carw, OE heorot, etc. 'stag, deer' (3.75).

all orig. 'horned' : OE horn, Lat. cornū, Grk. κέρας 'horn'. Walde-P. 1.406 ff.

5. Skt. vaçā-, above, 2.

3.24. Most of the words for 'calf' are specialized from 'young of an animal', this from 'young', 'yearling', etc.

1. Grk. μόσχος : Arm. mozi 'calf', root connection? Walde-P. 2.309. Boisacq 646.

2. Lat. vitulus (dim. vitellus > It. vitello, Fr. veau, Rum. vițel), orig. 'yearling' : Grk. dial. ἔτελον, ἔταλον 'yearling', ἔτος 'year', Skt. vatsa- 'year', etc. Walde-P. 1.251. Ernout-M. 1118.

Sp. ternero, deriv. of tierno 'young', Lat. tener 'soft, tender'. REW 8645.

Sp. becerro, perh. fr. Lat. ibex 'chamois' (Korominas).

3. Ir. lāeg, lōeg, NIr. laogh, W. llo, Br. leue, prob. fr. *lāpego- : Alb. lopë 'cow'. Pedersen 2.22. Loth, RC 44.267 ff.

4. Goth. kalbō 'female calf', ON kālfr, OE cealf, etc., same word as ON kālfr 'calf of the leg', fr. *gel-bh- an extension of *gel- in Skt. gula- 'ball', Lat. galla 'gallnut', parallel to *gel-t- in Goth. kilþei 'womb', OE cild 'child', and with a similar semantic development, in this case 'swelling' to 'womb', 'fetus', 'young of an animal', 'calf'. But in part perh. blended with *gʷelbh- in Grk. δελφύς, Skt. garbha- 'womb', etc. In any case 'calf' is a specialization of 'young of an animal'. Walde-P. 1.615, 692. Feist 305 f.

5. Lith. telias, Lett. tel'š, ChSl. telę, dim. telĭcĭ, SCr. tele, Boh. tele, Pol. cielę, Russ. telenok (pl. teljata), perh. as 'born' fr. *tel- 'raise, carry' (Lat. tollere, etc.), like Goth. barn 'child' fr. *bher- 'carry'. Walde-P. 1.740, top.

Lith. veršis, OPruss. werstian : Lett. vērsis 'ox' (3.22).

6. Skt. vatsa-, above, 2.

	3.25 SHEEP	3.26 RAM	3.27 WETHER	3.28 EWE	3.29 LAMB
Grk.	*οἶς, πρόβατον*	*κριός*	*τομίᾱς*	*οἶς*	*ἀμνός, ἀρήν*
NG	*πρόβατο*	*κριάρι*	*μουνουχισμένο κριάρι*	*προβατῖνα*	*ἀρνί, ἀρνάκι*
Lat.	*ovis*	*ariēs*	*vervex*	*ovis*	*agnus*
It.	*pecora*	*montone*	*castrone*	*pecora*	*agnello*
Fr.	*mouton*	*bélier*	*mouton*	*brebis*	*agneau*
Sp.	*carnero, oveja*	*morueco*	*carnero llano*	*oveja*	*cordero*
Rum.	*oaie*	*berbec*	*berbec castrat*	*oaie*	*miel*
Ir.	*cāera, ōi, cit*	*reithe*	*molt (lon)*	*ōi, cāira; ōisc*	*uan, dīnu*
NIr.	*caora*	*reithe*	*molt*	*fōisc*	*uan*
W.	*dafad*	*hwrdd, maharen*	*mollt, gwedder*	*dafad, mamog*	*oen*
Br.	*dañvad*	*maout-taro, -tourc'h*	*maout*	*dañvadez*	*oan*
Goth.	*lamb*	....	....	....	*lamb, wiþrus*
ON	*sauðr, fær, smali* (coll.)	*hrūtr, veðr*	*geldingr*	*ær*	*lamb*
Dan.	*faar*	*vædder*	*bede*	*faar*	*lam*
Sw.	*får*	*bagge, vädur, gumse*	*gällgumse*	*tacke*	*lamm*
OE	*scēap*	*ramm, weðer*	*weðer*	*eowu*	*lamb*
ME	*schepe*	*ram, wether*	*wether*	*ewe*	*lamb*
NE	*sheep*	*ram*	*wether*	*ewe*	*lamb*
Du.	*schaap*	*ram*	*hamel*	*ooi*	*lam*
OHG	*scāf*	*ram(mo), widar*	*widar (hamal)*	*ou (ouwi)*	*lamp*
MHG	*schāf*	*wider, ram*	*hamel*	*ouwe*	*lamp*
NHG	*schaf*	*widder, schafbock*	*hammel, schöps*	*mutterschaf*	*lamm*
Lith.	*avis*	*tekis, avinas*	*avinas*	*avis*	*ėras, avinėlis*
Lett.	*aita, avs*	*auns, tekulis*	*auns*	*avs*	*jērs*
ChSl.	*ovĭca*	*ovĭnŭ*	....	*ovĭca*	*agnę, agnĭcĭ*
SCr.	*ovca*	*ovan*	*škopac ovan*	*ovca*	*jagnje*
Boh.	*ovce*	*beran*	*skopec, beran*	*ovce, bahnice*	*jehně, beranek*
Pol.	*owca*	*baran*	*skop, baran*	*owca*	*jagnię, baranek*
Russ.	*ovca*	*baran*	*baran*	*ovca*	*jagnenok*
Skt.	*avi-*	*meṣa-, uraṇa-*	*petva-*	*avi-, meṣī-, urā-*	....
Av.	*anumaya-*	*maēša-*	....	*maēšī-*	....

3.25. Generic words for 'sheep', several of them also or only 'ewe'.

1. IE **owi-*, nom. sg. **owis*. Walde-P. 1.167. Ernout-M. 717 f.

Grk. *ὄϝις* (Arg. acc. pl. *ὄϝινς*), *ὄϊς* (Hom.), *οἶς*, the reg. word in Homer and most dialects, but replaced in Att. by *πρόβατον*; Lat. *ovis* (> OFr. *oue*, Rum. *oaie*), late dim. *ovicula* (> Sp. *oveja* 'ewe' but also generic); Ir. *ōi* generic and 'ewe', Ir. *ōisc*, NIr. *fōisc* (*f* by sentence phonetics) 'ewe', (W. *ewig* 'hind'); (Goth. *awēþi* 'herd of sheep', *awistr* 'sheepfold', but *lamb* 'sheep', cf. Jn. 10.15, 16), ON *ær*, OE *eowu*, ME, NE *ewe*, Du. *ooi*, OHG *ou, ouwi*, MHG *ouwe* (NHG dial. *aue*), all 'ewe'; Lith. *avis*, Lett. *avs*, 'sheep' or 'ewe', derivs. Lith. *avinas*, Lett. *auns* 'male sheep' ('ram' or 'wether'), Lith. *avinėlis* 'lamb', Lett. *aita, aitin'a* 'sheep'; ChSl. *ovĭca*, SCr. *ovca*, etc., all the Slavic words for 'sheep' or 'ewe', deriv. ChSl. *ovĭnŭ*, SCr. *ovan* 'ram'; Skt. *avi-* 'sheep', 'ewe'.

2. Att., NG *πρόβατον*, specialized fr. 'cattle, small cattle' (3.15).

3. It. *pecora*, fr. Lat. *pecora* pl. of *pecus* 'cattle, small cattle, sheep' (3.15).

Fr. *mouton*, orig. 'wether', 3.27.

Sp. *carnero*, orig. 'wether', see 3.27.

For the distribution of Lat. *ovis, pecora, fēta, vervex* in Romance, cf. Wartburg, Abh. Preuss. Akad. 1918, no. 10.

4. Ir. *cāera*, NIr. *caora*, deriv. of Ir. *cāer* 'berry, lump, clod', hence 'sheep' from its characteristic droppings. Thurneysen, Z. celt. Ph. 13.107.

Ir. *cit, cetnait* 'sheep' or 'lamb' : Arm. *xoy* 'wether', *očxar* 'sheep', NIcel. *hjeða* 'sheep, sheepshead'. Walde-P. 1.384. Pedersen 1.120. Johannesson, KZ 67.220.

W. *dafad*, Br. *dañvad* : Ir. *dam* 'ox', Grk. *δαμάλης* 'young ox', Skt. *damya-* 'to be tamed, young bull', Skt. *dam-*, Grk. *δάμνημι* 'tame', etc., orig. 'tamed animal' specialized in different ways. Walde-P. 1.789. Pedersen 1.132.

5. Goth. *lamb*, see 3.29.

ON *sauðr* (Norw. *sau*, Sw. dial. *sö*) : Goth. *sauþs* 'sacrifice', orig. the boiled mutton offered in pagan sacrifices : ON *sjōða*, OE *sēoþan* 'boil'. Walde-P. 2.471. Falk-Torp 952. Feist 413.

ON *fær* (rare), Dan. *faar*, Sw. *får* (Norw. riksmål *får* 'mutton' vs. *sau* 'sheep') : Grk. *πόκος* 'fleece', etc. Walde-P. 2.17. Falk-Torp 199.

OE *scēap*, NE *sheep*, OHG *scāf*, etc., the regular West Gmc. word, with no generally accepted etym., but perh. as orig. 'creature' : Goth. *ga-skap-jan*, etc. 'create'. Holthausen IF 39.74. Cf. Dan., Sw. *kreatur*, NE dial. *creature, critter* for 'cattle, livestock' (3.15), and the specialization of 'cattle' to 'sheep' in It. *pecora*, Grk. *πρόβατον* (above, 2, 3).

6. Balto-Slavic words, above, 1.

7. Av. *anu-maya-*, adj. in *pasu-anumaya-* 'pecus ovillum', and as sb. the usual word for 'sheep', orig. 'bleating' : Skt. *mā-* 'bleat', etc. Barth. 128.

3.26. 'Ram'. 1. Grk. *κριός* (Byz. *κριάριον* > NG *κριάρι*), orig. 'horned' : Grk. *κέρας*, 'horn', etc. Walde-P. 1.406.

2. Lat. *ariēs* (> Rum. dial. *arete*), Umbr. *erietu* : Grk. *ἔριφος* 'kid', Ir. *heirp* 'she-goat', all prob. fr. IE **er-* in words of motion, as Grk. *ὄρνῡμι*, Skt. *ṛ-*, etc. (Walde-P. 1.135, 136 without connecting the two groups). G. S. Lane, Language 7.281 ff.

It. *montone*, orig. the same word as dial. *molton*, like Fr. *mouton* fr. Celtic (below, 3.27), but remade fr. *montare* 'mount, cover (the female)'. REW 5739.

It. also *pecoro*, new masc. to *pecora*.

Fr. *bélier*, OFr. *belin*, deriv. of Gmc. word for 'bell', as in Du. *belhamel*, NE *bellwether*. REW 1022a. Wartburg 1.318.

Sp. *morueco*, of Basque orig.(?). REW 5374.

Rum. *berbec*, fr. Lat. *vervex* 'wether' (3.27).

3. Ir. *reithe*, fr. *rethim* 'run', like Lith. *tekis* fr. *tekėti* 'run' (below, 5). G. S. Lane, Language 7.281.

W. *hwrdd*, same word as *hwrdd* 'push, thrust', used for 'ram' by semantic borrowing from NE *ram*.

W. *maharen*, MW *maharaen*, cpd. of *oen* 'lamb', first part : Lat. *mās* 'male'(?) Morris Jones 114.

Br. *maout-taro*, or *maout-tourc'h* cpds. of *maout* 'wether' (3.27) and *taro* 'bull' (3.21) or *tourc'h* 'boar'.

4. ON *hrūtr*, orig. 'horned' : Grk. *κέρας* 'horn', etc. Walde-P. 1.407.

On *veðr*, Dan. *vædder*, Sw. *vädur*, OE *weðer* (also 'wether'), OHG *widar* (also 'wether'), NHG *widder* : Goth. *wiþrus* 'lamb', orig. 'yearling', like Lat. *vitulus* 'calf', etc. (3.24) : Grk. *ἔτος* 'year', etc. Walde-P. 1.251. Shift from 'lamb' to the grown male, either 'ram' or 'wether'.

Sw. *bagge* : ON *bǫggr*, ME *bagge* 'bag'. Orig. applied to various fat, clumsy animals. Hellquist 46.

Sw. *gumse*, formed with *-se* fr. stem of older *gummarlamb* 'male lamb', etc., but further history dub. Hellquist 312 f.

OE *ramm*, ME, NE, Du., OHG, MHG *ram*, prob. : ON *ramr* 'strong', from the ram's strength in butting (rather than its strong smell). Walde-P. 2.371. Falk-Torp 874.

5. Lith. *tekis*, fr. *tekėti* 'run'. Cf. Lett. *tekulis* also used for 'ram' or 'boar'.

Boh. *beran*, Pol., Russ. *baran* 'male sheep' ('ram', or 'wether') : Grk. *βάριχοι· ἄρνες, βάριον· πρόβατον* (Hesych.), Alb. *berr* 'wether, livestock', ultimate source dub. Berneker 43.

6. Skt. *meṣa-*, Av. *maēša-* (alone or with *varšni-* 'male') 'ram', Skt. *meṣī-*, Av. *maēšī-* 'ewe', NPers. *mīš* 'sheep' : ChSl. *měchŭ* 'bag made of skin', etc., orig. 'sheepskin' or 'skin'(?), root connection dub. Walde-P. 2.303. Berneker 2.246.

Skt. *uraṇa-*, with *urā-* 'ewe' : Lat. *vervex* 'wether' (3.27), Grk. *ἀρήν* 'lamb', etc. (3.29).

3.27. 'Wether'. The castration of male sheep for fattening is an old and almost universal practice, and the 'wether' (understood here in the technical sense of NE *wether* 'castrated sheep') is the grown sheep par excellence. Hence the generic word for 'sheep', where it is not a distinctively feminine form, may be commonly applied to the 'wether', even though distinctive terms for the latter exist. Some of these are unfamiliar to the layman (as NE *wether* except in *bellwether*). Conversely some words that were originally specific for 'wether' have become generic (as Fr. *mouton*) or through generic use have acquired a new specialization (as Fr. *brebis* 'ewe', fr. Lat. *vervex* 'wether').

In some languages, however, 'wether' is expressed by the same word as that for 'ram', that is, the same word was used for 'male sheep' whether 'ram' or 'wether' (as OE *weðer*, Russ. *baran*, etc.).

1. In ancient Greek there is no quotable specific word. Covered by *ὄϊς ὁ*, *ὄϊς ἄρσην* in Homer, in Att. by *τομίᾱς* 'castrated animal' (3.14) or specifically *τῶν προβάτων τομίᾱς* (cf. *βοῶν τομίαι*, Aristot. HA 575[b]).

NG *μουνουχισμένο κριάρι* 'castrated ram', with pple. of *μουνουχίζω* 'castrate' (3.14).

2. Lat. *vervex* (specific meaning clear from Varro, LL 5.98, *quoniam si cui ovi mari testiculi deempti vervex declinatum*) : Skt. *urā-* 'ewe', Grk. *ἀρήν* 'lamb', *ἔριον* 'wool', etc. (3.29) going back to a word for 'wool' or the wool-bearing 'sheep', with various specializations. Walde-P. 1.268 ff.

Late Lat. *vervex, berbex* was used generically for 'sheep' (examples in Marc. Emp., 4th cent. A.D., etc.), in Gaul also specialized to 'ewe' (examples from about 800 A.D.). Hence Fr. *brebis* 'ewe' (but generic *berger* 'shepherd' fr. **berbicārius*; so Rum. *berbecar*); Rum. *berbec* 'ram', *berbec castrat* 'wether' (or *berbec batut*, with pple. of *bāte* 'beat', here 'castrate'), but generic in *carne de berbice* 'mutton'; meaning 'wether' retained in some Rum. and Rhaet. dialects. REW 9270. Gamillscheg 99. Wartburg, op. cit., p. 28 ff.

It. *castrone* (MLat. *castronus*, MHG *kastrūn*), deriv. of Lat. *castrāre* 'castrate' (3.14).

Fr. *mouton*, orig. 'wether' and still covering it, though felt as generic, fr. a Gallic form (cf. MLat. *multo, -onis* partly 'wether' but also generic 'sheep'; cf. Wartburg op. cit.) : Ir. *molt*, etc. 'wether' (below, 3). REW 5739.

Sp. *carnero* now generic, but orig. 'wether' (now *carnero llano* with *llano* 'plain'), as the fatted sheep, deriv. of *carne* 'flesh'. REW 1706.

3. Ir. *molt*, W. *mollt*, Br. *maout*, a general Celtic word for 'wether' and prob. fr. **mel-* 'grind, crush' (Ir. *melim*, Lat. *molere*, etc.), here in the sense of 'castrate' (cf. 3.19). Stokes 212. (Doubted in Walde-P. 2.287, where the meaning 'wether' is wrongly questioned.)

Ir. *lon* (rare) : Skt. *lūna-* pass. pple. of *lu-* 'cut'. Stokes 258. Walde-P. 2.407.

W. *gwedder*, fr. NE *wether*.

4. ON *geldingr*, fr. *gelda* 'castrate' (3.14).

Dan. *bede*, fr. *bede* 'castrate' beside *bøde* 'spay', fr. MLG *bōten* 'heal, castrate' (3.14). Falk-Torp 67.

Sw. *gällgumse*, cpd. of *gäll-* fr. *gälla* 'castrate' (3.14) and *gumse* 'ram' (3.26).

OE *wether* (also 'ram'), etc., see 3.26).

OHG *hamal* (late in this sense), MHG, Du. *hamel*, NHG *hammel*, fr. OHG *hamal* 'maimed', deriv. of *ham* 'maimed' : Goth. *hamfs* 'maimed', ON *hamla*, OE *hamelian* 'maim' (NE *hamble* obs. or dial.). Falk-Torp 377. Weigand-H. 1.803.

NHG *schöps*, fr. Boh. *skopec*, below, 6. Weigand-H. 2.780.

5. Lith. *avinas*, Lett. *auns* 'male sheep' either 'ram' or 'wether', deriv. of *avs* 'sheep' (3.25).

6. SCr. *škopac*, Boh. *skopec*, Pol. *skop* (ChSl. *skopĭcĭ* 'eunuch'), fr. the verb for 'castrate', ChSl. *skopiti*, etc. (3.14).

SCr. *ovan* (3.25) is used for 'ram' and 'wether', likewise Boh. *beran*, Pol., Russ. *baran* (3.26).

7. Skt. *petva-* (cf. Zimmer, Altind. Leben 229) : *pī-* 'swell', *pīvan-* 'fat', etc., hence 'wether' as the 'fatted' sheep. Uhlenbeck s.v.

3.28. Most of the words for 'ewe' reflect the inherited generic word, IE **owi-* (3.25), completely specialized to 'ewe' in Gmc., elsewhere generic and 'ewe', or belong with other words already discussed in 3.25–3.27. The few remaining are:

1. W. *mamog*, orig. 'pregnant sheep', same word as *mamog* 'womb', deriv. of *mam* 'mother' (*y fam* 'the womb').

2. Sw. *tacke*, fr. the calling cry. Hellquist 1156.

3. Boh. *bahnice*, fr. *bahniti se* 'produce lambs', this fr. **ob-agniti* : ChSl. *agnę*, Boh. *jehne*, etc. 'lamb' (3.29). Berneker 24.

4. Lat. *fēta* 'breeding female' (*fēta ovis* 'ewe', etc.) is specialized to 'ewe' in various Romance dialects. REW 3269. Wartburg op. cit. 23 ff.

3.29. 'Lamb'. 1. IE **ag^w(h)no-*. Walde-P. 1.39. Ernout-M. 24. Walde-H. 1.23.

Grk. *ἀμνός*; Lat. *agnus*, dim. *agnellus* (> It. *agnello*, Fr. *agneau*, Rum. *miel;* REW 284); Ir. *uan*, W. *oen*, Br. *oan;* Gmc. only in verb, OE *ēanian* 'bring forth lambs'; ChSl. *agnę, agnĭcĭ*, etc., the general Slavic word (Berneker 24).

2. Grk. *ἀρήν* (Cret. *ϝαρήν*), gen. *ἀρνός*, dim. *ἀρνίον*, NG *ἀρνί, ἀρνάκι* : Skt. *urā-* 'ewe', *uraṇa-* 'ram', Lat. *vervex* 'wether', Grk. *ἔριον* 'wool', Aeol. *ἔπερος* lit. 'having wool on' used for 'male sheep' (*ἔπεροι καὶ ἀρνηάδες* 'male sheep and ewes'), all going back to a word for 'wool' or the wool-bearing animal. Walde-P. 1.268 ff.

3. Sp. *cordero*, deriv. of Lat. *c(h)ordus* 'late-born'. Cf. Varro, RR 2.1.29, *dicuntur agni chordi qui post tempum nascuntur*. So (Diez, REW 1883 in first ed.) much better than deriv. fr. *chorda*, as 'led on a rope' (Gouchat, REW 1881 in new ed.). For Lat. *cordus*, cf. Walde-H. 1.273.

4. Ir. *dīnu*, fr. *dīnim* 'suck' : Grk. *θῆσθαι* 'suck', etc. Pedersen 1.183. Walde-P. 1.830.

5. Goth., ON, OE *lamb*, etc., the general Gmc. word, perh. : Grk. *ἔλαφος* 'stag' and other animal names, but root

connection and primary sense dub. Walde-P. 1.154. Feist 321.

Goth. *wiþrus*, see 3.26, OE *weðer*, etc.

6. Lith. *ėras*, Lett. *jērs*, orig. 'yearling', like SCr. *jare* 'kid', etc. : Goth. *jēr* 'year', etc. Walde-P. 1.135 (to be added 1.105).

ChSl. *agnę*, etc., above, 1.

Boh. *beranek*, Pol. *baranek*, dim. of *beran*, *baran* 'male sheep' (3.26).

7. In Sanskrit and Avestan no special words are quotable for 'lamb', which was presumably expressed as 'young sheep'.

	3.31 SWINE	3.32 BOAR	3.33 BARROW	3.34 SOW	3.35 PIG
Grk.	ὗς, χοῖρος	κάπρος	ὗς ὁ, τομίᾱς	ὗς ἡ	χοιρίδιον, δέλφαξ
NG	γουρούνι, χοῖρος	κάπρος, καπρί	μουνουχισμένο, γουρούνι	γουρούνα, σκρόφα	γουρουνάκι, γουρουνόπουλο, χοιρίδιον
Lat.	sūs, porcus	verrēs	maiālis	sūs, scrofa, porca	porcus, porcellus
It.	porco	verre	maiale	scrofa, troia	porcello
Fr.	cochon, porc, pourceau	verrat	porc (châtré)	truie	cochon (de lait), porcelet
Sp.	puerco, cerdo, marrano	verraco	puerco (castrado)	puerca, marrana	cochinillo
Rum.	porc	vier	porc (castrat)	scroafă, purcea	purcel
Ir.	mucc, orc	(muc-)cullach	. . . .	mucc, crāin	banb, orcān
NIr.	muc, orc	collach	(muc choillte)	crāin	banbh
W.	moch	baedd, twrch	(mochyn dis-baidd)	hwch	porchell
Br.	moc'h, houc'h	tourc'h	(penmoc'h spaz)	gwiz	porc'hell
Goth.	swein	. . . .	. . . .	. . . .	. . . .
ON	svīn	gǫltr	bǫrgr	sȳr	grīss
Dan.	svin	orne	galt	so	gris
Sw.	svin	fargalt	galt	sugga, so	gris
OE	swīn	bār	bearg	sū, sugu	fearh
ME	swine, hogge	bore	barowe, hogge	sow	pigge
NE	(swine), hog, pig	boar	barrow	sow	pig
Du.	zwijn	beer	barg	zeug	varken, big
OHG	swīn	bēr	barug (barh)	sū	farah, farhelī(n)
MHG	swīn	eber, bēr	barc (barch)	sū	varch, värchel(in)
NHG	schwein	eber (bär)	barch (borg, etc.)	sau	ferkel
Lith.	kiaulė	kuilys	paršas	kiaulė	paršelis
Lett.	cūka	kuilis	vepris	cūka	sivēns
ChSl.	svinija	. . . .	. . . .	svinija	prasę
SCr.	svinja, krme	nerast	brav	krmača, svinja	prase
Boh.	svině, prase	kanec	vepř	svině	sele
Pol.	świnia	kiernoz	wieprz	świnia	prosię
Russ.	svin'ja	kaban	borov	svin'ja	porosenok
Skt.	sūkara-	varāha-	. . . .	sūkarī-	. . . .
Av.	hū-	varāza-	. . . .	. . . .	. . . .

3.31–3.35. Note that in the headings and translations either *swine* or *hog*, is used as the generic term, *barrow* for the castrated, and *pig* for the young animal, that is, in accordance with its original (and still mainly U.S.) use, in contrast to the now current British generic use.

3.31. Here are discussed the generic words for 'swine' and also groups of cognates which include several of the words listed under the other headings. Swine were domesticated in Europe from the earliest times, but not in ancient India and Iran (the Skt. and Av. words listed

refer to the wild species). Schrader, Reallex. 2.359 ff.

1. IE **sū-*, prob. of imitative orig. Walde-P. 2.512 f. Ernout-M. 100 f. Feist 465. Kretschmer, Glotta 3.132 f.

Grk. ὗς and σῦς (sentence-doublets, not to be separated as in Walde-P.); Lat. *sūs*, Umbr. *sif* 'sues'; W. *hwch* 'sow' (formerly generic), Br. *houc'h* 'hog'; ON *sȳr*, OE *sū*, etc., all the Gmc. words for 'sow'; and fr. **swīno-* (orig. adj. like Lat. *suīnus*) the generic words, Goth. *swein*, OE *swīn*, etc.; Lett. *suvēns*, *sivēns* 'pig'; ChSl. *svinija*, etc., the Slavic words, fr. a fem. deriv. of **swīno-*; Skt. *sūkara-* (fem. *sūkarī-* 'sow'), Av. *hū-*; Alb. *thí*; Toch. B. *suwo*.

2. IE **porḱo-*. Walde-P. 2.78. Ernout-M. 780 f. REW 6660, 6666.

Lat. *porcus* (in Varro, RR the regular word for 'pig', as 2.1.20 with co-ordinate *agni, haedi, porci;* but also generic as 2.4.20 *porcorum gregem*), whence It. *porco*, Fr., Rum. *porc*, Sp. *puerco;* Lat. *porca* 'sow' (> It. *porca*, Sp. *puerca*), Umbr. *porca* 'porcas'; Lat. dim. *porculus*, *porcellus* 'pig' (> It. *porcello*, Rum. *purcel*, W. *porchell*, Br. *porc'hell* 'pig'; but Fr. *pourceau* = *porc;* new dim. *porcelet* still dial. for 'pig', Gamillscheg 713), with fem. *porcella* (> Rum. *purcea* 'female pig' and 'sow'); Ir. *orc* 'hog', *orcān* 'pig'; OE *fearh* (ME, NE *farrow* 'litter of pigs,' whence vb. *farrow* still used by farmers), Du. *varken*, OHG *far(a)h*, *farhelī(n)*, NHG *ferkel* 'pig'; Lith. *paršas* 'barrow', dim. *paršelis*, *paršiukas* 'pig'; SCr., Boh. *prase*, Pol. *prosię*, Russ. *porosenok*, all 'pig' (Boh. *prase* also generic).

3. Grk. χοῖρος sometimes 'pig' but mostly generic 'swine' (so Hom. once and later; reg. in NT where ὗς does not occur; lit. NG), dim. χοιρίδιον 'pig', etym. dub. Walde-P. 610. Boisacq 1065.

NG γουρούνι (the usual pop. word), with fem. γουρούνα 'sow', dim. γουρουνάκι or γουρ(ου)νόπουλο 'pig' : γρωνάδες· σύες θήλειαι (Hesych.), formed fr. the grunting sound γρῦ, seen also in γρύζω, Lat. *grunnīre*, NE *grunt*, etc. Hatzidakis, Μεσ. 1.105, 2.294.

4. Fr. *cochon* 'hog', Sp. *cochino* 'hog', *cochina* 'sow', *cochinillo* 'pig', in OFr. 'pig', dial. forms 'wood louse', prob. connected with late Lat. *cutiones* 'wood lice', with the frequently observed relation between the names of such animals and words for 'pig', 'sow', etc., as in Lat. *porcelliō* 'wood louse', NE *sow*, *sow bug*, *hog louse*, but ultimate source dub. (fr. a calling cry?). Gamillscheg 233. REW 4745. Bloch 1.157.

Sp. *cerdo* 'hog', prob. of Basque orig. REW 9696 f.

Sp. *marrano* 'hog', *marrana* 'sow', fr. Arab. *muharrama* 'forbidden' (a form of the same word that is the source of NE *harem*), applied to the 'forbidden' pork, later to the animal.

5. Ir. *muc(c)*, W. *moch* (sg. *mochyn*) Br. *moc'h* (sg. *pen-moc'h*), etym.? Stokes 219. Walde-P. 2.253.

6. ME *hogge* used generically, but also defined in some passages as the castrated male (*an Hogge, maialis, est enim porcus carens testiculis*), NE *hog* generic but in dial. applied also to young sheep, etc., orig. dub. NED s.v. *hog*. Björkman, IF 30.262.

In NE both *hog* and *pig* (3.35) are used generically in the plural in place of *swine*, which (though sometimes appearing in U.S. livestock reports beside the more usual *hogs*) has disappeared from common use among farmers. The former is the usual U.S. word (but in New England *pig* is also frequently generic, cf. Linguistic Atlas, Map 205), while in British usage *pig* is now definitely the common generic term (cf. NED s.v.

pig, sb.[1] 2; and the heading *pig* as generic in the Encyclopaedia Britannica).

7. Lith. *kiaulė*, Lett. *cūka* 'swine, sow', Lith. *kuilys*, Lett. *kuilis* 'boar', relations and orig. dub. Walde-P. 1.467. Mühl.-Endz. 1.398.

8. SCr. *krme* 'swine' (with *krmača* 'sow'), deriv. of *krma* 'fodder' (5.12), *krmiti* 'feed animals', hence orig. the animal fattened for slaughter, but completely specialized to 'swine'. Berneker 668.

3.32. 'Boar'. Words that are used only of the 'wild boar' are not included (except the Sanskrit and Avestan) unless they belong with others which are used for the domestic boar. Thus Lat. *aper* is considered, but not Fr. *sanglier*, etc.

1. IE **epero-*(?). Walde-P. 1.121. Ernout-M. 59. Walde-H. 1.56.

Lat. *aper* (only 'wild boar', but the Umbr. forms refer to domestic boars offered as sacrifice, e.g. *abrof trif* 'three boars' beside *porca trif* 'three sows'); OE *eofor* 'wild boar', OHG *ebur* ('wild boar'), MHG, NHG *eber;* ChSl. (late) *veprĭ*, SCr. *vepar*, Russ. *vepr'* 'wild boar'; Lett. *vepris*, Boh. *vepř*, Pol. *wieprz* 'barrow'.

2. Grk. κάπρος : Lat. *caper*, ON *hafr* 'he-goat', etc., root connection dub. Walde-P. 1.347. Walde-H. 1.157.

3. Lat. *verrēs* (> Romance words) : Skt. *vṛṣan-* 'male' (2.23), Lett. *vērsis* 'ox', etc., with various special applications of 'male'. Walde-P. 1.269. Erout-M. 1090 f. REW 9239.

4. Ir. *(muc-)cullach*, NIr. *collach* (used also for 'stallion', 'he-ass', etc., but esp. 'boar'), like Ir. *(ech-)cullach*, Br. *marc'h kalloc'h* 'stallion' (3.42), lit. 'with testicles, uncastrated' (like Grk. ἔνορχος fr. ὄρχις 'testicle'), deriv. of word for testicle, W. *caill*, Br. *kell* (4.49). Stokes 72. Henry 50.

Ir. *torc* 'wild boar', but W. *twrch*, Br. *tourc'h* 'domestic boar', prob. a blend of *orc* 'hog' (3.31) with some other word, perh. **trogos* : late Lat. *troia* 'sow' (3.34). Walde-P. 2.642. Vendryes, RC 35.220.

W. *baedd*, Corn. *baedh* (OCorn. *bahet*, Pedersen 1.16), etym.?

5. ON *gǫltr*, Dan., Sw., ME, NE (dial.) *galt* 'male swine' ('boar' or 'barrow'), Sw. *fargalt* 'boar' (*far-* : OE *fearh* 'pig', Lat. *porcus* 'swine', etc., 3.31) with fem. OE *gilte*, NE *gilt*, OHG *galza* 'young sow', NHG *gelze* 'spayed sow', etym. dub., but perh. : ON *gelda* 'castrate' (3.14), with shift from the castrated animal no more difficult to credit than that seen in Lat. *vervex* 'wether' > 'sheep' > 'ewe' (3.27). Walde-P. 1.628 f. Falk-Torp 298. Hellquist 269. NED s.v. *gilt*, sb.[2].

Dan. *orne* 'boar', Sw. dial. *orne* 'boar' or 'barrow' : Lat. *verrēs* 'boar', etc. (above, 3) Falk-Torp 867. Hellquist 737.

OE *bār*, ME *bore*, NE *boar*, Du. *beer*, OHG, MHG *bēr*, NHG dial. *bār*, etym.?

6. Lith. *kuilys*, Lett. *kuilis* : Lith. *kiaulė* 'swine' (3.31).

7. SCr. *nerast*, cpd. of neg. *ne* and *rasti* 'grow', lit. 'one that does not grow', applied to a tree that will not grow and to the 'boar' as the swine that will not fatten, in contrast to the castrated hog. Rječnik Akad. 8.46.

Boh. *kanec*, fr. Hung. *kan* 'male animal'. Berneker 479.

Pol. *kiernoz* = ORuss., Ukr. *knoroz* : ChSl. *krŭnŭ* 'mutilated', perh. compounded with a word for testicle cognate with Grk. ὄρχις, the whole meaning orig. 'castrated', with shift to 'boar'. Berneker 663 f. Brückner 229.

Russ. *kaban*, fr. Turk. Berneker 464. Lokotsch 975.

8. Skt. *varāha-*, Av. *varāza-* (but both only 'wild boar') etym.?

3.33. Special terms for the 'barrow' are often lacking or unfamiliar, the generic terms being commonly used in reference to the swine that is neither 'boar' nor 'sow'; or with added 'castrated' (cf. 3.14), as NE *castrated hog*, Fr. *porc châtré*, NHG *verschnittenes schwein*, NG μουνουχισμένο γουρουνι, etc.

1. Grk. τομίᾱς 'castrated animal' (3.14) was the technical term, just as for 'wether' (3.27), but usually simply ὗς or σῦς with ὁ or ἄρσην (as in Hom., Od. 14, 13 ff., where the 360 hogs used for eating, contrasted with the 600 sows, were, of course, castrated males).

NG μουνουχόχοιρος, cpd. of χοῖρος 'hog' with μουνοῦχος 'castrated' (3.19).

2. Lat. *maiālis* (Varro, RR 2.4.21 *castrantur verres—quo facto nomen mutant atque e verribus dicuntur maiales*), hence It *maiale*, perh fr. *Maia* (or only pop. etym.?), in any case prob. influenced by *maior* 'larger', with reference to the greater growth of the castrated animal. Walde-H. 2.13. Ernout-M. 582.

In Fr., Sp., Rum. only the generic words in common use, though the words for 'castrated' may be added.

3. In Celtic, only the generic words or with the addition of the words for castrated (3.14).

4. ON *bǫrgr*, OE *bearg*, ME *baru*, *barowe*, NE *barrow*, Du. *barg*, OHG *barug*, *barh*, NHG *barch* (*borch*, *barg*, *borg*), prob. fr. the root of ON *berja* 'strike', Lat. *ferīre* 'strike, cut', etc., here in the sense of 'castrate'. Walde-P. 2.160.

Dan., Sw. *galt* 'male swine', both also used alone for 'barrow', see 3.32.

5. Lith. *paršas* : Lat. *porcus*, etc. (3.31).

Lett. *vepris*, Boh. *vepř*, Pol. *wieprz* : ChSl. *veprĭ*, Lat. *aper* 'wild boar', etc. (3.31).

6. SCr. *brav* (also 'sheep'), Russ. *borov*, etc., with various applications in Slavic (Boh. *brav* 'small cattle, sheep, swine') prob. from the root of ChSl. *brati* 'fight', orig. 'strike', Lat. *ferīre* 'strike, cut', etc., here as 'castrate'. Cf. ON *bǫrgr*, etc. (above, 4). Walde-P. 2.161. Berneker 75.

7. There are naturally no Skt. or Av. words for the castrated hog, since swine were not domesticated in India or Iran.

3.34. Most of the words for 'sow' reflect the inherited generic word, IE **sū-* (3.31), in this form completely specialized to 'sow' in Gmc., or belong to other groups discussed in 3.31 or 3.32. The others are:

1. Lat. *scrōfa* (> It. *scrofa*, Rum. *scroafă*, NG σκρόφα), loanword fr. an Italic dialect (hence the medial *f*), and perh. fr. a root **skerb(h)-* in OE *sceorpan* 'scratch', Lett. *skrabt* 'scratch, hollow out', Lat. *scrobis* 'ditch', etc. (Walde-P. 2.582, without inclusion of *scrōfa*), hence 'sow' as 'rooter'.

2. It. *troia*, Fr. *truie*, fr. late Lat. *troia*, this prob. fr. **trogyā-* : ON *þrekkr*, MHG *drec* 'filth', etc. Walde-P. 2.642.

3. Ir. *crāin*, fr. **krākni-* : Lat. *crōcīre* 'croak', Lith. *krokti* 'grunt', etc., hence orig. 'grunter'. Walde-P. 1.414.

4. Br. *gwiz*, OBr. *gues*, Corn. *guis* : Lat. *vitulus* 'calf', Skt. *vatsa-* 'calf, yearling', etc., all orig. 'yearling'. Walde-P. 1.251. Stokes 268.

3.35. 'Pig' is understood here as the young animal. Only the most general terms are included, with omission of others like NE *shote*, 'pig after it is weaned' (common in U.S.; cf. Linguistic Atlas of New England, Map 205).

Most of the words listed have been included in the discussion of 3.31. The few others are:

Grk. δέλφαξ : δελφύς, Skt. garbha- 'womb', etc., with shift from 'womb' through 'fetus' to 'young of an animal', as often (cf. NE calf, etc., 3.24), then specialization to 'pig'.

Ir. banb, NIr. banbh, W. banw (obs.) 'pig', OCorn. baneu 'sus', Br. bano 'sow with litter', etym.? Pedersen 1.47. Loewenthal, Wört. u. Sach. 9.188.

ON griss (> Scotch grice), Dan., Sw. gris, etym. dub., perh. : OHG gris 'gray', etc. Walde-P. 1.602 f. Falk-

Torp 348, 1473. Hellquist 300 (imitative orig.).

ME pigge (prob. OE *picga, like docga, frocga), NE pig, MLG bigge, Du. big, prob. : Dan. pig, Sw. pigg 'spike', etc. beside OE pīc 'pick, pike', etc. (cf. Falk-Torp. 823), and orig. an epithet referring to the shape. Björkman, IF 30.266 f. NED s.v. pig. Franck-v. W. 64.

Boh. sele, orig. 'suckling', deriv. of ssáti 'suck'.

	3.36 GOAT (Generic or feminine)	3.37 HE-GOAT	3.38 KID
Grk.	αἴξ (χίμαιρα)	τράγος	ἔριφος
NG	γίδι, fem. γίδα	τράγος, τραγί	κατσίκι
Lat.	capra	hircus, caper	haedus
It.	capra	becco, capro	capretto
Fr.	chèvre, bique	bouc	chevreau, biquet
Sp.	cabra, chiva	cabrón	cabrito
Rum.	capră	ţap	caprioară
Ir.	gabor	bocc	menn(ān)
NIr.	gabhar	boc	mionnān
W.	gafr	bwch	myn
Br.	gaor	bouc'h	gaorig
Goth.	gaits	....	....
ON	geit	hafr (bukkr)	kið
Dan.	ged	buk	kid
Sw.	get	bock	kid
OE	gāt	bucca, hæfor	ticcen, hēcen
ME	gote	bucke	kide
NE	goat	he-goat	kid
Du.	geit	bok	geitje
OHG	geiz, ziga	boc	zickī(n), kizzī(n)
MHG	geiz, zige	bock	zickelīn
NHG	ziege, geiss	bock	zicklein
Lith.	ožka	ožys	oželis, ožkutis
Lett.	kaza	āzis	kazlens
ChSl.	koza	kozĭlŭ	kozĭlę
SCr.	koza	jarac	jare, kozlić
Boh.	koza	kozel	kůzle
Pol.	koza	kozioł	koźlę
Russ.	koza	kozel	kozlenok
Skt.	aja-; fem. ajā-	aja-, chāga-	....
Av.	....	būza-	....

3.36. 'Goat'. The generic and feminine words are taken together, since the latter are generally those used in generic sense.

Meillet, Rev. ét. sl. 5.8 f., brings together under a series of alternating forms groups that are here given separately, namely αἴξ etc. (1), OHG ziga etc. (4), Lith. ožys, Skt. aja- (7), and ChSl. koza (6).

1. Grk. αἴξ (mostly ἡ, rarely also ὁ) : Arm. aic 'goat', Av. izaēna- 'of (goat's) skin', perh : Skt. ejati 'stirs, moves', etc. Walde-P. 1.8 f., 11.

Hence dim. αἰγίδιον 'kid', whence NG γίδι generic for 'goat' (τὰ γίδια), with new fem. γίδα 'she-goat'.

Grk. χίμαρος (ὁ, also ἡ), χίμαιρα, orig. 'yearling' : Skt. himā- 'winter', Lat. bīmus (*bi-himos) 'two years old', etc. Walde-P. 1.547.

2. Lat. capra (> It., Sp. capra, Fr. chèvre, Rum. capră), fem. to caper 'he-goat' (3.37).

Fr. bique, prob. fr. a calling cry REW 1099. Wartburg 1.358 ff.

Sp. chiva, masc. chivo, source?

3. Ir. gabor, NIr. gabhar, W. gafr, Br. gaor, gavr, perh. with unexplained init. variation : Lat. caper, etc. So Thurneysen, Gram. 139, Z. celt. Ph. 13.103 ff. Otherwise Walde-P. 1.533, 547.

4. Goth. gaits, ON geit, OE gāt, etc., the general Gmc. word : Lat. haedus 'kid', perh. Lith. žaidžiu, žaisti 'play' as orig. 'jump, gambol'. Walde-P. 1.527. Feist 186.

OHG ziga, MHG zige, NHG ziege with dim. OE ticcen, OHG zickīn), MHG zickelīn, NHG zicklein, perh. : Grk. δίζα· αἴξ. Λάκωνες (Hesych.), Arm. tik 'leather bag', root connection? Walde-P. 1.814.

5. Lith. ožka, new fem. fr. ožys 'he-goat' : Skt. aja-, etc. (below, 7).

6. ChSl. koza, etc., the general Slavic word, with Lett. kaza fr. Russ., perh. : OE hēcen, MLG hōken 'kid', root connection? Walde-P. 1.336. Berneker 595.

7. Skt. aja-, fem. ajā- : Lith. ožys, Lett. āzis, perh., through notion of rapid motion, fr. root of Skt. aj-, Grk. ἄγω, etc. 'drive'. Walde-P. 1.38.

3.37. 'He-goat'. 1. Grk. τράγος (hence fr. dim. form, NG τραγί) : τρώγω, aor. ἔτραγον 'nibble'. Walde-P. 1.732. Boisacq 978.

2. Lat. caper : ON hafr, OE hæfor 'he-goat', Grk. κάπρος 'boar', root connection dub. Walde-P. 1.347. Ernout-M. 146 f. Walde-H. 1.157. It. capro, Sp. cabrón, formed anew fr. fem. capra, cabra.

Lat. hircus (so, not caper, in Varro, RR, as 2.3.10 ad denas capras singulos parent hircos, and in general much more common than caper) perh. : Lat. hirtus, hirsūtus 'shaggy', etc. Walde-P. 1.610. Ernout-M. 454. Walde-H. 1.649 f.

Lat. bucca occurs as 'he-goat' in the description of the game "buck, buck", Petron. 64. Cf. Ullman, Cl. Ph. 38.94 ff. But it seems more likely to be a loanword adopted in this game than an inherited cognate of OE, Ir. bocc, OE buoca, etc. (below, 3.4).

It. becco, prob. of imitative orig. REW 1020a.

Fr. bouc, loanword fr. Gmc. or Celtic (below, 3, 4). REW 1378. Wartburg 1.590.

Rum. ţap : Alb. cjap and a widespread group of pop. or dial. terms for 'he-goat', based on a calling cry. Cf. esp. CGL 5.503.27 hyrcus caper zappu dicitur. REW 9599. Rohlfs, Z. rom. Ph. 45.664 f. Walde-H. 1.157.

3. Ir. bocc, W. bwch, Br. bouc'h, loanword fr. (or cognate with?) the Gmc. group (below, 4). Walde-P. 2.189.

4. ON bukkr, OE bucca, OHG boc,

NHG bock, etc., the most general Gmc. word (but NE buck no longer so used, now mostly for 'male deer') : Av. būza- 'he-goat', NPers. buz 'goat', root connection dub., perh. of imitative orig. Walde-P. 2.189. Rohlfs, Z. rom. Ph. 45.671.

5. Lith. ožys, Lett. āzis : Skt. aja- (3.36).

6. ChSl. kozĭlŭ, deriv. of fem. koza (3.36). Berneker 595.

SCr. jarac, deriv. of jare 'kid' (3.38).
7. Skt. aja-, see 3.36.

Skt. chāga- (fem. chāgā- rare), etym.? Walde-P. 1.336.

Av. būza- : OE bucca, etc., above, 4.

3.38. 'Kid' is often expressed by diminutive forms of words for 'goat'. So the Romance; Br. gaorig; OE ticcen, OHG zickī(n), NHG zicklein (also bocklein), Du. geitje; and the Balto-Slavic words.

1. Grk. ἔριφος : Lat. ariēs 'ram', etc. (3.26).

NG κατσίκι (with fem. κατσίκα), dim. fr. Alb. kats 'goat', ultimate source dub., perh. fr. a calling cry. G. Meyer, Alb. Etym. Wtb. 185.

2. Lat. haedus : Goth. gaits, etc. (3.36).

3. Ir. menn(ān), NIr. mionnān, W. myn, Br. menn (obs.), etym.? Taken as 'suckling' (Stokes 311, rejected by Walde-P. 2.232); or perh. : Ir. menb 'small' (Macbain with query) but all dub.

4. ON kið, Dan., Sw. kid, ME kide (fr. ON), NE kid, OHG kizzi(n), NHG kitze, kitzlein, prob. fr. a calling cry. Walde-P. 1.527 ff. Falk-Torp 506.

5. SCr. jare, see 3.36, ChSl. koza.

5. SCr. jare, orig. 'yearling' : Russ. ChSl. jarŭ 'spring', Goth. jēr 'year', etc. Walde-P. 1.105, 135. Berneker 446 ff.

	3.41 HORSE (Generic)	3.42 STALLION	3.43 GELDING	3.44 MARE	3.45 FOAL, COLT
Grk.	ἵππος	ἵππος ὁ, ὀχεῖον	ἵππος ἐκτεμνό-μενος	ἵππος ἡ	πῶλος
NG	ἄλογο	βαρβᾶτο ἄλογο, ἄτι	ἄλογο μουνουχισμένο	φοράδα	πουλάρι
Lat.	equus	(equus) admissā-rius	cantērius	equa	pullus (eculus)
It.	cavallo	stallone	cavallo castrato	cavalla	puledro
Fr.	cheval	étalon	hongre	jument	poulain
Sp.	caballo	caballo padre	caballo castrado	yegua	potro
Rum.	cal	armăsar	jugan	iapă	mînz
Ir.	ech, marc (capall)	(ech-)cullach	gerrán	lāir	serrach
NIr.	capall, marc	stail	gillīn, gearrān	lāir	searrach
W.	march, ceffyl	march, ystalwyn	adfarch	caseg	ebol
Br.	marc'h	marc'h kalloc'h	(marc'h) spaz	kazeg	ebeul
Goth.	....	....	....	....	fula
ON	hross, hestr (marr, jōr)	(stōð-)hestr, stōð-hross	geldhestr	merr (hross)	foli, fyl
Dan.	hest	hingst	vallak	hoppe	føl
Sw.	häst	hingst	vallack	märr, sto	föl, fåle
OE	hors, mearh, eoh	stēda	hengest	mere (myre)	fola, colt
ME	hors	stalon	geldyng	mere	fole, colte
NE	horse	stallion, studhorse	gelding	mare	foal, colt
Du.	paard	hengst	ruin	merrie	veulen
OHG	(h)ros, marah	reinno, scelo	hengist	mer(i)ha	folo, fulin, colo
MHG	pfert, ros (ross, gaul)	schele, reine	heng(e)st	merhe	vole, vülin
NHG	pferd (ross)	hengst	wallach	stute, mähre	füllen
Lith.	arklys, žirgas	eržilas, drigantas	volokas	kumelė	kumelys
Lett.	zirgs	ērzelis, drigants	izrūnīts zirgs	k'ève	kumelš
ChSl.	konjĭ	....	....	kobyla	žrěbę
SCr.	konj	ždrijebac, pastuh, ajgir	uštrojen konj	kobila	ždrijebe
Boh.	kůň	hřebec	valach	klisna, kobyla	hříbě
Pol.	koń	ogier, drygant, stadnik	wałach	klacz, kobyla	źrebię
Russ.	lošađ' (kon')	žerebec	merin	kobyla	žerebenok
Skt.	açva-, haya-	açva-, marya-	....	açvā-, vaḍabā-	kiçora-
Av.	aspa-	....	....	aspā-	....

3.41. While the agreement in most of the IE languages pointing to an IE word for 'horse' and its great frequency in personal names do not prove the IE domestication of the horse (cf. the similar situation for 'wolf'), there is strong probability on other grounds that the horse was at least partially domesticated in the IE period, and further that the use of the horse for drawing war chariots and for riding came to western Asia and Egypt through the medium of IE-speaking peoples of Asia Minor. Schrader, Reallex. 2.170 ff. For Celtic cf. also Loth, Mém. de l'institut de France 43.113 ff.

1. IE *eḱwo-, root connection wholly obscure. Walde-P. 1.113. Ernout-M. 307.

Grk. ἵππος, dial. also ἵκκος (but with some unexplained phonetic features and taken as an Illyr. loanword by Kretschmer, Glotta 22.120); Lat. equus (with fem. equa 'mare'); Ir. ech, Gall. *epo- in names Eporedia, etc. (W. ebol, Br. ebcul 'colt'); ON jōr (poet.), OE eoh 'warhorse' (Goth. aihwa-tundi 'bramble bush', lit. 'horse-tooth'); Lith. (obs.) ešva, ašva 'mare'; Skt. açva-, Av., OPers.

aspa- (OPers. also *asa-*); Toch. A *yuk*, B *yakwe*.

Thus the word is attested in all the main branches of the IE family except Slavic, and it is still that in use in most of the modern Iranian languages (NPers. *asp*, etc.). But in all the European languages it has sooner or later been displaced by other terms (but cf. Sp. *yegua*, Rum. *iapă* 'mare'). Likewise in the Indic vernaculars, mostly by forms answering to the late and obscure *ghoṭa-*, *ghoṭaka-*, on which cf. Sommer, IF 31.363 ff.

2. NG ἄλογο, fr. neuter of Grk. ἄλογος 'unreasoning', not with primary application to the horse, to which it would be relatively inappropriate, but through the medium of 'animal' (so τὰ ἄλογα 'animals' in Plato, etc.) with specialization starting in military parlance, in which one commonly coupled ἄνθρωποι and ἄλογα 'men and beasts', that is, 'men and horses'. Hatzidakis, Μεσ. 1.142.

Byz. φάρας, φαρίον, MHG *vārīs*, etc., rather widespread medieval word for 'horse, steed', fr. Arab. *fāris* 'rider'. Lokotsch 591. Berneker 279.

3. Lat. *caballus*, in part attested as 'gelding', mostly 'work horse' (cf. καβάλλης· ἐργάτης ἵππος Hesych.), sometimes pejorative 'old nag', but eventually simply 'horse', in VLat. displacing *equus*, and so the source of the Romance words, also Ir. *capall*, W. *ceffyl* (Pedersen 1.226, Vendryes, De hib. voc. 121). Cf. also late Lat. *cabō, ōnis* in glosses (*caballus, caballus magnus, equus castratus*), Grk. κάβηλος 'castrated' (Hesych.), ChSl. *kobila* 'mare', etc. Certainly a loanword, but precise source dub. Prob. orig. 'gelding' and of ethnic orig. (Anatolian or Balkan) like Fr. *hongre*, NHG *wallach*, etc. (3.43). Walde-H. 1.125. Ernout-M. 124. Maas, Rh. M. 74.469. Kretschmer, Glotta 16.191, 20.248. Grégoire, Etud. Horat. 81 f., Byzantion 11.615 (: Grk. κόβαλος 'rogue', orig. 'porter'; rejected by Kretschmer, Glotta 27.232).

4. Ir. *marc*, W. *march*, Br. *marc'h*, ON *marr*, OE *mearh*, OHG *marah*, with Gmc. fem. forms for 'mare' (3.44), orig.? Walde-P. 2.235. Walde-H. 1.79.

5. ON *hross*, OE, ME *hors*, NE *horse*, OHG *(h)ros*, MHG *ros*, *ors* (esp. 'war horse', beside *pfert* for common 'horse'), NHG *ross* (mostly lit., but in some dialects still the common word for 'horse') : Lat. *currere* 'run' (*rr* fr. *rs) or Skt. *kūrd-* 'jump'. Walde-P. 1.428. Falk-Torp 421.

ON *hestr* (also 'stallion'), Dan. *hest*, Sw. *häst*, with OE *hengest*, OHG *hengist* 'gelding', NHG *hengst* 'stallion' (> Dan., Sw. *hingst* 'stallion'), orig. a superl. form, perh. : Lith. *šankus* 'swift', *šokti* 'jump', etc. Walde-P. 1.334. Falk-Torp 402.

OHG *parafrid*, MHG *pfert*, NHG *pferd*, Du. *paard*, fr. late Lat. (Cod. Just.) *paraverēdus* 'extra post horse' (whence also with dissim. OFr. *palefrei*, ME, NE *palfrey*), cpd. of Grk. παρά 'beside' and *verēdus* (Martial., Cod. Just.), the latter a Celtic word like Lat. *rēda* 'carriage'. Weigand-H. 2.408. NED s.v. *palfrey*.

NHG *gaul* 'nag', in some dialects the common word for 'horse', MLG *gūl* 'war horse', etc. (cf. Weigand-H. s.v.), etym.? Sommer, IF 31.362.

For the local distribution of NHG *pferd*, *ross*, *gaul*, cf. Kretschmer, Wortgeogr. 61, 600.

6. Lith. *arklys*, deriv. of *arklas* 'plow', this fr. the root of *arti* 'plow' : Grk. ἀρόω, Lat. *arāre* 'plow', etc., hence orig. 'plow horse'. Walde-P. 1.78.

Lith. *žirgas* (esp. 'riding-horse, steed'), Lett. *zirgs* (OPruss. *sirgis* 'gelding') : Lith. *žergiu*, *žergti* 'stretch the legs

apart', hence lit. a 'wide-stepper'. Leskien, Ablaut 358.

7. ChSl. *konjĭ*, etc., the general Slavic word, etym. much disputed. Perh. fr. **komnjo-* : ORuss. *komon'*, OPruss. *camnet* 'horse', (here also Lith. *kumelys*, Lett. *kumel̦š* 'foal', Lith. *kumelė* 'mare'?), and further fr. **kobnjo-* : ChSl. *kobyla* 'mare', Lat. *caballus*, etc. Walde-H. 1.125. Berneker 561, 555. Brückner 253 f. Junker, KZ 50.249 ff. Pokorny, KZ 56, 133.

Russ. *lošad'*, now the usual word (*kon'* esp. 'charger, steed'), Pol. *łoszak* still specific for the small Tartar horse, fr. Turk. *alaša* 'pack horse'. Berneker 734. Lokotsch 55.

8. Skt. *açva-*, Av. *aspa-*, above, 1.

Skt. *haya-* : *hi-* 'set in motion, impel'. Walde-P. 1.546.

3.42. 'Stallion'. 1. Grk. (beside ὁ ἵππος, usual in Aristot., etc.), ὀχεῖον (also 'cock', both in Aristot.) : ὀχεύω, the technical word for 'cover, mount' (of the male), this : ἔχω 'hold', Skt. *sah-* 'overpower', etc. Walde-P. 2.481 f.

NG βαρβᾶτο ἄλογο, fr. βαρβᾶτος 'uncastrated', this fr. Lat. *barbātus* 'bearded' and orig. applied to the bearded uncastrated man in contrast to the eunuch. Cf. Rum. *bărbat* 'man' (2.21).

NG ἄτι, fr. Turk. *at* 'horse'. So ORum., SCr. *at* 'horse' or 'stallion'. Lokotsch 128.

2. Lat. *(equus) admissārius* (> VLat. *armissarius* > Rum. *armăsar*), deriv. of *admittere* 'give access to' in its special sense of 'put the male to the female'.

It. *stallone*, OFr. *estalon* (> ME *stalon*, NE *stallion* > NIr. *stail*, W. *ystalwyn*), Fr. *étalon*, deriv. of the Gmc. word for 'stable', OHG *stal*, etc. (3.19), hence used for the horse kept in the stable for serving mares. REW 8219.

Sp. *caballo padre*, lit. 'father horse', with *padre* as often for the male animal.

3. Ir. *ech-cullach*, or simply *cullach*, Br. *marc'h-kalloc'h*, with deriv. of word for 'testicle', W. *caill*, Br. *kell*. Cf. Ir. *(muc-)cullach* 'boar' (3.32). Also Br. *marc'h-kalc'h* with *kalc'h* 'penis'.

4. ON *hestr* (3.41) also 'stallion', for which also *stōð-hestr* and *stōð-hross* cpds. with *stōð* 'stud of horses' : OE *stōd* (NE *stud*, whence *studhorse*), OHG *stuot* (NHG *stute* 'mare'), all meaning ('place for', then coll.) 'horses kept for breeding', orig. 'standing place', deriv. of IE * *stā-* 'stand'.

OE *stēda* (NE *steed*), deriv. of OE *stōd* (above).

ON *reini* (rare), OS. *wrēnio*, OHG *reinno*, MHG *reine* : OE *wrǣne* 'lascivious', Dan. *vrinske* 'neigh', Sw. dial. *vrensk* 'stallion', all from the characteristic lip motion of the stallion in heat. Walde-P. 1.277. Falk-Torp 1397.

OHG *scelo*, MHG *schele*, NHG *schellhengst*, *beschäler* (cf. *beschälen* 'cover the mare'), Dan. *beskeler* : MHG *schel* 'springing', Skt. *çalabha-* 'grasshopper', etc. Walde-P. 1.600. Falk-Torp 62.

NHG *hengst* (> Dan., Sw. *hingst*), with shift of meaning from MHG *hengest*, OHG *hengist* 'gelding' : ON *hestr* 'horse', etc. (3.41).

5. Lith. *eržilas*, Lett. *ērzelis* : Grk. ὄρχις 'testicle', etc. Walde-P. 1.183. Mühl.-Endz. 1.577.

Lith. *drigantis*, Lett. *drigants*, loanword fr. Pol. *drygant*. Mühl.-Endz. 1.498.

6. SCr. *ždrijebac*, Boh. *hřebec*, Russ. *žerebec*, derivs. of the word for 'foal', ChSl. *žrěbę*, etc. (3.46).

SCr. *pastuh* : ChSl. *pastuchŭ* 'herdsman, shepherd', (3.18), hence 'stallion' as protector of the stud(?).

SCr. *ajgir*, Pol. *ogier*, loanword fr.

Turk. *aygır* 'stallion'. Berneker 26. Lokotsch 40.

Pol. *drygant*, orig.? Brückner 99.

Pol. *stadnik*, deriv. of *stado* 'herd, stud' : OE *stōd*, etc. (above, 4).

7. Skt. for 'stallion' mostly simply *açva-* (3.41) or rarely *açva-vṛṣa-* (*vṛṣan-* 'male').

Skt. *marya-* 'young man' (: Grk. μεῖραξ 'girl' or 'boy') in RV also 'stallion'.

3.43. 'Gelding' is in part expressed only by phrases 'castrated horse', with words for 'castrate' (3.14), hence requiring no further comment here.

1. Xen. Cyrop. 7.5.62 refers to ἵπποι ἐκτεμνόμενοι. But Aristot., who uses τομίᾶς (3.14) for the castrated ox, sheep, or swine (3.14), does not use it of a horse or make any reference to the castration of horses (cf. HA 6.22), which Strabo 7.4.8 says was peculiar to the Scythians and Sarmatians. Apparently it was not a common practice in ancient Greece.

2. Lat. *cantērius*, loanword fr. Grk. κανθήλιος 'pack-ass', with change of meaning fr. 'beast of burden, old hack' to 'gelding'. Ernout-M. 145. Walde-H. 1.155.

Fr. *hongre*, orig. 'Hungarian'. Cf. NHG *wallach*, etc. (below, 4).

Rum. *jugan* : *jugăni* 'castrate' (3.14).

3. Ir. *gerrān* (glosses Lat. *caballus*, here as 'gelding'), NIr. *gearrān*, deriv. of Ir. *gerraim* 'cut', *gerr* 'short'. Walde-P. 1.605.

NIr. *gillīn* (also 'eunuch'), prob. early loanword fr. ME *geldyng*, NE *gelding*, which were formerly also used for 'eunuch'.

W. *adfarch*, cpd. of *march* 'horse, stallion' and *ad-*, like *adfwl* 'castrated bull', with the depreciatory use of *ad-* as in *adfyw* 'half alive', *adfyd* 'adversity', etc.

4. ON *geldhestr*, ME *geldyng*, NE *gelding* (ON *geldingr* 'wether') : ON *gelda*, ME *gelde* 'castrate' (3.14).

OE *hengest*, OHG *hengist* : ON *hestr* 'horse', etc. (3.41).

Du. *ruin*, MLG *rūne*, NHG dial. *raun* (cf. also Lett. *rūnit* 'castrate', 3.14), prob. fr. the root of Skt. *ru-* 'break in pieces', Lith. *rauti* 'tear out', etc. Walde-P. 1.352. Franck-v. W. 563.

MLG *wallache* (> Dan. *vallak*, Sw. *vallack*), NHG *wallach* (> Boh. *valach*, Pol. *wałach*, Lith. *volokas*), all orig. 'Wallachian'. The castration of horses as a general practice spread from Eastern Europe. Hence for 'gelding' also MLat. *equus Hunnicus*, Fr. *hongre* orig. '*Hungarian*', early NHG *reuss* orig. 'Russian'.

5. Russ. *merin*, fr. Mongol. *morin* 'gelding'. Berneker 2.37.

6. Skt. *vadhri-* 'castrated' (3.14) not quotable with reference to horses.

3.44. 'Mare'. 1. Expressed by fem. forms of word discussed under 'horse' (3.41), as Grk. ἡ ἵππος, Lat. *equa* (> OFr. *ive*, Sp. *yegua*, Rum. *iapă*), It. *cavalla*, ON *merr*, OE *mere*, etc., Skt. *açvā-*, Av. *aspā-*.

2. Grk. φορβάς 'grazing' (: φέρβω 'feed'), as sb. 'mare' late and lit. NG.

NG pop. φοράδα, fr. Grk. φοράς 'fruitful' (sb. 'mare' in Hesych. and late pap.).

3. Fr. *jument*, fr. Lat. *iūmentum* 'beast of burden' ('mare' in Lex Salica). The interchange started in country districts where the work horses on the farm were in fact the mares. REW 4613. Meillet, Arch. glott. it. 147 f.

4. Ir. *lāir*, etym.? (Stokes 240 **plāreks* : Alb. *pelë* 'mare').

W. *caseg*, Br. *kazeg*, MW, OCorn. *cassec*, perh. : OHG *hengist*, etc. Pedersen 2.29. Loth, op. cit. 130.

5. Dan. *hoppe*, orig. 'pacer' : *hoppe* 'hop', NE *hop*, *hobble*, etc. Cf. ME *hobyn* 'ambling horse, pacer, pony' (NE *hobbyhorse*). Falk-Torp 417.

Sw. *sto*, NHG *stute*, fr. ON *stōð*, OHG *stuot*, coll. 'horses kept for breeding'. Cf. under 'stallion' (3.42).

6. Lith. *kumelė*, see 3.41, ChSl. *konjĭ*.

Lett. *k'eve* (fr. Lith. *kėvė* 'bad mare, jade'), OPruss. *kajwe*, perh. : Lith. *kaimenė* 'herd'. BB 27.168.

7. ChSl. *kobyla*, etc., the general Slavic word, fr. the same source as Lat. *caballus* (3.41).

Boh. *klisna* : ChSl. *kljusę* 'beast of burden', SCr. *kljuse* 'nag', Boh. *klusati* 'trot', etc. Berneker 529 f.

Pol. *klacz*, loanword fr. Russ. *klajača* 'nag, pack horse' (Ukr. 'mare') : ChSl. *klęčati* 'kneel', SCr. *klecati* 'stagger', etc. Berneker 515. Brückner 231.

8. Skt. (beside *açvā-*) *vaḍabā*; etym.?

3.45. 'Foal, colt'. Technically NE *foal* is applied to the young of the horse while still with the dam, *colt* to the young horse up to four years or more (cf. NED). But in U.S. *colt* is now the word even for the newborn, *foal* being in common use only as the vb.

1. Grk. πῶλος, dim. πωλάριον (> NG πουλάρι); Lat. *pullus* 'young of an animal, chicken, foal' ('foal' regularly in Varro, RR 2.7.11 ff.), with derivs. *pulliter* (Niedermann, Mnemos. 3.3.270 f., MLat. *poledrus* Du Cange) whence OIt. *poltro*, Sp. *potro*, It. *puledro* (REW 6825) and VLat. *pullāmen* > Fr. *poulain* (Gamillscheg 712. Bloch 2.174), Goth. *fula*, OE *fola*, etc., the general Gmc. word, all fr. the same root as Grk. παῦρος, Lat. *paucus* 'little, few', Grk. παῖς, Lat. *puer* 'child', etc. Walde-P. 2.75 f. Feist 170 f.

2. Lat. *eculus*, dim. of *equus* (*ecus*), in Varro, RR 2.7.12, 13 is 'colt' as distinguished from 'foal' which is regularly *pullus*.

Rum. *mînz* : Alb. *mcz* 'foal', It. *manzo* 'yearling bullock', *manza* 'heifer', etc., generally regarded as of Illyr. origin. REW 5289. Densusianu 29. G. Meyer, Alb. Etym. Wtb. 270. Otherwise, as fr. **mandius*, deriv. of *mandere* 'chew', Pușcariu 1092.

3. Ir. *serrach*, NIr. *searrach* : Ir. *serr* 'timid' (and 'proud'), NIr. *searr* 'timid and flighty young animal that follows the dam, child at the mother's heels' (Dinneen), this fr. **ster-p-* (Lith. *stirpti* 'grow up') beside **ster-t-* in NE *start*, *startle*, etc. Loth. RC 43.147. Pedersen 1.94. Walde-P. 1.631. The development of 'foal' through the notion of 'timid, startled' is much more probable than either of the stages assumed by Pedersen or Walde-P. G. S. Lane, Language 13.26 f.

W. *ebol*, Br. *ebeul* : Gall. **epo-*, Lat. *equus* 'horse' (3.41).

4. OE *colt*, used for the young of a horse, ass, or even a camel, ME *colte*, NE *colt* : Sw. *kull* 'brood, litter', Sw. dial. *kult* 'pig, overgrown boy', Norw. *kult* 'thick round shape, block', Skt. *gaḍi-* 'young ox', Goth. *kilþei* 'womb', OE *cild* 'child', etc. Walde-P. 1.614. Falk-Torp 593, 430. Cf. ON *hūnn* 'block' and 'young bear', NE *cub* : Norw. *kubbe* 'block, stump'.

5. Lith. *kumelys*, Lett. *kumel̦š*, see 3.41, under ChSl. *konjĭ*.

6. ChSl. *žrěbę*, etc., the general Slavic word : Grk. βρέφος 'fetus, babe, young of an animal'. Walde-P. 1.689. Brückner 666.

7. Skt. *kiçora-*, etym.?

3.46 ASS, DONKEY

Grk.	ὄνος	Goth.	asilus	Lith.	asilas
NG	γαΐδαρος, γαϊδούρι	ON	asni	Lett.	ēzelis
	γομάρι	Dan.	æsel	ChSl.	oslŭ
Lat.	asinus	Sw.	åsna	SCr.	osao, magarac
It.	asino, somaro	OE	assa, esol	Boh.	osel
Fr.	âne	ME	asse	Pol.	osiol
Sp.	asno, burro	NE	donkey, ass	Russ.	osel
Rum.	asin, măgar	Du.	ezel	Skt.	gardabha-, rāsabha-
Ir.	asan	OHG	esil	Av.	xara-, kaθwā-
NIr.	asal	MHG	esel		
W.	asyn	NHG	esel		
Br.	azen				

The majority of the European words for 'ass, donkey' are derived, mostly through Latin, from some Asiatic name for this animal, the appearance of which in Europe was relatively late. Other words reflect the function of the ass as 'beast of burden', or sometimes other characteristics such as 'lascivious' or 'harsh braying'. Schrader, Reallex. 1.271.

1. Grk. ὄνος (prob., see below), Lat. asinus, loanwords fr. some Asiatic source, ultimately prob. the same word as Sumerian anšu 'ass'. Schrader l.c. Ernout-M. 79. Walde-H. 1.72 ff.

Lat. asinus, or in part dim. asellus, is the source of the common European words, the Romance, Celtic, Gmc. (ON asni, Sw. asna fr. OFr. asne; Dan. œsel fr. LG or HG; OE assa perh. fr. Ir. asan) and, through Gmc., the Balto-Slavic.

2. Grk. ὄνος is prob. fr. the same source as Lat. asinus, though the precise phonetic relation is obscure. The old view that it belongs with Lat. onus 'load, burden' (cf. NG γομάρι, It. somaro, below) has recently been revived by Grégoire, Byzantion 13.288 ff.

NG γαΐδαρος, γαϊδάρι, γαϊδούρι, fr. γαϊδάριον occurring in pap. of the 6th to 8th cent. A.D., parallel to a gaydor in a 4th cent. Talmudic text, with somewhat

similar forms in other Semitic writings, doubtless a word of Asiatic origin, precise source uncertain. Hatzidakis Μεσ. 2.560 with references.

NG γομάρι, fr. neut. of adj. γομάρις, deriv. (suffix fr. Lat. -ārius) of class. Grk. γόμος 'load'. Cf. It. samaro (below, 3), NG dial. βασταγό(ς), βασταγούρι, and φορτίκι 'donkey', fr. adjs. βασταγός (: βαστάζω 'carry') and φορτικός (: φορτίον 'load'). G. Meyer, Alb. Etym. Wtb. 127. D. Georgacas, Ἀθηνᾶ 51.71 ff.

3. It. somaro 'donkey' in parts of Italy; cf. R. A. Hall, Jr., Language 19.136), like Fr. sommier, OE sēamere, OHG saumari 'pack horse' or 'mule', fr. late Lat. sagmārius (> Byz. σαγμάριος), deriv. of sagma, late sauma (> OE sēam 'pack-horse load', etc.) fr. Grk. σάγμα 'packsaddle' (: σάττω 'pack'). REW 7512.

Sp. burro, back-formation fr. borrico = It. brico 'ass, mule, old horse', Fr. bourrique 'she-ass', fr. late Lat. burricus 'small horse', this fr. burrus 'red'(?). REW 1413.

4. NE donkey, replacing ass in common use (ass for the animal still used in

Ireland, otherwise lit.; now commonly applied to a person), orig. dialect or slang term, but precise orig. uncertain. NED s.v.

5. Skt. gardabha-, deriv. of gardha- 'desire', gṛdh- 'be eager', hence the 'lascivious' beast. Walde-P. 1.614.

Skt. rāsabha-, deriv. of rāsa- 'noise', rā- 'howl', hence the 'brayer'.

Av. xara- (NPers. xar) : Skt. khara- 'harsh', also 'ass', 'mule', 'crow', etc. fr. their harsh cries. Barth. 531.

Av. kaθwā- 'she-ass', etym.? Barth. 435.

3.47 MULE

Grk.	ἡμίονος	Goth.	. . . .	Lith.	mulas, asilénas
NG	μουλάρι	ON	mūll	Lett.	mūlis
Lat.	mūlus	Dan.	muldyr, mulæsel	ChSl.	mĭskŭ
It.	mulo	Sw.	muldsna	SCr.	mazga
Fr.	mulet	OE	mūl	Boh.	mezek
Sp.	mulo	ME	mule	Pol.	mul
Rum.	catîr	NE	mule	Russ.	mul, lošak, išak
Ir.	mūl	Du.	muilezel	Skt.	açvatara-
NIr.	mūil	OHG	mūl	Av.	. . . .
W.	mul	MHG	mūl		
Br.	mul	NHG	maultier, maulesel		

Most of the words for 'mule' go back ultimately, most of them through Lat. mūlus, to non-IE sources. A few are derived from words for 'ass' or 'horse'.

1. Grk. ἡμίονος, cpd. of ἡμι- 'half' and ὄνος 'ass'.

2. Lat. mūlus (*muḫslo-?) : Grk. dial. μυχλός 'stallion-ass' (Hesych.), Alb. mushk, late ChSl. mĭskŭ, SCr. mazga, Boh. mezek (Russ. mesk obs.) 'mule', all prob. fr. some Anatolian source. Walde-P. 2.311 f. Ernout-M. 640.

Hence most of the European words, some of the Gmc. now with the addition of words for 'ass' or 'animal', as NHG maultier, maulesel.

3. Rum. catîr, like Bulg. katur, fr.

Turk. katir 'mule'. Berneker 495. Lokotsch 1131.

4. Lith. asilénas (neolog.), deriv. of asilas 'ass'.

5. ChSl. mĭskŭ etc., above, 2.

Russ. lošak : lošad' 'horse', Pol. loszak 'Tartar horse', of Turk. orig. (3.41).

Russ. išak, fr. Tartar išek 'ass', this fr. Arm. ēš 'ass' (: Lat. asinus, etc.). Berneker 438. Lokotsch 565.

6. Skt. açvatara- (with Iran. forms of similar orig., Pahl., NPers. astar, etc.; Horn 86), fr. açva- 'horse' with suffix -tara- as in vatsatara- 'calf that has been weaned' fr. vatsa- 'calf', in both cases giving the force of 'something different, not quite', hence 'kind of, sort of (horse, calf)'. Cf. Lat. mātertera 'aunt' as orig. 'a kind of mother'.

	3.51 HEN, CHICKEN (Generic)	3.52 COCK	3.53 CAPON	3.54 HEN	3.55 CHICKEN
Grk.	ἀλέκτωρ, ὄρνις	ἀλεκτρυών, ὁ ὄρνις	. . . .	ἀλεκτορίς, ἡ ὄρνις	ὀρνίθιον, νεοσσίον
NG	πουλί	κόκκορας, πετεινός	καπώνι	ὄρνιθα, κόττα	πουλί, κοττόπουλο
Lat.	gallina	gallus	capō	gallina	pullus
It.	pollo	gallo	cappone	gallina	pulcino
Fr.	poule	coq	chapon	poule	poulet, poussin
Sp.	gallina	gallo	capon	gallina	pollo, polluelo
Rum.	găină	cocoș	clapon	găină	puiu de găina
Ir.	cerc	cailech	. . . .	cerc	. . . .
NIr.	cearc	coileach	cābūn	cearc	sicín
W.	iar	ceilog	capwllt, capwrn	iar	cyw
Br.	yar	kilhog, kog	kabon	yar	poñsin
Goth.	. . . .	hana	. . . .	. . . .	. . . .
ON	h·ns	hani	. . . .	hœna	ungi, kjúklingr
Dan.	høns	hane	kapun	høne	kylling
Sw.	hóns	tupp, hane	kapun	hóna	kyckling
OE	hen, henn	hana, coc(c)	capūn	henn	cicen
ME	. . . .	cocke	capon	henne	chicken
NE	hen, chicken	cock (U.S. rooster)	capon	hen	chicken
Du.	hoen	haan	kapoen	henna, hanin	kuiken
OHG	huon	hano	cappo	henna	huonichlin
MHG	huon	han, hane	kappe, kappūn	henne	huonlin, hüenel
NHG	huhn	hahn	kapaun	henne	hühnchen, küchlein
Lith.	višta	gaidys	romytas gaidys	višta	vištytis, viščiukas
Lett.	vista	gailis	ramits gailis	vista	cālis, cālitis
ChSl.	. . . .	kurŭ, kokotŭ, pětelŭ	. . . .	kokošĭ	kurę, pŭtenĭcĭ
SCr.	kokoš	pijetao, kokot	kopun	kokoš	pile
Boh.	slepice, kuře	kohout	kapoun	slepice	kuře
Pol.	kura, kokosz	kogut, pietuch	kaplon	kura, kokosz	kurcze
Russ.	kura	petuch	kaplun	kurica	cyplenok
Skt.	. . . .	kukkuṭa-, kṛkavāku-	. . . .	. . . .	kukkuṭī-
Av.	. . . .	parōdarš, kahrkatāš, karstōdqsuš	. . . .	. . . .	. . . .

3.51–3.55. These are most conveniently discussed together. The words entered as generic are mostly those for the much more numerous female, the 'hen', in a few cases those for the young, the 'chicken'. Thus NE hen and chicken are both used generically, with varying local usage (in New England one used to keep hens, but now generally in U.S., chickens, chicken farm). Only occasionally is there a distinctively generic word, as NHG huhn, in common use. Some of the words listed under 'chicken' are used mainly of the very young 'chick'.

The majority of the terms are connected with words meaning 'sing, cry out', etc., or are of imitative origin, reflecting the characteristic cries. Some are in origin words for 'bird' or 'young of an animal'.

1. Grk. ἀλεκτρυών, orig. a personal name (Hom. Ἀλεκτρυών : ἀλέξω 'ward off'), then applied (cf. Fr. renard 'fox', etc.) to (at first the fighting) 'cock', secondarily, also 'hen'. Walde-P. 1.89. Also ἀλέκτωρ 'cock', and reg. fem. ἀλεκτορίς 'hen', freq. in Aristot. (where also generic τὸ τῶν ἀλεκτορίδων γένος).

Grk. ὄρνις 'bird' (3.64), in Att. also the usual word for the 'cock' (ὁ) or 'hen' (ἡ). Hence NG ὄρνιθα 'hen', still the common word in some regions.

Grk. ὀρνίθιον, dim. of ὄρνις, 'small bird', later also 'chicken'.

Grk. dial. καλαῖς 'hen' and 'cock' (IG 4.914), prob. fr. *καλαϝίς : καλέω 'call' (cf. Ir. cailech 'cock', below, 3). Bechtel, Gr. Dial. 2.510.

Grk. νεοσσός 'young bird' (deriv. of νέος 'young'), dim. νεοσσίον, νοσσίον, may be used of the domestic 'chick, chicken' as NT, Mt. 23, 37; νεοττίς Aristot. is 'young hen'.

NG πουλί 'chicken' and generic, also, but in this case secondarily, 'bird' (3.64), fr. late Grk. πουλλίον (ὀρνιθοπούλλιον 'chicken' in pap. of 6th or 7th cent. A.D.; Byz. πουλλίον common), loanword fr. Lat. pullus 'chicken' (below, 2). Hence also the dim. πουλάκι 'chicken' but mostly as endearing term 'darling'.

NG κόκκορας 'cock', a blend of Grk. κόρκορα: ὄρνις (Hesych.) belonging with Ir. cerc, etc. (below, 3) and a *κόκκος belonging with MLat. coccus, etc. (below, 2).

NG πετεινός 'cock', sb. use of old πετεινός 'winged', like πετεινόν 'bird' (3.64).

NG κόττα 'hen', fem. of κόττος: ὄρνις (Hesych.) this with reference to the cock's comb : κοττίς 'head', προκοττίς 'mane'. Cf. Hesych. (s.v. πρόκοττα) αἱ ἀλεκτρυόνιτε κοττοί διὰ τὸν ἐπὶ τῇ κεφαλῇ λόφον. Kukules, quoted in Glotta 5.285. Here also NG κοττόπουλο, κοττοπούλι 'chicken'.

2. Lat. gallus 'cock' (> It., Sp. gallo), etym. disputed. Perh. orig. 'Gallic' (cf. Grk. Περσικός and Μῆδος for 'cock'), on the assumption that the Romans became acquainted with the cock from Gaul, where it was brought by the Phoenicians; or, as a native word,

'crier' (like the Gmc. words, etc.) fr. *galso- : ChSl. glasŭ 'voice', OE callian 'call', etc. Walde-P. 1.538, Ernout-M. 409 f. Walde-H. 1.580 f. (but for Grk. καλαῖς, see above).

Hence fem. gallina 'hen' (> It., Sp. gallina, OFr. geline, Rum. găină, etc. REW 3661).

Lat. pullus 'young of an animal', esp. 'chicken', fr. the same root as Grk. πῶλος, Goth. fula 'foal' (3.45), Grk. παῦρος, Lat. paucus 'little, few', Grk. παῖς, Lat. puer 'child', etc. Walde-P. 1.75 ff. Ernout-M. 822 f.

Hence It. pollo 'fowl', Sp. pollo 'chicken'; fr. new fem. forms Sp. polla 'pullet', Fr. poule 'hen'; and the various derivs. It. pulcino, Fr. poulet, poussin, etc., only partially listed under 'chicken'. REW 6828, 6818a, 6820, 6826.

MLat. coccus, Fr. coq, ON kokkr (rare), OE coc(c), ME cocke, NE cock, ChSl. kokotŭ, etc. (below, 6), Skt. kukkuṭa- 'cock', a group of imitative orig. reflecting the cries like Grk. κόκκυ, Lat. coco. Walde-P. 1.455 ff.

Rum. cocoș 'cock', loanword fr. Slavic, SCr. kokoš 'hen', etc. (below, 6).

Lat. cāpus (Varro), usually cāpō, -ōnis 'capon' : ChSl. skopiti 'castrate', etc. (3.14). Ernout-M. 151. Walde-H. 1.161.

Hence all the words listed under 'capon', except the Baltic (where it is expressed as 'castrated cock'; Lith. kaplunas fr. Pol. kapłon is quoted in an old Lith. dictionary; Lett. kapauns in Drawneek, but not in Mühl.-Endz.). It was an article of the Roman table that the capon spread over Europe.

3. Ir. cerc, NIr. cearc 'hen' : Grk. κερκίς, κέρκαξ, κόρκορα, etc. (Hesych., as names of birds), Skt. kṛkara- 'a kind of partridge', Lith. karkti, kirkti, 'croak, cackle', etc., all of imitative orig. Walde-P. 1.413 ff. Pedersen 1.126.

W. *iar*, Br., OCorn. *yar* 'hen', Ir. *eirin* 'pullet', outside connections? Walde-P. 1.199. Pedersen 1.65. Stokes 223.

Ir. *cailech*, NIr. *coileach*, W. *ceilog*, Br. *kilhog* 'cock' : Grk. καλέω 'call', Lat. *clāmāre* 'call', Skt. *uṣa-kala-* 'cock' (lit. 'crying at dawn'), etc. Walde-P. 1.443 ff. Stokes 73. Br. also *kog* fr. Fr. *coq*.

NIr. *sicín*, fr. NE *chicken*.

W. *cyw* 'chicken' (also 'young bird', and in North Wales 'the young of animals'), prob. : Grk. κύος 'fetus', Skt. *çāva-* 'young of an animal', etc. (Walde-P. 1.365 ff., but without W. *cyw*). G. S. Lane, Language 7.280.

Br. *poñsin* 'chicken', fr. Fr. *poussin*. Henry 226.

4. Goth., OE *hana*, ON *hani*, OHG *hano*, etc. 'cock', with fem. ON *hœna*, OE *henn*, OHG *henna*, *hanīn*, etc., and generic (orig. coll.) ON *hœns*, Dan. *hóns*, Sw. *hóns*, Du. *hoen*, OHG *huon*, NHG *huhn*, all : Lat. *canere*, Ir. *canim* 'sing', etc. Here also Grk. ἠί-κανος· ἀλεκτρυών (Hesych.). Walde-P. 1.351. Falk-Torp 453. Feist 243 f.

Sw. *tupp* 'cock', named from its 'crest, comb', by-form of *topp* 'top' : NE *top*, etc. Hellquist 1245 f.

OE *coc(c)*, etc. : MLat. *coccus*, etc. (above, 2). In U.S. *cock* is commonly replaced by *rooster*, for which *roost-cock* (cf. NED s.v.) is quotable earlier.

ON *kjúklingr* (rare; mostly *ungi* : *ungr* 'young', Dan. *kylling*, Sw. *kyckling*, OE *cicen*, NE *chicken*, Du. *kuiken*, NHG *küchlein*, the most widespread Gmc. words for 'chicken', derivs. of words belonging with MLat. *coccus*, etc. (above, 2).

OHG *huonichlīn*, MHG *huonlīn*, *hüenel*, NHG *hühnchen* 'chicken', dims. of OHG *huon*, NHG *huhn*.

ME *pultrie*, NE *poultry* (fr. OFr. *pouletrie* : *poule* 'hen', etc.) is used as coll. for domestic fowls, but not limited to the genus Gallus. NED. s.v. *poultry*.

NE *fowl*, orig. 'bird' (3.65), now mostly for domestic birds, esp. 'cock' or 'hen', but in U.S., at least, includes ducks, geese, etc.

NE *hen* and *chicken* both used also generically, see above.

5. Lith. *višta*, Lett. *vista* 'hen', with dim. Lith. *vištytis*, *visčiukas* 'chicken', perh. as orig. 'house bird' : Skt. *viç-*, Grk. οἶκος 'house', Lith. *vieš-pats* 'lord' ('housemaster'), etc. Mühl.-Endz. 4.626.

Lith. *gaidys*, Lett. *gailis* : Lith. *giedoti* 'sing', ORuss. *gajati* 'crow', etc. Walde-P. 1.527. Mühl-Endz. 1.585.

Lett. *cālis*, *cālītis* 'chicken', etym.?

6. ChSl. *kurŭ* 'cock' (Cod. Zogr., etc.; for the distribution of ChSl. *kurŭ*, *kokotŭ*, *pětelŭ*, cf. Jagić, Entstehungsgesch. 355), Boh., Pol., Russ. *kur* 'cock' (but less common than the following), Boh., Pol., Russ. *kura*, ChSl., Russ. *kurica* 'hen', ChSl. *kurę*, Boh. *kuře*, Pol. *kurcze* 'chicken', prob. of imitative orig. like Skt. *kāuti* 'cries', etc. Walde-P. 1.331 f. Berneker 650.

ChSl. *kokotŭ* (Cod. Mar.). Scr. *kokot*, Boh. *kohout*, Pol. *kogut* 'cock', with fem. ChSl. *kokoši*, SCr. *kokoš*, Pol. *kokosz* 'hen' : MLat. *coccus*, OE *cocc*, etc. (above, 2). Berneker 540 f.

ChSl. *pětelŭ*, SCr. *pijetao*, Russ. *petuch* (> Pol. *pietuch*) 'cock' : ChSl. *pěti* 'sing'. Brückner 404.

ChSl. *pŭtenĭcĭ* 'young bird', dim. of *pŭta* 'bird' (3.64), also 'chicken' like νοσσίον which it renders (Mt. 23.37).

Boh. *slepice* 'hen' (similar forms in Polabian), deriv. of *slepý* 'blind' (4.97), based on the hen's blinking eyes? Miklosich 307.

SCr., Bulg. *pile* 'chicken' : Upper

Sorb. *pilo* 'duckling', Lower Sorb. *pile* 'gosling', Lett. *pīle* 'duck', Lith. *pypti*, Lat. *pīpāre* 'peep', etc., all of imitative orig. Oljinskij, KZ 43.178. Walde-P. 2.70.

Russ. *cyplenok* 'chicken', of imitative orig.

7. Skt. *kukkuṭa* 'cock', *kukkuṭī-* 'hen', of imitative orig., like MLat. *coccus*, etc. (above, 2).

Skt. *kṛka-vāku-* 'cock' (second part : *vāc-* 'voice'), Av. *kahrkatās* 'cock' (vulgar term), NPers. *kark* 'fowl', belonging to the same imitative group as Ir. *cerc* 'hen', etc. (above, 3). Barth. 452.

Av. *parōdarš* 'cock' (ceremonial term), cpd. of *parō* 'in front, before' and *daras-* 'see', hence lit. 'seeing ahead', that is, announcing the day. Barth. 859. On the pair *parōdarš* and *kahrkatās*, cf. Benveniste, Studia Indo-Iranica, Ehrengabe für W. Geiger, 219 ff.

Av. *karətōdąsuš* 'cock', cpd. of *karəta-* 'knife' and adj. **dąsu-* : Skt. *daṅç-* 'bite', hence lit. 'biting with knives' with reference to the spurs. Barth. 454.

3.56 GOOSE

Grk.	χήν	Goth.	....	Lith.	žąsis
NG	χήνα	ON	gās	Lett.	zass
Lat.	ānser	Dan.	gaas	ChSl.	*gąsĭ, gusĭ
It.	oca	Sw.	gås	SCr.	guska
Fr.	oie	ON	gōs	Boh.	husa
Sp.	gausa, oca	ME	goos	Pol.	gęś
Rum.	gĭscă	NE	goose	Russ.	gusʹ
Ir.	gēd, giugrann	Du.	gans	Skt.	haṅsa-
NIr.	gē	OHG	gans	Av.	....
W.	gwydd	MHG	gans		
Br.	gwaz	NHG	gans		

1. IE **ĝhans-*, prob. fr. the root seen in Grk. χάσκω, ἔχανον 'yawn, gape', with reference to the goose's characteristic squawk with wide open bill. Walde-P. 1.536. Ernout-M. 56. Walde-H. 1.52. Berneker 342.

Grk. χήν, Dor. χάν; Lat. *ānser* (for **hānser*); (Ir. *gēis* 'swan'); ON *gās*, OE *gōs*, OHG *gans*, etc., general Gmc.; Lith. *žąsis*, ChSl. **gąsĭ*, (*gusĭ*), etc., general Balto-Slavic (Slavic *g* fr. Gmc.?); Skt. *haṅsa-* (also 'swan', etc.

2. It., Sp. *oca*, Fr. *oie*, fr. late Lat. *auca*, a back-formation fr. *avicula*, *aucula*, dim. of *avis* 'bird', with specialization to 'goose', parallel with that of Grk. ὄρνις 'bird' to 'hen' (3.51). Walde-H. 1.79. REW 826.

Sp. *gansa* (with *ganso* 'gander'), fr. Goth. **gans* = OHG *gans*, etc.

Rum. *gĭscă*, fr. Slavic (late ChSl. *gąsika*, SCr. *guska*, dim. of *gąsĭ*, above, 1).

3. Ir. *gēd*, NIr. *gē*, W. *gwydd*, Br. *gwaz*, fr. **gegdā-* or the like : Lith. *gagéti* 'quack', MHG *gāgen* 'quack', etc., all of imitative orig. Walde-P. 1.526.

Ir. *giugrann*, likewise of imitative orig., either with the preceding or with Lat. *gingrīre* 'quack', etc. Walde-P. 1.526, 592.

3.57 DUCK

Grk.	νῆσσα	Goth.	....	Lith.	antis
NG	πάπια	ON	ǫnd	Lett.	pīle
Lat.	anas	Dan.	and	ChSl.	ǫty
It.	anatra	Sw.	and	SCr.	patka, raca, utva
Fr.	canard	OE	ened (duce)	Boh.	kachna
Sp.	anade, pato	ME	ducke, (h)ende	Pol.	koczka
Rum.	raţă	NE	duck	Russ.	utka
Ir.	lacha	Du.	eend	Skt.	....
NIr.	lacha	OHG	anut	Av.	....
W.	hwyad	MHG	ant		
Br.	houad	NHG	ente		

1. IE **anəti-*, **ǝ̄ti-*. Walde-P. 1.60. Ernout-M. 48. Walde-H. 1.44. REW 439.

Grk. νῆσσα (Att. νῆττα, Boeot. νᾶσσα); Lat. *anas*, gen. (*anitis* and) *anatis* (> It. *anatra*, Sp. *anade*, OFr. *ane*); ON *ǫnd*, OE *ened*, OHG *anut*, etc., general Gmc.; Lith. *antis*; ChSl. *ǫty*, SCr. *utva*, Russ. *utka*; (Skt. *āti-* a kind of water bird).

2. NG πάππια, imitative like It. *papero* 'gosling', Sp. *parpar* 'quack'.

3. Fr. *canard*, fem. *cane*, the latter a blend of OFr. *ane* (above, 1) with an imitative syllable. REW 4671a.

Sp. *pato*, *pata*, like SCr. *patka* 'duck', Alb. *patë* 'goose', NPers. *bat* 'duck', etc., all of imitative orig. (calling cry?). REW 6301. G. Meyer, Alb. Etym. Wtb. 324. Rohlfs, Z. frz. Spr. 49.108 f.

Rum. *raţă*, fr. Slavic, SCr. *raca*, etc. (below, 7).

4. Ir., NIr. *lacha*, etym.?

W. *hwyad*, *hwyaden*, Br. *houad*, OCorn. *hoet*, etym. dub. Pedersen 1.55 f. Walde-P. 1.21.

5. OE *duce* (rare), ME *ducke*, NE *duck*, fr. the vb. OE **dūcan*, NE *duck* : OHG *tūhhan*, NHG *tauchen*, etc. 'dive, dip'. NED s.v. *duck*, sb.

6. Lett. *pīle* : SCr. *pile* 'chicken' (3.55).

7. SCr. *patka* : Sp. *pato*, etc. (above, 3). SCr., *raca* (> Rum. *raţă*), *rosë*, etc., like NHG dial. *rätsche*, of imitative orig. G. Meyer, Alb. Etym. Wtb. 368. Rohlfs, Z. frz. Spr. 49.111 f.

Boh. *kachna*, Pol. *kaczka* : Boh. *kachati*, Lith. *kagenti* 'quack', imitative. Berneker 465.

3.61 DOG

Grk.	κύων	Goth.	hunds	Lith.	šuo
NG	σκυλί	ON	hundr	Lett.	suns
Lat.	canis	Dan.	hund	ChSl.	pĭsŭ
It.	cane	Sw.	hund	SCr.	pas
Fr.	chien	OE	hund (docga)	Boh.	pes
Sp.	perro (can)	ME	hound, dogge	Pol.	pies
Rum.	ciine	NE	dog	Russ.	sobaka (pes)
Ir.	cū, matad	Du.	hond	Skt.	çvan-
NIr.	madra(dh), gadhar	OHG	hunt	Av.	span-
W.	ci	MHG	hunt		
Br.	ki	NHG	hund		

The dog is the earliest and most widespread of all domestic animals. Evidence of its domestication goes back at least to the earliest neolithic period, and from neolithic times on the dog was common throughout Europe, Asia (whence it was brought to America) and Egypt. Cf. Ebert, Reallex. and Schrader, Reallex. s.v. Hund. Hence familiarity with the dog in the IE period could be taken for granted, even without the confirmatory evidence of an IE word for 'dog'.

1. IE **k̑uon-*, *k̑un-*, root connection much disputed and dub. Walde-P. 1.465 ff. Ernout-M. 142 f. Walde-H. 1.152 f. Feist 276.

Grk. κύων; Lat. *canis* (phonetic development peculiar, but connection not to be questioned), whence It. *cane*, Fr. *chien*, Sp. *can* (now mostly obs.), Rum. *ctine*; Ir. *cū* (NIr. 'hound'), W. *ci*, Br. *ki*; Goth. *hunds*, OE *hund*, etc., general Gmc.; Lith. *šuo*, Lett. *suns*, OPruss. *sunis* (Pol., Russ. *suka* 'bitch' here?); Skt. *çvan-*, Av. *span-*, Median σπάκα (Hdt.), and fr. an Iran. form like the last, Russ. *sobaka*; Arm. *šun*; Toch. *ku*, *kū*.

2. NG σκυλί, fr. dim. form of late σκύλ(λ)ος, (σκύλλον· τὴν κύνα λέγουσιν, Hesych.) = Grk. σκύλαξ 'whelp, puppy', sometimes simply 'dog', for which see 3.612.

3. Sp. *perro*, orig. unknown (Iberian?). REW 6449.

4. Ir. *matad*, NIr. *madadh*, *madradh* etym.? Macbain 238.

NIr. *gadhar*, fr. ON *gagarr* 'dog', the latter : ON *gaga* 'mock', Lith. *gagéti* 'quack', etc. Macbain 238. Marstrander, Bidrag 158. Falk-Torp 302.

5. OE *docga* (once, in a gloss), ME *dogge*, NE *dog*, orig. unknown. Displaces *hound* as the generic term, the latter being specialized to 'hunting dog', esp. 'foxhound'. NED s.v. *dog*, sb.

6. ChSl. *pĭsŭ*, etc., the general Slavic word, etym. wholly dub. Walde-P. 2.9. Osthoff, Parerga 265 ff. (as orig. 'herd dog', a deriv. of IE **pek̑u-*).

Note on 'bitch'. Of the preceding words, Grk. κύων, Lat. *canis*, and sometimes others were used of the male and female dog, without distinction except as shown by the gender of the agreeing word. But for the female 'bitch' there are usually special terms. Some of these are simply new fem. forms of words for 'dog', as NG σκύλα, VLat. **cania* (> It. *cagna*, MFr. *caigne*, Fr. *chienne*), Sp. *perra*, Br. *kiez*, Sw. *hynda*, NHG *hündin*, Skt. *çunī-*, also SCr. *kučka* (fr. *kučak*, a less common word for 'dog', based on a calling cry. Berneker 636 f.). Many more are quite unrelated. Rum. *caţea*, fr. Lat. *catella* 'female puppy' (REW 1763). ON *bikkja*, Norw. *bikje*, Sw. dial. *bicka*, OE *bicce*, ME *bicche*, NE *bitch*, etym. dub., perh. : Skt. *bhaga-* 'cunnus' (Walde-P. 2.148. Falk-Torp 72). OE *tīfe*, Du. *teef*, MLG *teve* (> Dan. *tœve*) etym. dub. (Falk-Torp. 1313. Franck-v. W. 690). OHG *zōha*, MHG *zohe*, NHG dial. *zope*, *zauche*, perh. as orig. 'bearer' : OHG *ziohan* 'draw, nourish' (Walde-P. 1.781. Falk-Torp. 1297).

7. Lith. *kale* : Ir. *cuilēn* 'puppy', NE. (3.612). Among others, either of imitative orig. or obscure, are Fr. *lice* (now obs. or dial.), Br. *gart*, ON *tik*, Norw., Sw. dial. *tik*, Lett. *kun'a*, Boh. *čubka*, Pol., Russ. *suka* (see above, 7).

3.612 PUPPY

Grk.	σκύλαξ	Goth.	....	Lith.	šunytis
NG	σκυλάκι, κουτάβι	ON	hvelpr	Lett.	sunītis
Lat.	catulus, catellus	Dan.	hvalp	ChSl.	štenę
It.	cagnuolo	Sw.	valp	SCr.	štene
Fr.	petit chien	OE	hwelp	Boh.	štěně
Sp.	cachorro, perrillo	ME	whelpe	Pol.	szezenie
Rum.	cațel	NE	puppy (whelp)	Russ.	ščenok
Ir.	cuilēn	Du.	jonge hond		
NIr.	coileān	OHG	welf		
W.	cenau (colwyn)	MHG	welf		
Br.	kolen-ki	NHG	junger hund		

Many of the words listed are applied not only to the 'puppy' but also to the young of other animals, and in this connection it will be convenient to notice some of the other terms used for the young of various wild animals (those for the young of domestic animals already have been noted under 'calf', 'lamb', etc.). These can always be denoted by words for 'young' or 'little', adj. or sb., and this is the usual method in some languages where the old special terms have been lost, e.g. Fr. *petit, le petit*, NHG *jung, das junge*. Or dim. forms of the animal names may be preferred.

1. Grk. σκύλαξ, NG σκυλάκι, Ir. *cuilēn*, NIr. *coileān*, W. (obs.) *colwyn*, OCorn. *coloin* (gl. *catulus*), Br. *kolen* (only in cpds. like *kolen-ki* 'puppy', etc.), beside Lith. *kalė* 'bitch', Alb. *kulish* 'puppy' (*këlüš* in G. Meyer, Alb. Etym. Wtb.), all prob. belonging together, but root connection? Walde-P. 1.445 f. Pedersen 1.104. Osthoff, Parerga 274 ff. Words of this group, though mostly 'puppy', are also used for the young of other animals, e.g. Grk. σκύλαξ for the young of the fox, weasel, dolphin, bear.

Grk. σκύμνος (etym.?), esp. the 'lion's cub' (Hom. +), is also used for the young of the fox, wolf, bear, and elephant (cf. Aristot. HA 511ᵇ30, 578ᵃ22, for the last two).

NG κουτάβι, fr. κουτός 'stupid, silly' (17.22).

2. Lat. *catulus* (used for the young of the dog and many other animals, as lion, tiger, wolf, etc., even serpent), dim. *catellus* (> Rum. *cațel*, OIt. *catello*, OFr. *chael*, Fr. *cheau* now obs.), perh. : ON *haðna* 'young goat, kid', Russ. *kotit'sja*, Pol. *kocić się*, etc. 'give birth to young' (of various 'animals'; cf. Berneker 589 f.). Walde-P. 1.338 f. Walde-H. 1.183. Osthoff, Parerga 250. REW 1763. Wartburg 2.496 ff.

Lat. *fētus* (used for the young of various animals), fr. the same root as in *fēmina* 'woman', *fēlāre* 'suck', etc., IE *dhē(i)-* 'suck' (5.16). Ernout-M. 354 f. Walde-H. 1.490.

It. *cagnuolo*, fr. *cagna* 'bitch'.

Fr. *petit chien*, and so in general *petit* 'little' adj. and sb. for the young of other animals.

Sp. *cachorro*, of Basque orig. REW 5959a. Diez 435.

Sp. *perrillo*, dim. of *perro* 'dog'.

3. Ir. *cuilēn*, etc., above, 1.

W. *cenau, ceneu* 'puppy' and 'lion's, wolf's cub', etc. with Ir. *cano* 'wolf's cub' : Skt. *kanīna-* 'young', Grk. καινός 'new' (14.13, 14.14), also prob. ChSl. *štenę*, etc. (below, 6). Walde-P. 1.398. Pedersen 1.121.

4. ON *hvelpr*, Dan. *hvalp*, Sw. *valp*, OE *hwelp*, ME *whelpe*, NE *whelp* (now arch.), Du. *welp* (now esp. 'lion's cub'), OHG–NHG *welf* (now obs. or arch. revival) : OE *hwelan* 'roar, bellow', ON

hvellr 'making a shrill sound'. Falk-Torp 437. These words, like Lat. *catulus*, were used for the young of the dog and many other animals. Cf. NED s.v. *whelp*, sb.

NE *whelp* is now replaced in common use by *puppy* (orig. 'toy dog', fr. Fr. *poupée*, Lat. *pūpa* 'doll'; NED s.v.) in the case of dogs, and by *cub* (: Dan. *kubbe* 'block, stump'; Falk-Torp 430) in the case of foxes, lions, tigers, wolves, while *calf* (3.24) is applied not only to the young of any bovine animal (bison, etc.), but also to that of various large animals, as the moose, elephant, whale.

Du. *jonge hond*, NHG *junger hund*, now the usual term for 'puppy' (in place of the old *welp, welf*), and so in general

Du. *jong*, NHG *jung* 'young', adj. and sb., for the young of other animals.

5. Lith. *šunytis*, Lett. *sunītis* dims. of the words for 'dog'.

6. ChSl. *štenę, štenĭcĭ*, SCr. *stene*, Boh. *štěně*, Pol. *szezenie*, Russ. *ščenok*, prob. (*sken* beside *ken-*) : W. *cenau*, Ir. *cano* (above, 3) and Skt. *kanīna-* 'young', Grk. καινός 'new', etc. Walde-P. 1.398. Osthoff, Parerga 268 f. Otherwise Brückner 543. These words were formerly used also for the young of other animals, 'lion's cub', etc., but except as 'puppy' are now replaced either by words for 'young', as sbs. SCr. *mlado*, Boh. *mládě*, or by dim. forms of the animal's names, e.g. Russ. *l'venok*, Pol. *lwiatko*, 'lion's cub'.

3.62 CAT

Grk.	αἰέλουρος, αἴλουρος	Goth.	....	Lith.	katė
NG	γάτα	ON	kǫttr	Lett.	kak'is, kak'e
Lat.	fēlēs	Dan.	kat	ChSl.	kotŭka
It.	gatto	Sw.	katt	SCr.	mačka
Fr.	chat	OE	catte, catt	Boh.	kočka
Sp.	gato	ME	cat	Pol.	kot
Rum.	pisică	NE	cat	Russ.	koška
Ir.	catt	Du.	kat	Skt.	mārjara-, biḍāla-
NIr.	cat	OHG	kazza	Av.	....
W.	cath	MHG	katze		
Br.	kaz	NHG	katze		

In marked contrast to the prehistoric and general domestication of the dog, the domestic cat was relatively late and for a long time only local. It appears in Egypt from about 2000 B.C., and hence became known to the Greeks and Romans. But it was not a familiar household animal in the classical period, and only after the beginning of our era did it become common and spread over Europe, together with its general European name.

1. Grk. αἰέλουρος, αἴλουρος, prob., as lit. 'wavy-tail', cpd. of αἰόλος 'quick moving' and οὐρά 'tail'. So Et. Mag.,

Buttmann, and J. Schmidt, KZ 32.324. Otherwise Walde-P. 1.287, Boisacq 22.

The word is used in Hdt. 2.66 with reference to the Egyptian cat, but elsewhere it refers to some native small animal, weasel, ferret, or marten, similar to the γαλῆ or ἴκτις, as clearly in Aristoph. Ach. 879. As domestic cat evidently in Aristot. HA 540ᵇ10, Plut. Mor. 2.144c, and later, until the word was replaced by κάττα, quotable from 6th cent. A.D.

2. Lat. *fēlēs*, possibly : W. *beleu* 'marten'. Walde-P. 2.177. Walde-H. 1.474. In Plaut. Rud. 3.4.43 'mouser', prob.

marten or ferret, as in Varro. Used for 'cat' in Cic. with reference to Egypt and later (Pliny, etc.) common, until its displacement by *cattus*.

3. Late Lat. (4th cent. A.D.) *cattus, catta, gattus*, in Grk. form κάττος, κάττα, γάττος, of dub. orig. Ernout-M. 163. Walde-H. 1.182 f. Hence (or from the same source), with variation of init. *c/g* and medial *tt/t*, nearly all the European words. These are listed in the forms that are commonly used generically, whether the masculines, as the Romance (Fr. *chat*, It. *gatto*, Sp. *gato* with fem. *chatte, gatta, gata*), and the Scandinavian (ON *kǫttr*, Dan. *kat*, Sw. *katt*, with fem. ON *ketta*, Norw., Sw. *katta*), or the feminines as NG γάτα, the West Gmc. (OE *catte*, OHG *kazza*, NHG *katze*, with masc. *kater*) and Balto-Slavic (Lith. *katė*, ChSl. *kotŭka*, Boh. *kočka*,

Russ. *koška*; but Pol. *kot* masc. and generic, fem. *kotka*).

4. Rum. *pisică*, deriv. of *pis* a callword for cats similar to Lith. *puž*, LG *puus*, Du. *poes* of NE *puss*. Cf. the use of NE *puss, pussy* as a common noun.

5. Lett. *kak'is, kak'e*, loanword? Mühl.-Endz. 2.139.

6. SCr. *mačka*, Boh. *macka* (obs.), orig. a pet-name form of *Maria*, like NHG *Mieze, Mies* also used for 'cat' (Weigand-H. s.v.), NE *Malkin*, pet-name form of *Matilda*, used for 'cat' (NED s.v. 5), also *Gray-Malkin* (Shaks.), *Grimalkin* (NED s.v.). The masculines, SCr. *maček*, Boh. *macek*, are, of course, by this view formed secondarily to the feminines. Berneker 2.1.

7. Skt. *mārjara-* : *mṛj-* 'wipe, clean'. Skt. *biḍāla-*, prob. from a non-Aryan source.

3.63 MOUSE

Grk.	μῦς	Goth.	....	Lith.	pelė
NG	ποντίκι	ON	mūs	Lett.	pele
Lat.	mūs	Dan.	mus	ChSl.	myšĭ
It.	topo (sorcio)	Sw.	mus	SCr.	miš
Fr.	souris	OE	mūs	Boh.	myš
Sp.	ratón	ME	mūs	Pol.	mysz
Rum.	șoarece	NE	mouse	Russ.	myš'
Ir.	luch	Du.	muis	Skt.	mūṣ-
NIr.	luch	OHG	mūs	Av.	....
W.	llygoden	MHG	mūs		
Br.	logodenn	NHG	maus		

1. IE *mūs-*. Walde-P. 2.312. Ernout-M. 645 f.

Grk. μῦς; Lat. *mūs*; ON, OE, OHG *mūs*, etc., all the Gmc. words; ChSl. *myšĭ*, etc., all the Slavic words; Skt. *mūṣ-*, NPers. *muš*; Arm. *mukn*; Alb. *mì*.

2. NG ποντικός, pop. ποντίκι fr. μῦς Ποντικός 'Pontic mouse' (Aristot. HA 600ᵇ14, Pliny 8.82, etc.).

3. It. *sorcio*, Rum. *șoarece*, fr. Lat. *sōrex* 'shrewmouse'. Fr. *souris* fr. *sōrīcius*. REW 8098, 8101.

It. *topo* 'mouse' or 'rat', fr. Lat. *talpa* 'mole'. REW 8545.

Sp. *ratón*, formed fr. *rata* 'rat', and 'she-mouse'. Similar confusion between 'rat' and 'mouse' in Fr. dialects (REW 7089a), likewise in NG ποντίκι and It. *topo*.

4. Ir. *luch*, W. *llygoden*, Br. *logodenn* (new sg. to pl. *llygod, logod*, old sg. *llyg, log*), perh. : W. *llwg* 'livid'. Stokes 244. Pedersen 1.376.

5. Lith. *pelė*, Lett. *pele*, orig. 'the gray one' : Lith. *pilkas* 'gray', Grk. πελιός 'livid', etc. Walde-P. 2.54.

3.64 BIRD

Grk.	ὄρνις, πτηνόν, πετεινόν	Goth.	fugls	Lith.	paukštis
NG	πουλί	ON	fugl	Lett.	putns
Lat.	avis	Dan.	fugl	ChSl.	pŭta, pŭtica
It.	uccello	Sw.	fågel	SCr.	(p)tica
Fr.	oiseau	OE	fugol	Boh.	pták
Sp.	ave, pájaro	ME	fowl, brid	Pol.	ptak
Rum.	pasăre	NE	bird	Russ.	ptica
Ir.	ēn	Du.	vogel	Skt.	vi-, pakšin-
NIr.	ēan	OHG	fogal	Av.	vi-, mərəɣa-
W.	aderyn, edn	MHG	vogel		
Br.	labous, evn	NHG	vogel		

1. Grk. ὄρνις (in Att. mostly the domestic 'cock' or 'hen', 3.51) : Goth. *ara*, Lith. *erelis* 'eagle', etc., prob. as 'quickly moving' fr. the root *er-* in Grk. ὄρνῡμι 'set in motion', Lat. *orīrī* 'rise', Skt. *ṛ-* 'move, rise', etc. Walde-P. 1.135.

Grk. πτηνόν, πετεινόν (in NT reg. τὰ πετεινά 'birds', not ὄρνιθες) sb. use of πτηνός, πετεινός 'winged', fr. root of πέτομαι 'fly'.

NG πουλί 'chicken' (3.51) is also the common word for 'bird' (τὰ πουλιά).

2. Lat. *avis* : Skt., Av. *vi-* 'bird'. Hence Sp. *ave*, and fr. dim. *aucellus* (cf. fem. *avicella, aucella*) It. *uccello*, Fr. *oiseau*. Walde-P. 1.21. Ernout-M. 90 f. REW 828.

Sp. *pájaro*, Rum. *pasăre*, fr. Lat. *passer* 'sparrow'. REW 6268.

3. Ir. *ēn*, NIr. *ēan*, W. *edn*, Br. *evn*, also W. *aderyn*, OW *eterin*, all fr. *pet-* 'fly' in Grk. πέτομαι, etc. Walde-P. 2.21. Pedersen 1.90.

Br. *labous*, fr. MBr. *lapous* 'bird' but also 'injurious insect' and so prob. fr. VLat. *lacusta = locusta* ('lobster' and) 'locust', with unexplained *p* for *c* as in

OE *lopystre* 'lobster'. Ernault, Glossaire 353. Henry 177. (Not in Loth, Mots lat.)

4. Goth *fugls*, OE *fugol*, etc., general Gmc., etym. disputed. Perh. : Lith. *paukštis* 'bird' (below, 5); or with dissim. fr. Gmc. *flug-la-* : OHG *fliugan*, OE *flēogan* 'fly'. Walde-P. 2.76. Feist 170. Falk-Torp 280, 1464. Wiegand-H. 2.1178.

ME *brid*, NE *bird*, now the usual generic term in place of the specialized *fowl* (3.51), fr. OE *brid* 'young bird', etym.? NED s.v.

5. Lith. *paukštis*, Lett. *putns*, ChSl. *pŭta, pŭtica*, etc., all the Slavic words, fr. the same root as Lat. *pullus* 'young of an animal, chicken' and other words for 'small, young', with the same extension to 'bird' as in NG πουλί. Walde-P. 2.76.

6. Skt., Av. *vi-* : Lat. *avis* (above, 2). Skt. *pakšin-*, deriv. of *pakša-* 'wing' (4.392).

Av. *mərəɣa-* used of large birds (Barth. 1172), NPers. *murgh* 'bird' : Skt. *mṛga-* 'wild animal' (3.11).

3.65 FISH

Grk.	ἰχθΰς	Goth.	fisks	Lith.	žuvìs
NG	ψάρι	ON	fiskr	Lett.	zivs
Lat.	piscis	Dan.	fisk	ChSl.	ryba
It.	pesce	Sw.	fisk	SCr.	rȉba
Fr.	poisson	OE	fisc	Boh.	ryba
Sp.	pez	ME	fisch	Pol.	ryba
Rum.	peşte	NE	fish	Russ.	ryba
Ir.	iasc	Du.	visch	Skt.	matsya-
NIr.	iasg	OHG	fisc	Av.	masya-
W.	pysgodyn	MHG	visch		
Br.	pesk	NHG	fisch		

1. Grk. ἰχθΰς, Lith. žuvìs, Lett. zivs, OPruss. suckis, Arm. jukn, root connection? Walde-P. 1.664.

2. Lat. piscis, Ir. íasc, NIr. iasg, Goth. fisk, etc., all the Gmc. words, root connection? Walde-P. 2.11. Pokorny, KZ 54.307. Cuny, Mélanges Glotz, 268 f.

From Lat. piscis all the Romance words, also W. pysg (old coll., whence pl. pysgod with new sg. pysgodyn), Corn. pisc, Br. pesk.

3. NG ψάρι, fr. Grk. ὀψάριον dim. of

ὄψον 'dainty', at Athens especially 'fish food' (cf. ὄψον ποντίων Eur.). ὀψάριον for 'fish' as food in NT in Jn. (6.9, 11; 21.9, 10, 13; but ἰχθΰς for fish in the sea 21.6, 9, 11; in the other gospels only ἰχθΰς in both senses) and often in the pap. The definite extension to the living fish is later.

4. ChSl. ryba, etc., all the Slavic words, etym.?

5. Skt. matsya-, Av. masya-, fr. an IE *mad- 'be wet' in Grk. μαδάω, Lat. madēre, etc.? Walde-P. 2.230.

3.66 FISHERMAN

Grk.	ἁλιεύς	Goth.	fiskja	Lith.	žvejys
NG	ψαρᾶς	ON	fiskimaðr, fiskikarl	Lett.	zvejnieks, zvejs
Lat.	piscātor	Dan.	fisker	ChSl.	rybarĭ
It.	pescatore	Sw.	fiskare	SCr.	rȉbar
Fr.	pêcheur	OE	fiscere	Boh.	rybář
Sp.	pescador	ME	fisher	Pol.	rybak
Rum.	pescar	NE	fisherman	Russ.	rybak, rybolov
Ir.	iascach	Du.	visscher	Skt.	kāivarta-, dhīvara-,
NIr.	iascaire	OHG	fiscāri		matsyajīvat-, etc.
W.	pysgotwr	MHG	vischære		
Br.	pisketaer	NHG	fischer		

Nearly all the words for 'fisherman' are derivatives of the words for 'fish' (2.65) through the corresponding verbs, or in some cases compounds, like NE fisherman which has displaced fisher in current use, Russ. rybolov 'fish-catcher'.

Thus Lat. piscātor (> Romance words, except Rum. pescar, fr. Lat. piscārius 'fishmonger', favored by the suffix of the Slavic word, ChSl. rybarĭ, etc.), Ir. iascach, NIr. iascaire, Goth. fiskja, OE fiscere, OHG fiscāri, Lith.

žvejys, ChSl. rybarĭ, etc.
Exceptions are:
Grk. ἁλιεύς, fr. ἅλς 'sea' and in Homer also 'sailor'. But NG pop. ψαρᾶς 'fisherman' and 'fishmonger', fr. ψάρι 'fish'.

Skt., beside occasional matsya-jīvat- lit. 'one who makes a living from fish', matsya-bandha- (bandh- 'bind, catch'), and mātsyika- (Pān.), more commonly kāivarta-, prob. orig. a term of opprobrium (cf. kev- 'serve' Dhātup.), and dhīvara-, prob. : dhīvan- 'skilful'.

3.71 WOLF

Grk.	λύκος	Goth.	wulfs	Lith.	vil̃kas
NG	λύκος	ON	ulfr, vargr	Lett.	vìlks
Lat.	lupus	Dan.	ulv	ChSl.	vlŭkŭ
It.	lupo	Sw.	varg, ulv	SCr.	vûk
Fr.	loup	OE	wulf	Boh.	vlk
Sp.	lobo	ME	wolf	Pol.	wilk
Rum.	lup	NE	wolf	Russ.	volk
Ir.	fáel, brech, cū allaid	Du.	wolf	Skt.	vŕka-
NIr.	cū allaidh, faol(chū),	OHG	wolf	Av.	vǝhrka-
	mactíre	MHG	wolf		
W.	blaidd	NHG	wolf		
Br.	bleiz				

1. IE *wl̥kwo- and *luko-. Here belong all the words listed except the Celtic and the ON vargr, Sw. varg. Lat. lupus is a loanword fr. a rural dialect, like Lat. bōs. Walde-P. 1.316 f. Ernout-M. 588. Walde-H. 1.836 f.

2. Ir. fáel, NIr. faol, also faolchū (with cū 'dog'), etym.? Walde-P. 1.213.
Ir. brech (K. Meyer, Contrib. 252; NIr. brēach in place names), etym.?
Ir. cū allaid, NIr. also madradh allaidh, both lit. 'wild dog'.

NIr. mactíre, lit. 'son of the land', like the many popular phrases with mac (Dinneen s.v.) but here without any obvious point to the special application.

W. blaidd, Br. bleiz = Ir. bled 'sea monster, whale', but etym.? Stokes 188. Henry 37. Against connection with Lat. bellua, cf. Walde-H. 1.100.

3. ON vargr, Sw., Norw. varg : OE wearg, OHG warg 'villain, criminal', etc. Walde-P. 1.273. Falk-Torp 1354. Hellquist 1314 f.

3.72 LION

Grk.	λέων	Goth.	...	Lith.	liūtas, levas
NG	λέων, λιοντάρι	ON	leō, leōn	Lett.	lauva
Lat.	leō	Dan.	løve	ChSl.	livŭ
It.	leone	Sw.	lejon	SCr.	lav
Fr.	lion	OE	lēo	Boh.	lev
Sp.	león	ME	lioun	Pol.	lev
Rum.	leu	NE	lion	Russ.	lev
Ir.	leo	Du.	leeuw	Skt.	siṅha-
NIr.	leomhan	OHG	leo, lio, lewo	Av.	....
W.	llew	MHG	lewe, louwo		
Br.	leon	NHG	löwe		

1. The European words (except Lith. liūtas) go back by a series of borrowings, through the medium of Lat. leō, to Grk. λέων, which is probably itself a loanword fr. some pre-Greek source. The development of the Gmc. w-forms, as OHG lewo, NHG löwe (> Dan. løve), is obscure. From such come the Slavic forms

and fr. the latter (Pol. or Russ.) the Lith. levas, while Lett. lauva is fr. MLG louwe. Walde-H. 1.785.

2. Lith. liūtas, fr. Russ. ljutyj 'fierce'. Berneker 756, 759.

3. Skt. siṅha-, without outside connection unless Arm. inj 'leopard'. Walde-P. 2.508.

3.73 BEAR

Grk.	ἄρκτος	Goth.	....	Lith.	lokys, meška
NG	ἀρκούδα	ON	bjǫrn	Lett.	lācis
Lat.	ursus	Dan.	bjørn	ChSl.	medvědĭ
It.	orso	Sw.	björn	SCr.	medvjed
Fr.	ours	OE	bera	Boh.	medvěd
Sp.	oso	ME	bere	Pol.	niedźwiedź
Rum.	urs	NE	bear	Russ.	medved
Ir.	art, mathgamain	Du.	beer	Skt.	ŕkṣa-
NIr.	mathghamhain	OHG	bero	Av.	arša-
W.	arth	MHG	ber		
Br.	ourz	NHG	bär		

1. IE *r̥k̂þo-, possibly as the 'destroyer' (of beehives): Skt. rakṣas- 'harm, injury.' Walde-P. 1.322. Benveniste, BSL 38.141.
Grk. ἄρκτος, NG pop. ἀρκούδα; Lat. ursus, whence the Romance forms, also Corn. ors, MBr. urs (Br. ourz = Fr.); Ir. art, W. arth (Pedersen 1.89); Skt. ŕkṣa-, Av. arša-.

2. Ir. mathgamain, NIr. mathghamhain, cpd. of gamain 'calf', first part fr. old math 'bear' (RIA Contrib. s.v.), perh. : maith 'good' as a euphemistic term. Stokes 199.

3. ON bjǫrn, OE bera, OHG bero, etc.,

the general Gmc. word : Lith. bėras 'brown', OE brūn 'brown', etc. Walde-P. 1.166. Falk-Torp 77.

4. Lith. lokys, Lett. lācis, OPruss. clokis, all fr. *tlākis, this perh. as 'hairy, shaggy' : SCr. dlaka 'hair'. Brückner, KZ 46, 207. Mühl.-Endz. 2.434. Otherwise Meillet, Ling. hist. 284.
Lith. meška fr. a Slavic (ORuss. mešika, Pol. Mieszka) pop. abbr. of the following. Berneker 2.30. Brückner 335.

5. ChSl. medvědĭ, etc., all the Slavic words, lit. 'honey-eater', cpd. of medŭ 'honey' and ěd- 'eat'. Berneker 2.30.

3.74 FOX

Grk.	ἀλώπηξ	Goth.	fauhō	Lith.	lapė
NG	ἀλεποῦ	ON	refr (m.), fóa (f.)	Lett.	lapsa
Lat.	vulpēs	Dan.	ræv	ChSl.	lisŭ
It.	volpe	Sw.	räv	SCr.	lis, lisica
Fr.	renard	OE	fox	Boh.	liška
Sp.	zorra, raposa	ME	fox	Pol.	lis
Rum.	vulpe	NE	fox	Russ.	lisa
Ir.	sinnach	Du.	vos	Skt.	(lopāça-)
NIr.	sionnach, mada ruadh	OHG	fuhs	Av.	(raopi-)
W.	cadno, llwynog	MHG	vuhs		
Br.	louarn	NHG	fuchs		

1. Grk. ἀλώπηξ, NG ἀλεποῦ, Lat. vulpēs (> It. volpe, Rum. vulpe), Br. louarn, Lith. lapė, Lett. lapsa : Skt. lopāça- 'jackal', Av. raopi- 'a kind of dog' (Barth. 1496), NPers. rōbāh 'fox'. But phonetic relations complicated and obscure. Walde-P. 1.317.

2. Fr. renard fr. OHG Reginhard, the name of the fox in fables (cf. the LG

poem Reinke de Vos), orig. 'strong in council, wily'. REW 7172.
OFr. goupil, fr. a blend of Lat. dim. vulpēcula, VLat. vulpīcula with Gmc. hwelp 'whelp'. REW 4248, 9463.
Sp. zorra (masc. zorro), fr. Basque azaria 'fox'.
Sp. raposa, fr. (*rapo >) rabo 'tail', this fr. Lat. rāpum 'turnip'. REW 7065.

3. Ir. sinnach, NIr. sionnach, etym.? NIr. also mada (or madra) ruadh, lit. 'red dog'.
W. cadno, etym.?
W. llwynog, deriv. of llwyn 'bush' (like draenog 'hedgehog' fr. draen 'thorn'), with reference to the bushy tail.

4. Goth. fauhō (fem.), ON fóa (fem.), OE fox, OHG fuhs, etc., the usual

Gmc. word, prob. : Skt. puccha- 'tail'. Walde-P. 2.82. Falk-Torp 281. Feist 144. Cf. Sp. raposa and W. llwynog.

ON refr (masc.), Dan. ræv, Sw. räv, perh. as 'red' : ON jarpr 'brown ', OE eorp 'darkish', etc. Walde-P. 1.146. Falk-Torp 931. Hellquist 871.

5. ChSl. lisŭ, etc., the general Slavic word, etym.? Berneker 724.

3.75 DEER

Grk.	ἔλαφος	Goth.	....	Lith.	elnis, briedis
NG	ἔλαφος, (ἐ)λάφι	ON	hjǫrtr	Lett.	alnis, briedis
Lat.	cervus	Dan.	hjort	ChSl.	jelenĭ
It.	cervo	Sw.	hjort	SCr.	jelen
Fr.	cerf	OE	heorot	Boh.	jelen
Sp.	ciervo	ME	hert, dere	Pol.	jelen
Rum.	cerb	NE	deer (hart)	Russ.	olen
Ir.	oss (sed, seg)	Du.	hert	Skt.	mŕga-, hariṇa-, etc.
NIr.	fiadh	OHG	hiruz	Av.	....
W.	carw, hydd	MHG	hirz		
Br.	karo	NHG	hirsch		

Only the generic words for 'deer', which are mostly also those for the male, are considered here. There is a notably extensive vocabulary of more specific terms according to sex, age, and particular species, as NE buck, stag, doe, hind, fawn, roe, elk, moose, etc. Schrader, Reallex. s.v. Hirsch.

1. Grk. ἔλαφος (also ἐλλός 'fawn'), Lith. elnis, Lett. alnis, ChSl. jelenĭ, etc., all the Slavic forms, also W. elain 'doe', OE elch 'elk', Arm. eln 'doe', etc., all fr. *el- perh. orig. denoting the reddish color. Walde-P. 1.154.

2. Lat. cervus (> Romance words), W. carw, Br. karo, ON hjǫrtr, OE heorot, OHG hiruz, etc. the general Gmc. word (but NE hart specialized and then poetic), OPruss. sirwis : Grk. κέρας, Lat. cornū, OE horn 'horn', etc. Walde-P. 1.406. Ernout-M. 181.

3. Ir. oss : W. ych, Goth. auhsa 'ox', etc. (3.22). Walde-P. 1.248 f. Pedersen 1.36.

Ir. sed, seg, W. hydd : Ir. segas 'forest'? Loth, RC 35.86 f.
Ir. dam allaid or ag allaid, lit. 'wild ox (cow)'.

NIr. fiadh = Ir. fiad 'wild animal, beast, deer', W. gwydd 'wild' (: Ir. fid 'tree' or ON veiðr 'the hunt'? Walde-P. 1.230, 314. Pedersen 1.111 f.). Specialization as in NE deer. Loth, RC 35.35.

4. ME dere, NE deer, from OE dēor 'wild animal' (3.11), with specialization (occasional even in OE, common in ME, now complete; cf. NED s.v.) to the favorite animal of the hunt.

5. Lith., Lett. briedis, OPruss. braydis, perh. : Sw. dial. brind 'elk', Messap. βρένδον 'deer'. Trautmann, Altpreuss. 313. Idg. Jhb. 5.193.

6. Skt. mŕga- 'wild animal' (3.11) used esp. for 'deer'.
Skt. hariṇa-, deriv. of hari- 'reddish brown'.

3.76 MONKEY

Grk.	πίθηκος	Goth.	....	Lith.	bezdžionė
NG	πίθηκος, μαϊμοῦ	ON	api	Lett.	pērtik'is
Lat.	sīmia	Dan.	abe	ChSl.	(pitikŭ)
It.	scimmia	Sw.	ape	SCr.	majmun, opica
Fr.	singe	OE	apa	Boh.	opice
Sp.	mono	ME	apa	Pol.	opica
Rum.	maimuță	NE	monkey (ape)	Russ.	obez'jana
Ir.	....	Du.	aap	Skt.	kapi-
NIr.	apa	OHG	affo	Av.	....
W.	epa	MHG	affe		
Br.	marmouz	NHG	affe		

Here is understood the generic name for the simians, NE monkey in current popular usage, but formerly and still sometimes ape, though the latter now generally denotes the tailless species. Cf. NED s.v. ape.

1. Grk. πίθηκος, etym.? Walde-P. 2.186. This is the generic term, while κῆπος, κῆβος (cf. below, 6) is specific. Cf. Aristot. HA 502ᵃ ὁ μὲν κῆβος πίθηκος ἔχων οὐράν.

Byz. μῑμώ : μῑμέομαι 'mimic'.

NG μαιμοῦ, fr. Turk., Arab. maimūn. Lokotsch 1365.

2. Lat. sīmia (> It. scimmia, Fr. singe), deriv. of sīmus, loanword fr. Grk. σῑμός 'snub-nosed'. First used as a nickname and prob. based on the name Σῑμίας, Simia. Kretschmer, KZ 33, 563.

OIt., OFr. maimon, Rum. maimuță, also OIt. monna, Sp. mono, -a, fr. Arab. maimūn. Lokotsch 1365. REW 5242.

3. NIr. apa, W. ab (arch.), fr. ME ape, OE apa (below, 4), W. epa late loanword fr. NE ape.

Br. marmouz, fr. OFr. marmot or marmouset, both used for 'monkey' (also

'small child', etc.), history dub. Henry 196. REW 5587. Gamillscheg 593.

4. ON api, OE apa, OHG affo, etc., the general Gmc. word, orig. unknown, perh. Celtic. Walde-P. 1.51 ff.

From Gmc. come the Slavic forms, Boh. op, opice, SCr., ORuss. opica, etc. Stender-Petersen 361.

NE monkey, prob. fr. a MLG moneke (Moneke as name attested), dim. of the word that appears as Sp. mono, etc. (above, 2). NED s.v.

5. ChSl. (late) pitikŭ fr. Grk. πίθηκος. Boh. opice, etc. from Gmc. (above, 4). Russ. obez'jana (> Lith. bezdžionė), fr. Turk. ebuzine. Lokotsch 556.

Lett. pērtik'is, fr. Esth. pertik (or conversely?). Mühl.-Endz. 3.210.

SCr. majmun fr. Turk., Arab. maimūn.

Pol. małpa fr. NHG maul-affe. Brückner 320.

6. Skt. kapi- : kapila- 'brownish, reddish', fr. 'smoke-colored, Grk. καπνός, etc.? Walde-P. 1.379. Prob. source of Egypt. qephi, Grk. κῆπος, κῆβος, etc. Schrader, Reallex. 1.16.

3.77 ELEPHANT

Grk.	ἐλέφας	Goth.	....	Lith.	dramblys
NG	ἐλέφας	ON	fíll	Lett.	elefants
Lat.	elephantus, elephās	Dan.	elefant	ChSl.	....
It.	elefante	Sw.	elefant	SCr.	slon
Fr.	éléphant	OE	elpend, ylp	Boh.	slon
Sp.	elefante	ME	olifant, elefant	Pol.	słoń
Rum.	elefant	NE	elephant	Russ.	slon
Ir.	elefant	Du.	olifant	Skt.	hastin-, gaja-, etc.
NIr.	elephant	OHG	elafant, helfant	Av.	....
W.	eliffant, cawrfil	MHG	elefant, (h)elfant		
Br.	olifant	NHG	elefant		

3.78 CAMEL

Grk.	κάμηλος	Goth.	ulbandus	Lith.	kupranugaris, kupris, verbliudas
NG	κάμηλος	ON	ulfaldi		
Lat.	camēlus	Dan.	kamel	Lett.	kamiēlis
It.	cammello	Sw.	kamel	ChSl.	velĭbǫdŭ
Fr.	chameau	OE	olfend (camel)	SCr.	deva, kamila
Sp.	camello	ME	camel	Boh.	velbloud
Rum.	cămilă	NE	camel	Pol.	wielbłąd
Ir.	camall	Du.	kameel	Russ.	verbljud
NIr.	camall	OHG	olbanta	Skt.	uṣṭra-
W.	camel	MHG	olbent(e), kembel, ka(m)mel	Av.	uštra-
Br.	kañval	NHG	kamel		

3.77, 3.78. Nearly all the European words for 'elephant' and 'camel' are from Grk. ἐλέφας or κάμηλος, which again are based upon Egyptian or Semitic words respectively. But the name of the elephant, known in southern Europe since Hannibal, was subject to great distortion and some confusion in application with the camel in northern and northeastern Europe, where both animals were long known only by hearsay as strange beasts.

1. Grk. ἐλέφας, -αντος 'ivory' (Hom. +) and 'elephant' (Hdt. +), to be analyzed as ἐλ-έφας, the second part, like Lat. ebur 'ivory' fr. Egypt. āb 'elephant, ivory', but first part disputed. Schrader, Reallex. 1.242. Ernout-M. 297 f. Walde-H. 1.389.

Hence most of the Eur. words for elephant, except the Balto-Slavic.

Hence also (though doubted by some), with shift to 'camel', Goth. ulbandus, ON ulfaldi, OE olfend, OHG

olbanta, MHG olbente, olbende, and, through Gmc. and in form influenced by velĭ- 'great', ChSl. velĭbǫdŭ, late -blǫdŭ, Boh. velbloud, Pol. wielbłąd, Russ. verbljud (> Lith. verbliudas). Feist 515. Stender-Petersen 358 ff. Brückner 616. For the confusion note also that MIr. camall is used for 'elephant' in Book of Leinster (K. Meyer, Contrib. 311).

My colleague Gelb reports a Hitt. hieroglyph for 'ox', in this case prob. for some kind of wild ox, with accompanying cuneiform name u-lu-pa-ta-sa, which may be normalized as ulupantas or ulpantas and seems to belong to the same group.

2. Grk. κάμηλος, 'camel', loanword fr. Semitic, Hebr. gāmāl, etc. Hence through Lat. camēlus (VLat. also -ēllus, -ellus, REW 1544) the Eur. words (OE camel in Lindisf. vs. olfend in WSax. Gospels), except those fr. 'elephant'

(above, 1) and SCr. deva fr. Turk. (Lokotsch 510).

3. W. cawrfil 'elephant', cpd. of cawr 'giant' and mil 'animal' (3.11).

4. ON fíll 'elephant' (still the common word in Icel.; ODan. fil), loanword through Slavic fr. some oriental source, Arab. fil, NPers. pīl, etc. Falk-Torp 217. Lokotsch 605. Schrader, Reallex. 1.245.

5. Lith. dramblys 'fat-belly' and 'elephant' (NSB, etc., neolog. in this sense) : dribti 'roll down, tumble', etc. (Leskien, Ablaut 324 without dramblys), hence 'elephant' as the clumsy animal.

Lith. kupranugaris and kupris 'camel' (NSB, etc., neolog. for verbliudas) : kupra 'hump'.

6. SCr. slon, etc., the general Slavic word for 'elephant' (whence also obs. Lith. slonis, Lett. zilonis) : ChSl. sloniti

'lean', reflecting the popular notion that the elephant cannot bend its legs and sleeps leaning on a tree, a notion that is apparently referred to by Aristot. HA 498ᵃ and persisted in medieval and modern times (cf. Sir Thomas Browne, Pseudodoxia 3.1). Brückner 500.

7. Skt. hastin- (at first adj. with mṛga- 'wild animal') 'elephant', deriv. of hasta- 'hand', with reference to the elephant's trunk as 'hand'.

Other Skt. words for 'elephant' are gaja- (: gaj- 'roar'), kariṇ- (deriv. of kara- 'doer' in its special use as 'elephant's trunk') and vāraṇa- (prob. fr. vṛ- in sense of 'ward off').

Skt. uṣṭra-, Av. uštra- 'camel', perh. with Skt. usra- 'ox, bull' as orig. 'male animal' fr. IE *wes- 'moisten' as 'impregnate', like Skt. vṛṣan- 'male', Lat. verrēs 'boar', etc. : Skt. varṣa- 'rain', etc. Walde-P. 1.308. Uhlenbeck 32.

3.79 HUNT (vb.)

Grk.	θηρεύω, θηράω, κυνηγετέω, κυνηγέω	Goth.	....	Lith.	medžioti
NG	κυνηγῶ	ON	veiða	Lett.	medīt
Lat.	vēnārī, sectārī	Dan.	jage	ChSl.	loviti
It.	cacciare	Sw.	jaga	SCr.	loviti
Fr.	chasser	OE	huntian, wǣpan	Boh.	loviti
Sp.	cazar, montear	ME	hunte	Pol.	polować
Rum.	vîna	NE	hunt	Russ.	ochotit'sja
Ir.	adclaidim	Du.	jagen	Skt.	mṛgaya-
NIr.	fiadhachaim	OHG	weidōn, jagōn	Av.	....
W.	hela	MHG	jagen		
Br.	hemolc'hi, chaseal	NHG	jagen		

Some of the verbs for 'hunt' (wild animals) are from the more general notion of 'try to seize, chase' or the like. Others, more distinctive from the outset, are derived from words for 'wild animal' or 'woods', or (in Grk.) connected with the use of dogs.

Nouns for the 'hunt' and 'hunter' are obvious cognates of the verbs.

1. Grk. θηράω, θηρεύω, fr. θήρ 'wild beast' (3.11).

Grk. κυνηγετέω, κυνηγέω, fr. the earlier κυνηγέτης (Hom.), κυνηγός 'hunter', cpds. of κύων 'dog' and ἄγω 'drive'.

2. Lat. vēnārī (> Rum. vîna), prob. (with grade *wēn- beside *wen-) : Skt. van- 'seek, desire', OE winnan 'strive, fight', etc. Walde-P. 1.230. Ernout-M. 1085.

Lat. sectārī 'follow, pursue' also used for 'hunt' animals, fr. *sectus, old pple. of sequī 'follow' (10.52).

It. cacciare, Fr. chasser, Sp. cazar fr. VLat. *captiāre for Lat. captāre 'try to seize, chase' (frequent. of capere 'seize, take'). REW 1662.

Sp. montear, fr. monte 'mountain, woods'.

3. Ir. adclaidim (also 'fish'), cpd. of claidim 'dig' (8.22) Pedersen 2.492.

NIr. fiadhachaim, fiadhuighim, fr. Ir. fiadhach 'hunt' (sb.), this fr. fiadh 'wild animal', now 'deer' (3.75). But for the sbs., cf. also Ir. selg, NIr. sealg, seilg 'hunt' and NIr. sealgaire 'hunter', belonging with the following.

W. hela, Br. hemolc'hi (for *emholc'hi), Ir. selg 'hunt' (sb.) : Skt. sṛj- 'loose, emit, shoot'. Semantic development in Celtic through loosing the hunting dogs (cf. Skt. sṛjati çunas). Walde-P. 2.508. Pedersen 1.106.

Br. chaseal fr. Fr. chasser (above, 2).

4. ON veiða, OE wǣpan (with nouns for 'the hunt' ON veiðr, OE wǣþ), OHG weidōn (also 'pasture', NHG weiden, 3.15), fr. an extension of *wei- in Lith. veju, vyti 'pursue', Skt. veti 'seeks, follows', Av. vayeiti 'pursues', etc. Walde-P. 1.230. Falk-Torp 1361 f.

OE huntian (and hunta 'hunter'), ME hunte, NE hunt : OE hentan 'seize',

Goth. fra-hinþan 'capture', Sw. hinna 'reach', upphinna 'overtake' (10.54) fr. parallel root forms (*ken-d-, *ken-t-?), but outside connections dub. Walde-P. 1.460. Feist 161. NED s.v. hunt.

OHG jagōn, MHG, NHG jagen (> Dan. jage, Sw. jaga), Du. jagen, etym. dub., but perh. : Skt. yahu-, yahva- 'restless, active, swift', (pra-)yakṣ- 'hasten, press on', Grk. ἰχανάω 'desire', etc. Walde-P. 1.195 f. Weigand-H. 1.940.

5. Lith. medžioti, Lett. medīt, fr. Lith. medis 'tree', older sense 'woods', Lett. mežs 'woods' (1.41). Mühl.-Endz. 2.590, 611. Cf. Sp. montear, above, 2.

6. ChSl. SCr., Boh. loviti, Pol. łowić, polować, deriv. of ChSl. lovŭ 'hunting, booty' : Grk. λεία 'booty', Lat. lucrum 'gain', Goth. laun, OHG lōn 'reward, pay', etc. Walde-P. 2.379 f. Berneker 735 ff.

Russ. ochotit'sja refl. (with na 'on' when used transitively) fr. ochata 'desire, will, hunt, chase, sport' : chotět', ChSl. chotěti 'wish' (16.61). For the change 'desire' > 'hunt', cf. Skt. lubdha- 'greedy', as sb. 'hunter'. Berneker 398 f.

7. Skt. mṛgaya-, fr. mṛga- 'wild animal, game' (3.11).

3.81 INSECT

Most of the European words for 'insect' (generic, but of somewhat changing scope; sometimes including worms, etc.) are of learned origin, going back ultimately to Aristotle's naming of insects from the notches in their bodies. But there are some others which either have become the accepted technical terms (so Lith. vabzdys, Boh. hmyz, Pol. owad) or are colloquial expressions used much like bug in U.S.

1. Grk. ἔντομα (sc. ζῷα), the term used by Aristot. (e.g. HA 487ᵃ33 καλῶ δ'

ἔντομα ὅσα ἔχει κατὰ τὸ σῶμα ἐντομάς), fr. ἐντέμνω 'cut in', with reference to the incisions, notches. Translated by the Lat. insecta (: insecāre 'cut in') in Pliny, with later sg. insectum. Hence the widespread Eur. words, mostly borrowed directly, but translated in W. trychfil (fr. trychu 'cut', mil 'animal'), SCr. zareznik (fr. cpd. of rezati 'cut'), Russ. nasekomoe (fr. cpd. of seč', sekat' 'cut').

2. NE bug (the pop. word in U.S.; in British use 'bedbug'), prob. the same word as ME bugge 'scarecrow, bugbear'

and ultimately connected with Lith. *bužys* 'scarecrow', *būžys* 'insect' (so separated in NSB), etc. Bugs are unpleasant creatures. Walde-P. 2.117. Endzelin, KZ 44.64. NED s.v. *bug¹*, *bug²*.

Lith. *vabzdys*, now the accepted term (whence *vabzdėdžiai* 'insectivora'), neolog. introduced by Javlonskis in 1908 and based on *vabalas* 'beetle', as I am informed by Senn.

Boh. *hmyz* : *hemzati*, SCr. *gmizati* 'crawl', etc. (12.41). Berneker 367.

Pol. *owad* = late ChSl. *obadŭ*, *ovadŭ*.

SCr. *obad*, Boh. *ovád* 'gadfly', fr. **obwado-*, orig. 'something that pesters, annoys' : Boh. *vaditi* 'harm, hinder, trouble', Pol. *wadzić* 'make quarrel, hinder' (= ChSl. *vaditi* 'accuse', 21.31). Brückner 387.

Some words which normally denote a particular insect or a worm are also used generically, as NE *fly* (NED s.v. *fly*, sb.; cf. *butterfly*), W. *pryf*, Pol. *robak*, both 'worm' (3.84).

Of the numerous Skt. insect names (Zimmer, Altind. Leben 97 f.) none seems to be generic.

3.82 BEE

Grk.	μέλισσα	Goth.	....	Lith.	bitė, bitis
NG	μέλισσα	ON	bȳfluga	Lett.	bite
Lat.	apis	Dan.	bi	ChSl.	bĭčela
It.	ape, pecchia	Sw.	bi	SCr.	pčela
Fr.	abeille	OE	bēo	Boh.	včela
Sp.	abeja	ME	be	Pol.	pszczoła
Rum.	albină	NE	bee	Russ.	pčela
Ir.	bech	Du.	bei	Skt.	bhramara-, ali-
NIr.	beach	OHG	bīa, bini	Av.	....
W.	gwenynen	MHG	bine		
Br.	gwenanenn	NHG	biene		

Familiarity with the bee in the IE period, if not proved by the partial European agreement in words for 'bee', is clearly shown by the more complete agreement in the old words for 'honey' and 'mead' (5.84, 5.85).

1. IE(?) **bhī-*, etc., root connection dub., perh. of imitative orig. Walde-P. 2.184 f.

ON *bȳfluga* (cpd. with *fluga* 'fly'), OE *bēo*, OHG *bīa*, *bini*, etc., all the Gmc. words; Lith. *bitė*, *bitis*, Lett. *bite*, OPruss. *bitte*; Ir. *bech*, NIr. *beach*; ChSl. *bĭčela*, etc., all the Slavic forms.

2. Grk. μέλισσα, Att. μέλιττα, deriv. of μέλι 'honey'.

3. Lat. *apis*, dim. *apicula*, etym.? Hence It. *ape*, OFr. *ef* (Fr. dial. *e*, etc.); fr. dim., It. *pecchia*, Fr. *abeille*, Sp. *abeja*. (Fr. dial. also *mouche à miel* lit. 'honey fly'). Ernout-M. 61. Walde-H. 1.57. REW 523, 525.

Rum. *albină*, fr. late Lat. *alvīna* = *alveārium* 'beehive' (Keil, Gram. Lat. 7.107). Development fr. 'beehive' to coll. 'swarm of bees', then 'bee'. REW 393. Pușcariu 59.

4. W. *gwenynen*, Br. *gwenanenn*, OCorn. *guenenen* (new sgs. to coll. W. *gwenyn*, Br. *gwenan* 'bees'), fr. W. *gwan*, Corn. *gwane* 'thrust, stick, stab', this : Goth. *wunds* 'wound', etc. Walde-P. 1.212 (without mention of the words for 'bee'). Henry 150.

5. Skt. *bhramara-*, of imitative orig. here 'buzzing', but prob. the same as in Lat. *fremere*, OHG *breman* 'growl, mutter', NHG *bremse* 'gadfly', etc. Walde-P. 2.202.

Skt. *ali-*, etym.? Uhlenbeck 15.

Skt. *bambhara-* (rare), of imitative orig. : Grk. πεμφρηδών 'a kind of wasp', etc. Walde-P. 2.161.

3.83 FLY (sb.)

Grk.	μυῖα	Goth.	....	Lith.	musė
NG	μυῖγα	ON	fluga	Lett.	muša
Lat.	musca	Dan.	flue	ChSl.	mucha
It.	mosca	Sw.	fluga	SCr.	muha
Fr.	mouche	OE	flēoge	Boh.	moucha
Sp.	mosca	ME	flye	Pol.	mucha
Rum.	muscă	NE	fly	Russ.	mucha
Ir.	cuil	Du.	vlieg	Skt.	makṣa-
NIr.	cuil	OHG	fliuga	Av.	maxšī-
W.	gwybedyn, cylionyn	MHG	oliege		
Br.	kelienenn	NHG	fliege		

Of words for the 'fly' there is a widespread cognate group, probably of imitative origin. Another group, but only Gmc., is derived from the verb for 'fly', with early specialization.

1. IE **mu-*, **mus-*, prob. of imitative orig., with reference to the humming. Walde-P. 2.311. Ernout-M. 646. Falk-Torp 744.

Grk. μυῖα (**μυσια), NG pop. μῦγα; Lat. *musca* (> Romance words); here, but as 'midge' ON *mȳ*, OE *mycg*, OHG *mucca*, etc. (NHG *mücke* also locally 'fly'); Lith. *musė*, Lett. *muša*, OPruss. *muso*; ChSl. *mucha*, etc., general Slavic.

2. Ir. *cuil*, W. *cylionyn*, Br. *kelienenn* : Lat. *culex* 'midge', prob. Skt. *çūla-* 'spit, pike', etc. Walde-P. 1.33. Pedersen 1.147.

W. *gwybedyn*, coll. pl. *gwybed*, early *gwȳgbed* (Morris Jones 180), etym.?

3. ON *fluga*, OE *flēoge*, OHG *fliuga*, etc., general Gmc., fr. the Gmc. vb. for 'fly', OE *flēogan*, etc. (10.37), with early and general (though not complete) specialization.

4. Skt. *makṣa-*, Av. *maxšī-* prob. of imitative orig., like the group above, 1. Uhlenbeck 209.

3.84 WORM

Grk.	σκώληξ	Goth.	maþa (waurms)	Lith.	kirmėlė
NG	σκουλήκι	ON	ormr, maðkr	Lett.	tārps
Lat.	vermis	Dan.	orm	ChSl.	črŭvĭ
It.	verme	Sw.	mask	SCr.	crv
Fr.	ver	OE	wyrm, wurm	Boh.	červ
Sp.	verme	ME	werm, wurm	Pol.	robak
Rum.	vierme	NE	worm	Russ.	červ'
Ir.	cruim	Du.	worm	Skt.	kṛmi-
NIr.	cruimh, cnuimh	OHG	wurm	Av.	(kərəma-), NPers.
W.	pryf	MHG	wurm		kirm
Br.	preñv	NHG	wurm		

The majority of the words for 'worm' belong to one or the other of two groups, alike in suffix but from different roots. One of these groups and a few other words are based on the notion of 'turning around, winding'. A few are connected with verbs for 'bore' or 'rustle, gnaw' and must have applied at first to the woodworm.

Several of the words were also used frequently of, some even specialized to, the 'snake'.

1. IE **wṛmi-*, fr. **wer-* in words for 'turn, twist', seen esp. in the extension **wer-t-*, in Lat. *vertere*, etc. (10.12). Walde-P. 1.271. Ernout-M. 1090. NED s.v. *worm*, sb.

Lat. *vermis* (> Romance words);

Goth. *waurms*, ON *ormr*, OE *wyrm*, OHG *wurm*, etc., general Gmc., but in older period esp. 'snake', as Goth. *waurms* quotable only in this sense, ON *ormr* mostly 'snake' but also 'worm' (Fritzner s.v.v.), and Sw. *orm* now only 'snake'.

2. IE **kʷṛmi-*. Walde-P. 1.523. Ernout-M. 1090. Pedersen 1.43. Berneker 169, 172 f.

Skt. *kṛmi*, NPers. *kirm* (here prob. Av. *kərəma-* used with *star-* of a shooting star); Ir. *cruim*, NIr. *cruimh*, *cnuimh*, W. *pryf*, Br. *preñv*; OLith. *kirmis*, now *kirmėlė* (Lett. *cerms* 'maw-worm'); here also, with different suffix, ChSl. *črŭvĭ*, SCr. *crv*, Boh. *červ*, Pol. *czerw* (mostly 'grub, maggot'), Russ. *červ'*.

3. Grk. σκώληξ, NG σκουλήκι : σκολιός 'curved, bent, winding', σκέλος 'leg', and many other words based on the notion of 'curved, bent'. Walde-P. 2.598.

Grk. ἕλμις (in Aristot. used of intestinal worms) and εὐλή (mostly 'maggot'),

both : εἰλέω, ἴλλω 'turn around, wind'. Walde-P. 1.299.

4. Goth. *maþa* (for σκώληξ Mk. 9.44 ff.; *waurms* only for ὄφις; ON *maðkr*, OE *maþa*, OHG *mado*, these mostly 'maggot' (ME, NE dial. *mathe*, Sc. *mad* also 'earthworm', NED s.v.v. *mad*, sb.¹ and *mathe*; NHG *made*, etc.), but Sw. *mask* now reg. word for 'worm', possibly : OE *moppe* 'moth', Skt. *matkuṇa-* 'bug', etc. Walde-P. 2.228. Falk-Torp 700. Hellquist 634.

5. Lett. *tārps*, prob. as the 'borer' fr. an extension of the root seen in Lat. *terere* 'rub', Grk. τετραίνω 'bore' (cf. τερηδών 'woodworm'), etc. Walde-P. 1.732. Mühl.-Endz. 4.150.

6. Pol. *robak*, older *chrobak* = Boh. *chrobák* : Pol. *chrobotać* 'rustle', Sloven. *hrobati* 'gnaw', of imitative orig., with development in Pol. presumably through the 'gnawing' woodworm. Berneker 403. Brückner 459.

3.85 SNAKE

Grk.	ὄφις (ἔχις)	Goth.	waurms, nadrs	Lith.	gyvatė (angis, žaltys)
NG	ὄφις, φίδι	ON	ormr, naðr, snákr	Lett.	čū ka
Lat.	anguis, serpēns,	Dan.	slange, snog	ChSl.	zmija
	colubra	Sw.	snok, orm	SCr.	zmija
It.	serpe	OE	wyrm, nædre, snaca	Boh.	had
Fr.	serpent	ME	worme, snake, serpent, (n)addre	Pol.	wąż žmija)
Sp.	culebra, serpiente			Russ.	zmeja (už)
Rum.	șarpe	NE	snake, serpent	Skt.	ahi-, sarpa-, uraga-
Ir.	nathir	Du.	slang	Av.	aži-
NIr.	nathair	OHG	nāt(a)ra, wurm, slan-		
W.	neidr, sarff		go		
Br.	aer	MHG	slange, wurm		
		NHG	schlange		

1. Grk. ὄφις (NG φίδι fr. dim. ὀφίδιον), beside ἔχις, ἔχιδνα 'viper' (less generic than ὄφις cf. Aristot. HA 511ᵃ14 ff.), Lat. *anguis*; Lith., OPruss. *angis*; ChSl. **ążĭ*, Pol. *wąž*, Russ. *už*; Skt. *ahi-*, Av. *aži-*; fr. parallel forms with and without nasal, but phonetic relations in part obscure. Walde-P. 1.63 ff. Ernout-M. 52. Walde-H. 1.48.

2. Lat. *serpēns*, pple. of *serpere* 'creep', like Skt. *sarpa-* fr. *sṛp-* 'creep'. Walde-P. 2.502. Ernout-M. 931.

Hence the Romance forms and ME, NE *serpent* fr. OFr., also W. *sarff*. REW 7855. Loth, Mots lat. 205.

Lat. *colubra* (> Sp. *culebra*) prob. : Grk. κυλλός 'crooked', κυλίνδω 'roll', etc. Walde-P. 2.598. Walde-H. 1.248.

'ing', with curious specialization, doubtless through 'animal' (cf. *gyvolis* 'animal', 3.11). This is the generic word, while *angis* (above, 1) and *žaltys*, fr. *žalias* 'green', are mostly 'viper, adder'.

Lett. *čūska*, from a poor imitation of the hissing sound? Mühl.-Endz. 1.425.

6. ChSl., SCr. *zmija*, Pol. *žmija*, Russ. *zmeja*, derivs. of word for 'earth', ChSl. *zemlja*, etc., hence for the animal that crawls on the earth. Walde-P. 1.663. Brückner 665.

Boh. *had* : ChSl. *gadŭ* 'reptile, harmful animal', *gadinŭ* 'foul, hateful', SCr., Pol., Russ. *gad* 'reptile, anything loathsome', Lith. *gėda* 'shame', Lett. *gŭat* 'filth' (NHG *kot*), etc. A term of loathing applied to the snake in many Slavic dialects. Berneker 289. Walde-P. 1.695.

Pol. *wąž*, Russ. *už*, above, 1.

7. Skt. *ahi-*, Av. *aži-*, above, 1.

Skt. *sarpa-* : *sṛp-* 'crawl', like Lat. *serpēns*.

Skt. also often *uraga-*, lit. 'breast-going', cpd. of *uras-* 'breast' and *gam-* 'go'.

3. Ir. *nathir*, NIr. *nathair*, W. *neidr*, Br. *aer* (MBr. *azr* for **nazr*, Pedersen 1.255), Goth. *nadrs* (ἔχιδνα) ON *naðr*, OE *næd(d)re*, ME *(n)addre* (NE *adder* with restriction of use), OHG *nāt(a)ra* (NHG *natter* with restriction of use), here also Lat. *nātrix* 'water snake' (though doubtless felt as derived fr. *nāre* 'swim'), perh. fr. a root **(s)nē-* 'turn, twist' in words for 'spin', etc. (6.31). Walde-P. 2.327 f., 694.

4. Goth. *waurms*, ON *ormr*, Sw. *orm*, OE *wyrm*, ME *worme* (NE *worm* now obs. for 'snake'), OHG, NHG *wurm* (now rarely for 'snake' except in *lind-wurm* 'dragon'), all orig. 'worm'. See 3.84.

ON *snákr*, Dan. *snog*, Sw. *snok*, OE *snaca*, ME, NE *snake* (displacing *serpent* in pop. use) : OHG *snahan* 'crawl', OE *snægl* 'snail', etc. Walde-P. 1.697 ff. Falk-Torp 1098.

OHG *slango*, MHG, MLG *slange* (> Dan. *slange*), Du. *slang*, NHG *schlange* : OHG *slingan* 'turn, wind', refl. 'crawl', OE *slingan* 'crawl', Lith. *slinkti* 'crawl', etc. (10.41). Walde-P. 2.714.

5. Lith. *gyvatė*, deriv. of *gyvas* 'liv-

CHAPTER 4

PARTS OF THE BODY; BODILY FUNCTIONS AND CONDITIONS

4.11–4.49. Words for parts of the body, of which a rather large selection is included here, form a distinctive class, many of them of added importance because of their extensive secondary uses. They have been exhaustively discussed for certain fields[1], especially the Romance, where it has been noted that, with the inclusion of the dialects, there are some four hundred words answering to about eighty in Latin.

Many of the words belong to inherited groups reflecting definite IE terms for parts of the body both external and internal. A considerable familiarity with the latter, gained through the dissection of animals for food or sacrifice, is common among primitive peoples and is not surprising for the IE period.

In the case of such inherited words the root connection, and so the semantic source, is in large measure obscure. So far as we can judge from the words whose etymology is clear, the underlying notion is more often relating to the position or shape of the part than to its function. The inherited words for 'eye', 'ear', 'nose', 'mouth', 'foot' are not derived from any of the usual verbs for 'see',

'hear', 'smell', 'speak' (or 'eat'), 'walk', and so far as some cognates of the former are applied to function this is probably, and in most cases certainly, secondary. On the other hand, the derivation of the IE word for 'tooth' from the participle of the IE root for 'eat' seems too obvious on the formal side to be discarded, though even this situation may possibly be the result of a secondary association (see 4.27). The application of words for 'tongue' to 'speech, language' is almost universal, but the latter use is always secondary.

However, there are also examples enough of words for parts of the body derived from a function, as 'hand' from 'grasp, gather' (4.33), etc. and, regardless of priority, a relation between organ and function is widely observed.

There is frequent shift of application between words for parts of the body that are adjacent, of similar relative position, associated in function, or through common figurative uses with reference to the emotions. So between 'head'–'horn' (from 'summit'); 'head'–'skull'–'brain'; 'mouth'–'jaw', 'throat', 'cheek', 'chin', 'lip'; 'neck'–'throat'; 'shoulder'–'shoulder blade'–'back'–'arm'; 'hand'–'arm'; 'foot'–'leg'; 'finger'–'toe'; 'belly'–'womb'; 'breast' as front of the chest–'woman's breasts'; 'heart' from 'soul' (Rum. *inimă*, 4.44) or 'bowels' (W. *calon*, 4.44).

With such obvious exceptions as

---

[1] Schrader, Reallex. s.v. Körperteile.
Zauner, Die romanischen Namen der Körperteile, Rom. Forsch. 14.339–430.
Meyer-Lübke, Neubenennungen von Körperteilen im Romanischen, Wört. u. Sach. 12.1–16.
Tappolet, GRM 14.295 ff.
F. Thöne, Die Namen der Körperteile bei den Angelsachsen, Diss. Kiel, 1912.
W. T. Arnoldson, Parts of the Body in Older Germanic. Diss. Chicago, 1915.

'hand' or 'horn, tail, claw', the parts of the body correspond for man and beast and are generally expressed by the same word. But in some cases the etymology indicates that the original application was to one or the other. Words for 'head' that are based on the notion of 'top, summit' were most distinctly applicable to the head of man. Of the words for 'back', those connected with the notion of 'rear, behind' were applicable to man, those connected with 'ridge' or the like to animals. There are also some words which in actual use are applied primarily to animals and only contemptuously or facetiously to man, as NE *muzzle* or *snout*, Fr. *gueule*, NHG *maul*, etc. But words of this type, and in general vulgar expressions, of which there is a luxuriant growth, especially for certain parts (cf. Goldberger, Glotta 18.16 ff.), may in part become the accepted terms.

There are a few instances (some of the words for 'liver', 4.45) in which the name of the organ was originally one applied to it only as an article of food, parallel to the case of 'fish' as an animal from 'fish food' (NG ψάρι, 3.65).

4.11 BODY

Grk. σῶμα	Goth. leik	Lith. kūnas
NG σῶμα	ON līk, līkamr (līkami)	Lett. miesa, kūnis
Lat. corpus	Dan. legeme, krop	ChSl. tĕlo
It. corpo	Sw. kropp	SCr. tijelo
Fr. corps	OE līchama, līc (bodig)	Boh. tĕlo
Sp. cuerpo	ME body, cor(p)s, līkam(e)	Pol. ciało
Rum. corp	NE body	Russ. telo
Ir. corp, colinn, crī	Du. lichaam	Skt. çarīra-, deha-, tanū-
NIr. corp	OHG līchamo	Av. kəhrp-, tanū-
W. corff	MHG līch, līch(n)am(e), līp	
Br. korf	NHG leib, körper	

Words for 'body' may also be used, as NE *body*, for the 'dead body, corpse', but those that are used distinctively in this latter sense are considered separately (4.77).

Several of the words must have been applied originally to the main part of the body, the 'trunk' as distinguished from the extremities (as sometimes NE *body*, cf. NED s.v., 5) and reflect notions like 'swelling, curved, bulging shape'. Some go back to 'covering', or 'surface', whence 'form, shape, body'. Some words for 'flesh' were also used for 'body', as Grk. σάρξ, Lat. *carō*, ME, NE *flesh* in *ills of the flesh*, etc., as conversely words for 'body' may be used for 'flesh', as Lat. *corpus*.

1. Grk. σῶμα (in Hom. only of the dead body), fr. *twō-mn̥- : Grk. τύλη 'swelling, lump', Lat. *tumēre* 'swell', etc. (σ-fr. *tw-* as in σ́ós : Skt. *tva-*). Walde-P. 1.706 ff. Boisacq 935.

Grk. δέμας, in Hom. 'stature, living body' : δέμω 'build'.

2. Lat. *corpus* (> It. *corpo*, OFr. *cors*, ME *cor(p)s*, NE *corpse*, Fr. *corps*, Sp. *cuerpo*, Rum. *corp*, Ir. *corp*, W. *corff*, Br. *korf*, NHG *körper*), Ir. *crī* (? Stokes 97), Av. *kəhrp-* ('body, corpse'; MPers. *karp* 'body') : Skt. *kr̥p-* (only instr. sg. *kr̥pā*) 'shape, beauty', and perh. OE *hrif* 'womb, belly', OHG *(h)ref* 'body, abdomen, womb', root connection dub. Walde-P. 1.486f. Ernout-M. 222f. Walde-H. 1.277 f.

3. Ir. *colinn* (renders Lat. *carō*, but in the sense of 'body'), often also 'dead body, corpse' . ON *hold* 'flesh', OE *hold* 'carcass', W. *celain* 'corpse', best taken as, whether orig. 'body' or 'flesh', fr. 'covering' : Ir. *celim* 'hide', Grk. καλύπτω 'cover', etc. (12.26). Otherwise for root connection Walde-P. 2.592 and Falk-Torp 427.

4. Goth. *leik* ON *līk* (Dan. *lig*, Sw. *lik* 'corpse'), OE *līc* (oftener 'corpse', as mostly ME *lich*), OHG *līh*, MHG *lich* (NHG *leiche* only 'corpse') : Goth. *galeiks*, OE *gelīc* 'like', etc., Lith. *lygus* 'equal', etc. The semantic sequence seems to be 'like' (attested also in Alb., cf. Jokl, Wört. u. Sach. 12.83), whence 'likeness, form, body', but 'like' in the Gmc. cpds. secondary fr. 'having same form'. Walde-P. 2.398 f. Feist 327. Falk-Torp 642.

ON *līkama*, *līkami*, Dan. *legeme*, OE *līchama*, ME *likam(e)*, Du. *lichaam*, OHG *līchamo*, MHG *lich(n)ame* (NHG *leichnam* 'corpse', cpd. of preceding and Gmc. *haman-* 'covering' (OE *hama* 'covering', ON *hamr* 'skin, husk', Dan., Sw. *ham* 'skin, husk', etc.). Walde-P. 1.386. Falk-Torp 631.

Dan. *krop*, Sw. *kropp* : ON *kroppr* 'crop' (of birds), later 'trunk, body', OE *cropp* 'head' (of plants, etc.), 'crop' (of birds), OHG *kropf* 'crop' (of birds), bunch, swelling', OE *crēopan* 'creep', *cryppan* 'curve, bend', Grk. γρυπός 'curved, hook-nosed', all with notion of 'curved shape, bunch'. Walde-P. 1.598. Falk-Torp 582. Hellquist 513.

OE *bodig* 'stature, trunk, body', ME, NE *body* : OHG *botah*, MHG *botech* 'trunk, corpse', prob. (though disputed) the same word as OHG *botahha*, NHG *bottich* 'tub, vat', fr. MLat. *but(t)a*, *buttis*, *butica*, *butagium*, etc., with application to the bulging 'trunk' of the body, then 'body'. NED s.v. Falk-Torp 89.

NHG *leib*, fr. MHG *līp* 'life' then 'living mass, body', fr. OHG *līp* 'life' : OE *līf* 'life', Goth. *liban* 'live', etc. (4.74). Weigand-H. 2.43.

5. Lith. *kūnas*, Lett. *kūnis*, perh. as orig. 'trunk' fr. IE *keu-* in words denoting curved shape as Lat. *cumulus* 'heap', Lith. *kaukas* 'boil', etc. (Walde-P. 1.370 ff., without mention of these words for 'body'). Otherwise (as fr. a *skeu-* 'cover'). Charpentier, Monde Or. 2.23.

Lett. *miesa* 'flesh' (4.17) is also the usual word for 'body'.

6. ChSl. *tĕlo*, etc., the general Slavic word, prob. through 'surface, form' : ChSl. *tĭlo*, 'ground', Skt. *tala-* 'surface', etc. Walde-P. 1.740. The assumption, after Lewy, of development through 'carved image' is unnecessary. ChSl. *tĕlo* in the Gospels renders σῶμα regularly, in two passages (Mt. 6.27, Lk. 12.25) ἡλικία where this means 'stature' not 'age'. Later often *plŭtĭ* 'flesh' used for 'body'. Jagić, Entstehungsgesch. 407.

7. Skt., Av. *tanū-* : Skt. *tan-*, Grk. τείνω 'stretch', Skt. *tanu-*, Lat. *tenuis* 'thin', etc. Development of 'body' through notion of 'surface, form'. Walde-P. 1.724.

Skt. *çarīra-*, prob. as orig. 'covering' : Skt. *çarman-* 'protection, shelter, etc.', Grk. καλύπτω 'cover', Ir. *celim* 'hide', etc. Charpentier, Monde Or. 2.23.

Skt. *deha-* 'form, shape, body', fr. the root seen in Skt. *dih-*, Lat. *fingere* 'fashion', etc. Walde-P. 1.833.

4.12 SKIN; HIDE

Grk.	*δέρμα, χρώς; σκῦτος*	Goth.	*-fill*	Lith.	*oda; skūra*
NG	*δέρμα, πετσί*	ON	*hūð, skinn (hǫrund)*	Lett.	*āda*
Lat.	*cutis; pellis (corium)*	Dan.	*hud; skind*	ChSl.	*koža*
It.	*pelle, cute*	Sw.	*hud, skin*	SCr.	*koža*
Fr.	*peau (cuir)*	OE	*hȳd; fell*	Boh.	*kůže, pokožka*
Sp.	*cutis (cuero); pellejo*	ME	*hide, skinn; fell*	Pol.	*skóra*
Rum.	*piele*	NE	*skin; hide (fell)*	Russ.	*koža; škura*
Ir.	*cness; croccenn, seche*	Du.	*huid, vel*	Skt.	*tvac-; carman-, ajina-*
NIr.	*cneas, croiceann; seithe*	OHG	*hūt, fel*	Av.	*(surī-); čarəman*
W.	*croen (cen)*	MHG	*hūt, vel*		
Br.	*kroc'hen (kenn)*	NHG	*haut; fell*		

Most of the words listed may be used, like NE *skin*, for the skin of man or beast, a few, like Grk. χρώς, only for human skin, and several (placed after a semicolon), like NE *hide*, only or mainly for the skin of animals. Several of the words are used also or mainly for 'leather' (6.29).

The semantic sources are partly 'covering, surface' of the 'body', but oftener 'cut, tear' or the like, orig. referring to the hide detached from the body. But such difference in origin is not reflected in actual difference in usage. A few show generalization from the skin of a particular animal, namely 'goatskin'.

1. Grk. δέρμα (in Hom. mostly 'hide', later the regular word for 'skin'; also δορά 'hide') : δέρω, Lith. *dirti*, etc., 'flay, skin' (9.29), OE *teran* 'tear', Skt. *dṛ-* 'split, tear', etc. Walde-P. 1.797.

Grk. χρώς (only of human skin and, mostly poet., also 'complexion, color') beside χροα (χροιά, Ion. χροιή), χρῶμα 'skin, complexion, color', all orig. 'surface' : χραύω 'graze, scrape', fr. an extension of IE **gher-*, parallel to that in Skt. *ghṛṣ-* 'rub'. Walde-P. 1.648 ff. Boisacq 1071.

Grk. σκῦτος 'hide, leather' : OE *hȳd*, etc. (below, 4).

NG πετσί, fr. It. *pezzo* 'piece', *pezza* 'piece of cloth'. G. Meyer, Neugr. Stud. 4.70.

2. Lat. *cutis* (> It. *cute*, Sp. *cutis*) : ON *hūð*, OE *hȳd*, etc. (below, 4).

Lat. *pellis* 'hide' (> It. *pelle*, Fr. *peau*, Rum. *piele* 'skin, hide', Sp. *piel* 'pelt'; fr. dim. also Sp. *pellejo* 'hide'), Goth. *þruts-fill* 'leprosy', ON *berfjall* 'bearskin', OE *fell*, ME, NE *fell*, Du. *vel*, OHG *fel*, MHG *vel*, NHG *fell* : Grk. ἐρυσί-πελας 'inflammation of the skin', Lith. *plėvė* 'film', etc., prob. fr. a **pel-* 'cover', an extension of which may be seen in Goth. *filhan* 'hide, bury' (4.78). Walde-P. 2.58 f. (adversely to this root connection). Ernout-M. 749. Falk-Torp 217. Persson, Beiträge 226, 946.

Lat. *corium* 'hide, leather' (> It. *cuoio*, Fr. *cuir*, Sp. *cuero* all mostly 'leather', but sometimes 'skin, hide'), Pol. *skóra*, Russ. *škura*, Skt. *carman-*, Av. *čarəman-*, all fr. IE **(s)ker-* 'cut' in Grk. κείρω 'shear', etc. Walde-P. 2.573 ff. Ernout-M. 220. Walde-H. 1.274.

3. For the following, and some other, less important, Celtic words (as Ir. *codal*, *bīan* 'hide') cf. esp. Vendryes, Les noms de la "peau" en celtique, Wört. u. Sach. 12.241 ff.

Ir. *cness*, NIr. *cneas*, W. *cnes* (rare), perh. fr. **knid-tā-* : Ir. *cned* 'wound', Grk. κνίζω 'scrape, chafe', OE *hnītan* 'strike', etc. (Walde-P. 1.395, without inclusion of Ir. *cness*, etc.). Vendryes, loc. cit.

Ir. *croccenn*, NIr. *croiceann*, W. *croen*,

Br. *kroc'hen*, fr. **krokno-*, perh., like Lat. *corium* (above, 2) fr. IE **(s)ker-* 'cut'. Morris Jones 165. Vendryes, loc. cit.

W. *cen*, Br. *kenn* (both now mostly in cpds.), Corn. *cennen* (Ir. *cenni* 'scales') : ON *hinna* 'membrane' and ON *skinn*, etc. (below, 4). Walde-P. 2.563.

Ir. *seche*, NIr. *seithe* : Lat. *secāre* 'cut', etc. Walde-P. 2.475.

4. ON *hūð*, OE *hȳd*, OHG *hūt*, etc., the general Gmc. word for 'skin' (NE *hide* now properly only of animals) : Grk. σκῦτος 'hide, leather', Lat. *cutis* 'skin', Lith. *kiautas* 'hull, husk', OPruss. *keuto* 'skin', Ir. *codal* 'hide'; Grk. κεύθω, OE *hȳdan* 'cover, hide', etc., fr. IE **(s)keu-* with various extensions. Walde-P. 2.546 ff. Ernout-M. 249. Falk-Torp 425.

ON *skinn* (> ME *skinn*, NE *skin*), Dan. *skind*, Sw. *skin* : MHG *schint* 'fruit skin', Du. dial. *schinde* 'hide, bark', OHG *scintan*, NHG *schinden* 'remove the skin or bark', ON *hinna* 'membrane', W. *cen* 'skin', etc. (above, 3), fr. an IE **(s)ken-* 'cut off', perh. an extension of **sek-* 'cut'. Walde-P. 2.563 f. Falk-Torp 997.

ON *hūð* and *skinn* are both applied to the skin of man or beast. The distinction prevailing in Dan., less markedly in Sw., is secondary (cf. Falk-Torp 997), like the opposite distinction in NE.

For ON *hǫrund* 'flesh, skin' (of a human being, but even here not the usual word), see 4.13.

5. Lith. *oda*, Lett. *āda*, etym.?

ChSl., SCr. *koža* (> Rum. *coaje* 'bark, rind'), Boh. *kůže*, *pokožka*, Russ. *koža*, orig. 'goatskin', fr. *koza* 'goat'. Cf. Skt. *ajina-*, below, 6. Walde-P. 1.336. Berneker 597 f. Brückner 263.

Pol. *skóra*, Russ. *škura* (WhRuss. *skura* > Lith. *skūra*) : Lat. *corium*, etc., above, 2.

6. Skt. *tvac-*, *-tvacas-* : Grk. σάκος 'shield', root connection? Walde-P. 1.747.

Skt. *carman-*, Av. *čarəman-* 'hide' : Lat. *corium*, etc., above, 2.

Skt. *cyavi-*, fr. IE **(s)keu-* 'cover'? Walde-P. 2.546.

Av. *surī-* (once, Barth. 1586), etym.?

Skt. *ajina-* 'hide' : ChSl. *jazno* 'leather', derivs. of word for 'goat', Skt. *aja-*, etc. Walde-P. 1.38.

4.13 FLESH

Grk.	*σάρξ, κρέας*	Goth.	*mimz, mammō*	Lith.	*mėsa*
NG	*σάρκα, κρέας*	ON	*hold, hǫrund*	Lett.	*miesa*
Lat.	*carō*	Dan.	*kød*	ChSl.	*plŭtĭ, męso*
It.	*carne*	Sw.	*kött*	SCr.	*meso*
Fr.	*chair*	OE	*flǣsc*	Boh.	*maso*
Sp.	*carne*	ME	*fleshe*	Pol.	*mięso*
Rum.	*carne*	NE	*flesh*	Russ.	*mjaso*
Ir.	*fēoil, cūa*	Du.	*vleesch*	Skt.	*mānsa-, mās-*
NIr.	*feoil*	OHG	*fleisk*	Av.	*gav-* (NPers. *gušt*)
W.	*cig, cnawd*	MHG	*vleisch*		
Br.	*kig*	NHG	*fleisch*		

Most of the words for 'flesh', though not all, are also used for flesh as food, 'meat' (5.61). Words for 'flesh' are also used, esp. in eccl. writings, for 'body', and conversely some words for 'body' are also used for 'flesh'. Cf. 4.11. The semantic sources, where clear, are partly 'covering, surface', referring to 'flesh' vs. 'bone', but oftener 'cut', or 'raw, bloody', or name of an animal, in all these cases referring to the flesh of an animal cut off for food or sacrifice.

1. IE **mēmso-*, **mēs-*, root connection? Walde-P. 2.262. Feist 361.

Goth. *mimz* (once, here 'meat'; also *mammō* prob. related); Lith. *mėsa*, Lett. *miesa*, OPruss. *mensā*; ChSl. *męso*, etc., general Slavic: Skt. *mānsa-*, *mās-*; Arm. *mis*; Alb. *mish*; Toch. B *misa* (pl. tantum); with other meanings, Grk. μηρός 'thigh', Lat. *membrum* 'part of the body', Ir. *mīr* 'portion, morsel', etc.

2. Grk. σάρξ : Av. *θwares-* 'cut', with development as in Lat. *carō* (below, 3). Walde-P. 1.751. Boisacq 854.

Grk. κρέας (but mostly 'meat') : Skt. *kravis-* 'raw flesh, carrion', *krūra-* 'bloody, raw', Av. *xrū-* 'raw flesh', Lat. *cruor* 'blood from a wound', OE *hrēaw* 'raw', Lith. *kraujas* 'blood', etc. (4.14). Walde-P. 1.478 ff. Walde-H. 1.295.

3. Lat. *carō*, gen. *carnis* (> It., Sp., Rum. *carne*, Fr. *chair*) : Umbr. *karu* 'pars' (but also *karne*, etc. 'flesh'), Osc. *carneis* 'partis', Umbr. *kartu* 'distributo', Grk. κείρω 'shear', OE *sceran* 'cut, shear', etc., IE **(s)ker-* 'cut'. Development in Italic to 'portion' in general, then esp. 'portion, cut of the flesh, flesh'. Walde-P. 2.575. Ernout-M. 156. Walde-H. 1.170.

4. Ir. *fēoil*, etym.? Pedersen 1.139 compares W. *gwanu* 'pierce', OE *wund* 'wound', etc. (Walde-P. 1.212, Stokes 259, both without *fēoil*).

Ir. *cūa* (K. Meyer, Contrib. 540), etym.?

W. *cig*, Br. *kig*, OCorn. *chic* (Ir. *cīch* 'female breast'), outside connections? Pedersen 1.51. Walde-P. 1.334.

W. *cnawd*, prob. fr. **knō-to-* : Grk. κνάω 'scrape, scratch', ultimately connected with Ir. *cness* 'skin' (4.12) in both cases orig. 'surface'. Vendryes, Wört. u. Sach. 12.243.

5. ON *hold* : OE *hold* 'carcass', Ir. *colinn* 'body', etc. (4.11).

ON *hǫrund* 'flesh, skin' (for actual uses, cf. Fritzner, and Vigfusson) : Lat. *corium* 'hide, leather', Lat. *carō* (above, 2), etc., fr. IE **(s)ker-* 'cut'. Walde-P. 2.576.

ON *kjǫt* (occurs only as 'meat'), Dan. *kød*, Sw. *kött*, prob. : MLG *kūte* 'entrails', Du. *kuit* 'calf of the leg', Skt. *guda-* 'intestine', etc. Walde-P. 1.559. Falk-Torp 522, 1496.

OE *flǣsc*, etc., the WGmc. word for 'flesh' (ON. *flesk* 'pork, bacon', Dan. *flesk*, Sw. *fläsk* 'bacon'), prob. : ON *flikki*, OE *flicce* 'flitch of bacon', Lith. *plėšti* 'tear', all perh. from various extensions of IE **(s)pel-* 'split'. Walde-P. 2.98 ff. Falk-Torp 235.

6. ChSl. *plŭtĭ*, in the Gospels (where *męso* does not occur; also less common than *plŭtĭ* in Supr.) reg. for σάρξ (whether 'flesh' or 'flesh' for 'body'), Russ. *plot'* 'flesh' = 'body' eccl., 'scurf on the skin' : Lith. *pluta* 'crust of bread', Lett. *pluta* 'flesh, skin', all prob. from the notion of a filmy, 'floating' covering, and so, with Russ. *plot* 'float, raft', Skt. *pluta-* 'floating', etc., fr. IE **pleu-* 'flow, float' (Walde-P. 2.94 ff., without inclusion of the group here in question). Mühl.-Endz. 3.359. Brückner 420 f.

7. Av. *gav-* 'ox, cow' (3.20) is also used for 'flesh' and 'meat'. Barth. 507–8. Extension of 'ox flesh, beef' to 'flesh, meat' in general, as confirmed by NPers. *gūšt* 'flesh, meat' and similar forms in the other Iran. languages (Horn 944).

4.14 HAIR

(Partly distinguished as a) of the Head, b) of the Body, of Animals)

Grk.	*θρίξ*, pl. *τρίχες*, *κόμη* (a)	Goth.	*tagl, skuft* (a)	Lith.	*plaukas, gauras* (b)
NG	*τρίχα*, pl. *τρίχες* (b), *μαλλιά* (a)	ON	*hār, skopt* (a)	Lett.	*mats, spalva* (b)
Lat.	*capillus* (a), *crīnis* (a), *coma* (a), *pilus* (b)	Dan.	*haar*	ChSl.	*vlasŭ*
It.	*capello* (a), *pelo* (b)	Sw.	*hår*	SCr.	*vlas, kosa* (a), *dlaka* (b)
Fr.	*cheveu* (a), *poil* (b)	OE	*hǣr, feax* (a)	Boh.	*vlas*
Sp.	*pelo, cabello* (a)	ME	*here, fax* (a)	Pol.	*włos*
Rum.	*păr*	NE	*hair*	Russ.	*volos*
Ir.	*folt* (a), *find*	Du.	*haar*	Skt.	*keça-* (a), *roman-* (b)
NIr.	*gruaig* (a), *folt* (a), *fionn*	OHG	*hār, fahs* (a)	Av.	*varəsa-* (a), *gaona-* (b)
W.	*gwallt* (a), *flew*	MHG	*hār, vahs* (a)		
Br.	*fleo*	NHG	*haar*		

Some of the words listed have the same wide scope as NE *hair*. Some are used only or mainly for the hair of the head (a), others for that of the human body or an animal (b). Words for the long hair of a horse's mane or tail often go with a. The distribution may be fluctuating, so that the designation by a or b is only approximate. Special words for the hair of particular parts of the body are ignored except those for 'beard' (4.142).

'The hair' is expressed partly by singular collectives, more commonly by plural forms, some without singular in use, most of them with singular used for 'a hair' (in such cases the words are listed in the singular, as Fr. *cheveu*).

1. Grk. θρίξ, pl. τρίχες : Ir. *gairb-driuch* 'brush', further connections? Walde-P. 1.876. Pedersen 1.100.

Hence NG τρίχα 'a hair', pl. τρίχες, the latter commonly only of 'animal's hair, bristles'.

NG μαλλιά pl., the usual word for the human 'hair of the head', fr. dim. form of Grk. μαλλός 'lock of wool', rarely 'lock, tress of hair' : Lith. *milas* 'cloth', etc. Walde-P. 2.294.

Grk. κόμη (a), etym.? Boisacq 489.

2. Lat. *capillus* (a; > It. *capello*, Fr. *cheveu*, Sp. *cabello*), etym. dub. Walde-P. 1.347. Ernout-M. 147. Walde-H. 158.

Lat. *crīnis* (a, mostly pl. or sg. coll.; > It. *crine* 'hair' lit. word, Fr., Sp. *crin* 'horsehair, mane'), fr. **cris-ni-* : Lat. *crista* 'tuft on the head of animals', Goth. *-hrisjan*, OE *hrisian* 'shake', etc. Walde-P. 2.572. Ernout-M. 233. Walde-H. 1.292.

Lat. *coma* (a; > It. *chioma* lit. word, Rum. *coamă* 'horse's mane, ridge'), fr. Grk. κόμη (above, 1).

For the relative frequency of Lat. *capillus*, *coma*, *crīnis* in different authors, cf. Thesaurus s.v. *capillus*.

Lat. *pilus*, mostly 'single hair on the body' (> It. *pelo*, Fr. *poil* 'hair of the body', but Fr. dial. *pel*, Sp. *pelo*, Rum. *păr* generic), perh. : Lat. *pilleus* 'felt cap', Grk. πῖλος 'felt'. Walde-P. 2.71.

3. Ir. *folt* (mostly a, but also 'the long hair of a horse's tail', etc.), W. *gwallt* (a), OBr. *guolt*, all coll., prob. : OPruss. *wolti* 'ear of corn', SCr. *vlat* 'blade of grass', etc., fr. the same root as Lat. *vellus* 'fleece', *lāna* 'wool', etc. Walde-P. 1.297.

Ir. *find* 'a hair', pl. *finda* 'hair', NIr. *fionn* 'a hair', *fionnadh* 'hair' (b) : Grk. ἴονθος 'young hair', OHG *wint-brāwa* 'eyelash', etc. Walde-P. 1.262. Pedersen 1.114.

NIr. *gruaig* 'hair of head, or of horse's mane', perh.?

For still other NIr. words for 'hair' in special applications, cf. McKenna s.v. hair.

W. *blew*, Br. *bleo* (both coll. with sg. *blewyn*, *blevenn* 'a hair'), perh. fr. *ml-eu-* beside *ml-* in Grk. μαλλός, etc. (above, 1). G. S. Lane, Language 7.279.

4. Goth. *tagl* ('the single hair of the head' and once 'camel's hair') : ON *tagl* 'hair of horse's tail', OE *tœgl* 'tail', etc. (4.18).

Goth. *skuft* (Jn. 11.2, etc. dat. sg. *skufta* coll. = θριξί 'with her hair'), ON *skopt* (poet.), OHG *scuft*, MHG *schopf*, all coll. for 'hair' of the head (NHG 'top of the head, tuft of hair', etc.) : ON *skauf* 'fox's brush', OE *scēaf*, OHG *scoub*, etc. 'sheaf'. Walde-P. 2.555. Feist 435.

ON, OHG *hār*, OE *hǣr*, etc., general Gmc., etym. much disputed, perh. : Lith. *šerys* 'brush' and other words for 'stiff, bristly'. Walde-P. 1.427. Falk-Torp 369. Weigand-H. 1.783.

OE *feax*, OS, OHG *fahs* (ON *fax* 'mane') : Grk. πόκος 'fleece, wool', etc. Walde-P. 2.17. Falk-Torp 201. NED s.v. fax.

5. Lith. *plaukas*, pl. *plaukai* (mostly a) : Lett. *plauki* 'snowflakes, fluff, dust', *plūkt* 'pluck', further relations disputed. Walde-P. 2.97. Persson, Beiträge 238 ff. Lett. *mats*, pl. *mati* (mostly a), etym.?

(: *mest* 'throw' as orig. 'hair arranged in a particular way'? Mühl.-Endz. 2.567).

Lett. *spalva* 'hair of quadrupeds, feathers, etc.' : Lat. *spolium* 'hide stripped off', OHG *spaltan* 'split', etc. Walde-P. 2.679. Mühl.-Endz. 3.983.

Lith. *gauras*, mostly pl. *gaurai* 'hair on the body, tuft of hair' : Lett. *gauri* 'hair on private parts', NIr. *guaire* 'rough hair, bristle', Norw. *kaur* 'lamb's wool', also with different suffix Av. *gaona-* 'hair', root *geu-*, perh. the same as in Grk. γυρός 'round, curved', etc. Walde-P. 1.557.

6. ChSl. *vlasŭ*, pl. *vlasi*, etc., general Slavic : Av. *varəsa-* 'hair', Skt. *valça-* 'shoot, twig', fr. *wol-ko-*, with the same root as in Ir. *folt* 'hair', Lat. *vellus* 'fleece', *lāna* 'wool', etc. Walde-P. 1.297.

SCr. *kosa* 'hair' (a), Pol., Russ. *kosa*, Lith. *kasa* 'tress, braid of hair' : ChSl. *česati* 'comb', etc. Walde-P. 1.449. Berneker 580.

SCr. *dlaka* 'hair' (b), etym.? Berneker 208.

7. Skt. *keça-* (a) : Lith. *kaišti* 'shave, rub, make smooth', OPruss. *coipsnis* 'comb'. Walde-P. 1.328.

Skt. *roman-*, *loman-* (b), prob. : Ir. *ruamnae*, gl. *lodix* (meaning here?), NIr. *rūaimneach* 'long hair, horsehair, fishing line', also Ir. *rūainne* 'a hair', *rōn*, W. *rhawn* 'horsehair', Br. *reun* 'coarse hair, bristles'. Walde-P. 2.361.

Av. *varəsa-* (mostly a, but also b) : ChSl. *vlasŭ*, etc., above, 6.

Av. *gaona-* (b, also 'color', NPers. *gūn* 'color') : Lith. *gauras*, above, 5.

4.142 BEARD

Grk.	πώγων, γενειάς	Goth.	....	Lith.	barzda
NG	γένεια, γενειάδα	ON	skegg	Lett.	bārda
Lat.	barba	Dan.	skeg	ChSl.	brada
It.	barba	Sw.	skägg	SCr.	brada
Fr.	barbe	OE	beard	Boh.	vous (brada)
Sp.	barba	ME	berd	Pol.	broda
Rum.	barbă	NE	beard	Russ.	boroda
Ir.	fēsōc	Du.	baard	Skt.	çmaçru-
NIr.	fēasōg	OHG	bart	Av.	....
W.	barf	MHG	bart		
Br.	barv	NHG	bart		

For 'beard' there is a group common to Lat., WGmc., and Balto-Slavic, prob. cognate with words for 'bristle', 'point', etc. Several of these are used also for 'chin', as in the Romance languages (REW 944) and Slavic (SCr., Boh. *brada*, Russ. *boroda*), and the interchange between 'beard' and 'chin' is seen in several outside this group (below, 2 and 6).

An interesting secondary development rests on the similarity in shape between the beard and the blade of an ax, hence OHG *barta* etc. 'ax' (9.25).

1. IE *bhardhā-*, prob. fr. the same root as ON, OHG *burst*, OE *byrst* 'bristle', Skt. *bhṛṣṭi-* 'point, edge', etc. Walde-P. 2.135. Ernout-M. 103. Walde-H. 1.96. Berneker 72 f.

Lat. *barba* (> Romance forms and W. *barf*, Br. *barv*); OE *beard*, OHG *bart*, etc., general WGmc. (ON *barð* only in secondary senses, 'edge, brim, prow', etc.); Lith. *barzda*, ChSl. *brada*, etc. general Balto-Slavic.

2. Grk. πώγων, perh. cpd., -γων : γένυς

'jaw', etc., but first part difficult. Walde-P. 1.587.

Grk. γένειον 'chin' (4.209) and sometimes 'beard', and so reg. in NG, esp. pl. γένεια. Hence also Grk. γενειάς, NG γενειάδα 'beard'.

3. Ir. *fēsōc*, NIr. *fēasōg*, deriv. of *fēs* beside *find* 'hair' (4.14). Pedersen 1.86.

4. ON *skegg*, Dan. *skœg*, Sw. *skägg* : OE *sceaga* (once as gl. to Lat. *coma*), ME, NE *shag* 'rough hair' (whence the more common NE *shaggy*), ON *skagi* 'promontory' (with vb. *skaga* 'project'), *skōgr* 'woods', etc. Walde-P. 2.557. Falk-Torp 1000. Hellquist 970.

5. Boh. *vous* (more common for 'beard' than *brada*, which is mostly 'chin') = Pol. *was*, Russ *us* 'mustache', ChSl. *(v)ǫsŭ* (quotable only late *usŭ*, *vusŭ*) : Grk. ἴονθος 'young hair', Ir. *find* 'hair', etc. Walde-P. 1.262. Miklosich 223. Brückner 604.

6. Skt. *çmaçru-* (by assim. fr. *smaçru-*) : Arm. *maurukⁱ* 'beard', Ir. *smech*, Lith. *smakras* 'chin'. Walde-P. 2.689.

4.15 BLOOD

Grk.	αἷμα (ἔαρ)	Goth.	blōþ	Lith.	kraujas
NG	αἷμα	ON	blōð	Lett.	asins
Lat.	sanguis, cruor	Dan.	blod	ChSl.	krŭvĭ
It.	sangue	Sw.	blod	SCr.	krv
Fr.	sang	OE	blōd	Boh.	krev
Sp.	sangre	ME	blode	Pol.	krew
Rum.	sînge	NE	blood (gore)	Russ.	krov'
Ir.	fuil, crú	Du.	bloed	Skt.	asan- (Ved.), rakta-,
NIr.	fuil, crō	OHG	bluot		rudhira-, etc.
W.	gwaed (crau)	MHG	bluot	Av.	vohunī-
Br.	gwad	NHG	blut		

Of the two principal groups of cognates (1, 2, below) the first reflects an IE word for 'blood', of which nothing can be said as to any remoter semantic source. In the second the prevailing sense is 'raw flesh, raw', or 'blood outside the body, gore', whence simply 'blood' in some languages. Other words are from such sources as 'red' (notably in Sanskrit), 'wound', 'vein'(?), and probably 'flow, gush' or the like.

1. IE *ēsen-*, nom.-acc. -ṛ, a typical r/n stem neuter. Walde-P. 1.162. Ernout-M. 80 f., 893. Walde-H. 1.72.

Grk. poet. ἔαρ, εἶαρ (ἦαρ Hesych.); OLat. *aser*, *assyr* (Paul. Fest., with *asarātum* 'drink of wine and blood mixed'); Lett. *asins*; Skt. *asṛk*, gen. *asnas*; Arm. *ariun*; Hitt. *eshar* (with derivs., Sturtevant, Hitt. Gloss. 37); Toch. *ysār* (SSS, 6).

2. IE *krew-*, *krū-*, etc. Walde-P. 1.478. Ernout-M. 234 f. Walde-H. 1.294 f.

Lat. *cruor* 'blood from a wound, gore' (as distinguished from generic *sanguis*; cf. also *cruentus* 'bloody'); Ir. *crū*, NIr. *crō*, W. *crau* (obs.), Corn. *crow*, all used mostly like Lat. *cruor*; Lith. *kraujas*, OPruss. *craujo*, *krawia*, ChSl. *krŭvĭ*, etc., the general Balto-Slavic (except Lett.) word for 'blood' : Grk. κρέας 'meat', Skt. *kravis-* 'raw flesh', Av. *xrū-* 'raw flesh', Skt. *krūra-* 'raw, bloody', Av. *xrūra-* 'bloody, fierce', OE *hrēaw* 'raw', etc.

3. Grk. αἷμα, etym.? Possibly connected with certain words meaning

'drip' or 'juice'. Walde-P. 2.464 f. Boisacq 24.

4. Lat. *sanguis* (early neut. *sanguen*) *-inis* (> the Romance words), etym.? Connection with Skt. *asṛk*, *asnas*, etc. (above, 1) too complicated to be convincing. Cf. refs. in 1, above.

5. Ir. *fuil* (beside *fuili* 'bloody wounds') : W. *gweli*, Corn. *goly*, MBr. *gouli* 'wound' (W. *gweli* formerly also 'blood', as still in Ir. *rhed-weli* 'artery', cpd. with *rhed* 'course', Lat. *vulnus* 'wound', ON *valr*, OE *wœl* 'the slain on the battlefield', etc. Walde-P. 1.304 ff. Pedersen 1.139, 162. Loth, RC. 41.208.

W. *gwaed*, Corn. *gwad*, Br. *gwad*, perh. as 'blood' fr. 'vein' : W., Corn. *gwyth* 'vein', Ir. *fēith* 'fibre' etc. (Walde-P. 1.224, without inclusion of the words for 'blood'). Henry 146.

6. Goth. *blōþ*, OE *blōd*, etc., general Gmc., prob. as 'that which bursts out' : Goth. *blōma* 'flower', etc. Walde-P. 1.177. Falk-Torp 83 f. Feist 101.

NE *gore*, used much like Lat. *cruor*, fr. OE, ME *gor(r)e* 'dung, filth'. NED s.v.

7. Lith. *kraujas*, ChSl. *krŭvĭ*, etc., above, 2.

Lett. *asins*, above, 1.

8. Skt. (Vedic) *asan-*, *asṛk*, above, 1. Skt. *rakta-* neut., sb. use of *rakta-* 'red', pple. of *raj-* 'be colored, be red'. Likewise for 'blood' neuter forms of other words for 'red', as *rudhira-*, *lohita-*, *çoṇita-*. Cf. also ON *roðra* 'sacrificial blood' beside *rjōðr* 'red'.

Av. *vohunī-* (NPers. *xūn* 'blood'), etym.? Barth. 1434.

4.16 BONE

Grk.	ὀστέον	Goth.	....	Lith.	kaulas
NG	κόκκαλο	ON	bein	Lett.	kauls
Lat.	os	Dan.	ben, knogle	ChSl.	kostĭ
It.	osso	Sw.	ben	SCr.	kost
Fr.	os	OE	bān	Boh.	kost'
Sp.	hueso	ME	bone	Pol.	kość
Rum.	os	NE	bone	Russ.	kost'
Ir.	cnāim	Du.	been, knok	Skt.	asthi-
NIr.	cnāimh	OHG	bein	Av.	ast-
W.	asgwrn	MHG	bein		
Br.	askourn	NHG	knochen (-bein)		

Apart from the inherited group, words for 'bone' come by generalization from or through terms denoting a particular bone, esp. 'knuckle-bone', or by extension of 'hollow stalk', to the long bone of arm or leg, or by extension of the hard 'kernel' of fruits to the analogous parts of the body.

1. IE *ost-*, etc. Walde-P. 1.185 f. Ernout-M. 716.

Grk. ὀστέον; Lat. *os*, gen. *ossis*, also *ossu*, *ossum* (> It. *osso*, Sp. *hueso*, Fr., Rum. *os*); W. *asgwrn*, Br. *askourn*, Corn. *ascorn*; Skt. *asthi-*, gen. *asthnas*, Av. *ast-*, *asti-*; Arm. *oskr*; Alb. *asht*. Here also ChSl. *kostĭ*, etc.? See below, 6.

2. NG κόκκαλο neut., fr. Grk. κόκκαλος 'kernel of the pine cone', deriv. of κόκκος 'kernel, grain, seed'.

3. Ir. *cnāim*, NIr. *cnāimh* : Grk. κνήμη 'leg between knee and ankle', OE *hamm* 'hollow at the back of the knee', etc. Walde-P. 1.460. Pedersen 1.53. Development of 'bone' through 'knuckle'.

4. ON *bein*, OE *bān*, etc., general Gmc. (but NHG *bein* for 'bone' now only in cpds. as *elfenbein* 'ivory', origin obscure. Falk-Torp 69.

NHG *knochen*, fr. MHG *knoch knoche*, 'knuckle, knot', this with dim. MLG *knokel* 'bone, knuckle' (> Dan. *knokkel*, *knogle* 'bone'), ME *knokel*, NE *knuckle*, NHG *knöchel* 'knuckle' : ON *knjūkr* 'round summit', Ir. *gniauzti* 'close the fist', etc. Walde-P. 1.582. Falk-Torp 69. The meaning 'knuckle' is the more general and earlier, whence 'bone' only by later extension (not 'knuckle' from 'bone', as in NED).

5. Lith. *kaulas*, Lett. *kauls*, OPruss. acc. *kaulan* : Grk. καυλός, Lat. *caulis* 'stalk', Ir. *cuaille* 'post, stake', also Skt. *kulyā-* 'canal, channel, ditch' (hence neut. *kulya-* 'receptacle for bones', rarely 'bone', no direct connection with the Baltic use), with common notion 'long, hollow shape'. Walde-P. 1.332. Doubtless applied first to the long bone of arm or leg. Cf. Lat. *caulis* used by Pliny of the 'bony part of an ox's tail'; also the use of ON *leggr* (4.35).

6. ChSl. *kostĭ*, etc., general Slavic : Lat. *costa* 'rib'. Further analysis of both as *k-ost-*, with relation to IE *ost-* (above, 1) is attractive but dub. Walde-P. 1.186. Ernout-M. 225, 716. Berneker 582 f.

4.162 RIB

Grk.	πλευρόν	Goth.	....	Lith.	šonkaulis
NG	πλευρόν	ON	rif	Lett.	riba
Lat.	costa	Dan.	ribben	ChSl.	rebro
It.	costa	Sw.	revben	SCr.	rebro
Fr.	côte	OE	rib	Boh.	žebro
Sp.	costilla	ME	rib	Pol.	žebro
Rum.	coastă	NE	rib	Russ.	rebro
Ir.	asna	Du.	rib	Skt.	parçu-, pṛšṭi-
NIr.	easna	OHG	rippa	Av.	parəsu-
W.	asen	MHG	rippe		
Br.	kostezen	NHG	rippe		

The largest group of words for 'rib' is connected with words for 'cover with a roof', 'a roof' and were evidently applied to the plural 'ribs' as forming a sort of roof over the interior of the thorax. Some are connected with words for 'bone'. The secondary use as 'side', etc. is widespread.

1. Grk. πλευρόν, etym.? Boisacq 794.

2. Lat. costa (> It. costa, Fr. côte, Rum. coastă; Sp. cueste as 'rib' replaced by deriv. costilla) : ChSl. kostĭ 'bone' (4.16). Walde-P. 1.464. Ernout-M. 225. Walde-H. 1.281.

3. Ir. asna, NIr. easna, W., Corn. asen : Grk. ὀστέον 'bone' etc. (4.16). Pedersen 1.85.

Br. kostezen, fr. VLat. *costātum

(source of Fr. côté 'side'), deriv. of Lat. costa (above, 2). Henry 77.

4. ON rif, OE rib, OHG rippa, etc. general Gmc. (but Dan., Sw., rev and 'rib' replaced by Dan. ribben, Sw. revben, cpds. with ben 'bone') : ChSl. rebro 'rib', etc. general Slavic, fr. the root seen in Grk. ἐρέφω 'roof over', ὄροφος 'roof', etc. Walde-P. 2.371. Falk-Torp 896.

5. Lith. šonkaulis, cpd. of šonas 'side' and kaulas 'bone'.

Lett. riba, fr. MLG ribbe. Mühl.-Endz. 3.521.

6. ChSl. rebro, etc., general Slavic: OE rib, etc., above, 4.

7. Skt. parçu-, pṛšṭi-, Av. parəsu- : ChSl. prŭsi (pl.) 'breast' (as region of the ribs), root connection? Walde-P. 2.44.

4.17 HORN

Grk.	κέρας	Goth.	haurn	Lith.	ragas
NG	κέρατο	ON	horn	Lett.	rags
Lat.	cornū	Dan.	horn	ChSl.	rogŭ
It.	corno	Sw.	horn	SCr.	rog
Fr.	corne	OE	horn	Boh.	roh
Sp.	cuerno (asta)	ME	horn	Pol.	róg
Rum.	corn	NE	horn	Russ.	rog
Ir.	adarc, benn	Du.	hoorn	Skt.	çṛṅga-
NIr.	adharc	OHG	horn	Av.	srū-, srvā-
W.	corn	MHG	horn		
Br.	korn	NHG	horn		

Most of the words for 'horn' belong to a single group of cognates which includes words for 'horn, head, summit', etc. with the common notion of 'top'. Originally denoting an animal's horn

and so considered here, most of them are also applied, like NE horn, to 'horn' as material and to objects of similar shape, esp. 'drinking-horn' or 'horn' for blowing. But such uses may also be distin-

guished by different forms, as Fr. corne, but cor.

1. IE *ḱer- in a variety of formations meaning 'top, summit, head, horn'. Walde-P. 1.403 ff. Ernout-M. 221 f. Walde-H. 1.276.

Here as 'horn' : Grk. κέρας (cf. esp. Skt. çiras-, Av. sarah- 'head', Att. gen. κέρᾱτος, dat. κέρᾱτι, etc., whence NG κέρατο (> Lat. cornū (> It. corno, etc. general Romance; also Ir. corn 'drinking-horn', W. corn, Br. korn); Goth. haurn, OE horn, etc., general Gmc.; Skt. çiras-, Av. srū-, srvā- (NPers. surū 'horn'); in other senses, Grk. κάρᾱ, Skt. çiras- 'head', etc. (4.21), Lat. cerebrum 'brain', Grk. κορυφή 'summit', etc.

2. Sp. asta 'lance' (fr. Lat. hasta) also 'horn' of deer, etc.

3. Ir. adarc, NIr. adharc, an old continental loanword with Celtic suffix (cf. Gallo-Lat. adarca 'spongy growth on sedge') fr. Basque adar 'horn'. Walde-H. 1.12. Pokorny, Z. celt. Ph. 14.273, 16.112.

Ir. benn (also 'point, peak', as NIr. beann), perh. : OE pinn 'pin, peg', MLG pint 'penis', etc. Walde-P. 2.109.

4. Lith. ragas, Lett. rags (OPruss. ragis 'hunting-horn'), ChSl. rogŭ, etc., general Balto-Slavic, without outside connections. Walde-P. 2.367.

4.18 TAIL

Grk.	οὐρά	Goth.	....	Lith.	uodega
NG	οὐρά	ON	hali (tagl, rōfa, etc.)	Lett.	aste (l'ipa, uodega)
Lat.	cauda	Dan.	hale (svans)	ChSl.	opaši, očesŭ, ošibŭ
It.	coda	Sw.	svans	SCr.	rep
Fr.	queue	OE	tægl (steort)	Boh.	ocas, ohon, chvost
Sp.	cola, rabo	ME	tail	Pol.	ogon (chwost)
Rum.	coadă	NE	tail	Russ.	chvost
Ir.	err, erball	Du.	staart	Skt.	puccha-, lāṅgūla-
NIr.	earball	OHG	zagal	Av.	duma-
W.	cynffon	MHG	zagel, swanz, sterz		
Br.	lost	NHG	schwanz (schweif)		

Words for 'tail' are from such notions as 'projection', 'long slender shape', 'pointed shape' (or after particular objects of such shape), 'swinging motion'. Several are obscure. There are often special words for the 'tail' of different kinds of animals, some of which are mentioned beside the more generic.

1. Grk. οὐρά : ὄρρος, OE ears, OHG ars, Hitt. arras 'rump, arse', Skt. ṛšva- 'high', all from the notion of 'what stands out, projects', root as in Skt. ṛ- 'move, rise', Grk. ὄρνῡμι 'stir up', Lat. orīrī 'rise', etc. Here also Ir. err 'tail' (also 'end', etc., as NIr. earr), and Ir. erball, NIr. earball 'tail', cpd. with ball

'part of the body'. Walde-P. 1.138. Pedersen 1.83.

2. Lat. cauda, cōda (> Romance words), etym.? Ernout-M. 164. Walde-H. 1.185. REW 1774.

Sp. rabo, fr. Lat. rāpum 'turnip, radish', as applied first to the similar shaped pig's tail, etc. REW 7065.

3. Ir. err, erball, above, 1.

W. cynffon, cpd. of cyn(t) 'former, earlier' but here 'hind' and ffon 'stick, staff'. Morris Jones 246.

Br., Corn. lost : W. llost 'spear', arch. also 'tail', Ir. loss 'point, end' rarely 'tail', ON ljōstr 'fish-spear', all with the notion of 'pointed object', and

perh. fr. the root seen in Skt. lu- 'cut off', etc. Walde-P. 2.408. Pedersen 1.80.

4. ON hali, Dan. hale : Ir. cail 'spear', Grk. κῆλον 'shaft, arrow', OPruss. kelian 'spear', etc. Walde-P. 1.431. Falk-Torp 373.

ON rōfa 'bony part of horse's tail' (in NIcel. 'tail' of cats and dogs; for the many different words for 'tail', cf. Vigfusson s.v. hali), Norw. rōve 'tail' : OHG ruoba, NHG rübe 'turnip, etc.'. Falk-Torp 914.

ON tagl 'horse's tail' (Sw. tagel 'horsehair', Goth. tagl 'hair', OE tægl, ME, NE tail, OHG zagal, MHG zagel (NHG zagel now 'penis') : Skt. daçā- 'fringe of cloth', all with common notion of 'long slender shape', whence also Goth. tahjan 'tear, scatter' through 'shred, tear in shreds'. Walde-P. 1.785. Falk-Torp 1242. Feist 470.

ON stertr 'bony part of horse's tail' (Dan. stjært mostly 'handle', Sw. stärt mostly 'arse'), OE steort, Du. staart, MHG sterz (NHG sterz also dial. 'tail'; but of this group only Du. staart now the normal word) : Grk. στόρθη, στόρθυγξ 'point, spike', etc., from extensions of *ster- in Grk. στερεός, NHG starr 'stiff', etc. Walde-P. 2.640. Falk-Torp 1170.

MHG swanz, MLG swans (> Dan., Sw. svans; Dan. in secondary uses), NHG schwanz, fr. MHG swanzen 'move to and fro', intensive of swanken beside swingen 'swing, throw', etc. (Walde-P. 2.526). Weigand-H. 2.812. Kluge-G. 549. Hellquist 1121.

NHG schweif ('tail' of large animals), fr. MHG sweif 'swinging motion', fr. sweifen 'turn around', ON sveipa 'stroke,

wrap', etc. (Walde-P. 2.520). Weigand-H. 2.817.

Thus NHG schwanz and schweif are of the same semantic origin, but the former is generic while the latter is still restricted to the swishing tail of large animals (or the similar tail of a comet).

5. Lith., Lett. uodega (in Lett. of limited scope), etym. dub. Walde-P. 1.175. Mühl.-Endz. 4.412.

Lett. aste, prob. : ass 'sharp', Lith. aštrus, etc. Cf. Lith. ašutas 'horsehair'. Mühl.-Endz. 1.145.

Lett. l'ipa 'tail' of some small animals, fr. Esth. lipp 'tail'. Mühl.-Endz. 2.540 f.

6. ChSl. opaši (Supr.) : ChSl. pachati 'toss, fan', Russ. pachát' 'blow', etc. Walde-P. 2.67. Miklosich 230. Brückner 389.

ChSl. (late) očesŭ, Boh. ocas, etym.?

ChSl. (late) ošibŭ : ChSl. *šiba 'rod', attested by šibati 'scourge', Slov. šiba 'rod', outside connections? Scheftelowitz, IF 33.142.

SCr. rep : Pol. rząp 'stump of the tail', Boh. řap 'handle of a spoon', but outside connections? Brückner 474.

Pol. ogon, Boh. ohon : ChSl. goniti, Pol. gonić, Boh. honiti 'drive, chase', hence 'tail' as swishing away flies, etc. Berneker 328.

Boh., Russ. chvost, Pol. chwost, etym.? Berneker 409 ff. Brückner 187 f.

7. Skt. puccha-, perh. as orig. 'bushy' : Pol., Russ. puch 'down, thin hair'. Walde-P. 2.82 ff.

Skt. lāṅgula- : Lith. lingoti 'move to and fro', etc. Walde-P. 2.436.

Av. duma- (NPers. dum 'tail') : OHG zumpfo 'penis'. Walde-P. 1.816.

4.19 BACK

Grk.	νῶτον	Goth.	....	Lith.	nugara
NG	ράχη (νῶτα)	ON	bak	Lett.	mugura
Lat.	dorsum, tergum	Dan.	ryg	ChSl.	(chribŭtŭ)
It.	dosso, dorso, schiena	Sw.	rygg	SCr.	leda
Fr.	dos	OE	hrycg, bæc	Boh.	hřbet, záda
Sp.	espalda(s)	ME	bak, rugge	Pol.	grzbiet (plecy)
Rum.	spate, dos	NE	back	Russ.	spina
Ir.	cúl, druimm	Du.	rug	Skt.	pṛštha-
NIr.	druim	OHG	(h)rucki	Av.	paršta-
W.	cefn	MHG	rücke		
Br.	kein	NHG	rücken		

Both as regards origin and secondary uses of words for 'back', there are different associations for the horizontal back of an animal (with ridge, etc.) and the back of man as the hind-part. Many of the words were doubtless first applied only to the former or the latter, and later extended. But there is rarely historical evidence of actual distinction in usage (some in the case of Lat. dorsum). Some come from notions like 'bent', 'projecting part', 'ridge', 'hind-part', etc. In several cases 'back' rests on an extension from 'backbone', spine', 'shoulder', 'rump, anus', 'loins'.

1. Grk. νῶτον (also νῶτος, coll. pl. νῶτα (so NG νῶτα in certain phrases), perh. : Lat. natēs 'rump'. Walde-P. 2.340. Ernout-M. 656.

NG ράχη, the usual pop. word, fr. Grk. ῥάχις 'spine'.

2. Lat. tergum (> It. tergo), coll. pl. terga, also tergus, -oris, etym. dub. Walde-P. 2.629. Ernout-M. 1031 f.

Lat. dorsum, pop. form dossum (cf. dossennus 'hunchback')—whence It. dosso (beside dorso), Fr., Rum. dos—prob. fr. deorsum 'turned down', through some such stages as 'sloping, steep' (cf. abruptus 'steep' fr. 'broken down') 'mountain ridge' or 'back' of animals, later of men. Ernout-M. 284. Otherwise (rejecting above as only pop. etym.) Walde-H. 1.372.

It. schiena 'back' fr. 'spine' (cf. Sp.

esquena 'spine'), loanword fr. Gmc., OHG scina 'thin strip, shin', NE shin, etc. REW 7994.

Sp. espalda(s) fr. Lat. spatula 'flat piece, shoulder blade, shoulder' (as Fr. épaule, etc. 4.30), dim. of spatha 'spattle, sword' (fr. Grk. σπάθη 'flat blade', whence Rum. spată 'shoulder blade', pl. spate 'back'. REW 8128, 8130.

3. Ir. cúl (NIr. cúl mostly 'back of the head', W. cil 'back' in phrases and of objects, Br. kil 'backside' of an object) : Lat. cūlus 'anus', etc. Walde-P. 2.547. Ernout-M. 240. Pedersen 1.50.

Ir. druimm, NIr. druim, drom (W. trum 'ridge', Br. adreñv 'behind'), etym. dub., perh. with 'back' fr. 'anus' : Grk. τόρμος, τρῆμα 'hole', τράμις· τρῆμα τῆς ἕδρας, ὁ ὄρρος, etc. (Hesych.), ON þarmr, OE þearm, OHG daram 'gut, colon', etc. Walde-P. 1.733, 734 (top). Pedersen 1.170.

W. cefn, Br. kein (older kevn), etym.? Pedersen 1.117. Henry 57.

4. ON bak (Dan. bag, Sw. bak adv. 'behind' and in cpds. for 'hind-'), OE bæc, ME bak, NE back (NHG bah NHG hinterbacke 'buttock', Du. bakbord 'larboard'), outside connections dub., but perh. from a root meaning 'bend'. Walde-P. 2.148. Falk-Torp 41.

ON hryggr 'backbone, spine', as 'back' Dan. ryg, Sw. rygg, OE hrycg, ME rugge (NE ridge now obs. in this sense), Du. rug, OHG (h)rucki, MHG *rücke*, NHG *rücken*, prob. with notion of 'curved' : Skt. *kruñc-* 'be crooked', W. *crug* 'heap', etc. Walde-P. 2.573. Falk-Torp 926. Hellquist 857 f.

5. Lith. *nugara*, cpd. of *nu-* 'down', second part : ChSl. *gora* 'mountain', etc. (1.22), hence first 'mountain ridge', then 'back'. Walde-P. 1.682. Berneker 329. Here also Lett. *mugura* (also *mugara*) fr. **nugara* (> Liv. *nugār*), with unexplained init. *m.* Mühl.-Endz. 2.661.

6. SCr. *leđa* (pl.) : ChSl. *lędvíję*, etc., general Slavic as 'loins'. Berneker 705 f.
Boh. *záda*, pl. of *zad* = ChSl. *zadŭ*

'back part' in phrases, beside prep. *za* 'behind' (like *nadŭ* 'above' beside *na* 'on', etc.).

Boh. *hřbet*, Pol. *grzbiet* : ChSl. *chrŭbĭtŭ* 'neck', also late *chribŭtŭ* 'back', SCr. *hrbat* 'hump, back', Boh. *chřib* 'hill', etc. Berneker 404. Brückner 160 f.

Pol. *plecy* 'shoulder' (4.30), used in phrases for 'carry on the back', etc.

Russ. *spina*, fr. Lat. *spīna* 'spine'.

7. Skt. *pṛṣṭha-*, Av. *paršta-* (NPers. *pušt* 'back'), cpd. of **pṛ-* 'forth' (Lat. *por-*, etc.; beside **pro* in Grk. *πρό*, Skt. *pra*, etc.) and **st(h)ā-* 'stand', so lit. 'that which stands out'. Walde-P. 2.53.

4.20 HEAD

Grk.	κεφαλή, κάρᾱ (poet.)	Goth.	haubiþ	Lith.	galva
NG	κεφάλι	ON	hǫfuð, haufuð	Lett.	galva
Lat.	caput	Dan.	hoved	ChSl.	glava
It.	testa, capo	Sw.	hufvud	SCr.	glava
Fr.	tête	OE	hēafod, hafela	Boh.	hlava
Sp.	cabeza	ME	heved, hed	Pol.	głowa
Rum.	cap	NE	head	Russ.	golova
Ir.	cend, cenn	Du.	hoofd	Skt.	çiras-, çīrṣan-, mūrdhan-
NIr.	ceann	OHG	houbit		
W.	pen	MHG	houbet, kopf	Av.	sarah-, sāra-, vaγδana-, kamərəδa-
Br.	penn	NHG	kopf, haupt		

Words for 'head' are from the notion of 'top, summit' (as conversely often 'head' for 'top'), or through 'skull' from 'bowl, cup', 'potsherd' or 'bald'. No account is taken of the countless slang words for 'head' (NE *bean*, *nut*, etc.), except where such have become the standard words.

1. IE **ḱer-* in various formations meaning 'top, summit, head, horn'. Walde-P. 1.403 ff. Ernout-M. 177.

Grk. poet. κάρ, κάρᾱ, κάρη; Skt. *çiras-*, *çīrṣan-*, Av. *sarah-*, *sāra-*; cf., in other senses, Grk. κορυφή 'summit', Grk. κέρας, Lat. *cornū* 'horn', etc. (4.17), Lat. *cerebrum*, OHG *hirni* 'brain', etc.

2. IE **kap-* in various formations meaning 'head, bowl', etc., root connection dub. Walde-P. 1.346 ff. Ernout-M. 151 f. Walde-H. 1.163. Falk-Torp 422.

Lat. *caput* (> It. *capo*, Rum. *cap*, etc.); ON *hǫfuð*, Dan. *hoved*, Sw. *hufvud*, and with different suffix OE *hafela*; cf. Skt. *kapucchala-* (**kaput-çala-*) 'hair on the back of the head', *kapāla-* 'cup, bowl, skull', Lat. *capis* 'bowl', etc.

3. Grk. κεφαλή (NG κεφάλι fr. dim. form) : Goth. *gibla* 'gable', etc. Walde-P. 1.571.

4. From Lat. *caput* (above, 2) the meaning 'head' of the body persists in

Rum. *cap*, in part in It. *capo*, and in various dialects, while Fr. *chef* (> NE *chief*) and Sp. *cabo* (> Fr. *cap*, NE *cape*) have only secondary uses. But Sp. *cabeza* 'head', fr. Lat. deriv. *capitium*. REW 1668, 1637.

Lat. *testa* 'potsherd' was used in late Lat. for 'skull' and became a common colloquial word for 'head', partly displacing *caput* in this sense. Hence It. *testa*, Fr. *tête* as the standard words, while Sp. *testa* is still only colloquial for *cabeza*. REW 8682.

5. Ir. *cend*, *cenn*, NIr. *ceann*, W. *pen*, Br. *penn* (cf. also *Alpes Penninae*, the Apennines), etym.? Walde-P. 1.398. Pedersen 1.157 f.

Ir. *calb* (rare), fr. Lat. *calva* 'skull' (4.202). Pedersen 1.215.

6. ON *hǫfuð*, etc., above, 2. The more widespread forms with diphthongal first syllable, Goth. *haubiþ*, ON *haufuð*, OE *hēafod*, ME *heved*, NE *head*, Du. *hoofd*, OHG *houbit*, NHG *haupt*, are explained by some as a blend of this group

with another represented by Skt. *kakubh-* 'summit', Lith. *kaupas* 'heap', etc. Walde-P. 1.346. Falk-Torp 422. Feist 248. Kluge-G. 237.

MHG *kopf* 'drinking-cup', hence sometimes 'skull, head' (cf. Lat. *testa*, above, 4), NHG *kopf* displacing *haupt* (now mostly wholly in secondary uses) : OE *cuppe* 'cup', etc. (5.35). Weigand-H. 1.1118 f.

7. Lith., Lett. *galva*, ChSl. *glava*, etc. general Balto-Slavic : ChSl. *golŭ*, Russ. *gol* 'naked, bare, bald', NHG *kahl* 'bald', etc. (4.93). For the development of 'bald' through 'skull' to 'head', cf. Lat. *calva*, *calvāria* 'skull' fr. *calvus* 'bald'. Berneker 324.

8. Skt. *çiras-*, Av. *sarah-*, etc., above, 1.

Skt. *mūrdhan-*, also Av. *ka-mərəδa-* (only for 'head' of evil beings) : OE *molda* 'top of the head', Grk. βλωθρός 'tall'. Walde-P. 1.295. Barth. 440.

Av. *vaγδana-*, etym.? Barth. 1336.

4.202 SKULL

Grk.	κρᾱνίον	Goth.	hwairnei	Lith.	kiaušė, kaukolė
NG	κρανίο, καύκαλο	ON	hauss	Lett.	kauss
Lat.	calva, calvāria	Dan.	hovedskal, hjerneskal	ChSl.	kranijevŭ (adj.), lŭbŭ
It.	cranio	Sw.	huvudskalle, skalle	SCr.	lubanja
Fr.	crâne	OE	hēafodpanne (-bān)	Boh.	leb, lebka
Sp.	craneo (calavera)	ME	skulle, pan	Pol.	czaszka
Rum.	craniu	NE	skull	Russ.	čerep
Ir.	clocenn	Du.	schedel	Skt.	mastaka-, kapāla-, karpara-
NIr.	cloigeann	OHG	hirniscala		
W.	penglog	MHG	schedel, hirneschal	Av.	mastrəγan- (in pl.)
Br.	klopenn	NHG	schädel, hirnschale		

Of the words for 'skull', some are cognate with words for 'head' or cpds. of such with words for 'stone' (so the Celtic) or 'shell, bowl, pan' (latter also with words for 'brain'). A few (like some for 'head' through 'skull') are based on the notion of 'bald'. But the most frequent

relation is with words for 'bowl, cup', owing to the similarity in shape and the once widespread use of skulls as drinking-vessels. Cf. Scheftelowitz, BB 28.143 ff. (where are many less common words not included here).

1. Grk. κρᾱνίον (> MLat. *cranium* >

Romance words, etc., fr. **κρασ-νιον* : κάρᾱ 'head', κέρας 'horn', etc. Walde-P. 1.405.

NG pop. also καύκαλο, fr. Byz. καῦκος 'drinking-cup'.

2. Lat. *calva* and later *calvāria* (> Sp. *calavera* mostly 'skull' of a dead person, 'death's head', influenced by *cadāvar* 'corpse'? REW 1529), fr. *calvus* 'bald' (4.93). Ernout-M. 137. Walde-H. 1.143.

3. Ir. *clocenn* (K. Meyer, Contrib. 390), NIr. *cloigeann*, W. *penglog*, Br. *klopenn*, cpds. of words for 'stone' (Ir. *cloch*, W. *glog*, 1.44) and head (Ir. *cenn*, W. *pen*, etc., 4.20). Pedersen 1.418.

4. Goth. *hwairnei* : ON *hverna* 'cooking-vessel', ON *hverr*, OE, OHG *hwer*, Skt. *caru-* 'caldron, pot, kettle', etc. Walde-P. 1.518. Feist 280.

ON *hauss* (so also Norw. *haus*, Sw. dial. *hös*) : Grk. κύστις 'bladder, pouch', etc., fr. an *s*-extension of IE **(s)keu-* 'cover', parallel to a *k*-extension in Lith. *kiaušė* (below, 5). Walde-P. 2.551. Falk-Torp 385.

Norw., Sw. *skalle* (both used alone for 'skull'), fr. the same root as Dan., Sw. *skal* 'shell' and Dan. *skaal*, Sw. *skal* 'bowl, cup'. Here also cpds. with words for 'head' or 'brain', Dan. *hovedskal*, *hjerneskal*, Sw. *huvudskalle*, *huvudskal*. Walde-P. 2.293. Falk-Torp 981 f.

OE *hēafodpanne*, *hēafodbān*, cpds. of *hēafod* 'head' with words for 'pan' or 'bone'. ME *pan* also used alone for 'skull', NED s.v. 6.

ME *skulle* (*scolle*, *sculle*), NE *skull*, loanword fr. some Scand. form belonging with Sw. *skalle*, etc. (above). NED s.v. *skull*. Falk-Torp 982.

OHG *hirniscala*, MHG *hirneschal*, NHG *hirnschale*, cpd. of *hirni* 'brain' and *scala* 'covering, shell'.

MHG *schedel*, NHG *schädel* (> Du. *schedel*) = MLG *schedel* 'box, case', MDu. *scedel*, Du. *scheel* 'cover, lid', root connection dub. Walde-P. 2.543. Falk-Torp 982. Weigand-H. 1.665. Franck-v. W. 576.

5. Lith. *kiaušė*, Lett. *kauss* (latter mostly with gen. sg. of *galva* 'head') : Skt. *koça-* 'case, box' (i.e. 'container'), fr. **keu-k-* extension of IE **(s)keu-* 'cover', parallel to **keu-s-* in ON *hauss* (above, 4). Walde-P. 2.548 f. Mühl.-Endz. 2.178.

Lith. *kaukolė*, etym.? Scheftelowitz, op. cit. 148, takes as loanword fr. the rare Lat. *caucula*, dim. of *caucus* 'drinking-cup', but medium of borrowing?

6. ChSl. in Gospels only adj. in *kranijevo město* = κρανίου τόπος, based on the Grk. κρᾱνίον, for which later *lŭbovo* (or *lŭbĭnoje*) *město* (Jagić, Entstehungsgesch. 312).

Late ChSl. *lŭbŭ* (whence adj. *lŭbovo*, etc., above), SCr. *lubanja*, Boh. *leb*, *lebka* (Pol. *łeb*, Russ. *lob* 'forehead'), prob. : Russ. *lub* 'bark', etc., either through the notion of 'peeled off, bald' (as in Lat. *calva*, above 2), or 'drinking-vessel'. Walde-P. 2.418. Berneker 749.

Pol. *czaszka*, fr. *czasza* : ChSl. *čaša* 'cup', etc. Berneker 137.

Russ. *čerep* = ChSl. *črěpŭ* 'potsherd' : OPruss. *kerpetis* 'skull', OHG *scirbi*, NHG *scherbe* 'potsherd', Skt. *karpara-* 'potsherd, pot' also 'skull'. Walde-P. 2.580. Berneker 147.

7. Skt. *mastaka-*, Av. *mastrəγan-* (in pl.), prob. : Skt. *majjan-* 'marrow', ChSl. *mozgŭ* 'brain', etc. (4.203). Walde-P. 2.309.

Skt. *kapāla-* 'cup, bowl, potsherd' and 'skull', fr. the same root as Lat. *caput* 'head'. Walde-P. 1.346.

4.203 BRAIN

Grk.	ἐγκέφαλος	Goth.	. . . .	Lith.	smegenys (pl.)
NG	μυαλό	ON	hjarni	Lett.	smadzenes
Lat.	cerebrum	Dan.	hjerne	ChSl.	mozgŭ
It.	cervello	Sw.	hjarna	SCr.	mozak
Fr.	cerveau	OE	brægen	Boh.	mozek
Sp.	cerebro	ME	brain, hernes (pl.)	Pol.	mózg
Rum.	creieri (pl.)	NE	brain	Russ.	mozg
Ir.	inchinn	Du.	hersenen (pl.), brein	Skt.	mastiṣka-
NIr.	inchinn	OHG	hirni	Av.	mastrəγan- (in pl.)
W.	ymennyd	MHG	herne		
Br.	empenn	NHG	hirn, gehirn		

Most of the words for 'brain' are cognate with words for 'head' or 'marrow'. Sometimes the plural used as coll., like NE *brains*, is the usual form.

1. Derivs. of **ḱer(ə)s-*, etc. seen in Skt. *çiras-* 'head', Grk. κέρας 'horn', etc. Walde-P. 1.403 ff. Ernout-M. 177. Walde-H. 1.203. Falk-Torp 410. REW 1826, 1827.

Lat. *cerebrum* (> Sp. *cerebro*, Rum. *creier* used mostly in pl. *creieri*), *cerebellum* (> It. *cervella*, Fr. *cerveau*); ON *hjarni*, OHG *hirni*, etc., general Gmc. (except English, where ME *hernes*, Sc. *harns* fr. Norse).

2. Grk. ἐγκέφαλος phrase cpd. fr. ἐν 'in' and κεφαλή 'head'.

NG μυαλό, often pl. τὰ μυαλά, fr. Grk. μυελός, late μυαλός 'marrow'. Cf. Aristot. PA 652ᵃ25 πολλοῖς γὰρ καὶ ὁ ἐγκέφαλος δοκεῖ μυελὸς εἶναι 'for many think the brain is really marrow'.

3. Ir. *inchinn*, W. *ymennyd*, Br. *empenn*, cpds. (like Grk. ἐγκέφαλος) fr. words for 'in' and 'head' (Ir. *cenn*, etc., 4.20).

4. OE *brægen*, ME, NE *brain*, Du. *brein*, prob. : Grk. βρεχμός, βρέγμα 'front part of the head'. Walde-P. 2.314. NED s.v. *brain*. Franck-v. W. 91.

5. Lith. *smegenys* (pl.), Lett. *smadzenes* (or pl. *-is*), ChSl. *mozgŭ*, etc. (all the Slavic words) : Skt. *majjan-*, ON *merg*, OE *mearg*, NE *marrow*, OHG *mar(a)g*, NHG *mark*, etc., all 'marrow' (Av. *mazga* once, 'marrow' or 'brain'? NPers. *mayz* both), root connection? For the association of 'marrow' with 'brain', see above, 2. Walde-P. 2.309.

6. Skt. *mastiṣka-* : *mastaka-* 'skull' (4.202).

Av. *mastrəγan-* in pl. 'skull' (4.202) and 'brains' (Yt. 10.72). Barth. 1155.

4.204 FACE

Grk.	*πρόσωπον*	Goth.	*andwairþi, wlits, andawleizn, ludja*	Lith.	*veidas*
NG	*πρόσωπο*	ON	*andlit*	Lett.	*vaigs*
Lat.	*faciēs*	Dan.	*ansigt*	ChSl.	*lice*
It.	*faccia* (*viso*)	Sw.	*ansikte* (*anlete*)	SCr.	*lice*
Fr.	*visage*	OE	*ansȳn, andwlīta*	Boh.	*tvář*
Sp.	*cara* (*rostro*)	ME	*face*	Pol.	*twarz*
Rum.	*faţă, obraz*	NE	*face*	Russ.	*lico*
Ir.	*agad, enech*	Du.	*gezicht*	Skt.	*anīka-*
NIr.	*aghaidh*	OHG	*gesiht, antlutti, annuzzi*	Av.	*ainika-, čiϑra-*
W.	*wyneb*	MHG	*gesiht, antlitze*		
Br.	*dremm*	NHG	*gesicht* (*angesicht, antlitz*)		

The face is the most distinguishing and expressive portion of the body, and the words for 'face' are most commonly based on the notion of 'appearance, look', most of these derived from verbs for 'see, look', or in some cases on the notion of 'form, shape'. There is sometimes interchange between 'face' and 'cheek' in the same word or group.

Included in the list (in parentheses) are some words that are synonyms of those given in first place, either popular (but not vulgar, as NE *mug*), as It. *viso*, Sp. *rostro*, or now restricted to a lofty style, as NHG *angesicht, antlitz*.

1. Grk. *πρόσωπον* (in Hom. always pl.), fr. *πρός* 'toward' and deriv. of *ὀπ-* (IE **okʷ-*) in *ὄψομαι* fut. of *ὁράω* 'see, look', *ὄσσε* 'eyes', *ὤψ* also 'face', etc. (15.51). Hence orig. the 'appearance, look'.

2. Lat. *faciēs*, orig. 'form, shape', then esp. 'face', fr. *facere* 'make'. Hence, through VLat. **facia*, It. *faccia*, Fr. *face* (> ME, NE *face*), Rum. *faţă* (Port. *face* 'cheek', Sp. *haz, faz* fig.). But the use of Fr. *face* for the 'face' of a person was given up in the 17th cent. (Wartburg 3.356). Ernout-M. 322. Walde-H. 1.439. REW 3130.

Fr. *visage*, fr. older *vis* (now only in *vis-à-vis*) = It. *viso* (pop. for *faccia*), fr. Lat. *vīsus* 'sight'. REW 9384. Gamillscheg 893.

Sp. *cara* (the once quoted *ante caram*, Corippus in laud. Justini 2.413, is a false reading of *ante casam* now in the editions of Partsch and of Petschenig), OFr. *chiere* (> ME *chere*, NE *cheer*, NED s.v.), generally taken as fr. Grk. *κάρα* 'head'. The difficulties are (1) the fact that *κάρα* is only found in poets, (2) the change in sense (but *κάρα* used for 'face' in Soph. El. 1310), (3) the restriction of the group to the West. Apparently one would have to assume a literary poetical borrowing as the starting point, or else that the Grk. word was in ordinary prose use among those who founded the colonies in Spain and southern Gaul. REW 1670. Diez 87. Wartburg 2.350.

Sp. *rostro* (pop. word for 'face', not vulgar), fr. Lat. *rōstrum* 'beak'. REW 7386.

Rum. *obraz*, fr. Slavic, ChSl. *obrazŭ* 'form, shape, image' (12.57), SCr. *obraz* 'cheek', etc. Tiktin 1072 f.

3. Ir. *agad*, NIr. *aghaidh*, etym.? Pedersen 1.129.

Ir. *enech*, MW, MBr. *enep*, W. *wyneb*, (Br. *enep, eneb* 'the opposite'), a cpd. of IE **okʷ-* 'see', like Grk. *πρόσωπον* (above, 1) and *ἐνώπιος* 'facing', Skt. *anīka-* 'face'? Walde-P. 1.171 (adversely). Pedersen 1.38. Morris Jones 154.

Br. *dremm* = W. *drem* 'sight, look', fr. **dṛksmā-* : Skt. *dṛç-*, Grk. *δέρκομαι*, etc. 'see' (15.51).

4. Goth. *andwairþi*, fr. adj. *andwairþs* 'present', renders appropriately *πρόσωπον* where it means 'presence', but also where it means 'face' (as Mt. 6.16, Mk. 14.65, Lk. 9.29).

Goth. *andaugi* (twice for *πρόσωπον*), cpd. of *and* 'along, over', second part : *augō* 'eye'.

Goth. *ludja* (only acc. sg. Mk. 6.17), OHG *antlutti, analutti* and (Otfr., Tat.) *annuzzi*, MHG *antlütte, antlütze* (beside *antlitze*, etc., see foll.) : Goth. *liudan* 'grow', etc. Cf., fr. the same root, Av. *raoδa-* 'appearance' (Barth. 1495), NPers. *rūy* 'face'. Walde-P. 2.416. Feist 337.

Goth. *wlits, andawleizn*, ON *andlīt* (Sw. *anlete* arch.), OE *andwlīta*, MHG *antlitze*, NHG *antlitz*, fr. the root seen in ON *līta*, OE *wlītan* 'see, look' (15.51). Walde-P. 1.293. Falk-Torp 28. Feist 48, 571 f. Weigand-H. 1.73.

OE *ansȳn* (usual word), OHG *anasiuni* ('face' in Notker, etc.; cf. Goth. *anasiuns* 'visible'), OHG, MHG *gesiht*, NHG *gesicht*, also (but less common in this sense) OHG *anasiht*, MLG *ansichte* (> Dan. *ansigt*, Sw. *ansikte*) and MHG *angesihte*, NHG *angesicht*, all fr. the root of OE *sēon*, OHG *sehan* 'see' (15.51). Weigand-H. 1.61, 704. Paul, Deutsches Wtb. s.v. *Gesicht*. Falk-Torp 26. Hellquist 24.

5. Lith. *veidas*, fr. the root **weid-* in Grk. *εἶδον* 'saw', *εἶδος* 'appearance, form, kind', Lat. *vidēre* 'see', Lith. *veizdėti* 'look', etc. (15.51). Walde-P. 1.239.

Lett. *vaigs* 'face' and 'cheek', see under latter, 4.208.

6. ChSl., SCr. *lice*, Russ. *lico* (Boh. *lice*, Pol. *lice* mostly 'cheek'; Boh. *obličej*, Pol. *oblicze* 'face' but not the usual words) : OPruss. *laygnan* 'cheek', root connection? Walde-P. 2.395 f. Berneker 719 f.

Boh. *tvář*, Pol. *twarz* (the common words for 'face'), fr. the root of ChSl. *tvoriti*, etc. 'do, make' (9.11), hence orig. 'creation, form, kind' (attested for older Boh. and Pol.; cf. also ChSl. *tvarĭ* 'creation, work, deed', SCr. *tvar* 'material', *stvar* 'thing', Boh. *tvar* 'form, shape', Russ. *tvar'* 'creature'), with further semantic development like that in Lat. *facies* (above, 2). Brückner 586.

7. Skt. *anīka-* (RV 'face' lit. and fig.), Av. *ainika-* (Barth. 125), also Skt. *pratīka-* 'front' and sometimes 'face' cpds. with *-īka-*, fr. a form of IE **okʷ-* 'see' as in Skt. *īkṣ-* 'see, look' (15.51). Cf. Grk. *πρόσωπον* (above, 1).

Av. *čiϑra-* 'look, sight' and 'face' (NPers. *čihr* 'face'), fr. adj. *čiϑra-* 'visible, bright' = Skt. *citra-* id. Barth. 586.

4.205 FOREHEAD

Grk.	*μέτωπον*	Goth.	. . . .	Lith.	*kakta*
NG	*μέτωπο, κούτελο*	ON	*enni*	Lett.	*piere*
Lat.	*frōns*	Dan.	*pande*	ChSl.	*čelo*
It.	*fronte*	Sw.	*panna*	SCr.	*čelo*
Fr.	*front*	OE	*forhēafod*	Boh.	*čelo*
Sp.	*frente*	ME	*forhe(ue)de*	Pol.	*czoło*
Rum.	*frunte*	NE	*forehead* (*brow*)	Russ.	*lob* (*čelo*)
Ir.	*ētan, tul*	Du.	*voorhoofd*	Skt.	*bhāla-*
NIr.	*clār a ēadain*	OHG	*stirna, tinna, andi*	Av.	*ainika-*
W.	*talcen*	MHG	*stirn(e), tinne*		
Br.	*tal*	NHG	*stirn*		

Words for 'forehead' have such semantic sources as 'between the eyes', 'front part', 'flat surface', 'high', etc.

1. Grk. *μέτωπον*, cpd. of *μετά* 'between', second part as in *πρόσωπον* 'face' (4.204), hence as if 'between the eyes', and so described by Aristot., HA 491b12.

NG *κούτελο*, prob. (through 'skull'), deriv. of class. Grk. *κοτύλη* 'hollow vessel'. Amantos, 'Αθηνᾶ 28, *παραρτ.* 128 f.

2. Lat. *frōns, frontis* (> Romance words), etym. dub. Walde-H. 1.551.

3. Ir. *ētan* (also *cend-ētan*, with *cend* 'head'), NIr. (*ēadain* 'front') *clār a ēadain* (with *clār* 'surface') : ON *enni*, OHG *andi* 'forehead', all as orig. the 'front side', derivs. of **anti* in Grk. *ἀντί*, etc., 'over against, opposite'. Walde-P. 1.67. Falk-Torp 193.

Ir. *tul* (also *tul cind*, with gen. of *cend* 'head'), W., Br. *tal*, W. now *tal-cen* (with *cen* fr. Ir. *tul cind*) : Ir. *talam* 'earth', Skt. *tala-* 'surface', etc., with development of 'forehead' fr. 'flat surface'. Walde-P. 1.740. Pedersen 1.132.

4. ON *enni*, OHG *andi*, see under Ir. *ētan*, above, 3.

Dan. *pande*, Sw. *panna* = ON *panna*, OE *panne*, etc. 'pan' (5.28), with sense of 'forehead' fr. old Dan. *hovedpande*, old Sw. *hovudhpanna* 'head-pan' = 'skull'. Falk-Torp 813. Hellquist 747.

OE *forhēafod*, ME *forhe(ue)de*, NE *forehead*, Du. *voorhoofd*, cpds. of words for 'fore, front' and 'head'.

NE *brow* (poet. or rhet.), orig. a word for 'eyebrow' (4.206).

OHG *stirna*, MHG *stirn(e)*, NHG *stirn* (cf. OE *steornede* gl. *frontalis*), fr. the root of Grk. *στόρνυμι*, Lat. *sternere*, etc. 'spread out', with development, as in Grk. *στέρνον* 'breast', fr. 'flat surface'. Walde-P. 2.639.

OHG *tinna* (in gl.), MHG *tinne* (cf. OHG *dunwengi*, OE *þunwange*, etc. 'temple'), fr. IE **ten-* in words for 'stretch' and 'thin'. Walde-P. 1.724. Falk-Torp 1262.

5. Lith. *kakta*, prob. : *kaktas* 'bow' (obs.), Lett. *kakts* 'corner'. Leskien, Bildung d. Nom. 542.

Lett. *piere*, etym. dub. Mühl.-Endz. 3.284.

6. ChSl. *čelo*, etc. general Slavic (but Russ. *čelo* as 'forehead' obs.), fr. IE **kel-* in Lith. *kelti* 'raise', *kalnas* 'mountain', Lat. *celsus* 'high', *collis* 'hill' etc. Walde-P. 1.434. Berneker 140. Brückner 80.

Russ. *lob*, orig. 'skull' like late ChSl. *lŭbŭ*, Boh. *leb*, etc. (4.202).

7. Skt. *bhāla-* : ChSl. *bělŭ* 'white', Alb. *ballë* 'forehead', OPruss. *ballo* (correction of *balto*) 'forehead', etc. fr. **bhel-* beside **bhā-* in Skt. *bhā-* 'shine', etc. Walde-P. 2.175 f.

Av. *ainika-* 'face' (4.204) is rendered 'forehead' in Yt. 14.9. Barth. 125.

4.206 EYEBROW

Grk.	*ὀφρῦς*	Goth.	. . . .	Lith.	*antakis*
NG	*φρύδι*	ON	*brūn*	Lett.	*uzacs*
Lat.	*supercilium*	Dan.	*øjenbryn*	ChSl.	*brŭvĭ*
It.	*ciglio*	Sw.	*ögonbryn*	SCr.	*obrva*
Fr.	*sourcil*	OE	*ofarbrū*	Boh.	*obrv, obočí*
Sp.	*ceja*	ME	*eyebrowe* (*browes* pl.)	Pol.	*brwi* (pl.)
Rum.	*sprînceană*	NE	*eyebrow* (*brows*, pl.)	Russ.	*brov'*
Ir.	*brai* (dual), *mala*	Du.	*wenkbrauw*	Skt.	*bhrū-*
NIr.	*mala*	OHG	*brāwa, ubarbrāua, oucbrā*	Av.	*brvat-*
W.	*ael y llygad*	MHG	*brā, oug(e)brā, oberbrā*		
Br.	*abrant*	NHG	*augenbraue*		

The majority of the words for 'eyebrow' belong to an inherited group. Of the others, some are based on the notion of 'covering', and some are compounds of words for 'eye' and 'on, upon'. There is some interchange of 'eyebrow' with 'eyelid' or 'eyelash', and even 'forehead' (NE *brow*). Several show the figurative sense seen in NE *brow of a hill*.

1. IE **bhrū-*; also **bhrēu-* (disputed, see below). Walde-P. 2.206 f. (and 2.169). Brugmann, Grd. 2.1.137. Hirt, Idg. Gram. 2.96. Pedersen 2.93. Falk-Torp 44, 109. NED s.vv. *brow*, sb.[1] and *bree*, sb.[1]. Weigand-H. 1.113, 280. Franck-v. W. 787. Berneker 91 f.

Grk. *ὀφρῦς, -ύος*, NG *φρύδι* (fr. late dim. *ὀφρύδιον*); Ir. *brai, brœ* (nom. du.), *brūad* (gen. du.), also *for-brū* (gen. pl., gl. *superciliorum*); ON *brūn*, pl. *brynn*, Dan. *øjenbryn*, Sw. *ögonbryn* (with words for 'eye'), OE *brū* 'eyelash', *ofarbrū* 'eyebrow' cf. OHG *ubarbrāwe*), ME *eyebrowe*, NE *eyebrow*, also pl. ME *browes*, NE *brows* 'eyebrows', but NE sg. *brow* only 'forehead'; Lith. *bruvis* (obs.); ChSl. *brŭvĭ*, SCr. *obrva*, Boh. *obrv*, Pol. *brwi* (pl.; sg. *brew* only in phrases with secondary sense), Russ. *brov'*; Skt. *bhrū-* (nom. *bhrūs*, gen. *bhruvas*), Av. *brvat-*, NPers. *abrū, barū*; Maced. *ἀβροῦτες* (Hesych.); Toch. *parwān-* in dual forms (SSS, 128).

The following Gmc. group is taken by many as of wholly different origin and only secondarily mixed with the preceding (so Walde-P., Falk-Torp, NED, etc.) but more probably is based upon a different grade of the stem, namely **bhrēu-* beside **bhrū-* (so Noreen, Brugmann, Hirt, etc.).

ON *brā* 'eyelash' (so Fritzner, Falk-Torp; 'eyelid' Vigfusson, NED), OE *brǣw* 'eyelid' (later forms also 'eyelash' and esp. 'eyebrow', as still Scottish *bree;* NED s.v. *bree* sb.[1]), OHG *brāwa, brā* 'eyelid, eyebrow', *ubarbrāwa* 'eyebrows' (gl. to *supercilia*), MHG *brā*, pl. *brāwen*, NHG *braue*, also (with words for 'eye') OHG *oucbrā*, MHG *oug(e)brā*, NHG *augenbraue*, also OHG *wintbrāwa* 'eyelash' (NHG *wimper*) with *wint-* prob. : Ir. *find, finn* 'hair', so MDu. *wintbrauwe*, but now Du. *wenkbrauw* 'eyebrow' influenced by *wenk* 'wink'.

2. Lat. *supercilium* (> Fr. *sourcil*, Rum. *sprînceană*, latter by a blend with Lat. *gena* 'cheek', Rum. *geană* 'eyelid, eyelash'), cpd. of *cilium* 'eyelid' (> It. *ciglio*, Sp. *ceja* 'eyebrow', Fr. *cil* 'eyelash'), this later than and perh. abstracted fr. *supercilium* (hence *cil-*), in any case fr. the root **kel-* in Lat. *occulere*, *cēlāre* 'hide', Grk. *καλύπτω* 'cover', etc. Ernout-M. 186. Walde-H. 1.215. REW 1913, 8459.

3. Ir., NIr. *mala*, prob. : Lett. *mala* 'edge', Alb. *mal* 'mountain', etc. Walde-P. 2.795. Pedersen 2.99. Stokes 203.

W. *ael*, or esp. *ael y llygad* (with *llygad* 'eye'), OBr. *ail*, *guor-ail*: Ir. *āil*, *ōil* 'cheek' (4.208)? Stokes 3.

Br. *abrant* ('sourcil', Ernault, Vallée; not 'eyelid' as Pedersen) = Ir. *abra*, nom. pl. *abrait* 'eyebrow, eyelid' (K. Meyer, Contrib. 7), W. *amrant* 'eyelid', etym. dub. Pedersen 1.119 (: Lat. *frōns*, *frontis* 'forehead'). Henry 3.

4. Lith. *antakis*, Lett. *uzacs*, Boh. *oboči*, cpds. of words for 'eye' (4.21) and 'on, upon, about'.

	4.207 JAW	4.208 CHEEK	4.209 CHIN
Grk.	σιᾱγών, γνάθος, γένυς	παρειά, γένυς, σιᾱγών	γένειον
NG	σαγόνι, μασέλλα	παρειά, μάγουλο	πιγούνι
Lat.	*maxilla, māla*	*gena, bucca*	*mentum*
It.	*mascella*	*guancia*	*mento*
Fr.	*mâchoire*	*joue*	*menton*
Sp.	*quijada*	*mejilla, carrillo*	*barba*
Rum.	*falcă*	*obraz, bucă*	*barbie*
Ir.	*carpat*	*grūad, lecconn, āil*	*smech*
NIr.	*giall (carbad, corrān)*	*gruadh, leaca, pluc*	*smeig*
W.	*gen, cern*	*grudd, boch, cern*	*gen*
Br.	*karvan*	*boc'h, jod*	*elgez*
Goth.	....	*kinnus*	....
ON	*kjǫptr*	*kinn, vangi*	*haka*
Dan.	*kæve*	*kind*	*hage*
Sw.	*käk*	*kind*	*haka*
OE	*cēace, ceafl*	*wange, cēace*	*cin*
ME	*iowe, chavel*	*cheke, wonge*	*chinne*
NE	*jaw*	*cheek*	*chin*
Du.	*kaak*	*wang*	*kin*
OHG	*chinnibahho*	*wanga (baccho)*	*kinni*
MHG	*kinnebacke, kiver, kivel*	*wange, backe*	*kinne*
NHG	*kinnbacken, kiefer*	*wange, backe(n)*	*kinn*
Lith.	*žandas*	*skruostas*	*smakras*
Lett.	*žuokls, zuods*	*vaigs*	*zuods, smakrs*
ChSl.	*čeljustĭ*	*lanita*	....
SCr.	*čeljust, vilica*	*obraz*	*brada*
Boh.	*čelist*	*líce*	*brada*
Pol.	*szczęka*	*lice*	*podbrodek*
Russ.	*čeljust'*	*ščeka*	*podborodok*
Skt.	*hanu-*	*gaṇḍa-*	*civuka-*
Av.	*zānu-*	....	....

4.207–4.209. There is considerable interchange between 'jaw', 'cheek' and 'chin', notably in a widespread cognate group. This is not surprising, for the 'chin' is the prominent part of the lower jaw and the 'cheek' corresponds in position to the side of the jaw. Cf. Aristot., HA 492b22 ἔτι σιαγόνες δύο τούτων τὸ πρόσθιον γένειον, τὸ δ' ὀπίσθιον γένυς 'furthermore there are two jaws; of these the front part is the chin, the hinder part the cheek'. There is also some interchange with 'mouth' and with 'face', and between 'chin' and 'beard'.

4.207. Several of the words for 'jaw' owe this use to some resemblance in shape, as that of a 'sickle' to the lower jaw in side view, of a 'wagon, cart' to the palate or upper jaw, of a 'box' to the jaw as a box for the teeth, of a 'fork', and prob. of 'angle' to that of the jaw in the large cognate group. Some are derived from verbs for 'chew' or 'bite'. One (the modern Polish) seems to have started as a slang term for the 'chattering' jaw. Several are obscure in their ultimate root connection.

1. IE *$\hat{g}$enu- in words for 'jaw', 'cheek', and 'chin'. Orig. sense 'jaw' and ultimate connection with the word for 'knee', IE *$\hat{g}$enu- (neut.), Grk. γόνυ, Lat. *genū*, etc. (4.36), through some common notion like 'angle', is probable. Walde-P. 1.587. Ernout-M. 414. Walde-H. 1.589 f.

Grk. γένυς 'jaw' (so always in Hom.) and 'cheek', γένειον 'chin' (and 'beard'); Lat. *gena* 'cheek' (mostly in pl.; stem *genu-* in *genuīnī dentēs* 'back teeth'); W. *gen* 'jaw, chin' (Ir. *gin*, W. *geneu*, Br. *genou* 'mouth'); Goth. *kinnus*, ON *kinn*, Dan., Sw. *kind* 'cheek', OE *cin*, OHG *kinni*, etc. (all WGmc. words) 'chin' (but in early period traces of use for 'jaw', as OHG *chinne* 'jaws' Notker, Ps. 31.9, OHG *chinnibacho* 'jaw', OE *cinbān* 'jawbone'); Skt. *hanu-* 'jaw' (*h* for *j* secondary), Av. *zānu-* 'jaw' or 'chin' (in cpd., Barth. 1689), NPers. *zanax* 'chin'; Toch. *śanweṃ* 'jaws' (dual, SSS, 3, ftn.).

Here also, fr. an extension *$\hat{g}$on(ə)dh-, Grk. γνάθος, Lith. *žandas* 'jaw', Lett. *zuods* (mostly 'chin', in some places 'jaw', Mühl.-Endz. 4.759).

2. Grk. σιᾱγών (the usual prose word), NG σαγόνι, etym.? Boisacq 862.

Aristot. uses σιαγών, γνάθος, γένυς (above, 1) in this order of frequency.

NG μασέλλα, fr. It. *mascella* (below, 3).

3. Lat. *māla* (mostly in pl.) and *maxilla* (> It. *mascella* 'jaw', but Sp. *mejilla* 'cheek', Rum. *maseă* 'back tooth'), belonging together like *vēlum-vexillum*, *āla-axilla*, with *māla*, perh. fr. *makslā and : Ir. *smech*, Lith. *smakras* 'chin', Skt. *çmaçru-* 'beard'. Walde-P. 2.689. Ernout-M. 582. Walde-H. 2.15.

Fr. *mâchoire*, fr. *mâcher* 'chew'.

For Fr. dial. words and their distribution, cf. H. Kahane, Bezeichnungen der Kinnbacken im Galloromanischen, in Berl. Beitr. z. rom. Ph. 2.2.

Sp. *quijada*, deriv. of Lat. *capsa* and *capsus* 'box', as if 'box for the teeth'. Cf. Prov. *cais* 'jaw' and 'cheek'. Port. *queixo*, formerly 'jaw', now 'chin'. REW 1659c. Zauner, Rom. Forsch. 14.400. Wartburg 2.316. Malkiel, Language 21.151 ff.

Rum. *falcă*, fr. *falca for Lat. *falx*, *falcis* 'sickle' (8.33), hence 'jaw' from the similar shape of the lower jaw in side view. REW 3175. Pușcariu 575.

4. Ir. *carpat*, NIr. *carbad* 'chariot, wagon' (10.75) used also for the 'upper jaw, palate' (cf. NIr. *fiacla carbaid* 'teeth of the upper jaw'), apparently from the resemblance in shape. Here also Br. *karvan* 'beam of a loom' and reg. word for 'jaw' (upper or lower), and W. *car yr ên* 'jawbone'. Pedersen 1.118, 494.

NIr. *corrān* 'sickle' (8.33) is used for the lower 'jaw'.

NIr. *giall*, prob., like Gael. *ciobhal*, fr. forms of OE *ceafl*, NE *jowl* (below, 5). Macbain 193.

W. *gen*, above, 1.

W. *cern*, also 'cheek', see 4.208.

5. ON *kjǫptr* (Dan. *kæft*, Sw. *käft* now more like 'mug'), OE *ceafl*, ME *chavel*, NE *jowl* (in part), MHG *kiver*, *kivel*, NHG *kiefer*, LG *keve* (> Dan. *kæve*) : Av. *zafar-* 'mouth' (of evil beings). Walde-P. 1.570 f. Falk-Torp 518, 521. Hellquist 544. Weigand-H. 1.103. NED s.v. *jowl*, sb.[1].

OE *cēace*, *cēce* (also and later reg. 'cheek', but 'jawbone' in Chaucer's *an asses cheek;* and *cēacbān*, NE *cheek bone* = 'jawbone' in all early uses, present

use only since 19th cent., cf. NED s.v.), fr. the root in OE *cēowan*, OHG *kiuwan* 'chew' (: ChSl. *žĭvati* 'chew'), not (as NED s.v. *cheek*) fr. *kākā = Du. *kaak*, etc. (below), though it may have the added guttural by a blend with such form. Falk-Torp 1307. Franck-v. W. 283.

OHG *chinnibahho*, MHG *kinnebacke*, NHG *kinnbacken*, cpd. of OHG *kinni* (above, 1, here as 'jaw') and *baccho* 'jaw, cheek' (4.208).

Du. *kaak*, MLG *kake*, and with different vowel-grade MLG *keke*, Norw. *kjake*, Sw. *käk*, perh. fr. a root seen in NPers. *gazīdan* 'bite'. Falk-Torp 513. Hellquist 545. Franck-v. W. 283.

ME *iow*, *iowe*, *iawe*, NE *jaw*, etym. disputed. Now taken by many as fr. *chowe : OE *cēowan* 'chew', like MHG *kiuwe* 'jaw' fr. the same root (OHG *chiwa*, like OE *cīan* 'gills'). But the old deriv. fr. a form of Fr. *joue* 'cheek' is less difficult, despite the objection made in NED. For OFr. *ioe*, *ioue* must have been pronounced with [owe], not [ū], and the phonetic history would be parallel to that of ME *powe*, *pawe*, NE *paw*, fr. OFr. *poe*, *poue* = Prov. *pauta*. The transition fr. 'cheek' to 'jaw' may have started in 'cheek bone' = 'jawbone', which is in fact the sense in the earliest ME quotation (*iow* in Wyclif, see NED).

6. Lith. *žandas*, Lett. *zuods*, see above, 1.

Lett. *žuokls*, perh. with *žākle* 'fork of a tree', fr. the root in Lith. *-žioti* 'yawn, gape', etc. (4.52). Mühl.-Endz. 4.839.

7. ChSl. *čeljustĭ*, etc., general Slavic (but Pol. *czeluść* obs. in this sense), etym. dub. but prob. cpd. with second part : ChSl. *usta* 'mouth' (4.24). Berneker 142. Brückner 75.

SCr. *vilica* 'fork' (5.39, 8.26) also 'jaw'.

Pol. *szczęka*, early *szczeka* (Russ. *ščeka* 'cheek'), beside sb. *szczęk* 'clash, clatter', vbs. *szczekać* 'bark', *szczękać* 'clash, clatter', of imitative origin. Brückner 543, 544.

8. Skt. *hanu-*, Av. *zānu-*, above, 1.

4.208. In several of the words for 'cheek' this sense is clearly secondary to 'jaw', and in some it is a specialization of 'face'. Others are mostly based on a notion of swollen or curved rounded surface.

1. Grk. γένυς 'jaw' and 'cheek', see 4.207.

Grk. παρειά (Hom. in pl. only; sg. παρήϊον), Ion. παρήϊον, Aeol. παραύα, mostly a poet. word, but revived in lit. NG, fr. *παρ-αυσ-ιᾱ-, cpd. of παρά 'beside' and a form of either the word for 'mouth' (Lat. *ōs*, etc., 4.24), or that for 'ear' (Grk. οὖς, Lat. *auris*, etc., 4.22). Walde-P. 1.168. Boisacq 747.

Grk. σιᾱγών, usually 'jaw' (4.207), but 'cheek' in NT (Mt. 5.39, Lk. 6.29) and several pap. (Moulton-Milligan, s.v.).

Byz. μάγουλον (also in text of Melampus, but prob. Byz.) 'jaw' in κατωμάγουλον (Const. Porph.) and 'cheek', in NG reg. pop. word for 'cheek', orig. dub. G. Meyer, IF 3.68 f., Neugr. St. 3.40. Walde-H. 2.12.

2. Lat. *gena* : Grk. γένυς 'jaw, cheek', etc. See 4.207.

Lat. *bucca* (> Rum. *bucă* 'cheek', but other Romance forms 'mouth', 4.24), fr. an imitative *bu-* (beside *bhu-*) seen in many words based on the notion 'blow up, puff out', as OE *pohha* 'bag', (*ā-*)*pyffan* 'blow out, puff out', etc. Walde-P. 2.114 ff. Walde-H. 2.120.

It. *guancia*, fr. Gmc., OHG *wanga*, etc. (below, 5). REW 9499.

It. *gota* ('cheek' in phrases, but not the usual word), Prov. *gauta*, Fr. *joue* (OFr. *iou*, *ioue*), fr. a Celtic form like (if not the same as) Gall.-Rom. *gabata*

'dish'. REW 3706a. Gamillscheg 541. Meyer-Lübke, Einführung[3] 243.

For the numerous It. dial. words and their distribution, cf. H. Kahane, Language 17.212 ff.

Sp. *mejilla*, fr. Lat. *maxilla* 'jaw' (4.207). REW 5443.

Sp. *carrillo*, dim. of *carro* 'cart', and used, doubtless first as slang, for the lower jaw or cheek, with reference to the up-and-down movement in eating. Spitzer, Riv. fil. esp. 11.316.

Rum. *obraz* 'face' and 'cheek', fr. Slavic, ChSl. *obrazŭ* 'form, shape, image', SCr. *obraz* 'cheek', etc. Tiktin 1072 f.

3. Ir. *grūad*, NIr. *gruadh*, W. *grudd* : OE *grēada* 'bosom', with common notion of curved surface, but root connection? Walde-P. 1.658.

Ir. *lecconn*, NIr. *leaca*, prob. cpd. of *leth* 'side' and *conn* = *cenn* 'head'. Thurneysen, KZ 48.67 (rejecting the usual comparison with ChSl. *lice* 'face', etc., Pedersen 1.159, etc.).

Ir. *āil*, *ōil* : W. *ael* 'eyebrow' (4.206). Stokes 3. Otherwise (: Grk. οἶδος 'swelling') W. Lehman, Z. celt. Ph. 6.438.

NIr. *pluc* 'lump, knob' (beside *ploc* and prob. like W. *ploc* fr. NE *block* in sense of 'lump', as NED s.v. 11), hence also 'cheek'.

W. *boch*, Br. *boc'h*, fr. Lat. *bucca* (above, 2). Loth, Mots lat. 138.

W. *cern* 'side of the head' and so 'cheek' or 'jaw' (cf. NT, Lk. 6.29 *cern* vs. *grudd* Mt. 5.39) = Ir. *cern* 'corner' : ChSl. *črěnovĭnaja* 'molar teeth', Slovak. *čren* 'jaw', etc. Walde-P. 1.427. Loth, RC 42.354. Berneker 147.

Br. *jod*, fr. some early form of Fr. *joue*. Loth, Mots lat. 180.

4. Goth. *kinnus*, ON *kinn*, Dan., Sw. *kind*, see 4.207.

ON *vangi* (cf. Goth. deriv. *waggareis* 'pillow'), OE *wange*, *wenge*, ME *wonge*, Du. *wang*, OHG *wanga*, MHG, NHG *wange*, prob. : OE *wang* 'field', etc., with common notion of curved surface, and fr. the root seen in Skt. *vañc-* 'move crookedly', etc. Walde-P. 1.218. Falk-Torp 1350 f. Feist 540.

OE *cēace* (WSax.), *cēce* (Angl.) 'jaw' (4.207), also 'cheek' (so Mt. 5.39, Lk. 6.29 in Lindisf. vs. *wenge* in WSax. versions), and so reg. later, ME *cheke*, NE *cheek*. NED s.v. *cheek*.

OHG *baccho* (rare, gl. to *mandibula*, *mala;* cf. *chinnibahho* 'jaw'), MHG *backe*, NHG *backe* or *backen*, in early period partly 'jaw', now the popular word for 'cheek' vs. *wange*, except locally (Kretschmer, Wortgeogr. 100 ff.), etym. dub., perh. : OE *bæc* 'back', etc. Walde-P. 2.148. Falk-Torp 41, 44. Or as 'jaw' fr. 'eater' fr. the root seen in Grk. φαγεῖν 'eat', φαγών 'glutton' and (Hesych.) 'jaw'? So, after Much, Weigand-H. 1.136, Kluge-G. 33. But the sense 'eat' in Grk. is secondary.

5. Lith. *skruostas* : *skrosti* 'split open'? Buga in Mühl.-Endz. 3.900.

Lett. *vaigs* (also 'face'), perh. as orig. 'curved surface' (cf. OE *wange*, etc., above, 4), fr. the root seen in ON *veikja* 'bend', etc. (Walde-P. 1.235). Mühl.-Endz. 4.435. Buga, Kalba ir Senovė 73.

6. ChSl. *lanita* (Boh. *lanita*, *lanitva* obs.), fr. *olnita : Grk. ὠλένη 'forearm'; OE *eln* 'ell', *elnboga* 'elbow', etc. (4.32). Development through 'jaw' with its angle or 'cheek' as 'bent, curved surface'? Walde-P. 1.157. Torbiörnsson, Liq. Met. 68.

SCr. *obraz* : ChSl. *obrazŭ* 'form, shape, image', with development through 'face' (cf. the loanword Rum. *obraz* in both senses).

Boh. *líce*, Pol. *lice*, orig. 'face' as ChSl. *lice*, etc. (4.204). Cf. OPruss. *laygnan* 'cheek'.

Russ. *ščeka*, prob. orig. 'jaw', as Pol. *szczęka*, earlier *szczeka* (4.207).

7. Skt. *gaṇḍa-*, mostly 'cheek', but also 'boil, pimple' and orig. 'swelling', fr. **goldno-*(?) or some form of the root **gel-* seen in numerous words for round or swollen objects (Goth. *kilþei* 'womb', etc.) Walde-P. 1.614.

4.209. Some of the words for 'chin' belong to the group of cognates in which 'jaw', 'cheek' and 'chin' interchange (4.207). Some reflect the 'shape 'as 'something projecting' or a 'hook'. Several belong with words for 'beard' (4.142), for just as 'chin' may give the word for 'beard', so conversely a word for 'beard' or 'behind the beard', 'what has a beard on it', may be used also for the 'chin', and, once so established, no incongruity is felt in applying the term equally to a woman's chin.

1. Grk. *γένειον* : *γένυς* 'jaw, cheek', etc. (4.207).

NG *πιγούνι*, with haplology fr. *ἐπι-(πω)γώνιον* 'that which has a beard on it' : *πώγων* 'beard' (4.142). Cf. Russ. *podborodok* 'chin', lit. 'what is under the beard'. Kretschmer, Glotta 9.231.

2. Lat. *mentum* (> It. *mento*; Fr. *menton* in form fr. *mentō, -ōnis* 'person with a long chin') : W. *mant* 'jaw, mouth' (and prob. Goth *munþs*, etc. 'mouth', 4.24), fr. root **men-* in Lat. *ē-minēre, prōminēre* 'stand out, project', *mōns, montis* 'mountain', etc. Walde-P. 2.263. Ernout-M. 608. Walde-H. 2.72 f.

Sp. *barba*, also and orig. 'beard', and Rum. *barbie* deriv. (**barbīlia?* Tiktin 158) of *barbă*, Lat. *barba* 'beard' (4.142).

3. Ir. *smech*, NIr. *smeig, smig* : Lith. *smakras*, Lett. *smakrs* 'chin', Skt. *çmaçru-* 'beard', etc. (4.142). Walde-P. 2.689. Pedersen 1.86.

W. *gen* : Lat. *gena* 'cheek', etc.

Br. *elgez*, W. *elgeth* (obs.), OCorn. *elgeht* (gl. *mentum*) : OBr. *ail*, W. *ael* 'eyebrow' (4.206). Ernault, Dict. étym. 281.

4. ON, Sw. *haka*, Dan. *hage*, orig. 'hook' (as still Dan. *hage*, Sw. *hake*) : OE *haca, hōc*, etc. (12.75). Falk-Torp 371. Hellquist 327.

OE *cin*, OHG *kinni*, etc., general WGmc. for 'chin' = Goth. *kinnus*, ON *kinn*, etc. 'cheek' : Grk. *γένυς* 'jaw, cheek', etc. (4.207).

5. Lith. *smakras*, Lett. *smakrs* : Ir. *smech* 'chin', etc. (above, 3). Mühl.-Endz 3.950.

Lett. *zuods*, mostly 'chin' but in some places 'jaw' : Lith. *žandas*, Grk. *γνάθος* 'jaw' (4.207). Mühl.-Endz. 4.759.

6. SCr., Boh. *brada*, also and orig. 'beard' (4.142), and fr. same source Pol. *podbrodek*, Russ. *podborodok*, lit. 'what is under the beard', fr. *pod* 'under' and *broda, boroda* 'beard'. Berneker 72.

7. Skt. *chubuka-* (RV), *cubuka-, cibuka-, civuka-* (cf. BR s.vv.), wholly obscure. Uhlenbeck 91. Looks like a word of imitative orig., but why 'chin'?

4.21 EYE

Grk.	ὀφθαλμός, ὄμμα	Goth.	augō	Lith.	akis	
NG	μάτι	ON	auga	Lett.	acs	
Lat.	oculus	Dan.	øje	ChSl.	oko	
It.	occhio	Sw.	öga	SCr.	oko	
Fr.	oeil	OE	ēage	Boh.	oko	
Sp.	ojo	ME	eʒe (eghe, eye)	Pol.	oko	
Rum.	ochiu	NE	eye	Russ.	glaz	
Ir.	súil, rosc	Du.	oog	Skt.	akṣi, cakṣus-, locana-,	
NIr.	súil	OHG	ouga		netra-	
W.	llygad	MHG	ouge	Av.	čašman-, dōiϑra-, aši	
Br.	lagad	NHG	auge			

Most of the words for 'eye' belong to an inherited group. The others are from such notions as 'see, look, bright, sun(?), shining ball'.

1. IE **okʷ-* in various formations. There are also verbal forms for 'see', as Skt. desid. *īkṣ-*, Grk. fut. *ὄψομαι*, perf. *ὄπωπα*, etc., but these are much less widespread than the nouns for 'eye'. Walde-P. 1.169 ff. Ernout-M. 697 f. Falk-Torp 1417 f. Feist 64 f.

Grk. *ὄσσε* (dual, poet.); *ὄμμα* mostly poet., but also sometimes in NT and pap., whence through dim. *ὀμμάτιον* the NG *μάτι*; *ὀφθαλμός*, the usual prose form, prob. a cpd. with second part related to *θάλαμος* 'inner room' and orig. used for the socket of the eye; dial. *ὄκταλλος, ὀπτίλος*, formation unexplained; Lat. *oculus*, whence the Romance words (also the rare Ir. *ugail* 'eyes'); Goth. *augō*, OE *ēage*, etc., all the Gmc. words (diphthong explained in part by influence of word for 'ear', Goth. *ausō*, etc.? but connection with this group denied by some); Lith. *akis*, Lett. *acs*, ChSl. etc. *oko* (obs. in Russ.); Skt. *akṣi*, gen. sg. *akṣṇas*; Av. nom. dual *aši* (*š* for *xš* after *uši* 'ears'), used only of evil beings; Arm. *akn*; Toch. A *ak*, B *ek*.

2. Ir., NIr. *súil*, prob. : W. *haul*, Lat.

sōl, etc. 'sun' (1.52). Walde-P. 2.446. Pedersen 1.62. Stokes 692.

Ir. *rosc*, fr. **pro-sc-*, deriv. of *sech-* (only in cpds.), IE **sekʷ-* 'point out, say, see'. Walde-P. 2.366, 377 ff. Pedersen 2.621.

W. *llygad*, Br. *lagad*, prob. (with Br. *a* for *u* by assim.) : W. *llwg* 'bright', *go-lwg* 'sight', Grk. *λεύσσω* 'see', Skt. *lok-, loc-* 'look, see', *locana-* 'eye', etc. Walde-P. 2.381, 411. Pedersen 2.36.

3. Russ. *glaz* (displacing the obs. *oko*), orig. 'bright ball or stone' (cf. Pol. *galy* 'eyes', pl. of *gała* 'ball') : ORuss. *glazokŭ* 'little ball', Pol. *głaz* 'stone', *glaźny* 'smooth', prob. loanword fr. Gmc., OHG *glas* 'amber, glass', etc. Berneker 301. Brückner 143.

4. Skt. *akṣi*, Av. *aši*, above, 1.

Skt. *cakṣus-*, Av., OPers. *čašman-* (NPers. *čašm* 'eye') : Skt. *cakṣ-* 'see', Av. *čaš-* 'teach', etc. Walde-P. 1.510.

Skt. *locana-* : Skt. *lok-, loc-* 'see', Grk. *λεύσσω* 'see', *λευκός* 'bright', etc. Walde-P. 2.411.

Skt. *netra-, nayana-* 'guide, guiding', also 'eye', fr. *nī-* 'lead'.

Av. *dōiϑra-, daēman-* (NPers. *dīm* 'face'), fr. Av., OPers. *dī-* 'see' (NPers. *dīdan* 'see') : Skt. *dhī-* 'perceive, think', etc. Walde-P. 1.831. Barth. 667, 744, 724 ff.

4.22 EAR

Grk.	οὖς	Goth.	ausō	Lith.	ausìs	
NG	αὐτί	ON	eyra, hlust	Lett.	auss	
Lat.	auris	Dan.	øre	ChSl.	ucho	
It.	orecchio	Sw.	öra	SCr.	uho	
Fr.	oreille	OE	ēare	Boh.	ucho	
Sp.	oreja, oído	ME	ere	Pol.	ucho	
Rum.	ureche	NE	ear	Russ.	ucho	
Ir.	au, clúas	Du.	oor	Skt.	karṇa-	
NIr.	cluas	OHG	ōra	Av.	gaoša-, karəna-,	
W.	clust	MHG	ōr(e)		uši (dual)	
Br.	skouarn	NHG	ohr			

Most of the words for 'ear' belong to an inherited group. These and the others, so far as their origin is clear, are related to words for 'perceive, hear' (15.11, 15.41).

1. IE **aus-* (also **ōus-, *ous-*, to account for the Grk. forms) in various formations, esp. *i-, n-*, and *s-* stems; beside IE **au-* in Skt. *āvis* 'evidently', Grk. *αἰσθάνομαι* 'perceive', etc. Walde-P. 1.17 f. Ernout-M. 93. Walde-H. 1.85 f.

Grk. *οὖς* (fr. **ούσος*, cf. ChSl. *ucho*), gen. *οὔατος*, Att. *ὠτός*, dim. form *ὠτίον*, used for *οὖς* sometimes in NT, etc., whence (through *τὰ ὠτία* > *τ'αὐτία*, Hatzidakis, Μεσ. 2.322) NG *αὐτί*; Lat. *auris*, in VLat. replaced by dim. *auricula, ōricla*, whence It. *orecchio*, Fr. *oreille*, Sp. *oreja*, Rum. *ureche*, etc. (REW 793); Ir. *au, ō*; Goth. *ausō*, OE *ēare*, etc., general Gmc.; Lith. *ausìs*, Lett. *auss*, OPruss. *ausins* (acc. pl.) ; ChSl. *ucho* (*s*-stem; but *i*-stem in dual, nom. *uši*, etc.); Av. nom. dual *uši* (NPers. *hoš* 'ear'); Arm. unkn.

2. Sp. *oído* 'hearing' and 'ear' as organ of hearing (but not used for the ex-

ternal ear), deriv. of *oír* 'hear', fr. Lat. *audīre* 'hear'.

3. Ir. *clúas*, NIr. *cluas*, W. *clust* : ON *hlust* 'ear' (beside *eyra*, cf. Vigfusson s.v.), OE *hlyst* 'hearing', *hlystan* 'hear, listen' (NE *listen*), etc. fr. IE **kleu-s-*, beside **kleu-* in Skt. *çru-*, Grk. *κλύω* 'hear', etc., from which root also Skt. *çrotra-* 'hearing, ear', Toch. A *klots*, B *klautso* 'ear' (SSS, 128, 129). Walde-P. 1.494 f. Pedersen 1.80.

Br. *skouarn*, Corn. *scovarn*, W. *ysgyfarn* (obs.), etym. dub., but perh. fr. a **skeu-* beside IE **keu-* in Grk. *κοέω* 'perceive, hear', Lat. *cavēre* 'beware', Goth. *hausjan* 'hear', OE *scēawian* 'look at', etc. (15.41, 15.52). Henry 243. Windisch ap. Ernault, Dict. étym. 377. Less probably Pedersen 2.53.

4. Skt. *karṇa-*, Av. *karəna-* (of evil beings), etym.? Walde-P. 1.412, 495.

Av. *gaoša-*, OPers. *gauša-* (NPers. *goš* 'ear') : Av. *gūš-* 'hear', Skt. *ghoṣa-* 'noise', *ghoṣati* 'sounds, calls'. Walde-P. 1.569.

Av. *uši* (dual), above, 1.

4.23 NOSE

Grk.	ῥίς	Goth.	. . . .	Lith.	nósis	
NG	μύτη	ON	nasar	Lett.	deguns	
Lat.	nāsus	Dan.	næse	ChSl.	nosŭ	
It.	naso	Sw.	näsa	SCr.	nos	
Fr.	nez	OE	nosu	Boh.	nos	
Sp.	nariz	ME	nose	Pol.	nos	
Rum.	nas	NE	nose	Russ.	nos	
Ir.	srón	Du.	neus	Skt.	nās-, ghrāṇa-	
NIr.	srón	OHG	nasa	Av.	nāh-	
W.	trwyn	MHG	nase			
Br.	fri	NHG	nase			

Most of the words for 'nose' belong to an inherited group. The others are partly of obscure origin.

1. IE **nas-, nās-*. Walde-P. 2.318. Ernout-M. 653, 655. Falk-Torp 779 f.

Lat. *nāsus* (> It. *naso*, Fr. *nez*, Rum. *nas*), also pl. *nārēs* 'nostrils', late sg. *nāris* (> Sp. *nariz*); ON sg. *nǫs* 'nostril', pl. *nasar* 'nostrils, nose', OE *nosu, nasu*, OHG *nasa*, etc., general Gmc.; Lith. *nósis*, OPruss. *nozy*; Skt. *nas-, nās-* (in RV only dual, nom. *nāsā*, gen. *nasos*), Av., OPers. *nāh-* (sg. and dual in Av., sg. in OPers.). The meaning 'nostril' is implied by the early use of dual or pl. forms, but is not necessarily older than 'nose'. For it may be abstracted from the latter, and the dual was favored by its frequency in the case of 'eyes', 'ears', 'hands', etc.

2. Grk. *ῥίς*, gen. *ῥῑνός*, also pl. *ῥῖνες* 'nostrils, nose' (like Lat. *nārēs*), etym.? The explanation as 'running', either : Skt. *sr-* 'flow', etc. (Boisacq 842) or : Skt. *ri-* 'flow', etc. (Walde-P. 1.140 with query) is possible, the word being

then orig. a vulgar epithet, displacing the IE word, like the following which displaced it in turn.

NG *μύτη*, fr. Grk. *μύτις* used by Aristot. (HA 524ᵇ15 ff.) for an organ of the cuttlefish connected with the ink sac, and attested as a vulgar term for 'snout, nose' by Eust., Comm. 950 (*οἱ τὴν ῥῖνα μύτιν καλέσαντες*), prob. : Lith. *mute*, Skt. *mukha-* 'mouth', etc. (4.24). Walde-P. 2.310.

3. Ir. *srón* = W. *ffroen*, Br. *fron* 'nostril' (here in some way Br. *fri* 'nose', MBr. *fry*), fr. **skrok-nā-*, prob. : Skt. *srakva-* 'corner of the mouth', and fr. the root in Ir. *srennim*, Grk. *ῥέγκω, ῥέγχω* 'snore, snort', of imitative origin. Walde-P. 2.705. Pedersen 1.82. Lewis-Pedersen 22.

W. *trwyn*, OCorn. *trein*, perh. fr. an imitative group parallel to the preceding (cf. Grk. *ῥύγχος* 'pig's snout'). Pedersen 1.82. Morris Jones 156.

4. Lett. *deguns*, etym.?

5. Skt. *ghrāṇa-* 'smell' and 'nose', fr. *ghrā-* 'smell' (15.21).

4.24 MOUTH

Grk.	στόμα	Goth.	munþs	Lith.	burna
NG	στόμα	ON	munnr (múðr)	Lett.	mute
Lat.	ōs	Dan.	mund	ChSl.	usta
It.	bocca	Sw.	mun	SCr.	usta
Fr.	bouche	OE	mūþ	Boh.	ústa
Sp.	boca	ME	mouthe	Pol.	usta, gęba
Rum.	gurā	NE	mouth	Russ.	rot
Ir.	gin, bēoil	Du.	mond	Skt.	mukha-, ās-, etc.
NIr.	bēal	OHG	mund	Av.	āh-, zafar-
W.	geneu	MHG	munt		
Br.	genou	NHG	mund		

The IE word for 'mouth' persisted in several languages in the literal sense, in some others in secondary uses, but was to a large extent replaced by other words. Most of these were originally expressions applied to the mouth of animals and vulgarly of persons, like Lat. rōstrum, NHG maul, NE jaw, snout, mug, and many others (not included in the list, except where they have become standard words for 'mouth'). There is frequent association between 'mouth' and 'throat', 'jaw', 'cheek', 'chin' or 'lip'.

1. IE *ō(u)s-, *əus-. Walde-P. 1.168. Ernout-M. 714 f.

Lat. ōs (also ōstium 'door, entrance, river-mouth', ōra 'edge, coast'); Ir. ā (rare); OPruss. austo (Lith. uostas 'river-mouth'); Lith. usta, etc., general Slavic (but Russ. usta obs.); Skt. ās-, āsan-, āsya-, Av. āh- (also Skt. oṣṭha-, Av. aoṣta- 'lip'); cf. also ON ōss 'river-mouth', ON ōr 'beginning', ōra 'edge, bank', etc. But Hitt. aiš, gen. iššaš 'mouth (Sturtevant, Hitt. Gloss. with refs.) points to a parallel *ōis-.

2. Grk. στόμα : Av. staman- 'dog's mouth', W. safn 'mouth, jaws' (of animals), MBr. staffn, Br. staoñ 'palate', root connection? Walde-P. 2.648. Pedersen 1.78.

3. It. bocca, Fr. bouche, Sp. boca, fr. Lat. bucca 'puffed-out cheek' (4.208) and also a pop. substitute for ōs (cf. Thes.

s.v.). Ernout-M.110. Walde-H. 2.120. REW 1357.

Rum. gurā (so Alb. gojë 'mouth', Fr. gueule 'mouth, jaws' of animals, in some dial. common word for 'mouth'), fr. Lat. gula 'throat, gullet' (4.29).

Lat. gurges 'whirlpool', late gurga, has through 'throat' (Fr. gorge) given dial. words for 'mouth'; likewise Lat. rōstrum 'beak, snout, mouth' (of animals, vulgarly of persons), as ORum. rost. REW 3921, 7386.

4. Ir. gin, W. geneu (beside gen 'chin'), Br. genou : Lat. gena, Goth. kinnus 'cheek', etc. (4.207).

Ir. bēoil, NIr. bēal, see bēl 'lip' (4.25).

5. Goth. munþs, OE mūþ, OHG mund, etc., general Gmc., prob. : Lat. mentum 'chin', etc. (4.209), rather than : Lat. mandere 'chew', as preferred in Walde-P. 2.270, Falk-Torp 738. Feist 368. Ernout-M. 608.

6. Lith. burna : Bulg. bŭrna 'lip', Arm. beran 'mouth', Ir. bern 'cleft, gap', Grk. φάραγξ 'cleft, ravine', φάρυγξ 'throat', etc. Walde-P. 2.159. Trautmann 40.

Lett. mute : Skt. mukha- 'mouth', etc. (below, 8).

7. ChSl. usta, etc., above, 1.

Pol. gęba : Boh. huba, SCr. gubica (both 'mouth' only in derogatory sense, 'mug'), Russ. guba 'lip', ChSl. gǫba 'sponge', Lith. gumbas 'swelling, protu-

berance', Lett. gumba 'tumor', etc. Walde-P. 1.568. Brückner 138 ff. (Berneker 340 makes two separate groups.)

Russ. rot : ChSl. rŭtŭ 'peak', SCr. rt 'promontory', Boh. ret 'lip', etc., these prob. as orig. 'projection' (whence 'mouth' or 'lip' through 'snout' of animals) : Lat. orīrī 'rise', Skt. ṛṣva- 'high', etc. G. S. Lane, AJPh. 54.64.

8. Skt. (beside ās-, etc., above, 1)

mukha- : Lett. mute 'mouth', OHG mūla, NHG maul 'mouth' (of animals, vulgarly of persons), Lett. maut 'roar', etc., an imitative group based on an utterance like Grk. μῦ, Lat. mu. Walde-P. 2.309 ff.

Skt. vadana-, vaktra- 'mouth' as organ of speech, fr. vad-, vac- 'speak' (18.21).

Av. zafar- 'mouth' (of evil beings) : OE ceafl, NHG kiefer 'jaw'. Walde-P. 1.570 f. Barth. 1657.

4.25 LIP

Grk.	χεῖλος	Goth.	wairilōm (dat. pl.)	Lith.	lūpa
NG	χεῖλος, χεῖλι	ON	vǫrr	Lett.	lūpa
Lat.	labrum	Dan.	læbe	ChSl.	ustina
It.	labbro	Sw.	läppe	SCr.	usne
Fr.	lèvre	OE	weler, lippa	Boh.	vet (pysk)
Sp.	labio	ME	lippe	Pol.	warga
Rum.	buzā	NE	lip	Russ.	guba
Ir.	bēl	Du.	lip	Skt.	oṣṭha-
NIr.	bēal, puisīn	OHG	leffur, lefs	Av.	aoṣta
W.	gwefus (gwefl)	MHG	lefs(e)		
Br.	gweuz, muzell	NHG	lippe		

Some of the words for 'lip' are from the notion of 'hanging down' or 'projecting'. Several are connected with words for 'mouth', the lips being the visible part of the mouth.

1. Grk. χεῖλος, Dor. χῆλος, Aeol. χέλλος (*χελνος; cf. also χελύνη), NG χεῖλι (based on pl. τά χείλη) : ON gjǫlnar 'gills', root connection? Walde-P. 1.632. Falk-Torp 319.

2. Lat. labrum (> It. labro), pl. labra, late as fem. sg. (> Fr. lèvre), labium (> Sp. labio) : OE lippa, NE lip, OHG leffur, lefs, NHG lippe (fr. LG), etc. (see list), root connection uncertain, but more prob. : Skt. lamb- 'hang down', Lat. labāre 'slip', etc. (on semantic side, cf. below, 5) than : Lat. lambere 'lick'. Walde-P. 2.384. Ernout-M. 513. Walde-H. 1.738 f. REW 4808, 4813. Falk-Torp 672.

Rum. buzā, fr. or like Alb. buzë 'lip' (cf. below, 3).

3. Ir. bēl 'lip', pl. bēoil 'lips, mouth', NIr. bēal 'mouth, lip, etym.? Walde-P. 1.671. Pedersen 1.117.

W. gwefl 'lip of animals' = MBr. gueff 'mouth of animals', etym.? Stokes 335 (vs. 175).

Ir. bus 'lip' (rare), NIr. pus 'lips, mouth' (derogatory term), whence regular word puisīn, W. gwefus (fr. *gwe-bus; or *gwef-us : gwefl?), Br. gweuz : Alb. buzë, Rum. buzā 'lip', NE buss, NHG bus 'a kiss', etc., of imitative orig. Walde-P. 2.113 ff. Thurneysen, Kelto-Rom. 86.

Br. muzell, fr. Prov. muzel (Fr. museau 'snout, muzzle', dim. of *mūsus, It. muso, etc. Henry 208. REW 5784.

4. OE lippa, etc., above, 2.

Goth. wairilōm (dat. pl.), ON vǫrr, OFris. were, OE weler (fr. *werel) : OPruss. warsus 'lip', and perh. through notion of 'protuberance' : OE wearr 'callous skin', Lat. verrūca 'height' and

'wart', Skt. varṣman- 'height', etc. Walde-P. 1.266 ff. Feist 545.

5. Lith., Lett. lūpa : LG lobbe 'hanging lip', Fris. lobbe 'hanging lump of flesh', NE lob (NED lob, sb.²), etc., with common notion of 'loosely hanging'. Walde-P. 2.710.

6. ChSl. ustĭna, SCr. usne, deriv. of usta 'mouth' : Skt. oṣṭha-, Av. aoṣta- 'lip', Lat. ōstium 'door, entrance, river-mouth', etc., all derivs. of word for 'mouth' (4.24). Walde-P. 1.168 ff.

Boh. ret : ChSl. rŭtŭ 'peak', SCr. rt 'promontory', Russ. rot 'mouth' (4.24).

Boh. pysk = Pol. pysk 'snout' : Boh. puchnouti, Pol. puchnąć 'swell', Grk. φῦσάω 'blow', etc. Walde-P. 2.81. Brückner 449 f.

Pol. warga, perh. : OPruss. warsus 'lip', etc. (above, 4). Brückner 602.

Russ. guba : Pol. gęba 'mouth', etc. (4.24), with shift to 'lips' in pl. guby, whence sg. in same sense.

7. Skt. oṣṭha-, Av. aoṣta-, see above, 6.

4.26 TONGUE

Grk.	γλῶσσα	Goth.	tuggō	Lith.	liežuvis
NG	γλῶσσα	ON	tunga	Lett.	mēle
Lat.	lingua	Dan.	tunge	ChSl.	językŭ
It.	lingua	Sw.	tunga	SCr.	jezik
Fr.	langue	OE	tunge	Boh.	jazyk
Sp.	lengua	ME	tounge	Pol.	język
Rum.	limbā	NE	tongue	Russ.	jazyk
Ir.	tenge	Du.	tong	Skt.	jihvā-
NIr.	teanga	OHG	zunga	Av.	hizvā-, hizū-
W.	tafod	MHG	zunge		
Br.	teod	NHG	zunge		

The majority of the words for 'tongue' belong to an inherited group, of unknown root connection. Secondary association with words for 'lick' is shown by some. Most of the words for 'tongue' are also used for 'language' (see 18.24).

1. IE *dn̥ĝhwā- or the like, but various phonetic difficulties involved. Walde-P. 1.792. Ernout-M. 553. Walde-H. 1.806 f.

Lat. lingua (> the Romance words), with dial. l (supported by association with lingere 'lick') fr. old dingua (quoted by grammarians); Ir. tenge, NIr. teanga, W. tafod, Br. teod all with unexplained init. t; Pedersen 1.88 assumes init. zd); Goth. tuggō, OE tunge, OHG zunga, etc., general Gmc.; OPruss. in-zuwis, Lith. liežuvis (re-formed by association with liežiu 'lick'), ChSl. językŭ,

etc., general Slavic (all with unexplained loss of init. d, as in Lith. ilgas 'long' for *dilgas; here also (with metathesis) Toch. A käntu, B. käntwa (Pisani, KZ 64.100 f.; Benveniste, Hirt Festschrift 2.235).

2. Grk. γλῶσσα, Att. γλῶττα, Ion. γλάσσα : γλωχίς 'point', γλῶχες 'beard of corn', outside connection dub. Walde-P. 1.662.

3. Lett. mēle, etym.? Mühl.-Endz. 2.614. Berneker 2.72, 74.

4. Skt. jihvā-, Av. hizvā-, hizū-, OPers. acc. sg. h(i)zbānam (for reading, cf. Kent, Language 19.226 f.), NPers. zabān, all as if fr. an IE *sighwā- (init. s > Iran. h; Skt. j by assim. to following palatal), and so possibly a blend of IE *dn̥ĝhwā- (above, 1) with some other word. Barth. 1815 with references.

4.27 TOOTH

Grk.	ὀδούς	Goth.	tunþus	Lith.	dantis
NG	δόντι	ON	tǫnn	Lett.	zuobs
Lat.	dēns	Dan.	tand	ChSl.	zǫbŭ
It.	dente	Sw.	tand	SCr.	zub
Fr.	dent	OE	tōþ	Boh.	zub
Sp.	diente	ME	tothe	Pol.	zǫb
Rum.	dinte	NE	tooth	Russ.	zub
Ir.	dēt, fiacail	Du.	tand	Skt.	dant-
NIr.	fiacal (dēad)	OHG	zan(d)	Av.	dāta- dantan-
W.	dant	MHG	zan(t)		
Br.	dant	NHG	zan(t)		

Most of the words for 'tooth' belong to an inherited group.

1. IE *dont-, *dn̥t-, prob. a pple. form of *ed- 'eat'. But some think this is only a secondary association and connect with the root of Grk. δάκνω 'bite', OE tang 'tongs', etc. Walde-P. 1.120. Ernout-M. 260 f. Walde-H. 1.340 f. Feist 483.

Grk. ὀδών, ὀδούς, gen. -όντος (ὀδοντ-, fr. ἐδοντ-, as Aeol. ἔδοντες, and this prob. by reassociation with ἔδω, rather than an inherited form) NG δόντι fr. dim. form; Lat. dēns, dentis (> the Romance forms); Ir. dēt (NIr. dēad coll. 'teeth'), W., Br. dant; Goth. tunþus, OE tōþ, OHG zan(d), etc., general Gmc.; Lith. dantis; Skt. dant-, Av. dantan-, dātā- (Barth. 683, 728); Arm. atamn.

2. Ir. fiacail, NIr. fiacal, deriv. of a rare fec 'tooth' (Windisch 538), NIr. feac (Dinneen), this perh. in orig. identical with Ir. fec, NIr. feac 'spade' (though differing in decl. and gender), of which the etym. is dub. (Pedersen 1.159. Walde-P. 1.316). But cf. also Zupitza, KZ 36.208.

3. Lett. zuobs, ChSl. zǫbŭ, etc., general Slavic : Lith. žambas 'edge of a beam', Grk. γόμφος 'bolt, pin, etc.', γομφίος 'molar tooth', Skt. jambha- 'tooth, tusk', Alb. dhëmp 'tooth', OE comb 'comb', etc., all with common notion of 'tooth' or 'toothlike object'. Walde-P. 1.575 ff. (with needless division of Grk. γόμφος into two words). Here also Toch. A kam, B keme 'tooth'.

4.28 NECK

Grk.	αὐχήν, τράχηλος, δίρη	Goth.	hals	Lith.	kaklas
NG	λαιμός	ON	hals, svíri	Lett.	kakls
Lat.	collum	Dan.	hals	ChSl.	vyja, šija
It.	collo	Sw.	hals	SCr.	vrat (šija)
Fr.	cou	OE	heals, sweora	Boh.	krk
Sp.	cuello	ME	hals, swere, necke	Pol.	szyja, kark
Rum.	gīt	NE	neck	Russ.	šeja
Ir.	brāge, muin, muinēl	Du.	hals	Skt.	grīvā-, kaṇṭha-
NIr.	muinēal, brāgha	OHG	hals	Av.	manaoθri-, grīvā-
W.	gwddf, mwnwgl	MHG	hals, krage		
Br.	gouzoug	NHG	hals		

Some words for 'neck' originally denoted only the 'back (nape) of the neck' (cf. NE neck : NHG nacken), and rest on the notion of 'projection, ridge'.

Others, denoting from the outset the whole round neck, are connected with words for 'circle', 'column', or 'turn, wind'. Some were originally words for 'throat', with extension from the internal throat (cf. 4.29), the latter being the front of the neck, hence 'neck'. In general, words for 'throat' are sometimes used for 'neck', as conversely (cf. NHG *halsweh* 'sore throat', etc.).

1. Grk. αὐχήν (Hom.+, regular word in Aristot. and not at all restricted to 'nape of the neck'), perh.: Arm. *awj-* in *awji-k* 'collar'. N. Adontz, Mélanges Boisacq 1.10.

Grk. τράχηλος (Hdt.+, displacing αὐχήν in Hellenistic Grk., as always in NT), prob. : τροχός 'wheel', τρέχω 'run', etc. Walde-P. 1.874 f. (with query, but favored by analogies).

Grk. δέρη (poet.), see below, 7.

Grk. λαιμός 'throat' (4.29) is in NG also the usual word for 'neck' (τράχηλος lit.). Cf. also σβέρκος (= Alb. *zverk*) and σνίχι 'nape of the neck', loanwords but ultimate source?

2. Lat. *collum* (> It. *collo*, Fr. *cou*, Sp. *cuello;* Fr. *col* 'neck' of bottles, dresses, etc.) : Goth. *hals*, OE *heals*, etc., general Gmc. word for 'neck', all prob. fr. IE **kʷel-* 'turn around' in Skt. *car-*, Grk. πέλομαι, etc., also Lith. *kaklas* 'neck' (below, 5), rather than fr. **kel-* 'rise, project' in *celsus* 'high', *collis* 'hill', etc., though either connection is possible phonetically, and semantically according as the words orig. denoted the '(round) neck' or the 'nape of the neck'. Ernout-M. 204. Walde-H. 1.245 (vs. Walde-P. 1.434). Feist 242.

Rum. *gît*, orig. 'throat' (hence *gîtlej* 'throat'), loanword fr. Slavic, SCr. *gut* 'throat' (obs., but *gutati* 'swallow'), Slov. *golt* 'throat', Bulg. *gŭltŭk* 'a swallow', etc., these : Lat. *gula* 'throat', etc. (4.29). Tiktin 684. Berneker 309.

3. Ir. *brāge* 'neck' and rarely (inner) 'throat' (cf. K. Meyer, Contrib. s.v.), NIr. *brāgha* mostly 'throat' : MHG *krage* (below, 4), Grk. βρόχθος 'throat', Skt. *gr-* 'swallow', Lith. *gerti* 'drink', etc. Walde-P. 1.683. Pedersen 1.100, 183.

Ir. *muin*, *muinēl* 'nape of the neck', NIr. *muinēal* 'neck', W. *mwn* (arch.), *mwnwgl* 'neck' : ON *men*, OE *mene* 'necklace' (also OE *manu* 'mane', etc.), Lat. *monīle* 'necklace, collar', Skt. *manyā-* 'nape of the neck', Av. *minu-* 'necklace', *manaoθri-* 'neck' (both words in Yt. 5.127, cf. Barth. 1126), all prob. fr. IE **men-* 'project' in Lat. *ēminēre*, *prominēre* 'project', *mōns* 'mountain', etc. Walde-P. 2.305, 265. Pedersen 1.33.

W. *gwddf*, Br. *gouzoug* (both also 'throat'), etym.? Pedersen 1.63. Henry 142. Morris Jones 145 (cf. Loth, RC 36.170).

4. Goth. *hals*, etc., above, 2.

ON *svīri*, OE *swēora*, *swīra* (so, not *heals*, always in the Gospels), ME *swere* (cf. NED s.v. *swire*) : OE *swer*, *sweor* 'column', Skt. *svaru-* 'post', etc. Walde-P. 1.528.

ME *necke*, NE *neck*, fr. OE *hnecca* 'nape of the neck' : ON *hnakki*, OHG *hnac*, NHG *nacken*, etc. general Gmc. for 'nape of the neck', prob. : Ir. *cnoc* 'hill', etc. Walde-P. 1.391. Falk-Torp 754.

MHG *krage* 'neck, throat, collar' (NHG *kragen* 'collar', rarely 'neck', Du. *kraag* 'collar'; ME *crawe*, NE *craw* with only specialized meaning) : Ir. *brāge*, etc. above, 3.

5. Lith. *kaklas*, Lett. *kakls* : Grk. κύκλος 'circle', Skt. *cakra-* 'circle, wheel', OE *hweol* 'wheel', etc., fr. IE **kʷel-* 'turn', as prob. also Lat. *collum*, Goth. *hals*, etc. (above, 2). Walde-P. 1.515.

6. ChSl. *vyja* (so always in Gospels, Supr., etc., *šija* only in later texts), etym.? Löwenthal, Z. sl. Ph. 8.129, connects with Av. *uyamna-* 'lacking, deficient' (Walde-P. 1.108) as if orig. 'neck-hole' (in a garment).

ChSl. (late) *šija* (SCr. *šija* 'neck' of geese, etc.), Boh. *šije*, Pol. *szyja*, Russ. *šeja*, etym.? Wiedemann, BB 27.261 connects with Lat. *sinus* 'fold' fr. a doubtful root meaning 'bend'. Better (cf. Miklosich, Lex. s.v.) : Skt. *si-*, Lith. *sieti*, Lett. *siet* 'bind', ChSl. *sětĭ* 'cord', Lith. *sija* 'joist', etc. (Walde-P. 2.463 ff., without *šija*). Form (with *š* for *s* fr. a parallel form with *śj-*) like Lith. *sija*, semantic development like that in Lat. *iugulum* 'throat' (4.29).

ChSl. *vratŭ* (late), SCr. *vrat*, fr. the root of ChSl. *vrŭtěti*, *vratiti*, Lat. *vertere* 'turn', etc. (10.12). Walde-P. 1.275. Cf., fr. the same root, NPers. *gardan* 'neck' (**vartana-*). Horn 903.

Boh. *krk*, Pol. *kark* (latter esp. 'nape of the neck') : Skt. *kṛkāṭa-* 'joint of the neck', prob. fr. same root as ChSl. *sŭkrŭčiti* 'contract', etc. Walde-P. 2.569. Berneker 667 f.

7. Skt. *grīvā-* (in Vedic only pl. 'vertebrae of the neck'), Av. *grīvā-* (Vend. 3.7, of a mountain called here the 'neck'; elsewhere also 'head' or 'back' of *Arəzura*, name of a fiend; NPers. *garīva* 'hill') : Grk. δέρη, δειρή 'neck' (poet.), Arc. δέρϝα 'ridge' (so δειράς 'ridge'), ChSl. *griva* 'mane', all prob. as orig. 'throat' : Skt. *gr-* 'swallow', Lith. *gerti* 'drink', Grk. βιβρώσκω 'devour', etc. Walde-P. 1.683.

Skt. *kaṇṭha-*, prob. a Middle Indic form of a **kartra-* (> **kaṭṭa*, **kaṭṭha-*, then *kaṇṭha-* with the secondary nasalization frequent in Middle Indic), fr. **kʷol-tlo-*, deriv. of the same IE **kʷel-* 'turn' as in Lith. *kaklas*, Lat. *collum*, Goth. *hals*, etc. (above, 2). Tedesco (to appear in JAOS).

Skt. *çirodharā-*, lit. 'head-supporter', cpd. of *çiras-* 'head' and *dhṛ-* 'hold'.

Av. *manaoθri-* : Ir. *muin*, etc., above, 3.

4.29 THROAT

Grk.	*λαιμός, σφαγή*	Goth.	....	Lith.	*gerklė*
NG	*λαιμός*	ON	*kverkr* (pl.), *strjūpi*	Lett.	*rīkle*
Lat.	*faucēs, iugulum, gula*	Dan.	*strube*	ChSl.	*grŭlo*
It.	*gola, strozza*	Sw.	*strupe*	SCr.	*grlo*
Fr.	*gorge*	OE	*ceole, hrace þrotu*	Boh.	*hrdlo*
Sp.	*garganta, gola*	ME	*throte* (*rake*)	Pol.	*gardło*
Rum.	*gîtlej, beregată*	NE	*throat*	Russ.	*gorlo*
Ir.	*brāge*	Du.	*keel, strot*	Skt.	*gala-*
NIr.	*scōrnach*	OHG	*kela, drozza*	Av.	*garəman-* (in pl.), *garō* (pl.)
W.	*gwddf*	MHG	*kele, drozze*		
Br.	*gouzoug*	NHG	*kehle*		

Most of the words listed are used for both the internal and external throat. But the Latin terms are differentiated, there being no single word with the broad scope of NE *throat*. The commonest semantic source is 'swallow', which with some others, as 'gurgle', 'abyss', 'round shape', 'narrow opening', indicate primary application to the internal throat. In a few cases the opposite is true, as in Lat. *iugulum* and the group including NE *throat*. Extension from 'throat' to 'neck' has been noted in 4.28.

1. Derivs. of vbs. for 'swallow, devour' either 1) IE **gel-* in Ir. *gelim*, etc.; or 2) IE **gʷer-* in Skt. *gṛ-*, Grk. βιβρώσκω, Lat. *vorāre*, etc.

IE **gel-*. Walde-P. 1.621. Ernout-M. 437. Walde-H. 1.625 f.

Lat. *gula* 'throat (internal), gullet'

(> It., Sp. *gola* 'throat', but Fr. *gueule* 'jaws', Rum. *gură* 'mouth'; REW 3910); OE *ceole*, Du. *keel*, OHG *kela*, MHG *kele*, NHG *kehle*.

IE **gʷer-*. Walde-P. 1.682 ff. Ernout-M. 438. Walde-H. 1.627 f. Falk-Torp 605. Berneker 369.

Lat. *gurges* 'abyss, whirlpool' (also 'gullet' to be inferred fr. *ingurgitāre* 'gorge oneself'), VLat. **gurga* (> Fr. *gorge* 'throat'; REW 3921); ON *kverkr* (pl.); Lith. *gerklė*, OPruss. *gurkle;* ChSl. *grŭlo*, SCr. *grlo*, Boh. *hrdlo*, etc., general Slavic (**gŭrdlo*, Berneker 369); here (or in preceding group?) Skt. *gala-*, Av. *garō* (pl.), *garəman-* (in pl.), NPers. *gulū*.

2. Grk. λαιμός, prob. (as fr. *λαμμος) : λάμια 'abysses', λαμυρός 'greedy', also λαμία 'monster', Lat. *lemurēs* 'ghosts'. Walde-P. 2.377, 434. Otherwise Boisacq 551.

Grk. σφαγή or pl. σφαγαί (both in Aristot.) 'throat', this prob. the earliest meaning of the word, whence σφάζω 'cut the throat, slay' (cf. Lat. *iugulāre* 'slay' fr. *iugulum* 'throat') and the resulting common use of σφαγή as 'slaughter'. No accepted etym., but prob. connected, by a series of parallel root-forms, with σφήξ, Dor. σφᾶξ (gen. -κός) 'wasp', σφήν, Dor. σφάν 'wedge', σφίγγω 'bind tight, constrict', all with common notion of 'narrow'. Cf. Dan. *strube*, etc., below, 4. (Different combinations in Walde-P. 2.651–53, 658.)

Grk. στόμαχος 'throat, gullet' (Hom., and reg. word for 'gullet' in Aristot., who does not use λαιμός at all), only later 'stomach', fr. στόμα 'mouth', hence the passage from the mouth to the stomach, cf. Aristot. HA 595ᵇ19 ff. ὁ δὲ στόμαχος ἤρτηται μὲν ἄνωθεν ἀπὸ τοῦ στόματος, ... τελευτᾷ δὲ . . . . εἰς τὴν κοιλίαν.

3. Lat. *faucēs* (sg. *faux* rare), 'throat' (internal, esp. upper part), etym.? Walde-P. 1.565. Ernout-M. 339 f.

Lat. *iugulum* 'throat' (external), orig. the collarbone, joining the breastbone and shoulder blade : *iugum* 'yoke', *iungere* 'join'. Walde-P. 1.201. Ernout-M. 502. Walde-H. 1.737 f.

Lat. *gula*, etc., above, 1.

Lat. *guttur* 'throat' (internal), prob. : Hitt. *kuttar* 'neck, strength' and a large group of words denoting diverse objects of a round or curved shape. Walde-P. 1.560. Ernout-M. 439 f. Walde-H. 1.629.

It. *strozza* (whence *strozzare* 'throttle'), fr. a Langobard form like MLG *strozze* (below, 5).

Fr. *gorge*, above, 1.

Sp. *garganta*, deriv. of *garg* in words for 'gurgle, gargle', mostly of imitative orig., but partly mixed with derivs. of Lat. *gurges* (above). Here with dissim. Rum. *beregată*. REW 3685.

Rum. *gîtlej*, deriv. of *gît* 'neck', orig. 'throat' (4.28).

4. Ir. *brāge* 'neck' (4.28), sometimes 'throat'.

Ir. *scōrn* in cpds. (*scōrn-chailbhe* 'epiglottis', etc.), NIr. *scōrnach*, etym.?

W. *gwddf*, Br. *gouzouk* 'neck' (4.28) also 'throat'.

5. ON *kverkr*, above, 1.

ON *strjūpi* (rare), Dan. *strube*, Sw. *strupe*, orig. 'narrow opening' (as Norw. dial. *strop*) : OHG *strūben* 'be stiff', etc. Walde-P. 2.635. Falk-Torp 1183. Hellquist 1089.

OE *ceole*, OHG *kela*, etc., above, 1.

OE *hrace*, ME *rake*, cf. OHG *racho* 'sublinguium', NHG *rachen* 'pharynx, (open) jaws', of imitative orig., fr. the sound of 'hawking, or clearing the throat' : OE *hrǣcan* 'spit', OHG *rachisōn* 'hawk', Skt. *kharj-* 'creak', Grk. κρώζω 'croak, caw', etc. Walde-P. 1.415.

OE *þrotu*, ME *throte*, NE *throat*, OHG *drozza*, MHG *drozze* (NHG *drossel* 'Adam's apple') : OE *þrūtian*, ON *þrūtna* 'swell', etc., beside parallel forms with init. *s*, as MLG *strotte*, Du. *strot*, MHG *strozze* 'throat', ME *strouten* 'bulge, swell' (OE *strūtian* once, meaning dub., cf. NED s.v. *strut*), etc., remoter root connections uncertain, but immediate semantic source of 'throat' doubtless 'bulge, swell', applied first to the external throat. Walde-P. 2.634. NED s.v. *throat*.

6. Lith. *gerklė*, ChSl. *grŭlo*, etc., above, 1.

Lett. *rīkle* (Lith. *ryklė* dial. or vulgar), fr. the root of Lett. *rīt*, Lith. *ryti* 'swallow'. Mühl.-Endz. 3.537.

7. Skt. and Av. words, above, 1.

4.30 SHOULDER

Grk.	*ὦμος*	Goth.	*amsans* (acc. pl.)	Lith.	*petys*
NG	*ὦμος*	ON	*herðr, ǫxl*	Lett.	*plecs, kamiēsis*
Lat.	*umerus*	Dan.	*skulder*	ChSl.	*ramo, plešte*
It.	*spalla, omero*	Sw.	*axel, skuldra*	SCr.	*rame, pleća*
Fr.	*épaule*	OE	*eaxl, sculdor*	Boh.	*rameno, plece*
Sp.	*hombro*	ME	*schulder*	Pol.	*ramię, plecy* (pl.)
Rum.	*umăr*	NE	*shoulder*	Russ.	*plečo*
Ir.	*gūalu, formna*	Du.	*schouder*	Skt.	*skandha-, aṅsa-* (*çupti-*)
NIr.	*guala*	OHG	*scultira, ahsala*	Av.	*supti-* (*daoš-*)
W.	*ysgwydd*	MHG	*schulter, ahsel*		
Br.	*skoaz*	NHG	*schulter, achsel*		

Many of the words for 'shoulder' belong to an inherited group, of which the semantic source is unknown. Several were originally words for 'shoulder blade', these mostly from the notion of 'flat, broad', but also from 'joint'.

1. IE **om(e)so-s*, root connection? Walde-P. 1.178. Ernout-M. 1123.

Grk. ὦμος, NG also νῶμος (ν from forms of the article); Lat. *umerus* (> It. *omero*, Sp. *hombro*, Rum. *umăr*), Umbr. *ose* 'in umero'; Goth. *amsans* (acc. pl.); Skt. *aṅsa-;* Arm. *us*.

2. It. *spalla*, Fr. *épaule* (Sp. *espalda* 'back', 4.19), fr. Lat. *spatula* 'flat piece, shoulder of an animal', dim. of *spatha* 'spattle, sword' (fr. Grk. σπάθη 'flat blade'). REW 8130.

3. Ir. *gūalu*, NIr. *guala*, etym. disputed, but possibly : Grk. γύαλον 'hollow', OHG *kiol*, OE *cēol*, ON *kjöll* 'keel, vessel', Skt. *gōla-* 'ball', etc. Walde-P. 1.571 (but rejected 1.556). Otherwise Pedersen 1.117 and Stokes 115.

Ir. *formna* (fr. **for-monyo-*) : *muin*, *muinēl* 'neck' (4.28). Walde-P. 2.305.

W. *ysgwydd*, Br. *skoaz*, OCorn. *scuid* : Ir. *scīath* 'shoulder blade, wing', as 'flat piece' fr. the root in Br. *skeja* 'cut', Lat. *scindere*, Grk. σχίζω 'split'. Walde-P. 2.544. Pedersen 1.76.

4. Goth. *amsans*, above, 1.

ON *herðr*, usually pl. *herðar* (Dan. arch. and dial. *hærde*) : OHG *harti*, *herti* 'shoulder blade', also OHG *skerti* id., prob. fr. **sker-dh-* an extension of **(s)ker-* in Grk. κείρω, OE *sceran* 'cut, shear', etc. G. S. Lane, JEGPh. 32.293 f.

ON *ǫxl*, Sw. *axel*, OE *eaxl*, OHG *ahsala*, MHG *ahsel*, NHG *achsel* : Lat. *āla* 'armpit, upper arm' whence regularly 'wing', Du. *oksel*, OHG *uochisa*, etc. 'armpit', all orig. 'shoulder joint' : Skt. *akṣa-*, Lat. *axis*, etc. 'axle'. Walde-P. 1.37. Falk-Torp 18.

OE *sculdor*, NE *shoulder*, Du. *schouder* (MLG *schulder* > Dan. *skulder*, Sw. *skuldra*), OHG *scultir(r)a*, MHG, NHG *schulter*, prob. through 'shoulder blade' from 'flat piece' : Goth. *skildus* 'shield', Grk. σκαλίς 'hoe' (8.25), σκάλλω 'scrape, hoe', ON skilja 'divide, separate', Lith. skilti 'split', etc. Walde-P. 2.593. Solmsen, Beiträge 198 (but the assumed development first to 'shoulder blade as implement for digging' with closer relation to Grk. σκαλίς is not necessary; cf. the derivation of Fr. épaule, etc., and W. ysgwydd, above).

5. Lith. petys, OPruss. pettis, pette, prob. through 'shoulder blade' fr. the notion 'flat, spread out' : Grk. πετάννυμι 'spread out', Lat. pandere 'spread, open', Av. paθana- 'broad'. Walde-P. 2.18.

Lett. plecs, mostly pl. pleci, either loanword fr. Russ. pleči (below, 6), or as native word : Lett. plāce 'shoulder blade', plakt 'become flat', Grk. πλάξ 'flat surface', etc. Walde-P. 2.90 Mühl.-Endz. 332 ff., 328.

Lett. kamiēsis, OPruss. caymois (*cammoys), perh. : Arm. k'amak 'back'. Lidén, Arm. Stud. 30. Mühl.-Endz. 2.151.

6. ChSl. ramo, ramę, SCr. rame, see under Lat. armus, 4.31.

ChSl. plešte, SCr. pleća, Boh. plece, Pol. plecy (pl.), Russ. plečo, prob. fr. *plet-yo- : Lith. platus, Grk. πλατύς 'broad, flat', but could also be fr. *plek-tyo- : Lett. plāce 'shoulder blade', plakt 'become flat', Grk. πλάξ 'flat surface', etc., in either case fr. parallel extensions of the same root and fr. the notion of 'flat'. Walde-P. 2.100.

7. Skt. skandha-, etym.? Uhlenbeck 341.

Skt. aṅsa-, above, 1.

Skt. çupti- (only once, RV 1.51.5), Av. supti- (NPers. suft) : Alb. supë 'shoulder', MLG schuft, Du. schoft 'buttock, rump, shoulder (of animals)'. Walde-P. 1.467.

Av. daoš- 'upper arm, shoulder' (NPers. doš 'shoulder') : Skt. doṣ- 'forearm', Ir. dōe 'arm', etc. Walde-P. 1.782. Pedersen 2.104.

4.31 ARM

Grk.	βραχίων, πῆχυς, χείρ	Goth.	arms	Lith.	ranka
NG	χέρι, μπράτσο	ON	armr, handleggr, hǫnd	Lett.	ruoka
Lat.	bracchium	Dan.	arm	ChSl.	myšĭca
It.	braccio	Sw.	arm	SCr.	ruka (mišica)
Fr.	bras	OE	earm	Boh.	rámě, paže
Sp.	brazo	ME	arm	Pol.	ramię, ręka
Rum.	braţ	NE	arm	Russ.	ruka
Ir.	lām, dōe	Du.	arm	Skt.	bāhu-, bhuja-
NIr.	lāmh	OHG	arm	Av.	bāzu-
W.	braich	MHG	arm		
Br.	brec'h	NHG	arm		

Many of the words for 'arm' belong to an inherited group, derived from the notion of 'joint', and applied to both 'arm' and 'shoulder'. In several languages the words for 'hand' are extended to include, and in some are the usual terms for, 'arm' (cf. 'foot' for 'leg', 4.35).

1. IE *arəmo-s, *r̥mo-s, fr. IE *ar(ə)- in Grk. ἀραρίσκω 'fit', ἄρθρον 'joint', Lat. artus 'joint', etc. Walde-P. 1.73. Ernout-M. 74. Walde-H. 1.69.

Lat. armus mostly 'shoulder, forequarter' of animals, rarely 'arm' of men; Goth. arms, etc., general Gmc.; OPruss. irmo 'arm'; ChSl. ramo, ramę, SCr. rame 'shoulder', Boh. rámě, rameno, mostly 'arm', Pol. ramię, 'shoulder, arm'; Skt. īrma- 'forequarter' of an animal; Av. arəma- in arəmō-šūta- 'thrown by the arm'; Arm. armuka 'elbow'.

2. IE *bhāĝhu-. Walde-P. 2.130.

Grk. πῆχυς, Dor. πᾶχυς, mostly 'forearm', but also 'arm' (as Hom., Il. 5.314); Skt. bāhu-, Av. bāzu- (NPers. bāzū) 'arm'; ON bōgr, OE bōg, OHG buog 'shoulder' (mostly of animals); Toch. A poke 'arm' (SSS, p. 3, ftn. 1).

3. Grk. βραχίων, in part 'upper arm' (e.g. vs. πῆχυς in Plat. Tim. 75a; but also = πῆχυς in Aristot. HA 698^{b2}), but mostly generic (cf. esp. Aristot. HA $493^{b}26$ f. with subordinate sequence ὦμος, ἀγκών, ὠλέκρανον, πῆχυς, χείρ 'shoulder, upper arm, elbow, forearm, hand'), an old comparative of βραχύς 'short', to be understood as first applied to the upper arm as 'shorter' than the forearm (including the hand; less prob. as shorter than the leg). Bechtel, Lexilogus zu Homer 83.

Hence Lat. bracchium > It. braccio (> NG μπράτσο), Fr. bras, Sp. brazo, Rum. braţ, W. braich, Br. brec'h. Ernout-M. 116. Walde-H. 1.114. REW 1256. Loth, Mots lat. 140.

Grk. χείρ 'hand' (4.33) is also used for 'arm' (Hom.; the double use is noted by Rufus, Onom. 82 χεὶρ δὲ τὸ ὅλον ἀπὸ τοῦ ὤμου καὶ ᾧ κρατοῦμεν), and NG χέρι is the usual pop. word for 'arm' as well as 'hand'.

4. Ir. lām, NIr. lāmh 'hand' (4.33), also 'arm'.

Ir. dōe : Skt. dōṣ- 'forearm', Av. daoš- 'upper arm, shoulder' (4.30).

W. braich, Br. brec'h, fr. Lat. bracchium (above, 3).

5. Goth. arms, etc., above, 1.

ON handleggr (so reg. NIcel. handleggur replaces old armr), also armleggr, cpds. of 'hand' and 'arm' with leggr 'hollow bone of foot or arm', esp. 'leg' (4.35).

ON hǫnd 'hand' (4.33), also 'arm'.

6. Lith. ranka, Lett. ruoka, SCr., Russ. ruka, Pol. ręka 'hand' and 'arm', but orig. only the former. Cf. ChSl. rąka 'hand' (4.33).

ChSl. myšĭca (SCr. mišica 'arm' and 'muscle'), deriv. of ChSl. myšĭ 'mouse' in transferred sense 'muscle' (from the resemblance between the muscle of upper arm especially and a mouse). Cf. Lat. mūsculus 'little mouse, muscle', Grk. μῦς 'mouse' and 'muscle', etc. Walde-P. 1.312 f. Ernout-M. 645 f.

Boh. rámě, rameno, Pol. ramię, above, 1.

Boh. paže : Russ. pacha 'armpit', pach 'groin', paz 'groove, joint', Skt. pakṣa- 'wing, side', all prob. fr. the root *pāg- in Grk. πήγνυμι 'fix', OHG fuoga 'joint', etc. Walde-P. 2.3 f. Brückner 400.

7. Skt. bāhu-, Av. bāzu-, above, 2.

Skt. bhuja- : Skt. bhuj-, Goth. biugan, OHG biogan 'bend', etc. Walde-P. 2.145 f.

4.32 ELBOW

Grk.	ἀγκών, ὠλέκρᾱνον	Goth.	. . . .	Lith.	alkūnė
NG	ἀγκῶνας	ON	ǫlnbogi	Lett.	elkuons
Lat.	cubitus	Dan.	albue	ChSl.	lakŭtĭ
It.	gomito	Sw.	armbåge	SCr.	lakat
Fr.	coude	OE	elnboga	Boh.	loket
Sp.	codo	ME	elbowe	Pol.	łokieć
Rum.	cot	NE	elbow	Russ.	lokot'
Ir.	uilind	Du.	elleboog	Skt.	aratni-
NIr.	uille	OHG	e(l)linbogo	Av.	arəθna-
W.	elin	MHG	e(l)lenboge		
Br.	ilin	NHG	ellenbogen		

Words for 'elbow' are regularly from the notion of 'bend'. There is frequent interchange between 'elbow' and 'forearm', the latter also as a measure 'ell, cubit'.

1. Derivs. of IE *el-, *ele-, etc. 'bend' (but primary verbal forms lacking) in words for 'forearm' (as measure 'ell, cubit'), and 'elbow'. Walde-P. 1.156 ff. Ernout-M. 1120. Pedersen 2.59.

Grk. ὠλένη 'forearm', ὠλλόν· τὴν τοῦ βραχίονος καμπήν Hesych., ὠλέκρᾱνον 'elbow' (so reg. in Aristot., where ἀγκών is 'upper arm', as HA $493^{b}27$, etc.), fr. *ὠλενο-κρᾱνον, cpd. with second part 'tip' : κάρα 'head, top', etc.; Lat. ulna 'forearm' as measure 'ell'; Ir. uilind, NIr. uille, W. elin, Br. ilin 'elbow'; Goth. aleina, ON ǫln, eln, OE eln, OHG elina 'ell', in cpds. for 'elbow', ON ǫlnbogi, Dan. albue, OSw. alboghi (Sw. armbåge by popular connection with arm; Hellquist 32), OE elnboga, ME elbowe, NE elbow, Du. elleboog, OHG e(l)linbogo, MHG e(l)lenboge, NHG ellenbogen, ellbogen, with final member : ON bogi, etc. 'bend, bow'; Lith. alkūnė, Lett. elkuons (beside Lith. uolektis, Lett. uolekts 'ell', OPruss. woaltis, woltis 'ell, forearm'); ChSl. lakŭtĭ ('πῆχυς, ell'), SCr. lakat, Boh. loket, Pol. łokieć, Russ. lokot' 'elbow, ell'; Skt. aratni-, Av. arəθna- 'elbow' (Av. frārāθni- 'ell').

2. Grk. ἀγκών ('elbow' Hom.+, but 'upper arm' in Aristot.), NG pop. ἀγκῶνας : ἀγκύλος 'bent', Skt. añc- 'bend', etc. Walde-P. 1.60 f.

3. Lat. cubitus, cubitum (> It. gomito, Fr. coude, Sp. codo, Rum. cot; REW 2354) : Lat. cubāre 'recline, lie down' (as orig. 'bend'), Goth. hups, etc. 'hip', OE hoppian, etc. 'hop', Grk. κύβος 'hollow above the hips on cattle', fr. IE *keub-, beside *keu-, *keup-, etc. in words for 'bend, hollow'. From Lat. cubitum (or a similar Italic form) through Sicilian (not conversely, as Bechtel, Griech. Dial. 2.284, Ernout-M. 237), comes Grk. κύβιτον 'elbow' in Hippoc., etc. Walde-P. 1.374. Walde-H. 1.297.

4.33 HAND

Grk.	χείρ	Goth.	handus	Lith.	ranka
NG	χέρι	ON	hǫnd, mund	Lett.	ruoka
Lat.	manus	Dan.	haand	ChSl.	rąka
It.	mano	Sw.	hand	SCr.	ruka
Fr.	main	OE	hand, mund	Boh.	ruka
Sp.	mano	ME	hand	Pol.	ręka
Rum.	mînă	NE	hand	Russ.	ruka
Ir.	lām	Du.	hand	Skt.	hasta-, kara-, pāṇi-
NIr.	lāmh	OHG	hant, munt	Av.	zasta-, gu-
W.	llaw	MHG	hant		
Br.	dourn	NHG	hand		

Several of the words for 'hand' are from roots meaning 'seize, take, collect' or the like. Some are from words meaning orig. a part of the hand, 'palm' or 'fist'. Several are without any clear root connection. For extension of 'hand' to 'arm', cf. 4.31.

1. Grk. χείρ, gen. χειρός and χερός (Dor. χήρ, Aeol. χερρ-; NG χέρι), formerly taken as fr. *χερ-σ- : Skt. hr̥- 'hold, carry', haras- 'grip, power', etc. (Walde-P. 1.603), but now as fr. *χεσρ- : Hitt. kessar and kessras 'hand' (also, with loss or assimilation of s, Arm. jeṙn, Alb. dorë 'hand'), Toch. A tsar, B šar, Sturtevant, Hitt. Gram. 89. Duchesne-Guillemin, BSL 39.211 ff.

2. Lat. manus (> It., Sp. mano, Fr. main, Rum. mînă), Osc. manim 'manum', Umbr. mani 'manu', etc. : ON mund 'hand', OE mund, OHG munt 'hand' (but more usually 'protection, guardianship'), Grk. μάρη 'hand' (Pind.; cf. εὐμαρής), IE *mər-, *mən- (or *mr̥-, *mn̥-), *mn̥t- (orig. an r/n stem). Walde-P. 2.272. Ernout-M. 591 f. Walde-H. 2.34 f.

3. Ir. lām, NIr. lāmh, W. llaw : OE folm 'palm, hand', folme 'hand', OS folmōs pl. 'hands', OHG folma 'palm', Lat. palma 'palm', Grk. παλάμη 'palm' (Grk. and Lat. forms also used for 'hand'), Skt. pāṇi- 'hand' (*parni-), Av. pərənā- 'cupped hollow hand', all with orig. application to the '(flat) palm' only, fr. the root in Lat. palam 'openly', plānus 'smooth, flat', etc. Walde-P. 2.62. Ernout-M. 725.

Br. dourn = Corn. dorn, W. dwrn, Ir. dorn 'fist' : Lett. dūre, dūris 'fist', orig. 'fist' in striking, fr. dūrt 'sting, thrust' (cf. Lat. pugnus 'fist' : pungere 'sting', orig. 'thrust'). Walde-P. 1.794 f. Stokes 148. Mühl.-Endz. 2.529. (Otherwise Preveden, Language 5.149, fr. IE *dher- 'hold'; but cf. RC 47.496).

4. Goth. handus, etc., general Gmc., etym. disputed, but prob. : Goth. frahinþan 'seize, pursue', Sw. hinna 'reach', OE huntian 'hunt' (fr. parallel root forms *ken-t-, *ken-d-) with development of 'hand' fr. 'seize'. Walde-P. 1.460. Falk-Torp 366. Feist 244 f.

ON, OE mund, OHG munt, above, 2.

5. Lith. ranka, Lett. ruoka, ChSl. rąka, etc., the general Balto-Slavic word : Lith. renkti 'collect'. Walde-P. 2.373.

6. Skt. hasta-, Av. zasta-, OPers. dasta- : Lith. pažastis, pažastė 'space under the arm, armpit'. Walde-P. 1.541. Perh. ultimately : Grk. χείρ, etc. (above, 1), i.e., *ĝhos-to- beside *ĝhes-r-. Duchesne-Guillemin, loc. cit.

Skt. kara- = kara- adj. 'doing, making', fr. kr̥- 'do, make'.

Skt. pāṇi-, see above, 3.

Av. gu- in dual gava, etc. (of evil beings) prob. : Grk. ἐγ-γύη 'pledge, surety', ἐγγύς 'near' (both as orig. 'in the hand'), etc. Walde-P. 1.636 f. Barth. 505.

4.34 FINGER

Grk.	δάκτυλος	Goth.	figgrs	Lith.	pirštas
NG	δάχτυλο	ON	fingr	Lett.	pirksts
Lat.	digitus	Dan.	finger	ChSl.	prŭstŭ, prĭstŭ
It.	dito	Sw.	finger	SCr.	prst
Fr.	doigt	OE	finger	Boh.	prst
Sp.	dedo	ME	finger	Pol.	palec
Rum.	deget	NE	finger	Russ.	palec (perst)
Ir.	mēr	Du.	vinger	Skt.	aṅguli-
NIr.	mēar	OHG	fingar	Av.	ərəzu-, angušta-
W.	bys	MHG	vinger		
Br.	biz	NHG	finger		

There is no inherited group pointing to an IE word for 'finger', but mostly agreement within the several branches, as Gmc., Balto-Slavic, etc. These independent terms are in most cases of doubtful, if not wholly obscure, etymology.

1. Grk. δάκτυλος, also neut. pl. δάκτυλα (Theoc. +) hence NG neut. δάχτυλο, prob. fr. *δατ-κυλος (cf. Boeot.

δακκύλιος), but etym. dub. Perh. orig. 'tip' (whence 'finger' and 'toe') : ON *tindr* 'point, mountain peak', OE *tind*, OHG *zinna* 'prong', etc., though for these there are other possible connections. Walde-P. 1.120 ff. Boisacq 164.

2. Lat. *digitus* (> the Romance words), prob. fr. IE *deiĝ̂-* than *taikns* 'sign', etc., beside *deik-* in Grk. δείκνῡμι, Skt. *diç-* 'point out', Lat. *dīcere* 'say' (fr. 'point out'), *index* 'index finger', prob. also OE *tā* 'toe', etc. (as orig. 'finger'). Walde-P. 1.776 f. Ernout-M. 268, 271. Walde-H. 1.351.

3. Ir. *mēr*, NIr. *mēar*, etym. dub. Walde-P. 2.221, 223. Pedersen 1.134.

W. *bys*, Br. *biz*, possibly : ON *kvistr* 'twig'. Walde-P. 1.694. Pedersen 1.79.

4. Goth. *figgrs*, OE *finger*, etc., general Gmc., perh. fr. *penkʷrós* : Ir. *cōicer* 'number of five', fr. IE *penkʷe* 'five'. Walde-P. 2.26. Falk-Torp 218. Feist 150.

4.342 THUMB

Grk.	μέγας δάκτυλος, ἀντίχειρ	Goth.	....	Lith.	nykštis
NG	μεγάλο δάχτυλο	ON	þumalfingr	Lett.	īkstis
Lat.	pollex	Dan.	tommelfinger	ChSl.	(palĭcĭ)
It.	pollice	Sw.	tumme	SCr.	palac
Fr.	pouce	OE	þūma	Boh.	palec
Sp.	pulgar	ME	thoum(b)e	Pol.	wielki palec
Rum.	degetul cel gros, policar	NE	thumb	Russ.	bol'šoj palec
Ir.	ordu	Du.	duim	Skt.	aṅguṣṭha-
NIr.	ordóg	OHG	dūmo	Av.	....
W.	bawd, bodfys	MHG	dūme		
Br.	meud	NHG	daumen		

In some of the IE languages there is no single word for 'thumb', which is called the 'big finger', like NE *big toe*. Many of the single words are of similar semantic origin, being based on the notion of 'stout, thick'. Just as the same word may be used for 'finger' or 'toe', so many of the forms listed here are used for either 'thumb' or 'big toe' (NE *thumb* obs. in latter sense). Several were also used for a measure of length, the 'thumb's breadth' (cf. NED s.v. *thumb*, sb.[4]) and in some cases came to be restricted to this use, with derivatives or compounds for 'thumb', as Dan. *tomme* vs. *tommelfinger*, Sw. *tum* vs. *tumme*.

1. Grk. μέγας δάκτυλος, NG μεγάλο δάχτυλο, the 'big finger'.

Grk. ἀντίχειρ (sc. δάκτυλος), as what is opposite the fingers.

2. Lat. *pollex* (> It. *pollice*, Fr.

---

pouce), adj. *pollicāris* (> sbs. Sp. *pulgar*, Rum. neolog. *policar*), prob. (formed on the analogy of *index* 'forefinger') : Lat. *pollēre* 'be strong', Skt. *phala-* 'fruit, kernel, testicle', with a common notion of 'swelling, thickening'; here prob. also ChSl. *palĭcĭ*, SCr. *palac* 'thumb' (below, 6). Walde-P. 2.102. Ernout-M. 785 f.

3. Ir. *ordu*, NIr. *ordóg*, Gael. *ordag*, prob.: *ord* 'hammer' (9.49). Macbain 269.

W. *bawd* (also *bodfys*, cpd. with *bys* 'finger'), OW *maut*, Br. *meud*, fr. *mōto-*, perh.: Arm. *matu* 'finger', root connection? Walde-P. 2.221. Henry 200 f.

4. ON *þumi*, *þumalfingr*, Dan. (*tomme* formerly 'thumb', now only 'inch') *tommelfinger*, Sw. (*tum* 'inch') *tumme*, OE *þūma*, ME *thoum(b)e*, etc., NE *thumb*, Du. *duim*, OHG *dūmo*,

MHG *dūme*, NHG *daumen*, orig. the 'stout or thick (finger)': Lat. *tumēre* 'swell', *tumor* 'swelling', Skt. *tu-* 'be strong', etc. Walde-P. 1.708. Falk-Torp 1270. NED s.v. *thumb*, sb.

5. Lith. *nykštis*, OLith. *inkstys*, Lett. *īkstis*, OPruss. *instixs*, prob. : Lith. *inkstas*, Lett. *īkst* 'kidney' : Lat. *inguen* 'swelling in the groin', Grk. ἀδήν 'gland', the various applications being based on the common notion 'swelling'. Mühl.-Endz. 1.835. Walde-H. 1.701.

6. Late ChSl. *palĭcĭ*, SCr. *palac*, Boh. *palec*, prob.: Lat. *pollex* 'thumb' (above, 2). But Pol., Russ. *palec* now 'finger' and Pol. *wielki palec*, Russ. *bol'šoj palec* 'thumb', lit. the 'big finger'.

7. Skt. *aṅguṣṭha-* = Av. *aṅgušta-* 'finger, toe', beside Skt. *aṅguli-* 'finger, toe' (4.34).

4.35 LEG

Grk.	σκέλος	Goth.	....	Lith.	koja
NG	σκέλι (πόδι)	ON	leggr, fótr, fótleggr	Lett.	kāja
Lat.	crūs		(bein)	ChSl.	golěnĭ
It.	gamba	Dan.	ben	SCr.	noga
Fr.	jambe	Sw.	ben	Boh.	noha
Sp.	pierna	OE	sceanca, scía	Pol.	noga
Rum.	picior	ME	leg	Russ.	noga
Ir.	cos	NE	leg	Skt.	jaṅghā-
NIr.	cos	Du.	been	Av.	paitištāna-
W.	coes	OHG	bein, gibeini		
Br.	gar	MHG	bein, gebeine		
		NHG	bein		

Some words which meant originally only 'foot' have been extended to designate the 'leg' also (like 'hand' > 'arm', 4.31). Sometimes the original sense was 'bone' of the leg 'either above or below the knee'. Often (as in the case of 'hand', 'arm', and 'shoulder') the original term seems to have applied to various members of the body or to their articulations.

1. Grk. σκέλος, NG pop. σκέλι : σκολιός 'curved, bent', OHG *scelah* 'crooked,' Lat. *scelus* 'wickedness' (fr.

'crookedness'), prob. also (fr. *kel-*, beside *skel-*) Lith. *kelys*, Lett. *celis*, ChSl. *kolěno* 'knee', Lat. *calx*, Lith. *kulnis* 'heel'. Walde-P. 2.598.

NG πόδι, ποδάρι 'foot' (4.37), also sometimes 'leg'.

2. Lat. *crūs*, etym.? Walde-P. 1.489. Ernout-M. 236. Walde-H. 1.295.

It. *gamba*, Fr. *jambe* (OSp. *camba*), fr. late Lat. *gamba* 'hoof or hock of a horse', orig. only a veterinary's term, then applied to persons; this from Grk. καμπή 'bend', used in Aristot. for the joints of

---

various parts. Ernout-M. 410. Walde-H. 1.581. REW 1539.

Sp. *pierna*, fr. Lat. *perna* 'ham, haunch' (esp. of pork) : Grk. πτέρνα 'heel, ham', Skt. *pārṣṇi-*, Av. *pāšna-*, Goth. *fairzna* 'heel', etc. Walde-P. 2.50 f. Ernout-M. 757. REW 6418.

Rum. *picior*, orig. only 'foot' (4.37).

3. Ir. *coss* (also 'foot'), NIr. *cos* : Lat. *coxa* 'hip' (in VLat. replaces *femur* 'thigh', hence Fr. *cuisse*, etc., REW 2292; > W. *coes* 'leg'), Skt. *kakṣa-*, Av. *kaša-* 'armpit', OHG *hahsa* 'bend of the knee', with varied specializations fr. a common notion of 'joint, articulation of the limbs'. Walde-P. 1.456 f. Ernout-M. 226. Walde-H. 1.283. Pedersen 1.34, 78.

Br., Corn. *gar* = W. *gar* 'thigh, ham', Ir. *gairri* 'calves' of the leg (cf. Fr. *jarret* 'hock' fr. Gallic *garr-*), etym. obscure. Henry 129. Connection with Lett. *gurni* 'groins, hips' (as Bezzenberger in Stokes 107) apparently untenable (cf. Walde-P. 1.557, Mühl.-Endz. 1.684).

4. ON *leggr* 'hollow bone of arms and legs' but also 'leg' (> ME, NE *leg*), esp. in latter sense *fótleggr* (as *handleggr* 'arm', 4.31), Dan. *læg*, Sw. *lägg* 'calf (of the leg)', no certain outside connection, but prob. fr. an IE *lek-* 'bend'(?) in Skt. *lakuṭa-* 'cudgel', Lat. *lacertus* 'muscle of the upper arm', and numerous other words with partial application to parts of the body, etc. Walde-P. 2.421. Falk-Torp 631.

ON *fótr* 'foot' (4.37) used of the entire 'leg'.

ON *bein* (but mostly 'bone'), Dan.,

Sw. *ben*, Du. *been*, OHG, MHG *bein* 'bone, leg' (also coll. OHG *gibeini*, MHG *gebeine* in both senses), NHG *bein* 'leg' = OE *bān*, NE *bone* (4.16).

OE *sceanca* (dust. esp. the leg below the knee, 'the shank', gl. Lat. *crus*) = Dan. *skank* 'shank', Sw. *skank* 'thigh- or shinbone', MLG *schenke* 'thigh' (dim. MHG, NHG *schenkel*, etc. 'thigh'), perh. fr. the notion of 'crooked' (cf. Grk. σκέλος : σκολιός, above, 1) : OHG *hinkan*, NHG *hinken*, Skt. *khañj-* 'limp', *kañja-* 'lame'. Walde-P. 2.564. Falk-Torp 984 f.

OE *scía*, gl. Lat. *crus*, perh. only 'shin' : OE *scinu*, OHG *scina*, etc. 'shin, shinbone', perh. fr. the root in Skt. *chyati* 'cuts off', Grk. σχάω 'slit, rend', as orig. 'flat piece split off', then applied to the 'shinbone?'. Walde-P. 2.542.

5. Lith. *koja*, Lett. *kāja* 'leg, foot', etym. obscure (Arm. *k'ayl* 'step, foot'??). Mühl.-Endz. 1.288.

6. ChSl. *golěnĭ* renders σκέλος in Jn. 19, 31 ff., 'breaking the (bones of the) legs', the modern Slavic forms meaning 'shinbone, shin', etym. uncertain. Berneker 320 ff.

SCr. *noga*, etc. the common modern Slavic word for 'leg', but properly, and ChSl. *noga* in Gospels only, 'foot' (4.37).

7. Skt. *jaṅghā-* (mostly 'lower leg'; Av. *zanga-* 'ankle') : Lith. *žengti* 'step, stride', Goth. *gaggan*, ON *ganga* etc. 'walk, go', IE *ĝhengh-*. Walde-P. 1.588.

Av. *paitištāna-*, lit. 'what one stands on, support', fr. cpd. of *štā-* 'stand'. Barth. 837.

4.36 KNEE

Grk.	γόνυ	Goth.	kniu	Lith.	kelys
NG	γόνατο	ON	knē	Lett.	celis
Lat.	genū	Dan.	knæ	ChSl.	kolěno
It.	ginocchio	Sw.	knä	SCr.	koljeno
Fr.	genou	OE	cnēo(w)	Boh.	koleno
Sp.	rodilla (hinojo)	ME	kne	Pol.	kolano
Rum.	genunchiu	NE	knee	Russ.	koleno
Ir.	glún	Du.	knie	Skt.	jānu-
NIr.	glún	OHG	kniu, kneo	Av.	žnu-
W.	glin	MHG	knie (kniu)		
Br.	glin	NHG	knie		

1. IE *ĝenu-* 'knee', root connection? Walde-P. 1.586 f. Ernout-M. 419 f. Walde-H. 1.592 f.

Grk. γόνυ, gen. γόνατος (hence NG γόνατο); Lat. *genū* (VLat. dim. *genuculum* > It. *ginocchio*, Fr. *genou*, Sp. *hinojo*, Rum. *genunchiu*); Goth. *kniu*, etc., general Gmc.; Skt. *jānu-* Av. *žnu-*, NPers. *zānū*; Arm. *cunr*; Hitt. *genu*; Toch. A *kanwem*, B *kenīne* (dual; SSS 128 f.); here also prob. the Celtic group Ir. *glún*, W. Br. *glin* (*gnū-nes* > *glū-

nes by dissim., Vendryes quoted by Loth, RC 40.149). Otherwise for the Celtic words Walde-P. 1.618.

2. Sp. *rodilla* = It. *rotella*, Port. *rodella* 'kneepan', fr. Lat. *rotella* 'little wheel' (dim. of *rota*). REW 7389.

3. Lith. *kelys*, Lett. *celis*, ChSl. *kolěno*, etc., general Balto-Slavic : Grk. κωλήψ 'hollow of the knee', κῶλον 'limb', σκέλος 'leg', etc. (4.35). Walde-P. 2.599. Berneker 545 f.

4.37 FOOT

Grk.	πούς	Goth.	fótus	Lith.	koja
NG	πόδι, ποδάρι	ON	fótr	Lett.	kāja
Lat.	pēs	Dan.	fod	ChSl.	noga
It.	piede	Sw.	fot	SCr.	noga
Fr.	pied	OE	fót	Boh.	noha
Sp.	pie	ME	fote	Pol.	noga
Rum.	picior	NE	foot	Russ.	noga
Ir.	traig, coss	Du.	voet	Skt.	pad-, caraṇa-
NIr.	troigh	OHG	fuoz	Av.	pad-, paiδyā-, zbar-
W.	troed	MHG	vuoz		aθa-, dvariθra-
Br.	troad	NHG	fuss		

Aside from the inherited group, concerning the root connection of which nothing can be said, words for 'foot' may come from 'move, run, walk', or through 'claw' from 'nail'. As noted above (4.35), words for 'foot' have often been extended to 'leg'.

1. IE *ped-*. Walde-P. 2.23 ff. Ernout-M. 761.

Grk., Dor. πώς, Att. πούς (ου unexplained), gen. ποδός, NG πόδι, ποδάρι (fr.

the dims. πόδιον, ποδάριον); Lat. *pēs*, *pedis* (> It. *piede*, Fr. *pied*, Sp. *pie*), Umbr. *peři*, *persi* *pede*; Goth. *fótus*, ON *fótr*, etc., general Gmc.; Skt. *pad-*, Av. *pad-*, deriv. *paiδyā-*; Arm. *otn*, Toch. A *pe* (SSS 2), B *pai*; here also Lith. *pėda* 'foot-track', Lett. *pēda* 'sole of the foot, foot-track', ChSl. *pěšĭ* 'on foot', *podŭ* 'ground', etc.

Here prob. also Rum. *picior* 'foot, leg', fr. *peciolus*, this by syncope for a dim.

Lat. *pediciolus. REW 6324a. Puşcariu 1305.

2. Ir. traig (gen. traiged), NIr. troigh, W. troed, Br. troad : Gall. ver-tragus 'swift-footed dog', SCr. trag 'footstep', perh. Goth. þragjan 'run', etc. Walde-P. 1.752 f. Pedersen 1.39. But cf. H. Lewis, BBCS 9.34 f.

Ir. coss 'leg, foot', NIr. cos 'leg' (4.35).

3. Lith. koja, Lett. kāja 'foot, leg' (4.35).

4. ChSl., etc. noga, the regular Slavic word for 'foot' (and by extension 'leg') : OPruss. nage 'foot', Lith. naga 'hoof', all

orig. 'claw', coll. formation to Lith. nagas, Lett. nags 'nail (on finger or toe), claw' (4.39). Walde-P. 1.180 f.

5. Skt., Av. pad-, above, 1.

Skt. caraṇa- fr. car- 'go, move, wander'.

Av. zbaraθa-, fr. zbar- 'walk' (of evil beings) : Skt. hvar, hval- 'go crookedly, go astray, err', etc. Barth. 1699. Walde-P. 1.643.

Av. dvariθra-, fr. dvar- 'go, hasten' (of evil beings), prob. : Skt. dhur- 'run' (only Dhātup.), further connections still more dub. Walde-P. 1.842. Otherwise Barth. 765.

4.38   TOE

Grk.	δάκτυλος	Goth.	....	Lith.	pirštas (kojos)
NG	δάχτυλο (τοῦ ποδιοῦ)	ON	tā	Lett.	(kājas) pirksts
Lat.	digitus	Dan.	taa	ChSl.	prŭstŭ(?)
It.	dito (del piede)	Sw.	tå	SCr.	prst (od noge)
Fr.	orteil, doigt du pied	OE	tā	Boh.	prst (na nahou)
Sp.	dedo (del pie)	ME	to	Pol.	palec (u nogi)
Rum.	deget de la picior	NE	toe	Russ.	palec (na noge)
Ir.	mēr (coise)	Du.	teen	Skt.	aṅguli-, pādāṅguli-
NIr.	mēar (coise)	OHG	zaha	Av.	aṅguṣṭa-
W.	bys troed	MHG	ze(he)		
Br.	biz troad	NHG	zehe		

'Toe' is usually expressed by the word for 'finger' (4.34) with or without the addition of 'of the foot'. The use of parentheses in the list attempts to show the situation. The distinctive words for 'toe' are:

1. Fr. orteil, fr. OFr. arteil, fr. Lat. articulus 'joint, knuckle, limb', also of

the fingers (articulus manus), but crossed with Gall. ordiga 'big toe' (Cassel Glosses). REW 687. Wartburg 1.149 f.

2. ON tā, etc., all the Gmc. words, prob. orig. 'finger' as 'pointer' : Lat. index 'index finger', digitus 'finger' (4.34). Walde-P. 1.776. Falk-Torp 1237. Walde-H. 1.351.

4.39   NAIL

Grk.	ὄνυξ	Goth.	....	Lith.	nagas
NG	νύχι	ON	nagl	Lett.	nags
Lat.	unguis	Dan.	negl	ChSl.	nogŭtĭ
It.	unghia	Sw.	nagel	SCr.	nokat
Fr.	ongle	OE	nægl	Boh.	nehet
Sp.	uña	ME	nail	Pol.	paznokieć
Rum.	unghie	NE	nail	Russ.	nogot'
Ir.	ingen	Du.	nagel	Skt.	nakha-
NIr.	ionga	OHG	nagal	Av.	srū-, srvā-
W.	ewin	MHG	nagel		
Br.	ivin	NHG	nagel		

1. IE *(o)nogh- (with wide variation of root grade and suffixes in different IE languages). Walde-P. 1.180 f. Ernout-M. 1125.

Hence all the words listed except Av. srū, srvā (below), but represented in Iranian by NPers. nāxun (Skt. also nakha-, with unexplained kh for gh). NG νύχι fr. dim. ὀνύχιον; the Romance

forms fr. the Lat. dim. ungula (REW 9071); Pol. paznokieć, cpd. with prefixed paz-: pazur 'claw', pazucha 'breast', Boh. paže 'arm' (4.31), etc. (Brückner 400).

2. Av. srū, srvā, also 'horn' (the earlier meaning) : Grk. κέρας, etc. 'horn' (4.17). Walde-P. 1.404. Barth. 1647 f.

4.392   WING

Grk.	πτέρυξ	Goth.	....	Lith.	sparnas
NG	φτερούγα	ON	vængr	Lett.	spārns
Lat.	āla, penna	Dan.	vinge	ChSl.	krilo
It.	ala	Sw.	vinge	SCr.	krilo
Fr.	aile	OE	fipere, feþera (pl.)	Boh.	křídlo
Sp.	ala	ME	wenge, winge	Pol.	skrzydło
Rum.	aripă	NE	wing	Russ.	krylo
Ir.	ette, scíath	Du.	vleugel	Skt.	pakṣa-, pattra-
NIr.	eite, eiteog, sciathán	OHG	federah, fettach	Av.	parəna-
W.	adain, asgell	MHG	vlügel, vedrach		
Br.	askell	NHG	flügel		

Many of the words for 'wing' are derived from verbs for 'fly', whence also many of those for 'feather', in this case a secondary sense, which are then included in the discussion here. Several words for 'wing' denoted originally the joint or axis (of arm or wing), hence relations with words for 'shoulder blade, shoulder'.

1. Derivs. of IE *pet- in Grk. πέτομαι, Skt. pat- 'fly' (10.37), including here words for 'feather'. Walde-P. 2.19 ff. Ernout-M. 752 f. Pedersen 1.90, 160.

Grk. πτέρυξ 'wing' (dim. πτερύγιον > NG φτερούγα; Hatzidakis, Μεσ. 2.99), πτερόν 'feather', pl. often 'wings'; Lat.

penna 'wing, feather' (> It. penna, Rum. pană 'feather'); Ir. ette 'wing', NIr. eite, eiteog 'wing, pinion, feather', W. adain 'wing'; ON fjǫðr, OE feþer (pl. also 'wings'), OHG federa, etc., general Gmc. for 'feather', with derivs. for 'wing' OE fipere (cf. NED s.v. feather, sb.), OHG federah, MHG vedrach, also OHG fettach, MHG vettach (NHG fittich, Weigand-H. s.v.); Skt. pattra- (also patra-) 'wing, feather, leaf, blade'.

2. Forms fr. *per-, ultimately *pter- and belonging with preceding? Walde-P. 2.21.

Skt. parṇa-, Av. parəna- 'feather' (Av.

also 'wing', Barth. 870); ChSl. pero, etc. general Slavic for 'feather', Lith. sparnas, Lett. spārns 'wing'.

3. Lat. āla (> It., Sp. ala, Fr. aile), fr. *axlā (cf. dim. axilla), orig. the joint of wing or arm : OE eaxl, OHG ahsala, etc. 'shoulder', Lat. axis 'axle', etc. Walde-P. 1.37. Ernout-M. 30 f. Walde-H. 1.25. REW 304.

Rum. aripă : Calabr. alapa, Fr. aube 'a sweep', fr. Lat. alapa 'blow with the hand on the face' (of obscure orig.), with common notion of swinging. REW 310.

4. Ir. ette, etc., W. adain, above, 1.

Ir. scíath 'shoulder blade, wing' (W. ysgwydd 'shoulder'), NIr. sciathán 'wing', fr. the root in Grk. σχίζω, Lat. scindere 'split'. Walde-P. 1.544. Pedersen 1.76, 112.

W. asgell, Br. askell, Corn. ascall (Ir. ascall 'armpit') fr. late Lat. ascella ('wing' in Itala, etc.) for axilla dim. of āla (above, 3). Loth, Mots lat. 134, RC 41.395 ff.

5. ON vængr (pl. > ME wengen, win-

gen, wenge, first used in pl., NE wing; NED s.v. wing, sb.), Dan., Sw. vinge, fr. IE *wē- in Skt. vā-, Grk. ἄημι, Goth. waian, etc. 'blow', prob. through a secondary 'flutter'. Falk-Torp 1384. Hellquist 1350. (Not included in Walde-P. 1.220 ff.)

OE fipere, OHG federah, above, 1.

MHG vlügel, NHG flügel, Du. vleugel, fr. vbs. for 'fly', MHG vliegen, etc. (10.37).

6. Lith. sparnas, Lett. spārns, above, 2.

7. ChSl. krilo, etc., general Slavic, fr. *krī-dlo (dl preserved in Boh., Pol.) : Lith. skrieti 'run or fly in a circle', skritulys 'circle', OHG scrītan 'stride', also Lith. kreivas, ChSl. *krivŭ (SCr. kriv, etc.), Lat. curvus, etc. 'crooked', fr. a root *(s)ker- with various extensions. Development of 'wing' fr. 'fly' or like that in Lat. āla? Walde-P. 2.570. Berneker 615 f. Brückner 497 f.

8. Skt. pakṣa-, see under Boh. paže, 4.31.

Skt. pattra-, above, 1.

4.393   FEATHER

Grk.	πτερόν	Goth.	....	Lith.	plunksna
NG	φτερό	ON	fjǫðr	Lett.	spalva
Lat.	penna	Dan.	fjeder, fjer	ChSl.	pero
It.	penna, piuma	Sw.	fjäder	SCr.	pero
Fr.	plume	OE	feþer	Boh.	péro
Sp.	pluma	ME	fether	Pol.	pióro
Rum.	pană	NE	feather	Russ.	pero
Ir.	cleite, clūm	Du.	feder, feer	Skt.	parṇa-, pattra-
NIr.	cleite, clūm	OHG	fedara	Av.	parəna-
W.	pluen	MHG	veder(e)		
Br.	pluenn	NHG	feder		

The majority of the words for 'feather' are cognate with words for 'wing' and have been included in the preceding discussion, 4.392. Here only the following:

1. Lat. plūma, denoting the fine, soft feathers covering the body, vs. the penna

of wing or tail, but eventually displacing the latter in part (hence It. piuma, Fr. plume, Sp. pluma) prob. (fr. *plus-mā) : MLG vlūs, OE flēos, etc. 'fleece', also(?) Lith. plunksna 'feather' (see below). Walde-P. 2.96. Ernout-M. 781.

2. Ir., NIr. cleite, etym.?

3. Ir., NIr. clūm (coll. 'feathers'), W., Br. plu (coll.; sg. -en, enn), fr. Lat. plūma (above, 2). Vendryes, De hib. voc. 127. Loth, Mots lat. 196.

4. Lith. plunksna (old also pluksna,

plusna), either : plaukas 'hair', Lett. plūkt 'pluck', or, with k fr. this group, fr. old plusna, this : Lat. plūma (above, 1). Walde-P. 2.96. Thurneysen IF 14.127 f.

4.40   BREAST[1]
(Front of Chest)

Grk.	στῆθος (στέρνον)	Goth.	brusts (pl.)	Lith.	krūtinė
NG	στῆθος	ON	brjóst	Lett.	krūts
Lat.	pectus	Dan.	bryst	ChSl.	prĭsi (pl.), grudĭ
It.	petto	Sw.	bröst	SCr.	prsa (pl.), grudi (pl.)
Fr.	poitrine, sein	OE	brēost	Boh.	prsa (pl.), hrud'
Sp.	pecho	ME	breste	Pol.	piers
Rum.	piept	NE	breast	Russ.	grud'
Ir.	bruinne, ucht	Du.	borst	Skt.	uras-, vakṣas-
NIr.	ucht, bruinne	OHG	brust	Av.	varah-
W.	bron, dwyfron	MHG	brust		
Br.	brennid	NHG	brust		

Words for 'breast' as front part of the chest and for 'breast' as woman's breast are in part the same, and where they are normally different there may be some overlapping. There is also overlapping on the other side with 'chest'. In fact, except where the distinctive Grk. θώραξ (the whole 'trunk' in Aristot., later 'chest') has been borrowed, 'breast' as the front of the chest, and the whole 'chest' are generally not distinguished but covered by the same word. (So Lat. pectus, It. petto, Fr. poitrine and most of of the words listed here.)

Omitted from the list are a number of words which, like NE bosom, are sometimes used of the breast in a literal sense but are generally poetical, or with emotional connotation. So Grk. κόλπος, Lat. sinus, Goth. barms (which renders κόλπος in this sense), Dan., Sw. barm, OE bearm, OHG barm, OE bōsm, NE bosom, NHG busen, etc.

The chief semantic source is the notion of 'curved shape, swelling'.

1. Grk. στῆθος, prob. related in some way (perh. a blend with some other word

in -θος) to στήνιον στῆθος (Hesych.), this : Skt. stana- 'woman's breast', etc. (4.41). Walde-P. 2.663.

Grk. στέρνον (in Hom. only of males), specialization of 'flat surface', fr. the root of στόρνῡμι, etc. 'spread out' (9.34). Cf. OHG sterna 'forehead', fr. the same root. Walde-P. 2.639. Boisacq 931.

2. Lat. pectus (> It. petto, Sp. pecho, Rum. piept; Fr. pis once 'breast', now 'udder'; deriv. Fr. poitrine; REW 6335, 6332), perh. as denoting first the hairy breast of man (cf. Grk. λάσια στήθη) : Lat. pectere 'comb', Grk. πόκος 'fleece', etc. Walde-P. 2.17.

Fr. sein (It., Sp. seno, Rum. sîn 'bosom, lap') fr. Lat. sinus 'fold, bosom, lap', itself of dub. etym. Ernout-M. 946. REW 7950.

3. Ir. bruinne, W. bron (also dwyfron orig. 'the two breasts'), Br. brennid : Ir. brū 'belly, womb', W. bryn 'hill', Goth. brusts, etc., all fr. a common notion of 'swelling'. Walde-P. 2.197 ff.

Ir. ucht, prob. fr. *puptu- : VLat. puppa, It. poppa, Lett. pups 'woman's breast' (4.41). Walde-P. 2.81. Stokes 55. Otherwise (: Lat. *pectus*) Pedersen 1.90, etc. (cf. Walde-P. 2.17).

4. Goth. *brusts* (pl. = στῆθος), OE *brēost*, etc., general Gmc. : Ir. *bruinne*, etc., above, 3.

5. Lith. *krūtis* (mostly 'woman's breast'), *krūtinė*, Lett. *krūts* : NIr. *cruit*, W. *crwth* 'hump' and a kind of 'violin', fr. common notion of 'curved, bent'. Walde-P. 1.489. Mühl.-Endz. 2.293.

6. ChSl. *grądǐ* (quotable only in late form *grudǐ*), SCr. *grudi* (pl.), Boh. *hrud*, Russ. *grud'*, perh. : Grk. βρένθος 'arrogance', Lat. *grandis* 'large', fr. a common

notion of 'swelling'. Walde-P. 1.699. Berneker 356. Walde-H. 1.351.

ChSl. *prǔsi* (pl.), SCr., Boh. *prsa* (pl.) or *prsi*, *prsy* (pl.), Boh. sg. *prs* 'woman's breast', Pol. *pierś* : Skt. *parçu-*, *pr̥ṣṭi-*, Av. *parəsu-* 'rib'. Slavic shift from 'ribs' through 'chest' to 'breast', or 'ribs' and 'chest' fr. a common notion of 'inclosing'; uncertain which, since root connection doubtful. Walde-P. 2.44 f.

7. Skt. *uras-*, Av. *varah-* (rare, Barth. 1365, but NPers. *bar* 'breast') : Skt. *uru-*, Grk. εὐρύς 'wide, broad', etc. Walde-P. 1.285.

Skt. *vakṣas-* : Skt. *vakṣ-*, *ukṣ*, Goth. *wahsjan* 'grow', etc. Walde-P. 1.22 ff.

4.41 BREAST[2]
(Of Woman)

Grk.	μαστός	Goth.	(brusts pl.)		Lith.	krūtis	
NG	στῆθος, βυζί	ON	brjōst		Lett.	pups, krūts	
Lat.	mamma, mamilla	Dan.	bryst		ChSl.	sǔsǔ, sǔsǐcǐ	
It.	poppa, mamella	Sw.	brōst		SCr.	sisa, dojka	
Fr.	sein, mammelle	OE	brēost		Boh.	prs	
Sp.	teta, mama	ME	breste		Pol.	piers'	
Rum.	ṭâṭă	NE	breast		Russ.	grud'	
OIr.	cích	Du.	borst		Skt.	stana-	
NIr.	cíoch, mama	OHG	brust		Av.	fštāna-	
W.	bron	MHG	brust				
Br.	bronn	NHG	brust				

Words for woman's (or the corresponding man's) 'breast' are in part the same as those listed and discussed in 4.40. They are naturally most frequent occurrence in the plural (or originally dual), but may be used in the singular and are so entered. Words for 'teat, nipple' are frequently used, especially in vulgar speech, for woman's 'breast', but these are not considered here, except where they have become serious terms in the latter sense. Numerous other vulgar terms, like Fr. *nichon*, etc. are likewise omitted.

1. Grk. μαστός, Ion. μαζός, late μασθός : Lat. *madēre* 'be moist' (Grk. μαδάω

only with secondary meaning), Skt. *mad-* 'bubble, be glad', *matta-* 'drunk', OHG *manzon* 'udders', Alb. *mënd* 'suckle', etc. Walde-P. 2.230 f. Walde-H. 2.7.

Grk. στῆθος (4.40) only rarely for woman's 'breast', but in NG preferred as polite term, esp. in pl. pop. τὰ στήθια, to the following.

NG pop. βυζί, fr. late βυζίον (Test. Solom. +; cf. also βίζιν, βίζια in CGL), whence also Byz., NG βυζάνω 'suck', fr. adj. βυζός (Hesych. βυζόν· πυκνόν, κτλ.· belonging with βύζην 'closely', βύω, βύζω 'be full') and applied to the full, large breasts of women. Hatzidakis, Glotta 15.144 f.

2. NG μαστάρι, deriv. of Grk. μαστός 'breast', and βυζί 'breast' (4.41) also 'udder'.

3. It. *poppa*, *mammella*, same as for 'woman's breast'.

Fr. *pis*, fr. Lat. *pectus* 'breast' (4.40).

4. Ir. *uth*, NIr. *ūth*, perh. fr. *puta-* : Lith. *pusti* 'blow up', *putlus* 'puffed up', Lett. *pute* 'blister, pustule', etc. Walde-P. 2.80. Stokes 54.

4.43 NAVEL

Grk.	ὀμφαλός	Goth.	....		Lith.	bamba	
NG	ἀφαλός	ON	nafli		Lett.	naba	
Lat.	umbilīcus	Dan.	navle		ChSl.	pǫpǔkǔ, pǫpǔ	
It.	bellico	Sw.	navle		SCr.	pupak	
Fr.	nombril	OE	nafola		Boh.	pupek	
Sp.	ombligo	ME	navele		Pol.	pępek	
Rum.	buric	NE	navel		Russ.	pupok	
Ir.	imbliu, imlecan	Du.	navel		Skt.	nābhi-	
NIr.	imleacán	OHG	nabalo		Av.	nāfa-	
W.	bogail	MHG	nabel(e)				
Br.	begel	NHG	nabel				

Most of the words for 'navel' belong to an inherited group. A recurring secondary sense of such words is 'center'.

1. IE *ombh-*, *nobh-*, etc. with various grades of the root syllable and different suffixes. Walde-P. 1.130. Ernout-M. 1122.

Grk. ὀμφαλός, NG pop. ἀφαλός, ἀφάλι; Lat. (*umbō* 'boss, knob') *umbilīcus* (> It. *bellico*, Sp. *ombligo*, Rum. *buric*; dim. form *umbilīculus* > OFr. *lombril*, Fr. *nombril*; REW 9044–45); MIr. *imlecan*, NIr. *imleacán*; ON *nafli*, OE *nafola*, etc., general Gmc.; Lett. *naba*, OPruss. *nabis*; Skt. *nābhi-*, Av. *nāfa-*, NPers. *nāf*.

2. W. *bogail*, Br. *begel*, fr. Lat. *buc-*

W. *pwrs* (also 'bag, purse') fr. ME *purs* 'purse'. Parry-Williams 160. Cf. the similar use of NE *bag* for 'udder' (NED s.v. *bag*, sb. 10).

Br. *tez* : Fr. *tette* 'teat', etc. Cf. 4.41, Rum. *ṭâṭă*.

5. Lith. *tešmuo*, Lett. *tesmins* : Lith. *tešia* 'swells up', *tešla* 'dough', etc. Mühl.-Endz. 4.168. Leskien, Ablaut 351.

4.42 UDDER
(Of Animals)

Grk.	οὖθαρ	Goth.	....		Lith.	tešmuo	
NG	μαστάρι, βυζί	ON	jūgr		Lett.	tesminis	
Lat.	ūber	Dan.	yver		ChSl.	....	
It.	mammella, poppa	Sw.	juver		SCr.	vime	
Fr.	pis	OE	ūder		Boh.	výmě	
Sp.	ubre	ME	udere		Pol.	wymię	
Rum.	uger	NE	udder		Russ.	vymja	
Ir.	uth	Du.	uier		Skt.	ūdhar-	
NIr.	ūth	OHG	ūtar(o)		Av.	....	
W.	pwrs (cader)	MHG	ūter (inter)				
Br.	tez	NHG	euter				

Words for an animal's 'udder' are usually distinct from those for a woman's 'breast', but there is some overlapping. Aristotle uses μαστός as a general term of all animals, and its deriv. NG μαστάρι is 'udder', as Fr. *pis* from Lat. *pectus* is now 'udder'.

1. IE *ūdhr/n-*, etc., with different grades of root syllable and the neuter r/n

cela 'little buckle'? So Henry 29, Thurneysen, Keltorom. 40. Doubted by Loth, Mots lat. 139.

3. Lith. *bamba* : Lett. *bamba* 'ball', Skt. *bimba-* 'disk, sphere', Grk. βέμβιξ 'a top, whirlpool', etc., a large group prob. based on an imitative expression for the puffed-out cheeks similar to that in words for a booming sound, as Grk. βόμβος (> Lat. *bombus*), etc. Walde-P. 2.107 f.

4. ChSl. *pǫpǔ*, *pǫpǔkǔ*, etc., general Slavic : Lith. *pumpuras* 'bud', Lett. *pumpt* 'swell', etc., another group of similar orig. to the preceding. Walde-P. 2.108.

stem. Walde-P. 1.111. Ernout-M. 1076 f.

Grk. οὖθαρ, gen. -ατος; Lat. *ūber* (> Sp. *ubre*, Rum. *uger*, latter with g from *suge* 'suck'; REW 9026); ON *jūgr*, OE *ūder*, OHG *ūtar*, etc., general Gmc.; Skt. *ūdhar*, gen. *ūdhnas*; here also (from *ūdh-men-*) ChSl. *vymę* (not quotable), SCr. *vime*, etc., general Slavic.

4.44 HEART

Grk.	καρδία	Goth.	hairtō		Lith.	širdis	
NG	καρδιά	ON	hjarta		Lett.	sirds	
Lat.	cor	Dan.	hjerte		ChSl.	srǔdǐce	
It.	cuore	Sw.	hjärta		SCr.	srce	
Fr.	cœur	OE	heorte		Boh.	srdce	
Sp.	corazón	ME	herte		Pol.	serce	
Rum.	inimă	NE	heart		Russ.	serdce	
Ir.	cride	Du.	hart		Skt.	hr̥d-, hr̥daya-	
NIr.	croidhe	OHG	herza		Av.	zərəd-	
W.	calon	MHG	herze				
Br.	kalon	NHG	herz				

Most of the words for 'heart' belong to an inherited group. Words for 'heart' or their derivatives may be used for the 'middle, center' and for such various emotions as 'courage', 'love', 'anger', etc. (chapter 16).

1. IE *ḱerd-*, etc., with gradation. Walde-P. 1.423 ff. Ernout-M. 219 f.

Grk. καρδία, poet. κῆρ; Lat. *cor* (> It. *cuore*, Fr. *cœur*, OSp. *cuer*; Sp. *corazón*, Port. *coração* fr. deriv.); Ir. *cride*, NIr. *croidhe* (W. *craidd*, Br. *kreis* 'center'); Goth. *hairtō*, OE *heorte*, etc., general Gmc.; Lith. *širdis*, Lett. *sirds*,

ChSl. *srǔdǐce*, etc., general Slavic; Arm. *sirt*; here also Skt. *hr̥d*, *hr̥daya-*, Av. *zərəd-*, but with init. as if IE *ǵh*, due to a blend with some other word; Hitt. *kartis* (Sturtevant, Hitt. Gram. 106).

2. Rum. *inimă*, fr. Lat. *anima* 'soul', with shift through common figurative uses of 'soul' and 'heart'. REW 475.

3. W., Corn., MBr. *calon*, Br. *kaldun*, loanword fr. a form like OFr. *caudun*, *chaudun* 'bowels' (deriv. of Lat. *caldus* 'warm'), with shift through common figurative uses of 'bowels' and 'heart'. Pedersen 1.147.

4.45 LIVER

Grk.	ἧπαρ	Goth.	....		Lith.	kepenys, jaknos (pl.)	
NG	συκώτι	ON	lifr		Lett.	aknas (pl.)	
Lat.	iecur	Dan.	lever		ChSl.	jętro	
It.	fegato	Sw.	lever		SCr.	jetra	
Fr.	foie	OE	lifer		Boh.	jātra	
Sp.	hígado	ME	liver		Pol.	wątroba	
Rum.	ficat	NE	liver		Russ.	pečenka, pečen'	
Ir.	ōa, trommchride	Du.	lever		Skt.	yakr̥t	
NIr.	ae	OHG	libara		Av.	yākarə	
W.	afu	MHG	leber(e)				
Br.	avu	NHG	leber				

Several of the words for 'liver' belong to an inherited group. But the IE word has been largely replaced by others, partly within the historical period. Many of the new words denoted at first only the liver as an article of food.

1. IE *yēk(ʷ)r/n-*, a typical neuter r/n stem. Walde-P. 1.205. Ernout-M. 472. Walde-H. 1.673.

Grk. ἧπαρ, gen. -ατος; Lat. *iecur* (later *iocur*), gen. -*oris*, -*inoris*; Lith. *jaknos* (or *jeknos*, OLith. *jekanas*, all pl.), Lett. *aknas* (pl.); Skt. *yakr̥t*, gen. *yaknas*, Av. *yākarə*, NPers. *jigar*.

2. NG συκώτι, dim. form of late Grk. συκωτόν, neut. of συκωτός (fr. σῦκον 'fig'), in ἧπαρ συκωτόν, denoting the liver of animals fed on dried figs, as explained in

Gal. 6.679, 704. Hence the Latinized form *fīcātum* (fr. *fīcus* 'fig'), whence (but with fluctuation of accent and of vowel of first syllable; cf. REW 8494), It. *fegato*, Fr. *foie*, Sp. *hígado*, Rum. *ficat*.

3. Ir. *ōa*, NIr. *ae*, W. *afu*, Br. *avu*, general Celtic word, etym.? Pedersen 1.313.

Ir. *trommchride*, cpd. of *tromm* 'heavy' and *cride* 'heart'. Pedersen 1.56.

4. ON *lifr*, OE *lifer*, etc., general Gmc., prob. : Grk. λίπος 'fat', λιπαρός 'fatty', etc., and at first applied to the 'liver' as an article of food (cf. Fr. *foie gras*). Walde-P. 1.205. Falk-Torp 639 (but with a less probable view of the semantic relation).

5. Lith. *kepenys*, fr. *kepti* 'bake, roast', as (and prob. in imitation of) Russ. *pečen'*, *pečenka* fr. *peč'* 'bake, roast', orig., of course, the cooked liver.

6. ChSl. *jętro*, SCr. *jetra*, Boh. *játra*, Pol. *wątroba* (like ChSl. *ątroba* 'womb') : ChSl. *ątrĭ*, Lat. *inter*, Skt. *antar* 'within', Grk. ἔντερα 'entrails', etc. Walde-P. 1.127. Berneker 269. Brückner 605.

4.46 BELLY; STOMACH

Grk.	*γαστήρ, κοιλία; (στόμαχος)*	Goth.	*wamba; qiþus*	Lith.	*pilvas; skilvis, pilvėlis*
NG	*κοιλιά; στομάχι*	ON	*kviðr, vǫmb; magi*	Lett.	*vēders; pazirds*
Lat.	*venter; stomachus*	Dan.	*bug; mave*	ChSl.	*črěvo, ątroba*
It.	*ventre; stomaco*	Sw.	*buk; mage*	SCr.	*trbuh; želudac*
Fr.	*ventre; estomac*	OE	*wamb, innoþ; maga*	Boh.	*břich(o), život; žaludek*
Sp.	*vientre; estómago*	ME	*wombe, beli; mawe, stomak*	Pol.	*brzuch, żywot; żołądek*
Rum.	*pîntece; stomac*	NE	*belly; stomach*	Russ.	*brjucho, život; želudok*
Ir.	*brū, bolg; eclas, gaile*	Du.	*buik; maag*	Skt.	*udara-, jaṭhara-*
NIr.	*bolg; goile*	OHG	*wamba, būh; mago*	Av.	*udara-, maršū-*
W.	*bol, bola; cylla*	MHG	*būch, wambe; mage*		
Br.	*kof; poulgalon*	NHG	*bauch; magen*		

Words for 'belly' were used alike for the external 'belly' and the internal 'belly, stomach', and most of them are still familiar in the latter sense, in biblical language ("the whale's belly") and in common, partly vulgar, speech. Either the external or internal application may be the more original etymologically. Many of the same or related words were also used for 'womb' (4.47).

Words that denote more specifically the internal organ, the 'stomach', are added in the list after a semicolon. Some of these, like the Gmc. group, ON *magi*, etc. are old and have always been in common use. Some are less common, except in medical use, than the old words for 'belly', while NE *stomach* has virtually replaced *belly* in polite use.

Words that properly denote 'big belly, paunch', like It. *pancia*, Fr. *panse*, Sp. *panza*, NHG *wanst*, Russ. *puzo*, are not included in the list, except where such a word has become the usual one for 'belly', as Rum. *pîntece*.

1. IE *udero-, *wedero-. This is at least a convenient heading for a group of words for 'belly' or 'womb' which are obviously related, though showing phonetic disparity which must be due in part to analogical influence. Root connection wholly uncertain. Walde-P. 1.190 f. Ernout-M. 1085, 1141.

Skt. *udara-*, Av. *udara-* (in a cpd.) 'belly'; Lett. *vēders*, OPruss. *weders* 'belly' (Lith. *vėdaras* 'fish entrails', 'a kind of sausage', also 'stomach' in Donalit.?); Grk. ὅδερος· γαστήρ (Hesych.); Lat. *venter* 'belly' (> It., Fr. *ventre*, Sp. *vientre* 'belly'; Rum. *vintre* now 'abdomen'), Lat. *uterus* 'womb' (> It. *utero*, etc. only as learned words), in which the *t* of both forms is easily explained as due to the influence of words with suffix *-ter*, *-tero-*, like Lat. **interus* (*interior*) 'inner', Grk. ἔντερα 'entrails', etc., and perh. the *n* of *venter* likewise.

2. Grk. γαστήρ (in Hom. 'belly' in connection with wounds, most frequently 'stomach' in connection with hunger, once 'womb'; in Aristot. 'belly' and 'womb', while κοιλία is 'stomach'), by dissim. fr. *γραστήρ : γράω 'gnaw, eat', γράστις 'fodder', Skt. *gras-* 'devour'. Walde-P. 1.657 f. Otherwise Boisacq 141.

Grk. κοιλία, used for various cavities in the body, but esp. 'belly' (not in Hom.; in Aristot. the technical word for the 'stomach' as organ; in NT more common than γαστήρ for both 'belly' and 'womb'; so in NG), fr. κοῖλος 'hollow' : Lat. *cavus* 'hollow', etc. Walde-P. 1.366 f.

Grk. στόμαχος, deriv. of στόμα 'mouth' (4.24), hence, as orig. the passage from the mouth, 'throat, gullet' (see 4.29), later 'orifice of the stomach' and finally 'stomach' (στόμαχος occurs only once in NT, namely 1 Tim. 5.23, likewise the only occurrence of *stomach* in the English Bible; elsewhere, as Mt. 12.40 'whale's belly', κοιλία, likewise in the translations NE *belly*, NHG *bauch*, Lith. *pilvas*, etc.). Hence Lat. *stomachus* > It. *stomaco*, Sp. *estómago*, Rum. *stomac*, Fr. *estomac* > ME *stomak*, NE *stomach*.

3. Lat. *venter*, etc., above, 1.

Rum. *pîntece* 'belly, womb', like It. *pancia*, OFr. *panche* (> ME *paunche*, NE *paunch*), *pance*, Fr. *panse*, Sp. *panza* 'big belly, paunch', fr. Lat. *pantex*, mostly pl. *pantices* 'entrails, bowels'. REW 6207.

4. Ir. *brū* 'belly, womb', NIr. *brū* mostly 'womb', W. *bru* 'womb' : Ir. *bruinne*, W. *bron* 'breast', W. *bryn* 'hill', Goth. *brusts* 'breast', etc., all with common notion of 'swelling'. Walde-P. 2.197 f.

Ir. *bolg* 'bag, bellows, belly', NIr. *bolg* 'belly, bag', W. *bol*, *bola* 'belly' : Goth. *balgs* 'leather bag' (Grk. ἀσκός), ON *belgr* 'skin, leather bag', OHG *balg*, OE *bælg* 'husk, pod', ME *bali*, *beli* 'belly', NE *belly* (and *bellows*), all fr. IE **bhelĝh-*, extension of **bhel-* in Lat. *follis* 'leather bag', Lat. *flāre*, OE *blāwan* 'blow', etc. Walde-P. 2.182 f., 2.177 f.

Br. *kof* 'belly, womb', obs. W. *coff* 'hollow trunk' (Pughe), also 'belly' (Evans), etym.? On Henry's deriv. fr. Lat. **cofus*, *cophinus* 'basket', see Loth, Mots lat. 151.

OIr. *eclas* 'stomach' (Thes. 1.687), NIr. *eaglais* 'bird's stomach', etym.?

MIr. *gaile*, NIr. *goile* 'stomach' : Ir. *gelim* 'devour', Lat. *gula*, OE *ceole* 'throat', etc. (4.29)? So Macbain 200, but phonetically difficult and not included in Stokes 112 or Walde-P. 1.621 ff.

W. *cylla* (arch. *cwll*) 'stomach', etym.?

Br. *poullkalon*, *poulgalon* (cf. Vallée s.v. *estomac*), cpd. of *poull* 'hole, hollow' and *kalon* 'heart' (4.44).

5. Goth. *wamba* 'belly, womb', ON *vǫmb* 'belly', OE *wamb*, *womb*, ME *wambe*, *wombe* 'belly, womb', in latter sense NE *womb*; OHG *wamba*, MHG *wambe* 'belly, womb', NHG *wamme* 'belly of animal's skin', dial. 'belly', outside connections? Walde-P. 1.191. Feist 549.

Goth. *qiþus* 'womb', once 'stomach', ON *kviðr* 'belly, womb', OE *cwiþ* 'womb' : ON *koddi* 'pillow', OE *codd* 'bag, pod' (ME *cod* rarely 'belly' or 'testicle'), prob. Lat. (fr. Oscan) *botulus* 'sausage', all with common notion of 'swollen, rounded' object. Walde-P. 1.671. Falk-Torp 606. Feist 390.

Dan. *bug*, Sw. *buk* (ON *būkr* 'trunk'),

OE *būc* (rarely 'belly', mostly 'jug'), Du. *buik*, OHG *būh*, MHG *būch*, NHG *bauch*, all 'belly', root connection disputed, either : Skt. *bhuj-*, Goth. *biugan* 'bend', etc., IE **bheug-*, **bheugh-*, or : words denoting 'swelling', etc. containing a syllable **bhu-*. Walde-P. 2.146 (with preference for latter connection, that is, with 2.114 ff.). Falk-Torp 113.

OE *innoþ* 'belly, womb', lit. 'inner part' : OE *innan* 'within', etc.

ME *bali*, NE *belly* : Ir. *bolg*, etc. (above, 4).

ON *magi*, Dan. *mave*, Sw. *mage*, OE *maga*, ME *mawe* (NE *maw* only of animals), Du. *maag*, OHG *mago*, NHG *magen* 'stomach', prob. : Lith. *makas* 'purse', W. *megin* 'bellows'. Walde-P. 2.225.

6. Lith. *pilvas* 'belly', etym.? Leskien, Ablaut 359 : Lith. *pilti* 'pour', *pilnas* 'full'. Better (though ultimately perh. the same root) : Lat. *pēlvis* 'basin', Grk. πέλλα 'bowl, pail', etc. (Walde-P. 2.56 ff., without *pilvas*). Cf. the modern anatomical application of *pelvis*.

Lett. *vēders*, above, 1.

Lith. *skilvis* 'stomach' (so in translations of NT, 1 Tim. 5.23; cf. also Kurschat, Lalis, Gailius-Šlaža, etc.), perh. (cf. Lett. *škilva*, 'maw of birds') : Lith. *skelti* 'split', etc. Walde-P. 2.594.

Lith. *pilvėlis*, *pilvukas* (given for 'magen' by Senn, Lit. Sprachl., pp. 42, 267), dims. of *pilvas* 'belly'.

Lett. *pazirds* 'stomach', cpd. of *pa* 'under' and *zirds* 'heart'. Mühl.-Endz. 3.98.

7. ChSl. *črěvo* 'belly, womb', Boh. *střevo*, SCr. *crijevo*, Pol. *trzewo* 'intestine', OPruss. *kermens* 'body', root connection? Walde-P. 2.577. Berneker 150. Brückner 581.

ChSl. *ątroba* 'belly'(?), 'womb' (much less frequent than *črěvo*, Jagić, Entstehungsgesch. 421; the examples are where Grk. κοιλία is 'womb', but this may be accidental), SCr., Bulg., Russ. *utroba* 'womb' (in church language), Pol. *wątroba* 'liver', all : ChSl. *jętro* 'liver', etc. (4.45).

SCr. *trbuh* 'belly', Pol. dial. *telbuch* id., Russ. *trebucha* 'intestine', etc., etym.? Miklosich 364. Brückner 567.

Boh. *břich*, *břicho*, Pol. *brzuch*, Russ. *brjucho* 'belly' : Goth. *brusts* 'breast', etc. (4.40), orig. 'swelling'. Walde-P. 2.198. Berneker 95 ff.

Boh. *život*, Pol. *żywot* 'belly, womb', Russ. *život* 'belly' (Lith. *žyvatas* 'womb' fr. Pol. or Russ.), same as the word for 'life', ChSl. *životŭ*, Boh. *život*, etc. (4.74), applicable to either 'belly' (as 'stomach') or 'womb', as the source of life.

ChSl. (late) *želądŭkŭ*, SCr. *želudac*, etc., general Slavic for 'stomach', etym.? Against deriv. fr. *żelądĭ* 'acorn' (Brückner 665), see Meillet, Etudes 322 ff.

8. Skt., Av. *udara-*, above, 1.

Skt. *jaṭhara-* 'belly, womb' : Goth. *kilþei* 'womb', OE *cild* 'child', fr. IE **gel-t-*, beside **gel-* in words for round objects. Walde-P. 1.614. Feist 311.

Av. *maršū-* 'belly', perh. orig. 'bag' (cf. Ir. *bolg*, etc., above, 4), and the source, or from the same source as, Grk. μάρσιπος 'bag, pouch'. Buck, IF 25.257.

4.47 WOMB

Grk.	*ὑστέρα, γαστήρ, κοιλία,* etc.	Goth.	*wamba, qiþus, kilþei*	Lith.	*žyvatas*
NG	*κοιλιά, μήτρα*	ON	*kviðr*	Lett.	*mātes miesas, mātes klēpis*
Lat.	*uterus, vulva*	Dan.	*moderliv*	ChSl.	*črěvo, ątroba*
It.	*matrice, madre, utero*	Sw.	*moderlif*	SCr.	*materica*
Fr.	*sein, matrice, utérus*	OE	*hrif, innoþ*	Boh.	*život, matka*
Sp.	*matriz, madre, utero*	ME	*wombe*	Pol.	*żywot, łono*
Rum.	*pîntece*	NE	*womb*	Russ.	*matka*
Ir.	*brū*	Du.	*baarmuoder*	Skt.	*garbha-, yoni-*
NIr.	*brū*	OHG	*(h)ref, wamba*	Av.	*garəwa-, barəθrī-*
W.	*croth, bru*	MHG	*barmuoter, muoterlīp (wambe)*		
Br.	*kof*	NHG	*mutterleib, gebärmutter, schoss*		

The majority of the words for 'womb' are related to those for 'belly' and so have been discussed in 4.46. Of the others the commonest source is 'mother', while some are words for 'body' or 'lap' used in specialized sense, or of various other sources.

1. Grk. μήτρα (in Aristot. HA 510[b] distinguished from ὑστέρα or δελφύς 'womb' as the 'tube and opening of the womb'; in NG the technical word for 'womb', pop. κοιλιά); Lat. *mātrīx* 'breeding animal', late 'womb' (> It. *matrice*, etc.); SCr. *materica*, all derivs. of word for 'mother', as It., Sp. *madre*, Dan. *moder*, Boh., Russ. *matka* 'mother' also used for 'womb'. Cf. also NHG *mutterleib*, *gebärmutter*, etc.

Grk. ὑστέρα (the most usual technical term, Hipp., Aristot., etc.; cf. also ὕστρος· γαστήρ Hesych.), apparently : ὕστερος 'latter, behind', Skt. *uttara-* 'upper', *ud* 'upwards', so orig. 'back part' or 'upper part'? Or perh. ultimately : Skt. *udara-* 'belly', etc. (4.46) with analogical re-formation. Walde-P. 1.191. Boisacq 1008.

Grk. δελφύς (rare) : Skt. *garbha-*, etc., below, 7.

2. Lat. *volva*, *vulva*, prob. : Lat. *volvere* 'roll', *vola* 'hollow of the hand or foot', Grk. εἴλῡμα 'wrapper', etc. Walde-P. 1.301.

Fr. *sein* 'breast' (fr. Lat. *sinus* 'fold, bosom, lap') also the common expression for 'womb'.

3. W. *croth* (formerly also 'belly') : W. *crwth*, NIr. *cruit* 'hump', Lith. *krutis* 'breast', etc. (4.40). Walde-P. 1.489.

4. OE *hrif* (also sometimes 'belly'; cf. NE *midriff*), OHG (*h*)*ref*, prob. : Lat. *corpus*, Skt. *kṛp-* 'body', etc. (4.41). Walde-P. 1.486.

MHG *muoterlīp*, NHG *mutterleib*, Dan. *moder(s)liv*, *livmoder*, Sw. *moderlif*, *lifmoder*, cpds. of words for 'mother' and 'body' (4.11), the latter also used alone for 'womb' (as NHG *leib* in Luther).

MHG *barmuoter*, NHG *gebärmutter*, Du. *baarmuoder*, cpds. of words for 'bear' and 'mother'.

NHG *schoss* 'lap' (orig. part of a garment), also used for 'womb'. Weigand-H. 2.782.

5. Lett. *mātes miesas* or *mātes klēpis*, lit. 'mother's body' or 'mother's lap', translations of NHG *mutterleib*, *mutterschoss*.

6. Pol. *łono* 'lap' (ChSl. *lono* 'bosom, lap', etc.) also used for 'womb', like NHG *schoss*.

7. Skt. *garbha-*, Av. *garəwa-* : Grk. δελφύς 'womb' (rare), ἀδελφός 'brother' (2.44), with parallel forms in Goth. *kalbō* 'calf' (3.24), and with *r* in Grk. βρέφος 'foetus', etc. Walde-P. 1.692.

Skt. *yoni-* : Skt. *yu-* 'unite'? Uhlenbeck s.v.

Av. *barəθrī-* 'bearer' and 'womb' : Skt. *bhartrī-* 'supporter, mother', fr. Av. *bar-*, Skt. *bhṛ-* 'bear'. Barth. 946.

4.48 EGG

Grk.	*ᾠόν*	Goth.	*ada*	Lith.	*kiaušinis*
NG	*αὐγό*	ON	*egg*	Lett.	*uola*
Lat.	*ōvum*	Dan.	*æg*	ChSl.	*ajĭce*
It.	*uovo*	Sw.	*ägg*	SCr.	*jaje*
Fr.	*œuf*	OE	*ǣg*	Boh.	*vejce*
Sp.	*huevo*	ME	*ey, egg*	Pol.	*jaje, jajo*
Rum.	*ou*	NE	*egg*	Russ.	*jajco*
Ir.	*og*	Du.	*ei*	Skt.	*aṇḍa-*
NIr.	*ubh*	OHG	*ei*	Av.	(**āvaya-*)
W.	*wy*	MHG	*ei*		
Br.	*vi*	NHG	*ei*		

The majority of the words for 'egg' belong to an inherited group.

1. IE **ōwo-, *ōw(e)yo-, *ō(w)yo-*(?). The words grouped here, despite some phonetic problems, prob. reflect an IE word for 'egg' derived fr. the word for 'bird' seen in Lat. *avis*, Skt. *vi-* (3.64). Walde-P. 1.21 ff. Ernout-M. 718. Pedersen 1.66. Falk-Torp 182. Berneker 26.

Grk. **ὠϝεον* (ὤβεα· ὠά. Ἀργεῖοι, Hesych.), ὤεον (Epich.), Lesb. ὤιον, Att. ᾠόν, NG αὐγό (arising in τὰ ᾠά > τ'αυγά like τὰ ὠτία > τ'αυτία, whence αὐτί 'ear'; Hatzidakis Μεσ. 2.322); Lat. *ōvum* (> It. *uovo*, Fr. *œuf*, Sp. *huevo*, Rum. *ou*); Ir. *og*, NIr. *ubh*, W. *wy*, Br. *vi;* Crim. Goth. *ada*, ON *egg*, Dan. *æg*, Sw. *ägg*, OE *ǣg*, ME *ey* (ME, NE *egg* fr. ON), Du., OHG, MHG, NHG *ei;* ChSl. **(j)aje, ajĭce*, SCr. *jaje*, Boh. *vejce*, Pol. *jaje, jajo*, Russ. *jajco;* Av. **āvaya-*, NPers. *xāya-;* Arm. *ju*.

2. Lith. *kiaušinis* (also *kiaušis*) : Lith. *kiaušė* 'skull', Skt. *koça-* 'container, cup, pod' (also rarely 'egg'), *sku-* 'cover', etc. Walde-P. 2.549.

Lett. *uola* (also 'round stone, pebble'; Lith. *uola* 'whetstone, rock') : Lett. *velt*, Lat. *volvere* 'turn', Lith. *apvalus*, ON *valr* 'round', etc. (Walde-P. 1.298 ff., without *uola*). Mühl.-Endz. 4.416.

Lith. *pautas*, Lett. *pauts*, formerly 'egg', now 'testicle' (Lett. dial. 'egg') : Lith. *pusti* 'blow, swell up', Lett. *pūte* 'blister, pustule', etc. Walde-P. 2.80. Mühl.-Endz. 3.130.

3. Skt. *aṇḍa-* (also 'testicle'), etym.? Possibly fr. **andra-* and : ChSl. **jędro, jadro* 'kernel, testicle' (but cf. 4.49). So Uhlenbeck, s.v., Barth., IF 3.175.

4.49 TESTICLE

Grk.	ὄρχις	Goth.	....	Lith.	*pautas*
NG	ὄρχις (lit.), ἀρχίδι	ON	*eista, bǫllr* (*hreðjar* pl.)	Lett.	*pauts*
Lat.	*testiculus, testis* (*cāleus*)	Dan.	*testikel, sten, rædder* (pl.)	ChSl.	*isto, *mądo, lono*
It.	*testicolo, coglione*	Sw.	*testikel, sten*	SCr.	*mudo, jajce*
Fr.	*testicule, couille*	OE	*herþan, sceallan, beallucas* (all pl.)	Boh.	*varle, mudo, kulka*
Sp.	*testiculo, cojon*	ME	*ballok, stone*	Pol.	*mudo, jądra* (pl.)
Rum.	*testicul, boş, coĭŭ*	NE	*testicle* (*ballock, ball*)	Russ.	*mudo, jajco*
Ir.	*macraille, uirge*	Du.	*teelbal, zaadbal*	Skt.	*aṇḍa-, muṣka-*
NIr.	*magairle*	OHG	*hodo*	Av.	*ərəzi* (du.)
W.	*caill*	MHG	*hode*		
Br.	*kell*	NHG	*hode*		

The words for 'testicle', though naturally they are used mostly in the plural (or old dual), are listed in the singular unless otherwise noted. The Irish forms are singular collectives 'scrotum, testicles'. Of the numerous slang terms, only a few that seemed the most important are included in the list. The commonest are words for 'balls, stones, nuts, eggs'.

1. IE **orĝhi-*, etc. Walde-P. 1.182 f.

Grk. ὄρχις, late dim. ὀρχίδιον (> NG ἀρχίδι); Ir. *uirge* (prob.); Av. *ərəzi* (dual, sg. 'scrotum'); Arm. *orjikʽ* (pl.); Alb. *herdhe;* cf. Skt. *āvir-ṛjīka-* 'with protruding testicles'.

2. Lat. *testiculus* (whence the literary Romance words, It. *testicolo*, etc., and Dan., Sw. *testikel*, NE *testicle*), dim. of *testis* also 'testicle' (Plaut., etc.), but the same word as *testis* 'witness'. This peculiar use of *testēs* is prob. in imitation of Grk. παραστάται 'testicles' (Plaut. Com., etc.), wrongly associated with the legal sense of παραστάτης 'supporter, defender' and so with (cf. *superstes* =) *testis* 'witness', instead of with the use of παραστάται for twin 'supporting pillars', 'props of a mast', etc., hence 'testicles', just as δίδυμοι 'twins' was also used in this sense (Galen, etc.). Cf. (but without the semantic explanation proposed here), Keller, Zur lat. Sprachgeschichte 144, Niedermann I Anz. 19.35, the latter assuming direct application of 'witness' to 'testicle'(!) and quoting Fr. slang *témoins* 'testicles' (student's slang influenced by Latin associations?).

Lat. *cōleus* (> Fr. *couille*, Rum. *coĭŭ;* VLat. **cōleō, -ōnis* > It. *coglione*, Sp. *cojon*), etym. dub. Walde-H. 1.244. REW 2036, 2038.

Rum. *boş* (or *boaşe* pl. tant.), orig. 'scrotum', fr. VLat. **bursa* 'leather bag' (> It. *borsa*, etc.), Grk. βύρσα 'hide, leather'. REW 1432. Puşcariu 210.

3. Ir. *macraille*, NIr. *magairle*, prob. cpd. of which the first member is related to Ir. *macc*, W. *mab* 'son', etc., but final member? Pedersen 1.128.

Ir. *uirge* 'testicle', not 'penis' (K. Meyer, Ber. Preuss. Akad. 1912.800), see above, 1 and Pedersen 2.662.

W. *caill*, Br. *kell* : OE *sceallan*, OFris. *skal* 'testicles', possibly as 'scrotum' fr. 'leather bag', fr. the root **skel-* 'cut, split' (cf. ON *hreðjar*, etc., below, 4). Walde-P. 2.592.

4. ON *eista*, prob. : ChSl. *isto*, below, 6.

ON *bǫllr*, usually 'ball' but also 'testicle', OE *beallucas* (pl.), ME *ballok*, NE *ballock* (but more commonly *balls* in vulgar speech) : OHG *ballo, balla*, etc., 'ball', Lat. *follis* 'leather bag, bellows', Grk. φαλλός 'phallic emblem', all from a root **bhel-* 'swell'. Walde-P. 2.177 ff.

ON *hreðjar* (pl.) 'scrotum with testicles' (NIcel. 'testicles'), Dan. *rædder*, OE *herþan* 'testicles', prob. orig. 'scrotum' as 'leather bag' : OE *heorþa* 'deerskin', OHG *herdo* 'vellus', Lat. *cortex* 'bark, rind', *scortum* 'skin, hide' (here also late *scrōtum?*). Walde-P. 2.578. Falk-Torp 931.

OE *sceallan* : W. *caill*, above, 3.

Dan., Sw. *sten*, as also ME, NE *stone* frequently used for 'testicle'.

Du. *teelbal, zaadbal*, cpds. of *telen* 'beget', and *zaad* 'seed' with *bal* 'ball' (cf. above).

OHG *hodo*, MHG, NHG *hode*, prob. : W. *cwd* 'scrotum', Grk. σκῦτος 'leather', Lat. *cutis* 'skin', OE *hyd* 'skin, hide', etc., fr. IE **skeu-t-* 'cover' (semantic development from 'leather bag', 'scrotum' as in ON *hreðjar* and W. *caill*, etc., above). Walde-P. 2.549. Falk-Torp 425.

5. Lith. *pautas*, Lett. *pauts*, orig. 'egg' (4.48).

6. ChSl. *isto* (pl. *istesa* 'kidneys', ORuss. du. *jestesě* 'testicles'), prob. : ON *eista* 'testicle' (both combined under

**id-s-to-, *oid-s-to-*) and Grk. οἶδος 'swelling, tumor', οἶδμα 'swelling', etc. Walde-P. 1.166. Berneker 434 f.

ChSl. **jędro*, Russ.-ChSl. *jadro* 'kernel, testicle', Pol. *jądro* 'kernel', pl. *jądra* 'testicles' (Boh., Russ. *jadro* 'kernel'), etym.? Perh. as orig. 'swelling' and fr. a nasalized **ind-* : ChSl. *isto*, etc., above, but other combinations, as with Skt. *aṇḍa-* 'egg, testicle', possible. Walde-P. 1.166. Berneker 455 f.

ChSl. *lono* 'bosom, lap' (as in Russ., Pol., etc.), late ChSl. also 'testicle', etym. dub. Walde-P. 1.158. Berneker 732.

ChSl. **mądo*, late *mudo*, SCr., Russ. (> Pol.) *mudo*, Boh. *moud*, etym. dub. Walde-P. 2.232. Miklosich 201.

SCr. *jajce* 'little egg', Russ. *jajco*, 'egg' (4.48), also testicle.

Boh. *varle*, etym.?

Boh. *kulka* (also esp. 'bullet'), dim. of *koule* 'ball', fr. LG *kūle*. Berneker 641.

7. Skt. *aṇḍa-* (du. *aṇḍāu* in AV.), same word as for 'egg' (4.48).

Skt. *muṣka-*, apparently dim. to *mūṣ-* 'mouse', from the shape (cf. Lat. *musculus* 'muscle', etc.). Walde-P. 2.313.

Av. *ərəzi*, above, 1.

4.492 PENIS

It would be futile to repeat in a list the usual euphemistic phrases like Lat. *membrum virīle*, Fr. *membre viril*, NE *male organ*, NHG *männliches glied*, Russ. *mužkoj člen*, etc.; and it would be difficult to make a selection from the innumerable vulgar terms in common or occasional use, many of which, moreover, are of obscure origin. Here are noted those of an inherited group and some others.

1. IE **pes-, *pesos-*. Walde-P. 2.68. Ernout-M. 752.

Grk. πέος (Aristoph. +); Lat. *pēnis* (fr. **pes-ni-s*, otherwise Walde-P.); Skt. *pasas-* (AV); prob. OHG *faselt*, MHG *visel;* perh. here Grk. πόσθη ('penis' in Aristoph., 'foreskin' in medical writers) analyzed as πόσ-θη.

2. Grk. αἰδοῖον (Hom. αἰδοῖα 'private parts'; αἰδοῖον in Aristot. the regular word for either male or female part), fr. αἰδώς 'shame'. Cf. NHG *schamteil*, etc.

3. Among the semantic sources of vulgar terms are:

'Pointed object'. Dan. *pik*, Sw. *pick* (Hellquist 760); NE *prick* (NED *prick*, sb. 17); W., Corn. *cal*, Br. *kalc'h* (: W. *col* 'sting', Ir. *colg* 'sword', Pedersen 1.105); W. *llost* ('sting, dart, penis'); Ir. *gae* 'spear' (20.26) and 'penis' (Laws, Gloss. 438); OE *pintel* (NE *pintle* 'a kind of pin or bolt'), MLG *pint, pitte*, Sw. dial. *pitt* (Falk-Torp 861); OHG *zumpfo*, MHG *zumpfe* (prob. : MLG *timpe*, Du. dial. *tump* 'tip, point', nasalized form of that in NE *tip*); Russ. *chuj* perh. : *chvoj* 'pine needle' (Berneker 408); Skt. *çepa-, çepas-* (: Lat. *cippus* 'stake, post', etc., Walde-H. 1.219); Sp. *carajo* (prob. fr. VLat. **caracium*, Grk. χαράκιον, dim. of χάραξ 'pointed stake' (REW 1862); perh. here W. *pidyn*, Br. *pidenn* (Henry 223).

'Rod' or 'stalk'. Lat. *verpa* (cf. Grk. ῥαπίς 'rod', Walde-P. 1.276); Lat. *virga*, Fr. *verge;* NIr. *slat;* ME *zerde*, NE *yard* (NED *yard*, sb.[2] 11); Du. *roede*, NHG *rute;* ChSl. *kočanŭ*, Alb. *kotsh* (Berneker 536); Av. *fravaxs-* (Barth. 99.).

'Swelling.' Lett. *pimpis* (: *pempt* 'swell', Mühl.-Endz. 2.218); Boh. *pyj* (prob. : Lith. *pusti* 'swell', Lat. *praepūtium* 'foreskin', Walde-P. 2.80 f.); VLat. *pūtium* (abstracted fr. *praepūtium*) > Rum. *puţă*, NG πούτσα (REW 6881).

'Tail' (4.18). Lat. *cauda;* ME *tayl* (but oftener 'pudendum', NED *tail* sb. 5c); NHG *schwanz, zagel*.

'Cock' (3.52, but prob. through the secondary sense of 'stopcock, tap' or 'cock' of a gun). NE *cock* (NED s.v. 20), NHG *hahn* (Grimm s.v. 4), SCr. *kurac, kokot*, Pol. *kurek* (Berneker 650).

'Tool'. NE *tool* (NED *tool* sb. 21), NIr. *glēas* ('means, instrument').

'Weapon'. OE *wǣpen* 'weapon' (20.21) and 'penis', whence *wǣpned* 'male'.

'Power'. OHG *gimaht*, MHG *gemaht*, NHG *gemacht* (: OHG *maht* 'power', Weigand-H. 1.671).

'Creation, form.' ON *skǫpin* (pl., with article, of *skap* 'state, condition'), OE *(ge)sceap* 'private parts' of either sex (NE dial. *shape* 'female parts', NED s.v. 16). Falk-Torp 976.

'Organ for urinating'. Skt. *medhra-* (AV +), fr. *mih-* (4.65), Lith. *mizius*, Lett. *mīslis* (Leskien, Ablaut 279).

Miscellaneous and doubtful. Lat. *mūtō*, Ir. *moth* (Walde-P. 2.312. Ernout-M. 649); Lat. *mentula* (> It. *minchia*), etym. dub. (Walde-H. 2.72. REW 5513) : It. *cazzo* (: *cazza* 'crucible'?); Rum. *pulă* (Tiktin 1277 f.); Ir. *bīach* (Walde-P. 1.667); Ir. *bot*, NIr. *bod* : W. *both* 'nave of a wheel, boss of a shield', perh. ChSl. *gvozdĭ* 'nail' (Pokorny, Z. celt. Ph. 16.405. Walde-H. 1.574); OE *teors*, ME, NE *terse, tarse* (NED *tarse* sb.[1]), OHG, MHG *zers* (perh. : OE *teran* 'tear,' etc. Walde-P. 1.802); Lith. *bybis;* Pol. *kutas* ('tassle', Berneker 653) : Skt. *çiçna-* (Walde-P. 1.402); Skt. *kapṛt(h)-* (Walde-P. 1.348, 2.49).

4.51 BREATHE; BREATH

Grk.	πνέω; πνεῦμα, πνοή	Goth.	*anan*	Lith.	*kvėpuoti; kvapas*
NG	ἀναπνέω; ανασαίνω; πνοή, ἀνάσα	ON	*anda; ǫnd, andi*	Lett.	*dvašuot, elpūt; dvaša, elpe*
Lat.	*spīrāre; anima, spīritus*	Dan.	*aande; ande*	ChSl.	*dychati; dychanĭje, duchŭ*
It.	*respirare, fiatare; fiato, respiro*	Sw.	*andas; ande*	SCr.	*disati, dihati; dah*
Fr.	*respirer; haleine, souffle*	OE	*orþian, ēþian; oroþ, ǣþm*	Boh.	*dýchati; dech*
Sp.	*respirar, resollar; aliento, huelgo*	ME	*brethe; bre(e)th*	Pol.	*dychać; dech*
Rum.	*răsufla; răsuflare*	NE	*breathe; breath*	Russ.	*dyšat'; dychanie*
Ir.	*doberim anāl; anāl*	Du.	*ademen; adem*	Skt.	*an-, çvas-; ana-, çvāsa-, ātman-*
NIr.	*anāluighim; anāl*	OHG	*ātumōn; ātum*	Av.	(*ånti-, parånti-*)
W.	*anadlu; anadl*	MHG	*ātemen; ātem*		
Br.	*alanat; alan*	NHG	*atmen; atem, hauch*		

A few of the words listed apply only to the exhalation of breath, as NHG *hauch* in contrast to *atem*, or are mostly so used. This was originally true of most, and probably all, of the others, as shown by the usual associations with 'blow, exhale, pant', etc.

Noun and verb are usually parallel, but not always, and both are listed.

1. IE **an-*. Walde-P. 1.56 ff. Ernout-M. 53 f. Walde-H. 1.49. Falk-Torp. 5.

Lat. *anima;* Ir. *anāl*, W. *anadl*, Br. *alan* (with metathesis), whence the verbs Ir. *anāluighim*, W. *anadlu*, Br. *alanat;* Goth. *anan* (only *uz-anan* ἐκπνεῖν Mk. 15.37, 39), ON *anda*, Dan. *aande*, Sw. *andas* (refl.), with nouns ON *ǫnd, andi*, Dan. *aande*, Sw. *ande;* OE *orþian* (fr. *oroþ* 'breath', this fr. **uz-anþ-*); Skt. *an-* but mostly cpd. *pra-an-*, with nouns *ana-, prāṇa-*, Av. *ånti, parånti-* 'inhalation', 'exhalation' (fr. **anti-* 'breath' with *ā* and *parā-*) : Grk. ἄνεμος 'wind', ChSl. *vonja* 'odor', *ąchati* 'odorari', etc.

Here also Fr. *haleine*, fr. late Lat. *alēna;* Sp. *aliento* fr. *alentar* 'breathe, encourage' (fr. *alēnitāre) derivs. (with metathesis) of Lat. anhēlāre 'breathe hard, puff, pant', fr. an- + *anslā- (cf. hālāre 'breathe out, exhale', with unetymological h-). REW 472, 473.

2. Grk. πνέω (ἀναπνέω 'take breath', in NG the usual form for 'breathe'; cf. Fr. respirer, etc., below) with the sbs. πνεῦμα, πνοή : ON fnȳsa 'sneeze, snort', OE fnēosan 'sneeze', etc., IE *pneu- in words for 'puff, pant, breathe, etc.'. Walde-P. 2.85 (with other similar groups with initial *pn-, all of imitative orig.).

NG ἀνασαίνω (with sb. ἀνάσα, backformation), deriv. of class. Grk. ἄνεσις 'relaxation' (: ἀνίημι 'let go'), through ἀνεσαίνω, then ἀνα- by pop. etym. 'Relax' > 'catch one's breath', then also simply 'breathe'. Hatzidakis, Μεσ. 2.58, ftn.

3. Lat. spīrāre (cpd. respīrāre 'breathe again, take breath, etc.') > It. respirare, Fr. respirer, Sp. respirar), with sb. spīritus (It. respiro fr. respīrāre) prob. : ChSl. piskati 'whistle', SCr. pištati 'hiss', ON fīsa 'pedere' (4.64), etc., IE *(s)peis- (imitative). Walde-P. 2.11.

It. fiatare, deriv. of fiato, fr. Lat. flātus 'blowing, snorting, breeze' sometimes also 'breath' : flāre 'blow', etc. REW 3359.

Fr. souffle (also 'wind, blast') backformation fr. souffler 'blow, pant' (= Sp. sollar, Rum. sufla, etc.) fr. Lat. sufflāre 'blow' (10.38); Sp. resollar, Rum. răsufla (whence sb. răsuflare), fr. new cpd. parallel to Lat. respīrāre. REW 8430. Puşcariu 1447.

Sp. huelgo (Port. folego), back-formation to Sp. holgar (Port. folgar) 'rest, cease from labor', orig. 'stop for breath' from 'pant', fr. VLat. follicāre 'swell or move as a bellows', deriv. of Lat. follis 'bellows'. REW 3417.

4. Ir. do-berim anál lit. 'give breath'; for anál, etc., see above, 1.

5. Goth. anan, OE orþian, etc., above, 1.

OE ǣþm, Du. adem, OHG ātum, MHG, NHG atem, whence the vbs. OE ēþian, Du. ademen, OHG ātumōn, etc. : Skt. ātman- 'breath, soul, life', root connection? Walde-P. 1.118.

ME breth, breeth, NE breath (whence vb. ME brethe, NE breathe), fr. OE brǣþ 'odor, smell, scent' : OHG brādam 'exhalation, heat' (fr. the root in ON brāðr 'heated', OE brǣdan, OHG brātan 'bake', etc.). The meaning 'breath' comes by specialization, either of 'exhalation' (the sense 'exhalation, vapor, steam' common in ME). Walde-P. 2.158. NED s.v. breath.

NHG hauch, fr. hauchen, MHG hūchen 'blow the breath, breathe out', of imitative orig. Weigand-H. 1.820.

6. Lith. kvėpuoti, kvapas : kvėpti 'blow the breath', kvepéti 'smell, emit an odor', Lett. kvēpt 'steam, smoke', Grk. καπνός 'smoke', Lat. vapor 'steam', etc. Specialization of 'exhalation'. Walde-P. 1.380.

Lett. dvašuot, dvaša (Lith. dusti 'get out of breath', dvēsti 'expire, die', dvēsuoti 'pant', dvasia 'spirit' also 'breath'), ChSl. dychati (duchati 'blow') with sbs. dychanǐje, duchŭ, etc., general Slavic, fr. IE *dhwes-, *dhus-, extension of *dheu- with base *dhū- 'shake, agitate', Grk. θύω 'rage, seethe', etc. Walde-P. 1.846. Berneker 234 ff., 249.

Lett. elpēt, fr. the noun elpe, this prob. through 'weak breath' or 'pant' (cf. also Lett. alpa 'moment of time') : Lith. alpti 'faint', alpnas 'weak', this perh. : Skt. alpa- 'small'. Mühl.-Endz. 1.568.

7. Skt. an-, ana-, Av. ånti-, parånti-, above, 1.

Skt. çvas-, çvāsa- : Av. suši- 'the lungs', Lat. querī 'lament, bewail', ON hvǣsa, OE hwǣsan 'pant', etc. Walde-P. 1.474.

Skt. ātman-, : OE ǣþm, etc., above, 5.

4.52 YAWN, GAPE

Grk.	χάσκω, χασμάομαι	Goth.	....	Lith.	žiovauti, -žioti
NG	χάσκω, χασμουριοῦμαι	ON	gīna, gapa	Lett.	žāvāties
Lat.	hiāre	Dan.	gabe	ChSl.	zinǫti, zijati
It.	sbadigliare	Sw.	gapa	SCr.	žijevati
Fr.	bâiller, bayer	OE	gīnan, ginian, gānian	Boh.	zívati
Sp.	bostezar	ME	ȝone, yane, gape	Pol.	ziewać
Rum.	căsca	NE	yawn, gape	Russ.	zevat'
Ir.	mēnaigim	Du.	gapen, geeuwen	Skt.	jr̥mbh-.
NIr.	doghním mēanfadhach	OHG	ginēn, giēn, giwēn, etc.	Av.	....
W.	dylyfu gen	MHG	ginen, geinen, gewen, etc.		
Br.	dislevi gen, bazailhat	NHG	gähnen, gaffen		

The primary notion of the words listed here is 'open the mouth wide'. Many of them may be extended to 'open wide' in general (of the earth, etc.). Nearly all of them show secondary associations with mental attitudes of which the action is indicative, namely wonder, stupidity, or fatigue. In such secondary associations they may be differentiated, as NE yawn (with fatigue) and gape (indicating wonder or stupidity; hence also 'stare at' with open mouth, as usually NHG gaffen; but gape formerly and still locally 'yawn'), or be restricted to one or another of these notions.

1. IE *ĝhē(i)-, *ĝhī-, *ĝhiā-. Walde-P. 1.548 ff. Ernout-M. 453 f. Walde-H. 1.648.

Grk. χάσκω (late χαίνω), χασμάω, -άομαι (through χάσμα 'open mouth, yawning space, chasm', or *χασμός), NG χάσκω now 'gape', χασμοῦμαι (lit.) or χασμουριοῦμαι (as if from a *χασμοῦρα, like κλεισοῦρα 'gorge', etc.) now 'yawn'; Lat. hiāre; ON gīna, OE gīnan, ginian, gānian, ME ȝone, yane, gane, NE yawn (NED s.vv. gane, vb. and yawn, vb.), Du. geeuwen, OHG ginēn, ginōn, giēn, giwēn, etc., MHG ginen, geinen, gewen, etc., NHG gähnen; Lith. žiovauti, in cpds. -žioti, Lett. žāvāties; ChSl. zinǫti, zijati (pres. zējǫ and zijajǫ), etc., general Slavic; Toch. A śew (G. S. Lane, Language 21.21).

Here prob. also ON, Sw. gapa, Dan. gabe (ME, NE gape fr. Norse), Du. gapen, MHG, NHG gaffen, fr. an extension of the same root, as if IE *ghǝ-b- (*ghǝ- as in Grk. χάσκω). Walde-P. 2.552. Falk-Torp 293 f.

2. OFr. baaillier, Fr. bâiller, fr. a late Lat. bataclāre (gl.), also It. sbadigliare, with different formation, but both derivs. of VLat. *batāre (> OFr. baer, beer, Fr. bayer 'gape', etc.) fr. an imitative ba. REW 986, 988. Wartburg 1.281 ff., 287.

Sp. bostezar, a differentiated form (with unexplained st, Cuervo, s.v.; perh. by a blend with a VLat. *ōsticāre by transposition fr. Lat. ōscitāre 'yawn') of bocezar formerly 'yawn' (now 'move the lips', of animals eating), Port. bocejar 'yawn' : It. boccheggiare 'gasp' (of fish out of water), dial. boccheare 'yawn', all derivs. of bo(c)ca 'mouth' (4.24).

Rum. căsca, fr. Grk. χάσκω (above, 1). Tiktin 305.

3. Ir. mēnaigim, NIr. mēanfuighim (not used; rather doghním mēanfadhach 'make a yawn', deriv. of mēn, NIr. mēan 'mouth' (4.24).

W. dylyfu gen, Br. dislevi gen, phrases with gen 'jaw, chin' (4.207), the verbs, used only in these phrases, being cpds. with prefix W. dy-, Br. di(s)-, but second

part obscure (: W. llyfu 'lick' and so first used of animals licking their jaws??). Henry 101.

Br. bazailhat, fr. some Romance form of bataclāre (above, 2), cf. OProv. badal-har, Gascon badalar, etc. Ernault, Glossaire 225.

4. Skt. jr̥mbh-, etym.? (Uhlenbeck 102 : ChSl. glǫbokŭ 'deep', but cf. Berneker 307).

4.53 COUGH (vb.)

Grk.	βήσσω	Goth.	....	Lith.	koséti
NG	βήχω	ON	hōsta	Lett.	kāsēt, klepuot
Lat.	tussīre	Dan.	hoste	ChSl.	kašĭljati
It.	tossire	Sw.	hosta	SCr.	kašljati
Fr.	tousser	OE	hwōstan	Boh.	kašlati
Sp.	toser	ME	coghe, host	Pol.	kaszlać
Rum.	tuşi	NE	cough	Russ.	kašljat'
Ir.	casachtach (sb.)	Du.	hoesten	Skt.	kās-.
NIr.	casachtach (sb.)	OHG	huosten	Av.	....
W.	pesychu	MHG	huosten		
Br.	pasaat	NHG	husten		

Some of the words for 'cough' are clearly of imitative origin, and so probably several of the others in which the appropriateness is less apparent (in some cases 'cough' may be a secondary specialization of an imitative expression applied to various sudden involuntary actions). Noun and verb are regularly parallel, in most cases the verb being derived from the noun. Only the verbal forms are listed, except for Irish, where the verbal notion is expressed only by a phrase containing the noun.

1. IE *kʷās-, prob. of imitative orig. Walde-P. 1.506.

Ir. casachtach 'a cough' (NIr. doghním casachtach 'cough', lit. 'make a cough'), W. pesychu beside peswch 'a cough' (derivs. of arch. pas id.), Br. pasaat (fr. sb. pas); ON hōsta, Dan. hoste, Sw. hosta, OE hwōstan, ME host (NE hoast), Du. hoesten, OHG huosten, MHG huosten, NHG husten; Lith. koséti, Lett. kāsēt, late ChSl. kašĭljati (fr. sb. *kašĭl, kašeli), SCr. kašljati, etc., general Slavic; Skt. kās-.

2. Grk. βήσσω (with sb. βήξ, gen. βηχός), NG βήχω (new pres. to aor. ἔβηξα, with sb. βήξας), perh. of imitative orig., though only the χ seems appropriate.

3. Lat. tussīre (> It. tossire, OFr. toussir, Sp. toser, Rum. tuşi; Fr. tousser fr. the sb.; REW 9015–16) deriv. of tussis 'a cough', prob. : Lat. tundere 'pound, beat', Skt. tud- 'pound, thrust, prick', Goth. stautan, OHG stōzan, etc. 'thrust'. Cf. the use of NE hack (NED s.v. hack, sb.¹ 5) and cough. Walde-P. 2.618.

4. ME co(u)ghe, cowe, NE cough : Du. kuchen, MDu. kuchen, kichen 'cough slightly', NHG keuchen, MHG kīchen 'breathe with difficulty, pant', MHG kūchen 'blow (the breath) hard', Sw. kikna 'choke'; all prob. of imitative orig. NED s.v. Weigand-H. 1.1028.

5. Lett. klepuot (sb. klepus), prob. : klapstēt 'clatter', Lith. klepterēti 'clap', ChSl. klepati 'knock', etc., all of imitative orig. (cf. NE clap, etc.). Mühl.-Endz. 2.214, 223.

4.54 SNEEZE (vb.)

Grk.	πτάρνυμαι	Goth.	....	Lith.	čiaudéti
NG	φτερνίζομαι	ON	hnjōsa-, fnȳsa	Lett.	šk'aut
Lat.	sternuere	Dan.	nyse	ChSl.	....
It.	starnutare	Sw.	nysa	SCr.	kihati
Fr.	éternuer	OE	gefnēsan	Boh.	kýchati
Sp.	estornudar	ME	nese, fnese, snese	Pol.	kichać
Rum.	strănuta	NE	sneeze	Russ.	čichat'
Ir.	sreod (sb.)	Du.	niezen (fniezen)	Skt.	kṣu-
NIr.	sraoth (sb.)	OHG	niosan, niesan	Av.	....
W.	tisian	MHG	niesen		
Br.	strevia	NHG	niesen		

All the words for 'sneeze' are of imitative origin. Noun and verb are regularly parallel. Only the verbal forms are listed, except for Irish, where the verbal notion is expressed only by a phrase containing the noun.

1. IE *pster-, imitative. Walde-P. 2.101. Ernout-M. 974.

Grk. πτάρνυμαι, NG φτερνίζομαι; Lat. sternuere (frequent. sternūtāre > It. starnutare, Fr. éternuer, Sp. estornudar, Rum. strănuta); MIr. sraod, NIr. sraoth (sb.); verb rendered by doghním 'make', cuirim 'put' with sraoth), W. (arch.) trewi, ystrewi, Br. strevia; Arm. p'rnčem.

2. IE *ksneu-(?), as common source of following, all imitative. Walde-P. 1.501 ff., 2.551.

*kseu-, *skeu- in Skt. kṣu-, Lith. čiaudéti, Lett. šk'aut, šk'audēt; *kneus-in ON hnjōsa, ME nēse (NE dial. neeze), Du. niezen, OHG niosan, niesan, MHG,

NHG niesen; *keu-s- (*kūs-) in SCr.-ChSl. kuchnovenije (sb.), SCr. kihati, Boh. kýchati, Pol. kichać; but also with i-vowel, Russ. čichat', etc. Berneker 165, 658.

3. ON fnȳsa, OE gefnēsan (*fnēosan attested in fnēosung 'sternutatio'), ME fnese, Du. fniezen : Grk. πνέω 'breathe, blow', etc., all of imitative orig. Walde-P. 2.85. Falk-Torp 247.

ME snese, NE sneeze, perh. due in part to a misreading of fnese, but supported by new imitative association (or, as Walde-P. 2.551, an inherited form representing *sneus- beside *kneus-, etc., above, 2). NED s.v. sneeze, vb.

4. W. tisian, orig. dub. Formerly (Rhys) considered a loanword fr. Lat. tussīre 'cough' (4.53), but rejected by Loth, Mots lat. 211. Perh. an independent imitative formation?

4.55 SWEAT (sb.)

Grk.	ἱδρώς	Goth.	....	Lith.	prakaitas
NG	ἱδρωτας	ON	sveiti	Lett.	sviedri
Lat.	sūdor	Dan.	sved	ChSl.	potǔ
It.	sudore	Sw.	svett	SCr.	znoj (pot)
Fr.	sueur	OE	swāt	Boh.	pot
Sp.	sudor	ME	swot, swet	Pol.	pot
Rum.	sudoare, năduşeală	NE	sweat	Russ.	pot
Ir.	allas	Du.	zweet	Skt.	sveda-
NIr.	allus	OHG	sveiz	Av.	xᵛaēša-
W.	chwys	MHG	sveiz		
Br.	c'houez	NHG	schweiss		

The majority of the words for 'sweat' belong to an inherited group pointing to an IE word for this notion. In most of the others 'sweat' is a specialization of 'heat'. Noun and verb are regularly parallel, and in this case it is the nouns that are listed.

1. Derivs. of IE *sweid- (in part with r-suffix). Walde-P. 2.521. Ernout-M. 997.

Grk. ἱδρώς, NG ἱδρῶτας (for accent, cf. Hatzidakis, Μεσ. 1.190, 2.91); Lat. sūdor (> It. sudore, Fr. sueur, Sp. sudor, Rum. sudoare); W. chwys, Br. c'houez; ON sveiti, OE swāt, etc., general Gmc. (ME swet, NE sweat fr. the vb. ME swete, OE swǣtan); Lett. sviedri (pl.); Skt. sveda-, Av. xᵛaēδa-; Arm. k'irtn, Alb. dirsë, djersë.

2. Rum. nădușeală, fr. năduși 'make sweat, sweat', fr. năduf 'sultriness, closeness, asthma', this a loanword fr. Slavic, SCr. neduh 'asthma', etc. (neg. ne + duh beside dah 'breath', 4.51). Tiktin 774, 1030.

3. Ir. allas, NIr. allus, etym.? (Macbain 162 as *yas-l- : W. ias 'boiling, seething', Grk. ζέω 'boil', etc.; not in Walde-P. 1.208, Stokes 223).

4. Lith. prakaitas : kaisti, Lett. kaist 'become hot', etc., OHG heiz, ON heitr, OE hāt 'hot' (parallel t- and d-extensions of an IE *kǎi-). Walde-P. 1.327.

5. ChSl. potŭ, etc., general Slavic, (but SCr. only dial.) fr. *poktŭ : ChSl. pekŭ 'heat', pešti, pekǫ 'bake', Lat. coquere, Skt. pac- 'cook', etc. Walde-P. 2.18. Brückner 432.

SCr. znoj = ChSl., Boh., Russ. znoj, Pol. znój 'sultry heat, etc.'. Brückner 655.

4.56 SPIT (vb.)

Grk. πτύω	Goth. speiwan	Lith. spiauti
NG φτύνω	ON hrækja, spýta	Lett. spl'aut
Lat. spuere	Dan. spytte	ChSl. pljivati
It. sputare	Sw. spotta	SCr. pljuvati
Fr. cracher	OE spǣtan, hrǣcan, spyttan	Boh. plivati
Sp. escupir	ME spete, spitte (reche)	Pol. pluć
Rum. scuipa	NE spit	Russ. plevat'
Ir. saile (sb.)	Du. spuwen	Skt. ṣṭhīv-
NIr. sailighim	OHG spīwan	Av. spāma- (sb.)
W. poeri	MHG spī(w)en	
Br. skopa, tufa	NHG speien, spucken	

The majority of the words for 'spit' are of imitative origin, and most of these belong to an inherited group, which, though partly affected by new imitative associations, clearly reflect an IE expression.

1. IE *spyēu-, spyū-, etc. Most of the forms included here are derivable by regular phonetic processes from init. *spy-, but some owe their form to new associations. Walde-P. 2.683. Ernout-M. 969.

Grk. πτ῟ω, NG pop. φρύνω, φτυ῟, φτ῟; Lat. spuere, frequent. spūtāre (> It. spu-tare, OFr. espuer); Goth. spuwen, Du. spuwen, OHG spīwan, spīan, MHG spī(w)en, spüen, NHG speien (in the older language also 'spew, vomit', as chiefly OE spīwan, ON spȳja, cf. 4.57); ON spȳta, Dan. spytte, Sw. spotta, OE spyttan, ME spitte, NE spit, OE spǣtan, ME spete, NHG spucken (Weigand-H. 2.936, Falk-Torp 1137, 1138); Lith. spiauti, Lett. spl'aut; ChSl. pljǐvati, etc., general

Slavic; Skt. ṣṭhiv-, ṣṭhīv- (Av. spāma- 'spittle, slime'); Arm. t'k'anem.

2. Fr. cracher, fr. an imitative *krak, but prob. blended with a Gmc. form belonging with OE hrācan, etc. (below, 4). REW 4752.

Sp. escupir, OFr. escopir (> Br. sko-pa), Rum. scuipa (Maced.-Rum. ascu-pi), history much disputed, but prob. fr. some VLat. deformation (with metathesis of c-sp to sc-p) of Lat. conspuere (cf. Port. cuspir). REW 8014. Pușcariu 1566.

3. Ir. saile, NIr. seile 'spittle', fr. Lat. salīva 'spittle'. Pedersen 1.211. Hence denom. NIr. seilighim, but in older language vb. 'spit' rendered by locutions as do-biur (fo-cerdim, láim, etc.) mo saile, and commonly also NIr. gabhaim (cui-rim, caithim) mo sheile lit. 'put (cast, etc.) my spit'.

W. poeri (poer sb.), orig.?

Br. skopa, fr. OFr. escopir (above, 2). Henry 243.

Br. tufa, prob. of imitative orig. Henry 274.

4. ON hrækja, OE hrǣcan, ME reche (NE retch, reach), also 'hawk, clear the throat' (as mostly OHG rachisōn, MHG rächsenen) : OE hrǣca, ON hrāka 'spittle', OE hraca, OHG rahho 'throat', etc., all of imitative orig. (cf. Skt. kharj- 'creak', etc.). Walde-P. 2.415. Falk-Torp 381, 867.

4.57 VOMIT (vb.)

Grk. ἐμέω	Goth.	Lith. vemti
NG ξερνῶ	ON spȳja	Lett. vemt
Lat. vomere	Dan. brække sig	ChSl. bljivati
It. vomitare, recere	Sw. krakas	SCr. bljuvati
Fr. vomir	OE spīwan	Boh. dáviti, blíti
Sp. vomitar	ME spewe (vomyte)	Pol. womitować
Rum. vărsa, vomita	NE vomit, spew	Russ. blevat', izrygat'
Ir. scēim	Du. braken	Skt. vam-, chṛd-
NIr. scēithim	OHG (ar)spīwan	Av. vam-
W. cyfogi, chwydu	MHG spīwen, (sich brechen)	
Br. c'houeda, dislonka	sich (er)brechen	

Beside the usual word for 'vomit', generally avoided in polite speech, there are in most of the modern languages a number of euphemistic expressions corresponding to NE throw up, as Dan. kaste op, Sw. kasta upp, NHG auswerfen, Boh. vrhnouti, Pol. womitować, etc., or 'reject, give back, return' as Fr. rejeter, rendre (la gorge), NIr. ūrlacaim, and especially in Slavic 'turn back, return', SCr. povraćiti, Boh. zvrátiti, etc., and 'tear, pull out' as Russ. rvat', vyrvat'. Such locutions (except some that have lost all association with the more literal meaning and are used only for 'vomit', like It. recere in contrast to Fr. rejeter), are not included in the list.

1. IE *wem-. Walde-P. 1.262 f. Ernout-M. 1133 f.

Grk. ἐμέω; Lat. vomere (> Fr. vomir; Lat. frequent. vomitāre > It. vomitare, Sp. vomitar, Rum. vomita); Lith. vemti, Lett. vemt; Skt., Av. vam-.

2. NG ξερνῶ, fr. Grk. ἐξ-εράω 'evacuate (by purge or vomit)', 'disgorge' (-εράω only in cpds., cf. ἀπ-εράω 'pour out a fluid', etc.), fr. the root in Skt. rasa- 'sap, fluid', Lat. rōs 'dew', etc. Walde-P. 1.149. Hatzidakis, Μεσ. 1.292.

3. It. recere, fr. Lat. reicere 'throw back' (iacere 'throw'). REW 7183.

Rum. vărsa (and refl. se vărsa), lit. 'pour' (= Fr. verser, etc.), fr. Lat. versāre 'turn'. REW 9242. Pușcariu 1861.

4. Ir. scēim, NIr. scēithim (fr. vbl. n. scēith), W. chwydu, Br. c'houeda, c'houedi : ON skíta, OE scītan, NE shit, etc. (4.66), fr. extensions of IE *skēi- 'divide, separate', in Skt. chyati 'cuts off', Lat. scīre 'know, decide' (orig. 'separate'), etc. Walde-P. 2.541 f. Pedersen 1.77.

W. cyfogi, prob. cpd. cyf-ogi : MBr. heugel 'belch', Br. heug 'aversion, repugnance', perh. orig. imitative (fr. glottal contraction as NE hic). Henry 162.

Br. dislonka, lit. 'un-swallow', cpd. of lonka : W. llyncu, Ir. slucim 'swallow' Walde-P. 2.711. Pedersen 1.151.

5. ON spȳja, OE spīwan, ME spewe, NE spew, OHG spīwan, arspīwan, MHG spīwen, spīen, see under 'spit', 4.56.

Dan. brække sig, fr. LG sik bräken = MHG sich brechen (once 'vomere' in Lexer s.v.), NHG sich (er)brechen (cf. OE brecan, refl. 'retch, hawk', lit. 'break one's self'. Falk-Torp 110.

Sw. krakas of imitative orig. Hellquist 518.

NE vomit, late ME vomyte, either fr. the sb. (quotable somewhat earlier), this fr. OFr. vomit(e), Lat. vomitus, or directly fr. an OFr. form of Lat. vomitāre (above, 1). NED s.v.

Du. braken : breken 'break' (= NHG brechen, etc., above). Franck-v. W. 89.

6. ChSl. bljǐvati (late bljuvati), SCr. bljuvati, Boh. blíti (old blvati), Russ. blevat' : Grk. φλύω 'boil over, bubble', φλέω 'teem with', Lith. bliauti 'roar, bleat', etc. (extension of *bhel- 'puff, swell', in Lat. follis 'bellows', etc.). Walde-P. 2.212. Berneker 64.

Boh. dáviti (and refl. dáviti se), also 'oppress, strangle' (ChSl. daviti, SCr. daviti), 'choke, strangle' (the regular meaning in all the Slavic languages), Lith. dovyti 'torment', etc. Walde-P. 1.823. Berneker 181 f.

Pol. womitować fr. Lat. vomitus : vomere (above). Brückner 630.

Russ. izrygat', izrugnut', cpd. of rygat' 'belch' : ChSl. rygati sę, Lith. raugéti, Lat. ructāre, Grk. ἐρεύγομαι 'belch', etc. Walde-P. 2.357. Trautmann 244 f.

7. Skt., Av. vam-, above, 1.

Skt. chṛd- : MIr. sceirdim 'spew out', perh. also Grk. σκῶρ 'excrement', etc. Walde-P. 2.587.

4.58 BITE (vb.)

Grk. δάκνω	Goth. beitan	Lith. kąsti
NG δαγκάνω	ON bíta	Lett. kuost
Lat. mordēre	Dan. bide	ChSl. grysti, kusati
It. mordere	Sw. bita	SCr. gristi
Fr. mordre	OE bītan	Boh. kousati (hrýzti)
Sp. morder	ME bite	Pol. kąsać (gryźć)
Rum. mușca	NE bite	Russ. kusat' (gryzt')
Ir. greim (sb.)	Du. bijten	Skt. danç-
NIr. greamuighim	OHG bizan	Av. (dǫs-)
W. cnoi	MHG bizen	
Br. danta	NHG beissen	

Words for 'bite' are cognate with others meaning 'gnaw, crush, rub, scrape, split', of which the most original application is sometimes doubtful. A few are derived from words for 'tooth' or 'snout, mouth'.

1. Grk. δάκνω, late and NG δαγκάνω (new pres. to aor. ἔδακον after λαμβάνω,

etc.), Skt. danç-, Av. dąs- in tiži-dąstra- 'with sharp bite' (Barth. 635) : OHG zangar 'sharp, biting', ON tǫng, OE tang(e), OHG zanga 'tongs', etc. Walde-P. 1.790.

2. Lat. mordēre (> It. mordere, Fr. mordre, Sp. morder) : Skt. mṛd- 'crush, rub to pieces', Av. marəd- 'destroy', etc., IE *mer-d-. Walde-P. 2.278 f. (Hardly to be questioned on semantic grounds as Ernout-M. 631; cf. introd. note, above).

Rum. mușca, like Sp. dial. mottsikare, etc. 'bite', deriv. of VLat. *mucceus : Lat. mūcus, muccus 'snot', through its use for 'snout, mouth' (of animals) as in Maced.-Rum. muts. REW 5707 (assuming blend with morsicāre). Pușcariu 1136.

3. NIr. greamuighim, fr. Ir., NIr. greim 'bite, piece, morsel', etym.? (As *gresmen : Skt. gras- 'eat, devour', Grk. γράω 'gnaw, eat', etc. Stokes 118; rejected by Walde-P. 1.658).

W. cnoi, etym.? Perh. : MIr. cnáim 'gnaw, chew', Grk. κνῆν 'scrape', etc. (Stokes KZ 41.385, Walde-P. 1.392, both without W. cnoi).

Br. danta, fr. dant 'tooth' (4.27).

4. Goth. beitan, etc., general Gmc. : Lat. findere, Skt. bhid- 'split', IE *bheid-. Walde-P. 2.138.

5. Lith. kąsti, kandu (kandis sb.), Lett. kuost, ChSl. *kǫsati, late kusati, Boh. kousati, Pol. kąsać, Russ. kusat' : Grk. κνώδων 'tooth on a hunting spear', κνώδαξ 'pin, pivot', prob. fr. an extension of the root in Grk. κνῆν 'scrape', etc. Walde-P. 1.392 f. Berneker 601.

6. ChSl. grysti, SCr. gristi (Boh. hrýzti, Pol. gryźć also 'gnaw' as mostly Russ. gryzt') : Lith. graužti, Arm. krcem 'gnaw', Grk. βρύχω 'gnash, grind the teeth'. Walde-P. 1.697 f. Berneker 359.

4.59 LICK (vb.)

Grk. λείχω	Goth. -laigōn	Lith. laižyti (liežti)
NG γλείφω	ON sleikja	Lett. laizīt
Lat. lingere	Dan. slikke	ChSl. lizati
It. leccare	Sw. slicka	SCr. lizati
Fr. lécher	OE liccian	Boh. lizati
Sp. lamer	ME licke	Pol. lizać
Rum. linge	NE lick	Russ. lizat'
Ir. ligim	Du. likken	Skt. lih-
NIr. lighim	OHG leccōn	Av. raēz-
W. llyfu, llyw	MHG lecken	
Br. lipat	NHG lecken	

Most of the words for 'lick' belong to an inherited group, pointing to an IE word of this meaning. The others are connected with words for 'lip' or 'lap up'.

1. IE *leiĝh-. Walde-P. 2.400. Ernout-M. 552. Walde-P. 1.806.

Grk. λείχω, NG γλείφω fr. ἐκλείχω (γλ as in γλυτώνω, 'rescue', deriv. of ἔκλυτος; aor. *ἔγλειξα > ἐγλειφω by dissim., hence new pres. γλείφω; Pernot, Recueil 46); Lat. lingere (> Rum. linge); Ir. ligim, NIr. lighim, W. llyfu, llyw (nonetym. f; Pedersen 1.100); Goth. -laigōn (in bi-laigōn ἐπιλείχειν), OE liccian, ME licke, NE lick, Du. likken, OHG leccōn, MHG, NHG lecken; Lith. liežti, iter. laižyti, Lett. laizīt; ChSl. lizati, etc., general Slavic; Skt. lih-, rih-, Av. raēz-; Arm. lizum, lizanem.

Here also prob. ON sleikja, MLG slicken (> Dan. slikke, Sw. slicka), late MHG slecken, NHG schlecken 'eat daintily', fr. a parallel root form with initial *s-*. Falk-Torp 1063.

Here also It. *leccare*, Fr. *lécher*, either as deriv. of a VLat. **ligicāre* intensive to *lingere*, or else fr. the Gmc., OHG *leccōn*, etc. REW 5027. Gamillscheg 555.

2. Sp. *lamer*, Port. *lamber* fr. Lat. *lambere* 'lap up, lick up' : OE *lapian*, OHG *laffan*, Grk. λάπτω 'lap'. Walde-P. 2.384. Ernout-M. 519 f. REW 4865.

3. Br. *lipat*, deriv. of borrowing fr. Fr. *lippe* '(thick) lower lip', *lippée* 'mouthful', etc. Henry 187.

4.61 SLEEP (vb.; sb.)

Grk.	*καθεύδω, κοιμάομαι; ὕπνος*	Goth.	*slēpan; slēps*	Lith.	*miegoti; miegas*
NG	*κοιμοῦμαι (-ᾶμαι); ὕπνος*	ON	*sofa; svefn*	Lett.	*mieguot; miegs*
Lat.	*dormīre; somnus*	Dan.	*sove; søvn*	ChSl.	*sŭpati; sŭnŭ*
It.	*dormire; sonno*	Sw.	*sova; sömn*	SCr.	*spavati; san, spavanje*
Fr.	*dormir; sommeil*	OE	*slǣpan, swefan; slǣp, swefn*	Boh.	*spáti; spaní, spánek*
Sp.	*dormir; sueño*	ME	*slepe; slepe*	Pol.	*spać; sen, spanie*
Rum.	*dormi; somn*	NE	*sleep; sleep*	Russ.	*spat'; son, span'e*
Ir.	*con-tulim (foaim); sūan, cotlud*	Du.	*zlapen; zlaap*	Skt.	*svap-, drā-; svapna-, nidrā-*
NIr.	*codlaim; codladh, suan*	OHG	*slāfan; slāf*	Av.	*x^vap-; x^vafna-*
W.	*cysgu, huno; hun, cwsg*	MHG	*slāfen; slāf, swep*		
Br.	*kousket, huni; kousk, hun*	NHG	*schlafen; schlaf*		

Many of the words for 'sleep' belong to an inherited group reflecting an IE verbal root and an established substantive form for 'sleep'. Others are cognate with words meaning 'lie, rest, quiet, slack, blink'. Verb and noun are generally parallel, but not in Greek or Latin, and both forms are listed. The verbal forms listed are those that mean 'be asleep', beside which there are distinctive types for 'fall asleep' and 'put to sleep'. Several of the nouns are used also for 'dream' (4.62).

1. IE **swep-*, sb. **swep-no-s*, **swop-no-s*, **sup-no-s*. Walde-P. 2.523 f. Ernout-M. 954 f. Falk-Torp 1109 f.

ON *sofa*, Dan. *sove*, Sw. *sove*, OE *swefan;* ChSl. *sŭpati*, etc., general Slavic verbs; Skt. *svap-*, Av. *x^vap-*; beside forms for 'put to sleep', as Lat. *sōpīre*, ON *svefja*, OE *swebban*, OHG *antswebjan, -swebban*, MHG *entsweben;* or 'fall asleep', as ON *sofna*, ChSl. *usŭnąti*, etc.

Grk. ὕπνος; Lat. *somnus* (> It. *sonno*, Sp. *sueño*, Rum. *somn*, OFr. *somme* [now 'nap']; Fr. *sommeil* fr. dim. **somniculus*); Ir. *sūan*, W., Br. *hun* (denom. vbs. W. *huno*, Br. *huni*, *hun(i)a*); ON *svefn*, Dan. *søvn*, Sw. *sömn*, OE *swefn;* (Lith. *sapnas*, Lett. *sapnis*, *sapns* 'dream'); ChSl. *sŭnŭ*, SCr. *san*, Pol. *sen*, Russ. *son* (all these also, and Boh. *sen* only, 'dream'); Skt. *svapna-*, Av. *x^vafna-* (also Iran. **x^vāpa-*, NPers. *x^vāp*, cf. Beneveniste, BSL 30.75 ff.); Arm. *k'un;* Alb. *gjum;* Toch. A *ṣpäṃ*, *spän-*, *säpn-*.

Lat. *sopor*, of different formation (**swepōs*, like *amor*, etc.), mostly poet. and esp. 'overpowering sleep', sometimes personified.

ChSl. (late) *sŭpanĭje*, SCr. *spavanje*, Boh. *spaní*, *spánek*, Pol. *spanie*, Russ.

span'e, vbl. nouns 'sleeping', fr. the vbs. ChSl. *sŭpati*, etc.

2. Grk. εὕδω, καθεύδω, etym.? Boisacq 293. Otrębski, KZ 66.248.

Grk. κοιμάομαι (mostly in aor. 'fall asleep'; act. 'put to sleep'), NG κοιμοῦμαι (or -ᾶμαι) : Grk. κεῖμαι 'lie', Skt. *çī-* 'lie, rest', also 'sleep, fall asleep', Av. *sāy-* 'rest', etc. Walde-P. 1.358 f.

3. Lat. *dormīre* (> Romance vbs.) : ChSl. *drěmati* 'slumber, drowse', Skt. *drā-* 'sleep', Hom. aor. ἔδραθον 'sleep', late pres. δαρθάνω, etc. Walde-P. 1.821. Ernout-M. 283 f. Walde-H. 1.372.

4. OIr. *con-tulim*, MIr. *cotlaim*, NIr. *codlaim*, vbl. n. OIr. *cotlud*, NIr. *codladh*, also rarely uncompounded e.g. 3 sg. pret. *toilis*, etc. : ChSl. *toliti* 'pacify, quiet, still (hunger, thirst)', Lith. *tilti* 'become quiet, silent'. Walde-P. 1.740 f. Pedersen 2.655 f.

Ir. *foaim* ('sleep' as 'pass the night'), perh. : Skt. *vas-* 'dwell', etc. Pedersen 2.524.

W. *cysgu*, Br. *kousket*, Corn. *cusce*, fr. Lat. *quiēscere*, VLat. *quēscere* 'rest, repose'. The sbs. W. *cwsg*, Br. *kousk* are back-formations. Loth, Mots lat. 155.

5. Goth. *slēpan, slēps*, OE *slǣpan, slǣp*, OHG *slāfan, slāf*, etc. (common to Goth. and WGmc.) : MLG, Du. *slap*, OHG *slaf(f)*, NHG *schlaff* 'slack, loose, lax', ChSl. *slabŭ*, Lith. *slabnas* 'weak', etc. Walde-P. 2.432. Falk-Torp 1056.

6. Lith. *miegoti, miegas, miegojimas*, Lett. *mieguot, miegs* (Lith. *migti*, Lett. *migt* 'go to sleep') : ChSl. *mĭgnąti*, *mĭzati*, Russ. *migat'* 'blink, twinkle', etc. Walde-P. 2.246. Berneker 2.56 f.

7. Skt. *svap-*, Av. *x^vap-*, etc., above, 1. Skt. *drā-*, sb. *nidrā-* : Lat. *dormīre*, above, 3.

4.62 DREAM (sb.)

Grk.	*ὄνειρος, ἐνύπνιον*	Goth.	. . . .	Lith.	*sapnas*
NG	*ὄνειρο*	ON	*svefn, draumr*	Lett.	*sapnis, sapns*
Lat.	*somnium, insomnium*	Dan.	*drøm*	ChSl.	*sŭnŭ*
It.	*sogno*	Sw.	*dröm*	SCr.	*san*
Fr.	*rêve, songe*	OE	*swefn, mæting*	Boh.	*sen*
Sp.	*ensueño, sueño*	ME	*sweven, drem(e), meting*	Pol.	*sen*
Rum.	*vis*	NE	*dream*	Russ.	*son*
Ir.	*aisling*	Du.	*droom*	Skt.	*svapna-*
NIr.	*brionglōid, taidhbhreadh, aisling*	OHG	*troum*	Av.	. . . .
W.	*breuddwyd*	MHG	*troum*		
Br.	*huñvre*	NHG	*traum*		

Many of the nouns for 'dream' are the same as, or derived from, those for 'sleep'. Other sources are notions like 'sight, appearance, revelation', or 'deceit'.

1. IE **swep-no-s*, etc. 'sleep' (4.61) or derivs. of it.

Grk. ἐνύπνιον; Lat. *somnium* (> It. *sogno*, Fr. *songe*, Sp. *sueño*), later also *insomnium* (> Sp. *ensueño*, etc.) modeled on Grk. ἐνύπνιον; Br. *huñvre* (fr. *hun* 'sleep'); ON *svefn*, OE *swefn* (also 'sleep'), ME *sweven;* Lith. *sapnas*, Lett. *sapnis, sapns;* ChSl. *sŭnŭ*, SCr. *san*, etc. (also 'sleep', except Boh. *sen*); Skt. *svapna-* (also 'sleep'); Toch. A. *ṣpäm* (also 'sleep').

2. Grk. ὄνειρος and ὄναρ (nom.-acc. only), NG ὄνειρο : Arm. *anurǰ*, Alb. *andërë* 'dream', root connection? Walde-P. 1.180.

3. Fr. *rêve*, beside vb. *rêver* 'dream' also 'be delirious, mad', etym. much disputed. Derivation fr. VLat. **rabia*,

Lat. *rabiēs* 'madness', with some, orig. local, differentiation from *rage* (so Diez 669; cf. also NED s.v. *rave*, vb.[1]) is semantically the most attractive, but is now generally rejected. REW 4210. Gamillscheg 762.

Rum. *vis*, fr. Lat. *vīsum* 'sight, appearance, vision'. REW 9383.

4. Ir. *aisling*, etym. dub., perh. cpd. : *sellaim* 'look' (15.52). Stokes ap. Macbain 12.

NIr. *brionglōid* fr. MIr. *brinnglōid* 'a vision' (K. Meyer, Contrib. 262) : MIr. *brinda* 'vision', NIr. *brionn* 'fiction, dream', but outside connection? Macbain 50.

NIr. *taidhbhreadh*, vbl. n. of vb. *taidhbhrighim* 'dream', cpd. of MIr. *brigaim* 'show, declare' beside *bricht* 'spell, charm, incantation'. A deriv. of this root **brig-* is prob. also the final member of Br. *huñ-vre* (above, 1) and the first of W. *breu-ddwyd*, older *breiddwyd*, MW *breiđwyt* (the final member obscure). Loth, RC 40.362 f.

5. ON *svefn*, OE *swefn*, above, 1.

ON *draumr*, Dan. *drøm*, Sw. *dröm*, (OE *drēam* only 'joy, music'), ME *drem*, *dreme*, NE *dream*, OS *drōm*, Du. *droom*, OHG, MHG *troum*, NHG *traum*, prob. (as Gmc. **draugma-*) : OS *bidriogan*, OHG *triogan* 'deceive', Skt. *druh-* 'seek to harm, injure', Av. *druž-* 'lie, deceive', etc. Walde-P. 1.874. Falk-Torp 161.

OE *mǣting*, ME *meting* (e.g. Chaucer), with the more common vbs. OE *mǣtan*, ME *mete*, etym.? NED s.v. *mete*, vb.[2]

6. Balto-Slavic and Skt. words, above, 1.

4.63 WAKE (a, trans., b, intr.)

Grk.	*ἐγείρω* (a, mid. b)	Goth.	*uswakjan* (a), *gawaknan* (b), *wakan* (b)	Lith.	*budinti* (a), *busti*, *budėti* (b)
NG	(*ἐ*)*ξυπνῶ* (a, b)	ON	*vekja* (a), *vakna* (b), *vaka* (b)	Lett.	*muodināt* (a), *muodīt* (a), *muost* (b)
Lat.	*excitāre* (a, pass. b), *expergiscī* (b)	Dan.	*vække* (a), *vaagne* (b), *vaage* (b)	ChSl.	*buditi* (a), *bŭděti* (b)
It.	*destare* (a, refl. b), *svegliare* (a, refl. b)	Sw.	*väcka* (a), *vakna* (b), *vaka* (b)	SCr.	*probuditi* (a, refl. b)
Fr.	(*r*)*éveiller* (a, refl. b)	OE	*weccan* (a), *onwæcnan* (b), *wacian* (b)	Boh.	*probuditi* (a, refl. b), *bdíti* (b)
Sp.	*despertar* (a,b, refl. b)	ME	*wecche* (a), *wake* (a, b)	Pol.	*obudzić* (a, refl. b), *czuwać* (b)
Rum.	*deștepta* (a, refl. b)	NE	*wake* (a, b)	Russ.	(*raz*)*budit'* (a, refl. b), *prosnut'sja* (b)
Ir.	*do-fūiscim* (a, b)	Du.	(*op*)*wekken* (a), (*ont-*)*waken* (b)	Skt.	*budh-* (b, caus. a), *jāgr̥-* (b, caus. a)
NIr.	*dūisighim* (a, b), *mūsclaim* (a, b)	OHG	(*ar*)*wecchan* (a), *wachēn*	Av.	*gar-* (b, caus. a)
W.	*dihuno* (a, b), *deffroi* (b)	MHG	(*er*)*wecken* (a), (*er*)*wachen* (b)		
Br.	*dihuna* (a, b)	NHG	(*er*)*wecken* (a), (*er*)*wachen* (b)		

Transitive 'wake' (a) and intransitive (b) 'be awake' or 'become awake, awake' are generally expressed by different formation of the same root. There are two inherited groups (1 and 2, below), of which one may surmise that their primary values were still partially distinct in IE, as perhaps 1) 'be or make physically lively, awake', 2) 'be mentally conscious, awake'. The other words rest on such notions as 'stir up, rouse, call up' or 'be lively, vigorous', with a few from the absence of or emergence from 'sleep'.

1. IE **ger-*. Walde-P. 1.598 f.

Grk. ἐγείρω (trans.; intr. in perf. act. ἐγρήγορα 'am awake' and aor. mid. or pass.); Skt. intens. *jāgr̥-* (intr.; trans. in caus.), Av. *gar-* (perf. *ǰagāra* 'is awake'; trans. in caus. *a-garaya-*, *frāγrāγrāya-*, *frāγrāraya-*); Alb. *ngréhë* 'raise up'.

2. IE **bheudh-*. Walde-P. 2.147 f.

Lith. *budėti* 'be awake', (*pa*)*busti* 'awake', ChSl. *bŭděti* 'be awake, watch' (Boh. *bdíti;* SCr. *bdjeti*, Russ. *bdjet'* mostly obs.); trans. Lith. *budinti*, ChSl. *buditi*, etc., general Slavic (but more usually in cpd. perfect. forms, the more important of which are given in the list), with reflexive forms for intr. 'awake'; Skt. *budh-* intr. 'be awake, awake', also 'be conscious of, perceive', trans. in caus.; in derived senses, Av. *bud-* (*baod-*, Barth. 917), 'be aware of, perceive, smell', Grk. πεύθομαι, πυνθάνομαι 'learn of', Goth. *ana-biudan* 'command', etc.

3. NG (ἐ)ξυπνῶ, aor. (ἐ)ξύπνισα), with new pres. formation fr. late Grk. ἐξυπνίζω (Hatzidakis, Μεσ. 2.599 ff.), deriv. of late adj. ἔξυπνος 'awake', a phrase-cpd. of ὕπνος 'sleep' (4.61).

4. Lat. *excitāre* (also *suscitāre*) 'stir up, rouse' and so, like NE *rouse*, in phrases or situations involving 'sleep', equivalent to 'wake' (trans.), cpd. of *citāre* frequent. of *cīre* 'put in motion' : Grk. κινέω 'move', etc. Ernout-M. 184 ff. Hence VLat. **de-excitāre*, It. *destare*, Rum. *deştepta* (with *p* after *aştepta*). REW 2515. Puşcariu 528.

Lat. *expergiscī* (intr.; trans. OLat. *expergere*, Lat. *expergēfacere*), much disputed, but prob. fr. *pergere* (cpd. of *regere* 'direct'; Grk. ὀρέγω 'stretch out') in an early sense of 'stretch out' (like *porgere;* *pergere* also 'awaken' according to Festus, but usual development > 'start up, go on' > 'proceed, continue'). Walde-H. 1.429 f. Otherwise (: Grk. ἐγείρω, etc., above, 1, and only secondary association with *pergere*) Walde-P. 1.599. Ernout-M. 315.

It. *svegliare*, Fr. *éveiller* (more commonly deriv. *réveiller*), VLat. **exvigilāre*, cpd. of Lat. *vigilāre* 'stay awake, keep watch' (> Fr. *veiller*, etc.), deriv. of *vigil* 'awake, lively' : *vigēre* 'be lively, vigorous', etc. (cf. the Gmc. group, below, 6). REW 3114. Ernout-M. 1064 f.

Sp., Port. *despertar*, fr. Sp. *despierto*, Port. (*d*)*esperto* 'awake', deriv. of Lat. *expergīscī* (above, 1). REW 3043.

5. Ir. *do-fūiscim* (e.g. 3 sg. *do-fūsci*, *nī diuschi*, etc.), NIr. *dūisighim*, *dūisim* fr. *di-*, *od-*, and *sech-* (cpds. only e.g. *dofar-siged* 'significatum est') : Grk. ἐνέπω 'tell, relate', Lat. *inseque* imperat. 'tell', W. *heb* 'says', etc. Semantic development fr. 'call up' or the like to 'wake' (trans., then also intr.). Walde-P. 2.477 ff. Pedersen 2.620. Here also (**imm-od-sc-al-*) NIr. *mūsclaim*, Gael. *mosgail*. Macbain 254.

W. *dihuno*, Br. *dihuna*, *dihuni*, lit. 'unsleep', neg. *di-* and *huno*, etc. 'sleep' (4.62).

W. *deffroi*, older *effroi*, fr. adj. *effro* 'awake', etym.? (Morris Jones, by dissim. fr. **eks-pro-gr-*, with root as above, 1; but cf. Loth, RC 36, 168 f.).

6. Goth. *us-wakjan*, etc. all the Gmc. words : Lat. *vigēre* 'be lively, vigorous', *vegēre* 'move, excite', Skt. *vāja-* 'strength, vigor', etc., IE **weĝ-*. Walde-P. 1.246 f. Falk-Torp 1338 f.

The original distribution of the Gmc. forms is seen in Goth. *wakan*, ON *vaka* 'be awake, watch', inchoative Goth. *gawaknan*, ON *vakna* 'become awake, wake up', caus. Goth. *uswakjan*, ON *vekja* 'cause to wake', and similarly in OE (where there are also a number of cpds. with *on-*, *a-* not given in the list); but the simple inchoative OE *wæcnan*, *wæcnian* means 'come into being', and only the cpd. *onwæcnan* is regularly 'become awake'. In ME the forms of the strong OE (*wæcnan*), *wōc*, *wōcon* coalesced with the weak OE *wacian* and ME (*a*)*wake*, (*a*)*wakene* are used indiscriminately for 'be awake, become awake', and also with causative sense superseding ME (*a*)*wecche*, OE *weccan*. Hence NE *wake*, *awake*, *waken*, *awaken* trans. and intr., but in common use *wake* 'become awake', *awake* only adj., whence *be awake* for the state. Cf. NED s.vv. *wake*, vb. and *waken*, vb.

7. Lett. *muodināt*, *muodēt*, *muost* : *muodrs* 'lively, gay', Lith. *mandrus*, *mundrus* 'lively, arrogant', OHG *muntar* 'zealous, lively' (NHG *munter*), etc. Walde-P. 2.270 f.

8. Pol. *czuwać* (only 'be awake') : ChSl. *čuti* 'feel, notice', Russ. *čujat'* 'experience, feel', Slov. *čuti* 'hear, wake', etc., Grk. κοέω 'notice', Lat. *cavēre* 'take heed', Goth. *hausjan*, etc. 'hear', etc., IE **keu-*. Walde-P. 1.368 ff. Berneker 162.

Russ. *prosnut'sja* (refl.), apparently new formation after *usnut'* 'fall asleep', ChSl. *usŭnąti*, etc. id. : Russ. *son*, ChSl. *sŭnŭ* 'sleep', etc. (4.62).

4.64 BREAK WIND, FART (vb.)

Grk.	*πέρδομαι, βδέω*	Goth.	. . . .	Lith.	*persti; bezdėti*
NG	*κλάνω, πορδίζω*	ON	*freta, fīsa*	Lett.	*pirst, bezdēt*
Lat.	*pēdere (vissīre)*	Dan.	*fjerte; fise*	ChSl.	. . . .
It.	*spetezzare*	Sw.	*fjärta; fisa*	SCr.	*prditi*
Fr.	*péter, vesser*	OE	*feortan;* sb. *fīsting*	Boh.	*prděti, bzditi*
Sp.	*peer*	ME	*ferte, fyste*	Pol.	*pierdzieć, bzdzieć*
Rum.	*băşi*	NE	*fart*	Russ.	*perdet', bzdet'*
Ir.	*braigim*	Du.	*veesten*	Skt.	*pṛd-*
NIr.	*broimnighim*	OHG	*ferzan*	Av.	*pərəd-*
W.	*bramu, rhechain*	MHG	*verzen; visten*		
Br.	*bramma*	NHG	*farzen, furzen; fisten*		

The majority of the words belong to one of the two inherited groups, both prob. of imitative origin. The others are either likewise of imitative origin or from the notion of 'break'.

Phrases with the noun, like It. *tirar peti*, Rum. *da băşini*, etc., are omitted, though these are more or less popular in all languages and in some are in more common use than the verbs listed.

1. IE **perd-*. Walde-P. 2.49.

Grk. πέρδομαι, aor. ἔπαρδον (sb. πορδή, hence NG πορδίζω); W. *rhechain* (denom. of *rhech* fr. **pṛd-kā-*); ON *freta*, Dan. *fjerte*, Sw. *fjärta*, OE *feortan*, ME *ferte*, NE *fart*, OHG *ferzan*, MHG *verzen*, late MHG *varzen*, and denom. *vurzen*, NHG *farzen*, *furzen*; Lith. *persti*, Lett. *pirst*, SCr. *prditi*, Boh. *prděti*, Pol. *pierdzieć*, Russ. *perdet'*; Skt. *pṛd-* (Dhātup.; now quotable *pardate*), Av. *pərəd-* (3 pl. *pərədən*); Alb. *pjerth* (sb. *pordhë* fr. NG πορδή).

2. IE **pezd-*, **bzd-*, of imitative orig., but prob. through 'blow' (as in words pointing to IE **pes-* 'blow'). Walde-P. 2.68 f. Ernout-M. 748. Brückner 54.

Grk. βδέω; Lat. *pēdere* (> OIt. *pedere*, OFr. *poire*, Sp. *peer*; It. *spetezzare*, Fr. *péter*, derivs. of the nouns *peto*, *pet*, Lat. *pēditum*; REW 6345, 6358); Lith. *bezdėti*, Lett. *bezdēt* (*bezd-* for *pezd-* by assim. or by blend with **bzd-*), Slov. *pezdeti*, Boh. *bzditi*, Pol. *bzdzieć*, Russ. *bzdet'*.

3. NG κλάνω = Byz. κλάνω 'break', fr. Grk. κλάω id. Cf. NE *break wind*.

4. Lat. *vissīre*, sb. *vi(s)siō*, *vissium* (all only in glosses), prob. of imitative orig., like ON *fīsa*, etc. (below, 6). Hence Rum. *băşi*, Fr. sb. *vesse*, vb. *vesser*. Ernout-M. 1116. REW 9382.

5. Ir. *braigim*, NIr. *broimnighim* (fr. sb. *broimm*), W. *bramu*, Br. *bramma* (fr. sb. W. *bram*, Br. *bramm*) : Lat. *frangere* 'break', *fragor* 'breaking, crash, din', ON *braka* 'creak', etc. Walde-P. 2.193. Walde-H. 1.539.

6. ON *fīsa*, Dan. *fise*, Sw. *fisa*, OE sb. *fīsting*, ME vb. *fyste* (cf. NED s.v. *fist*, sb.[2], vb.[2]), Du. *veesten*, MHG *vīsten*, *visten*, NHG *fisten*, of imitative orig., prob. through 'blow' (cf. also Lat. *spīrāre* 'breathe', ChSl. *piskati* 'whistle'). Walde-P. 2.11. Falk-Torp 220 f.

4.65 URINATE; URINE

Grk.	*οὐρέω, ὀμείχω; οὖρον, ὄμειχμα*	Goth.	. . . .	Lith.	*myžti; myzalai* (pl.), *šlapumas*
		ON	*mīga*		
NG	*κατουρῶ; κάτουρο*	Dan.	*pisse; urin*	Lett.	*mīzt; mizali* (pl.)
Lat.	*mingere, meiere; ūrīna*	Sw.	*pissa; urin*	ChSl.	*sĭcati; sĭčĭ*
		OE	*mīgan; mīgoþa, mīgþa*	SCr.	*mokriti, pišati; mokraća*
It.	*urinar, pisciare; orina*				
Fr.	*uriner, pisser; urine*	ME	*pisse; pisse, urine*	Boh.	*scáti, močiti; moč*
Sp.	*orinar, mear; orina*	NE	*urinate, piss; urine, piss*	Pol.	*szczać, moczyć; mocz, uryna*
Rum.	*urina, pişa; urina*				
Ir.	*mūnaim; fūal, mūn*	Du.	*pissen; urine*	Russ.	*scat', močit'sja; moča*
NIr.	*mūnaim; fual*	OHG	*seichan; haran, seich*	Skt.	*mih-, mūtraya-; mūtra-, metra-*
W.	*piso, troethi; pis, troeth*	MHG	*harmen, seichen; harn, seiche*		
				Av.	*miz-; maēsma-, maēsman-*
Br.	*staota, troaza; staot, troaz*	NHG	*harnen, pissen; harn*		

Several of the more respectable verbs, like NE *urinate*, etc., are derived from Lat. *ūrīna* 'urine'. Among the more euphemistic but still common terms, many (though not entered in the list) are parallel to NE *make water*, as Fr. *faire de l'eau*, Rum. *lăsa udul*, Dan. *lade vandet*, NG κάνω (dial. χύνω) τὸ νερό μου.

Among those listed there is a widely distributed inherited group reflecting an IE root with this meaning. Another group, widespread through loanwords, is of imitative origin. Other words are connected with such notions as 'wet, pour, drip' or 'filth'. In several cases there are cognates meaning 'filth', 'lye', or 'wash', reflecting the common notions of either 'filth' or 'acidity', esp. the primitive use of urine as acid in washing.

1. IE **meiĝh-*. Walde-P. 2.245 f. Ernout-M. 602, 616.

Grk. ὀμείχω (so prob. for ὀμῑχέω, etc. codd.; cf. Solmsen, IF 31.468), with ὄμειχμα 'urine'; Lat. *mingere*, *meiere*, late *meiāre*, *miāre* (> Sp. *mear*); ON *mīga*, OE *mīgan*; Lith. *myžti* (1 sg. *mężu*, OLith. *minžu*), Lett. *mīzt*, with sbs. Lith. *myzalai* (pl.), Lett. *mizali* (pl.) 'urine'; SCr. (obs.) *mižati*; Skt. *mih-*, Av. *miz-* (with *maēsma-* 'urine'); Arm. *mizem*; Toch. B *miṡo*.

2. Grk. οὐρέω, NG (lit. οὐρῶ) κατουρῶ, with sbs. οὖρον, NG κάτουρο 'urine'; Lat. *ūrīna* 'urine' (source of the most widespread Eur. words): Skt. *varṣa-* 'rain', *var-*, *vāri-* 'water', etc. (1.31, 1.75). Walde-P. 1.268 f. Ernout-M. 1137.

3. It. *pisciare*, Fr. *pisser* (> ME *pisse*, NE *piss*, reg. biblical words, also as sbs.; Dan. *pisse*, Sw. *pissa*, Du., NHG *pissen*), Rum. *pişa* (SCr. *pišati* fr. Rum. or It.), all fr. a VLat. **pissiāre* (or the like), of imitative orig. REW 6544. Puşcariu 1324. Falk-Torp 830.

4. Ir. *mūnaim*, *mūnigim*, NIr. *mūnaim*, with Ir. *mūn* 'urine' : Skt. *mūtra-* id. (whence denom. *mūtraya-*, but usually *mūtram kṛ-* lit. 'make urine'), Av. *mūθra-* 'filth, dung', MLG *modder*, NE *mud*, etc., also Lith. *maudyti* 'bathe', ChSl. *myti* 'wash', fr. IE **meu-*, **meu-d-*, etc. Walde-P. 2.249 f.

Ir. *fūal*, NIr. *fual* 'urine', perh. with prefix *wo-* : W. *eulon* 'dung', this : Goth. *fūls*, OE *fūl* 'foul', Lat. *pūs* 'pus', Skt. *pū-* 'stink', etc. Loth, RC 45.190 f. (vs. Stokes 266).

W. *troethi*, Br. *troaza*, fr. W. *troeth* 'lye, urine, wash', Br. *troaz* 'urine' ("mot plus relevé," Vallée) : W. *trwnc* 'urine, lye', perh. Lat. *stercus* 'dung', etc. Walde-P. 2.641. But Pedersen 1.124 as 'lessive, lye' (for washing) : MBr. *gouzroncquet* 'bathe', Ir. *fo-thrucud* id., Lith. *trinkti* 'wash'.

W. *piso*, with sb. *pis*, fr. ME *pisse*, NE *piss*. Parry-Williams 141.

Br. *staota*, deriv. of *staot*, MBr. *staut* 'urine' (esp. of animals, but also of men), loanword fr. Gmc., Dan. *stalle*, Sw. *stalla*, MLG, NHG *stallen* (OFr. *estaler*), NE *stale*, all 'urinate' (of horses, NHG *stallen* dial. also of men), these perh. (with special application to horses influenced by the words for 'stall, stable') : Grk. σταλάσσω 'drip'. Walde-P. 2.642. Henry 252. Loth, Rom. 19, 593.

5. OHG *seichan*, MHG *seichen* (NHG dial. id.), LG *sēken* (sbs. OHG *seih*, MHG *seich*), fr. IE **seig-*, beside **seik-* in ChSl. *sĭcati*, Boh. *scáti*, Pol. *szczác*, Russ. *scat'* : OE *sēon*, OHG *sīhan*, NHG *seihen* 'strain, filter', Skt. *sic-* 'pour out, shed', Lat. *siat*: οὐρεῖ ἐπὶ βρέφους (gl.). Walde-P. 2.466 f. Weigand-H. 2.835. Brückner 545.

MHG *harmen*, *hermen*, NHG *harnen*, fr. sbs. NHG *harn*, MHG *harm*, *harn*, OHG *haran*, 'urine' cf. MHG vb. *hurmen* 'manure', prob. : Lith. *šarmas* 'lye from ashes', Lett. *sarms*, OPruss. *sirmes* 'lye'. Walde-P. 1.463.

6. Lith. *myžti* etc., above, 1.

Lith. *šlapumas* 'wetness' (: *šlapias* 'wet', 15.83) and, esp. pl., *šlapumai*, 'urine'.

7. ChSl. *sĭcati*, etc. : OHG *seichan*, etc. (above, 5).

SCr. *mokriti*, Boh. *močiti*, etc., with sbs. SCr. *mokraća*, Boh. *moč*, etc. : ChSl. *mokrŭ* 'wet' (15.83).

8. Skt. *mih-*, Av. *miz-*, etc., above, 1.

Skt. *mūtraya-*, *mūtra-* : Ir. *mūn*, 'urine', etc., above, 4.

4.66 VOID EXCREMENT; EXCREMENT, DUNG

Grk.	*κακκάω, χέζω; κάκκη, κόπρος, σκῶρ*	Goth.	. . . . ; *maihstus, smarna*	Lith.	*šikti; šudas, mėšlas*
				Lett.	*dirst; sūds, mēsls*
NG	*χέζω; σκατά, κόπρος, κόπρανα* (pl.)	ON	*skīta, drīta; drit, skītr, myki, skarn*	ChSl.	. . . . ; *gnojĭ, govno, lajĭno*
Lat.	*cacāre; stercus, merda, fimus, excrēmentum*	Dan.	*skide; skidt, møg*	SCr.	*srati; govno, gnoj, balega*
		Sw.	*skita; skit, dynga, träck*		
It.	*cacare; merda, sterco*			Boh.	*sráti; hovno, lejno, hnůj*
Fr.	*chier; merde, fumier, fiente*	OE	*scītan; meox, cwēad, scearn, dung, tord*	Pol.	*srać; gowno, łajno, gnój*
Sp.	*cagar; mierda, estiércol*	ME	*schite, drite; schit, dung, mix, tord*	Russ.	*srat'; govno, kal, pomet*, etc.
Rum.	*căca; căcat*	NE	*shit; shit, dung, turd, manure*		
Ir.	*caccaim; cacc*			Skt.	*had-; çakṛt-, purīṣa-, viṣṭhā-, gūtha-*
NIr.	*cacaim; cac*	Du.	*schijten, drijten; mest, drek, dreet*		
W.	*cachu, caca; cach, caca, tom*			Av.	*ri-; mūθra-, gūθa-, sairya-, šāman-*
		OHG	*scīzan; mist, quāt, tunga*		
Br.	*kac'hout; kac'h, mon*				
		MHG	*schīzen; schīze, mist, drec, quāt, tunge*		
		NHG	*scheissen; scheisse, mist, dreck, kot, dünger*		

Many of the verbs listed, and some of the nouns, belong to inherited groups reflecting a variety of roots, in part, of the imitative or nursery type, which were apparently applied already in the IE period to this bodily function. In the Gmc. group and several of the other words the development is from 'separate', whence 'discharge from the body'. The countless euphemistic expressions are mostly ignored, as for example those meaning lit. 'discharge, empty one's self, ease one's self, do one's need', and especially the widespread use of the simple verbs for 'do'. The current NE medical term *defecate* shows a recent specialization of 'cleanse of dregs, purify' (Fr. *déféquer*, Lat. *dēfaecāre*, fr. *faecēs* 'dregs'; NED s.v.).

The nouns for 'excrement, dung' are so numerous that a selection is sometimes difficult. The notion is often a specialization of 'filth', but the converse relation is also seen (as in NE *dirt*). A distinction between human excrement and animal dung is partly observed, though this is not indicated in the list and many words for 'manure' are not entered. The etymology of certain words reflects the use of dung for fertilizing the land.

1. IE **kakka-*, orig. nursery word. Walde-P. 1.336. Ernout-M. 125. Walde-H. 1.127. Falk-Torp. 484. Berneker 470.

Grk. κακκάω (sb. κάκκη 'human excrement'); Lat. *cacāre* (> It. *cacare*, Fr. *chier*, Sp., Port. *cagar*, Rum. *căca*, deriv. sb. Rum. *căcat*); Ir. *caccaim*, NIr. *cacaim*, sbs. Ir. *cacc*, NIr. *cac*, W. *cach*, Br. *kac'h* (hence vbs. W. *cachu*, Br. *kac'hout*); Arm. *k'akor* 'manure'; still as nursery words in Slavic, SCr. *kakati*, *kakiti*, Boh. *kakati*, Pol. *kakać*, Russ. *kakat'*; disputed whether the Gmc. words, NE *cack* (rare, but OE *cac-hūs* 'latrina'), Du. *kakken*, Dan. *kakke*, NHG *kacken* (nursery words) are native of the same popular type (Walde-P., Walde-H., etc.) or through student slang fr. Lat. *cacāre* (NED, Kluge-G., Weigand-H., Falk-

Torp). Re-formed to the original type apparently W. *caca* (vb. and sb.) like It. *cacca*, Fr. *caca*, etc.

2. IE **ĝhed*-. Walde-P. 1.571.

Grk., NG χέζω (also χοδιτεύειν· ἀποπατεῖν ('retire to ease oneself', Hesych.); Skt. *had*-, Alb. *dhjes* 'cacare'; Av. *zadah*- 'rump', Grk. χόδανον· τὴν ἕδραν Hesych. etc.

3. IE **k̂ekʷ*-. Walde-P. 1.381.

Grk. κόπρος (NG κόπρανα, pl., medical term), Lith. *šikti*, Skt. *çakṛt*- (gen. *çaknas*).

4. IE **gʷou*-, **gʷu*- in words for 'excrement, dung, filth' (orig. 'cow dung' : IE **gʷou*- 'ox, cow'?). Walde-P. 1.694 ff. Falk-Torp 600. Berneker 339.

ChSl. *govno* (**govĭno*), etc., general Slavic word for 'excrement'; Skt. *gūtha*-, Av. *gūθa*-, Arm. *ku*, *koy* 'dung'; with *d*-extension OE *cwēad*, OHG *quāt*, MHG *quāt*, *kōt*, *kāt*, NHG *kot*.

5. Derivs. of IE *sk̂er*- partly neut. *r*/*n* stem (or, with separation of Slavic and Av. forms, **sker*-, same as in vbs. for 'cut, cut off, separate', as OE *sceran*, Lat. *cernere*, Lith. *skirti*, etc.?). Walde-P. 2.587. Falk-Torp 986. Benveniste, Origines de la formation des noms 9.

Grk. σκῶρ, gen. σκατός, hence NG σκατό, usually pl. σκατά; Lat. *mūscerda* 'mouse dung', *sucerda* 'swine dung', etc.; OE *scearn*, ON *skarn*; Slavic vbs., SCr. *srati*, etc.; Av. *sairya*- (Barth. 1567); Hitt. *sakkar*, gen. *saknas* (Sturtevant, Hitt. Gloss. 128).

6. Lat. *stercus* (> It. *sterco*; Sp. *estiércol* 'dung, manure', back-formation to *estercolar* fr. Lat. *stercorāre* 'to dung, manure'), perh.: W. *trwnc* 'urine, lye' (but Br. *stronk* 'excrement' : *strinka* 'spurt out'), Lith. *teršti* 'to soil, dirty', also Grk. στεργάνος, MHG *drec*, etc. (below, 8), but all doubtful combinations. Walde-P. 2.641 f.

Lat. *merda* (> It. *merda*, Fr. *merde*, Sp. *mierda*), prob. : Lith. *smirdėti*, Lett. *smirdēt*, ChSl. *smrŭděti* 'stink'. Walde-P. 2.691. Ernout-M. 609.

Lat. *excrēmentum* (whence the learned technical words Fr., NE *excrement*, etc., general European), deriv. of *excernere* 'separate', also 'discharge from the body', cpd. of *cernere* 'separate' : Grk. κρῖνω 'separate, judge', OE *sceran* 'cut, shear', etc. (cf. also Skt. *ava*-, *apa-skara*- 'excrement'). Walde-P. 2.573 f., 584. Ernout-M. 178 f.

Lat. *fimus*, *fimum* (hence through derivs. Fr. *fumier* and *fiente*. REW 3307a, 3309), etym? Walde-P. 1.836. Ernout-M. 360. Walde-H. 1.499 f.

Fr. *ordure* ('filth' in general and 'excrement'), deriv. of *ord* 'filthy', Lat. *horridus* 'rude, rough'. REW 4187.

7. W. *tom*, esp. 'horse dung', orig. as 'ball of dung' : Ir. *tomm* 'small hill', Grk. τύμβος 'burial mound', etc. Vendryes, RC 48.398. Walde-P. 1.708.

Br. *mon*, perh. fr. OFr. *moun* 'yolk of an egg'. Henry 204.

8. Goth. *maihstus* (κοπρία), OE *meox*, ME *mix*, Du. *mest*, OS, OHG, MHG, NHG *mist* : ON *mīga*, OE *mīgan*, etc. 'mingere' (4.65), hence orig. 'liquid excrement'. Walde-P. 2.245 f. Feist 340.

Goth. *smarna* (only nom. pl. *smarnos* for σκύβαλα 'refuse, dung'), prob. : ON *smjǫr*, OE *smeoru*, OHG *smero* 'grease, fat', Ir. *smiur*, W. *mer* 'marrow' (semantic development as in NHG *schmierig*, Du. *smerig* 'greasy' > 'filthy, dirty'). Walde-P. 2.690. Feist 439.

ON *skīta*, OE *scītan*, etc., the reg. Gmc. vb., and the corresponding sbs., ON *skītr*, etc., orig. 'separate' (as in Lat. *excrēmentum*, above) : Lith. *skeisti*, Lett. *šk'iest* 'separate, divide', Lat. *scindere*, Grk. σχίζω 'split', etc., fr. IE **skei-d*- beside **skei-t*- in Ir. *sceithim* 'vomit' (4.57), Goth. *skaidan* 'separate', etc. Walde-P. 2.544. Falk-Torp 992.

ON *drīta*, Norw. *drite*, OE *gedrītan* (rare), ME *drite* (NE *drite* obs., NED s.v.), Du. *drijten*, LG *drīten*, sbs. ON *drit*, ME *drit*, *dyrte* (NE *dirt*), Du. *dreet*, etc. : Russ. dial. *dristat'*, SCr. *driskati*, Boh. *dřístati* 'have diarrhœa', fr. IE **dhreid*-, prob. extension of **dher*- in Lat. *foria* pl. 'diarrhœa'. Walde-P. 1.861 f. Falk-Torp 156.

ON *myki*, *mykr* (ME *muk* 'dung, manure', NE *muck*), Dan. *møg*, prob. (from the notion of 'soft, damp') : ON *mjūkr*, Dan. *myg*, etc. 'soft', ON *mugga* 'fine rain'. Walde-P. 2.253. Falk-Torp 748.

Sw. *träck* (but also 'filth, mire' as mostly ON *þrekkr*), Du. *drek*, late OHG, MHG *drec*, NHG *dreck* : Grk. στεργάνος· κοπρών Hesych., τρύξ, τρυγός 'must, dregs', etc., IE **sterg*- (cf. **sterk*- in Lat. *stercus*, above, 6). Walde-P. 2.642. Falk-Torp 159 f. On the dialectal distribution of NHG *kot* and *dreck* in this sense (vs. 'mud, filth'), cf. Kretschmer, Wortgeogr. 178 f.

OE-NE *dung*, Sw. *dynga* (Dan. *dynge* 'heap'), OHG *tunga* ('manuring'), MHG *tunge*, NHG *dünger* (ON *dyngja*, OHG, MHG *tunc* 'underground room') : Lith. *dengti* 'cover', *danga* 'a cover', IE **dhengh*-. Development fr. 'covering' to 'dung' as fertilizer, and also (independently or through 'dung') to 'heap, underground room'. Walde-P. 1.854. Falk-Torp 171.

For the development of 'dung' through its aspect as fertilizer, cf. NE sb. *manure*, fr. the verb, this fr. Anglo-Fr. *maynoverer* = OFr. *manouvrer* 'work with the hands', hence 'till, cultivate' and 'fertilize' (NED s.v.). Also Dan. *gødsel*, Sw. *gödsel* 'manure', fr. vbs. *gøde*, *göda* 'manure' = ON *gœða* 'improve', fr. *goð* 'good'.

OE *cwēad*, OHG *quāt*, etc., above, 4.

OE *scearn*, etc., above, 5.

OE, ME *tord*, NE *turd*, ON *torð* in *torð-yfill* 'dung beetle', MHG *zurch* 'dung' : Lett. *dirsti* 'void excrement', fr. the root in Lith. *dirti*, Grk. δέρω 'flay', OE *teran* 'tear', etc., with development through the notion of 'cast off, separate'. Walde-P. 1.798. Falk-Torp 1273. Mühl.-Endz. 1.470.

9. Lith. *šikti*, above, 3.

Lett. *dirsti* : OE *tord*, etc. (above, 8).

Lith. *mėšlas*, Lett. *mēsls*, beside vbs. Lith. *mėžti*, Lett. *mēzt* 'manure', etym.? Mühl.-Endz. 2.621–22.

Lith. *šudas*, Lett. *sūds*, perh. : Grk. (Hesych.) ὑσ-κυθά· ὑὸς ἀφόδευμα and κυθώδεος· δυσόσμου. Walde-P. 1.467. Boisacq 530.

10. ChSl. *gnojĭ* ('κοπρία'; also 'σῆψις, putrefaction'), SCr. *gnoj*, Pol. *gnój*, Boh. *hnůj* (also 'pus, matter, etc.', as Russ. *gnoj*, dial. also 'dung') : ChSl. etc. *gniti* 'rot', ChSl. *gnesĭ* 'dirt, filth', outside connections obscure. Berneker 314.

ChSl. *govno*, etc., above, 4.

ChSl. (late) *lajĭno* (pl. *lajĭna* 'bricks'), SCr. dial. *lajno*, Boh. *lejno*, Pol. *łajno* : Skt. *lī*- 'cling to, adhere, lie upon', Grk. ἀλίνω 'anoint', Lat. *linere* 'daub, smear', *līmus* 'slime, mud, mire', etc. Berneker 687. Brückner 306.

SCr. *balega* 'dung', fr. Rum. *baligar* 'horse or cow dung', Alb. *bagelë* id., fr. It. *bagola* 'bilberry', in North It. dial. also used for the berry-like excrement of certain animals (sheep, goats, etc.). G. Meyer, IF 6.116. Berneker 41.

Russ. *kal* = SCr. *kao* 'mud, excrement' (not popular), ChSl. *kalŭ* 'mud, mire', prob. : Grk. κηλίς 'spot', Ir. *caile* id., Skt. *kāla*- 'blue-black'. Walde-P. 1.441.

Russ. *pomet*, back-formation to *pometat'* 'throw away'. Cf. for sense NE *droppings*.

11. Skt. *had*-, above, 2.

Skt. *gūtha*-, Av. *gūθa*-, above, 4.

Skt. *çakṛt*-, above, 3.

Skt. *purīṣa*-, also 'earth, land' (as opposed to water), 'rubbish', perh. as orig. 'filling' fr. the root *pṛ*- 'fill'. Uhlenbeck 170.

Skt. *viṣṭhā*-, also *viṣ*- : *viṣa*-, Av. *viš*-, Grk. ἰός 'poison', Lat. *vīrus* 'slime, semen, poison, stench', etc. Walde-P. 1.243 f.

Av. *ri*- (only with prefix), NPers. *rīdan* 'cacare' : Skt. *rī*- 'let go, release', *raya*- 'flow', etc. Barth. 1511. Horn 639.

Av. *šāman*-, adj. *fra-šāimna*-, etym.? Barth. 1008, 1708.

Av. *mūθra*- : Skt. *mūtra*- 'urine', etc. (4.65).

Av. *sairya*-, above, 5.

Av. *hixra*- ('liquid excrement') : *haek*-, Skt. *sic*- 'pour', Serb.-ChSl. *sĭcati* 'mingere', etc. (4.65). Barth. 1812.

Also Skt. *uccar*- (*ud-car*-), lit. 'move out', frequent as euphemistic expression for 'void excrement' (also 'pronounce'). Hence *uccāra*- 'pronunciation' and 'excrement'.

4.67 HAVE SEXUAL INTERCOURSE

Grk.	ὁμιλέω, βινέω, οἴφω; ὀχεύω, -ομαι	Goth.	. . . .	Lith.	*prigulėti, pisti, žaisti*
NG	γαμῶ	ON	*liggja hjā*	Lett.	*piegulēt, pist*
Lat.	*coīre, futuere*	Dan.	*ligge hos, kneppe, knolde*	ChSl.	. . . .
It.	*fottere*	Sw.	*ligga hos, knulla*	SCr.	*jebati*
Fr.	*foutre*	OE	*hǣman*	Boh.	*jebati*
Sp.	*hoder*	ME	*swive*	Pol.	*jebać*
Rum.	*fute*	NE	*sleep (lie) with, fuck*	Russ.	*et', ebat'*
Ir.	*goithimm, conricim*	Du.	*bijslapen*	Skt.	*yabh*-
NIr.	*comluighim*	OHG	*ubarligan*	Av.	*miθ*-
W.	*cydio*	MHG	*bīslāfen, serten*		
Br.	*en em bara*	NHG	*beischlafen, ficken*		

Perhaps for no other notion is there such a boundless wealth of both euphemistic and vulgar expressions. In the former class are words meaning literally 'come together, have relations or intercourse with, be familiar or intimate with, lie or sleep with, know', etc. (cf. NE bibl. *lie with*, while *sleep with* is just now the popular expression).

Only a few of these, which are quite definitely specialized in the sexual sense, are included in the list. For the vulgar terms in most general use in the modern languages the selection must depend chiefly on information from native speakers, since the words are taboo and often unrecorded in the dictionaries. Those recorded by H. Sperber, Imago 1.405 ff., 429 ff., include a variety of dialect expressions, but the collection is, of course, incomplete (e.g. What are the NIr. and W. vulgar terms?).

The only indication of an IE term (there were doubtless several) is the agreement between a Greek, Slavic, and Sanskrit word.

1. IE **yebh*-(?). Walde-P. 1.198. Berneker 452.

Grk. οἴφω (Cret., Lac., Ther.; οἰφέω or -άω in late Attic) : SCr., Boh. *jebati*, Pol. *jebać*, Russ. *et'* (1 sg. *ebu*), *ebat'*; Skt. *yabh*- (AV+).

2. Grk. ὀχεύω of animals, act. of male 'cover', pass. of female 'be covered' (Hdt. +, regular technical terms in Aristot. HA), orig. 'be master of' or the like: ἔχω 'hold, have', Skt. *sah*- 'prevail, overcome', Goth. *sigis* 'victory', etc. Walde-P. 2.481 ff.

Grk. ὁμιλέω, lit. 'consort with', is the usual euphemistic term for human sexual relations, with sb. ὁμιλία '(sexual) intercourse'.

Grk. βινέω (Aristoph., etc., prob. the commonest Attic term; also El. βενέοι), prob. : βία 'violence', etc. Boisacq 119. Otherwise Walde-P. 1.667 after Lid'n.

Grk. γαμέω 'marry' (2.33) rarely used for mere sexual intercourse until late (Lucian), but Byz. and NG regularly in this sense.

Grk. βατέω 'cover' of animals (cf. LS s.v.) and so NG βατεύω, orig. 'tread on' : βαίνω 'walk, step'.

NG πηδῶ 'leap, jump' (10.43), also 'cover' of animals.

3. Lat. *coīre* lit. 'come together', the commonest euphemistic term, with sb. *coitus*.

Lat. *futuere* (> It. *fottere*, Fr. *foutre*, Sp. *hoder*, Rum. *fute*) etym. dub. Walde-P. 2.126. Ernout-M. 406. Walde-H. 1.574. REW 3622.

For Fr. *ficher* 'fix' used for *foutre*, cf. Wartburg 3.511.

4. Ir. *goithimm* (gl. *futuo*, Thes. 2.184) : W. *god* 'adulterous', *godineb* 'adultery, fornication', outside connection? Pedersen 2.34. Stokes 113.

MIr. *conricim*, lit. 'come together' (cpd. *com-ro-icc*-, Pedersen 2.556), in the Laws used also, like Lat. *coīre*, of sexual intercourse.

NIr. *comluighim*, lit. 'lie with' (cpd. of *com*-, *luighim* 'lie'), cf. also Ir. *coblige* 'coitus'. Pedersen 2.560. NIr. vulgar term?

W. *cydio*, deriv. of *cyd* 'union, copulation' : *cy*-, *cyf*-, Br. *ke*-, *ked*-, etc. Loth, RC 37.27 (vs. Morris Jones 264).

Br. *en em bara*, reflex. of *para* 'to pair, couple', deriv. of *par*, loanword fr. Lat. *pār* 'equal, mate, spouse'.

5. ON *liggja hjā* (or *með*) 'lie with', the common expression for sexual intercourse; so also Dan. *ligge hos*, Sw. *ligga hos*; Dan. also *have samleje med*.

ON *serða* 'stuprare' (> OE *serðan* 'violate', Mt. 5.27 Lindisf.), MHG *serten* 'futuere, stuprare' also 'beat, strike, torment', etc., etym. dub. Walde-P. 2.500. Wood, Mod. Ph. 5.283.

Dan. *kneppe* prob. same word as *kneppe* 'give a pinch, slight blow'. Dahlerup s.v. *kneppe*, I1.5.

Dan. *knolde*, Sw. *knulla* : ON *knylla*, OE *cnyllan* 'beat, knock'. Falk-Torp 554. Dahlerup s.v. *knolde*, II. Ordbok Akad. s.v. *knulle*.

OE *hǣman* : *hām* 'dwelling, home' (7.122), hence orig. 'take home' then 'cohabit' with vulgar sense definitely prevailing over 'marry', just as in the current use of NE *cohabit*. Direct connection with the sense of the orig. root, namely 'lie' (as Walde-P. 1.359) is unlikely.

ME *swive* : OE *swīfan* 'move lightly over, sweep' (beside *swift*, NE *swift*), ON *svīfa* 'rove, ramble', OHG *sweibōn* 'sway, swing', etc. Walde-P. 2.520. NED s.v.

NE *copulate*, now the usual term with reference to animals, formerly 'couple, link together' in general, like its source Lat. *cōpulāre*.

NE *fuck* (the most notorious "four-letter word", taboo even for the NED, but quotable in print from the early 16th cent. A. W. Read, American Speech 9.267 ff.; a much earlier date is evidenced by the name *John le Fucker* quoted from 1278 A.D.) may be only a variant of ME, NE (esp. Sc.) *fyke*, *fike* 'move restlessly, fidget', also 'dally, flirt' (NED s.v. *fike*, vb., with quot. under 1b). Cf. NHG *ficken* (below) with dial. *fucken* (Grimm, s.v. *ficken*), and semantically ME *swive* (above).

OHG *ubarligan*, lit. 'lie over', sometimes 'coire' (Graff).

MHG **bīslāfen* (not quotable, but *bīslāfe* 'beischläferin', *bīslāfunge* 'coniugium'; *beslāfen* is 'get with child'), NHG *beischlafen*, Du. *bijslapen*, etc., all lit. 'sleep beside'.

NHG *ficken* 'make quick movements to and fro, flick', earlier 'itch, scratch', vulgar sense quotable from 16th cent. Weigand-H. 1.528.

6. Lith. *priguléti*, Lett. *piegulēt*, lit. 'lie with', the usual euphemistic terms.

Lith. *pisti*, Lett. *pist*, the vulgar terms (Lith. also *žaisti* 'play') : ChSl. *pĭchati* 'strike', Boh. *pichati* 'prick', Russ. *pichat'* 'push, shove' (refl. *pichat'sja* also 'futuere'), Lat. *pīnsere* 'crush', etc. Walde-P. 2.1.

7. SCr. *jebati*, etc., general Slavic, above, 1.

8. Skt. *yabh-*, above, 1.

Av. *miϑ-* (inf. *maēϑmanəm* of dogs, Barth. 1107; cf. also *mayah-* 'coitus' Barth. 1141) : Av. *miϑwa-*, *miϑwara-* 'paired', Skt. *mith-* 'meet, alternate, etc.', *mithuna-* 'paired, pairing, copulation', etc. Walde-P. 2.247 f.

4.71 BEGET (of Father)

Grk.	*τίκτω, γεννάω*	Goth.	. . . .	Lith.	*gimdyti, gaminti*
NG	*γεννῶ*	ON	*geta, ala*	Lett.	*dzemdināt*
Lat.	*gignere, generāre*	Dan.	*avle*	ChSl.	*roditi*
It.	*generare*	Sw.	*avla*	SCr.	*roditi*
Fr.	*engendrer*	OE	*gestrȳnan, (ge)cennan*	Boh.	*zploditi*
Sp.	*engendrar*	ME	*begete, gete*	Pol.	*spłodzić*
Rum.	*naşte*	NE	*beget*	Russ.	*rodit'*
Ir.	*do-fuismim*	Du.	*verwekken, voortbringen, telen*	Skt.	*jan-, sū-*
NIr.	*geinim*	OHG	*giberan, kindōn, gikennan*	Av.	*us-zan-*
W.	*cenhedlu*	MHG	*gebern, kinden*		
Br.	*engehenta*	NHG	*zeugen*		

'Beget' of the father and 'bear' of the mother (4.72) are partly differentiated, partly expressed by the same terms with a common relation to 'be born' or 'offspring'. Several words originally belonging to this latter type have become restricted to either 'beget' or 'bear'. A few meaning properly 'bear' are sometimes used also for 'beget'.

Apart from the inherited groups (1, 2, 3, below), words for 'beget' are mostly specializations of 'get, obtain' or derivatives of words meaning 'child, offspring'.

1. IE **ĝen-* (**ĝenə-*, **ĝnē-*, **ĝnō-* **ĝn̥-*) in words for 'beget' or 'bear', 'be born', 'birth', 'race', etc. Walde-P. 1.576 f. Ernout-M. 415 ff. Walde-H. 1.597 ff.

Grk. *γεννάω* mostly 'beget' but also 'bear', NG *γεννῶ* 'beget, bear'; Lat. *gignere, generāre* 'beget' (> It. *generāre;* Fr. *engendrer*, Sp. *engendrar* fr. Lat. *ingenerāre*), *nāscī* 'be born', also (mostly late) *nāscere* (> It. *nascere*, Fr. *naître*, Sp. *nacer* 'be born', but Rum. *naşte* act. 'beget, bear', reflex. 'be born'; REW 5832, Puşcariu 1155); W. *geni* 'bear', Br. *genel* 'bear, be born', Ir. *geinim* 'beget' (: Ir. *gein* 'birth'); OE *cennan* 'beget, bear', OHG *gikennan* 'beget'; Skt. *jan-* 'beget, bear' esp. in older language, later mostly 'be born', caus. *janaya-* 'beget, bear', Av. *zan-* 'bear', *us-zan-* 'beget'; Arm. *cnanim* 'beget, bear, be born'.

2. IE **sū-* in words for 'beget, bear' and esp. 'son'. Walde-P. 2.469 f.

Skt. *sū-* 'bear' and 'beget' esp. in earlier language (in the later language

for 'beget' *pra-sū-*, *sam-pra-sū-*), Av. *hu-* 'bear' (of evil beings), with Skt. *suta-*, *sūnu-* 'son', Av. *hunu-*, Goth. *sunus*, etc. id. (2.41).

3. IE **tek-*. Walde-P. 1.715.

Grk. *τίκτω* 'beget, bear' of both parents, cf. *οἱ τεκόντες* 'parents', *τέκνον* 'child' : Skt. (gramm.) *takman-* 'offspring, child', ON *þegn* 'freeman, free subject', OE *þegn* 'nobleman, warrior', OHG *degan* 'boy, servant, hero'.

4. Ir. *do-fuismim* 'beget, bear', NIr. *tuismim* 'bear, be descended from', cf Ir. *tuistidi* pl. 'parents', fr. **to-od-sem-*, root *sem-* 'pour' (only in cpds. e.g. *doesmet* 'they pour out', etc.) : Lith. *semti* 'dip, draw water'. Walde-P. 2.487. Pedersen 2.624 f. The orig. Ir. application only 'beget' (from the pouring out of semen)?

Ir. *geinim*, above, 1.

W. *cenhedlu*, fr. *cenedl* 'nation, tribe, kindred' : Ir. *cenēl* 'race, lineage, kind', *cinim* 'arise, spring from', ChSl. *na-čęti* 'begin' (*za-čęti* also 'conceive'), etc. Walde-P. 1.397 f.

Br. *engehenta* (cf. MBr. *engue hentadur* 'coitus', NBr. *engehentadur* 'conception'), fr. a cpd. of *em-* (reciprocal or reflexive), *ke-* ('co-'), and MBr. vb. *hentaff* 'visit, frequent' (fr. *hent* 'way, road'). Influence of Fr. *engendrer* is possible in both form and meaning. Henry 114.

5. ON *geta*, ME *gete, begete*, NE *beget* : OE *(be)gietan* only in lit. sense 'get, obtain (11.16)', Goth. *bigitan* 'find', OHG *bigezzan* 'obtain', OS *bigetan* 'seize', etc. Walde-P. 1.589. Falk-Torp 308.

ON *ala* mostly 'bear', but also 'beget' (esp. in speaking of both parents together), properly 'nourish, rear' : Lat. *alere*, Ir. *alim* 'nourish, rear', etc. Walde-P. 1.86.

Dan. *avle*, Sw. *avla*, in ODan., OSw. also 'acquire, earn', in the latter sense ON, NIcel. *afla*, fr. ON *afl* 'strength' : OE *afol* id., Lat. *opus*, Skt. *apas-* 'work', etc. Walde-P. 1.175 f. Falk-Torp 37 f.

OE *gestrȳnan*, lit. 'gain, obtain' = OHG *gistriunan* 'gain', denom. of OE *(ge)strēon* 'gain, treasure', OHG *gistriuni* 'gain' (11.73).

OE *(ge)cennan*, OHG *gikennan*, above, 1.

Du. *verwekken*, cpd. of *wekken* 'wake' (4.63).

Du. *voortbringen*, lit. 'bring forth', used for both 'beget' and 'bear' in contrast to NE *bring forth* only of the mother.

Du. *gewinnen* 'gain' (: NE *win*, etc.), also (esp. bibl.) 'beget'.

Du. *telen*, 'beget, bear', fr. MDu. *tēlen* 'produce, care for, attend' : OE *tilian* 'strive, cultivate land' (NE *till*), OHG *zīlon* 'hasten, aim', etc., root connection dub. Walde-P. 1.809. Franck-v. W. 692 f.

OHG *giberan*, MHG *gebern* 'bear' of the mother (4.72), but also 'beget' of the father (for OHG cf. esp. Mt. 1.2 ff. in Tat.).

OHG *kindōn*, MHG *kinden, kindeln* (NHG *kindern*) 'beget, bear', fr. *kind* 'child' (: OHG *gikennan*, etc., above, 1).

NHG *zeugen*, fr. MHG *zuigen* 'produce, prepare' late and isolated 'beget, bear' (of both parents), deriv. of *zuic* 'implement, equipment' (NHG *zeug*). Paul, Deutsches Wtb. 668. Weigand-H. 2.1320 f.

6. Lith. *gimdyti* 'beget, bear', Lett. *dzimdēt* 'bear' with new caus. *dzimdināt* 'beget', OPruss. *gemton* 'bear' : Lith. *gimti*, Lett. *dzimt* 'be born'; also Lith. *gaminti* 'prepare, produce' and 'beget' (: *gamas* 'nature, innate being'); outside root connection dub. Same root as IE **gʷem-* 'come', with development 'come into the world, be born', or related to

**gem-* in Grk. *γάμος* 'marriage', etc.? Walde-P. 1.676. Feist 387.

7. ChSl., SCr. *roditi*, Russ. *rodit'* 'beget, bear', Boh. *roditi*, Pol. *rodzić* 'bear' : ChSl. *rodŭ* 'offspring, birth, race, etc.' (19.23).

Boh. *(z)ploditi*, Pol. *(s)płodzić* 'beget' : Boh. *plod*, Pol. *płod*, ChSl. *plodŭ*, etc. 'fruit (in wide sense), product, offspring', root connection dub. Walde-P. 2.103. Brückner 421.

8. Skt. and Av. words, above, 1, 2.

4.72 BEAR (of Mother)

Grk.	*τίκτω γεννάω*	Goth.	*gabairan*	Lith.	*gimdyti*
NG	*γεννῶ*	ON	*ala, fœða (bera)*	Lett.	*dzemdēt*
Lat.	*parere*	Dan.	*føde*	ChSl.	*roditi*
It.	*partorire*	Sw.	*föda*	SCr.	*roditi*
Fr.	*enfanter*	OE	*beran, cennan (fēdan)*	Boh.	*roditi*
Sp.	*parir*	ME	*bere*	Pol.	*rodzić*
Rum.	*naşte*	NE	*bear*	Russ.	*rodit'*
Ir.	*do-fuismim, biru*	Du.	*baren*	Skt.	*jan-, sū*
NIr.	*beirim, tuismim*	OHG	*(gi)beran, kindōn*	Av.	*zan-, hu-*
W.	*planta, geni*	MHG	*(ge)bern, kinden*		
Br.	*genel*	NHG	*gebären*		

The words discussed in 4.71 which are used for both 'beget' and 'bear' are not repeated here, except (in the list) where there are no special terms for 'bear'. Others are from 'bear, carry', 'feed, nourish' or, like 'beget', from 'obtain, get'.

Phrases like NE *bring into the world*, *be delivered of*, It. *metter al mondo*, Fr. *mettre au monde, accoucher de*, Sp. *dar a luz*, etc., are omitted, though some of these are perhaps in more common use than the words listed, e.g. Fr. *mettre au monde* than *enfanter*.

For all except the following, see 4.71.

1. Lat. *parere* 'bear' (> Sp. *parir*), *parturīre* 'be in labor' (> It. *partorire*), cf. *parentēs* 'parents' : Lat. *parāre* 'prepare, produce, obtain, get', Lith. *perėti* 'hatch, brood', etc. Semantic development prob. fr. the general meaning 'produce, get' seen in Lat. *parāre* and often in *parere* (and always in its cpds.) with specialization to 'produce offspring' in Lith. and partially in Lat. *parere* (so Ernout-M. 734 f.), rather than conversely (as Walde-P. 2.41 f.).

Fr. *enfanter* fr. *enfant* 'child'.

2. Ir. *biru*, NIr. *beirim;* Goth. *(ga)bairan*, ON *bera* (but chiefly of animals, cf. Dan. *bære*, Sw. *bära* 'calve'), OE *beran*, ME *bere*, NE *bear*, Du. *baren* (MDu. *ghebaren* prob. loanword fr. MHG, cf. Franck-v. W. 33), OHG *(gi)beran*, MHG *(ge)bern*, NHG *gebären*, all orig. 'bear, carry' : Grk. *φέρω*, Lat. *ferre*, etc. IE **bher-* (10.61), with specialization through 'bear, carry the child in the womb' (cf. Lat. *gerere* 'bear, carry' and 'be pregnant with').

3. ON *fœða*, Dan. *føde*, Sw. *föde* also 'feed, nourish, rear', as mostly OE *fēdan* (rarely also 'bear', cf. Bosworth-Toller s.v.) = OS *fōdian* 'nourish, beget, bear', OHG *fuotan*, Goth. *fōdjan* 'feed, nourish' : ON *fōðr*, OE *fōþer, fōdor*, OHG *fuotar* 'food, nourishment', etc. (5.12).

4.73 PREGNANT

Grk.	*ἔγκυος*	Goth.	*inkilþō, qiþuhaftō*	Lith.	*neščia*
NG	*(ἐγ)γαστρωμένη, ἔγκυος*	ON	*þunguð, ūlētt, hafandi, með barni*	Lett.	*grūta*
Lat.	*praegnāns, gravida; inciēns*	Dan.	*frugtsommelig, svanger; drægtig*	ChSl.	*neprazdĭna*
It.	*gravida, incinta, pregna*	Sw.	*havande; dräktig*	SCr.	*trudna, bređa, noseća*
Fr.	*enceinte, grosse; pleine*	OE	*geēacnod, bearn-ēacen, mid cilde*	Boh.	*těhotná; březí*
Sp.	*preñada, encinta*	ME	*with childe, with barne*	Pol.	*brzmienna, ciężarna*
Rum.	*însărcinată, grea*	NE	*pregnant, with child*	Russ.	*beremennaja*
Ir.	*torrach*	Du.	*zwanger; drachtig*	Skt.	*garbhiṇī-, garbhavatī-,* etc.
NIr.	*bruinneach, toircheasach*	OHG	*swangar*	Av.	*puϑrā-*
W.	*beichiog*	MHG	*swanger, trehtec, swære*		
Br.	*brazez, dougerez*	NHG	*schwanger; trächtig*		

Beside the words for 'pregnant' as applicable to woman there are in some languages special words for 'pregnant' of animals. These are given last, preceded by a semicolon. But there is no attempt to include all the technical words or phrases for particular animals, like Lith. *veršinga* of a cow (*veršis* 'calf'), *kumelinga* of a mare (*kumelė* 'mare'), etc., so also NE *with calf, with foal*, etc.

The words for 'pregnant' are mostly derivatives of nouns for 'womb, offspring, son, burden' or adjectives meaning literally 'heavy, swollen, big, full, carrying'.

1. Grk. *ἔγκυος* (with *κυέω* 'be pregnant'), Lat. *inciēns* (only of animals) : Skt. *cvayate* 'swells up, becomes strong', Grk. *κοῖλος*, Lat. *cavus* 'hollow', etc., IE **k̂eu-*. Walde-P. 1.366. Ernout-M. 483 (suggesting that Lat. *inciēns* may be an adaptation of Grk. *ἔγκυος* with substitution of suffix). Walde-H. 1.690.

NG *(ἐγ)γαστρωμένη*, pple. of *ἐγγαστρώνω* 'make pregnant', fr. Grk. *γαστήρ* 'belly, womb' (4.46).

2. Lat. *praegnāns, -antis*, with secondary pple. form, beside more orig. *praegnās, -ātis*, this prob. a phrase-cpd. 'in face of birth', second part deriv. of *gnā-* in *nāsci* 'be born' (4.71), *(g)nātus* 'born, son'. Ernout-M. 803. Schwyzer, KZ 56.10 f. Hence Fr. *prégnante*, NE *pregnant*. But VLat. **praegnis* > It. *pregna*, OFr. *prein*, deriv. Sp. *preñarse* 'become pregnant', pple. *preñada*. REW 6720. Gamillscheg 716.

Lat. *gravida* (> It. *gravida*), fr. *gravis* 'heavy' (15.81) also 'pregnant'. VLat. **grevis* > Rum. *grea* 'heavy' and 'pregnant'. Ernout-M. 415.

It. *incinta*, Fr. *enceinte*, Sp. *encinta*, fr. VLat. *incincta*, by popular etym. 'girdled' or 'ungirdled' (Isid.), but perh. really based on an **incienta*, formed fr. *inciēns* (cf. *clienta* : *cliēns*). Walde-H. 1.690. Schwyzer, KZ 56.11, 22.

Fr. *grosse*, lit. 'big' (12.55).

Fr. *pleine* (of animals only), lit. 'full', so also formerly NE *full* (cf. NED s.v.).

Rum. *însărcinată* lit. 'burdened', pple. of *însărcina* 'load, burden'.

3. Ir. *torrach* (NIr. *torrach, tarrach* 'big-bellied, pregnant'), NIr. *toircheasach* (cf. *toircheas* 'pregnancy') : Ir. *tarr* 'rear part, belly', NIr. *tarr* 'bottom, lower side, belly', W. *tor* 'bulge, belly, boss', etc. Pedersen 1.83.

NIr. *bruinneach, bruinnteach*, same word as Ir. *bruinnech* 'mother' (K. Meyer, Contrib. 277), deriv. of *bruinne* 'breast' (4.40), hence orig. 'with swelling breasts' or the like.

W. *beichiog*, arch. also in literal sense 'burdened', fr. *baich* 'burden, load'.

Br. *brazez*, fr. *bras* 'big, large'.

Br. *dougarez*, fem. of *douger* 'bearer', fr. *dougen* 'bear'.

4. Goth. *inkilþō* ('ἔγκυος'), fr. *kilþei* 'womb' (4.47).

Goth. *qiþuhaftō* ('ἐν γαστρὶ ἔχουσα'), cpd. of *qiþus* 'belly, womb' (4.47) and *hafts* 'bound'.

ON *þunguð*, lit. 'loaded', pple. of *þunga* 'load', fr. *þungr* 'heavy' (fr. the same root as Boh., Pol. words, below, 6).

ON *ūlētt*, lit. 'not light' (*lēttr* 'light'), cf. *verða lēttari* 'give birth' lit. 'become lighter'.

ON *hafandi*, Sw. *havande*, fem. pple. of *hafa*, *hava* 'have', hence lit. 'having' (i.e. a child in the womb). Cf. Grk. ἔχουσα Hdt. 5.41 beside the full ἔχουσα ἐν γαστρί id. 3.32. Hellquist 341.

ON *með barni*, OE *med cilde*, ME *with cilde, with barne*, NE *with child* are also usual. In ME no other expression quotable, and still common in NE, regular in NIcel.

ON frequently *ekki heil*, lit. 'not well'.

Dan. *frugtsommelig* extended from ODan. *frugtsom* 'fruitful' (fr. LG *vrugtsam*). Falk-Torp 278.

OE *geēacnod* pple. of *(ge)ēacnian* 'conceive', lit. 'increase' : *ēacan* 'increase, augment' (pple. *ēacen* 'increased' with *bearn* 'child', in *bearn-ēacen* 'pregnant'), Goth. *aukan*, ON *auka* 'increase', etc.

NE *pregnant*, above, 2.

Du. *zwanger*, OHG *swangar*, MHG *swanger*, NHG *schwanger* (> Dan. *svanger*) = OE *swangor* 'heavy, slow' : Lith. *sunkus* 'heavy', *sunkti* 'become heavy', older Lith. *sunkinga* 'pregnant'. Walde-P. 2.525. Falk-Torp 1210.

Du. *drachtig*, LG *drechtig* (> Dan. *drægtig*, Sw. *dräktig*), MHG *trehtec*, NHG *trächtig* (of animals, MHG also of women), fr. MHG *traht*, MLG *dracht* 'burden' : OHG *tragan*, etc. 'carry'. Weigand-H. 2.1057. Falk-Torp 159.

MHG *swære* sometimes 'pregnant' (as also MLG *swār*), lit. 'heavy' (NHG *schwer*, etc.).

5. Lith. *neščia*, fr. *nešti* 'carry'.

Lett. *grūta* lit. 'heavy'.

6. ChSl. *neprazdĭna* (cf. Jagić, Entstehungsgesch. 369), lit. 'not empty', cpd. of neg. *ne-* and *prazdĭnŭ* (see 13.22). So also Bulg. *neprazdna*.

SCr. *trudna*, fem. of *trudan* 'tired, feeble' : ChSl. *trudŭ* 'labor, toil'.

SCr. *bređa*, late ChSl. *brěžda*, Russ. *berežaja* (of the mare), Slov. *brėja*, Boh. *březí* (of animals), prob. fr. the root **bher-* 'carry' in ChSl. *berą*, *bĭrati* 'gather, take', etc. Cf., fr. this root, Lat. *forda* in *bos forda quae fert in ventre*, Varro LL 6.15, etc. Walde-P. 2.157. Berneker 49.

SCr. *noseća*, fr. *nositi* 'carry'.

Boh. *těhotná*, Pol. *ciężarna*, derivs. of *tihota*, *ciężar* 'burden' : ChSl. *tęgota*, *tęgostĭ* 'burden', *težikŭ* 'heavy', Lith. *tingus* 'lazy', ON *þungr* 'heavy' (cf. above, 4), etc. Walde-P. 1.726 f. Brückner 64.

Pol. *brzemienna*, Russ. *beremennaja*, fr. Pol. *brzemię*, older Russ. *beremja*, ChSl. *brěmę* 'load, burden' : ChSl. *bĭrati* 'gather, take', etc. (cf. above SCr. *bređa*). Berneker 50.

7. Skt. *garbhiṇī-*, *garbhavatī-* fr. *garbha-* 'womb' (4.47).

Av. *puθrā-*, deriv. of *puθra-* 'son'. Barth. 910.

4.732. Verbs for 'conceive' or 'be pregnant' are in part derivatives of the same root as 'pregnant', as for example Grk. κυέω, OE *(ge)ēacnian*. But more commonly they are expressions for 'receive, take' like Grk. συλλαμβάνω, Lat. *concipere* which served as models for the greater part of the European terms, NIr. *gabhaim*, Goth. *ganiman*, OHG *intfahen*, NHG *empfangen*, Du. *ontvangen*, Dan. *undfange* (from MLG), Lett. *ien'emt*, etc. Others mean essentially 'begin', Lith. *pradėti*, ChSl. *začęti*, Russ. *začat'*, etc.

4.74 LIVE (= BE ALIVE); LIVING, ALIVE; LIFE

Grk.	ζῶ; ζῶν, ζωός, ἔμψυχος; ζωή, βίος	Goth.	*liban; qius; libains*	Lith.	*gyvas buti, gyventi; gyvas; gyvastis, gyvenimas*, etc.
NG	ζῶ; ζωντανός; ζωή	ON	*lifa; kvikr, lifandi, līfs; līf, fjǫr*	Lett.	*dzīvuot; dzīvs; dzīvība*
Lat.	*vīvere; vīvus; vīta*	Dan.	*leve; levende, i live; liv*	ChSl.	*žiti; živŭ; životŭ, žiznĭ*
It.	*vivere, campare; vivo, vivente; vita*	Sw.	*leva; levande, i livet; liv*	SCr.	*živjeti; živ; život, žiće*
Fr.	*vivre; vivant, vif; vie*	OE	*libban, lifian; cwicu, lebbende; līf, feorh*	Boh.	*žíti; živý, živoucí; život*
Sp.	*vivir; vivo; vida*	ME	*live; living, on live, quik; lif*	Pol.	*żyć; żywy, żyjący; życie, żywot*
Rum.	*trăi (vieţui); viu, în viaţă; viaţă*	NE	*live; living, (a)live; life*	Russ.	*žit'; živaj; žizn'*
Ir.	*am bēo, maraim; bēo, im-bethu; bethu, bēo*	Du.	*leven; levend, in leven; leven*	Skt.	*jīv-; jīva-, jīvant-*, etc.; *jīvana-, jīvita-*, etc.; *asu-*
NIr.	*tāim beo, mairim; beo; beatha*	OHG	*lebēn; lebentīg, lebenti, quec; līb*	Av.	*jīv-; jīva-, jīvya*, etc.; *gaya-, jīti-, jyātu-*, etc., *aŋhu-*
W.	*byw; byw; bywed*	MHG	*leben; lebendic, lebende, quec; līp*		
Br.	*beva; beo; buhez*	NHG	*leben; lebend, lebendig; leben*		

In some languages the verb 'live' is expressed preferably by 'is living, alive', and in fact there are few languages where it may not be so expressed. But this locution is entered in the list only in case the language has a decided preference for it, as against the simple verb forms (as notably in Irish and Lithuanian). Likewise in many cases the original adjective forms are superseded by participial forms of the verb or by phrases 'in life' (so notably in Germanic). These are also omitted from the list where their competition with the adjective is not strong.

Most of the words belong to an inherited group reflecting IE words for 'live, alive', etc. The few others are from the notion of 'remain', or 'be', or are obscure.

In many languages the verbs for 'live, be alive' are also those commonly used for 'live, dwell' (7.11).

1. IE **gʷei-* (*gʷeyə-*, *gʷyē/ō-*, etc.), adj. **gʷīwo-*. Walde-P. 1.668 f. Ernout-M. 1118 f.

Grk. **ζήω* (Att. ζῶ, ζῇ, pple. ζῶν), dial. also ζώω, adj. ζωός, sb. ζωή, and βίος (but the latter mostly 'mode of life', cf. βιόω 'pass one's life' as opposed to ζῶ 'be alive'); Lat. *vīvere, vīvus, vīta* (and the derived Romance group); Ir. *bēo, bethu*, NIr. *beo, beatha*, and the W., Br. forms; in Gmc. only as adjs. in the earliest dialects, Goth. *qius*, ON *kvikr*, OE *cwic(u)*, ME *quik*, OHG, MHG *quec*; all the Balto-Slavic and Indo-Iranian words; Toch. A *śo-*, B *śau-*, *śai-*.

2. Grk. ἔμψυχος 'alive, animate', fr. ἐν 'in' and ψυχή 'breath of life, soul'.

3. Rum. *trăi* 'live', fr. the Slavic, cf. SCr. *trajati* 'last, continue', Bulg. *traja* 'last', etc. Tiktin 1634.

This replaced ORum. *vie* (fr. Lat. *vīvere*), homonymous with *vie* 'come', also *vieţui* (fr. sb. *viaţa*), the latter revived by modern writers. Tiktin 1734, 1738.

4. Ir. *maraim*, NIr. *mairim* 'remain' (12.16), also 'live'.

5. Goth. *liban, libains*, etc., the regular Gmc. group (the old adj. forms from IE **gʷei-* being replaced by participles and forms derived from participles and

by phrases 'in, on life'), generally and satisfactorily explained (though disputed by some who set up an independent IE **leibh-* 'live' for which there is no good outside evidence) as 'live' from 'remain, be left' (perh. through 'be left alive after battle'), with the same root as Goth. *bileiban*, OE *belīfan*, OHG *bilīban* 'be left, remain', ON *leifa* 'leave' and *lifa* 'be left' as well as 'live', etc. (12.16, 12.18). Walde-P. 2.403. Falk-Torp 638, 648. Feist 330.

ON *fjǫr*, OE *feorh* 'life' : OS, OHG *ferh, ferah* 'soul, spirit, life', Goth. *fairhwus* 'world', OE *fīras*, ON *firar* pl., OHG *firahim*, OS *firihun* dat. pl. 'men', outside connections? Walde-P. 2.45. Feist 139.

6. Skt. *asu-*, Av. *aŋhu-* 'life', fr. *as-*, Av. *as-*, IE **es-* 'be'.

4.75 DIE; DEAD; DEATH

Grk.	(ἀπο)θνῄσκω; τεθνηκώς; θάνατος	Goth.	*(ga)swiltan, gadauþnan; dauþs; dauþus*	Lith.	*mirti; numiręs; mirtis*
NG	πεθαίνω; πεθαμένος; θάνατος	ON	*deyja, svelta; dauðr, dāinn; dauði*	Lett.	*mirt; nuomiris; nāve (mira, mirte)*
Lat.	*morī; mortuus; mors, nex*	Dan.	*dø; død; død*	ChSl.	*(u)mrěti; mrŭtvŭ; sŭmrŭtĭ*
It.	*morire; morto; morte*	Sw.	*dö; död; död*	SCr.	*umrijeti; mrtav; smrt*
Fr.	*mourir; mort; mort*	OE	*sweltan, steorfan, cwelan; dēad; dēaþ, swylt*	Boh.	*(u)mříti; mrtvý; smrt*
Sp.	*morir; muerto; muerte*	ME	*deye, swelte, sterve, quele; deed; deeth*	Pol.	*umiérać, umrzeć; umorty; śmierć*
Rum.	*muri; mort; moarte*	NE	*die; dead; death*	Russ.	*umirat', umeret'; mertvyj; smert'*
Ir.	*at-balim, bā-; marb; bās, ēc, bath*	Du.	*sterven; dood; dood*	Skt.	*mṛ-; mṛta-; mṛti-, maraṇa-, mṛtyu-*
NIr.	*do-gheibhim bās, ēagaim; marbh; bās, ēag*	OHG	*sterban, touwen; tōt; tōd*	Av.	*mar-, riθ-; mərəta-, məša-; arista-*, etc.; *(ava)mərəti-, mərəθyu-, mahrka-*, etc.
W.	*marw; marw; angeu*	MHG	*sterben, touwen; tōt; tōt*		
Br.	*mervel; maro; maro*	NHG	*sterben; tot; tod*		

The plain bald words for 'die' are listed, with omission of the numerous euphemistic expressions like NE *pass away, depart, expire, perish*, Grk. (βίον) τελευτάω lit. 'end one's life, come to an end', Lat. *ex-, inter-, per-īre*, lit. 'go from, etc.', *dē- ex-cēdere* lit. 'depart', etc., and likewise of vulgar expressions like NE *croak*, with the parallel Fr. *crever*, It. *crepare* (from Lat. *crepāre* 'crack, creak, rattle') and NG ψοφῶ (Grk. ψοφέω 'make a noise, knock, rattle').

Most of the common words, except in Greek and Germanic, belong to an inherited group, reflecting an IE root for 'die', whatever its ultimate semantic source. Others are originally euphemistic substitutes, cognate with words meaning 'be extinguished, endure pain', 'burn slowly, become stiff', etc.

1. IE **mer-* 'die', perh. ultimately the same as **mer-* in words for 'rub, crush'. Walde-P. 2.276. Ernout-M. 631 f.

Lat. *morī*, adj. *mortuus*, sb. *mors* (hence all the Romance forms); Ir. *marb*, NIr. *marbh* 'dead', W. *marw* 'die, dead', Br. *maro* 'dead, death' (hence *mervel* 'die'); Lith. *mirti*, pple. (perfect.) *numiręs*, sb. *mirtis*, Lett. *mirt*, pple. *nuomiris*, sbs. *mira*, *mirte* (but both rare); ChSl. *mrěti, umrěti*, adj. *mrŭtvŭ*, sb. *sŭmrŭtĭ*, and the other Slavic words (chiefly perfect. forms for the verb); Skt. *mṛ-* (3 sg. pres. *mriyate*, and *marate*), Av. 3 sg. pres. *mairyeiti*, etc., OPers 3 sg. imperf. *amariyatā*, pples.

Skt. *mṛta-*, Av. *mərəta-*, *məša-*; sbs. Skt. *mṛti-*, *maraṇa-*, *mṛtyu-*, Av. *(ava-) mərəti-*, *mərəθyu-*; Arm. *meŕanim* 'die'; Grk. βροτός 'mortal', ἄμβροτος 'immortal'; OHG *mord*, OE, ON *morð* 'murder', etc.

2. Grk. θνῄσκω, ἀποθνῄσκω, perf. pple. τεθνεώς, τεθνηκώς 'dead', sb. θάνατος, NG (ἀποθνῄσκω, τεθνηκώς lit.) πεθαίνω (new pres. to aor. ἀπέθανε), pple. πεθαμένος 'dead' prob. (cf. NG σκοτώνω 'kill', 4.76) : Skt. *dhvan-* 'be extinguished', pple. *dhvānta-* 'dark' and 'darkness', pointing to an IE **dhwenə-*, but further root connections uncertain. Walde-P. 1.841. Otherwise (: θείνω 'strike', etc.) Kent, Language 11.207 ff.

3. Lat. *nex* 'violent death' (vs. *mors*, above, 1), late sometimes also for natural 'death' : Grk. νεκρός, νέκυς Av. *nasu-* 'corpse' (4.77), Skt. *naç-*, Av. *nas-* 'vanish, perish', Ir. *ēc*, etc. (below, 4) 'death'. Walde-P. 2.326. Ernout-M. 669 f.

4. Ir. *at-balim* (e.g. 3 sg. *at-bail*) = **as-t-bal-* (with infixed pronoun, cf. Thurneysen, Gram. 267), OE *cwelan*, ME *quele* : W. *aballu* 'fail, perish', OHG, OS *quelan* 'endure torment', Lith. *gelti* 'sting, cause violent pain', *gelia* 'it hurts', *galas* 'end', OPruss. *gallan* 'death', etc., IE **gʷel-*. Walde-P. 1.690. Pedersen 2.459 f. Vendryes, RC 40.433 ff.

Ir. *bā-* 'die' (forms in Lewis-Pedersen 339, Thurneysen Gram. 461), vbl. n. *bās* 'death', also MIr. *bath* 'death', etym. disputed. As orig. 'go (forth)' : Grk. ἔβην, Skt. *agāt* 'went', IE **gʷā-* 'go', Pedersen 2.458. Otherwise, as a Celtic root *bās-* (with separation of MIr. *bath*), Thurneysen, KZ 37.112, 120 (Gram. 450, 461), Walde-P. 1.677 (with added suggestion of **bās-* : ChSl. *gasiti* 'extinguish', etc.).

NIr. *do-ghcibhim bās* reg. for 'die', lit. 'get death'.

Ir. *ēc*, NIr. *ēag* (hence vb. *ēagaim*), W. *angeu*, Corn. *ancou* 'death' (Br. *ankou* 'death' personified) : Lat. *nex* 'violent death', etc. (above, 3). Pedersen 1.46. Thurneysen, Gram. 127.

5. Goth. *(ga)swiltan*, ON *svelta* poet. (esp. 'die of hunger, starve', so NIcel., Dan., Sw.), OE *sweltan*, ME *swelte* 'die' (ME also 'be oppressed with heat', as NE *swelter*), OE *swylt* 'death' (ON *sultr* 'hunger'), cf. OHG *swelzan*, MHG *swelzen* 'burn up (with hot love), dissolve in fire', Crim. Goth. *schuualt* 'death', all with *d*-extension of **swel-* in OE *swelan* 'burn slowly', Lith. *svilti* 'be scorched', etc. Walde-P. 1.531 f. Falk-Torp 1204, 1208. Feist 468.

Goth. *gadauþnan*, *dauþs*, *dauþus*, ON *deyja* (pple. *dāinn*), *dauðr*, *dauði*, and the Dan. and Sw. words, OE *dēad*, *dēaþ* (vb. lacking in OE, hence ME *deye* prob. fr. Norse), Du. *dood*, OHG *touwen*, *tōt*, *tōd*, etc. : Goth. *diwans* 'mortal', fr. an IE **dheu-*, perh. connected further with **dhwenə-* in Grk. θάνατος, etc. (above, 2), but ultimate relations of the various **dheu-*groups uncertain. Walde-P. 1.835 f. Falk-Torp 175. Feist 118.

OE *steorfan*, ME *sterve* (NE *starve*), Du. *sterven*, OHG *sterban*, MHG, NHG *sterben* : ON *starfa* 'work, tire', *stjarfi* 'tetanus', LG *starfen* 'become stiff, coagulate', Lat. *torpēre* 'be stiff, numb', Lith. *tirpti* 'be numb', etc., labial extensions of IE **ster-* in Grk. στερεός 'stiff, firm', etc. Walde-P. 2.632. Falk-Torp 1159.

6. Lett. *nāve* 'death' : *nāvēt* 'kill', ChSl. *navĭ*, Goth. *naus*, ON *nār* 'corpse' (4.77), Lith. *novyti* 'torture, kill', ChSl., Boh. *naviti* 'tire', etc. Walde-P. 2.316. Mühl-Endz. 2.703 f.

7. Av. *riθ-* (3 sg. pres. *iriθyeiti*), pple. *irista-*, euphemistic terms for 'die, dead' always used of good beings (leaving forms of the inherited root, above, 1, for

evil beings) : Goth. -leipan, ON líða, etc. 'go, pass', cf. ON pple. liðinn 'dead', leiði 'burial place', IE *leit(h)- 'go (away)'. Walde-P. 2.401 f. Barth. 1480 f.

4.76 KILL

Grk.	(ἀπο)κτείνω (ἔπεφνον)	Goth.	usqiman, -daupjan, afslahan	Lith.	užmušti, žudyti
NG	σκοτώνω			Lett.	nuokaut, nuonāvēt
Lat.	interficere, occidere, necāre	ON	deyða, drepa, slā, vega	ChSl.	ubiti, umoriti
		Dan.	dræbe	SCr.	ubiti, usmrtiti
It.	uccidere, ammazzare	Sw.	döda (dräpa)	Boh.	zabiti, usmrtiti
Fr.	tuer	OE	cwellan, slēan, (a)dȳdan	Pol.	zabić, uśmiercić
Sp.	matar			Russ.	ubit'
Rum.	omorî, ucide	ME	sley, culle, quelle	Skt.	han-, vadh-
Ir.	marbaim, gonim, or-gim	NE	kill (slay)	Av.	jan-, fra-kuš-, mərəč-, etc.
NIr.	marbhaim	Du.	dooden		
W.	lladd	OHG	tōtan, (ir)slahan		
Br.	laza,	MHG	tœten, (er)slān		
		NHG	tōten, erschlagen, um-bringen		

Words for 'kill' are often originally the same as, or derived from, words for 'strike' (9.21). Frequently, as in Balto-Slavic, the perfective form of 'strike' is 'kill'. Some are derivatives of words for 'dead', 'death', or causatives of those for 'die'. Some are originally euphemistic expressions from such diverse sources as 'put in darkness', 'deprive of (life)', 'extinguish', etc.

1. Grk. ἀποκτείνω, less frequently (Hom., poet.) κτείνω : Skt. kṣan- 'hurt, wound'. Walde-P. 1.505.

Hom. aor. ἔπεφνον, perf. pass. πέφαται (pres. θείνω 'strike', sb. φόνος 'slaughter, murder', with vb. φονεύω mostly 'murder') : Ir. gonim 'wound, kill', Skt. han- 'strike, kill' (esp. with ni-, abhi-, etc., Av., OPers. jan- 'strike, kill' (esp. with ava-), Hitt. kwen-, kun- 'strike, kill'; Arm. ganem 'strike, beat', Lat. dē-fendere 'ward off', of-fendere 'strike', etc., IE *gʷhen- 'strike'. Walde-P. 1.679 f. Ernout-M. 344. Walde-H. 1.332 f.

Grk. σφάζω, mostly 'slaughter' (in Hom. only of animals), beside σφαγή

'slaughter, throat', root connection? See 4.29.

NG σκοτώνω, fr. class. Grk. σκοτόω 'make dark', Byz. 'kill', deriv. of σκότος 'darkness' (1.62).

2. Lat. interficere, cpd. of inter 'between' (but here in secondary use seen in interīre 'perish, die', interimere 'take away, destroy, kill') and facere 'to make, hence 'do away with, take away' (Plautus, Merc. 832 f. usus, fructus, victus, cultus iam mihi harunc aedium interemptust, interfectust, alienatust), 'deprive of' (Plautus, Truc. 518 salve qui me interfecisti paene vita et lumine), then specialized to 'deprive of life, kill' (also in Plautus). Ernout-M. 324 f., 481. Walde-H. 1.409.443. Thierfelder, Glotta 20.172.

Lat. occīdere (> It. uccidere, OFr. ocire, Rum. ucide), cpd. of ob- and caedere 'cut, strike', also 'kill', perh. : Skt. khid- 'strike, tear, press'. Walde-P. 2.538. Ernout-M. 128 f. Walde-H. 1.129.

Lat. necāre : nex 'violent death', etc. (4.75).

It. ammazzare, orig. 'beat, maul', deriv. of mazza 'club' : OFr. masse (> ME, NE mace), Sp. maza, etc. REW 5425.

Fr. tuer, fr. Lat. tūtāre, tūtārī 'make safe (tūtus), protect', also 'protect oneself against, allay' (inopiam tūtārī Caes.), with development in certain phrases (e.g. famem tūtārī or focum tūtārī) to 'quench, smother, extinguish' as in OIt. stūtare, Prov. tudar, etc. and still in Fr. tuer le feu, hence finally 'kill' already in 12th. cent. French. REW 9018. Gamillscheg 872.

Sp. matar, fr. Pers. māt 'dead' (through the use in the game of chess of Pers. šāh māt 'the king is dead', NE checkmate). REW 5401. Lokotsch 1443.

Rum. omorî, loanword fr. Slavic, ChSl. umoriti, etc. (below, 6).

3. Ir. marbaim, NIr. marbhaim fr. Ir. marb 'dead' (4.75).

Ir. gonim : Grk. ἔπεφνον, etc., above, 1.

Ir. orgim 'strike, kill, injure, hurt'), with a (presumably secondary) Gall. gl. orgē 'occide' (CGL 5.376.29) OBr. gl. orgiat 'caesar', Gall. Orgeto-rīx, perh. : Arm. harkanem 'strike', fr. *perg- an extension of *per- in ChSl. perq, pĭrati 'beat', etc. Walde-P. 2.43. Pedersen 2.587, 590.

W. lladd (old also 'strike'), Br. laza : Ir. slaidim 'strike', outside connections? Walde-P. 1.439. Pedersen 2.630.

4. Goth. af-, ga-daupjan (render θανα-τόω 'put to death'), ON deyða, Sw. döde, OE (a)dȳdan, Du. dooden, OHG tōtan, MHG tōten, fr. the adjs. Goth. daups, ON dauðr, etc. 'dead' (4.75).

Goth. usqiman, cpd. of us- 'out, off', and qiman 'come', hence 'come to the end' (as once = ἀποκτανθῆναι 'be killed',

Lk. 9.22), then, mostly with dat., 'come to an end with, bring an end to, kill'. Cf. Delbrück, Vergl. Syntax 1.262.

Goth. af-slahan (slahan 'strike'), ON slā 'strike', later 'strike to death, kill', OE slēan, ME sley 'strike, kill', NE slay (now with rhetorical flavor, commonly replaced by kill), OHG (ir-)slahan, MHG (er)slān, NHG erschlagen, the simplex mostly 'strike, kill by striking', see under 'strike', 9.21.

ON drepa 'strike, kill', Dan. dræbe, Sw. dräpa 'kill' : OE drepan 'strike', OHG treffan 'strike, hit' (9.21). Falk-Torp 159. Hellquist 158.

ON vega, orig. 'fight' (20.11), also 'kill'.

OE cwellan, ME quelle (NE quell), caus. of OE cwelan 'die' (4.75).

ME culle, kille, also (earlier) 'strike, beat, knock', NE kill, orig. dub. The earlier meaning is against the supposition of OE *cyllan (Gmc. *kuljan) as an ablaut variant of cwellan, etc. NED s.v. kill, vb.

NHG umbringen, earlier 'destroy', MHG umbebringen 'avert, prevent, spoil, squander'. Weigand-H. 2.1107. Paul, Deutsches Wtb. 567.

5. Lith. užmušti, cpd. of už- 'on' (with perfect force) and mušti 'strike'.

Lith. žudyti (Lett. zaudēt 'lose'), caus. of žūti 'perish', perh. : OE gētan 'destroy'. Walde-P. 1.564. Leskien, Ablaut 314.

Lett. nuokaut, perfect. of kaut 'strike, hew'.

Lett. nuonāvēt, perfect. of nāvēt 'kill, murder', fr. nāve 'death' (4.75).

6. ChSl. ubiti (iter. ubivati), SCr. ubiti, Boh. zabiti, Pol. zabić, Russ. ubit', perfect. of ChSl. biti, etc. 'strike'. Berneker 117.

ChSl. umoriti caus. to (u)mrěti 'die', etc. (4.75).

Late ChSl. usŭmrŭtiti, SCr. usmrtiti,

Boh. usmrtiti, Pol. ušmiercić, fr. ChSl. sŭmrŭtŭ, etc. 'death'.

7. Skt. han-, Av. jan- 'strike, kill' : Grk. ἔπεφνον, etc., above, 1.

Skt. vadh- 'smite, kill' (mostly in tenses supplementing han-), beside vadha- 'killing, murder', vadhar- 'Indra's weapon', Av. vadar- 'weapon, club' (20.22) : Grk. ὠθέω 'thrust, push'. Walde-P. 1.254 f.

4.77 CORPSE

Grk.	νεκρός, σῶμα, πτῶμα	Goth.	leik, naus	Lith.	lavonas
NG	πτῶμα, νεκρός	ON	lik, nár	Lett.	lik'is, miruonis
Lat.	cadāver, corpus	Dan.	lig	ChSl.	tĕlo, trupŭ, navĭ
It.	cadavere	Sw.	lik	SCr.	leš, mrtvac
Fr.	cadavre	OE	lic	Boh.	mrtvola
Sp.	cadáver	ME	cor(p)s, liche, body	Pol.	trup, ciało
Rum.	cadavru, leş	NE	corpse, body	Russ.	trup, telo
Ir.	marb, marbán	Du.	lijk	Skt.	çava-, çarīra-
NIr.	marbhám, corp, cor-pán	OHG	lîh, lîhhamo	Av.	nasu-, kəhrp
W.	corff	MHG	lich, lich(n)ame		
Br.	korf-maro	NHG	leichnam, leiche		

Most, though not all, of the words for 'body' (4.11) may be used for the 'dead body', corpse, even where there are also specific terms for this, just as NE body is often used in preference to corpse. Several of the old words for 'body' have even been specialized to 'dead body', as NE corpse, Dan. lig, NHG leichnam, etc. All these have been discussed in 4.11.

Again, words for 'the dead' are often used in preference to specific words for 'corpse' (as NG pop. πεθαμένος for lit. πτῶμα, It. morto for cadavere, etc.), and in some languages words for 'dead' or derivs. of them are the usual terms for 'corpse'. So Ir. marb, marbán, Lett. mir-uonis, SCr. mrtvac, Boh. mrtvola, all obvious derivs. of IE *mer- 'die' (4.75) and so needing no further discussion here. The inclusion, in the list, of words for 'body' or 'dead' beside the other specific terms

is inconsistent, since they might be added in many other cases, but may indicate roughly their relative importance.

Words that are restricted to the dead body of an animal, as OE hold, NE carcass, NHG aas, Lith., Lett. maita, SCr. strvina, Russ. sterva, etc. are not included.

1. Grk. νεκρός, νέκυς, Av. nasu- : Skt. naç-, Av. nas- 'perish, vanish', Lat. nex 'violent death', etc. Walde-P. 2.326.

Grk. πτῶμα 'a fall' (: πίπτω 'fall'), hence esp. 'fallen body, corpse'.

2. Lat. cadāver, deriv. of cadere 'fall', analogous to Grk. πτῶμα. Hence as late loanwords It. cadavere, Fr. cadavre, Sp. cadáver, Rum. cadavru; also NHG kadaver now used only as 'carcass'. Ernout-M. 126.

Rum. leş, fr. SCr., Bulg., Turk. leš (below, 5).

3. Goth. naus (acc. pl. nawins), ON nār, OE nēo- in nēo-bedd 'bed for a

---

corpse', etc. : ChSl. navĭ 'corpse', Lett. nāve 'death' (4.75), Lith. novyti 'torture, kill', ChSl. naviti 'tire', prob. also Goth. naups 'necessity', OE nēad 'violence, constraint, necessity' (NE need), etc. Walde-P. 2.316. Feist 372.

4. Lith. lavonas : Lith. liauti 'cease', OPruss. au-laut 'die', Russ. dial. luna 'death', etc. Walde-P. 2.405. Berneker 745.

Lett. lîk'is, loanword fr. MLG lîk 'corpse'.

5. ChSl. trupŭ (renders πτῶμα 'corpse'

or 'carcass', while tĕlo renders σῶμα 'body', whether living or dead), Pol., Russ. trup 'corpse' (SCr., Boh. trup 'trunk, block', etc.) : ChSl. truplĭ 'hollow', Lith. trupėti 'crumble', Grk. τρῡ-πάω 'bore', etc. Walde-P. 1.732. Brückner 578.

SCr., Bulg. leš (likewise Rum. leş, Alb. lesh), fr. Turk. leš 'corpse, carcass'. Berneker 702. Lokotsch 1306.

6. Skt. çava-, prob. : çū- 'swell', as orig. 'swollen mass, body'.

Av. nasu- : Grk. νεκρός, etc., above, 1.

4.78 BURY (the Dead)

Grk.	θάπτω	Goth.	ga-, us-filhan, gana-wistrōn	Lith.	(pa)laidoti, pakasti
NG	θάφτω, θάβω			Lett.	aprakt, apbedît
Lat.	sepelire (humāre)	ON	jarða, heygja, grefta, grafa	ChSl.	pogreti
It.	sotterrare, seppellire			SCr.	pokopati, sahraniti
Fr.	enterrer, ensevelir	Dan.	begrave, jorde	Boh.	pochovati, pohřbiti
Sp.	enterrar, sepultar	Sw.	begrava, jorda	Pol.	pochować, pogrzebać
Rum.	inmorminta, îngropa	OE	byr(i)gan	Russ.	(s)choronit', pogrebat'
Ir.	adnaicim	ME	burie, enter	Skt.	ni-khan-
NIr.	cuirim, adhlacaim	NE	bury, inter	Av.	(nasu-spaya- 'burial')
W.	claddu, daearu	Du.	begraven		
Br.	douara, bezia	OHG	bigraban, (bi)felahan		
		MHG	begraben, bevelhen		
		NHG	begraben, beerdigen, bestatten		

In the disposal of the dead both burial (inhumation) and cremation have been practiced, either at different periods or contemporaneously, among nearly all the peoples of IE speech. The Zoroastrian custom, attested also for some other Iranian peoples, was the exposure of the corpse to be devoured by dogs and vultures. Cf. Schrader, Reallexicon s.v. Bestattung. Even where cremation was practiced this was generally followed by burial of the bones or ashes.

Cremation was denoted by the usual verbs for 'burn', as Grk. καίω (καίειν νεκρούς in Hom.), Lat. ūrere (XII Tab. hominem mortuom in urbe ne sepelito neve urito), cremāre (the technical term in class. Lat., whence NE cremate, etc.),

Skt. dah- (RV 10.15.14 ye agnidagdhā ye anagnidagdhā 'those who are and those who are not burned with fire' AV 18.2.34 ye nikhātā . . . . ye dagdhā 'those who are buried and those who are burned'), uš- (hence upoṣana- 'cremation').

The words listed here are those for 'bury'—with the following reservations. Grk. θάπτω, while probably originally 'bury' and appropriate to the actual burial of Mycenaean times, is in Homer 'honor with funeral rites', which were normally those of cremation, and only rarely specifically 'bury' (as Od. 11.52 ἐτέθαπτο ὑπὸ χθονός), later usually 'bury', but cf. also πυρὶ θάπτειν 'cremate'. NHG bestatten, though commonly felt as 'bury with ceremony', is used in scientific writings as a convenient general term to cover burial, cremation, etc.

Many of the words for 'bury' are from those for 'dig' (8.22), in part differentiated from the latter by prepositional compounds with perfective sense. Some are from the notion of 'cover, hide' (12.26, 12.27), and some are derivatives of words for 'earth', 'grave', or 'corpse'.

1. Grk. θάπτω, with sbs. τάφος 'burial, grave', ταφή mostly 'burial', τάφρος 'ditch' : Arm. *damban*, *dambaran* 'grave, tomb', further connections dub. Walde-P. 1.852. Boisacq 334.

2. Lat. *sepelīre* (> It. *seppellire*, OFr. *sevelir*, OSp. *sebellir;* Fr. *ensevelir* generic 'bury' in literary use, but commonly 'prepare the corpse for burial'; Sp. *sepultar* new deriv. of *sepolto* 'buried', Lat. *sepultus*), generally combined on the basis of a **sepelyo-* with Skt. (Ved.) *saparyati* 'honors', which clearly belongs with Skt. *sap-* 'serve, honor, love', Grk. ἕπω in ἀμφέπω, ἀμφιέπω 'be busy with, honor', ἐφέπω 'follow', etc. Walde-P. 2.487. Ernout-M. 925. But since Lat. *sepelīre* is expressly 'bury' (cf. *ne sepelito neve urito*, etc. quoted above), a more probable analysis is *se-pelīre* (*se-* as in *solvere* fr. **se-luere*) with a root **pel-* 'cover' inferred fr. Lat. *pellis*, OE *fell*, etc. 'skin, hide' and Goth. *filhan* 'hide, bury' (see below, 4).

Lat. *humāre* (not common), fr. *humus* 'earth'. Still less common *tumulāre* fr. *tumulus* 'mound, tomb'.

It. *sotterrare* (Sp. *soterrar* 'bury, hide' in wide sense), deriv. of phrase Lat. *sub terrā*.

Fr. *enterrer* (> ME *enter*, NE *inter*), Sp. *enterrar* (It. *interrare* 'put in the earth, cover with earth', not used for 'bury the dead'), late Lat. *interrāre*, deriv. of phrase *in terrā*.

Rum. *înmormînta*, fr. *mormînt* 'grave' (4.79).

Rum. *îngropa*, fr. *groapă* 'pit, grave' (4.79).

3. Ir. *ad-naicim* (for OIr. **ad-anagim*, but re-formed in MIr. after vbl. n. *adnacul*, cf. OIr. *co adanastais* gl. 'ut mandarentur terrae'), also 'accompany', NIr. *adhlacaim* for *adhnaclaim* (fr. the vbl. n. *adhnacal*, OIr. *adnacul*, above), cpd. of *ad-* and *anagim* 'protect' (root connection dub., Pedersen 2.457, 558 n. 3). The senses 'bury' and also 'protect' are prob. fr. 'accompany', in the former case applied to attending the corpse to the burial place.

NIr. *cuirim* 'put' (12.12), elliptical for 'put away, put in the earth', now the reg. current term for 'bury'.

W. *claddu*, lit. 'dig' : Ir.*cladi m*, Br. *klaza* 'dig'.

W. *daearu*, Br. *douara*, fr. W. *daear*, Br. *douar* 'earth'.

Br. *bezia*, fr. *bez* 'grave' = W. *bedd* (4.79).

4. Goth. *ga-*, *us-filhan*, cpds. of *filhan* 'hide' (also 'bury' Mt. 8.22), OHG *felahan* 'hide, bury', usually *bifel(a)han*, MHG *bevelhen* 'give up, yield, intrust', and 'bury' (chiefly in the latter sense MHG *der erde bevelhen*), OS *bifehlan* 'yield, bury', ON *fela* 'hide, cover', OE *befēolan* 'commit, deliver, grant', semantic relations peculiar and outside connections dub., but prob. as orig. 'cover', fr. an extension of a root to be seen also in Lat. *pellis*, OE *fell*, etc. 'skin, hide' (4.12). Walde-P. 2.59 (adversely to above). Falk-Torp 227. Feist 151. Weigand-H. 1.178.

Goth. *ganawistrōn*, fr. *naus* 'corpse' (4.77).

ON *jarða*, Dan. *jorde*, Sw. *jorda*, fr. ON *jǫrð*, Dan., Sw. *jord* 'earth' (cf. early Sc. *to earth* in same sense, NED s.v.).

ON *heygja* fr. *haugr* 'mound, burial mound, cairn'.

ON *grefta*, fr. *grǫftr* 'burial, grave' (4.71) : *grafa* (below).

ON *grafa* 'dig', also 'bury', Dan. *begrave*, Sw. *begrava* (*be-* after the German forms), Du. *begraven*, OHG *bigraban*, MHG, NHG *begraben* (but Goth. *bigraban* 'dig around'), cpds. of the Gmc. word for 'dig', Goth., OHG *graban*, etc. : ChSl. *grebą*, *greti* 'scrape', *pogreti* 'bury' (below, 6).

OE *byrigan*, *byrg(e)an*, etc., ME *burie*, NE *bury* (also OE *byrgels*, OS *burgisli* 'burial') : Goth. *bairgan*, ON *bjarga*, OE *beorgan*, OHG *bergan* 'save, keep'. Walde-P. 2.172. NED s.v. *bury*.

NHG *beerdigen*, first 17th. cent., fr. *erde* 'earth'.

NHG *bestatten*, MHG *bestaten* 'put in (the correct) place' also 'permit, equip, prepare for marriage, bury', fr. *statt* 'place, room'. Weigand-H. 1.219.

5. Lith. *laidoti*, *palaidoti* (as orig. 'commit to earth'?) : *pa-laidas* 'loose', *leidžu*, *leisti* 'let, let loose' : Goth. *lētan*, etc. 'let, leave'. Leskien, Ablaut 276 f. Walde-P. 2.395.

Lith. *pakasti*, fr. *kasti* 'dig'.

Lett. *apbedīt*, fr. *bedīt* 'dig' also 'bury' : *best*, Lith. *besti* 'dig', Lat. *fodere* 'dig', etc. Walde-P. 2.188.

Lett. *aprakt*, fr. *rakt* 'dig' : Lith. *rakti* 'poke, scratch, prick', cf. Lith. *rakštis* 'grave' (4.79).

6. ChSl. *pogrebą*, *pogreti*, Boh. *pohřbiti*, Pol. *pogrzebać*, Russ. *pogrebat'* : ChSl. *grebą*, *greti* 'scrape', Goth. *graban* 'dig', etc. (above, 4). Berneker 347 f.

SCr. *pokopati*, fr. *kopati* 'dig'.

SCr. *sahraniti*, Russ. *schoronit'*, *pochoronit'*, fr. SCr. *hraniti* 'keep, nourish', Russ. *choronit'* 'hide, conceal', also in simplex 'bury' : ChSl. *chranq*, *chraniti* 'watch, guard', etc. Berneker 397 f.

Boh. *pochovati*, Pol. *pochować*, fr. Boh. *chovati*, Pol. *chować* 'keep, take care of' (11.24).

7. Skt. *ni-khan-*, cpd. of *ni-* 'down' and *khan-* 'dig'; used of 'burying' any object (treasure, etc.) but also of the dead (e.g. AV 18.2.34 quoted above), though burial in India was only an occasional practice beside the usual cremation (Oldenberg, Religion des Veda 570).

Av. *nasu-spaya-*, *nasu-spā-* 'burial, burier of corpses', cpds. of *nasu-* 'corpse' (4.77) and the root of *spayeiti*, etc. 'take away, remove'. These words occur only with reference to a sin, a violation of the prescribed Zoroastrian practice of exposing the corpse. Cf. Vd. 3.41 *daēna mazdayašniš . . . . spayeiti nasuspaēm* "the Mazdayasnian law removes the (sin of) corpse-burial". Barth. 1059 f., 1615.

4.79 GRAVE

Grk.	*τάφος, σῆμα*	Goth.	*hlaiw*	Lith.	*kapas*
NG	*τάφος*	ON	*grǫf, grǫftr*	Lett.	*kaps*
Lat.	*sepulcrum*	Dan.	*grav*	ChSl.	*grobŭ*
It.	*sepoltura, fossa (tomba)*	Sw.	*grav*	SCr.	*grob*
Fr.	*tombe (tombeau)*	OE	*byrgen, græf*	Boh.	*hrob*
Sp.	*sepultura*	ME	*grave, tumbe*	Pol.	*grób*
Rum.	*mormînt (groapă)*	NE	*grave (tomb)*	Russ.	*mogila (grob)*
Ir.	*fert, lecht*	Du.	*graf*	Skt.	*(çmaçāna-)*
NIr.	*uaigh*	OHG	*grab*	Av.	*(uzdāna-)*
W.	*bedd*	MHG	*grap*		
Br.	*bez*	NHG	*grab*		

The words listed are those commonly employed for the burial place of the dead without necessary implication of its precise form. Most of them are cognate with those for 'bury' (4.78) or meant originally 'ditch, trench' or 'mound'. Words for 'memorial, monument' are often used for 'burial monument, tomb', but in most cases are not among the common words for 'grave'.

1. Grk. τάφος 'burial, funeral' (Hom. +), later the usual word for 'grave' (ταφή mostly 'burial', rarely 'burial place') : θάπτω 'bury', τάφρος 'ditch', etc. (4.78).

Grk. σῆμα 'sign, mark' (12.94), hence also 'burial mound' (so in Hom., where τάφος is only 'burial'), 'grave, tomb' (Hdt., Thuc., etc., freq. in inscriptions, e.g. Ditt. Syll. 1218).

Grk. θήκη 'box, chest', also 'tomb, vault' for the dead (Aesch.+) : τίθημι 'place, put'.

2. Lat. *sepulcrum* (> It. *sepolcro*, OFr., ME, NE *sepulcre*, Sp. *sepulcro*, not popular words) : *sepelīre* 'bury'.

It. *sepoltura*, Sp. *sepultura* (also 'burial' as Fr. *sépulture*), fr. Lat. *sepultūra* 'burial' : *sepelīre* 'bury'.

Fr. *tombe* (> ME *tumbe*, NE *tomb*, formerly more generic than now) beside the less generic *tombeau* 'tomb', It. *tomba* 'tomb', fr. late Lat. *tumba*, this fr. Grk. τύμβος 'burial mound' : Lat. *tumulus* 'mound, burial mound', *tumēre* 'be swollen', Ir. *tomm* 'hillock', etc. Walde-P. 1.708. Ernout-M. 1063, -64. REW 8977.

Rum. *mormînt* fr. Lat. *monumentum*, *monimentum* 'memorial, monument' sometimes 'tomb', prob. influenced by *mort* 'dead'. REW 5672. Pușcariu 1109. Cf. the similar occasional use of Grk. μνῆμα, and of Lat. *memoria* in late times (Peregrinatio).

Rum. *groapă* ('ditch' and 'excavation for burial', 'grave' in narrower sense than *mormînt*), prob. through Alb. *gropë* 'grave, hole in the earth' fr. Slavic *grobŭ* (below). G. Meyer, Alb. Etym. Wtb. 131. Tiktin 703.

It. *fossa*, 'ditch' and pop. for 'grave' (as formerly Sp. *fosa* now obs. for 'grave'; Fr. *fosse* used only in the original narrow sense, the excavation, cf. *tombe de fosse*), fr. Lat. *fossa* 'ditch, trench', late 'grave' : *fodere* 'dig'.

3. Ir. *fert*, prob. (either as 'covering' or 'protected inclosure') : *fern* 'shield', Goth. *warjan*, ON *verja* 'protect', Skt. *vṛ-* 'cover', etc., cf. Alb. *vorr* 'grave' (**wornā*), IE **wer-*. Walde-P. 1.282. Stokes 271.

Ir. *lecht* (NIr. *leacht* 'grave, cairn, monument'), prob. fr. Lat. *lectus* 'bed, couch' also 'funeral couch, bier'. Vendryes, De hib. voc. 150. Walde-P. 2.424. (Otherwise, as cognate, Stokes 245).

NIr. *uaigh*, also 'den, cave', MIr. *uag* 'hole, grave' (rare), outside connections? Walde-P. 1.171.

W. *bedd*, Br. *bez*, Corn. *bedh* : Lett. *bedīt* 'dig, bury' (4.78), Lith. *besti* 'dig', Lat. *fodere* 'dig'. Walde-P. 2.188.

4. Goth. *hlaiw* = OE *hlāw*, *hlǣw* 'mound, burial mound', OHG *hlēo* 'burial mound' : Lat. *clīvus* 'hill, slope', etc., fr. the root of OE *hlinian*, Lat. *clīnāre* 'lean', etc. Walde-P. 1.491. Feist 261.

ON *grǫf*, *grǫftr*, OE *græf*, OHG *grab*, etc., general Gmc. (but Goth. *graba* only 'trench') : ON *grafa* 'dig, bury', OHG *graban* 'dig', *begraban* 'bury', etc.

OE *byrgen* : *byrigan*, NE *bury*, etc.

ME *tumbe*, NE *tomb*, fr. Fr. *tombe* above, 2.

5. Lith. *kapas*, Lett. *kaps* : OPruss. *enkopts* 'buried', Lett. *kapāt*, Lith. *kapoti* 'hew, chop', ChSl. *kopati* 'dig' (8.22), SCr. *pokopati* 'bury', etc. Mühl.-Endz. 2.159. Walde-P. 2.561.

6. ChSl. *grobŭ*, etc., general Slavic : ChSl. *greti* 'scrape', *pogreti* 'bury', Goth. *graban*, ON *grafa* 'dig', etc. (cf. above ON *grǫf*). Berneker 353.

Russ. *mogila* (replaces *grob* in popular use) = ChSl. *mogyla*, Pol. *mogiła* 'burial mound', Bulg. *mogila*, Alb. *magulë* 'hill', source unknown. Berneker 2.68 f.

7. The nearest approach to a Skt. word for 'grave' is *çmaçāna-* 'place for burning the corpse and collecting the bones', etym. dub. Walde-P. 1.387. Charpentier, IF 28.157 ff.

The nearest approach to an Av. word for 'grave' is *uzdāna-* 'place for deposit of the bones' (Vd. 6.50), fr. *uz-* 'up' and *dā-* 'place'.

4.81 STRONG, MIGHTY, POWERFUL

Grk.	*ἰσχῡρός, κρατερός, δυνατός*	Goth.	*swinþs, mahteigs, abrs*	Lith.	*stiprus, galingas*
NG	*δυνατός (ἰσχυρός, κρατερός)*	ON	*sterkr, styrkr, māttugr*	Lett.	*stiprs, spēcīgs*
Lat.	*validus, valēns, fortis, potēns*	Dan.	*stærk, mægtig, kraftig*	ChSl.	*krěpŭkŭ, silĭnŭ*
It.	*forte, potente*	Sw.	*stark, mäktig, kraftig*	SCr.	*jak, snažan, silan*
Fr.	*fort, puissant*	OE	*swīþ, strang, mæhtig*	Boh.	*silný, mocný*
Sp.	*fuerte, potente*	ME	*strong, stark, myghty*	Pol.	*silny, mocny*
Rum.	*tare, puternic*	NE	*strong, powerful, mighty*	Russ.	*sil'nyj, moštnyj*
Ir.	*trēn, lāidir, adbol*	Du.	*sterk, machtig, krachtig*	Skt.	*balin-, çūra-, ojasvant-*
NIr.	*trean, lāidir, nearthmar*	OHG	*strengi stark, mahtig, kreftig, giwaltig*	Av.	*sūra-, aojahvant-, amavant-*
W.	*cryf, cadarn, nerthol, galluog, grymus*	MHG	*starc, strenge, swint, mehtec, kreftec, gewaltec*		
Br.	*kréñv, nerzek, galloudek*	NHG	*stark, mächtig, kräftig, gewaltig*		

'Strong' is understood here in its application to bodily strength. But such words have a much wider range, being used also of mind, feelings, etc., and of inanimate things. Furthermore there is no sharp line between 'strong' and 'powerful, mighty', which are applied to bodily strength with more emphasis on the active quality.

While only the adjectives are listed, the nouns for 'strength' are mostly parallel, either the sources of or derived from the adjectives, and so are covered in the comments—where are added a few important nouns not so related.

Among the semantic sources are notions such as 'stiff, hard', 'hold', 'be able, have power', and various others.

1. Grk. ἰσχῡρός, fr. ἰσχύς 'strength', Lac. acc. sg. βίσχυν and γισχύν· ἰσχύν (Hesych.), fr. *ϝι-σχῡς, first part : Skt. *vi-* 'apart' (or possibly : ἴς, *ϝῖς, Lat. *vīs* 'strength') and the second from the weak grade of IE **seĝh-* in Skt. *sah-* 'vanquish, overcome, be able' (cf. *vi-sah-* 'overcome, have in one's power'), Grk. ἔχω 'have, hold', etc. Walde-P. 2.482. Boisacq 386. Brugmann, IF 16.494.

Grk. κρατερός, καρτερός (Hom. also κρατύς) with sb. κράτος, κάρτος 'strength', etc. : Goth. *hardus*, ON *harðr*, etc. 'hard', prob. also Skt. *karkara-* 'rough, hard', etc. Walde-P. 1.354. Boisacq 510 f.

Grk. δυνατός, properly 'able, powerful' but also 'strong' in body, in NG the common word for 'strong' : δύναμαι 'be able', δύναμις 'power', etym. obscure. Boisacq 204.

Grk. σθένος 'strength', perh. σθ-ένος fr. the weak grade of the root in Skt. sagh- 'be a match for', etc. IE *seǵh- beside *seǵh- in ἔχω, etc. Walde-P. 2.482 f. Bolling, AJPh. 21.316.

Grk. ῥώμη 'strength' : ῥώννῡμι 'strengthen', perf. mid., 'have strength', outside connections? Boisacq 847.

2. Lat. vīs, the commonest noun for 'strength' : Grk. ἴς 'strength', Skt. vayas- 'strength, vigor, etc.'. Walde-P. 1.229 f. Ernout-M. 1115.

Lat. valēns pple. of valēre 'be strong', whence also validus : Ir. faln-, foln- 'rule', flaith 'sovereignty, prince', OHG waltan, ON valda, ChSl. vlasti 'rule', etc. (19.31). Walde-P. 1.219. Ernout-M. 1071.

Lat. rōbustus, orig. 'oaken, of oak', fr. rōbur, old rōbus 'oak' (: ruber, dial. rōbus 'red'). Ernout-M. 867.

Lat. fortis (more commonly of mental strength, 'brave', but also and orig. used of physical strength and in this sense > It. forte, Fr. fort, Sp. fuerte), fr. forctis (Festus), prob. : Av. dražaite 'holds', ChSl. drŭžati 'hold', guttural extensions of IE *dher- in Skt. dhṛ- 'hold, support', etc. Walde-P. 1.859. Ernout-M. 382 f. Otherwise (fr. *bherǵh- in Skt. bṛhant- 'great, mighty, high', Av. bərəzant- 'high', etc.) Walde-H. 1.535 ff.

Lat. potēns (> It., Sp. potente) pple. of *potēre (= posse 'be able', 9.95), whence OFr. poer, povoir, Fr. pouvoir vb. and sb. (> sb. ME, NE power, whence adj. NE powerful), Rum. putere 'power', whence adj. puternic; Fr. adj. puissant fr. OFr. puis 1 sg. of vb. Ernout-M. 796. REW 6682. Gamillscheg 725.

Rum. tare, fr. Lat. tālis 'such' in the pregnant use as tālis vir 'such a man'.

Cf. SCr. jak, below, 6. REW 8543. Puşcariu 1713.

3. Ir. trēn (also 'brave', cf. Lat. fortis), NIr. trēan and (orig. comp.) treis, : ON þrekr, þrek 'strength, bravery', OE þrece 'force, oppression', etc. Walde-P. 1.755 f. Pedersen 1.296.

Ir. lāidir, etym.?

Ir. adbol (ind adbol gl. valde), adbal (also 'vast'), etym. dub., perh. fr. Celtic ad-velo-, IE *ad-upelo- : Goth. ubils 'bad', through sense of 'extreme, excessive'. Pokorny, Streitberg Festgabe 292.

NIr. nearthmar, W. nerthol, Br. nerzek, nerzus, fr. Ir. nert, NIr. neart, W. nerth, Br. nerz 'strength, power' : Grk. ἀνήρ, Skt. nar- 'man', etc. (2.21). Walde-P. 2.332. Pedersen 1.136.

W. cryf, Br. krénv, etym. dub., perh. fr. *kṛp- beside *krēp- in ChSl. krĕpŭ, etc. (below, 6). Walde-P. 1.487 (adversely). Stokes 96. Henry 81 (:Skt. kram- 'advance, walk', etc.).

W. cadarn (= Br. kadarn 'brave') beside cadr (arch.) 'mighty, handsome', OBr. cadr, Br. kaer 'beautiful' : Gall. catu-, Ir. cath, W. cad, etc. 'battle'. Walde-P. 1.339, 340. Pedersen 1.323, 2.50, 53.

W. galluog, Br. galloudek, through sbs. W. gallu, Br. galloud, fr. vbs. W. gallu, Br. gallout 'be able' (9.95).

W. grymus, fr. grym 'power' = Ir. greim id. : Ir. in-grennim 'pursue' (*ghrend- : Lat. gradī 'step', etc.) Pedersen 2.548 f. Stokes 118.

4. Goth. swinþs, OE swīþ, MHG swint, swinde (also 'violent, cunning', etc.) : ON svinnr 'wise', OS swīdi, swīð 'strong, violent', etc., perh. also OHG gisunt, etc. 'healthy', outside connections disputed. Walde-P. 2.525 f. Feist 468 f.

Goth. abrs (cf. abraba 'very', bi-

abrjan 'be astonished'), etym.? Walde-P. 1.177 f. Feist 1 f.

Goth. mahteigs, ON máttugr, OE mæhtig, OHG mahtig, etc. general Gmc. (Dan., Sw. fr. MLG) fr. sb. Goth. maht, etc. 'might', this fr. vb. Goth. magan, etc. 'be able' (9.95). Walde-P. 2.227. Falk-Torp 690.

ON sterkr, Dan. stærk, Sw. stark (OE stearc 'hard, rigid, harsh, stern, violent', ME, NE stark also 'strong', now obs. in this sense), Du. sterk, OHG star(a)ch, stark, MHG starc, NHG stark (Gmc. *starku-), weak grade in ON styrkr (*sturku-) : Goth. ga-staurknan 'stiffen', ON storkna 'curdle', guttural extension of IE *ster- in Grk. στερεός 'stiff, hard', ON starr, NHG starr 'stiff', etc. Walde-P. 2.629. Falk-Torp 1159.

OE strang, strong, ME, NE strong, OHG strengi, MHG strenge (NHG streng 'severe'), cf. ON strangr 'hard, severe', and 'strong' (of a current), prob.: ON strengr, OE streng (NE string), OHG stranc 'rope, cord, string', Ir. srengim 'pull', with a common notion of 'stiff, taut', and ultimately connected with *ster- in Grk. στερεός 'stiff, hard', OE stearc, etc. (above; cf. NE dial. stark 'taut', NED s.v. 4e). Walde-P. 2.650. Falk-Torp 1179.

OE þrӯþfull (not common), fr. þrӯþ 'strength' (mostly in pl. 'forces', but common in cpds., esp. proper names) : ON þrúðr and þrúð- in cpds., OHG proper names in Thrud- : OHG triuwen 'bloom, grow'. Walde-P. 1.754. Holthausen 371.

OHG kreftig, NHG kräftig, Dan., Sw. kraftig, Du. krachtig, fr. sb. OHG kraft, etc. 'strength, power' (OE cræft mostly 'intellectual power, skill'), outside connections? Walde-P. 1.596. Falk-Torp 572.

OHG giwaltig, MHG gewaltec NHG gewaltig, fr. OHG giwalt 'power' (= OE

geweald id.), fr. OHG waltan 'rule' (19.31), this fr. the same root as Lat. validus (above, 2).

5. Lith. stiprus, Lett. stiprs : Lith. stipti, Lett. stipt 'stiffen', OE stīf, MHG stīf 'stiff', Lat. stīpāre 'press together', etc. Walde-P. 2.647.

Lith. galingas, gale 'strength, power', galéti 'be able', W. gallu 'be able' (9.95). Walde-P. 1.539.

Lett. spēcīgs, fr. spēks 'power, strength' (Lith. spėka, spėkas less common) : spēt 'be able, capable', Lith. spėti 'keep up with, guess', ChSl. spěti 'succeed, progress', OE spōwan 'succeed', Sk. sphā- 'fatten', etc. Walde-P. 2.657. Mühl.-Endz. 3.991–93.

Lith. jiga (also nuo-, pa-) 'power, might' : Grk. ἥβη 'vigor of youth, youth'. Walde-P. 1.206 f.

Lett. vara 'power, might', OPruss. warrin (acc. sg.) id. : varit 'be able' (9.95).

6. ChSl. krěpŭkŭ (reg. in Gospels for ἰσχυρός; SCr. krepak, Boh. krepký, Pol. krzepki, Russ. krepkij, mostly 'powerful, robust' or 'firm, solid', etym. dub., perh. : ON hráfa 'tolerate, bear', W. craff 'fast, secure' (W. cryf 'strong'? cf. above, 3). Walde-P. 1.487. Berneker 614.

SCr. jak = ChSl. jakŭ 'qualis' (Pol. jaki, Boh. jaký 'what sort of', etc.). Semantic development like Rum. tare fr. Lat. tālis (above, 2). Leskien, Serbokroat. Gram. 406.

SCr. snažan fr. snaga 'strength' : ChSl. snaga 'work, zeal', Boh. snaha 'effort', etc., outside connections? Miklosich 312.

ChSl. silĭnŭ, Boh. silný, Pol. silny, Russ. sil'nyj, fr. the sbs. for 'strength', ChSl. sila, etc. : OPruss. seilin 'industry, zeal', ON seilask 'seek for, stretch out the hand', further root connections dub. Walde-P. 2.460 f. Brückner 490 f.

Boh. mocný, Pol. mocny, Russ. moštnyj, fr. sbs. for 'might', Boh. moc, etc. = ChSl. moštĭ, fr. vbs. for 'be able' ChSl. mošti, mogǫ, etc. : Goth. magan 'be able', etc. (above, 4). Walde-P. 2.227. Berneker 2.67 f., 70.

7. Skt. balin-, fr. bala- 'strength' : ChSl. boljĭjĭ 'larger', bolje 'more', Lat. dē-bilis 'weak', Grk. βελτίων 'better', etc. Walde-H. 1.327. Walde-P. 2.119 f. Berneker 72.

Skt. çūra-, Av. sūra-, also Skt. çavas 'strength' : Grk. ἄκυρος 'without authority', κύριος 'lord, ruler', prob. fr.

the root *keu- 'swell' in Skt. çvayate, etc. Walde-P. 1.365 f.

Skt. ojasvant-, Av. aojah-, aojahvant-, fr. Skt. ojas-, Av. aojas- 'strength' : Skt. vakṣ-, ukṣ-, Av. vaxš-, uxš- 'grow, make grow', Goth. wahsjan 'grow', Lat. augēre 'increase', etc. Walde-P. 122. f.

Av. amavant-, fr. ama- 'strength, power' : Skt. ama- 'onset, am- 'press on, injure', ON ama 'vex, annoy,' etc. Walde-P. 1.178. Barth. 141.

Av. zavah-, zāvar- 'strength, power' (NPers. zōr > Turk. zor > NG ζόρι 'force, violence') : Skt. javas- 'speed', jū- 'be swift', etc. Walde-P. 1.555. Barth. 1690.

4.82   WEAK

Grk.	ἀσθενής, ἄρρωστος	Goth.	lasiws	Lith.	silpnas
NG	ἀδύνατος	ON	veikr	Lett.	vājš, nestiprs
Lat.	dēbilis, invalidus, in-firmus	Dan.	svag	ChSl.	slabŭ
		Sw.	svag	SCr.	slab
It.	debole	OE	wāc	Boh.	slabý
Fr.	faible	ME	woke, waike	Pol.	slaby
Sp.	débil	NE	weak	Russ.	slabyj
Rum.	slab	Du.	zwak	Skt.	durbala-, ni-bala-, abala-
Ir.	lobur, lacc, fand	OHG	weich, kümig		
NIr.	lag, fann	MHG	weich, swach, kume	Av.	asūra-
W.	gwan	NHG	schwach		
Br.	gwan				

'Weak' as the opposite of 'strong' is often expressed simply as 'not strong', with negative compounds of words for 'strong' or 'strength'. The other words are from diverse notions such as 'loose, slack', 'pliant', 'yielding', 'lamentable or plaintive', etc.

1. Grk. ἀσθενής, neg. cpd. of σθένος 'strength' (4.81).

Grk. ἄρρωστος, neg. cpd. of *ῥωστός, vbl. adj. of ῥώννῡμι 'strengthen' (4.81).

NG ἀδύνατος (in class. Grk. 'unable, weakly'), neg. of δυνατός 'able, strong' (4.81).

2. Lat. dēbilis (> It. debole, Sp. débil), cpd. of dē- here 'without' (as in dēmēns, dēformis, etc.), second part : Skt. bala-

'strength' (4.81). Ernout-M. 255. Walde-H. 1.327.

Lat. invalidus, neg. of validus 'strong' (4.81).

Lat. infirmus, neg. of firmus 'fast, solid, firm, strong' : Skt. dhṛ-, Av. dar- 'hold, support', etc. (cf. Lat. fortis 'strong', 4.81). Walde-P. 1.859. Ernout-M. 364.

Fr. faible, OFr. feble (> ME feble, NE feeble), fr. Lat. flēbilis (: flēre 'weep') 'tearful, plaintive' and 'to be wept over, lamentable', both of which meanings are naturally associated with weakness. REW 3362.

Rum. slab fr. Slavic (below, 6).

3. Ir. lobur (NIr. lobhar 'leprous') :

lobraim 'putresco', W. llwfr 'timid', MBr. lofr 'leprous', these perh. : Lat. labāre 'waver, be ready to fall', etc. and the Slavic group below, 6. Walde-P. 2.432. (Otherwise Pedersen 1.116 f. : Grk. λώβη 'outrage, mistreatment', Lith. slogus 'burdensome', etc., cf. Walde-P. 2.714.)

Ir. lacc, NIr. lag (W. lacc 'slack, loose') : Grk. λήγω 'cease', λαγαρός 'slack', ON slakr, NE slack 'loose, slack', etc. Walde-P. 2.712. Pedersen 1.161.

Ir. fand, fann, NIr. fann (usually 'infirm, weak willed, etc.'), W., Br. gwan, etym.? Walde-P. 1.259. Pedersen 1.178.

4. Goth. lasivs : OE lyso, lyswen 'corrupt, evil', OHG erleswen 'become weak', ON las-meyrr 'decrepit', Bulg. loš 'bad, ugly', SCr. loš 'bad, unfortunate', all from the notion of 'slack'(?). Walde-P. 2.439. Feist 322. Falk-Torp 625.

ON veikr (> ME waike, NE weak), OE wāc, ME woke, OHG, MHG weich (also 'soft' as NHG) : ON vīkja 'drive away, move', OE wīcan 'yield, give way', OHG wīhhan 'yield', fr. *weig- beside *weik- in Grk. εἴκω 'yield, give way', etc. Walde-P. 1.235. Falk-Torp 1360.

Du. zwak, MLG swak (> Dan., Sw. svag), MHG swach, NHG schwach (in the earlier dialects also 'pliant, poor',

etc.) : Norw. dial. svaga 'vacillate', ON sveggja 'turn (a ship)', (with nasal) OHG etc. swingan 'swing', OE swancor, MHG swank 'pliant, slender', Skt. svaj- 'embrace', fr. a root meaning 'bend, pliant' or the like. Walde-P. 2.527. Falk-Torp 1208.

OHG kūmīg (also 'ill, sick'), MHG kūm(e), as orig. 'complaining' or 'lamentable' (cf. on Fr. faible, above, 2) : OHG cūma 'lamentation', kūmen 'complain', OHG gikewen 'name, call', Grk. γοάω 'lament', etc. Walde-P. 1.635.

5. Lith. silpnas, cf. silpti 'become weak', etym.? Walde-P. 1.92, 2.432.

Lett. vājš, with sb. vājums : Lith. vojes pple. 'suffering', outside connections dub. (Skt. vāyati 'becomes exhausted'?). Walde-P. 1.213 f. Mühl.-Endz 4.493 f.

Lett. nestiprs, neg. of stiprs 'strong' (4.81).

6. ChSl. slabŭ, etc., general Slavic : OHG slaf(f), NHG schlaff, MLG slap 'loose', and without s-, Icel. lapa 'hang loose', Lat. labāre 'waver, be ready to fall', etc. (cf. above, 3, Ir. lobur). Walde-P. 2.432. Walde-H. 1.739.

7. Skt. durbala-, nirbala-, abala-, neg. cpds. of bala- 'strength' (4.81).

Av. asūra-, neg. of sūra 'strong' (4.81).

4.83 WELL; HEALTH

Grk.	*ὑγιής; ὑγίεια*	Goth.	*hails*	Lith.	*sveikas; sveikata*
NG	*ὑγιής, γερός; ὑγεία*	ON	*heill; heilsa*	Lett.	*vesels, sveiks; veselība*
Lat.	*sānus*, etc.; *sānitās*, etc.	Dan.	*rask, sund; helbred, sundhed*	ChSl.	*sŭdravŭ, cělŭ; sŭdravĭje*
It.	*sano; salute*	Sw.	*frisk, sund; hälsa, sundhet*	SCr.	*zdrav; zdravlje*
Fr.	*sain; santé*			Boh.	*zdravý; zdraví*
Sp.	*sano; salud (sanidad)*	OE	*hāl, gesund; hǣlþ, hǣlu*	Pol.	*zdrowy; zdrowie*
Rum.	*sănătos; sănătate*			Russ.	*zdorovyj; zdorov'e*
Ir.	*slān; slāntu*	ME	*hole (hale), (i)sunde; helthe*	Skt.	*svastha-, kuçalin-; kuçala-, aroga-*, etc.
NIr.	*slān, follāin; slāinte*				
W.	*iach; iechyd*	NE	*well, healthy; health*		
Br.	*yac'h; yec'hed*	Du.	*gezond; gezondheid*	Av.	*drva-, abanta-; drvatāṯ-*
		OHG	*heil, gisunti; heilī, gisuntī*		
		MHG	*heil, gesunt; heil, gesunde*		
		NHG	*gesund; gesundheit*		

Words for 'well' (in body) are from such notions as 'well-living, whole, strong, firm, in good condition, lively, fresh', etc.

The nouns for 'health' are mostly derivatives of adjectives for 'well' (in a few cases conversely), but the adj. and sb. forms in most common use are not always parallel (cf. It., Dan., NE, etc.).

Several of the words for 'health' in its original sense of 'good health' were extended to connote bodily condition, so as to include also (mostly with adj. for 'bad' or 'weak') 'bad health', e.g. Lat. *valētūdō*, Fr. *santé*, Dan. *helbred* (in contrast to *sundhed* only 'good health'), NE *health*, SCr. (*slabo*) *zdravlje*, etc.

1. Grk. ὑγιής (also ὑγιηρός > NG γερός), hence ὑγίεια, NG ὑγεία 'health' (hence the pop. greeting γειά σου), fr. **su-g*ʷ*iyēs*, cpd. of IE **su-* 'well' (Skt. *su-*, Av. *hu-*, etc.) and deriv. of IE **g*ʷ*ei-* 'live' in Grk. ζῶ etc. (4.74). Walde-P. 1.669.

But the NG phrase εἶναι καλά or στέκει καλά is the most common way of saying that a person 'is well'.

2. Lat. *sānus* (> It., Sp. *sano*, Rum. dial. *sîn*, *sar*, Fr. *sain*; NE *sane* restricted to 'mentally sound' after its opposite *insane*, Lat. *insānus* 'insane'; hence also present use of *sanity*), hence *sānitās* (> Fr. *santé*, Sp. *sanidad*, Rum. *sănătate*; VLat. **sānitōsus* > Rum. *sănătos*), outside connection? Walde-P. 2.452. Ernout-M. 893 f. REW 7584.

Lat. *salūs* 'welfare, safety' and 'health' (> It. *salute*, Sp. *salud* esp. 'health'), deriv. of *salvus* 'unharmed, sound, safe' (> It. *salvo*, Fr. *sauf*, etc. 'safe') : Umbr. *saluom* 'salvum', Skt. *sarva-* 'whole, all', Av. *haurva-* 'whole', Grk. ὅλος, Hom. οὖλος 'whole', Toch. A *salu*, adv. 'entirely' (SSS 278). Walde-P. 2.510 f. Ernout-M. 890 f.

Lat. *validus* 'strong' (4.81), also frequently 'sound, well', and *valētūdō* (fr. *valēre* 'be strong') wholly specialized to 'bodily health', orig. 'good health', later often 'bad health, sickness' (hence *valētūdinārius* 'sickly', NE *valetudinarian*).

3. Ir. *slān*, NIr. also *follāin* (deriv. with *fo-*), hence *slāntu*, NIr. *slāinte* 'health', etym. dub. Direct equation with Lat. *salvus* (Pedersen 1.53; Brugmann, Grd. 1.477) is phonetically difficult. Cf. Walde-P. 2.511 (bottom). Perhaps *slān* results from a blend in a Celtic formula corresponding to Lat. *sānus et salvus* (cf. Ernout-M. 890).

W. *iach*, Br. *yac'h* (hence W. *iechyd*, Br. *yec'hed* 'health'), Corn. *yagh* : Ir. *īcc* 'healing, payment', Grk. ἄκος 'cure', ἀκέομαι 'heal'. Walde-P. 1.195. Pedersen 1.65.

4. Goth. *hails*, ON *heill* (> ME *hail*), OE *hāl*, ME *hole* (NE *whole*; but *hale* fr. North. dial. used for 'well, vigorous'), OHG, MHG *heil* (hence derivs. and cpds. for 'health', ON *heilsa*, Sw. *hälsa*, Dan. *helbred*, OE *hǣlþ*, *hǣlu*, ME *helthe*, NE *health* with new adj. *healthy*, OHG *heilī*, MHG *heil*), orig. 'whole, intact' (and so mostly in modern dialects, NE *whole*, NHG *heil*, Dan., Sw. *hel*, etc.) : ChSl. *cělŭ* 'whole, unharmed, well', *cěliti* 'heal', Russ. *celyj* 'whole, entire', etc. Walde-P. 1.329. Falk-Torp 393 f. Feist 232 f.

Dan. *rask* ('quick, active, brisk' but also the popular term for 'well', instead of *sund*) = Sw. *rask* 'quick, brisk', fr. MLG *rasch* = OHG *rasc*, NHG *rasch* 'quick, brisk', prob. : ON *ras* 'haste', Grk. ἐρωή 'quick motion, rush', etc. Walde-P. 1.150 n. 3. Falk-Torp 881 f.

Sw. *frisk* ('fresh', but also the popular word for 'well') = Dan. *frisk* 'fresh' (also 'well, hale') fr. MLG *frisch* = OHG *frisc*, NHG *frisch* 'fresh, cool', etc. : Lith. *prieskas* 'unleavened, fresh', ChSl. *prěsĭnŭ* id. Walde-P. 2.89. Falk-Torp 274 f. Hellquist 238 f.

OE *gesund*, ME *isunde*, *sunde* (NE *sound*), Du. *gezond* (MLG *gesunt*, *sunt* > Dan., Sw. *sund*), OHG *gisunt*, *gisunti*, MHG *gesunt*, NHG *gesund*, prob. : Goth. *swinþs*, OE *swīþ* 'strong' (4.81). Walde-P. 2.525. Falk-Torp 1205.

NE *well* (used chiefly predicatively, in U.S. also attributively with *man*, *person*, etc.) = *well* 'bene' (used predicatively with dat. in OE, cf. Beowulf 186 *wel biþ þæm* 'bene erit eis') : ON, Icel. *vel*, OHG *wela*, etc. 'bene'. Cf. NED s.v. Cf. the similar use of Fr. *bien portant*, Sp. *bueno*, etc.

5. Lith. *sveikas* (hence *sveikata* 'health'), Lett. *sveiks*, perh. fr. **su-ei-kas*, cpd. of *su-* = Skt. *su-* 'well' (16.71) and deriv. of root in *eiti-* 'go'. Fraenkel, Mélanges Pedersen 448 ff.

Lett. *vesels* (hence *veselība* 'health'): ChSl. *veselŭ* 'joyful, gay' (16.22).

6. ChSl. *sŭdravŭ*, SCr. *zdrav*, etc., general Slavic words (with the deriv. nouns ChSl. *sŭdravĭje*, etc.), cpd. of prefix *sŭ-* = Skt. *su-* 'well' and **dorvŭ* : Skt. *dhruva-* 'firm, stable', Av. *drva-* 'well', OPers. *duruva-* 'secure, safe', Lat. *dūrus* 'hard', etc. Walde-P. 1.804 ff. Berneker 214.

ChSl. *cělŭ* : Goth. *hails* (above, 4). Berneker 123 f.

7. Skt. *svastha-* (hence *svāsthya-* 'health', not common), lit. 'self-abiding, being in one's natural state', cpd. of refl. pron. *sva-* and *-stha-* : *sthā-* 'stand'.

Skt. *kuçala-*, adj. 'appropriate, fitting, well, etc.' as neut. sb. 'good condition, health' (hence also adj. *kuçalin-*), etym. dub. Uhlenbeck 60.

Skt. *aroga-* (hence adj. *arogin-*), cpd. of *a*-privative and *roga-* 'disease' (4.84).

Av. *drva-* (hence sb. *drvatāṯ-*) : ChSl. *sŭdravŭ*, above, 6.

Av. *abanta-* cpd. of *a*-privative and *banta-* 'sick' (4.84).

4.84 SICK; SICKNESS

Grk.	*ἀσθενής; νόσος, ἀσθένεια*	Goth.	*siukks; siukei, sauhts*	Lith.	*sergas, nesveikas; liga, sirgimas*
NG	*ἄρρωστος (ἀσθενής); ἀρρώστια (ἀσθένεια, νόσος)*	ON	*sjūkr; sōtt, sjūkleiki (-dōmr)*	Lett.	*slims, nevesels; slimība, neveselība, liga*
		Dan.	*syg; sygdom*		
Lat.	*aeger; morbus*	Sw.	*sjuk; sjukdom*	ChSl.	*bolĭnŭ; bolěznĭ, nedągŭ, jędza*
It.	*malato; malattia*	OE	*sēoc; suht, sēocness, ādl*		
Fr.	*malade; maladie*			SCr.	*bolestan; nemocan; bolest, nemoć*
Sp.	*enfermo; enfermidad*	ME	*sik(e), sek(e); sikness, disese*		
Rum.	*bolnav; boală*			Boh.	*nemocný; nemoc*
Ir.	*lobur; serg*	NE	*sick, ill; sickness, illness*	Pol.	*chory; choroba*
NIr.	*tinn, breoidhte; tinneas, aicīd*			Russ.	*bol'noj; bolezn'*
		Du.	*ziek, krank; ziekte*	Skt.	*asvastha-, ātura-; vyādhi-, roga-*
W.	*claf; clefyd*	OHG	*sioh; siohī, suht*		
Br.	*klañv; kleñved*	MHG	*siech; suht(s), siechtuom (-heit, -tac)*	Av.	*banta-, bazda; yaska-*
		NHG	*krank; krankheit*		

'Sick, sickness' are preferred, in the heading and translations, to 'ill, illness', since NE *sick* is the old unambiguous word and the one still in most common use in U.S. *Ill* is now preferred in British usage (*sick* being especially 'sick at the stomach, nauseated') and by many in U.S. as a more refined expression.

Many of the words are from the notion of 'weak, without strength or power', or that of 'bad, evil'. Some were doubtless applied originally to a special form of ailment and so may be from the most diverse sources, as 'burning' (> 'feverish' > 'sick'), 'bent, twisted' (> 'deformed or abnormal' > 'weakly' > 'sick'), perhaps 'worried' or 'angry' as applied first to mental illness. But a considerable number of the words are of uncertain origin.

Most of the nouns for 'sickness' are derivatives of the adjectives for 'sick'. These are entered in the list, but generally not repeated in the discussion. But there are also some important nouns without parallel adjectives.

1. Grk. ἀσθενής 'weak' (4.82), also 'sick', but this often expressed rather by pple. of ἀσθενέω 'be sick' (aor. 'become sick'), or of νοσέω (below).

Grk. ἄρρωστος 'weak' (4.82), increasingly common for 'sick' in Hellenistic times (inscr., pap., NT, etc.) and the NG common word (ἀσθενής more lit.).

Grk. νόσος, Hom. νοῦσος 'sickness', whence νοσέω 'be sick', pple. often for 'sick', etym. much disputed and altogether doubtful. Walde-P. 2.333. Boisacq 672.

2. Lat. *aeger* : Toch. A *ekro*, B *aik(a)re* 'sick' (SSS, 11), also (?) ChSl. *jędza* 'sickness', root connection dub. Walde-P. 1.9. Ernout-M. 16. Walde-H. 1.16.

Lat. *morbus* 'sickness', etym. dub., perh. : Grk. μαραίνω 'quench', mid. 'waste away' (σῶμα), 'dry up' (αἷμα), 'wither', Skt. *mṛ-* 'crush', etc. Walde-P. 2.277. Ernout-M. 630.

It. *malato*, Fr. *malade*, fr. Lat. *male habitus*, lit. 'ill conditioned', parallel to *sē habēre bene*, *male* 'be well, ill'. REW 5264.

Sp. *enfermo*, fr. Lat. *infirmus* 'weak' (4.82).

Rum. *bolnav*, fr. Slavic (below, 6).

3. Ir. *lobur* 'weak, sick', see 4.82.

Ir. *serg* 'sickness' : Lith. *sergas* 'sick', *sirgti* 'be sick', Lett. *serga* 'pestilence', perh. Goth. *saurga* 'care', etc. (16.14). Walde-P. 2.529. Feist 413.

NIr. *tinn* = MIr. *tind* 'sore, painful' (so still Munster), etym.? (Macbain 367 : Ir. *tinaim* 'disappear').

NIr. *breoidhte*, *breoite* 'sick' (chiefly Munster, Dinneen s.v.), pple. adj. of *breodhaim* 'oppress, sicken, enfeeble', intr. 'wither, decline', etym.?

NIr. *aicīd* 'sickness, calamity' (for **aicidhid*), fr. Lat. *accidentia* (> OIr. *accidit* grammatical term). Pedersen 1.234 n. 3.

W. *claf*, Br. *klañv* : Ir. *clam* 'leprous', Grk. κλαμαράν· πλαδαράν, ἀσθενῆ Hesych., Skt. *klam-* 'be weary'. Walde-P. 1.498. Pedersen 1.163.

W. *clwyf* 'disease' (obs. or of special diseases), perh. : Skt. *klība-* 'emasculated, impotent, eunuch', fr. an extension of the root **kel-* in Lith. *kalti* 'strike', Gr. κλάω 'break', etc. (Walde-P. 1.436 ff.). G. S. Lane, Language 13.23.

4. Goth. *siuks*, ON *sjūkr*, OE *sēoc*, etc., general Gmc. (but NHG *siech* 'sickly', as 'sick' replaced by *krank*) with sbs. Goth. *siukei*, *sauhts*, ON *sōtt*, OE *suht*, etc., later replaced by new derivs. of the adjectives, as ON *sjūkleiki*, *sjūkdōmr*, OE *sēocness*; outside connections dub., but perh. through 'careworn, worried' : Lith. *saugus* 'cautious', *saugoti* 'pay attention to'. Walde-P. 2.472 f. Falk-Torp 1125. Feist 426.

OE *ādl* 'sickness', early ME *adle* (Ormulum), prob. as orig. 'fever' : OE *ād*, OHG *eit* 'funeral pile', Grk. αἴθω, Skt. *idh-* 'kindle', etc. NED s.v. *adle*. Otherwise Uhlenbeck, PBB 26.568 : Lith. *aitrus* 'bitter' (Walde-P. 1.3).

ME *disese* 'discomfort' and esp. 'sickness', NE *disease* (but now mostly of a specific, esp. organic disease), fr. OFr. *desaise*, cpd. of *des-* 'dis' and *aise* 'comfort'. NED s.v.

NE *ill*, now preferred to *sick* in British usage, a specialized use of *ill* 'bad, evil' (16.72). NED s.v.

NHG, Du. *krank*, fr. MHG, MLG *kranc* 'weak (bodily or mentally), bad, slim' (cf. also ON *krankr* 'weakly', OFris. *kronk* 'deathly weak'), prob. as orig. 'bent, twisted' : OE *cranc-stæf* 'implement of weaving', NE *crank* 'handle for turning', Lith. *gręsti* 'turn'. Walde-P. 1.594. Falk-Torp 575. Weigand-H. 1.1137.

5. Lith. *sergas* : *sirgti* 'be sick', Ir. *serg* (above, 3).

Lith. *nesveikas*, lit. 'unwell' (see 4.83).

Lith., Lett. *liga* 'sickness' : Grk. λοιγός 'ruin, mischief', Alb. *lig* 'evil, lean'. Walde-P. 2.398. Mühl.-Endz. 2.466.

Lett. *slims* 'sick, evil' (hence *slimība* 'disease'), fr. MLG *slim* 'ill, miserable' (= NHG *schlimm*). Mühl-Endz. 3.932.

Lett. *nevesels*, lit. 'unwell' (see 4.83).

6. ChSl. *bolĭnŭ* (and *bolěti* 'be sick, feel pain'), SCr. *bolestan*, Russ. *bol'noj* (with sbs., ChSl. *bolěznĭ*, SCr. *bolest*, Russ. *bolezn'*) prob. : Goth. *balwa-weisi* (ON *bǫlviss*) 'evil, wickedness', Goth. *balwjan* 'torment', ON *bǫl*, OE *bealu* 'evil' (NE *bale*), though doubted by Berneker 71 f. and Walde-P. 2.189.

ChSl. *nedągŭ* 'sickness' (frequent beside *bolěznĭ*, cf. Jagić, Entstehungsgesch. 327), neg. cpd. of a **dągŭ* 'power, strength' (cf. Boh. *duh* 'thriving', *neduh* 'sickness', etc.) : Ir. *daingen* 'firm, hard', Skt. *dagh-* 'attain', etc. Walde-P. 1.791. Berneker 217 ff.

ChSl. *jędza* 'sickness' (renders mostly μαλακία, but also νόσος, cf. Jagić, op. cit. 420) : SCr. *jeza* formerly 'sickness' now 'horror', Pol. *jędza* 'fury, witch', Lett. *īgt* 'feel inward pain, be peevish', *īgnis* 'peevish person', also (?) Lat. *aeger*. Walde-P. 1.9. Berneker 268 f. Brückner 208.

SCr. *nemocan*, Boh. *nemocný* (ChSl. *nemoćnŭ* for ἀσθενής 'weak'), neg. cpds.

of *mocan, mocný* 'mighty, strong' (as sbs. *nemoć, nemoc* fr. *moć, moc* 'might'; ChSl. *nemoštĭ* late for 'sickness', Jagić, op. cit. 327).

Pol. *chory* (Boh. *chorý, churavý*, Russ. *chvoryj* 'sickly') : Av. *x*ᵛ*ara-* 'wound', OHG *sweran* 'pain, fester, swell', OHG sb. *swero* 'pain, sore, boil' (NHG *geschwür*), etc. Berneker 409. Brückner 183.

7. Skt. *asvastha-* (hence sb. *asvāsthya-* 'sickness'), neg. cpd. of *svastha-* 'well' (4.84).

Skt. *ātura-*, cpd. of prefix *ā-* and *tura-* 'hurt' (RV) : Grk. τείρω 'rub, exhaust', Lat. *terere* 'rub', etc. Walde-P. 1.728 f.

Skt. *vyādhi-* 'sickness', lit. 'displacement', cpd. of *vi-ā-* and *dhā-* 'place, put'. Uhlenbeck 299.

Skt. *roga-* 'sickness' (hence *rogīn-, rogārta-* 'sick'), also *ruj-* 'pain, sickness' : *ruj-* 'break, cause pain', Lat. *lūgēre* 'mourn', etc. Walde-P. 2.412. Walde-H. 1.830.

Av. *banta-*, pass. pple. of *ban-* 'be sick' in caus. *banaya-* 'make sick' (also *bazda-*, pass. pple. of *band-* id.) : Goth. *banja*, ON *ben*, etc. 'wound', OE *bana* 'murderer', OHG *bano* 'death, murderer'. Walde-P. 2.149. Barth. 926.

Av. *yaska-* 'sickness', perh. for **yakska-* : Skt. *yakṣma-* 'an emaciating disease, consumption', further connection obscure. Walde-P. 1.10. Barth. 1269.

4.85 WOUND (sb.)

Grk.	*τραῦμα, ἕλκος, ὠτειλή*	Goth.	*banja*	Lith.	*žaisda, rona*
NG	*πληγή, λαβωματιά*	ON	*sār, und, ben*	Lett.	*vāts, ievainuojums*
Lat.	*vulnus*	Dan.	*saar*	ChSl.	*strupŭ, jazva, rana*
It.	*ferita*	Sw.	*sår*	SCr.	*rana*
Fr.	*blessure, plaie*	OE	*wund, ben*	Boh.	*rána*
Sp.	*herida*	ME	*wound*	Pol.	*rana*
Rum.	*rană*	NE	*wound*	Russ.	*rana*
Ir.	*crēcht, cned*	Du.	*wond*	Skt.	*vraṇa-, kṣata-*
NIr.	*goin, cneadh, crēacht*	OHG	*wunta*	Av.	*x*ᵛ*ara-*
W.	*archoll, gweli, briw*	MHG	*wunde*		
Br.	*gloaz, gouli*	NHG	*wunde*		

The distinction between a 'wound' resulting from an external blow, and a 'sore' which may result from a wound or from an internal source, is generally observed, but with some overlapping or shift. The words for 'wound' are mostly from roots denoting 'strike' or other actions (as 'pierce' or 'tear') from which the wound resulted. But some, without such reference to a causal action and not originally distinguished from 'sore', are connected with notions of 'pain', 'foulness', etc.

1. Grk. τραῦμα, Dor., Ion. τρῶμα : Grk. τρώω 'pierce, wound', τιτρώσκω 'wound, harm', τρῶσις 'wounding, injury', τρύω 'rub down, wear out', fr. an extension of IE **ter-* in Grk. τείρω 'rub, pierce, distress', τορός 'piercing, loud', Lat. *terere* 'rub', etc. Walde-P. 1.730. Boisacq 972.

Grk. ἕλκος 'wound' (Hom.+), but chiefly 'sore' (so in NT), cf. ἕλκανα· τραύματα Hesych., ἑλκαίνω 'be wounded' : Lat. *ulcus* 'sore', Skt. *arças-* 'hemorrhoids'. Walde-P. 1.160. Ernout-M. 1120.

Grk. ὠτειλή 'wound' (Hom., Hipp.) and 'scar' (fr. *ὀϝατελνᾱ, cf. γατάλαι· οὐλαί Hesych.; οὐτάω the regular Hom. vb. for 'wound' clearly belongs here, though the ου is unexplained) : Lett. *vāts* 'wound', Lith. *votis* 'ulcer, boil', fr. IE **wā-* beside **wen-* in OE *wund*, etc. (below, 4). Walde-P. 1.211. Solmsen, Unters. 298 f.

Grk. πληγή 'blow, stroke', NG 'wound', Doric πλāγά, whence prob. (though it could be native) Lat. *plāga* 'blow', also 'wound', late also 'plague' (> Fr. *plaie* 'sore, wound', also OFr., ME *plage*, NE *plague;* It. *piaga*, Sp. *llaga* 'sore', Rum. *plaga* mostly 'plague') : Grk. πλήσσω 'strike', Lat. *plangere* 'strike, beat the breast, lament', etc. Walde-P. 2.91 f. Ernout-M. 774.

NG pop. λαβωματιά, fr. λαβώνω 'wound', this fr. λαβή 'handle, grip' in the sense 'hold, grip' in wrestling. Hatzidakis, Μεσ. 1.145.

2. Lat. *vulnus* (earlier *volnus*), W. *gweli*, Br. *gouli* : Ir. *fuil* 'blood', *fuili* 'bloody wounds', Grk. οὐλή 'scar', ON *valr* 'corpses of the slain', OHG *wuol* 'defeat, pestilence', OPruss. *ulint* 'fight', Hitt. *walh-* 'strike, defeat, destroy' (Sturtevant, Hitt. Gloss. 75 f.), Toch. A *wäl-* 'die'. All fr. a root **wel-* (ultimately the same as in Lat. *vellere* 'pluck, tear out', etc.?). Walde-P. 1.304 f. Ernout-M. 1129.

It. *ferita*, Sp. *herida*, fr. It. *ferire*, Sp. *herir* 'wound, hit', fr. Lat. *ferīre* 'strike, beat'.

Fr. *blessure*, fr. vb. *blesser* 'wound', OFr. *blecier* 'bruise, crush, injure, wound', fr. deriv. of a Frank. **blēta* (*freobleto* in Lex Salica 'running wound'?) : OHG *bleizza* gl. *livor*, OE *blāt* 'livid, pale', hence a 'bruise' or 'wound' fr. its 'livid' (that is, 'black and blue') appearance. REW 1168. Gamillscheg 115. Wartburg 1.406.

Rum. *rana*, fr. Slavic (below, 6).

3. Ir. *crēcht*, NIr. *crēacht* : W. *creithen*, MBr. *creizenn*, NBr. *kleizenn* 'scar', perh. as orig. 'scab' (cf. NE *scar* fr. OFr. *escare* 'scab') : ON *skrā* 'dry piece of skin, scroll', etc. (Falk-Torp 1021), G. S. Lane, Language 13.23 f.

Ir. *cned*, NIr. *cneadh* : Grk. κνίζω 'scrape, scratch', ON *hnīta* 'strike, wound to death', OE *hnītan* 'strike, thrust', etc. Walde-P. 1.395.

NIr. *goin* : Ir. *guin* 'a wounding', vbl. n. of *gonim* 'wound, kill' (4.76).

W. *archoll*, prob. (with irregular mutation) cpd. of *ar-* 'fore-' and *coll* 'destruction, loss' : Goth. *halts*, OE *healt*, etc. 'lame' (4.94). Morris Jones 264.

W. *gweli*, Br. *gouli*, Corn. *goly* : Lat. *vulnus*, above, 2.

W. *briw*, Corn. *brew*, prob. fr. some form of the root seen in Ir. *brīum*, OE *brȳsan* 'crush, bruise'. Pedersen 1.54 f. But cf. also Loth, RC 42.74 f.

Br. *gloaz* = W. *gloes* 'pang, ache', etym.?

4. Goth. *banja* (renders πληγή 'blow, wound' and ἕλκος 'sore'), ON, OE *ben* : ON *bani* 'death', OE *bana*, OHG *bano* 'murderer', Av. *banta-* 'sick' (4.841), etc., all prob. fr. a root **bhen-* 'strike'. Walde-P. 2.149. Feist 80.

ON *sār*, Dan. *saar*, Sw. *sår* = OE *sār* 'pain, sore', rarely 'wound' (ME, NE *sore* also sometimes 'wound', now only in dial.), Goth. *sair*, OHG, OS *sēr* 'pain', *ro*-formation to a root **sai-* in Ir. *sāeth* 'injury, trouble, sickness', Lat. *saevus* 'raging, fierce'. Walde-P. 2.445. Falk-Torp 941.

ON *und*, OE *wund*, etc., general Gmc. words (with adjs. Goth. *wunds*, OE, OHG, etc. *wund* 'wounded'), prob. : W. *gwanu* 'pierce, thrust, stab', *ym-wan* 'fight', fr. IE **wen-* beside **wā-* in Grk. ὠτειλή etc. (above, 1). Walde-P. 1.212. Falk-Torp 1399.

5. Lith. *žaisda* perh. : Ir. *gōite* 'wounded' (**ĝhoizd-*), Skt. *hiṅs-* 'injure', fr. IE **ĝheis-*, extension of the root in Skt. *hi-* 'set in motion, hurl'. Walde-P. 1.546.

Lith. *rona* fr. Pol. *rana* (below, 6).

Lett. *vāts* : Grk. ὠτειλή, etc. (above, 1).

Lett. *ievainuojums* fr. *ievainuot* 'injure, wound', cpd. of *vaināt* 'accuse, blame, injure, wound' (physical from

mental), deriv. of *vaina* 'fault, blame' : Lith. *vainoti* 'scold', ChSl. *vina* 'accusation', etc. Mühl.-Endz. 4.438 f.

6. ChSl. *strupŭ* (Lk. 10.34 renders τραῦμα Mar., Glag.; *jazva* Sav.), cf. Russ., Bulg. *strup* 'scab', Pol. *strup* 'scurf', etc., prob. : Grk. ῥύπος 'filth' ῥυπόω 'make foul', IE **sreup-*. Walde-P. 2.703. (Otherwise Brückner 521, but ??).

ChSl. *jazva* (also 'blow' and 'plague') = Russ. *jazva* 'cleft, wound, ulcer', Bulg. *jazva* 'wound', Boh. *jízva* 'scar, wound' : OPruss. *eyswo* 'wound', Lett. *aiza* 'crack (in the ice)', Lith. *aižyti* 'husk', etc., further connections dub. Berneker 276 f. Walde-P. 1.9.

ChSl. *rana* (also 'blow' and 'plague'), etc., the modern Slavic words : Skt. *vraṇa-* 'wound, sore, flaw', Alb. *varrë* 'wound', fr. a root **wer-* meaning 'tear' or the like(?). Walde-P. 1.286. For distribution of the three preceding ChSl. words see Jagić, Entstehungsgesch. 392.

7. Skt. *vraṇa-* : ChSl. *rana*, etc. (above, 6).

Skt. *kṣata-*, fr. *kṣan-* 'wound, injure' : Grk. (ἀπο)κτείνω 'kill' (4.76). Walde-P. 1.505.

Av. *x*ᵛ*ara-* : OHG *swero* 'pain, sore, boil', NHG *geschwür* 'sore, ulcer', *schwären* 'fester', root connection? Walde-P. 2.529.

4.86 CURE, HEAL

Grk.	*ἰάομαι, θεραπεύω, ἰᾱτρεύω*	Goth.	*hailjan, lēkinōn*	Lith.	*gydyti*
NG	*γιατρεύω, θεραπεύω*	ON	*lækna, bæta*	Lett.	*dziedēt, ārstēt*
Lat.	*sānāre, cūrāre, medērī*	Dan.	*helbrede, læge*	ChSl.	*cěliti (lěčiti)*
It.	*sanare, guarir*	Sw.	*bota, hela, läka*	SCr.	*liječiti,*
Fr.	*guérir*	OE	*hǣlan, lācnian*	Boh.	*hojiti, léčiti*
Sp.	*curar, sanar*	ME	*hele, cure (lechne)*	Pol.	*leczyć, goić*
Rum.	*vindeca, tămădui*	NE	*cure, heal*	Russ.	*lečit', celit'*
Ir.	*īccaim, fris-ben* (3 sg.)	Du.	*genezen, heelen*	Skt.	*bhiṣaj-, bhiṣajya-, cikitsa-*
NIr.	*leigheasaim*	OHG	*heilen, lāchinōn, giarzinōn*	Av.	*bišaz-*
W.	*iachau*	MHG	*heilen, erzenen*		
Br.	*yac'haat, parea*	NHG	*heilen*		

Most of the words listed may be used for 'cure' with either the person or the disease or wound as the object, but a few only with reference to the person, and this was the primary application in nearly all cases.

Some of the words are in origin '(make) well, whole, alive, vigorous, etc.', or 'protect, rescue, save', and in all such the notion of 'cure' is inherent.

Others are from 'care for, attend to', specialized to medical care, or are derivatives of words for 'physician'. These then meant properly only 'treat medically', but generally acquired the optimistic implication of successful treatment and so came to be used for 'cure' just like those of the preceding type.

1. Grk. ἰάομαι : ἰαίνω (**isn̥yō*) 'heat, warm, cheer', Skt. *iṣ-* 'set in motion, urge, animate', *iṣira-* 'refreshing, active, vigorous', ON *eisa* 'dash forward', etc., all prob. fr. a root meaning 'animate, enliven' or the like. Walde-P. 1.106. Boisacq 262 f.

Grk. θεραπεύω 'attend, do service, take care of', hence esp. 'treat medically, cure' : Grk. θεράπων 'servant, attendant' (19.43). Walde-P. 1.857. Boisacq 340 f.

Grk. ἰᾱτρεύω 'doctor, treat medically', NG γιατρεύω 'cure', fr. ἰᾱτρός 'physician' (4.87).

2. Lat. *sānāre* (> It. *sanare*, Sp. *sanar*), fr. *sānus* 'well, healthy' (4.83).

Lat. *cūrāre*, fr. *cūra* 'care', hence 'take care of' and in medical language 'treat medically, cure'. Hence Sp. *curar* 'cure' and (through OFr. *curer* 'care for, clean') ME *cure* 'care for' and 'cure', NE *cure*.

Lat. *medērī* 'give (medical) attention to, cure' (with dat., rarely acc.), beside *medicus* 'physician' (whence also poet. and late Lat. *medicāre*), *medicīna* 'medicine', *remedium* 'remedy, medicine', etc. : Av. *vī-mad-* 'physician', *vī-mādaya-* 'act as physician', prob. an early specialization of the root **med-* in Grk. μέδομαι 'be mindful of', Lat. *meditārī* 'reflect on', Ir. *miduir* 'judge', etc. Walde-P. 2.260. Ernout-M. 599. Walde-H. 2.54 f.

It. *guarir*, Fr. *guérir*, OSp. *guarir*, etc. fr. the Gmc. vb. seen in Goth. *warjan*, OE *werian*, etc. 'ward off, prevent, defend.' REW 9504.

Rum. *vindeca*, fr. Lat. *vindicāre* 'lay claim to, avenge, set free, restore, rescue', with further specialization of 'restore, rescue' to 'cure'. REW 9347. Puşcariu 1893.

Rum. *tămădui*, fr. Hung. *tamad* 'arise, come into being'. Tiktin 1554 f.

3. Ir. *īccaim*, W. *iachau*, Br. *yac'haat*, fr. Ir. *īcc* 'healing, remedy', W. *iach*, Br. *yac'h* 'well, healthy' (4.83).

Ir. *fris-ben* (3 sg.), common in early glosses, prob. cpd. of *fri(s)* 'to, towards, against' and *ben-* 'strike', through 'touch' in healing (cf. *benim fri* often simply 'touch'). This semantically better than cpd. of *ben-* 'be' (as Pedersen 2.443), though there is confusion here as elsewhere in the forms of the two roots.

NIr. *leigheasaim*, fr. *leigheas* 'cure, medicine' (4.88).

Br. *parea*, fr. *pare* 'healed', fr. Fr. *paré* 'prepared'. Henry 218.

4. Goth. *hailjan* (but ON, NIcel. *heila* 'make good, restore'), Sw. *hela*, OE *hǣlan*, ME *hele*, NE *heal*, Du. *heelen*, OHG–NHG *heilen*, fr. Goth. *hails*, etc. 'well, healthy, whole' (4.83).

Goth. *lēkinōn*, ON *lækna*, Dan. *læge*, Sw. *läka*, OE *lācnian*, ME (early) *lechne*, OHG *lāchinōn* (MHG *lāchenen* 'treat with remedies, conjure') : Goth. *lēkeis*, OE *lǣce*, etc. 'physician' (4.87).

ON *bæta*, Sw. *bota*, fr. ON *bōt*, Sw. *bot* 'remedy' : Goth. *bōtjan* 'be of use, improve', fr. *bōta* 'use', OE *bētan* 'better, compensate', fr. *bōt* 'betterment, amends', etc., fr. the root in Goth. *batiza* 'better', etc. Feist 103.

Dan. *helbrede*, fr. *helbred* 'health' (4.83).

ME, NE *cure* fr. Lat. *cūrāre* (above, 2).

Du. *genezen* = NHG *genesen* 'get well', OHG *ginesan*, OE *genesan*, Goth. *ganisan* 'be saved' : Skt. *nas-* 'associate with, unite in love', Grk. νέομαι 'go, come, return', νόστος 'return home', IE **nes-*, perh. with an original sense 'arrive safely' or the like. Walde-P. 2.335. Franck-v. W. 187 f.

OHG *giarzinōn*, MHG *erzenen*, MLG *arsten* (> Lett. *ārstēt*), fr. OHG *arzāt*, etc. 'physician' (4.87), with form influenced by *lāchenōn*, etc. (above). Weigand-H. 1.90.

5. Lith. *gydyti* (perfect. *išgydyti*), Lett. *dziedēt, dziedināt* : Lith. *gyti*, Lett. *dzīt* (intr.) 'heal over', fr. the root **g*ᵘ*ei-* in Lith. *gyvas* 'alive', *gyventi* 'live', etc. (4.74). Walde-P. 2.668.

Lett. *ārstēt*, fr. MLG *arsten* (above, 4).

6. ChSl. *cěliti*, Russ. *celit'*, fr. ChSl. *cělŭ*, etc., 'whole, well' (4.83).

Late ChSl. *lěčiti, lěkovati*, SCr. *liječiti*, Boh. *léčiti*, Pol. *leczyć*, Russ. *lečit'* fr. ChSl. *lěkŭ*, etc. 'remedy' (cf. also *lěkarĭ* 'physician'), early Slavic borrowing from the Gmc. group in Goth. *lēkinōn*, etc. (above, 4). Berneker 710. Stender-Petersen 330 f.

Boh. *hojiti*, Pol. *goić* = SCr. *gojiti* 'care for, rear', caus. to ChSl. *žiti*, etc. 'live', (4.74.) Walde-P. 2.668. Berneker 319.

7. Skt. *bhiṣaj-* (only RV 8.79.1), and *bhiṣajya-* (fr. *bhiṣaj-* 'physician'), Av. *bišaz-*, etym.? Walde-P. 2.449. Barth. 966 f.

Skt. *cikitsa-* 'aim at, care for, etc.', then also 'treat medically, cure' (cf. also *cikitsā-* 'medical practice'), desiderative of *cit-* 'perceive, intend, attend to, etc.'

4.87 PHYSICIAN

Grk.	*ἰατρός*	Goth.	*lēkeis*	Lith.	*gydytojas*
NG	*γιατρός*	ON	*læknir*	Lett.	*ārsts*
Lat.	*medicus*	Dan.	*læge*	ChSl.	*balĭji, vračĭ, lěkarĭ*
It.	*medico*	Sw.	*läkare*	SCr.	*liječnik, lijekar*
Fr.	*médecin*	OE	*lǣce*	Boh.	*lékař*
Sp.	*médico*	ME	*leche, fisicien*	Pol.	*lekarz*
Rum.	*medic*	NE	*physician, doctor*	Russ.	*vrač, lekar'*
Ir.	*līaig (midach)*	Du.	*arts*	Skt.	*bhiṣaj-, vāidya-, cikitsaka-*
NIr.	*liaigh*	OHG	*lāchi, arzāt*		
W.	*meddyg*	MHG	*arz(e)t*	Av.	*vīmad-*
Br.	*medesin*	NHG	*arzt*		

The majority of the words for 'physician' are connected with the verbs for 'cure', discussed in 4.86. Some are words for 'teacher' or 'learned person' used in specialized sense. Several, according to their probable etymological connections (cf. below, 3, on Ir. *līaig*, etc., and 6 on ChSl. *balĭji* and *vračĭ*), reflect the primitive antecedent of the physician, the 'conjurer' or 'medicine man'. Cf. also under 'medicine' (4.88), and Schrader, Reallex. 1.58 f.

1. Grk. *ἰατρός*, Hom. and dial. *ἰατήρ* : *ἰάομαι* 'cure' (4.86).

2. Lat. *medicus* (> It. *medico*, OFr. *mie, miege;* and learned borrowings Sp. *médico*, Rum. *medic;* Fr. *médecin*, back formation to *médecine* 'medicine', 4.88), also poet. and late Lat. *medēns* pple. : *medērī* 'cure' (4.86).

3. Ir. *līaig*, NIr. *liaigh*, prob. fr. **lēp-agi-* 'conjurer' : W. *llef* 'voice', MW *llefein* 'cry', Br. *leñv* 'groan', Skt. *lap-* 'chatter, talk, whisper', etc. Hence prob. (though also disputed) the Gmc. group, Goth. *lēkeis*, OE *lǣce* (> ODan. *læke*, Dan. *læge*), ME *leche* (NE *leech* arch.), OHG *lāchi*, and (re-formed after the verbs) ON *læknir*, Sw. *läkare;* fr. Gmc. the Slavic group, late ChSl. *lěkarĭ*, SCr. *lijekar* (reformed *liječnik*), Boh. *lékař*, Pol. *lekarz*, Russ. *lekar'*. Walde-P. 2.429. Falk-Torp 673. Feist 329. Pedersen 1.311. Stokes 251. Berneker 710. Otherwise for Gmc. group (: Grk. *λέγω* 'speak', etc.) Holthausen, IF 39.71, Stender-Petersen 330.

W. *meddyg*, Br. *mezec* (obs.), also (rare) Ir. *midach*, fr. Lat. *medicus* (above, 2). Pedersen 1.239.

Br. *medesin* fr. Fr. *médecin*.

4. Goth. *lēkeis*, etc., above, 3.

ME *fisicien*, NE *physician* (also ME and earlier NE 'student of physics') fr. OFr. *fisicien* 'médecin' (Godefroi), deriv. of Lat. *physica* 'physics' (fr. Grk. *φυσικός* 'natural'), but which came to be used extensively in medieval Latin for *medicina* (Du Cange). NED s.v.

NE *doctor*, the usual term in common

use, found also in ME in the special sense (cf. Chaucer's *Doctur of Phesike*), fr. OFr. *doctor*, Lat. *doctor* 'teacher'. Similar usage is found more or less colloquially in all the European languages : It. *dottore*, Fr. *docteur*, etc., Dan., Sw., NHG (esp. northern dials.) *doktor* (and hence Lith. *daktaras*, Lett. *dakteris*), and in the modern Slavic languages.

OHG *arzāt*, MHG *arzet*, *arzt*, NHG *arzt*, MLG *arste*, Du. *arts*, fr. late Lat. *archiater*, Grk. *ἀρχ-ιᾱτρός* (both frequent in late inscrr.) 'chief, (and hence court) physician'. Weigand-H. 1.90. Kluge-G. 25.

5. Lith. *gydytojas* : *gydyti* 'heal' (4.86).

Lett. *ārsts*, *ārste* fr. MLG *arste* (above, 4).

6. ChSl. *balĭji* (cf. *balĭstvo* 'medicine', *balovati* 'curare'), as orig. 'conjurer' : late ChSl. *bajati* 'relate, conjure, heal', SCr. *bajati* 'enchant, conjure', etc., fr. the root in Grk. *φημί* 'say', etc. Berneker 42.

ChSl. *vračĭ*, Russ. *vrač* = SCr. *vrač* 'sorcerer, fortuneteller', etc., orig. 'conjurer' : Russ. *vorčat'* 'growl, grumble, mutter', *vraka* 'nonsense, idle talk', etc., fr. the root **wer-* in Grk. *εἴρω* 'say', Skt. *vrata-* 'command, vow', etc. Walde-P. 1.283. Solmsen, Unters. 263.

ChSl. (late) *lěkarĭ*, SCr. *lijekar*, *liječnik*, etc., fr. the Gmc. (above, 3).

7. Skt. *bhiṣaj-* : *bhiṣaj-*, *bhiṣajya-* 'cure' (4.86).

Skt. *vāidyá-*, lit. 'one versed in science (*vidyā-* : *vid-* 'know'), learned', then, like the current European adoption of Lat. *doctor*, (above, 4), 'one skilled in medical science, doctor'.

Skt. *cikitsaka-*, fr. *cikitsa-* 'heal, cure' (4.86).

Av. *vīmad-* : Lat. *medērī* 'cure', etc. (4.86). Barth. 1450.

4.88 MEDICINE, DRUG

Grk.	*φάρμακον*	Goth.	*(lubja-)*	Lith.	*vaistas, gydyklas*
NG	*γιατρικό, φάρμακο*	ON	*lyf, lækningarlyf, læknisdōmr*	Lett.	*zāles*
Lat.	*medicāmen(tum), remedium*	Dan.	*medicin, lægemiddel*	ChSl.	*balĭstvo, lěkŭ*
It.	*medicina, droga*	Sw.	*medicin, läkemedel, drog*	SCr.	*lijek, ljekarije*
Fr.	*médicament, drogue*			Boh.	*lék*
Sp.	*medicamento, droga*	OE	*lybb, lǣcedōm*, etc.	Pol.	*lekarstwo, lek*
Rum.	*medicament, leac, doctorie*	ME	*medicine, drogges* (pl.)	Russ.	*lekarstvo*
Ir.	*leiges*	NE	*medicine, drug*	Skt.	*āuṣadha-, bheṣaja-*
NIr.	*leigheas, īoc*	Du.	*artsenij, geneesmiddel, drogerij*	Av.	*baēšaza-*
W.	*meddyginiaeth, cyffur*	OHG	*lāchin, lāchintuom*, etc.		
Br.	*louzou*	MHG	*arzenīe, arzātīe, lāchen*		
		NHG	*arznei, heilmittel, medizin, droge*		

The words listed cover the wider 'medicine', as any medicinal substance or preparation, and the narrower 'drug', as a simple medicinal substance or ingredient. The majority are connected with those for 'cure' or 'physician', discussed 4.86, 4.87. Some are the result of specialization, as from 'herb' through 'healing herb', from 'substance' to 'medicinal substance', from 'dry wares'(?) to 'drugs', from 'knowledge' through 'magic'.

1. Grk. *φάρμακον* (also 'poison, enchantment, etc.'), prob. : Lith. *burti* 'practice sorcery', Lett. *burt* 'enchant', root connection dub. Walde-P. 2.161.

NG *γιατρικό*, neut. of adj. *ἰατρικός*, deriv. of *ἰατρός* 'physician' (4.87).

2. Lat. *medicāmen(tum)*, *medicīna* (also 'medical science'), *remedium* (but with extension beyond medical sense, as likewise its derivs. Fr. *remède*, NE *remedy*, etc.) : *medērī* 'heal' (4.86). Hence It. *medicina*, Fr. *médicament* (OFr. *medecine* > ME, NE *medicine*), Sp. *medicamento*, Rum. *medicament*, W. *meddyginiaeth*, Dan., Sw. *medicin*, NHG *medizin*, also more or less common in Slavic, SCr. *medicina*, Boh. *medecina*, Pol. *medycyna*, Russ. *medicina*, *medicament*.

It., Sp. *droga*, Fr. *drogue* (> NHG *droge*, Sw. *drog;* Fr. *droguerie* > Du. *drogerij*), ME *drogges* pl. (fr. Fr. or earlier from same source?), NE *drug*, formerly and still in part (esp. Fr.) used for chemical ingredients in general, later esp. for ingredients of medicine, prob. fr. Du. *droog* 'dry', either through a frequently attested commercial phrase MDu. *droge vate* 'dry barrels' for 'goods in packing barrels' (Baist, Z. frz. Spr. 32, 298 f.), or simply through *droge waere* lit. 'dry wares', but used for 'drugs, spices', just as Lat. *speciēs*, in late Lat. 'wares', was specialized to spices (Fr. *épice*, NE *spice*) or drugs (It. *spezieria* 'pharmacy'). REW 2776a. Gamillscheg 327. Deriv. fr. Arab. *dūrawā* 'chaff', preferred by Lokotsch 549, Franck v. W. 136 (also Wartburg 3.189 in heading, but see 190) is less likely.

Rum. *leac* fr. ChSl. *lěkŭ* (below, 6).

Rum. *doctorie* (pop.), fr. *doctor* in sense 'physician'.

3. Ir. *leiges*, NIr. *leigheas*, properly 'cure, healing', also 'medicine', fr. *līaig* 'physician' (4.87).

NIr. *īoc* fr. Ir. *īcc* 'cure, healing' : *īccaim* 'cure' (4.86).

W. *cyffur* 'substance, matter' (orig.?), also 'drug' (cf. *cyfferïwr* 'druggist').

Br. *louzou* lit. 'plants, herbs', orig. pl. of sg. form in W. *llys*, Ir. *lus* 'plant, herb'. Henry 190.

4. ON *lyf* esp. 'herb with healing or magic power', cpd. *lækningarlyf*, *læknislyf* (: *lækna* 'heal'), OE *lybb* also 'poison' = OHG *luppi* 'poison, charm, sorcery', Goth. *lubja-* in *lubja-leisei* '*φαρμακεία*, sorcery' : Ir. *luib*, NIr. *luibh* 'herb, plant'. Walde-P. 2.418. Falk-Torp 679.

ON *læknisdomr*, OE *lǣcedōm* 'cure, medicine', fr. ON *læknir*, OE *lǣce* 'physician' (4.87).

Dan. *lægemiddel*, Sw. *läkemedel* lit. 'healing agent' : Dan. *læge*, Sw. *läka* 'heal' (4.86).

MHG *arzenīe* (> Du. *artsenij*), *erzenīe*, NHG *arznei*, MHG *arzātīe*, fr. MHG *erzenen* 'treat medically' (4.86), OHG *arzāt* 'physician' (4.87).

Du. *geneesmiddel*, NHG *heilmittel*, lit. 'healing agent', fr. Du. *genesen*, NHG *heilen* 'heal' (4.86).

OHG *lāchin*, MHG *lāchen*, cpd. OHG *lāchintuom* : OHG *lāchi* 'physician' (4.87).

5. Lith. *vaistas*, prob. (as 'supernatural knowledge, magic') : OPruss. *waist* 'know' (*waidimai* 'we know', etc.), *waidleimai* 'we enchant', ORuss. *vědĭ* 'knowledge, magic', ChSl. *vědĕ* 'report', Grk. *οἶδα* 'know', etc. Trautmann 338.

Lith. *gydyklas*, fr. *gydyti* 'cure' (4.86).

Lett. *zāles* fr *ārstējamās zāles* 'healing herbs' : *zāle* 'herb, grass', Lith. *žolė* 'grass', etc.

6. ChSl. *balĭstvo* : *balĭji* 'physician' (4.87).

ChSl. *lěkŭ*, etc., general Slavic : ChSl. *lěčiti* 'heal', *lěkarĭ* 'physician', etc. (4.86, 4.87).

7. Skt. *āuṣadha-*, fr. *oṣadhi-* 'herb, plant'.

Skt. *bheṣaja-* (and *bhāiṣajya-*), Av. *baēšaza-*, lit. 'healing', fr. Skt. *bhiṣaj-*, Av. *bišaz-* 'heal' (4.86).

4.89 POISON (sb.)

Grk.	*φάρμακον, ἰός*	Goth.	. . . .	Lith.	*nuodai*
NG	*φαρμάκι*	ON	*eitr*	Lett.	*nāveklis, nāves zāles*
Lat.	*venēnum, vīrus*	Dan.	*gift*	ChSl.	*jadŭ, otrava*
It.	*veleno, tossico*	Sw.	*gift*	SCr.	*otrov (jed)*
Fr.	*poison, venin*	OE	*ātor, lybb*	Boh.	*jed, otrova*
Sp.	*veneno, ponzoña, tósigo*	ME	*venim, poison, atter*	Pol.	*trucizna, jad*
		NE	*poison (venom)*	Russ.	*jad, otrava*
Rum.	*otravă, venin*	Du.	*gif(t), vergif(t)*	Skt.	*viṣa-, gara-, garala-*
Ir.	*neim, fī*	OHG	*eitar, luppi (gift)*	Av.	*viš-, vīša-*
NIr.	*neimh*	MHG	*eiter, gift (lüppe)*		
W.	*gwenwyn*	NHG	*gift*		
Br.	*kontamm, binim*				

Words for 'poison', apart from an inherited group, are in some cases the same as those for 'drug' (4.88). Several are euphemistic expressions from 'drink' or 'gift'. Some are from verbs meaning 'injure, pollute, consume' or the like. Other sources are 'love (potion)', '(poison) of arrow', 'swelling' (through 'pus'), '(means of) death'.

1. IE **wīs-o-*, root connection dub. (possibly an IE specialization of 'fluid' to 'poisonous fluid', but evidence of an IE **weis-* 'flow' meager). Walde-P. 1.243 f. Ernout-M. 1114.

Grk. *ἰός* (poet.); Lat. *vīrus* (also 'slimy liquid, sperm'); Ir. *fī;* Skt. *viṣa-*, Av. *viš-*, *vīša-*.

2. Grk. *φάρμακον* 'drug' (4.88) and 'poison', hence, fr. dim. form, NG *φαρμάκι* 'poison'.

3. Lat. *venēnum*, earlier (ante-classical) 'potion, drug', then (like Grk. *φάρμακον*) 'poison' (> It. *veleno*, Sp. *veneno*, Rum. *venin*, Fr. *venin*, OFr. *velin*, *venim*, latter > ME *venim*, NE *venom*), prob. (as 'love potion') fr. **wenes-no-* : *Venus* 'love', Skt. *van-* 'wish, desire, gain', etc. Ernout-M. 1083. REW 9195.

It. *tossico*, Sp. *tósigo*, fr. Lat. *toxicum* 'poison on arrows' and also 'poison' in general, fr. Grk. *τοξικὸν* (*φάρμακον*) 'poison for smearing arrows' (: *τόξον* 'bow').

Fr. *poison* (> ME, NE *poison*), OSp. *pozon* fr. Lat. *pōtiō* 'drink'; also OSp. *ponçoña*, Sp. *ponzoña* by influence of Sp. *punzar* 'punch, prick, stick' (fr. VLat. **punctiāre*). REW 6699.

Rum. *otravă*, fr. Slavic (below, 7).

4. Ir. *neim*, NIr. *neimh*, prob. : Grk. *νέμω* 'deal out, distribute', Goth. *niman* 'take', etc., with development similar to that of NHG *gift* (below, 5). Macbain 262.

W. *gwenwyn* fr. Lat. *venēnum* (above, 3). Loth, Mots lat. 175.

Br. *kontamm*, back-formation fr. vb. *kontammi* 'poison' fr. Lat. *contamināre* 'corrupt, pollute'. Henry 75.

Br. *binim*, fr. OFr. *venim* (above, 3).

5. ON *eitr*, OE *ātor*, *āttor*, ME *atter*, OHG *eitar*, MHG *eiter* (NHG *eiter* 'pus') : OHG *eiz* 'abscess, boil', Grk. *οἰδέω*, Arm. *aitnum* 'swell', prob. also ChSl. *jadŭ*, etc. 'poison' (below, 7). Walde-P. 1.166. Falk-Torp 180.

OE *lybb* 'drug, poison', OHG *luppi* 'poison', MHG *lüppe* 'astringent fluid, poisoning, sorcery' : ON *lyf* 'drug', etc. (4.88).

OHG *gift* (pl. *die gifte* 'venena', Boeth. De Consol. Phil.), MHG *vergift*, *gift*, NHG *gift*, identical with OHG, MHG *gift* 'gift' (NHG *mit-gift*, etc.), fr. OHG *geban* 'give'. Hence the sense of 'poison' in the Du., Dan., Sw. forms. The euphemistic use for 'poison' may have been aided by imitation of Grk. *δόσις* 'gift, portion, dose of medicine'. Falk-Torp 308. Weigand-H. 1.727 f. Kluge-G. 206. Franck-v. W. 199.

ME *venim*, NE *venom* (now mostly restricted to poison of snakes, etc.), fr. OFr. *venim* (above, 3).

ME, NE *poison* fr. OFr. *poison* (above, 3).

6. Lith. *nuodai* (pl.) : OLith. *nuodžia* 'sin', both cpds. of *nuo-* 'down, from', second part : *dėti* 'put'. Trautmann 47. Semantic development 'put away' through 'injure' to 'poison' and 'sin'(?).

Lett. *nāveklis*, fr. *nāve* 'death' (4.75); likewise *nāves zāles* 'drugs of death'.

Lett. *g'ipte, g'ifts*, pop. (not in Mühl.-Endz.), fr. NHG *gift*. Sehwers, Lehnwörter 148.

7. ChSl. *jadŭ*, SCr., Boh. *jed*, Pol., Russ. *jad* (but SCr. now mostly 'bile, anger') prob. : ON *eitr*, etc. (above, 5). Berneker 271 f.

ChSl. *otrava*, etc. (late, but deriv. in Supr.), SCr. *otrov*, Boh. *otrova*, Pol. *trucizna*, Russ. *otrava* : vbs. ChSl. *otruti*, Pol. *otruć*, Russ. (iter.) *otravit'* 'poison', cpds. of ChSl. *truti* 'spend, consume', Pol. *truć* 'waste, poison', etc.; Grk. τραῦμα 'wound', etc. (4.85). Trautmann 327. Brückner 577.

8. Skt. *viṣa-*, Av. *viš-*, above, 1.

Skt. *gara-* 'drink, fluid, poison', hence *garala-* 'poison' : *gṛ-* 'swallow', Lith. *gerti* 'drink', etc. Uhlenbeck 77. Walde-P. 1.682 f.

4.91 TIRED, WEARY

Grk.	(ἀπο)καμών, etc.	Goth.	*afmauiþs*	Lith.	*pailsęs, pavargęs*
NG	κουρασμένος	ON	*mōðr*	Lett.	*piekusis, nuoguris, gurds*
Lat.	*fatīgātus, fessus, lassus*	Dan.	*træt*	ChSl.	*truzdŭ sę, trudĭnŭ*
It.	*stanco*	Sw.	*trött*	SCr.	*umoran*
Fr.	*las, fatigué*	OE	*wērig, mēþe*	Boh.	*unavený, mdlý*
Sp.	*cansado (fatigado, laso)*	ME	*weri, tyred*	Pol.	*zmęczony, strudzony*
Rum.	*obosit*	NE	*tired, weary*	Russ.	*ustavšij, utomljennyj*
Ir.	*scīth*	Du.	*moede*	Skt.	*çrāṁta-, khinna-*
NIr.	*tuirseach, cortha*	OHG	*muodi*	Av.	. . . .
W.	*blin, lluddedig*	MHG	*muede*		
Br.	*skuiz*	NHG	*müde*		

Several of the words for 'tired' are based upon the causal action 'work, toil', as one who has toiled hard and is therefore 'tired'. Some are based upon various actions or conditions which may be associated with weariness, as 'rest, keep still, leave off, cease', or 'weak, faint, slow, wretched, sad'. Some are from a transitive 'tire', which itself may be from 'vex, torment, oppress' (these again from 'press, beat, shave, etc.'), 'break' or even 'kill'.

1. Grk. (ἀπο)καμών, κεκμηκώς, Hom. κεκμηώς, aor. and perf. pples. of Grk. κάμνω 'work, toil, be weary', ἀποκάμνω 'be weary' : Skt. *çam-* 'toil, labor', etc. Walde-P. 1.387.

Grk. κοπιάω 'be tired' (hence perf. pple. κεκοπιακώς 'tired' as NT, Jn. 4.6), fr. κόπος 'toil, trouble, weariness,' orig. 'beating' : κόπτω 'strike, beat'.

NG κουρασμένος, pple. of κουράζω 'tire, fatigue', attested in Byz., meaning prob. 'punish' (cf. also *kuradzo* 'beat, flog' in dial. Bova), prob. fr. κουρά 'a shearing, tonsure', with semantic development similar to that in NHG *scheren* 'cut, shear' and 'vex, torment', *schererei* 'vexation, annoyance'. Kretschmer, Byz. Zt. 7.403. Hatzidakis, Μεσ. 2.513. Psaltes, Gram. d. Byz. Chron. 42. Cf. Fr. *raser* 'shave', also 'demolish' (cf. NE *raze*), and colloq. 'tire, bore'.

2. Lat. *fatīgātus* (> Fr. *fatigué*, Sp.

fatigado), pple. of *fatīgāre* 'tire' (trans.), 'vex', deriv. of *fatis* in *ad fatim* 'sufficiently, enough', whence also *fatīscere* 'fall apart, become weak, faint', adj. *fessus* 'weak, weary', outside connections dub. Walde-P. 1.829. Ernout-M. 336. Walde-H. 1.463.

Lat. *lassus* (> Fr. *las*, Sp. *laso*), fr. **ləd-to-* : Grk. ληδεῖν 'be tired', Goth. *lētan* 'leave, let', *lats*, ON *latr*, OHG *laz* 'lazy', etc. (4.92). Walde-P. 2.395. Ernout-M. 525 (with uncalled-for doubt), Walde-H. 1.767 f.

It. *stanco*, cf. Rum. *stîng* 'left', OFr. *estanc* 'weak, dry', etc., orig. dub. REW 8225. Gamillscheg 390.

Sp. *cansado*, pple. of *cansar* 'tire' (now trans.; refl. 'get tired'), this (not : Fr. *casser* 'break', fr. Lat. *quassāre* 'shake', as Diez 91, REW 6939, but) = It. *cansare* 'avoid', fr. Lat. *campsāre* 'turn aside from', fr. Grk. κάμψαι aor. of κάμπτω 'bend' (9.14). So Körting, Menéndez Pidal, C. C. Rice, Language 13.18 f., 19.154. Leo Spitzer, Language 14.205 f., Wartburg 2.156. Lat. *campsāre* occurs in Ennius in the nautical sense of doubling a headland (frequent in Grk.), then only in late Latin in more general sense of 'turn aside from' e.g. *ut de via campsemus* Peregrinatio 10.8 and in many glosses. The semantic development in Spanish was prob. (otherwise Rice) 'avoid' > 'cease' > 'get tired'. Although a sequence 'get tired' > 'cease' is the easier, the association is there, and one may compare esp. Russ. *ustavat'* 'get tired', Boh. *ustati* 'get tired, cease' = ChSl. *ustati, ustaviti* 'cease' (below, 6).

Rum. *obosit* pple. of *obosi* 'tire' (trans. or intr.), fr. Slavic, SCr. *obositi* (deriv. of *bos* 'barefoot') 'be barefoot' or of horses 'be unshod', with development from application to horses (since they tire more easily when unshod) to intr. 'tire'. Tiktin 1072. Densusianu 367.

3. Ir. *scīth*, Gael. *sgith*, Br. *skuiz*, etym.? (Pedersen 1.76 · Grk. ἀσκηθής 'unharmed', Goth. *skaþjan* 'harm', but?). Walde-P. 2.558.

NIr. *tuirseach*, also 'depressed, sorrowful', fr. *tuirse* 'grief, fatigue' : Ir. *torsi* 'sadness', outside connections?

NIr. *cortha*, pple. of *coraim* 'tire out, weary', etym.?

W. *lluddedig*, fr. *lludded* 'fatigue', *lludd* 'faint', prob. : ON *lūta*, OE *lūtan* 'bow, stoop', OHG *luzeda* 'infirmatio', Lith. *liusti* 'become sad, grieve', etc., with common notion of 'bend down, be downcast'. Walde-P. 2.415 f. (with much wider grouping). Falk-Torp 658 f.

W. *blin*, cf. OBr. pl. *blinion* 'inert', Gael. *blian* 'lean, insipid' etym. dub., perh. (fr. IE **mlēno-* or **mlīno-*): Skt. *mlāna-* 'faded, withered, exhausted, languid', pple. of *mlā-* 'fade, wither, grow weary', SCr. *mlitav* 'tepid, listless', etc. fr. extensions of IE **mel-* 'rub, grind' (Walde-P. 2.284 ff.). G. S. Lane, Language 13.21 f.

4. ON *mōðr*, OE *mēþe*, OS *mōði*, Du. *moede*, OHG *muodi*, MHG *muede*, NHG *müde* : Goth. *af-mauiþs* (only nom. pl. *afmauidai* 'ἐκλυόμενοι, wearied', pple. of **afmōjan*), OHG *muojan, muoan* 'disturb, torment', Russ. *majat'* 'fatigue, harass', prob. Grk. μῶλος 'toil, moil', Lat. *mōles* 'large mass', *molestus* 'troublesome'. Walde-P. 2.302. Feist 9. Weigand-H. 2.225, 227.

Dan. *træt*, Sw. *trött* = (NIcel. *þreyttur* also 'tired') ON *þreyttr* 'exhausted, worn out', pple. of *þreyta* 'strive, struggle, exert one's strength', denom. of *þraut* 'struggle, exertion' : ChSl. *trudŭ* 'toil, exertion, hardship', *truditi* 'labor, become tired' (etc., below, 6), Lat. *trūdere* 'thrust, press', IE **treud-* prob. extension of **ter-* in Grk. τείρω, etc. 'rub'. Walde-P. 1.755. Falk-Torp 1294. Hellquist 1238.

OE *wērig*, ME *weri*, NE *weary* : OS *wōrag, wōrig* id., OHG *wuorag* 'drunken', OE *wōrian* 'wander, totter', ON *ōrar* pl. 'stupor', root connections dub. Walde-P. 1.316 (also 1.20). Falk-Torp 1420.

ME *tyred*, NE *tired*, pple. of ME *tyre*, OE *teorian* 'fail, give out, become weak, exhausted', perh. as Gmc. **teuz-*, IE **deus-* : Skt. *doṣa-* 'fault, lack', Grk. δέω, Hom. δεύω 'lack', etc. Holthausen, IF 20.324. Walde-P. 1.782.

5. Lith. *pailsęs*, pple. of *pa-ilsti*, perfect. of *ilsti* 'get tired', beside *alsas* 'fatigue', *ilsėtis* 'rest', perh. : Skt. *il-* 'keep still, be quiet', Grk. ἐλινύω 'keep quiet, take a rest', IE **el-* (?). Persson, Beiträge 743. Walde-P. 1.152.

Lith. *pavargęs*, pple. of *pavargti*, perfect. of *vargti* 'exhaust oneself, suffer want' : *vargas* 'distress, want, misery', OPruss. *wargs* 'bad', ChSl. *vragŭ*, etc. 'enemy'. Walde-P. 1.320. Trautmann 342.

Lett. *piekusis*, pple. of *piekusti*, perfect. of *kust* 'become tired' : ChSl. *kŭsněti* 'delay', *kŭsnŭ* 'slow, sluggish', etc., further connections dub. Mühl.-Endz. 2.328. Berneker 672. Walde-P. 1.468 (further combination with Slavic *kyselŭ* 'sour', cf. NHG *faul* 'foul', and 'lazy').

Lett. *nuoguris*, pple. of *nuogurt* 'tire', cpd. of *gurt* 'weaken, decrease' : *gurds* 'exhausted, tired', Lith. *gursti* 'die' (of animals), perh. Goth. *qairrus* 'gentle', ON *kvirr* 'still, quiet'. Mühl.-Endz. 1.684. Walde-P. 1.685 (further root connection with Grk. βαρύς 'heavy', etc.).

6. ChSl. *truždŭ sę* 'κεκοπιακώς' (Gospels, Jn. 4.6), pple. of *truždati sę* 'exhaust oneself', iter. of *truditi* 'toil', also adj. ChSl. (later attested) *trudĭnŭ*, Pol. *strudzony* (SCr. *trudan* now mostly 'feeble' or 'pregnant'), all derivs. of ChSl. *trudŭ*, SCr., Pol. *trud* 'toil, exertion', etc. (see under Dan. *træt*, above, 4).

SC. *umoran*, fr. *umoriti* 'tire, kill' = ChSl. *umoriti* 'kill' (4.76). Berneker 2.80.

Boh. *unavený* fr. *unaviti* 'tire, fatigue', cpd. of *naviti* id., fr. *nýti* 'waste away, languish' : ChSl. *-nyti* 'be sluggish', Lith. *novyti* 'torment, oppress', apparently from the same root as Lett. *nave* 'death', etc. (4.75). Walde-P. 2.316. Miklosich 218.

Boh. *mdlý*, also 'faint' : Pol. *mdły* 'faint, weak', ChSl. *mŭdlŭ* 'slow', Pol. *mudzić* 'delay, pass the time', ChSl. *muditi* 'loiter', etc:, outside connections? Brückner 347 f.

Pol. *zmęczony*, fr. *zmęczyć* 'exhaust, fatigue', cpd. of *męczyć* 'torture, harass' : Pol. *męka*, ChSl. *mąka*, etc. 'torture', ChSl. *mękŭkŭ* 'soft', Lith. *minkyti* 'knead', Grk. μάσσω 'press, knead', OE *mengan* 'mix', etc. Walde-P. 2.268. Berneker 2.43. Brückner 328.

Russ. *ustavšij*, perf. act. pple. of *ustavat'* 'get tired' : Boh. *ustati* 'get tired, cease', Pol. *ustać* 'cease' (also sometimes 'get tired'), ChSl. *ustati, ustaviti* 'cease' (14.28). Brückner 596.

Russ. *utomljennyj* perf. pass. pple. of *utomljat'* 'fatigue, tire', cpd. of *tomit'* 'oppress, make weary, overcome', Russ.-ChSl. *tomiti* 'torment', prob. fr. the root in Skt. *tam-* 'faint, be exhausted, lose the breath', Lat. *tēmētum* 'intoxicating drink', MIr. *tām* 'death'. Walde-P. 1.720.

7. Skt. *çram-* 'get tired', pple. *çrāṁta-* 'tired', also *klam-, klāṁta-* id. : Ir. *clam* 'leprous', W. *claf*, Br. *klañv* 'sick' (4.83). Walde-P. 1.498.

Skt. *khid-* 'tear, press', pple. *khinna-* 'oppressed, exhausted, tired', perh. : Lat. *caedere* 'cut, beat, strike down'. Walde-P. 2.538.

4.92 LAZY

Grk.	ἀργός, ἄπονος	Goth.	*lats*	Lith.	*tingus, vangus (slinkas)*
NG	τεμπέλης, (ὀκνηρός)	ON	*latr*	Lett.	*kūtrs, slinks, laisks*
Lat.	*piger, ignāvus*	Dan.	*doven, lad*	ChSl.	*lěnŭ*
It.	*pigro, infingardo*	Sw.	*lat*	SCr.	*lijen*
Fr.	*paresseux, fainéant*	OE	*slāw, slæc*	Boh.	*líný, lenivý*
Sp.	*perezoso*	ME	*slouthful, slak*	Pol.	*leniwy*
Rum.	*leneş, trîndav*	NE	*lazy (slothful)*	Russ.	*lenivyj*
Ir.	*lesc*	Du.	*lui, traag*	Skt.	*alasa-, manda-*
NIr.	*leisceamhail*	OHG	*laz, trāgi*	Av.	*avərəzika-*
W.	*diog*	MHG	*laz, træge, lezzic*		
Br.	*diek, lezirek*	NHG	*faul, träge (lässig)*		

Words for 'lazy' are mostly from notions like 'not working, inactive, idle' or 'weak, sluggish, slow, tired', with acquired derogatory connotation. But in some, cognate with words for 'bad, evil, foul', the derogatory sense is earlier, specialized to 'lazy'.

1. Grk. ἀργός, Hom. ἀεργός, neg. cpd. of ἔργον, ϝέργον 'work' (9.12).

Grk. ἄπονος 'untroubled' and 'lazy', neg. cpd. of πόνος 'toil, work' (9.12).

NG τεμπέλης, fr. Turk. *tembel* 'lazy'.

NG (lit.) ὀκνηρός 'lazy', so also in NT, but class. Grk. 'shrinking, timid' : ὄκνος 'shrinking, hesitation', ὀκνέω 'shrink from, hesitate'. Walde-P. 1.169.

2. Lat. *piger* (> It. *pigro*), also 'slow', beside *piget* 'it irks, is displeasing', prob. as opprobrious terms: OE *fācen* 'fraud, evil' etc. (cf. OHG *trāgi* 'lazy' = OE *trāg* 'evil, bad', below, 4). Walde-P. 2.10. Otherwise Ernout-M. 766 (without outside connections and taking 'slow' as the earlier sense).

Hence *pigritia* 'laziness' > Fr. *paresse*, Sp. *pareza* id., whence adj. Fr. *paresseux*, Sp. *perezoso* 'lazy'. REW 6493.

Lat. *ignāvus*, neg. of *nāvus* (old *gnāvus*) 'industrious, active': W. *go-gnaw* 'activity, active', prob. belonging with IE **ĝnō-* 'know' in Lat. (*g*)*nōscere*, etc. (cf. 'be able' fr. 'know how', in NE *can*, etc., 9.95). Walde-P. 1.580. Ernout-M. 657.

It. *infingardo*, Fr. *fainéant* (transformed fr. OFr. *feignant*, by connection with *faire* and *néant*), fr. It. *fingere*, Fr. *feindre* 'feign' (OFr. *soi feindre* 'be lazy'), fr. Lat. *fingere* 'form, shape' but in the transferred sense 'contrive, feign' (as commonly the pple. *fictus* 'feigned, false'). REW 3313. Gamillscheg 403.

Rum. *leneş* fr. *lene* 'laziness', fr. Slavic, ChSl. *lěnĭ*, etc. 'laziness' : *lěnŭ* 'lazy' (below, 6).

Rum. *trîndav*, fr. *trînd* 'slow, ponderous', fr. Slavic, cf. ChSl. *trądŭ* name of some disease (Pol. *trąd* 'leprosy, scurf', Boh. *trud* 'pimples'). Tiktin 1650. Densusianu 254.

3. Ir. *lesc*, NIr. *leisceamhail* (cpd. with *amhail* 'like, as') : W. *llesg* 'weak, feeble, faint', perh. from **legh-sko-* fr. the root **legh-* 'lie'. Walde-P. 2.425. Walde-H. 1.768. Otherwise (: ON *lǫskr* 'slack') Pedersen 1.147, Falk-Torp 625.

W. *diog*, Br. *diek*, cf. OCorn. *diauc* gl. *segnem*, cpd. of neg. *di-*, second part : Lat. *ōcior* 'swifter', Grk. ὠκύς, Skt. *āçu-* 'swift'. Walde-P. 1.172. Pedersen 1.48.

Br. *lezirek*, fr. MBr. *lezir* fr. Fr. *loisir* 'leisure'. Henry 185.

4. Goth. *lats*, ON *latr*, Dan. *lad*, Sw. *lat*, OHG, MHG *laz*, MHG *lezzic* (NHG *lass, lässig*), the common Gmc. term for 'lazy, slow' (but OE *læt* 'slow, late', NE *late*) : Lat. *lassus* (**ləd-to-*) 'tired, weary' (4.91), Grk. ληδεῖν 'be tired', Goth. *lētan*, ON *lāta* 'leave, let', ChSl. *lěnŭ* (**lēd-no-*) 'lazy', prob. also Lat. *lēnis* 'soft'. Walde-P. 2.395. Falk-Torp 616. Feist 323.

Dan. *doven* = ON *dofinn* 'dull, drowsy' : ON *dofna* 'become dull, lose strength', OE *dofian* 'be silly, stupid', OHG *tobēn*, NHG *toben* 'rage', prob. fr. the root *dheubh- in Goth. *daufs* 'deaf', etc. (4.95). Walde-P. 1.840. Falk-Torp 149 f.

OE *slāw* 'dull, sluggish' and 'slothful' (= 'lazy', so Mt. 25.26), ME *slow* partly in this sense, hence *slowthe* 'sloth' and adj. *slouthful*, NE *slothful* (now commonly replaced by *lazy*) : ON *sljōr*, *slǣr* 'dull', OHG *sleo* 'exhausted, dull, weak', etc., outside connections dub. Walde-P. 2.378. Falk-Torp 1075. NED s.vv. *sloth*, etc.

OE *slæc*, ME *slak* (NE *slack*) = ON *slakr*, OHG *slah* 'loose, slack', etc. : Ir. *locc* 'weak' (4.82). Walde-P. 2.712.

NE *lazy*, orig. dub., but prob. fr. MLG *lasich*, *losich* 'lazy, loose', cf. early Du. *leuzig* 'idle', fr. the root in Goth. *lasiws*, OE *leswe* 'weak' (4.82). Falk-Torp 625. NED s.v.

Du. *traag*, OS *trāg*, OHG *trāgi*, etc. = OE *trāg* 'evil, bad', fr. a lengthened grade of the root in Goth. *trigō* 'grief, repugnance', ON *tregi* 'grief, hindrance', perh. : Skt. *drāgh-* 'be tired', Av. *drigu-*, *drəgu-* 'poor, needy, weak'. Walde-P. 1.821. Falk-Torp 1291 f.

NHG *faul*, fr. MHG *vūl* 'rotten, weak' (also 'lazy'), OHG *fūl* 'rotten' = Goth. *fūls*, OE *fūl*, ON *fūll* 'foul, rotten' (: Lat. *pūtēre* 'stink, rot'). Walde-P. 2.82. Paul, Deutsches Wtb. s.v., assumes development from 'rotten' through 'physically incapacitated, weak' to 'lazy'. But perh. rather through the well-attested secondary sense 'worthless', applied as an opprobrious epithet to the 'lazy'.

Du. *lui* = MLG *loi*, *loie* id., etym. dub., perh. as Gmc. *hlu-ja- : *hlēw-a- in Du. *lauw*, OHG *lāo*, NHG *lau* 'tepid', etc., fr. IE *k̑leu-, extension of *k̑el- in Lat. *calidus* 'warm', etc. Franck-v. W. 400 f. (372). Walde-P. 2.709 (1.430). Otherwise Falk-Torp 680.

5. Lith. *tingus* : ChSl. *tęžĭkŭ* 'heavy', *tęgostĭ* (deriv. of *tęgŭ) 'weight', ON *þungr* 'heavy', etc. Walde-P. 1.726.

Lith. *vangus* : *vengti* 'shun', OHG *winchen*, MHG *winken* 'move aside, waver', OHG *wankōn*, NHG *wanken* 'rock, waver', etc. Walde-P. 1.218, 260. Mühl.-Endz. 3.470.

Lett. *kūtrs* : *kavēt* 'delay, tarry', this possibly ('reflect, ponder' > 'hesitate, delay') : Lat. *cavēre* 'heed, take care', Grk. κοέω 'notice', etc. Walde-P. 1.370. Mühl.-Endz. 2.338.

Lett. *laisks* : *laist* 'let go', etc., Lith. *leisti* 'let, permit' (: Goth. *lētan*, etc., above, 4; see 19.47). Mühl.-Endz. 2.411.

Lith. *slinkas* (Buga, KZ 52.296; not in Kurschat, Lalis, but cf. *slinka* 'sluggard'; *slankus* 'slow, lazy' in Busch-Chowskas), Lett. *slinks* : Lith. *slinkti* 'crawl, slink', OE *slingan* 'wind, crawl', etc. Walde-P. 2.714. Mühl.-Endz. 3.933.

6. ChSl. *lěnŭ*, etc. general Slavic : Goth. *lats*, etc. (above, 4). Berneker 711.

7. Skt. *alasa-* : *il-* 'keep still, be quiet', Lith. *ilsti* 'become tired', cf. *pailsęs* 'tired, weary' (4.91). Walde-P. 1.152.

Skt. *manda-* : ChSl. *mǫditi* 'delay, linger', *mǫdĭnŭ* 'slow', etc. Walde-P. 2.305. Meillet, MSL 14.372.

Av. *ə-vərəzika-*, lit. 'not working', fr. *varəz-* 'work, do, make' (9.13). Barth. 347.

4.93 BALD

Grk.	φαλακρός	Goth.	....	Lith.	*plikas*
NG	φαλακρός	ON	*skǫllōttr*	Lett.	*pliks, kails*
Lat.	*calvus*	Dan.	*skaldet*	ChSl.	*vŭzlysŭ, plěšivŭ*
It.	*calvo*	Sw.	*skallig, kal*	SCr.	*ćelav, plešiv*
Fr.	*chauve*	OE	*calu*	Boh.	*lysý, plešivý, plešatý*
Sp.	*calvo, pelón*	ME	*balled, calouh*	Pol.	*łysy*
Rum.	*chel, pleșuv*	NE	*bald*	Russ.	*lysyj, plešivyj*
Ir.	*mael*	Du.	*kaal*	Skt.	*khalati-, muṇḍa-*
NIr.	*maol*	OHG	*kalo*	Av.	*kaurva-*
W.	*moel*	MHG	*kal*		
Br.	*moal*	NHG	*kahl*		

Most of the words listed may be used either of the head or of the person having a bald head (NE *his head is bald* or *he is bald*), though the latter may also be called 'bald-headed', and so usually NHG *kahlköpfig*.

The words for 'bald' seldom have any connection with those for 'hair', words meaning literally 'hairless' being used otherwise. The commonest source, where this is clear, is the notion of 'bright, shiny' or 'smooth'.

1. Grk. φαλακρός (NG pop. also, with metathesis, καραφλός) : φαλός· λευκός Hesych., φαλιός, φαλᾱρός 'having a white spot', Ir. *ball* 'spot', Lith. *baltas* 'white', Skt. *bhāla-* 'splendor, forehead' (cf. also ME *balled*, below, 4). Walde-P. 2.175 f.

2. Lat. *calvus* (> It., Sp. *calvo*, Fr. *chauve*) : Av. *kaurva-*, NPers. *kal* 'bald', Skt. *ati-kulva-*, *-kūlva-* 'entirely bald', prob. also, Skt. *khalati-*, *khalvāta-* 'bald-headed'. Walde-P. 1.447. Ernout-M. 137. Walde-H. 1.144.

Sp. *pelón*, fr. *pelo* 'hair' (4.14), through ironical use of 'hairy' for the opposite, or through a derogatory sense common alike to 'hairy' and 'bald'(?).

Rum. *chel*, fr. Turk. *kel* 'bald'. Lokotsch 1152.

Rum. *pleșuv*, fr. the Slavic, cf. ChSl. *plěšivŭ*, etc. (below, 6).

3. Ir. *mael* (also 'dull, without horns'), NIr. *maol*, W. *moel* (OW *mail* 'mutilum'), Br. *moal*, perh. (as *mai-los) fr. the root *mai- 'cut off, hew', in Goth. *maitan* 'hew, cut', ON *meita* 'cut', etc. Walde-P. 2.222. Otherwise Stokes 204.

4. ON *skalli* (sb. 'a baldhead'), adj. *skǫllōttr*, Dan. *skaldet*, Sw. *skallig*, perh. fr. *s*-form of the root in Lat. *calvus*, etc. (above, 2). Ernout-M. 137. Falk-Torp 980 (but combined with the following).

OE *calu*, ME *calouh* (NE *callow*), Du. *kaal* (LG *kal* > Sw. *kal*), OHG *kalo*, MHG *kal*, NHG *kahl* : ChSl. *golŭ* 'naked', etc. (4.99). Walde-P. 1.537 f. Berneker 325 f. Combined by some with Lat. *calvus*, etc. (above, 2) on the basis of IE variant initial *k/g*, or even as loanword from it (cf. Walde-P. 1.538).

ME *balled*, NE *bald* (cf. also Dan. *bældet* 'bald, callow', of birds), prob. fr. *ball* 'white spot' on the forehead (in spite of the fact that this is not quotable as early as *balled*), this (whether or not through Celtic) : Grk. φαλᾱρός, etc. (above, 1). Walde-P. 2.175. Falk-Torp 123. NED s.v.

5. Lith. *plikas*, Lett. *pliks* (also 'naked'), ChSl. *plěšivŭ*, SCr. *plešiv*, Boh. *plešivý*, *plešatý*, Russ. *plešivyj* (also Lith. *pleikas* 'bald spot', Lett. *plaikums* 'spot') : Lith. *plynas* 'plain, even, smooth', *plynė* 'plain, open field', Norw. dial. *flein* 'bald, naked', Sw. dial. *flen* 'naked', but further root connection dub. Walde-P. 2.93. Mühl.-Endz. 3.344. Falk-Torp 235.

Lett. *kails* 'bald, naked, bare' : Ir. *cōil* 'thin, slender', W., Corn. *cul* 'lean, narrow'. Walde-P. 1.455.

6. ChSl. *vŭz-lysŭ*, Boh. *lysý*, Pol. *łysy*, Russ. *lysyj* : Skt. *ruçant-* 'bright, shining', IE *leuk̑-, beside *leuk- in Lat. *lūx* 'light', etc. Walde-P. 2.411. Berneker 752.

ChSl. *plěšivŭ*, above, 5.

SCr. *ćelav*, fr. Turk. *kel* id. (cf. above, 2, Rum. *chel*).

7. Skt. *khalati-*, Av. *kaurva-* : Lat. *calvus*, above, 2.

Skt. *muṇḍa-* 'with shaven head' (also 'hornless, blunt'), perh. : Skt. *mṛd-* 'crush, rub', etc. Walde-P. 2.288 (287).

4.94 LAME

Grk.	χωλός	Goth.	*halts*	Lith.	*raišas, šlubas*
NG	κουτσός	ON	*haltr (lami)*	Lett.	*tizls, klibs, slums*
Lat.	*claudus*	Dan.	*halt, lam*	ChSl.	*chromŭ*
It.	*zoppo, ranco*	Sw.	*halt, lam*	SCr.	*hrom, šepav*
Fr.	*boiteux*	OE	*healt (lama)*	Boh.	*chromý, kulhavý*
Sp.	*cojo*	ME	*halt, lame*	Pol.	*chromy, kulawy*
Rum.	*șchiop*	NE	*lame (halt)*	Russ.	*chromoj*
Ir.	*bacach, losc*	Du.	*kreupel, lam, mank*	Skt.	*çrōṇa-, srāma-, pañgu-*, etc.
NIr.	*bacach*	OHG	*halz (lam)*		
W.	*cloff*	MHG	*lam, halz, hinkende*	Av.	....
Br.	*kamm*	NHG	*lahm, hinkend*		

The words listed are those used primarily for 'lame' in the leg or foot (as in NE *he is lame*), but most of them are or were also used for 'lame' in wider sense, 'crippled' in any limb.

They are from diverse notions such as 'break, bend, twist', some from the name of a part affected (as 'hip'), some probably of imitative origin (from the clumping sound of a lame person), several quite obscure.

1. Grk. χωλός, etym.? Boisacq 1072.

NG κουτσός, Byz. κουτζός (κοτσός Chron. Mor.), orig. 'crippled' as in cpds. κουτζοδάκτυλος 'stump-fingered' (Byz.), κουτζομύτης 'snub-nosed', κουτσοχέρης 'with crippled hand', κουτσαύτης 'crop-eared', etc. (G. Meyer, Neugr. Stud. 2.97 ff.), now plausibly explained as fr. κοψο- (: κόπτω 'cut') in cpds., the change of πσ to τσ perh. first by dissim. in cases like κοψο-πόδης > κοτσο-πόδης. Amantos, Αθηνᾶ 28, παραρτ. 124 f. Georgacas, Ἀρχ. Θρᾳκ. Θησ. 14.227, n. 4. The Slavic words, Bulg. *kuc* 'lame', etc. (Berneker 636), are then loan words.

2. Lat. *claudus*, history obscure, but prob. connected in some way with *claudere* 'shut'—either directly through 'shut off, prevent' (as *fugam claudere*) and hence 'hamper', or more remotely through the underlying root of *claudere* and *clāvis* 'key', with the notion of 'bend, hook'. Walde-P. 1.492. Walde-H. 1.231.

It. *zoppo*, blend of *zanca* 'leg' and VLat. *cloppus* 'lame' (see below). REW 9598.

It. *ranco*, through Cat. or Prov. *ranc* fr. Frank. *rank (= MLG *rank* 'twisted') : NHG *renken*, NE *wrench*, etc. REW 7044. Weigand-H. 2.570.

Fr. *boiteux* (beside *boiter* 'limp'), OFr. *boisteux*, apparently a deriv. of OFr. *boiste*, Fr. *boîte* 'box', also 'bone-socket' (fr. MLat. *buxida*, Grk. πυξίς, -ίδα 'box'), hence orig. 'club-footed' (perh., but not necessarily, influenced by *bot* 'club-footed'). REW 6892. Gamillscheg 119.

Sp. *cojo* (Cat. *coix*, Port. *coxa*), fr. VLat. *coxus* 'claudus' (gl.), fr. Lat.

coxa 'hip, hipbone'. REW 2292a. Ernout-M. 226.

Rum. *șchiop* fr. VLat. *cloppus* 'lame' (gl.), cf. *cloppicāre in Fr. *clocher*, Prov. *clopchar* 'limp', Alb. *shqep* 'lame', prob. of imitative orig. Ernout-M. 199. Walde-H. 1.237. REW 1997. Pușcariu 1550.

3. Ir. *losc*, etym. dub., perh. : Grk. λοξός 'slanting, oblique', etc. Stokes 244. (Walde-P. 1.157 with query.)

Ir. *bacach* (= W. *bachog* 'hooked, crooked'), fr. Ir. *bacc*, W. *bach* 'hook' (orig. dub. Walde-P. 2.105).

W. *cloff*, fr. VLat. *cloppus* (cf. above, 2, Rum. *șchiop*). Pedersen 1.238. Loth, Mots lat. 150.

Br. *kamm* 'crooked' (12.74), also 'lame'.

4. Goth. *halts*, ON *haltr*, OE *healt* etc. the old Gmc. group for 'lame' (NE *halt* arch.) : Ir. *coll* 'destruction, loss, ruin', W. *coll* 'loss, damage', prob. fr. *d*-formations of the root *kel- in Grk. κλάω 'break', Lat. *per-cellere* 'strike, beat, destroy' (cf. *clādēs* 'destruction'), Lith. *kalti* 'beat, hammer', etc. Walde-P. 1.439. Falk-Torp 375. Feist 242 f.

ON *lami*, OE *lama*, OHG *lam*, etc., in the older periods 'maimed, crippled' and esp. 'paralytic, palsied' (so still commonly in Dan., Sw., Du.) : OHG *lemmian*, OE *lemian* 'lame', ON *lemja* 'strike, hit', ChSl. *lomiti*, OPruss. *limtwei* 'break', etc., IE *lem-. Walde-P. 2.434. Falk-Torp 621.

Du. *kreupel*, MLG *kröpel* (> MHG, NHG *krüppel*) = OE *crypel* 'a cripple', etc., fr. the root of OE *crēopan*, MLG *krūpen* 'creep, crawl' : Grk. γρυπός 'crooked', etc. (extensions of IE *ger- 'twist, turn'). Walde-P. 1.598. Franck-v. W. 348.

Du. *mank* (MDu. *manc*, MLG *mank*) fr. Lat. *mancus* 'maimed, infirm, defective' orig. 'crippled in the hand' : *manus* 'hand'. Ernout-M. 585., Walde-H. 2.23. Franck-v. W. 413. Falk-Torp 694.

MHG *hinkende*, NHG *hinkend*, pple. of *hinken* 'limp' (= ON *hinka*, etc.) : Skt. *khañj-* 'limp', *khañja-* 'lame', Grk. σκάζω 'limp', ON *skakkr* 'awry, twisted', IE *(s)keng-. Walde-P. 2.564. Falk-Torp 406.

5. Lith. *raišas* : Grk. ῥοικός 'crooked, bent', Av. *urvaēsa-* 'turning, whirl', *urvisyeiti* 'turns', etc., IE *wreik-, extension of *wer- 'turn'. Walde-P. 1.279.

Lith. *šlubas* (whence *šlubuoti* 'limp'), *šlumas*, Lett. *slums*, history dub. Not directly : Skt. (RV) *çrōṇa-* 'lame' (so W. Schulze, Berl. Sitzungsber. 1910 p. 801, Mühl.-Endz. 3.941), since this is rather a deriv. of *çrōṇi-* 'hip, buttock' (name of the defect from the part of the body affected, cf. VLat. *coxus* 'lame', above, 2). The Baltic words may be independent derivatives of a root *k̑leu- 'crack, break'(?) assumed as underlying the words for 'hip', Skt. *çrōṇi-*, Lith. *šlaunis*, W. *clun*, etc. Walde-P. 1.499 f.

Lett. *tizls*, etym.? Mühl.-Endz. 4.199.

Lett. *klibs*, cf. Lith. *klibas* 'bowlegged, tottering' : Lith. *klibėti* 'shake, totter', Lith. *klebėti*, Lett. *klabāt* 'shake, rattle', outside root connection? Mühl.-Endz. 2.225.

6. ChSl. *chromŭ*, etc., general Slavic : Skt. (Ved.) *srāma-* 'crippled, lame', root connection? Walde-P. 2.706. Berneker 403.

SCr. *šepav*, cf. *šepati* 'limp, hobble', Ukr. *šepast* 'lame', etc., outside connections? Miklosich 338.

Boh. *kulhavý*, Pol. *kulawy*, with vbs. Boh. *kulhati*, Pol. *kulać* 'limp', history difficult. Brückner 281 derives Pol. *kulawy* fr. *kula* 'staff, crutch' (this fr. NHG dial. *küle* = *keule* 'club'),—attractive for the Polish, but not for group as a whole, for which cf. Berneker 642 f.

7. Skt. çrōṇa-, see under Lith. šlubas (above, 5).

Skt. srāma- : ChSl. chromŭ, etc. (above, 6).

Skt. paṅgu-, etym.? Uhlenbeck 152.

Skt. khañja- : MHG hinken 'limp', etc. (above, 4).

Skt. khora- (also khoḍa-, khola-), perh. : Lat. scaurus 'clubfooted' (cf. Scaurus). Ernout-M. 904. Walde-P. 2.538.

4.95 DEAF

Grk.	κωφός	Goth.	baups	Lith.	kurčias, kurtinas
NG	κουφός	ON	daufr	Lett.	kurls, kurns
Lat.	surdus	Dan.	døv	ChSl.	gluchŭ
It.	sordo	Sw.	döv	SCr.	gluh
Fr.	sourd	OE	dēaf	Boh.	hluchý
Sp.	sordo	ME	deaf	Pol.	głuchy
Rum.	surd	NE	deaf	Russ.	gluchoj
Ir.	bodar	Du.	doof	Skt.	badhira-
NIr.	bodhar	OHG	toub (tumb)	Av.	karəna-, asruṭ-gaoša-
W.	byddar	MHG	toup		
Br.	bouzar	NHG	taub		

The common words for 'deaf' are not from such a logical source as 'not hearing', but rather from more general notions such as 'dull' or 'mutilated', as are likewise several of the words for 'dumb' or even 'blind'. 'Deaf' and 'dumb' were expressed by the same word in Greek, and OHG tumb was sometimes used in both senses.

1. Grk. κωφός, in Hom. 'dull, blunt' (κωφὸν βέλος 'blunt missile') and 'mute, noiseless' (κύματι κωφῷ 'with noiseless wave'), later both 'dumb' and 'deaf' (so still in NT), but NG κουφός only 'deaf', prob. : κηφήν 'drone', ChSl. chabiti 'spoil', pochabŭ 'foolish', Boh. ochabiti 'make loose, weak'. Walde-P. 1.348. Boisacq 452.

2. Lat. surdus (> Romance words) also 'dull (of sound), indistinct (also of smell and color), inaudible', prob. (as orig. 'indistinct' of sound) fr. the root in susurrus 'muttering, whisper', susurrāre 'hum, mutter, whisper', Skt. svar- 'sound', ON svarra 'roar'. Walde-P. 2.528. Ernout-M. 1007.

3. Ir. bodar, NIr. bodhar, W. byddar, Br. bouzar, prob. (with IE o) : Skt.

badhira- 'deaf'. Stokes 176. Pedersen 1.111, 363. Thurneysen, Gram. 74. Otherwise Walde-P. 2.190, with attempt to combine with Goth. baups.

4. Goth. baups, etym. dub. Possibly as orig. 'blunt' : MDu. bot 'dull, stupid', LG butt 'blunt, coarse', Norw. dial. butt 'blunt', cf. also Arm. bot 'blunt'. Persson, Beiträge 256. Feist 86. Otherwise Walde-P. 2.190 (cf. above, 3).

ON daufr, OE dēaf, OHG toub, etc., general Gmc. (in most cases also in the sense of 'dull, slow' of mind or body; Goth. only in this sense, daubata hairtō 'dulled heart', Mk. 8.17) : ON deyfa 'blunt, stupefy', ofinn 'dull, drowsy' (Dan. doven 'lazy' 4.92), MHG touben 'stupefy', etc., Grk. τύφω 'raise a smoke, stupefy with smoke', τυφλός 'blind' (4.97), etc., here also Goth. dumbs 'dumb', etc., OHG tumb 'stupid, dumb, deaf' (4.96), fr. *deu-bh- extension of IE *dheu- in Skt. dhū- 'shake', dhūma- 'vapor, smoke', Grk. θύω 'rush, rage' and numerous other formations, with a common notion of 'whirling, rapid, dizzy motion', applied to various physical and mental phenomena, and including some

---

words for 'deaf', 'dumb', and 'blind'. Walde-P. 1.840. Falk-Torp 179.

5. Lith. kurčias, kurtinas, Lett. kurls, kurns : ChSl. krŭnŭ 'having a mutilated ear or nose' (cf. also Russ. kur-guzyj 'short-tailed', Ukr. kur-nosyj 'snub-nosed'), prob. also Av. karəna- 'deaf', Skt. karṇa- 'short-eared', all with common notion of mutilated and presumably fr. IE *(s)ker- 'cut'. Mühl.-Endz. 2.323. Berneker 669.

6. ChSl. gluchŭ, etc., general Slavic, outside connections? Berneker 308, 309. Brückner 145 (unconvincing).

7. Skt. badhira- : Ir. bodar (above, 3). Av. karəna- (so NPers. kar 'deaf'), see above, 5 and Barth., IF 3.169.

Av. asruṭ-gaoša-, lit. 'having unhearing ears' (cpd. of a- privative with sru- 'hear' and gaoša- 'ear'). Barth. 223.

4.96 DUMB

Grk.	κωφός, ἄφωνος	Goth.	dumbs, baups	Lith.	nebylys, bežadis
NG	βουβός, μουγγός	ON	dumbr	Lett.	mēms
Lat.	mūtus	Dan.	stum	ChSl.	nēmŭ
It.	muto, mutolo	Sw.	stum	SCr.	nijem
Fr.	muet	OE	dumb	Boh.	němý
Sp.	mudo	ME	dumb	Pol.	niemy
Rum.	mut	NE	dumb	Russ.	nemoj
Ir.	amlabar, balb	Du.	stom	Skt.	mūka-
NIr.	balbh	OHG	stum (tumb)	Av.	afravaoča-
W.	mud	MHG	stum (tump)		
Br.	mud	NHG	stumm		

Of the words for 'dumb', only a few are from such a logical source as 'not speaking'. Some are from the general notion of 'dull', with the same word or cognates used also for 'deaf' (4.95). The majority are from 'stammer' or the like, most of these being of imitative origin.

1. Grk. κωφός, same as for 'deaf' (4.95).

Grk. ἄφωνος (often merely 'silent', but also 'dumb', neg. cpd. of φωνή 'voice').

Late Grk. βωβός (quotable as 'dumb' from Plut., etc., in Hesych. 'lame'), common in Byz. Grk., NG βουβός, prob. in origin a mere derogatory epithet of the same type as Sp. bobo 'stupid', NE boob, booby, OFr. bobu 'simpleton', etc. G. Meyer, IF 6.109.

NG μουγγός, see below, 2.

2. Lat. mūtus (> It. muto, Sp. mudo, Rum. mut, OFr. mu; derivs. It. mutolo, Fr. muet), fr. the imitative syllable mū,

sound made with closed lips (cf. non facere mu 'say not a word', Grk. μῦ λαλεῖν 'mutter'). So also Skt. mūka-, Grk. μυν-δός, and the forms of Hesych. μύδος, μυκός, μυναρός, μυττός, μύτης, Byz. μογγός (Leont. Cypr., 7th cent.), NG μουγγός and Arm. munj. Walde-P. 2.309 ff. Ernout-M. 650.

3. Ir. amlabar, cpd. of neg. am- and labar 'loquacious' : W. llafar 'speech', Br. lavar 'word', dilavar 'silent, speechless'. Pedersen 2.7.

Ir. balb, NIr. balbh, fr. Lat. balbus 'stammering' (this sense also in Irish). Vendryes, De hib. voc. 115.

W., Br. mud fr. Lat. mūtus. Loth., Mots lat. 188.

4. Goth. dumbs, ON dumbr, OE-NE dumb, but OHG tumb mostly 'stupid', rarely 'dumb, deaf', MHG tump 'stupid', rarely 'dumb' (NHG dumm in LG form), fr. a nasal form of the root in ON daufr,

---

etc., 'deaf' (4.95). Walde-P. 1.840. Feist 129.

Goth. baups 'deaf' (4.95) once (Mt. 9.32), also for κωφός as 'dumb'.

Du. stom (MLG stum > Dan., Sw. stum), OHG, MHG stum, NHG stumm : OHG stam(m)alōn, MHG stammeln, ON stama, OE stamorian 'stammer', Lett. stuomities 'stammer, stumble, stop', stumt 'push', Lith. stumti 'shove'. Walde-P. 2.626. Falk-Torp 1189 f.

5. Lith. nebylys, neg. cpd., second part : byloti formerly the common word for 'speak' (18.21).

Lith. bežadis, cpd. of privative prefix be- and žadas 'voice, sound'.

Lett. mēms, prob. fr. an imitative syllable mē- (like *mū- in Lat. mūtus, etc., above, 2). Mühl.-Endz. 2.615 f.

6. ChSl. nēmŭ, etc., general Slavic, prob. by dissimilation of *mēmŭ : Lett. mēms (above), or, in any case, of similar imitative orig. Schulze, KZ 50.129. Grünenthal, Arch. sl. Ph. 39.290 f.

7. Skt. mūka- : Lat. mūtus, etc. (above, 2).

Av. afravaoča-, neg. cpd., second part : fra-vač- 'speak out, announce'. Barth. 101.

4.97 BLIND

Grk.	τυφλός	Goth.	blinds	Lith.	aklas
NG	τυφλός, στραβός	ON	blindr	Lett.	akls, neredzīgs
Lat.	caecus	Dan.	blind	ChSl.	slěpŭ
It.	cieco, orbo	Sw.	blind	SCr.	slijep
Fr.	aveugle	OE	blind	Boh.	slepý
Sp.	ciego	ME	blind	Pol.	ślepy
Rum.	orb	NE	blind	Russ.	slepoj
Ir.	dall, goll	Du.	blind	Skt.	andha-
NIr.	caoch, dall	OHG	blint	Av.	anda-
W.	dall	MHG	blint		
Br.	dall	NHG	blind		

Of the words for 'blind' only a few are connected with those for 'eye' or 'see'. Some have come through 'squinting, one-eyed', and this was probably the sense of the inherited group, Lat. caecus, etc., (below, 2). Some are from such general notions as 'mixed, confused' or 'bereft'.

1. Grk. τυφλός, also of objects 'dim, obscure' : τύφω 'stupefy with smoke', Goth. daufs 'insensible' (of the heart), ON daufr 'deaf' (4.95). Walde-P. 1.840.

NG στραβός 'crooked' (12.74), also (through 'squint-eyed') 'blind'.

2. Lat. caecus (> It. cieco, Sp. ciego) : Ir. caech 'one-eyed', 'squinting, blind' (K. Meyer, Contrib. 297), NIr. caoch 'blind, dim-eyed' ('blind' by influence of Latin?), W. coeg 'empty, foolish' (coeg-

ddall 'half blind'), Goth. haihs 'one-eyed', cf. Skt. kekara- 'squinting'. Walde-P. 1.328. Ernout-M. 128. Walde-H. 1.129.

It. orbo (but also 'bereft, orphaned'), OFr., Rum. orb, fr. Lat. orbus 'bereft, deprived', with late Lat. specialization fr. phrases like orbus lumine, perh. assisted by association with orbis in the sense of 'eye'. Ernout-M. 710. REW 6086.

Fr. aveugle, OIt. avocolo, fr. a late Lat. *ab-oculus, a medical term like and prob. modelled on Byz. ἀπόμματος 'blind'. REW 33. Wartburg 1.7.

3. Ir., W., Br. dall, prob. : Goth. dwals 'silly', OE dol, OHG tol 'foolish', Grk. θολός 'mud, dirt' (esp. in water), θολόω 'make turbid (of water)', con-

---

found', fr. *dhwel-, extension of *dheu- also in Grk. τυφλός 'blind', ON daufr 'deaf', etc. (4.95). Walde-P. 1.842. Pedersen 1.60.

MIr. goll (secondary media), OIr. coll (once, Thes. 1.236.3 gl. 'luscum' but prob. 'blind'), perh. : Lat. kāṇa 'perforated, one-eyed', Grk. κελλάς· μονόφθαλμος Hesych., root *kel- 'prick'(?). Walde-P. 1.436. Pedersen 1.157.

NIr. caoch : Lat. caecus (above, 2).

4. Goth. blinds, etc., general Gmc., prob. (as 'confused, troubled', cf. Ir. dall, Grk. τυφλός, etc.) fr. OHG blandan 'mix with', ON blanda, OE blandan, OHG blantan 'mix, trouble', ChSl. blędą,

blęsti 'go astray', etc. Walde-P. 2.216. Falk-Torp 82. Feist 100.

5. Lith. aklas, Lett. akls apparently fr. the name of the affected organ, Lith. akis, Lett. acs 'eye' (4.21). Mühl.-Endz. 1.63. Walde-P. 1.34.

Lett. neredzīgs, neg. cpd., second part : redzēt 'see'.

6. ChSl. slěpŭ, etc., general Slavic (cf. also vb. ChSl. oslīpnqti, OBoh. oslnúti 'make blind') outside connections? Miklosich 307. Brückner 531.

7. Skt. andha-, Av. anda-, cf. Ved. andha- 'darkness', perh. : Lat. umbra 'shade'. Walde-P. 1.182. Ernout-M. 1123.

4.98 DRUNK

Grk.	μεθύων	Goth.	drugkans	Lith.	girtas
NG	μεθυσμένος	ON	drukkinn, ǫlr, ǫlvaðr	Lett.	pilns, piedzēriēs
Lat.	ēbrius	Dan.	drukken, fuld	ChSl.	pijanŭ
It.	(ub)briaco, briaco	Sw.	drucken, full	SCr.	pijan
Fr.	ivre	OE	druncen	Boh.	opilý
Sp.	borracho (ebrio, beodo)	ME	drunken	Pol.	pijany
Rum.	beat	NE	drunk(en)	Russ.	p'janyj
Ir.	mesc	Du.	dronken	Skt.	matta-
NIr.	meisceamhail	OHG	truncan	Av.	mað- 'get drunk'
W.	meddw	MHG	trunken		
Br.	mezo	NHG	(be)trunken		

The words listed are the commonplace words for a person who is 'drunk', with omission of the more elegant expressions parallel to NE intoxicated, inebriated, etc. and of the boundless variety of colloquial and slang terms parallel to NE full, soaked, lit up, etc. (but Lett. pilns lit. 'full', used for 'drunk' in version of NT, and Dan. fuld, Sw. full not felt as slang).

Many are in origin participial forms of verbs for 'drink' (5.13). Some are derived from the name of an intoxicating drink 'mead, beer', and some are in origin similar to NE full or soaked.

1. Grk. μεθύων, NG μεθυσμένος (pples. of μεθύω 'get drunk'), W. meddw, Br. mezo, and prob. Ir. mesc (-sko-forma-

tion, cf. Grk. μεθύσκω), fr. Grk. μέθυ 'wine' (orig. 'mead'), OIr. mid, W. medd, Br. mez 'mead' (5.85). Walde-P. 2.261. Pedersen 1.63, 367. Otherwise for Ir. mesc, as *mik-sko- 'mixed' : Lat. miscere, etc. Pokorny, Hist. Reader of OIr p. 40.

2. Lat. ēbrius (> OIt ebbro, Fr. ivre, Sp. ebrio), hence late Lat. ēbriācus (> It. (ub)briaco), obviously related to its opposite sōbrius 'sober', both presumably cpds. with a common second part, but this, and consequently the precise analysis, is entirely obscure. Ernout-M. 292. Walde-H. 1.387 f. REW 2818, 2820.

Sp. borracho, as sb. 'drunkard', orig. a facetious epithet 'wine flask', masc. to *borracha* 'leather wine flask' (= It. *borraccia*, of dub. orig., REW 1411).

Sp. *beodo*, Rum. *beat*, fr. Lat. *bibitus* 'drunk' pple. of *bibere* 'drink'. REW 1080.

3. Ir. *mesc*, NIr. *meisceamhail* (cpd. with *amhail* 'like'), W. *meddw*, Br. *mezo*, see above, 1.

4. Goth. *drugkans* (I Cor. 11.21), OE *druncan* etc., the regular Gmc. expression, pples. of Goth. *drigkan*, OE *drincan*, etc. 'drink'.

ON *ǫlr*, later *ǫlvaðr*, fr. *ǫl* 'ale, beer' (5.92).

Dan. *fuld*, Sw. *full* (so also NIcel. *fullur*, Scotch *fou*, and NE slang *full*), lit. 'full (of strong drink)'.

5. Lith. *girtas* (old pple., Leskien, Ablaut 326), Lett. *pasigeres*, Lett. *piedzēriēs* (pples. of refl. perfect. forms) : Lith. *gerti*, Lett. *dzert* 'drink'.

Lett. *pilns*, lit. 'full', but also 'drunk' (like Dan. *fuld*, etc., above). Mühl.-Endz. 3.216.

6. ChSl. *pĭjanŭ* (deriv. *pĭjanica ὁ μεθύων*, Mt. 24.49), SCr. *pijan*, Pol. *pijany*, Russ. *p'janyj* (old mid. pple.? Cf. Meil-

let, Études, 438), Boh. *opilý, zpilý* (pples.) : ChSl. *piti*, etc. 'drink'.

7. Skt. *matta-* 'drunk', pple. of *mad-* 'be drunk, rejoice' = Av. *maδ-* 'get drunk' (pple. *masta-* happens not to be quotable in this sense, but cf. NPers. *mast* 'drunk') : Lat. *madēre* 'be wet', also 'be drunk' (whence *madidus* 'wet, soaked, drunk'; *mattus*, Petr. Sat. 41 and in glosses 'drunk' fr. **maditus*), Grk. *μαδάω* 'be moist, flaccid' (of a disease of fig trees), 'fall out' (of hair), *μαδαρός* 'wet'. Walde-P. 2.230 f. Walde-H. 2.6 f.

Ernout-M. 578 reject the connection between the Latin (and Greek) and the Indo-Iranian forms, on formal and semantic grounds. But the Skt. *mand-* forms make no serious difficulty, and on the semantic side, the secondary sense of 'be drunk' (whence *madidus* 'wet, also U.S. slang *soaked*) may well have developed in part in the IE period, and prevailed to the exclusion of 'be wet' in the Indo-Iranian period, with some new extension in Sanskrit ('be exhilarated, glad'). Separation seems entirely uncalled for.

6.222); Lat. *nūdus*, whence (or fr. derivs.) It. *nudo, ignudo*, Fr. *nu*, Sp. *desnudo*; Ir. *nocht*, NIr. *nocht, nochttha*, W. *noeth*, Br. *noaz*; Goth. *naqaþs* ON *nǫkviðr, nǫktr*, rarely (but reg. NIcel.) *nakinn*, Dan. *nøgen*, Sw. *naken*, OE *nacod*, ME, NE *naked*, OHG *nachut*, MHG *nacket, nackent*, NHG *nackt*; Lith. *nuogas*, ChSl. *nagŭ*, SCr. *nag*, Boh. *nahý*, Pol. *nagi*, Russ. *nagoj*; Skt. *nagna*, Av. *maγna-* (for *m-*, cf. Barth. 1112); cf. Hitt. *nekumanz* 'naked', *nekuzi* 'goes to bed', *nekus* 'evening' (Sturtevant, Hitt. Gram. 122 f.).

2. NG *γδυμνός*, fr. *γυμνός* by association with *γδύνω* 'undress'.

3. Rum. *gol*, fr. Slavic (below, 7).

4. Ir. *lomm*, NIr. *lom* (also frequently cpd. *lomnocht* with *nocht*, above, 1), W. *llwm* 'bare' : OIr. *lommar* 'callow, bare', MIr. *lommraim* 'strip, peel', prob. fr. the root **leu-bh-* in Russ. *lub* 'bast', Lith. *luobas* 'tree bark', etc., beside

*leu-p in Skt. *lup-* 'break, injure, plunder', Lith. *lupti* 'peel'. Walde-P. 2.418.

5. ON *berr*, Dan., Sw. *bar*, OE *bær*, ME, NE *bare*, OHG, MHG *bar* (NHG *bar* in old sense in cpds. *barfuss, barhaupt* and readopted in the modern lit. language) : Lith. *basas*, Lett. *bass*, ChSl. *bosŭ* 'barefoot', with guttural suffix Arm. *bok* id. Walde-P. 2.189.

Du. *bloot*, MHG *blôz*, NHG *bloss* (OHG *blôz* 'proud', fr. 'empty, vain'?) : OE *blēat* 'miserable', ON *blautr* 'soft', also OE *blēap*, ON *blauðr* 'timid', prob. from extensions of **bhlau-* seen in Grk. *φλαῦρος* 'petty, trivial'. Walde-P. 2.208. Falk-Torp 85 f.

6. Lett. *pliks* and *kails*, both also 'bald' (4.93).

7. ChSl. *golŭ*, SCr. *go*, Boh. *holý*, Pol. *goli*, Russ. *golyj* : OE *calu*, OHG *kalo*, etc. 'bald' (4.93). Walde-P. 1.537 f. Berneker 325 f.

4.99 NAKED, BARE

Grk.	γυμνός	Goth.	naqaþs	Lith.	nuogas
NG	γυμνός, γδυμνός	ON	nǫkviðr, nǫktr; berr	Lett.	pliks, kails
Lat.	nūdus	Dan.	nøgen; bar	ChSl.	nagŭ; golŭ
It.	nudo, ignudo	Sw.	naken; bar	SCr.	go, nag
Fr.	nu	OE	nacod; bær	Boh.	nahý; holý
Sp.	desnudo	ME	naked; bare	Pol.	nagi; goli
Rum.	gol	NE	naked; bare	Russ.	nagoj; golyj
Ir.	nocht; lomm	Du.	naakt; bloot	Skt.	nagna-
NIr.	nocht; lom	OHG	nachut; bar	Av.	maγna-
W.	noeth; llwm	MHG	nacke(n)t; bar, blôz		
Br.	noaz	NHG	nackt; bloss		

A distinction of usage between the common word for a wholly 'naked' person or body, and one that applies more commonly to some 'bare' part of the body (and objects quite apart from the body) exists in some languages and is indicated by a semicolon in the table,

but even in these is not strictly observed and in others is wholly absent.

The majority of the words for 'naked' belong to an inherited group.

1. IE **nog^u-*, with various suffixes. Walde-P. 2.339. Ernout-M. 684.

Grk. *γυμνός* (cf. Sturtevant, Language

CHAPTER 5
FOOD AND DRINK; COOKING AND UTENSILS

5.11 EAT

Grk.	ἐσθίω, ἔδω, aor. ἔφαγον	Goth.	matjan, itan	Lith.	valgyti (ésti)
NG	τρώγω, aor. ἔφαγα	ON	eta	Lett.	ēst
Lat.	ésse, edere	Dan.	spise (æde)	ChSl.	jasti
It.	mangiare	Sw.	äta	SCr.	jesti
Fr.	manger	OE	etan	Boh.	jisti
Sp.	comer	ME	ete	Pol.	jeść
Rum.	mînca	NE	eat	Russ.	jest' (kušat')
Ir.	ithim	Du.	eten	Skt.	ad-, aṣ-, bhuj-, ghas-
NIr.	ithim	OHG	ezzan	Av.	xᵛar-, gah-
W.	bwyta	MHG	ezzen		
Br.	dibri	NHG	essen, spᵣisen		

A majority of the words for 'eat' belong to an inherited group representing an IE **ed-*. A few of these survive only as homely words used of animals 'feeding' or vulgarly of men. The substitutes are partly words meaning originally 'chew, nibble, swallow', etc., which were used of animals 'feeding' and also as colloquial or slang expressions with reference to men (cf. NE *where'll we feed?*), until they finally became the standard words for 'eat'. Others are derivatives of nouns meaning 'food, meal' (these of various sources discussed under 'food', etc.), that is, 'take food, a meal'; or again from the notion of 'partake of', with specialization to 'partake of food', as frequently in NE.

1. IE **ed-*. Walde-P. 1.118. Ernout-M. 294 f. Walde-H. 1.392 f.

Grk. *ἔδω* (poet.), Att. *ἐσθίω*; Lat. *ésse*, late *edere*, Osc. *edum*; Ir. subj. *estar*, pple. pass. *eisse*, etc. (supplying parts of *ithim*; cf. Pedersen 2.559; Thurneysen, Gram. 471), W. *ysu* 'devour'; Goth. *itan*, etc. general Gmc.; Lith. *ésti*, Lett. *ēst*, OPr. *īst*; ChSl. *jasti*, etc., general Slavic; Skt. *ad-*; Arm. *utem*, Hitt. *et-*. But Dan. *æde* (regular for 'eat' in Dan. Bible) and Lith. *ésti* are now used only of animals (or vulgarly of men). Falk-Torp 1411. NSB s.v.

Cf. cpd. Goth. *fra-itan* (for *κατεσθίω* 'eat up, devour'), OE *fretan*, OHG *frezzan* 'devour', whence NHG *fressen*, used

of animals, etc. (NE *fret* with total loss of any relation to food).

2. Grk. *τρώγω* 'gnaw, nibble, feed on' (perh. : Lat. *tergēre* 'rub off', *terere* 'rub', etc. Walde-P. 1.732), used mostly of animals, but also of men, and in late times simply 'eat'. In the NT, while less common than *ἐσθίω*, it is usual in the Fourth Gospel and must have there a fully respectable standing, for it is put in the mouth of Jesus (Jn. 13.18, etc.). For other examples in pap., cf. Moulton-Milligan s.v. NG *τρώ(γ)ω* is the reg. word for 'eat' in the present.

Grk. aor. *ἔφαγον*, still persisting in NG *ἔφαγα*, fut. *θὰ φά(γ)ω*, etc. : Skt. *bhaj-* 'give or receive a portion', *bhakṣ-* 'partake of, eat or drink'. Locr. *παματοφαγεῖσται* 'have one's property confiscated' is a relic of the more general meaning. Walde-P. 2.127.

Grk. *βιβρώσκω* 'devour, eat up' and simply 'eat', *βέβρωκα, ἐβρώθην* being used in Hellenistic Greek as tenses of *ἐσθίω*, fr. IE **gʷer-* 'swallow, devour' (cf. Grk. *βάραθρον* 'pit' in Skt. *vorāre*, Lat. *vorāre*, ChSl. *žrěti* etc. Walde-P. 1.682 ff.

3. Lat. *comedere* (> Sp., Port. *comer*) cpd. of *edere*.

Lat. *mandūcāre* 'chew' (beside older *mandere*), used colloq. for 'eat' and freq. in this sense from Varro on (esp. Petronius, Peregrinatio, Itala, etc.). Hence OIt. *manicare*, Fr. *manger* (> It.

mangiare), Rum. *mînca*, etc. Ernout-M. 585. Walde-H. 2.24. REW 5292.

4. Ir. *ithim* : Skt. *pitu-* 'food, drink', ChSl. *pitěti* 'feed', etc. (5.12). Pedersen 2.559.

W. *bwyta*, fr. *bwyd* 'food' (5.12).

Br. *dibri*, MBr. *dibriff*, OBr. sb. *diprim* 'food', Corn. *dibry.*, prob. fr. a cpd. **di-prim-* : NIr. *creimim* 'gnaw, chew' (Ir. vbl. n. *creim*, K. Meyer, Contrib. 511). Henry 95. Loth, Vocab. vieux-breton 105. (Otherwise, but to be rejected, Pedersen 1.111).

5. Goth. *matjan* (more common than *itan*), fr. *mats* 'food' (5.12).

Dan. *spise*, fr. sb. *spise*, loanword fr. MLG *spise* 'food' (5.12). As the polite term this has displaced the old *æde* (above, 1), as NHG *speisen* has encroached on *essen*, but without displacing it (Kretschmer, Wortgeogr. 469).

6. Lith. *valgyti* (displacing *ėsti*, above, 1), fr. *valgis* 'food, meal' (5.12).

7. Russ. *kušat'*, polite term 'partake of' food or drink : ChSl. = *kusiti* 'taste', etc. (15.31).

8. Skt. *aç-* 'eat, devour', etym. dub. Walde-P. 1.112.

Skt. *bhuj-* 'enjoy', esp. 'enjoy food, eat', prob. : Lat. *fungī* 'be engaged in, perform'. Walde-H. 1.566 (with refs.).

Skt. *ghas-*, Av. *gah-* 'eat, devour' (Av. only of evil beings), etym.? Walde-P. 1.640. Barth. 517.

Skt. *khād-* 'chew', colloq. for 'eat' and in MIndic mostly displacing *ad-*. Wackernagel-Debrunner, KZ 67.158.

Av. *x^var-* 'consume, eat or drink' (cf. NPers. *xurdan*, the reg. word for 'eat') points to a root **swer-* or **swel-*, and under the latter head may be connected with the Gmc. group, OE *swelgan* 'swallow', NE *swallow*, etc. Walde-P. 2.530. Barth. 1865 f. For 'eat' fr. 'swallow', cf. Grk. *βιβρώσκω*, above, 2.

5.12 FOOD

Grk.	*τροφή, βρῶμα, ἐδωδή, σῖτία*	Goth.	*mats, fōdeins*	Lith.	*valgis, maistas*
NG	*τροφή, φαγί*	ON	*matr, fœða, āt, vist*	Lett.	*barība*
Lat.	*cibus, ēsca, penus*, etc.	Dan.	*mad, føde, spise*	ChSl.	*pišta, jadĭ, brašĭno, krŭma*
It.	*cibo, mangiare, vitto*	Sw.	*mat, föda, spis*	SCr.	*hrana, jelo*
Fr.	*nourriture, aliment*	OE	*mete, fōda, wist, feorm*	Boh.	*jídlo, pokrm, potrava*
Sp.	*alimento, comida*	ME	*mete, fọde*	Pol.	*jadło, pokarm, potrawa*
Rum.	*hrană, mîncare*	NE	*food*		
Ir.	*biad, tūare*	Du.	*voedsel, spijs*	Russ.	*pišča, jastva*
NIr.	*biadh*	OHG	*muos, maz, spīsa, āz, wist*	Skt.	*anna-, pitu-*
W.	*bwyd*	MHG	*muos, spīse, maz, āz*	Av.	*x^varəθa-, pitu-*
Br.	*boed*	NHG	*speise, essen, nahrung, kost*		

Many of the words listed cover 'food' for man or beast. Words that are used only of food for animals ('fodder') are not included in the list, though several of these belong to the same cognate groups and are mentioned in the discussion.

The commonest derivation is naturally from words for 'eat' or 'feed'. But some of the verbs for 'feed' and many more of the nouns for 'food' are the result of specialization from meanings that originally had no specific reference to food, such as 'means of life, a living', 'rear, nourish, preserve, save', 'portion', 'expense, outlay', 'provisions', etc. In some cases a word originally denoting some special kind of food comes to be

used for food in general—the opposite of the specialization seen in NE *meat*.

1. Derivs. of IE **ed-* 'eat' (5.11). Grk. *ἐδωδή, ἔδεσμα*, Hom. *εἶδαρ*; Lat. *ēsca;* ON *āt*, OE *ǣt*, OHG, MHG *āz;* Lett. *ēdiens* ('an article of food'); ChSl. *jadĭ*, SCr. *jelo*, Boh. *jídlo*, Pol. *jadło, jedzenie*, Russ. *jastva;* Skt. *anna-*. But some of these are among the less common words for 'food', and still others are used only in a specialized sense, e.g. OE *ǣs*, OHG *ās*, NHG, Du. *aas* 'carrion, bait', Lith. *ėdesis* 'fodder, bait', etc.

2. Derivs. of IE **pā-* (cf. Lat. *pāscere*, ChSl. *pasti* 'feed cattle, pasture'), **pī-*, (relationship between **pā-* and **pĭ-* on the basis of **pāi-* prob.; otherwise Walde-P. 2.73). Walde-P. 2.72 ff. Ernout-M. 737 f. Feist 157.

Lat. *pābulum* 'fodder'; the Gmc. group represented by NE *food* and *fodder* (below, 6); Skt. *pitu-* 'food, drink', Av. *pitu-* 'food'; ChSl. *pišta* 'food', Boh. *pice* 'fodder', Russ. *pišča* 'food' (cf. ChSl. *pitěti* 'feed').

3. Grk. *τροφή*, fr. *τρέφω* 'make thrive, nourish, rear' (Walde-P. 1.876), with the same specialization to 'food' as in Lat. *alimentum* fr. *alere*.

Βρῶμα, *βρῶσις*, fr. *βιβρώσκω* 'devour, eat'. (5.11)

Σῖτος 'grain' (8.42) is also used for 'food', and so especially *σῖτα* or *σῖτία* (neut. pl.), also *σῖτησις*.

NG *τὸ φαγί*, fr. the old aor. infin. *φαγεῖν* 'eat'. Cf. It. *il mangiare*, NHG *das essen*. NG *φαγητό* is mostly 'an article of food'.

4. Lat. *cibus* (> It. *cibo* 'food', but Sp. *cebo* 'fodder'), etym. dub. Ernout-M. 183. Walde-H. 1.210.

Lat. *penus* 'food supply, provisions' : Lith. *penas* 'food, fodder', *penėti* 'feed, fatten'. Walde-P. 2.25. Ernout-M. 753 f.

Lat. *alimentum* (> It., Sp. *alimento*, Fr. *aliment*), fr. *alere* 'nourish'. Walde-P. 1.86. Ernout-M. 36 ff.

Lat. *nūtrīmentum* (> It. *nutrimento*, etc.; so with different suffix Fr. *nourriture*, fr. *nourrir*), fr. *nūtrīre* 'nourish, feed, suckle' : Skt. *snu-* 'drip, give milk'. Walde-P. 2.623. Ernout-M. 689 f.

Derivs. of Lat. *vīvere* 'live'. Lat. *vīctus* (> It. *vitto*), late *vīctuālia* (> OFr. *vitaile* > ME *vitaile*, NE *victuals*), *vīvenda* (> Sp. *vianda*, OFr. *viande* > NE *viands;* Fr. *viande* now 'meat'), It. *vivere* infin. used as sb., pl. *viveri*. Cf. NHG *lebensmittel* and the Celtic forms below.

Rum. *hrană*, fr. SCr., Bulg. *hrana* (below, 8).

Rum. *mîncare*, old infin. form of *mînca* 'eat'.

5. Ir. *biad*, NIr. *biadh*, W. *bwyd*, Br. *boed*, OCorn. *buit*, fr. IE **g^wei-* 'live' in Lat. *vīvere*, etc. (4.74). Walde-P. 1.668 ff. Pedersen 1.58.

Ir. *tūare*, deriv. of *tūar* 'preparation, provision', vbl. n. to *do-ferim* 'establish', like *fūar* 'preparation', vbl. n. to *foferim*. 'Food' as specialization of 'provision'. K. Meyer, Ber. Preuss. Akad. 1918.628.

6. Goth. *fōdeins* (renders *τροφή*, vs. *mats* = *βρῶμα*; but in OE Gospels *mete* for both), ON *fœða*, Dan. *føde*, Sw. *föda*, OE *fōda*, ME *fọde*, NE *food*, Du. *voedsel;* beside OE *fōder*, NE *fodder*, OHG *fuotar*, NHG *futter* 'fodder'; see above, 2.

Goth. *mats*, ON *matr*, Dan. *mad*, Sw. *mat*, OE, ME *mete* (NE *meat*, still 'food' in NT, King James version, but now specialized to flesh-food), OHG, MHG *maz*, and with different grade of the root and with *s-* suffix, OE *mōs*, OHG *muos, muas* (the usual word in Tat. and Otfr.), MHG *muos* (NHG *mus* 'stewed fruit', etc.) etym. disputed. From **mad-* in Lat. *madēre* 'be moist', Skt. *medas* 'fat', etc., through 'moist or fatty food'

(cf. Lith. *valgis*, below, 7); or fr. **med-* in Goth. *mitan* 'measure', etc. through 'portion', like Lat. *carō* 'flesh' fr. 'portion', Grk. *φαγ-* 'eat' fr. 'partake'. Walde-P. 2.232. Falk-Torp 638. Feist 349.

ON *vist*, OE, OS, OHG *wist* (in OE one of the commonest words for 'food') : Goth. *waila wisan, bi-wisan* 'be merry', *wailawizn* 'food, feasting', *frawisan* 'spend, waste', Ir. *feis*, W. *gwest* 'feast', Skt. *vas-* 'consume' (rare), Av. *vāstra-* 'fodder, pasture'. Walde-P. 1.307 f. Falk-Torp 1403. Feist 568.

OE *feorm* 'food, provisions' (also 'feast, meal', 5.41), prob. fr. Lat. *firma*, as a 'fixed amount, ration'. NED s.v. *farm*, sb.[1].

OHG *spīsa*, MHG *spīse*, NHG *speise*, Du. *spijs* (Dan. *spise*, Sw. *spis*, fr. MLG), fr. MLat. *spē(n)sa* (Lat. *expēnsa*) 'outlay, expense' (cf. It. *spesa* > NHG *spesen*), specialized to 'outlay for provisioning', then 'provisions, food', and now used mostly of prepared food. Falk-Torp 1124. Weigand-H. 2.907.

NHG *kost* 'food, fare, board' (MLG *koste* > Dan., Sw. *kost*), fr. OHG *chosta* 'expense' (cf. NHG pl. *kosten*, NE *cost*, etc. 11.72).

MHG *nar, narunge, nerunge*, NHG *nahrung* (MLG *neringe* > Dan. *næring*, Sw. *näring*) : NHG *nähren* 'nourish', this fr. OHG *nerjan* = OE *nerian*, Goth. *nasjan* 'heal, make well', caus. of *nes-* in Goth. *ganisan*, OHG *genesan*, etc. 'get well'. Walde-P. 2.334 f. Weigand-H. 2.270.

For other examples of partial specialization to 'food', cf. NE *fare* in *good fare, bill of fare*, fr. *fare* 'journey' through 'provisions for journey'; *(good) board*, fr. *board* 'table'; *provisions;* NHG *gericht* 'article of food, dish', fr. *richten* 'arrange, prepare'.

7. Lith. *valgis*, used of prepared food, also 'an article of food' : *vilgyti* 'moisten', Lett. *valgs* 'moist', SCr. *vlaga* 'moisture', Russ. *vologa* used of rich soup and various dainties. Development through 'moist food, dainty' to 'article of food, food'. Walde-P. 1.306. Brückner, KZ 45.104.

Lith. *maistas* 'food, provisions' (Lith., Lett. *maita* 'carrion' with specialization fr. 'food', like NHG *aas*) : *maitinti* 'feed', *misti* 'feed on, live on, get one's living', Lett. *mist* 'live on, get one's living, thrive', *mitināt* 'support, provide maintenance', all with the underlying notion of 'living, maintenance' and prob. connected with Av. *mit-, miθ-* 'dwell', *maēθana-* 'dwelling'. Walde-P. 2.247.

Lett. *barība*, beside *baruōt* 'feed, fatten', prob. : Russ. dial. *bor* 'millet', fr. **bhar-* beside **bhars-* in ChSl. *brašĭno* 'food', etc. (below, 8). Mühl.-Endz. 1.265.

8. ChSl. *jadĭ*, etc. above, 1.

ChSl. *pišta* (in Gospels = *τροφή*), Russ. *pišča*, above, 2.

ChSl. *brašĭno* (in Gospels = *βρῶμα*) : SCr. *brašno* 'meal', Russ. *borošno* 'ryemeal', Lat. *far* 'spelt', Goth. *barizeins* 'made of barley', etc. Walde-P. 2.134. Berneker 74. Cf. the use of Grk. *σῖτος* 'grain' for 'food' (above, 3).

ChSl. *krŭma* 'food, fodder', SCr. *krma*, Pol. *karm*, Russ. *korm* 'fodder' but Pol. *pokarm*, Boh. *pokrm* 'food', perh. (despite the *k*) : Lith. *pašaras* 'fodder', *šerti*, 'feed cattle', etc. Brückner 220. Osthoff, Parerga 62. Berneker 668 f.

Late ChSl. *chrana*, SCr., Bulg. *hrana* 'food, provisions' (> Rum. *hrană*) = Russ. *chorona* 'protection', Boh. *chrana* 'place of refuge' : ChSl. *chraniti* 'guard, preserve, keep', Lat. *servāre*, etc. For the semantic development, cf. NHG *nahrung* (above, 6). Walde-P. 2.498. Berneker 397 f.

For distribution of ChSl. forms, cf. Jagić, Entstehungsgesch. 327, 378.

Boh. *potrava*, Pol. *potrawa, strawa* : ChSl. *trava* 'grass', fr. the root in *truti* 'consume', *na-truti*, 'nourish, feed', *tryti* 'rub', etc. Walde-P. 1.731. Trautmann 327. Brückner 518, 575.

9. Skt. *anna-*, Skt., Av. *pitu-*, above, 1, 2.

Av. *x^varəθa-*, fr. **x^var-* 'consume' (5.11). Hence Arm. *χor* 'food' (Hübschmann, Arm. Gram. 160).

5.13 DRINK (vb.)

Grk.	*πΐνω*	Goth.	*drigkan*	Lith.	*gerti*
NG	*πίνω*	ON	*drekka*	Lett.	*dzert*
Lat.	*bibere*	Dan.	*drikke*	ChSl.	*piti*
It.	*bere*	Sw.	*dricka*	SCr.	*piti*
Fr.	*boire*	OE	*drincan*	Boh.	*piti*
Sp.	*beber*	ME	*drinken*	Pol.	*pić*
Rum.	*bea*	NE	*drink*	Russ.	*pit'*
Ir.	*ibim*	Du.	*drinken*	Skt.	*pā-*
NIr.	*ōlaim*	OHG	*trinkan*	Av.	*x^var-*
W.	*yfed*	MHG	*trinken*		
Br.	*eva*	NHG	*trinken*		

Most of the words for 'drink', apart from the Gmc. group, are inherited from IE **pō(i)-* 'drink', of which any further relations are problematical. Some are from 'swallow, devour' with specialization to 'drink', as in other cases to 'eat'.

1. IE **pō(i)-*, **pī-*. Walde-P. 2.71. Ernout-M. 109. Walde-H. 1.103 f.

Grk. *πΐνω;* Lat. *bibere* (pple. *pōtus*), whence It. *bere*, Fr. *boire*, Sp. *beber*, Rum. *bea;* Ir. *ibim* (vbl. n. *oul, ōl*, whence NIr. *ōlaim*), W. *yfed*, Br. *eva;* OPruss. *poutwei;* ChSl. *piti*, etc., general Slavic; Skt. *pā-;* Alb. *pi*.

2. Goth. *drigkan*, OE *drincan*, etc., general Gmc., etym. disputed. Semantically the deriv. fr. 'draw' (cf. NE *take a draught*, Lat. *dūcere pōcula, sucōs*, etc.) is the most attractive, and so ultimate connection with OE *dragan* 'draw', etc., through a nasalized form of a parallel root (**dhreg-* perh. seen in Skt. *dhraj-* 'move, glide'). Cf. also Toch. A *tsuk-* 'drink' : Lat. *dūcere* 'draw, lead', etc. Walde-P. 1.874. Feist 125. G. S. Lane, Language 14.27.

3. Lith. *gerti*, Lett. *dzert* : ChSl. *žrěti*, Skt. *gr-*, Lat. *vorāre*, Grk. *βιβρώσκω*, IE **g^wer-* 'swallow, devour'. Walde-P. 1.682 ff.

4. Av. *x^var-* 'consume, eat, drink', *x^vāšar-* 'a drinker', see 5.11.

The words for the sb. 'drink' are nearly all obvious derivs. of the roots appearing in the verbs, as Grk. *πῶμα, πόσις*, Lat. *pōtiō, pōtus*, NHG *getränk*, etc. Those of different orig. are as follows:

Ir. *deog*, NIr. *deoch*, W. *diod*, MW *diawt*, OCorn. *diot*, MBr. *diet*, orig. obscure. Walde-P. 1.786. Stokes 146.

Ir. *lind* (NIr. *lionn* 'ale'), W. *llyn*, prob. the same word as Ir. *lind* (*s*-stem), W. *llyn* 'lake, pond' (1.43). Pedersen 1.37. Persson, Beiträge 878. But separated by Walde-P. 2.438.

5.14 HUNGER (sb.)

Grk.	λῑμός, πεῖνα	Goth.	hūhrus, grēdus	Lith.	alkis, badas
NG	πεῖνα	ON	hungr	Lett.	izalkums, bads
Lat.	famēs	Dan.	hunger	ChSl.	gladŭ
It.	fame	Sw.	hunger	SCr.	glad
Fr.	faim	OE	hungor	Boh.	hlad
Sp.	hambre	ME	hunger	Pol.	głód
Rum.	foame	NE	hunger	Russ.	golod
Ir.	gorte	Du.	honger	Skt.	kṣudh-, kṣudhā-
NIr.	ocras, gorta	OHG	hungar	Av.	šud-
W.	newyn	MHG	hunger		
Br.	naon	NHG	hunger		

Words for 'hunger' come by specialization from either 'want, distress, wasting away' or 'desire, longing'. Cf. the specialization of NE starve from OE steorfan 'die'.

1. Grk. λῑμός : λοιμός 'plague', λιάζομαι 'withdraw, shrink', Goth. aflinnan 'depart', ON linna 'cease', etc., IE *lei-. Walde-P. 2.388. Whatever the ultimate relations of the various IE roots *lei-, the immediate Greek development is fr. 'waste away' to 'hunger'.

Grk. πεῖνα, Ion. πείνη, fr. *πένϳα : Grk. πενία 'poverty', πένης 'poor', πένομαι 'toil, be poor', πόνος 'toil', outside connections dub. Walde-P. 2.8 f., 661.

2. Lat. famēs (> Romance words) etym. dub. Walde-P. 1.829. Ernout-M. 328 f. Walde-H. 1.451.

3. Ir. nūna, NIr. naoine 'famine', W. newyn, Br. naon 'hunger, famine', OCorn. naun (gl. famis), prob: Goth. nauþs, OHG nōt, OE nēad 'necessity, distress' (NE need). Walde-P. 2.316. Pedersen 1.61. Stokes 193.

Ir. gorte, NIr. gorta : Ir. goirt 'bitter, painful', fr. the root of gorim 'heat', ChSl. gorěti 'burn', etc. (1.85). Walde-P. 1.688. Pedersen 1.33.

NIr. ocras, cpd. of od- and root of caraim 'love'. 'Hunger' fr. 'desire'. Pedersen 1.476.

4. Goth. hūhrus, ON hungr, OE hungor, etc. general Gmc. : Grk. κέγκω· πεινᾶ (Phot.), κέγχει ἐπιδάκνει (Hesych.), Lith. kenkia 'it hurts', kanka 'pain', ON hā 'vex, distress'. Walde-P. 1.401. Falk-Torp 432. Feist 273.

Goth. grēdus (once = λῑμός) with adj. grēdags : ON grāðr 'hunger, greed', OE grǣdig 'hungry, greedy' (NE greedy, whence greed), fr. *ghrēdh-, prob. an extension of *gher-, in Goth. gairnjan, OE giernan 'desire' (NE yearn), fr. IE *gher-. Walde-P. 1.601. Feist 220. Walde-H. 1.658. Otherwise Falk-Torp 339.

5. Lith. alkis, Lett. izalkums : Lith. alkti, Lett. alkt, ChSl. alkati 'be hungry', outside connections dub. Walde-P. 1.159.

Lith. badas, Lett. bads, prob. : Skt. bādh- 'press, urge', bādha- 'distress'. But cf. Mühl.-Endz. 1.248.

6. ChSl. gladŭ, etc., general Slavic : ChSl. žlŭděti 'long for, desire', also(?) Skt. gṛdh- 'be eager, long for', gardha- 'desire'. Walde-P. 1.633. Berneker 320.

7. Skt. kṣudh-, kṣudhā-, Av. šud-, NPers. šud : Skt. kṣudh- 'be hungry', outside connections?

5.15 THIRST (sb.)

Grk.	δίψα, δίψος	Goth.	þaurstei	Lith.	troškulys, troškimas
NG	δίψα	ON	þorsti	Lett.	slāpes
Lat.	sitis	Dan.	tørst	ChSl.	žęžda
It.	sete	Sw.	törst	SCr.	žed
Fr.	soif	OE	þurst, þyrst	Boh.	žízeň
Sp.	sed	ME	thurst, thirst	Pol.	pragnienie
Rum.	sete	NE	thirst	Russ.	žažda
Ir.	itu, tart	Du.	durst	Skt.	tṛṣṇā-
NIr.	tart, íota	OHG	durst	Av.	taršna-
W.	syched	MHG	durst		
Br.	sec'hed	NHG	durst		

Words for 'thirst' come, through the verb, from 'be dry, parched', or, like those for 'hunger', by specialization from 'wasting away, growing weak' or 'desire, longing' (as also conversely 'long for' from 'thirst for').

1. Derivs. of IE *ters- in Grk. τέρσομαι 'become dry', Lat. torrēre 'make dry', Goth. þaursjan 'be thirsty', OHG derran 'make dry', Skt. tṛṣ- 'be thirsty, etc. Walde-P. 1.737 f. Ernout-M. 1048. Pedersen 1.81.

Ir. tart; Goth. þaurstei, OE þurst, etc. general Gmc.; Lith. troškulys, troškimas (trokšti 'be thirsty', troškus 'thirsty'); Skt. tṛṣṇā-, Av. taršna-.

2. Grk. δίψα, δίψος, with vb. διψάω, etym.? Boisacq 192.

3. Lat. sitis (> Romance words) prob.: Grk. φθίσις 'wasting away, decay', Skt. kṣiti- 'disappearance, destruction'. Walde-P. 1.506. REW 7961.

4. Ir. ĩtu, NIr. íota, etym. dub. Pedersen 1.65. Walde-P. 1.197, 2.8.

W. syched, Br. sec'hed fr. W. sych, Ir. secc 'dry', loanwords fr. Lat. siccus 'dry' (: sitis? see 15.84). Loth, Mots lat. 209.

5. Goth. þaurstei, etc., above, 1.

6. Lett. slāpes : slāpt 'be thirsty, become weak', Lith. slopti 'become weak or choke with thirst' prob. fr. a parallel form of the root (*slap- in ON slafast 'slacken'): Lith. slabnas, ChSl. slabŭ 'weak', etc. (Walde-P. 2.432, but without inclusion of Lett. slāpes, etc.). Mühl.-Endz. 3.924.

7. ChSl. žęžda (vb. žęždati), SCr. žed, Boh. žízeň, Russ. žažda : Lith. pasigesti 'long for', godas 'greed', Grk. θέσσασθαι 'pray for', πόθος 'longing', etc. IE *gʷhedh-. Walde-P. 1.673.

Pol. pragnienie, fr. pragnąć 'be thirsty' : Boh. prahnouti 'be parched' (as with thirst), Pol. pražyć, etc. 'roast' (5.18). Brückner 434.

8. Skt. tṛṣṇā-, Av. taršna-, above, 1.

5.16 SUCK (vb.)

Grk.	θηλάζω (θῆσθαι), μυζάω	Goth.	(daddjan)	Lith.	žįsti, čiulpti
NG	βυζαίνω, θηλάζω (lit.)	ON	sūga	Lett.	zīst, dēt (sūkt)
Lat.	sūgere, fēlāre	Dan.	suge, die	ChSl.	sŭsati
It.	succiare, sugere	Sw.	suga, dia	SCr.	sisati
Fr.	sucer, téter	OE	sūcan, sūgan	Boh.	ssati
Sp.	chupar, mamar	ME	suke	Pol.	ssać
Rum.	suge	NE	suck	Russ.	sosat'
Ir.	sūgim, denim	Du.	zuigen	Skt.	dhā- (cūṣ-)
NIr.	sūghaim	OHG	sūgan (tāen)		
W.	sugno, dyfnu	MHG	sūgen, dien		
Br.	suna, dena	NHG	saugen		

Most of the verbs for 'suck' belong to one of two considerable groups of cognates. Some are derived from the nouns for a woman's 'breast' or 'teat', and some are of imitative origin reflecting the sound of sucking.

The notion 'give suck, suckle' is mostly expressed by the same form (e.g. Grk. θηλάζω) or by related forms, as NE suckle vs. suck, NHG säugen vs. saugen. Cf. also ChSl. dojiti (of the inherited group, below, 1) in the Gospels only for θηλάζω as 'suckle' vs. sŭsati for θηλάζω as 'suck' (Lk. 11.27).

1. IE *dhēi- (*dhē-, *dhī-, etc.). Walde-P. 1.829 f. Ernout-M. 341. Walde-H. 1.476. Pedersen 1.111, 2.505. Falk-Torp 141. Berneker 205.

Grk. aor. θήσατο, θῆσθαι (Hom.+, poet.), with sb. θηλή 'teat', whence θηλάζω 'suckle' and 'suck' (usual prose word, Aristot., etc.); Lat. fēlāre; Ir. denim, Corn., Br. dena, also W. dyfnu (R. A. Fowkes, Language 21.96); Goth. daddjan (in one occurrence = θηλάζω as 'suckle', but the passage Lk. 11.27, where θηλάζω is 'suck', is lacking), OHG tāen (rare and only 'suckle'), MHG dīen, Dan. die, Sw. dia; Lett. dēt; ChSl., SCr. dojiti 'suckle' (but 'milk' vb. in Boh., Pol., Russ.; 5.87); Skt. dhā- (3 sg. pres. dhayati, 3 sg. aor. adhāt, pple. dhīta-).

2. IE *seug, *seuk, and *seup-, *seub-, extensions of *seu- in Skt. su- 'press out', etc. Walde-P. 2.469. Ernout-M. 999. Falk-Torp 1202. Brückner 514 f.

Lat. sūgere (> It. sugere, Rum. suge), VLat. *sūctiāre (> It. succiare, Fr. sucer; It. succhiare fr. *sūculāre; REW 8415, 8417, but see also 2452); Ir. sūgim, NIr. sūghaim, W. sugno, Br. suna; ON sūga, OE sūcan, sūgan, OHG sūgan, etc. general Gmc. (except Goth.); Lett. sūkt (now used only of the leech, Mühl.-Endz, 3.1132); ChSl. sŭsati, etc. general Slavic, prob. fr. *sup-s- : OE sūpan, OHG sūfan 'sip, sup'.

3. Grk. μυζάω (late medical), μύζω (once Xen.) : μύδος 'damp, decay', NE mud (1.214), ChSl. myti 'wash', and many other words with common notion of 'moisture' or 'filthy moisture'. Walde-P. 2.249 ff.

Byz. βυζάνω, NG βυζαίνω ('suck' and 'suckle'), fr. late Grk. βυζίον, NG βυζί 'woman's breast' (4.41).

4. Fr. téter (Sp. tetar 'suckle'), fr. Fr. tette, Sp. teta 'teat'. REW 8759.

Sp. chupar of imitative orig. REW 2452.

Sp. mamar, fr. mama 'woman's breast'.

5. Celtic and Gmc. words, above, 1, 2.

6. Lith. žįsti, žindu (cf. caus. zindyti 'suckle'), Lett. zīst, zīdu, perh. : Grk. νεογιλλός (or -γῑλος) 'newborn'. Walde-P. 1.552. Mühl.-Endz. 4.736.

Lith. čiulpti, of imitative origin. Cf. interj. čiulpt.

7. ChSl. sŭsati, etc., above, 2.

8. Skt. cūṣ- (infrequent beside usual dhā-, above, 1), of imitative origin.

5.17 MIX

Grk.	μείγνῡμι, κεράννῡμι	Goth.	blandan	Lith.	maišyti
NG	ἀνακατεύω (or -όνω)	ON	blanda	Lett.	maisīt
Lat.	miscēre	Dan.	blande, mænge	ChSl.	(sŭ-)mĕsiti
It.	mischiare	Sw.	blanda, mänga	SCr.	miješati
Fr.	mêler	OE	mengan, miscian,	Boh.	michati, smísiti
Sp.	mezclar		blandan	Pol.	mieszać
Rum.	amesteca	ME	menge, blende	Russ.	mešat'
Ir.	mescaim	NE	mix (mingle)	Skt.	mikṣ-, çrī-
NIr.	meascaim	Du.	mengen	Av.	raēθwa-
W.	cymysgo	OHG	miskan		
Br.	meska	MHG	mischen, mengen		
		NHG	mischen, mengen		

The majority of verbs for 'mix' belong to an inherited group, and in this the primary application was probably to food or drink.

1. IE *meik-, *meig-. Walde-P. 2.244 f. Ernout-M. 619 f. Berneker 2.52 f.

Grk. μείγνῡμι (μιγ- in codd.), μίσγω; Lat. miscēre, (VLat. miscere > It. mescere, mostly 'pour out'); deriv. *misculāre > It. mischiare, Fr. mêler, Prov., Cat. mesclar > Sp. mezclar; *mixticāre > Rum. amesteca; REW 5604, 5606, 5617); Ir. mescaim, NIr. meascaim, W. mysgu, now cpd. cymysgo, Br. meska; OE miscian, OHG miskan, etc. prob. fr. Lat. rather than cognate, as certainly NE mix, back-formation fr. pple. mixt fr. Fr. mixte, Lat. mixtus; Lith. maišyti (also miešti), ChSl. (sŭ-)mĕsiti, etc., general Balto-Slavic; Skt. mikṣ- beside adj. miçra- 'mixed'.

2. Grk. κεράννῡμι, κίρνημι, κιρνάω 'mix', but mostly of mixing wine and water (hence NG κερνῶ 'pour, treat to a drink') : Skt. çrī- 'mix', prob. also OE hrēran 'move, stir', etc. (10.11). Walde-P. 1.419 f.

NG ἀνακατεύω or -όνω, fr. adv. ἀνάκατα 'topsy-turvy, pell-mell' (ἀνά 'up' and κατά 'down'), hence (through 'move up and down') 'stir, mix'.

3. Lat. confundere, lit. 'pour together', cpd. of fundere 'pour' (9.35) is used for 'mix', but most commonly in a harmful manner, 'confound, confuse'.

4. Goth. blandan, ON, Sw. blanda, Dan. blande, OE blandan (rare), ME, NE blend (prob. fr. Norse) : Goth. blinds, etc. 'blind', Lith. blįsti 'grow dim', blēsti 'cease to burn, go out' (of fire), etc., hence through 'make a liquid dim, turbid by mixing, to 'mix' in general. Walde-P. 2.216. Feist 98.

OE mengan, ME menge (NE mingle), MLG, Du. mengen (MLG > Dan. mænge, Sw. mänga, MHG, NHG mengen), fr. the root of OE gemang 'mingling, crowd' and 'among', this perh. : Lith. minkyti 'knead', etc. (5.54). NED s.vv. meng, vb., and among. Walde-P. 2.268. Falk-Torp 747.

5. Av. raēθwa- etym.? Barth. 1482 f.

	5.21 COOK (vb.)	5.22 BOIL	5.23 ROAST, FRY	5.24 BAKE
Grk.	πέσσω (μαγειρεύω)	ἕψω	ὀπτάω, φρῡ́γω, φώγω	ὀπτάω, πέσσω
NG	μαγειρεύω	βράζω	ψήνω; τηγανίζω	ψήνω
Lat.	coquere	coquere	torrēre, frīgere, assāre	coquere, torrēre (in furnō)
It.	cocere	lessare	arrostire; friggere	cocere (in forno)
Fr.	cuire	faire bouillir	rôtir; frire	cuire (au four)
Sp.	cocer, cocinar, guisar	cocer, hervir	asar; freir	cocer (en horno)
Rum.	găti, coace	fierbe	frige, prăji	coace (in cuptor)
Ir.	fo-no-	berbaim	(fo-no-)	fo-no-
NIr.	fuinim	beirbhim, bruithim	rostaim, grīoscaim	fuinim
W.	coginio	berwi	rhostio, crasu; ffrio	pobi, crasu
Br.	poaza (darevi)	birvi	rosta; frita	poba
Goth.	. . . .	. . . .	. . . .	. . . .
ON	matbūa	sjōða, vella	steikja	baka
Dan.	lave mad, koge	koge	stege	bage
Sw.	tillaga, koka	koka	steka	baka
OE	gegearwian	sēoþan, wiellan	brǣdan, hyrstan	bacan
ME	coke	sethe, boile	roste; frye	bake
NE	cook	boil	roast; fry	bake
Du.	koken, bereiden	koken	roosten, braden	bakken
OHG	kochōn	siodan, kochōn	brātan, harstan, rōstan	backan
MHG	kochen	kochen, sieden	brāten, ræsten	backen
NHG	kochen	kochen	braten, rösten	backen
Lith.	virti	virti	kepti, spirginti	kept
Lett.	vārīt	vārīt	cept	cept
ChSl.	variti	variti	pešti, pražiti	pešti
SCr.	kuhati	variti, kuhati	peći, pržiti	peći
Boh.	vařiti	vařiti	peci, smažiti	peci
Pol.	warzyć	warzyć	piec, smażyć, prażyć	piec
Russ.	varit'	varit'	žarit'	peč'
Skt.	pac-, çrā-	pac-, çrā-	pac-, bhrajj-	pac-
Av.	pač-	pač-	pač-	pač-

5.21. Words for 'cook', that is, general terms for preparing food by the use of heat, covering boiling, roasting, baking, etc., belong mostly to an inherited group representing an IE *pek^w-. The forms of this root in Indo-Iranian, Tocharian, Greek, and Latin have the general meaning 'cook' (also 'ripen' fruit in Skt., Grk., Toch.; in Lat. also 'prepare anything by heat', as 'bake' (bricks), but in Balto-Slavic (also Alb.) are specialized to 'roast, bake' (Russ. only 'bake', as also W., Br.), and in several languages are used most commonly for 'boil' (conversely 'boil' for 'cook' in Balto-Slavic).

With the spread of the Roman art of cookery, the Lat. derivs. *coquus* 'a cook' and *coquīna* 'kitchen' were widely borrowed in Celtic and Gmc., and through the latter in Slavic; much less widely the verb *coquere* and mostly in the sense of 'boil'. But in some cases new verbs for 'cook' were formed from the noun.

Some languages have no distinctive general word for 'cook', but use the more specific terms for 'boil', 'roast', etc., as the case may be, or in a phrase like 'cook a meal' use words meaning 'prepare, make ready', some of these latter being almost specialized in this direction.

1. IE *pek^w-. Walde-P. 2.17 f. Ernout-M. 218 f. Walde-H. 1.270 f.

Skt. *pac-*, Av. *pač-* 'cook'; Toch. *päk-* 'cook' (SSS 448); Grk. πέσσω, Att. πέττω, πέπτω, fut. πέψω 'cook, bake'; Lat. *coquere*, with its derivs. (below); Br. *poba*, W. *pobi* 'bake',

Br. *poaza* 'cook' (formed to the pple. *poaz* 'cooked' = W. *poeth* 'hot', Lat. *coctus* 'cooked'); Lith. *kepti*, ChSl. *peką*, *pešti*, etc., general Balto-Slavic 'bake, roast'; Alb. *pjékë* 'bake, roast, ripen'.

Lat. *coquere* > It. *cocere*, Fr. *cuire*, Sp. *cocer*, Rum. *coace* (esp. 'bake'); also Du., MLG *koken* (> Dan. *koge*, Sw. *koka*), OHG *kochōn*, MHG, NHG *kochen*, all mostly 'boil' but also 'cook' (cf. NHG *gekochtes fleisch* 'boiled meat', but *ungekochtes fleisch* 'uncooked meat').

Lat. *coquus* 'a cook' > It. *cuoco*, Ir. *cōic*, NIr. *cōcaire*, W. *cog*, *cogydd* (whence vb. *coginio*, but ending influenced by *cegin* 'kitchen', below), OE *cōc*, NE *cook*, Du. *kok*, OHG *coch*, NHG *koch* (> Dan. *kok*, Sw. *kock*). From *cōc* comes the later verb ME *coke*, NE *cook*.

Lat. *coquīna* 'kitchen' > Sp. *cocina*, It. *cucina*, Fr. *cuisine*, whence the vbs. Sp. *cocinar*, It. *cucinare*, Fr. *cuisiner*, and new nouns for 'a cook', Fr. *cuisinier*, Sp. *cocinero;* NG κουζίνα, fr. Venetian *cusina* = It. *cucina;* W. *cegin;* OE *cycen*, NE *kitchen;* OHG *kuchina*, MHG *küchen*, NHG *küche*, whence most of the Slavic words for 'kitchen' and 'a cook', as SCr. *kuhinja* 'kitchen', *kuhar* 'a cook', and vb. *kuhati* 'boil' and 'cook (a meal)', Boh. *kuchyně*, *kuchař*, Pol. *kuchnia*, *kucharz*.

2. Grk. μαγειρεύω (late, but reg. NG word), fr. μάγειρος 'a cook' : μάσσω, aor. ἐμάγην 'knead', μάγις, μάκτρα 'kneading-trough', Br. *meza* 'knead', ChSl. *mazati* 'smear, anoint', etc. Walde-P. 2.226. Hence μάγειρος was orig. the 'kneader' of bread, etc. But cf. Meillet, BSL 33.41.

3. Sp. *guisar* 'arrange, prepare', but esp. 'prepare food, cook', fr. *guisa* 'manner', loanword fr. Gmc. *wīsa* (NHG *weise*) 'manner'. REW 9555.

Rum. *găti* 'make ready, prepare', whence also 'dress' and esp. 'prepare food, cook', fr. *gata* 'ready', loanword fr. Slavic, SCr. *gotovŭ*, etc. 'ready' (14.29).

Rum. *bucătar* 'a cook', *bucătărie* 'kitchen', fr. *bucată* 'bit' (pl. *bucate* 'viands') = It. *boccata*, Fr. *bouchée* 'mouthful', fr. VLat. **buccāta*, deriv. of Lat. *bucca* 'cheek', later 'mouth'. REW 1358. Tiktin 230 f.

4. Ir. *fo-no-*, NIr. *fuinim* 'cook, bake', perh. as orig. 'prepare' fr. a genuine cpd. **fo+gnī* > **fōni* (later treated as separable **fo-ni-* by analogy) : *gnīu* 'do, make', cf. *air-fogni* 'prepares (food)'. Pedersen 2.586.

Br. *darevi* 'prepare, ripen, cook', fr. *darev* 'ready, ripe, cooked' (14.29).

5. In the Gmc. languages there is a dearth of distinctive words for 'cook', apart from NE *cook*, which is derived from the noun (above, 1). OHG *kochōn*, MHG, NHG *kochen* may be used in the general sense, though usually 'boil'. Otherwise 'cook' is expressed by words meaning 'prepare' as OE *gegearwian* (cf. NHG *garkochen*, *garkoch*, etc.), NHG *zubereiten*, Dan. *lave mad*, Sw. *tillaga*, ON *būa til matar* or cpd. *matbūa*, also *matgera*, NIcel. *matreiða* (with *matr* 'food').

6. In Balto-Slavic 'cook' may be expressed by the words that mean also and orig. 'boil', as Lith. *virti*, ChSl. *variti*, etc. (5.22). This wider use is confirmed by derivs. like Lith. *virėjas*, Lett. *pavars* 'a cook', Lith. *virtuvė* 'kitchen', Russ. *povar'* 'a cook'.

7. Skt. *pac-*, Av. *pač-*, above, 1.

Skt. *çrā-*, esp. 'boil' but also 'roast, bake' (cf. *çr̥ta-* 'cooked' vs. *āma-* 'raw') : Grk. κεράννῡμι, 'mix'. Walde-P. 1.419.

5.22. Words belonging under IE *pek^w- 'cook' (5.21) serve also in several languages for the specific 'cook by boiling', e.g. Lat. *coquere*, NHG *kochen*,

Skt. *pac-*. The other words for this are mostly the same as those for the intransitive 'boil' (10.31), used transitively, or made transitive as Fr. *faire bouiller*, OE *wiellan*, caus. of *weallan*. The few others are as follows:

1. Grk. ἕψω (only 'cook by boiling' vs. ζέω 'boil' intr.) : Arm. *ephem* 'boil', further connections unknown. Walde-P. 1.124. In later Greek 'cook' and then 'roast, bake' (5.23).

2. It. *lessare* fr. late Lat. *ēlixāre*, fr. Lat. *ē-lixus* 'thoroughly boiled' : Lat. *liquēre* 'be fluid'. Ernout-M. 556. REW 2848.

5.23. Words belonging under IE *pek^w- 'cook' (5.21) may also serve for the specific 'roast', and in Balto-Slavic are used only for 'roast' or 'bake'.

Most of the words listed cover also 'fry', 'broil', 'grill', and 'toast'. Some specific words for 'fry' are added, separated by a semicolon if clearly differentiated.

1. Grk. ὀπτάω (used of all kinds of cooking by means of fire or dry heat as opposed to ἕψω 'boil'), fr. ὀπτός 'roasted, baked', this prob. (though not generally accepted) fr. *o-pk^w-to- (*pek^w-), like ὄζος 'branch' fr. *o-zdo- (*sed- 'sit'). Prellwitz 364. Boisacq 708 (adversely).

Grk. φρῡ́γω; Lat. *frīgere*, whence It. *friggere*, Fr. *frire* (> Br. *frita*, ME *frye* [> W. *ffrio*], NE *fry*), Sp. *freir*, Rum. *frige;* Skt. *bhrajj-*, all with various extensions of *bher-, prob. the same as in Lat. *fervēre* 'boil', etc. Walde-P. 2.165 ff. Ernout-M. 390. Walde-H. 1.548.

Grk. φώγω : ON *baka*, OE *bacan*, OHG *backan* 'bake', etc. fr. an extension of *bhē- in OHG *bāen*, NHG *bähen* 'soften by warm applications' and 'toast (bread)', OE *bæþ* 'bath', etc. Walde-P. 2.187. Falk-Torp 42.

NG ψήνω, new present formed to ἔψησα, ψητός, etc. of Grk. ἕψω 'boil' (5.22), with shift (prob. through a generalized 'cook') to 'roast, bake' (but still 'boil' or 'cook' in some phrases, as ψήνω καφέ, also ψημένος 'well done').

NG τηγανίζω 'fry' (already in LXX) fr. τήγανον 'frying-pan' : OE *þeccan* 'burn', etc. Walde-P. 1.717. Boisacq 936.

2. Lat. *torrēre*, lit. 'make dry', hence 'roast' or 'bake' : Grk. τέρσομαι, Goth. *gaþairsan* 'dry up', Skt. *tr̥ṣ-* 'thirst', etc. (5.15). Walde-P. 1.737 ff. Ernout-M. 1047 f.

Lat. *assāre* (> Sp. *asar*), late deriv. of *assus* 'roasted' : Lat. *ārēre* 'be dry', Gr. ἄζω 'dry up', Skt. *āsa-* 'ashes, dust', etc. Ernout-M. 80. Walde-H. 1.65. REW 716.

It. *arrostire*, OFr. *rostir* (> ME *roste*, NE *roast* [> NIr. *rostaim*, W. *rhostio*], Br. *rosta*), Fr. *rôtir*, all fr. Gmc., OHG *rōstan*, etc. (below, 4). REW 7098.

Rum. *prăji*, fr. Slavic, ChSl. *pražiti*, etc. (below, 5).

3. Ir. *fo-no-* general 'cook' (5.21), but MIr. pple. *fonaithe* 'roasted' (cf. Atkinson, Passions and Homilies 714).

NIr. *grīoscaim*, fr. *grīos*, MIr. *grīs* 'fire, embers'.

W. *crasu* 'roast, bake, toast', Br. *kraza* 'dry up, broil', fr. W. *cras* 'parched, baked', Br. *kraz* 'dried up, broiled', outside connections dub. Henry 80. Loth, Mots lat. 153. Morris Jones 137.

4. ON *steikja* (with sb. *steik* > ME *steke*, NE *steak*), Dan. *stege*, Sw. *steka*, lit. 'stick' (on a spit) : Goth. *stiks* 'point', OE *stician* 'stick, stab', etc. Falk-Torp 1155. Hellquist 1070.

OE *brǣdan*, Du. *braden*, OHG *brātan*, NHG *braten* : ON *brǣða* 'melt', OE *bræþ* 'odor, exhalation' (NE *breath*), all fr. *bhrē- beside *bhrō- in MHG *bruot*

'heat, hatching, brood' (OE *brōd*, NE *brood*) and ultimately connected with other extensions of *bher- as in Goth. *brinnan* 'burn', Lat. *fervēre* 'boil', etc. Walde-P. 2.158. Falk-Torp 96.

OE *hyrstan*, OHG *harstan*, fr. OE *hyrste*, OHG *harst* 'gridiron' (OE *hearstepanne* 'frying-pan') : Lith. *karštas* 'hot', *kurti* 'to heat', ON *hyrr* 'fire', etc. Walde-P. 1.418.

OHG *rōstan*, MHG *ræsten*, NHG *rösten*, Du. *roosten*, fr. OHG *rōst*, etc. 'gridiron', Weigand-H. 2.610. Franck-v. W. 560.

5. Lith. *spirginti*, ChSl. *pražiti*, SCr. *pržiti*, Boh. *pražiti* : Lith. *spragėti* 'crackle', *sprogti* 'burst, explode', Skt. *sphurj-* 'crackle, rumble', Lat. *spargere* 'scatter, strew', etc. Walde-P. 2.673. Brückner 434.

Boh. *smažiti*, Pol. *smażyć* : Boh. *smah* 'fire, brand', *smahlý* 'dried up', ChSl. *smaglŭ* 'dark colored', outside connections? Brückner 502 compares Lith. *smogis* 'blow', *smogti*, *smagiu* 'strike', but semantic relation?

Russ. *žarit'*, fr. *žar* 'heat, glow' : ChSl. *gorěti*, etc. 'burn' (1.84).

5.24. Most of the words for 'bake' have been discussed under 'cook' or 'roast'. The most distinctive group is the Gmc., ON *baka*, OE *bacan*, etc., which regularly have the specific force of 'bake', but are related to Gr. φώγω 'roast' (5.23). Others are the general words for 'cook', the application to baking being apparent from the object (as 'bread') or directly expressed by a phrase (as It. *in forno*); or words used for both 'roast' and 'bake', which are very commonly undifferentiated.

Among the derivatives of IE *pek^w-, the Balto-Slavic forms mean 'roast' and 'bake', but Russ. *peč'* now only 'bake'; and 'bake' is dominant in Gr. πέσσω, Rum. *coace*, W. *pobi*, Br. *poba*.

5.242. Words for 'baker' are derived from the words for 'bake' or from those for 'bread' or 'oven'.

From 'bake', OE *bæcere*, NE *baker*, OE *bæcestre* (orig. fem.), NE dial. *baxter*, NHG *bäcker*, etc.; NIr. *fuinneadōir*, W. *pobydd;* Lith. *kepėjas*, SCr. *pekar*, Russ. *pekar'*, etc.

From 'bread' (5.51) Gr. ἀρτο-κόπος (-κόπος : πέσσω), ἀρτο-ποιός, NG ψωμᾶς; Sp. *panadero;* NIr. *arānōir*(?). So Fr. *boulanger*, OFr. *bolenc*, formed fr. a MLG *bolle* 'round cake', this prob. fr. It. *bolla*, Lat. *bulla* 'knob'. Wartburg 1.427 ff. Rum. *brutar*, fr. *brut* used of coarse, black bread (loanword fr. NHG *brot*, Tiktin 229).

From 'oven' (5.25). Late Lat. *furnārius* (earlier *furnāria* 'baker's trade'), NG φούρναρης, Sp. *hornero*, It. *fornaio*. REW 3601.

But Lat. *pistor*, orig. 'miller' (fr. *pīnsere* 'pound, crush'), then the reg. word for 'baker', hence in this sense OIt. *pistore*, OFr. *pesteur*. Ernout-M. 770. REW 6539.

5.25 OVEN

Grk.	ἰπνός (κλίβανος)	Goth.	auhns	Lith.	pečius
NG	φοῦρνος	ON	ofn	Lett.	ceplis
Lat.	furnus, fornāx	Dan.	(bage-, stege-)ovn	ChSl.	peštĭ
It.	forno	Sw.	(bag-, steg-)ugn	SCr.	peć
Fr.	four	OE	ofen	Boh.	pec
Sp.	horno	ME	oven	Pol.	piec
Rum.	cuptor	NE	oven	Russ.	peč'
Ir.	(sornn, fulacht)	Du.	oven	Skt.	āpaka-
NIr.	bācūs	OHG	ovan	Av.	....
W.	ffwrn, popty	MHG	oven		
Br.	forn	NHG	(back)ofen		

Words for 'oven' are derived from verbs for 'bake', from words for 'hot', or are in origin words for some kind of a 'pot' or 'pan' (an earthen pot sunk in coals is the primitive antecedent of the cooking oven). Several of these words have come to be used for 'stove' (7.32), and then the 'oven' for cooking may be expressed more specifically by a compound, as NHG backofen.

1. From IE *pekʷ- (5.21), mostly where the derivs. of this root are used especially for 'bake'. Rum. cuptor (Lat. *coctōrium); W. popty, properly 'bakehouse' (ty 'house'); all the Balto-Slavic words, as Lett. ceplis, ChSl. peštĭ, SCr. peć, Russ. peč' (> Lith. pečius), etc.; Skt. āpaka-.

2. Grk. ἰπνός, Goth. auhns, ON ofn, Dan. ovn, Sw. ugn, OE ofen, ME oven, OHG ovan, etc. : Skt. ukhā- 'pot' (for cooking), Lat. aulla, ōlla 'pot'. These words almost certainly belong together, though their phonetic history is complicated. Walde-P. 1.24 f. Ernout-M. 91 f. Walde-H. 1.84. Falk-Torp 808. Feist 65 f.

Grk. κλίβανος, (Att. κρίβανος) in earliest use 'an earthen pot for baking bread', later 'furnace, kiln' and 'oven', an old loanword, perh. related to Goth. hlaifs 'bread'. Walde-P. 1.499. Boisacq 470.

3. Lat. furnus, fornāx : Lat. formus, Grk. θερμός 'hot', etc. (15.85). Walde-P. 1.687 ff. Ernout-M. 380. Walde-H. 1.533 f.

Hence NG φοῦρνος, It. forno, Fr. four, Sp. horno; Ir. sornn 'furnace, kiln', also 'oven' for cooking?), W. ffwrn, Br. forn. Pedersen 1.221.

4. Ir. fulacht 'act of cooking' and 'cooking-pit' (nearest approach to an oven?) : fo-sligim 'smear over'? Laws, Gloss. 433.

NIr. bācūs, fr. NE bakehouse.

5. Gmc. words, above, 2.

6. Balto-Slavic and Skt. words, above, 1.

5.26–5.39. Utensils for cooking, eating, and drinking are so multifarious, and so different according to the country and the period, that only the crudest classification is possible. There are so many kinds of 'pot', 'kettle', 'bowl', etc., and the terms are so vaguely definable, that the words grouped under each head are only roughly synonymous, and the choice may often seem arbitrary.

Noteworthy is the extensive European borrowing of Latin words for such utensils. Several oriental words have passed through Turkish into the Balkan languages and even further.

5.26 POT

Grk.	χύτρα	Goth.	....	Lith.	puodas
NG	τσουκάλι	ON	grȳta, pottr	Lett.	puods
Lat.	aulla, ōlla	Dan.	gryde, potte	ChSl.	grŭnĭcĭ
It.	pentola	Sw.	gryta	SCr.	grnac
Fr.	pot, marmite	OE	crocca, pott	Boh.	hrnek, hrnec
Sp.	olla, pote, puchero	ME	potte	Pol.	garnek
Rum.	oală	NE	pot	Russ.	goršok
Ir.	crocān	Du.	pot	Skt.	kumbha-, ukhā-,
NIr.	corcān	OHG	hafan		sthāli-
W.	pot, crochan	MHG	haven, topf	Av.	xumba-, dišta-
Br.	pod	NHG	topf		

1. Grk. χύτρα, fr. the root of Grk. χέω 'pour' (9.35).

NG τσουκάλι, dim. of τσούκα, fr. It. zucca 'gourd' and 'gourd-shaped vessel' (as sometimes NE gourd, cf. NED s.v.), this fr. VLat. cucutia 'a fruit'. G. Meyer, Neugr. Stud. 4.93. REW 2369.

2. Lat. aulla, pop. ōlla (> OIt. oglia, OFr. oule, Sp. olla, Rum. oală) : Skt. ukhā- 'pot, boiler', Goth. auhns 'oven', etc. (5.25). Ernout-M. 91 f. Walde-H. 1.84. REW 6059.

It. pentola, dim. of It. pinta (> Fr. pinte > ME pynt, NE pint 'a liquid measure'), the same word as Sp. pinta 'spot, mark' fr. late Lat. pincta for picta 'painted, marked'. REW 6512.

Fr. pot (> Sp. pote), fr. Gmc.? See below, 4.

Fr. marmite, etym. dub. Gamillscheg 593. Bloch 2.45 ('étym. inconnue').

Sp. puchero, fr. Lat. pultārius 'a kind of pot or jar', orig. 'a vessel for pottage', fr. puls, pultis 'pottage made of meal, pulse' : Grk. πόλτος 'pottage', πάλη 'fine meal', Lat. pollen 'fine flour', etc. Walde-P. 2.60. Ernout-M. 785. REW 6840.

3. Ir. crocān, NIr. corcān, W. crochan, fr. OE crocca (below, 4). Thurneysen, Keltorom. 97.

W. pot fr. NE pot. Br. pod, fr. Fr. pot.

4. Late OE pott, ME potte, NE pot, Du. pot (MLG pot > late ON pottr, Dan. potte [Sw. potta 'chamber-pot'],

NHG dial. pott), perh. fr. Gmc. *putta-, IE *budno-, and related to numerous words having the notion of 'swell up' applied to shape, etc. If so, that is, if in spite of its late appearance it is a genuine Gmc. word, it is the source of MLat. pottus, Fr. pot (> Sp. pote). But much disputed. Walde-P. 2.116. Falk-Torp 845. Franck-v. W. 518. REW 6705. NED s.v. pot.

ON grȳta, Dan. gryde, Sw. gryta, deriv. of ON grjōt 'stones, gravel, soapstone': OE grēot 'sand, gravel' (NE grit), etc. Orig. a pot made of soft stone. Falk-Torp 354. Hellquist 305.

OE crocca ('earthenware pot', often glosses Lat. olla; NE crock now in specialized use): OE crōg 'small vessel', OHG kruog 'pitcher', etc. (5.34).

OE grēofa (greoua twice glosses olla) = OHG griobo 'roasting pan', etym.? Falk-Torp 346, 358.

OHG hafan, MHG haven (NHG hafen dial. = topf; Kretschmer, Wortgeogr. 531 ff.), lit. 'holder' : Lat. capere 'take', Goth. hafjan 'raise', etc. Kluge-G. 225.

MHG, NHG topf : MLG dop(pe) 'shell, husk', further connection dub. Falk-Torp 148. Weigand-H. 2.1053.

5. Lith. puodas, Lett. puods : OE fæt 'vessel' (NE vat), OHG vaz 'vessel', OHG fazzōn 'hold, contain', etc. Walde-P. 2.22. Falk-Torp 200.

6. ChSl. grŭnĭcĭ, SCr. grnac, Boh.

hrnek, hrnec, Pol. garnek, Russ. goršok: Lat. furnus 'oven', Skt. ghṛṇa-, gharma-'heat', Grk. θερμός 'hot', ChSl. gorěti 'burn', etc. Berneker 371.

SCr. lonac (Bulg. lonec, late ChSl. lonĭcĭ), perh. : ChSl. lono 'bosom, lap', both from notion of curved shape, and fr. *loksno- : Grk. λεκάνη 'pot, pan', etc. Walde-P. 1.158. Berneker 732.

7. Skt. kumbha-, Av. xumba- (NPers. xumb) : Grk. κύμβος 'vessel, goblet', W.

cwmm 'valley', NE hump, etc. with common notion of curved shape. Walde-P. 1.376.

Skt. ukhā-, above, 2.

Skt. sthālī- : sthal- 'stand' (Dhātup.), Grk. στέλλω 'set up', etc. Walde-P. 2.643. Uhlenbeck 347.

Av. dišta- : Av. diz- 'heap up', Skt. dih- 'smear', Lat. fingere 'form, mould', hence 'earthen pot'. Walde-P. 1.833. Barth. 747.

5.27 KETTLE

Grk.	λέβης, χαλκίον	Goth.	katilē (gen. pl.)	Lith.	katilas
NG	τέντζερες	ON	ketill, hverr	Lett.	katls
Lat.	lebēs, caldāria (late)	Dan.	kedel	ChSl.	kotĭlŭ
It.	paiuolo, caldaia	Sw.	kittel	SCr.	kotao
Fr.	bouilloire, chaudron	OE	cetel, hwer	Boh.	kotel
Sp.	caldera, perol	ME	kettel	Pol.	kocieł
Rum.	căldare	NE	kettle	Russ.	kotel
Ir.	coire, scaball	Du.	ketel		
NIr.	citeal (coire, scabhal)	OHG	chezzil (h)wer		
W.	crochan (callor, pair)	MHG	kezzel		
Br.	kaoter	NHG	kessel		

The words listed under 'pot' (5.26) may include pots for boiling. Here under 'kettle' are added those that are applied more specifically to vessels for boiling, usually of metal.

1. Grk. λέβης (> Lat. lebēs), of unknown source, prob. an old loanword (Aegean?). Boisacq 563.

Grk. χαλκίον, fr. χαλκός 'copper', is often 'kettle'.

NG τέντζερες, fr. Turk. tencere 'kettle, stewpan'. So Rum. tingire 'stewpan', etc. Lokotsch 2066 (without the NG word).

2. Late Lat. caldāria, fr. Lat. caldus 'hot' (15.85). Hence It. caldaia (derivs. calderone 'large kettle', calderotto 'small kettle'), Fr. chaudière (deriv. chaudron 'small kettle'), Sp. caldera, Rum. căldare, also Br. kaoter, W. callor (obs.). REW 1503.

It. paiuolo, Sp. perol, fr. VLat. *pariolum, dim. of *parium, this of

Celtic orig. (cf. W. pair, below, 3). REW 6245, 6246.

Fr. bouilloire, fr. bouillir 'boil' (5.22).

3. Ir. coire, W. pair (both now 'caldron, boiler'), OCorn. per, ON hverr, OE hwer, OHG (h)wer (cf. Goth. hwairnei 'brainpan, skull') : Skt. caru- 'a kind of pot'. Walde-P. 1.518. Pedersen 1.69.

Ir. scaball, scabell ('caldron, large cooking pot'; Laws, Gloss. 641), NIr. scabhal fr. Lat. scaphula, dim. of scapha 'small boat' (fr. Grk. σκάφη 'trough, tub'). Pedersen 1.236.

NIr. citeal, fr. NE kettle. Cf. W. tegell, tecell, fr. NE teakettle.

W. crochan 'pot' (5.26), also commonly used for 'kettle'.

4. Goth. *katils or *katilus (only gen. pl. katilē quotable), OE cetel, etc., general Gmc., whence also the Balto-Slavic words, Lith. katilas, ChSl. kotĭlŭ, etc., fr. Lat. catīnus (5.31) a kind of bowl for food, also (Pliny) a 'crucible' for

melting metals, and also (Vitruv. 10.7) the 'water-tank' of a pumping-engine. The view that it was just in this last use that the word was first borrowed, and then extended to any metal 'kettle', is propounded in the most recent discus-

sion, namely Brüch, Kretschmer Festschrift, 6 ff. For other discussions, cf. Feist 308, Walde-H. 1.182.

5. The Skt. and Av. words listed under 'pot' cover in part a 'boiling pot, kettle'.

5.28 PAN

Grk.	τήγανον, τάγηνον	Goth.	....	Lith.	keptuvas, skaurada
NG	τηγάνι	ON	panna	Lett.	panna
Lat.	patina, patella, sartāgō	Dan.	pande	ChSl.	skovrada
It.	padella, cazzerola	Sw.	panna	SCr.	tava, tiganj
Fr.	poêle, casserole	OE	panne	Boh.	pánev
Sp.	sartén, cazuela	ME	panne	Pol.	panew, patelnia
Rum.	tigaie, tingire, cratiţă	NE	pan	Russ.	skovoroda
Ir.	aigen	Du.	pan	Skt.	kaṭāha- bhrāṣṭa-
NIr.	oighean	OHG	pfanna	Av.	....
W.	padell, pan	MHG	pfanne		
Br.	pillig	NHG	pfanne		

Several of the words listed here have not the wide range of NE pan, some being applied only to a 'frying-pan', others to a 'saucepan, stewpan'.

1. Grk. τήγανον, τάγηνον 'frying-pan' : OE peccan 'burn', etc. Walde-P. 1.717. Hence dim. τηγάνιον, NG τηγάνι, SCr. tiganj, Rum. tigaie.

2. Lat. patina, fr. Grk. πατάνη 'flat dish' (: πετάννῡμι 'spread out'). Hence dim. patella. Ernout-M. 741.

Lat. patella > It. padella, Fr. poêle, Sp. padilla, W. padell, Pol. patelnia (earlier patela). REW 6286.

Lat. patina > MLat. panna, OE panne, NE pan (> W. pan), OHG pfanna, etc. (all the Gmc. words), and, through Gmc., Lett. panna, late ChSl. pany, Boh. pánev, Pol. panew, etc. Falk-Torp 813. Pol. brytfanna 'frying-pan' fr. NHG bratpfanne.

Lat. sartāgō, -inis (> Sp. sartén), prob. : sarcīre 'patch, mend'; Grk. ἕρκος 'fence, inclosure', and first used of a covered receptacle(?). Ernout-M. 895. REW 7613.

It. cazzerola, Fr. casserole, Sp. cazuela 'stewpan', dim. fr. VLat. cattia, this prob. fr. Lat. cyathus, fr. Grk. κύαθος 'ladle'. Ernout-M. 249. Walde-P. 1.182. REW 2434.

Rum. tigaie, through Slavic fr. NG τηγάνι (above, 1).

Rum. tingire, through Slavic fr. Turk. tencere 'kettle, stewpan'. Lokotsch 2066. Tiktin 1598.

Rum. cratiţă ('deep stewpan'), prob. through Slavic krata fr. It. grata 'grating', Lat. crātis 'wickerwork'. Berneker 608 f. Tiktin 431.

3. Ir. aigen, NIr. oighean : Grk. ἄγγος, ἀγγείον 'vessel'? Walde-P. 1.38. Stokes 7.

Br. pillig, dim. fr. Lat. pīla 'mortar', through 'trough'. Cf. It., Sp. pila 'trough, basin, font'. Henry 223.

4. Lith. keptuvas, fr. kept 'roast, bake' (5.23).

Lith. skaurada, fr. Slavic (below, 5). Brückner, Sl. Fremdwörter 132.

5. ChSl. skovrada (Supr.), Russ. skovoroda, fr. skver- (prob. imitative) in

ChSl. *raskvrěti* 'melt', Boh. *škvařiti* 'sizzle', etc. Miklosich 305.

SCr. *tava*, fr. Turk. *tava* 'frying-pan'.

SCr. *tiganj* fr. NG τηγάνι (above, 1).

6. Skt. *kaṭāha-*, perh. orig. a basket-work receptacle and so : *kaṭa-* 'straw mat', Grk. κάρταλος 'basket', etc. Walde-P. 1.421 (without inclusion of *kaṭāha-*).

Skt. *bhrāṣṭa-* 'roasting pan', fr. *bhrajj-* 'roast' (5.23).

5.31 DISH

Grk.	λέκος, λεκάνη	Goth.	....	Lith.	*bliūdas*
NG	πιάτο	ON	....	Lett.	*bl'uoda*
Lat.	*catīnus, lanx*	Dan.	*fad*	ChSl.	(*misa, bljudo*)
It.	*piatto*	Sw.	*fat*	SCr.	*zdjela*
Fr.	*plat*	OE	*disc*	Boh.	*mísa*
Sp.	*plato*	ME	*disch*	Pol.	*misa*
Rum.	*farfurie*	NE	*dish*	Russ.	*bljudo*
Ir.	*tesc, mias*	Du.	*schotel*	Skt.	*bhājana-, pātra-, carāva-*, etc.
NIr.	*mias*	OHG	*scuzzila*	Av.	....
W.	*dysgl*	MHG	*schüzzel*		
Br.	*plad*	NHG	*schüssel*		

Generic words for 'dish', that is, with the scope of NE *dish*, which may be applied to all kinds of eating or even drinking utensils (cf. *wash the dishes, dish-closet*), are lacking in most of the other IE languages. The notion is covered, but still more broadly, by words for 'vessel' or 'utensil' like Lat. *vās* or NG σερβίτσιο πιαττικά, NHG *geschirr* (cf. *tischgeschirr, tischgerat*).

The words listed here are such as are applied to a wide variety of dishes and furnish some approximation to a generic 'dish'. Several of them are the same as those listed also under 'plate' (5.32) or 'bowl' (5.33).

1. Grk. λέκος, λεκάνη, Lat. *lanx*, perh. fr. **lek-*, **lenk-* 'bend' in Lith. *lenkti* 'bend', etc. Walde-P. 1.158, 2.435. Ernout-M. 522. Walde-H. 1.761.

2. Lat. *catīnus*, dim. *catillus* prob. : Grk. κότυλος, κοτύλη 'cup' (also 'hollow'), fr. the common notion of 'hollow'. Walde-H. 1.182. Otherwise Meringer, Wört. u. Sach. 7.16.

Rum. *farfurie*, usually 'plate' (5.32), also 'dish' (cf. *dulap pentru farfurie* 'dish-closet, cupboard').

Fr. *plat*, It. *piatto*, NG πιάτο, etc., also and orig. 'plate, platter'. (5.32).

3. Ir. *tesc* 'lanx' (for *t* cf. Pedersen 1.224), W. *dysgl*, OE *disc* ('platter' and 'dish', ON *diskr* 'platter'), NE *dish*, fr. Lat. *discus*, Grk. δίσκος 'quoit'. Used for a flat serving-tray, hence 'platter' and 'dish' (and, with development in another direction, NE *desk*, NHG *tisch* 'table').

4. Ir. *mias* 'table, dish', NIr. 'dish', Goth. *mēs* 'table, platter', ChSl. *misa* 'platter', Boh. *mísa*, Pol. *misa* 'bowl, dish', Russ. *misa, miska* 'soup-dish', etc. fr. VLat. *mēsa*, Lat. *mēnsa* 'table' (7.44). Feist 355. Stender-Petersen 404.

5. Dan. *fad*, Sw. *fat* (ON *fat*, OE *fæt* 'vessel', NE *vat*) : Lith. *puodas* 'pot', etc. (5.26). Falk-Torp 200.

OE *scutel* 'catinus' (NE *scuttle*), Du. *schotel*, OHG *scuzzila*, NHG *schüssel* 'platter, bowl, dish' (cf. *schüssel-brett, -schrank*, etc.), fr. Lat. *scutella* 'platter' (5.32, 5.33).

6. Lith. *bliūdas*, Lett. *bl'uoda* 'bowl, dish', fr. Russ. *bljudo* 'platter, dish' = ChSl. *bljudo* 'platter', loanword fr. Gmc., Goth. *biuþs* 'table', etc., orig. 'serving-tray' (7.44) Berneker 64. Stender-Petersen 404.

SCr. *zdjela*, fr. **sdjeti*, ChSl. *sŭ-děti* 'put together, make'.

7. Skt. *bhājana-* used for various dishes, fr. *bhaj-* 'partake of' (cf. *bhakṣ-* 'eat, drink', Grk. φαγεῖν 'eat', etc.).

Skt. *pātra-* used for 'cup, bowl, plate' or any receptacle. As 'cup' it may be = Lat. *pōculum*, fr. IE **pō(i)-*, Skt. *pā-* 'drink', but in wider use, and so perh. even when 'cup', fr. Skt. *pā-* 'protect, guard', hence orig. 'container'. Walde-P. 2.71, 72.

Skt. *carāva-* 'shallow dish', also 'cover' : *carman-* 'shelter', etc., fr. IE **kel-* 'cover' in Ir. *celim*, OE *helan*, Lat. *occulere* 'hide', etc. Walde-P. 1.432.

5.32 PLATE

Grk.	πίναξ	Goth.	*mēs*	Lith.	*lėkštė, torėlius, torielka*
NG	πιάτο	ON	*diskr, skutill*	Lett.	*telek'is, šk'īvis*
Lat.	(*lanx, scutella*)	Dan.	*tallerken*	ChSl.	*misa, bljudo*
It.	*piatto*	Sw.	*tallrik*	SCr.	*tanjir*
Fr.	*assiette, plat*	OE	*disc*	Boh.	*talíř*
Sp.	*plato*	ME	*disch, plate*	Pol.	*talerz*
Rum.	*farfurie* (*taler*)	NE	*plate*	Russ.	*tarelka*
Ir.	....	Du.	*bord*		
NIr.	*plāta*	OHG	*disc*		
W.	*plat*	MHG	*tallar, teller*		
Br.	*asied*	NHG	*teller*		

The ancestor of the modern individual plate is the serving 'platter', originally a piece of flat board. The words listed here from earlier periods mean 'platter' and in part other forms of dishes. Several of them have been discussed under 'dish'.

1. Grk. πίναξ 'board, plank, tablet' and 'platter' : Skt. *pināka-* 'staff', ChSl. *pĭnĭ*, Russ. *pen'*, etc. 'tree-trunk' or 'stump'. Walde-P. 2.71.

2. Lat. *lanx*, in part a deep platter, see 5.31.

Lat. *scutella* (also *scutra, scutula*) 'flat tray, platter', etym.? Ernout-M. 912 f. Hence ON *skutill* 'platter' and many words for 'dish' (5.31) or 'bowl' (5.33).

Fr. *plat* (> Br. *plad* 'platter', It. *piatto* [> NG πιάτο], Sp. *plato*, ME, NE *plate* [> NIr. *plāta*, W. *plat*]), fr. VLat. *plattus*, Grk. πλατύς 'flat'. REW 6586.

Fr. *assiette* (> Br. *asied*) in OFr. 'assignment, place', hence 'assigned portion at table', fr. OFr. *aseter* 'set', VLat. **asseditāre* : Lat. *sedēre* 'sit'. REW 722.

Rum. *farfurie*, orig. 'porcelain' and, like similar Slavic words, fr. vulg. Turk. *farfuri* 'porcelain' = *fağfuri*, fr. *fağfur* (through Arab. fr. Pers. *bagpūr*, a title of the Chinese emperor). Lokotsch 569. Berneker 279.

3. Goth. *mēs*, see 5.31.

ON *diskr*, OE, OHG *disc*, see 5.31.

Du. *bord* 'plate' and 'board' : OE *bord* 'board, table', etc. (7.44).

MHG *tallar, teller*, NHG *teller*, whence Lett. *telek'is*, Dan. *tallerken*, Sw. *tallrik* (fr. NLG dim. *talloreken*), Boh. *talíř*, Pol. *talerz*, Rum. *taler* ('wooden or earthenware plate'), SCr. *tanjir* (through Hung.), Russ. (with metathesis) *tarel*, *tarelka* (> Lith. *torėlius, torielka*), fr. It. *tagliere* 'kitchen chopping-board', this fr. Fr. *tailloir*, fr. *tailler* 'cut'. REW 8542. Falk-Torp 1244. Brückner 564.

4. Lith. *lėkštė* (neolog. for 'plate'), fr. *lėkštas* 'flat' (12.71).

Lett. *šk'īvis*, Lith. dial. *skyvis*, fr. MLG *schīve* 'disk, plate' (NHG *scheibe*). Mühl.-Endz. 4.50.

5. ChSl. *misa, bljudo*, see 5.31.

6. For Skt. words, see under 'dish' (5.31).

5.33 BOWL

Grk.	κρᾱτήρ, φιάλη, etc.	Goth.	....	Lith.	*bliudas*
NG	σκουτέλι	ON	*bolli, skāl*	Lett.	*bl'uoda*
Lat.	*crāter, catīnus*, etc.	Dan.	*bolle, skaal*	ChSl.	....
It.	*scodella*	Sw.	*bål, skål*	SCr.	*zdjela*
Fr.	*bol, écuelle*	OE	*bolla*	Boh.	*mísa*
Sp.	*escudilla*	ME	*bolle*	Pol.	*misa*
Rum.	*strachină, bol*	NE	*bowl*	Russ.	*čaša* (*misa*)
Ir.	*cūach*	Du.	*schaal, kom*		
NIr.	*bulla, scāla*	OHG	*scāla*		
W.	*cawg, powl*	MHG	*schale*		
Br.	*bolenn, skudell*	NHG	*napf, schale, schüssel*		

Under 'bowl' are listed some of the more common words for a (usually) round dish of some depth in contrast to the flat 'plate'. But some are used only of shallow, others only of deep, bowls, while some cover a wider range and have also been listed and discussed under 'dish'. Some of the words rest on the notion of hollow or rounded shape, but in some cases what was originally a flat dish has become a deep platter or bowl.

1. Grk. κρᾱτήρ 'mixing-bowl' (> Lat. *crāter*), fr. κεράννῡμι 'mix' (5.17).

Grk. φιάλη 'shallow bowl', etym.?

NG σκουτέλι, see below, 2.

2. Lat. *catīnus*, see 5.31.

It. *scodella*, Fr. *écuelle*, Sp. *escudilla*, Br. *skudell*, NG σκουτέλι, (ON *skutill* 'platter', OE *scutel* 'catinus', Du. *schotel*, OHG *scuzzila*, etc. 'platter, dish', 5.31), fr. Lat. *scutella* 'platter' (5.32), with partial development through 'deep platter' to 'bowl'.

Fr. *bol* (> Br. *bolenn*, Rum. *bol*), fr. NE *bowl* (below, 4).

Rum. *strachină* ('shallow bowl'), fr. Grk. ὀστρακινά 'earthenware'. Tiktin 1505.

3. Ir. *cūach*, W. *cawg*, fr. late Lat. *caucus, caucum* 'drinking-vessel', beside Byz. καῦκα, καῦκος, καυκίον 'a kind of cup', orig. dub. Walde-H. 1.184 f. Vendryes, De hib. voc. 133.

NIr. *scāla, bulla* fr. ON *skāl, bolli* (below, 4).

Br. *bolenn, skudell*, (above, 2).

4. ON *bolli*, Dan. *bolle*, OE *bolla*, ME *bolle*, NE *bowl* (> W. *powl*, Sw. *bål*, Fr., Rum. *bol*) : OHG *ballo*, NHG, NE *ball*, etc., all fr. notion of rounded shape. Falk-Torp 91.

ON *skāl*, Dan. *skaal*, Sw. *skål*, Du. *schaal*, OHG *scāla*, MHG, NHG *schale* : OE *scealu* 'husk, scale', Dan. *skal* 'husk', *skalle* 'skull', NHG *schale* 'husk', etc. Walde-P. 2.593. Falk-Torp 975.

Du. *kom* : MLG *kumm, kump*, MHG *kumpf* 'round vessel, cup', etc., fr. an extension of IE **geu-* in Grk. γύαλον 'cavity', Skt. *gola-* 'ball', etc. Walde-P. 1.555 ff., 562. Franck-v. W. 333.

NHG *napf*, fr. MHG *napf*, OHG (*h*)*napf* 'drinking-vessel' : OE *hnæp* 'drinking-vessel, Du. *nap* 'bowl, basin', etc., root connection dub. The extension fr. 'drinking-vessel' to 'bowl' for food begins in MHG, and the present wide use dates from the 15th cent. Weigand-H. 1.272.

NHG *schüssel*, used for a shallow bowl or locally any bowl, see under 'dish' (5.31). On the local distribution of *napf* and *schüssel*, see Kretschmer, Wortgeogr. 350 f.

5. For Balto-Slavic words, see under 'dish' (5.31), or for Russ. *čaša* under 'cup' (5.35).

6. For Skt. words, see under 'dish' (5.31).

5.34 PITCHER, JUG

Grk.	χοῦς, ἀμφορεύς, κάλπις, ὑδρία	Goth.	*aurkjē* (gen. pl.)	Lith.	*ąsočius, izbonas*
NG	κανάτα, σταμνί	ON	*krukka*	Lett.	*krūza*
Lat.	*urceus*	Dan.	*krukke*	ChSl.	*krŭčagŭ, čĭvanŭ* (*vrŭčĭ*)
It.	*boccale, brocca*	Sw.	*kruka, krus*	SCr.	*krčag, vrč*
Fr.	*cruche, broc*	OE	*crōg, crūce*	Boh.	*džbán*
Sp.	*cántaro, jarro, jarra*	ME	*picher*	Pol.	*dzban*
Rum.	*urcior*	NE	*pitcher, jug*	Russ.	*kuvšin, kružka*
Ir.	*cilornn*	Du.	*kruik*	Skt.	*kalaça-*
NIr.	*crūiscīn* (*ciolarn*)	OHG	*kruog*	Av.	....
W.	*piser*	MHG	*kruoc*		
Br.	*brog*	NHG	*krug*		

Many of the words listed here under 'pitcher' are applied to a great variety of vessels, covering what in NE would be called a *jug* or *mug*, or in part a *jar* or *can*.

1. Grk. χοῦς, mostly used of a specific liquid measure, fr. χέω 'pour'.

Grk. ἀμφορεύς, fr. Hom. ἀμφιφορεύς (ἀμφί 'on both sides', φέρω 'bear') a jar with two handles.

Grk. ὑδρία fr. ὕδωρ 'water'.

Grk. κάλπις, κάλπη : Ir. *cilornn* 'pitcher' (K. Meyer, Contrib. 369), NIr. *ciolarn* 'pitcher, bucket', W. *celwrn* 'milk-pail', etc. Walde-P. 1.447. Pedersen 1.94.

Late Grk. ξέστης, fr. Lat. *sextārius*, a Roman measure, is in NT (Mk. 7.8) a 'pitcher'.

NG κανάτα, fr. MLat. *cannata* beside *canna* 'a drinking-vessel', this generally taken as loanword fr. Gmc., OHG *channa*, etc., (OE *canne*, NE *can*). Walde-P. 1.535. Ernout-M. 144. Walde-H. 1.154. But otherwise, and better, as Lat. *canna* 'reed' applied to a vessel with long spout, and the source of the Gmc. group. Wartburg 2.204, 208. Frings, Germania Romania 129 f.

NG στάμνα, σταμνί fr. class. Grk. στάμνος, σταμνίον 'wine-jar' : ἵστημι 'stand'.

2. Lat. *urceus* (> It. *orcio* 'large oil-jar'), dim. *urceolus* (> Rum. *urcior*), beside *orca* 'tun' with Grk. ὕρχη 'a kind of jar', perh. an old loanword. Lat. *urceus* or *orca* > OE *orc*, Goth. *aurkjus* (only *aurkjē* gen. pl.). Ernout-M. 1136 f. Feist 68.

It. *boccale*, fr. late Lat. *baucālis*, Grk. βαυκάλις 'vessel for cooling wine', orig.? REW 1002.

It. *brocca*, Fr. *broc* (> Br. *brog*), late Lat. *broci*, fr. Grk. βροχίς 'a kind of vessel for liquids', deriv. of βρέχω 'wet'. REW 1320. Wartburg 1.549. Vendryes, BSL 25.40.

Fr. *cruche* fr. Gmc. (see below, 4).

Sp. *cántaro*, fr. Lat. *cantharus*, fr. Grk. κάνθαρος 'large drinking-cup'. REW 1614.

Sp. *jarra, jarro*, Fr. *jarre* (> NE *jar*), fr. Arab. *ǧarrah* 'earthen water-vessel'. REW 3944. NED s.v. *jar*, sb.[2].

3. Ir. *cilornn*, NIr. *ciolarn* : Grk. κάλπις, above, 1.

NIr. *crūiscīn*, fr. ME *cruskyn*, this like OFr. *creusequin* fr. MFlem. *kruyseken* dim. of *kruyse* (NE *cruse*, etc., below, 4). NED s.v. *cruskyn*.

W. *piser* fr. NE *pitcher*.

4. The Gmc. group, ON *krukka* (rare), Dan. *krukke*, Sw. *kruka*, OE *crōg, crūce, crocca*, Du. *kruik*, OHG *kruog*, NHG *krug*, is of obscure source (possibly some connection with Grk. κρωσσός 'water-pail, pitcher') and shows a great variety of parallel forms, including some with *s* as MHG *krūse*, MLG

krūs (Du. *kroes* 'cup, mug'), NE *cruse*, etc. Walde-P. 1.487, 594, 597. Falk-Torp 583, 584.

From one or another of the Gmc. forms come Fr. *cruche* (cf. MHG *krūche*), NIr. *crūiscīn* (above, 3), Lith. *kragas*, OPruss. *kragis*, Lett. *krūza* (fr. MLG *krūs*), Russ. *kružka*.

ME *picher*, NE *pitcher* (in British usage now somewhat arch. or dial., but in U.S. the usual word), fr. OFr. *pichier*, MLat. *picārium*, *bicārium* 'a drinking-vessel' (whence also OHG *pechari*, *behhari*, NHG *becher*, NE *beaker*, etc.), this fr. Grk. βῖκος 'wine-jar, drinking-bowl', this again a loanword of unknown source. NED s.v. *pitcher*[1]. REW 1081a. Weigand-H. 1.173.

NE *jug*, in U.S. usually denoting a large earthenware vessel with stopper and no spout, but in current British speech displacing *pitcher*, e.g. *jug* (U.S. *pitcher*) *of cream*, prob. fr. the female pet name *Jug* = *Joan*. NED s.v.

5. Lith. *ąsočius*, *ąsotis*, fr. *ąsa* 'handle' : Lat. *ānsa* 'handle'.

Lith. *izbonas* (also *uzbonas*, *zbonas*), fr. WhRuss. *žban* (see below, 6). Brückner, Sl. Fremdwörter 155. Skardžius 88, 241.

Lett. *krūza*, fr. MLG *krūs* (above, 4).

6. ChSl. *krŭčagŭ* (Mk. 7.8 Zogr.), SCr. *krčag*, etym.? Berneker 665.

ChSl. *čivanŭ* (Mk. 7.8 Mar.), Boh. *čban*, *džban*, Pol. *dzban* (Russ. *žban* 'wooden jug, tub'), obscure. Berneker 165. Brückner 107.

ChSl. *vrŭčĭ* (late), SCr. *vrč*, prob. through Gmc., fr. Lat. *urceus* (above, 2) or fr. the same source. Miklosich, Lex. Palaeoslov. s.v.

Russ. *kuvšin* beside *kovš* 'scoop, ladle' : Lith. *kaušas* 'ladle', Lett. *kauss* 'bowl', Skt. *koça-* 'pail, cup', etc. Berneker 594.

Russ. *kružka* fr. the Gmc., MHG *krūse*, etc. (above, 4). Berneker 628.

7. Skt. *kalaça-* (vessel for holding liquids, esp. the soma) : Grk. κύλιξ, Lat. *calix* 'cup' (5.35).

5.35 CUP

Grk.	ποτήριον, κύλιξ, κύπελλον	Goth.	*stikls*	Lith.	*puodelis, puodukas*
NG	φλιτζάνι, κούπα, κύπελλο	ON	*koppr*	Lett.	*tase*
Lat.	*pōculum, calix*	Dan.	*kop*	ChSl.	*čaša*
It.	*tazza, coppa*	Sw.	*kopp*	SCr.	*fildžan, čaša*
Fr.	*tasse, coupe*	OE	*calic, cuppe*	Boh.	*šalek, číše*
Sp.	*taza, copa*	ME	*cuppe, coupe*	Pol.	*filiżanka, czarka*
Rum.	*ceașcă, cupă*	NE	*cup*	Russ.	*čaška*
Ir.	*airidech, copān, cailech*	Du.	*kop*	Skt.	*caṣaka-, pātra-*
NIr.	*cupān*	OHG	*kelih, kopf, behhare*	Av.	*tašta-*
W.	*cwpan*	MHG	*kopf, becher*		
Br.	*tas, kop*	NHG	*tasse, becher*		

Some of the words listed have the broad range of NE *cup*. But some are used only for the modern small cup for serving tea, coffee, etc., while different words are employed for the larger drinking-vessels.

1. Grk. κύλιξ, Lat. *calix* 'goblet' : Skt. *kalaça-* 'pot, pitcher', root connection? Walde-P. 1.442. Ernout-M. 135. Walde-H. 1.138 f.

Grk. ποτήριον (NG ποτήρι 'a glass') : πῑνω 'drink', etc. Walde-P. 271 ff.

Grk. κύπελλον 'large drinking-cup, beaker' (> NG κύπελλο) : Lat. *cūpa* 'tub, cask', Skt. *kūpa-* 'hole, pit, cavity', OE *hȳf* 'beehive', fr. IE **keu-p-* in words for curved shape. Walde-P. 1.372. Ernout-M. 243. Walde-H. 1.310 f.

NG φλιτζάνι (φιλτζάνι less common), SCr. *fildžan*, Pol. *filiżanka*, fr. Turk. *fincan*, *filcan* 'cup'. Berneker 281. Brückner 121 f. Lokotsch 608. Orig. used only of the small Turkish coffee cup, but no longer so restricted.

2. Lat. *pōculum* : Lat. *bibere* 'drink', pple. *pōtus*, etc. (5.13). Ernout-M. 800. Walde-H. 1.103 f.

MLat. *cuppa*, a late form of *cūpa* 'tub, cask' : Grk. κύπελλον, etc., above, 1. Hence It. *coppa*, Fr. *coupe* (> ME *coupe*), Sp. *copa*, Rum. *cupă*, etc., now used for a large drinking-vessel and otherwise replaced by *tazza* etc.; NG κούπα; Ir. *copp*, *copān*, etc. (Vendryes, De hib. voc. 130), NIr. *cupān*, W. *cwpan*, Br. *kop;* and so prob. the Gmc. group, ON *koppr*, OE *cuppe*, OHG *kopf*, etc. (otherwise, as genuine Gmc., fr. IE **geu-*, parallel to **keu-*. Persson, Beiträge 104, Falk-Torp 564, Walde-P. 1.562). Walde-H. 1.311. REW 2409. Weigand-H. 1.118 f. NED s.v. *cup*.

It. *tazza*, Fr. *tasse* (> Br. *tas;* NHG *tasse*, this > Lett. *tase*), Sp. *taza*, fr. Arab. *tassah* 'bowl, basin'. REW 8594.

Rum. *ceașcă* fr. Slavic *čaša* (below, 6).

3. Ir. *airidech*, *airdech*, apparently a cpd. of *air-* 'for', but second part obscure (the late spelling *irdeoch*, as if fr. *deoch* 'drink' only a pop. etym.). Thurneysen, Z. celt. Ph. 8.71 f.

Ir. *cailech*, fr. Lat. *calix* (above, 1).

Ir. *copān*, etc., fr. MLat. *cuppa* (above, 2).

4. Goth. *stikls* (reg. for ποτήριον), orig. the pointed drinking-horn : ON *stikill* 'pointed end of a horn', OE *sticel* 'sting, goad', Goth. *stiks* 'point', Skt. *tij-* 'be sharp', etc. Walde-P. 2.612 ff. Feist 453.

ON *koppr*, OE *cuppe*, etc., see above, 2.

OE *calic* (reg. word for 'cup' in Gospels, as also Lat. *calix* in Vulgate), OHG *kelih*, NHG *kelch*, etc., fr. Lat. *calix* (above, 1).

OHG *behhare*, MHG, NHG *becher*, like NE *beaker*, fr. the same source as NE *pitcher* (5.34).

5. Lith. *puodelis*, *puodukas*, dims. of *puodas* 'pot' (5.26).

6. ChSl., SCr. *čaša*, Boh. *číše*, Russ. *čaška* (Russ. *čaša* 'bowl or large drinking-cup'), Skt. *caṣaka-*, Arm. *čašak*, all perh. fr. Iranian (cf. NPers. *čašidan* 'taste'). Berneker 137.

Boh. *šalek*, dim. fr. NHG *schale* 'bowl'.

Pol. *czarka*, dim. of *czara* 'drinking-bowl' (cf. Russ. *čar*, *čarka* 'drinking-glass'), prob. fr. Turk. dial. *čara* 'large bowl'. Berneker 136. Brückner 72.

7. Skt. *caṣaka-*, above, 6.

Skt. *pātra-*, as 'cup' apparently fr. *pā-* drink, IE **pō(i)-*, like Lat. *pōculum*. But see under 'dish' (5.31).

Av. *tašta-* 'cup' or 'bowl' (NPers. *tašt* 'bowl, saucer'), fr. Av. *taš* 'cut out, fashion' : Skt. *takṣ-* 'fashion', etc. Walde-P. 1.717. Barth. 646.

5.36. Saucer. Words for the modern saucer placed under the cup are mostly compounds of 'under' and 'cup', or diminutives of the words for 'dish' or 'plate'.

1. Cpds. of 'under' and 'cup'. It. *sottocoppa*, after which was modeled Fr. *soucoupe* (earlier *soutecouppe*), NIr. *fochupān* (*fo*+*cupān*), Icel. *undirskāl*, Dan. *underkop*, NHG *untertasse*, Lett. *apakštase*. Cf. Boh. *spodní šalek*, lit. 'lower cup', Pol. *spodek* (*od filiżanki*), dim. of *spod* 'under part'.

2. Dims. of 'dish', 'bowl', 'plate'. NG πιατάκι, πιατέλο, It. *piattello*, Sp. *platillo*, Rum. *farfurioară*, Du. *schoteltje*, NHG

dial. *köppchen*, *schälchen*, *plättchen*, etc. (Kretschmer, Wortgeogr. 522), Lith. *lėkštelė*, *torielkėlė*, SCr. *tanjirić*, Pol. *miseczka*, Russ. *bljudečko*.

3. Others. NE *saucer* (> W. *soser*), formerly a 'saucedish' fr. OFr. *saussier*, deriv. of *sausse* 'sauce'.

Sw. *tefat*, lit. 'tea-dish'.

5.37 SPOON

Grk.	μυστῖλη, μύστρον, κοχλιάριον	Goth.	. . . .	Lith.	*šaukštas*
NG	κουτάλι, χουλιάρι	ON	*spōnn (skeið)*	Lett.	*kar'uote*
Lat.	*cochleāre, ligula*	Dan.	*ske*	ChSl.	*lŭžica*
It.	*cucchiaio*	Sw.	*sked*	SCr.	*žlica, kašika*
Fr.	*cuiller, cuillière*	OE	*cuc(e)ler*	Boh.	*lžíce*
Sp.	*cuchara*	ME	*spone*	Pol.	*łyżka*
Rum.	*lingură*	NE	*spoon*	Russ.	*ložka*
Ir.	*liag*	Du.	*lepel*	Skt.	*darvī-, camasa-*
NIr.	*liach*	OHG	*leffil*	Av.	. . . .
W.	*llwy*	MHG	*leffel*		
Br.	*loa*	NHG	*löffel*		

Spoons of wood, bone, or clay are known from neolithic times, and of metal in the orient and in classical antiquity. Some of the North European words reflect the development of the wooden spoon from a flat chip. Others are from roots for 'lick, gulp, drink', or of miscellaneous sources.

1. Grk. μυστῖλη, also μύστρον, μυστιλάριον, orig. a piece of bread hollowed out for supping soup or gravy, later used also of metal spoons (μύστρων χρυσῶν Athen. 128c), etym.? Boisacq 653.

Grk. κοχλιάριον, the usual word in late writers (Diosc.+), fr. Lat. *cochleārium* (below, 2). Hence NG χουλιάρι (with assim. of gutturals and subsequent dissim. loss of the second). Hatzidakis, Μεσ. 1.328, 2.284.

NG κουτάλι (κουτάλιν 'spoon' quotable from 12th cent. A.D.), also κουτάλα 'ladle' and dial. 'shoulder blade', belongs (for ου fr. ο, ω, cf. Hatzidakis, Μεσ. 2.281 ff.) with Byz. κώταλις 'ladle' (Suidas, λάκτιν τὴν λεγομένην κώταλιν, τορύνην, ὅ ἐστι ζωμήρυσιν) and 'winnowing-fan' (Eust. 1675.57), all having in common the notion of shovel-shape. The deriv. fr. Lat. *scuta* 'platter' (G. Meyer, Neugr. Stud. 2.99, 3.61, but with no mention of κώταλις) is unsatisfactory.

2. Lat. *coc(h)leāre*, *coc(h)leārium*, a small spoon with one end pointed, used for eating snails and eggs (Mart. 14.121 *sum cochleis habilis, sed non minus ovis. Numquid scis potius cur cochleare vocor*), deriv. of *coc(h)lea* 'snail', this fr. Grk. κοχλίας. Hence It. *cucchiaio*, Fr. *cuiller*, *cuillière*, Sp. *cuchara*, also OE *cuc(e)ler*. Walde-H. 1.241. Ernout-M. 201. Walde-H. 1.241. REW 2012.

Lat. *ligula*, also *lingula* (> Rum. *lingură*) fr. the root of Lat. *lingere* 'lick'. Ernout-M. 552. REW 5036.

3. Ir. *liag*, NIr. *liach*, W. *llwy*, Br. *loa*, fr. the root of Ir. *ligim*, etc. 'lick'. Walde-P. 2.400. Pedersen 1.101.

4. ON *spānn*, *spōnn*, 'chip', also 'spoon', OE *spōn* 'chip', ME *spone* 'spoon', NE *spoon* : OHG *spān*, NHG *span*, Sw. *span* 'chip', and, fr. the same root, Grk. σπάθη 'broad, flat blade', OE *spadu* 'spade', etc. Walde-P. 2.652 ff. Falk-Torp 1110. Development of 'spoon' fr. flat piece of wood, as also in the next following.

ON *skeið* 'weaver's rod, etc.', also 'spoon' (so NIcel.), Dan. *ske*, Sw. *sked* :

Goth. *skaidan* 'separate, Grk. σχίζω, Lat. *scindere* 'split', etc. Walde-P. 2.543 ff. Falk-Torp 990. Hellquist 930.

Du. *lepel*, OHG *leffil*, MHG *leffel*, NHG *löffel* : OE *lapian* 'lap, drink', OHG *laffan* 'lick', Lat. *lambere* 'lick', etc. Walde-P. 2.384. Weigand-H. 2.77 f.

5. Lith. *šaukštas*, prob. : Lith. *šukė* 'shred', *šiukšmės* 'sweepings', etc. Cf. 'spoon' fr. 'chip', above, 4. So, with query, Leskien, Ablaut 318. Bezzenberger, BB 27.170, connects with Grk. κυκάω 'stir, mix', in which case 'spoon' fr. 'stirrer, mixer'. But cf. Walde-P. 1.377.

Lett. *kar'uote*, perh. : ChSl. *koryto* 'trough', with development through 'scoop, ladle'. Mühl.-Endz. 2.166.

6. ChSl. *lŭžica*, SCr. *žlica* (fr. **lžica*), Boh. *lžíce*, Pol. *lyžka*, Russ. *ložka*, dim. of **lŭga* (cf. Alb. *lugë* 'spoon'), prob. orig. 'chip' (cf. above, 4) : Lith. *lūžti* 'break', Skt. *ruj-* 'break', *lu-* 'cut', etc. (IE **leu-*, **leug-*, Walde-P. 2.407, 412). Mikkola ap. Berneker 750. Brückner 316. Jokl, Ling.-kulturhist. Unters. 150 f.

SCr. *kašika*, fr. Turk. *kaşik* 'spoon'. Lokotsch 1120.

7. Skt. *camasa-*, a kind of ladle, fr. *cam-* 'sip, drink'.

Skt. *darvī-* 'ladle' : *dāru-* 'wood', etc.

5.38 KNIFE

Words for 'knife' as a table utensil are the same as those for 'knife' in general (9.23).

5.39 FORK

The use of a fork for eating is still far from world-wide and in Europe became common only in the 15th and 16th centuries, having spread from Italy. Cf. Schrader, Reallex. s.v. *Gabel* and NED s.v. *fork*, sb. 2. Roman forks used in cooking are mentioned by Petronius, passim. But small bronze and silver forks like our modern table forks have also been found (so my colleague Ullman informs me), though there seems to be no literary reference to the use of forks for eating.

The words are mostly either the same as or diminutives of those used for the much earlier farm implement (8.26), but a few are from other sources.

1. Same as words listed in 8.26. Lat. *furca* (Petronius for the fork used in cooking, and so also for the smaller forks; or for these an unattested dim. form?), NE *fork* (in this sense > NIr. *forc*, W. *fforc* vs. *fforch*), NHG *gabel*, Dan., Sw. *gaffel*.

2. Dims. of words listed in 8.26. It. *forchetta*, Fr. *fourchette* (> Br. *fourchetez*), Rum. *furculiță;* Lith. *šakutė* (or *-ės* pl.), Lett. *dakšina* (or *-as* pl.); SCr. *viljuška*, *vilica*, Boh. *vidlička*, Pol. *widelec*, Russ. *vilka*.

3. Grk. κρεάγρα 'hook for taking meat out of the pot' (the nearest approach to a 'fork'), cpd. of κρέας 'meat' and ἄγρα : ἀγρέω, 'seize'.

4. NG πιρούνι, fr. late Grk. περόνιον, dim. of περόνη 'pin, brooch', fr. the root of πείρω 'pierce'. Doubtless first used of a single pronged utensil and then extended to the modern 'fork'. But in this form (*er* > *ir* in contrast to the normal *ir* > *er*) and sense prob. through the medium of Venetian *pirun* 'fork'. REW 6366. Rohlfs, Etym. Wtb. d. unterital. gräzität 1673a.

5. Sp. *tenedor*, also and orig. 'holder', fr. *tener* 'hold'.

5.41 A MEAL

Grk.	δαίς, δεῖπνον, τράπεζα	Goth.	*-mats*	Lith.	*valgis*
NG	φαγί	ON	*verðr, māl, maltīð*	Lett.	*maltite*
Lat.	*epulum, daps, cibus*	Dan.	*maaltid*	ChSl.	(*obědŭ*)
It.	*pasto*	Sw.	*mål, måltid*	SCr.	*ručak*
Fr.	*repas*	OE	*mǣl, feorm*	Boh.	*jídlo*
Sp.	*comida*	ME	*mele, farme*	Pol.	*jedzenie, jadło*
Rum.	*masă, mîncare*	NE	*meal*	Russ.	*stol*
Ir.	*dithat*	Du.	*maal, maaltyd*	Skt.	*bhojana-*
NIr.	*bēile*	OHG	*gouma*	Av.	. . . .
W.	*pryd*	MHG	*māl, mālzīt*		
Br.	*pred*	NHG	*mahlzeit, mahl*		

Words for 'a meal' are words for 'food, portion of food'; 'portion'; 'time' specialized to 'mealtime, meal'; 'table'; words usually applied to a particular meal.

1. Hom. δαίς 'meal, feast', orig. 'portion', fr. δαίομαι 'divide', IE **dā(i)-* Walde-P. 1.763.

Grk. δεῖπνον in Hom. used of any meal, later mostly 'dinner', etym. dub. Walde-H. 1.324.

Grk. τράπεζα 'table' (7.14) also used for 'meal' or 'course'.

NG φαγί 'food' (5.12), also 'meal'.

2. Lat. *epulum* (also pl. *epulae*), mostly 'a sumptuous meal, feast' on religious or public festivals, prob. as orig. ritual term: Lat. *opus* 'work', Skt. *āpas-* 'religious act', OHG *uoba* 'festival'. Ernout-M. 306, 709. Walde-H. 1.410.

Lat. *daps* 'religious feast, feast', sometimes a simple 'meal' : Grk. δαπάνη 'expense', δάπτω 'devour, rend', fr. an extension of IE **dā(i)-* 'divide'. Walde-P. 1.764. Ernout-M. 253. Walde-H. 1.323.

Lat. *cibus* 'food' (5.12), also 'meal' (Suet., Isid.).

Lat. *mēnsa* 'table' (7.44) also 'meal, course'. Hence Rum. *masă* 'table, meal'.

It. *pasto*, fr. Lat. *pāstus* 'fodder, food'. Fr. *repas*, fr. *repaître*, late Lat. *repāscere* 'feed'. REW 6283, 7216.

Sp. *comida* 'food' (5.12) and 'meal'.

Rum. *mîncare* 'food' (5.12) and 'meal'.

3. Ir. *dithat* (K. Meyer, Contrib. 661), prob. a deriv. of (*do-* +) *ithim* 'eat' (5.11). But not mentioned in Pedersen 2.558 f.

NIr. *bēile*, fr. *bēil* 'mouth' (4.24).

W. *pryd*, Br. *pred* 'time' (14.11) and 'meal'. Cf. Gael. *trāth* 'time' and 'meal'.

4. Goth. *-mats* 'food' (5.12), also 'meal' in cpds. *undaurni-, nahta-mats* (5.42–45).

ON *verðr* (also in cpds *dagverðr*, etc., 5.42, 5.45) prob. : Goth. *wairdus*, OHG *wirt* 'host' (19.57), with sense 'meal' fr. 'portion offered'. Falk-Torp 1371. Hellquist 693, 1393.

ON *māl*, Norw. *maal*, Sw. *mål*, OE *mǣl*, ME *mele*, NE *meal*, Du. *maal*, MHG *māl*, NHG *mahl*, same word as Goth. *mēl*, ON, OHG *māl*, OE *mǣl*, etc. 'time' (14.11). Hence also, with addition of another word for 'time' (14.11) MLG *māltīt* (> late ON *māltīð*, Dan. *maaltid*, Sw. *måltid*), Du. *maaltijd*, MHG *mālzīt*, NHG *mahlzeit*. Falk-Torp 685. Hellquist 674.

OE *feorm* 'food, provisions' (5.12), also 'feast, meal', translating ἄριστον, *prandium* in Mt. 22.4 and δεῖπνον, *cēna* in Mk. 6.21, Lk. 14.12, 16, hence ME *farme* 'meal' (*this hasty farme had bene a feast*, Chaucer). NED s.v. *farm*, sb.[1].

OHG *gouma* : *goumen* 'give attention to, protect', Goth. *gaumjan* 'perceive, see', OE *gīman* 'take care of, heed', also 'provide' (cf. Bosworth-Toller, Supplement s.v. *gīman*), outside root connections dub., but 'meal' fr. 'caring for, provision for'. Walde-P. 1.635 f. Falk-Torp 314. Feist 207.

5. Lith. *valgis* 'food' (5.12) and 'meal'. Lett. *maltite*, fr. MLG *māltīt* (above, 4).

6. ChSl. *obědŭ*, etc., see under 'dinner' (5.42–45).

SCr. *ručak*, fr. *ručati* 'take a meal' : *ručiti* 'reach out the hands', denom. of *ruka* 'hand'. Development in the vb. fr. 'reach out' or 'handle' with specialized reference to food.

Boh. *jídlo*, Pol. *jedzenie*, *jadło* '(article of) food' (5.12), also 'meal'.

Russ. *stol* 'table' (7.44) and 'meal'.

See also words listed under 'dinner'.

7. Skt. *bhojana-* 'eating, food, meal', fr. *bhuj-* 'enjoy', esp. 'enjoy food, eat' (5.11).

	5.42 BREAKFAST	5.43 LUNCH	5.44 DINNER	5.45 SUPPER
Grk.	ἀκράτισμα (ἄριστον)	ἄριστον	δεῖπνον	δεῖπνον
NG	πρωινό, κσλατοιό, καφές	πρόγευμα	γεῦμα, δεῖπνον	δεῖπνον
Lat.	*ientāculum*	*prandium*	*cēna*	*cēna*
It.	*colazione*	*colazione*	*pranzo, desinare*	*cena*
Fr.	*petit déjeuner*	*déjeuner*	*dîner*	*souper*
Sp.	*desayuno*	*almuerzo*	*comida*	*cena*
Rum.	*prînşisor*	*dejun*	*prînz, masă*	*masă de seară, cină, ojina*
Ir.	. . . .		*praind*	. . . .
NIr.	*bricfeasta* (*cēadbhēile*)		*dinnēar* (*proinn*)	*suipēar* (*seire*)
W.	*boreufwyd, brecwast*		*cinio*	*swper*
Br.	*predbeure*		*lein, merenn*	*koan*
Goth.	. . . .		*undaurnimats*	*nahtamats*
ON	*dagverðr*		. . . .	*nāttverðr*
Dan.	*morgenmad, frokost*	*frokost*	*middag*	*aftensmad*
Sw.	*frukost*	*andrafrukost*	*middag*	*aftonmåltid, kvällsvard*
OE	*morgenmete*		*undernmete*	*æfenmete*
ME	*brekfast*		*diner*	*soper*
NE	*breakfast*	*luncheon*	*dinner*	*supper*
Du.	*ontbijt*	*tweede ontbijt*	*middagmaal(-eten)*	*avondmaal(-eten)*
OHG	. . . .	*imbīz, gouma*	*gouma*	
MHG	*vruoessen, vruostücke*		*mittag(s)essen, -mahl*	*ābentessen, -māl, -brōt*
NHG	*frühstück*	*zweites frühstück*	*mittag(s)essen, diner*	*abendessen, -brot*
Lith.	*pusryčiai*		*pietūs*	*vakarienė*
Lett.	*bruokastis, azaids*	*azaids*	*azaids, pusdienas*	*vakarinas*
ChSl.	. . . .		*obědŭ*	*večerja*
SCr.	*doručak*		*objed, ručak*	*večera*
Boh.	*snídaně*		*oběd*	*večeře*
Pol.	*sniadanie*		*obiad*	*kolacja*
Russ.	*čaj, zavtrak*	*zavtrak*	*obed*	*užin*
Skt.	*prātarāça-*		(*bhojana-*)	(*bhojana-*)
Av.	*sūirya-*		. . . .	*xšafnya-*

The words for the principal meals are discussed together because of the frequent fluctuation in application due to local and social differences of custom, in modern times especially between city and country. Words for 'breakfast' may shift to 'lunch', with substitutes for 'breakfast' such as 'first' or 'little breakfast', or merely 'coffee' or 'tea'. 'Dinner', that is, the principal meal, may be a midday or evening meal. In the former case the three regular meals are 'breakfast', 'dinner', and 'supper', while 'lunch' is a slight, casual meal. In the latter case the three regular meals are 'breakfast', 'lunch', and 'dinner', while

'supper' is an extraordinary, late evening meal. Grk. δεῖπνον, Lat. *cēna*, both used of the principal meal, but shifting in time, are commonly rendered by 'dinner', but regularly the 'Lord's Supper'.

For detailed discussion of the distribution in Romance, cf. Herzog, Die Bezeichnungen der täglichen Mahlzeiten in den romanischen Sprachen und Dialekten.

1. Grk. ἄριστον, orig. 'breakfast' as in Hom., later 'lunch' : ἦρι 'early', Goth. *air* 'early', NE *ere*, etc.; *-στο-* fr. *-d-to-*, pple. of **ed-* 'eat'. Walde-P. 1.3.

Grk. ἀκράτισμα, the later word for 'breakfast' : ἀκρᾱτίζομαι 'drink unmixed wine' (ἄκρᾱτος 'unmixed') = 'take breakfast', the breakfast consisting of bread dipped in wine (cf. Ath. 11c ff.).

Grk. δεῖπνον, in Hom. any 'meal' (5.41), later 'dinner'.

Grk. δόρπον, in Hom. 'evening meal' (in later epic 'meal', but in prose displaced by δεῖπνον) : Alb. *darke* 'evening, evening meal', *dreke* 'midday meal', prob. fr. an extension of **der-* 'flay, split' (Grk. δέρω 'flay', δρέπω 'pluck', etc.) with development fr. 'part split off' to 'portion, meal'. Cf. sources of Grk. δαίς (5.41), Lat. *cēna* (below), etc. Walde-P. 1.801. Boisacq 197.

NG γεῦμα 'dinner', fr. class. Grk. γεῦμα 'a taste, food' (fr. γεύομαι 'taste'). Hence NG πρόγευμα 'lunch'; for 'breakfast' πρωινό, fr. adj. πρωινός 'in the morning', κολατσιό (fr. It. *colazione*, below, 2) or simply καφές 'coffee'.

2. Lat. *ientāculum, iantāculum* 'breakfast', fr. vb. *ientāre, iantāre* 'take breakfast' : *iēiūnus, iāiūnus* 'hungry', further etym.? Ernout-M. 472. Walde-H. 1.674 f.

Lat. *prandium* 'lunch' (> It. *pranzo* 'dinner', Rum. *prînz* 'midday meal', dim. *prînşisor* 'breakfast'), prob. fr. **prām-(e)dio-m* lit. 'early eating', with **prāmo-* : Lith. *pirmas* 'first', Dor. πράν 'formerly', etc., and **ed-* 'eat'. Walde-P. 2.37. Ernout-M. 806. REW 558.

Lat. *cēna* 'dinner' fr. **kert-snā-* 'portion' (cf. Osc. *kerssnaís* 'cenis'), fr. IE **kert-*, in Skt. *kṛt-* 'cut', Lith. *kertu, kirsti* 'hew', etc. Walde-P. 2.578. Ernout-M. 173. Walde-H. 1.198.

Hence It., Sp. *cena*, OFr. *cene*, Rum. *cină* 'supper' (Fr. *cène* 'Lord's Supper'), W. *cwyn* (obs.), Corn. *coyn*, Br. *koan* 'supper', W. *cinio* 'dinner'. Wartburg 2.576 f. Loth, Mots lat. 149, 150.

It. *colazione* 'breakfast' or 'lunch', fr. OFr. *colation* 'evening meeting and meal of the monks' (NE *collation*, cf. NED s.v. II.8, 9), Lat. *collātiō* 'bringing together'. REW 2043.

VLat. **disiēiūnāre* 'to breakfast' (fr. *dis-* and *iēiūnāre* 'fast'), OFr. *desiuner* and *disner*, whence, used also as sb., (1) Fr. *déjeuner* 'breakfast', later 'lunch' (> Rum. *dejun*, neolog.), Sp. *desayuno* 'breakfast', (2) Fr. *dîner*, ME *diner*, NE *dinner* (> NIr. *dinnēar*), NHG *diner*, It. *desinare* 'dinner'. REW 2670.

Fr. *souper* 'supper' (OFr. *soper* > ME *soper*, NE *supper*), sb. use of *souper* 'sup' deriv. of *soupe* in its earlier sense of 'sop', orig. a Gmc. word (5.64).

Sp. *almuerzo* 'lunch', formerly and still locally 'breakfast', orig. 'a bite', fr. VLat. **admordium* (with substitution of Arab. *al-*), fr. Lat. *ad-mordēre* 'bite'. REW 182.

Sp. *comida* 'food' (5.12) used for 'meal' and esp. the principal meal 'dinner'.

Rum. *masă* 'table, meal' (5.41), also 'dinner'.

Rum. *ojina* 'supper', fr. Slavic, cf. SCr. *užina* 'vespers', Russ. *užin* 'supper'.

For the Rum. usage in names of meals, cf. especially Tiktin s.v. *prînz*.

3. NIr. *cēadbhēile* 'breakfast', lit. 'first meal', from *cēad* 'first' and *bēile* 'meal' (5.41).

Ir. *praind, proind*, NIr. *proinn* 'dinner', fr. Lat. *prandium* (above, 2). Vendryes, De hib. voc. 169. The early application was to the chief meal of the day, taken in the evening. Thurneysen, Heldensage 82.

NIr. *seire* 'supper', fr. Ir. *sēre, sēir*, 'food, meal', source?

But the preceding NIr. words (though given in Dinneen) are no longer in use, being replaced by the NE words in the form *bricfeasta, dinnēar, suipēar*.

W. *boreufwyd* or *boreubryd* 'breakfast', cpd. of *bore* (old also *boreu*) 'morning' and *bwyd* 'food' or *pryd* 'meal'. But now mostly *brecwast* fr. NE *breakfast*.

W. *cinio* 'dinner' fr. Lat. *cēna* (above, 2). W. *swper* fr. NE *supper*.

Br. *pred-beure* 'breakfast', cpd. of *pred* 'meal' and *beure* 'morning'. Cf. W. *boreubryd*.

Br. *lein* 'dinner', MBr. *leiff*, etym.? Henry 182.

Br. *koan* 'supper', fr. Lat. *cēna*.

Br. *merenn* 'dinner' and (dialects) 'afternoon lunch', fr. Lat. *merenda* 'afternoon lunch' (deriv. of *merēre* 'earn, gain'). Loth, Mots Lat. 187.

4. Goth. *undaurnimats* = ἄριστον, OE *undernmete* = *prandium* : OE *undern* 'third hour of the day', later 'sixth hour, midday' (cf. NED s.v. *undern*), MLG *undern*, etc.; Goth. *nahtamats* = δεῖπνον : Goth. *nahts* 'night'. Both cpds. with *mats* 'food', here 'meal'.

ON *dagverðr*, lit. 'day-meal', in time 'breakfast', but the principal meal (cf. Vigfusson s.v.), *nāttverðr*, lit. 'night-meal' (Dan. *nadver*, Sw. *nattvärd* 'Lord's Supper'), both cpds. of *verðr* 'meal' (5.41).

Dan. *morgenmad*, but Dan., Sw. simply *middag* ('dinner', regardless of time), Dan. *aftensmad*, Sw. *aftonmåltid*, lit. 'morning-, midday-, evening-food (meal)'.

Dan. *frokost*, Sw. *frukost* 'breakfast' or 'lunch', fr. MLG *vrōkost*, fr. *vrō* 'early' and *kost* 'food' (5.12).

Sw. *kvällsvard* 'supper' fr. *kväll* 'evening' = ON *kveld*, and *vard* = ON *verðr* 'meal' (5.41).

OE *morgenmete, undernmete* (cf. above), *æfenmete*, lit. 'morning-, noon-, evening-food (meal)'.

OE *wist* 'food' (5.12) and *feorm* 'food, meal' (5.12, 5.41) are used for *prandium* and *cēna* respectively in Lk. 14.12.

ME *diner*, NE *dinner* fr. Fr. *dîner* (above, 2).

ME *soper*, NE *supper*, fr. OFr. *soper* (above, 2).

ME (late) *brekfast*, NE *breakfast*, cpd. of *break* (ME *breke*) and *fast*. Cf. VLat. **disiēiūnāre*, Fr. *déjeuner*, above, 2.

NE *lunch*, of which *luncheon*, though quotable from a few years earlier, is an extension, was first used of a 'hunch, hunk' (of bacon, bread, etc.), and was prob. a colloq. blend of *lump* and *hunch*. Cf. NED s.v.

Du. *ontbijt* 'breakfast', fr. MDu. *ontbīten*, like OE *onbītan* 'partake of', cpd. of *bītan* 'bite'. Similarly OHG *imbīz* (gl. Lat. *prandium*), cpd. of *bīzan* 'bite', whence NHG *imbiss* 'smack, lunch'.

OHG *gouma* 'meal' (5.41) also renders Lat. *prandium* and *cēna*.

MHG *vruostücke* (also *vruoessen*), NHG *frühstück* 'breakfast', fr. *vruo* 'early' and *stücke* 'bit'.

MHG, NHG *mittag(s)essen, -mahl* 'midday meal', MHG *ābentessen, -māl, -brōt*, NHG *abendessen, -brot* 'evening meal' (*abendmahl* mostly for the Lord's Supper), all obvious cpds. of 'midday' or 'evening' with 'food, meal, bread'. For the NHG local usage, cf. Kretschmer, Wortgeogr. 63 ff., 336 f.

5. Lith. *pusryčiai* (pl.) 'breakfast', cpd. of *pusė* 'half' (13.34) and *rytas* 'morning' (14.34), so lit. 'midmorning' (meal).

Lett. *bruokastis* 'breakfast', fr. MLG *vrōkost* (above, 4). Mühl-Endz. 1.342.

Lett. *azaids* 'midday meal', also locally 'breakfast' or 'lunch', etym.? Mühl.-Endz. 1.233.

Lith. *pietūs* (pl.) 'midday meal, dinner', orig. 'food' : ChSl. *pitěti* 'feed', *pišta* 'food', Skt. *pitu-* 'food, drink', etc. (5.12).

Lett. *pusdiena* 'midday, noon' (14.45), hence pl. *pusdienas* 'midday meal'. Mühl.-Endz. 3.425.

Lith. *vakarienė*, Lett. *vakarinas* 'supper', fr. Lith. *vakaras*, Lett. *vakars* 'evening'.

6. SCr. *zajutrak* 'breakfast', Russ. *zavtrak* 'breakfast' or 'lunch' (in which case 'the first meal' is *pervyj zavtrak* 'first breakfast', or often simply *čaj* 'tea'), cpd. of *za* 'at, for' etc. and *jutro* 'morning' (14.34).

Boh. *snidane*, Pol. *śniadanie* 'breakfast', cpd. of *sŭn-* 'with' and *jad-*, IE **ed-* 'eat'. Berneker 273.

ChSl. *obědŭ* (in Gospels renders Grk. ἄριστον 'the midday meal', while Grk. δεῖπνον 'the evening meal' is rendered by *večerja;* but it is entered in the list under 'dinner', since it is the principal meal in Slavic, as in) SCr. *objed*, Pol. *obiad*, Russ. *obed*, all fr. *ob(ŭ)jad-*, perfect. cpd. of *jad-*, IE **ed-* 'eat'. Berneker 273.

SCr. *ručak* 'meal' (5.41), also esp. the principal meal, the noon 'dinner'. Hence also *doručak* 'breakfast', cpd. with *do-* 'until, beside'.

ChSl. *večerja*, SCr. *večera*, Boh. *večeře*, 'supper' (Pol. *wieczerza*, Russ. *večerja* now mostly of the Lord's Supper), fr. ChSl. *večerŭ*, etc. 'evening' (14.36).

Pol. *kolacya* 'supper', fr. Lat. *collātiō*, through a special use among the monks. Cf. It. *colazione*, above, 2. Brückner 244.

Russ. *užin* 'supper' : SCr. *užina*, Pol. *juzyna* 'afternoon or evening lunch', orig. at noon, fr. *jug* 'south' in sense of 'noon' (cf. NHG *mittag* for 'south'). Brückner 210.

7. Skt. *prātarāça-* 'breakfast', cpd. of *prātar* 'early morning' and *aç-* 'eat'. But in general Skt. *bhojana-* 'meal' (5.41) was used for any meal.

Av. *sūirya-*, *xšafnya-* 'morning, night meal', fr. *sūr-* 'morning', *xšapan-* 'night'. Barth. 550, 1586.

5.51 BREAD

Grk.	*ἄρτος*	Goth.	*hlaifs*	Lith.	*duona*
NG	*ψωμί*	ON	*brauð*	Lett.	*maize*
Lat.	*pānis*	Dan.	*brød*	ChSl.	*chlěbŭ*
It.	*pane*	Sw.	*bröd*	SCr.	*kruh, hljeb*
Fr.	*pain*	OE	*hlāf (brēad)*	Boh.	*chléb*
Sp.	*pan*	ME	*brede*	Pol.	*chleb*
Rum.	*pîine*	NE	*bread*	Russ.	*chleb*
Ir.	*bairgen, arān*	Du.	*brood*	Skt.	*(apūpa-, pūpa-)*
NIr.	*arān*	OHG	*hleib, brōt*	Av.	. . . .
W.	*bara*	MHG	*brōt*		
Br.	*bara*	NHG	*brot*		

Words for 'bread', as being the most important food, the "staff of life", may come by specialization from 'food' or 'grain'. Some are from 'bit, piece'. Several denoted primarily the shaped loaf of bread baked in a pan, and this may be reflected in their source. Relation to the use of yeast in leavening bread is commonly assumed for the Gmc. group NE *bread* etc., but this is doubtful.

1. Grk. ἄρτος, generally called obscure. But the deriv. fr. ἀρ- in ἀραρίσκω 'join, fit, prepare' is possible, either through the general sense of 'prepared' (Prellwitz), or through the literal sense as applied to the loaf 'fitted' in the baking pot (κλίβανος). For ἄρτος is, from Homer down, distinctively the 'loaf', pl. ἄρτοι 'loaves', normally of wheat bread (in Hdt. 2.92 of Egyptian loaves made from lotus-root).

The more common diet of the populace (cf. Ath. 137e, etc.) was the μᾶζα 'barley-cake' (5.52).

In NG ἄρτος is used of the consecrated bread in the church, but otherwise displaced by ψωμί, fr. late Grk. ψωμίον, dim. of ψωμός 'bit, piece' : ψῆν 'rub'. ψωμίον is already a 'bit of bread' dipped in wine, 'sop' in the NT, Jn. 13.26 ff., and ψωμία occurs frequently in the papyri, where it is commonly translated 'cakes' or 'dainties', but in part at least is already simply 'bread'. Cf. passages quoted in Moulton-Milligan, s.v., also Kretschmer, Glotta 15.60 ff. Cf. Alb. *bukë* 'bread', fr. Lat. *bucca* 'mouth' through 'mouthful, morsel' (as Byz. βούκκα, NG μπουκιά), G. Meyer, Alb. Etym. Wtb. 51.

2. Lat. *pānis* (> Romance words), orig. 'food' fr. the root of Lat. *pāscere* 'feed', *pābulum* 'fodder', NE *food*, etc. (5.12). Ernout-M. 729.

3. Ir. *bairgen*, W., Br. *bara* : OE *bere* 'barley', Lat. *far* 'spelt', etc. Walde-P. 2.134. Walde-H. 1.455. Pedersen 1.101.

Ir. *arān*, prob. : Ir. *arbor* 'grain', root connection? Stokes 16 (but resemblance to Grk. ἄρτος accidental).

4. Goth. *hlaifs*, OE *hlāf* (NE *loaf*), OHG *(h)leib* (NHG *laib*), etc., the old Gmc. word for (loaf of) 'bread', orig. 'loaf' as in ON *hleifr* 'loaf' *brauð-hleifr* 'loaf of bread', etym. dub., perh. : Grk. κλίβανος, 'earthen pot for baking bread', without known root connection. Walde-P. 1.499. Feist 260.

Hence as loanword (less prob. fr. a common source) the general Slavic word, ChSl. *chlěbŭ*, etc., also Lith. *kliepas* (from WhRuss.), Lett. *klaips* (fr. LG) 'large loaf of bread'. Berneker 389. Stender-Petersen 297 ff.

ON *brauð*, OE *brēad*, OHG *brōt*, etc., becoming the general Gmc. word at the expense of the preceding, is commonly derived fr. the root of OE *brēowan* 'brew', etc., as if connected with the use of yeast. So Walde-P. 2.168, Falk-Torp 112, Schrader, Reallex. 1.166, etc. But more probable is the view preferred in NED s.v. *bread*, that the development is from 'bit, morsel' (cf. OE gl. *brēadru* 'frusta' and the Northumbrian *brēad* = OE *bitan*, Vulgate *buccella*, Grk. ψωμίον in Jn. 13.27, 30; also = ἄρτον, Vulgate *panem* in Jn. 6.23), just as in Grk. ψωμίον (above, 1), SCr. *kruh* (below, 6), and Sc. *piece bread* (NED s.v. *piece*, sb. 3b). In this case the word may be connected with OE *brēotan* 'break', through a parallel extension of IE **bhreu-* (Walde-P. 2.196).

Before 1200 A.D. *brēad* had replaced *hlāf* as the general word for 'bread' as a substance, while ME *loof*, NE *loaf*, and similarly MHG *leip*, NHG *laib*, remained in the sense of 'loaf of bread'. For the present local use of NHG *brot*

and *laib*, cf. Kretschmer, Wortgeogr. 150 ff.

5. Lith. *duona* (Lett. *duona* 'bit of bread') perh. : Skt. *dhānās* (pl.), *dhānya-* 'grain' (8.42). Trautmann 58. Mühl.-Endz. 1.534. Otherwise (as orig. 'gift of God' : Lith. *duoti* 'give') Walde-P. 1.831.

Lett. *maize* : *miezis* 'barley'. Mühl.-Endz. 2.553.

6. ChSl. *chlěbŭ*, etc. fr. Gmc. (above, 4).

SCr. *kruh*, orig. 'bit, piece' : ChSl. *kruchŭ* 'bit', Boh. *kruch* 'lump', etc. Berneker 628.

7. Skt. *apūpa-* and *pūpa-*, a kind of meal- or rice-cake (cf. Macdonell-Keith 1.26), the nearest equivalent of 'bread', etym.?

5.52 CAKE

Grk.	*πλακοῦς, μᾶζα*	Goth.	. . . .	Lith.	*pyragas*
NG	*πίττα*	ON	. . . .	Lett.	*rausis, pīrags*
Lat.	*lībum, placenta*	Dan.	*kage*	ChSl.	*(kolačĭ)*
It.	(*focaccia*, etc.)	Sw.	*kaka*	SCr.	*kolač*
Fr.	*gâteau*	OE	*cicel*	Boh.	*koláč*
Sp.	*pastel*	ME	*cake*	Pol.	*placek, ciastko*
Rum.	*plăcintă, prăjitură*	NE	*cake*	Russ.	*pirog*
Ir.	*bairgen*	Du.	*koek*	Skt.	*apūpa-, piṣṭaka-*
NIr.	*bairghean*	OHG	*kuocho*	Av.	*(draonah-)*
W.	*teisen*	MHG	*kuoche*		
Br.	*kouign, gwastell*	NHG	*kuchen*		

A 'cake' is understood here in the earlier sense of NE *cake*, distinguished from *bread* more in form than composition (NED s.v. 1.a,b), though the usual implication of a richer composition than the ordinary bread (NED s.v. 1c, whence 2) is common also to many of the words listed.

The commonest source is the notion of flat or round shape (cf. NE *roll*, *bun*, etc.).

1. Grk. πλακοῦς, gen. -οῦντος (> Lat. *placenta*), fr. πλακόεις 'flat' : πλάξ 'anything flat', ON *flaga* 'slab of stone', NE *flagstone*, Lett. *plakt* 'become flat', etc., fr. an extension of the root seen in Lat. *plānus* 'flat', etc. (12.71). Walde-P. 2.90. After πλακοῦς was formed a whole series, τυροῦς 'cheese-cake', οἰνοῦττα 'wine-cake', etc.

Grk. μᾶζα 'barley-cake', fr. μάσσω 'knead' (5.54).

NG πίττα > Alb. *pitë*, SCr. *pita*, etc., perh. through an Italianized form of a VLat. **picta*, fr. Grk. πηκτή fem. of πηκτός 'fixed'. Cf. Dor. πᾱκτά 'cream-cheese'. G. Meyer, Alb. Etym. Wtb. 340, BB 19, 153. Rohlfs, Wtb. d. unterit. Gräzität 1714 (adversely).

2. Lat. *lībum*, most commonly a 'sacrificial cake', and prob. a back-formation : Lat. *lībāre*, 'make an offering' (not restricted to liquids), Grk. λείβω 'pour a libation', etc. Walde-H. 1.796.

In Italian there is no single popular word for 'a cake'.

Italian scholars render Grk. πλακοῦς, Lat. *lībum* by *focaccia*, which in actual use denotes a very special kind of cake, orig. a sort of 'ash-cake', like Fr. *fouace*, fr. **focācea* (cf. *focācius* Isid. 20.2.15), deriv. of *focus* 'hearth'. REW 292. The Sprach- und Sach-Atlas Italiens und der Südschweiz, Karte 1007 (vol. 5) also gives *focaccia* (*schiacciata*) as the heading = NHG *Kuchen*, Fr. *gâteau*. The *schiacciata* is a flat, brittle cake, fr. *schiacciare* 'break, crack'.

Among other approximations are *torta* 'pie, tart' and *pasta* 'piece of pastry' (see below), or *dolce* 'a sweet'.

Fr. *gâteau* 'cake', OFr. *gastel*, Br. *gwastell*, fr. Gmc. **wastil*, dim. of OS, OE *wist* 'food' (5.12). REW 9514. Gamillscheg s.v.

Sp. *pastel*, NG παστέλλι 'a cake of sesame and honey', fr. It. *pastello*, Lat. *pastillum*, *pastillus* 'small loaf, cake', dim. of *pasta* 'dough' (5.52). REW 6274.

Other derivs. of *pasta* show the extension of 'dough' to 'pastry, pastry-cake, pie', etc., as It. *pasta*, Fr. *pâte*, ME *paste*, NE *pasty*, *pastry*.

Rum. *plăcintă*, fr. Lat. *placenta*.

Rum. *prăjitură*, fr. *prăji* 'roast, toast' (5.23).

Late Lat. *tōrta* 'loaf of bread' (Vulgate, glosses) is the source of the widespread group applied mostly to a large cake or pie, It., Sp. *torta*, Rum. *turtă*, Fr. *tourte*, NHG *torte*, etc. Ernout-M. 1049. REW 8802.

3. Ir. *bairgen* 'bread' (5.51), also 'cake', as NIr. *bairghean*.

W. *teisen*, Corn. *tesan*, etym.?

Br. *kouign*, fr. OFr. *cuignet* kind of 'cake', fr. dim. of *cuneus* 'wedge', in MLat. also 'loaf of bread' (Du Cange s.v.). Henry 77. Gamillscheg s.v. *quignon*.

Br. *gwastell*, see under Fr. *gâteau* (above, 2).

4. NIcel., Norw., Sw. *kaka*, Dan. *kage*, OE dim. *cicel*, ME, NE *cake* (fr. Norse), Du. *koek*, OHG *kuocho*, NHG *kuchen*, the general Gmc. word for 'cake', orig. prob. 'something round, lump', like Norw. *kok* 'lump', perh. : Lith. *guoge* 'head of cabbage', *guoga* 'cudgel'. Walde-P. 1.530 f. Falk-Torp 483. Weigand-H. 1.1163.

5. Lith. *pyragas*, Lett. *pīrags*, fr. Russ. *pirog* (below, 6).

Lett. *rausis* fr. *raust* 'poke, rake (the fire)', as a cake baked on the hearth. Mühl.-Endz. 3.488.

6. Late ChSl. *kolačĭ*, SCr., Boh. *kolač*, (Pol. *kołacz*, Russ. *kolač* 'white bread roll'), deriv. of *kolo* 'circle, wheel'. Berneker 541. Brückner 247.

Pol. *placek*, fr. MHG *placz* 'thin, flat cake' (NHG *plätzchen* 'lozenge'), deriv. of *plat* 'flat' (12.71). Weigand-H. 2.439.

Pol. *ciastko*, fr. *ciasto* 'dough' (5.53), pl. *ciasta* 'cakes'.

Russ. *pirog*, deriv. of *pir* 'feast' (: *pit'* 'drink'). Brückner 410.

7. Skt. *apūpa-*, *pūpa-*, see 5.51.

Skt. *piṣṭa-* (also 'meal'), *piṣṭaka-*, fr. *piṣ-* 'crush, pound'.

Av. *draonah-* 'portion, offering', later the sacred 'cake' : Skt. *dravinas-* 'wealth, property'. Barth. 770.

5.53 DOUGH

Grk.	*φύρᾱμα*	Goth.	*daigs*	Lith.	*minklė, tešla*
NG	*ζύμη, ζυμάρι*	ON	*deig*	Lett.	*mīkla*
Lat.	*massa*	Dan.	*dej*	ChSl.	*těsto*
It.	*pasta*	Sw.	*deg*	SCr.	*tijesto*
Fr.	*pâte*	OE	*dāg*	Boh.	*těsto*
Sp.	*pasta, masa*	ME	*dogh, paste*	Pol.	*ciasto*
Rum.	*aluat*	NE	*dough*	Russ.	*testo*
Ir.	*tāis*	Du.	*deeg*	Skt.	. . . .
NIr.	*taos*	OHG	*teig*	Av.	*gunda-*
W.	*toes*	MHG	*teig*		
Br.	*toaz*	NHG	*teig*		

1. Grk. φυρᾱμα, fr. φῡράω, φῡρω 'mix' : Skt. *bhur-* 'move rapidly', Lat. *fervēre* 'boil', etc. Walde-P. 2.157.

NG ζὑμη, ζυμάρι, fr. class. Grk. ζὑμη 'leaven' : Lat. *iūs*, Skt. *yūṣá-* 'soup', etc. (5.64).

2. Lat. *massa* 'lump, mass, dough' (> Sp. *masa* also 'dough', fr. Grk. μᾶζα 'barley-cake' (5.52). Ernout-M. 594. REW 5396.

It., Sp. *pasta*, OFr. *paste* (> ME *paste*), Fr. *pâte*, fr. late Lat. *pasta* 'dough', this fr. Grk. παστά 'porridge', neut. pl. of παστός 'salted' : πάσσω 'sprinkle'. REW 6272.

Rum. *aluat* fr. Lat. *allevātum* 'raised, leavened', pple. of *levāre* 'lighten, raise' (cf. NE *leaven*), denom. of *levis* 'light'. REW 360.

3. Ir. *tāis*, NIr. *taos*, W. *toes*, Br. *toaz*; ChSl. *tĕsto*, etc., general Slavic (whence also Lith. *tešla*) : OHG *theismo, deismo*, OE *þǣsma* 'leaven', prob. fr. the root of ChSl. *tajati*, Grk. τἡκω 'melt', etc. Walde-P. 1.702. Pedersen 1.56.

4. Goth. *daigs*, OE *dāg*, etc., general Gmc. : Goth. *digan* 'mold, form', Lat. *fingere* 'mold', Skt. *dih-* 'smear' ('fashion, form' implied by *dehī-* 'wall', like Grk. τεῖχος 'wall'), IE *dheiĝh-*. Walde-P. 1.833 ff.

5. Lith. *minklė* (NSB), Lett. *mīkla* : Lith. *minkyti*, Lett. *mīcit* 'knead' (5.53).

6. ChSl. *tĕsto*, etc., above, 3.

7. Av. *gunda-* (NPers. *gunda* 'lump of dough'), etym.? Barth. 525.

tāre 'break into fragments'. REW 3473. (Not fr. Lat. *fermentāre*, as Tiktin and formerly Puşcariu.)

3. NIr. *fuinim*, same word as *fuinim* 'cook, bake' (orig. 'prepare'? see 5.21).

W. *tylino*, etym.? (fr. *tyle* 'mound, hill', as 'form a mound'?).

Br. *meza*, dial. *meat*, deriv. through sb. (Van. *me*) of OFr. *maie, mait* 'kneading-trough' (fr. Lat. *magis*, fr. Grk. μαγίς : μάσσω). Ernault, Glossaire 414.

Br. *merat* 'touch, feel' and 'knead', same word as *mera* 'handle, administer', MBr. *maerat, merat*, fr. Lat. *mairer* 'master, control', fr. *maire* 'chief, master' (Lat. *maior*). Ernault, Glossaire 383 f.

4. ON *knođa*, OE *cnedan*, etc., general Gmc., also Boh. *hnísti* ('press' and 'knead') : ChSl. *gnetǫ, gnesti* 'press', OPruss. *gnode* 'trough for kneading of bread', etc. Walde-P. 1.580 ff. Falk-Torp 543. Berneker 311 f.

ON. *elte* : ON *elta*, Sw. *älta* 'press, stamp' and 'drive away, pursue', this perh. fr. an extension of the root of Grk. ἐλαὑνω 'drive', etc. Walde-P. 1.156. Falk-Torp 188.

5. Lith. *minkyti*, Lett. *mīcit* : Skt. *mac-* 'pound, grind', perh. OE *mengan* 'mix', etc. (5.17). Walde-P. 2.268.

ChSl. *u-mĕsiti*, SCr. *mjesiti*, Pol. *miesić*, Russ. *mesit'*, the usual Slavic word for 'knead', orig. 'mix', as ChSl. *mĕsiti*, etc. (5.17).

6. In Skt. there is no word for 'knead' or for 'dough', but only words for crushing the grain. So *piṣ-* 'crush, pound' : Lat. *pīnsere*, etc. (Walde-P. 2.1); or *mr̥d-* 'crush, pound, rub' : Lat. *mordēre* 'bite', etc. (Walde-P. 2.278 ff.).

5.54 KNEAD

Grk.	μάσσω, aor. ἐμάγην	Goth.	....	Lith.	minkyti
NG	ζυμώνω	ON	knođa	Lett.	mīcit
Lat.	subigere, depsere	Dan.	elte	ChSl.	umĕsiti
It.	impastare	Sw.	knāđa	SCr.	mjesiti
Fr.	pétrir	OE	cnedan	Boh.	hnísti
Sp.	amasar	ME	knede	Pol.	miesić
Rum.	frămînta	NE	knead	Russ.	mesit'
Ir.	....	Du.	kneden	Skt.	....
NIr.	fuinim	OHG	knetan	Av.	....
W.	tylino	MHG	kneten		
Br.	meza, merat	NHG	kneten		

Words for 'knead' are mostly cognate with words for 'mix, press, break, crush, mold, handle', of which 'knead' is an easy specialization. A few are derived from nouns for 'dough' or 'kneading-trough'.

1. Grk. μάσσω, prob. new present for *μάζω, aor. ἐμάγην (cf. sbs. μαγίς, μαγεύς, μᾶζα, etc.) : ChSl. *mazati* 'anoint', etc. Walde-P. 2.226 (but separating μάσσω, taken, 2.268, with Lith. *minkyti* 'knead', etc.).

NG ζυμώνω, fr. class. Grk. ζῡμόω, denom. of ζῡμη 'leaven', now 'dough' (5.52).

2. Lat. *subigere* 'turn up, break up (land)' is also 'knead' (Cato, Pliny).

Lat. *depsere* (rare), fr. Grk. δέψω 'soften by working' (as leather), beside δέψω, this perh. : SCr. *depati* 'hit'. Walde-P. 1.786. Ernout-M. 262. Walde-H. 1.342.

It. *impastare*, fr. *pasta* 'dough' (5.53).

Fr. *pétrir*, fr. VLat. *pistrīre* or *pistūrīre*, deriv. of Lat. *pistor* 'baker', *pīnsere* 'crush, pound'. REW 6542. Gamillscheg 690.

Sp. *amasar*, denom. of *masa* 'dough' (5.52).

Rum. *frămînta*, fr. VLat. *fragmen-*

5.55 MEAL, FLOUR

Grk.	ἄλευρον	Goth.	....	Lith.	miltai
NG	ἀλεὑρι	ON	mjǫl	Lett.	milti
Lat.	farina	Dan.	mel	ChSl.	mǫka
It.	farina	Sw.	mjöl	SCr.	brašno
Fr.	farine	OE	melu	Boh.	mouka
Sp.	harina	ME	mele, flour	Pol.	mąka
Rum.	făină	NE	meal, flour	Russ.	muka
Ir.	men	Du.	meel	Skt.	piṣṭa-
NIr.	min	OHG	melo	Av.	pištra-
W.	blawd	MHG	mel		
Br.	bleud	NHG	mehl		

Words for 'meal' are mostly from verbs for 'grind' (5.56) or 'crush', one group from the name of a cereal.

1. From IE *mel-* 'grind' (5.56). Walde-P. 2.284 ff.

W. *blawd*, Br. *bleud*, OCorn. *blot* (Pedersen 1.52); ON *mjǫl*, OE *melu*, etc., general Gmc.; Lith. *miltai*, Lett. *milti*, OPruss. *meltan*; Hitt. *memal*.

2. Grk. ἄλευρον, NG ἀλεὑρι, fr. ἀλέω 'grind', as Arm. *aleur* 'meal', *ałauri* 'mill', fr. *ałam* 'grind' (5.56). Walde-P. 1.89.

3. Lat. *farīna* (> Romance words), SCr. *brašno* (ChSl. *brašĭno* 'food', 5.12) : Lat. *far* 'spelt, grain', Goth. *barizeins* 'made of barley', OE *bere* 'barley', etc. Walde-P. 2.134. Ernout-M. 330. Walde-H. 1.455.

4. Ir. *men*, NIr. *min* : Lith. *minti* 'tread, break flax, prepare skins', ChSl. *mǫti*, 'compress', etc. Walde-P. 2.263.

5. ME, NE *flour*, the same word as *flower*, came to be used of the flower or finest part of the meal, then especially though not exclusively for the fine meal

of wheat, leaving *meal* for the coarser products. NED s.v.

6. ChSl. *mǫka*, Boh. *mouka*, Pol. *mąka*, Russ. *muka* : ChSl. *mękŭkŭ* 'soft', Lith. *minklė* 'knead', etc. (5.54). Walde-P. 2.268. Brückner 327.

7. Skt. *piṣṭa*, Av. *pištra-* : Skt. *piṣ-*, Lat. *pīnsere* 'crush', etc. (5.56).

5.56 GRIND

Grk.	ἀλέω	Goth.	malan	Lith.	malti
NG	ἀλέθω	ON	mala	Lett.	malt
Lat.	molere	Dan.	male	ChSl.	mlěti
It.	macinare	Sw.	mala	SCr.	mlijeti
Fr.	moudre	OE	grindan	Boh.	mlíti
Sp.	moler	ME	grinde	Pol.	mleć
Rum.	măcina	NE	grind	Russ.	molot'
Ir.	melim	Du.	malen	Skt.	(piṣ-)
NIr.	meilim	OHG	malan	Av.	....
W.	malu	MHG	maln, malen		
Br.	mala	NHG	mahlen		

The earliest process of converting grain into meal was 'crushing' by pounding, whence later the 'grinding' between two stones. For the earlier process there is a distinctive group of cognates, namely Grk. πτίσσω (also 'winnow'), Lat. *pīnsere*, Skt. *piṣ* (Walde-P. 2.1. Ernout-M. 770). But such was also the more original force of IE *mel-*, which furnishes most of the European words for 'grind' and 'mill', but shows its earlier sense in Arm. *malen* 'pound, bruise', Skt. *mr̥-, mr̥d-* 'crush', Lat. *mollis* 'soft', Toch. A *malyw-, B mely-* 'press, tread' (SSS 454).

1. IE *mel-*. Walde-P. 2.284 ff. Ernout-M. 626 f.

Lat. *molere* (> Fr. *moudre*, Sp. *moler*); Ir. *mèlim*, NIr. *meilim*, W. *malu*, Br. *mala*; Goth. *malan*, ON *mala*, etc.,

general Gmc. except in English; Lith. *malti*, Lett. *malt*; ChSl. *mlěti*, etc., general Slavic; Hitt. 3 sg. *mallai*, 3 pl. *mallanzi* (Sturtevant, Hitt. Gram. 243 f.).

2. Grk. ἀλέω, late ἀλήθω, NG ἀλέθω : Arm. *ałam* 'grind', *ałauri* 'mill', *aleur*, 'meal', Skt. *aṇu-* 'fine, thin'. Walde-P. 1.89. Boisacq 43.

3. It. *macinare*, Rum. *măcina*, fr. VLat. *machināre* a new denom. of Lat. *machina* 'machine', with specialization to 'grind'. REW 5206.

4. OE *grindan*, ME *grinde*, NE *grind* : Du. *grind, grint* 'gravel, coarse meal', Lat. *frendere* 'crush, bruise, gnash the teeth', Lith. *grendu, grȩsti* 'rub, scrape', etc. Walde-P. 1.656 ff. Walde-H. 1.545.

5. Skt. *piṣ-* 'crush', representing the earlier process, whence *piṣṭa-* 'meal', see above.

5.57 MILL
(Words in parentheses 'Handmill')

Grk.	μὑλη, μὑλος	Goth.	-qairnus	Lith.	malunas (girnos)
NG	μὑλος	ON	kvern, mylna	Lett.	sudmalas (dzirnavas)
Lat.	molae, molina	Dan.	mølle (kvern)	ChSl.	žrŭnŭvi, žrŭny
It.	mulino	Sw.	kvarn	SCr.	mlin (žrvanj)
Fr.	moulin	OE	cweorn, mylen	Boh.	mlýn (žerna)
Sp.	molino	ME	mylne, mille (quern)	Pol.	młyn (žarna)
Rum.	moară (rîşniţă)	NE	mill (quern)	Russ.	mel'nica
Ir.	brāo, mulenn	Du.	molen	Skt.	(peṣaṇa-)
NIr.	muileann (brō)	OHG	mulī(n) (quirn)	Av.	(suduš-)
W.	melin (breuan)	MHG	mul(e) (kürne)		
Br.	milin (breo)	NHG	mühle		

'Mill' is understood here in the original sense of 'grist-mill, flour-mill', not in the extended sense of NE *mill* in *sawmill, woolen-mill*, etc., which is foreign to the other words for 'mill' and is expressed rather by words for 'factory', 'workshop', or the like.

Most of the words for 'mill' are derivatives of IE *mel-* 'crush, grind', but in large part through the medium of Latin.

1. From IE *mel-* 'crush, grind' (5.56). Walde-P. 2.284 ff. Ernout-M. 626.

Grk. μὑλη (Hom.), later μὑλος 'mill' or 'millstone', also μυλών 'mill' (as the place), NG μὑλος 'mill' : Lat. *mola* 'millstone' (> Fr. *meule*, Sp. *muela* 'millstone', Rum. *moară* 'mill'), pl. *molae* 'millstones' = 'mill'.

Late Lat. *molīna, molīnum*, whence It. *mulino*, Fr. *moulin*, Sp. *molino*; Ir. *mulenn*, NIr. *muileann*, W. *melin*, Br. *milin*; ON *mylna*, Dan. *mølle*, OE *mylen, myln*, ME *mylne, mille*, etc., NE *mill*, Du. *molen*, OHG *mulī(n)*, NHG *mühle*; Lith. *malunas*, OPruss. *malunis*; SCr. *mlin*, Boh. *mlýn*, Pol. *młyn*, Russ. *mel'nica*. REW 5644. Pedersen 1.194. Falk-Torp 749.

Lett. *sudmalas*, cpd. of which the first part *sud-* is obscure, possibly fr. *suta* 'vapor, steam, seapage', with first appli-

cation of the word to a water-mill(?). Mühl.-Endz. 3.1114.

2. Rum. *rîşniţă* 'handmill', fr. a Slavic deriv. of the word for 'hand', ChSl. *rǫka*, etc. Tiktin 1329.

3. Goth. *-qairnus* (*asilu-qairnus* lit. trans. of μὑλος ὀνικός used of the upper 'millstone'), ON *kvern*, Sw. *kvarn*, OE *cweorn*, ME, NE *quern*, etc.; Ir. *brāo*, W. *breuan*, Br. *breo*; Lith. *girnos* (pl.), Lett. *dzirnavas* (pl.), OPruss. *girnoywis*, ChSl. *žrŭnŭvi* (pl.), also *žrŭny*, etc. : Skt. *grāvan-* 'stone for pressing the soma', Arm. *erkan* 'millstone' and prob. Skt. *guru-*, Grk. βαρύς 'heavy', IE *gʷer-*. Walde-P. 1.685. Feist 59. Meillet, Mélanges Boyer 1 ff. The words of this group meant first 'millstone', then especially in plural (like Lat. *molae*) 'mill'. After the spread of Lat. *molīna* (above, 1), they mostly survived only in the sense of 'handmill' or sometimes 'millstone'. Only Sw. *kvarn* is still the usual general word for 'mill', but frequently in general sense also Icel. *kvörn* and Lett. *dzirnavas* (Mühl.-Endz. 1.555).

4. Skt. *peṣaṇa-*, quoted as 'handmill' (BR s.v.), but mostly the act of 'crushing', fr. *piṣ-* 'crush' (5.56).

Av. *suduš-*, but meaning and etym. dub. Barth. 1583.

5.61 MEAT

Grk.	κρέας	Goth.	mimz	Lith.	mėsa
NG	κρέας	ON	kjǫt	Lett.	gaľa
Lat.	carō	Dan.	kød	ChSl.	męso
It.	carne	Sw.	kött	SCr.	meso
Fr.	viande	OE	flǣsc	Boh.	maso
Sp.	carne	ME	fleshe	Pol.	mięso
Rum.	carne	NE	meat	Russ.	mjaso
Ir.	feōil, cūa	Du.	vleesch	Skt.	māṅsa-
NIr.	feoil	OHG	fleisk	Av.	gav-
W.	cig	MHG	vleisch		
Br.	kig	NHG	fleisch		

Words for 'meat' are mostly the same as those for 'flesh' (4.13). The exceptions are:

Fr. *viande*, 'meat' (*chair* 'flesh'), orig. 'food' (cf. NE *viands*) fr. Lat. *vīvenda* 'means of life, sustenance'. REW 9410.

ON *kjǫt* always 'meat' (*hǫrund* 'flesh') but orig. also 'flesh', as Dan. *kød*, Sw. *kött* (4.13).

NE *meat*, orig. 'food' (5.12). NED s.v. Lett. *gaľa* 'meat' (*miesa* 'flesh'), possibly as orig. 'raw meat' : Slav. *golŭ* 'naked'. Mühl.-Endz. 1.598. Or better (suggestion of F. K. Wood) as orig. 'portion' (like Lat. *carō* 'flesh, meat' fr. 'portion', 4.13) : Lett. *gals*, Lith. *galas* 'end', the latter used also for 'piece' (of bread, etc.).

5.612 BUTCHER

Grk.	κρεοπώλης	Goth.	....	Lith.	mėsininkas
NG	μακελλάρης, καοάπης, κρεοπώλης	ON	....	Lett.	miesnieks
Lat.	lanius, macellārius	Dan.	slagter	ChSl.	....
It.	macellaro, beccaio	Sw.	slaktare	SCr.	mesar
Fr.	boucher	OE	hyldere, cwellere	Boh.	řezník
Sp.	carnicero	ME	bo(u)cher, slaghter-man	Pol.	rzeźnik
Rum.	măcelar			Russ.	mjasnik
Ir.	....	NE	butcher	Skt.	māṅsika-
NIr.	bûistēir	Du.	slager	Av.	....
W.	cigydd	OHG	slahtari		
Br.	kiger	MHG	vleischslachter, vleisch-houwer, metzjære		
		NHG	fleischer, metzger, schlächter		

The 'butcher' was primarily the one who slaughters large domestic animals for their meat, then the one who cuts up the meat in the shop and sells it, simply a dealer in 'meat'.

Several of the words are derived from verbs for 'slaughter' or 'cut' (a 'cutter' may be specialized to 'butcher' or 'tailor'). The majority are derived from words for 'flesh, meat' (4.13, 5.61). A small group shows generalization from 'one who slaughters goats or deals in goat's flesh'.

1. Grk. σφαγεύς (: σφάζω 'slaughter', esp. animals for sacrifice) is used for 'slayer, murderer' and technically for the one who slaughters the sacrificial victims, but is not quotable as a tradesman's name. Instead we have κρεο-κόπος, -ποιός (both rare), and esp. κρεο-, κρεω-πώλης (as in NG), cpds. of κρέας

'flesh, meat' with words for 'cut', 'make', and 'sell'.

NG χασάπης, fr. Turk. *kasap* 'butcher'.

2. Lat. *lanius*, late *laniō*, beside vb. *laniāre* 'tear in pieces, mangle', perh. of Etruscan origin. Walde-P. 2.434. Ernout-M. 522. Walde-H. 1.759 f.

Lat. *macellārius* (> It. *macellaro*, *macelaio*, Rum. *măcelar*, NG μακελλάρης), fr. *macellum* 'market', esp. 'meat-market', this fr. Grk. μάκελλον 'inclosure' (IG 4².1.102, etc., 4th cent. B.C.; pl. in Hesych.; late μάκελλος as 'market' after Lat.), this again of Semitic orig. (cf. Hebr. *miklā* 'inclosure'). Ernout-M. 575. Walde-H. 2.1.

Fr. *boucher* (OFr. *bochier, bouchier* > ME *bocher, boucher*, NE *butcher*), fr. *bouc*, OFr. *boc* 'he-goat', hence orig. 'one who slaughters he-goats' (young he-goats were regularly killed for their meat except for a few reserved for breeding). REW 1378. Wartburg 1.587 f. Otherwise Gamillscheg 125.

It. *beccaio*, fr. *becco* 'he-goat'.

Sp. *carnicero*, fr. *carne* 'flesh, meat'.

3. NIr. *bûistēir*, fr. NE *butcher* (for transposition of *tš*, cf. Pedersen 1.230).

W. *cigydd*, Br. *kiger*, fr. W. *cig*, Br. *kig* 'flesh, meat'.

4. Dan. *slagter*, Sw. *slaktare*, ME *slaghterman*, Du. *slager*, OHG *slahtari* (killer of sacrificial victims), MHG *vleischslahter*, NHG *schlächter* (or *schlach-*

ter), all fr. vbs. for 'slaughter' (: Goth. *slahan*, etc. 'strike, slay' 9.21).

OE *hyldere* (fr. *hyldan* 'flay', 9.29) and *cwellere* (: *cwellan* 'kill', 4.76) occur as glosses to Lat. *laniō*, *macellārius*.

ME *bo(u)cher*, NE *butcher*, fr. OFr. *bo(u)chier* (above, 2).

MHG *vleischhouwer*, NHG *fleischer* (locally also *fleischhauer, fleischhacker*), fr. *fleisch* 'flesh, meat'.

MHG *metzeler*, fr. *metzeln* 'slaughter', this fr. late Lat. *macellāre* 'slaughter' (cf. *macellārius*, above, 2).

MHG *metzjære*, NHG *metzger*, perh. in form fr. MLat. *matiārius* 'sausage-dealer', fr. *matia* 'intestine' (CGL 6.684 *matia intestina, unde matiarii dicuntur qui eadem tractant vel vendunt*), but influenced by *metzjen* beside *metzeln* 'slaughter' (above). Weigand-H. 2.178. Kluge-G. 390. Kretschmer, Wortgeogr. 416, ftn. On the distribution of the NHG words, cf. Kretschmer, op. cit. 412 ff.

5. Lith. *mėsininkas*, Lett. *miesnieks*, fr. Lith. *mėsa* 'flesh, meat', Lett. *miesa* 'flesh'.

6. SCr. *mesar*, Russ. *mjasnik*, fr. SCr. *meso*, Russ. *mjaso* 'flesh, meat'.

Boh. *řezník*, Pol. *rzeźnik*, fr. Boh. *řezati*, Pol. *rznǫć* 'cut' (9.22).

7. Skt. *māṅsika-* (rare), fr. *māṅsa-* 'flesh, meat'.

5.62 BEEF

Grk.	βό(ε)ιον κρέας	Goth.	....	Lith.	jautiena
NG	βοδινό	ON	oxakjǫt	Lett.	versu gaľa
Lat.	būbula	Dan.	oxeksød	ChSl.	....
It.	carne de bue	Sw.	oxkött	SCr.	govedina
Fr.	bœuf	OE	hrīðeren flǣsc	Boh.	hovězina
Sp.	carne de vaca	ME	boef	Pol.	wolowina
Rum.	carne de vitǎ	NE	beef	Russ.	govjadina
Ir.	martfeōil	Du.	rundvleesch	Skt.	gomāṅsa-
NIr.	mairtfheoil	OHG	rinderin	Av.	gao-
W.	cig eidion, biff	MHG	rintvleisch		
Br.	bevin	NHG	rindfleisch		

Words for 'beef' are chosen as typical of the names of meats in general. These are regularly from the animal names, (1) without change (cf. NE *lamb, chicken*, and the whole Fr. series *bœuf, veau, mouton, agneau, porc*), (2) with a derivative suffix (so regularly in Lith. and Slavic), or (3) cpds. or phrases with the words for 'meat' (5.61). In English a difference has been established by the fact that the Fr. words, used for the animal and the meat, were borrowed and restricted (in the main) to the latter sense in contrast to the native animal names. So NE *beef, veal, mutton, pork*. Cf. also Norw. *sau* 'sheep', but *får* (Dan. *faar* 'sheep') 'mutton'. NHG *rindfleisch, kalbfleisch*, but for 'mutton' not *schaffleisch* but *hammelfleisch* or locally *schöpsenfleisch*, fr. words for 'wether'. Kretschmer, Wortgeogr. 228 f. Cf. It. *castrato* 'mutton'.

1. Words for 'beef' connected with those for 'cattle', 'ox', or 'cow' (3.21–3.23).

(1) Without change. Fr. *bœuf* (> ME *boef*, NE *beef* > W. *biff*), Av. *gao-* (cf. Barth. 507–8).

(2) With suffix. NG βοδινό, Lat. *būbula*, Br. *bevin* (fr. Lat. *bovīnum*), OHG *rinderīn*, Lith. *jautiena*, SCr. *govedina*, Pol. *wolowina*, etc.

(3) Cpds. ON *oxakjǫt*, Dan. *oxeksød*,

Sw. *oxkött*, Du. *rundvleesch*, MHG *rintvleisch*, NHG *rindfleisch*, Skt. *gomāṅsa-*.

(4) Phrases. Grk. βό(ε)ιον κρέας (quotable only in pl.; the sg. would be 'piece of beef'; cf. ἄρνεια κρέα, etc.), It., Sp., Rum. *carne de bue, de vaca, de vitǎ* respectively, W. *cig eidion*, OE *hrīðeren flǣsc* (cf. NED s.v. *rotheren*), Lett. *versu gaľa*.

2. Ir. *martfeōil*, NIr. *mairtfheoil*, cpds. of word for 'flesh, meat' with *mart* 'the carcass of an ox or cow slain for food' (cf. Laws, Gloss. s.v.), orig. 'dead body', fr. the root in *marbh*, Lat. *mortuus* 'dead' (4.75). Loth, RC. 41.56.

There are some names for meats that are from a different source, the result of specialization, as for example:

The old Gmc. word for 'flesh, meat' is specialized to 'pork, bacon' in the Scand. languages, as ON, Dan. *flesk*, Sw. *fläsk*.

A word denoting a certain part of any animal may be used specifically for the meat of that part of a particular animal. So words for 'ham' mainly that of swine, as NE *ham*, once 'hollow back of the knee', 'back of the thigh, buttock' (cf. NED s.v.), NHG *schinken* (: *schenkel* 'thigh'), Fr. *jambon* (: *jambe* 'leg'), Russ. *okorok* (: SCr. *krak* 'thigh'), etc. Cf. also NE *bacon* (: *back*), NHG *speck* 'bacon' (: OE *spic* 'fat, fat meat or bacon', etc.).

5.63 SAUSAGE

Grk.	ἀλλᾶς	Goth.	....	Lith.	dešra
NG	λουκάνικο	ON	mǫr-bjūga	Lett.	desa
Lat.	farcīmen, lūcānica, botulus	Dan.	pølse	ChSl.	....
It.	salsiccia	Sw.	korv	SCr.	kobasica
Fr.	saucisse, boudin	OE	mearh(?)	Boh.	jitrnice (klobása)
Sp.	salchicha	ME	sausige	Pol.	kiełbasa
Rum.	cîrnaţ	NE	sausage	Russ.	kolbasa
Ir.	mar, maróc	Du.	worst		
NIr.	maróg	OHG	wurst		
W.	selsig	MHG	wurst		
Br.	silzig	NHG	wurst		

1. Grk. ἀλλᾶς, fr. *ἀλλᾶεις, *ἀλλᾶϝευτ-, of Italiot Doric orig., with ἀλλᾶ- (cf. Hesych. ἀλλήν· λάχανον Ἰταλοί) borrowed fr. an Italic dialect form of Lat. *alium* 'garlic'. Kretschmer, Glotta 1.323 ff. Walde-H. 1.30.

NG λουκάνικο, see below, 2.

2. Lat. *farcīmen*, fr. *farcīre* 'stuff'.

Lat. *lūcānica* (also *-cus, -cum*, and *lūcāna*) a kind of sausage invented by the Lucanians. Hence dialect words in northern Italy, etc. and NG λουκάνικο. Ernout-M. 563. REW 5134. G. Meyer, Neugr. Stud. 3.39.

Lat. *botulus* (source of Fr. *boudin*? REW 1192. Wartburg 1.423), loanword fr. an Osc.-Umbr. dial. (with labial for orig. labio-velar, as in *popīna*, etc.) : Goth. *qiþus* 'belly, womb', Grk. γύαλον 'hollow', etc. Walde-P. 1.560, 671. Ernout-M. 116. Walde-H. 1.112.

It. *salsiccia* (> Sp. *salchicha*), OFr. *saussiche* (> ME *sausige*, NE *sausage*), Fr. *saucisse*, W. *selsig*, Br. *silzig*, fr. late Lat. *salsicia* (neut. pl. > fem. sg.), prob. cpd. of *salsus* 'salt' and *(in)sicium* 'mincemeat'. REW 4551. Gröber, Arch. lat. Lex. 3.272 f. Loth, Mots lat. 206.

Rum. *cîrnaţ*, fr. VLat. **carnāceus* 'made of meat'. REW 1701. Puşcariu 374.

3. Ir. *mar*, dim. *maróc*, NIr. *maróg*, loanword fr. ON *mǫrr* (below, 4). K. Meyer, RC 12.461.

4. ON *mǫrbjūga*, cpd. of *mǫrr* 'fat', suet' (by-form of *smǫr* 'fat, butter' : OE *smeoru* 'fat, suet', etc. Falk-Torp 1086) and *bjūga* (also once 'sausage') : *bjūgr* 'crooked, bent', etc.

Dan. *pølse* : LG *pole*, Du. *peul* 'pod, husk', NE *pulse* (otherwise NED), Lat. *bulla* 'knob'. Hence 'sausage' fr. its podlike container. Falk-Torp 863.

Sw. *korv*, Norw. *kurv* : Norw. dial. *kurva* 'to bend, crook'. Falk-Torp 597. Hellquist 501.

OE *mearh* 'marrow' (: ON *mergr*, Skt. *majjan-*, Av. *mazga-* 'marrow', ChSl. *mozga* 'brain', etc. Walde-P. 2.309) once glosses Lat. *lucānica*, but there seems to be no confirmation for this use for 'sausage'. NED s.v. *marrow*.

OHG-NHG *wurst*, Du. *worst*, etym. disputed, but prob. a deriv. of OHG *werdan*, etc., in its orig. meaning 'turn' (Lat. *vertere*, etc.), applied to the bent roll of a sausage, like ON *bjūga* and Sw. *korv* (above). Other views in Weigand-H. and Kluge-G. s.v.

5. Lith. *dešra*, Lett. *desa*, etym.? SCr. *kobasica*, Boh. *klobása*, Pol. *kiełbasa*, Russ. *kolbasa*, perh. a loanword, through Jewish butchers, fr. Hebr. *kolbāsar* 'all kinds of meat'. Berneker 542.

Boh. *jitrnice*, orig. 'liver-sausage' (fr. *játra* 'liver'), now generalized at the expense of *klobása*.

5.64 SOUP, BROTH

Grk.	*ζωμός*	Goth.	. . . .	Lith.	*sriuba*
NG	*σούπα, ζουμί*	ON	*broð*	Lett.	*zupa, strēbiens*
Lat.	*iūs*	Dan.	*suppe*	ChSl.	*jucha*
It.	*zuppa, minestra, brodo*	Sw.	*soppa*	SCr.	*juha, supa, čorba*
		OE	*broþ*	Boh.	*polévka*
Fr.	*soupe, potage, bouillon*	ME	*broth*	Pol.	*zupa, rosół, polewka*
		NE	*soup, broth*	Russ.	*sup (ucha)*
Sp.	*sopa, caldo*	Du.	*soep*	Skt.	*yūṣa-, sūpa-*
Rum.	*supă, ciorbă*	OHG	*prod*	Av.	. . . .
Ir.	*enbruithe*	MHG	*brüeje, suppe*		
NIr.	*anbhruith, brachān*	NHG	*suppe, brühe*		
W.	*potes, cawl*				
Br.	*soubenn*				

Most of the words listed cover what in current use is partly distinguished, as NE *soup* vs. *broth*, Fr. *soupe* vs. *bouillon*, etc.

1. Derivs. of IE **yeu-* 'mix', ultimately the same as **yeu-* 'unite'. Walde-P. 1.199. Ernout-M. 508. Walde-H. 1.734. Pedersen 1.65.

Grk. *ζωμός*, NG *ζουμί* ('juice' and 'broth'); Lat. *iūs;* (Ir. *īth*, OW *iot*, Br. *yod* 'porridge'); Lith. *jūšė* ('fish soup'), OPruss. *juse;* ChSl. *jucha*, SCr. *juha* (Boh. *jicha* 'sauce, gravy'), Russ. *ucha* ('fish soup'); Skt. *yūṣa-*.

2. The widespread modern Eur. group goes back, mostly through Fr. *soupe*, to a Gmc. *suppa*, attested in MLat. *suppa* 'sop' (Oribas. trans., cf. Thomas, Mél. Havet 525), ON *soppa* 'wine-soup', OE *soppe* 'sop', OHG *sopha, soffa* 'broth with softened bread' : ON *sūpa*, OE *sūpan* 'sup', Skt. *sūpa-* 'soup', fr. **seup-*, **seub-*, extensions of **seu-* in Skt. *su-* 'press out juice', etc., perh. ultimately of imitative orig. Thus Fr. *soupe*, in 13th cent. 'sop, bit of bread softened with broth or wine' (still surviving in the phrase *ivre comme une soupe*), then 'soup', is in the latter sense the source of ME *soupe*, NE *soup*, Du. *soep*, Br. *soubenn*, Rum. *supă* (recent), Russ. *sup*, and semantically at least (some of the forms go back to the Gmc. *suppa*) of It. *zuppa* (> NG *σοῦπα*), Sp. *sopa*, Dan. *suppe*, Sw. *soppe*, late MHG, NHG *suppe* (> Lett. *zupa*, SCr. *supa*, Pol. *zupa*). Walde-P. 2.468 f. REW 8464. Falk-Torp 1205.

3. It. *minestra, minestrone* (esp. 'vegetable soup'), orig. any 'prepared food', fr. *minestrare*, Lat. *ministrāre* 'serve'. REW 5590.

It. *brodo*, Sp. *brodio, bodrio*, MLat. *brodum, brodium*, fr. OHG *brod* (below, 5).

Fr. *bouillon*, fr. *bouillir* 'boil' (10.31).

Fr. *potage* (> ME *potage* > W. *potes*), orig. a 'stew', fr. *pot* 'pot' (5.26).

Sp. *caldo* 'broth', orig. 'hot' fr. Lat. *calidus* (15.85).

Rum. *ciorbă*, SCr. *čorba*, fr. Turk. *çorba* 'soup'. Berneker 159 f. Lokotsch 440.

4. Ir. *enbruithe*, NIr. *anbhruith* : Ir. *berbaim*, W. *berwi*, Lat. *fervēre* 'boil', etc. (10.31). Walde-P. 2.167 f. Pedersen 1.115.

NIr. *brachān* 'broth, gruel', orig. 'fermented matter' : *brachaim* 'ferment', Ir. *mraich, braich* 'malt', Lat. *marcēre* 'wither', etc. Walde-P. 2.282. Pedersen 1.163.

W. *cawl*, orig. 'cabbage' (5.70), hence through 'cabbage-soup' now 'soup, broth'.

5. ON *broð*, OE *broþ*, ME, NE *broth*, OHG *prod*, also MHG *brüeje*, NHG *brühe* 'broth' : OHG *briuwan*

'brew', Lat. *fervēre*, MIr. *berbaim* 'boil', etc. Walde-P. 2.157, 168. On distribution of NHG *brühe* vs. *suppe*, cf. Kretschmer, Wortgeogr. 156 f.

6. Lith. *sriuba*, Lett. *strēbiens* : Lith. *sriopti, srėbti*, Lett. *strebt* 'sup, sip, suck', Lat. *sorbēre*, Grk. *ῥοφέω* 'sup up, gulp down', etc. Walde-P. 2.704. Mühl.-Endz. 3.1087.

Boh. *polévka*, Pol. *polewka*, fr. Boh. *polívati*, Po. *polewać*, ChSl. *polivati* 'pour on', iter. cpd. of *liti* 'pour'. Berneker 709.

Pol. *rosół* : Russ. *razsol*, SCr. *rasol* 'brine, pickle', cpd. of *raz-*, Pol. *roz-* and *sol* 'salt'. Brückner 463, 506 f.

7. Skt. *yūṣa-, sūpa-*, above, 1, 2.

5.65 VEGETABLES

Grk.	*λάχανα*	Goth.	*gras*	Lith.	*daržovės*
NG	*λάχανα, χόρτα*	ON	*urt*	Lett.	*dārzaji*
Lat.	*(h)olus*	Dan.	*grøntsager*	ChSl.	*zelĭje*
It.	*legumi, verdura*	Sw.	*grönsaker*	SCr.	*povrce*
Fr.	*légumes*	OE	*wyrte*	Boh.	*zelenina*
Sp.	*legumbres, verdura*	ME	*wortes*	Pol.	*jarzyna, warzywo*
Rum.	*legume, zarzavat*	NE	*vegetables*	Russ.	*zeleń, ovošč*
Ir.	. . . .	Du.	*groenten*	Skt.	*çāka-*
NIr.	*glasraidh*	OHG	*wurzī*	Av.	. . . .
W.	*llysiau*	MHG	*gemuese*		
Br.	*louzou(-kegin*, etc.)	NHG	*gemüse*		

The words for 'vegetables' are partly singular collectives, partly words that are used nearly always in the plural, though some of these may be used also in the singular for 'a vegetable'.

'Vegetables' are simply edible plants and are sometimes denoted only by the general word for 'plant, herb' (8.53). The commonest source is words for 'green' or 'growing'; some are from words for 'garden'; some are specialized from 'food' or 'fruit'.

1. Lat. *(h)olus*, early *helus*, ChSl. *zelĭje*, Boh. *zelenina*, Russ. *zeleń* : Lat. *helvus* 'yellowish red', Lith. *žalias* 'green', *žolė* 'grass', ChSl. *zelenŭ* 'green', etc. (15.68), words applied to the 'green' or 'yellow' of growing things. Walde-P. 1.624 f. Ernout-M. 456. Walde-H. 1.654.

2. Grk., NG *λάχανα* (NG sg. 'cabbage') : Grk. *λαχαίνω* 'dig' (8.22).

NG *χόρτα*, esp. 'greens' but also 'vegetables', pl. of *χόρτο* 'herb', fr. class. Grk. *χόρτος* 'fodder, grass' (8.51).

3. It. *legumi*, Fr. *légumes*, Sp. *legumbres*, Rum. *legume*, fr. Lat. *legūmen* 'leguminous plant', etym. dub. Ernout-M. 538. Walde-H. 1.781. REW 4972.

It., Sp. *verdura* properly 'verdure', but also 'vegetables, deriv. of It., Sp. *verde*, Lat. *viridis* 'green'. REW 9368a.

Rum. *zarzavat*, fr. Turk. *zerzavat* 'vegetables'. Tiktin 1797. Lokotsch 1747.

4. NIr. *glasraidh*, deriv. of *glass* 'green' (15.68).

W. *llysiau*, Br. *louzou* 'plants, herbs' (8.53), also 'vegetables', in Br. esp. cpds. with *kegin* 'kitchen', *pod* 'pot', or *taol* 'table'.

5. Goth. *gras* (for *λάχανα* Rom. 14.2; gen. pl. *grasē* Mk. 4.32) = ON *gras*, OE *græs*, etc. 'grass' (8.51).

ON *urt*, OE *wyrt*, OHG *wurz* 'plant, herb' (8.53) served also for 'vegetable', and OE *wyrte* (pl.), OHG *wurz*, pl. *wurzī* frequently gloss Lat. *olus* or *olera*. Cf. also OE *wyrt-mete*, lit. 'plant-food'.

Dan. *grøntsager*, Sw. *grönsaker*, lit. 'green things', fr Dan. *grøn*, Sw. *grön*

'green' and Dan. *sag*, Sw. *sak* 'thing'. So Du. *groenten*, fr. *groen* 'green'.

NE *vegetables*, sb. use of adj. *vegetable*, fr. OFr. *vegetable* 'capable of growing', Lat. *vegetābilis* 'animating, vivifying', deriv. of *vegetāre*, iter. of *vegēre* 'move, quicken' beside *vigēre* 'be lively' : Skt. *vāja-* 'strength', etc. Walde-P. 1.246 f. Ernout-M. 1079, 1107.

MHG (late) *gemüese*, NHG *gemüse*, orig. 'cooked food of garden produce', then the 'garden produce itself', collective of OHG, MHG *muos* 'food' (5.12). Weigand-H. 1.674.

6. Lith. *daržovės*, Lett. *dārzaji*, fr. Lith. *daržas*, Lett. *dārzs* 'garden' (8.13), hence lit. 'garden produce'. Cf. SCr. *povrce* (below). Mühl.-Endz. 1.448.

ChSl. *zelĭje*, etc., above, 1.

SCr. *povrce*, fr. **po-vrt-je*, lit. 'what is in the garden' : *vrt* 'garden' (8.13).

Pol. *warzywo* (Boh. *vařivo* 'eatables') : *warzyć* 'boil, cook' (5.21). Brückner 633.

Pol. *jarzyna*, fr. *jarz* 'spring', hence lit. 'product of spring'. Brückner 199.

Russ. *ovošč* = ChSl. *ovoštĭ*, Pol. *owoc* 'fruit', a loanword fr. Gmc., OHG *obaz*, NHG *obst* 'fruit' (5.71). Brückner 388.

7. Skt. *çāka-* : Lith. *šėkas*, Lett. *sēks* 'green hay', OPruss. *schokis* 'grass', root connection? Walde-P. 1.381.

5.66 BEAN

Grk.	*κύαμος, φάσηλος*	Goth.	. . . .	Lith.	*pupa*
NG	*κουκκί, φασούλι*	ON	*baun*	Lett.	*pupa*
Lat.	*faba, phasēlus*	Dan.	*bønne*	ChSl.	*bobŭ*
It.	*fava, fagiuolo*	Sw.	*böna*	SCr.	*grah, bob, pasulj*
Fr.	*fève, haricot*	OE	*bēan*	Boh.	*bob, fazol*
Sp.	*haba, frijol, judía*	ME	*bene*	Pol.	*bób, fasola*
Rum.	*fasole*	NE	*bean*	Russ.	*bob, fasol'*
Ir.	*seib*	Du.	*boon*	Skt.	*māṣa-*
NIr.	*pōnaire* (pl.)	OHG	*bōna*	Av.	. . . .
W.	*ffäen*	MHG	*bōne, fasōl*		
Br.	*favenn*	NHG	*bohne, fasole*		

Both the unripe pod and the grown seeds of the 'bean' are common articles of food. In several languages, instead of a comprehensive term like NE *bean*, there are two words, distinguished according to the variety. The commonest source is the notion of 'swelling'.

1. Grk. *κύαμος* : *κυέω* 'be pregnant', orig. 'be swollen' : Skt. *çvā-, çū-* 'swell', etc. This etym., questioned by Walde-P. 1.366, is perfect formally (*κυα-* from dissyllabic root, parallel to *πρια-* in *πρίαμαι* : Skt. *krī-*) and semantically.

Grk. *φάσηλος* (> Lat. *phasēlus*), of obscure formation, and possibly a pre-Greek loanword, but the first syllable *φα-* is prob. the same as that of Lat. *faba*, etc. (below, 2). Later forms *φασήολος*, *φασίολος*, whence NG *φασόλι, φασούλι* (> Rum. *fasole*, SCr. *pasulj*), Lat. *phaseolus* (> It. *fagiuolo*, Sp. *frijol*, MHG *fasōl*, NHG *fas(e)ole* > Boh. *fazol*, Pol. *fasola*, Russ. *fasol'*). REW 6464. Berneker 280. Kretschmer, Wortgeogr. 135 ff., 603.

NG *κουκκί* fr. Grk. *κοκκίον*, dim. of *κόκκος* 'kernel, berry' (5.80).

2. Lat. *faba* (> It. *fava*, Fr. *fève*, Sp. *haba;* Ir. *seib*, etc., below, 3); OPruss. *babo*, ChSl. *bobŭ*, SCr., Boh. *bob*, Russ. *bob*, perh. fr. a reduplicated form **bha-bha-* with the notion of 'swelling'. Walde-P. 1.131. Ernout-M. 318 f. Walde-H. 1.436. Berneker 65.

Fr. *haricot*, fr. Mexican *ayacotli*

'bean'. REW 847. Gamillscheg 508. Wartburg 1.190.

Sp. *judía*, fr. *haba Judía* 'Jewish bean'. Cf. NE *lima bean*, NHG *türkische bohne*, etc. Rohlfs, Z. rom. Ph. 40.340.

3. Ir. *seib*, W. *ffa* (coll.; sg. *ffäen*), Br. *fao, fā* (coll. pl.; sg. *favenn*) fr. Lat. *faba*. Vendryes, De hib. voc. 176. Loth, Mots lat. 166.

NIr. *pōnaire* (pl.) fr. ON *baunir*, pl. of *baun* 'bean' (below, 4). Marstrander, Bidrag 59, 96.

4. ON *baun*, OE *bēan*, etc., general Gmc., prob. : Goth. *ufbauljan* 'cause to swell up, blow up', OHG *būlla*, OE *byle* 'boil', and other words containing **bhu-*, **bheu-* with the notion of 'swelling' (Walde-P. 2.114 ff.). But some derive from a reduplicated form like Lat. *faba*, etc. (above, 2), which amounts to the same thing semantically. So Walde-P. 2.131.

5. Lith., Lett. *pupa* : Lett. *paupt* 'swell', *pups* 'woman's breast', Lat. *pūpus* 'small child', and other words containing **pū-*, **peu-*, with notion of 'swelling'. Walde-P. 2.79 ff. Against the view of borrowing fr. Slavic *bob* (accepted in Walde-P. 2.131 in contrast to 2.81) cf. Persson, Beiträge 246, ftn.

6. ChSl. *bobŭ*, etc., above, 2.

SCr. *grah*, orig. 'pea' (5.77).

7. Skt. *māṣa-* : NPers. *māš*, Pamir dial. *max* 'pea', prob. a loanword on one side or the other, and without known root connection. Uhlenbeck 223. Horn 960.

5.67 PEA

Grk.	*πίσος (ἐρέβινθος)*	Goth.	. . . .	Lith.	*žirnis*
NG	*(μ)πιζέλι (ρεβίθι)*	ON	*ertr* (pl.)	Lett.	*dzirnis*
Lat.	*pisum (cicer)*	Dan.	*ært*	ChSl.	. . . .
It.	*pisello*	Sw.	*ärt*	SCr.	*grašak*
Fr.	*pois*	OE	*pise*	Boh.	*hrách*
Sp.	*guisante*	ME	*pese*	Pol.	*groch*
Rum.	*mazăre*	NE	*pea (pease)*	Russ.	*goroch* (coll.)
Ir.	*piss*	Du.	*erwt*	Skt.	*kalāya-, satīna-*
NIr.	*pis*	OHG	*araweiz*	Av.	. . . .
W.	*pysen*	MHG	*arweiz*		
Br.	*pizenn*	NHG	*erbse*		

Most of the words for 'pea' are loanwords the ultimate source of which is obscure. But the Baltic and the Slavic words are connected with words in other IE languages meaning 'grain' or 'what is ground, rubbed'.

1. Grk. *πίσος, πίσον*, prob. of pre-Greek, Aegean orig. Hence, or from the same source, Lat. *pisum*. Boisacq 787. Ernout-M. 772.

Lat. *pisum* is the source of Fr. *pois*, Ir. *piss*, NIr. *pis*, W. *pysen*, Br. *pizenn*, OE *pise*, ME *pese*, NE *pease*, *pea* (new sg. fr. *pease* conceived as pl.). Lat. dim. *pisellum* > It. *pisello* > NG *(μ)πιζέλι*. Here also Sp. *guisante*, with complicated history, through an Arab. form fr. *pisum sapidum*. Corominas, Romance Ph. 1.87 ff.

2. Grk. *ἐρέβινθος* 'chick-pea' (> NG *ρεβίθι*), Lat. *ervum* 'vetch', and the Gmc. group ON *ertr* (pl.), Dan. *ært*, Sw. *ärta*, Du. *erwt*, OHG *araweiz*, NHG *erbse*, are prob. loanwords fr. some common but unknown source. Boisacq 273. Walde-H. 419 f. Falk-Torp 196.

3. Grk. *κριός*, Lat. *cicer* 'chick-pea' (> It. *cece*, OFr. *chiche* > ME *chick*, NE *chick-pea*), OPruss. *keckers* 'pea', also prob. loanwords fr. a common source. Walde-H. 1.212.

4. Rum. *mazăre* : Alb. *modhullë*, loan-

word of unknown source. G. Meyer. Alb. Etym. Wtb. 284 f.

5. Lith. *žirnis*, Lett. *dzirnis* : ChSl. *zrŭno*, Goth. *kaurn*, Lat. *grānum* 'grain', etc. (8.42). Walde-P. 1.599 f.

SCr. *grah* (but now 'bean', with deriv. *grašak* 'pea'), Boh. *hrách*, Pol. *groch*, Russ. *goroch* (coll.; *gorošina* 'a pea') : Skt. *ghṛṣ-* 'rub', etc. Walde-P. 1.605 f. Berneker 331 f.

6. Skt. *kalāya-*, *satīna-*, both obscure. Uhlenbeck 48, 326.

5.68 ONION

Grk.	κρόμμυον	Goth.	. . . .	Lith.	*svogūnas, cibulė*
NG	κρομμύδι, κρεμμύδι	ON	. . . .	Lett.	*sīpuols*
Lat.	*cēpa, ūniō*	Dan.	*rødløg*	ChSl.	. . . .
It.	*cipolla*	Sw.	*rödlök*	SCr.	*luk*
Fr.	*oignon*	OE	*cīpe, ynnelēac*	Boh.	*cibule*
Sp.	*cebolla*	ME	*unyon*	Pol.	*cebula*
Rum.	*ceapă*	NE	*onion*	Russ.	*luk*
Ir.	. . . .	Du.	*ui*	Skt.	*palāṇḍu-*
NIr.	*inniun*	OHG	*zwibolla*	Av.	. . . .
W.	*wynwynyn*	MHG	*zwibolle*		
Br.	*ognonenn*	NHG	*zwiebel*		

1. Grk. κρόμυον (Hom.), κρόμμυον (κρέμυον Hesych.), dim. κρομμύδιον > NG κρομμύδι, κρεμμύδι : Ir. *crem*, W. *craf*, OE *hramsa*, Lith. *kremušė* 'wild garlic'. Walde-P. 1.426. Boisacq 520.

2. Lat. *cēpa* (> Rum. *ceapă*, OFr. *cive*, Ir. *ciap* in *foltchep* 'porrum, capillosa cepa', OE *cīpe;* late dim. *cēpulla* > It. *cipolla*, Sp. *cebolla*, OHG *zwibolla*, etc. [pop. association with words for 'two' and 'ball']; MHG *zibolle* > Lith. *cibulė*, Boh. *cibule*, Pol. *cebula;* MLG *sipolle* > Lett. *sīpuols*), with Grk. dial. κάπια· τὰ σκόροδα (Hesych.), loanword fr. unknown source. Ernout-M. 176. Walde-H. 1.201. REW 1817, 1820. Vendryes, De hib. voc. 124. Weigand-H. 2.1355.

Late Lat. *ūniō* (> OE *ynne* in *ynnelēac*, cpd. with *lēac* 'leek'; Fr. *oignon* > ME *unyon*, etc. > NIr. *inniun*, W. *wynwyn* coll., sg. *wynwynyn;* Br. *ognon* coll., sg. *ognonenn*, fr. Fr.; Du. dial. *ajuin, juin*, etc. whence, as if pl., new sg. *ui*), prob. (though disputed) the same word as *ūniō* (fr. *ūnus* 'one') commonly applied to a single large pearl, and so not improbably by farmers to the onion. Ernout-M. 1126. REW 9073. Pedersen 1.207. Franck–v. W. 12,716.

3. Dan. *rødløg*, Sw. *rödlök*, cpd. of words for 'red' (15.66) and 'leek' (ON *laukr*, OE *lēac*, etc.).

4. Lith. *svogūnas* (now preferred to *cibulė*, NSB), fr. some Asiatic form belonging with Turk. *svogan* 'onion'. Hehn, Kulturpflanzen[7] 205.

5. SCr., Russ. *luk*, fr. Gmc. word for 'leek', ON *laukr*, etc. Berneker 744. Stender-Petersen 302 f.

6. Skt. *palāṇḍu-*, cpd., first part dub., second part : *aṇḍa-* 'egg' (cf. *āṇḍīka-* name of a plant with edible bulbs). Uhlenbeck 159.

5.69 CABBAGE

Grk.	ῥάφανος, κράμβη	Goth.	. . . .	Lith.	*kopustas*
NG	λάχανο	ON	*kāl*	Lett.	*kāpuosts*
Lat.	*brassica, caulis*	Dan.	*kaal*	ChSl.	. . . .
It.	*cavolo*	Sw.	*kål*	SCr.	*kupus*
Fr.	*chou*	OE	*cawel*	Boh.	*kapusta, zelí*
Sp.	*berza, col*	ME	*cole, caboche*	Pol.	*kapusta*
Rum.	*varză*	NE	*cabbage*	Russ.	*kapusta*
Ir.	*cāl, braissech*	Du.	*kool*		
NIr.	*cabāiste (cāl)*	OHG	*cōl*		
W.	*bresychen (cawl)*	MHG	*kōl*		
Br.	*kaolenn*	NHG	*kohl (kraut)*		

1. Grk. κράμβη, fr. the appearance of 'curled, wrinkled' : κράμβος 'dry, crackly', sb. 'blight in grapes when they shrivel', OE *hrympel* 'wrinkle', etc. Walde-P. 2.588 f. Boisacq 507.

Grk. ῥάφανος (Att. for κράμβη), beside ῥαφανίς 'radish' : ῥάπυς, ῥάφυς 'a kind of turnip', Dor. ῥάφα 'a kind of radish', Lat. *rāpum* 'rape, turnip', OHG *ruoba*, NHG (*weisse*) *rübe* 'turnip', *rote rübe* 'beet', *gelbe rübe* 'carrot'. Walde-P. 2.341. Ernout-M. 852.

NG λάχανο, sg. of λάχανα 'vegetables' (5.65).

2. Lat. *brassica*, etym.? Mostly replaced in VLat. by *caulis*, but the source of It. *brasca* (arch.), Ir. *braissech* 'cabbage' (NIr. *praiseach* 'pottage') W. *bresych* 'cabbages' (coll.; sg. *bresychen*), SCr. *broskva* 'cabbage-turnip', also NG μπράσκα 'toad'. Ernout-M. 117. Walde-H. 1.114. REW 1278. Pedersen 1.226. Vendryes, De hib. voc. 118. Berneker 87.

Lat. *caulis* 'stalk', esp. 'cabbage-stalk', then 'cabbage' : Grk. καυλός 'stalk', etc. Hence It. *cavolo*, Fr. *chou*, Sp. *col*, Ir. *cāl*, Br. *kaol* (coll.; sg. *kaolenn*), ON *kāl*, OE *cawel*, OHG *cōl*, etc. general Gmc. (NE *cole* obs.; U.S. *coleslaw*, or with pop. etym. *coldslaw*, fr. Du. *koolsla* shortened form of *koolsalade*). Walde-P. 1.332. Ernout-M. 165. REW 1778. NED s.v. *cole*, sb.[1].

Sp. *berza*, Rum. *varza*, fr. Lat. *viridia* 'green plants', fr. *viridis* 'green', REW 9367.

3. Ir. *braissech*, W. *bresychen*, fr. Lat. *brassica* (above, 2).

NIr. *cabāiste*, fr. NE *cabbage* (below, 4). Pedersen 1.230.

4. ON *kāl*, OE *cawel*, etc., above, 2.

ME *caboche, cabache*, NE *cabbage*, fr. OFr. (Pic., Norm.) *caboce* (Fr. *caboche*) 'head' beside *cabosse*, deriv. of OFr. *boce, boche, bosse* 'swelling, boil, bump', prob. influenced by derivs. of Lat. *caput* 'head' NED s.v. *cabbage*, sb.[1] REW 1191a. Gamillscheg 164. Wartburg 1.469.

Late OHG *cabuz, capuz*, MHG *kappuz*, NHG dial. *kappus, kappes* (Kretschmer, Wortgeogr. 565), like Fr. *cabus* in *chou cabus*, fr. deriv. of *caput* 'head'. REW 1668. Weigand-H. 1.988.

NHG *kraut* 'herb, plant' (8.53) is usual for 'cabbage' in South Germany, and generally in *sauerkraut*. Kretschmer, Wortgeogr. 566 ff.

5. Boh., Pol., Russ. *kapusta* (> Lith. *kopustas*, Lett. *kāpuosts*), SCr. *kupus*, fr. deriv. of *caput* 'head' (like Fr. *cabus*, etc., above, 4), but in form apparently influenced by MLat. *compos(i)ta*, It. *composta* 'compost'. Berneker 486. Brückner 218.

Boh. *zelí* : ChSl. *zelĭje* 'vegetables' (5.65).

5.70 POTATO

NG	πατάτα	Dan.	*kartoffel*	Lith.	*bulvė, ropuṫė*
It.	*patata*	Sw.	*potatis*	Lett.	*kartupelis (bulbe)*
Fr.	*pomme de terre*	NE	*potato*	SCr.	*krumpir*
Sp.	*patata*	Du.	*aardappel*	Boh.	*brambor, zemák*
Rum.	*cartof*	NHG	*kartoffel (erdapfel)*	Pol.	*ziemniak, kartofel*
NIr.	*prāta*			Russ.	*kartofel'*
W.	*taten*				
Br.	*avaldouar*				

The potato was introduced into Europe from the Western Hemisphere, first the sweet potato from the West Indies, then the common potato from Peru. The native Haitian name of the former was widely adopted and extended to the second. Cf. NED s.v. *potato.*

Other designations arose, and spread either by direct borrowing or literal translation, such as those meaning 'earth-apple', 'earth-pear', or words for 'bulb' or the like that were applied to the new product. There is a wealth of local dialect words that are not considered here. Cf. Spitzer, Wört. u. Sach. 4.147 ff., Niedermann, ibid. 8.33 ff., Kretschmer, Wortgeogr. 256 ff.

1. Haitian *batata*, through Sp. *patata*, is the source of It. *patata* (> NG πατάτα), NE *potato*, whence NIr. *prāta* (explanation of *r?*), W. *tatws* (pl. fr. NE *'tatoes*), new sg., *taten*, Sw. *potatis* (fr. NE pl. *potatoes*, cf. Hellquist s.v.).

2. Fr. *pomme de terre*, lit. 'earth-apple', and similarly, mostly by imitation of the French, Br. *aval-douar*, Du. *aardappel*, NHG *erdapfel* (OHG *erdaphul*, MHG *ertapfel* 'melon, cucumber'), Icel. *jarðepli*, NG γεώμηλον (only literary and clearly a translation of the French).

3. Sw. dial. *jordpäron* lit. 'earth-pear', and so NHG dial. *erdbirne, grundbirne*, the latter the source of SCr. *krumpir*. Berneker 622.

4. NHG *kartoffel* (> Rum. *cartof*, Dan. *kartoffel*, Lett. *kartupelis*, Pol. *kartofel*, Russ. *kartofel'*), by dissim. fr. older *tartuffel*, this fr. It. *tartufolo* 'truffle', used also for 'potato'. REW 8966. Weigand-H. 1.199. Kretschmer, Wortgeogr. 256 f. Berneker 491.

5. Lith. *bulvė, bulbė*, Lett. *bulbe*, fr. Pol. *bulba, bulwa*, dial. 'potato', this fr. Lat. *bulbus* 'bulb'. Berneker 100. Niedermann, Wört. u. Sach. 8.67 ff.

Lith. *roputė*, dim. of *ropė* 'turnip' : ChSl. *rěpa*, OHG *ruoba*, Lat. *rāpum*, Grk. ῥάπυς 'turnip'. Walde-P. 2.341.

Boh. *zemák*, Pol. *ziemniak*, derivs. of *země, ziemia* 'earth'.

Boh. *brambor*, fr. *bramburk* = Brandenburg as the source of export. So Rum. dial. *bandraburcă* 'potato'. Berneker 81 ff. Tiktin 154.

5.71 FRUIT

Grk.	μῆλον, ὀπώρα	Goth.	. . . .	Lith.	*vaisiai*
NG	φροῦτο, (ὀ)πωρικό	ON	*aldin*	Lett.	*auglis*
Lat.	*pōmum, mālum*	Dan.	*frugt*	ChSl.	*ovoštĭ*
It.	*frutto*	Sw.	*frukt*	SCr.	*voće*
Fr.	*fruit*	OE	*ofet*	Boh.	*ovoce*
Sp.	*fruto*	ME	*frut*	Pol.	*owoc*
Rum.	*poamă, fruct*	NE	*fruit*	Russ.	*frukt*
Ir.	*torad*	Du.	*vrucht*	Skt.	*phala-*
NIr.	*toradh*	OHG	*obaz*	Av.	. . . .
W.	*ffrwyth, aeron*	MHG	*obez*		
Br.	*frouez*	NHG	*obst*		

'Fruit' is understood here in the current sense of the NE *fruit* as a generic name for 'tree fruit', covering apples, pears, etc. This notion is commonly, but not always, the result of specialization from 'fruit, product' in the widest sense.

1. Grk. μῆλον, Dor. μᾶλον, whence Lat. *mālum*, both used for 'apple' and other fruits, prob. of pre-Greek orig. See 5.72.

Grk. ὀπώρα 'late summer, fruit season', hence also 'fruit' (cf. LS s.v.), cpd. of ὀπι- as in ὄπι-θεν 'behind, after' and perh. *ὀ(σ)αρα : Goth. *asans* 'harvest-time, summer', ChSl. *jesenĭ*, etc. 'autumn' (14.67). Schulze, Quaest. Ep. 474 f. Walde-P. 1.161 f. Boisacq 709 (but Dor. ὀπᾰρα very dub.). Hence, through adj. ὀπωρικός NG (ὀ)πωρικό.

NG φροῦτο, the usual word, fr. It. *frutto.*

2. Lat. *pōmum*, orig. dub., loanword? Osthoff, IF 5.317 ff. Ernout-M. 786 f. Hence Rum. *poamă* 'fruit' (also 'apple', dial. 'grape'), *pom* 'fruit tree', It. *pomo* 'fruit, fruit tree', and other Romance words for 'fruit' or 'apple'. REW 6645.

Lat. *frūctus* 'product, fruit' in widest sense, fr. *fruī* 'enjoy' : Goth. *brūkjan*, OE *brūcan* 'use', etc. Walde-P. 2.208. Ernout-M. 393 f. Walde-H. 1.552. Hence with special though not exclusive application to 'tree fruit', It. *frutto*, coll. *frutta*, Fr. *fruit* (> ME *frut*, NE *fruit*), Sp. *fruto*, coll. *fruta*, Rum. *fruct*, W. *ffrwyth*, Br. *frouez*, MLG *vrucht* (> Dan. *frugt*, Sw. *frukt*), Du. *vrucht* (OHG *fruht*, NHG *frucht* only in wider sense 'product, fruit'), Russ. *frukt.*

3. MIr. *torad*, NIr. *toradh*, also 'product, fruit' in widest sense, (as always W. *toreth*), cpd. *to-rad* fr. **to-ret* : Ir *rethim* 'run', hence 'that which comes to one, in-come'. Pedersen 2.600, 677.

W. *aeron* : Ir. *āirne*, MBr. *irin* 'wild plum', Goth. *akran* 'fruit' (in widest sense, καρπός), etc. Walde-P. 1.173. Pedersen 1.103.

4. ON *aldin* : ON *ala*, Goth., OE *alan*, Lat. *alere*, etc. 'nourish, feed'. Walde-P. 1.86 f. Falk-Torp 789 f.

OE *ofet*, OHG *obaz*, MHG *obez*, NHG *obst*, whence (Brückner 388) ChSl. *ovoštĭ*, SCr. *voće*, Boh. *ovoce*, Pol. *owoc*, (Russ. *ovošč* 'vegetables'), orig. 'fruit' in wider sense, as esp. OE *ofet*, etym. dub. Prellwitz, BB 25.158. G. S. Lane, JEGPh. 32.486 f.

5 Lith. *vaisius* 'fruit' in widest sense (cf. *vaisa* 'fertility', *veislus* 'fruitful', etc.), also but esp. pl. *vaisiai* 'fruit' as intended here : *veisti* 'propagate, produce', Lett. *viest* 'nurture, increase', refl. *viesties* 'thrive', prob. also Gmc. group OE *wīse* 'sprout, stalk', etc. Walde-P. 1.242. Mühl.-Endz. 4.670.

Lett. *auglis*, fr. Lett. *augt*, Lith. *augti* 'grow' (12.53). Mühl.-Endz. 1.216.

6. Skt. *phala-*, fr. *phal-* 'burst', hence also 'ripen, bear fruit'. Walde-P. 2.102

5.72 APPLE

Grk.	μῆλον	Goth.	*apel*	Lith.	*obuolys*
NG	μῆλο	ON	*epli*	Lett.	*ābuols*
Lat.	*mālum*	Dan.	*æble*	ChSl.	*jablŭko*
It.	*mela*	Sw.	*äpple*	SCr.	*jabuka*
Fr.	*pomme*	OE	*æppel*	Boh.	*jablko*
Sp.	*manzana*	ME	*appel*	Pol.	*jabłko*
Rum.	*măr*	NE	*apple*	Russ.	*jabloko*
Ir.	*ubull*	Du.	*appel*		
NIr.	*ūbhall*	OHG	*apful*		
W.	*afal*	MHG	*apfel*		
Br.	*aval*	NHG	*apfel*		

Most of the words for 'apple' belong to a single group, the ultimate source of which is obscure.

1. Ir. *ubull*, NIr. *ūbhall*, W. *afal*, Br. *aval*; Crimean Goth. *apel*, ON *epli*, etc. general Gmc.; Lith. *obuolas*, *obuolys*, Lett. *ābuols*; ChSl. *jablŭko*, etc. general Slavic. The name of the Campanian city *Abella*, which was famous for its apples, is perh. derived fr. an otherwise unattested Italic form of this group. Walde-P. 1.50 f. Ernout-M. 5. Walde-H. 1.3. Falk-Torp 1411. Berneker 25. Mühl.-Endz. 1.235.

2. Grk. μῆλον, Dor. μᾶλον, whence Lat. *mālum* (both also 'fruit'), prob. of pre-Greek origin. But Lat. *mālum* was replaced by VLat. *mēlum* (Pallad., etc.) reborrowed fr. the common Grk. μῆλον, hence It. *melo* 'apple tree', with new *mela* 'apple', Rum. *măr*. Ernout-M. 583. Walde-H. 1.218 f. REW 5272.

3. Fr. *pomme*, fr. Lat. *pōmum* 'fruit' (5.71). REW 6645.

Sp. *manzana* (*manzano* 'apple tree'), fr. Lat. *māla Matiāna*, supposed to be named from a person (so Pliny 15.15.1) or a place (so Isid. 17.7.3). REW 5247.

5.73 PEAR

Grk.	ἄπιον	Goth.	....	Lith.	kriaušė
NG	ἀπίδι, ἀχλάδι	ON	pera	Lett.	bumbieris
Lat.	pirum	Dan.	pære	ChSl.	....
It.	pera	Sw.	päron	SCr.	kruška
Fr.	poire	OE	pere, peru	Boh.	hruška
Sp.	pera	ME	pere	Pol.	gruszka
Rum.	pară	NE	pear	Russ.	gruša
Ir.	....	Du.	peer		
NIr.	piorra	OHG	bira		
W.	gelleigen, peran, rhwnen	MHG	bire, bir		
		NHG	birne		
Br.	perenn				

1. Grk. ἄπιον, NG ἀπίδι, perh. (as *apiso-?) : Lat. *pirum*, both fr. a pre-IE, Mediterranean source. Lat. *pirum* is the source of the Romance and Gmc. forms, also of Br. *per* (coll.; sg. *perenn*), and (prob. through NE *pear*) NIr. *piorra*, W. *peran*. Walde-P. 2.75. Ernout-M. 772. REW 6524. Falk-Torp 862.

2. NG ἀχλάδι, fr. late Grk. ἀχλάς = ἀχράς, -άδος 'wild pear', beside ἄχερδος 'wild pear', etym.? Walde-P. 1.608.

3. W. *gelleigen*, pl. *gellaig*, also *gelly-gen*, pl. *gellyg*, perh. fr. (old cpd. of?) *gell* 'yellow'.

W. *rhwnen*, etym.?

4. Lith. *kriaušė*, OPruss. *crausios* (pl.), SCr. *kruša*, Boh. *hruška*, Pol. *grusza* (> Lith. *grūšia*), *gruszka*, Russ. *gruša*, all borrowed from some oriental source (cf. Kurd. *korēši*, *kurēši* 'pear'). Berneker 358. Trautmann 140. Brückner 160.

Lett. *bumbieris*, fr. Baltic-German *bumbeere*, like NE *pomepear*, fr. Fr. *pomme poire*. Mühl.-Endz. 1.349.

5.74 PEACH

Grk.	μῆλον περσικόν	Goth.	....	Lith.	persikas
NG	ροδάκινο	ON	....	Lett.	firsikis
Lat.	mālum Persicum	Dan.	fersken	ChSl.	....
It.	pesca	Sw.	persika	SCr.	breskva
Fr.	pêche	OE	persoc	Boh.	broskev
Sp.	durazno, melocotón	ME	peche	Pol.	brzoskwinia
Rum.	piersică	NE	peach	Russ.	persik
Ir.	....	Du.	persik		
NIr.	peitseog	OHG	....		
W.	eirinen wlanog, afal gwlanog	MHG	pfersich		
		NHG	pfirsche, pfirsiche		
Br.	pechezenn				

Nearly all the words for 'peach' come eventually from 'Persian', indicating the oriental source of the peach, which is native to China. Cf. Schrader, Reallex. 2.180 f.

1. Grk. μῆλον περσικόν, Lat. *mālum Persicum*. From the latter as *persicum* or *persica* (orig. neut. pl., used as fem. sg.) come It. *pesca*, Fr. *pêche* (> ME *peche*, NE *peach* > NIr. *peitseog*; also > Br. *pechez* coll., sg. *pechezenn*), Sp. *prisco*, *persigo* (not the usual words). Rum. *piersică*; OE *persoc*, MLG *persik* (> Sw. *persika*), MHG *pfersich*, NHG *pfirsche* (pl. > Dan. *fersken*), *pfirsiche* (> Lett. *firsikis*), etc. Russ. *persik* (> Lith. *persikas*) directly fr. the Grk. or Lat. form. The other Slavic forms, SCr. *breskva*, Boh. *broskev*, etc., prob. through MHG *pfersich*. REW 6427. Falk-Torp 214. Berneker 51. Brückner 45.

2. Lat. *dūracinus* 'hard-berried', cpd. of *dūrus* 'hard' and *acinus* 'berry', was applied to fruit with stones, as grapes, peaches, cherries. Hence words in various Romance dialects specialized to 'grape', 'cherry' or 'peach', the latter in Sp. *durazno*. Hence also late Grk. δωράκινον (also δορ-) and ροδάκινον (LS s.vv., without connecting them), the latter (reg. NG word) with transposition supported by association with ρόδον 'rose', owing to the rosy bloom of the peach. Ernout-M. 291. Walde-H. 1.384. REW 2803.

3. Sp. *melocotón* : It. *melo cotogno*, Grk. μῆλον κυδώνιον 'quince', but in Spanish 'peach'. REW 2436.

4. W. *eirinen wlanog*, *afal gwlanog*, lit. 'woolly plum, woolly apple', fr. the fuzzy skin of the peach.

5.75 FIG

Grk.	σῦκον	Goth.	smakka	Lith.	fyga
NG	σῦκο	ON	fikja	Lett.	vigs
Lat.	ficus	Dan.	figen	ChSl.	smoky
It.	fico	Sw.	fikon	SCr.	smokva
Fr.	figue	OE	fic, fic-æppel	Boh.	fík, smokva, smokev
Sp.	higo	ME	figge	Pol.	figa
Rum.	smochină	NE	fig	Russ.	figa
Ir.	fic	Du.	vijg		
NIr.	fige	OHG	figa		
W.	ffigysen	MHG	vige		
Br.	fiezenn	NHG	feige		

1. Grk. σῦκον, (Boet. τῦκον), Lat. *ficus*, and also Arm. *t'uz* 'fig', prob. fr. a common Mediterranean source. Lat. *ficus* is the source of all the other European words except the group given under 2. Schrader, Reallex. 1.306. Ernout-M. 356. Walde-H. 1.492. Falk-Torp 215. Pedersen 1.228. Berneker 281.

2. Goth. *smakka*, ChSl. *smoky*, SCr. *smokva*, etc. (once the general Slavic word, quotable from all the Slavic languages, but now partly replaced by the representatives of Lat. *ficus*; fr. Slavic also Rum. *smochină*), prob. fr. some oriental (Caucasian?) source. But some regard Goth. *smakka* as a Gmc. word (: NHG *smecken* 'taste', etc.), which was adopted by the Slavs. Schrader, Reallex. 1.306. Feist 439. Stender-Petersen 363 (with full Slavic material; for Gmc. orig.).

5.76 GRAPE

Grk.	βότρυς, σταφυλή (ῥάξ)	Goth.	weinabasi	Lith.	keke̊ vynuogė
NG	σταφύλι (ῥῶγα)	ON	vīnber	Lett.	k'ekars, vīnuoga
Lat.	ūva	Dan.	drue	ChSl.	grozdŭ, groznŭ
It.	uva	Sw.	druva	SCr.	grozd
Fr.	raisin	OE	winber(i)ge	Boh.	hrozen
Sp.	uva	ME	grape	Pol.	winogrono
Rum.	strugure	NE	grape	Russ.	vinograd
Ir.	fīn	Du.	druif	Skt.	drākṣā-
NIr.	fīonchaor	OHG	trūbo, winberi	Av.	....
W.	gwinronyn	MHG	trūbe, winber		
Br.	rezinenn	NHG	traube, weinbeere		

Some of the words listed, as Grk. βότρυς, σταφυλή, are collectives meaning 'a bunch of grapes, grapes', the single 'grape' being expressed by a different word, as Grk. ῥάξ (also 'berry'). Many others were originally used only in this way, and in general the notion of 'bunch, cluster' is a frequent source of the words for 'grape'. Several are connected with words for 'wine' or 'vine'.

1. Grk. βότρυς, without convincing etym. and perh. a loanword fr. a pre-Greek source. Meillet, MSL 15.163. Walde-H. 1.113.

Grk. σταφυλή, whence σταφύλιον, NG σταφύλι 'grape', ἀσταφύλι 'pressed olives or grapes', ἀσταφής 'firm, solid', Skt. *stambh-* 'make firm', OE *stempan* 'stamp', etc. Hence named from the pressing process. Walde-P. 2.624. Boisacq 903.

2. Lat. *ūva* (> It. Sp. *uva*, ORum. and dial. *auă*) etym. disputed, but prob., despite a phonetic question (*ōugʷā-, ōgʷā-?) : Lith. *uoga* 'berry' (5.80). Adversely, Lidén, IF 18.500, followed by Walde-P. 1.165, with refs. for the view preferred here.

Fr. *raisin* (> Br. *rezin*, coll.; sg. *rezinenn*), fr. Lat. *racēmus* 'bunch of grapes' : Grk. ῥάξ, ῥαγός (later ῥώξ, ῥωγός, NG ῥῶγα) the single 'grape berry', both perh. fr. a pre-Greek source. Boisacq 835. Ernout-M. 849. REW 6984. OFr. also > ME *raysyn*, NE *raisin*, once 'grape', now only the dried fruit. NED s.v. *raisin*.

Rum. *strugure* orig. 'bunch' (ORum. *strugur de vie*, Mold. *strugur de poamă*) etym. much disputed, but perh. fr. a VLat. *stribulus*, *strubulus* 'crooked' (cf. Lat. *strebula*, *stribula* 'flesh about the haunches', Gr. στρεβλός 'crooked', etc.). Densusianu, Grai și Suflet 5.175 ff.

3. Ir. *fīn* 'wine' apparently used also for grapes. Cf. Thes. 1.45, 19.

NIr. *fīonchaor*, W. *gwinronyn*, both lit. 'wine-berry' (*fīon*, *gwin* 'wine' + *caor*, *gronyn* 'berry').

4. Goth. *weinabasi*, ON *vīnber*, OE *winber(i)ge*, MHG *winber*, NHG *weinbeere*, cpds. of words for 'vine' or 'wine' and 'berry' (OE *berie*, etc., 5.80).

Dan. *drue*, Sw. *druva*, Du. *druif*, OHG *trūbo*, *drūbo*, MHG *trūbe*, NHG *traube* : EFris. *drūve*, *drūf*, LG *drubbel* 'clump, heap, etc. So orig. the 'bunch' of grapes. Falk-Thorp 158. Franck-v. W. 138.

ME, NE *grape*, fr. OFr. *grape*, *grappe* 'bunch of grapes', a back-formation fr. *graper* 'gather grapes with a vine-hook' fr. *grape* 'hook'. NED s.v. Gamillscheg 483.

5. Lith. *keke̊*, Lett. *k'ekars*, orig. 'bunch' : Lett. *cekulis* 'mop of hair', Boh. *čečeriti* 'ruffle', etc. Walde-P. 1.452. Berneker 138. Mühl.-Endz. 1.368, 2.361.

Lith. *vynuogė*, Lett. *vīnuoga*, both lit. 'wine-berry' (*vynas*, *vīns* 'wine' + *uoga* 'berry'). Cf. ChSl. *vinjaga*, etc. 'vine'. Berneker 25.

6. ChSl. *grozdŭ*, *groznŭ*, SCr. *grozd*, Boh. *hrozen* (Russ. *grozd* 'bunch, cluster'), etym. dub., perh. fr. *gras-d(h)o-*, *gras-nu-* : Goth. *gras* 'grass, herb', etc. Berneker 355. Walde-P. 1.646.

Pol. *winogrono*, cpd. of *wino* 'wine', and *grono* 'bunch, cluster', the latter either belonging to the above group (OPol. *grozno*) or more directly : SCr. *grana* 'branch', etc. Berneker 346. Brückner 158.

Russ. *vinograd*, orig. 'vineyard' like SCr. *vinograd*, then coll. for 'grapes' and now the usual word for 'grape'.

7. Skt. *drākṣā-* 'vine' and 'grape', perh. as 'running vine' fr. *drā-* 'run' (cf. adv. *drāk* 'quickly'). Other views Walde-P. 1.803, 862.

5.77 NUT

Grk.	κάρυον	Goth.	....	Lith.	riešutys
NG	καρύδι	ON	hnot	Lett.	rieksts
Lat.	nux	Dan.	nød	ChSl.	orěchŭ
It.	noce	Sw.	nöt	SCr.	orah
Fr.	noix	OE	hnutu	Boh.	ořech
Sp.	nuez	ME	nute	Pol.	orzech
Rum.	nucă	NE	nut	Russ.	orech
Ir.	cnū	Du.	noot	Skt.	(phala-)
NIr.	cnō	OHG	(h)nuz		
W.	cneuen	MHG	nuz		
Br.	kraonenn	NHG	nuss		

1. Lat. *nux* (> Romance words) : *knu-k-*; Ir. *cnū*, NIr. *cnō*, W. *cneuen*, Br. *kraonen* (MBr. *knoen*); ON *hnot*, OE *hnutu*, etc. general Gmc., fr. *knu-d-* : ON *hnūtr*, Norw. *nut* 'knot, gnarl', etc., all fr. *kneu-*, an extension of *ken-* in words for 'lump, knuckle', etc. Walde-P. 1.391. Ernout-M. 690.

2. Grk. κάρυον, NG καρύδι : Lat. *carīna* 'nutshell, ship's keel, ship', Skt. *karaka-* 'cocoanut', Goth. *hardus* 'hard',

Grk. κρατύς 'strong', etc. Walde-P. 1.354. Walde-H. 1.168.

3. Lith. *riešutys*, Lett. *rieksts* (OPruss. *buccareisis* 'beechnut'), ChSl. *orěchŭ*, SCr. *orah*, Boh. *ořech*, Pol. *orzech*, Russ. *orech*. The Baltic and Slavic words plainly belong together, but their precise relationship and root connection are obscure. Trautmann 241. Mühl.-Endz. 3.545.

4. Skt. *phala-* 'fruit' (5.71) covers 'nut' (*jāti-phala-* 'nutmeg') for which there is no special word.

5.78 OLIVE

Grk.	ἐλαία	Goth.	(alēwabagms 'olive	Lith.	alyva
NG	ἐλιά		tree')	Lett.	oliva
Lat.	oliva, olea	ON	oliva	ChSl.	(maslina)
It.	uliva	Dan.	oliven	SCr.	maslina
Fr.	olive	Sw.	oliv	Boh.	olivka
Sp.	aceituna	OE	eleberge	Pol.	oliwka
Rum.	măslină	ME	olive	Russ.	olivka
Ir.	....	NE	olive		
NIr.	....	Du.	olijf		
W.	olif	OHG	oliberi		
Br.	olivezenn	MHG	ŏlber		
		NHG	olive		

'Olive' is understood here as the fruit, though this and the olive tree were originally, and still are in part, expressed by the same word.

1. Most of the words are directly or indirectly fr. Lat. oliva, itself a loanword fr. Grk. ἐλαί(f)α 'olive tree, olive', this again prob. fr. some Mediterranean source. Schrader, Reallex. 2.130 ff. Ernout-M. 700.

Many of the forms are comparatively recent introduction. It was only the oil of the olive that was exported to the north in early times, and several of the words for 'olive' are derived from the name of the better known olive oil (5.79), as OE eleberge, OHG oliberi lit. 'oil-berry'; likewise Goth. alēwabagms 'olive tree'. In Ireland olives are virtually unknown, but if occasion arose the English word would doubtless be used.

2. Sp. aceituna fr. Arab. zaitūna, like aceite 'oil' fr. Arab. zait. REW 9612. Lokotsch 2186.

3. ChSl. maslina (quotable only for the tree), SCr. maslina (fruit and tree), Russ. maslina (now mostly of the tree), fr. Slavic like Rum. măslin (tree), măslină (fruit) : ChSl., Russ. maslo 'oil', etc. (5.79).

5.79 OIL

Grk.	ἐλαιον	Goth.	alēw	Lith.	aliejus
NG	λάδι	ON	olea	Lett.	el'l'a
Lat.	oleum, olivum	Dan.	olie	ChSl.	olěji, maslo
It.	olio	Sw.	olja	SCr.	ulje, zejtin
Fr.	huile	OE	ele	Boh.	olej
Sp.	aceite	ME	oli, oile	Pol.	olej, oliwa
Rum.	uleiu	NE	oil	Russ.	maslo
Ir.	ola	Du.	olie	Skt.	tāila-, sneha-
NIr.	ola	OHG	ol(e)i	Av.	....
W.	olew	MHG	ŏl(e), ŏl(e)		
Br.	eol	NHG	ŏl		

'Oil' was originally olive oil, an important article of food in southern regions, used also for cleansing the body (cf. under 'soap' 6.95), and as an illuminating fluid in lamps, while in most recent times its use as a lubricant or fuel dwarfs all others in magnitude. In general, the same word has remained in use, with all the extension in application.

1. Most of the Eur. words are directly fr. Lat. oleum (beside olivum), itself a loanword fr. Grk. ἐλαι(f)α 'olive' (5.78). Goth. alēw, precise history much disputed, Feist 35 f. ON olea, prob. fr. Lat. olea. Celtic forms, Pedersen 1.194. ME olie, oile (in place of OE ele), fr. OFr. olie, oile (Fr. huile), whence also Br. eol. Lith. aliejus

fr. Slavic (ChSl. olěji, etc.); Lett. el'l'a fr. LG ŏlje. Rum. uleiu fr. Slavic. NG λάδι fr. late dim. ἐλάδιον.

2. Sp. aceite, fr. Arab. zait 'oil'. So SCr. zejtin, through Turk., fr. Arab. zaitūn 'olives'. REW 9611. Lokotsch 2187.

3. ChSl. maslo (like olěji also translates ἐλαιον), Russ. maslo 'oil' and 'butter', in other Slavic languages 'butter' or 'grease' : ChSl. mazati 'anoint', Grk. μαγ-, in forms of μάσσω 'knead' (5.54), etc. Berneker 2.23, 29. Walde-P. 2.226 ff.

4. Skt. tāila- 'oil' (used as food and for lamps, like the Eur. group), deriv. of tila- the Indian sesame plant.

Skt. sneha- also 'oil' in both uses, fr. snih- 'be sticky'. Walde-P. 2.695.

5.80 BERRY

Grk.	(κόκκος, ῥάξ)	Goth.	-basi	Lith.	uoga
NG	κόκκος(?)	ON	ber	Lett.	uoga
Lat.	bāca	Dan.	bær	ChSl.	jagoda
It.	bacca	Sw.	bär	SCr.	jagoda, boba
Fr.	baie	OE	berie	Boh.	jagoda
Sp.	baya	ME	bery	Pol.	jagoda
Rum.	boabă	NE	berry	Russ.	jagoda
Ir.	cáer	Du.	bes	Skt.	....
NIr.	caor	OHG	beri	Av.	....
W.	aeronen	MHG	ber		
Br.	hugenn	NHG	beere		

Although there is a word for 'berry' in most of the Eur. languages, it is only in the Gmc. group that the word furnishes a long series of cpds. denoting the special kinds of berry. Thus NE berry, whence strawberry, raspberry, blackberry, blueberry, cranberry, gooseberry, etc., formerly also wineberry (OE weinberige, like Goth. weinabasi), now replaced by grape. Similarly, NHG beere, with erdbeere, himbeere, etc., and in the other Gmc. languages. Elsewhere the names of 'strawberry', 'raspberry', etc., are unrelated to each other, e.g. Fr. fraise 'strawberry' (with the other Romance words, fr. Lat. fragum), but framboise 'raspberry' (fr. a Frank. *brombasi 'blackberry' like NHG brombeere, first part : NE bramble, etc.); Russ. zemljanika 'strawberry' (fr. zemlja 'earth', like NHG erdbeere), but malina 'raspberry' (: Grk. μέλας, Lett. melns 'black', etc.).

1. In class. Grk. there is no distinctive word for 'berry' in common use. But κόκκος 'grain, seed' is rarely also 'berry' and so reg. in NG. Grk. ῥάξ, ῥώξ 'grape' (5.76), also sometimes 'berry'.

2. Lat. bāca or bacca (> It. bacca, Fr. baie, Sp. baya), prob. a loanword fr. a Mediterranean source, and perh. related to the Thracian Βάκχος. Ernout-M. 98. Walde-H. 1.91.

Rum. boabă, fr. SCr. boba 'berry'.

3. Ir. cáer, NIr. caor, W. pl. ceirios, perh. : Grk. καρπός 'fruit' in wide sense. Pedersen 1.23.

W. aeronen (coll. aeron) : Goth. akran 'fruit', etc. (5.71). Walde-P. 1.173. Pedersen 1.103.

Br. hugenn (mostly 'uvula', but also 'berry'), deriv. of Lat. ūva 'grape'. Ernault, Glossaire 328.

4. Goth. -basi (in weinabasi 'grape'), ON ber, OE berie, etc., general Gmc., root connection? Falk-Torp 124. Feist 559.

5. Lith., Lett. uoga, ChSl. jagoda, etc. general Slavic, prob. : Lat. ūva 'grape' (5.76). Berneker 25.

SCr. boba, fr. bob 'bean'.

5.81 SALT

Grk.	ἅλας	Goth.	salt	Lith.	druska
NG	ἁλάτι	ON	salt	Lett.	sāls
Lat.	sāl	Dan.	salt	ChSl.	solĭ
It.	sale	Sw.	salt	SCr.	so
Fr.	sel	OE	sealt	Boh.	sŭl
Sp.	sal	ME	salt	Pol.	sól
Rum.	sare	NE	salt	Russ.	sol'
Ir.	salann	Du.	zout	Skt.	lavaṇa-
NIr.	salann	OHG	salz	Av.	....
W.	halen	MHG	salz		
Br.	holen	NHG	salz		

1. Nearly all the Eur. words for 'salt', also Arm. ał and Toch. sāle, go back to an IE *sal- 'salt'. Walde-P. 2.452 f. Ernout-M. 887 f.

2. Lith. druska : Lett. druska 'crumb, scrap', Grk. θραύω 'break, smash', Goth. drauhsnōs 'crumbs, fragments', etc., IE *dhreu-. Cf. Alb. kripë 'salt', fr. Slavic, ChSl. krupa 'crumb' (G. Meyer, Alb. Etym. Wtb. 206). Walde-P. 1.872 ff. Walde-H. 1.553.

3. Skt. lavaṇa-, prob. with Skt lavańga- 'clove', as orig. 'cutting, sharp',· fr. Skt. lu- 'cut' (9.22). Reichelt, Streitberg Festgabe 297.

Skt. ūṣaka- 'salt' or 'pepper', with ūṣa- 'salt-pit', ūṣaṇa- 'black pepper', ūṣara- 'salty', fr. uṣ- 'burn' (1.84). Reichelt, op. cit.

There is no quotable Av. or OPers. word for 'salt'. For the modern Iranian words, cf. Reichelt, op. cit. 295 ff.

5.82 PEPPER

Grk.	πέπερι	Goth.	....	Lith.	pipirai
NG	πιπέρι	ON	piparr	Lett.	pipari
Lat.	piper	Dan.	pebber	ChSl.	pĭperŭ
It.	pepe	Sw.	peppar	SCr.	pepeř
Fr.	poivre	OE	pipor	Boh.	pepř
Sp.	pimienta	ME	peper	Pol.	pieprz
Rum.	piper	NE	pepper	Russ.	perec
Ir.	scibar, pipur	Du.	peper	Skt.	pippala-, etc.
NIr.	piobar	OHG	pfeffer	Av.	....
W.	pupur	MHG	pfeffer		
Br.	pebr	NHG	pfeffer		

1. Nearly all the Eur. words for 'pepper' are fr. Lat. piper, itself a loanword fr. Grk. πέπερι, this being, like the article 'pepper', of Indian orig. Cf. Skt. pippala-, pippali-, 'berry, pepper'. Schrader, Reallex. 2.164. Boisacq 769. Ernout-M. 771.

For Ir. scibar cf. Pedersen 1.235, Ven-dryes, De hib. voc. 175. SCr. biber fr. Turk. biber, this fr. NG πιπέρι.

2. Sp. pimiento, -a fr. Lat. pigmentum 'pigment' and (late) 'juice of plants', in the middle ages used for all sorts of salves and spices. REW 6488. Schrader, Reallex. 2.165.

3. Skt. pippala-, etc., above, 1. Also marica-, etym.?

5.83 VINEGAR

Grk.	ὄξος	Goth.	aket	Lith.	uksusas, actas, rūgpyvė
NG	ξίδι, γλυκάδι	ON	....	Lett.	etik'is
Lat.	acētum	Dan.	eddike	ChSl.	octĭ
It.	aceto	Sw.	ättika	SCr.	ocat, sirće
Fr.	vinaigre	OE	eced	Boh.	ocet
Sp.	vinagre	ME	vinaigre	Pol.	ocet
Rum.	oțet	NE	vinegar	Russ.	uksus
Ir.	(fín) acét	Du.	azijn	Skt.	(çukta-)
NIr.	fíneagra	OHG	ezzih	Av.	....
W.	finegr, gwinegr	MHG	ezzich		
Br.	gwinegr	NHG	essig		

Words for 'vinegar' go back to expressions for 'sharp, sour, acid', sometimes in combination with words for 'wine'.

1. Grk. ὄξος (> Russ. uksus > Lith. uksusas), late dim. ὀξείδιον, NG ξίδι : Grk. ὀξύς 'sharp, pointed, acid' (cf. εὖρος 'breadth' : εὐρύς 'broad'), Lat. acidus 'acid', ācer 'sharp', etc. Walde-P. 1.28 ff.

NG γλυκάδι fr. late Grk. γλυκάδιον 'vinegar' (EM, Choerob.), this fr. γλυκύς 'sweet'.

2. Lat. acētum, orig. pass. pple. of acēre 'be sour', beside acidus 'sour, acid' : ācer 'sharp', etc. Walde-P. 1.28 ff. Ernout-M. 8. Walde-H. 1.6.

Hence It. aceto, OFr. aisil, aisin (> Du. azijn); Ir. acét (also fín acét with fín 'wine'); Goth. aket, OE eced, and, with transposition of consonants, LG edik, etik (> Icel. edik, Dan. eddike, Sw.

ättika, also Lett. etik'is), OHG ezzih, NHG essig; ChSl. octĭ (> Rum. oțet), SCr. ocat, Boh., Pol. ocet (> Lith. actas). Falk-Torp 180. Feist 32. Brückner 373.

3. Fr. vinaigre (> Br. gwinegr, with influence of gwin 'wine'); ME vinaigre, NE vinegar > NIr. fíneagra, W. finegr, also W. gwinegr with influence of gwin 'wine'), Sp. vinagre, cpd. of Lat. vīnum 'wine' and ācer 'sharp'. REW 9356.

4. Lith. rūgpyvė (Kurschat's word for 'vinegar', as in Pruss. Lith.), cpd. of rūg- (as in rūgti 'sour, ferment') and pyvas 'beer'.

SCr. sirće fr. Turk. sirke 'vinegar'.

5. Skt. çukta- (not strictly 'vinegar', but used of any sour, acid liquid), fr. çuc- 'gleam, burn' and 'burn with pain'. Uhlenbeck 313.

5.84 HONEY

Grk.	μέλι	Goth.	miliþ	Lith.	medus
NG	μέλι	ON	hunang	Lett.	medus
Lat.	mel	Dan.	honning	ChSl.	medŭ
It.	miele	Sw.	honing	SCr.	med
Fr.	miel	OE	hunig	Boh.	med
Sp.	miel	ME	huni, honi	Pol.	miód
Rum.	miere	NE	honey	Russ.	med
Ir.	mil	Du.	honing	Skt.	madhu-
NIr.	mil	OHG	hona(n)g	Av.	*paēna-
W.	mêl	MHG	honec, honic		
Br.	mel	NHG	honig		

Honey was the old IE sweet, and so among the Greeks and Romans and in Europe generally until the introduction of sugar (5.85). From it was made the oldest IE intoxicating drink, the 'mead' (5.91).

Most of the words for 'honey' belong to one of two inherited groups. In Gmc. one of these is represented in Gothic, the other in words for 'mead', otherwise 'honey' is expressed by a new word derived from its yellow color.

1. IE *melit- 'honey'. Walde-P. 2.296. Ernout-M. 602. Grk. μέλι; Lat. mel (> Romance words); Ir. mil, W., Br. mel; Goth. miliþ (cf. OE mil-dēaw 'honey-dew, nectar', milisc 'honeyed'); Arm. mełr, Alb. mjall.

2. IE *medhu- 'honey' and 'mead'. Walde-P. 2.261. Here as 'honey', Lith., Lett. medus, OPruss. meddo, ChSl. medŭ, etc., general Slavic; Skt. madhu-, Toch. mit. Elsewhere as 'mead' or for some other intoxicating drink (5.91).

3. ON hunang, OE hunig, etc., general Gmc. (except Goth.) : Skt. kāñcana- 'golden', kanaka- 'gold', Grk. κνηκός 'pale yellow' etc. Walde-P. 1.400; Falk-Torp 417.

4. Av. *paēna-, implied by paēnaēna- 'prepared from honey', NPers. angubīn 'bee-honey', prob. as (bee's) 'milk' or 'juice' : Av. payah-, paēman- 'milk', Skt. payas- 'milk, juice', Lith. pienas 'milk' (5.87). Barth. 817.

5.85 SUGAR

Grk.	σάκχαρι, etc. (late)	Goth.	....	Lith.	cukrus
NG	ζάχαρι	ON	....	Lett.	cukurs
Lat.	saccharum (late)	Dan.	sukker	ChSl.	....
It.	zucchero	Sw.	socker	SCr.	šećer
Fr.	sucre	OE	....	Boh.	cukr
Sp.	azúcar	ME	sucere, sugure, etc.	Pol.	cukier
Rum.	zahăr	NE	sugar	Russ.	sachar
Ir.	....	Du.	zucker	Skt.	çarkarā-
NIr.	siúicre	OHG	zucura	Av.	....
W.	siwgr	MHG	zucker		
Br.	sukr	NHG	zucker		

The home of sugar and its European names is India. The companions of Alexander the Great told of the Indian cane which produced 'honey without bees' (περὶ τῶν καλάμων, ὅτι ποιοῦσι μέλι μελισσῶν μὴ οὐσῶν, Strabo 15.694). The native Indian name appears in Greek and Latin transcriptions in the first century A.D. (μέλι τὸ καλάμινον τὸ λεγόμενον σάκχαρι, Peripl. 14; σάκχαρον εἶδός ὄν μέλιτος ἐν Ἰνδίᾳ καὶ τῇ εὐδαίμονι Ἀραβίᾳ πεπηγότος, εὑρισκόμενον ἐπὶ τῶν καλάμων, Diosc. 2.104; Saccharon et Arabia fert, sed laudatius India, est autem mel in harundibus collectum, Plin. 12.32), but

the article was then only an exotic product used for medical purpose. The cultivation of the sugar cane was introduced in Sicily and Spain by the Arabs, and it was only after the crusades that sugar became the common sweetening in place of the older honey. The majority of European forms of the name come through Arabic via Spanish or Italian. Schrader, Reallex. 2.705 ff.

Skt. çarkarā- 'gravel, grit' (AV +) later 'sugar' : Grk. κρόκη, κροκάλη 'pebble'. Walde-P. 1.463.

Hence, through a later Prakrit form like Pāli sakkharā-, the following:

1. Grk. σάκχαρι, σάκχαρον, σάκχαρ, whence Lat. saccharum, NG ζάχαρι, Rum. zahăr, Russ. sachar.

2. NPers. šakar, Arab. sukkar, whence Sp. azúcar, It. zucchero, and, through these, OFr. çucre, sukere, etc. (> ME sucere, sugure, etc., NE sugar), Fr. sucre, the Celtic (W. siwgr fr. ME sugre) and Gmc. forms, and through the latter the Balto-Slavic forms, except Russ. sachar (above), and SCr. šećer, which is fr. Turk. sheker, this fr. NPers. šakar. Lokotsch 1855. REW 8441a. NED, s.v. sugar.

5.86 MILK (sb.)

Grk.	γάλα	Goth.	miluks	Lith.	pienas
NG	γάλα	ON	mjolk	Lett.	piens
Lat.	lac	Dan.	melk	ChSl.	mlěko
It.	latte	Sw.	mjölk	SCr.	mlijeko
Fr.	lait	OE	meolc, milc	Boh.	mléko
Sp.	leche	ME	melk	Pol.	mleko
Rum.	lapte	NE	milk	Russ.	moloko
Ir.	mlicht, ass, lacht	Du.	melk	Skt.	payas-, kṣīra-
NIr.	bainne	OHG	miluh	Av.	payah-, xšvīd-
W.	llaeth, blith	MHG	milich, milch		
Br.	laez	NHG	milch		

1. Grk. γάλα, γάλακτος, Lat. lac, lactis (> Romance words, also Ir. lacht, W. llaeth, Br. laez), without certain root-connection. Walde-P. 1.659. Ernout-M. 514. Walde-H. 1.741 f. REW 4817. Pedersen 1.228.

2. Ir. mlicht, blicht, W. blith; Goth. miluks, OE meolc, etc., general Gmc.; ChSl. mlěko (*melko), etc., general Slavic; Toch. A malke, B malkwer. These are put together here despite the dispute as to their relationship. Certainly some and prob. all : Grk. ἀμέλγω, Lat. mulgēre, Ir. melgim, OE melcan, etc., the general Eur. vb. for 'milk' (5.87). In the Gmc. group the second vowel of Goth. miluks, OHG miluh is puzzling, and some think that the relationship to the vb. is only secondary, due to the assimilation of an originally different word related to Grk. γάλα, Lat. lac (above, 1). The Slavic words were once regarded as Gmc. loanwords, but that is now generally given up. They are separated by many from the above group, but as a *melk- beside *melĝ- is attested by Lat. mulcēre, this is unnecessary, and the various substitute

connections that have been suggested seem less probable. Walde-P. 2.298. Feist 360 f. Berneker 2.34. Stender-Petersen 42 ff. F. A. Preveden, Language 5.152 ff.

3. Ir. ass (K. Meyer, Contrib. 138) etym.?

NIr. bainne, fr. MIr. banne 'drop', rarely 'milk' (K. Meyer, Contrib. 177) = Corn. banna, banne, Br. banne 'drop' : Skt. bindu- 'drop'. Walde-P. 2.110. Pedersen, 1.116.

4. Lith. pienas, Lett. piens, Skt. payas-, Av. payah- (also paēman- 'mother's milk') : Skt. pī-, pyā- 'swell, fatten', pīna- 'fat', Grk. πῖαρ 'fat', etc. Walde-P. 2.73 ff.

5. Skt. kṣīra-, NPers. šīr, etc. : Alb. hirrë 'whey'. Walde-P. 1.503.

Av. xšvīd-, perh. : Lith. sviestas, Lett. sviests 'butter'. Walde-P. 2.521.

Skt. dadhi, gen. dadhnas 'thick sour milk' : OPruss. dadan 'milk', Alb. djathē 'cheese', redupl. form fr. the root of Skt. dhayati 'sucks' (cf. dhenu- 'giving milk'), etc. (5.16). Walde-P. 1.829.

5.87 MILK (vb.)

Grk.	ἀμέλγω	Goth.	....	Lith.	milžti
NG	ἀμέλγω, ἀρμέγω	ON	mjolka	Lett.	slaukt
Lat.	mulgēre	Dan.	malke	ChSl.	mlěsti
It.	mungere	Sw.	mjölka	SCr.	musti
Fr.	traire	OE	melcan, meolcian	Boh.	dojiti
Sp.	ordeñar	ME	mylke	Pol.	doić
Rum.	mulge	NE	milk	Russ.	dojit'
Ir.	bligim, crudim	Du.	melken	Skt.	duh-
NIr.	crúdhaim, blighim	OHG	melchan	Av.	....
W.	godro	MHG	melchen		
Br.	goro	NHG	melken		

The verbs for 'milk' are unrelated to the nouns for 'milk' in the same language, except in Irish and the Gmc. group.

1. Grk. ἀμέλγω (> NG pop. ἀρμέγω through ἀλμέγω with transposition); Lat. mulgēre (> It. mungere, Rum. mulge, OFr. moudre); Ir. mligim, bligim; OE melcan, OHG melchan, etc., general Gmc. (but OE meolcian, ME mylke, NE milk, fr. the sb. OE meolc, etc.); Lith. milžti, melžu; ChSl. mlěsti, mlŭzą, SCr. musti, muzem; Alb. mjellë; the old general Eur. vb. for 'milk' : Skt. mṛj- 'wipe, stroke', Av. marəz- 'touch', IE *melĝ-, with Eur. specialization of 'wipe, stroke' or the like to 'milk'. Walde-P. 2.298 ff. Ernout-M. 637.

2. Fr. traire, fr. Lat. trahere 'draw'.

Sp. ordeñar, fr. VLat. *ordināre beside *ordinium 'implement', fr. Lat. ordināre 'arrange'. Development prob. through 'manipulate'. REW 6091.

3. MIr. crudim, cruthaim, with sb. crud 'milk' (cf. K. Meyer, Contrib. 535, 538), NIr. crúdhaim, etym.?

W. godro, MBr. gozro, Br. goro, cpd. *go-dro : W. troi 'turn, twist', Lat. trahere 'draw' etc. Walde-P. 1.752. Pedersen 1.97.

4. Lett. slaukt : Lith. šliaukti 'sweep', both fr. a common notion of 'wipe, stroke'. Mühl.-Endz. 3.919.

Boh. dojiti, Pol. doić, Russ. dojit' : ChSl. dojiti 'suckle', Skt. dhayati 'sucks', etc. (5.16). Berneker 205.

5. Skt. duh-, NPers. duxtan, dušidan, the Indo-Iranian verb for 'milk' (though not quotable fr. Av.). Connection with Grk. τεύχω 'make, build', τυγχάνω 'hit the mark, meet, happen', Goth. daug, OE dēag, OHG toug 'is of advantage, avails', etc. is generally rejected on semantic grounds. Walde-P. 1.847. Feist 128. But in view of the perfect formal correspondence, one must consider the possibility of deriving the divergent meanings (which even in the Eur. group offer some problems) from some common source, even if the attempt involves speculation falling short of conviction. For example, the Indo-Iranian 'milk' may be from 'stroke', like the Eur. 'milk' (above, 1); 'stroke' and 'strike' may be from a common source (cf. NE strike : NE stroke, NHG streicheln); and 'strike' may lead to 'hit, hit the mark', the earliest use of Grk. τυγχάνω (whence also 'meet, happen, be fortunate', etc.), from which 'suit, be good for, avail', etc. in Gmc.

5.88 CHEESE

Grk.	τῡρός	Goth.	....	Lith.	sūris, kiežas
NG	τυρί	ON	ostr	Lett.	siers
Lat.	cāseus	Dan.	ost	ChSl.	syrŭ
It.	formaggio, cacio	Sw.	ost	SCr.	sir
Fr.	fromage	OE	ciese, cēse	Boh.	sýr (tvaroh)
Sp.	queso	ME	chese	Pol.	ser (twaróg)
Rum.	brînză	NE	cheese	Russ.	syr (t·orog)
Ir.	cáise	Du.	kaas	Skt.	(dadhi-ja-, kṣīra-ja-)
NIr.	cáise	OHG	chāsi	Av.	fšutā- (tūiri-)
W.	caws	MHG	kæse		
Br.	fourmaj	NHG	käse		

1. Grk. τῡρός, dim. τῡρίον, NG τυρί, Av. tūiri- 'milk that has become like cheese', prob. : Lat. ob-tūrāre, re-tūrāre 'stop up, stuff, fill up', turunda 'pellet for fattening poultry', Skt. tura- 'abundant, strong', etc., all fr. the root seen in Grk. τύλη 'swelling', Lat. tumēre 'be swollen', etc. Here also probably the much disputed Boh. tvaroh, Pol. twaróg, Russ. tvorog 'curds' or soft 'cheese', whence MHG twarc, quarc, NHG quark 'curds'. Walde-P. 1.710 f. (with refs. to other views).

2. Lat. cāseus : ChSl. kvasŭ 'leaven', Skt. kvath- 'seethe, boil', Goth. hwapjan 'foam', etc. Hence It. cacio, Sp. queso, Rum. cas ('fresh sheep's milk cheese'); Ir. cáise, W. caws; OE ciese, cēse, ME chese, NE cheese, Du. kaas, OHG chāsi, MHG kæse, NHG käse (> Lith. kiežas). Walde-P. 1.468. Walde-H. 1.176 f. REW 1738. Pedersen 1.49, 202.

Fr. fromage (> Br. fourmaj), It. formaggio, fr. MLat. formāticum, deriv. of Lat. forma 'shape, form, mold' (cf.

MLat. casei forma, and Prov. furmo 'cheese'). REW 3441.

Rum. brînză (cf. It. brinze, NHG local (Austrian) primsenkäse, for which see Kretschmer, Wortgeogr. 564), orig. dub. REW 1272.

3. ON ostr, Dan., Sw. ost : Grk. ζωμός, Lat. iūs, Skt. yūṣa-, etc., 'soup' (5.64), Grk. ζύμη 'leaven'. Walde-P. 1.199. Falk-Torp 803.

4. Lith. sūris, Lett. siers (ie instead of u by association with siet 'bind' in sieru siet 'make cheese', ChSl. syrŭ, etc., general Slavic : ChSl. syrŭ 'moist', SCr. sirov 'raw, fresh', Lith. suras 'salted', ON sūrr, OHG, OE sūr 'sour', etc. Walde-P. 2.513. Trautmann 293 f. Mühl.-Endz. 3.859.

5. Skt. dadhi-ja-, kṣīra-ja-, lit. 'milk-born', cpds. of dadhi- or kṣīra- 'milk' (5.86) are used for 'curds', whether formed 'cheese' is not clear.

Av. fšutā-, fr. fšu-'fatten'? Barth. 1029.

Av. tūiri- above, 1.

5.89 BUTTER

Grk.	βούτῡρον (late)	Goth.	....	Lith.	sviestas
NG	βούτυρον	ON	smjǫr	Lett.	sviests
Lat.	būtyrum (late)	Dan.	smør	ChSl.	....
It.	burro	Sw.	smör	SCr.	maslac
Fr.	beurre	OE	butere	Boh.	máslo
Sp.	manteca	ME	butere	Pol.	masło
Rum.	unt	NE	butter	Russ.	maslo
Ir.	imb	Du.	boter	Skt.	ghṛta-, navanīta-
NIr.	im	OHG	ancho, butera	Av.	(raoγna-)
W.	ymenyn	MHG	buter, anke		
Br.	amann	NHG	butter		

Butter was a common article of food from early times in India and Iran ('melted butter') and in northern Europe, but not among the ancient Greeks and Romans, who first heard of it as a Scythian product. It is first reported by Herodotus (4.2), who describes the process of churning, later by Hippocrates (4.20), who first introduces the word βούτῡρον. Pliny (28.133) tells of *butyrum, barbararum gentium lautissimus cibus*. Schrader, Reallex. 1.175 ff.

1. Grk. βούτῡρον, lit. 'cow-cheese', but either a translation or an adaptation of a native Scythian word (πῖον, ὃ βούτυρον καλέουσι, Hipp. 4.20). Hence Lat. būtyrum, and fr. this OFr. burre (> It. burro), Fr. beurre, OE, ME butere, NE butter, Du. boter, OHG (late) butera, MHG buter, NHG butter.

2. Sp. manteca (also 'fat, lard'), prob. of pre-Roman orig. REW 5324a.

Rum. unt (also 'oil') : It. unto, OFr. oint 'fat', fr. Lat. ūnctum 'ointment', pple. of unguere 'smear, anoint', REW 9057.

3. Ir. imb, imm, NIr. īm, W. ymenyn, Br. amann, OHG ancho, MHG anke, OPruss. anctan : Lat. unguen 'fat, oint-ment', unguere 'smear, anoint', Skt. añj- 'anoint, adorn'. Walde-P. 1.181. Pedersen 1.46.

4. ON smjǫr, Dan. smør, Sw. smör, OHG chuo-smero (lit. 'cow-grease') : Goth. smairþr 'fat', OE smeoru, OHG smero 'fat, grease' (NE smear), Ir. smir 'marrow', etc. Walde-P. 2.690 f. Falk-Torp 1086 f.

5. Lith. sviestas, Lett. sviests, perh. : Av. xšvīd- 'milk'. Walde-P. 2.521.

SCr. maslac (beside maslo 'grease'), Boh. máslo, Pol. masło, Russ. maslo ('butter' and 'oil') : ChSl. maslo 'ointment, oil', mazati 'anoint', Grk. μάσσω 'knead', etc. Walde-P. 2.226. Berneker 2.23, 28.

6. Skt. ghṛta- 'clarified butter, ghee' : Skt. ghṛ- 'besprinkle', further connections dub. Uhlenbeck 85, 100. Walde-P. 1.407.

Skt. navanīta- 'fresh butter', lit. 'fresh drawn' cpd. of nava- 'new' and pple. of nī- 'lead, bring'.

Av. raoγna-, raoγnya- 'butter' (? So Barth. 1488) or 'oil' (Darmesteter) : NPers. rauγan 'oil, grease', outside connections unknown.

5.91 MEAD

Grk.	μελίτειον	Goth.	*midus	Lith.	midus
NG	ὑδρόμελι	ON	mjǫðr	Lett.	medus
Lat.	hydromeli	Dan.	mjød	ChSl.	(medŭ)
It.	idromele	Sw.	mjöd	SCr.	medovina
Fr.	hydromel	OE	medu, medo	Boh.	medovina
Sp.	hidromel	ME	mede	Pol.	miód
Rum.	hidromel, mied	NE	mead	Russ.	med
Ir.	mid	Du.	mee		
NIr.	miodh	OHG	metu		
W.	medd	MHG	met(e)		
Br.	mez	NHG	met		

Mead was the oldest IE intoxicating drink, made from honey, and remained a common drink among the Celtic, Germanic, and Balto-Slavic peoples, but not among the Greeks and Romans. It is regularly expressed by a word for 'honey' or a derivative of it.

1. IE *medhu- 'honey' and 'mead'. Walde-P. 2.261. Here, only for the drink, Ir. mid, etc., all the Celtic words; ON mjǫðr, OE medu, etc., all the Gmc. words (Goth. *midus not quotable, but inferred fr. a Grk. transcription μέδος, referring to a drink taking the place of wine at the Hunnish court; cf. NED s.v. mead). The Balto-Slavic words are partly the same as for 'honey' (hence also Rum. mied), partly derivs., as SCr., Boh. medovina; but Lith. midus is fr. Goth. *midus, and ChSl. medŭ is quotable only as 'honey' or late for 'wine'.

Skt. madhu- was used for any sweet intoxicating drink, especially the soma juice. Av. maδu- was a kind of wine or beer (Barth. 1114. NPers. mai 'wine', Horn 1003). Grk. μέθυ occurs only as a poetical word for 'wine', but is the source of the common prose words μεθύω, μεθύσκω 'be drunk, make drunk', whence NG μεθυσμένος 'drunk'.

2. Grk. μελίτειον (Plut. Mor. 672b of the drink of the barbarians), deriv. of μέλι 'honey'.

3. Late Grk. ὑδρόμελι, cpd. of ὕδωρ 'water' and μέλι 'honey', whence Lat. hydromel(i), It. idromele, Fr. hydromel (> Rum. hidromel), Sp. hidromel (also aguamel, with substitution of agua 'water'). These words are those employed to denote the 'mead' of other peoples, though also used of an unfermented mixture of honey and water.

5.92 WINE

Grk.	οἶνος	Goth.	wein	Lith.	vynas
NG	κρασί	ON	vin	Lett.	vīns
Lat.	vīnum	Dan.	vin	ChSl.	vino
It.	vino	Sw.	vin	SCr.	vino
Fr.	vin	OE	wīn	Boh.	vino
Sp.	vino	ME	wine	Pol.	wino
Rum.	vin	NE	wine	Russ.	vino
Ir.	fín	Du.	wijn	Skt.	drākṣarasa-
NIr.	fíon	OHG	wīn	Av.	maδu-, xšudra-(?)
W.	gwin	MHG	wīn		
Br.	gwin	NHG	wein		

The intensive cultivation of the vine and the use of wine as the customary alcoholic drink had its home in the eastern Mediterranean region, whence it spread over Europe, mainly through the Romans. In ancient India and Iran wine was not one of the common alcoholic drinks. Schrader, Reallex. 2.642 ff.

1. Grk. οἶνος, early ϝοῖνος, Lat. vīnum (prob. fr. *woinom, like vīcus, vīdī : ϝοῖκος, ϝοῖδα; in which case Umbr. vinu must be a Lat. loanword), Alb. venë, Arm. gini, together with the Semitic words, Arab. wain, Hebr. yayin, all prob. loanwords fr. some prehistoric Mediterranean source. So Meillet, MSL 15.163, Ernout-M. 1111. But even so, the source could be some IE language of that region. For if we assume that the orig. sense was 'vine', it is attractively derived fr. the same root as Lat. vītis 'vine' (IE *wei- in words for 'twist, wind', see 8.67). Walde-P. 1.226. Schrader, Reallex. 2.643 f.

Lat. vīnum is the source of all the other Eur. words, except the Greek and Albanian.

2. NG κρασί, fr. dim. of Grk. κρᾶσις 'mixture', its use arising from the common Greek practice of mixing wine and water. The use of οἶνος for the wine of the sacrament may have been a factor in its disappearance from common speech.

3. Skt. drākṣarasa- (rare), cpd. of drākṣā- 'vine, grape' (5.76) and rasa- 'juice'.

Av. maδu- : Skt. madhu-, etc. See 5.91.

Av. xšudra-, 'liquid, semen' also an 'alcoholic drink' ('wine'? So Barth. 555) : xšusta- 'liquid', xšaošah- 'stream, flood', Skt. kṣoda- 'swell' (of the waves). Walde-P. 1.502.

Among other Indo-Iranian words for alcoholic drinks are: Skt. soma-, Av. haoma- 'juice of the soma plant' : Skt. sū- 'press, extract' (Walde-P. 2.468); Skt. mada- 'intoxication' and Av. maδa- 'intoxicating drink' : Skt. mad- 'be glad, be drunk', Lat. madēre, 'be wet', etc. (Walde-P. 2.230 f.). See also under 'beer' (5.93).

of Egyptian beer (which Hdt. 2.77 refers to as οἶνῳ ἐκ κριθέων πεποιημένῳ), and quoted as if an Egyptian word (τὸ ἐν Αἰγύπτῳ καλούμενον ζῦθος, Theophr., CP 6.11.2; κατασκευάζουσι δὲ καὶ ἐκ τῶν κριθῶν Αἰγύπτιοι πόμα, ὃ καλέουσι ζῦθος, Diod. 1.34), but perh. a genuine Grk. word related to ζύμη 'leaven', etc. Walde-H. 1.734. Boisacq 311.

2. Ir. cuirm, W. cwrw, OCorn. coref, coruf, an old Celtic word represented in late Grk. authors by κοῦρμι, κόρμα, κερβησία, in Pliny by cerea or cervesia (> Sp. cerveza), perh. : Lat. cremor 'thick broth', Skt. karambha- 'groats, porridge'. Walde-P. 1.419 f. Pedersen 1.168. Walde-H. 1.207.

Ir. laith (Corn. lad 'liquid', W. llaid 'mud') : Grk. λάταξ 'drop of wine'. Walde-P. 2.381. Walde-H. 1.770.

NIr. lionn (leann), fr. Ir. lind 'a drink' ('wine' or 'beer') : W. llyn 'a drink', etc. (5.13). Pedersen 1.37.

3. OE bēor (> ON bjórr, Ir., NIr. beoir), ME bere, NE beer, Du. bier, OHG bior, MHG, NHG bier (> It.

birra > NG μπίρα; Fr. bière > Br. bier; Rum. bere), orig. much disputed, perh. an old loanword fr. MLat. biber a 'drink' (fr. Lat. infin. bibere 'drink'). Kluge-G. 56. For other views cf. Walde-P. 2.118, Weigand-H. 1.236, NED s.v. beer, sb.¹.

4. ON ǫl, Dan. øl, Sw. öl, OE ealu, ME, NE ale (the differentiation from beer is recent, cf. NED s.v.), and (fr. Gmc.) Lith., Lett. alus (OPruss. alu 'mead'), ChSl., ORuss. olu : Grk. ἀλύδοιμος 'bitter' (Sophr.), Lat. alūmen 'alum'. Walde-P. 1.91. Falk-Torp 1419 f. Stender-Petersen 294 ff.

5. ChSl. pivo, etc., general Slavic (> Lith. pyvas), orig. 'a drink' : ChSl. piti 'drink', etc. (5.13).

6. Skt. yavasurā-, cpd. of yava- 'grain, millet, barley' and surā- itself perh. 'beer' (KZ 35.314) = Av. hurā- 'milk-wine' (Barth. 1837), fr. the same root as Skt. soma-, Av. haoma- (5.92), or more directly : OE sūr 'sour', etc. Walde-P. 2.513.

5.93 BEER

Grk.	(βρῦτος, ζῦθος)	Goth.	....	Lith.	alus, pyvas
NG	μπίρα (ζῦθος lit.)	ON	bjórr, ǫl	Lett.	alus
Lat.	(zythum, cervesia)	Dan.	øl	ChSl.	pivo, olŭ
It.	birra	Sw.	öl	SCr.	pivo
Fr.	bière	OE	bēor, ealu (alu)	Boh.	pivo
Sp.	cerveza	ME	bere, ale	Pol.	piwo
Rum.	bere	NE	beer	Russ.	pivo
Ir.	cuirm, laith, beoir	Du.	bier	Skt.	yavasurā-
NIr.	lionn, beoir	OHG	bior	Av.	(hurā-)
W.	cwrw	MHG	bier		
Br.	bier	NHG	bier		

Beer was a common drink among most of the European peoples, as well as in Egypt and Mesopotamia, but was known to the Greeks and Romans only as an exotic product. Schrader, Reallex. 1.142 ff.

1. Grk. βρῦτος or -ον, first used (Archil.) with reference to Thracian or Phrygian beer and properly a Thracian form : OE brēowan 'brew', etc. Walde-P. 2.168.

Grk. ζῦθος (> Lat. zythum), first used

CHAPTER 6
CLOTHING; PERSONAL ADORNMENT AND CARE

6.11 CLOTHE, DRESS

Grk.	ἕννῡμι, ἐνδύω	Goth.	wasjan	Lith.	apvilkti, aprėdyti,
NG	ἐνδύω, ντύνω	ON	klæða		aprengti, etc.
Lat.	vestire, induere	Dan.	klæde	Lett.	apg'ērbti, g'erbt
It.	vestire	Sw.	klāda	ChSl.	oděti, oblěšti
Fr.	habiller, (re)vêtir	OE	scrȳdan, gewǣdian	SCr.	odjesti, oblačiti
Sp.	vestir	ME	clothe, dresse	Boh.	odíti, oblékati, ošatiti
Rum.	îmbrăca	NE	dress, clothe	Pol.	ubrać, odziać, oblec
Ir.	ētim, intuigur	Du.	kleeden	Russ.	odet'
NIr.	cōirighim, ēaduighim	OHG	werien, wāten	Skt.	vas-
W.	gwisgo, dilladu	MHG	wæten, kleiden	Av.	vah-
Br.	gwiska	NHG	kleiden		

Most of the verbs listed are used for the trans. 'dress, clothe' (a), with mid., pass., or refl. forms for the intr. 'dress', 'be clothed' (b), e.g. Grk. ἕννῡμι vs. ἕννυμαι, Fr. habiller vs. s'habiller, ChSl. oděti vs. oděti sę. Less commonly the same form is used in both ways, as NE dress (e.g. dresses well), Goth. wasjan, and occasionally others. Again, 'be clothed' may become 'be clothed in, wear', with the garment as direct object, as regularly OE werian, NE wear, now hardly felt as 'be clothed in' and answering to the use elsewhere of verbs for 'carry', as NHG kleider tragen, Fr. porter des vêtements, NG φορῶ ροῦχα.

Aside from the inherited group (IE *wes-, below, 1), many of the verbs are derived from the nouns for 'clothing' or some article of clothing. Others are from 'cover', 'arrange, put in order', or 'put (or draw) on (or about)'. These last, e.g. Grk. ἐνδύω, Lat. induere, ChSl. oděti, oblěšti, were naturally at first used with the garment as direct object, but as the literal sense weakened were construed also with the person clothed, first as the subject of pass. or refl. forms and finally as the object of trans. forms. Cf. the partial development in this direction of NHG anziehen 'draw on, pull on' used with especial reference to clothes, then sich anziehen 'be dressed, dress' (intr.), but not with another person as object or subject of passive (though Luther used such a construction; Paul, Deutsches Wtb. s.v.).

1. IE *wes-, perh. an extension of *eu- in Lat. ind-uere, etc. (below, 3). Walde-P. 1.309. Ernout-M. 1098. Feist 553.

Grk. ἕννῡμι (Ion. εἵνῡμι), fr. *ϝέσ-νῡμι; Lat. (fr. sb. ves-tis) vestire (> It. vestire, Fr. vêtir, revêtir, Sp. vestir); W. gwisgo, Br. gwiska (fr. sbs. W. gwisg, Br. gwisk, formed with -sk- suffix; Pedersen 2.18); Goth. (ga-)wasjan, ON verja (but mostly 'cover, wrap', etc., not the usual word for 'clothe'), OE werian (but reg. 'be clothed in, wear'), OHG werien; Skt. vas- (mid. b, caus. a), Av. vah- (act. and mid., both b); Arm. z-genum (b); Alb. vesh; Toch. was- (SSS 471); Hitt. wess-, wass- (Sturtevant, Hitt. Gloss. 182).

The Gmc. forms of this group, except Goth. wasjan, were homonyms of the vb. for 'prevent, ward off, protect' (Goth. warjan, OE werian, etc.), and this was prob. a factor in their early displacement in most of the Gmc. languages. For the modern vocabulary they survive only in Icelandic (and here only pple. varinn 'clad' in common use) and NE wear with its wide extension from the orig. sense.

2. Grk. ἐνδύω ('put on', mid. 'be clothed in': cf. ἐκδύω 'take off'), NG pop. ντύνω, cpd. of δύω 'sink, plunge, enter' : Skt. upā-du- 'put on'. Walde-P. 1.777.

3. Lat. induere (that is, ind-uere, cf. Umbr. an-ouihimu 'induitor'), like exuere 'take off', fr. IE *eu- in Lith. auti, ChSl. ob-uti 'put on shoes', etc. Walde-P. 1.109. Ernout-M. 317. Walde-H. 1.434 f.

Fr. habiller, orig. sense 'prepare, arrange' (OFr. abiller, fr. bille 'log, block of wood', etc.), specialized under influence of habit 'dress' (6.12). REW 1104. Wartburg 1.366, 368.

Rum. îmbrăca, fr. Lat. braccae, brācae 'trousers' (6.48), REW 4281. Puşcariu 780.

4. Ir. in-tuigur, and ētim both fr. *in-tog-, *in-teg- cpds. of IE *(s)teg- in Grk. στέγω, Lat. tegere 'cover', toga 'gown'. Pedersen 2.655. Hence vbl. nouns ētach and ētiuth, NIr. ēadach 'clothing', with vb. NIr. ēaduighim.

NIr. cōirigim 'arrange, prepare' (fr. cōir 'suitable, right') now used like, and doubtless influenced by, NE dress (McKenna).

W. dilladu, fr. dillad 'clothes' (6.12).

---

5. ON klæða, OE clāpian, clǣpan (both rare), ME, NE clothe, MHG, NHG kleiden, etc., all derivs. of the words for 'cloth' or 'clothes', ON klæði, OE clāp (6.12). NED s.v. clothe.

OE gewǣdian, OHG wāten, MHG wæten, fr. the words for 'clothes', OE gewǣde, OHG wāt, giwāti, MHG wāt (6.12).

OE scrȳdan, ME schride fr. OE scrūd 'garment, clothing' (6.12). ON skrȳða less common for 'dress'.

ME dresse, NE dress, in Chaucer still merely 'prepare, get ready', fr. OFr. dresser 'arrange', Lat. *dīrēctiāre, fr. dīrēctus 'straight'. NED s.v. REW 2645.

6. Lith. aprėdyti, fr. rėdas 'order', this fr. WhRuss. rēd = Pol. rząd, ChSl. rędŭ 'order'. Brückner, Sl. Fremdwörter 125. Skardžius 188.

Lith. aprengti, cpd. of rengti 'arrange, prepare'.

Lith. apdaryti, cpd. of daryti 'do, make', which is also used for 'put on, wear' (NSB s.v., 2; Fraenkel IF 52.297).

Lith. apvilkti, Lett. apvilkt, beside Lith. vilkéti, Lett. valkāt 'be clothed in, wear' : Lith. vilkti, Lett. vilkt 'draw' (9.33). Leskien, Ablaut 354 f.

Lit!.. apgerbti, Lett. apg'ērbt, g'erbt (the Lett. prob. fr. Lith., cf. Mühl.-Endz. 1.698) : Lith. gerbti 'praise, treat honorably', Lith. garbé 'honor', Lett. garbāt 'care for, attend'. Semantic development apparently fr. 'honor' through 'adorn, decorate' to 'dress'. Leskien, Ablaut 362.

7. ChSl. oděti, SCr. odjesti, Boh. odíti, Pol. odziać, Russ. odet', with the iter. forms ChSl. odějate, etc., cpd. of obŭ- (o-) 'about' and ChSl. děti 'place, put' (12.12). Cf. Lith. děvěti 'wear' (clothing). Berneker 191 f.

ChSl. oblěšti, SCr. oblačiti, Boh. oblékati, Pol. oblec, fr. *ob-wlek-, cpd. of ChSl. vlěšti, etc. 'draw' (9.33).

Boh. ošatiti, fr. šaty 'clothes' (6.12).

Pol. ubrać, iter. ubierać, cpd. of u 'at, on, by' and brać 'take' (11.13). Cf. rozbierać 'take apart' and 'undress', and Russ. u-birat' 'take away' and 'arrange, put in order, adorn' (a room, a dress, one's hair, etc.). Berneker 57.

6.12 CLOTHING, CLOTHES

Grk.	ἐσθής, εἵματα, ἱμάτια	Goth.	wasʼjōs	Lith.	drabužis, drapanos
NG	ροῦχα, ἐνδύματα, φορέματα	ON	klæði, būningr, fot		rubai
		Dan.	klæder	Lett.	drēbes
Lat.	vestis, vestitus, vestimentum	Sw.	kläder, klädning	ChSl.	odežda, riza
		OE	clāpes, gewǣde, rēaf, scrūd, hrægl	SCr.	odjeća, odijelo, ruho, haljine
It.	vestiti, abiti	ME	clothes, iwede	Boh.	šaty, oděv, oblek
Fr.	vêtements, habits	NE	clothes, clothing, dress	Pol.	suknie, odzież, odzienie
Sp.	vestidos, ropa	Du.	kleederen, kleeding	Russ.	odežda, plat'e
Rum.	îmbrăcăminte, haine	OHG	wāt, giwāti	Skt.	vasana-, vastra-, vāsas-, cela-
Ir.	dillat, ētach, ētiuth	MHG	kleit, kleidunge, wāt		
NIr.	ēadach	NHG	kleider, kleidung	Av.	vaṅhana-, vastra-
W.	dillad, gwisg				
Br.	gwiskamant				

The generic 'clothing, clothes' is expressed by collectives, or by plurals the singular of which denotes an article of clothing, a 'garment' (but sometimes also coll.) or in some cases 'cloth'.

Many of the words are derived from the verbs for 'clothe' and several from nouns for 'cloth'.

1. Derivs. of IE *wes- in ἕννῡμι 'clothe' (6.11).

Grk. ἐσθής, Dor. ἐσθάς, sg. coll., orig. a fem. abstract in -τητ-, -τᾱτ-, with θ fr. the neut. ἔσ-θος (formed like πλῆ-θος, etc.), Schwyzer, IF 30, 443. Buck, Cl.Ph. 12.178 f.; Grk. εἷμα, Aeol. ἔμμα, Cret. ϝῆμα, fr. *ϝέσ-μα (Cret. ϝῆμα coll. 'clothing', elsewhere mostly pl. as εἵματα). Grk. ἱμάτιον, Ion. εἱμάτιον, sg. 'garment', esp. 'cloak', pl. 'clothes', fr. εἷμα; Lat. vestis (> It. veste, etc.), hence (through vb. vestīre) vestītus, vestīmentum (> It. vestito, Sp. vestido, Fr. vêlement, sg. 'garment' or coll., pl. 'clothes'); W. gwisg 'garment, clothing', pl. 'clothes', Br. gwisk 'swaddling clothes', formerly 'clothes', in this sense now replaced by gwiskamant (coll.; formed after Fr. vêtement); Skt. vāsas-, vasana-, Av. vaṅhana- (cf. Hom. ἑανός 'robe, garment', fr. *ϝέσανος), Skt. vastra-, Av. vastra-, pl. 'clothes' (for *ϝέσ-τρα-); Toch. A wsāl (SSS 6, 471).

2. Grk. ἔνδῡμα 'garment', NG id., also sg. coll. or pl. 'clothes', fr. ἐνδύω 'clothe' (6.11).

NG ροῦχα 'clothes' (the pop. word), sg. 'garment', fr. Slavic (below, 7). G. Meyer, Neugr. Stud. 2.55.

NG φόρεμα 'garment', esp. 'woman's dress', pl. 'clothes', late form of Grk. φόρημα 'burden, that is worn', fr. Grk. φορέω 'carry' also 'wear' (as reg. NG φορῶ), frequent of φέρω 'carry'.

It. abito, Fr. habit 'garment', pl. 'clothes', fr. Lat. habitus 'garment', earlier 'state, condition' fr. habēre 'have'. REW 3964.

Sp. ropa, fr. Gmc., cf. OE rēaf (below, 5). REW 7090.

Rum. îmbrăcăminte 'clothing' (pl. seldom used), fr. îmbrăca 'clothe' (6.11).

Rum. hainā 'garment', pl. 'clothing', fr. SCr. haljina (below, 7).

3. Lat. vestis, etc., above, 1.

4. Ir. dīllat (borrowed fr. W. dillad, word for 'clothe'), OE werian (but reg. Pedersen 1.24), W., Br. dillad, OCorn. dillat 'clothes', etym.? Henry 98.

Ir. ētach, ētiud 'clothes', NIr. ēadach 'cloth, clothes', fr. Ir. in-tuigur, ētim 'clothe' (6.11). Pedersen 2.514, 655.

W. gwisg, Br. gwisk, gwiskamant, above, 1.

5. Goth. wasti, above, 1.

ON klæði, Dan. klæder, Sw. kläder (pl.) 'clothes', sg. 'cloth' or 'garment', Sw. klädning 'garment', coll. 'clothes', OE clāpes, etc. (pl.) 'clothes', sg. 'cloth', MHG kleit, NHG kleid, Du. kleed 'garment, dress', pl. 'clothes', MHG kleidunge, NHG kleidung, Du. kleeding (coll.) 'clothing', fr. words orig. meaning 'cloth' (6.21).

ON būningr, būnaðr 'equipment' and esp. 'clothing', fr. būa 'equip, prepare, dwell' : Goth. bauan 'till, dwell', OHG OE būan 'dwell', IE *bheu- 'become, be'. Walde-P. 2.140 ff.

ON fot, pl. of fat 'vessel' = OE fæt, OS fat, OHG faz 'vessel', cf. Goth. fētjan 'adorn', ga-fēteins 'adornment' : Lith. puodas 'pot', OHG fazzōn 'hold, contain, prepare'. also 'dress'. Walde-P. 2.22. Falk-Torp 200.

OE gewǣde, ME iwede, wede (NE widow's weeds), OHG giwāti, wāt, MHG wāt (coll.) 'clothing', orig. 'cloth', cf. ON vāð 'cloth' (6.21).

OE rēaf 'spoils, booty', but esp. 'garment', pl. 'clothes' : OHG roub 'booty', etc. 20.48).

OE hrægl 'garment, robe, cloak', etc. (NE rail, night-rail, NED), OHG hregil 'garment' (rare), perh. through 'woven piece' : ON hræl 'weaver's reed', Grk. κρέκω 'strike, weave', κρόκη 'woof', etc. Walde-P. 1.483.

OE scrūd 'dress, clothing, garment', ME schroud sometimes also general for 'clothing' (NE shroud) = ON skrūð 'ornament, furniture' : OE scrēadian 'cut off, prune' (NE shred), OHG scrōtan, etc. Walde-P. 2.586. NED s.v. *shroud*, sb.[1].

NE *dress*, fr. vb. *dress* (6.11).

ME *garnement*, NE *garment* 'an article of clothing', pl. 'clothes' (now rather rhetorical, but *garment-makers' union*), fr. OFr. *garnement* 'equipment', deriv. of *garnir* 'furnish, equip'.

6. Lith. *drabužis* 'garment', sg. coll. or pl. 'clothes', Lett. *drēbe* 'cloth, garment', pl. 'clothes' : Lith. *drobė* 'linen cloth', Boh. *z-draby* 'rags, tatters', prob. fr. an extension of IE *der-, in ChSl. *dirati*, OE *teran*, etc. 'tear' (9.28), with development fr. 'rag' to 'cloth', then 'garment'. Mühl.-Endz. 1.497. Buga, Kalba ir Senovė 228. Berneker 219.

Lith. *drapanos* (pl.; sg. rare) 'clothes' : Skt. *drāpi-* 'cloak, mantle', Av. *drafša-* 'banner', ChSl. *drapati* 'scratch, tear', fr. an extension of IE **der-* in words for 'tear'. Here also perh. late Lat. *drappus* (Fr. *drap*) 'cloth'. Walde-P. 1.802. Berneker 220. Walde-H. 1.373. REW 2765.

Lith. *rubai* (pl.) 'clothes' (formerly the usual word), fr. WhRuss. *rub* = ChSl. *rąbŭ* 'cloth' (6.21). Brückner, Sl. Fremdwörter, 128.

Lith. *aprėdas*, *aprėdalas* (sg. as coll.) 'clothing', fr. *aprėdyti* 'clothe' (6.11).

Lett. *apg'ērbs* (sg. as coll.) 'clothing, costume', fr. *apg'ērbt* 'clothe' (6.11). Also Lith. *abgerbas* 'a suit of clothing'.

7. ChSl. *odežda* (*oděja*, *oděnije*), SCr. *odjeća*, *odijelo*, Boh. *oděv*, Pol. *odzież*, *odzienie*, Russ. *odežda* (coll.), fr. ChSl. *oděti*, *oděјati*, etc. 'clothe' (6.11).

ChSl. *riza*, translating ἔνδυμα, ἱμάτιον, ἐσθής, χιτών, and ὀθόνιον 'linen cloth' (Jagić, Entstehungsgesch. 392) : Russ. *riza* 'chasuble', Bulg. *riza* 'shirt', Boh. *říza* 'a long garment', Lith. *ryzai* 'rags' (borrowed), otherwise obscure. Miklosich 279.

SCr. *ruho*, Boh. *roucho*, Pol. *rucho* 'garment, clothing' (OPruss. *rūkai* 'clothes' fr. Pol.), Bulg. *roucha* 'cloth', late ChSl. *rucho* 'load, cloth, spoils', as orig. 'spoils', fr. the root in ChSl. *rušiti* 'wreck, destroy', Lith. *rausti* 'root up', etc., IE **reu-s-*, extension of **reu-*. Walde-P. 2.356. Brückner 467. Hence NG ροῦχα 'clothes', Rum. *rufă*, 'soiled clothes'.

SCr. *haljina* 'garment', pl. 'clothes' : *halja* 'dress, coat', Bulg. *halina* 'long upper garment', fr. Turk. *halı* 'carpet, rug'. Berneker 383.

Boh. *šat*, Pol. *szata* 'garment', pl. 'clothes' (now more common in Boh. than in Pol.) orig.? Brückner 542.

Boh. *oblek* 'garment, suit of clothes', fr. *oblékati* 'clothe' (6.11).

Pol. *suknia* 'garment', pl. 'clothes', fr. *sukno* 'cloth' (6.21).

Russ. *plat'e* (also esp. woman's dress) : ChSl. *platŭ* 'cloth' (6.21).

8. Skt. *vasana-*, Av. *vaŋhana-*, Skt., Av. *vastra-*, above, 1.

Skt. *cela-* 'garment, clothes', fr. *cil-* (rare) 'put on clothes', etym. dub., perh. : Lith. *kailis* 'hide, pelt'. Uhlenbeck 93.

6.13 TAILOR

Grk.	**ἱματιουργός*, *ῥάπτης* (late)	Goth.	. . . .	Lith.	*siuvėjas*
NG	*ῥάφτης*	ON	*skraddari*	Lett.	*drēbnieks*, *skruoderis*
Lat.	(*vestītor*, *sartor*)	Dan.	*skrædder*	ChSl.	. . . .
It.	*sarto*	Sw.	*skräddare*	SCr.	*krojač*, *šnajder*
Fr.	*tailleur*	OE	*sēamere*	Boh.	*krejči*
Sp.	*sastre*	ME	*taillour*	Pol.	*krawiec*
Rum.	*croĭtor*	NE	*tailor*	Russ.	*portnoj*
Ir.	. . . .	Du.	*kleermaker*	Skt.	*sūcika-*, *sāucika-*
NIr.	*tāilliūr*	OHG	*scrōtari*	Av.	. . . .
W.	*teiliwr*	MHG	*schrōtære*, *snīdære*		
Br.	*kemener*	NHG	*schneider*		

Words for 'tailor', as a general term for one who makes clothes, are partly derivatives or compounds of words for 'clothes' or 'cloth', but mostly words that originally were used more specifically of the 'cutter', 'sewer', or 'mender'.

1. Grk. *ἱματιουργός, lit. 'clothes-maker', not directly attested, but cf. ἱματιουργική (sc. τέχνη) the 'tailor's art'.

Late Grk. (5th cent. A.D.+) ῥάπτης, NG ῥάφτης, fr. ῥάπτω 'sew' (6.35).

2. Late Lat. *vestītor*, fr. *vestīre* 'clothe', *vestis* 'garment' (6.11).

Late Lat. *sartor*, (> It. *sarto*, Sp. *sastre*), fr. *sarcīre* 'mend' : Grk. ἕρκος 'inclosure'. Walde-P. 2.502. Ernout-M. 895. REW 7614.

Fr. *tailleur*, OFr. *tailleor* (> ME *taillour*, NE *tailor*), fr. *tailler* 'cut' (9.22). Through the English also NIr. *tāilliūr*, W. *teiliwr*. The latter was divided by pop. etym. *teili-wr*, as if from *gwr* 'man' (older pl. *teili-wyr*, cf. *gwyr* 'men').

Rum. *croĭtor*, fr. *croi* 'cut out', esp. 'cut out a garment', fr. Slavic (below, 6).

3. Br. *kemener*, i.e. *kem-ben-er*, lit. 'one who cuts and puts together' : MBr. *quemenas* (pret.) 'cut', cpd. of **kom-* (= Lat. *con-*) and *bena* 'cut, hew' : Ir. *benim* 'strike' (9.21). Pedersen 2.463. Henry 60.

4. ON *skraddari*, Dan. *skrædder*, Sw. *skräddare*, fr. MLG *schrāder*, orig. 'cutter', fr. *schrāden* 'cut'. Falk-Torp 1033.

OHG *scrōtari*, MHG *schrōtære*, orig. 'cutter', fr. OHG *scrōtan* 'cut', a parallel form to MLG *schrāden* (above), both fr. extensions of **sker-* in OE *sceran* 'cut', etc. (9.22). Walde-P. 2.586. Falk-Torp 1033.

OE *sēamere*, fr. *sēam*, NE *seam* : ON *sauma* 'sew' (6.35).

Du. *kleermaker*, for *kleeder-maker* 'clothes-maker'.

MHG *snīdære*, NHG *schneider* (in MHG also 'mercer, plowman'), orig. 'cutter', fr. OHG *snīdan* 'cut' (9.22).

5. Lith. *siuvėjas*, : Lith. *siūti* 'sew' (6.35).

Lett. *drēbnieks*, fr. *drēbe* 'cloth, garment' (6.12).

Lett. *skruoderis*, fr. MLG *schrāder* (above, 4). Mühl.-Endz. 3.900.

6. SCr. *krojač*, Boh. *krejči*, Pol. *krawiec* : ChSl. *krojiti*, etc. 'cut' (9.22). Berneker 620.

SCr. *šnajder*, fr. NHG *schneider* (above, 4).

Russ. *portnoj* : *porty* 'clothes' (obs.), *portki* 'drawers', ChSl. *prŭtŭ* 'piece of cloth', Pol. *part* 'coarse hempen cloth', etc., root connection? Miklosich 243. Brückner 397.

7. Skt. *sūcika-*, *sāucika-*, lit. 'needle-worker', fr. *sūci-* 'needle' (6.36).

6.21 CLOTH

Grk.	*ὕφασμα*, *ῥάκος*	Goth.	*fana*	Lith.	*milas*, *gelumbė*
NG	*ὕφασμα*, *πανί*	ON	*klæði*, *vāð*, *dūkr*	Lett.	*vadmala*, *drēbe*, *drāna*, *mila*
Lat.	*textum*, *textīle*, *pannus*	Dan.	*klæde*, *tøi*	ChSl.	*platŭ*, *sukno*, *rąbŭ*
It.	*panno*, *stoffa*, *tela*	Sw.	*kläde*, *tyg*	SCr.	*sukno*, *čoha*, *latak*
Fr.	*étoffe*, *tissu*, *drap*, *toile*	OE	*clāþ*, *clǣþ*	Boh.	*sukno*, *látka*
Sp.	*paño*, *tela*	ME	*cloth*	Pol.	*sukno*, *płat*, *chusta*
Rum.	*stofă*, *postav*, *pănură*	NE	*cloth*	Russ.	*tkan'*, *sukno*, *materija*
Ir.	*brēit*	Du.	*laken*	Skt.	*vasana-*, *vastra-*
NIr.	*ēadach*, *brēid*	OHG	*fane*, *tuoh*	Av.	*ubdaēna-*.
W.	*brethyn*	MHG	*tuoch*, *lachen*		
Br.	*mezer*	NHG	*tuch*, *zeug*, *stoff*		

'Cloth' is considered here primarily as the generic term for fabrics like wool, cotton, linen, etc., but also as a piece of such fabric, 'a cloth', some of the words being used mainly or only in the latter sense.

Several of the words for 'cloth' reflect the process of 'weaving', 'spinning', and in one important group (NE *cloth*, etc.) probably 'felting'. Some result from specialization of words for 'material' or 'equipment'. A 'piece of cloth' may be something 'torn off, cut off' or the like.

Some of the words listed are less generic than NE *cloth*, with differentiation between woolen and linen or cotton cloth.

1. Grk. ὕφασμα : ὑφαίνω 'weave' (6.33).

Grk. ῥάκος (in Hom. 'ragged garment', pl. 'rags', then 'piece of cloth' as in NT), Aeol. βράκος 'garment' : ῥακόω 'tear in strips', Skt. *vṛkṇa-* 'torn', ChSl. *vraska* 'fold, wrinkle', etc. Walde-P. 1.286 f. Boisacq 833.

NG πανί, fr. Lat. *pannus* (below, 2).

2. Lat. *textum*, *textīle* fr. *texere* 'weave' (6.33), whence also (**tex-lā-*) *tēla* (also 'warp, loom'; > It., Sp. *tela*, Fr. *toile*), and Fr. *tisser* whence sb. *tissu*. Ernout-M. 1038. REW 8620.

Lat. *pannus* ('piece of cloth', esp. 'rag'), Goth. *fana* (reg. for ῥάκος), OHG *fano* (NHG *fahne* like OE *fana*, ON *fani* specialized to 'banner') : Grk. πήνη 'thread on the bobbin, woof', pl. 'web', πῆνος· ὕφασμα (Hesych.). Walde-P. 2.5. Ernout-M. 729. Feist 142.

Hence It. *panno*, Sp. *paño*, NG πανί; Rum. *pănură* fr. the dim. Lat. **pannula* (*pannulus* attested). REW 6204, 6203.

It. *stoffa*, Fr. *étoffe* (Sp. *estofa*), Rum. *stofă*, fr. the Gmc. word seen in NHG *stoff*, this fr. Lat. *stuppa* 'coarse linen, tow', fr. Grk. στύππη (perh. : Skt. *stupa-* 'tuft of hair', Walde-P. 2.620). This is preferable to the usual deriv. of Gmc. fr. Romance, though the ins and outs of borrowing are complicated. REW 8332.

Fr. *drap* (It. *drappo* 'silk cloth', Sp. *trapo* 'rag, sail'), fr. late Lat. *drappus* 'cloth', perh. a Gallic word : Lith. *drapanos* 'clothes', etc. (6.12). REW 2765. Wartburg 3.156.

Rum. *postav* (esp. 'woolen cloth'), fr. Slavic, cf. ChSl. *postavŭ* 'loom, products of the loom', Bulg. *postavŭ* 'lining', etc. (6.34).

3. Ir. *brēit* (NIr. *brēid*), W. *brethyn* : Ir. *brat* 'cloak', Br. *broz* 'skirt', perh. Grk. φᾶρος 'cloak'. G. S. Lane, Language 7.279 f.

NIr. *ēadach* 'clothing' (6.12), also 'cloth'.

Br. *mezer*, fr. **māderia*, Lat. *māteria* 'material'. Loth, Mots lat. 187.

4. OE *clāþ* (> ME. NE *cloth*), rarely *clǣþ* (> ON *klæði*, Dan. *klæde*, Sw. *kläde*), more widespread in the secondary sense 'garment', pl. 'clothes' (6.12) :

OE *æt-clīþende* 'sticking to', *clīþa* 'plaster', etc., fr. IE **glei-t-*, extension of **glei-*, in Grk. γλία, Lat. *glūs* 'glue', OE *clǣg*, MLG *klei* 'clay', etc. As a name for 'cloth' it apparently referred orig. to the early process of felting. Walde-P. 1.620. Falk-Torp 540. NED s.v. *cloth*.

ON *vāð* : OE *gewǣde*, OHG *giwāti* 'clothes' (6.12), IE **wedh-*, extension of **au-* 'weave' (6.33). Falk-Torp 1340 f.

ON *dūkr* (Dan. *dug*, Sw. *duk* now mostly 'tablecloth') fr. MLG *dōk*, *dūk* (Du. *doek*) = OHG *tuoh*, MHG *tuoch*, NHG *tuch*, etym.? Falk-Torp 164.

Dan. *tøi*, Sw. *tyg* (also 'gear, tackle', late ON *tȳgi* 'equipment, implement'), apparently borrowed fr. MLG *tūch* 'implement, armor, article of clothing' : NHG *zeug* (OHG *gi-ziuc* 'equipment', etc.), MLG *tūgen* 'make', MHG *ziugen* 'prepare, produce'. The transfer from 'equipment' to 'clothes, cloth' was through the application in warfare to 'armor'. Falk-Torp 1314 f. Weigand-H. 2.1320 f.

Du. *laken* (> ME *lake* 'fine linen'), OS *lacan* = MHG *lachen* (OHG *lahhan* usually 'a cover of cloth') : MLG *lak*, Lat. *laxus*, Ir. *lace* 'loose', hence orig. 'something pliant' or 'loose hanging'(?). Walde-P. 2.712 f. Falk-Torp 619. Franck-v. W. 368.

5. Lith. *milas*, Lett. *mila* (both usually 'woolen homespun'; OPruss. *milan* 'gewant') perh. : Grk. μαλλός 'tuft of hair'. Walde-P. 2.294.

Lith. *gelumbė*, orig. 'blue cloth' now esp. 'manufactured cloth' : ChSl. *goląbyjŭ*, Russ. *golubyj*, OPruss. *golimban* 'blue' (15.67).

Lett. *vadmala*, of Scand. orig., cf. Icel. *vaðmāl*, Sw. *vadmal* 'homespun', ON *vāð-māl*, lit. 'a measure of cloth', a unit of legal tender at fairly late date in the north. The orthography indicates a direct borrowing rather than through LG *wātmāl*, *wammāl*, *wātman*, etc. as Mühl.-Endz. 4.430.

Lett. *drēbe*, in pl. 'clothes', see 6.12.

Lett. *drāna*, prob. fr. **der-* in *dirāt* 'tear' (cf. Lith. *drabužis* 'clothes', etc., 6.12). Mühl.-Endz. 1.494.

6. ChSl. *sukno* (Supr. with or without *vlaśeno* for τρίχινον ῥάκος 'hair-cloth'), etc., general Slavic for 'cloth', orig. 'what is spun' : ChSl. *sukati*, Boh. *soukati*, etc. 'turn, wind' and (like Lith. *sukti*) used also for 'spin' (as 'spin' often fr. 'turn', 6.31). Walde-P. 2.470. Miklosich 333. Brückner 525.

ChSl. *platŭ* (reg. for ῥάκος in Gospels, etc.), Pol. *płat* 'piece of cloth, rag'), Russ. *platok* 'handkerchief', *plat'e* 'dress', prob. : Lith. *platus*, Grk. πλατύς, Skt. *pṛthu-* 'broad', as orig. 'something spread out'. Miklosich 249. Brückner 420. Otherwise (: OHG *spaltan* 'split', etc.) Walde-P. 2.678.

Late ChSl. *rąbŭ* (Pol. *rąb* 'seam, hem', Boh. *rub* 'wrong side' of cloth, etc.; cf. SCr. *rubača*, Russ. *rubaška* 'shirt') : Pol. *rąbać*, Russ. *rubit'* etc. 'cut, hew' (outside root connections?), hence orig. 'piece cut off' like Grk. ῥάκος (above, 1). Brückner 455. Miklosich 281.

SCr. *čoha* fr. Turk. *çuha* 'cloth'. Berneker 159.

SCr. *latak*, Boh. *látka* : Boh., Pol. *lata*, Russ. *latka* 'patch, rag', outside connection? Berneker 693. Brückner 291.

Pol. *chusta* (mostly 'linen cloth'), etym.? Brückner 186 (: ChSl. *skutŭ* 'edge of a garment', etc., but??).

Russ. *tkan'*, fr. *tkat'* 'weave' (6.33).

7. Skt. *vasana-*, *vastra-* 'clothing' (6.12) also 'cloth'.

Av. *ubdaēna-*, fr. IE **webh-* 'weave' (6.33). Barth. 401.

6.22 WOOL

Grk.	ἔριον	Goth.	wulla	Lith.	vilnos
NG	μαλλί	ON	ull	Lett.	vilna
Lat.	lāna	Dan.	uld	ChSl.	vlŭna
It.	lana	Sw.	ull	SCr.	vuna
Fr.	laine	OE	wull, wulle	Boh.	vlna
Sp.	lana	ME	wolle	Pol.	welna
Rum.	lînă	NE	wool	Russ.	šerst'
Ir.	olann	Du.	wol	Skt.	ūrṇā-
NIr.	olann	OHG	wolla	Av.	varanā-
W.	gwlan	MHG	wolle		
Br.	gloan	NHG	wolle		

1. IE *wḷnā-, *wlənā-, etc. fr. *wel- in words for 'hair, wool, grass, etc.', prob. the same as in Lat. vellere, etc. 'tear, pluck'. Walde-P. 1.296 f. Ernout-M. 521, 1081. Walde-H. 1.756 f. Feist 476 f.

Lat. lāna (> Romance words); Ir. olann, W. gwlan, Br. gloan; Goth. wulla, ON ull, OE wull, wulle, etc., general Gmc.; Lith. vilnos (pl. coll.), Lett. vilna; ChSl. vlŭna, etc. general Slavic (but Russ. volna old or dial.); Skt. ūrṇā-, Av. varanā-; cf. Grk. (rare) λῆνος, Dor. λᾶνος 'fillet, fleece', Lat. vellum 'fleece', Grk. οὖλος 'woolly'.

2. Att. ἔριον, Ion. εἶρος, εἴριον, fr.

IE *wer-, in ἀρήν 'lamb', Lat. vervex 'wether', Skt. urā- 'sheep', all wool-bearing animals, perh. the same as IE *wer- 'cover', in Skt. vṛ- 'protect, cover', etc. Walde-P. 1.269 f.

3. NG μαλλί, fr. Grk. μαλλός 'tuft of hair' : Lith. milas 'cloth' (6.21).

4. Late ChSl., obs. SCr., Russ. jarina : Grk. ἔριφος 'kid', Lat. ariēs 'ram', Lith. éras 'lamb'. Walde-P. 1.135. Berneker 447.

5. Russ. šerst' : ChSl. srŭstĭ, Pol. sier(ś)ć, Boh. srst' 'animal hair', Lith. šerys 'bristle', OHG hrusti 'crest', etc. Walde-P. 1.427. Brückner 490.

6.23 LINEN; FLAX

Grk.	λίνον	Goth.	lein	Lith.	audeklas, drobė; linai
NG	λινὸ πανί; λινάρι	ON	lin, lērept, hörr	Lett.	audekls; lini
Lat.	linum, linteum	Dan.	lærred, linned; hør	ChSl.	platno; linŭ
It.	tela (di lino), lino	Sw.	lärft, linne; lin	SCr.	platno, bez; lan
Fr.	toile (de lin); lin	OE	linen; lin, fleax	Boh.	plátno; len
Sp.	lienzo, lino	ME	linen; lin, flex	Pol.	płotno; len
Rum.	pînză; in	NE	linen; flax	Russ.	polotno, cholst; len
Ir.	lín	Du.	linnen, lijnwaad; vlas	Skt.	kṣāuma-; kṣumā-
NIr.	lliain; llin	OHG	linin; lin, flahs, haru		
W.	lliain; llin	MHG	linnen, linwāt; lin,		
Br.	lien; lin		vlahs, har		
		NHG	leinen, leinwand;		
			flachs, lein		

Linen, considered here as a material for clothing parallel to wool, cotton, etc., was originally denoted by the same word as that for the raw material, flax. But 'linen' and 'flax' are now generally differentiated, partly by parallel forms of the old word, including the use of derivative adjectives, compounds, or phrases for 'linen', and partly by the restriction of the old word to one sense and the substitution of different words for the other. The situation is shown in

the list by giving first the words for 'linen', or 'linen' and 'flax', and adding those for 'flax' alone if different.

1. Eur. *līno- 'flax, linen'. Walde-P. 2.440 f. Schrader, Reallex. 1.323 ff. Ernout-M. 555. Walde-H. 1.810.

Grk. λίνον 'flax, linen', NG λινὸ πανί 'linen cloth', λινάρι 'flax'.

Lat. līnum, whence It., Sp. lino 'flax, linen', Fr. lin, Rum. in 'flax'. For It. tela, Fr. toile 'cloth', see 6.21. Fr. linge 'linen' (clothes, etc.), fr. Lat. adj. lineus 'of linen'. REW 5060. Gamillscheg 563.

Ir. lín 'linen', NIr. líon 'flax, linen', W. llin, Br. lin 'flax', fr. Lat. līnum (Vendryes, De hib. voc. 151; Loth, Mots lat. 182), but W. lliain, Br. lien 'linen' are perh. cognate, though the formation is obscure.

Goth. lein 'linen', ON līn 'flax, linen', Norw., Sw. lin, OE, OHG līn, ME lin, NHG lein 'flax'. Hence OE līnen, OHG līnīn, etc., orig. adjs. 'flaxen, linen'.

ON lērept, Dan. lærred, Sw. lärft 'linen (goods)', for *līn-rept, cpd. of ript 'piece of cloth' : ON ripti 'veil' (6.59). Dan. linned (with -d after lærred), Sw. linne, fr. MLG linne = OHG līnīn (above). Falk-Torp 636, 646. Hellquist 577, 609.

Du. lijnwaad, MHG līnwāt, NHG leinwand (transformed after ge-wand 'garment') : ON vāð 'cloth' (6.21).

Lith. linai, Lett. lini, ChSl. linŭ, SCr. lan, Boh., Pol. len, Russ. len 'flax'.

2. Lat. linteum textum, or simply linteum (> Sp. lienzo), the proper term for 'linen fabric', obscure, blend of līnum

with some other word? Ernout-M. 555. Walde-H. 1.811.

Rum. pînză, fr. *pandia : Lat. pandere 'spread out', i.e. from its use on table, bed, etc. REW 6190.

3. ON hörr 'flax, linen', Dan. hør, OHG haru, MHG har, OFris. her 'flax', etym. dub. Walde-P. 1.356. Falk-Torp 454.

OE fleax, ME flex, NE flax, Du. vlas, OHG flahs, MHG vlahs, NHG flachs, prob. fr. the root of Grk. πλέκω, Lat. plectere, OHG flehtan 'plait, braid' (9.75). Walde-P. 2.97. NED s.v. flax.

4. Lith. audeklas, Lett. audekls 'linen cloth' : Lith. austi, Lett. aust 'weave' (6.33).

Lith. drobė 'fine linen cloth', see 6.12.

5. ChSl. platĭno, SCr. platno, Boh. plátno, Pol. płotno, Russ. polotno, perh. : ON feldr 'sheepskin, cloak', Skt. paṭa- 'rag', Lat. pellis 'hide', etc. Walde-P. 2.58 f.

ChSl. prŭtŭ (for λίνον, Mt. 12.20, Mar., Zogr., where platŭ Assem.; Jagić, Entstehungsgesch. 378) : Russ. porty 'clothes' (obs.), portki 'drawers', etc., root connection? Miklosich 243. Brückner 397.

Russ. cholst '(coarse) linen' : Pol. chełst 'roar of waves, rustling of reeds', vb. chełścić 'roar, rustle', etc., hence stiff linen as 'rustling'. Berneker 411. Brückner 178.

SCr. bez, fr. Turk. (orig. Arab.) bez 'linen or cotton cloth'. Lokotsch 280.

6. Skt. kṣāuma- 'linen', fr. kṣumā- 'flax', perh. : kṣu-pa- 'shrub, bush', Russ. chmyz 'brush', chvorost 'bush', all dub. H. Petersson, KZ 46, 145 f. Walde-P. 1.501.

6.24 COTTON

NG	μπαμπάκι	Dan.	bomuld	Lith.	medvilnė, bovelna
It.	cotone	Sw.	bomull	Lett.	kuokvilna
Fr.	coton	ME	cotoun, coton	SCr.	pamuk
Sp.	algodón	NE	cotton	Boh.	bavlna
Rum.	bumbac	Du.	katoen, boomwol	Pol.	bawelna
NIr.	canach, cadás	MHG	kattun, boumwolle	Russ.	chlopok
W.	cotwm	NHG	baumwolle	Skt.	kārpāsa-
Br.	kotoñs				

European names for cotton are mostly borrowed with the plant from oriental sources.

1. Arab. quṭn, quṭun (Sp.-Arab. qoṭun). Schrader, Reallex. 1.84. Lokotsch, 1272. REW 4796a.

It. cotone, Fr. coton (> Br. kotoñs), Sp. algodón, ME cotoun, coton (> W. cotwm), NE cotton, Du. katoen, MHG kattūn (NHG kattun 'calico').

2. An oriental word, perh. orig. Iranian, represented by Pahl. pambak, Osset. bambag, NPers. panba, Arm. bambak. Schrader, loc. cit. Berneker 100 f.

Hence late Lat. bombax 'linteorum aut aliae quaevis quisquiliae' (Du Cange), bombacium (> NE bombasine, bombast, Fr. bombasin, etc.), and apparently Grk. βόμβυξ (> Lat. bombyx) 'silkworm, silk'.

Here also NG μπαμπάκι, Rum. bumbac, SCr. pamuk, but by the mediation of different Turkish forms (cf. Berneker, loc. cit.).

MHG boumwolle, bounwolle, boumwol, etc., NHG baumwolle, LG bōmwolle, Du. boomwol, lit. 'tree wool'. Cf. Hdt. 3.106 (of Indian cotton) τὰ δὲ δένδρεα τὰ ἀπ' αὐτόθι φέρει καρπὸν εἴρια. But possibly the first part was orig. bamb or bomb fr.

the same source as Lat. bombax, etc. (above) and transformed by popular connection with baum 'tree'. Falk-Torp 92.

Dan. bomuld, Sw. bomull, fr. LG bōmwolle with translation of the final member.

Lith. medvilnė, Lett. kuokvilna, lit. 'tree wool', semantic borrowings fr. NHG baumwolle.

Pol. bawełna (> Lith. bovelna), Boh. bavlna, fr. NHG baumwolle with ba- for baum- and translation of final (cf. Dan. bomuld, above). Brückner 18.

3. NIr. canach (also Gael.) : Ir. canach 'down, fuzz', etym.? Macbain 68.

NIr. cadás (also by McKenna s.v. cotton), fr. ME cadas (NE caddis) a sort of coarse cotton or wool used in padding, fr. OFr. cadaz, cadas, further orig. unknown. NED s.v. caddis. Macbain 74.

4. Russ. chlopok : chlop'e 'flocks (of wool), flakes (of snow)', Boh. chlupatý 'hairy', Pol. dial. chłupy 'tufts', otherwise obscure. Berneker 390 f.

5. Skt. kārpāsa-, loanword fr. the same source as Grk. κάρπασος, Lat. carbasus 'fine cotton cloth', Arab. kerpas, etc. Walde-H. 1.165.

6.25 SILK

Grk.	σηρικόν	Goth.	....	Lith.	šilkai
NG	μέταξα, μετάξι	ON	silki	Lett.	zids
Lat.	sēricum	Dan.	silke	ChSl.	šelkŭ, godovablĭ, svila
It.	seta	Sw.	silke, siden	SCr.	svila
Fr.	soie	OE	sioloc, seoloc	Boh.	hedvábí
Sp.	seda	ME	selk	Pol.	jedwab
Rum.	mătase	NE	silk	Russ.	šelk
Ir.	síta, síric	Du.	zijde	Skt.	kāuçeya-
NIr.	síoda	OHG	sīda, serih, silecho	Av.	....
W.	sidan	MHG	sīde		
Br.	seiz	NHG	seide		

Many of the words for 'silk', like the article, are of oriental origin.

1. An oriental word represented by Manchurian sirghe, Mongolian sirkek. The ultimate source is dub., the old identification with a Chinese word being unsubstantiated. Cf. Schrader, Reallex. 2.382; Laufer, Sino-Iranica 538 ff., who thinks the word of Iranian origin.

Grk. σηρικός adj., σηρικόν (σήρ 'silkworm', Σῆρες being later back-formations), Lat. sēricus adj., sēricum, whence Ir. síric, OHG serih. The earliest Grk. reference to 'silk', but without the word, is supposed to be Aristot. HA 551ᵇ13. Miss Richter, AJA 1929, 27 ff., argues for much earlier use of silk.

ChSl. šelkŭ, Russ. šelk, Lith. šilkai, OPruss. silkas, borrowed independently from the Orient (rather than through σηρικόν, etc.) fr. same form with l for s. The Balto-Slavic form then passed, through the Baltic trade, into Gmc., ON silki, Dan., Sw. silke, OE sioloc, seoloc, ME selk, NE silk, etc. Berneker 390 f.

2. An oriental word, prob. by metathesis fr. the Arab. name of Damascus (source of NE damask, etc.). Lokotsch, 476. Schrader, op. cit., 383. Hence late

Grk. μέταξα, μάταξα, NG μέταξα, μετάξι, mataxa 'silk', Fr. matasse 'raw silk'.

3. Late Lat. sēta (fr. saeta 'coarse hair, bristles'), elliptical for sēta sērica. Hence It. seta, Fr. soie, Sp. seda; Ir. síta, NIr. síoda, W. sidan, Br. seiz; OHG sīda, MHG sīde, NHG seide, Du. zijde, MLG zīde (> Sw. siden, Lett. zīds). REW 7498. Vendryes, De hib. voc. 178.

4. Late ChSl., SCr., ORuss. svila, for *sŭvila, fr. sŭviti, cpd. of viti 'wind' (10.14). Orig. a participial formation meaning 'wound', perh. referring to the cocoon of the silkworm.

Russ.-ChSl. godovablĭ, Boh. hedvábí (> Pol. jedwab) fr. Gmc., cf. OHG gotawebbi 'any fine expensive cloth', gl. also sericum, ON guðvefr, OE godweb 'velvet, purple, fine cloth', perh. lit. 'God's cloth', i.e. fine cloth suitable for use in God's service, though the first member may be transformed fr. Arab. quṭn 'cotton' (6.24). Berneker 316. Brückner 204.

5. Skt. kāuçeya-, fr. koça- 'cask, vessel', then applied to the 'cocoon' of the silkworm; cf. koça-kara- 'silkworm', lit. 'cocoon-maker'.

6.26 LACE

NG	δαντέλλα	Dan.	kniplinger	Lith.	karbatkos
It.	trina, merletto	Sw.	spets	Lett.	spice
Fr.	dentelle	NE	lace	SCr.	čipka
Sp.	encaje	Du.	kant	Boh.	krajky, čipky
Rum.	dantelă	NHG	spitzen	Pol.	koronki
NIr.	lása			Russ.	kruževo
W.	ysnoden				
Br.	dantelez				

Lace as a well-known fabric dates from the 16th century A.D. (incipiently somewhat earlier; cf. Encycl. Brit. s.v. lace) so that words for 'lace' are confined to the modern languages.

They are mostly based on words for 'point, edge, tooth, peg, notch', with obvious relation to the appearance of the fabric. A few are from words for 'cord, thread' or 'bobbin', or verbs for 'fit' or 'turn around'.

1. It. trina, fr. Lat. trīnus 'triple', presumably first applied to lace with groups of three points. REW 8910.

It. merletto, dim. of merli 'pinnacles, battlements' of a wall, this prob. (like a row of blackbirds perched on a wall) pl. of merlo 'blackbird'. Hornung, Z. rom. Ph. 21, 456. REW 5534a.

Fr. dentelle, dim. of dent 'tooth'. Hence Rum. dantelă, NG δαντέλλα, Br. dantelez.

Sp. encaje, fr. encajar 'fit, join' (in woodwork), cpd. of caja 'sheath, case', Lat. capsa 'repository, box'. A semantic parallel is seen in NE insertion, usually used of lace set in the body of a garment in contrast to that put on the borders.

2. W. ysnoden 'band, lace' and 'lace' as fabric (like NE lace) : Ir. snáth, Br. neud 'thread', W. nyddu 'spin' (6.31).

3. Dan. kniplinger (pl.), fr. kniple 'make lace', fr. MLG knuppeln (with dissim.) = NHG klöppeln : LG knuppel, NHG klöppel 'bobbin'. Falk-Torp, 549.

NE lace (> NIr. lása) same word as lace in shoelace, etc. (fr. OFr. las, laz, Lat. laqueus 'noose'), which came to be used esp. for ornamental braid (cf. gold lace) and (first through the similar function of lace ruffles?) 'lace' as the fabric in general. NED s.v.

Du. kant, lit. 'edge', fr. OFr. cant 'corner'. Franck-v. W. 291.

NHG spitzen (> Sw. spets), pl. of spitze 'point' (12.352).

4. Lith. karbatkos (pl., NSB; karbatkai Lalis), fr. karbas 'notch, dent', karbuoti 'notch, indent', fr. Pol. karb 'notch', karbować 'notch, indent', fr. NHG kerbe, kerben id. Brückner, Sl. Fremdwörter 90.

Lett. spice, fr. LG or NHG spitze.

Lett. knipele (Dravneek; not in Mühl.-Endz.), fr. MLG knuppeln 'make lace' (above, 3).

5. SCr. čipka, Boh. čipky (pl.), fr. dim. of SCr., Boh. čep 'peg' (cf. Boh. čipek 'little peg').

Boh. krajky (pl.), dim. of kraj, ChSl. krajь 'edge' (12.353). Cf. NE edging sometimes 'lace' (NED s.v. 4).

Pol. koronka or pl. koronki, dim. of korona (fr. Lat. corōna) 'crown' with development through 'coronet, chaplet, rosary', etc. Brückner 257.

Russ. kruževo (cf. ChSl. krąživo 'suturae genus') : Russ. krug, ChSl. krągъ 'circle' (12.82), Russ. kružiti 'turn around'. Miklosich 142. Berneker 626 (without kruževo).

6.27 FELT (sb.)

Grk.	πῖλος	ON	þōfi, flōki	Lith.	tūba
NG	κετσές	Dan.	filt	Lett.	tūba
Lat.	coācta	Sw.	filt	ChSl.	plъstъ
It.	feltro	OE	felt	SCr.	pust
Fr.	feutre	ME	felt	Boh.	plst
Sp.	fieltro	NE	felt	Pol.	pilśń, pilść
Rum.	pîslă	Du.	vilt	Russ.	vojlok
NIr.	feilt, bēabhar	OHG	filz		
W.	llawban	MHG	vilz		
Br.	feltr	NHG	filz		

Words for 'felt', made of pressed hair or wool, are mostly from words denoting the process of manufacture as 'press', 'pound', etc.

1. IE *pil-so- : Lat. pilus 'hair'. Walde-P. 2.71.

Grk. πῖλος, also 'anything made of felt, cap, shoe, etc.' (NG 'hat'), Lat. pilleus 'felt hat, cap', prob. also ChSl. plъstъ (on the formation cf. J. Schmidt, KZ 32, 387 f.), SCr. pust, Boh. plst, Pol. pilśń, pilść. Hence Rum. pîslă (through *pъlsta, *pъstla, cf. Tiktin, s.v.). But the Slavic forms may also be combined with the following group.

2. From *peld- (Gmc. *felt-), prob. an extension of *pel- in Lat. pellere (*pel-d- or pel-n-), perf. pepulī 'strike, drive'. Walde-P. 2.57. Falk-Torp 217. REW 3305.

OE–NE felt, (> NIr. feilt, McKenna), OHG, NHG filz, Du. vilt, etc.; Dan., Sw. filt fr. MLG vilt. Hence MLat. filtrum, It. feltro, Fr. feutre (OFr. feltre > Br. feltr), Sp. fieltro.

3. NG κετσές, like SCr. ćeča, etc. fr. Turk. keçe 'felt, coarse carpet'. Lokotsch 1148.

4. Lat. coācta ('felt' in Caesar BC 3.41; cf. also Plin. NH 8.73 lanae et per se coactae vestem faciunt), fr. pple. of cōgere 'compress'. Hence also late Lat. adj. coāctilis 'made of felt' (Edict. Diocl.), sb. coāctile 'felt', coāctiliārius 'felt-maker'.

5. NIr. bēabhar 'beaver, beaver hat' and 'felt' (Dinneen) fr. NE beaver, used also of a sort of felted cloth in 18th cent. (cf. NED s.v. 4).

W. llawban, back-formation to vb. llawbannu 'felt', lit. 'full by hand', cpd. of llaw 'hand' and pannu 'full (cloth)'.

6. ON þōfi : þœfa 'press', cf. þōf 'crowd, throng', Skt. vi-, sam-tap-'press'. Hence, or at least fr. some Gmc. form of this group, Lith., Lett. tūba, OPruss. tubo. Falk-Torp 1250. Mühl.-Endz. 4.277.

ON flōki (the usual word in NIcel.) : OE flōcan 'clap', Goth. flōkan 'lament', i.e. 'beat the breast', Lat. plangere 'beat, lament'. Walde-P. 2.92. Falk-Torp 239.

7. Russ. vojlok, cf. Pol. wojłok 'felt saddle-blanket', fr. Tartar ojlik 'covering'. Brückner 629.

6.28 FUR

Grk.	(δέρμα, δορά)	ON	(skinn), loð-	Lith.	kailis, kailiniai
NG	γοῦνα	Dan.	pels	Lett.	kažuoks
Lat.	(pellis)	Sw.	pels	ChSl.	kožuchъ, krъzno
It.	pelliccia	OE	pels	SCr.	krzno
Fr.	fourrure	ME	furre	Boh.	kožešina
Sp.	pelliza	NE	fur	Pol.	futro
Rum.	blană	Du.	bont	Russ.	mech
Ir.	(crocenn)	OHG	(fel), pelliz		
NIr.	fionnadh	MHG	belliz		
W.	ffwr	NHG	pelz		
Br.	feur, foulinenn				

Animals' skins provided man's earliest clothing and even after the use of woven cloth continued to play some part. Some of the words for 'skin, hide' (4.12) that are most frequently quotable as applied to clothing are repeated in the list, without further comment below. There are many other obscure terms for garments of skin among various people, as the Gmc. rēno, etc. Cf. Schrader, Reallex. 2.156 ff.

Considered here mainly are the words applied to the dressed skins with fine hair, the 'fur' of medieval and modern times. Some of these are derived from words for 'skin', but several are of quite different origin.

1. NG γοῦνα (esp. 'fur coat', with γουναρικός 'made of fur') = Byz. γοῦνα 'fur coat' (cf. Const. Porph., Cer. 381.11, as worn by the Goths inside out, Achmet ed. Drexl p. 118, 11.9–18), MLat. gunna id. (St. Boniface, 8th cent.; also Schol. Bern. ad Verg. Buc. et Georg., ed. Hagen, p. 946), whence OFr. gonne, goune 'long coat' (> ME goune, NE gown > W. gwn, 6.42). Here also (through Grk.) Bulg. guna 'cloak of goat's hair', etc. (Berneker 363), Alb. gunë 'woolen or fur cloak'. Ultimate orig. unknown (not Celtic), perh. non-IE. Pokorny, Z. sl. Ph. 4.103 f. NED s.v. gown.

2. From Lat. pellis (4.12) comes the late Lat. adj. pellicius, -eus 'of skins', fem. sb. pellīcia > It. pelliccia (Fr. pelisse 'fur cloak', Sp. pelliza (ON piliza, OE pylece 'fur cloak', NE obs. pilch), OHG pelliz, MHG belliz, NHG pelz, MLG pels (> Dan., Sw. pels). REW 6375. Weigand-H. 2.392.

Fr. fourrure (OFr. forreure 'fur lining'), fr. OFr. forrer 'line, line with fur', fr. OFr. fuerre 'sheath', fr. Gmc., cf. Goth. fōdr 'sheath' (NHG futter also 'lining'). But OFr. fuerre must itself have been used also for 'fur lining', though this is not attested. For it is the source of Br. feur both 'sheath' and 'fur' and ME furre, NE fur only in the secondary sense. REW 3405a. Wartburg 3.672 ff., NED s.v. fur.

Rum. blană, fr. Slavic, cf. Boh. blana 'membrane, fine fur', etc. (Berneker 69 f.). Tiktin 197 f.

3. Ir. crocenn 'skin' used of the 'golden fleece' (K. Meyer, Contr. 524).

NIr. fionnadh (used for the fine hair of the face and the hair of animals; but also for fur garments?) fr. MIr. findfad 'hair', cpd. of find 'hair' (4.14) and -bod 'be', with the sense of the composition entirely obscure. Pedersen 2.14.

W. ffwr, older ffwrri, etc., fr. ME furre, NE fur. Parry-Williams 157.

Br. feur 'sheath' and 'fur', fr. OFr. fuerre (above, 2).

Br. foulinenn, orig. 'cured fur' (cf. Le Gonidec, s.v.), fr. MBr. fouliff (fr. Fr. fouler) 'full'.

4. In ON most of the words for articles of clothing made of fur are compounds of loð-, fr. loðinn 'hairy, shaggy' (actually a past pple. 'overgrown with', cf. Goth. liudan 'grow up', etc. 12.53), e.g. loðbrœkr 'fur breeches', loðkápa 'fur cloak', etc., cf. NIcel. loðskinn 'fur'.

Du. bont, fr. MLG = MHG bunt 'multicolored fur' (in contrast to grā 'gray fur'), fr. adj. bunt 'with white and black stripes', this prob. fr. Lat. pūnctus 'dotted'. Weigand-H. 1.308. Kluge-G. 87. Franck-v. W. 82.

5. Lith. kailis, kailiniai (the latter usually 'fur garment'), etym. dub. (see 6.12, Skt. cela- 'clothes').

6. SCr.–ChSl. kožuchъ, Boh. kožešina, fr. koža 'hide' (4.12). Hence Lett. kažuoks. Berneker 597.

SCr.–ChSl. krъzno, SCr. krzno (Boh. krzno 'fur coat'), etym. disputed, perh. cognate with Ir. crocenn, etc. 'hide' (4.12). Hence MHG kursina, late OE crusne, MLat. crusna, crusina 'fur coat', borrowed through Slavic fur trade. Berneker 671.

Russ. mech (pl. mecha) : ChSl. měchъ 'leather bottle', Russ. mech (pl. mechi) 'bellows', Boh. měch, Pol. miech 'sack', Lett. maiss 'sack', Skt. meṣa- 'ram, fleece' perh. orig. 'sheepskin'. Walde-P. 2.303. Berneker 2.46.

Pol. futro (also 'lining'), 16th cent. borrowing fr. NHG futter 'lining' (: Goth. fōdr, cf. Fr. fourrure, above, 2). Brückner 130.

6.29 LEATHER

Grk.	σκῦτος	Goth.	(skauda-, filleins)	Lith.	skūra
NG	πετσί, τομάρι	ON	leðr	Lett.	āda
Lat.	corium	Dan.	læder	ChSl.	koža, azno
It.	cuoio	Sw.	läder	SCr.	koža
Fr.	cuir	OE	leþer	Boh.	kůže
Sp.	cuero	ME	lether	Pol.	skóra
Rum.	piele	NE	leather	Russ.	koža
Ir.	lethar	Du.	lēer	Skt.	carman-
NIr.	leathar	OHG	leder	Av.	čaroman-
W.	lledr	MHG	leder		
Br.	ler	NHG	leder		

Words for 'leather' originate mostly in words for 'hide, skin', etc. Some, many of them loanwords, show specialization from 'piece', 'cut', etc.

1. Grk. σκῦτος, orig. 'hide' (: OE hyd, etc., 4.12), but usually 'leather'. Cf. σκῡτοτόμος 'leather-cutter' (Hom.), 'shoemaker', etc.

Grk. δέρμα 'skin, hide' (4.12) rarely used for 'leather', but often adj. δερμάτινος 'made of leather'.

NG πετσί, fr. It. pezza 'piece of cloth, piece' = Fr. pièce, NE piece, fr. a Gallic *pettia : Br. pez 'piece', W. peth

'part, thing'. Meyer, Neugr. Stud. 4.70. REW 6450.

Byz. τομάριον, NG τομάρι, dim. of τόμος 'slice' (: τέμνω 'cut'), thence 'tome, scroll'. Development through 'scroll' to the 'parchment' or 'skin' of the scroll and finally generalized to 'skin' and 'leather'.

2. Lat. corium (> It. cuoio, Fr. cuir, Sp. cuero), Skt. carman-, Av. čaroman-, all orig. 'hide' (4.12).

Rum. piele, fr. Lat. pellis 'hide' (4.12).

3. Ir. lethar, NIr. leathar, W. lledr : Br. ler beside ON leðr, OE leþer, OHG

leder, etc., uncertain whether cognate groups (**letro-*) or orig. Celtic (**letro-* fr. **pletro-* : Lat. *pellis?*) with early Gmc. borrowing. Pedersen 2.45. Or as orig. 'smoothed skin' (**letro-* fr. **lēitro-*) : Grk. λεῖος, Lat. *lēvis* 'smooth'? Kluge-G. 350.

4. Goth. *skauda-* in *skaudaraip* (acc. sg.) 'thong' : Grk. σκῦτος, etc. (above, 1). Feist 430.

Goth. *filleins* (adj. translating δερμάτινος 'leathern') : OHG *fel*, Lat. *pellis* 'hide' (4.12). Feist 152.

5. Lith. *skūra*, Lett. *āda*, orig. 'hide' (4.12).

6. ChSl., SCr., Russ. *koža*, Boh. *kůže*, orig. 'hide' (4.12).

Pol. *skóra* orig. 'hide' (4.12) or esp. *skóra wyprawna*, lit. 'tanned hide'.

ChSl. *azno*, *jazno* (**azĭno*) : Skt. *ajina-* 'hide, skin' (4.12). Berneker 35.

6.31 SPIN

Grk.	*νέω, νήθω, κλώθω*	Goth.	*spinnan*	Lith.	*verpti*
NG	*γνέθω*	ON	*spinna*	Lett.	*vērpt, prest, sprest*
Lat.	*nēre*	Dan.	*spinde*	ChSl.	*pręsti*
It.	*filare*	Sw.	*spinna*	SCr.	*presti*
Fr.	*filer*	OE	*spinnan*	Boh.	*příst i*
Sp.	*hilar*	ME	*spinne*	Pol.	*prząść*
Rum.	*toarce*	NE	*spin*	Russ.	*prjast', sprjast'*
Ir.	*snī-*	Du.	*spinnen*	Skt.	*kṛt-*
NIr.	*snīomhaim*	OHG	*spinnan*		
W.	*nyddu*	MHG	*spinnen*		
Br.	*neza*	NHG	*spinnen*		

Words for 'spin' are mostly based on the notions of either 'turn' or 'stretch', in one group derived from the noun for 'thread'.

1. IE *(*s*)*nē-*, *(*s*)*nēi-* in words for 'spin', 'sew' (Gmc.), 'thread', 'needle' beside **sneu-* in words for 'sinew', primary sense 'turn, wind' or 'stretch'(?). Walde-P. 9.694. Ernout-M. 665 f. Pedersen 1.68, 2.633.

Grk. νέω (*σνήιω, cf. 3 sg. pres. νῇ, 3 sg. imperf. ἔννη, etc.), νήθω, NG pop. γνέθω; Lat. *nēre;* Ir. *snī-*, NIr. *snīomhaim*, W. *nyddu*, Br. *neza* : OHG *nājan* 'sew'; Lett. *snāt* 'twist lightly' (as in spinning or esp. plaiting, cf. Mühl.-Endz. 3.974), Skt. *snāyu-* and *snāvan-*, Grk. νεῦρον 'sinew'.

2. Grk. κλώθω, root connections? Walde-P. 1.464.

3. It. *filare*, Fr. *filer*, Sp. *hilar*, fr. VLat. *fīlāre* (CGL 5 passim), fr. Lat. *fīlum* 'thread' (6.38). REW 3293. Wartburg 3.539.

Rum. *toarce*, fr. VLat. **torcere*, Lat. *torquēre* 'turn around, twist' (10.13). REW 8798.

4. Goth. *spinnan*, etc., general Gmc., fr. IE *(*s*)*pen-* in OHG *spannan* 'stretch', Lith. *pinti* 'plait', ChSl. *pęti* 'stretch', etc. Walde-P. 2.660 ff. Falk-Torp 1122.

5. Lith. *verpti*, Lett. *vērpt*, with sbs. Lith. *varpstis* 'spool', *varpstė* 'spindle' : Grk. ῥάπτω 'sew', fr. **wer-p-*, an extension of IE **wer-* 'turn, bend'. Walde-P. 1.276 f.

6. ChSl. *prędą*, *pręsti*, etc., general Slavic (Russ. *prjast'*, *sprjast'* > Lett. *prest*, *sprest*), prob. : Lith. *spręsti* formerly 'span, measure' (now 'judge'), sb. *sprindis* 'span' (Leskien, Ablaut 346), perh. also ChSl. *prędati* 'spring, quiver' (common element 'be taut, tense'). Persson, Beiträge 873. Trautmann 278. Brückner 440.

7. Skt. *kṛt-* (3 sg. *kṛṇatti*) : Grk. κάρταλος 'basket', Lat. *crātis* 'wickerwork', etc., with interchange between notions of plaiting and spinning. Walde-P. 1.421.

6.32 SPINDLE

Grk.	*ἄτρακτος*	ON	*snælda*	Lith.	*varpstė*
NG	*ἀδράχτι*	Dan.	*ten*	Lett.	*sprēslica*
Lat.	*fūsus*	Sw.	*spindel*	ChSl.	*vreteno*
It.	*fuso*	OE	*spinel*	SCr.	*vreteno*
Fr.	*fuseau*	ME	*spindle*	Boh.	*vřeteno*
Sp.	*huso*	NE	*spindle*	Pol.	*wrzeciono*
Rum.	*fus*	Du.	*spil*	Russ.	*vereteno*
Ir.	*fertas*	OHG	*spinnila, spilla*	Skt.	*tarku-*
NIr.	*fearsad*	MHG	*spinnel, spindel*		
W.	*gwerthyd*	NHG	*spindel*		
Br.	*gwerzid*				

Most of the words for 'spindle' are from verbs for 'turn' or 'spin'. One is cognate with words for 'twig, branch' with specialized application to the stick forming the 'spindle'.

1. Grk. ἄτρακτος, NG pop. ἀδράχτι, Skt. *tarku-*, fr. the root in Lat. *torquēre* 'twist, turn' (10.13), OHG *drāhsil* 'roller', etc. Walde-P. 1.735.

2. Lat. *fūsus* (> Romance words), etym. dub. Connection with *fundere* 'pour' difficult semantically. Ernout-M. 405. Walde-H. 1.574.

3. Ir. *fertas* 'distaff, spindle, axle' (cf. Laws, Gloss. s.v.), NIr. *fearsad* (by metathesis), W. *gwerthyd*, Br. *gwerzid*, ChSl., SCr. *vreteno*, Boh. *vřeteno*, Pol. *wrzeciono*, Russ. *vereteno* : Skt. *vartulā-*, MHG *wirtel* 'spinning-ring' fr. IE **wert-* in Skt. *vṛt-*, Lat. *vertere*, etc. 'turn' (10.12). Walde-P. 1.274 f. Pedersen 1.137.

4. ON *snælda*, Norw. *snelde*, Gmc. **snādla-*, fr. IE *(*s*)*nē-* in words for 'spin' (6.31). Falk-Torp 1093.

Dan. *ten* : ON *teinn* 'twig, sprout, spit', OE *tān* (cf. NE *mistletoe*), Goth. *tains* 'twig, branch', root connection? Falk-Torp 1253. Feist 473.

OE *spinel*, ME, NE *spindle*, Du. *spil*, *spinnila*, *spilla*, MHG *spinnel*, *spindel*, *spille*, NHG (> Sw.) *spindel* : Goth. *spinnan*, etc. 'spin' (6.31). NED s.v. *spindle*.

5. Lith. *varpstė* : *verpti* 'spin' (6.31).

Lett. *sprēslica* 'spindle' beside *prēslica* 'distaff' (cf. *sprest* beside *prest* 'spin'), fr. Slavic, Pol. *przęślica*, Russ. *prjaslica*, etc. 'distaff', fr. the root in ChSl. *pręsti*, etc. 'spin' (6.31). Mühl.-Endz. 3.1018. Brückner 440.

6. ChSl., SCr. *vreteno*, etc., general Slavic, above, 3.

7. Skt. *tarku-*, above, 1.

6.33 WEAVE

Grk.	*ὑφαίνω*	Goth.	....	Lith.	*austi*
NG	*ὑφαίνω*	ON	*vefa*	Lett.	*aust*
Lat.	*texere*	Dan.	*væve*	ChSl.	*tŭkati*
It.	*tessere*	Sw.	*väva*	SCr.	*tkati*
Fr.	*tisser*	OE	*wefan*	Boh.	*tkáti*
Sp.	*tejer*	ME	*weve*	Pol.	*tkać*
Rum.	*ţese*	NE	*weave*	Russ.	*tkat'*
Ir.	*figim*	Du.	*weven*	Skt.	*u-*
NIr.	*fighim*	OHG	*weban*		
W.	*gweu*	MHG	*weben*		
Br.	*gwea*	NHG	*weben*		

The process of weaving is similar to that of the more primitive plaiting in basketwork, etc., and plaiting is in fact the ancestor of weaving. Beside the widespread inherited group of verbs for 'plait' (9.75), there is also a considerable group of cognates pointing to a probable IE verb for 'weave'. Schrader, Reallex. 2.632 ff.

1. IE **au-*, with extensions, a. **webh-*, b. **audh-*, *wedh-*, c. *(*a*)*weg-*. Walde-P. 1.16 f., 247 f., 257.

Skt. *u-* (3 sg. *vayati*, past pass. pple. *ŭta-*, inf. *otum;* cf. Wackernagel, Altind. Gram. 1.94.)

a. Grk. ὑφαίνω, ON *vefa*, OE *wefan*, etc., general Gmc. Cf. Skt. *ūrṇa-vābhi* 'spider', lit. 'wool-weaver'.

b. Lith. *austi*, Lett. *aust* : ON *vāð* 'cloth'.

c. Ir. *figim*, NIr. *fighim*, W. *gweu*, Br. *gwea* : Skt. *vāgura-* 'net', perh. Lat. *vēlum* (**vexlom*) 'curtain, veil, sail', OE *wēoce*, NE *wick*, etc.

2. Lat. *texere*, also 'build' (> It. *tessere*, Fr. *tisser*, Sp. *tejer*, Rum. *ţese*), fr. IE **tek̑ᵖ-*, in Skt. *takṣan-*, Grk. τέκτων 'carpenter', Lith. *tašyti*, ChSl. *tesati* 'hew', etc. Latin alone has specialized the root in this sense, but here also the primary sense was prob. 'construct artfully'. Walde-P. 1.717. Ernout-M. 1037 f.

3. ChSl. *tŭkati*, etc., general Slavic, prob. fr. the same root as ChSl. *tŭkati*, *tŭknąti*, Russ. *tknuti*, etc. 'prick, stab, hit', whence 'weave' with reference to the manipulation of the shuttle(?). Trautmann 331. Brückner 571. Otherwise Walde-P. 1.716.

6.34 LOOM

Grk.	*ἱστός*	Goth.	....	Lith.	*staklės*
NG	*ἀργαλειός*	ON	*vefstaðr, vefstöll*	Lett.	*stelles, stāve, kangas*
Lat.	*tēla*	Dan.	*vævestol*	ChSl.	*postavŭ*
It.	*telaio*	Sw.	*vävstol*	SCr.	*krosna, stan, razboj*
Fr.	*métier*	ME	*lome*	Boh.	*stav*
Sp.	*telar*	NE	*loom*	Pol.	*krosna, warsztat*
Rum.	*războiu*	Du.	*weefgetouw*	Russ.	*stanok*
Ir.	*garmain*	MHG	*gezouwe, weberstuol*	Skt.	*veman-*
NIr.	*seol*	NHG	*webstuhl*		
W.	*gwŷdd*				
Br.	*stern*				

Words for 'loom' are most frequently derived from IE **stā-* 'stand', but with independent formations. Such derivation obviously confirms the priority of the upright loom. Otherwise the word is specialized from a general designation 'tool, instrument, equipment'. Some of the words are used also for the 'beam of the loom', as Grk. ἱστός, ME *lome* (NED s.v. *loom*, sb.[1] 3).

1. Grk. ἱστός, also 'mast', lit. 'anything which stands upright' : ἵστημι 'stand'.

NG ἐργαλειός, pop. ἀργαλειός, fr. Grk. ἐργαλεῖον 'tool' (9.422).

2. Lat. *tēla* ('web, warp' and 'loom') : *texere* 'weave' (6.33). Hence MLat. *telārium*, It. *telaio*, Sp. *telar*. Ernout-M. 1038. REW 8620.

Fr. *métier*, usually 'trade, craft', fr. Lat. *ministerium* 'service, occupation'. OFr. *mestier* was used also for various utensils, whence specialized to 'loom'. REW 5589. Bloch 2.61.

Rum. *războiu*, fr. Bulg., SCr. *razboj* (below, 6).

3. Ir. *garmain* (quotable only for 'weaver's beam', but perh. used also for the whole 'loom', like Grk. ἱστός, etc.) : ON *karmr* 'breastwork', Dan. *karm* 'frame'. Pedersen 1.494.

NIr. *seol*, identical with *seol* 'course, guidance', this = *seol* 'sail' (10.88), in sense back-formation fr. *seolaim* 'steer, guide'.

W. *gwŷdd*, orig. 'wooden frame', hence also 'plow', MW 'mast', and so not connected with *gweu* 'weave', but identical with *gwŷdd* 'trees, woods' (1.41).

Br. *stern*, orig. 'frame' : W. *ystarn* 'harness, packsaddle', lit. 'that which is spread out', prob. fr. Lat. *sternere* 'spread'. Loth, Mots lat. 217.

4. ON *vefstaðr*, or *vefr*, the older name for the loom, cpd. of *vefa* 'weave' and *staðr* 'that which is set up, stand' (IE **stā-*).

ON *vefstöll*, Dan. *vævestol*, Sw. *vävstol*, MHG *weberstuol*, NHG *webstuhl*, lit. 'weaving support or equipment', Gmc. **stōla-* (OE *stōl* 'chair', etc., 7.43) retaining its more primitive force. Falk-Torp 1172. Hellquist 1403.

ME *lome*, NE *loom*, fr. OE *gelōma* 'utensil, implement' (fr. the adv. *gelōme* = OHG *gilōmo* 'often', hence orig. 'a thing of frequent use'?) NED s.v.

Du. *weefgetouw*, cpd. of *getouw* = MLG *getouwe*, MHG *gezouwe* 'tool, equipment, loom' : Goth. *taujan* 'do, make'. Falk-Torp 1267. Franck-v. W. 192, 704 f.

5. Lith. *staklės* (pl.), cf. Lett. *stakle* 'post, fork', OPruss. *stakle* 'support', fr. IE **stā-*. Walde-P. 2.606. Mühl.-Endz. 3.1040 f.

Lett. *stāve* : *stāvs* 'upright, standing', *stāvēt* 'stand', fr. IE **stā-*. Mühl.-Endz. 3.1052 f.

Lett. *stelles*, fr. MLG *stelle* 'rack, frame, weaver's rack' : OS *stellian*, OHG *stellen*, etc. 'place'. Mühl.-Endz. 3.1060.

Lett. *kangas*, fr. Liv. *kāṅgas* 'tissue, web'. Mühl.-Endz. 2.154.

6. ChSl. *postavŭ* (also 'web, cloth'), Boh. *stav*, SCr. *stan* (spec. *tkalački stan*), Russ. *stanok* (spec. *tkackij stanok*), all derivs. of IE **stā-*.

SCr. *krosna*, Pol. *krosna*, Russ. (arch.) *krosny* (pl.) prob. : Lith. *krėslas*, *krasė*, Russ. *kreslo*, etc. '(arm)chair' (7.43) fr. a common notion of 'frame'. Walde-P. 1.485. Berneker 623 f.

SCr., Bulg. *razboj* (> Rum. *războiu*) fr. *razbiti* 'strike apart, break up' (cpd. of ChSl. *biti* 'strike', 9.21) prob. with reference to the division of the warp and woof on the loom.

Pol. *warsztat* (spec. *warsztat tkacki* lit. 'weaver's workshop'), fr. NHG *werkstatt*. Brückner 603.

7. Skt. *veman-* : *u-* 'weave' (6.33).

6.35 SEW

Grk.	*ῥάπτω*	Goth.	*siujan*	Lith.	*siūti*
NG	*ράβω*	ON	*sauma, *sȳja*	Lett.	*šūt*
Lat.	*suere*	Dan.	*sy*	ChSl.	*šiti*
It.	*cucire*	Sw.	*sy, sömma*	SCr.	*šiti*
Fr.	*coudre*	OE	*sīwian*	Boh.	*šíti*
Sp.	*coser*	ME	*sewe*	Pol.	*szyć*
Rum.	*coase*	NE	*sew*	Russ.	*šit'*
Ir.	*uagim*	Du.	*naaien*	Skt.	*sīv-*
NIr.	*fuaghaim*	OHG	*siuwan, nājan*		
W.	*gwnïo*	MHG	*siuwen, næjen*		
Br.	*gwriat*	NHG	*nähen*		

The majority of the verbs for 'sew' belong to an inherited group.

1. IE *syū-, *sīw-, *sū-. Walde-P. 2.514 ff. Ernout-M. 1003. Feist 425.

Lat. suere; Goth. siujan, ON *sȳja (only in pl. pret. sēðu, and past pple. sȳðr), Dan., Sw. sy, OE sīwian, sēowian, ME sewe, sowe, NE sew, OHG siuwan, MHG siuwen; Lith. siūti, Lett. šūt; ChSl., SCr. šiti, Boh. šíti, Pol. szyć, Russ. šit'; Skt. sīv-, syū-.

ON sauma, Sw. sömma, denom. fr. ON saumr = OHG soum, OE sēam 'seam', fr. a Gmc. variant of the same root.

It. cucire, Fr. coudre, Sp. coser, Rum. coase, fr. the Lat. cpd. con-suere 'sew together'. REW 2174.

2. Grk. ῥάπτω, NG pop. ῥάβω (new pres. to aor. ἔρραψα, like κόβω 'cut', etc. : Lith. verpti 'spin' (6.31).

6.36 NEEDLE

Grk.	ῥαφίς, βελόνη	Goth.	nēpla	Lith.	adata
NG	βελόνι	ON	nāl	Lett.	adata
Lat.	acus	Dan.	naal	ChSl.	*igŭla (adj. igŭlinŭ)
It.	ago	Sw.	nål	SCr.	igla
Fr.	aiguille	OE	nǣdl	Boh.	jehla
Sp.	aguja	ME	nedle	Pol.	igła
Rum.	ac	NE	needle	Russ.	igla
Ir.	snáthat	Du.	naald	Skt.	sūci-
NIr.	snáthad	OHG	nādela	Av.	sūkā-
W.	nodwydd	MHG	nādele		
Br.	nadoz	NHG	nadel		

Words for 'needle' are mostly either derived from verbs for 'sew', or cognate with words denoting sharp pointed objects.

1. Grk. ῥαφίς, fr. ῥάπτω 'sew' (6.36).

Grk. βελόνη (replacing ῥαφίς in Att.), NG βελόνα, βελόνι : ὀβελός 'spit', Lith. gelti 'sting, ache', etc. Walde-P. 1.689 f. Boisacq 118.

2. Lat. acus (> It. ago, Rum. ac; Fr. aiguille, Sp. aguja fr. MLat. dim. acūcula) : ācer 'sharp', aciēs 'sharp edge or point', Grk. ἄκρος 'topmost', ἀκίς 'sharp object' ('needle' in Hipp.), Skt. açri-

'edge', etc. Walde-P. 1.28 ff. Ernout-M. 8. Walde-H. 1.11. REW 130.

3. Ir. snáthat, NIr. snáthad, W. nodwydd, Br. nadoz, fr. IE *snō- as in words for 'thread' (Ir. snáthe, etc., 6.38) beside *snē- in words for 'spin' (6.31). Walde-P. 2.694 f. Pedersen 1.85.

4. Goth. nēpla, ON nāl, OE nǣdl, OHG nādela, etc., general Gmc., fr. *snē- in words for 'spin', but in Gmc. 'sew', as OHG nājan, etc. (6.35).

Lith., Lett. adata : Lith. adyti 'darn, mend', Lett. adīt 'knit', outside root connection dub. Mühl.-Endz. 1.11.

---

3. Ir. uagim, NIr. fuaghaim, of disputed etym., perh. : Lat. augēre, Grk. αὔξω, Goth. aukan 'increase', ON auka 'increase, add'. A similar semantic change fr. 'add to' to 'fasten together', hence 'sew', is partially effected in NIcel. auka saman 'piece together'. Pedersen 1.54 (rejected by Walde-P. 1.22).

W. gwnīo, Br. gwriat (for n > r in Br. cf. Pedersen 1.155), specialized fr. 'make' : Ir. do-gnīu 'do, make' (9.11). Pedersen 1.60.

4. OHG nājan, MHG næjen, NHG nähen, Du. naaien : Grk. νέω, Lat. nēre, etc. 'spin' (6.31). The use of this root in the sense of 'sew' (cf. also Goth. nēpla, etc. 'needle', 6.36) instead of 'spin' is peculiar to Gmc. Cf. Grk. ῥάπτω 'sew' : Lith. verpti 'spin'.

5. ChSl. *igŭla (adj. igŭlinŭ, Gospels), SCr., Russ. igla, Boh. jehla, Pol. igła, OPruss. ayculo, etym. dub. Berneker 423. Brückner 189, 208.

6. Skt. sūci- : Skt. çūka- 'beard of grain, sting', Av. sūkā- 'needle', with Skt. s for ç, perh. influenced by the init. of sīv-, syū- 'sew' (6.35). Barth. 1582. Wackernagel-Debrunner, KZ 67.174 f.

6.37 AWL

Grk.	ὄπεας	Goth.	....	Lith.	yla
NG	σουβλί	ON	alr	Lett.	ilens
Lat.	sūbula	Dan.	syl	ChSl.	šilo
It.	lesina	Sw.	syl	SCr.	šilo
Fr.	alêne	OE	al	Boh.	šidlo
Sp.	lesna	ME	al, aule	Pol.	szydło
Rum.	sulă	NE	awl	Russ.	šilo
Ir.	menad	Du.	els, priem	Skt.	ārā-
NIr.	meanadh (-aithe)	OHG	āla, alansa, siula	Av.	....
W.	mynawyd	MHG	āle, pfriem(e)		
Br.	menaoued	NHG	ahle, pfriem		

The 'awl', though used for other purposes, is primarily a shoemaker's tool, and many of the words for 'awl' are derived from the root for 'sew'. Others are connected with words for 'hole' or for 'prick'.

1. Root *ēlā-, *ōlā-, without other known connections. Walde-P. 1.156. Falk-Torp 4. Kluge-G. 7.

Skt. ārā-; ON alr, OE æl, eal, al, ME al but mostly aule, oule (in form fr. OE awul 'fork', prob. a different word : ON sōð-āll 'meat-fork', Lat. aculeus 'sting, spur', etc.), whence NE awl; OHG āla, MHG āle, NHG ahle; OHG alansa, fr. *alesna (> It. lesina, Fr. alêne, Sp. lesna, alesna; REW 346), Du. els (NHG else 'sailmaker's awl'); Lith. yla, OPruss. ylo, Lett. ilens, all prob. fr. a Goth. *ēla (Mühl.-Endz. 1.836).

2. Derivs. of IE *syū- (6.35). Walde-P. 2.515. Falk-Torp 1226.

Lat. sūbula (> Rum. sulă, NG σουβλί); Dan., Sw. syl, OHG siula (NHG säule dial. as 'awl'); ChSl. (late), SCr., Russ. šilo, Boh. šidlo, Pol. szydło.

3. Grk. ὄπεας, gen. -ατος, dim. ὀπήτιον : ὀπή 'hole' (orig. 'eye', cf. 4.21), as orig. *ὀπᾰ-ϝατ- neut. of adj. (cf. ὀπήεις), used with ὀστέον 'bone' or the like, for the well-known type of awl with hole in the end, like a heavy needle. Schwyzer, KZ 60.224 ff.

NG σουβλί, fr. Lat. sūbula (above, 2). G. Meyer, Neugr. Stud. 3.61 ff.

4. Lat. sūbula, Rum. sulă, above, 2. It. lesina, Fr. alêne, Sp. lesna, fr. Gmc., above, 1.

5. Ir. menad, etc., general Celtic, etym.? Walde-P. 2.222. Stokes 216.

6. ON alr, OE æl, etc., above, 1. OHG siula, etc., above, 2.

MHG, NHG pfriem : ON prjònn 'knitting-needle', OE prēon 'pin' (6.63), Du. priem 'puncher, etc.', outside connection? Falk-Torp 848. Weigand-H. 2.415.

7. Baltic words, above, 1.

8. Slavic words, above, 2.

9. Skt. ārā-, above, 1.

6.38 THREAD

Grk.	νῆμα, κλωστήρ	Goth.	....	Lith.	siūlas
NG	νῆμα, γνέμα, κλωστή	ON	þrāðr	Lett.	pavediens
Lat.	fīlum	Dan.	traad	ChSl.	nitĭ, nĭšta
It.	filo	Sw.	tråd	SCr.	nit
Fr.	fil	OE	þrǣd	Boh.	nit'
Sp.	hilo	ME	threde	Pol.	nić
Rum.	fir	NE	thread	Russ.	nit', nitka
Ir.	snáthe	Du.	draad	Skt.	sūtra-
NIr.	snáth	OHG	fadam		
W.	edau	MHG	vadem		
Br.	neud	NHG	faden		

1. Derivs. of IE *(s)nē-, *(s)nēi- in words for 'spin' (6.31). Walde-P. 2.694 f.

Grk. νῆμα, NG pop. γνέμα; Ir. snáthe, NIr. snáth, Br. neud; ChSl. nitĭ, nĭšta, etc., general Slavic.

2. Grk. κλωστήρ, NG κλωστή : κλώθω 'spin' (6.31).

3. Lat. fīlum (> Romance words) : Lith. gysla, Lett. dzīsla, OPruss. -gislo, ChSl. žila 'vein', etc. Walde-P. 1.670. Ernout-M. 360. Walde-H. 1.497 f.

4. W. edau, MW adawed (pl.), OW etem (gl. instita), OHG fadam, MHG vadem, NHG faden, orig. 'a measure of thread from tip to tip of the outstretched arms' : Ir. aitheamh, OE fæþm 'fathom', orig. 'embrace', ON faðmr 'embrace' (IE *pet- in Grk. πετάννυμι 'spread out', Lat. patēre 'stand open', etc.). The

parallel semantic development in Welsh and German is remarkable. Walde-P. 2.18. Pedersen 1.132. Falk-Torp 208 f.

5. ON þrāðr, Dan. traad, Sw. tråd, OE þrǣd, ME threde, NE thread, Du. draad (NHG draht 'wire'), fr. a Gmc. *þrēðu- : OE þrāwan, OHG drājan, etc. 'turn around, twist' (10.13). Walde-P. 1.729. NED s.v. thread.

6. Lith. siūlas, and with different suffix Skt. sūtra-, fr. Lith. siūti, Skt. sīv- 'sew' (6.35).

Lett. pavediens, prob. formed with agent-noun suffix -iens (cf. Endz., Gr. 235 f.) fr. pavedu, pavest 'lead a distance' (cpd. of vest, Lith. vesti 'lead'), with development of sense 'thread' through a measure (as in NHG faden, etc., above, 4), or through the notion of guidance (in stories like the myth of Ariadne)?

7. ChSl. nitĭ, etc., above, 1.

6.39 DYE (vb.)

Grk.	βάπτω	Goth.	....	Lith.	dažyti, parvuoti
NG	βάφω	ON	lita	Lett.	krāsuot (pervēt)
Lat.	tingere, inficere	Dan.	farve	ChSl.	....
It.	tingere	Sw.	färga	SCr.	bojadisati (farbati)
Fr.	teindre	OE	dēagian, telgan	Boh.	barviti
Sp.	teñir	ME	dye	Pol.	farbować (barwić)
Rum.	boi, văpsi	NE	dye	Russ.	krasit'
Ir.	(dathaigim)	Du.	verven	Skt.	rañjaya-
NIr.	dathuighim	OHG	farawen		
W.	lliwio	MHG	verwen		
Br.	liva	NHG	färben		

Many of the verbs listed mean simply 'color' and are used alike for 'dye' (cloth) and 'paint' (a board, house, etc.). But several are from the notion of 'dip', specifically applicable to the process of dyeing cloth.

1. Grk. βάπτω 'dip' (Hom.+), hence 'dye', cf. βαφή 'dipping, dye', βαφεύς 'dyer', NG βάφω (new pres. to aor. ἔβαψα) : ON kv(v)efja 'submerge, overwhelm', OSw. kvaf 'depth of the sea', etc. Walde-P. 1.674. Boisacq 114. Falk-Torp 504.

2. Lat. tingere 'dip, soak', hence 'dye' > It. tingere, Fr. teindre, Sp. teñir 'dye, stain', cf. tīnctus 'a dipping, dyeing', tinctor 'dyer' : Grk. τέγγω 'wet, moisten', OHG thunkōn, dunkōn 'dip, soak'. Walde-P. 1.726. Ernout-M. 1041. REW 8750.

Lat. inficere, lit. 'put into', hence esp. 'put into a dyeing vat, dye, color' (cf. infector 'dyer'), cpd. of facere 'do, make'. Ernout-M. 324.

Lat. fūcāre, rarely 'dye' (wool), mostly 'paint the face', deriv. of fūcus name of a plant and the dye made from it, 'rouge', borrowed fr. Grk. φῦκος id. Ernout-M. 396.

Rum. boi (cf. boiangiu 'dyer') : boia 'dye' fr. Turk. boya 'dye, paint'. Lokotsch 328.

Rum. văpsi, reg. vb. for 'paint', but also and orig. 'dye', fr. Grk. aor. infin. βάψαι (above, 1), perh. through Slavic (late ChSl. vapĭsati 'stain', etc.). Tiktin 1713.

3. Ir. dathaigim (quotable?), NIr. dathuighim deriv. of Ir. dath 'color, dye' (15.61).

W. lliwio, Br. liva both also 'paint', derivs. of W. lliw, Br. liou 'color, dye, paint' : Ir. lí 'color', Lat. līvor 'bluish color', etc. Walde-P. 2.715. Pedersen 1.51.

4. ON lita, deriv. of litr 'color', orig. 'complexion, appearance' : Goth. wlits, OE wlite 'appearance, form'. Walde-P. 1.293. Falk-Torp 679.

OHG farawen, MHG verwen, NHG färben, Du. verven, Dan. farve, Sw. färga, derivs. of sbs. OHG farawa, etc. (MLG verwe > Dan. farve, Sw. färg) 'dye, paint, color' : OHG faro 'colored', Grk. περκνός 'dark, livid', Skt. prçni- 'speckled', etc. Walde-P. 2.45. Falk-Torp 206.

OE dēagian, ME, NE dye, derivs. of OE dēah, dēag 'dye', NE dye, prob. : OE dēagol, OHG tougal 'secret, hidden', but root connection and semantic sequence dub. (see 17.36). Walde-P. 1.838.

OE telgan (only in gl.) deriv. of telg 'dye, paint', etym.?

5. Lith. parvuoti, Lett. pervēt, Boh. barviti, Pol. barwić, farbować, SCr. farbati, derivs. of the nouns for 'dye, paint', these loanwords of different periods fr. MHG varve, MLG verwe, or NHG farbe (above, 4).

Lith. dažyti, orig. 'dip' hence 'dye' (cf. dažas 'dye, color), etym.? Walde-P. 1.786.

Lett. krāsuot, deriv. of krāsa 'dye, paint', loanword fr. Slavic (cf. Russ. krasit', below, 6).

6. SCr. bojadisati, also 'paint', deriv. of boja 'dye, paint', this from Turk. boya id.

Russ. krasit', 'adorn' hence 'dye, paint', fr. krasa 'beauty, adornment' : late ChSl. krasa 'beauty' OBoh. krasa 'light, splendor', etc. Berneker 607. Walde-P. 1.418 ff.

7. Skt. ra(ñ)jaya-, caus. of ra(ñ)j-'be bright, colored, red' (cf. rāga-'coloring, dyeing', rakta- 'colored, red') : Grk. ῥέζω 'dye', ῥεγεύς or ῥαγεύς 'dyer' (all rare). Walde-P. 2.366.

6.41–6.59. The attempt to set up even approximate synonyms meets with more than the usual difficulty in the case of articles of dress, owing to the radical differences in the costume of various peoples and periods. Thus there are so many kinds of cloaks and coats with their distinctive names that it is difficult to select the most important, and in the case of some words even the assignment to one or the other group is arbitrary. Conversely, there is nothing in early periods like the modern trousers, which evolved from the short breeches or the long stockings or leggings. The early Cretan figurines show a remarkably modern woman's costume with separate jacket and skirt, but there was nothing similar among the Greeks or Romans of the classical period. Their 'tunic', a jersey-like garment, might from the point of view of function be called a 'coat' (and is in fact generally rendered by words for 'coat' in modern versions of the NT, e.g. Lk. 6.29 ἱμάτιον–χιτών, 'cloak'–'coat'), or a 'shirt'. A long coat may become the modern man's 'coat' or the woman's 'skirt' (NHG *rock*). There is overlapping between 'shoes' and 'stockings' and between 'stockings' and 'trousers', so that words of the same cognate group may denote any one of the three (as derivs. of Lat. *calceus* 'shoe').

Loanwords are notably numerous, several of oriental origin, and often showing a radical change of application.

A mine of information on medieval and later European costume is Viollet-le-Duc, Dict. rais. du mobilier français, vols. 3, 4.

6.41 CLOAK

Grk.	ἱμάτιον, χλαῖνα, φᾶρος	Goth.	*wasti, hakuls*	Lith.	*apsiaustas, ploščius*
NG	μανδύας (lit.)	ON	*feldr, skikkja, kāpa, mǫttull*	Lett.	*mētelis*
Lat.	*toga, pallium, paenula, lacerna, mantellum*	Dan.	*kaabe, kappe*	ChSl.	*plaštĭ, riza*
It.	*mantello, cappa*	Sw.	*kappa, mantel*	SCr.	*plašt, kabanica*
Fr.	*manteau*	OE	*hacele, sciccels, wǣfels, mentel, pæll*	Boh.	*plášt'*
Sp.	*manto, capa*	ME	*cloke, mantel, pall*	Pol.	*płaszcz*
Rum.	*manta*	NE	*cloak*	Russ.	*plašč*
Ir.	*lenn, brat, mattal*	Du.	*mantel*	Skt.	*drāpi-, prāvāra-*
NIr.	*clōca, brat*	OHG	*hachul, mantal*		
W.	*mantell, cochl, clog*	MHG	*mantel*		
Br.	*mantell*	NHG	*mantel*		

Under 'cloak' are grouped the more important words for a loose outer garment, without defining their more special form, even where this is known, and without attempting to include all the special varieties of cloaks, some of which are rather 'shawls' or 'capes'. For the great variety of Greek and Roman cloaks, cf. Daremberg et Saglio s.v. *pallium*.

1. Grk. ἱμάτιον 'garment' (6.12), esp. 'cloak'.

Grk. χλαῖνα (> Lat. *laena* 'rough woolen cloak', perh. through Etruscan), χλανίς, orig.? Boisacq 1062. Ernout-M. 518. Walde-H. 1.749.

Grk. φᾶρος φάρος, : φάραι· ὑφαίνειν, πλέκειν Hesych., φορμός 'woven basket', Lith. *burva* 'a sort of garment', *burė* 'sail' Walde-P. 2.164.

Grk. μανδύα (Aesch. of a Liburnian cloak), later μανδύας as Byz. and NG (lit.; but μαντύα 'military cloak or overcoat'), doubtless a loanword, but source?

2. Lat. *toga* : *tegere* 'cover' (12.26).

Lat. *pallium* (> OE *pæll*, ME, NE *pall*, cf. NED s.v. *pall*, sb.[1] 5), perh. fr. **par(u)lā-* dim. of a borrowing fr. Grk. φᾶρος (above). Walde-P. 2.58. Ernout-M. 724.

Lat. *paenula*, fr. Grk. φαινόλα (Rhinthon) = late Grk. φαινόλης (by metathesis also φελόνης NT, pap., etc.), this perh. orig. 'a bright-colored or shining garment' : φαινόλις 'light-bringing, light-giving', φαίνω 'show forth, reveal'. Ernout-M. 722. E. Fraenkel, KZ 42, 115.

Lat. *lacerna*, perh. fr. *lacer* 'torn, mangled' : Grk. λακίς 'rag', λακίζω 'tear up', Pol. *łach*, Russ. *lochma* 'rag'. Walde-P. 2.419 f. Walde-H. 1.743. Ernout-M. 515 ("only pop. etym.").

Late Lat. *mantellum*, dim. of a Celto-Iberian *mantum*, whence Sp. *manto*. Hence It. *mantello*, OFr. *mantel* (> ME *mantel*, NE *mantle*), Fr. *manteau* (> Rum. *manta*); Ir. *mattal*, *matal* (fr. ON *mǫttull*), W., Br. *mantell* (Loth, Mots lat. 184); ON *mǫttull*, OE *mentel*, OHG *mantal*, Du., MHG, NHG *mantel* (> Sw. *mantel*, Lith. *mantelis;* Lett. *mētelis* through ORuss. *mjatĭlĭ;* also Slavic words, most in specialized sense. Ernout-M. 589. Walde-H. 2.32 f. REW 5326, 5328. Berneker 2.17.

It. *cappa*, Sp. *capa*, fr. late Lat. *cappa* 'sort of head-covering' (Isid.), whence also words for 'cap' (6.55), connection with *caput* 'head' dub. Hence also Dan. *kappe*, Sw. *kappa* (through MLG *kappe*). Another form of *cappa* is *cāpa* in ON *kāpa*, Dan. *kaabe*, ME *cape*, NE *cope*, NE *cape* (through OFr. *cape*). Ernout-M. 150. Walde-H. 1.162. REW 1642. Falk-Torp 480, 494.

3. Ir. *lenn* (OW *lenn*, Gall. *linna*), etym.? Walde-P. 2.53. Stokes 252.

Ir., NIr. *brat* : Ir. *brēit* 'cloth' (6.21). Pedersen 1.160.

W. *cochl*, fr. Ir. *cochull* 'cowl', fr. Lat. *cucullus* (> W. *cwcwll* 'cowl, chasuble') 'cap, hood', orig. dub. Walde-H. 1.298 f. Pedersen 1.227.

4. Goth. *wasti* 'garment', pl. 'clothes' (6.12), commonest word for ἱμάτιον also where it means 'cloak' (as Mt. 5.40, Lk. 6.29).

Goth. *hakuls* 'φελόνης', OE *hacele*, OHG *hachul* (ON *hǫkull* 'priest's cope') prob. : OE *hēcen*, MLG *hōken* 'young goat', ChSl. *koza* 'goat', etc. Walde-P. 1.336 f. Feist 238 f.

ON *feldr* : Lat. *pellis*, OE *fell*, etc. 'hide' (4.12). Walde-P. 2.58 f. Falk-Torp 1457 f.

ON *skikkja*, with other suffixes OE *sciccels*, *sciccing* : OHG *scecho* 'stragulum', MHG *schecke* 'corslet', root connection? Walde-P. 1.400 f.

OE *wǣfels* 'covering' and 'cloak' (e.g. Mt. 5.40), fr. the root of OE (*bi-*)*wǣfan*, Goth. *bi-waibjan* 'wrap about, clothe' : ON *veifa* 'vibrate', Skt. *vip-* 'tremble', etc. Walde-P. 1.240. Feist 97.

ME *cloke* (> W. *clog*, Parry-Williams 181, 241), NE *cloak* (> NIr. *clōca*), fr. OFr. *cloke*, *cloche*, MLat. *clo(c)ca* 'cape worn by horsemen and travelers' so called fr. its bell-shape, being the same word as the earlier and more widespread MLat. *clo(c)ca*, OFr. *cloche*, etc., 'bell', prob. fr. Celtic (see under 'clock', 14.43). NED s.v. *cloak*. REW 1995. Wartburg 2.290 ff.

5. Lith. *apsiaustas* (neolog. for 'cloak' or 'overcoat'), fr. *ap-siausti* 'wrap around'.

6. ChSl. *riza* (6.12) is the usual rendering of both ἱμάτιον and χιτών (but *riza* vs. *sračica* Lk. 6.29, conversely Mt. 5.40). Cf. also Jagić, Entstehungsgesch. 296, 322.

ChSl. *plaštĭ* (Supr.), SCr. *plašt*, Boh. *plášt'*, Pol. *płaszcz* (> Lith. *ploščius*), Russ. *plašč* : OPruss. *ploaste* 'sheet', Lith. *ploštė* 'sort of shawl', Russ. *plast* 'layer', ChSl. *platŭ* 'cloth' (6.21). Brückner 420.

SCr. *kabanica*, fr. It. *gabbano* 'raincoat', fr. Pers., Arab. *ḳabā* 'upper garment, cloak'. Berneker 464. REW 4648. Lokotsch 971.

7. Skt. *drāpi-*, perh. orig. 'a piece of cloth' : Av. *drafša-* 'banner', Lith. *drapanos* 'clothes' (6.12).

Skt. *prāvāra-*, fr. *vṛ-* 'cover', with *pra-ā-* 'cover over, put on'.

6.412 OVERCOAT

NG	ἐπανωφόρι, παλτό	Dan.	*overfrakke*	Lith.	*apsiaustas*
It.	*palto*	Sw.	*overrock*	Lett.	*virssvārks*
Fr.	*pardessus, paletot*	NE	*overcoat*	SCr.	*ogrtač*
Sp.	*sobretodo (paletó, gabán, abrigo)*	Du.	*overjas*	Boh.	*srchník*
Rum.	*pardesiu, palton*	NHG	*überzieher, überrock*	Pol.	*palto*
NIr.	*cōta mōr, casōg mhōr*			Russ.	*pal'to*
W.	*cot uchaf, cot fawr*				
Br.	*mantell*				

The modern 'overcoat', which has so largely displaced the 'cloak' in men's attire, is commonly expressed by words for 'over' or 'top', esp. in phrases with words for 'coat', etc. Thus Fr. *pardessus* (> Rum. *pardesiu*), sb. use of adv. *pardessus* 'above, over'; Boh. *svrchník*, fr. *svrchní* 'upper' (: *vrch* 'top', 12.33); Sp. *sobretodo*, NE *overcoat*, NHG *überrock*, Du. *overjas*, Dan. *overfrakke*, Sw. *overrock;* Lett. *virssvārks* (*virsus* 'top'); NG ἐπανωφόρι (-φόρι : φορέω 'wear', φόρεμα 'garment', 6.12); NHG *überzieher* fr. *überziehen* 'pull over'; SCr. *ogrtač* fr. *ogrtati* 'hang about' (Berneker 372).

Fr. *paletot*, fr. (instead of conversely, as formerly assumed) the earlier attested ME *paltock* a kind of short coat (NED s.v.), perh. fr. *pall* 'cloak' (Lat. *pallium*). Baist, Z. rom. Ph. 32.430 ff. REW 6178. Gamillscheg 661. Hence, in the very different modern use of the Fr. *paletot* as a loose outer coat or cloak, It. *palto*, NG παλτό, Sp. *paletó*, Rum. *palton*, Pol. *palto*, Russ. *pal'to* 'overcoat'.

Sp. *gabán*, orig. the peasant's heavy coat, but kept in part for the modern 'overcoat', fr. Pers., Arab. *ḳabā* a kind of cloak. REW 4648. Lokotsch 971.

Sp. *abrigo* 'protection, shelter' (REW 560), used also for 'overcoat'.

NIr. *cōta mōr*, *casōg mhōr*, W. *cot fawr*, all 'greatcoat', W. also *cot uchaf* (*uchaf* 'upper' fr. *uch* 'above, over').

Lith. *apsiaustas*, see 6.41.

6.42 WOMAN'S DRESS

This is most commonly expressed by more generic words for 'clothing, garment' (6.12), used (with or without 'woman's') in this special application, as NE *dress* (now the most common use), NHG *kleid*, Russ. *plat'e*, etc. A full list would be in large measure a repetition of words included in 6.12. But a few others that apply mainly to a woman's dress are given here.

1. Grk. πέπλος (sometimes 'covering', also man's 'cloak', but esp. the long robe worn by women), reduplicated form (πε-πλο-) of IE **pel-* in Lat. *pellis*, OE *fell*, etc. 'hide', ON *feldr* 'cloak', etc. Less prob., since 'covering' seems to be the earlier sense, fr. **pel-* in words for 'fold'. Walde-P. 2.56, 58. Boisacq 769.

NG pop. φουστάνι (beside φόρεμα 'garment', 6.12, esp. woman's 'costume, dress'), fr. It. *fustagno* 'fustian', fr. Arab. *Fustat* name of a suburb of Cairo where the cloth was made. Lokotsch 621 (where φουστάνι is wrongly defined, as if = φουστανέλλα 'kilt').

2. Lat. *stola* (in earliest use not restricted to women), fr. Grk. στολή 'equipment', esp. 'clothing, garment' : στέλλω 'order, arrange'.

Fr. *robe* (= It. *roba* 'thing, stuff, wares', Sp. *ropa* 'clothes, dry goods', etc.) fr. Frank. **rauba* = OHG *roub*, pl. *rouba* 'booty', OE *rēaf* 'booty, clothes' (6.12, 20.48). REW 7090. Gamillscheg 768.

Rum. *rochie*, through SCr. *roklja* fr. dim. form of NHG *rock* 'coat, skirt' (6.43). Tiktin 1333.

3. Br. *sae* = W. *sae*, Fr. *saie* 'say' (a kind of cloth), Ir. *sāi* (gl. *tunica, lacerna*), all fr. late Lat. *saia* for Gallo-Lat. *sagum* 'coarse blanket or cloak', Walde-P. 2.448. Ernout-M. 887. Pedersen 1.216. Loth, Mots lat. 203 (Br. fr. Fr.).

4. Dan. *kjole*, shortened form of *kjortel* = ON *kyrtill* 'kirtle, tunic', fr. ON **kortr*, Dan. *kort* 'short' (12.59). Falk-Torp 518.

ME *goune*, NE *gown* (> W. *gwn*, cf. Loth, RC 20.353), in 18th cent. the usual word, later less common than *dress*, but revived in fashionable use (cf. NED s.v.; the statement that in U.S. "it has always been the current word" is not correct), fr. OFr. *gonne*, *goune* 'long coat', this fr. MLat. *gunna* 'fur coat', for which see 6.28 under NG γοῦνα 'fur'.

Du. *japon*, fr. Fr. *jupon* 'petticoat, skirt' (6.46).

6.43 COAT

Grk.	(χιτών)	Goth.	*paida*	Lith.	*švarkas*
NG	σακκάκι	ON	*rokkr*	Lett.	*svārki*
Lat.	(*tunica*)	Dan.	*frakke*	ChSl.	*riza, sračica*
It.	*giacca, giacchetta (giubba)*	Sw.	*rock*	SCr.	*kaput*
Fr.	*veston, paletot*	OE	*pād, rocc*	Boh.	*kabát*
Sp.	*americana (saco, chaqueta)*	ME	*cote*	Pol.	*surdut, suknia*
Rum.	*haină*	NE	*coat*	Russ.	*pidžak (kaftan)*
Ir.	*fūan, inar*	Du.	*jas*	Skt.	*kañcuka-, uttarīya-*
NIr.	*casōg*	OHG	*roc*		
W.	*cot*	MHG	*roc*		
Br.	*jupen*	NHG	*rock*		

1. Grk. χιτών, Ion. κιθών, Lat. *tunica* (see above, p. 416), borrowed independently fr. the Semitic, cf. Hebr. *kᵉtōnet*, Akkad. *kittinu* 'linen garment'. LS s.v. Ernout-M. 1064 f.

NG σακκάκι, lit. 'a little sack', dim. of σάκκος 'sack', orig. 'coarse cloth of hair'. fr. Hebr.-Phoen. *śaq* 'haircloth, sack'. Boisacq 849.

2. It. *giacchetta* (whence *giacca*), Sp. *chaqueta*, fr. Fr. *jaquette* (OFr. *jaquet* > ME *jaket*, NE *jacket*), dim. of *jaque*, fr. Sp. *jaco* 'short jacket', fr. Arab. *šakk* 'coat of mail'. REW 7519d. Gamillscheg 536.

It. *giubba* (old word for 'coat', now mostly specialized), fr. Arab. *ǧubbah* 'cotton undergarment' (whence also Fr. *jupe* 'skirt'). REW 3951. Lokotsch 737.

Fr. *veston*, dim. of *veste* 'waistcoat, round jacket', fr. Lat. *vestis* 'garment' (6.12).

Fr. *paletot* (6.412) is now, as my colleague Professor Vigneron informs me, often used for the ordinary coat of a business suit.

Sp. *americana* 'the American', the current term in Spain for the coat of a business suit.

Sp. *saco* 'sack' and 'coat' (in Am. Sp. esp. the usual word), fr. Lat. *saccus*, Grk. σάκκος 'sack' (above, 1).

Rum. *haină* 'garment' (6.12), also 'coat' according to informant and some dictionaries.

3. Ir. *fūan*, perh. cpd. (**wo-ouno-*, **wo* fr. **upo*), fr. the root of Lat. *ind-uere* 'dress' (6.11). Walde-P. 1.109. Stokes 281.

Ir. *inar* (with *i-* for *e-* by connection with *i-n* 'in') : Ir. *anart* 'shirt', Grk. ἔναρα 'spoils'. Pedersen 1.178. Adversely Walde-P. 2.5.

NIr. *casōg*, fr. NE *cassock*, fr. Fr. *casaque*, orig. a military cloak and perh. belonging with Fr. *cosaque* 'cossack'. NED s.v. Lokotsch 1143.

W. *cot*, fr. NE *coat*.

Br. *jupen*, fr. Fr. *jupon* 'skirt', formerly (Molière) 'man's coat reaching to the knees', dim. of *jupe* 'skirt' (6.46).

4. Goth. *paida* (reg. for χιτών), OE *pād* (mostly in cpds., as *here-pād* 'coat of mail'), early loanword fr. the same source (Thracian?) as Grk. βαίτη 'coat of skins'. Walde-P. 2.104. Feist 381 f.

OE *rocc*, OHG, MHG, *roc*, NHG *rock* (ON *rokkr* in this sense rare and Sw. *rock* fr. MLG), with Ir. *rucht* 'tunic', MW *rhuch* a kind of coat, prob. : ON *rokkr*, OHG *rocko*, NHG *rocken*, NE *rock*, etc. 'distaff', both groups fr. some root meaning 'spin'(?). Walde-P. 2.374. Falk-Torp 909 f. Loth, RC 42.62 ff.

But more commonly OE *tuneca*, OHG *tunihha*, etc. fr. Lat. *tunica* (as in NT, Lk. 6.29, etc.).

Dan. *frakke*, through NHG *frack*, fr. Fr. *frac* 'dress coat', this prob. fr. NE *frock* (cf. NED s.v. 5), itself fr. Fr. *froc* 'monk's garment', this perh. fr. OHG *hroc* beside *roc* (above). Falk-Torp 271. Gamillscheg 437, 444. Weigand-H. 1.572. REW 4212.

ME *cote*, NE *coat*, fr. OFr. *cote* (Fr. *cotte* now 'petticoat'), MLat. *cotta*, fr. Gmc., cf. OHG *chozzo*, OS *cot* 'coarse woollen stuff, woollen garment' (further etym. dub., Walde-P. 1.671). REW 4747. NED s.v. *coat*, sb.

Du. *jas* : Fris. *jas*, MLG *jesse*, orig. unknown. Franck-v. W. 279.

5. Lith. *švarkas*, Lett. *svārki*, etym. dub. Mühl.-Endz. 3.1144. Buga, Kalba ir Senovė 289.

6. ChSl. *riza*, usual rendering of χιτών (but also ἱμάτιον etc.), see 6.12.

ChSl. *sračica* (renders χιτών, less commonly ἱμάτιον; Jagić, Entstehungsgesch. 322), beside less common *sraky* (cf. also Russ. *soročka* 'chemise'), perh. loanword fr. Gmc. word for 'shirt', OE *serc*, etc. (6.44). So Falk-Torp 960. Not mentioned by Stender-Petersen.

SCr. *kaput*, through Turk. *kaput* 'cloak with sleeves', fr. It. *capotto* 'raincoat with cowl', fr. MLat. *cappa* 'cloak' (6.41).

Boh. *kabát*, fr. Byz. καβάδης, καβάδιον 'a sort of long cloak', this fr. Pers. *qabā* id. Berneker 464. Lokotsch 971.

Pol. *surdut*, fr. Fr. *surtout*, lit. 'overall', formerly used for 'overcoat' (hence NE *surtout*, cf. NED s.v.).

Pol. *suknia* 'garment' (6.12), also used for 'coat'.

Russ. *kaftan* (the old word for 'coat', now the peasant's coat), fr. Turk. *kaftān* 'long coat'. Berneker 468. Lokotsch 774.

Russ. *pidžak* (now the reg. word), fr. NE *pea-jacket* = Du. *pij-jakker* 'short heavy coat' worn esp. by sailors (cpd. of ME *pee*, Du. *pij* id., etym. unknown, cf. NED s.v. *pee*, sb.[1], Franck-v. W. s.v. *pij*), evidently introduced after Peter the Great's return from Holland and England.

7. Skt. *kañcuka-*, fr. *kañc-* 'bind' : Lat. *cingere* 'gird'. Walde-P. 1.400.

Skt. *uttarīya-*, fr. *uttara-* 'upper'.

6.44 SHIRT

Grk.	(*χιτών*)	ON	*serkr, skyrta*	Lith.	*marškiniai*
NG	*ποκάμισο*	Dan.	*skjorte*	Lett.	*krekls*
Lat.	(*tunica*), late *camisia*	Sw.	*skjorta*	ChSl.	*riza, sračica, košulja*
It.	*camicia*	OE	*serc, scyrte, hemeþe*	SCr.	*košulja, rubača*
Fr.	*chemise*	ME	*sherte*	Boh.	*košile*
Sp.	*camisa*	NE	*shirt*	Pol.	*koszula*
Rum.	*cămașă*	Du.	*hemd*	Russ.	*rubaška*
Ir.	*lēne, caimmse, anart*	OHG	*hemidi*	Skt.	*çāmulya-*
NIr.	*lēine*	MHG	*hemde*		
W.	*crys*	NHG	*hemd*		
Br.	*krez*				

Grk. χιτών, Lat. *tunica*, already given under 'coat', were the nearest equivalents of 'shirt' in the classical period. Grk. χιτωνίσκος and χιτώνιον were applied to a short χιτών or woman's shift. Grk. ὑπένδυμα, ὑπενδύτης 'undergarment', Lat. *tunica interior* and Lat. *subūcula* (fr. **sub-uere*, parallel to *ind-uere*, *exuere*) would be a sort of undershirt. But the use of a linen shirt under a woollen tunic first appears in the 4th century A.D. Cf. Marquardt, Röm. Privatleben 470, 552.

1. Derivs. of IE **k̑em-* seen also in words for 'covering', 'sky', etc. But the Gallo-Lat. form prob. fr. Gmc. Walde-P. 1.386 f. Walde-H. 1.147 f. OE *hemeþe*, OHG *hemidi*, MHG *hemde*, NHG, Du. *hemd;* Gallo-Lat. *camisia* (> Romance forms and Ir. *caimmse*, Byz. καμίσιον, NG ὑπο-κάμισο; Fr. > NE *chemise*, now only for woman's undergarment, replacing *smock* and *shift*); Skt. *çāmulya-*.

2. Ir. *lēne*, NIr. *lēine*, etym. dub., perh. : OW *liein*, W. *lliain*, etc. 'linen' (6.23), though the exact relation is obscure. Pedersen 1.311. Pokorny, KZ 45, 361 f.

Ir. *anart* : *inar* 'coat' (6.43). Pedersen 1.178.

W. *crys*, Br. *krez* = Ir. *criss* 'girdle' : Russ. *čerez*, Pol. *trzos* 'money-belt'. Walde-P. 1.423. Pedersen 1.42 f.

3. ON *serkr* (Dan. *særk*, Sw. *särk* not the usual words), OE *serc*, ME *serke* (Sc. *sark* still the usual word for 'shirt'), prob. : Skt. *sraj-*, Toch. A *sark* 'wreath' (fr. an extension of IE **ser-*, in Lat. *serere* 'join', etc.). Falk-Torp 959 f. K. Schneider, KZ 66.252.

ON *skyrta*, Dan. *skjorte*, Sw. *skjorta*, OE *scyrte* (gl. *praetexta*, where perh. the Lat. word was misunderstood), ME *sherte*, NE *shirt*, derivs. of adj. for 'short', OE *sceort*, etc. (12.59). Falk-Torp 1007. NED s.v. *shirt*, sb.

OE *smoc*, (OHG *smoccho*, ON *smokkr* rare), only for woman's undergarment : OE *smūgan* 'slip, slide into', Lett. *smaugs* 'slender', etc. Walde-P. 2.254 f. Falk-Torp 1083, 1085.

4. Lith. *marškiniai* (pl.) : *marška* 'piece of linen cloth', also 'fishing-net' (perh. : ChSl. *mrěža* 'net', etc.). Walde-P. 2.273. Berneker 2.39.

Lett. *krekls*, prob. : Lith. *kreklas*, OPruss. *kraclan* 'breast'; or : OE *hrægel* 'garment', etc. (6.12). Leskien, Bildung d. Nom. 453. Walde-P. 1.483. Mühl.-Endz. 2.272.

5. ChSl. *riza*, *sračica*, *sraky* (rendering χιτών), see 6.12 and 6.43.

Late ChSl., SCr. *košulja*, Pol. *koszula*, fr. MLat. *casula* 'cloak with a hood' (orig. 'little hut', dim. of *casa* 'hut'), whence also Boh. *košile* through MHG *kāsele* 'part of a priest's garment'. Berneker 586.

SCr. *rubača*, Russ. *rubaška* (Boh. *rubáš* 'short underskirt') : ChSl. *rąbŭ* 'cloth' (6.21).

6. Skt. *çāmulya-*, above, 1.

6.45 COLLAR

NG	*κολλάρο, γιακᾶς*	ON	(late) *kragi*	Lith.	*apikaklė* (*kalnierius*)
It.	*collo, colletto, collare*	Dan.	*krave, flip*	Lett.	*apkakle*
Fr.	*col, collet*	Sw.	*krage*	SCr.	*ogrlica, jaka*
Sp.	*cuello*	ME	*coler*	Boh.	*límec*
Rum.	*guler, guleraș*	NE	*collar*	Pol.	*kołnierz*
NIr.	*coilēar, bōna*	Du.	*kraag, boord(je)*	Russ.	*vorotnik, vorotniček*
W.	*coler*	MHG	*krage, gollier*		
Br.	*gouzougenn*	NHG	*kragen*		

In the older languages there are no words for 'collar' as part of a garment, but only as an article of adornment, 'necklace' (6.75). Most of the words are from those for 'neck', a few from words for other circular forms or for 'hem, border, flap'.

1. Derivs. of Lat. *collum* 'neck' (4.28), either directly or fr. Lat. *collāre* 'band or chain for the neck'. REW 2042, 2053.

a. It. *collo*, Fr. *col*, Sp. *cuello*, also 'neck' (obsolete as 'neck' in French, being replaced by *cou*), hence the dims. It. *colletto*, Fr. *collet*.

b. It. *collare* (> NG κολλάρο); Rum. *guler*, dim. *guleraș*, perh. through MHG *goller*, *koller* (variants of *gollier*, etc.) or Hung. *galler* (cf. Tiktin 707); ME *coler*, NE *collar* (> NIr. *coilēar*, W. *coler*); MHG *gollier*, *kollier*, etc., fr. Fr. *collier;* Pol. *kołnierz* (> Lith. *kalnierius*), through MHG dial. *kolner* for *koller* (Brückner 247).

2. NG γιακᾶς, fr. Turk. *yaka* 'collar', whence also SCr., Bulg. *jaka*. Miklosich, Turk. Elem. 1.314.

3. NIr. *bōna*, *pōna*, also 'inclosure, pound for cattle', prob. orig. in the latter sense and so fr. ME, NE *pound* id., which was usually of circular shape, hence the sense 'collar'.

Br. *gouzougenn*, dim. of *gouzoug* 'neck' (4.28).

4. ON *kragi* (late and only on armor), Dan. *krave*, Sw. *krage*, fr. MLG *krage* = MHG *krage* (also 'neck, gullet'), NHG *kragen*, Du. *kraag*, all orig. 'neck' (4.28).

Dan. *flip*, lit. 'a flap', fr. LG, cf. EFris. *flabbe*, *flebbe*, Du. *fleb*, *flep* 'woman's headdress with hanging ends' : Norw. *flipa* 'hang the lips, pout', etc. Falk-Torp 237.

Du. *boord* 'edge, border' (= OHG *bort*, etc.), also (or *boordje*) 'collar'.

5. Lith. *apikaklė*, Lett. *apkakle*, cpds. of *api* 'around' and Lith. *kaklas*, Lett. *kakls* 'neck' (4.28).

6. SCr. *ogrlica* fr. *grlo* 'throat' (4.29). Berneker 369.

Boh. *límec*, fr. *lem* 'border, hem', a loanword of disputed orig. Berneker 700. Brückner 290.

Russ. *vorotnik*, dim. *vorotniček*, fr. word for 'neck', ChSl. *vratŭ*, etc. (4.28).

6.46 SKIRT

NG	*φοῦστα*	Dan.	*skørt*	Lith.	*marginė*
It.	*gonnella, sottana*	Sw.	*skört*	Lett.	*lindraki, kedele*
Fr.	*jupe*	ME	*skyrt*	SCr.	*suknja*
Sp.	*falda*	NE	*skirt*	Boh.	*sukně*
Rum.	*fustă*	Du.	*rok*	Pol.	*spodnica*
NIr.	*sciorta*	NHG	*rock*	Russ.	*jubka*
W.	*sgyrt*				
Br.	*broz, lostenn*				

The Cretan representations of the Minoan female dress show a distinct skirt, but there is nothing corresponding in classical Greek or Roman costume.

Several of the words entered are used for 'skirt' in general, including 'underskirt, petticoat', but those used only for the latter are not included.

1. NG φοῦστα (> Rum. *fustă*), a shortened form of NG φουστάνι 'dress' (6.42).

2. It. *gonnella*, in earliest use a long coat with skirts (cf. Encycl. Ital. s.v.) dim. of *gonna*, fr. MLat. *gunna* 'fur coat' (see under NG γοῦνα 'fur', 6.28). REW 3919.

It. *sottana* (whence the Fr., NE *soutane* of Roman Catholic priests), fr. MLat. *subtana*, fr. Lat. *subtus* 'below, under'. REW 8402.

Fr. *jupe*, dim. *jupon*, fr. Arab. *ǧubbah* 'cotton undergarment'. REW 3951. Lokotsch 737.

Sp. *falda*, through OProv. fr. Gmc., OHG *falt* 'fold', etc. through use like that of ON *faldr* 'hem of a garment'. REW 3162. Brüch, Z. frz. Spr. 52.427 f.

3. NIr. *sciorta*, W. *sgyrt*, fr. NE *skirt*.

Br. *broz* : Ir. *brat* 'cloak', *brēit* 'cloth' (6.21).

Br. *lostenn*, fr. *lost* 'tail' (4.18).

4. Dan. *skørt*, Sw. *skört* (ODan. also 'apron'), fr. MLG *schorte* = MHG *schurz* 'apron', ON *skyrta* 'shirt' (6.44), whence borrowed ME *skyrt*, NE *skirt*. The apparently conflicting meanings 'shirt' and 'skirt' are readily explained by the form of the Icelandic *skyrta*, which is essentially a long garment, the tails of which fall outside the trousers. Falk-Torp 1007, 1015.

Du. *rok*, NHG *rock*, the same word as OHG *roc*, etc. 'coat' (6.43), orig. a long coat, in the case of women the whole dress, then restricted to the skirt. Cf. Kretschmer, Wortgeogr. 389, and the similar former use of NE *coat* (NED s.v. 2) still in *petticoat*.

5. Lith. *marginė*, orig. 'cloth of many colors', fr. *margas* 'many-colored' : *mirgėti* 'glitter', etc. (Walde-P. 2.275).

Lett. *lindraki*, fr. NHG dial. *lintrock* 'skirt with linen strings'. Mühl.-Endz. 2.471.

Lett. *kedele* (Lith. *kedelys* 'petticoat'), fr. MLG *kedele* = MHG *kitel*, *kittel*, NHG *kittel* 'a shirtlike upper garment, smock', orig. dub. Mühl.-Endz. 2.359. Weigand-H. 1.1042.

6. SCr. *suknja*, Boh. *sukně*, through more general sense (as in Pol. *suknia* 'garment', esp. 'woman's dress'), fr. common Slavic *sukno* 'cloth' (6.21).

Pol. *spodnica*, also and orig. 'undershirt', fr. adj. *spodni* 'under' (fr. *spod* 'bottom', fr. prep. *pod* = ChSl. *podŭ* 'under'). Brückner 424 f.

Russ. *jubka*, through Turk. and Pers., fr. Arab. *ǧubbah* 'cotton undergarment', whence also Fr. *jupe* (above, 2). Berneker 460.

6.47 APRON

NG	*ποδιά*	ON	(*svunta*)	Lith.	*prijuostė*
It.	*grembiule*	Dan.	*forklæde*	Lett.	*priekšauts*
Fr.	*tablier*	Sw.	*förkläde*	SCr.	*pregača, kecelja*
Sp.	*delantal*	ME	*napron*	Boh.	*zástěra*
Rum.	*șorț*	NE	*apron*	Pol.	*fartuch*
NIr.	*aprūn, prāiscin*	Du.	*schort, voorschoot*	Russ.	*fartuk, perednik*
W.	*ffedog, barclod*	NHG	*schürze*		
Br.	*tavañcher, diaraogenn*				

'Apron', as 'an article of dress worn in front of the body to protect the clothing from dirt or injury', is evidently to be found only in the modern languages.

1. NG *ποδιά* (Byz. *ποδέα* 'skirts of a garment') : Grk. *ποδεῶνες* 'ragged ends of the skin of an animal where the feet and tail have been', sg. 'the corner of a sail', 'neck of a skin bag', etc., fr. *πούς*, gen. *ποδός* 'foot'.

2. It. *grembiule*, fr. *grembo*, Lat. *gremium* 'lap, bosom'. REW 3861.

Fr. *tablier*, in OFr. 'napkin', fr. *table* 'table'. REW 8514. Gamillscheg 827.

Sp. *delantal*, fr. *delante* 'in front', replacing the older and widespread *devantal* (OSp. also *avantal*) = OFr. *devantel*, etc., cpd. of *de* and MLat. *abante* 'before'. REW 4335. Wartburg 1.2.

Rum. *şorţ*, fr. NHG *schurz* (below, 4).

3. NIr. *aprūn*, fr. NE *apron* (below, 4).

NIr. *prāiscīn* (usually of coarse material), fr. *prāisc* 'filth' (with dim. suffix *-īn*).

W. *ffedog*, for older *arffedog*, fr. *arffed* 'lap'.

W. *barclod*, fr. ME *barm-cloth* 'apron', cpd. of *barm* 'bosom, lap'. NED s.v. *barm*, sb.[1] Parry-Williams 34.

Br. *tavañcher* (or *-jer*), fr. arch. Fr. *devantier* 'apron' (cf. OFr. *devantel*, etc., above).

Br. *diaraogenn*, deriv. of *diaraog* 'front'.

4. Late ON, NIcel. *svunta*, East Icel. *svinta* (in Norw. dial. 'mop'), as orig. something 'flapping, swinging' : Norw. *svinta* 'move quickly, wave, flutter', *svint* 'quick'. Torp, Nynorsk 757.

Dan. *forklæde*, Swed. *förkläde*, lit. 'forecloth'.

ME *napron*, NE *apron* (*a napron* > *an apron*), fr. OFr. *naperon*, dim. of *nape*, *nappe* 'tablecloth', fr. Lat. *mappa* 'napkin' (6.83). NED s.v.

Du. *schort*, (MHG *schurz* 'apron' as protective armor, NHG mostly 'man's apron'), NHG *schürze*, fr. OHG *scurz*, etc. 'short'. Cf. ON *skyrta* 'shirt', etc. (6.44).

Du. *voorschoot*, cpd. of *schoot* 'lap, bosom' : NHG *schoss* 'lap', Goth. *skauts* 'hem', ON *skaut* 'corner', NE *sheet*, etc.

5. Lith. *prijuostė* (Senn, Hermann, etc.), fr. *prijuosti*, cpd. of *juosti* 'gird' (cf. *juosta* 'girdle', etc. 6.57).

Lett. *priekšauts*, lit. 'forecloth', cpd. of *priekš* 'before' and *auts* 'a cloth, foot clouts' (: Lett. *aut* 'put on shoes', cf. Lat. *induere* 'dress', etc., 6.11).

6. SCr. *pregača* : *pregnuti* 'bend', *zapregnuti* 'stretch, span', etc.

SCr. *kecelja*, fr. Hung. *kecele*, *köcölye*. Rječnik Akad. 4.930 f.

Boh. *zástěra* : *zastirati*, *zastříti* 'cover, veil' (cf. SCr. *zastor* 'curtain'), cpd. of *za-* 'over' and *stříti* 'spread, cover'.

Pol. *fartuch*, Russ. *fartuk*, fr. NHG *vortuch* lit. 'forecloth', used locally for 'apron' (cf. *fürtuch*, Kretschmer, Wortgeogr. 20).

Russ. *perednik*, fr. *pered* 'fore, front'.

6.48 TROUSERS

Grk.	(*ἀναξυρίδες, θύλακοι, βράκαι*)	ON	*brækr*	Lith.	*kelinės*
NG	*πανταλόνι, βρακί*	Dan.	*bukser*	Lett.	*bikses*
Lat.	(*brācae*)	Sw.	*byxor*	ChSl.	*nadragy*
It.	*pantaloni* (*calzoni, brache*)	OE	*brēc*	SCr.	*hlače, čakšire*
Fr.	*pantalon(s)*, (*culotte(s)*), *braies*	ME	*brech*	Boh.	*spodky, kalhoty*
Sp.	*pantalones* (*calzones, bragas*)	NE	*trousers, pants* (*breeches*)	Pol.	*spodnie, portki*
Rum.	*pantaloni*	Du.	*broek*	Russ.	*štany* (*pantalony, brjuki*)
Ir.	*brōc*	OHG	*bruch*		
NIr.	*brīste*	MHG	*bruoch*		
W.	*llodrau, trowsus*	NHG	*hosen, beinkleid(er)*		
Br.	*bragou, lavreg*				

In the evolution of costume, the short breeches were a development of the loincloth, and the long trousers a development of the short breeches, in part by a union with the long stockings or leggings (hence the relation of some of the words to those for 'stockings'). But in classical Greek and Roman costume there was neither loincloth (*διάζωμα* once worn by athletes at Olympia, Thuc. 1.6) nor any form of breeches.

The Greeks knew the trousers worn by oriental peoples, which they called *ἀναξυρίδες*, a foreign word, or *θύλακοι* 'sacks'; and the Romans became acquainted with the *brācae* worn by the peoples of north Europe, which they eventually, despite even legal opposition to this barbarian garment, adopted.

1. ON *brækr* (sg. *brōk*), OE *brēc* (sg. *brōc* rare), ME *brech*, NE *breeches* (double pl.), Du. *broek*, OHG *bruoh*, MHG *bruoch*; prob. fr. Gmc. Gallo-Lat. *brācae*, *braccae* (> Grk. *βράκαι*, NG *βρακί*, cf. also *ἰσώβρακα* 'drawers'; It. *brache*, Sp. *bragas*, Fr. *braies*; Br. *bragou*); MIr. *brōc* fr. ON sg. *brōk* (Zimmer, KZ 30.87 f.); Russ. *brjuki* fr. LG; NIr. *brīste*, fr. NE *breeches*. Etym. dub. The application of the word to the part of the body covered, the 'breech', often assumed to be the original sense, is certainly attested only in NE (see NED s.v. 4). Schrader, Reallex. 1.512. Falk-Torp 104. REW 1252.

Although the early North European 'breeches' were in part long trousers (cf. figures in Schrader, Reallex. 1.510 f.), many of the modern words of this group are used mainly of short breeches (as in NE *knee-breeches*), but locally without such restriction. So NE *breeches* was in U.S. the usual term before the introduction of the popular *pants* (c. 1840), and locally long after.

2. It. *pantaloni*, Fr. *pantalon(s)*, Sp. *pantalones*, NE *pantaloons* (now obs. in this form; but the abbr. *pants* is the commonest term, though regarded as vulgar), NG *πανταλόνι*, Rum. *pantaloni*, Russ. *pantalony* (formerly common, but not in current use), all based on It. *pantalone* name of the buffoon in It. comedy, supposedly Venetian in origin and a nickname derived from the name of a local saint, *San Pantal(e)one*. The application to the characteristic tights of the costume and subsequent extension spread from France. REW 6206. NED s.vv. *pantaloon* and *pants*.

It. *calzoni*, Sp. *calzones* (both now rural terms; It. *calzone* source of Fr. *caleçon* 'drawers') fr. MLat. *calcea (fem. of *calceus* 'shoe', 6.51), whence also Fr. *chausse* 'short breeches', It. *calza* 'stocking', etc. REW 1495.

Fr. *culotte(s)*, now vulgar term, fr. *cul* 'rump, buttocks', (Lat. *cūlus*). Gamillscheg 285.

Rum. *nadragi*, fr. the Slavic, cf. ChSl. *nadragy* (below, 6). Tiktin 1030.

For detailed history and distribution of the Romance words (also for 'stocking'), cf. Jaberg, Wört. u. Sach. 9.137 ff.

3. Ir. *brōc*, NIr. *brīste*, Br. *bragou*, above, 1.

W. *llodrau*, arch. sg. *llawdr* : Br. *loer* 'sock', Ir. *lāthar* 'disposition', NIr. *lāthair* 'place, site, plan', orig. 'basis, foundation', hence 'that which is below'. Walde-P. 2.61. Pedersen 2.45.

W. *trowsus*, fr. NE *trousers*.

Br. *lavreg*, Corn. *lafroc*, arch. W. *llafrog* : W. *llafr* 'spreading, the breech' (Pughe) : *llafru* 'spread, stretch'. G. S. Lane, Language 7.281.

4. ON *brækr*, OE *brēc*, etc., above, 1.

Dan. *bukser*, Sw. *byxor* (pl.), fr. MLG *buxe*, *boxe* contracted fr. *buck-hose, i.e. 'trousers of buckskin' (cf. NHG *hosen*, below). Falk-Torp 115.

NE *trousers*, earlier *trouses*, pl. of *trouse*, this fr. Ir. or Gael. *triubhas* (pronounced as NIr. *triūs*, Sc. *trews*), this prob. fr. OFr. *trebus*, MLat. *tubrūcus* a sort of 'leggings' (Isid. 22.30), this again fr. a Gmc. form like OHG *deohproh*, cpd. of words for 'thigh' and 'breeches'. NED s.v. REW 8967. Jaberg, op. cit. 159.

NHG *hosen*, fr. MHG *hose*, OHG *hosa* 'long stocking or legging' = OE *hosa*, etc. id. (6.49). Weigand-H. 1.893. Kluge-G. 256.

NHG *beinkleid(er)* lit. 'leg-clothes', in some localities used as a more refined term than the usual *hosen*. Kretschmer, Wortgeogr. 112.

5. Lith. *kelinės*, *kelnės*, fr. *kelys* 'knee', orig. therefore 'knee-breeches'.

Lett. *bikses*, fr. MLG *buxe*, *boxe*, pl. *büxen*, cf. Dan. *bukser* (above). Mühl.-Endz. 1.295.

6. Late ChSl. *nadragy*, Pol. *nadragi* (obs.), perh. : Pol. *droga*, Russ. *doroga* 'way, road, journey', etc., but semantic history difficult. Brückner 97.

SCr. *hlače*, fr. MLat. *calcea (cf. It. *calzoni*, above, 2). Berneker 387.

SCr. *čakšire*, fr. Turk. *çakşir* 'wide trousers tied about the ankle'. Lokotsch 385.

Boh. *spodky*, Pol. *spodnie*, fr. Boh. *spod*, Pol. *spodni* 'under, below' : ChSl. *podŭ* 'below'. Brückner 424 f.

Boh. *kalhoty*, OBoh. *kalihoty*, *galihoty*, *kalioty*, etc., representing an It. *caligotte, dim. of Lat. *caliga* 'boot, shoe'. (6.52). Berneker 473.

Pol. *portki*, fr. Russ. *portki* (now 'drawers') : ChSl. *prŭtŭ* 'linen', Pol. *part* 'coarse hempen cloth, sacking', Russ. (obs.) *porty* 'clothes', etc. Brückner 397.

Russ. *štany*, prob. loanword, source?

6.49 STOCKING, SOCK

NG	*κάλτσα*	ON	*hosa; sokkr*	Lith.	*kojinė*
It.	*calza*	Dan.	*strømpe, hose; sok*	Lett.	*zeke*
Fr.	*bas; chaussette*	Sw.	*strumpa; socka*	SCr.	*čarapa*
Sp.	*media; calcetin*	OE	*hosa*	Boh.	*punčocha*
Rum.	*ciorap*	ME	*hose; socke*	Pol.	*pończocha*
NIr.	*stoca; giosān*	NE	*stocking, hose; sock*	Russ.	*čulok*
W.	*hosan; socas*	Du.	*kous; sok*		
Br.	*loer*	OHG	*hosa*		
		MHG	*hose; socke*		
		NHG	*strumpf; socke*		

The 'stocking' was unknown to the classical peoples. In medieval times it is not yet clearly defined, being confused with 'shoe' or 'leggings, breeches', of one or the other of which it originally formed a part.

In some of the modern languages a distinction is made between the long 'stocking' as now worn by women (or men in sporting costume) and the short stocking, half-hose, 'sock' of the ordinary men's wear. So Fr. *bas* vs. *chaussette*, NE *stocking* vs. *sock* (such words for 'sock' being added in the list after a semicolon). But in many languages the old words for 'stocking' continued to be used comprehensively, either generally or locally, e.g. It. *calza*, NE *stocking* (in parts of New England at least; I still normally call what I wear *stockings*), NHG *strumpf* (cf. Paul, Deutsches Wtb. s.v.).

1. It. *calza* (> NG *κάλτσα*) = Fr. *chausse* 'short breeches', dim. *chaussette* 'sock', fr. MLat. *calcea fem. of *calceus* 'shoe' (6.51).

Fr. *bas* for *bas de chausses* : *bas* 'low' (12.32). Gamillscheg 85.

Sp. *media* (orig. *media calza*), fem. of *medio*, Lat. *medius* 'middle', hence 'the middle garment', i.e. between shoe and breeches. REW 5462.

Sp. *calcetin*, through *calceta*, fr. *calza* 'hose, leggings' = It. *calza* 'stocking' (above).

Rum. *ciorap*, SCr. *čarapa*, fr. Turk. *çorap* 'stocking'. Lokotsch 439.

2. NIr. *stoca*, abbr. fr. NE *stocking*.

NIr. *giosān*, W. *hosan*, fr. ME *hosen*, pl. (below. 3).

W. *socas* (pl., sg. rare), fr. NE *socks*.

Br. *loer* : W. *llodrau* 'breeches' (6.48).

3. ON *hosa*, Dan. *hose*, OE *hosa*, ME, NE *hose* (now rather elegant for 'stockings', but reg. *hosiery*), orig., like OHG *hosa*, 'long stocking or legging', prob. as 'covering' fr. *kus- as in Goth. *huzds* 'hoard', etc., extension of IE *(s)keu- in Skt. *sku-* 'cover', etc. Walde-P. 2.551. Falk-Torp 421. NED s.v. *hose*, sb.

ON *sokkr*, Dan. *sok*, Sw. *socka*, OE *socc*, ME *socke*, NE *sock*, Du. *sok*, OHG *soc*, MHG *soc*, *socke*, NHG *socke*, fr. Lat. *soccus* 'a low-heeled, light shoe' (6.51), as also the rare OE *socc*, OHG *soc*, hence the short stocking, 'sock'.

NE *stocking*, fr. the somewhat earlier *stock* in this sense (cf. *legging* fr. *leg*), a special use of *stock* 'trunk' (NED *stock*, sb.[1] 40).

Du. *kous* (MDu. *couse* 'breeches, leggings'), fr. Picard *cauce* = OFr. *chauce*, Fr. *chausse* 'short breeches' (above, 1). Franck-v. W. 341.

NHG *strumpf* = MLG *strump* (fr. the plural of which are borrowed Dan. *strømpe*, Sw. *strumpa*), the same word as MLG *strump*, MHG *strumpf* 'trunk, stump'. The present use arose fr. ellipsis of the first member of the cpd. *hosenstrumpf* 'trunk of the hose', occurring already in the 16th cent. Falk-Torp 1186 f. Weigand-H. 2.993.

4. Lith. *kojinė* (neolog., replacing loanwords, *štriumpa*, fr. NHG, *pančeka*, fr. Pol.), fr. *kojinis* 'of the foot', adj. fr. *koja* 'foot'.

Lett. *zeke*, fr. LG *söcke*, pl. of *socke* (above, 3). Mühl.-Endz. 4.703.

5. SCr. *čarapa*, see Rum. *ciorap* (above, 1).

Boh. *punčocha* (> Pol. *pończocha*), fr. MHG *puntschuch* = *buntschuoch*, lit. 'bound-shoe', a sort of 'coarse laced peasant's shoe'. Brückner 686. Grimm s.v. *buntschuh*.

Russ. *čulok* (Bulg. *čulka*), fr. Turk. dial., cf. Kasan. *čolgau* 'rags for wrapping the feet' : Osman. Turk. *çolak* 'crippled in the arm'. Berneker 163. Lokotsch 437.

6. Av. *ā̆θravana-* 'stocking'(?), etym.? Barth., IF 11.125 ff.

6.51 SHOE

Grk.	*ὑπόδημα, πέδῖλον, κρηπίς*	Goth.	*skōhs*	Lith.	*kurpė*
NG	*ὑπόδημα, παπούτσι*	ON	*skōr*	Lett.	*kurpe*
Lat.	*calceus (soccus)*	Dan.	*sko*	ChSl.	*sapogŭ, črěvĭjĭ*
It.	*scarpa, calzatura*	Sw.	*sko*	SCr.	*obuća, cipela, postola*
Fr.	*chaussure, soulier*	OE	*scōh*	Boh.	*střevíc, obuv*
Sp.	*zapato, calzado*	ME	*sho*	Pol.	*trzewik, obuwie*
Rum.	*gheată, încalţaminte*	NE	*shoe*	Russ.	*sapog, bašmak, obuv'*
Ir.	*brōc (accrann, cūarān, assa)*	Du.	*schoen*	Skt.	*upānah-, pādukā-*
NIr.	*brōg*	OHG	*scuoh*	Av.	*aoθra-*
W.	*esgid*	MHG	*schuoch*		
Br.	*botez, arc'henad*	NHG	*schuh*		

Under 'shoe' are considered the words of most general application to footwear, with omission of many that denote special types of shoes. For the great variety of such special types among the Greeks and Romans, cf. Pauly-Wissowa s.v. *Schuh*, with references.

1. Grk. *ὑπόδημα* : *ὑποδέω* 'bind under', *δέω* 'bind' (9.16).

Grk. *πέδῖλον* (in Hom. 'sandal') : *πούς*, gen. *ποδός* 'foot'.

Grk. *κρηπίς* (> Lat. *crepida*), Lith. *kurpė*, Lett. *kurpe* : Ir. *cairem*, W. *crydd*, Br. *kere* 'cobbler', SCr. *krplje* 'snowshoe', prob. fr. a **kerep-* beside **(s)ker-* 'cut'. Walde-P. 1.425.

NG pop. *παπούτσι*, fr. Turk. *pabuç* (Pers. *pāpūš*, lit. 'foot-covering', cpd. of *pā-* 'foot' and *pūš* fr. *pūšīdan* 'cover'). Lokotsch 1625.

2. Lat. *calceus*, whence or fr. MLat. **calcea* and other derivs., It. *calzatura*, Fr. *chaussure*, Sp. *calzado*, Rum. *încalţaminte* 'footwear' : Lat. *calx*, *-cis* 'heel'. Ernout-M. 138. REW 1496–98.

Lat. *soccus*, a sort of low shoe worn by Greeks and comic actors (important only for the borrowed Gmc. words for 'sock' 6.49), loanword, like *σύκχος*, *συκχάς* (Hesych.) 'a sort of shoe'. Ernout-M. 948.

It. *scarpa*, perh. as 'leather shoe' fr. OHG *scharpe* 'leather purse'. Brüch, Z. rom. Ph. 40.647. REW 7981c.

Fr. *soulier*, with change of suffix fr. OFr. *souler*, Prov. *sotlar*, fr. MLat. **subtelāre*, fr. *subtel* 'hollow of foot'. REW 8397. Gamillscheg 812.

Sp. *zapato* (It. *ciabatta*, Fr. *savate* 'worn-out shoe'), fr. Pers. *čabat* 'bast shoe'. Hence also WhRuss. *čebot* 'boot', etc. REW 2448. Lokotsch 379.

Rum. *gheată* (pl. *ghete*), through It. *ghetta* fr. Fr. *guêtre* 'gaiter', fr. Gmc., cf. MHG, NHG *rist* 'instep', OE *wryst* 'wrist'. REW 9577.

3. Ir. *accrann*, prob. (with metathesis for *arcc-*) : W. *archen* 'clothing, shoe', OW *archenatou* 'shoes', Br. *arc'hena* 'put shoes on', *arc'henad* 'shoe', perh. through notion of 'covering, protection' : Lat. *arcēre* 'inclose, prevent'. Stokes KZ 41.381. Walde-P. 1.80.

Ir. *cūarān* : MW *curan* 'boot', perh. fr. the root **(s)keu-* 'cover' as W. *esgid*, Goth. *skōhs*, etc. (below). Walde-P. 2.547. Otherwise Pedersen 1.176 (: ChSl. *črěvĭjĭ*, etc., below, 6).

Ir. *as(s)a*, *ass* (K. Meyer, Contrib. 138), etym.? Walde-P. 2.3. Walde-H. 1.99.

Ir. *brōc*, NIr. *brōg*, prob. fr. ON *brōk*, pl. *brœkr* 'breeches' (6.48), which were sometimes provided with feet, called specifically *leistabrœkr* (in contrast to *leistalausar brœkr*). Leather breeches of this sort are still used by Icelandic and Faroese fishermen. Zimmer, KZ 30.87 f.

Falk, Altwestnordische Kleiderkunde 118.

W. *esgid*, perh. fr. **ped-skūto-*, cpd. of IE **pĕd-* 'foot' and **skeu-t-* fr. **(s)keu-* 'cover' as in Grk. *σκῦτος* 'leather', etc. (6.29). Walde-P. 2.549. Osthoff, Z. celt. Ph. 6.398 ff.

Br. *botez*, fr. Fr. *botte* 'boot' (6.52).

4. Goth. *skōhs*, ON *skōr*, OE *scōh*, OHG *scuoh*, etc., general Gmc., prob. fr. **skōu-ko-*, IE **skeu-* 'cover'. Walde-P. 2.548. Falk-Torp 1016. Feist 434.

5. Lith. *kurpė*, Lett. *kurpe* : Grk. *κρηπίς*, etc. (above, 1).

6. ChSl. *sapogŭ* (usual word for *ὑπόδημα* in Gospels, etc.; Jagić, Entstehungsgesch. 393), Russ. *sapog* (esp. 'boot', but also used for 'shoe', instead of *bašmak* regarded as somewhat vulgar), etym.?

ChSl. *črěvĭjĭ*, Boh. *střevíc*, Pol. *trzewik*, SCr. dial. *crevlja* (cf. *crevljar* 'cobbler'), ORuss. *čereviji* (pl.), Bulg. *crěve* (pl.), perh. as orig. 'leather, hide', fr. IE **(s)ker-* 'cut'. Berneker 151.

SCr. *postola*, fr. Turk. *postol* 'soldier's shoe'. Lokotsch 1667.

SCr. *cipela* (cf. Slov. *cipele* 'ladies' shoes'), fr. Hung. *cipö*, *cipellö* 'shoe'. Berneker 130.

Russ. *bašmak*, fr. Turk. *başmak* 'shoe, sandal' (cf. SCr. *pašmag*, Pol. arch. and dial. *baszmag* 'sort of shoe'). Berneker 45.

ChSl. *obuvĭ* (rare), SCr. *obuća*, Boh. *obuv*, Pol. *obuwie*, Russ. *obuv'* : ChSl. *obuti*, Lith. *auti* 'wear shoes', Av. *aoθra-* 'shoe', IE **eu-*, in Lat. *ind-uere* 'dress' (6.11).

7. Skt. *upānah-*, fr. *upa-nah-* 'tie under' (cf. Grk. *ὑπόδημα*).

Skt. *pādukā-* (rarely *pādū-*) fr. *pad-* 'foot'.

Av. *aoθra-* : Lith. *auti*, ChSl. *ob-uti* 'wear shoes', etc. (above, 6). Barth. 42.

6.52 BOOT

Grk.	*κόθορνος, ἐνδρομίς*	ON	*bōti, styfill*	Lith.	*batas, čebatas, sopagas*
NG	*στιβάλι, μπότα*	Dan.	*støvle*	Lett.	*zābaks*
Lat.	*cothurnus, pērō, caliga*	Sw.	*stövel*	SCr.	*čizma*
It.	*stivale*	ME	*bote*	Boh.	*bota*
Fr.	*botte*	NE	*boot*	Pol.	*but*
Sp.	*bota*	Du.	*laars*	Russ.	*sapog*
Rum.	*cizmă*	OHG	*stiful*		
NIr.	*buatais*	MHG	*stival*		
W.	*botas*	NHG	*stiefel*		
Br.	*heuz*				

1. Grk. *κόθορνος*, whence Lat. *cothurnus* (esp. 'tragedian's boot'), a loanword, perh. of Lydian orig. J. S. Jongkees, JHS 55.80.

Grk. *ἐνδρομίς* : *ἔνδρομος* 'running'.

2. Lat. *pērō* (esp. 'soldiers' and waggoners' boot') : Grk. (Hom., etc.) *πήρα* 'leather bag, wallet' (whence late Lat. *pēra* 'wallet'), *πηρῖν* 'scrotum', root connection? Boisacq 781.

Lat. *caliga*, perh. (but difficulties), fr. cpd. **calco-liga* : *calx* 'heel', *calceus* 'shoe', and *ligāre* 'bind'. Kent, BSL 26.110 ff. Ernout-M. 134. Walde-H. 1.138.

It. *stivale*, fr. Prov. *estibal* = OFr. *estivel* 'boot', fr. *estive* 'pipe', Lat. *stīps* 'stake'? So REW 8264.

But the objection to the old deriv. fr. MLat. *aestīvālia*, lit. 'belonging to the summer' (fr. Lat. *aestīvus*, fr. *aestus* 'summer'), but actually described as 'high boots', is invalid. Cf. esp. Kretschmer, Wortgeogr. 487 f.

Hence NG *στιβάλι*, late ON *styfill*, Dan. *støvle*, Sw. *stövel*, late OHG *stiful*, MHG *stival*, NHG *stiefel* (cf. Falk-Torp 1201).

OFr. *bote* (> ME *bote*, NE *boot*), Fr. *botte*, Sp. *bota*, orig. much disputed, but prob. belongs with Fr. *pied bot* 'club-foot', fr. Gmc., LG *butt* 'stumpy', etc. Wartburg 1.667 f. Gamillscheg 123. REW 1239a.

Hence NG *μπότα*, Boh. *bota*, Pol. *but*, older *bot* > Lith. *batas* (Berneker 77); late ON *bōti* fr. ME *bote* (cf. Falk, Altwestnordische Kleiderkunde 137 f.); NIr. *buatais*, W. *botas(en)* prob. fr. ME *botes* (pl.).

Rum. *cizmă* (through Hung. *csizma*), SCr., Bulg. *čizma*, fr. Turk. *çizme* 'boot'. Tiktin 370. Lokotsch 431. Berneker 158.

Rum. *ciobotă* (Mold.), Lith. *čebatas*, through Slavic, cf. Russ. dial. *čebot*, etc. fr. Turk., cf. Kasan. *čabata* 'boot' (whence also Sp. *zapato* 'shoe', 6.51). Lokotsch 379. Berneker 159.

3. Br. *heuz*, through OFr. *house* fr. Gmc., cf. OHG *hosa* 'legging, stocking' etc. (6.49). Henry 162.

4. Du. *laars* = MLG *lērse*, contracted fr. **lēder-hose*, cf. OHG *lederhosa* 'leather-stocking'. Franck-v. W. 366.

5. Russ. *sapog* (> Lith. *sopagas*, Lett. *zābaks*), see 6.51.

6.53 SLIPPER

NG	*παντόφλα*	Dan.	*tøffel*	Lith.	*šliurė, pantaplis*
It.	*pantofola*	Sw.	*toffel*	Lett.	*tupele*
Fr.	*pantoufle*	NE	*slipper*	SCr.	*papuča*
Sp.	*pantufla, zapatilla*	Du.	*pantoffel*	Boh.	*pantofel*
Rum.	*papuc, pantof*	NHG	*pantoffel*	Pol.	*pantofel, patynek*
NIr.	*slipēir*			Russ.	*tuflja, tufel'*
W.	*yslopan*				
Br.	*arc'henad-kambr, pantouflenn*				

For the 'slipper' intended for house wear only modern words are listed. For earlier periods the nearest approximation would be words for 'sandal', as Grk. *σάνδαλον*, Lat. *solea* (> Goth. *sulja*), or for a light 'shoe', some of which are included in 6.51.

1. MLat. *pantofla* (1482, Du Cange), It. *pantofola* (> NG *παντόφλα*), Fr. *pantoufle* (> NE *pantofle* now obs.), Sp. *pantufla*, prob. the creation of a 15th cent. humanist, based upon a fictitious Grk. **παντό-φελλος* 'all-cork' (no such cpd. is quotable for any period). Hence also, through Fr. or It., NHG *pantoffel* (> Boh., Pol. *pantofel*, Lith. *pantaplis*, Rum. *pantof*), Du. *pantoffel*, and the shortened early Du., LG *toffel*, *tuffel* (> Dan. *tøffel*, Sw. *toffel*, Lett. *tupele*, Russ. *tufel'*, *tuflja*). REW 6208a. Franck-v. W. 488. Falk-Torp 1314.

Sp. *zapatilla*, dim. of *zapato* 'shoe' (6.51).

Rum. *papuc*, SCr. *papuča*, fr. Turk. *pabuç*, source of NG *παπούτσι* 'shoe' (6.51).

2. NIr. *slipēir*, fr. NE *slipper*.

W. *yslopan*, evidently the same word as the archaic *llopan*, *llop* 'boot, buskin, shoe' (for preservation of initial *s-* by prothetic *y-* cf. *ysnoden* 'lace', 6.26), fr. ME *sloppe*, *slop* an unidentified form of footwear, the name of which seems identical with *sloppe* for other articles of clothing 'loose jacket, gown, wide breeches, etc.' (cf. NED s.v.).

Br. *arc'henad-kambr* (Vallée, who gives also *pantouflenn*), lit. 'chamber-shoe'.

3. ME *slypper*, NE *slipper*, fr. the OE vb. *slip*, cf. the rare OE *slīpe-scōh* 'slip-shoe', NE *slip*.

4. Lith. *šliurė*, fr. LG dial. *schlorre*, *schlurre* 'slipper', fr. *schlorren*, *schlurren* 'shuffle in walking' (Weigand-H. 2.740).

5. Pol. *patynek*, *patynka*, fr. It. *pattino* 'sort of shoe', now 'skate', fr. Fr. *patin* 'shoe with wooden sole, skate', fr. *patte* 'paw'. Brückner 399. REW 6301.

6.54 SHOEMAKER, COBBLER

Grk.	*ὑποδηματαποιός, σκῦτοτόμος, νευρορράφος*	ON	*skōari*	Lith.	*kurpius, kurpininkas*
NG	*τσαγγάρης, παπουτσῆς*	Dan.	*skomager*	Lett.	*kurpnieks*
Lat.	*sūtor, calceolārius*	Sw.	*skomakare*	ChSl.	*sapogošĭvĭcĭ, sapožĭnikŭ*
It.	*calzolaio, ciabattino*	OE	*scōhere, scōhwyrhta, sūtere*	SCr.	*postolar, obućar, čizmar*
Fr.	*cordonnier, savetier*	ME	*scomakere, cobelere*	Boh.	*švec, obuvník*
Sp.	*zapatero*	NE	*shoemaker, cobbler*	Pol.	*szewc*
Rum.	*cizmar*	Du.	*schoenmaker*	Russ.	*sapožnik, bašmačnik*
Ir.	*cairem*	OHG	*sūtāri, scuohbuozo*	Skt.	*pādūkṛt-, pādūkāra-, carmakāra-*
NIr.	*grēasaidhe, coiblēir*	MHG	*schuochwürhte, schuochsūtære*		
W.	*crydd*	NHG	*schuhmacher, schuster*		
Br.	*kere*				

A distinction between 'shoemaker' and 'cobbler' as 'one who mends shoes' is rarely maintained and is ignored here. Most of the words are based on some of those for 'shoe' or 'boot', either derivs. or cpds. with agent-nouns of vbs. for 'make' or 'sew'. A few are words for 'leatherworker', or simply 'sewer' in specialized application.

1. Grk. *ὑποδηματοποιός* (IG 2^2.1559.48, etc., also lit. NG), cpd. of *ὑπόδημα* 'shoe' (6.51) and *-ποιός* 'maker'.

Grk. *σκῦτοτόμος*, cpd. of *σκῦτος* 'leather' (6.29) and *-τομος* 'cutter' (: *τέμνω* 'cut'), used for 'leatherworker' in general (cf. Hom. Il. 7.221), but esp. 'shoemaker', as also the deriv. *σκυτεύς*.

Grk. *νευρορράφος*, lit. 'cord-sewer', cpd. of *νεῦρον* 'nerve, fibre, cord' and *-ραφος* fr. *ῥάπτω* 'sew' (6.36).

Late Grk. *τζαγγάριος* (6th cent. pap., Byz.; *σαγγάριος* Hesych.), NG *τσαγγάρης*, fr. late *τζάγγα* (also *τζαγγίον*, freq. Byz.) a kind of 'shoe', through Syrian fr. a Persian word = Av. *zanga-* 'ankle' : Skt. *jañghā-* 'leg from ankle to knee'. G. Meyer, Z. rom. Ph. 16.525 f.

NG *παπουτσῆς*, fr. *παπούτσι* 'shoe' (6.51).

2. Lat. *sūtor*, fr. *suere* 'sew' (6.36). Hence OFr. *sueur*, OE *sūtere*, OHG *sūtāri*, MHG cpd. *schuoch-sūtære*, whence NHG *schuster*.

Lat. *calceolārius* (> It. *calzolaio*), fr. *calceolus*, dim. of *calceus* 'shoe' (6.51).

It. *ciabattino*, Fr. *savetier*, Sp. *zapatero*, fr. It. *ciabatta*, Fr. *savate* 'worn-out shoe', Sp. *zapato* 'shoe' (6.51).

Fr. *cordonnier*, OFr. *cordouanier*, fr. *cordouan* 'leather from Cordova'. REW 2230. Gamillscheg 255.

Rum. *cizmar*, fr. *cizmă* 'boot' (6.52).

3. Ir. *cairem*, NIr. (obs.) *caiream*, W. *crydd*, Br. *kere*, *kereour* : Grk. *κρηπίς*, Lith. *kurpė* 'shoe' (6.51).

NIr. *grēasaidhe* (Dinneen, etc.; McKenna gives only the borrowed *coiblēir*), also in general 'artisan, skilled worker', fr. *grēas* 'design, art, craft', esp. 'needlework', Ir. grēss 'art', of dub. etym. (cf. Macbain 205).

4. ON skōari, OE scōhere (both rare), fr. ON skōr, OE scōh 'shoe' (6.51).

Dan. skomager, Sw. skomakare, ME scomakere, NE shoemaker, Du. schoen-maker, NHG schuhmacher, all obvious cpds. of words for 'shoe' and 'maker'.

OE scōhwyrhta, MHG schuochwürhte, cpds. of words for 'shoe' and agent-nouns of OE wyrcan, OHG wurchen 'make' (9.11).

ME cobelere, NE cobbler, etym.? NED s.v.

OHG scuohbuozo, scuohbuzare, cpds. of word for 'shoe' and agent-nouns fr. buozen 'make better' = Goth. bōtjan 'avail, profit' (cf. OE bōt 'help, remedy').

5. Lith. kurpius, kurpininkas, Lett. kurpnieks, fr. Lith. kurpė, Lett. kurpe 'shoe' (6.51).

6. ChSl. sapogošivĭcĭ (late), cpd. of sapogŭ 'shoe' and šivĭcĭ 'sewer' = Boh. švec, Pol. szewc 'shoemaker', agent-nouns of ChSl. šiti 'sew', etc. (6.36).

ChSl. sapožĭnikŭ (late), Russ. sapož-nik, fr. ChSl. sapogŭ, Russ. sapog 'shoe', 'boot' (6.51).

SCr. postolar, fr. postola 'shoe' (6.51).

SCr. obućar, Boh. obuvnik, fr. SCr. obuća, Boh. obuv 'footwear, shoe' (6.51).

SCr. čizmar, fr. čizma 'boot' (6.52),

Russ. bašmačnik, fr. bašmak 'shoe' (6.51).

7. Skt. pādūkṛt-, pādūkāra-, cpds. of pādū- = pādukā- 'shoe' (6.51) and agent-nouns of kṛ- 'do, make'.

Skt. carmakāra-, also 'leatherworker' (in general), fr. carman- 'hide, leather' (6.29) and kāra- (as above).

6.55 HAT; CAP

Grk.	πέτασος, πῖλος; κυνῆ	ON	hǫttr; hūfa	Lith.	skrybėlė; kepurė
NG	καπέλλο; σκοῦφος, κασκέτο	Dan.	hat, hue; kasket	Lett.	cepure
		Sw.	hatt; mössa	SCr.	šešir, klobuk; kapa, šapka
Lat.	pilleus, petasus	OE	hætt, cæppe		
It.	cappello; berretto	ME	hat; cappe	Boh.	klobouk; čepice, čapka
Fr.	chapeau; casquette	NE	hat; cap	Pol.	kapelusz; czapka
Sp.	sombrero; gorra	Du.	hoed; muts, pet	Russ.	šljapa; šapka
Rum.	pǎlǎrie; șapcǎ ·	OHG	huot	Skt.	(çirahṣāṭaka-, çiras-tra-)
Ir.	(culpait)	MHG	huot; mütze		
NIr.	hata; caipin, bairēad	NHG	hut; mütze	Av.	xaoδa-
W.	het; cap				
Br.	tok; kalabousenn				

'Hat' and 'cap' are given in this order in the list, where a clear distinction can be made. In most cases 'cap' or 'hood', according to the modern notion, would better describe the types of headgear worn in ancient and medieval times.

1. Derivs. of MLat. cappa 'a sort of headgear' (cf. It. cappa, Sp. capa 'cloak', 6.41).

It. cappello (> NG καπέλλο), Fr. cha-peau, fr. dim. MLat. cappellus; OE cæppe, ME cappe, NE cap (> W. cap, NIr. caipin with dim. suffix); SCr. kapa,

kapice, SCr., Russ. šapka, Boh. čapka, Pol. czapka (czapa), the Slavic forms with š- and č- perh. through Fr. chape 'cope' (cf. Berneker 483 f.); Pol. kapelusz fr. It. cappellucio deriv. (now depreciatory, 'old worn-out hat') of cappello; Rum. șapcǎ fr. Slavic.

2. Grk. πέτασος (> Lat. petasus) fr. πετα- of πετάννῡμι 'spread out'. Walde-P. 2.18.

Grk. πῖλος, Lat. pilleus, orig. words for 'felt' (6.27).

6. ChSl. sapogošivĭcĭ ... [see above]

Grk. κυνῆ, orig. 'cap of dog's skin', fem. of adj. κύνεος, fr. κύων, gen. κυνός 'dog'.

NG σκοῦφος, σκούφια, fr. It. scuffia, cuffia 'sort of headdress', MLat. cofea 'hood' (Fr. coiffe), prob. fr. Gmc., cf. OHG chuppha 'head-covering used un-der helmet', also 'woman's headgear'. REW 2024. Brüch, Z. rom. Ph. 38.676. Wartburg 2.838.

3. It. berretto (Fr. béret), fr. OProv. beret, OFr. barrete, derivs. of Lat. birrus 'cloak with cowl', perh. of Gall. orig. (Ir. berr 'short', etc.). REW 1117a. Ernout-M. 110. Walde-H. 1.107.

Hence fr. one or the other of the Ro-mance forms NIr. bairēad.

Fr. casquette (> NG κασκέτο, Dan. kasket), dim. of casque 'helmet', fr. Sp. casco 'skull, crown (of hat), helmet', orig. 'potsherd', fr. cascar 'break'. REW 6941.

Sp. sombrero, fr. sombra 'shade' (1.63).

Sp. gorra, fr. Basque gorri 'red'. REW 3822.

Rum. pǎlǎrie, of dub. orig., perh. by dissim. for *pǎrǎrie fr. pǎr 'hair' (Lat. pilus). Tiktin 1110.

4. Ir. culpait (NIr. culpaid) 'hood', most common sort of head-covering, fr. Lat. culcita 'sack of feathers, cushion'. Vendryes, De hib. voc. 134.

Br. tok, tog fr. Fr. toque a kind of 'cap', fr. Sp. toca (orig. Basque?). Henry 265. REW 8601a. Gamillscheg 849.

Br. kalabousenn, also kara- (cf. Er-nault, Vallée), apparently, as named for its shape, fr. early Fr. calabasse, Cat. carabassa, etc. (REW 1623, Gamillscheg 172) 'calabash'.

5. ON hǫttr, Dan. hat, Sw. hatt, OE hætt, ME hat, NE hat, and, with different vowel grade, OHG, MHG huot, NHG hut, Du. hoed (= OE hōd, NE hood), fr. IE *kādh- 'cover, protect' in Lat. cassis 'helmet', OHG huoten 'protect', etc. Walde-P. 1.341 f. Falk-Torp 384. Walde-H. 1.177.

ON hūfa, Dan. hue : OE hūfe, OHG hūba, NHG haube 'hood', etc., perh. orig. for its rounded shape, fr. IE *keu-bh-, in Grk. κῡφός 'bent', or *keu-p- in Grk. κύπελλον 'cup', etc. Walde-P. 1.375. Falk-Torp 426.

Du. muts (MLG mutze, musse > Sw. mössa), MHG, NHG mütze, earlier MHG armuz, almuz, fr. MLat. almutia, armutia 'cloak with cowl' (> Sp. almu-cio, Fr. aumusse, NE amice), through Arab. al-mustakah, fr. Pers. muša 'fur cloak with wide sleeves'. Lokotsch 1520. Falk-Torp 750. Weigand-H. 2.249.

Du. pet : OFris. pet, LG petzel, MHG bezel, NHG betzel 'sort of hood', orig. un-known. Franck-v. W. 498.

6. Lith. skrybėlė : skrebai 'hatbrim', this : skrebėti 'rustle'(?). Leskien, Ablaut 343.

Lith. kepurė, Lett. cepure, Boh. čepice 'cap' (Boh., Russ. čepec 'hood') : Grk. σκέπας 'cover, envelope', IE *(s)kep-. Walde-P. 2.559. Berneker 143 f.

7. SCr. klobuk, Boh. klobouk (Russ. klobuk 'monk's hood', Pol. kłobuk 'high cap'), early borrowings fr. a Turk. *kal-buk, beside kalpak 'high cap, hat' (whence later Russ. kalpak 'nightcap', Pol. kołpak 'high fur cap', etc.). Berneker 474 f. Brückner 237.

SCr. šešir, prob. loanword, but source?

Russ. šljapa, fr. NHG schlappe 'broad-brimmed hat' (fr. vb. schlappen 'flap'). Weigand-H. 2.722.

8. In India the turban took the place of the Western hat. Skt. çirahṣāṭaka-, lit. 'head-cloth' (çaṭa- 'cloth'); Skt. çirastra- 'helmet', çiras- 'head'.

Av. xaoδa- (OPers. xauda- in tigra-xauda- 'with pointed cap'), perh. : Lat. cūdō 'skin helmet', IE *(s)keudh-, ex-tension of *skeu- 'cover'. Walde-P. 2.550. Walde-H. 1.301.

6.57 BELT, GIRDLE

Grk.	ζώνη, ζωστήρ	Goth.	gairda	Lith.	juosta
NG	ζώνη	ON	gjǫrð, gyrðill, lindi, belti	Lett.	juosta
Lat.	cinctus, cingulum, balteus			ChSl.	pojasŭ
		Dan.	bælte	SCr.	pojas
It.	cintura	Sw.	bälte, gördel	Boh.	pás
Fr.	ceinture	OE	gyrdel, belt	Pol.	pas
Sp.	cinturon	ME	belt, girdel	Russ.	pojas, kušak
Rum.	cingǎtoare, curea, colan	NE	belt, girdle	Skt.	kāñcī-, mekhalā-, raçanā-
		Du.	gordel		
Ir.	ferenn, criss	OHG	gurtil, balz	Av.	yāh-, kamarā-
NIr.	crios	MHG	gürtel		
W.	gwregys	NHG	gürtel		
Br.	gouriz				

1. Derivs. of *yōs- 'gird' (perh. orig. *yōu-s-, extension of *yeu- 'bind') in Grk. ζώννῡμι, ζωστός, Lith. juosti, ChSl. po-jasati, Av. yāh-, pple. yāsta-. Walde-P. 1.209.

Grk. ζωστήρ, ζώνη; Lith., Lett. juosta; ChSl. pojasŭ, SCr., Russ. pojas, Boh. pás, Pol. pas; Av. yāh-.

2. Derivs. of IE *kenk- in Lat. cin-gere 'gird', Skt. kañc- 'bind' (Dhātup.), etc. Walde-P. 1.400. Ernout-M. 187. Walde-H. 1.216 f.

Lat. cinctus, cingulum, late cīnctūra (> It. cintura, Fr. ceinture, Sp. cintura, cinturon); Rum. cingǎtoare new forma-tion); Skt. kāñcī-.

3. Lat. balteus (esp. 'sword-belt'), ac-cording to Varro an Etruscan word. Walde-H. 1.95. Ernout-M. 102. Hence ON belti, Dan. bælte, Sw. bälte, OE–NE belt, OHG balz. Falk-Torp 124.

Rum. curea ('strap' and the usual word for the common leather 'belt'), fr. Lat. corrigia 'strap'. REW 2253.

Rum. colan (esp. for women), fr. Turk. kolan 'saddle-girth'. Lokotsch 1195.

4. Ir. ferenn : fern 'shield' (20.34), and so prob. at first 'sword-belt'.

Ir. criss, NIr. crios = W. crys 'shirt' (6.44); cpds. in W. gwregys (for *gwe-

grys), Br. gouriz : Pol. trzos, Russ. čerez 'money-belt'. Walde-P. 1.423. Pedersen 1.42 f.

5. Goth. gairda, ON gjǫrð, gyrðill, Sw. gördel, OE gyrdel, ME girdel, NE girdle, Du. gordel, OHG gurtil, MHG, NHG gürtel, perh. fr. IE *gherdh- 'sur-round'(?), as in Goth. gards 'house, court', OHG gart 'inclosure', etc. Walde-P. 1.608 f. Feist 185.

ON lindi (orig. of 'linden bast'), fr. ON lind 'linden tree', so named fr. its flexible bast (OHG lindi, OE līpe 'mild', Lat. lentus 'flexible, slow', etc.). Falk-Torp 646.

6. Lith., Lett. juosta, ChSl. pojasŭ, etc., above, 1.

Russ. kušak, fr. Turk. kuşak 'belt'. Berneker 652.

7. Skt. kāñcī-, above, 2.

Skt. mekhalā-, perh. as me-kha-lā- fr. IE *mei- 'bind, join'(?) in Skt. mitra-, Av. miθra- 'friend', Hom. μίτρη 'metal waist-guard (Hom.), girdle'. Walde-P. 2.241 f.

Skt. raçanā- ('strap' and esp. 'wom-an's girdle', beside raçmi- 'strap'), etym. dub. Walde-P. 2.362. Uhlenbeck 246.

Av. kamarā- (NPers. kamar) : Grk. καμάρα 'vault', etc. Walde-P. 1.349 f.

6.58 GLOVE

Grk.	χειρίς	ON	glófi, hanzki	Lith.	pirštinė
NG	γάντι, χειρόχτι	Dan.	handske	Lett.	cimds, pirkstaine
Lat.	(manica)	Sw.	handske	ChSl.	rǫkavica
It.	guanto	OE	glóf	SCr.	rukavica
Fr.	gant	ME	glove	Boh.	rukavice
Sp.	guante	NE	glove	Pol.	rękawica
Rum.	mǎnușǎ	Du.	handschoen	Russ.	perčatka
Ir.	lámind, lámann	OHG	hantscuoh		
NIr.	lámhainn	MHG	hantschuoch		
W.	maneg	NHG	handschuh		
Br.	maneg				

Most of the words for 'glove' are de-rived from those for 'hand' (4.33) or 'finger' (4.34).

1. Grk. χειρίς, covering for the hand, 'glove' (Hom., etc.), or for the arm, 'sleeve', fr. χείρ 'hand'.

NG χειρόχτι (also χερ-), fr. Byz. χερόρτι (Chron. Mor.), χειρόρτιον (Du Cange), this, with haplology and vowel change, fr. *χειραρίδια (cf. ἀρτάρια 'felt shoes' Suid.), cpd., second part fr. root of ἀραρίσκω 'fit'. Koraes, Ἄτακτα 2.429. Hatzidakis, Ἀθηνᾶ 22.205 f.

2. Lat. manica, 'long sleeve of a tunic covering arm and hand', fr. manus 'hand'. Hence (Romance words for 'sleeve', but) W., Br. maneg 'glove'. Pedersen 1.193. Loth, Mots lat. 184.

Fr. gant (> It. guanto, Sp. guante, NG γάντι), ON vǫttr 'mitten', fr. the root of OHG wintan, OE windan etc. 'turn around, wind'. The name must orig. have applied to a strip of cloth wrapped about the hand to protect it from sword-blows, a frequent practice in the Icelandic sagas. This is further in-dicated by the compound ON band-vett-

lingar, lit. 'band-mittens'. REW 9500. Falk-Torp 1351 f.

Rum. mǎnușǎ (also 'handle'), deriv. of Lat. manus (Rum. mîna) 'hand'.

3. Ir. lámind, lámann, NIr. lámhainn, fr. Ir. lám 'hand'.

4. ON glófi, OE glóf, ME, NE glove, fr. *ga-lófi, *ga-lōf : ON lófi, ME love, Goth. lōfa 'flat of the hand'. Falk-Torp 657.

OHG hantscuoh, NHG handschuh (OE handscíó only a proper name; see now Bosworth-Toller, Suppl. s.v.), Du. handschoen, MLG hantsche (> late ON hanzki, Dan., Sw. handske), cpd. of words for 'hand' and 'shoe'. Falk-Torp 380.

5. Lith. pirštinė, Lett. pirkstaine, fr. Lith. pirštas, Lett. pirksts 'finger'.

Lett. cimds, etym. dub., perh. fr. IE *kem- in words for 'covering', etc., like OHG hemidi 'shirt', etc. (6.44). Mühl.-Endz. 1.383.

6. ChSl. rǫkavica, SCr., Russ. ruka-vica (in Russ. 'mitten'), Boh. rukavice, Pol. rękawica, fr. ChSl. rǫka, etc. 'hand'.

Russ. perčatka (perstjatka, peršcatka), fr. perst 'finger'.

6.59 VEIL

Grk.	κάλυμμα	ON	lín	Lith.	šy̆ras, šy̆das, nometas
NG	βέλο	Dan.	slør	Lett.	škidrauts, plīvurs
Lat.	(vēlum)	Sw.	flor, slöja	SCr.	veo, koprena
It.	velo	ME	veile	Boh.	závoj
Fr.	voile	NE	veil	Pol.	kwef, welon
Sp.	velo	Du.	sluier	Russ.	vual'
Rum.	văl	MHG	sloier, sleier		
Ir.	caille, fíal	NHG	schleier		
NIr.	caille				
W.	gorchudd				
Br.	gwel				

Words for 'veil' are partly based on the notion of 'covering', 'something wrapped about', or 'dragging, trailing'. But several are in origin names of some fine fabric such as is used for veils.

1. Grk. κάλυμμα, fr. καλύπτω 'cover' (12.26).

2. Lat. vēlum, mostly 'curtain' or 'sail', rarely if ever quotable as woman's 'veil', but in this sense the source of It. velo (> NG βέλο, SCr. veo; Pol. welon fr. It. velone), Fr. voile (> ME veile, vail, NE veil, Russ. vual'), Sp. velo, Rum. văl (cf. Tiktin 1710), Ir. fíal, Br. gwel; prob. fr. *vexlom, cf. dim. vexillum, fr. IE *weg-, in Ir. figim 'weave' (6.33). Walde-P. 1.247. Ernout-M. 1082. REW 9184. Pedersen 1.208. Vendryes, De hib. voc. 141 f.

3. Ir. caille, fr. Lat. pallium 'covering', esp. 'cloak' (6.41). Pedersen 1.235. Vendryes, De hib. voc. 119.

W. gorchudd, cpd. of gor- 'on' (= Ir. for-, fr. *upor) and cudd 'covering' : cuddio 'hide' (12.27).

4. ON lín 'linen' (6.23), also 'bridal veil'.

ON blœja 'cloth used for covering, burial sheet, bed-covering', etc., but reg. word for 'veil' in NIcel. : Norw. blœje 'swaddling clothes', Dan. ble 'sheet', Lat. floccus 'flock of wool', etc. Walde-P. 2.217. Falk-Torp 80.

MLG slöier (> Dan. slør), MHG sloier, sleier, NHG schleier, Du. sluier,

also the shorter form MDu. slöie, (> Sw. slöja) : MDu. sloien 'drag', ON slœða 'drag', slœðar 'trailing gown' (Gmc. *slōd-). Falk-Torp 1073, 1074. Franck-v. W. 621. Hellquist 998.

Sw. flor, 'fine cloth, crepe, gauze', used also commonly for 'veil', fr. LG flor 'crepe, gauze', fr. Fr. velours 'velvet' (fr. Prov. velos id., Lat. villōsus 'hairy'). Falk-Torp 240. REW 9334.

5. Lith. šy̆ras 'crepe', used also for 'veil' (Lalis, Kurschat), fr. NHG dial. schïr 'fine cloth' (: adj. schier, NE sheer, etc.). Alminauskis 126.

Lith. šy̆das (fr. LG sïde 'silk'), also used for 'veil' (Lalis, Gailius-Šlaža).

Lith. nometas 'headdress or veil of married women' (cf. Lalis and NSB s.v.), cpd. of nuo 'down, from, away' and deriv. of mesti 'throw', i.e. something 'thrown over and down' from the head.

Lett. škidrauts, lit. 'a thin cloth', cpd. of škidrs 'thin, loose woven' and auts 'piece of cloth' (cf. priekšauts 'apron', 6.47). Mühl.-Endz. 4.39, 1.231.

Lett. plīvurs : plīvuot 'flutter, flicker', plīva 'thin dry skin, thin layer'.

6. SCr. koprena 'gauze, crepe', used also for 'veil' = ChSl., ORuss., Bulg. koprina 'sort of silk'. Berneker 564.

Boh. závoj : zaviti 'wrap up, swathe', cpd. of viti 'wind' (10.14).

Pol. kwef, fr. Fr. coiffe 'headdress'. Brückner 287.

6.61 POCKET
(In a Garment)

NG	τσέπη	Dan.	lomme	Lith.	kišené (delmonas)
It.	tasca	Sw.	ficka	Lett.	k'eša
Fr.	poche	ME	poket, pouche	SCr.	džep
Sp.	bolsillo	NE	pocket	Boh.	kapsa
Rum.	buzunar	Du.	zak	Pol.	kieszeń
NIr.	póca	MHG	tasche	Russ.	karman
W.	llogell	NHG	tasche		
Br.	godell				

Words for 'pocket' in a garment, unknown in ancient costume, are from those for 'bag, sack' or the like.

1. NG τσέπη, SCr. džep, through Turk. cep id., fr. Arab. ǵaib 'pocket, wallet, sack'. Lokotsch 641.

2. It. tasca, fr. Gmc., cf. MHG tasche (below, 4).

Fr. poche (> ME pouche, NE pouch), fr. Frank. *pokka > OE pocca 'bag' (cf. ME poket, below, 4). REW 6631.

Sp. bolsillo, dim. of bolsa 'purse, pouch, bag' = Fr. bourse, It. borsa, fr. MLat. byrsa 'hide, leather, leather bag', fr. Grk. βύρσα 'hide'. REW 1432.

Rum. buzunar, orig.? Tiktin 248.

3. NIr. póca, fr. OE-ME poke 'bag', cf. ME poket (below, 4).

W. llogell, also 'chest, receptacle', fr. Lat. locellus, dim. of locus 'place'. Loth, Mots lat. 182.

Br. godell, fr. god 'fold in a garment' = W. cod 'bag, pouch, purse, scrotum', fr. OE codd 'bag'. Henry 136.

4. Dan. lomme (Sw. dial. lomma, Fris. lomm), perh. loanword fr. Celtic, cf. Ir. lumman 'covering', NIr. luman 'coarse cover, bag, pod' : Ir. lomm, W. llwm 'bare, naked'. Walde-P. 2.418. Falk-Torp 654. Hellquist 588.

Sw. ficka (Dan. fikke 'a little pouch'), fr. MLG vicke, back-formation to ficken 'stick on, fasten', fr. It. ficcare 'fix' (MLat. *fīgicāre for Lat. fīgere 'fix, fasten'). Falk-Torp 215. Hellquist 207.

ME poket, NE pocket, fr. Anglo-Norm. pokete (13th cent. Godefroy), dim. of

ONorm.Fr. poke = ON poki, OE pocca, pohha 'bag', etc., these prob. (with common notion of 'blown up, swollen') : Lat. bucca 'cheek', etc. Walde-P. 2.116 f. NED s.v. pocket.

Du. zak, MDu. sack (NHG sack also locally 'pocket' or 'wallet'; Kretschmer, Wortgeogr. 514) = MLG sak, OHG sac(ch), OE sæcc, etc. 'sack', fr. Lat. saccus, fr. Grk. σάκκος 'coarse cloth, sack', a Semitic loanword (cf. NG σακκάκι 'coat', 6.43).

MHG tasche, tesche, NHG tasche, fr. OHG tasca, dasca 'pouch, bag', orig. dub. Walde-P. 1.766. Falk-Torp 1249.

5. Lith. kišené, kišenius 'stick (for earlier kešené), i after kišti 'stick in, thrust in'), Lett. k'eša (for *kešene felt as dim. form), fr. Pol. kieszeń (below, 6). Brückner, Sl. Fremdwörter 92. Mühl.-Endz. 2.371.

Lith. delmonas, dalmonas (old word for 'pocket', but not in NSB), fr. Pol. dolman 'Hussar's jacket' (orig. Turk.; Berneker 206), with curious shift of sense.

6. SCr. džep, see under NG τσέπη (above, 1).

Boh. kapsa (Pol. kapsa 'box, sack, wallet'), fr. Lat. capsa 'case, chest, repository'. Berneker 485.

Pol. kieszeń, prob. (fr. its shape) : kiszka, Russ. kiška 'gut, intestine'. Berneker 503, 679. Brückner 229.

Russ. karman, fr. Turk. dial. karman 'pocket'. Lokotsch 1097. Otherwise Berneker 490.

6.62 BUTTON

NG	κουμπί	Dan.	knap	Lith.	saga, knypkis (guzikas)
It.	bottone	Sw.	knapp	Lett.	puoga
Fr.	bouton	ME	botoun	SCr.	puce, dugme
Sp.	botón	NE	button	Boh.	knoflík
Rum.	nasture	Du.	knoop	Pol.	guzik
NIr.	cnaipe	NHG	knopf	Russ.	pugovica
W.	botwm				
Br.	nozelenn				

Ornamental buttons have been found dating back even to prehistoric times (e.g. perforated tin buttons from Italy). But it was apparently not till the 14th or 15th cent. A.D. that they came into use as fastenings for garments, eventually replacing in large measure the pins or lacings of earlier dress.

The words for 'button' originate mostly in those meaning originally 'knob, knot' or the like.

1. NG κουμπί, fr. κουμβίον, dim. of Byz. κόμβος 'knot, roll, band', prob. : σκαμβός, Ir. camm 'crooked', etc. (12.74). Walde-P. 2.539 f.

2. Fr. bouton, whence It. bottone, Sp. botón, ME botoun (> W. botwm), NE button, fr. Fr. bout 'end, point' (12.35). REW 1228c.

Rum. nastur(e), fr. It. nastro 'band, ribbon', MLat. nastola, fr. Gmc., cf. OHG nestila, NHG nestel 'lace' for fastening clothing, with Rum. shift fr. such 'lace' to the 'button' serving the same purpose. REW 5840.

3. NIr. cnaipe (MIr. cnap 'button, lump, stud', fr. ON knappr (below, 4). K. Meyer, Contrib. 397.

Br. nozelenn, fr. MLat. nōdellus, dim. of nōdus 'knot'. Henry 213.

4. Dan. knap, Sw. knapp (ON knappr 'knob', OE cnæpp 'point', LG knapp

'summit of a mountain'), likewise NHG knopf (Dan. knop, MLG knoppe, Du., NE knop 'bud'), Du. knoop, all through 'knob, knot', fr. various extensions of *gen- in words for 'press together', etc. Walde-P. 1.581 ff. Falk-Torp 544.

5. Lith. saga, dim. sagutė (now preferred, cf. NSB s.v. guzikas; formerly a kind of fastening for the washing) : segti 'fasten', sagtis, Lett. sagts, OPruss. sagis 'buckle', Skt. saj- 'hang on', etc. Walde-P. 2.480 f. Leskien, Ablaut 365. Trautmann, Altpreuss. 416 f.

Lith. knypkis, fr. MLG knoepke, dim. of knoppe (above, 4).

Lith. guzikas, fr. Pol. guzik (below, 6).

Lett. puoga, fr. the same source as ChSl. pągy 'knob', etc.

6. SCr. puce (*pug-ce), Pol. pągwica (obs.), Russ. pugovica, fr. ChSl. pągy 'knob, tassel, cluster', prob. a Gmc. loanword, cf. Goth. puggs, OE pung, etc. 'money wallet'. Brückner 401. Feist 385. Stender-Petersen 396.

SCr. dugme, fr. Turk. düğme 'button'. Lokotsch 540.

Boh. knoflík, Pol. (arch.) knaflík, dim. of MHG knofel, knoufel, itself dim. of knopf (above, 4). Berneker 530.

Pol. guzik, dim. of guz 'knob, bruise' = SCr. guz, Boh. huze 'rump, breech' : Lith. gūžys 'Adam's apple, crop', etc. Berneker 342 f. Brückner 164.

6.63 PIN

Grk.	περόνη, πόρπη, ἐνετή	ON	dálkr, nesti	Lith.	spilka
NG	καρφίτσα; πόρπη	Dan.	naal	Lett.	kniepe
Lat.	acus; fibula	Sw.	nål	SCr.	čioda
It.	spillo	OE	dalc, prēon	Boh.	špendlík
Fr.	épingle	ME	preen, pynn	Pol.	szpilka
Sp.	alfiler	NE	pin	Russ.	bulavka
Rum.	ac (cu gămălie)	Du.	speld	Skt.	sūci-
Ir.	delg, sē̆t	OHG	spinula		
NIr.	biorán, dealg	MHG	spenel, stecknölde		
W.	pin	NHG	stecknadel		
Br.	spilenn				

The 'pin' for fastening clothing, though in ultimate origin a simple pointed object like a thorn or pointed piece of bone, was in ancient (even prehistoric) Greece, Italy, and other parts of Europe mostly of the 'safety-pin, clasp-pin' form, ornamental as well as practical (cf. Ebert, Reallex. s.v. Fibel; J. L. Myres, Who Were the Greeks? 405 ff.). This is now often distinguished by the use of the Lat. fibula (so archeologists) or terms like Fr. broche, NE brooch, etc. (fr. Lat. adj. broccus used of 'projecting' teeth), NHG spange (OE spang 'clasp'), etc. But the modern words listed are those which are used for the common straight pin (though many are also used more comprehensively, like NE pin for breastpin, etc.).

A few of the words are from verbs for 'pierce', 'fasten', or 'set in'. But more are cognate with words for other pointed objects such as 'needle', 'thorn', 'awl', 'spit'.

1. Grk. περόνη, περονίς, πόρπη, fr. the root of πείρω 'pierce'. Walde-P. 2.39. Boisacq 757 f.

Grk. (Hom.) ἐνετή : ἐν-ίημι 'put in'. Walde-P. 1.199. Boisacq 253.

NG καρφίτσα, dim. of καρφίον, dim. of Grk. κάρφος 'dry stick'.

2. Lat. acus 'needle' (6.36) and 'pin'. Hence Rum. ac (cu gămălie), lit. 'needle (with a head)'.

Lat. fibula, fr. fīgere 'fasten, fix'. Ernout-M. 355, 358 f. Walde-H. 1.492.

It. spillo, spilla, Fr. épingle, Br. spilenn, fr. Lat. spīnula, dim. of spīna 'thorn'. Hence also prob. (rather than cognate, as Walde-P. 2.634) OHG spinula, MHG spenel, Du. speld (MDu. spelle fr. *spenle). REW 8154. Falk-Torp 1122. Franck-v. W. 643.

Sp. alfiler, fr. Arab. al ḥilēl 'needle'. REW 4129b. Lokotsch 865.

3. Ir. delg, NIr. dealg, ON dálkr, OE dalc, dolc, orig. 'thorn' (as still also in Irish) : Lith. dilgé 'nettle', dilgus 'pricking, burning'. Walde-P. 1.865 f. Pedersen 1.106.

Ir. sē̆t, see under NIr. seod 'jewel' (6.72).

NIr. biorán, dim. of bior 'spit, lance, point' (bior- in cpds. 'pointed'), Ir. bir, W. ber 'spit, lance' : Lat. veru 'spit, dart', etc. Pedersen 1.144.

4. ON nesti (NIcel. nisti 'disk-shaped brooch'), fr. nesta 'fasten' : MHG nesten 'stitch, fasten' (IE *ned-, in Lat. nōdus 'knot', etc.). Walde-P. 2.328.

Dan. naal, Sw. nål 'needle' (6.36), also 'pin', for which also esp. Dan. knappenaal, Sw. knappnål, lit. 'button-needle'.

OE prēon, ME preen, prene : ON prjōnn 'knitting needle', MLG prīn, prēne, MHG pfrieme 'awl' (6.37), orig.? Falk-Torp 827.

ME pynn, NE pin, in modern use since latter part of 14th cent., fr. OE pinn = late ON pinni, OS pin, Du. pin 'peg, point' perh. : Ir. bonn 'horn, point'. Walde-P. 2.109 f. Falk-Torp 827.

Du. *speld*, OHG *spinula*, MHG *spenel*, fr. Lat. *spīnula* (above, 2).

Late MHG *stickenālde*, *stecknōlde*, NHG *stecknadel*, cpd. of *stecken* 'stick' and *nādel* 'needle' (6.36). Weigand-H. 2.958.

5. Lith. *spilka*, fr. Pol. *szpilka* (below, 6).

Lett. *kniepe*, *kniepis*, fr. MLG *knöpe* pl. 'buttons' (6.62). Mühl.-Endz. 2.249.

6. SCr. *čioda*, dial. *špioda*, fr. MHG *spilte* 'splinter'(?). Rječnik Akad. 2.38.

SCr. *bačenka*, *babljača*, *batuška* (all given in Rječnik Akad.; which is common?), etym.?

Boh. *špendlík* (dim.), fr. NHG *spännadel*, a pop. transformation of OHG *spinula* (above) through connection with *spannen* 'stretch' (cf. Grimm s.v.).

Pol. *szpilka*, dim. of *szpila*, MHG *spille* 'spindle' (6.32), but confused with MHG *spenel* 'pin' (above, 2). Brückner 554.

Russ. *bulavka*, dim. of *bulava* 'club' (= Pol. *buława* id.) : Slov. *bula*, Boh. *boule* 'boil', prob. fr. Gmc., cf. OHG *biule* 'swelling', Goth. *uf-bauljan* 'swell up'. Berneker 100.

6.71 ADORNMENT
(Personal)

Grk.	*κόσμος*	ON	*skraut, prȳði*	Lith.	*papuošalas*
NG	*στολίδι*	Dan.	*smykke, prydelse*	Lett.	*ruota, greznums*
Lat.	*mundus, ōrnātus, ōrnāmentum*	Sw.	*prydnad, smycke*	ChSl.	*ukrašenĭje*
It.	*ornamento*	OE	*gearwe*	SCr.	*nakit, ures, ukras*
Fr.	*parure*	ME	*ornement*	Boh.	*okrasa*
Sp.	*adorno*	NE	*adornment*	Pol.	*ozdoba, okrasa*
Rum.	*podoabă*	Du.	*versiering*	Russ.	*ukrašenie*
Ir.	*cumtach, ōrnaid*	OHG	*garawi*	Skt.	*bhūṣaṇa-, alaṁkāra-*
NIr.	*ōrnaidheācht, sciamhacht*	MHG	*gerwe, gesmuc*	Av.	*pis-, paēsa-*
W.	*addurnaid, trwsiad*	NHG	*schmuck*		
Br.	*kinklou, bragerezou*				

Collective terms for articles of 'adornment' are mostly based on still more comprehensive notions, like 'arrangement', 'equipment', 'preparation', or what is 'suitable', 'beautiful', 'clean'.

1. Grk. κόσμος, orig. 'orderly arrangement', then specialized in two directions, 'adornment' and 'world'. See 1.1.

NG στολίδι, στόλισμα, fr. class. Grk. στολίς (gen. - ίδος), στόλισμα 'garment' : στόλος 'equipment', στέλλω 'make ready, equip'. Walde-P. 2.643. Boisacq 907 f.

2. Lat. *mundus* (usually in this sense only 'woman's adornment'; the sense 'world' borrowed fr. Grk. κόσμος, see 1.1) : adj. *mundus* 'clean, elegant' (15.87).

Lat. *ōrnātus*, *ōrnāmentum* (both words are used in the sense of 'personal adornment, embellishment' as well as 'furnishings, equipment'), fr. *ōrnāre* 'put in order, equip, adorn', for **ōrdināre* : *ōrdō* (*-inis*) 'order, row', this perh. fr. the root **ar-* 'fit' in Grk. ἀραρίσκω, Lat. *artus*, etc., but details dub. Hence, directly or new formations fr. vbs. derived fr. Lat. *ōrnāre*, It. *ornamento*, Sp. *adorno*, Ir. *ōrnaid*, NIr. *ōrnaidheacht*, W. *addurnaid*, ME *ornement* (fr. OFr. *ornement*), NE *adornment* (fr. OFr. *aournement*, with spelling-pronunciation by approximation to Latin). Walde-P. 1.76. Ernout-M. 711 f.

Fr. *parure*, fr. OFr. *parer* 'adorn, deck out' (It. *parare*), fr. Lat. *parāre* 'prepare'. REW 6229. Gamillscheg 673.

Rum. *podoabă*, fr. Slavic, cf. ChSl. *podoba* and Pol. *ozdoba* (below, 6).

3. Ir. *cumtach*, lit. 'building, construction', vbl. n. of *conutgim* 'build, erect'. Pedersen 2.506.

NIr. *sciamhacht* (also 'beauty'), fr. *sciamh* 'form, appearance', Ir. *sciam*, fr. Lat. *schēma*, fr. Grk. σχῆμα 'shape, form'. Pedersen 1.208.

W. *trwsiad* (also 'dress, apparel'), fr. *trwsio* 'dress, deck out, trim, adorn' beside early *trws* 'ornament, dress', *trwsa* 'pack, bundle', fr. ME *trusse* 'pack, bundle' (fr. Fr. *trousse*). Cf. the specialization in Fr., NE *trousseau*, orig. 'bundle' fr. the same source. Parry-Williams 95, 161.

Br. *kinklou* (pl.), *kinkladur*, with vb. *kinkla* 'adorn', fr. some deriv. of OFr. *cliquer*, *clinquer* 'ring, clink' (fr. Du. *klinken*) like *clinquant* 'gold leaf'. Henry 67. NED s.v. *clinquant*.

Br. *bragerezou* (pl., sg. *bragerez*), fr. *bragal* 'parade, show off one's clothes', orig. 'put on breeches', fr. *bragou* 'breeches' (6.48). Henry 42.

4. ON *skraut* with vb. *skreyta* 'adorn', perh. : Sw. *skyrta* 'boast', Dan. *skryde* 'bray, boast'. Falk-Torp 1033.

ON *prȳði*, Dan. (*pryd* arch.) *prydelse*, Sw. *prydnad*, with vbs. ON *prȳða*, Dan. *pryde*, Sw. *pryda* 'adorn', fr. adj. ON *prūðr* 'valiant, magnificent in appearance' (= OE *prūd* 'proud', whence *prȳde* 'pride'), fr. OFr. *prud*, *prod* (nom. *prouz*, Fr. *preux*), 'capable, valiant', fr. late Lat. *prōde* abstracted fr. *prōd-esse* 'be of use'. Falk-Torp 851 (but wrong Lat. source). Hellquist 791. REW 6766.

OE *gearwe* (pl.), OHG *garawī*, MHG *gerwe* 'gear, equipment', hence also 'armor', 'clothing', and 'adornment' : OE *gierwan*, OHG *garawen* 'prepare', ON *gǫrva*, Dan. *gøre*, Sw. *göra* 'do'. Falk-Torp 323. NED s.v. *gear*, s.b.

Du. *versiering*, deriv. of (*ver*)*sieren* 'adorn', fr. MHG *zieren*, OHG *zierōn* id. : OHG *ziari* 'precious, beautiful', ON, OE, OS *tīr* 'honor, fame', etc. Falk-Torp 970. Franck–v. W. 608.

MHG *gesmuc*, NHG *schmuck* in this sense a back-formation fr. vb. MHG *smucken*, *smücken* orig. 'press closely, draw together' (: MHG *smiegen* id.), hence 'put on clothing, ornaments', 'adorn'. MLG *smucken* > Dan. *smykke*, Sw. *smycka* 'adorn', whence sb. Dan. *smykke*, Sw. *smycke* influenced by NHG *schmuck*. Weigand-H. 2.754. Kluge-G. 532. Falk-Torp 1085.

5. Lith. *papuošalas*, fr. *pa-puošti* 'adorn' = Lett. *puosti* 'clean, adorn' : ON *fāga* 'clean, polish', etc. Walde-P. 2.16. Mühl.-Endz. 3.458.

Lett. *ruota*, perh. orig. 'something notched', i.e. 'a trinket' : *ruotīt* 'cut on bias, notch, indent', Lith. *rentas*, *rintys* 'notch'. Mühl.-Endz. 3.583 f.

Lett. *greznums* (also 'trinket, beauty') fr. *grezns* 'beautiful' (16.81). Mühl.-Endz. 1.651.

6. ChSl.(Supr.) *ukrašenĭje* (hence Russ. form), SCr. *ukras*, Boh., Pol. *okrasa*, with vb. ChSl. (*u*)*krasiti* 'adorn' : ChSl. *krasa* 'beauty', *krasĭnŭ* 'beautiful', etc. (16.81). Berneker 607 f.

SCr. *nakit*, with vb. (*na*)*kititi* 'adorn' : *kita* 'tassel, tuft', etc. (a large Slavic group with similar meanings) etym.? Berneker 679.

SCr. *ures*, with vb. *uresiti* 'adorn' : *resa* 'fringe', ChSl. *ręsa* 'catkin, ornament', Boh. *řása*, Pol. *rzęsa* 'eyelash', Slov. *ŕesa* 'bud', orig.? Miklosich 276 f. Brückner 477.

Pol. *ozdoba*, with vb. *ozdobić* 'decorate' : ChSl. *po-doba* 'what is suitable', *dobrŭ* 'good', etc. (16.71). Berneker 203 f. Brückner 91.

7. Skt. *bhūṣaṇa-*, fr. *bhūṣ-* 'be busy with, attend upon', caus. 'adorn', extension of *bhū-* 'become, be'. Walde-P. 2.141.

Skt. *alaṁkāra-*, fr. *alaṁ-kr̥-* 'prepare', lit. 'make sufficient', cpd. of *alam* 'enough' and *kr̥-* 'do, make'.

Av. *pis-*, *paēsa-* : Skt. *piç-*, *peças* 'ornament', fr. vb. Av. *pis-* 'color, adorn', Skt. *piç-* 'adorn' : Lat. *pingere* 'paint', Grk. ποικίλος 'many-colored'. Walde-P. 2.9. Barth. 818, 907.

6.72 JEWEL

Grk.	*λίθος*	ON	*gimsteinn, gørsemi*	Lith.	*brangenybė, brangus akmuo*
NG	*κόσμημα, διαμαντικό, τζοβαΐρι*	Dan.	*juvel*	Lett.	*dārgums*
Lat.	*gemma*	Sw.	*juvel*	SCr.	*dragulj*
It.	*gioiello*	OE	*gimstān, gim*	Boh.	*klenot, drahokam*
Fr.	*bijou, joyau*	ME	*iuele, gemme*	Pol.	*klejnot*
Sp.	*joya, alhaya*	NE	*jewel, gem*	Russ.	*dragocennost'*
Rum.	*giuvaer*	Du.	*juweel, kleinood*	Skt.	*ratna-, maṇi-*
Ir.	(*sēt*)	OHG	*gimma*		
NIr.	*seod*	MHG	*gimme, kleinōt*		
W.	*gem, tlws*	NHG	*juwel, kleinod*		
Br.	*braoig*				

A 'jewel' (mostly 'precious stone', now esp. with its setting, but in part including gold and silver ornaments) may be expressed simply as '(precious) stone', but more commonly by specialization of something 'valuable, costly', 'beautiful', 'giving pleasure', an 'ornament' or a 'plaything'. In a few cases the name of a specific ornament or gem has been generalized (cf. Fr. *bijou*, NG διαμαντικό, below).

1. Grk. λίθος 'stone' (1.44), used also for 'precious stone', likewise NG πέτρα.

Grk. κόσμημα 'ornament', NG id. and also in pl. 'jewels', fr. κοσμέω 'adorn', fr. κόσμος 'adornment' (6.71).

NG διαμαντικό, fr. διαμάντι 'diamond'.

NG τζοβαΐρι, τζοβαερικό, Rum. *giuvaer*, fr. Turk. *cevahir* 'jewel' (orig. Pers.). Lokotsch 694.

2. Lat. *gemma*, also and orig. 'bud' on vines and trees, etym. dub., perh. fr. **gembh-nā-* : Lith. *žembėte* 'sprout', Skt. *jambha-*, ChSl. *zǫbŭ*, etc. 'tooth'. Hence W. *gem*, OE *gim*, ME *gemme*, NE *gem*, OHG *gimma*, MHG *gimme*, also, with 'stone', ON *gimsteinnr*, OE *gimstān*. Ernout-M. 413 f. Walde-H. 1.587 f.

Fr. *joyau* (OFr. *joel* > It. *gioiello*, ME *iuel*, NE *jewel*, Du. *juweel*, NHG *juwel* > Dan., Sw. *juvel*), deriv. (cf. MLat. pl. *iocālia*) of Lat. *iocus* 'jest, sport', Fr. *jeu* 'play'. REW 4588. Gamillscheg 543.

Fr. *bijou*, fr. Br. *bizou* 'finger-ring' (*biz* 'finger'). REW 1142. Wartburg 1.389.

Sp. *alhaya*, fr. Arab. *hāja* 'necessaries, clothing, furniture, etc.'. Lokotsch 775.

Sp. *joya*, through OFr. *joi*(*e*), fr. Lat. *gaudium* 'joy'. REW 3705.

3. NIr. *seod* fr. Ir. *sēt* 'a valuable' covering a wide range of objects (cf. Laws, Gloss. s.v.), but including 'pin, brooch', its earliest attested sense (cf. *sēt argait* 'silver brooch' Thes. 2.345) = Lat. (orig. Gall.?) *sentis* 'thornbush', MLat. 'brooch', etym.? Schrader, Reallex. 2.335. Walde-P. 1.450.

W. *tlws* : Ir. *tlus* 'cattle', but further connections? Loth, RC. 34.150.

Br. *braoig*, deriv. of *brao* 'beautiful' (16.81).

4. ON *gørsemi*, apparently fr. an adj. *gørsamr* 'precious' : *gørr* 'ready, skilled', *gørva* 'do, make', etc. Cf. OE *gearwe* 'adornment' (6.71). Falk-Torp 323.

Du. *kleinood*, MHG *kleinōt*, NHG *kleinod*, older 'a valuable' (in general), esp. (MHG) 'a gift', cpd. of *klein* in earlier meaning 'pure, elegant, fine' (OHG *kleini*, OE *clǣne*, NE *clean*) and OHG *-ōd*, in *al-ōd* 'free possession' (MLat. *allōdium*), OS *ōd* 'possession', OE *ēad*, ON *auðr* 'riches'. Hence Lith. *kleinotas* (Kurschat, but not in NSB), Boh. *klenot*, Pol. *klejnot*.

5. Lith. *brangenybė* 'a valuable' and 'jewel' (cf. NSB s.v.), deriv. of *brangus* 'dear, costly' (11.88). Also *brangus akmuo* 'costly stone'.

Lett. *dārgums*, fr. *dārgs* 'dear, costly' (11.88).

6. SCr. *dragulj*, Boh. *drahokam* (cf. *kámen* 'stone'), Russ. *dragocennost'*, fr. ChSl. *dragŭ*, etc. 'dear, costly' (11.88).

7. Skt. *ratna-* (also 'treasure, goods'), perh. fr. **r̥tno-* : Ir. *rēt* 'thing' (**rentu*). Walde-P. 2.374. Uhlenbeck 243.

Skt. *maṇi-*, esp. 'pearl', etym.? Walde-P. 2.295.

6.73 RING
(For Finger)

Grk.	*δακτύλιος*	Goth.	*figgragulþ*	Lith.	*žiedas*
NG	*δαχτυλίδι*	ON	*hringr*	Lett.	*gredzens*
Lat.	*ānulus*	Dan.	*ring*	ChSl.	*prŭstenĭ*
It.	*anello*	Sw.	*ring*	SCr.	*prsten*
Fr.	*bague*	OE	*hring*	Boh.	*prsten*
Sp.	*sortija*	ME	*ring*	Pol.	*pierścień*
Rum.	*inel*	NE	*ring*	Russ.	*kol'co*
Ir.	*āinne, ordnasc*	Du.	*ring*	Skt.	*añgulīya-*
NIr.	*fāinne*	OHG	*ring*		
W.	*modrwy*	MHG	*ring*		
Br.	*bizou*	NHG	*ring*		

Most of the words for 'ring' (for the finger) are based on either words for 'ring' in the wider sense of circular form, or those for 'finger' (4.34). A few are from words for 'berry, bud' or the like and must have applied first to a ring with setting. One was in origin a magic ring.

1. Grk. δακτύλιος, NG δαχτυλίδι, fr. δάκτυλος 'finger'.

2. Lat. *ānulus*, fr. *ānus* 'ring, anus', root connection? Here also (loanwords or cognate?) Ir. *āinne*, *ānne*, NIr. *fāinne* (*f-* by sentence phonetics). Walde-H. 1.55.

It. *anello*, Rum. *inel* (Fr. *anneau* now 'ring' in wider sense or 'wedding ring'), fr. Lat. *ānellus*, dim. of *ānulus* (above). REW 452.

Fr. *bague*, fr. Prov. *baga*, Lat. *bāca*, *bacca* 'any small round fruit, berry, a pearl' (Fr. *baie* 'berry'). REW 859. Wartburg 1.196.

Sp. *sortija* (cf. MLat. *sortelia*, Du Cange s.v.), fr. Lat. *sortīcula* 'a little lot, a small tablet or ticket' (apparently for casting lots etc.), dim. of *sors*, *sortis* 'lot'. Evidently therefore first applied to a magic ring, then generalized. REW 8108.

3. Ir. *ordnasc* 'thumb-ring', cpd. of *ordu* 'thumb' and *nasc* 'ring, band' (: *nascim* 'tie', Lat. *nōdus* 'knot', etc., Walde-P. 2.328).

W. *modrwy*, cpd. of OW *maut* (W. *bawd* with *b-* by sentence phonetics) 'thumb' and an obscured deriv. of the root in *rhwyme* 'bind' (Ir. *con-riug* 'bind together', Lat. *corrigia* 'strap', etc.). Morris Jones 136, 163.

Br. *bizou*, fr. *biz* 'finger'.

4. Goth. *figgragulþ*, lit. 'finger-gold'.

ON *hringr*, OE *hring*, OHG *ring*, etc., general Gmc. (except Goth.) : ChSl. *krągŭ* 'circle', Umbr. *cringatrō* 'shoulder band', etc. Walde-P. 2.570.

5. Lith. *žiedas*, also 'bloom, blossom', pl. 'menses'. Orig. perh. 'bud', as the semantic source for all the meanings, and therefore first applied to a ring with a setting (cf. Lat. *gemma* 'bud, gem', Fr. *bague* fr. Prov. *baga* 'berry') : Lith. *žydėti* 'bloom', *žysti* 'open (of flowers)'. Walde-P. 1.544.

Lett. *gredzens*, perh. : ON *krākr*, *krōkr* 'hook, bend', *kraki* 'pole with hook on end, anchor'. Walde-P. 1.593 ff. Mühl-Endz. 1.646.

6. ChSl. *prŭstenĭ*, SCr. *prsten*, Boh. *prsten*, Pol. *pierścień* (Russ. *persteń* now replaced by *kol'co*), fr. ChSl. *prŭstŭ*, etc. 'finger'.

Russ. *kol'co*, dim. of *kolo* 'circle, wheel' (obs. or dial.) = ChSl. *kolo* 'wheel' (10.76). Berneker 548.

7. Skt. *añgulīya-*, *añgulīyaka-*, fr. *añguli-* 'finger, toe'.

6.74 BRACELET

Grk.	ψέλιον, ἕλιξ	ON	*baugr*	Lith.	*apyrankė*
NG	βραχιόλι	Dan.	*armbaand*	Lett.	*apruoce*
Lat.	*brachiāle, armillae*	Sw.	*armband*	SCr.	*narukvica, grivna*
It.	*braccialetto*	OE	*bēag*	Boh.	*náramek*
Fr.	*bracelet*	ME	*beg*	Pol.	*naramiennik, bransoletka*
Sp.	*brazalete, pulsera*	NE	*bracelet*	Russ.	*braslet'*
Rum.	*brăţară*	Du.	*armband*	Skt.	*kañkaṇa-, karabhūṣaṇa-*
Ir.	*foil, fail*	OHG	*boug*		
NIr.	*brāislēad*	MHG	*bouc*		
W.	*breichled*	NHG	*armband*		
Br.	*trovrec'h*				

Words for 'bracelet' are mostly derived from those for 'arm' (4.31), a few from verbs for 'turn, wind around', or 'bend'.

1. Grk. ψέλιον orig.? Boisacq 1075.

Grk. ἕλιξ used for various objects of spiral shape, prob. 'armlet' in Hom. Il. 18.401, fr. the root of ἑλίσσω, Lat. *volvere*, etc. 'turn around' (10.13).

Late Grk., Byz. βραχιόνιον, fr. βραχίων 'arm'. Hence also (but through Lat. *brachiāle*) late Grk. βραχιάλιον and βραχιόλιον, the latter Byz. and NG (βραχιόλι).

2. Lat. *brachiāle*, fr. *brachium* 'forearm' (fr. Grk. βραχίων). Hence Rum. *brăţară* and the dims. It. *braccialetto*, Fr. *bracelet* (> NE *bracelet*, Russ. *braslet'*; also Pol. *bransoletka*, Brückner 38), Sp. *brazalete*. Ernout-M. 116. REW 1254.

Lat. *armillae* (pl.; sg. late), fr. *armus* 'upper arm, shoulder'. Ernout-M. 74.

Sp. *pulsera*, fr. *pulse* 'pulse' and 'wrist' (where pulse is felt), Lat. *pulsus* 'blow, push'.

3. Ir. *foil, fail* : Grk. ἕλιξ (above, 1). Windisch, IF 3.76.

NIr. *brāislēad*, fr. NE *bracelet*, whence also W. *breichled* but prob. influenced by *breichiau* pl. of *braich* 'arm'.

Br. *trovrec'h*, cpd. of *tro* 'turn' and *brec'h* 'arm'.

4. ON *baugr*, OE *bēag* (also 'ring, collar'), ME *beg*, OHG *boug*, MHG *bouc* : OE *būgan*, Goth. *biugan* 'bend' (9.14).

NHG, Du. *armband* (Dan. *armbaand*, Sw. *armband*, by semantic borrowing), lit. 'arm-band'.

5. Lith. *apyrankė*, Lett. *apruoce* (also

'cuff, ruffle at wrist') fr. *api-*, *ap-* 'about' and *ranka*, *ruoka* 'hand, arm'.

6. SCr., Bulg. *grivna* = ChSl. *grivĭna* 'necklace' (6.75).

SCr. *narukvica*, Boh. *náramek*, Pol. *naramiennik*, all dim. cpds. of *na-* 'on' and the words for 'arm', SCr. *ruka*, Boh. *rámě*, Pol. *ramię*.

7. Skt. *kañkaṇa-*, perh. orig. as 'the clinking ornament' (cf. *kānkanī-* 'adornment with little bells') fr. IE **kan-*, in Lat. *canere* 'sing', etc. Walde-P. 1.351. Uhlenbeck 38.

Skt. *karabhūṣaṇa-*, lit. 'hand-adornment', cpd. of *kara-* 'hand' and *bhūṣaṇa-* 'adornment' (6.71).

6.75 NECKLACE

Grk.	ὅρμος, στρεπτός, περιδέραιον	ON	*men, hālsgjọrð*	Lith.	*kaklaryšis, karieliai*
NG	περιδέραιο	Dan.	*halsbaand*	Lett.	*kakla ruota*
Lat.	*monīle, torquēs*	Sw.	*halsband*	ChSl.	*monisto, grivĭna, ožrělĭ*
It.	*collana*	OE	*mene, healsbēag, sig(e)le*	SCr.	*đerdan*
Fr.	*collier*	ME	*coler*	Boh.	*náhrdelník*
Sp.	*collar*	NE	*necklace*	Pol.	*naszynik*
Rum.	*colier, ghiordan*	Du.	*halssnoer*	Russ.	*ožerel'e* (*monisto*)
Ir.	*muince, muintorc, basc*	OHG	*menni, halsboug, halsgolt*	Skt.	*kaṇṭhikā-, kaṇṭhabhūṣā-*
NIr.	*muince*	MHG	*halsbouc, halsgolt*	Av.	*minu-*
W.	*gwddfdorch, gleindorch*	NHG	*halsband*		
Br.	*tro-c'houzoug*				

Most of the words for 'necklace' are derivs. or cpds. of those for 'neck' or 'throat' (4.28, 4.29) and so often parallel to those for 'collar' or 'necktie'. A few are from verbs for 'string together', 'turn around'.

1. Grk. ὅρμος, fr. the root of εἴρω 'string together', Lat. *serere* 'bind together, entwine', etc. Cf. ON *sørvi* 'necklace of stones, pearls, or the like'. Walde-P. 2.499 f.

Grk. στρεπτός and στρεπτόν, sb. use of vbl. adj. of στρέφω 'turn, roll, twist'. Walde-P. 2.632.

Grk. περιδέραιον, περιδερίς, deriv. of περί 'about' and δέρη 'neck'.

2. Lat. *monīle* : Ir. *muince*, OW *mince*, ON *men* (also *hāls-men*), OE *mene*, *myne* (also *heals-mene*), OHG *menni*, Av. *minu-*, ChSl. *monisto* (cf. Berneker 2.76), Gallo-Grk. μανιάκης, μαννιάκιον, μάννος 'Celtic necklace' : Ir. *muin*, OW *mwn*, Skt. *manya-* 'neck', ON *mọn*, OE *manu*, OHG *mana* 'mane'. Walde-P. 2.305. Ernout-M. 628.

Lat. *torquēs* : *torquēre* 'turn around, twist' (10.13). Hence Ir. *torc*, W. *torch* in Ir. *muin-torc*, W. *gwddf-dorch*, *gleindorch* (W. *gwddf* 'neck', *gleiniau* 'gems, beads'). Ernout-M. 1047. Vendryes, De hib. voc. 183.

It. *collana*, fr. *collo* (Lat. *collum*) 'neck'.

Fr. *collier* (> Rum. *colier*), Sp. *collar*, fr. Lat. *collāre* 'band or chain for the neck' (for captives, animals, etc.), fr. *collum* 'neck'. ME *coler* (also 'collar'), fr. OFr. *coller*, *collier*.

Rum. *ghiordan*, SCr. *đerdan*, fr. Turk. *gerdan* 'neck, necklace', fr. Pers. *gardan* 'neck'. Lokotsch 675. Tiktin 675.

3. Ir. *muince*, *muintorc*, above, 2.

Ir. *basc*, perh. : W. *baich* 'burden, load', Lat. *fascis* 'bundle', etc. Pedersen 1.77. Walde-H. 1.459.

W. *gwddfdorch*, *gleindorch*, see above, 2.

Br. *tro-c'houzoug* (Vallée), cpd. of *tro* 'twisted' and *gouzoug* 'neck'.

4. ON *men*, OE *mene*, OHG *menni*, above, 2.

ON *hālsgjọrð*, lit. 'neck-girdle' (cf. 6.57).

OE *sig(e)le* 'necklace' beside *sig(e)l* 'brooch', fr. Lat. *sigillum* 'little image, seal'. Generalized first through 'signet-ring' to other pieces of jewelry? Falk-Torp 953 f. NED s.v. *seal*, sb.[2].

OE *healsbēag*, OHG *halsboug*, *halspouc*, MHG *halsbouc*, lit. 'neck-ring', cf. ON *baugr* 'bracelet' (6.74).

NE *necklace*, cpd. of *lace* (6.26), but here used in older sense 'noose, cord'. NED s.v.

Du. *halssnoer*, lit. 'neck-cord', cpd. of *snoer* = NHG *schnur* 'cord'.

OHG, MHG *halsgolt*, lit. 'neck-gold'. (Cf. Goth. *figgragulþ* 'finger-ring', 6.73).

NHG *halsband* (Dan. *halsbaand*, Sw. *halsband* by semantic borrowing), lit. 'neckband'.

5. Lith. *kaklaryšis* (also 'necktie'), fr. *kaklas* 'neck'.

Lith. *karieliai*, pl. of *karielis* 'bead' (orig. 'coral'), used for '(bead) necklace' (NSB, Lalis).

Lett. *kakla* (gen. sg. of *kakls* 'neck') with *ruota* 'adornment' (6.71), or *bante* 'band' (fr. NHG).

6. ChSl., Russ. *monisto* (Russ. arch. or local) : Lat. *monīle* (above, 2).

ChSl. *grivĭna*, fr. *griva* 'mane' : Skt. *grīvā-* 'neck', etc. Berneker 352.

ChSl. (late) *ogrŭlĭ*, *ožrělĭ*, Russ. *ožerel'e* : ChSl. *grŭlo*, Russ. *gorlo*, etc. 'throat' Miklosich 63.

Boh. *náhrdelník*, Pol. *naszynik*, dim. cpds. of *na-* 'on' and the words for 'throat, neck', Boh. *hrdlo*, Pol. *szyja*.

7. Skt. *kaṇṭhikā-* (rare), fr. *kaṇṭha-* 'neck'. Also *kaṇṭha-bhūṣā-* cpd. with *bhūṣ-* in caus. 'adorn' (cf. *bhūṣaṇa-*, 6.71).

6.81 HANDKERCHIEF

NG	μαντίλι	Dan.	*lemmetørklæde*	Lith.	*nosinė*
It.	*fazzoletto, pezzuola*	Sw.	*näsduk*	Lett.	*slaucis*
Fr.	*mouchoir*	NE	*handkerchief*	SCr.	*maramica*
Sp.	*pañuelo*	Du.	*zakdoek*	Boh.	*kapesník*
Rum.	*batistă, basma*	NHG	*taschentuch, schnupftuch*	Pol.	*chustka*
NIr.	*ciarsūr*			Russ.	*platok*
W.	*cadach (poced), hances*				
Br.	*mouchouer, mouched*				

Words for 'handkerchief' are listed only for the modern languages. For such words as Grk. χειρόμακτρον, Lat. *mantēle*, etc., which might have served also as handkerchiefs, see 'towel' (6.82).

But Lat. *sūdārium*, lit. 'sweat-cloth' (: *sūdor* 'sweat'), used esp. for wiping the face, was in fact much like a 'handkerchief'. Cf. Daremberg et Saglio s.v. *orarium*. Hence Grk. σουδάριον (NT, etc.) rendered lit. as 'sweat-cloth' in OE *swāt-lin*, OHG *sueiz-lahhan*, *-tuoh*, but Goth. dat. sg. *auralja* (: OE *orel* 'garment, veil', etc. fr. Lat. *ōrārium* 'a kind of handkerchief', deriv. of *ōs*, *ōris* 'mouth'; Feist 68), ChSl. *ubrusŭ* (: SCr. *brusiti* 'whet', *ubrisati* 'wipe off', etc.; Berneker 89 f.). The rendering *napkin* in Tyndale and King James version represents a now unfamiliar use of this word (see below).

1. NG μαντήλι, μαντίλι (Byz. μαντήλιον, -ίλιον mostly 'towel') fr. Lat. *mantēle*, *mantīle* 'towel' (6.82).

2. It. *fazzoletto*, fr. late Lat. *faciāle* 'face-cloth, towel' (gl. to προσόψιον, etc., cf. NG προσόψι, 6.82), deriv. of *faciēs* 'face'. REW 3128a.

It. *pezzuola*, dim. of *pezza* 'piece of cloth'.

Fr. *mouchoir*, fr. *moucher* 'blow the nose', MLat. *mūccāre*, fr. Lat. *mūcus* 'snot'. REW 5706.

Sp. *pañuelo*, dim. of *paño* 'cloth' (6.21).

Rum. *batistă*, also 'cambric (cloth)', fr. Fr. *batiste* 'cambric' (named for a certain Bâtiste de Cambrai, who developed a famous linen factory in the 13th cent.).

Rum. *basma* (also 'kerchief'), fr. Turk. *basma* 'printed cloth'. Lokotsch 264.

3. NIr. *ciarsūr* (also 'kerchief'), borrowed fr. NE *kerchief* in some dial. pronunciation.

W. *cadach (poced)*, lit. 'pocket-cloth', cf. *cadach* 'cloth, rag, kerchief' (= NIr. *cadach* 'calico', prob. : W. *cadas*, NIr. *cadās*, fr. ME *cadas* (NE *caddis*), with suffix after NIr. *canach* 'cotton' (?). See under 'cotton' (6.24).

W. *hances*, fr. a vulgar form of NE *handkerchief* (cf. *hanky*).

Br. *mouchouer*, *mouched*, borrowed (and the latter adapted) fr. Fr. *mouchoir*.

4. Dan. *lemmetørklæde*, cpd. of *lomme* 'pocket' and *tørklæde* 'kerchief, neckcloth' (cpd. of *tør* 'dry' and *klæde* 'cloth').

Sw. *näsduk*, lit. 'nose-cloth'.

NE *napkin* (6.83), formerly used also, and still Sc., for 'handkerchief,' NED s.v. 2.

NE *handkerchief*, cpd. of *kerchief*, ME *curchef*, fr. OFr. *couvre-chief*, lit. 'cover-head', a cloth for covering the head, a sort of woman's headgear. NED s.v.

Du. *zakdoek*, NHG *taschentuch*, lit. 'pocket-cloth'.

NHG *schnupftuch*, fr. *schnupfen* 'snuff', MHG *snupfen* 'puff, blow, snort'.

5. Lith. *nosinė*, fem. of adj. *nosinis* 'of the nose'.

Lett. *slaucis* : *slaucīt* 'wipe off'.

6. SCr. *maramica*, dim. of *marama*, *mahrama* 'rag, cloth', orig. 'veil (of a married woman)', through Turk. fr. Arab. *maḥrama* 'holy, forbidden, wife' : Arab. *ḥarām* 'forbidden'. Lokotsch 1361.

Boh. *kapesník*, fr. *kapsa* 'pocket'.

Pol. *chustka*, dim. of *chusta* '(linen) cloth' (6.21).

Russ. *platok* : ChSl. *platŭ* 'cloth, rag', etc. (6.21).

6.82 TOWEL

Grk.	χειρόμακτρον	ON	*handklæði, þurka*	Lith.	*rankšluostis (abrūsas)*
NG	προσόψι, πετσέτα	Dan.	*haandklæde*	Lett.	*dvielis*
Lat.	*mantēle*	Sw.	*handduk*	ChSl.	*ręčĭnikŭ*
It.	*asciugamano*	OE	*handclāþ*	SCr.	*ručnik, peškir*
Fr.	*essuie-main*	ME	*towaille*	Boh.	*ručník*
Sp.	*toalla*	NE	*towel*	Pol.	*ręcznik*
Rum.	*prosop, peşchir*	Du.	*handdoek*	Russ.	*polotence*
NIr.	*tuāille*	OHG	*dwahilla*	Skt.	*gātramārjanī-*
W.	*lliain, tywel*	MHG	*dwehel*		
Br.	*lien*	NHG	*handtuch*		

1. Grk. χειρόμακτρον, cpd. of χείρ 'hand' and μάκτρον, also 'towel' (but quotable only late) : μάσσω 'knead' (5.54).

NG προσόψι (> Rum. prosop), lit. 'for the face', fr. ὄψις 'face'.

NG πετσέτα (pop. for 'towel' or 'napkin', latter in urban use), fr. It. pezzetta 'piece of cloth', dim. of pezza 'piece'.

2. Lat. mantēle ('towel, napkin', late 'tablecloth'), fr. *man-terg-sli-, cpd. of manus 'hand' and deriv. of tergēre 'wipe off'. Ernout-M. 589. Walde-H. 2.32.

It. asciugamano, Fr. essuie-main, cpds. of It. asciugare, Fr. essuyer 'wipe' (Lat. exsūcāre 'deprive of juice') and It. mano, Fr. main 'hand'.

Sp. toalla, fr. Gmc. (see below, 4, OHG dwahilla, etc.).

Rum. peşchir, SCr. peškir, fr. Turk. peşkir 'towel' (orig. Pers.). Lokotsch 1660.

3. W. lliain, Br. lien, lit. 'linen' (6.23).

4. ON handklæði, Dan. haandklæde, OE handclāþ, Sw. handduk, Du. handdoek, NHG handtuch, all lit. 'hand-cloth'.

ON þurka : þurka 'wipe off', þurr, Goth. þaursus 'dry'.

OHG dwahilla, twehilla, MHG dwehel, twehel, zwehel, etc., fr. OHG dwahan, Goth. þwahan, etc. 'wash' (9.36). Hence MLat. toacula, (It. tovaglia 'tablecloth'), OFr. toaille (> ME towaille > NIr. tuáille, NE towel > W. tywel), Sp. toalla (fr. Prov. toalha). Lett. dvielis fr. MLG dwele (Mühl.-Endz. 1.538). REW 8720.

5. Lith. rankšluostis, cpd. of ranka 'hand', and deriv. of šluostyti 'wipe off'.

Lith. abrūsas (now replaced by preceding, NSB s.v.), fr. WhRuss. obrus (ChSl. obrusŭ 'sudarium', 6.83). Brückner, Sl. Fremdwörter 66.

Lett. dvielis, above 4.

6. ChSl. rǫčĭnikŭ, SCr. ručnik, Boh. ručník, Pol. ręcznik, fr. the words for 'hand', ChSl. rǫka, etc.

SCr. peškir, see Rum. peşchir (above, 2).

Russ. polotence, fr. polotno 'linen' (6.23).

7. Skt. gātramārjanī- (rare), lit. 'limb-rubber', cpd. of gātra- 'limb' and deriv. of mṛj- 'rub, wash'.

6.83 NAPKIN

Grk.	χειρόμακτρον	Dan.	serviet	Lith.	serveta
NG	πετσέτα	Sw.	servet	Lett.	serveta
Lat.	mappa, mantēle	ME	napkin	SCr.	ubrus, ubrusac
It.	tovagliuolo, salvietta	NE	napkin	Boh.	ubrousek
Fr.	serviette	Du.	servet	Pol.	serweta
Sp.	servilleta	NHG	serviette	Russ.	salfetka
Rum.	şervet				
NIr.	naipcín				
W.	napcyn				
Br.	servietenn				

Words listed under 'towel' (6.82) would in earlier periods cover the 'napkin' wherever such an article was in use, and so definitely Grk. χειρόμακτρον and Lat. mantēle. Cf. Daremberg et Saglio s.v. mantēle and mappa.

The majority of the mod. Eur. words

---

are borrowed from the Fr. serviette, orig. 'service-cloth'.

1. For Grk. χειρόμακτρον, Lat. mantēle, and NG πετσέτα see 6.82.

2. Lat. mappa, according to Quintilian a Punic word. Ernout-M. 592. Walde-H. 2.36.

It. tovagliuolo, dim. of tovaglia 'tablecloth', fr. Prov. toalha 'towel' (6.82).

Fr. serviette, fr. servir 'serve' in its special sense of 'serve the table', hence 'service-cloth', prob. first applied to the cloth under the dish served. Cf. NHG tellertuch lit. 'plate-cloth', used for 'napkin' (Grimm s.v., now obs.?). Hence It. salvietta (> NHG dial. salvet, Russ. salfetka), Rum. şervet, Br. servietenn, Dan. serviet, Sw., Du. servet, NHG servet, Lith. serveta, Lett. serveta.

---

serviette (> Lett. servjete, Pol. serweta > Lith. serveta). REW 7874. Gamillscheg 799. Weigand-H. 2.854.

Sp. servilleta, either a direct or a semantic borrowing fr. Fr. serviette.

3. ME, NE napkin (> NIr. naipcín, W. napcyn), dim. of OFr. nappe (Fr. nappe 'tablecloth'), by dissim. fr. Lat. mappa (above, 2). NED s.v.

4. SCr. ubrus, ubrusac, Boh. ubrousek : ChSl. obrusŭ 'sudarium' (see 6.81).

6.91 COMB

Grk.	κτείς	ON	kambr	Lith.	šukos
NG	χτένι	Dan.	kam	Lett.	kemme
Lat.	pecten	Sw.	kam	ChSl.	grebenĭ, česlŭ, česalo
It.	pettine	OE	camb	SCr.	češalj
Fr.	peigne	ME	comb	Boh.	hřeben
Sp.	peine	NE	comb	Pol.	grzebień
Rum.	pieptene	Du.	kam	Russ.	greben', grebenka
Ir.	cír	OHG	kamb	Skt.	prasādhanī-, kaṅkata-
NIr.	cíor	MHG	kamp		
W.	crib	NHG	kamm		
Br.	krib				

1. Grk. κτείς (fr. *πκτευς), Lat. pecten, fr. the root of Grk. πέκω 'shear'. Lat. pectere 'comb', etc. Hence NG χτένι (fr. late κτένιον), It. pettine, Fr. peigne (12th cent. pigne; modern form influenced by peigner), Sp. peine, Rum. pieptene (older piepten). Walde-P. 2.10. Ernout-M. 745. REW 6328.

2. Ir. cír, NIr. cíor (*kēs-rā-), ChSl. česlŭ, česalo, SCr. češalj (with l-formation, cf. Berneker 152) : ChSl. česati 'comb', Lith. kasyti 'scratch, shave', Grk. ξέω 'shave', ξυρόν 'razor' (6.93), etc. Walde-P. 1.449 f.

W. crib, Br. krib = Ir. crích 'border, boundary', orig. 'edge' : Grk. κρίνω 'judge, decide', Lat. cernere 'separate, distinguish', Grk. κείρω, OE sceran 'cut, shear', etc. Walde-P. 2.574. Pedersen 2.33.

3. ON kambr, OE camb, etc., general Gmc. : Skt. jambha-, ChSl. zǫbŭ, Lett.

---

zuobs 'tooth', Grk. γόμφος 'bolt, spike', etc. Walde-P. 1.575. Falk-Torp 488 f.

4. Lith. šukos (pl.), fr. šukė 'notch' beside Lett. suka 'brush', perh. : Skt. çūka- 'beard of grain, sting', Av. sūkā- 'needle', and even SCr. četka 'brush', etc. (6.92), but all dub. Walde-P. 1.470 (quite otherwise). Trautmann 309 f. Mühl.-Endz. 3.1116 f.

Lett. kemme, fr. MLG kam with e fr. plural supported by the verb kemmēt 'comb' fr. MLG. kämmen. Mühl.-Endz. 2.363.

5. ChSl. grebenĭ, Boh. hřeben, Pol. grzebień, Russ. greben', dim. grebenka (SCr. greben 'crest, ridge') : ChSl. grebǫ, greti 'scratch, dig, scrape', etc., Goth., OHG graban 'dig'. Walde-P. 1.653 f. Berneker 347.

6. Skt. prasādhanī-, fr. pra-sādh- 'set in order, arrange, subject' (sādh- 'attain, succeed').

Skt. kaṅkata-, etym.? Uhlenbeck 38.

6.92 BRUSH

Grk.	(κόρημα)	ON	bursti	Lith.	šepetys
NG	βούρτσα	Dan.	børste	Lett.	suka, suseklis
Lat.	pēniculus	Sw.	borste	SCr.	četka, kefa
It.	spazzola	ME	brusshe	Boh.	kartáč
Fr.	brosse	NE	brush	Pol.	szczotka
Sp.	cepillo, bruza	Du.	borstel	Russ.	ščetka
Rum.	perie	MHG	bürste	Skt.	ágharṣaṇi-
NIr.	bruis	NHG	bürste		
W.	brws				
Br.	barr-skuber, palouer				

Most of the words for 'brush' are based on words denoting some material which was used for the utensil, such as 'brushwood, bristles, tails of animals, feathers'. A few are from verbs for 'sweep' or 'rub'.

1. Grk. κόρημα 'broom', see 9.38.

NG βούρτσα, through βρούτσα fr. some Romance form of the group Fr. brosse, etc. (below, 2). G. Meyer, Neugr. Stud. 4.20.

2. Lat. pēniculus, dim. of pēnis 'penis' (4.492) and 'tail', here in latter sense, reflecting the use of animals' tail for a brush.

It. spazzola, fr. spazzare 'sweep' (9.37).

Fr. brosse (OFr. > ME brusshe, NE brush > NIr. bruis, W. brws), Sp. bruza, same word as OFr. brosse, broce, MLat. bruscia, brossa, etc. (cf. Du Cange) 'brush' = 'brushwood', with secondary application to the utensil made therefrom—orig. dub.; borrowing fr. a word of the Gmc. group (ON bursti, etc., below, 4) now generally rejected. REW 1340a (but Sp. bruza fr. Goth., 1417). Wartburg 1.572 ff.

Sp. cepillo (also 'carpenter's plane', dim. of cepo 'bough of a tree', etc., fr. Lat. cippus 'post, stake, pillar'. REW 1935.

Rum. perie, fr. ChSl. perĭje 'feathers'. Tiktin 1146.

---

3. NIr. bruis, W. brws, fr. NE brush (above, 2).

NIr. scúab, see under 'broom' (9.38).

Br. barr-skuber, fr. barr 'branch' and skuba 'sweep' (9.37).

Br. palouer, orig. dub., perh. by dissim. fr. a deriv. of OFr. parer 'adorn'. Henry 216.

4. ON bursti, Dan. børste, Sw. borste, Du. borstel dim., MHG, NHG bürste : ON burst, OE byrst, borst 'bristle', Skt. bhṛṣṭi- 'point, edge', etc. Walde-P. 2.131 f. Falk-Torp 129.

5. Lith. šepetys (usually of bristles tied together at one end), etym.? (suffix in -eti-s, Leskien, Bildung d. Nom. 571, but root connection?).

Lett. suka, doubtless orig. 'comb' : Lith. šukos 'comb' (6.91). Hence perh. as a dim. Lett. suseklis by assim. fr. *suceklis (Mühl.-Endz. 3.1125.

6. SCr. četka : Russ. ščet, Pol. szczotka, Russ. ščetka : Russ. ščet', Polab. sacét 'bristle', Pol. szczeć 'bristle, teasel', etc. Outside connections dub. See refs. under Lith. šukos 'comb' (6.91).

SCr. kefa, fr. Hung. kefe id. (this fr. Turk.). Berneker 499.

Boh. kartáč, fr. NHG kardätsche 'currycomb, wool-comb with steel bristles', fr. Fr. cardasse 'carding-comb' (through It. fr. Lat. carduus 'thistle'). Berneker 489 f.

7. Skt. ágharṣaṇi- (rare), fr. ghṛṣ-'rub, polish, brush' (9.31).

6.93 RAZOR

Grk.	ξυρόν	Dan.	barberkniv	Lith.	skutiklis, britva
NG	ξυράφι	Sw.	rakkniv	Lett.	bārdas nazis
Lat.	novācula	OE	scearseax	ChSl.	britva, brič
It.	rasoio	ME	rasor, rasour	SCr.	britva
Fr.	rasoir	NE	razor	Boh.	břitva
Sp.	navaja	Du.	scheermes	Pol.	brzytwa
Rum.	briciu	OHG	scarasahs	Russ.	britva
Ir.	altan	MHG	scharsahs, schermezzer	Skt.	kṣura-
NIr.	rāsūr	NHG	rasiermesser, schermesser		
W.	ellyn				
Br.	aotenn				

Words for 'razor' are derived from verbs for 'cut, shear, shave' or 'scrape', or from words for 'knife', or both together.

1. Grk. ξυρόν, NG ξυράφι, Skt. kṣura-, fr. *ksu- in Grk. ξύω 'scrape, scratch', etc., an extension of *kes- in ChSl. česati 'comb, scrape', sb. česlŭ 'comb', etc. (6.91). Here also prob. Lat. novācula (> Sp. navaja), apparently formed fr. a lost vb. *novāre based on a parallel extension with nasal infix, namely *ks-n-eu- seen in Skt. kṣṇu- 'whet'. Walde-P. 1.450. Ernout-M. 679.

2. It. rasoio, Fr. rasoir (OFr. > ME rasor, rasour > NIr. rāsūr, NE razor), fr. MLat. rāsōrium : Lat. rādere 'shave, scrape'. REW 7076.

Rum. briciu, fr. Slavic, cf. ChSl. brič (below, 6).

3. Ir. altan, W. ellyn, Br. aotenn, prob. as orig. 'jointed (knife)' : Ir. alt 'joint', Goth. falþan 'fold', etc. Pedersen 1.137. Otherwise (: OHG spaltan 'split', etc.) Walde-P. 2.678, Stokes 21.

---

4. OE scearseax, OHG scarasahs, MHG scharsahs, also Du. scheermes, MHG schermezzer, NHG schermesser, all cpds. of vbs. for 'cut' (OE sceran, etc., 9.22) and words for 'knife' (OE seax, OHG sahs, MHG mezzer, etc., 9.23).

NHG rasiermesser, cpd. of rasieren (fr. Fr. raser) 'shave' and messer 'knife'.

Dan. barberkniv, lit. 'barber-knife'.

Sw. rakkniv, lit. 'shave-knife' (raka 'rake, shave').

5. Lith. skutiklis, fr. skusti 'shave, scrape' (perh. fr. IE *ksu-, above, 1, with initial metathesis, or fr. extension of *sek- in Lat. secāre 'cut', etc. Walde-P. 1.450.

Lith. britva, fr. Russ. (below, 6).

Lett. bārdas nazis, lit. 'beard-knife'.

6. ChSl., SCr., Russ. britva, Boh. břitva, Pol. brzytwa, also late ChSl. brič : Russ.-ChSl. briti, Russ. brit', Boh. bříti, etc. 'shave', fr. *bhrei-, extension of *bher- in Lat. ferīre, OHG berjan, etc. 'strike' (9.21). Walde-P. 2.194. Berneker 94.

6.94 OINTMENT

Grk.	ἄλειμμα, ἀλοιφή	Goth.	salbōns	Lith.	tepalas, mostis
NG	ἀλοιφή	ON	smyrsl	Lett.	smēre
Lat.	unguentum, unguen	Dan.	salve	ChSl.	mastĭ
It.	unguento	Sw.	salva	SCr.	mast, pomast
Fr.	onguent	OE	sealf, smyrels	Boh.	mast
Sp.	unguento	ME	oignement, salve	Pol.	mast́
Rum.	unsoare, alifie	NE	ointment (salve)	Russ.	maz'
Ir.	ongain	Du.	zalf	Skt.	añjana-, añjas-, lipti-
NIr.	ungadh	OHG	salba		
W.	ennaint, eli	MHG	salbe		
Br.	traet	NHG	salbe		

1. Grk. ἄλειμμα, ἀλοιφή (> Rum. alifie), fr. ἀλείφω 'anoint', as Skt. lipti- fr. lip- 'anoint' : Grk. λίπος 'fat', Lith. lipti 'stick', etc. Walde-P. 2.403.

Grk. χρῖμα, χρῖσμα, fr. χρίω 'anoint', outside connections dub. Walde-P. 1.646.

2. Lat. unguentum, unguen, Skt. añjana-, añjas- (cf. OHG ancho, Ir. imb, etc. 'butter', 5.89) : Lat. unguere 'anoint', Skt. añj- 'rub, anoint'. Walde-P. 1.181. Ernout-M. 1126.

Hence, fr. Lat. unguentum, or new derivs. of unguere, It., Sp. unguento, Fr. onguent, Rum. unsoare (fr. perf. stem of unge), Ir. ongain, NIr. ungadh (Ir. ongad 'an anointing', fr. ongim, Lat. unguere), W. ennaint (fr. OFr. enoint, past pple. of enoindre, Lat. in-unguere; cf. Pedersen 1.224), ME oignement (OFr. oignemont, MLat. *unguimentum), NE ointment (with -t- from anoint).

3. W. eli : OBr. eli 'redolent', fr. Lat. olēre 'smell'(?). Pedersen 1.197. Loth, Mots lat. 163.

Br. traet, abstracted fr. the borrowed

Fr. traiter in the sense 'médicamenter'. Henry 270.

4. Goth. salbōns, OE sealf, ME salve, OHG salba, MHG, NHG salbe, Du. zalf, MLG salve (> Dan. salve, Sw. salva) : Skt. sarpis- 'clarified butter', sṛpra- 'fatty, smooth', Toch. A ṣalyp 'fat, oil'. Walde-P. 2.508. Feist 407 f. NED s.v. salve, sb.¹.

ON smyrsl, OE smyrels (Dan. smørelse 'grease', Sw. smörjelse 'unction') : ON smyrva, smyrja, OE smierwan 'anoint', ON smør 'butter, fat', Ir. smiur, W. mer 'marrow', etc. Walde-P. 2.690 f. Falk-Torp 1086 f.

5. Lith. tepalas, fr. tepti 'smear, grease, oil', Lett. tept id. Trautmann 319. Lith. mostis, fr. WhRuss. mast' = ChSl. mastĭ (below, 6).

Lett. smēre, fr. MLG smer 'grease' : ON smør 'butter' (cf. ON smyrsl, above).

6. ChSl. mastĭ, SCr. mast, pomast, Boh. mast, Pol. mast́, Russ. maz' : ChSl. mazati 'ἀλείφειν', Grk. μαγῆναι 'knead', etc. Walde-P. 2.226 f. Berneker 2.23 f.

7. Skt. lipti- and añjas-, above, 1, 2.

6.95 SOAP

NG	σαπούνι	ON	þvál, lauðr	Lith.	muilas
Lat.	sāpō (late)	Dan.	sæbe	Lett.	ziepes
It.	sapone	Sw.	sāpa, tvāl	SCr.	sapun
Fr.	savon	OE	sāpe, lēapor	Boh.	mýdlo
Sp.	jabon	ME	sope	Pol.	mydło
Rum.	săpun	NE	soap	Russ.	mylo
NIr.	galluanach	Du.	zeep		
W.	sebon	OHG	seipfa, seifa		
Br.	soavon	MHG	seife		
		NHG	seife		

Soap was unknown to the Greeks and Romans of the classical period, its place being taken by ointment or special kinds of earth as agents, for any of which in Greek might be used ῥύμμα fr. ῥύπτω 'cleanse, wash' or σμῆμα, σμῆγμα fr. σμάω 'wipe, wash'. Cf. Pauly-Wissowa s.v. Seife.

Pliny mentions sāpō as a Gallic invention for coloring the hair red, used also by the Germans (HN 28.191, prodest et sapo; Gallorum hoc inventum rutilandis capillis; fit ex sebo et cinere . . . . duobus modis, spissus et liquidus, uterque apud Germanos maiore in usu viris quam feminis), but the word is of Germanic origin; whence it was widely borrowed. The few other words for 'soap' are mostly derived from verbs for 'wash'.

1. OE sāpe (> Icel. sāpa, Norw. saapa, Sw. såpa), OHG seipfa, seifa, MHG, NHG seife, Du. zeep, MLG sēpe (> Dan. sæbe, Lett. ziepes), fr. Gmc. *saip(i)ōn (cf. Finn. loanword saippio), prob. : OE sīpian 'drip', with reference

to the process of manufacture (or through an intermediate 'resin', the cognate OE sāp). Walde-P. 2.468. Falk-Torp 1229 f. Hence late Lat. sāpō, -ōnis, It. sapone (> NG σαπούνι > Turk. sabun > SCr. sapun), Fr. savon (> Br. soavon), Sp. jabon, Rum. săpun, W. sebon (learned borrowing).

2. NIr. galluanach, gallūnach, apparently fr. gall 'stone' and uanach 'foaming, frothing'.

3. ON þvál, Sw. tvāl = OE þwēal, OHG dwahal, Goth. þwahl 'washing, purification' : Goth. þwahan, OE þwēan, ON þvā, etc. 'wash' (9.36). Hellquist 1253.

ON lauðr, OE lēapor 'washing-soda', fr. *lou-tro- : Ir. luaith, W. lludw, Br. ludu 'ashes' and Lat. lavāre, Grk. λούω 'wash'. Walde-P. 2.441. Falk-Torp 568. NED s.v. lather, sb.

4. Boh. mýdlo, Pol. mydło, Russ. mylo (> Lith. muilas) : ChSl. myti 'wash' (9.36).

6.96 MIRROR

Grk.	κάτοπτρον, κάτροπτον	Goth.	skuggwa	Lith.	veidrodis (zerkolas)
NG	καθρέφτης	ON	skuggsjā, spegill	Lett.	spuogulis, spiegelis
Lat.	speculum	Dan.	spejl	ChSl.	zrĭcalo, *oględalo
It.	specchio	Sw.	spegel	SCr.	ogledalo (zrcalo)
Fr.	miroir	OE	glæs	Boh.	zrcadlo
Sp.	espejo	ME	mirour, glas	Pol.	zwierciadlo
Rum.	oglindă	NE	mirror, glass	Russ.	zerkalo
Ir.	scáthán	Du.	spiegel	Skt.	ādarça-, darpaṇa-
NIr.	scáthán	OHG	spiegal, scūcar		
W.	drych	MHG	spiegel		
Br.	melezour	NHG	spiegel		

Words for 'mirror' are mostly from verbs for 'look', with a few from words for 'shadow' or other sources. The common use of the word for the material 'glass' in the sense of 'mirror' seems to be peculiar to English.

1. Grk. κάτοπτρον beside κατόπτης 'spy', etc., deriv. of κατά and the root of ὄψομαι, ὄπωπα fut. and aor. to ὁράω 'see'. Hence also, with transposition, Att. κάτροπτον, NG καθρέφτης (for θ cf. καθορᾶω).

2. Lat. speculum, fr. *spec- 'look' in cpds. -spicere, etc. (15.52). Hence It. specchio, Sp. espejo, OHG spiegal, MHG, NHG, Du. spiegel, MLG spēgel (> ON spegill, Dan. spejl, Sw. spegel, Lett. spiegelis). Ernout-M. 961. REW 8133. Falk-Torp 1115.

OFr. miradoir, mireor, mirour (> ME mirour, NE mirror), fr. miroir, fr. *mīrātōrium, deriv. of Lat. mīrāre (mīrārī) 'wonder at' in the later sense of 'look' as in It. mirare, Fr. mirer, etc. (15.52). REW 5603. NED s.v. mirror.

Rum. oglindă, fr. Slavic, see below, 6.

3. Ir. scáthán : scáth 'shade, shadow' (1.63). Cf. Goth. skuggwa, etc. (below, 4).

W. drych (also 'sight, appearance') : Ir. drech 'face, appearance', Grk. δέρκομαι, Skt. dṛç- 'see', etc. (15.51). Walde-P. 1.807. Pedersen 1.42.

Br. melezour, with dissim. of liquids,

fr. OFr. miredoir or the same source (above, 2). Loth, Mots lat. 186. Pedersen 1.491.

4. Goth. skuggwa, ON skuggsjā, OHG scūcar : ON skuggi, OE scūa, etc. 'shade, shadow' (1.63). Falk-Torp 1045. Feist 435.

OE glæs 'glass' as material (9.74), also as 'mirror', and so NE glass (with or without looking-) commonly to the present day (look in the glass). Similarly NG dial. γυαλί and τηρογυαλί (τηρῶ 'look').

OHG spiegal, etc., above, 2.

ME mirour, NE mirror, above, 2.

5. Lith. veidrodis (neolog., replacing zerkolas fr. Russ. zerkalo), fr. veidas 'face' and rodyti 'show'.

Lett. spuogulis, fr. spuogat 'shine', but a blend with spiegelis (fr. LG, above, 2).

6. ChSl. zrĭcalo (Supr.), SCr. zrcalo, Boh. zrcadlo, Pol. zwierciadło, Russ. zerkalo, fr. the root of ChSl. zĭrĕti, etc. 'look' (15.52).

ChSl. *oględalo (not quotable, but cf. Rum. oglindă), SCr. ogledalo, fr. ChSl. ględati, etc. 'look' (15.52). Berneker 302.

7. Skt. ādarça-, fr. ā-dṛç- cpd. of dṛç- 'see' (15.51). Also ātmadarça- with ātman- 'self'.

Skt. darpaṇa- : Grk. δρωπάζω 'gaze at'. Walde-P. 1.803. Uhlenbeck 122. Otherwise BR s.v.

CHAPTER 7

DWELLING, HOUSE, FURNITURE

7.11 DWELL

Grk.	οἰκέω, κατοικέω	Goth.	bauan	Lith.	gyventi
NG	κατοικῶ, κάθομαι	ON	būa	Lett.	dzīvuôt, majuôt
Lat.	habitāre, incolere (vīvere)	Dan.	bo	ChSl.	žiti, obitati
		Sw.	bo	SCr.	živjeti, stanovati, prebivati
It.	abitare, dimorare, stare di casa	OE	wunian, būan, eardian, sittan	Boh.	bydleti, obývati
Fr.	habiter, demeurer	ME	wone, dwelle (live)	Pol.	mieszkać
Sp.	vivir, habitar, morar	NE	live, dwell, reside	Russ.	žit', obitat'
Rum.	locui, şedea (trăi)	Du.	wonen	Skt.	vas-, kṣi-
Ir.	atreba (3 sg.)	OHG	būan, wonēn	Av.	ši-
NIr.	comhnuighim, áitighim	MHG	wonen		
W.	trigiannu, byw, preswylio	NHG	wohnen		
Br.					

Words for 'dwell' (really live in present spoken English, but 'dwell' is used here to avoid ambiguity) are from such notions as 'be, exist', and especially 'live' = 'be alive' of this various sources (cf. 4.74); through 'remain, abide' from 'sit', 'delay, linger, go slowly', etc.; 'possess, be busy with, cultivate'. Some are denominatives from words for 'house' or 'place'.

1. Grk. οἰκέω, fr. οἶκος 'house' (7.12). Hence also κατοικέω.

Grk. κάθημαι 'sit' (cpd. of ἧμαι 'sit',

12.13), in LXX and NT also 'dwell'. Hence, with shift to the common thematic type, NG pop. κάθομαι (ποῦ κάθεται; 'where does he live?').

2. Lat. habitāre (> It. abitare, Fr. habiter, Sp. habitar) frequent. of habēre 'have, possess', which is itself sometimes used for 'occupy, dwell in' and simply 'dwell'.

Lat. incolere 'dwell in, inhabit', and 'dwell', but with reference to country or town rather than to one's house, fr. colere 'cultivate' and 'dwell in' : Grk.

πέλομαι 'be in motion, be', Skt. *car-* 'move, perform', etc., IE *k^wel-. Development fr. 'turn, move' through 'be busy with'. Cf. Lat. *versārī* 'remain, dwell', fr. *vertere* 'turn'. Walde-P. 1.514 f. Ernout-M. 204 ff. Walde-H. 1.246.

Lat. *sedēre* 'sit, remain', whence Rum. *şedea* 'sit' and also 'dwell'; cpd. *residēre* 'remain, abide', rarely 'dwell', whence Fr. *résider* (> NE *reside*), Sp. *resider* 'reside'.

Lat. *morārī, dēmorārī* 'delay' (14.24), in VLat. also 'dwell' (so *morārī* and *commorārī* in Peregrinatio), whence Sp. *morar* 'dwell', It. *dimorare*, Fr. *demeurer* 'remain' and 'dwell'. Wartburg 3.38 f.

Lat. *vīvere* 'live' is occasionally used for 'dwell' (e.g. *extra urbem* Cic.). So sometimes It. *vivere*, Fr. *vivre;* and Sp. *vivir* is the usual spoken form, like NE *live*. See below, 5.

It. *stare di casa*, lit. 'be at home', as in *dove sta di casa?* 'where do you live?'

Rum. *locui*, the reg. word for 'dwell', formerly *lăcui*, fr. Hung. *lak* 'dwell', but with present spelling as if derived fr. *loc*, Lat. *locus*. Tiktin 921. Densusianu 1.375.

Rum. *trăi* 'live' (4.74), also used for 'dwell'.

3. Ir. 3 sg. *atreba* 'habitat', NIr. *aitreabhaim*, cpd. of *ad-* and *trebaim* 'inhabit, cultivate', NIr. *treabhaim* 'cultivate, plow' : Ir., OW, OBr. *treb* 'dwelling', Osc. *trííbum* (**trēbo-*) 'building', Umbr. *trebeit* 'versatur', Lat. *trabs* 'beam', Lith. *troba* 'building', OE *þorp*, OHG *dorf* 'village'. Walde-P. 1.757.

NIr. *comhnuighim*, fr. *comhnaidhe* 'dwelling, abiding', Ir. *comnaide*, beside *irnaide*, NIr. *urnaidhe* 'waiting, watching', vbl. n. of Ir. *ar-neut* 'I expect', this a cpd. of **ni* 'down' and **sed-* 'sit'. Thurneysen, Gram. 523. Lewis-Pedersen 385 (vs. Pedersen 2.584).

NIr. *āitighim*, fr. *āit* 'place' (12.11).

W. *trigiannu*, older also *trigo*, Corn. *trega, trige* (with sbs. W. *trig*, MCorn. *trig-se* 'abode'), prob. orig. 'delay', fr. VLat. *trīcāre*, Lat. *trīcārī* 'trifle, dally, play tricks'. Loth, Mots lat. 212.

W. *preswylio*, fr. *preswyl* 'dwelling' : adj. *preswyl* 'constant, ready', OW *presuir* gl. *adfixa*, prob. fr. a deriv. of Lat. *pressus* 'pressed, firm, fixed' (pple. of *premere* 'press'). Loth, Mots lat. 198 f.

W. *byw* 'live' and also commonly 'dwell', due in part to the corresponding use of NE *live*.

Br. *chom* 'remain' and 'dwell', fr. Fr. *chômer* 'rest during heat, lay off work, be idle' (this fr. Grk. καῦμα 'burning heat'. REW 1779). Henry 168.

4. Goth. *bauan*, ON *būa*, Dan., Sw. *bo*, OE, OHG *būan* (NHG *bauen* 'build'), fr. forms of IE **bheu-* 'be'. Walde-P. 2.142. Feist 83 f. Cf. Boh. *obývati* 'dwell', etc. fr. the same root, below, 5.

OE *wunian*, ME *wone* (NE dial. *won*), Du. *wonen*, OHG *wonēn*, MHG *wonen*, NHG *wohnen*, fr. IE **wen-* 'strive for, desire, gain', etc. (NE *win, wish*, etc.). Walde-P. 1.258 ff. But the precise semantic development is uncertain. Prob. through 'be satisfied with, accustomed to', which is also a widespread meaning in Gmc. (ON *una* 'be satisfied with', *vanr* 'accustomed', OE *gewun* 'accustomed', OE *wunian*, OHG *wonēn* also sometimes 'be wont', NE *wont*, etc.), whence 'be at home in, dwell'. But possibly independently of this, directly fr. 'gain, win' to 'occupy, dwell in, dwell' (cf. Lat. *habitāre*). Still otherwise Meringer IF 16. 179, KZ 40. 232, but with no evidence that **wen-* meant orig. 'plow'.

OE *eardian*, fr. *eard* 'native land, country, home', this prob. like OHG *art*

'plowed land' : OE *erian*, Lat. *arāre* 'plow', etc. Walde-P. 1.78.

OE *sittan* 'sit' is also frequently 'dwell'. Cf. Grk. κάθημαι, Lat. *sedēre, residēre*, above, 1, 2.

ME *dwelle*, NE *dwell*, fr. OE *dwellan* 'lead astray, stupefy, hinder, delay' : ON *dvelja* 'delay, put off', refl. *dveljask* 'stay', Sw. *dväljas* 'dwell', OHG *twellan* 'delay', all caus. forms of Gmc. **dwel-* in OHG *twelan* 'be benumbed, torpid', OE *gedwolen* 'gone astray', Goth. *dwals* 'foolish', IE **dhwel-* in Grk. θολός 'dirt', Ir. *dall* 'blind', etc. The development is fr. 'confuse, lead astray' to 'hinder, delay', then intr. 'delay, linger', whence 'dwell' as often. Walde-P. 1.842 f. Falk-Torp 169. NED s.v. *dwell*, vb.

ME, NE *live* 'live' = 'be alive' (4.74), also 'live' = 'dwell' fr. the 13th cent. and now virtually displacing *dwell* in spoken use.

5. Lith. *gyventi*, Lett. *dzīvuōt*, ChSl. *žiti*, SCr. *živjeti*, Russ. *žit'*, all meaning 'live' = 'be alive' (4.74) and also 'live' = 'dwell'.

Lett. *majuōt*, fr. *māja* 'house' (7.12).

6. ChSl. *vitati* (cf. Mt. 13. 32 of birds 'lodging'), *obitati* (**obŭ-vitati*), Russ. *obitat'* 'dwell' (Russ. *vitat'* 'soar', Boh. *vitati*, Pol. *witać* 'welcome') : Lith. Lett. *vieta* 'place' (12.11), root connection? Trautmann 345.

ChSl. *prěbyvati* 'remain', SCr. *prebivati* 'dwell', Boh. *obývati* 'dwell', Russ. *prebyvati* 'sojourn, reside', cpds. of ChSl. *byvati* iter. of *byti* 'be' (9.91); Boh. *bydleti*, denom. of *bydlo* 'dwelling', fr. the same root.

SCr. *stanovati*, fr. *stan* 'dwelling', this : ChSl. *stanŭ* 'camp', Boh. *stan* 'tent', Skt. *sthāna-* 'place', fr. IE **stā-* 'stand'. Walde-P. 2.606.

Pol. *mieszkać*, now the usual word for 'dwell', formerly 'delay, linger, tarry' (so Boh. *meškati*, Russ. *meškat'*), fr. **mieszka* (*Mieszka* as a name) a pop. abbr. of the Slavic word for 'bear' (3.73). Development fr. 'move clumsily like a bear' (so the borrowed Lith. dial. *meškiuoti*) to 'move slowly, linger', etc. Berneker 2.30. Brückner 335.

7. Skt. *vas-*, the usual word for 'dwell', Av. *vah-* (less common) : Goth. *wisan*, OE, OHG *wesan* 'be' and 'abide, remain', IE **wes-*, of which the primary sense was prob. 'abide, dwell'. Walde-P. 1.306 ff. Feist 567.

Skt. *kṣi-* (less usual than *vas-*), Av. *ši-* (the usual word for 'dwell') : Grk. κτίζω 'build, found', κτίσις 'foundation', etc. Walde-P. 1.504.

7.12 HOUSE

Grk.	*οἰκία, οἶκος, δόμος*	Goth.	*gards, razn*	Lith.	*namai, butas*
NG	*σπίτι*	ON	*hūs, rann*	Lett.	*māja, nams*
Lat.	*domus*	Dan.	*hus*	ChSl.	*domŭ, chramŭ, chyzŭ*
It.	*casa*	Sw.	*hus*	SCr.	*kuća, dom*
Fr.	*maison*	OE	*hūs, ærn*	Boh.	*dům*
Sp.	*casa*	ME	*hus, hous*	Pol.	*dom*
Rum.	*casă*	NE	*house*	Russ.	*dom*
Ir.	*tech*	Du.	*huse*	Skt.	*gṛha-, dama-*
NIr.	*teach*	OHG	*hūs*	Av.	*nmāna-*
W.	*ty*	MHG	*hūs*		
Br.	*ti*	NHG	*haus*		

'House' is understood here as 'dwelling house'. There is overlapping, on the one hand, with 'building' in general, on the other, with 'dwelling', 'home'. The former notion is more dominant etymologically, the majority of the words reflecting the notion of 'build', 'cover', or some other feature of the construction. But some come from 'remain, rest, stand, dwell', etc. Regardless of their etymology, words for 'house' may also be used for 'building', but still more generally for 'home' and for 'household, family'. They commonly supply the phrases answering to NE *at home*, as Gr. οἴκοι, NGr. στὸ σπίτι, It. *a casa*, Fr. *chez moi*, etc. (*chez* fr. Lat. *casa*), NHG *zu hause*, Lith. *namie*, Russ. *doma*, etc. Hence the common dictionary definition 'house, home' for most of the words listed here. But they do not correspond to NE *home* in its widest sense. Cf. below 7.122. Words for 'dwelling', derived from the verbs for 'dwell' (7.11), though they cover 'dwelling house', like Lat. *habitātiō*, Rum. *locuinţă*, NHG *wohnung*, NE *dwelling*, Skt. *veçman-*, etc. are not included in the list, unless they are the common words for 'house', as Grk. οἶκος.

1. IE **domo-, *domu-* 'house', fr. **dem-* 'build' in Gr. δέμω, etc. (9.44). Walde-P. 1.786 ff. Ernout-M. 281 ff. Gr. δόμος (mostly poet.); Lat. *domus;* ChSl. *domŭ*, etc., general Slavic; Skt. *dama-* (Vedic), Av. *dəmāna-, nmāna-*.

2. IE **weiḱ-, *wiḱ-, *woiḱo-*. Walde-P. 1.231. Ernout-M. 1103.

Grk. οἶκος, οἰκία 'house', Lat. *vīcus* 'group of houses, village', Goth. *weihs* 'village', ChSl. *vĭsĭ* 'village', Skt. *viç-* 'settlement, house, clan, people', Av. *vis-* 'dwelling, village', OPers. *viθ-* 'royal court, palace, family', Skt. *veçman-*, Av. *vaēsma* 'dwelling'. In this group the notion of 'house' as a building is subordinate to that of 'home, settlement, family'. But whether the latter is also more original or a secondary development from 'house', the ultimate root connection is too doubtful to determine.

3. NG σπίτι, the reg. word for 'house' in the spoken language, fr. Lat. *hospitium* 'lodging, inn', VLat. 'house'. Cf. Arch. lat. Lex. 8.194; Peregrinatio 25.7 *vadent se unusquisque ad ospitium suum*.

4. It., Sp. *casa*, Rum. *casă* (cf. Fr. *chez moi*, etc. 'at home'), fr. Lat. *casa* 'cottage, hut', (7.13).

Fr. *maison*, fr. Lat. *mansiō* 'staying' later 'stopping place, station, lodging', fr. *manēre* 'remain' (12.16).

5. Ir. *tech*, NIr. *teach*, W. *ty*, Br. *ti* : Grk. στέγος, τέγος 'roof', στέγω, Lat. *tegere* 'cover', NHG *dach* 'roof', etc. (7.15). Walde-P. 1.620 ff. Pedersen 1.98 f. Cf. Cret. στέγα 'house' (so in Law Code, where οἰκία is 'household'), Lat. *tectum* 'roof' and frequently 'house'. Cf. also Grk. ὄροφος 'roof', at Cyrene 'house'.

6. Goth. *-hūs* (*gudhūs* 'temple'), ON, OE, OHG *hūs*, etc., general Gmc., etym. much disputed, but prob. : Grk. κεύθω, OE *hȳdan* 'hide', IE **keudh-*, or fr. a parallel **keut-* (Lat. *cutis*, OHG *hūt* 'skin'), or **keus-* (OE *hosa* 'husk' and 'leg-covering, hose', etc.), all extensions of IE **(s)keu-* 'cover'. Walde-P. 2.546 ff., 551. Falk-Torp 433. Feist 223.

Goth. *gards* ('house', rarely 'court') : ON *garðr* 'yard, court', OE *geard*, NE *yard*, etc. (7.15).

Goth. *razn*, ON *rann* (poet.), OE *ærn* (esp. 'place' in cpds., but also 'house') : Goth. *rasta* 'mile', OHG *rasta*, OE *ræst* 'rest', NE *rest*, etc. Walde-P. 1.144. Falk-Torp 878, 882.

7. Lith. *namai* (pl.), less frequently sg. *namas*, the usual word for 'house' as 'home' (cf. *namie* 'at home', *namo eiti* 'go home'), Lett. *nams* 'kitchen', etc., also 'house' (but less usual than *māja*), etym. dub. Possibly : Grk. δόμος, etc. (above, 1), with partial assimilation of the initial *d* to the following nasal (cf. Grk. dial. νύναμαι = δύναμαι), or influenced by a form with *nm-* from *dm-* like Av. *nmāna-* (so J. Schmidt, Pluralbildung 222). Walde-P. 1.788 with refs.

Lith. *butas*, the individual 'house', OPruss. *buttan* 'house' : ON *būð* 'booth', ON, OE, OHG *būan* 'dwell', W. *bod* 'dwelling', Ir. *both* 'hut', etc. Walde-P. 2.140 ff.

Lett. *māja*, the usual word for 'house', loanword fr. Esth. *māja* 'house' or conversely? Mühl.-Endz. 2.577 f.

8. ChSl. (beside usual *domŭ*) *chramŭ* 'house' : SCr. *hram* 'temple', etc., etym.? Berneker 397.

ChSl. *chyzŭ* 'house' (Supr.), ORuss. *chyz* 'hut, house', etc., loanword fr. Gmc. (Goth. *hūs*, etc.). Berneker 415. Stender-Petersen 240 ff.

SCr. *kuća* 'house', Bulg. *kŭšta* 'house, hut' : ChSl. *kąšta* 'tent', *sukątati* 'prepare for burial', Russ. *kutat'* 'wrap in', etc. perh. fr. a nasalized form of IE **(s)keu-t-* 'cover', in Grk. σκῦτος, Lat. *cutis* 'hide', etc. Berneker 603. Walde-P. 2.550.

9. Skt. *gṛha-*, the usual word for 'house' : Av. *gərəδa-* 'cavern', and prob. Goth. *gards* 'house, court', at least fr. the same root. See 7.15 under Goth. *gards*, etc.

Skt. *dama-*, Av. *nmāna-*, above, 1.

Skt. *çālā-* 'house, stall, hut' (cf. also *çālam* 'at home'), see 7.13.

7.122. 'Home' in the full range and feeling of NE *home* is a conception that belongs distinctively to the word *home* and some of its Gmc. cognates and is not covered by any single word in most of the IE languages. In the prevailing sense of one's own dwelling house it is commonly expressed by the words for 'house' (7.12), or sometimes by various words for 'dwelling, abode', mostly connected with the verb 'dwell'. As applied to one's home town or country it is mostly expressed by quite distinct words or phrases involving 'town' or 'country' (for 'native country', see 19.12).

The Gmc. group is as follows: Goth. *haims* 'village', ON *heimr* 'abode, world', Dan. *hjem*, Sw. *hem*, both 'home' in wide sense, OE *hām* 'home', mostly as 'dwelling house', ME, NE *home*, OS *hēm* (Du. *heem* is a loanword fr. LG and of restricted use), OHG, MHG *heim* (NHG mostly adverbial), OHG *heimuoti*, MHG *heimuote*, NHG *heimat* 'home' as native town or country : Lett. *saime* 'household, family', Lith. *šeimyna* 'family', Lat. *cīvis* 'citizen', etc., fr. IE *ḱei-* 'lie' in Grk. κεῖμαι etc. 'Place of abode' specialized in different directions to 'dwelling house', 'household', 'village', etc. Walde-P. 1.358 ff. Falk-Torp 409. Feist 233 f.

From other languages the following may be mentioned as approximating 'home' and not listed under 'house'.

Words for 'fireplace, hearth' (7.31) as symbolic of the 'home' (cf. NE *fight for their firesides*). So often Grk. ἑστία, Rum. *cămin*, etc.

NIr. *baile* 'town, village' (19.16), also 'home', as in *ag baile* 'at home'.

W. *cartref* 'home', *gartref* 'at home', cpd. of MW *gar* beside *ger, ker* 'at' and *tref* 'home, town' (: Ir. *trebaim* 'inhabit, cultivate', 7.11).

7.13 HUT

Grk.	*καλύβη, καλία, κλισίη*	Goth.	. . . .	Lith.	*bakužė, gryčia*
NG	*καλύβα, καλύβη*	ON	*kofi, kot*	Lett.	*būda*
Lat.	*casa, tugurium*	Dan.	*hytte*	ChSl.	. . . .
It.	*casupola, tugurio, capanna*	Sw.	*hydda*	SCr.	*koliba*
		OE	*cot*	Boh.	*chatrč, chalupa*
Fr.	*hutte, cabane*	ME	*cot, hutte*	Pol.	*chałupa, chata, buda*
Sp.	*huta, cabaña, choza*	NE	*hut*	Russ.	*chižina, lačuga*
Rum.	*colibă, bordeiu*	Du.	*hut*	Skt.	*kuṭī-, çālā-*
Ir.	*both, bothān*	OHG	*hutta*	Av.	. . . .
NIr.	*both, bothān*	MHG	*hütte*		
W.	*bwth, cwt*	NHG	*hütte*		
Br.	*log, logell*				

Words for 'hut' are from those denoting 'cover', 'rounded or hollow shape', or some special manner or material of construction. Some are diminutives of those for 'house'.

1. Grk. *καλύβη* fr. the stem of *καλύπτω* 'cover', also *καλία* and Skt. *çālā-* 'house, stall, hut' fr. the same root, IE **k̂el-* 'cover, hide' in Lat. *occulere, cēlāre,* Ir. *celim*, OE *helan*, etc. (12.26, 12.27). Walde-P. 1.432 ff.

NG *καλύβα* is, through Turk., the source of SCr. *koliba*, Rum. *colibă*, etc. Berneker 546.

Grk. *κλισία*, Hom. *κλισίη* ('hut', also 'couch') : *κλῑνω* 'incline, recline', *κλίνη* 'couch', Goth. *hleiþra* 'tent' (7.14), etc., IE **k̂lei-*. Walde-P. 1.490. Boisacq 470 f.

2. Lat. *casa*, etym. dub., perh. as orig. 'wickerwork', fr. **kat-* in Lat. *catēna* 'chain', *cassis* 'net', etc. Walde-P. 1.338. Walde-H. 1.175 f.

It. *casupola*, dim. of *casa*, after it had become 'house'. REW 1752.

Lat. *tugurium* (> It. *tugurio*), *tegurium*, fr. *tegere* 'cover' (12.26). Ernout-M. 10.20.

Late Lat. *capanna* (Isid. 15.12.2 *tugurium casula est . . . . hunc rustici capannam vocant*), orig. dub., perh. fr. *cannaba* 'booth' with form influenced by *capere*. Hence It. *capanna*, Sp. *cabaña*, NE *cabin*, etc. Ernout-M. 146. Walde-H. 1.156. REW 1624.

Fr. *hutte*, Sp. *huta*, fr. Gmc. (below, 4).

Sp. *choza, chozo,* fr. Lat. *pluteum* 'shed'. REW 6619. Otherwise (fr. Arab. *ḫuṣṣ* 'straw hut') Lokotsch 887.

OFr. *borde* 'booth, hut', *bordel* 'hovel, brothel' (> ME *bordel,* It. *bordello* 'brothel') fr. Gmc. *bord* 'board'. Here also prob. (but through Bulg. *bordej*) Rum. *bordeiu* 'mud hut'? REW 1216.

3. Ir., NIr. *both, bothān* : W. *bod* 'dwelling', ON *būð* 'dwelling', ME *bōþe, bōthe* 'hut, tent', NE *booth* (> W. *bwth*), NHG *bude* 'booth' (> Pol., Russ. *buda* 'booth, hut' > Lith. *būda* 'booth, tent', Lett. *būda* 'hut'), Lith. *butas* 'house', Goth. *bauan* 'dwell', etc. (7.11). Walde-P. 2.142. Pedersen 1.35.

W. *cwt*, fr. OE, ME *cot* (below, 4).

Br. *log, logell*, fr. Fr. *loge* (OFr. 'arbor, bower', also 'hut', cf. Godefroy), this fr. Gmc. *laubja* (NHG *laube*). Loth, Mots lat. 182. REW 4936.

4. ON *kofi* : OE *cofa* 'a room' (also 'hollow in the rock', later 'recess on the coast', NE *cove*), MHG *kobe* 'stall, cage', Grk. *γύπη* 'hole, cave, hut' (Hesych.), fr. an extension of IE **geu-*, as in the following. Walde-P. 1.561. Falk-Torp 570, 1500.

ON *kot* (ODan. *kod* 'hovel'), OE, ME *cot* (also *cote*, NE *dovecote*, etc.), MLG *kot, kote* (NHG *kot, kote* 'hovel', Du. *kot* 'hovel, sty, kennel'; fr. Gmc., OFr. *cotage* > NE *cottage*), fr. an extension of IE **geu-* in words denoting hollow or

rounded shape. Walde-P. 1.555 ff., 560. Falk-Torp 570.

OHG *hutta*, MHG, NHG *hütte* (> Fr. *hutte* > ME *hutte,* NE *hut,* Sp. *huta;* also > Dan. *hytte*), also ODan. *hudde,* Sw. *hydda,* all : Grk. *κεύθω,* OE *hȳdan* 'hide', etc. and so ultimately connected with OE *hūs* 'house' etc. (7.12). Walde-P. 2.546 ff., 551. Falk-Torp 445.

5. Lith. *bakužė* (NSB, etc.), fr. MLG *backhūs* 'bakehouse'. Alminauskis 28.

Lith. *gryčia, grinčia,* shortened form of old *gryničia* 'servants hall', 'smokehouse' fr. WhRuss. **gridnica.* Berneker 139. Skardžius 78.

6. Boh. *chatrč* beside dial. *chat'* = Pol., Russ. dial. *chata*, loanword fr. Iran., Av. *kata-* 'chamber, storeroom', NPers. *kad* 'house'. Berneker 385 f.

Boh. *chalupa*, Pol. *chałupa*, orig. dub. Berneker 383. Brückner 175 f.

Russ. *chižina,* dim. of *chiža* : Ukr. *chyža* 'hut', ChSl. *chyzŭ* 'house', Bulg. *hiža* 'hut', etc., early loanword fr. Gmc., OHG *hūs*, etc. (7.12). Berneker 414. Stender-Petersen 240 ff.

Russ. *lačuga,* older *alačuga,* fr. Turk. *alačuk* 'hut of cloth or bark'. Berneker 682. Lokotsch 49.

7. Skt. *kuṭi-, kuṭī-* fr. **kṛtī-* : Skt. *kṛt-* 'twist', Grk. *κάρταλος* 'basket', Lat. *crātis* 'wickerwork', etc. Walde-P. 1.421.

Skt. *çālā-*, above, 1.

7.14 TENT

Grk.	*σκηνή*	Goth.	*hleiþra, hlija*	Lith.	*palapinė, šėtra*
NG	*σκηνή, τέντα*	ON	*tjald*	Lett.	*telts*
Lat.	*tabernāculum, tentōrium*	Dan.	*telt*	ChSl.	*skinĭji, kąšta*
		Sw.	*tält*	SCr.	*šator*
It.	*tenda, padiglione*	OE	*(ge)teld*	Boh.	*stan*
Fr.	*tente, pavillon*	ME	*tente, teld, pavilon*	Pol.	*namiot, szater*
Sp.	*tienda, pabellón*	NE	*tent*	Russ.	*palatka, šater*
Rum.	*cort, şatră*	Du.	*tent*	Skt.	*vastragṛha-*
Ir.	*pupall*	OHG	*(gi)zelt*	Av.	. . . .
NIr.	*pailliūn, puball*	MHG	*(ge)zelt*		
W.	*pabell*	NHG	*zelt*		
Br.	*telt, tinell*				

Words for 'tent' come from those denoting 'cover', 'stretch', 'shade', or simply 'dwelling'. Some denoted, at first, the military headquarters' tent. One group reflects the 'butterfly' appearance of the open tent.

1. Grk. *σκηνή*, Dor. *σκᾱνά* : *σκιά* 'shade' (1.63), etc. Walde-P. 2.535. Boisacq 874 f.

2. Lat. *tabernāculum*, dim. of *taberna* in its earlier sense of 'dwelling, hut', this prob. fr. **trabernā-* : Lat. *trabs* 'beam', Osc. *trííbúm* 'building', Umbr. *trebeit* 'versatur', Ir. *atreba* 'dwells', (7.11). Walde-P. 1.757. Ernout-M. 1011, 1050.

Lat. *tentōrium*, fr. *tendere* 'stretch', pple. *tentus* (19.32). Replaced by MLat. *tenta,* fem. of pple., whence Byz., NG *τέντα*, Fr. *tente* (> ME *tente,* NE *tent,* Du. *tent*); also MLat. *tenda* (with *d* from *tendere*), whence It. *tenda* 'tent, awning', Sp. *tienda* 'tent, shop', Rum. *tindă* 'forecourt, vestibule'. Ernout-M. 1026. REW 8639.

Lat. *pāpiliō* 'butterfly' and a kind of open 'tent' : OE *fīfalde* 'butterfly', etc., prob. fr. IE **pel-* in Grk. *πάλλω* 'shake', etc. Hence It. *padiglione*, Fr. *pavillon* (> ME *pavilon* > NIr. *pailliūn*, NE *pavilion*), Sp. *pabellón;* also Ir. *pupall*, NIr. *puball*, W. *pabell.* Walde-P. 2.52. Ernout-M. 730. REW 6211. Vendryes, De hib. voc. 170.

Rum. *cort,* fr. Byz. *κόρτη* 'military

headquarters, emperor's tent', this fr. Lat. *cors, cortis* 'court' (7.15).

Rum. *şatră*, see below, 6, SCr. *šator,* etc.

3. Ir. *pupall*, etc., above, 2.

Br. *telt*, fr. OE *teld* (below, 4). Henry 262.

Br. *tinell,* fr. Fr. *tonnelle* 'arbor, bower'.

4. Goth. *hleiþra, hlija* : Grk. *κλισία* 'hut' (7.13), *κλῑνη* 'couch', *κλῑνω* 'incline, recline', Lat. *inclīnāre* 'incline', Umbr. *kletram* 'litter', etc. Walde-P. 1.490. Feist 263.

ON *tjald*, Dan. *telt*, Sw. *tält*, OE *teld, geteld*, ME *teld, tild* (NE *tilt*), MLG *telt* (> Lett. *telts*), OHG *(gi)zelt*, MHG *(ge)-zelt*, NHG *zelt* : OE *beteldan* 'cover' (but this prob. fr. *teld*), outside root connection dub. Walde-P. 1.811. Falk-Torp 1253.

5. Lith. *palapinė,* neolog. for loanword *šėtra*, 'tent', used also for 'arbor' and formed fr. *lapas* 'leaf' under influence of NHG *laube, laubhütte.* Fraenkel, Z. sl. Ph. 6.87.

Lith. *šėtra*, fr. Russ. *šater* (below, 6).

6. In ChSl. the Grk. *σκηνή* is taken over as *skinĭji*, once is rendered by *krovŭ* 'roof' (7.26), once (Supr.) by *kąšta* : Bulg. *kŭšta,* SCr. *kuća* 'house' (7.12).

SCr. *šator*, Pol. *szater,* Russ. *šater,* Rum. *şatră,* fr. Turk. *çadır*, NPers. *čādar* 'tent'. Berneker 133. Lokotsch 380.

Boh. *stan* : ChSl. *stanŭ* 'camp', SCr. *stan* 'dwelling', Skt. *sthāna-* 'place', fr. IE **stā-* 'stand'. Walde-P. 2.606. Development of 'tent' through the military 'headquarters' tent', as in Rum. *cort*, above, 2.

Pol. *namiot* : Russ. *namet* 'cover, roof, large tent', etc., cpd. of *na-* 'upon' and *met-* 'throw'. Berneker 2.40. Brückner 354.

Russ. *palatka*, dim. of *palata* 'official chamber, palace', fr. Byz. *παλάτιον*, fr. Lat. *palātium.* Development through 'headquarters' tent'.

7. Skt. *vastragṛha-* (rare), lit. 'cloth-house', cpd. of *vastra-* 'cloth, dress' and *gṛha-* 'house'.

7.15 YARD, COURT

Grk.	*αὐλή*	Goth.	*rōhsns, gards*	Lith.	*kiemas*
NG	*αὐλή*	ON	*garðr*	Lett.	*pagalms*
Lat.	*cohors, aula*	Dan.	*gaard*	ChSl.	*dvorŭ*
It.	*cortile*	Sw.	*gård*	SCr.	*avlija, dvor(ište)*
Fr.	*cour*	OE	*geard*	Boh.	*dvůr*
Sp.	*patio*	ME	*ȝerd, hawe*	Pol.	*dziedziniec, podwórze*
Rum.	*curte*	NE	*yard*	Russ.	*dvor*
Ir.	*cuirt*	Du.	*hof, binnenplaats*	Skt.	*añgana-*
NIr.	*bannrach*	OHG	*hof*	Av.	. . . .
W.	*iard*	MHG	*hof*		
Br.	*porz*	NHG	*hof*		

The words listed here, while not altogether synonymous in their range, are intended to cover those commonly applied to the enclosed area attached to a house, whether outside or an inner court. Many of the words for 'court' have developed secondary meanings such as 'hall, palace, estate' and, with Fr. *cour* leading the way, 'royal retinue', 'assembly of judges', etc. Some are now used only in such secondary senses and no longer applied to a 'courtyard', and so are omitted from the list.

Some that originally belonged to this group have come to denote the cultivated 'garden' (as Lat. *hortus,* NE *gar-*

den cognate with NE *yard*, etc.), and so are entered under that head (8.13).

1. Grk. *αὐλή* (> Lat. *aula;* NG > Turk. *avlu* > SCr. *avlija*), prob. at first an enclosed space near the house where the cattle slept, a 'cattleyard' : *αὖλις* 'place for sleeping', *αὔλιον* 'cottage, fold, stable', fr. the root of *ἰαύω* 'sleep'. Walde-P. 1.19 ff. Boisacq 100.

2. Lat. *cohors, cohortis* (later *cōrs, cōrtis*, also *curs* or *curtis*) : Lat. *hortus* 'garden', Grk. *χόρτος* 'farmyard', Ir. *gort* 'field of grain', W. *garth* 'enclosure, garden', Br. *garz* 'hedge', Skt. *hṛ-* 'take, hold, carry', Osc. *heriiad* 'capiat', etc. Hence OFr. *cort, curt, court* (> ME *curt, court*, NE *court*), Fr. *cour*, Rum. *curte* (It., Sp. *corte* in secondary senses), deriv. It. *cortile*. Walde-P. 1.603. Ernout-M. 461. Walde-H. 1.242 f. REW 2032.

Sp. *patio*, prob. orig. a learned deriv. of Lat. *patēre* 'lie open'.

3. Ir. *cuirt*, fr. Lat. *cors, cortis.* Vendryes, De hib. voc. 134.

NIr. *bannrach* (with *b* fr. *m*, as often), fr. Ir. *mainder* (guttural stem, e.g. gen. pl. *mandrach*) 'enclosure, pen, fold', this, through MLat. *mandra*, fr. Grk. *μάνδρα* 'fold, pen for animals'.

W. *iard*, fr. NE *yard*.

Br. *porz*, fr. Lat. *porta* 'gate'. Loth, Mots lat. 197. Cf. the relation of 'door' and 'court' in Slavic, below, 6.

4. Goth. *rōhsns*, etym.? Feist 400.

Goth. *gards*, rarely 'court', mostly 'house' (6.12), ON *garðr*, Dan. *gaard*, Sw. *gård*, OE *geard*, ME *ȝerd*, NE *yard* (OHG *garto*, MHG, NHG *garten* 'garden'), uncertain whether fr. IE **ghordho-* : Skt. *gṛha-* 'house', or fr. **ghortó-* : Lat. *cohors* 'court', *hortus* 'garden', etc. (above, 2), in either case fr. the same root. Walde-P. 1.608. Walde-H. 1.243. Falk-Torp 292 f. Feist 197 f.

ME *hawe* ('yard' e.g. in Chaucer, NE obs. *haw*), fr. OE *haga* 'hedge, hedged or fenced-in enclosure', OHG *hag* 'enclosure', beside OE *hegg*, etc. 'hedge'. Walde-P. 1.337. NED s.v. *haw*, sb.[1].

OHG–NHG *hof* (Du. *hof* 'court' and 'garden'; 'yard' also expressed by *plaats* 'place' or *binnenplaats;* ON *hof* 'temple', Norw. *hov* 'small hill', OE *hof* 'house, building'), etym. dub., perh. : OHG *hubil* 'hill', etc. Walde-P. 1.373. Falk-Torp 414. Weigand-H. 877.

5. Lith. *kiemas* : Lith. *kaimas*, Lett. *ciems* 'village', all loanwords fr. Gmc. or (with confusion of gutturals) cognate with Goth. *haims* 'village', etc., fr. IE **k̂ei-* 'lie'. Walde-P. 1.360.

Lett. *pagalms*, prob. as orig. 'open space' : ChSl. *golŭ* 'bare', OHG *kalo* 'bald', etc. Cf. OPol. *gola* 'open place'. Mühl.-Endz. 3.27.

6. ChSl. *dvorŭ*, etc., general Slavic (but Pol. *dwór* 'court' only in secondary senses, as also Lith. *dvaras* fr. Pol. or Russ.; for 'courtyard' Pol. *podwórze*, cpd. with *po* 'in, about') : Lat. *forum* 'public place, market-place', both prob., as orig. the 'doorway with the adjacent court', related to the words for 'door', Lith. *durys*, ChSl. *dvĭri*, Lat. *forēs*, Grk. *θύρα*, etc. (7.22). Berneker 241. Ernout-M. 377 f., 383. Walde-P. 1.871 (but with separation of Lat. *forum*, as also Walde-H. 1.537 f.).

Pol. *dziedziniec*, formerly only 'court of a palace' : Pol. *dziedzina*, Boh. *dědina* 'inherited property, inheritance', deriv. of ChSl. *dědĭ*, Boh. *děd*, etc. 'grandfather'. Berneker 191. Otherwise (: ChSl. *dětę* 'child', etc.) Brückner 108 f.

7. Skt. *añgana-* 'walking' and (as place for walking) 'court, yard', fr. *añg-* 'go'.

7.21 ROOM (In a House)

Grk.	*οἶκος, δῶμα*, etc.	Goth.	. . . .	Lith.	*kambarys* (*stuba*)
NG	*δωμάτιο(ν), κάμαρα*	ON	*stofa*	Lett.	*istaba* (*kambaris*)
Lat.	*conclāve* (*cubiculum*, etc.)	Dan.	*værelse, stue*	ChSl.	. . . .
It.	*stanza, camera*	Sw.	*rum*	SCr.	*soba* (*odaja, komora*)
Fr.	*chambre*	OE	*cofa*	Boh.	*světnice, pokoj* (*jizba, komnata*)
Sp.	*cuarto* (*pieza*)	ME	*chambre, roume*	Pol.	*pokój, izba* (*komnata*)
Rum.	*odaie, cameră*	NE	*room* (*chamber*)	Russ.	*komnata, pokoj*
Ir.	*camra*	Du.	*kamer*	Skt.	*veçman-, çālā*
NIr.	*seomra*	OHG	*camara, chemināta*	Av.	. . . .
W.	*ystafell*	MHG	*stube, gemach, kamer*		
Br.	*kambr*	NHG	*zimmer, stube, gemach*		

Words for 'a room' come in part by specialization from those denoting 'dwelling, abode', 'building', 'covering', 'space', etc.; in part by extension from those denoting originally a special room, as a 'bathroom, heated room', 'rest-room', 'light-room'.

1. In Greek 'a room' is generally expressed by words that are also used for 'house, dwelling' (7.12), as *οἶκος, οἴκημα δόμος, δῶμα, δωμάτιον, τέγος* (properly 'roof' 7.62), or words denoting a special room, as *ἀνδρών* 'man's room, *γυναικών* 'woman's room', *θάλαμος* mostly 'bedroom' (: *θόλος* 'vaulted building', etc. Walde-P. 1.864), *μέγαρον* 'large hall' (etym.? Walde-P. 1.590), etc. Of these, *δωμάτιον*, the NG lit. word for 'room', has been taken over in the pop. language (hence *δωμάτιο* not *δωμάτι*) and is now more common than *κάμαρα* (below, 2) for 'room' in general (as *πόσα δωμάτια*; 'how many rooms?').

2. Lat. *conclāve*, cpd. of *clāvis* 'key' (7.24), hence a place that can be locked up. Otherwise only words for special rooms, as *cubiculum* mostly 'bedroom', fr. *cubāre* 'recline'; *triclinium* 'dining-room', orig. the couch on three sides of the table, fr. Grk. *τρικλίνιον*.

Lat. *camera* (also *camara*) 'vaulted roof', fr. Grk. *καμάρα*, was used in VLat. for 'room'. Hence Byz., NG *κάμαρα, κάμερα*, It. *camera*, Fr. *chambre* (> ME *chambre*, NE *chamber* now esp. 'bedroom', etc.; ME > NIr. *seomra;* Fr. > Br. *kambr*), Rum. *cameră;* Ir. *camra;* OHG *camara*, MHG, Du. *kamer* (MLG > Lith. *kambarys*, Lett. *kambaris*), NHG *kammer*, Dan. *kammer*, Sw. *kammare;* SCr., Boh., Pol. *komora*, etc. Many of these are no longer common words for 'room', but are used for 'bedroom', 'storeroom', 'pantry', 'small room', 'official chamber', etc. REW 1545. Falk-Torp 489. Berneker 555 ff.

It. *stanza*, fr. **stantia*, like *substantia*, etc., fr. Lat. pple. *stāns, stantis*, hence lit. a 'standing place'. REW 8231.

Sp. *pieza* 'piece' also frequently used for 'room', of Celtic orig. REW 6450.

Sp. *cuarto*, 'a fourth' and commonly 'room', fr. Lat. *quartum* 'fourth'. Development through 'region, district, dwelling place', as in NE *quarter* in local sense and *quarters, headquarters*, etc. (NED s.v. III).

Rum. *odaie* through Slavic fr. Turk. *oda* 'room' (see below, 6).

3. Ir. *camra*, NIr. *seomra*, Br. *kambr*, above, 2.

W. *ystafell*, fr. Lat. *stabulum* 'standing-place, stall'. Pedersen 1.219.

4. ON *stofa* 'sitting-room, main room', OE *stofa* 'bathroom' (gl. Lat. *balneum*), OHG *stuba* 'bathroom, heated room', MLG *stove* 'bathroom, heated room' (> ME *stove*, 7.32), MHG *stube* 'bathroom, dining-room, etc., NHG *stube* 'room', Dan. *stue* 'room'. Generalization fr. 'bathroom' to any 'heated room', then any 'room'. Prob. an old loanword fr. the group It. *stufa*, Fr. *étuve* 'hothouse, stove' (7.32), though some regard it as a native Gmc. word related to OHG *stioban*, NHG *stieben* 'be dusty' as if used of steam. Falk-Torp 1188 f. Weigand-H. 2.995. REW 3108 (against connection of Gmc. and Romance words). Meringer, IF 18.273 ff. Kretschmer, Wortgeogr. 507.

From Gmc. come Lith. *stuba* (the reg. word in Pruss. Lith., as in Kurschat, Leskien's Lesebuch, etc.), Lett. *istaba* (through ORuss. *istŭba*, Mühl.-Endz. 1.711), Boh. *jizba*, Pol. *izba*, SCr. *soba* (through Hung. *szoba*), etc. Berneker 436 ff. Stender-Petersen 247 ff.

Goth., ON, OE, OHG *rūm* 'space, place' (: Av. *ravah-* 'space', Lat. *rūs* 'country', etc. Walde-P. 2.356), hence also 'a room' in ME *roume*, NE *room*, Sw. *rum*.

Dan. *værelse*, orig. 'abode', fr. *være* 'be', cf. ON sb. *vera* 'dwelling', etc. Falk-Torp 1403.

OE *cofa*, esp. in cpds. *bed-cofa* 'bedroom', etc. : ON *kofi* 'hut', etc. (7.13). NED s.v. *cove* sb.[1].

OHG *chemināta*, MHG *kemenate* 'room with a fireplace' (> Boh., Pol., Russ. *komnata* 'room'), fr. MLat. *camīnāta*, deriv. of *camīnus* 'furnace, fireplace' (7.31).

MHG, NHG *gemach* : OHG *gimah* 'quiet, comfort', OE *gemæc*, ON *makr* 'suitable', fr. the same root as OE *macian* 'make', etc. Walde-P. 2.226. Weigand-H. 1.671.

NHG *zimmer*, fr. OHG *zimbar* 'timber, building' = OE *timber* id. : Grk. *δέμω* 'build', *δόμος* 'house', etc. (7.12). Walde-P. 1.786 ff. Weigand-H. 2.1327.

5. Lith. *kambarys*, SCr. *komora*, etc., above, 2.

6. Boh., Pol., Russ. *pokoj*, orig. and still also 'quiet, rest' : ChSl. *pokojĭ* 'rest'. Cf. NHG *gemach*. Berneker 538 f.

Lith. *stuba*, Lett. *istaba*, SCr. *soba*, Boh. *jizba*, etc., above, 4.

Boh., Pol., Russ. *komnata*, above, 4.

Bulg., SCr. *odaja* (> Rum. *odaie*), fr. Turk. *oda* 'room'. Lokotsch 1584.

Boh. *světnice* (fr. *světlnice, světlice*), deriv. of *svět* 'light', adj. *světly*, hence orig. a 'light room'.

7. Skt. *veçman-* 'dwelling, house' (7.12), and *çālā-* 'house, hut' (7.13) may also be used for a 'room' (BR s.vv.).

7.22 DOOR; GATE

Grk.	*θύρα; πύλη*	Goth.	*daur, haurds*	Lith.	*durys* (pl.); *vartai* (pl.)
NG	*πόρτα, θύρα; ἐξώπορτα*	ON	*dyrr* (pl.), *hurð; hlið, grind*	Lett.	*duris* (pl.); *vārti* (pl.)
Lat.	*forēs* (pl.), *ōstium, iānua; porta*	Dan.	*dør; port*	ChSl.	*dvĭrĭ; vrata* (pl.)
It.	*porta, uscio*	Sw.	*dörr; port*	SCr.	*vrata* (pl.); *vrata, kapija*
Fr.	*porte*	OE	*duru; geat, dor, port*	Boh.	*dveře* (pl.); *vrata* (pl.), *brána*
Sp.	*puerta*	ME	*dore; ȝet*	Pol.	*drzwi* (pl.); *brama, wrota*
Rum.	*ușă; poartă*	NE	*door; gate*	Russ.	*dver'; vorota* (pl).
Ir.	*dorus* (*comla*)	Du.	*deur; poort*	Skt.	*dvar-, dvāra-*
NIr.	*cōmhla, doras; geata*	OHG	*turi; tor, pforta*	Av.	*dvar-*
W.	*drws, dor; porth*, etc.	MHG	*tür; tor, pforte*		
Br.	*dor*	NHG	*tür; tor, pforte*		

The 'door' of a house and the 'gate' of a wall or fence are often expressed by the same word, and even where commonly expressed by different words, separated by a semicolon in the list, the applications overlap. In several cases the word given first as 'door' may also be used for 'gate', even when there is another word for the latter.

1. IE **dhwer-*, with gradation. Some of the words are used mainly in the dual or plural. Walde-P. 1.870 ff. Ernout-M. 377 f. Walde-H. 1.529 f.

Grk. *θύρα;* Lat. *forēs* (pl.); Ir. *dorus*, NIr. *doras*, W. *drws* (Pedersen 2.20), W., Br. *dor;* Goth. *daur*, OE *duru*, OHG *turi*, etc., general Gmc. for 'door', beside OE *dor* 'gate' (but not always distinguished fr. *duru* 'door'), OHG–NHG *tor* 'gate'; Lith. *durys* (pl.), ChSl. *dvĭrĭ* (mostly pl. *dvĭri*), etc., general Balto-Slavic; Skt. *dvar-* (mostly in dual or pl.; *d* for *dh* by analogy of *dvāu* 'two'), *dvāra-*, Av. *dvar-*, OPers. *duvara-*, NPers. *dar;* Arm. *duṙn;* Alb. *derë*.

2. Grk. *πύλη* 'gate' (mostly pl. *πύλαι*) : Skt. *gopura-* 'town-gate', also(?) Skt. *pur-* 'fortress, town', Grk. *πόλις* 'city'. Walde-P. 2.51. Boisacq 826.

3. Lat. *porta* 'gate', orig. 'passage' : Av. *pərətu-* 'passage, bridge', OE *ford* 'ford', Grk. *πόρος* 'passage, ford', *περάω* 'pass through', Skt., Av. *par-* 'pass through, carry across', etc., IE **per-*. Walde-P. 2.39 ff. Ernout-M. 792, 794. Hence, with extension to 'door' in VLat., NG *πόρτα* 'door', *ἐξώπορτα* 'gate', It. *porta*, Fr. *porte*, Sp. *puerta*, 'door' and 'gate'; as 'gate' Rum. *poartă*, W. *porth*, OE, Dan., Sw. *port*, MLG *porte*, Du. *poort*, OHG *pforta*, MHG, NHG *pforte*.

Lat. *ōstium* 'door, entrance' : Lat. *ōs*, Skt. *ās-* 'mouth' (4.24). Hence VLat. *ūstium*, It. *uscio*, Rum. *ușă*, OFr. *huis* 'door' (Fr. *à huis clos* 'with closed doors, secretly'). Walde-P. 1.168. Ernout-M. 716 f. REW 6117.

Lat. *iānua* 'door, entrance' : Skt. *yāna-* 'going, course', *yā-* 'go', IE **yā-* beside **ei-* 'go'. Walde-P. 1.104. Walde-H. 1.669. Ernout-M. 469 (adversely).

4. Ir. *comla* 'door, shutter', NIr. *cōmhla* partly distinguished as the 'door' itself vs. *doras* 'doorway', perh. **com-plā-*, fr. **pel-* 'fold' in OE *fealda* 'fold', Grk. *ἁπλοῦς*, Lat. *simplus* 'simple', etc. Macbain 98.

NIr. *geata* 'gate' fr. NE *gate*.

W. words for 'gate', all loanwords, *porth* fr. Lat. *porta;* *llidiart* fr. Norse, ON *hlið*, below, 5; *iet* fr. ME *yet; gat* fr. NE *gate*.

5. Goth. *haurds*, ON *hurð*, orig. a door of 'lattice work' : OE *hyrdel* (NE *hurdle*), OHG *hurt*, Lat. *crātis* 'wicker-work', Grk. *κάρταλος* 'basket', Skt. *kaṭa-* 'straw mat', *kṛt-* 'wind', etc., IE **kert-*. Walde-P. 1.421. Feist 250.

ON *hlið* 'gate' : OE *hlid*, OHG *hlit* 'cover' (NE *lid*, NHG *augenlid*), with vb. OE *hlīdan* 'cover', fr. the same root as OE *hlinian*, Grk. *κλίνω* 'lean', etc., IE **k̂lei-*. Walde-P. 1.490 f. Falk-Torp 629.

ON, Dan., Sw. *grind* 'lattice-work door or gate' : OE *grindlas* 'gratings', OHG *grinlit*, Du. *grendel* 'bolt', Lith. *grinda* 'flooring board', etc. Walde-P. 1.657. Falk-Torp 348.

OE *geat* 'gate', ME *ȝet, yet* (> W. *iet*), NE *gate* (> NIr. *geata*, W. *gat*) : ON, OS, Du. *gat* 'hole, opening' (12.85), root connection dub., but English sense clearly a specialization. NED s.v. *gate* sb.[1].

6. Lith. *vartai*, Lett. *vārti*, OPruss. *warto*, ChSl., SCr., Boh. *vrata*, Pol. *wrota*, Russ. *vorota*, all pl., general Balto-Slavic for 'gate' (but SCr. *vrata* also the usual word for 'door'; *dveri* 'doors of an altar') : Osc. *veru* (pl.), Umbr. *uerofe* (acc. pl.) 'gate', Lith. *verti* 'open or shut', ChSl. *vrěti* 'shut', Lat. *aperīre, operīre* 'open, shut' (**ap-*, **op-verīre*), Skt. *vṛ-* 'cover', Goth. *warjan*, OE *werian* 'hinder', etc., IE **wer-*. Walde-P. 1.280 ff. Walde-H. 1.56 f.

Bulg., SCr. *kapija* 'gate', fr. Turk. *kapı* 'gate'. Berneker 484.

Boh. *brána*, Pol. *brama* 'gate', orig. 'defense' as Bulg., SCr. *brana* : ChSl. *branĭ* 'war', *braniti* 'hinder, forbid', Boh. *braniti* 'hinder, defend', fr. the same root as ChSl. *brati* 'fight', Lat. *ferīre* 'strike', etc. Berneker 74.

7.23 LOCK (sb.)

Grk.	*κλεῖθρον, μοχλός, ὀχεύς*	Goth.	. . . .	Lith.	*jutrina, spyna*
NG	*κλειδαριά, κλειδωνιά*	ON	*lāss, loka*	Lett.	*atslēga*
Lat.	*claustrum, pessulus, sera*	Dan.	*laas*	ChSl.	(*zamka*)
It.	*serratura, toppa*	Sw.	*lås*	SCr.	*brava*
Fr.	*serrure*	OE	*loc, clūstor*	Boh.	*zámek*
Sp.	*cerradura, cerraja*	ME	*loke*	Pol.	*zamek*
Rum.	*broască*	NE	*lock*	Russ.	*zamok*
Ir.	*glass*	Du.	*slot*	Skt.	*tāla-, tālaka-*
NIr.	*glas*	OHG	*sloz*	Av.	. . . .
W.	*clo*	MHG	*sloz*		
Br.	*krogen-alc'houez, potaith*	NHG	*schloss*		

In the primitive method of fastening a door, still familiar in a farmer's barn or a rude cabin, the wooden bar and catch represent the 'lock', while the 'key' is the wooden peg which serves to release the bar. Or the bar may be secured by a peg driven through it, and in this case the 'key' is a kind of hook used for pulling out the peg (Grk. *βαλανάγρα*). Cf. Schrader 2.325 f. and, for the Greek and Roman mechanism, Diels, Antike-Technik[2] 45 ff. Several of the words listed under 'lock' mean simply 'bar', and the most widespread group listed under 'key' has cognates meaning 'peg', 'nail', or 'hook' and originally applied to such a primitive type of 'key'. Some forms of this latter group are used for 'lock'.

1. Grk. *μοχλός* 'bar', etym. dub., is used especially of the bar used to fasten gates. It was held in place by a *βάλανος* or wooden peg. The *βαλανάγρα* was a hook for pulling out the peg, so that the bar was released. But the Hom. term for the 'bar' is *ὀχεύς* : *ἔχω* 'hold'.

Ion. *κληΐθρον* (not in Hom.), Att. *κλῇθρον, κλεῖθρον*, deriv. of *κλῄω, κλείω* 'shut', this belonging with Grk. *κλείς* 'key', etc. (7.24).

NG *κλειδαριά*, new deriv. of *κλειδί* 'key'. Also *κλειδωνιά* fr. *κλειδώνω* 'lock'.

2. Lat. *claustrum*, most general term covering 'bar, bolt' etc., fr. *claudere* 'shut', this belonging with *clāvis* 'key' (7.24).

Lat. *pessulus*, 'bolt' for fastening doors, fr. Grk. *πάσσαλος* 'peg'. Ernout-M. 762.

Lat. *sera*, 'bar' for fastening doors : Lat. *serere* 'join', etc., or : Skt. *svaru-* 'post, stake', OE *swer* 'pillar', etc.? Hence VLat. *serra* (explanation of *rr* dub., influence of *serra* 'saw'?), whence *serrāre* 'shut, fasten' (Fr. *serrer*, etc.), and fr. this the words for 'lock', It. *serratura*, Fr. *serrure*, Sp. *cerradura, cerraja*.

Walde-P. 2.500, 528. Ernout-M. 927. REW 7867.

It. *toppa*, 'patch' and 'lock', beside *toppo* 'block', loanword fr. Gmc., MLG, NE *top*, etc. Cf. NE *top* in sense of 'cover' of a utensil, as *top* of a kettle.

Rum. *broască* 'frog' (etym.? REW 1329. Tiktin 227), applied first to a kind of hasp (from resemblance in shape; cf. NE *frog* on a garment), then to any lock.

3. Ir. *glass*, NIr. *glas* : (or fr.?) ME *clasp* 'fastening'. Pedersen 1.75.

W. *clo* : Lat. *clāvis* 'key', etc. (7.24).

Br. *krogen-alc'houez*, fr. *krogen* 'shell' and *alc'houez* 'key' (7.24), lit. 'shell of the key'. Cf. *krogen ar penn* 'shell of the head' = 'skull'.

Br. *potailh*, *potenn*, prob. a loanword fr. Fr. *poteau* 'post, stake', with semantic development through 'barrier' or 'bar' to 'lock'. Henry 226.

4. ON *lāss*, Dan. *laas*, Sw. *lås*, perh., as orig. a metal plate used as a bolt, fr. Gmc. **lamsa-* : ON *lamar* 'hinges', Lat. *lammina* 'thin metal plate', etc. Walde-P. 2.385. Falk-Torp 614. Adversely Walde-H. 1.755.

ON *loka* (*lok* 'cover, lid'), OE *loc*, ME *loke*, NE *lock* : Goth. *galūkan*, ON *lūka*, OE *lūcan* 'shut, fasten, lock' (12.25). NED s.v. *lock* sb.[2].

OE *clūstor*, fr. Lat. *claustrum* (above, 2).

Du. *slot*, OHG *sloz*, etc. beside Du. *sleutel* 'key', etc., see 7.24.

5. Lith. *jutrina* ('lock' built into doors, etc. in contrast to a 'padlock'), fr. Russ. *nutrina* 'inner part' (Senn).

Lith. *spyna* (in part esp. 'padlock') : Lett. *spīne* 'iron clamp' and 'padlock', perh. loanword fr. or cognate with Lat. *spīna* 'thorn, spine' and orig. applied to the pin fastening a hasp. Walde-P. 2.653.

Lett. *atslēga* 'lock' or 'key', see 7.24.

6. Late ChSl. *zamka*, Boh., Pol. *zamek*, Russ. *zamok* (SCr. *zamka* 'trap') : ChSl. *zamknąti*, Russ. *zamknut'* 'shut', cpd. of ChSl. *mŭknąti sę* 'move' : Lith. *mukti* 'flee', Skt. *muc-* 'release', etc. Walde-P. 2.254. Brückner 644.

SCr., Bulg. *brava*, Alb. *bravë*, orig.? Berneker 82.

7. Skt. *tāla-*, *tālaka-*, rarely 'lock, bar', *tāla-* usually 'fan-palm' : Lat. *tālea* 'rod, bar', etc. Walde-P. 1.705.

7.24 KEY

Grk.	*κλείς*	Goth.	. . . .	Lith.	*raktas*
NG	*κλειδί*	ON	*lykill*	Lett.	*slēdzeklis, slēdzamais*
Lat.	*clāvis*	Dan.	*nøgle*	ChSl.	*ključĭ*
It.	*chiave*	Sw.	*nyckel*	SCr.	*ključ*
Fr.	*clef*	OE	*cǣg*	Boh.	*klíč*
Sp.	*llave*	ME	*keie*	Pol.	*klucz*
Rum.	*cheie*	NE	*key*	Russ.	*ključ*
Ir.	*eochair*	Du.	*sleutel*	Skt.	*kuñcikā-*
NIr.	*eochair*	OHG	*sluz(z)il*	Av.	. . . .
W.	*allwedd (agoriad)*	MHG	*slüzzel*		
Br.	*alc'houez*	NHG	*schlüssel*		

1. IE **klāu-*, *klāwi-*, denoting the wooden peg which was the primitive 'key', cognate with words meaning 'peg' or 'nail' as Lat. *clāvus*, Ir. *clō*, and with verbs meaning 'hook' as Lith. *kliuti*, or 'shut' as Lat. *claudere*. Walde-P. I, 492 ff. Ernout-M. 194 f. Walde-H. 1.229 f. Falk-Torp 1070. Berneker 526, 528.

Here belong (with the meaning 'key', unless otherwise noted) Grk. **κλᾱϝίς*, -*ιδος*, Dor. *κλᾱΐς* (also *κλᾱΐξ*), Att. *κλῄς*, later *κλείς*, dim. *κλειδίον*, NG *κλειδί* (also Ion. *κλήϊθρον*, Att. *κλῇθρον*, *κλεῖθρον* the 'bar' used for fastening the door, 'lock'); Lat. *clāvis* (with *clāvus* 'nail', *claudere* 'shut') and its Romance derivs.; Ir. *clō* 'nail', W. *clo* 'lock', MBr. *clou* 'iron tool'; Gmc. words with init. *s*-(*skl-* > *sl-*), OS *slutil*, Du. *sleutel*, OHG *sluzzil*, MHG *slüzzel*, NHG *schlüssel*, also for 'lock', MLG, Du. *slot* (> ME *slot* 'bar, bolt'), OHG, MHG *sloz*, NHG *schloss*, also the verb for 'shut' MLG *slūten*, OHG *sliozan*, NHG *schliessen*, etc.; ChSl. *ključĭ*, etc., general Slavic, all dim. forms of *kljuka* (SCr. *kljuka*, Boh. *klika*, Pol. *kluka*, etc.) 'hook, crook'.

2. Ir., NIr. *eochair* : W. *agori* 'open' (whence *agoriad* 'opening', also 'key' in North W.), root-connection? Pedersen 1.123. Morris Jones 151 (cf. Loth, RC 36.173 f.).

W. *allwedd*, Corn. *alwedh*, Br. *alc'houez*, etym.? Pedersen 1.77. Morris Jones 150 ("bien invraisemblable" Loth, RC 36.173). Henry 7. Ernault, Dict. étym. s.v. *alhuez*.

3. ON *lykill*, later with dissim. *nykill*, Dan. *nøgle*, Sw. *nyckel* : Goth. *galūkan*, ON *lūka*, OE *lūcan* 'shut, fasten, lock' (as OE *loc* 'lock', 7.23). Falk-Torp 784. Hellquist 709.

OE *cǣg*, ME *keie*, NE *key*, OFris. *kei*, *kay*, etym.?

4. Lith. *raktas* : *rakti* 'dig, pick' (cf. NE *pick a lock*).

Lett. *slēdzamais*, *slēdzeklis* : *slēgt* 'shut, lock' (12.25). Here also Lett. *atslēga* 'lock' or 'key', also distinguished as *atslēgas mate* 'lock', *atslēgas berns* 'key' (lit. 'mother' or 'child' of the *atslēga*). Mühl.-Endz. 1.193, 3.927, 928.

5. Skt. *kuñcikā-* : *kuñc-* 'make crooked'.

7.25 WINDOW

Grk.	*θυρίς*	Goth.	*augadaurō*	Lith.	*langas*
NG	*παράθυρο, παραθύρι*	ON	*vindauga, gluggr*	Lett.	*luogs*
Lat.	*fenestra*	Dan.	*vindue*	ChSl.	*okno*
It.	*fenestra*	Sw.	*fönster*	SCr.	*prozor, pendžer*
Fr.	*fenêtre*	OE	*ēagduru, ēagþyrel*	Boh.	*okno*
Sp.	*ventana*	ME	*windowe, fenestre, eythurl*	Pol.	*okno*
Rum.	*fereastră (geam)*	NE	*window*	Russ.	*okno*
Ir.	*senister, fuindeōc*	Du.	*venster*	Skt.	*vātāyana-, gavākṣa-, etc.*
NIr.	*fuinneog*	OHG	*venstar, augatora*	Av.	*raočana-*
W.	*ffenestr*	MHG	*venster*		
Br.	*prenest(r)*	NHG	*fenster*		

In contrast to the door, which belongs to the most primitive house, the window is a later development, a very early one in the Mediterranean region, even with panes of glass or similar transparent material, but long unknown in northern Europe, and in parts of Scandinavia not earlier than the 16th century. Cf. Ebert, Reallex. and Schrader, Reallex. s.v. *Fenster*. With the spread of the Roman type of window, the Lat. *fenestra* was widely adopted, while in other cases the native word persisted. Cf., for example, Dan. *vindue*, but Sw. *fönster* (dial. *vindoga* used of the small window for throwing out dung), or ME *fenestre* beside *windowe*, with eventual victory of the latter, itself a loanword from Norse.

Words for 'window' are connected with those for 'door', 'light', 'wind', and 'eye'.

1. Grk. *θυρίς* dim. of *θύρα* 'door' (7.22). Cf. Port. *janella* fr. dim. of Lat. *iānua* 'door'.

NG *παράθυρο*, *παραθύρι*, fr. class. Grk. *παράθυρος* 'side door'.

2. Lat. *fenestra*, orig. dub., perh. loanword for Etruscan. Ernout-M. 344 f. Walde-H. 1.478.

Hence It. *fenestra*, OFr. *fenestre* (> ME *fenestre;* Br. *prenest(r)*, influenced by *prenna* 'shut', Henry s.v.), Fr. *fenêtre*, OSp. *piniestra*, Rum. *fereastră;* Ir. *senister*, W. *ffenestr;* Sw. *fönster*, OHG *venstar*, NHG *fenster*. REW 3242. Pedersen 1.221.

Sp. *ventana*, deriv. of Lat. *ventus* 'wind'. REW 9212. Cf. the uses of NE *vent*.

Rum. *geam* properly 'pane of glass', but also used for 'window', fr. Turk. (orig. Pers.) *cam* 'glass'. Cf. NG *τζάμι* 'window pane'. Lokotsch 650.

3. Celtic words fr. Lat. *fenestra*, above, 2, or from ON *vindauga*, below, 4.

4. Goth. *augadaurō*, OE *ēagduru*, OHG *augatora*, lit. 'eye-door', cpd. of words for 'eye' and 'door'.

OE *ēagþyrel*, ME *eythurl*, lit. 'eye-hole', cpd. of *þyrel* 'hole', ME *thurl* also used alone for 'window'.

ON *vindauga* (> ME *windowe*, NE *window;* Ir. *fuindeōc*, NIr. *fuinneog*, Marstrander, Bidrag 90), Dan. *vindue*, lit. 'wind-eye', cpd. of the words for 'wind' and 'eye'. Falk-Torp 1383.

ON *gluggr* (Sw. *glugg* 'hole, opening'), fr. Gmc. **glū-* beside *glō-* in ON *glōa*, OE *glōwan* 'glow', hence orig. 'opening for light' (cf. ON *ljōre* 'opening in the roof' : *ljōs* 'light'). Walde-P. 1.627. Hellquist 288.

5. Lith. *langas*, Lett. *luogs*, OPruss. *lanxto*, etym.? Possibly orig. a swinging window and so : Lith. *linguoti* 'swing back and forth' (Leskien, Ablaut 334 with?).

Late ChSl. *okno*, etc., general Slavic (but SCr. *okno* 'window pane') : ChSl. *oko*, Lith. *akis* 'eye', etc. Walde-P. 1.171. Brückner 377.

SCr. *prozor*, fr. *pro-zirati* 'look through'.

SCr. *pendžer*, fr. Turk. *pencere* 'window'. Lokotsch 1648.

6. Skt. *vātāyana-*, lit. 'wind-passage', cpd. of *vāta-* 'wind' and *ayana-* 'going, course'.

Skt. *gavākṣa-*, lit. 'ox-eye' (cf. NE *bull's-eye*), cpd. of *gava-* 'ox' and *akṣa-* 'eye'. Also *gṛhākṣa-* (rare) lit. 'house-eye'.

Skt. *jāla-* 'net', also 'lattice-work window'.

Av. *raočana-* (NPers. *rōzan*) : Skt. *rocana-* 'bright', *locana-* 'eye', etc. Barth. 1489.

7.26 FLOOR

Grk.	*ἔδαφος, δάπεδον (οὖδας)*	Goth.	. . . .	Lith.	*asla*
NG	*πάτωμα*	ON	*golf*	Lett.	*grīda*
Lat.	*pavīmentum, solum*	Dan.	*gulv*	ChSl.	*(podŭ)*
It.	*pavimento*	Sw.	*golv*	SCr.	*pod, patos*
Fr.	*plancher*	OE	*flōr*	Boh.	*podlaha*
Sp.	*suelo*	ME	*flore*	Pol.	*podloga*
Rum.	*pardoseală, duşumea*	NE	*floor*	Russ.	*pol*
Ir.	*lār*	Du.	*vloer*	Skt.	*bhūmi-*
NIr.	*urlār*	OHG	*dilla, astrīh, arin*	Av.	. . . .
W.	*llawr*	MHG	*dille, esterīch, ern*		
Br.	*leur*	NHG	*(fuss)boden (diele, estrich)*		

Words for 'floor' are mostly from general notions like 'bottom, ground', 'flat surface', but some reflect a particular material, especially 'board', or form of construction.

1. Grk. *ἔδαφος* 'bottom, ground', and 'floor' (Hdt.+, Att. and Delian inscriptions), also poet. *οὖδας* 'surface of the earth', 'ground', and 'floor' (as Hom. Od. 23.46), both words prob. cognate, but root connection dub. Walde-P. 1.254. Boisacq 215, 726.

Grk. *δάπεδον* 'ground, plain' and 'floor' (prose use for 'floor' attested in IG 4.823, 43, 45 and 952.44), cpd. of *δα-*, fr. **dm̥-* : *δόμος* 'house', etc. and *πέδον* 'ground'. Walde-P. 1.787.

Grk. *πάτος* 'path', Byz. (with new meaning fr. *πατῶ* 'tread') 'floor' (> SCr. *patos* 'floor'), NG 'bottom'. Hence also, or better fr. the verb *πατῶ* 'tread', after the analogy of other derivs. in -*ωμα*, Byz., NG *πάτωμα* 'floor'.

2. Lat. *pavīmentum*, the normal technical word for the Roman 'floor', fr. *pavīre* 'beat, tread down' : Lith. *piauti* 'cut', etc. Hence It. *pavimento* 'floor', while other Romance derivs. mean 'pavement' or Rum. *pămînt* 'earth' (1.21). Walde-P. 2.12. Ernout-M. 743. REW 6312.

Lat. *solum* 'bottom, ground, soil' (1.212), also 'floor'. Hence Sp. *suelo*, reg. word for 'floor'. REW 8079.

Fr. *plancher*, fr. *planche* 'board, plank'. REW 6455.

Rum. *pardoseală*, deriv. of (?Byz. *πάτος* 'floor', influenced by) *pardos* 'leopard', orig. a 'mosaic floor' fr. its resemblance to a leopard's skin. Tiktin 1122.

Rum. *duşumea*, fr. Turk. *döşeme* 'floor' and 'furniture'. Tiktin 590. Lokotsch 534.

3. Ir. *lār*, NIr. *urlār*, W. *llawr*, Br. *leur;* OE *flōr*, ME *flore*, NE *floor*, Du. *vloer* (ON *flōrr* only 'floor' of a stall; MHG *vluor*, NHG *flur* 'field, plain' and 'vestibule'); all orig. 'flat surface', fr. the same root as Lat. *plānus* 'flat', etc. Walde-P. 2.61 f.

4. ON *golf*, Dan. *gulv*, Sw. *golv*, in ON also 'an apartment', etym.? Falk-Torp 361. Hellquist 293.

OE *flōr*, etc., above, 3.

OHG *dil*, *dilla*, MHG *dil*, *dille*, NHG *diele* 'board' and 'wooden floor' : OPruss. *talus* 'floor', ChSl. *tĭlo* 'bottom, ground', Skt. *tala-* 'surface', etc. Walde-P. 1.740. Weigand-H. 1.354.

OHG *astrīh*, MHG *esterīch*, NHG *estrich* 'stone floor' or 'cement floor', fr. MLat. *astracum* 'floor', this fr. Grk. *ὄστρακον* 'potsherd'. Kluge-G. 140. REW 6118.

NHG *boden* 'bottom, ground' (12.34), commonly used for 'floor' where the context or situation makes this sense clear, or more specifically *fussboden*.

OHG *arin*, MHG *ern*, fr. Lat. *arēna*. Walde-P. 1.79.

For the distribution of NHG (*fuss*)-*boden* and *diele*, cf. Kretschmer, Wortgeogr. 174 f.

5. Lith. *asla*, etym.? (connection with L. *ārea* or OHG *astrīh*, BB 16.207, unlikely).

Lett. *grīda* : Lith. *grinda* 'board', pl. *grindos* 'flooring, wooden floor', SCr. *greda* 'beam', ON *grind* 'lattice work', etc. Walde-P. 1.657. Berneker 348 f.

6. SCr. *pod* : ChSl. *podŭ* 'bottom, floor' (rare), Russ. *pod* 'bottom', Lith. *padas* 'sole of the foot', Grk. *πέδον* 'ground', etc. Walde-P. 2.24.

SCr. *patos*, fr. Byz. *πάτος* 'floor' (above, 1).

Boh. *podlaha*, Pol. *podloga*, cpd. of *po-* and **dolga* in Boh. *dlaha* 'splint, board', *dlažiti* 'pave', Pol. *dłażić* 'press, trample' : OE *telga* 'branch', Ir. *dluigim* 'split', etc. fr. an extension of IE **del-* 'split'. Berneker 207.

Russ. *pol* : ChSl. *polica* 'board, shelf', Boh. *police*, Russ. *polka* 'shelf', etc. (widespread Slavic group), Skt. *phalaka-* 'board, plank', ON *fjǫl* 'thin board', Grk. σφέλας 'footstool, pedestal', Skt. *phal-* 'burst, split', OHG *spaltan* 'split', etc. Walde-P. 2.677 ff. Brückner 429.

7. Skt. *bhūmi-* 'earth, ground' (1.21), also used for 'floor'. Other more specific words?

7.27 WALL (Of a Town; Partition Wall)

Grk.	*τεῖχος; τοῖχος, τειχίον*	Goth.	*-waddjus*	Lith.	*mūras; siena*
NG	*τοῖχος*	ON	*mūrr; veggr*	Lett.	*mūris; siena*
Lat.	*mūrus, moenia* (pl.); *pariēs*	Dan.	*mur; væg*	ChSl.	*zidŭ, stěna*
It.	*muro; parete*	Sw.	*mur; vägg*	SCr.	*zid, stijena*
Fr.	*mur, muraille*	OE	*weall; wāg*	Boh.	*zed'; stěna*
Sp.	*muro; pared*	ME	*wall (waw)*	Pol.	*mur; ściana*
Rum.	*zid; părete*	NE	*wall*	Russ.	*stena*
Ir.	*mūr; fraig*	Du.	*muur; wand*	Skt.	*dehī-, prākāra-; kuḍya-*
NIr.	*mūr; falla (fraigh)*	OHG	*mūra; want*	Av.	*uzdaēzi-*
W.	*mur, gwal, magwyr; pared*	MHG	*mūr(e); want*		
Br.	*moger*	NHG	*mauer; wand*		

While the notion of the outer 'wall' of a town, fortress, etc. does not properly belong in this chapter, it must be considered in connection with the partition 'wall' of a house, which may be expressed by the same word, as in NE *wall*.

Where there is a distinctive word for the partition 'wall', like NHG *wand*, this is separated in the table by a preceding semicolon. But even in several of these cases, the distinction is not rigorous, and the word preceding the semicolon may also be used for the partition wall, e.g. OE *weall*, which glosses both Lat. *mūrus* and Lat. *pariēs*. For the outside wall of a house there is the greatest fluctuation, e.g. Lat. *pariēs*, less commonly *mūrus*, but It. *muro*, not *parete*.

Most of the words for 'wall' reflect in their origin some special type of construction.

1. Grk. τεῖχος (σ- stem), τοῖχος (ο-stem; both forms and uses merged in NG τοῖχος) : Osc. acc. pl. *feíhúss* 'walls', Skt. (Ved.) *dehī-* 'wall, mound', OPers. *didā-* 'fortress', Av. *uzdaēzi-* 'wall', Toch. A *tseke* 'piece of sculpture', fr. IE **dheiĝh-* in Skt. *dih-* 'smear', Lat. *fingere* 'mold', etc. (9.72). Here also prob., with metathesis, ChSl. *zĭdati* 'build', *zidŭ*, *zĭdŭ* 'wall', SCr. *zid* (> Rum. *zid*), Boh. *zed'*, etc. (also OPruss. *seydis* 'wall'). Walde-P. 1.833 ff. Walde-H. 1.501 f.

2. Lat. *mūrus* (early *moerus*) and *moenia* (pl.) : Skt. *mi-* 'fix, build', etc. Walde-P. 2.239 f. Ernout-M. 624 f., 645 (without etym.).

From Lat. *mūrus* come It., Sp. *muro*, Fr. *mur*, *muraille;* Ir. *mūr*, W. *mur;* ON *mūrr*, Dan., Sw. *mur;* OE *mūr* (rare), MLG *mūre* (> Lith. *mūras*, Lett. *mūris*, Pol. *mur*), Du. *muur*, OHG *mūra*, MHG *mūr(e)*, NHG *mauer*.

Lat. *pariēs*, etym. dub., perh. : Lith. *tvora* 'fence', vb. *tverti* 'grasp, form', etc.; or : ChSl. *podŭ-pora* 'a prop', *za-prěti* 'shut', OHG *sparro* 'beam', etc., and so orig. the supporting struts of a wall. Walde-P. 1.750 f., 2.655 f. Ernout-M. 734.

Hence It. *parete* (Fr. *paroi* not common; generally *mur*), Sp. *pared*, Rum. *părete*, W. *pared*.

3. Ir. *fraig* (NIr. *fraigh* 'panel, side wall', etc.) : Skt. *vṛjana-* 'enclosure', Grk. ἔργω, Att. εἴργω 'shut in or out', etc. Walde-P. 1.290. Pedersen 1.97.

NIr. *falla* or *balla*, W. *gwal*, fr. NE *wall*. Pedersen 1.214.

W. *magwyr*, Br. *moger*, fr. Lat. *māceria* 'garden wall'. Pedersen 1.199. Loth, Mots lat. 183 f.

4. Goth. *-waddjus* (*grunduwaddjus* 'foundation', *baurgswaddjus* 'town wall'), ON *veggr*, Dan. *væg*, Sw. *vägg*, OE *wāg*, ME *waw*, fr. IE **wei-*, *wei-k-* in Skt. *vi-* 'weave', Lat. *viēre* 'twist, plait, weave', *vincīre* 'bind', Lith. *vyti* 'twist, wind', etc. So orig. a wall made of wattle-work. Walde-P. 1.224. Falk-Torp. 1400. Feist 538 f.

OE *weall*, ME, NE *wall*, OFris., OS, MLG *wal* (> Du. *wal*, Sw. *vall*, NHG *wall* 'rampart, embankment'), fr. Lat. *vallum* 'wall of palisades', coll. of *vallus* 'stake, palisade' : Goth. *walus* 'staff', Grk. ἧλος 'nail', etc. Walde-P. 1.301. NED s.v. *wall*, sb.[1].

OHG, MHG *want*, NHG, Du. *wand* : Goth. *wandus*, Dan. *vaand* 'rod' (ME, NE *wand* fr. Norse), fr. the root of Goth., OE *windan* 'turn, wind, plait'. So orig. a wall of wattle-work, like ON *veggr*, etc., above. Falk-Torp 1339, 1382. Walde-P. 1.261.

5. Lith., Lett. *siena* : Lith. *sieti*, Lett. *siet* 'bind', Skt. *sā-*, *si-* 'bind', etc. Walde-P. 2.463 ff.

6. ChSl. *zidŭ*, etc., above, 1.

ChSl. *stěna*, etc., general Slavic : Goth. *stains* 'stone', etc. Walde-P. 2.611. Trautmann 281. Otherwise Brückner 529.

7. Skt. *dehī-*, Av. *uzdaēzi-*, above, 1.

Skt. *prākāra-*, cpd. of *pra-* 'in front' and *ākāra-* 'form, shape', fr. *ā-kṛ-* 'make'.

Skt. *kuḍya-*, etym.? Uhlenbeck 57.

7.28 ROOF

Grk.	*(σ)τέγος, στέγη, ὀροφή*	Goth.	*hrōt*	Lith.	*stogas*
NG	*στέγη, σκεπή*	ON	*þak (hrōt)*	Lett.	*jumts*
Lat.	*tēctum*	Dan.	*tag*	ChSl.	*krovŭ, strěcha*
It.	*tetto*	Sw.	*tak*	SCr.	*krov*
Fr.	*toit*	OE	*þæc, hrōf*	Boh.	*střecha, krov*
Sp.	*techo, techado*	ME	*rofe*	Pol.	*dach, strzecha*
Rum.	*acoperiș*	NE	*roof*	Russ.	*kryša*
Ir.	*(tuige)*	Du.	*dak*	Skt.	*chadis-*
NIr.	*ceann*	OHG	*dah*	Av.	. . . .
W.	*to*	MHG	*dach*		
Br.	*to*	NHG	*dach*		

Most of the words for 'roof' are from verbs meaning 'cover' (12.26). But a few reflect a special material or type of structure, and conversely a general word for 'roof' may become restricted to a special type, as NE *thatch*.

1. From IE **(s)teg-* 'cover', in Skt. *sthag-*, Grk. στέγω, Lat. *tegere*, etc. Walde-P. 2.620 f. Ernout-M. 1020. Pedersen 1.97.

Grk. στέγος, τέγος, στέγη; Lat. *tēctum* (> It. *tetto*, Fr. *toit*, Sp. *techo*, *techado*); Ir. *tuige* 'straw, thatch' and prob. used for the 'thatched roof', W. *to*, Br. *to;* ON *þak*, Dan. *tag*, Sw. *tak*, OE *þæc* (NE *thatch*), Du. *dak*, OHG *dah*, MHG, NHG *dach* (> Pol. *dach*); Lith. *stogas*, OPruss. *stogis*.

2. Grk. ὀροφή (so, not στέγη, in Hom. and early Att. inscriptions IG 1².373 and 374; cf. also at Epidaurus ὀροφά IG 4².1.106.46, 106. II. 136 f., vs. στέγα ib. 102.293) : ἐρέφω, ἐρέπτω 'cover with a

roof', OHG *hirni-reba* 'skull', OHG *rippa*, OE *ribb* 'rib', etc. Walde-P. 2.371.

NG σκεπή (or σκέπη) 'cover, shelter', also used for 'roof'.

3. Rum. *acoperiș*, fr. *acoperi* 'cover', Lat. *cooperīre* 'cover'.

4. NIr. *ceann* 'head' (4.20), 'top' and 'roof'.

5. Goth. *hrōt*, ON poet. *hrōt* : OE, OS *hrōst* 'framework of the roof', NE *roost* (in Sc. 'inner roof of a cottage', cf. NED s.v., 3), MHG *rāz* 'funeral pile', ChSl. *krada* 'funeral pile', root connection? Walde-P. 1.485 f. Feist 270 f.

OE *hrōf*, ME *rofe*, NE *roof* : ON *hrōf* 'boat-shed', MLG *rōf*, Du. *roef* 'deck-house', further connections (MIr. *crō* 'stall, hovel', etc., Pedersen 1.92) dub. Walde-P. 1.477. Falk-Torp 917.

6. Lett. *jumts*, fr. *jumt* 'cover', root connection? Mühl.-Endz. 2.119.

ChSl. *krovŭ*, SCr., Boh. *krov*, Russ. *kryša* : ChSl. *kryti* 'cover, hide'. Berneker 632.

ChSl. *strěcha* (Supr.), Boh. *střecha*, Pol. *strzecha* (SCr. *streha* 'gutter') : ChSl. *strojiti* 'prepare', Russ. *stroit'* 'build', etc. (9.44). Brückner 522.

7. Skt. *chadis-*, fr. *chad-* 'cover'.

7.31 FIREPLACE (Hearth)

Grk.	*ἑστία, ἐσχάρα*	Goth.	. . . .	Lith.	*ugniavietė, židinys*
NG	*ἑστία* (lit.), *γωνιά, τζάκι*	ON	*arinn*	Lett.	*pavards, ugunskurs*
Lat.	*focus (camīnus)*	Dan.	*arne, ildsted*	ChSl.	*ognište*
It.	*focolare*	Sw.	*eldstad*	SCr.	*ognjište*
Fr.	*foyer, âtre*	OE	*heorþ*	Boh.	*ohniště, ohnisko*
Sp.	*hogar, chimenea*	ME	*herth, chimney*	Pol.	*ognisko*
Rum.	*vatră, cămin*	NE	*fireplace (hearth)*	Russ.	*kamin*
Ir.	*tenlach, tellach*	Du.	*haard*	Skt.	*(agnikuṇḍa-)*
NIr.	*teallach*	OHG	*herd*	Av.	. . . .
W.	*aelwyd*	MHG	*hert, kamīn, viurstat*		
Br.	*oaled*	NHG	*feuerstätte, kamin, herd*		

Words of this group are traditionally rendered by 'hearth', but mostly cover what in present NE usage is the *fireplace*, of which the *hearth* is only the floor with its extension in front.

The majority are from notions like 'fire', 'burn', 'shine', 'heat'; a few from 'corner', 'pavement', etc.

Many of them are also used symbolically for the family dwelling house, the 'home' (cf. NE *fight for their firesides*), as very commonly Grk. ἑστία (cf. ὁμέστιος 'of the same household'), Rum. *cămin*, NHG *herd*, etc.

1. Grk. ἑστία, dial. ἱστία : Lat. *Vesta*, both prob. fr. IE **wes-* in Skt. *vas-* 'shine', *uṣas-* 'dawn', etc. rather than fr. IE **wes-* in Skt. *vas-* 'dwell', etc. Walde-P. 1.307. Buck, IF 25.259. Boisacq 289 f., 1110.

Grk. ἐσχάρα, in Homer 'fireplace', later 'brazier, grate, altar', etym. dub. Boisacq 290.

NG γωνιά 'corner' (12.76) also common for 'fireplace'. But also τζάκι, fr. Turk. *ocak*.

2. Lat. *focus* : Arm. *boç* 'flame'? Walde-P. 2.186 ff. Ernout-M. 373. Walde-H. 1.521. VLat. *focus* was 'fire' replacing *ignis* (1.81), and 'fireplace' was expressed by derivs., whence It. *focolare*, Fr. *foyer*, Sp. *hogar*. REW 3398, 3400.

Lat. *camīnus*, covering the whole apparatus, consisting of fireplace and chimney, used in smelting, baking, and

also for heating a room (cf. Daremberg et Saglio, s.v.), fr. Grk. κάμῑνος 'furnace, kiln', this prob. fr. the same root as Grk. καμάρα 'vault', etc. Walde-P. 1.349. Walde-H. 1.147, 149.

Hence, besides words for 'stove' (7.32) and 'chimney' (7.33), for 'fireplace' Rum. *cămin*, MHG, NHG *kamin* (also 'fireplace mantle' and 'chimney', with local-variation in use), Russ. *kamin;* and, through a deriv. VLat. *camīnāta*, OFr. *cheminée* (> ME *chimney* also 'fireplace', cf. NED), Sp. *chimenea*. REW 1548–49. Falk-Torp 489. Berneker 553.

Fr. *âtre*, OFr. *astre*, fr. MLat. *astracum* 'floor' (7.26). REW 6118.

Rum. *vatră*, loanword fr. Slavic *vatra* 'fireplace, fire' (1.81).

3. Ir. *tenlach*, *tellach*, NIr. *teallach*, deriv. of Ir. *tene* 'fire' (1.81), with suffix *-lach* 'place of' (fr. IE **legh-* 'lie'). Loth, MSL 18.352.

W. *aelwyd*, OCorn. *oilet*, Br. *oaled*, fr. OE *ǣled* 'fire' (1.81). Walde-P. 1.5. Parry-Williams 34.

4. ON *arinn*, Dan. *arne* : Lat. *āra*, Osc.-Umbr. *āsā-* 'altar' (orig. 'fire-altar'), *ārēre* 'be dry', Grk. ἄζω 'dry up', Goth. *azgō* 'ashes', etc., IE **ăs-*. Reichelt, KZ. 46.315. Falk-Torp 33.

Dan. *ildsted*, Sw. *eldstad*, lit. 'fireplace', cpds. of *ild*, *eld* 'fire' (1.81).

OE *heorþ*, ME *herth*, NE *hearth*, Du. *haard*, OHG *herd* (also 'floor, ground'), MHG *hert*, NHG *herd* : Goth. *hauri* 'coal', ON *hyrr* 'fire', Lith. *kurti* 'heat', etc., IE **ker-*. Walde-P. 1.418. Feist 250.

NE *fireplace* (1702+, NED), now the common term, *hearth* being used only in a more restricted sense (above).

MHG *viurstat*, NHG *feuerstätte*, in origin and use like NE *fireplace*.

5. Lith. *ugniavietė*, cpd. of *ugnis* 'fire' and *vieta* 'place' (12.12).

Lith. *ugniakuras* (Lalis), Lett. *ugunskurs*, cpds. of Lith. *ugnis*, Lett. *uguns* 'fire' and the root of Lith. *kurti*, Lett. *kurt* 'heat', OE *heorþ*, etc. (above, 4).

Lith. *židinys*, fr. the root of *žiesti* 'construct, build', ChSl. *zĭdati* 'build', etc. (9.44).

Lett. *pavards*, etym.?

6. ChSl. *ognište*, etc., general Slavic, fr. *ognĭ* 'fire' (1.81). But Russ. *ognišče* now obs. and replaced by *kamin* (above, 2). Russ. *očag* 'hearth' in symbolic sense, fr. Turk. *ocak* 'fireplace'.

7. Skt. *agnikuṇḍa-*, cpd. of *agni-* 'fire' and *kuṇḍa-* 'pot, vessel for coals', is used of a receptacle for the sacred fire, but there is no word for a household fireplace.

7.32 STOVE

Grk.	*(ἰπνός, θερμάστρα)*	Goth.	. . . .	Lith.	*kakalys, krosnis, pečius*
NG	*θερμάστρα* (lit.), *σόμπα*	ON	*(ofn)*	Lett.	*krāsns*
Lat.	*(furnus, fornāx, camīnus)*	Dan.	*kakkelovn*	ChSl.	. . . .
It.	*stufa*	Sw.	*ugn, kamin*	SCr.	*peć*
Fr.	*poêle (fourneau)*	OE	*(ofen)*	Boh.	*kamna*
Sp.	*estufa, hornillo*	ME	*(oven)*	Pol.	*piec*
Rum.	*sobă*	NE	*stove*	Russ.	*peč'*
Ir.	*(sornn)*	Du.	*kachel*	Skt.	*(açmanta-, culli-)*
NIr.	*stōv*	OHG	*(ovan)*	Av.	. . . .
W.	*stof*	MHG	*oven*		
Br.	*fornigell*	NHG	*ofen*		

Much later than the 'fireplace, hearth' (7.31), which, succeeding the fire in the open, dates from the primitive house, and the 'oven' for cooking (5.25), is the heating by a 'brazier' of live coals or by a closed apparatus which became the modern 'stove'. This developed in southern Europe primarily for heating the bath. The Greek and Latin words and others listed from an early period (as the Ir., ON, OE, and OHG words) are generally rendered by 'furnace'. Most of these and many of the modern words for 'stove' are the same as those for 'oven'.

1. Words already discussed under 'oven' (5.25). Grk. ἰπνός, Lat. furnus (> Ir. sornn, NIr. sorn; dim. Sp. hornillo, Fr. fourneau, Br. fornigell), ON ofn, Sw. ugn, OE ofen, OHG ovan, NHG ofen, SCr. peć, Pol. piec, Russ. peč' (> Lith. pečius).

2. MLat. stufa (stuba, stupa), It. stufa, Fr. étuve, Sp. estufa, used for 'hot bath, hothouse', etc. and finally (It., Sp.) for 'stove', OE stofa 'hot bath', OHG stuba 'bathroom, heated room', MLG stove (> ME stove 'hot-air bath, sweating-room', also 'heated sitting-room or bedroom'; NE stove in present sense since about 1600; > NIr. stōv, W. stof, etc.) The continental Gmc. forms developed in the direction of 'room' and spread to Balto-Slavic mostly in this sense (cf. 7.21). But the development to 'stove', as in NE and Romance, shows itself in some of the Balkan derivs., namely (in form through Hung. szoba, now only 'room') Turk., Bulg. soba, Rum. sobǎ, NG σόμπα (soba). Stender-Petersen 249.

The ultimate origin of this group (and

even its unity, though this seems obvious) is much disputed, but it prob. rests on a back-formation fr. VLat. *extūfāre (It. stufare, OFr. estuver, NE stew, etc.), this fr. *tūfus, Grk. τῦφος 'vapor'. Cf. REW 3108 (with separation of the Gmc. words), and other references given in 7.21.

3. Grk. θερμάστρα 'furnace' (Callim., Euphor.), lit. 'heater', fr. θερμαίνω 'heat' fr. θερμός 'hot' (15.85). Hence NG θερμάστρα 'stove', mostly in the literary language, the common word being σόμπα (above, 2).

4. Lat. camīnus 'forge', etc., also used for heating a room (7.31). Hence, besides words for 'fireplace' (7.31) or 'chimney' (7.33), also some for 'stove', as It. camino mostly 'cookstove', Sw. kamin 'iron stove', Boh. kamna 'stove'.

Fr. poêle, formerly 'heated room', fr. Lat. (balneae) pēnsilēs, lit. 'hanging-bath', used of a bathroom with the floor heated from underneath. REW 6392. Gamillscheg 704.

5. Dan. kakkelovn, now any 'stove', orig. 'stove of tile', like Sw. kakelugn, MLG, MHG kacheloven, NHG kachelofen, cpd. of Dan. kakkel, Sw. kakel, MLG kachel 'glazed tile' (> Du. kachel 'stove', Lith. kakalys 'stove'), fr. OHG kachala 'earthen pot', further orig. dub. Falk-Torp 484. Meringer, Wört. u. Sach. 3.156 ff.

6. Lith. krosnis, Lett. krāsns, orig. 'stove made of stones', 'heap of stones', prob. : Lett. krāt 'collect': Buga, Kalba ir Senovė 178. Mühl.-Endz. 2.268.

7. Skt. açmanta-, fr. açman- 'stone', and Skt. culli-, etym. unknown, are both rare, but rendered by 'ofen' in BR.

7.33 CHIMNEY

Grk.	καπνοδόκη, κάπνη	ON	reykberi, -hāfr, skorsteinn	Lith.	kaminas
NG	καπνοδόχη (lit.), καμινάδα, φουγάρο	Dan.	skorsten	Lett.	skurstenis
Lat.	(camīnus)	Sw.	skorsten	SCr.	dimnjak (odžak)
It.	camino	ME	chimney	Boh.	komin
Fr.	cheminée	NE	chimney	Pol.	komin
Sp.	chimenea	Du.	schoorsteen	Russ.	truba
Rum.	cos	OHG	scor(en)stein		
NIr.	simnē	MHG	schor(n)stein		
W.	simdde, simnai	NHG	schornstein (kamin, rauchfang)		
Br.	siminal				

The 'chimney' is no part of the primitive house, from which the smoke escaped by the door or an opening in the roof, and is relatively late in northern Europe. But it was known in ancient Greece and Rome, as attested by literary references, vase paintings, and actual remains. Cf. Daremberg et Saglio 1.860 ff.

The words are partly compounds or derivatives of those for 'smoke' (1.83), but come also from words for 'fireplace with chimney', or for 'pipe', 'basket', 'prop-stone'.

1. Grk. καπνοδόκη (later -δόχη), lit. 'smoke-receptacle', cpd. of καπνός 'smoke' and δέκομαι (δέχομαι) 'receive'. Hence the abbreviated κάπνη in the comic poets.

NG φουγάρο, fr. It. dial. fogaro, fugaro, deriv. of fogo = fuoco 'fire'. G. Meyer, Neugr. Stud. 4.97.

NG καμινάδα, see below, 2.

2. Lat. camīnus (7.31) included the 'chimney', but is not quotable as applied to the 'chimney' only. Its derivs. are used for 'fireplace' (7.31), 'stove' (7.32), and 'chimney'. So as 'chimney' It. camino, MHG, NHG kamin (> Boh., Pol. komin > Lith. kaminas); through VLat. camīnāta 'room with heating apparatus', NG καμινάδα, Fr. cheminée (> ME, NE chimney > NIr. simnē,

W. simdde, simnai; Br. siminal fr. Fr.), Sp. chimenea. REW 1548. Gamillscheg 215.

Rum. cos, orig. 'basket', loanword fr. Slavic, ChSl. košĭ 'basket', etc. Berneker 586. Tiktin s.v.

3. ON reykberi, reykhāfr, cpds. of reykr 'smoke' and bera 'carry', hafa 'hold'. Cf. NHG rauchfang. Both words rare, usually ljóri 'opening in the roof' : ljós 'light' (Falk-Torp 650).

MLG scor(en)stein, scorstēn (> late ON skorsteinn, Dan., Sw. skorsten, Lett. skurstenis), Du. schoorsteen, MHG schor(n)stein, NHG schornstein (> Lith. šiurkštainis in Pruss. Lith.), orig. the 'propstone' upon which the chimney rested, first part of the cpd. : ON skorða, MLG, ME schore 'prop' (NE shore in a shipyard): Falk-Torp 1019. Weigand-H. 2.781.

NHG rauchfang, lit. 'smoke-catcher', is the usual word for 'chimney' in Austria. For the local distribution of NHG schornstein, kamin, rauchfang (also esse, schlot), cf. Kretschmer, Wortgeogr. 436 ff.

4. Lith. kaminas, Boh., Pol. komin, above, 2.

Lith. dūmalaidė, dūmatakis (NSB, but book words only?), cpds. of dūmas 'smoke' with -laidė : leidžu, leisti 'let' and -takis : teku, tekéti 'run'.

SCr. dimnjak, deriv. of dim 'smoke'.

SCr. odžak, common in eastern area, from Turk. ocak 'fireplace, chimney'. Lokotsch 1587.

Russ. dymovaja truba 'smoke-pipe' or commonly truba 'pipe, trumpet' used alone for 'chimney' : ChSl. trǫba 'pipe,

trumpet', loanword fr. OHG trumba 'trumpet' (It. tromba, etc., REW 8952).

5. Skt. dhūmanirgama- (rare and no evidence of an actual chimney) lit. 'smoke-outlet', cpd. of dhūma- 'smoke' and nirgama- 'outgoing'.

7.41 FURNITURE

Grk.	ἔπιπλα	Goth.	....	Lith.	baldai, rakandai
NG	ἔπιπλα	ON	hūsbūnaðr, -būningr	Lett.	istabas lietas, mebele
Lat.	supellex	Dan.	møbler, husgeraad	ChSl.	....
It.	mobili, supellettile	Sw.	möbler, husgerǎd	SCr.	namještaj, pokućstvo
Fr.	meubles	OE	īdisc, inorf	Boh.	nabytek
Sp.	muebles	ME	(houshold, mobles)	Pol.	mebel, sprzęt
Rum.	mobile	NE	furniture	Russ.	mebel, obstanovka
Ir.	intreb, fointreb	Du.	meubelen, huisraad	Skt.	(upakaranāni)
NIr.	troscǎn	OHG	(giziugali, giziawi)	Av.	....
W.	dodrefn	MHG	hūsrāt, hūsgeræte		
Br.	annez, arrebeuri	NHG	möbel, hausgerat		

'Furniture' is understood here in the now prevailing sense of NE furniture (NED s.v., 7), that is as 'house furniture'. Some of the words are connected with those for 'house, dwelling'. But the majority had originally, and some still have, a wider scope, covering all sorts of movable property, equipment, utensils, etc.

The words are partly plural, partly singular forms used collectively.

1. Grk. ἔπιπλα (also 'utensils, fittings', but usually not so general as σκεύη) : ἐπιπολή 'surface' : ἐπιπόλαιος 'on the surface' (cf. Cret. ἐπιπόλαια χρήματα = ἔπιπλα), ἐπιπέλομαι 'come upon', etc., IE *kʷel-. Walde-P. 1.514 f.

2. Lat. supellex, gen. -lectilis (> It. supellettile), prob. fr. *super-lecti-(li-) 'what lies or is laid over' : lectus 'bed', Goth. ligan 'lie', etc. Ernout-M. 1004 (with doubt).

It. mobili, Fr. meubles (sg. meuble > Dan. møbel, Sw. möbel, Du. meubel 'piece of furniture', pl. 'furniture', NHG coll. möbel, Lett. mebele, Pol. mebel, Russ. mebel'), Sp. muebles, Rum. mobile,

plurals of It. mobile, Fr. meuble, etc. 'piece of furniture', fr. Lat. mōbile 'movable' (cf. mōbilia 'movable goods, chattels', deriv. of movēre 'move'.

3. Ir. intreb, fointreb, (NIr. intreabh 'property, wealth', cpds. of ind- 'in', fo- 'under', and treb 'dwelling' (7.11).

NIr. troscǎn 'implements, baggage, clothes' (Gael. trusgan 'clothes') and 'furniture' (or more specifically troscǎn tighe 'furniture of the house'), loanword fr. ME trusse 'bundle, baggage', with added suffix. Macbain 378.

W. dodrefn, MW deodreven, cpd. of dy-to' (often intensive), go 'sub', and trefn 'arrangement, order, system'.

Br. annez fr. MBr. anhez 'dwelling', back-formation fr. anhezaff 'establish, dwell in' (Br. anneza 'furnish'), fr. *ansed-, cpd. of IE *sed- 'sit'. Ernault, Glossaire 30.

Br. arrebeuri, fr. arre 'anew' and peuri 'pasture' (3.16), with extension fr. 'farm accessories'. Henry 17.

4. ON hūsbūnaðr, hūsbūningr, cpds. of hūs 'house' and būnaðr, būningr 'equipment', deriv. of būa 'prepare'.

OE īdisc(e), inēddisc (gl. Lat. supellex), deriv. of ēad 'property, riches' (11.42).

OE inorf, inirfe, cpds. of orf 'cattle, livestock' (but orig. 'inheritance'), yrfe, ierfe 'property, inheritance' : Goth. arbi, NHG erbe 'inheritance', etc. Falk-Torp 34.

OE andlōman and gelōma sometimes gloss. supellex, but here in their usual sense of 'utensil(s), tool(s)', whence NE loom (6.34).

ME houshold was sometimes used for 'household furniture' (NED s.v., 2).

ME mobles, fr. OFr. mobles) 'movable property' covered 'furniture' but never became specialized like the Fr. word.

NE furniture, formerly of more general scope, 'furnishing, furnishings, implements', etc., fr. Fr. fourniture 'furnishing, provision', deriv. of fournir 'supply, provide', this fr. OHG frummen 'perform, accomplish', deriv. of fram 'further'. Wartburg 3.829 ff. NED s.v.

OHG giziugali, caziucali (gl. Lat. supellex), deriv. of giziug 'material' (NHG zeug); OHG gizawi (also gl. supellex), whence NHG gezähe 'miner's tools' : OE geatwe 'trappings, ornaments', etc., Goth. taujan 'make', etc. Falk-Torp 1267. Walde-P. 1.779. But whether these OHG words were used for 'house furniture' is doubtful.

MHG hūsrāt, hūsgeræte, MLG husgerāt (> Dan. husgeraad, Sw. husgerǎd),

NHG hausrat, hausgerat, cpds. of hūs 'house' and rāt 'provision', coll. geræte 'utensils', fr. OHG rātan 'prepare, counsel' : OE rēdan 'counsel', etc. Falk-Torp 433, 865.

5. Lith. baldai, etym.? There is no apparent semantic connection with OLith. baldas 'pestle', baldyti, bildéti 'knock, make a noise' (Leskien, Ablaut 320). But cf. the curious history of NE knickknacks used of small ornaments, connected with knack 'trick' and this with the verb knack 'strike, knock', etc.

Lith. rakandai, orig. 'utensils', pl. of rakandas a kind of 'vessel' or 'utensil' beside rakanda a kind of 'basket', root connection? Leskien, Bildung d. Nom. 588 f.

Lett. istabas lietas, lit. 'things, implements' (lietas) of the room (istaba).

Lett. mebele (given by Drawneek, but not in Mühl.-Endz. or Ulmann), fr. NHG möbel (above, 2).

6. SCr. namještaj, fr. namjestiti 'set up, place', deriv. of mjesto 'place'.

SCr. pokućstvo, fr. a verbal deriv. of kuća 'house' (7.12).

Boh. nabytek, fr. nabyti 'obtain, acquire', hence lit. 'acquisition'.

Pol. sprzęt 'utensils' and 'furniture' : sprzątać 'put a room in order', ChSl. oprętati 'take care of', etc. Brückner 436.

Russ. obstanovka : obstavit' 'put around, set up'.

7. Skt. upakaranāni, mostly 'utensils', fr. upa-kr- 'bring near, prepare'.

7.42 BED

Grk.	*κλίνη, κοίτη, λέχος, εὐνή*	Goth.	*ligrs, badi*	Lith.	*lova, patalas*
NG	*κρεββάτι*	ON	*rekkja, hvīla, sǣing, beðr*	Lett.	*gulta*
Lat.	*lectus*	Dan.	*seng*	ChSl.	*odrŭ, lože*
It.	*letto*	Sw.	*säng, bädd*	SCr.	*postelja, krevet*
Fr.	*lit*	OE	*bedd*	Boh.	*lože, postel*
Sp.	*cama, lecho*	ME	*bed*	Pol.	*łóżko*
Rum.	*pat*	NE	*bed*	Russ.	*postel'* (*lože*)
Ir.	*lebaid, lige*	Du.	*bed*	Skt.	*talpa-, çayyā-, çayana-*
NIr.	*leabaidh*	OHG	*be(t)ti*	Av.	*stairiš-*
W.	*gwely*	MHG	*bette, bet*		
Br.	*gwele*	NHG	*bett*		

The majority of the words for 'bed' mean literally 'place for lying', from roots meaning 'lie' (12.13). Others are from various notions, like 'spread out', 'ground, floor', 'dug out', etc., applicable to the bed or to the more primitive resting places which were antecedent to the frame bed as a piece of furniture.

1. From IE **legh-* in Goth. *ligan* 'lie', etc. Walde-P. 2.424 f. Ernout-M. 534. Walde-H. 1.777 f.

Grk. *λέχος*; Lat. *lectus* (> It. *letto*, Fr. *lit*, Sp. *lecho*); Ir. *lige*, W. *gwely*, Br. *gwele* (with prefix *gwe-* fr. *gwo-*, IE **upo-*); Goth. *ligrs;* ChSl., Boh. *lože*, Pol. *łóżko* (Russ. *lože* in restricted use).

2. Grk. *κλίνη* : *κλίνομαι* 'recline, lie', *κλίνω*, Lat. *-clīnāre* 'cause to lean', etc. Walde-P. 1.490.

Grk. *κοίτη*, Skt. *çayyā-*, *çayana-* : Grk. *κεῖμαι* 'lie', Skt. *çete* 'lies', IE **k̑ei-*. Walde-P. 1.358.

Grk. *εὐνή*, etym. dub. Walde-P. 1.110. Boisacq 295 f.

NG *κρεββάτι*, fr. dim. of *κράββατος* (*κράβακτος*, etc.), first in comic poets, freq. in NT and later, orig. a kind of 'mean bed, pallet', prob. a loanword, but of unknown source. Cf. Moulton-Milligan s.v. Hence (through Turk.) SCr. *krevet*.

3. Sp. *cama* (cf. Isid. 20.11.2 *cama est brevis et circa terram*), either fr. Grk. *χαμαί* 'on the ground', or an old Iberian word. Walde-H. 1.145. REW 1537.

Rum. *pat* fr. Byz. *πάτος* 'floor' (7.26).

4. Ir. *lige*, etc. above, 1.

Ir. *lebaid*, NIr. *leabaidh*, etym.? Macbain 224.

5. Goth. *badi*, ON *beðr* ('bed' and 'pillow'; Dan. *bed* only 'bed' in the garden), Sw. *bädd*, OE *bedd*, ME, NE, Du. *bed*, OHG *betti*, *beti*, MHG *bette*, *bet*, NHG *bett*, the most widespread Gmc. word, best explained as orig. 'dug-out place, den, lair' for man and beast : Lat. *fodere* 'dig', W. *bedd* 'grave', etc. Walde-P. 2.188. Walde-H. 1.542. Falk-Torp 66. Feist 73. NED s.v. *bed*, sb.

ON *sǣing*, Dan. *seng*, Sw. *säng* (OE *sæccing*, *song*, fr. Norse), etym. dub. Falk-Torp 959. Hellquist 1148.

ON *rekkja*, fr. *rekja* 'spread out' : Goth. *ufrakjan*, OE *reccan* 'stretch out', etc. (Walde-P. 2.364).

ON *hvīla* ('bed' fr. 'rest') : Goth. *hweila* 'time', OE *hwīl* (NE *while*), etc. Falk-Torp 440.

6. Lith. *lova* : Lith. *lāva*, Russ. *lava* 'bench', perh. ON *lōfi* 'threshing floor', orig. a 'piece of board', fr. **leu-* in Skt. *lunāti* 'cuts off'? Walde-P. 2.407. Berneker 695.

Lith. *patalas* : OPruss. *talus* 'floor', Skt. *tala-* 'flat surface', etc. Walde-P. 1.740. Buga, Kalba ir Senovė 262.

Lett. *gulta*, fr. the root of *gult*, Lith. *gulti* 'lie down, go to bed'. Cf. also Lith. *guolis* 'bed, lair', Lett. *guol'a* 'nest, lair'. Mühl.-Endz. 1.679.

7. ChSl. *odrŭ* (in Gospels most common word for *κράββατος* and *κλίνη*) = Russ. *odr* 'couch, bier', Boh. *odr* 'post, scaffolding', etym. dub., perh. : OE *eodor* 'hedge, fence', etc. Walde-P. 1.121.

SCr. *postelja* (ChSl. rare), Boh. *postel*, Russ. *postel'* : ChSl. *po-steljq*, *-stĭlati* 'spread out', Lat. *lātus* 'broad', etc., IE **stel-*. Walde-P. 2.843. Trautmann 286.

ChSl., Boh. *lože*, Pol. *łóżko*, Russ. *lože*, above, 1.

8. Skt. *çayyā*, *çayana-*, above, 2.

Skt. *talpa-*, perh. : Lith. *talpa* 'spatial capacity, room for', *telpu*, *tilpti* 'have room for'. Walde-P. 1.741. Cf. ON *rūm* 'space', Av. *gātu-* 'place', both sometimes used for 'resting place, bed'.

Av. *stairiš-* (prob. only a 'carpet, rug' on which one lies or sits), fr. *star-* 'spread out' (9.34). Barth. 1599. Cf. Lat. *strātum* sometimes 'bedding' or 'bed', SCr. *postelja*, etc., above, 7.

7.43 CHAIR

Grk.	*καθέδρα, ἕδρα*	Goth.	*sitls* (*stōls*)	Lith.	*krėslas, kėdė*
NG	*καρέκλα*	ON	*stōll*	Lett.	*krēsls*
Lat.	*sella, cathedra*	Dan.	*stol*	ChSl.	*sědalište*
It.	*seggiola, sedia*	Sw.	*stol*	SCr.	*stolica*
Fr.	*chaise*	OE	*stōl*	Boh.	*sedadlo, stolice*
Sp.	*silla*	ME	*stole, chaire*	Pol.	*krzesło*
Rum.	*scaun*	NE	*chair*	Russ.	*stul*
Ir.	*cathair*	Du.	*stoel*	Skt.	*pīṭha-*
NIr.	*cathaoir*	OHG	*stuol*	Av.	(*gātu-*)
W.	*cadair*	MHG	*stuol*		
Br.	*kador*	NHG	*stuhl*		

Under 'chair' are listed the common words for the individual seat, as an article of furniture, whether one with or without back or arms, that is, without regard to the present differentiation of NE *chair* and *stool*. Not included are words which may denote any kind of 'seat', or those denoting some special form of chair.

But of the latter there may be noted here certain interesting words applied to a ceremonial chair or the modern 'armchair'.

Grk. *θρόνος*, in Hom. a high ornate chair, in part (but by no means restricted to) the 'seat, throne' of gods and princes (hence the Eur. words for 'throne'), with *θρᾶνος* 'bench, beam' and Hom. *θρῆνυς* 'footstool', fr. the root **dher-* in Skt. *dhṛ-* 'hold, support', etc. (11.15). Walde-P. 1.857. Boisacq 349.

It. *poltrona* (beside OIt. *poltro* 'bed', Fr. *poutre* 'beam') fr. a deriv. of Lat. *pullus* 'colt, foal' (3.45), applied with reference to the horse-head decorations, in this case of the arms. REW 6825. Hence NG *πολτρόνα*, now by pop. etym. *πολυθρόνα*, as if fr. *θρόνος* (above). G. Meyer, Neugr. Stud. 4.72.

Fr. *fauteuil*, OFr. *faudestuel*, fr. Frank. **faldistōl* = OHG *faltstuol*, OE *fyldestōl*, lit. 'folding chair' and so in fact, but an ornate one (cf. Chanson de Roland 115 'of pure gold, there sits the king of France'). The early forms and the transition to an armchair are illustrated

in Viollet le Duc 1.109 ff. REW 3161. Wartburg 3.385.

With a few exceptions, the general words for 'chair' are from roots meaning either 'sit' or 'place, set'.

1. From IE **sed-* 'sit' in Lat. *sedēre*, Goth. *sitan*, Skt. *sad-*, etc. (12.13). Here besides numerous words for 'seat', as Grk. *ἕδος*, Skt. *sadas-*, belong Grk. *ἕδρα*, *καθέδρα*; Lat. *sella* (> Sp. *silla*), It. *sedia* (OIt. *seggia*), *seggiola* (new formations fr. the vb., as also Fr. *siège* 'seat', REW 7780, 7782); Goth. *sitls;* ChSl. *sědalište*, *sědalo*, *sědanĭje*, Boh. *sedadlo*.

Grk. *καθέδρα* is the source of Lat. *cathedra*, whence OFr. *chaire* (> ME *chaire*, NE *chair*), Fr. *chaise*, Ir. *cathair*, NIr. *cathaoir*, W. *cadair*, Br. *kador;* also (through the medium of OVenetian *charegla*) NG *καρέγλα*, *καρέκλα* (both forms heard; also *καθέκλα*, a blend with *καθέδρα*). REW 1768. Pedersen 1.191.

2. From IE **stel-* 'place, set up' beside **stā-* 'stand', hence orig. 'something set up, support'. The alternative deriv. fr. **stā*, *stə-* with *l*-suffix amounts to the same thing semantically. Walde-P. 2.607, 643. Falk-Torp 1172. Feist 455 f.

Goth. *stōls* (only for *θρόνος*), OE *stōl*, etc. general Gmc. (NE *stool* with restricted application); ChSl. *stolŭ*, *prěstolŭ* (mostly 'throne'), SCr. *stolica*, Boh. *stolice*. Russ. *stul* fr. NHG *stuhl*. Other Slavic cognates mean 'table' (7.44).

3. Rum. *scaun*, fr. Lat. *scamnum* 'bench, stool' (> NG *σκαμνί* 'stool') : Skt. *skabh-* 'prop, support', sb. *skambha-* 'post, prop'. Walde-P. 2.539. Ernout-M. 901.

4. Lith. *krėslas*, Lett. *krēsls*, OPruss. *creslan*, Boh. *křeslo*, Pol. *krzesło*, Russ. *kreslo*, all esp. and orig. 'armchair', but in part the most nearly generic words, prob. : SCr. *krosna* 'loom', etc. (6.34), fr. a common notion of 'frame'. Walde-P. 1.485. Berneker 614 f. Mühl.-Endz. 2.276.

Lith. *kėdė*, *kedė*, prob. as orig. 'spinning stool', with Lett. *k'eda* 'spindle' fr. Esth. *kedr* 'spindle'. Leskien, Bildung der Nom. 265. On this and *krėslas*, cf. esp. Buga, Kalba ir Senovė 136 ff. Both words are now used for the common 'chair' (Senn).

5. Skt. *pīṭha-*, etym.?

Av. *gātu-*, OPers. *gāθu-* 'place' and 'seat, throne' : Skt. *gā-* 'go'. Walde-P. 1.677.

7.44 TABLE

Grk.	*τράπεζα*	Goth.	*biuþs, mēs*	Lith.	*stalas*
NG	*τράπεζα, τραπέζι*	ON	*borð* (*bjōð*)	Lett.	*galds*
Lat.	*mēnsa*	Dan.	*bord*	ChSl.	*trapeza*
It.	*tavola*	Sw.	*bord*	SCr.	*stol* (*trpeza*)
Fr.	*table*	OE	*bord, bēod*	Boh.	*stůl*
Sp.	*mesa*	ME	*borde, table*	Pol.	*stół*
Rum.	*masă*	NE	*table*	Russ.	*stol*
Ir.	*mias, bordd*	Du.	*tafel*	Skt.	(*phalaka-*)
NIr.	*bōrd*	OHG	*tisc, mias*	Av.	. . . .
W.	*bwrdd, bord*	MHG	*tisch*		
Br.	*taol*	NHG	*tisch* (*tafel*)		

A regular 'table' for serving meals and for other purposes (Grk. *τράπεζα* also 'bank'), was a common article of furniture in Greece and Rome. Previous to its introduction into northern Europe, food was served on small individual tables (as also in Homer), such a table being properly a serving tray and in part consisting only of a piece of board. Cf. Schrader Reallex. 2.536.

This situation has an important bearing on the history of the words.

1. Grk. *τράπεζα* (> ChSl. *trapeza*, SCr. *trpeza*), fr. **τρα-πεδια* 'four-footed', cpd. of forms of *τέσσαρες*, *τετρα-* 'four' and *πούς*, *ποδός* 'foot'. Also Boeot. *τρίπεζα* (*τρέπεδδα*), lit. 'three-footed'.

2. Lat. *mēnsa*, fem. of *mēnsus*, pple. of *mētīrī* 'measure', fr. IE **mē-* 'measure'. Orig. 'portion' applied to the antecedent small individual table (cf. above) and to the 'meal, course, food', the latter use also surviving in Latin beside 'table'. Walde-P. 2.237. Ernout-M. 607. Walde-H. 2.70.

Hence (through VLat. *mēsa*) Sp. *mesa*, Rum. *masă*, Ir. *mias* ('table' and 'dish'), Goth. *mēs* ('table' and 'platter'), OHG *mias*, *meas*, OE *mēsa*, *myse*. Hence also, as applied to the small individual table or serving tray of the Celts, Germans, and Slavs, numerous words for 'platter' or 'dish' (5.31, 5.32).

It. *tavola*, Fr. *table* (> ME, NE *table*), Br. *taol*, Du. *tafel*, fr. Lat. *tabula* 'board, tablet' (9.52). As suggested by Meyer-Lübke, this was first used for 'table' by the Franks, as equivalent to the Gmc. terms for their small table (below, 4). That is, semantic borrowing in Fr. fr. Gmc., then fr. Fr. in It., etc., and in NHG *tafel* (> Dan., Sw. *taffel*) when used for 'dining-table'.

3. Ir. *bordd*, NIr. *bōrd*, W. *bwrdd*, *bord*, fr. Gmc., OE or Norse, below, 4.

4. Goth. *biuþs*, ON *bjōð* (rare), OE *bēod*, OHG *beot*, *biet*, fr. the root of Goth. *-biudan*, OE *bēodan*, OHG *biotan* 'offer'. Orig. 'offering, portion' (cf. Lat. *mēnsa*, above, 2), applied to the 'serving tray, platter' (whence Balto-Slavic words for 'platter, dish, bowl', 5.31–5.33), which was the old Gmc. 'table'. Walde-P. 2.147. Feist 97.

ON *borð*, Dan., Sw., OE *bord*, ME *borde*, all meaning also and orig. 'board' (cf. Goth. *fōtu-baurd* 'footstool', MHG *bort* 'board', etc.), fr. an extension of an IE **bher-* 'cut'(?). Walde-P. 2.174, 159. Falk-Torp 94.

OHG *tisc* (*disc*), MHG, NHG *tisch*, fr. Lat. *discus*, Grk. *δίσκος* 'quoit', this also first applied to the 'serving tray, platter' (whence words for 'platter, dish', 5.31, 5.32). Weigand-H. 2.1047.

5. Lith. *stalas*, OPruss. *stalis* (acc. sg. *stallan*), SCr. *stol*, etc., the general Slavic word : ChSl. *stolŭ* 'throne', Goth. *stōls* 'chair', etc. See 7.43.

Lett. *galds*, also and orig. 'piece of board', etym. dub., possibly : Norw. dial. *kult* 'stump', Skt. *gaḍu-* 'hump', etc. (Walde-P. 1.614, without the Lett. form). Mühl.-Endz. 1.590 f.

6. Skt. *phalaka-* 'board, tablet, gaming-table', perh. the nearest thing to a 'table', fr. *phal-* 'burst, split'.

7.45 LAMP

Grk.	*λύχνος* (*λαμπάς*)	Goth.	*lukarn*	Lith.	*liampa*
NG	*λάμπα, λυχνάρι*	ON	*lampi, ljōsker*	Lett.	*lampa*
Lat.	*lucerna* (*lampas*)	Dan.	*lampe*	ChSl.	*světilĭnikŭ*
It.	*lampada, lucerna*	Sw.	*lampa*	SCr.	*lampa, svjetiljka*
Fr.	*lampe*	OE	*lēohtfæt*	Boh.	*lampa*
Sp.	*lampara*	ME	*lampe*	Pol.	*lampa*
Rum.	*lampă*	NE	*lamp*	Russ.	*lampa*
Ir.	*lōcharnn*	Du.	*lamp*	Skt.	*dīpa-*
NIr.	*lōchrann, lampa*	OHG	*liohtfaz*	Av.	. . . .
W.	*lamp, llusern*	MHG	*liehtvaz, lampe*		
Br.	*kreuzeul*	NHG	*lampe*		

Oil lamps made of stone date from prehistoric times in Greece, followed by the common earthenware and the ornamental bronze lamps. From Greece they were introduced into Rome, where candles, unknown in ancient Greece, were in earlier use. From Greece and Rome they spread to the rest of Europe, where the earlier illumination had been from the light of the fire on the hearth or from pine torches. Cf. Daremberg et Saglio and Pauly-Wissowa s.v. lucerna, Schrader, Reallex. 2.6 ff.

Like the article itself, the Greek and Latin words were largely adopted. But there are some early Gmc. and Slavic terms, derived from words for 'light'.

1. Grk. λύχνος (> early Lat. lucnus, lucinus; NG λυχνάρι), Lat. lucerna (> It. lucerna, Ir. lōcharnn, NIr. lōchrann, W. llusern, Goth. lukarn), fr. the root of Grk. λευκός 'bright', Lat. lūx 'light', lūcēre 'be light', OE lēoht 'light', etc. (1.61). Walde-P. 2.408ff. Ernout-M. 573.

2. Grk. λαμπάς, -άδος 'torch', fr. λάμπω 'give light, shine' : OPruss. lopis 'flame', etc. Walde-P. 2,383. Only 'torch' in class. Grk., but later 'lamp' (so, beside λύχνος, in NT, as Mt. 25.1 ff.). Hence Lat. lampas, -adis 'torch', later 'lamp', the source of the present almost universal mod. Eur. word for 'lamp', in large part through Fr. lampe.

3. Br. kreuzeul fr. OFr. croisel 'night-lamp', this ultimately fr. a Celt.-Gmc. word for 'earthenware pot' (OE crocca, MIr. crocan, etc., 5.26). Henry 81. Gamillscheg 277.

4. ON ljōsker, OE lēohtfæt, OHG liohtfaz, MHG liehtvaz, all cpds. of words for 'light' (1.61) and 'vessel' (ON ker, OE fæt, etc.).

5. ChSl. světilǐniku, fr. světiti 'give light', denom. of světǔ 'light' (1.61). Similarly SCr. svjetiljka.

6. Skt. dīpa-, fr. dīp- 'shine', an extension of dī- 'shine'. Walde-P. 1.772 ff.

7.46 CANDLE

Grk.	....	Goth.	....	Lith.	žvakė
NG	κερί	ON	ljōs, kerti	Lett.	svece
Lat.	candēla	Dan.	lys	ChSl.	(svěšta)
It.	candela	Sw.	ljus	SCr.	sveča
Fr.	bougie (chandelle)	OE	lēoht, candel, tapor	Boh.	svíce
Sp.	vela (bujia, candela)	ME	candel, taper	Pol.	swieca
Rum.	luminare	NE	candle	Russ.	sveča
Ir.	caindel	Du.	kaars		
NIr.	coinneal	OHG	kerza, lioht		
W.	cannwyl	MHG	kerze, lieht		
Br.	goulou, kantol	NHG	kerze, licht		

Candles were unknown in ancient Greece (besides lamps there were various kinds of torches) but were common from very early times among the Romans and the Etruscans. Cf. Daremberg et Saglio, s.v. candēla.

Most of the words are derived from those for 'light' or 'shine', with specialization to 'candle'. Some are from other sources, as 'vigil, watch', name of a town, some material used, as wax. But several words for 'wax candles' are used only for those in ceremonial, not in domestic, use.

1. NG κερί, fr. Grk. κηρίον, dim. of κηρός 'wax' (κηροί 'wax candles' from 3d cent. A.D.), whence Lat. cēra 'wax', cēreus 'wax-candle' (> It. cero, Sp. cirio, OFr. cirge > ME cerge). Ernout-M. 176. Walde-H. 1.202. REW 1829.

---

2. Lat. candēla, the common tallow candle, fr. candēre 'be bright, shine' : Skt. cand- 'shine', etc. Walde-P. 1.352. Hence It., Sp. candela, Fr. chandelle, Ir. caindel, NIr. coinneal, W. cannwyl, Br. kantol, OE ME candel, NE candle; NG καντήλι a kind of small lamp with disk floating in oil. Late Lat. candēla also 'chandelier' (candelae vitreae ingentes pendent, Peregrinatio 247). REW 1578. Vendryes, De hib. voc. 120.

Port. lume de Bugia, Sp. bujia, OFr. chandelle de Bougie, Fr. bougie (It. bugia 'candlestick'), fr. the name of the Algerian town Bugia, and referring orig. to the 'wax', of which much was imported from Algeria. REW 1375. Wartburg 1.600.

Sp. vela 'vigil, watch' and 'candle' (vela de sebo, de cera) : It. veglia 'watch', etc., denom. of Lat. vigilāre 'keep awake, watch'. REW 9326.

Rum. luminare, fr. Lat. lūmināre used in late Latin of a small lamp, deriv. of lūmen 'light'.

3. Br. goulou 'light' (1.61) and 'candle', also with koar 'wax' or soav 'tallow'.

4. ON ljōs, OE lēoht, OHG lioht, etc.

'light' (1.61) were also applied to any form of artificial light, as still NE light (put out the light), NHG licht, etc., but especially the 'candle', for which Dan. lys, Sw. ljus are the current words. For this use in OE and ME cf. NED s.v. light, sb. 5.b and for NHG, cf. Kretschmer, Wortgeogr. 326 f.

MLG kerte (> late ON kerti, Dan. kjerte), Du. kaars, OHG kerza, MHG, NHG kerze, beside OHG charz 'wick', prob. fr. Lat. charta 'papyrus', the pith of the papyrus being used for the wick of a candle, though charta is not quotable in such connection, as is papyrus. The latter is glossed by weoce and taper in OE vocabularies (Wright 126.29, 267.12), and is the source of Sp. pabilo, etc., 'wick' (REW 6218.3), and prob. of OE tapor, ME taper. Falk-Torp 517. Kluge-G. 296. NED s.v. taper, sb.[1].

5. Lith. žvakė : Lat. fax, facula 'torch'. Walde-P. 1.645.

6. SCr. sveča, Boh. svíce, Pol. swieca, Russ. sveča (ChSl. svěšta 'light, lamp, torch'), fr. světiti 'give light', denom. of světǔ 'light' (1.61). Hence Lett. svece, but perh. blended with a native word. Mühl.-Endz. 3.1145.

CHAPTER 8

AGRICULTURE, VEGETATION[1]

8.11 FARMER

Grk.	γεωργός	Goth.	(airþōs) waurstwja	Lith.	ūkininkas, laukininkas, būras
NG	γεωργός, χωρικός, χωριάτης	ON	bōndi, akrmaðr, etc.	Lett.	laucinieks, zemnieks
Lat.	agricola	Dan.	dyrker, landmand, bonde	ChSl.	dělatelǐ, težatelǐ
It.	agricoltore, coltivatore, contadino	Sw.	åkerman, jordbrukare, bonde	SCr.	ratar, težak, seljak
Fr.	agriculteur, cultivateur, paysan	OE	(eorð)tilia, æcerman, gebūr, etc.	Boh.	rolnik, sedlák
Sp.	labrador, agricultor	ME	husbond(man), acreman	Pol.	rolnik, chłop
Rum.	agricultor, țăran	NE	farmer (husbandman)	Russ.	zemledelec, krest'janin, mužik
Ir.	briugu, brugaid	Du.	landbouwer, boer	Skt.	kṣetrakarṣaka-, kṣetrapati-
NIr.	feirmeoir	OHG	accarbigango, accharman, gibūr(o)	Av.	vāstrya-
W.	amaethwr, ffermwr	MHG	ackerman, lantman, būr		
Br.	gounideg, kouer	NHG	ackermann, bauer		

[1] Names of various vegetables and fruits under Food, Chap. 5, pp. 370 ff.

'Farmer' is understood in the present common use of NE farmer (NED s.v. 5), that of Lat. agricola. Dictionaries of other languages are apt to take this in an older sense and render it by Fr. fermier, métayer, NHG pächter, etc. Such words for special classes of farmers, according to form of tenure, are not included. On the other hand, words for 'peasant', lit. 'countryman', since the peasant and farming class coincide in large measure, may be those in common use for 'farmer', while the stricter equivalents are more or less learned or archaic (cf. Fr. paysan vs. agriculteur, NHG bauer vs. ackermann, etc.). Hence several words for 'peasant' which are commonly so used are included in the list. Many of these have also a derogatory use, which does not concern us here.

1. Grk. γεωργός, fr. *γηοργός, beside Boeot. γᾱϝεργός, Lac. γᾱβεργόρ, cpd. of γῆ 'earth, land' (1.21) and the root of ἔργον 'work' (9.12).

NG (beside γεωργός) χωρικός, χωριάτης, prop. 'peasant', derivs. of χώρα 'country', χωρίον 'village'.

2. Lat. agricola, cpd. of ager 'field' (8.12) and the root of colere 'cultivate, inhabit'. Ernout-M. 22.205. Walde-H. 1.247.

It. agricoltore, Fr. agriculteur, Sp., Rum. agricultor, learned borrowing fr. Lat. agricultor (late), agrī cultor, with the same elements as the old agricola.

It. coltivatore, Fr. cultivateur, deriv. of It. coltivare, Fr. cultiver, MLat. cultivāre, this through late cultīvus fr. Lat. cultus, pple. of colere.

It. contadino 'peasant', deriv. of contado 'country region', once 'county' : Fr. comté etc., deriv. of Lat. comes, -itis in its later sense of 'count'. REW 2078.

Fr. paysan 'peasant' (OFr. paisant > ME peysant, NE peasant), deriv. of pays 'country' (19.11). REW 6145.

Sp. labrador, fr. labrar 'work, make', esp. 'cultivate, till' (8.15).

Rum. țăran 'peasant', deriv. of țara 'land, country' (1.21).

3. Ir. briugu, brugaid 'landowner, farmer, yeoman' (K. Meyer, Contrib. 263, 275. Laws, Gloss. 109) fr. bruig 'inhabited land, country, district' (19.14).

NIr. feirmeoir, W. ffermwr, farmwr, fr. NE farmer (below).

W. amaethwr, older amaeth (Laws 'plowman') : Gallo-Lat. ambactus 'servant, dependent' (orig. perh. this sense in Welsh, whence 'farm-laborer', 'plowman', 'farmer') : Ir. imm-agim 'drive, go about', Lat. agere, etc. Walde-P. 1.35.

Br. gounideg fr. gounid 'profit', vb. gounit 'gain, earn' and 'cultivate' (8.15).

Br. kouer 'peasant', perh. fr. OFr. coillier 'gatherer', in sense of 'harvester'. Henry 77.

4. Goth. waurstwja deriv. of waurstw 'work' (9.12), renders ἐργάτης 'workman' and also reg. γεωργός (once with airþōs 'of the earth').

ON bōndi (older būandi) 'settled landowner, head of a household', Dan., Sw. bonde 'peasant', fr. ON būa 'dwell, inhabit' (7.11).

ON akrmaðr, Sw. åkerman, OE æcerceorl, æcerman, ME acreman, OHG accharman, MHG ackerman, NHG ackermann, (also Du. akkerman) cpds. of akr, etc. 'field' and words for 'man'.

ON akrgerðarmaðr, akrverksmaðr lit. 'field-work's man'.

Dan. dyrker fr. dyrke 'cultivate, till' (8.15).

Dan. landmand, Sw. landtman, Du. landman, MHG lantman, NHG landmann, cpd. of land 'country' and 'man'.

Sw. jordbrukare, cpd. of jord 'earth, land' and brukare fr. bruka 'use'.

OE tilia (also eorð-tilia Gospels, Jn. 15.1; Lindisf. lond-buend) : tilian 'labor, strive for, attend to', late also 'cultivate, till' (see 8.15).

OE *gebūr*, MDu. *ghebuur*, Du. *boer*, OHG *gibūr(o)*, MHG *būr*, *gebūr(e)*, NHG *bauer*, cpd. of *ge-*, *gi-* here 'with' and OE *būr*, OHG *būr*, etc. 'house', fr. OE, OHG *būan* 'dwell, inhabit' (7.11). Weigand-H. 1.168, 169. Franck-v. W. 77.101.

ME *husbonde*, *husbondman*, NE *husbandman* (so reg. in our Bible, but now arch.), fr. late OE *hūsbonda* 'master of a house', this fr. ON *hūsbōndi* 'master of a house, husband' (in the latter sense also ME *husbonde*, NE *husband*, 2.33), cpd. of *hūs* 'house' and *bōndi* (above).

NE *farmer*, earlier 'one who rents land for the purpose of cultivation', fr. ME *fermour* 'one who undertakes the collection of taxes or revenues, etc. by payment of a fixed sum for the proceeds', Anglo-Fr. *fermer* (Fr. *fermier*), fr. MLat. *firmārius* lit. 'one who fixes, makes fast', fr. *firmus* 'fast, firm'. However, the word is felt in modern speech to be the agent noun of the vb. *farm*. NED s.v.

Du. *landbouwer*, cpd. of *land* 'land' and *bouwer* fr. *bouwen* 'dwell, cultivate'.

OHG *accarbigango*, *accarbigengiri* ('agricola' reg. in Tatian), fr. *acchur* 'field' and *bigango* 'cultor' : *bigangan* 'go over, frequent, till'.

5. Lith. *ūkininkas* (the preferred word in Lalis, Senn, Lit. Sprachl., and Hermann, Lit.-deutsches Gesprächs. 120 f.) fr. *ūkis* 'farm, farming' (: *junkti* 'be accustomed'. Walde-P. 1.111).

Lith. *laukininkas*, Lett. *laucinieks*, fr. Lith. *laukas*, Lett. *lauks* 'field' (1.23).

Lith. *žemdirbis*, cpd. of *žemė* 'earth' and root of *dirbti* 'work' (9.13).

Lith. *būras*, fr. MLG *būr* (= NHG *bauer*, etc., above, 4).

Lett. *zemnieks*, fr. *zeme* 'land, earth'.

6. ChSl. *dělatelĭ* (freq. in Gospels for ἐργάτης and γεωργός), fr. *dělati* 'work' (9.13).

ChSl. *tęžatelĭ*, *tęžarĭ*, SCr. *težak* (Boh. *těžař* 'cultivator, miner'), fr. ChSl. *tęžati* 'work', etc. : ChSl. *tęgnąti* 'pull, draw' (9.33). Semantic development through 'stretch, strain' to 'work, work in the field'. Miklosich 350. For ChSl. distribution, cf. Jagić, Entstehungsgesch. 342.

Late ChSl. *ratajĭ*, SCr. *ratar*, *rataj*, lit. 'plow-man' : ChSl. *orati* 'plow', etc. (8.21).

SCr. *seljak*, fr. *selo* 'village, country' : ChSl. *selo* 'field', etc. Similarly also Boh. *sedlák*, orig. fr. *selo* 'village, field', but in form as if from *sedlo* 'saddle', orig. 'seat' (see under *selo*, 8.12).

Boh. *rolník*, Pol. *rolnik*, fr. Boh. *role*, Pol. *rola* 'field' (8.12).

Pol. *chłop* : Russ. *cholop* 'serf', Boh. *chlap* 'churl, fellow', ChSl. *chlapŭ* 'serving man, servant', etc., ultimate origin obscure. Berneker 394.

Russ. *zemledelec*, fr. *zemlja* 'earth' and *-delec* fr. *delat'* 'do, work'.

Russ. *krest'janin*, earlier 'Christian', then 'man (in general)', whence 'peasant', ChSl. *krĭstĭjanŭ*, *krĭstĭjaninŭ* 'Christian', through OHG *christjāni* fr. Grk. χριστιανός. Berneker 635.

Russ. *mužik* 'peasant', deriv. of *muž* 'man'.

7. Skt. *kṣetrakarṣaka-*, *kṣetrapati-* fr. *kṣetra-* 'field' with *karṣaka-* 'plowing, cultivating' (fr. *kṛṣ-* 'plow') and *pati-* 'owner, master'.

Av. *vāstrya-*, sb. form of adj. *vāstrya-* 'pertaining to husbandry, agriculture' : *vāstra-* 'pasture, field'. Barth. 1416.

8.12 FIELD

(For Cultivation)

Grk.	ἀγρός, ἄρουρα	Goth.	*akrs*	Lith.	*dirva, laukas*
NG	ἀγρός, χωράφι	ON	*akr*	Lett.	*tīrums, druva*
Lat.	*ager, arvum*	Dan.	*mark, ager*	ChSl.	*selo, niva*
It.	*campo*	Sw.	*åker, mark*	SCr.	*njiva, oranica*
Fr.	*champ*	OE	*æcer*	Boh.	*role*
Sp.	*campo*	ME	*aker, feeld*	Pol.	*rola, grunt*
Rum.	*cîmp*	NE	*field*	Russ.	*niva, pole*
Ir.	*gort*	Du.	*akker, veld*	Skt.	*kṣetra-, urvarā-*
NIr.	*gort*	OHG	*acchar*	Av.	*karšū-, yavan-*
W.	*cae, maes*	MHG	*acker*		
Br.	*park, maez*	NHG	*acker, feld*		

'Field' is understood here as a tract of land for cultivation, in distinction from 'field' in a broader sense, without special reference to agriculture, which has been considered with 'plain' (1.23). But several of the words entered here cover both notions, and in such cases reference is made to the previous discussion. Even some of those in which the agricultural sense is dominant are sometimes used also in a wider sense, as Grk. ἀγρός, Lat. *ager* for 'open country' vs. 'town' (19.13).

1. IE *_aĝro-_, prob. fr. *_aĝ-_ 'drive' in Lat. *agere*, etc., and so orig. 'place where the cattle were driven, pasture' (cf. OHG *trift* 'pasture' : *trīben* 'drive'), whence, with the advance of the agricultural stage, the common Eur. use. Walde-P. 1.37. Ernout-M. 22 f. Walde-H. 1.22. Feist 33. Specht, KZ 66.17.

Grk. ἀγρός; Lat. *ager*; Goth. *akrs*, ON *akr*, OE *æcer*, etc., general Gmc.; but Skt. *ajra-* (RV) 'open field' without reference to cultivation.

2. Grk. ἄρουρα, Lat. *arvum* 'arable land' prob. : Skt., Av. *urvarā-* (below, 8), and both : Grk. εὐρύς 'wide', Skt. *varas-* 'width'. Specht, KZ 66.246 f.

NG χωράφι fr. Grk. χωράφιον (Theophr; freq. in Byz.), dim. of χώρα 'land, country'. Petersen, Grk. Dim. in -ιον 277, 279.

3. It., Sp. *campo*, Fr. *champ*, Rum. *cîmp*, fr. Lat. *campus* 'plain, open field' (1.23).

4. Ir. *gort*, esp. 'field sown to grain' : W. *garth* 'enclosure, garden', Br. *garz* 'hedge', Lat. *hortus* 'garden' (8.13), etc. Walde-P. 1.603. Pedersen 1.136.

W. *cae*, the common word for an 'enclosed field' (cf. Evans, Welsh Dict. s.v.), orig. 'fence, hedge' (about the field) : Br. *kae* 'enclosure, hedge', OHG *hecka*, OE *hecg* 'hedge', etc. Walde-P. 1.337.

W. *maes*, Br. *maez*, also 'field (in broad sense), plain' (1.23).

Br. *park*, fr. Fr. *parc* 'park', orig. 'inclosed tract of land' (orig. dub., REW 6253).

5. Dan. *mark*, Sw. *mark* (but the latter largely 'land, ground') : ON *mǫrk* 'forest' (1.41), Goth. *marka* 'boundary', OE *mearc* 'borderland' (NE *march*), Lat. *margō* 'border', etc. Walde-P. 2.283 ff. Falk-Torp 699 f.

ME *feeld*, NE *field*, Du. *veld*, NHG *feld*, orig. only 'field' in the broad sense, OE, OHG *feld*, etc. (1.23).

6. Lith. *dirva*, Lett. *druva* : Russ. *derevnja* 'village, landed property', dial. 'small field', prob. Skt. *dūrvā-* 'panic-grass', Du. *tarwe* 'wheat', all perh. fr. an extension of IE *_der-_ in Lith. *dirti*, Lett. *dirāt*, OE *teran* 'tear', etc. Walde-P. 1.800, 803. Berneker 186. Specht, KZ 66.18.

Lith. *laukas* 'field' but chiefly in broad sense (1.23).

Lett. *tīrums*, orig. 'a cleared field (for

cultivation)' : *tīrs* 'clean, pure' (cf. *tīri lauki*, Lith. *tyrai laukai* 'cleared land'). Mühl.-Endz. 204.

7. ChSl. *selo* (in Gospels reg. for ἀγρός, later sometimes 'village' as SCr., Russ. *selo*, Pol. *sioło*), prob. : OHG *sal* 'dwelling, hall', ON *salr* 'hall, room', Lat. *solum* 'bottom, soil', etc. (but in Slavic partly mixed with the deriv. of IE *_sed-_ 'sit', Slov. *sedlo* 'seat', etc.). Walde-P. 2.503. Ernout-M. 953. Meillet, Études 419. Trautmann 248. Brückner 491 f.

ChSl. *niva* (in Gospels for χώρα 'earth, ground', later for ἀγρός; cf. Jagić, Entstehungsgesch. 393), SCr. *njiva*, Russ. *niva* (also Boh. *niva* 'field, plain') : Grk. νειός 'fallow land' (fr. 'depression'), νείατος 'lowest', Skt. *ni-*, OHG *nidar*, OE *niþer* 'down', etc. Walde-P. 1.335.

SCr. *oranica* 'plow-land', fr. *orati* 'plow'.

Boh. *role*, Pol. *rola*, late ChSl. *ralija* : ChSl. *orati*, etc. 'plow' (8.21). Miklosich 225. Brückner 462.

Pol. *grunt*, fr. NHG *grund* 'ground, soil'. Brückner 160.

Russ. *pole*, also 'field' in broad sense as reg. in the other Slavic languages, ChSl. *polje*, etc. (1.23).

8. Skt. *kṣetra-*, also 'place' but esp. 'field' = Av. *šōiθra-* 'dwelling-place' : Skt. *kṣi-*, Av. *ši-* 'dwell' (7.11).

Skt. *urvarā-* : Av. *urvarā-* 'plant', see under Grk. ἄρουρα, above, 2.

Av. *karšū-* 'field' (? Barth. 458) : Skt. *karṣu-* 'furrow', Av. *karš-*, Skt. *kṛṣ-* 'plow' (8.22). Walde-P. 1.429.

Av. *yavan-*, *yəvin-* 'field of grain', fr. *yava-* 'grain' : Skt. *yava-* id., etc. (8.42).

8.13 GARDEN

Grk.	κῆπος	Goth.	*aurtigards*	Lith.	*daržas*
NG	κῆπος, περιβόλι	ON	*-garðr*	Lett.	*dārzs*
Lat.	*hortus*	Dan.	*have*	ChSl.	*vrŭtŭ, vrŭtogradŭ (ogradŭ)*
It.	*giardino; orto*	Sw.	*trädgård*	SCr.	*vrt, bašča*
Fr.	*jardin*	OE	*ortgeard, wyrttūn*	Boh.	*zahrada*
Sp.	*jardin, huerta*	ME	*garden, orchard*	Pol.	*ogród*
Rum.	*grădină*	NE	*gardin*	Russ.	*sad, ogorod*
Ir.	*lubgort, garda*	Du.	*tuin*	Skt.	*vāṭikā-, udyāna-*
NIr.	*garrdha, gāirdīn*	OHG	*garto*	Av.	*(pairidaēza-)*
W.	*gardd*	MHG	*garte*		
Br.	*liorz*	NHG	*garten*		

'Garden' is often a specialization of 'yard', and several of the words entered here belong to groups already discussed under that head (7.15). Most of the others are from a similar notion of 'enclosure'. There may be specialization of 'garden' to 'flower garden', 'vegetable garden', or 'tree garden, orchard'. A converse generalization is seen in Sw. *trädgård*, lit. 'tree-garden'.

1. Grk. κῆπος, Dor. κᾶπος : OHG *huoba*, 'piece of land' (NHG *hufe*, *hube*), Alb. *kopsht* 'garden', root connection? Walde-P. 1.345 f.

NG περιβόλι, fr. dim. of Grk. περίβολος 'circuit, enclosure' : περιβάλλω 'surround, put about'.

2. Lat. *hortus* (> It. *orto* 'vegetable garden', Sp. *huerto* 'orchard', *huerta* 'vegetable garden'), Osc. *húrz* 'hortus, lucus' : Lat. *cohors* 'yard, court', Grk. χόρτος 'farmyard', Ir. *gort* 'field', *lub-gort* 'garden' (cpd. with *luib* 'plant'), Br. *liorz* 'garden' (by contraction, cf. MCorn. *lowarth* id., Pedersen 1.116), prob. also OE *geard* 'yard' (7.15), OHG *garto* 'garden', etc. (below, 4), all as orig. 'enclosure' fr. IE *_ĝher-_ in Osc.

heriiad 'capiat', Skt. *hṛ-* 'seize, hold', etc. Walde-P. 1.603 f. Ernout-M. 461. Walde-H. 1.242 f.

Fr. *jardin* (> It. *giardino*, Sp. *jardin* esp. 'flower garden'; fr. a North Fr. form also ME *gardin*, NE *garden*) fr. OHG *garto* 'garden' (below, 4). REW 3684.

Rum. *grădină*, fr. Slavic (below, 6).

3. Ir. *lubgort*, Br. *liorz*, see above, 2.

Ir. *garda*, NIr. *garrdha*, W. *gardd*, fr. ON *garðr* (below, 4). Pedersen 1.110.

NIr. *gāirdīn* fr. NE *garden*.

4. In Gmc. mostly words for 'yard', alone or in cpds. ON *-garðr*, as in *kālgarðr* 'cabbage garden' (NIcel. *garður* alone 'garden'); Goth. *aurtigards*, OE *ortgeard*, ME *orchard* (OE, ME also and NE only 'orchard'), first part prob. old loanword fr. Lat. *hortus* (Feist 68, Stender-Petersen 370 f.; otherwise, namely : Goth. *waurts* 'root', OE *wyrt* 'plant', Walde-P. 1.288, Falk-Torp 1336); Sw. *trädgård*, cpd. with *träd* 'tree', and so orig. 'a pleasure garden with trees, park', like the NHG *lustgarten* (Hellquist 1233); OHG *garto*, MHG *garte*, NHG *garten* (with the loanwords Fr. *jardin*, NE *garden*, etc.); all : Goth. *gards* 'house, court,' OE *geard* 'yard', etc., and prob., fr. the same root as Lat. *hortus*, etc. See above, 2 and 7.15.

Dan. *have*, fr. ODan. *hage* 'hedged-in piece of land' : OE *haga* 'hedge, hedged-in piece of land' (NE *haw*), etc. Falk-Torp 386.

OE *wyrttūn*, cpd. of *wyrt* 'plant' and *tūn* 'enclosure', also Du. *tuin* 'garden' : OHG *zūn*, NHG *zaun* 'hedge', Ir. *dūn* 'castle, fort', etc. Walde-P. 1.778.

5. Lith. *daržas*, Lett. *dārzs*, perh. : OHG *targa* 'circumference, border', Grk. δράσσομαι 'grasp', etc. (the group in Walde-P. 1.807; but transposition fr. *_žardas_ is preferred, 1.859). Mühl.-Endz. 1.449. Trautmann 45 (: ON *draga* 'draw').

6. For the various ChSl. renderings of κῆπος, cf. Jagić, Entstehungsgesch. 330, 428.

ChSl. *vrŭtogradŭ*, loanword fr. Goth. *aurtigards* (above, 4).

ChSl. *vrŭtŭ*, SCr. *vrt*, either abstracted fr. the preceding (Miklosich and others), or fr. a Goth. simplex. Stender-Petersen 371.

Late ChSl. *ogradŭ*, Pol. *ogród*, Russ. *ogorod* ('vegetable garden'), Boh. *zahrada*, cpds. of ChSl. *gradŭ*, etc. 'city' (19.15), reflecting an earlier meaning 'enclosure', regardless of whether or not this is a loanword fr. the Gmc. group (above, 4). Late ChSl. and Bulg. also deriv. *gradina* 'garden' (> Rum. *grădină*). Berneker 330.

Russ. *sad* (Pol. *sad* 'orchard', Boh. *sad* 'park, orchard, plantation') = ChSl. *sadŭ* 'plant, tree, shrub' (late also for κῆπος), fr. vb. *saditi* 'plant' : Skt. *sādaya-*, Goth. *satjan* 'set', caus. of IE *_sed-_ 'sit'. Trautmann 258 f.

SCr. *bašča* fr. Turk. *bahçe* 'garden' (orig. Pers.). Berneker 39. Lokotsch 169.

7. Skt. *vāṭikā-*, *vāṭaka-*, fr. *vāṭa-* 'enclosure, enclosed piece of land' : *vṛti-* 'hedge, fence', *vṛ-* 'cover, surround', etc. Uhlenbeck 281 (Walde-P. 1.281 without *vāṭikā-*, etc.).

Skt. *udyāna-*, *udyānaka-*, esp. 'pleasure garden, park', fr. *ud-yā-* 'go out', cpd. of *yā-* 'go, walk'.

Av. *pairidaēza-* 'hedged-in place', perh. 'garden' (cf. NPers. *pālēz* 'garden', and loanwords Grk. παράδεισος, Arm. *partēz* 'enclosed garden') : *pairi-daēzaya-* 'wall about', Skt. *dēhī-*, Grk. τεῖχος 'wall', etc. (7.27). Walde-P. 1.833. Barth. 865.

8.14 BARN

Grk.	*σιτοβολών, ἀποθήκη*	Goth.	*bansts*	Lith.	*daržinė, skūnė*
NG	*σιταποθήκη, σιτοβολών*	ON	*hlaða*	Lett.	*šk'ūnis*
Lat.	*horreum, grānāria*	Dan.	*lade*	ChSl.	*žitĭnica*
It.	*granaio*	Sw.	*lada*	SCr.	*štagelj, žitnica, ambar*
Fr.	*grenier, grange*	OE	*berern, beren*	Boh.	*stodola*
Sp.	*granero*	ME	*bern*	Pol.	*stodoła*
Rum.	*şură, hambar*	NE	*barn*	Russ.	*žitnica, ambar*
Ir.	*saball*	Du.	*schuur*	Skt.	*kuçūla-*
NIr.	*sciobōl*	OHG	*sciura, scugin, stadal*	Av.	*yavan-*
W.	*ysgubor*	MHG	*schiur(e); schiune, stadel*		
Br.	*granch*	NHG	*scheune, scheuer (stadel)*		

Words for 'barn', as a storehouse for grain or other farm produce, are partly specializations of 'storehouse' and partly from words for 'grain' (or some particular kind of grain, as 'barley' in the case of NE *barn*). But since the farmer's barn may also be the place where the farm animals are kept, there is sometimes confusion with the notion of 'stable'. So a few of the words for 'barn' probably rest on this latter notion (Goth. *bansts*, Ir. *saball*). Conversely in NE *barn* in U.S. usage the secondary association with the place where the cattle and horses are kept is so strong that in the country it is the common word covering 'stable', and it is by this analogy (rather than the notion of 'storehouse') that one uses *car barn* of the place where street cars stand when not on their run.

Some of the words included in the list denote any storage place for grain, with no resemblance to our *barn*, for which there may be no good equivalent.

1. Grk. *ἀποθήκη* 'storehouse' in general, including one for grain (as reg. in NT, Mt. 6.26, etc.), fr. *ἀποτίθημι* 'put away, store up', cpd. of *τίθημι* 'put, place'. NG *σιταποθήκη*, cpd. with *σῖτος* 'grain' (8.42).

Grk. *σιτοβολών* (so NG), also *-βολεῖον*, *-βόλιον*, *-βολον*, cpds. of *σῖτος* 'grain', with derivs. of *βάλλω* 'throw'.

Grk. *καλιά* 'hut' (7.13), also 'barn' (Hes.).

2. Lat. *horreum*, etym.? Ernout-M. 461. Walde-H. 1.659 f.

Lat. *grānārium* (> It. *granaio*, Sp. *granero*, Fr. *grenier*), usually in pl. *grānāria*, fr. *grānum* 'grain' (8.42), whence also Fr. *grange* (> Br. *granch*) fr. VLat. *grānica*, fem. of an adj. **grānicus* 'pertaining to grain'. REW 3839, 3845. Gamillscheg 482.

Rum. *şură* (see illustration in Dict. Enc. 1262), fr. MHG *schiure* or *schūr* (below, 4). Tiktin 1537.

Rum. *hambar*, SCr., Russ. *ambar* 'storage place for grain', fr. Turk. *ambar*, Pers. *anbar* id. Berneker 28. Lokotsch 71.

3. Ir. *saball*, NIr. *sabhall* (obs.), fr. Lat. *stabulum* 'stall, stable'. Pedersen 1.219.

NIr. *sciobōl*, etym.?

W. *ysgubor*, OW *scipaur* gl. *horrea*, Corn. *scibor*, perh. fr. VLat. **scōpārium* (deriv. of Lat. *scōpa* 'besom of twigs', 9.38). Loth, Mots lat. 216.

4. Goth. *bansts* : LG *banse* 'grain-chamber', ON *bāss* 'cow-stall' (NE dial. *boose*), derivs. of stem *band-* : *bindan* 'bind'. The more orig. meaning is prob. 'stable' (for tying cattle, etc.). Walde-P. 2.152. Feist 80 f. Falk-Torp 40.

ON *hlaða*, Dan. *lade*, Sw. *lada* : ON *hlaða*, Goth. *hlaþan* 'load, pile up, store', Lith. *klōti* 'spread out', ChSl. *klasti* 'load, lay'. Walde-P. 1.489. Falk-Torp 617.

OE *berern*, *beren*, ME *berne*, *bern*, NE *barn*, fr. **bere-ærn*, cpd. of *bere* 'barley' (8.45) and *ærn* 'house', in cpds. 'place' : ON *rann*, Goth. *razn* 'house', etc. (7.12). NED s.v. *barn*.

Du. *schuur*, MLG *schūr(e)*, OHG *sciura*, *scūra*, MHG *schiur(e)*, NHG *scheuer* (*schauer*) : OHG *scūr*, MHG *schūr* 'cover, shelter', fr. the same root as OHG *scugin*, *scugina*, MHG *schiune*, NHG *scheune*, all derivs. of IE *(*s*)*keu-* 'cover', in Skt. *skunāti* 'protects', Grk. *σκῦτος* 'hide', Lat. *obscūrus* 'dark', etc. Walde-P. 2.548. Weigand-H. 2.700.

OHG *stadal*, MHG *stadel* (NHG dial. *stadel*; Kretschmer, Wortgeogr. 408) : ON *stǫðull* 'milking-pen', OE *staþol* 'place, foundation', etc., derivs. of IE **stā-* 'stand'. Walde-P. 2.606. Falk-Torp 1199. Possibly through notion of 'standing-place' for animals, but there is no trace of this in the actual usage, and a direct development of 'standing-place' to 'storage place' is easy.

5. Lith. *daržinė*, fem. of adj. *daržinis* 'pertaining to a garden', deriv. of *daržas* 'garden' (8.13), hence orig. a storehouse for garden produce.

Lith. *skūnė*, Lett. *šk'ūnis*, fr. MLG *schune* = NHG *scheune* (above, 4).

6. ChSl. *žitĭnica*, SCr., Russ. *žitnica*, fr. ChSl. *žito* 'grain' (8.42).

Boh. *stodola*, Pol. *stodoła*, prob. also SCr. *štagelj*, fr. OHG *stadal*, MHG *stadel* (above, 4). Miklosich 323. Brückner 516.

7. Skt. *kuçūla-*, etym. dub., but perh. : *koça-* 'container', fr. extension of *(*s*)*keu-* in OHG *sciura*, etc. (above, 4). Uhlenbeck 60.

Av. *yavan-* fr. *yava-* 'grain' (8.42). Barth. 1.267.

8.15 CULTIVATE, TILL

Grk.	*γεωργέω*	Goth.	....	Lith.	*apdirbti*
NG	*γεωργῶ, καλλιεργῶ*	ON	*yrkja, vinna*	Lett.	*apstrādāt*
Lat.	*colere*	Dan.	*dyrke*	ChSl.	*dělati*
It.	*coltivare*	Sw.	*bruka, odla*	SCr.	*obraditi*
Fr.	*cultiver, labourer*	OE	*būan, tilian*	Boh.	*vzdělavati*
Sp.	*cultivar, labrar*	ME	*tille*	Pol.	*uprawić*
Rum.	*cultiva*	NE	*cultivate, till*	Russ.	*pachat'*
Ir.	*airim*	Du.	*bebouwen*	Skt.	*kṛṣ-* (?)
NIr.	*oibrighim, saothruighim*	OHG	*būan*	Av.	*aiwi-vərəz-*
		MHG	*bouwen*		
W.	*diwyllio, trin, amaethu*	NHG	*bebauen, ackern*		
Br.	*gounit*				

Verbs for 'work' (9.13) may be used transitively with objects like 'land, soil' in the special sense of 'cultivate', like NE *work the land*. Several of these, or their compounds, are the usual, or at least very common, expressions for this notion. Some verbs for 'plow' (8.21) are also used in the broader sense 'cultivate', partly by extension from 'plow', partly from a common source. Two important groups, formally unrelated, have the twofold sense of 'dwell, inhabit' and 'cultivate', through a common notion of 'be busy with, be accustomed', or the like. Among other semantic sources are 'strive, gain, attain', 'make use of', 'make unwild', 'make valuable'.

1. Grk. *γεωργέω*, deriv. of *γεωργός* 'farmer' (8.11).

NG *καλλιεργῶ* (late Grk. 'make beauti-

ful', in pass. 'be well cultivated', fr. *καλλι-εργής*, cpd. of *κάλλος* 'beauty' and the root of *ἔργον* 'work'.

2. Lat. *colere* 'inhabit' and 'cultivate' : Skt. *car-* 'move, go, be busy with', Grk. *πέλομαι*, *τέλλομαι* 'become', *ἀνατέλλω* 'rise', *πόλος* 'axis, pole', *κύκλος* 'circle', etc., IE **kʷel-*, orig. sense 'turn', with development through 'be busy with' (cf. Lat. *versārī* 'be busy with' : *vertere* turn). Walde-P. 1.514 ff. Ernout-M. 204 ff. Walde-H. 1.245 ff. Hence, fr. pass. pple. *cultus*, MLat. adj. *cultīvus*, vb. *cultivāre*, whence It. *coltivare*, Fr. *cultiver* (> NE *cultive*, now obs.), Sp. *cultivar*, Rum. *cultiva*.

Fr. *labourer* 'cultivate' and esp. 'plow', Sp. *labrar* 'cultivate', fr. Lat. *labōrāre* 'labor, toil', deriv. of sb. *labor* 'labor, toil' (9.12). REW 4810.

3. Ir. *airim* 'plow' (8.21), also in wider sense 'cultivate'. Hessen s.v.

NIr. *oibrighim* 'work' (8.13) and 'cultivate.'

NIr. *saothruighim* 'labor, toil' and 'cultivate', deriv. of Ir. *sāeth* 'labor, toil' (9.12).

W. *di-wyllio* (with *tir* 'land', etc. 'cultivate', but also 'worship') : *gwyllt* 'wild', Goth. *wilþeis*, OE *wilde* 'wild', with neg. force of *di-*, hence lit. 'make unwild'. Morris Jones 167.

W. *trin* 'handle, manage, cultivate' : sb. *trin* 'fight, toil', this : Lat. *strēnuus* 'active, vigorous', etc. Walde-P. 2.628. Stokes 137.

W. *amaethu*, fr. *amaeth* 'farmer, plowman' (8.11).

Br. *gounit* 'gain, earn' and 'cultivate' : W. *gweini* 'serve', Corn. *gonys* 'work', also 'cultivate' (Williams, Lexicon s.v.), Ir. *fo-gnīu* 'serve', *gnīu* 'do, make'. Pedersen 2.545.

4. ON *yrkja* 'work' (= OE *wyrcan* 'work', etc. 9.13), but often esp. 'cultivate'.

ON *vinna* 'work, gain' (9.13), also sometimes 'cultivate'.

Dan. *dyrke* = ON *dȳrkja* 'glorify, exalt', fr. *dȳrr* 'dear, costly'. Falk-Torp 173.

Sw. *bruka* 'use' (9.423), also with *jorden*, etc. 'cultivate'.

Sw. *odla*, fr. *odal*, ON *ōðal* 'property, homestead' : OE *ōþel*, *ēþel* 'home, native country', etc. Hellquist 724, 723. Falk-Torp 787.

OE *būan*, mostly 'dwell, inhabit', sometimes 'cultivate' (cf. Bosworth-Toller, Suppl. and *lond-buend* 'agricola' in Lindisf. Gospels, Jn. 15.1), OHG *būan*, MHG, Du. *bouwen* 'dwell, inhabit' and 'cultivate', in latter sense now mostly NHG *bebauen*, Du. *bebouwen*, all ultimately fr. IE **bhū-* 'become, be'. See under 'dwell' (7.11). Walde-P. 2.140 f. Feist 83 f.

NHG *ackern*, fr. *acker* 'field' (8.12).

OE *tilian* 'labor, strive, attend to', late (c. 1200+) 'till, cultivate', as ME *tille* mostly and NE *till* now only in this sense : Du. *telen* 'breed, raise, cultivate', Goth. *gatilōn* 'attain', OHG *zilōn* 'strive', etc., outside root connections dub. Walde-P. 809. Feist 477. NED s.v. *till*, vb.[1].

NE *cultivate*, fr. pass. pple. of MLat. *cultivāre* (above, 2).

5. Lith. *apdirbti*, Lett. *apstrādāt*, cpds. of Lith. *dirbti*, Lett. *strādāt* 'work' (9.13).

6. ChSl. *dělati* 'work' (9.13), also 'cultivate' (cf. *dělatelĭ* 'farmer'). Here also Boh. *vz-dělavati*.

SCr. *obraditi*, cpd. of *raditi* 'work' (9.13).

Pol. *uprawić*, cpd. of *prawić*, but in the earlier sense seen in ChSl. *praviti* 'set right', etc.

Russ. *pachat'* 'plow' (8.21), also used in wider sense 'cultivate'.

7. Skt. *kṛṣ-* 'plow' (8.21), also 'cultivate'(?).

Av. *aiwi-vərəz-*, cpd. of *vərəz-* 'work, do' (9.13). Barth. 1376.

8.21 PLOW

(vb.; sb.)

Grk.	*ἀρόω; ἄροτρον*	Goth.	*arjan; hōha*	Lith.	*arti; plūgas, arklas, žagrė*
NG	*ὀργώνω, ζευγαρίζω; ἀλέτρι*	ON	*erja, plœgja; arðr, plōgr*	Lett.	*art; arkls*
Lat.	*arāre; arātrum*	Dan.	*pløje; plov*	ChSl.	*orati; ralo*
It.	*arare, solcare; aratro*	Sw.	*plöja; plog*	SCr.	*orati; plug*
Fr.	*labourer; charrue*	OE	*erian; sulh*	Boh.	*orati; pluk*
Sp.	*arar; arado*	ME	*ere; plogh*	Pol.	*orać; pług*
Rum.	*ara; plug*	NE	*plow; plow*	Russ.	*pachat' (orat'); plug, socha*
Ir.	*airim; arathar, cēcht*	Du.	*ploegen; ploeg*		
NIr.	*treabhaim; cēachta*	OHG	*erren; pfluog*	Skt.	*kṛṣ-; lāñgala-, sīra-, hala-*
W.	*aredig; aradr*	MHG	*pfluegen, ern; pfluoc*		
Br.	*arat; arar*	NHG	*pflūgen; pflug*	Av.	*karš-; aēša-*

The verbs and nouns for 'plow' ('plough') go together in large measure, but not always. In the inherited group the verbs have, on the whole, been the more persistent. In the evolution of the implement, from the primitive crooked stick to the modern plow, the old name may persist, or new words may arise (hence again, in part, new verbs) and spread as loanwords. In several languages there are different words for the modern plow and a more primitive wooden plow still used by peasants.

1. IE **ar-* (**arā-*, **arə-*) in vbs. and sbs. common to the European languages and Armenian, but unknown in Indo-Iranian. Walde-P. 1.78. Ernout-M. 75. Walde-H. 1.69.

Vbs. : Grk. *ἀρόω*; Lat. *arāre* (> It. *arare*, Sp. *arar*, Rum. *ara*); Ir. *airim*, W. *aredig*, Br. *arat*; Goth. *arjan*, ON *erja*, OE *erian*, ME *ere*, OHG *erren*, MHG *ern*; Lith. *arti*, Lett. *art*; ChSl., SCr., Boh. *orati*, Pol. *orać* (Russ. *orat'* arch.).

Sbs. : Grk. *ἄροτρον*, NG *ἀλέτρι*, dial. *ἄλετρον* by dissim. (Hatzidakis, Μεσ. 1.328); Lat. *arātrum* (> It. *aratro*, Sp. *arado*); Ir. *arathar*, W. *aradr*, Br. *arar*; Lith. *arklas*, Lett. *arkls*; ChSl. *ralo* fr. **radlo*, **ordlo* (but SCr. *ralo*, Boh. *radlo*, Pol. *radło*, Russ. *ralo*, *oralo*, now used only of a primitive plow, or 'plow-handle', 'plowshare', otherwise replaced by the Gmc. word); Arm. *araur*; Toch. A *āre*.

2. NG *ὀργώνω*, fr. *ὄργον* dial. = *ἔργον* 'work'. Similarly, *καματεύω*, fr. *κάματος* 'labor', is locally (Sparta, etc.) the common verb for 'plow'. Cf. Fr. *labourer*.

NG *ζευγαρίζω*, fr. *ζευγάρι* 'team of oxen', class. Grk. *ζευγάριον*, dim. of *ζεῦγος* 'team'.

3. It. *solcare*, fr. Lat. *sulcāre* 'furrow, plow' (poet.), deriv. of *sulcus* 'furrow' (8.212).

Fr. *labourer*, also in wider sense 'cultivate, till'. See 8.15.

Fr. *charrue*, fr. Gallo-Lat. *carrūca* 'wagon, wheeled plow', deriv. of Gallo-Lat. *carrus* 'wagon'. REW 1720. Gamillscheg 210. Wartburg 2.424 ff.

Rum. *plug*, through Slavic fr. Gmc. (below, 5).

4. NIr. *treabhaim* = MIr. *trebaim* 'inhabit, cultivate', beside *treb* 'dwelling place', etc. (7.11).

Ir. *cēcht*, NIr. *cēachta* : W. *cainc* 'branch', ChSl. *sąkŭ* 'branch', Skt. *çañku-* 'stake, post', also (forms without nasal) Skt. *çākhā-* 'branch', Goth. *hōha* 'plow', OHG *huohili* 'aratiuncula', perh. also Slavic *socha* (below, 7). 'Plow' fr. 'branch, stick'. Walde-P. 1.335. Pedersen 1.126. Feist 266.

5. Goth. *hōha*, see just above.

ON *plōgr*, Dan. *plov*, Sw. *plog*, ME *plogh* (this sense perh. fr. Norse, cf. OE *plōg* 'a certain measure of land'), NE *plow*, Du. *ploeg*, OHG *pfluog*, *pfluoh*,

MHG *pfluoc*, NHG *pflug;* hence the vbs. ON *plœgja*, etc.; now general Gmc. for sb. and vb., the sb. also widely spread as loanword in eastern Europe (Lith. *plūgas*, Russ. *plug*, etc.). Origin much disputed and quite uncertain. Walde-P. 1.812. Falk-Torp 838. Schrader, Reallex. 2.186 f. Kluge-G. 442.

OE *sulh* : Lat. *sulcus* 'furrow', etc. (8.212).

6. Lith. *plūgas*, fr. Gmc., for the modern plow. For wooden plow either the old *arklas* (above, 1), or *žagrė* : *žagaras* 'dry limb', OHG *kegil* 'peg, stake', Sw. *kage* 'tree-stump'. Walde-P. 1.569 f.

7. ChSl. *orati, ralo*, etc., above, 1.

SCr. *plug*, etc., general Slavic for the modern plow, loanword fr. Gmc. (above, 5).

Russ. *socha* 'wooden plow' : ChSl. *socha* 'cudgel' (Boh., Pol. 'forked stick plow-handle', etc.), outside connection disputed, perh. : Skt. *çākhā-* 'branch', Goth. *hōha* 'plow', etc. (above, 4). Walde-P. 1.335. Stender-Petersen 409 f.

Russ. *pachat'* (also *pašnja* 'plow-land') : late ChSl. *pachati* 'shake, fan', Russ. *pachnút'* 'blow', *páchnut'* 'smell', etc. Brückner 389. 'Plow' fr. 'shake up' or the like.

8. Skt. *kṛṣ-*, Av. *karš-*, both also 'draw, pull', beside : Skt. *karṣū-*, Av. *karša-* 'a furrow', outside connections dub. Walde-P. 1.429. Barth. 456 f.

Skt. *lāñgala-* (RV+) perh. with *lāñgula-* 'tail, penis' : Lith. *linguoti* 'swing, rock'. Walde-P. 2.436. Otherwise, as loanword fr. a pre-Aryan language, Przyluski, BSL 22.118 f.

Skt. *sīra-* (RV+), perh., with *sīta-* 'furrow', fr. IE **sē(i)-* 'throw' and 'sow' (8.31), and denoting a kind of 'drill-plow' (i.e. for plowing and sowing) such as is attested for ancient Mesopotamia and modern India. Bloch, La charrue védique, Bull. School of Or. Studies 8.414 ff.

Skt. *hala-*, perh. : Arm. *jol* 'post, stake', Lith. *žuolis* 'stick, tree-trunk'; or : Arm. *jlem* 'plow' (vb.), all of dub. root connection. Walde-P. 1.629.

Av. *aēša-*, NPers. *xeš* prob. : Skt. *īṣā-* 'pole of a plow or wagon', Grk. *οἴᾱξ* 'rudder-handle', etc. (Walde-P. 1.167, without *aēša-*). Barth. 32.

8.212 FURROW

Grk.	*αὖλαξ*	Goth.	. . . .	Lith.	*vaga*
NG	*αὐλάκι*	ON	*for*	Lett.	*vaga*
Lat.	*sulcus*	Dan.	*fure*	ChSl.	*brazda*
It.	*solco*	Sw.	*fåra*	SCr.	*brazda*
Fr.	*sillon*	OE	*furh*	Boh.	*brázda*
Sp.	*surco*	ME	*forwe*	Pol.	*brózda*
Rum.	*brazdă*	NE	*furrow*	Russ.	*borozda*
Ir.	*etrech*	Du.	*voor*	Skt.	*sītā-, karṣū-*
NIr.	*clais (eitre)*	OHG	*furh, furuh*	Av.	*karša-*
W.	*rhych*	MHG	*vurch, vurich*		
Br.	*ero, erv*	NHG	*furche*		

Words for 'furrow' (here, of course, that made by the plow) are in part derived from verbs for 'draw', 'dig', or 'sow'(?). But in the case of Fr. *sillon* and probably some of the others the development was through the ridge of the furrow.

1. Grk. *αὖλαξ*, fr. **ἀϝλακ-* (beside **ἀϝολκ-*, **ἀϝλοκ-* in Hom. *ὦλξ*, Att. *ἄλοξ*) : Lith. *vilkti, velku*, ChSl. *vlěšti, vlěką* 'draw' (9.33). Hence NG *αὐλάκι*. Walde-P. 1.306.

2. Lat. *sulcus* (> It. *solco*, Sp. *surco*) : Grk. *ἕλκω* 'draw' (9.33), *ὁλκός* 'track,

trace', etc. (but not 'furrow' made by the plow), OE *sulh* 'plow'. Walde-P. 2.507. Ernout-M. 999.

Fr. *sillon*, in its earlier use 'heaped-up earth', fr. a vb. meaning 'heap up earth', prob. of Gallic orig. Hence used for the ridge of earth between furrows, then for the furrow itself. REW 7797a. Gamillscheg 801.

Fr. *raie*, 'furrow' in OFr. and still in local use more widespread than *sillon* (cf. Atlas linguistique, Carte 1234), fr. a Gallic word represented by W. *rhych*, etc. (below, 3). REW 7299. Gamillscheg 736. Bloch 2.204.

Rum. *brazdă*, fr. Slavic (below, 6).

3. Ir. *etrech*, NIr. *eitre*, W. *rhych*, OBr. *rec* : OE *furh*, etc. (below, 4). Pedersen 1.122. Thurneysen, Keltorom. 74 f.

NIr. *clais*, also 'groove, trench' as Ir. *class* : *claidim* 'dig' (8.22).

Br. *ero, erv* = OCorn., W. *erw* 'field' : OHG *ero* 'earth', etc. (1.21). Walde-P. 1.142. Pedersen 1.63.

4. ON *for*, OE, OHG *furh*, etc., general Gmc. : Lat. *porca* 'ridge between furrows', W. *rhych* 'furrow', etc., perh. Skt. *parçāna-* 'chasm'. Walde-P. 2.47. Falk-Torp 283.

5. Lith., Lett. *vaga*, etym. dub. Mühl.-Endz. 4.431.

6. ChSl. *brazda*, etc., general Slavic, prob. (as orig. the ridge between furrows) : Skt. *bhṛṣṭi-* 'point, edge', OE *brerd* 'edge, brim', etc. Walde-P. 2.133. Berneker 75.

7. Skt. *sītā-*, perh. fr. IE **sē(i)-* 'throw' and 'sow' (8.31). See under Skt. *sīra-* 'plow' (8.21).

Skt. *karṣū-*, Av. *karša-*, fr. Skt. *kṛṣ-*, Av. *karš-* 'draw' and 'plow' (8.21).

8.22 DIG

Grk.	*σκάπτω, ὀρύσσω, λαχαίνω*	Goth.	*graban*	Lith.	*kasti*
NG	*σκάβω*	ON	*grafa*	Lett.	*rakt*
Lat.	*fodere*	Dan.	*grave*	ChSl.	*kopati, ryti*
It.	*vangare (scavare)*	Sw.	*gräva*	SCr.	*kopati, riti*
Fr.	*creuser (fouir, fouiller)*	OE	*grafan, delfan*	Boh.	*kopati, ryti*
		ME	*grave, digge, delve*	Pol.	*kopać, ryć*
		NE	*dig (delve)*	Russ.	*kopat', ryt'*
Sp.	*cavar*	Du.	*graven (delven)*	Skt.	*khan-*
Rum.	*săpa*	OHG	*graban, telban*	Av.	*kan-*
Ir.	*claidim*	MHG	*graben, telben*		
NIr.	*rōmharaim*	NHG	*graben*		
W.	*cloddio, palu*				
Br.	*klaza, kava*				

1. Grk. *σκάπτω* (NG pop. *σκάβω*) ChSl., SCr., Boh. *kopati*, Pol. *kopać*, Russ. *kopat'* : Lith. *kapas* 'grave, mound', Lett. *kaps* 'grave', Grk. *σκάπετος, κάπετος* 'grave, ditch', IE *(*s*)*kăp-*. Walde-P. 2.560 f. Berneker 562 f.

Grk. *ὀρύσσω* : Lat. *runcāre* 'root up, weed', Skt. *luñc-* 'tear out, pluck', fr. an extension of IE **reu-* in Lith. *rauti* 'root out', etc. Walde-P. 2.353. Ernout-M. 877.

Grk. *λαχαίνω* (not common) : Ir. *laige* 'spade', W. *llain* 'blade'. Walde-P. 2.381.

2. Lat. *fodere* (> Fr. *fouir*) : ChSl. *bodą, bosti* 'stick, prick', Lith. *bedu, besti* 'stick into', Lett. *bedu, best* 'bury', W. *bedd* 'grave', Goth. *badi* 'bed', etc. Walde-P. 2.188. Ernout-M. 373. Walde-H. 1.521 f.

It. *vangare*, fr. *vanga* 'spade' (8.23).

It. *scavare* (tech. 'excavate'), Sp.

cavar, fr. Lat. (*ex-*)*cavāre* 'make hollow, excavate, deriv. of *cavus* 'hollow' (12.72), REW 1788, 2964.

Fr. *creuser*, fr. *creux* 'hollow' (12.72).

Fr. *fouiller* ('dig', but mostly as archeological term for 'excavate'; the pop. sense of the word is 'rummage'), fr. **fodiculāre* extended fr. Lat. *fodicāre* 'dig, pierce', fr. *fodere* (above). REW 3404. Wartburg 3.666 f.

Rum. *săpa* (cf. Fr. *saper* 'undermine', It. *zappare* 'dig up'), deriv. of *sapă* 'hoe', MLat. *sappa* (8.25).

3. Ir. *claidim* (NIr. *claidhim* 'excavate', W. *claddu* 'bury', old 'dig'; now for 'dig' W. *cloddio*, fr. *clawdd* 'mine, quarry', arch. 'ditch'), Br. *klaza* : Lat. *clādēs* 'injury', *-cellere* 'strike', etc. fr. an extension of **kel-* in words for 'strike, cut, etc.'. Walde-P. 1.439. Walde-H. 1.225.

NIr. *rōmharaim* (W. arch. *rhyforio*), fr. NIr. *rōmhar*, MIr. *ruamor* 'effossio' : ChSl. *ryti* 'dig' (below, 6). Walde-P. 2.352. Stokes 234. Otherwise Loth, RC 34.146 f. (taking as cpd. of *ro-* and *mor-*, *mār-* : Fr. *marre* 'hoe', Lat. *marra*, but this is not a Gallic word, cf. Walde-H. 2.43).

W. *palu*, fr. *pal* 'spade' (8.23).

Br. *kava*, fr. *kao, kav* 'cellar, cave', fr. Fr. *cave* 'cellar' (Lat. *cavus* 'hollow', cf. Sp. *cavar* 'dig', above). Henry 54, 56.

4. Goth. *graban*, OE *grafan*, etc., general Gmc. : Lett. *grebt* 'scrape, hollow out', ChSl. *po-greti* 'bury', etc., IE **ghrebh-*. Walde-P. 1.653 f. Feist 218 f.

ME *digge* (14th cent.), NE *dig*, prob. fr. OFr. *diguer* 'make a dike, hollow out the earth', fr. *digue* 'dike', loanword from Gmc., as Du. *dijk* 'dam, dike, bank' = OE *dīc*, NE *ditch* (this : Lat. *fīgere* 'fix', etc. Walde-P. 1.832 f.). NED s.vv. *ditch, dig*.

OE *delfan*, ME *delve* (NE *delve* still dial. for 'dig' in literal sense), Du. *delven*, OHG *telban*, MHG *telben* : Russ. *dolbat'*, *dolbit'* 'chisel, hollow out', Lett. *dalbs* 'fish-prong, sort of hay-fork', etc. Walde-P. 1.866 f. Berneker 250 f.

5. Lith. *kasti* : Lett. *kast* 'scrape, rake', ChSl. *česati* 'scratch, comb', Grk. *ξέω* 'shave', IE **kes-*. Walde-P. 1.449 f.

Lett. *rakt* : Lith. *rakti* 'scratch, prick', *rakštas* 'grave', otherwise obscure. Mühl.-Endz. 3.475.

6. ChSl. *kopati*, etc., general Slavic, above, 1.

ChSl. *ryti*, etc., general Slavic : Lith. *rauti* 'tear out', ON *rȳja* 'tear out wool', Skt. *ru-* 'break to pieces', etc., IE **reu-*. Walde-P. 1.352.

7. Skt. *khan-*, Av., OPers. *kan-*, without certain Eur. connections. Walde-P. 1.399.

8.23 SPADE

Grk.	*ἄμη, σκαφεῖον*(?)	Goth.	. . . .	Lith.	*spatas, kasiklis*
NG	*φτυάρι, πατόφτυαρο*	ON	*pāll, reka*	Lett.	*lāpsta*
Lat.	*pāla*	Dan.	*spade*	ChSl.	*rylo*
It.	*vanga*	Sw.	*spade*	SCr.	*ašov, lopata*
Fr.	*bêche*	OE	*spadu, pāl*	Boh.	*rýč, lopata*
Sp.	*laya*	ME	*spade*	Pol.	*rydel*
Rum.	*lopată*	NE	*spade*	Russ.	*zastup, lopata*
Ir.	*rāme, laige*	Du.	*spade*	Skt.	*khanitra-*
NIr.	*rāmhan, lāighe*	OHG	*scūvala(?)*	Av.	*kąstra-*
W.	*pal, rhaw*	MHG	*grabeschīt*		
Br.	*pal*	NHG	*spaten (grabscheit)*		

For some of the ancient names of digging implements, especially the Greek, it is impossible to distinguish certainly between the 'spade' and some form of 'hoe'. On the other hand, 'spade' and 'shovel', though the latter is not a digging implement, are from their similar shape sometimes expressed by the same word.

1. Grk. *ἄμη* (that this was properly a 'spade' rather than a 'shovel' is indicated by the definition *τὸ ἐργαλεῖον ἐν ᾧ ὀρύττουσι τὴν γῆν*, and by *ἀμάρα* 'trench', *ἐξαμάω* 'dig out'), prob. : ChSl. *jama* 'pit', etc. Walde-P. 1.198. Solmsen, Beiträge 194 f.

Grk. *σκαφεῖον*, fr. the root of *σκάπτω*, aor. *ἐσκάφην* 'dig' (8.22), is the commonest word for a digging tool, but whether 'spade', 'hoe', or 'mattock' is not clear.

In modern Greece the common digging tool has been the *τσάπα*, a kind of heavy hoe (8.25). For the true spade, only recently introduced, *φτυάρι*, also and orig. 'shovel' (8.24), is commonly used. But a more distinctive term has also been coined, namely *πατόφτυαρο*, cpd. with first part : *πατῶ* 'step on, tread', hence 'shovel that one pushes with the foot', an excellent description. Cf. Russ. *zastup* (below, 6).

Grk. *λίστρον* is often translated 'spade' or 'hoe', but was some kind of a smoothing tool, a 'scraper' (cf. esp. Hom. Od. 22.455 and *λείστριον* Ditt. Syll. 972.119 with note), the source of NG *γλιστρῶ* 'slip, slide' (10.42). Prob. : Lett. *līst* 'grub up, level off'. Walde-P. 2.879. Boisacq 584. Mühl.-Endz. 2.490.

2. Lat. *pāla*, also and more persistent as 'shovel' (8.24), fr. **pāg-slā-* : *pangere* 'fix, drive in, sink in', Grk. *πήγνῡμι* 'fix', etc. Ernout-M. 723.

It. *vanga*, fr. late Lat. *vanga* 'spade with crossbar', a loanword but source uncertain (Gmc.?). Ernout-M. 1072. REW 9137.

Fr. *bêche*, OFr. *besche*, back-formation fr. OFr. *beschier* 'dig up', deriv. of a *bessos* 'hoe', Fr. dial. *besse*, this fr. a VLat. **bissus* 'double'(?). Wartburg 1.381, 382 f. Gamillscheg 93.

Sp. *laya*, loanword fr. Basque. REW 4957.

Rum. *lopată*, loanword fr. Slavic (below, 6).

3. Ir. *rāme* (rare in this sense), NIr. *rāmhan*, W. *rhaw*, orig. 'oar' as Ir. *rāme*, etc. (10.85). Stokes 39.

Ir. *laige*, NIr. *lāighe* 'spade' with narrow blade (> Anglo-Ir. *loy*, NED s.v.) : Grk. *λαχαίνω* 'dig'. Walde-P. 2.381. Stokes 238.

W., Br. *pal*, prob. loanword fr. Lat. *pāla* (above, 2). Pedersen 1.204. But cf. Walde-P. 1.435.

4. ON *pāll*, OE *pāl* fr. Lat. *pāla* (above, 2). Falk-Torp 862.

ON *reka*, also 'shovel' (reg. 'spade' in NIcel.), see 8.24.

OE *spadu*, ME, NE *spade*, Dan., Sw. *spade*, Du. *spade*, NHG *spaten* (fr. LG) : Grk. *σπάθη* 'flat blade', OE *spōn* 'chip, splinter', etc. Walde-P. 2.652 f. Falk-Torp 1110.

OHG *scūvala*, which reg. glosses Lat. *pāla*, is 'shovel' (8.24); also used for 'spade'?

MHG *grabeschīt*, NHG *grabscheit*, cpd. of *graben* 'dig' and OHG *scīt* 'wooden billet'.

5. Lith. *spatas* fr. NHG *spaten*.

Lith. *kasiklis, kastuvas* (neolog. for *spatas*), fr. *kasti* 'dig' (8.22).

Lett. *lāpsta*, also 'shovel', see 8.24.

6. ChSl. *rylo* (Supr.), Boh. *rýč*, Pol. *rydel* : ChSl. *ryti*, etc. 'dig' (8.22). Brückner 471.

SCr. *lopata*, etc. reg. 'shovel' (8.24), in part also 'spade' (> Rum. *lopată* 'spade, shovel').

SCr. *ašov*, fr. Hung. *ásó* 'spade, shovel' (: Hung. *ás* 'dig, mine').

Russ. *zastup* (but *lopata* usual for 'spade' as well as 'shovel'), fr. *zastupit'* 'tread on' (secondarily 'replace'), cpd. of *stupit'* 'tread, step' (ChSl. *stąpiti*), applied to the spade with reference to

the fact that one steps on it to push it into the ground.

7. Skt. *khanitra-*, Av. *kąstra-* : Skt. *khan-*, Av. *kan-* 'dig' (8.24).

8.24 SHOVEL

Grk.	πτύον	Goth.	-skaurō	Lith.	šiupelė, lopeta
NG	φτυάρι	ON	reka	Lett.	lâpsta
Lat.	pāla	Dan.	skovl	ChSl.	lopata
It.	pala	Sw.	skovel	SCr.	lopata
Fr.	pelle	OE	scofl	Boh.	lopata
Sp.	pala	ME	schovel	Pol.	lopata, szufla
Rum.	lopată	NE	shovel	Russ.	lopata
Ir.	slūasat	Du.	schop	Skt.	khanitra-
NIr.	sluasad	OHG	scūvala (scora)	Av.	....
W.	rhaw, siefl	MHG	schüvele, schüfel		
Br.	pal		(schor)		
		NHG	schaufel		

'Shovel' and 'spade', though implements of different purpose, are, from their similar shape, in part expressed by the same words. According as one or the other application seems the earlier, they are discussed in 8.23 or here.

1. Grk. πτύον 'winnowing-shovel', late dim. πτυάριον, whence NG φτυάρι (φκυάρι) 'shovel', perh. (with unexplained πτ as in πτόλις beside πόλις, and orig. sense of 'purifier' hence 'winnowing-shovel') : Lat. *pūrus* 'pure', Skt. *pū-* 'cleanse', OHG *fowen* 'sift grain', etc. Walde-P. 2.13. Boisacq 824.

2. Lat. *pāla* 'spade' (8.23), later 'shovel', whence in latter sense It., Sp. *pala*, Fr. *pelle*.

Rum. *lopată*, fr. Slavic (below, 5).

3. Ir. *slūasat*, NIr. *sluasad*, etym.? W. *rhaw*, also 'spade' (8.23). W. *siefl*, fr. NE *shovel*. Br. *pal*, also 'spade' (8.23).

4. Goth. *skaurō* in *winþi-skaurō* 'win-

nowing-shovel', OHG *scora* (rare), MHG *schor* (also 'hoe') : ON *skora* 'make an incision, score'. Walde-P. 2.552. Feist 566.

ON *reka* ('shovel' also in Norw.) : OE *racu*, etc. 'rake', Goth. *rikan* 'heap up'. See 8.27.

Dan. *skovl*, Sw. *skovel*, OE *scofl*, ME *schovel*, NE *shovel*, OHG *scūvala*, MHG *schüvele*, *schüfel* (LG > Lith. *šiupelė*, Pol. *szufla*), NHG *schaufel*, also with different suffix, Du. *schop* (like NHG *schüppe* 'scoop') : ON *skúfa*, OE *scūfan*, OHG *scioban*, etc. 'shove' (10.67). Walde-P. 2.556. Falk-Torp 1020 f.

5. Lith. *lopeta*, Lett. *lâpsta* (also 'spade'), OPruss. *lopto* 'spade', Slavic *lopata* (in part also 'spade') : Lith. *lopa*, Russ. *lapa* 'paw', Goth. *lōfa*, OE *lōf* 'palm of hand', etc. Walde-P. 2.428. Berneker 733.

6. Skt. *khanitra-* 'spade' or 'shovel', see 8.23.

8.25 HOE

Grk.	σκαπάνη, σμινύη, etc.	Goth.	....	Lith.	matikas, kaplys
NG	τσάπα, σκαλιστήρι	ON	....	Lett.	kaplis
Lat.	ligō, sarculum	Dan.	hakke	ChSl.	motyka
It.	zappa	Sw.	hacka	SCr.	motika
Fr.	houe	OE	mattuc	Boh.	motyka
Sp.	azada	ME	howe	Pol.	motyka
Rum.	sapă	NE	hoe	Russ.	motyka
Ir.	....	Du.	houweel	Skt.	....
NIr.	grafán, grafóg	OHG	houwa	Av.	....
W.	hof	MHG	houwe, hacke		
Br.	pigell	NHG	hacke, haue		

The numerous types of 'hoe' have this in common, that with them one hacks the soil and pulls toward one (in contrast to the spade, which one pushes). A crude hoe was man's earliest agricultural implement. Some of the words listed cover the combination tool, with transverse hoe-like blade at one end, at the other either a pick or a narrow ax-like blade, the 'mattock' (but to me a *pickax*, *mattock* being only a book word).

1. Grk. σκαπάνη, prob. 'hoe' or 'mattock' (NG lit. σκαπάνη is 'mattock'), fr. σκάπτω 'dig' (9.22).

Grk. σκαλίς, late σκαλιστήριον, NG σκαλίδα, σκαλιστήρι (a small weeding hoe vs. τσάπα, the heavy hoe in common use) : σκάλλω 'stir up, hoe', ON *skilja* 'divide', etc. From a by-form of the same root also δί-κελλα 'two-pronged hoe'. Walde-P. 2.591, 1.436.

Grk. σμινύη 'hoe' or 'mattock'(?) : σμίλη 'chisel', OE *smiþ* 'smith', etc. Walde-P. 2.686.

Grk. μάκελλα 'mattock', etym.? Boisacq 602. Prellwitz 116.

NG τσάπα, fr. It. *zappa* (below, 2).

2. Lat. *ligō* (> Sp. *legón*, a tool used in mining), perh. : late Grk. λίσγος (*λιγ-σκος ?), λισγάριον, NG dial. λισγάρι, 'a kind of spade', OE *slicc* 'hammer', etc., but all dub. Walde-P. 2.707. Ernout-M. 550. Walde-H. 1.800.

Lat. *sarculum* 'weeding hoe', fr. *sarrīre* 'weed', etym.? Ernout-M. 896.

Lat. *bidēns*, lit. 'with two teeth', used of a 'heavy two-pronged hoe'.

It. *zappa* (> NGr. τσάπα, Fr. *sape*), Rum. *sapă*, prob. fr. a pop. term for a 'he-goat' appearing as *zappu* in a gloss, Rum. *ţap*, etc. (3.37), hence applied first to the two-pronged grub-hoe, from its resemblance to the he-goat's horns. REW 9559. Rohlfs, Z. rom. Ph. 45.662 ff.

Fr. *houe*, fr. the Gmc. (below, 4).

Sp. *azada* (also augment. *azadón*) fr. VLat. *asciata*, deriv. of *ascia* 'adze', late also 'hoe' : Grk. ἀξίνα, Goth. *aqizi* 'ax', etc. (9.25). REW 697.

3. NIr. *grafán*, *grafóg*, fr. *grafaim* 'write, scrape, carve', *graf* 'mark', of the same orig. as *graifnim* 'write' (18.51).

W. *hof*, fr. ME *howe*, NE *hoe*, dial. *how*.

Br. *pigell*, dim. of *pik*, fr. Fr. *pic* 'pickax' (of obscure origin, cf. Gamillscheg 692). Henry 223.

4. OE *mattoc*, *mattuc* (simple 'hoe' or already the combination tool like NE *mattock?*), prob. fr. a VLat. *matteūca* (> Fr. *massue* 'club', etc. REW 5426), NE *mace*, etc., REW 5425; cf. Lat. *mateola* 'mallet'), this : ChSl. *motyka* 'mattock', Skt. *matya-* 'harrow', etc. Pokorny, Z. sl. Ph. 5.393 f. Walde-P. 2.229 (but taking OE *mattoc* as Gmc. cognate). Walde-H. 2.49.

OHG *houwa* (> Fr. *houe* > ME

howe, NE *hoe*), MHG *houwe*, NHG *haue* (still the usual word for 'hoe' in the south, *hacke* in the north; cf. Kretschmer, Wortgeogr. 223), Du. *houweel*, fr. OHG *houwan* (NHG *hauen*), etc. 'strike, hew' (9.22). NED s.v. hoe sb.².

MHG, NHG *hacke* (MLG > Dan. *hakke*, Sw. *hacka*) : vb. MHG *hacken* 'hack'. Cf. also NED s.v. hack, sb.¹.

8.26 FORK

Grk.	δίκρανον	Goth.	....	Lith.	šakės
NG	δικράνι	ON	kvisl, tjúga	Lett.	dakša
Lat.	furca	Dan.	greb, tyv, gaffel	ChSl.	....
It.	forcone, forca	Sw.	gaffel, grep(e)	SCr.	vile
Fr.	fourche	OE	geafel, forca	Boh.	vidle
Sp.	horca	ME	forke	Pol.	widły
Rum.	furcă	NE	fork	Russ.	vily
Ir.	forc	Du.	vork	Skt.	....
NIr.	pice	OHG	gabala, furka	Av.	..
W.	fforch	MHG	gabel(e), furke		
Br.	forc'h	NHG	gabel		

Several of the words for 'fork' as an agricultural implement, 'pitchfork', are connected with words for 'branch', or as orig. 'two-pronged' derived fr. words for 'two'.

1. Grk. δίκρανον (rare, but δικρανίζω in pap., and NG δικράνι in common use), sb. of δίκρανος 'two-headed' : κάρα 'head' (4.20).

2. Lat. *furca* (> Romance words), etym.? Ernout-M. 403 f. Walde-H. 1.569 f.

3. Ir. *forc*, W. *fforch*, Br. *forc'h* fr. Lat. *furca*. Vendryes, De hib. voc. 144. Loth, Mots lat. 169.

NIr. *píce*, also 'pike, long spear' fr. NE *pike*, used also in the sense 'pitchfork' (cf. NED pike, sb.¹ 3b).

4. ON *kvisl* (esp. *myki-kvísl* 'dung-fork'), also 'branch or fork of a tree or river', prob. (with initial *k* for *t*) : OE *twisla* 'branch of a river', OHG *zwisila* 'forked object, branch', derivs. of ON *tveir*, etc. 'two'. Falk-Torp 607 f.

ON *tjúga*, Dan. *tyv* (usually cpd.

heytjúga, *høtyv* 'pitchfork'), deriv. of ON *tveir*, etc. 'two'. Falk-Torp 450 f.

Dan. *greb*, Sw. *grep(e)* : Sw. *gribe*, Sw. *gripa* 'grasp, seize'. Falk-Torp 343.

OE *geafel*, OHG *gabala*, MHG, NHG *gabel*, MLG *gaffel* (> Dan., Sw. *gaffel*) : Ir. *gabul* 'fork', esp. 'forked branch', W. *gafl* 'fork', Gallo-Lat. *gabalus* 'gallows', root connection? Walde-P. 1.533. Falk-Torp 294 (deriving Gmc. words fr. Celtic).

OE *forca*, *force*, ME *forke*, NE *fork*, Du. *vork*, OHG *furka*, MHG *furke*, fr. Lat. *furca*.

5. Lith. *šakės* (pl.) : Lith. *šaka* 'branch', Lett. *sakas* (pl.) 'hames', Skt. *çākhā-* 'branch', etc. Walde-P. 1.335.

Lett. *dakša*, perh. : MLG *tagge*, NHG *zacke* 'prong, point', Du. *tak* 'branch'. Mühl.-Endz. 1.433 f.

6. SCr. *vile*, Boh. *vidle*, Pol. *widły*, Russ. *vily* (all pl.) : ChSl. *viti* 'wind, twist', *vĕja* 'branch', etc. Brückner 613.

7. There seem to be no Skt. or Av. references for a 'fork'.

8.27 RAKE

Grk.	ἁρπάγη	Goth.	....	Lith.	grėblys
NG	τσουγκράνα	ON	hrífa	Lett.	grābeklis
Lat.	rāstrum, rastellus	Dan.	rive	ChSl.	....
It.	rastrello	Sw.	rāfsa	SCr.	grablje
Fr.	râteau	OE	racu, raca	Boh.	hrábě
Sp.	rastrillo, rastro	ME	rake	Pol.	grabie
Rum.	greblă	NE	rake	Russ.	grabli
Ir.	rastal	Du.	hark	Skt.	....
NIr.	raca, rastal	OHG	rehho, recho	Av.	....
W.	cribin, rhaca	MHG	reche		
Br.	rastell	NHG	rechen, harke		

1. Grk. ἁρπάγη 'hook' and 'rake' (rare) : ἁρπάζω 'snatch away', ἅρπαξ 'robber', ἅρπη 'sickle', Lat. *sarpere* 'prune', etc. Walde-P. 2.501.

NG τσουγκράνα, orig.? Reminds one of NG τσουγκρίζω, dial. τσουγκρῶ 'strike together', etc., of imitative origin (G. Meyer, Neugr. Stud. 2.90), but no apparent connection.

2. Lat. *rāstrum* (> Sp. *rastro*), dim. *rāstellus* (> Fr. *râteau*), and, by crossing with *rāstrum*, It. *rastrello*, Sp. *rastrillo*) : Lat. *rādere* 'shave, scrape, scratch', W. *rhathu* 'rub, smooth', etc. Walde-P. 2.369. Ernout-M. 849 f. REW 7078-79.

Rum. *greblă* fr. Slavic (below, 5).

3. Ir. *rastal*, Br. *rastell*, fr. Lat. *rāstellus* (above, 2).

NIr. *raca*, W. *rhaca*, fr. NF *rake* (below, 4).

W. *cribin* (cf. *crib* 'comb, crest, ridge') : Ir. *crích* 'border', Grk. κρίνω 'judge', Lat. *cernere* 'separate, distinguish', etc., fr. an extension of IE *(s)ker-* 'cut'. Walde-P. 2.584.

4. ON *hrífa*, Dan. *rive*, Sw. dial. *riva* : ON *hrífa* 'snatch after, scratch',

East Fris. *rīfen*, Du. *rijven* 'rake', Lat. *scrībere* 'write', fr. extensions of IE *(s)ker-* 'cut'. Walde-P. 2.586. Falk-Torp 906.

Sw. *rāfsa* : *rafsa* 'scratch, rummage', Dan. *rapse* 'snatch away, scrape together', OHG *raspōn* 'scrape together'. Falk-Torp 880. Hellquist 867.

OE *racu*, *raca*, ME, NE *rake*, OHG *recho*, *rehho*, MHG *reche*, NHG *rechen* : ON *reka* 'shovel', Goth. *rikan* 'heap up, collect', OHG *rehhan* 'scrape together'; perh. fr. the same root as OHG *richten*, Lat. *regere* 'direct', Grk. ὀρέγω 'stretch out', etc., with development fr. 'stretch out the hand' to 'collect'. Walde-P. 2.364 ff. Falk-Torp 870.

Du. *hark*, NHG *harke* (in the north, elsewhere *rechen*; cf. Kretschmer, Wortgeogr. 231) : LG *harken* 'scrape, scratch', ON *harka* 'drag with a scraping sound', prob. Skt. *kharj-* 'creak', etc. Walde-P. 1.415. Falk-Torp 381.

5. Lith. *grėblys*, Lett. *grābeklis*, SCr. *grablje*, Boh. *hrábě* (pl.), Pol. *grabie*, Russ. *grabli* (pl.) : Lith. *grėbti*, Lett. *grābt*, ChSl. *grabiti* 'snatch, seize, tear away', etc., IE *grebh-*. Walde-P. 1.653. Berneker 344.

8.28 HARROW

Grk.	*ὀξίνα, ἀγρεῖφνα*	Goth.	. . . .	Lith.	*akėčios, ekėčios*
NG	*βωλοκόπος, σβάρνα*	ON	*herfi*	Lett.	*ecēša*
Lat.	*irpex, occa, crātis*	Dan.	*harv*	ChSl.	. . . .
It.	*erpice*	Sw.	*harv*	SCr.	*brana, drljača*
Fr.	*herse*	OE	*egeþe, fealh*	Boh.	*brany, vlačidlo*
Sp.	*grada*	ME	*harwe*	Pol.	*brona*
Rum.	*grapă*	NE	*harrow*	Russ.	*borona*
Ir.	*clīath*	Du.	*eg, egge*	Skt.	*matya-*
NIr.	*brāca*	OHG	*egida*	Av.	. . . .
W.	*og, oged*	MHG	*egede, egde, ege*		
Br.	*oged*	NHG	*egge*		

1. A related group, prob. fr. IE **ak̂-* in words for 'sharp, pointed', Grk. ἄκρος, ὀξύς, Lat. *ācer*, etc. Walde-P. 1.31 f. Schrader, Reallex. 1.215. Ernout-M. 695. Weigand-H. 1.404 f.

Grk. ὀξίνα (Hesych.); Lat. *occa;* W. *oged*, *og*, Br. *oged;* OE *egeþe*, OHG *egida*, MHG *eg(e)de* (later *ege*, NHG *egge*, Du. *eg*, *egge* formed after deriv. vbs.); Lith. *akėčios*, *ekėčios*, Lett. *ecēša*.

2. Grk. ἀγρῖφη, ἀγρεῖφνα (both rare, and uncertain whether 'harrow' or 'rake'), prob. (with ἁ- cop.) : γριφᾶσθαι (Hesych.) 'write, scrape, scratch'. Walde-P. 1.607.

NG βωλοκόπος, in class. Grk. adj. 'clod-breaking', cpd. of βῶλος 'clod' and the root of κόπτω 'strike, cut'.

NG pop. σβάρνα, fr. Slavic, SCr. *brana*, etc. (below, 6). G. Meyer, Neugr. Stud. 2.56.

3. Lat. *irpex* (**hirpex*, also **herpex*, *erpica* > It. *erpice*, Fr. *herse* > ME *herse*, now *hearse* in different sense), orig. dial. word, deriv. of Samnite *hirpus* 'wolf', hence 'harrow' from its sharp teeth, like Lat. (*frēnum*) *lupātum* 'curb with sharp teeth' fr. *lupus* 'wolf'. Ernout-M. 455. Walde-H. 1.651. REW 4141.

Lat. *crātis* 'wickerwork, hurdle', and (as orig. a frame of wickerwork with teeth, *crātēs dentātae*) 'harrow' (> Sp. *grada*) : OHG *hurt* 'wickerwork', Goth. *haurds* 'door', Grk. κάρταλος 'basket', etc. Walde-P. 1.421. Ernout-M. 228. REW 2304.

Lat. *occa*, above, 1.

Rum. *grapă*, orig. 'hook' : It. *grappa* 'clamp', Sp. *grapa* 'clamp', etc., all loanwords fr. Gmc., OHG *crapfo* 'hook, claw', etc. Tiktin 697. REW 4760.

4. Ir. *clīath* 'wickerwork' (: W. *clwyd* 'hurdle', etc. Walde-P. 1.490 ff.), also 'harrow' (cf. K. Meyer, Contrib., s.v.), a semantic borrowing fr. Lat. *crātis*.

NIr. *brāca* (also a carding implement), fr. NE *brake* 'instrument for breaking flax' and 'harrow' (NED *brake*, sb.[3]).

W. *og*, *oged*, Br. *oged*, above, 1.

5. ON *herfi*, Dan. Sw. *harv*, ME *harwe* (loanword fr. Norse?), NE *harrow* prob. : Lat. *carpere* 'pluck', Lett. *kārpīt* 'scrape', etc., fr. an extension of *(*s*)*ker-* 'cut'. Walde-P. 2.581. Walde-H. 1.172. Falk-Torp 383. Hellquist 339.

OE *fealh* (gl. *occa*), perh. fr. notion of 'crooked, bent' : OE *felg*, OHG *felga* 'rim of a wheel' (NE *felloe, felly*), of which the further root connection is disputed. Walde-P. 1.516. Falk-Torp 288.

6. Lith., Lett. forms, above, 1.

7. SCr. *brana*, etc., general Slavic, fr. **borchna*, **bhorsnā* : ON *burst*, OE *byrst* 'bristle', Skt. *bhṛṣṭi-* 'point, edge', etc.; or fr. **borna* : ON *barmr* 'edge', Grk. φάρος 'furrow', etc. Walde-P. 2.132. Berneker 73 f.

SCr. *drljača*, fr. *drljati* 'to harrow', extension of Slavic *dĭrati* 'tear' : Goth. *-tairan*, Grk. δέρω etc. Berneker 255.

Boh. *vlačidlo*, fr. *vláčeti* 'drag, trail' : ChSl. *vlačiti* iter. of *vlěšti* 'draw'. Walde-P. 1.306.

8. Skt. *matya-* : Lat. *mateola* 'mallet', OE *mattoc*, ChSl. *motyka* 'hoe', etc. (8.25).

8.31 SOW; SEED

Grk.	*σπείρω; σπέρμα*	Goth.	*saian; fraiw*	Lith.	*sėti; sėkla*
NG	*σπέρνω; σπόρος*	ON	*sā; frjō*	Lett.	*sēt; sēkla*
Lat.	*serere, sēmināre; sēmen*	Dan.	*saa; frø*	ChSl.	*sěti; sěmę*
It.	*seminare; seme, semenza*	Sw.	*så; frö*	SCr.	*sijati; sjeme*
Fr.	*semer; graine, semence*	OE	*sāwan; sǣd*	Boh.	*síti; semeno*
Sp.	*sembrar; semilla*	ME	*sowe; sede*	Pol.	*siać; siemię, nasienie*
Rum.	*semăna; sămînța*	NE	*sow; seed*	Russ.	*sejat'; semja*
Ir.	*sīlaim; sīl*	Du.	*zaaien; zaad*	Skt.	*vap-; bīja-*
NIr.	*cuirim; sīol*	OHG	*sāen; sāmo*	Av.	. . . .; *taoxman-, čiϑra-*
W.	*hau; had*	MHG	*sæjen; sāme*		
Br.	*hada; had*	NHG	*säen; same*		

1. IE **sē-* 'sow' in verbs and nouns in all the European branches except Greek. The primary verbs are often displaced by derivatives of the noun. Doubtless the same root as **sē-*, **sēi-* 'throw', seen in Skt. *sāyāka-*, *senā-* 'missile' (for indirect evidence of the sense 'sow' also in Skt., cf. Bloch, Bull. School of Or. Stud. 8.414). Walde-P. 2.459 ff. Persson, Beiträge 361 ff. Ernout-M. 929 f. Feist 404.

Lat. *serere* (*serō* fr. **si-sō*, perf. *sēvī*), *sēmen* (> It. *seme;* **sēmentia* > It. *semenza*, Fr. *semence*, Rum. *sămînță;* dim. > Sp. *semilla*), whence again *sēmināre* (> It. *seminare*, Fr. *semer*, Sp. *sembrar*, Rum. *semăna*); Ir. *sīl*, NIr. *sīol* 'seed', whence Ir. *sīlaim* 'sow'—W., Br. *had* 'seed', whence W. *hadu* 'go to seed', Br. *hada* 'sow'; Goth. *saian*, ON *sā*, OE *sāwan*, etc., general Gmc. vb. for 'sow'—sbs. OE *sǣd*, ME *sede*, NE *seed*, Du. *zaad* (Goth. *-sēþs* in *manasēþs* 'mankind'; ON *sāð*, *sǣði*, Dan. *sæd*, Sw. *säd* mostly in secondary uses 'crop', 'semen', 'offspring', OHG *sāt*, NHG *saat* 'crop'), and (with suffix as in Lat. *sēmen*) OHG *sāmo*, NHG *same;* Lith. *sėti*, Lett. *sēt*, ChSl. *sěti*, *sějati*, etc., with sbs. Lith. *sėkla*, Lett. *sēkla*, ChSl. *sěmę*, etc., general Balto-Slavic; Toch. A *sāry-* 'sow' (SSS 477).

2. Grk. σπείρω, NG σπέρνω, with sbs. Grk. σπέρμα 'seed', σπόρος mostly 'sowing', but in NG 'seed', prob. : Arm. *p'arat* 'scatter, separate', MHG *spræjen* 'sprinkle, spray', etc. Walde-P. 2.670. Boisacq 894.

3. Fr. *graine* 'seed', fr. VLat. *grāna* sg. coll., orig. pl. of Lat. *grānum* 'grain, kernel' (8.42).

4. NIr. *cuirim* 'place, put' (12.12), hence esp. 'place seed, sow'.

W. *hau* 'sow', deriv. of MW *se, he* 'seed' : Lat. *seges* 'field of grain, crop'. Walde-P. 2.480. Pedersen 1.99.

5. Goth. *fraiw*, ON *frjō*, Dan. *frø*, Sw. *frö* (the usual Scand. word for 'seed' for planting; for ON *sāð*, etc., see above, 1), etym.? Feist 163. Falk-Torp 280.

6. Skt. *vap-* 'strew, scatter', esp. 'sow' : Av. aor. *vīvapat* 'laid waste', outside connections? Walde-P. 1.256.

Skt. *bīja-* (NPers. *bīdž*, Baluchi *bidz*), obscure. Uhlenbeck 190.

Av. *čiϑra-* (NPers. *čihr* 'origin'), etym.? Barth. 587.

Av. *taoxman-* (NPers. *tuxm* 'seed, race') : Skt. *tokman-* 'young barley stalk', *tuc-* 'children, offspring', perh. fr. an extension of IE **teu-* 'swell'. Walde-P. 1.713. Barth. 623.

8.32 MOW, REAP

Grk.	*θερίζω, ἀμάω*	Goth.	*sneiþan*	Lith.	*piauti*
NG	*θερίζω*	ON	*slā*	Lett.	*pl'aut*
Lat.	*metere*	Dan.	*slaa, meje*	ChSl.	*žęti*
It.	*mietere, segare, falciare*	Sw.	*slå, meja*	SCr.	*žeti, kositi*
Fr.	*moissoner (faucher)*	OE	*māwan, rīpan*	Boh.	*žíti, síci, kositi*
Sp.	*segar, guadañar*	ME	*mowe, repe*	Pol.	*żąć, siec, kosić*
Rum.	*secera, cosi*	NE	*mow (reap)*	Russ.	*žat', kosit'*
Ir.	*bongaim*	Du.	*maaien*	Skt.	*lū-, dā-*
NIr.	*buanaim, spealaim*	OHG	*mājan, māen*	Av.	. . . .
W.	*medi, pladuro*	MHG	*mæjen*		
Br.	*medi, falc'hat*	NHG	*mähen*		

Words for 'mow' or 'reap' (in the old specific sense, now uncommon, of NE *reap*) are mostly from 'cut', or in some cases 'strike', with partial or complete specialization to 'cut grain' (and besides the words listed here the common words for 'cut' may be freely used in equivalent expressions, as NE *cut*, NHG *schneiden*, etc.). In one group the specific 'mow' is common to Greek, Latin, Celtic, and Germanic. Owing to the natural association, words for 'mow, reap' may be used for 'gather the crop, harvest', and this may become the dominant sense (as in NE *reap*). Conversely, words in which the latter sense is the more original may serve also for the specific 'mow, reap', and so are included here (but not those which are used only in the broad sense 'reap' = 'harvest', as OHG *arōn*, NHG *ernten*, for which see under 'harvest', 8.41).

1. IE **mē-* **met-*. Walde-P. 2.259. Ernout-M. 613.

**mē-*. Grk. ἀμάω (poet.), OE *māwan*, ME *mowe*, NE *mow*, Du. *maaien*, MLG *mējen* (> Dan. *meje*, Sw. *meja*), OHG *mājan*, *māen*, MHG *mæjen*, NHG *mähen*.

**met-*. Lat. *metere* (> It. *mietere*), W., Br. *medi*, cf. also NIr. *meitheal* 'a party of reapers', OHG *mad* 'swath', OE *mæþ* 'mowing, mown hay'.

2. Grk. θερίζω, fr. θέρος 'summer' and hence also 'harvest' (8.41).

3. It. *segare*, Sp. *segar*, fr. Lat. *secāre* 'cut' (9.22).

It. *falciare*, Fr. *faucher*, derivs. of It. *falce*, Fr. *faux*, Lat. *falx* 'scythe' (8.33).

Fr. *moissoner*, fr. *moisson* 'harvest', fr. Lat. *messiō* 'reaping' : *metere* 'mow' (above, 1). REW 5542.

Sp. *guadañar* (*guadaña* 'sickle' is a back-formation), as orig. 'harvest', fr. a Gmc. (Frank., Langob.?) **waidanjan* = OHG *weidenen* 'hunt, go out in search of food', *weidōn* 'pasture, hunt', ON *veiða* 'hunt, fish', etc. REW 9483.

Rum. *secera*, fr. *secere* 'sickle' (8.33).

Rum. *cosi*, fr. Slavic (below, 7).

4. Ir. *bongaim* (general sense 'break'), with vbl. n. *buain*, whence NIr. *buanaim* : Skt. *bhañj-* 'break'. Walde-P. 2.149 ff.

NIr. *spealaim*, fr. *speal* 'scythe' (8.33).

W. *pladuro*, fr. *pladur* 'scythe' (8.33).

Br. *falc'hat*, fr. *falc'h* 'scythe' (8.33).

5. Goth. *sneiþan* (prob. general 'cut', but renders θερίζω) = ON *snīða*, OE *snīþan* 'cut', etc. (9.22).

ON *slā*, Dan. *slaa*, Sw. *slå* 'strike' (9.21), used also for 'mow'.

OE *rīpan*, ME *repe*, NE *reap* (no longer a farm term, at least in United States, but cf. *reaper* for the machine) : Norw. *ripa* 'tear off, strip off' (as berries from a bush), OS *rīpi*, OE *rīpe*, OHG *rīfi* 'ripe' (orig. 'ready for reaping'), beside ON *rīfa* 'tear', etc., all prob. fr. extensions of IE **rei-* in words for 'tear, scratch', etc. Walde-P. 2.343. Falk-Torp 902, 906.

6. Lith. *piauti* ('cut' and 'mow'), Lett. *pl'aut* (specialized to 'mow, reap') : Lat. *pavīre* 'strike, pound', *putāre* 'cut', Grk. παίω 'beat', etc. Walde-P. 2.12.

7. ChSl. *žęti*, etc., general Slavic : Lith. *genėti* 'trim, prune', Skt. *han-* 'strike, kill', Grk. θείνω 'strike', etc., IE **gʷhen-*. Walde-P. 1.679 ff.

SCr., Boh. *kositi*, Pol. *kosić*, Russ. *kosit'*, fr. *kosa* 'scythe' (8.33), and used esp. of cutting grass in contrast to preceding group. Berneker 581.

Boh. *síci*, Pol. *siec* : ChSl. *sěšti*, Lat. *secāre* 'cut' (9.22).

8. Skt. *lū-* 'cut' and 'mow' (cf. *lavitra-* 'sickle') : Grk. λύω 'loose', ON *lē* 'sickle', etc. Walde-P. 2.407.

Skt. *dā-* (3 sg. *dāti*, *dyati*) 'cut off, divide' and 'mow' (cf. *dātra-* 'sickle') : Grk. δαίομαι 'divide, share', etc. Walde-P. 1.763 ff.

8.33 SICKLE; SCYTHE

Grk.	*δρέπανον, ἅρπη*	Goth.	*gilþa*	Lith.	*piautuvas; dalgis*
NG	*δρεπάνι; κόσα*	ON	*sigðr; lē*	Lett.	*cirpa, sirpis; izkapts*
Lat.	*falx*	Dan.	*segl; le*	ChSl.	*srŭpŭ; kosa*
It.	*falce*	Sw.	*skära; lie*	SCr.	*srp; kosa*
Fr.	*faucille; faux*	OE	*sicol; sīðe*	Boh.	*srp; kosa*
Sp.	*hoz; guadaña, dalle*	ME	*sikel; sithe*	Pol.	*sierp; kosa*
Rum.	*secere; coasă*	NE	*sickle; scythe*	Russ.	*serp; kosa*
Ir.	*corrān (serr); spel*	Du.	*sikkel; zeis*	Skt.	*dātra-, sṛṇī-, lavitra-*
NIr.	*corrān; speal*	OHG	*sihila; segansa*	Av.	. . . .
W.	*cryman; pladur*	MHG	*sichel; segens(e)*		
Br.	*fals; falc'h*	NHG	*sichel; sense*		

'Sickle' (the older implement) and 'scythe' are sometimes expressed by the same word, notably Lat. *falx*, covering 'sickle' (*falx messōria*), 'scythe' (*falx faenāria*), and also 'pruning hook' (Grk. δρέπανον is 'sickle' but is also used of the 'scythes' on the Persian chariots). But in general they are denoted by different words, of distinct formal, though similar semantic, origin, namely, the notion of 'cut' or the like. Cf. Niedermann, Essais d'étym. 17 ff.

1. Grk. ἅρπη, MIr., OW *serr* (but taken as loanword fr. Lat. *serra* 'saw' by Vendryes, De hib. voc. 177, Loth, Mots lat. 206, Niedermann, op. cit. 17), Lett. *sirpis*, ChSl. *srŭpŭ*, etc., general Slavic : Lat. *sarpere* 'prune', fr. **serp-*, prob. extension of **ser-* in Skt. *sṛṇī-* 'sickle'. Walde-P. 2.500 ff. Ernout-M. 896.

2. Grk. δρέπανον : δρέπω 'break off, pluck', SCr. *drpati* 'tear', etc. fr. **drep-* extension of **der-* in Grk. δέρω 'flay', Skt. *dṛ-* 'burst, tear', Goth. *dis-tairan* 'tear', etc. Walde-P. 1.801.

NG κόσα 'scythe', fr. Slavic (below, 7). G. Meyer, Neugr. Stud. 2.34.

3. Lat. *falx* (> It. *falce*, Fr. *faux*, dim. *faucille*, Sp. *hoz*), perh. loanword fr. a (Ligurian?) form preserved in Sicilian ζάγκλον 'sickle' (Thuc. 6.4.5, etc.),

Σάγκλα, Δάνκλη. Niedermann, op. cit. 24. Ernout-M. 327. Walde-H. 1.449 f.

Sp. *dalle*, Cat. *dalla*, OFr. *dail, daile* (Fr. dial. *dal*, etc.), late Lat. *daculum* (in glosses), perh. of the same ultimate origin as Lat. *falx*. Niedermann, op. cit. 29 ff. REW 2458.

Sp. *guadaña*, back-formation to *guadañar* 'mow' (8.52).

Rum. *secere* fr. VLat. **sicilis*, fr. *sīcīlis* (Ennius), influenced by *secāre* 'cut'(?). Cf. also Lat. *secula* > OE *sicol*, etc. (below, 5). Ernout-M. 896. REW 7900.

Rum. *coasă*, fr. Slavic (below, 7).

4. Ir. *corrān* : *cirrim* 'cut off', Grk. καρπός 'harvest', Lat. *carpere* 'pluck', OE *hærfest* 'harvest', Lith. *kirpti* 'cut with shears', etc. Walde-P. 2.581. Pedersen 1.94.

Ir. *spel*, NIr. *speal*, etym. dub., perh. (*sp/ps*) : Grk. ψαλίς 'shears'. Stokes ap. Macbain 338.

W. *cryman*, fr. *crwm* 'bent, crooked' (cf. Ir. *cromān* 'a crooked surgical instrument', fr. *cromm* = W. *crwm*). Pedersen 2.27.

W. *pladur*, MW *paladur*, with agent suffix *-adur* (fr. Lat. *-ātōrem*), perh. first applied to a sharp digging instrument of some sort, fr. *palu* 'dig', cf. *pal* 'spade' (8.23).

Br. *fals* fr. OFr. *fals* (> Fr. *faux*); Br. *falc'h*, fr. Lat. *falx* (*falcem*). Henry 120.

5. Goth. *gilþa*, perh. : OE *gielm* 'sheaf', Arm. *jelm* 'furrow', Skt. *hala-* 'plow', fr. an IE **ĝhel-* 'cut'(?). Walde-P. 1.629. Feist 215.

ON *lē*, Dan. *le*, Sw. *lie*, MLG *lē* (**lewan*) : Skt. *lavitra-* 'sickle', *lū-* 'cut off, mow' (3.32). Walde-P. 2.407. Falk-Torp 650.

ON *sigðr*, OE *sīðe*, ME *sithe*, NE *scythe*, and with different suffix OHG *segansa*, MHG *segens(e)*, NHG *sense*, Du. *zeis*, fr. Gmc. **seg-*, IE **sek-* in Lat. *secāre* 'cut', etc. (9.22). Walde-P. 2.475. Falk-Torp 963.

OE *sicol*, OHG *sihila*, etc., general WGmc. (and Dan. *segl* fr. MLG *sekele*), fr. Lat. *secula* 'sickle' (Varro), deriv. of *secāre* 'cut'. Walde-P. 2.475. Falk-Torp 953. Kluge-G. 561.

Sw. *skära*, fr. vb. *skära* 'cut' = NE *shear*, NHG *scheren*, etc. (9.22).

6. Lith. *piautuvas*, OLith. *piuklas* (now 'saw'), OPruss. *piuclan* : *piauti* 'cut, mow' (8.32).

Lith. *dalgis* (> Lett. dial. *dalgs, dalg'is*), OPruss. *doalgis* : Ir. *dlongim*, MIr. *dluigim* 'split', ON *telgja* 'whittle', fr. **delgh-* (**dlegh-*), extension of **del-* in Skt. *dal-* 'split, burst', etc. Walde-P. 1.812. Berneker 207.

Lett. *cirpa*, through Esth. *tsirp*, fr. ORuss. *sĭrpŭ* (ChSl. *srŭpŭ*, above, 1). Leskien, Bildung d. Nom. 269. Thomsen, Beröringer 78. Walde-P. 2.582. Otherwise (fr. *cirpt* 'shear') Mühl.-Endz. 1.386.

Lett. *sirpis*, above, 1.

Lett. *izkapts*, fr. *iz-kapāt* 'hew, cut out' : Lith. *iskapoti* 'chop', ChSl. *iskopiti* 'dig out', cpd. of *kopati* 'dig' (8.22). Mühl.-Endz. 1.748.

7. ChSl. *srŭpŭ*, etc., above, 1.

Slavic *kosa* (> Rum. *coasă*, NG κόσα), prob. (with *k* fr. *k̂* by dissim.) : Skt. *ças-* 'cut', *çastra-* 'knife', Lat. *castrāre* 'castrate', etc. Meillet, Études 178. Walde-P. 1.448. Berneker 581.

8. Skt. *dātra-*, fr. *dā-* 'mow' (8.32).

Skt. *sṛṇī-*, above, 1.

Skt. *lavitra-*, above, 5 (ON *lē*, etc.).

8.34 THRESH

Grk.	*ἀλοάω, τρῖβω*	Goth.	*þriskan*	Lith.	*kulti*
NG	*ἀλωνίζω*	ON	*þreskja*	Lett.	*kult*
Lat.	*terere*	Dan.	*tærske*	ChSl.	*mlatiti, vrěšti*
It.	*battere, tribbiare*	Sw.	*tröska*	SCr.	*mlatiti, vrijeći*
Fr.	*battre*	OE	*þerscan*	Boh.	*mlatiti*
Sp.	*trillar*	ME	*thresche*	Pol.	*młócić*
Rum.	*treera*	NE	*thresh* (*thrash*)	Russ.	*molotit'*
Ir.	*do-fuaircc* (3 sg.)	Du.	*dorschen*	Skt.	*mṛ-, prati-han-*
NIr.	*buailim*	OHG	*drescan*	Av.	x^v*asta-* 'threshed'
W.	*dyrnu*	MHG	*dreschen*		
Br.	*dourna*	NHG	*dreschen*		

Words for 'thresh' are (apart from the Grk. derivs. of 'threshing-floor') from the notions of 'rub', 'beat', or (rarely) 'drag', orig. applied to different methods, namely, (1) the rubbing with the hands (most primitive of all methods), extended to the treading by oxen, etc., (2) the beating with a flail, and (3) the use of a dragging implement, a kind of threshing-sled, such as is still used by peasants in various parts of Europe. Cf. Meyer-Lübke, Wört. u. Sach. 1.211 ff. (with details of word distribution in Romance). Schrader, Reallex. 1.204 ff. Pauly-Wissowa s.v. *dreschen*.

1. Grk. ἀλοάω, NG ἀλωνίζω, derivs. of words for 'threshing-floor' (8.35).

Grk. τρῖβω 'rub' (9.31), used for 'thresh' (by oxen) in Hom. Il. 20.496.

2. Lat. *terere* 'rub' (9.31) is the usual expression. But also, for certain processes, *tundere* 'beat' and *excutere* 'shake out'.

It. *tribbiare*, Sp. *trillar*, Rum. *treera* (*triera*), fr. Lat. *trībulāre* 'press, oppress', deriv. of *trībulum* 'threshing-sled' (in form like a harrow), fr. root of *terere* (above). Ernout-M. 1033. REW 8885.

It. *battere*, Fr. *battre*, lit. 'beat', fr. Lat. *battuere* 'beat' (9.21).

3. Ir. 3 sg. *do-fuaircc* (Wb. 10d6) lit. 'crushes', cpd. of *to- fo-* and *org-* 'strike, destroy'. Pedersen 2.250, 590. Thurneysen, Gram. 532.

NIr. *buailim* 'strike, beat' (9.21) and 'thresh'.

W. *dyrnu*, Br. *dourna*, orig. 'beat with the hand', fr. W. *dwrn* 'fist', Br. *dourn* 'hand' (4.33).

4. Goth. *þriskan*, OE *þerscan*, OHG *drescan*, etc., general Gmc. (in lit. NE tendency to differentiate *thresh* in old sense from *thrash* in secondary, but latter also the usual form among farmers), perh. : Lith. *traškėti* 'crack, rattle', ChSl. *trěskŭ* 'crash'; or/and fr. the root **ter-* in Lat. *terere* 'rub' (cf. above, 2), etc. Walde-P. 1.730. Falk-Torp 1255. Feist 503. NED s.v. *thrash*.

5. Lith. *kulti*, Lett. *kult*, lit. 'strike, beat' : Lith. *kalti*, Lett. *kalt* 'strike, hammer, forge', ChSl. *kolją, klati*, 'stick, slaughter', Lat. *percellere* 'strike down', etc. Walde-P. 1.436 ff. Walde-H. 1.226.

6. ChSl. *mlatiti*, etc., general Slavic : *mlatŭ* 'hammer', *mlěti* 'grind', Lith. *malti*, Lat. *molere* 'grind', etc. (5.56). Walde-P. 2.284 ff. Berneker 2.73.

Late ChSl. *vrěšti, vrŭchą*, SCr. *vrijeći* (cf. also ChSl. *vrachŭ* 'threshing', Russ. *voroch* 'heap of grain'), prob. as orig. applied to threshing by dragging : Lat. *verrere* 'sweep', etc. Walde-P. 1.292. Miklosich 383.

7. Skt. *mṛ-* 'crush' (: Lat. *molere* 'grind', etc., 5.56) is the technical expression for 'thresh' in Çat. Br. 1.6.1.3,

following the words for 'plow', 'sow', and 'reap'. Macdonell-Keith 1.182.

Skt. *pratihan-*, cpd. of *han-* 'strike', occurs in RV 10.48.7 with play on 'thresh' and 'thrash'.

Av. x^v*asta-* 'threshed', *a*x^v*asta-* 'unthreshed' (cf. NPers. *pai-*x^v*asta* 'trodden by foot'), fr. x^v*ah-* 'press'. Otherwise Barth. 874 f. ("Et.?"), Suppl. 246 (fr. root ending in dental), but the deriv. fr. x^v*ah-* (Aryan **svas-*) seems perfect in form and sense.

8.35 THRESHING-FLOOR

Grk.	*ἅλως*	Goth.	*gaþrask*	Lith.	*klojimas, kluonas, klaimas*
NG	*ἀλώνι*	ON	*lāfi* (*lōfi*)	Lett.	*piedarbs, kluons*
Lat.	*ārea*	Dan.	*lo*	ChSl.	*gumĭno*
It.	*ara*	Sw.	*loge*	SCr.	*gumno*
Fr.	*aire*	OE	*þirsceflōr*	Boh.	*mlat*
Sp.	*era*	ME	*thresschinge floore*	Pol.	*klepisko*
Rum.	*arie*	NE	*threshing-floor*	Russ.	*gumno, tok*
Ir.	*ithland*	Du.	*dorschvloer*	Skt.	*khala-*
NIr.	*urlār an bhuailte*	OHG	*tenni*	Av.	. . . .
W.	*llawr dyrnu*	MHG	*tenne*		
Br.	*leur*	NHG	*tenne*		

Words for 'threshing-floor' are in part derived from verbs for 'thresh' (mostly in combination with 'floor'). Most of them are from the notions of 'open space', 'floor', 'flat surface', with specialization.

1. Grk. ἅλως, Hom. ἀλωή (also 'garden, cultivated land', and so Cypr. ἄλϝον), late ἅλων (LXX, NT), dim. ἀλώνιον, NG ἀλώνι, etym.? Relation to ON *lāfi*, etc. (below, 4) dub. Walde-P. 2.407. Boisacq 48.

2. Lat. *ārea* 'open space' and 'threshing-floor' (>Romance words), etym.? Walde-P. 1.79. Ernout-M. 70. Walde-H. 1.65.

3. OIr. dat. *ithlaind* gl. *in area*, MIr. *ithla*, cpd. of *ith* 'grain' (8.42) and *-land* = MW *lann* 'area, yard' : Goth. *land* 'land', etc. Walde-P. 2.438. Pedersen 1.3.

NIr. *urlār an bhuailte*, W. *llawr dyrnu*, Br. *leur*, the words for 'floor' (7.26), the first two (perh. after NE *threshing-floor*) with those for 'thresh' (8.34).

4. Goth. *gaþrask* : *þriskan* 'thresh' (8.34).

ON *lāfi* (*lōfi*), Dan. *lo*, Sw. *loge*, perh. : Russ. *lava* 'bench', Lith. *lova* 'bedstead', etc., with dub. root connection. Walde-P. 2.407. Falk-Torp 650.

OE *þirsceflōr* (also *þerscelflōr*, with *þerscel* 'flail'), Du. *dorschvloer*, cpds. of derivs. of OE *þerscan*, Du. *dorschen* 'thresh' (8.34) and words for 'floor.' ME *thresschinge floore* (Trevisa; *corne floore* Wyclif), NE *threshing-floor*.

OHG *tenni* (*danea* 'area' in Reichenau gl.), MHG, NHG *tenne* = Du. (obs.) *denne* 'flooring' and 'den', OE *denn* 'den', etc., with orig. notion of 'flat surface' : Grk. θέναρ, OHG *tenar* 'palm of the hand', etc. Walde-P. 1.853. Kluge-G. 617.

5. Lith. *klojimas, kluonas*, Lett. *kluons*, fr. Lith. *kloti*, Lett. *klāt* 'spread out' (9.34). Walde-P. 1.489. Mühl.-Endz. 2.238.

Lith. *klaimas*, orig. dub. Leskien, Bildung d. Nom. 422. Berneker 518.

Lett. *piedarbs* : *pie-darīt* 'fill, load full' (cpd. of *darīt* 'do, make'). Mühl.-Endz. 3.242 f.

6. ChSl. *gumĭno* (for ἅλων in Gospels, Supr.), SCr., Russ. *gumno* (Boh. *humno*,

Pol. *gumno* now mostly 'barnyard'), perh. an obscured cpd. **gu-mĭno*, the first part : Skt. *gāus*, Grk. βοῦς, etc. 'ox', and the second : ChSl. *męti* 'press', Lith. *minti* 'tread'. Berneker 362. Schrader, Reallex. 1.206.

Boh. *mlat* : *mlatiti* 'thresh' (8.34).

Pol. *klepisko* : *klepać*, ChSl. *klepati* 'strike, pound'. Berneker 512 f.

Russ. *tok* 'current, stream' (1.36), also used locally for 'threshing-floor' (hence Pol. *tok* sometimes in this sense).

7. Skt. *khala-* (RV, etc.), etym.? Pedersen, KZ 38.203, 39.380.

8.41 CROP, HARVEST

Grk.	*καρπός, θέρος, συγκομιδή*	Goth.	*akran, asans*	Lith.	*piūtis*
NG	*θέρος, συγκομιδή*	ON	*lōð, āvǫxtr*	Lett.	*pl'āvums*
Lat.	*frūgēs, seges, messis*	Dan.	*høst, grøde*	ChSl.	*plodŭ, žętva*
It.	*messe, raccolta*	Sw.	*gröda*	SCr.	*žetva, prirod*
Fr.	*moisson, récolte*	OE	*wæstm, rīp*	Boh.	*žeň, úroda*
Sp.	*mies, cosecha*	ME	*frut(es), crop, ripe*	Pol.	*żniwo, urodzaj*
Rum.	*seceriș, recoltă*	NE	*crop, harvest*	Russ.	*žatva, urožaj*
Ir.	*torad, buain*	Du.	*oogst*	Skt.	*sasya-*
NIr.	*barr, toradh, fōghmar*	OHG	*wahsmo, aran*	Av.	. . . .
W.	*cnwd, cynhaeaf*	MHG	*erne*		
Br.	*eost*	NHG	*ernte, ertrag*		

Many of the words listed originally denoted 'harvest' as the act or season of harvesting and only secondarily (some only occasionally, others commonly) were extended to cover the resulting 'crop, harvest'. These are mostly derivs. of vbs. for 'mow, reap' (8.32). But association between the harvest and its season also accounts for several. The words that are used only for 'harvest' as 'crop' are from the general notions of 'fruit, product, growth, gathering', applied esp. to 'fruits of the field'.

1. Grk. καρπός 'fruit' in general, also 'crop, harvest' : OE *hærfest*, OHG *herbist* 'harvest time', etc. (below, 4), Lat. *carpere* 'pluck'. Walde-P. 2.581. Ernout-M. 157. Walde-H. 1.179. Falk-Torp 454 f.

Grk. θέρος 'summer' and also 'crop, harvest' (NG pop. ὁ θέρος), whence, through θερίζω (8.32), θερισμός 'harvest' in both senses, all through identification of 'hot season' with 'harvest-season' : θερμός 'hot', etc. (15.85). Walde-P. 1.687 f. Boisacq 341.

Grk. συγκομιδή, fr. συγκομίζω 'bring together, gather'.

2. Lat. *frūgēs, frūctus* 'product' and esp. 'fruits of the field' : *fruī* 'enjoy', Goth. *brūkjan*, OHG *brūhhan*, OE *brūcan*, etc. 'use, enjoy'. Walde-P. 2.208. Ernout-M. 395. Walde-H. 1.552.

Lat. *seges* 'grain-field', later 'crop' : W. *he* 'seed', *hau* 'sow', fr. a root **seg-* (related to **sē-* 'sow'?). Walde-P. 2.480. Ernout-M. 920.

Lat. *messis* (> It. *messe*, Sp. *mies*) and *messiō* (> Fr. *moisson*), orig. the act of 'reaping', but also for the resulting 'crop', fr. *metere* 'reap' (8.32). Ernout-M. 613. REW 5542–43.

It. *raccolta* (> Fr. *récolte*), Rum. *recoltă*, fr. pple. of Lat. *recolligere* 'gather up'. REW 7127.

Sp. *cosecha*, fr. MLat. *collēcta* 'harvest', fr. pple. of Lat. *colligere* 'collect'. REW 2045.

Rum. *seceriș*, fr. *secera* 'mow, reap' (8.32).

3. Ir. *torad*, NIr. *toradh*, in general 'fruit, product', cpd. *to-rad, to-ret-* :

rethim 'run', hence orig. sense 'income'. Pedersen 2.600, 677.

Ir. *buain*, vbl. n. of *bongaim* 'reap' (8.32).

NIr. *barr*, also and orig. 'top, tip' (12.33), with development similar to, and perh. influenced by, that in NE *crop* (below, 4).

NIr. *fōghmar*, also and orig. 'autumn' (14.67).

W. *cynhaeaf* 'harvest-time, autumn' (14.67), now sometimes 'harvest'.

W. *cnwd*, orig.?

Br. *eost* orig. 'August' (the 'harvest month'), as also Du. *oogst* (below, 4). Henry 115.

4. Goth. *akran* (= καρπός) : ON *akarn* 'wild fruit, mast', OE *æcern* 'acorn', prob. deriv. of Goth. *akrs* 'field', etc. (8.12). Falk-Torp 16. Feist 32 f. Otherwise Walde-P. 1.173.

Goth. *asans* (= θερισμός, once θέρος 'summer'), OHG *aran*, MHG *erne*, NHG *ernte*, all orig. with reference to the 'harvest-season' : OE *earnian*, OHG *arnen* 'earn', *arnōn* 'reap', ChSl. *jesenĭ* 'autumn'. Walde-P. 1.161. Feist 58 f.

ON *ǭvǫxtr*, OE *wæstm*, OHG *wahsmo*, all orig. 'growth', fr. ON *vaxa*, OE *weaxan*, OHG *wahsan* 'grow' (12.53).

ON *lōð* : ON *lāð* 'land', Goth. *unlēds*, OE *unlǣd* 'poor', all fr. notion of 'property'. Walde-P. 2.394. Falk-Torp 650. Feist 521.

Dan. *grøde*, Sw. *gröda* : Dan., Sw. *gro*, OE *grōwan* 'grow', etc. (12.53). Falk-Torp 356. Hellquist 307.

OE *rīp*, ME *ripe*, fr. OE *rīpan* 'reap' (8.32).

OE *hærfest*, OHG *herbist*, NHG *herbst*, Du. *herfst*, Sw. *höst*, all used mainly or only for the 'harvest season, autumn', but NE *harvest* and Dan. *høst* for 'crop, harvest', all : Grk. καρπός, etc. (above, 1).

ME *frut(es)*, NE *fruit(s)*, reg. for καρπός in Bible from Wyclif on, but now arch. in this sense.

ME, NE *crop*, fr. OE *crop(p)* 'top of a plant', as 'ear of corn', etc., orig. 'bunch, lump', identical with *crop* (of fowls) : NHG *kropf*, etc. Falk-Torp 582. NED s.v.

Du. *oogst*, orig. 'August' the harvest month (now *Oogst-maand*), fr. Lat. *Augustus*. Franck-v. W. 474.

NHG *ertrag* 'income, yield', but esp. 'crop', fr. *ertragen* in older sense 'yield' (now 'bear, suffer'), cpd. of *tragen* 'carry'. Weigand-H. 1.471. Cf. NE *yield* in *a good yield*, etc.

5. Lith. *piūtis*, Lett. *pl'āvums* fr. Lith. *piauti*, Lett. *pl'aut* 'mow, reap' (8.32).

Lett. *auglis*, in general 'fruit, growth', fr. Lett. *augt* 'grow' (12.53).

6. ChSl. *plodŭ* (= καρπός, and the general Slavic word for 'fruit, product'), outside connections dub. Walde-P. 2.103.

ChSl. *žętva* (= θερισμός), SCr. *žetva*, Boh. *žeň*, Pol. *żniwo*, Russ. *žatva*, fr. the root of ChSl. *žęti*, etc. 'reap' (8.32).

SCr. *prirod*, Boh. *úroda*, Pol. *urodzaj*, Russ. *urožaj* : ChSl. *rodŭ* 'birth, race, family' etc. (19.23).

7. Skt. *sasya-* 'grain' (8.42), also used for 'crop, harvest'.

8.42 GRAIN

(Generic = British Corn)

Grk.	*σῖτος*	Goth.	*kaurn*	Lith.	*grūdai, javai*
NG	*γεννήματα, σιτηρά*	ON	*korn*	Lett.	*labība*
Lat.	*frūmentum*	Dan.	*korn*	ChSl.	*žito*
It.	*grano, frumento, biada*	Sw.	*säd, korn*	SCr.	*žito*
		OE	*corn*	Boh.	*obilí*
Fr.	*blé, grain*	ME	*corn, greyn*	Pol.	*zboże*
Sp.	*grano*	NE	*corn* (Brit.), *grain*	Russ.	*chleba*
Rum.	*grîne*	Du.	*graan, koren*	Skt.	*yava-, dhānya-, sasya-*
Ir.	*ith, arbar*	OHG	*korn*	Av.	*yava-* (*dāna-, hahya-*)
NIr.	*arbhar*	MHG	*korn*		
W.	*yd*	NHG	*getreide*		
Br.	*ed*				

The words for 'grain, corn' (in the older and still British use of *corn*), as the generic name for the cereal products, include a few that reflect an IE word denoting 'grain', or more probably some particular kind of 'grain', the one best known in the IE period. Many more reflect an IE word denoting 'a grain, kernel', which as esp. characteristic of the cereals, led to the generic 'grain'. Similarly some other words orig. denoted 'a grain' or 'seed'. Several come from such notions as 'food, means of life, bread, fruit of the soil, good', with specialized application to the cereals from their prime importance as food products.

The widespread literary words coming from Lat. *cereālis* 'pertaining to Ceres', as Fr. *céréales*, NE *cereals*, etc., are omitted from the list.

The generic words are often specialized to denote a particular kind of grain, the one that is the chief product of a given region, as to 'wheat' (NG σῖτος, Fr. *froment*, in part It. *frumento, grano*, Fr. *blé*, SCr. *žito*), to 'rye' (Boh. *žito*, Pol. *żyto*, NHG *korn* in many parts of Germany), to 'barley' (later Skt. *yava-*, Sw. *korn* in part), to 'maize' (NE *corn* in U.S.).

Of the several grains the names of which are discussed in 8.43–8.48, wheat and barley were those prized for human food in Greek and Roman antiquity, and in this order of preference (in Greece the bread par excellence, ἄρτος, was made of wheat, while the μᾶζα 'barley-cake' was the inferior diet of the common people), while in India rice and barley held the corresponding rank. The earliest food of the Romans was the *far* 'spelt', and its former importance is reflected in the use of pl. *farra* for 'grain' and esp. *farīna* 'meal'. Rye and oats were North European products, the former unknown in classical antiquity, the latter only as wild oats in Greece, in Italy as weeds or used for fodder. Rice, of first importance in India as in the whole Orient, was in Europe an importation little used until late times. Maize is a native American product, introduced into Europe by the Spaniards. Schrader, Reallex. under *Weizen, Gerste*, etc. Jardé, Les céréales dans l'antiquité grecque.

1. IE **yewo-*. Walde-P. 1.202 ff.

Skt. *yava-* 'grain' in RV, later 'barley'; Av. *yava-* 'grain', NPers. *jav* 'barley'; Lith. *javai* (pl.) 'grain'; Grk. ζειαί (pl.) 'spelt'.

2. IE **ĝr̥no-* in Eur. (except Grk.) words for 'a grain, kernel', with widespread development to generic 'grain'. These agree phonetically with Skt. *jīrṇa-* 'old, worn out', fr. the root seen in Skt. *jr̥-* 'grow old, wear out', Grk. γέρων 'old man', and ultimate relationship, perh. fr. a notion of 'rub' (whence 'rub down, wear out' in Skt. and Grk.; elsewhere 'something rubbed fine, grain'), though disputed, is probable. Walde-P. 1.599 f. Ernout-M. 432. Feist 309 f.

Lat. *grānum* 'a grain', but generic 'grain' reflected in *grānārium* 'granary', and common to the derivs., It., Sp. *grano*, Fr. *grain* (> ME *greyn, grayn*, NE *grain*), Rum. *grîne* (pl.; sg. *grîu* 'wheat'), also Du. *graan*; Goth. *kaurn*, OE *corn*, etc., general Gmc. (but NE *corn* specialized to 'maize' in U.S.; NHG *korn* mostly 'rye', Sw. *korn* esp. 'barley'); but Ir. *grān*, W. *grawn* only in older sense, likewise ChSl. *zrŭno*, SCr. *zrno*, while Lith. *žirnas*, Lett. *zirnis* are specialized to 'pea'.

3. Grk. σῖτος 'grain' (also 'bread, food'), but already 'wheat' in Hellenistic times (NT, pap.) as in NG (pop. σιτάρι), orig.? Walde-P. 1.470. Boisacq 866 ff. Hence adj. σιτηρός, whence σιτηρά 'cereal products' (also lit. NG).

Grk. γέννημα 'product' (fr. γεννάω 'beget, bear', 4.71), hence pl. γεννήματα 'fruits of the field' (Polyb., NT, etc.), NG esp. 'cereals, grain'.

4. Lat. *frūmentum* (> It. *frumento*, generic esp. in pl., sg. mostly 'wheat', Fr. *froment* 'wheat'), fr. the same root as *frūgēs* 'fruits of the field' (8.41), *frūctus* 'fruit', *fruī* 'enjoy', etc. Walde-P. 2.208. Ernout-M. 393.

Fr. *blé* (both generic, esp. pl. *les blés*, and 'wheat'; cf. *ce mot de bled .... est prins généralement pour tous les grains, jusques aux légumes bons à manger. En plusieurs endroits de ce roiaume, par le bled est entendu le pur froment*, quoted from early 17th cent.), It. *biada* ('fodder', esp. 'oats', pl. *biade* more generic), MLat. *bladum*, fr. a Frank. **blād* = OE *blǣd*, MDu. *blāt* 'fruit of the field', this fr. the same root as OHG *blat* 'leaf', etc. (8.56). REW 1160. Wartburg 1.391 f.

5. Ir. *ith*, W. *yd*, Br. *ed*, orig. 'nourishment, food' (hence Ir. *ithim* 'eat') : Skt., Av. *pitu-* 'food', ChSl. *pitěti* 'feed, nourish', etc. (5.12). Walde-P. 2.73 f. Pedersen 1.41.

Ir. *arbar*, NIr. *arbhar*, esp. 'unthreshed or standing grain' : Lat. *arvum*, Grk. ἄρουρα 'plow-land, field' (8.12). Walde-P. 1.78 f. Pedersen 1.63.

6. Goth. *kaurn*, etc., also NE *grain*, Du. *graan*, see above, 2.

Sw. *säd* = Dan. *sæd* 'seed, semen', OE *sǣd* 'seed', etc. (8.31).

NHG *getreide*, fr. MHG *getregede*, deriv. of *tragen* 'carry, bear, wear' and used with diverse applications, 'clothing, burden', etc. and esp. what is born of the earth, whence the present application. Weigand-H. 1.712. Kluge-G. 204.

7. Lith. *grūdai*, pl. of *grūdas* 'a grain' = Lett. *grūds* = SCr. *gruda* 'clod, lump' : ON *grjōt* 'stones, gravel', OHG *grioz* 'sand, shore-gravel', NE *grit*, etc. Walde-P. 1.648 f.

Lith. *javai* (pl.), above, 1.

Lett. *labība* lit. 'goods, the good', deriv. of *labs* 'good' (16.71).

8. ChSl. *žito* (in Gospels once = γεννήματα 'fruits of the field'; as 'grain' in derivs. *žitĭnica* 'granary, barn', etc.; reg. *pĭšenica* for σῖτος, but here prob. understood as 'wheat', cf. 8.43), SCr. *žito*, orig. 'food, nourishment, means of life' : OPruss. *geits* 'bread', OCorn. *buit* 'food', W. *bwyd* 'victuals', etc., fr. the root of ChSl. *žiti*, Lat. *vīvere*, etc. 'live' (4.74). Walde-P. 1.669.

Boh. *obilí* : ChSl. *obilĭje* 'abundance', *obilŭ* 'abundant', etym. dub. Meillet, Études 413.

Pol. *zboże*, 'grain' for earlier 'wealth, income', cf. Boh. *zboží* 'goods, commodity, wares' : ChSl. *bogatŭ*, etc. 'rich',

Skt. *bhaj-* 'part, divide', *bhaga-* 'share, welfare', etc. Berneker 67.

Russ. *chleba*, pl. of *chleb* 'bread' (5.51).

9. Skt., Av. *yava-*, above, 1.

Skt. *dhānya-*, deriv. of *dhānā-*, pl. *dhānās* 'grains', Av. *dāna-* (NPers. *dāna* 'grain') in *dānō-karš-* 'ant', lit. 'grain-stealer', root connection? Walde-P. 1.831. Barth. 734.

Skt. *sasya-*, Av. *hahya-* (in cpd., Barth. 1800) : Gall. acc. *(s)asiam* 'rye', W. *haidd*, Br. *heiz* 'barley'. Walde-P. 2.454.

8.43 WHEAT

Grk.	*πῡρός*	Goth.	*hwaiteis*	Lith.	*kviečiei, pūrai*
NG	*σῖτος, σιτάρι*	ON	*hveiti*	Lett.	*kvieši, pūr'i*
Lat.	*trīticum*	Dan.	*hvede*	ChSl.	*pĭšenica*
It.	*frumento, grano*	Sw.	*hvete*	SCr.	*pšenica*
Fr.	*froment, blé*	OE	*hwǣte*	Boh.	*pšenice*
Sp.	*trigo*	ME	*whete*	Pol.	*pszenica*
Rum.	*grîu*	NE	*wheat*	Russ.	*pšenica*
Ir.	*cruitnecht, tuirend*	Du.	*tarwe, weit*	Skt.	*godhūma-*
NIr.	*cruithneacht*	OHG	*weizzi*	Av.	*gantuma-*
W.	*gwenith*	MHG	*weizze*		
Br.	*gwiniz*	NHG	*weizen*		

Several of the words for 'wheat' are from those for 'grain' with specialization to the most important of the cereals. Some are from '(grain) for threshing, grinding or winnowing'. Some originally applied to particular species, reflecting some characteristic of form or color.

1. Grk. πῡρός, Lith. *pūrai*, Lett. *pūr'i* (in Baltic esp. 'winter wheat') : ChSl. *pyro* 'spelt', Boh. *pýr*, Russ. *pyrej* 'spear-grass', OE *fyrs* 'furze', root-connection? Walde-P. 2.83.

NG σῖτος, pop. σιτάρι, see 8.42.

2. Lat. *trīticum* (> Sp. *trigo*) : *terere* (*trīvī, trītum*) 'rub, thresh' (8.34), so orig. 'grain for threshing'. Cf. ChSl. *pĭšenica*, below, 6. Ernout-M. 1033.

It. *frumento*, Fr. *froment*, fr. Lat. *frūmentum* 'grain' (8.42).

Fr. *blé*, formerly and still in part 'grain' (8.42).

It. *grano*, Rum. *grîu* (in pl. 'grain'), fr. Lat. *grānum* (8.42).

3. Ir. *cruitnecht*, NIr. *cruithneacht*, W. *gwenith*, Br. *gwiniz*, cpds. with final member Ir. *-necht*, W. *-nith*, Br. *-niz* : W. *nithio*, Br. *niza* 'winnow' (this : Lith. *n(i)ekoti* 'winnow in a trough', etc. Walde-P. 2.321), hence 'wheat' as 'grain for winnowing', like Lat. *trīticum* as 'grain for threshing'. First part of Ir. *cruitnecht* : Ir. *cruth* 'red', with reference to the old red wheat of Ireland. First part of W. *gwenith*, Br. *gwiniz* prob. (despite the *n* for *nn*) : *gwynn*, Br. *gwenn* 'white' (cf. Goth. *hwaiteis* : *hweits*, below, 4). For full discussion, cf. Loth, RC 41.193 ff.

Ir. *tuirend*, etym. dub., perh. a cpd. of *rind* 'point' and first used of a special kind of wheat. Loth, RC 41.199 ff.

4. Goth. *hwaiteis*, OE *hwǣte*, etc., general Gmc., so called from the white meal therefrom : Goth. *hweits*, etc. 'white' (15.64). Walde-P. 1.469 f. Feist 280.

Du. *tarwe* (more popular than *weit*), MDu. *tarewe*, prob. (as first applied to some rank species of wheat?) : ME, NE *tare* 'vetch, weed', Skt. *dūrva-* 'panic-grass', also prob. Lith. *dirva* 'field' (8.12). Walde-P. 1.803. Franck-v. W. 689.

5. Lith. *kviečiei*, Lett. *kvieši*, fr. Gmc. (Goth. *hwaiteis*, etc., above, 4).

Lith. *pūrai*, Lett. *pūr'i*, above, 1.

6. ChSl. *pĭšenica*, SCr., Russ. *pšenica*, Boh. *pšenice*, Pol. *pszenica*, orig. 'grain destined for grinding' : ChSl. *pĭchati* 'strike', *pĭšeno* 'meal', Lat. *pinsere* 'crush', etc. Walde-P. 2.1.

7. Skt. *godhūma-*, by pop. etym. (as cpd. of *go-* 'cow' and *dhūma-* 'smoke') for *gandhuma- = Av. *gantuma-*, NPers. *gandum* 'wheat', root connection? Barth. 493. Hübschmann, Pers. Stud. 95.

8.44 BARLEY

Grk.	κρīθή	Goth.	*barizeins* (adj.)	Lith.	*miežiai*
NG	κριθάρι	ON	*bygg, barr*	Lett.	*mieži*
Lat.	*hordeum*	Dan.	*byg*	ChSl.	*jęčĭnĕnŭ, jęčĭnŭ* (adj.)
It.	*orzo*	Sw.	*bjugg, korn*	SCr.	*ječam*
Fr.	*orge*	OE	*bere, bærlic* (*bēow*)	Boh.	*ječmen*
Sp.	*cebada*	ME	*bere, barli*	Pol.	*jęczmień*
Rum.	*orz*	NE	*barley*	Russ.	*jačmen'*
Ir.	*eorna*	Du.	*gerst*	Skt.	*yava-*
NIr.	*eorna*	OHG	*gersta*	Av.	....
W.	*haidd*	MHG	*gerste*		
Br.	*heiz*	NHG	*gerste*		

Apart from the inherited group, and some with specialization from 'grain' or 'fodder, crop', several words for 'barley' are from sources reflecting its sharp, prickly form.

1. IE *ĝherzd(h)-, *ĝhr̥zd(h)-, root connection uncertain and phonetic development in part obscure. Walde-P. 1.611. Ernout-M. 459. Walde-H. 1.657.

Grk. κριθή, NG κριθάρι; Lat. *hordeum* (> It. *orzo*, Fr. *orge*, Rum. *orz*); Du. *gerst*, OHG *gersta*, MHG, NHG *gerste*; (Alb. *dridhë* 'grain').

2. Sp. *cebada*, orig. 'fodder', fr. *cebar* 'feed, fatten animals', Lat. *cibāre* id., fr. *cibus* 'food'. REW 1894.

3. Ir. *eorna*, etym. dub. Pokorny, Z. celt. Ph. 17.304 ff. takes as *es-orniā : Goth. *asans* 'harvest' (8.41). (Connection with Skt. *yava-*, etc., as Pedersen 1.65, Stokes 223, now rejected.)

W. *haidd*, Br. *heiz* : Skt. *sasya-*, Av. *hahya-* 'grain' (8.42). Walde-P. 2.454. Pedersen 1.69.

4. Goth. *barizeins* adj. 'κρίθινος', ON *barr* (also 'pine needles'), OE *bere*, *bærlic*, ME *bere*, *barli*, NE *barley*, dial. *bear* : Lat. *far*, *farris*, 'spelt', prob. so-called fr. the spikes of the grain, and fr. the root in Skt. *bhr̥ṣṭi-* 'point, tip', ON *burst*, OE *byrst*, etc. 'bristle'. Walde-P. 2.134. Walde-H. 1.455 f. Feist 81.

ON *bygg*, Dan. *byg*, Sw. *bjugg*, OE *bēow* (rare) = OS *beo* 'crop, produce', fr. the root of ON *būa* 'till, dwell', Goth. *bauan* 'dwell', etc. Hence orig. 'the cultivated crop' and then specialized to 'barley'. Falk-Torp 121. Hellquist 74.

Sw. *korn*, also and orig. 'grain' (8.42).

5. Lith. *miežiai*, Lett. *mieži* (pl.), OPruss. *moasis*, beside Lett. *maize* 'bread', etym.? Mühl.-Endz. 2.553, 657.

6. ChSl. *jęčĭnĕnŭ*, *jęčĭnŭ* adj. 'κρίθινος', SCr. *ječam*, etc., general Slavic, prob. (as 'prickly, bearded') : ChSl. *ąkotĭ* 'hook', Lat. *uncus* 'bent, hook', etc. Berneker 268. Walde-P. 1.61.

7. Skt. *yava-*, earlier 'grain' (8.42).

8.45 RYE

Grk.	(βρίζα)	Goth.	....	Lith.	*rugiai*
NG	σήκαλη, βρίζα	ON	*rugr*	Lett.	*rudzi*
Lat.	*secale, centēnum*	Dan.	*rug*	ChSl.	(*rŭžĭ*)
It.	*segale*	Sw.	*råg*	SCr.	*raž*
Fr.	*seigle*	OE	*ryge*	Boh.	*žito, rež*
Sp.	*centeno*	ME	*rye*	Pol.	*żyto, reż*
Rum.	*secară*	NE	*rye*	Russ.	*rož'*
Ir.	*secul*	Du.	*rog*	Skt.	....
NIr.	*seagal*	OHG	*rocko, roggo*	Av.	....
W.	*rhyg*	MHG	*rocke, rogge*		
Br.	*segal*	NHG	*roggen*		

1. Rye was unknown in ancient Greece. βρίζα, quoted by Galen as the native name of 'rye' raised in Thrace and Macedonia, is a Thracian word. Connection with ON *rugr*, etc. (below, 4) is assumed by Hirt, Idg. Gram. 2.94, but doubtful.

Byz. σήκαλις, NG σήκαλη fr. Lat. (below, 2).

2. Rye was likewise unknown in ancient Italy, and *secale* (Pliny), *sicale* (Edict. Diocl.) is doubtless a loanword, of unknown source. Hence It. *segale*, Fr. *seigle*, Rum. *secară*, also Ir. *secul*, NIr. *seagal*, Br. *segal*, NG σήκαλη, Alb. *thekërë*. REW 7763.

Sp. *centeno*, Port. *centeio*, fr. late Lat. *centēnum* 'rye' (Edict. Diocl.), fr. *centērī* 'hundred each', because of the alleged 'hundred-fold yield' (Pliny, NH 18.16, 40 *nascitur* (*secale*) *qualicumque solo cum centesimo grano*). Ernout-M. 1746. REW 1811.

3. Ir. *secul*, etc., fr. Lat. *secale* (above, 2).

W. *rhyg*, fr. OE *ryge* (below, 4).

4. ON *rugr*, OE *ryge*, OHG *rocko*, etc. general Gmc., Lith. *rugiai*, Lett. *rudzi* (pl., sg. 'grain of rye'), late ChSl. *rŭžĭ*, SCr. *raž*, etc., general Slavic, all plainly connected, but perh. loanwords fr. some unknown source. Walde-P. 2.374 f. Weigand-H. 1.599. Kluge-G. 484 f.

5. Boh. *žito*, Pol. *żyto*, also gen. 'grain' (8.42).

8.46 OATS

Grk.	βρόμος	Goth.	....	Lith.	*avižos* (pl.)
NG	βρόμη	ON	*hafri*	Lett.	*auzas*
Lat.	*avēna*	Dan.	*havre*	ChSl.	*ovĭsŭ*
It.	(*a*)*vena*	Sw.	*havre*	SCr.	*zob, ovas*
Fr.	*avoine*	OE	*āte*	Boh.	*oves*
Sp.	*avena*	ME	*ote*	Pol.	*owies*
Rum.	*ovăs*	NE	*oats*	Russ.	*oves*
Ir.	*coirce*	Du.	*haver*	Skt.	....
NIr.	*coirce*	OHG	*habaro, evina*	Av.	....
W.	*ceirch*	MHG	*haber*(*e*)		
Br.	*kerc'h*	NHG	*hafer*		

1. Grk. βρόμος, NG βρόμη, orig. unknown.

2. Lat. *avēna* (among the Romans a weed, or good only for fodder; but Pliny comments on its use for porridge among the Germans). Hence It. *avena*, pop. *vena*, Fr. *avoine*, Sp. *avena*, also OHG *evina* : Lith. *avižos*, Lett. *auzas*, ChSl. *ovĭsŭ*, SCr. *ovas*, etc. (> Rum. *ovăs*), general Balto-Slavic for 'oats'. Root connection? Walde-P. 1.24. Ernout-M. 87. Walde-H. 1.81. REW 818.

3. Ir. *coirce*, W. *ceirch*, Br. *kerc'h*, etym. uncertain, but possibly : Sw. and Norw. dial. *hagre* 'oats'. Walde-P. 1.348. Pedersen 1.188.

4. ON *hafri* (ME *hafyr*, NE *haver* fr. Norse), Dan., Sw. *havre*, Du. *haver*, OHG *habaro*, MHG *haber(e)*, NHG *hafer* (LG for HG *haber*), perh. as 'goats' food' (cf. Grk. αἰγίλωψ a kind of 'wild oats' : αἴξ 'goat') : ON *hafr* 'he-goat', Lat. *caper*, etc. Walde-P. 1.348. Falk-Torp 387 f. Hellquist 341.

OE *āte*, ME *ote(s)*, NE *oats*, orig. denoting the single grain (cf. NED s.v.) and prob. : ON *eitill* 'nodule in stone, iron, etc.', Norw. *eitel* 'knot in a tree', Pol. *jądro*, Russ. *jadro* 'kernel' (cf. also Russ. *jadrica* 'porridge of oats or barley'), fr. the root seen in Grk. οἰδάω 'swell', etc. Skeat, Etym. Dict. s.v., further supported by Binz, Z. deutsch. Ph. 38.369 ff. Walde-P. 1.106.

5. Lith. *avižos*, Lett. *auzas*, above, 2.

6. ChSl. *ovĭsŭ*, etc., above, 2.

SCr. *zob* = Boh. *zob* 'bird-feed', Russ. *zob* 'crop, goiter, chopped straw with barley', prob. back-formation to SCr. *zobati* 'eat grain' : ChSl. *zobati* 'eat', Lith. *žėbti* 'eat slowly', Walde-P. 1.570. Brückner 655 f.

8.47 MAIZE, (U.S.) CORN

NG	ἀραβόσιτος, καλαμπόκι	Dan.	*majs*	Lith.	*kukuruza*
It.	*granturco*	Sw.	*majs*	Lett.	*kukuruza*
Fr.	*maïs, blé de Turquie*	NE	*maize*, (U.S.) *corn*	SCr.	*kukuruz*
Sp.	*maíz*	Du.	*mais*	Boh.	*kukuřice*
Rum.	*porumb*	NHG	*mais*	Pol.	*kukurydza*
NIr.	*arbhar Indiach*			Russ.	*kukuruza*
W.	*indrawn*				
Br.	*ed Turki*				

Maize (in U.S. *corn*) is an American product. Its first European cultivation was in Spain, whence it spread first to northern Africa and the other Mediterranean lands and thence to central and northern Europe. Cf. J. W. Harshberger, The Maize (Philadelphia, 1892), and Leo Spitzer, Wört. u. Sach. 4. 122 ff. (with discussion of the numerous Romance dialect terms).

1. A West Indian form of the native name was adopted by the Spanish as *mahiz*, *mayz*, now *maíz*, whence it spread to other Eur. languages, Fr. *maïs*, NE *maize*, NHG *mais*, etc.

2. In North America it was known by the French as *bleds d'Inde* (quoted from Champlain; also as *mil gros* 'large millet', Cartier), by the English as *Indian corn*, and so in England, whence NIr. *arbhar Indiach* (*arbhar*, 8.42), W. (Spurrell, old. ed.) *gwenith India* (*gwenith* 'wheat', 8.43) or now (Spurrell-Anwyl) *indrawn* (abbr. *ind-* + *grawn* 'grain'); later in U.S. simply *corn* at the expense of its old generic use.

3. Owing to the early cultivation of maize in Mediterranean lands and its reputed oriental origin, coupled with the vague use of Turkey in connection with things exotic (cf. NE *turkey*, the bird), arose such names as It. *granturco*, Fr. *blé de Turquie*, Br. *ed Turki*, NE *Turkey wheat* (cf. NED), NHG *türkischer weizen*. Similarly NG ἀραβόσιτος, ἀραβοσίτι, lit. 'Arabian corn', with which one may compare Fr. *blé sarrasin* 'buckwheat' and Turk. *mısır* (*buğday*) 'maize', lit. 'Egyptian (wheat)'. For many other terms based on fanciful geographic origin, cf. Spitzer, op. cit. 133 ff.

4. Rum. *porumb*, also and orig. 'dove' (Lat. *palumbēs*, VLat. *palumbus*). Cf. Montenegrin *kolomboć* 'maize', deriv. of Lat. *columba* 'dove', and Bulg. *gŭlŭbĭ* 'maize' fr. *gŭlŭb* 'dove'. Here also NG καλαμπόκι, a blend with κάλαμος 'reed' (cf. also καλαμο-σίταρο 'maize'). Due to the dove-like appearance of the ear of corn with its folded sheath (so Tiktin 1207; cf. also Mold. *păpuşoiŭ* fr. *păpuşă* 'doll'), or to a resemblance in color (so Meyer-Lübke, Arch. sl. Ph. 36.591, after Weigand). In It. dial. *columbine*, used of the white popping corn, the association with doves is more obvious.

5. SCr. *kukuruz*, etc., general Slavic, whence also the Lith. and Lett. terms, prob. not loanword fr. Turkish (as in Miklosich, Türk. Elem. 1.334, Lokotsch 1230), perh. related to certain Slavic plant names, but uncertain. Berneker 640. Brückner 280.

8.48 RICE

Grk.	ὄρυζα	Goth.	....	Lith.	*rysai*
NG	ρύζι	ON	....	Lett.	*rīsi*
Lat.	*oryza*	Dan.	*ris*	ChSl.	....
It.	*riso*	Sw.	*ris*	SCr.	*riža, oriz*
Fr.	*riz*	OE	....	Boh.	*rýže*
Sp.	*arroz*	ME	*rys*	Pol.	*ryż*
Rum.	*orez*	NE	*rice*	Russ.	*ris*
Ir.	....	Du.	*rijst*	Skt.	*vrīhi-*
NIr.	*rīs*	OHG	....	Av.	....
W.	*reis*	MHG	*rīs*		
Br.	*riz*	NHG	*reis*		

Rice is of oriental origin, and likewise without doubt Grk. ὄρυζα, which is the source of all the European words. This is prob. a distorted form (through Iran.) of the word seen in Skt. *vrīhi-* (AV+), Afghan *vrižē*, etc. Boisacq 712. Schrader, Reallex. 2.230.

8.51 GRASS

Grk.	πόα, χόρτος	Goth.	*hawi*	Lith.	*žolė*
NG	χορτάρι	ON	*gras*	Lett.	*zāle*
Lat.	*herba, grāmen*	Dan.	*græs*	ChSl.	*trava*
It.	*erba*	Sw.	*gräs*	SCr.	*trava*
Fr.	*herbe*	OE	*græs, gærs*	Boh.	*tráva*
Sp.	*hierba*	ME	*gras*	Pol.	*trawa*
Rum.	*iarbă*	NE	*grass*	Russ.	*trava*
Ir.	*fēr*	Du.	*gras*	Skt.	*tr̥ṇa-*
NIr.	*fēar*	OHG	*gras*	Av.	(*vāstra-*)
W.	*gwellt, glaswellt*	MHG	*gras*		
Br.	*geot*	NHG	*gras*		

Words for 'grass' are from such notions as 'green, growing, fat, blade', but in part also from 'fodder', since the fodder was usually grass.

1. Grk. πόα, Ion. ποίη, Dor. ποία, fr. *ποίϝα : πῖων 'fat', Lith. *pėva* 'meadow', Skt. *pīvas-*, Av. *pīvah-* 'fat', etc. Walde-P. 2.74.

Grk. χόρτος, orig. 'enclosure', esp. 'feeding place for cattle', whence 'fodder, grass, hay' : Lat. *hortus* 'garden' (8.13), Ir. *gort* 'field' (8.12), etc. Walde-P. 1.603. Hence NG χορτάρι.

2. Lat. *herba* (> It. *erba*, Fr. *herbe*, Sp. *hierba*, *yerba*, Rum. *iarbă*), etym.

dub. Walde-P. 1.646. Ernout-M. 448. Walde-H. 1.639 f.

Lat. *grāmen*, prob. as orig. 'fodder', fr. **grasmen-* : Grk. γράω 'gnaw', Skt. *gras-* 'devour', etc. Ernout-M. 430 f. Otherwise (: Goth. *gras*, etc.) Walde-P. 1.645, Walde-H. 1.616.

3. Ir. *fēr*, NIr. *fēar* = W. *gwair* 'hay' (OW *gweir*), prob. fr. **wegro-* : Lat. *vigēre* 'be fresh and strong', *vegetus* 'lively, vigorous', Skt. *vāja-* 'strength', etc. Walde-P. 1.247. Pedersen 1.103.

W. *gwellt*, Br. *geot* (older *guelt*), prob. : W. *gwallt*, Ir. *folt* 'hair', OPruss. *wolti*, SCr. *vlat* 'ear (of corn)', etc. Walde-P. 1.297. Otherwise (as orig. 'fodder' : Ir. *gelim* 'graze', etc.) Pedersen 1.96.

W. *glaswellt*, lit. 'green grass', cpd. of *glas* 'green' and *gwellt*.

4. Goth. *hawi*, reg. for 'grass', see under 'hay' (8.52).

Goth. *gras* (but only for χόρτος as 'fruit of the field' or mostly λάχανον 'herb, vegetable'), OE *græs*, etc., general Gmc. (and OE *gærs*, Flem. *gers* with metathesis) : MHG *gruose* 'young plant, shoot', ON *grōa*, OE *grōwan* 'grow', etc. Walde-P. 1.646. Feist 220. Otherwise (: Skt. *ghṛṣ-* 'rub') Falk-Torp 355.

5. Lith. *žolė*, Lett. *zāle* : Lith. *žalias*, Lett. *zal'š*, ChSl. *zelinŭ* 'green', Grk. χόλος 'gall', χλόη 'young green plant or grass', χλωρός 'green', etc. Walde-P. 1.625.

6. ChSl. *trava*, etc., general Slavic, orig. 'fodder', fr. the root of ChSl. *truti* 'use up', *natruti* 'feed', etc. : *tryti* 'rub', etc. (9.31). Walde-P. 1.731. Trautmann 327. Brückner 575.

7. Skt. *tṛṇa-* : Goth. *þaurnus*, ON, OE *þorn*, ChSl. *trŭnŭ* 'thorn', ChSl. *strŭnĭ* 'stalk, blade', perh. fr. the root **ster-* seen in Grk. στερεός 'stiff, firm', NHG *starr* 'rigid, stiff', etc. Walde-P. 2.641.

Av. *vāstra-* 'pasture' (3.17), hence also 'fodder, grass'.

8.52 HAY

Grk.	χόρτος	Goth.	*hawi*	Lith.	*šienas*
NG	χορτάρι, σανός	ON	*hey*	Lett.	*siens*
Lat.	*fēnum*	Dan.	*hø*	ChSl.	*sěno*
It.	*fieno*	Sw.	*hö*	SCr.	*sijeno*
Fr.	*foin*	OE	*hēg, hīg*	Boh.	*seno*
Sp.	*heno*	ME	*hey, hay*	Pol.	*siano*
Rum.	*fîn*	NE	*hay*	Russ.	*seno*
Ir.	(*fēr*)	Du.	*hooi*	Skt.	(*tṛṇa-*)
NIr.	*fēar tirim*	OHG	*hewi, houwi*	Av.	. . . .
W.	*gwair*	MHG	*höuwe*		
Br.	*foenn*	NHG	*heu*		

'Hay' is sometimes undistinguished from 'grass', as in the case of Grk. χόρτος 'fodder, grass, hay', or is from 'grass' with secondary differentiation, as Welsh *gwair*. But usually there are distinctive words.

1. Grk. χόρτος, NG χορτάρι, the same as for 'grass' (8.51).

NG σανός, fr. Slavic (below, 5).

2. Lat. *fēnum* (> Romance words), etym. dub., perh. as **fend-snom* : *defendere* 'defend', *offendere* 'repulse', Grk. θείνω, Skt. *han-* 'strike', etc. ('hay' as grass cut down, cf. the Gmc. group, below, 4); or with specialization fr. 'product' like *fēnus* 'interest on capital' fr. the same root as *fēcundus*, *fēlix* 'fruitful'. Walde-P. 1.680. Ernout-M. 345. Walde-H. 1.479.

3. Ir. *fēr* also 'grass', NIr. *fēar tirim* lit. 'dry grass', W. *gwair* 'hay', see under 'grass' (8.51).

Br. *foenn*, fr. Fr. *foin*.

4. Goth. *hawi*, ON *hey*, OE *hēg*, etc., general Gmc., in earlier period also 'grass' (so in Gospels Goth. *hawi* Jn. 6.10, OE *ofer grēne hīg* Mt. 6.39), prob. as orig. 'mown' or 'to be mown' : OE *hēawan*, OHG *houwan* 'hew' (9.22). Walde-P. 1.330, 381. Feist 252.

5. Lith. *šienas*, Lett. *siens*, ChSl. *sěno*, etc., general Balto-Slavic : Grk. κοινά· χόρτος (Hesych.), root connection? Walde-P. 1.455.

6. Skt. *tṛṇa-* 'grass' (8.51), also used for 'hay'?

8.53 PLANT

Grk.	φυτόν, βοτάνη	Goth.	. . . .	Lith.	*augalas, žolė*
NG	φυτό, βοτάνη	ON	*urt*	Lett.	*augs, zāle*
Lat.	*herba*	Dan.	*plante, urt*	ChSl.	*sadŭ*
It.	*pianta, erba*	Sw.	*planta, ört*	SCr.	*biljka, trava*
Fr.	*plante, herbe*	OE	*wyrt*	Boh.	*rostlina, bylina, zelina*
Sp.	*planta, hierba*	ME	*wort, erbe*	Pol.	*roślina, ziele*
Rum.	*plantă, iarbă*	NE	*plant, herb*	Russ.	*rastenie, trava*
Ir.	*luib, luss*	Du.	*plant, kruid*	Skt.	*vīrudh-, oṣadhi-*
NIr.	*plannda, luibh, lus*	OHG	*pflanza, wurz, krūt*	Av.	*urvarā-*
W.	*planhigyn, llysieuyn*	MHG	*pflanze, wurz, krūt*		
Br.	*plantenn, louzaouenn*	NHG	*pflanze, kraut*		

Although words like NE *plant* are used by botanists to cover the whole vegetable vs. animal kingdom, in common use they are applied to the smaller varieties, to the exclusion of trees and shrubs. Many of the words listed in second place have an even more restricted scope, being applied only to certain types of plants, like NE *herb* (see NED s.v.), etc.

Several of the words are from the notion of 'grow', as, conversely, some of the words for 'grow' were primarily applied to plant life (cf. 12.53). Some show extension from 'cutting, shoot' or connection with words for 'root'.

1. Grk. φυτόν : φύω 'grow, produce', Skt. *bhū-* 'become, be', etc. Walde-P. 2.140 ff. Hence φυτεία 'planting', late also a 'plant' (NT, etc.).

Grk. βοτάνη 'pasture, fodder' (: βόσκω 'feed'), also 'plant, herb, weed'.

2. Lat. *herba*, same as for 'grass' (8.51), but general for 'growing vegetation, plant'. Hence the Romance words for 'grass' and 'herb', and ME *erbe*, NE *herb*. These have a less broad scope than the descendants of Lat. *planta* (below), but differ considerably in their particular applications.

Lat. *planta* 'cutting, shoot, slip' (in this sense always Varro, RR), never 'plant', but the source of the modern Romance, Celtic, and Gmc. words in the latter sense (but OE, ME *plante* in sense of Lat. *planta*), same word as *planta* 'sole of the foot'? Some suggest a back-formation fr. the vb. *plantāre* 'plant' taken as fr. *planta* 'sole of the foot'. But, beside the fact that the vb. is late, this would suit the later better than the early sense. Ernout-M. 775.

3. Ir. *luib*, NIr. *luibh* (cf. Ir. *lubgort* 'garden', 8.13) : Goth. *lubja-leis* 'skilled in poison', ON *lyf* 'herb', OE *lybb*, OHG *luppi* 'poison, witchcraft', these prob. also : Goth. *laufs* 'leaf', etc. (8.56). Walde-P. 2.418. Pedersen 1.116.

Ir. *luss*, NIr. *lus*, W. *llysieuyn*, Br. *louzaouenn* (sg. fr. pl. *llysiau*, *louzaou*, old sg. W.-*lys* in plant-names = '-wort'), OCorn. *les* 'herba', perh. (as **lud-su-*) : Skt. *rudh-*, Goth. *liudan* 'grow'. Walde-P. 2.417. Otherwise (**lubh-stu-* : *luib*) Pedersen 1.378, 2.19.

4. ON, Dan. *urt*, Sw. *ört*, OE *wyrt*,

ME *wort*, MLG *wurt*, OHG, MHG *wurz*, all : Goth. *waurts* 'root', etc. (8.54).

Du. *kruid*, OHG, MHG *krūt*, NHG *kraut*, used for 'plant, herb' or with specialization (esp. 'cabbage'), prob. : Grk. βρύω 'well, teem' (cf. γῆ φυτοῖς βρύουσα 'earth teeming with plants', Aristot.). Walde-P. 1.689. Weigand-H. 1.1142. Franck-v. W. 353.

5. Lith. *augalas*, *augmuo*, Lett. *augs* : Lith. *augti*, Lett. *augt* 'grow', Lat. *augēre*, Grk. αὔξω 'increase', etc. Walde-P. 1.22 f.

Lith. *žolė*, Lett. *zāle* 'grass' (8.51), also 'plant, herb' (cf. esp. Mühl-Endz. 4.696 ff.).

6. ChSl. *sadŭ* (Gospels Mt. 15.13, Supr.) = Russ. *sad* 'garden' (8.13), fr. *saditi* 'set' = 'plant', caus. of *sędą*, *sěsti* 'sit' (cf. also Lith. *sodįti* 'set, plant'), IE **sed-* 'sit'. Walde-P. 2.483.

ChSl. *bylĭje* (Supr. for βοτάνη and φάρμακον 'drug'), SCr. *biljka*, Boh. *bylina*, derivs. of *bylŭ* pple. of *byti* 'be' (cf. Grk. φυτόν, above, 1). Berneker 112.

Boh. *rostlina*, Pol. *roślina*, Russ. *rastenie* : ChSl. *rasti* 'grow', etc. (12.53).

SCr., Russ. *trava* 'grass' (8.51), also 'herb'.

Boh. *zelina*, Pol. *ziele* : ChSl. *zelenŭ* 'green' (15.68), *zelĭje* 'vegetables' (5.65), Lith. *žolė* 'grass' and 'herb', etc.

7. Skt. *vīrudh-*, fr. *vi-rudh-* 'sprout, grow' (*vī-* as in other cpds., like *ānu-* beside *anu-*).

Skt. *oṣadhi-*, esp. 'healing herb' (in contrast to more generic *vīrudh-*; cf. Macdonell - Keith 1.125), apparently a cpd., second part : *dhā-* 'place, put', but first part obscure. Uhlenbeck 37.

Av. *urvarā-* (usually pl.) : Skt. *urvarā-* 'field' (8.12). Barth. 401 ff.

8.54 ROOT

Grk.	ῥίζα	Goth.	*waurts*	Lith.	*šaknis*
NG	ρίζα	ON	*rōt*	Lett.	*sakne*
Lat.	*rādīx*	Dan.	*rod*	ChSl.	*korenĭ*
It.	*radice*	Sw.	*rot*	SCr.	*korijen*
Fr.	*racine*	OE	*wyrttruma, wyrtwala*	Boh.	*kořen*
Sp.	*raíz*	ME	*rote*	Pol.	*korzen*
Rum.	*rădăcină*	NE	*root*	Russ.	*koren'*
Ir.	*frēm*	Du.	*wortel*	Skt.	*mūla-*
NIr.	*frēamh*	OHG	*wurzala*	Av.	*varəšaji-*
W.	*gwreiddyn*	MHG	*wurzel*		
Br.	*gwrizienn*	NHG	*wurzel*		

For 'root' there is a widespread inherited group, which includes also several words denoting 'branch' or 'plant', and community between 'root' and 'branch' is observed in another group. But the root connection and underlying notion is uncertain.

1. IE **wṝd-*, **wṛd-*, etc. in words for 'root', also 'plant, branch', etc., prob. fr. a **werd-* beside **werdh-* in Skt. *vṛdh-* 'grow'. Walde-P. 1.288. Ernout-M. 849. Falk-Torp 907, 1336. REW 6995, 7000.

Lat. *rādīx* (> It. *radice*, OFr. *raiz*, Sp. *raíz;* late deriv. *rādīcīna* > Fr. *racine*, Rum. *rădăcină*), beside Grk. ῥάδῑξ 'branch' and Lat. *rāmus* (**rādmo-*) 'branch'; Ir. *frēm* (early *frēn*, cf. Z. celt. Ph. 12.409), NIr. *frēamh*, W. *gwreiddyn* (beside *gwrysgen* 'branch'), Br. *gwrizienn;* Goth. *waurts* 'root', but OE *wyrt*, OHG *wurz* alone mostly 'plant, herb' (8.53), with cpds. for 'root', OE *wyrt-truma* (*truma* 'support'), OE *wyrt-wala*, *wyrtwalu*, OHG *wurzala*, MHG, NHG *wurzel*, Du. *wortel* (final member : Goth. *walus*, ON *vǫlr* 'staff, stick'), ON

rōt (> ME *rote*, NE *root*), Dan. *rod*, Sw. *rot*.

Grk. ῥίζα, Lesb. βρίσδα belongs here despite the difficult ρι. See refs. in Feist 556.

2. Lith. *šaknis*, Lett. *sakne*, OPruss. *sagnis* : Lith. *šaka* 'branch, twig', Skt. *çākhā* 'branch', etc. (8.55).

3. ChSl. *korenĭ*, etc., general Slavic: Lith. *keras* 'old weatherworn tree-stump, shrub', Lett. *cers* 'bush, knotty root', Lith. *kerėti* 'take root', root connection uncertain. Berneker 570. Walde-P. 1.412.

4. Skt. *mūla-*, perh. (as the plant's organ of drinking; cf. *pādapa-* 'tree, plant', lit. 'drinking with the foot') : OHG *mūla* 'mouth, snout', etc. (4.24) Wackernagel, Berl. Sitzb. 1918.410.

Av. *varəšaji-* (taken as 'stem, trunk' by Darmesteter, but prob. 'root' as Barth.), cpd. of *varəša-* 'tree', and the root of *gaya-* 'life', etc., hence lit. 'what gives life to the tree'. Barth. 1379.

8.55 BRANCH

Grk.	κλάδος, ὄζος	Goth.	*asts*	Lith.	*šaka*
NG	κλάδος, κλαδί	ON	*grein, kvistr*	Lett.	*zars*
Lat.	*rāmus*	Dan.	*gren*	ChSl.	*větvĭ, věja*
It.	*ramo, rama*	Sw.	*gren*	SCr.	*grana*
Fr.	*branche, rameau*	OE	*telga, bōg, twig*	Boh.	*větev, haluz*
Sp.	*rama, ramo*	ME	*bow(e), braunche, twist*	Pol.	*gałąź*
Rum.	*ramură, cracă*			Russ.	*suk, vetv'*
Ir.	*crāib, gēsca*	NE	*branch, bough*	Skt.	*çākhā-, vayā-*
NIr.	*gēag, craobh*	Du.	*tak*	Av.	*yaxšti-, fraspara*γ*a-*
W.	*cangen, cainc*	OHG	*ast, zwelge, zwīg*		
Br.	*brank, barr*	MHG	*ast, zelge (zwīc)*		
		NHG	*ast, zweig*		

Some words for 'branch' are cognate with words for 'root' (8.54). Others are from diverse sources, but esp. from the notion of 'split, fork, divide', or with transferred application from words for animal parts, as 'paw, arm, leg'. Words for 'twig' are not included, except as they are also used for 'branch'. Where two words are listed as current in the same modern language, aside from other differences in scope or feeling, one of these is definitely preferred for the widespread figurative uses, as NE *branch* vs. *bough*, NHG *zweig* vs. *ast*, Russ. *vetv'* vs. *suk*.

1. IE **ozdos*, that is, **o-zd-o-s* with weak grade of **sed-* 'sit', like **ni-zd-o-s* 'nest', and likewise used orig. with reference to birds, namely, as 'place to sit on, perch'. M. Bloomfield, Language 3.213 ff. Walde-P. 1.186, 95 (with different semantic view). Feist 60.

Grk. ὄζος, Goth. *asts*, OHG–NHG *ast*, Arm. *ost*.

2. Grk. κλάδος, orig. the 'broken-off' branch : κλαδαρός 'frail, easily broken', Lat. *percellere* 'strike down', *clādēs* 'destruction', Lith. *kalti* 'strike', also OE *holt*, OHG *holz* 'wood, woods', ChSl. *klada* 'beam, block', etc. Walde-P. 1.438 f. Walde-H. 1.225 f.

3. Lat. *rāmus* (> It., Sp. *ramo*, or, as orig. coll., It., Sp. *rama;* dim. forms > Fr. *rameau*, Rum. *ramură*) : *rādix* 'root', etc. (8.54). Ernout-M. 849. REW 1033, 7055.

Fr. *branche* (> ME *braunche*, NE *branch;* also Norm. Fr. form > Br. *brank*), fr. late Lat. *branca* 'paw of an animal' (> Rum. *brîncă*, It. *branca* 'paw, claw'), orig.? REW 1271. Wartburg 1.498. Gamillscheg 139 f.

Rum. *cracă*, fr. Slavic, cf. Bulg. *krak*, *kraka* 'leg, foot', SCr. *krak* 'long leg', etc., also in ChSl. *dlŭgo-krakŭ* 'sort of insect' (lit. 'long-leg'). Tiktin 429. Berneker 571 f.

4. Ir. *crāib*, NIr. *craobh* (also a 'tree', as in Gael.), etym.? Macbain 104.

Ir. *gēsca*, *gēc*, NIr. *gēag*, W. *cangen*, *cainc*, Lith. *šaka*, Russ. *suk* (ChSl. *sąkŭ* 'twig', Boh. *suk* 'knot' in wood), Skt. *çākhā-*, Arm. *çax* : Skt. *çañku-* 'peg', Lith. *šaknis*, Lett. *sakne*, OPruss. *sagnis* 'root', Goth. *hōha*, Ir. *cēcht* 'plow' ('forked stick'), etc. Walde-P. 1.335. Pedersen 1.126, 494.

Br. *barr* 'top' (12.33), also 'branch' (as 'tip', cf. Du. *tak*, below, 5).

Br. *brank*, fr. a dial. form of Fr. *branche* (above, 3).

5. Goth. *asts*, OHG *ast*, etc., above, 1.

ON *kvistr*, mostly 'small branch, twig' (Dan. *kvist*, Sw. *qvist* 'twig'), ME *twist*, *twyste* (cf. NED s.v.), cf. ON *kvīsl* 'fork, branch' (of a river, etc.), fr. Gmc. *twis-* (Goth. *twis-* 'apart'), IE **dwis* in Lat. *bis*, early Lat. *duis* 'twice' : IE *dwōu-* 'two' (cf. below, OE *twig*, etc.). Walde-P. 1.820. Falk-Torp 607 f.

ON *grein*, Dan., Sw. *gren* : Sw. *gren* 'fork between two branches', Sw. dial. *grena* 'spread the legs', MHG *griten*, id., Goth. *griþs* 'step', etc., connections outside Gmc. uncertain, but semantic development clearly 'fork, angle' > 'branch'. Falk-Torp 345. Walde-P. 1.652.

OE *telga*, OHG *zwelge* (with *zw-* for *z-* fr. *zwīg*), MHG *zelge*, *zelch* (ON *tjalga* 'thin limb, long arm', rare) : ON *telgja* 'whittle', Ir. *dlongim*, *dluigim* 'split', Lith. *dalgis* 'scythe'. Walde-P. 1.812. Falk-Torp 1252.

OE *bōg*, *bōh*, ME *bow(e)*, NE *bough*, same word as OE *bōg* 'shoulder' : OHG *buog* 'shoulder', Skt. *bāhu-*, Grk. πῆχυς 'arm', etc. (4.31). Early and usual specialization to 'bough' of a tree. NED s.v. *bough*, sb.

OE *twig*, *twigge* (ME, NE *twig* 'small branch, twig', but in OE general 'branch', cf. Gospels, Mk. 13.28, Mt. 24.32, of the branches of the fig tree, also Jn. 12.13 *palm-treowa twigu*), Du. *twijg*, OHG *zwīg* (mostly 'twig', cf. Graff 5.729; but also 'branch', cf. Tatian 116.4, 5), MHG *zwīc* (likewise mostly 'twig, sprout, cutting'), NHG *zweig*, all derivs. of IE **dwi-*, **dwei-* : **dwōu* 'two', like ON *kvistr*, etc., above. Here also OHG *zuog*, OS *tōg*, with vowel from the numeral. Walde-P. 1.819. Note the opposite tendencies of usage in English ('branch' > 'twig') and German ('twig' > 'branch').

ME *braunche*, NE *branch*, fr. Fr. *branche* (above, 3).

Du. *tak*, fr. MDu. *tacke*, *tac* 'point, branch' = MHG *zacke*, NHG *zacken* 'point, prong', NE *tack*, etc. root connection dub. Franck-v. W. 685. Walde-P. 1.785.

6. Lith. *šaka*, above, 4.

Lett. *zars*, prob. : Lith. *žaras* 'beam of light' (Lalis), *žėrėti* 'shine, glitter', etc. Cf. the opposite semantic development in OE *bēam*, NE *beam* for 'beam of light' (NED s.v. 19). Mühl.-Endz. 4.691.

7. ChSl. *větvĭ*, Boh. *větev*, Russ. *vetv'* : Lith. *vytis* 'osier', Lett. *vitvols*, OPruss. *witwan*, ON *viðir*, OHG *wīda* 'willow', etc., *t*-formations of IE **wei-* in ChSl. *věja*, Skt. *vayā-* 'branch', Ir. *fē* 'rod, measuring-rod', Lat. *viēre* 'plait, weave', Lith. *vyti* 'twist', ChSl. *viti* 'wind, twist', etc. Jokl, Arch. sl. Ph. 29.44. Walde-P. 1.224, 225.

SCr. (Bulg., Slov.) *grana*, Ukr. *hranok* (Russ. *granka* 'tuft, wisp') : Russ. *gran'* 'facet, limit', *granica* 'frontier', Pol. *grań*, Boh. *hrana* 'corner, edge', etc., all from the notion of 'point' : ON *grǫn*, Ir. *grend* 'beard', OHG *grani* 'bearded', etc. Walde-P. 1.606. Berneker 346.

Pol. *gałąź*, Boh. *haluz*, Ukr. *háluź*, Russ. dial. *galjuka*, as **galą-zĭ* : Russ. *gol'ja* (rare) 'bough', Boh. *hůl* 'staff, stick', etc., Arm. *kołr* 'branch', root connection? Berneker 292, 326. Brückner 133.

Russ. *suk*, above, 4.

8. Skt. *çākhā*, above, 4.

Skt. *vayā* : ChSl. *věja*, etc. (above, 7).

Av. *yaxšti-* (in cpds. *θri-yaxšti-*, etc.) = Skt. *yaṣṭi-* 'staff, stick', root connections dub. Walde-P. 1.443. Barth. 809, 1236.

Av. *frasparəγa-*, lit. 'that which shoots forth' (cpd. of *fra* = Skt. *pra*, and *sparəγa* : Skt. *spūrj-* 'burst forth, roar') and *fravāxš-* (cpd. of *fra* and *vaxš-* 'grow') in this sequence, Yasna 10.5, are taken as 'branch'–'twig' by Darmesteter and Mills (also *frasparəγa* rendered by *çākhā-* in Skt. translation), but as 'twig'–'stem, branch' by Barth. (*frasparəγa-* rendered by *spīk* 'twig' in Pahlavi translation). Barth. 991, 1003.

8.56 LEAF

Grk.	*φύλλον*	Goth.	*laufs*	Lith.	*lapas*
NG	*φύλλο*	ON	*laufsblað (lauf, blað)*	Lett.	*lapa*
Lat.	*folium*	Dan.	*blad (løv)*	ChSl.	*listŭ*
It.	*foglia*	Sw.	*blad (löf)*	SCr.	*list*
Fr.	*feuille*	OE	*lēaf (blæd)*	Boh.	*list*
Sp.	*hoja*	ME	*leef*	Pol.	*liść*
Rum.	*frunză (foaie)*	NE	*leaf*	Russ.	*list*
Ir.	*duille*	Du.	*blad (loof)*	Skt.	*parṇa-, pattra-*
NIr.	*duilleog, bileog*	OHG	*blat, loub*	Av.	*varəka-*
W.	*deilen, dalen*	MHG	*blat, loup*		
Br.	*delienn*	NHG	*blatt (laub)*		

Words for 'leaf' are connected with words for 'bloom, flower' (orig. 'swell'?), for 'peel, strip off', and for 'wing, feather', the last reflecting the notion of lightness, fluttering.

1. From a root **bhel-*, seen also in words for 'flower' (5.57), and perh. ultimately the same as that in words resting on the notion of 'swell' (Lat. *follis* 'leather bag', Grk. φαλλός 'phallic emblem', NE *ball*, etc.). Walde-P. 2.176 f. Ernout-M. 374. Walde-H. 1.523 f. Falk-Torp 79.

Grk. φύλλον; Lat. *folium* (pl. *folia*, late coll. sg. > It. *foglia*, Fr. *feuille*, Sp. *hoja*, Rum. *foaie*, the last mostly 'leaf' of paper); Gael. *bile* 'blade' of grass, etc., dim. Ir. *billeōc*, NIr. *bileog*; ON *blað* (rare in this sense), *laufsblað*, Dan., Sw. *blad*, OE *blæd* (but rare in this sense, ME, NE *blade* never in this sense, and only late ME in modern sense of 'blade' of grass, etc., cf. NED s.v.), OHG, MHG *blat*, NHG *blatt*, Du. *blad*.

2. Rum. *frunză*, fr. MLat. *frondia* formed after the analogy of *folia* fr. Lat. *frōns*, *frondis* 'leafy branch, foliage', itself of dub. orig. Pușcariu 659. REW 3530.

3. Ir. *duille*, *duillen*, NIr. *duilleog*, W. *deilen* (and *dalen*, coll. *dail*), Br. *delienn* (coll. *deil*), OCorn. *delen* gl. *folium*, cf. Gall. πεμπε-δουλα 'πεντάφυλλον' : Grk. θάλλω 'bloom, flourish, abound', θαλλός 'sprout, young twig', Alb. *dal* 'sprout, go forth', Arm. *dalar* 'green, fresh', etc. Walde-P. 1.825. Pedersen 1.375. Lat. *folium* could also be put with this group, instead of as above, 1. Cf. Ernout-M. s.v.

4. Goth. *laufs*, pl. *laubōs*, also *lauf* coll. 'φύλλα', as likewise ON *lauf*, Dan. *løv*, Sw. *löf* 'foliage'; OE *lēaf* sg. and pl., ME *lefe*, *leef*, etc., NE *leaf*, OHG *loub*, MHG *loup* either 'leaf' (pl. OHG *loubir* 'leaves'), or coll. 'foliage' as NHG *laub*, Du. *loof*, prob. : Lith. *lupti*, Lett. *lupt* 'flay, peel', Russ. *lupit'* 'peel, bark', etc. with the same semantic relation as Lith. *lapas* : Grk. λέπω (below, 5). Walde-P. 2.418. Feist 323 f. Falk-Torp 683.

ON *blað*, etc., above, 1.

5. Lith. *lapas*, Lett. *lapa* : Slov. *lépen*, Sorb. *łopjëno* 'leaf', Russ. *lepen'* 'piece, scrap', etc., fr. the root seen in Grk. λέπω 'peel off', λέπος 'bark', etc. Walde-P. 2.429 f. Berneker 701 f.

6. ChSl. *listŭ* (coll. *listvĭje*), etc., general Slavic : Lith. *laiškas* formerly 'leaf' (esp. of a book), now 'sheet of paper, letter' (as also Boh., Pol. *list*), OPruss. *lāiskas* 'book', root connection? Berneker 723 f.

7. Skt. *pattra-*, also and orig. 'wing, feather' (4.392).

Skt. *parṇa-*, also and orig. 'wing, feather' (4.392).

Av. *varəka-*, cf. MPers. *varg*, NPers. *barg*. etym.? Barth. 1367.

8.57 FLOWER

Grk.	*ἄνθος*	Goth.	*(blōma)*	Lith.	*gėlė (kvietka, žiedas)*
NG	*ἄνθος, λουλούδι*	ON	*blōm, blōmstr*	Lett.	*puk'e (zieds)*
Lat.	*flōs*	Dan.	*blomst*	ChSl.	*cvětŭ, cvětĭcĭ*
It.	*fiore*	Sw.	*blomma, blomster*	SCr.	*cvijet*
Fr.	*fleur*	OE	*blōstma*	Boh.	*květina*
Sp.	*flor*	ME	*blosme, flour, blome*	Pol.	*kwiat*
Rum.	*floare*	NE	*flower*	Russ.	*cvetok*
Ir.	*blāth, scoth*	Du.	*bloem*	Skt.	*puṣpa-, kusuma-*
NIr.	*blāth*	OHG	*bluomo*	Av.	. . . .
W.	*blodeuyn, blodyn*	MHG	*bluome*		
Br.	*bleunienn, boked*	NHG	*blume*		

Words for 'flower' are mostly connected with others for 'bloom, sprout thrive', these latter notions being of diverse origin, as 'swell, shine', etc. One or two are probable examples of extension from the name of a particular flower. Most of the words in the older period, and some still, cover both 'flower' and 'blossom'.

1. From **bhlō-*, **bhlē-*, extension of **bhel-* in words for leaf (8.56) and perh. orig. 'swell'. Walde-P. 2.176 ff. Ernout-M. 370. Walde-H. 1.518. Falk-Torp 85.

Lat. *flōs*, *flōris* (> Romance words; OFr. *flour* > ME *flour*, NE *flower*); Ir. *blāth*, W. *blodeuyn*, *blodyn* (pl. *blodau*, arch. sg. *blawd*), Br. *bleunienn* (coll. *bleuñ*); Goth. *blōma* (quotable only as acc. pl. 'τὰ κρίνα' Mt. 6.28), ON *blōm*, *blōmstr* (*blōmi* 'bloom, prosperity', pl. *blōmar* 'flowers'; hence ME *blome*, NE *bloom*), Dan. *blomst* (older *blomster*), Sw. *blomster*, *blomma* (Dan. *blomme* arch.), OE *blōstma*, ME *blosme* (NE *blossom*), Du. *bloem*, OHG *bluomo*, MHG *bluome*, NHG *blume*.

2. Grk. ἄνθος (hence ἀνθέω 'bloom', etc.) : Skt. *andhas-* 'an herb', further connection dub. Walde-P. 1.67 f.

NG λουλούδι, fr. Alb. *lule* 'flower', this perh. fr. Lat. *lilium* 'lily'. G. Meyer, Neugr. Stud. 2.68, Alb. Etym. Wtb. 250.

3. Ir. *scoth*, etym.? Perh. : Lith. *skėsti* 'spread out, unfold'. Lidén, Mélanges Vising (cf. Idg. Jhrb. 11.364). Otherwise (: Lat. *scatere* 'gush, spring forth') Stokes, KZ 33.69.

Br. *boked* (also 'bouquet'), fr. Fr. *bouquet*.

4. Goth. *blōma*, ON *blōm*, *blōmstr*, etc., above, 1.

ME *flour*, NE *flower*, above, 1.

5. Lith. *gėlė* (now the preferred word, cf. NSB s.v. *kvietka*) prob. (orig. applied to a particular flower?) : Lith. *geltas*, *geltonas*, Lett. *dzeltāns*, ChSl. *žlŭtŭ*, etc. 'yellow' (15.69).

Lith. *kvietka*, fr. WhRuss. *kvetka* : ChSl. *cvětŭ*, etc., (below, 6). Brückner, Sl. Fremdw. 101.

Lith. *žiedas* (also 'ring'), Lett. *zieds* (mostly 'bloom' or fig. 'flower') : Lith. *žydėti*, Lett. *ziedēt* 'bloom', Goth. *keinan*, OHG *chīnan* 'sprout', OE *cīnan* 'burst, stand open', etc. Walde-P. 1.544. Mühl.-Endz. 4.738 ff. Leskien, Ablaut 290.

Lett. *puk'e*, fr. Liv. *puk'k'* 'flower'. Mühl.-Endz. 3.405 f.

6. ChSl. *cvětŭ*, *cvětĭcĭ*, etc., general Slavic (the simple words partly replaced as the popular terms by dims.) : ChSl. *pro-cvisti*, Russ. *cvesti*, etc. 'bloom', Lett. *kvitēt* 'shine, glimmer', prob. fr. IE **kweit-*, beside **k̑weit-* in ChSl. *svĭtěti* 'shine', *světŭ*, Goth. *hweits* 'white', etc. Walde-P. 1.470. Berneker 656 f.

7. Skt. *puṣpa-* : *puṣ-* 'thrive, flourish, prosper', Grk. φυσάω, ChSl. *puchati* 'blow', etc. Walde-P. 2.81.

Skt. *kusuma-*, orig.? Uhlenbeck 61.

8.58 ROSE

Grk.	*ῥόδον*	Goth.	. . . .	Lith.	*rožė*
NG	*τριαντάφυλλο*	ON	*rōs, rōsa*	Lett.	*ruoze*
Lat.	*rosa*	Dan.	*rose*	ChSl.	. . . .
It.	*rosa*	Sw.	*ros*	SCr.	*ruža*
Fr.	*rose*	OE	*rōse*	Boh.	*růže*
Sp.	*rosa*	ME	*rose*	Pol.	*róża*
Rum.	*trandafir*	NE	*rose*	Russ.	*roza, rozan*
Ir.	*rōs*	Du.	*roos*	Skt.	*(japa-, oḍra)*
NIr.	*rōs*	OHG	*rōsa*	Av.	*varəδa-(?)*
W.	*rhosyn*	MHG	*rōse*		
Br.	*rozenn*	NHG	*rose*		

'Rose' is chosen as a conspicuous example of specific flower names. The agreement does not rest upon inheritance from an IE form, but upon borrowing, the name spreading with the cultivation of the flower.

1. Lat. *rosa*, the source of most of the other European forms, is itself a loanword, either fr. some dialect form of Grk. ῥόδον, or with the latter fr. a common East Mediterranean source. Grk. ῥόδον, ϝρόδον belongs further with (Av. *varəδa-* 'rose'? Barth. 1369), Arm. *vard*, NPers. *gul* 'rose', whether orig. an Iranian word, or all from some common unknown source. Schrader, Reallex. 2.267 ff. Ernout-M. 870 f.

2. NG τριαντάφυλλο, displacing ῥόδον as the common word (hence Rum. *trandafir*, Alb. *trëndafil*), was orig. the rose 'of thirty petals'. Cf. the parallel ἑκατοντάφυλλα (Theophr.) and *rosa centifolia* (Pliny), and the reference to ῥόδα, ἓν ἕκαστον ἕχον ἑξήκοντα φύλλα (Hdt. 8.138).

3. Skt. *japā-* and *oḍra-*, said to denote the 'Chinese rose', are both of unknown origin.

8.60. 'Tree' = 1.42.

	8.61 OAK	8.62 BEECH	8.63 BIRCH	8.64 PINE (Pinus)	8.65 FIR (Abies)
Grk.	δρῦς, φηγός	ὀξύα	σημύδα(?)	πεύκη, πίτυς	ἐλάτη
NG	βελανιδιά	ὀξυά	σημύδα	πεύκη, πεύκο	ἐλάτη, ἔλατο
Lat.	*quercus* (*rōbur*)	*fāgus*	*betu(l)la*	*pīnus*	*abies*
It.	*quercia* (*rovere*)	*faggio*	*betula*	*pino*	*abete*
Fr.	*chêne* (*rouvre*)	*hêtre*	*bouleau*	*pin*	*sapin*
Sp.	*roble*	*haya*	*abedul*	*pino*	*abeto*
Rum.	*stejar*	*fag*	*mesteacăn*	*pin*	*brad*
Ir.	*daur*	*faghvile*	*bethe*	*gius*, *ochtach*	. . . .
NIr.	*dair*	*fāigh*	*beith*	*pēine*, *giūs*	*giūs*
W.	*derwen*	*ffawydden*	*bedwen*	*pin*(*wydden*)	*ffynidwydden*, *sybwydden*
Br.	*dervenn*	*favenn*	*bezvenn*	*pin*	*saprenn*
Goth.	. . . .	. . . .	. . . .	. . . .	. . . .
ON	*eik*	*bōk*	*bjǫrk*	*fura*	*grǫn*
Dan.	*eg*	*bøg*	*birk*	*fyr*	*gran*
Sw.	*ek*	*bok*	*björk*	*tall*, *fura*	*gran*
OE	*āc*	*bēce*	*beorc*	*pīnbēam*, *furh*	*sæppe*, *gyr*
ME	*oke*	*beche*	*birch*	*pine*	*fyrre*
NE	*oak*	*beech*	*birch*	*pine*	*fir*, *spruce*
Du.	*eik*	*beuk*	*berk*	*pijn*(*boum*)	*den*
OHG	*eih*	*buohha*	*bircha*, *birihha*	*pīnboum*, *forha*, *fiohta*	*tanna*
MHG	*eich*(*e*)	*buoche*	*birke*, *birche*	*vorhe*	*tanne*, *viehte*
NHG	*eiche*	*buche*	*birke*	*kiefer*, *föhre*	*tanne*, *fichte*
Lith.	*ąžuolas*	*skroblus*, *skirpstas*	*beržas*	*pušis*	*eglė*
Lett.	*uōzuols*	*vīksna*	*berzs*	*priede*	*egle*
ChSl.	. . . .	. . . .	. . . .	(*borŭ*)	*jela*
SCr.	*hrast*, *dub*	*bukva*	*breza*	*bor*	*jela*
Boh.	*dub*	*buk*	*bříza*	*sosna*, *smrk*	*jedle*
Pol.	*dąb*	*buk*	*brzoza*	*sosna*	*jodła*
Russ.	*dub*	*buk*	*bereza*	*sosna*	*el'*
Skt.	. . . .	. . . .	*bhūrja-*	*pītudāru*, *devadāru-*, etc.	. . . .
Av.	. . . .	. . . .	. . . .	. . . .	. . . .

8.61–8.65. As illustrative of specific tree names are chosen those for 'oak', 'beech', 'birch', 'pine', and 'fir'. For these and some others (as 'elm', 'yew', 'willow') there are cognate groups common to several of the European branches of IE, but only in a few cases extending to Indo-Iranian. The root connections are mostly obscure. The interest of such tree names lies mainly in their bearing on the moot question of the IE flora and the IE home, and further in the shift of application, connected with differences in the flora of different regions. So of 'beech' to 'oak' in Grk. φηγός (8.62), of 'oak' to 'fir' in Gmc. words for 'fir' (8.65), of 'yew' to 'willow' (OE *īw*, etc. 'yew', but Slavic *iva* 'willow'), between 'pine' and 'fir' (8.64, 8.65), 'beech' and 'oak' or 'elm' (8.62), etc.

Noteworthy is the primacy of the oak, as shown in mythology and in the recurring use of 'oak', as the tree par excellence, for 'tree', also in some derivatives for 'mountain' and 'forest'.

Schrader, Reallex. 2.629 ff. and in separate items, *Eiche*, etc. Hoops, Waldbäume und Kulturpflanzen.

8.61. 'Oak'. 1. IE *derwo-, *dru-*, etc. in words for 'oak' and for 'tree, wood' (1.42), the former, specific, use being probably the earlier. Walde-P. 1.804 ff. Osthoff, Parerga 169 ff.

Grk. δρῦς, Ir. *daur*, NIr. *dair*, W. *derwen* (pl. *derw*), Br. *dervenn*, all 'oak' (and so also *dru-* in Ir. *drūi* 'druid', Gall. *Druides*, Thurneysen Z. celt. Ph. 16.277) : Grk. δόρυ 'tree' (rare), 'beam, shaft, spear', OE *trēow* 'tree, wood', ChSl. *drěvo* 'tree', Skt. *dāru*, *dru-* 'wood', *druma-* 'tree', etc.

2. Grk. φηγός, orig. 'beech', see 8.62.

NG pop. βελανιδιά, fr. βελανίδι 'acorn' (8.66).

3. Lat. *quercus* (adj. *querceus*, fem. *quercea* > It. *quercia*), fr. *perkʷu- (assim. as in *quīnque* fr. *penkʷe, etc.) : OHG *fereh-eih*, Langob. *fereha*, NHG *vereiche* 'oak', Swiss *ferch* 'oak wood' (Weigand-H. 1.566), OHG *furha*, etc. with shift to 'pine' or 'fir' (8.64, 8.65), also Goth. *fairguni*, OE *firgen* 'mountain' (1.22). Walde-P. 2.47 ff. Ernout-M. 838.

Lat. *rōbur*, a special kind of oak (as It. *rovere*, Fr. *rouvre*, but Sp., Port. *roble* generic 'oak'), early form *rōbus* (whence *rōbustus* 'of oak, hard, strong'), named from its reddish heart-wood, and with dial. *ō* : Lat. *ruber* 'red', etc. Walde-P. 2.358. Ernout-M. 867.

Fr. *chêne*, OFr. *chaisne* (influenced by *fraisne*, *frêne* 'ash'), *chasne*, fr. a Gall. *cassanus (orig. Celtic?). REW 1740. Wartburg 2.459 ff. Gamillscheg 215.

Rum. *stejar* 'oak' beside *steajer* 'pole, stake' (in a threshing floor), fr. parallel forms of the same Slavic word, ChSl. *stežerŭ* 'prop', Bulg. *stožar* 'pole' (of a hayrick), 'mast', SCr. *stožer* 'doorpost', etc., with Rum. shift fr. '(oaken) pole' to 'oak'. Tiktin 1490.

4. ON *eik*, OE *āc*, OHG *eih*, etc., general Gmc. (in Iceland, where there are no trees, used for 'tree') : Grk. αἰγίλωψ 'sort of oak tree', perh. Lat. *aesculus* 'species of oak sacred to Jupiter'. Walde-P. 1.10. Falk-Torp 182.

5. Lith. *ąžuolas*, Lett. *uōzuols*, OPruss. *ansonis*, etym.? Walde-P. 1.83. Mühl.-Endz. 4.427.

6. (ChSl. *dąbŭ* 'tree'), SCr., Boh., Russ. *dub*, Pol. *dąb* (orig. meaning 'oak'; ChSl. 'tree' secondary), etym. dub., possibly, with reference to the dark heart-wood (cf. Lat. *rōbur*), fr. *dhumbh- : Ir. *dub* 'black', Grk. τῦφος 'smoke, steam', etc. Berneker 216 f.

SCr. *hrast* : ChSl. *chvrastije*, Russ. *chvorost*, Boh. *chrasti*, Pol. *chróst*, etc. 'brushwood'. Berneker 408 f.

8.62. 'Beech'. 1. IE *bhāgo-s. Walde-P. 2.128 f. Ernout-M. 326. Walde-H. 1.445 f. Falk-Torp 126.

Grk. φηγός, Dor. φāγός with shift to 'oak', there being no beeches in Greece proper; Lat. *fāgus* (> Rum. *fag*, OFr. *fou*; adj. *fāgeus* > It. *faggio*, Sp. *haya*; REW 3142, 3145); fr. Lat. also the Celtic words (Vendryes, De hib. voc. 139. Loth, Mots lat. 167) Ir. *faghvile* (cpd. with *bile* 'tree'), NIr. *fāigh*, W. *ffawydden* sg. of *ffawydd* coll. 'beeches' (cpd. with *gwydd* 'wood'), Br. *favenn* (pl. *fao*, *fav*); ON *bōk*, OE *bēce*, OHG *buohha*, etc., general Gmc.; fr. Gmc. the Slavic (Berneker 99 f., Stender-Petersen 450 f.) SCr. *bukva*, Boh., Pol., Russ. *buk*.

2. Grk. ὀξύα, ὀξύη, NG ὀξυά prob. (in form influenced by ὀξύς 'sharp') : ON *askr*, OE *æsc*, etc. 'ash', Alb. *ah* 'beech', etc. Walde-P. 1.185.

3. Fr. *hêtre*, fr. a Frank. form like MLG *hēster* 'young tree' (esp. beech or oak) = MHG *heister* 'young beech'. The stem *heis-* is seen in OLG *hēsiwald*, MLat. *Silva Caesia*. REW 4121. Gamillscheg 514. Weigand-H. 1.841 f.

4. Lith. *skroblus* 'white beech, hornbeam' and *skirpstas* (or *-us*) 'red beech, elm' (OPruss. *skerptus* 'rustere'), both perh. : Lat. *carpinus* 'hornbeam' and

more remotely Russ. *grab* 'hornbeam', etc. Walde-H. 1.171.

Lett. *vīksna* 'elm' and 'beech' : Lith. *vinkšna*, SCr. *vez*, Russ. *vjaz*, OE *wice* (NE *witch*), LG *wīeke* 'elm'. Walde-P. 1.314.

8.63. 'Birch'. 1. Derivatives of *bherəĝ- (*bhrēĝ-, *bhr̥̄ĝ-) in Skt. *bhrāj-* 'shine', Goth. *bairhts*, OE *beorht* 'bright', etc., applied to the 'birch' on account of its white bark. Walde-P. 2.170 f. Walde-H. 1.544. Falk-Torp 74.

ON *bjǫrk*, OE *beorc*, OHG *birihha*, *bircha*, etc., general Gmc.; Lith. *beržas*, Lett. *berzs*, SCr. *breza*, etc., general Slavic; Skt. *bhūrja-*, Osset. *bärz*; here also prob. Lat. *farnus*, *fraxinus* 'ash'.

2. Grk. σημύδα (Theophr. HP 3.14.4, 5.7.7), formerly taken as 'birch' (but identification uncertain) and hence NG use to render the (foreign) birch; prob. a loanword of unknown source.

3. Lat. *betu(l)la* (> It. *betula*, OFr. *beoul*, deriv. Fr. *bouleau*, Sp. *abedul*; REW 1068, 1069), Gallic word : Ir. *bethe*, NIr. *beith*, W. *bedwen*, Br. *bezvenn* 'birch'; so named according to Pliny (HN 15.75) because *bitumen ex ea Galli excoquunt*, therefore may be connected with Lat. *bitūmen* 'bitumen, mineral pitch', this (as based on a Gallic or Osc.-Umbr. form) : Skt. *jatu-* 'lac, gum', OE *cwudu* 'cud' (*hwīt cwudu* 'white cud, mastich'), OHG *cuti* 'gluten'. Walde-P. 1.672. Ernout-M. 108, 111. Walde-H. 1.103, 107.

Rum. *mesteacăn*, fr. late Lat. *masticinus* 'of mastic', applied to the 'birch', which yields a sap used for a drink (cf. NE *birch beer*, *birch wine*), like that of the mastic tree. Tiktin 970.

8.64. 'Pine'. There is some confusion between 'pine' (*pinus*) and 'fir' (*abies*), as of the coniferous trees in general, and some of the words listed differ in application according to the period and region.

1. Derivs. of *pī̆- in words for 'fat, sap, pitch', as Grk. πῖων, Skt. *pīna-* 'fat' (adj.), Grk. πῖαρ, Skt. *pīvas* 'fat' (sb.), Grk. πίσσα, Lat. *pix* 'pitch', etc., applied to the very resinous 'pine'. Walde-P. 2.73 ff.

Grk. πίτυς; Skt. *pītu-dāru-*; Lat. *pīnus* (also *picea*, fem. of adj. *piceus*, fr. *pix* 'pitch'), whence It., Sp. *pino*, Fr., Rum. *pin*, also OE *pīn-bēam*, *pīn-trēow*, ME, NE *pine* (> NIr. *pēine*), OHG *pīnboum* (usual gl. to Lat. *pinus*), Du. *pijn* (*-boum*), W., Br. *pin*, W. also *pin-wydden* (with *gwydd* 'woods', 1.41).

2. Grk. πεύκη, NG pop. also πεύκα and τὸ πεύκο, OHG *fiohta* (Steinmeyer-Sievers, Ahd. Glossen 4.63.19; cf. ib. 3.195.63 *pinus pinbom vel viechtech vel chien*), MHG *viehte*, NHG *fichte* (but 'spruce'), Lith. *pušis*, OPruss. *peuse*, perh. also Ir. *ochtach* (cf. Stokes KZ 33.73) : Grk. ἐχε-, περι-πευκής 'sharp', hence 'pine' fr. its needles. Walde-P. 2.15.

3. Ir. *gius* (*crand gius* gl. *pinus*), NIr. *giūs* 'pine' or 'fir', etym.?

W. *ffynidwydden*, cpd. like *pin-wydden*, first part deriv. of *ffon* 'stick' (with reference to the needles).

4. ON, Sw. *fura*, Dan. *fyr*, OE *furh*, *furh-wudu* (gl. *pinus*; but ME *fyrre*, *fyrre-tre* glosses *abies* in 15th cent., Wright Vocab. 560.7, 646.20, etc.; cf. also *fyrre* 'sappin' in 16th cent.; this shift complete in NE *fir*, except that in Scotland the native pine is still called *fir*; ME > W. *ffyr* 'pine' or 'fir'), OHG *forha* (usual gl. to Lat. *picea*), MHG *vorhe*, NHG *föhre* (dial. = *kiefer*), all with transfer to 'pine' fr. 'oak' : Lat. *quercus* 'oak' (8.61).

NHG *kiefer*, fr. *kien-föhre*, cpd. of preceding with *kien* 'resinous wood, pine resin'. Cf. also OHG *chien*, *kinboum*

(gl. to Lat. *pinus*), MHG *kienboum*, NHG *kienbaum*. Weigand-H. 1.1030, 1032.

Sw. *tall* (ON *þǫll*, Norw. *tall* 'young pine') orig. dub., but perh. as orig. 'tall' fr. the root of Lat. *tollere* 'raise', etc. Hellquist 1161 f. Falk-Torp 1244.

5. Lith. *pušis* : Grk. πεύκη, above, 2.

Lett. *priede*, obscure. Mühl.-Endz. 3.392.

6. Late ChSl. (beside *peuga* fr. πεύκη) *borŭ*, coll. *borije*, SCr., Bulg. *bor* (Boh., Russ. *bor* 'pine forest', Pol. *bór* 'forest') : ON *bǫrr*, OE *bearo* 'forest', perh. fr. *bher- in words for 'pointed'. Berneker 76. Walde-P. 2.164. Stender-Petersen 271 (Slavic fr. Gmc.).

Boh. *smrk* : late ChSl. *smrěčĭ* 'cedar'.

Boh., Pol., Russ. *sosna* (also late ChSl.), fr. *soksnā : ChSl. *sokŭ* 'sap', Lith. *sakau* 'resin'. Wiedemann BB 29.315. Or fr. *sopsna : OE *sæp*, OHG *saf* 'sap'. Mikkola, IF 23.126.

7. Skt. names of pinelike trees include : *deva-dāru-*, lit. 'god-tree', the 'deodar' tree, *pītu-dāru-*, also the 'deodar' (?) : Grk. πίτυς (above, 1); *sarală-* : *sarala-* 'straight, outstretched'.

8.65. 'Fir' (including 'spruce-fir, spruce'). 1. Grk. ἐλάτη, NG pop. τὸ ἔλατο, etym. dub., perh. : OHG *linta* 'linden', or : Russ. *jalavoc* 'juniper'. Walde-P. 1.152, 2.437. Boisacq 237 f.

2. Lat. *abies* (> It. *abete*, Sp. *abeto*) : Grk. (?) ἄβιν· ἐλάτη, οἱ δὲ πεύκην (Hesych.), otherwise obscure. Ernout-M. 5. Walde-H. 1.4.

Fr. *sapin*, fr. Lat. *sa(p)pīnus* 'sort of pine or fir', this formed (with suffix *-īno-*, or cpd. of *pīnus*?) fr. *sapo- or some such shorter form reflected by OFr. *sap*, OE *sæppe*, W. *syb-wydden*, Corn. *sib-uit*, MBr. *sap*, Br. *saprenn* (after *prenn* 'tree'). Walde-P. 2.515. Ernout-M. 895. REW 7592.

Rum. *brad*, fr. Alb. *breth* 'fir', itself obscure. Tiktin 219. G. Meyer, Alb. Etym. Wtb. 45.

3. W. *sybwydden*, Br. *saprenn*, above, 2.

NIr. *giūs*, W. *ffynidwydden*, defined as 'pine' or 'fir', see under 'pine' (8.64).

W. *pyrwydden*, cpd. of *gwydd* 'wood', first part perh. from ME with init. treated as if mutated *p*?

4. ON *grǫn*, Dan., Sw. *gran*, same word as ON *grǫn*, OE *granu*, OHG *grana* 'mustache, beard', Ir. *brend* 'beard', etc., with common notion of 'pointed', appropriate to (the foliage of) any of the 'nadelhölzer' (cf. Grk. πεύκη 'pine' 8.64), actually in this case the 'fir, spruce'. Walde-P. 1.606. Falk-Torp 1244. Hellquist 295 f.

OE *sæppe*, above, 2.

OE *gyr*, *gyr-trēow* (gl. *abies*, Wright, Vocab. 1.138.11, 269.14), perh. : Lat. *horrēre* 'bristle', etc. Hoops, Waldbäume und Kulturpflanzen 365.

ME *fyrre*, *firr*, NE *fir*, orig. 'pine', see 8.64.

NE *spruce*, short for *spruce fir*, orig. 'Prussian fir', fr. *Spruce* beside *Pruce* 'Prussia'. NED s.v.

OHG *tanna*, MHG, NHG *tanne*, Du. *den*, perh. : Skt. *dhanvan-* 'bow', reflecting some inherited tree name (cf. ON *almr* and *ȳr* 'bow', orig. of elm or yew, respectively), with transfer in Gmc. from 'oak' (?) to 'fir'. Walde-P. 1.825, 853. Hoops, Waldbäume und Kulturpflanzen 115 f.

OHG *fiohta*, etc. : Grk. πεύκη 'pine' (8.64).

5. Lith. *eglė*, Lett. *egle*, OPruss. *addle*, ChSl. (late), SCr. *jela*, Boh. *jedle*, etc., general Balto-Slavic, perh. : Lat. *ebulus* 'dwarf-elder'. Berneker 261 f. Ernout-M. 292. Walde-H. 1.388 f.

8.66 ACORN

Grk.	βάλανος	Goth.	....	Lith.	gilė
NG	βελανίδι	ON	(akarn)	Lett.	dzile
Lat.	glāns	Dan.	agern	ChSl.	želądĭ
It.	ghianda	Sw.	ekollon	SCr.	žir
Fr.	gland	OE	œcern	Boh.	žalud
Sp.	bellota	ME	akern	Pol.	żołądź
Rum.	ghindă	NE	acorn	Russ.	žolud'
Ir.	daurgne	Du.	eikel	Skt.	....
NIr.	daraighe, measōg	OHG	eihhila	Av.	....
W.	mesen	MHG	eichel		
Br.	mezenn	NHG	eichel		

Of the words for 'acorn' only a few are derived from those for 'oak'. Most of them either belong to an independent inherited group or represent a specialization of 'fruit of the field' or 'food' through 'mast' (nuts, acorns, etc., esp. as food for swine) to 'acorns'.

1. IE *gʷel- in various forms, ultimate root connection and underlying sense dub. Walde-P. 1.690. Ernout-M. 424. Walde-H. 1.604 f.

Grk. βάλανος, NG pop. βελανίδι, βελάνι (also βαλ-); Lat. glāns, glandis (> It. ghianda, Fr. gland, OSp., Port. lande, Rum. ghindă; REW 3778); Lith. gilė, OPruss. gile, Lett. dzīle; ChSl. želądĭ, etc., general Slavic (but SCr. želud replaced by žir); Arm. kaɫin.

2. Sp. bellota, fr. Arab. ballūṭ 'acorn'. REW 1025. Lokotsch 206.

3. Ir. daurgne (K. Meyer, Contrib. 593), NIr. daraighe, deriv. of Ir. daur 'oak' (8.61). NIr. also cnō darach 'nut of the oak'.

NIr. measōg, W. mesen, Br. mezenn : Ir. mess 'mast', i.e. 'nuts, acorns', etc.

(cf. Laws, Gloss. 559), OE mæst 'mast', etc. Walde-P. 2.231. Henry 201.

4. ON akarn ('fruit of wild trees, mast', including but not restricted to acorns), Dan. agern, OE œcern (rarely 'fruit' or 'mast', mostly 'acorn'), ME akern, NE acorn (numerous forms influenced by pop. etym.) : Goth. akran 'fruit of the field, harvest' (8.41). Falk-Torp 16. NED s.v. acorn.

OHG eihhila, MHG, NHG eichel, Du. eikel, derivs. of words for 'oak', OHG eih, etc. (8.61).

Sw. ekollon, cpd. of ek 'oak' and ollon 'mast, acorn' : ON aldin 'fruit of trees', fr. the root of ON ala 'bear, feed', Lat. alere 'nourish', etc. Falk-Torp 789 f. Hellquist 728 f.

5. Lith. gilė, ChSl. želądĭ, etc., above, 1.

SCr. žir in form = late ChSl. žirŭ 'pasturage', Pol. żer 'fodder' fr. root of žiti 'live', with successive specializations of 'means of life' > 'fodder' > 'mast' > 'acorns'. Miklosich 411 f. Brückner 669.

8.67 VINE

Grk.	ἄμπελος	Goth.	weinatriu	Lith.	vynmedis
NG	ἀμπέλι	ON	vīntrē (-viðr)	Lett.	vīna kuoks
Lat.	vītis	Dan.	vinranke (-stok)	ChSl.	loza
It.	vite, vigne (pl.)	Sw.	vinranka (-stock)	SCr.	loza
Fr.	vigne	OE	wīngeard, wīntrēow	Boh.	réva, vinný keř
Sp.	vid	ME	vyne, vynetree	Pol.	winorośl
Rum.	viṭa	NE	vine	Russ.	vinograd
Ir.	fínemain	Du.	wijnstok	Skt.	drākṣā-
NIr.	fíneamhain	OHG	(win)reba	Av.	....
W.	gwinwydden	MHG	(win)rebe, winstok		
Br.	gwinienn	NHG	weinstock, rebe		

For the 'vine' there are a few old distinctive words, which, so far as the etymology is clear, are connected with verbs for 'twist, wind', 'creep', or 'run'(?) and so were not confined to the grapevine, though this was the most conspicuous and important vine. But many are based on the words for 'wine' (5.92), mostly compounds with words for 'tree' (1.42), 'stem, stalk, tendril, growth'. In several cases words for 'vineyard' have come to be used for 'vine'.

1. Grk. ἄμπελος, NG ἀμπέλι, etym.? Boisacq 55.

2. Lat. vītis (> It. vite, Sp. vid), fr. IE *wei- in Lat. viēre 'twist, plait', Lith. vyti, ChSl. viti 'twist, wind', Lith. vytis 'willow twig', Grk. ἰτέα 'willow', etc. Hence adj. viteus, fem. vītea (> Rum. viṭa). Walde-P. 1.224. Ernout-M. 1107, 1116 f. REW 9388, 9395.

It. vigna 'vineyard', pl. vigne 'vines', Fr. vigne 'vineyard', and 'vine', fr. Lat. vīnea 'vineyard', deriv. of vīnum 'wine'. REW 9350.

3. Ir. fínemain (OIr. gen. pl. fínime), NIr. fíneamhain 'vineyard' and 'vine', fr. Lat. vīndēmia 'grape-gathering, vintage', cpd. of vīnum 'wine', with second part fr. demere 'take away'. Ernout-M. 1111. Pedersen 1.214. Vendryes, De hib. voc. 142.

W. gwinwydden, cpd. of gwin 'wine' and gwydd 'woods, trees' (1.41).

Br. gwinienn, deriv. of gwin 'wine'.

4. Goth. weinatriu, ON vīntrē, vīnviðr, OE wīntrēow, ME vintrē, vynetree, cpds. of words for 'wine' and 'tree'.

OE wīngeard, cpd. with geard 'yard' and so properly 'vineyard', but also usual word for 'vine' (e.g. Gospels, Jn. 15.1, 5, etc., where Lindisf. has wīntrēo).

Dan. vinranke, Sw. vinranka, cpds. with ranke, ranka 'tendril', fr. MLG ranke id. : OE wrencan 'twist', etc. Falk-Torp 878.

MHG wīnstok, NHG weinstock, Du. wijnstok, Dan. vinstok, Sw. vinstock, cpds. with words for 'stem, stalk', OHG stoc, etc.

OHG reba, MHG, NHG rebe (also OHG wīnreba, etc.), prob. : Lat. rēpere 'creep', etc. (10.41). Falk-Torp 894. Walde-P. 1.277. Kluge-G. 473. Otherwise (: OHG ribba 'rib', etc.) Weigand-H. 2.544.

ME vyne, NE vine, fr. OFr. vine, vigne (above, 2).

5. Lith. vynmedis, Lett. vīna kuoks, both fr. words for 'wine' and 'tree'.

6. ChSl., Bulg., SCr. loza = Pol. łoza, Russ. loza 'switch, willow', Russ. vinogradnaja loza or even loza alone (e.g. NT Jn. 15.5) 'vine' (Berneker 736), prob. : NPers. raz 'vine'. Tedesco, JAOS 63.149 ff.

Boh. réva, fr. MHG, NHG rebe (above, 4).

Boh. vinný keř, Pol. krzew winny,

---

words for 'shrub, bush' with adjs. of words for 'wine'.

Pol. winorośl (according to informant the best current word; many others in dicts.), cpd. with rośl old word for 'growth' : róść, ChSl. rasti, etc. 'grow' (12.53).

Russ. vinograd, fr. ChSl. vinogradŭ 'vineyard', also sometimes 'vine', fr. Gmc., Goth. weinagards, 'vineyard', etc. Stender-Petersen 366 f.

7. Skt. drākṣā- (also 'grape'), prob. as 'running vine', fr. drā- 'run'. See 5.76.

8.68 TOBACCO

NG	καπνός	Dan.	tobak	Lith.	tobakas
It.	tobacco	Sw.	tabak	Lett.	tabaka
Fr.	tabac	NE	tobacco	SCr.	duhan, tabak
Sp.	tabaco	Du.	tabak	Boh.	tabak
Rum.	tutun	NHG	tabak	Pol.	tytun
NIr.	tobac			Russ.	tabak
W.	tybaco, baco, myglys				
Br.	butun				

Tobacco, which to many ranks not far below food and drink, was introduced into Europe from America and with it its most widespread name. The smoking habit is more directly traceable from Virginia to England to Europe.

1. A supposedly Haitian word, represented by Sp. tabaco was adopted with various spellings in most of the European languages. See NED s.v. tobacco.

2. Another Indian name, believed to be of Brazilian origin, but current also in North America, appears as bittin in a German (Hans Stade, 1557) and betum in Portuguese accounts of Brazil; petun or petum in Spanish, French, and English writings. Lescarbot, Histoire de la Nouvelle France has petun with vb. petuner, and un calumet ou petunoir for 'pipe'. Although now otherwise obsolete

(after having given the name to the plant petunia), it has survived as the regular word in Breton, in the form butun (cf. the spelling bittin quoted above).

3. NG καπνός 'smoke' (1.83), also 'tobacco', in this sense with pl. καπνά for the various kinds.

4. Rum. tutun, Pol. tytun (also SCr. tutun, Russ. tjutjun, but not the usual words), fr. Turk tütün 'tobacco', orig. 'smoke'. Lokotsch 2121. Tiktin 1669.

5. W. myglys (beside common tybaco, baco) : myg 'smoke' (1.83), myglyd 'smoky'.

6. SCr. duhan (also duvan) through Turk. fr. Arab. duhān 'smoke'. Lokotsch 539. Berneker 234. Rječnik Akad. s.v.

8.69 SMOKE (Tobacco)

NG	καπνίζω (φουμάρω, πίνω καπνό)	Dan.	ryge	Lith.	rūkyti
It.	fumare	Sw.	rōka	Lett.	smēk'ēt
Fr.	fumer	NE	smoke	SCr.	pušiti, duhaniti
Sp.	fumar	Du.	rooken	Boh.	kouřiti
Rum.	bea tutun	NHG	rauchen	Pol.	kurzyć
NIr.	caithim tobac, ōlaim tobac			Russ.	kurit'
W.	smocio				
Br.	butunat				

1. Most of the verbs for 'smoke' (tobacco) are derived from the usual nouns for 'smoke' (1.83), as NG καπνίζω, It. fumāre (> NG φουμάρω), Fr., Sp. fumer, NE smoke, NHG rauchen, Du. rooken, etc.

2. Some are of similar ultimate origin, but loanwords rather than derivs. of the native nouns, as W. smocio fr. NE smoke, Lett. smēk'ēt, fr. LG smoken (Mühl.-Endz. 3.960), Lith. rūkyti (cf. NSB s.v. kuryti) fr. some LG form like Du. rooken.

3. Derivs. of or phrases with 'tobacco'. Derivs. Br. butunat, SCr. duhaniti. Phrases with 'drink', as NG πίνω καπνό, Rum. bea tutun, SCr. dial. piti duvan (Rječnik, Akad. 9.900), Ir. ōlaim tobac (or caithim tobac 'use tobacco'), NHG obs. or dial. taback trinken, tabac sauffen (Weigand-H. 2.538).

4. SCr. pušiti : puhati 'blow' (10.38).

5. Boh. kouřiti, Pol. kurzyć, Russ. kurit', all used also with reference to literal smoke or dust : Lith. kurti 'heat', etc. Berneker 651 f. Brückner 284.

CHAPTER 9

MISCELLANEOUS PHYSICAL ACTS AND THOSE PERTAINING TO CERTAIN SPECIAL ARTS AND CRAFTS,[1] WITH SOME IMPLEMENTS, MATERIALS, AND PRODUCTS; OTHER MISCELLANEOUS NOTIONS

9.11	Do, Make	9.44	Build
9.12	Work (sb.)	9.45	Hew
9.13	Work (vb.)	9.46	Bore
9.14	Bend (vb. trans.)	9.47	Auger
9.15	Fold (vb. trans.)	9.48	Saw (sb.)
9.16	Bind (vb. trans.)	9.49	Hammer
9.17	Bond	9.50	Nail
9.18	Chain	9.51	Beam
9.19	Rope, Cord	9.52	Board
9.192	Knot (sb.)	9.53	Mason
9.21	Strike (Hit, Beat)	9.54	Brick
9.22	Cut (vb.)	9.55	Mortar
9.23	Knife	9.60	Smith
9.24	Scissors, Shears	9.61	Forge (vb.)
9.25	Ax	9.62	Anvil
9.26	Break (vb. trans.)	9.63	Cast (Metals)
9.27	Split (vb. trans.)	9.64	Gold
9.28	Tear (vb. trans.)	9.65	Silver
9.29	Flay, Skin	9.66	Copper, Bronze
9.31	Rub	9.67	Iron
9.32	Stretch	9.68	Lead
9.33	Draw, Pull	9.69	Tin; Tin-Plate
9.34	Spread out, Strew	9.71	Potter
9.342	Press (vb.)	9.72	Mold (Clay, etc.)
9.35	Pour	9.73	Clay
9.36	Wash	9.74	Glass
9.37	Sweep	9.75	Plait (vb.)
9.38	Broom	9.76	Basket
9.41	Craft, Trade	9.81	Carve
9.412	Art	9.82	Sculptor
9.42	Artisan, Craftsman	9.83	Statue
9.422	Tool	9.84	Chisel
9.423	Use (vb.)	9.85	Paint (vb., as Artist)
9.43	Carpenter		

[1] Namely (in 9.41–9.89), carpentry, masonry, metal-work, pottery, sculpture, and painting. Words pertaining to the making of cloth and clothing, as 'weave', 'spin', 'sew', etc., are discussed in the chapter on clothing (6); those for 'cook', 'bake', etc., in the chapter on food and drink (5). Numerous words for manual actions of wide application, important in various crafts, as 'bend', 'fold', 'cut', etc., are discussed here in 9.14 ff.

9.86	Painter (as Artist)	9.942	Duty
9.87	Painting, Picture	9.943	Fitting, Suitable
9.88	Paint (sb.)	9.95	Can, May
9.89	Paint (vb. 'Paint a House')	9.96	Easy
9.90	Thing	9.97	Difficult
9.91	Be	9.98	Try[1] (Make Trial of, Test)
9.92	Become	9.99	Try[2] (Attempt, Endeavor)
9.93	Need, Necessity	9.992	Way, Manner
9.94	Ought, Must	9.993	Happen

9.11 DO, MAKE

Grk.	πράσσω, ποιέω	Goth.	taujan, waurkjan	Lith.	(pra)daryti, veikti
NG	κάνω, φτιάνω	ON	gǫr(v)a	Lett.	darīt
Lat.	facere, agere	Dan.	gøre	ChSl.	tvoriti (dělati)
It.	fare	Sw.	göra	SCr.	činiti, raditi, praviti
Fr.	faire	OE	dōn, (ge)wyrcan,	Boh.	činiti, robiti, dělati
Sp.	hacer		macian	Pol.	czynić, robić, działać
Rum.	face	ME	do(ne), make, wirche	Russ.	delat', tvorit'
Ir.	dogniu	NE	do, make	Skt.	kṛ-
NIr.	do(gh)nim	Du.	doen, maken	Av.	kərə-, varəz-
W.	gwneuthur, gwneud	OHG	tuon, wirken, mahhōn		
Br.	ober (1 sg. gran)	MHG	tuon, machen		
		NHG	tun, machen		

Words for 'do' and 'make' are treated together because these most generic notions of action are so commonly expressed by the same word; and where there are pairs of words, roughly distinguished by the feeling for the action itself or the implication of result respectively, the idiomatic differentiation is never quite the same for different languages and periods, not even in the case of such closely allied pairs as NE do, make—NHG tun, machen; (cf. NHG Was macht er? = NE What is he doing?)

Words for 'do, make' rest on generalization from a great variety of notions, as 'place, put', 'set straight', 'make ready', 'arrange', 'fit', 'get through', 'cause to be born', and 'work'.

For a wider survey, including many of the less common alternative expressions not mentioned here, cf. Yoshioka, Verbs of Doing and Making in the Indo-European Languages (Chicago diss.).

1. From IE *dhē- 'place, put', in Skt. dhā-, Grk. τίθημι, Lith. dēti, ChSl. děti, etc. In these the prevailing meaning is still 'place, put', but the sense of 'make' is occasional in Indo-Iranian, rather frequent in Greek, and develops in Slavic. 'Do, make', prevails from the earliest times in Italic, and also in the WGmc. group, though here with considerable survival of 'put'. Walde-P. 1.826 ff. Ernout-M. 325. Walde-H. 1.440 ff. Berneker 194.

Lat. facere (> Romance words), Osc. fakiiad, Umbr. façia 'faciat'; OE dōn, ME done, don, do, NE do, Du. doen, OHG, MHG tuon, NHG tun; ChSl. (fr. děti) dělo 'work', whence vb. dělati 'work', later 'do, make' (below, 7).

2. Grk. ἔρδω and ῥέζω, in Hom. the commonest verbs for 'do', fr. the same root as ἔργον, ϝέργον 'work', OE weorc 'work', etc. (9.12), Av. varəz- 'work, do'.

Grk. δράω, in Hom. 'do service' (cf. δρηστήρ 'laborer'), elsewhere 'do' (hence δρᾶμα 'act'), but mostly poet.: Lith. daryti, Lett. darīt 'do'. Walde P. 1.803.

Grk. πράσσω, Att. πράττω, Ion. πρήσσω,

in Hom. 'pass through' (the sea), 'accomplish', in Attic 'act, do' (with emphasis on the action): πέρα, πέραν 'beyond, across', etc. Walde-P. 2.32.

Grk. ποιέω, ποιϝέω, in Hom. esp. 'construct, build' but also 'make', eventually the commonest word for 'make, do', deriv. of a *ποι-ϝο-: Skt. ci- 'arrange, gather construct, build', ChSl. činŭ 'arrangement', činiti 'arrange', with similar development to 'do, make' in the modern Slavic languages, SCr., Boh. činiti, Pol. czynić, etc. Walde-P. 1.509 ff. Berneker 156 f.

NG κάνω fr. Grk. κάμνω 'work, toil' (9.13), in Hom. already aor. κάμε, κάμον 'wrought, built', and in Byz. period frequent for 'make, do'.

NG φτιάνω, φκιάνω 'make, fix' (ἐφτιάσ-τηκα serves as aor. pass. of κάνω), fr. a late εὐθειάζω 'set right', deriv. of εὐθύς 'straight'. Hatzidakis, Einleitung 407.

3. Lat. agere 'drive' (10.65), hence also 'pursue a course of action, act, do', with more emphasis on the action than facere (above, 1), which in VLat. absorbed these uses of agere. Ernout-M. 24 ff.

4. Ir. do-gniu (less freq. gniu), NIr. do(gh)nīm : Grk. γίγνομαι 'be born', Lat. gignere 'beget, bear', with development through 'give birth to, create'. Walde-P. 1.576. Pedersen 2.544.

W. gwneuthur, gwneud, fr. the same root as the preceding, but with init. gw for g under the influence of supplementary forms fr. *upo-aĝ-. Pedersen 2.545.

Br. ober, fr. sb. ober = W. ober 'work, deed', fr. Lat. opera. But Br. infin. only, finite forms fr. gra-, as 1sg. gran, MBr. graf = Corn. guraf, connected with preceding group. Pedersen 2.545 f.

5. Goth. taujan (renders πράσσω and ποιέω), pret. tawida, sb. taui 'deed' : ON (runic) tawido 'made', OE tawian 'pre-

pare' (NE taw), getawa 'instruments', MHG zouwen 'prepare', etc., outside connections dub. Walde-P. 1.779. Feist 474 f.

Goth. waurkjan (renders ἐργάζομαι 'work' and ποιέω), OE (ge)wyrcan 'work' and 'make, do' (pret. worhte > NE wrought), OHG wirken, wurchen 'work, make, do' : OE weorc 'work', Grk. ἔργον, ῥέζω, etc. (above, 2).

ON gǫr(v)a, Dan. gøre, Sw. göra, orig. 'make ready' : OHG garawen 'prepare', OE gierwan 'prepare, cook', ON gǫrr, OHG garo, OE gearu 'prepared, ready', this last group, perh. as orig. 'prepared' of food, fr. 'hot' : Grk. θερμός 'hot', etc. Walde-P. 1.688. Falk-Torp 322 f. Hellquist 323.

OE macian (less common than gewyrcan), ME, NE make, Du. maken, OHG mahhōn, MHG, NHG machen (OS makōn 'build'), prob. fr. an IE *maĝ- in Grk. μάσσω, aor. ἐμάγην 'knead', etc. (5.54), with development through 'mold, build with clay'. Walde-P. 2.226. Falk-Torp 689. Weigand-H. 2.102.

OE dōn, OHG tuon, etc., above, 1.

6. Lith. (pa-)daryti, Lett. darīt : Grk. δράω, above, 2.

Lith. veikti : Lett. veikt 'struggle, accomplish', Lith. viekas 'strength, power', Lat. vincere 'conquer', Goth. weihan 'fight', etc. Walde-P. 1.232 f. Mühl.-Endz. 4.524 f.

7. ChSl. (sŭ-)tvoriti (in Gospels reg. for ποιέω 'do' or 'make'), Russ. tvorit' 'make' (SCr. tvoriti 'create, fashion', etc.) : Lith. tverti 'comprise' and 'create', tvora 'fence, hedge', turēti 'have', Lett. tvert 'seize, comprise, hold', outside connections dub. Walde-P. 1.750 f.

ChSl. (sŭ-)dělati, deriv. of dělo 'work' (cf. above, 1), in Gospels for ἐργάζομαι, later freq. for ποιέω (cf. Jagić, Entstehungsgesch. 400, 405), and so for 'do,

make' Boh. dělati (also 'work'), Pol. dziełać, Russ. delat'. Berneker 194.

SCr., Boh. činiti, Pol. czynić : Grk. ποιέω (above, 2).

SCr. raditi 'work' (9.13), also 'do, make'.

Boh. robiti, Pol. robić, derivs. of rob, ChSl. rabŭ 'servant' : Goth. arbaips 'toil, labor', etc. Walde-P. 1.184.

Bulg. pravja (the common verb for 'do, make'), SCr. praviti (Boh. spraviti 'mend, repair', Russ. praviti 'govern',

etc.) : ChSl. praviti 'direct', deriv. of pravŭ 'straight, right' (12.73).

8. Skt. kṛ- (kṛṇoti, karoti, kṛta-, etc.), Av. kərə- (kərənaoiti, karta-, etc.), OPers. kar- (akunavam, karta-, etc.), general Indo-Iranian (still the common word in modern Indic and Iranian languages), perh. : W. peri 'cause', Ir. cruth 'form', Lith. kurti 'build'. Walde-P. 1.517 f. Uhlenbeck 63.

Av. varəz- : Grk. ἔρδω, ἔργον, etc., above, 2.

9.12 WORK, LABOR, TOIL (sb. abstr.); WORK (sb. concr.)

Grk.	ἐργασία, πόνος; ἔργον
NG	δουλειά, ἐργασία; ἔργο
Lat.	(opus) opera, labor; opus
It.	lavoro; opera
Fr.	travail; œuvre, ouvrage
Sp.	trabajo; obra
Rum.	lucru, muncă; operă
Ir.	opair, lubair; opair
NIr.	obair, saothar; obair
W.	gwaith, llafur; gwaith
Br.	labour; ober
Goth.	arbaips; waurstw
ON	verk, vinna, erfiði; verk
Dan.	arbejde; værk
Sw.	arbete; verk
OE	weorc, swinc; weorc
ME	worke, swinke, labour; worke
NE	work, labor, toil; work
Du.	werk, arbeid
OHG	wer(a)h, arabeit; wer(a)h
MHG	werc, arbeit; werc
NHG	arbeit; werk
Lith.	darbas
Lett.	darbs
ChSl.	trudŭ; dělo
SCr.	rad; djelo
Boh.	práce; dílo
Pol.	robota, praca; dzieło
Russ.	rabota; delo
Skt.	karman-, çrama-; kṛta-
Av.	varəzya-; kərəta-

9.13 WORK, LABOR, TOIL (vb., intr.)

	ἐργάζομαι, κάμνω
	δουλεύω
	operāri
	lavorare
	oðvailler
	trabajar
	lucra, munci
	opraim, phrase with sb.
	oibrighim
	gweithio, llafurio
	labourat
	wyrcan, swincan
	worcke, swinke, laboure
	work, labor, toil
	werken, arbeiden
	wirken, arabeiten
	wirken, arbeiten
	arbeiten
	dirbti
	strādāt
	(sŭ)dělati
	raditi
	pracovati, dělati
	pracować, robić
	rabotat'
	çam-
	varəz-

9.12, 9.13. Words for 'work, labor' (sb.) as the activity (abstr.) may also be used for 'work' as the result, product of labor (concr.), or the two notions may be more or less differentiated. The attempt to indicate this in the table, by the use of the semicolon, is only a convenient approximation to the facts, applying to a usual but seldom rigid differentiation.

The aspect of 'hard work, toil' is present in the actual usage of several of the words and in the history of still more. In fact, while two groups reflect notions of vigorous activity or power (those represented by Grk. *ἔργον*, NE *work*, etc., and by Lat. *opus*, etc.), the majority are from notions of 'struggle, distress, slavery' or the like.

The verbs for 'work', though listed separately (9.13), are included in the discussion here, since nearly all of them are connected with the nouns.

Several words for 'work' became specialized, especially to 'till, plow', as ON *yrkja*, Fr. *labourer*, Sp. *labrar*.

1. From IE *werĝ- in Grk. *ἔρδω*, *ῥέζω* 'do', Av. *varəz-* 'work, do', etc. (9.11). Walde-P. 1.290 ff. Feist 555, 556.

Grk. *ἔργον*, *ϝέργον*, 'deed' or 'work' as product, *ἐργασία* 'work' as 'labor' (with *ἐργάτης* 'workman', *ἐργάζομαι* 'work'); Goth. *waurstw* (*ἔργον*), ON *verk*, OE *weorc*, etc., general Gmc., with vbs. OE *wyrcan*, OHG *wirken*, etc. (but NHG *wirken* now only trans.; so Goth. *waurkjan*).

2. Grk. *πόνος* 'toil', with vb. *πονέομαι* (Hom. in past tenses also 'worked, wrought'), later *πονέω* : *πένομαι* 'toil, be poor', *πένης* 'poor', outside connections? Walde-P. 2.661. Boisacq 767.

Grk. *κόπος* 'toil', with vb. *κοπιάω* (esp. common in LXX and NT) : *κόπτω* 'strike, beat' (9.21).

NG *δουλειά* (the pop. sb. for 'work') fr. Grk. *δουλεία* 'slavery', deriv. of *δοῦλος* 'slave'. Similarly, Grk. *δουλεύω* 'be a slave', but NG 'work'.

Grk. *κάμνω* 'work, toil, be weary' : Skt. *çam-* 'work, toil'. Walde-P. 1.387.

3. Lat. *opus* (sometimes abstr., mostly concr.), *opera* (mostly abstr., but concr. in derivs. It., Rum. *opera*, Fr. *œuvre*, Sp. *obra*), whence vb. *operārī*, late *operāre* (> It. *operare*, Sp. *obrar*, and Fr. *ouvrer*, whence *ouvrage* 'work' abstr. and concr.) : *ops*, *opis* 'power, wealth', Skt. *apas-*, *āpas-* 'work, act', esp. 'sacred act', Av. *hv-apah-* 'good deed', ON *afl*, OE *afol* 'power', OE *æfnan* 'perform', OHG *uoba* 'festival', etc. Walde-P. 1.175 f. Ernout-M. 708 f.

Lat. *labor*, prob. : *labāre* 'slip' and first used as 'tottering under a burden', hence 'toil', also 'fatigue, distress, suffering'. Walde-P. 2.432. Ernout-M. 513. Walde-H. 1.739 f. Hence, with or without continued emphasis on the aspect of 'toil, distress', It. *lavoro*, OFr. *labor*, *labour* (> ME, NE *labo(u)r*, Br. *labour*), Fr. *labeur*, Ir. *lubair*, W. *llafur*. From Lat. *labor* also vb. *laborāre* 'work', whence It. *lavorare*, OFr. *labourer* (> ME *laboure*, NE *labor*), but mostly with specialization as in Fr. *labourer* 'till, plow', Sp. *labrar* 'till, embroider, etc.'. REW 4810.

Fr. *travail*, Sp. *trabajo*, back-formations to vbs. *travailler*, *trabajar*, fr. VLat. **tripāliāre*, deriv. of **tripālium* (*trepalium* 6th. cent. A.D.) 'an instrument of torture' : Lat. *tripālis* 'of three stakes' (*pālus* 'stake'). Development in vb. fr. 'torture' to 'distress, trouble, weary', refl. 'distress, trouble, weary oneself, toil' (cf., through OFr., ME *travail* with this sense and also with new semantic development 'travel'), finally in Fr. and Sp. simply 'work'. REW 8911. Gamillscheg 860. NED s.v. *travail*, *travel*.

Rum. *lucru* 'work' (abstr.; and concr. > 'thing'), fr. Lat. *lucrum* 'gain, profit', as also (and prob. first in this sense), vb. *lucra* 'work' fr. Lat. *lucrārī* 'gain, acquire'. REW 5145, 5146. Cf. the relation of 'gain' and 'work' in the group OE *winnan*, etc. (below, 5).

Rum. *muncă* 'toil', vb. *munci* 'toil', fr. Slavic, ChSl. *mąka* 'torment', vb. *mąčiti*. Tiktin 1021. Densusianu 270.

4. Ir. *sāethar*, NIr. *saothar* (esp. 'toil') : Ir. *sāeth* 'trouble, suffering',

Goth. *sair*, OE *sār* 'pain', etc. Walde-P. 2.445. Pedersen 2.45.

Ir. *lubair*, fr. Lat. *labor* (above, 3).

Ir. *opair*, NIr. *obair*; hence vbs. Ir. *opraim* (rare; pret. *robair* RC 25.388; verbal notion mostly expressed by phrase with sb.), NIr. *oibrighim*, fr. Lat. *opera* (above, 2). Vendryes, De hib. voc. 161 f.

W. *gwaith* (abstr. and concr.; vb. *gweithio*) : Ir. *fecht* 'expedition, journey', Lat. *vehere* 'carry', etc. Walde-P. 1.250. Pedersen 1.123 f. Development through 'undertaking', or perh. a case of semantic borrowing, influence of ME *travail* in its two senses 'toil' and 'travel' (above, 3).

Br. *labour* fr. OFr. *labour*; Br. *ober* fr. Lat. *opera*.

5. Goth. *waurstw*, OE *weorc*, etc., above, 1.

Goth. *arbaiþs* (renders *κόπος* 'toil'), ON *erfiði* (cf. adj. *erfiðr*, OE *earfeþe* 'hard, difficult'; OE *earfoþ* 'hardship'), OHG *ar(a)beit*, MHG, NHG *arbeit*, Du. *arbeid* (MLG > Dan. *arbejde*, Sw. *arbete*), with vbs. Goth. *arbaidjan*, etc., all prob. : Grk. *ὀρφανός* 'orphan', Lat. *orbus* 'bereft', ChSl. *rabŭ* 'slave', etc., with development fr. 'condition of an orphan' to one of 'slavery, drudgery, toil'. Walde-P. 1.183 f. Falk-Torp 31. Feist 55. Kluge-G. 22.

ON *vinna* (with vb. *vinna*, also 'gain') :Goth. *winnō* 'suffering', *winnan* 'suffer', OE *winnan* 'labor, toil', later 'win, gain', OHG *winnan* 'strive, fight', Skt. *van-* 'desire, gain', etc. Walde-P. 1.260. Falk-Torp 1382 f. NED s.v. *win*, vb.

OE *swinc*, ME *swinke*, with vb. *swincan*, *swinken* (NE *swink*, arch. or dial.), parallel form to OE *swingan* 'flog, beat, strike, fling' and 'fling oneself, rush', OHG *swingan* 'fling, rush', etc. Walde-P. 2.526. NED s.v. *swink* vb.

NE *toil* (and vb. *toil*), fr. ME *toyle* 'dispute, fight, struggle', fr. OFr. *toil*, *touil* 'dispute, fight', back-formation to *toiler*, *toillier* 'dispute, stir up' (Fr. *touiller* 'stir, mix'), fr. Lat. *tudiculāre* 'stir' or 'bruise', deriv. of *tudicula* 'machine for bruising olives', fr. the root of *tundere* 'strike, beat'. REW 8971. Gamillscheg 852. NED s.v.

6. Lith. *darbas*, Lett. *darbs*, with vb. Lith. *dirbti* : OE *deorf* 'toil, trouble', vb. *deorfan*, further connections dub. Walde-P. 1.863. Mühl.-Endz. 1.439.

Lett. vb. *strādāt*, fr. Russ. *stradat'* 'suffer, endure'.

7. ChSl. *trudŭ* (renders *κόπος* 'toil'), with vb. *truditi* 'toil, struggle' (so Boh., Russ., Pol. *trud* 'toil, trouble, etc.', with vbs. for 'toil') : Lat. *trūdere* 'thrust, push', Goth. *us-þriutan* 'trouble', OE *þrēotan* 'trouble, weary', *þrēat* 'throng, pressure, distress', *þrēatian* 'press, urge, threaten' (cf. NE *threat*, *threaten*), etc. Walde-P. 1.755. Brückner 577.

ChSl. *dělo* (renders *ἔργον*), etc., general Slavic for concrete 'work' : *děti* 'put', etc. (9.11, 12.13). Hence vb. ChSl. (*sŭ-*)*dělati* in Gospels reg. for *ἐργάζομαι*, later for *ποιέω*, Boh. *dělati* 'do, make' and 'work' (Pol., Russ. 'do', 9.11).

SCr. *rad*, back-formation to vb. *raditi* 'work' : ChSl. *raditi* 'care for', Goth. *garēdan* 'care for', OHG *rātan* 'advise', Skt. *rādh-* 'prepare, perform, succeed', etc. Walde-P. 1.74. Trautmann 235. SCr. development fr. Slavic 'care for' through 'attend to, be busy with' to 'work'.

Boh. *práce*, Pol. *praca* (with vbs. *pracovati*, *pracować*), prob. : SCr., Slov. *pratiti* 'accompany', Bulg. *pratja* 'send', with development through 'errand' to 'business, occupation', then 'work' in general. Cf. SCr. *posao* (gen. *posla*) 'one's occupation, work' : *poslati* 'send'. Brückner 434.

Pol. *robota*, Russ. *rabota* (Boh. *robota* 'toil, drudgery'; with vbs. Boh. *robotiti*, Pol. *robić*, Russ. *rabotat'*) : ChSl. *rabota* 'slavery' (cf. NG *δουλειά*, above, 2), deriv. of *rabŭ* 'slave', this : Goth. *arbaiþs*, etc., above, 5.

8. Skt. *karman-* 'act, activity' and 'work' (cf. *karma-kāra-* 'workman') : *kṛ-* 'do' (9.11).

Skt. *çrama-* 'fatigue, toil' (with vb. *çram-* 'be weary, toil'), etym.? Walde-P. 2.426, 498.

Skt. *çam-* : Grk. *κάμνω*, above, 2.

Av. *vərəzya-* : *varəz-* 'do, work', Grk. *ἔργον*, etc. (above, 1).

For 'work' concr. mostly Skt. *kṛta-*, Av. *kərəta-*, OPers. *karta-* : Skt. *kṛ-* 'do, make' (9.11).

9.14 BEND (vb. trans.)

Grk.	*κάμπτω* (*λυγίζω*)	Goth.	*(ga)biugan*	Lith.	*lenkti*
NG	*λυγίζω* (*κάμπτω*)	ON	*sveigja, benda*	Lett.	*liekt, luocīt*
Lat.	*flectere, curvāre*	Dan.	*bøje*	ChSl.	*sŭlęšti*
It.	*piegare, incurvare*	Sw.	*böja, kröka*	SCr.	*pregnuti, pregibati*
Fr.	*courber, fléchir, plier*	OE	*bȳgan*	Boh.	*ohnouti, ohybati*
Sp.	*encorvar*	ME	*bowe, bende*	Pol.	*giąć, nagiąć*
Rum.	*încovoia, pleca*	NE	*bend*	Russ.	*gnut', sgibat'*
Ir.	*crommaim, fillim*	Du.	*buigen*	Skt.	*añc-, nam-, bhuj-*
NIr.	*camaim, lūbaim*	OHG	*biogan, bougen*	Av.	*nam-*
W.	*plygu*	MHG	*biegen, bögen, lenken*		
Br.	*kromma, plega*	NHG	*biegen, beugen*		

Words for 'bend' are derived, either directly or through words for 'bent, crooked' (12.74), from a considerable variety of roots which had already in the parent speech the notion of 'bend' (or in part 'turn, wind', etc.), though these were doubtless originally differentiated according to the object involved.

The association between 'bend' (a stick, etc.) and 'fold' (cloth, etc.) is such that there may be extension or shift in either direction. Thus Lat. *plicāre* 'fold' has furnished common words for 'bend' (Fr. *plier*, etc.), and conversely several words for 'fold' are cpds. of those for 'bend'.

Semantically related groups, not in the list, are those for such notions as 'bend the head or body, bow' (for this specialization of 'bend', cf. also NE *bow*), 'stoop, incline, lean', esp. in two important groups of cognates, namely:

1) IE *kneigʷh-, in Goth. *hneiwan* 'decline, wane', *anahneiwan* 'stoop', OE *hnīgan* 'bend (intr.), bow', OHG *hnīgan*, NHG *neigen* 'incline, bow', Lat. *cōnīvēre* 'close the eyes', etc. Walde-P. 1.476. Ernout-M. 213. Walde-H. 1.261.

2) IE *k̑lei-, in Grk. *κλίνω* 'cause to slope, incline, recline, decline, lean', Lat. *inclīnāre* 'cause to bend, incline', *dēclīnāre* 'bend down, turn aside', etc., OE *hlinian* 'recline', *hlǣnan* 'cause to incline, NE *lean*, etc. (general Gmc.), Skt. *çri-* 'lean', etc. Walde-P. 1.490 f. Ernout-M. 197 f. Walde-H. 1.234 f.

1. Grk. *κάμπτω*, with sb. *καμπή* 'bending, turning' : Lith. *kumpas* 'bent, crooked', etc., fr. IE *kamp-, prob. an extension of *kam- in Skt. *kmarati* (Dhātup.) 'is crooked', Av. *kamarā-* 'girdle, Grk. *καμάρα* 'vault', etc. Walde-P. 1.350.

Grk. *λυγίζω* 'bend, twist' like a withe (cf. *λύγος* 'withe'), in NG the usual pop. word for 'bend' (trans. and intr.) : Lith. *lugnas* 'pliable', ON *lykna* 'bend the knee', ON *lokkr*, OE *locc* 'lock of hair, curl'. Walde-P. 2.413 f.

2. Lat. *flectere* (hence **flecticāre* > OFr. *flechier*, Fr. *fléchir*), etym.? Ernout-M. 367 f. Walde-H. 1.514 f. REW 3366. Gamillscheg 424.

Lat. *curvāre* (> It. *curvare*, Fr. *courber*, Sp. *encorvar*), deriv. of *curvus* 'bent, curved' : Grk. *κορωνός*, *κυρτός*, Lith. *kreivas*, Russ. *krivoj*, etc. 'bent, curved, crooked', with widespread root connections. Walde-P. 2.568 ff. Ernout-M. 248. Walde-H. 1.317 f.

It. *piegare*, Fr. *plier* (both also 'fold'), Rum. *pleca*, fr. Lat. *plicāre* 'fold' (9.15).

Rum. *încovoia*, fr. Slavic, cf. ChSl. *kovati* 'hammer, forge' (9.61), Russ. *pod-kova*, SCr. *pot-kova* 'horseshoe', Rum. development through 'bend in the form of a horseshoe'. Tiktin 790.

3. Ir. *crommaim*, Br. *kromma* derivs. of Ir. *cromm*, Br. *kromm* 'crooked, bent' (12.74).

Ir. *fillim*, also and orig. 'fold' (9.15).

NIr. *camaim* deriv. of *camm* 'crooked, bent' (12.74).

Ir., NIr. *lūbaim* deriv. of Ir. *lūb* 'a loop, bend', formerly taken as loanword fr. NE *loop*, but by Zupitza, KZ 36.244, as cognate with ON *laupr*, OE *lēap* 'basket'.

W. *plygu*, Br. *plega*, also and orig. 'fold' (9.15).

4. Goth. *(ga)biugan* (OE *būgan* 'bow' intr.), ME *bowe* (trans. and intr. due to confusion with forms of OE *bȳgan*, cf. NED s.v. *bow*, vb.), Du. *buigen*, OHG *biogan*, MHG, NHG *biegen* fr. IE *bheugh-, beside *bheug- in Skt. *bhuj-* 'bend', *bhuja-* 'arm', Ir. *fid-bocc* 'wooden bow', here also prob. Grk. *φεύγω*, Lat. *fugere* 'flee'. Walde-P. 2.145 f. Falk-Torp 127. Walde-H. 1.556.

Here also, with caus. formation, ON *beygja* (rare), Dan. *bøje*, Sw. *böja*, OE *bȳgan* (*bīgan*, *bēgan*), OHG *bougen*, MHG *böugen*, NHG *beugen* (with idiomatic, though not rigid, differentiation from *biegen*; cf. Paul, Deutsches Wtb. s.v. *biegen*).

ON *sveigja* : *sveigr* 'flexible', *svigna* 'give way', fr. an extension of IE *swei- in words with the notion of 'bend, turn, swing'. Walde-P. 2.518 ff. Falk-Torp 1212.

ON *benda* 'bend a bow, bend' (OE *bendan* 'bind, bend a bow'), ME *bende*, NE *bend*, fr. Gmc. **bandjan*, deriv. of **bandja-* (OE *bend*, ON *band* 'band'), fr. the root of Goth., OE *bindan* 'bind', etc. (9.16). The semantic development is then 'bind', 'restrain with a bond', 'restrain a bent bow', 'bend a bow', 'make bow-shaped', 'bend'. NED s.v. *bend*, vb.

Sw. *kröka* deriv. of *krok* 'a hook, curve, bend' : Dan. *krog*, ON *krōkr* 'hook' (> ME, NE *crook*), OHG *krāko* 'hooked tool', etc. Walde-P. 1.593 f. Falk-Torp 581.

MHG *lenken* : ON *hlekkr* 'ring, link', OE *hlencan* pl. 'chain-armor', etc. Walde-P. 1.498. Falk-Torp 676.

5. Lith. *(pa)lenkti*, Lett. *liekt*, frequent. *luocīt*, ChSl. *sŭ-lęšti*, *-lęką* (prob. *lęceti* 'set snares', etc.) : Lith. *linkti* 'bend' intr., Lett. *likt* id., *liks* 'curved', ChSl. *ląkŭ* 'a bow', ON *lengja*, OE *-lōh* 'strap', fr. IE *lenk-. Walde-P. 2.435. Berneker 707 f.

6. (ChSl. *sŭ-gŭnąti*, *prě-gybati* 'fold'), SCr. *pregnuti*, *pregibati*, Boh. *ohnouti*, *ohybati*, Pol. *giąć*, *nagiąć*, Russ. *gnut'*, *sgibat'*, fr. a Slavic root *gŭb-, *gyb- : Lett. *gubt* 'bend' (intr.), perh. OE *gēap* 'crooked', etc. (or *gub-* by transposition fr. *bhug-* in Skt. *bhuj-*?). Walde-P. 1.567 f. Berneker 366, 373. Brückner 140.

7. Skt. *añc-* (cf. *aṅka-* 'bend, hook') : Grk. *ἀγκών* 'elbow', *ἀγκύλος* 'curved', Lat. *uncus* 'hook', OE *angel* 'hook', etc. (12.75). Walde-P. 1.60 f. Walde-H. 1.46.

Skt. *namati* mostly intr., Av. *nəmaiti* intr., caus. Skt. *nāmayati*, Av. *nāmayeiti* trans., Skt. *namas-*, Av. *nəmah-* 'bending, homage', Toch. *näm-* 'incline, bow' (SSS 446), further connections dub. Walde-P. 2.331 f.

Skt. *bhuj-* : Goth. *biugan*, etc. (above, 4).

9.15 FOLD (vb. trans.)

Grk.	*πτύσσω*	Goth.	*falþan*	Lith.	*stulpuoti*
NG	*διπλώνω*	ON	*falda*	Lett.	*saluocīt*
Lat.	*plicāre*	Dan.	*folde*	ChSl.	*sŭgŭnąti, sŭgybati*
It.	*piegare*	Sw.	*vika*	SCr.	*saviti*
Fr.	*plier*	OE	*fealdan*	Boh.	*skladati, zahýbati*
Sp.	*plegar, doblar*	ME	*folde*	Pol.	*fałdować*
Rum.	*îndoi*	NE	*fold*	Russ.	*skladyvat'*
Ir.	*fillim*	Du.	*vouwen*	Skt.	. . . .
NIr.	*fillim*	OHG	*faldan, faltan*	Av.	. . . .
W.	*plygu*	MHG	*valten*		
Br.	*plega*	NHG	*falten*		

For relations between 'fold' and 'bend', see 9.14. Among other semantic sources are 'double, turn, wind, put together'.

1. Grk. *πτύσσω*, with *πτυχή* 'a fold', perh. fr. **πι-υχ-*, a cpd., like Skt. *pyukṣna-* 'bow-case', with prefix **pi* beside **epi* (Skt. *api*, Grk. *ἐπί*), second part : Skt. *ūh-* 'move, roam'. Walde-P. 1.122, 189. Boisacq 824.

NG *διπλώνω* fr. class. Grk. *διπλόω* 'double', deriv. of *διπλόος*, *διπλοῦς* 'twofold'. Semantic development as in some uses of NE *double* (*over, up*) for 'fold' (NED s.v. *double*, vb. 8).

2. Lat. *plicāre* (> It. *piegare*, Fr. *plier* 'fold' or 'bend', Sp. *plegar* 'fold', Rum. *pleca* 'bend'; also W. *plygu*, Br. *plega* 'fold' or 'bend'. REW 6601. Loth, Mots. lat. 196), for **plecāre* (with *i* fr. cpds.) : Grk. *πλέκω*, Lat. *plectere*, OE *fleohtan*, etc. 'plait' (9.75), these prob. also (as parallel extensions of **pel-*) : Goth. *falþan*, etc. 'fold' (below, 4). Walde-P. 2.97. Ernout-M. 778 f.

Sp. *doblar*, deriv. of *doble* 'a fold' = *doble* 'double' fr. Lat. *duplus*.

Rum. *îndoi* 'fold, bend, doubt', fr. prefix *în-* and *doi* 'two'. Tiktin 801.

3. Ir. *fillim* (also 'bend', in gram. 'decline'), NIr. *fillim* : Skt. *val-* 'turn' intr., Grk. *ἑλίσσω*, Lat. *volvere* 'wind', etc., fr. IE **wel-*. Walde-P. 2.539. Pedersen 2.522.

W. *plygu*, Br. *plega*, fr. Lat. *plicāre*, above, 2.

4. Goth. *falþan*, OE *fealdan*, etc., general Gmc. (Du. *vouwen* fr. MDu. *vouden*; cf. also Goth. *ain-falþs*, OE *ān-feald*, etc. 'onefold, single'), fr. a deriv. or extension of **pel-*, seen in Grk. *διπλόος*, Lat. *duplus* 'twofold', etc. Here prob. Skt. *puṭa-* 'fold, pocket'. Walde-P. 2.55 f. Falk-Torp 249.

Sw. *vika* : OE *wīcan* 'yield, give way', ON *víkja* 'move', Skt. *vij-* 'move quickly, recede', Grk. *εἴκω* 'yield, shrink', fr. IE **weig-* *weik-*, prob. an extension of **wei-* in Lat. *viēre* 'plait', Lith. *vyti* 'wind', etc. Walde-P. 1.223, 233 ff. Hellquist 1341.

5. Lith. *stulpuoti* 'set posts, furnish with pillars', also 'fold', deriv. of *stulpas* 'post, pillar' (fr. Russ. *stolp* id.), which developed secondary meanings 'beam of light' and 'fold', the latter from the column-like appearance of vertical folds (pleats).

Lett. *saluocīt*, cpd. of *luocīt* 'bend' (9.14).

6. ChSl. *sŭgŭnąti* (perf.), *sŭgybati* (imperf.), Boh. *zahýbati*, cpds. of root in words for 'bend' (9.14).

SCr. *saviti*, cpd. of *viti* 'wind'.

Boh. *skladati*, Russ. *skladyvat'*, cpds. of *s-* = ChSl. *sŭ-* 'with, together', and Boh. *klasti* 'lay', Russ. *klast'* 'put, place' (12.12).

Pol. *fałdować*, deriv. of *fałda* 'a fold', loanword fr. MHG *valde* (NHG *falte*) 'a fold'. Berneker 278.

7. Skt. verb for 'fold'? The root *puṭ-* (beside *puṭa-* 'fold, pocket', cf. above, 4) is not quotable in this sense. The adj. *dvi-guṇa-* 'twofold' occurs with *vāsas-* 'clothing' in sense of 'folded'.

9.16 BIND (vb. trans.)

Grk.	*δέω*	Goth.	*(ga)bindan*	Lith.	*rišti*
NG	*δένω*	ON	*binda*	Lett.	*siet, rist*
Lat.	*vincīre, ligāre, nectere*	Dan.	*binde*	ChSl.	*sŭvęzati, povrěsti*
It.	*legare*	Sw.	*binda*	SCr.	*(s)vezati*
Fr.	*lier*	OE	*bindan, tīgan*	Boh.	*vazati*
Sp.	*ligar, atar*	ME	*binde, tye*	Pol.	*wiązać*
Rum.	*lega*	NE	*bind, tie*	Russ.	*svjazat'*
Ir.	*con-rigim, nascim, cenglaim*	Du.	*binden*	Skt.	*bandh-, sā-, nah-, dā-*
NIr.	*ceanglaim (naiscim)*	OHG	*bintan*	Av.	*band-, hā(y)-, dərəz-*
W.	*rhwymo*	MHG	*binden*		
Br.	*eren, staga*	NHG	*binden*		

A great variety of roots show the notion 'bind' either in verbs or in nouns for 'bond, chain, rope, knot', etc. But only one of these is common to the most usual verbs for 'bind' in more than one of the main branches, namely, to those of Gmc. and Indo-Iranian.

1. IE **bhendh-*. Walde-P. 2.152. Feist 93.

Goth., OE *bindan*, etc., with Goth. *bandi*, etc. 'bond', both vb. and sb. general Gmc.; Skt. *bandh-*, Av. *band-* with sbs. Skt. *bandha-*, *bandhana-*, Av. *banda-*; the same root in Grk. *πεῖσμα* (**πενθσμα*) 'ship's cable', Lat. *offendix*, *offendimentum* 'knot, band' (of the priest's cap, only a ritual term), Ir. *buinne* 'band', etc.

2. Grk. *δέω* (fut. *δήσω*), NG *δένω*, with *δεσμός* 'bond' : Skt. *dā-*, *di-* 'bind' (3sg. *dyati*, pple. *dita-*), *samdāna-*, *dāman-* 'bond, rope', fr. IE **dē(i)-*, **də-*. Walde-P. 1.771.

3. Lat. *vincīre*, with *vinculum* 'bond' (> It. *vincolo*, Sp. *vínculo*), prob. nasalized form of IE **weik-*, **weig-*, in Sw. *vika* 'fold', etc. (9.15), extension of **wei-* in Lat. *viēre* 'plait', Lith. *vyti* 'wind', etc. Walde-P. 1.233 ff.

Lat. *ligāre* (> It. *legare*, Fr. *lier*, Sp. *ligar*, Rum. *lega*) with derivs. *ligāmen* (> It. *legame*), *ligātūra* (> Rum. *legătură*), etc. : Alb. *lidh* 'bind', ON *līk*, Du. *lijk* 'leech-line', etc. Walde-P. 2.400. Ernout-M. 549 f. Walde-H. 1.800.

Lat. *nectere*, perh., reformed after *plectere*, fr. IE **ned-* or **nedh-* in Skt. *nah-*, Ir. *nascim* 'bind', Lat. *nōdus* 'knot', etc. (below, 4). Walde-P. 2.328. Ernout-M. 662 f.

Sp. *atar*, fr. Lat. *aptāre* 'fit, adapt, apply' (hence in Sp. 'tie to, fasten, bind'), deriv. of *aptus* 'fitted, adapted', pple. of the rare *apere* 'bind' (cf. *apīscī* 'seize, attain') : Skt. *āp-* 'reach, attain'. Walde-P. 1.46. Ernout-M. 60 f. Walde-H. 1.57.

4. Ir. *con-rigim*, W. *rhwymo*, Br. *eren* (**en-rig-*), with sbs. Ir. *cuimrech*, W. *rhwym*, Br. *ere* 'bond' : Lat. *corrigia*

'shoelace' (or loanword fr. Gall.?), root connections dub. Walde-P. 2.347. Pedersen 2.592 f. Ernout-M. 223. Walde-H. 1.278 f.

Ir. *nascim*, NIr. *naiscim* : Lat. *nōdus* 'knot', Goth. *nati*, ON, OE *net* 'net', ON *nesta* 'fasten', Skt. *nah-* 'bind', pple. *naddha-*, fr. IE **ned-* or **nedh-* (?). Walde-P. 2.328. Ernout-M. 662 f.

Ir. *cenglaim*, NIr. *ceanglaim*, deriv. of Ir. *cengal* 'bond' fr. Lat. *cingulum* 'girdle'. Vendryes, De hib. voc. 124.

Br. *staga*, fr. OFr. *estachier* beside *atachier* 'fasten', based on a Gmc. word like OE *staca* 'stake'. REW 8218. Ernault, Dict. étym. 384.

5. Goth. *bindan*, etc., above, 1.

OE *tīgan*, ME *tye(n)*, NE *tie*, deriv. of OE *tēah*, *tēag* 'bond' : ON *taug* 'rope', etc., fr. the same root as Goth. *tiuhan*, Lat. *dūcere* 'draw', etc. Walde-P. 1.780 f. NED s.v. *tie* sb. and vb.

6. Lith. *rišti*, Lett. *rist*, with Lith. *ryšys*, *raištis* 'bond', perh. : Grk. *ῥοικός* 'crooked', OE *wrēon* 'enshroud', *wrīgian* 'turn, wend', etc., fr. IE **wreik-* an extension of **wer-* 'turn, bend'. Walde-P. 1.278 f.

Lett. *siet*, Lith. *sieti* (rare) 'bind', with Lett. *saite*, Lith. *saitas* 'bond' : Grk. *ἱμάς* 'strap', ON *sīmi* 'rope', OE *sīma* 'bond', Skt. *sā-*, *si-*, Av. *hā(y)-* 'bind', Av. *hinu-* 'bond', fr. IE **sē(i)-*, **sī-*. Walde-P. 2.463 f.

7. ChSl. *sŭvęzati* (so reg. for *δέω* in Gospels; *vęzati* for *δεσμεύω*), SCr. *(s)vezati*, Boh. *vazati*, etc., general Slavic, with derivs. for 'bond' (9.17), prob. with prothetic *v* : ChSl. *ązìti* 'crowd, press', *ąza* 'bond' (so reg. for *δεσμός* in Gospels), *ązŭkŭ* 'narrow', Av. *qz-* 'lace, hem in', Grk. *ἄγχω* 'strangle', Lat. *angere* 'bind, oppress', ON *ǫngr*, OE *enge*, etc. 'narrow', fr. IE **anĝh-*. Walde-P. 1.62. Miklosich 56 f. Brückner 611.

ChSl. *povrěsti*, *-vrŭzą* (Supr.; not in Gospels) : Lith. *veržti* 'draw tight', *viržis* 'rope', ON *virgill* 'hangman's rope', OE *wyrgan* 'strangle', etc. Walde-P. 1.273.

8. Skt. *bandh-*, Av. *band-*, above, 1.

Skt. *sā-*, *si-*, Av. *hā(y)-* : Lett. *siet*, etc., above, 6.

Skt. *nah-* : Ir. *nascim*, etc., above, 4.

Skt. *dā-*, *di-* : Grk. *δέω*, above, 2.

Av. *dərəz-*, with sb. *dərəzā-* : Skt. *dṛh-* 'make firm, fix', Lith. *diržas* 'strap', etc. Walde-P. 1.859. Barth. 698.

9.17 BOND

Grk.	*δεσμός*	Goth.	*bandi*	Lith.	*ryšys, raištis*
NG	*δεσμός*	ON	*band*	Lett.	*saite*
Lat.	*vinculum, ligāmen(tum)*	Dan.	*baand*	ChSl.	*ąza*
It.	*legame, vincolo*	Sw.	*band*	SCr.	*(s)veza, vez*
Fr.	*lien*	OE	*bend, tēah*	Boh.	*úvazek, vazadlo*
Sp.	*lazo, vínculo*	ME	*band, bond, bend*	Pol.	*wiązadło,*
Rum.	*legătură*	NE	*bond*	Russ.	*svjaz', svjazka*
Ir.	*cuimrech*	Du.	*band*	Skt.	*bandha(na)-, saṁdāna-*
NIr.	*ceangal*	OHG	*gibenti, bant*	Av.	*banda-, hinu-, dərəzā-*
W.	*rhwym*	MHG	*gebende, bant*		
Br.	*ere*	NHG	*band*		

'Bond' is intended here to cover the generic notion 'anything with which one binds', though NE *bond* and several of the words listed are now less used in this way than in various secondary senses. In common speech one is more likely to use the more specific terms for 'rope, chain', or the like.

Most of the words are connected with, and have been included in the discussion of, the verbs for 'bind' (9.16). An exception is

Sp. *lazo* (esp. and orig. 'noose' but also generic), fr. Lat. *laqueus* 'noose, snare' : *lacere* 'attract, seduce', *lax* 'deception'. Ernout-M. 523 f., 532. Walde-H. 1.745. REW 4909.

9.18 CHAIN

Grk.	*ἅλυσις*	Goth.	*naudibandi, eisarnabandi*	Lith.	*grandinė, retėžis*
NG	*ἀλυσίδα*	ON	*rekendr, hlekkir*	Lett.	*k'ēde*
Lat.	*catēna*	Dan.	*kæde, lænke*	ChSl.	*ąže želězno*
It.	*catena*	Sw.	*kedja*	SCr.	*lanac, verige*
Fr.	*chaîne*	OE	*racente, racenttēah*	Boh.	*řetěz*
Sp.	*cadena*	ME	*chayne, rakenteie, rakand*	Pol.	*łańcuch,*
Rum.	*lanț*	NE	*chain*	Russ.	*cep'*
Ir.	*slabrad, rond*	Du.	*keten*	Skt.	*çṛṅkhalā-*
NIr.	*slabhradh*	OHG	*ketina*	Av.	. . . .
W.	*cadwyn*	MHG	*keten(e), lanne*		
Br.	*chadenn*	NHG	*kette*		

1. Grk. *ἅλυσις*, NG *ἀλυσίδα* (fr. dim. form), orig.?

2. Lat. *catēna* (> It. *catena*, Fr. *chaîne*, Sp. *cadena*; also Celt. and Gmc. words, below), etym. dub., but perh. : *cassis* (**cat-sis*) 'hunting net', Skt. *çasta-* 'sort of belt'. Walde-P. 1.338. Walde-H. 1.177 f. Ernout-M. 162. (Etruscan orig.?)

Rum. *lanț*, fr. Slavic, cf. SCr. *lanac* (below, 6). Tiktin 888.

3. Ir. *slabrad*, NIr. *slabhradh*, formed with suffix *-rad* (Pedersen 2.52 f.), fr. a *slab-*, which might be fr. **slagʷ-* (so Macbain 326) in OE *læccan* 'seize, grasp', etc. (Walde-P. 2.707), or as easily fr. **slabh-* (?) in Skt. *labh-* 'grasp, seize', etc. (Walde-P. 2.385).

Ir. *rond* (NIr. *ronn* 'chain, tie or bond, an ornamental chain, wire', etc., Dinneen), etym.?

W. *cadwyn*, fr. Lat. *catēna*. Loth, Mots lat. 142.

Br. *chadenn*, fr. an OFr. **chadene* > *chaeine*, Fr. *chaîne*. Loth, loc. cit.

4. Goth. *naudibandi* (alone renders *ἅλυσις* Mk. 5.4, 2 Tim. 1.16, otherwise with adj. *eisarneins* 'of iron', Mk. 5.3, 4; cf. also cpd. *eisarnabandi*, Lk. 8.29), lit. 'bond of necessity', cpd. of *nauþs* 'necessity, distress' (9.93) and *bandi* 'bond' (9.17).

ON *rekendr* pl. fem., rarely sg. *rekendi*, OE *racente*, ME *rakand*, cpd. OE *racenttēah*, ME *rakenteie*, *rakentyne*, etc. (with OE *tēah* 'bond') : ON *rakki* 'ring fastening sailyard to mast', OE *racca* 'part of a ship's rigging', fr. IE **reĝ-* beside **rek-* in Skt. *raçana-* 'cord, rope, strap, bridle', *raçmi-* 'cord, rope, rein', etc. Walde-P. 2.362. Falk-Torp 872.

ON *hlekkir*, pl. of *hlekkr* 'ring, link', Dan. *lænke* 'link, chain' : OE *hlence* 'link', MHG *gelenk* 'a bend', *lenken* 'bend', etc. Walde-P. 1.498. Falk-Torp 676.

Dan. *kæde*, Sw. *kedja*, fr. MLG *kede*, beside *kedene*, Du. *keten*, OHG *ketina*, MHG *keten(e)*, NHG *kette*, fr. Lat. *catēna*, in part through VLat. **cadena*. Falk-Torp 518. Franck-v.W. 302 f. Kluge-G. 297.

ME *chayne*, *cheyne*, NE *chain*, fr. OFr. *chaeine*, Fr. *chaîne*.

MHG *lanne*, *lan* (NHG *lanne* 'a sort of shaft'), orig.? Weigand-H. 2.18?

5. Lith. *grandinė*, *grandinis* (neolog. in this sense) : *grandis* 'ring, link of a chain', OPruss. *grandis* 'ring' on a plow, Lett. *gruods* 'tight twisted', these : OHG *kranz* 'wreath', etc. Walde-P. 1.595. Trautmann 94 f.

Lith. *retėžis*, fr. Russ. *retjaz'* (below, 6). Brückner, Sl. Fremdwörter 126.

Lith. *lenciugas* (but see NSB s.v.), fr. the Slavic, cf. WhRuss. *łancúh*, Pol. *łańcuch* 'chain' (below). Brückner, Sl. Fremdwörter 102.

Lett. *kēde*, fr. MLG *kede* (above, 4). Mühl.-Endz. 2.373.

6. ChSl. *ąže želězĭno*, lit. 'iron bond', *ąže* : *ąza* 'bond' (9.17).

SCr. *lanac*, beside Boh. *lano* 'rope', Pol. *lanwy* 'traces', fr. MHG *lanne* 'chain' (above, 4); Pol. *łańcuch*, fr. a cpd. MHG **lann-zug*. Berneker 689. Brückner 306.

SCr. *verige*, pl. of *veriga* id., ChSl. *verigy* (Supr.), Russ. *verigi* 'chains, irons, fetters' : ChSl. *vrŭvĭ* 'rope, cord' (9.19). Walde-P. 1.263. Trautmann 352.

Boh. *řetěz* (Pol. *rzeciądz*, *wrzeciądz* now 'chain or bolt of a door'), Russ. *retjaz'* (obs.), etc., etym. dub. Brückner 633. Miklosich 385.

Russ. *cep'* : *pri-cepit'sja* 'fasten upon, stick to', *cepkij* 'tenacious', outside root connections? Berneker 125 f.

7. Skt. *çṛṅkhalā-* (or *a-*), etym. dub., perh. fr. **k̂er-* in Arm. *sarikʻ* (pl.) 'bond, cord', Grk. *καῖρος* 'row of thrums for attaching thread to loom'; or : ON *hlekkir* (above, 4). Walde-P. 1.409, 499. Uhlenbeck 315.

9.19 ROPE, CORD

Grk.	*κάλως, σχοῖνος, σπάρτον*	Goth.	....	Lith.	*virvė, viržis*
NG	*σκοινί*	ON	*reip, taug, strengr, seil, sīmi, līna*	Lett.	*virve, valgs*
Lat.	*fūnis, restis*	Dan.	*reb, tov, snor, snøre, line*	ChSl.	*vrŭvĭ*
It.	*corda, fune*	Sw.	*rep, tåg, lina, snöre*	SCr.	*uže, konop*
Fr.	*corde, cordon*	OE	*rāp, sāl, streng, sīma, līne*	Boh.	*provaz, lano*
Sp.	*cuerda, soga, cordel*	ME	*roop, cord, streng, line*	Pol.	*powróz, sznur*
Rum.	*frînghie, funie, şnur*	NE	*rope, cord*	Russ.	*verevka, kanat, šnur*
Ir.	*sūanem, tēt, loman*	Du.	*touw, reep, snoer*	Skt.	*rajju-, guṇa-, dāman-*
NIr.	*tēad, cōrda*	OHG	*seil, stric, reif, strang, snuor, līna*	Av.	....
W.	*rhaff, cord*	MHG	*seil, stric, stranc, reif, snuor, līne*		
Br.	*kordenn, fun*	NHG	*seil, tau, strick, schnur*		

The gradation by size in the current use of NE *cable* (orig. 'halter'), *hawser* (orig. 'hoister'), *rope*, *cord*, and *string* or *twine* is one that is secondary and in part locally variant and cannot be equated with the differentiations of similar words elsewhere, which are too complex to be described briefly. It is intended here to give the principal words for 'rope' or 'cord'.

The smaller 'string, twine' is partly covered by words included in the list, or expressed more precisely by their dim. forms, e.g. Russ. *verevočka*, Pol. *sznurek*. Some of the words are cognate with those for 'thread', as Fr. *ficelle* (dim. of *file*), NHG *bindfaden*. Among others are MLat. *spagum*, It. *spago* (> NG *σπάγγος*), of unknown orig. (REW 8113; KZ 66.259), NE *twine* (OE *twīn*, fr. *twi-* 'two', hence orig. 'twisted').

1. Grk. *κάλος* (Hom.+), Att. *κάλως*, perh. : Du. *halen*, ME *hale* 'pull', NE *haul*, etc. Boisacq 401.

Grk. *σχοῖνος*, orig. 'rush, reed', then 'rope or cord' made by plaiting rushes together, dim. *σχοινίον*, NG *σκοινί* 'rope, cord', etym. dub. Boisacq 934.

Grk. *σπάρτον*, dim. *σπαρτίον*, orig. = *σπάρτος* a kind of rush or broom (like the Sp. *esparto*) : *σπεῖρα* 'anything twisted', also 'rope, cord' fr. **sper-* beside **sperg-* in *σπάργω* 'wrap', *σπάργανα* 'swaddling-clothes'. Walde-P. 2.667. Boisacq 892.

2. Lat. *fūnis* (> It. *fune*, Rum. *funie*), etym. dub. Walde-P. 1.670, 868. Ernout-M. 402 f. Walde-H. 1.567 f.

Lat. *restis* : Skt. *rajju-* 'rope, cord', OE *resc*, *risc*, MHG *rusc* 'rush', Lith. *regsti* 'plait, knit, bind', Lett. *režg'is* 'wicker'. Walde-P. 2.374. Ernout-M. 862 f.

It. *corda*, Fr. *corde* (> ME, NE *cord*), dim. *cordon*, Sp. *cuerda*, dim. *cordel* (fr. Prov.), fr. Lat. *chorda* 'string on a musical instrument', this fr. Grk. *χορδή* 'gut, tripe, string of a musical instrument (made of gut)'. REW 1881.

Sp. *soga* (also Port., Cat., etc.), OFr. *soue*, VLat. **sōca*, of Gall. orig.? REW 8051.

Rum. *frînghie*, fr. Lat. *fimbria* 'shred, fiber, fringe'. REW 3308. Puşcariu 653.

Rum. *şnur*, fr. NHG *schnur* (below, 4). Tiktin 1449.

3. Ir. *sūanem*, prob. : *sōim* 'turn, wind', hence orig. 'twisted cord'. Pokorny in Walde-P. 2.481. Otherwise Pedersen 1.103.

Ir. *tēt*, NIr. *tēad*, in older language esp. 'string of a musical instrument', cf. W. *tant* 'chord, string' : Lat. *tendere* 'stretch', etc. Walde-P. 1.723.

Ir. *loman*, cf. W. *llyfan* 'string, rope' (not in last ed. of Spurrell), Br. *louan* 'strap', etym.? Pedersen 1.33, 164.

NIr. *cōrda*, W. *cord*, fr. English. Macbain 101. Parry-Williams 185.

W. *rhaff*, orig.? Loth, RC 43.410 (: ON *reip*, OE *rāp*, etc. below 4, but phonetically difficult).

Br. *kordenn*, fr. Fr. *corde*. Henry 75.

Br. *fun*, fr. Lat. *fūnis*. Loth, Mots lat. 171.

4. ON *reip*, Dan. *reb*, Sw. *rep*, OE *rāp*, ME *roop*, NE *rope*, Du. *reep*, OHG, MHG *reif* (esp. 'loop, circle, circular band', NHG *reifen* 'hoop, tire'), Goth. *-raip* (in *skauda-raip* 'shoe-lace') : ON *ript* 'piece of cloth', OE *rift* 'garment', etc., root connection dub., but perh. (as orig. 'shreds'?) : ON *rīfa*, etc. 'tear'. Falk-Torp 884, 893. Walde-P. 2.345.

ON *taug*, Dan. *tov*, Sw. *tåg* (OE *tēah*, *tēag* 'bond'), orig. 'rope' as instrument for pulling, fr. the same root as Goth. *tiuhan*, Lat. *dūcere* 'draw', etc. Walde-P. 1.781. Falk-Torp 1250.

ON *strengr*, OE, ME *streng* (NE *string*), OHG *strang*, MHG *stranc* (NHG *strang*) : ON *strangr* 'violent, strong, hard', OE *strang* 'strong, hard', etc., fr. IE **stren-k-*, beside **stren-g-* in Grk. *στραγγός* 'twisted', Ir. *srengim* 'pull', NIr. *sreang* 'string, cord, strap', etc. Walde-P. 2.650. Falk-Torp 1179.

ON *seil*, OE *sāl*, OHG, MHG, NHG *seil* (Goth. **sail* in denom. *in-sailjan* 'let down' by ropes = OE *sǣlan*, OHG

seilen 'fasten with a cord') : Lith. *at-sailė* 'coupling-pole on a wagon', with different formation ON *sīmi*, OE *sīma*, OS *sīmo* 'rope, cord', Grk. *ἱμάς* 'strap', etc., fr. the root in Skt. *sā-*, Av. *hā(y)-* 'bind' (9.16). Walde-P. 2.463 f. Falk-Torp 956. Feist 294 f.

ON *snœri* 'twisted rope', Dan. *snøre*, Sw. *snöre*, Dan. *snor*, Du. *snoer*, OHG, MHG *snuor*, NHG *schnur* : Goth. *snōrjō* 'plaited basket', OE *snēr* 'harp-string', all either : Lith. *nerti* 'to noose, thread', *narys* 'knot, loop, link, joint', etc.; or : Skt. *snāvan-* 'band, sinew', Grk. *νεῦρον* 'sinew', etc. Walde-P. 2.699. Falk-Torp 1098. Feist 441.

ON *līna*, Dan. *line*, Sw. *lina*, OE *līne*, ME *line* (NE *line* nautical and 'fishing line, clothes line'), OHG *līna*, MHG *līne* (NHG *leine*), all orig. 'linen-rope', fr. ON, OE, OHG *līn* 'linen'. Falk-Torp 646.

ME, NE *cord*, fr. OFr. *corde* (above, 2).

Du. *touw* = MHG *tou(we)* 'tool, equipment' esp. of a ship, hence 'cable, rope' (NHG *tau* fr. LG) : Goth. *taujan* 'do, make' (9.11). Walde-P. 1.779. Falk-Torp 1267.

OHG, MHG *stric*, NHG *strick* : OHG *strickan* 'stitch, tie fast, knit', OE *gestrician* 'repair (nets)', perh. Lat. *stringere* 'draw tight, draw together'. Walde-P. 2.649. Weigand-H. 2.990.

5. Lith. *virvė*, Lett. *virve*, OPruss. *wirbe*, ChSl. *vrŭvĭ*, Russ. *verevka* : Lett. *vērens* 'thread', Lith. *virtinis* 'sling', *apivaras* 'shoe-string', etc., fr. a root **wer-* perh. the same as **wer-* 'turn', in Skt. *vṛj-*, Lat. *vertere*, Skt. *vṛt-*, etc. (10.12). Hence orig. 'twisted cord'. Walde-P. 1.263, 280.

Lith. *viržis* : *veržti* 'draw together', ChSl. *povrěsti* 'bind', Pol. *powróz*, etc. (below, 6).

Lett. *valgs* : Skt. *valgā-* 'bridle', perh. orig. 'twisted cord', fr. the root in OE *wealcan* 'roll', etc. Walde-P. 1.304. Mühl.-Endz. 4.454.

6. ChSl. *vrŭvĭ*, Russ. *verevka*, above, 5.

SCr. *uže* : ChSl. *ąže* 'chain', *ąza* 'bond' (9.18).

SCr. *konop* (Bulg. *konopéc*, Slov. *konòp*), orig. 'rope of hemp' : SCr. *konoplja* 'hemp', etc. Berneker 559.

Boh. *provaz* (OBoh. *povraz*), Pol. *powróz* (cf. Russ. *pavoroz* 'drawstring' on purse, etc.) : ChSl. *po-vrěsti* 'bind', etc. (9.16). Walde-P. 1.273. Trautmann 355. Gebauer 1.34.

Boh. *lano* : SCr. *lanac* 'chain', etc. fr. MHG *lanne* 'chain' (9.18).

Pol. *sznur*, Russ. *šnur*, fr. NHG *schnur* (above, 4).

Russ. *kanat* (esp. 'heavy rope'), perh. fr. a Byz. deriv. of *κάννα* 'reed'. A Byz. *καννάτα* 'funis' is quoted by Berneker 479 (after Vasmer) but on dub. evidence.

7. Skt. *rajju-* : Lat. *restis* (cf. above, 2).

Skt. *guṇa-*, esp. the individual 'strand' of a rope or cord (cf. *dvi-*, *tri-guṇa* 'two-, three-ply'), fr. **gr-no-* : Grk. *γυργαθός* 'basket (of wickerwork)', etc., fr. the root **ger-* 'turn, wind'. Walde-P. 1.593.

Skt. *dāman-* 'cord, band' : *dā-*, *di-*, Grk. *δέω* 'bind' (9.16).

Skt. *saṁnahana-* (Macdonell-Keith 2.423) : *nah-* 'bind' (9.16).

9.192 KNOT (sb.)

Grk.	*ἅμμα*	Goth.	....	Lith.	*mazgas*
NG	*κόμπος*	ON	*knūtr*	Lett.	*mazgs*
Lat.	*nōdus*	Dan.	*knude*	ChSl.	(*ązlŭ*)
It.	*nodo*	Sw.	*knut*	SCr.	*uzao*
Fr.	*noeud*	OE	*cnotta*	Boh.	*uzel*
Sp.	*nudo*	ME	*knotte*	Pol.	*węzeł*
Rum.	*nod*	NE	*knot*	Russ.	*uzel*
Ir.	*snaidm*	Du.	*knoop*	Skt.	*granthi-*
NIr.	*snaidhm*	OHG	*knodo, knoto, knopf*	Av.	....
W.	*clwm*	MHG	*knode, knote, knopf*		
Br.	*koulm, skoulm*	NHG	*knoten*		

A 'knot' in a rope, cord, etc., is a means of tying, and the words are mostly cognate with others denoting 'tie, fasten' or some form of fastening. The application to a lump or protuberance in the body or on a tree is clearly secondary in Lat. *nōdus*. For the Gmc. group as a whole the view that the latter sense is the earlier (cf. Paul, Deutsches Wtb. s.v. *Knoten*, "bedeutet ursprünglich 'ründliche Anschwellung an einem Gegenstand' ") is favored by the nearest cognates like OHG *knopf* 'knob, knot', OE *cnoll* 'hilltop', etc. But in the history of OE *cnotta*—NE *knot*, this sense is chronologically later (NED s.v. *knot*, sb[1]. 13–16) and for the prevailing earlier use, cf. the derivative OE *cnyttа* 'tie with a knot' (NE *knit*).

1. Grk. *ἅμμα* (anything for tying, covering 'knot', but more comprehensive), fr. *ἅπτω* 'fasten'.

NG *κόμπος*, fr. late Grk. *κόμβος* 'roll, band', perh. : *σκαμβός* 'crooked', etc. Walde-P. 2.539 f. Boisacq 488.

2. Lat. *nōdus* (> Romance words), fr. a root **ned-* seen in Ir. *naidm* 'bond', *nascim* 'bind', Goth. *nati* 'net', etc. Walde-P. 2.328. Ernout-M. 662 f., 674.

3. Ir. *snaidm*, NIr. *snaidhm*, perh. fr. some by-form of **snē(i)-* in Skt. *snāyu-* 'bond, sinew', Lat. *nēre* 'spin', Ir. *snāthe* 'thread', etc. Walde-P. 2.329, 694 f.

W. *clwm*, *cwlwm*, Corn. *colmen*, Br. *koulm*, *skoulm*, prob. : Ir. *colum* 'skin' and 'sinew' (cf. *columne* gl. *nervus*), reflecting the old use of sinews for binding. Loth, RC 41.375 ff.

4. ON *knūtr*, OE *cnotta*, OHG *knodo*, *knoto*, etc. general Gmc., fr. the root seen in Lith. *gniutu*, *gniusti* 'press' and with a different extension in OHG *knopf* 'knot' (NHG 'knob, button'), etc. Walde-P. 1.582 f. Falk-Torp 553. Kluge-G. 314.

Du. *knoop* ('knot' and 'button') = OHG *knopf* (above).

5. Lith. *mazgas*, Lett. *mazgs* : Lith. vb. *mezgu*, *megsti* 'knot, knit', OE *max* 'net', OHG *masca* 'mesh', etc. Walde-P. 2.301. Mühl.-Endz. 2.572.

6. ChSl. *ązlŭ* ('fastening', beside *ąza* = *δεσμός*), SCr. *uzao*, Boh., Russ. *uzel*, Pol. *węzeł*, deriv. of *ąza* 'bond' (9.16). Brückner 609 f.

7. Skt. *granthi-* : *grath-* 'tie', this perh. : OE *cradel* 'cradle', OHG *kratto* 'basket', fr. an extension of **ger-* in words based on the notion of 'twist, wind'. Walde-P. 1.593 ff. (595).

9.21 STRIKE (Hit, Beat)

Grk.	τύπτω, κρούω, κόπτω, θείνω, παίω	Goth.	slahan, stautan, bliggwan	Lith.	mušti, ištikti, daužti
NG	χτυπῶ, βαρῶ, δέρνω	ON	slā, ljōsta, berja, drepa	Lett.	sist, dauzīt, pērt
Lat.	ferīre, percutere, caedere, percellere, tundere	Dan.	slaa	ChSl.	biti, udariti, tlěšti, uraziti
It.	colpire, percuotere, battere	Sw.	slå	SCr.	udariti, biti, lupiti, tući
Fr.	frapper, battre, heurter	OE	slēan, bēatan, drepan	Boh.	uhoditi, udeřiti, biti, tlouci
Sp.	golpear, pegar, batir	ME	sleye, smite, strike, hitte, bete	Pol.	uderzyć, bić, razić
Rum.	lovi, bate	NE	strike (smite), hit, beat	Russ.	bit', udarit', kolotit', razit'
Ir.	benim, sligim, slaidim, būalim	Du.	slaan	Skt.	han-, taḍ-
NIr.	buailim	OHG	slahan, bōzan, berjen, bliuwan	Av.	ǰan-, snaθ-
W.	taro, curo	MHG	slōn, bōzen, bern, bliuwen		
Br.	skei, kanna, dourna	NHG	schlagen		

'Strike' is a broad notion, represented by several IE roots and by a great variety of words in many of the IE languages. These are partly differentiated, esp. according to the kind of instrument or object involved. But the differentiation is too diverse and fluctuating to permit any general classification or fixed arrangement in the table. Just as NE hammer and ram may be used as verbs, so a few of the more general verbs for strike are derived from the name of the instrument used. Several, mostly of imitative origin, were first used with reference to the sound made by a blow (cf. NE knock, Fr. frapper, NG χτυπῶ, below). Some are used esp. for 'strike with a sharp instrument', and so overlap with 'cut'. Some are used esp. for 'strike to death', and so overlap with 'kill'. The notion of repeated action is usually, though not always, present in NE beat and pound, and elsewhere may be brought out by the use of cpds. or iteratives.

1. IE *gʷhen- in words for 'strike', and esp. 'strike to death, wound, kill' (4.76). Walde-P. 1.679 ff. Ernout-M. 344. Walde-H. 1.332 f.

Grk. θείνω 'strike' (poet.), fut. θενῶ, aor. ἔθεινα, beside aor. ἔπεφνον 'kill', φόνος 'murder', etc.; Lat. dē-fendere 'ward off', of-fendere 'strike against'; Skt. han-, Av. ǰan- 'strike, slay'; Arm. ganem 'strike'; Hitt. kwen, kun- 'strike, defeat, kill' : Ir. gonim 'wound, kill'; Lith. ginti, ChSl. gŭnati 'drive' (fr. 'strike'), etc.

2. IE *bher-. Walde-P. 2.159 f. Ernout-M. 348. Walde-H. 1.481 f.

Lat. ferīre 'strike, beat, knock, slay' (> Sp. herir 'wound, hurt, strike', Fr. férir 'strike, smite', obs.); ON berja 'strike, beat', OHG berjen, MHG berjen, bern 'strike, pound', also 'knead, mold'; ChSl. borją, brati 'fight', Av. tižibāra- 'with a sharp cutting edge'; prob. also Lat. forāre, ON bora, OE borian, etc. 'bore' (9.46).

3. IE *bhei-. Walde-P. 2.137 f. Berneker 117.

Ir. benim 'strike, cut' (W. bidio 'trim a hedge', MBr. benaff 'cut', etc.); ChSl. bĭją, biti, SCr., Boh. biti, Pol. bić, Russ. bit' 'strike, beat'.

4. Grk. τύπτω, beside τύπος 'blow, imprint, form, image' : Skt. tup-, tump- 'hurt' (Dhātup.), pra-stumpati (gramm.), Lat. stupēre 'stand stiff, be stupefied', ChSl. tŭpati 'palpitare', tŭpŭtati 'palpitare, calcare', etc., fr. *(s)teu-p-, beside *(s)teu-d- in Lat. tundere 'strike, beat,

pound', Skt. tud- 'beat, push', Goth. stautan 'strike', OHG stōzan 'hit', NHG stossen 'hit, push', etc., *(s)teu-g- in Skt. tuj- 'strike, push, urge', Ir. tuagaim 'strike with an axe (tuag)', etc., extensions of IE *(s)teu-. Walde-P. 2.618. Boisacq 991 f. Ernout-M. 1064. Falk-Torp 1198.

Grk. κρούω, cf. Hom. κροαίνω 'stamp, strike with the hoof' : Lith. krušti 'pound, bruise, crush', ChSl. sŭ-krušiti 'break to pieces', IE *kreus-. Walde-P. 1.480 f. Boisacq 522.

Grk. κόπτω 'strike', and 'cut with a blow', with κοπίς 'cleaver', κοπεύς 'chisel', etc. : Lat. capus 'capon' (= 'cut'), Lith. kapoti 'chop up', ChSl. kopati 'dig', skopiti 'castrate', etc. Walde-P. 2.559 ff. Boisacq 492 f. Ernout-M. 151. Walde-H. 1.161 f.

Grk. παίω 'strike' (post-Hom. and poet.), perh. : Lat. pavīre 'strike, beat', but disputed. Schwyzer, IF 30.443 f. Walde-P. 1.12.

Grk. κτυπέω 'crash, resound' (: κτύπος 'crash, noise'), and trans. 'make resound', NG χτυπῶ 'strike, knock, hit', with development through 'strike with a sounding blow, knock', as in ἐχτύπησε τὴν πόρτα 'knocked on the door'.

Grk. βαρέω 'weigh down' (: βαρύς 'heavy'), with NG βαρῶ 'strike, hit', development through 'bring down' (a bird in hunting).

Grk. δέρω, 'flay' (9.28), colloq. also 'beat, trash' (LS s.v. III) and so reg. NG δέρνω.

5. Lat. percutere (> It. percuotere, Sp. percutir), cpd. of quatere 'shake' (10.26). The earlier sense is 'strike through', this from 'shake through and through'. Ernout-M. 834 f.

Lat. caedere 'strike (esp. with a cutting instrument), cut, strike to death, kill' (esp. in latter sense cpd. occīdere), prob. : Skt. khid- 'press, tear, pound', perh. also Skt. chid- 'cut off', Grk. σχίζω 'split', Lat. scindere 'tear', etc., but with complicated and difficult root relations. Walde-P. 2.538. Ernout-M. 128 f., 906. Walde-H. 1.129.

Lat. per-cellere 'strike', esp. 'strike down, destroy' (cf. clādēs 'destruction') : Grk. κλάω 'break', Lith. kalti, Lett. kalt 'hammer, forge', etc. Walde-P. 1.436 ff. Ernout-M. 171. Walde-H. 1.225 f.

Lat. pavīre 'strike', esp. 'beat, tread down', prob. : Lith. piauti 'cut'. Walde-P. 1.12.

Lat. tundere, see under Grk. τύπτω (above, 4).

Lat. īcere (rare and arch. except for pple. ictus and tenses formed with it), beside sb. ictus 'blow, beat', etym. dub. but perh. : Grk. ἰκτέα· ἀκόντιον Hesych., αἶκλοι· αἱ γωνίαι τοῦ βέλους Hesych., Cypr. ἰκμαμένος 'wounded'. Walde-P. 1.7 f. Ernout-M. 470. Walde-H. 1.670.

It. colpire, Sp. golpear (Fr. couper 'cut', OFr. 'strike'), fr. It. colpo (Fr. coup, Prov. colp >) Sp. golpe 'blow', VLat. *colpus for Lat. colaphus fr. Grk. κόλαφος 'buffet, slap' (: κολάπτω 'pick, carve with a chisel'. Walde-P. 1.440. REW 2034. Wartburg 2.865 ff.

Lat. battuere, late battere (> It. battere, Fr. battre, Sp. batir, Rum. bate), rare word in literature, though apparently old and popular (already in Plautus), perh. Gall. loanword, cf. Gall. anda-bata 'gladiator who fought with closed helmet'. Walde-P. 2.126. Walde-H. 1.99.

Fr. frapper, prob. of imitative orig., like NE rap, flap, clap, slap, etc. (cf. NG χτυπῶ, above, 4). Wartburg 3.763. Otherwise REW 3173.

Fr. heurter 'strike', esp. 'hit, knock', deriv. of a Gmc. noun = ON hrūtr 'ram', hence orig. like NE vb. ram. REW 4244.

Sp. pegar, also and orig. 'stick, fasten', fr. Lat. picāre 'daub with pitch', fr. pix 'pitch'. REW 6477.

Rum. lovi, fr. Slavic loviti 'hunt, catch' (3.79). Tiktin 923.

6. Ir. benim, above 3.

Ir. sligim : W. lliasu (arch.) 'slay, kill', perh. fr. a root *sleg- beside *slak- in Ir. slacc 'sword', Goth. slahan 'strike', etc. (below, 7).

Ir. slaidim : W. lladd, Br. laza 'kill', earlier 'strike', outside connections? Walde 1.439. Pedersen 2.630.

Ir. būalim, NIr. buailim, prob. fr. *boug-l- : NHG pochen 'knock', NE poke, etc., fr. an imitative bu-. Walde-P. 2.113. Stokes 180.

W. taro, cf. OBr. toreusit 'attrivit', prob. fr. an extension of *ter- in Grk. τείρω, Lat. terere 'rub', Grk. τρώω, τιτρώσκω 'wound', etc. Walde-P. 1.730.

W. curo, fr. cur 'blow', properly 'anxiety, care, affliction', fr. Lat. cūra 'care, trouble, anxiety'. Loth, Mots lat. 155.

Br. skei, MBr. squey, beside sko 'blow', etym. dub. Henry 240. Ernault, Glossaire 384.

Br. kanna, orig. 'bleach cloth (by beating it)', whence 'beat' in general, fr. kann 'white, shining'. Henry 53. Ernault, Dict. étym. 242.

Br. dourna 'strike with the hand', fr. dourn 'hand' (4.33).

7. Goth. slahan, ON slā, OE slēan, etc. general Gmc. (but specialized in NE slay, and largely already in ME sleye, sleie to 'strike so as to kill', a sense also present in most of the other Gmc. forms) : MIr. slachta 'stricken', slacc 'sword', NIr. slacaire 'batterer', slacairt 'beating', etc. Walde-P. 2.706. Feist 436. Falk-Torp 1048.

Goth. stautan : Lat. tundere, etc. (above, 4).

Goth. bliggwan (renders δέρειν, μαστιγοῦν, κατακόπτειν), OHG bliuwan, MHG bliuwen (NHG bleuen), OS ūtbliuwid 'excudit', MDu. blouwen (here prob. NE sb. blow), etym. dub. Walde-P. 2.217. Feist 100.

ON ljōsta, esp. 'hit, strike with a spear', cf. ljōstr, Dan. lyster, Sw. ljuster 'fish-spear', beside ON lustr 'cudgel' : W. llost 'spear', MIr. loss 'point of anything' (both secondarily 'tail'), root connection dub., but perh. as orig. '(los)-schlagen' fr. root in Goth. fra-liusan, OHG far-liosan 'loose', etc. Walde-P. 2.408. Falk-Torp 671.

ON berja, etc., above, 2.

ON drepa 'strike, kill' (Dan. dræbe, Sw. dräpa 'kill'), OE drepan 'strike', OHG treffan 'strike, hit, touch' (NHG treffen 'hit'), fr. a root *dhreb- beside *dhrebh- in Goth. gadraban 'hew out', ChSl. drobiti 'break in pieces'. Walde-P. 1.875. Falk-Torp 159. NED s.v. drepe.

OE bēatan, ME bete, NE beat, OHG bōzan, MHG bōzen 'beat' (ON bauta id., rare), perh. fr. a by-form of the root in Lat. con-fūtāre 'repress, confute'. Walde-H. 1.259. Falk-Torp 120.

ME, NE smite (now only rhet. or poet.), fr. OE smītan 'smear' : OHG (be)smīzan, MHG smīzen 'stroke, smear', MHG also 'strike', NHG schmeissen 'throw, hurl', dial. 'strike', Goth. bi-smeitan, ga-smeitan 'annoint', prob. fr. an extension of *smē(i)- in Grk. σμάω, σμήχω 'wipe off, cleanse', etc. Walde-P. 2.685 f. Falk-Torp 1081. Feist 95. Semantic development in Gmc. complicated and difficult (for 'throw' in NHG schmeissen cf. Paul, Deutsches Wtb. s.v.), but 'strike' prob. fr. 'smear' through 'stroke'. Cf. the following and also the current slang use of NE smear in U.S. sports reporting (= 'knock out, put out of action').

ME, NE strike, fr. OE strīcan 'stroke, smoothe, rub, wipe' = OHG strīhhan, NHG streichen 'stroke', perh. : Lat. stringere 'touch, touch lightly, graze, strip off', striga 'swath, winrow, furrow', root *streig-. Walde-P. 2.637.

ME hitte 'meet, reach with a blow, hit', then 'strike' as NE hit (now the most pop. word, at least in U.S.), fr. late OE hyttan 'come upon, meet with', prob. loanword fr. ON hitta 'meet, find'. NED s.v. hit, vb. Falk-Torp 407. Walde-P. 1.364.

OE cnucian, ME knokke, NE knock, orig. 'strike with a sounding blow' (as knock on the door), then also 'strike, hit' (as knocked him down), of imitative orig. NED s.v. knock vb.

8. Lith. mušti, etym. dub. Walde-P. 2.255.

Lith. ištikti, cpd. of iš- 'out' (but here with mere perfective force) and tikti 'fit, suit'; semantic development from 'fit' to 'hit the mark', hence 'hit'. Cf. the reverse semantic development in NE it doesn't strike me right 'doesn't suit me', Rum. lovi 'strike', but popular 'correspond to, match' (cf. Tiktin s.v.), etc.

Lith. daužti, Lett. dauzīt (frequent. of dauzt 'strike in two') : Slov. duzati 'shove, press', MHG tuc 'blow, shove'? Berneker 239 f. Mühl.-Endz. 1.445.

Lett. sist, etym. dub. Walde-P. 1.339. Mühl.-Endz. 3.850.

Lett. pērt also 'bathe' : Lith. perti 'strike with a besom in bathing, bathe' also general 'strike', ChSl. perą, pĭrati 'strike with a mallet in washing, wash' (general Slavic), Skt. pṛt-, pṛtanā-, Av. pərət-, pəšanā- 'battle', Arm. hari, e-har 'struck'. Walde-P. 2.42. Mühl.-Endz. 3.210.

9. ChSl. biti, etc., above, 3.

ChSl., SCr. udariti, Russ. udarit', Boh. udeřiti, Pol. uderzyć, perfect. cpds. of the root in ChSl. derą, dĭrati 'tear, flay' : Grk. δέρω 'flay' (but also 'cudgel, thrash', so often in NT), Goth. distairan 'tear to pieces', etc., IE *der-. Berneker 179 f., 185. Walde-P. 1.799.

ChSl. tlŭką, tlěšti (reg. for κρούω 'knock' on the door), SCr. tući, Boh. tlouci (Russ. toloč' 'pound, grind', tolkot' 'push') : Lith. aptilkti 'be tame', perh. W. talch 'fragment, grist', OCorn. talch 'furfures', all with a common notion of 'pound'. Walde-P. 1.741. Trautmann 321 f.

ChSl. uraziti, Pol. razić, Russ. razit', beside Boh., Pol., Russ. raz 'a blow' : Grk. ῥάσσω, Ion. ῥήσσω 'strike down, beat'. Walde-P. 1.318. Brückner 454 f.

SCr. lupiti : Russ. lupit' 'peel, scale off', also 'flog, drub, beat', Boh. loupiti 'peel', lupati 'slap, beat, flog', Pol. łupić 'scale off, plunder' and 'give a hard blow', etc., Lith. laupyti 'break, crumb', Lett. laupīt 'peel, skin, rob', Skt. lup- 'break, injure, rob', IE *leup-. Walde-P. 2.417 f. Berneker 746.

Boh. uhoditi, perfect. cpd. of hoditi 'throw' fr. 'aim, fit, suit', the general Slavic sense (ChSl. ugoditi 'please', etc.). Semantic development as in Lith. ištikti, above, 8. Berneker 317.

Russ. kolotit', esp. 'hammer, pound, beat' (ChSl. klatiti 'move, shake', SCr. klatiti 'shake up, rock', Pol. kłócić 'stir, shake', etc.), etym. dub., perh. : ChSl. klati 'prick', Russ. kolotit' 'prick, split, slaughter', Lith. kalti, Lett. kalt 'forge, hammer', etc. Walde-P. 1.438. Berneker 550 f.

10. Skt. han-, Av. ǰan-, above, 1.

Skt. taḍ- (3sg. tāḍayati), cf. tāḍa-, tāḍana- 'a blow', taḍit- 'lightning', etym.? Uhlenbeck 111. Walde-P. 2.646.

Av. snaθ-, beside snaiθiš- 'weapon for striking or hewing' : Skt. çnath- 'pierce, strike, injure, kill', further connections dub. Walde-P. 1.402. Uhlenbeck 317. Barth. 1627.

9.22 CUT (vb.)

Grk.	*τέμνω, κόπτω*	Goth.	*maitan, sneiþan*	Lith.	*piauti, kirsti, rėžti*
NG	*κόβω*	ON	*skera, sniða, telgja, hǫggva, meita*	Lett.	*griezt, cirst*
Lat.	*secāre, caedere*	Dan.	*skære, hugge*	ChSl.	*rězati, sěšti (-krojiti)*
It.	*tagliare*	Sw.	*skära, hugga*	SCr.	*rezati, sjeći*
Fr.	*couper, tailler, trancher*	OE	*sceran, ceorfan, snīþan, hēawan*	Boh.	*řezati, krájeti, sekati*
Sp.	*cortar, tajar*	ME	*schere, cerve, hewe, cutte*	Pol.	*krajać, rznąć, ciąć, rąbać, siec*
Rum.	*tăia*	NE	*cut*	Russ.	*rezat', rubit', seč'*
Ir.	*tescaim, snaidim, scothaim*	Du.	*snijden, houwen*	Skt.	*kṛt-, chid-, lu-, ças-*
NIr.	*gearraim, snoighim*	OHG	*snīdan, houwan, meizan*	Av.	*kərət-, θwarəs-, brī-*
W.	*torri, naddu, trychu*	MHG	*snīden, houwen, meizen*		
Br.	*trouc'ha, skeja*	NHG	*schneiden*		

'Cut' is an extremely broad notion, represented by several IE roots and by a great variety of words in many of the IE languages. As in various non-IE languages there is no generic word for 'cut' but only special words according to the instrument used or the object cut, so even in IE there is only partial generalization. There is often a partial distinction between 'cut' with a knife, etc., and 'cut' by blows of an ax, etc., the latter use overlapping with 'strike' (as in Grk. *κόπτω*, Lat. *caedere*, etc.). There may be special expressions for 'cut wood or stone, hew or carve' (9.45, 9.81), for 'cut grass or grain, mow, reap', (8.32), for 'cut hair or wool, shear', for 'cut garments' (cf. sbs. for 'tailor', partly = 'cutter', 6.13), for 'cut apart', 'split' (9.27) or 'separate' (12.23), etc., so that the same roots appear here and under many other headings. Where there is widespread agreement in a particular special use, as in certain groups for 'hew' in carpentry and for 'mow' and so not listed here, the presumption is that this is inherited. In certain other cases the special use is clearly the result of specialization, as in the current use of NE *shear* (cf. its history in NED s.v.). But most often the same formal group shows such interchange of generic and various special uses that it is impossible to determine whether the IE root in question carried some one of the special senses or was already generic. If the number of IE roots set up for 'cut' seems extravagant (some fifteen in Walde-P.), it is because 'cut' is merely a convenient common denominator for the historical uses.

From the preceding it is obvious how difficult is the selection and order of importance of words to be listed here, apart from those that are obviously the most generic, like NE *cut* and some others.

1. IE *sek-. Verbal forms in Italic, Celtic, and Balto-Slavic. Walde-P. 2.474 ff. Ernout-M. 913 ff.

Lat. *secāre* (> It. *segare*, Fr. *scier* 'saw', Sp. *segar* 'mow'); Ir. *tescaim* (cpd. *to-in-sec-*, Pedersen 2.612; NIr. *teascaim* 'chop off'); ChSl. *sěšti*, SCr. *sjeći*, Boh. *sekati* (OBoh. *sěkati*, *sieci*, Gebauer 1.41), Pol. *siec*, Russ. *seč'* : ON *sǫg*, OE *sagu*, OHG *sega*, *saga* 'saw', ON *sax*, etc. 'knife'.

2. IE *(*s*)*ker-*, with extensions *(*s*)*kert-*, *(*s*)*krei-*, etc. Walde-P. 2.573 ff. Falk-Torp 1010. Berneker 172, 620. But labiovelar in Hitt. *kwer-*, *kur-*. Sturtevant, Hitt. Gr. 119.

ON *skera*, Dan. *skære*, Sw. *skära*, OE *sceran*, ME *schere* (NE *shear* specialized 'cut wool, hair', as already OHG *sceran* 'tondere', MHG, NHG *scheren*); Lith. *kertu*, *kirsti*, Lett. *cērtu*, *cirst* 'hew, hack'; Russ.-ChSl. *črĭtu*, *črešti* 'cut'; Skt. *kṛt-*, Av. *kərət-* (3sg. Skt. *kṛntati*, Av. *kərəntaiti*); ChSl. *ras-krojiti*, Boh. *krájeti*, Pol. *krajać* (Russ. *krojit'*, SCr. *krojiti*, Pol. *kroić* mostly 'cut' as of a tailor) : Grk. *κείρω* 'shear', Lat. *curtus* 'shortened, mutilated', Ir. *scaraim* 'separate', Lith. *skirti* 'separate, divide', etc.

3. IE *tem-. Walde-P. 1.719 f. Boisacq 954. Brückner 60.

Grk. *τέμνω*; Pol. *tnę*, *ciąć* (OBoh. *tnu*, *tieti* 'hew', ORuss. *tinu*, *tjąti* 'strike'); Lith. *tinti* 'sharpen by hammering'.

4. Grk. *κόπτω* 'strike, cut with a blow' (9.21), hence NG pop. *κόφτω* or more commonly (with new present to aor. *ἔκοψα*) *κόβω* 'cut'.

5. Lat. *caedere* 'strike, cut' (9.21).

It. *tagliare*, Fr. *tailler*, Sp. *tajar*, Rum. *tăia*, fr. VLat. *tāliāre* 'cut', deriv. of Lat. *tālea* 'rod, stick', in agriculture 'cutting, scion'. Ernout-M. 1013. REW 8542.

Fr. *couper*, orig. 'strike', hence 'divide by a blow, cut', fr. *coup* 'blow' (see under It. *colpire* 'strike', etc. 9.21).

Fr. *trancher* 'cut off', fr. Lat. *truncāre* 'cut off, maim', fr. *truncus* 'maimed'. REW 8953.

Sp. *cortar*, fr. Lat. *curtāre* 'shorten', denom. of *curtus* 'shortened, mutilated', fr. the root *(*s*)*ker-* (above, 2). Ernout-M. 248. REW 2418.

6. Ir. *tescaim*, above, 1.

Ir. *snaidim*, NIr. *snoidhim*, *snoighim*, W. *naddu*, all esp. 'hew, chip', beside W. *neddyf* 'adze', Br. (*n*)*eze* 'twibill' : MHG *snat*(*t*)*e* 'weal, welt', Swab. *schnatte* 'cut in wood or flesh', Swiss *schnätzen* 'carve in wood', root *snadh-. Walde-P. 2.694. Otherwise Pedersen 2.29, 633.

Ir. *scothaim* 'cut off' : Ir. *scoth* 'flower, young shoot' (8.57). Cf. VLat. *tāliāre* : *tālea*, above, 5.

NIr. *gearraim*, fr. MIr. *gerraim* 'cut off, shorten', fr. *gerr* 'short' (12.59).

W. *torri*, also 'break', as Br. *terri* 'break', see 9.26.

W. *trychu*, Br. *trouc'ha*, beside W. *trwch* 'broken, maimed', MCorn. *trehy* 'hew', prob. fr. *truk-s- : Lith. *trukti* 'rend, break, burst', OE *þrycean* 'press', etc. (Walde-P. 1.731). G. S. Lane, Language 13.27 f. (vs. Walde-P. 1.758, etc.).

Br. *skeja* 'cut, split' : Grk. *σχίζω* 'split' (9.27). Walde-P. 2.544.

7. Goth. *maitan*, ON *meita*, OHG *meizan*, MHG *meizen*, beside sbs. ON *meitill*, OHG *meizil* 'chisel', OHG *meizo* in *stein-meizo* 'stonecutter', perh. fr. an extension of a root *mai- in Ir. *mael* 'bald, hornless', OW *mail* 'mutilum' (**mai-los* 'cut off'), ON *meiða* 'injure, mutilate', beside *smī-* in Grk. *σμίλη* 'knife for carving', OE *smiþ* 'smith', etc. Walde-P. 2.222. Feist 341 f. Falk-Torp 709.

Goth. *sneiþan* (renders *θερίζω* 'reap', but *uf-sneiþan* 'kill' for sacrifice), ON *sniða*, OE *snīþan* (early ME *sniþen*, NE dial. *snithe*), Du. *snijden*, OHG *snīdan*, MHG *snīden*, NHG *schneiden*, beside OHG *snit* 'cut', MHG *snitzen* 'carve (wood)', OE *snǣs*, ON *sneis* 'spit', outside root connections dub. Walde-P. 2.695 f. Feist 440. Falk-Torp 1097.

ON *telgja* : Ir. *dlongim* 'split' (9.27), fr. an extension of *del- in Lat. *dolāre* 'hew' (9.45). Walde-P. 1.812. Falk-Torp 1252.

ON *hǫggva*, Dan. *hugge*, Sw. *hugga*, OE *hēawan*, ME *hewe*, NE *hew*, Du. *houwen*, OHG *houwan*, MHG *houwen*, NHG *hauen* (common Gmc. use 'strike with a cutting instrument, cut by a blow', whence in part 'hew, carve', also 'hoe', 8.25) : ChSl. *kovati* 'forge', Russ.

kovat' 'forge, hammer', etc., Lith. *kauti* 'beat, hew', refl. 'fight', Lat. *cūdere* 'pound, knock, forge', Toch. A *ko-*, B *kau-* 'kill' (SSS 434). Walde-P. 1.330. Falk-Torp 426. Walde-H. 1.300 f.

OE *ceorfan*, ME *cerve* (NE *carve*) : OHG *kerban*, NHG *kerben* 'notch, cut', Grk. *γράφω* 'scratch, write', IE *gerbh-. Walde-P. 1.607.

ME *cutte*, NE *cut*, prob. loanword fr. Norse, cf. Norw. *kutte* 'cut', Sw. *kåta* 'whittle', Icel. *kuta* 'cut with a knife', Sw. dial. *kute*, *kytte*, Icel. *kuti* 'knife', outside connections? NED s.v. *cut*, vb. Falk-Torp 598. Hellquist 514.

8. Lith. *piauti*, prob. : Lat. *pavīre* 'beat, tread, stamp down', perh. Grk. *παίω* 'strike' (9.21). Walde-P. 2.12.

Lith. *kirsti*, Lett. *cirst*, above, 2.

Lith. *rėžti*, ChSl. *rězati*, SCr. *rezati*, Boh. *řezati*, Russ. *rezat'*, Pol. *rznąć*, root connection dub. Walde-P. 2.344. Trautmann 245. Brückner 476 f.

Lett. *griezt*, iter. *graizīt* : Lith. *griėžti* 'cut in a circle', further connection? Mühl.-Endz. 1.662.

9. ChSl. *rězati*, etc., above, 8.

ChSl. *sěšti*, etc., above, 1.

ChSl. *-krojiti*, Boh. *krájeti*, Pol. *krajać*, above, 2.

Pol. *ciąć*, above, 3.

Pol. *rąbać*, Russ. *rubit'* (both esp. 'cut wood, fell trees'; Boh. *roubiti* 'hew'), ChSl. *rąbŭ* 'pannus', Pol. *rąb*, *rąby* 'seam' etc. (as 'cut off piece'), but outside connections dub. Miklosich 281. Brückner 455.

10. Skt. *kṛt-*, Av. *kərət-*, above, 2.

Skt. *chid-* : Grk. *σχίζω* 'split', etc. (9.27), cf. Br. *skeja*, above, 6.

Skt. *lu-* prob. : Grk. *λύω* 'loose, free', Lat. *luere* 'atone, pay', etc., with development fr. 'cut, separate', to 'loose', etc. Walde-P. 2.407. Walde-H. 1.834.

Skt. *ças-* (cf. *çastra-* 'knife, sword') : Lat. *castrāre* 'castrate'. Walde-P. 1.448. Ernout-M. 160. Walde-H. 1.179.

Av. *θwarəs-* : Grk. *σάρξ* 'flesh', perh. OHG *dwerah* 'across' (as 'cut across'?), root *twerk̑-. Walde-P. 1.751.

Av. *brī-* (only with *pairi-* 'cut around'), NPers. *burrīdan* 'cut' : Skt. *bhrī-* 'injure', ChSl. *briti* 'shear', *britva* 'razor'. Walde-P. 2.194.

9.23 KNIFE

Grk.	*μάχαιρα*	Goth.	. . . .	Lith.	*peilis*
NG	*μαχαίρι*	ON	*knīfr*	Lett.	*nazis, peilis*
Lat.	*culter*	Dan.	*kniv*	ChSl.	*nožĭ*
It.	*coltello*	Sw.	*knif*	SCr.	*nož*
Fr.	*couteau*	OE	*seax, cnīf*	Boh.	*nůž*
Sp.	*cuchillo*	ME	*knife*	Pol.	*nóż*
Rum.	*cuțit*	NE	*knife*	Russ.	*nož*
Ir.	*scian*	Du.	*mes*	Skt.	*çastra-, kṛti-churikā-*
NIr.	*scian*	OHG	*mezzisahs, mezzira(h)s*	Av.	*karəta-*
W.	*cyllell*	MHG	*me(z)zer*		
Br.	*kontell*	NHG	*messer*		

Many of the words for 'knife' are from roots for 'cut', most of these appearing in the verbs discussed in 9.22. Others are connected with words for 'fight, sharpen, pierce, pinch(?)', etc., the orig. application being in part obscure.

Although 'knife' as an implement is primarily intended here, most of the words are used also, and some occur most frequently, for 'knife' as a weapon. But words used only for a special type of knife are not listed, as for 'penknife' NG

σουγιάς (fr. Turk.), Fr. *canif* (fr. Gmc.), Rum. *briceag* (fr. blend of Turk. and Slavic), etc.

1. Grk. *μάχαιρα*, dim. *μαχαίριον*, NG *μαχαίρι* : Grk. *μάχομαι* 'fight', *μάχη* 'battle', but root connection dub. See 20.11.

2. Lat. *culter*, dim. *cultellus* (> It. *coltello*, Fr. *couteau*, Sp. *cuchillo*, also W. *cyllell*, Br. *kontell*), either by dissim. fr. *(*s*)*ker-* in words for 'cut' (9.22), or fr. *(*s*)*kel-* in words for 'split, cut', like Lith. *skelti* 'split', etc. Walde-P. 2.592. Ernout-M. 240. Walde-H. 1.304. REW 2381. Loth, Mots lat. 152, 156.

Rum. *cuțit*, fr. a **cōtītus* 'sharpened', deriv. of Lat. *cōs*, *cōtis* 'whetstone' (Rum. *cute*). Cf. Rum. *ascuți* 'whet, sharpen' fr. **excōtīre*. Tiktin 471. Pușcariu 41.

3. Ir., NIr. *scian*, fr. an extension of *sek- in Lat. *secāre* 'cut', etc. (9.22). Walde-P. 2.542. Pedersen 1.68.

4. ON *knīfr*, Dan. *kniv*, Sw. *knif*, OE *cnīf* (later than *seax* and prob. fr. Scand.), ME, NE *knife*, MLG *knīf* (> NHG *kneif* 'short curved knife'; fr. Gmc. also Fr. *canif* 'penknife'), prob. (as orig. 'pruning knife'?) with MLG *knīpen* 'pinch' : Lith. *gnybti* 'pinch', etc. Walde-P. 1.581 f. Falk-Torp 550, 548.

OE *seax* : ON *sax*, OHG *sahs* 'large knife, short sword', Lat. *saxum* 'stone', fr. the same root as Lat. *secāre* 'cut', etc. (9.22). Hence cpds. with word for 'food', orig. 'knife for cutting food' but not so restricted in actual use, OE *meteseax*, OHG *mezzi-sahs*, *mezzira*(*h*)*s*, *mezers*, etc., MHG *mez*(*z*)*er*, NHG *messer*, Du. *mes*. Weigand-H. 2.171 f. Kluge-G. 388.

5. Lith., Lett. *peilis* (also OPruss. *peile*, *-peilis*), prob. with Slavic *pila* 'saw' (9.48), fr. OHG *fīla* 'file'. Buga, Kalba ir Senovė 187.

Lett. *nazis*, prob. fr. Russ. *nož* 'knife' (cf. foll.), rather than cognate with it. Mühl.-Endz. 2.697.

6. ChSl. *nožĭ*, etc., general Slavic : ChSl. *pro-noziti* 'pierce through', etc., outside connections? Walde-P. 2.326 f. Brückner 364, 367. Miklosich 214.

7. Skt. *kṛti-* (RV), Av. *karəta-* and *karəti-* (NPers. *kārd* 'knife'), fr. Skt. *kṛt-*, Av. *kərət-* 'cut' (9.22). Barth. 454. Wackernagel-Debrunner, KZ 67.157.

Skt. *çastra-* 'knife, dagger, sword', fr. Skt. *ças-* 'cut' (9.22).

Skt. *churikā-*, with MInd. *ch*, fr. *kṣurikā-* : *kṣura-*, Grk. *ξυρόν* 'razor', etc. Walde-P. 1.450. Uhlenbeck 95.

9.24 SCISSORS, SHEARS

Grk.	*ψαλίς*	Goth.	. . . .	Lith.	*žirklės*
NG	*ψαλίδι*	ON	*skæri, sǫx*	Lett.	*šk'ēres, zirkles*
Lat.	*forficēs*	Dan.	*saks*	ChSl.	. . . .
It.	*forbici, cesoie*	Sw.	*sax*	SCr.	*škare, nožice, makaze*
Fr.	*ciseaux, cisailles*	OE	*scēara*	Boh.	*nůžky*
Sp.	*tijeras*	ME	*sisours, schere*	Pol.	*nożyce*
Rum.	*foarfeci*	NE	*scissors, shears*	Russ.	*nožnicy*
Ir.	*demess*	Du.	*schaar*	Skt.	*kartarī-, kṛpāṇī-*
NIr.	*siosūr, deimheas*	OHG	*scār(a),*	Av.	. . . .
W.	*siswrn, gwellaif*	MHG	*schær(e)*		
Br.	*sizailhou, gweltre*	NHG	*schere*		

Words for 'scissors, shears' are mostly from roots for 'cut' or esp. 'shear'. Some are pl. or deriv. forms of the word for 'knife'. One group is a cpd. of the word for 'hair'.

1. Grk. *ψαλίς, -ίδος*, late dim. *ψαλίδιον*, NG *ψαλίδι*, Aeol. *σπαλίς* : *σφαλάσσειν· τέμνειν, κεντεῖν* Hesych., Skt. *phal-* 'burst'. Walde-P. 2.677. Boisacq 890.

2. Lat. *forfex*, esp. pl. *forficēs* (> OIt. *forfice*, It. *forbici*, Rum. *foarfeci*, pl.), history complicated and disputed. Prob. fr. *forceps* 'pair of tongs, forceps' (cpd. of *formus* 'warm' and root of *capere* 'take') with phonetic changes (through an intermediate *forpex* by dissim.) and shift of application from 'tongs' to 'shears' owing to the similarity of shape. Walde-H. 1.526 f. (with full refs.). REW 3435.

It. *cesoie* (not common), OFr. *cisoires* fr. VLat. **caesōrium, *cisōrium*, fr. *caedere* 'cut down, strike' (9.21). REW 1475.

Fr. *ciseaux*, pl. of *ciseau* 'chisel', fr. VLat. **cisellum* for **caesellum* : *caedere* (cf. above). REW 1474.

Fr. *cisailles*, esp. 'metal-shears', fr. VLat. **cisālia* for *caesālia*, pl. of adj. *caesālis* : *caedere* (above). REW 1472.

Sp. *tijeras*, more usual than sg. *tijera* (Port. *tesoura*, OFr. *tesoir*), fr. Lat. *tōnsōria* (sc. *ferrāmenta*) 'barber's instruments', fr. *tōnsor* 'barber' : *tondēre* 'shear, shave'. REW 8784.

3. Ir. *demess*, NIr. *deimheas*, lit. 'double knife', fr. prefix *de-* beside *dē-* 'two' (Thurneysen, Gram. 246) and deriv. of root in Lat. *metere*, Br. *medi* 'reap, harvest', etc. Walde-P. 2.259. Pedersen 1.162 f., 2.127.

NIr. *siosūr*, W. *siswrn*, fr. English (below, 4).

W. *gwellaif*, OW *guillihim*, Br. *gweltre*, *gwentle*, MBr. *guelteff*, cpds. of the words for 'hair' seen in W. *gwallt* (lost in Br.), second member dub. Pedersen 2.29 (without mention of the Br. word, which seems clearly connected with the W., though taken otherwise by Henry 150).

Br. *sizailhou* pl., fr. Fr. *cisailles* (above, 2).

4. ON *skœri* pl., OE *scēara* (pl., rarely sg. *scēar*), ME *schere*, NE *shears* (Sc. and dial. still 'scissors', but usually applied only to the larger implement), Du. *schaar*, OHG *scār, scāra, scera*, MHG *schœr, schære*, NHG *schere* : ON *skera*, OE *sceran* 'cut, shear', etc. (9.22). Weigand-H. 2.697. NED s.v. *shear*, sb.

ON *sǫx* pl., as orig. also Dan. *saks*, Sw. *sax*, in sg. ON *sax* 'large knife, short sword' = OE *seax* 'knife', etc. (9.23). Falk-Torp 944. Hellquist 890.

ME *sisours*, NE *scissors*, fr. OFr. *cisoires* (above), but influenced in NE spelling by fancied deriv. fr. Lat. *scissor* 'one who cleaves, divides' (: *scindere* 'split, cut, rend'). NED s.v.

5. Lith. *žirklės*, Lett. *zirkles*, perh. with dissim. fr. IE **ĝhḷtlo-*, beside **ĝhelto-* in Goth. *gilþa* 'sickle'. Walde-P. 1.629. Otherwise Mühl.-Endz. 4.728.

Lett. *šk'ēres*, fr. MLG *schere* (: MHG *schœre*, etc., above). Mühl-Endz. 4.34.

6. SCr. *nožice*, Boh. *nůžky*, Pol. *nożyce*, Russ. *nožnicy*, all pl. derivs. of the Slavic words for 'knife', SCr. *nož*, etc. (9.23).

SCr. *škare*, Slov. *škarje*, fr. OHG *skāri*, pl. of *scār* (above). Miklosich 298.

SCr. *makaze* fr. Turk. *makas* 'scissors'. Berneker 2.9.

7. Skt. *kartarī-* 'shears' or 'dagger, knife', see 9.23.

Skt. *kṛpāṇī-* 'shears' or 'dagger', beside *kṛpāṇa-* 'sword' : Lith. *kirpti* 'cut with shears', Lat. *carpere* 'gather, pluck', etc., fr. extension of **sker-* 'cut' (9.22). Walde-P. 2.580. Uhlenbeck 64.

Skt. (Vedic) *bhurijāu* (du.), meaning 'scissors' dub. (Macdonell-Keith 2.107). Walde-P. 2.181.

9.25 AX

Grk.	*πέλεκυς, ἀξίνη*	Goth.	*aqizi*	Lith.	*kirvis*
NG	*τσεκούρι*	ON	*øx (barða)*	Lett.	*cirvis*
Lat.	*secūris (bipennis, ascia)*	Dan.	*økse*	ChSl.	*sěkyra (brady)*
It.	*ascia, scure*	Sw.	*yxa*	SCr.	*sjekira (bradva)*
Fr.	*hache*	OE	*æx*	Boh.	*sekera (topor)*
Sp.	*hacha (segur)*	ME	*ax, ex*	Pol.	*siekiera (topór)*
Rum.	*topor, secure,*	NE	*ax*	Russ.	*topor*
Ir.	*biail, tūag*	Du.	*bijl*	Skt.	*paraçu-, kuṭhāra*
NIr.	*tuagh, biail*	OHG	*acchus, bīhal, barta*	Av.	*taša-*
W.	*bwyall*	MHG	*aches, bīl, barte*		
Br.	*bouc'hal*	NHG	*beil, axt*		

For 'ax' there is one inherited group, of obscure root connection. The Grk. and Skt. words reflect a prehistoric borrowing from a non-IE, Asiatic, source. The other words are from various roots for 'cut' or 'strike'.

While 'ax' as an implement is primarily intended here, the same words serve also in older periods for the weapon, the 'battle-ax' (cf. 20.222).

The primitive celt served as either 'ax' or 'adze' (i.e. with blade at right angles to the handle) according to the way it was mounted. Some of the older IE words probably covered both types, and many of the distinctive terms for 'adze' are either compounds of those for 'ax' (e.g. NHG *krummaxt, zimmeraxt*) or cognate with others for 'ax', as Lat. *ascia* (below, 1), Ir. *tāl*, ON *þexla*, Russ. *tesla*, etc. (below, 8). Among other words for 'adze' are Grk. *σκέπαρνον*, NG *σκεπάρνι*, prob. : Russ. *ščepat'* 'chip, split' (Walde-P. 2.559, Boisacq 873); Fr. *herminette*, deriv. of *hermine*, based on the resemblance of the animal's muzzle to the adze-blade; OE *adesa*, ME *adese*, NE *adze*, orig. unknown (NED s.v.).

1. IE form and root connection dub., but clearly a cognate group. Walde-P. 1.39. Ernout-M. 74 f. Walde-H. 1.71 f. Feist 54. REW 696.

Grk. *ἀξίνη* (but NG *ἀξίνα, ξινάρι* 'mattock'); Lat. *ascia* (an adze-shaped tool of carpenters, masons, etc., Daremberg et Saglio s.v.; > OFr. *aisse*, It. *ascia*, the latter now 'ax' including but not restricted to the 'adze'; derivs. Fr. *aisseau, aissette*, Sp. *azuela* 'adze'); Goth. *aqizi*, ON *øx*, OE *æx*, OHG *acchus*, etc.

2. Grk. *πέλεκυς* : Skt. *paraçu-* (below, 8), both early loanwords fr. a source represented by Akkad. *pilakku*, Sumer. *balag* 'ax'. Boisacq 761. Schrader, Reallex. 1.68.

NG *τσεκούρι* (Byz. *σικούριον, τζικούριον*), fr. Lat. *secūris* (below, 3). G. Meyer, Neugr. Stud. 3.67.

3. Lat. *secūris* (> It. *scure*, Rum. *secure*; Sp. *segur* obs.) : ChSl. *sěkyra*, etc. (below, 7), fr. the root of Lat. *secāre* 'cut', etc. (9.22). Walde-P. 474 f. Ernout-M. 914.

Lat. *bipennis* 'two-edged ax' (both tool and weapon), cpd. of *bi-* 'two-' and *penna* 'wing'. Ernout-M. 753.

Fr. *hache* (dim. *hachette* > ME *hachet*, NE *hatchet*), Prov. *apcha* (> Sp. *hacha*, OIt. *accia*), fr. a Gmc. **hapja* (MLat. *hapia*) seen in OHG *happa, heppa* 'sickle-shaped knife', this prob. : Grk. *κόπτω* 'strike, cut', *κοπίς* 'cleaver', etc. (9.21). Walde-P. 2.560. REW 4035. Gamillscheg 502.

Rum. *topor*, fr. Bulg. *topor* (below, 7).

4. Ir. *biail*, W. *bwyall*, Br. *bouc'hal* : ON *bildr, bilda* 'cutting tool', OE *bill* 'kind of broadsword', OHG *bīhal* (**bīpl-*), MHG *bīl*, NHG *beil*, Du. *bijl* 'ax', fr. the root in Ir. *benim* 'strike cut',

ChSl. *biti* 'strike' (9.21). Walde-P. 2.137. Pedersen 1.67. Falk-Torp 73. Walde-H. 1.503. Otherwise on Gmc. words (fr. the root of Lat. *findere*, Skt. *bhid-* 'split') Weigand-H. 1.190. Kluge-G. 47. Pisani, KZ 67.226 f.

Ir. *tūag*, NIr. *tuagh* : Ir. *tuagaim* 'hack, chop', Skt. *tuj-* 'strike', ON *þoka* 'move, change', etc. Walde-P. 2.616.

5. Goth. *aqizi*, OE *æx*, etc., above, 1.

ON *barða*, OS *barda*, OHG *barta*, MHG *barte*, derivs. of words for 'beard' (OHG *bart*, OE *beard*), fr. the resemblance of the projecting ax-head to the shape of a beard. Walde-P. 2.135. Falk-Torp 395.

OHG *bīhal*, etc., above 4. On the distribution of NHG *beil* and *axt*, see Kretschmer, Wortgeogr. 108 f.

6. Lith. *kirvis*, Lett. *cirvis* : Skt. *kṛvi-* 'a weaver's instrument' (prob. also Skt. *kuṭhāra-* 'ax'), Russ. (dial.) *červ'* 'sickle', fr. IE **(s)ker-* in Grk. *κείρω* 'shear', OE *sceran* 'cut', etc. (8.22). Walde-P. 2.576. Berneker 172.

7. ChSl. *sěkyra*, etc., general Slavic (Russ. *sekira* obs. for tool, but used for 'battle-ax') : Lat. *secūris* (above, 3).

Late ChSl. *brady*, SCr. *bradva*, loanword fr. Gmc., cf. OHG *barta*, etc. (above, 5). Berneker 73. Stender-Petersen 222 f.

Late ChSl. *toporŭ*, Boh., Pol., Russ. *topor* (in Russ. now the regular word for the common ax; in Boh., Pol. special kinds, partly 'adze'), widespread loanword (cf. also ON *tapar-øx* 'battle-ax', OE *taper-æx* 'small ax') corresponding to Finno-Ugrian and Iranian words (e.g. Finn. *tappara*, NPers. *tabar*), ultimate source dub. Lokotsch 1264. Brückner 573. Jacobsohn, Arier. und Ugro-Finnen 204. Specht, KZ 61.34.

8. Skt. *paraçu-*, fr. same source as Grk. *πέλεκυς* (above, 2).

Av. *taša-* (so NPers. *taš* 'ax') : Ir. *tāl* (**tōkslo-*), ON *þexla*, OHG *dehsa(la)*, NHG *dechsel*, SCr., Boh., Russ. *tesla* (> Rum. *teslă*), all 'adze', fr. the root of Skt. *takṣ-*, Av. *taš-* 'hew' (9.45). Walde-P. 1.717.

9.26 BREAK (vb. trans.)

Grk.	*ῥήγνῡμι, κατ-ἄγνῡμι, κλάω, θραύω*	Goth.	*brikan*	Lith.	*laužti*
NG	*σπάζω, τσακίζω*	ON	*brjōta (rjūfa)*	Lett.	*lauzt*
Lat.	*frangere, rumpere*	Dan.	*bryde, brække*	ChSl.	*lomiti*
It.	*rompere, spezzare*	Sw.	*bryta, bräcka*	SCr.	*lomiti*
Fr.	*casser, rompre, briser*	OE	*brecan (brēotan, rēofan)*	Boh.	*lamati, lomiti*
Sp.	*romper, quebrar*	ME	*breke*	Pol.	*łamać*
Rum.	*sparge, frînge (rupe)*	NE	*break*	Russ.	*lomat'*
Ir.	*brissim, conboing (3 sg.)*	Du.	*breken*	Skt.	*bhañj-*
NIr.	*brisim*	OHG	*brehhan*	Av.	*sčand-*
W.	*torri*	MHG	*brechen*		
Br.	*terri*	NHG	*brechen*		

Among the several words for 'break' in some of the languages, one or the other may be preferred in particular phrases (according to the kind of object broken, whether broken into two or into many pieces, etc.), but such differentiation is too vague and diverse to be taken account of here.

Even between 'break' and 'tear' or 'split', owing to a similarity in result, there is some overlapping and shift.

1. Grk. *ῥήγνῡμι* (*ϝρηγ-* attested in Lesb. *ϝρῆξις*) : Arm. *ergic-uçanem* 'break', other connections dub. Walde-P. 1.319.

Grk. *ἄγνῡμι* (mostly poet., or cpd. *κατ-*), etym.? Walde-P. 1.319. Boisacq 8.

Grk. *κλάω* : Lith. *kalti* 'hammer, forge', Lat. *per-cellere* 'strike down', etc. (9.21).

Grk. *θραύω*, etym. dub. Walde-P. 1.872. Walde-H. 1.553.

NG *σπάζω* or *σπάνω* (with new presents to aor. *ἔσπασα*), fr. class. Grk. *σπάω* 'draw' (9.33), also 'tear, rend' whence the NG 'break'.

NG *τσακίζω*, prob. of imitative origin. Pernot, Recueil, p. 4.

2. Lat. *frangere* (> It. *frangere* not common, OFr. *fraindre*, Rum. *frînge*, etc.; REW 3482) : Goth. *brikan*, OE *brecan*, etc. (below, 4). Walde-P. 2.200. Ernout-M. 386 f. Walde-H. 1.541. Feist 105.

Lat. *rumpere* (> It. *rompere*, Fr. *rompre*, Sp. *romper;* Rum. *rupe* now mostly 'tear') : ON *rjūfa*, OE *rēofan* 'break', Skt. *rup-* 'feel spasms', Lith. *rupėti* 'be anxious', etc., fr. **reup-*, prob. an extension of **reu-* in Lat. *ruere* 'fall down', Skt. *ru-* 'break into pieces', etc. Walde-P. 2.354 f. Ernout-M. 876 f.

It. *spezzare*, deriv. of *pezza* 'piece'. REW 6450.

Fr. *casser*, fr. Lat. *quassāre* 'shake, shatter'. REW 6939. Gamillscheg 192.

Fr. *briser*, fr. a Gallic form answering to Ir. *brissim* 'break' (below, 3). REW 1306. Gamillscheg 150. Wartburg 1.534 f.

Sp. *quebrar*, fr. Lat. *crepāre* 'rattle, crack', through 'burst' (cf. It. *crepare*, Fr. *crever*, Rum. *crăpa* 'burst, die'). REW 2313.

Rum. *sparge*, fr. Lat. *spargere* 'strew, scatter' (9.34), whence first (and still esp.) 'break into small pieces'. REW 8120. Tiktin 1465 f.

3. Ir. *brissim*, NIr. *brisim* (cf. Fr. *briser*, fr. a corresponding Gallic form; also Corn. *bresel* 'strife', MBr. *bresel*, Br. *brezel* 'war') : Skt. *bhrī-* 'injure', Av. *brī-* 'cut', ChSl. *briti* 'shear', etc. Walde-P. 2.194, 206.

Ir. *con-boing* (3sg.), cf. *bong-* (vbl. n. *buain*) 'reap, break' : Skt. *bhañj-* 'break' (see below, 7). Walde-P. 2.150. Pedersen 2.477. Stokes 177.

W. *torri* (older *torri*), cf. W. *tor*, Br. *torr* 'a break, cut', perh. fr. *torp-* : Lith. *tarpas* 'interval, interstice' (i.e. 'a break'), *trapus* 'fragile', etc. (Walde-P. 1.732). G. S. Lane, Language 13.27.

4. Goth. *brikan*, OE *brecan*, etc., general WGmc. (Dan. *brække*, Sw. *bräcka*, fr. MLG *breken*) : Lat. *frangere*, above, 2.

ON *brjōta*, Dan. *bryde*, Sw. *bryta*, OE *brēotan* (cf. also OHG *brōdi* 'fragile', ON *broma* 'fragment', OE *bryttian* 'divide, dispense', etc.), fr. IE **bhreu-*, perh. an extension of **bher-* in Lat. *ferīre* 'strike', etc. (9.21). Walde-P. 2.195 f. Hellquist 105.

ON *rjūfa*, OE *rēofan* : Lat. *rumpere*, above, 2.

5. Lith. *laužti*, Lett. *lauzt* : Skt. *ruj-* 'break, destroy', Grk. *λυγρός* 'mournful', Lat. *lūgēre* 'mourn', OE *tōlūcan* 'break in pieces', OHG *liohhan* 'pull, tear out', fr. IE **leug-*. Walde-P. 2.412 f. Walde-H. 1.830 f.

6. ChSl., SCr., Boh. *lomiti*, Pol. *łomić*, Russ. *lomat'*, and with different grade ChSl. *prělamati*, Boh. *lamati*, Pol. *łamać* : ON *lami*, OE *lama*, etc. 'lame, crippled', ON *lemja* 'beat, flog', Lett. *l'imt* 'break down under a load', OPruss. *limtwei* 'break', etc., fr. IE **lem-*. Walde-P. 2.433 f. Berneker 688, 731.

7. Skt. *bhañj-* : Arm. *bekanem* 'break', Ir. *bong-* 'break, reap', *con-boing* 'breaks' (above, 3), Lith. *banga* 'wave, billow'. Walde-P. 2.149 f.

Av. *sčand-* (in caus. form *sčandaya-, sčindaya-*; cf. sb. *skənda-*; Barth. 1586 f.), perh. : Ir. *scandaim* 'split', ON *skinn* 'skin, hide', etc. Walde-P. 2.563 f.

9.27 SPLIT (vb. trans.)

Grk.	*σχίζω*	Goth.	....	Lith.	*skelti*
NG	*σχίζω, σκίζω*	ON	*kljūfa*	Lett.	*šk'elt*
Lat.	*findere*	Dan.	*spalte, kløve, splitte*	ChSl.	*cěpiti*
It.	*fendere, spaccare*	Sw.	*splittra, klyva*	SCr.	*cijepati*
Fr.	*fendre*	OE	*clēofan*	Boh.	*štipati*
Sp.	*hender, rajar*	ME	*cleve*	Pol.	*łupać, szczepać*
Rum.	*despica*	NE	*split (cleave)*	Russ.	*kolot', ščepat'*
Ir.	*dlongim*	Du.	*splijten*	Skt.	*bhid- (dṛ-, chid-)*
NIr.	*scoiltim*	OHG	*spaltan, klioban*	Av.	*dar- (sid-)*
W.	*hollti*	MHG	*spalten*		
Br.	*faouta*	NHG	*spalten*		

In words for 'split' the distinctive notion is 'cut in two along the length, the grain, etc.', though they may also be used more broadly for 'sever, divide'. Many are from roots that appear also in words for 'cut', 'tear', 'flay', etc.

1. Grk. *σχίζω* : Skt. *chid-* 'cut off, split', Av. *sid-* 'split, destroy', Lat. *scindere*, sometimes 'split' (*cuneis lignum*, etc.), mostly 'tear', Goth. *skaidan* 'separate', Lith. *skiesti*, Lett. *šk'iest* 'separate', etc., with numerous and complicated root connections. Walde-P. 2.543 f. Ernout-M. 905 f.

2. Lat. *findere* (> It. *fendere*, Fr. *fendre*, Sp. *hender*) : Skt. *bhid-* 'split', Goth. *beitan*, ON *bīta*, OE *bītan*, etc. 'bite', fr. IE **bheid-*. Walde-P. 2.138. Ernout-M. 360 f. Walde-H. 1.500 f.

It. *spaccare*, fr. Gmc. (Langob. **spahhan*), cf. MHG *spachen* 'split', OHG *spahha* 'dry twig', of which further connections are dub. Walde-P. 2.652. REW 8114.

Sp. *rajar*, deriv. of *raja* 'a crack, slice', this fr. Lat. *rādula* 'scraper'? REW 7001.

Rum. *despica*, fr. late Lat. *dēspīcāre* 'break apart, break open' (*despicatis foribus, tectis*, Rönsch, Coll. phil. 295 f.; *despicatis* glossed by *patefactis, disruptis, incisis*, also *spiculatis decoriatis*, CGL 6.331.), same word as *dēspīcāre* (cf. Du Cange s.v.) used with *bladum* for 'pluck grain', that is 'break off the ears', deriv. of Lat. *spīca* 'ear of grain'. REW 2600 (but "Vögel rupfen"?). Puşcariu 524. Candrea-Hecht, Romania 31.307.

3. Ir. *dlongim, dluigim* : ON *telgja* 'whittle', OE *telga* 'branch, bough', Lith. *dalgis*, Lett. *dalgs* 'scythe', fr. **delgh-*, **dlegh-*, an extension of **del-* in Skt. *dal-* 'burst', Lat. *dolāre* 'hew', etc. Walde-P. 1.809 f., 812. Pedersen 1.43, 2.507.

NIr. *scoiltim*, W. *hollti*, Br. *faouta*, derivs. of Ir. *scoilt*, W. *hollt*, Br. *faout* 'a cleft, split' : Lith. *skelti* 'split', ON *skilja* 'divide', Grk. *σκάλλω* 'stir up, hoe', MIr. *scāilim* 'let loose, scatter', etc. Walde-P. 2.590 ff. Pedersen 1.77. Otherwise for the W. and Br. forms (fr. **spolto-* : OHG *spaltan*, etc.) Loth, RC 32.420.

4. ON *kljūfa*, Dan. *kløve*, Sw. *klyva*, OE *clēofan*, ME *cleve*, NE *cleave* (arch.), Du. *klieven*, OHG *klioban*, NHG *klieben* : Grk. *γλύφω* 'carve', Lat. *glūbere* 'peel', etc. Walde-P. 1.661. Walde-H. 1.610 f. Falk-Torp 542.

Du. *splijten* (MHG *splīzen*, NHG *spleissen*) and *splitten* (MDu. > NE *split*; MLG > Dan. *splitte*), MHG *splitteren* (> Sw. *splittra*), NHG *splittern*, all fr. a **spleid-*, prob. connected with **sp(h)el-* of the following group. Walde-P. 2.684. Falk-Torp 1126. NED s.v. *split* vb.

OHG *spaltan*, MHG, NHG *spalten*, with Goth. *spilda* 'tablet', etc. (prob. also, with secondary meaning, the group ON *spilla*, OE *spildan*, *spillan* 'destroy')

: Skt. *sphuṭ-* (*ṭ* fr. *lt*) 'burst, split open', *phal-* 'burst, ripen', Grk. *σφαλάσσειν· τέμνειν, κεντεῖν* (Hesych.), etc., fr. a root **(s)p(h)el-*. Walde-P. 2.677 f. Falk-Torp 1111.

5. Lith. *skelti*, *skaldyti*, Lett. *šk'elt*, *skaldīt* (cf. ChSl. *skala* 'cliff, stone', Russ. *ščel'* 'a cleft', etc.) : NIr. *scoiltim*, etc., above, 3.

6. Late ChSl. *cěpiti*, SCr. *cijepati* (cf. Russ. dial. *cepinka* 'stick, staff', etc.) perh. : Grk. *σκῖπων*, Lat. *scīpiō* 'staff', ON *skīfa* 'slice', and by parallel root extensions, Grk. *σχίζω*, etc. (above, 1). Walde-P. 2.545 (cf. also 1.364). Berneker 125.

Boh. *štipati*, Pol. *szczepać*, Russ. *ščepat'* : ChSl. *skopiti* 'castrate', Grk. *σκάπτω* 'dig', etc. Walde-P. 2.559 ff. Brückner 543.

Pol. *łupać* (also Ukr. *łupaty* 'split') : *łupić* 'peel, flay, plunder', Boh. *loupati*, *-iti* 'peel, plunder', Russ. *lupit'* 'peel', SCr. *lupiti* 'strike a blow', Lith. *lupti* 'peel, flay', Goth. *laufs* 'leaf', etc., perh. Skt. *lup-* 'break'. Walde-P. 2.417 f. Berneker 746.

Russ. *kolot'* : ChSl. *klati* 'stab, slay', Boh. *klati* 'stab, split', Lith. *kalti*, Lett. *kalt* 'strike, forge', etc. Walde-P. 1.438. Berneker 551 f.

7. Skt. *bhid-* : Lat. *findere*, above, 2.

Av. *dar-* : Skt. *dṛ-* 'burst, tear, split', Grk. *δέρω* 'flay', OE *teran* 'tear', etc., IE **der-*. Walde-P. 1.797 ff.

Skt. *chid-*, Av. *sid-* : Grk. *σχίζω*, above, 1.

9.28 TEAR (vb. trans.)

Grk.	*σπαράσσω*	Goth.	*tahjan, distairan*	Lith.	*plėšti, drėksti*
NG	*ξεσχίζω*	ON	*rīfa, slīta*	Lett.	*plēst, draskāt*
Lat.	*scindere*	Dan.	*rive*	ChSl.	*dĭrati*
It.	*stracciare*	Sw.	*riva, slita*	SCr.	*kidati, trgati*
Fr.	*déchirer*	OE	*teran, slītan*	Boh.	*trhati, rvati*
Sp.	*rasgar, desgarrar*	ME	*tere, rende, ryve*	Pol.	*drzeć, rwać*
Rum.	*rupe*	NE	*tear (rend)*	Russ.	*rvat', drat'*
Ir.	*rēbaim*	Du.	*scheuren*	Skt.	*dṛ-*
NIr.	*rēabaim, s(t)racaim*	OHG	*slīzan, zerran, rīzan*	Av.	*niš-dar*
W.	*rhwygo*	MHG	*slīzen, zerren, rīzen*		
Br.	*regi*	NHG	*reissen*		

Words for 'tear' are used, partly distinguished by prefixes, for 'tear in two, in pieces' or for 'tear off' (from the main body). In the latter sense they overlap with 'flay, pull, snatch, pluck, etc.' But many words that may be rendered 'tear off' as an emphatic expression for 'pull off with violence' and do not cover the other use of 'tear' are not considered here. Several of the words, though listed in the simplex, are more commonly used in cpds., as NHG *zerreissen*, Russ. *raz-dirat'*, etc., lit. 'tear apart'.

1. IE **der-* in words for 'tear' and 'flay' (9.29). Walde-P. 1.797 ff. Feist 120. Berneker 185.

Here as 'tear' : Goth. *dis-tairan* 'tear, burst' (leather bottles, where Grk. *ῥήγνυμι*; also *ga-tairan* 'destroy, break'), OE *teran*, ME *tere*, NE *tear*, OHG *zerran*, MHG *zerren* (NHG 'tear off, pull, tug'; OHG *fir-zeran* 'destroy', NHG *verzehren* 'consume'); ChSl. *dĭrati*, Pol. *drzeć*, Russ. *drat'*, *dirat'* (SCr. *derati*, Boh. *drati* mostly in secondary uses); Skt. *dṛ-* 'burst, tear' Av. *niš-dar-* 'tear out' (Barth. 689). Cf. also Toch. *tsär-* 'separate' (SSS 483).

2. Grk. *σπαράσσω* (*σπαραγ-* as in *σπάραγμα* 'a piece torn off', *σπαραγμός* 'a tearing, rending') prob. with connection through 'noise of tearing' : Skt. *sphūrj-* 'rumble, crash', Lith. *spragėti* 'crackle', etc. (Walde-P. 2.672 ff., but *σπαράσσω* separated, 2.668). Persson, Beiträge 869.

NG *ξεσχίζω*, cpd. (with *ξε-* for *ἐξ-* as reg., fr. *ἐξε-* in augmented forms) of *σχίζω* 'split' (9.27).

3. Lat. *scindere* (also 'split') : Grk. *σχίζω* 'split', etc. (9.27).

It. *stracciare*, with OFr. *estracier* 'tear', fr. **extractiāre* (influenced in use by *dis-*) : Lat. *extrahere*, *distrahere*, cpds. of *trahere* 'draw, pull'. REW 2692. Wartburg 2.331.

Fr. *déchirer*, cpd. form of OFr. *eschirer*, prob. fr. a Frank. **skīran* : OE *scīran* 'make clear' (: OE *scīr* 'clear, bright', etc., 15.57), ON *skīra*, OFris. *skīrja* 'cleanse, purify', EFris. *schiren* also 'smooth off', etc., with development through 'scrape off' to 'tear off'. Cf. on Lith. *bielyti* 'flay', 9.29. Braune, Z. rom. Ph. 20.355 ff. Gamillscheg 295. Otherwise REW 7990.

Sp. *rasgar* (beside *rascar* 'scratch'), fr. **rāsicāre*, deriv. of Lat. *rādere* 'scrape, scratch' (pple. *rāsus*). REW 7074.

Sp. *desgarrar*, deriv. of *garra* 'a claw', prob. fr. Gallic, cf. W. *gar* 'thigh', Br. *gar* 'leg'. REW 3690.

Rum. *rupe* (also 'break'), fr. Lat. *rumpere* 'break' (9.26).

4. Ir. *rēbaim*, NIr. *rēabaim*, etym.? (Stokes 228 : ON *rīfa*, etc., below, 5).

NIr. *stracaim* (*sracaim*, Dineen), Gael. *srac* etym.?

W. *rhwygo*, MBr. *roegaff* : Skt. *rikh-*, *likh-* 'rend, scratch', Lith. *rekti* 'cut bread', Grk. *ἐρείκω* 'rend', etc., fr. IE **reik(h)-* an extension (parallel to **reip-* in ON *rīfa*, etc., below, 5) of **rei-*. Walde-P. 2.343 f. Pedersen 1.122.

Br. *regi*, prob. a variant of *rega* 'to furrow', a deriv. of OBr. *rec* = W. *rhych* 'furrow' (8.212). Henry 231.

5. Goth. *distairan*, OE *teran*, OHG *zerran* etc., above, 1.

Goth. *tahjan* (for *σπαράσσω* 'tear', also for *σκορπίζω* 'scatter') : Goth. *tagl* 'hair', OE *tægl* 'tail', etc. (4.18), Skt. *daçā-* 'fringe of cloth'. Goth. development through 'shred, tear in shreds'. Walde-P. 1.785. Feist 470 f. (with alternative view).

ON *rīfa*, Dan. *rive*, Sw. *riva* (ME *rive*, *ryve* fr. Norse) : Grk. *ἐρείπω* 'tear down', fr. IE **reip-*, an extension of **rei-*. Walde-P. 2.345. Falk-Torp 906.

ON *slīta*, Sw. *slita*, OE *slītan* (NE *slit*), OHG *slīzan*, MHG *slīzen* (NHG *schleissen* 'slit'), prob. fr. an extension of **skel-* in Lith. *skelti* 'split', etc. (9.27). Walde-P. 2.595 f.

OE *rendan*, ME *rende*, NE *rend*, OFris. *renda*, not elsewhere in Gmc. and outside connections dub. Walde-P. 2.374, 578. NED s.v. *rend*, vb.[1].

Du. *scheuren*, MDu. *scoren* (cf. Du. *scheur*, MDu. *score* 'a rent, tear', ON *skor* 'notch, cleft' (> OE *scoru*, NE *score*) : ON *skera*, OE *sceran* 'cut', etc. (9.22). Franck-v.W. 584. Walde-P. 2.576.

OHG *rīzan* (mostly 'cut into, write', but also 'tear'), MHG *rīzen*, NHG *reissen*, esp. *zerreissen* : OE *wrītan* 'carve, write', etc., but both phonetic (parallel forms with or without init. *w*?) and semantic relations complicated. Walde-P. 1.287, 2.344. Weigand-H. 2.563. Falk-Torp 897. Feist 574.

6. Lith. *plėšti*, Lett. *plēst* : ON *flā*, OE *flēan*, etc. 'flay' (9.29). Walde-P. 2.98.

Lith. *drėksti*, *draskyti*, Lett. *draskāt* : OBoh. *z-dřieskati* 'break in pieces', Boh. *dřizhati* 'slice, split', etc., fr. IE **dre-sk-*, an extension of **der-* (above, 1). Walde-P. 1.803. Berneker 220 f., 224.

7. ChSl. *dĭrati*, etc., above, 1.

ChSl. *trŭgnǫti*, *trugati*, *trŭzati* (mostly in cpds. meaning 'tear off, pluck', SCr. *trgati*, Boh. *trhati* (both also 'pluck'), prob. (with variants of final guttural) : Lat. *tergēre* 'wipe off', Skt. *tṛh-* 'crush'. Walde-P. 1.732.

SCr. *kidati* : Russ. *kidat'* 'throw', ChSl. *iskydati* 'throw out', ON *skjōta*, OE *scēotan*, OHG *sciozan* 'shoot', etc. Walde-P. 2.554. Berneker 676.

Boh. *rvati*, Pol. *rwać*, Russ. *rvat'* : ChSl. *rŭvati* 'tear off, pluck', Lith. *rauti* 'root out', Lett. *raut* 'pluck, carry off, etc.', perh. Lat. *ē-ruere* 'tear out, pluck out' (but history of Lat. *ruere* and cpds. difficult), Skt. *ru-* 'break in pieces', etc. Walde-P. 2.352. Brückner 470.

8. Skt. *dṛ-*, Av. *niš-dar-* above, 1.

9.29 FLAY, SKIN

Grk.	*δέρω*	Goth.	....	Lith.	*dirti, bielyti, lupti*
NG	*γδέρνω*	ON	*flā*	Lett.	*dīrāt*
Lat.	*dēglūbere*	Dan.	*flaa*	ChSl.	*(dĭrati)*
It.	*scorticare*	Sw.	*flå*	SCr.	*derati, guliti*
Fr.	*écorcher*	OE	*flēan, hyldan*	Boh.	*dřiti*
Sp.	*desollar*	ME	*fle(n)*	Pol.	*zdzierać, łupić*
Rum.	*jupui*	NE	*flay, skin*	Russ.	*sdirat'*
Ir.	*fennaim*	Du.	*villen*	Skt.	....
NIr.	*feannaim*	OHG	*scintan, fillen*	Av.	*vī-naθ-*
W.	*blingo, digroeni*	MHG	*schinden, villen*		
Br.	*digroc'henna*	NHG	*schinden, häuten*		

Words for 'flay' are mostly from roots seen also in words for 'tear' or 'peel' or are derivs. of words for 'skin, hide'.

Secondary uses, as 'flog, despoil, plunder', etc., are widespread, and in some languages 'flay' in the old literal sense is now more commonly expressed by new derivs. of words for 'skin' (so NE *skin*, not *flay*, in common use), or by phrases containing them (Russ. *sdirat' kožu*, etc.), though such phrases are not entered in the list.

1. IE **der-* in words for 'flay' and 'tear' (9.28). Walde-P. 1.797 ff.

Here as 'flay' : Grk. *δέρω* (with *δέρμα*, *δορά* 'skin, hide'), NG *γδέρνω* (fr. *ἐκδέρω*); Lith. *dirti*, Lett. *dīrāt*, ChSl. *dĭrati* (quotable as 'flay'?), SCr. *derati*, Boh. *dřiti*, Pol. *drzeć*, (z)*dzierać*, Russ. *drat'*, *sdirat'*, etc.; Arm. *teřem*.

2. Lat. *dēglūbere*, cpd. of *glūbere* 'peel' : Grk. *γλύφω* 'carve, engrave', OE *clēofan* 'split, cleave', etc. (9.27). Walde-P. 1.661. Ernout-M. 426 f. Walde-H. 1.610 f.

It. *scorticare*, Fr. *écorcher*, fr. late Lat. *excorticāre* 'flay' (so used in Form. Andec., e.g. Pirson, Merow. und Karol. Formuläre, No. 7), deriv. of Lat. *cortex* 'bark'. REW 2988. Gamillscheg 340.

Sp. *desollar*, cpd. of *des-* = Lat. *dis-* and a deriv. of Lat. *follis* 'leathern bag'. REW 3422.

Rum. *jupui*, etym.? Tiktin 880 f.

3. Ir. *fennaim*, NIr. *feannaim*, etym. dub. G. S. Lane, Language 13.24.

W. *blingo*, etym. dub., perh. fr. a variant form of the root seen in Dan. *flænge* 'slash' and without nasal in ON *flā* 'flay', etc. (below, 4). Loth, RC 41.229 f.

W. *digroeni*, Br. *digroc'henna* cpd. of *di-* priv. and W. *croen*, Br. *kroc'henn* 'skin, hide' (4.12).

4. ON *flā*, Dan. *flaa*, Sw. *flå*, OE *flēan*, ME *fle(n)*, NE *flay* : Lith. *plėšti* 'tear'

(9.28), etc. Walde-P. 1.98. Falk-Torp 228.

OE (*be-*)*hyldan*, fr. *hold* 'carcass' = ON *hold* 'flesh' (4.13).

NE *skin* = sb. *skin* used verbally.

Du. *villen*, OHG *fillen*, MHG *villen* (but mostly in OHG and often in MHG 'flog, scourge'), derivs. of Du. *vel*, etc. 'skin, hide' (4.12).

OHG *scintan*, MHG, NHG *schinden*, deriv. of OHG **scind* : ON *skinn* 'skin, hide', etc. (4.12).

NHG *häuten*, deriv. of *haut* 'skin, hide' (4.12).

5. Lith. *dirti*, Lett. *dīrāt*, above, 1.

Lith. *bielyti*, fr. WhRuss. *běliti* 'flay' = Russ. *belit'* 'whiten, bleach' : ChSl. *bělŭ* 'white', etc. (15.64). Cf. Bulg. *bělja* 'bleach', also 'peel' and 'flay' (Gerof s.v.), Sorb. *bělić* also 'peel'. Development apparently through 'cleanse' > 'scrape off' > 'peel, flay', (cf. history of Fr. *déchirer* 'tear', 9.28). Buga, Kalba ir Senovė 28. Berneker 55.

Lith. *lupti* (but mostly and orig. 'peel') : Lett. *lupt* 'peel', Russ. *lupit'*, etc. 'peel' (Pol. *łupić* also 'flay'), Goth. *laufs*, etc. 'leaf', perh. Skt. *lup-* 'break'. Walde-P. 2.417 f. Berneker 746.

6. SCr. *derati*, etc., above, 1.

SCr. *guliti*, etym.? Berneker 362.

Pol. *łupić* : Lith. *lupti*, above, 5.

7. Skt. *dṛ-* not quotable for 'flay'. Other words?

Av. *vī-naθ-*, root connection? Barth. 1038.

9.31 RUB

Grk.	*τρῑβω*	Goth.	*bnauan*	Lith.	*trinti*
NG	*τρίβω*	ON	*gnūa*	Lett.	*berzt, trit*
Lat.	*fricāre, terere*	Dan.	*gnide*	ChSl.	*trěti*
It.	*fregare*	Sw.	*gnida*	SCr.	*trljati, ribati*
Fr.	*frotter*	OE	*gnīdan*	Boh.	*třiti*
Sp.	*frotar, fregar*	ME	*gnīde* (*gnodde*), *rubbe*	Pol.	*trzeć*
Rum.	*freca*	NE	*rub*	Russ.	*teret'*
Ir.	*commelim*	Du.	*wrijven*	Skt.	*ghṛṣ-*
NIr.	*cuimlim*	OHG	*gnītan, rīban*	Av.	. . . .
W.	*rhwbio*	MHG	*gnīten, rīben*		
Br.	*frota*	NHG	*reiben*		

For 'rub' there is one considerable inherited group. There are more or less probable connections with words for such various notions as 'scrape', 'gnaw', 'grind', 'turn around' (hence first 'rub with a circular motion'), 'strike, break' (hence first 'rub to pieces'), etc.

1. IE **ter-*, with extensions **trī-*, **treu-*. Here kept apart fr. **ter-*, etc. in words for 'bore' (9.46), though generally thought to be ultimately the same, fr. an orig. notion of 'rub with circular motion'. Walde-P. 1.728 ff. Ernout-M. 1032 ff.

Grk. *τρῑβω* (*τρῑ-β-*, cf. Lat. *trīvī, trītus;* the common word for 'rub' down to the present day; in secondary uses *τείρω*, *τρύω* 'wear out, distress', *τρῦχω* 'waste, consume'); Lat. *terere* (*trīvī, trītus*); Lith. *trinti*, Lett. *trit;* ChSl. *trěti* (**terti*), SCr. *trti* (with deriv. *trljati*), Boh. *třiti*, Pol. *trzeć*, Russ. *teret'*.

2. Lat. *fricāre* (> It. *fregare*, Sp. *fregar*, Rum. *freca*), VLat. also **frictāre* (> Fr. *frotter* > Sp. *frotar*, Br. *frota;* but explanation of *o* dub.; REW 3505, Gamillscheg 445 f., Wartburg 3.787) : *friāre* 'rub to pieces', this perh. : Skt. *bhrī-* 'hurt, injure', ChSl. *briti* 'shear', and ultimately Lat. *ferīre* 'strike', etc. Walde-P. 2.194. Ernout-M. 389. Walde-H. 1.549.

Lat. *terere* (much less common than *fricāre* for plain 'rub'; used esp. for 'thresh' and mostly 'wear out, waste'), above, 1.

3. Ir. *commelim*, NIr. *cuimlim*, cpd. of *com-* and *melim* 'grind' : Lat. *molere* 'grind', etc. (5.56). Pedersen 2.577.

W. *rhwbio*, fr. NE *rub*. Parry-Williams 160.

Br. *frota*, fr. Fr. *frotter*. Henry 126.

4. Goth. *bnauan*, ON *bnūa* (rare), prob. cpd. *bi-*, but root connection dub. (ON *nūa*, OHG *nūan* here or to foll.?), Feist 101. Falk-Torp 335.

ON *gnūa* (Norw. *gnu*), also *gniða* (rare), OE *gnīdan*, ME *gnīde* (*gnodde*), OHG *gnītan*, MHG *gnīten*, MLG *gnīden* (> Dan. *gnide*, Sw. *gnida*), perh. with various extensions : Grk. *χναύω* 'gnaw, nibble', OE *gnagan* 'gnaw', etc., or with variant init. : Grk. *κνάω*, *κνίζω* 'scrape', etc., all uncertain. Walde-P. 1.584 f. Falk-Torp 334, 335.

ME *rubbe*, NE *rub*, with East Fris. *rubben* 'scrape, rub', Dan. *rubbe* 'rub, scour', Sw. *rubba* 'move from one place to another', prob. : OE *rēofan* 'break, rend', etc. (9.26). Walde-P. 2.355. Falk-Torp 915.

OHG *rīban*, MHG *rīben*, NHG *reiben*, Du. *wrijven*, perh. as orig. 'turn around', then 'rub with circular motion, rub' : Grk. *ῥίψ* 'wickerwork', *ῥίπτω* 'throw' (cf. 10.25), fr. an extension of **wer-* in words for 'turn, twist', etc. (10.13). Walde-P. 1.280. Franck-v. W. 806 f. Otherwise (with ON *rīfa* 'tear' : Grk. *ἐρείπω* 'tear down') Falk-Torp 906.

5. Lith. *trinti*, Lett. *trit*, above, 1.

Lett. *berzt*, prob. through 'break in pieces, rub to pieces', with intr. *birzt* 'break in pieces, crumble', fr. an extension of **bher-* in Lat. *ferīre* 'strike', etc. Walde-P. 2.195. Mühl.-Endz. 1.280.

6. ChSl. *trěti*, etc., above, 1.

SCr. *ribati*, fr. NHG *reiben*.

7. Skt. *ghṛṣ-* : Russ. *goroch* 'pea' (fr. 'rubbed down, kernel'), etc., and, with different root extensions, Grk. *χρίω* 'rub the body, anoint', *χράω*, fut. *χραύσω* 'scrape, graze', etc. Walde-P. 1.605, 646, 648 f.

Av. word for 'rub'? NPers. *mālīdān* 'rub, polish' : Av. *marəz-* 'touch lightly', Skt. *mṛj-* 'wipe, rub, polish'. Barth. 1152 f.

9.32 STRETCH

Grk.	*τείνω*	Goth.	*uf-þanjan*	Lith.	*tęsti, tempti*
NG	*τεντώνω* (*ἐκτείνω* lit.)	ON	*þenja*	Lett.	*stiept*
Lat.	*tendere*	Dan.	*strække spænde*	ChSl.	*rastęšti*
It.	(*s*)*tendere*	Sw.	*sträcka, spänna* (*tänja*)	SCr.	*rastegnuti*
Fr.	(*é*)*tendre*	OE	*þennan, streccan*	Boh.	*roztáhnouti, napínati*
Sp.	*tender*	ME	*strecche*	Pol.	*rozciągnąć*
Rum.	*întinde*	NE	*stretch*	Russ.	*rastjanut'*
Ir.	*sīnim*	Du.	*strekken, spannen*	Skt.	*tan-*
NIr.	*sīnim*	OHG	*dennen, strecchan, spannan*	Av.	*tan-*
W.	*estyn*	MHG	*den(n)en, strecken, spannen*		
Br.	*astenn*	NHG	*dehnen, strecken, spannen*		

The majority of the words for 'stretch' belong to an inherited group. In this group and in some of the other words there are frequent relations between 'stretch' and 'draw, pull' (9.33), and, besides the words listed, there are others for 'pull out' virtually equivalent to 'stretch', as It. *stirare*, Sp. *estirar*, etc.

From the central notion of 'stretch' involving tension come a great variety of special uses, as 'stretch out, put forth' (the hand, etc.), 'reach for, tend', 'spread out, extend, lengthen', etc., with considerable divergence in this respect between the different words (as 'tend, strive' esp. in Lat. *tendere*, 'extend, lengthen' dominant in NHG *dehnen*). Conversely, some one of these notions may be the more original, as in the case of NE *stretch* (cf. below, 5), or if a word for 'lengthen' is used for 'stretch', as It. *allungare*.

1. IE **ten-*, with extensions. Walde-P. 1.722 ff., also 721, 726, 727. Ernout-M. 1026 f. Brückner 61.

Grk. *τείνω* (**τέν-ι̯ω*); Lat. (*ten-d-* beside *ten-* in *tenēre* 'hold', *tenuis* 'thin', and *tentus*, old pple. of *tendere*) *tendere* (> It. *tendere*, Fr. *tendre*, Sp. *tender*), *extendere* (> It. *stendere*, Fr. *étendre*), *intendere* (> Rum. *întinde*); W. *estyn*, Br. *astenn*, fr. Lat. *extendere*, beside W. *tynnu*, Br. *tenna* 'pull' fr. Lat. *tendere* (but cf. also Loth, Mots lat. 165); Goth. *uf-þanjan*, ON *þenja* (Norw. dial. *tenja;* Sw. *tänja*, nearly obs.), OE *þennan*, OHG *dennen*, MHG *denen*, NHG *dehnen;* Lith. *tęsti* (**ten-s-*, cf. Skt. *taṅs-* 'shake', Goth. *at-þinsan* 'draw', etc.) and *tempti* (**tem-p-*, cf. Lat. *tempus* 'time', etc.); ChSl. *rastęšti*, *rastęgnąti*, cpd. of *raz-* 'apart' and *tęgnąti* 'draw' (this prob. fr. a guttural extension of **ten-;* cf. 9.33) and so (or in part with other prefixes) SCr. *rastegnuti*, Boh. *roztáhnouti*, Pol. *rozciągnąć*, Russ. *rastjanut';* Skt., Av. *tan-*.

2. NG (beside lit. *ἐκτείνω*) *τεντώνω*, orig. 'pitch a tent' (so in Chron. Morea, etc.), deriv. of Byz. *τέντα*, fr. MLat. *tenta* 'tent' (7.14), this fr. Lat. *tendere*, *tentus* (above, 1).

3. Lat. *tendere*, etc., above, 1.

4. Ir., NIr. *sīnim*, perh. : ON *seilask* 'stretch out the hands or arms', and as orig. 'throw out (the hands, etc.) : Skt. *sāyaka-* 'missile' and numerous words commonly grouped under an IE **sēi-* 'throw' and 'sow'. Walde-P. 2.459 ff., esp. 460 (bottom) f.

W. *estyn*, Br. *astenn*, above, 1.

5. Goth. *uf-þanjan*, ON *þenja*, etc., above, 1.

OE *streccan*, ME *strecche*, NE *stretch*, OHG *strecchan*, MHG, NHG *strecken* (MLG > Dan. *strække*, Sw. *sträcka*), Du. *strekken*, all in the early period (so OE, OHG), and still mostly in NHG 'stretch out the body or limbs' and so as orig. 'make stiff, straighten out' : OE *stræc* 'severe, stern' (fig. use of 'rigid'), OHG *strach* 'stiff, rigid, straight', beside OE *stearc* 'stiff, strong', OHG *stark* 'strong, great', Grk. *στερεός* 'hard, stiff'. Walde-P. 2.629. Falk-Torp 1185. NED s.v. *stretch*, vb.

OHG *spannan* 'draw tight, stretch' (a bow, etc.), also 'fasten', MHG, NHG *spannen*, Du. *spannen*, Dan. *spænde*, Sw. *spänna*, all partly 'stretch', but in many other uses : OE *spannan* 'fasten', Grk. *σπάω* 'draw', etc. Walde-P. 2.655 f. Falk-Torp 1139.

6. Lith. *tęsti* and *tempti*, above, 1.

Lett. *stiept* : Lith. *stiepti* 'stretch the body, stand on tiptoe', *stīpti* 'become stiff' (with death or cold), OE *stīf* 'stiff', Lat. *stīpāre* 'press together', etc. Semantic development as in NE *stretch* (above, 5). Walde-P. 2.646 ff.

7. ChSl. *rastęšti*, etc., above, 1.

ChSl. *pęti* in *ras-(pro-)pęti* 'stretch out, crucify', Boh. *pnouti*, *na-(roz-)pínati*, etc. : Lith. *pinti* 'plait' (9.75), Goth. *spinnan* 'spin' (6.31), etc., IE *(*s*)*pen-*. Walde-P. 2.660 f. Trautmann 219.

8. Skt., Av. *tan-*, above, 1.

9.33 DRAW, PULL

Grk.	*ἕλκω, σπάω, ἐρύω*	Goth.	*atþinsan*	Lith.	*traukti*
NG	*σέρνω, τραβῶ*	ON	*draga, toga*	Lett.	*vilkt*
Lat.	*trahere* (*dūcere*)	Dan.	*trække, drage*	ChSl.	*vlěšti* (*tęgnąti*)
It.	*tirare* (*trarre*)	Sw.	*draga*	SCr.	*vući*
Fr.	*tirer*	OE	*tēon, dragan*	Boh.	*táhnouti*
Sp.	*tirar, sacar*	ME	*drawe*	Pol.	*ciągnąć*
Rum.	*trage*	NE	*draw, pull*	Russ.	*tjanut'*
Ir.	*srengim tairrngim*	Du.	*trekken*	Skt.	*kṛṣ-*
NIr.	*tarraingim*	OHG	*ziohan, dinsan*	Av.	*θanj-, karš-*
W.	*tynnu*	MHG	*ziehen*		
Br.	*tenna*	NHG	*ziehen*		

Only the more generic words for 'draw' are listed, with exclusion of many others, like NE *drag*, *trail*, *tug*, *tow*, etc. (and so for other languages), which fall under the general notion and in many cases are cognate with the generic words (or even orig. identical as NE *draw* and *drag*), but are used with more restricted application.

1. Grk. *ἕλκω* : Lat. *sulcus* 'furrow', OE *sulh* 'furrow, plow', Alb. *helk*, *hek* 'pull, tear off', fr. IE **selk-*, beside **welk-* in Lith. *vilkti*, etc. (below, 5), both fr. **swelk-* (?). Walde-P. 2.507. Ernout-M. 999 f.

Grk. *σπάω* : OE, OHG *spanan* 'entice, attract' (fr. 'draw'), *spannan* 'fasten', perh. Av. *spā-* 'throw' (fr. 'draw forth'?), with common notion of 'draw' and root forms **spā-*, **spə-*, **spen-*. Walde-P. 2.655 f.

Grk. *ἐρύω* (**ϝερύω*), etym. dub., perh. **weru-* remotely connected with **wers-* in Lat. *verrere* 'sweep', etc. Walde-P. 1.293.

NG *σέρνω* (lit. *σύρω*), fr. class. Grk. *σύρω* 'drag, trail', etym. dub. Walde-P. 2.530. Boisacq 849.

NG *τραβῶ* (*τραυῶ*), with metathesis fr. *ταυρῶ* = Byz. *ταυρίζω* 'pull', a deriv. of *ταῦρος* 'bull'. Cf. NE colloq. *pull like a steer.* Hatzidakis, Μεσ. 1.85 f.

2. Lat. *trahere* (> Rum. *trage* still the common word for 'draw', but It. *trarre* less common than *tirare;* Fr. *traire* specialized to 'milk'; Sp. *traer* 'lead, bring, wear', etc.; deriv. VLat. *tragīnare* > Fr. *traîner;* REW 8837, 8841), prob. with variant initial (*t, dh*) : OE *dragan*, etc. (below, 4). Walde-P. 1.752 f., 862. Ernout-M. 1050 f.

Lat. *dūcere*, mostly 'lead' but also and orig. 'draw' : Goth. *tiuhan*, etc. (below, 4).

It. *tirare*, Fr. *tirer*, Sp. *tirar*, etym. much disputed, but best explained as based on a pop. aphetic form of VLat. *martyrare* 'make a martyr of, torture' with special reference to the stretching on the rack. Serra, Dacoromania 5.437. (REW 8755, adversely).

Sp. *sacar* 'pull out', fr. *saco* 'sack, bag' (Lat. *saccus*) and 'plunder'. REW 7489.

3. Ir. *srengim*, with cpd. *do-srenga* (3sg.), vbl. n. *tarraing*, whence *tairrngim*, NIr. *tarraingim* : Grk. *στραγγός* 'twisted', Lat. *stringere* 'draw tight, OE *streng* 'string, cord', etc. Walde-P. 2.650. Pedersen, 1.81, 2.637.

W. *tynnu*, Br. *tenna*, fr. Lat. *tendere*

'stretch'. Pedersen 1.198. Loth, Mots lat. 213.

4. Goth. *tiuhan* (but mostly 'lead'; ON **tjūga*, pple. *toginn*), OE *tēon*, OHG *ziohan*, MHG, NHG *ziehen*, also caus. ON *teygja*, and fr. weak grade (cf. ON *tog* 'rope, cord') ON *toga*, OE *togian* (NE *tow*) : Lat. *dūcere* 'draw, lead', Grk. δαι-δύσσεσθαι· ἕλκεσθαι (Hesych.), fr. IE **deuk-*. Walde-P. 1.780 f. Ernout-M. 287. Walde-H. 1.377. Falk-Torp 1315. Feist 478 f.

Goth. *at-þinsan*, OHG *thinsan*, *dinsan* : Lith. *tęsti* 'stretch', etc. (9.32). Walde-P. 1.727. Feist 62.

ON *draga*, Dan. *drage*, Sw. *draga*, OE *dragan*, ME *drawe*, *drage*, NE *draw*, *drag*, also Goth. *ga-dragan* 'bring together', OHG *tragan* 'bear, carry', prob. with variant initial : Lat. *trahere* (above, 2), other connections remote and dub. Walde-P. 1.862. Feist 123. Falk-Torp 151.

MLG *trecken* (> Dan. *trække*), Du. *trekken* = OHG *trehhan* 'shove, etc.', perh. : Lett. *dragāt* 'tear, shake', and fr. an extension of **der-* in words for 'tear'. Walde-P. 1.801. Falk-Torp 1292. Franck-v.W. 708.

OE *(a)pullian*, ME *pulle*, NE *pull*, in early period 'pluck, snatch, pull with violence', and still with something of this feeling, but often only a colloq. equivalent of *draw*. Etym. ? NED s.v. *pull*, vb.

5. Lith. *traukti* : Lett. *traukt* 'strike, knock down', Lith. *trūkti* 'tear, break' (intr.), perh. : ON *þrūga*, OHG *drucken* 'press', etc. Walde-P. 1.731. Mühl.-Endz. 4.225.

Lith. *vilkti* (now 'drag', but once 'draw' whence refl. or *vilkėti* 'put on clothes, wear'), Lett. *vilkt*, ChSl. *vlěšti*, *vlěką* (in Gospels *pri-vlěšti*), SCr. *vući* ('draw' or 'drag'; but Boh. *vleci*, Pol. *wlec*, Russ. *voloč'*, *voločit'* 'drag') : Grk. αὖλαξ (*ἀϝλακ-) 'furrow', Av. *varək-* 'draw' in cpds. (Barth. 1366), all fr. **welk-*. (cf. **selk-* in Grk. ἕλκω, etc., above, 1). Walde-P. 1.306.

6. ChSl. *vlěšti*, etc., above, 5.

ChSl. (late) *tęgnąti*, SCr. *-tegnuti*, Boh. *táhnouti*, Pol. *ciągnąć*, Russ. *tjanut'*, all with cpds. meaning 'stretch', and prob. fr. a guttural extension of **ten-* 'stretch', though taken by some as a wholly different root **theng(h)-* on account of Av. *θanj-* 'draw', etc. Walde-P. 1.726 f. (with many dub. connections). Brückner 61.

7. Skt. *kṛṣ-*, Av. *karš-*, both 'draw' (so Av. only in cpds.; NPers. *kašīdan* 'draw') and 'draw furrows, plow', with Skt. *karṣū-*, Av. *karša-* 'furrow', etc., outside connections dub. Walde-P. 1.429.

Av. *θanj-*, apparently, but with unexplained initial (also in *θanvan-*, *θanvar-* 'bow') : ChSl. *tęgnąti*. See above, 6.

9.34 SPREAD OUT, STREW

Grk.	*στόρνῡμι, στρώννῡμι*	Goth.	*straujan*	Lith.	*ištiesti, kloti, berti, kreikti*
NG	*στρώνω*	ON	*breiða, strā*	Lett.	*klāt, kaisīt, bērt*
Lat.	*sternere, spargere*	Dan.	*brede ud, strø*	ChSl.	*postĭlati, rasypati*
It.	*stendere, spargere, spandere*	Sw.	*breda ut, strö*	SCr.	*sterati, prostrijeti, sipati*
Fr.	*étendre, répandre*	OE	*(ge)brǣdan, strēowian, stregdan*	Boh.	*prostříti, stláti, sypati, trousiti*
Sp.	*tender, esparcir*	ME	*sprede, strewe*	Pol.	*słać, sypać*
Rum.	*aşterne, împrăştia*	NE	*spread, strew*	Russ.	*stlat', razstilat', sypat'*
Ir.	*sernim, assrēdim*	Du.	*uitbreeden, strooien, spreiden*	Skt.	*stṛ-*
NIr.	*leathnuighim, sprēidhim*	OHG	*streuwen, breiten, spreitan*	Av.	*star-*
W.	*taenu, chwalu*	MHG	*breiten, ströuwen, spreiten*		
Br.	*astenn, streoui, skuilh*	NHG	*ausbreiten, streuen (spreiten)*		

The somewhat disparate notions suggested by the English words of the heading, with their widely different areas of usage, are combined here because they are interwoven and virtually one in the early uses of the widespread cognate group to which NE *strew* belongs (below, 1). In this the central notion seems to be 'spread out over a surface', with two types of application which have tended to become differentiated, namely *a*) 'spread bedding over a bed, a garment on the ground' or the like, and *b*) with small detached objects 'spread branches, leaves, flowers, sand over the ground' or the like, as NE *strew*—both conveniently illustrated in the NT, Mt. 21.8, Mk. 11.8, where the people spread their garments and strewed branches in the way, expressed alike by Grk. *στρωννύω*, Lat. *sternere* in the Vulgate, Goth. *straujan*, OE *streōwian* (so *strew* in Wyclif, but separated in Tyndale). Both types of application are common in Greek (down to the present day), Latin, and Indo-Iranian, and in part elsewhere. So Goth. *straujan* and in part OHG *streuwen*, but with a tendency in Gmc. to restrict the application to type *b* 'strew', as in present English. For type *a* are employed other words for 'spread out, stretch out' or the like, too numerous to be fully noted here.

From phrases of type *b*, 'strew' absorbed the notional element of dispersal and so came into a certain relation with 'scatter', in which this is the dominant element, without becoming identical in range with the latter. Thus NE *strew* and *scatter* may be used indifferently in many connections (as *strew* or *scatter* stones on the ground), but the old element of 'over the surface' is still felt in *strew* as contrasted with the more generic *scatter*. On the other hand, several of the words entered here to cover 'strew' are used without any such feeling of difference between 'strew' and 'scatter', though the latter is most apt to be expressed by cpds. or intensive forms, as Lat., It. *dispergere*, Fr. *disperser*, NHG *zerstreuen*, Russ. *razsypat'*, Lith. *išberti* or intens. *barstyti*. But it is not intended to cover here the general notion of 'scatter' for which there are numerous other words of totally different connections, e.g., Grk. *σκεδάννῡμι* and NE *scatter* (both resting on the notion of 'split', Walde-P. 2.558), Grk. *διασκορπίζω* (prob. : Lat. *carpere* 'pluck'), Goth. *distahjan* (cpd. of *tahjan* 'tear'), ChSl. *rastočiti*

(lit. 'make run apart' : *teką*, *tešti* 'run'), etc.

Apart from the inherited group, the connections are mostly with words for 'stretch', 'throw', 'pour', and 'broad'.

1. IE **ster-*, *streu-*, etc. Walde-P. 2.638 ff. Ernout-M. 973 f.

Grk. *στόρνῡμι*, *στρώννῡμι*, *στρωννύω*, NG *στρώνω*; Lat. *sternere* (hence or with *ad-*, Rum. *aşterne*, OFr. *esternir*, etc.; REW 8248, Puşcariu 151), and in different use *struere* 'pile up, construct'; Ir. *sernim*, Br. *streoui;* Goth. *straujan*, OE *strēowian*, etc., general Gmc. (also perh. with different extension or by some analogy OE *stregdan*); SCr. *sterati*, *prostrijeti*, Boh. *prostříti* (but ChSl. *prostrěti*, Russ. *prostirat'*, etc. rather 'stretch out, extend'); Skt. *stṛ-*, Av. *star-*.

2. Lat. *spargere* 'strew, scatter, sprinkle' (> It. *spargere*, Sp. *esparcir*), prob. fr. an extension of **sp(h)er-* in Grk. *σπείρω* 'scatter seed, sow', Arm. *spʿrem* 'scatter', etc. (Walde-P. 2.670 ff.), rather than (as Walde-P. 2.673) more directly to Skt. *sphūrj-* 'roar, crash, burst forth', etc., which seem to be of imitative origin. Walde-P. l.c. Ernout-M. 959 f.

It. *stendere*, Fr. *étendre*, Sp. *tender*, all lit. 'stretch, stretch out', fr. Lat. *tendere* 'stretch' (9.32) or cpds. REW 3083.

It. *spandere*, Fr. *répandre*, fr. cpds. of Lat. *pandere* 'unfold, expand, lay open' (: *patēre* 'stand open', Grk. *πετάννῡμι* 'spread out, apart, open', etc. Walde-P. 2.18). REW 3030.

Rum. *împrăştia*, deriv. of *praştie* 'a sling', fr. ChSl. *prašta* id., orig. then 'sling, throw'. Cf. Ir. *as-srēdim* (below, 3).

3. Ir. *sernim*, Br. *streoui*, above, 1.

Ir. *assrēdim*, cpd. of *srēdim* 'throw', prob., with unoriginal *d-*, fr. *srēim* 'throw, hurl', this fr. the root **ster-* in *sernim* 'strew, spread', etc. (above, 1). Pedersen 2.626.

NIr. *sprēidhim*, fr. ME *sprede*, NE *spread*.

NIr. *leathnuighim*, fr. *leathan* 'broad, wide'.

W. *taenu*, fr. *taen* 'a spreading, sprinkling', perh. fr. **(s)tagnā* : Br. *ster* 'river, brook' (**stagrā*), Grk. *στάζω* 'drip', *σταγών* 'drop', Lat. *stagnum* 'pool'. 'Spread' in general sense from 'sprinkle (water) over'. Walde-P. 2.612.

W. *chwalu*, Br. *skuilh* (Ir. *scāilim* 'let loose, scatter') : ON *skilja* 'divide, separate', Lith. *skelti* 'split', etc. (9.27). Walde-P. 2.592.

Br. *astenn*, fr. Lat. *extendere* 'stretch out, extend'. Loth, Mots lat. 165 f.

4. ON *breiða*, Dan. *brede ud*, Sw. *breda ut*, OE *(ge)brǣdan*, Du. *uitbreeden*, OHG, MHG *breiten*, NHG *ausbreiten* (in the older languages orig. 'broaden, make wider'), fr. the words for 'broad, wide', ON *breiðr*, OE *brād*, OHG *breit*, etc. Walde-P. 2.194. Falk-Torp 100.

OE *sprǣdan*, only in cpds. *tosprǣdan* 'extend, expand' (wings, fingers, etc.), *ge-sprǣdan* 'extend (the hand)', *ofer-sprǣdan* 'cover (a bed)', ME *sprede*, NE *spread*, Du. *spreiden*, OHG *spreiten*, MHG, NHG *spreiten*, fr. an extension of the root **s(p)her-* seen in Grk. *σπείρω* 'sow', Lat. *spargere*, etc. (above, 2). Walde-P. 2.671.

5. Lith. *ištiesti*, lit. 'stretch out', cpd. of *tiesti* 'straighten, stretch' : *tiesus* 'straight' (12.73).

Lith. *kloti*, Lett. *klāt* : ChSl. *klasti*, *kladą* 'lay, put' (12.12), ON *hlaða*, OE, OHG *hladan* 'load', etc. Walde-P. 1.489. Mühl.-Endz. 2.218.

Lith. *berti*, Lett. *bērt* : Grk. *φέρω*, etc. 'carry', IE **bher-*, with sense 'strew, scatter' taken over from cpds. Hermann, Studi baltici 3.65 ff. Trautmann 31. Mühl.-Endz. 1.292. Otherwise Walde-P. 2.165 and Meillet, Streitberg Festgabe 258 ff.

Lith. *kreikti*, intens. *kraikyti*, beside *kreikimas* 'strewing, spreading', *kraikas* 'litter', *kraika* 'spread of flax', Lett. *kreiki* 'litter' (Mühl.-Endz. 2.270), etym.?

Lett. *kaisīt*, etym. dub. Mühl.-Endz. 2.134.

6. ChSl. *stĭlati*, *stelją* (rare in simplex; in Gospels *postĭlati* = *στρωννύω* in both uses, Mt 21.8, etc.), Boh. *stláti*, Pol. *słać*, Russ. *stlat'*, *razstilat'*, fr. a root **stel-* to be recognized also in Lat. *stlatta* 'genus navigii latum magis quam altum et a latitudine sic appellatum', *lātus* 'wide' (**stlātos*). Walde-P. 2.643. Ernout-M. 527 f.

ChSl. *rasypati*, SCr. *sipati*, Boh. *sypati*, Pol. *sypać*, Russ. *sypat'* 'pour out, shake out, strew, scatter' : Lith. *supti* 'swing, rock', Lat. *supāre* 'throw' (Festus), cpd. *dissipāre* 'scatter'. Walde-P. 2.524. Trautmann 293. Ernout-M. 1005. Walde-H. 1.356 f.

Boh. *trousiti*, Russ. *trusit'*, through sb. fr. the root of ChSl. *tręsti*, etc. 'shake' (10.26). Miklosich 360. Trautmann 330.

7. Skt. *stṛ-*, Av. *star-*, above, 1.

9.342 PRESS (vb.)

Grk.	*πιέζω (θλῑβω)*	Goth.	*þreihan*	Lith.	*spausti*
NG	*πιέζω, ζουλίζω, σφίγγω*	ON	*þryngva*	Lett.	*spiest*
Lat.	*premere*	Dan.	*trykke, presse*	ChSl.	*(tiskati, žęti, gnesti)*
It.	*premere (stringere)*	Sw.	*trycka, pressa*	SCr.	*pritisnuti*
Fr.	*presser*	OE	*þryccan*	Boh.	*tisknouti, tlačiti*
Sp.	*prensar*	ME	*presse*	Pol.	*cisnąć, scisnąć*
Rum.	*presa*	NE	*press*	Russ.	*žat', davit'*
Ir.	*fāiscim*	Du.	*drukken, persen*	Skt.	*pīd-*
NIr.	*fāiscim*	OHG	*drucchen, pressōn*	Av.	....
W.	*gwasgu*	MHG	*drucken, pressen*		
Br.	*gwaska*	NHG	*drücken, pressen*		

Verbs for 'press' are of diverse sources. Their importance is augmented by the fact that they or their compounds have given the words for many other notions, as 'express, impress, oppress, print', etc.

1. Grk. *πιέζω*, Skt. *pīd-*, fr. **pi-sed-*, **pi-zd-*, cpd. of **pi-* beside **epi* 'upon' (Grk. *ἐπί*, Skt. *api*) and **sed-* 'sit'. Walde-P. 2.486. Brugmann, Grd. 2.2.839.

Grk. *θλῑβω* (but mostly in somewhat different senses than simple 'press'), beside *θλάω* 'crush, bruise', etym. dub. Walde-P. 1.877. Boisacq 347.

NG *πιέζω*, although strictly a lit. word (the pop. development in aor. *ἔπιασα*, whence new pres. *πιάνω* 'seize', 11.14), is generally familiar.

NG *ζουλῶ*, *ζουλίζω* ('press, crush, bruise'), etym. dub., possibly fr. a pop. form of *διυλίζω* 'filter' and first used of squeezing fruits to extract the juice. Philintas, *γλωσσογνωσία* 1.146.

NG *σφίγγω* 'bind tight', also sometimes 'press, squeeze' (esp. the hand), fr. class. Grk. *σφίγγω* 'bind tight', fr. a parallel extension of the root in Lat. *spissus* 'thick, compact'. Walde-P. 2.658.

2. Lat. *premere* (> It. *premere*), perf. *pressī*, pple. *pressus*, with frequent. *pressāre* (> Fr. *presser*, Sp. *prensar;* Rum. *presa*, fr. Fr.), fr. parallel stems **prem-* and **pres-* (cf. **trem-*, **tres-* in words for 'tremble'), outside connections dub. Walde-P. 2.43. Ernout-M. 807 f. REW 6738, 6741.

3. Ir. *fāiscim*, W. *gwasgu*, Br. *gwaska*

: Grk. *ὠθέω* 'push', Skt. *vadh-* 'strike, slay', *vāh-* 'press'. Walde-P. 1.255. Pedersen 2.515. Stokes 260.

4. Goth. *þreihan*, ON *þryngva*, OE *þringan*, OHG *dringan*, etc., all of these mostly 'press around, throng', prob. : Lith. *trenkti* 'throw violently, clash', *trankus* 'jolting', Av. *θraxta-* 'crowded together' (Barth. 801.). Walde-P. 1.758 f. Falk-Torp 1293 f. Feist 501 f.

OE *þryccan*, OHG *drucchen*, MHG *drucken*, NHG *drücken* (vs. *drucken* 'print'), Du. *drukken*, Dan. *trykke*, Sw. *trycka* : Lith. *trukti* 'rend, break'. Walde-P. 1.731. Falk-Torp 1288, 1290.

OHG *pressōn*, MHG, NHG *pressen* (> Dan. *presse*, Sw. *pressa*), ME *presse*, NE *press*, Du. *persen*, fr. Lat. *pressāre* or Fr. *presser* (above, 2). Falk-Torp 848. Franck-v. W. 497.

NE *squeeze* 'press hard', etym. dub. NED s.v.

5. Lith. *spausti* : Grk. *σπεύδω* 'urge on, hasten' (14.23), Walde-P. 2.659. Trautmann 273 f.

Lett. *spiest*, prob. : *spiest*, Lith. *spiesti* 'swarm', Lat. *spissus* 'thick, compact' (12.64), etc. Walde-P. 2.658. Trautmann 274. Otherwise Mühl.-Endz. 3.1006.

6. ChSl. *tiskati* (rare; *tisnąti* 'push out'), SCr. *pritisnuti*, *pritiskivati*, Boh. *tisknouti* (*tisniti* 'oppress'), Pol. (*ciskać* 'throw') *cisnąć*, *scisnąć*, Russ. (but not the usual words for 'press') *tiskat'*, *tisnut'*, prob. fr. the same root as ChSl. *těsto*, etc. 'dough' (5.53). Walde-P. 1.702.

ChSl. *žęti*, *žimą* (late), Russ. *žat*, 1sg. *žmu* (also, but not common, SCr. *žeti*, *žmem*, Boh. *ždimati*, Pol. *żąc*, *żme*) : Grk. *γέμω* 'be full', *γένῑο* 'seized', etc. Walde-P. 1.572 ff. Miklosich 408.

ChSl. *gnesti*, *gnetą* (late, but iter. *ugnětati* 'crowd upon', Ostrom.), Boh. *hnisti* (esp. 'knead'), Russ. *gnesti* (now esp. 'oppress'), etc. : OE *cnedan*, OHG *knetan*, etc. 'knead' (5.54) Walde-P. 1.580. Berneker 311 f.

Boh. *tlačiti* : *tlouci*, ChSl. *tlŭką*, *tlěsti* 'knock, beat, strike' (9.21). Miklosich 349.

Russ. *davit'* (also 'choke, strangle') : ChSl. *daviti*, etc. 'choke', perh. : Goth. *dauþs* 'dead', etc. Berneker 181 f. Feist 118.

7. Skt. *pīd-* : Grk. *πιέζω* (above, 1).

9.35 POUR

Grk.	*χέω*	Goth.	*giutan*	Lith.	*pilti, lieti*
NG	*χύνω*	ON	*hella, skenkja*	Lett.	*liet, gāzt*
Lat.	*fundere*	Dan.	*hælde, gyde, skænke*	ChSl.	*lĭjati*
It.	*versare*	Sw.	*hälla, gjuta, skänka*	SCr.	*liti*
Fr.	*verser*	OE	*gēotan (scencan)*	Boh.	*líti*
Sp.	*verter*	ME	*gete, poure, skynke, schenche*	Pol.	*lać*
Rum.	*vărsa, turna*	NE	*pour*	Russ.	*lit'*
Ir.	*teismim, doirtim*	Du.	*gieten, schenken*	Skt.	*sic-*
NIr.	*doirtim*	OHG	*giozan, scenken*	Av.	*hič*
W.	*tywallt*	MHG	*giezen, schenken, schüten*		
Br.	*skuilh, dinaoui*	NHG	*giessen, schütten, schenken*		

Apart from the inherited group, words for 'pour' rest on such notions as 'turn', 'tip up' (the vessel), 'shake', 'make flow'.

1. IE **ĝheu-*, with extension **ĝheud-*. Walde-P. 1.563 f. Ernout-M. 440 f. Walde-H. 1.563.

Grk. *χέω*, NG *χύνω* (new present to aor. *ἔχυσα*); Lat. *fundere* (also 'cast' metals and specialized in this sense in Romance; 9.63); Goth. *giutan*, OE *gēotan*, OHG *giozan*, etc., general Gmc. (but ON *gjōta* 'cast, drop young, etc.'); Skt. *hu-*, specialized to 'pour a libation, sacrifice'.

2. It. *versare*, Fr. *verser*, Rum. *vărsa*, fr. Lat. *versāre* 'turn, wind' (fr. *vertere* 'turn'). REW 9242.

Sp. *verter*, fr. Lat. *vertere* 'turn'. REW 9249.

Rum. *turna* (esp. 'pour in', as opposed to *vărsa* 'pour out'), fr. Lat. *tornāre* 'turn (in a lathe)', but general Romance 'turn'. REW 8796.

3. Ir. *teismim* (3pl. *doesmet*, 2sg. imperat. *tessim*, etc.), fr. a cpd. **to-eks-sem-* : Lith. *semti* 'draw, dip (water)', Lett. *smelt* id. (root **sem-*). Walde-P. 2.487. Pedersen 2.624.

Ir. *doirtim* (older mostly 'pour out, spill'), fr. a cpd. **de-fort-* : Lat. *vertere* 'turn', etc., with semantic development of Sp. *verter*, etc. (cf. above, 2). Pedersen 2.526. Walde-P. 1.274.

W. *tywallt*, MW *dywallaw*, cpd. of *dy-* (intensive) and *gwallaw* 'draw, pour, serve', lit. 'empty' : Br. *goullo* 'empty', etc. Morris Jones 266. Pedersen 1.34.

Br. *skuilh*, also 'spread, strew' (9.34).

Br. *dinaoui* 'tip over, pour out', MBr. *dinou* = W. (obs.) *dineu* 'pour out, spill', Corn. *denewy* 'pour out', cpd. of *di-* (cf. MW *dywallaw*, above), second part perh. : Ir. *snāim*, Br. *neui* Lat. *nāre*, Grk. *νέω* 'swim' (10.35). Ernault, Dict. étym. s.v. *dinou*. Otherwise (: Ir. *snigim* 'drop, rain') Stokes 316.

4. ON *hella*, Dan. *hælde*, Sw. *hälla*, lit. 'lean (the vessel)', hence 'pour out' : ON *halla* 'lean, slope', OHG *haldōn* 'stoop', ON *hallr*, OE *heald* 'inclined', etc. Walde-P. 1.430. Falk-Torp 394.

ON *skenkja*, OHG *scenken*, etc., general Gmc. (ME *skynke*, fr. Du. or LG, cf. NED s.v.) special term for 'pour out drink' (hence OE *scencan* mostly merely 'give to drink', and in later MHG, NHG, also simply 'give'), prob. (with same semantic development as ON *hella*, above) : ON *skakkr* 'oblique', etc. Walde-P. 2.564. Falk-Torp 1004.

ME *poure*, NE *pour*, orig. obscure. Cf. NED s.v.

MHG *schüt(t)en*, NHG *schütten*, in MHG also 'shake hard, move violently', in this sense OHG *scutan* : OE *scūdan* 'shake, tremble', OS *scuddian* 'shake', Lith. *kutėti* 'shake up', etc. Weigand-H. 2.805 f. Walde-P. 2.601.

5. Lith. *pilti* : Lett. *pilt* 'drip, trickle', prob. fr. the root in Skt. *pṛ-*, Grk. *πίμπλημι* 'fill', Lith. *pilnas*, Skt. *pūrṇa-*, etc. 'full'. Walde-P. 2.54 f. Mühl.-Endz. 3.217.

Lith. *lieti*, Lett. *liet*, ChSl. *lĭjati*, iter. *-livati*, SCr. *liti*, etc., general Slavic : Goth. *leiþu* (acc.) 'wine', ON *līð* 'strong drink', W. *lliant* 'flood, stream', Ir. *lia* 'flood', Alb. *lum* 'river'. Walde-P. 2.392. Berneker 709 f.

Lett. *gāzt* : Lith. *gožti* 'overthrow', also 'pour out' (NSB s.v.), root connection dub. Mühl.-Endz. 1.620.

6. Skt. *sic-*, Av. *hič-* : ChSl. *sicati* 'urinate', OHG *sīhan* 'filter', *sīgan* 'drip down, trickle', etc. Walde-P. 2.466. Barth. 1727.

'Pour' also expressed in Skt. by causatives of *sru-* 'flow' or *pat-* 'fly, fall'.

9.36 WASH

(a, The Body or Certain Parts of the Body; b, Clothes or the like; otherwise Generic)

Grk.	*λούω* (a), *νίζω* (a), *πλύνω* (b)	Goth.	*þwahan*	Lith.	*mazgoti*
NG	*πλένω*, *νίβω* (a), *λούζω* (a)	ON	*þvā, vaska*	Lett.	*mazgāt*
Lat.	*lavāre*	Dan.	*vaske, tvætte*	ChSl.	*myti, plakati* (b)
It.	*lavare*	Sw.	*tvätta, vaska*	SCr.	*prati, miti* (a)
Fr.	*laver*	OE	*þwēan* (a), *wæscan* (b), *swillan*	Boh.	*mýti, práti* (b)
Sp.	*lavar*	ME	*wasche, swyle*	Pol.	*myć, prać* (b)
Rum.	*spăla, la* (a)	NE	*wash*	Russ.	*myt', stirat'* (b)
Ir.	*nigim, folcaim, indaim* (a)	Du.	*wasschen*	Skt.	*nij-, dhāv-*
NIr.	*nighim* (*folcaim*)	OHG	*wascan, dwahan* (a)	Av.	*snā-, niž-*
W.	*golchi*	MHG	*waschen, twahen* (a)		
Br.	*gwelc'hi*	NHG	*waschen*		

In several of the IE languages, as often in non-IE, there are different words for 'wash' according to the object, whether the body (but, except for Grk. *λούω*, special words for 'bathe' are not included), or certain parts of the body as hands, feet, face, head (sometimes with differentiation even here), or clothing or the like. Such special uses may be original but are often only survivals in special connections of once generic use, as Rum. *la* now 'wash the hair', from Lat. *lavāre* 'wash' and similarly in many other cases.

But the idiomatic differentiation is so varied, even between corresponding words in the same group (as Gmc. or Slavic), that it cannot be fully shown in the following discussion, still less in the summary notation adopted in the list. Thus, for example, Boh. *mýti*, Pol. *myć*, Russ. *myt'* are used for washing parts of the body, but also dishes, etc., that is, are generic except with reference to clothes, for which there is a different word. Conversely, SCr. *prati* (= Boh. *práti*, Pol. *prać* 'wash clothes') is virtually generic, while *miti* is restricted to use with reference to the head, or hands and feet, etc. according to the local dialect (cf. Rječnik Akad. s.v.). In the Munster dialect of Irish three different words are used with reference to the hand, head, and foot, respectively (cf. Atkinson, Passions and Homilies 711). OE *wæscan* is used for washing clothes or the like (nets in Gospels, Lk. 5.2), *þwēan* (and likewise OHG *dwahan*) for washing parts of the body (also dishes, cf. Gospels, Mk. 7.8), but otherwise one or the other of the two Gmc. words is the usual generic term in nearly all connections, the former in West Gmc. and Dan., the latter in Goth., ON, Sw. and NIcel. (where *vaska* survives only in *vaska fisk*).

There are two groups pointing to IE roots which probably already had the meaning 'wash' with some, not now determinable, differentiation of application. Others reflect, on the one hand, the use of water, by connections with words for 'water, wet, flow' or the like; on the other, the process of rubbing or beating, the latter especially applicable to the old method of washing clothes.

1. IE **neig^w-*. Walde-P. 2.322.

Grk. *νίζω* (fut. *νίψω*, etc., hence), later *νίπτω*, only of parts of the body, as likewise NG *νίφτω* and *νίβω* (Hatzidakis, Μεσ. 1.282); Ir. *nigim* (of parts of the body, but also generic), NIr. *nighim*

(Thurneysen, Gram. 115); Skt. *nij-* (3sg. intens. *nenekti*), Av. *niž-* (3sg. *naēnižaiti*).

2. IE **lou-*. Walde-P. 2.441. Ernout-M. 528 ff. Walde-H. 1.773 ff.

Grk. *λούω* (Hom. *λόω*, *λοέω*, fr. **λόϝω*) 'wash the body, bathe' (cf. *λουτρόν*, Hom. *λοετρόν* 'bath'), NG *λούζω* (Hatzidakis, Μεσ. 1.276) now esp. 'wash the hair'; Lat. *lavāre* (> It. *lavare*, Fr. *laver*, Sp. *lavar*; Rum. *la* arch. except as 'wash the hair', cf. Tiktin s.v.); Arm. *loganem* 'bathe' : ON *lauðr*, OE *lēaþor* 'foam' (NE *lather*), ON *laug* 'bath (water)', OE *lēah*, NE *lye*, etc.

3. Grk. *πλύνω*, only of clothing, but NG *πλύνω*, pop. *πλένω* (Hatzidakis, Μεσ. 1.295) also of face, etc., generic : *πλέω* 'sail', Skt. *plu-* 'float, swim, sail', OE *flōwan* 'flow', etc.; with like semantic development OHG *flewen* ('wash' nets, Tat. 19.4 = Lk. 5.2), Arm. *luanam* 'wash'. Walde-P. 2.94 f.

4. Rum. *spăla*, fr. Lat. **experlavāre*, cpd. of *lavāre* (above, 2). REW 3044. Puşcariu 1613.

5. Ir. *folcaim* (NIr. esp. 'bathe, dip, steep'), W. *golchi*, Corn. *golhy* Br. *gwelc'hi* : Ir. *folc* 'deluge', Lett. *valks* 'damp', Lith. *vilgyti* 'moisten', OHG *welh* 'damp, limp'. Walde-P. 1.306. Pedersen 1.59.

Ir. *ind-aim*, of hands or feet, vbl. n. *indmat*, also *indlat*, etym. dub. Lewis-Pedersen 337 f. (revision of Pedersen 2.574 f. and suggesting possible connection with Skt. *yam-* 'hold, hold together').

6. Goth. *þwahan*, ON *þvā* (Dan. *to*, Sw. *två* mostly replaced by *tvætte*, *tvätta*, derivs. of corresponding nouns for 'washing', Dan. *tvæt*, Sw. *tvätt*, ON *þvāttr*; ON *þvætta* rare, NIcel. 'talk nonsense'), OE *þwēan*, OHG *dwahan*, MHG *twahen* (for differences in use, cf. above), without clear outside connections except OPruss. *twaxtan* 'scrubbing brush for the bath'. Walde-P. 1.747. Falk-Torp 1267 f., 1306. Feist 506.

ON *vaska*, OE *wæscan* (reg. of clothes), OHG *wascan* (generic), etc., general Gmc., prob. as **wat-sk-* : Goth. *watō*, ON *vatn*, OE *wæter*, etc. 'water'; or : Ir. *fāiscim*, MW *gwascu*, Br. *gwaska* 'press', Skt. *vadh-* 'beat', as originally 'beat clothes in washing' (cf. below, 8). Walde-P. 1.253, 255. Falk-Torp 1356.

OE *swillan*, ME *swyle* (NE *swill*), outside connection dub. Walde-P. 2.530. Falk-Torp 1213. NED s.v. *swill*, vb.

7. Lith. *mazgoti*, Lett. *mazgāt* : Skt. *majj-* 'dip, sink', Lat. *mergere* 'dip, immerse', IE **mezg-*. Walde 2.300 f. Mühl.-Endz. 2.572.

8. ChSl. *myti* (esp. *u-myti* in Gospels for *νίπτω* and *λούω*), etc., general Slavic (mostly generic except for washing clothes, but of more restricted use in SCr.) : Lett. *maut* 'dive, swim', MLG *mūten* 'wash the face', Lith. *maudyti*, Lett. *maudāt* 'bathe'. Walde-P. 2.249 ff. Trautmann 191 f.

ChSl. *plakati*, used of washing nets (Lk. 5.2), orig. 'beat' and same word as *plakati* 'weep, lament, beat the breast' : Lith. *plakti* 'beat, whip', Grk. *πλήσσω* 'smite, strike', Lat. *plangere* 'beat the breast, lament', etc. Walde-P. 2.92.

ChSl. *oprati* (rare for *νίπτω*, cf. Jagić, Entstehungsgesch. 531), cpd. of *pĭrati* 'beat', esp. 'beat with mallet in washing', Boh. *práti*, Pol. *prać* (both of clothes), SCr. *prati* (generic) : Lith. *perti* 'bathe, strike with a besom in washing', Lett. *pērt* 'bathe, beat', etc. Walde-P. 2.42. Trautmann 215.

Russ. *stirat'*, only of washing clothes, lit. 'rub off, clean by rubbing', cpd. of *teret'* 'rub' (9.31).

9. Skt. *nij-*, Av. *niž-*, above, 1.

Skt. *dhāv-*, prob. as 'cleanse, make shine' : *dhavala-* 'shining white', Av.

fra-dav- 'rub off', Grk. *θοός· . . . . λαμπρός, θοῶσαι· . . . . λαμπρῦναι* Hesych., etc., *θέω* 'shine' (Hes., Theoc., etc.). Walde-P. 1.835.

Av. *snā-*, esp. cpd. *fra-snā-* (quotable with reference to body, hands, and clothes) : Skt. *snā-* 'bathe, perform the rite of bathing', Grk. *νήχω*, Lat. *nāre* 'swim', etc. Walde-P. 2.692 f. Barth. 1628.

9.37 SWEEP

Grk.	*κορέω, σαίρω*	Goth.	*usbaugjan*	Lith.	*šluoti*
NG	*σαρώνω, σκουπίζω*	ON	*sōpa*	Lett.	*mēzt (slaucīt)*
Lat.	*verrere*	Dan.	*feje*	ChSl.	*pomesti*
It.	*spazzare, scopare*	Sw.	*sopa*	SCr.	*mesti*
Fr.	*balayer*	OE	*swāpan*	Boh.	*mésti*
Sp.	*barrer*	ME	*swepe, swope*	Pol.	*zamiatać*
Rum.	*mătura*	NE	*sweep*	Russ.	*mesti*
Ir.	*scōpaim*	Du.	*vegen*	Skt.	*mṛj-*
NIr.	*scuabaim*	OHG	*kerren*	Av.	*mərəz-*
W.	*ysgubo*	MHG	*keren*		
Br.	*skuba*	NHG	*fegen, kehren*		

Several of the words for 'sweep' are derived from those for 'broom', one from the word for 'floor'. In most of the others, so far as there are clear cognates, 'sweep' is a specialization of either 'cleanse, adorn' or various motions like 'turn, throw', etc., applicable to the removal of dirt.

1. Grk. *κορέω* (whence *κόρημα* 'sweepings' and 'broom'; cf. also *κόρος· . . . . κάλλυντρον*, Hesych., *νāο-κόρος* 'caretaker of a temple', etc.), etym. dub. Walde-P. 1.462. Boisacq 495 f.

Grk. *σαίρω* (cf. *σάρματα* 'sweepings', etc.), later *σαρόω* (whence Byz. *σάρωτρον*, NG *σάρωθρον* 'broom'), NG *σαρώνω*, perh. : *σύρω* 'drag', *συρφετός* 'sweepings', but root connection dub. Walde-P. 2.530. Boisacq 849.

NG *σκουπίζω*, deriv. of *σκοῦπα* 'broom' (9.38).

2. Lat. *verrere* (> Sp., Port. *barrer*) : ChSl. *vrŭchą, vrěšti* 'thresh' (fr. 'drag', cf. 8.34), perh. Grk. *ἔρρω* 'walk with difficulty, go to destruction, perish', dial. *ϝέρρω* 'be exiled'. Walde-P. 1.292. Ernout-M. 1091.

It. *spazzare*, fr. OIt. *spazzo* 'floor' (Lat. *spatium* 'space'). REW 8121.

It. *scopare*, fr. late Lat. *scōpāre*, deriv. of *scōpa* 'broom' (9.38). REW 7735.

Fr. *balayer*, fr. *balai* 'broom' (9.38).

Rum. *mătura*, fr. *mătură* 'broom' (9.38).

3. Ir. *scōpaim*, NIr. *scuabaim*, W. *ysgubo*, Br. *skuba*, fr. late Lat. *scōpāre* (above). Vendryes, De hib. voc. 176. Loth, Mots lat. 216.

4. Goth. *us-baugjan*, prob. fr. caus. of *biugan* 'bend', with specialization from 'make bend, turn aside'. Cf. 'sweep' fr. 'swing' in OE *swāpan*, fr. 'throw' in Slav. *mesti*, etc. Feist 529 (with other views). Walde-P. 2.145 (otherwise).

ON *sōpa* (with *sōfl* 'broom'), Sw. *sopa* (older Dan. *sobe*), prob. fr. a root **sweb-* beside **swep-* in ChSl. *sypati*, etc. 'strew, scatter' (9.34), Lat. *dis-sipāre* 'scatter'. Walde-P. 2.524. Falk-Torp 1108.

Dan. *feje* (Sw. *feja*, ON *fægja* 'clean, polish'), prob. influenced by the German group, Du. *vegen*, NHG *fegen* (MHG *vegen* 'clean, polish', still the ordinary meaning in most of South Germany) : ON *fāga* 'adorn, cleanse', Lith. *puošti* 'adorn', Lett. *puost* 'clean, tidy up, sweep'. Walde-P. 2.16. Falk-Torp 210 f.

OE *swāpan*, ME *swope*, also ME *swepe*, NE *sweep* (prob. fr. a mutated form, but cf. NED s.v.) : ON *sveipa* 'stroke, sweep over, wrap about', OHG *sweifan* 'swing', etc., root **swei-* with numerous extensions in words for 'swing, bend'. Walde-P. 2.520. Falk-Torp 1223.

OHG *kerren*, MHG *ker(e)n*, NHG *kehren*, OLG *kerren*, cf. OHG *uberkara* 'sweepings', Norw. *kare*, Sw. *kara* 'scrape', perh. : Lith. *žerti* 'scrape, scratch'. Falk-Torp 496. Kluge-G. 293. Weigand-H. 1.1017. On the distribution of NHG *kehren* and *fegen*, cf. Kretschmer, Wortgeogr. 194 ff.

5. Lith. *šluoti*, Lett. *slaucīt*, beside Lith. *šluota*, Lett. *sluota* 'broom' : Grk. *κλύζω* 'rinse', OLat. *cluere* 'cleanse' (cf. *cloāca*), Goth. *hlutrs* 'bright, clean', etc. Walde-P. 1.495.

Lett. *mēzt*, also 'to dung, clear away manure' : Lith. *mėžti* 'work the dung', root connection dub. (Mühl.-Endz. 2.622. Walde-P. 2.246), but Lett. 'sweep' clearly generalized fr. 'sweep up the dung'.

6. ChSl. *mesti*, *pomesti* (*σαρόω*, Lk. 15.8), etc., general Slavic (with SCr. *metla*, etc. 'broom', also general Slavic) = ChSl. *mesti*, etc. 'throw' ('sweep', fr. 'throw the sweepings'). Berneker 2.41.

7. Skt. *mṛj-* 'wipe off, cleanse', Av. *mərəz-* 'touch' (: Grk. *ἀμέλγω* 'milk', etc., 5.87) serve for 'sweep away'. Cf. BR s.v. and Barth. 1152 (*fra-mərəz-*), also Skt. *saṁmārjana-* 'sweeping' and esp. *saṁmārjanī-* 'broom' (BR s.v.).

9.38 BROOM

Grk.	*κόρημα*	Goth.	. . . .	Lith.	*šluota*
NG	*σκοῦπα, σάρωθρον*	ON	*sōfl*	Lett.	*sluota*
Lat.	*scōpae*	Dan.	*kost*	ChSl.	. . . .
It.	*granata, scopa*	Sw.	*kvast*	SCr.	*metla*
Fr.	*balai*	OE	*bes(e)ma*	Boh.	*koště, pometlo*
Sp.	*escoba*	ME	*besum, brome*	Pol.	*motła*
Rum.	*mătură*	NE	*broom*	Russ.	*metla*
Ir.	*scūap*	Du.	*bezem*	Skt.	*saṁmārjanī-*
NIr.	*scuab*	OHG	*besamo*	Av.	. . . .
W.	*ysgub*	MHG	*beseme*		
Br.	*skubell, balaenn*	NHG	*besen*		

Many of the words for 'broom' are derived from those for 'sweep' and have been cited with the latter (9.37). Others reflect the material of which the broom was made as 'twigs, leaves' and in two instances the plant 'broom'.

1. Lat. *scōpae*, lit. 'twigs' (sg. *scōpa* not common) : *scōpiō* 'stalk or pedicle of a bunch of grapes', *scāpus* 'shaft', etc. Hence It. *scopa*, Sp. *escoba;* NG *σκοῦπα*; Ir. *scūap*, NIr. *scuab*, W. *ysgub*, Br. *skubell.* Walde-P. 2.562. Ernout-M. 908. REW 7734. G. Meyer, Neugr. St. 3.60 f. Vendryes, De hib. voc. 176. Loth, Mots lat. 216.

It. *granata*, deriv. of Lat. *grānum* 'grain', prob. through a plant name. REW 3846.

Fr. *balai*, OFr. *balain(s)*, fr. Gall. **banatlo* (> **balatno* by metathesis), cf. W. *banadl*, Br. (V.) *benal, bonal* 'broom' (the plant); Fr. dial. (Lyon) *balan*, *balain* still used for plant also. Wartburg 1.232 f. REW 897. Hence Br. *balaenn.* Henry 24.

Rum. *mătură*, generally derived fr. Lat. *mētula*, dim. of *mētā* 'post, cone, pyramid', but its use as 'broom' doubtless helped by Slavic word SCr. *metla*, etc. (9.37) if not actually derived fr. it

(as Miklosich, Berneker). Puşcariu 1053. Tiktin 963.

2. Dan. *kost* (ODan. *kvost*, fr. *kvast*), Sw. *kvast* : MLG, MHG *quast* 'cluster, wisp' (of foliage, straw, etc.); OSCr. *gvozd* 'woods', etc. Walde-P. 1.644. Falk-Torp 568 f. Hellquist 534.

OE *bes(e)ma*, ME *besum* (NE *besom* still the generic word in Scotland), OHG *besamo*, etc., general West Gmc., also (OE, OHG) 'rod, switch (esp. for punishing)', hence orig. prob. a bundle of twigs used as a broom, but root connection dub. Walde-P. 2.136.

ME *brome*, NE *broom*, from the name of the plant (OE *brōm* 'genesta'), from which brooms were frequently made. Cf. above Fr. *balai.*

3. Boh. *koště*, contracted fr. older *chvostišče* id., fr. *chvost* 'tail' (4.18). Berneker 409.

9.41 CRAFT, TRADE

Grk.	*τέχνη*	Goth.	. . . .	Lith.	*amatas*
NG	*τέχνη, δουλειά*	ON	*(iðn, iðja)*	Lett.	*amats*
Lat.	*ars, artificium*	Dan.	*haandværk*	ChSl.	*chytrostĭ, remĭstvo, kŭznĭ*
It.	*mestiere (arte)*	Sw.	*handtverk*		
Fr.	*métier*	OE	*cræft, handcræft*	SCr.	*zanat, obrt*
Sp.	*oficio*	ME	*craft, handcraft*	Boh.	*řemeslo*
Rum.	*meşteşug, meserie*	NE	*(handi)craft, trade*	Pol.	*rzemiosło*
Ir.	*cerd*	Du.	*handwerk, ambacht*	Russ.	*remeslo, masterstvo*
NIr.	*ceard*	OHG	*hantwerch*	Skt.	*çilpa-*
W.	*crefft*	MHG	*hantwerc*	Av.	. . . .
Br.	*micher*	NHG	*handwerk, gewerbe*		

Although the beginnings of various crafts go back to remote prehistoric periods, they long remained merely household crafts. Such was the situation in the IE period, as still to a considerable extent in the Homeric period of Greece and in the early periods of the other lands of IE speech. The development of professional crafts with the distinct classes of craftsmen is a later outgrowth. Cf. Schrader, Reallex. 1.392 ff.

Hence, as to be expected, there are no inherited groups pointing to IE words for 'craft' or 'craftsman' in general, or for a particular craft or craftsman, with the exception of the group Grk. *τέκτων*, Skt. *takṣan-*, Av. *tašan-*, which reflects an IE word, though the earliest scope of its application is not entirely clear, 'fashioner, builder', or 'carpenter' (see under 'artisan').

Most of the words listed have a wider application than 'manual craft' and cover also either 'skill, art' or 'business, occupation', and etymologically they are mostly connected with general notions of either 'work, skill', etc. or 'occupation', these being of diverse sources.

1. Grk. *τέχνη* 'skill, art, craft, trade' : *τέκτων* 'artisan, carpenter' (9.42).

NG *ἐπάγγελμα* 'profession' (class. Grk. 'announcement' and 'profession' : *ἐπαγγέλλω* 'announce', mid. also 'make profession of'), used also for one's 'trade'. But the pop. term is simply *δουλειά* 'work' (9.12).

2. Lat. *ars, artis* 'skill, art, craft, trade' (> It. *arte* still in part 'craft'), esp. *ars sordida* as opposed to the liberal arts; *artificium* (cpd. with *facere* 'do, make'; cf. *artifex* 'artisan') fr. the notion of 'fit together' : Lat. *artus* 'joint', *armus* 'shoulder, Grk. *ἀραρίσκω* 'fit', etc. Walde-P. 1.71 f. Ernout-M. 76. Walde-H. 1.70.

Fr. *métier* (OFr. *mestier* > It. *mestiere*), fr. Lat. *ministerium* 'office, occupation, service', fr. *minister* 'servant, minister'. REW 5589.

Sp. *oficio*, fr. Lat. *officium* 'service, function, business', fr. **opificium*, cpd. of *opus* 'work, deed' and *facere* 'do, make'.

Rum. *meşteşug*, fr. Hung. *mesterség* 'trade, craft', this a deriv. of *mester* 'master', loanword fr. NHG *meister*. Tiktin 971.

Rum. *meserie*, prob. connected with *meserere* 'mercy, favor' (fr. Lat. *miserēre* 'pity') through its secondary meaning 'honor, office', perh. also influenced in its use by the group It. *mestiere*, etc. (above). Tiktin 970.

3. Ir. *cerd* 'skill, art, craft, trade', NIr. *ceard* : W. *cerdd* 'art, poetry', Grk. *κέρδος* 'gain, profit' (whence Lat. *cerdō* 'petty craftsman'), pl. 'wiles', *κερδαλέος* 'crafty', etc. Walde-P. 1.423. Pedersen 1.36.

W. *crefft*, fr. OE *cræft* (below, 4). Parry-Williams 25.

Br. *micher*, fr. Fr. *métier* (above, 2). Henry 197.

4. ON *iðn, iðja* 'occupation, business' : *īð* 'a doing, working', *iðinn* 'diligent, active', root connection dub. Walde-P. 1.5. Falk-Torp 457.

Dan. *haandværk*, Sw. *handtverk*, Du. *handwerk*, OHG *hantwerch*, MHG *hantwerc*, NHG *handwerk*, lit. 'handwork', cpds. of words for 'hand' and 'work'.

OE *cræft* 'strength, ability, skill, art, craft', ME, NE *craft*, also OE *handcræft*, ME *handcraft*, NE *handicraft* : ON *kraptr*, OHG *kraft* 'power, strength', etc. (4.81). Walde-P. 1.596. Falk-Torp 572.

NE *trade*, orig. 'path, course', hence 'regular course of action, manner of life' and then 'business, occupation, craft', perh borrowed fr. MLG *trade* 'track' : OHG *trata*, OE *trod* 'track, path', OHG *tretan*, OE *tredan* 'step, tread'. Walde-P. 1.796. NED s.v.

Du. *ambacht*, with preservation of the older form (the reg. development in Du. *ambt* 'office') : OHG *ambahti*, OE *ambiht*, Goth. *andbahti* 'service, office', derivs. of OHG *ambaht*, OE *ambeht*, Goth. *andbahts* 'servant' (19.43). Falk-Torp 189. Franck-v. W. 16.

NHG *gewerbe* 'business, vocation, trade', MHG 'activity, business' : *werben*, OHG *hwerfan* 'turn, move about, be busy', OE *hweorfan* 'turn, go about, roam', Goth. *hwairban* 'wander, roam', etc. Walde-P. 1.472. Weigand-H. 1.717.

5. Lith. *amatas*, Lett. *amats*, fr. MLG *am(m)et* 'office, position' : OHG *ambahti*, etc. (above, 4). Mühl.-Endz. 1.70.

6. ChSl. *remĭstvo* (Supr., etc.), Boh. *řemeslo*, Pol. *rzemiosto* (*-iesto*), Russ. *remeslo* : Lith. *remesas*, Lett. *remesis* 'craftsman, carpenter', OPruss. *romestud* 'ax', all prob. fr. the root of Lith. *ramtyte* 'cut, carve', Lett. *ramstīt* 'hew, saw' (with a blunt tool), further connections dub. Mühl.-Endz. 3.509 f. Brückner 475. Buga, Kalba ir Senovė 279.

ChSl. *chytrostĭ* (Jagić, Entstehungsgesch. 415), deriv. of *chytrŭ* 'skilled, crafty' : Russ. *chitryj* 'cunning, crafty', Bulg. *hitur* 'wise', SCr. *hitar* 'quick, experienced, skilled', etc. Berneker 414.

ChSl. *kŭznĭ* (Supr., etc.) : *kovati* 'forge' (9.61). Berneker 675.

SCr. *zanat*, fr. Turk. (orig. Arab.) *san'at* 'craft'. Miklosich, Turk. El. 2.151.

SCr. *obrt* 'turning' (: *obrnuti, obrtati* 'turn around', cpds. of *ob* 'around' and root of *vrtjeti* 'turn', 10.12) and 'occupation, craft', with the same development as NHG *gewerbe* (above, 4).

Russ. *masterstvo*, deriv. of *master* 'master, maker', used esp. in phrases for various craftsmen, fr. Lat. *magister* 'master'. Berneker 2.3.

7. Skt. *çilpa-*, adj. 'variegated', sb. 'variegated appearance, decoration, work of art, art, craft', etym.?

9.412. 'Art'. Phrases like NE *arts and crafts*, NHG *kunst und gewerbe* represent a differentiation that is modern and still not rigidly defined, though the terms for 'art' and 'artist' are most commonly used with reference to painting and sculpture. Formerly the various types of work demanding special skill were covered by the same word, as by Grk. τέχνη, Lat. *ars*, Skt. *çilpa-* (9.41). The differentiation began with such phrases as Fr. *beaux arts*, NE *fine arts*. The descendants of Lat. *ars, artis* (It., Sp. *arte*, Rum. *artă*, Fr. *art* > ME, NE *art*) have come to be used mainly in this more restricted sense (It. *arte* also 'craft').

Other terms for 'art' are as follows:

1. Ir. *elatha, elada* ('skill, art', cf. Laws, Gloss. 300), NIr. *ealadha*, etym.? Macbain 149.

W. *celf* (cf. *celfydd* 'skilful') : OBr. *celmed* gl. *efficax*, Ir. *calma* 'brave', root connection? Pedersen 1.168.

2. Du., NHG *kunst* (> Dan. *kunst*, Sw. *konst*), orig. 'knowledge, skill', fr. the root of NHG *kennen* 'know', *können* 'know how, be able'. Kluge-G. 336.

3. Lith. *menas* (cf. NSB s.v.), orig. 'understanding' : *minti*, *menu* 'think, remember'. Leskien, Ablaut 336. Neolog. in this sense, influenced by NHG *kunst*, etc.

Lith. *dailė*, with *dailininkas* 'artist' : *dailus* 'beautiful' (16.81).

Lett. *māksla* : *mācēt* 'be able' = Lith. *mokėti* 'be able', beside Lith. *mokyti*, Lett. *mācīt* 'teach (17.25). Mühl.-Endz. 2.579.

4. SCr. *umjetnost*, Boh. *umění*, orig. 'understanding', fr. *umjeti*, *uměti* 'know how, be able'. Cf. ChSl. *umŭ*, *raz-umŭ* 'intelligence' (17.12), *razuměti* 'understand' (17.16), etc.

Pol. *sztuka* 'piece' (fr. NHG *stuck*), also 'work of art' and 'art' (*sztuka malarska* 'art of painting'), for which also *kunszt*, directly fr. NHG *kunst*. Brückner 555 f.

Russ. *iskusstvo* = late ChSl. *iskusĭstvo* 'trial', fr. *iskusiti* 'try' (9.98). Berneker 653.

Russ. *chudožestvo* = late ChSl. *chądožĭstvo* 'art, science', fr. **chądogŭ*, *chudogŭ* 'wise', loanword fr. a Gmc. form **handags* beside Goth. *handugs* 'wise' (17.21). Berneker 400. Stender-Petersen 334.

9.42 ARTISAN, CRAFTSMAN

Grk.	*τεχνίτης*	Goth.	(*-smiþa*)	Lith.	*amatininkas*
NG	*τεχνίτης, μάστορας*	ON	*smiðr, iðnarmaðr*	Lett.	*amatnieks*
Lat.	*faber, artifex*	Dan.	*haandværker*	ChSl.	*chytrĭcĭ, kŭznĭnikŭ*
It.	*artigiano*	Sw.	*handtverkare*	SCr.	*zanatlija, obrtnik*
Fr.	*artisan*	OE	*wyrhta, cræftiga*	Boh.	*řemeslník*
Sp.	*artesano*	ME	*wright, craftiman*	Pol.	*rzemieślnik*
Rum.	*meşteşugar, meseriaş*	NE	*artisan, craftsman*	Russ.	*remeslennik, masterovoj*
Ir.	*sāer, cerd*	Du.	*handwerker, ambachtsman*	Skt.	*çilpin-, kāru-*
NIr.	*saor, ceard*	OHG	*wurhto, wercmeistar*	Av.	. . . .
W.	*saer, crefftwr*	MHG	*wercmeister, hantwerker*		
Br.	*micherour*	NHG	*handwerker*		

The majority of words for 'artisan, craftsman' are derivs., cpds., or root connections of those for 'craft', discussed in 9.41. Others are mostly of similar semantic sources, notions like 'work, fit, know'. In several there is an early tendency toward specialization, chiefly to 'carpenter' or 'metalworker' (9.43, 9.60).

1. Derivs. and cpds. of words for 'craft'.

Derivs. : Grk. τεχνίτης (cf. also τέκτων 'carpenter' with wider sense in Hom. 9.43); It. *artigiano* (> Fr. *artisan* in place of *artiste* formerly 'craftsman'; Fr. > Sp. *artesano*, NE *artisan*; REW 679. Gamillscheg 52), Rum. *meşteşugar*, *meseriaş*; W. *crefftwr*, Br. *micherour*; OE *cræftiga*, Dan. *haandværker*, Sw. *handtverkare*, Du. *handwerker*, MHG *hantwerker*, NHG *handwerker*; Lith. *amatininkas*, Lett. *amatnieks*; ChSl. *kŭznĭnikŭ*, SCr. *zanatlija*, *obrtnik*, Boh. *řemeslník*, Pol. *rzemieślnik*, Russ. *remeslennik*; Skt. *çilpin-*.

Cpds., the second part meaning 'doer, maker', 'man' or 'master' : Lat. *artifex* (cf. *facere* 'do, make'); ON *iðnarmaðr*, ME *craftiman*, NE *craftsman* (earlier *craftes man*), Du. *ambachtsman*; OHG *wercmeistar*, MHG *wercmeister* (lit. 'work-master'); also NHG *handwerksman*, Dan. *haandværksman*, Du. *handwerksman*, and NHG *handarbeiter*.

2. NG μάστορας, μάστορης, used for 'master-workman' and one who is master of a trade, 'artisan', fr. Lat. *magister* 'master'. G. Meyer, Neugr. Stud. 3.43. Cf. OHG *meistar* (in *wercmeistar*, above, 1), Russ. *masterovoj*, fr. the same source.

3. Lat. *faber*, general term for worker in hard materials, including metals, also used with descriptive adjectives to apply to particular crafts (cf. 9.43, 9.60), but in the majority of cases when standing alone 'carpenter', prob. fr. an orig. idea of 'one who fits, makes fitting' : Goth. *gadaban* 'be fitting, happen', OE *gedēfe* 'fitting, proper', *gedafnian* 'be fitting', ChSl. *po-doba jestŭ* 'is fitting', *dobrŭ* 'good', etc., (here perh. also Arm. *darbin* 'smith', fr. **dhabhro-*), IE **dhabh-*. Walde-P. 1.824. Ernout-M. 319. Walde-H. 1.436 f.

4. Ir. *sāer*, NIr. *saor*, W. *saer* 'craftsman' and esp. 'carpenter', fr. **sapero-* : Lat. *sapere* 'taste, perceive, know', OHG *intseffen* 'perceive'. Walde-P. 2.450. Pedersen 1.92.

Ir. *cerd* 'craftsman', also 'smith, artist, poet', NIr. *ceard* : Ir. *cerd* 'craft' (9.41).

5. Goth. *-smiþa* only in *aiza-smiþa* 'coppersmith' and so uncertain whether still generic 'craftsman' or 'smith', ON *smiðr* 'craftsman, woodworker or metal-worker' (cf. *gull-*, *jārn-*, *trē-smiðr*) : OE *smiþ*, OHG *smid* 'smith', etc. (9.60), fr. the root in Goth. *gasmiþōn* 'effect', ON *smiða* 'make, forge', etc. (9.61).

OE *wyrhta* (cf. *īsern-*, *stān-*, *trēow-wyrhta*), ME (with metathesis) *wright*, OHG *wurhto*, MHG (only in cpds.) *-würhte*, *-worhte* : OE *weorc*, OHG *werc*, etc. 'work' (9.12).

6. ChSl. *chytrĭcĭ*, deriv. of *chytrŭ* 'skilled, crafty' (cf. 9.41).

Russ. *masterovoj*, deriv. of 'master, maker' (9.41).

7. Skt. *kāru-* 'doer, maker', but esp. craftsman' : *kṛ-* 'do, make'.

9.422 TOOL

Grk.	*ἐργαλεῖον, ὄργανον*	Goth.	. . . .	Lith.	*įnagis, įrankis*
NG	*ἐργαλεῖο*	ON	*tōl* (pl.)	Lett.	*rīks*
Lat.	*instrūmentum*	Dan.	*værktøj, redskab*	ChSl.	(*orądĭje*)
It.	*ordigno, utensili* (pl.)	Sw.	*verktyg, redskap*	SCr.	*oruđe, alat*
Fr.	*outil, instrument*	OE	*tōl*	Boh.	*náčin, nástroj*
Sp.	*herramienta*	ME	*tole*	Pol.	*narzędzie*
Rum.	*unealtă*	NE	*tool*	Russ.	*orudie*
Ir.	*airnisi* (pl.)	Du.	*werktuig*	Skt.	*karaṇa-*
NIr.	*uirlis, oirnēis, acra*	OHG	*giziuc*	Av.	. . . .
W.	*arf*	MHG	*ziuc, wercziuc*		
Br.	*benveg*	NHG	*werkzeug*		

Many of the words listed have a wider range than NE *tool* in its usual application and may cover any 'instrument, implement'.

1. Grk. ἐργαλεῖον, deriv. (perh. through *ἔργα-λον, cf. ἐργά-της, ἐργά-νη) of ἔργον 'work' (9.12).

Grk. ὄργανον : ἔργον 'work'.

2. Lat. *instrūmentum* (> It. *strumento*, Fr., NE, NHG, Pol. Russ. *instrument*), deriv. of *instruere* 'provide, equip', orig. 'set in order', cpd. of *struere*, 'arrange, prepare', fr. the same root as Lat. *sternere* 'spread out', etc. (9.34). Ernout-M. 989 f.

It. *ordigno*, fr. VLat. **ōrdinium*, deriv. of Lat. *ōrdō, -inis* 'arrangement, order', *ōrdināre* 'arrange'. REW 6092.

It. *utensili* (pl.), Fr. *outil*, fr. Lat. *ūtensilia*, VLat. *usitilia* 'utensils', deriv. of *ūtī* 'use'. Ernout-M. 1141. REW 9101.

Sp. *herramienta*, deriv. (through vb. *herrar*) of *hierro*, Lat. *ferrum* 'iron'.

Rum. *unealtă*, fr. *unealte* 'of many kinds', pl. of *una alta* (cf. Lat. *ūnus alter*) 'one, the other'. Tiktin 1685.

3. Ir. *airnēis* 'cattle, wealth' also pl. *airnisi* 'tools', NIr. *oirnēis*, prob. fr. ME *harneis* 'equipment'. K. Meyer, Contrib. 64. Laws, Gloss. 44.

NIr. *uirlis*, orig. dub., a variant of the preceding word?

NIr. *acra* (given as 'tool' by McKenna and Dinneen), also and orig. 'use, service', same word as Ir. *acra* 'suing, claim' vbl. n. to *ad-gairim* 'sue, claim', cpd. of *gairim* 'call' (18.41). K. Meyer, Contrib. 12.

W. *arf* 'weapon' and 'tool', fr. Lat. *arma* 'arms'. Pedersen 1.241.

Br. *benveg* = W. *benffyg*, *benthyg* 'loan', fr. Lat. *beneficium* 'favor, service'. Loth, Mots lat. 138. Henry 31.

4. ON *tōl* (pl.), OE *tōl*, ME *tole*, NE *tool*, fr. the root of OE *tawian* 'prepare', Goth. *taujan* 'do, make' (9.11). NED s.v. *tool*, sb.

OHG *giziuc* 'equipment, tools', MHG *ziuc* (NHG *zeug* 'material, cloth', 6.21) : MLG *tūgen* 'make', etc. Weigand-H. 2.1320 f. Hence also, with words for 'work', MHG *wercziuc*, NHG *werkzeug*, and (prob. semantic borrowing) Du. *werktuig*, Dan. *værktøj*, Sw. *verktyg*.

Dan. *redskab*, Sw. *redskap*, fr. MLG *redeschap* 'readiness, equipment'. Falk-Torp 886. Hellquist 822.

5. Lith. *įnagis*, *įrankis*, cpds. of *į-* 'in' with *nagas* 'nail' (of finger or toe, 4.39), pl. 'fingers, hands' (cf. NSB s.v. *nagas*), and with *ranka* 'hand' (4.33).

Lett. *rīks* = Lith. *rykas* 'vessel, tool', root connection dub. Mühl.-Endz. 537.

6. ChSl. *orądĭje* ('affair, business', late 'implement'), SCr. *oruđe*, Russ. *orudie* : ChSl. *rędŭ* 'order, arrangement'. Walde-P. 2.368 f. Pedersen, KZ 38.310. Otherwise Miklosich 226, Brückner 381 (loanword fr. OHG *ārunti* 'embassy'; but cf. Pedersen l.c.)

SCr. *alat* (also Alb. *alat*, Rum. dial. *halat*), fr. Turk. *alet* 'tool'. Miklosich, Türk. El. 1.246.

Boh. *náčin* : *činiti* 'do, make' (9.11).

Boh. *nástroj* : *nastrojiti* 'prepare, equip', *strojiti* id.

Pol. *narzędzie* : *rząd*, *rzęd* 'row, set, order', ChSl. *rędŭ* 'order, arrangement'. Brückner 356, 474.

7. Skt. *karaṇa-* (neut.), mostly act of 'doing, making', fr. *kṛ-* 'do, make' (9.11), but also means of making, 'instrument, tool'.

9.423 USE

(vb. = Make Use of)

Grk.	*χρῶμαι*	Goth.	*brūkjan*	Lith.	*vartoti, naudoti*
NG	*μεταχειρίζομαι, χρησιμοποιῶ*	ON	*njōta, nyta*	Lett.	*lietuōt*
Lat.	*ūtī*	Dan.	*bruge, benytte, anvende*	ChSl.	. . . .
It.	*servirsi di, usare, adop(e)rare*	Sw.	*bruka, begagna, nyttja, använda*	SCr.	*upotrijebiti*
Fr.	*se servir de, employer, user de*	OE	*brūcan, nyttian*	Boh.	*užiti*
Sp.	*emplear, usar, servirse de*	ME	*brouke, use (nytten)*	Pol.	*użyć*
Rum.	*întrebuința, se servi de, se folosi de, uza*	NE	*use (employ)*	Russ.	*upotrebit'*
Ir.	*airbiur biuth*	Du.	*gebruiken*	Skt.	*upayuj-, prayuj-*
NIr.	*ūsāidhim*	OHG	*(ge)brūchan, niuzan, nuzzan*	Av.	. . . .
W.	*iwsio*	MHG	*(ge)brūchen, nuzzen*		
Br.	*ober gant*	NHG	*gebrauchen, benutzen, anwenden*		

'Use' is understood here as 'make use of', not in the secondary sense of 'make or be accustomed to', which developed in Romance and English (now mostly in past tense or pple. *used*). This latter started in the sb. Lat. *ūsus* 'use' and 'usage, custom' (so also in NHG *gebrauch*, but not in the vb. *gebrauchen*). 'Use' and 'enjoy' may be parallel senses in the same word or in cognate groups (below, 4); also 'use' and 'need' (below, 1, 6). Other connections are with words for 'turn' (through 'turn to, apply') and for 'live' (through 'live through, experience'), 'work' ('work at, operate'), 'fold' ('enfold, involve'), 'advantage' ('take advantage of'), 'serve' ('serve oneself of').

1. Grk. χρῶμαι (*χρηέομαι, cf. inf. χρῆσθαι, Boeot. χρειεῖσθαι), in various senses, 'have need of', whence both 'desire' and 'make use of', fr. the latter also the freq. technical 'consult an oracle' : χρεία 'need', χρή 'needs, must, ought', etc. (see 9.93). Hence χρήσιμος 'useful', whence cpd. NG χρησιμοποιῶ 'make use of'.

Grk. μεταχειρίζομαι (: χείρ 'hand') 'take in hand, practice', NG 'use'.

2. Lat. *ūtī*, OLat. *oetier* (cf. also Osc. *úíttiuf* 'usus', Pael. *oisa* 'usa'), etym.? Walde-P. 1.103. Ernout-M. 1141 f.

Hence, formed fr. pple. or sb. *ūsus*, MLat. *ūsāre*, It. *usare*, Fr. *user* (> ME, NE *use*), Sp. *usar* (Rum. *uza* neolog. fr. Fr.).

It. *servirsi di*, Fr. *se servir de*, etc., lit. 'serve oneself of', fr. Lat. *servīre* 'serve' deriv. of *servus* 'slave'.

Fr. *employer* (> ME, NE *employ*, in part = *use*, NED s.v. *employ*, vb. 1), Sp. *emplear*, fr. Lat. *implicāre* 'enfold, involve, engage', cpd. of *plicāre* 'fold' (9.15). Ernout-M. 778. REW 4312.

It. *adop(e)rare*, cpd. of *op(e)rare* 'work, do, make'.

Rum. *întrebuinţa*, cpd. fr. sb. *trebuinţa* 'need' (of Slavic orig., 9.93), with sense influenced by NHG *gebrauchen* (so Tiktin 840), or by the similar Slavic cpds. as SCr. *upotrijebiti*, etc. (below, 6).

Rum. *se folosi de*, fr. sb. *folos* 'gain, advantage', this fr. Byz. φελός, Grk. ὄφελος 'furtherance, advantage, help'. Tiktin 641 f.

3. Ir. *airbiur*, cpd. of *berim* 'carry', followed by *biuth* (dat. of *bith* 'world') glosses Lat. *fruī*, *ūtī*, etc., e.g. imperat. *airbir biuth* = *utere* of Vulgate, 1. Tim. 5.23 (Wb. 29a25). Pedersen 2.464 f. Thurneysen, Gram. 162. K. Meyer, Contrib. 113.

Ir. *caithim* 'consume, spend, waste', also 'use' (K. Meyer, Contrib. 326, Laws, Gloss. s.v.), etym.? Walde-P. 1.112. Pedersen 2.479.

Ir. *torbe* 'use, profit' (11.73) is used in phrases rendering Lat. *ūtilis*, also *torbatu* 'utilitas', but the vb. *torbenim* seems quotable only for 'be of use', not 'make use of'. Cf. Windisch, Wtb. 840.

NIr. *ūsāidhim*, W. *iwsio*, through sbs. *ūsāidh*, *iws*, fr. NE sb. *use*.

Br. *ober gant*, lit. 'do with' (*ober* 'do', 9.11; *gant* 'with').

4. Goth. *brūkjan*, OE *brūcan*, ME *brouke* (NE *brook* obs. or arch. in this sense; NED s.v.), LG *brūken* (> Dan. *bruge*, Sw. *bruka*), OHG *(ge)brūchan*, MHG *(ge)brūchen*, NHG (*brauchen* now 'need'; Paul, Deutsches Wtb. s.v.) *gebrauchen*, Du. *gebruiken* : Lat. *fruī* 'enjoy', *frūx*, *frūctus* 'fruit', etc. Walde-P. 2.208. Falk-Torp 106. Feist 107.

ON *njōta*, *nyta* ('use' and 'enjoy'; Dan. *nyde* 'enjoy', *nytte* 'be of use', *benytte* 'use'), Sw. *nyttja*, OE *nēotan*, *nyttian*, ME *nytten*, OHG *niuzan*, *nuzzan*, MHG *nuzzen*, NHG (*nutzen* mostly 'be of use') *benutzen* : Goth. *niutan* 'attain, enjoy', *ganiutan* 'catch', Lith. *nauda* 'use, profit'. In this group the sense of advantageous use is dominant, and the early forms also mean 'enjoy'. Walde-P. 2.325. Falk-Torp 774, 777. Feist 379.

NHG *anwenden* (> Dan. *anvende*, Sw. *använda*), cpd. of *wenden* 'turn', hence 'turn to, apply, use' for a particular purpose.

5. Lith. *vartoti*, fr. the root of *versti*, Lat. *vertere*, etc. 'turn'. Cf. NHG *anwenden*.

Lith. *naudoti*, fr. *nauda* 'use, profit' : OE *nēotan*, etc. (above, 4).

Lett. *lietuōt*, fr. *lieta* 'thing' (9.90), also 'tool', etc. Mühl.-Endz. 2.505 f.

6. ChSl. (?), SCr. *upotrijebiti*, Russ. *upotrebit'*, cpds. with root seen in ChSl. *trěbovati* 'need', sb. *potrěba* 'need', etc. (9.93).

Boh. *užiti*, Pol. *użyć*, cpds. of *žiti*, *żyć* 'live' (4.74), hence through 'live through, experience' (cf. NHG *erleben*) > 'use'.

7. Skt. *upayuj-*, *prayuj-*, cpds. of *yuj-* 'join, unite'.

9.43 CARPENTER

Grk.	*τέκτων*	Goth.	*timrja*	Lith.	*dailidė*
NG	*μαραγκός, ξυλουργός*	ON	*trēsmiðr*	Lett.	*remesis*
Lat.	*faber*	Dan.	*tømrer*	ChSl.	*tektonŭ, drěvodělja*
It.	*falegname*	Sw.	*timmerman*	SCr.	*tesar, drvodjelja*
Fr.	*charpentier*	OE	*trēowwyrhta*	Boh.	*tesař*
Sp.	*carpintero*	ME	*carpenter*	Pol.	*cieśla*
Rum.	*dulgher, teslar*	NE	*carpenter*	Russ.	*plotnik*
Ir.	*sāir*	Du.	*timmerman*	Skt.	*takṣan-, rathakāra-*
NIr.	*saor*	OHG	*zimbarman, zimbarāri*	Av.	. . . .
W.	*saer*	MHG	*zimberman*		
Br.	*kalvez*	NHG	*zimmermann*		

Words for 'carpenter' are in part identical with those for 'artisan' (9.42) used, either with or without a defining adjective or phrase, in the specialized sense. Others are derivatives of words for 'wood, timber', often as cpds. meaning literally 'woodworker'. Some are extensions from a more specific idea of 'carriage-maker', 'ship's carpenter'.

Words that are used only of those who do the finer work in wood, like NE *joiner*, *cabinetmaker*, NHG *tischler*, *schreiner*, etc., are not considered here.

1. Grk. τέκτων, in Hom. more than 'carpenter' (builds houses, ships, wagons, furniture, carves horn and ivory, etc., but most frequently the reference is to woodwork) : Skt. *takṣan-* 'carpenter' (often esp. 'wagon-builder'), Av. *tašan-* 'creator', fr. the root in Skt. *takṣ-*, Av. *taš-* 'cut, hew, fashion', etc. (9.45). Walde-P. 1.717. Schrader, Reallex. 1.394. Blümner, Gewerbe und Künste 2.165.

NG μαραγκός, fr. It. *marangone* 'diver', esp. 'one who repairs ships under water', deriv. of Lat. *mergus* 'diver'. G. Meyer, Neugr. Stud. 4.49. REW 5528.

Grk. ξυλουργός 'woodworker' (cf. ξύλον 'wood', ἔργον 'work'), late and rare (Pollux 7.101), but the NG lit. word for 'carpenter'.

2. Lat. *faber* (see 9.42), spec. *faber tignārius*, *faber lignārius* (also late *lignārius* alone), cf. *tignum* 'timber', *lignum* 'wood'.

It. *falegname*, cpd. of *fare* 'do, make' and *legname* 'woodwork, articles made of wood' (deriv. of Lat. *lignum* 'wood').

Fr. *charpentier* (> ME, NE *carpenter*), Sp. *carpintero*, fr. Lat. *carpentārius* 'carriage-maker', deriv. of *carpentum* 'carriage, coach', a Gallic word. REW 1709. Walde-H. 1.171.

Rum. *dulgher*, fr. Turk. *dülger* 'carpenter'. Lokotsch 553.

Rum. *teslar*, fr. Slavic, SCr. *tesar*, etc. (below, 6), with *l* fr. *teslă* 'adze', this also fr. Slavic. Tiktin 1581 f.

3. Ir. *sāir*, NIr. *saor*, W. *saer* (cf. 9.42), or esp. NIr. *saor adhmaid*, *saor crainn*, cf. *adhmad* 'timber, wood', *crann* 'tree, wood'; W. *saer coed*, cf. *coed* 'wood, timber'.

Br. *kalvez*, MBr. also *calmez* : OBr. *calmed* gl. *efficax*, W. *celfydd* 'skilful', Ir. *calma* 'brave'. Ernault, Glossaire 556.

4. Goth. *timrja* 'carpenter, builder', Dan. *tømrer*, OHG *zimbarāri*, derivs. of Goth. **timrs*, ON *timbr*, Dan. *tømmer*, Sw., Du. *timmer*, OHG *zimbar*, etc. 'wood for building, timber' (whence also cpds. Sw., Du. *timmerman*, OHG *zimbarman*, MHG *zimberman*, NHG *zimmermann*) : Grk. δέμω 'construct, build', etc. (9.44). Falk-Torp 1317.

ON *trēsmiðr*, also *hūssmiðr*, cpds. of *trē* 'tree, wood', *hūs* 'house, building' and *smiðr* 'craftsman' (9.42).

OE *trēowwyrhta*, cpd. of *trēow* 'tree, wood' and *wyrhta* 'craftsman' (9.42).

ME, NE *carpenter*, fr. Fr. *charpentier* (above, 2).

5. Lith. *dailidė* (orig. for the finer work 'joiner', but also more general) : *dailus* 'beautiful' (16.81), *dailinti* 'adorn, beautify'.

Lett. *remesis* (Lith. *remesas* 'craftsman, carpenter' obs.) : ChSl. *remĭstvo* 'craft', etc. (9.41). Mühl.-Endz. 3.509 f.

6. SCr. *tesar*, Boh. *tesař*, Pol. *cieśla* : ChSl. *tesati* 'hew', etc. (9.45). Miklosich 355. Brückner 63.

ChSl. *tektonŭ* (Gospels), fr. Grk. τέκτων (above, 1).

ChSl. *drěvodělja* (Supr.), SCr. *drvodjelja*, cpds. of ChSl. *drěvo*, SCr. *drvo* 'tree, wood' and ChSl. *dělati* 'work', SCr. *djeljati* 'carve, fashion'.

Russ. *plotnik*, fr. *plotit'* 'join, put together' : *plest'* 'plait' (9.75).

7. Skt. *takṣan-* = Grk. τέκτων, above, 1.

Skt. *rathakāra-*, lit. 'carriage-maker' (cpd. of *ratha-* 'carriage' and a form of *kṛ-* 'make'), but in actual use 'carpenter'. Cf. F. Edgerton, Proceedings Am. Philosoph. Soc. 79.707.

9.44 BUILD

Grk.	*οἰκοδομέω*	Goth.	*timrjan*	Lith.	*budavoti*
NG	*κτίζω, χτίζω*	ON	*gørva, timbra*	Lett.	*būvēt*
Lat.	*aedificāre*	Dan.	*bygge*	ChSl.	*zĭdati (graditi)*
It.	*edificare*	Sw.	*bygga*	SCr.	*graditi, zidati*
Fr.	*bâtir*	OE	*timbrian, bytlian*	Boh.	*stavěti, budovati*
Sp.	*edificar*	ME	*bylde*	Pol.	*budować (wystawić)*
Rum.	*clădi, zidi*	NE	*build*	Russ.	*stroit', sozidat'*
Ir.	*cunutgim*	Du.	*bouwen*	Skt.	*nir-mā-*
NIr.	*foirgnighim*	OHG	*zimberen*	Av., OPers.	*kar-*
W.	*adeiladu*	MHG	*zimbern, būwen*		
Br.	*sevel*	NHG	*bauen*		

Words for 'build', primarily used for building houses, are in part connected with verbs for 'dwell' through the notion of making a dwelling place, or derivs. and cpds. of nouns for 'dwelling, house'. Words for 'make' when used with an object like 'house', 'wall', etc., are naturally equivalent to 'build', and are often (though generally not entered in the list) the common colloquial expressions for 'build' (cf. NG ἔκαμε ἕνα σπίτι, lit. 'made a house', etc.). In some cases they are the source of the standard words for 'build'. Others reflect more specific actions originally applicable to particular methods of construction, as 'mold, fashion' for work in clay, 'plait' for wickerwork construction (see also under 'plait', 9.75), 'join, put together, arrange' and 'set up, erect', both appropriate to work in wood or stone.

1. Grk. οἰκοδομέω 'build' in general, deriv. of οἰκοδόμος 'builder', or a like cpd. (cf. also οἰκοδομία 'act of building, a building') of οἶκος 'house, dwelling', and the root of δέμω 'construct, build' (not a common prose word), δόμος 'house' : ON *timbr* 'wood for building' (cf. below, 4), Skt. *dama-*, Lat. *domus*, etc. 'house', IE **dem-* 'build', perh. orig. 'join, fit together', as in Goth. *gatiman*, OHG *zeman* 'be fitting, becoming'. Walde-P. 1.786 f.

NG κτίζω or χτίζω 'build', class. Grk. κτίζω mostly 'settle, found' a city, etc. (cf. κτίσις 'a founding', Hom. ἐϋκτίμενος 'well-built') : Skt. *kṣi-* 'dwell, inhabit', Av. *ši-* 'dwell', Lat. *situs* 'situated', *situs*, *-ūs* 'situation', etc. Walde-P. 1.504. Boisacq 525 f.

2. Lat. *aedificāre* (> It. *edificare*, Sp. *edificar*), deriv. of a cpd. (cf. *aedificium* 'building') of *aedēs* 'building, house' (pl. of *aedēs* 'temple', 22.13) and the root of *facere* 'do, make'.

Fr. *bâtir*, OFr. *bastir*, fr. a Gmc. **bastjan* : OHG *bestan* 'bind', deriv. of OHG *bast*, OE *bæst* 'bast, inner bark of trees used for plaiting and building', hence orig. meaning 'work with bast, plait', then 'build houses by plaiting, build'. REW 981. Wartburg 1.278.

Rum. *clădi* 'lay in order, arrange' and hence 'build', fr. Slavic, ChSl. *klasti*, *kladą*, etc. 'lay, put' (12.12). Tiktin 371.

Rum. *zidi*, fr. Slavic, SCr. *zidati*, etc. (below, 6). Tiktin 1820.

3. Ir. *cunutgim* 'build, erect', fr. **con-od-ding-* (cf. *digen* 'firm') : Lat. *fingere* 'mold, fashion', etc. (9.72). Pedersen 2.505 f.

NIr. *foirgnighim*, cpd. of *for-* (: Grk. ὑπέρ) and *gni-* in *do-gnīm* 'do, make'.

W. *adeiladu*, deriv. of *adail*, *adeilad* 'building', prob. cpd. of *ail* 'wattling, plaited work' (whence *eilio* 'wattle, plait, construct'). Morris Jones, 390.

Br. *sevel* 'set up, raise' and hence 'build' : W. *sefyll* 'stand', Ir. *samaigim* 'place', fr. an *m*-formation of IE **stā-* 'stand'. Walde-P. 2.606. Pedersen 1.79.

4. Goth. *timrjan*, ON *timbra*, OE *timbr(i)an*, OHG *zimberen*, *zimbarōn*, MHG *zimbern* (also 'hew' as NHG *zimmern*), derivs. of Goth. **timrs*, ON *timbr*, OE *timber*, OHG *zimbar*, MHG *zimber* 'wood for building, timber' : Grk. δέμω, etc. (above, 1). Falk-Torp 1317. Feist 478.

ON *gørva* 'do, make' (9.11) and in phrases like *gørva hūs*, *skip*, etc., the most common expression for 'build'.

Du. *bouwen*, MHG *būwen*, NHG *bauen* 'cultivate, build' : OHG *būan* 'dwell, inhabit, till', Goth. *bauan*, OE *būan* 'dwell, inhabit', ON *būa* 'dwell, arrange, prepare', also (late) *byggja*, Dan. *bygge*, Sw. *bygga* 'settle, found, build'; with *-*þlo* suffix OE *botl* 'dwelling' (whence OE *bytlian*), with metathesis *bold* (whence ME *bylde*, *bulde*, NE *build*), fr. IE **bheu-* 'be' (9.91). Walde-P. 2.142. Falk-Torp 88, 121.

5. Lith. *budavoti*, fr. Pol. *budować* (below, 6). Brückner, Sl. Fremdwörter 74.

Lett. *būvēt*, fr. MLG *būwen* : Du. *bouwen*, etc. (above, 4). Mühl.-Endz. 1.30.

6. ChSl. *zĭdati*, *sŭzĭdati*, SCr. *zidati*, Russ. *sozidat'* : Lith. *žiesti* 'form, shape, build', prob. with metathesis fr. IE **dheiĝh-* in Lat. *fingere* 'mold, fashion', etc. (9.72). Walde-P. 1.834. Trautmann 367.

ChSl. *graditi* (late, cf. Jagić, Entstehungsgesch. 348, 440), SCr. *graditi* : Boh. *hraditi*, Pol. *grodzić*, Russ. *gorodit'* 'fence in', ChSl. *gradŭ*, etc. 'town' orig. 'enclosure' (19.15). Berneker 330. Stender-Petersen 259.

Boh. *stavěti*, Pol. *wystawić* : *staviti*, Pol. *stawić* 'set, place, erect'.

Boh. *budovati*, Pol. *budować*, derivs. of Boh. *bouda* (older *buda*), Pol. *buda* 'booth, hut', fr. MHG *buode*, NHG *bude* id. Berneker 96.

Russ. *stroit'* 'set in order, arrange' and hence 'build' = ChSl. *stroiti* 'prepare, arrange', etc., fr. **strei-*, perh. an extension of *ster-* in ChSl. *-strěti*, Lat. *sternere*, etc. 'spread out' (9.34). Walde-P. 2.639.

7. Skt. *nir-mā-* 'form, create, fashion, build', cpd. of *mā-* 'measure, mete out, fashion, make'. (9.72).

But 'build' also expressed by Skt. *kr-* 'make', and so regularly by the corresponding Av. and OPers. forms. Cf. OPers. *imam tačaram* (*imām hadiš*) *akunauš* 'built this palace'.

9.45 HEW

Grk.	πελεκάω	Goth.	(*maitan*)	Lith.	*tašyti*
NG	πελεκῶ	ON	*hǫggva, telgja*	Lett.	*tēst*
Lat.	*dolāre*	Dan.	*hugge*	ChSl.	*tesati*
It.	*tagliare*	Sw.	*hugga*	SCr.	*tesati*
Fr.	*tailler* (*doler*)	OE	*hēawan*	Boh.	*tesati*
Sp.	*tajar, dolar, hachear*	ME	*hewe*	Pol.	*ciesać*
Rum.	*tăia* (*dura*)	NE	*hew*	Russ.	*tesat'*
Ir.	*snaidim*	Du.	*houwen*	Skt.	*takṣ-*
NIr.	*snoidhim*	OHG	*houwan*	Av.	*taš-*
W.	*naddu*	MHG	*houwen, zimbern*		
Br.	*trouc'ha, bena*	NHG	*zimmern, behauen*		

'Hew', as distinguished from the more generic 'cut' (9.22), is understood here as applying to cutting with an ax or adze, either the cutting down of trees or especially the skilled trimming of wood in carpentry or of stone. Many of the words listed here are those that are still or have been used for 'cut' in general, and so have been discussed in 9.22. But there are some derivatives of words for 'ax', and one inherited group in which the specific sense of 'hew' is clearly the primary one.

1. IE *$te\hat{k}^{p}$-. Walde-P. 1.717.

Skt. *takṣ-*, Av. *taš-*; Lith. *tašyti*, Lett. *tēst;* ChSl. *tesati*, etc., general Slavic. The same root is still more widespread in words for 'ax', 'adze' (9.25), or 'artisan, carpenter' (9.42, 9.43).

2. Grk. πελεκάω, deriv. of πέλεκυς 'ax' (9.25).

3. Lat. *dolāre* (> OIt. *dolar*, Fr. *doler*, Sp. *dolar*, Rum. *dura;* REW 2718) : Skt. *dal-* 'split, burst', Grk. δαίδαλος 'artfully wrought', with extension, Ir. *dluigim* 'split' (9.27), ON *telgja* 'cut' (9.22), also Ir. *delb* 'form, image', *dolbaim* 'form, mold', Lat. *dōlium* 'vase, jar', IE **del-*. Walde-P. 1.810. Ernout-M. 280. Walde-H. 1.364 f.

Sp. *hachear*, deriv. of *hacha* 'ax' (9.25).

4. Br. *bena*, esp. 'hew stone' : Ir. *benim* 'strike' (9.21).

5. MHG *zimbern*, NHG *zimmern*, see under 'build' (9.44).

For the other words listed see 9.22.

9.46 BORE

Grk.	τετραίνω, τρῡπάω	Goth.	....	Lith.	*grę̃žti* (*skverbti*)
NG	τρυπῶ	ON	*bora*	Lett.	*urbt*
Lat.	*perforāre, terebrāre*	Dan.	*bore*	ChSl.	....
It.	*forare*	Sw.	*borra*	SCr.	*bušiti, vrtjeti*
Fr.	*percer*	OE	*borian*	Boh.	*vrtati*
Sp.	*taladrar, barrenar*	ME	*bore*	Pol.	*swidrować, wiercić*
Rum.	*găuri*	NE	*bore*	Russ.	*buravit', sverlit'*
Ir.	*tollaim*	Du.	*boren*	Skt.	*vidh-, çnath-*
NIr.	*tollaim*	OHG	*borôn*	Av.	....
W.	*tyllu*	MHG	*born*		
Br.	*toulla*	NHG	*bohren*		

Words for 'bore' are often from the notion of 'turn', appropriate to the rotary motion employed in boring a hole, but also through 'pierce' from 'strike' or the like, or 'separate'. Several are derivatives of words for 'auger' or 'hole'.

1. Grk. τετραίνω (cf. τρητός 'perforated', τρῆμα 'perforation, hole', τέρετρον 'auger', Hom. ἔτορε 'pierced') : τείρω 'wear out', Lat. *terere*, Lith. *trinti*, ChSl. *trěti* 'rub', OE *þrāwan* 'twist, turn' (NE *throw*), OHG *drāen* id. (NHG *drehen*), etc., fr. a root **ter-* (**trē-*, etc.), perh. orig. 'rub with a rotary motion', with divergent development to 'rub' or to 'twist, turn' whence 'bore', the last mostly in Grk., but also in Lat. *terebra* 'auger' and the Celtic words for 'auger' (9.47). From an extension of the same root also Grk. τρῡ́ω 'wear out', τρῡπάω 'bore', τρῡ́πανον 'auger', Lith. *trupėti* 'break in pieces', etc. Walde-P. 1.728 ff.

2. Lat. *forāre* (> It. *forare;* but Fr. *forer* only of machine boring), more frequently *perforāre* (> Fr. *perforer*) 'bore, pierce' (cf. *forāmen* 'hole') : ON *bora*, etc. (below, 4), prob. also (otherwise Ernout-M. 381) Lat. *ferīre*, ON *berja* 'strike', etc. (9.21), fr. IE **bher-*, perh. 'strike' as applied to various uses of sharp tools. Walde-P. 2.159 f. Walde-H. 1.481 f.

Lat. *terebrāre*, deriv. of *terebra* 'auger' (above, 1).

Fr. *percer* (It. *pertugiare* 'perforate'), fr. VLat. **pertūsiāre* 'perforate' (cf. *pertūsiō* 'perforation'), deriv. of Lat. *pertundere*, pple. *pertūsus*, 'strike through, pierce', fr. *tundere* 'strike, beat' (9.21). REW 6436.

Sp. *taladrar*, *barrenar*, derivs. of *taladro, barrena* 'auger' (9.47).

Rum. *găuri*, deriv. of *gaură* 'hole', fr. VLat. **cavula*, deriv. of Lat. *cavum* 'hollow, hole'. REW 1795.

3. Ir. *tollaim*, W. *tyllu*, Br. *toulla*, derivs. of Ir. *toll*, W. *twll*, Br. *toull* 'hole' : OE *þēon* (*þēowan*) 'press, stab', ChSl. *tŭknąti* 'prick, push', etc. Walde-P. 2.615.

4. ON *bora*, OE *borian*, etc., general Gmc. : Lat. (*per*)*forāre* (above, 2). Falk-Torp 94.

5. Lith. *grę̃žti* (also 'turn') : Lett. *griezt* 'turn', ON *krōkr* 'a bend, hook', *kringr* 'ring, circle', OHG *krāgo* 'hook', etc. Walde-P. 1.594. Mühl.-Endz. 1.662 f.

Lith. *skverbti* (now mostly 'force in, insert'), etym.? Walde-P. 2.602.

Lett. *urbt* : Lith. *urbti, urbinti* 'pierce with an awl', Lett. *irbs* 'knitting-needle', *urbulis* 'awl', outside connections? Walde-P. 1.146. Mühl.-Endz. 4.302.

6. SCr. *bušiti* (*búšiti*, with different accent from *bùšiti* 'strike down'), etym.?

SCr. *vrtjeti* 'turn, bore', Boh. *vrtati* 'bore', Pol. *wiercić* (*-cieć*) 'turn, bore' : ChSl. *vrŭtěti*, Boh. *vrtěti*, etc. 'turn' (10.12).

Pol. *swidrować*, Russ. *buravit'*, *sverlit'*, derivs. of Pol. *swider*, Russ. *burav, sverlo* 'auger' (9.47).

7. Skt. *vidh-* 'pierce', prob. : Lat. *dī-videre* 'separate, divide', fr. an IE **weidh-* 'separate' (perh. fr. **wi-* 'apart' and **dhē-* 'put, place'). Walde-P. 1.239. Ernout-M. 274.

Skt. *çnath-* 'pierce, thrust through' : Av. *snaθ-* 'strike', outside connections dub. Walde-P. 1.402.

9.47 AUGER

Grk.	τρύπανον, τέρετρον	Goth.	....	Lith.	*grąžtas*
NG	τρυπάνι	ON	*nafarr*	Lett.	*svarpsts*
Lat.	*terebra*	Dan.	*bor*	ChSl.	*svrŭdlŭ*
It.	*trapano, succhiello*	Sw.	*borr, navare*	SCr.	*svrdao, burgija*
Fr.	*tarière*	OE	*na(b)fogār, bor*	Boh.	*vrtak, nebozez*
Sp.	*taladro, barrena*	ME	*navegar, nauger*	Pol.	*świder*
Rum.	*sfredel, burghiu*	NE	*auger*	Russ.	*burav, sverlo*
Ir.	*tarathar*	Du.	*boor, avegaar*	Skt.	(*vedhaka-*)
NIr.	*tarathar*	OHG	*nabagēr, bora*	Av.	....
W.	*taradr, ebill, trwyddew*	MHG	*nabeger*		
		NHG	*bohrer*		
Br.	*tarar*				

Words for 'auger', that is, the more generic words for a boring instrument (special terms for a small borer, like NE *gimlet*, are ignored) are partly from the verbs for 'bore' (or roots of similar source, 'turn, whirl'), partly connected with words for 'sharp' or some sharp instrument. A few are from various other sources, and there are several loanwords.

1. Derivs. of **ter-*, etc. in words for 'bore' (9.46).

Grk. τρύπανον (cf. τρῡπάω 'bore'), whence MLat. *trepanum*, OIt. *trepano* (cf. Fr. *trépan* as surgical instrument), It. *trapano*, NG τρυπάνι; Grk. τέρετρον (Hom.); Lat. *terebra;* Ir. *tarathar*, W. *taradr*, Br. *tarar*, *talar*, Latinized Gall. *taratrum*, whence OFr. *tarere*, Fr. *tarière* (with suffix change), Sp. *taladro*. Ernout-M. 1033. REW 8570, 8959.

2. It. *succhiello* (less commonly *succhio* in this sense) : *succhiare* 'suck', from the notion of sucking out the chips. REW 8417.

Sp. *barrena*, fr. Lat. *veruīna* 'spit, javelin' and later 'auger', deriv. of *veru* 'spit, javelin' : Ir. *bir* 'spit', Goth. *qairu* 'stake, thorn', etc. Walde-P. 1.689. REW 9261.

Rum. *sfredel*, fr. Slavic (below, 6).

Rum. *burghiu*, fr. Turk. *burgu* 'auger' (cf. SCr. *burgija*, below, 6). Lokotsch 363.

3. Ir. *tarathar*, etc., above, 1.

W. *ebill* (MBr. *ebil* 'peg, nail') : Lat. *aculeus* 'sting, spur, spine', *ācer* 'sharp', OE *awel* 'awl', etc. Walde-P. 1.29. Walde-H. 1.11. Stokes 5.

W. *trwyddew* : *trwyddedu* 'penetrate, pass' (now 'license'), deriv. of *trwy* 'through'.

4. ON *nafarr*, Sw. *navare*, OE *na(b)fogār*, ME *navegar*, *nauger*, NE *auger* (*a nauger > an auger*), Du. *avegaar*, OHG *nabagēr*, *nabugēr*, MHG *nabeger*, also (with metathesis through influence of OHG *nagal*, MHG *nagel* 'nail') OHG *nagabēr*, MHG *nageber*, fr. a Gmc. cpd. (**naba-gaiza-*, **nabō-gaiza-*) of the elements seen in ON *nǫf*, OE *nafu*, OHG *naba* 'nave of a wheel' and ON *geirr*, OE *gār*, OHG *gēr* 'spear, pointed instrument', with orig. meaning 'sharp tool for boring through the nave of a wheel'. Falk-Torp 757. NED s.v. *auger*.

Dan. *bor*, Sw. *borr*, OE *bor*, Du. *boor*, OHG *bora*, NHG *bohrer* : ON *bora* 'bore', etc. (9.46).

5. Lith. *grąžtas* (cf. OPr. *granstis* id.) : *grę̃žti* 'turn, bore' (9.46).

Lett. *svarpsts*, prob. : W. *chwerfu* 'whirl', ON *svarfa* 'displace, turn', OHG *swerban* 'whirl', ME, NE *swerve*, etc. Mühl.-Endz. 3.1144. Walde-P. 2.529 f. (without Lett. *svarpsts*).

6. ChSl. *svrŭdlŭ*, SCr. *svrdao*, Pol. *świder*, Russ. *sverlo*, prob. fr. **svrŭb-dlo-* and either (IE *sw-*) : OHG *swerban* 'whirl', or (IE *k̂w-*) : Goth. *hvairban* 'wander', OE *hweorfan* 'wander, turn', etc. (orig. 'turn around'). Walde-P. 1.473. Brückner 535.

SCr. *burgija* 'small auger', fr. Turk. *burgu* 'auger'. Miklosich, Türk. El. 1.269. (Lokotsch 363).

Boh. *vrtak* : *vrtati* 'bore' (9.46)

Boh. *nebozez*, early Gmc. loanword, cf. OHG *nabagēr*, etc. (above, 4). Stender-Petersen 292 f.

Russ. *burav*, prob. fr. a Turk. **burav* beside *burgu* (> SCr. *burgija*, above). Berneker 102.

7. Skt. *vedhaka-*, *vedhanikā-* 'instrument for piercing pearls' : *vidh-* 'pierce' (9.46).

9.48 SAW (sb.)

Grk.	πρίων	Goth.	....	Lith.	*piuklas*
NG	πριόνι	ON	*sǫg*	Lett.	*zāg'is*
Lat.	*serra*	Dan.	*sav*	ChSl.	*pila*
It.	*sega*	Sw.	*såg*	SCr.	*pila, testera*
Fr.	*scie*	OE	*sagu, snid*	Boh.	*pila*
Sp.	*sierra*	ME	*sawe*	Pol.	*piła*
Rum.	*ferestrău*	NE	*saw*	Russ.	*pila*
Ir.	*tuiresc* (*serr*)	Du.	*zaag*	Skt.	*krakaca-, karapatra-*
NIr.	*sābh* (*toireasc*)	OHG	*saga*	Av.	....
W.	*llif*	MHG	*sage*		
Br.	*heskenn*	NHG	*säge*		

The saw is a special form of cutting instrument (though its evolution as a distinct tool goes back to neolithic times), and the majority of words for 'saw' are from roots meaning 'cut'. Imitative origin, a rough imitation of the noise of sawing, is probable for several. Some loanwords reflect the resemblance between a fine saw and a file.

1. Grk. πρῑ́ων, NG πριόνι, fr. vb. πρῑ́ω 'saw' (cf. πριστός 'sawn' Hom., ἐπρίσθην, etc.), *πρῑσ-, prob. of imitative origin. Walde-P. 2.89.

2. Lat. *serra* (> Sp. *sierra*), perh. of imitative orig. (*rr*, with *s* fr. *secāre*). Walde-P. 2.501.

It. *sega*, Fr. *scie* : It. *segare*, Fr. *scier* 'to saw', fr. Lat. *secāre* 'cut'. REW 7764.

Rum. *ferestrău*, fr. Hung. *füresz* 'saw'.

3. Ir. *tuiresc*, NIr. *toireasc*, prob. fr. **tar-thesc*, a cpd. of *tar-* 'across' and a deriv. of *tescaim* 'cut' (9.22). Macbain 381.

Ir. *serr*, fr. Lat. *serra* (above, 2). Vendryes, De hib. voc. 177. See also under 'scythe, sickle', 8.33.

NIr. *sābh*, fr. NE *saw*.

W. *llif*, fr. Lat. *līma* 'file'. Loth, Mots lat. 182.

Br. *heskenn* : *hesk* a kind of reed with sharp edges, W. *hesg* 'sedges', reduplicated formations fr. the root **sek-* 'cut' of Lat. *secāre*, etc., and in the Gmc. word for 'saw' (below, 4). Henry 161. (Walde-P. 2.475 for *hesk*, etc.).

4. ON *sǫg*, OE *sagu*, *sage*, OHG *saga*, *sega*, etc., general Gmc., fr. IE **sek-* in Lat. *secāre*, ChSl. *sěšti* 'cut', etc. (9.22). Walde-P. 2.475. Falk-Torp 942.

OE *snid* : *snīþan*, ON *snīða*, Goth. *sneiþan* 'cut' (9.22). Walde-P. 2.695.

5. Lith. *piuklas* : *piauti* 'cut', etc. (9.22). Walde-P. 2.12.

Lett. *zāg'is*, fr. MLG *sage* : OHG *saga*, etc. (above, 4). Mühl.-Endz. 4.695.

6. ChSl. *pila*, etc., general Slavic word for 'saw', with dimin. forms for 'file', also (perh. through Slavic) Lith.

piela 'saw, file' (obs.), *pielyčia* 'file', *pelyti* 'to file', loanword fr. the Gmc., word for 'file', OHG *fīhala*, *fīla*, MHG *vīle*, NHG *feile*. Brückner 414. Buga Kalba ir Senovė 68, 187. (Trautman 210 assumes orig. connection with Lith. *peilis* 'knife', but this is another loanword.)

SCr. *testera*, fr. Turk. *testere* 'saw'. Miklosich, Türk. El. 1.176.

Skt. *krakaca-*, of imitative orig., cf. *krakṣ-* 'roar, crash', etc., *kṛkara-* 'a kind of partridge', etc. Walde-P. 1.413.

Skt. *karapatra-*, lit. 'hand-blade', cpd. of *kara-* 'hand' and *pattra-* 'wing, feather, blade' (4.392).

9.49 HAMMER (sb.)

Grk.	*σφῦρα*	Goth.	....	Lith.	*plaktukas* (*kujis*)
NG	*σφυρί*	ON	*hamarr*	Lett.	*āmars, veseris*
Lat.	*malleus*	Dan.	*hammer*	ChSl.	*mlatŭ*
It.	*martello*	Sw.	*hammar(e)*	SCr.	*čekić*
Fr.	*marteau*	OE	*hamor, bȳtl*	Boh.	*kladivo*
Sp.	*martillo*	ME	*hamer*	Pol.	*młot*
Rum.	*ciocan*	NE	*hammer*	Russ.	*molot*
Ir.	*ordd*	Du.	*hamer*	Skt.	*mudgara-, ghana-*
NIr.	*casūr*	OHG	*hamar*	Av.	(*čakuš-*)
W.	*morthwyl*	MHG	*hamer*		
Br.	*morzol*	NHG	*hammer*		

Words for 'hammer' (sb.) are mostly from roots meaning 'strike, beat, crush', but some are based on the material (as the Gmc. group reflects the primitive hammer of stone) or shape (as probably the Grk. *σφῦρα*).

1. Grk. *σφῦρα*, NG *σφυρί*, prob. fr. Grk. *σφυρόν* 'ankle' through similarity of appearance. Walde-P. 2.668 f. Boisacq 931.

2. Lat. *malleus* (> Romance words meaning 'mall, mallet', etc.), with which is connected *martulus* (by dissim. fr. **malltlo-*), late *martellus* (> It. *martello*, Fr. *marteau*, Sp. *martillo*), prob. : ChSl. *mlatŭ*, etc. (below, 6), and fr. the root of Lat. *molere* (cf. Umbr. *maletu* 'molitum'), ChSl. *mlěti* 'crush, grind', but much disputed in details. Walde-P. 2.287. Ernout-M. 582, 592. Walde-H. 2.16, 37.

Rum. *ciocan*, fr. Turk. *çakan* 'battle-ax', prob. through Slavic, cf. Bulg. *čekan* 'hammer', Russ. *čekan* 'punch, stamp' earlier 'battle-ax'. Tiktin 355. Lokotsch 384. Berneker 134 f.

3. Ir. *ordd* (NIr. *ord*, W. *gordd* 'sledge-hammer', Br. *horz* 'mallet'), etym.? Pedersen 1.114. Stokes 52. Macbain 269.

NIr. *casūr*, prob. loanword fr. some unattested deriv. of NE *cass* or Fr. *casser* 'break'.

W. *morthwyl*, Br. *morzol*, fr. Lat. *martulus*, *martellus* (above, 2). Pedersen 1.239. Loth, Mots lat. 188.

4. ON *hamarr*, OE *hamor*, etc., general Gmc., orig. 'stone tool' (this meaning preserved in ON) : Skt. *açman-*, Lith. *akmuo*, ChSl. *kamy* 'stone' (1.44). Walde-P. 1.29 f. Falk-Torp 377 f.

OE *bȳt(e)l* : MLG *botel* 'hammer', MHG *bœzel* 'flail', fr. the root of OE *bēatan*, OHG *bōz(z)an* 'strike, beat', etc. (9.21). Walde-P. 2.127.

5. Lith. *plaktukas* : *plakti* 'beat, whip', Lat. *plangere* 'beat (the breast), wail', Grk. *πλήσσω* 'strike', etc. Walde-P. 2.92.

Lith. *kugis*, *kujis* ('heavy hammer'), OPruss. *cugis* : late ChSl. *kyjĭ* 'hammer, mallet', fr. root of Lith. *kauti* 'strike, beat, fight', ChSl. *kovati* 'hammer, forge', etc. (9.61). Walde-P. 1.330. Berneker 676.

Lett. *āmars*, *āmurs*, fr. MLG *hamer* : ON *hamarr*, etc. (above, 4). Mühl.-Endz. 1.238 f.

Lett. *veseris*, fr. Esth. *wasar* 'hammer'. Mühl.-Endz. 4.544.

6. ChSl. *mlatŭ*, Pol. *młot(ek)*, Russ. *molot* (cf. SCr. *mlat* 'threshing flail', Boh. *mlat* 'mallet'), fr. the root of ChSl. *mlěti* 'crush, grind'. Berneker 2.73.

SCr. *čekić*, through Turk. *çekiç* fr. NPers. *čakuš* (below, 7). Berneker 135.

Boh. *kladivo* (also late ChSl.), prob. : Grk. *κλαδαρός* 'fragile', Lat. *clādēs* 'harm, injury', etc., fr. a dental extension of the root in Lith. *kalti* 'hammer, forge', etc. (9.61). Walde-P. 1.438 f. Berneker 506 f.

7. Skt. *mudgara-*, etym.? Walde-P. 2.312. Uhlenbeck 227.

Skt. *ghana-*, adj. 'striking', sb. 'hammer, club' : *han-*, Av. *jan-* 'strike, kill'. Grk. *θείνω* 'strike', etc. (9.21). Walde-P. 1.679 f.

Av. *čakuš-* (quotable only as a weapon, but cf. NPers. *čakuš* 'hammer'), etym.? Walde-P. 1.381.

9.50 NAIL

Grk.	*ἧλος*	Goth.	(*ga-nagljan*, vb.)	Lith.	*vinis*
NG	*καρφί, πρόκα*	ON	*nagli, saumr* (coll.)	Lett.	*nagla*
Lat.	*clāvus*	Dan.	*søm*	ChSl.	*gvozdĭ*
It.	*chiodo*	Sw.	*spik*	SCr.	*čavao*
Fr.	*clou*	OE	*nægel*	Boh.	*hřeb*
Sp.	*clavo*	ME	*nayl*	Pol.	*g(w)óźdź*
Rum.	*cuiu*	NE	*nail*	Russ.	*gvozd'*
Ir.	*clō, tairnge*	Du.	*spijker*	Skt.	(*çan̄ku-*)
NIr.	*tairnge*	OHG	*nagal*	Av.	....
W.	*hoel*	MHG	*nagel*		
Br.	*tach*	NHG	*nagel*		

The ancestor of the metal 'nail' was a wooden peg, and several of the words listed were also used for the latter in the early periods, while still others have cognates pointing to this as the earlier use. The identity with the 'nail' of fingers and toes is characteristic of Germanic.

1. Grk. *ἧλος* (in Hom. 'nail-head, stud' as an ornament), Dor. *ἇλος*, Aeol. **ϝάλλος* (cf. *γάλλοι· ἧλοι*, Hesych.), prob. : Lat. *vallum* 'stake, palisade', this perh. with Goth. *walus* 'staff', ON *vǫlr* 'round staff', etc., fr. IE **wel-* in Lat. *volvere*, Goth. *-walwjan* 'roll', etc. Walde-P. 1.301. Ernout-M. 1072.

Byz. *καρφίον*, NG *καρφί*, dim. of Grk. *κάρφος* 'dry stalk' : *κάρφω* 'dry up'.

NG *πρόκα* ('shoemaker's peg', 'tack', but also common for 'nail'), earlier *μπρόκα*, fr. It. *brocca* 'forked stick'. G. Meyer, Neugr. Stud. 4.64.

2. Lat. *clāvus* (whence, partly through VLat. **claus*, It. *chiodo*, Fr. *clou*, Sp. *clavo*) : Ir. *clō* 'nail', Lat. *clāvis*, Grk. *κλείς*, ChSl. *ključĭ* 'key', orig. 'peg for fastening' (7.24). Walde-P. 1.492. Ernout-M. 194. Walde-H. 1.229 f. REW 1984.

Rum. *cuiu*, fr. Lat. *cuneus* 'wedge'. REW 2396.

3. Ir. *clō* : Lat. *clāvus* (above, 2).

MIr., NIr. *tairnge* : Gall. *tarinca*, *taringa* 'iron spike', fr. the same root as Ir. *tarathar* 'auger' (9.47). Marstrander, Festskr. til Alf Torp 242 f.

W. *hoel*, perh. fr. **soghlā-*, deriv. of IE **segh-* 'hold' in Grk. *ἔχω*, etc. Walde-P. 2.482. Stokes 297.

Br. *tach*, fr. OFr. *tache* 'fibula, gros clou' (Godefroi), belonging with MLG *tacke*, MHG *zacke* 'prong', ME *takke*, NE *tack*, and prob. of Gmc. origin (though relations with the group OFr. *estache*, etc., are complicated). Henry 258. Falk-Torp 1241. REW 8218. Gamillscheg 828.

4. (Goth. *ga-nagljan*, vb., 'nail on'), ON *nagli*, OE *nægel*, ME *nayl*, NE *nail*, OHG *nagal*, MHG, NHG *nagel*, the same words as for 'nail' of the finger or toe (except that ON *nagli* and *nagl* are differentiated), this latter sense being the orig., as in the cognates, Grk. *ὄνυξ*, Lat. *unguis*, etc. (4.39).

ON *saumr* 'seam, sewing' (: OE *sēam* 'seam', etc., fr. the root for 'sew'), also coll. 'nails' (esp. in shipbuilding), whence Dan. *søm* 'nail', Sw. *söm* 'hobble nail, horseshoe nail'. By analogy to the 'seam' of a garment the word was applied to the 'seam' of a ship (as in OE and NE), then to the row of nails marking the seam. This does not necessarily reflect directly the primitive method of binding the planks together by thongs (for which cf. the passages quoted by Falk, Wört. u. Sach. 4.50) as is assumed by Falk-Torp 1234 and Hellquist 942.

Sw. *spik* (also Norw.), Du. *spijker* (ON *spīkr* 'spike') : ON *spīk* 'splinter, peg', Lat. *spīca* 'point, spear of grain', *spīna* 'thorn', etc. Walde-P. 2.654. Falk-Torp 1120. Hellquist 1041.

5. Lith. *vinis* : OPruss. *winis* 'peg, bung'; further connections? Trautmann, Altpreuss. 462.

Lett. *nagla*, fr. MHG *nagel* : OHG *nagal*, etc. (above, 4). Mühl.-Endz. 2.687.

6. ChSl. *gvozdĭ*, *gvozdĭjĭ*, Pol. *g(w)óźdź*, Russ. *gvozd'*, perh. : Ir. *bot* 'penis', W. *both* 'nave of a wheel, boss'. Pokorny, Z. celt. Ph. 16.405. Walde-H. 1.574. Otherwise (: Lat. *hasta* 'spear'). Berneker 365 f., Brückner 166.

SCr. *čavao*, fr. the Venetian form (cf. Meyer-Lübke, It. Gram. 112) of It. *chiavo*, a by-form (now only poetic) of *chiodo* (above, 2). Berneker 138.

Boh. *hřeb*, fr. OHG *grebil* 'peg'? So Miklosich 412. Otherwise Gebauer 1.518 (same word as *hřebí*, ChSl. *žrěbĭjĭ* 'lot', but semantic relation?).

7. Skt. *çan̄ku-* '(wooden) stake, peg' (no evidence of the use of metal nails in construction) : ChSl. *sąkŭ* 'twig', W. *cainc* 'branch', Skt. *çākhā-*, Lith. *šaka* 'branch', etc. (8.35). Walde-P. 1.335.

9.51 BEAM

Grk.	*δοκός*	Goth.	*ans*	Lith.	*balkis, sija, rąstas*
NG	*δοκάρι* (*πατερό, γρεντιά*)	ON	*āss, bjalki, trē*	Lett.	*bal'k'is*
Lat.	*trabs*	Dan.	*bjælke*	ChSl.	*brŭvŭno*
It.	*trave*	Sw.	*bjälke*	SCr.	*greda*
Fr.	*poutre*	OE	*bēam, balca* (*trēow*)	Boh.	*trám, břevno*
Sp.	*viga*	ME	*beem, balke*	Pol.	*belka, bierwiono*
Rum.	*bîrna, grinda*	NE	*beam*	Russ.	*brevno, balka*
Ir.	*trost* (*crann*)	Du.	*balk*	Skt.	*sthūṇā-*
NIr.	*sail*	OHG	*balco, boum*	Av.	*fra-skəmba-*
W.	*trawst*	MHG	*balke*		
Br.	*treust*	NHG	*balken*		

The supporting or carrying element in the construction of wooden buildings, originally the squared timber of a tree, is often denoted by the word for 'tree', or some kind of tree (Ir. *sail* 'willow') or 'timber'. Or it may be named for its function as the 'supporter, carrier', or 'binder'.

1. Grk. *δοκός*, NG *δοκάρι*, orig. 'supporter, holder' : *-δοκος*, in *ἰο-δόκος* 'holding arrows', *οἰνο-δόκος* 'holding wine', etc., *δοχή* 'receptacle', *δέκομαι*, *δέχομαι* 'receive, hold'. Walde-P. 1.783.

NG *πατερό* (or *πάτερο*), deriv. of *πάτος* 'bottom, floor'. G. Meyer, Neugr. Stud. 2.86.

NG also *γρεντιά* fr. Slavic (SCr. *greda*, etc., below, 6), and *τράβα* fr. Ital. *trave*.

2. Lat. *trabs* (> It. *trave*, OFr. *tref*, Sp. *trabe* obs.), prob. : Osc. *trííbúm* 'house, building', Umbr. *trebeit* 'abides, is stationed', Ir. *treb* 'dwelling', *atreba* 'dwells', Lith. *troba* 'building', OE *þorp*, OHG *dorf* 'village', etc., but the semantic relation of Lat. *trabs* to the other words is far from clear. Walde-P. assumes that the primary meaning was 'beam', whence 'beam-construction, building'. But the meaning 'beam' is confined to the Latin word and more likely secondary. Possibly to be explained either as part for the whole applied to the main structural element of a building, or as though the notion 'dwell' (as in Irish), 'be stationed' (as Umbr. *trebeit*) applied to the most substantial part of the structure. Walde-P. 1.757. Ernout-M. 1050.

Fr. *poutre*, earlier meaning (in OFr. and into 16th. cent.) 'young mare', fr. VLat. *pulliter* (cf. Niedermann, Mnemos. 1936.270 f.), deriv. of Lat. *pullus* 'young of animals, foal' (3.45). The semantic change prob. reflects the practice of ornamenting the ends of beams with carved horses' heads, etc., as similarly OIt. *poltro* 'bed' and *poltrona* 'armchair'. REW 6825. Sperber, Wört. u. Sach. 2.190 ff. Otherwise, comparing the secondary uses of animal names, like Fr. *chèvre*, *bélier*, etc. (cf. also NE *sawhorse*, *clotheshorse*, etc.). Bloch 2.176.

Sp. *viga*, fr. Lat. *bīga* 'pair, team of horses' (cf. *bijugus* 'yoked two together') through 'wooden yoke'. REW 1095.

Rum. *bîrna*, *grinda*, both fr. Slavic, cf. ChSl. *brŭvŭno*, etc., SCr. *greda*, etc. (below, 6).

3. Ir. *trost* (NIr. *trost* 'staff'), W. *trawst*, Br. *treust*, fr. Lat. *trānstrum* 'cross-beam', deriv. of *trāns* 'across'. Pedersen 1.203.

Ir. *crann* 'tree, wood' (1.42), hence also 'beam'.

Ir. *sail* 'willow', NIr. also 'beam, club' : Lat. *salex*, OE *sealh*, etc. 'willow'. Walde-P. 2.454.

4. Goth. *ans*, ON *āss* : MHG *ans-boum* 'bridge-beam', further connections dub. Walde-P. 1.133. Falk-Torp 9. Feist 52.

ON *bjalki* (rare), Dan. *bjælke*, Sw. *bjälke*; with different grade OE *balca*, ME *balke*, Du. *balk*, OHG *balco*, MHG *balke*, NHG *balken* : ON *bolr* 'tree-trunk', Grk. *φάλαγξ* 'log, block, line of battle', Lith. *balžiena* 'beam on a harrow', Russ. (dial.) *bolozno* 'thick board'; root connection dub. Walde-P. 2.181. Falk-Torp 76 f.

OE *bēam* 'tree, pillar, beam', ME *beem*, NE *beam*, OHG *boum* 'tree, pole, beam' (NHG *baum* 'tree') : Goth. *bagms* 'tree', etc. (1.42).

ON *trē*, OE *trēow* 'tree, wood' (1.42), hence also 'beam' (cf. NE *axletree*, *singletree*, etc.).

5. Lith. *balkis*, Lett. *bal'k'is*, fr. MLG *balke* : NHG *balken*, etc. (above, 4).

Lith. *sija* : Lett. *siet*, etc. 'bind' (9.16).

Lith. *rąstas*, prob. : *ręsti* 'cut, notch',

as something 'cut off' or 'trimmed'. H. Petersson, IF 24.277.

6. ChSl. *brŭvŭno, brŭno*, Boh. *břevno*, Pol. *bierwiono*, Russ. *brevno*, prob. : ON *brū*, OE *brycg*, OHG *brucka*, Gall. *briva* 'bridge', root connection? Walde-P. 2.207 f. Berneker 92.

ChSl. **gręda* (Russ.-ChSl. *grjada*), SCr. *greda* : Boh. *hřada* 'pole', Lith. *grinda* 'floor-board', Lat. *grunda, suggrunda* 'eaves', ON *grind* 'latticework, door', etc., root connection? Walde-P. 1.657. Walde-H. 1.623 f. Berneker 348 f.

Boh. *trám* (Pol. *tram* 'architrave'), fr. NHG (dial.) *tram* 'beam', MHG *drām(e), trām(e)* 'beam, bar' : OHG *dremil* 'beam, bar', MHG *drum* 'end-piece, splinter', prob. as 'something rubbed or hewn', fr. IE **ter-* 'rub' (9.31). Weigand-H. 1060. Brückner 574 f.

Pol. *belka*, Russ. *balka*, fr. NHG *balken* (above, 4). Brückner 20.

7. Skt. *sthūṇā-* 'post, pillar' and perh. also 'beam' : Av. *stūna-* 'pillar', Grk. στῦλος 'pillar, style', OE *studu* 'pillar, prop', etc., fr. IE **stāu-*, beside **stā-* 'stand' in Skt. *sthā-*, Grk. ἵστημι, etc. Walde-P. 2.608.

Av. *fra-skəmba-, fra-sčimbana-* 'supporting beam' : Skt. *skambha(na)-* 'prop, pillar', *skambh-* 'support', Av. *(frā-) skamb-* 'fix'. Walde-P. 2.539. Barth. 1002.

9.52 BOARD

Grk.	*σανίς*	Goth.	*(-baurd)*	Lith.	*lenta*
NG	*σανίδι, τάβλα*	ON	*borð*	Lett.	*dēlis*
Lat.	*tabula, assis*	Dan.	*bræt*	ChSl.	*dŭska*
It.	*asse, tavola*	Sw.	*bräde*	SCr.	*daska*
Fr.	*planche*	OE	*bord*	Boh.	*prkno, deska*
Sp.	*tabla*	ME	*bord, planke*	Pol.	*deska*
Rum.	*scîndură*	NE	*board, plank*	Russ.	*doska*
Ir.	*clār*	Du.	*plank*	Skt.	*phalaka-*
NIr.	*clār*	OHG	*bret*	Av.	....
W.	*astell*	MHG	*bret*		
Br.	*planken*	NHG	*brett*		

Words for 'board' or 'plank' (the differentiation of NE *board* and *plank* according to its thickness may generally be ignored) are from notions like 'flat surface', 'piece of wood', 'something split off'. As 'piece of board' they are used also in various specialized senses, as 'tablet, table, slab, shelf, plate, shield', etc.

1. Grk. σανίς, -ίδος (in Hom. mostly pl. 'folding doors'), NG σανίδι, -ίδα etym. dub. Walde-P. 1.709. Boisacq 851.

Grk. πίναξ, in Hom. for boards or planks of ships, but usually 'tablet' or 'platter' (see 5.32).

Byz., NG τάβλα, fr. Lat. *tabula* (below, 2). G. Meyer, Neugr. Stud. 3.64 f.

2. Lat. *tabula* (> It. *tavola*, Sp. *tabla*), Umbr. *tafle* 'in tabula', etym. dub., perh. fr. **tal-dhlā-* : Skt. *tala-* 'surface', OHG *dil* 'boarding', etc. (below, 4). Walde-P. 1.740.

Lat. *assis*, also written *axis* (> It. *asse*, Fr. *ais*) : *asser* 'stake, beam', *assula* 'splinter, chip', outside connections dub. Ernout-M. 80. Walde-H. 1.74. REW 732.

Late Lat. *planca* (> Fr. *planche*; ONorth.Fr. *planke* > ME *planke*, NE *plank*, Du. *plank*, Br. *planken*), fem. of *plancus* 'flat-footed' (only in Festus, but source of cognomen Plancus) : Grk. πλάξ 'flat surface', Lett. *plakt* 'become flat', etc. Ernout-M. 774.

Rum. *scîndură*, fr. Lat. *scandula* (*scindula*) 'shingle', this prob. : OHG *scinten* 'flay' (NHG *schinden*), Ir. *scandraim* 'split', etc., with orig. notion of 'split', and in the form *scindula* associated with *scindere* 'split'. Walde-P. 2.563 f. REW 7652.

3. Ir. *clār* : W. *clawr* 'surface, lid', etc., Br. *kleur* 'shaft', Grk. κλῆρος 'piece of wood for casting lots', κλῆμα 'twig, cutting', κλάω 'break (off)', etc. Walde-P. 1.437. Pedersen 2.49.

W. *astell*, fr. late Lat. *astella*, Lat. *assula* (*astula*) : *assis* (above, 2). Loth, Mots lat. 134.

Br. *planken*, fr. Lat. *planca* (above, 2).

4. Goth. *-baurd* (in *fotubaurd* 'footstool'), ON *borð* (Dan., Sw. *bord* mostly 'table'), OE, ME *bord*, NE *board*, OHG, MHG, MLG *bret* (> Dan. *bræt* and prob. Sw. *bräde*), prob. as orig. 'piece cut off' from either the *to-* pple. or a *dh-* extension of IE **bher-* in Lat. *ferīre* 'strike', etc. Walde-P. 2.174. Falk-Torp 94, 111. Hellquist 107.

ON *þili* 'board wall, flooring', *þilja* 'planking on a ship', OE *þel* 'thin plate of wood or metal', *þille* 'flooring', OHG *dil* 'boarding', *dilla* 'board, boarding, deck', NHG *diele* 'long board, floor, etc.', MLG *dele* 'plank, flooring' (> NE *deal*), etc., widespread Gmc. group, but mostly in some specialized sense of 'board, plank' (and so not entered in the list) : Skt. *tala-* 'surface', Grk. τηλία a kind of 'board' or 'tablet', Ir. *talam* 'earth', etc., all from notion of flat surface. Walde-P. 1.740. Falk-Torp 1261.

ME *planke*, NE *plank*, Du. *plank*, fr. Lat. *planca* (above, 2).

5. Lith. *lenta*, prob. orig. 'board of linden-wood' : ON, OE *lind*, OHG *linta* 'linden-tree' also 'shield'. Walde-P. 2.437. Otherwise Falk-Torp 645.

Lett. *dēlis* (*dēle*), fr. MLG *dele* (above, 4). Mühl.-Endz. 1.462, 463.

6. ChSl. *dŭska*, etc., general Slavic, an early Gmc. loanword, cf. ON *diskr*, OE *disc* 'plate', OHG *tisc* 'plate, table', this fr. Lat. *discus* 'discus, plate' (fr. Grk. δίσκος 'quoit, discus'). The word was used in Gmc. for a flat piece of board, then specialized in its use for 'plate' or 'table', but in Slavic becoming the word for 'board' in general. Berneker 246. Stender-Petersen 405 f.

Boh. *prkno*, etym.? Miklosich 242. Possibly as orig. 'something laid across' : ChSl. *prěkŭ* (**perkŭ*) 'crosswise'.

7. Skt. *phalaka-* : *phal-* 'burst, split', OHG *spalten* 'split', etc. (9.27), Grk. σφέλας 'footstool, pedestal', σφαλ(λ)ός 'a kind of discus', late ChSl. *polica* 'board', ON *fjǫl*, Dan. *fjæl* 'thin board', etc. Walde-P. 2.677 ff.

9.53 MASON

Grk.	*τέκτων, λιθουργός*	Goth.	*timrja*	Lith.	*murininkas*
NG	*χτίστης, μάστορας*	ON	*steinsmiðr*	Lett.	*mūrnieks*
Lat.	*(faber)*	Dan.	*murer*	ChSl.	....
It.	*muratore*	Sw.	*murare*	SCr.	*zidar*
Fr.	*maçon*	OE	*stānwyrhta*	Boh.	*zednik*
Sp.	*albañil*	ME	*machun*	Pol.	*mularz*
Rum.	*zidar*	NE	*mason*	Russ.	*kamenščik*
Ir.	*sāir*	Du.	*metselaar*	Skt.	*lepaka-*
NIr.	*saor cloiche*	OHG	*mūrāri*	Av.	....
W.	*saer maen, saer cerrig*	MHG	*mūrære*		
Br.	*mañsoner*	NHG	*maurer*		

'Mason', the one who builds with stone or brick, is often expressed by words for 'artisan' or 'builder', either used alone in specialized sense or with defining noun or adjective forms. Several of the more distinctive words are derivs. of those for '(stone) wall'. Some derivs. of words for 'stone' are used for 'mason', but most of these apply rather to the 'stonecutter' who prepares the stone or does fine work in stone.

1. Grk. τέκτων 'artisan', including 'mason', see 9.42.

Grk. λιθουργός, general term for 'worker in stone' (cf. λίθος 'stone', ξυλουργός 'woodworker', 9.43); less frequent, but with more technical significance, λιθολόγος, lit. 'one who picks out (and builds with) stone' (λέγω 'pick out, select'), λιθοδόμος 'one who builds with stone' (δέμω 'construct, build', 9.44).

NG χτίστης 'builder', also spec. 'mason' : κτίζω 'build' (9.44).

NG μάστορας 'artisan', also spec. 'mason', see 9.42.

2. Lat. *faber* 'artisan', including 'mason', see 9.42.

Late Lat. *lapidārius* (fr. *lapis, -idis* 'stone') is rather 'stonecutter, lapidary' than 'mason'.

It. *muratore*, deriv. of *murare* 'build in stone', fr. *muro* '(stone) wall' (Lat. *mūrus* 'wall').

Fr. *maçon* (> ME *machun*, NE *mason*), MLat. *macio, machio, matio* 'mason', prob. a Latinized form of a Gmc. **makō* : OE *macian* 'make', OHG *mahhōn* 'accomplish, make, construct', etc., reflecting an assumed earlier meaning of the Gmc. verb, namely 'build with clay' (see 9.11). REW 5208. Meyer-Lübke, Wört. u. Sach. 9.67 f. Sofer, Isidorus 142. Walde-H. 2.4.

Sp. *albañil*, fr. Arab. *bannā* 'architect'. Lokotsch 216.

Rum. *zidar*, fr. Slavic, SCr. *zidar* (below, 6).

3. Ir. *sāir*, NIr. *saor*, W. *saer* 'artisan' (9.42), including 'mason'; more specifically NIr. *saor cloiche*, W. *saer maen, saer cerrig*, with words for 'stone' (1.44).

Br. *mañsoner*, fr. Fr. *maçon* (above, 2) with added agent suffix.

4. Goth. *timrja* 'carpenter, builder' (9.43), also 'builder in stone' (Mk. 12.10).

ON *steinsmiðr*, cpd. of *steinn* 'stone' and *smiðr* 'artisan' (9.42); also *steinmeistari*, lit. 'stone-master'.

Dan. *murer*, Sw. *murare*, OHG *mūrāri*, MHG *murære*, NHG *maurer*, derivs. of Dan., Sw. *mur*, OHG *mūra*, MHG *mūre*, NHG *mauer* 'stone wall', fr. Lat. *mūrus* 'wall'. Falk-Torp 741.

OE *stānwyrhta*, both 'stonecutter' and 'mason', cpd. of *stān* 'stone' and *wyrhta* 'artisan' (9.42).

ME *machun, macon, mason*, NE *mason*, fr. Fr. *maçon* (above, 2). NED s.v.

Du. *metselaar*, deriv. of *metselen* 'build in stone', fr. MDu. *mets(e), maets(e)* 'mason' : OHG *stein-meizo*, NHG *steinmetz* 'stonecutter', fr. a Gallo-Rom. **matsio* = MLat. *macio* (above, 2). Meyer-Lübke, Wört. u. Sach. 9.67 f. Sofer, Isidorus 142.

5. Lith. *murininkas*, Lett. *mūrnieks*, derivs. of Lith. *muras*, Lett. *mūris* 'stone wall', fr. MLG *mure* : OHG *mūra*, etc. (above, 4). Mühl.-Endz. 2.678 f.

6. SCr. *zidar*, Boh. *zednik* : ChSl. *zĭdati*, SCr. *zidati* 'build', etc. (9.44).

Pol. *mularz*, by dissim. fr. *murarz*, deriv. of *mur* 'wall', fr. Gmc., cf. OHG *mūra*, etc. (above, 4). Brückner 348.

Russ. *kamenščik*, deriv. of *kamen'* 'stone' (1.44).

7. Skt. *lepaka-* (also *lepakara-*, prob. by influence of *kṛ-* 'do, make') 'smearer, plasterer' and hence with reference to building with clay or mortar 'mason' : *lip-* 'smear' (Grk. λίπος 'fat', etc. Walde-P. 2.403).

9.54 BRICK

Grk.	*πλίνθος*	Goth.	*(skalja)*	Lith.	*plyta*
NG	*τοῦβλο*	ON	*tigl*	Lett.	*kieg'elis*
Lat.	*later*	Dan.	*mursten, tegl*	ChSl.	*plinŭta*
It.	*mattone*	Sw.	*tegel*	SCr.	*opeka, cigla*
Fr.	*brique*	OE	*tigele*	Boh.	*cihla*
Sp.	*ladrillo*	ME	*tyle*	Pol.	*cegła*
Rum.	*cărămidă*	NE	*brick (tile)*	Russ.	*kirpič*
Ir.	*later*	Du.	*baksteen, tegel*	Skt.	*iṣṭakā-*
NIr.	*brice*	OHG	*ziagal*	Av.	*ištya-*, OPers. *išti-*
W.	*priddfaen, bricsen*	MHG	*ziegel*		
Br.	*brikenn*	NHG	*ziegel (-stein), backstein*		

Some of the words for 'brick' were probably applied originally to a slab of stone (as Grk. πλίνθος actually so used) and only later to the substituted 'brick'. Such may go back to the idea of 'a fragment, piece broken off', or simply 'flat'. Others, as meaning from the outset 'baked bricks', are connected with words for 'burn, bake'. An extensive group of loanwords from Latin shows an extension from 'roof-tile', orig. 'covering', to 'tile, brick' (several of the words listed were or are still used for both 'brick' and 'tile') in general.

1. Grk. πλίνθος, possibly, like many words with νθ, fr. a pre-Grk. source, but may be IE : OE *flint*, OHG *flins* 'flint, rock', etc., fr. IE **(s)plei-* 'split' in Dan. *splitte*, NE *split*, MHG *splīzen*, etc. Walde-P. 2.684.

NG τοῦβλο, Byz. τούβουλον, τοῦβλον also 'brick' (cf. DuCange), fr. Lat. *tubulus* 'pipe, tube' through the notion of 'hollow or curved tile'. G. Meyer, Neugr. Stud. 3.65.

2. Lat. *later*, prob. as orig. 'flat piece' : *latus, -eris* 'side', this again prob. : *lātus* 'wide' (neither connection accepted by Ernout-M.). Walde-P. 2.643.

It. *mattone*, deriv. of It., late Lat. *matta* 'mat' (whence also OFr. *maton* 'curds' and 'cheesecake', in Norm. Fr. 'brick'). Diez 208. (REW 5424, but without It. *mattone*, which is given 5271 under *maltha*, but with doubt).

Fr. *brique* (OFr. and dial. also 'piece, fragment'), fr. MDu. *bri(c)ke* 'brick', prob. also 'piece, fragment' (cf. MLG *bricke* 'disk, plate, piece used in games') : Du. *breken* 'break', etc. (9.26). REW 1300. Wartburg 1.522 f. NED s.v. *brick*.

Sp. *ladrillo*, deriv. of Lat. *later* (above).

Rum. *cărămidă*, fr. NG κεραμίδα 'tile', fr. Grk. κεραμίς 'roof-tile' : κέραμος 'clay, pottery, tile' (9.73). Tiktin 290.

3. Ir. *later*, fr. Lat. *later* (above, 2). Vendryes, De hib. voc. 149.

NIr. *brīce* 'brick, tile', fr. NE *brick* (below, 4).

W. *priddfaen*, cpd. of *pridd* 'earth, clay' (9.73) and *maen* 'stone'.

W. *bricsen*, pl. *brics*, fr. NE pl. *bricks* (below, 4). Parry-Williams 104, 138.

Br. *brikenn*, fr. Fr. *brique* (above, 2).

4. Goth. *skalja* 'roof-tile' : ON *skel*, OE *sciell*, OHG *scala* 'shell', Lith. *skala* 'splinter, fragment', etc., fr. IE **(s)kel-* in ON *skilja* 'separate', etc. Walde-P. 2.593. Feist 427.

ON *tigl*, Dan. *tegl*, also *teglsten* (cf. *sten* 'stone'), Sw. *tegel, tegelsten*, OE *tigele*, ME *tyle, tile* 'brick, tile', NE *tile*, Du. *tegel, tegelsteen*, OHG *ziagal*, MHG *ziegel*, NHG *ziegel, ziegelstein* 'brick, tile' (NHG also *mauerziegel* 'brick', cf. *mauer* 'wall'), all fr. Lat. *tēgula* 'roof-tile' : *tegere* 'cover, roof over'. Falk-Torp 1251. NED s.v. *tile*, sb.[1].

ME (late) *bryke, brike*, NE *brick*, fr. Fr. *brique* (above, 2).

Dan. *mursten*, fr. MLG *mūrstēn*, cpd. of *mūr* 'wall' and *stēn* 'stone'. Falk-Torp 741.

Du. *baksteen*, NHG *backstein*, cpds. of words for 'bake' and 'stone'.

5. Lith. *plyta*, fr. Pol. *płyta* 'slab' (below, 6). Brückner, Sl. Fremdwörter 119.

Lett. *kieg'elis*, prob. by assim. fr. *tieg'elis* (dial.), fr. MLG *tegel* : MHG, NHG *ziegel* (above, 4). Mühl.-Endz. 2.390, 4.209.

6. Late ChSl. *plinŭta, plita* (Pol., Ukr. *płyta* 'slab' > Lith. *plyta* 'brick'), fr. Grk. πλίνθος (above, 1). Brückner 423.

SCr. *opeka* : *opeći* 'burn', *peći* 'bake'.

SCr. *cigla*, Boh. *cihla*, Pol. *cegła*, fr. MHG, NHG *ziegel* (above, 4). Brückner 57.

Russ. *kirpič* (SCr. *čerpić* 'unbaked brick'), fr. Turk. *kerpiç* 'unbaked brick'. Berneker 501. Lokotsch 1184.

7. Skt. *iṣṭakā-*, Av. *ištya-*, OPers. *išti-* (Dar. Sus. f 29), NPers. *xišt*, prob. fr. **idh-s-to-* : Skt. *idh-*, Grk. αἴθω 'kindle', etc. Walde-P. 1.6. Johansen, IF 19.136.

9.55 MORTAR

Grk.	(πηλός, κονία)	Goth.	. . . .	Lith.	*kalkių glaistas*
NG	λάσπη	ON	. . . .	Lett.	*mertelis*
Lat.	*calx arēnātus, mortārium*	Dan.	*mørtel*	ChSl.	. . . .
It.	*calcina, malta*	Sw.	*murbruk*	SCr.	*malter*
Fr.	*mortier*	OE	. . . .	Boh.	*malta*
Sp.	*argamasa, mezcla, mortero*	ME	*morter*	Pol.	*zaprawa wapienna,* etc.
Rum.	*tencueală*	NE	*mortar*	Russ.	*izvestkovyj rastvor*
Ir.	. . . .	Du.	*mortel*	Skt.	(*lepa-, sudhā-*)
NIr.	*moirtēal*	OHG	. . . .	Av.	. . . .
W.	*cymrwd*	MHG	*morter*		
Br.	*priraz*	NHG	*mörtel*		

Mortar in the technical sense of a mixture of lime and sand was known to the Greeks and Romans, and spread thence, with brick construction, to northern Europe. The majority of the European words are of Latin origin. Several contain the words for 'lime' or 'sand' or both. But as mortar was a substitute for clay, previously used for the same purpose, some words for 'clay, mud' or the like came to be used also for 'mortar'. Some languages have no single word for 'mortar' but make use of expressions meaning lit. 'mason's sauce', 'lime-cement', etc.

1. Grk. πηλός 'clay' (9.73), used for clay serving as mortar and then prob. for true mortar, for which also πηλὸς ἠχυρωμένος 'clay mixed with chaff', IG 2².463.42.

Grk. κονία 'dust', also 'lime, plaster' (hence κονιάω 'to plaster', κονίᾱσις 'plastering, stucco-work' in building inscriptions), also 'mortar'(?); ἀμμοκονία (rare) 'sand mixed with lime, cement' (cf. ἄμμος 'sand') : κόνις 'dust, ashes', Lat. *cinis* 'ashes', etc. Walde-P. 1.392.

NG λάσπη 'mud' (1.214), also 'mortar'.

2. Lat. *calx (h)arēnātus* 'lime mixed with sand, mortar', also *(h)arēnātum* alone as sb. 'mortar', cf. *calx* 'lime' and *(h)arēna* 'sand'.

Lat. *mortārium* 'a mortar' in which substances are pounded and crushed, hence also 'that which is crushed in a mortar' and 'mortar for building' (> Fr. *mortier*, Sp. *mortero* in both senses), prob. fr. the root seen in Skt. *mṛ-* 'crush, destroy', ON *merja* 'bruise, crush', etc. Walde-P. 2.276.

It. *calcina*, deriv. of Lat. *calx* 'lime'.

It. *malta*, fr. Lat. *maltha* 'a kind of cement' (Pliny), borrowed fr. Grk. μάλθη 'a mixture of wax and pitch' : μαλθακός 'soft', Goth. *mulda*, OE *molda* 'dust, earth', Skt. *mṛd-* 'clay, loam' (9.73). Walde-P. 2.289. Walde-H. 2.17.

Sp. *argamasa* (Cat., Port. *argamassa*), cpd. of *masa* 'mass, dough, mortar', but first part dub. (relation to Lat. *argilla* 'clay' difficult).

Sp. *mezcla* 'mixture' (5.17), commonly used by the workmen for 'mortar'.

Rum. *tencueală* 'plaster, mortar', deriv. of *tencui* 'cover with plaster or mortar', fr. NHG *tünchen* 'cover with lime, whitewash, plaster' through Pol. *tyncować*. Tiktin 1577.

3. NIr. *moirtēal*, with dissim. fr. NE *mortar* (below, 4).

W. *cymrwd*, etym.? (cpd. of *cym-* 'together' and *rhwd* 'sediment, rust, dung water'?).

Br. *priraz*, cpd. of *pri* 'clay' (9.73) and *raz* 'lime'.

4. MHG *morter*, with dissim. Dan. *mørtel*, Du. *mortel*, NHG *mörtel*, fr. Lat. *mortārium* (above, 2) in second sense only.

ME *morter*, NE *mortar* (both senses), fr. Fr. *mortier* (above, 2).

Sw. *murbruk*, cpd. of *mur* 'wall' and *-bruk*, this prob. the same word as *bruk* 'use'. Hellquist 102.

5. Lith. *kalkių glaistas* (NSB, s.v. *kalkės*), lit. 'lime-cement'. Also Lith. *murininko košė*, lit. 'mason's pap', like Pol. *zaprawa mularska* (below, 6).

Lett. *mertelis*, fr. NHG *mörtel* (above, 4).

6. Boh. *malta*, SCr. *malta* (obs.), now *malter*, fr. It. *malta* (above, 2). Berneker 2.12 f.

Pol. *zaprawa mularska*, lit. 'mason's sauce', and *zaprawa wapienna* 'lime sauce'.

Russ. *izvestkovyj rastvor*, lit. 'lime solution'.

7. Whether true mortar was known in ancient India may be doubted, but the following words that are used for 'plaster' may be noted:

Skt. *lepa-* 'smearing, plaster' : *lip-* 'smear, etc.'.

Skt. *sudhā-* 'nectar, milk' hence 'whitewash, plaster', cpd. of *su-* 'well, good' and *dhā-* 'suck, drink'.

9.60 SMITH

Grk.	χαλκεύς	Goth.	*aizasmiþa*	Lith.	*kalvis*
NG	γύφτος (σιδηρουργός)	ON	(*jārn-*)*smiðr*	Lett.	*kalejs*
Lat.	*faber* (*ferrārius*)	Dan.	*smed*	ChSl.	*kovačĭ*
It.	*fabbro*	Sw.	*smed*	SCr.	*kovač*
Fr.	*forgeron*	OE	*smiþ*	Boh.	*kovař*
Sp.	*herrero*	ME	*smith*	Pol.	*kowal*
Rum.	*făurar, fierar*	NE	*smith*	Russ.	*kuznec*
Ir.	*goba*	Du.	*smid*	Skt.	*kārmāra-, lohakāra-*
NIr.	*gabha*	OHG	*smid*	Av.	. . . .
W.	*gof*	MHG	*smit*		
Br.	*gov*	NHG	*schmied*		

Words for 'smith, metalworker' are in part derived from the verbs for 'hammer, forge'. Some are the words for 'artisan' or 'worker' in specialized use, while others show generalization from worker in a particular metal, as copper or iron.

1. Grk. χαλκεύς, orig. 'worker in copper', generalized, already in Hom., to 'worker in any metal, smith', deriv. of χαλκός 'copper, bronze' (9.66).

Grk. σιδηρουργός (rare) 'ironworker', NG lit. in part also 'smith', cpd., like ξυλουργός 'woodworker', of σίδηρος 'iron' (9.67).

NG pop. γύφτος 'gypsy' (fr. Αἰγύπτιος 'Egyptian'; D. Georgacas, Glotta 27.159) and hence 'smith', since the gypsies were the common tinkers (as, conversely, NE *tinker* is the common name for a gypsy in Scotland, cf. NED s.v.).

2. Lat. *faber* (> It. *fabbro*, Rum. *făur, făurar*), see 9.42; also *faber ferrārius* or simply *ferrārius* (> It. *ferraio*, Sp. *herrero*, Rum. *fierar*), deriv. of *ferrum* 'iron' (9.67). REW 3120, 3257.

Fr. *forgeron*, deriv. of *forger* 'forge' (9.61).

3. Ir. *goba* (stem *gobann-*), NIr. *gabha*, W. *gof*, Br. *gov* (cf. Gall. *Gobannio*, *Gobannilo*), etym.? Thurneysen, Gram. 209. Pedersen 2.112.

4. Goth. *aizasmiþa* 'smith' (cf. *aiza* 'bronze'), ON *smiðr* 'artisan', also 'metalworker' (also *jārnsmiðr*, with *jārn* 'iron'), Dan., Sw. *smed*, OE *smiþ*, ME, NE *smith* (also *goldsmith, coppersmith*, etc., and *blacksmith* 'worker in black metal', i.e. iron), Du. *smid*, OHG *smid*, *smeidar* (also *ēr-, gold-, isarn-smid*), MHG *smit*, NHG *schmied* : ON *smīða* 'make, forge', etc. Prob. specialization of generic 'artisan' (as in ON). See 9.42 and NED s.v. *smith*.

5. Lith. *kalvis*, Lett. *kalejs* : Lith. *kalti*, Lett. *kalt* 'hammer, forge' (9.61).

6. Late ChSl. *kovačĭ, kovalĭ*, SCr. *kovač*, Boh. *kovař*, Pol. *kowal*, Russ. dial. *koval'*, *kovač*, with different formation Russ. *kuznec* : ChSl. *kovati* 'hammer, forge', etc. (9.61). Berneker 593, 655.

7. Skt. *kārmāra-* 'smith' (as opposed to 'woodworker', cf. RV 9.112.2, 10.72.2), prob. as specialized fr. 'worker' : *karma-* 'work, deed, etc.', *kṛ-* 'do, make'. Uhlenbeck 47.

Skt. *lohakāra-*, cpd. of *loha-* 'copper' (9.66) and *-kāra-* : *kṛ-* 'do, make'.

9.61 FORGE (vb.)

Grk.	χαλκεύω	Goth.	. . . .	Lith.	*kalti*
NG	σφυρηλατῶ	ON	*smīða*	Lett.	*kalt*
Lat.	*fabricāre, cūdere*	Dan.	*smede*	ChSl.	*kovati*
It.	*fabbricare*	Sw.	*smida*	SCr.	*kovati*
Fr.	*forger*	OE	*smiþian*	Boh.	*kouti, kovati*
Sp.	*forjar, fraguar*	ME	*smithe, forge*	Pol.	*kuć, kować*
Rum.	*făuri*	NE	*forge*	Russ.	*kovat'*
Ir.	. . . .	Du.	*smeden*	Skt.	(*ghaṭaya-*)
NIr.	*oibrighim*	OHG	*smidōn*	Av.	. . . .
W.	*morthwylio*	MHG	*smiden*		
Br.	*govelia*	NHG	*schmieden*		

The principal activity of a smith, that of shaping and fashioning articles from heated metals by hammering or beating, is usually denoted by verbs for 'strike, beat', or by derivatives of words for 'hammer' or 'smith'.

1. Grk. χαλκεύω, deriv. of χαλκεύς 'smith' (9.60).

Grk. (rare), NG σφυρηλατῶ 'hammer, beat out, forge', deriv. of σφυρήλατος 'wrought with the hammer', cpd. of σφῦρα 'hammer' and the vbl. adj. of ἐλαύνω 'drive, strike, forge'.

2. Lat. *fabricāre* (> It. *fabbricare* 'make, build, forge', Fr. *forger*, Sp. *fraguar*), general word for 'make of wood, stone, metal' but often spec. 'forge' (cf. *fabrica* 'trade, workshop', esp. 'smithy'), deriv. of *faber* 'artisan, smith' (9.42).

Lat. *cūdere* 'strike, hammer, forge', also *procūdere, excūdere* 'beat out, forge' : ChSl. *kovati*, etc. (below, 6). Ernout-M. 238 f. Walde-H. 1.300 f.

Sp. *forjar*, deriv. of *forja* 'smithy', fr. Fr. *forge*, this fr. Lat. *fabrica* (above). REW 3121.

Rum. *făuri*, deriv. of *făur* 'smith' (9.42).

3. NIr. *oibrighim* 'work, work on' (9.13), also spec. 'work on metals, forge'.

W. *morthwylio* 'hammer, beat, forge', deriv. of *morthwyl* 'hammer' (9.49).

Br. *govelia*, deriv. of *govel* 'smithy', fr. *gov* 'smith' (9.60).

4. ON *smīða* 'make, forge', Dan. *smede*, Sw. *smida* 'forge', OE *smiþian* 'make of wood or metal', ME *smithe*, Du. *smeden* 'forge', OHG *smidōn* 'make, forge', MHG *smiden*, NHG *schmieden* 'forge' : Goth. *gasmiþōn* 'effect, cause', all perh. first used of woodwork (cf. also 9.42, 9.60) and fr. a root **smēi-* 'cut, hew'(?) seen in Grk. σμῑλη 'knife for carving', σμινύη 'hoe' or 'mattock'. Walde-P. 2.686. Falk-Torp 1077 f. Feist 31 f.

ME, NE *forge*, fr. Fr. *forger* (above, 2).

5. Lith. *kalti, nukalti*, Lett. *kalt* 'hammer, forge' : Lith. *kulti* 'thrash', Lett. *kult* 'beat, thrash', Grk. κλάω 'break', ChSl. *klati* 'prick, pierce, kill', etc. Walde-P. 1.437.

6. ChSl., SCr. *kovati*, Boh. *kouti, kovati*, Pol. *kuć, kować*, Russ. *kovat'* 'hammer, forge' : Lat. *cūdere* (above, 2), Lith. *kauti* 'strike, beat, fight', ON *hǫggva* 'cut, hew', etc. (9.22). Walde-P. 1.330. Berneker 593.

7. Skt. *ghaṭaya-* 'unite, fashion, make', sometimes used for making something of metal, caus. of *ghaṭ-* 'strive, unite, take place'. Apparently no technical word for 'forge'.

9.62 ANVIL

Grk.	ἄκμων	Goth.	. . . .	Lith.	*priekalas*
NG	ἄκμων, ἀμόνι	ON	*steði*	Lett.	*lakta*
Lat.	*incūs*	Dan.	*ambolt*	ChSl.	*nakovalo*
It.	*ancudine*	Sw.	*städ*	SCr.	*nakovanj*
Fr.	*enclume*	OE	*anfilt*	Boh.	*kovadlo*
Sp.	*yunque*	ME	*anvelt* (*stithi*)	Pol.	*kowadło*
Rum.	*nicovală*	NE	*anvil*	Russ.	*nakoval'nja*
Ir.	*indēin*	Du.	*aanbeeld*	Skt.	. . . .
NIr.	*inneoin*	OHG	*anafalz, anabōz*	Av.	. . . .
W.	*ein(g)ion*	MHG	*anebōz*		
Br.	*anneo*	NHG	*amboss*		

Most of the words for 'anvil' belong to roots for 'strike, beat', in part the same as for 'forge'. One small group is based on the notion of 'stationary, firmly fixed', and another word probably on that of 'raised place'. The Greek word reflects a primitive anvil of stone.

1. Grk. ἄκμων, NG pop. ἀμόνι (fr. ἀκμόνιον) : Skt. *açman-*, Lith. *akmuo*, ChSl. *kamy*, etc. 'stone'. (1.44).

2. Lat. *incūs, -ūdis* (VLat. **incūdine* > It. *incudine, ancudine*, Fr. *enclume*, Sp. *yunque*) : *(in)cūdere* 'strike, hammer, forge' (9.61). Ernout-M. 238. REW 4367.

Rum. *nicovală*, fr. Slavic, ChSl. *nakovalo* (below, 6).

3. Ir. *indēin, indeoin*, NIr. *inneoin*, W. *ein(g)ion*, Br. *anneo*, fr. a cpd., first part Ir. *ind-*, etc., second part dub. Thurneysen, IF 4.274 f. Pedersen 1.114.

4. ON *steði* (> ME *stithi*), Sw. *städ*, through the notion of 'something firmly fixed', fr. IE **stā-* 'stand'. Walde-P. 2.605. Falk-Torp 1155. Hellquist 1103.

The other Gmc. words are from cpds. of *ana-* 'on' with roots meaning 'strike'. They are thus similar to, and perh. modeled upon, Lat. *incūs* (above, 2).

OE *anfilt*, ME *anvelt*, NE *anvil*, OHG *anafalz*, MLG *anebelte, ambolt* (> Dan. *ambolt*), Du. *aanbeeld* : Lat. *pellere* 'strike, beat, drive', etc. Walde-P. 2.57, 184. Franck-v.W. 3. NED s.v. *anvil*.

OHG *anabōz*, MHG *anebōz*, NHG *amboss* : OHG *bōzan*, OE *bēatan* 'strike, beat', etc. (9.21). Walde-P. 2.127. Weigand-H. 1.49.

5. Lith. *priekalas* : *kalti* 'hammer, forge' (9.61).

Lett. *lakta*, prob. the same word as *lakta* 'perch' (: *lekt* 'fly') and 'raised place'. No etym. in Mühl.-Endz. 2.417.

6. ChSl. *nakovalo, nakovalĭno*, SCr. *nakovanj*, Boh. *(na)kovadlo, (na)kovadlina*, Pol. *(na)kowadło*, Russ. *nakoval'nja* : ChSl. *kovati* 'hammer, forge', etc. (9.61). Berneker 593.

9.63 CAST (Metals)

Grk.	χοανεύω	Goth.	. . . .	Lith.	*lieti*
NG	χύνω	ON	*steypa*	Lett.	*liet*
Lat.	*fundere*	Dan.	*støbe*	ChSl.	. . . .
It.	*fondere, gettare*	Sw.	*gjuta, stöpa*	SCr.	*liti*
Fr.	*fondre*	OE	*gēotan*	Boh.	*líti*
Sp.	*fundir*	ME	*gete, caste*	Pol.	*lać*
Rum.	*turna*	NE	*cast (found)*	Russ.	*lit'*
Ir.	. . . .	Du.	*gieten*	Skt.	*sic-*
NIr.	*teilgim*	OHG	*giozan*	Av.	*hič-*
W.	*bwrw*	MHG	*giezen*		
Br.	*teuzi*	NHG	*giessen*		

Words for 'cast' in the technical sense of forming metal objects by pouring the molten metal into molds are mostly the same as, or related to, those for 'pour' (9.35). But some are from 'throw, cast' (into the mold).

1. Grk. χοανεύω, χωνεύω, deriv. of χόανος 'smelting pot, mold for casting', fr. the root of χέω 'pour' (9.35), whence also NG χύνω 'pour' and 'cast'.

2. Lat. *fundere* 'pour' (9.35), also 'cast', and specialized to 'cast, smelt, melt' in It. *fondere*, Fr. *fondre*, Sp. *fundir*.

It. *gettare* 'throw, cast (metals)', fr. VLat. **iectāre*, Lat. *iactāre* 'throw, hurl'. REW 4568.

Rum. *turna* 'pour in' (9.35) and 'cast'.

3. NIr. *teilgim* 'throw, cast' (10.25), and by semantic borrowing fr. NE *cast* also 'cast metals'. Walde-P. 2.396 f. Pedersen 2.564 f.

W. *bwrw* 'throw' and by semantic borrowing fr. NE *cast* also 'cast metals' : Ir. *di-bairgim* 'throw'. Walde-P. 2.165. Pedersen 2.476.

Br. *teuzi* 'melt, dissolve', and by influence of Fr. *fondre* (above, 2) also 'smelt, cast' : W. *toddi* 'melt, dissolve', Ir. *tām* 'tabes', Lat. *tābēs* 'wasting away', Grk. τήκω 'melt', etc. Walde-P. 1.701. Pedersen 1.68.

4. ON *steypa* 'make stoop, overthrow, pour out', hence also 'cast metals', Dan. *støbe*, Sw. *stöpa* 'cast', caus. to ON *stūpa*, OE *stūpian*, NE *stoop*. Walde-P. 2.619. Falk-Torp 1198. Hellquist 1108.

Sw. *gjuta*, OE *gēotan*, ME *gete*, Du. *gieten*, OHG *giozan*, MHG *giezen*, NHG *giessen*, same as for 'pour' (9.35).

ME *caste*, NE *cast* 'throw', hence 'throw into a mold, cast metals', fr. ON *kasta* 'throw'. NED s.v. *cast*, vb.

NE *found* 'smelt, cast metals' (now little used, but cf. *foundry*), fr. Fr. *fondre* (above, 2).

5, 6. Lith. *lieti*, Lett. *liet*, SCr. *liti*, etc. general Balto-Slavic, same as for 'pour' (9.35).

7. Skt. *sic-*, Av. *hič-* 'pour' (9.35), both also 'cast' (cf. AV 11.10, 12; Yt. 10.96.3).

9.64–9.69. Schrader, Sprachvergleichung und Urgeschichte 2.10 ff., Reallex. s.v. Metalle, Erz, Gold, etc. V. Bradke, Methode und Ergebnisse der arischen Altertumswissenschaft 28 ff. Hirt, Indogermanen 684 ff. Feist, Kultur, Ausbreitung und Herkunft der Indogermanen 196 ff.

Among the metal names the one most certainly inherited group is that pointing to an IE word for 'copper', with subsequent extension to 'bronze' or in part transference to 'iron'. For 'gold' and 'silver' there are certain widespread groups within which there is agreement in root and partially in suffix, an agreement not sufficient to determine a precise IE form but too great to be accidental. For this and other reasons it is now generally believed (otherwise Schrader) that gold and silver, as well as copper, were known in the IE period.

Some of the other words for metals are derived from names of places that were important centers of production and export. Some are loanwords, their precise source unknown.

It is noticeable that the old metal names are regularly neuters, except in Greek.

A generic word for 'metal' is relatively late. The source of the European generic words is Lat. *metallum*, fr. Grk. μέταλλον 'mine', later 'metal'.

Note on words for 'mine':

Grk. μέταλλον 'mine', later 'metal' (> Lat. *metallum* 'mine, metal'), orig. dub. Boisacq 630.

Fr. *mine* (> ME *myne*, NE *mine*, Rum. *mină*, Dan., NHG *mine*, etc.) It., Sp. *mina* (It. now *miniera*, fr. Fr. *minière*, in sense intended here), prob. fr. a Gallic word for 'ore'. Cf. Gael. *mèin* 'ore, metal', Ir. *mianach* 'ore, mine', W. *mwn, mwyn* 'ore', *mwnglawdd* 'mine', Br. *mengleuz* 'mine, quarry'. REW 5465. Thurneysen, Keltorom. 67 ff. Gamillscheg 613. NED s.v. *mine*, sb. (doubtful of above connection).

MHG *bercwerc*, NHG *bergwerk* (Dan. *bjærgværk* after NHG), cpd. of *berg* 'mountain, mountainous region' (1.22) and 'work'.

NHG *grube* (> Dan. *grube*, Sw. *gruva*) 'pit' and 'mine' (or for latter spec. *erzgrube*), fr. OHG *gruoba* 'pit', fr. *graben* 'dig' (8.22). Cf. Boh. *důl* 'pit' and (prob. after NHG) 'mine' = ChSl. *dolŭ*, Pol. *dół* 'pit', Russ. *dol* 'valley' : ChSl. *dolě* 'under'. Berneker 208 f.

From verbs for 'dig' (8.22). Lith. *kasykla*, Lett. *raktuve*, Pol. *kopalnia* (but for 'miner' *gornik*, fr. *gora* 'mountain', prob. after NHG *bergmann*), Skt. *khani-*.

SCr., Boh. Russ. *rudnik*, fr. *ruda*, 'ore', orig. 'red ore' : ChSl. *rŭdrŭ* (15.66).

9.64 GOLD

Grk.	χρῦσός	Goth.	*gulþ*	Lith.	*auksas*
NG	χρυσός, χρυσάφι, μάλαμα	ON	*gull*	Lett.	*zelts*
		Dan.	*guld*	ChSl.	*zlato*
Lat.	*aurum*	Sw.	*guld*	SCr.	*zlato*
It.	*oro*	OE	*gold*	Boh.	*zlato*
Fr.	*or*	ME	*gold*	Pol.	*złato*
Sp.	*oro*	NE	*gold*	Russ.	*zoloto*
Rum.	*aur*	Du.	*goud*	Skt.	*hiraṇya-, jātarūpa-*
Ir.	*ōr*	OHG	*gold*	Av.	*zaranya-*, OPers. *daranya-*
NIr.	*ōr*	MHG	*golt*		
W.	*awr*	NHG	*gold*		
Br.	*aour*				

1. Derivs. of IE **ĝhel-* in words for 'yellow' like Skt. *hari-*, Av. *zari-*, Lat. *helvus*, etc. (15.69). Agreement in suffix between Gmc. and Slavic, and within Indo-Iranian. Walde-P. 1.624 ff. Falk-Torp 360. Feist 224.

Goth. *gulþ*, OE *gold*, etc., general Gmc.; Lett. *zelts*, ChSl. *zlato*, etc., general Slavic; Skt. *hiraṇya-*, Av. *zaranya-*, OPers. *daranya-* (Dar. Sus. f. 35), all neuters.

2. Lat. *aurum* (> Romance and Celtic words, also Alb. *ar*), fr. **ausom* (Sab. *ausum*, Festus); OPruss. *ausis*, OLith. *ausas*, Lith. *auksas;* here also prob. Toch. A *wäs* 'gold' beside *wsi* 'yellow'; all prob. as 'reddish' fr. **aus-* (*wes-*) in words for dawn, Grk. ἠώς, Lat. *aurōra*, Skt. *uṣas-*, etc. The view that the Baltic words were borrowed in very ancient times fr. Lat. **ausom* is improbable. Walde-P. 1.27. Ernout-M. 94. Walde-H. 1.86.

3. Grk. χρῦσός, loanword fr. Semitic (cf. Akkad. *ḫurāšu*, Hebr.-Phoen. *ḥārūṣ*), doubtless through Phoenician. Lewy, Fremdwörter 59 f. Schrader, Reallex. 1.404.

Hence NG χρυσός and χρυσάφι.

NG pop. also μάλαμα, fr. Grk. μάλαγμα 'soft material'.

4. Skt. *jātarūpa-*, lit. 'having native beauty', is also used for 'gold'. Macdonell-Keith 1.281.

9.65 SILVER

Grk.	ἄργυρος	Goth.	*silubr*	Lith.	*sidabras*
NG	ἀσήμι	ON	*silfr*	Lett.	*sidrabs*
Lat.	*argentum*	Dan.	*sølf*	ChSl.	*s(ŭ)rebro*
It.	*argento*	Sw.	*silver*	SCr.	*srebro*
Fr.	*argent*	OE	*siolfor, seolfor*	Boh.	*stříbro*
Sp.	*plata*	ME	*sylver*	Pol.	*srebro*
Rum.	*argint*	NE	*silver*	Russ.	*serebro*
Ir.	*argat, airged*	Du.	*zilver*	Skt.	*rajata-*
NIr.	*airgead*	OHG	*sil(a)bar*	Av.	*ərəzata-*, OPers. *ardata-*
W.	*arian*	MHG	*silber*		
Br.	*arc'hant*	NHG	*silber*		

1. Derivs. of IE **arĝ-* in words for 'bright, white' like Grk. ἀργός, Skt. *arjuna-*, etc. Some variation in form of root and of suffix. Walde-P. 1.82 f. Ernout-M. 71. Walde-H. 1.66, 848.

Grk. ἄργυρος; Lat. *argentum* (> It. *argento*, Fr. *argent*, Rum. *argint*), Osc. abl. sg. *aragetud;* Gall. *arganto-* in *Arganto-marus*, etc., Ir. *argat, airged*, NIr. *airgead*, W. *arian*, Br. *arc'hant;* Skt. *rajata-*, Av. *ərəzata-*, OPers. *ardata-* (Dar. Sus. f. 40), all neuter; Arm. *arcat'*.

2. Loanwords from some common source, perh. to be sought in Asia Minor. Feist 421.

Goth. *silubr*, OE *siolfor*, OHG *sil(a)bar*, etc., general Gmc.; OPruss. *siraplan*, Lith. *sidabras*, Lett. *sidrabs;* ChSl. *sŭrebro, srebro*, etc., general Slavic.

3. NG ἀσήμι, dim. of Grk. ἄσημον fr. ἄσημος 'without mark, uncoined', used freq. with χρῦσός or ἄργυρος for gold or silver bullion, and ἄσημον finally specialized to 'silver' (LXX and freq. in pap.).

Sp. *plata*, Port. *prata*, through 'silver plate', fr. Prov. *plata* 'plate' : Fr. *plat*, It. *piatto*, etc., all fr. Grk. πλατύς 'flat'. REW 6586.

9.66 COPPER, BRONZE

Grk.	χαλκός	Goth.	*aiz*	Lith.	*varis, žalvaris, bronza*
NG	χαλκός, μπακίρι, μπροῦντζος	ON	*koparr, eir*	Lett.	*kapars, varš, bronza*
		Dan.	*kobber, bronze*	ChSl.	*mědĭ*
Lat.	*aes*	Sw.	*koppar, brons*	SCr.	*mjed, bakar, bronza*
It.	*rame, bronzo*	OE	*copor, ār, bræs*	Boh.	*měd', bronz*
Fr.	*cuivre, bronze, airain*	ME	*coper, bras*	Pol.	*miedź, bronz, spiż*
Sp.	*cobre, bronze*	NE	*copper, bronze*	Russ.	*med', bronza*
Rum.	*cupru, aramă, bronz*	Du.	*koper, brons*	Skt.	*loha-, ayas-*
Ir.	*umae, crēdumae*	OHG	*kupfar, ēr*	Av.	*ayah-*
NIr.	*umha, prās*	MHG	*kupfer, ēr*		
W.	*copr, efydd, pres*	NHG	*kupfer, erz, bronze*		
Br.	*kouevr, arem*				

Grk. χαλκός and Lat. *aes* covered both 'copper' and its alloy with tin, 'bronze'. Their actual reference in the majority of cases would be to bronze, since this was so much more extensively employed than pure copper. So Goth. *aiz* (which renders χαλκός as the 'copper', really bronze coin, also in *aiza-smiþa* for χαλκεύς 'coppersmith'), ON *eir*, OE *ār*, OHG *ēr*, all cognate with Lat. *aes* and orig. words for 'copper', were applied mainly to what was really bronze. A new, specific name for 'copper', which spread over nearly all of western and central Europe, was furnished by a late Lat. derivative of the name of the copper-producing Cyprus. The old words survived in part for 'bronze', but for this another new word, which spread over nearly all Europe, was furnished by It. *bronzo*, the source of which is disputed.

Brass, the alloy with zinc, was unknown in classical antiquity. Of its names, NE *brass* (whence Ir. *prās*, W. *pres*) originally applied to bronze and must still be so understood in the English Bible and in old references to classical antiquity (cf. NED s.v.). MHG *messinc*, NHG *messing* represent a widespread Gmc. group (OE *mæsling*, NE dial. *maslin*, cf. NED), whence also the Lith., Lett., Boh., Pol. words for 'brass', but of uncertain origin (cf. Schrader, Reallex. 1.269, 2.62). The group Fr. *laiton* (> Russ. *latun'*), It. *ottone*, etc., is also difficult (REW 4933). 'Brass' is 'yellow copper' in Du. *geel koper*, SCr. *žuta mjed*. Grk. ὀρείχαλκος lit. 'mountain copper' (whence Lat. *aurichalcum* with spelling after *aurum*), an alloy of unknown character, later used for 'brass', as in NG.

1. IE **ayes-*. Walde-P. 1.4. Ernout-M. 19. Walde-H. 1.19.

Lat. *aes*, gen. *aeris* (cf. *aēnus, ahēnus*, fr. **ayes-no-*, Umbr. *ahesnes* 'ahenis'), whence late *aerāmen*, **arāmen* (> It. *rame*, Rum. *aramă* 'copper', OFr. *arain*, Br. *arem*, Fr. *airain* 'bronze'); Goth. *aiz*, ON *eir*, OE *ār*, OHG *ēr;* Skt. *ayas-*

prob. 'bronze' in Rigveda (Zimmer, Altind. Leben 51 f. Macdonell-Keith 1.31 f.), later 'iron', Av. *ayah-* 'bronze' (as shown by epithets 'yellow, golden'; cf. Geiger, Ostiran. Kultur 148), later 'iron' as NPers. *āhan.*

2. Grk. χαλκός, prob. a loanword and possibly fr. the same source as Lith. *geležis* 'iron', etc. (9.67). Walde-P. 1.629. Boisacq 1049.

NG pop. μπακίρι, like SCr. *bakar,* fr. Turk. *bakır* 'copper'. Lokotsch 193. Berneker 40.

3. Lat. *aes Cyprium* 'aes from Cyprus', like *aes Corinthium, aes Campānum* (cf. *vāsa Campāna* 'vessels of Campanian bronze', source of It. *campana* 'bell'). Hence late Lat. *cuprum* 'copper', whence Fr. *cuivre* (> Br. *kouevr*), Sp. *cobre,* Rum. *cupru,* and the Gmc. words, OE *copor* (rare), OHG *kupfar,* etc., also W. *copr* (fr. ME) and Lett. *kapars* (fr. LG).

4. It. *bronzo,* whence NG μπροῦντζος, Fr. *bronze,* and similar forms in nearly all the present European languages, orig. disputed, best derived, not fr. Pers. *biring* (as REW 1113, etc.), but fr. *aes Brundisium.* The best bronze mirrors were made at Brundisium (*specula Brundisina,* Pliny 33.130) and Byz. βροντήσιον 'bronze' occurs in the works of the alchemists (e.g. Berthelot, Alchimistes grecs 376.25). Berthelot, Rev. arch. 1888.295 ff. Wartburg 1.373 says "Aes Brundisium wäre sachlich gerecht-

fertigt, aber lautlich unmöglich". But the phonetic difficulty seems less than that in the deriv. fr. Pers. *biring,* esp. in the *o-* vowel admittedly unexplained.

5. Ir. *umae* (also *crēdumae,* cpd. of *crēd* 'tin', Windisch, Wtb. s.v., K. Meyer, Contrib. 509, 511), NIr. *umha,* OW *emid,* W. *efydd :* Ir. *om,* W. *of* 'raw', hence orig. 'raw ore'. Pedersen 1.166.

6. OE *bræs* (both this and *ār* render Lat. *aes.* Cf. Aelfric, Gram. *aes, bræs oððe ar*), ME *bras* (> NIr. *prās,* W. *pres*), NE *brass* with change of application, etym.?

OHG *aruz(zi), erizze,* MHG *arze, erze,* NHG *erz* 'raw metal, ore', now often 'bronze', etym. dub. Schrader, Reallex. 1.262. Walde-P. 2.360.

7. Lith. *varis,* Lett. *varš,* OPruss *wargien* 'copper', also Lith. *žalvaris* 'bronze' (cpd. of *žalias* 'green'), perh. loanword from a language of the Finnish group. Schrader, Reallex. 1.262. Mühl.-Endz. 4.484.

8. ChSl. *mědi,* etc., general Slavic (SCr. also *bakar,* see above, 2), etym. dub. Berneker 46. Walde-P. 2.222.

Pol. *spiž* 'bronze', fr. MHG *spīse* 'food' and also 'metal ready for casting' as in NHG *glockenspeise* 'bell-metal'. Brückner 509. Weigand-H. 2.908.

9. Skt. *loha-, lohāyasa-, lohitāyasa-* 'copper' (cf. Macdonell-Keith 1.31 f.) : *loha-* 'red' beside *rohita-, rudhira-* 'red', etc. Walde-P. 2.358 f.

Skt. *ayas-,* Av. *ayah-,* above, 1.

9.67 IRON

Grk.	σίδηρος	Goth.	eisarn	Lith.	geležis
NG	σίδερο	ON	īsarn, jārn	Lett.	dzelzs
Lat.	ferrum	Dan.	jærn	ChSl.	železo
It.	ferro	Sw.	järn	SCr.	željezo, gvozde
Fr.	fer	OE	īsern, īsen, īren	Boh.	železo
Sp.	hierro	ME	īren	Pol.	żalazo
Rum.	fier	NE	iron	Russ.	železo
Ir.	iarn	Du.	ijzer	Skt.	ayas-
NIr.	iarann	OHG	īsarn, īsan	Av.	ayah-
W.	haearn	MHG	īsern, īsen		
Br.	houarn	NHG	eisen		

The use of iron is comparatively late in history, long after the period of IE unity. Most of the words are of obscure origin. The only agreement between the different branches of IE is that between Celtic and Gmc., which reflects prehistoric borrowing.

1. The Celtic and Gmc. group. Walde-P. 1.4. Schrader, Reallex. 1.235 f. Feist 131. Pokorny, KZ 46.292 ff., 49.126. Walde-H. 1.19 f.

Ir. *iarn,* NIr. *iarann,* W. *haearn,* Br. *houarn,* fr. a Celt. **īsarnon* (cf. Gall. *Isarnus,* etc.), whence the Gmc. group, Goth. *eisarn,* ON *īsarn* (the more common ON *jārn* by later borrowing fr. Ir. *iarn*), OE *īsern, īsen,* OE, ME *īren,* NE *iron,* OHG *īsarn, īsan,* NHG *eisen,* etc. The Celt. **īsarnon* perh. itself of Illyrian origin (there is a similar Illyr. river name, and the Hallstatt iron finds are earlier than the Celtic) and : Skt. *iṣira-* 'strong'.

2. Grk. σίδηρος, NG pop. σίδερο neut., prob. a loanword, but source unknown. Schrader, Reallex. 1.239.

3. Lat. *ferrum* (> Romance words), orig. dub., loanword fr. Semitic (?). Schrader, Reallex. 1.240. Ernout-M. 352. Walde-H. 1.486.

4. Lith. *geležis,* Lett. *dzelzs,* OPruss. *gelso,* ChSl. *železo,* general Balto-Slavic word, perh. with Grk. χαλκός 'copper, bronze' as loanwords fr. some common source. Walde-P. 1.629. Schrader, Reallex. 1.236.

SCr. also *gvozde,* deriv. of old *gvozd* 'nail' (9.51), hence orig. 'nail material'. Berneker 366.

5. Skt. *ayas-,* Av. *ayah-* : Lat. *aes,* etc. See 9.66.

Skt. *çyāma-* 'black' is used with *ayas-* or alone for 'iron'. Macdonell-Keith 1.31 f.

9.68 LEAD

Grk.	μόλυβδος	Goth.	. . . .	Lith.	švinas
NG	μολύβι	ON	blȳ	Lett.	svins
Lat.	plumbum	Dan.	bly	ChSl.	olovo
It.	piombo	Sw.	bly	SCr.	olovo
Fr.	plomb	OE	lēad	Boh.	olovo
Sp.	plomo	ME	lede	Pol.	ołów
Rum.	plumb	NE	lead	Russ.	svinec
Ir.	luaide	Du.	lood	Skt.	sīsa-
NIr.	luaidhe	OHG	blīo	Av.	srva-
W.	plwm	MHG	blī		
Br.	ploum	NHG	blei		

Lead dates from the bronze age in the eastern Mediterranean region and possibly in Britain, but in most of Europe it is contemporaneous with iron. Among the words for 'lead' there is a group common to Celtic and Gmc., resting on borrowing, and probably the Greek and Latin words are from a common, unknown source. There is some confusion between 'lead' and 'tin'. Schrader, Reallex. 1.149 ff.

1. Grk. μόλυβδος (with variants μόλιβος, βόλιμος, βόλιβος), NG μολύβι (also βολίμι), doubtless a loanword, but source unknown. Boisacq 644.

2. Lat. *plumbum* (> Romance words, also W. *plwm,* Br. *ploum*), prob. a loanword fr. the same source as the Grk. word. Ernout-M. 781.

3. Ir. *luaide,* NIr. *luaidhe;* OE *lēad,* ME *lede,* NE *lead,* Du. *lood* (MHG *lōt,* NHG *lot* 'lead' as 'solder' or 'plummet'; so also Dan., Sw. *lod,* fr. MLG). The Gmc. words are prob. borrowed from Celtic, and the latter perh. deriv. of IE

*pleu- in words for 'flow, float', etc., as applied to the quickly melting lead. Walde-P. 2.442. Franck-v. W. 396 f.

4. ON *blȳ,* Dan., Sw. *bly,* OHG *blīo* (gen. *blīwes*), MHG *blī,* NHG *blei,* pointing to a Gmc. **blīwa-,* perh. : Lith. *blyvas* 'violet colored', etc. Walde-P. 2.210. Falk-Torp 86.

5. Lith. *švinas,* Lett. *svins,* Russ. *svinec,* etym. dub. Persson, Beiträge 745.

OPruss. *alwis* 'lead', Lith. *alvas* 'tin', Lett. *alvs, alva* 'tin', ChSl., SCr., Boh. *olovo,* Pol. *ołów* all 'lead', but Russ. *olovo* 'tin', orig. a color word (with characteristic *-wo-*suffix) with application to either 'lead' or 'tin' and subsequent varying distribution in this respect. But root connection dub. (OHG *elo* 'yellow', etc.?). Walde-P. 1.159, 2.442.

6. Skt. *sīsa-* neut. (AV+, cf. Macdonell-Keith 2.452), etym.?

Av. *srva-* neut. (Barth. 1649), NPers. *surb,* etym.?

9.69 TIN; TIN-PLATE

Grk.	κασσίτερος	Goth	. . . .	Lith.	cinas, alvas; skardis
NG	καλάι; τενεκές	ON	tin	Lett.	alvs, alva; skārds
Lat.	plumbum album	Dan.	tin; blik	ChSl.	kositerŭ
It.	stagno; latta	Sw.	tenn; bleck	SCr.	kalaj, kositer (cin); lim
Fr.	étain; fer-blanc	OE	tin		
Sp.	estaño; lata	ME	tin	Boh.	cin; plech
Rum.	cositor; tinichea	NE	tin	Pol.	cyna; blacha
Ir.	stān, crēd	Du.	tin; blik	Russ.	olovo; žest'
NIr.	stān	OHG	zin	Skt.	trapu-
W.	ystaen, tyn	MHG	zin	Av.	. . . .
Br.	stean	NHG	zinn; blech		

NE *tin* covers both the raw metal and the more familiar tin-plate, for which in many languages different words are used. The latter (from which usually the words for 'tinner') are from notions like 'thin strip, plate', shining', 'white iron', 'hard'. But most of the old words for 'tin' as the metal are of obscure origin. Schrader, Reallex. 2.696 ff.

1. Grk. κασσίτερος (> ChSl. *kasiterŭ, kositerŭ,* SCr. *kositer,* Rum. *cositor*), orig.? Boisacq 420.

NG καλάι, SCr. *kalaj,* etc., general Balkan word, fr. Turk. *kalay,* this from *Qualah* name of a city in Malacca, which produces tin in large quantities. Schrader, loc. cit. Lokotsch 1021.

NG τενεκές 'tin-plate' or 'tin vessel',

Rum. *tinichea,* Bulg. *tenekija,* fr. Turk. *teneke* id. Lokotsch 2065.

2. Lat. *plumbum album,* lit. 'white lead'.

Lat. *stagnum (stannum)* 'an alloy of silver and lead', late 'tin', whence It. *stagno,* Fr. *étain,* Sp. *estaño,* also Ir. *stān,* W. *ystaen* (but now mostly *tyn* fr. NE), Br. *stean,* orig.? Ernout-M. 971.

It. *latta,* Sp. *lata* 'tin-plate', the latter also 'lath' as Fr. *latte,* loanword fr. Gmc., OHG *latta* 'lath', etc. REW 4933.

Fr. *fer-blanc* 'tin-plate', lit. 'white iron'.

Rum. *cositor,* through Slavic fr. Grk. (above, 1).

3. Ir. *stān,* etc., above, 2.

Ir. *crēd* (cf. Windisch, Wtb. s.v., K. Meyer, Contrib. 509), orig.?

4. ON, OE *tin,* OHG *zin,* etc., general Gmc., orig.?

OHG *bleh,* MHG, NHG *blech* 'thin plate of metal', now esp. 'tin' (> Boh.

plech, Pol. *blacha*), more spec. *weissblech,* MLG *bleck* (> Dan. *blik,* Sw. *bleck*), Du. *blik,* as orig. 'shining, bright' : ON *blik* 'gleam', OE *blican* 'shine', etc. Weigand-H. 1.249. Falk-Torp 82.

5. Lith. *alvas,* Lett. *alva, alva,* Russ. *olovo* = ChSl. *olovo,* etc. 'lead'. See 9.68.

Lith. *skardis,* Lett. *skārds* 'tin-plate', perh. fr. Liv. *kārda,* Finn. *karta* id. (or conversely, and the Baltic forms fr. MHG *schart* 'iron pan', etc.?). Walde-P. 2.601. Endzelin, KZ 52.120.

6. Lith. *cinas,* SCr. Boh. *cin,* Pol. *cyna,* fr. NHG *zinn* (above, 4). Berneker 130.

SCr. *lim,* perh. fr. Ital. *lama* 'metal strip, blade', but vowel change unexplained. Rječnik Akad. s.v.

Boh. *plech,* Pol. *blacha,* fr. NHG *blech* (above, 4).

Russ. *žest'* : *žestkij* 'hard', ChSl. *žestŭ, žestokŭ* id. (17.54).

7. Skt. *trapu-* (AV+, Macdonell-Keith, 1.326), orig.?

9.71 POTTER

Grk.	κεραμεύς	Goth.	kasja	Lith.	puodžius
NG	ἀγγειοπλάστης, τσουκαλᾶς	ON	(leirsmiðr)	Lett.	puodnieks
		Dan.	pottemager	ChSl.	grinčari
Lat.	figulus	Sw.	krukmakare	SCr.	lončar
It.	stovigliaio, vasaio	OE	croc-, lāmwyrhta	Boh.	hrnčíř
Fr.	potier	ME	pottere	Pol.	garncarz, zdun
Sp.	alfarero, ollero	NE	potter	Russ.	goršečnik, gončar
Rum.	olar	Du.	pottenbakker	Skt.	kumbhakāra-, kulāla-
Ir.	cerd, doīlbthid	OHG	havanāri, leimwurhto	Av.	. . . .
NIr.	criadoir	MHG			
W.	crochenydd	NHG	töpfer		
Br.					

The majority of the words for 'potter' are derivs. or cpds. of words for 'earthenware vessel, pot' (5.26) or 'vase, vessel'. Others are connected with those for 'mold' (9.72) or for 'clay' (9.73).

Words for 'pottery' (collective, or for the art or place of manufacture) are related to those for 'potter' or 'clay', and a separate list is superfluous.

1. Grk. κεραμεύς, fr. κέραμος 'clay, pottery' (9.73).

NG ἀγγειοπλάστης, cpd. of ἀγγεῖον 'vessel' and πλάστης : πλάσσω 'form, mold' (9.72).

NG τσουκαλᾶς, fr. τσουκάλι 'pot'.

2. Lat. *figulus* (cf. *fictīlia* 'earthenware, pottery') : *fingere* 'mold, form' (9.72).

It. *vasaio* (the term used in archeology), deriv. of *vaso* 'vase, pot' (also *vasello*, whence *vasellame* 'pottery'), Lat. *vāsum*.

It. *stovigliaio* 'pot-maker' and 'pot-seller', deriv. of *stoviglie* 'pottery', this fr. VLat. *testuīle, deriv. of Lat. *testu* beside *testa* 'earthen pot, tile, etc.'. REW 8688.

Fr. *potier*, deriv. of *pot* 'pot', whence also *poterie* 'pottery' > Br. *poderi*, *poderez*, NE *pottery*.

Sp. *alfarero* (cf. *alfareria* 'pottery'), fr. *alf(ah)ar* 'pottery', this fr. Arab. *faḫḫār* 'potter'. Lokotsch 570.

Sp. *ollero*, Rum. *olar* (cf. Rum. *olläne* 'pottery, potter's shop'), fr. Lat. *ollārius*, adj. 'pertaining to pots', later 'potter', deriv. of *ōlla* 'pot'.

3. Ir. *cerd* 'artisan' (9.42) also spec. 'potter' (cf. Ml. 18a12, 18b4).

Ir. *doilbthid* (Wb. 4c29), deriv. of *dolbaim* 'mold' (9.72). Pedersen 2.17.

NIr. *criadoir*, fr. *criad(h)a* 'pottery', deriv. of *crē* 'clay' (9.73).

W. *crochenydd*, deriv. of *crochan* 'pot'.

Br. *poder*, deriv. of *pod* 'pot', fr. Fr. *pot*.

4. Goth. *kasja*, deriv. of *kas* 'vessel, jar' : ON *ker*, OHG *kar* id., of dub. orig. Falk-Torp 496. Feist 308.

Late ON *leirsmiðr*, OE *lāmwyrhta*, OHG *leimwurhto*, cpds. of words for 'clay' (9.73) and 'artisan' (9.42).

Dan. *pottemager*, Sw. *krukmakare*, cpds. of Dan. *potte* (: OE *pott*, below), Sw. *kruk* (: OE *crocca*, below) and 'maker'.

OE *crocwyrhta*, cpd. of *crocca* 'pot, crock' and *wyrhta* 'artisan' (9.42).

ME *pottere*, NE *potter*, derivs. of ME, NE *pot*, OE *pott* 'pot'.

Du. *pottenbakker*, cpd. of *pot* (: OE *pott*, above) and *bakken* 'bake'.

OHG *havanāri*, MHG *havenære*, NHG dial. *hafner*, derivs. of OHG *hafan*, MHG *haven* 'pot'.

NHG *töpfer* (whence *töpferei* 'pottery'), deriv. of MHG, NHG *topf* 'pot'.

5. Lith. *puodžius*, Lett. *puodnieks*, derivs. of Lith. *puodas*, Lett. *puods* 'pot'.

6. ChSl. *grŭnĭčarĭ*, Boh. *hrnčíř*, Pol. *garncarz*, Russ. *gončar*, *goršečnik*, derivs. of ChSl. *grŭnĭcĭ*, etc. 'pot'.

SCr. *lončar*, deriv. of *lonac* 'pot'.

Pol. *zdun* (cf. late ChSl. *zĭdŭ* 'potter's clay') : ChSl. *zĭdati* 'build', orig. 'mold, fashion' (cf. 9.44). Brückner 650.

7. Skt. *kumbhakāra-*, cpd. of *kumbha-* 'pot' and a deriv. of *kṛ-* 'do, make'.

Skt. *kulāla-* (whence *kāulālaka-* 'pottery'), orig.? Uhlenbeck 59.

8. Cf. Toch. A *kuntis-tsek*, B *lwaksā-tsaik* 'potter' (= Skt. *kumbhakāra-*), cpds. of (presumably words for 'pot', with) *tsek-*, *tsaik-* 'form, fashion' (9.72).

9.72 MOLD (Clay, etc.)

Grk.	πλάσσω	Goth.	*digan*	Lith.	(*daryti*)
NG	πλάθω	ON	*mynda*	Lett.	(*taisīt*)
Lat.	*fingere*	Dan.	*forme, danne*	ChSl.	. . . .
It.	*modellare, plasmare, formare*	Sw.	*forma, dana*	SCr.	(*tvoriti*)
Fr.	*modeler, former*	OE	*hīwian*	Boh.	(*tvařiti*)
Sp.	*formar, modelar*	ME	*fourme*	Pol.	*ulepić*
Rum.	*forma, modela*	NE	*mo(u)ld*	Russ.	*lepit'* (*delat'*)
Ir.	*dolbaim, cummaim*	Du.	*vormen*	Skt.	(*mā-, saṁskṛ-*)
NIr.	*foirmighim, cumaim*	OHG	*scaf(f)ōn*	Av.	(*mā-*)
W.	*ffurfio, llunio*	MHG	*formen, schaffen*		
Br.	*aoza*	NHG	*formen, bilden*		

For the process of forming articles from clay or other plastic material by molding with the hands, only a few of the IE languages show distinctive technical terms, and even these came to be used also in a more general sense 'form, fashion, make', etc. There was an IE root, namely *dheiĝh-, of which the primary application was probably to just this process, together with the similar one of kneading dough, but such special use survived in only a small part of its derivs. Some derivs. of a word for 'a mold' were used first for 'form in a mold' and then by extension for molding with the hands. In the majority of cases the words commonly employed are those of general scope, meaning 'form, shape, make, etc.', and especially derivs. of Lat. *fōrma* 'shape, form'. From these it has been in part difficult to make a selection for the list.

1. IE *dheiĝh-, prob. used primarily for the molding of clay and the kneading of dough. Walde-P. 1.833 f. Ernout-M. 361 f. Walde-H. 1.501 f.

Here as 'mold', Lat. *fingere* (with *figulus* 'potter'), Goth. *digan* in *kasa digana* 'clay vessels', *þamma digandin* 'τῷ πλάσαντι', *daigs* 'lump of clay' (Rom. 9.21; but usually 'dough'); as 'knead' in the Gmc. word for 'dough', Goth. *daigs*, OE *dāg*, etc.; Skt. *dih-* 'smear'; words for 'wall', Skt. *dehī*, Grk. τεῖχος, Osc. *feíhúss* (acc. pl.); Toch. A *tsek-*, B *tsaik-* 'form, fashion' in *kuntis-tsek* 'potter', etc. (SSS 2,484).

2. Grk. πλάσσω, πλάττω (cf. also πλάστης 'molder', πλάσμα 'molded figure'), fr. *πλάθιω (cf. κοροπλάθος 'molder of small figures', πηλοπλάθος 'molder of clay'), NG πλάθω (also 'knead'), perh. with semantic development through the notion of flattening out the clay in the process of molding, fr. an extension of IE *pelə-, *plā- in Lat. *plānus* 'flat', etc. Walde-P. 2.63.

3. Lat. *fingere*, above, 1.

Derivs. of Lat. *fōrmāre* 'shape, form' (fr. *fōrma* 'shape, form', 12.51), or new verbs formed fr. the noun, occurring in most of the modern European languages, may be used to cover the notion of molding clay, and in many languages are the most usual expressions for this. Cf. Fr. *former* (OFr. *fourmer* > ME *fourme*, NE *form*), Sp. *formar*, Rum. *forma*, NIr. *foirmighim*, W. *ffurfio*, Dan. *forme*, Sw. *forma*, Du. *vormen*, MHG, NHG *formen*, also, although prob. less common, Lith. *formuoti*, Lett. *formēt*, Boh. *formovati*, Pol. *formować*, Russ. *formovat'*.

Lat. *modulus* 'a measure' yields words for 'a mold', as OFr. *modle* (Fr. *moule*), whence ME, NE *mo(u)ld*, and fr. this the vb., orig. 'shape in a mold' (as Fr. *mouler*), then extended to molding with the hands (clay, etc., or dough); also, through *modellus, words for 'model', whence again vbs. as It. *modellare*, Fr. *modeler*, Sp. *modelar*, Rum. *modela*, NE *model*, which may also be used for molding clay. NED s.v. *mould*, sb.[3] and vb.[2].

It. *plasmare*, Sp. *plasmar*, deriv. of *plasma* fr. Grk. πλάσμα 'molded figure' (above, 2).

4. Ir. *dolbaim* 'form, fashion artfully' : *delb* 'form, image', Lat. *dolāre* 'hew', etc. (9.45).

Ir. *cummaim*, NIr. *cumaim* 'form, shape, make', derivs. of Ir. *cumma* 'a shaping', vbl. abstract of *com-benim*, cpd. of *benim* 'strike' (9.21). Pedersen 2.461.

W. *llunio*, deriv. of *llun* 'form, shape, figure', etym.?

NIr. *foirmighim*, W. *ffurfio*, above, 3.

Br. *aoza* 'form, fashion, arrange, prepare', deriv. of *aoz* 'fashion, manner', MBr. *neuz* 'form, nature' : W. *naws* 'nature, temperament', Ir. *gnās*, NIr. *nos* 'custom' (19.61). Henry 14, 211. Ernault, Glossaire 343.

5. Goth. *digan*, above, 1.

ON *mynda* 'shape, form', deriv. of *mynd* 'shape, form, image' (12.51).

Dan. *danne* (> Sw. *dana*), both now common for 'form' with widest scope, deriv. of adj. *dan* (seen in Dan. *saadan*, *hvordan*, etc.), fr. MLG *dān*, pple. of *dōn* 'do, make' : OE *dōn*, OHG *tuon*, etc. (9.11). Falk-Torp 136. Hellquist 134.

OE *(ge)hīwian* 'form, fashion, shape' ('fingere' Aelfric), deriv. of OE *hīw* 'shape, form, appearance, color' (12.51).

NE *mold*, *model*, above, 3.

OHG *scaf(f)ōn*, MHG *schaffen* 'form, shape, arrange', derivs. of OHG *scaf* 'form, arrangement' : ON *skap* 'form, condition', Goth. *gaskapjan*, ON *skapa*, OHG *sceffan* 'create, form'. Walde-P. 2.562. Weigand-H. 2.667.

NHG *bilden* 'form, fashion', OHG *bilidōn* 'represent, form after a model', derivs. of OHG *biladi*, NHG *bild* 'image, picture' (9.87).

6. Lith. *daryti* 'do, make' (9.11) also used in sense of 'make, form something of clay'.

Lett. *(iz)taisīt* 'make, prepare, form' : Lith. *taisyti* 'make, prepare, repair', *tiesus* 'straight', *tiesti* 'straighten'. Mühl.-Endz. 4.124.

7. SCr. *tvoriti*, Boh. *tvařiti* 'make, form, shape' (= ChSl. *tvoriti* 'make', 9.11) also applied to work in clay.

Pol. *ulepić*, Russ. *lepit'* 'stick together' (: ChSl. *pri-lěpiti* id., Skt. *lip-* 'smear', etc.; Berneker 712), also 'model in clay' (cf. Russ. *lepšik* 'modeler').

Russ. *delat'* 'do, make' (9.11), also 'make from clay'.

8. Skt. *mā-* 'measure, mete out', hence also 'prepare, arrange, fashion, form' (cf. *nir-mā-* 'construct, build', 9.44), Av. *mā-* 'measure, make, form' (12.54).

Skt. *saṁskṛ-* 'put together, compose', etc., cpd. of *sam-* 'together' and *(s)kṛ-* 'do, make'.

9.73 CLAY

Grk.	πηλός, ἄργῖλος	Goth.	*þāhō*	Lith.	*molis*
NG	πηλός, γλίνα	ON	*leir*	Lett.	*māls*
Lat.	*argilla, crēta*	Dan.	*ler*	ChSl.	*glina*
It.	*argilla, creta*	Sw.	*lera*	SCr.	*glina, ilovača*
Fr.	*argile, glaise*	OE	*clǣg, lām*	Boh.	*hlina, jil*
Sp.	*arcilla, barro*	ME	*clai*	Pol.	*glina*
Rum.	*argilă, lut, humă*	NE	*clay*	Russ.	*glina*
Ir.	*crē*	Du.	*klei, leem*	Skt.	*mṛd-, mṛttikā-*
NIr.	*crē*	OHG	*dāha, leim*	Av.	. . . .
W.	*clai, pridd*	MHG	*dāhe, leim*		
Br.	*pri*	NHG	*ton, lehm*		

Words for the potter's 'clay' are from notions of color ('gray, white', or 'dark'), consistency ('sticky, thick'), 'mixture', 'mud'. Many of the common words for 'earth', though not included in the list, are also used for 'earth' as potter's material, as in Lat. *Samia terra*, It. *terra cotta*, NHG *töpfererde*, NE *potter's earth*, etc., cf. also NE *earthenware*, Du. *aardewerk* 'pottery', etc.

1. Grk. πηλός, also 'mud', etym. dub. See under 'mud' (1.214).

Grk. κέραμος, sometimes 'potter's clay' but mostly the product, 'pottery, earthen vessel, tile', also κεραμίς 'tile', γῆ κεραμίς 'potter's earth', κεραμεύς 'potter', possibly through the idea of mixing and molding the clay : κεράννῡμι 'mix'; or loanword fr. some Anatolian source?

Walde-P. 1.419. Kretschmer, Glotta 11.284.

Grk. ἄργῖλος, ἄργιλλος (latter infrequent, but source of Lat. *argilla*) : ἀργός, ἀργής 'bright, white', ἄργυρος 'silver', Skt. *arjuna-* 'white, bright', Lat. *argentum* 'silver', etc. Walde-P. 1.82. Ernout-M. 71. Walde-H. 1.66.

NG γλίνα (also 'fat, dirt', etc.) fr. class. Grk. γλίνα : γλία 'glue', OE *clǣg* 'clay', etc. (below, 4).

2. Lat. *argilla* (> It. *argilla*, Fr. *argile*, Sp. *arcilla*, Rum. *argilă*), fr. Grk. ἄργιλλος (above, 1).

Lat. *crēta* 'chalk, white earth or clay' (> It. *creta*), also spec. *crēta figlīna* 'potter's clay', etym. dub., perh. through *terra crēta* 'sifted earth', fr. *cernere* 'sift, separate'; or : Ir. *crē*, etc. (below, 3)? Walde-H. 1.290 f.

Fr. *glaise*, also *terre glaise* 'potter's clay', fr. Gall., cf. *glisomarga* 'a kind of marl' (Plin.). REW 3788. Gamillscheg 471.

Sp. *barro* 'clay, mud' (It. *barro*, a special kind of clay), orig.? REW 965. Wartburg 1.265.

Rum. *lut*, fr. Lat. *lutum* 'mud, potter's clay' (1.214).

Rum. *humă*, fr. Bulg. *huma* 'clay', this fr. Grk. χῶμα 'earth'. Tiktin 743.

3. Ir. *crē* (gen. *criad*), W. *pridd*, Br. *pri* : Lat. *crēta*? See above, 2.

W. *clai*, fr. ME *clai* (below, 4).

4. Goth. *þāhō*, OE *þōhe* (rare), OHG *dāha*, MHG *dāhe*, *tāhe*, NHG *ton* : ON *þā* 'loam', ON *þéttr*, NHG *dicht* 'dense, compact', Lith. *tankus* 'frequent, thick', Skt. *tañc-* 'contract'. Walde-P. 1.725 f. Feist 488.

ON *leir*, Dan. *ler*, Sw. *lera* (cf. Dan. *lervare*, Sw. *lerkärl* 'pottery'), with different suffix OE *lām* (cf. *lǣmina* 'pottery'), Du. *leem*, OHG, MHG *leim*, NHG *lehm* (LG form) 'mud, earth, clay' : Lat. *līmus* 'slime, mud', OPruss. *layso* 'clay', Lat. *linere* 'besmear', etc. Walde-P. 2.389. Falk-Torp 635.

OE *clǣg*, ME *clai*, NE *clay*, Du. *klei* : ChSl. *glina*, etc. (below, 6), Grk. γλία, γλίνα, Lat. *glūten* 'glue', Ir. *glenim*, OHG *klenan*, *klebēn* 'stick, adhere', etc. Walde-P. 1.619. Walde-H. 1.611 f.

5. Lith. *molis*, Lett. *māls*, prob. : Lith. *mėlynas* 'blue', Lett. *melns*, Grk. μέλας 'black', Skt. *malina-* 'dirty, dark', etc. Walde-P. 2.294. Berneker 2.12.

6. ChSl. *glina* (cf. *glinĭnŭ* 'of clay', Supr.), etc., general Slavic : OE *clǣg*, etc. (above, 4). Berneker 304.

SCr. *ilovača*, Boh. *jil* 'mud, clay' : ChSl. (late) *ilŭ* id., Lett. *īls* 'pitch-dark', Grk. ἰλύς 'mud, slime'. Walde-P. 1.163. Berneker 424.

Skt. *mṛd-*, *mṛttikā-* 'clay, loam, earth' (cf. *mṛnmaya-* 'pottery', cpd. with *mā-* 'form', 9.72) : Goth. *mulda* 'dust', OE *molde* 'loose earth, soil', fr. dental extensions of IE *mel- in Lat. *molere*, etc. 'grind' (5.56). Walde-P. 2.288.

9.74 GLASS

Grk.	ὕαλος	Goth.	. . . .	Lith.	*stiklas*
NG	γυαλί	ON	*gler*	Lett.	*stikls, glāze*
Lat.	*vitrum*	Dan.	*glas*	ChSl.	*stĭklo*
It.	*vetro*	Sw.	*glas*	SCr.	*staklo*
Fr.	*verre*	OE	*glæs*	Boh.	*sklo*
Sp.	*vidrio*	ME	*glas*	Pol.	*szklo*
Rum.	*sticlă*	NE	*glass*	Russ.	*steklo*
Ir.	*glain(e)*	Du.	*glas*	Skt.	*kāca-*
NIr.	*gloine*	OHG	*glas*	Av.	*yama-*
W.	*gwydr*	MHG	*glas*		
Br.	*gwer*	NHG	*glas*		

The manufacture of glass goes back to remote antiquity in Egypt, and also became a flourishing industry in Phoenicia. In Greece and Italy glass was known only from imported objects (glass beads, etc., in the Mycenaean period) until a comparatively late period. From the Greco-Roman world it spread to northern Europe, where its predecessor in objects of ornament was amber. In its early uses colored glass was more common than the transparent. Schrader, Reallex. and Pauly-Wissowa s.v. Glas. Mary L. Trowbridge, Philological Studies in Ancient Glass, Univ. of Illinois Studies in Language and Literature 13. Nos. 3–4.

Most of the IE words for 'glass', if not obscure, are connected with words for some color or for 'bright, shining'. But, as words for 'glass' as material came to be used also for a 'glass drinking vessel', so conversely the Balto-Slavic words for 'glass' are from a Gmc. word for 'drinking vessel'.

1. Grk. ὕαλος, ὕελος, NG γυαλί, prob. a loanword, but of unknown source. The word occurs first in Hdt. 3.24, but here refers to some kind of transparent stone and is quotable only later for 'glass'. An earlier expression for true glass, namely 'poured stone' is reflected in ἀρτήματα λίθινα χυτά, Hdt. 2.69.

2. Lat. *vitrum* (> It. *vetro*, Fr. *verre;* VLat. **vitrium* > Sp. *vidrio*), prob., as appropriate to the familiar blue-green Roman glass, the same word as *vitrum* 'woad' (a plant furnishing a blue dye), this again related in some fashion to OHG *weit*, OE *wād* 'woad'. Walde-P. 1.236. Ernout-M. 1074 f.

Rum. *sticlă*, fr. Slavic, ChSl. *stĭklo*, etc. (below, 6).

3. Ir. *glain(e)*, NIr. *gloine* : W. *glain* 'gem, bead', Ir., W., Br. *glan* 'bright, pure', Ir. *gel* 'white', fr. IE **ĝel-* or **ĝhel-* in numerous color names (for 'gray', 'blue', 'green', 'yellow'). Walde-P. 1.622 f., 624 ff.

W. *gwydr*, Br. *gwer*, fr. Lat. *vitrum* (above, 2). Pedersen 1.233. Loth, Mots lat. 176.

4. ON *gler*, OE *glæs*, OHG *glas*, etc., general Gmc. (Dan., Sw. *glas* fr. MLG), orig. used of 'amber' (as OE *glær* and in part OHG *glas*) : Ir. *glass* 'green, gray, blue', W. *glas* 'blue', Br. *glaz* 'green', ON *glæsa* 'make shine, adorn', ME, MLG *glaren* 'gleam', all prob. fr. an *s*-extension of IE **ĝhel-* in color names (cf. above, 3). Walde-P. 1.626. Falk-Torp 325.

5. Lith. *stiklas*, Lett. *stikls*, OPruss. *sticlo*, fr. Slavic (below, 6).

Lett. *glāze* fr. MLG *glas* (above, 4). Mühl.-Endz. 1.624.

6. ChSl. *stĭklo* (quotable only late), etc., general Slavic, fr. Goth. *stikls* 'drinking cup' (ποτήριον), which became known to the Slavs as a glass drinking cup (prob. their first acquaintance with glass, at least as a useful product, hence used also for the material), but which orig. applied to the old Gmc. 'drinking horn', and so : ON *stikill* 'pointed end of a drinking horn', OE *sticel*, OHG *stichil* 'point, prick', etc. Brückner 549. Stender-Petersen 398 f.

7. Skt. *kāca-* : *khac-* 'shine through' (?). Uhlenbeck 51.

Av. *yama-*, *yāma-* (Barth. 1264, 1286; NPers. *jām*), etym.?

9.75 PLAIT (vb.)

Grk.	*πλέκω*	Goth.	*uswindan*	Lith.	*pinti*
NG	*πλέκω*	ON	*flētta*	Lett.	*pīt, režg'īt*
Lat.	*plectere*	Dan.	*flette*	ChSl.	*plesti*
It.	*intrecciare*	Sw.	*fläta*	SCr.	*ples i*
Fr.	*tresser*	OE	*bregdan, fleohtan*	Boh.	*plešti*
Sp.	*trenzar*	ME	*breide*	Pol.	*pleść*
Rum.	*împleti*	NE	*plait, braid*	Russ.	*plest'*
Ir.	*figim*	Du.	*vlechten*	Skt.	*u-*
NIr.	*dualaim*	OHG	*flehtan*	Av.	. . . .
W.	*plethu*	MHG	*vlehten*		
Br.	*plañsona*	NHG	*flechten*		

The construction of dwellings, fences, walls, etc., and the manufacture of various articles like mats, baskets, etc., by plaiting together twigs, reeds, etc., antedates the more technical crafts. Moreover, plaiting is the ancestor of the more specialized and refined weaving (cf. 6.33) and is basic to at least some of the earliest pottery (as made by smearing clay on a wickerwork frame). Apart from the existence of an IE root for 'plait' (**pleḱ-*, below, 1), the early importance of wickerwork construction is reflected in the history of certain words for 'build', 'house' (?) and for various objects which have long since ceased to be associated with such construction. Cf. Fr. *bâtir* 'build' (9.44), Lat. *crātis* 'harrow' (8.28), Goth. *haurds* 'door' (7.22), etc. But several of the examples commonly assumed are doubtful. Thus the assumption of an IE **gherd-*, **ĝherd-*, in the sense of 'plait' (Walde-P. 1.608) is highly speculative, since all the words involved may rest on the notion of 'hold, inclose'.

Plaiting naturally declined in relative importance with the advance of other crafts, and survives in only a very limited role in modern industry. Furthermore, when more important than now, it did not call for the special skill, implements, and workshops characteristic of other crafts, and remained longer, what all the crafts were at the outset, merely one of the numerous activities of the household. Hence it did not develop much of a technical terminology. Words for the workman and generic terms for the product are mostly artificial rather than popular.

The one cognate group that comes nearest to representing a generic term for the product, though the words are used mostly for various more specific products, is the following:

Grk. κάρτα(λ)λος 'a kind of basket', κύρτη 'fish-basket', κυρτία 'wickerwork shield' (all rare words), Lat. *crātis* (esp. pl. *crātēs*) 'wickerwork, hurdle, harrow', OE *hyrdel*, OHG *hurd* 'hurdle', Goth. *haurds*, ON *hurð* 'door' (7.22), Skt. *kaṭa-* (**kṛta-*) 'straw mat' : Skt. *kṛt-* 'twist thread, spin'. Walde-P. 1.421.

Other expressions for the product may be based on the current verbs for 'plait', as Grk. πλέγμα, NHG *geflecht*, *flechtwerk*, It. *lavoro intrecciato*, or on some special material or product, as NE *wickerwork* (*wicker* 'pliant twig', fr. Scand., cf. ODan. *viger* 'willow'), *basketwork*, *lattice-work* (*lattice* deriv. of word for 'lath'), Fr. *claie* (fr. Celtic, cf. Ir. *clīad* 'hurdle'), *clayonnage*, etc. Cf. also OE *watul*, NE *wattle*, *wattling* (of dub. orig.; NED s.v. *wattle*). But only a few of these are truly generic.

Apart from the inherited groups, in which 'plait' is based on 'fold', words for

'plait' are from other roots meaning 'fold, twist, wind' or the like, or derivatives of nouns for 'trees, braid'. A few are identical with the words for 'weave' (6.33), and in most languages the words for 'weave' are freely used with an object like 'basket, mat' or 'reeds, twigs', so that they thus cover 'plait'.

1. IE **pleḱ-* in words for 'plait' and 'fold', an extension of **pel-* in other words for 'fold'. Cf. Lat. *plicāre*, Goth. *falþan*, etc. 'fold' (9.15). Walde-P. 2.97. Ernout-M. 777 ff.

Grk. πλέκω; with *t*-extension Lat. *plectere* (> W. *plethu;* Loth, Mots lat. 196) and ON *flētta*, OE *fleohtan*, OHG *flehtan*, etc., once general Gmc.; here also (or fr. **plet-*, a parallel extension of **pel-*?) ChSl. *plesti*, *pletą*, etc., general Slavic (whence Rum. *împleti*).

2. It. *intrecciare*, Fr. *tresser*, Sp. *trenzar*, derivs. of It. *treccia*, Fr. *tresse*, Sp. *trenza* 'tress, braid', fr. VLat. **trichea*, orig. dub. REW 8893. Gamillscheg 863.

Rum. *împleti*, fr. Slavic (above, 1).

3. Ir. *figim*, same as for 'weave' (6.33).

NIr. *dualaim* 'plait, fold, braid', deriv. of Ir. *dūal* 'fold, fringe, plait, lock of hair' (**doklo*) : Goth. *tagl* 'hair', OE *tægl* 'tail', Skt. *daçā-* 'fringe, border', etc. Walde-P. 1.785. Stokes 152.

Br. *plañsona*, deriv. of *plañson* 'braid (of hair)', fr. Fr. *plançon* (deriv. of Lat. *planta*) 'young plant, shoot'; the meaning 'braid' fr. that of 'plant, shoot' through similarity of appearance. Henry 224.

4. Goth. *us-windan* (Mk. 15. 17, etc. for πλέκω), cpd. like *bi-windan* 'wrap' : OE *windan* 'wind', etc. (10.14).

OE *bregdan* 'make a quick movement, draw a sword', hence from the motions in the process (cf. the throwing of the shuttle in weaving) also 'plait, braid', ME *breide*, NE *braid* (now mostly with reference to hair, but cf. *braided rugs*) : ON *bregða* 'move quickly, draw a sword, etc.', OS *bregdan* 'plait', OHG *brettan* 'jerk, weave', these further : ON *brjā* 'sparkle, shine', *braga* 'flame, burn', etc. (for such relations cf. the uses of NE *flash*). Walde-P. 2.169. Falk-Torp 56.

NE *plait*, *plat* (in southern U.S. one *plats* hair), deriv. of *plait* 'a fold, crease', fr. OFr. *pleit*, Lat. *plicitum* : *plicāre* 'fold', *plectere* (above, 1). NED s.v.

5. Lith. *pinti*, Lett. *pīt* : Goth., OE *spinnan* 'spin', ChSl. *pęti* 'stretch', fr. IE *(*s*)*pen-* 'stretch, draw' and hence from the stretching involved in twisting together the fibers, etc., 'spin, plait'. Walde-P. 2.660 f.

Lett. *režg'īt* : *režg'is* 'wickerwork', Lith. *regsti* 'knit, plait', Skt. *rajju-*, Lat. *restis* 'cord, rope', OE *resc*, *rysc* 'rush' Walde-P. 2.374.

6. ChSl. *plesti*, *pletą*, etc., see above, 1.

7. Skt. *u-* (*vayate*, *uta-*), same as for 'weave' (6.33).

9.76 BASKET

Grk.	*κόφινος, κάλαθος*, etc.	Goth.	*tainjō, snōrjō*	Lith.	*gurbas*
NG	*καλάθι, κοφίνι*	ON	*laupr, teina*	Lett.	*kurvis, gruozs*
Lat.	*corbis, calathus*, etc.	Dan.	*kurv*	ChSl.	*košĭ, krabĭjĭ*
It.	*cesta, canestra, paniere, corba*	Sw.	*korg*	SCr.	*koš, kotarica* (*korpa*)
		OE	*tǣnel, windel, wilige*	Boh.	*koš, košik*
Fr.	*panier, corbeille*	ME	*windle, basket*	Pol.	*kosz*
Sp.	*cesta, canasta*	NE	*basket*	Russ.	*korzina, kuzov, korob*
Rum.	*coş, paner*	Du.	*korf, mand*	Skt.	*piṭa(ka)-, peṭa(ka)-*
Ir.	*cliab*	OHG	*zeinna, corb, cratto*	Av.	. . . .
NIr.	*cliabh, basc(a)eid*	MHG	*korp, krebe, krezze*		
W.	*basged, cawell, cest*	NHG	*korb*		
Br.	*paner, kavell*				

'Basket' is chosen here as a conspicuous product of the process of plaiting and one that has remained familiar in all periods. But there are so many kinds of baskets with their special names that it is difficult to select the most important, especially from the earlier periods, when there was no generic term like NE *basket*.

Despite the factual relation between 'basket' and 'plait', none of the words for 'basket' are derived from the regular words for 'plait' as listed in 9.75. But, like some of these latter, they may reflect an action like 'twist, wind' or a material like 'twig' or 'reed'. French *panier* shows generalization from 'bread container'. Many of the words are of wholly obscure origin.

1. Grk. κόφινος (> late Lat. *cophinus* > OFr. *coffin* > ME *coffyn* 'basket', NE *coffin* in spec. sense), NG κοφίνι, orig. dub., perh. loanword fr. a pre-Greek source. Walde-P. 2.540. Boisacq 504.

Grk. κάλαθος (> Lat. *calathus*), NG καλάθι, orig. dub., but perh. : κλώθω 'spin' (cf. Lith. *pinti* 'plait' : Goth. *spinna* 'spin', 9.75). Walde-P. 1.464.

Grk. κάνεον, deriv. of κάννα 'reed', whence also Lat. *canna*. Hence also (with chronological relations between Grk. and Lat. forms uncertain) Grk. κάναστρον (> Sp. *canasta*), κάνιστρον (prob. fr. Lat.), Lat. *canistrum* (> It. *canestra*). Ernout-M. 143. Walde-H. 1.154. REW 1594.

Grk. κίστη (> Lat. *cista* > It. Sp. *cesta*, W. *cest*) : Ir. *cess* 'basket' (K. Meyer, Contrib. 353), *cisse* 'twisted'. Walde-P. 1.452. Walde-H. 1.223. Vendryes, MSL 19.61.

Grk. σπυρίς, -ίδος (> Lat. *sporta*, dim. *sportula*, It. *sporta*, etc.) : σπεῖρα 'anything twisted, coil, cord', σπάρτον 'rope', etc. Walde-P. 2.667.

Grk. ἄρριχος (Ion. ἄρσιχος), orig. dub. Walde-P. 2.374.

Grk. σαργάνη (in NT, 2 Cor. 11.33 clearly a 'rope-basket'; cf. the Goth. rendering *snōrjō;* so prob. in the papyri, where the word is frequent beside κόφινος), Att. ταργάνη (Hesych., EM), etym.? Walde-P. 1.751. Boisacq 853.

NG πανέρι fr. It. *paniere* (below, 2).

2. Lat. *corbis* (> It. *corba;* late dim. *corbicula* > Fr. *corbeille*), orig. dub., possibly with notion of plaiting from bending : Russ. *korobit'* 'bend', ON *herpask* 'contract', etc.; or may be a loanword fr. some Mediterranean source. Lat. *corbis* is the source of the Gmc. words, Dan. *kurv*, Sw. *korg*, Du. *korf*, OHG *corb*, NHG *korb*, and these again of the Balto-Slavic words, Lith. *gurbas*, Lett. *kurvis*, ChSl. *krabĭjĭ*, Russ. *korob*. Walde-P. 2.588. Walde-H. 1.272. Ernout-M. 220. Berneker 568.

Lat. *quālum* (**quaslom*, cf. *quasillus* 'small basket') : ChSl. *košĭ* 'basket', etc. (below, 6), also ChSl. (late) *košara* 'hurdle, sheep inclosure', SCr. *košara* 'stall of wickerwork', with no known root connection. Walde-P. 1.507. Ernout-M. 832. Berneker 586 f.

Lat. *fiscus* (orig. 'basket' for olives, etc., then 'money-basket' hence 'public treasury'), perh. : Grk. πίθος 'wine-vessel', Lat. *fidēlia* 'earthen jar', as orig. a woven basket covered with clay. Ernout-M. 364. Walde-H. 1.492 f., 506.

It., Sp. *cesta*, see Grk. κίστη, above, 1.

It. *canestra*, Sp. *canasta*, see Grk. κάνεον, above, 1.

It. *paniere*, Fr. *panier* (> Br. *paner*), Rum. *paner*, fr. Lat. *pānārium* 'bread-basket', deriv. of *pānis* 'bread'.

Rum. *coş*, fr. Slavic, ChSl. *košĭ*, etc.

3. Ir. *cliab*, NIr. *cliabh*, perh. orig. 'basket-shield' : ON *hlīf* 'shield', *hlīfa* 'protect'. Pedersen 1.116.

NIr. *basc(a)eid*, W. *basged*, fr. NE *basket* (below, 4).

W. *cawell*, Br. *kavell*, fr. a late Lat. *cavellum* : *cavea* 'cage, hive, inclosure of lattice-work', this fr. *cavus* 'hollow'(?). Loth, Mots lat. 146. Walde-H. 1.188 (vs. Walde-P. 1.337).

Br. *paner*, fr. Fr. *panier* (above, 2).

4. Goth. *tainjō*, OE *tǣnel*, OHG *zeinna* 'basket', ON *teina* 'fish-basket', derivs. of Goth. *tains*, OE *tān*, OHG *zein*, ON *teinn* 'branch, reed, twig'. Falk-Torp 1252. Feist 473.

Goth. *snōrjō* (for σαργάνη, see above, 1) : OE *snēr* 'string of a musical instrument', ON *snœri* 'twisted rope', OHG *snuor* 'cord' (9.19). Walde-P. 2.700. Falk-Torp 1098. Feist 441.

ON *laupr* 'basket, bucket', OE *lēap* 'basket, a certain measure' : OHG *louft* 'bark, bast', Goth. *laufs*, OE *lēaf*, OHG *loub* 'leaf'. Falk-Torp 678. Walde-P. 2.418.

OE *windel*, ME *windle* : OE *windan* 'wind', etc. (10.14).

OE *wilige*, prob. deriv. of *welig* 'willow', at any rate from the same root, that of *wil(w)ian* 'roll, twist together, join', Goth. *-walwjan*, Lat. *volvere* 'roll', etc., IE **wel-*. Walde-P. 1.298 ff.

OE *mand* (NE dial. *maund*), Du. *mand*, orig.? Franck-v. W. 411.

ME, NE *basket*, fr. a Celtic word appearing in Martial and Juvenal as *bascauda*, this prob. : Lat. *fascia* 'bundle'. Walde-H. 1.97. Doubted in NED s.v., but cf. Weekley s.v.

OHG *corb*, etc., above, 2 under Lat. *corbis*.

MHG *krebe* : OHG *krippa*, OE *cribb* 'crib, manger', MLG *kerve* 'fish-basket, net', ON *kjarf* 'bundle'; OHG *cratto*, *krezzo*, MHG *krezze* : OE *cræt* 'wagon-basket', OHG *kranz* 'wreath', OE *cradol* 'cradle'; both groups perh. from extensions of an IE **ger-* 'twist, wind' (?) assumed as the basis of numerous words. Walde-P. 1.593 ff.

5. Lith. *gurbas*, Lett. *kurvis*, above, 2 under Lat. *corbis*.

Lett. *gruozs* : *griezt*, *gruōzīt* 'turn, twist' (Walde-P. 1.594). Mühl.-Endz. 1.672.

6. ChSl. *košĭ*, SCr. *koš*, Boh. *koš(ik)*, Pol. *kosz* (Russ. *koš* 'fish-basket', *košel* 'small basket, bag, wallet') : Lat. *quālum* (above, 2).

ChSl. *krabĭjĭ*, Russ. *korob*, above, 2, under Lat. *corbis*.

SCr. *kotarica* : Bulg. *kotara* 'hurdle', Russ. *koty* (pl.) 'fishweir', root connections dub. Walde-P. 1.338. Berneker 588 f.

Russ. *korzina*, perh. fr. Sw. dial. *kars(e)* 'basket, creel' : ON *kass* id., Grk. γέρρον 'wicker shield, screen, etc.', these perh. from the root of MHG *kerren*, OE *cierran* 'turn'. Berneker 578. Walde-P. 1.609.

Russ. *kuzov* : Pol. *kożub*, *każub*, Slov. *kozoł* 'a sort of basket', etc., prob. a non-IE loanword. Berneker 596.

7. Skt. *piṭa(ka)-*, *peṭa(ka)-*, orig.? Uhlenbeck 175.

9.81 CARVE

Grk.	γλύφω	Goth.	....	Lith.	*iškalti*
NG	γλύφω	ON	*skera, grafa*	Lett.	*tēluot*
Lat.	*scalpere (sculpere)*	Dan.	*udhugge*	ChSl.	*vajati*
It.	*scolpire*	Sw.	*uthugga*	SCr.	*vajati*
Fr.	*sculpter, tailler*	OE	*ceorfan, grafan*	Boh.	*vytesati*
Sp.	*esculpir*	ME	*kerve, grave*	Pol.	*wyciosać*
Rum.	*sculpta*	NE	*carve, sculp*	Russ.	*vajat'*
Ir.	*snaidim*	Du.	*uithouwen*	Skt.	....
NIr.	*snoighim*	OHG	*graban*	Av.	....
W.	*cerfio*	MHG	*ergraben*		
Br.	*kizella, bena*	NHG	*aushauen, ausmeisseln*		

Words for 'carve', as applied to the sculptor's work in stone (and usually also to the carving of wood) are mostly such as are also used with wider scope for 'cut' or 'hew' or are cognate with words which in other languages are non-technical words for 'cut, scrape, scratch, split', etc. A few are derivs. of words for 'chisel' or for 'statue', hence 'carve' through 'use the chisel' or 'make a statue'. Some of the forms listed for the older Gmc. languages are not certainly quotable in the technical sense.

1. Grk. γλύφω 'cut out, carve' in wood, stone, metals (cf. γλύπτης 'sculptor', γλύφανος 'knife, chisel', γλυφή 'a carving') : Lat. *glūbere* 'peel', ON *kljūfa*, OE *clēofan* 'split', etc., IE **gleubh-*. Walde-P. 1.661. Ernout-M. 426 f. Walde-H. 1.610.

2. Lat. *scalpere* 'scratch, scrape', and also the proper classical form for 'carve' in technical sense, and only in late times replaced in this sense by *sculpere*, fr. the cpds., thus resulting in a late differentiation in use from *scalpere* (whence confusion in the MSS and introduction of *sculpere, sculptor, sculptura*, in our texts in place of *scalpere, scalptor, scalptura*, while *scalprum* 'knife, chisel', dim. *scalpellum*, remain), prob. fr. an extension of the root seen in Grk. σκάλλω 'scrape, hoe', Lith. *skelti* 'split', ON *skilja* 'separate, divide', etc. Walde-P. 2.595. Ernout-M. 900 f.

It. *scolpire*, Sp. *esculpir*, fr. VLat. **sculpīre* : Lat. *sculpere* (above); Fr. *sculpter*, Rum. *sculpta*, back-formations to Fr. *sculpteur*, Rum. *sculptor* 'sculptor'.

Fr. *tailler* 'cut' (9.22), also used technically for 'carve'.

3. Ir. *snaidim*, NIr. *snoighim*, see under 'cut' (9.22).

W. *cerfio*, fr. ME *kerve*, NE *carve* (below, 4). Parry-Williams 115.

Br. *kizella*, fr. *kizell* 'chisel' (9.84).

Br. *bena*, see under 'hew' (9.45).

4. ON *skera*, see under 'cut' (9.22).

Dan. *udhugge*, Sw. *uthugga*, Du. *uithouwen*, NHG *aushauen*, lit. 'hew out', cpds. of Dan. *hugge*, etc. (9.22).

OE *ceorfan*, ME *kerve*, *carve*, NE *carve*, see under 'cut' (9.22).

ON *grafa* 'dig, bury, engrave', OE *grafan* 'dig, dig out, engrave, carve', ME *grave* 'engrave, carve' (NE *engrave* after Fr. *engraver*, this with *graver* 'engrave', *graveur* 'engraver' fr. Gmc.), OHG *graban* 'dig, engrave', MHG *graben* id., *ergraben* 'engrave, cut out' : Goth. *graban* 'dig', Lett. *grebt* 'scrape, hollow out', ChSl. *pogreti* 'bury', etc., IE **ghrebh-*. Walde-P. 1.653.

NE *sculp*, fr. Lat. *sculpere*, but now felt as a whimsical back-formation to *sculpture*, *sculptor*. NED s.v.

NHG *ausmeisseln*, lit. 'chisel out', deriv. of *meissel* 'chisel'.

5. Lith. *iškalti* 'beat out, chisel out, carve', cpd. of *kalti* 'hammer, forge' (9.61).

Lett. *(iz)tēluot* 'represent' hence spec. 'represent by carving in wood, stone, etc.', deriv. of *tēls* 'form, statue' (9.83).

6. ChSl. *vajati* (late, but deriv. *vajanije* 'sculpture', Supr.), SCr. *vajati*, Russ. *vajat'*, etym.?

Boh. *vytesati*, Pol. *wyciosać*, lit. 'hew out', cpds. of Boh. *tesati*, Pol. *ciosać* 'hew' (9.45).

7. Sculpture was highly developed in the pre-Aryan civilization disclosed by the discoveries at Mohenjodaro and elsewhere in northwest India. But in Aryan India there is no evidence of sculpture before the Buddhistic statues of about 300 B.C. There is likewise no reference to sculpture in the Avesta. Hence the lack of quotable words in this group, except the Skt. (late) and OPers. words quoted under 'statue' (9.83).

9.82 SCULPTOR

Grk.	ἀγαλματοποιός	Goth.	....	Lith.	*skulptorius*
NG	γλύπτης	ON	....	Lett.	*tēlnieks*
Lat.	*scalptor (sculptor)*	Dan.	*billedhugger*	ChSl.	....
It.	*scultore*	Sw.	*bildhuggare*	SCr.	*kipar, vajar*
Fr.	*sculpteur*	OE	*(grafere)*	Boh.	*sochař, řezbář*
Sp.	*escultor*	ME	*(graver), kerver*	Pol.	*rzeżbiarz*
Rum.	*sculptor*	NE	*sculptor*	Russ.	*vajatel', skul'ptor*
Ir.	....	Du.	*beeldhouwer*	Skt.	....
NIr.	*snoigheadōir*	OHG	*(grabari)*	Av.	....
W.	*cerflunydd*	MHG	*(grabære)*		
Br.	*kizeller, bener*	NHG	*bildhauer*		

Words for 'sculptor' are derived from those for 'carve' (9.81) or 'statue' (9.83).

1. Grk. ἀγαλματοποιός, also ἀνδριαντοποιός, cpds. of words for 'statue' (9.83) and -ποιός : ποιέω 'do, make'.

Late Grk., NG γλύπτης : γλύφω 'carve'.

2. Lat. *scalptor*, later *sculptor* (> Romance words) : *scalpere*, *sculpere* 'carve'.

3. NIr. *snoigheadōir* : *snoighim* 'cut, carve'.

W. *cerflunydd*, deriv. of *cerflun* 'piece of sculpture, statue' (9.83).

Br. *kizellèr*, *bener*, derivs. of *kizella*, *bena* 'carve'.

4. Dan. *billedhugger*, Sw. *bildhuggare*, Du. *beeldhouwer*, NHG *bildhauer*, cpds. of Dan. *billede*, etc. 'picture, image' and Dan. *hugger*, etc., agent nouns of *hugge*, NHG *hauen*, etc. 'cut, hew' (9.22).

OE *grafere*, *græfere*, ME *graver*, OHG *grabari*, MHG *grabære*, prop. 'engraver' : ON *grafa*, OE *grafan*, etc. 'dig, engrave'.

ME *kerver* 'carver, sculptor' : ME *kerve*, *carve*, OE *cēorfan* 'cut, carve'.

NE *sculptor*, fr. Lat. *sculptor*.

5. Lith. *skulptorius*, fr. Lat. *sculptor*. Lett. *tēlnieks*, deriv. of *tēluot* 'carve'.

6. SCr. *kipar*, deriv. of *kip* 'statue'.

SCr. *vajar*, Russ. *vajatel'*, derivs. of SCr. *vajati*, Russ. *vajat'* 'carve'.

Boh. *sochař*, deriv. of *socha* 'statue' (9.83).

Boh. *řezbář*, Pol. *rzeżbiarz* : Boh. *řezati*, Pol. *rznąć* 'cut, carve' (9.22).

Russ. *skul'ptor*, fr. Lat. *sculptor*.

9.83 STATUE

Grk.	ἄγαλμα, ἀνδριάς	Goth.	*(manleika)*	Lith.	*statula (stovyla)*
NG	ἄγαλμα, ἀνδριάς	ON	*mannlīkan, līkneski*	Lett.	*statuja, t ls*
Lat.	*statua (signum)*	Dan.	*statue, billedstøtte*	ChSl.	*tělo*
It.	*statua*	Sw.	*staty, bildstod*	SCr.	*kip*
Fr.	*statue*	OE	*manlīca*	Boh.	*socha*
Sp.	*estatua*	ME	*licness, statue*	Pol.	*statua, posąg*
Rum.	*statue*	NE	*statue*	Russ.	*statuja, izvajanie*
Ir.	*(delb)*	Du.	*standbeeld*	Skt.	*pratimā-, dāivata-*
NIr.	*dealbh, iomāigh*	OHG	*manalīho, sūl*	OPers.	*patikara-*
W.	*delw, cerflun*	MHG	*sūl, sūel*		
Br.	*delouenn, skeudenn*	NHG	*statue, bildsäule*		

Generic words for 'sculpture', either as the art or the product, are regularly parallel to those for 'sculptor' and need no further comment. Instead of these, 'statue' is chosen as the most characteristic product.

Words for 'statue' are only rarely connected with those for 'carve'. Most of them come by specialization from 'ornament', 'what is set up', 'pillar, column', 'form, figure, likeness', etc. Several of those listed cover 'statue' but have a wider range, 'image'.

1. Grk. ἄγαλμα, -ατος, orig. an 'ornament', as in Hom., and sometimes used in inscriptions for any votive offering (e.g. a modest pottery slab, a bronze vase, etc.), but esp. for a divine 'statue', which became its established use : ἀγάλλω 'adorn' and 'glorify', ἀγλαός, 'bright, splendid', etc. Walde-P. 1.623. Boisacq 5.

Grk. ἀνδριάς, -άντος, orig. 'image of a man' and reg. applied to statues of men or women, only rarely to those of the gods (as on the base of an archaic statue of Apollo at Delos), deriv. of ἀνήρ, ἀνδρός 'man'.

2. Lat. *statua*, usually of men : *statuere* 'cause to stand, set up', fr. *stāre* 'stand' (cf. pple. *status*, and *status*, *-ūs* 'a standing, position, attitude'); *statua* appears as a general European loanword in It. *statua*, Fr. *statue*, Sp. *estatua*, Rum. *statue*, Dan. *statue*, Sw. *staty*, ME, NE *statue*, NHG *statue*, Lett. *statuja*, Pol. *statua*, Russ. *statuja*.

Lat. *signum* 'mark, sign' (12.94), hence also 'military standard' and 'image, statue' (usually of a god). Ernout-M. 939.

3. Ir. *delb* 'form, image', NIr. *dealbh*, W. *delw* 'form, image, statue' (also W. *cerfddelw* 'carved image', cf. *cerfio* 'carve', 9.81), Br. *delouenn* (so Vallée for 'statue', not in Ernault) : Ir. *dolbaim* 'form, mold' (9.72), Lat. *dolāre* 'hew', etc. (9.45). Walde-P. 1.810. Pedersen 1.64.

NIr. *iomāigh* 'image, statue', fr. Lat. *imāgō* 'image, representation'. Vendryes, De hib. voc. 146 f.

W. *cerflun* 'piece of sculpture, carving, statue', cpd. of *cerf* 'carving, sculpture' (: *cerfio* 'carve', 9.81) and *llun* 'form, picture' (9.87).

Br. *skeudenn* 'image, statue' (Ernault), deriv. of *skeud* 'shadow' (1.63).

4. Goth. *man(n)leika* 'image' (in the only occurrence renders εἰκών, the image on a coin), ON *mannlīkan* 'human image, idol', OE *man(n)līca* 'human image, statue', OHG *manalīho*, etc. (Graff 2.118), cpds. of words for 'man' and those for 'like', Goth. *(ga)leiks*, etc., whence also ON *līkneski*, ME *licness* 'likeness, image, statue'.

Dan. *billedstøtte*, Sw. *bildstod*, cpds. of Dan. *billede* 'image, picture', Sw. *bild* 'picture, representation, statue' (9.87) and Dan. *støtte*, Sw. *stod* 'pillar'.

Du. *standbeeld*, cpd. of *stand* : *staan* 'stand' and *beeld* 'image, picture'.

OHG *sūl*, MHG *sūl*, *süel* 'post, pillar' hence also 'statue', NHG *bildsäule* 'statue' (cf. *bild* 'image, picture', 9.87) : ON *sūl*, *sūla*, OE *sȳl*, Goth. *sauls* 'pillar, column'. Falk-Torp 1233. Walde-P. 2.503.

5. Lith. *statula* (now preferred to *stovyla*, fr. Wh. Russ., formerly in common use), fr. weak grade of IE **stā-* 'stand', as in *statymas* 'building', etc. Cf. OE *staþol* 'foundation, support'. Buga, Kalba ir Senovė 172 f.

Lett. *tēls* 'form, image, statue', prob. fr. ORuss. *tělo* 'image, idol, statue' (below, 6). Mühl.-Endz. 4.171.

6. ChSl. *tělo* 'body, form' (9.11), hence later 'image, statue' as also ORuss. *tělo*, etc.

SCr. *kip* 'form, image, statue', fr. Hung. *kép* 'appearance, form, picture, image'. Berneker 504.

Boh. *socha* 'handle, pole, pillar' hence also 'statue' : ChSl. (late) *socha* 'club, cudgel', Russ. *socha* 'wooden plow', etc. (8.55). Walde-P. 1.335.

Pol. *posąg* 'statue', orig. 'wooden pillar', fr. *sąg* 'cord of wood', this as orig. a measure (cf. *sążeń*, ChSl. *sęžĭnĭ* 'fathom', i.e. 'the distance to which the arms can be stretched') : ChSl. *sęgnąti* 'stretch out (the arm)', Pol. *sięgać* 'reach, stretch'. Brückner 483.

Russ. *izvajanie* 'piece of sculpture, statue' : *(iz)vajat'* 'carve' (9.81).

7. Skt. *pratimā-* 'image, picture, statue' : *prati-mā-* 'imitate, copy', cpd. of *prati* 'over against' and *mā-* 'measure' (12.54) 'mete out, fashion, build', etc.

Skt. *dāivata-* 'statue of a god, idol' (so freq. in Manu, etc.), deriv. of *deva-* 'god'.

OPers. *patikara-* used of the figures sculptured in relief (NPers. *paikar* 'face, form, portrait'), cpd. of *pati-* 'over against' and *kar-* 'make', hence lit. 'something made in likeness'.

9.84 CHISEL (sb.)

Grk.	σμῖλη	Goth.	....	Lith.	*kaltas*
NG	σμίλη, σμιλάρι	ON	*meitill*	Lett.	*kalts*
Lat.	*scalprum*	Dan.	*mejsel, bejtel*	ChSl.	*dlato*
It.	*scalpello, cesello*	Sw.	*mejsel*	SCr.	*dlijeto*
Fr.	*ciseau*	OE	*græfsex*	Boh.	*dláto*
Sp.	*escoplo*	ME	*chisell*	Pol.	*dłóto*
Rum.	*daltă*	NE	*chisel*	Russ.	*doloto*
Ir.	....	Du.	*beitel*	Skt.	....
NIr.	*siséal*	OHG	*meizil*	Av.	....
W.	*cyn, gaing*	MHG	*maizel*		
Br.	*kizell*	NHG	*meissel*		

Words for 'chisel' (sculptor's or carpenter's) are from verbs for 'cut, hew, carve', 'split', or 'hollow out'. The Welsh words denoted originally 'wedge', whence 'chisel' from the similar shape.

1. Grk. σμῖλη, NG also σμιλάρι : OE *smiþ* 'smith', etc. and prob. Goth. *maitan* 'cut, hew', OHG *meizil* 'chisel', etc. Walde-P. 2.686.

2. Lat. *scalprum* (> Fr. *échoppe*, Sp. *escoplo;* dim. *scalpellum* > It. *scalpello*), fr. *scalpere* 'carve' (9.81). Ernout-M. 901. REW 7642, 7645.

It. *cesello*, OFr. *cisel* (> Br. *kizell*), *chisel* (> ME *chisell*, NE *chisel* > NIr. *siséal*), Fr. *ciseau*, fr. late Lat. **caesellum*, *cīsellum*, deriv. through **cīsum* (cf. *cīsōrium* 'cutting tool') of *caedere* 'cut'. REW 1474. Wartburg 2.40. NED s.v. *chisel* sb.[1].

Rum. *daltă*, fr. Slavic (below, 6).

3. W. *cyn*, also and orig. 'wedge', fr. Lat. *cuneus* 'wedge'. Loth, Mots lat. 157. Morris Jones 91.

W. *gaing*, also and orig. 'wedge' = Ir. *geind*, OBr. *gen* 'wedge' : ON *gandr* 'magic staff', root connection dub. Walde-P. 1.680. Stokes 110. Falk-Torp 299.

4. ON *meitill*, OHG *meizil*, MHG *maizel*, NHG *meissel* (> Dan., Sw. *mejsel*), fr. the root of Goth. *maitan*, OHG *meizan*, etc. 'cut' (9.22). Walde-P. 2.222. Weigand-H. 2.162.

OE *græfsex*, fr. *grafan* 'carve' (9.81) and *seax*, *sex* 'knife' (9.23).

ME *chisell*, NE *chisel*, above, 2.

Du. *beitel* (MLG > Dan. *bejtel*), fr. the root of *bijten*, Goth. *beitan*, etc. 'bite', orig. 'split', Lat. *findere*, Skt. *bhid-* 'split' (9.27). Franck-v. W. 44.

5. Lith. *kaltas*, Lett. *kalts*, fr. vbs. Lith. *kalti*, Lett. *kalt* 'hammer, forge' (9.61), also to 'chisel' (NSB s.v.).

6. ChSl. (late) *dlato*, Boh. *dláto*, Pol. *dłóto*, Russ. *doloto*, fr. **dolb-to-*, beside SCr. *dlijeto* with *e*-grade, fr. the root of Russ. *dolbat'*, *dolbit'* 'hollow out', OE *delfan* 'dig', etc., IE **delbh-*. Walde-P. 1.866 f. Berneker 183, 208, 250 f.

9.85 PAINT

(vb., As Artist)

Grk.	ζωγραφέω	Goth.	....	Lith.	*tapyti, piešti*
NG	ζωγραφίζω	ON	*fā, skrifa*	Lett.	*gleznuot*
Lat.	*pingere, depingere*	Dan.	*male*	ChSl.	....
It.	*dipingere*	Sw.	*måla*	SCr.	*slikati*
Fr.	*peindre*	OE	*mētan, ātīefran*	Boh.	*malovati*
Sp.	*pintar*	ME	*peynte*	Pol.	*malować*
Rum.	*picta*	NE	*paint*	Russ.	*pisat'*
Ir.	....	Du.	*schilderen*	Skt.	*likh-*
NIr.	*pīnteālaim*	OHG	*mālōn, mālēn*	Av.	....
W.	*paentio*	MHG	*malen*		
Br.	*liva, penta*	NHG	*malen*		

The verbs for 'paint' as an artist are in most cases (unlike those for 'paint' a house, etc., 9.89) not based on a notion of color, but are rather from notions like 'scratch, draw, adorn', 'mark, represent', and were used at first for any form of graphic delineation, then especially for 'paint' since the use of color was usual.

1. Grk. γράφω (: OE *ceorfan* 'cut, carve', 9.22) 'scratch, mark', hence usual 'write', but also 'draw, depict' (cf. γραφεύς sometimes for 'painter'), hence ζῷα γράφω 'depict live creatures', ζωγράφος 'painter', and fr. the latter, the usual verbs ζωγραφέω, NG ζωγραφίζω.

2. Lat. *pingere* 'adorn, embroider' and esp. 'paint' (> Fr. *peindre*, It. *pingere*, but mostly *dipingere*, fr. Lat. *dēpingere;* VLat. **pinctāre* > Sp. *pintar;* Rum. *picta* back-formation to *pictor* 'painter', this a literary loanword fr. Lat.) : Skt. *piñj-* 'paint' (gram.), *piñga-*, *piñjara-* 'reddish brown, tawny', ChSl. *pěgŭ* 'speckled, dappled', fr. IE **peig-* beside **peiḱ-* in Grk. ποικίλος 'speckled, dappled, many-colored', Skt. *piç-* 'carve, fashion, adorn', ChSl. *pĭsati* 'write', OPers. *piš-* 'write', Lith. *piešti* 'sketch, draw' (cf. below, 5), Goth. *filu-faihs* 'manifold' (πολυποίκιλος), OE *fāh*, *fāg*, OHG *fēh* 'colored', etc. whence again the verbs OE *fāgian* 'grow dark, vary', OHG *fēhen* 'color' and with these ON *fā* 'draw, paint'; here also Toch. *pik-*

'write, paint' (SSS 451). Walde-P. 2.9 ff. Ernout-M. 769.

3. NIr. *pīnteālaim*, with *pīnteāil* 'painting', *pīntēar* 'painter', *pēint* 'paint', all (with various spellings) based on NE *paint*.

W. *paentio*, also *peintio*, fr. ME *peynte*, NE *paint* (below, 4).

Br. *penta*, fr. Fr. *peint*, 3sg. and pple. of *peindre* (above, 2).

Br. *liva* 'dye, paint' ('paint' in artistic sense secondary), deriv. of *liv* 'color, dye, paint' (9.88).

4. ON *fā*, see above, 2.

ON *skrifa* 'write, paint', fr. Lat. *scrībere* 'write'. Walde-P. 2.586. Falk-Torp 1028.

OE *mētan*, deriv. of an OE **mōt* : EFris. *mōt* 'mark, spot', ON *mōt* 'mark, stamp'.

OE *ā-tīefran* (cf. *tīfrung* 'painting'), fr. *tēafor* 'red color' (NE dial. *tiver*, NED) : ON *taufr*, OHG *zoubūr* 'magic'. Holthausen 343, 347.

ME *peynte*, NE *paint*, fr. Fr. *peint*, 3sg. and pple. of *peindre* (above, 2).

OHG *mālōn*, *mālēn* 'trace, draw, paint', MHG, MLG *mālen* (> Dan. *male*, Sw. *måla*), NHG *malen* : Goth. *mēljan* 'write', OE *mǣlan* 'spot, soil', derivs. of Goth. *mēl*, OE *mǣl*, OHG *māl* 'spot, mark, sign', these prob. fr. the root seen in Skt. *malina-* 'dirty, dark', Grk. μέλας, Lett. *melns* 'black', etc. But the immediate development in German is fr. 'make a mark' to 'draw', hence also 'paint', and has no direct connection with a color notion. Walde-P. 2.293. Falk-Torp 691.

Du. *schilderen* (cf. NHG *schildern* 'portray, describe', formerly also 'paint'; *schilderei* formerly 'a painting'), deriv. of obs. *schilder* 'painter', orig. 'shield-maker, shield-painter', as MLG *schilder*, MHG *schiltære*, derivs. of the words for 'shield', OHG *scilt*, etc. Falk-Torp 994. Franck-v. W. 587. Paul, Deutsches Wtb. s.v. *schildern*.

5. Lith. *tapyti* (now best word, Senn; formerly in different sense) : Lith. *tepti*, Lett. *tept* 'smear', ChSl. *tepą*, *teti* 'strike, beat' (Trautmann 319).

Lith. *piešti*, lit. 'draw, sketch', but *piešti paveikslą* 'paint' (Lalis, cf. also Hermann, Lit.-deutsches Gesprächsb. 131), see under Lat. *pingere*, above 2.

Lett. *gleznuot* : Lith. *gleznoti* (dial. 'paint'), derivs. of Lett. *glezns*, Lith. *gležnus* 'weak, tender, delicate', with development through 'do delicate work, adorn'. Mühl.-Endz. 1.626.

6. SCr. *slikati*, deriv. of *slika* 'painting, picture' : *lik* 'form, appearance'. Berneker 719.

SCr. *malati* (dial.), Boh. *malovati*, Pol. *malować*, fr. MHG, NHG *malen* (above, 4). Berneker 2.11.

Russ. *pisat'* 'write, draw, paint' (hence *živopis'* 'painting', *živopisec* 'painter', cpds. with *živoj* 'alive'; cf. Grk. ζωγράφος, above, 1) : ChSl. *pĭsati* 'write', etc. (above, 2).

7. Skt. *likh-*, earlier *rikh-* 'scratch, write, draw, engrave, paint' (cf. *lēkha-*, *rēkha-* 'mark, stroke, line, figure') : Grk. ἐρείκω 'bruise, tear', W. *rhwygo* 'tear', Lith. *riekti* 'slice, cut, etc.'. Walde-P. 2.344.

9.86 PAINTER

(As Artist)

Grk.	ζωγράφος (γραφεύς)	Goth.	....	Lith.	*tapytojas*
NG	ζωγράφος	ON	*(skrifari)*	Lett.	*gleznuotojs*
Lat.	*pictor*	Dan.	*maler*	ChSl.	....
It.	*pittore*	Sw.	*målare*	SCr.	*slikar*
Fr.	*peintre*	OE	*mētere*	Boh.	*malíř*
Sp.	*pintor*	ME	*peyntour*	Pol.	*malarz*
Rum.	*pictor*	NE	*painter*	Russ.	*živopisec*
Ir.	....	Du.	*schilder*	Skt.	*citrakāra-*
NIr.	*pīntēar*	OHG	*mālari*	Av.	....
W.	*paentiwr*	MHG	*mālære*		
Br.	*livour, penter*	NHG	*maler*		

The words for 'painter' as an artist are obvious derivatives of the verbs for 'paint' (9.85), or conversely in the case of Du. *schilder*. For Russ. *živopisec*, see *živopis'* 'painting' (9.87). The only exception among the words listed here is:

Skt. *citrakāra-*, cpd. of *citra-* in the sense of 'picture' (9.87) and deriv. of *kṛ-* 'make'.

But the 'painter' in this sense may also, especially where the word is ambiguous (as NE *painter*, etc.), be expressed by the more generic 'artist' (cf. 9.412), as NE *artist*, NHG *künstler*, Lith. *dailininkas*, etc.

9.87 PAINTING, PICTURE

Grk.	γραφή, ζωγράφημα, πίναξ, εἰκών	Goth.	....	Lith.	*paveikslas*
NG	ζωγραφιά, πίνακας (εἰκονα)	ON	*(skrifan, pentan)*	Lett.	*gleznojums*
Lat.	*pictūra, tabula*	Dan.	*maleri, billede*	ChSl.	*obrazŭ*
It.	*pittura, quadro*	Sw.	*målning, tavla, bild*	SCr.	*slika*
Fr.	*peinture, tableau*	OE	*mēting, tīfrung*	Boh.	*malba; obraz*
Sp.	*pintura, cuadro*	ME	*peyntyng, peynture, pycture*	Pol.	*malowidło; obraz*
Rum.	*pictură, tablou*	NE	*painting, picture*	Russ.	*živopis', kartina*
Ir.	....	Du.	*schilderij, beeld*	Skt.	*citra-, citrakarman-*
NIr.	*pīnteāil, pictiūir*	OHG	*gimālidi, gimāli (biladi)*	Av.	....
W.	*llun, pictiwr*	MHG	*gemælde, gemæle, bilde*		
Br.	*taolenn, livadur*	NHG	*gemälde, bild*		

Nearly all the words for 'a painting', involving the use of color, and some of those for the more comprehensive 'picture' (e.g. NE *picture*, fr. Lat. *pictūra* 'painting' vs. *painting* fr. vb. *paint*), are derived from (or in the case of SCr. *slika*, are the source of) the verbs for 'paint', and so have been covered by the discussion in 9.85. Other words for 'picture', which cover and often are the more common expressions for 'a painting', are of various sources.

1. Grk. γραφή sometimes 'picture', ζωγράφημα rare; ζωγραφία 'art of painting', NG ζωγραφιά 'picture'.

Grk. πίναξ 'board, tablet', rarely 'picture' (like Lat. *tabula*), hence late πινακοθήκη 'picture-gallery'.

Grk. εἰκών 'a likeness' (: ἔοικα 'be like'), used of a picture or a statue, NG εἰκόνα 'holy picture' (whence Russ. *ikon* id.).

2. Lat. *tabula picta* 'painted tablet', hence also *tabula* alone for 'painting, pic-

ture', whence in this sense also Sw. *tavla*, Br. *taolenn*, and, through dim. form, Fr. *tableau* (> Rum. *tablou*).

It. *quadro*, Sp. *cuadro*, fr. Lat. *quadrum* 'a square'.

3. W. *llun* 'form, shape, figure, picture', as 'picture' also cpds. *arlun*, *darlun*, etym.?

4. OHG *bilade*, *bilidi*, MHG *bilde* (MLG > Dan. *billede*, Sw. *bild*), NHG *bild* (also *bildniss*), Du. *beeld*, a general word for 'likeness, image' (as mostly in OHG), whence 'picture', or in part 'statue' (9.83), prob. : OHG *billīch*, NHG *billig* 'fitting, seemly', OE *bilewit* 'simple, honest', Ir. *bil* 'good', perh. Grk. φίλος 'dear'. Walde-P. 2.185. Falk-Torp 73 f. Weigand-H. 1.238. Kluge-G. 57.

5. Lith. *paveikslas*, general 'picture, image, example' : *į-vykti* 'happen', perh. Grk. εἰκών 'picture', etc. (above, 1). Walde-P. 1.233. For current use cf. *aliejiniais dažais piešlas paveikslas* (lit. 'picture drawn with oil paints' = *ölgemälde*), Hermann, Lit.-deutsches Gesprächsb. 131).

6. ChSl. *obrazŭ* 'form, kind, image' (reg. word for εἰκών; Jagić, Entstehungsgesch. 309), Boh., Pol. *obraz* (Pol. > Lith. *abrozas* 'holy picture, ikon'), orig. 'an outline', fr. **ob-raziti* 'cut around' beside *u-raziti* 'strike', *rězati* 'cut' (9.22). Brückner 371 f.

Russ. *živopis'*, cpd. of *živoj* 'alive' and the root of *pisat'* 'paint'. Cf. Grk. ζωγραφέω, ζωγράφος, etc. (9.85).

Russ. *kartina*, deriv. of *karta* 'card, map', this fr. Lat. *charta* 'paper'. Berneker 491.

7. Skt. *citra-* 'bright, clear' (: OHG *heitar* id., Walde-P. 2.537), neut. sb. 'ornament' and 'picture', likewise *citrakarman-*, cpd. with *karman-* 'work'.

9.88 PAINT (sb.)

Grk.	χρῶμα	Goth.	. . . .	Lith.	*dažai*
NG	μπογιά, χρῶμα	ON	*steinn*	Lett.	*krāsa*
Lat.	*pigmentum, color*	Dan.	*maling (farve)*	ChSl.	. . . .
It.	*colore*	Sw.	*färg*	SCr.	*boja*
Fr.	*couleur*	OE	. . . .	Boh.	*barva*
Sp.	*pintura, color*	ME	*peynture*	Pol.	*farba, barwa*
Rum.	*văpsea*	NE	*paint*	Russ.	*kraska*
Ir.	. . . .	Du.	*verf*	Skt.	*varṇa-*
NIr.	*pēint*	OHG	*farawa*	Av.	. . . .
W.	*paent (lliw)*	MHG	*varwe*		
Br.	*liv*	NHG	*farbe*		

The majority of the words for 'paint' (sb.) are the same as those for 'color', discussed in 15.61, and cover any coloring matter, 'paint' or 'dye'. Most of the others are obvious derivs. of the verbs for 'paint' discussed in 9.85 or 9.89. Only the following need further comment:

1. NG pop. μπογιά 'dye, paint', fr. Turk. *boya* id., whence also SCr. *boja* 'paint' and secondarily 'color', and Rum. *boia* 'dye'. Miklosich, Turk. Elem. 1.265 f. Lokotsch 328.

2. ON *steinn* 'dye, paint, stain', prob. same word as *steinn* 'stone', and orig. some special kind of mineral dye.

3. Lith. *dažai* (pl.), with vb. *dažyti*, etym. dub. Walde-P. 1.786.

4. Russ. *kraska*, deriv. of *krasa* 'beauty, adornment', whence also *krasit'* 'dye, paint', and Lett. *krāsa* also 'color', see 15.61.

9.89 PAINT

(vb. 'Paint a House', etc.)

Grk.	χρωματίζω	Goth.	. . . .	Lith.	*dažyti*
NG	χρωματίζω, μπογιατίζω	ON	*steina (penta)*	Lett.	*nuokrāsuot*
Lat.	*fūcāre (pingere)*	Dan.	*male*	ChSl.	. . . .
It.	*colorire*	Sw.	*måla*	SCr.	*obojiti (bojadisati)*
Fr.	*peindre*	OE	. . . .	Boh.	*barviti, natirati*
Sp.	*pintar*	ME	*peynte*	Pol.	*malować*
Rum.	*văpsi, zugrăvi*	NE	*paint*	Russ.	*krasit'*
Ir.	. . . .	Du.	*verven (schilderen)*	Skt.	*varṇaya-*
NIr.	*pīnteālaim*	OHG	*(farawen)*	Av.	. . . .
W.	*paentio, lliwio*	MHG	*(verwen)*		
Br.	*liva*	NHG	*anstreichen*		

In several languages the verbs for 'paint' in the artistic sense (9.85) have come to be used also with reference to painting a house, board, etc., as NE *paint*, Fr. *peindre*, etc. But most of those used in this latter sense are derived from the nouns for 'paint' orig. 'color', and may also cover 'dye'. Apart from these two classes, of obvious connection with the words discussed in 9.85 or 9.88, are the following:

1. Lat. *fūcāre* 'paint, dye, rouge', deriv. of *fūcus* 'rouge', fr. Grk. φῦκος id., orig. the kind of seaweed from which the dye was obtained. Ernout-M. 396. Walde-H. 1.555.

2. Rum. *văpsi* 'dye, paint', fr. Grk. ἔβαψα, aor. of βάπτω 'dip, dye'. Tiktin 1713.

3. Rum. *zugrăvi* (earlier *zografisi*), fr. NG ζωγραφίζω 'paint' in artistic sense (9.85). Tiktin 1830.

4. NHG *anstreichen*, cpd. of *streichen* 'stroke, touch', also used alone for 'paint'.

5. Boh. *natirati*, lit. 'rub on', hence also 'paint', cpd. of *třiti* 'rub' (9.31).

9.90 THING

Grk.	πρᾶγμα, χρῆμα	Goth.	*waihts*	Lith.	*daiktas*
NG	πρᾶγμα (pop. πρᾶμα)	ON	*hlutr*	Lett.	*lieta*
Lat.	*rēs*	Dan.	*ting, sag*	ChSl.	*veštĭ*
It.	*cosa*	Sw.	*sak, ting*	SCr.	*stvar*
Fr.	*chose*	OE	*þing*	Boh.	*věc*
Sp.	*cosa*	ME	*thing*	Pol.	*rzecz*
Rum.	*lucru*	NE	*thing*	Russ.	*vešč', delo*
Ir.	*nī, rēt*	Du.	*ding, zaak*	Skt.	*vastu-*
NIr.	*nī, rud*	OHG	*dinc, sacha*	Av.	. . . .
W.	*peth*	MHG	*dinc, sache*		
Br.	*tra*	NHG	*sache, ding*		

There can hardly be a more vague general notion than that of 'thing', covering any act, event, or material object. It is based on a variety of specific notions, and most commonly the generalization to an act, event, or affair is earlier than that to a material object. A few of the words listed are still not used for 'thing' as a material object.

In several cases, partly due to semantic borrowing, the development has been through 'subject of litigation'. Other sources are 'act, deed, work, share, thing needed, property', etc. The use of the neuter of the indefinite pronoun for 'anything, something' and, with negative, 'nothing' (Grk. τι, οὔτι, Lat. *quid*, *aliquid*, *nē quid*, etc.), has led

to an independent word for 'thing' in Irish.

1. Grk. πρᾶγμα (notion of 'act, affair', etc., dominant) : πράσσω, Att. πράττω 'do' (19.11). NG πρᾶγμα, pop. πρᾶμα also of material objects and as generic as NE *thing*.

Grk. χρῆμα (in pl. also 'goods, property') orig. 'what is needed' : χρεία 'need', χρή 'needs, ought, must', etc. (see 9.93). Cf. Osc. *egmo* 'thing' : Lat. *egēre* 'have need', prob. semantic borrowing fr. Grk. χρῆμα. Kretschmer, Glotta 10.157 f.

2. Lat. *rēs* ('property' and 'affair, thing'), Umbr. *re-per* 'pro re' : Skt. *rās*, gen. sg. *rāyas*, Av. gen. sg. *rāyō* 'riches', Skt. *rā-* 'give, grant'. Walde-P. 2.343. Ernout-M. 822 f. Lat. acc. sg. *rem* > Fr. *rien* 'thing', mostly 'nothing' fr. neg. phrases, like NG τίποτε 'something', 'nothing'. Otherwise replaced by the following:

It., Sp. *cosa*, Fr. *chose*, fr. Lat. *causa* 'cause' and esp. 'lawsuit', whence 'affair, thing'. Root connection unknown. Ernout-M. 166 f. Walde-H. 1.190.

Rum. *lucru* 'work, act' and 'thing', fr. Lat. *lucrum* 'gain'. Sense of 'work' through vb. *lucra* (Lat. *lucrārī*) 'gain' (by work) > 'work', but generic 'thing' by Slavic influence. Cf. Bulg. *dělo* and *rabota* both 'work' and 'thing'. Tiktin 927 f. REW 5146.

3. Ir. *nī*, NIr. *nī*, pl. *neithe*, orig. neut. of pronominal *nech* 'someone' (**ne-kʷo-*, with change fr. negative to positive, as in Lith. *ne-kas* 'something'. Pedersen 1.212. Thurneysen, Gram. 309, 311.

Ir. *rēt* (cf. also *crę̄t* 'what?' for *ce rēt*), NIr. *rud*, perh. : Skt. *ratna-* 'riches'. Walde-P. 2.374. Stokes 232. Thurneysen, Gram. 127.

W. *peth* : Br. *pez* 'piece, bit', Ir. *cuit* 'share, part', etc. (13.23). Pedersen 1.160.

Br., Corn. *tra* (W. *tra* as 'thing' obs.), etym. dub., connected with Br., Corn., W. *tro* 'turn, course, occasion, occurrence'? Henry 269.

4. Goth. *waihts* : ON *vættr* 'creature', esp. supernatural, *ekki vætta* 'nothing', OE *wiht* 'creature' (NE *wight*), *ǣnig wiht* 'anything' (NE *aught*), *ne wiht*, *nā wiht* 'nothing' (NE *naught* and *not*), OHG *wiht* 'creature' (cf. NHG *bösewicht*), *ni wiht* 'nothing' (NHG *nicht*)—further ChSl. *veštĭ*, Boh. *věc*, etc. 'thing', but root connections unknown. Walde-P. 1.246. Falk-Torp 1372. Feist 543.

ON *hlutr* 'lot, share' and 'thing' : OE *hlot* (NE *lot*), etc. Walde-P. 1.493. Falk-Torp 650 f.

OE *þing* 'judicial assembly, court', 'matter before the court', then any 'matter, affair, thing', with generic sense as ME, NE *thing* = ON *þing* 'public assembly', Dan., Sw. *ting* 'judicial court' and 'thing', OHG *dinc* (*ding*, *thing*) 'assembly, council', and 'thing' as MHG *dinc*, NHG *ding*—all : Goth. *þeihs* 'time' (14.11). Semantic development 'appointed time' > judicial assembly > subject of debate > 'affair, thing'. Walde-P. 1.725. Falk-Torp 1263. NED s.v. *thing*.

MHG, NHG *sache*, fr. OHG *sacha* 'cause', sometimes 'affair, thing' : OE *sacu* 'strife, dispute, lawsuit' (NE *sake*), Goth. *sakjō* 'strife', etc. (19.62). Similarly Du. *zaak*, Dan. *sag*, Sw. *sak*, with sense 'thing' perh. due to NHG influence. Falk-Torp 942 f. Weigand-H. 2.633.

5. Lith. *daiktas* (also 'place') : *dygti* 'sprout' (fr. 'stick up'), *diegti*, Lett. *diegt* 'prick', Lat. *fīgere* 'pierce, fix', etc. Semantic development 'something sticking up, point', whence both 'definite place' (cf. NE *point* in this sense) and 'item, matter' (cf. NE *a point in his favor*, etc., NED s.v. *point* II 5), hence any 'matter, thing'. Walde-P. 1.832 f.

Lett. *lieta*, perh. : Lith. *lytis* 'form, shape'. Mühl.-Endz. 2.506.

6. ChSl. *veštĭ*, Boh. *věc*, Russ. *vešč'* : Goth. *waihts*, etc. (above, 4).

SCr. *stvar* : ChSl. (*sŭ*)*tvoriti* 'make, do' (9.11), *tvarĭ* 'creation, work, deed', etc. Miklosich 366. Brückner 586.

Pol. *rzecz*, also and in early period only 'speech' = ChSl. *rěčĭ* : *resti* 'say' (18.22). Hence 'subject matter' and further generalization. Brückner 475.

Russ. *delo* 'deed, work' and generic 'thing' as 'affair, matter', etc. (but not used of material objects) = ChSl. *dělo*, etc. 'work' (9.12). Berneker 194.

7. Skt. *vastu-*, fr. *vas-* 'remain, dwell' (7.11), hence orig. the 'abiding, existing' (thing).

9.91 BE

Grk.	εἰμί, ἐστί, etc.	Goth.	*wisan, ist, was*	Lith.	*būti, esu, yra*
NG	εἶμαι, εἶναι, etc.	ON	*vera, er, var*	Lett.	*būt, esmu, ir*
Lat.	*esse, est, fuī*, etc.	Dan.	*være, er, var*	ChSl.	*byti, jestŭ*
It.	*essere, é, fui, stato*	Sw.	*vara, är, var*	SCr.	*biti, jest*
Fr.	*être, est, fus, été*	OE	*wesan, bēon, bēo(m), is, wæs*	Boh.	*býti, je(st)*
Sp.	*ser, estar, es, fuí, sido, estado*	ME	*be(n), is, was*	Pol.	*być, jest*
Rum.	*fi, ĭeste, fuĭ*	NE	*be, is, was*	Russ.	*byt', est'*
Ir.	*-tāu, biuu, buith*	Du.	*zijn, ben, is, was*	Skt.	*as-, bhū-*
NIr.	*tāim, bīm, beith*	OHG	*wesan, bim, ist, was*	Av.	*ah-, bū-*
W.	*bod, ys, yw*	MHG	*wesen, bin, ist, was*		
Br.	*beza, bez*	NHG	*sein, bin, ist, war*		

Words for 'be', denoting existence and serving as the copula, are mostly derived from two IE roots, of which one (**es-*) was the most colorless, while the other (**bheu-*, **bhū-*) evidently had the primary sense of 'come into being, become'. Other roots, meaning 'remain, stay', 'stand', or 'sit', have furnished some of the forms. Nearly everywhere two or more of these roots supplement each other in the complete verb.

The forms given in the list are merely illustrative of the different roots. The details of distribution and the precise history of particular forms (e.g. Lat. 1sg. *sum*, Grk. 3pl. εἰσί, OE 3pl. *aron*) are too complicated for discussion here and irrelevant to our general purpose. For Celtic cf. Pedersen 2.418 ff., and for English and Germanic in general NED s.v. *be*.

1. IE **es-*, weak grade **s-*. Walde-P. 1.160 f. Ernout-M. 1001.

Grk. εἰμί, Aeol. ἔμμι (**esmi*), 3sg. ἐστί, NG εἶμαι (mid. starting fr. forms like imperf. ἤμην NT), 3sg., pl. εἶναι (fr. ἔνι = ἔνεστι; vowels after εἶμαι); Lat. *esse*, *sum*, *est*, etc., with Romance pres. forms; infin. *esse* > VLat. **essere* after *legere*, etc., hence It. *essere*, Fr. *être*, Sp. *ser*; Celt. 3sg. (as copula) Ir. *is*, W. *ys*, *yw*, Br. *es*, etc. (Pedersen 2.422 ff.); Gmc. 3sg. Goth., OHG–NHG *ist*, OE–NE *is*, ON, Dan. *er*, Sw. *är*; OLith. 1sg. *esmi* (now *esu*), Lett. *esmu*, OPruss. *asmai*, 3sg. OLith. *esti* (now *yra*, as Lett. *ir*), OPruss. *ast*; ChSl. 1sg. *jesmĭ*, 3sg. *jestŭ*, SCr *jest*, Boh. *je(st)*, Pol. *jest*, Russ. *est'*; Skt. *as-*, 1sg. *asmi*, 3sg. *asti*, Av. *ah-*, 1sg. *ahmi*, 3sg. *asti*; Hitt. *es-* (3sg. *eszi*, 3 pl. *asanzi*).

2. IE **bheu-*, **bhū-*, primarily 'come into being, become', this sense prevailing, on the whole, in Indo-Iranian, frequent also in early (and partly modern) Slavic, and wholly dominant in Grk., as

φύομαι, aor. ἔφῦν 'come into being', esp. 'grow' (φύω 'bring forth, beget'), φύσις 'nature', φυτόν 'plant', etc., and in a Lat. differentiated form (*fierī, fīō*). Walde-P. 2.140 f. Ernout-M. 1001. Walde-H. 1.557 f.

Lat. perf. *fuī*, etc. (early Lat. also infin. *fore*, imperf. subj. *forem*, Osc. *fusíd* 'esset'), It., Sp. *fui*, Fr. *fus*, Rum. *fuī*, Rum. infin. *fi*, etc.; Ir. *biuu*, NIr. *bīm* (consuetud. pres.), infin. Ir. *buith*, NIr. *beith*, W. *bod*, Br. *beza* (MBr. *bout*), Br. 3sg. *bez*, etc. (Pedersen 2.437 ff.); OE infin. *bēon*, ME *be(n)*, NE *be*, 1sg. OE *bēo(m)*, NE *be* (subj. and dial. indic.), OHG *bim*, MHG, NHG *bin*, Du. *ben;* Lith. *būti*, Lett. *būt*, pret. Lith. *buvau*, Lett. *biju;* ChSl. *byti*, SCr. *biti*, Boh. *býti*, Pol. *być*, Russ. *byt'*, pret. ChSl. *bychu*, pple. pret. ChSl. *bylŭ*, Russ. *byl*, etc.; Skt. *bhū-*, Av., OPers. *bū-* (3sg. Skt. *bhavati*, Av. *bavati*, OPers. 3sg. pret. *abava*, etc.) 'become' and simply 'be'. (NPers. *būdan* 'be').

3. IE **wes-*, primary notion 'remain, abide, dwell', as in Skt. *vas-*, Av. *vah-* (7.11). Walde-P. 1.306 f. Feist 567.

Infin. Goth. *wisan*, ON *vera*, Dan. *være*, Sw. *vara*, OE, OHG *wesan*, MHG *wesen;* pret. Goth., OHG, MHG *was* (NHG *war*), ON, Dan., Sw. *var*, OE *wæs*, ME, NE *was*, etc.

4. IE **stā-* 'stand'.

From Lat. *stāre*, pple. It. *stato*, Fr. *été*, Sp. *estado*, also Sp. *estar* with pres. forms, etc.; Ir. *-tāu-*, NIr. *tāim* fr. *atāim* (Pedersen 2.431. Thurneysen, Gram. 477 f.).

Cf. derivs. of the same root for the stronger 'exist', sometimes hardly more than 'be', as Lat. *ex-istere* (> Fr. *exister*, NE *exist*, etc.), NHG *bestehen* (also *entstehen* 'come into being, arise'), and for 'become' (9.92).

5. Forms of Lat. *sedēre* 'sit' are mixed with those of *esse* in the inflection of Sp. *ser*. Hanssen, Sp. Gram. p. 76.

6. Lith. 3sg., pl. *yra*, Lett. *ir* (old *ira*) is prob. an old noun meaning 'existence', but etym. unknown (OE 2sg. *eart*, pl. *aron*, NE *art*, *are*, prob. fr. **es-*, cf. NED). J. Schmidt KZ 25.595.

9.92 BECOME

Grk.	γίγνομαι, γίνομαι	Goth.	*wairþan*	Lith.	*tapti*
NG	γίνομαι	ON	*verða*	Lett.	*tapt*
Lat.	*fierī*	Dan.	*blive*	ChSl.	*byti*
It.	*divenire, diventāre, farsi*	Sw.	*bliva*	SCr.	*postati*
Fr.	*devenir*	OE	*weorþan, becuman*	Boh.	*státi se*
Sp.	*devenir, hacerse*	ME	*worthe, become*	Pol.	*(zo)stać się*
Rum.	*deveni, să face*	NE	*become*	Russ.	*stanovat'sja, stat', (s)delat'sja, byt'*
Ir.	. . . .	Du.	*worden*	Skt.	*bhū-*
NIr.	*tigim, ēirghim* (both impers.)	OHG	*werdan*	Av.	*bū-*
W.	*dyfod*	MHG	*werden*		
Br.	*dont (mont) da veza*	NHG	*werden*		

As already stated in 9.91, one of the two IE roots for 'be' denoted primarily 'come into being, become', this sense prevailing or frequent in some of the IE languages.

Other sources of 'become' are 'be born, come, turn (cf. also NE *turn pale*, etc.), remain, stand', and reflexive forms of 'make, do'. Apart from the words included in the list, 'become' with predicate complement, as 'become warm' may also be expressed by 'grow' (NE *grow warm*, but most commonly *get warm*), or by inchoative derivatives, e.g. Lat. *calēscere* 'become warm', Russ. *sogrevat'sja* 'become warm'.

1. Grk. γίγνομαι, later γίνομαι also and orig. 'be born' : γένος 'race', Lat. *gignere* 'beget, bear', pass. 'be born', Skt. *jan-* 'beget, bear', etc. (4.71).

2. Lat. *fierī* : *fuī* 'was', Skt. *bhū-* 'be, become', etc. (9.91).

It. *divenire, diventare*, Fr., Sp. *devenir*, Rum. *deveni* (fr. Fr.), fr. Lat. *dēvenīre* 'arrive'. REW 2612.

'Become' is also commonly expressed by the reflexive of 'make', It. *farsi*, Sp. *hacerse*, Rum. *să face*.

3. Ir. 'become' prob. expressed impersonally by phrases as in NIr.

NIr. *tigim* 'come' (10.48) used impersonally, e.g. *tāinig formad agam leo*, lit. 'envy came to me toward them' = 'I became envious of them'.

NIr. *ēirghim* 'rise, arise' (10.21), used impersonally in the same way, e.g. *d'ēirigh buile dhō*, lit. 'rage arose to him' = he became furious'.

W. *dyfod* 'come' (10.48), and more orig. (as cpd. of *bod* 'be') 'become'.

Br. *dont* (or *mont*) *da* (*veza*), i.e. *dont* 'come' (10.48) or *mont* 'go' (10.47) with softening *da* or *da veza* (= *beza* 'being, be', 9.91).

4. Goth. *wairþan*, ON *verða* (Dan. *vorde*, Sw. *varda* arch.), OE *weorþan*, ME *worthe*, OHG *werdan*, MHG, NHG *werden*, Du. *worden* : Lat. *vertere*, Skt. *vṛt-*, etc. 'turn' (10.12). Cf. NE *turn* (= *become*) *pale*, etc. Walde-P. 1.274 f. Falk-Torp 1393.

Dan. *blive*, Sw. *bliva*, fr. MLG *bliven* = Goth. *bileiban*, OHG *biliban*, NHG *bleiben* 'remain' (12.16). Falk-Torp 83. Hellquist 79.

OE *becuman* 'arrive, come', also (late) 'become', ME, NE *become*, cpd. of *cuman* 'come'.

5. Lith. *tapti*, Lett. *tapt*, perh. : OE *þafian* 'consent, permit', Grk. τόπος 'place'. Walde-P. 1.743. Mühl.-Endz. 4.132.

Other expressions for 'become', Lith. *darytis* (reflex. of *daryti* 'do, make'; cf. It. *farsi*, etc.), *pastoti* (like Slavic, cf. below), *pavirsti* (cpd. of *virsti* 'turn'); Lett. *iznākt* (lit. 'come out', cpd. of *nākt* 'come', 10.48).

6. ChSl. *byti* 'be' (9.91), also 'become'. So sometimes in modern Slavic, esp. SCr. *biti*, Russ. *byt'*.

SCr. *postati*, Boh. *státi se*, Pol. *(zo)stać się*, Russ. *stat'*, *stanovat'sja* : ChSl. *stati*, etc. 'stand'.

Russ. *(s)delat'sja*, refl. of *(s)delat'* 'do, make'.

7. Skt. *bhū-*, Av., OPers. *bū-* 'be' (9.91), but esp. 'become'.

9.93 NEED, NECESSITY

Grk.	χρεία, ἀνάγκη	Goth.	*þaurfts, nauþs*	Lith.	*reikalas*
NG	χρεία, ἀνάγκη	ON	*þǫrf, þurft, nauð(r)*	Lett.	*vajadzība*
Lat.	*opus, necessitās*	Dan.	*behov, nød, nødvendighet*	ChSl.	*potrěba, nąžda, nevolja*
It.	*bisogno, necessità*	Sw.	*behov, nöd, nödvändighet*	SCr.	*potreba, nužda, nevolja*
Fr.	*besoin, necessité*	OE	*þearf, nēad*	Boh.	*potřeba, nouze*
Sp.	*necesidad*	ME	*nede, necessite*	Pol.	*potrzeba, konieczność*
Rum.	*trebuinţă*	NE	*need, necessity*	Russ.	*potrebnost', nadobnost' nužda, neobchodimost'*
Ir.	*ēcen*	Du.	*behoefte, nood*	Skt.	*kartavya-, āvaçyaka-*
NIr.	*gābhadh, riachtanag, ēigin*	OHG	*durft, nōt*	Av.	. . . .
W.	*angen, rhaid*	MHG	*durft, nōt*		
Br.	*ezomm, red*	NHG	*bedürfnis, bedarf, not, notwendigkeit*		

Words for 'need' and 'necessity' are taken together, since there is much overlapping and no sharp demarcation. The same word, or words of the same cognate group, may cover both. Or the dominant sense may shift, as OE *nēad* mostly 'necessity' (also 'violence, compulsion') vs. *þearf* 'need', but NE *need* vs. *necessity*. However, whenever there are several words in the same language, they are listed in the order which corresponds most nearly to 'need' and 'necessity', that is, in the order of increasing urgency.

Some of the words for 'necessity' are often used in the sense of 'distress', as Grk. ἀνάγκη, OHG *nōt*, this sense being dominant in NHG *not* vs. the unambiguous deriv. *notwendigkeit*.

'Need' implies the 'lack' or 'want' of something, and words which have primarily this sense may sometimes express 'need', as NE *want* in *attend to his wants*, etc. (NED s.v. *want*, sb[2].5). Cf. Grk. δέω, primarily 'be lacking, be without', but also 'need' and esp. impers. δεῖ 'it is necessary, must'.

Many of the words listed are without any certain root connection which might determine the ultimate underlying sense. But in one large group (the one including NE *need*) 'violence' or 'distress' seems to be the primary notion. Other sources are 'work, unyieldingness, care, what is of use, what comes, purpose, what is against one's will, what one cannot get round'.

1. Grk. χρεία (beside impers. vb. χρή 'needs, must'), with χρέος 'debt', χρῆμα 'thing', pl. 'property', etc., extensive Grk. group, primary sense prob. 'lack, need' and so best : χερείων, χέρηες 'inferior', Skt. *hrasva-* 'short, small', Ir. *gair* 'short', etc. Walde-P. 1.604. Boisacq 1069 f. Otherwise Brugmann, IF 37.239 f.

Grk. ἀνάγκη : Ir. *ēcen*, NIr. *ēigin*, W. *angen* 'necessity, need' (Br. *anken* 'distress), root connection? Walde-P. 1.60. Benveniste, Origines 155.

2. Lat. *opus* 'work' (9.12), hence *opus est* 'there is work' = 'there is need'. Hence It. *uopo* and other dial. Romance forms, but not the usual word for 'need'. Ernout-M. 708. REW 6079.

Lat. *necessitās* (> It., Fr., Sp. forms), fr. *necesse* 'necessary' (in phrases with *esse* or *habēre*), neg. cpd. : *cēdere* (**cezd-*, Walde-H. 1.193), 'yield'. Hence orig. 'what is unyielding'. Ernout-M. 661.

Although Lat. *egēre* is the reg. vb. for 'need', the sense of 'be in need, be poor' (prevailing in Plaut. and Ter.) is dominant in its deriv. *egestās*.

It. *bisogno* (MLat. *bisonium*), Fr. *besoin*, prob. fr. a Gmc. cpd. (Goth. **bisunja* assumed fr. adv. *bisunjane* 'round about') of the word (like OS *sunnea* 'care') which is the source of Fr. *soin* 'care' (16.14). REW 8089a. Gamillscheg 804.

Rum. *trebuinţă*, fr. *trebui* 'be necessary', 3sg. *trebue* 'must', this fr. Slavic (cf. 9.94).

3. Ir. *ēcen*, NIr. *ēigin*, W. *angen* : Grk. ἀνάγκη (above, 1).

NIr. *gābhadh* (also and orig. 'danger'), fr. Ir. *gābud* 'danger' (16.54).

NIr. *riachtanag*, fr. *riachtain* 'attaining', vbl. n. of Ir. *riccim* 'reach, attain' (10.55). Development fr. a fatalistic 'what comes to one'.

W. *rhaid*, Br. *red*, prob. : Lat. *ratiō* 'reckoning, manner, cause', etc. Pedersen 1.69. Henry 231.

Br. *ezomm*, Corn. *ethom* : Ir. *adamna* 'terror' (not 'hunger', cf. Hessen s.v.), root connection dub. Walde-P. 1.12 (vs. Pedersen 1.169).

4. Goth. *þaurfts* (χρεία, ἀνάγκη), ON *þǫrf*, *þurft*, OE *þearf*, OHG, MHG *durft*, NHG *bedürfnis* (new formation fr. vb. *bedürfen*), with vbs. Goth. **þaurban*, ON *þurfa*, OE **þurfan*, OHG *durfan* (NHG *dürfen*. now mostly 'may'; as 'need' replaced by *bedürfen*), esp. pret.-pres. Goth., ON *þarf*, OE *þearf*, *þarf*, OHG–NHG *darf;* outside root connections dub. (: Skt. *tṛp-* 'be satisfied, pleased', Grk. τέρπω 'delight', Lith. *tarpti* 'thrive' ??), but prob. : ChSl. *trěbovati* 'need', sb. *potrěba*, etc. (below, 6), with variant final. Walde-P. 1.737. Falk-Torp 1248 f. Feist 491 f.

Goth. *nauþs* (ἀνάγκη), ON *nauð(r)*, Dan. *nød*, Sw. *nöd*, OE *nēad*, ME *nede*, NE *need*, Du. *nood*, OHG, MHG *nōt*, NHG *not;* meaning also 'violence, compulsion, distress' in early periods and so still e.g. NHG *not* vs. the deriv. *notwendigkeit* 'necessity' (through the adj. *notwendig;* hence Dan. *nødvendig*, *nødvendighet*, Sw. *nödvändig*, *nödvändighet*) : OPruss. *nautin* (acc. sg.) 'necessity, distress', Boh. *nyti* 'languish', *unaviti* 'tire' (trans.), etc. prob. also ChSl. *nąžda*, *nužda*, etc. (below, 6). Walde-P. 2.316. Falk-Torp 782 f. Weigand-H. 2.312. Feist 372.

Dan., Sw. *behov*, fr. MLG *behōf* = Du. *behoef*, OE *behōf*, NHG *behuf*, 'use, advantage'. Du. *behoefte* fr. *behoef*, with same development of 'need' fr. 'what is of use'. So OE *behōfian* 'have need of', later 'be proper' (NE *behoove*). All ultimately : Goth. *hafjan* 'raise', Lat. *capere* 'take', etc. Cf. NHG *brauchen* 'make use of' and now also 'need'. Falk-Torp 58, 455. Hellquist 61. NED s.v. *behoof*.

5. Lith. *reikalas*, fr. *reikia* 'is necessary, must', OLith. *reika* 'necessity', root connection? Meringer, IF 18.220.

Lett. *vajadzība*, fr. vb. *vajadzēt*, this fr. *vajaga* 'need, necessity' in *vajaga* (*ir*) 'is necessary', fr. Liv. *vajāg* 'need, needful, necessary'. Mühl.-Endz. 4.445.

6. ChSl. *potrěba* (χρεία, ἀνάγκη in Gospels), SCr. *potreba*, Boh. *potřeba*, Pol. *potrzeba*, Russ. *potrebnost'*, cpds. fr. root of vbs. ChSl. *trěbovati*, SCr. *trebati* 'need', prob. with variant final : Goth. *þaurfts* 'need', etc. (above, 4).

ChSl. *nąžda* (ἀνάγκη in Gospels), also *nužda* (Supr., etc.), SCr., Russ. *nužda*, Boh. *nouze* (Pol. *nędza* 'misery, distress', as the others in part, *nuda* 'weariness'), with difficult phonetic relations, but prob. : Goth. *nauþs*, etc. (above, 4). Brückner 358. Osthoff, Parerga 355.

ChSl. *nevolja* (ἀνάγκη, e.g. Mt. 18.7 vs. *nąžda* Lk. 14.18), SCr. id. (but mostly 'misery'; cf. Boh. *nevole* 'dislike, disgust', Russ. *nevolja* 'bondage'), lit. 'un-will', neg. cpd. of *volja* 'will'.

Pol. *konieczność*, through adj. *konieczny* 'needful' fr. *koniec* 'end' (12.35) and 'purpose'. Brückner 252.

Russ. *nadobnost'*, fr. *nadobno* 'it is necessary' (9.94).

Russ. *neobchodimost'* (the strongest word), through adj. *neobchodimyj*, fr. neg. cpd. of *obchoditi* 'go round, pass over', hence lit. what one cannot 'get round', i.e. 'evade, escape'.

7. Apparently there is no common Skt. noun for 'need', which is expressed by gerundives of particular verbs, of which perh. the most nearly generic is *kartavya-* adj. and neut. sb. 'what is to be done'. Also *kartavyatā-* and *-tva-m* 'obligation, necessity'.

Skt. *āvaçyaka-*, adj. and neut. sb., also *āvaçyakatā-*, fr. *avaçya-* in adv. *avaçyam* 'necessarily, certainly' and cpds. like *avaçya-karman-* 'necessary action', *avaçya-kārya-* 'necessary to be done', etc., *avaçya-* being lit. 'against one's will', fr. *a-* privative and *vaç-* 'wish, will'. Cf. ChSl. *nevolja*, above, 6.

9.94 OUGHT, MUST (3sg.)

Grk.	*χρή, δεῖ, ὀφείλει, ἀνάγκη ἐστί*	Goth.	*skal*	Lith.	*reikia, tur,* phrase with fut. of 'be'
NG	*πρέπει, ἀνάγκη εἶναι*	ON	*skal, verðr, ā*	Lett.	*vajaga (ir),* phrase with fut. of 'be'
Lat.	*opus est, oportet, dēbet, necesse est*	Dan.	*bør, skal, maa*	ChSl.	*dlŭžĭnŭ jestŭ, podobajetŭ*
It.	*dovrebbe, deve, bisogna*	Sw.	*bör, måste*	SCr.	*treba, mora*
Fr.	*devrait, doit, il faut*	OE	*sceal, mōt*	Boh.	*musí, má*
Sp.	*debiera, debe, hay que, tiene que, ha de*	ME	*shal, oughte, mote*	Pol.	*powinieneś, trzeba, musi*
Rum.	*trebue*	NE	*ought, should, must, has to*	Russ.	*dolžen, nado, nadobno*
Ir.	*is ēcen*	Du.	*(behoort) moet*	Skt.	*(arh-)*
NIr.	*ba cheart, ba chōir, is ēigin*	OHG	*scal, muoz*	Av.	. . . .
W.	*dylai, rhaid (i)*	MHG	*sol, muoz*		
Br.	*dle, renk, red eo*	NHG	*sollte, darf, muss*		

The expressions for 'ought, must' are cited in the third singular. Some of them are only so used, that is, impersonally, as Grk. δεῖ, Lat. *oportet*, Lith. *reikia*. Others may also be used personally ('I ought, must', etc.).

'Ought' (implying obligation, whether or not fulfilled) and the more urgent 'must' (implying compulsion, whether from within oneself or from outward circumstances) are taken together, since the distinction is often ignored (the same word covering both) or brought out by different forms of the same verb. What was originally 'ought' may become virtually 'must' in the present indicative, the weaker 'ought' being expressed by a modal form, e.g. Fr. *doit* (fr. Lat. *dēbet*) 'is to, must' vs. condit. *devrait* 'ought' (similarly in It., Sp.). Cf. also NE *ought, should*, NHG *sollte* originally pret. subj. forms; Russ. *dolžen by, nadobno by* (*by* the old conditional) weaker than the plain *dolžen* or *nadobno*.

Most of the words that meant primarily 'ought' are from verbs for 'owe' (11.63).

Of the other words listed, many are connected with those for 'need, necessity' (9.93). In several cases 'may' has become 'must', probably starting in negative phrases ('may not' = 'must not'). Another source is 'is fitting, proper', strengthened to 'ought' or even 'must'.

Widespread is the use of verbs for 'have' as 'must' ('has it to do' > 'has to do it'). So in late Grk., late Lat. and the Romance languages, Br., NHG, Lith., Slavic. Such forms are only partially entered in the list, namely, under Sp., Lith., Boh. and NE, where they are most important.

The notion of obligation or necessity with reference to a particular action is also expressed by verbal derivatives like the Grk. -τέος and the Lat. and Skt. gerundives. Only the last are included in the list, as the usual method of expression, there being no special Skt. verb in common use for 'ought, must'.

A widespread substitute for 'ought, must' is seen in phrases like NE *it is to be noted*, more commonly with act. infin. (so formerly in English), as Fr. *c'est à remarquer*, Sp. *es de notar*, NHG *es ist zu bemerken*. In Lith. and Lett. the future 'it will be' is so used.

1. Grk. χρή (reg. Hom. term; δεῖ only once), see under χρεία 'need' (9.93).

Grk. δεῖ impers. (usual prose term), fr. δέω 'lack, miss, need', Aeol. δεύω : Skt. *doṣa-* 'lack, fault, guilt, harm'. Walde-P. 1.782. Boisacq 180.

Grk. ὀφείλει, fr. ὀφείλω 'owe' (11.63), used also personally as 'ought', esp. in imperf. and aor.

Grk. ἀνάγκη ἐστί (NG εἶναι), phrase with ἀνάγκη 'necessity' (9.93).

Grk. πρέπει 'is fitting' (9.943), in NG (and sometimes Byz.), also 'ought, must' (the usual pop. expression).

Grk. ἔχει 'has' in late Grk. = 'must' (incipiently in NT, common Byz., also used as future).

2. Lat. *opus est, necesse est*, phrases with *opus* 'work, need' and *necesse* 'necessary' (9.93).

Lat. *oportet*, impers. 'is proper, ought', perh. fr. **op-vortet* : *vortere, vertere* 'turn'. Walde-P. 1.122. Ernout-M. 704 f.

Lat. *dēbet*, fr. *dēbēre* 'owe' (11.63), used also personally as 'ought'. Hence It. *deve*, Fr. *doit*, Sp. *debe*, now stronger vs. It. *dovrebbe*, Fr. *devrait*, Sp. *debiera* (or imperf. indic. *debía*).

Lat. *habet* 'has', late 'must', e.g. *ipsam vallem nos traversare habebamus* 'we had to cross this valley' (Peregrin. 2.1). Hence It. *ha*, Fr. *a*, Sp. *ha de* (also *hay que* impers.), Rum. *are*, and similarly Sp. *tiene que* fr. *tener* 'have' (11.11).

It. *bisogna* : *bisogno* 'need' (9.93).

Fr. *il faut*, impers., fr. Lat. *fallit*, fr. *fallere* 'deceive, escape notice', esp. in phrases like *mē fallit* 'is unknown to me' (mostly with neg.), hence 'fails me'. Development 'fails' > 'is lacking' > 'is needed, is necessary'. REW 3167. Gamillscheg 402. Wartburg 3.389.

Rum. *trebue*, fr. Slavic, cf. ChSl. *trěbuetŭ* 'needs' (below, 6).

3. Ir. *is ēcen*, NIr. *is ēigin* 'is necessary', phrases with nouns for 'need, necessity' (9.93).

NIr. *ba cheart, ba chōir*, phrases with *ba* 'was' and *ceart* or *cōĭr* 'right, just, proper' (16.73), hence orig. 'was right, proper', then = 'ought' as past, now also as present.

W. *dylai*, Br. *dle*, fr. W. *dylwn* 'ought' orig. 'owe' (cf. *dyled* 'debt'), Br. *dleout* 'owe, ought'.

W. *rhaid* (*i*), Br. *red eo*, phrases with nouns for 'need, necessity' (9.93).

Br. *renk, rank*, fr. *renkout, rankout* 'be obliged', this prob. : Ir. *riccim* 'reach, attain' (cf. pret. *ranac*, etc., Pedersen 2.556), *riccim less* 'need'. Henry 232.

Br. also phrases *a dlean, a renkan* (: preceding) and with forms of *beza* 'be', as *eo* (*da*) 'is to', or *kaout* 'have'. Vallée s.v. *devoir*.

4. Goth., ON *skal*, OE *sceal*, ME *s(c)hal*, NE *shall*, Du. *zal*, OHG *scal*, MHG *sol*, NHG *soll* (but NE *shall*, Du. *zal*, NHG *soll* mostly in other uses; as 'must' bibl., e.g. *thou shalt not steal*, or uncommon) pret.-pres. of Goth. *skulan*, OE, OHG *sculan* 'owe' (11.63). Hence for 'ought' NE *should*, NHG *sollte*, orig. pret. subj. NED s.v. *shall*.

ON *verðr*, special use of *verða* 'become, happen' (9.92).

Dan. *bør*, Sw. *bör* : ON *byrja*, 'behave, be suitable', OE *gebyrian*, OHG *giburien* (NHG *gebühren*) 'be suitable, happen' (9.993). Cf. OE *gebyraþ* in Gospels Jn. 9.4 (δεῖ, *oportet;* the Lindisf. version has *gedæfnaþ* : Goth. *gadaban* 'be fitting, happen', 9.993), and Du. *behoort* 'belongs, is proper' sometimes 'ought'. Falk-Torp 118. Hellquist 125.

ON *ā*, OE *āh*, ME *owe*, fr. ON *eiga*, OE *āgan* 'own' (11.12), sometimes 'ought', but in this sense replaced by pret. ME *oughte*, NE *ought*. NED s.v. *owe* and *ought*.

Dan. *maa* 'may' and 'must' (Sw. *må* 'may', as 'must' replaced by *måste*, below) = ON *mā*, Goth. *mag*, OE *mæg*, etc. 'can' (9.95). Falk-Torp 687 f. Hellquist 670.

OE *mōt*, ME *mote* 'may' and must', as 'must' displaced by ME *moste*, NE *must*, orig. pret. or esp. the pret. subj.—Du. *moet* 'ought' and 'must', OHG, MHG *muoz* 'may' and 'must', NHG *muss* 'must' : Goth. *ga-mōt* 'has room for' (χωρεῖ), OHG *muoza*, NHG *musse* 'free time, leisure', perh. fr. the root of Goth. *mitan*, etc. 'measure'. Sw. *måste* 'must' fr. (or old *må* reformed fr.) MLG pret. *moste*. Semantic development 'has (or there is) room or time for' > 'be permitted, may' (cf. Grk. συγχωρέω 'assent to, agree', συγχωρεῖ 'it is agreed, may be done') > 'must'. Walde-P. 2.260. NED s.v. *mote* and *must*. Franck-v. W. 437. Weigand-H. 242 f. Hellquist 678.

OE *nēodaþ*, ME *nedeth*, NE *needs* (: OE *nēad* 'need', 9.93), also used with notion of obligation or necessity. NED s.v. *need* vb.

NHG *darf* orig. 'needs' (9.93), now 'may' and esp. with neg. 'must'.

NE *has to*, now the most common expression for 'must' (barring perhaps the more colloq. *has got to;* cf. even U.S. vulgar *I gotta*) and favored by the fact that, in contrast to *must*, it has a past tense in same use (*had to do it*). Similarly NHG *hat* (*er hat abzuwarten* 'he must wait'), but much less important for this sense than NE *has*.

5. Lith. *reikia* (impers.), cf. *reikalas*, 9.93.

Lith. *tur*, fr. *turėti* 'have' (11.11), the common expression for 'must'.

Lett. *vajaga* (*ir*) impers., cf. *vajadzība*, 9.93.

'Ought, must' also expressed by fut. of verb 'be', lit. 'it will be', e.g. Lith. *rytoj bus i giria važiuoti* 'tomorrow we must ride into the forest' (NSB p. 93; cf. Senn, Lit. Sprachlehre p. 58), Lett. *tev nebūs zagt* 'thou shalt not steal' (Mühl.-Endz. 1.359).

6. ChSl. *dlŭžĭnŭ jestŭ* (ὀφείλει both as 'owes' and 'ought', latter e.g. Jn. 19.7), SCr. *dužan je*, Russ. *dolžen* (without copula) and the weaker *dolžen by*, phrase with adj. ChSl. *dlŭžĭnŭ* 'in debt', fr. *dlŭgŭ* 'debt' (11.63).

ChSl. *podobajetŭ* (in Gospels for δεῖ, Supr. also for χρή, ὀφείλει, πρέπει), fr. *podoba* in *podoba jestŭ* (Supr. δεῖ, πρέπει, etc.), orig. *po-doba* 'what is timely, suitable' : *doba* 'point of time, time' (not quotable in ChSl., but SCr., Boh., etc., 14.11), Goth. *gadaban* 'be suitable', etc. Similarly Russ. *na-doba*, whence *nadobno* or shortened *nado* impers. 'it is necessary' and the weaker *nado*(*bno*) *by*. Berneker 203 f.

SCr. *treba*, Pol. *trzeba* (impers.), Boh. *treba jest*, all orig. sb. 'need' : ChSl. *potrěba* 'need', vb. *trěbovati*, 3sg., *trěbuetŭ* 'needs' (9.93).

SCr. *mora* 'must' (also Slov.) : *more* = *može* 'can' (*ž* > *r*, Leskien SCr. Gram. p. 105, Vondrak, Slav. Gram. p. 459) = ChSl. *možetŭ* 'can' (9.95). Development fr. 'can' > 'must' (like 'may' > 'must' in Gmc., above, 4) and differentiated form, spreading fr. Slov. and Croat. territory. Rječnik Akad. 7.1 f. Miklosich 199. Berneker 2.67.

Boh. *musí*, Pol. *musi*, fr. NHG *muss*. Brückner 348 f. Stender-Petersen 318.

Pol. *powinieneś*, usual expression for 'ought', fr. adj. *powinien* 'obliged' (: *wina* 'fault, guilt', 16.76) with vb. 'to be'.

SCr. *ima*, Boh. *má*, Pol. *ma*, Russ. *imejet* 'has', all used sometimes like NE *has to*, most commonly the Boh. *má* (or *měl jest, měl by*).

7. Skt. *arhati* 'deserves, may', sometimes 'ought', beside *argha-* 'worth, price' : Av. *arəjaiti* 'is worth', Grk. ἀλφή 'produce, gain', ἀλφάνω 'bring in, yield'. Walde-P. 1.91.

But in Indo-Iranian the notion of obligation or necessity is commonly expressed by the gerundives or modal forms of particular verbs.

9.942 DUTY

Grk.	(ὃ *ὀφείλει, καθήκει,* etc.); *καθῆκον*	Goth.	(phrase with 'ought')	Lith.	*pareiga*
NG	*καθῆκον, χρέος*	ON	(phrase with 'ought')	Lett.	*pienākums*
Lat.	*officium*	Dan.	*pligt*	ChSl.	(phrase with 'ought')
It.	*dovere*	Sw.	*pligt*	SCr.	*dužnost*
Fr.	*devoir*	OE	(phrase with 'ought')	Boh.	*povinnost'*
Sp.	*deber*	ME	*duetee*	Pol.	*powinność*
Rum.	*datorie*	NE	*duty*	Russ.	*dolg*
Ir.	*dliged*(?)	Du.	*plicht*	Skt.	(*dharma-, kṛtya-*)
NIr.	*dualgar*	OHG	(phrase with 'ought')	Av.	. . . .
W.	*dyled*	MHG	(phrase with 'ought')		
Br.	*dlead*	NHG	*pflicht*		

'Duty', understood here in the most usual present sense of NE *duty*, namely as moral obligation, is most commonly expressed by words connected with the verbs for 'ought', 'owe' (9.94, 11.63), in fact, in several languages by phrases containing such verbs, 'what one ought', rather than by nouns. Other semantic sources are 'performance, activity', 'care' and 'what comes to one, becomes one, concerns one'. Some of the words were used primarily for the financial duty, 'debt', but the two notions are generally distinguished.

1. In the earlier Grk. writers there is no single distinctive sb. for 'duty'. It was expressed by phrases with vbs. for 'ought' as ὃ ὀφείλει (sb. ὀφείλημα only 'debt'), χρή, δεῖ (with pple. δέον); by simple genitive with forms of εἰμί, as πολίτου ἐστί 'is the part of, the duty of, a citizen'; by phrases like καθήκει μοι, προσήκει μοι 'belongs to, concerns me, is my duty'. With these last, also the pples. used substantively, esp. καθῆκον which became the technical term of the Stoics. Cf. περὶ καθήκοντος, title of a work by Zeno, and Cic. ad Att. *non dubito quin* καθῆκον *"officium" sit*. Grk. χρέος 'debt' (11.64), NG also 'duty', as ἔκαμα τὸ χρέος μου 'I did my duty'.

2. Lat. *officium*, fr. **opi-ficiom*, cpd. of *opus* 'work' and *facere* 'do' (cf. *opifex, artifex, artificium*), earliest sense 'performance, activity', hence the usual 'duty'. Ernout-M. 700. Skutsch, Glotta 2.161 ff.

It. *dovere*, Fr. *devoir*, Sp. *deber*, infins., used as sbs., of vbs. for 'owe' and 'ought' (9.94).

Rum. *datorie* 'debt' (11.64) and 'duty'.

3. Ir. *dliged* 'right, law', also 'duty'(?), W. *dyled* 'debt' and 'duty', Br. *dlead* 'duty' beside *dle* 'debt', see 11.64.

NIr. *dualgar*, fr. *dual* 'fit, proper', etym.? Macbain 145.

4. In older Gmc. 'duty' was expressed by phrases with vbs. for 'owe, ought', Goth. *skulan*, etc. (9.94, 11.63), e.g. Goth., OE in Lk. 17.10 (where verbal phrase also in Grk. and Vulgate). The corresponding sbs., OE *scyld*, etc., were used for 'debt' or 'guilt', but not 'duty'.

ME *duetee*, NE *duty*, fr. Anglo-Fr. *dueté*, formed (like *beauté* 'beauty', etc.) fr. *du* 'due', pple. of *devoir* 'owe'. In ME the more usual sense was that of deference, or financial duty, 'debt' (cf. the present customs *duties*). NED sv.. *duty*.

NHG *pflicht* (as moral 'duty' only since 16th cent.) fr. OHG *pfliht* 'intercourse, care', formed fr. *pflegan* 'be answerable for, care for'. Same development or semantic borrowing in Du., MLG *plicht* (> Dan., Sw. *pligt*), Weigand-H. 2.413. Paul, Deutsches Wtb. 394.

5. Lith. *pareiga*, formed like *eiga* 'course', fr. *pareiti* 'come back', 'come to', hence 'what comes to, becomes one'. Leskien, Bildung d. Nom. 523.

Lett. *pienākums*, fr. *pie-nākt* 'come to, reach, concern'. Mühl-Endz. 3.275.

6. ChSl., only verbal phrase for 'ought'.

SCr. *dužnost*, deriv. of adj. *dužan* 'in debt' = ChSl. *dlŭžĭnŭ* id., fr. *dlŭgŭ* 'debt'.

Boh. *povinnost'*, Pol. *powinność*, fr. adj. *povinný*, *powinny* 'obliged, due' derivs. of ChSl. *vina*, etc. 'fault, guilt' (16.76).

Russ. *dolg* 'debt' (11.64), also 'duty'.

7. Skt. *dharma-* 'custom, law' (21.11) may cover 'duty'; or *kṛtya-* 'what is to be done, proper'.

9.943 FITTING, SUITABLE

Grk.	*ἐπιτήδειος, εὔθετος, πρέπων*	Goth.	*gadōb* (neut.), *fagrs*	Lith.	*pritinkas*
NG	*κατάλληλος*	ON	*fallinn, hentr, hæfr*	Lett.	*derīgs*
Lat.	*conveniēns, aptus, idōneus, habilis*	Dan.	*passende*	ChSl.	*upravlenŭ, podobĭnŭ*
It.	*convenevole, conveniente, proprio*	Sw.	*passande, lämplig*	SCr.	*priličan, shodan*
Fr.	*convenable, propre*	OE	*gedafen, gerisene, gelimplīc*	Boh.	*vhodný*
Sp.	*conveniente, propio*	ME	*able, propre, sutely*	Pol.	*stosowny*
Rum.	*convenabil*	NE	*suitable, fitting, proper*	Russ.	*priličnyj*
Ir.	*comadas, oiremain, oiremnach*	Du.	*gepast, voegzaam*	Skt.	*yogya-*
NIr.	*oireamhnach, ion-*	OHG	*biquāmi, gilumpflīh, gifuoglīh*	Av.	. . . .
W.	*addas, cyfaddas*	MHG	*bequæme, gefuege*		
Br.	*dereat*	NHG	*passend, angemessen*		

The notion 'fitting, suitable' is expressed by a great variety of terms, with semantic sources too diverse to summarize.

1. Grk. *ἐπιτήδειος*, fr. adv. *ἐπίτηδες*, Dor. *ἐπίτᾱδες* 'purposely, fittingly', this of dub. etym. The old view that it is based on a phrase *ἐπὶ *τᾶδε* is attractive semantically, but a nom.-acc. pl. neut. in -ᾰ (= Vedic -ā) is otherwise unknown. However, there could be an adv. *τᾶδε* 'in this way' (of instrumental orig.), parallel to Lac. *ταυτᾶ*, Delph., Cret. *ἇδε*, etc. For a quite different, but unconvincing, suggestion, cf. Brugmann, Demonstrativpronomina 141 f.

Grk. *εὔθετος* 'well placed', sometimes 'convenient, suitable'.

Grk. *πρέπων*, pres. pple., or more commonly 3sg. impers. *πρέπει* 'is fitting', fr. *πρέπω* 'be conspicuous', prob. : Ir. *richt*, W. *rhith* 'form, appearance', etc. Walde-P. 2.89. Boisacq 810.

Grk. *κατάλληλος* 'corresponding, appropriate', NG 'suitable, fitting', fr. *κατά* 'according to' and *ἀλλήλους, ἄλληλα* 'one another'.

2. Lat. *conveniēns*, fr. *convenīre* 'come together', 3sg. impers. *convenit* 'is suitable', whence also the Romance forms, It. *convenevole*, etc. (see list).

Lat. *idōneus*, based on some pronominal form like *id*, etc., but precise analysis dub. Ernout-M. 471. Walde-H. 1.671 f.

Lat. *aptus*, orig. 'fastened', but mostly fig. 'suitable', pass. pple. of the rare *apere* 'bind' beside *apiscī* 'reach, obtain' : Skt. *āp-* 'reach, obtain', etc. Ernout-M. 60 f. Walde-H. 1.57 f.

Lat. *habilis* 'easy to handle', hence also 'fit, suitable' (and skilful), fr. *habēre* (11.11).

Lat. 3sg. impers. *decet* 'is fitting' : Grk. *δέκομαι*, Att. *δέχομαι* 'receive', etc. Walde-P. 1.783 f. Ernout-M. 256 f. Walde-H. 1.330 f.

It. *proprio*, Fr. *propre* (> ME *propre*, NE *proper*), Sp. *propio* (with dissim.), all also and orig. 'what is one's own', fr. Lat. *proprius* 'one's own', this fr. a phrase *prŏ prīvō* (*prīvus* 'single, one's own'). Ernout-M. 846. For uses, cf. NED s.v. *proper*.

3. Ir. *comadas*, OW *cimadas*, W. *addas, cyfaddas*, with Ir. *ad* 'law, custom' (NIr. *ādh* 'good luck', perh. : Umbr. *arsie* 'sancte', *arsmor* 'ritus' (also Goth. *ga-tils*, etc.?). Vendryes, RC 35.212 ff., 42.401 ff. Walde-H. 1.12. Devoto, Mélanges Pedersen 224.

Ir. *oiremain, oiremnach*, NIr. *oireamhnach*, fr. *oirim* 'fit, suit', this denom. fr. *or* 'border, edge' (12.353)?

NIr. cpds. with prefix *ion-, in-* (Pedersen 2.11), as *ion-miachair* 'fit for marriage', etc. (Dinneen s.v. *ion-, in-*), formerly very common, but not in current use (M. Dillon).

Br. *dereat*, fr. MBr. *deren* 'rule, guide' (cf. W. *dyre* 'come!'), cpd. of *de-* and *ren* 'rule, guide'. Henry 92. Ernault, Dict. étym. 264.

4. Goth. *gadōb*, neut. sg. (*gadōb ist* = *πρέπει*) beside *gadaban* 'be fitting' and 'happen', OE *gedafen, gedafenlīc, gedēfe*, beside *gedafnian* 'be fitting' : ChSl. *podoba jestŭ, po-dobajetŭ* 'ought' (9.94), SCr. *doba* 'point of time' (14.11), ChSl. *dobrŭ* 'good', etc., prob. Lat. *faber* 'artisan' (9.42). Walde-P. 1.284 f. Walde-H. 1.436 f. Feist 176 f. Berneker 203 f.

Goth. *fagrs* (neut. *fagr* = *εὔθετον*, Lk. 14.35) = ON *fagr*, OE *fæger* 'fair, beautiful', fr. the same root as OHG *fuogan* 'join, fit together'. Falk-Torp 201. Feist 424.

Goth. *gatils* (renders *εὔκαιρος* 'timely, convenient', but also *εὔθετος*, Lk. 9.62) : OE *til* 'capable, apt', OHG *zil* 'object', etc., outside root connections dub. Walde-P. 1.809. Falk-Torp 1565. Feist 205, 477. See also above, 3.

ON *fallinn*, esp. *til fallinn*, or *fallinn til*, pple. of *falla* 'fall' (10.23), here in its sense of 'agree, suit' (cf. NHG *gefallen* 'please').

ON *hentr*, lit. 'handy' (: *hǫnd* 'hand'), but esp. 'serviceable, suitable'.

ON *hæfr*, fr. *hæfa* 'aim, fit, be suitable', deriv. of *hōf* 'moderation, fairness' : OE *behōfian* 'have need of' (see Dan. *behov*, 9.93). Falk-Torp 455.

Dan. *passende*, Sw. *passande*, fr. vbs. Dan. *passe*, Sw. *passa*, these fr. MLG *passen* = NHG *passen* (see below). Falk-Torp 817. Hellquist 752.

Sw. *lämplig*, fr. *lämpa* 'suit, fit', this fr. MLG **lempen* beside *limpen* 'make suitable' : OE (*ge*)*limpan* 'take place, happen', OHG (*gi*)*limfan* 'be suitable', OE *gelimplīc*, OHG *gilumpflīh* (freq. in Otfr.) 'suitable', prob. ultimately fr. the same root as NE *limp* 'walk lamely', Skt. *lamb-* 'hang down', the sense 'suitable' coming fr. the prefix *ge-*. Walde-P. 1.740. Falk-Torp 634. Hellquist 607.

OE (beside *gedafen*, etc., above) *gerisene, gerisenlīc*, fr. *gerīsan* 'suit, be fitting', cpd. of *rīsan* 'rise' (10.21).

ME *able* (as 'fit, suitable' Wycliff, Lk. 9.62, freq. in Chaucer, etc.), through OFr. (*h*)*able* fr. Lat. *habilis* (above, 2). NED s.v.

ME *sutely* (rare), NE *suitable*, fr. vb. *suit* (in senses 10, 14 NED), this fr. sb. *suit* (cf. senses 21, 23 in NED), fr. OFr. *suite*, orig. 'what follows, consequence', fr. deriv. of Lat. *sequī* 'follow'. REW 7839. Gamillscheg 821. NED s.vv. *suit*, vb., *suit*, sb.

NE *fitting*, fr. vb. *fit*, this fr. adj. *fit*(?), both : MDu. *fitten* 'fit', etym.? NED s.v. *fit*, vb. Franck-v. W. 164, 745.

OHG *biquāmi* (OE *gecwēme* 'pleasing, acceptable'), MHG *bequæme* (NHG *bequem* sometimes 'suitable, convenient, but mostly 'comfortable, easy'), fr. OHG *biqueman* 'come to, attain'. Weigand-H. 1.204 f.

OHG *gifuoglīh* (Tat. = *aptus*), MHG *gefuege* (NHG *gefügig*), fr. OHG *fuogan* 'join, fit together'. Similarly Du. *voegzaam*, fr. *vuegen*.

Du. *gepast*, NHG *passend*, fr. vb. Du. (> NHG) *passen* 'suit', this fr. Fr. *passer* 'pass', VLat. *passāre*, deriv. of Lat. *passus* 'step'. Development, first in Du., through 'pass through to one's goal, attain' to 'be suitable'. Kluge-G. 434. Paul, Deutsches Wtb. 390. Franck-v. W. 491.

NHG *angemessen*, lit. 'measured up to', fr. *messen* 'measure'.

MHG *geschicket* 'arranged, ready', also 'suitable', pass. pple. of *schicken* 'create, arrange, make'. Hence NHG *geschickt* formerly more common than now for 'suitable' (so e.g. Luther, Lk. 9.62). Weigand-H. 697. Paul, Deutsches Wtb. 204.

5. Lith. *pritinkas* : *tikti*, *tinku* 'fit, suit', *tikras* 'right, sure', *tikėti* 'believe', etc. (17.15).

Lett. *derīgs*, fr. *deret* 'bargain, be of use, suit' = Lith. *derėti* 'bargain' : Skt. *dhṛ* 'hold', etc.(?). Walde-P. 1.858. Mühl.-Endz. 1.456.

6. ChSl. *upravlenŭ* (Gospels, Lk. 9.62 = *εὔθετος*), pple. pret. pass. of *upraviti*, cpd. of *praviti* 'set right', fr. *pravŭ* 'straight, right' (12.73, 16.73).

ChSl. *podobĭnŭ* (mostly 'similar', 12.82, but *podobno jestŭ* = *πρέπον ἐστίν* Gospels, Mt. 3.15) : Goth. *gadōb*, etc. (above, 4).

SCr. *priličan*, Russ. *priličnyj*, cpds. : ChSl. *lice* 'face' (4.204). Berneker 719 f.

SCr. *shodan*, fr. *sahoditi* 'go together', cpd. of *hoditi̯* 'go' (10.47).

Boh. *vhodný* : *vhod* 'at the right time', *hoditi se* 'be suitable', ChSl. *godŭ* 'time', etc. Berneker 316 ff.

Pol. *stosowny*, fr. *stos* 'a hit, thrust' (now mostly 'a pile, heap'), fr. NHG *stoss* 'a hit, thrust' (also 'pile, heap'). Brückner 517.

7. Skt. *yogya-*, fr. *yoga-* 'yoke', *yuj-* 'join' (12.22).

9.95 CAN, MAY (3 sg.)

Grk.	*δύναται, ἔξεστι*	Goth.	*mag*	Lith.	*gal*
NG	*μπορεῖ*	ON	*mā*	Lett.	*var, lai*
Lat.	*potest, licet*	Dan.	*kan, maa*	ChSl.	*možetŭ*
It.	*può*	Sw.	*kan, må*	SCr.	*može, smije*
Fr.	*peut*	OE	*mæg, mōt*	Boh.	*může, smí*
Sp.	*puede*	ME	*may, can, mote*	Pol.	*može*
Rum.	*poate*	NE	*can, may*	Russ.	*možet*
Ir.	*conic, fētar*	Du.	*kan, mag*	Skt.	*çaknoti*
NIr.	*fēadann, tig leis*	OHG	*mag, muoz*	Av.	*tavaiti*
W.	*gall*	MHG	*mac, kan, muoz*		
Br.	*gall, gell*	NHG	*kann, mag, darf*		

Despite the difference between 'can', implying physical or mental power, ability, and 'may', implying permission or possibility, these notions are very commonly merged in their linguistic expression. That is, they are covered by the same word, either in accepted usage or at least in popular usage. Even in English, the teacher who conscientiously corrects the pupil's *can I?* to *may I?* is engaged in a hopeless struggle. Furthermore, the Gmc. group represented by NE *may* meant 'can' in the early period.

The strictly permissive 'may' finds more distinctive expression in some forms like the Lat. impers. *licet*, NHG *darf*. More generally as 'is permitted', with pass. forms of the verbs for 'permit' (19.47), e.g. NG *μοῦ ἐπιτρέπεται*; 'is it permitted me, may I?' These obvious expressions are not repeated in the list.

Most of the words are connected with others for 'might, power', for which no earlier ultimate sense is attainable. Words for 'know' are in many languages used as 'know how' and so virtually 'can', like Fr. *il sait lire* 'he (knows how to) can read'. The full development in this direction, displacing the older meaning 'know' and the old words for 'can', is characteristic of the Gmc. group, NE *can*, etc.

1. Grk. *δύναται*, with *δυνατός* 'strong, powerful' and *δύναμις* 'strength, power', etym. dub. (4.81). NG *δυνατός* and *δύναμις* are still the common words, but *δύναται* (*δύναμαι*, etc.), while lit. and familiar to most, is commonly replaced by the following:

NG *μπορεῖ* (also *ἠμπορεῖ*; late Byz. spelling varied), certainly fr. *εὐπορεῖ* 'prospers, has plenty', sometimes with infin. 'finds a way, is able, can' (Aristot.), and in this sense well attested in late Grk. (e.g. Jo. Moschus). The only question is the precise formal development, which is much disputed. Regularly *εὐπορεῖ* > *ἐπορεῖ, πορεῖ* (Hatzidakis, Glotta 22.131). Then nasal introduced (causing change of *p* > *b*), either by influence of *ἔμπορος* 'merchant' (so Hatzidakis, l.c., but?); or from neg. phrase *δὲν πορεῖ* pronounced *δεμπορεῖ* with subsequent detachment of (*ἐ*)*μπορεῖ* (so Jannaris, Hist. Greek Gram. §§ 130, 132b); or (another possibility not previously considered) the influence of opposite cpds. like *ἔμμορφος* vs. *ἄμορφος* (that is, *ἐμπορεῖ* vs. *ἀπορεῖ* sometimes = 'is unable').

Grk. *ἔξεστι*, lit. 'it is' (for some one to), used as 'it is permitted'. So often, and in NT, where it is rendered by *licet* in the Vulgate, in other versions by phrases meaning 'is due' (Goth. *skuld ist*), 'is proper' (ChSl. *dostojitŭ*, NHG *sich ziemet* Luther), 'is lawful' (King James), or by pass. forms of the verbs for 'permit' (OE *alȳfed is*, etc.).

2. Lat. *potest* (> Romance forms), fr. *potis est* and *pote est*, phrase with *potis*, neut. *pote* 'able, possible' : Skt. *pati-* 'master, husband', Grk. *πόσις* 'husband', Goth. *faþs* in *brūþ-faþs* 'bridegroom', *hunda-faþs* 'master of a hundred, centurion', Lith. *patis* 'husband', etc. Walde-P. 2.77 f. Ernout-M. 796.

Lat. *licet*, impers. 'it is permitted, may' (Osc. *licitud* 'liceto') : *licēre, licērī* 'be or offer for sale, bid on, appraise', this perh. : Lett. *līkt* 'agree in trade' (adversely Mühl.-Endz. 2.487). Walde-P. 2.395. Ernout-M. 547 f. Walde-H. 1.797.

3. Ir. *conic*, cpd. of *com-* 'with' and *icc-* in other cpds. 'cause, find, come' (cf. *do-iccim*, 10.48). Pedersen 2.554. Thurneysen, Gram. 503.

Ir. *ēta* 'gets' and, after neg., 'can', more freq. pres. pass. *fētar* (cf. Laws, Gloss. 353), NIr. *fēadann, fēadtar* (1sg. *fēadaim*) or phrase *is fēidir*, cpd. of *-tā-* in *attā* 'is' (9.91), *ad-co-ta* 'obtains, gets' (11.16), etc., IE **stā-* 'stand'. Pedersen 2.638. (Otherwise Stokes 323.)

NIr. *tig leis*, lit. 'comes with him', frequent expression for 'can' (*tig liom* 'I can', etc.).

W. *gall*, Br. *gall, gell* : Corn. *gallos*, OBr. *gol* 'might', Ir. *gal* 'bravery', Lith. *galėti* 'be able', 3sg. *gal* 'can', *galia* 'might', etc. Walde-P. 1.539. Pedersen 1.156 f.

4. Goth. *mag*, ON *mā*, OE *mæg*, OHG *mag*, all 'can' (with sbs. Goth. *mahts*, OE *meaht*, OHG *maht* 'power, might'), but in later use 'may', as NE *may*, NHG, Du. *mag*, Sw. *må* (Dan. also 'must') : ChSl. *mošti*, *mogą*, 3sg. *možetŭ*, etc., general Slavic, prob. Grk. μῆχος 'means, remedy'. Walde-P. 2.227. Falk-Torp 687 f. NED s.v. *may*.

OE *mōt*, ME *mote*, OHG, MHG *muoz* 'may' and 'must', see 9.94.

ME, NE *can*, MHG, Du., Dan. *kan*, NHG *kann*, all orig. 'know', as Goth., ON, OHG *kann*, OE *can* : Grk. γιγνώσκω, Lat. *(g)nōscere*, etc. 'know' (17.17), with development through 'knows how' (to do something).

NHG *darf*, orig. 'needs' (9.93), now usual for the permissive 'may'.

5. Lith. *gal* (*galiu*, *galėti*) : W. *gall*, etc. (above, 3).

Lett. *var* (*varu*, *varēt*), with sb. *vara*, OPruss. *warrin* (acc. sg.) 'might, power', etym.? Mühl.-Endz. 4.475, 477. Lett. *var* covers 'can' and 'may', but the latter is also expressed by the particle *lai*, orig. imperat. of *laist* 'leave, let'. Mühl.-Endz. 2.400.

6. ChSl. *možetŭ* (*mogą*, *mošti*), SCr. *može*, etc., general Slavic : Goth. *mag* 'can', etc. (above, 4).

SCr. *smije*, Boh. *smí* (*smjeti*, *smiti*), now used like NHG *darf*, that is, 'may' or with neg. 'must', orig. 'dare' : ChSl. *sŭměti* 'dare' (16.51).

7. Skt. *çaknoti* (*çak-*), reg. word for 'can', beside desid. *çiks-* 'learn' : Av. *sač-* 'take note of', desid. *sixš-* 'learn', caus. 'teach' (Barth. 1551 f.), development perh. through 'know how', but outside connections dub. Walde-P. 1.333. Uhlenbeck 301.

Av. *tavaiti*, with *tavah-* 'might, power' : Skt. *tavīti*, *tāuti* 'is strong', *tavas-*, *tura-* 'strong, powerful', perh. ultimately the same root as in Lat. *tumēre* 'swell', etc. Walde-P. 1.706 ff. Barth. 638 f.

9.96 EASY

Grk.	ῥᾴδιος, εὔκολος	Goth.	*azetizō* (comp.)	Lith.	*lengvas*
NG	εὔκολος	ON	*auð-*	Lett.	*viegls*
Lat.	*facilis*	Dan.	*let*	ChSl.	*udobĭ*
It.	*facile*	Sw.	*lätt*	SCr.	*lak*
Fr.	*facile*	OE	*ēaþe, ēaþelīc, lēoht*	Boh.	*snadný*
Sp.	*fácil*	ME	*ethe, light, aisy*	Pol.	*łatwy*
Rum.	*ușor, lesne*	NE	*easy*	Russ.	*legkij*
Ir.	*asse, rēid, soirb*	Du.	*gemakkelijk*	Skt.	*su-kara-*, etc.
NIr.	*furus*	OHG	*ōdi*	Av.	. . . .
W.	*hawdd*	MHG	*æde*		
Br.	*aes*	NHG	*leicht*		

Of words for 'easy' the most widespread source is 'light' in weight, developing through phrases like 'light burden, light work', etc. Other sources are the notion of something that is 'at hand, convenient, suitable, do-able', and probably in one group 'uninhabited, empty', with development through 'free from difficulties'. In Greek a word originally applied to a person 'good natured, of easy disposition' was extended to things and eventually became the regular word for 'easy'.

1. Grk. ῥᾴδιος, Ion. ρηΐδιος, Aeol. βρᾴδιος (βρᾴδιον EM), that is, *ϝρᾱ-ίδιος, based on the form seen in the adv. ῥᾶ, ῥῆα, Hom. ῥεῖα, Aeol. βρᾶ and in comp. ῥᾴων, superl. ῥᾷστος, but root connection and orig. sense dub. Wackernagel, Vermischte Beiträge 11 ff. Hermann, Gött. Nachrichten 1918, 281. Schwyzer, IF 45.259 f. (: ἀπο-ϝρᾱ- in Hom. ἀπηύρα, ἀπούρας 'take away, rob'; semantic development through 'tearing', 'quick').

Grk. εὔκολος, mostly of persons 'easily satisfied, good-natured', then also of things 'easy' (Plato; but common in this sense only later; reg. Byz. and NG); taken by some (e.g. LS) as orig. 'contented with one's food' (attested late) : κόλον 'intestine', but more prob. belongs with other cpds. in -κολος, -πολος 'turning, tending', etc. (IE *k^wel- in πέλομαι, Lat. *colere*, etc.; κ reg. after εὐ-, whence also δύσ-κολος as opposite). Walde-P. 1.431 (top; not repeated 514). Still otherwise Boisacq 294.

2. Lat. *facilis* (> It., Fr. *facile*, Sp. *fácil*, all late borrowed forms), lit. 'do-able', fr. *facere* 'do'.

Lat. *levis* 'light' (15.82), though only rarely quotable as 'easy' (cf. *id eo levius ferendum*, Cic.), was prob. common in VLat. in this sense and the usual term in Romance before the borrowing of Lat. *facilis*. This sense is attested for It. *lieve* in Dante, Petrarch, etc. (Accad. della Crusca), OFr. *legere*, *legiere* (cf. Godefroy), Sp. *legero* in early period (cf. Juan Ruiz); and Rum. *ușor* (deriv. of *levis*, Pușcariu 1844) is still the usual word for 'easy' as well as 'light'.

Rum. *lesne* (with verbal phrases, e.g. *lesne a zice* 'easy to say'), fr. Bulg. *lesen* 'easy'. Tiktin 905. Berneker 755.

3. OIr. *asse*, prob. fr. **ad-sta-yo-* 'standing by', hence 'at one's disposal, easily attainable'. Hence MIr. *ussa* and with intensive prefix (: Lat. *per*, etc.) *irussa*, lit. 'very easy' (both forms used as 'easy' and 'easier'), NIr. *furus*, *furas*. Pokorny, KZ 45.138, 143 ff.

Ir. *soirb* (gl. *facilis*; NIr. *soirbh* 'favorable, pleasant'), with *doirb* 'difficult' (NIr. *doirbh* 'unfavorable'), plainly cpds. of *so-* and *do-* (= Skt. *su-* and *dus-*), second part perh. : *srib* 'stream' K. Meyer, Ber. Preuss. Akad. 1917, 626.

Ir. *rēid*, NIr. *rēidh* 'level, smooth, clear', and so sometimes 'easy', orig. of a road 'passable' : Ir. *riadaim* 'ride'. Pedersen 1.58. Hence Ir. *so-rēid*, *so-raid*, but mostly 'happy, successful', NIr. *soraidh*, and its opposite *do-raid*, NIr. *doraidh* sometimes 'difficult'.

W. *hawdd*, perh. : W. *hedd*, Ir. *sīd* 'peace', with different grades of the root **sed-* 'sit', W. *hawdd* fr. the *ā* (IE *ō*) grade as in Ir. *con-sādu* 'compono'. Loth, RC 36.162 (vs. Morris Jones 135, 247). Another suggestion (: Skt. *sādhu-* 'effective, well-disposed, correct, good'), G. S. Lane, Language 13.25.

Br. *aes*, fr. sb. *aez*, fr. Fr. *aise* 'ease, comfort' (cf. below, ME *aisie*, NE *easy*). Henry 5.

4. Goth. *azetizō*, comp. 'easier', beside *azetaba* 'gladly' and **azeti* in *wizondei in azetjam* 'living in pleasure', etym.? Feist. 71.

ON prefix *auð-*, as in *auð-sær* 'easy to see', *auð-sōttr* 'easy to get', etc., OE *ēaþe*, *ēaþelīc*, ME *ethe*, OHG *ōdi*, MHG *æde*, prob. same word as Goth. *auþs* (or *auþeis*), ON *auðr*, OHG *ōdi* 'uninhabited, empty' (NHG *öde*), with development through 'free from difficulties'. NED s.v. *eath*. Weigand-H. 2.330. Otherwise (as orig. 'willing' : Skt. *av-* 'favor, help', Lat. *avēre* 'desire eagerly', etc.) Falk-Torp 1407 (Walde-P. 1.19 with doubt).

OE *lēoht*, ME *light* (often as predicate 'it is easy', now only in phrases like *light burden*, *light work*, etc., which are felt as appropriate to the prevailing sense of *light = not heavy;* NED s.v. *light*, adj. 18), Dan. *let*, Sw. *lätt*, NHG *leicht* (OHG forms rarely quotable for 'easy', barring the intermediate 'light burden', etc.), all orig. 'light in weight' (15.82), with development of 'easy' through phrases 'light work', etc.

ME *aisie*, *aisy*, *esy*, etc., NE *easy*, fr. OFr. *aisié* (Fr. *aisé*), pple. of *aisier* 'put at ease', deriv. of *aise* 'comfort, ease, opportunity' (> ME *eise*, etc., NE *ease* sb.), this fr. Lat. *adiacēns* 'lying near, neighboring', but mainly through 'what is at hand, convenient'. REW 168. Gamillscheg 23. Wartburg 1.31 ff.

Du. *gemakkelijk*, fr. *gemak* 'comfort, ease' = OHG *gimah* 'quiet, comfort', fr. adj. *gimah* 'suited, convenient' = OE *gemæc* 'suited, well-matched', etc. Franck-v. W. 185.

5. Lith. *lengvas*, Lett. *viegls* 'light' (15.82) and 'easy'.

6. ChSl. *udobĭ*, adj. and adv. (on form, cf. Leskien, Altbulg. Gram. 97.3; in Gospels *ne udobĭ* δύσκολον, δυσκόλως and comp. *udoběje*, in Supr. adv. = ῥᾳδίως, εὐκόλως), cpd. of form seen in *doba* 'proper time', ChSl. *pa-doba jestŭ* 'is proper', etc. : Goth. *ga-daban* 'happen', perf. *gadōb* 'is proper', etc. Berneker 203 f.

SCr. *lak*, Russ. *legkij* 'light' (15.82) and 'easy'.

Boh. *snadný* = Pol. *snadny* 'convenient, easy' (but not the usual word) : Pol. *snadź* adv. 'apparently, perhaps', Russ. *snast'* 'tool, implement', *snadit'* 'provide, supply', late ChSl. adv. *snadĭ* 'superficially', all apparently fr. some such notion as 'on the surface', whence 'apparent' or 'convenient', but without any known root connections. Miklosich 312. Brückner 504.

Pol. *łatwy* (*łacwy*, *łacny*) : Boh. *laciný*, *lacný* 'cheap', formerly 'easy', *láce* 'cheapness', formerly 'insignificance, trifle', root connection dub. Berneker 694. Brückner 307 (: SCr. *latiti*, *laćati* 'seize, undertake').

7. In Skt. 'easy' and 'difficult' are expressed by cpds. of *su-* 'well' and *dus-* 'ill', e.g. *sukara-* (*duşkara-*) 'easy (hard) to do', *sudarça-* (*durdarça-*) 'easy (hard) to see', etc.

9.97 DIFFICULT

Grk.	χαλεπός, δύσκολος	Goth.	*aglus*	Lith.	*sunkus*
NG	δύσκολος	ON	*tor-, erfiðr*	Lett.	*grūts*
Lat.	*difficilis*	Dan.	*vanskelig*	ChSl.	*ne udobĭ*
It.	*difficile*	Sw.	*svår*	SCr.	*težak*
Fr.	*difficile*	OE	*earfeþe, unēaþe*	Boh.	*těžký*
Sp.	*difícil*	ME	*hard, difficile* (*unethe*)	Pol.	*trudny*
Rum.	*greu, dificil*			Russ.	*trudnyj*
Ir.	*anse, doirb, decair*	NE	*difficult, hard*	Skt.	*duş-kara-*, etc.
NIr.	*deacair*	Du.	*moeilijk*	Av.	. . . .
W.	*anodd*	OHG	*unōdi*		
Br.	*diez*	MHG	*swære*		
		NHG	*schwer, schwierig*		

Many of the words for 'difficult' are simply formal opposites of those for 'easy', as Grk. δύσκολος vs. εὔκολος, Lat. *difficilis* vs. *facilis*, ON *tor-* vs. *auð-*, Skt. *dus-* vs. *su-*. Even where there are other words for 'difficult', neg. cpds. or phrases with words for 'easy' may also be in common use, e.g. (besides NE *not easy*, NHG *nicht leicht*, etc.) Lith. *nelengvas*, Boh. *nesnadný*.

Others are semantic opposites, esp. 'heavy' vs. 'light', with parallel development, starting from phrases like 'heavy burden, heavy work', etc., in which most words for 'heavy' may be used with a suggestion of 'difficult'. But those which occur only in such transitional use, but have not gone the full way to 'it is difficult to', are not included in the list.

Another source is 'hard' vs. 'soft', through the notion of 'resistant', notably in ME, NE *hard*, but incipiently elsewhere (e.g. Lat. *dūrum est* 'it is difficult', freq. in Horace; less clearly in NHG *hartes leben*, etc.).

Several are in origin 'toilsome, laborious', derivs. of words for 'toil, labor'.

1. Grk. χαλεπός, in Hom. mostly 'hard to hear, painful, severe', etym.? Boisacq 1048.

Grk. δύσκολος 'hard to please, discontented', later 'difficult' (so NT as in NG), formed as opposite to εὔκολος and with similar semantic development (9.96).

2. Lat. *difficilis* (> It., Fr., Sp. forms; Rum. *dificil* fr. Fr.), cpd. of *facilis* 'easy' (9.96) with the separative-negating *dis-*.

Rum. *greu* 'heavy' (11.81) and 'difficult'.

3. Ir. *anse*, cpd. of *asse* 'easy' (9.96) with neg. prefix. Pedersen 1.47.

Ir. *doirb*, see *soirb* 'easy' (9.96).

Ir. *decair* (adj. and sb.; K. Meyer, Contrib. 595), NIr. *deacair*, prob. neg. cpd. opp. to *socair* 'smooth, calm, quiet, easy' (Dinneen), second part prob. : *cuirim* 'put'. Macbain 124, 334.

W. *anodd*, older *anhawdd*, neg. cpd. of *hawdd* 'easy' (9.96). Morris Jones 247.

Br. *diez*, neg. of *aez* 'easy' (9.96). Henry 96.

4. Goth. *aglus* : *agls* 'shameful', OE *egle* 'loathsome, troublesome', etc., with development similar to that in Grk. δύσκολος. Walde-P. 1.41. Feist 15.

ON prefix *tor-* (: Goth. *tuz-*, Grk. δυσ-, Skt. *dus-*), opp. of *auð-* (9.96) and used in parallel cpds., e.g. *tor-fyndr* 'hard to find', *tor-sōttr* 'hard to come at or do'.

ON *erfiðr*, OE *earfeþe*, *earfoþe* (e.g. Aelfric Gram. *earfoþe* = Lat. *difficilis*), orig. 'burdensome, toilsome', deriv. of ON *erfiði* 'toil, labor', OE *earfoþ* 'hardship' = Goth. *arbaiþs* 'toil', etc. (9.12).

ON *vandr* 'particular, choice, requiring pains to attain', also 'difficult', Dan. *vanskelig* 'difficult' (Sw. *vansklig* 'changeable, fickle, risky', in some phrases 'difficult') : ON *vinda*, Goth., OE *windan*, etc. 'turn', with development through 'turning, twisting, eluding one's efforts'. Walde-P. 1.261. Falk-Torp 1339.

Sw. *svår*, see below under MHG *swære*, etc.

OE *unēaþe*, more common in adv. OE *unēaþe*, ME *un(n)ethe*, NE dial. *uneath* (NED s.v.), neg. cpd. of *ēaþe* 'easy' (9.96).

Late ME, NE *difficile*, fr. Fr. id. (above, 2). Replaced by *difficult*, back-formation fr. sb. *difficulty* (Lat. *difficultās*).

ME, NE *hard*, orig. only 'hard' vs. 'soft' (15.74), hence 'difficult' through the notion of 'resisting', and now even more common in this sense than 'difficult'.

Du. *moeilijk*, deriv. of MDu. *moeye* 'trouble, pains, burden' = NHG *mühe*, etc. Franck-v. W. 436.

OHG *unōdi*, neg. cpd. of *ōdi* 'easy' (9.96).

MHG *swære*, NHG *schwer*, also and orig. 'heavy' (15.81). Hence NHG *schwierig* unambiguously 'difficult', but still less common than *schwer*. Dan. *svær* (fr. NHG? Falk-Torp 1222) sometimes, but less commonly 'difficult'. Sw. *svår* formerly 'heavy', now only 'difficult' (*tung* 'heavy').

5. Lith. *sunkus* 'heavy' (15.81) and 'difficult'.

Lett. *grūts*, orig. and still locally 'heavy' : Grk. βαρύς, Lat. *gravis*, etc. 'heavy' (15.81). Mühl.-Endz. 1.669 f.

6. ChSl. *ne udobĭ* (Gospels, Mk. 10.24

kako ne udobĭ = πῶς δύσκολόν ἐστι), neg. phrase with *udobĭ* 'easy' (9.96).

SCr. *težak*, Boh. *těžký* (or *obtížný*) 'heavy' (15.81) and 'difficult' (Pol. *ciężki*, Russ. *tjaželyj* in phrases with 'work, task, problem', etc., but not in phrases 'it is difficult to').

Pol. *trudny*, Russ. *trudnyj*, derivs. of forms = ChSl. *trudŭ* 'toil, pains' : Lat. *trūdere* 'thrust, press', OE *þrēat* 'throng, oppression, distress', etc. (cf. NE *threaten* 18.44). Walde-P. 1.755. Brückner 577.

7. Skt. *duṣ-kara-*, etc., opp. of *su-kara-*, etc. 'easy' (9.96).

9.98 TRY[1]

(= Make Trial of, Test)

Grk.	δοκιμάζω, πειράω	Goth.	*kiusan, kausjan, fraisan*	Lith.	*bandyti, mėginti*
NG	δοκιμάζω	ON	*reyna, freista*	Lett.	*mēg'ināt, mēdzināt*
Lat.	*experīrī, temptāre, probāre*	Dan.	*prøve*	ChSl.	*iskusiti*
It.	*provare, tentare*	Sw.	*pröva*	SCr.	*pokušati, probati*
Fr.	*essayer, éprouver, tenter*	OE	*fandian, costian*	Boh.	*skoušeti, pokusiti*
Sp.	*probar*	ME	*fonde, prove, assay, essay, trie*	Pol.	*próbować*
Rum.	*încerca*	NE	*try*	Russ.	*probovat'*
Ir.	*promaim*	Du.	*probeeren, beproeven*	Skt.	*parīkṣ-*
NIr.	*fromhaim, triailim*	OHG	*corōn, costōn*	Av.	. . . .
W.	*profi*	MHG	*prueven, versuochen*		
Br.	*esaat*	NHG	*probieren, prüfen, versuchen*		

'Try' is understood here as 'make trial of, test', though many of the words, like NE *try*, came to be used with the infinitive in the sense of 'attempt, endeavor' (9.99). For the sake of brevity these two notions may be referred to as 'try'[1] and 'try'[2]. The semantic sources are various, as 'get through' (through 'experience' to 'try'), 'approve', 'weigh', 'try to find out, seek, ask', 'separate, sift', 'look around, inspect'.

Several of the words cover also 'approve', partly secondary (as make a test with favorable result), but the earlier sense in the case of Lat. *probāre* with its derivs., which, in addition, show the sense 'prove' = 'establish as true'.

Many of the words came to be used for 'tempt', especially in biblical language and in the bad sense; in some this became the dominant use and without necessarily bad sense. In fact, the majority of the words for 'tempt' are the same as, or cognate with, some of those listed here. There are, of course, others of quite different origin, based on notions like 'lead into, invite, attract, allure, entice'.

Several of the words are also used more specifically with reference to food, that is, as 'taste' (15.31).

1. Grk. δοκιμάζω, fr. δόκιμος 'approved' : δοκέω 'seem, seem good', Lat. *decet* 'is proper', and, with different semantic development, Grk. διδάσκω 'teach', Lat. *discere* 'learn', *docēre* 'teach', all prob. fr. notion of 'receive' (hence 'acceptable') as in Grk. δέκομαι 'receive'. Walde-P. 1.782 ff. Boisacq 172, 194.

Grk. πειράω ('try' in both senses Hom.+), πειράζω (mostly 'try'[1], later also 'tempt' and sometimes 'try'[2]) : πεῖρα 'trial, attempt', Lat. *experīrī* 'try, experience', *perīculum* 'trial, experiment, danger', prob. the same root **per-* as in Grk. πέρᾶν 'beyond, across', πείρω 'pierce', Lat. *per* 'through', etc. Walde-P. 2.88 ff. Boisacq 756 f. Ernout-M. 756 f.

2. Lat. *experīrī* : Grk. πειράω, etc. (above, 1).

Lat. *temptāre* (later spelling *tentāre*) 'feel of', mostly 'try'[2], also 'attack, incite' (> It. *tentare*, Fr. *tenter*, Sp. *tentar* in various senses including 'try' and 'tempt'), prob. : Lith. *tempti* 'stretch' (cf. Lat. *tempus* 'time'), fr. an extension of IE **ten-* in Grk. τείνω, Lat. *tendere*, Skt. *tan-* 'stretch', Lat. *tenēre* 'hold', etc. Walde-P. 1.721 f. Ernout-M. 1024.

Lat. *probāre* 'approve, find good', 'try'[1], and 'prove', first sense the earliest, Osc. *prúfatted* 'approved', deriv. of *probus* 'good, upright', fr. **pro-bhwo-* (cf. *superbus*) : Skt. *pra-bhu-*, 'excelling, eminent, mighty', orig. 'being in front'. Hence It. *provare*, OFr. *prover* (Fr. *prouver* 'prove'; as 'try' replaced by *éprouver*, but this also 'prove' and esp. 'experience'), Sp. *probar*, and similar forms (partly through Fr., also partly through sb. MLat. *proba*, a back-formation to *probāre*) in Celtic, Gmc., and Slavic. Walde-P. 2.37. Ernout-M. 812 f. REW 6764.

It. *assaggiare* (now esp. 'taste'), OFr. *a(s)sayer*, Fr. *essayer*, derivs. of It. *saggio*, OFr. *assai*, *essai* 'trial', fr. late Lat. *exagium* 'weighing, balance' (: *exigere* 'weigh, try' with recomposition). REW 2932. Gamillscheg 384 f. Wartburg 3.255 ff.

Rum. *cerca*, orig. 'seek' (= It. *cercare*, Fr. *chercher*, 11.31), now mostly 'try', for which esp. *încerca*.

3. Ir. *promaim*, NIr. *fromhaim*, W. *profi*, fr. Lat. *probāre* (above, 2). Vendryes, De hib. voc. 169. Loth, Mots lat. 1991.

NIr. *triailim*, fr. sb. *triail*, this for NE *trial*, but helped by native *triall*, *triallaim* (9.99).

Br. *esaat*, fr. sb. *esa(e)*, this fr. Fr. *essai*. Henry 116.

4. Goth. *(ga)kiusan* (reg. for δοκιμάζω; also *us-*, but mostly for ἀποδοκιμάζω 'disapprove, reject'), OE *costian*, OHG *corōn*, *costōn*, MHG, NHG *kosten* (now mostly 'taste') : OE *cēosan* 'choose', Goth. *kausjan* (with gen. for γεύομαι, but with acc. for δοκιμάζω), Grk. γεύομαι, Lat. *gustāre* 'taste, enjoy' (15.31), Skt. *juṣ-* 'enjoy', IE **ĝeus-*, orig. sense 'try' > 'taste', 'choose' and 'enjoy', or conversely 'taste' > 'try', 'choose' and 'enjoy'? Walde-P. 1.568 f. Ernout-M. 439. Walde-H. 1.628 f. Feist 312 f.

Goth. *fraisan* (reg. for πειράζω, partly 'make trial of', but esp. 'tempt'), ON *freista*, ODan. *freste*, Sw. *fresta* ('try', but esp. 'tempt') : OE *frāsian* 'ask, tempt', OHG *freisōn* 'be in danger'; perh. : Grk. πειράω, etc. (above, 1), but various other possibilities. Walde-P. 1.29. Falk-Torp 275 f. Feist 162.

ON *reyna*, deriv. of *raun* 'trial' : Grk. ἔρευνα 'inquiry, search', ἐρέω 'ask', etc. Walde-P. 2.356. Falk-Torp 936.

OE *fandian*, ME *fonde* (OHG *fantōn* rare) : OE *findan* 'find', etc. (11.32). Walde-P. 2.27. NED s.vv. *fand*, *fond*.

ME, NE *prove* (usual word for 'try'[1] in Bible, and still in technical use with reference to guns, etc. (e.g. *proving grounds*); but also old and now mostly 'establish as true'), fr. OFr. *prover* (above, 2), whence also MLG *prōven* (> Dan. *prøve*, Sw. *pröva*), Du. *proeven* (now mostly 'taste'), *beproeven*, MHG *prueven*, NHG *prüfen* (esp. 'examine'). Cf. also, fr. Lat. *probāre* (in part through sb. MLat. *proba*, back-formation to *probāre*), Du. *probeeren*, NHG *probieren* (> Dan. *probere*, Sw. *probera*), NHG *proben*, *erproben*, NE *probe*, etc. NED

s.v. *prove*. Falk-Torp 850, 851. Weigand-H. 2.476, 485.

ME *assay*, *essay*, fr. Fr. *a(s)sayer*, *essayer* (above, 2). NED s.vv. *assay* and *essay*.

ME *trie*, NE *try*, in earliest use 'separate' the good, 'sift', etc. (as still in *try out fat*, etc.), fr. OFr. *trier* 'separate', this prob. (despite Prov. *triar*) fr. VLat. **trītāre* (It. *tritare* 'rub down, pulverize, cut into small pieces', formerly also 'thresh' grain), this fr. Lat. *terere*, pple. *trītus* 'rub' (9.31) and also 'thresh' (8.34). NED s.v. *try*. REW 8922. Gamillscheg 863.

NE *test*, first used with reference to metals; now more generic but stronger than *try*, fr. sb. *test* 'cupel for treating metals' (cf. *test tube*), fr. Lat. *testum* = *testa* 'potsherd, earthen vessel'. NED s.v.

MHG *versuochen*, NHG *versuchen* (in various senses, but esp. 'try'[1] and 'tempt', now also 'try'[2], cpd. of *suochen*, *suchen* 'seek' (11.31). Weigand-H. 1166. Paul, Deutsches Wtb. 603.

5. Lith. *bandyti* : OPruss. *perbanda* 'tempts', *perbandan* (acc. sg.) 'temptation', outside connection?

Lith. *mėginti* (> Lett. *mēg'ināt*), Lett. *mēdzināt* : Lith. *mėgti* 'be pleasing to', now trans. 'like, be fond of', Lett. *mēgt* 'be able, be accustomed', outside connections dub. Walde-P. 2.256. Mühl.-Endz. 2.612, 613.

6. ChSl. *iskusiti* (in Gospels reg. for both δοκιμάζω and πειράζω; also *okušati*, *pokušati; vŭkusiti* reg. for 'taste' lit. and fig.), SCr. *(po)kušati*, Boh. *zkoušeti* (also *zkusiti*, *pokusiti*, but mostly 'taste' or 'perceive, experience, suffer', *pokoušeti* 'tease, tempt'; Pol. *kusić* with cpds., and Russ. *iskusit'* 'tempt'), cpds. of *kusiti*, loanword fr. Goth. *kausjan* (above, 4). Berneker 652 f. Stender-Petersen 372 f. Otherwise Brückner 285.

SCr. *probati*, Pol. *próbować*, Russ. *probovat'*, through sb. (= late Lat. *proba*) fr. Lat. *probāre* (above, 2).

7. Skt. *parīkṣ-*, lit. 'look around', hence 'inspect, examine, try', cpd. of *īkṣ-* 'see, look' (15.51).

9.99 TRY[2]

(Try to = Attempt, Endeavor)

Grk.	πειράω, ζητέω	Goth.	*sōkjan*	Lith.	*bandyti, mėginti*
NG	προσπαθῶ, δοκιμάζω, πασκίζω	ON	*leita við*	Lett.	*raudzīt*
Lat.	*cōnārī*	Dan.	*forsøge*	ChSl.	*iskati*
It.	*provare, tentare, procurare, cercare*	Sw.	*försöka*	SCr.	*pokušati*
Fr.	*essayer, tâcher, tenter, chercher*	OE	*sēcan, onginnan*	Boh.	*pokusiti se, snažiti se*
Sp.	*procurar*	ME	*seke, endover, fonde*	Pol.	*starać się*
Rum.	*încerca, cauta, umbla*	NE	*try (endeavor, attempt, seek, essay)*	Russ.	*starat'sja*
Ir.	*triallaim*	Du.	*pogen, trachten*	Skt.	*yat-*
NIr.	*tabhraim iarracht ar*	OHG	*suohhen*	Av.	. . . .
W.	*ceisio*	MHG	*suochen*		
Br.	*esaat*	NHG	*versuchen*		

Many of the words for 'try'[2] = 'attempt, endeavor' are the same as those for 'try'[2] = 'make trial of, test', which came to be used with the infinitive, like NE *try to*.

Many are words for 'seek', which came to be used with the infinitive, like NE *seek to* (now mostly lit.). Other sources are 'take care of, attend to', 'reflect upon, consider', 'begin, undertake', 'yearn for', and 'make an effort'. But some words in which the strenuous effort is still felt are omitted, e.g. NG πολεμῶ orig. 'make war', now pop. 'struggle, try hard', NE *strive* orig. 'contend', NHG *bemühen*.

1. Words for 'try'[1] (9.98) used also for 'try'[2].

Grk. πειράω, NG δοκιμάζω (often 'try'[2] in pop. speech), It. *provare* (use for 'try'[2] not in most dicts., but common according to informants), *tentare*, Fr. *essayer*, *tenter*, Rum. *încerca*, Br. *esaat*, ME *fonde* (NED s.v. *fand*, 5), NE *try* (*try to* since 17th. cent.), NHG *versuchen* (with infin. since 16th. cent.; hence the similar use of Dan. *forsøge*, Sw. *försöka*), Lith. *bandyti*, *mėginti*, SCr. *pokušati*, Boh. *skoušeti*, but esp. refl. *pokusiti se* in this sense.

2. Words for 'seek' (11.31), used also (some of the preceding also belong here in orig.) with infin. for 'try'[2].

Grk. ζητέω (with infin. Hdt.+; reg. word for this sense in NT, and rendered by words for 'seek' in the Vulgate, Goth., OE and ChSl. versions); It. *cercare*, Fr. *chercher*, Rum. *cauta*, W. *ceisio*, Goth. *sōkjan*, ON *leita (við)*, OE *sēcan*, ME *seke*, NE *seek*, OHG *suohhen*, MHG *suochen*, ChSl. *iskati* (SCr. *tražiti*, Boh. *hledati* so used in NT).

3. Grk. προσπαθέω 'feel passionate love for' (: πάθος 'emotion, passion,' 16.12), NG with νά clause (= old infin.) 'try to'.

Similarly, fr. the same root, NG pop. πασκίζω, deriv. of πάσκω (πάσχω) 'suffer, experience'.

4. Lat. *cōnārī*, etym. dub. Walde-P. 1.398 f. Ernout-M. 213. Walde-H. 1.262.

It. *procurare*, Sp. *procurar*, fr. Lat. *prōcūrāre* 'take care of, attend to' (whence also Fr. *procurer* > ME, NE *procure* with different semantic development), deriv. of *cūra* 'care' (16.14).

Fr. *tâcher*, deriv. of *tâche* 'task', or blend of **tastāre* 'feel' (It. *tastare*, Fr. *tâter*) with Fr. *chercher* 'seek'. REW 8595. Gamillscheg 828.

Rum. *umbla* 'walk' (10.45) also used with *să* for 'try'[2]. Tiktin 1676. Șaineanu s.v. *tâcher*.

5. Ir. *triallaim* : *triall* 'attempt, purpose', orig. 'journey' (?), fr. **tre-ell-* cpd. of *ell-* 'go, set in motion' (10.47). Pedersen 2.511.

NIr. *tabhraim* (or *tugaim*) *iarracht ar*, lit. 'give effort to', phrase with *iarracht* 'attempt, effort' : *iarraim* 'seek' (11.31).

6. OE *onginnan* 'begin' (14.25), sometimes with infin. 'attempt, try' and glossing Lat. *cōnārī*.

NE *endeavor*, fr. late ME *endevoir*, *endover*, *endever* 'exert oneself', fr. *en-* and *devoir* 'duty', hence orig. 'take on as one's duty'. NED s.v.

Du. *pogen*, etym.? Franck-v. W. 514.

Du. *trachten* = NHG *trachten* (with *nach* or *danach*), fr. OHG *trahtōn* 'consider, reflect upon' (cf. NHG *betrachten*), fr. Lat. *tractāre* 'handle, manage, treat' and 'consider'. Franck-v. W. 705. Weigand-H. 2.1057.

7. Lett. *raudzīt* 'see, look at, pay attention to' and with infin. 'try' : *raugs* 'pupil of the eye' and perh. : Russ. *ruž'* 'face', *na-ruzy* 'outside'. Mühl.-Endz. 3.486.

8. Pol. *starać się*, Russ. *starat'sja* = SCr., Boh. *starati se* 'be anxious, take care of, be concerned with, busy with', orig. 'grow old', derivs. of word for 'old', ChSl. *starŭ*, etc. (14.15). Old age was associated with care (cf. Boh. *starost* in both senses), and the latter notion became dominant. Miklosich 320. Brückner 513, 514. Otherwise (fr. **ster-* in Grk. στερεός, NHG *starr*, etc. 'firm, stiff') Walde-P. 2.628; Persson, Beiträge 430.

Boh. *snažiti se* (Pol. *snażyć się* obs.), fr. *snaha* 'effort' = SCr. *snaga* 'strength', etc. Miklosich 312. Brückner 504.

9. Skt. *yat-* used in various senses, but esp. 'exert oneself, be eager for, strive for' (followed by case-forms or infin.) = Av. *yat-* 'set in motion, be active, zealous' : W. (arch.) *add-iad, add-iant* 'longing', Ir. *ēt* 'zeal, jealousy', many other connections dub. Walde-P. 1.197.

9.992 WAY, MANNER

Grk.	*τρόπος*	Goth.	*haidus*	Lith.	*būdas*
NG	*τρόπος*	ON	*-vīs*	Lett.	*veids, vīse*(?)
Lat.	*modus*	Dan.	*maade* (*vis, sæt*)	ChSl.	*obrazŭ*
It.	*modo, maniera*	Sw.	*sätt* (*vis*)	SCr.	*način*
Fr.	*façon, manière, mode*	OE	*wīse* (*weg*)	Boh.	*způsob*
Sp.	*modo, manera, forma*	ME	*wise, weie, manere*	Pol.	*sposób*
Rum.	*chip, fel*	NE	*way, manner* (*wise*)	Russ.	*obraz*
Ir.	*mod, conar*	Du.	*wijze*	Skt.	*prakāra-*
NIr.	*modh*	OHG	*wīsa*	Av.	. . . .
W.	*modd*	MHG	*wīse*		
Br.	*doare*	NHG	*weise, art*		

Several of the words for 'way, manner' (of doing something) are also used for the 'kind, sort' (of things), and still others must have passed through this stage, especially those based upon 'form, appearance' or the like. The diverse notions which have been generalized to 'manner' include 'turn, direction', 'way' (= 'road'), 'measure', 'handling, conduct, performance', 'arrangement, order', and 'form, appearance'.

The use of such words has spread at the expense, but by no means to the exclusion, of the old adverbs of manner formed from adjectives or pronouns, in such well-known types as Grk. *καλῶς*, Lat. *bene*, Goth. *waila*, NE *well*, ChSl. *dobrě*, all 'in a good manner, well', or Lat. *ita*, Skt. *tathā*, OE *þus*, etc. 'in this manner, thus'. Conversely, NE *wise* has become virtually an adverbial ending in *likewise, otherwise*, etc., and late Lat. phrases with *mente*, abl. of *mēns* 'mind, disposition', have given rise to the new adverbial ending, It., Sp. *-mente*, Fr. *-ment*.

1. Grk. *τρόπος*, orig. 'turn, direction' : *τρέπω* 'turn' (10.12).

2. Lat. *modus* (> It., Sp. *modo*, Fr. *mode*), earliest sense 'measure', fr. the root of Lat. *medērī* 'care for, heal', *meditārī* 'think about', Grk. *μέδομαι* 'be mindful of', Goth. *mitan* 'measure', etc. Walde-P. 2.259 f. Ernout-M. 599, 622 ff. Walde-H. 2.56.

It. *maniera*, Fr. *manière*, Sp. *manera*, fr. form of Lat. *manuārius* 'belonging to the hand', deriv. of *manus* 'hand'. Semantic development through '(way of) handling'. REW 5332. Gamillscheg 586.

Fr. *façon*, fr. Lat. *factiō* 'party, class' (also rarely 'conduct') fr. *facere* 'do, make'. REW 3133. Gamillscheg 401.

Sp. *forma* 'form' (12.51), also 'manner'.

Rum. *chip*, in earliest use 'statue, portrait', hence 'form, appearance' and finally 'kind' and 'manner', through Slavic (SCr. *kip*), fr. Hung. *kep* 'statue, portrait, form'. Tiktin 343 f. Berneker 504.

Rum. *fel* ('kind, sort', and 'manner'), fr. Hung. *fel* in phrases like *minden féle* 'all kinds of'. Tiktin 614 f.

3. Ir. *mod*, NIr. *modh*, W. *modd*, fr. Lat. *modus* (above, 2). Vendryes, De hib. voc. 157. Loth, Mots lat. 188.

Ir. *conar* 'road' (10.71), also 'way, manner' (Laws, Gloss. 174).

Br. *doare*, also and orig. 'appearance' : W. *dwyrain* 'east' (through 'sunrise'), perh. fr. a cpd. of the root in Ir. *rigim* 'stretch out', etc. Pedersen 1.526, 2.596 with 677. Henry 103 f. (with different root connection).

4. Goth. *haidus* : ON *heiðr* 'honor', OE *hād* 'rank, condition, kind', Skt. *ketu-* 'brightness, light, appearance, form'. Semantic development 'brightness' > 'appearance, kind' > (Goth.) 'manner'. Walde-P. 2.537. Feist 231.

ON *vīs* (in phrase *oðru vīs* 'otherwise'), Dan., Sw. *vis* (in phrases for 'likewise', 'in this wise', etc.), OE *wīse*, ME, NE *wise* (NE archaic except in *likewise, otherwise*, etc.), Du. *wijze*, OHG *wīsa*, MHG *wīse*, NHG *weise*, all orig. 'appearance' : Grk. *εἶδος* 'appearance, form, kind', fr. root **weid-* 'see'. Walde-P. 1.239. Weigand-H. 2.1231.

Dan. *maade*, orig. (and still bibl.) 'measure' : Goth. *mitan*, etc. 'measure', semantic development as in Lat. *modus*. Falk-Torp 684.

Dan. *sæt*, Sw. *sätt* (Dan. in phrases, Sw. usual word) : Dan. *sætte*, Sw. *sätte* 'set', with development through 'how a thing is set, arrangement'. Cf. NE *set* of a garment, etc. Falk-Torp 1231.

ME *weie, waye*, NE *way* (OE *weg* once in this sense), orig. 'road' (10.71). Extension from 'way' by which one goes to 'way' in which one does anything. NED s.v. *way*.

ME *manere*, NE *manner*, fr. Anglo-Fr. *manere* = Fr. *manière* (above, 2).

MHG *art* 'birth, descent, nature', NHG 'kind, sort' (of thing) and 'manner' (of doing something), prob. (but disputed) fr. Lat. *ars, artis* 'skill, art' in its secondary sense of 'character, conduct'. Falk-Torp 33. Weigand-H. 1.88. Kluge-G. 24.

5. Lith. *būdas*, also and earliest sense 'character', fr. the root of *būti* 'be'. Cf. Grk. *φύσις* 'nature, character' fr. the same IE root.

Lett. *veids* 'appearance, form' and 'kind, manner' (Dravneek) = Lith. *veidas* 'face' : Grk. *εἶδος* 'appearance, kind', etc. Mühl.-Endz. 4.522.

Lett. *vīse* (Ulman; not in Mühl.-Endz.), fr. MHG or MLG *wise* (above, 4).

6. ChSl. *obrazŭ* 'form, kind, image' (Pol. *obraz* 'image, picture', etc. 9.87), freq. also for *τρόπος* in Supr. (in the Gospels the passages with *τρόπος* are rendered by advs. or conjs. of manner, e.g. Mt. 23.37), Russ. *obraz* also 'manner'.

SCr. *način*, cpd. of *čin* 'form, rank, act' = ChSl. *činŭ* 'arrangement, order'. Berneker 156.

Boh. *způsob*, Pol. *sposób*, cpds. of stem seen in dat. sg. of refl. pron., ChSl. *sebě*, Boh. *sobě*, Pol. *sobie*. Cf. ChSl. *sobĭstvo* 'substance', Boh. *osoba* 'person', etc. Miklosich 331. Brückner 510.

7. Skt. *prakāra-* (also 'means, sort, kind') fr. *pra-kṛ-* 'perform, effect', cpd. of *kṛ-* 'do make'.

9.993 HAPPEN

Grk.	*τυγχάνω, συμβαίνω, συμπίπτω*	Goth.	*gadaban*	Lith.	*atsitikti*
NG	*τυχαίνω, συμβαίνω*	ON	*bera, henda*	Lett.	*nuotikt*
Lat.	*accidere, contingere, ēvenīre*	Dan.	*hænde, tildrage sik, ske*	ChSl.	*prikljutiti sę, (sŭ-)lučiti sę*
It.	*accadere, avvenire, darsi*	Sw.	*hända, inträffa, ske*	SCr.	*dogoditi se, zbiti se* (*slučiti se*)
Fr.	*arriver, advenir, se passer*	OE	*gebyrian, gelimpan, gescēon*	Boh.	*přihoditi se, státi se*
Sp.	*acontecer, suceder, pasar, sobrevenir, ocurrir*	ME	*happe, happene*	Pol.	*trafić się, wydarzyć się, stać się*
Rum.	*se întîmpla*	NE	*happen*	Russ.	*slučit'sja, prikljutit'sja*
Ir.	*tecmaing* (3sg.)	Du.	*gebeuren*	Skt.	*nipat-, udpad-*
NIr.	*teagmhaim*	OHG	*giburien, gascehan*	Av.	. . . .
W.	*digwydd, damweinio*	MHG	*geschehen*		
Br.	*c'hoarvezout, darvezout, digouezout*	NHG	*geschehen, sich ereignen, sich treffen*		

NE *happen* by etymology and early use referred to a chance occurrence, as still felt in phrases like *I happened to be there.* But it became also the most general verb to express any event, with no necessary implication of chance. Cf. NED s.v. It is in this wider sense that the heading is to be understood. But in several languages there is no equally common general term, and the notion may be expressed in a variety of ways with some slight difference of nuance. The selection listed is somewhat unbalanced (cf. the numerous NIr. phrases in McKenna).

The most frequent connections are with verbs for 'fall' (Grk., Lat., W., Br., Skt.; cf. also NE *befall* now arch.) or 'come' ('out', 'to' or 'together'). In several cases 'be fitting' is the immediate antecedent. Some are reflexives of verbs for 'stand', 'put' (cf. also NE *take place*, NHG *stattfinden*), or 'hit'. But there are still other sources.

1. Grk. *τυγχάνω*, aor. *ἔτυχον*, NG *τυχαίνω* (new pres. fr. aor.), beside *τύχη* 'fortune, good fortune', prob. : *τεύχω* 'make, prepare', Goth. *daug*, OE *deag*, OHG *toug* 'is of use', etc. Walde-P. 1.847. LS s.v. *τυγχάνω*, end.

Grk. *συμβαίνω*, cpd. of *συν-* 'together' and *βαίνω* 'go, walk'.

Grk. *συμπίπτω* 'fall together', also 'happen'.

2. Lat. *accidere*, cpd. of *cadere* 'fall' (10.23), whence also the re-formation It. *accadere*, and Sp. *suceder* (Lat. *succidere*) 'follow, succeed', impers. 'happen'. Ernout-M. 126. REW 61.

Lat. *contingere* (> Sp. *acontecer*), cpd. of *con-* 'together' and *tangere* 'touch' (15.71). Ernout-M. 1016 f. REW 2184.

Lat. *ēvenīre*, cpd. of *ē-* 'out' and *venīre* 'come', whence also (Lat. *advenīre* 'come to, arrive'), It. *avvenire*, Fr. *avenir*, now *advenir*, and Sp. *sobrevenir*, Ernout-M. 108. REW 216.

It. *darsi*, refl. of *dare* 'give'.

Fr. *arriver*, also and orig. 'arrive' (10.55).

Fr. *se passer*, refl. of *passer* 'pass', fr. VLat. **passare*, deriv. of *passus* 'step'. Sp. *pasar* 'pass' and impers. 'happen'. Cf. NE *come to pass*. Ernout-M. 728. REW 6267.

OFr. *occurrir*, NE *occur*, Sp. *ocurrir*, fr. Lat. *occurrere* 'run into, meet', cpd. of *currere* 'run'. NED s.v. *occur*, vb.

Rum. *se întîmpla*, deriv. of Lat. *tempus* 'time', through a parallel VLat.

**templum* in this sense? Tiktin 835. Puşcariu 884.

3. Ir. *tecmaing, donecmaing* (3sg.), etc., NIr. *teagmhaim*, cpd. (*to-in-com-*) of *icc-* in *do-iccim, ticim* 'come' (10.48) Pedersen 2.555.

NIr. *imthighim* 'go' (cpd. of *tēighim* 'go', 10.47) also 'happen', as *cad d'imthigh air* 'what happened to him'.

W. *digwydd*, Br. *digouezout*, cpds. of W. *cwyddo*, Br. *koueza* 'fall' (10.23).

W. *damweinio*, fr. sb. *damwain*, cpd. of *chwaen* 'change, hap.'

Br. *darvezout, darvout*, cpd. of *dar-* (*d-ar-*) and *beza* 'be', like W. *darfod* 'finish'. Pedersen 2.442.

Br. *c'hoarvezout, c'hoarvout*, Corn. *wharfos*, cpds. of the vb. 'be', first part seen also in simplex MW *chweris, chweiris*, Corn. *whyris* 'it happened', perh. : NHG *schwer* 'heavy', etc. with development through 'fall'(?). Loth RC 49.372 ff. (vs. Pedersen 2.442). H. Lewis, BBCS 4.136 f.

4. Goth. *gadaban* 'be fitting' (9.943) and 'happen' (Mk. 10.32).

ON *bera* 'bear, carry' (10.61), often impers. 'happen'.

ON *henda*, orig. 'seize, catch', like OE *gehendan* (both: ON *hǫnd*, OE *hand* 'hand,' with parallel forms in Goth. *frahinþan*, OE *hentan* 'seize'), hence also 'take an interest in, concern', etc. and sometimes 'happen', as reg. Dan. *hænde*, Sw. *hända*. Falk-Torp. 447. Hellquist 386.

Dan. *tildrage sik*, cpd. of *drage* 'draw', but in this sense after MLG *sik tōdragen* (Du. *zich toedragen*) = NHG *sich zutragen*. Falk-Torp 1259.

Dan., Sw. *ske*, fr. MLG *schēn* : NHG *geschehen*, etc. (below). Falk-Torp 989.

Sw. *inträffa* 'arrive' and 'happen', fr. NHG *eintreffen* 'arrive' and 'be realized'. Falk-Torp 1291.

OE *gebyrian*, Du. *gebeuren*, OHG *giburien* (NHG *gebühren* 'be proper, belong') : OE *beran*, etc. 'bear, carry'. Cf. the use of Grk. *συμφέρω* 'bring together', 'be useful, fitting' and sometimes 'happen', with sb. *συμφορά* 'event, hap, mishap'. Walde-P. 2.156. Falk-Torp 118. Franck-v. W. 57.

OE *gelimpan*, cpd. of *limpan* 'happen' and 'pertain to', beside *gelimplīc* 'suitable' : OHG (*gi*)*limfan* 'be fitting', etc. (see 9.943).

OE *gescēon*, OHG *gascehan*, MHG, NHG *geschehen*, cpds. of OE *scēon* 'go quickly' (also 'fall to one's lot'), OHG *scehan*, MHG *schehen* 'move quickly' : ChSl. *skočiti* 'spring, jump', etc. Walde-P. 2.556. Weigand-H. 1.695.

ME *happe, happene*, NE *happen*, fr. sb. *hap* 'chance, fortune', this fr. ON *happ* id. (16.17).

NHG *sich ereignen*, fr. MHG *erougnen, erougen*, OHG *irougen* 'show', deriv. of *ouga* 'eye'. Weigand-H. 1.459. Kluge-G. 136.

NHG also *sich treffen, sich zutragen*, refl. of *treffen* 'hit', *tragen* 'carry'; *begegnen* 'meet' (*ist ihm begegnet* 'happened to him'), *vorkommen* 'come forth' (*das kann vorkommen* 'that may happen').

5. Lith. *atsitikti*, Lett. *nuotikt*, cpds. of Lith. *tikti* 'fit, suit', Lett. *tikt* 'be pleasing' (see 9.943).

6. ChSl. *prikljutiti sę* 'fall to one's lot', 'fit', and 'happen' (Lk. 24.14; cf. also *po prikljutaju* 'by chance' Lk. 10.31), Russ. *prikljutit'sja* (less common than *slučit'sja*), deriv. of *kljuka* 'hook, crutch', with development through 'hook into', 'fit', etc. Berneker 528.

ChSl. *lučiti sę, sŭlučiti sę* (freq. for 'happen' in Supr.), SCr. *slučiti se*, Russ. *slučit'sja* (Boh. *lučiti* 'shoot, throw', Pol. *luczyt'* 'shoot, hit'), prob. : Lith. *laukti* 'wait for', OPruss. *laukīt* 'seek', Grk. λεύσσω, Skt. *loc-* 'look', with development 'look' > 'aim at' > 'fit' > 'happen'? Walde-P. 2.411. Berneker 742 f. Brückner 313 f.

ChSl. *byti* 'be' sometimes 'happen' (e.g. Mk. 10.32), and so reg. SCr. *zbiti se*. SCr. *dogoditi se*, Boh. *přihoditi se* : ChSl. *u-goditi* 'be pleasing', *godŭ* 'time', Russ. *godit'sja* 'be suitable', etc. Berneker 316 ff.

Boh. *státi*, Pol. *stać się*, refl. of vbs. for 'stand', hence 'take place, happen'.

Boh. *dīti se*, Pol. *dziać się* refl. of vbs. for 'put, do' (ChSl. *děti*, etc. 12.12, 9.110).

Pol. *wydarzyć się*, refl. cpd. of *darzyć* 'present with, bestow', deriv. of *dar* 'gift' (ChSl. *darŭ* : Grk. δῶρον 'gift').

Pol. *trafić się*, refl. of *trafić* 'hit', fr. NHG *treffen*, and whole phrase like NHG *sich treffen*. Brückner 574.

7. Skt. *nipat-*, cpd. of *ni-* 'down' and *pat-* 'fly, fall'.

Skt. *udpad-*, cpd. of *ud* 'up, out' and *pad-* 'fall, go'.

CHAPTER 10

MOTION; LOCOMOTION, TRANSPORTATION, NAVIGATION

10.11	Move (vb.)	10.54	Overtake
10.12	Turn (vb.)	10.55	Arrive, Reach
10.13	Turn Around	10.56	Approach (vb.)
10.14	Wind, Wrap (vb.)	10.57	Enter
10.15	Roll (vb.)	10.61	Carry (Bear)
10.21	Rise (vb.)	10.62	Bring
10.22	Raise, Lift	10.63	Send
10.23	Fall (vb.)	10.64	Lead (vb.)
10.24	Drop (sb., of Liquid)	10.65	Drive (vb. trans.)
10.25	Throw (vb.)	10.66	Ride (vb.)
10.26	Shake (vb. trans.)	10.67	Push, Shove (vb.)
10.31	Boil (vb. intr.)	10.71	Road
10.32	Flow (vb.)	10.72	Path
10.33	Sink (vb.)	10.73	Street
10.34	Float (vb.)	10.74	Bridge
10.35	Swim (vb.)	10.75	Carriage, Wagon, Cart
10.36	Sail (vb.)	10.76	Wheel
10.37	Fly (vb.)	10.77	Axle
10.38	Blow (vb. intr.)	10.78	Yoke
10.41	Creep, Crawl	10.81	Ship
10.42	Slide, Slip (vb.)	10.82	Sailor
10.43	Jump, Leap (vb.)	10.83	Boat
10.44	Dance (vb.)	10.84	Raft
10.45	Walk (vb.)	10.85	Oar
10.46	Run (vb.)	10.852	Row (vb.)
10.47	Go	10.86	Rudder
10.48	Come	10.87	Mast
10.49	Go Away, Depart	10.88	Sail (sb.)
10.51	Flee	10.89	Anchor
10.52	Follow	10.90	Harbor, Port
10.53	Pursue		

10.11 MOVE (vb.)

Grk.	κῑνέω	Goth.	(wagjan, wipōn)	Lith.	judin!i, judēti
NG	κῑνῶ, κουνῶ, σαλεύω	ON	hreyfa, hrœra	Lett.	kustināt, kustēt
Lat.	movēre	Dan.	bevæge (røre)	ChSl.	dvignǫti
It.	m(u)overe	Sw.	röra	SCr.	maknuti, gibati
Fr.	mouvoir, remuer, bouger	OE	styrian, hrēran	Boh.	hnouti, hýbati
		ME	move, styre	Pol.	ruszyć
Sp.	mover	NE	move (stir)	Russ.	dvinut'
Rum.	mișca	Du.	bewegen	Skt.	car-, ṛ-
Ir.	-luur, luadaim	OHG	ruoren, weggen,	Av.	(čar-, ar-)
NIr.	corruighim		wegan		
W.	symud, ysgogi	MHG	rüeren, bewegen		
Br.	finval, flacha	NHG	bewegen (rühren)		

The nouns for 'motion' are not listed, as they are derivatives of the verbs listed here. In these the transitive 'move' = 'put in motion' (the commonest transitive use of NE *move* = 'change the position of', as in *move a chair*, is secondary and of course not intended here, this notion being expressed quite differently in most other languages) and the intransitive 'move' = 'be in motion' are generally expressed by the same, or by differentiated forms of the same, verb. In the majority of cases the transitive use is the primary, with intransitive expressed by middle, passive, or reflexive forms. But the Skt. and Av. roots listed are intransitive, with the transitive expressed by causative forms. A few of the words listed could be, overcome.

Verbs for 'move' are often related to those for 'turn, bend', 'raise', 'carry', 'stir', 'mix', etc. The sense 'move' may result from extension of one of these senses as the more original, or in some cases 'move' may be the more original, and the other uses be due to specialization.

1. Grk. κῑνέω: κίω 'go', Lat. *ciēre, cīre* 'set in motion, excite, summon', IE **kei-*, beside extension **ky-eu* in Grk. σείω 'set in swift motion, drive, chase', mid. 'rush, hasten', Skt. *cyu* in mid. 'move, move away' intr., OPers. *ašiyava* 'set out, marched'. Walde-P. 1.361 ff. Ernout-M. 186. Walde-H. 1.213 f.

Hence NG lit. κῑνῶ, but pop. κουνῶ by blend with κουνῶ 'rock' (a cradle), deriv. of κουνί, κοίνια 'cradle' (fr. Lat. *cunae*). G. Meyer, Neugr. Stud. 3.35.

Grk. σαλεύω 'shake, toss' (10.26), in NG 'stir', 'wag' (as of a dog's tail), also simply 'move' (intr.).

2. Lat. *movēre* (> It. *muovere*, Fr. *mouvoir*, Sp. *mover*; Anglo-Fr. *mover* > ME, NE *move*) : Skt. *mīv-* 'push, press', Av. *ava-mīvāmahi* 'we deprive', Grk.

ἀμεύσασθαι 'pass over, surpass' (also ἀμύνω 'ward off'?). Walde-P. 2.252. Ernout-M. 634 f. REW 5703.

Fr. *remuer*, cpd. of OFr. *muer* 'change' (fr. Lat. *mūtāre*). REW 5785.

Fr. *bouger* (orig. and now only intr.), fr. VLat. **bullicāre* (cf. It. *bulicare*), deriv. of *bullīre* 'bubble' (10.31), whence 'be agitated, move'. REW 1388. Wartburg 1.617 f.

Rum. *mișca*, etym.? Tiktin 995 ("sicherlich Erbwort, aber dunklen Ursprungs"). Not in REW or Pușcariu. Development fr. some deriv. of Lat. *miscēre* 'mix', through the notion of 'stir up, agitate' (as seen in It. *mestare* 'stir', **miscitāre*; cf. OE *hrēran*, etc., below, 4) would be attractive if the phonetic difficulties could be, overcome.

3. Ir. *-luur* (e.g. in *dana-m-luur* 'when I rouse myself'), vbl. n. *luud*, whence Ir. *luadaim, luathaim*, prob. fr. IE **pleu-* in Grk. πλέω 'sail, float', OE *flēotan*, NE *float*, etc. Walde-P. 2.94 f. Pedersen 2.571 f.

NIr. *corruighim*, deriv. of MIr. *corrach* 'uneven, unsteady', this fr. *corr* 'uneven, odd, pointed', prob. fr. IE **kwerp-* in Grk. κρανπός 'turn', etc. (10.12–13). Walde-P. 2.472, (without *corruighim*). Macbain 71.

W. *symud*, fr. MW *symudau* 'change' (for change as in Fr. *remuer*), fr. Lat. *sub-mūtāre* 'change, interchange'. G. S. Lane, Language 8.298.

W. *ysgogi* : Br. *di-skogella* 'shake', ChSl. *skočiti* 'jump', OE *scacan* 'shake', etc., IE **(s)kek-, (s)keg-*. Walde-P. 2.556. Pedersen 1.125.

Br. *finval*, MBr. *fifual* : W. *chwifio* 'stir, wave, brandish', perh. ON *svimma*, OE *swimman*, etc. 'swim' (10.35). Walde-P. 2.524. Henry 122. Stokes 304.

Br. *flacha* (intr.), fr. OFr. *fleschier* (Fr. *fléchir*) 'bend, turn aside' (fr. Lat. *flexicāre*). Henry 123.

---

4. Goth. *ga-wigan*, OHG *wegan* whence caus. Goth. *wagjan*, -*wagjan* (but Goth. forms mostly for σαλεύω 'shake'; OE *wecgan, wagian* also 'shake'), NE *waw, wag*), OHG *weggen*, MHG, NHG *bewegen* (> Dan. *bevæge*) : Skt. *vah-*, Av. *vaz-*, Lat. *vehere*, etc. 'carry, ride', etc., IE **wegh-* (10.66). Walde-P. 1.250. Feist 212. The assumption of two distinct roots **wegh-* (Meillet, BSL 35.2.116) is uncalled for.

Goth. *wipōn* (Mk. 15.29, the only extant Goth. passage where Grk. has κῑνέω, but here also 'shake, wag') : Skt. *vyath-* 'waver, stagger'. Walde-P. 1.318.

ON *hreyfa*, Norw. *røyva*, fr. an IE **kreu-p-*, prob. related to Skt. *krunc-* 'bend' (**kreu-k-*), Lith. *kreipti* 'twist, turn' (**krei-p*), etc., parallel extensions of IE **(s)ker-* in words for 'twist, turn, bend'. Falk-Torp 879 (Walde-P. 2.568 ff. without *hreyfa*).

ON *hrœra*, Sw. *röra*, Dan. *røre*, OE *hrēran*, OHG *ruoren*, MHG *rüeren* (NHG *rühren* now more specialized; cf. Paul, Deutsches Wtb. s.v.), deriv. of IE **(s)ker-* in words for 'twist, turn, bend': Skt. *çrī-*, Grk. κεράννῡμι 'mix', etc. Walde-P. 1.419 f. Falk-Torp 937, 1536. Hellquist 875.

OE *styrian*, ME *styre* (NE *stir*) : ON *styrr* 'tumult', NHG *stören* 'disturb', *zerstören* 'destroy', and with *m*-suffix ON *stormr*, OE, NE *storm*, etc., perh. related to forms without *s*-, Skt. *tvar-* 'hurry', Lat. *turbāre* 'disturb, agitate', OHG *dveran* 'whirl rapidly', IE **twer-*. Walde-P. 1.749. Falk-Torp 1194.

5. Lith. *judinti*, intr. *judēti* : Av. *yuz-*, OPers. *yud-* 'be in commotion', Skt. *yudh-* 'fight', Lat. *iubēre* 'command', IE **yeudh-*. Walde-P. 1.203 f. Ernout-M. 500. Walde-H. 1.725.

Lett. *kustināt, kustēt*, cf. Lith. *kusēti* 'rouse oneself' : Russ. *kiset'* 'swarm', Grk. κῡκάω 'mix'. Berneker 672. Mühl.-Endz. 2.329.

6. ChSl. *dvignǫti* (reg. for κῑνέω and σαλεύω in Gospels; cf. *dviženĳe* = κῑνησις), Russ. *dvinut', dvigat'* (the other Slavic cognates mostly 'raise, lift'), outside connections dub. Berneker 240 suggests *d-vignǫti*, with prefix *d-* (zero grade to Lat. *ad*) and **vignǫti* : Skt. *vij-* 'start up, flee from, tremble', Av. *vij-* 'swing, throw', ON *vīkja* 'recede, give way'. Doubted by Walde-P. 1.235.

SCr. *gibati*, Boh. *hnouti, hýbati*, orig. 'bend' as the other Slavic cognates (9.14). Berneker 366, 373.

SCr. *maknuti, micati* : ChSl. *mŭknǫti sę* 'transire', Pol. *mknąć (się)* 'move away quickly', Lith. *mukti* 'escape, free oneself', Skt. *munc-* 'let loose', IE **meuk-*. Brückner 339. Trautmann 189 f.

Pol. *ruszyć, ruszać* : Boh. *rušiti* 'touch, spoil', Russ. *rušit'*, ChSl. *rušiti* 'destroy', Boh., Russ. *ruch* 'movement', IE **reu-s*-, beside **reu-* in Skt. *ru-* 'break to pieces', Lat. *ruere* 'tear up, dig up'. Brückner 466 f. Walde-P. 2.356 f.

7. Skt. *car-* (and esp. in this sense *cal-*), also 'wander, go about, drive, etc' : Av. *čar-* 'move about, be occupied', Grk. πέλομαι 'come', etc. Skt. *ṛ-* (*ṛṇoti, ṛṇvati*), Av. *ar-* (ərə-, *iyar-, īr-*) 'move', but also 'raise, reach', etc. : Grk. ὄρνῡμι 'rouse, move', Arm. *y-arnem* 'rise', Lat. *orīrī* 'arise, have an origin in', with *s*-extension Goth. *-reisan*, etc. 'rise' (10.21). Walde-P. 1.136 f. Barth. 183.

	10.12 TURN (vb.)	10.13 TURN AROUND (vb.) (Besides those in 10.12)	10.14 WIND, WRAP (vb.)	10.15 ROLL (vb.)
Grk.	*τρέπω, στρέφω*		*ἑλίσσω, τυλίσσω*	*κυλίνδω, κυλίω*
NG	*στρέφω, γυρίζω*		*τυλίγω*	*κυλῶ*
Lat.	*vertere*	*torquēre*	*amicīre*	*volvere*
It.	*voltare, volgere*	*girare, torcere*	*av-(in-)volgere, inviluppare*	*rotolare*
Fr.	*tourner*	*tordre*	*(en)rouler, envelopper*	*rouler*
Sp.	*volver*	*torcer*	*devanar, envolver*	*rodar*
Rum.	*întoarce*	*învîrti*	*încolăci, înfăşura, depăna*	*rostogoli*
Ir.	*sōim*	*impōim*		
NIr.	*iompuighim*	*casaim*	*casaim, cornaim*	*rolaim*
W.	*troi*		*dirwyn*	*rholio, treiglo*
Br.	*trei*		*rodella*	*ruilha*
Goth.	*wandjan*		*-windan*	*-walwjan, waltjan*
ON	*venda, hverfa, snūa*	*rīða*	*vinda, vefja*	*velta*
Dan.	*vende*	*dreje, sno*	*vinde, svøbe, vikle*	*rulle*
Sw.	*vända*	*vrida, sno*	*vinda, veckla*	*rulla*
OE	*wendan*	*þrāwan, wrīþan, tyrnan*	*windan*	*wielwan, wieltan*
ME	*turne*	*writhe*	*winde, wrappe*	*walwe, rolle*
NE	*turn*	*twist*	*wind, wrap*	*roll*
Du.	*wenden, keeren*	*draaien*	*winden, wikkelen*	*wentelen, rollen*
OHG	*wenten, kēran*	*drājen, rīdan*	*wintan*	*welzen, wellen*
MHG	*wenden, kēren*	*dræjen, rīden*	*winden*	*welzen, rollen*
NHG	*wenden, kehren*	*drehen*	*winden, wickeln*	*wälzen, rollen*
Lith.	*kreipti, versti*	*sukti, gręžti*	*vyti, vynioti*	*risti*
Lett.	*verst, griezt*		*tīt, vīt*	*velt, ritināt*
ChSl.	*obratiti*	*krǫtiti*	*(sŭ)viti*	*valiti*
SCr.	*obratiti, okrenuti*	*vrtjeti*	*viti, (o)motati*	*valjati, kotrljati*
Boh.	*obratiti*	*točiti, kroutiti, vrtěti*	*viti, ovinouti*	*váleti*
Pol.	*obrocić*	*kręcić*	*wić, obwinąć*	*toczyć*
Russ.	*povernut'*	*vertet', krutit'*	*vit', zavernut'*	*katit', katat'*
Skt.	*vṛt-, vṛj-, val-*		*vī-*	*vṛt-*
Av.	*urvis-*			

10.12–10.15. Only a partial differentiation is practicable between (10.12) 'turn' in the widest sense 'change the direction of', and (10.13) 'turn around, rotate, revolve, twist' (covering motion around an axis), and again between the latter and certain other more specialized notions involving circular motion, as (10.14) 'turn something about an object', 'wind' thread on a spool, 'wrap' a garment about a person, whence also with change of construction 'wrap' (NE *wind* only rarely so) an object with, as a bundle with twine, a person with a garment, and (10.15) 'roll' in which the central notion seems to be that of progressive movement (not merely around an axis) of, or like that of, a circular or spherical object. These notions doubtless started from quite specific images, such as, for example, the winding of thongs about something, the rolling of a stone, etc. But actually derivatives of the same root may serve for several of these notions in different languages or in the same language. Even where there is a fairly clear difference in dominant value, the idiomatic choice for specific phrases varies from one language to another or even in the same language.

In many languages the same words are used for 'turn' in general and commonly for 'turn around' (often, in fact, the primary sense), even where there are

special words for the latter notion. Thus NE *turn* is far more common for the circular motion than *twist*, which is felt as somewhat strenuous; so Fr. *tourner* vs. *tordre*, etc. But in some languages the circular turning is normally expressed by distinctive words, as Lat. *torquēre* vs. *vertere*, NHG *drehen* vs. *wenden, kehren*. There is considerable interchange between 'turn around, twist' and 'wind' and 'roll'. Definitions are mostly omitted in the following discussion. But the grouping in the lists, despite the overlapping, is roughly approximate for the dominant uses in the several languages.

Most of the forms listed are used transitively, the intransitive being expressed by middle, passive, or reflexive forms, or without change. In a few cases the simple verbs are intransitive, with causative forms or phrases for the transitive use. The difference is ignored in the lists.

1. IE **wert-*, also **werg-*, **werĝh-*, **wreiḱ-*, **wreit-*, all prob. parallel extensions of a simpler **wer-* seen in words for 'worm' (3.84) and others. Walde-P. 1.270 ff. Ernout-M. 1091 ff.

Lat. *vertere;* Lith. *versti*, Lett. *verst;* ChSl. *vrŭtěti* (> Rum. *învîrti*), *vratiti*, esp. (cpd. with *obŭ* 'round') *obratiti* (reg. in Gospels for *στρέφω*), general Slavic, either simplex (now mostly as 'turn around') or cpds. as SCr., Boh. *obratiti*, Pol. *obrocić* (Russ. *obratit'*, but less usual for 'turn' in the literal sense), Russ. *povernut'*, etc.; Skt. *vṛt-* (intr. in act. and mid. forms, trans. in caus.), Av. *varət-* (rare); Goth. *wairþan*, OE *weorþan*, OHG *werdan*, etc. 'become' fr. 'turn' (9.92).

**werg-*. Skt. *vṛj-* (3sg. *vṛṇakti, varjati*); ChSl. *vrĭgą, vrěšti* 'throw', Lat. *vergere* 'bend, incline, turn', Du. *werken* 'warp' (of wood), etc.

**werĝh-*. Lett. *vērzt;* Lith. *veržti* 'squeeze, draw fast, bind', ChSl. *-vrŭzą, -vrěsti* 'bind', with nasal OE *wringan* 'twist, squeeze', etc.

**wreiḱ-*. Av. *urvis-*, (caus. *urvaēsaya-*); Grk. *ῥοικός* 'crooked, bent', OE *wrigian* 'move, wend, turn' (intr., ME also 'turn', trans.), etc.

**wreit-*. ON *rīða*, Sw. *vrida*, OE *wrīþan*, ME, NE *writhe*, OHG *rīdan*, MHG *rīden;* Lith. *risti, riesti*, Lett. *ritināt* (*rietēt* intr.).

2. IE **wel-*, esp. in words for 'roll', 'wind', or 'wrap'. Walde-P. 1.298 ff. Ernout-M. 1132 f. Falk-Torp 1366. Feist 13.

Grk. *εἰλέω, εἰλύω, ἑλίσσω*; Lat. *volvere* (> OIt. *volvere*, It. *volgere, avvolgere*, Sp. *volver, envolver;* VLat. **volvitāre* > It. *voltare, avvoltare*); Ir. *fillim* (mostly 'fold, bend'); Goth. *-walwjan* (cpds. only), *walwisōn*, OE *wielwan*, intr. *wealwian*, ME *walwe* (NE *wallow*); OHG *wellen*; Goth. *waltjan*, ON *velta*, OE *wieltan, wyltan*, Du. *wentelen* (for **weltelen*, Franck-v. W. 787), OHG, MHG *welzen*, NG *wälzen* (caus. to ON *velta*, OHG *welzan, wialz*, etc.); Lett. *velt* (Lith. *velti* 'to feel, felt'); ChSl. *valiti, valjati*, SCr. *valjati*, Boh. *váleti, valiti;* Arm. *gelum* 'twist, wind', etc. For late Skt. *val-*, perh. a Middle Indic form of *vṛt-*, and Av. *var-*, cf. now Tedesco, JAOS 67.100 ff.

3. IE **wei-*, esp. in words for 'wind'. Walde-P. 1.223 ff. Ernout-M. 1106 f.

Lith. *vyti, vynioti;* ChSl. *vĭją, viti, sŭviti*, SCr. *viti*, Boh. *viti, (na)vinouti*, Pol. *wić*, Russ. *vit';* Skt. *vī-* (3sg. pres. *vyayati*, pple. *vīta-);* Lat. *viēre* 'bend, plait', etc.

4. IE **seu-, *seu-k-*. Walde-P. 2.470. Pedersen 2.635 ff.

Ir. *sōim*, cpd. *imbsōim, impōim* (*imb-* 'about', but cpd. not exclusively 'turn around'), NIr. *iompuighim;* Lith. *sukti* 'turn around, twist', ChSl. *sukati*, Boh.

soukati 'wind, twist' (thread, wool, etc.), Russ. *skatat'* 'roll up', *skatit'* 'roll down' etc.; also **seu-p-* in Lith. *supti* 'swing, rock'.

5. Grk. *τρέπω* (Lat. *trepit* 'vertit' only in Festus and prob. fictitious after Grk.) : Skt. *trap-* 'be ashamed or perplexed' (cf. Grk. *ἐντρέπομαι* 'hesitate, feel awe', etc., late and NG 'be ashamed'). Walde-P. 1.756 f.

Grk. *στρέφω* (in late times ousting *τρέπω*, which does not occur in the NT or in NG) : *στρεβλός* 'twisted, bent', *στρόφος* 'string' (fr. 'twisted'?), etc., outside root connection? Boisacq 919.

Grk. *τυλίσσω*, NG *τυλίνω* : *τύλος* 'knot, callus, bolt', *τύλη* 'callus, cushion', ON *þollr* '(young) tree, peg', OE *þol* 'peg', Skt. *tūla-* 'tuft, wisp, cotton', etc., IE **teu-* 'swell'. Walde-P. 1.709 f. Boisacq 990.

Grk. *κυλίνδω, κυλινδέω*, Att. also *κυλῑ́ω*, NG *κυλίω, κυλῶ* : Grk. *κύλινδρος* 'cylinder', *κυλλός* 'twisted, lame', Skt. *kuṇḍala-* 'earring, ring', OHG *scelah*, OE *sceolh* 'oblique, crooked', Lat. *scelus* 'crime, evil deed' (as 'crookedness'), etc. Walde-P. 2.598.

NG *γυρίζω*, fr. *γῦρος* 'ring, circle', *γυρός* 'round, curved' : Arm. *kor* 'crooked, bent', *kuṙn* 'back', etc., SCr. *gura* 'hump', *guriti se* 'contract, hump up (with cold)', etc. Walde-P. 1.556 f. Boisacq 159.

6. Lat. *torquēre* (VLat. **torcere* > It. *torcere*, Fr. *tordre*, Sp. *torcer;* Rum. *toarce* 'spin', cpd. *întoarce* 'turn') : Grk. *ἄτρακτος*, Skt. *tarku-* 'spindle', OHG *drahsil* 'roller', etc. Walde-P. 1.735. REW 8798.

Lat. *amicīre*, usual for 'wrap (oneself) in a garment, throw a garment about (oneself)', cpd. of *am(b)-* 'about' and *iacere* 'throw'. Ernout-M. 43 f. Walde-H. 1.39.

It. *girare* (= Sp. *girar* intr. only), fr. late Lat. *gyrāre*, deriv. of *gyrus* 'circle, circuit', fr. Grk. *γῦρος* (above, 5). Ernout-M. 440. REW 3937.

It. *rotolare*, fr. VLat. **rotulāre*, deriv. of *rotulus*, dim. of *rota* 'wheel'. REW 7396.

Fr. *rouler, enrouler*, OFr. *roeler*, deriv. of Fr. *rouelle* 'round, (round) slice', fr. Lat. *rotella*, dim. of *rota* 'wheel'. REW 7389.

Fr. *tourner*, fr. Lat. *tornāre* 'turn in a lathe, round off', deriv. of *tornus* 'lathe', fr. Grk. *τόρνος* id. (: Grk. *τείρω* 'rub', cf. Boisacq 976 f.). REW 8794.

Fr. *envelopper*, OFr. *envoluper* (> ME *envolupe*, NE *envelop*) : It. *inviluppare* 'wrap', *viluppo* 'bundle, tangle', *faloppa* 'husk', late Lat. gl. *faluppa* prob. 'husk'. REW 3173.3. Gamillscheg 368. Wartburg 3.395 ff.

Sp. *devanar*, Rum. *depăna* = It. *dipanare* 'unwind', fr. VLat. *dēpānāre*, deriv. of *pānus* 'thread wound on a bobbin'. REW 2569. Wartburg 3.44.

Sp. *rodar* (intr.; *hacer rodar* trans.), fr. Lat. *rotāre* 'rotate, turn as a wheel', fr. *rota* 'wheel'. REW 7388.

Rum. *încolăci*, deriv. of *colac* 'ring, circle', this fr. Slavic. Tiktin 389. Berneker 541.

Rum. *înfăşura*, fr. VLat. **infasciolāre*, deriv. of Lat. *fasciola* 'band', dim. of *fascia* id. REW 3212.

Rum. *rostogoli* (also *răs-*), prob. Slavic, cpd. of prefix *raz-* 'apart' and **trukolo* (cf. Bulg. *tarkolo* 'circle'), blended with *okolŭ* 'circle'. Tiktin 1339.

7. NIr. *casaim*, deriv. of *cas* 'curl, fold', MIr. adj. *cass* 'curly, crooked', etc. (root connection dub. Walde-P. 1.450).

NIr. *cornaim*, deriv. of *corn* 'roll, coil, cylinder', prob. = *corn* 'goblet' (fr. Lat. *cornu* 'horn').

NIr. *rolaim*, W. *rholio*, fr. NE *roll;* also NIr. *rothlaim* by influence of *roth* 'wheel'.

W. *troi*, Br. *trei*, etym. dub., perh. : Lat. *trahere* 'draw', Goth. *þragjan* 'run', also the Celtic words for 'foot' W. *troed*, Ir. *traig*, etc. Walde-P. 1.752. Stokes 136.

W. *dirwyn*, cpd. of older *rhwyno* id., etym.?

W. *treiglo, treillio* deriv. of *treigl* 'turn, path, track', etym.?

Br. *rodella*, deriv. of *rodell* 'curl (of hair)', dial. also 'little wheel', fr. Lat. *rotella* (cf. Fr. *rouler*, etc., above, 6). Loth, Mots lat. 202.

Br. *ruilha*, prob. fr. OFr. *roeler* (Fr. *rouler*, above, 6). Henry 236.

8. Goth. *wandjan*, ON *venda*, Dan. *vende*, Sw. *vända*, OE *wendan*, ME *wende* (NE *wend*), OHG *wenten*, Du., MHG, NHG *wenden*, causatives to Goth. *-windan* (*biwindan* 'wrap', *uswindan* 'plait'), ON, Sw. *vinda*, Dan. *vinde*, OE *windan*, ME *winde*, NE *wind*, OHG *wintan*, Du., MHG, NHG *winden* 'wind' : Umbr. *aha-uendu* 'avertito', Skt. *vandhura-* 'hamper (of wickerwork)', Arm. *gind* 'ring'. Walde-P. 1.261. Falk-Torp 1367, 1382. Feist 98, 550.

ON *snūa*, Dan., Sw. *sno* : OE *snēowan*, Goth. *sniwan* 'hurry' (as 'turn'), ChSl. *snuti* 'warp', Russ. *snovat'* 'warp, go to and fro', Skt. *snāvan-* 'band, tendon', etc. Walde-P. 2.696. Falk-Torp 1097.

ON *hverfa*, OE *hwēorfan*, OHG *(h)werban*, all mostly intr. 'turn' or in secondary senses : Goth. *hvairban* 'wander about', prob. Grk. *καρπός* 'wrist' (as 'pivot'). Walde-P. 1.472 f. Falk-Torp 438 f. Feist 279 f.

ON *vefja* : *vefa*, OE *wefan*, OHG *weban* 'weave, plait', Grk. *ὑφαίνω* 'weave', etc. Walde-P. 1.257. Falk-Torp 1405.

Dan. *svøbe* (Sw. *svepa* 'shroud, wrap up') : ON *sveipa* 'stroke, sweep, swathe, swaddle', OE *swāpan* 'swing, sweep', OHG *sweifan* 'swing, set in turning motion, wriggle', Goth. *midja-sweipains* 'deluge' (lit. 'middle-sweeping'). Walde-P. 2.520. Falk-Torp 1223 f.

OE *tyrnan, turnian*, ME *turne*, NE *turn*, fr. Lat. *tornāre* OFr. *torner, turner*, Fr. *tourner* (above, 6). NED s.v. *turn*, vb.

ME *wrappe*, NE *wrap*, perh. (*pp* fr. *pn*) : Lith. *verpti* 'spin', Grk. *ῥάπτω* 'sew, patch', *ῥέπω* 'bow, stoop', etc. Walde-P. 1.277 (top). Falk-Torp 1399.

ME *rolle*, NE *roll*, MLG (> Dan. *rulle*, Sw. *rulla*), Du., MHG, NHG *rollen*, fr. OFr. *roeler*, Fr. *rouler* (above, 6). Falk-Torp 918 f. Weigand-H. 2.602.

NE *twist*, fr. ME *twiste* 'separate, divide' and 'combine, unite', whence esp. (early NE) 'plait, interlace, combine by interlacing' and eventually the modern general sense; fr. *twi-* : *two*. Cf. Du., LG *twisten* 'quarrel' (fr. 'divide'), Icel. *tvistra* 'scatter' and older Flem. *twisten*, Dan. dial. *tviste, tveste* 'twine'. NED s.v.

OHG *kēran*, MHG *kēren*, NHG *kehren*, etym. dub. Walde-P. 1.546. Weigand-H. 1.1015. Kluge-G. 293.

OE *þrāwan* ('turn, twist, torture', hence in altered sense NE *throw*), Du. *draaien* (LG *dreien* > Dan. *dreje*), OHG *drājan*, MHG *dræjen*, NHG *drehen* : Grk. *τείρω*, Lat. *terere*, Lith. *trinti*, ChSl. *trěti* 'rub'. Walde-P. 1.729. Weigand-H. 1.376.

Du. *wikkelen*, late MHG, NHG *wickeln* (> Dan. *vikle*, Sw. *vekla*), deriv. of NHG *wickel*, MHG *wickel(īn)*, OHG *wicchili, wichel*, etc., orig. 'roll of flax or wool on the distaff to be spun' : OE *wice, wecca*, OHG *wekko* 'wick', Ir. *figim*, W. *gweu* 'weave', Skt. *vāgurā-* 'snare, noose'. Walde-P. 1.248. Falk-Torp 1377.

9. Lith. *kreipti* : ChSl. *krěsŭ* 'turn, change of weather', *vŭskrěsiti* 'raise' (from the dead), ON *hreifi* 'wrist' (as

'pivot'), etc. Walde-P. 2.571. Berneker 615.

Lith. *grę̃žti* (but chiefly 'bore'), Lett. *griezt* : ON *kringr*, MHG *krinc* 'ring', MHG *kranc* 'circle, region', etc., also OE *cranc* (in *crancstæf* 'a weaver's tool'), NE *crank*, etc., IE **greng̑(h)-*. Walde-P. 1.594. Mühl.-Endz. 1.662 f.

Lett. *tīt* : Lith. *tinti* 'swell' (as 'stretch'), Goth. *uf-þanjan* 'stretch' (intr.), OE *þenian*, Lat. *tendere*, Grk. τείνω 'stretch', etc. Walde-P. 1.724. Mühl.-Endz. 4.205 f.

10. Late ChSl. *krǫtiti* (*krętati* 'plait'), Boh. *kroutiti*, Russ. *krutit'*, SCr. *okrenuti*, *okretati*, Pol. *kręcić* : Lat. *crātis* 'wicker-work, hurdle', Grk. κάρταλος 'basket', Skt. *kṛt-* (3sg. *kṛṇatti*) 'twist thread together, spin'. Walde-P. 1.421. Berneker 612 f., 627.

SCr. *kotrljati*, Russ. *katit'*, *katat'*, cf. Pol. dial. *kocić się* intr. refl., Boh. *kotiti* 'overturn', refl. 'rush', *kotrlčiti* 'tumble, roll head over heels', etc. (large group with similar meanings), etym. dub. Berneker 591 f.

SCr. *motati*, *omotati*, etc. (Boh. *motati*, Pol. *motać*, Russ. *motat'* in more restricted or secondary uses) : ChSl. *metą mesti* 'throw' (10.25). Berneker 2.40 f. Brückner 345. Miklosich 203.

Boh. *točiti*, Pol. *toczyć* (ChSl. *točiti* 'drive') : ChSl. *tokŭ* 'flow, issue', *tešti*, Lith. *tekėti* 'run' (10.32). Brückner 573. Walde-P. 1.716.

11. Skt. and Av. words, above, 1, 2, 3.

10.21 RISE (vb.)

Grk.	ἀνίσταμαι	Goth.	*urreisan, usstandan*	Lith.	*kilti, keltis*
NG	σηκώνομαι	ON	*rīsa, stīga upp*	Lett.	*celties*
Lat.	*surgere*	Dan.	*staa op, rejse sig*	ChSl.	*vŭstaniti*
It.	*levarsi, alzarsi, sorgere*	Sw.	*stå upp, resa sig*	SCr.	*ustati, dignuti se*
Fr.	*se lever, monter*	OE	*rīsan, up stīgan*	Boh.	*povstati, zvedati se*
Sp.	*levantarse, alzarse*	ME	*rise*	Pol.	*(pow)stać, wznieść się*
Rum.	*se scula, se ridica*	NE	*rise*	Russ.	*vstat', podnjat'sja*
Ir.	*ērigim*	Du.	*opstaan, opstijgen*	Skt.	*utthā-*
NIr.	*ēirghim*	OHG	*ar-, uf-stantan*	Av.	*usstā-, usar-*
W.	*codi (cyfodi, cynnu)*	MHG	*ufstān*		
Br.	*sevel*	NHG	*aufstehen, sich erheben, (auf)steigen*		

There is often a distinction between 'rise' = 'get up from a sitting or lying posture' and 'rise' = 'ascend, mount (from a lower to a higher position)'.

Several words not included in the list are common for 'rise' in certain connections, as for the rising of the sun Grk. (ἀνα)τέλλω, Lat. *orīrī*.

1. Cpds. and phrases with IE **stā-* 'stand' (12.15).

Grk. ἀνίσταμαι, mid. of ἀνίστημι 'make stand upright, erect'; Goth. *us-standan*, Dan. *staa op*, Sw. *stå upp*, Du. *op-staan*, OHG *ar-*, *uf-stantan*, MHG *uf-stān*, NHG *auf-stehen*; ChSl. *vŭ-staniti*, SCr. *u-stati*, Boh. *pov-stati*, Pol. *pow-stać*, Russ. *v-stat'*, Skt. *ut-thā* (= *ud-sthā*), Av. *us-stā-*. Barth, 1602.

2. NG σηκώνομαι, mid. of σηκώνω 'lift' (10.22).

3. Lat. *surgere* (> It. *sorgere*, etc., REW 8475), fr. *sub-r(e)gere*, cpd. of *regere* 'make straight, direct, rule'; Ir. *ērigim*, NIr. *ēirghim*, fr. **ess-rig-*, cpd. of *rigim* 'stretch out', all fr. IE **reĝ-* in Goth. *raihts*, OHG *reht*, Skt. *ṛju-*, Av. *ərəzu-* 'right, exact'. Walde-P. 2.363. Ernout-M. 856 f.

It. *levarsi*, Fr. *se lever*, Sp. *levantarse*, refl. of It. *levare*, etc. 'lift' (10.22).

It. *alzarsi*, Sp. *alzarse*, refl. of It. *alzare*, Sp. *alzar* 'lift' (10.22).

Fr. *monter* (general 'go up, mount'), fr. VLat. **montāre* deriv. of Lat. *mons*, *montis* 'mountain'. Gamillscheg 620.

Rum. *se scula* ('rise, get up', also 'wake'), refl. of *scula* 'rouse, awaken', fr. VLat. **excubulāre*, fr. Lat. *cubāre* 'lie down, sleep'. Puşcariu 1559. Tiktin 1396.

Rum. *se ridica*, refl. of *ridica* 'raise' (10.22).

4. Ir. *ērigim*, NIr. *ēirghim*, see above, 3.

W. *cyfodi* > *codi*, etym.? Morris Jones 382 (but cf. Loth, RC 37.45 f.)

W. *cy-chwynnu* 'start, rise', *cynnu* (*cwnnu*) 'rise' : Ir. *scendim*, *scinnim* 'spring, start'. Pedersen 2.617. Morris Jones 86. Evans s.v. *cwnnu*.

Br. *sevel* (also 'erect, construct') = W. *sefyll* 'stand' (12.15).

5. Goth. *ur-reisan*, ON *rīsa*, OE *rīsan*, ME, NE *rise* (OHG *rīsan* mostly 'fall', MHG *rīsen* 'rise' or 'fall') : Grk. ὀρῑ́νω 'arouse, move', Arm. *ari* 'climb', IE **erei-*, extension of **er-* in Skt. *ṛ-* (*ṛṇoti*), Av. *ar-* 'move', *us-ar* (inf. *uzīrəidyai*) 'rise', Grk. ὄρνῡμι 'stir up, arouse' (mid. 'arise, rise' in various phrases), etc. Hence the caus. refl. Dan. *rejse sig*, Sw. *resa sig* (nonrefl. mostly 'erect, set up'), fr. ON *reisa* 'lift, raise', etc. (10.22). Walde-P. 1.140. Falk-Torp 888.

Goth. *us-standan*, etc., above, 1.

ON *stīga upp*, OE *up stīgan*, Du. *opstijgen*, NHG *(auf)steigen* (the simplex in the older Gmc. dialects mostly a general word for 'go, come, ascend, descend', cf. Goth. *steigan* 'ἀναβαίνειν', *at-steigan* 'καταβαίνειν', etc.) : Grk. στείχω 'stride, go', Ir. *tiagu* 'go', IE **steigh-*. Walde-P. 2.614.

NHG *sich erheben*, refl. of *(er)heben* 'lift' (10.22).

6. Lith. *kilti*, and *keltis*, Lett. *celties* (refls. of Lith. *kelti*, Lett. *celt* 'lift', 10.22) : Lat. *ex-cellere* 'be eminent, excel,' *celsus* 'high,' *collis* 'hill', etc. (1.22).

7. ChSl. *vŭstaniti*, etc., above, 1.

SCr. *dignuti se*, Boh. *zvedati se*, Pol. *wznieść się*, Russ. *podnjat'sja*, all refls. of words for 'raise, lift' (10.22).

8. Skt. *utthā-*, Av. *usstā-*, above, 1.

Av. *usar-*, above, 5.

10.22 RAISE, LIFT

Grk.	αἴρω	Goth.	*hafjan*	Lith.	*kelti*
NG	σηκώνω	ON	*hefja, lypta, reisa*	Lett.	*celt*
Lat.	*tollere, levāre*	Dan.	*løfte, hæve*	ChSl.	*vŭzęti, vŭzdvignąti, vŭznesti*
It.	*alzare, (sol)levare*	Sw.	*lyfta, höja (häva)*	SCr.	*dignuti*
Fr.	*(sou)lever*	OE	*hebban, rǣran*	Boh.	*zdvihnouti, zvednouti*
Sp.	*alzar, levantar*	ME	*heve, reise, rere, lyfte*	Pol.	*podnieść, (po)dźwignąć*
Rum.	*ridica*	NE	*raise, lift*	Russ.	*podnjat'*
Ir.	*conucbaim*	Du.	*(op)heffen, (op)tillen*	Skt.	*tul-*, caus. of *ut-thā-*
NIr.	*togaim*	OHG	*heffen*	Av.	*us-grab-*
W.	*codi*	MHG	*heben*		
Br.	*sevel*	NHG	*(auf)heben*		

Words for 'raise, lift' are but rarely causatives of those for 'rise', like NE *raise*, or related to them except as the latter are reflexives. They are mostly from notions like 'weigh', 'make light', 'make high', 'take up', 'move up', etc.

1. Grk. αἴρω, ἀείρω, prob. (otherwise Solmsen, Unters. 290 ff.) same word as ἀείρω 'bind together, join' (in συν-αείρω, συν-ήορος, παρήορος, etc.), mid. 'hang' (Hom. ἄωρτο 'hung', ἄορ 'sword', etc.), and this perh. fr. *ἀ-ϝερι̯ω : Lett. *vert* 'to

string, thread' (a needle), Lith. *virvė* 'string', etc., IE **wer-*. But the semantic relation is not clear. Walde-P. 1.264. Boisacq, 15 f.

Grk. ἐγείρω 'wake' (4.63), 'rouse', hence also late (esp. NT) 'raise', mid. 'rise'.

NG σηκώνω, Byz. σηκόω = class. Grk. σηκόω 'weigh, balance', beside σήκωμα 'weight in a balance'. Further connection with σηκός 'pen, fold, enclosure' ('weight' only late and fr. the vb.) through an unattested use of the latter for the scale pan of a balance? Walde-P. 1.747.

2. Lat. *tollere* : Skt. *tul-* 'lift, weigh', *tulā-* 'balance', Grk. τάλαντον 'balance', τελαμών 'strap for holding shield or sword, pedestal, pillar' (all fr. 'supporter'), ταλάσσαι, τλῆναι 'support, bear' in figurative sense = 'endure', as also Goth. *þulan*, OE *þolian* (NE dial. *thole*), OHG *dolēn*, NHG *dulden*, etc., IE **tel-*. Walde-P. 1.738 ff. Ernout-M. 1043 f.

Lat. *levāre*, deriv. of *levis* 'light' (15.82) and mostly 'lighten, relieve' but also 'raise, lift' in poetry and post-Aug. prose. Hence in this sense (or fr. *sublevāre*) It. *(sol)levare*, Fr. *(sou)lever*, deriv. Sp. *levantar*. REW 5000.

It. *alzare*, Sp. *alzar* (Rum. cpd. *înălţa* 'erect, elevate'), fr. VLat. **altiāre*, deriv. of *altus* 'high'. REW 385.

Rum. *ridica*, fr. Lat. *ērādīcāre* 'root out'? Tiktin 1322. Puşcariu 1424.

3. Ir. *conucbaim* (OIr. 3pl. *co-ta-ucbat*, etc.), fr. **com-od-gaib-* beside MIr. *tōcbaim*, NIr. *tōgaim* (also 'take'), fr. **to-od-gaib-*, cpds. of *gaibim* 'take' (11.13). Pedersen 2.530 f.

W. *codi*, Br. *sevel*, both also 'rise', see 10.21.

4. Goth. *hafjan*, ON *hefja*, Dan. *hæve*, Sw. *häva*, OE *hebban*, ME *heve* (NE *heave*), OHG *heffen*, etc., general Gmc. words : Lat. *capere* 'take', etc. Walde-P. 1.343. Walde-H. 1.159. Falk-Torp 450. Feist 230.

ON *lypta* (> ME *lyfte*, NE *lift*), Dan. *løfte*, Sw. *lyfta*, fr. ON *lopt* 'air' (cf. ON *hefja ā lopt* 'lift in the air'). Falk-Torp 680.

ON *reisa* (> ME *reise*, NE *raise*, mostly replacing the following native forms), OE *rǣran*, ME *rere* (NE *rear*), beside Goth. *ur-raisjan* 'rouse, wake', caus. to *urreisan*, ON *rīsa* 'rise', etc. (10.21).

Sw. *höja*, deriv. of *hög* 'high'.

Du. *(op)tillen*, OFris. *tilla*, orig. dub., perh. : OE *ā-*, *ge-tillan* 'touch, reach, attain'. Franck-v. W. 697.

5. Lith. *kelti*, Lett. *celt* : Lith. *kilti* 'rise' (10.21).

6. ChSl. *vŭzęti*, Russ. *podnjat'*, cpds. of ChSl. *jęti*, etc. 'take' (11.13). Berneker 426 f.

ChSl. *vŭzdvignąti*, Boh. *zdvihnouti*, SCr. *dignuti*, Pol. *(po)dźwignąć*, cpds. of or = ChSl. *dvignąti* etc. 'move' (10.11). Berneker 240.

ChSl. *vŭznesti*, Boh. *povznésti*, Pol. *podnieść*, cpds. of ChSl. *nesti*, etc. 'carry' (10.61).

Boh. *zvednouti* cpd. of root *ved-* in *vésti* 'lead, guide' (10.64).

7. Skt. *tul-* : Lat. *tollere*, above, 2.

Skt. *ut-thāpaya-* (mostly 'raise' = 'make stand up'), caus. of *ut-thā-* 'rise' (10.21).

Av. *us-grab-*, cpd. of *us-* (cf. *us-stā-* 'rise') and *grab-* 'seize' (11.14). Barth. 527.

10.23 FALL (vb.)

Grk.	πίπτω	Goth.	*driusan*	Lith.	*pulti, kristi*
NG	πέφτω	ON	*falla*	Lett.	*krist*
Lat.	*cadere*	Dan.	*falde*	ChSl.	*pasti, padati*
It.	*cadere*	Sw.	*falla*	SCr.	*pasti, padati*
Fr.	*tomber*	OE	*feallan, drēosan*	Boh.	*padnouti*
Sp.	*caer*	ME	*falle, droppe*	Pol.	*paść, padać*
Rum.	*cădea*	NE	*fall, drop*	Russ.	*past', padat'*
Ir.	*do-tuit*	Du.	*vallen*	Skt.	*pad-, pat-*
NIr.	*tuitim*	OHG	*fallan*	Av.	*pat-*
W.	*cwympo, syrthio*	MHG	*vallen*		
Br.	*koeza*	NHG	*fallen*		

In words for 'fall' the central notion is that of free, rapid, downward motion, as that of an object falling by its own weight. But in many of them the 'downward' element, though become dominant, is of secondary origin, a specialization from some notion of rapid movement. This is especially obvious in the case of the root which serves for both 'fall' and 'fly' in Indo-Iranian and also, though with differentiated forms of it, in Greek (below, 1). Some are probably of imitative origin, based on expressive syllables analogous to NE *plump*, *thud*, etc.

1. IE **pet-*. Walde-P. 2.19.

Grk. πίπτω 'fall', NG pop. πέφτω (πτ > φτ regular; ε from aor. ἔπεσα, cf. Hatzidakis, Μεσ. 2.503), beside πέτομαι 'fly'; Skt., Av. *pat-* 'fall' and 'fly', OPers. *ud-apatatā* 'made an uprising, rebellion'; Lat. *petere* 'go after, seek', etc. The sense 'fly' is the most widespread, notably in the derivs. for 'wing, feather', and was probably the primary use of the root. Cf. 10.36. But the notion of rapid motion unites all the uses.

2. Lat. *cadere* (> It. *cadere*, Sp. *caer*, Rum. *cădea*, OFr. *cheoir*) : Skt. *çad-* 'fall off, out', MIr. *casar* 'hail, lightning', IE **k̑ad-*. Walde-P. 1.339. Ernout-M. 127. Walde-H. 1.128.

Fr. *tomber*, replacing *cheoir* (above) in 18th cent., OFr. *tomber*, *tumber* 'leap, dance, stagger, make tumble', prob. with OFr. *tumer* 'leap', loanword fr. the Gmc. group seen in OHG *tūmōn* 'turn around', NHG *taumeln* 'stagger', OE *tumbian* 'tumble, dance', NE *tumble*, etc., all prob. of imitative origin. REW 8975. Gamillscheg 847.

3. Ir. *do-tuit* (3sg.), NIr. *tuitim*, prob. through 'hit the ground' : Lat. *tundere* 'beat, pound', Skt. *tud-* 'push, thrust, prick', Goth. *stautan* 'smite', etc. Walde-P. 2.618. Pedersen 2.656 ff.

W. *cwympo*, cf. MW *cwymp* 'a fall', of imitative orig.?

W. *syrthio*, perh. (with reg. *s* fr. *st*, as in *seren* 'star', etc.) : OE *styrte* 'jump, leap' (NE *start*). Loth. RC 43.148 f.

Br. *koeza* (*koueza*), W. *cwyddo* (arch.), Corn. *codhe*, etym. dub., perh. : ON *hitta* 'hit upon, meet', etc. Walde-P. 1.364. Falk-Torp 407.

4. ON *falla*, OE *feallan*, OHG *fallan*, etc., the main Gmc. group : Lith. *pulti*, Lett. dial. *pult* 'fall', Arm. *p'lanim* 'fall in'. Walde-P. 2.103. Falk-Torp 202.

Goth. *driusan*, OE *drēosan*, ME *drese* (rare), OS *driosan* : OHG *trōren* 'drip, trickle', Grk. θραύω 'break up, shatter', IE **dhreus-*. Walde-P. 1.873. Feist 126.

ME *droppe*, NE *drop*, orig. like OE *dropian* 'fall in drops' (see 10.24), but extended, so that in its intr. use it is common in the sense of *fall*, without by any means displacing it, and in its trans. use is generally substituted for the phrase *let fall*, NHG *fallen lassen*, Fr. *laisser tomber*, etc., e.g. *drop a pencil, a handkerchief*, etc.

5. Lith. *pulti*, above, 4.

Lith. *kristi*, Lett. *krist;* prob. : Lith. *krėsti*, Lett. *krest* 'shake, shake off'. Leskien, Ablaut 333. Mühl.-Endz. 2.281. Otherwise (: Lith. *kirsti*, Lett. *cirst* 'hew, hack') Walde-P. 2.579.

6. ChSl., SCr. *pasti, padati*, etc., general Slavic : Skt. *pad-* 'fall, go', Av. *pad-, paδ-* 'move downward, plunge down', prob. the same root as in Skt. *pad-*, Grk. πούς, etc. 'foot'. Walde-P. 2.23.

7. Skt. *pad-*, above, 6.

Skt. *pat-*, Av. *pat-*, above, 1.

10.24 DROP (sb., of Liquid)

Grk.	σταγών	Goth.	. . . .	Lith.	*lašas*
NG	σταγόνα	ON	*dropi*	Lett.	*lase*
Lat.	*gutta*	Dan.	*draabe*	ChSl.	*kaplja*
It.	*goccia, gocciola*	Sw.	*droppe*	SCr.	*kaplja*
Fr.	*goutte*	OE	*dropa*	Boh.	*kapka*
Sp.	*gota*	ME	*drope*	Pol.	*kropla*
Rum.	*picătură, strop (gută)*	NE	*drop*	Russ.	*kaplja*
Ir.	*banna, brōen*	Du.	*drop*	Skt.	*bindu-*
NIr.	*braon*	OHG	*tropfo*	Av.	. . . .
W.	*dafn, diferyn*	MHG	*tropfe*		
Br.	*banne, bannec'h*	NHG	*tropfen*		

The extension of 'fall in drops' to 'fall' in general, as seen in NE *drop* (10.23), leads us to consider here the nouns for a 'drop'—despite the fact that in these the notion of motion, the 'dropping', is subordinate in feeling to that of (small) amount (of a liquid), so that the inclusion in this chapter seems illogical.

1. Grk. σταγών, with vb. στάζω 'drip' (*στάγιω), prob. : Lat. *stagnum* 'stagnant water, pool', OBr. *staer*, NBr. *ster* 'river', W. *taen* 'a sprinkling'. Walde-P. 2.612. Pedersen 1.103.

2. Lat. *gutta* (> It. *gotta* 'gout'; deriv., through a vb. **guttiāre, goccia, gocciola* 'drop'; Fr. *goutte*, Sp. *gota* 'drop' and 'gout'; Rum. *gută* 'gout', dial. 'drop'), etym.? Ernout-M. 439. Walde-H. 1.629. REW 3928, 3929. For the sense 'gout', see NED s.v. *gout*, sb.[1].

Rum. *pic* (also 'a little, a bit'), for 'drop' more commonly *picătură*, fr. vb. *pica* 'drip', this fr. an imitative syllable seen in It. *piccolo* 'small', etc. (1.256). REW 6494. Puşcariu 1304. Tiktin 1154.

Rum. *strop*, back-formation fr. vb. *stropi* 'sprinkle', prob. corruption of a Slavic **sŭ-kropiti* (cf. ChSl. *kropiti*, SCr. *škropiti* 'sprinkle', Berneker 623). Tiktin 1519.

3. Ir. *banna* (K. Meyer, Contrib. 177), Br. *banne, bannec'h*, OCorn. *banne* (MCorn. 'a jot, bit') : Skt. *bindu-* 'drop', root connection? Walde-P. 2.110. Pedersen 1.116. A. Mayer, Glotta 29.69 f.

Ir. *brōen* (also 'rain, shower, spot', K. Meyer, Contrib. 266), NIr. *braon*, etym.? Walde-P. 1.268 (vs. Stokes 271).

W. *dafn* (with vb. *dafnu* 'drip'), etym.?

W. *diferyn*, with vb. *diferu* = Corn. *devery, dyvery* 'drip', etym.?

4. ON *dropi*, OE *dropa*, OHG *tropfo*, etc., general Gmc., beside vbs. ON *drjūpa*, OE *drēopan*, OHG *triufan*, etc., also OE *dropian, dryppan*, etc. (NE *drop, drip*, beside *dreep* fr. OE *drēopan*, and *droop* fr. ON *drūpa*), with Ir. *drucht*

'dew', fr. **dhreub-* beside **dhreubh-* in Grk. θρύπτω (ἐτρύφην) 'break in pieces', θρύμμα, τρύφος 'bit, lump', and **dhreus-* in Goth. *driusan*, OE *drēosan* 'fall'. Walde-P. 1.873. Falk-Torp 150, 159.

5. Lith. *lašas*, Lett. *lase*, perh. : Russ. *lasa, lasina* 'spot'. Mühl.-Endz. 2.441. Berneker 691. Buga, Kalba ir Senovė 193.

6. ChSl., SCr., Russ. *kaplja*, Boh. *kapka*, beside vb. ChSl. *kapati* 'drip', etc., perh. fr. an imitative syllable. Berneker 487.

Pol. *kropla* (ChSl. *kroplja* 'stream' of tears, Supr.), fr. the root of ChSl. *kropiti*, etc. 'sprinkle', based on an imitative syllable like that in Lat. *crepere* 'rattle, clatter', etc. Walde-P. 1.416. Berneker 623. Brückner 270.

7. Skt. *bindu-* : Ir. *banna* (above, 3).

10.25 THROW (vb.)

Grk.	βάλλω (ῥίπτω, ἵημι)	Goth.	*wairpan*	Lith.	*mesti*
NG	ρίχνω, πετῶ	ON	*verpa, kasta*	Lett.	*mest*
Lat.	*iacere*	Dan.	*kaste*	ChSl.	*mesti, vrěšti*
It.	*gettare*	Sw.	*kasta*	SCr.	*baciti*
Fr.	*jeter*	OE	*weorpan*	Boh.	*hazeti, hoditi, vrhnouti*
Sp.	*arrojar (tirar, echar)*	ME	*thrawe*	Pol.	*rzucić, ciskać*
Rum.	*arunca*	NE	*throw*	Russ.	*brosit'*
Ir.	*focerdaim, srēdim, dolēicim*	Du.	*werpen*	Skt.	*kṣip-, as-*
NIr.	*caithim, teilgim*	OHG	*werfan*	Av.	*ah-, spā-*
W.	*taflu*	MHG	*werfen*		
Br.	*teurel*	NHG	*werfen*		

Besides the words listed as the most generic for 'throw', there are numerous others which are usually expressive of greater violence or are more restricted as to their objects, as NE *fling, hurl, cast*, It. *lanciare*, Fr. *lancer*, Sp. *lanzar* (extended from 'throw a lance', but still less generic than others), ChSl. *kydati*, Pol. *kidać*, Russ. *kidat'* (: SCr. *kidati* 'break, tear', Boh. *kydati* 'clean out dung'; Berneker 676), etc. The once generic word has sunk to a subordinate position in the case of Sp. *echar* in contrast to It. *gettare*, Fr. *jeter*, or Boh. *metati*, Russ. *metat'*, etc., in contrast to ChSl. *mesti*.

Most of the words are cognate with others denoting some kind of quick motion, as 'turn', 'roll', 'gush', etc. A few come from the notion of 'aim at' or 'draw' (through 'shoot').

1. From various extensions of **wer-* parallel to *wert-* in words for 'turn', as Lat. *vertere*, etc. (10.12). Cf. NE *throw*, orig. 'turn around'. Walde-P. 1.271 ff. Falk-Torp 1370 f.

Grk. ῥίπτω (NG ρίχνω, also ρίφτω, ρίχτω, cf. Hatzidakis, Μεσ. 1.291) fr. **wrīp-*; Goth. *wairpan*, ON *verpa*, OE *weorpan*, OHG *werfan*, etc., fr. **wer-b-*; ChSl. *vrŭgą, vrěšti* (*vrŭgnąti, vrŭzati*), Boh. *vrhnouti, vrhati*, fr. **wer-g-* (in Skt. *vṛj-* 'turn', 10.12).

2. Grk. βάλλω, Arc. δέλλω, with βολή, βόλος 'a throw', βέλος 'missile', etc., all pointing to IE **gʷel-*, prob. the same as in Skt. *gal-* 'drip', OHG *quellan* 'gush forth', etc. Walde-P. 1.690 f. Semantic connection through a common 'fall, let fall'. Cf. Hom. ποταμὸς . . . . εἰς ἅλα βάλλων 'river falling into the sea', and the extended use of NE *drop* (10.23) beside *drip*. Otherwise Wackernagel-Debrunner, KZ 67.159 f.

NG πετῶ 'fly' (10.37), also 'let fly, throw'.

3. Lat. *iacere, iēcī* : Grk. ἵημι, aor. ἧκα 'send', also 'throw'. Walde-P. 1.199. Ernout-M. 466 ff. Walde-H. 1.666 f. (with full refs. on the disputed ἵημι). Hence frequent. *iactāre*, **iectāre* > It. *gettare*, Fr. *jeter*, Sp. *echar* (the last esp. in manifold secondary senses). REW 4568.

Sp., Port. *arrojar*, fr. VLat. **rotulāre* 'roll' (10.15). REW 7396.

Sp. *tirar* 'draw' (9.33), hence also 'shoot' and 'throw'.

Rum. *arunca*, fr. Lat. *ēruncāre* 'weed out'. REW 2908. Tiktin 100.

4. Ir. *focerdaim* (OIr. 3sg. *foceird*) 'throw' and 'put' (for uses cf. Laws, Gloss. 372), fr. **upo-kerd-* perh. : Skt. *kūrd-* 'leap', Grk. κόρδαξ 'gay dance' (in comedy), W. *cerdded* 'walk', fr. an extension of *(*s*)*ker-* in Grk. σκαίρω 'jump, hop', etc. Walde-P. 2.567. (For OIr. *cuirethar*, suppl. vb. to *fo-ceird*, cf. NIr. *cuirim* 'place, put', 12.12.)

Ir. *srēdim*, see under *as-srēdim* 'spread out', 9.34.

Ir. *dolēicim, teilcim*, NIr. *teilgim*, cpd. of *lēicim* 'leave' (12.18). Pedersen 2.564.

NIr. *caithim* (also and MIr. mostly 'consume, spend, use') : Lat. *quatere* 'shake'? Walde-P. 1.511. Pedersen 2.479.

W. *taflu*, Br. *teurel* (old infin. *taoli*), deriv. of the word seen in W. *taf(o)l* 'scales, balance', *ffon dafl* 'sling', orig. a 'staff-sling', fr. Lat. *tabula* 'tablet'. Loth, Mots lat. 210. Pedersen 1.491.

5. Goth. *wairpan*, ON *verpa*, etc., above, 1.

ON *kasta* (> ME *caste*, NE *cast*), Dan. *kaste*, Sw. *kasta*, etym.? Connection with Lat. *gestāre* 'carry', *gerere* 'carry, conduct' (Falk-Torp 502) dub. Ernout-M. 421. Walde-H. 1.595.

ME *thrawe*, NE *throw*, fr. OE *þrāwan* 'turn around, twist' (10.13). NED s.v. *throw*, vb. For semantic development cf. Grk. ῥίπτω etc. (above, 1).

6. Lith. *metu, mesti*, Lett. *mest*, ChSl. *metą, mesti*, iter. *metati* (Russ. *metat'*, Boh. *metati*, Pol. *miotać* 'fling, cast', etc., in more restricted applications; SCr. *metati* mostly 'put, place'), characteristic old Balto-Slavic word for 'throw', but outside connections dub. That with Lat. *metere* 'reap' is generally rejected (cf. Walde-P. 2.259, Berneker 2.40 f.). E. Hermann, IF 50.238, connects with words for 'measure', Grk. μέτρον, Lat. *mētīrī*, Skt. *mā-*, etc.

7. ChSl. *vrěšti*, etc., above, 1.

SCr. *baciti* : Boh. *baciti*, Russ. *bacnut'* 'slap', of imitative orig., cf. Boh., Russ. *bac!* 'bang!' Berneker 37.

Boh. *hazeti, hoditi* 'throw', fr. 'aim at' : ChSl. *u-goditi* 'please', Russ. *godit'sja* 'be fitting', SCr. *gađati* 'aim', etc., with ChSl. *godŭ* '(fitting) time' (14.11). Berneker 290, 317.

Pol. *rzucić*, cf. Boh. *řititi* 'throw down, dash', Slavic **rjut-*, outside connections? Brückner 477. Gebauer 1.274.

Pol. *ciskać* : SCr. *tiskati*, etc. 'press' (9.342). Brückner 64.

Russ. *brosit'*, cf. Ukr. *brosyty* 'throw away' (with general 'throw' from letting refuse fall in shaving, scraping, etc.) : Russ.-ChSl. *brŭsnuti* 'shave, scrape', etc., and (**bhreu-k-* vs. **bhreu-ḱ-* in Slavic) Lett. *brukt* 'peel off', Lith. *braukti* 'wipe, stroke'. Walde-P. 2.197. Berneker 90 f.

8. Skt. *kṣip-*, cf. *kṣipra-* 'swift', fr. IE **kseip-* beside **kseib-* in ChSl. *o-šibati* 'turn away from, desert', Russ. *šibit'* 'throw' (rare word), *šibkij* 'swift'. Walde-P. 1.501.

Skt. *as-* (3sg. *asyati*), Av. *ah-* (3sg. *aŋhyeiti*), outside connections? Walde-P. 1.134 f.

Av. *spā-* (3sg. *spayeiti*), perh. : Grk. σπάω 'draw, rend, wrench', OHG *spanan* 'entice', Icel. *spenja* 'charm', all fr. a more orig. meaning 'stretch', IE **spē(i)-*? Walde-P. 2.655. Barth. 1615.

10.26 SHAKE (vb. trans.)

Grk.	σείω, τινάσσω, πάλλω, σαλεύω	Goth.	*-hrisjan, gawigan, wagjan*	Lith.	*kratyti, purtyti*
NG	τινάζω, σείω	ON	*hrista, skaka*	Lett.	*purināt, kratīt*
Lat.	*quatere, quassāre*	Dan.	*ryste*	ChSl.	*tręsti*
It.	*scuotere*	Sw.	*skaka*	SCr.	*tresti*
Fr.	*secouer*	OE	*hrysian, sceacan*	Boh.	*třásti*
Sp.	*sacudir*	ME	*schake, rese*	Pol.	*trząść*
Rum.	*scutura*	NE	*shake*	Russ.	*trjast'*
Ir.	*crothim*	Du.	*schudden*	Skt.	*dhū-*
NIr.	*crothaim*	OHG	*scut(t)an, scutilōn*	Av.	. . . .
W.	*siglo*	MHG	*schüten, schüteln*		
Br.	*heja*	NHG	*schütteln*		

1. Grk. σείω, with sb. σεισμός fr. **tweis-* : Skt. *tviṣ-* 'be aroused', *tveṣa-* 'violent', Av. *θwyant-* pple. 'causing fear', etc. Walde-P. 1.748.

Grk. τινάσσω, NG pop. τινάζω, etym.? Boisacq 971.

Grk. πάλλω ('brandish, swing, toss', also 'shake'), etym. dub. (init. π fr. IE *p* or *kʷ*?). Walde-P. 2.52. Boisacq 744. Palmer, Glotta 27, 134 ff. (: ChSl. *kolěbati*, Russ. *kolebat'* 'shake', Berneker 545).

Grk. σαλεύω ('shake, toss', esp. by wind or sea; NG 'stir, move'), with sb. σάλος ('shaking motion' of earth or sea), prob. (**twḷ-* or **twəl-*) : τύλη, τύλος 'swelling, hump, knob', fr. extension of **teu-* in words for 'swell'. Walde-P. 1.709. Boisacq 850.

2. Lat. *quatere, quassāre* : Ir. *caithim* 'throw'? Walde-P. 1.511. Ernout-M. 834 f. Hence fr. cpds. It. *scuotere* (fr. *ex-cutere*), Fr. *secouer*, OFr. *secourre*, Sp. *sacudir* (fr. *succutere*), Rum. *scutura* (fr. **ex-cutulāre*, fr. *ex-cutere*). REW 2998, 3000, 8413.

3. Ir. *crothim*, NIr. *crothaim*, prob. : Lith. *kresti, kratyti* 'shake', etc. (below, 5), ON *hræða* 'frighten'. Walde-P. 1.484. Stokes 99. Falk-Torp 928.

W. *siglo*, etym.?

Br. *heja, hejal*, MBr. *hegaff*, fr. Fr. *hocher*, this fr. Du. *hotsen* 'shake'. Henry 159. REW 4203. Franck-v. W. 264.

4. Goth. *af-hrisjan* ('ἀποτινάσσειν'), *us-hrisjan* ('ἐκτινάσσειν') OE *hrysian*, ME *rese*, ON *hrista* (dental pres.), Dan. *ryste* : Skt. *krīḍ-* 'play, frolic' (**kriz-d-*), IE *(*s*)*krei-s-*, extension of *(*s*)*ker-* 'turn, bend', cf. Lith. *kreipti* (10.12). Walde-P. 2.572. Falk-Torp 904, 928. Feist 7.

Goth. *gawigan, wagjan* (render σαλεύω), OE *wecgan, wegan*, see under 'move,' 10.11.

ON, Sw. *skaka*, Norw. *skage*, OE *sceacan, scacan*, ME *schake*, NE *shake* : Skt. *khaj-* 'stir about', IE *(*s*)*keg-* beside *(*s*)*kek-*, in ChSl. *skokŭ* 'a leap, bound', W. *ysgogi* 'move' (10.11), Br. *diskogella* 'secouer pour arracher'. Walde-P. 2.557. Falk-Torp 979.

Du. *schudden*, OHG *scut(t)an*, MHG *schüt(t)en* (NHG *schütten*), with iter. forms OHG *scutilōn*, MHG *schüt(t)eln*, NHG *schütteln* (also NHG *schüttern* 'tremble, shiver' and *schaudern* 'shudder', NE *shudder*) : Lith. *kutėti* 'rouse', Lett. *kutēt* 'tickle', ON *hossa* 'toss' (a child on the knees). Walde-P. 2.601 f. Weigand-H. 2.806. Franck-v. W. 602 f.

5. Lith. *kresti*, Lett. *krest*, with the more common iter. *kratyti, kratīt*, see above, 3.

Lith. *purtyti*, Lett. *purēt, purināt* : Lith. dial. *iš-purti*, Russ. *pyrit'* 'ruffle (feathers) up', perh. also Boh. *pufeti*, *pouřiti se* 'blow oneself up', SCr. *puriti* 'blow', etc., these as orig. 'kindle' : Boh.

pyř 'embers', Grk. πῦρ 'fire', etc.? Trautmann 232. Štrekelj, Arch. sl. Ph. 27.56 f.

6. ChSl. *tręsti*, etc., general Slavic, fr. **trems-*, a blend of **trem-* in Grk. τρέμω, Lat. *tremere* 'tremble', ON *þramma* 'trample', and **tres-* in Skt. *tras-* 'tremble', Grk. τρέω 'flee'. Walde-P. 2.758, 760.

7. Skt. *dhū-* : Grk. θύω 'rage, blow', Slavic *duti* 'blow', the same root as in Skt. *dhūma-*, Lat. *fūmus*, ChSl. *dymŭ* 'smoke', Grk. θῡμός 'spirit, anger', all with a common notion of 'agitation'. Walde-P. 1.837.

10.31 BOIL (vb. intr.)

Grk.	ζέω	Goth.	wulan	Lith.	virti
NG	βράζω	ON	vella	Lett.	virt
Lat.	fervēre	Dan.	koge (syde)	ChSl.	vĭrěti
It.	bollire	Sw.	koka (sjuda)	SCr.	vreti
Fr.	bouillir	OE	weallan	Boh.	vříti
Sp.	hervir, bullir	ME	boile, welle, sethe	Pol.	warzyć się, wrzeć
Rum.	fierbe	NE	boil (seethe)	Russ.	kipet', varit'sja
Ir.	berbaim, fichim	Du.	koken, zieden	Skt.	kvath-, yas-
NIr.	beirbhim, fiuchaim, bruithim	OHG	wallan	Av.	yah-
		MHG	wallen, sieden		
W.	berwi	NHG	kochen (sieden)		
Br.	birvi				

'Boil' is understood here as the intransitive verb, as in NE *water boils*, in contrast to the transitive 'boil' in cooking (5.22). Most, though not all, of the words in the two groups are the same or related.

1. Grk. ζέω : Skt. *yas-*, Av. *yah-* 'boil, foam' (cf. Grk. ζεστός, Skt. *yasta-*, Av. *yašta-*), W. *ias* 'boiling, seething', ON *jastr*, OE *giest*, NE *yeast*, etc., IE **yes-*. Walde-P. 1.208.

NG βράζω, fr. late Grk. βράζω 'boil, froth up, ferment' beside βράσσω, Att. βράττω 'shake violently', 'throw up (on the shore of the sea)', perh. : Lett. *murdēt* 'bubble, gush', Lith. *murdynas* 'springy spot of ground', etc. Walde-P. 2.280.

2. Lat. *fervēre*, also *fervere* (> Sp. *hervir*, Rum. *fierbe*), Ir. *berbaim*, NIr. *beirbhim*, W. *berwi*, Br. *birvi*, also NIr. *bruithim* : Skt. *bhurvaṇi-* 'wild, restless', Russ. *bruja* 'streaming, current', OHG *briuwan*, etc. 'brew', IE **bheru-*. Walde-P. 2.167 f. Ernout-M. 352 f. Walde-H. 1.437.

It. *bollire*, Fr. *bouillir* (> ME *boile*, NE *boil*), Sp. *bullir*, fr. Lat. *bullīre* 'bubble, be in bubbling motion', deriv. of *bulla* 'bubble' (also 'knob', etc.) : Grk. βολβός 'bulb', Lith. *bulbė* 'potato', etc. Walde-P. 2.111, 115. Ernout-M. 121. Walde-H. 1.122. REW 1389.

3. Ir. *berbaim*, NIr. *beirbhim*, above, 2.

Ir. *fichim*, NIr. *fiuchaim*, same word as *fichim* 'fight', with development through idea of 'quick, restless motion'? Pedersen 2.521.

4. Goth. *wulan*, ON *vella*, OE *weallan*, OHG *wallan*, MHG *wallen*, all 'bubble up, well up, boil', prob. through idea of 'rolling' (of the water, waves, etc.) : Lat. *volvere*, Goth. *-walwjan*, OE *wielwan* 'roll', etc. (10.15). Walde-P. 1.302. Falk-Torp 1401 (otherwise). Feist 575 f.

Du. *koken* (MLG > Dan. *koge*, Sw. *koka*), NHG *kochen*, orig. 'boil' trans. = 'prepare (food) by boiling' fr. Lat. *coquere* (5.22).

Dan. *syde*, Sw. *sjuda*, ME *sethe*, NE *seethe*, Du. *zieden*, MHG, NHG *sieden* (all now more or less archaic), orig. only

'boil' trans., like ON *sjōða*, OE *sēoþan*, OHG *siodan* (5.22), root connections dub. Walde-P. 2.471 f. Falk-Torp 1225. Feist 413.

ME *boile*, NE *boil*, above, 2.

5. Lith. *virti*, Lett. *virt*, ChSl. *vĭrěti*, SCr. *vreti*, Boh. *vříti*, Pol. (caus. refl.) *warzyć się* beside *wrzeć* (this mostly 'bubble, boil violently'), Russ. (caus. refl.) *varit'sja* all prob. fr. IE **wer-* 'turn' (cf. Lat. *vertere*, ChSl. *vrŭtěti*, 10.12), with same semantic development as in Goth. *wulan*, etc. (above, 4). Walde-P. 1.269, 270.

6. ChSl. *vĭrěti*, etc., above, 5.

Russ. *kipet'* = ChSl. *kypěti* 'well up, run over', SCr. *kipjeti*, Boh. *kypěti*, Pol. *kipieć*, mostly 'bubble, well up' : Skt. *kup-* 'be agitated, become angry', etc. Walde-P. 1.380. Berneker 677 f.

7. Skt. *kvath-* : Goth. *hwaþjan* 'foam', OE *hwæþerian* 'foam, rage', ChSl. *vŭ(s)kysnąti* 'become sour', etc. Walde-P. 1.468.

Skt. *yas-*, Av. *yah-*, above, 1.

10.32 FLOW (vb.)

Grk.	ῥέω	Goth.	rinnan	Lith.	tekėti, bėgti
NG	τρέχω	ON	renna, fljōta	Lett.	tecēt
Lat.	fluere	Dan.	flyde, rinde	ChSl.	tešti, pluti
It.	scorrere, fluire	Sw.	flyta, rinna	SCr.	teći
Fr.	couler	OE	flōwan, irnan	Boh.	téci
Sp.	fluir, correr	ME	flowe, renne	Pol.	płynąć
Rum.	curge	NE	flow, run	Russ.	teč'
Ir.	rethim	Du.	vloeien	Skt.	sru-, sṛ-, kṣar-
NIr.	rithim	OHG	fliozan, rinnan	Av.	γžar-, rud-, tač-
W.	llifo, rhedeg	MHG	vliezen, rinnen		
Br.	bera, redek	NHG	fliessen, rinnen		

Among verbs for 'flow' there is one group which clearly reflects a distinctive IE root for this notion, though its survival is more widespread in derivatives than in the verbs. Some are cognate with verbs for 'gush forth, swell' or 'pour' or 'float', or come through 'drip', from 'filter'.

But the commonest situation is the extension of words for 'run' (10.46) to cover 'flow'. Nearly everywhere the words for 'run' may, at least occasionally or colloquially, be applied to liquids. So in NE, despite *flow*, the brook *runs*, water is *running* (in the tap), etc. In many languages they are the regular words for 'flow', either for both 'flow' and 'run' (as NG τρέχω, Lith. *bėgti*) or specialized to 'flow' (as mostly *tek-* in Balto-Slavic). Or the older distinctive word for 'flow' may survive only in technical or literary use, as It. *fluire* beside *scorrere*.

1. IE **sreu-*. Walde-P. 2.702 f.

Grk. ῥέω, Skt. *sru-*, Av. *rud-* (pres. stem *raoδa-*, caus. *raodaya-*; cf. also *raoδah-* 'stream') beside *urvant-* (**sruvant-*) pple. 'flowing'; more widespread in derivs., esp. words for 'river' or 'stream' (1.36).

2. From 'run' (10.46). Grk. τρέχω 'run', NG 'run' and 'flow'; Lat. *currere* 'run', as 'flow' mostly poet., It. *(s)correre*, Sp. *correr* 'run, flow', Rum. *curge* (re-formed after *merge* 'go') formerly 'run, flow', now reg. 'flow'; Ir. *rethim*, NIr. *rithim*, W. *rhedeg*, Br. *redek* 'run, flow'; Goth. *rinnan*, ON *renna*, OE *irnan*, OHG *rinnan*, etc. 'run, flow' (NHG *rinnen* mostly 'flow in a small stream, trickle'); Lith. *bėgti* 'run, flow'; Lith. *tekėti* 'flow, run , Lett. *tecēt* mostly

'flow' (as 'run' only special uses, cf. Mühl.-Endz. s.v.), ChSl. *tešti* 'run, flow', SCr. *teći*, Boh. *téci*, Russ. *teč'* 'flow' (sense 'run' entirely lost), Av. *tač-* 'run, flow'.

3. Lat. *fluere* (> It. *fluire*, Sp. *fluir*), perf. *flūxī* (cf. also *con-flugēs*) : Grk. οἰνό-φλυξ 'wine-drunk', φλύζω 'boil up, bubble over', fr. an extension of **bhleu-* in words for 'swell (up), burst (out)', etc., cf. Grk. φλέω 'teem', ChSl. *bl'ivati* 'spit, vomit', etc. Walde-P. 2.213 f. Ernout-M. 370 ff. Walde-H. 1.519 f.

Fr. *couler*, fr. Lat. *cōlāre* 'filter, strain' (fr. *cōlum* 'strainer'), with development of 'flow' through 'drip'. REW 2035.

4. W. *llifo*, cf. *llif* 'a stream, flood', Br. *livaden* 'flood', prob. fr. **līb-* : Grk. λείβω, Lat. *lībāre* 'pour a libation', with extension of the root in Lith. *lieti*, ChSl. *liti* 'pour', W. *lliant* 'stream', Ir. *lia* 'flood', etc. (Walde-P. 2.392 f., without W. *llifo*, etc.) G. S. Lane, Language 8.297.

Br. *bera* 'flow' beside W. *beru* 'drip', prob. fr. **bher-* in Ir. *topur* 'spring, well', Skt. *bhur-* 'quiver', *bhurvan-* 'surging, etc. (Walde-P. 2.157 f., without the Br., W. forms). G. S. Lane, Language 8.297.

5. OE *flōwan*, ME *flowe*, NE *flow*, Du. *vloeien* (= ON *flōa* 'flow over, flood'), ChSl. *pluti* 'sail, flow', Pol. *płynąć* 'flow' (but other Slavic cognates mostly 'float, swim, sail', as also Grk. πλέω, Skt. *plu-*, etc.) fr. IE **pleu-*, with extension **pleu-d-* in ON *fljōta*, Dan. *flyde*, Sw. *flyta*, OHG *fliozan*, MHG *vliezen*, NHG *fliessen* (= OE *flēotan*, ME *flete* 'float' (ME also sometimes 'flow'), Lith. *plausti* 'swim'). Cf. 10.34–36. Walde-P. 2.94 f. Falk-Torp 242.

6. Lith. *tekėti*, *bėgti*, ChSl. *tešti*, etc., above, 2.

ChSl. *pluti*, Pol. *płynąć*, above, 5.

7. Skt. *sru-*, Av. *rud-*, above, 1.

Skt. *sṛ-* 'flow, run' : Grk. ὁρμή 'onrush, onset', etc. Walde-P. 2.497. Uhlenbeck 330.

Skt. *kṣar-*, Av. γžar- (by metathesis *žgar-*) : Arm. *jur* 'water', Grk. φθείρω 'destroy' (as 'let perish, pass away'). Walde-P. 1.700.

Av. *tač-* above, 2.

10.33 SINK (vb.)

(a = trans., b = intr.)

Grk.	(κατα-)δύω (a, b, mid. b), βυθίζω (a, mid. b)	Goth.	siggan (b), saggjan (a)	Lith.	grimsti (b), gramzdinti (a)
NG	βουλιάζω (a, b), βυθίζω (a, mid. b)	ON	søkkva (st. b, wk. a)	Lett.	grimt (b), gremdēt (a)
Lat.	(sub)mergere (a, pass. b)	Dan.	synke (b), sænke (a)	ChSl.	pogręznąti (b), pogrąžati (b), topiti (a, refl. b), tonąti (b)
It.	affondare (a, refl. b)	Sw.	sjunka (b), sänka (a)	SCr.	potopiti (a, refl. b), tonuti (b)
Fr.	couler (a, b), enfoncer (a, refl. b), plonger (a, refl. b)	OE	sincan (b), sencan (a)	Boh.	(po)topiti (a, refl. b), tonouti (b)
Sp.	hundir (a, refl. b)	ME	sinke (a, b), senche (a)	Pol.	(za)topić (a), (za)tonać (b)
Rum.	scufunda (a, refl. b)	NE	sink (a, b)	Russ.	potopit' (a, refl. b), (po)tonut' (b)
Ir.	bāidim (a, pass. b)	Du.	zinken (b), laten zinken (a)	Skt.	majj- (b, caus. a)
NIr.	bāidhim (a), tēighim fē (b)	OHG	sinkan (b), senkan (a)	Av.	. . . .
W.	suddo, soddi (a, b)	MHG	sinken (b), senken (a)		
Br.	goueledi (a, b)	NHG	sinken (b), senken (a)		

In verbs for 'sink' the primary notion is taken here as 'become or cause to be submerged', as of a ship in the sea, though many of the words are used also for 'sink' in wider sense = 'go down', 'lower', etc. Several are connected with words for 'bottom' or 'depth'. But in many cases the relations are obscure, and in part a notion of movement downward or into may be earlier than the specific.

The transitive and intransitive 'sink' are expressed by related forms of the same verb, or in part by the same form, as NE *sink*. The primary forms are entered first in the list, whether transitive or intransitive.

1. Grk. δύω (pres. also δύνω), esp. καταδύω, same root as in ἐν-δύω 'put on' (clothing), ἐκ-δύω 'take off', perh. : Skt. *upā-du-* 'put on'; but primary sense of root obscure. Walde-P. 1.777 f. Boisacq 206.

Grk. βυθίζω (rare in classical, common from Hellenistic times, Polyb., NT, etc., Byz., NG), deriv. of βυθός 'depth' (esp. of the sea).

NG βουλιάζω, fr. late Grk. βολίζω 'heave the lead, sound' (NT, Byz.), mid. 'sink' (Geop.), deriv. of βολίς 'a missile, a casting-lead' (: βάλλω 'throw', 10.25). Koraes, Ἄτακτα 4.58. Cf. Fr. *plonger*, below, 2.

2. Lat. *mergere*, esp. *sub-mergere* : Skt. *majj-* 'sink', Lith. *masgoti*, Lett. *masgot* 'wash' (through 'dip, plunge into water'), IE **mezg-*. Walde-P. 2.300 f. Ernout-M. 610. Walde-H. 2.76 f.

Derivs. of Lat. *fundus* 'bottom'. It. *affondare* (cf. *affondo* 'deep'); Fr. *enfoncer* (cf. OFr. *fons*, Fr. *fond* 'bottom'), Sp. *hundir* (*hondo* 'bottom'), Rum. *scufunda* (also *cufunda*, fr. **con-fondāre*; *s-* from *ex-* or by blend with *sub-*). REW 269, 3585, 8437.

Fr. *couler* = *couler* 'flow', fr. Lat. *cōlāre* 'filter, strain' (10.32).

Fr. *plonger*, fr. **plumbicāre*, deriv. of *plumbum* 'lead' through its nautical sense. REW 6613.

3. Ir. *bāidim* ('drown' and 'sink', cf. K. Meyer, Contrib. 161), NIr. *bāidhim*, *bādhaim* : W. *boddi*, Br. *beuzi* 'drown', Skt. *gāh-* 'plunge (into)', *gāha-* 'depth', IE **gʷādh-*. Walde-P. 1.665. Pedersen 2.458 f.

NIr. (for intr.) *tēighim fē* (or *faoi*), lit. 'go under'.

W. *suddo*, *soddi*, perh. fr. forms of IE **sed-* 'sit', with semantic development as in NE *settle* (of a ship), but there are phonetic difficulties. Morris Jones 78, 154 (but untenable explanation of the *u*-form).

Br. *goueledi*, fr. *goueled* 'bottom'.

4. Goth. *siggan*, ON *søkkva* (strong vb.), Dan. *synke*, Sw. *sjunka*, OE *sincan*, etc., whence caus. Goth. *saggqja* (= **saggjan*, cf. *ufsaggjan*), ON *søkkva* (weak vb.), OE *sencan*, etc. (caus. forms lost in NE and Du.), general Gmc. group, but outside connections dub. Walde-P. 2.496. Falk-Torp 1228.

5. Lith. *grimsti*, *gramzdėti*, caus. *gramzdinti*, Lett. *grimt*, caus. *gremdēt*, fr. a root **gremd-*, beside **grenĝ-* in ChSl. *pogręznąti*, *pogrąžati* 'sink', further connections dub. Walde-P. 1.654 ff. Berneker 350.

6. ChSl. *topiti*, *tonąti* (fr. **topnąti*), attested late (in Gospels only *pogrąžati*, etc.), but general Slavic : Arm. *t'at'avem* 'dip, plunge', *t'on* 'dampness, wet'. Walde-P. 1.705. Otherwise Brückner 573 (: ChSl. *teti*, *tepą* 'strike', for which see Trautmann 319).

7. Skt. *majj-*, above, 2.

10.34 FLOAT (vb.)

Grk.	πλέω	Goth.	....	Lith.	plaukti, pludurioti
NG	ἐπιπλέω	ON	fljóta	Lett.	pluduot
Lat.	fluitāre	Dan.	flyde	ChSl.	pluti, plavati
It.	galleggiare	Sw.	flyta	SCr.	ploviti, plivati
Fr.	flotter, surnager	OE	flēotan, flotian	Boh.	plouti, plovati
Sp.	flotar	ME	flete, flote	Pol.	pływać
Rum.	pluti	NE	float	Russ.	plyt', plavat'
Ir.	snāim	Du.	drijven	Skt.	plu-
NIr.	snāmhaim	OHG	swebēn, fliuzan	Av.	....
W.	nofio	MHG	sweben, vliezen		
Br.	neuñvi, neuī	NHG	schwimmen		

The notions of 'float', 'swim', and 'sail' are so closely related that in many cases two of them are expressed by the same word or even all three by forms of the same root.

1. IE *pleu-, also *pleu-d-, *pleu-k-, in words for 'float', 'swim', and 'sail', also 'flow' (10.32), and 'rain' (Lat. pluere). Walde-P. 2.94 ff. Ernout-M. 781 f.

Grk. πλέω, mostly 'sail', also 'float', ἐπιπλέω 'sail upon', also 'float', NG 'float', ON fljōta, Dan. flyde, Sw. flyta 'flow, float', OE flēotan, flotian (rare), ME flete, flote, NE float 'float', OHG fliuzan, MHG vliezen mostly 'flow', sometimes 'float'; Lith. plaukti 'swim, float, sail', pludurioti, Lett. pluduot 'float'; ChSl. pluti, plavati, SCr. ploviti, plivati, Boh. plaviti se (refl.), plovati, plouti, Pol. pływać, Russ. plyt', plavat', all 'float, swim' and, except Pol., 'sail'; Skt. plu- 'float, swim, sail' : Av. fru- in caus. 'cause to flow' (Vd. 5.16, 18), also 'overflow, extinguish, fly, etc.' (Barth. 990).

2. Lat. fluitāre, frequent. of fluere 'flow' (10.32).

It. galleggiare, deriv. of galla 'gall-apple, air-bubble, light object' (cf. a galla 'floating'), fr. Lat. galla 'gall-apple'. REW 3655.

OFr. floter, Fr. flotter (> Sp. flotar), prob. deriv. of flot 'wave', this fr. an OFrank. form corresponding to OE flōd 'flowing, flood'. Wartburg 3.638 ff. Somewhat otherwise, as to the precise Gmc. source, REW 3383, Gamillscheg 426.

Fr. surnager, cpd. of sur 'on' and nager 'swim' (10.35).

Rum. pluti, fr. the Slavic (above, 1).

3. Ir. snāim, etc., general Celtic for 'swim' (10.35) and 'float'.

4. ON fljōta, OE flēotan, etc., above, 1. OHG swebēn, MHG sweben 'float' in water or air, NHG schweben 'soar' : OHG sweibōn 'move to and fro', OE swīfan 'move, sweep' etc. Walde-P. 2.520. Weigand-H. 2.815.

Du. drijven 'drive' (10.65), also 'drift, float'. Cf. the similar use of NE drive (NED s.v. 26) and esp. (through sb.) drift, NHG auf dem Wasser treiben.

MHG swimmen, NHG schwimmen 'swim' (10.35), also 'float' (for purposes of definition obenauf schwimmen).

5. Lith. pludurioti, Lett. pluduot, Lith. plaukti, above, 1.

6. ChSl. pluti, etc., general Slavic, above, 1.

7. Skt. plu-, above, 1.

10.35 SWIM (vb.)

Grk.	νήχω, νέω	Goth.	....	Lith.	plaukti, plaukyti
NG	κολυμπῶ	ON	svimma, synda	Lett.	peldēt
Lat.	nāre, natāre	Dan.	svømme	ChSl.	pluti, plavati
It.	nuotare	Sw.	simma	SCr.	ploviti, plivati
Fr.	nager	OE	swimman	Boh.	plouti, plovati
Sp.	nadar	ME	swymme	Pol.	pływać
Rum.	înota	NE	swim	Russ.	plyt', plavat'
Ir.	snāim	Du.	zwemmen	Skt.	plu-
NIr.	snāmhaim	OHG	swimman	Av.	....
W.	nofio	MHG	swimmen		
Br.	neuñvi, neuī	NHG	schwimmen		

1. IE *snā-, also *snāu-, *sneu-, in words for 'swim' also 'bathe', 'drip', 'wet', etc. Walde-P. 2.692 f. Ernout-M. 673 f. Pedersen 1.85.

Grk. νήχω, νέω, aor. ἔνευσα; Lat. nāre, natāre (> Sp. nadar), VLat. also *notāre (> It. nuotare, Rum. înota, OFr. noer, REW 5846); Ir. snāim, NIr. snāmhaim, W. nofio (fr. sb. nawf, nofion), Br. neuñvi, neuī; cf. Skt. snā- 'bathe', snāuti 'drips', etc.

2. NG κολυμπῶ, fr. class. Grk. κολυμβάω 'dive, plunge', deriv. of κόλυμβος 'diver', name of a bird. Already Hellenistic for 'swim', cf. Moeris νεῖν καὶ νήχεσθαι Ἀττικοί, κολυμβᾶν Ἕλληνες.

3. Fr. nager, fr. Lat. nāvigāre 'sail' (10.36). REW 5861.

4. ON svimma, OE, OHG swimman, etc., general Gmc., also ON, NIcel. synda (deriv. of sund 'swimming, strait', cf. NE sound, etc., fr. *sumtó-), perh. : W. chvyfio 'stir, wave, brandish'. Walde-P. 2.524. Falk-Torp 1224.

5. Lith. plaukti, plaukyti (the latter in Hermann, Lit.-deutsches Gesprächsb., p. 148), see 10.34.

Lett. peldēt : Grk. πλάδος 'dampness, foulness', πλαδᾶν 'be wet', prob. fr. an extension of the root in Lith. pilti 'pour', Lett. pilēt 'drip', etc. Walde-P. 2.66 (54). Mühl.-Endz. 3.195.

6. ChSl. pluti, etc., general Slavic, see 10.34.

7. Skt. plu-, see 10.34.

10.36 SAIL (vb.)

Grk.	πλέω	Goth.	farjan	Lith.	plaukti
NG	πλέω	ON	sigla	Lett.	kug'uot, zēg'elēt
Lat.	nāvigāre	Dan.	sejle	ChSl.	jachati, pluti, plavati
It.	navigare	Sw.	sigla	SCr.	jedriti, ploviti
Fr.	naviguer	OE	siglan lipan, rōwan	Boh.	plaviti se, plouti, plovati
Sp.	navegar	ME	seile		
Rum.	naviga	NE	sail	Pol.	żeglować
Ir.	immrāim	Du.	zeilen, varen	Russ.	plyt', plavat'
NIr.	seolaim	OHG	ferien	Skt.	plu-
W.	hwylio, morio, mordwyo	MHG	schiffen, sigelen, vern	Av.	....
Br.	mordeī	NHG	schiffen, segeln		

The verbs for 'sail' are partly from the same root that is widespread also in those for 'float' and 'swim' (cf. 10.34). Others are derivs. of nouns for 'sail', 'ship', or 'sea'. Some are words for 'row' extended to 'travel by water, sail', and some are general words for 'travel, go', used for 'sail'.

1. Grk. πλέω, see 10.34.

2. Lat. nāvigāre (> Romance words)

deriv. of nāvis 'ship' (10.81). Ernout-M. 624.

3. Ir. immrāim, lit. 'row about', but reg. also 'sail, go by ship' (cf. vbl. n. imrām 'voyage'), cpd. of rāim 'row' (10.852). Pedersen 2.591.

NIr. seolaim, W. hwylio, derivs. of Ir. seol, W. hwyl 'sail' (10.88).

W. morio, deriv. of mor 'sea'.

W. mordwyo, Br. mordeī, cpds. of mor 'sea' and last part : Ir. tiagu 'go' (10.47). Pedersen 2.648.

4. Goth. farjan (πλέω Lk. 8.23, also ἐλαύνω 'row' Jn. 6.19), OHG ferien, MHG vern = OS ferian 'voyage', OE ferian 'transport (esp. by water), ferry, go, travel', ON ferja (trans.) 'carry, transport (esp. by sea), ferry' : Goth. faran 'go (about)', OHG, OE faran, ON fara 'go, travel', all used frequently of travel by sea, and so esp. Du. varen (10.47).

ON sigla, Dan. sejle, Sw. segla, OE siglan, seglian, ME seile, NE sail, Du. zeilen, MHG sigelen, NHG segeln, derivs. of ON, OE segl, etc. 'sail' (10.88). Falk-Torp 955.

OE lîpan 'travel', but esp. 'travel by sea, sail' : ON lîða 'go, travel', etc. (10.47).

OE rōwan 'row' (10.852), but also 'travel by ship, sail', cf. ic rowe = navigo (Aelfric, Gram.), þa hig reowon 'navigantibus illis' (Lk. 8.23).

MHG, NHG schiffen, deriv. of schiff 'ship' (10.81).

5. Lith. plaukti, see 10.34.

Lett. kug'uot, deriv. of kug'is 'ship' (10.81).

Lett. zēg'elēt, fr. MLG segelen (cf. above, 4).

6. ChSl. pluti, plavati, etc., general Slavic, see 10.34.

ChSl. jachati (jadą), lit. 'go, ride' (10.66), but renders πλέω Lk. 8.23 (likewise prě-jachati καταπλέω Lk. 8.26).

SCr. jedriti, deriv. of jedro 'sail' (10.88).

Pol. żeglować, fr. NHG segeln (above, 4).

10.37 FLY (vb.)

Grk.	πέτομαι	Goth.	....	Lith.	lėkti, skristi
NG	πετῶ	ON	fljúga	Lett.	laisties, skriet
Lat.	volāre	Dan.	flyve	ChSl.	poletěti
It.	volare	Sw.	flyga	SCr.	letjeti
Fr.	voler	OE	flēogan	Boh.	letěti
Sp.	volar	ME	fleie	Pol.	lecieć
Rum.	sbura	NE	fly	Russ.	letet'
Ir.	foluur, etelaigim	Du.	vliegen	Skt.	pat-
NIr.	eiteallaim	OHG	fliugan	Av.	dvan-, vay-, pat-
W.	ehedeg	MHG	vliegen		
Br.	nijal	NHG	fliegen		

Words for 'fly' are cognate with others applied to various other forms of rapid motion. But in one group the meaning 'fly' is dominant and widespread and, though also extended, was probably the primary sense of the IE root.

1. IE *pet-. Walde-P. 2.19 ff.

Grk. πέτομαι, NG πετῶ (Hatzidakis Μεσ. 1.413); Skt., Av. pat- (also 'fall'; OPers. ud-apatatā 'made an uprising, rebellion'); OW hedant, W. hed, hedeg 'flying', whence ehedeg 'fly' (cpd. of eh- : Lat. ex, Pedersen 1.91). In sense of 'fly' more widespread in the derivs. for 'wing, feather', as Skt. pattra-, Lat. penna, etc. (4.392). Cf. also Lat. petere 'go after, seek' and words for 'fall' (10.23).

2. Lat. volāre (> It. volare, Fr. voler, Sp. volar; Rum. sbura, OIt. svolare fr. *exvolāre; REW 9431, 3115), cf. volucer 'winged, swift', perh. (fr. a root *gʷel-) : Skt. garut-mant- 'winged, bird'. Ernout-M. 1131. Pedersen, KZ 36.92 f.

3. Ir. foluur, cpd. of -luur 'move' (10.11).

MIr. etelaigim, NIr. eiteallaim, deriv. of Ir. ette, NIr. eite 'wing, feather', (cpd. with laigim 'lie'?).

W. ehedeg, cf. above, 1.

Br. nijal : MCorn. nyge 'fly' (also 'float'), W. neidio 'jump, leap', these prob. : Lat. natāre 'swim, float'. Loth, RC 46.154.

4. ON fljúga, OE flēogan, etc., general Gmc. : Lith. plaukti, plaukyti 'float, sail, swim', IE *pleu-k-, extension of *pleu- in Grk. πλέω 'sail, float, Skt. plu- 'swim', etc. (cf. 10.34).

5. Lith. lėkti (= Lett. lēkt 'jump, hop'), ChSl. po-letěti (simplex only in iter. lětati), SCr. letjeti, etc., general Slavic (let- fr. *lek-t- as in pletą 'plait' : Lat. plectere, etc.; Leskien, Altbulg. Gram. 57) : Grk. λακτίζω 'kick', ON leggr 'leg, joint', etc. Walde-P. 2.421. Berneker 703 f. Brückner 292.

Lett. skriet, mostly 'run rapidly, etc.' (= Lith. skrieti 'move or fly in a circle'), Lith. skristi 'fly, circle' : ChSl. krilo 'wing', Lith. kreipti 'turn around' (10.13), ON skrīða 'creep, crawl', etc., fr. *(s)krei-, etc., extensions of *(s)ker-. Walde-P. 2.570 f. Mühl.-Endz. 3.897.

Lett. laisties, also used of other quick movements 'hurry, go rapidly, ride', orig. 'let oneself out', refl. of laist 'let'; Lith. leisti 'let', etc. (19.47). Mühl.-Endz. 2.411 ff.

6. ChSl. poletěti, SCr. letjeti, etc., above, 5.

7. Skt., Av. pat-, cf. above, 1.

Av. vay- (only with ā, āvayeinti 3pl., of gods), cf. Skt. (RV) vēvīyatē 'flutters' : Skt. vī- (veti) 'seek, approach eagerly', Lith. vyti 'pursue', etc., IE *wei-. Walde-P. 1.228 ff. Barth. 1355.

Av. dvan- (only with preverbs, Barth. 763) : dvąnman- 'cloud', Lett. dvans, dvanums 'vapor, steam', n-extensions of IE *dheu- in Skt. dhū- 'shake' (10.26), etc. Walde-P. 1.841.

10.38 BLOW (vb. intr.)

Grk.	πνέω, φῡσάω, ἄημι	Goth.	waian (-blēsan)	Lith.	pūsti (dumti)
NG	φυσῶ, πνέω	ON	blása	Lett.	pūst
Lat.	flāre	Dan.	blæse	ChSl.	duchati, vějati
It.	soffiare	Sw.	blåsa	SCr.	puhati, duvati
Fr.	souffler	OE	blāwan, wāwan	Boh.	váti, douti
Sp.	soplar	ME	blawe, blowe	Pol.	wiać, dąć
Rum.	sufla	NE	blow	Russ.	dut', vejat'
Ir.	sétim	Du.	blazen, waaien	Skt.	vā-, dham-
NIr.	séidim	OHG	blāsan, wājan	Av.	vā-
W.	cwythu	MHG	blāsen, wajen		
Br.	c'houeza	NHG	blasen, wehen		

Many of the verbs for 'blow', including perhaps the inherited group, are of imitative origin. Sometimes there are two common words for 'blow', one in a strong, the other in a weak sense, as NHG blasen vs. wehen, Russ. dut' vs. vejat'.

1. IE *wē-, much more widely preserved in the deriv. sb. for 'wind', Lat. ventus, Goth. winds, Lith. vėjas, ChSl. větrŭ, Av. vāta- (1.72). Walde-P. 1.220 f. Feist 541 f.

Grk. ἄημι (poet.); Goth. waian, OE wāwan (much less common than blā-

wan), Du. *waaien*, OHG *wājan*, MHG *wæjen*, NHG *wehen;* ChSl. *vějati* (in Gospels *vŭz-vějati* Mt. 7.25, 27 for πνέω, beside more common *duchati* Lk. 12.55, etc.), Boh. *váti*, Pol. *wiać*, Russ. *vejat'*.

2. Grk. πνέω 'breathe' and the usual word for 'blow', see 4.51.

Grk. φῡσάω, NG φυσῶ (now the usual pop. word), fr. an imitative syllable **bhū̆* beside **pū̆* in Lith. *pūsti*, Lett. *pūst*, SCr. *puhati* 'blow' (Boh. *puchati* 'swell up, stink', *pychati* 'be puffed up', Russ. *puchnut'* 'swell up', *pychnout'* 'breathe hard, pant', etc.), Lat. *pustula* 'blister', etc. Walde-P. 2.81. Trautmann 233.

3. Lat. *flāre* (cpd. *sufflāre* > Romance words; REW 8430), fr. **bhlā-* beside **bhlē-* in OE *blāwan*, ME *blawan*, NE *blow*, OHG *blājan*, MHG *blæjen* (NHG *blähen* mostly 'cause flatulence', refl. 'be puffed up'); and **bhlēs-* in Goth. *-blēsan* (only in *ufblēsan* 'be puffed up'), ON *blása*, Dan. *blæse*, Sw. *blåsa*, Du. *blazen*, OHG *blāsan*, etc., all fr. various extensions of an imitative syllable. Walde-P. 2.179. Ernout-M. 369. Walde-H. 1.517. Feist 512.

4. Ir. *sētim*, NIr. *sēidim*, W. *cwythu*, Br. *c'houeza*, fr. **sweizd-*, **swizd-*, with parallel, though not identical, forms in Skt. *kṣvid-* 'hum', Grk. σίζω, Lat. *sībilāre*, ChSl. *svistati* 'hiss', etc., all of imitative origin. Walde-P. 2.517 f. Ernout-M. 936. Pedersen 2.627.

5. Gmc. words, above, 1 and 3.

6. Lith. *pūsti*, Lett. *pūst*, SCr. *puhati*, above, 2.

7. ChSl. *duchati*, *dušą* (reg. in Gospels for πνέω 'blow'), SCr. *duhati*, beside ChSl. *dŭchnąti*, *dychati* (in Gospels *vŭz-* 'sigh'), SCr. *dihati*, etc. 'breathe' (4.51) : Lith. *dusti* 'get out of breath', *dvėsti* 'expire, die', etc., fr. IE **dhwes-*, extension of **dheu-* in Skt. *dhū-* 'shake', etc. (cf. ChSl. *dunąti*, etc., below). Walde-P. 1.846. Berneker 234 f.

ChSl. *dąti*, *dŭmą* (Supr. 'be puffed up'), SCr. *duti*, *dmem* (old), Boh. *douti*, Pol. *dąć*, Russ. *dut'* (here in part) : Lith. *dumti*, Skt. *dham-* 'blow', etc. Walde-P. 1.851 f. Berneker 244.

ChSl. *dunąti*, *duną*, SCr. (old *duti*, *dujem*) *duvati*, Russ. *dul'*, *duvat'*, *dunut'* : Skt. *dhū-* 'shake, agitate', Grk. θύω 'rage, seethe', etc. In part confused with preceding group (where *ą* and *u* were merged). Walde-P. 1.835 f. Berneker 236.

ChSl. *vějati*, etc., above, 1.

8. Skt., Av. *vā-*, above, 1.

Skt. *dham-* : Lith. *dumti*, ChSl. *dąti* 'blow' (above, 7).

10.41 CREEP, CRAWL

Grk.	*ἕρπω*	Goth.	....	Lith.	*lįsti, slinkti*
NG	*σέρνομαι, ἕρπω*	ON	*skrīða, krjūpa*	Lett.	*list*
Lat.	*serpere, rēpere*	Dan.	*krybe kravle*	ChSl.	*plŭziti, (prě)smykati sę*
It.	*strisciare, serpeggiare*	Sw.	*krypa kräla*	SCr.	*puzati gmizati*
Fr.	*ramper, se traîner*	OE	*crēopan snīcan, smūgan*	Boh.	*plaziti se, lézti*
Sp.	*arrastrarse*	ME	*crepe, craule*	Pol.	*pełzać, czołgać się*
Rum.	*se tîrî*	NE	*creep, crawl*	Russ.	*presmykat'sja, polzat'*
Ir.	....	Du.	*kriupen*	Skt.	*sṛp-*
NIr.	*snāighim, snāmhaim*	OHG	*chriochan, slīhhan*	Av.	....
W.	*ymlusgo, cropian*	MHG	*kriechen, slīchen*		
Br.	*en em stleja*	NHG	*kriechen, schleichen*		

Words for 'creep' in the literal sense are also extended to denote slow or stealthy motion, and, conversely, the latter is the primary notion in some of the words included in the list. Apart from an inherited group, several of the words are reflexive or middle forms of those for 'drag', while others are cognate with words denoting such diverse actions as 'slip', 'stroke', 'climb', 'scratch', 'turn', etc.

1. IE **serp-*. Walde-P. 2.502. Ernout-M. 931.

Grk. ἕρπω; Lat. *serpere* (pple. *serpens* 'serpent' > It. *serpe*, whence vb. *serpeggiare*); Skt. *sṛp-* (with *sarpa-* 'serpent'); Alb. *gjarpën* 'serpent'. Clearly an IE root with the dominant sense of 'creep' though in the last analysis, if taken as **ser-p-* beside **ser-* in Skt. *sṛ-* 'flow, hasten, etc.', this would be an early specialization.

2. Grk. ἕρπω (NG esp. fig. 'cringe'), above, 1.

NG σέρνομαι (or with μὲ τὴν κοιλιά 'with the belly'), mid. of σέρνω 'draw, drag' (9.33). Cf. late Grk. σύρεσθαι γαστέρι (LS s.v. σύρω), and σύράμενος 'crawling' (Pallad., Migne 34.1084).

3. Lat. *serpere*, above, 1.

Lat. *rēpere* : Lith. *rėplioti*, *roploti*, Lett. *rāpuot* 'creep on all fours', perh. fr. **srēp-* beside **serp-* (above, 1). Walde-P. 2.370. Ernout-M. 861, 931. Mühl.-Endz. 3.497.

It. *strisciare*, also and orig. 'touch lightly, stroke', of imitative orig. REW 8309.

It. *serpeggiare*, above, 1.

Fr. *ramper*, formerly 'climb' (cf. also *rampant* 'with raised paws' > NE *rampant*) : It. *rampare* 'clamber up', *rampa* 'claw', etc., all through 'claw, paw', fr. Gmc. **hrampa-* 'hook' (cf. MLG *ramp* 'cramp, misfortune', Du. *ramp* 'misfortune') related to OHG *hrimpfan* 'pull together, wrinkle'. REW 7032. Gamillscheg 739. Falk-Torp 875.

Fr. *se traîner*, refl. of *traîner* 'drag', fr. VLat. **tragīnāre*, fr. **tragere* for *trahere* 'draw' (9.27). REW 8837. Gamillscheg 856.

Sp. *arrastrarse*, refl. of *arrastrar* 'drag' : *rastra* 'track, trail, harrow', fr. Lat. *rāstrum* 'rake'.

Rum. *se tîrî*, refl. of *tîrî* 'drag' (fr. Slavic, ChSl. *trěti*, *tĭrą* 'rub', 9.25). Tiktin 1606.

4. NIr. *snāighim*, fr. root seen in OHG *snahan* 'creep' (rare), OE *snaca* 'snake', etc. Falk-Torp 1098.

NIr. *snāmhaim* 'swim, float' (10.35), also 'creep, crawl'.

NIr. *lāmacān* (sb.), deriv. of *lām* 'hand', is the word used for the child's 'creeping on all fours'.

W. *ymlusgo*, cpd. of refl. *ym-* and *llusgo* 'drag', etym.? Morris Jones 139 (but cf. Loth, RC 36.166).

W. *cropian*, fr. NE (dial.) *crope*, pret. of *creep* (below). But same form in sense of 'grope' fr. NE *grope*. Fynes-Clinton, W. Voc., Bangor Dist., 298. Parry-Williams 182, 220.

Br. *en em stleja*, refl. of *stleja* 'drag', etym.? (Henry 254 : Ir. *slōet* 'a slide', OE *slīdan* 'slide', etc.)

5. ON *skrīða* = OE *scrīþan* 'go, go about, glide', OHG *scrītan*, NHG *schreiten* 'stride' : Lith. *skristi*, Lett. *skriet* 'fly' (10.37). Walde-P. 2.571. Falk-Torp 1027.

ON *krjūpa*, Dan. *krybe*, Sw. *krypa*, OE *crēopan*, ME *crepe*, *creep*, NE *creep*, Du. *kriupen*, fr. IE **greu-b-* (: Lith. *grubineti* 'stumble'); OHG *chriochan*, MHG, NHG *kriechen*, fr. IE **greu-g-* (: Ir. *grug* 'wrinkle'); extensions of IE **ger-* in Lett. *griezt* 'turn' (10.13–14), Lith. *gręžti* 'turn around, bore', etc. Walde-P. 1.597 f. Falk-Torp 585.

Dan. *kravle*, Sw. *kräla* (ME *craule*, NE *crawl*, fr. Norse), ON *krafla* 'paw, scramble', Sw. *kravla* 'crawl, scramble': MLG *krabben* 'scratch, scrape', NHG *krabbeln* 'crawl, grope', Grk. γράφω 'scratch, write', etc. Walde-P. 1.607. Falk-Torp 577 f., 572. Hellquist 507, 519. NED s.v. *crawl* vb.[1].

OE *snīcan*, early ME *snīken* (NE *sneak* fr. a parallel form) : ON *snīkja* 'hanker after', Dan. *snige*, Sw. *snika* 'sneak', Gmc. **snik-* beside **snak-* in OE *snaca* 'snake', etc. Walde-P. 1.697 f. Falk-Torp 1095.

OE *smūgan* (ON *smjūga* esp. 'crawl through a hole') : ChSl. *smykati sę*, etc. (see below, 7).

OHG *slīhhan*, MHG *slīchen*, NHG *schleichen* : ON *slīkr* 'smooth', Ir. *sligim* 'smear', etc., IE **sleig-*, fr. **(s)lei-* in words for 'slimy, slippery, etc.' (Grk. ἀλίνω, Lat. *linere* 'smear', etc.). Walde-P. 2.391.

6. Lith. *lįsti*, Lett. *list*, prob. fr. forms of IE **sleidh-* 'slip' (in Grk. ὀλισθάνω, etc., 10.42) without initial *s-* (in Lith. also nasalized). Walde-P. 2.708, 715.

Lith. *slinkti* : OHG *slingan* 'wind, swing', OE *slingan* 'creep' (rare word), OHG *slango* 'snake', etc. Walde-P. 2.714.

7. ChSl. *plŭziti*, SCr. *puzati*, Boh. *plaziti se*, Pol. *pełzać*, Russ. *polzat'*, etym. dub., perh. (as orig. 'turn, twist') : OE *fealh*, *fulgon* pret. of **felgan* 'turn' (intr.), OHG *felga*, OE *felg(e)* 'felloe' (on a wheel), fr. **pel-k-* (the Slavic words fr. **pel-ĝ-*). Walde-P. 1.516. Brückner 402.

ChSl. *(prě)smykati sę*, Russ. *presmykat'sja* : Boh. *smykati* 'drag', Pol. *smykać*, Lith. *mukti*, *smukti* 'slip away', OE *smūgan* 'crawl', Skt. *muñc-* 'loose, let go', Grk. ἀπομύσσω, Lat. *ēmungere* 'blow the nose'. Walde-P. 2.254. Ernout-M. 641 f.

Late ChSl. *gŭmŭzati*, SCr. *gmizati* : Russ. *gomozit'sja* 'swarm', Boh. *hemzati* 'crawl', *hemzeti* 'swarm', etc. (a large Slavic group), outside connections dub. Berneker 367.

Boh. *lézti* : ChSl. *vŭz-lěsti* 'ascend', *sŭ-lěsti* 'descend', Russ. *lezt'* 'climb', Lett. *lēžuot* 'go slowly, drag oneself', ON *lāgr* 'low', IE **lēgh-*, **ləgh-*. Walde-P. 2.426. Berneker 716.

Pol. *czołgać się*, also 'crouch, grovel', as orig. 'touch the forehead' fr. *czoło* 'forehead' (4.205).

8. Skt. *sṛp-*, above, 1.

10.42 SLIDE, SLIP (vb.)

Grk.	*ὀλισθάνω*	Goth.	*(sliupan)*	Lith.	*slysti, čiaužti*
NG	*γλιστρῶ*	ON	*skreppa, skriðna*	Lett.	*slīdēt*
Lat.	*lābī*	Dan.	*glide*	ChSl.	....
It.	*sdrucciolare, scivolare*	Sw.	*glida (slippa)*	SCr.	*klizati se*
Fr.	*glisser*	OE	*slīdan, slūpan*	Boh.	*klouznouti*
Sp.	*deslizar, resbalar*	ME	*slide, slippe*	Pol.	*pośliznać się*
Rum.	*aluneca*	NE	*slide, slip*	Russ.	*skol'zit'*
Ir.	....	Du.	*glijden, slippen*	Skt.	*sṛp-*
NIr.	*sleamhnuighim*	OHG	*slīfan, slupfan*	Av.	....
W.	*llithro*	MHG	*glīten, slüpfen, slīten*		
Br.	*rikla*	NHG	*gleiten, schlüpfen*		

1. From extensions of IE **(s)lei-*. Walde-P. 2.391 f., 707 f.

**(s)lei-dh-*, Grk. ὀλισθάνω, OE *slīdan*, ME, NE *slide*, MHG *slīten*, Lith. *slysti*, Lett. *slīdēt*, prob. also W. *llithro* (formation as in Grk. ὀλισθηρός 'slippery'); cf. also Lett. *list*, Lith. *lendu*, *lįsti* 'crawl, creep' (10.41).

**(s)lei-b-*. NIr. *sleamhnuighim* (cf. MIr. *slemon* 'lubricus', W. *llyfu* 'level, even'), OHG *slīfan* (NHG *schleifen*), Sw. *slippa*, ME *slippe*, NE *slip* (OE adj. *slipor* 'slippery'), Du. *slippen*, etc.

**(s)lei-ĝ-*. SCr. *klizati se*, Boh. *klouznouti*, Pol. *pośliznać się*, *ślizgać się*, Russ. *skol'zit'*, *skol'znut'* : ChSl. *slĭzŭkŭ*, SCr. *klizak*, Russ. *slizkij* 'slippery', etc. (cf. OHG *slīhhan* 'crawl', etc., 10.41). Brückner 531. Miklosich 300.

2. NG γλιστρῶ, fr. ἐκ-λιστρῶ (Eust. 1119.53), deriv. of Grk. λίστρον 'tool for smoothing, scraper (cf. 8.23). Hatzidakis, Μεσ. 1.160.

3. Lat. *lābī* : *labāre* 'waver, be ready to fall', prob. Ir. *lobor* 'weak' and (with *s-*) ChSl. *slabŭ* 'weak', Goth. *slēpan* 'sleep', etc., fr. a root in words for 'loose, weak, hang down' and the like. Walde-P. 2.431 ff. Ernout-M. 512 f. Walde-H. 1.734.

It. *sdrucciolare*, fr. **dis-roteolāre*, deriv. of Lat. *rota* 'wheel'. REW 2686.

It. *scivolare*, of imitative orig., belonging with the group Lat. *sībilāre* 'hiss, whistle', Fr. *siffler*, etc. REW 7890.

Fr. *glisser*, blend of OFr. *glier* 'slip' with OFr. *glacier* 'slip out' (fr. *glace* 'ice'); OFr. *glier* fr. the Gmc., cf. OE *glīdan*, etc. below, 5. REW 3789. Gamillscheg 472.

Sp. *deslizar*, deriv. of *liso* 'smooth, even' (15.77).

Sp. *resbalar*, etym. dub. Wartburg 1.221.

Rum. *aluneca*, *luneca*, fr. Lat. *lūbricāre* 'make smooth, lubricate' (cf. below, 5, OE *slūpan*, etc.). Puşcariu 997.

4. NIr. *sleamhnuighim*, W. *llithro*, above, 1.

Br. *rikla* (Vallée, Ernault), prob. fr. earlier *riskla* beside *riska* (both in Le Gonidec), fr. Fr. *risquer* 'risk'?

5. ON *skreppa* (sense 'slip' fr. 'disappear', orig. 'contract, draw together') = MHG *schrimpfen* 'draw together, wrinkle' : ON *skorpinn* 'shrunken', fr. an extension of **(s)ker-* 'twist, turn'. Walde-P. 21.588. Falk-Torp 1032.

ON *skriðna* : *skrīða* 'creep, crawl' (10.41).

(OE *glīdan*) ME, NE *glide* (only rarely 'slide'), MLG *glīden* (> Dan. *glide*, Sw. *glida*), Du. *glijden*, MHG *glīten*, NHG *gleiten*, perh. fr. **ghleidh-*, beside **ghlend-*, *ghlādh*, etc. in words for 'shining, smooth', etc. (through 'smooth' to 'slippery', cf. OE *glæd* 'shining, bright, glad' : OHG *glat* 'smooth', fr. **ghlədh-*). Walde-P. 1.627. Franck-v. W. 203.

OE *slūpan*, OHG *slupfan*, MHG *slüpfen*, NHG *schlüpfen* : Goth. *sliupan*, OHG *sliofan* 'slip, creep in', IE **(s)leub-* in Lat. *lūbricus* 'slippery', etc. Walde-P. 2.710 f. Feist 438.

6. Lith. *slysti*, Lett. *slīdēt*, above, 1.

Lith. *čiaušti*, *čiuožti*, prob. of imitative origin.

7. SCr. *klizati se*, etc., the Slavic group, above, 1.

8. Skt. *sṛp-*, nearest equivalent, but chiefly 'creep, crawl' (10.41).

10.43 JUMP, LEAP (vb.)

Grk.	*ἅλλομαι, πηδάω*	Goth.	*-hlaupan*	Lith.	*šokti*
NG	*πηδῶ*	ON	*støkkva, hlaupa*	Lett.	*lēkt*
Lat.	*salīre*	Dan.	*hoppe, springe*	ChSl.	*skočiti*
It.	*saltare*	Sw.	*hoppa*	SCr.	*skočiti*
Fr.	*sauter*	OE	*hlēapan, springan*	Boh.	*skočiti*
Sp.	*saltar, brincar*	ME	*lepe, springe*	Pol.	*skoczyć*
Rum.	*sări*	NE	*jump, leap, spring*	Russ.	*prygnut', skočit*
Ir.	*lingim*	Du.	*springen*	Skt.	*skand-, pru-*
NIr.	*lēimim, lingim*	OHG	*springan*	Av.	. . . .
W.	*neidio, llamu*	MHG	*springen*		
Br.	*lammet*	NHG	*springen*		

1. IE *sel- or *sal-. Walde-P. 2.505. Ernout-M. 888 f. REW 7540, 7551.

Grk. *ἅλλομαι*; Lat. *salīre* 'jump' (> Rum. *sări*), *saltāre* 'dance' (> It. *saltare*, Fr. *sauter*, Sp. *saltar* 'jump'), Toch. A *sāl-* 'hop, jump' (SSS 477); perh. Skt. *ucchalati* (*ud-sal-) 'rushes up'.

2. Grk. *πηδάω*, NG *πηδῶ* : Skt. *pad-* 'go, fall', ChSl. *pasti* 'fall' (10.23), fr. the same root as Grk. *πούς, ποδός*, Skt. *pad-*, etc. 'foot'. Walde-P. 2.23.

3. Lat. *salīre*, etc., above, 1.

Sp. *brincar* : Cat. *vinclar, blincar* 'bend' (intr.), deriv. of Lat. *vinculum* 'chain, bond'. REW 9341.

4. Ir. *lingim*, vbl. n. *lēim* = W. *llam*, Br. *lamm* 'a leap' (*lŋg-smen), whence NIr. *lēimim*, W. *llamu*, Br. *lammet* (-at, -out) : Skt. *laghu-, raghu-* 'quick, swift', Grk. *ἐλαχύς* 'small, little', IE *legʷh-. Walde-P. 2.426. Pedersen 2.368.

W. *neidio* : Br. *nijal*, MCorn. *nyge* 'fly' (10.37).

5. Goth. *-hlaupan* (only cpd. *us-hlaupan* 'jump up'), ON *hlaupa*, OE *hlēapan*, ME *lepe*, NE *leap* = OHG *hlaufan*, NHG *laufen* 'run' (this meaning also in OE and late ON), etym. dub., perh. : Lith. *šlubas* 'limping', *šlubuoti* 'limp', IE *k̑lou-b-, extension of *k̑lou- in Skt. *çroṇa-* 'lame', Lith. *šlumas* 'limping'. Walde-P. 1.473 f. Feist 532 f.

ON *støkkva*, also 'burst, spring apart, spurt' : Goth. *stigqan* 'hit, collide with', OE *stincan*, OHG *stincan* 'smell' (15.21). Walde-P. 2.617. Falk-Torp 1168.

Dan. *hoppe*, Sw. *hoppa* (ON *hoppa* 'hop') = OE *hoppian*, NE *hop*, etc. : Goth. *hups*, OE *hype*, OHG *huf* 'hip', Lat. *cubitum* 'elbow', Grk. *κύβος* 'hollow above the hips of cattle', etc. Walde-P. 2.374. Falk-Torp 418.

Dan. *springe* (ON *springa* 'burst', rare and poet. 'leap', Sw. *springa* 'run'), OE *springan* (also 'burst forth, spurt'), ME *springe*, NE *spring*, Du. *springen*, OHG *springan*, MHG, NHG *springen*, fr. IE *spreng̑h- : *sperg̑h- in Skt. *spṛh-* 'be jealous of, emulate', Grk. *σπέρχομαι* 'move rapidly, be in haste'. Walde-P. 2.675. Falk-Torp 1133.

NE *jump*, of imitative orig., like *bump*. Cf. also NHG dial. *gumpen* 'jump, hop', etc. NED s.v.

6. Lith. *šokti* : Grk. *κηκίω* 'gush, bubble forth', Lith. *šankinti* 'cause (a horse) to mount', OHG *hengist* 'stallion', etc. Walde-P. 1.334. Otherwise (: ChSl. *skočiti*, etc. below) Brückner 494.

Lett. *lēkt* : Lith. *lēkti* 'fly' (10.37).

7. ChSl. *skočiti*, iter. *skakati*, etc., general Slavic, beside *skokŭ* 'a leap' : Br. *diskogella* 'shake', W. *ysgogi* 'move, stir' (10.11), also OE *scacan* 'shake', etc. IE *skek-, *skeg- Walde-P. 2.556 f.

Russ. *prygnut', prygat'*, perh. fr. a guttural extension of IE *preu- in Skt. *pru-* (below). Walde-P. 2.88. Otherwise Miklosich 266 (: ChSl. *pręgą, pręšti* 'span, stretch'), Brückner 436 (with other connections).

8. Skt. *skand-* : Lat. *scandere* 'climb, mount', MIr. *scendim* 'spring, burst out', Grk. *σκάνδαλον* 'trap, snare', etc. Walde-P. 2.540. Ernout-M. 902.

Skt. *pru-* : ON *frār* 'swift, light-footed', etc. Walde-P. 2.87 f.

10.44 DANCE (vb.)

Grk.	*ὀρχέομαι, χορεύω*	Goth.	*plinsjan*	Lith.	*šokti*
NG	*χορεύω*	ON	*hoppa, dansa*	Lett.	*dancuot (diet)*
Lat.	*saltāre*	Dan.	*danse*	ChSl.	*plęsati*
It.	*ballare, danzare*	Sw.	*dansa*	SCr.	*plesati, igrati*
Fr.	*danser*	OE	*sealtian*	Boh.	*tancovati*
Sp.	*bailar, danzar*	ME	*daunse*	Pol.	*tańcować*
Rum.	*dansa, juca*	NE	*dance*	Russ.	*tancovat', pljasat'*
Ir.	. . . .	Du.	*dansen*	Skt.	*nṛt-*
NIr.	*rinncim*	OHG	*salzōn*	Av.	. . . .
W.	*dawnsio*	MHG	*tanzen*		
Br.	*dañsal*	NHG	*tanzen*		

Several of the verbs for 'dance' are connected with words for 'jump, leap', or other notions of quick motion; one rests on a specialization of 'enclosure' to 'place for dancing'. Interchange between 'dance' and 'play' is seen in Slavic and by semantic borrowing in Rumanian. Most conspicuous is the extent of loanwords—the Gothic word from Slavic, the OE and OHG from Latin, late Latin from a Greek word, the French from a Gmc. word, and especially the spread from French to the majority of the modern European languages. In part the loanword from French is used mainly with reference to fashionable dancing while the older native word persists in use with reference to folk-dancing, as definitely Russ. *pljasat'* vs. *tancovat'*.

1. Grk. *ὀρχέομαι* (with *ὀρχηστής* 'dancer', *ὀρχήστρα* 'space for dancing', etc.) : Skt. *ṛghāya-* 'rave, rage, tremble', *ṛghāvant-* 'raging, violent', OHG *arag*, OE *earg* 'evil', NHG *arg*, etc., fr. an extension of IE *er- in Grk. *ὄρνυμι* 'stir up, arouse', etc. Walde-P. 1.147. For the semantic relationship, cf. Skt. *nṛt-* (below, 7).

Grk. *χορεύω*, esp. 'dance the choral dance', but in NG the reg. general word, fr. *χορός* 'choral dance', also 'place for dancing', the more original application : *χόρτος* 'enclosed place, courtyard', Lat. *hortus* 'garden', etc. Walde-P. 1.603.

2. Lat. *saltāre* : *salīre* 'jump' (10.43).

Fr. *danser*, OFr. *dancier*, whence the main European words, It. *danzare*, Sp. *danzar*, Rum. *dansa*, Br. *dañsal*, late ON *dansa*, Dan. *danse*, Sw. *dansa*, ME *daunse* (> W. *dawnsio*), NE *dance*, Du. *dansen*, MLG *danzen* (> Lett. *dancuot*), MHG, NHG *tanzen* (> Boh. *tančiti*, *tancovati*, with Pol. and Russ. forms). Doubtless a loanword from Gmc., perh. a Low Frank. *dintjan = Fris. *dintje* 'tremble, quiver'. REW 2644b. Wartburg 2.82.

It. *ballare*, OFr. *baler* (cf. sb. *bal* > NE *ball*), and also Sp. *bailar* (by a blend with another word), fr. late Lat. *ballāre* 'dance' (Augustine, etc.), loanword fr. Grk. *βαλλίζω* 'dance' (which *ballō* glosses, CGL 2.255.43, and which is quoted by Athenaeus from Epicharmus and Sophron). Wartburg 1.221. Walde-H. 1.95. Ernout-M. 102. Otherwise REW 909.

Rum. *juca*, orig. 'play' like Fr. *jouer*, etc. (16.27), but used also for 'dance', influenced by the double use of Slavic *igrati* (below, 6).

3. There was apparently no dancing in ancient Ireland (cf. O'Curry 2.406 f.).

NIr. *rinncim*, used also for 'spin' (of a top), and so prob. orig. and fr. *rinn* 'point'.

W. *dawnsio*, Br. *dañsal*, above, 2.

4. Goth. *plinsjan*, fr. the Slavic, cf. ChSl. *plęsati* (below, 6). Feist 384. Stender-Petersen 530.

ON *hoppa*, used of the dance, but mostly 'hop, jump about', cf. Dan. *hoppe* 'jump' (10.43).

ON *dansa*, etc., above, 2.

OE *sealtian, saltian*, OHG *salzōn*, fr. Lat. *saltāre* (above, 2).

5. Lith. *šokti*, also regularly 'jump' (10.43).

Lett. *diet* (used for 'dance' in NT translation, now obs.) : Skt. *dī-* 'soar, fly', Grk. *δινέω* 'whirl', Ir. *dīan* 'swift'. Walde-P. 1.775. Mühl.-Endz. 1.483.

Lett. *dancuot*, above, 2.

6. ChSl. *plęsati*, SCr. *plesati*, Russ. *pljasat'* (Boh. *plesati*, Pol. *pląsać* 'frolic') : OLith. *plęsti* 'dance, frolic', further connections disputed. Walde-P. 2.100 (: ChSl. *plesna* 'sole of the foot'). Brückner 417, KZ 45.323 (: ChSl. *pleksati* 'clap the hands'). Trautmann 225. Specht, KZ 57.159 (IE *plenk̑-).

ChSl. *igrati* 'leap, spring, dance', SCr. *igrati* 'dance', refl. 'play', general Slavic word for 'play' (16.27) : Skt. *ej-* 'stir, move, tremble', ON *eikenn* 'wild, raging', etc. Walde-P. 1.11. Berneker 422.

Boh. *tancovati*, Pol. *tańcować*, Russ. *tancovat'*, above, 2.

7. Skt. *nṛt-*, cf. *nṛti-* 'dance, play', etc., perh. : Lith. *į-nirtęs* 'enraged', OPruss. *er-nertimai* 'we become angry', etc., through a common notion of violent motion or emotion. Walde-P. 2.333.

10.45 WALK (vb.)

Grk.	*βαδίζω, βαίνω*	Goth.	*gaggan*	Lith.	*eiti, vaikščioti*
NG	*περ(ι)πατῶ*	ON	*ganga*	Lett.	*staigāt, iet*
Lat.	*ambulāre, gradī*	Dan.	*gaa*	ChSl.	*iti, choditi*
It.	*camminare*	Sw.	*gå*	SCr.	*ići, hoditi*
Fr.	*marcher*	OE	*gangan, gān*	Boh.	*jeti, choditi*
Sp.	*andar, caminar, marchar*	ME	*go, walke*	Pol.	*iść, chodzić*
Rum.	*umbla, merge*	NE	*walk*	Russ.	*idti, chodit'*
Ir.	*cingim, tiagu*	Du.	*wandelen, gaan*	Skt.	*gam-*
NIr.	*siubhalaim*	OHG	*gān, gangen*	Av.	*gam-*
W.	*cerdded, rhodio*	MHG	*gēn, gān, wandeln*		
Br.	*kerzet, bale*	NHG	*gehen*		

'Walk' is most widely expressed by the words for 'go', either alone or in phrases 'go on foot', as Fr. *aller à pied*, NHG *zu fuss gehen*, etc. Rarely is there so specific a word as NE *walk*, clearly distinguished from both *go* and *run* (cf. NED s.v. *walk*, vb.[1] 7). Even where the words for 'go' are not repeated in the list for 'walk', they may be so used. Conversely, some of the other words entered here, as Fr. *marcher*, Sp. *marchar*, may be used in the wider sense of 'go'.

Expressions that are used only for 'take a walk', as Fr. *se promener*, NHG *spazieren gehen*, are not included.

1. Grk. *βαδίζω*, mostly 'walk leisurely, stroll', *βαίνω* also 'go', see under 'go' (10.47).

Grk. *περιπατέω* 'walk about, walk up and down', later simply 'walk' (cf. NT, Mt. 11.5 'the lame walk'), NG. pop. *περπατῶ*, cpd. of *πατέω* 'tread, trample' : *πάτος* 'path', Skt. *panthā-*, ChSl. *pątĭ* 'way', etc. Walde-P. 2.26.

2. Lat. *ambulāre*, Umbr. *amboltu* 'ambulato', cpd. of *amb-* 'about' and a root *el-, prob. : Grk. *ἀλάομαι, ἀλαίνω* 'wander about', Lett. *aluot* 'stray, go astray'. Ernout-M. 43. Walde-H. 1.38. Hence Rum. *umbla* 'walk, go', Fr. *aller* 'go' (see 10.47).

Lat. *gradī* ('step, walk') : ChSl. *grędą, gręsti* 'come', Ir. *in-grennim* 'pursue', Av. *aiwi-gərəδmahi* 'we pursue'. Walde-P. 1.652. Ernout-M. 430. Walde-H. 1.615.

It. *camminare*, Sp. *caminar*, derivs. of It. *cammino*, Sp. *camino* (Fr. *chemin*) 'road' (10.71).

Fr. *marcher* (> Sp. *marchar*), orig. 'tread' with foot, prob. fr. Gallorom. *marcāre 'beat, stamp', deriv. of Lat. *marcus* 'hammer', first in the military language as 'beat time (with feet)' = 'march'. Gamillscheg 590. Otherwise REW 5364 and Bloch 2.42 f.

Sp. *andar*, Rum. *merge*, see under 'go' (10.47).

3. Ir. *cingim*, vbl. n. *cēim* = W. *cam*, Br. *kamm* 'a step', outside connections dub. Walde-P. 1.588.

Ir. *tiagu*, see under 'go' (10.47).

NIr. *siubhalaim*, fr. *siubhal* 'march, gait, walk', etym. dub., perh. for *suimhal, fr. *swemul : W. *chwyfio* 'move, wave', OE *swimman* 'swim', etc. (10.35). Walde-P. 2.524. Stokes 323.

W. *cerdded*, Br. *kerzet* : Ir. *ceird* 'a stepping', *fō-ceird* 'throws' (10.25).

W. *rhodio*, also 'stroll', perh. fr. *rhod* 'wheel, circle' (semantic development 'go in a circle', 'go about', 'walk'?).

Br. *bale*, fr. *bal* 'swing, dance' (fr. Fr. *bal* 'dance', cf. It. *ballare* 10.44), with generalization to 'rhythmic motion' whence 'walk'. Henry 24.

4. Goth. *gaggan*, ON *ganga*, Dan. *gaa*, OE *gangan, gān*, etc., all general words for 'go' (10.47).

ME *walke*, NE *walk*, fr. OE *wealcan* 'roll, toss' = OHG *walkan*, MHG, NHG *walken* 'full' (cloth) : Skt. *valgati* 'hops', IE *wal-g-, extension of *wel- in Goth. *-walwjan*, OE *walwian* 'roll' (10.15). Walde-P. 1.304. NED *walk*, vb.[1].

Du. *wandelen*, MHG (NHG) *wandeln*, = OHG *wantelōn* 'change, roll', fr. *wantal* (NHG *wandel*) 'a change' : Goth. *wandjan*, NHG *wenden* 'turn', etc. (10.12). Walde-P. 1.261. Weigand-H. 2.1209. Franck-v. W. 774.

5. Lith. *eiti*, Lett. *iet*, see under 'go' (10.47).

Lith. *vaikščioti*, but also 'stroll, go for a walk' : *vaikyti* 'hunt, chase, drive about', further connections? Leskien, Ablaut 289.

Lett. *staigāt* : *steigt*, Lith. *steigtis* 'hurry', Grk. *στείχω* 'stride, advance', Ir. *tiagu* 'go' (10.47), etc. Walde-P. 2.615.

6. ChSl. *iti, choditi*, etc., see under 'go' (10.47).

7. Skt., Av. *gam-*, see under 'go' (10.47).

10.46 RUN (vb.)

Grk.	*τρέχω*, aor. *ἔδραμον, θέω*	Goth.	*rinnan, þragjan*	Lith.	*bėgti, tekėti*
NG	*τρέχω (πιλαλῶ)*	ON	*renna, hlaupa*	Lett.	*skriet*
Lat.	*currere*	Dan.	*løbe*	ChSl.	*tešti*
It.	*correre*	Sw.	*springa, ränna (löpa)*	SCr.	*trčati*
Fr.	*courir*	OE	*irnan, rinnan, þrǣgan*	Boh.	*běžeti*
Sp.	*correr*	ME	*renne*	Pol.	*biedz*
Rum.	*alerga*	NE	*run*	Russ.	*bežat'*
Ir.	*rethim*	Du.	*loopen*	Skt.	*dhāv-, dru-, drā-*
NIr.	*rithim*	OHG	*loufan, rinnan*	Av.	*tač-, dru-*
W.	*rhedeg*	MHG	*loufen, rinnen*		
Br.	*redek*	NHG	*laufen, rennen*		

Words for 'run' are often related to those for 'flee'. Other affinities are with those for 'jump', 'turn', and 'flow'.

1. IE **drem-*, **drā-*, **dreu-*, apparently extensions of a root **der-* not found in monosyllabic form. Other cognates mean mostly 'step, trample, stumble, etc.'. Walde-P. 1.795 ff.

**drem-*. Grk. aor. ἔδραμον, perf. δέδρομα (poet.), cf. δρόμος 'course'; Skt. *dram-* 'run about, wander'.

**drā-*. Skt. *drā-* (3sg. *drāti*); Grk. ἀποδιδρᾱ́σκω 'run away', aor. ἀπέδρᾱν.

**dreu-*. Skt. *dru-* (3sg. *dravati*), Av. *dru-* (caus. *drāvaya-*, pple. *drūta-*, but only of Daevic beings); Goth. *trudan* 'tread, step', etc.

2. Grk. τρέχω, fut. θρέξω, with τροχός 'wheel'; Ir. *droch* 'wheel', Arm. *durgn* 'potter's wheel', fr. **dhregh-* beside **tregh-*(?) in Goth. *þragjan*, OE *þrægan* 'run' (root relations complicated). Walde-P. 1.753 f., 874 f. Feist 500.

Grk. θέω, with θοός 'swift' : Skt. *dhāv-* 'run, flow', *dhāuti-* 'spring, brook', ON *dǫgg*, OE *deaw* 'dew', IE **dheu-*. Walde-P. 1.834.

Byz., NG πιλαλῶ, widespread pop. word for 'run, run hard,' fr. ἐπιλαλῶ (πι- as in πιγούνι 'chin', 4.209), cpd. of λαλῶ (cf. 18.21) in its sense of 'shout' to domestic animals, and so make them run (πιλαλῶ in Patmos, according to an informant, is reg. used for 'drive' sheep, goats, etc.) Korais, Ἄτακτα 1.303 f. Pernot, Phonétique des parlers de Chio 319. Βασ. Φάβης, Ἀθηνᾶ 29, παράρτ. 39 ff.

3. Lat. *currere* (> It. *correre*, Fr. *courir*, Sp. *correr*) : *cursus* 'course', *currus* 'wagon', Gallic *carrus*, Ir. *carr*, Br. *karr* 'vehicle, wagon', further connections (as with OE *hors* 'horse', etc.) dub. Walde-P. 1.428. Ernout-M. 247 f. Walde-H. 1.315 f.

Rum. *alerga* : It. dial. *alargarse* 'withdraw', VLat. **allargāre*, deriv. of Lat. *largus* 'abundant' in its later sense 'wide' (as in It. *largo*, etc., 10.61). REW 352, 4912.

4. Ir. *rethim*, NIr. *rithim*, W. *rhedeg*, Br. *redek* : Ir. *roth*, W. *rhod*, OHG *rad*, Lat. *rota* 'wheel', Skt. *ratha-* 'chariot'. Walde-P. 2.368, Pedersen 2.600 f.

5. Goth. *rinnan*, ON *renna*, OE *irnan*, *rinnan*, ME *rinne*, *renne*, NE *run*, OHG *rinnan*, MHG *rinnen* (NHG *rinnen*); hence NHG *rennen*, Sw. *ränna*, orig. caus. = OHG *rennan*, ON *renna* (pret. *rende*) 'cause to run', Goth. *ur-rannjan* 'cause (the sun) to rise' : Skt. *ṛ-* (3sg. *ṛṇoti*, *ṛṇvati*) 'move, stir' (10.11), Grk. ὄρνῡμι 'rouse, move', etc. Walde-P. 1.138. Falk-Torp 890, 901. Feist 398 f.

Goth. *þragjan*, OE *þrǣgan*, see under Grk. τρέχω, above, 2.

ON *hlaupa* (late in this sense, earlier mostly 'leap'), Dan. *løbe* (Sw. *löpa* 'run' in many phrases, but mostly replaced by *springa*; Hellquist 1051), Du. *loopen*, OHG *hlaufan*, *loufan*, MHG *loufen*, NHG *laufen*, see ON *hlaupa*, OE *hlēapan* 'leap, jump' (10.43).

Sw. *springa*, orig. 'leap, jump', as ON *springa*, OE *springan*, etc. (10.43). Hellquist 1051.

6. Lith. *bėgti*, Boh. *běžeti*, *běhati*, Pol. *biedz*, *biegać*, Russ. *bežat'*, *begat'*, also or orig. 'flee', like Lett. *bēgt*, etc. See 10.51.

Lett. *skriet*, see under 'fly' (10.37).

Lett. dial. *vert*, prob. fr. **wer-* underlying words for 'turn' (10.12). Walde-P. 1.271. Persson, Beiträge 956.

7. ChSl. *tešti*, *tekǫ* 'run, flow', whence the Slavic words for 'flow' (cf. 10.32) : Lith. *tekėti* 'flow, run', Lett. *tecēt* 'flow', Ir. *techim* 'flee' (10.51), Av. *tač-* (3sg. *tačaiti*) 'run, flow', Skt. *tak-* (3sg. *takti*) 'rush'. Walde-P. 1.715.

SCr., Slov. *trčati* : ChSl. *trŭkŭ* 'course, flight', Ir. *trice*, NIr. *tric* 'quick, nimble', root **trek-* : **trek̑-* in Av. *udaro-θrąsa-* 'moving on the belly, creeping' (of snakes)? Walde-P. 1.755.

Boh. *běžeti*, etc., above, 6.

8. Skt. and Av. words, above, 1, 2, 7.

10.47 GO

Grk.	εἶμι, βαίνω	Goth.	*gaggan*, *-leiþan*, *-steigan*	Lith.	*eiti*
NG	πάω, πηγαίνω	ON	*ganga*, *fara*, *līða*	Lett.	*iet*, pret. *gaju*
Lat.	*īre* (*cēdere*, late *vādere*, *ambulāre*)	Dan.	*gaa* (*fare*)	ChSl.	*iti*, *choditi*
It.	*andare* (*ire*), *vado*	Sw.	*gå* (*fara*)	SCr.	*ići*, *hoditi*
Fr.	*aller*, *vais*, *irai*	OE	*gangan*, *gān*, *faran*, *wadan*	Boh.	*jiti*, *choditi*
Sp.	*ir*, *voy*	ME	*go*, *gonge*, *fare*	Pol.	*iść*, *chodzić*
Rum.	*merge*, *umbla*	NE	*go*, *went*	Russ.	*idti*, *chodit'*
Ir.	*tiagu* (*lod*, *-rega*, *dul*)	Du.	*gaan*, *varen*	Skt.	*i-*, *yā-*, *gam-*, *gā-*
NIr.	*tēighim* (*chuaidh*, *raghaidh*)	OHG	*gangan*, *gān*, *faran*, *līdan*	Av.	*jam-*, *i-*, *yā-*, *dvar-*
W.	*myned* (*a*, *aeth*, *el*, etc.)	MHG	*gēn*, *gān*, *varn*, *līden*		
Br.	*mont* (*a*, *eas*, *yelo*, etc.)	NHG	*gehen* (*fahren*)		

'Go' is understood here as covering the most generic verbs denoting locomotion, without necessary implication of direction or goal. In so far as they are used for 'go away, go from', it is only by contrast to those for 'come', as in NE *come and go*, etc.

In NE *come* and the other European words listed under 'come' (10.48) there is the implication of approach toward or arrival at a goal (which is often felt as the real or imagined position of the speaker or another; but any such definition is too narrow).

It is probable that this situation fairly reflects the difference in value between the two important IE roots **ei-* and **gʷem-*, as essentially one of aspect. The former expressed the action of going *per se*, while the latter involved the implication of a definite goal. But such a relation is only partially maintained in their derivatives. Skt. *i-* and *gam-* are both used where we must translate 'go' or 'come' according to the situation or the prefix employed (especially *ā-* for 'come', *sam-* for 'come together'), and similarly in Iranian, only that Av. *i-* is rare, *gam-* (*jam-*) frequent and without prefix mostly 'come'. Grk. βαίνω is 'go, walk', and εἶμι sometimes 'come'. The Balto-Slavic words for 'come' (except Lett. *nākt*) are compounds of IE **ei-* with prefixes meaning 'to' or the like (cf. Grk. εἴσ-ειμι 'go to, come').

Grk. ἔρχομαι, aor. ἦλθον, though listed only under 'come', in accordance with what eventually became their prevailing use, are also frequently 'go', especially in Homer, and regularly in ἀπέρχομαι 'go away'.

On the Celtic words for 'go' and 'come', cf. esp. Vendryes, RC 46.217 ff.

1. IE **ei-*, extended **yā-*. Walde-P. 1.102 ff. Ernout-M. 303 ff. Walde-H. 1.406 ff.

**ei-*. Grk. εἶμι (but mostly fut. in sense); Lat. *īre* (> Sp. *ir*, Fr. fut. *irai*, It. inf. *ire*, imperat. *ite*, etc.); Lith. *eiti*, Lett. *iet*, ChSl. *iti*, SCr. *ići*, Boh. *jiti*, Pol. *iść*, Russ. *idti*, Skt. *i-* (3sg. *eti*), Av. *i-* (3sg. *aeiti*, OPers. *aitiy*); Hitt. imperat. 2sg. *it*, 2pl. *iten* (Sturtevant, Hitt. Gram. 95).

**yā-*. Skt., Av. *yā-* : Lith. *joti*, Lett. *jāt*, ChSl. *jachati* 'ride', etc.; uncertain Goth. *iddja*, OE *ēode* 'went', which, moreover, do not coincide (Feist 288 f.); Toch. A *yā-* 'go' (SSS 423, 458); Hitt. *ya-* 'go, march' (Sturtevant, Hitt. Gloss. 184).

2. IE **gʷem-*, **gʷā-*. Walde-P. 1.675 ff. Ernout-M. 1083 ff.

**gʷem-*. Grk. βαίνω 'go, walk'; Lat. *venīre* 'come' (> the Romance words); Goth. *qiman*, OE *cuman*, etc., general Gmc. for 'come'; Skt., Av., OPers. *gam-* 'go, come' (Skt. *gacchati*, Av. *jasaiti*, *sk̑o-* presents like Grk. βάσκω; Av. *jam-* without prefix mostly 'come'; also Av., OPers. *ā-jam-* 'come', whence NPers. *āmadan* 'come'); Toch. *käm-*, *kum-*, etc. 'come' (SSS 428 f.).

**gʷā-*. Grk. aor. ἔβην, Dor. ἔβᾱν; Skt. aor. *agām*, pres. *jigāti*; Av. aor. *gāt*; Lett. *gaju* 'went' (pret. to *iet*).

3. Grk. ἕρπω 'creep, crawl' (10.41), in many dialects simply 'go'. Buck, Grk. Dial. 333.

NG pop. πάω, fr. Grk. ὑπ-άγω 'lead, bring (up, under)', intr. 'go slowly away, retire, withdraw' (of an army, etc.), in NT simply 'go away'. Hence also NG πηγαίνω new pres. to aor. πῆγα = old imperf. ὑπῆγον.

Grk. βαίνω, in NG only in cpds., μπαίνω 'go in', βγαίνω 'go out', fr. ἐμβαίνω, ἐκβαίνω.

4. Lat. *īre*, Sp. *ir*, etc., above, 1.

Lat. *cēdere*, perf. *cessī* (mostly 'go away', but 'go' in cpds., perh. fr. **ce-zd-* with weak grade of **sed-* in ChSl. *choditi*, etc. (below, 8). Walde-P. 2.486. Walde-H. 1.193. Ernout-M. 168 f.

Lat. *vādere* 'go rapidly, rush, advance', in late Lat. simply 'go' (e.g. frequently in Peregrinatio) : Lat. *vadum* 'ford', ON *vaða* 'wade, rush', OHG *watan* 'wade', OE *wadan* 'go, advance' (NE *wade*). Hence the present forms like It. *vado*, *va*, Fr. *vais*, Sp. *voy*, Rum. 3sg. *va*, etc. Walde-P. 1.217. Ernout-M. 1069. REW 9117.

Lat. *ambulāre* 'walk' (10.45), used colloquially for 'go' in Plautus (*quo ambulas tu*, *bene ambula*) and regularly in late Latin. Hence Fr. *aller*, Rum. *umbla*. REW 412. Wartburg 1.86 f.

It. *andare*, Sp. *andar* (latter mostly 'walk'), much disputed. Apparently fr. a VLat. **ambitāre* (: Lat. *ambīre* 'go around', sb. *ambitus*), but in late Lat. texts there is no trace of such a form beside the common *ambulāre;* hence one suspects some, not precisely explained, reformation of the latter. REW 409, 412.

Rum. *merge*, fr. Lat. *mergere* 'sink, plunge' (10.33). Semantic development perh. 'sink' > 'disappear' > 'withdraw' (cf. Alb. *mërgonj* 'withdraw') > 'go away' > 'go' (so Pușcariu 1058), but may be simply fr. the pop. use of *mergere* for impetuous going, like NE *plunge* into the woods, into the crowd, etc. Cf. *immersit sese in ganeum* 'plunged into a gaming-house', etc. (Plaut.), and *immargebam* in a Roman epitaph from Bulgaria. REW 5525.

5. Ir. *tiagu*, NIr. *tēighim* : Grk. στείχω 'stride, advance, walk' (in Lesb. dial. 'go'), Goth. *steigan*, *-steigan* used for various cpds. of Grk. βαίνω, ON *stīga*, OE, OHG *stīgan*, all used for 'go, go up, go down', Lett. *steigt* 'hasten', etc. Walde-P. 2.614.—Ir. imperat. *eirg*, fut. *-rega*, NIr. *raghaidh*, etc., etym. disputed. Walde-P. 2.364 (: *rigim* 'stretch out'). Pedersen 2.648, Thurneysen, Gram. 473. (: Grk. ἔρχομαι 'come' 10.48).—Ir. pret. *luid* : Grk. ἐλεύσομαι, ἤλυθον (10.48). Walde-P. 2.417. Pedersen 2.378.—NIr. pret. *chuaidh*, Ir. perf. *docuaid*, perh. **dicom-vad-* : Lat. *vādere* (above, 4). Pedersen 2.648.—Ir. inf. *dul*, etym.? (Pedersen l.c. : Alb. *dálë* 'go out, sprout').

W. *myned*, Br. *mont*, *monet*, Corn. *mones* : ChSl. *minąti* 'pass' (of time), Lat. *meāre* 'wander, go', IE **mei-*. Walde-P. 2.241. Pedersen 2.454.—The finite indicative Britannic forms chiefly fr. the root **ag̑-* (in Lat. *agere*, etc.), e.g. (only 3sg. forms quoted) W. pres. *a* (OW *agit*), imperf. *ai*, perf. *aeth;* Br. pres. *a*, imperf. *ae*, pret. *eaz*. Pedersen 2.353, 451 f. (Walde-P. 1.35).—W. subj. (3sg.) *el*, *elo*, Corn. *ello*, Br. fut. *y-elo* : Ir. *adella* 'goes to, visits', either fr. IE **pel-* in Lat. *pellere* 'drive', or fr. **el-* in Grk. ἐλαύνω 'drive'. Walde-P. 1.156. Pedersen 2.353. Thurneysen, Gram. 95.

6. Goth. *gaggan*, ON *ganga*, OE *gangan*, ME *gonge*, OHG *gangan* : Lith. *žengti* 'step, stride', Skt. *jangha-* 'lower leg', Av. *zanga-* 'ankle'. Walde-P. 1.588. Feist 182.

Goth. *-leiþan* (only in cpds.), ON *līða*, OHG *līdan*, MHG *līden* (OE *līþan* 'go by sea, sail', the latter sense prominent in other dialects also) : Av. *riθ-* (3sg. *iriθyeiti*) 'die' (as 'go away'), IE **leit(h)-*. Walde-P. 2.401. Feist 8.

Goth. *steigan*, etc. : Ir. *tiagu*, above, 5.

Goth. *faran* (but only Lk. 10.7, for μεταβαίνω; *farjan* 'row, sail'), ON *fara*, Dan. *fare*, Sw. *fara*, OE *faran* (also *fēran*, in form = OHG *fuoren* 'lead', but in use = *faran;* NED s.v. *fere*, vb.[1]), ME, NE *fare*, OHG *faran*, MHG *varn* (NHG *fahren*, Du. *varen*), in the modern Gmc. languages mostly 'travel' (but NIcel. *fara* 'go, go away') : Skt. *pṛ-* 'bring across, deliver', Grk. πορεύω 'carry, convey', Lat. *portāre* 'carry', etc. Walde-P. 2.39. Feist 142 f.

Dan. *gaa*, Sw. *gå*, OHG, MHG *gān*, Du. *gaan*, fr. IE **ghē-*, beside OE *gān*, ME, NE *go*, OHG, MHG *gēn*, NHG *gehen*, fr. IE **ghēi-*, prob. : Skt. *hā-*, *hī-* 'leave, give up', in mid. 'go forth, give way' and cpds. 'go up, down, after', etc., Grk. κιχάνω 'reach'. Walde-P. 1.543. Falk-Torp 292.

OE *wadan* : Lat. *vādere*, above, 4.

NE *went*, orig. past of *wend*, OE *wendan* 'turn' (10.12).

7. Lith. *eiti*, Lett. *iet*, above, 1.

8. ChSl. *iti*, SCr. *ići*, etc., above, 1.

ChSl. *choditi*, SCr. *hoditi*, etc., general Slavic (iter. to *iti*, etc.) with sb. ChSl. *chodŭ*, etc. : Grk. ὁδός 'road', ὁδεύω 'wander', Skt. *ā-sad-* 'arrive at, reach', *ut-sad-* 'go away, withdraw', fr. IE **sed-* ultimately identical with **sed-* 'sit' (Lat. *sedēre*, etc.). The sense 'go' might have arisen first by derivation with prefixes (as in Skt.). Walde-P. 2.486. Berneker 392. Otherwise Brückner 181.

9. Skt., Av. *i-*, *yā-*, above, 1.

Skt., Av. *gam-*, *gā-*, above, 2.

Av. *dvar-* 'go' (of Daevic beings) : Skt. *dhorati* 'trots', Grk. ἀ-θύρω 'play', etc., IE **dhwer-* : **dhwen-* in Av. *dvan-* 'fly' (10.37), extensions of **dheu-* in Skt. *dhu-* 'shake' (10.26). Walde-P. 1.842.

10.48 COME

Grk.	ἔρχομαι, aor. ἦλθον	Goth.	*qiman*	Lith.	*ateiti*
NG	ἔρχομαι, aor. ἦρθα	ON	*koma*	Lett.	*nākt* (*atiet*)
Lat.	*venīre*	Dan.	*komme*	ChSl.	*priti*, *gręsti*
It.	*venire*	Sw.	*komma*	SCr.	*doći*
Fr.	*venir*	OE	*cuman*	Boh.	*přijíti*, *přicházeti*
Sp.	*venir*	ME	*come*	Pol.	*przyjść*, *przychodzić*
Rum.	*veni*	NE	*come*	Russ.	*pridti*, *prichodit'*
Ir.	*doiccim*, *ticim*	Du.	*komen*	Skt.	(*ā-*)*gam-*, (*ā-*)*i-*, etc.
NIr.	*tigim*	OHG	*queman*, *coman*	Av.	(*ā-*)*jam-*
W.	*dyfod* (*daw*, *daeth*, *del*, etc.)	MHG	*komen*, *kumen*		
Br.	*don(e)t*	NHG	*kommen*		

1. For the Latin, Romance, Germanic, and Indo-Iranian words, representing IE *gʷem-, and for the general relation of 'come' to 'go', see under 'go' (10.47).

2. Grk. ἔρχομαι, etym. dub. Boisacq 287 with refs. Perh. fr. an extension of IE *er- in Grk. ὄρνῡμι 'rouse', Skt. ṛṇoti 'moves' (10.11); or more closely : ὀρχέομαι 'jump, dance'. Persson (cf. Boisacq). McKenzie, Cl. Q. 15.44.

Grk. aor. ἦλθον, ἤλυθον, fut. ἐλεύσομαι : Ir. lod 'I went' (pret. to tiagu 'go', 10.47), further connection with Skt. rudh- 'grow, mount', Goth. liudan 'grow', dub. Walde-P. 1.417.

3. Ir. do-iccim, ticim, NIr. tigim, cpd. of icc- (fr. *ṇk̑-?) : Skt. aç-, naç-, Av. nas- 'attain', Lat. nancīrī, nancīscī 'attain, obtain', Grk. ἤνεγκα, Lith. nešti, ChSl. nesti 'carry, bring'. Walde-P. 1.128 f. Ernout-M. 652. Pedersen 2.557 f. Thurneysen, Gram. 126, 130.

W. dyfod, cpd. of dy- (*to-) and bod 'be'. Here also Br. donet, dont, but blended with monet, mont 'go'. The finite Welsh forms are fr. cpds. (*to-aĝ-, *to-el-) of the roots *aĝ-, *el- discussed under 'go' (10.47). The modern Breton has constructed a regular conjugation on the stem deu-, after MBr. 1sg. d-euaff, etc. (*to-aĝ-). Pedersen 2.446, 452 ff.

4. Lith. ateiti = Lett. atiet, but the latter mostly 'come back', cpds. of prefix at- 'back, hither', and eiti, iet 'go' (10.47).

Lett. nākt : Lith. nokti 'mature', pranokti 'overtake', perh. fr. a *nek- beside *nek̑- in Skt. naç-, Av. nas- (above, 3). Walde-P. 1.129. Mühl.-Endz. 2.698.

5. ChSl. priti (= pri-iti), SCr. doći (= do-ići), etc., also ChSl. pri-choditi, Boh. při-chdzeti (orig. iter. form to při-choditi, rare), etc., all cpds. of the Slavic preverbs pri- or do- 'to, at', and words for 'go', ChSl. iti, choditi, etc. (10.47).

ChSl. gręda, gręsti (more frequent than forms of iti in present; Jagić, Entstehungsgesch. 337) : Av. aiwi-gərəδmahi 'we begin', Lat. gradī 'step, walk', Ir. in-grennim 'pursue' (10.53). Walde-P. 1.652. Berneker 349.

6. Skt. (ā-)i-, cf. 'go' (10.47).

10.49 GO AWAY, DEPART

Grk.	ἀπ-(ἐξ-)ἔρχομαι, ἀνα-(ἀπο-)χωρέω	Goth.	afleiþan, usgaggan	Lith.	išeiti, nueiti
NG	ἀναχωρῶ, φεύγω, μισσεύω	ON	ganga af, ganga brott	Lett.	aiziet
		Dan.	gaa bort, drage bort	ChSl.	otiti, iziti
Lat.	ab-(ex-)īre, discēdere	Sw.	gå bort	SCr.	otići
It.	partire, andarsene	OE	gewītan, ūtgān	Boh.	odejeti
Fr.	partir, sortir, s'en aller	ME	go away, depart	Pol.	odejść
		NE	go away, depart, leave	Russ.	vyiti
Sp.	partir, salir, irse	Du.	weggaan, vertrekken	Skt.	apagam-
Rum.	pleca	OHG	ūzgangan, argangan	Av.	apajam-
Ir.	immthigim	MHG	ūzgān		
NIr.	imthigim	NHG	weg-(fort-)gehen		
W.	ymadael				
Br.	mont kuit				

'Depart' is simply to 'go away' and is most commonly so expressed (NE depart is mostly in literary use). But there are also some terms of different origin.

1. Verbs for 'go' are often used alone for 'go away', as NE go!, begone!, he's gone, It. andarsene, Fr. s'en aller, Sp. irse, etc. Cf. OE ferde, Gospels Mk. 5.20 = eode Lindisf. = Vulgate abiit, Goth. galaiþ, ChSl. ide in same passage.

2. Verbs for 'go' in compounds or phrases with words for 'away, forth, out', etc. Grk. ἀπ-, ἐξ-ἔρχομαι, Lat. ab-, ex-īre, abs-, dē-, dis-cēdere (also cēdere alone), Ir. immthigim (orig. 'go about' but also 'go away', as NIr.; cf. Windisch 629), W. ymadael, ymadaw (: dyfod 'come', 3sg. daw, etc.), Br. mont kuit (kuit 'free', fr. Fr. quitte, sense influenced by kuitaat 'quit, leave', fr. Fr. quitter; Henry 84), ON afleiþan, usgaggan, ON ganga af, ganga brott, Dan. gaa bort, Sw. gå bort (brott, bort : ON braut 'way, road', 10.71. Falk-Torp 95; Dan. also drage bort with drage 'draw' 9.33, also 'go'; Falk-Torp 151), OE ūtgān, OHG ūzgangan, argangan, NHG weggehen, fortgehen, Lith. išeiti, nueiti, ChSl. otiti, iziti, Skt. apagam-, etc.

3. Grk. ἀναχωρέω (also ἀπο-), cpd. of χωρέω 'make room, withdraw', fr. χῶρος 'space'.

NG φεύγω 'flee' (10.51), also the most common pop. word for 'go away', e.g. ἔφυγε 'he's gone'.

Byz., NG μισσεύω, in earliest use 'dismiss', then 'be dismissed, depart', fr. μίσσα, eccl. Lat. missa 'dismissal' (source of NE mass, etc.). G. Meyer, Neugr. Stud. 3.45.

4. It. partire, Fr. partir (also OFr. departir > ME, NE depart), Sp. partir, fr. Lat. partīre 'divide' (fr. pars, partis 'part'), with semantic development through the use, first in refl., for 'separate oneself' (cf. NE they parted). REW 6259. Gamillscheg 673.

Fr. sortir ('go forth'), etym. disputed. REW 8110. Gamillscheg 809.

Sp. salir fr. Lat. salīre 'jump, leap' (10.43). REW 7540.

Rum. pleca (as trans. 'bend'), fr. Lat. plicāre 'fold', with sense 'depart' prob. starting in phrase for folding the tents. Note the contrast with Sp. llegar 'arrive', fr. the same source (10.55). REW 6601. Puşcariu 1334.

5. OE gewītan (usual word for 'depart'), apparently cpd. of wītan 'impute' (: Goth. fra-weitan 'avenge', OHG wīzan 'impute', these : Goth., OE witan, etc. 'know'), but semantic development obscure (cf. also OS giwītan 'go', OHG arwīzan 'depart' in Tat.). Walde-P. 1.238.

Du. (beside weggaan, etc.) vertrekken, cpd. of trekken 'draw' (9.33) and 'march, go'.

NE leave (12.18) in phrases like left the house is equivalent to 'depart from', hence now also without object, perhaps the most common popular expression, as he is leaving, he has just left.

10.51 FLEE

Grk.	φεύγω	Goth.	þliuhan	Lith.	bégti
NG	φεύγω	ON	flýja	Lett.	bēgt
Lat.	fugere	Dan.	flygte, fly	ChSl.	běžati
It.	fuggire	Sw.	fly	SCr.	bježati
Fr.	fuir, s'enfuir	OE	flēon	Boh.	utéci, prchnouti
Sp.	huir	ME	flee	Pol.	uciec
Rum.	fugi	NE	flee	Russ.	bežat'
Ir.	techim	Du.	vluchten, vlieden	Skt.	palāy-
NIr.	teichim	OHG	fliohan	Av.	frā-nam-
W.	ffoi	MHG	vliehen		
Br.	tec'het	NHG	fliehen		

A frequent and obvious relation of words for 'flee' is to those for 'run', just as NE run away is the colloquial substitute for flee, which is now rather literary. Some are related to those for 'bend', with development through 'bend aside'.

1. Grk. φεύγω, Lat. fugere : Lith. bugti 'take flight', buginti 'frighten', fr. IE *bheug-, prob. identical with *bheug(h)-in Skt. bhuj-, Goth. biugan, 'bend' etc. (9.14). Walde-P. 2.144. Ernout-M. 397 (with different view of the words for 'bend'). Walde-H. 1.556. VLat. fugīre > It. fuggire, Fr. fuir (but mostly s'enfuir), Sp. huir, Rum. fugi. REW 3550.

2. Ir. techim, NIr. teichim, Br. tec'het, tec'hout : Av. tač-, ChSl. tešti 'flow, run', Lith. tekéti 'flow', etc. (10.32, 10.46). Walde-P. 1.715. Pedersen 1.128.

W. ffoi fr. fo 'flight', this fr. Lat. fuga 'flight'. Loth, Mots lat. 169.

3. Goth. þliuhan, ON flýja, Dan., Sw. fly, OE flēon, ME flee(n), fley, NE flee, Du. vlien (but usually vlieden), OHG fliohan, MHG vliehen, NHG fliehen, fr. a Gmc. root *þleuh-, without clear outside connections. Falk-Torp 242. Feist 499. Weigand-H. 1.553. The view that Goth. þl- is from fl- and the whole group connected with that for 'fly' (ON fljūga, etc. 10.37), as Zupitza, Gutt. 131, is generally rejected. But there was much later confusion between the two groups. Cf. NED s.v. flee.

Du. vluchten (MLG > Dan. flygte) = NHG flüchten 'rescue (by flight)', refl. sich flüchten 'flee, escape', deriv. of NHG flucht, Du. vlugt 'flight' : OHG fliugan, NHG fliegen 'fly', etc. (10.37). Falk-Torp 243.

4. Lith. bégti, Lett. bēgt, ChSl. běžati, běgati, SCr. bježati, bjegati, Russ. bežat', begat (the Lith. and Russ. words also 'run', as reg. Boh. běžeti, Pol. biedz, 10.46) : Grk. φέβομαι 'flee in terror', φόβος 'panic flight' (Hom.), 'fear', IE *bhegʷ-. Walde-P. 1.148 f. Berneker 54 f.

5. Boh. utéci, Pol. uciec cpds. of root in ChSl. teka, tešti 'run, flow' (10.32, 10.46; Boh. and Pol. simplex now only 'flow' or 'leak').

Boh. prchnouti (Pol. pierzchnać also 'flee', but less common) : SCr. prhati 'fly up', Russ. porchat' 'flutter', poruch 'dust', etc. Walde-P. 2.50. Miklosich 241. Brückner 411.

6. Skt. palāy- = i- 'go' (10.47) with preverb palā- for parā- 'away, forth'.

Av. frā-nam-, cpds. of nam- 'bend' (: Skt. nam- id., etc.) with frā- 'forward, forth', and apa- 'away'.

In words of the inherited group are combined the notions of 'go (come) after, behind' and 'go (come) with, accompany, attend', with dominance of the latter in Indo-Iranian and generally in derivatives. The notion of 'follow aggressively, pursue' was originally foreign to them, though it developed in Latin. Apart from this group, the words for 'follow' are mostly derived from words for 'track, way', but in Celtic (except Br.) from words for 'adhere, stick'.

The literal phrases for 'go after' may also be used everywhere and may even be the more usual popular expressions for 'follow', especially in Slavic.

1. IE *sekʷ-. Walde-P. 2.476 f. Ernout-M. 927.

Grk. ἕπομαι; Lat. sequī (late sequere > It. seguire, Fr. suivre, Sp. seguir); Ir. sechur; Lith. sekti, Lett. sekt, sekuot; Skt. sac-, Av. hač-.

2. Grk. ἀκολουθέω (Thuc.+, and displacing ἕπομαι in the κοινή, so always in NT), NG ἀκολουθῶ (pop. also ἀκλουθῶ), deriv. of ἀκόλουθος 'accompanying, follower', cpd. of ἀ-copulative and κέλευθος 'way' (: Lith. kelias 'way'). Walde-P. 1.446.

3. Rum. urma, fr. urmă 'foot-track, track, trace' = It. orma 'foot-track', Sp. husma, husmo 'scent', fr. Grk. ὀσμή 'smell'. REW 6112. Puşcariu 1835. Densusianu 201.

4. Ir. sechur, above, 1.

NIr. leanaim = Ir. lenim 'hang to, adhere' : Lat. līnere 'daub, besmear', Grk. ἀλίνω 'smear' (IE *lei-. Walde-P. 2.389). Pedersen 2.565.

W. dilyn, canlyn, cpds. of di- intensive or can (gan) 'with' and glynu 'adhere, stick' (: Ir. glenim id., Grk. γλία, Lat. glūten 'glue', etc.). Pedersen 2.539. Walde-P. 2.389, 1.619.

Br. heulia, fr. OBr. ol = W. ol 'track' (etym.? Henry 162 connects with ON fylgja, etc., below).

5. Goth. laistjan, OE lǣstan 'follow, perform, last') = OHG leisten, NHG leisten 'accomplish, perform', etc., derivs. of Goth. laists, OE lāst, lǣst, OHG leist 'track' (OE, OHG also shoemaker's 'last' : OHG -leise, MHG leise 'track', ChSl. lěcha 'garden-bed', Lat. līra 'ridge between two furrows', etc. Walde-P. 2.404. Falk-Torp 636. NED s.v. last vb.¹.

ON fylgja, OE folgian, fylgean, etc., general Gmc., etym. dub. Falk-Torp 291. Kluge-G. 169.

6. Lith. sekti, Lett. sekt, sekuot, above, 1.

7. ChSl. vŭ slědŭ iti (gręsti, choditi) lit. 'go (come, walk) in the track', regularly renders Grk. ἀκολουθέω in the Gospels, similarly in modern Slavic, SCr. ići za (kim), Boh. jíti za (kym), Pol. iść za (kim) 'go behind (someone)'.

ChSl. po-slědovati (renders παρακολουθέω), slěditi (mostly in secondary sense), SCr. sljediti, Boh. (ná-)slědovati (Pol. na-slědować mostly 'imitate'), Russ. sledit', sledovat', derivs. of Sl. slědŭ 'track' (: Lith. slysti, Lett. slidēt 'slip, slide', etc. 10.42). Walde-P. 2.708.

8. Skt. sac-, Av. hač-, above, 1.

10.52 FOLLOW

Grk.	ἕπομαι, ἀκολουθέω	Goth.	laistjan	Lith.	sekti
NG	ἀκολουθῶ	ON	fylgja	Lett.	sekt, sekuot
Lat.	sequī	Dan.	følge	ChSl.	vŭ slědŭ iti, po-slědovati
It.	seguire	Sw.	följa		
Fr.	suivre	OE	folgian, lǣstan	SCr.	sljediti, ići za
Sp.	seguir	ME	folwe	Boh.	(ná)slědovati, jíti za
Rum.	urma	NE	follow	Pol.	iść za
Ir.	sechur	Du.	volgen	Russ.	sledit', (pre)sledovat'
NIr.	leanaim	OHG	folgēn, folgōn	Skt.	sac-
W.	dilyn, canlyn	MHG	volgen	Av.	hač-
Br.	heulia	NHG	folgen		

10.53 PURSUE

Grk.	διώκω	Goth.	wrikan	Lith.	persekinéti, vyti
NG	διώχνω, κυνηγῶ	ON	elta	Lett.	vajât
Lat.	(in-, per-)sequī	Dan.	forfølge	ChSl.	izgŭnati, goniti
It.	inseguire	Sw.	förfölja	SCr.	(pro)goniti, (pro)-ganjati
Fr.	poursuivre	OE	ēhtan, folgian		
Sp.	perseguir	ME	pursue, chace	Boh.	pronâsledovati, sti-hati
Rum.	urmari, goni	NE	pursue, chase		
Ir.	ingrennim, dosennim	Du.	vervolgen, najagen	Pol.	ścigać, gonić
NIr.	tōruighim	OHG	āhten, arfolgēn, jagōn	Russ.	presledovat, gnat'
W.	erlidio, ymlid	MHG	æchten, vervolgen, jagen	Skt.	anu-dhāv-, etc.
Br.	redek warlerc'h			Av.	3sg. vayeiti, etc.
		NHG	verfolgen, nachjagen		

Many of the words for 'pursue' are connected with, mostly compounds of, those for 'follow'. So in Latin and Romance, and, probably by semantic borrowing, in modern Germanic languages (NHG verfolgen, etc.), hence again in Lithuanian and West Slavic.

Some are words that were used primarily of the 'hunt, chase' of animals (3.79) or the 'driving' of cattle. Some are from roots that appear elsewhere in words for 'go', 'run', 'stride', etc., and everywhere the literal phrases for 'run after' or the like may be popular expressions of 'pursue'.

The older European words for 'pursue' and many of the modern cover the more malignant 'persecute', which is the sense of Grk. διώκω in the Gospels, with its translations in Gothic, etc. Less commonly 'persecute' is differentiated either by a new formation as Fr. persé-cuter (> NE persecute), back-formation fr. sbs. Lat. persecūtiō, persecūtor, or by specialization in this direction of an old word for 'pursue', as Pol. prześladować (below, 6).

1. Grk. διώκω (NG pop. διώχνω), perh. pres. formation fr. a perf. *δεδίωκα : δίω 'fly', δίομαι 'drive away', δινέω 'whirl', Skt. dīyate 'flies, soars'. Walde-P. 1.775. Boisacq 192.

NG κυνηγῶ properly 'hunt' (3.79), but also 'pursue'.

2. Lat. in-sequī, per-sequī (late -se-quere > It. inseguire, Sp. perseguir, with change of prefix Fr. poursuivre, OFr. porsivre, porsuire), cpds. of sequī 'follow' (10.52).

Rum. urmari, fr. urma 'follow' (10.52).

Rum. goni (also 'drive'), fr. the Slavic (below, 6).

3. Ir. ingrennim, cpd. of the vbl. stem -grenn- (not found as simplex), fr. *grendn- : Lat. gradī 'walk', ChSl. gręsti 'come'. Walde-P. 1.652. Walde-H. 1.615. Pedersen 2.549. Thurneysen, Gram. 353.

Ir. do-sennim (e.g. 3pl. du-m-sennat, etc.), etym. dub., perh. as orig. 'start, frighten (game, etc.) by a noise' : Skt. svan- 'sound', Lat. sonāre, etc. (15.44). Pedersen 2.625.

NIr. tōruighim : Ir. toracht 'pursuit, success' prob. fr. *to-ro-saig-, cpd. of saig- 'go after, claim' (cf. 3sg. doroich 'attains', etc.). Pedersen 2.610. Laws, Gloss. 739.

W. erlidio, ymlid, perh. fr. same root as dilyn, canlyn 'follow' (10.52). Morris Jones 391. Lloyd-Jones, BBCS 2.108.

Br. redek warlerc'h 'run after' (war-lerc'h 'after' fr. war 'on' and lerc'h 'track').

4. Goth. wrikan = ON reka, OE wre-can 'drive, avenge' (NE wreak), OHG rehhan 'punish, avenge' : Lat. urgēre 'press, impel', Skt. vraj- 'stride, go'. Walde-P. 1.319. Feist 574.

ON elta : Grk. ἐλαύνω 'drive', etc. (10.65). Walde-P. 1.156. Falk-Torp 188.

Dan. forfølge, Sw. förfölja, prob. modeled on NHG verfolgen, MHG vervolgen (but not ordinarily in this sense), Du. vervolgen, OHG arfolgēn, cpds. of the words for 'follow' (10.52).

OE ēhtan, OHG āhten, MHG œchten (NHG ächten), fr. OE ōht 'hostile pursuit, enmity', OHG āhta (NHG acht) 'hostile pursuit', outside connections dub. Walde-P. 1.60. Falk-Torp 17, 1430.

ME, NE pursue, fr. Anglo-Fr. pur-suer = OFr. porsivre, porsuire (above, 2). NED s.v.

ME chace, NE chase, fr. OFr. chacier 'hunt out, pursue', Fr. chasser 'drive (away), hunt' (3.79).

Du. najagen, NHG nachjagen, cpds. of na, nach 'after' and jagen 'hunt', OHG jagōn, MHG jagen 'hunt, pursue' (3.79).

5. Lith. persekinéti, cpd. of per- 'through' and frequent. form of sekti 'follow' (10.52).

6. ChSl. izgŭnati (commonest for διώκω in Gospels), pogŭnati, goniti, SCr. (pro)goniti, (pro)ganjati, Boh. honiti, Pol. gonić, Russ. gnat' (also refl. with za 'after'), all of these also or mainly 'drive' and 'chase' : Skt. han- 'strike, kill', Grk. θείνω 'strike', Ir. gonim 'wound, kill', etc., IE *gʷhen-. Walde-P. 2.615. Berneker 328.

Boh. stíhati, Pol. ścigać : SCr. stizati, ChSl. stignąti 'arrive', Lett. staigāt 'walk' (10.45), Ir. tiagu 'go' (10.47), Grk. στείχω 'stride, advance', etc., IE *steigh-. Walde-P. 2.615.

Boh. pronâsledovati (Pol. prześlado-wać 'persecute'), Russ. presledovat', cpds. of words for 'follow' (10.52).

7. Skt. anu-dhāv-, lit. 'run after', cpd. of dhāv- 'run' (10.46), similarly other cpds. of words for 'run' or 'go'.

Av. vayeiti, above, 5.

10.54 OVERTAKE

Grk.	καταλαμβάνω, φθάνω	Goth.	....	Lith.	pavyti
NG	φτάνω, προφτάνω	ON	nā	Lett.	panākt
Lat.	ad-, con- sequī	Dan.	indhente	ChSl.	postignąti
It.	raggiungere	Sw.	upphinna	SCr.	(do)stići
Fr.	rattraper	OE	offaran	Boh.	dohoniti, přistihnouti
Sp.	alcanzar	ME	oftake, overtake	Pol.	dogonić, doścignąć
Rum.	ajunge	NE	overtake	Russ.	dogonjat'
Ir.	dogrennim	Du.	inhalen	Skt.	āp-
NIr.	beirim (suas) ar	OHG	arfolgēn(?)	Av.	ap-
W	goddiwedydd	MHG	erfolgen		
Br.	tizout	NHG	einholen		

Many of the words for 'overtake' are merely compounds of those already considered under 'follow' and 'pursue'. Others are words for 'seize, catch', or 'arrive, reach', which, either in compounds or without change, are also used for 'overtake'. Cf. NE catch or catch up with.

1. Grk. καταλαμβάνω 'seize, lay hold of' and 'overtake' (Hdt., etc.), cpd. of λαμ-βάνω 'take, seize' (11.13).

Grk. φθάνω 'be beforehand, get ahead of, overtake, arrive', NG φτάνω 'overtake, arrive', and 'be enough', etym.? Boisacq 1025. Cpd. Grk. προφθάνω 'an-

ticipate', NG προφτάνω (or -αίνω) 'be in time for, overtake, arrive'.

2. Lat. ad-sequī, con-sequī, cpds. of sequī 'follow' (10.52).

It. raggiungere, fr. giungere 'arrive, reach' (10.55).

Fr. rattraper, fr. attraper 'catch', deriv. of trappe 'trap', Gmc. loanword. REW 8863. Gamillscheg 859.

Sp. alcanzar, prob. metathesis for OSp. encalzar, cf. It. incalzare 'follow up closely', VLat. *incalciāre, deriv. of calx, calcis 'heel'. REW 4338.

Rum. ajunge, see under 'arrive, reach', 10.55.

3. Ir. dogrennim, cpd. of the root -grenn- in ingrennim 'pursue' (10.53). Cf. also rosaigim, etc. 'arrive at, reach' (10.55).

NIr. beirim ar, also 'seize, catch' (11.14), lit. 'carry on' (beirim 'carry, bring, take', 10.61), also beirim suas ar, with suas 'up' (prob. copied from NE catch up with).

W. goddiweddydd, re-formed infin. from 1sg. goddiweddaf, old infin. goddiwes, MW gorδiwes, prob. = *upor-di-wedd- (cf. di-wedd 'close, conclusion') fr. IE *wedh- 'lead', in Ir. fedim, etc. (10.65). Morris Jones, 251, 372.

Br. tizout, also 'attain, obtain', MBr. tizaff : Ir. techtaim 'own' (11.12), Lith. tekti 'reach, suffice', ON þiggja 'accept'. Walde-P. 1.715. Henry 265.

4. ON nā (Dan. naa, Sw. nå 'reach') = NHG nahen 'approach' : Goth. nēh-wjan 'approach', fr. the root of ON nær,

Goth. nēhwa, OE nēar 'near', etc. Falk-Torp 751.

Dan. indhente, cpd. of hente 'fetch' : ON heimta 'fetch, demand', Gmc. *haim-atjan 'bring home' (deriv. of *haimaz > ON heimr, Dan. hjem, etc.). Falk-Torp 398. In the sense 'overtake' prob. modeled on NHG einholen (below).

Sw. upphinna, cpd. of hinna 'reach' (10.55).

OE offaran, cpd. of of- and faran 'go, journey' (10.47). Rarely also OE offyl-gan with fylgan 'follow' (cf. OHG arfol-gēn, below).

ME oftake (with of- as above), later overtake, cpds. of take. NED s.v. over-take.

Du. inhalen, NHG einholen (the former perh. modeled on the latter), cpds. of in-, ein-, and holen 'fetch'; orig. perh. with the application 'bring in' the game pursued. Cf. Paul, Deutsches Wtb. s.v.

OHG arfolgēn, MHG erfolgen, in OHG also merely 'pursue' (10.53), cpds. of folgēn 'follow'.

5. Lith. pavyti, and Lett. panākt, cpds. of vyti 'pursue', nākt 'come'.

6. ChSl. postignąti, SCr. (do)stići, Boh. přistihnouti, Pol. doścignąć all cpds. of ChSl. stignąti, SCr. stići 'arrive', Boh. stíhati, Pol. ścigać 'pursue' (10.53).

Boh. dohoniti, Pol. dogonić, Russ. dogonjat', etc., cpds. of Boh. honiti, etc. 'pursue' (10.53).

7. Skt. āp- 'get, obtain' (11.16) also 'attain' and 'overtake'. So Av. ap-, esp. with avi- or a- (Barth. 71).

10.55 ARRIVE (intr.) and ARRIVE AT, REACH (trans.)

Grk.	ἀφικνέομαι, φθάνω	Goth.	(anaqiman)	Lith.	atvykti, ateiti
NG	φτάνω, προφτάνω	ON	koma at, nā	Lett.	atnākt, pienâkt
Lat.	advenīre, pervenīre	Dan.	ankomme, naa	ChSl.	priti, prispěti
It.	arrivare, giungere	Sw.	framkoma, anlända, hinna, nå	SCr.	(na)doći, prispjeti
Fr.	arriver			Boh.	přijiti, pristati
Sp.	llegar	OE	ancuman	Pol.	przybyć
Rum.	ajunge, sosi	ME	aryve, reche	Russ.	pridti, pribyt'
Ir.	roiccim, rosaigim	NE	arrive, reach	Skt.	gam-, ā-gam-, ā-sad-
NIr.	sroichim	Du.	inhalen	Av.	jam-, aibi-jam-, hant-
W.	dyfod, cyrraed	OHG	anaqueman, gilangōn		
Br.	don(e)t	MHG	anekomen, gelangen		
		NHG	ankommen, gelangen		

'Arrive' is most widely expressed by verbs for 'come' or compounds of these. But several new terms have arisen, of diverse sources.

1. Grk. ἀφικνέομαι (or simple ἱκνέο-μαι), mostly 'arrive at, reach' with acc., but also intr. 'arrive' : ἵκω 'come' also 'reach', prob. : Lith. siekti 'reach out with the hand, take oath'. Walde-P. 2.465. Boisacq 372.

Grk. φθάνω in part 'arrive', NG φτάνω usual for 'arrive' (cf. waiter's ἔφτασα lit. 'I have arrived' = 'immediately'), also προφτάνω, see under 'overtake', 10.54.

2. Lat. advenīre, pervenīre, cpds. of venīre 'come'.

Fr. arriver (> It. arrivare), in the older language 'reach the shore, land', fr. VLat. *adrīpāre, deriv. of Lat. rīpa 'bank' (1.27). REW 675. Wartburg 1.146 f.

It. giungere, fr. Lat. iungere 'join', late refl. 'arrive'. Cf. iunximus nos denuo ad mare rubrum Peregrinatio 6.3. Similarly Rum. ajunge 'arrive' and 'overtake', fr. Lat. cpd. adiungere. REW 171, 4620.

Sp. llegar, fr. Lat. plicāre 'fold', in late Lat., esp. refl., 'turn, approach'. Cf. in Peregrinatio ut .... sic plicavimus nos ad montem Dei (2.4), plicavimus nos ad mare (6.3), cum iam prope plicarent civitati (19.9). So, not fr. applicāre as REW 548.

Rum. sosi, fr. Grk. σώζω, aor. ἔσωσα 'save', also 'bring safe to', Byz. and NG (new pres. σώνω) also simply 'arrive'. Cf., fr. same source, Alb. sos 'finish, arrive' and Bulg. sosaja 'come'. Densusi-anu 358.

3. Ir. roiccim, riccim ('reach', trans.; cf. Laws, Gloss. 614 f.), NIr. roichim, sroichim, fr. same root as do-iccim 'come' (10.48).

Ir. rosaigim, dorochim, cpds. of saigim 'seek' (11.31). Pedersen 2.609 ff. From the same root also W. cyrraed, cyr-haed (cy-r-haed) 'attain, reach, arrive at', Br. direza 'attain'. Pedersen 2.28. Loth, RC 30.260.

W. dyfod 'come' (10.48), also 'arrive'.

Br. don(e)t 'come' (10.48), also 'arrive'.

4. Goth. anaqiman (but quotable only as 'come upon, appear', Lk. 2.9), ON koma at, Dan. ankomme (fr. LG or HG), Sw. framkoma, OE ancuman, Du. aankomen, OHG anaqueman, MHG anekomen, NHG ankommen, all cpds. or phrases with words for 'come'.

ON nā, Dan. naa, Sw. nå : Goth. nēhwjan 'draw near', advs. Goth. nēhw, OE nēah, etc., 'near' (12.43).

Sw. anlända, orig. 'come to land', now in extended sense like Fr. arriver. Hell-quist 607.

Sw. hinna : Goth. fra-hinþan 'capture', OE hentan 'pursue, follow', hun-

tian 'hunt', outside root connections? Walde-P. 1.460. Hellquist 354.

ME *aryve*, NE *arrive*, fr. Fr. *a(r)river* and in ME mostly in its older sense (see above, 2). NED s.v. *arrive*.

ME *reche*, NE *reach* (OE *ræcan* = OHG-NHG *reichen*), orig. 'stretch out the hand', hence 'seize, obtain, attain' (as also NHG *erreichen*), further 'arrive at', as *reached home*, etc. NED s.v. *reach*, vb.

OHG *gilangōn*, MHG, NHG *gelangen*, fr. *lang* 'long', with development through 'stretch out, seize', similar to that in NE *reach*. Weigand-H. 1.663, 2.15. Paul, Deutsches Wtb. 195, 311.

5. Lith. *atvykti* (beside *įvykti* 'happen') : Lett. *vīkt* 'succeed, prosper', Lith. *veikti* 'act, do', *veikus* 'quick, ready', outside root connections dub. Walde-P. 1.235. Leskien, Ablaut 289.

Lith. *at-* (or *nu-*)*eiti*, *-joti*, *-važiuoti*, cpd. of vbs. for 'go, come' (10.47) or 'ride' (10.66).

Lett. *atnãkt*, *pienãkt*, cpds. of *nãkt* 'come' (10.48).

6. Slavic verbs for 'come' (10.48), also 'arrive'.

ChSl. *prispěti* (Supr.), SCr. *prispjeti* ('be in time, arrive') = Pol. *przyspiać* 'come in time, be in a hurry', cpd. of verb seen in ChSl. *spěti* 'make progress, succeed', Boh. *spěti* 'hasten', etc. : Skt. *sphā-* 'grow, increase', OE *spōwan* 'succeed', *spēd* 'success', etc. Walde-P. 2.656 f. Brückner 509.

Boh. *přistati*, cpd. of *stati* 'stand'.

Pol. *przybyć*, Russ. *pribyt'*, cpds. of verb for 'be'.

7. Skt. *gam-*, Av. *jam-*, 'go, come' (10.47), also used for 'arrive', or cpds. with Skt. *ā-*, *abhi-*, Av. *aibī-*, OPers. *abiy-ā-* (Barth. 496). OPers. also *abiy upa-i-* (*abiy bābirum yaθā naiy upāyam* 'when I had not yet reached Babylon'). Barth. 150.

Skt. *ā-sad-* 'arrive at, reach, approach, meet', cpd. of *sad-* 'sit', with notion of motion developed in cpds. Cf. Grk. *ὁδός* 'road', ChSl. *choditi* 'go' (10.47). Walde-P. 2.486.

Av. *hant-* : OHG *sinnan* 'travel', *sint* 'course, way', etc. Walde-P. 2.496 f. Barth. 1771.

The majority of the verbs for 'approach' are based on adverbs for 'near' (12.43). A few are compounds of verbs for 'come' or 'go', or from various other sources.

1. Grk. *πλησιάζω*, *πελάζω* fr. *πλησίον*, *πέλας* 'near'.

Grk. *ἐγγίζω*, fr. *ἐγγύς* 'near'. But NG *ἀγγίζω* 'touch'.

NG *ζυγώνω*, fr. class. Grk. *ζυγόω* 'join'. Cf. Lat. *iungere* 'join', late refl. 'approach', It. *giungere* 'arrive' (10.55).

NG *σιμώνω*, fr. *σιμά* 'near'.

NG *κοντεύω* (fr. *κοντά* 'near') is rarely used for 'approach' in the literal sense, but reg. in phrases like *κοντεύει νὰ πεθάνη* 'comes near dying'.

2. Lat. *adpropinquāre*, fr. adj. *propinquus* 'near', deriv. of adv. *prope* 'near'. Similarly, late *adproximāre* (> Sp. *aproximar*), through *proximus*; late *adpropiāre* (> OFr. *aprochier*, Fr. *approcher*, Rum. *apropia*). Ernout-M. 815. REW 557–59.

Lat. *accēdere*, cpd. of *cēdere* 'go' (10.47).

Sp. *acercar*, cpd. of *cercar* 'circle, surround' (: Lat. *circāre*, REW 1938).

Sp. *allegar* (also 'gather, collect'), fr. Lat. *adplicāre* 'attach, apply', cpd. of *plicāre* 'fold'. Cf. *llegar* 'arrive' (10.55). Ernout-M. 778. REW 548.

3. OIr. *adcosnaim*, *ascnaim* 'strive for', MIr. *ascnaim*, *tascnaim* 'approach, visit' (Laws, Gloss.), cpds. of *sni-* orig. 'spin' (6.31), but also 'make an effort'. Pedersen 2.634.

NIr. *druidim* ('close, shut' and 'come close to, approach') : Ir. sb. *drut*, *druit* 'closing' (*druzd-?*), outside connections? Thurneysen, Idg. Anz. 33.25. Macbain 144.

NIr. *tarraingim* ('draw, pull' and 'draw near to, approach'), fr. Ir. *tairngim*, cpd. of *srengim* 'draw, pull' (9.33). Pedersen 2.637.

W. *nesu*, *dynesu*, *neshau*, Br. *nesaat*, *dinesaat*, derivs. of W. *nes* 'nearer', Br. *nes* 'near'.

Br. *tostaat*, fr. *tost* 'near'.

4. Goth. *nēhwa wisan* (*nēhwa was* = *ἤγγισεν* Lk. 19.41), *nēhwa qiman* (= *προσεγγίσαι* Mk. 2.4), ON *ganga nær*, *nākvæma*, Dan. *nærme sig*, Sw. *närma sig*, OE *nēahlǣcan* (*lǣccan* 'seize', 11.14), Du. *naderen*, OHG *nāhan* (also *nāhlīhhōn* frequent in Tat.), fr. adv. in *-līh*), MHG *nāhen*, NHG *nahen* and *sich nähern* (*nähern* 'bring near'), all derivs., cpds., or phrases with the Gmc. words for 'near'.

ME *aproche*, NE *approach*, fr. OFr. *aprochier* (above, 2).

5. Lith. *artintis*, refl. of *artinti* 'bring near', fr. *arti* 'near'.

Lett. *tuvoties*, fr. *tuvu* 'near'.

6. ChSl. *približiti sę*, etc., general Slavic, fr. ChSl. *blizĭ*, etc. 'near'.

7. Skt. *abhi-gam-* and other cpds. of *gam-* 'go' or 'come'.

Skt. *upa-sthā* 'stand by' and 'approach', cpd. of *sthā-* 'stand'.

10.56 APPROACH (vb.)

Grk.	πλησιάζω, πελάζω, ἐγγίζω	Goth.	nēhwa wisan, nēhwa qiman	Lith.	artintis
NG	πλησιάζω, ζυγώνω, σιμώνω	ON	ganga nær, nākvæma	Lett.	tuvoties
		Dan.	nærme sig	ChSl.	približiti sę
Lat.	adpropinquāre, accēdere	Sw.	närma sig	SCr.	približiti se
		OE	nēahlǣcan	Boh.	približiti se
It.	avvicinarsi	ME	aproche	Pol.	zbližyć się
Fr.	approcher, s'approcher	NE	approach	Russ.	približat'sja
Sp.	acercar(se), allegar-(se), aproximar(se)	Du.	naderen	Skt.	abhi-gam-, upa-sthā-
Rum.	apropia	OHG	nāhan, nāhlīhhōn	Av.	....
Ir.	ascnaim, tascnaim	MHG	nāhen		
NIr.	druidim, tarraingim	NHG	nahen, sich nähern		
W.	dynesu				
Br.	tostaat, (di)nesaat				

10.57 ENTER

Grk.	εἰσέρχομαι	Goth.	galeiþan, inn-(at-)gaggan	Lith.	įeiti
NG	μπαίνω	ON	gagga inn	Lett.	ieiet, iemit
Lat.	intrāre, introīre, ingredī	Dan.	intræde	ChSl.	vъniti
		Sw.	inträda	SCr.	uci, ulaziti, stupiti u
It.	entrare	OE	ingān, infaran	Boh.	vstoupiti, vejiti
Fr.	entrer	ME	entre	Pol.	wejść
Sp.	entrar	NE	enter	Russ.	voiti, vstupit'
Rum.	intra	Du.	binnen gaan (-komen, -treden)	Skt.	viç-
Ir.	inodtiagu			Av.	....
NIr.	téighim isteach	OHG	ingangan		
W.	myned (or dyfod) i mewn	MHG	ingān		
Br.	mont ebarz	NHG	hineingehen, eintreten		

'Enter' is simply to 'go or come in' and is most commonly so expressed, but also in part by compounds of verbs for 'tread, step' or the like, or by a direct derivative of a word for 'within'.

1. Cpds. or phrases with verbs for 'go' or 'come'.

Grk. *εἰσέρχομαι*, Lat. *introīre*, Ir. *inod-tiagu* (Pedersen 2.645), NIr. *téighim isteach* (*isteach* 'into', orig. 'into the house' : *tech* 'house'; Pedersen 1.264), W. *myned* (or *dyfod*) *i mewn* (*mewn* 'within' : Ir. *medōn* 'middle', Pedersen 1.112), Br. *mont ebarz* (*ebarz* 'within' : *parz* 'part', Henry 2,109), Goth. *inngag-gan*, *atgaggan*, *galeiþan*, OE *ingān*, *infaran*, OHG *ingangan* (NHG *eingehen* formerly so used, now replaced in this sense by *hineingehen* or *eintreten*; but still *eingang* 'entrance'), Lith. *įeiti*, ChSl. *vъniti*, etc.

2. Cpds. of words for 'tread, step, walk', as Lat. *ingredī* (*gradī*, 10.45), NG *μπαίνω* (fr. *ἐμβαίνω*, in class. Grk. mostly 'embark'), NHG *eintreten* (*treten* : OE *tredan* 'step upon, tread', etc., outside connections dub. Walde-P. 1.796, Falk-Torp 1291), Dan. *intræde*, Sw. *inträda* (semantic borrowing?), SCr. *stupiti u*, Boh. *vstoupiti*, Russ. *vstupit'* (: ChSl. *stąpiti* 'tread').

3. Lat. *intrāre* (> It. *entrare*, Sp. *entrar*, Rum. *intra*, Fr. *entrer* > ME *entre*, NE *enter*), deriv. of *intrā* (*inter*, *intrō*) 'within'. Ernout-M. 482. REW 4511.

4. SCr. *ulaziti* (with sb. *ulaz* 'entrance' : ChSl. *vъlazъ* id.) : ChSl. *u-laziti* 'descend', etc., this : ChSl. *-lězq*, *-lěsti* in words for 'ascend, descend'. Berneker 697, 715.

5. Skt. *viç-*, the usual word for 'enter', but this sense perh. extension fr. 'enter the house or home' (cf. NIr. *isteach* 'into', above) in view of the widespread cognate nouns, like Skt. *viç-* 'settlement, dwelling place, house', Grk. *οἶκος* 'house', Goth. *weihs* 'village', etc. Walde-P. 1.231.

10.61 CARRY (BEAR)

Grk.	φέρω (οἴσω, ἤνεγκα), ἄγω	Goth.	bairan	Lith.	nešti
NG	φέρω, φέρνω, βαστῶ	ON	bera	Lett.	nest
Lat.	ferre (tuli, lātus), por-tāre	Dan.	bære, føre	ChSl.	nesti, nositi
		Sw.	bära, föra	SCr.	nositi (nijeti, nesti)
It.	portare	OE	beran, ferian	Boh.	nésti, nositi
Fr.	porter	ME	bere, carie	Pol.	nieść, nosić
Sp.	llevar	NE	carry (bear)	Russ.	nesti, nosit'
Rum.	purta, duce	Du.	dragen	Skt.	bhṛ-
Ir.	biru, immchuirim	OHG	beran, tragan	Av.	bar-, nāš-
NIr.	beirim, iomcharaim	MHG	tragen		
W.	cludo, cario	NHG	tragen		
Br.	dougen				

The majority of the old words for 'carry' belong to an inherited group pointing to an IE root of this meaning. Some of this group, like NE *bear*, have ceased to be the common generic words for 'carry' and are used only in more specialized applications. In certain other inherited groups the generic 'carry' is much less widespread and apparently secondary to other notions, such as 'reach', 'support, lift', 'carry by a vehicle'. For the group in which this last is the dominant sense, though sometimes extended to generic 'carry', namely Lat. *vehere*, OE *wegan*, Skt. *vah-*, etc., see under 'ride' (10.66). In the historical period there is development of 'carry' from 'lift', 'carry in a vehicle', 'lead', and 'put, place'.

1. IE *bher-*. Walde-P. 2.153 ff. Ernout-M. 348 ff. Walde-H. 1.483 ff.

Grk. *φέρω*, NG also *φέρνω*; Lat. *ferre*; Ir. *biru*, *berim*, NIr. *beirim*; Goth. *bairan*, OE *beran*, etc., once general Gmc. for 'carry', now in part restricted (Du. *baren*, NHG *gebären* 'bear' children, NE *bear* in this sense, also = 'endure', and in many phrases, as *bear in mind*, but no longer generic 'carry' in common speech); Skt. *bhṛ-*, Av., OPers. *bar-*; Arm. *berem*; Alb. *bie* 'bring'; Toch. *pär-* 'carry, bring' (SSS 448); but ChSl. *berq*, *bĭrati* 'bring together, collect' (12.21).

2. IE *enk̑-*, *nek̑-*, *n̥k̑-*. Walde-P. 1.1286. Ernout-M. 652.

Grk. aor. *ἤν-εγκα* (cf. Skt. perf. *ān-ança*); Lith. *nešti*, Lett. *nest*, ChSl. *nesti*, *nositi*, etc., general Slavic for 'carry'; Skt. *aç-*, *naç-* 'reach, attain' (cf. Grk. *ποδ-ηνεκής* 'reaching to the feet', Av. *nas-* 'reach, attain', *nāš-* 'carry' (*s*-extension, Barth. 1067); Lat. *nanciscī* 'obtain, receive'; Goth. *ga-nōhs* 'enough', etc.; Ir. *do-iccim* 'come' (10.48). The meaning 'reach, attain' appears to be the primary one and 'carry' a secondary, in part already IE, prob. through 'cause to reach' hence 'bring'.

3. Grk. *ἤνεικα* or *ἤνικα* = *ἤνεγκα* in most dialects except Attic, fr. *ἐν-* and the root of *ἴκω*, *ἱκνέομαι* 'come, reach, arrive at' (10.55). Walde-P. 2.465.

Grk. fut. *οἴσω*, also aor. in infin. *ἀν-οῖσαι* etc., etym.? Walde-P. 1.103. Boisacq 694. Possibly : *εἶμι* 'go', *οἶμος* 'way', through a caus. notion. Cf. Cret. *ἐπ-ελευσεῖ* 'will bring', *ἐπ-ηλευσαν* 'brought' : *ἐλεύσομαι* 'will come'.

Grk. *ἄγω* 'lead', orig. 'drive' (10.65), also used for 'carry, bring', but mostly of living creatures.

Grk. *βαστάζω* 'lift, raise', also 'carry' (Aesch.+, freq. in NT), NG *βαστάζω* pop. *βαστῶ* 'support, carry, and 'bear' = 'endure', etym.? Boisacq 116.

4. Lat. perf. *tulī*, old *tetulī*, pple. *lātus*

(*tlātos) : Lat. tollere 'raise, lift', etc. (10.22); the primary sense of the root *tel- being prob. 'support'. Ernout-M. 1044.

Lat. portāre (> It. portare, Fr. porter, Rum. purta) : Skt. pr̥- 'lead across, rescue', para- 'beyond, far', Grk. πείρω 'pierce', περάω 'pass across', Goth., OHG, OE faran 'go, travel' (10.47), OE ferian 'carry' (Dan. føre, Sw. föra 'carry and 'lead', 10.64), IE *per-. Walde-P. 2.39. Ernout-M. 793 f.

Lat. vehere, sometimes generic 'carry' but mostly 'carry' on a horse, vehicle, ship, cf. pass. vehī 'be carried, ride' and cognates (10.66).

Lat. gerere, sometimes 'carry', but mostly 'carry on one's person, wear, conduct oneself, act', etc., root *ges- (cf. gessī, gestus) but etym. dub., perh. as *ĝ-es- : *aĝ-in agere 'drive', etc. Walde-P. 1.37. Ernout-M. 420 f. Walde-H. 1.595 f.

Sp. llevar = It. levare, Fr. lever 'lift', fr. late Lat. levāre 'lift, lighten, alleviate' (10.22).

Rum. duce, fr. Lat. dūcere 'lead' (10.64).

5. Ir. biru, NIr. beirim, above, 1.

Ir. immchuirim, NIr. iomcharaim, cpd. of cuirim 'place, put' (12.2). Pedersen 2.500.

W. cludo, orig. 'carry by a vehicle' : clud 'a vehicle, baggage', outside connections?

W. cario, fr. NE carry (or independent deriv. of car 'car, vehicle'?).

Ir. ru-ucc- (perfect. stem in conjugation of berim), beside Ir. to-ucc- (perfect. stem to do-biur 'bring'), W. dwyn 'bring' (1sg. dygaf), Br. dougen 'carry', etym. dub. Walde-P. 1.111. Pedersen 2.474, 475.

6. Goth. bairan, ON bera, etc., above, 1.

OE ferian, Dan. føre, Sw. föra, see under Lat. portāre (above, 4).

ME carie, NE carry, orig. 'carry' by a vehicle, fr. ONorthFr. carier (Fr. charrier 'cart, haul'), fr. late Lat. carricāre derived fr. carrus 'cart' (Gallic; cf. currere 'run', 10.46). NED s.v.

OHG tragan, MHG, NHG tragen, Du. dragen (Goth. dragan for ga-dragan 'heap up'), prob. (but disputed) : ON draga, OE dragan 'draw, drag' (9.33). Walde-P. 1.862. Franck-v. W. 130. Feist 91. Falk-Torp 150 f. (separating OHG tragen, from ON draga, etc.).

7. Lith. nešti, Lett. nest, ChSl. nesti, nositi, above, 2.

8. Skt. bhr̥-, Av. bar-, above, 1.
Av. nāš-, above, 2.

10.62 BRING

Grk.	φέρω, etc.	Goth.	briggan	Lith.	atnešti
NG	φέρω, φέρνω	ON	færa, koma (with dat.)	Lett.	atnest
Lat.	ferre, adferre, etc.			ChSl.	prinesti
It.	portare	Dan.	bringe	SCr.	donositi
Fr.	apporter	Sw.	bringa	Boh.	přinesti
Sp.	traer	OE	bringan, brengan, fetian	Pol.	przynieść
Rum.	aduce			Russ.	prinesti
Ir.	biru, dobiur (to-ucc-)	ME	bringe, fecche	Skt.	bhr̥-, hr̥-
NIr.	beirim, dobeirim	NE	bring (fetch)	Av.	bar-, ā-yās-
W.	dwyn, cyrchu	Du.	brengen, halen		
Br.	digas, dizougen	OHG	bringan, halōn		
		MHG	bringen, holen		
		NHG	bringen, holen		

The relation of 'bring' to 'carry' is similar to that of 'come' to 'go' (cf. 10.47). While 'carry' denotes the action without regard to direction, 'bring' involves the implication of a definite goal, often the position of the speaker, but not necessarily so. Generally this notion is either undistinguished from 'carry', as in Grk. φέρω, Lat. ferre, etc., which cover both 'carry' and 'bring', or is expressed by compounds of the verbs for 'carry' with prefixes meaning 'to' or the like. For these, as already discussed in 10.47, or obvious compounds of the same, no further comment is needed.

It is only in Germanic that there is a distinctive independent group for 'bring'. But some other words of various primary meanings are also used for 'bring', and the most important of these are listed.

1. Sp. traer, fr. Lat. trahere 'pull, draw' (9.33).

2. Ir. to-ucc- (perfect. to do-biur), W. dwyn, Br. dizougen (= di + dougen), see under Ir. ro-ucc-, Br. dougen 'carry', 10.61.

W. cyrchu 'approach', but also (prob. through 'go for, go get') 'bring', fr. Lat. circāre 'go around' and 'seek', the latter meaning attested by It. cercare, Fr. chercher 'seek', etc. (11.31). Loth, Mots lat. 157.

Br. digas, cpd. of di- 'to' and kas 'send, lead' (10.63).

3. Goth. briggan, OE bringan, ME bringe, NE bring, MLG bringen (> Dan.

---

bringe, Sw. bringa), OHG bringan, MHG, NHG bringen, beside OE brengan, OS brengian, MLG, Du. brengen (fr. *brang-jan) : W. he-brwng 'lead, conduct, bring', MCorn. hem-bronk 'will lead', MBr. ham-brouc, NBr. ambrouk 'lead'. Walde-P. 2.204. Falk-Torp 102. Feist 105.

ON færa (Dan. føre, Sw. föra 'carry' and 'lead', NHG führen 'lead', 10.64), caus. to ON fara, Goth. faran 'go, travel' (10.47).

ON koma 'come' (10.48) with dat. of object, and so reg. NIcel. koma með, for 'bring'.

OE fetian, ME fecche, NE fetch (still common locally), prob. as orig. 'go after' : ON fet 'a step', feta 'find one's way', Grk. πέδον 'ground', etc. Walde-P. 2.24. NED s.vv. fet and fetch.

OHG halōn, halōn, MHG, NHG holen, Du. halen (also 'draw', cf. ME hale, NE haul) : OE ge-holian 'get', perh. Arm. k'atem 'collect, take away', Toch. käl-'lead, bring' (SSS 430). The old comparison with Lat. calāre, Grk. καλέω 'call', etc. (Falk-Torp 373, Walde-P. 1.141) is based on the frequent use as 'call' in OHG. But the evidence as a whole indicates that this sense is secondary. Mansion, PBB 33.547 ff. Franck-v. W. 226.

4. Skt. hr̥- 'hold, carry, take' and (esp. with ā-) 'bring' : Osc. heriiad 'capiat', Lat. hortus 'garden', etc., IE *ĝher-. Walde-P. 1.603.

Av. ā-yās-, cpd. of yās- 'desire, ask for, order'; outside connections dub. Walde-P. 1.197. Barth 1288 f.

10.63 SEND

Grk.	πέμπω	Goth.	sandjan	Lith.	siųsti
NG	στέλλω, στέλνω	ON	senda	Lett.	sūtīt
Lat.	mittere	Dan.	sende	ChSl.	(po-)sŭlati
It.	mandare, inviare	Sw.	sända	SCr.	(po-)slati
Fr.	envoyer	OE	sendan	Boh.	(po-)slati
Sp.	enviar, mandar	ME	sende	Pol.	(po-)słać
Rum.	trimite	NE	send	Russ.	(po-)slat'
Ir.	fóidim	Du.	zenden	Skt.	pra-iṣ-
NIr.	cuirim	OHG	sentan	Av.	maēθ-(?)
W.	anfon	MHG	senden		
Br.	kas	NHG	schicken, senden		

Several of the words for 'send' are derived from words for 'road', with development through an intermediate 'go, travel' to 'cause to go' = 'send'. Some show specialization from 'let go, throw', or 'put, place, prepare, arrange' (an expedition, etc.). Some are connected with words for 'know', 'warn', 'command', and must then have been used first for 'send a message'.

1. Grk. πέμπω, etym.? Boisacq 765.

NG στέλλω, στέλνω, fr. Grk. στέλλω 'make ready, equip, arrange, dispatch' (an expedition), esp. ἀποστέλλω 'send off, dispatch' (an embassy, expedition, etc.) : OE stellan, 'set, establish', etc. (12.12).

2. Lat. mittere (orig. sm-? cf. cosmittere Paul. Fest.), etym. wholly uncertain (Av. maēθ- 'mittere' Barth 1105, but?), but meaning 'send' specialization of 'let go, throw', etc., which is also found at all periods and is dominant in the cpds. and in VLat. (whence Fr. mettre 'put', etc.). Walde-P. 2.688. Ernout-M. 621 f.

It. mandare, Sp. mandar (also 'command') = Fr. mander 'send word, summon', fr. Lat. mandāre 'commit, enjoin', also late 'send word', fr. man- = manus 'hand' (cf. man-ceps, etc.) and dare 'give'. Ernout-M. 586. REW 5286.

It. inviare, Fr. envoyer, Sp. enviar, fr. VLat. *inviāre beside late Lat. viāre

---

'travel', deriv. of via 'road' (10.71). REW 9295.

Rum. trimite, fr. Lat. trāmittere = trans-mittere 'send across'. REW 8849. Pușcariu 1763.

3. Ir. fóidim, prob. : Skt. vēdaya-caus. of vid- 'know' (IE *weid- in Grk. οἶδα 'know', Lat. vidēre 'see', etc.), with semantic development 'inform' to 'send (a message)' and 'send' in general. Pedersen 1.359, 2.525.

NIr. cuirim 'put, place' (12.12; cf. Ir. fo-ceird 'throws' 10.25), also 'send'.

W. anfon (and danfon, with dy- 'to'), perh. fr. *ndhi-mon- : Lat. monēre 'warn', caus. of the root *men- in Lat. meminī 'remember', Skt. man- 'think'. Pedersen 2.301.

Br. kas (also 'lead'), fr. Norm. Fr. casser = Fr. chasser 'hunt, drive away'. Henry 56.

4. Goth. sandjan, OE sendan, OHG sentan, etc., general Gmc., caus. of the root seen in OHG sinnan 'travel, go', OE sīð, OHG sint 'journey, course, way', etc., hence orig. 'cause to go'. From the same root prob. also Lith. siųsti, Lett. sūtīt. Walde-P. 2.496 f. Feist 410 f.

NHG schicken, earlier meaning 'prepare, suit, adapt', so MHG schicken = ON skikka 'arrange' : OHG scehen, NHG geschehen 'happen', etc. Weigand-H. 2.702. Kluge-G. 516.

---

5. Lith. siųsti, Lett. sūtīt, see under Goth. sandjan, etc. (above, 4).

6. ChSl. sŭlati, more commonly perfect. poslati (iter. sylati), etc., general Slavic, perh. : Goth. saljan 'offer', ON selja 'give over, sell', OE sellan 'give, sell'. Walde-P. 2.504 f. Brückner 499.

7. Skt. pra-iṣ- in preṣyati and caus.

---

preṣayati (so also OPers. frāišayam 'I sent'; but Av. fraēšya- 'impel' and 'promise', not quotable as 'send'), cpd. of pra- 'forth' and iṣ- 'impel, hurl' = Av. iš- 'set in rapid motion' : ON eisa 'start violently', Lat. īra 'anger', etc., IE *eis-. Walde-P. 1.106 f.

Av. maēθ- 'mittere', Barth. 1105, but this sense dub.

10.64 LEAD (vb.)

Grk.	ἄγω, ἡγέομαι	Goth.	tiuhan	Lith.	vesti
NG	ὁδηγῶ	ON	leiða	Lett.	vest
Lat.	dūcere	Dan.	lede, føre	ChSl.	vesti
It.	menare, condurre, guidare	Sw.	leda, föra	SCr.	voditi
		OE	lǣdan	Boh.	vésti
Fr.	mener, conduire, guider	ME	lede	Pol.	prowadzić
		NE	lead	Russ.	vesti, vodit'
Sp.	llevar, conducir, guiar	Du.	voeren, leiden	Skt.	ni-
Rum.	duce, conduce	OHG	leiten	Av.	ni-, vāðaya-
Ir.	fedim	MHG	leiten, vueren		
NIr.	treōruighim	NHG	führen, leiten		
W.	arwain, tywys				
Br.	kas				

Apart from an inherited group in which 'lead' seems to be the primary sense, words for 'lead' are cognate with others for 'draw', 'seek', 'road', 'carry', 'go' (as 'cause to go'), and 'drive'. Strictly, one 'leads' from in front and 'drives' from behind, but in situations where both have in common the notion of 'conduct' the difference may be lost sight of, with resulting interchange.

1. IE *wedh-. Walde-P. 1.255. Pedersen 2.515 f.

Ir. fedim; Lith. vedu, vesti, Lett. vedu, vest; ChSl. vedǫ, vesti, iter. voditi, SCr. voditi, Boh. vésti, Pol. prowadzić (cpd. replacing largely wieść, wodzić), Russ. vesti, vodit', Av. vāðaya- (caus.).

2. Grk. ἄγω : Lat. agere, Skt. aj-'drive' (10.65).

Grk. ἡγέομαι (cf. ἡγεμών 'leader, chief') : Lat. sāgīre 'perceive keenly', Goth. sōkjan 'seek', etc. (11.31). Walde-P. 2.449. Boisacq 314. Ernout-M. 887.

Grk. ὁδηγέω 'show the way, guide', NG ὁδηγῶ 'guide, lead', deriv. of ὁδηγός 'guide', cpd. of ὁδός 'way, road' and the root of ἄγω.

3. Lat. dūcere (also 'draw', OLat. doucere) : Goth. tiuhan 'lead' and 'draw', OHG ziohan, OE tēon, etc. 'draw' (9.33). Walde-P. 1.780 f. Ernout-M. 285 f. Walde-H. 1.377 f.

Hence Rum. duce both 'carry' and 'lead' (cf. Sp. llevar); and, fr. the cpd. Lat. condūcere 'draw, bring together, assemble', It. condurre (OIt. conducere), Fr. conduire, Sp. conducir, Rum. conduce. REW 2127.

It. menare, Fr. mener (both also used for 'drive' animals) = Rum. mīna 'drive' animals, fr. late Lat. mīnāre 'drive' animals, deriv. of minae 'threats' (cf. minae 'threats'). Ernout-M. 615. REW 5585.

It. guidare, Fr. guider (OFr. guier), Sp. guiar, fr. Gmc., prob. a Frank. witan : OE gewītan 'see, look' and 'take a certain direction'. REW 9528. Gamillscheg 498.

Sp. *llevar* 'carry' (10.61), also 'lead'.

4. Ir. *fedim*, above, 1.

NIr. *treōruighim*, deriv. of *treōir* 'guide, direction, conduct, strength' : Ir. *treōir* 'vigor', *treōrach* 'strong' (Windisch), further etym.?

W. *arwain*, earlier 'carry', fr. **ariwegn-* : Ir. *fēn*, OE *wægn* 'wagon', Lat. *vehere* 'carry', *vehī* 'ride', Skt. *vah-* 'carry, ride', etc. (10.66). Walde-P. 1.250.

W. *tywys* (cf. also *tywysog* 'leader, prince') : Ir. *tuus, tossach* 'beginning', *tōisech* 'leader', fr. IE **weid-* 'know' in Skt. *vid-*, Grk. *οἶδα*, etc., with development of 'know' to 'know the way, lead'. Walde-P. 1.238, 256. Pedersen 1.308 (vs. 136).

Br. *kas* 'send' (10.63), also 'lead'.

5. Goth. *tiuhan*, see under Lat. *dūcere*, above, 3.

ON *leiða*, Dan. *lede*, Sw. *leda*, OE *lǣdan*, ME *lede*, NE *lead*, Du. *leiden*, OHG, MHG, NHG *leiten*, Gmc. **laidjan*, caus. to ON *līða*, Goth. *leiþan*, etc. 'go' (10.47). Walde-P. 2.401. Falk-Torp 629.

Dan. *føre*, Sw. *föra* (also 'carry'), Du. *voeren*, MHG *vueren*, NHG *führen*, but ON *fœra* 'bring' (10.62), OHG *fuoren* 'convey, cause to go', etc., Gmc. **fōrjan*, caus. to ON *fara*, Goth. *faran*, etc. 'go' (10.47). Walde-P. 2.39. Falk-Torp 291.

6. Lith. *vesti*, ChSl. *vesti*, etc. (the Balto-Slavic group), above, 1.

7. Skt. *ni- nī-* (*nayati, nīta-*), Av., OPers. *ni-* (Av. 3sg. pres. *nayeiti*, OPers. 3sg. imperf. *anaya*, etc.); cf. Skt. *netar-* 'guide', perh. : Ir. *nēath* (Ogam gen. *netas*) 'hero'. Walde-P. 2.321.

Av. *vāδaya-*, above, 1.

10.65 DRIVE (vb. trans.)

Grk.	*ἐλαύνω*	Goth.	*dreiban, draibjan*	Lith.	*varyti, ginti*
NG	*διώχνω, βγάζω*, etc.	ON	*reka, keyra*	Lett.	*dzīt*
Lat.	*agere, pellere*	Dan.	*drive*	ChSl.	*gŭnati, goniti*
It.	*spingere, cacciare*	Sw.	*driva, köra*	SCr.	*tjerati, goniti*
Fr.	*pousser, chasser*	OE	*drīfan, wrecan*	Boh.	*hnáti, honiti, puditi*
Sp.	*arrear, echar*	ME	*drive*	Pol.	*gnać, gonić, pędzić*
Rum.	*goni, mîna*	NE	*drive*	Russ.	*gnat', gonit'*
Ir.	3sg. *ad-aig, imm-aig*	Du.	*drijven*	Skt.	*aj-, nud-*
NIr.	*tiomāinim*	OHG	*trīban*	Av.	*az-*
W.	*gyrru*	MHG	*trīben*		
Br.	*kas*	NHG	*treiben*		

Apart from the inherited group, some words for 'drive' are cognate with words for 'strike' or 'push', but many are of doubtful origin. Several were clearly used first of driving cattle.

'Drive' is understood here as 'force to move on or away' (from in front of one, action from behind), virtually the opposite of 'lead'. But the words listed, like NE *drive*, have many other, and quite disparate, uses.

Where the object is a horse or a vehicle, NE always uses *drive* (so Grk. *ἐλαύνω*, e.g. Hom. Il. 23.334, and Lat. *agere*), but the majority of other modern languages use rather a verb for 'lead' (10.64) or 'guide', e.g. NG *ὁδηγῶ*, It. *guidare, condurre*, Fr. *conduire*, Sp. *guiar, conducir*, NHG *lenken* (but *vieh treiben*), Russ. *pravit'* ('rule, direct', etc. : *pravyj* 'right').

1. IE **aĝ-*, widespread root in words with primary meaning 'drive' but with highly developed secondary uses. Walde-P. 1.35 ff. Ernout-M. 24 ff. Walde-H. 1.23 f. Pedersen 2.451.

Grk. *ἄγω* 'lead'; Lat. *agere* 'drive, carry on, act, do', etc.; Ir. 3sg. *ad-aig*, MIr. *imm-aig*, with vbl. n. *immāin*, whence NIr. *iomāinim, tiomāinim*; Skt. *aj-*, Av. *az-*; Arm. *acem* 'bring, lead'; ON *aka* 'ride' (in a vehicle); Toch. *āk-* 'lead, conduct' (SSS 422).

2. Grk. *ἐλαύνω* : Arm. *elanem* 'come out, mount' (Celtic *el-* in W. *elo* 'go', etc. here or fr. **pel-*?; 10.47). Walde-P. 1.156.

NG *ἐλαύνω* 'drive' is a lit. word. The pop. survivals are *λάμνω* 'row' (10.852) and *ἔλα* 'come!' fr. imperat. of *ἐλάω* in intr. sense.

NG *διώχνω* 'pursue' (10.53) is used also for 'drive away', e.g., *τοὺς ἔδιωχνε ἀπὸ κοντά του*.

NG *βγάζω*, aor. *ἔβγαλα*, used in many senses but including 'drive out', fr. Grk. *ἐκβάλλω* (cpd. of *βάλλω* 'throw'; for pres. *βγάζω*, see *βάζω* 'put', 12.12), which in the NT is the usual word for 'drive out', as Mt. 21.12, Mk. 11. 15, etc. (rendered literally as 'throw out' in Goth. *uswairpan*, as *cast out* in K. James version, but as 'drive out' in OE, Luther, ChSl., etc.).

For 'drive' domestic animals, *ὁδηγῶ* may be used (as for a vehicle, cf. above), and there are various pop. local terms, as *πιλαλῶ* (see 10.46), *σαλαγῶ* (beside *σάλαγο* 'noise'; cf. *σαλαγή βοή* Hesych.).

3. Lat. *agere*, above, 1.

Lat. *pellere* 'drive, drive out, strike', with *pulsus* 'a blow', Umbr. *ař-peltu* 'adpellito, admoveto', root connections much disputed and various combinations possible. Walde-P. 2.57. Ernout-M. 750. Walde-H. 1.59. Cpd. *impellere* > It. *impellere*, Sp. *impeler*, obs. Fr. *impeller* > NE *impel*, all only rarely used in the literal sense of 'drive'.

It. *spingere*, also 'push, shove' (cf. Fr. *pousser*), fr. VLat. *expingere* 'drive out', cpd. of *pangere* 'drive in, fix'. REW 3048.

It. *cacciare*, Fr. *chasser* 'drive away, drive', also 'hunt' (3.81), fr. VLat. **captiāre* : *capere* 'seize, take'. REW 1662.

Fr. *pousser* (also 'push, shove'), fr. Lat. *pulsāre* 'push, strike, beat' (: *pulsus* 'blow', *pellere* 'drive', above). REW 6837.

Of the numerous Sp. words which may correspond to NE *drive* in special connections, as *guiar, conducir* (for vehicles, see above), *impeler* (so in lit. sense NT, Lk. 8.29, but now only fig.) may be mentioned *arrear* (usual word for driving domestic animals), fr. the driver's cry *arre* (cf. Acad. Esp. Dicc. Hist. 1.777); *echar*, esp. 'drive away', orig. 'throw' (10.25).

Rum. *goni*, fr. Slavic, ChSl. *goniti*, etc. (below, 6).

Rum. *mîna* 'drive' (animals), fr. late Lat. *mināre* id., see Fr. *mener* 'lead', etc., 10.64.

4. Ir. *ad-aig-*, NIr. *tiomāinim*, above, 1.

W. *gyrru*, beside *gyrr* 'drove (of cattle)', etym. dub. Walde-P. 1.609. Falk-Torp 524, 1496. Morris Jones 137.

Br. *kas*, apparently the pop. word in this sense, but also 'lead', and 'send', see 10.63.

5. Goth. *dreiban, draibjan*, Dan. *drive*, Sw. *driva*, OE *drīfan*, OHG *trīban*, etc. (but ON *drīfa* 'drive' of spray, 'drift, let drift'), outside cognates dub. Walde-P. 1.872. Feist 124 f.

ON *reka*, OE *wrecan* (the latter largely 'drive away, banish, venge') = Goth. *wrikan* 'pursue' (10.53).

ON *keyra*, Sw. *köra*, see under Dan. *køre* 'ride', 10.66.

6. Lith. *varyti* prob. : Lett. dial. *vert* 'run' (10.46) and = ChSl. *variti* 'go before, outstrip, anticipate'. Trautmann

353. Buga, Kalba ir Senovė 298. Otherwise Walde-P. 1.281.

Lith. *ginti*, Lett. *dzīt*, ChSl. *gŭnati, goniti* (for *ἐλαύνω* but also for *διώκω* 'pursue, persecute'), etc., general Slavic : Skt. *han-*, Grk. *θείνω* 'strike', Ir. *gonim* 'wound', etc., IE **gʷhen-* (semantic development through 'strike' to 'urge cattle, etc., forward', whence 'drive', then 'pursue'). Walde-P. 1.680 f. Berneker 328. Brückner 146.

7. SCr. *tjerati* = late ChSl. *tĕrjati* 'pursue, chase' (Miklosich 356), clearly fr. Grk. *θηράω* 'hunt, chase' (3.81). For *t*, cf. *temelĭ* fr. *θεμέλιον*.

Boh. *puditi*, Pol. *pędzić* (beside *pęd* 'impulse, speed', *piądz* 'span') = ChSl. *pǫditi* 'press, drive' (beside *pędĭ* 'span'), this possibly (semantic development through 'lead cattle by attached rope'?) : Lat. *pendēre* 'hang' (i.e. 'hang by a stretched cord'), Lith. *spęsti* 'set a snare', OLith. *spandyti* 'stretch', IE *(*s*)*pend-*. Walde-P. 2.662. Meillet, Études 264.

8. Skt. *aj-*, Av. *az-*, above, 1.

Skt. *nud-* in this sense mostly 'drive away', also 'push, thrust' (cf. also Romance words), etym. dub., but perh. as *d*-present : Grk. *νεύω*, Lat. *nuere* 'nod, beckon', etc., also Skt. *nāuti* 'turns, twists' (intr.), fr. a root **neu-* having the notion of 'short, quick motion', whence 'shove', 'nod', etc. Walde-P. 2.323 (316).

10.66 RIDE (vb.)

(a = on a Horse, etc.; b = in a Vehicle)

Grk.	*ὀχέομαι, ἐλαύνω* (a, b), *ἱππεύω* (a)	Goth.	. . . .	Lith.	*joti* (a), *važiuoti* (b)
NG	*πηγαίνω καβάλλα* (a), *πηγαίνω μὲ ἅμαξα* (b)	ON	*rīða* (a), *aka* (b)	Lett.	*jāt* (a), *braukt* (b)
Lat.	*vehī* (a, b), *equitāre* (a)	Dan.	*ride* (a), *køre* (b)	ChSl.	*jachati* (b), *voziti sę* (b)
It.	*andare a cavallo* (a), *in carozza* (b)	Sw.	*rida* (a), *åka* (b)	SCr.	*jahati* (a), *voziti se* (b)
Fr.	*aller à cheval* (a), *en voiture* (b)	OE	*rīdan* (a)	Boh.	*jeti* (a, b)
Sp.	*ir a caballo* (a), *en coche* (b)	ME	*ride* (a, b)	Pol.	*jechać* (a, b)
Rum.	*umbla (merge) călare* (a), *cu trăsura* (b)	NE	*ride* (a, b), *drive* (b)	Russ.	*jachat'* (a, b)
Ir.	*rīadaim* (a?, b)	Du.	*rijden* (a, b)	Skt.	*vah-* (a, b)
NIr.	*marcuighim* (a, b)	OHG	*rītan* (a, b)	Av.	*bar-* (a), *vaz-* (b)
W.	*marchogaeth* (a, b)	MHG	*rīten* (a, b)		
Br.	*mont war varc'h* (a), *en eur c'harr* (b)	NHG	*reiten* (a), *fahren* (b)		

'Ride' on a horse or other animal (a) and 'ride' in a vehicle (b) are expressed in part by the same, in part by different, words, as shown in the list. Apart from an inherited group, several are derivatives of the words for 'horse' (3.41), some of these used only in sense (a), some extended to cover sense (b). Some are words for 'drive', which from such phrases as 'drive horses, drive a vehicle' have come to be used intransitively not merely of the person doing the driving but also of anyone being driven in a vehicle (as NE *drive*). Some are words for 'go, travel' used also, or specifically, for 'ride'. In the Romance languages (also NG) 'ride' is expressed only by phrases with words for 'horse' or 'carriage'.

1. IE **weĝh-*, widespread in words for 'carry' or 'be carried' in a vehicle and in those for 'vehicle, wagon', so that this, rather than generic 'carry', is to be assumed as the dominant IE sense. Walde-P. 1.249 f. Ernout-M. 1079 f.

Grk. *ϝέχω* 'carry, bring' (Cypr., Pamph.; lost in most dial.), *ὄχος* 'wagon', *ὀχέομαι* 'be carried' (by wagon, chariot, horses, ship, etc., these usually expressed), sometimes alone 'ride', 'float'; Lat. *vehere* 'carry' (mostly by animal or vehicle), pass. *vehī* 'be carried, ride'; Goth. *ga-wigan*, OHG *wegan* 'move', OE *wegan* 'carry, bear, weigh' (NE *weigh*); Lith. *vežti* 'carry' in a vehicle, *važiuoti* 'ride'; ChSl. *vesti* (*vezą*), *voziti* 'vehere', refl. 'vehī', etc.; Skt. *vah-*, Av. *vaz-* 'carry in a vehicle' and 'ride'.

2. Grk. *ἐλαύνω* 'drive' (10.65), also intr. 'drive, ride'.

Grk. *ἱππεύω*, deriv. of *ἱππεύς* 'horseman' : *ἵππος* 'horse'.

NG *πηγαίνω καβάλλα* (*καβάλλα* used as adv. 'on horseback, muleback', etc.), also *καβαλλικεύω* (mostly 'mount a horse, mule', etc., but also 'ride'), derivs. of Lat. *caballus* 'horse'. G. Meyer, Neugr. Stud. 3.22.

NG for 'ride' (b) only phrases, *πηγαίνω μὲ ἅμαξα*, etc.

3. Lat. *vehī*, above, 1.

Lat. *equitāre*, deriv. of *eques* 'horseman' : *equus* 'horse'.

In the modern Romance languages only phrases for 'ride', for which see the list. Rum. *călare* is fr. late Lat. *caballārius*.

4. Ir. *rīadaim* : OE *rīdan*, etc., below, 5.

Ir. **marcaigim* (cf. *marcaigecht* 'horsemanship'), NIr. *marcuighim*, W. *marchogaeth*, fr. Ir. *marc*, W. *march* 'horse' (on formation, see Loth, RC 37.46). Here also Br. *marc'hekaat*, but replaced now largely by phrases *mont war var'ch, mont en eur c'harr* 'go on a horse, in a vehicle' copied after the French. The Irish and Welsh words are now generalized (perh. after the NE *ride*) to both sense (a) and sense (b).

5. ON *rīða*, OE *rīdan*, OHG *rītan*, etc., Gmc. group (chiefly in sense (a) in the older period, but OHG *rītan*, MHG *rīten* also (b)) : Ir. *rīadaim* 'ride', but further connections dub. Walde-P. 2.348 (but on Lett. *raidīt* 'urge', cf. Mühl.-Endz. 3.470, Trautmann 243).

ON *aka*, Sw. *åka* (Dan. *age* mostly replaced by *køra*), orig. 'drive' : Lat. *agere*, Skt. *aj-* 'drive', etc. (10.65).

Dan. *køre* orig. 'drive' (horses, a vehicle, etc.), like Sw. *köra*, ON *keyra* (these only rarely intr.), the latter also 'whip, lash' (horses), 'fling, thrust', outside connections dub., but perh. : SCr. *žuriti se* 'hurry', *gurati* 'shove, press'. Falk-Torp 524, 1496 f. Hellquist 551.

NE *drive* (10.65), used in *drive a horse, carriage, automobile*, hence also intr. in the same connection (but not for *ride* in a railway car, etc.), e.g. *go driving* vs. *go riding*. NED s.v. B5c.

NHG *fahren* also 'go, travel', etc., cf. Goth. *faran* 'go', etc. (10.47).

6. Lith. *joti*, Lett. *jāt*, ChSl. *jadą, jachati*, etc., general Slavic : Skt. *yā-*, Av. *yā-* 'go' (10.47). Walde-P. 1.104. Berneker 442.

Lith. *važiuoti*, ChSl. *voziti sę*, etc., above, 1.

Lett. *braukt*, also 'stroke' = Lith. *braukti* 'stroke, wipe' : Lett. *brukt* 'crumble', *bruzināt* 'whet (a scythe)', fr. **bhreu-k̂-* : **bhreu-k̂-* in Russ.-ChSl. *brusnuti* 'shave, scrape' (cf. under Russ. *brosit'* 'throw away', 10.25). Walde-P. 2.197, Mühl.-Endz. 1.326, 339. (For a semantic parallel cf. NHG *streichen* 'stroke, rove, wander').

7. Skt. *vah-*, Av. *vaz-*, above, 1.

Av. *bar-* 'bear' also act. and mid. 'ride'. Barth. 936 and 942, note 14, suggesting confusion of *bar-* 'bear' with *bar-* 'move rapidly' (of wind, water).

10.67 PUSH, SHOVE (vb.)

Grk.	*ὠθέω*	Goth.	*afskiuban*	Lith.	*stumti*
NG	*σπρώχνω*	ON	*skȳfa*	Lett.	*stumt*
Lat.	*trūdere, impellere, pulsāre*	Dan.	*puffe, skubbe, støde*	ChSl.	. . . .
It.	*spingere*	Sw.	*skjuta, stöta*	SCr.	*gurati, turati*
Fr.	*pousser*	OE	*scūfan*	Boh.	*strkati, šoupati*
Sp.	*empujar*	ME	*shoue, thrist, pusshe, putte*	Pol.	*pchać, sunąć*
Rum.	*împinge, îmbrînci*	NE	*push, shove (thrust)*	Russ.	*tolkat', pichat'*
Ir.	. . . .	Du.	*duwen, stooten*	Skt.	*tud-*
NIr.	*sāithim*	OHG	*scioban*	Av.	. . . .
W.	*gwthio, hyrddu*	MHG	*schieben*		
Br.	*poulza*	NHG	*stossen, schieben*		

The notion intended by the heading is that of forcing back either by a sharp impact or by gradual pressure. These two aspects are sometimes distinguished, at least roughly, as in NHG *stossen* vs. *schieben*. But, in general, the former is the earlier, as shown by the frequent connection with words for 'strike, hit', 'drive', or 'shoot', or others for 'swift' motion.

1. Grk. *ὠθέω* : Skt. *vadh-* 'strike, kill', Av. *vādāya-* 'force back'. Walde-P. 1.254 f. Boisacq 1080.

NG *σπρώχνω*, fr. cpd. of preceding, namely **εἰσ-προ-ωθέω* (cf. class. *προωθέω*) > **σπρώθω*, whence *σπρώχνω* after the *-νω* presents and with guttural fr. aor. *ἔσπρωξα* for *ἔσπρωσα* (cf. class. *ὦσα* and *ἔπρωσα*; for spread of *ξ-* vs. *σ-* aor. cf. Hatzidakis Einleitung 136). Cf. NG dial. *ἀμπώθω*, *ἀμπώχνω*, etc. fr. *ἀπωθέω* (Ἱστ. Λεξ. 1.550).

2. Lat. *trūdere* : Goth. *us-þriutan* 'make trouble for, annoy', OE *(ā)þrēotan* 'make weary', OHG *driozan* 'press, oppress', ChSl. *trudŭ* 'trouble', vb. *truditi* 'trouble', etc. Walde-P. 1.755. Ernout-M. 1060.

Lat. *pellere* 'drive, strike' (10.65) and cpds., esp. *impellere*, sometimes 'push'. Hence also, through *pulsus* 'blow', *pulsāre* (> Fr. *pousser*) and *impulsāre* (> Sp. *empujar*). Ernout-M. 750. REW 4323, 6837.

Lat. *impingere* (> Rum. *împinge*), **expingere* (> It. *spingere*), cpds. of *pangere* 'drive in, fix'. Ernout-M. 728 f. REW 3048, 4309. Tiktin 764.

Rum. *îmbrînci*, deriv. of *brînca* 'paw, hand' (etym. dub., REW 1271).

3. NIr. *sāithim*, fr. Ir. *sāidim* 'drive in, fix', caus. of *saidim* 'sit'. Pedersen 2.605.

W. *gwthio*, beside sb. *gwth* 'a push, thrust', etym.?

W. *hyrddu*, beside sb. *hwrdd* 'a push', etym.? Loth, RC 36.175 (vs. Morris Jones 153).

Br. *poulza*, fr. an early form of Fr. *pousser*, fr. Lat. *pulsāre* (above, 2).

4. Goth. *afskiuban* (renders *ἀπωθέω*), ON *skȳfa*, Norw. *skyve* (Dan. *skubbe* fr. a different but related form), OE *scūfan*, ME *shoue*, NE *shove* (Du. *schuiven* now less common in this sense), OHG *scioban*, MHG, NHG *schieben*, prob. : Lith. *skubus* 'swift, quick', ChSl. *skubati* 'pull' (cf. also Skt. *kṣubh-* 'a jerk'), with common notion of quick motion. Walde-P. 2.556. Feist 9. Falk-Torp 1035, 1047. Weigand-H. 2.703.

Dan. *støde*, Sw. *stöta*, Du. *stooten*, NHG *stossen*, all also 'hit, strike' as mostly in earlier times (Goth. *stautan* only in this sense) : Lat. *tundere* 'strike, beat, pound', Skt. *tud-* 'hit, push', etc. Walde-P. 2.618. Feist. 451. Falk-Torp 1198.

Dan. *puffe*, fr. MLG *puffen, buffen* 'hit, pop' (Du. *poffen, boffen*), of imitative orig. (cf. NE *puff*, etc.). Falk-Torp 854.

Sw. *skjuta* (also 'shoot') : ON *skjōta* 'put in motion, shoot', etc. (with *bātr* 'boat' = 'shove off'), OE *scēotan* 'move or cause to move swiftly or suddenly, shoot', etc. (cf. NE *shoot the bolt*), OHG *sciozan* (NHG *schiessen*), etc. Falk-Torp 1044.

Early ME *þrusten, þristan*, ME *thrist*, NE *thrust* (now mostly a lit. word), fr. ON *þrysta* 'thrust, press,' this perh. : Lat. *trūdere* (above, 2). Walde-P. 1.755. Falk-Torp 1294. NED s.v. *thrust*, vb.

ME *pusshe*, NE *push*, fr. Fr. *pousser* (above, 2). NED s.v. *push*, vb.

ME *putte* 'put, place' (12.12), also 'push', NED s.v. *put*, vb.B1.

Du. *duwen* : OHG *dūhan*, OE *þȳn* 'press', prob. : Grk. *τύκος* 'mason's hammer', ChSl. *tŭknąti* 'prick, stab' and with other extensions, Lat. *tundere*, Goth. *stautan*, etc. (above), Grk. *τύπτω* 'strike, hit, beat'. Walde-P. 2.615 ff. Frank-v. W. 144.

5. Lith. *stumti*, Lett. *stumt*, fr. another extension of the root **(s)teu-* seen in Goth. *stautan*, NHG *stossen*, etc. (above, 4). Mühl.-Endz. 3.1106.

6. SCr. *gurati*, deriv. of *gura* 'hump'? Berneker 363 (but without this vb.).

SCr. *turati, turiti* (also 'throw') : Russ. *turit'* 'urge, drive away', outside connections? Miklosich 365.

Boh. *strčiti, strkati* (with sb. *strk* 'a thrust') : Pol. *sterczeć* 'jut out, project', etc., outside connections? Miklosich 322. Brückner 513.

Boh. *šoupati*, fr. sb. *šoup* 'a shove', this fr. NHG *schub* id. (: *schieben*, above, 4).

Pol. *pchać*, Russ. *pichat'* : ChSl. *pĭchati* 'strike' (with the fist or the foot), Boh. *pichati* 'prick', Skt. *piṣ-*, Lat. *pīnsere* 'pound, crush'. Walde-P. 2.1. Ernout-M. 770 f. Brückner 401.

Pol. *sunąć*, *suwać* = Russ. *sunut'*, *sovat'* 'thrust, poke, put in', ChSl. *sovati* 'throw, hurl' : Lith. *šauti* 'shoot', Walde-P. 2.552. Brückner 526.

Russ. *tolkat'*, *tolknut'* : ChSl. *tlŭką*, *tlěsti*, *tlŭknąti* 'strike, knock' (9.21).

7. Skt. *tud-* : Lat. *tundere* 'strike, beat, pound', Goth. *stautan* 'hit', NHG *stossen*, etc. (above, 4).

10.71 ROAD

Grk.	*ὁδός (κέλευθος)*	Goth.	*wigs*	Lith.	*kelias*
NG	*δρόμος*	ON	*vegr, braut, gata*	Lett.	*cel'š*
Lat.	*via*	Dan.	*vej*	ChSl.	*pǫtĭ, cěsta*
It.	*strada, cammino, via*	Sw.	*väg*	SCr.	*put, cesta*
Fr.	*chemin, route, voie*	OE	*weg, stræt*	Boh.	*cesta*
Sp.	*camino, via*	ME	*weie, strete, gate*	Pol.	*droga*
Rum.	*drum, cale*	NE	*road (way)*	Russ.	*doroga, put'*
Ir.	*slige, sēt, rōt, conar, bōthar*	Du.	*weg*	Skt.	*path-, mārga-, adhvan-*
NIr.	*bōthar, rōd, bealach*	OHG	*weg, strāza*	Av.	*paθ-, advan-, frayana-*
W.	*ffordd*	MHG	*wec, strāze*		
Br.	*hent*	NHG	*weg, strasse*		

1. Grk. *ὁδός* : ChSl. *chodŭ* 'gait, walk', *choditi* 'walk, go' (10.45). Walde-P. 2.486.

Grk. *κέλευθος* (mostly poet., but also for 'road' in Arc. dial.) : Lith. *keliauti*, Lett. *cel'uot* 'travel', Lith. *kelias*, Lett. *cel'š* 'road'. Walde-P. 1.446.

NG *δρόμος* = class. Grk. *δρόμος* 'course, race' : Grk. aor. *ἔδραμον* 'ran' (10.46). Hence SCr.–ChSl. *drumŭ, dromŭ*, Bulg.,

SCr. *drum* (esp. 'highway') > Rum. *drum* 'road'. Berneker 231. Tiktin 578.

2. Lat. *via* (> It., Sp. *via*, Fr. *voie*) generally both 'road' and 'street', Osc. *víú*, Umbr. (abl.) *vea, via*, perh. : Skt. *vī-thi-* 'row', also 'street', *vī-* 'approach eagerly, seek, etc.', Lith. *vyti* 'pursue' (10.53). Walde-P. 1.229. The old deriv. fr. **weĝh-yā-* : Lat. *vehere*, etc., still mentioned in Ernout-M. 1101 and most attractive semantically (cf. Goth. *wigs*, etc., below, 4), seems phonetically impossible.

Lat. *(via) strāta* 'paved road' (*strātus* pple. of *sternere* 'spread, pave') > It. *strada* (> Rum. *stradă* 'street'), Byz., NG *στράτα* (now mostly 'course, way'), Ir. *srāt*, NIr. *srāid* (see 10.73), OE *stræt* (> ON *stræti*), ME *strete*, NE *street*, Du. *straat*, OHG *strāza*, MHG *strāze*, NHG *strasse*. For the varying use of these as 'road' or 'street', see the lists and NED s.v. *street*.

It. *cammino*, Fr. *chemin*, Sp. *camino*, fr. Gallo-Lat. *cammīnus* : Ir. *cingim* 'walk, stride' (10.45). REW 1552. Thurneysen, Keltorom. 52.

Fr. *route*, fr. Lat. *(via) rupta* (*ruptus* pple. of *rumpere* 'break') 'broken road', i.e. one that has been broken through, opened up. Gamillscheg 775.

Rum. *drum*, see above, 1, NG *δρόμος*.

Rum. *cale* (= Sp. *calle* 'street'), fr. Lat. *callis* 'path' (10.72). Puşcariu 262.

3. Ir. *slige* (NIr. *slighe* 'way, avenue'), with *sluicht* 'a following', MIr. *slicht* 'track' : Ir. *sligim* 'strike'(?). Pedersen 2.103. Adversely Walde-P. 2.706.

Ir. *sēt*, Br. *hent* (= W. *hynt* 'way, journey') : OE *sīð*, OHG *sind* 'journey, course, way, time', Goth. *sinþs* 'time', etc. Walde-P. 2.496. Pedersen 1.138.

Ir. *conar* 'road, path (*conaraib* gl. *semitis* Ml. 143b2), journey', also 'way, manner' (K. Meyer, Contrib. 460. Laws, Gloss. 174), etym.? Pedersen 2.51.

Ir., NIr. *bōthar*, perh. orig. 'ox-track, ox-run', deriv. of *bō* 'ox, cow'. Pedersen 2.51.

Ir. *rōt*, NIr. *rōd*, fr. OE *rād*, NE *road* (below, 4). Pedersen 1.21.

NIr. *bealach* chiefly Ulster in this sense, otherwise 'mountain pass, inlet, passage', fr. *beal* 'lip, mouth', also 'entrance, opening' (cf. *Beal Feirste* 'Belfast' : *fearsad* 'sand bar').

W. *ffordd*, fr. OE *ford*. Parry-Williams 34. Morris Jones 227 f.

4. Goth. *wigs*, ON *vegr*, OE, OHG *weg*, etc., general Gmc. (NE *way* now rare in this sense except in *highway*, *railway* beside *railroad*, but still common in 18th cent. and even later; in U.S. colonial records Sir William Craigie finds that *way* is the usual word until about 1700) : Goth. *gawigan*, OHG *wegan* 'move', Skt. *vah-*, Lat. *vehere*, *vehī* 'carry, ride', etc. (10.66). Walde-P. 1.250.

ON *braut*, fr. *brjōta* 'break', like Fr. *route*, above 2. Falk-Torp 95.

ON *gata* (> ME *gate*), cf. Goth. *gatwo* 'street' (10.73).

OE *stræt* 'street' and 'road', but used especially in earliest period of certain (chiefly Roman) roads, ME *strete*, OHG *strāza*, MHG *strāze*, NHG *strasse* 'street, road', see above, 2.

NE *road*, fr. OE *rād*, ME *rode* 'act of riding, journey' : OE *rīdan* 'ride (10.66). NED s.v.

5. Lith. *kelias*, Lett. *cel'š* : Grk. *κέλευθος*, above, 1.

6. ChSl. *pǫtĭ*, SCr. *put*, Russ *put'* : OPr. *pintis* 'road', Skt. *path-* (nom. *panthās*, etc.), Av. *paθ-* (nom. *pantå*, etc.; OPers. acc. *paθim*) 'way' (in general), whether 'road, street' or 'path', Grk. *πάτος* 'path', *πόντος* 'sea', Lat. *pons* 'bridge', etc. (10.74), Goth. *finþan*, ON *finna*, etc. 'find, experience', OS *fāthi* 'going', OHG *fendeo* 'walker'. Walde-P. 2.26 f.

ChSl. *cěsta*, SCr., Boh. *cesta*, etym. dub., but perh. (as 'smoothed way') : Lith. *kaišti* 'shave, rub, smooth', OPruss. *coysnis* 'comb'. Walde-P. 1.328. Berneker 127. (Cf. semantic source of Grk. *τρίβος* 'path', 10.72.)

Pol. *droga*, Russ. *doroga* = SCr. *draga* 'valley', Boh. *dráha* 'way, track' (old 'lane between fields') : Russ. *dergat'* 'pull, draw', etc. (9.33). Semantic development through 'something drawn out, a stretch'. Berneker 212. Brückner 97.

7. Skt. *path-*, Av. *paθ-*, see above, 6.

Skt. *mārga-*, orig. 'path of wild animals', deriv. of *mṛga-* 'wild animal, deer' (3.11). Uhlenbeck 222.

Skt. *adhvan-*, Av. *advan-* : Pali *andhati* 'goes', further connections dub. Walde-P. 1.130.

Av. *frayana-*, cpd. of *fra* + *ayana* (Skt. *prāyana-* 'entrance, beginning'): *i-*, Skt. *i-* 'go' (10.47). Barth. 989.

10.72 PATH

Grk.	*πάτος, ἀτραπός, τρίβος*	Goth.	*staiga*	Lith.	*takas*
NG	*μονοπάτι*	ON	*stīgr*	Lett.	*teka, taks, stiga*
Lat.	*sēmita, callis*	Dan.	*sti*	ChSl.	*stĭza, stĭdza*
It.	*sentiero*	Sw.	*stig*	SCr.	*staza*
Fr.	*sentier*	OE	*stīg, pæþ*	Boh.	*stezka*
Sp.	*senda, sendero, vereda*	ME	*path, sti*	Pol.	*ścieżka*
Rum.	*cărare*	NE	*path*	Russ.	*stezja, tropa*
Ir.	*cassān (conar)*	Du.	*pad*	Skt.	*path-, mārga-*
NIr.	*cosān*	OHG	*pfad, stīga*	Av.	*paθ-, advan-*
W.	*llwybr*	MHG	*pfat, stīc*		
Br.	*gwenodenn, ravent*	NHG	*pfad, steig*		

Although several of the words discussed under 'road' are used to cover any sort of 'way', there are usually other words for the less pretentious 'path'.

1. Grk. *πάτος* : ChSl. *pǫtĭ* 'road, street', Skt. *path-*, Av. *paθ-* 'way, road, path', etc. (10.71). Hence Byz. *μονοπάτιον*, NG *μονοπάτι*, cpd. with *μόνος* 'alone, single'.

Grk. *ἀτραπός*, Hom. *ἀταρπός*, lit. 'trodden (path)', cpd. of *ἁ*-cop. and the root of *τραπέω* 'tread grapes' : Russ. *trepat'* 'crush, peel, strip', *tropat'* 'stamp', *tropa* 'path' (cf. below, 6). Walde-P. 1.756.

Grk. *τρίβος*, lit. a 'worn, beaten' path : *τρίβω* 'rub'.

2. Lat. *sēmita* (> OFr. *sente*, Sp. *senda*), etym.? Ernout-M. 922. Hence adj. *sēmitārius* > Fr. *sentier*, Sp. *sendero*. REW 7813. Gamillscheg 796.

Lat. *callis* (> Sp. *calle* 'street', Rum. *cale* 'road'), etym. disputed, perh. : Bulg. *klánik* 'space between hearth and wall', SCr. *klánac* 'narrow passage', etc., NHG *helle*, *hölle* 'chimney-corner'. Walde-P. 1.356 f., Walde-H. 1.140.

Sp. *vereda*, fr. MLat. *verēda*, properly a road for the *verēdī* 'post-horses'. REW 9226. Du Cange s.v. *veredus*.

Rum. *cărare* (= Sp. *carrera* 'course, avenue', etc.), fr. VLat. **carrāria* 'wagon road', deriv. of *carrus* 'wagon'. REW 1718.

3. MIr. *cassān* 'foot-path', NIr. *cosān*, fr. *coss* 'foot'. K. Meyer, Contrib. 323.

Ir. *conar*, see under 'road' (10.71).

W. *llwybr*, etym.? (Morris Jones 127 : Grk. *λείπω*, Lat. *linguere* 'leave'.)

Br. *gwenodenn*, etym. dub., but perh. fr. *gwen* 'pliant, flexible' (from the winding course?). Henry 151.

Br. *ravent*, etym. dub., but perh. for

rao-hent, cpd. of *rao* 'pole-chain' (on vehicles, etc.) and *hent* 'road' (in sense of 'twisted road'?). Henry 230.

4. Goth. *staiga;* ON *stīgr,* Dan. *sti,* Sw. *stig,* OE *stīg,* ME *sti,* OHG *stīga,* MHG *stīc,* NHG *steig;* Lett. *stiga,* ChSl. *stĭza, stĭdza,* etc., general Slavic : Goth. *steigan,* ON *stīga* 'climb, mount', Lett. *staigāt* 'walk' (10.45), ChSl. *stignąti* 'arrive', Ir. *tiagu* 'go' (10.47), etc. Walde-P. 2.615. Falk-Torp 1160. Feist 447.

OE *pæþ,* ME, NE *path,* Du. *pad,* OHG, NHG *pfad,* much disputed. Possibly (but historically difficult) an early WGmc. loanword of either Grk. (πάτος) or Iran. (cf. Av. *paθ-,* 10.71) origin. Other etymologies unconvincing. Walde-P. 2.26 f. Weigand-H. 2.401. Kluge-G. 438. Franck-v. W. 485.

5. Lith. *takas,* Lett. *teka, taks* : Lith. *tekėti* 'run', etc. (10.46).

Lett. *stiga,* above, 4.

6. ChSl. *stĭza, stĭdza,* SCr. *staza,* Boh. *stezka,* Pol. *ścieżka,* Russ. *stezja,* above, 4.

Russ. *tropa,* dim. *tropinka* (Pol. *trop* 'track'), see under Grk. ἀτραπός, above, 1.

7. Skt. Av. words for 'path', see under 'road' (10.71).

10.73 STREET

Grk.	*ὁδός, ἄγυια, πλατεῖα*	Goth.	*gatwō, plapja*	Lith.	*gatvė (ulyčia)*
NG	*ὁδός, δρόμος*	ON	*stræti, gata*	Lett.	*iela, gatva*
Lat.	*via, platēa*	Dan.	*gade*	ChSl.	*raspątije, pątĭ, cěsta*
It.	*via*	Sw.	*gata*	SCr.	*ulica*
Fr.	*rue*	OE	*stræt*	Boh.	*ulice*
Sp.	*calle, rua*	ME	*strete, gate*	Pol.	*ulica*
Rum.	*stradă, uliţă*	NE	*street*	Russ.	*ulica*
Ir.	*slige, srāt*	Du.	*straat*	Skt.	*rathyā-, vīthi-*
NIr.	*srāid*	OHG	*gazza, strāza*	Av.	. . . .
W.	*heol (ystryd)*	MHG	*gazze, strāze*		
Br.	*ru*	NHG	*strasse (gasse)*		

The distinction between 'road' and 'street' (in a town) is secondary and incomplete. Words for 'road' covered also 'street', and some came to be used mainly in the latter sense, like NE *street.* Several of the other words that are used mainly for 'street', and listed here only, are sometimes used also for 'road'.

1. Grk. ὁδός 'road' (10.71) also and in NG only 'street' (beside pop. δρόμος).

Grk. ἄγυια (sc. ὁδός), formed with the same suffix as the fem. perf. act. pple. in -υῖα (cf. also ὄργυια, etc.) fr. ἄγω 'lead'.

Grk. πλατεῖα (sc. ὁδός), fem. of πλατύς 'wide', in Hellenistic times the common word for 'street' (freq. in NT and pap.) but in NG the public 'square'.

Grk. ῥύμη 'force, rush' (fr. ἐρύω 'drag'), in Hellenistic times (LXX, NT, pap.) 'street' or 'alley', with development, fr. 'rush through', 'going, passage', like that in Fr. *allée* (> NE *alley*) fr. *aller* 'go'.

2. Lat. *via,* It. *via,* see 'road' (10.71).

Lat. *platēa,* fr. Grk. πλατεῖα (above, 1).

Fr. *rue* (> Sp. *rua* 'street in a village'), fr. Lat. *rūga* 'wrinkle, fold, crease'. REW 7462.

Sp. *calle,* fr. Lat. *callis* 'path' (10.72).

Rum. *stradă,* fr. It. *strada* 'road' (10.71).

Rum. *uliţă,* fr. the Slavic (below, 6). This is now used for the street in a village, but *stradă* for the city street.

3. Ir. *slige,* see 'road' (10.71).

Ir. *srāt,* NIr. *srāid,* fr. Lat. *strāta* (10.71), directly (Pedersen, Vendryes) or through OE (Marstrander, Bidrag 76); in either case the use affected by English. W. *ystryd* (used locally = *heol*) fr. ME *strete.* Parry-Williams 27.

W. *heol,* formerly also 'course, way' = Ir. *seol* 'course', etym.?

Br. *ru,* fr. Fr. *rue* (above).

4. Goth. *gatwō,* ON *gata* (> ME *gate*), Dan. *gade,* Sw. *gata,* OHG *gazza,* MHG *gazze,* NHG *gasse* (in the north mostly 'lane, alley', but cf. Kretschmer, Wortgeogr. 491 f.), etym. disputed and wholly dub. Walde-P. 1.543. Feist 205.

Goth. *plapja* (once) by assim. or mere error fr. Grk. πλατεῖα or Lat. *platēa* (above, 1, 2).

OE *stræt,* OHG *strāza,* etc., see under Lat. *strāta (via)* 'paved road' (10.71).

5. Lith. *gatvė,* Lett. *gatva,* fr. Gmc., above, 4. Buga, Kalba ir Senovė 114 f. Mühl.-Endz. 1.609.

Lith. *ulyčia* (now replaced by *gatvė* in lit. language), fr. Pol. *ulica* (below). Lett. *iela* : Lith. *eilė* 'row', Lett. *iet,* Lith. *eiti* 'go' (10.47). Mühl.-Endz. 2.35.

6. ChSl. *raspątije* (so reg. for πλατεῖα in Gospels; later also *pątĭ* or *cěsta;* Jagić, Entstehungsgesch. 415 f.) cpd. of *raz-* 'apart' and *pątĭ* 'road' (10.71).

SCr., Pol., Russ. *ulica,* Boh. *ulice,* as orig. 'narrow opening' : ChSl. *ulĭjĭ,* Lith. *aulys* 'beehive', orig. 'hollow' (tree), Grk. αὐλός 'flute, tube, pipe', Arm. *uł, uli* 'road', etc. Walde-P. 1.25. Brückner 593.

7. Skt. *rathyā-* 'carriage-road, highway, street', fem. of adj. *rathya-* 'belonging to a chariot' : *ratha-* 'chariot, car'.

Skt. *vīthi-* 'row' and 'road, street' : *vī-* 'approach eagerly, seek', etc.

10.74 BRIDGE

Grk.	*γέφῡρα*	Goth.	. . . .	Lith.	*tiltas*
NG	*γέφυρα*	ON	*brū*	Lett.	*tilts*
Lat.	*pōns*	Dan.	*bro*	ChSl.	*mostŭ*
It.	*ponte*	Sw.	*bro, brygga*	SCr.	*most*
Fr.	*pont*	OE	*brycg*	Boh.	*most*
Sp.	*puente*	ME	*brigge*	Pol.	*most*
Rum.	*pod*	NE	*bridge*	Russ.	*most*
Ir.	*drochet*	Du.	*brug*	Skt.	*setu-*
NIr.	*droichead*	OHG	*brucka*	Av.	*pəšu-, pərətu-*
W.	*pont*	MHG	*brucke, brugge*		
Br.	*pont*	NHG	*brücke*		

Words for 'bridge' are connected with words for 'beam, board-flooring', reflecting the structure, or with words for 'way, road, ford, band', reflecting the purpose of the bridge.

1. Grk. γέφῡρα (NG also τὸ γεφύρι), Boeot. βέφῡρα, Cret. δέφῡρα, earlier meaning (Hom., etc.) 'dam, dyke', etym.? Walde-P. 1.674. Boisacq 146.

2. Lat. *pōns, pontis* (> It. *ponte,* Fr. *pont,* Sp. *puente*) : Grk. πόντος 'sea', πάτος 'path', ChSl. *pątĭ,* Skt. *path-,* Av. *paθ-* 'road, way, path' (10.71). Ernout-M. 788. Cf. also Specht, KZ 62.245 f.

Rum. *pod,* fr. ChSl. *podŭ* 'ground, floor'. Tiktin s.v.

3. Ir. *drochet,* NIr. *droichead,* prob. as a coll. **druk-anto-* 'beams' : OE *trog* 'trough', ChSl. *drŭkolŭ* 'cudgel', *ko*-formations fr. IE **dreu-* in Grk. δρῦς 'tree, oak', etc. Walde-P. 1.805. Pedersen 2.47.

W., Br. *pont,* fr. Lat. *pōns (-tis).* Loth, Mots lat. 197.

4. ON *brū,* Dan., Sw. *bro,* Sw. *brygga* (Dan. *brygge* 'wharf, pier'), OE *brycg,* OHG *brucka,* etc., general Gmc. : Gall. *briva* 'bridge', ChSl. *brŭvŭno* 'beam',

SCr. *brv* 'beam, footbridge', etc., a group with primary meaning 'beam', whence 'bridge'. Walde-P. 2.207. Falk-Torp 103, 109.

5. Lith. *tiltas,* Lett. *tilts* : OPruss. *talas* 'floor' (of a room), ChSl. *tilo* 'ground', ON *þil,* OHG *dil* 'board-wall', Skt. *tala-* 'surface, plane', etc. Walde-P. 1.740.

6. ChSl. *mostŭ,* SCr. *most,* etc., general Slavic (cf. also Russ. *mostovaja* 'pavement, deck', *pomost* 'floor, scaffold') prob. as orig. 'beam' an early loanword fr. the Gmc. group OHG *mast* 'pole, flagstaff', esp. 'mast', OE *mæst,* ON *mastr* 'mast'. Stender-Petersen 282 f. Walde-P. 2.235 f. (rather as cognate with Gmc. group). Walde-H. 2.19.

7. Skt. *setu-,* lit. 'a band', as adj. 'binding' = Av. *haētu-* 'a dam' : Lat. *saeta* 'coarse hair', OHG *seid* 'string', etc., *t*-formations to Skt. *si-,* Av. *hi-,* Lett. *set* 'bind', etc. Walde-P. 2.464.

Av. *pəšu-, pərətu-,* also 'ford, passage' : OE *ford,* OHG *furt* 'ford', Lat. *portus* 'harbor', *porta* 'gate', etc. Walde-P. 2.40.

10.75 CARRIAGE, WAGON, CART

Grk.	*ἅμαξα, ἀπήνη, ὄχος*	Goth.	. . . .	Lith.	*vežimas, ratai*
NG	*ἅμαξα, καρρότσα, κάρρο*	ON	*reið, vagn, kartr*	Lett.	*rati, vāg'i, divriči*
Lat.	*vehiculum, raeda, carrus, plaustrum*	Dan.	*vogn, karre*	ChSl.	*kola, kolesa, vozŭ*
It.	*vettura, carro*	Sw.	*vagn, kärra*	SCr.	*kola, taljige*
Fr.	*voiture, chariot, charrette*	OE	*wægn, cræt*	Boh.	*vůz, povoz, kara*
Sp.	*coche, carruaje, carro*	ME	*carre, wain, cart(e)*	Pol.	*wóz, powóz*
Rum.	*trăsură, căruţă, car*	NE	*carriage, wagon, cart*	Russ.	*povozka, telega*
Ir.	*fēn, carpat, carr*	Du.	*wagen, kar*	Skt.	*yāna-, vāhana-, anas-*
NIr.	*carrāiste, carbad, fēan, cairt, carr*	OHG	*wagan, reita, carra*	Av.	*(vāša-, raθa-)*
W.	*cerbyd, ben, cart*	MHG	*wagen, karre*		
Br.	*karr*	NHG	*wagen, karre(n)*		

It is intended to cover here the most important words for a wheeled vehicle, whether for carrying persons or goods, whether four- or two-wheeled. The differentiation which prevails in the current use of NE *carriage, wagon, car, cart* (see NED) is secondary and still by no means rigid. Furthermore, there is a wealth of words for special types of vehicle, which must be ignored except as they have become more generic. So the specific words for 'chariot', like Grk. ἅρμα, Lat. *currus,* are omitted, although 'chariot' is included in the scope of many of those listed and is the usual sense of the only Avestan words quotable.

Many of the words, including those of the inherited group, are derived from verbs for 'carry in a vehicle' or 'ride', with isolated cases from 'draw, pull', 'turn', or 'go'. Others reflect characteristics of the structure, as, in general, the 'wheel' or some feature of special types. Several Gallic words for special types of vehicle were adopted in Latin, and one of these is the most prolific source of European loanwords.

1. Derivatives of IE **weĝh-,* in Grk. ὀχέομαι, Lat. *vehī,* Lith. *vežti,* ChSl. *voziti,* Skt. *vah-* 'ride', etc. (10.66). Walde-P. 1.249 f. Ernout-M. 1080.

Grk. ὄχος, ὄχημα; Lat. *vehiculum* (> It. *veicolo,* Fr. *véhicule,* NE *vehicle,* but not pop. words); Ir. *fēn,* NIr. *fēan;* ON

vagn, Dan. *vogn,* Sw. *vagn,* OE *wægn,* ME *wain,* MLG *wagen,* and *wage* (> Lett. *vāg'i,* pl. after *rati*), Du. *wagen* (> early NE *wagan, wagen,* NE *wagon*), OHG *wagan,* MHG, NHG *wagen;* Lith. *vežimas,* ChSl. *vozŭ* (mostly 'chariot'), Boh. *vůz, povoz,* Pol. *wóz, powóz,* Russ. *povozka;* Skt. *vāhana-, vāha-* (both also 'draught-animal').

2. Grk. ἅμαξα (NG also pop. τὸ ἁμάξι), in Hom. sometimes the 'framework, chassis' of the wagon, usually the four-wheeled wagon in contrast to the two-wheeled ἅρμα 'chariot', cpd. with second part: ἄξων, Lat. *axis,* etc. 'axle' (10.77), first part prob. : ἅμα 'together', hence a coll. for the '(wheels) with axles' making up the chassis. Kretschmer, KZ 39.549 ff., Glotta 9.216 ff., 12.216 ff. Otherwise, as orig. 'with one axle', Meringer, KZ 40.217 ff.

Grk. ἀπήνη, prob. as orig. 'wagon with a tentlike top' (the pioneer 'covered wagon' in U.S.), a cpd. ἀ-πήνη with ἀ-cop. (cf. also Thess. καπάνα for *κατ-πάνα) : πῆνος· ὕφασμα Hesych., Lat. *pannus,* Goth. *fana* 'cloth', etc. Bezzenberger, BB 27.149. Meringer, KZ 40.228. Walde-P. 2.5.

NG καρρότσα 'carriage', κάρρο 'cart', see Lat. *carrus* (below, 3).

3. Lat. *vehiculum,* above, 1.

Lat. *raeda (rēda, rhēda),* Gallic word : ON *reið,* OHG *reita* 'carriage', Ir. *rīadaim,* ON *rīða,* etc. 'ride' (10.66). Walde-P. 2.348.

Lat. *carrus,* Gallic word = Ir., MW *carr,* Br. *karr* : Lat. *currus* 'chariot', *currere* 'run', etc. (10.46). Walde-P. 1.427 f. Ernout-M. 157. Walde-H. 1.174.

Hence It., Sp. *carro* 'cart', Fr. *char* (mostly 'chariot', etc., now in military use for armored car or 'tank'), dim. *charrette* 'cart', Rum. *car* 'heavy wagon', NG κάρρο 'cart' (ON *kerra* 'chariot'), Sw. *kärra,* ME *carre* (fr. ONorthFr.), NE *car,* Du. *kar,* MLG *kar(r)e* (> Dan. *karre*), OHG *carra, carro,* MHG, NHG *karre* (> Lith. *karas,* Lett. *k'erra,* Pol. *kara* 'pushcart', Boh. *kara* 'cart'); derivs., It. *carrozza* 'coach' (> NG καρρότσα), Rum. *căruţă* 'light wagon', Fr. *chariot,* Sp. *carruaje,* etc. REW 1721. Wartburg 2.426 ff. Falk-Torp 499, 520. NED s.v. *car,* sb. Berneker 448.

Lat. *plaustrum,* etym. dub. Walde-P. 2.90. Ernout-M. 777.

It. *vettura,* Fr. *voiture,* fr. Lat. *vectūra* 'transportation, carrying' : *vehere* 'carry', *vehī* 'drive', *vehiculum* 'carriage' (above, 1).

Sp. *coche,* the same word as, but in much more generic application than, the general Eur. word Fr. *coche,* NE *coach,* NHG *kutsche,* etc., 'coach' fr. Hung. *kocsi* 'carriage, wagon, cart' (fr. *Kocs* a place-name). Wartburg 2.830. NED s.v. *coach,* sb.

Rum. *trăsură,* deriv. of *tras,* pple. of *trag* 'pull, draw'. Tiktin 1638.

4. Ir. *fēn,* NIr. *fēan,* above, 1.

Ir. *carpat,* NIr. *carbad* (> W. *cerbyd*), the reg. word also for 'chariot', cognate with or reloaned from Gallo-Lat. *carpentum* 'two-wheeled carriage or cart' : Lat. *corbis* 'basket' (with reference to the body of wickerwork). Pedersen 1.118. Vendryes, De hib. voc. 122. Walde-H. 1.171.

Ir. *carr,* NIr. *cārr,* Br. *karr* : Lat. *carrus* (above, 3).

NIr. *cairt,* W. *cart, ceirt,* fr. ME *cart(e)* (below, 5).

NIr. also *carrāiste* fr. NE *carriage,* and *cōiste* fr. NE *coach.*

W. *ben (men)* : Gall. *benna* 'genus vehiculi', Grk. φάτνη 'crib, manger', orig. of wickerwork, fr. IE **bhendh-* in Skt. *bandh-,* Goth. *bindan* 'bind', etc. Walde-P. 2.152.

5. ON *vagn*, OE *wægn*, etc., general Gmc., above, 1.

ON *reið*, OHG *reita*, see Lat. *raeda* (above, 3).

ON *kartr*, OE *cræt*, ME *carte* (this form perh. fr. Norse), NE *cart*, perh. orig. with body of basket-work and so : MHG *krenze* 'basket', OHG *kratto*, *krezzo* 'basket', OE *cradol* 'cradle', etc. Walde-P. 1.595. Falk-Torp 499. NED s.v. *cart* sb.

Dan. *karre*, Sw. *kärra*, ME *carre*, etc., see Lat. *carrus* (above, 3).

ME, NE *chariot* (fr. OFr. *chariot*, above, 3), formerly more generic than now. NED s.v.

NE *carriole* (fr. Fr. dim. *carriole*), used only of a special type, but interesting because of the resulting old New England (by pop. etym.) *carryall*.

NE *carriage*, fr. ME *cariage* 'act of carrying' and 'thing carried, burden', fr. ONorthFr. *cariage*, deriv. of *carier* 'carry', this again deriv. of Lat. *carrus* (above, 3). Used for 'wheeled vehicle' since 16th. cent., now esp. one for carrying persons. NED s.v.

6. Lith. *vežimas*, above, 1.

Lith. *ratai*, Lett. *rati*, lit. 'wheels', pl. of *ratas*, *rats* 'wheel' (10.76). Cf. ChSl. *kola* (below, 7) and Toch. A *kukäl*, B *kokale* 'wagon' : Skt. *cakra-*, Grk. κύκλος 'wheel' (10.76).

Lett. *vāg'i*, above, 1.

Lett. *divriči* (esp. 'two-wheeled cart', also *riči*, Mühl.-Endz. 3.522), cpd. of *div-* for *divi* 'two' and form related to *ritenis* 'wheel' (10.76). Likewise *divritenis* 'bicycle' and 'two-wheeled cart'. Mühl.-Endz. 1.473.

7. ChSl. *kola*, *kolesa*, SCr. *kola* (Pol. *kolasa*, *kolaska*, Russ. *koljaska* dim. 'calash'), pl. of *kolo* 'wheel' (10.76). Berneker 548.

ChSl. *vozŭ*, Boh. *vůz*, *povoz*, etc., above, 1.

SCr. *taljige*, Russ. *telega* 'cart' (Pol. *telega*, etc., not ordinary word), fr. Turk. *talika* 'light four-wheeled carriage'. Miklosich, Türk. Elemente 2.46. Brückner 568.

8. Skt. *vāhana-*, *vāha-*, above, 1.

Skt. *yāna-* : *i-* 'go' (10.47).

Skt. *anas-* (mostly 'draught-wagon, cart') : Lat. *onus* 'load'. Walde-P. 1.132 f. Ernout-M. 703.

Skt. *ratha-*, Av. *raθa-* 'chariot' : Lat. *rota*, Lith. *ratas* 'wheel' (10.76).

Av. *vāša-* : *varət-* 'turn' (10.13–14). Barth. 1418.

10.76 WHEEL

Grk.	τροχός (κύκλος)	Goth.	....	Lith.	*ratas, tekinis*
NG	τροχός, ρόδα	ON	*hvel, hjōl, hvēl*	Lett.	*rats, ritenis, skritulis*
Lat.	*rota*	Dan.	*hjul*	ChSl.	*kolo*
It.	*ruota*	Sw.	*hjul*	SCr.	*kolo, točak, kotač*
Fr.	*roue*	OE	*hwēol*	Boh.	*kolo*
Sp.	*rueda*	ME	*hwele, whele*	Pol.	*koło*
Rum.	*roată*	NE	*wheel*	Russ.	*koleso*
Ir.	*droch, roth*	Du.	*wiel*	Skt.	*cakra-*
NIr.	*roth*	OHG	*rad*	Av.	*čaxra-*
W.	*olwyn, rhod*	MHG	*rat*		
Br.	*rod*	NHG	*rad*		

Words for 'wheel' include an inherited group derived from a root for 'turn' and others from roots meaning 'run' or 'roll'.

1. IE **kʷelo-s*, **kʷolo-s*, redupl. **kʷekʷlo-s*, fr. **kʷel-* in Skt. *car-* 'move, wander', Grk. πέλομαι 'be in motion', etc. Walde-P. 1.514 ff. Falk-Torp 413.

ON *hvel;* OPruss. *kelan;* ChSl., SCr., Boh. *kolo*, Pol. *koło*, Russ. *koleso;* Grk. κύκλος 'ring, circle', also rarely 'wheel'

(sg. Hom. Il. 23.340, mostly in pl. κύκλα); ON *hvēl*, *hjōl*, Dan., Sw. *hjul*, OE *hweogul*, *hweowol*, *hwēol*, ME *hwele*, *whele*, NE *wheel*, Du. *wiel;* Skt. *cakra-*, Av. *čaxra-;* Toch. A *kukäl*, B *kokale* 'wagon'.

2. Derivs. of IE **reth-* in Ir. *rethim*, W. *rhedeg* 'run', etc. (10.46). Walde-P. 2.368. Ernout-M. 871.

Lat. *rota* (> Romance forms); Ir. *roth*, W. *rhod*, Br. *rod;* OHG *rad*, MHG *rat*, NHG *rad;* Lith. *ratas*, Lett. *rats;* Skt. *ratha-*, Av. *raθa-* 'chariot' (10.75). Here NG ρόδα fr. Ven. *roda* = It. *ruota*. G. Meyer, Neugr. Stud. 2.77.

3. Grk. τροχός = Ir. *droch* : Grk. τρέχω 'run', etc. (10.46). Walde-P. 1.874 f.

4. Ir. *roth*, W. *rhod*, Br. *rod*, above, 2. Ir. *droch*, above, 3.

W. *olwyn*, etym. dub. Walde-P. 1.301.

5. Lith. *ratas*, Lett. *rats*, above, 2.

Lith. *tekinis* : *tekėti* 'run', (10.46).

Lett. *ritenis* : *ritināt*, *rietet*, *rist* 'roll' (10.15). Mühl.-Endz. 3.532.

Lett. *skritulis* : Lith. *skritulys* 'circle, knee-pan', *skrytis*, OPruss. *scritayle* 'felloe', Lith. *skriesti* 'make a circle', OE *scriþe* 'course', *scrid* 'carriage', fr. extensions of **sker-* in words for 'turn, bend'. Mühl.-Endz. 3.894. Walde-P. 2.571.

6. SCr. *točak* : *tok*, ChSl. *tokŭ* 'flow', but through the sense of 'run' as in ChSl. *tekq*, *tešti* 'run, flow' (10.46).

SCr. *kotač* : *kotrljati*, Russ. *katit'*, etc. 'roll' (10.15). Berneker 591.

7. Skt. *cakra-*, Av. *čaxra-*, above, 1.

10.77 AXLE

Grk.	ἄξων	Goth.	....	Lith.	*ašis*
NG	ἄξων, ἄξωνας	ON	*ǫxull, ǫxultrē*	Lett.	*ass*
Lat.	*axis*	Dan.	*aksel*	ChSl.	*osĭ*
It.	*sala, asse*	Sw.	*axel*	SCr.	*osovina, os*
Fr.	*essieu*	OE	*eax*	Boh.	*náprava*
Sp.	*eje*	ME	*ax, axletre, axtre*	Pol.	*oś*
Rum.	*osie*	NE	*axle*	Russ.	*os'*
Ir.	*fertas*	Du.	*as*	Skt.	*akṣa-*
NIr.	*acastōir*	OHG	*ahsa*	Av.	....
W.	*echel*	MHG	*ahse*		
Br.	*ahel*	NHG	*achse*		

With few exceptions, the words for 'axle' belong to an inherited group.

1. Derivs. of IE **ak̂s-*, this prob. fr. **aĝes-* : **aĝ-* 'drive' in Skt. *aj-*, Lat. *agere*, etc. (10.65). Walde-P. 1.37. Ernout-M. 97. Walde-H. 1.89.

Grk. ἄξων; Lat. *axis* (> It. *asse*, Sp. *eje*), It. *sala* (fr. VLat. **axalis*), Fr. *essieu* (fr. VLat. **axilis*); OE *eax*, ME *ax*, *ax-tre* (*tre* here as 'beam'), NE dial. *ex* (usual pop. form in New England), Du. *as*, OHG *ahsa*, MHG *ahse*, NHG *achse;* Lith. *ašis*, Lett. *ass;* ChSl. *osĭ*, SCr. *osovina*, rarely *os* (Boh. *osa* 'axis'), Pol. *oś*, Russ. *os'*; Skt. *akṣa-* (Av. *aša-* 'shoulder'); ON *ǫxull*, *ǫxul-trē* (> ME *axle-tre*, NE *axle*), Dan. *aksel*, Sw. *axel* (Gmc. **ahsulaz*); W. *echel*, Br. *ahel* (fr. **aksilā*); Rum. *osie* fr. Slavic.

In late Lat. *axis* became identical with *assis* 'board', whence the two meanings of It. *asse* and the prevalence of derivs. in most Romance dialects. Wartburg 1.160 f., 190.

2. Ir. *fertas* 'distaff, spindle' (6.32), also 'axle' (Laws, Gloss. s.v.).

NIr. *acastōir* (Dinneen, etc.; *acaistēar* McKenna), fr. ME *axtre*.

3. Boh. *náprava*, also 'restoration, repairing', abstract to *napraviti* 'set right, repair', with specialization to 'axle' as the part that breaks down and needs repairing?

10.78 YOKE

Grk.	ζυγόν	Goth.	*jukuzi*	Lith.	*jungas*
NG	ζυγός	ON	*ok*	Lett.	*jūgs*
Lat.	*iugum*	Dan.	*aag*	ChSl.	*igo, jarĭmŭ*
It.	*giogo*	Sw.	*ok*	SCr.	*jaram*
Fr.	*joug*	OE	*geoc, gioc*	Boh.	*jařmo, jho*
Sp.	*yugo*	ME	*ȝoke, yocke*	Pol.	*jarzmo*
Rum.	*jug*	NE	*yoke*	Russ.	*jarmo*
Ir.	*cuing*	Du.	*juk*	Skt.	*yuga-*
NIr.	*cuing*	OHG	*joh, juh*	Av.	....
W.	*iau*	MHG	*joch*		
Br.	*yeo*	NHG	*joch*		

Most of the words for 'yoke' reflect an IE word for 'yoke' derived from a root for 'yoke, join'. In Slavic this has been mostly replaced by a derivative of another root for 'fit, join'.

1. IE **yugo-m*, deriv. of **yeug-* in verbs for 'yoke, join', as Skt. *yuj-*, Av. *yuj-*, Grk. ζεύγνυμι, Lat. *jungere*, Lith. *junkti*, etc. (this an extension of IE **yeu-*, in Skt. *yu-* 'yoke, harness, bind, fasten', etc.). Walde-P. 1.201 f. Ernout-M. 501 f. Feist 304. Berneker 421 f.

Grk. ζυγόν, also ζυγός, NG ζυγός; Lat. *iugum* (> Romance words); Ir. *cuing* (**com-yung-*), W. *iau*, Br. *yeo;* Goth. *jukuzi* (*juk* only for ζεῦγος 'yoke of oxen'), ON *ok*, OE *geoc*, etc., general Gmc.; Lith. *jungas* (*-n-* fr. *junkti*), Lett. *jūgs;* ChSl. *igo* (**jĭgo* fr. **jŭgo*), Boh. *jho* (Pol. *igo-* in place-names; Russ. *igo* now only fig.); Skt. *yuga-m* (Av. form not quotable, but NPers. *ȷ̌uγ*, etc.); Hitt. *yugan*, *yukan*.

2. ChSl. *jarĭmŭ* (late, cf. Jagić, Entstehungsgesch. 348), SCr. *jaram*, Pol. *jarzmo* (> Boh. *jařmo*), Russ. *jarmo* (Slavic **arĭmŭ*, **arĭmo*) : Grk. ἀρμός 'joint, fastening', ἅρμα 'chariot', Lat. *arma* 'equipment, arms, etc.', *m*-formations to IE **ar-* in Grk. ἀραρίσκω 'join together', etc. Berneker 31. Walde-P. 1.73.

10.81 SHIP

Grk.	ναῦς, πλοῖον	Goth.	*skip*	Lith.	*laivas*
NG	πλοῖο, καράβι	ON	*skip* (*nōr, fley*)	Lett.	*kug'is*
Lat.	*nāvis, nāvigium*	Dan.	*skib*	ChSl.	*korabljĭ, ladĭji*
It.	*nave, vascello, bastimento*	Sw.	*skepp*	SCr.	*brod, lađa*
		OE	*scip*	Boh.	*lod', koráb*
Fr.	*navire, vaisseau, bâtiment*	ME	*schip, vessel*	Pol.	*okręt, statek*
		NE	*ship, vessel*	Russ.	*korabl', sudno*
Sp.	*buque, nave, navio*	Du.	*schip*	Skt.	*nāu-*
Rum.	*corabie*	OHG	*scif, scef*	Av.	(*nāvaya-*, adj.)
Ir.	*nau, long* (*lestar*)	MHG	*schif, schef*		
NIr.	*long*	NHG	*schiff*		
W.	*llong*				
Br.	*lestr*				

'Ship' is understood here as a seagoing vessel of some size in contrast to the smaller 'boat', with disregard of the more specific technical use of NE *ship* and the fact that NE *boat* is also a popular generic term. Furthermore, the IE 'ship', that is, what was denoted by the word which yielded the widespread group for 'ship', was rather a 'boat', and ultimately only a 'dugout'. There is

evidence of IE words for 'oar' and 'row', but not for 'mast' or 'sail'. Cf. Schrader, Reallex. 2.295 ff.

Apart from the inherited group, the most common connection, in part reflecting the primitive 'dugout', is with words denoting some sort of hollow object, as 'vessel' (in orig. sense of *vessel*), 'pot', 'tub', 'trough', 'belly', etc. A late Grk. word for a kind of boat is a prolific source of European loanwords denoting a special type of ship or generic 'ship'. Specialization of 'something built' to 'ship' occurs. Connection with verbs for 'sail, float' is exceptional.

Words for the modern steamship are combinations of those for 'steam' and 'ship' or 'boat', as NE *steamship*, *steamboat*, NHG *dampschiff*, Fr. *navire* (*bâtiment*, *bateau*, etc.) *à vapeur*, NG ἀτμόπλοιο, Russ. *parovoe sudno*, or simply those for 'steam' or derivs., as NE *steamer*, NHG *dampfer*, Fr. *vapeur*, It. *vapore* (> NG pop. βαπόρι), Russ. *parochod*.

1. IE **nāu-*, root connection wholly uncertain. Walde-P. 2.315. Ernout-M. 656 f. REW 5863.

Grk. ναῦς; Lat. *nāvis* (> It., Sp. *nave*, obs. Rum. *naie*, *navă*), *nāvigium* (> Fr. *navire*, Sp. *navio*); Ir. *nau*, *nō;* ON (poet.) *nōr;* Skt. *nāu-*, NPers. *nāv* (OPers. *nāviyā* 'navigable'? Av. *nāvaya-* 'navigable'), Arm. *nav*.

2. Grk. πλοῖον = ON *fley* (poet.) : Grk. πλέω 'sail, float', Slav. *ploviti* 'float', etc. (10.34, 10.36).

NG pop. καράβι, fr. καράβιον, dim. of κάραβος 'horned beetle, crayfish' (: κέρας 'horn'), which came to be applied to a kind of boat, apparently from its crab-like appearance (cf. Hesych. ἐφόλκια· μικρὰ καράβια) and is a common Byz. word. Hence also late Lat. *carabus* 'wicker boat covered with hide' (Isid.), It. *caravella*, NE *caravel*, etc., also the Slavic group (below, 7). For the application of other Grk. animal names to certain types of ships (κύκνος, δόρκων, κριός, τράγος) cf. Gelzer, Leont. v. Neap., p. 128.

3. Lat. *nāvis* and derivs., above, 1.

Derivs. of Lat. *vascellum*, dim. of *vās* 'vessel, dish, utensil', show specialization to 'seagoing vessel, ship', as It. *vascello*, OFr. *vessel* (> ME, NE *vessel* in current speech mainly in this sense, cf. NED s.v.), Fr. *vaisseau*, Sp. *bajel*. REW 9163.

It. *bastimento*, Fr. *bâtiment*, derivs. of It. *bastire*, Fr. *bâtir* 'build' (9.44). REW 981.

Sp. *buque*, fr. Cat. *buc* 'belly, ship's hull, ship', this fr. Gmc., OE *būc*, OHG *būh* 'belly'. REW 1376.

Rum. *corabie*, fr. the Slavic (below, 7).

4. MIr., NIr. *long*, W. *llong*, usually considered loanwords fr. Lat. *longa* (*nāvis*), cf. Vendryes, De hib. voc. 152, Pedersen 1.195; but Loth, RC 43.133 ff., takes as Celtic **lungā* : Ir. *luighe* 'caldron, kettle, pan', *coblach* 'fleet'.

Br. *lestr*, also 'vessel, pot' (as Ir. *lestar* mostly, but also 'ship'; Laws, Gloss, s.v.), Corn. *lester* 'ship' (OCorn. gl. *nāvis*), W. *llestr* 'vessel, pot', fr. the root **les-* in Goth. *lisan*, ON *lesa* 'pick up, collect' (12.21). Walde-P. 2.440. Thurneysen, KZ 37.95.

5. Goth., ON *skip*, OE *scip*, etc., general Gmc. (OHG also 'vessel' in older sense), prob. as 'hewn-out, hollowed log' : Lett. *šk'ibīt* 'hew, cut', ON *skipa* 'arrange, divide', fr. IE **skei-b-*, extension of **skēi-* in Skt. *chyati* 'cuts off', etc. Walde-P. 2.545. Falk-Torp 992. Feist 434.

ME, NE *vessel*, above, 3.

6. Lith. *laivas* 'ship', Lett. *laiva* 'boat' (Russ. dial. *lajba*, Pol. dial. *łajba*), fr. Finn. *laiva* 'ship'. Berneker 686.

Lett. *kug'is*, fr. MLG *kogge* = MHG *kocke*, late OHG *kocho* 'sort of boat' (broad with round bow and stern), Icel. *kuggur* 'barge'. Berneker 537. Mühl.-Endz. 2.300.

7. ChSl. *korablĭ*, Boh. *koráb*, Russ. *korabl'* (Pol. *korab* 'boat, skiff'), an old general Slavic loanword (despite *b* for expected *v*) fr. late Grk. καράβιον (above, 2). Berneker 567. Brückner 256. Otherwise Preveden, Language 6.279 ff.

ChSl. *ladĭji, aldĭji* (less common than *korablĭ*, cf. Jagić, Entstehungsgesch. 358), SCr. *lađa*, Boh. *lod'* (Pol. *łódź, łódka*, Russ. *lodka* 'boat'), perh. as orig. 'hollow vessel' : ON *alda* 'wave', Dan. *olde* 'trough', OE *ealdoþ* 'trough, tub'. Walde-P. 1.92. Brückner 310.

SCr. *brod*, also and orig. 'a ford', as general Slavic (Russ., Boh. *brod*, Pol. *bród*, etc., Berneker 86 f.), hence as means of crossing it 'boat', extended to 'ship', Rječnik Akad. s.v.

Pol. *okręt*, cpd. of *kręt* 'a twist' : *kręcić, krącić* 'twist' (ChSl. *krątiti* 'turn', etc. 10.14). Semantic development prob. through 'plaited vessel' of some kind, cf. SCr. dial. *okrut* 'cask', Boh. *krutina* 'knot, cradle'. Berneker 627. Brückner 377 f.

Pol. *statek*, formerly 'property, equipment, implements' (cf. expressions like NHG *fahrzeug*, Dan. *fartøj*, etc.), fr. the root of *stać* 'stand', etc. Brückner 514.

Russ. *sudno* 'vessel' ('ship' or 'boat') : *sosud* 'vessel, vase', Pol. *sąd*, SCr., Boh. *sud* 'vat, tub', etc. Brückner 483. Walde-P. 1.827.

8. Skt. *nāu-* (in Av., OPers. only derivs. quotable), above, 1.

10.82 SAILOR

Grk.	*ναύτης*	Goth.	. . . .	Lith.	*jūreivis, jūrininkas*
NG	*ναύτης*	ON	*skipari, skipamaðr, sjōmaðr*	Lett.	*jūrnieks, kug'inieks*
Lat.	*nauta*			ChSl.	(*morjaninŭ*)
It.	*marinaio, marinaro*	Dan.	*sømand, matros*	SCr.	*mornar, brodar*
Fr.	*marin, matelot*	Sw.	*sjöman, matros*	Boh.	*námořník, plavec*
Sp.	*marinero, marino*	OE	*scipmann, scipere, sǣlīþend*	Pol.	*żeglarz, marynarz, majtek*
Rum.	*marinar, matelot*				
Ir.	*nōaire, loingseach*	ME	*schipman, seman, mariner*	Russ.	*morjak, matros*
NIr.	*mairnēalach*			Skt.	*nāvika-*
W.	*morwr, llongwr*	NE	*sailor, seaman (mariner)*	Av.	. . . .
Br.	*merdead, martolod*				
		Du.	*zeeman, matroos*		
		OHG	*scifman, sēolīdanti*		
		MHG	*schifmann, marnære*		
		NHG	*seemann, matrose*		

Most of the words for 'sailor' are derivatives or compounds of words for 'ship' or 'sea'; a few are from 'sail, navigate'.

1. Grk. ναύτης (> Lat. *nauta*), Ir. *nōaire, noere*, Skt. *nāvika-*, derivs. of Grk. ναῦς, etc. 'ship' (10.81).

2. Fr. *marin*, Sp. *marino*, fr. Lat. *marīnus* adj. 'marine', deriv. of *mare* 'sea'. It. *marinaio, marinaro*, OFr. *mariner* (> ME, NE *mariner*, now poet.), Sp. *marinero*, Rum. *marinar*, fr. MLat. *marīnārius*. REW 5359.

Fr. *matelot* (> Rum. *matelot;* pl. > Du. *matroos* > Dan., Sw. *matros*, NHG *matrose*, Russ. *matros*), fr. OFr. *matenot* 'comrade', fr. ON *mǫtunautr* 'mess-companion' (cpd. of *matr* 'food, meal' and *nautr* 'companion'). Gamillscheg 599. Falk-Torp 705. Franck-v. W. 417.

3. Ir. *nōaire*, above, 1.

Ir. *loingseach*, deriv. of *long* 'ship' (10.81).

NIr. *mairnēalach*, cf. *mairnēalacht* 'navigation', apparently fr. Sc. and North E. *marinal* 'mariner, sailor', fr.

OFr. *marinal*, MLat. *marīnālis* (cf. NED s.v.).

W. *morwr* and W. *llongwr*, cpds. of *mor* 'sea' and *llong* 'ship' with *gwr* 'man'.

Br. *merdead*, cf. W. *mordwyad* '(sea) voyage' : MBr. *mordeiff*, Br. (*merdei*) *mordei*, W. *mordwyo* 'navigate, sail' (10.36).

Br. *martolod*, fr. Fr. *matelot*, with *r* fr. *merdead*. Henry 196.

4. ON *skipari*, OE *scipere* (MLG, MDu. *schipper* > NE *skipper* 'captain of a small vessel'), derivs. of *skip*, etc., 'ship' (10.81).

ON *skipamaðr, skipmaðr*, OE *scipmann*, ME *schipman*, OHG *scifman*, MHG *schifmann*, cpds. of words for 'ship' and 'man'.

ON (NIcel.) *sjōmaðr*, Dan. *sømand*, Sw. *sjöman*, ME *seman*, NE *seaman*, Du. *zeeman*, NHG *seemann*, cpds. of words for 'sea' and 'man'.

OE *sǣlīþend*, OHG *sēolīdanti* lit. 'seagoing', cpds. of word for 'sea' and pple. of OE *līþan*, OHG *līdan* 'go'.

Dan., Sw. *matros*, Du. *matroos*, NHG *matrose*, above, 2.

NE *sailer*, agent noun of vb. *sail* (10.36), now written *sailor* after the agent nouns of Lat. origin, as distinguished from *sailer* used of a ship (*a fast sailer*).

MHG *marnære*, fr. MLat. *marīnārius* or It. *marinaro* (above, 2).

5. Lith. *jūreivis, jūrininkas*, Lett. *jūrnieks*, derivs. of Lith. *jūra*, Lett. *jūr'a* 'sea'.

Lett. *kug'inieks*, deriv. of *kug'is* 'ship'.

6. Late ChSl. *morjaninŭ*, Boh. *námořník*, Russ. *morjak*, derivs. of ChSl. *morje*, etc. 'sea'.

SCr. *mornar, mrnar*, Boh. (old) *marinář*, Pol. *marynarz*, fr. It. *marinaro* (above, 2). Berneker 2.19 f.

SCr. *brodar*, fr. *brod* 'ship'.

Boh. *plavec*, fr. *plouti* 'sail' (10.36).

Pol. *żeglarz*, fr. NHG *segler* 'sailer', also 'sailor' (: *segeln* 'sail'). Brückner 660 f.

Pol. *majtek*, fr. Du. *maat* 'mate, comrade'. Brückner, 318.

Russ. *matros*, fr. Du. *matroos*, see Fr. *matelot*, above, 2.

7. Skt. *nāvika-*, above, 1.

10.83 BOAT

Grk.	*λέμβος, σκάφη, κύμβη*	Goth.	*skip*	Lith.	*laivelis, valtis*
NG	*βάρκα*	ON	*bātr, nǫkkvi*	Lett.	*laiva*
Lat.	*linter, cymba, scapha*	Dan.	*baad*	ChSl.	*korablĭ*
It.	*barca, battello*	Sw.	*båt*	SCr.	*čamac, čun*
Fr.	*bateau, barque*	OE	*bāt, naca*	Boh.	*člun, lod'ka*
Sp.	*bote, barca, barco*	ME	*bote*	Pol.	*łódka, łódź*
Rum.	*luntre, barcă*	NE	*boat*	Russ.	*lodka*
Ir.	*curach, bāt*	Du.	*boot*	Skt.	*nāu-, plava-*
NIr.	*bād*	OHG	*scif, nacho*	Av.	. . . .
W.	*bad, cwch*	MHG	*nache, nāwe*		
Br.	*bag*	NHG	*boot (kahn, nachen)*		

'Boat' is understood here as a small craft in contrast to the larger 'ship' (10.81). But there is no sharp line, and the words entered here are of diverse scope. Some are the same as those entered under 'ship'. Thus Grk. πλοῖον and dim. πλοιάριον are used in NT without distinction for the fishing boats (e.g. πλοιάριον Mk. 3.9, πλοῖον Mk. 4.1) and rendered by Goth. *skip*, OHG *scif*, ChSl. *korablĭ*. Conversely, some of those entered here, as NE *boat*, Fr. *bateau*, are sometimes also used as generic terms, with reference to even

the largest vessels. Some cover rowboats and small sailing craft, some only the former, and some only still more specific types of small boats. For the scope of the Greek and Latin terms, only a few of which are included here, cf. Torr, Ancient Ships 105 ff., and for the Old Norse, cf. Falk, Wört. u. Sach. 4.85 ff.

1. Grk. λέμβος (> Lat. *lembus*), so Byz. and lit. NG, etym.? Boisacq 568.

Grk. σκάφη (> Lat. *scapha*) also 'trough, tub' : σκάφος 'hollow vessel', σκάπτω 'dig'.

Grk. κύμβη (> Lat. *cymba*), also 'drinking cup, bowl' : Skt. *kumbha-* 'pot', MIr. *comm* 'vessel', W. *cwmm* 'valley', etc., fr. **kum-b-*, extension of IE **keu-* in words for 'swelling, round', etc. Walde-P. 1.376. Boisacq 534.

NG βάρκα, fr. late Lat. *barca* (below, 2).

2. Lat. *lunter* (> Rum. *luntre*), *linter*, also 'washtub, trough', etc., etym.? Walde-P. 2.437, 440. Ernout-M. 567. Walde-H. 1.809 f.

Lat. *cymba, scapha*, fr. Grk., above, 1.

Late Lat. *barca*, fr. **bārica*, deriv. of *bāris*, fr. Grk. βᾶρις 'flat-bottomed boat', in origin an Egypt. word (Copt. *barī*). Hence Byz., NG βάρκα; It. *barca* (> Fr. *barque* > NE *bark*), Fr. *barge* (> NE *barge*), Sp. *barca, barco*, Rum. *barcă;* MIr. *bārc;* late ON *barki*, MHG *barke*, etc. The words of this group are applied in different languages and periods to the most diverse types, from a small rowboat (only, or covering small sailboat) to a large three-masted vessel (as NE *bark* in the technical sequence according to the rigging, *ship, bark, brig, brigantine*). Ernout-M. 103. Walde-H. 1.96. Wartburg 1.251. NED s.vv. *bark* and *barge.*

Fr. *bateau*, OFr. *batel* (> It. *battello*), deriv. of Anglo-Norm. *bat* fr. OE *bāt* (below, 4). REW 985. Wartburg 1.281.

Sp. *bote*, fr. NE *boat.*

3. Ir. *curach* = NIr. *curach*, W. *corwg, corwgl* 'coracle, boat of wickerwork covered with a hide' (in OIr. the regular type of boat) : Grk. κώρυκος 'leather bag', Lat. *corium* 'leather', Skt. *carman-* 'hide, leather'. Pedersen 1.332. Walde-P. 2.574.

MIr. *bāt*, NIr. *bād*, fr. OE *bāt* or ON *bātr* (below). Marstrander, Bidrag 127.

W. *bad*, fr. OE *bāt.* Parry-Williams 34.

W. *cwch*, also 'hive, crown of a hat' : Br. *kouc'h* 'lid of a hive', perh. fr. a MLat. **coccus* for *cocca* 'strong boat', of uncertain origin. Loth, Mots lat., 155. Thurneysen, Keltorom. 55.

Br. *bag*, fr. Fr. *bac* 'ferry, ferryboat', also 'trough', of Gallic origin? Henry 23. REW 862.

4. Goth. *skip*, OHG *scif* 'ship, boat' (10.81).

OE *bāt* (> ON *bātr*, Dan. *baad*, Sw. *båt*), ME *bote, boot* (> Du., LG *boot* > NHG *boot*), NE *boat* (> Russ. *bot*, esp. 'ship's boat') = ON *beit* poet. 'ship', orig. perh. as 'hollowed-out tree' : Skt. *bhid-*, Lat. *findere* 'split', Goth. *beitan*, OE *bītan*, etc. 'bite'. Walde-P. 2.139. Falk-Torp, 38 f. NED s.v. *boat.*

ON *nǫkkvi*, OE *naca*, OHG *nacho*, MHG *nache*, NHG *nachen*, as '(boat from hollow) tree trunk' : Skt. *naga-* 'tree, mountain'. Walde-P. 2.304. Falk-Torp 773.

MHG *nāwe* (NHG dial. *naue*), fr. Lat. *nāvis* 'ship' (10.81). Weigand-H. 2.281.

NHG *kahn* : MLG *kane*, Du. *kaan* (obs.) 'ship's boat, yawl', ON *kæna* 'sort of boat' (rare), Dan. *kane* 'sled', also ON *kanna*, etc., 'can', perh. cognate with MIr. *gann* 'vessel' (otherwise only Gmc.). Walde-P. 1.535. Kluge-G. 274. On the use and distribution of the NHG words, see Kretschmer, Wortgeogr. 245 ff.

5. Lith. *laivelis, laive* (NSB), Lett. *laiva* : Lith. *laivas*, now 'ship' (10.81).

Lith. *valtis*, prob. same word as the obs. *valtis* 'fishing net, seine' (: Russ. *volot* 'fiber', etc., Walde-P. 1.303), with transfer to 'fishing boat'. Cf. NE *seiner* (NED s.v.) and NG γρῖπος 'seine' and also 'seiner' (e.g. Pernot, Recueil p. 104.9). Otherwise (: OHG *wald* 'woods', etc.) Schrader, Reallex. 2.311.

6. ChSl. *korablĭ*, see 'ship' (10.81).

SCr. *čamac*, fr. *čam* 'pine tree', rarely 'boat', fr. Turk. *çam* 'pine tree'. Rječnik Akad. 1.885.

SCr. *čun*, Boh. *člun* (Pol. *czółno*, Russ. *čeln, čelnok* 'skiff, canoe'), as orig. 'dugout' : Lith. *kelmas* 'tree-stump', Lett. *celms* 'stump', OHG *scalm* 'navis' (Graff 6.491), Norw. *skolm* 'pod', etc., fr. IE **skel-* in words for 'cut, split, etc.'. Walde-P. 2.594. Berneker 167.

Boh. *lod'ka*, Pol. *łódka*, (also *łódź* larger 'boat'), Russ. *lodka* : ChSl. *ladĭji*, etc. 'ship' (10.81).

7. Skt. *nāu-* 'ship, boat', see 10.81.

Skt. *plava-* (also 'raft, float') : *plu-* 'float, swim' (10.34).

10.84 RAFT

Grk.	*σχεδία*	Goth.	. . . .	Lith.	*sielis*
NG	*σχεδία*	ON	*floti*	Lett.	*pluosts, pluts, sielains*
Lat.	*ratis*	Dan.	*flaade*	ChSl.	. . . .
It.	*zattera*	Sw.	*flotte*	SCr.	*splav*
Fr.	*radeau*	OE	. . . .	Boh.	*vor, plt'*
Sp.	*balsa*	ME	. . . .	Pol.	*tratwa, plet*
Rum.	*plută*	NE	*raft*	Russ.	*plot*
Ir.	*raith*	Du.	*vlot*	Skt.	*uḍupa-*
NIr.	*slaod*	OHG	*flōz*	Av.	. . . .
W.	*cludair*	MHG	*vlōz*		
Br.	*radell*	NHG	*floss*		

Many of the words for 'raft' are derived from the verbs for 'float'. A few are connected with verbs for 'slide, slip', here, too, doubtless through the notion of 'float'. Others reflect the construction of rafts of sticks or logs, as 'fastening together, bundle, pile', etc.

1. Grk. σχεδία, fr. fem. (sc. ναῦς) of σχέδιος 'casual, temporary' with reference to a light, hastily made construction. Cf. σχεδιάζω 'do offhand, improvise'. Boisacq 932.

2. Lat. *ratis*, often in pl. and defined as 'logs fastened together' (*rates vocantur tigna colligata, quae per aquam aguntur*, Paul. Fest.), and so perh. : OE *rōd*, OHG *ruota* 'rod, pole'. Walde-P. 2.638. Ernout-M. 852. Hence fr. dim. form (MLat. *radellus, rasellus, razellus*, Du Cange), Prov. *radel* > Fr. *radeau;* also Br. *radell, razell.* REW 7088.

It. *zattera* (Sp. *zata, zatara*, but not the usual word), fr. MHG *tatze* 'paw'? REW 8599.

Sp., Port. *balsa* 'raft' (also 'pool', in Port. also 'clump of briar bushes'). 'Raft' prob. based on the material used in its construction, but the ultimate source of the word is unknown (Iber.?). REW 917.

Rum. *plută*, also 'cork', fr. the Slavic, cf. Slov. *pluta*, SCr. *pluto* 'cork', Russ. *plot* 'raft' (below, 5). Tiktin 1193.

3. Ir. *raith*, fr. Lat. *ratis* (above, 2). RIA Contrib. s.v.

NIr. *slaod*, also 'swath, layer or pile, sliding mass' (Dinneen), hence the meaning of 'raft' (in this sense also *bāthshlaod* : *bata* 'stick, timber') = MIr. *slāet* 'a slide' (: OE *slīdan* 'slide', etc., 10.42). Walde-P. 2.707 f. Macbain 327.

W. *cludair*, also 'heap, pile' (Spurrell), hence the meaning 'raft' (fr. 'pile of wood') : *cludo* 'carry, convey', arch. 'heap' (10.61).

Br. *radell*, *razell*, see above, 2.

4. ON *floti*, Dan. *flaade* (both also 'fleet'), Sw. *flotte* (cf. *flotta* 'fleet'), NE *float* (rare in this sense, NED s.v. 7*a*), Du. *vlot*, OHG *flōz* (mostly 'flux, flow'), MHG *vlōz*, NHG *floss* : ON *fljōta*, OE *flēotan* 'float', etc. (10.34). Falk-Torp 229.

NE *raft*, arch. (ME) 'rafter, beam, spar', fr. ON *raptr* 'rafter', coll. 'roof, ceiling'. NED s.v.

5. Lith. *sielis*, Lett. *sielains*, prob. : Lett. *siet* 'bind'. Leskien, Bildung d. Nom. 275. Mühl.-Endz. 3.858.

Lett. *pluosts* (= Lith. *pluostas* 'ferry') : *plūst* 'overflow', OE *flēotan* 'float', etc. (above, 4). Mühl.-Endz. 3.364, 365.

Lett. *pluts*, fr. ORuss. **plŭtŭ*, Russ. *plot* 'raft' (below, 6). Mühl.-Endz. 3.359.

6. SCr. *splav*, cpd. **sŭ-plav*, cf. *plav* (poet.) 'navis, linter' (Rječnik Akad. 10.22) : *ploviti* 'float', etc.

Boh. *vor*, as orig. 'a binding-together' (of logs) : Pol. *wór* 'sack, bundle', ChSl. *vrŭvĭ*, Lith. *virvė* 'cord', Lith. *verti* 'to thread', etc. Walde-P. 1.263. Trautmann 352. Brückner 382, 634.

Pol. *tratwa*, earlier *trafta*, fr. early NHG *trift* 'a drive of logs' (14th cent., still in local use; cf. Weigand-H. 2.1071 and similar use of NE *drive* in U.S.) : *treiben* 'drive'. Brückner 575.

Russ. *plot*, Pol. *pɫet*, Boh. *plt'* : Russ. *plavat'*, Pol. *pɫywać*, Boh. *plovati* 'float'. Trautmann 224.

7. Skt. *uḍupa-*, also 'moon', particularly 'new moon' (whence the meaning 'raft, barge' as a 'flat, slightly curved boat'?), MIndic for Skt. **ṛtu-pa-*, lit. 'keeper of the (correct) time'. Wackernagel, Altind. Gram. 1.167 (Uhlenbeck 28, but with unconvincing explanation of the meaning 'raft').

10.85 OAR

Grk.	*κώπη, ἐρετμόν*	Goth.	....	Lith.	*irklas*
NG	*κουπί*	ON	*ār, ræði*	Lett.	*irkls*
Lat.	*rēmus* (*tōnsa*)	Dan.	*aare*	ChSl.	*veslo*
It.	*remo*	Sw.	*åra*	SCr.	*veslo*
Fr.	*rame, aviron*	OE	*ār, rōþer*	Boh.	*veslo*
Sp.	*remo*	ME	*ore*	Pol.	*wiosɫo*
Rum.	*vîslă, lopată*	NE	*oar*	Russ.	*veslo*
Ir.	*rāme*	Du.	*riem*	Skt.	*aritra-, kṣepaṇi-, nāu-daṇḍa-*
NIr.	*rāmha*	OHG	*ruodar, riemo*		
W.	*rhwyf*	MHG	*ruoder, ruodel, rieme*	Av.	....
Br.	*roeñv*	NHG	*ruder*		

Many of the words for 'oar' belong to an inherited group pointing to IE words for 'oar' and 'row'. Other connections are with words for 'carry, ride' or for 'rod, pole'.

1. IE **erə-*, **rē-*, **rō-* in words for 'oar, rudder, row' (perh. ultimately connected with IE **er-* in Skt. *ṛ-* 'move', Grk. *ὄρνῡμι* 'rouse, move', but this quite uncertain). Walde-P. 1.143 f. Ernout-M. 859. Pedersen 2.591. Stokes 39.

Grk. *ἐρετμόν* (cf. *ἐρέσσω* 'row', *ἐρέτης* 'rower'); Lat. *rēmus* (> It., Sp. *remo*, OFr. *reime*, W. *rhwyf*, Br. *roeñv;* Fr. *rame*, back-formation fr. deriv. vb. *ramer* 'row'); Ir. *rāme*, NIr. *rāmha;* OE *rōþer* (NE *rudder*), OHG *ruodar*, MHG *ruoder* (also 'rudder'), NHG *ruder;* Lith. *irklas*, Lett. *irkls*, *irklis* (cf. Lith. *irti*, Lett. *irt* 'row'); Skt. *aritra-* (cf. *aritar-* 'rower').

2. Grk. *κώπη*, NG lit. *κώπη, κωπίον*, pop. *κουπί*, orig. 'handle', hence the 'handle of

the oar', then the 'oar' itself : *κάπτω* 'gulp down' (fr. 'seize'), Lat. *capere* 'seize, take', Alb. *kap* 'grasp', etc. Walde-P. 1.342. Walde-H. 1.159.

3. Lat. *rēmus*, etc., above, 1.

Lat. *tōnsa* (poet.), etym. dub, perh. : Goth. *at-þinsan* 'draw on', OHG *dinsan* 'pull, drag', etc., IE **tens-* extension of **ten-* in Lat. *tendere* 'stretch', etc.; or else : Lat. *tondere* 'shear, crop, cut off' (as 'hewn-out stick'?). Walde-P. 1.720, 727.

Fr. *aviron*, fr. OFr. *avirer* 'turn about' (found only as refl.), cpd. of *virer* 'turn, change course, veer, tack'. Gamillscheg s.v.

Rum. *lopată*, also and orig. 'shovel', fr. Slavic *lopata* 'shovel' (8.24).

Rum. *vîslă*, fr. the Slavic, cf. ChSl. *veslo*, etc. (below, 7).

4. Ir. *rāme*, etc., cf. above, 1.

5. ON *ār*, Dan. *aare*, Sw. *åra*, *år*, OE *ār*, ME *ore*, NE *oar*, fr. Gmc. **airō-* (cf. Finn. loanword *airo*), without clear outside connections. Walde-P. 1.167. Falk-Torp 7, 1429.

ON *ræði*, prob. : MHG *ruote* 'rod, pole' also 'oar-shaft, oar' (NHG *rute*), OHG *ruota*, OE *rōd* 'rod, pole', etc. Falk-Torp 908 (against connection with OE *rōþer*, etc.).

OE *rōþer*, OHG *ruodar*, above, 1.

Du. *riem*, OHG *riemo*, MHG *rieme* (NHG dial. *riemen*), fr. Lat. *rēmus* (above, 1). Franck-v. W. 547. Weigand-H. 1.587.

6. Lith. *irklas*, Lett. *irkls*, above, 1.

7. ChSl. *veslo*, etc., general Slavic (fr. IE **weĝh-slo-*) : ChSl. *vožą*, *voziti*, Lat. *vehī* 'ride', etc. (10.66). Walde-P. 1.250.

8. Skt. *aritra-*, above, 1.

Skt. *kṣepaṇi-* (also *kṣepaṇī-*, *kṣipaṇi-*, etc.) : *kṣip-* 'throw, cast' (10.25), fr. the 'throwing motion' involved in rowing.

Skt. *nāudaṇḍa-*, *nāukādaṇḍa-* lit. 'boat-pole', cpd. of *nāu-* 'boat' and *daṇḍa-* 'stick, staff'.

10.852. 'Row' (vb.). Nearly all the verbs for 'row' are connected with the nouns for 'oar', mostly those of the widespread group 1 of 10.85—either from their roots or, more commonly, derivatives, compounds, or phrases with them. Thus Grk. *ἐρέσσω*; Lat. *rēm-igere* (cpd. with *agere*), VLat. **rēmāre* (It. *remare*, Fr. *ramer*, Sp. *remar;* Ir. *rāim* (Pedersen 2.591), NIr. *rāmhuighim*, W. *rhyfo*, Br. *roeñvi;* ON *rōa*, Dan., Sw. *ro*, OE *rōwan*, NE *row*, Du. *roeien*, OHG *ruoderōn*, NHG *rudern;* Lith. *irti*, Lett. *irt;* SCr. *veslati* (similarly Rum. *vîsli*, fr. *vîslă*), Boh. *veslovati*, Pol. *robić wiosɫem* (lit. 'act with the oar').

But there are a few of different origin.

NG pop. *λάμνω*, fr. *ἐλαύνω* 'drive' (10.65), which is used for 'row' in NT, Mk. 6.48, Jn. 6.19, and so rendered in the other versions (Vulgate, Goth., OE, ChSl., etc.).

Fr. *nager*, fr. Lat. *nāvigāre* 'sail' (10.36), now commonly 'swim' or 'float', is also sometimes used for 'row', esp. in phrase *nager de long* 'row with long strokes'.

It. *vogare*, Sp. *vogar*, fr. a Gmc. form like NHG *wogen*, deriv. of word for 'wave' (1.35). REW 9566.

Goth. *farjan* (for *ἐλαύνω* 'row' in Jn. 6.19; also for *πλέω* 'sail') : OE *faran*, etc. 'go' (10.47).

ChSl. *greti*, Russ. *gresti* (latter also 'rake') : Lith. *grėbti* 'rake', Skt. *grabh-* 'seize', etc. Walde-P. 1.652 f. Berneker 347.

10.86 RUDDER

Grk.	*πηδάλιον*	Goth.	....	Lith.	*vairas*
NG	*τιμόνι*	ON	*stȳri, ræðri*	Lett.	*stūre*
Lat.	*gubernāculum*	Dan.	*styr, ror*	ChSl.	*krŭma, krŭmilo*
It.	*timone*	Sw.	*styre, roder*	SCr.	*krmilo*
Fr.	*gouvernail*	OE	*stēor, stēorrōþor*	Boh.	*kormidlo*
Sp.	*timón, gobernalle*	ME	*stere, rother*	Pol.	*stér*
Rum.	*cîrmă*	NE	*rudder*	Russ.	*rul', kormilo*
Ir.	*lue*	Du.	*roer, stuur*	Skt.	*karṇa-, aritra-, kenipāta-*
NIr.	*failm, stiuir*	OHG	*ruodar, stiura, stiurruodar*		
W.	*llyw*			Av.	....
Br.	*stur*	MHG	*stiurruoder, stiur, ruoder*		
		NHG	*steuerruder*		

Many of the names of the 'rudder' are cognates with those for 'oar'. In the older languages they may be the same since the simplest form of 'rudder' is merely an 'oar' trailed in the water behind the boat. With a more advanced form of steering apparatus come special words for 'helm, tiller' (mostly connected with words for 'handle' or 'beam'), and these are sometimes extended to cover the whole 'rudder'. A few words for 'rudder' are from verbs for 'guide, steer'.

1. Grk. *πηδάλιον* : Hom. *πηδόν* 'blade of the oar', pl. *πηδά* also 'rudder', through notion of 'flat surface' : *πέδον* 'ground, earth', *πεδίον* 'plain', *πούς*, Lat. *pēs* 'foot', etc. Walde-P. 1.23 f.

NG *τιμόνι*, fr. It. *timone* (below, 2).

2. Lat. *gubernāculum* (> Fr. *gouvernail*, Cat. *governall* > Sp. *gobernalle*), deriv. of *gubernāre* 'steer, pilot a ship', fr. Grk. *κυβερνάω* 'act as pilot, steer'. Ernout-M. 437.

It. *timone*, Sp. *timón*, also 'helm, tiller, beam, pole' (so Fr. *timon*) fr. VLat. **tīmo*, for *tēmo* (*-ōnis*) 'beam, pole'. REW 8625.

Rum. *cîrmă*, fr. the Slavic, cf. ChSl. *krŭma* (below, 6).

3. Ir. *lue*, W. *llyw*, Corn. *leu*, fr. *[*p*]*luwo-* : Grk. *πλέω* 'sail, float', ON *fljōta* 'float, flow', etc. (10.34). Walde-P. 2.95. Pedersen 1.61 f.

NIr. *failm*, fr. Lat. *palma* 'blade of an oar', like *failm*, *pailm* 'palm-tree' fr. the same source.

NIr. *stiuir*, fr. ON *stȳri* (below, 4). Marstrander, Bidrag 73.

Br. *stur*, fr. Du. *stuur* 'helm, rudder' (below, 4). Henry 257.

4. ON *stȳri*, Dan. *styr*, Sw. *styre*, OE *stēor*, ME *stere*, MLG *stūr*(*e*), Du. *stuur* (mostly 'helm'), OHG *stiura*, MHG *stiur* (NHG *steuer*), and cpds. with words for 'oar' in OE *stēorrōþor*, OHG *stiurruodar*, etc.; the same word as OHG *stiura*, NHG *steuer*, MLG *stūr*(*e*) 'support, aid, contribution' (hence the orig. sense of the group was 'support, aid to the ship'; the vbs. ON *stȳra*, OE *stieran*, etc. 'steer' are secondary) : OHG *stūri*, and *stiuri* 'strong, magnificent', Skt. *sthūra-* 'strong, thick', etc. Walde-P. 1.609. Falk-Torp 1194. Franck-v. W. 682.

ON *ræðri*, Dan. *ror*, Sw. *roder*, (OE *rōþer* 'oar'), ME *rother*, NE *rudder*, Du. *roer*, OHG *ruodar*, MHG *ruoder*, NHG *ruder* (mostly 'oar', but in the earlier language 'rudder, oar' without distinction) : Grk. *ἐρετμόν*, Lat. *rēmus* 'oar', etc. (10.85).

5. Lith. *vairas*, with Lett. *airis* 'oar', fr. a Gmc. **airō* (through Finn. *airo?*), whence ON, OE *ār* 'oar', etc. (10.85). Walde-P. 1.167. Mühl.-Endz. 1.13.

Lett. *stūre*, fr. MLG *stūre* (above). Mühl.-Endz. 2.1109.

6. ChSl. *krŭma* (also 'stern, poop'),

SCr. *krma*, with suffix later ChSl. *krŭmilo*, SCr. *krmilo*, Boh. *kormidlo*, Russ. *kormilo*, perh. as 'hewn-off pole' : ChSl. *okrŭniti* 'cut off', etc. Walde-P. 2.577 (against connection with Grk. *πρύμνη* 'poop, stern', as Berneker 668 and others).

Pol. *stér*, older *styr*, Russ. (arch.) *styr*, fr. MLG *stūr* (above, 4).

Russ. *rul'*, with dissim. fr. Du. *roer* 'rudder', like many other Russ. nautical terms taken over from Dutch in time of Peter the Great. Preveden, Chicago Diss.

7. Skt. *karṇa-* 'ear' (4.22), also 'handle' and 'helm, rudder'. Cf. *karṇa-grāha-* and *karṇa-dhāra-*, also *nāu-karṇa-dhāra-* 'helmsman'.

Skt. *kenipāta-* (lexicog.), prob. a foreign word, Semitic? cf. Hebr. *kānāf* 'wing, tip'. Uhlenbeck 65.

10.87 MAST

Grk.	*ἱστός*	Goth.	....	Lith.	*stiebas*
NG	*κατάρτι*	ON	*sigla, siglutrē*	Lett.	*masts*
Lat.	*mālus*	Dan.	*mast*	ChSl.	*jadro*
It.	*albero*	Sw.	*mast*	SCr.	*jarbol, katarka*
Fr.	*mât*	OE	*mæst*	Boh.	*stěžeň, stožár*
Sp.	*mástil, palo, árbol*	ME	*mast*	Pol.	*maszt*
Rum.	*catart*	NE	*mast*	Russ.	*mačta*
Ir.	*seolchrand*	Du.	*mast*	Skt.	....
NIr.	*seolchrann, crann*	OHG	*mast*	Av.	....
W.	*hwylbren*	MHG	*mast*		
Br.	*gwern*	NHG	*mast*		

Words for 'mast' are mostly connected with those for 'tree' or 'pole'. There is also specialization from 'something standing, an upright', and from 'equipment'.

1. IE **mazdos*. Walde-P. 2.235. Ernout-M. 584. Walde-H. 2.19. Falk-Torp 704.

Lat. *mālus* (with dial. *l* for *d*); OE *mæst*, OHG *mast*, etc. general WGmc. (Dan., Sw. *mast* fr. MLG), whence also Fr. *mât*, Sp. *mástil* (REW 5397), and Lith. *mastas*, Lett. *masts*, Pol. *maszt*, Russ. *mačta;* cf. NIr. *maide* 'stick, staff', MIr. *admat* 'timber'.

2. Grk. *ἱστός* ('mast' Hom.+, but also 'beam of a loom, loom, pole'), orig. 'an upright' : *ἵστημι* 'stand'.

Byz. *κατάρτιον* (> NG *κατάρτι*, Rum. *catart*, SCr. *katarka*, ORuss. *katart*), orig. 'equipment' (so *καταρτεία*, *καταρθία* in pap.; cf. *παρέλαβον τὸ πλοῖον σὺν τῇ καταρθίῃ*) : *καταρτίζω* 'adjust, prepare, equip' (: *ἄρτι* 'just now', *ἄρτιος* 'suitable, perfect').

3. Lat. *mālus*, above, 1.

It. *albero* (Venetian *arboro* > NG *ἄρμπουρο*), Sp. *árbol*, lit 'tree' (cf. ON *siglutrē*, below, 5).

Fr. *mât*, Sp. *mástil*, above, 1.

Sp. *palo*, lit. 'pole, stake', fr. Lat. *pālus* 'stake'.

Rum. *catart*, above, 2.

4. Ir. *seolchrand*, NIr. *seolchrann*, W. *hwylbren*, cpds. of words for 'sail' (10.88) and 'tree' (1.42), prob. semantic borrowings fr. ON *siglutrē* (below, 5). Marstrander, Bidrag 46.

Br. *gwern*, fr. the name of the tree *gwern* 'alder'. Henry 152, n. 2.

5. ON *sigla*, and cpd. *siglu-trē* (*trē* here 'beam') : *segl* 'sail' (10.88).

OE *mæst*, etc., above, 1.

6. Lith. *mastas* (Kurschat; in this sense now replaced by *stiebas*, NSB s.v. *mastas*), Lett. *masts*, above, 1.

Lith. *stiebas* (in Kurschat as 'mast' of

small craft, but now apparently generic), also 'stake, pole' : ChSl. *stǐbljǐ* 'stalk', etc. Walde-P. 2.648.

7. ChSl. *jadro* (Supr. 400 for ἰστός, but mostly for κόλπος 'bosom'), beside *jadrilo*, SCr. *jedro* 'sail', see 10.88.

SCr. *jarbol, arbuo*, older *arbor*, etc., fr. Venet. *arbolo, arboro* = It. *albero* 'tree, mast' (above, 3). Berneker 30.

10.88 SAIL (sb.)

Grk.	ἰστίον	Goth.	....	Lith.	*buré* (*žéglius*)
NG	πανί	ON	segl	Lett.	*bur'a*
Lat.	*vēlum*	Dan.	sejl	ChSl.	*jadrilo*
It.	*vela*	Sw.	segel	SCr.	*jedro*
Fr.	*voile*	OE	segl	Boh.	*plachta*
Sp.	*vela*	ME	segl	Pol.	*żagiel*
Rum.	*pînză*	NE	sail	Russ.	*parus*
Ir.	*sēol*	Du.	zeil	Skt.	....
NIr.	*seol*	OHG	segal, segil	Av.	....
W.	*hwyl*	MHG	segel, sigel		
Br.	*gouel*	NHG	segel		

Most of the words for 'sail' meant originally 'piece of cloth', and several continued to be used in that sense also. This is true also of many colloquial terms for 'sail' that are not considered here. Cf. Lidén, Stud. 23. More isolated are certain instrument nouns from verbs for 'ride, go' and probable derivatives of nouns for 'mast' and 'wind'. There is no connection with verbs for 'sail' except as the latter are derived from the noun.

1. Grk. ἰστίον, mostly pl. ἰστία 'sails' already in Homer and so prob. deriv. of ἰστός 'mast'. One would prefer development through ἰστίον 'piece of cloth', but this use is attested only late and clearly secondary.

NG πανί, also and orig. 'cloth', fr. Lat. *pannus* 'cloth' (6.21).

2. Lat. *vēlum*, orig. 'cloth', as 'sail' mostly pl. *vēla* (> It., Sp. *vela*, Fr. *voile*), prob. fr. *weg-s-lo-m*, cf. *vexillum* dim. 'ensign, banner' : Ir. *figim* 'weave', etc., IE *weg-*. Walde-P. 1.247. Ernout-M. 1082.

Rum. *pînză*, also 'linen cloth' (cf. 6.23).

3. Ir. *sēol*, W. *hwyl*, either cognate with or early loanwords fr. Gmc., OE *segl*, etc. Walde-P. 2.475. Falk-Torp 955. Pedersen 1.103.

Br. *gouel*, fr. Lat. *vēla* (above, 2). Loth, Mots lat. 173.

4. ON, OE *segl*, etc., general Gmc. (MHG, NHG *segel* > Pol. *żagiel* > Lith. *žéglius*, formerly in use), fr. Gmc. *segla-*, IE *sek-lóm* as 'piece of cloth' : Lat. *secāre* 'cut', etc. Walde-P. 2.475. Falk-Torp 955.

5. Lith. *buré*, Lett. *bur'a*, cf. Lith. *burva* 'sort of garment', Lett. *burves* 'little sail', prob. : Grk. φᾶρος, φάρος 'cloth, cloak' (cf. Hom. Od. 5.258, where Calypso brings φάρεα to make sails), φορμός 'woven basket'. Walde-P. 2.164. Mühl.-Endz. 1.356.

6. ChSl. *jadrilo* 'sail' (*jadro* 'mast, bosom'), SCr. *jedro*, prob. derivs. of ChSl. *jati* 'ride', etc., IE *yā-* in Skt. *yā-* 'go', etc. (10.47, 10.66). Berneker 442.

SCr. *katarka*, above, 2.

Boh. *stěžeň*, lit. 'pole, tree', *stožár* also 'pole' (with a large Slavic group for 'pole, stick', etc.) : ON *staki*, OE *staca*, NE *stake*, etc. Miklosich 324. Walde-P. 2.622.

Pol. *maszt*, Russ. *mačta*, above, 1.

8. No Skt. or Av. words for 'mast' or 'sail'.

Boh. *plachta*, also 'a cloth, bed-sheet' = Pol. *płachta* 'coarse linen cloth' (: *plaszcz* 'cloak', etc., 6.41). Brückner 419.

Pol. *żagiel*, above, 4.

Russ. *parus*, generally taken as old loanword fr. Grk. φᾶρος (cf. above, 5).

Doubted by Lidén, Stud. 24, n. 2, on the ground that φᾶρος is mainly a poet. word. But its use in Hdt. 9.109 shows that it was a prose word somewhere, say in the Asia Minor region, and it may well have come into Russian from the Grk. colonies on the north shore of the Black Sea.

10.89 ANCHOR

Grk.	ἄγκῦρα	Goth.	....	Lith.	*inkaras*
NG	ἄγκυρα, σίδερο	ON	akkeri	Lett.	*enkurs*
Lat.	ancora	Dan.	anker	ChSl.	*kotŭka, ankvra*
It.	ancora	Sw.	ankare	SCr.	*sidro, kotva, lenger*
Fr.	ancre	OE	ancor	Boh.	*kotva*
Sp.	ancla	ME	ancre, ancer	Pol.	*kotwica, kotew*
Rum.	ancoră	NE	anchor	Russ.	*jakor'*
Ir.	ingor	Du.	anker	Skt.	....
NIr.	ancoire	OHG	senchil, anchar	Av.	....
W.	angor	MHG	anker		
Br.	eor	NHG	anker		

The majority of the words for 'anchor' are borrowed through the Latin from the Greek word, which itself is based on the notion of something bent, 'a hook'. Other connections are with 'cat', 'sink', 'iron'.

1. Grk. ἄγκῦρα : ἀγκύλος 'crooked', Skt. *añc-* 'bend', OHG *ango* 'hook', etc. Hence ChSl. *ankvra*, Lat. *ancora* and, fr. the latter, the other Eur. forms, as It. *ancora*, Fr. *ancre*, Sp. *ancla* and *áncora*, Rum. *ancoră*; Ir. *ingor*, MIr., NIr. *ancoire* (later borrowing), W. *angor*, Br. *eor*; ON *akkeri*, Dan. *anker*, Sw. *ankare* (> Lith. *inkaras*, Lett. *enkurs*, Russ. *jakor'*), OE *ancor*, etc., the Gmc. words. Walde-P. 1.60. Falk-Torp 30. Berneker 29.

2. NG σίδερο 'iron, iron bar' (fr. Grk.

σίδηρος 'iron'), also pop. nautical term for 'anchor', whence SCr. *sidro* in this sense only.

3. OHG *senchil, senchila*, the early word (replaced by late OHG *anchar*, cf. above) : *senken* 'sink' (10.33).

4. ChSl. *kotŭka*, SCr., Boh. *kotva*, Pol. *kotwica, kotew* : ChSl. *kotŭka*, Russ. *kot*, etc. 'cat'. The application to 'anchor', fr. the hooks resembling the claws of a cat, is paralleled in Du. *kat, katanka* 'small anchor, grapnel' (cf. also the nautical use of NE *cat*, NED s.v. 7), but need not be attributed to borrowing. Berneker 589 ff. Brückner 262.

SCr. *sidro*, fr. NG σίδερο, above, 2.

SCr. *lenger, lender*, fr. Turk. *lenger*. Berneker 29.

10.91 HARBOR, PORT

Grk.	λιμήν	Goth.	....	Lith.	*uostas*
NG	λιμάνι	ON	hǫfn	Lett.	*uosta*
Lat.	portus	Dan.	havn	ChSl.	*pristanište*
It.	porto	Sw.	hamn	SCr.	*luka*
Fr.	port	OE	hæfen, port	Boh.	*přístav*
Sp.	puerto	ME	haven, port, herberwe	Pol.	*port*
Rum.	port	NE	harbor, port	Russ.	*port, gavan'*
Ir.	cuan	Du.	haven	Skt.	....
NIr.	cuan	OHG	urfar, stad, stedi	Av.	....
W.	porthladd, porth	MHG	urvar, haben(e)		
Br.	porz	NHG	hafen		

The origin of words for 'harbor' reflects partly its function as a shelter for ships and partly some physical aspect.

1. Grk. λιμήν (in Thess. dial. 'market-place'), NG pop. λιμάνι (a fr. the Turk. loanword *liman*), beside λίμνη 'lake, pool', Λίμναι orig. the 'Marshes', λειμών 'meadow', all fr. the notion of 'a curve, hollow depression' in the shore or surface of the land, and prob. : Lat. *limus* 'askew, slanting', ON *limr* 'limb, twig' (orig. 'flexible'), m-formations of a root *(e)lei-* in words for 'bend, crooked', etc. Walde-P. 1.158. Boisacq 565 f.

2. Lat. *portus* (> Romance words), orig. 'passage' : Av. *pərətu-* 'passage, ford, bridge', Ir. *rith*, OHG *furt*, etc. 'ford'. Walde-P. 2.40. Ernout-M. 794.

3. Ir. *cuan*, prob. : ON *hǫfn*, etc. (below, 4). Pedersen 1.94.

W. *porth*, Br. *porz*, fr. Lat. *portus*. Loth, Mots lat. 197. W. *porthladd* apparently new sg. of *porthle*, pl. *porthloedd* (same meaning but not a common word), cpd. of *porth* and *lle* 'place'.

4. ON *hǫfn*, OE *hæfen*, etc., general Gmc. (NHG *hafen* fr. LG; NE *haven* now mostly fig.), prob. as orig. 'container (of ships)' : Goth. *hafjan* 'lift', Lat. *capere* 'seize, take', etc. Derivation fr. ON *haf* 'sea', though fr. the same root, is less probable. Walde-P. 1.342 f. Falk-Torp 387. NED s.v. haven.

OE, ME, NE, MHG *port*, fr. Lat. *portus*.

ME *herberwe* (but mostly 'shelter, lodging', etc.), NE *harbor*, fr. OE *her-*

beorg (orig. or fr. ON) : ON *herbergi* 'inn, lodgings', OHG *heriberga* 'camp, lodging', lit. 'army shelter', cpd. of ON *herr*, etc. 'army' and derivs. of root in OE *beorgan* 'save, shelter', etc. NED s.v. harbor.

OHG *urfar* gl. *portus*, MHG *urvar* 'landing-place, ford, etc.', cpd. of *ur-* (Goth. *us-*) 'out' and deriv. of root in OHG, OE, Goth. *faran* 'go, travel' (cf. above, 2).

OHG *stad* (*stat*), *stedi*, reg. 'shore', but also 'portus' : Goth. *staþa*, OE *stæþ*, etc. 'shore' (1.27).

5. Lith. *uostas*, Lett. *uosta, uosts*, both also 'mouth of a river', hence, as landing-place for ships, 'harbor' : Skt. *ōṣṭhas-*, Av. *aošta-* 'lip', Lat. *ōstium* 'river's mouth', further Lat. *ōs* 'mouth', ON *ōss* 'river's mouth', etc. Walde-P. 1.168.

6. ChSl. *pristanište* (Supr. reg. for λιμήν), Boh. *přístav* (Pol. *przystań*, Russ. *pristan'* mostly 'landing-place), cpds. of *pri* 'by, at, near' and derivs. of the root in ChSl. *stati, stanǫ* 'take a stand', *staviti* 'put, place', etc.

SCr. *luka*, also 'field near a river' (Boh. *louka* 'meadow', Russ. *luka* 'bend, meadow-land near a river bend') : SCr. *luk*, ChSl. *lǫkŭ* 'bow', fr. the root of ChSl. *na-lęšti* 'bend (the bow)', etc., with the same semantic relation as in Grk. λιμήν (above, 1). Berneker 739.

Pol., Russ. *port*, fr. Lat. *portus*.

Russ. *gavan'*, fr. Du. *haven*.

CHAPTER 11

POSSESSION, PROPERTY, AND COMMERCE

11.11 HAVE	11.55 MISER
11.12 OWN, POSSESS	11.56 STEAL
11.13 TAKE	11.57 THIEF
11.14 SEIZE, GRASP, TAKE HOLD OF	11.58 ROB, ROBBER
11.15 HOLD	11.61 LEND
11.16 GET, OBTAIN	11.62 BORROW
11.17 KEEP, RETAIN	11.63 OWE
11.21 GIVE	11.64 DEBT
11.22 GIVE BACK, RETURN	11.65 PAY (vb.)
11.23 RESTORE	11.66 ACCOUNT, RECKONING
11.24 PRESERVE, KEEP SAFE, SAVE	11.67 SECURITY, SURETY
11.25 SAVE, RESCUE	11.68 INTEREST
11.26 SAFE (adj.)	11.69 TAX (sb.)
11.27 DESTROY	11.71 INCOME
11.28 HARM, INJURE, DAMAGE (vb.)	11.72 EXPENSE, COST
11.29 SPOIL (vb. trans.)	11.73 PROFIT
11.31 SEEK	11.74 LOSS
11.32 FIND	11.75 LEASE, RENT (to Another)
11.33 LOSE	11.76 RENT, LEASE (from Another)
11.34 RELEASE	11.77 HIRE (vb., a Person)
11.41 PROPERTY	11.78 WAGES, PAY
11.42 WEALTH, RICHES	11.79 EARN
11.43 MONEY	11.81 BUY
11.44 COIN	11.82 SELL
11.45 PURSE	11.83 TRADE (vb.)
11.46 TREASURE	11.84 MERCHANT, TRADESMAN
11.47 BANK	11.85 MARKET (Place)
11.48 HEIR	11.86 STORE, SHOP
11.51 RICH	11.87 PRICE
11.52 POOR	11.88 DEAR (=Costly, Expensive)
11.53 BEGGAR	11.89 CHEAP
11.54 AVARICIOUS, STINGY	

11.11 HAVE

Grk.	*ἔχω*	Goth.	*haban* (*aigan*)	Lith.	*turėti*
NG	*ἔχω*	ON	*hafa*	Lett.	*būt* with dat.; *turēt*
Lat.	*habēre*	Dan.	*have*	ChSl.	*iměti*
It.	*avere*	Sw.	*hava*	SCr.	*imati*
Fr.	*avoir*	OE	*habban*	Boh.	*míti*
Sp.	*tener*	ME	*have*	Pol.	*mieć*
Rum.	*avea*	NE	*have*	Russ.	prep. *u* with gen., *imet'*
Ir.	phrase with 'be'	Du.	*hebben*	Skt.	*as-* or *bhū-* with gen.
NIr.	phrase with 'be'	OHG	*habēn*	Av.	*ah-* with gen.
W.	phrase with 'be'	MHG	*haben*		
Br.	phrase with 'be'; *kaout*	NHG	*haben*		

There is considerable overlapping of sense among the verbs listed in 11.11–11.17. There is no sharp line between the colorless 'have' and the stronger 'own, possess'. 'Have' is mostly from earlier 'seize, take hold of', 'hold', or 'take', which are again closely allied with each other and in part with 'get, obtain' and 'keep, retain'.

The oldest method of indicating simple possession, and doubtless that of the IE period, was by means of a phrase containing the verb 'be', expressed or implied, with an oblique case for the person. This is common enough even in languages which also have verbs for 'have' (Grk. μοί ἐστι, Lat. *mihi est*, etc.), and is the normal type in Indo-Iranian, and in the Celtic languages down to the present day.

The secondary use of verbs for 'have' as auxiliaries, esp. for past tenses, but also for future and 'must' (9.94), is not considered here.

Cf. Meillet, Le développement du verbe "avoir", Festschrift Wackernagel, 9 ff.

1. 'Have' regularly expressed by phrases. Ir. *rotbia less lōg dodaggnīma* lit. 'reward shall be to thee with him of thy well-doing' (Wb. 6a11), or using a prepositional phrase, *is ed inso fil lasuide* lit. 'it is this that is with him' (Ml. 63d4), or, taking NT, Jn. 4.17, οὐκ ἔχω ἄνδρα is rendered by NIr *nī fhuil fear agam*, W. *nid oes gennyf wr*, and Br. *n'em eus pried ebet* 'there is not a husband to me'; so also Lett. *man vīra nav*, Russ. *u menja net muža* 'there-is-not a husband to me'. Skt. *as-* or *bhū-* with the gen. may be 'have' or 'own', cf. *tasya çataṁ jāyā babhuvur* 'he had a hundred wives', or *manor ha vā ṛṣabha āsa* 'Manu had a bull' (cf. Delbrück, Altind. Syntax 162), and similarly, Av. *ašava dąna . . . . yā̊ hənti spəntahe mainyə̄uš* 'those creatures . . . . which the holy spirit possesses' (Yt. 6.2), also with omission of *ah-* : *vahišta īštiš srāvī zaraθuštrahē* 'Zarathustra has the best good known', lit. 'optimum bonum auditum (est) Zarathustri' (cf. Reichelt, Aw. Gramm. 253; Barth. 269).

2. Grk. ἔχω 'hold, possess, have' : Skt. *sah-* 'be able, be powerful, overcome, be victorious', Av. *haz-* 'take possession of, gain', Goth. *sigis*, etc. 'victory'. Walde-P. 2.481 f.

3. Lat. *habēre* (> It. *avere*, Fr. *avoir*, Rum. *avea*) earlier 'hold', whence 'occupy, possess' and finally 'have' : Umbr. *habitu*, *habetu* 'habeto', but the older sense in *haburent* 'ceperint', etc., Ir. *gaibim* 'take, seize', W. *gafaelu* 'hold, grasp' (10.14), perh. Lith. *gabenti* 'carry off, transport', IE **ghab(h)-*. Walde-P. 1.344 f. Ernout-M. 442. Walde-H. 1.630 f.

Sp. *tener* fr. Lat. *tenēre* 'hold' (11.15).

4. Br. *kaout* : *kavout* 'get, find', etc. See 11.16.

5. Goth. *haban*, etc., general Gmc. : Lat. *capere* 'seize, take', Goth. *hafjan*, ON *hefja*, etc. 'lift', Lett. *kampt* 'seize, grasp', IE **kap-*. Walde-P. 1.342 ff. Walde-H. 1.159. Falk-Torp 386. Feist 229.

Goth. *aigan* renders Grk. ἔχω in expressing relationship ('have as father' Lk. 3.8, 'have to wife' Lk. 20.33, Mc. 12.23), but represents the general Gmc. word for 'own', as ON *eiga*, etc. (11.12). Feist 20.

6. Lith. *turėti* = Lett. *turēt* 'hold, keep' (also 'have', dial. 'possess', cf. Mühl.-Endz. 4.270), OPruss. *turit* 'have' : Lith. *tverti* 'fence, inclose', *nutverti* 'seize', Lett. *tvert* 'grasp, seize', ChSl. *za-tvoriti* 'close, inclose'. Walde-P. 1.751.

7. ChSl. *iměti*, etc., the Slavic words (but Russ. *imet'* rather 'possess' than 'have') : ChSl. *imą*, *jęti* 'take', etc., general Slavic (11.13).

8. Skt. and Av., see above, 1.

11.12 OWN, POSSESS

Grk.	*κέκτημαι*	Goth.	*gastaldan*, *aigan*	Lith.	*turėti*
NG	*ἀνήκει* (*μου*, etc.)	ON	*eiga*	Lett.	phrase = have
Lat.	*possidēre*, *tenēre*	Dan.	*eje*, *besidde*	ChSl.	*pritężati*, *sŭtężati*
It.	*possedere*	Sw.	*äga*, *besitta*	SCr.	*posjedovati* (*imati*)
Fr.	*posséder*	OE	*āgan*, *āgnian*, *stealdan*	Boh.	*držeti* (*míti*)
Sp.	*poseer*	ME	*owe* (*ohne*)	Pol.	*posiadać*, *dzierżeć* (*mieć*)
Rum.	*poseda*	NE	*own*, *possess*	Russ.	*vladet'*, *obladat'*, *imet'*
Ir.	*techtaim*, *selbaim*	Du.	*bezitten*	Skt.	= 'have', *kṣi-*, *īç-*
NIr.	*sealbhuighim*	OHG	*bisizzan*, *eigan*	Av.	= 'have'
W.	*meddu*	MHG	*besitzen*		
Br.	*piaoua*	NHG	*besitzen*		

In most cases any expression for 'have' may be used also for 'own, possess' if the context shows that the relations ip is one of enduring (or legal, etc.) nature, as opposed to the temporary associative notion of 'have', which is often only a weakening of the stronger 'hold, possess'. In Sanskrit and Avestan it is not possible to distinguish between 'have' and 'own' except by context (and so largely still in Breton and Lettic), where both notions are expressed by a phrase (cf. 11.11). Likewise, most of the modern European languages show a distinct preference for expressing ownership by a phrase, as N.E. *it's mine*, or Fr. *c'est à moi*, even where there are also distinctive verbs for 'own'.

The latter are often from the notion of 'rule, have power over'. Several must have been used primarily with reference to lands or houses, as indicated by early usage or the cognates, so notably Lat. *possidēre* with semantic borrowings in Gmc. and (through Gmc.) Slavic.

1. Grk. κέκτημαι, lit. 'have acquired', perf. of κτάομαι 'get, obtain' : Skt. *kṣi-* 'possess, rule over', Av. *xši-* 'have might, rule, be able'. Walde-P. 1.504.

In NG 'own' is regularly expressed by a phrase with ἀνήκει 'it belongs' = class. Grk. ἀν-ήκει 'it comes to'.

2. Lat. *possidēre*, legal term first used in connection with real estate (cf. *uti nunc possidetis eum fundum*, etc., Festus), cpd. of *sedēre* 'sit', first part prob. *potis*, *pote* 'having power, powerful' (otherwise Sommer, Hdb. 266, *por-* as in *por-tendere*, etc.). Hence the borrowed Romance forms, It. *possedere*, Fr. *posséder*, Rum. *poseda*, and inherited forms, OIt. *posseer*, OFr. *posseoir*, Sp. *poseer*, etc. NE *possess* fr. OFr. *possessier*, formed fr. Lat. pple. Ernout-M. 795 f. REW 6683.

Lat. *tenēre* 'hold' (11.15), then 'occupy, possess'.

3. Ir. *techtaim* 'own' (esp. in legal use, cf. Laws, Gloss.) : Br. *tizout* 'attain, obtain', ON *þiggja*, OE *þicgan* 'take, receive, accept' (11.13).

Ir. *selbaim*, NIr. *sealbhuighim*, fr. *selb* 'property' (11.41).

W. *meddu*, with 'own' fr. 'rule, have power' : Ir. *midiur* 'judge' (cf. *conmidethar* 'rules, has power'), Lat. *medērī* 'be good for, remedy', *meditāre* 'consider, meditate', Grk. μέδομαι 'be mindful of, provide for', μέδων 'ruler', Goth. *mitan*, etc. 'measure', IE **med-*. Walde-P. 2.259 f. Walde-H. 2.56. Pedersen 2.580.

Br. *kaout* 'own, have' (11.11).

Br. *piaoua* (MBr. *biou*, *biaou* but without inflection), verbal form derived from the locution *piou euz?* 'to whom is (this)?', i.e. 'to whom does this belong?'. Likewise, W. *piau* 'belong' and 'possess', Corn. *pew*, *bew* 'own'. Pedersen 2.200.

4. Goth. *gastaldan*, renders κτάομαι and once ἔχω (*gastaldand* = ἔξουσιν, Cor. 7.28), cf. *andstaldan* 'supply with', OE *stealdan* 'possess' : OE *gesteald* 'dwelling', *hagu-steald*, OHG *hagu-stalt*, etc. 'one living in the lord's house, unmarried person', fr. an extension of the root **stel-* in OE *stellan*, OHG *stellen* 'put, place', etc. Walde-P. 2.646. Feist 50.

Goth. *aigan* (see 11.11), ON *eiga*, Dan. *eje*, Sw. *äga*, OE *āgan*, ME, NE *owe* (now obs. in this sense), OHG *eigan*; also OE *āgnian* 'get possession of, own' (= Goth. *ga-aiginōn* 'gain advantage over', OHG *eigenen* 'appropriate, make one's own', fr. Goth. *aigin*, etc. 'property'), ME *ohne* (rare), NE *own* : Skt. *īç-* 'own, rule, be master of', Av. *išti-* 'possession, riches, power'. Walde-P. 1.105. Falk-Torp 184. Feist 20.

OHG *bisizzan*, MHG, NHG *besitzen*, Du. *bezitten* (Dan. *besidde*, Sw. *besitta* by semantic borrowing fr. MLG) = OE *besittan* 'sit around, besiege, sit in session', rarely 'sit in possession of, possess', all starting fr. the notion of 'sit about' and undoubtedly influenced by Lat. *possidēre*.

5. Lith. *turėti* 'have, own' (11.11).

6. ChSl. *pritężati*, *sŭtężati* 'acquire, possess', perfect. of *tężati* 'work, till' : *tęgnąti* 'pull, stretch', etc. (9.33).

SCr. *posjedovati*, Pol. *posiadać*, cf. SCr. *posjed*, Pol. *posiad* 'property', cpds. of the words for 'sit', probably in imitation of NHG *besitzen*, *besitz* (above, 4).

Boh. *držeti*, Pol. *dzierżeć*, lit. 'hold, keep', hence also 'own' : ChSl. *drŭžati* 'hold', etc. (11.15).

Russ. *vladet'*, *obladat'* (*obŭ-v-*) 'own, rule, govern' : ChSl. *vlasti*, Lith. *valdyti*, Lett. *valdīt* 'rule', Goth. *waldan* id., etc., fr. the root in Lat. *valēre* 'be strong'. Walde-P. 1.219.

Russ. *imet'* 'have', but also 'possess', as less commonly also the corresponding Slavic words for 'have', ChSl. *iměti*, etc. (11.11).

7. Skt. and Av. 'possess' usually = 'have' expressed by 'be' with predicate gen. (cf. 11.11).

Skt. *kṣi-* : Grk. κέκτημαι (above, 1).

Skt. *īç-* : Goth. *aigan*, etc. (above, 4).

11.13 TAKE

Grk.	*λαμβάνω*, *αἱρέω*	Goth.	*niman*	Lith.	*imti*
NG	*παίρνω*, *λαβαίνω*	ON	*nema*, *taka*, *þiggja*	Lett.	*n'emt*, *jemt*
Lat.	*capere*, *sūmere*	Dan.	*tage*	ChSl.	*vŭzęti*, etc., *bĭrati*
It.	*prendere*	Sw.	*taga*	SCr.	*uzeti*
Fr.	*prendre*	OE	*niman*, *þicgan*	Boh.	*vzíti*, *bráti*
Sp.	*tomar*	ME	*take*, *nime*	Pol.	*wziąć*, *brać*
Rum.	*lua*	NE	*take*	Russ.	*brat'*, *vzjat'*
Ir.	*gaibim*, *air-fo-emim*	Du.	*nemen*	Skt.	*grabh-*, *rabh-*, *labh-*
NIr.	*tōgaim*, *gabhaim*	OHG	*neman*	Av.	*grab-*
W.	*cym(e)ryd*	MHG	*nemen*		
Br.	*kemer*	NHG	*nehmen*		

'Take' is mostly a weakening of 'take hold of, seize', and in some languages not distinguished from the latter.

1. Grk. λαμβάνω 'seize, take', aor. ἔλαβον, perf. Att. εἴληφα (cf. λάφῡρον 'booty'), prob. : Skt. *labh-*, *rabh-* 'seize, take'. Brugmann, Grd. 2.3.291. Walde-P. 2.385, 707 (with alternative of a root ending in a labiovelar, assumed for Ion. λάζομαι and OE *læccan* 'seize'). NG λαμβάνω or λαβαίνω (new pres. fr. aor.), aor. ἔλαβα, used esp. for 'receive' and in certain formal phrases.

Grk. αἱρέω 'seize, take, catch, etc.' (much less common than λαμβάνω for 'take'), etym. dub. Walde-P. 2.498. McKenzie, Cl. Quart. 15.46 f. Aeol. ἀγρέω : ἄγρα 'the hunt', etc. Walde-P. 1.36 f. Aor. ἑλεῖν prob. : caus. Goth. *saljan* 'offer', OE *sellan* 'give, sell', etc. (as orig. 'cause to take'). Walde-P. 2.504. Feist 408.

NG παίρνω, fr. Grk. ἐπαίρω 'lift up', cpd. of αἴρω 'lift' (10.22), which is itself used for 'take up' and 'take away'.

2. Lat. *capere* 'seize, take' : Goth. *hafjan*, ON *hefja* 'lift', Goth. *haban*, ON *hafa*, etc. 'have' (11.11). Walde-P. 1.342 ff. Ernout-M. 147 ff. Walde-H. 1.159.

Lat. *sūmere* 'take up', fr. **sus-(e)mere*, cpd. of *sub-s-*, *sus-* with *emere* orig. 'take' (attested in Festus; 'buy' secondary) : Ir. *em-* (in cpds., *air-fo-emim* 'take, receive', etc.), Lith. *imti* 'take', ChSl. *jęti* 'seize, take' (but 'take' usually cpds., see below), etc., *iměti* 'have' (11.11). Walde-P. 1.124 f. Ernout-M. 299 ff.; 1102. Pedersen 2.512. Berneker 426 f.

It. *prendere*, Fr. *prendre* (Sp. *prender* 'seize'), fr. Lat. *prehendere* 'seize' (11.14).

Sp. *tomar* (cf. Cat. *tomar* 'stretch out the hands'), much disputed, perh. belonging to the group Fr. *tomber* 'fall', NE *tumble*, etc. REW 8975.

Rum. *lua*, fr. Lat. *levāre* 'lift' (10.22). Cf. Sp. *llevar* 'take away, carry' (10.61) and NG παίρνω 'take' (above, 1). REW 5000.

3. Ir. *gaibim* 'take, seize', NIr. *gabhaim* but mostly replaced by the cpd. *tōgaim* (for *tōgbhaim*, MIr. *tōcbaim* 'lift', fr. **to-od-gab-*) : Lat. *habēre* 'have', etc. (11.11). Pedersen 2.531.

Ir. *air-fo-emim* : Lat. *emere*, *sūmere* (above, 2).

W. *cymeryd*, *cymryd*, MBr. *compret*, Br. *kemer*, *kemeret*, fr. cpd. of IE **bher-* in Ir. *berim*, Grk. φέρω, etc. 'carry'. Pedersen 1.119, 2.472.

4. Goth. *niman*, ON *nema*, OE *niman*, ME *nime*, OHG *neman*, etc., with Lett. dial. *nemt* 'take' (cf. below), prob. : Grk. νέμω 'share' (act. 'give a share', mid. 'receive a share'; secondary 'pasture'). For the semantic polarity see under Goth. *giban* 'give' (11.21). Walde-P. 2.330 f. Falk-Torp 762. Feist 376 (adversely). C. Paschall, Univ. of California Publications in Linguistics 1.3 ff.

ON *þiggja*, OE *þicgan* 'take, receive, accept' (Dan. *tigge*, Sw. *tigga* 'beg') : Lith. *tekti* 'suffice, fall to one's lot', Ir. *techtaim* 'own'. Walde-P. 1.715. Falk-Torp 1258.

ON *taka* 'seize', later 'take' replacing *nema* in this sense (> ME *take* 'seize, take', NE *take*), Dan. *tage*, Sw. *taga* 'take' : Goth. *tēkan* 'touch', outside connections dub., but primary sense apparently 'lay hands on'. Walde-P. 1.786. Falk-Torp 1241. NED s.v. *take* vb.

5. Lith. *imti*, OPruss. *īmt* 'take', ChSl. *jęti* 'seize, take', but mostly cpds. *vŭzęti*, *prijęti*, *vŭsprijęti*, etc. for λαμβάνω 'take' (cf. Jagić, Entstehungsgesch. 293), as also in modern Slavic, SCr. *uzeti*, Boh. *vzíti*, Pol. *wziąć*, Russ. *vzjat'* : Lat. *emere* 'take, buy', *sūmere* 'take' (above, 2). Here perh. also Lett. *jemt* with *j*- by influence of Lith. dial. *jimti*. Walde-P. 1.124 f. Otherwise for Lett *jemt* (: Skt. *yam*- 'hold up, sustain'). Mühl.-Endz. 2.110.

Lett. *n'emt*, prob. a blend of the (now only) dial. *nemt* (above, 4) with *jemt* (above.) Mühl.-Endz. 2.899. Walde-P. loc. cit.

6. ChSl. *vŭzęti*, etc., above, 5.

ChSl. *bĭrati* 'collect, take', Boh. *bráti*, Pol. *brać*, Russ. *brat'* 'take' : Lat. *ferre*, Grk. φέρω, Skt. *bhṛ*-, etc. 'carry' (10.61).

7. For Indo-Iranian forms, see under 'seize' (11.14).

11.14 SEIZE, GRASP, TAKE HOLD OF

Grk.	λαμβάνω, ἁρπάζω, δράσσομαι	Goth.	*fahan, greipan*	Lith.	*nutverti, griebti*
		ON	*taka, grīpa (fā)*	Lett.	*tvert, grābt, k'ert*
NG	πιάνω	Dan.	*gribe*	ChSl.	*jęti, chvatiti*
Lat.	*prehendere, capere*	Sw.	*gripa*	SCr.	*uhvatiti, zgrabiti*
It.	*afferare, agguantare*	OE	*grīpan, læccan, fōn*	Boh.	*uchopiti, uchvatiti, chytiti*
Fr.	*saisir*	ME	*take, sese, gripe, lache*		
Sp.	*asir, agarrar, coger*	NE	*seize, grasp*	Pol.	*uchwycić, pochopić*
Rum.	*apuca, prinde*	Du.	*grijpen, vatten*	Russ.	*chvatat'*
Ir.	*gaibim*	OHG	*fāhan, grīfan*	Skt.	*grabh-, rabh-, labh-*
NIr.	*beirim ar, glacaim*	MHG	*vāhen, vazzen, grīfen*	Av.	*grab-*
W.	*gafaelu*	NHG	*(er)greifen, fassen*		
Br.	*kregi*				

Verbs for 'seize, grasp', besides the usual notion of 'seize with the hand', may come by extension from 'seize by a claw', 'by a hook', 'catch birds', 'overtake', etc.

Several of these, or their compounds, have come to be used for 'understand' (17.16).

1. Grk. λαμβάνω 'take, seize', see 11.13.

Grk. ἁρπάζω 'snatch away, carry off, seize' : ἁρπαγή 'rape, robbery, booty', ἁρπάγη 'hook for drawing buckets up, rake', ἅρπη 'sickle, a certain bird of prey', ChSl. *srŭpŭ* 'sickle', etc. Semantic development fr. 'hook' to 'snatch, seize' as in Br. *kregi* (below, 3). Walde-P. 2.501. Boisacq, 81.

Grk. δράσσομαι 'grasp, clutch' : δράξ 'hand', δραχμή 'drachma' (orig. 'handful'), outside connections dub. Walde-P. 1.807. Boisacq 198 f.

NG πιάνω, new present formed to aor. ἔπιασα, fr. Grk. πιέζω, πιάζω 'press' (9.342), late 'seize' (cf. Theocr. 4.35 ταῦρον . . . πιάξας τᾶς ὁπλᾶς, and so reg. in NT and pap.).

2. Lat. *prehendere*, *prēndere* (> Rum. *prinde* 'seize, effect, begin', etc.; It. *prendere*, Fr. *prendre* 'take') fr. *praehendere* : Grk. χανδάνω 'hold, comprise, contain', Goth. *bi-gitan* 'find', OE *be-gietan* 'get', etc., W. *genni* 'be contained', etc., IE **ghend*-. Walde-P. 1.589. Ernout-M. 803 f.

Lat. *capere*, see 'take' (11.13).

Lat. *rapere* (but esp. 'snatch away, carry off, rob, plunder') : Lith. *aprėpti* 'seize, embrace', Alb. *rjep* 'flay, rob', Grk. ἐρέπτομαι 'browse on, feed on' (as orig. 'pluck'). Walde-P. 2.369 f. Ernout-M. 851 f.

It. *afferare*, also Sp. *aferrar* 'grasp, furl, anchor', fr. VLat. **afferrāre*, cpd. of **ferrāre* (It. *ferrare*, Sp. *herrar*, etc.), deriv. of Lat. *ferrum* 'iron, iron implement' (cf. *ferrātus* 'covered with iron'). REW 256, 3256.

It. *agguantare*, deriv. of *guanto* 'glove'. REW 9500.

Fr. *saisir*, Prov. *sazir* (> Sp. *asir*), etym. disputed, prob. as orig. a legal term (MLat. *sacire* 'make legal claim') fr. a Frank. **sakjan* : *gasacio* 'adversary' (Lex Salica), OS *saca*, OHG *sahha* 'litigation'. Gamillscheg 781. Otherwise, fr. an OHG **sazjan* > *sezzen* 'set' (likewise fr. the legal terminology), REW 7632, Bloch 2.250.

Sp. *agarrar*, fr. *garra* 'claw, talon, clutch', an Iber. word. REW 3690a.

Sp. *coger* ('catch, collect', etc., also 'seize, take hold of'), fr. Lat. *colligere* 'collect'. REW 2048.

Rum. *apuca*, prob. fr. Lat. *aucupārī* 'go fowling, catch birds, give chase', deriv. of *auceps*, *aucupis* 'fowler'. REW 776.

3. Ir. *gaibim* 'take, seize', see 11.13.

NIr. *beirim ar*, lit. 'bear upon', e.g. *beirim air* 'I lay hold of him', the usual locution.

NIr. *glacaim*, fr. *glac* 'half-open fist, grasp, clutch, etc.'.

W. *gafaelu*, fr. *gafael* 'hold, grasp, grip' = Ir. *gabāl*, vbl. n. of *gaibim* (above). Walde-P. 1.345. Pedersen 2.532.

Br. *kregi* and *krogein*, also (earlier) 'hook, bite' fr. *krog* 'hook'.

4. Goth. *fahan*, ON *fā*, OE *fōn*, OHG *fāhan*, MHG *vāhen*, *vān*, the older Gmc. word (but in ON largely 'capture, get', NIcel. *fā*, Dan. *faa*, Sw. *få* 'get', NHG *fangen* 'catch, capture') : Lat. *pangere* 'fasten, fix, infix', Grk. πήγνυμι 'make fast', Av. *pas*- 'fasten together, join', etc., IE **pāk̑*-, **pāĝ*-. Walde-P. 2.2 f. Falk-Torp 199. Feist 134.

Goth. *greipan*, ON *grīpa*, Dan. *gribe*, Sw. *gripa*, OE *grīpan*, ME *gripe*, Du. *grijpen*, OHG *grīfan*, MHG *grīfen*, NHG *(er)greifen* : Lith. *griebti* 'seize, grasp (at)', Lett. *gribēt* 'wish' (fr. 'grasp at'), IE **ghreib*-. Walde-P. 1.647. Falk-Torp 346. Feist 221.

ON *taka*, ME *take* 'seize, take', see 11.13.

OE *læccan*, ME *lache* (NE *latch*), perh. : Grk. Ion. λάζομαι 'take'. Walde-P. 2.707.

ME *sese*, NE *seize* fr. Fr. *saisir* (above, 2).

NE *grasp* : ME *graspe(n)* 'clutch (at)', for **grapsen* = LG *grapsen* 'grab, snatch' : Lett. *grābt*, etc. (below).

Du. *vatten*, MHG *vazzen*, NHG *fassen* : OHG *fazzōn* 'pack together, inclose', deriv. of OHG *faz* 'vessel', NHG *fass* 'cask, tub', etc. Weigand-H. 1.504.

5. Lith. *nutverti*, Lett. *tvert* : Lett. *turēt* 'hold', Lith. *turėti* 'have', etc. (11.11).

Lith. *griebti* : Goth. *greipan*, etc. (above, 4).

Lett. *grābt* : Lith. *grobti* 'snatch, rob', ChSl. *grabiti* 'snatch away, carry off', SCr. *zgrabiti* 'seize, snatch up', etc., Skt. *grabh*-, *grah*-, Av., OPers. *grab*- 'seize,

take', Sw. *grabba*, NE *grab* 'seize hastily', etc., IE **ghrebh*-. Walde-P. 2.652 f. Berneker 344.

Lett. *k'ert*, prob. for **kart* (in *aizkart* 'touch, stir') by a blend with *tvert* (above), etym. dub. Perh. : Russ.-ChSl. *črěnŭ* 'handle', W. *carn* id., Skt. *karṇa*- 'ear, handle'. Walde-P. 1.412. Mühl.-Endz. 2.369 f.

6. ChSl. *jęti* 'seize, take', see 11.13.

ChSl. *chvatiti*, *chvatati*, SCr. *uhvatiti*, Boh. *uchvatiti*, *chytiti*, Pol. *uchwycić*, Russ. *chvatat'*, etym.? Berneker 407, 414. Brückner 188.

Boh. *uchopiti*, Pol. *pochopić*, etc., other Slavic words for 'snatch, clutch', prob. sound imitative for quick clutching motion. Berneker 396. Brückner 182.

7. Skt. *grabh*-, *grah*-, Av., OPers. *grab*- : Lett. *grābt*, etc. (above, 5).

Skt. *rabh*-, *labh*- prob. : Grk. λαμβάνω (11.13).

11.15 HOLD

Grk.	ἔχω	Goth.	*haban*	Lith.	*laikyti*
NG	κρατῶ, βαστῶ	ON	*halda (hafa)*	Lett.	*turēt*
Lat.	*tenēre*	Dan.	*holde*	ChSl.	*drŭžati*
It.	*tenere*	Sw.	*hålla*	SCr.	*držati*
Fr.	*tenir*	OE	*healdan (habban)*	Boh.	*držeti*
Sp.	*tener*	ME	*holde*	Pol.	*trzymać*
Rum.	*ţine*	NE	*hold*	Russ.	*deržat'*
Ir.	*congaibim*	Du.	*houden*	Skt.	*dhṛ-*
NIr.	*congbhaim*	OHG	*habēn (haltan)*	Av.	*dar-, drag-, hap-*
W.	*dal*	MHG	*haben, halten*		
Br.	*derc'hel*	NHG	*halten*		

Several of the verbs for 'hold' are the same as those for the weaker 'have' (11.11). But there are other, and diverse, connections.

1. Grk. ἔχω 'hold, have', see 11.11.

Grk. κρατέω 'be strong, rule, be master of' (: κράτος 'strength'), hence also 'take hold of' and 'hold' (both senses in NT, etc.), NG κρατῶ 'hold'.

NG βαστῶ 'carry' (10.61) also 'hold'.

2. Lat. *tenēre* (> Romance words) : *tendere*, Skt. *tan*-, etc. 'stretch' (9.32). Semantic development prob. through 'extend, last, hold out'. Walde-P. 1.722 f. Ernout-M. 1028.

3. Ir. *congaibim*, NIr. *congbhaim*, cpds. of *gaibim* 'take' (11.13).

W. *dal*, *dala*, Br. *derc'hel* (for **delc'hel*, cf. pple. *dalc'het*) : Goth. *tulgus* 'firm', OS *tulgo* 'very', Grk. δολιχός, Skt. *dīrgha*-, etc. 'long' (12.57). (Cf. NHG *gelangen* 'reach, attain' : *lang* 'long', and NE *long for*.) Walde-P. 1.813. Pedersen 1.106.

4. Goth. *haban*, ON *hafa* (as *hafa ā hǫndum*), OE *habban* (*habban be honda*), OHG *habēn*, MHG *haben*, also the regular Gmc. words for 'have' (11.11).

ON *halda*, OE *healdan*, also 'keep, guard, pasture cattle', Dan. *holde*, Sw. *hålla*, ME *holde*, NE *hold*, Du. *houden*, MHG, NHG *halten*, but OHG *haltan* 'keep, guard, observe, pasture', Goth. *haldan* 'pasture', prob. the more orig. meaning : Skt. *kālaya*- 'drive', Grk. κέλλω 'drive (a ship onto land), land', etc. Walde-P. 1.443. Falk-Torp 415. Feist 239 f.

5. Lith. *laikyti*, cf. OPruss. *lāiku* 'they hold', *laikut* 'perform', caus. of Lith. *likti* 'be left, remain' ('hold' as 'cause to stay') : Grk. λείπω, Lat. *linquere* 'leave', etc. Walde-P. 2.397.

Lett. *turēt* : Lith. *turėti* 'have, possess' (11.11).

6. ChSl. *drŭžati*, SCr. *držati*, Boh. *držeti* (Pol. *dzierżeć*, obs.), Russ. *deržat'* : Av. *drag*- (3sg. mid. *dražaite* 'hold, have along, lead', *drang*- 'strengthen, make firm', fr. **dhergh*-, **dhregh*-, beside **dherĝh*- in Skt. *dṛh*-, Av. *darez* 'make fast, bind', prob. extensions of IE **dher*- in Skt. *dhṛ*- 'hold, bear, support', Av. *dar*- 'hold, hold fast, retain', etc. Walde-P. 1.856 ff. (807). Berneker 258. Barth. 771 f.

Pol. *trzymać* (replaces the older *dzierżeć*), etym.? Brückner 583.

7. Skt. *dhṛ*-, Av. *dar*-, *drag*-, above, 6.

Av. *hap*- 'hold (in the hand), support' : Skt. *sap*- 'seek after, follow, honor, serve', Grk. ἀμφι-έπω 'be busy with', etc. Walde-P. 2.487. Barth. 1.764.

11.16 GET, OBTAIN

Grk.	κτάομαι	Goth.	*gastaldan*	Lith.	*gauti*
NG	ἀποκτῶ (παίρνω)	ON	*fā, geta*	Lett.	*dabūt*
Lat.	*nancisci, adipisci, parāre*	Dan.	*faa*	ChSl.	*polučiti*
		Sw.	*få*	SCr.	*dobiti*
It.	*ottenere*	OE	*begietan*	Boh.	*dostati, dobyti*
Fr.	*obtenir*	ME	*gete, obteine*	Pol.	*dostać*
Sp.	*obtener, conseguir*	NE	*get, obtain*	Russ.	*polučit', dostat', dobyt'*
Rum.	*căpăta, obţine*	Du.	*krijgen, bekomen*	Skt.	*āp-*
Ir.	*adcota* (3sg.)	OHG	*(bi)gezan*	Av.	*fra-ap-*
NIr.	*faghaim*	MHG	*(er)krīgen (bekommen)*		
W.	*caffael, cael*				
Br.	*kavout*	NHG	*kriegen, bekommen*		

Few verbs in any language show such a variety of idiomatic uses as NE *get*. But it is understood here in its primary sense of 'obtain'. Many of the words listed correspond more nearly in feeling to NE *obtain* than to *get*, to which perhaps the nearest approach is the colloquial NHG *kriegen*.

Besides the words listed as the most important, 'get' is often expressed by the words for 'take', sometimes also by those for 'gain' (Fr. *gagner*, Sp. *ganar*, etc.), 'find', etc. Not included are several words in which the implication of special effort (orig. common to many others for 'obtain') is still dominant, though sometimes ignored (cf. NED s.v. *acquire*), as Sp. *adquirir*, Fr. *acquérir*, NE *acquire* (derivs. of Lat. *quaerere* 'seek'), NHG *erwerben* (: *werben* 'turn, be busy with, seek to obtain'), *erlangen* (MHG 'reach, attain' : *lang* 'long'), Fr. *procurer*, NE *procure* (fr. Lat. *prōcūrāre* 'care for, attend to'), and many other possible substitutes which would swell the list.

The main words are from such notions as 'have, seize, hold, possess, come to, reach, attain, strive for', etc.

1. Grk. κτάομαι, NG ἀποκτῶ, cf. Grk. κέκτημαι 'own, possess' (11.12).

Grk. τυγχάνω 'happen, hit on' (9.993) is sometimes simply 'get'.

NG παίρνω 'take' (11.13) is also frequently equivalent to NE *get* in certain uses.

2. Lat. *nancīscī*, inchoative of an obs. *nancīre*, *nancī* (Gramm.) : Skt. *naç*-, Av. *nas*- 'reach', Grk. aor. ἤνεγκα 'carry', etc. Walde-P. 1.128 f. Ernout-M. 652.

Lat. *adipīscī*, cpd. of *apīscī* 'reach, attain, get' (rare but class.), inchoative to *apere* 'fasten, join' : Skt. *āp*- 'attain, get', Av. *ap*- 'reach', cpd. *fra-ap*- 'reach' and rarely 'get', Hitt. *ēp*-, *app*- 'take' (Sturtevant, Hitt. Gloss. 35). Walde-P. 1.46. Ernout-M. 60 f. Walde-H. 1.57 f.

Lat. *parāre*, commonly 'prepare' but

also frequently and classical 'strive after, get', whence 'get with money, buy', prob. : Lat. *parere* 'give birth, bear' (perh. orig. 'produce'), Lith. *perėti* 'brood, hatch', etc. Walde-P. 2.41. Ernout-M. 734 f.

It. *ottenere*, Fr. *obtenir*, Sp. *obtener*, Rum. *obține*, all late borrowings fr. Lat. *obtinēre* 'get hold of, get possession of, acquire', cpd. of *tenēre* 'hold' (11.15).

Sp. *conseguir* (= It. *conseguire* 'reach'), fr. Lat. *cōnsequī* (VLat. *-sequere*) 'follow up, reach'.

Rum. *căpăta* (= It. *capitare* 'arrive'), fr. VLat. **capitāre*, deriv. (beside *captāre*) of *capere* 'take' (11.13). REW 1635.

3. Ir. *ad-cota* (3sg.), cpd. of *ad-* (pretonic for *en-*) *com-ta* fr. the IE root **stā-* 'stand'. Cf. Lat. *praestināre* 'buy', Arm. *stanam* 'acquire, earn'. Pedersen 2.638 f. Thurneysen, Gram. 351, 420.

NIr. *faghaim* for *faghbhaim* : Ir. *fogabim, fogbaim* 'find', cpd. of *gaibim* 'take, seize' (11.14). Pedersen 2.528.

W. *caffael, cael*, Br. *kavout* (also 'find') : Ir. *gaibim* 'take, seize', perh. by a blend with the root of Lat. *capere*, etc. Walde-P. 1.345. Pedersen 1.187, 2.532.

4. Goth. *gastaldan* 'possess' (11.12), also 'get, acquire' (*gastaistald* = ἐκτησάμην Neh. 5.16).

ON *fá* 'get, seize', Dan. *faa*, Sw. *få* : Goth. *fahan* 'seize' (11.14).

ON *geta* (but not the chief use of the word, cf. Vigfusson and Fritzner s.v.), OE *begietan*, ME *gete*, NE *get*, OHG *bigezzan* : Goth. *bigitan* 'find', OS *bigetan* 'seize', Lat. *prehendere* 'seize', etc. (11.14). Walde-P. 1.589. Falk-Torp 308. NED s.v. *get*, vb.

ME *obteine*, NE *obtain*, fr. Fr. *obtenir* (above, 2).

Du. *krijgen*, MHG (central) *krīgen*, *erkrīgen* 'strive for, acquire, get', hence NHG *kriegen* (now regarded as vulgar vs. *bekommen*, but everywhere heard), deriv. of MDu. *crijch*, MHG *kriec*, (central) *krīc, krīg* 'exertion, endeavor, enmity, conflict' (NHG *krieg* 'war'), outside connections dub. Weigand-H. 1.1151 f. Franck-v. W. 349 f. Paul, Deutsches Wtb. 302.

Du. *bekomen*, NHG *bekommen* : MHG *bekommen* 'arrive at, reach' with gen. 'acquire, win', OHG *biqueman* 'come up to, reach, etc.' = Goth. *biqiman* 'come upon', cpd. of *qiman*, OHG *queman*, etc. 'come'.

5. Lith. *gauti*, Lett. *gūt, gaut* (Lett. mostly 'catch, try to get', but locally 'get') : Av. *gūnaoiti* 'promotes', *gaona-* 'profit'. Mühl.-Endz. 1.687. Walde-P. 1.637.

Lett. *dabūt*, fr. Russ. *dobyt'* (below).

6. SCr. *dobiti*, Boh. *dobyti*, Russ. *dobyt'*, cpd. of *do-* 'until, up to' and *byti* 'be', with semantic development 'be up to' > 'reach, attain' > 'obtain', as in, and perh. influenced by, NHG *bekommen*.

Boh. *dostati*, Pol. *dostać*, Russ. *dostat'*, cpd. of *do-* and *stati* 'stand', semantic development as in preceding.

ChSl. *polučiti*, Russ. *polučit'* (SCr. *polučiti* 'attain, acquire'), cpd. of ChSl. *lučiti*, refl. *lučiti sę* 'happen, must', in Supr. 'hit, touch' (in modern Slavic often also 'aim, throw'), prob. : Skt. *lok-* 'see, behold, look at', Grk. λεύσσω 'see', etc., IE **leuk-*. Semantic development through 'reach, hit' fr. 'take aim, see'. Walde-P. 2.411. Berneker 742 f.

7. Skt. *āp-*, Av. *fra-ap-* : Lat. *adipīscī* (above, 2).

11.17 KEEP, RETAIN

Grk.	ἔχω	Goth.	*(ga)fastan*	Lith.	*išlaikyti*
NG	κρατῶ	ON	*halda*	Lett.	*paturēt*
Lat.	*tenēre*	Dan.	*beholde*	ChSl.	*drŭžati*
It.	*ritenere*	Sw.	*behålla*	SCr.	*(za)držati*
Fr.	*garder, retenir*	OE	*(ge)healdan*	Boh.	*držeti*
Sp.	*retener, guardar*	ME	*holde, kepe*	Pol.	*(za)trzymać*
Rum.	*ține*	NE	*keep, retain*	Russ.	*deržat'*
Ir.	*congaibim*	Du.	*behouden*	Skt.	*dhṛ-*
NIr.	*congbhaim*	OHG	*(gi)haltan, bihaltan*	Av.	*(dar-)*
W.	*cadw*	MHG	*behalten*		
Br.	*mirout*	NHG	*behalten*		

'Keep, retain' is for the most part expressed by words for 'hold' (11.15), or by compounds of these, e.g. Fr. *retenir* (> ME *reteyne*, NE *retain*), NHG *behalten*, Lith. *išlaikyti*, etc. Or words for 'preserve (from harm), keep safe' (11.24) are also used in the weakened sense of 'retain', as Fr. *garder*, W. *cadw*, etc. (and so sometimes NE *preserve*), and to this group belongs NE *keep* in which 'retain' is now the leading sense. Thus all the words listed belong with those discussed in 11.15 or 11.24.

11.21 GIVE

Grk.	δίδωμι	Goth.	*giban*	Lith.	*duoti*
NG	δίνω, δίδω	ON	*gefa*	Lett.	*duot*
Lat.	*dare*	Dan.	*give*	ChSl.	*dati*
It.	*dare, donāre*	Sw.	*giva*	SCr.	*dati*
Fr.	*donner*	OE	*giefan*	Boh.	*dáti*
Sp.	*dar*	ME	*give*	Pol.	*dać*
Rum.	*da*	NE	*give*	Russ.	*dat'*
Ir.	*do-biur*	Du.	*geven*	Skt.	*dā-, rā-*
NIr.	*tugaim, tabhraim*	OHG	*geban*	Av.	*dā-*
W.	*rhoi, rhoddi*	MHG	*geban*		
Br.	*rei*	NHG	*geben*		

Except in Celtic and Germanic, the words for 'give' belong to an inherited group.

1. IE **dō-*. Walde-P. 1.814 ff. Ernout-M. 274 ff. Walde-H. 1.360 ff.

Grk. δίδωμι, aor. ἔδωκα, NG δίδω and δίνω (blend of δίδω and δώνω, latter formed to aor. ἔδωσα; Hatzidakis, Einl. 408, note 1); Lat. *dare* (> It. *dare*, Sp. *dar*, Rum. *da;* Fr. *donner*, It. *donare* fr. Lat. *dōnāre* 'present, give as a gift', denom. of *dōnum* 'gift'), perf. *dedī*, Osc. *deded*, Umbr. *dede* 'dedit', Umbr. *dirsa* 'det', etc.; Lith. *duoti*, Lett. *duot;* ChSl. *dati*, etc., general Slavic; Skt., Av. *dā-;* Arm. *tam;* Alb. *dhanë;* Hitt. *dā-* 'take' (Sturtevant, Hitt. Gloss. 146 with refs.). Possibly here also W. *rhoi, rhoddi*, Br. *rei*, fr. **pro-d-*, cf. Ir. *do-rat* 'gave' (suppl. verb to *do-biur*, below) fr. **to-pro-d-* as also W. *dyry* imperat. 'give!', etc. Pedersen 2.380, 473.

There are also forms pointing to an extension **dōu-*, as OLat. subj. *duim, duam*, Umbr. *purdovitu* 'porricito', Cypr. opt. δυϝάνοι, Lith. *dovana* 'gift', etc.

2. Ir. *do-biur* 'give, bring', NIr. *dobheirim*, but commonly dependent *tabhraim*, cpd. of Ir. *berim* 'carry, bring' (10.61).

NIr. *tugaim*, generalized fr. the pret. 3sg. *tug*, Ir. *duic, tuic, tuc* 'brought', fr.

**to-ucc-*, etym. dub. See under Ir. *roucc-*, 10.61.

3. Goth. *giban*, etc., general Gmc., prob. : Lat. *habēre* 'have', Ir. *gaibim* 'take, seize' (11.13), despite the semantic polarity, for which there are some parallels. Thus Ir. *gaibim* 'take, seize' and ON *fá* 'seize, get' (11.14) are sometimes used in the sense of 'give', likewise ME *take* (NED s.v. 60), and Hitt. *dā-* 'take' = IE **dō-* 'give' (see above, 1). The relation is perh. explained by the common notion of stretching out the hands, hence 'take' or 'hand over, give'. Walde-P. 1.344. Falk-Torp 312. Kretschmer, Glotta 19.207. See also refs. under Goth. *niman* 'take' (11.13).

4. Skt. *rā-* (Av. *rā-* 'grant') : *rās* 'goods, riches', *rāyi-* 'gift, jewel', Lat. *rēs* 'thing' (early also 'property'). Walde-P. 2.343. Ernout-M. 861 f.

11.22 GIVE BACK, RETURN

Grk.	ἀποδίδωμι	Goth.	*atgiban*	Lith.	*atiduoti, atgrąžinti*
NG	ἐπιστρέφω, ἀποδίδω	ON	*gefa aptr*	Lett.	*atduot*
Lat.	*reddere (restituere)*	Dan.	*give tilbage*	ChSl.	*vŭ-, vŭz-, otŭ-dati*
It.	*restituire, rendere*	Sw.	*giva tilbaka, återgiva*	SCr.	*vratiti*
Fr.	*rendre, restituer*	OE	*agiefan, edgiefan*	Boh.	*vrátiti*
Sp.	*restituir, devolver*	ME	*gife again, restore*	Pol.	*wrócić, oddać*
Rum.	*înapoia*	NE	*give back, return*	Russ.	*otdat', vozvraščat'*
Ir.	*aisicim*	Du.	*teruggeven*	Skt.	*prati-dā-*
NIr.	*tabhraim, aisigim*	OHG	*argeban*	Av.	. . . .
W.	*rhoi*	MHG	*widergeben*		
Br.	*rei*	NHG	*zurückgeben*		

For the most part 'give back' is expressed as in English by the words for 'give' with prefixes or adverbs meaning 'again, back, etc.', or by the terms equivalent to the English 'return'.

1. Words belonging with verbs for 'give' (11.21). Grk. ἀποδίδωμι (ἀπο- 'from', but also 'back again'), NG ἀποδίδω; Lat. *reddere* (whence after *prendere* 'take' VLat. **rendere* > It. *rendere*, Fr. *rendre*, Sp. *rendir*); Goth. *at-giban*, etc., all the native Gmc. words and phrases; Lith. *atiduoti*, Lett. *atduot;* ChSl. *vŭdati, vŭzdati, otŭdati*, Pol. *oddać*, Russ. *otdat'*; Skt. *prati-dā-*. In the modern Celtic languages there is usually no distinction between 'give' and 'give back'. So NIr. *tabhraim* (also with *tar n-ais* 'back'), W. *rhoi*, Br. *rei*.

2. Words belonging with verbs for 'turn' (10.13). NG ἐπιστρέφω, γυρίζω; Sp. *devolver;* NE *return;* Lith. *atgrąžinti* (: *grę̃žti* 'bore', Lett. *griezt* 'turn'); SCr. *vratiti*, Boh. *vrátiti*, Pol. *wrócić*, Russ. *vozvraščat'* (ChSl. loanword).

3. Lat. *restituere* 'replace, restore' (11.23), also 'return', as It. *restituire*, Fr. *restituer*, Sp. *restituir*.

Rum. *înapoia*, fr. *înapoi* 'back, behind' (fr. *apoi* 'after, next').

4. Ir. *aisicim, aiscim* (K. Meyer, Contrib. 69. Laws, Gloss. 45 f.), NIr. *aisigim* (McKenna), *aiseagaim* (Dinneen), deriv. (cpd.?) of *ais* 'back'.

5. ME, NE *restore*, also 'bring back to a previous (or original) condition', now the usual sense (11.23).

11.23 RESTORE

Grk.	ἀποκαθίστημι, ἐπανορθόω	Goth.	*aftra gasatjan, aftra gabōtjan*	Lith.	*atitaisyti, atstatyti*
NG	ἐπιδιορθώνω, ἀποκαθιστῶ	ON	*endrbœta, endrreisa*	Lett.	*atjaunuot, atkal sataisīt*
Lat.	*restituere, reficere, restaurāre*	Dan.	*genoprette*	ChSl.	*ustrojiti, utvoriti, utvrŭditi*
It.	*restaurare, ristabilire*	Sw.	*återställa*	SCr.	*uspostaviti, obnoviti*
Fr.	*restaurer, rétablir*	OE	*geednīwian, geedstaþelian*	Boh.	*znovu zříditi, obnoviti*
Sp.	*restaurar, restablecer*	ME	*restore*	Pol.	*przywrócić, naprawić*
Rum.	*restaura, restabili*	NE	*restore*	Russ.	*vozstanovit', vozobnovit'*
Ir.	*aisicim*	Du.	*weerherstellen*	Skt.	*prati-sam-ā-dhā-*
NIr.	*aisigim*	OHG	*arsezzen*	Av.	. . . .
W.	*adfer*	MHG	*widermachen*		
Br.	*adsevel*	NHG	*wiederherstellen*		

Words for 'restore' are from 'set in place', 'make straight', 'make firm', 'renew', 'raise, erect', 'make better', etc.

1. Grk. ἀποκαθίστημι, NG lit. ἀποκαθιστῶ, cpds. of ἀπό, in same use as in ἀποδίδωμι 'give back' (11.22), and καθίστημι 'set in order, arrange', NG καθιστῶ 'establish', cpd. of Grk. ἵστημι 'make stand'.

Grk. ἐπανορθόω, NG ἐπανορθώνω, ἐπιδιορθώνω, cpds. of Grk. ὀρθόω 'set straight, right' deriv. of ὀρθός, straight'), NG ὀρθώνω, ὀρθῶ 'erect, straighten'.

2. Lat. *restituere*, orig. 'replace', fr. *statuere* 'set up' : *stāre* 'stand'. Ernout-M. 981.

Lat. *reficere*, fr. *facere* 'make, do'.

Lat. *restaurāre*, beside older *instaurāre* 'restore, renew, repeat', prob. (as denom. of a **stauro-*) : Grk. σταυρός, ON *staurr* 'stake', etc. Walde-P. 2.608. Ernout-M. 490 f. (no etym.).

Hence (lit. words) It. *restaurare*, Fr. *restaurer*, Sp. *restaurar*, Rum. *restaura*. REW 7249.

It. *ristabilire*, Fr. *rétablir*, Sp. *restablecer*, Rum. *restabili*, cpds. of It. *stabilire*, Fr. *établir*, Sp. *establecer*, Rum. *stabili*, fr. Lat. *stabilīre* 'make firm, fix, establish'. REW 8702.

3. Ir. *aisicim*, NIr. *aisigim*, but mostly 'restore' = 'give back', see 11.22.

W. *adfer*, cpd. of *ad-* and the root seen in Ir. *berim* 'carry'. Morris Jones 332.

Br. *adsevel*, cpd. of *ad-* and *sevel* 'lift (10.22).

4. Goth. *aftra gasatjan* (*aftra gasatiþs warþ* = ἀποκατεστάθη Mk. 8.25), lit. 'set again'.

Goth. *aftra gabōtjan* (*aftra gabōteiþ* = ἀποκαθιστᾷ Mk. 9.12), lit. 'better again'.

ON *endrbœta, endrreisa*, cpds. of *endr* 'again' with *bœta* 'better, mend' (: Goth. *bōtjan*) and *reisa* 'raise, erect, build'.

Dan. *genoprette*, lit. 'erect again'.

Sw. *återställa*, lit. 'set (up) again'.

OE *ge-ednīwian*, fr. *nīwe* 'new', with prefix *ed-* 're-'.

OE *ge-edstaþelian*, fr. *staþol* (*staþel*) 'foundation, fixed condition or position'.

ME, NE *restore* fr. OF *restorer*, Lat. *restaurāre* (above, 2).

Du. *weerherstellen*, NHG *wiederherstellen*, lit. 'set in place again'.

OHG *ir-* (or *ar-*) *sezzen* ('restore', Otfr., Tat.; NHG *ersetzen* 'make good, replace'), cpd. of *sezzen* 'set'.

MHG *widermachen*, lit. 'make again'.

5. Lith. *atstatyti*, lit. 'set (up) again'.

Lith. *atitaisyti*, cpd. of *taisyti* 'mend, repair' (: *tiesus* 'straight', etc., 12.73).

Lett. *atjaunuot*, lit. 'make young again, renew' (: *jauns* 'young').

Lett. *atkal sataisīt* (so in NT), lit. 'make, prepare again' (*atkal* 'again', 14.35).

6. ChSl. *ustrojiti* (*ustrojitŭ* = ἀποκα-

ταστήσει Mt. 17.11, *ἀποκαθιστᾷ* Mk. 9.12), also 'prepare, bring into order', cpd. of *strojiti* 'prepare, arrange'.

ChSl. *utvoriti* (*utvori sę* = *ἀποκατεστάθη* Mk. 8.25), cpd. of *tvoriti* 'make'.

ChSl. *utvrŭditi* (*utvrŭdi sę ἀποκατεστάθη* Mt. 12.13, Mk. 3.5, Lk. 6.10), also 'make firm, strengthen', cpd. of *tvrŭditi* id. (: *tvrŭdŭ* 'firm', etc.).

SCr. *uspostaviti*, Russ. *vozstanovit'*, lit. 'make stand up again'.

SCr., Boh. *obnoviti*, Russ. *vozobnovit'* lit. 'renew' (ChSl. *novŭ*, etc. 'new').

Boh. *znovu zříditi*, lit. 'establish, arrange anew' (*říditi* : ChSl. *rędŭ* 'arrangement').

Pol. *przywrócić*, lit. 'replace, put (back again)', cpd. of *wrócić* 'replace, give back' (11.22).

Pol. *naprawić*, lit. 'set right, repair', fr. *naprawa* 'betterment', cpd. of *prawy* 'right'.

7. Skt. *prati-sam-ā-dhā-* lit. 'put back together again', cpd. of *dhā-* 'place, put'.

11.24 PRESERVE, KEEP SAFE, SAVE

Grk.	*φυλάσσω, σώζω*	Goth.	*bairgan, (ga)fastan*	Lith.	*(ap)saugoti*
NG	*φυλάω, σώνω (σώζω)*	ON	*bjarga*	Lett.	*sargāt, glabāt*
Lat.	*(cōn)servāre, custōdīre*	Dan.	*bevare, bjærge*	ChSl.	*chraniti*
It.	*conservare*	Sw.	*bevara*	SCr.	*čuvati*
Fr.	*garder, conserver*	OE	*beorgan, healdan*	Boh.	*chovati, chraniti*
Sp.	*guardar, conservar*	ME	*kepe, berwe, save, preserve*	Pol.	*chować*
Rum.	*păstra*			Russ.	*chranit'*
Ir.	*conōim, comētaim*	NE	*preserve, save (keep)*	Skt.	*rakṣ-*
NIr.	*coimhēadaim*	Du.	*bewaren*	Av.	*θrā-*
W.	*cadw*	OHG	*biwarōn, bergan, haltan*		
Br.	*mirout*				
		MHG	*bewarn, bergen*		
		NHG	*bewahren*		

Words for 'preserve' are mostly connected with those for 'guard, watch, protect', etc. Some derivatives of words for 'safe' are used for 'keep safe, preserve' as well as for 'save, rescue' (11.25), and in some other words also the two groups overlap.

1. Grk. *φυλάσσω*, NG *φυλάω*, properly 'watch over, guard' (and so mostly in Hom., but Il. 16.30 'cherish' wrath, and Od. 5.208 'keep' i.e. 'remain in' the house), hence also 'preserve', fr. *φύλαξ* 'guard, watchman', etym.? Walde-P. 2.192.

Grk. *σώζω*, aor. *ἔσωσα*, Hom. *ἐσάωσα*, NG *σώνω*, used for 'save' both as 'keep safe, preserve' and 'rescue', fr. *σάος, σῶς* 'safe' (11.26).

2. Lat. *servāre*, whether or not a denom. of *servus* 'slave' in a supposed orig. sense 'guardian' (disputed, see 19.42), is clearly cognate with Av. *pasuš-haurva-* 'guarding the flock', *viš-haurva-* 'guarding the village', *nišhaurvaiti* 'watches over', IE **serw-*, extension of **ser-* in Av. *har-* 'give attention to, watch over', *harətar-* 'watcher'. Walde-P. 2.498 f. Ernout-M. 933.

Hence Lat. *cōnservāre*, with the literary borrowings, It. *conservare*, Fr. *conserver* (> NE *conserve*), Sp. *conservar*, also Fr. *préserver* (> ME, NE *preserve* now more common in this sense than the Fr.), etc.

Lat. *custōdīre*, orig. 'watch, guard' then, like Grk. *φυλάσσω*, also 'preserve, maintain, keep', fr. *custōs, -ōdis* 'watchman, guard' etym.? Walde-P. 2.551. Ernout-M. 248 f. Walde-H. 1.319.

Fr. *garder*, Sp. *guardar*, also 'guard', fr. 'observe, watch' (as It. *guardare*), fr. the Gmc., cf. OS *wardōn* 'care for, be on the watch', OE *weardian* 'guard, defend', OHG *wartēn* 'watch, wait for', etc. REW 9502.

Rum. *păstra* (cf. Bulg. *pastrja* id.), fr. NG *παστρεύω* 'cleanse', *πάστρα* 'cleanliness' (see 15.87), with easy sequence 'cleanse' to 'preserve'. Tiktin 1131.

3. Ir. *con-ōim* (K. Meyer, Contrib. 478) : W. *ewyllys*, Corn. *awell* 'desire', Lat. *avēre* 'desire greatly, be greedy', Skt. *av-* 'urge, favor, help'. Walde-P. 1.19. Walde-H. 1.81. Pedersen 2.586 f.

Ir. *comētaim*, NIr. *coimhēadaim*, fr. Ir. *comēt* 'servatio', vbl. n. of *com-em-* 'protect' (pret. 3pl. *comroitatar*), root *em-* also in *air-fo-emim* 'take', etc. (11.13). Ir. *comēt* serves also as vbl. n. for *con-ōim* (above). Pedersen 2.511 f., 586.

W. *cadw*, perh. : W. *cader* 'fort, stronghold', Ir. *cathir* 'city', OE *heaþorian* 'restrain', etc. G. S. Lane, Language 8.295 f. Otherwise (: W. *cad* 'troop, battle', Ir. *cath* 'battle', etc.) Loth, RC 42.84.

Br. *mirout*, also 'observe, keep' (a commandment, festival, etc.) = Corn. *miras* 'look at, observe', fr. Lat. *mīrāre* 'wonder at'. Loth, Mots lat. 188.

4. Goth. *bairgan*, ON *bjarga*, Dan. *bjærge*, OE *beorgan*, ME *berwe*, OHG *bergan*, MHG *bergen* (NHG rare in this sense) : ChSl. *brěga, brěšti* 'care for', Russ. *berec'* 'take care of, look after', etc., IE **bhergh-*. Walde-P. 2.172. Feist 76. Berneker 49.

Goth. *(ga)fastan* 'keep, watch, guard' (also to 'fast') : OE *fæstan*, ON *fasta*, OHG *fastōn, fastēn* 'make fast, fast', etc., fr. ON *fæst*, ON *fastr*, etc. 'fast, firm' : Arm. *hast* id., Skt. *pastya-* 'homestead' (i.e. 'fixed dwelling place'), IE **pasto-*. Walde-P. 2.7. Feist 143.

OE *healdan*, OHG *haltan* in both senses 'keep, preserve', showing the more orig. sense of the general Gmc. group for 'hold' (see 11.15).

ME *kepe*, mostly 'preserve, observe', NE *keep* with older sense in many phrases (*keep silence, keep guard*), but most commonly merely 'retain', fr. late OE *cēpan* 'watch, observe, regard' also 'take', orig. and history difficult, perh. : ON *kōpa* 'stare, gape'. Walde-P. 1.530. NED s.v. *keep*, vb.

ME, NE *save*, both 'keep safe, preserve' and 'rescue', see 11.25.

Du. *bewaren*, MLG *bewaren* (> Dan. *bevare*, Sw. *bevara*), OHG *biwarōn*, MHG *bewarn*, NHG *bewahren*, less usual also as simplex OHG *warēn*, MHG *warn*, NHG *wahren* = OE *warian* 'beware, warn, guard', ON *vara* 'warn, beware' : Grk. *ὁράω* 'see', Lat. *verērī* 'be anxious, fear', Lett. *vērt* 'look at, notice', IE **wer-*. Walde-P. 1.284 f.

5. Lith. *(ap)saugoti* 'watch, guard, keep', cf. *saugus* 'careful, cautious', etym. dub. The Gmc. group, Goth. *siuks*, etc. 'sick', if cognate (as Walde-P. 2.247 f.), has secondary meaning.

Lett. *sargāt* : Lith. *sergėti* 'watch, guard', *sargas* 'watcher', etc., prob. fr. a guttural extension of the root **ser-* in Av. *har-*, Lat. *servāre*, etc. (above, 2). Walde-P. 2.499.

Lett. *glabāt* : Lith. *glaboti* 'put away', Lett. *glābt, glēbt* 'save, help', Lith. *glebti* 'clasp, embrace', SCr. *globiti* 'lay together, join', etc., OE *clyppan* 'embrace', OHG *klāftra* 'measure of the outstretched arms', etc., perh. fr. a root meaning 'press, squeeze, put together' or the like. Walde-P. 1.616. Berneker 305.

6. ChSl. *chraniti*, Boh. *chraniti*, Russ. *chranit'*, perh. fr. the root **ser-* in Av. *har-*, Lat. *servāre*, etc. (above, 2). Walde-P. 2.498. Berneker 397 f.

SCr. *čuvati*, orig. iter. to *čuti* 'hear, feel', ChSl. *čuti*, etc. 'feel, notice' : Grk. *κοέω* 'notice', Lat. *cavēre* 'take care, watch over', OHG *scouwēn* 'regard', Skt. *kavi-* 'wise, seer', etc., IE **(s)keu-*. Walde-P. 1.370. Berneker 162 f.

Boh. *chovati*, Pol. *chować*, etym. dub. Berneker 399 f. Brückner 183 (: ChSl. *čuti*, OHG *scouwēn*, etc., above).

7. Skt. *rakṣ-* 'protect, preserve, save' : Grk. *ἀλέξω* 'ward off, defend', OE *ealgian* 'protect, defend'. Walde-P. 1.89.

Av. *θrā-*, see 11.25.

11.25 SAVE, RESCUE

Grk.	*σώζω*	Goth.	*(ga)nasjan*	Lith.	*išgelbėti*
NG	*γλυτώνω, σώνω*	ON	*hjalpa, frjālsa*	Lett.	*glābt*
Lat.	*servāre, ēripere (salvāre)*	Dan.	*redde, frelse*	ChSl.	*sŭpasti*
		Sw.	*rädda, frälse*	SCr.	*spasti, izbaviti*
It.	*salvare*	OE	*nerian, hreddan*	Boh.	*zachraniti*
Fr.	*sauver*	ME	*save, redde, reskowe*	Pol.	*ratować, ocalić*
Sp.	*salvar*	NE	*save, rescue*	Russ.	*spasti, izbavit'*
Rum.	*mîntui, scăpa*	Du.	*redden*	Skt.	*tāraya-, trā-*
Ir.	*tessurc, sōirim*	OHG	*rettan, (ge)nerian*	Av.	*būǰ-, θrā-*
NIr.	*saoraim, fuasclaim, sābhālaim*	MHG	*retten, (ge)nern*		
		NHG	*retten*		
W.	*achub*				
Br.	*savetei, salvi*				

Words for 'save, rescue' are in part derivatives of those for 'safe', but come also from various notions like 'let loose, snatch away, set free'.

1. Grk. *σώζω*, see 11.24.

NG *γλυτώνω* = *ἐκλυτώνω*, fr. class. Grk. *ἐκλυτός* 'let loose, relaxed', vbl. adj. of *ἐκλύω* 'let loose, free'. Hatzidakis, Μεσ. 1.160.

2. Lat. *servāre*, see 11.24.

Lat. *ēripere*, cpd. of *rapere* 'snatch away, carry off' (11.14).

Late Lat. *salvāre* (> It. *salvare*, Fr. *sauver*, Sp. *salvar*) deriv. of *salvus* 'safe, well' (11.26).

Rum. *mîntuĭ*, prob. through the Slavic (cf. SCr. *mentovati*) fr. Hung. *mend* id. Tiktin 989.

Rum. *scăpa* (also intr. 'escape' = Fr. *échapper*, It. *scappare*, etc.), fr. VLat. *excappāre*, lit. 'un-cloak', deriv. of *cappa* 'cloak'. REW 2952. Puşcariu 1542.

3. Ir. *tessurc*, MIr. *tessargim* (NIr. *teasargaim* Dinneen), cpd. of *to-ess-* with *orgim* 'kill, injure' (4.76). Pedersen 2.588.

Ir. *sōirim*, NIr. *saoraim*, fr. Ir. *sōir*, NIr. *saor* 'free' (19.44).

NIr. *fuasclaim*, fr. OIr. *dufualsci* (3sg.) 'undoes, releases', cpd. of *to-od-ess-* with *lēicim* 'let, leave, let go' (: Lat. *linquere*, etc.). Pedersen 2.564 f.

NIr. *sābhālaim*, prob. fr. NE *save*. K. Meyer ap. Macbain 299.

W. *achub* (older sense 'occupy, seize' hence 'rescue, save'), fr. Lat. *occupāre* 'take possession of, occupy'. Loth, Mots lat. 130.

Br. *savetei* deriv. of *savete* 'safety, security', fr. OFr. *savété(t), salvété(t)*, etc. id. (Lat. *salvitās, -ātis*).

Br. *salvi* deriv. of *salo, salv* 'safe', fr. Lat. *salvus* (11.26). Loth, Mots lat. 204.

4. Goth. *(ga)nasjan*, OE *nerian*, OHG *(ge)nerian*, MHG *(ge)nern, nerigen* (NHG *nähren* 'nourish', and so largely also in the older language) = OFris. *nera* 'nourish', caus. to Goth. *ga-nisan*, OE *genesan*, OHG *ginesan*, etc. 'be saved, healed', prob. : Grk. *νέομαι* 'go, return (safely)', Skt. *nas-* 'approach, embrace'. Semantic development not clear, but perh. 'be saved' fr. 'escape, go safely'. Walde-P. 2.335. Feist 196.

ON *hjalpa* 'help, save' : Goth. *hilpan*, etc. 'help' (19.58).

ON *frjālsa*, Dan. *frelse*, Sw. *frälse*, fr. ON *frjāls* 'free' (19.44). Falk-Torp 272. Hellquist 242.

OE *hreddan*, ME *redde*, Du. *redden* (MLG *redden* > Dan. *redde*, Sw. *rädda*), OHG *rettan* (also 'drive, move'), MHG, NHG *retten*, perh. as 'save' fr. 'move, thrust aside' : Lith. *krėsti*, Ir. *crothaim* 'shake'. The OHG word would then preserve the more orig. meaning. Cf. the semantic development of NE *rescue* (below). Walde-P. 1.484. Falk-Torp 885, 928.

ME, NE *save* fr. OFr. *salver, sauver* (above, 2).

ME *reskowe*, NE *rescue*, fr. OFr. *rescourre* 'to free', cpd. of *escourre* 'shake', fr. Lat. *ex-cutere* 'shake off'. NED s.v. REW 2998.

5. Lith. *išgelbėti*, also 'help' as usually the simple *gelbėti* (19.58).

Lett. *glābt* : *glabāt* 'preserve, lay up' (11.24).

6. ChSl. *sŭpasti*, SCr., Russ. *spasti*, perfect. cpd. of *pasti* 'pasture, tend (sheep)' : Lat. *pāscere* 'pasture, feed', etc. Walde-P. 2.72.

SCr. *izbaviti*, Russ. *izbavit'* = ChSl. *izbaviti* 'free, redeem', cpds. of *iz-* 'off, out' with caus. of Slav. *byti* 'become, be'. Berneker 46 f.

Boh. *zachraniti*, perfect. cpd. of *chraniti* 'preserve' (11.24).

Pol. *ratować*, cf. *rat, rata* 'rescue, help', loanword fr. NHG *retten* (above, 4). Brückner 454.

Pol. *ocalić*, fr. *cały* 'safe, whole' (11.26).

7. Skt. *tāraya-*, 'cause to cross' also 'rescue', caus. of *tṛ-* 'cross over', also 'escape', with Skt. *trā-*, Av. *θrā-* 'protect, save, rescue' : Lat. *trāns* 'across', *intrāre* 'enter', IE **ter(ə)-*, **trā-*, primary sense prob. 'cross, penetrate' or the like. Walde-P. 1.732 ff.

Av. *būǰ-, bunǰ-* 'loose, release, rescue', also *avi-būǰ-* 'rescue' (Barth. 916 f.), cf. NPers. *bōxtan* 'save, redeem' : Goth. *usbaugjan* 'sweep away', perh. also (**bheug-* beside **bheugh-*), Lat. *fungī* 'execute, perform, discharge', Skt. *bhuj-* 'enjoy'. Walde-P. 2.145. Ernout-M. 402. Walde-H. 1.566 (with separation of the two groups).

11.26 SAFE (adj.)

Grk.	*σῶς, ἀσφαλής*	Goth.	*(ga)hails (arniba, adv.)*	Lith.	*sveikas, čielas*
NG	*ἀσφαλής, σῶος*			Lett.	*druošs, vesels*
Lat.	*tūtus, salvus, sēcūrus*	ON	*ūhættr, heill*	ChSl.	*(sŭchranĭno, adv.), cělŭ*
It.	*salvo, sicuro*	Dan.	*sikker, tryg, uskadt*		
Fr.	*sauf (sûr)*	Sw.	*säker, trygg, oskadd*	SCr.	*siguran, čitav, cio*
Sp.	*salvo, seguro*	OE	*sicor, orsorg, hāl*	Boh.	*bezpečný, jistý, celý*
Rum.	*nevătămat, teafăr*	ME	*sauf, siker, sūre, hool, unharmed*	Pol.	*bezpieczny, cały, ocalony*
Ir.	*slān*				
NIr.	*sābhālta, slān*	NE	*safe, secure, unharmed*	Russ.	*bezopasnyj, celyj*
W.	*diogel, dianaf*			Skt.	*kṣema-, akṣata-*
Br.	*salo, diogel*	Du.	*veilig, zeker, onbeschadigd*	Av.	....
		OHG	*sichur, ursurgi, heil*		
		MHG	*sicher, heil, unversēret*		
		NHG	*sicher, unversehrt*		

Words for 'safe' as 'free from danger or harm' are of diverse sources. Several mean literally 'without care, anxiety' (hence first of persons who feel 'safe'), or 'without danger', 'without harm'. Many are words that mean primarily 'whole' or 'well, in good health' (4.83). Most of these are used for 'unharmed', but hardly for 'safe' as 'free from danger'. Other semantic sources are 'strong'(?), 'protected', 'true, trustworthy', 'unconcealed'.

Several words of this group come to mean also or mainly 'sure, certain' (17.37).

1. Grk. *σῶς*, *σῶος*, fr. *σάος* (cf. comp. *σαώτερος*), *σαϝος* (cf. Cypr. *Σαϝο-κλέϝης*), prob. fr. **twə-wo-* : Skt. *tāuti*, *tavīti* 'is strong, has power', Av. *tavah-* 'might, strength', etc. Walde-P. 1.706. Boisacq 852.

Grk. *ἀσφαλής*, lit. 'firm, solid, not liable to fall' neg. cpd. : *σφάλλω* 'cause to fall, overthrow', etym. dub. Walde-P. 2.599, 678. Boisacq 927.

2. Lat. *tūtus*, pple. (beside *tuitus*) of *tuērī* 'protect', also (poet.) 'look at, see', perh. : Ir. *tūath* 'left, north' (as orig. 'favorable'), Goth. *þiuþ* 'good', ON *þȳðr* 'mild, friendly', etc. Walde-P. 1.706. Otherwise Ernout-M. 1062 f. (as perh. : Skt. *tavīti* 'is strong', etc., above, 1).

Lat. *salvus* (> It., Sp. *salvo*, Fr. *sauf*) 'whole, unharmed, safe' : Skt. *sarva-* 'whole, all', Grk. *ὅλος* 'whole', etc. Walde-P. 2.510 f. Ernout-M. 891.

Lat. *sēcūrus* (> It. *sicuro*, OFr. *sure*, Fr. *sûr*, Sp. *seguro*), lit. 'without care', neg. cpd. of *cūra* 'care, concern, trouble', hence, but only later, 'safe'. Ernout-M. 246.

Rum. *nevătămat*, lit. 'not injured', neg. of pple. of *vătăma* 'injure, wound' (11.28).

Rum. *teafăr*, orig. ? Tiktin 1570.

3. Ir. *slān*, also 'well, in good health' (4.83).

NIr. *sābhālta*, pple. of *sābhālaim* 'save, rescue' (11.25).

W., Br. *diogel*, cpd. of prefixes *di-* (neg.), *o-* (= *go-*, cf. W. *di-o-ddef* : *go-deff* 'suffer') and the root seen in W. *celu* 'hide', *di-gelu* 'cease hiding, expose'. Cf. W. *digel* 'unconcealed, open'. Hence 'safe' because 'not hidden'.

W. *dianaf*, neg. cpd. of *anaf* 'blemish, defect, wound' : Ir. *anim* 'blemish, flaw', Grk. *ὄνομαι* 'scold, blame', etc. Pedersen 2.61. Walde-P. 1.180.

Br. *salo*, fr. Lat. *salvus* (above, 2). Loth, Mots lat. 204.

4. Goth. *hails*, *gahails*, ON *heill*, OE *hāl*, OHG, MHG *heil*, all also 'well, whole' (4.83).

ON *ūhœttr* (usually impers. as in *einhverjum er ūhœtt* 'it is safe for someone'), lit. 'not dangerous', neg. cpd. of *hœttr* 'dangerous' (*hœtta* 'danger', 16.54).

Goth. *arniba* adv. (renders *ἀσφαλῶς* Mk. 14.44) : ON *ern* 'brisk, vigorous', OE *eornost* 'zeal, earnestness', etc. perh. fr. the root in Skt. *ṛṇoti*, *ṛṇvati* 'arises, moves', Grk. *ὄρνῡμι* 'arouse, move', etc. Walde-P. 1.138. Feist 58.

OE *sicor*, ME *siker*, NE dial. *sicker*, OHG *sichur*, MHG, NHG *sicher*, MLG *seker* (> Dan. *sikker*, Sw. *säker*), Du. *zeker*, all fr. Lat. *sēcūrus* (above, 2). Falk-Torp 965. NED s.v. *sicker*.

Dan. *tryg*, Sw. *trygg* : ON *tryggr*, Goth. *triggws*, OE *trīewe*, OHG *gi-triuwi*, etc. 'true, trustworthy' (16.66). Falk-Torp 1290.

Dan. *uskadt*, Sw. *oskadd*, *oskadad*, neg. pple. of Dan. *skade*, Sw. *skada* 'harm, injure' (11.28).

OE *orsorg*, OHG *ursurgi* (Tat.), neg. cpd. of OE *sorg*, OHG *sorga* 'care' (16.14), a lit. rendering of Lat. *sēcūrus*, and (at least OE) used in both its orig. and later sense.

ME *sauf*, NE *safe* fr. Fr. *sauf* (above, 2).

ME *sūre* (NE obs. in this sense), fr. OFr. *sure* (above, 2).

ME, NE *unharmed*, neg. pple. of *harm*, OE *hearmian* 'injure, harm' (11.28).

NE *secure* fr. Lat. *sēcūrus* (above, 2).

Du. *veilig* = MLG *vēlich*, OFris. *fēlig* : ODu. *veile* id., OE *fǣle* 'faithful, true, good', root connection dub. Walde-P. 2.70 (top). Franck-v. W. 727.

Du. *onbeschadigd*, neg. pple. of *beschadigen* 'injure, harm' (11.28).

MHG *unversēret*, NHG *unversehrt*, neg. pple. of MHG *versēren* 'wound, injure' (NHG *versehren*), cpd. of MHG *sēren* 'cause pain' (fr. MHG *sēre*, OHG *sēro* 'painful', etc.). Weigand-H. 2.1127, 1163.

5. Lith. *sveikas*, Lett. *vesels*, both also 'well' (4.83).

Lith. *čielas*, also 'whole', fr. Russ. *celyj* (below).

Both these Lith. words (like OE *hāl*, ChSl. *cělŭ*, etc.) are used for 'safe' as 'unharmed', but hardly as 'free from danger', which might be expressed by a phrase *be pavojaus* 'without danger'.

Lett. *druošs*, orig. 'brave, bold' : Lith. *drąsus* 'bold, brave', Lett. *drīstēt*, *drīkstēt*, Lith. *drįstėti* 'dare'. Mühl.-Endz. 1.508.

6. ChSl. *sŭchranĭno* adv. (renders *ἀσφαλῶς* Mk. 14.44) : (*sŭ*)*chraniti* 'save, preserve' (11.24).

ChSl. *cělŭ*, SCr. *cio*, Boh. *celý*, Pol. *cały* (and *ocalony* fr. *ocalić* 'save'), Russ. *celyj*, all also 'whole, entire', ChSl. also 'well' (4.83).

SCr. *siguran*, Slov. *siguren*, like NG *σίγουρος* 'certain, safe', fr. Venet. *seguro* = It. *sicuro* (above, 2). Miklosich 296. G. Meyer, Neugr. Stud. 4.81.

SCr. *čitav*, prob. : Lith. *kietas* 'hard, firm'. Berneker 158.

Boh. *bezpečný*, Pol. *bezpieczny*, lit. 'without care' (Russ. *bezpečnyj* 'careless'), cpd. of *bez* 'without' and second member fr. Boh. *péče*, Pol. *piecza* 'care'.

Boh. *jistý* : ChSl. *istŭ* 'real, actual', *istina* 'truth', etc. Berneker 435.

Russ. *bezopasnyj*, cpd. of *bez* 'without, un-' and *opasnyj* 'dangerous' (cf. 16.54).

7. Skt. *kṣema-*, also 'comfortable, agreeable' : *kṣi-* 'dwell, abide, inhabit'. Uhlenbeck 72.

Skt. *akṣata-*, neg. *a-* with pple. of *kṣan-* 'hurt, wound, break'. Uhlenbeck 69.

11.27 DESTROY

Grk.	*φθείρω*, *ἀπόλλῡμι*	Goth.	*fraqistjan*	Lith.	(*su-*)*naikinti*, (*su-*) *griauti*
NG	*καταστρέφω*, *χαλῶ*	ON	*spilla*	Lett.	(*iz-*)*puostīt*, *iznīcināt*
Lat.	*perdere*, *abolēre*, *dēstruere*	Dan.	*ødelægge*	ChSl.	(*po-*, *iz-*)*gubiti*, *razoriti*
It.	*distruggere*	Sw.	*förstöra*	SCr.	*razoriti*, *uništiti*, *porušiti*
Fr.	*détruire*	OE	*spillan*, *spildan*	Boh.	(*z*)*ničiti*, (*z*)*bořiti*
Sp.	*destruir*	ME	*spille*, *destrui*(*e*)	Pol.	(*z*)*niszczyć*, (*z*)*burzyć*
Rum.	*distruge*	NE	*destroy*	Russ.	*uničtožit'*, *razorit'*, *razrušit'*
Ir.	*do-lega* (3sg.), *millim*, *collim*	Du.	*vernietigen*	Skt.	*nāçaya-*, *dhvaṁsaya-*, *kṣi-*
NIr.	*scriosaim*	OHG	*firquistan*, *furliosan*	Av.	*marək-*
W.	*dinistrio*, *distrywio*	MHG	*zerstœren*, *vernih-t*(*ig*)*en*		
Br.	*distruja*	NHG	*zerstören*, *vernichten*		

Words for 'destroy' reflect a variety of destructive actions, some of them originally applicable to particular kinds of objects, as 'tear down, wreck' (buildings), 'lay waste' (land), 'make perish' (living things), while others like 'scatter, disturb, put down, bring to naught' might be more generally applied, so that the precise history is obscure.

1. Grk. *φθείρω* (**φθέρϳω*) : Skt. *kṣar-* 'flow' also 'melt away, perish', Av. *γžar-* 'flow', cf. Grk. *φθορά* 'destruction' and also (as remnant of orig. meaning) 'mixing of colors in painting'. Walde-P. 1.700. Development fr. 'flow' prob. through 'melt away, dissolve' to 'perish' (as sometimes in Skt.), hence 'cause to perish, destroy', or possibly through 'mix' (> 'destroy the purity of, destroy'). Cf. Ir. *leg-* 'dissolve, melt', cpd. *dolega* 'destroys' (below, 3).

Grk. *ὄλλῡμι* (poet.), in prose usually *ἀπόλλῡμι*, beside *ὄλεθρος* 'destruction, death', *ὀλέκω* 'kill', with no clear outside connections.

Grk. *καταλύω*, among other uses also 'destroy' (so freq. in NT), cpd. of *λύω* 'loose, release' (11.34).

Grk. *ἀφανίζω*, orig. 'make unseen' (fr. *ἀφανής* 'unseen'), hence also 'destroy'.

Grk. *καταστρέφω* 'overturn, upset', sometimes 'ruin', NG 'destroy', cpd. of *στρέφω* 'turn'.

NG *χαλῶ*, see 11.29.

2. Lat. *perdere* ('destroy' and 'lose'; > Romance words with latter sense prevailing, 11.33), cpd. like *condere*, etc., of IE **dhē-* 'place, put', with development fr. 'put away' (cf. U.S. slang *put away* 'kill'), with *per-* as in *pervertere* 'turn aside, seduce', etc. Walde-P. 1.827. Ernout-M. 277. Walde-H. 1.362.

Lat. *abolēre*, prob. (not : Grk. *ὄλλῡμι*, but) a new transitive formation to *abolēscere* 'perish, grow old', this a pendant of *ad-olēscere* 'grow up', cpd. of *alere* 'nourish', etc. Walde-P. 1.87. Ernout-M. 5 f. Walde-H. 1.4 f.

Lat. *dēstruere*, mostly late in general sense, earlier 'tear down, demolish', cpd. of *struere* 'build'. Hence the Romance words It. *struggere* 'melt, destroy' (but in latter sense now new cpd. *distruggere* > Rum. *distruge*), Fr. *détruire*, Sp. *destruir*. Ernout-M. 989 f. REW 2606. Tiktin 553.

3. Ir. *do-lega* (3sg.), cpd. of *leg-* 'dissolve, melt' (e.g. 3sg. rel. *legas*, vbl. n. *legad*) : W. *llaith*, Br. *leiz* 'damp', ON *leka*, MHG *leken* 'leak', etc. Walde-P. 2.422 f. Pedersen 1.123, 2.562.

Ir. *millim* (also, as NIr. mostly, 'ruin, spoil'), etym. ? Macbain 249.

Ir. *collim* 'violate, destroy, ruin' (K. Meyer, Contrib. 425), fr. *coll* 'destruction, loss, ruin' = W. *coll*, Br. *koll* 'loss, damage' : Goth. *halts*, ON *haltr*, OE *healt* 'lame', prob. as 'broken' fr. the root **kel-* 'strike'. Walde-P. 1.439. Pedersen 1.114.

W. *dinistrio*, fr. *dinistr* 'destruction', older *dinustr*, etym.? Morris Jones 387 (but dub.).

W. *destrywio* fr. Lat. *dēstruere* (above). Loth, Mots lat. 161.

Br. *distruja*, likewise fr. Lat. *dēstruere* through an OFr. form.

4. Goth. *fraqistjan*, *usqistjan*, once simply *qistjan*, OHG *firquistan*, *arquistan*, etym. dub., perh. : Lith. *gesti* 'be quenched, go out' and 'spoil', Grk. *σβέννῡμι* 'quench', etc. Walde-P. 1.528, 668, 693. Feist 389.

ON *spilla*, OE *spillan*, ME *spille* 'destroy' and 'spoil' (sense obs. in NE *spill*), also OE *spildan* : OHG *spildan* 'waste', OS *spildian* 'ruin, spoil', prob. fr. the root in OHG *spaltan* 'split', etc. (9.27). Walde-P. 2.678. Falk-Torp 1121 f.

Dan. *ødelægge*, orig. 'lay waste' (but now in this sense *lægge øde*), cpd. of *øde* 'waste, desert' and *lægge* 'lay'.

Sw. *förstöra*, fr. MLG *vorstoren*, parallel to NHG *zerstören* (below). Hellquist 1109.

ME *destrui*(*e*), NE *destroy* fr. OFr. *destruire*.

Du. *vernietigen*, *vernieten*, MHG *vernihtigen*, *vernihten*, NHG *vernichten* (in MHG, MDu. also 'hold as naught; despise'), cpd. of Du. *niet*, MHG *niht*, NHG *nicht* 'not'. Franck-v. W. 735. Weigand-H. 2.1157.

OHG *furliosan*, *firliosan* 'lose' (11.33) also 'destroy' (both senses in Tat. and Otfr.), perh. influenced by Lat. *perdere* 'destroy' and 'lose'.

MHG *zerstœren*, NHG *zerstören*, lit. 'scatter completely', cpd. of MHG *stœren*, OHG *stōren* 'scatter' (NHG *stören* 'disturb') : OE *styrian* 'move, stir', NE *stir*, etc. Walde-P. 1.750. Weigand-H. 2.979.

5. Lith. (*su*)*naikinti*, Lett. *iznīcināt* : Lith. *nykti* 'disappear', Lett. *nīkt* 'be sickly, not thrive, perish', these prob. : Lett. *nīca* 'downstream', ChSl. *nicĭ* 'bent over', Skt. *nīca-* 'low', *ni* 'down', etc. Mühl.-Endz. 2.746, 747. Leskien, Ablaut 279.

Lith. (*su*)*griauti* : Lett. *g'raut* 'wreck, demolish', Lat. *in-gruere* 'break in, fall upon', *con-gruere* 'fall together, meet', Grk. (Hom.) *ἔχραον* 'fell upon, assailed'. Walde-P. 1.647. Walde-H. 1.700.

Lett. (*iz*)*puostīt*, in the simplex properly 'lay waste', fr. *puosts* 'waste, deserted', loanword fr. ORuss. *pustŭ* id. Mühl.-Endz. 3.459 f.

6. ChSl. *pogubiti*, *izgubiti*, less usually also simplex *gubiti* = SCr. *gubiti* 'lose', Russ. *gubit'* 'spoil', etc., caus. to ChSl. *gybati*, etc. 'perish', prob. = *gybati* 'bend'. Berneker 373 f. Walde-P. 1.567 f.

ChSl., SCr. *razoriti*, Russ. *razorit'*, Boh. (*z*)*bořiti* (fr. *ob-ořiti*, Gebauer 1.424), cpds. of Slavic *oriti* 'loosen, plunge down, demolish, etc.' : Lith. *irti* 'go to pieces, fall in ruins', Skt. *arma-* 'ruins'. Walde-P. 1.143.

SCr. *uništiti*, Boh. (*z*)*ničiti*, Russ. *uničtožit'*, fr. the words for 'nothing', SCr. *ništ*, Boh. *nic*, Russ. *ničto*. Cf. NHG *vernichten*.

SCr. *porušiti*, Russ. *razrušit'*, cpds. of Slavic *rušiti* 'tear asunder, loose' : Lith. *rausti* 'dig up, grub up', etc., fr. **reu-s-* extension of IE **reu-* in Lat. *ruere* 'tear up, dig up', Skt. *ru-* 'strike to pieces', etc. Walde-P. 2.356.

Pol. (*z*)*niszczyć*, fr. *nizki* 'low' : ChSl. *ništĭ* 'poor', *nizŭ* 'down', fr. **ni-* 'down' (cf. above, 5). Brückner 364.

Pol. (*z*)*burzyć* : Russ. *burit'* 'hurl, throw', *burja* 'storm', SCr. *buriti se* 'become angry', etc., outside connections disputed. Walde-P. 2.191. Berneker 103. Brückner 50.

7. Skt. *nāçaya-*, caus. of *naç* 'be lost, perish' : Av. *nas-* 'disappear', Lat. *necāre* 'kill', etc., IE **nek̑-*. Walde-P. 2.326. So also Toch. A *nāks-*, caus. of *nāk-* 'disappear, perish' (SSS 445).

Skt. *dhvaṁsaya-*, caus. of *dhvaṁs-* 'fall, go to pieces, perish', prob. : Grk. *θύω* 'blow, storm, smoke', Lat. *furere* 'rage', etc. Walde-P. 1.843 f.

Skt. *kṣi-* : Grk. *φθίνω* 'decay, wane, waste away', also trans. 'consume, destroy', Av. *xšyō* gen. of **xšī-* 'vanishing, misery, distress'. Walde-P. 1.505 f.

Av. *marək-* 'destroy, kill' : Skt. *mṛc-* 'hurt, injure', prob. fr. an extension of IE **mer-* in Skt. *mṛ-* 'crush', Grk. *μαραίνω* 'quench, make waste away', mid. 'waste away, decay, etc.'. Walde-P. 2.278.

11.28 HARM, INJURE, DAMAGE (vb.)

Grk.	*βλάπτω, λυμαίνομαι*	Goth.	*ga-skaþjan, ga-sleiþjan*	Lith.	*kenkti, iškadyti*
NG	*βλάπτω, ζημιώνω*	ON	*skeðja, skaða*	Lett.	*skādēt*
Lat.	*nocēre, laedere*	Dan.	*skade (beskadige)*	ChSl.	*vrěditi, otŭštetiti*
It.	*far male, nuocere*	Sw.	*skada*	SCr.	*oštetiti, (na-)škoditi*
Fr.	*faire mal, nuire*	OE	*hearmian, skeþþan*	Boh.	*ubližiti, (po-, u-)škoditi*
Sp.	*dañar*	ME	*harme, skathe, hurte*	Pol.	*(u-, za-)szkodzić*
Rum.	*face rău, vătăma*	NE	*harm, injure, damage, hurt*	Russ.	*vredit'*
Ir.	*fofichim, bronnaim*	Du.	*schaden, beschadigen, kwaad doen*	Skt.	*hiṅs-, riṣ-*
NIr.	*deanaim olc*, etc.	OHG	*scadōn*	Av.	*zyā-, iriš-*
W.	*niweidio*	MHG	*schaden, schadigen*		
Br.	*ober drouk*, etc.	NHG	*beschädigen, schaden*		

The majority of words for 'harm, injure' (and those for the corresponding nouns) were originally applied to living creatures, with reference to bodily (or sometimes mental) injury, coming from notions like 'strike, wound, hurt, cause grief', etc.,—and only secondarily applied to material things. An exception is Lat. *damnum* with its derivatives, like NE *damage*, mostly applied to material things.

1. Grk. βλάπτω, in Hom. mostly 'disable, hinder', later 'harm, injure', beside sb. βλάβη 'harm, injury', also π-forms, as Cret. βλοπία, καταβλάπεθαι, etym. dub. Connection with Skt. *mṛc-* 'hurt, injure' (through *μλαπ-, IE **mḷk*^{w}-), as Boisacq 120, is impossible if the analysis of Skt. *mṛc-* preferred in 10.27 under Av. *marək-* 'destroy, kill' is the correct one. Walde-P. 2.297.

Grk. λυμαίνομαι, in earliest use a strong expression 'outrage, maltreat', later also 'cause damage, harm, spoil' : λύμη 'outrage', λῦμα 'dirt, filth', Lat. *lutum* 'mud', *polluere* 'pollute'. Walde-P. 2.406.

NG ζημιώνω, fr. Grk. ζημιόω mostly 'penalize, fine, punish', deriv. of ζημία 'loss, damage', esp. 'penalty, fine', in NG the usual noun for 'harm, damage' and financial 'loss' (11.74).

2. Lat. *nocēre* with dat. 'do harm to' (> It. *nuocere*, Fr. *nuire*, etc., REW 5938), caus. of **neḱ-* in Lat. *nex* 'violent death, murder', *necāre* 'kill', Grk. νέκυς, νεκρός 'corpse', Av. *nasu-* 'corpse', Skt. *naç-* 'perish', caus. *nāçaya-* (11.27). Walde-P. 2.326. Ernout-M. 669.

Lat. *laedere*, esp. 'wound, hurt' but also 'injure', etym. dub., but orig. sense 'strike, hit' implied by cpds. *allīdere*, *collīdere*, etc. Ernout-M. 517. Walde-H. 1.749.

Lat. *damnum*, the regular noun for 'harm, injury' (> It. *danno*, OFr. *dam*, Sp. *daño*, Rum. *daună*; deriv. OFr. *damage*, Fr. *dommage*; REW 2468), also in early use 'loss, expense', prob. fr. **dap-no-* : Grk. δάπτω 'devour, rend, tear', δαπάνη 'expense', etc. Walde-P. 1.764. Ernout-M. 252 f. Walde-H. 1.322. Its deriv. *damnāre* is 'doom, condemn' (> It. *dannare*, etc.), the orig. sense 'harm' being only rare and early, so that the use of Sp. *dañar* for 'harm' is not inherited but restored from the noun.

Rum. *vătăma* 'injure, wound', etym. dub. Puşcariu 1865.

In the Romance languages generally 'to harm' is most commonly expressed by phrases, as It. *far male*, Fr. *faire (du) mal*, Rum. *face rău*, all lit. 'do ill' (cf. 'bad' 16.62). Similarly, after French, Br. *ober drouk*, etc. and Du. *kwaad doen*.

3. Ir. *fofichim* 'inflict (injury, damage)', cpd. of *fichim* 'fight' (20.11). Pedersen 2.521.

Ir. *bronnaim* : W. *briwo* 'break, hurt', OE *brȳsan* 'crush' (NE *bruise*), Lat. *frūstum* 'piece, bit', etc. Walde-P. 2.198 f. Pedersen 1.54 f.

Ir. *orgim* 'kill' (4.76), also 'injure, harm' (Laws, Gloss. 597).

NIr. *deanaim olc* 'do ill' and other phrases with *olc* 'bad' (16.62). For *loitim* see under 'spoil' (11.29).

W. *niweidio*, deriv. of *niwed* 'harm, injury', etym.? Morris Jones 106 (fr. **nwyet*, **nāw-yat* : Lith. *novyti* 'afflict, kill', etc., Walde-P. 2.316).

Br. *ober drouk*, *ober gwall* 'do ill' (like Fr. *faire mal*), phrases with words for 'bad' (16.62), also *ober gaou* 'do wrong' (like Fr. *faire tort*) with *gaou* 'false, wrong, a lie' (16.71).

4. Goth. *ga-skaþjan*, ON *skeðja*, *skaða* (> ME *skathe*, NE *scathe*), Dan. *skade*, Sw. *skada*, OE *skeþþan* (also *sceaþan*), OHG *scadōn*, *scadēn*, NHG *schaden*, *beschädigen*, etc., with sbs. OHG *scado*, etc., general Gmc. : Ir. *scathaim* 'mutilate, lame', Grk. ἀ-σκηθής 'unhurt, unscathed'. Walde-P. 2.557 f. Falk-Torp 978.

Goth. *ga-sleiþjan*, lit. 'endanger' : *sleiþs* 'dangerous, bad', *sleiþi* 'danger', OE *slīþe* 'dangerous, cruel', etc. (16.65).

OE *hearmian*, ME *harme*, NE *harm*, deriv. of OE *hearm* 'hurt, injury, harm' = ON *harmr* 'grief, sorrow', OHG *harm* 'hurt, injustice, grief', NHG *harm* 'grief', etc., prob. : ChSl. *sramŭ* 'shame', but root connection? Walde-P. 1.463. Falk-Torp 381.

NE *injure*, back-formation to *injury* fr. Lat. *iniūria* 'wrong, injustice' : *iūs* 'right, law'.

NE *damage*, fr. ME, NE *damage* (sb.), fr. OFr. *damage*, deriv. of OFr. *dam* fr. Lat. *damnum* (above, 2).

ME *hurte*, NE *hurt*, fr. OFr. *hurter* (Fr. *heurter*) 'strike, hit, knock' (9.21). English uses 'knock, dash', then 'cause bodily injury, pain to', then more generally 'injure', still mostly with reference to living creatures, but colloquially also with reference to material things. NED s.v. *hurt* vb.

5. Lith. *kenkti*, intr. (cf. *kenkia* 'it hurts, aches'), with dat. 'be harmful to', : Grk. κέγκει· ἐπιδάκνει (Hesych.), κένκω· πεινῶ (Phot.), OE *hungor*, etc. 'hunger' (5.14). Walde-P. 1.401.

Lith. *iškadyti* (NSB, but mostly obs.?), deriv. of sb. *iškadą* 'harm', this through Pol. *szkoda* fr. OHG *scado*, MHG *schade* id. (above, 4).

Lett. *skādēt*, fr. MLG *schaden* (above, 4). Mühl.-Endz. 3.879.

6. ChSl. *vrěditi* (Gospels, etc.), Russ. *vredit'*, derivs. of ChSl. *vrědŭ*, Russ. *vred* 'harm, injury' (ChSl. also 'wound', Boh. *vřed*, Pol. *wrzod* 'ulcer, sore'), outside connections dub., perh. : Skt. *vrad-* 'become soft'. Walde-P. 1.287.

ChSl. *otŭštetiti* (Supr., etc.), SCr. *oštetiti*, derivs. of ChSl. *tŭšteta*, SCr. *šteta* 'harm, injury' : ChSl. *tŭštĭ* 'empty' (13.22). Leskien, Serbo-Croat. Gram. 55.

Boh. *ubližiti*, deriv. of *bliz* 'near', through 'come near', cf. NHG *zu nahe treten* 'offend, injure'. Berneker 61.

SCr. *(na-)škoditi*, Boh. *(po-, u-) škoditi*, Pol. *(u-, za-)szkodzić*, derivs. of SCr., Boh. *škoda*, Pol. *szkoda* 'harm, injury', loanwords fr. OHG *scado*, MHG *schade* (above, 4). Brückner 549.

7. Skt. *hiṅs-*, prob. : *heṣa-* 'missile', fr. an extension of the root in Skt. *hi-* 'impel, hurl', Av. *zaēna-* 'weapon', etc. Walde-P. 1.546.

Av. *zyā-* (pres. *zi-nā-*) 'injure', esp. 'deprive of' (as OPers. *dī-*, 3sg. imperf. *adīnā*), with *fra-* 'lay waste', also sb. *zyāni-* 'harm, injury' : Skt. *jyā-* (3sg.

pres. *jināti*) 'oppress, deprive of', pointing to an IE **ĝyā-* beside **g*^{w}*yā-* in words for 'might, power', as Grk. βία, etc. Walde-P. 1.667. Barth. 1700.

Skt. *riṣ-*, Av. *iriš-* 'be injured' and 'injure' (cf. Av. *raēša-* 'injury', NPers. *rēš* 'wound'), etym. dub. Walde-P. 2.345 f. Uhlenbeck 250. Barth. 1485 f.

11.29 SPOIL (vb. trans.)

Grk.	*διαφθείρω*	Goth.	*frawardjan*	Lith.	*gadinti*
NG	*χαλῶ*	ON	*spilla*	Lett.	*maitāt*
Lat.	*corrumpere*	Dan.	*fordærve*	ChSl.	*tĭlěti*
It.	*guastare, sciupare*	Sw.	*fördärva*	SCr.	*pokvariti*
Fr.	*gâter*	OE	*spillan*	Boh.	*(z)kaziti*
Sp.	*echar a perder*	ME	*spille, corrupt*	Pol.	*(ze)psuć*
Rum.	*strica*	NE	*spoil, ruin*	Russ.	*(is)portit'*
Ir.	*loitim*	Du.	*bederven*	Skt.	*dūṣaya-*
NIr.	*loitim*	OHG	*farwarten*	Av.	. . . .
W.	*difetha*	MHG	*verderben*		
Br.	*gwasta*	NHG	*verderben*		

The notion 'spoil', as in the prevailing current use of NE *spoil* (vb.), that is, 'injure something seriously', mostly so as to make it useless without entirely destroying it, is midway between 'harm, injure' and 'destroy', so that there is some overlapping of usage. Several of the words listed here may be used also for 'destroy' or for 'injure', but in most there is a close approximation to the use of NE *spoil*.

The etymological connections are too diverse to summarize.

1. Grk. διαφθείρω, cpd. of φθείρω 'destroy' (11.27), orig. 'destroy utterly', then esp. 'corrupt, spoil, ruin'.

NG χαλῶ (or χαλνῶ), aor. ἐχάλασα, also 'destroy' but esp. 'spoil', fr. Grk. χαλάω 'loosen, let fall, drop', with development prob. fr. 'drop' through 'break to pieces, smash'. Earlier sense preserved in nautical use for 'lower' (the mast), 'drop' (the anchor).

2. Lat. *corrumpere* (also 'destroy'; in fig. sense 'corrupt', as mod. derivs. mostly; but ME *corrupt* also 'spoil', as NE in Bible, etc., NED s.v. *corrupt* vb.[1]), cpd. of *rumpere* 'break' (9.26), hence orig. 'break to pieces'. Ernout-M. 876.

It. *guastare*, Fr. *gâter* (It. and formerly Fr. also 'lay waste'; Sp. *gastar* 'waste, spend'), fr. a blend of Lat. *vastāre* and (init. fr.) Gmc. **wōstjan* (OS *āwōstian*, OHG *wuosten*), both 'lay waste', and derivs. of the adjs. Lat. *vastus* and OHG *wuosti*, etc. 'empty, waste', themselves cognate. REW 9168. Gamillscheg 461.

It. *sciupare* (also 'waste, squander'), perh. fr. **ex-sūpāre* 'drink up' second part fr. Gmc. (MLG *sūpen*, OE *sūpan*, NE *sup*, etc.). REW 3077. Or fr. a blend of this with Lat. *dissupare* (*dissipāre*) 'scatter, disperse, squander'?

Sp. *echar a perder*, phrase with *echar* 'throw' (10.25) and *perder* 'lose' (11.35).

Rum. *strica* 'break in pieces', also 'spoil, ruin, injure', etc. perh. fr. Lat. *ex-tricāre* 'untangle', but semantic development uncertain. Tiktin 1514. Puşcariu 1655.

3. Ir., NIr. *loitim* (also 'injure, hurt, wound', but esp. 'spoil') : Ir. *lot* 'destruction, wound, hurt', further connections dub. Macbain 233. Stokes 258.

W. *difetha*, perh. fr. **di-fed-ha*, cpd. of neg. prefix *di-* and *med-* in *meddu* 'possess'. Morris Jones 384.

Br. *gwasta* in use and orig. like Fr. *gâter*, etc. (above, 2).

4. Goth. *frawardjan* ('corrupt, spoil, disfigure', rendering φθείρω, διαφθείρω, ἀφανίζω), OHG *farwarten*, MHG *verwerten*, caus. of Goth. *frawairþan* 'be corrupted', OHG *farwerdan*, cpds. of Goth. *wairþan*, OHG *werdan* 'become' (cf. OE *forweorþan* 'come to naught, perish'). Walde-P. 1.275. Feist 166.

ON *spilla*, OE *spillan*, ME *spille*, see under 'destroy', 11.27.

NE *spoil*, in ME 'despoil', through OFr. fr. Lat. *spoliāre* 'despoil', deriv. of *spolium* 'booty, spoil'. Orig. sense kept in the noun *spoil*, while the verb took on the use of ME *spille* (above), as this became restricted to 'spill'. NED s.v.

NE *ruin*, orig. 'reduce to ruins', hence 'inflict great injury', often 'spoil', fr. Fr. *ruiner*, MLat. *ruīnāre*, deriv. of Lat. *ruīna* 'a falling-down, ruin', fr. *ruere* 'fall down'.

MHG, NHG *verderben*, MLG *vorderven* (> Dan. *fordærve*, Sw. *fördärva*), Du. *bederven*, caus. to MHG *verderben* (intr. str. vb.) 'come to naught, die', OFris. *forderva* 'perish', OE *(ge)deorfan* 'labor' and 'be in peril, perish', prob. : Lith. *darbas* 'labor', etc. Walde-P. 1.863, 2.631 (after v. Wijk, IF 24.230 f.).

5. Lith. *gadinti*, Lett. dial. *(sa-)gandēt* : Lith. *gesti*, pres. *gendu*, Lett. *g'int*, pres. *g'instu* 'spoil' (intr.), 'perish', Skt. *gandh-* (Dhātup.) 'hurt, injure', etc. Walde-P. 1.672 f.

Lett. *maitāt*, prob. as orig. 'cause to rot', deriv. of Lett. *maita* 'carrion'. Mühl.-Endz. 2.552. Otherwise Walde-P. 2.222 (: Goth. *maitan* 'cut', etc.).

6. ChSl. *tĭlěti* (Gospels, Supr.; also *ras-*), beside *tĭlja* 'corruption, rust, moth' = Russ. *tleti* 'be rotten', *tlja* 'rot', etc. (Miklosich 370), perh. : Grk. τῖλος 'thin stool' (in diarrhea), OE *þīnan* 'be moist', etc. Walde-P. 1.701.

SCr. *pokvariti*, beside *kvar* 'injury', etym.? Berneker 655.

Boh. *(z)kaziti* = ChSl. *(is)kaziti* 'destroy, spoil', Russ. *izkaziti* 'disfigure, distort, spoil', Pol. *zkasić* 'taint, corrupt, defile', etc., caus. of ChSl. *čeznąti* 'disappear', etc. Berneker 498, 153 f.

Pol. *(ze)psuć*, deriv. of *pies* (gen. *psa*) 'dog', like SCr. *psovati* 'scold, swear' likewise fr. *pas* 'dog', and NHG *verhunzen* 'spoil, botch, disfigure' fr. *hund* 'dog'. Brückner 445 f.

Russ. *(is)portit'* (late ChSl. *(is)prŭtiti*), beside *porča* 'damage, corruption', Pol. *zapartek* 'foul egg', etc., etym.? Miklosich 243. Brückner 397.

7. Skt. *dūṣaya-*, caus. of *duṣ-* 'become bad', fr. prefix *duṣ-* = Grk. δυσ- 'ill'.

For other Skt. and Av. words, see under 'destroy' (11.27).

11.31 SEEK

Grk.	*ζητέω*	Goth.	*sōkjan*	Lith.	*ieškoti*
NG	*γυρεύω, ζητῶ*	ON	*leita, sœkja*	Lett.	*meklēt*
Lat.	*quaerere, petere*	Dan.	*søge, lede (efter)*	ChSl.	*iskati*
It.	*cercare*	Sw.	*söka, leta (efter)*	SCr.	*tražiti, iskati*
Fr.	*chercher*	OE	*sēcan*	Boh.	*hledati*
Sp.	*buscar*	ME	*seke, seche*	Pol.	*szukać*
Rum.	*căuta (cerca)*	NE	*seek, look for*, etc.	Russ.	*iskat'*
Ir.	*sīrim, iarraim, saigim*	Du.	*zoeken*	Skt.	*anu-iṣ-*
NIr.	*loirgim, iarraim*	OHG	*suohhen*	Av.	*iš-*
W.	*ceisio*	MHG	*suochen*		
Br.	*klask(out)*	NHG	*suchen*		

Words for 'seek' reflect such notions as 'go about, go after, track, look for'.

1. Grk. ζητέω (Dor. ζᾱτέω) fr. *δι̯ᾱ-το-, beside δίζημαι fr. *δι-δι̯ᾱ-, also ζῆλος (Dor. ζᾶλος) 'zeal, jealousy', prob. fr. an orig. sense 'exert oneself', or the like : Hom. δίω 'flee', δίομαι 'drive away', Skt. *dīyati* 'flies, hovers', etc. Walde-P. 1.775.

NG pop. γυρεύω, deriv. of γῦρος 'circle' and formerly (like γυρίζω) 'go about', but now 'seek' (cf. Fr. *chercher*, etc., below, 2).

2. Lat. *quaerere*, fr. **quais-* (cf. pple. *quaestus* and desid. *quaessere, quaesere*), etym.? Ernout-M. 830 f.

Lat. *petere*, orig. 'direct oneself toward, attack, fall upon' then in weakened sense 'seek' (and later 'ask') : Grk. πέτομαι 'fly', πίπτω 'fall', Skt. *pat-* 'fly, fall', etc. (10.23, 10.37). Walde-P. 2.19 f. Ernout-M. 763 f.

It. *cercare*, Fr. *chercher* (Rum. *cerca* now mostly 'try, taste'), fr. VLat. *circāre* 'go about', fr. *circa* 'about'. REW 1938.

Sp., Port. *buscar*, deriv. of VLat. **būsca* 'firewood' (> OFr. *busche*, Fr. *bûche* 'stick of wood'), with semantic development through 'hunt for firewood'. REW 1420. Wartburg 1.650.

Rum. *căuta* fr. VLat. **cavitāre*, iter. formation to Lat. *cavēre* 'be on one's guard, take heed'. REW 1793. Puşcariu 325.

3. Ir. *sīrim*, perh. deriv. of *sīr* 'long' (cf. NHG *verlangen*, NE *long for*). Pedersen 2.628. Rejected by Bergin, Ériu 8.196, maintaining *sĭrim* (with short vowel) for OIr.

Ir. *iarraim*, also 'ask, demand' (and so mostly in NIr.), etym. dub. Walde-P. 2.29. Stokes 17,327.

Ir. *loirgim*, lit. 'to track', fr. *lorg* 'track, trace, footprint' (Walde-P. 2.439. Pedersen 1.104 f.).

Ir. *saigim* : Goth. *sōkjan*, etc. (below, 4).

W. *ceisio* 'seek, attempt', deriv. of *cais* 'attempt, quest', this fr. Lat. *quaestiō* 'inquiry, question'? Loth, Mots lat. 147.

Br. *klask, klaskout* (= W. *clasgu, casglu* 'gather'), perh. fr. a VLat. **quaesiculāre*, frequent. to *quaerere* (above). Henry 69. But doubted by Loth, Mots lat. 149 f.

4. Goth. *sōkjan*, ON *sœkja* (but largely used in sense 'go get, fetch' and also 'pursue, attack', and so chiefly in NIcel.), Dan. *søge*, Sw. *söka*, OE *sēcan*, etc., general Gmc. : Grk. ἡγέομαι 'go ahead, lead', Lat. *sāgīre* 'perceive acutely', Ir. *saigim* 'go after, seek'. Walde-P. 2.449. Feist 442. Pedersen 2.610.

NE *seek* is in colloquial speech mostly replaced by phrases, like *try to find, look for* or *hunt for*.

ON *leita* (with gen., or prep. *at* or *eptir*), Dan. *lede*, Sw. *leta* (*efter*) = Goth. *wlaitōn* 'look about', OE *wlātian* 'gaze' : OE *wlītan*, ON *līta* 'look', etc. Walde-P. 1.293. Falk-Torp 629.

5. Lith. *ieškoti* : ChSl., SCr. *iskati*, Boh. (old) *jiskati* (Pol. *iskać* old 'seek', now 'hunt lice, louse'), Russ. *iskat'*, Skt. *iṣ-* 'seek, wish' (esp. with *anu-* 'seek after'), Av. *iš-* 'seek', OHG *eiscōn* 'inquire, ask, demand', OE *āscian* 'attempt, demand, ask', etc. (18.31). Walde-P. 1.12. Berneker 432 f.

Lett. *meklēt*, etym. dub. Mühl.-Endz. 2.594.

6. ChSl. *iskati*, etc., above, 5.

SCr. *tražiti*, lit. 'to track', deriv. of *trag* 'track, trace'.

Boh. *hledati* = ChSl. *ględati*, SCr. *gledati* 'look at', etc. (15.52). Berneker 302.

Pol. *szukać*, fr. NHG *suchen*. Brückner 557.

7. Skt. *anu-iṣ-*, Av. *iš-* : Lith. *ieškoti*, etc. (above, 5).

11.32 FIND

Grk.	εὑρίσκω	Goth.	*bigitan*	Lith.	*rasti*
NG	βρίσκω	ON	*finna*	Lett.	*atrast*
Lat.	*invenīre, reperīre*	Dan.	*finde, hitte*	ChSl.	*obrěsti*
It.	*trovare*	Sw.	*finna, hitta*	SCr.	*naći, nalaziti*
Fr.	*trouver*	OE	*findan*	Boh.	*nalézti, najíti, nacházeti*
Sp.	*hallar, encontrar*	ME	*finde*	Pol.	*znaleźć*
Rum.	*găsi, afla*	NE	*find*	Russ.	*nachodit', naiti*
Ir.	*fogaibim, foriccim*	Du.	*vinden*	Skt.	*vid-, adhi-gam*, etc.
NIr.	*dogheibhim*	OHG	*findan*	Av.	*vid-*
W.	*caffael, cael*	MHG	*vinden*		
Br.	*kavout*	NHG	*finden*		

Words for 'find' reflect such notions as 'seize, get', 'come upon, go after', 'see, know' (through 'come to recognize'). Some originated in the language of the chase through 'stir up' or 'scent' (game).

1. Grk. εὑρίσκω, NG βρίσκω : OIr. pret. *fūar* 'found', *frīth* 'was found', Arm. *gerem* 'capture, seize', root **wer-*. Walde-P. 1.280. Thurneysen, Gram. 428, 471.

2. Lat. *invenīre*, lit. 'come upon, meet', whence the usual sense 'find, discover', cpd. of *venīre* 'come'. Ernout-M. 1084.

Lat. *reperīre* 'find out, discover' (but often synonymous with *invenīre*) and 'obtain', cpd. of *parere* (older *parīre*) 'give birth to' for orig. 'get' (cf. *parāre* 'prepare, get', 11.16). Ernout-M. 734.

Fr. *trouver* (> It. *trovare*), Prov. *trobar, trovar* ('find', hence also 'compose poetry'), etym. much disputed, but best fr. Lat. *turbāre* 'disturb' through use as a hunters' and fishermen's term, as actually attested in Sard. *turbare* 'stir up game' and 'frighten fish into a place where the water is poisoned'. REW 8992 (with refs., esp. Schuchardt, Wagner). Iordan-Orr, Introd. to Romance Linguistics 54.

Sp. *hallar*, Port. *achar*, Rum. *afla*, fr. Lat. *afflāre* 'breath upon', through use as a hunters' term, 'scent' (cf. Fr. *flairer*, etc.) game, hence 'track', 'find'. REW 261.

Sp. *encontrar* ('meet, happen on' and so 'find' without searching, in contrast to *hallar*) fr. Cat. *encontrar*, deriv. of *encontra* 'against' (Lat. *in+contrā*), like OFr. *encontrer* (> NE *encounter*). REW 4361.

Rum. *găsi*, etym. unknown. Tiktin 664.

3. Ir. *fogaibim*, NIr. *dogheibhim* (also in NIr. 'get', esp. in orig. dependent form *faghaim* 11.16), cpds. of *fo-* 'under' and *gaibim* 'take, seize' (11.14). Pedersen 1.265.

W. *caffael, cael*, Br. *kavout*, also 'get', see 11.16.

4. Goth. *bigitan* = OE *begietan*, ON *geta*, etc. 'get, obtain' (11.16).

ON, Sw. *finna*, Dan. *finde*, OE *findan*, etc., general Gmc. = Goth. *finþan* 'learn, find out' : OE *fandian*, OHG *fandōn* 'try, examine', OE *fundian*, OHG *funden* 'strive after, go forward, tend to', etc., prob. fr. the root in Skt. *panthās*, ChSl. *pątĭ* 'road, way', etc. (10.71). Walde-P. 2.27. Falk-Torp 218.

Dan. *hitte*, Sw. *hitta* = ON *hitta* 'meet with, hit upon, hit' (> late OE *hyttan*, ME *hitte*, NE *hit*) : W. *cwyddo* 'fall'. Walde-P. 1.364. Falk-Torp 407.

5. Lith. *rasti* (pres. *randu*), Lett. *atrast* (strictly 'find again' but usual for the simple *rast*), prob. : ChSl. *ob-rěsti* (pret. *ob-rětŭ*) 'find', *sŭ-rěsti* 'meet', fr. parallel root forms in *-d* and *-t*, these perh. **wrē-d-, wrē-t-* as extensions of the

root **wer-* in Grk. εὑρίσκω (above, 1). Walde-P. 1.280, 2.367. Otherwise (: Goth. *wrātōn* 'go, journey', ON *rata* 'go about', Walde-P. 1.274) Mühl.-Endz. 3.479, Trautmann 236.

6. ChSl. *obrěsti*, see above, Lith. *rasti*.

SCr. *naći*, Boh. *najíti, nacházeti*, Russ. *naiti, nachodit'* cpds. of *na-* 'on, upon' and words for 'go, walk', ChSl. *iti, choditi*, etc. (10.47).

SCr. *nalaziti* (iter. to *nalesti* 'catch (cold, disease, etc.)', dial. also 'find', Boh. *nalézti*, Pol. *znaleźć*, cpd. of Slav. *lěsti* in ChSl. *vŭz-lěsti* 'go up', *sŭ-lěsti* 'go down', etc. Berneker 697, 715.

7. Skt. *vid-* (pres. 3sg. *vindati*), Av. *vid-* (pres. 3sg. *vīnasti*, 3pl. *vindənti*), the same root as Skt., Av. *vid-* 'know', IE **weid-* 'see, know', with partial differentiation in the inflected forms, cf. Arm. *egit* 'found', *gtanem* 'find', Ir. *finn-* 'know, find out'. Walde-P. 1.237.

In Skt. 'find' is also often expressed by cpds. of *gam-* 'go' or *āp-* 'reach, obtain'.

11.33 LOSE

Grk.	ἀπόλλῡμι	Goth.	*fraliusan*	Lith.	*pamesti, prarasti, nustoti, netekti*
NG	χάνω	ON	*tȳna, tapa*	Lett.	*(pa)zaudēt* (*pamest*)
Lat.	*āmittere, perdere*	Dan.	*tabe*	ChSl.	*pogubiti*
It.	*perdere*	Sw.	*förlora, tappa*	SCr.	*(iz)gubiti*
Fr.	*perdre*	OE	*forlēosan*	Boh.	*ztratiti*
Sp.	*perder*	ME	*lese, lose*	Pol.	*stracić, zgubić*
Rum.	*pierde*	NE	*lose*	Russ.	*terjat', utratit'*
Ir.	(*ēiplid ūad*)	Du.	*verliezen*	Skt.	*hā-*, phrases with *bhraṅç-*
NIr.	*caillim*	OHG	*farliosan*	Av.	. . . .
W.	*colli*	MHG	*verliesen*		
Br.	*koll*	NHG	*verlieren*		

Words for 'lose' mostly reflect such notions as 'destroy, injure' or 'let loose, let go, throw away', in a few cases 'rub' (through 'rub out, wear out').

In a few languages there are two common verbs for 'lose', with some idiomatic, but not rigid, differentiation. Thus Lat. *āmittere* in part 'lose' by accident or without fault vs. the stronger *perdere* 'lose' so that the object is destroyed or utterly lost. But actually both verbs are quotable with the same objects ('life', 'property', 'a person' by death, etc.) and without difference unless rhetorical. (Cf. e.g. Cic. Fam. 5.16.3).

1. Grk. ἀπόλλῡμι 'destroy' (11.27), also 'lose'.

NG χάνω, new pres. to aor. ἔχασα fr. ἐχάωσα to late χαόω 'destroy, lose', deriv. of χάος 'abyss, chasm'. Hatzidakis, Μεσ. 1.104.

2. Lat. *āmittere*, in earliest use 'dismiss', then 'lose', cpd. of *mittere* 'let go, throw, send' (10.63).

Lat. *perdere* 'destroy' (11.27) and 'lose' (> Romance words for 'lose'). Ernout-M. 277. REW 6403.

3. In older Irish 'lose' is usually expressed by a phrase with *at-baill* 'perishes, dies', e.g. *at-baill a dligid*, lit. 'perishes his right' = 'he loses his right' (Laws 1.118. 4, 9), and more often with the conjunct. form used independently *ēiplid ūad ini dligis* 'perishes from him that which is due (him)' = 'he loses what is due him' (ibid. 1.10).

NIr. *caillim*, W. *colli*, Br. *koll* : Ir. *collim* 'destroy' (11.27).

4. Goth. *fraliusan*, OE *forlēosan* (pple.

forloren > NE *forlorn*), ME *lese*, Du. *verliezen*, OHG *farliosan*, MHG *verliesen*, NHG *verlieren* : Goth. *laus* 'empty, vain', *lausjan* 'release, rescue', ON *lauss* 'free, loose', etc. (NE *loose*), fr. the root in Grk. λύω 'loose, release', etc. (11.34). Walde-P. 2.408. Feist 163.

ON *tȳna* (Norw. *tyne* 'injure, spoil') = OE *tīenan* 'vex, annoy', deriv. of ON *tjōn* 'harm, injury', OE *tēona* 'harm, injustice', etc., perh. : Skt. *du-* 'burn, torment', Grk. δαίω 'kindle', etc. (In any case the Norse meaning 'lose' fr. 'injure, harm' as often.) Walde-P. 1.768. Falk-Torp 1309.

ON *tapa*, Dan. *tabe*, Sw. *tappa*, prob. fr. the root of Lat. *damnum* (**dap-no-*) 'harm, injury' (11.28). Walde-P. 1.765. Falk-Torp 1239 f.

Sw. *förlora* = Dan. (old) *forlore*, re-formations fr. Dan. *forloren* 'lost' (now 'false') fr. MLG *vorloren* pple. of *vorlēren* : Goth. *fraliusan*, etc. (above). Falk-Torp 258 f. Hellquist 260.

ME, NE *lose*, fr. OE *losian* 'perish, be lost', also Northumbr. twice trans. 'destroy, ruin', but trans. use not regular until 13th cent.; deriv. of *los* 'loss', fr. the root in Goth. *fraliusan*, etc. (above). NED s.v.

5. Lith. *pamesti*, Lett. *pamest* (but the latter mostly 'throw away') perfect. cpds. of Lith. *mesti*, Lett. *mest* 'throw' (10.25).

Lith. *prarasti*, cpd. of *pra-* expressing missing or failing and *rasti* 'find' (11.32).

Lith. *nustoti*, cpd. of *nuo* 'from' and *stoti* 'take a stand', hence 'cease' (14.28) and, with gen., 'lose' (NSB s.v.).

Lith. *netekti*, neg. cpd. of *tekti* 'fall to one's share, have enough' : OE *þicgan* 'take, receive', etc. Walde-P. 1.715. Falk-Torp 1258.

Lett. *(pa)zaudēt*, caus. of *zust* 'disappear, be lost' like Lith. *žudyti* 'kill' caus. of *žuti* 'perish, be lost', perh. : OE *(ā)gētan* 'injure, wound, kill'. Walde-P. 1.564.

6. ChSl. *pogubiti*, SCr. *(iz)gubiti*, Pol. *zgubić* (Pol. now 'lose' by accident, as money from one's pocket, etc.), in ChSl. also 'destroy'. See 11.27.

Boh. *ztratiti*, Pol. *stracić*, Russ. *utratit'* (*tratit'* 'spend, waste') : ChSl. *tratiti* 'consume, exhaust, ruin', Goth. *þrōþjan* 'exercise', prob. fr. an extension of the root **ter-* in Lat. *terere*, ChSl. *trěti*, *tĭrą*, etc. 'rub' (9.31), whence also Russ. *terjat'* 'lose'. Walde-P. 1.730. Brückner 575.

7. Skt. *hā-* 'leave' (12.18), 'give up', also 'lose'. But 'lose' mostly expressed as 'be lost by', e.g. *bhraṣṭa-*, pple. of *bhraṅç-* 'fall, fall away, be lost'.

11.34 RELEASE

Grk.	(ἀπο)λύω, ἀφίημι, ἀπαλλάσσω	Goth.	*fralētan, (ga)lausjan*	Lith.	*paleisti*
NG	ἀπολύω, ἀπαλλάσσω	ON	*lāta laust*	Lett.	*atlaist*
Lat.	*dīmittere, ēmittere, solvere*	Dan.	*løslade, slippe (løs)*	ChSl.	*(otŭ)pustiti, rěšiti*
It.	*(ri)lasciare*	Sw.	*(lös)släppa, lösgiva*	SCr.	*pustiti*
Fr.	*(re)lâcher*	OE	*forlǣtan*	Boh.	*(pro)pustiti*
Sp.	*soltar*	ME	*lete ga, relese*	Pol.	*puścić*
Rum.	*lăsa*	NE	*release, let go*	Russ.	*pustit'*
Ir.	*lēicim*	Du.	*loslaten*	Skt.	*muc-, sṛj-*
NIr.	*scaoilim*	OHG	*furlazzan, lōsen*	Av.	*harəz-, zā-*
W.	*gollwng*	MHG	*verlazzen, læsen*		
Br.	*leuskel*	NHG	*entlassen, loslassen*		

Words for 'release' reflect such notions as 'loose' (in lit. sense 'unbind'), 'loosen', 'let go, send forth, let slip', etc. There is frequent connection and some overlapping in use with words for 'leave' (12.18) and 'let, permit' (19.47).

1. Grk. ἀπολύω, cpd. of ἀπό 'away, from' and λύω 'loose, unbind', the latter sometimes also 'release' : Lat. *luere* 'expiate, pay a debt', *solvere* (fr. **seluere*) 'loose, unbind, release, solve', Skt. *lu-* 'cut off', etc. Walde-P. 2.408. Ernout-M. 954. Walde-H. 1.834.

Grk. ἀφίημι 'send forth, let go, release', cpd. of ἵημι 'let go, throw' (10.25).

Grk. ἀπαλλάσσω, cpd. of ἀλλάσσω 'change' (12.93).

2. Lat. *dīmittere*, *ēmittere*, cpds. of *dī-* (*dis-*) 'apart' and *ē-* (*ex*) 'from' with *mittere* 'let go, throw, send' (10.63).

It. (*ri*)*lasciare*, Rum. *lăsa*, also 'leave, let' (as Fr. *laisser*), fr. Lat. *laxāre* 'loosen, relax', deriv. of *laxus* 'slack, loose'. REW 4955.

Fr. (*re*)*lâcher*, deriv. of *lâche* 'loose, slack' = It. *lasco*, fr. **lascus* = Lat. *laxus* with cons. transposition. REW 4918.

Sp. *soltar*, deriv. of *suelto* 'loose, free', pple. of *solver* 'loosen, untie', Lat. *solvere*. REW 8081.

3. Ir. *lēicim*, also 'let, leave' : Grk. λείπω, Lat. *linquere* 'leave', etc. (12.18). Walde 2.396 f.

NIr. *scaoilim* = MIr. *scailim* 'scatter, strew, separate' : Lith. *skelti* 'split', ON *skilja* 'divide, separate' (cf. *skilja eptir* 'leave', 12.18), etc. Walde-P. 2.592.

W. *gollwng*, with secondary pref. *go-*, fr. MW *ellwng* id. = Ir. *inloing* 'claims' (i.e. 'puts in'), fr. IE **legh-* 'lie', in MIr. *laigid* 'lies down', Goth. *ligan*, etc. 'lie'. Walde-P. 2.424. Pedersen 2.570.

Br. *leuskel*, beside adj. *laosk* 'loose, slack', connected in some way with Lat. *laxus* or **lascus*. Loth, Mots lat. 180 f.

4. Goth. *fra-lētan*, *af-lētan*, ON *lāta laust*, Dan. *løslade*, OE *forlǣtan*, Du. *loslaten*, OHG *furlazzan*, NHG *entlassen*, *loslassen*, cpds. of Goth. *lētan*, etc. 'let, leave' (12.18).

Goth. (*ga*)*lausjan*, OHG *lōsen*, MHG *lœsen*, NHG *lösen* (but now mostly in secondary applications), fr. Goth. *laus* 'empty, vain', OHG *lōs* 'free', these fr. the root of Goth. *liusan* in *fraliusan* 'lose' (11.33), etc.

Dan. *slippe*, Sw. *släppa* : ON *sleppa* (str. vb.) 'slip, escape', *sleppa* (wk. vb.) 'let slip, drop', further relations (as with NE *slip*, etc., 10.42) uncertain. Walde-P. 2.433. Falk-Torp 1064.

Sw. *lösgiva* cpd. of *lös* 'loose, free' and *giva* 'give' (11.21).

ME *relese*, NE *release* fr. OFr. *relaisser* : It. *rilasciare*, etc. (above, 2).

5. Lith. *paleisti*, Lett. *atlaist*, cpds. of Lith. *leisti*, Lett. *laist* 'let loose, let', fr. a root with diphthong IE **lēid-*, beside **lēd-* in Goth. *lētan* 'leave, let', etc. Walde-P. 2.395.

6. ChSl. *pustiti*, *otŭpustiti*, iter. *puštati*, etc., general Slavic, derivs. of *pustŭ* 'empty, waste' = OPruss. *pausto* 'wild', perh. : Grk. παύω 'stop, cease' (?). Walde-P. 2.1 f. Semantic relation similar to that between NE sb. *desert*, fr. Lat. *dē-sertus* 'abandoned, left waste' and vb. *desert* 'abandon, forsake' also sometimes 'relinquish, give up' (cf. NED).

ChSl. *rěšiti* (not in Gospels, but freq. in Supr. = λύω 'loose, release'; SCr. *riješiti* 'solve, dispose of, acquit', Russ. *rešit'* 'solve, decide'), etym.? Walde-P. 2.346, 347. Miklosich 277.

7. Skt. *muc-* : Lith. *mukti* 'slip away', Lett. *mukt* 'strip oneself of, slip off', with *s-* Lith. *smukti* 'slide', ChSl. *smykati sę* 'crawl'. Walde-P. 2.254. Cf. the semantic development of Dan. *slippe* (above).

Skt. *sṛj-*, Av. *harəz-*, both also 'discharge, emit, send out' : MHG *selken* 'drip down', Ir. *selg* 'hunt' (sb.), W. *hela* 'to hunt' (3.79). Walde-P. 2.508.

Av. *zā-* : Skt. *hā-* 'leave, lose', etc. (11.33).

11.41 PROPERTY

Grk.	*χρήματα, κτήματα, οὐσία*	Goth.	*aihts, aigin, faihu*	Lith.	*turtas*
NG	*περιουσία, βιός*	ON	*eign, gōz, fē*	Lett.	*manta, īpašums*
Lat.	*bona, rēs, fortūnae*	Dan.	*ejendom, gods, formue, besiddelser*	ChSl.	*sŭtężanĭje, iměnĭje*
It.	*proprietà, beni*	Sw.	*egendom, gods, besittningar*	SCr.	*imanje, posjed, vlasništvo*
Fr.	*biens (propriété)*	OE	*ǣht, sceatt, feoh, gōd*	Boh.	*jmění, majetek, vlastnictví*
Sp.	*propiedad, bienes, haber(es)*	ME	*a(u)ght, godes, catel, possessiounes*	Pol.	*własność, posiadłość, majątek*
Rum.	*bun(uri), avere*	NE	*property, possessions*	Russ.	*imuščestvo, sobstvennost'*
Ir.	*selb*	Du.	*eigendom, bezit, goed, vermogen*	Skt.	*rāi-, vasu-, dhana-, dravya-, apnas-,* etc.
NIr.	*sealbh*	OHG	*ēht, guot, haba (eigan)*	Av.	*gaēθā-, īšti-*
W.	*meddiant*	MHG	*guot, habe (eigen)*		
Br.	*mad(ou), tra*	NHG	*eigentum, besitz, habe, gut, vermögen*		

Words for 'property' are mostly connected with verbs for 'own, possess', or 'have', or with adjectives for 'one's own', a few with words for 'need, use' or 'power'; several with words for 'good', not only in the European languages, where the influence of Lat. *bona* is suspected, but also in Sanskrit. Some are based on words for 'cattle', as conversely often 'property' > 'cattle'. See also 3.15, 11.43.

Several of the generic terms came to be specialized to 'money', 'movable property' or 'landed property'. 'Landed property' is popularly expressed by words for 'land' or 'lands and houses'. The technical terms are mostly combinations (cpds. or phrases) of words for 'property' with 'land, ground' (or sometimes 'immobile'), of such obvious make-up, that it does not seem worth while to list them in a separate group.

1. Grk. χρήματα, pl. of χρῆμα 'thing (of use), matter, affair' : χρή 'needs, must, ought' (9.94), χρέος, χρῆος 'debt' (11.64), χρῶμαι 'need, use' (9.423). Generic term, but also often spec. for 'money' and so reg. in NG.

Grk. κτήματα, sg. κτῆμα 'a piece of property' : κτάομαι 'obtain', perf. κέκτημαι 'own', etc. (11.12, 11.16). Generic term (in Homer more common than χρήματα), but specialized to 'landed property' in Hellenistic times, and so reg. in NG.

Grk. οὐσία, lit. 'the substance, being, essence', fr. οὖσα fem. pres. pple. of εἰμί 'am'. Hence Grk. περιουσία 'abundance, surplus', but in NG the reg. word for 'property' in general.

Grk. βίος (ὁ) 'life' (cf. 4.74) as 'mode of life' and esp. 'means of living, livelihood', late 'property', hence NG βιός (τό) 'property' and 'wealth'.

2. Lat. *bona*, nom. pl. neut. of *bonus* 'good'. Hence Rum. *bun* 'good', sb. 'property', pl. *bunuri*.

Lat. *rēs* (also general 'thing, affair, matter' but only secondarily) : Skt. *rāi-* (nom. sg. *rās*, gen. sg. *rāyas*) 'property,

wealth' (also *rayi-*), Av. *rāyō* (gen. sg.) 'wealth', *rayi-* 'splendor', Skt. *rā-* 'give'. Walde-P. 2.343. Ernout-M. 861 f.

Lat. *fortūnae*, pl. of *fortūna* 'chance, luck, fortune' (16.17), in sense of 'gifts of (good) fortune'.

Lat. *possessiōnēs*, orig. generic but in actual use 'landed property' (cf. *possessiones appellantur agri late patentes, publici privatique*, etc., Festus), sg. *possessiō* prop. 'acquisition, act of taking possession' : *possidēre* 'possess' (11.12).

It. *proprietà*, Fr. *propriété*, Sp. *propiedad* (*propriedad*) fr. Lat. *proprietās*, *-tātis* 'peculiarity, natural quality' (fr. *proprius* 'one's own, proper', fr. *prope* 'near'), in late use 'ownership, property'. But now Fr. *propriété* in the sense 'property' is mostly used of 'real estate, landed property', etc.

It. *beni*, Fr. *biens* (less usually *bien* sg.), Sp. *bienes*, used like Lat. *bona* but formed fr. the adv. It. *bene*, Fr., Sp. *bien* 'well' (Lat. *bene*).

Sp. *haberes* (less usually sg. *haber*), Rum. *avere*, fr. the vbs. Sp. *haber*, Rum. *avea* 'have' (11.11).

3. Ir. *selb*, esp. 'landed property' or 'cattle' (cf. Laws, Gloss. 652), NIr. *sealbh*, cpd. of *s-* (= *so-* 'well'), second part : NIr. *ealbh* 'flock, herd', W. *elw* 'profit', referring orig. to property in cattle. Cf. *dealbh* 'poor, destitute', fr. parallel cpd. with *d-* (= *do-* 'ill'). Loth. RC 45.187 ff.

W. *meddiant* : *meddu* 'possess, be able' (11.12).

Br. *mad* (pl. *madou*) = *mat* 'good, well', prob. influenced by Fr. *bien*(*s*), though not necessarily.

4. Goth. *aihts*, OE *ǣht*, ME *aght*, *aught*, etc. (Sc. *aucht*), OHG *ēht* (= Av. *īšti-*) : Goth. *aigin*, also 'property', but ON *eign*, OHG *eigan*, MHG *eigen* esp. 'property in land, estate' and particularly 'inherited estates', fr. the root of Goth. *aigan*, etc. 'own' (11.12). Here also Dan. *ejendom*, Sw. *egendom* (infl. of MLG *ēgendom*), Du. *eigendom*, NHG *eigentum*. Walde-P. 1.105. Falk-Torp 184 f.

Goth. *faihu* 'property, money', ON *fē*, OE *feoh* 'cattle, property, money' : OHG *fihu* 'cattle', Lat. *pecu* 'cattle', *pecūnia* 'property, riches, wealth', esp. 'money' (11.43), Skt. *paçu-*, Av. *pasu-* 'cattle', etc. (3.15). Walde-P. 2.16 f. Ernout-M. 746 f.

ON *gōz* (= *gōðs*), Dan., Sw. *gods* (old gen. sg.), OE *gōd* (neut. sg. and pl.), ME *godes* (NE *goods*, but no longer generic), Du. *goed*, OHG, MHG *guot*, NHG *gut*, fr. the adjs. ON *gōðr*, etc. 'good' (16.71). Falk-Torp 337.

Dan. *besiddelser*, Sw. *besittningar*, Du. *bezit*, NHG *besitz* : Dan. *besidde*, etc. 'possess' (11.12).

OE *sceatt*, also 'tribute, money' : Goth. *skatts* 'money', ON *skattr* 'tribute' (NIcel. 'tax'), OFris. *sket* 'money, cattle', OS *skat* 'money, wealth', OHG *skaz* 'money, coin', NHG *schatz* 'treasure', outside connections and orig. meaning dub. Falk-Torp 988. Feist 429.

ME *catel* fr. ONFr. *catel*, and ME *chatel* fr. OFr. *chatel*, both fr. Lat. *capitāle*, neut. of the adj. *capitālis* 'head-, chief-' used in medieval times for 'principal sum of money, property, etc.'. NED s.v. *chatel*.

ME *possessiounes*, NE *possessions*, pl. of *possession* 'act of possession' then 'piece of property' (but in the sg. usually in the abstract sense, the chief use in the modern Romance languages), fr. OFr. *possessiun* borrowed fr. Lat. *possessiō*, *-ōnis* (above, 2). Generic use for 'property' not directly fr. Lat. *possessiōnēs*, since this was 'landed property', but fr. the vb. *possess*.

NE *property*, ME *proprete* (but rarely in concrete sense before 17th. cent.), fr. OFr. *propriété* (above, 2).

NHG *vermögen* (= MLG *vermogen* > ODan. *formoge*, Dan. *formue*), lit. 'power', sb. fr. inf. *vermögen*, etc. 'be able'. Falk-Torp 260. Weigand-H. 1157.

OHG *haba*, MHG, NHG *habe*, fr. *haben* 'have' (11.11).

5. Lith. *turtas*, fr. *turėti* 'have' (11.11).

Lett. *manta* (= Lith. *manta* 'money') fr. LG *monte*, *munte* (= NHG *münze* 'coin', 11.45). Mühl.-Endz. 2.561 f.

Lett. *īpašums*, fr. *īpašs* 'own, peculiar, special' (: *pats* 'self'). Mühl.-Endz. 1.836.

6. ChSl. *sŭtężanĭje* : *sŭtężati* 'possess' (11.12).

ChSl. *iměnĭje*, SCr. *imanje*, *imutak*, *imovina*, Boh. *jmění*; Boh. *majetek*, Pol. *majątek* (the latter frequently 'estate'), Russ. (fr. ChSl.) *imuščestvo*, also Russ. *imenie* (but chiefly 'estate') : ChSl. *iměti*, etc. 'have' (11.11). Berneker 425.

SCr. *vlasništvo*, Boh. *vlastnictví*, Pol. *własność* : SCr. *vladati*, Boh. *vladiti*, Pol. *władać* 'rule', Russ. *vladet'* 'rule, own' (11.12), etc.

SCr. *posjed*, Pol. *posiadłość* : SCr. *posjedovati*, Pol. *posiadać* 'possess' (11.12).

Russ. *sobstvennost'*, fr. *sobstvennyj* 'own, belonging to' (: *sebja* 'self').

7. Skt. *rāi-* : Lat. *rēs*, above, 2.

Skt. *vasu-*, sb. fr. adj. *vasu-* 'good'.

Skt. *dhana-*, in Vedic mostly 'prize (of contest), stake, booty', whence also 'property, wealth', prob. : *dhā-* 'set, place', Grk. τίθημι, etc., cf. Grk. θέμα 'deposit of money, pledge'. Uhlenbeck 134. Walde-P. 1.828.

Skt. *dravya-*, also 'material, substance', this perh. as orig. 'building material', fr. *dru-* 'wood'. Uhlenbeck 132.

Skt. *apnas-*, also 'earnings' : *apas-* 'work', Lat. *opus* 'work', *ops* 'riches, wealth', Grk. ὄμπνη 'food', etc. Walde-P. 1.175. Uhlenbeck 10.

Av. *gaēθā-* (= OPers. *gaiθā-*), lit. 'being, material being, substance' then 'house and home', whence, in general, 'possessions' (esp. as 'worldly possessions'), fr. the root **gʷei-* 'live' in Av. *jīva-*, Skt. *jīva-* 'alive' (4.74). Cf. for semantic development Skt. *gaya-* 'house, household'. Barth. 476 f. Walde-P. 1.668.

Av. *īšti-* 'power, possession, property, wealth' (Barth. 376) : Goth. *aihts*, etc., above, 4.

11.42 WEALTH, RICHES

Grk.	*πλοῦτος*	Goth.	*gabei*	Lith.	*bagotystė*
NG	*πλοῦτος, πλούτη, βιός*	ON	*auðr, auðœfi (rīkdōmr)*	Lett.	*bagātība*
Lat.	*dīvitiae, opēs*	Dan.	*rigdom, formue*	ChSl.	*bogatĭstvo*
It.	*ricchezza*	Sw.	*rikedom, förmögenhet*	SCr.	*bogatstvo*
Fr.	*richesse*	OE	*wela, ēad*	Boh.	*bohatství*
Sp.	*riqueza*	ME	*welthe, richesse, wele*	Pol.	*bogactwo*
Rum.	*avere, bogaţie*	NE	*wealth, riches*	Russ.	*bogatstvo*
Ir.	*saidbre, somme*	Du.	*rijkdom, vermogen*	Skt.	*dhana-, vasu-, rāi-*
NIr.	*saidhbhreas, maoin*	OHG	*wolo, welida, rīchiduam*	Av.	*šaēta-, īšti-*
W.	*golud, cyfoeth*	MHG	*rīchtuom*		
Br.	*pinvidigez*	NHG	*reichtum, vermögen*		

The notion of 'wealth, riches' is not universally distinguished from that of 'property'. Words for 'property' may be used with emphasis implying 'much property, wealth', and in fact in primitive society any 'property' beyond household goods and a few domestic animals constitutes 'wealth'. But in the

European languages there are distinctive words for 'wealth', most of them derived from the adjectives for 'rich' (11.51; but sometimes conversely 'rich' from 'wealth'); and there are also certain of the words for 'property' which are most often used with the implication of 'wealth' and so are also entered here in second place, e.g. NHG vermögen.

1. Grk. πλοῦτος (ὁ, but in Byz. declined as neut. σ-stem, hence) NG pop. pl. πλούτη : πολύς 'much, many', πλεῖος, Att. πλέως 'full', etc. Walde-P. 2.64.

NG βίος, see 11.41.

2. Lat. dīvitiae, fr. dīves 'rich' (11.51). Lat. opēs : Skt. apnas- 'property', etc. (11.41).

It. ricchezza, Fr. richesse, Sp. riqueza, derivs. of It. ricco, etc. 'rich' (11.51).

Rum. avere, see 11.41.

Rum. bogație fr. the Slavic (below, 5).

3. Ir. saidbre, NIr. saidhbhreas and saidhbhreacht, fr. Ir. saidbir 'rich' (11.51).

Ir. somme, sb. use of adj. somme 'rich' (11.51). Cf. also somaine esp. 'profits' (Laws, Gloss. 672).

NIr. maoin fr. Ir. mōin, māin 'object of value, treasure' (11.46).

W. golud : Ir. folad 'substance', fr. a cpd. of W. gwo-, Ir. fo- (IE *upo-) and a deriv. of the root in Skt. lota- 'booty', Goth. laun, OHG lōn 'pay, reward', etc. (11.78). Walde-P. 2.380. Pedersen 1.54.

W. cyfoeth, also (and orig.) 'dominion, power', cf. OCorn. chefuidoc 'omnipotens' : Ir. cumachte 'power', con-iccim 'can', etc. Pedersen 1.124.

Br. pinvidigez, fr. pinvidig 'rich' (11.51).

4. Goth. gabei : giban 'give' (11.21).

ON auðr (also auðœfi, cpd. with second member deriv. of of 'excess, multitude'), OE ēad, OHG in al-ōd 'free possession' (hence MLat. allodium), OS ōd 'possession' : ON auðna 'fortune, fate' auðinn, OE ēaden 'granted by fate', Goth. audags 'μακάριος', etc., perh. of mythological origin, with reference to the weaving of the goddess of fate, fr. the root in Lith. austi 'weave', ON vāð 'piece of cloth', etc. Walde-P. 1.16 f. Falk-Torp 530. Feist 63.

Dan. formue, Du. vermogen, NHG vermögen, see 'property' (11.41).

Sw. förmögenhet, deriv. of förmögen 'powerful, wealthy', fr. MLG vormogen(de) pple. of vormogen 'be able' = Du. vermogen, etc. 'be able' as sb. 'power, wealth' (above).

OE wela, ME wele (NE weal), OHG wolo, welo, etc., with deriv. suffix ME welthe (not found in OE), NE wealth, OHG welida : OE wel(l), OHG wola, wela adv. 'well', etc.

ME richesse fr. OFr. richesse; then conceived as pl. form in ME, NE riches.

Du. rijkdom (MLG rīkedōm > late ON rīkdōmr, Dan. rigdom, Sw. rikedom), OHG rīchiduam, rīhtuom, MHG rīchtuom, NHG reichtum, orig. and in the earlier language mostly 'power, dominion' (OE rīcedōm only in this sense), fr. OHG rīchi, OE rīce, ON rīkr, etc. 'mighty', later 'rich' (11.51).

5. Lith. bagotystė, Lett. bagātība, ChSl. bogatĭstvo, etc., fr. the Baltic and Slavic words for 'rich' Lith. bagotas, Lett. bagats, ChSl. bogatŭ (11.51).

6. Skt. dhana-, vasu-, rāi-, Av. išti-, see 'property' (11.41).

Av. šaēta-, etym. dub. Barth. 1704 f.

11.43 MONEY

Grk.	ἀργύριον, χρήματα	Goth.	skatts, faihu	Lith.	pinigai
NG	χρήματα, παράδες, λεφτά	ON	fē, peningar (baugr)	Lett.	nauda
		Dan.	penge	ChSl.	
Lat.	pecūnia, aes, argentum	Sw.	pengar	SCr.	novac, novci
		OE	feoh, sceatt	Boh.	
It.	denaro	ME	mone(ye), fe	Pol.	pieniądze
Fr.	argent	NE	money	Russ.	den'gi
Sp.	dinero	Du.	geld	Skt.	(dhana-)
Rum.	bani, parale	OHG	scaz, gelt	Av.	(šaēta-)
Ir.	....	MHG	gelt, schaz		
NIr.	airgead	NHG	geld		
W.	arian				
Br.	arc'hant				

The chief standard of value in the IE period and in the history of the IE-speaking peoples before the introduction of actual 'money' based on coinage was cattle (in the old wide sense 'livestock'). This is amply attested for the several peoples by direct references and is also reflected in the interchange of 'cattle' with 'property' or 'money' in an inherited IE group and some others (3.15). Cf. Schrader, Reallex. 1.371 ff., and, especially for Celtic, Vendryes, RC 42.381 ff.

Among other standards of value preceding 'money' proper were horses, furs (ORuss. kuna 'martin skin, money, a small coin', whence Russ. kunec 'merchant'; cf. Berneker 644), linen (whence Slavic verb for 'pay', 11.65), articles of jewelry (Skt. niṣka- in RV, cf. Zimmer, Altind. Leben 259; Ir. sēt, see below), certain utensils (Grk. λέβης 'bronze kettle', in Crete also of a coin, πέλεκυς 'ax' in Cyprus name of a coin). The immediate precursor of coined money officially standardized and stamped was the use of precious metals in rings (cf. ON baugr, below, 4), bars (cf. Grk. ὀβολός 'spit, nail' and name of a small coin), or other forms.

Of the words for 'money', some are those for 'property' used to include or specialized to 'money'. More frequent is generalization from 'coin' or the

names of particular coins, the latter in part derived from the name of the metal used, especially 'silver'. In one group 'money' is from 'payment'.

1. Grk. ἄργυρος 'silver' (9.65), also 'money' (Aesch.+) as esp. the deriv. ἀργύριον (both forms as 'money' in Cretan Law-Code).

Grk. χρήματα 'property' (11.41), also and in NG reg. money.

NG pop. παράδες, pl. of παράς, fr. Turk. para, the small Turkish coin.

NG pop. λεφτά, pl. of λεπτόν 'centime'.

2. Lat. pecūnia, earlier 'wealth in cattle', then 'wealth, money' whence also 'coin' esp. in late Lat. 'copper coins', fr. pecu 'cattle', this also sometimes 'money' (like Goth. faihu, below).

Lat. aes 'bronze' (9.66), hence, since the early coins were of bronze, 'money' esp. in the expression aes aliēnum 'another's money' = 'debt' (11.64).

Lat. argentum 'silver' (9.65), used also of 'silver coin, money' (so already in Plautus), hence Fr. argent in both senses.

It. denaro, danaro (OIt. danaio), Sp. dinero, fr. VLat. dinarius for Lat. dēnārius, name of a Roman silver coin orig. worth ten asses, fr. dēnī distributive adj. to decem 'ten'. Ernout-M. 245. REW 2553.

Rum. bani, pl. of ban, name of a coin (11.44).

Rum. parale, pl. of para, name of a coin, fr. Turk. para (see above, 1).

3. In older Irish, the regular method of estimating value is by heads of cattle, chiefly by so many dairt 'yearling', or samaisc 'three-year-old heifer'. Another standard of value is the sēt probably orig. a jewel or brooch of some sort (see 6.72). Schrader, Reallex. 2.335. Laws, Gloss. 657 f.

NIr. airgead, W. arian (ariant), Br. arc'hant 'silver' (9.65) and 'money'.

4. Goth. skatts (also δηνάριον, μνᾶ), OE sceatt 'property, money, coin', OHG scaz 'money, coin' (also as in Goth. the name of certain coins, see under 'property', OE sceatt (11.41).

Goth. faihu (renders ἀργύριον Mk. 14.11), ON fē, OE feoh, ME fe, all 'property, money', see 11.41.

ON baugr 'ring' and, from the use of spiral-formed rings as a medium of payment, also 'money', esp. in cpds. as baug-gildi 'wergeld', etc. Vigfusson s.v.

ON peningr, Sw. penning 'coin', esp. a definite coin 'a penny', pl. ON peningar, Dan. penge, Sw. pengar 'money' : OE pening, pending, etc., OHG pfenning 'penny, small coin', orig. dub. Falk-Torp 821. Weigand-H. 2.407 f. NED s.v. penny. Hence borrowed Lith. pinigas, piningas 'coin', pl. 'money', ChSl. *pĕnęgŭ, pĕnęzĭ 'denarius' (whence pĕnęžĭnikŭ 'money-changer, banker' Jn. 2.14, Lk. 19.23). Stender-Petersen 385.

ME mone(ye) in both senses 'coin, money', NE money, fr. OFr. moneie, mon(n)oie 'coin', cf. Fr. monnaie (11.44).

OHG, MHG gelt, NHG, Du. geld, orig. 'payment, compensation', cf. OE gild 'payment, tribute, substitute, offering',

ON gjald 'tribute, payment', Goth. gild 'tax, tribute' : OHG geltan 'replace, pay', Goth. fra-, us-gildan 'repay', outside connections dub. Walde-P. 1.632. Feist 161.

5. Lith. pinigai, pl. of pinigas 'coin', fr. the Gmc., see above, 4.

Lett. nauda, cf. Lith. nauta 'use, profit', fr. the Gmc., cf. ON naut, OE nēat 'cattle, oxen' (3.20). Mühl.-Endz. 2.695 f.

6. ChSl. sĭrebro, sŭrebro 'silver' (9.65) reg. renders also Grk. ἀργύριον as 'money'.

SCr. novac 'coin, money', esp. in latter sense pl. novci, fr. nov 'new', orig. referring to the 'new coinage' as contrasted to the old, then extended. Rječnik Akad. 8.243 f.

Boh. peníze, Pol. pieniądze : ChSl. pĕnęzĭ 'denarius', fr. the Gmc., see above, 4.

Russ. den'gi, pl. of den'ga 'a copper coin' (> Pol. dzięga), loanword fr. a widespread oriental group of terms for 'money' or various coins, as Kasan. tenk'e, Kirg. tenge, etc. Berneker 183 f. Lokotsch 478.

7. Several of the Skt. words for 'property' or 'wealth' are sometimes rendered 'money', most commonly dhana- (11.41), but evidence of actual money is late. For early substitutes, see Zimmer, Altind. Leben 259.

Av. šaēta- 'wealth' (11.42) is in certain passages rendered 'Geld' by Bartholomae and 'argent' (also 'trésor') by Darmesteter, but there is no certain reference to actual money in the Avesta, and the payments enumerated in Vd. 7.41 ff. are in terms of domestic animals.

11.44 COIN

Grk.	νόμισμα	Goth.	(skatts)	Lith.	pinigas
NG	νόμισμα	ON	peningr, mynt	Lett.	naudas gabals
Lat.	nummus (monēta)	Dan.	mynt	ChSl.	sklęzĭ
It.	moneta	Sw.	mynt, penning	SCr.	novac
Fr.	monnaie	OE	mynet, sceatt	Boh.	mince
Sp.	moneda	ME	mynt, mone(ye), coyn	Pol.	moneta
Rum.	monedă, ban	NE	coin	Russ.	moneta
Ir.	....	Du.	munt		
NIr.	bonn, pĩosa	OHG	muniz(a), scaz		
W.	bath	MHG	münze		
Br.	moneiz	NHG	münze		

1. Grk. νόμισμα, orig. 'anything sanctioned by custom', then esp. (as 'legal tender') 'coin', deriv. of νομίζω 'practice as custom' : νόμος 'custom, law' (21.11). Walde-P. 2.330 ff.

2. Lat. nummus, prob. an early loanword fr. Grk. νόμιμος 'customary, legal' : νόμος, etc. (above). Sicil. Grk. νοῦμμος would then be in turn fr. the Italic form. Ernout-M. 686 f.

Late Lat. monēta, orig. a surname of Juno, then the temple where she was worshiped and where money was coined, hence 'place of coinage, mint', in later use also the 'die or stamp for coining' and esp. the 'coin' itself. Hence the common European words, It. moneta, Fr. monnaie (> Br. moneiz, ME moneye), Sp. moneda, Rum. monedă; OE mynet, ME mynt, MLG munt (> late ON, Dan., Sw. mynt), Du. munt, OHG muniza, muniz, MHG, NHG münze (> Boh. mince); Pol., Russ. moneta. Ernout-M. 628. Falk-Torp 745. Berneker 2.76.

Rum. ban, name of a coin and pop. 'coin', orig. a coin struck by the ban, a government official (fr. Hung. ban). Tiktin 151 f.

3. NIr. bonn (also 'medal', etc.), fr. Lat. pondo 'by weight'. Vendryes, De hib. voc. 117. Macbain 43.

NIr. pĩosa 'piece' and 'coin', fr. NE

piece, also used for a coin (NED s.v. piece, sb. 13).

W. bath 'stamp, emblem', also (with or without arian 'silver, money') 'coin' : vb. bathu 'coin', fr. Lat. batt(u)ere 'strike'. Loth, Mots lat. 137.

4. For ON peningr and Goth. skatts (quotable only for a particular coin; the passage Mt. 22.19 lacking), OE sceatt, OHG scaz, see under 'money' (11.43), and for OE mynet, OHG muniza, etc. above, 2.

ME coyn, NE coin, fr. Fr. coin 'wedge, corner, die, stamp', fr. Lat. cuneus 'wedge'. NED s.v. coin, sb.

5. Lith. pinigas, piningas 'coin', pl. 'money', see 11.43.

Lett. naudas gabals, lit. 'piece of money', paralleled by expressions in other languages (cf. Dan. pengestykke, NHG geldstück) but here apparently the usual expression.

6. ChSl. sklęzĭ (renders νόμισμα Mt. 22.19), cf. Pol. szelag name of different old Polish coins, Russ. šeleg 'counter', etc., fr. the Gmc., cf. Goth. skilliggs, ON skillingr, OE scilling, etc. 'shilling', name of various coins : ON skilja 'separate, divide', etc. (more directly : Goth. skildus 'shield'?). Walde-P. 2.593. Feist 433. Stender-Petersen 380 f.

SCr. novac 'coin, money', see 11.43.

For Indo-Iranian, see under 'money' (11.43).

11.45 PURSE

Grk.	*βαλλάντιον*	Goth.	*puggs*	Lith.	(*pinigų*) *ma*(*k*)*šna*
NG	*πουγγί*	ON	*sjōðr, pungr*	Lett.	*naudas maks*
Lat.	*marsupium, crumīna*	Dan.	*pung*	ChSl.	*vŭlagalište*
It.	*borsa*	Sw.	*pung*	SCr.	*novčarka*
Fr.	*bourse*	OE	*sēod, pung*	Boh.	*měšec, váček* (*na peníze*)
Sp.	*bolsa*	ME	*purs*		
Rum.	*pungă*	NE	*purse* (*cod*)	Pol.	*worek* (*na pieniądze*)
Ir.	. . . .	Du.	(*geld*)*buidel, beurs*	Russ.	*košelek*
NIr.	*sparān*	OHG	*seckil, scazfung, pfoso*	Skt.	*granthi-*
W.	*pwrs, cod*	MHG	*seckel, biutel*	Av.	. . . .
Br.	*yalc'h*	NHG	(*geld*)*beutel*		

The 'purse' of earlier times was simply a 'money bag' and so was regularly expressed by words for 'bag, pouch'. Some continued to be used for both 'bag' and 'purse', in the latter case with 'money' understood, or explicit as in NHG *geldbeutel*, etc. Others were definitely specialized to 'purse', as Fr. *bourse*, NE *purse*, etc.

1. Grk. *βαλλάντιον*, etym. dub., perh. fr. a **gʷel-* beside **gel-* in Lat. *gula* 'throat', etc. (cf. Walde-H. 1.625 f.).

NG *πουγγί*, Byz. *πουγγίον*, fr. Gmc., Goth. *puggs*, etc. (below, 4).

2. Lat. *marsup*(*p*)*ium*, fr. Grk. *μαρσύπ*(*π*)*ιον*, *-ίπ*(*π*)*ιον*, dim. of *μάρσυπος*, *μάρσιππος* 'pouch, bag', this prob. of oriental origin, cf. Av. *maršū-* 'belly'. Buck, IF 25.257.

Lat. *crumīna*, orig. dub., perh. (through Etruscan?) fr. Grk. *γρυμέα* 'bag, chest for old clothes, trash'. Walde-H. 1.294. Ernout-M. 234. Ernout, BSL 30.100.

It. *borsa*, Fr. *bourse*, Sp. *bolsa*, fr. late Lat. *byrsa, bursa*, this fr. Grk. *βύρσα* 'skin, hide, wineskin'. REW 1432.

Rum. *pungă*, fr. Gmc., Goth. *puggs*, etc. (below, 4), through Byz.? REW 6849.

3. NIr. *sparān*, Gael. *sporan*, etym.? Macbain 340 quotes MIr. *sboran*, and derives this by metathesis fr. late Lat. *bursa* (above).

W. *pwrs*, fr. ME *purs*(*e*).

W. *cod*, prob. fr. NE *cod* (below, 4). But see also Loth, RC 42.79 f.

Br. *yalc'h*, etym.? Henry 172 suggests deriv. fr. **pel-* in Lat. *pellis* 'skin', etc.

4. Goth. *puggs*, ON *pungr*, Dan., Sw. *pung*, OE *pung*, MLG *punge*, OHG (*p*)*fung* in *scazfung* (gl. *marsupium*, OHG Glosses 1.284 no. 10), prob. nasalized forms to ON *poki* 'pouch, sack', MHG *pfoch* 'pouch' and : Lat. *bucca* 'puffed-out cheek', etc., with guttural extensions of an imitative **b*(*h*)*u-*. Walde-P. 2.117. Otherwise Feist 385 and Stender-Petersen 396.

ON *sjōðr*, OE *sēod* = OHG *siut* 'seam' : ON *syja*, OE *sēowian*, etc. 'sew'. Walde-P. 2.515. Falk-Torp 1224. Semantic development perh. fr. piece of cloth or hide sewn together to form a bag, or else fr. a fold sewn in the garment.

OE *codd* 'bag', NE *cod* formerly freq. as 'purse' : Du. *kodde* 'testicle', ON *koddi* 'pillow', etc. Falk-Torp 558. NED s.v. *cod* sb.[1].

Late OE *pors*, ME *purs*, NE *purse*, Du. *beurs*, fr. late Lat. *bursa, byrsa* (above, 2).

Du. *buidel*, NHG *beutel* (also frequently in cpd. with *geld* ('money'), MHG *biutel* 'pouch, sack, purse', OHG *būtel* 'pouch, bag' (also for money?), cf. also NIcel. *budda* 'purse', prob. fr. a dental extension of **b*(*h*)*u-* in words for 'puff

out, swell', etc. Walde-P. 2.116. Franck-v. W. 97.

OHG *seckil*, MHG *seckel* (NHG *säckel*), dim. to OHG *sac*(*h*), NHG *sack*, etc., cf. Lat. *saccellum*, dim. to *saccus*. Weigand-H. 2.634.

OHG *pfoso* : OE *pusa, posa*, ON *posi, pūss* 'bag', prob. fr. the same root as Du. *buidel*, etc., above. Walde-P. 2.117. Falk-Torp 844.

5. Lith. (*pinigų*) *mašna* (fr. Russ. *mošna* 'bag, purse'), or *makšna*, of the same group as Lith. *makas* also 'bag, purse' (NSB), Lett. *maks* 'bag', *naudas* (gen. of *nauda* 'money') *maks* 'purse'. Walde-P. 2.225. Mühl.-Endz. 2.554.

6. ChSl. *vŭlagalište* : *vŭlagati* 'put in', iter. cpd. to *ložiti* 'lay'. Berneker 683.

SCr. *novčarka*, fr. *novac* 'money'.

Boh. *měšec*, dim. to *měch* 'sack, leather bag, bellows' (: ChSl. *měchŭ* 'leather bag', etc.).

Boh. *váček* (*na peníze*) dim. of *vak* 'bag, pouch'.

Pol. *worek* (*na pieniądze*) dim. of *wor* 'sack, bag'.

Russ. *košelek*, dim. of *košel'* 'basket, wallet' : *koš* 'basket'. Berneker 587.

7. Skt. *granthi-* 'knot' (9.192), used also of a knot in a corner of a garment for carrying coins, is the nearest approach to 'purse'.

11.46 TREASURE

Grk.	*θησαυρός*	Goth.	*huzd*	Lith.	*turtas*
NG	*θησαυρός*	ON	*hodd*	Lett.	*manta*
Lat.	*thēsaurus*	Dan.	*skat*	ChSl.	*sŭkrovište*
It.	*tesoro*	Sw.	*skatt*	SCr.	*blago*
Fr.	*trésor*	OE	*hord*	Boh.	*poklad*
Sp.	*tesoro*	ME	*tresor, hord*	Pol.	*skarb*
Rum.	*comoară*	NE	*treasure* (*hoard*)	Russ.	*sokrovišče, klad*
Ir.	*mōin*	Du.	*schat*	Skt.	*koça-, nidhi-, nidhāna-*
NIr.	*stōr, taisce*	OHG	*treso, hort*		
W.	*trysor*	MHG	*trese, hort, schaz*	Av.	*šaēta-*
Br.	*teñzor*	NHG	*schatz*		

The most widespread group consists of loanwords going back to Greek *θησαυρός* of unknown etymology. Several reflect the notion of something 'hidden' or 'stored up, deposited'. Some are old words for 'property, wealth' that are used also for, or definitely specialized to, 'treasure'.

1. Grk. *θησαυρός*, etym.? Hence as loanword Lat. *thēsaurus* > It., Sp. *tesoro*; Fr. *trésor* (> ME *tresor*, NE *treasure* > W. *trysor*) with anticipatory *r*, as also OHG *treso*, MHG *trese, tresen;* Br. *teñzor* lit. borrowing fr. Lat. *thensaurus* (orthographical variant of *thēsaurus* with *en* = *ē*). Boisacq 345. REW 8706. Gamillscheg 862 f.

2. Rum. *comoară*, fr. Slavic, cf. SCr. *komora* 'chamber, treasury', Slov. *komora* 'chamber', etc., fr. Lat. *camara, camera* 'vault, arch', in VLat. 'room', 'treasure room'. Tiktin 396. Berneker 555 f.

3. Ir. *mōin, māin*, cf. *dag-mōini* 'good gifts, benefits' : Lat. *mūnus* 'service, office, gift, etc.', *commūnis*, Goth. *gamains* 'common', etc. Walde-P. 2.241. Pedersen 1.57. Thurneysen, Gram. 43.

NIr. *stōr*, fr. NE *store*.

NIr. *taisce*, fr. *taiscim* 'store up, treasure, take care of' apparently = MIr. *taiscim* 'give notice' denom. of *tasc* 'notice, announcement' (cf. Laws 6.692), cf. OIr. *do-fa-r-siged* gl. 'significatum est', cpd. of IE **sekʷ-* 'see, say' (Walde-P. 2.478, Pedersen 2.619, but without mention of the NIr. words).

4. Goth. *huzd*, ON *hodd*, OE, ME *hord*, NE *hoard*, OHG, MHG *hort*, fr. IE **kus-dho-* (or **kudh-dho-* :) in Grk. *κύσθος* 'pudenda muliebria', i.e. 'hidden, covered' : Skt. *koça-, koṣa-* 'container' (whence 'treasure chest, chamber' and also applied to the 'treasure' itself), ON, OE *hūs* 'house', fr. the root *(*s*)*keu-* 'cover'. Walde-P. 2.551. Feist 278.

Dan. *skat*, Sw. *skatt*, Du. *schat*, MHG *schaz*, NHG *schatz* = OHG *scaz* 'money, coin', OE *sceatt* 'property, money, coin', etc. (11.41).

5. Lith. *turtas* and Lett. *manta*, both 'property' (11.41), cover also 'treasure'.

6. ChSl. *sŭkrovište*, Russ. *sokrovišče* (fr. ChSl.), cf. ChSl. *pokrovište* 'covering', *pokroviteli* 'protector', fr. *krovŭ*, Russ. *krov* 'roof', etc. : ChSl. *kryją, kryti* 'cover'. Berneker 625, 633.

SCr. *blago*, fr. *blag* = ChSl. *blagŭ*, etc. 'good'. Cf. also Bulg. *blágo* 'possessions, wealth'. Berneker 69.

Boh. *poklad*, Russ. *klad*, cf. ChSl. *pokladŭ* 'deposit', Ukr. *pokład* 'layer, treasure' : ChSl. *kladą, klasti*, etc. 'load, lay'. Berneker 507.

Pol. *skarb*, cf. Russ. *skarb* 'furniture, household utensils', etym? Brückner 493 (: SCr. *skrb* 'distress, care', etc.).

7. Skt. *koça-, koṣa-*, see under Goth. *huzd*, above, 4.

Skt. *nidhi-, nidhāna-*, both orig. 'receptacle', fr. *ni-dhā-* 'lay, put down'.

Av. *šaēta-* 'wealth' (11.42) is virtually 'treasure' in Yt. 13.67.

11.47 BANK

Grk.	*τράπεζα*			Lith.	*bankas*
NG	*τράπεζα*			Lett.	*banka*
Lat.	*argentāria*			SCr.	*banka*
It.	*banca*			Boh.	*banka*
Fr.	*banque*	Dan., Sw., NE, Du., NHG	*bank*	Pol.	*bank*
Sp.	*banco*			Russ.	*bank*
Rum.	*bancă*				
NIr.	*bannc*				
W.	*ariandy, banc*				
Br.	*bank*				

In Greece in early times the temples served for the safe deposit of money, private as well as public. But a regular banking business had evolved from the humble trade of the money changers by the fifth century B.C. Its flourishing state in fourth-century Athens appears in the frequent references in the orators. Hence it spread to Rome and eventually to the rest of Europe. It was in Italy, the home of the great European bankers (cf. the use of *Lombard* for 'banker' or 'bank'. NED s.v.), that the current European word for 'bank' began its career.

Of the terms for 'bank' a few are derivatives of words for 'money', but the more common source is the 'table' of the moneychangers.

1. Grk. *τράπεζα* 'table' (7.44), hence in special application the 'table' of the moneychangers, then 'bank', whence *τραπεζίτης* 'banker'. Cf., beside the many examples in the orators, the Boeot. *διὰ τραπέδδας τᾶς Πιστοκλεῖος* 'through the bank of Pistocles', Schwyzer, Dial. Graec. Ex. 523.170.

2. Lat. *mēnsa* 'table' was sometimes used in the special sense like Grk. *τράπεζα*. But more commonly *taberna argentāria* (*taberna* 'booth') and simply *argentāria*, with *argentārius* 'banker', fr. *argentum* 'money' (11.43). Similarly W.

ariandy (beside *banc*), fr. *arian* 'money' and *ty* 'house'.

3. It. *banco, banca*, with similar forms in other Romance languages, were borrowed fr. a Gmc. word *bank* 'bench' seen in OHG *banch*, NHG *bank*, OE *benc*, NE *bench*, etc. They were often applied to a 'table, counter' for the display of wares, and through that of the moneychangers became the regular words for 'bank' and in this sense spread to the rest of Europe (except Greece). It was the fem. form that most commonly prevailed in this sense, as It. *banca*, Fr. *banque*, etc.; but cf. also Sp. *banco*, Lith. *bankas* vs. Lett. *banka*, Pol., Russ. *bank* vs. SCr., Boh. *banka*. NED s.v. *bank*, sb. 3. Wartburg 1.235 ff.

4. One cannot, of course, expect to find words for 'bank' in the early period of the European languages other than Greek or Latin except as translations from the latter. The NT passage, Lk. 19.23, *ἐπὶ τὴν τράπεζαν*, Vulgate *ad mensam*, is rendered as follows.

Goth. *du skattjam*, dat. pl. of *skattja* deriv. of *skatts* 'money' (11.43), hence 'money-dealer, banker'. Similarly ChSl. *pěnęžĭnikomŭ*, dat. pl. of *pěnęžĭnikŭ* deriv. of *pěnęzĭ* 'denarius, money' (11.43), so here likewise 'to the money-dealers'.

OE *to hyre*, that is, a paraphrase giving the proper sense, 'to hire, on loan'. Lindisf. *to wege to disc*, with *disc* = Vulgate *mensam*. Wyclif uses *boord* 'table'.

OHG (Tat.) *zi mazzu*, clearly a distortion or mistranslation of the Vulgate *mensam* (cf. *maz* 'food', *gimazzo* 'table-companion').

11.48 HEIR

Grk.	*κληρονόμος*	Goth.	*arbja*	Lith.	*paveldėtojas, įpėdinis*
NG	*κληρονόμος*	ON	*arfi, erfingi, arftaki*	Lett.	*mantinieks*
Lat.	*hērēs*	Dan.	*arving*	ChSl.	*naslědĭnikŭ*
It.	*erede*	Sw.	*arvinge*	SCr.	*baštinik, nasljednik*
Fr.	*héritier*	OE	*ierfenuma*	Boh.	*dědic*
Sp.	*heredero*	ME	(*h*)*eir*, etc.	Pol.	*spadkobierca* (*dziedzic*)
Rum.	*moştenitor*	NE	*heir*		
Ir.	*orbam*	Du.	*erfgenaam*	Russ.	*naslednik*
NIr.	*oidhre*	OHG	*arpeo, erbo*	Skt.	*dāyāda-, rikthin-*, etc.
W.	*etifedd*	MHG	*erbe*	Av.	. . . .
Br.	*hêr*	NHG	*erbe*		

In general, words for 'heir' are derived from words for 'share' or 'property', or through the notion of 'patrimony' from words for 'father' or 'grandfather', or meant simply 'follower, successor'. But the notion of 'inheritor of property' common to these is, on the other hand, quite secondary in two important groups, which rest on the notion of 'bereaved', with cognates meaning 'orphan' or 'widow'.

1. Grk. *κληρονόμος*, cpd. of *κλῆρος* 'lot, share, heritage' (orig. 'piece of wood used in casting lots' : Ir. *clār*, etc. 'board') and the root of *νέμω* 'distribute', mid. 'have as one's share'. This is the reg. Attic term, but Cretan has *πατρωιῶχος* fr. **πατρωιό-οχος*, cpd. of *πατρώιος* 'inherited from the father' (cf. *τὰ πατρώια* 'patrimony') and *-οχος* : *ἔχω* 'hold, have'.

2. Lat. *hērēs, -dis* (hence It. *erede*, OFr. (*h*)*eir*, (*h*)*oir* > Br. *hêr*, ME, NE *heir;* Fr. *héritier*, Sp. *heredero*, fr. Lat. *hērēditārius* adj. 'hereditary'; REW 4114) : Grk. *χῆρος* 'bereft', *χήρα* 'widow', Skt. *hā-* 'leave, lose', etc. Walde-P. 1.543. Ernout-M. 448 f. Walde-H. 1.641.

Rum. *moştenitor*, fr. *moşteni* 'inherit', this again fr. arch. *moştean* 'heir', beside which also arch. *moşan* 'heir', all derivs. of *moş* 'grandfather, ancestor' (cf. *stramoşi* 2.56). Densusianu 354.

3. Ir. *orbam* (RAI Contrib. s.v.), also *comarbe* 'co-heir' (*comarbi*, gl. *coheredes* Wb. 19c20), fr. *orbe* 'inheritance' : Goth. *arbi* 'inheritance', etc., below, 4. Pedersen 1.32.

NIr. *oidhre*, fr. ME *heir*. Macbain 267.

W. *etifedd*, formerly 'child, offspring', MW *etyfed*, perh. : *tyfu* 'grow'. G. S. Lane, Language 7.280 f.

4. Goth. *arbja*, ON *arfi*, OHG *arpeo, erbo*, MHG, NHG *erbe* 'heir' (beside ON *arfr*, OE *ierfe*, Goth., OHG *arbi*, MHG, NHG *das erbe* 'inheritance', in cpds. ON *erfingi*, Dan. *arving*, Sw. *arvinge* (last member prob. *-gengi*), ON *arf-taki, -takari, arftǫkumaðr*, OE *ierfenuma*, Du. *erfgenaam* (: ON *taka*, OE *neman*, etc. 'take') : Ir. *orbe* 'inheritance', Grk. ὀρφα- νός 'bereft, orphan', Lat. *orbus* 'bereft', Arm. *orb* 'orphan', Skt. *arbha-* 'little, weak' sb. 'child'. Walde-P. 1.183. Falk-Torp 34.

5. Lith. *paveldétojas*, fr. *paveldéti* 'in-

herit', cpd. of *veldéti* id., beside *valdyti* 'rule' (19.31).

Lith. *įpédinis*, 'successor' and 'heir', fr. *péda* 'footstep, track'.

Lett. *mantinieks*, fr. *manta* 'property' (11.41).

6. ChSl. *naslědĭnikŭ*, SCr. *nasljednik*, Russ. *naslednik*, fr. ChSl. *naslěditi* 'in- herit', etc. cpd. of *na* 'on' and *slěditi* 'follow' (10.52).

SCr. *baštinik*, fr. *baština* 'patrimony', this fr. the rare *bašta* 'father'. Berneker 46.

Boh. *dědic* (Pol. *dziedzic* formerly the usual word, now mostly 'landed pro- prietor', Russ. *dedič* now obs.), fr. Boh. *děd*, etc. 'grandfather' (2.46). Berneker 191.

Pol. *spadkobierca*, cpd. of *spadek* 'a fall, that which falls by lot, heritage' (: *pasc*, ChSl. *pasti* 'fall', 10.23) and *brać* 'take'. Brückner 37,390.

7. Skt. *dāyāda-*, fr. *dāya-* 'share, in- heritance' (: *dāti* 'cuts off, divides, shares') and *-āda-* 'taking-, receiving-' (fr. *ā-dā-* 'receive').

Skt. *rikthin-* (adj. and sb.), fr. *riktha-* 'inheritance', whence also cpds. for 'heir', *rikthagraha-, rikthabhāj-, riktha- hāra-*, etc. : *ric-* 'leave', etc. (11.34).

11.51 RICH

Grk.	πλούσιος	Goth.	*gabigs*	Lith.	*bagotas, turtingas*
NG	πλούσιος	ON	*auðigr (ríkr)*	Lett.	*bagāts, turīgs*
Lat.	*dives, opulentus*	Dan.	*rig*	ChSl.	*bogatŭ*
It.	*ricco*	Sw.	*rik*	SCr.	*bogat*
Fr.	*riche*	OE	*welig, ēad(ig) (ríce)*	Boh.	*bohatý*
Sp.	*rico*	ME	*riche, welthy*	Pol.	*bogaty*
Rum.	*bogat*	NE	*rich, wealthy*	Russ.	*bogatyj*
Ir.	*somme, saidbir*	Du.	*rijk*	Skt.	*dhanin-, dravyavant-, revant-*
NIr.	*saidhbhir*	OHG	*ōtag, ēhtig (rīchi)*		
W.	*cyfoethog*	MHG	*rich(e)*	Av.	*šaētavant-, īštavant-*
Br.	*pinvidig*	NHG	*reich*		

While many of the words for 'rich' are derivatives of those for 'property' or 'wealth', others are of independent origin resting on broader notions such as 'mighty', 'fortunate', 'splendid', 'favored of the gods.'

1. Grk. πλούσιος, fr. πλοῦτος 'wealth' (11.42).

2. Lat. *dives, -itis*, prob. fr. *dīvus* 'god', reflecting the conception of the gods as the dispensers of wealth. Er- nout-M. 273. Walde-H. 1.358 f.

Lat. *opulentus*, fr. *opes* 'riches' (11.42).

It. *ricco*, Fr. *riche*, Sp. *rico*, fr. Gmc. (below, 4). REW 7315.

Rum. *bogat*, fr. Slavic (below, 6).

3. Ir. *somme* 'rich' and *domme* 'poor', cpds. of *so-* 'well' (IE *su-*) and *do-* 'ill' (IE *dus-*), second part dub., perh. *op- smio* fr. the root in Lat. *opēs* 'riches', etc. Walde-P. 1.176.

Ir. *saidbir*, NIr. *saidhbhir* 'rich' and *daidbir*, NIr. *daidhbhir* 'poor', cpds. of *so-* and *do-* (as above) with *adbar* 'ma- terial' (of dub. etym.). Pedersen 1.305, 2.9, 518 note.

W. *cyfoethog*, fr. *cyfoeth* 'power, wealth' (11.42).

Br. *pinvidig* by metathesis for *pindi- vig = W. *pendefig* 'prince, noble', deriv. of *penn* 'head, chief'. Pedersen 1.381. Henry 224. Ernault, Glossaire 492.

4. Goth. *gabigs*, fr. *gabei* 'wealth, riches' (11.42).

ON *auðigr*, OE *ēadig, ēad*, OHG *ōtag*, fr. ON *auðr*, OE *ēad* (OHG *-ōd* in *alōd*) 'wealth' (11.42).

ON *rīkr*, Dan. *rig*, Sw. *rik*, OE *rīce*, etc., but in the older period mostly 'mighty, noble' = Goth. *reiks* 'ruler', adj. 'honored', prob. old Gmc. loanword fr. Celtic, cf. Gall. *rīx* 'king' (e.g. in *Dumno-rīx*, etc.), Ir. *rī* (gen. *rīg*) id. = Lat. *rēx*, etc. Walde-P. 2.365. Falk- Torp 898.

OE *welig*, ME *welthy*, NE *wealthy*, fr. OE *wela*, ME *welthe* 'wealth' (11.42).

OHG *ēhtig*, fr. *ēht* 'property' (11.41).

5. Lith. *bagotas*, Lett. *bagāts*, loan- words fr. Slavic (below, 6). Mühl.- Endz. 1.249.

Lith. *turtingas*, fr. *turtas* 'property' (11.41).

Lett. *turīgs*, fr. *turēt* 'hold, keep, have' (11.11).

6. ChSl. *bogatŭ*, etc., general Slavic, fr. *bogŭ* 'share' in *ubogŭ, nebogŭ* 'poor' = *bogŭ* 'god' : Skt. *bhaga-* 'good for- tune, welfare' and 'dispenser', Av. *baγa-* 'share, good fortune, god', OPers. *baga- 'god', Skt. *bhaj-* 'share, distribute', etc. Walde-P. 2.128. Berneker 67. Brück- ner 33 f.

7. Skt. *dhanin-*, fr. *dhana-* 'property, wealth' (11.41).

Skt. *dravyavant-*, fr. *dravya-* 'property' (11.42).

Skt. *revant-* (also 'splendid' and so Av. *raēvant-*), fr. *rāi-* 'wealth' (11.41).

Av. *šaētavant-*, fr. *šaēta-* 'riches' (11.42).

Av. *īštavant-*, fr. *īšti-* 'property, riches' (11.41).

11.52 POOR

Grk.	πένης	Goth.	*unlēds*	Lith.	*biednas, neturtingas*
NG	φτωχός	ON	*fátœkr, ūauðigr*	Lett.	*nabags, mazturīgs*
Lat.	*pauper, inops*	Dan.	*fattig*	ChSl.	*ubogŭ, nebogŭ, ništĭ*
It.	*povero*	Sw.	*fattig*	SCr.	*ubog, siromašan*
Fr.	*pauvre*	OE	*wǣdla, þearfende, earm*	Boh.	*chudý, ubohý*
Sp.	*pobre*			Pol.	*ubogi, biedny*
Rum.	*sărac*	ME	*pou(e)re, arm*	Russ.	*bednyj, ubogyj*
Ir.	*bocht, domme, daidbir*	NE	*poor*	Skt.	*daridra-, nirdhana- etc.*
NIr.	*bocht, daidhbhir, dealbh*	Du.	*arm, behoeftig*		
		OHG	*arm, durftig, wādal*	Av.	*drigu-, ašaēta-*
W.	*tlawd*	MHG	*arm, durftic*		
Br.	*paour, tavantek*	NHG	*arm, (be)dürftig*		

Most of the common words for 'poor' as the opposite of 'rich' are also used with strong emotional value (depreciatory or affectionate) for 'unfortunate, wretched', etc., and this latter use is by no means al- ways the secondary one. That is, be- sides the words in which lack of wealth is the primary notion, as shown by their etymology (e.g. neg. cpds. of words for 'rich' or 'wealth'), there are many others in which, as the cognates show, the de- velopment has been in the opposite di- rection, namely from an expressive term for 'unfortunate' or the like to 'poor' = 'not rich'.

1. Grk. πένης (adj. 'poor' and sb. 'a poor man') : πένομαι 'toil, work' also 'be poor', πόνος 'toil, work', etc. (9.12).

The πένης was the one who toiled for a living, 'poor' by contrast to the rich, but distinct from the πτωχός 'beggar' (11.53) who had nothing (cf. Aristoph., Plutus 553). But already in the NT πτωχός has displaced πένης as the com- mon word for 'poor', hence NG φτωχός.

2. Lat. *pauper*, prob. an old cpd. *pau-paro-s* 'getting little' (cf. ON *fá- tœkr*, below, 4), first member : *paucus* 'little', Goth. *fawai*, ON *fár* 'few', and the second : *parāre* 'get, prepare' (11.16). Hence It. *povero*, Fr. *pauvre* (OFr. *povre* > Br. *paour*, ME *pou(e)re*, NE *poor*), Sp. *pobre*. Walde-P. 2.75. Ernout-M. 744. REW 6305.

Lat. *inops*, neg. cpd. of *opes* 'wealth' (11.42).

Rum. *sărac*, fr. Slavic, late ChSl. *si- rakŭ* (below, 6).

3. Ir. *bocht*, prob. orig. 'broken', pple. to *bong-* 'break'. Stokes 177.

Ir. *domme*, see under *somme* 'rich' (11.51).

Ir. *daidbir*, NIr. *daidhbhir*, see under *saidbir* 'rich' (11.51).

NIr. *dealbh*, see under *selb* 'property' (11.41).

W. *tlawd*, cf. Ir. *tláith* 'soft' : Grk. τλᾱτός 'suffering, patient', Lat. *lātus* 'born, carried', fr. the root *tel-* in words for 'lift, carry' and 'endure'. Walde-P. 1.739. Pedersen 1.132.

Br. *paour*, fr. OFr. *povre* (above, 2). Henry 217.

Br. *tavantek*, etym. dub. Henry 261. Ernault, Glossaire 683.

4. Goth. *unlēds* = OE *unlǣd* 'miser- able, unfortunate' sometimes also 'poor', lit. 'without possessions in land', neg. cpd. of OE *lǣþ* = ON *lāð* 'share of land'. Walde-P. 2.394. Feist 521.

ON *fátœkr*, Dan., Sw. *fattig*, lit. 'tak- ing little', cpd. of *fá* acc. of *fár* 'few' and *tœkr* : *taka* 'take'. Falk-Torp 208. Hellquist 203.

ON *ūauðigr*, neg. cpd. of *auðigr* 'rich'.

OE *wǣdla* (also sb. 'a poor man, beg- gar') beside *wǣdl* 'poverty', OHG *wādal*

'poor' beside *wādali* 'poverty', etym. dub. Walde-P. 1.15, 221.

OE *þearfende*, pple. of *þearfan* 'need'.

OE *earm* (but mostly 'miserable'), ME *arm* (rare), Du., OHG-NHG *arm* = Goth. *arms*, ON *armr* 'wretched, miser- able', etym. dub., perh. fr. *arb-ma-* : Lat. *orbus* 'bereft', Grk. ὀρφανός 'bereft, orphan', etc. Walde-P. 1.184. Falk- Torp 32 f.

ME *pouere, poure*, NE *poor*, fr. OFr. *povre* (above, 2).

Du. *behoeftig* : *behoeven* 'need, want'.

OHG *durftig*, MHG *durftic*, NHG (be)dürftig : OHG *durfan*, etc. 'need, want'.

5. Lith. *biednas*, fr. Pol. *biedny* (be- low).

Lith. *neturtingas*, neg. of *turtingas* 'rich' (11.51).

Lett. *nabags*, fr. Slavic *nebogŭ*, beside *ubogŭ* 'poor' (below). Mühl.-Endz. 2.685 f.

Lett. *mazturīgs*, cpd. of *maz* 'little' and *turīgs* 'wealthy' (11.51).

6. ChSl. *ubogŭ, nebogŭ*, SCr. *ubog*, Boh. *ubohý*, Pol. *ubogi*, Russ. *ubogyj*, neg. cpds. beside *bogatŭ* 'rich', etc. (11.51).

ChSl. *ništĭ* renders Grk. πτωχός more frequently than *ubogŭ*, mostly as sb.

'poor person, beggar' (Jagić, Entsteh- ungsgesch. 408; and so Russ. *nišči* mostly 'beggar'), fr. *nīstyo-* or *nīskyo-*, precise analysis uncertain but based on a form cognate with Skt *ni-* 'down', ChSl. *nizŭ* 'down', etc. Zubaty, KZ 31.58 ff. Meillet, Études 2.380 f. End- zelin, Z. sl. Ph. 13.78.

SCr. *siromašan*, cf. late (Serb.-)ChSl. *siromachŭ, sirakŭ* 'poor', fr. ChSl. *sirŭ* 'orphaned' (2.75).

Boh. *chudý* = Pol. *chudy* 'lean, wretched', SCr. *hud*, Russ. *chudoj* 'evil, bad' (Russ. also 'lean'), ChSl. *chudŭ* 'small, insignificant', etc. perh. : Skt. *kṣud-* 'crush, pound', *kṣudra-* 'small'. Walde-P. 1.502. Berneker 405.

Pol. *biedny*, Russ. *bednyj* (= Boh. *bidný*, SCr. *bijedan* 'wretched, miser- able', ChSl. *bědĭnŭ* 'maimed') : ChSl. *běda* 'necessity', *běditi* 'compel', etc. Berneker 54. Walde-P. 2.185 f.

7. Skt. *daridra-*, lit. 'wandering about, roving', hence 'poor' and as sb. 'beggar' : *daridrā-* intens. to *drā-* 'run'. Walde-P. 1.795. Uhlenbeck 121.

Skt. *nir-dhana*, neg. cpd. of *dhana- 'property, wealth' (11.41).

Av. *drigu-, driγu-*, etym.? Walde-P. 1.821. Barth. 777 f.

Av. *ašaēta-*, neg. cpd. of *šaēta-* 'wealth' (11.42).

11.53 BEGGAR

Grk.	πτωχός	Goth.	*bidagwa*	Lith.	*elgeta, ubagas*
NG	ζητιάνος, διακονιάρης	ON	*gǫngumaðr, ǫlmusu- maðr*	Lett.	*nabags, diedelnieks*
Lat.	*mendicus*			ChSl.	*ništĭ*
It.	*mendicante, accattone*	Dan.	*tigger*	SCr.	*prosjak*
Fr.	*mendiant*	Sw.	*tiggare*	Boh.	*žebrák*
Sp.	*mendigo, mendigante*	OE	*wǣdla*	Pol.	*żebrak*
Rum.	*(şoigde 'begging')*	ME	*begger(e)*	Russ.	*niščij*
Ir.	*bacach*	NE	*beggar*	Skt.	*bhikṣu-, daridra-, yācaka-*
NIr.	*bacach*	Du.	*bedelaar*		
W.	*cardotyn*	OHG	*betalāri*	Av.	*. . . . .*
Br.	*klaskerbara*	MHG	*betelære*		
		NHG	*bettler*		

The majority of the words for 'beggar' are from verbs for 'ask for' (18.35). But several are in origin opprobrious epithets (like NE *bum*), based in part upon certain physical or mental defects.

1. Grk. πτωχός : πτώξ 'timid, fearful, cowering', πτώσσω 'cower, cringe', πτήσσω 'cower, crouch', (these : πίπτω 'fall', πέπτωκα, etc.). Walde-P. 2.19. Boisacq 823.

NG ζητιάνος, fr. ζητῶ 'seek, ask for' (11.31, 18.35).

NG διακονιάρης, fr. διακονῶ 'serve' (formerly also 'beg', now διακονεύω), fr. διάκονος 'servant, deacon'.

2. Lat. *mendīcus* (> Sp. *mendigo*), prob. orig. 'defective, unsound' : *mendum* and *menda* 'physical defect, fault', W. *man* 'spot, mark (on the body)', Skt. *mindā-* 'physical defect' (fr. the same root also Lat. *mendāx* 'lying', etc., with divergent semantic development). Walde-P. 2.270. Ernout-M. 605. Walde-H. 2.69.

Hence vb. *mendīcāre* 'beg' > It. *mendicare*, Fr. *mendier*, Sp. *mendigar* with pples. for 'beggar', It. *mendicante*, Fr. *mendiant*, Sp. *mendigante*.

It. *accattone*, fr. *accatare* 'beg, go begging', fr. VLat. **accapitāre*, cpd. frequent. to *capere* 'seize, take'. REW 62.

It. *pitocco* (but now generally 'miserable', hardly used for 'a beggar'), fr. Grk. πτωχός. REW 6803.

Rum. *cerşetor*, fr. *cere* 'ask for' (cf. pple. *cerşit*, aor. *cerşui*, etc.). Tiktin 328. Puşcariu 337.

3. Ir. *foigde* 'begging' (related form for 'beggar' apparently not quotable), vbl. noun fr. cpd. of *guidim* 'ask for, pray' (22.17). Pedersen 2.551.

NIr. *bacach*, also and orig. 'cripple' = *bacach* 'lame' (4.94).

W. *cardotyn* : *cardota* 'beg', MW *cardotta*, deriv. of *cardawt* (W. *cardod*) 'charity' fr. Lat. *caritātem*. Loth, Mots lat. 144 f.

Br. *klaskerbara*, cpd. of *klasker* agent noun to *klask* 'seek' (11.31) and *bara* 'bread' (5.51).

4. Goth. *bidagwa* (read *bidaga*?), fr. *bida* 'prayer' : *bidjan* 'ask for', etc. Feist 89.

ON *gǫngumaðr*, cpd. of *ganga* 'walking, going' and *maðr* 'man'.

ON *ǫlmusumaðr*, lit. 'alms-man' (*ǫlmusa* 'alms').

Dan. *tigger*, Sw. *tiggare*, fr. *tigge*, Sw. *tigga* 'beg' (ON *þiggja* 'accept', Ir. *techtaim* 'own', etc. 11.12). Falk-Torp 1258. Hellquist 1181 f.

OE *wǣdla*, see under 'poor' (11.52).

ME *begger(e)*, NE *beggar*, fr. ME *begge(n)*, NE *beg* 'ask alms, beg' (of dub. orig. NED s.v.).

Du. *bedelaar*, OHG *betalāri*, MHG *betelære*, NHG *bettler*, fr. Du. *bedelen*, OHG *betalōn*, etc. 'beg', frequent. to Du. *bidden*, OHG *bitten* 'ask for'. Weigand-H. 1.224.

5. Lith. *elgeta* : Arm. *ałkałk* 'miserable, needy, bad', perh. also Lith. *alkti* 'be hungry', etc. Walde-P. 1.160 (159).

Lith. *ubagas*, Lett. *nabags*, fr. Slav. *ubogŭ*, *nebogŭ* 'poor' (11.52).

Lett. *diedelnieks* 'vagabond, beggar', fr. *diedelēt* 'bum around, beg', prob. : *diet* 'dance'. Mühl.-Endz. 1.479 (with another suggestion).

6. ChSl. *ništĭ*, Russ. *niščij*, see under 'poor', 11.52.

SCr. *prosjak*, fr. *prositi* 'beg' : ChSl. *prositi* 'ask', etc.

Boh. *žebrák*, Pol. *żebrak*, fr. early NHG *seffer* 'vagabond, tramp, beggar' (slang. Cf. Grimm s.v.). Brückner 663.

7. Skt. *bhikṣu-* : *bhikṣ-* 'beg', desid. to *bhaj-* 'share, divide'. Uhlenbeck 200.

Skt. *daridra-* sb. form of *daridra-* 'poor' (11.52).

Skt. *yācaka-* : *yāc-* 'ask for'.

11.54 AVARICIOUS, STINGY

Grk.	φιλάργυρος, φιλοχρήματος, φειδωλός	Goth.	*faihu-friks, -gairns*	Lith.	*godingas, godus, gabš(t)us, šykštus*
NG	φιλάργυρος, φειδωλός, σφιχτός	ON	*fē-gjarn, -frekr, hnøggr*	Lett.	*mantkārīgs, skuops, sīksts*
Lat.	*avārus, tenāx, sordidus*	Dan.	*gerrig, karrig*	ChSl.	*sŭrebroljubĭcĭ*
It.	*avaro, spilorcio*	Sw.	*girig, snål, njugg*	SCr.	*lakom, skup, škrt*
Fr.	*avare, chiche*	OE	*feoh-gīfre, -georn, hnēaw*	Boh.	*lakomý, lakotný, skoupý*
Sp.	*avaro, mezquino*	ME	*avarous, nigard*	Pol.	*chciwy, łakomy, skąpy*
Rum.	*sgîrcit, avar, scump*	NE	*avaricious, stingy*	Russ.	*korystoljubivyj, skupoj*
Ir.	*santach*	Du.	*gierig*	Skt.	*kadarya-, kṛpaṇa-, dhanārthin-*
NIr.	*sanntach*	OHG	*gīri, gītag*	Av.	*arāitivant-*
W.	*cybyddlyd, crintach*	MHG	*gīrisch, gītec*, etc.		
Br.	*piz*	NHG	*habsüchtig, geizig, karg*		

Although there is obviously a distinction between 'avaricious' and 'parsimonious, stingy', as excessively desirous of either accumulating wealth or retaining it, and the majority of the words listed belong under one or the other, either in actual use or in origin, nevertheless the two characteristics are so commonly associated that a single epithet, of whatever origin, is often applied without any conscious differentiation of the two notions. Hence they are united here.

Words for 'avaricious' may contain explicit reference to 'money', lit. 'fond of money', etc., or mean originally simply 'eager, grasping', in some cases related to those for 'greedy'. 'Stingy' may be euphemistically expressed as 'sparing, thrifty', or by terms analogous to NE colloquial *near*, *tight*, or *close*. Many are opprobrious epithets of the most diverse sources with specialized application, as Lat. *sordidus*, Fr. *chiche*, NE *stingy*, *mean*, NG *filzig*, and others too numerous to be included in the list.

1. Grk. φιλάργυρος, φιλοχρήματος, lit. 'money-loving', cpds. of φίλος 'friend' with ἄργυρος 'silver, money', and χρήματα 'property, money'.

Grk. φειδωλός, orig. 'sparing' without derogatory connotation : φείδομαι 'spare, be sparing', prob. as orig. 'separate oneself from something' : Lat. *findere*, Skt. *bhid-* 'split'. Walde-P. 2.138.

NG pop. σφιχτός (: σφίγγω 'bind tight') 'tight' in literal sense and also 'stingy', like NE *tight*.

2. Lat. *avārus* (> It., Sp. *avaro*, OFr. *aver*, Fr. *avare*, Rum. *avar*) : *avēre* 'desire vehemently', *avidus* 'greedy'. REW 814. Wartburg 1.187. Walde-P. 1.19. Ernout-M. 85 f. Walde-H. 1.79.

Lat. *tenāx*, lit. 'tenacious, grasping', fr. *tenēre* 'hold' (11.15).

Lat. *sordidus*, lit. 'dirty, filthy', fr. *sordēs* 'filth'. Ernout-M. 958.

Fr. *chiche* : Sp. *chico* 'small', etc. (12.56).

Sp. *mezquino* (= It. *meschino* 'wretched, paltry'), fr. Arab. *meskīn* 'poor, wretched'. REW 5539.

Rum. *sgîrcit*, fr. *sgîrci* 'draw together, cramp', fr. Slavic, cf. SCr.-ChSl. *sgrčiti sę* 'contract' (Berneker 369). Tiktin 1812 f.

Rum. *scump*, fr. Slavic, ChSl. *skąpŭ*, etc. (below, 6). Tiktin 1396, 1813.

3. Ir. *santach*, NIr. *sanntach*, fr. *sant* 'greed, avarice', loanword fr. W. *chwant* 'desire, appetite, lust', Br. *c'hoant* 'desire' (: Grk. χάτις 'need', etc.). Pedersen 1.24, 139 f.

W. *cybyddlyd*, fr. *cybydd* 'miser' (11.55).

W. *crintach*, apparently a popular term derived from *crin* 'withered, dry', arch. 'niggard' (cf. arch. *crinwas* 'niggard', cpd. with *gwas* 'youth, servant').

Br. *piz* 'stingy', prob. a semantic borrowing fr. Fr. *chiche* 'stingy' (above) taken to be the same word as *chiche* 'chick pea', i.e. Br. *piz* 'peas'. G. S. Lane, Language 13.26.

4. Goth. *faihu-friks*, ON *fē-frekr*, Goth. *faihu-gairns*, ON *fē-gjarn*, OE *feoh-georn*, OE *feoh-gīfre*, all cpds. of Goth. *faihu*, etc. 'property' (11.41) with words for 'greedy' (Goth. *-friks*, ON *frekr* = OE *frec*; OE *gīfre*) or 'eager' (Goth. *-gairns*, etc.).

ON *hnøggr*, Sw. *njugg*, OE *hnēaw* : MHG *nouwe* 'close, careful', cpd. MHG *genouwe*, NHG *genau* 'precise, exact', also ON *hnøggwa* 'strike, hit', Grk. κνύω 'scratch'. Walde-P. 1.396. Falk-Torp 335, 785. Hellquist 700.

Dan. *gerrig*, Sw. *girig*, fr. MLG *girich* = OHG *girīg* 'greedy' : Skt. *hṛ-* 'desire', Grk. χαίρω 'rejoice', etc. Walde-P. 1.601. Falk-Torp 316 f.

Dan. *karrig*, NHG *karg* : OHG *carag*, OE *cearig* 'sad', NE *chary* 'careful, sparing of', Goth. *kara*, OE *cearu* 'care', etc. Falk-Torp 499.

Sw. *snål* = Norw. *snaal(en)* 'greedy, stingy', lit. 'sniffing after' : Norw. *snaala* 'sniff after, rummage'. Falk-Torp 1088. Hellquist 1019.

ME *avarous*, fr. OFr. *averos*, deriv. of *aveir*, *avoir* 'possession' but confused with Fr. *avare* (above). NED s.v.

NE *avaricious* fr. OFr. *avaricieux*, deriv. of *avarice*, Lat. *avaritia* 'avarice'. NED s.v.

ME *nigard* (also sb. 'miser'), NE *niggard(ly)*, also ME *nigon* 'miser', *nig* 'niggardly or mean person'. NED s.vv. *nig*, sb.[1], *niggard* says "of obscure origin". But they are obviously based on some Scand. form belonging with Sw. *njugg*, etc. (above). Cf. esp. Skeat, Etym. Dict. s.v. *niggard*.

NE *stingy*, orig. 'having a sting' then 'mean, bad-tempered', fr. *sting*. NED s.v.

OHG *gīri* (generally renders *avārus*), MHG *gīric*, *gīrisch*, (cf. NHG *habgier* 'avarice'), Du. *gierig* : Goth. *faihu-geiro*, OS *fehu-girī* 'avarice', perh. through the notion of standing 'open, yawning', fr. the root in OHG *gīen*, etc. 'yawn'. Walde-P. 1.549. Franck-v. W. 198. Feist 136 f.

OHG *gītag*, MHG *gītec*, NHG *geizig*, fr. OHG *gīt*, MHG *gīte*, *gīze* 'avarice' : Lith. *geisti* 'desire, wish', ChSl. *žīdati* 'wait', etc., IE **gheidh-*. Walde-P. 1.553. Weigand-H. 1.661.

NHG *habsüchtig*, adj. to *habsucht* 'avarice', cpd. of *haben* 'have' and *sucht* 'sickness, disease' (: *siech* 'sickly'), with development of sense of 'tendency to, passion for', esp. in cpds. (cf. *trunksucht*, *sehnsucht*, etc.) and popular association with *suchen* 'seek'. Weigand-H. 1.785, 2.1006. Paul, Deutsches Wtb. s.v. *Sucht*.

NHG *filzig*, adj. to *filz* 'miser' (11.55).

5. Lith. *godingas*, *godus* : Lett. *(sa)gāds* 'supply, store', *gādāt* 'care for', Ir. *gataim* 'steal', Skt. *gadhya-* 'to be seized', etc. Walde-P. 1.532.

Lith. *gabštus*, *gabšus* (also *gobštus*, *gobšus*; see NSB) : *gobėtis* 'be avaricious, greedy' (*gobus* 'greedy'), WhRuss. *habáć* 'take, seize', etc. (11.11). Walde-P. 1.345. Berneker 287 f.

Lith. *šykštus* (*-as* Kurschat), Lett. *sīksts*, orig. 'hard' or 'tough'. Cf. NE *tight*, *close* for 'stingy'. Mühl.-Endz. 3.853.

Lett. *mantkārīgs*, cpd. of *manta* 'property' and *kārīgs* 'hankering (after), covetous', fr. *kārs* 'greedy' (: Lat. *cārus* 'dear', etc.).

Lett. *skuops*, fr. ORuss. *skupŭ*, Russ. *skupoj* (below). Mühl.-Endz. 3.910.

6. ChSl. *sŭrebroljubĭcĭ* (Gospels, Lk. 16.14), a lit. rendering of φιλάργυρος, cpd. of *sŭrebro*, *sĭrebro* 'silver, money' and deriv. of *ljubiti* 'love'. Berneker 757.

SCr. *lakom*, Boh. *lakomý*, Pol. *łakomy*, Boh. *lakotný* : ChSl. *lakomŭ* 'hungry', *lakati*, *alŭkati* 'be hungry', etc. Walde-P. 1.159. Trautmann 6 f.

Late ChSl. *skąpŭ*, SCr. *skup*, Boh. *skoupý*, Pol. *skąpy*, Russ. *skupoj*, etym. dub., perh. as orig. 'tight, pinched'(?) : Pol. *szczmić*, Russ. *štemit'* 'pinch', or as an opprobrious 'whining' : ChSl. *skomljati* 'howl', Pol. *skomleć* 'whine'. Brückner 493.

SCr. *škrt*, etym.?

SCr. *tvrd* 'hard' (15.74), also 'stingy'.

Pol. *chciwy*, fr. *chcieć* 'desire, wish'.

Russ. *korystoljubivyj*, fr. *korystoljubie* 'love of gain', cpd. of *koryst* 'interest, gain, profit' and deriv. of *ljubit'* 'love'.

7. Skt. *kadarya-*, cpd. of *kad-* in its derogatory use 'bad, little' and *arya-* 'faithful, kind', hence an opprobrious epithet specialized to 'avaricious, stingy'. Uhlenbeck 41.

Skt. *kṛpaṇa-*, lit. 'miserable' (cf. NE *miser*) : *kṛp-* 'lament'. Uhlenbeck 64.

Skt. *dhanārthin-*, lit. 'eager for wealth', cpd. of *dhana-* 'property, wealth' and *arthin-* 'busy, eager, desirous of'.

Av. *arāiti-*, *arāitivant-*, fr. *arāti-* 'stinginess', lit. 'not-giving', neg. cpd. of *rā-* 'give'. Barth. 188.

11.55 MISER

Grk.	φειδωλός, κίμβιξ, etc.	Goth.	....	Lith.	*gabas, godišius, šykštuolis*
NG	τσιγγούνης, (ἐ)ξηνταβελόνης, σπαγγοραμμένος	ON	....	Lett.	*skuopolis, mantrausis, sīkstulis*
Lat.	*homo avārus, tenāx*, etc.	Dan.	*gnier*	ChSl.	....
It.	*avaro, spilorcio*	Sw.	*girigbuk*	SCr.	*škrtac, tvrdica*
Fr.	*avare, ladre*	OE	*gītsere*	Boh.	*lakomec, skrbec, držgrešle*
Sp.	*avaro*	ME	*nigarde*	Pol.	*skąpiec*
Rum.	*sgîrcit, avar, scump*	NE	*miser, niggard*	Russ.	*skupec, skrjaga*
Ir.	*dībech*	Du.	*gierigaard, vrek*	Skt.	*kṛpaṇa-*
NIr.	*sprionnlōg*	OHG	....	Av.	....
W.	*cybydd*	MHG	*gītegære, vilz*		
Br.	*piz*	NHG	*geizhals, filz*		

The majority of the words for 'miser' are connected with those for 'avaricious' or 'stingy' (11.54), either the same in substantive use or derivatives or compounds. But several are contemptuous terms of different origin.

1. Grk. φειδωλός, sb. form of adj. for 'stingy' (11.54).

Grk. κίμβιξ, etym. dub. Boisacq 456.

Grk. κυμινοπρίστης, lit. 'a cummin seed splitter', cpd. of κύμινον 'cummin' and πρίστης : πρίω 'saw, cut to pieces'.

NG τσιγγούνης, fr. Turk. *çingâne* 'gypsy' and as adj. 'shameless, stingy'.

NG (ἐ)ξηνταβελόνης, lit. 'one who has sixty needles', hence, as one who saves small things, 'miser'. Cf. δὲν λείπει βελόνι 'nothing (lit. 'not a needle') is missing'.

2. In Latin 'miser' is expressed by *homo* with words for 'avaricious, stingy' *avārus*, *tenāx*, *sordidus*, etc.

It., Sp. *avaro*, Fr. *avare*, Rum. *avar*, sb. use of adj. for 'stingy'.

It. *spilorcio*, less usually *pilorcio*, prob. as a term of abuse = the obs. *pilorcio* 'scraps of waste leather'. Cf. NHG *filz* (below, 4).

Fr. *ladre* 'leper' and 'miser', fr. the biblical *Lazarus*. REW 4958.

Rum. *sgîrcit*, sb. use of adj. for 'stingy'.

3. Ir. *dībech*, also as adj. 'churlish, niggardly' (NIr. *dībheach* 'grudging' as sb. 'niggard'), fr. *dībe* 'a denying, refusing, churlishness, stinginess', vbl. n. of *do-benim*, cpd. of *benim* 'strike, slay'. K. Meyer, Contrib. 633–34.

NIr. *sprionnlōg* (also *spriūnlōg, sprionnlōir*, etc.), etym.?

W. *cybydd*, fr. Lat. *cupidus*. Loth, Mots lat. 155.

Br. *piz*, sb. use of adj. for 'stingy'.

4. Goth. and ON sbs. for 'miser' lacking. Presumably expressed by phrases analogous to Lat. *homō avārus*.

Dan. *gnier* = Sw. *gnidare* (but not the usual word), fr. Dan. *gnie*, Sw. *gnida*, Norw. *gni* 'be stingy, pinch and spare'. For the modern feeling the word appears as 'one who rubs his money' (cf. Dan. *gnide*, Sw. *gnida* 'rub[1]'). The connection is probably rather through the notion of 'tormenting and afflicting (oneself)' to save rather than directly from 'rub'. Falk-Torp 334 f.

Sw. *girigbuk*, lit. 'stingy-belly', where *buk* 'belly' is used for 'person' in pejorative sense. Hellquist 110.

OE *gītsere*, fr. *gītsian* 'covet, desire' (: MHG *gīt(e)sen* 'be greedy'); MHG *gītegære* fr. *gītec* 'avaricious'; NHG *geizhals* lit. 'greedy-neck' : OHG *gīt* 'avarice', *gītag* 'avaricious', etc.

ME *nigarde*, NE *niggard*, cf. ME *nigarde* 'stingy'.

NE *miser*, formerly also 'miserable' and 'a miserable, wretched person', fr. Lat. *miser* 'miserable, wretched'.

Du. *gierigaard*, fr. *gierig* 'stingy', with pejorative suffix *-aard* (fr. Fr. *-ard*). Franck-v. W. 198.

Du. *vrek*, sb. form fr. MDu. *vrec* 'covetous, greedy, evil' = OHG *freh* 'covetous, greedy', ON *frekr*, Goth. *-friks* in *faihu-friks* 'avaricious', etc. Franck-v. W. 762.

MHG *vilz*, NHG *filz* 'felt', in MHG also 'an uncouth person' and 'miser', NHG 'miser', with reference to one clad in felt or in felt slippers (as the miser was often pictured). Paul, Deutsches Wtb. s.v.

5. Lith. *gabas* (also *gobas*) : *gabštus, gabšus* 'avaricious'.

Lith. *godišius* : *godingas, godus* 'avaricious'.

Lith. *šykštuolis*, Lett. *sīkstulis*, fr. Lith. *šykštus*, Lett. *sīksts* 'stingy'.

Lett. *mantrausis*, lit. 'money-raker', cpd. of *manta* 'property' and deriv. of *raust* 'rake, poke together (the fire, etc.)'.

6. SCr. *škrtac*, fr. *škrt* 'stingy'.

SCr. *tvrdica*, fr. *tvrd* 'stingy'.

Boh. *lakomec*, fr. *lakomý* 'avaricious'.

Boh. *skrbec, skrblik*, beside vb. *skrbiti* 'be niggardly' : ChSl. *skrŭběti* 'be sad', *skrŭbĭ* 'grief', etc. (16.32). Brückner 493.

Boh. *držgrešle*, lit. 'pinch-penny', cpd. of *drzeti* 'hold' and *grešle* dim. of *groš* fr. older NHG *grosch* = *groschen*.

Boh. *skupec*, Pol. *skąpiec*, Russ. *skupec*, fr. Boh. *skoupý*, Pol. *skąpy*, Russ. *skupoj* 'stingy'.

Russ. *skrjaga*, etym.?

7. Skt. *kṛpaṇa-*, sb. use of adj. for 'stingy'.

11.56 STEAL

Grk.	*κλέπτω*	Goth.	*hlifan, stilan*	Lith.	*vogti*
NG	*κλέβω, κλέφτω*	ON	*stela*	Lett.	*zagt*
Lat.	*fūrārī*	Dan.	*stjæle*	ChSl.	*krastı*
It.	*rubare*	Sw.	*stjäla*	SCr.	*krasti*
Fr.	*voler*	OE	*stelan, stalian*	Boh.	*krásti*
Sp.	*hurtar, robar*	ME	*stele*	Pol.	*kraść*
Rum.	*fura*	NE	*steal*	Russ.	*krast', vorovat'*
Ir.	*gataim*	Du.	*stelen*	Skt.	*muṣ-* (*cur-*)
NIr.	*goidim*	OHG	*stelan*	Av.	*tarəp-*
W.	*dwyn, lladrata*	MHG	*stelen*		
Br.	*laerez*	NHG	*stehlen*		

Some of the words for 'steal' rest on notions like 'hide, carry off, collect'. Some seem to have first denoted various rascally actions, specialized to 'steal'.

For an important IE group, see under 'thief' (11.57).

1. Grk. *κλέπτω*, NG *κλέβω, κλέφτω*, Lat. *clepere* (rare and arch.), Goth. *hlifan*, fr. **k̑lep-*, prob. an extension of **k̑el-* in Lat. *oc-culere*, Ir. *celim*, OE *helan*, etc. 'hide'. Walde-P. 1.497. Ernout-M. 196. Walde-H. 1.232. Feist 263.

2. Lat. *fūrārī*, also *fūrāre* (> Rum. *fura*; It. *furare* obs. or poet., OFr. *furer*), fr. *fūr* 'thief' (11.57).

It. *rubare*, Sp. *robar*, fr. the Gmc., OHG *roubōn*, Goth. *biraubōn*, etc. 'rob, plunder'. REW 7092.

Fr. *voler* (as 'steal' since 16th cent.) = *voler* 'fly', through its trans. use 'make fly', then as slang term for 'steal, rob'. REW 9431. Gamillscheg 896. Dict. gén. s.v.

Sp. *hurtar*, deriv. of *hurto* 'theft', fr. Lat. *fūrtum* : *fūrārī* (above). REW 3606.

3. Ir. *gataim*, NIr. *goidim* : Lith. *godas* 'avarice', *godus* 'avaricious' (11.54). Walde-P. 1.532. Pedersen 1.160.

W. *dwyn*, lit. 'carry, bring' (10.62).

W. *lladrata*, Br. *laerez*, fr. W. *lleidr* (pl. *lladron*), Br. *laer* 'thief' (11.57).

4. Goth. *hlifan*, above, 1.

Goth. *stilan*, OE *stelan*, etc., general Gmc., outside connections dub. Walde-P. 2.636. Falk-Torp 1170. Feist 453 f.

5. Lith. *vogti* : Lat. *vagārī* 'roam, wander', ON *vakka* 'wander about', Skt. *vañg-* 'go, limp'. Walde-P. 1.218. Semantic development prob. through 'be a vagabond', perh. first in sb. *vagis* as 'vagabond, thief'.

Lett. *zagt* : Lith. *žagti* 'pollute, defile', refl. 'pollute oneself'. Development through 'commit a foul action', then specialized to 'steal'? Mühl.-Endz. 4.680.

6. ChSl. *krasti*, etc. general Slavic, prob. : Lett. *krāt* 'collect, heap up', with labial extension Lett. *krāpt*, Lith. *kropti* 'deceive', root **krā(u)-* in Lith. *krauti* 'heap up, load', etc. Walde-P. 1.477. Berneker 605. Brückner 264 f.

Russ. *vorovat'*, fr. *vor* 'thief' (11.57).

7. Skt. *muṣ-*, prob. : Frank. (Lex Sal.) *chreo-mōsido* 'corpse-robbery', and fr. an extension of IE **meu-* in Lat. *movēre* 'set in motion, move', Skt. *mīv-* 'shove, press', etc. Walde-P. 2.253.

Skt. *cur-*, etym.?

Av. *tarəp-* (*trəfya-*) : Skt. *tṛp-* in *paçu-tṛp-* 'cattle-stealing', root connection? Walde-P. 1.737. Barth. 643.

11.57 THIEF

Grk.	*κλέπτης, φώρ*	Goth.	*þiufs, hliftus*	Lith.	*vagis*
NG	*κλέφτης*	ON	*þjōfr*	Lett.	*zaglis*
Lat.	*fūr*	Dan.	*tyv*	ChSl.	*tatĭ*
It.	*ladro*	Sw.	*tjuf*	SCr.	*tat, kradljivac*
Fr.	*voleur* (*larron*)	OE	*þēof*	Boh.	*zloděj, kradce*
Sp.	*ladrón, hurtador*	ME	*theef*	Pol.	*złodziej*
Rum.	*hoț*	NE	*thief*	Russ.	*vor* (*tat'*)
Ir.	*tāid, merlech*	Du.	*dief*	Skt.	*stena-, cāura-, moṣaka-, tāyu-*, etc.
NIr.	*gadaidhe*	OHG	*diob*	Av.	*tāyu-*
W.	*lleidr*	MHG	*diep*		
Br.	*laer*	NHG	*dieb*		

Several of the words for 'thief' are derived from those for 'steal', as in part conversely. But more often there is no connection, as in the Gmc. group (NE *steal*, but *thief*). Several of the words for 'thief' were originally more general terms for 'evildoer, rascal, bandit, robber', etc.

1. IE group based on **(s)tāi-*. Walde-P. 2.610.

Ir. *tāid*; ChSl. *tatĭ*, etc.; Skt. *tāyu-* (RV), also *stāyu-*, Av. *tāyu-*, Skt. *stena-*; cf. ChSl. *taj* 'secretly', *tajiti* 'hide', Grk. *τητάομαι* 'be in want, bereft of', Hitt. *tāyēzzi* 'steals' (Sturtevant, Hitt. Gloss. 157).

2. Grk. *κλέπτης*, NG *κλέφτης* : *κλέπτω* 'steal' (11.56).

Grk. *φώρ* (Hdt.+), as 'one who carries off' : Grk. *φέρω*, Lat. *ferre* 'carry'. Walde-P. 2.154 ff.

3. Lat. *fūr*, either cognate with or loanword fr. Grk. *φώρ*. Ernout-M. 403. Walde-H. 1.569.

It. *ladro*, Fr. *larron*, Sp. *ladrón*, fr. Lat. *latrō* 'mercenary soldier' (so in Plaut., class. also), 'bandit, highwayman', loanword fr. Grk. *λάτρον* 'pay, wage', *λατρεύς* 'hired servant', etc. Ernout-M. 527. Walde-H. 1.771. REW 4931.

Fr. *voleur*, fr. *voler* 'steal' (11.56).

Sp. *hurtador*, fr. *hurtar* 'steal' (11.56).

Rum. *hoț*, also 'robber, rascal' and prob. orig. a general abusive term, but source unknown. Tiktin 739.

4. Ir. *tāid*, see above, 1.

Ir. *merlech*, fr. *merl* 'theft', etym. dub. (: *mairnim* 'betray'?). Pedersen 2.55.

NIr. *gadaidhe*, fr. *gadaim* 'steal' (11.56).

W. *lleidr*, Br. *laer*, fr. Lat. *latrō*. Loth, Mots lat. 181.

5. Goth. *þiufs*, OE *þēof*, OHG *diob*, etc., general Gmc. : Goth. *þiubjō* 'secretly', and so perh. as 'cowering, crouching' : Lith. *tupėti* 'cower, squat', Lett. *tupt* 'squat'. Walde-P. 1.714. Falk-Torp 1310 f. Feist 497.

Goth. *hliftus* : *hlifan* 'steal' (11.56).

6. Lith. *vagis* : *vagiu, vogti* 'steal' (11.56).

Lett. *zaglis* : *zagt* 'steal' (11.56).

7. ChSl. *tatĭ*, SCr. *tat*, Russ. *tat'* (obs.), see above, 1.

SCr. *kradljivac*, Boh. *kradce*, fr. Slavic *krasti* 'steal' (11.56).

Boh. *zloděj*, Pol. *złodziej* = Russ. *zlodej* 'villain, rascal, wretch', ChSl. *zŭloděĭ* 'evildoer' (*zŭlŭ* 'evil' and *děti* 'put, place'). Berneker 193. Brückner 654.

Russ. *vor* : Pol. *wór*, Boh. *vor* a kind of 'sack', SCr. *verati* 'stick away, hide' Lith. *verti* 'open or shut' (Trautmann 351 f., without Russ. *vor*), etc. Miklosich 382. Brückner 631.

8. Skt. *stena-*, *tāyu-*, *stāyu-*, Av. *tāyu-*, see above, 1.

Skt. *cāura-*, fr. *cur-* 'steal' (11.56).

11.58. 'Rob, robber'. These differ from 'steal, thief' by the implication of violence. But the distinction is often ignored. Many of the verbs listed under 'steal' (11.56) are used also for 'rob'. So It. *rubare*, Sp. *robar* (these two orig. 'rob'), Fr. *voler*, Rum. *fura*, Br. *laerez*, Lith. *vogti*, Skt. *muṣ-* (or cpds. for 'rob', as Boh. *o-krásti*, Pol. *o-kraść*). Of course the difference may always be brought out, when required (as in law), by the addition for 'rob' of a phrase expressing the violence involved, e.g. Fr. *voler à main armée*.

Or 'rob' may be included in the scope of verbs for 'seize, plunder', etc., as Grk. *ἁρπάζω* (11.14), *σῡλάω* (etym.?), Lat. *rapere* (11.14; source of NE *rape* and *ravish*), Lat. *spoliāre* (fr. *spolium* 'spoils, booty', 20.48), W. *ysbeilio* (fr. Lat. *spoliāre*, Loth, Mots lat. 216).

Owing to this situation a formal list is omitted, and further comment limited to the only distinctive and widespread group (the Gmc.) and a few other words.

1. Goth *biraubōn* (renders *ἐκδύω* Lk. 10.30 and *σῡλάω* 2 Cor. 11.8), (ON *raufa* 'break open'), Dan. *røve*, Sw. *röva* (fr. MLG *rōven*?), OE *rēafian*, ME *reve*, NE *reave* (now arch. or poet.; replaced by ME, NE *rob* through Fr.), Du. *rooven*, OHG *roubōn*, MHG *rouben*, NHG *rauben* : OE *rēofan*, ON *rjūfa*, Lat. *rumpere* 'break', etc. Walde-P. 2.354 f. Falk-Torp 914. NED s.v. *reave* vb.[1].

Hence as loanwords fr. OHG or NHG, OFr. *rouber, rober* (> ME, NE *rob*), It. *rubare*, Sp. *robar*, SCr. *robiti*, Boh. *rabovati*, Pol. *rabować*.

2. Grk. *λῃστής* 'robber, pirate', fr. the same root as *λεία* 'booty' (20.48), namely that in *ἀπολαύω* 'enjoy, take advantage of', Lat. *lucrum* 'gain, profit', etc. Walde-P. 2.379. In the NT the sense is clearly 'robber, highwayman' (cf. esp. Lk. 10.30), though rendered as 'thief' in the OE Lindisf., Wyclif, Tyndale, and K. James versions, that is in the extended but now obs. use of *thief* (NED s.v. b). It is rendered in the Vulgate by *latrō* (see It. *ladro* 'thief', 11.57), in Goth. by *waidedja* lit. 'evildoer' (cf. OE *wēa-dǣd* 'ill deed'; Feist 542), in OE mostly by *sceaþa* (: OE *sceaþan* 'harm', 11.28), in ChSl. by *razbojĭnikŭ* (similar forms in modern Slavic; fr. cpd. of *biti* 'strike', Berneker 68).

Grk. *λωποδύτης* 'clothes-stealer' (: *λῶπος, λώπη* 'robe'), also in more general sense 'robber', hence vb. *λωποδυτέω* also 'rob'. Cf. LS s.v.

3. Ir. *arcelim* 'take away, rob', cpd. of *celim* 'hide'. Cf. Grk. *κλέπτω* 'steal', fr. an extension of the same root (11.56). Pedersen 2.482.

NIr. *slaidim, sladaim*, fr. *slad*, MIr. *slat* 'robbery, plundering', etym.? Stokes 314. Walde-P. 2.636.

4. Lith. *plėšti* 'tear' (9.28), also 'rob'.

Lith. *grobti* 'seize, rob', Russ. *grabit'* 'rob' : ChSl. *grabiti* 'snatch away', Skt. *grabh-* 'seize', etc. (11.14). Berneker 344.

Lett. *laupīt*, Boh. *loupiti*, Pol. *łupić* 'peel' and 'rob, plunder' : Lith. *lupti*, Russ. *lupit* 'peel', Skt. *lup-* 'break' also 'rob, plunder, destroy', etc. Walde-P. 2.417 f. Berneker 746.

11.61 LEND

Grk.	δανείζω, κίχρημι	Goth. leihwan
NG	δανείζω	ON lją, lāna
Lat.	mūtuum dāre	Dan. laane
It.	(im)prestare	Sw. lāna
Fr.	prêter	OE lǣna, lēon
Sp.	prestar	ME len(d)e, lane
Rum.	imprumuta, da cu imprumut	NE lend, loan
Ir.	airléicim, oidim	Du. leenen
NIr.	airleagaim	OHG līhan, lehanōn
W.	echwyna, benthycio	MHG līhen, lēhenen
Br.	presta	NHG leihen, borgen (lehnen)

Lith.	skolinti
Lett.	aizduot, tapināt
ChSl.	vŭ zajĭmŭ dajati
SCr.	pozajmiti, posuditi
Boh.	půjčiti
Pol.	požyčić
Russ.	ssudit', odolžit'
Skt.	r̥ṇam dā-
Av.	(*nəmahya-)

Words for 'lend' are partly derivatives of nouns for 'loan' or 'debt', these of various sources, and partly from more general notions of 'furnish, provide, give', 'exchange', 'leave', etc.

1. Grk. δανείζω, fr. δάνος 'loan, debt', prob. fr. IE *də- weak grade of *dā(i)- in Grk. δαίομαι 'distribute', etc. Walde-P. 1.763. Boisacq 166.

Grk. κίχρημι, aor. ἔχρησα: χρή 'needs, must' (9.94), χρέος 'debt' (11.64), etc. For frequent use as 'lend', cf. refs. in LS 2001 (esp. Schwyzer, Dial. Graec. Ex. 324 for early technical use) and Moulton-Milligan 344.

2. Lat. usually phrase mūtuum (argentum, frumentum, etc.) dāre lit. 'give (silver, grain, etc.) loaned'; mūtuus : mūtāre 'change, exchange' (12.93) Ernout-M. 648.

It. prestare, imprestare, OFr. prester, Fr. prêter, Sp. prestar, fr. Lat. praestāre 'be at the disposition of, be responsible for, fulfill, furnish', with adv. praestō 'at hand', orig. much disputed, but perh. simply fr. prae 'in front of' and stāre 'stand', with divergent semantic development from that seen in prae-stāre 'surpass'. Ernout-M. 805, 982. REW 6725.

Rum. imprumuta, also 'borrow' = Fr. emprunter 'borrow', etc. (11.62). Also differentiated by da 'give' or lua 'take' with cu imprumut 'by way of loan'.

3. Ir. airléicim, NIr. airleagaim, cpd. of léicim 'leave, let' (12.18) with air- 'pre-, pro-'. Pedersen 2.563.

Ir. oidim, with sb. oin 'loan', etym. dub. Walde-P. 1.204. Pedersen 1.65, 2.587.

W. echwyna, also 'borrow', fr. sb. echwyn 'loan', this prob. fr. cwnnu, cynnu 'raise'. Evans W. Dict. s.v. Or more specifically for 'lend' rhoi echwyn 'give a loan'.

W. benthycio (with i 'to' = 'lend', with gan 'from' = 'borrow'), fr. benthyg 'a loan', older benffyg fr. Lat. beneficium 'favor'. Loth, Mots lat. 138. Or more specifically for 'lend' rhoi benthyg 'give a loan'.

Br. presta, fr. OFr. prester (above, 2).

4. Goth. leihwan, ON lją, OE lēon, ME lene, lende, NE lend, OHG līhan, MHG līhen, NHG leihen : Lat. linquere, Grk. λείπω 'leave'. Walde-P. 2.397. Falk-Torp 613 f. Feist 327.

ON lāna (> ME lane, NE loan), Dan. laane, Sw. lāna, OE lǣnan, OHG lehanōn, MHG lēhenen, NHG lehnen, fr. the sbs. ON lān, OE lǣn, OHG lēhan 'a loan' : Goth. leihwan, etc. (above). Falk-Torp 613 f.

MHG, NHG borgen 'borrow' (11.62), also 'lend'.

5. Lith. skolinti, skolyti, fr. skola 'debt' : skeléti 'owe', etc. (11.63).

Lith. žyčyti (Kurschat, NT, now replaced by preceding), fr. WhRuss. zyčić (cf. Pol. požyczać, below). Brückner, Sl. Fremdwörter 158.

Lett. aizduot, cpd. of duot 'give'.

Lett. tapināt, also 'borrow' caus. to tapt 'become, reach, arrive at' : Lith. tapti 'become' (9.92). Mühl.-Endz. 4.133 f.

6. ChSl. vŭ zajĭmŭ dajati (Lk. 6.34, etc.) lit. 'give in loan', SCr. po-(u-)zajmiti 'lend, borrow' : ChSl. zajęti 'borrow' (11.62).

SCr. posuditi (also 'borrow'), Russ. ssudit' : SCr. suditi, Pol. sądzić, ChSl. sǫditi 'judge', deriv. of ChSl. sǫdŭ 'judgment, decision' (sǫ-dŭ : Skt. samdhā- 'union, agreement', etc. Walde-P. 1.827), but with independent semantic development 'make a decision, arrangement, agreement', specialized to 'lend', as with a still different specialization

hence 'owe', or through 'withhold'(?). Ernout-M. 255. Walde-H. 1.326.

Lith. samdas 'hire, rent' vb. samdyti 'hire, let, rent'.

Boh. půjčiti, Pol. požyčić (latter also 'borrow'), cpds. : Pol. žyčyć 'wish well', Boh. žičiti 'grant', these : Boh. žiti, Pol. žyć, ChSl. žiti, etc. 'live'. Brückner 669. Miklosich 411.

Russ. odolžit', fr. dolg, ChSl. dlŭgŭ 'debt'. Berneker 244.

7. Skt. r̥ṇa dā-, lit. 'give a debt' (r̥ṇa- 'debt' 11.64), used for 'pay a debt', also with loc. 'lend' (cf. r̥ṇa-dātar- 'lender of money') and with abl. 'borrow'.

Skt. kusīda-, the technical term for 'lending of money at interest', but not appearing in verbal phrases, etym.? Uhlenbeck 61.

Av. *nəmahya- (cf. adj. nəmaɣhant- 'lending') fr. nəmah- 'a loan', prob. : Grk. νέμω 'divide, distribute', Goth. niman 'take', etc. (11.13). Walde-P. 2.330. Barth. 1069 f.

11.62 BORROW

Grk.	δανείζομαι	Goth. leihwan sis
NG	δανείζομαι	ON þiggja at lāni
Lat.	mūtuum sūmere, mū-	Dan. laane
	tuāri	Sw. lāna
It.	prendere in prestito	OE borgian
Fr.	emprunter	ME borwe
Sp.	tomar prestado	NE borrow
Rum.	imprumuta, lua cu	Du. borgen
	imprumut	OHG wehslōn
Ir.	....	MHG entlēhenen, borgen
NIr.	faghaim ar iasacht	NHG borgen, leihen, entleh-
W.	echwyna, benthycio	nen
Br.	empresta	

Lith.	skolinti
Lett.	aizn'emt, tapināt
ChSl.	zajęti
SCr.	posuditi, pozajmiti
Boh.	vypůjčiti se, služiti se
Pol.	požyczić
Russ.	zanjat'
Skt.	r̥ṇam kr̥-
Av.	....

The majority of the words for 'borrow' are akin to those for 'lend', already discussed (11.61). The verb may be in the same form, the difference in application being shown by construction (e.g. with 'to' = 'lend', but with 'from' = 'borrow'), or in a differentiated form (e.g. mid. or refl., or with prefix) for 'borrow'. Thus Grk. δανείζομαι, mid. of δανείζω 'lend'; Lat. mūtuārī fr. mūtuus

'lent, borrowed' (in mūtuum dāre 'lend', etc.); W. benthycio, echwyna 'borrow, lend'; Br. empresta (or empresta), a blend of presta 'lend' and Fr. emprunter; Goth. leihwan sis refl. (with af.); Dan. laane, Sw. lāna 'lend, borrow'; NHG leihen 'lend, borrow'; MHG entlēhenen, NHG entlēhenen fr. MHG lēhenen 'lend', etc.; Lith. skolinti 'lend, borrow'; Lett. tapināt 'lend, borrow'; SCr. posuditi, Pol.

---

požyczić 'lend, borrow'; Boh. vypůjčiti se refl. cpd. of půjčiti 'lend'.

Furthermore 'borrow' is frequently expressed by a phrase with words for 'loan, loaned, debt', and in some languages this is the usual locution. Thus Lat. mūtuum sūmere; It. prendere in prestito 'take in loan', Sp. tomar prestado 'take loaned', NIr. faghaim ar iasacht 'get on loan' (iasacht 'loan', etym.?), ON þiggja (nema) at lāni 'receive (take) as a loan', Skt. r̥ṇam kr̥- lit. 'make a debt' (r̥ṇa- 'debt' 11.64), also r̥ṇam dā- with abl. (cf. 11.61).

Of independent origin are the following:

1. Fr. emprunter, Rum. imprumuta (the latter also 'lend'), fr. VLat. *im-prōmūtuāre, deriv. of Lat. prōmūtuum 'a loan' (cpd. of mūtuum, cf. 12.61). REW 4319. Gamillscheg 354.

2. OE borgian, ME borwe, NE bor-

row, Du., MHG, NHG borgen (MHG also like OHG borgēn 'give heed to', etc.), fr. OE borg, borh 'pledge, surety', MHG borg, Du. borg 'pledge, loan', etc. (hence orig. 'take on pledge', or in MHG, NHG also 'give on pledge, lend'), fr. the root of OE beorgan, OHG bergan, ON bjarga 'keep, preserve', etc. (11.25). Walde-P. 2.172. NED s.v. borrow, vb.[1]

OHG wehslōn 'change, exchange' (12.93), also 'borrow' (Tat. Mt. 5.42).

3. Lett. aizn'emt, cpd. of n'emt 'take' (11.13), cf. aizduot 'lend' (11.61).

4. ChSl. zajęti, Russ. zanjat', cpds. of the Slavic verb for 'take', ChSl. jęti, etc. Hence the sb. ChSl. zajĭmŭ, etc. 'loan', and fr. this SCr. po-(or u-) zajmiti 'lend, borrow' and many phrases not entered in the list but frequently used for 'lend' or 'borrow', e.g. Russ. dat' vzaimy 'lend', vzjat' (or brat') vzaimy 'borrow'. Berneker 426.

11.63 OWE

Grk.	ὀφείλω	Goth. skulan
NG	χρ(ε)ωστῶ	ON vera skyldr, skyldugr
Lat.	dēbēre	Dan. skylde
It.	dovere	Sw. vara skyldig
Fr.	devoir	OE sculan (āgan)
Sp.	deber	ME oʒe, owe (schal)
Rum.	datori	NE owe
Ir.	dlegair domsa, etc.	Du. schuldig zijn
NIr.	dligim	OHG scolan
W.	bod mewn dyled(i)	MHG schulden, schuldec sin, suln
Br.	dleout	NHG schuldig sein, schulden

Lith.	kaltas (skolingas) buti, skeléti
Lett.	parāda būt
ChSl.	dlŭžĭnŭ byti
SCr.	biti dužan, dugovati
Boh.	býti dlužen
Pol.	byč winien
Russ.	byt' dolžnyj
Skt.	dhr̥-
Av.	....

'Owe' is frequently expressed as 'be in debt', that is by phrases containing words for 'debt' or adjectives derived from them, or more rarely by verbal derivatives therefrom. But in several cases the verb is conversely the source of the noun, or is unrelated. In some of these the underlying notion is 'have, hold' (something belonging to another).

1. Grk. ὀφείλω, Hom., Aeol., Arc.

ὀφέλλω, Cret. ὀφήλω, Arc. perf. pple. ϝοφληκόσι, etc., etym.? Boisacq 731 f.

Late Grk. χρεωστέω, NG pop. χρωστῶ, deriv. of χρεώστης 'debtor', this of χρέως 'debt' (11.64).

2. Lat. dēbēre (> It. dovere, Fr. devoir, Sp. deber), fr. dē-habēre, with semantic development through 'have (something) from (someone)', that is, 'have something belonging to another'

---

skilti 'get in debt', OPruss. skalisnan 'duty', without s- Lith. kaltas 'owing, obliged', kaltė 'debt', further root connections, as with Lith. skelti 'split' dub. Walde-P. 2.596. Falk-Torp 1038 f., 1045 f. Feist 435 f.

OE āgan (āgan to geldanne 'owe' in Lindisf. Gospels, Lk. 16.5, etc., but reg. 'own'), ME oʒe, owe, NE owe, cf. OE āgan 'own' (11.12). NED s.v. owe.

5. Lith. kaltas or skolingas buti, lit. 'be owing'; for kaltas, skolingas 'owing', and skeléti 'owe', see above, 4.

Lett. parādā būt, lit. 'be in debt', with loc. of parāds 'debt' (11.64).

6. ChSl. dlŭžĭnŭ byti, etc. 'be owing, in debt', with forms of adjs. ChSl. dlŭžĭnŭ, SCr. dužan, Boh. dlužen, Russ. dolžnyj, fr. ChSl. dlŭgŭ, SCr. dug, etc. 'debt' (11.64).

SCr. dugovati, fr. dug 'debt' (11.64).

Pol. byč winien 'be owing', with adj. winien 'owing, guilty' : wina, Boh. vina 'guilt, fault', etc. (16.76). Brückner 622.

7. Skt. dhr̥- 'hold' (11.15) is also used for 'owe' (with dat. or gen., BR s.v. 18). Cf. dēbēre, above, 2.

11.64 DEBT

Grk.	χρέος	Goth. dulgs
NG	χρέος	ON skuld
Lat.	dēbitum, aes aliēnum	Dan. gæld
It.	debito	Sw. skuld (gäld)
Fr.	dette	OE scyld
Sp.	deuda, débito	ME dette
Rum.	datorie	NE debt
Ir.	fiach	Du. schuld
NIr.	fiacha	OHG sculd
W.	dyled	MHG schult
Br.	dle	NHG schuld

Lith.	skola
Lett.	parāds
ChSl.	dlŭgŭ
SCr.	dug
Boh.	dluh
Pol.	dlug
Russ.	dolg
Skt.	r̥ṇa
Av.	....

1. Grk. χρέος (Arc., Cret. χρῆος, Hom. χρεῖος, Att. also χρέως) : χρή 'needs, ought, must' (9.94), χρήματα 'property, money' (11.41).

2. Lat. dēbitum (> Fr. dette, Sp. deuda, and as lit. borrowings It. debito,

Sp. débito), fr. dēbēre 'owe' (11.63). REW 2492.

Lat. aes aliēnum, lit. 'another's money', with aes 'bronze, money', Ernout-M. 19.

Rum. datorie, fr. datori 'owe' (11.63).

3. Ir. *fiach*, NIr. *fiacha*, prob. : Lat. *vicēs* 'change, return, recompense', ON (*gjafa-*)*vīxl* 'exchange (of gifts)', OHG *wehsal* 'change, exchange', etc., fr. the root in Grk. εἴκω 'yield, give way', etc. Walde-P. 1.235. Pedersen 1.174.

W. *dyled*, Br. *dle* : Ir. *dliged* 'law, right', *dligim* 'have a right to, claim upon', Br. *dleout* 'owe', etc. (11.63), Goth. *dulgs* 'debt' (loanword fr. Celtic?), ChSl. *dlŭgŭ*, etc. id. (prob. loanword fr. Gmc.). Walde-P. 1.868. Pedersen 1.100, 2.506 f. Vendryes, RC 40.428 ff. (: Lat. *indulgēre*, but cf. Walde-H. 1.695). Feist 128. Berneker 244. Stender-Petersen 319.

4. Goth. *dulgs*, see above, 3.

ON *skuld*, Sw. *skuld* (but Dan. *skyld* 'guilt'), OE *scyld*, OHG *sculd, sculda*, MHG *schult, schulte*, Du., NHG *schuld* : Goth. *skulan*, etc. 'owe' (11.63).

Dan. *gæld* (Sw. *gäld* less usual) = ON *gjald* 'payment', OHG *gelt* 'payment, compensation, money', etc. (11.43). Falk-Torp 318.

ME *dette*, fr. OFr. *dette* (above, 2), NE *debt* with *b* restored only in the spelling fr. Lat. *debitum*.

5. Lith. *skola* : *skelėti*, Goth. *skulan*, etc. 'owe' (11.63).

Lett. *parāds* (= Lith. *parodas* 'proof') : Lett. *parādīt* 'show, prove' (Lith. *parodyti*). Mühl.-Endz. 3.88 f.

6. ChSl. *dlŭgŭ*, etc., general Slavic, see above, 3.

7. Skt. *ṛṇa-* (also *ṛṇa-* adj. 'owing, guilty'), etym. obscure. Walde-P. 1.77. Uhlenbeck 34.

11.65 PAY (vb.)

Grk.	ἀποδίδωμι, ἀποτίνω	Goth.	*-gildan*	Lith.	*mokėti*
NG	πληρώνω	ON	*gjalda*	Lett.	*maksāt*
Lat.	*pendere, solvere*	Dan.	*betale*	ChSl.	*vŭzdati*
It.	*pagare*	Sw.	*betala*	SCr.	*platiti*
Fr.	*payer*	OE	*gieldan*	Boh.	(*za*)*platiti*
Sp.	*pagar*	ME	*paie, yelde*	Pol.	(*za*)*płacić*
Rum.	*plăti*	NE	*pay*	Russ.	(*za*)*platit'*
Ir.	*direnim, asrenim*	Du.	*betalen*	Skt.	*dā-*
NIr.	*dīolaim*	OHG	*geltan*	Av.	*či-*
W.	*talu*	MHG	*gelten*		
Br.	*paea*	NHG	(*be*)*zahlen*		

'Pay' may be expressed simply as 'give' or 'give back', as 'weigh out' or 'count out', or with primary reference to the debt or the creditor as 'release, discharge, fulfil, recompense, appease', etc. According to their source they would originally differ in construction, namely 'pay an amount to a person' if the source is 'give' or the like, but 'pay a debt or a person' if the source is 'fulfil, appease', etc. But as consciousness of the original meaning was lost, the words of the latter type came also to be used with the amount paid as the direct object, e.g. Grk. ἀποτίνω (no less than ἀποδίδωμι), Lat. *solvere*, Fr. *payer*, NE *pay*, etc.

1. Grk. ἀποδίδωμι 'give back, return' (11.22) is the most common term for 'pay'.

Grk. ἀποτίνω 'requite, repay', then 'pay' (as a penalty) and simply 'pay' (ἀργύριον, etc.), less commonly in this sense ἐκτίνω, cpds. of τίνω 'requite, atone for, repay' (rarely 'pay' money) : Skt. *ci-* (*cayate*) 'hate, punish', Av. *či-* 'atone for, pay' (see below, 7); common meaning of this root 'requite' in good or bad sense (cf. the derivs. Grk.

τιμή 'reward' or 'penalty', ποινή 'penalty', Av. *kaēna* 'penalty', ChSl. *cěna* 'reward'). Walde-P. 1.509.

Grk. τελέω 'finish, fulfil' (fr. τέλος 'end, fulfilment', 14.26), also sometimes 'pay' (Hom.+).

Grk. πληρόω 'fill, fulfil' (: πλήρης 'full'), also 'make good, supply' (with χρεία 'need', etc. Thuc.), and in late times 'pay' (pap.), hence NG πληρώνω.

2. Lat. *pendere*, orig. 'hang' (trans.) whence 'weigh' and 'pay' (from the weighing out of silver in payment), trans. to the intr. *pendēre* 'hang, be hanging'. Ernout-M. 750 ff.

Lat. *solvere*, 'loose, release' (11.34), then in legal terminology 'acquit oneself of, discharge' (*debitum, rem, vōtum*, etc.), 'pay'. Ernout-M. 954.

It. *pagare*, Fr. *payer* (> Br. *paea*, ME *paie*, NE *pay*), Sp. *pagar*, fr. Lat. *pācāre* 'pacify' (through 'appease' and esp. 'appease with pay'). REW 6132.

Rum. *plăti*, fr. Slavic (below, 6).

3. Ir. *direnim, asrenim* cpds. of *renim* 'sell' (11.82). Pedersen 2.596 f.

NIr. *dīolaim* (also 'sell' and 'betray') beside *dīoghlaim* 'betray', fr. Ir. *dīgalim* 'avenge' : Ir. *dīgal*, W. *dial* 'vengeance', cpd. of Ir. *gal* 'valor'. Pedersen 1.101. Macbain 134. Development of 'pay' through 'atone for, pay the penalty' (cf. Grk. ἀποτίνω, above, 1), and of 'sell' through 'betray' (as Judas betrayed Christ for thirty pieces of silver)?

W. *talu*, with *tal* 'payment, recompense, reward', prob. also Ir. *-tal* in *tuarastal* 'wages' (11.78), *taile* gl. *salarium*, MBr. *talvout* 'be worth, reward', etc., outside connections? (Stokes, 130 : Lat. *tollere* 'lift', etc.; rejected by Walde-P. 1.739).

Br. *paea*, fr. Fr. *payer* (above).

4. Goth. *-gildan* (only cpds. *fragildan, usgildan* 'repay'), ON *gjalda*, OE *gieldan*, *āgieldan*, ME *yelde*, OHG *geltan*, MHG *gellen*, beside Goth. *gild, gilstr* 'tribute, tax', OHG *gelt* 'payment, recompense, money', NHG *geld* 'money', etc., outside connections dub. Walde-P. 1.632. Feist 161. NED s.v. *yield* vb.

MLG *betalen* (> Dan. *betale*, Sw. *betala*), Du. *betalen*, NHG (*be*)*zahlen* (MHG *bezaln* rarely 'pay', mostly = *zaln* 'count, calculate, relate', OHG *zalōn* 'count'), fr. the sbs. LG *tal*, OHG *zala* 'number, series', NHG *zahl* 'number'; hence 'pay' fr. 'count out'. Falk-Torp 64, 1243. Paul, Deutsches Wtb. s.v. *zahl*.

ME *paie*, NE *pay*, fr. Fr. *payer* (above, 2).

5. Lith. *mokėti* 'understand, know how' ('can' in this sense, as 'can read') and 'pay' (*už-* only in this sense) : *mokti* 'learn', Lett. *māku, mācēt* 'understand, be able', *mācīt* 'teach', OPruss. *mukint* 'teach'. Mühl.-Endz. 2.575. Semantic development prob. 'know how' (to count), 'count out' > 'pay' (cf. NHG *zahlen*, above).

Lett. *maksāt*, fr. *maksa* 'payment' (Esth. or Liv. *maks* id.). Mühl.-Endz. 2.555.

6. ChSl. *vŭzdati* 'give back' (11.22), in Gospels reg. for ἀποδίδωμι also when it means 'pay, repay'.

SCr. *platiti*, etc., general Slavic (but not in old ChSl.), deriv. of word for linen (ChSl. *platŭ, platĭno*, 6.23). According to the chronicle of Helmold the Slavs used linen cloth as the standard of value in trade. Brückner 420. Schrader, Reallex. 1.325.

7. Skt. *dā-* 'give' (11.21) also the usual word for 'pay'.

Av. *či-* 'atone for' and so 'pay' (e.g. *čikayaṯ* Vd. 13.10; cf. Barth. 103 s.v. *afša-* and 464) : Grk. τίνω 'atone for', etc. (above, 1).

11.66 ACCOUNT, RECKONING

Grk.	λόγος, λογισμός	Goth.	*raþjō*	Lith.	*sąskaita*
NG	λογαριασμός	ON	*tal, tala, reikningr*	Lett.	*rēk'ins, rēk'ināšana*
Lat.	*ratiō*	Dan.	*regnskab, regning*	ChSl.	(*slovo*)
It.	*conto*	Sw.	*räkning*	SCr.	*račun*
Fr.	*compte*	OE	*gerād, riht*	Boh.	*účet*
Sp.	*cuenta*	ME	(*a*)*count, re*(*c*)*k*(*i*)*ning*	Pol.	*rachunek*
Rum.	*socoteală, cont*	NE	*account, reckoning*	Russ.	*sčet*
Ir.	*airem, comairem*	Du.	*rekening*	Skt.	*gaṇana-*
NIr.	*comhaireamh, cunntas*	OHG	*reda*	Av.	. . . .
W.	*cyfrif*	MHG	*rech*(*e*)*nunge*		
Br.	*kont*	NHG	*rechnung*		

Some of the words for 'account' are related to those for 'number' or 'count', while others are based on a more general notion of 'reason, right' or the like.

1. Grk. λόγος (also 'reason, word', etc.) : λέγω 'gather, recount, say', etc., Lat. *legere* 'gather, select, read', etc. Walde-P. 1.422. From same source also λογισμός : λογίζομαι 'count, reckon', and Byz., NG λογαριασμός : Byz. λογαριάζω 'calculate', fr. λογάριον dim. of λόγος.

2. Lat. *ratiō* : *reor, rērī, ratus* 'reckon, judge', etc., Goth. *raþjō* 'number, count', OHG *reda, radia* 'account, speech, tale', etc., fr. IE **rē-*, **rə-*, prob. related ultimately to the root of Grk. ἀραρίσκω 'join together, fit', Lat. *artus* 'joint', etc. Walde-P. 1.73 f. Ernout-M. 860 f. Feist 394.

It. *conto*, Fr. *compte*, Sp. *cuenta* (fr. *cuento*), Rum. *cont* (lit. loanword) fr. late Lat. *computus* 'computation', fr. *computāre* 'reckon', cpd. of *putāre* 'reckon, consider, think'. Ernout-M. 828. REW 2109.

Rum. *socoteală*, fr. *socoti* 'heed, pay attention to', fr. the Slavic, cf. Bulg. dial. *sokoti* 'guard'. Tiktin 1451 ff.

3. Ir. *airem, comairem* 'number, reckoning, account' (cf. Laws, Gloss. 37), NIr. *comhaireamh*, W. *cyfrif*, cpds. fr. *rīm-*, W. *rhif* 'number' (13.12), vb. Ir. *airmin* 'count' (*ad-rīm-*, Pedersen 2.602).

NIr. *cunntas*, fr. ME *counte*.

Br. *kont*, fr. OFr. *conte, cunte*.

4. Goth. *raþjō*, OHG *reda* (*radia, redia*) : Lat. *ratiō* (above, 2).

ON *tal, tala* (also 'number, tale, talk') : OE (*ge*)*tæl* 'tale, number, series', OHG *zala* id., NHG *zahl* 'number', etc. (13.12). Walde-P. 1.808. Falk-Torp 1243.

ON (late) *reikningr*, Dan. *regning*, Sw. *räkning*, fr. MLG *rekeninge* = Du. *rekening*, etc. (below).

Dan. *regnskab*, fr. *regne* 'reckon, calculate', fr. MLG *rekenen* (below).

OE *gerād* (also *gerādegode*; cf. Gospels, Mt. 18.23, 24, where Lindisf. *reht, rehtnis*) : adj. *gerād* 'well arranged, skilled', Goth. *garaiþs* 'appointed', MGH *gereit* 'ready', etc. (14.29).

OE *riht* 'right, justice, law' (21.11), also (esp. Northumbrian) 'account', as likewise *rehtnis*.

ME *acount, count*, NE *account*, fr. OFr. *a-conte, a-cunte, conte, cunte* (above, 2).

ME *re*(*c*)*k*(*i*)*ning*, NE *reckoning*, Du. *rekening* (MLG *rekeninge*), MHG *rech*(*e*)*nunge*, NHG *rechnung* (OHG *rechenunga* 'arrangement'), fr. OE *gerecenian*, MLG *rekenen*, OHG *rehhanōn*, etc. 'calculate', fr. the same root as OE *riht*, etc. (above). NED s.v. *reckoning*. Weigand-H. 2.546.

5. Lith. *sąskaita* (neolog.; *rokundas* now obs.), fr. *suskaityti* 'count', cpd. of *skaityti* 'read' (18.52) and 'count'.

Lett. *rēk'ins* (*rēk'ens, rēk'enis*), fr. MLG *rekinge, rekeninge* (above); Lett. *rēk'ināšana* fr. *rēkināt* 'reckon, consider,

fr. MLG *rekenen* 'reckon' (above). Mühl.-Endz. 3.520.

6. ChSl. *slovo* 'word' (18.26), reg. = Grk. λόγος 'word' is used also in the Gospels where λόγος is 'account', as Mt. 12.36 (both senses in same verse), 18.23, etc.

SCr. *račun*, fr. It. *razione* (now 'ration'), Lat. *ratiō* (above, 2). Miklosich 271.

Boh. *účet*, Russ. *sčet* cpds : ChSl. *čĭtą, čisti* 'count, read', etc. (18.52).

Pol. *rachunek*, fr. *rachować*, fr. NHG *rechnen*. Brückner 451.

7. Skt. *gaṇana-* : *gaṇaya-* 'count, enumerate, calculate', *gaṇa-* 'host, multitude'.

11.67 SECURITY, SURETY

Grk.	ἐνέχυρον, ἐγγύη, ἀρραβών	Goth.	*wadi*	Lith.	*užstatas*
NG	ἐνέχυρον, ἀρραβών	ON	*veð, pantr*	Lett.	*k'īla*
Lat.	*pignus* (*arrabō, arra*)	Dan.	*pant*	ChSl.	*zalogŭ*
It.	*pegno* (*arra*)	Sw.	*pant*	SCr.	*zalog*
Fr.	*gage* (*arrhes*)	OE	*wedd*	Boh.	*zástava*
Sp.	*prenda*	ME	*plege, wed*(*de*)*, surete*	Pol.	*zastawa*
Rum.	*amanet, zălog*	NE	*security, pledge, surety*	Russ.	*zaklad, zalog*
Ir.	*gell*	Du.	*pand*	Skt.	*nyāsa-, nikṣepa-, ādhi-*
NIr.	*geall*	OHG	*wet*(*t*)*i, pfant*	Av.	. . . .
W.	*adneu*	MHG	*pfant*		
Br.	*gouestl*	NHG	*pfand*		

Here is intended the material security offered, not the personal promise as in the now most common use of NE *pledge*.

1. Grk. ἐνέχυρον, cpd. of ἐν- 'in' and ἐχυρός 'strong, secure, safe' (: ἔχω 'hold, have').

Grk. ἐγγύη (cf. ἔγγυος the personal 'surety', ἐγγυάω 'give surety', etc.) : ἐγγύς 'near', both prob. orig. 'in the hand', cpds. of ἐν- 'in' and *γυ- : Av. *gu-* 'hand'. Walde-P. 1.637. Boisacq 211.

Grk. ἀρραβών 'earnest-money, pledge' (NG pop. ἀρραβῶνα id. and esp. 'betrothal ring', pl. 'betrothal'), loanword fr. Semitic, prob. a Phoen. word = Hebr. *ʿērābōn* 'pledge'. Hence Lat. *arrabō* and abbr. *arra* > It. *arra*, Fr. *arrhes*. Boisacq 82. Ernout-M. 75. Walde-H. 1.69. REW 665.

2. Lat. *pignus* (> It. *pegno*) perh. as 'mark (for remembering a contract)' : *pingere* 'embroider, paint'. Ernout-M. 766 f.

Fr. *gage*, OFr. also *wage*, fr. Gmc., Goth. *wadi*, etc. (below, 4). REW 9474. Gamillscheg 451.

Sp. *prenda*, fr. *prender* 'take'. Diez 646.

Rum. *amanet*, through NG ἀμανέτι 'pawn, pledge', fr. Turk. *emanet* 'security'. Lokotsch 66. Tiktin 56.

Rum. *zălog*, fr. Slavic, ChSl. *zalogŭ*, etc. (below, 6).

3. Ir. *gell* (cf. Thurneysen, Z. celt. Ph. 15.266 ff.), NIr. *geall* (hence vb. *gell-* 'promise, pledge'), fr. **ghislo-* : Ir. *gīall*, W. *gwystl* 'hostage', Br. *gouestl* 'pledge, security', ON *gīsl*, etc. 'hostage' (**gheislo-*), root connection dub. Walde-P. 1.554. Pedersen 2.537.

W. *adneu* : Ir. *aithne* gl. *depositum*, abstract of *aith-no-* 'entrust', perh. : Lat. *ad-nuere* 'nod to, assent'. Pedersen 1.441, 2.586.

4. Goth. *wadi*, ON *veð*, OE *wedd*, ME *wed*(*de*), OHG *we*(*t*)*ti* (NHG *wette* 'bet', cf. NE *wager* orig. 'pledge' : *wage*, Fr.

gage), OS *weddi* : Lat. *vas, vadis* 'surety' (the person), cpd. *praes, praedis*, Lith. *vaduoti* 'redeem, ransom (a pledge)'. Walde-P. 1.216. Feist 539. Ernout-M. 804, 1075.

ON *pantr*, Dan., Sw. *pant* (fr. MLG *pant*), Du. *pand*, OHG, MHG *pfant*, NHG *pfand* (cf. also MHG *pand* 'loss, damage', esp. by war, *panden* 'rob', MHG *pfenden* 'rob one of something, take a pledge'), orig. dub., but perh. of Romance origin, cf. OFr. *pan* 'pledge, security, surety' (> NE *pawn*), if this is the same word as *pan* 'piece' (orig. of cloth, fr. Lat. *pannus*) and not conversely fr. Gmc. as some think. Falk-Torp 813 f. Kluge-G. 439, Franck-v. W. 487 f.

ME *surete*, NE *surety* (in this sense fr. 14th cent., NED s.v. 5) fr. OFr. *surte*, fr. Lat. *sēcūritās* 'security, whence the now more common NE *security*.

ME *plege*, NE *pledge*, fr. OFr. *plege* 'surety' (Fr. *pleige*), MLat. *plevium, plebium, plivium*, etc. (cf. also MLat. *plevina*, OFr. *plevine*, NE *plevin*, *replevin*), beside vb. OFr. *plevir* 'warrant', prob. fr. a Gmc. form belonging with OHG, OS *plegan* 'take responsibility for'. REW 6592. Gamillscheg 701. NED s.v. *pledge*.

5. Lith. *užstatas* : *už-statyti* 'set up, place behind'; cf. Boh. *zástava* (below).

Lett. *k'ila* (*k'īls, k'ilis*), fr. Liv. *kīl* 'pledge'. Mühl.-Endz. 2.388.

6. ChSl. *zalogŭ*, SCr., Russ. *zalog*, cpds. with *za-* 'behind' and deriv. of root in *ložiti* 'lay', *ležati* 'lie', etc., IE **legh-*. Walde-P. 2.425. Berneker 727 f.

Boh. *zástava*, Pol. *zastawa*, cpds. of *za-* 'behind' and deriv. of the root in Boh. *státi*, Pol. *stać* 'stand'.

Russ. *zaklad*, fr. *za-* 'behind' and *kladu, klast'* 'put, place' (12.12).

7. Skt. *nyāsa-*, lit. 'a setting down', fr. *ni-as-* 'throw, lay, or put down' (*as-* 'throw', 10.25).

Skt. *nikṣepa-*, fr. *ni-kṣip-* 'throw down' (*kṣip-* 'throw', 10.25).

Skt. *ādhi-*, fr. *ā-dhā-* 'put in' (*dhā-* 'place, put').

11.68 INTEREST

Grk.	τόκος	Goth.	*wōkrs*	Lith.	*nuošimčiai, palūkanos*
NG	τόκος	ON	*āvǫxtr, okr*	Lett.	*auglis*
Lat.	*ūsūra, fēnus*	Dan.	*rente*	ChSl.	*lichva*
It.	*interesse*	Sw.	*ränta*	SCr.	*kamate* (*interes*)
Fr.	*intérêt*	OE	*gestrēon, hȳr, gafol*	Boh.	*úrok*
Sp.	*interés*	ME	*usure, gavel*	Pol.	*procent*
Rum.	*dobîndă, interes*	NE	*interest*	Russ.	*procent* (*interes*)
Ir.	*fuillem*	Du.	*rente* (*interest*)	Skt.	*vṛddhi-*
NIr.	*breis, gaimbīn*	OHG	*wuochar, phrasamo*	Av.	. . . .
W.	*llog*	MHG	*wuocher* (*zins*)		
Br.	*kampi, mad*	NHG	*zins*		

Words for 'interest' on money are specialized from more general notions like 'growth, produce, profit, income', also 'interest' (in wider sense). Several old words for 'interest' come to mean 'excessive interest, usury' (e.g. Fr. *usure*, NE *usury*, Dan. *aager*, NHG *wucher*, Russ. *lichva*) through their use by church writers to whom all 'interest' was 'usury'.

1. Grk. τόκος 'childbirth, offspring' and (as product of money) 'interest' : τίκτω 'beget, bear' (4.71) and 'produce'.

2. Lat. *ūsūra*, prop. 'use', then through specialization 'use of loaned money' > 'interest' (paid for the use) : *ūsus* 'use,

utility', *ūtor, ūtī* 'use, make use of'. Ernout-M. 1142.

Lat. *fēnus* : *fēlix, fētus* 'productive', etc. Ernout-M. 345. Walde-H. 1.479.

It. *interesse*, Sp. *interés*, Rum. *interes*, Fr. *intérêt*, fr. MLat. *interesse* (and 3sg. *interest*) 'concern' (lit. 'be between'). Hence NE *interest* (early NE also *interesse*), and other Eur. words, less commonly used in financial sense, a Sw. *intresse*, Du. *interest*, NHG *interesse*, SCr., Russ. *interes*. NED s.v. *interest* sb.

Rum. *dobîndă*, formerly 'profit, gain', fr. *dobîndi* 'earn, acquire', fr. Slavic *dobyti* 'get, obtain' (11.16). Tiktin 556.

3. Ir. *fuillem*, fr. **fo-slī-mo-* cpd. deriv. of the root *slī-* as in *adroilliu* 'earn' (**ad-ro-slī-*), IE **slē-*, perh. fr. the root **sel-* in Ir. *selb* 'property', etc. (11.41). Walde-P. 2.504. Pedersen 2.630 f.

NIr. *breis* : MIr. *breis* 'increase, profit' (K. Meyer, Contrib. 254), orig.? Perh. (orig. a comp.?) : Ir. *bress*, NIr. *breass* 'great'.

NIr. *gaimbīn* 'morsel, bit', also 'interest' or 'usury' (cf. Dinneen, s.v., McKenna 683), etym.?

W. *llog*, back-formation to *llogi* 'hire, engage, lend at interest', fr. Lat. *locāre* 'place, let, lease, hire'. Loth, Mots lat. 182.

Br. *kampi*, fr. MLat. *cambium* (> It. *cambio* 'exchange, rate of exchange', etc.), itself of Celt. orig. (cf. 12.93). Henry 52.

Br. *mad* 'property' (11.41) also 'interest'.

4. Goth. *wōkrs*, ON *okr* (partly 'usury', as Dan. *aager*, Sw. *ocker*, all fr. MLG *wōker*), OHG *wuochar* (but mostly 'increase, gain; offspring'), MHG *wuocher* (NHG *wucher* 'usury'), OFris. *wōker* (OE *wōcor* 'increase, fruit, offspring'), either fr. the root of Goth. *wahsjan*, OHG *wahsan*, etc. 'make grow', Goth. *aukan*, Lat. *augēre* 'increase', etc.; or fr. that of Goth. *wakan*, OE *wæcnan* 'wake' (cf. OE *wæcnian* 'be born', Lat. *vigēre* 'thrive'). The former connection is simpler semantically and without serious phonetic difficulty, but the latter is now preferred by many. Walde-P. 1.23, 247 (but cf. Walde-H. 1.479 s.v. *fēnus*). Feist 572. Falk-Torp 3. Hellquist 723. Weigand-H. 2.1287.

ON *āvǫxtr*, lit. 'growth, produce, fruit', cpd. of *ā* 'on' and *vǫxtr* 'growth' : *vaxa* 'grow', etc. Falk-Torp 3.

Dan. *rente*, Sw. *ränta* (late ON *renta* 'income'), fr. MLG *rente* 'income, yield, interest', also Du. *rente* 'interest' = MHG *rente* 'income' (11.71). Falk-Torp 891.

OE *gestrēon*, also 'gain, product, wealth,' etc. : (*ge*)*strēonan* 'gain, acquire', OHG *gistriuni* 'gain', etc. Walde-P. 2.640.

OE *hȳr*, also 'payment for any service' (ME, NE *hire*) but esp. 'payment for the use of money' : OE *hȳrian*, etc. 'hire' (11.77).

OE *gafol* (also 'tribute, tax'), ME *gavel*, fr. the root of OE *giefan* 'give' (11.21). NED s.v. *gavel*, sb.[1].

NE *interest*, etc., above, 2.

OHG *phrasamo* (Tat.), OLG *prisma*, (Grimm, Deutsche Gram. 2.142), orig.?

NHG *zins* (or pl. *zinsen*) : OHG. MHG *zins* 'tribute, tax' (11.69).

5. Lith. *nuošimčiai*, pl. of *nuošimtis* 'percentage' fr. *nuo* 'from' and *šimtas* 'hundred', neolog. modelled on Pol., Russ. *procent* (below).

Lith. *palūkanos* (pl.), fr. *palūkėti* 'wait for' (*lūkėti* beside *laukti* 'wait', NSB).

Lett. *auglis* 'fruit' and 'interest', fr. *augt* 'grow'. Mühl.-Endz. 1.216.

6. ChSl. *lichva* (in modern Slavic mostly 'usury' or archaic), fr. a Gmc.

(Goth.) **līχwa* : Goth. *leihwan*, OHG *līhen*, etc. 'lend' (11.61). Berneker 717. Stender-Petersen 320 f.

SCr. *kamate* (pl.), Russ. (old) *kamato* (Bulg. *kamato* 'debt'), fr. Byz. κάματον 'toil' and 'product of toil' (cf. NG μεροκάματο 'day's work' and 'day's wages'). Berneker 476.

Boh. *úrok*, lit. 'term', cpd. of *rok* 'year, set term', ChSl. *rokŭ* 'determined time, goal' : *rešti, reką* 'say'. Walde-P. 2.362. Miklosich 274.

Pol., Russ. *procent* 'percentage, rate of interest', hence also simply 'interest', prob. fr. NHG *prozent* = It. *per cento*, etc. 'by the hundred, percent' with substitution of *pro*, as if Lat. *prō centum*.

7. Skt. *vṛddhi-* 'growth' (fr. *vṛdh-* 'grow'), also 'gain, profit' and the technical term for 'interest'.

11.69 TAX (sb.)

Grk.	φόρος, τέλος, εἰσφορά	Goth.	*gild, gilstr, gabaur*	Lith.	*mokestis*
NG	φόρος	ON	*skattr, tollr*	Lett.	*nuoduoklis, mesls*
Lat.	*vectīgal, stipendium, tribūtum*	Dan.	*skat*	ChSl.	*danĭ*
It.	*imposta, tassa*	Sw.	*skatt*	SCr.	*porez* (*danak*)
Fr.	*impôt, taxe, contribution*	OE	*gafol, sceatt, toll*	Boh.	*daň* (*berně, poplatek*)
Sp.	*impuesto, contribución*	ME	*taxe*	Pol.	*podatek* (*pobór, taksa*)
Rum.	*impozit, taxă*	NE	*tax*	Russ.	*nalog, podat'*
Ir.	*cīs*	Du.	*belasting*	Skt.	*kara-, bali-, çulka-*
NIr.	*cāin*	OHG	*zins, zol, tribuz*	OPers.	*bāji-*
W.	*treth*	MHG	*zins, zol*		
Br.	*tell*	NHG	*steuer*		

Words for 'tax' (for older periods more appropriately 'tribute') are from words meaning 'carry, bring, contribute, pay' or 'put on, assess, rate'. NE *tax* is the most generic term and in U.S. covers virtually every form of tax except import *duties* and bridge or road *tolls* (many other *duties* in British usage which are *taxes* in U.S.; see NED s.vv. *tax* and *duty*). Elsewhere too, beside the most generic word, others may be used for special forms of 'tax', as the import duty (NHG *zoll*, etc.).

1. Grk. φόρος 'tribute' : φέρω 'carry, bring' (10.61).

Grk. τέλος, prob. the same word as τέλος 'fulfilment, completion, end' (14.26), with easy development fr. 'fulfilment' to 'expense' (cf. εὐτελής 'cheap', πολυτελής 'costly') and 'service, duty, dues, tax' (cf. ἀτελής 'free from tax'). Otherwise (: τλῆναι 'bear, endure', Lat. *tollere* 'lift', etc.) Walde-P. 1.739, Boisacq 953.

Grk. εἰσφορά 'contribution' and at Athens 'property-tax', fr. εἰσφέρω 'bring in'.

2. Lat. *vectīgal*, neut. subst. of *vectīgālis* 'pertaining to taxation, taxable', orig. in detail dub., but prob. based on a **vectis* 'delivery' : *vehere* 'carry'. Walde-P. 1.250. Ernout-M. 1078 (suggesting a loanword).

Lat. *stipendium* (also 'soldiers' pay'), fr. **stipi-pendium* (cf. Varro *militis stipendia ideo quod eam stipem pendebant*) cpd. of *stips* 'small piece of money' and deriv. of *pendere* 'pay' (11.65). Ernout-M. 977.

Lat. *tribūtum*, fr. *tribuere* 'assign, allot, yield, pay', deriv. of *tribus* 'tribe'. Ernout-M. 1056.

It. *imposta*, Fr. *impôt*, Sp. *impuesto*, Rum. *impozit*, fr. Lat. *imposita* (*-tum*), pple. of *impōnere* 'put on'. REW 4314. Gamillscheg 526.

It. *tassa*, Fr. *taxe* (> Rum. *taxă*), back-formation fr. It. *tassare*, Fr. *taxer* 'assess, tax', fr. Lat. *taxāre* 'censure, appraise, rate' loanword fr. Grk. τάσσω, aor. ἔταξα 'appoint, fix (a payment or tax)', lit. 'set in order, arrange'. Ernout-M. 1019. Gamillscheg 837.

Fr. *contribution*, Sp. *contribución*, fr. Lat. *contribūtiō, -ōnis* 'distribution, contribution' (: *tribuere*, etc. above, 2).

3. Ir. *cīs* 'tribute' (in Laws 'rent'), fr. Lat. *cēnsus* (cf. below OHG *zins*, etc.). Vendryes, De hib. voc. 126. Pedersen 1.209.

NIr. *cāin* 'law, rule' and 'tribute, tax', fr. Lat. *canōn* 'rule' (fr. Grk. κανών id., orig. 'rod') and under the emperors 'a tribute (in money or kind)'. Vendryes, De hib. voc. 119. Pedersen 1.193. Zimmer, KZ. 36.440 ff.

W. *treth*, orig.? Loth, Mots lat. 212 (rejecting deriv. fr. Lat. *tribūtum*, Stokes).

Br. *tell*, abbreviated fr. Lat. *telōnium* 'toll-house' (cf. ON *tollr*, etc., below). Henry 262.

4. Goth. *gild* = OHG *gelt* 'payment, money', etc. (11.43), fr. the root in Goth. (*fra*)-*gildan*, OHG *geltan* 'pay' (11.65). Hence also Goth. *gilstr*, OHG *ghelstar, kelstar* (also 'sacrifice'). Feist 214 f.

Goth. *gabaur* (renders φόρος Rom. 13.7, but otherwise λογία 'collection') : *ga-bairan* 'bring together', *bairan* 'bear'.

Goth. *mōta* (for τέλος and τελώνιον), OE *mōt* (only Gospels, Mt. 22.19, Lindisf.) = OHG *mūta* 'teloneum' (prob. fr. Goth.), ON *mūta* 'fee', orig. disputed, but prob. fr. MLat. *mūta* (cf. Du Cange) : Lat. *mūtāre* 'exchange'. Feist 365. Falk-Torp 703. Otherwise, as Gmc. word (whence MLat. *mūta*) : Goth. *mitan* 'measure', Walde-P. 2.260, Kluge-G. 383.

ON *skattr*, Dan. *skat*, Sw. *skatt*, OE *sceatt* : Goth. *skatts* 'money', etc. (11.43).

ON *tollr*, OE *toll*, OHG, MHG *zol*, all used esp. in the restricted sense of the modern words (Dan. *told*, Sw. *tull*, NHG *zoll*, NE *toll*) but also as general words for 'a tax' (cf. ON *sauða-tollr*, OE *cynelīc toll*, and OHG *zol* often gl. *vectigal*), fr. MLat. *tol*(*l*)*ōnium* by influence of *tollere* 'lift' for lat. Lat. *telōnium* 'tollhouse', fr. Grk. τελώνιον id. Falk-Torp 1269. NED s.v. *toll* sb.[1].

OE *gafol*, also 'interest' (11.68).

ME *taxe*, NE *tax*, fr. the verb ME *taxe*, fr. OFr. *taxer* (above, 2). NED s.v.

Du. *belasting*, lit. 'a loading', fr. *belasten* 'load, burden'.

OHG, MHG *zins* (general for 'any sort of tribute from the subject to the lord', MHG also in the modern sense 'interest'), fr. Lat. *cēnsus* 'census, register' (of citizens and property), late 'tax' (so Grk. κῆνσος in NT). Ernout-M. 173. Weigand-H. 2.1330. Kluge-G. 713.

OHG *tribuz* (Tat.), fr. Lat. *tribūtum*.

NHG *steuer* : MHG *stiur*(*e*), OHG *stiura* 'prop, support' (also 'rudder', 10.36). Weigand-H. 2.967 f. Paul, Deutsches Wtb. s.v.

5. Lith. *mokestis*, lit. 'payment' (beside *mokesnis*), fr. *mokėti* 'pay' (11.65).

Lett. *nuoduoklis*, fr. *nuoduot* 'give up, deliver' (: *duot* 'give').

Lett. *mesls* (pl. *mesli* 'dice, lot'), fr. *mesti* 'throw'. Mühl.-Endz. 2.603. Semantic development through 'that which is one's lot (to pay)'?

6. ChSl. *danĭ*, Boh. *daň*, SCr. *danak*; Pol. *podatek*, Russ. *podat'* : ChSl. *dati*, etc. 'give' (11.21). Berneker 179, 180.

ChSl. *myto* (not quotable for 'tax', but *mytarĭ* reg. for τελώνης and *mytĭnica* for τελώνιον in Gospels), Bulg. *mito*, Boh.

mýto, Pol. *myto*, etc. 'toll', fr. Gmc., Goth. *mōta*, etc. (above, 4). Stender-Petersen 324.

SCr. *porez*, lit. 'assessment' : *porezati* 'cut up, separate, divide' (*rezati* 'cut' 9.22). Miklosich 278.

Boh. *berně*, Pol. *pobór* : Boh. *bráti*, Pol. *brać* 'take' (11.13). Berneker 51, 75 f.

Boh. *poplatek*, also *plat* (but this mostly 'pay, payment') : *platiti* 'pay' (11.65).

Russ. *nalog*, cpd. of *na* 'on' and deriv. of root in Slavic *loziti* 'lay' (cf. *zalog* 'pledge', 11.67). Semantic borrowing fr. the Romance group (It. *imposta*, etc.) possible.

7. Skt. *kara-*, perh. (like *kara-* 'ray', but with independent semantic development), fr. *kar-*, *kir-* 'pour out, scatter' (as what is 'poured out' to the ruler). Uhlenbeck 45.

Skt. *bali-*, etym.? Uhlenbeck 188.

Skt. *çulka-* (in RV 'price', later 'tax'), etym.? Uhlenbeck 313.

OPers. *bāǰi-*, as orig. 'assessment' or more prob. 'contribution' : Av. *baǰ-* 'assign as a share', Skt. *bhaj-* 'divide, share, furnish', etc. Barth. 953.

11.71 INCOME

Grk.	*πρόσοδος*	Goth.	....	Lith.	*pajamos*
NG	*εἰσόδημα, ἔσοδο*	ON	*taka, tekja*	Lett.	*ienākšana, ienākums*
Lat.	*frūctus, reditus*	Dan.	*indtægt, indkomst*	ChSl.	(*dochodŭ*)
It.	*rendita*	Sw.	*inkomst*	SCr.	*dohod(ak), prihod*
Fr.	*rente*	OE	....	Boh.	*důchod, příjem*
Sp.	*renta*	ME	*rente*	Pol.	*dochód*
Rum.	*venit*	NE	*income*	Russ.	*dochod*
Ir.	....	Du.	*inkomst*	Skt.	*āya-, āgama-*
NIr.	*teacht isteach*	OHG	....	Av.	....
W.	*cyllid, incwm*	MHG	*rente, gülte, gelt*		
Br.	*leve*	NHG	*einkommen, einkünfte, einnahme, rente*		

Most of the words for 'income' (from property of any sort, more comprehensive than 'interest' on money, though sometimes specialized in this direction, and than produce of land) meant literally what 'comes in' or 'comes back' or is 'taken in'. From the older period of several languages quotable examples for financial 'income' seem to be lacking.

1. Grk. *πρόσοδος* 'approach' and 'income', cpd. of *πρός* 'to, toward' and a form of IE **sed-* in the sense shown by Grk. *ὁδός* 'way, road', ChSl. *choditi* 'go', etc. (10.47, 10.71).

NG *εἰσόδημα*, new formation to *εἴσοδος* 'entrance' (*εἴσοδος*, like *πρόσ-οδος*, above), the latter also sometimes 'income' in late times. Hence also NG *ἔσοδο* (mostly in pl.).

2. Lat. *frūctus* 'use, enjoyment', 'products' (in widest sense) and often 'income' : *frūgēs* 'fruit', *fruī* 'enjoy', Goth. *brūkjan* 'use', etc. Walde-P. 2.208. Ernout-M. 393 f. Walde-H. 1.552.

Lat. *vectīgal* 'tax, public revenues' (11.69), also used for private 'income'.

Lat. *reditus* (*u*-stem), a 'return' in lit. sense, later as commercial term 'return, revenue, income', deriv. of *red-īre* 'come back'. In this sense often written *redditus* (late inscr., Cassiod.) showing association with pple. of *reddere* 'give back, return'. Replaced in VLat. by *rendita* fr. pple. of VLat. **rendere* = *reddere* (11.22), hence It. *rendita*, Fr. *rente*, Sp. *renta*. REW 7141.

Rum. *venit*, fr. *veni* 'come'.

3. NIr. *teacht isteach*, lit. 'coming in' (*teacht* : *tigim* 'come', 10.48; *isteach* 'in, within', orig. 'into the house'), prob. semantic borrowing of NE *income*.

W. *cyllid*, orig.? Loth, Mots lat. 147.

W. *incwm*, fr. NE *income*.

Br. *leve*, fr. OFr. *levée*, fr. *lever* 'raise, lift' (10.22). Henry 185.

4. ON *taka*, late *tekja* (pl. *tekjur*, reg. in NIcel.), Dan. *indtægt*, fr. ON *taka*, Dan. *tage* 'take' (11.13).

Dan. *indkomst* (usually pl. *inkomster*), Sw. *inkomst*, NE *income*, Du. *inkomst*, NHG (pl.) *einkünfte*, more usually *einkommen*, all orig. 'in-come'. Also NHG *einnahme*, fr. *einnehmen* 'take in'.

ME, MHG, NHG *rente* (NE *rent* now obs. in this sense) fr. OFr. *rente* (above, 2). NED s.v. *rent*, sb.[1].

MHG *gülte*, *gelt*, lit. 'payment', but frequently also 'income' (cf. Lexer) : OHG *geltan*, etc. 'pay' (11.81).

5. Lith. *pajamos* (pl.; now definitely established, Senn, Sprachl.), fr. *paimti* 'take in', cpd. of *imti* 'take' (11.13).

Lett. *ienākšana*, *ienākums*, fr. *ie-nākt* 'come in'.

6. ChSl. *dochodŭ* (only late), SCr. *dohod(ak)*, *prihod*, Boh. *důchod*, Pol. *dochód*, Russ. *dochod*, cpds. of Slavic *do* 'to', *pri* 'at', and *chodŭ* : *choditi* 'go'.

Boh. *příjem* 'reception, receipt', and 'income' (so esp. pl. *příjmy*), fr. *přijati*, *přijmouti* 'accept, receive', cpd. of *jati* = ChSl. *jęti* 'take' (11.13).

7. Skt. *āya-*, *āgama-*, fr. *ā-i-*, *ā-gam-* 'come to, approach'.

11.72 EXPENSE, COST

Grk.	*ἀνάλωμα, δαπάνη*	Goth.	*manwiþa*	Lith.	*išlaidos, kaštas*
NG	*ἔξοδο* (*κόστος*)	ON	*kostnaðr, kostr*	Lett.	*izdevumi, maksa*
Lat.	*sūmptus, impendium, impēnsa*	Dan.	*omkostning, udgift*	ChSl.	*dovolŭ*
It.	*spesa, costo*	Sw.	*(om)kostnad, utgift*	SCr.	*trošak, rashod*
Fr.	*frais, dépense, coût*	OE	*andfengas, dægwine*	Boh.	*výdaj, náklad, výloha, útrata*
Sp.	*gasto, coste*	ME	*expence, cost*	Pol.	*wydatek, koszt*
Rum.	*cheltuială*	NE	*expense, cost, outlay*	Russ.	*raschod, izderžka*
Ir.	....	Du.	*kosten*	Skt.	*vyaya-*
NIr.	*costas*	OHG	*gifuori, chosta*	Av.	....
W.	*cost, traul*	MHG	*kost(e)*		
Br.	*miz, dispign, koust*	NHG	*spesen, ausgabe, kosten*		

Words for 'expense, cost' are partly from verbs for 'spend', 'pay', or 'cost' as originally 'stand at' (a price), and partly 'what goes out' or 'what is given out'. A few meant originally 'waste', hence 'excessive expense', then simply 'expense'.

Some of the words are used only as plural collectives (Fr. *frais*, NHG *spesen*, *kosten*) and many of the others, though listed in the singular, frequently so (NE *costs*, *expenses*, It. *spese*, Sp. *gastos*, NHG *ausgaben*, etc.).

1. Grk. *ἀνάλωμα*, deriv. of *ἀνᾱλίσκω* (fut. *ἀνᾱλώσω* etc.) 'use up, spend', cpd. of *ἀνα-* 'up, again' and *ἁλίσκω* mostly in mid. *ἁλίσκομαι* 'be seized' (dial. *ϝαλίσσκηται*, *ϝαλόντοις*) : Lat. *vellere* 'pluck, tear out', Goth. *wilwan* 'seize, rob', etc. Walde-P. 1.305. Boisacq 45.

Grk. *δαπάνη* : *δάπτω* 'rend, devour', Skt. *dāpayati* 'divides', etc., extension of the root **dā(i)-* in Grk. *δαίομαι* 'divide, share'. Walde-P. 1.764. Boisacq 166.

NG *ἔξοδο*, usually pl. *ἔξοδα*, fr. *ἔξοδος* 'exit, issue' also frequently (inscr., Polyb. and Byz.) 'outgoing of money, expenditure', cpd. of *ἐξ* 'out' and *ὁδός* 'way'.

2. Lat. *sūmptus*, fr. *sūmere* 'take, take up' (11.13) and 'spend'.

Lat. *impendium*, *impēnsa*, fr. *impendere* 'expend', cpd. of *pendere* 'pay' (11.65). Similarly late Lat. *expē(n)sa* > It. *spesa*, OFr. *espoise*, in learned form > Anglo-Fr. *expense* > ME, NE *expence*, *expense*; also MLat. *dispensa* or *-um* > Fr. *dépense*. Ernout-M. 751 f. NED s.v. *expense*. Wartburg 3.97.

It. *costo*, Sp. *coste* (*costo*, *costa*), OFr. *cost*, *coust* (> Br. *koust*, ME, NE *cost*) back-formations fr. vbs. It. *constare*, Sp. *costar*, OFr. *coster* 'cost', fr. Lat. *cōnstāre* 'stand fast, be settled, agreed', then in commerce (already in Plaut.) 'stand at (with abl. of price), cost'. Ernout-M. 982. REW 2170.

Hence also the loanwords in Gmc. and through Gmc. in Celtic and Slavic; also NG *κόστος* 'cost, price', but not in such common use as the vb. *κοστίζω*, e.g. *πόσο κοστίζει* 'how much does it cost, what is the price?'

Fr. *frais* (pl.), OFr. sg. *fret*, *frait*, pl. *fras*, fr. Lat. *fractum* 'broken'. Cf. OFr. *fret* 'damage by breaking', hence 'damage, expense', REW 3468. Wartburg 3.755 f.

Sp. *gasto*, also and orig. 'waste', fr. *gastar* 'waste, spend', this fr. Gmc., OHG *wuostan*, etc. 'lay waste'. REW 9168.

Rum. *cheltuială*, fr. *cheltui* 'spend, expend', fr. Hung. *költ* 'spend'. Tiktin 334.

3. NIr. *costas*, W. *cost*, fr. ME, NE *cost*.

W. *traul*, also and orig. 'wear, waste', perh. fr. a form of the root **ter-* 'rub' in Grk. *τείρω*, Lat. *terere*. Lloyd-Jones, Bull. of Celt. Stud. 2.292. G. S. Lane, Language 7.283.

Br. *miz* (and pl. *mizou*), fr. OFr. *mise* (*misse*, *mize*), lit. 'action of placing' (Fr. *mise*), but frequently found in sense of 'expense' (through notion of 'sum of money put out' for a thing), cf. Godefroy. G. S. Lane, Language 13.26.

Br. *dispign*, fr. Lat. *dispendium* (cf. above, 2). Loth, Mots lat. 161.

4. Goth. *manwiþa* (renders *δαπάνη* Lk. 14.28, but more precisely *ἑτοιμασία* 'preparation' Eph. 6.15), fr. *manwus* 'ready', *manwjan* 'prepare'. Feist 345.

ON *kostnaðr*, Dan. *omkostning* (also *be-*), Sw. *(om)kostnad*, fr. ON (late in this sense) *kostr*, older Dan., Sw. *kost* fr. MLG *kost(e)* = Du. *kosten*, OHG *chosta*, MHG *kost(e)*, NHG *kosten* (sg. *kost* obs.), derivs. of the vbs. MLG, MHG *kosten*, etc., fr. VLat. *costāre*, Lat. *cōnstāre* (above, 2). Falk-Torp 569. Weigand-H. 1.1127 f.

Dan. *udgift*, Sw. *utgift*, fr. MLG *ūtgift* 'what is given out', hence used like NHG *ausgabe*.

OE *andfengas* (Lk. 14.28 renders *sumptus*), pl. of *andfeng* 'assuming, reception, etc.' : *fōn* (*feng*) 'take, seize'. Semantic borrowing fr. Lat.?

OE *dæg-wine* 'day's pay' also glosses Lat. *expensa* and *impensum*.

ME, NE *cost*, fr. OFr. *cost*, (above, 2).

ME, NE *expence*, *expense*, fr. Anglo-Fr. *expense* (above, 2).

NE *outlay*, sb. fr. *lay out*.

OHG *gifuori* (renders *sumptus* Tat. 67.12), usually 'what is advantageous or fitting' (as *gifuari* Otfr. etc.) : OS *gifōri* 'use, advantage', ON *fœri* 'opportunity', etc., fr. the root in OHG *fuoran*, etc. 'bring, lead'. Falk-Torp 291.

NHG *spesen*, fr. It. *spese*, pl. of *spesa* (above, 2). Weigand-H. 2.912.

NHG *ausgabe*, mostly in pl. *ausgaben*, lit. 'what is given out'.

5. Lith. *išlaidos*, pl. of *išlaida* 'outlet', fr. *išleisti*, intens. *išlaidyti* 'let out' and 'give out, spend'.

Lith. *kaštas*, fr. Pol. *koszt* (below).

Lett. *maksa* (so Lk. 14.28; this sense not given by Mühl.-Endz., but cf. Ulmann-Brasche s.v. *kosten*), lit. 'payment, pay', fr. Liv. or Esth. *maks* 'pay'. Mühl.-Endz. 2.554 f.

Lett. *izdevumi* (so Drawneek), pl. of *izdevums* 'expenditure' fr. *iz* 'out' and *devums* 'giving, gift' (: *duot* 'give'), semantic borrowing of NHG *ausgabe(n)*.

6. ChSl. *dovolŭ* (for *δαπάνη* Lk. 14.28, otherwise *αὐτάρκεια* 'sufficiency') : *do-vĭlěti* 'suffice'. 'Cost' fr. 'sufficient amount'. Meillet, Études 224.

SCr. *trošak*, fr. *trošiti* 'spend, consume' = ChSl. *trošiti* id. : Boh., Pol. *trocha* 'a bit', root connection? Brückner 576. Miklosich 362.

SCr. *rashod*, Russ. *raschod*, cpd. of *ras-*, *raz-*, 'dis-' and *chodŭ* : *choditi* 'go, come' (opp. to SCr. *prihod*, *dohod*, etc. 'income', 11.75).

Boh. *výdaj*, *vydáni*, Pol. *wydatek*, fr. *vy-dati*, *wy-dać* 'give out, spend'.

Boh. *náklad* (also 'load'), fr. *na-klasti* 'put on' (*klasti*, 12.12). Berneker 507.

Boh. *výloha*, fr. *vy-* 'out' and the root of *lehnouti* 'lie down', ChSl. *legą*, *lešti* (12.14), hence like NE *outlay*.

Boh. *útrata* = Russ. *utrata* 'loss', cf. Boh. *stratiti* 'lose' fr. the root in ChSl. *tratiti* 'consume' (11.33).

Pol. *koszt*, fr. MHG *kost*. Brückner 260. Berneker 586.

Russ. *izderžka*, fr. *izderžat'* 'spend, consume', cpd. of *deržat'* 'hold, keep'.

7. Skt. *vyaya-*, lit. 'disappearance, loss' (as adj. 'passing away, liable to change'), fr. *vi-i-* 'disperse, be lost, perish', cpd. of *i-* 'go' (cf. Uhlenbeck 298 s.v. *vyayati*).

11.73 PROFIT

Grk.	*κέρδος*	Goth.	*gawaurki*	Lith.	*pelnas*
NG	*κέρδος*	ON	*ābati, āgōði*	Lett.	*pel'n'a*
Lat.	*lucrum*	Dan.	*gevinst, fortjeneste, udbytte*	ChSl.	*pribytŭkŭ*
It.	*profitto, guadagno*	Sw.	*vinst, förtjänst*	SCr.	*dobit(ak)*
Fr.	*profit, gain*	OE	*(ge)strēon*	Boh.	*zisk, výdělek*
Sp.	*ganancia*	ME	*profit*	Pol.	*zysk*
Rum.	*profit, cîștig, folos*	NE	*profit, gain*	Russ.	*pribyl'*
Ir.	*torbe, sochor, somaine*	Du.	*winst, gewin*	Skt.	*lābha-, prāpta-*
NIr.	*tairbhe, sochar*	OHG	*gistriuni, giwin*	Av.	*ǰōyā-*
W.	*elw, ennill*	MHG	*gewin*		
Br.	*gounid*	NHG	*gewinn*		

'Profit' is understood here as a commercial term, but most of the words listed are also used for 'gain, profit' in the wider sense. They are mostly from verbs for 'gain, earn, win' or the like. But in one case the underlying notion is 'skill' or 'craftiness'.

1. Grk. *κέρδος*, sense of 'profit' fr. 'skill' or (as first pejorative in feeling) 'craftiness', shown in pl. *κέρδεα* 'cunning arts, wiles' and *κερδαλέος* 'crafty, wily' : Ir. *cerd* 'art, handicraft', W. *cerdd* 'art, poetry, music'. Walde-P. 1.423.

2. Lat. *lucrum* (prob. fr. **lu-tlo-m*) : Ir. *lōg*, 'price', Goth. *laun*, etc. 'reward, wages', Grk. *ἀπο-λαύω* 'enjoy', *λεία* 'booty', ChSl. *loviti* 'hunt', etc. Walde-P. 2.379 f. Ernout-M. 564. Walde-H. 1.826.

Fr. *profit* (> It. *profitto*, Rum. *profit*), fr. Lat. *profectus* 'progress, increase, growth, success', fr. *proficere* 'advance, derive advantage, profit'. REW 6769.

It. *guadagno*, Fr. *gain*, fr. vbs. It. *guadagnare*, Fr. *gagner* (OFr. *gaaignier*) 'gain, earn', fr. a Gmc. (Langob. or

Frank.) *waidenjan* : OHG *weidenen* 'hunt, pasture', ON *veiða* 'hunt', etc. REW 9483. Gamillscheg 451.

Sp. *ganancia*, fr. *ganar* 'win, gain', orig. dub., perh. fr. a Goth. form belonging with OE *gīnan*, *gānian*, etc. 'yawn, gape' (4.52), with semantic development through 'open the mouth for, snap at'. Cf. the equally radical change in OE (Lindisf.) *gīwian* 'ask for' : OHG *gīwen* 'yawn' (Sievers, Anglia 16.98 f.). Diez 155, 175. REW 3637a.

Rum. *câștig*, fr. *câștiga* 'earn, win', dial. also 'be concerned about something, give attention to something', fr. Lat. *castigāre* 'punish, chastise, correct'. REW 1746. Pușcariu 377.

Rum. *folos*, fr. Byz. φελός, Grk. ὄφελος 'furtherance, advantage, help'. Tiktin 641.

3. Ir. *torbe*, NIr. *tairbhe*, fr. **to-ro-ben-* (e.g. 3sg. *dororban* gl. *proficit*), cpd. of *ben-* used in inflection of the vb. 'to be'. Pedersen 2.445 f. Otherwise Thurneysen, Gram. 529.

Ir. *sochor*, NIr. *sochar*, cpd. of prefix *so-* (Skt. *su-*, etc.) and vbl. noun of *cuirim* 'put, place, throw'. *Cor*, NIr. *car* is often used as a suffix with meanings like '-setting', 'arrangement', etc. (cf. Dinneen 164).

W. *elw*, older *helw*, orig. 'possession' : Ir. *selb* 'property', etc. (11.41).

W. *ennill* : OBr. *endlim* gl. *fenus*, Ir. *indile* 'increase, cattle', cpd. of prefix W. *an-*, *en-*, Ir. *ind-* (Gall. *ande-*, etc.) but second member obscure. Pedersen 1.115, 148.

Br. *gounid* (also 'victory') : W. *gweini*, Ir. *fo-gnīu* 'serve', cpd. of Br. *go(u)-*, W. *gw(a)-*, Ir. *fo-* (**upo*) with the root in Ir. *do-gnīu* 'do, make', etc. Pedersen 1.104.

4. Goth. *gawaurki* (renders κέρδος Ph. 1.21, 3.7, also πραγματεία, πορισμός 'occupation, providing') : *gawaurkjan* 'perform, prepare', perfect. of *waurkjan* 'work, do', etc. Feist 210.

ON *ābati* (so reg. in NIcel.), cpd. of *ā* 'on, to' and *bati* 'improvement, advantage' : ON *betri*, *bestr*, Goth. *batiza*, *batists* 'better, best', etc.

ON *āgōði*, cpd. of *ā* and *gōði* 'boon' : *gōðr*, Goth. *gōþs* 'good', etc.

Dan. *fortjeneste*, Sw. *förtjänst*, fr. Dan. *fortjene*, Sw. *förtjäna* 'earn' (11.79).

Dan. *gevinst*, Sw. *vinst*, fr. NHG *gewinst*, MLG *winst* : *gewinn*, (below). Falk-Torp 305. Hellquist 1351.

Dan. *udbytte*, fr. cpd. of *bytte* 'exchange'. Cf. NHG *ausbeute* 'share, profit'.

OE *(ge)strēon*, OHG *gistriuni*, with vbs. OE *(ge-) strēonan*, *strīnan*, 'gain, beget', OHG *gistriunan* 'gain', perh. : OE *strēowian* 'strew', Lat. *struere* 'pile up, construct'. Walde-P. 2.640.

ME, NE *profit*, fr. OFr. *profit* (above).

Late ME *gayne*, NE *gain*, fr. OFr. *gain* (above).

Du. *winst*, *(ge)win*, OHG *giwin*, MHG *gewin* (earlier also 'battle, exertion' then 'acquisition by battle, earnings, gain'), NHG *gewinn*, fr. Du. *winnen* 'gain, earn', OHG *giwinnan* 'acquire by battle, effort, etc.', NHG *gewinnan* 'gain, earn, etc.'. Weigand-H. 1.719.

5. Lith. *pelnas*, Lett. *pel'n'a*, beside Lith. *pelnyti*, Lett. *pelnīt* 'gain, earn' : ChSl. *plěnŭ* 'booty', Skt. *paṇa-* 'gaming, wager'. Walde-P. 2.51. Mühl.-Endz. 3.197.

6. ChSl. *pribytŭkŭ*, SCr. *dobit(ak)* : Bulg. *dobitŭk*, Boh. *dobytek* 'cattle', etc., SCr. *bitak*, Boh., Russ. *byt* 'being', fr. the root in ChSl. *byti* 'be' (cf. SCr. *dobyti* 'get', 11.16). Berneker 113 f.

Boh. *zisk*, Pol. *zysk*, fr. *ziskati*, *zyskać* 'gain', cpds. of *z-* and Boh. (old) *jiskati*, Pol. *iskać* 'seek' (old, now 'louse'), ChSl. *iskati* 'seek', etc. (11.31). Berneker 433.

Boh. *výdělek* ('earnings', also 'profit'), fr. *vydělati* 'earn (11.79), make, work'.

Russ. *pribyl'* : *pribyt'* 'arrive, come, increase', cpd. of *byt'* 'be', etc.

7. Skt. *lābha-* : *labh-* 'seize, grasp, get' (11.14).

Skt. *prāpta-*, pple. 'got, obtained', fr. *pra-āp-* 'reach, obtain', cpd. of *āp-* 'reach, obtain, attain' (11.16).

Av. *ǰōyā-*, fr. *ǰi-* 'gain', desid. *ǰiǰīš-* 'seek to get for oneself' : Skt. *ji-* 'win, conquer', Grk. βία 'force', etc. Walde-P. 1.666 f. Barth. 608, 503.

11.74 LOSS

Grk.	ζημία	Goth.	*sleiþa*	Lith.	*nuostolis*
NG	ζημία	ON	*(fjār)skaði, (fjār)tjōn*	Lett.	*zaudejums (skāde)*
Lat.	*damnum*	Dan.	*tab*	ChSl.	. . . .
It.	*perdita*	Sw.	*förlust*	SCr.	*gubitak*
Fr.	*perte*	OE	*lȳre, lor*	Boh.	*ztráta*
Sp.	*perdida*	ME	*loss(e), lore*	Pol.	*strata*
Rum.	*pierdere*	NE	*loss*	Russ.	*ubytok*
Ir.	*dīth, dochor*	Du.	*verlies*	Skt.	*hāni-, kṣaya-*
NIr.	*cailleamhain, dochar*	OHG	*farloranissa*	Av.	*afša-*
W.	*coll(ed)*	MHG	*verlust*		
Br.	*koll*	NHG	*verlust*		

To a great extent words for 'loss' of money, property, etc., are the same as those for 'loss' in general and are the usual nouns corresponding to the verbs for 'lose' already discussed (above, 11.33). Such are : It. *perdita*, Fr. *perte*, Sp. *perdida*, Rum. *pierdere* (: It. *perdere*, etc.); NIr. *cailleamhain*, W. *coll(ed)*, Br. *koll* (: NIr. *caillim*, W. *colli*, Br. *koll*); ON *tjōn*, esp. cpd. *fjār-tjōn* 'loss of money' (: *tȳna*), Dan. *tab* (: *tabe*); Sw. *förlust*, OE *lȳre*, OE *lor*, ME *lore*, ME *loss(e)*, NE *loss*, Du. *verlies*, OHG *farloranissa* ('damnum, perditio', but *forlust* 'perditio', cf. Graff 2.266), MHG *verlornisse*, *verlust*, NHG *verlust* (but Goth. *fralusts* 'destruction, ruin'); Lith. *nuostolis* (: *nustoti*), Lett. *zaudejums* (: *zaudēt*); SCr. *gubitak* (: *gubiti*); Boh. *ztráta*, Pol. *strata* (: Boh. *ztratiti*, etc.); Skt. *hāni* (: *hā-*).

There are however some other special terms used in this sense, mostly from notions like 'injury, damage, penalty'.

1. Grk. ζημία, Dor. ζāμία, also 'penalty, fine', perh. (as ζā-μία) : ζῆλος (ζā-λος) 'ardor, zeal, jealousy', ζητέω 'seek' (11.31), but semantic development not clear. Boisacq 309.

2. Lat. *damnum*, also 'harm, damage' see 11.28.

3. Ir. *dīth*, also 'destruction, ruin, death' : Arm. *di* 'corpse', OE *dwīnan* 'waste away', ON *dvīna* 'dwindle, pine away'. Walde-P. 1.835.

Ir. *dochor*, NIr. *dochar*, cpd. with *do-* 'ill-' (: Grk. δυσ-, etc.), opp. to *sochor* 'profit' (11.73).

NIr. *dīoghbhāil*, fr. Ir. *digbāil* 'diminution, injury, harm', vbl. n. of *di-gaibim* 'take away, diminish' (cpd. of *gaibim* 'take', 11.13).

4. Goth. *sleiþa* (renders ζημία Ph. 3.7, 8) : *sleiþei* 'danger', *sleiþs* 'bad, dangerous', ON *slīðr* 'fearful', OE *slīþe* 'dire, cruel, dangerous'. Walde-P. 1.401. Feist 437.

ON *fjārskaði*, *fēskaði*, cpd. of *fē*, gen. *fjār* 'money, property, cattle' and *skaði* 'harm, damage, destruction' (= OHG *scado*, NHG *schade*, etc.).

5. Lith. *nuostolis* (above), now reg. word for 'loss' of any kind, replacing

iškada (in NT versions) fr. Pol. *szkoda* 'damage' (11.28) and *blėdis* in this sense.

Lett. *skāde* (in NT, Ph. 3.7, 8 and Ulmann; Mühl.-Endz. 'damage, misfortune'), fr. MLG *schade* 'damage' (11.28). Mühl.-Endz. 3.879.

6. Russ. *ubytok*, cpd. formed with *u-* 'away' as opp. to *dobytok* 'acquisition, (acquired) possessions', ChSl. *pribytŭkŭ*, SCr. *dobitak* 'profit, gain', etc. (11.73). Berneker 113.

7. Skt. *kṣaya-*, lit. 'destruction, decrease' : *kṣi-* 'destroy' (11.27), etc. Walde-P. 1.505.

Av. *afša-* (Vd. 13.10 *aδāt̰ paiti afšə čikayat̰* 'then he shall pay for the loss', of one who has injured a watch-dog so that the property is stolen) : Skt. *apvā-* 'a disease' (RV), Lith. *opus* 'sensitive (to pain)'. Walde-P. 1.47. Barth. 103.

11.75 LEASE, RENT (To Another), LET

Grk.	μισθόω	Goth.	*anafilhan*	Lith.	*samdyti*
NG	ἐνοικιάζω	ON	*selja ā leigu*	Lett.	*izīrēt, iznuomāt*
Lat.	*locāre*	Dan.	*leje (ud)*	ChSl.	*vŭdati*
It.	*affittare, appigionare*	Sw.	*(ut)hyra*	SCr.	*iznajmiti, dati u najam*, etc.
Fr.	*louer*	OE	*lǣtan, gesettan*		
Sp.	*alquilar, arrendar*	ME	*let, hire, lese*	Boh.	*pronajmouti*
Rum.	*închiria*	NE	*lease, let, rent*	Pol.	*wynająć*
Ir.	*tabraim ar fochruic*	Du.	*verhuren*	Russ.	*otdat' vnaem*
NIr.	*leigim ar ghabhāil*	OHG	*befelahan*	Skt.	*ā-dhā-*(?)
W.	*ardrethu, rhentu*	MHG	*vermieten*	Av.	. . . .
Br.	*feurmi*	NHG	*vermieten*		

NE *lease* and *rent* (and several of the other words listed) are used both of the owner who lets out property and the one who receives it on rental, only *let* in connection with property being unambiguous. There is some tendency now to prefer *lease* in the former and *rent* in the latter use (though *rent* is the popular word for both), and we shall adopt this distinction as a matter of convenience in the following discussion, using 'lease' for the notion in 11.75 and 'rent' for that in 11.76.

For the most part, though not universally, 'lease' and 'rent' (as defined above) are expressed by the same or by differentiated forms (voice, cpds.) of the same word. In some cases the former, in some the latter, use is the original.

Only the more general terms which may refer to any kind of property rented are listed. Those which apply only to the rental or 'farming out' of land for agricultural purposes are omitted, e.g. words like Fr. *affermer*, NHG *pachten* (and *verpachten*), Eng. *farm* (in the older sense), Lith. *randuoti*, etc.

1. Grk. μισθόω, fr. μισθός 'wages, pay' (11.78).

Grk. ἐκδίδομαι, mid. of ἐκδίδωμι 'give out', is sometimes 'let out' for hire (Hdt.+, so NT).

Byz., NG ἐνοικιάζω, fr. ἐνοίκιον 'house-rent', sb. fr. adj. ἐνοίκιος 'in the house'.

2. Lat. *locāre* (> Fr. *louer*), orig. 'to place', fr. *locus* 'place'. Ernout-M. 559. Walde-H. 1.817. REW 5094.

It. *affittare*, fr. *affitto* 'rental' (esp. of land), cpd. of *fitto* 'rental' (now mostly 'horse-hire'), this sb. to adj. *fitto* 'thick, close', fr. Lat. *fīctus* (Varro) pple. of *fīgere* 'fix, infix'. REW 3280.

It. *appigionare* (or *dare a pigione*), fr. *pigione* 'rent', fr. Lat. *pēnsiō* 'payment' (fr. *pendere* 'pay', 11.65), late 'rent'. REW 6393.

Sp. *alquilar*, fr. *alquiler* 'wages, rent', loanword fr. Arab. *kirāʾ* 'pay, rent'. REW 4703a. Lokotsch 1181.

Sp. *arrendar* (but esp. 'lease land'), fr. Cat. *arrendar*, cpd. : Sp. *rendir*, etc. 'return, give back' (11.22). REW 7141.

Rum. *închiria*, fr. *chirie* 'rent, hire', fr. Arab. (through Turk.) *kirāʾ* 'pay, rent' (cf. Sp. *alquilar*, above). Tiktin 344. Lokotsch 1181.

3. Ir. *tabraim ar fochruic* (of land, Laws 3.127, 129, 131, etc.), lit. 'give on pay', with *fochricc* 'pay, reward, wage' (11.78).

NIr. *leigim ar ghabhāil*, lit. 'let on taking' with *gabhāil* vbl. n. of *gabhaim* 'take' (11.13).

W. *ardrethu*, fr. *ardreth* 'rent, toll, revenue', lit. 'over-tax', cpd. of *treth* 'tax' (11.69) with *ar* 'upon, over' (but often with mere intensive force).

W. *rhentu*, fr. NE *rent*. Parry-Williams 119.

Br. *feurmi*, fr. *feurm* 'rent', loanword fr. Fr. *ferme* 'leasing (of land), farming out'.

4. Goth. *anafilhan* (renders ἐκδίδομαι Mk. 12.1, Lk. 20.9 'let out', of the vineyard), so also OHG *bifelahan* ('locare' Tat. 124.1, 4), both mostly 'give over, entrust', cpds. of Goth. *filhan* 'hide, bury', OHG *felahan* 'bury' : OE *befēolan* 'commit, deliver, grant', ON *fela* 'hide, cover', etc. (4.78, 12.27).

ON *selja ā leigu*, lit. 'give (sell) on hire, rent', with *leiga* : *leiga* (vb.) 'rent' (11.76).

Dan. *leje (ud)*, see *leje* 'rent' (11.76).

Sw. *(ut)hyra*, ME *hire* (e.g. Wyclif Mk. 12.1 for 'let out'), Du. *verhuren*, see under 'hire' (11.77).

OE *lǣtan*, ME, NE *let* (in this sense quoted from 909 in NED s.v. *let*, vb.[1] 8) = OE *lǣtan* 'leave', etc. (11.34).

OE *gesettan* (with *mid* renders *locāre* Mk. 12.1, Lk. 20.9), lit. 'set, place'.

ME *lese*, NE *lease*, fr. OFr. *lesser*, Fr. *laisser* 'let, leave' (11.34).

NE *rent*, earlier (ME) 'provide with revenue, endow', fr. ME *rente* 'source of revenue, revenue, income' (11.71), later 'rent'.

MHG, NHG *vermieten*, cpd. of OHG *miaten*, etc. 'rent' (11.76).

5. Lith. *samdyti* : *samdas* 'hire, rental', cpd. of IE **som-* (Skt. *sam-*, etc.) 'together' and root **dhē-* 'place, put', cf. Skt. *samdha-* 'union', etc. Walde-P. 1.827, 2.490. Cf. SCr. *posuditi* 'lend', etc. (11.61).

Lett. *izīrēt*, *iznuomāt*, cpds. of *īrēt* and *nuomāt* 'rent' (11.76).

6. ChSl. *vŭdati* (for ἐκδίδομαι 'let out' Mk. 12.1, etc.; mostly for ἀποδίδωμι 'give over, pay', etc.), cpd. of *dati* 'give'.

SCr. *iznajmiti*, Boh. *pronajmouti*, Pol. *wynająć*, cpds. of SCr. *najmiti*, etc. 'rent' (11.76).

SCr. *dati u najam*, Russ. *otdat' vnaem*, SCr. *dati pod kiriju*, all lit. 'give in rent'.

7. Skt. *ā-dhā-* 'give, lend', etc., prob. used also for 'lease'. Cf. sb. *ādhi-* 'pledge', etc. used for 'rent' (Āpast. 1.18.20).

11.76 RENT, LEASE (From Another)

Grk.	μισθοῦμαι	Goth.	....	Lith.	pasamdyti
NG	ἐνοικιάζω	ON	leiga	Lett.	īrēt, nuomāt
Lat.	condūcere	Dan.	leje	ChSl.	(najeti)
It.	prendere a pigione	Sw.	hyra	SCr.	najmiti
Fr.	louer	OE	(hȳrian)	Boh.	najmouti
Sp.	alquilar, arrendar	ME	hire	Pol.	najać
Rum.	închiria	NE	rent, lease (hire)	Russ.	nanjat'
Ir.	(gaibim ar fochruic)	Du.	huren		
NIr.	gabhaim ar thuarastal	OHG	(gi)miaten		
W.	cyflogi, rhentu	MHG	mieten		
Br.	feurmi	NHG	mieten		

1. Grk. μισθοῦμαι, mid. of μισθόω 'lease' (11.75).

NG ἐνοικιάζω, also 'lease' (11.75).

2. Lat. condūcere, lit. 'lead, bring together', then 'hire' (laborers, servants, etc.) and extended to objects 'rent', cpd. of dūcere 'lead'. Ernout-M. 286.

It. prendere a pigione 'take on rent', cf. dare a pigione 'lease' (11.75).

Fr. louer, Sp. alquilar, arrendar, Rum. închiria, all also 'lease' (11.75).

3. Ir. gaibim ar fochruic (quotable?), lit. 'take on pay, wages' (cf. tabraim ar fochruic 'lease', 11.75).

NIr. gabhaim ar thuarastal, lit. 'take on wages' (tuarastal 'wages, salary', 11.78).

W. cyflogi, less usually uncompounded llogi, fr. Lat. locāre 'lease' (11.75). Loth, Mots lat. 182.

W. rhentu, also 'lease' (11.75).

Br. feurmi, also 'lease' (11.75).

4. ON leiga, Dan. leje 'rent, hire' (but Sw. lega mostly of persons) : ON ljā, etc. 'take, seize' (11.13).

Goth. leihwan 'lend', etc. (11.61). Falk-Torp 632.

OE hȳrian 'hire' a person, in 13th. cent. also 'hire' a ship, a mare, ME hire (also a house, etc.), NE hire (still mostly persons, but also a horse, carriage, etc.), Du. huren, Sw. hyra 'hire' and 'rent', see under 'hire' (11.77).

NE rent, lease, both also 'lease' (11.75).

OHG (gi)miaten, MHG, NHG mieten, earlier (and so mostly in OHG) 'pay, bribe, take into one's pay', cf. OHG miata, miete (NHG miete) 'pay' (11.78).

5. Lith. pasamdyti, cpd. of samdyti 'lease' (11.75).

Lett. īrēt, fr. MLG hüren 'hire' (11.77). Mühl.-Endz. 1.837.

Lett. nuomāt, fr. nuoma (sb.) 'rent' : nemt (dial. beside n'emt) 'take' (11.13). Mühl.-Endz. 2.818, 815.

6. SCr. najmiti, etc., general Slavic words (but ChSl. najeti in Gospels only of hiring persons), cpds. of ChSl. jęti, etc. 'take, seize' (11.13).

11.77 HIRE (vb., a Person)

Grk.	μισθοῦμαι	Goth.	....	Lith.	pasamdyti
NG	μισθώνω	ON	leiga	Lett.	derēt
Lat.	condūcere	Dan.	hyre, leie	ChSl.	najeti
It.	prendere a servizio, fissare	Sw.	hyra, lega	SCr.	najmiti
		OE	hȳrian	Boh.	najmouti
Fr.	louer, engager	ME	hire	Pol.	najać
Sp.	alquilar	NE	hire	Russ.	nanjat', rjadit'
Rum.	tocmi	Du.	huren		
Ir.	(gaibim ar faichill)	OHG	(gi)miaten (gileiten)		
NIr.	fostuighim	MHG	mieten, dingen		
W.	cyflogi, llogi, hurio	NHG	mieten, dingen		
Br.	gopra				

Verbs for 'hire' with reference to persons, are mostly used also in the sense 'rent' of objects, and have been already discussed (11.76). A few, which are used entirely in the former sense or belong here primarily, are discussed here.

1. NG μισθώνω, in form fr. Grk. μισθόω 'lease' (11.75), but semantically as if a new deriv. of μισθός 'wages', and used mostly for 'hire' (persons).

2. It. prendere a servizio (used of hiring servants, etc.), lit. 'take in service'.

It. fissare, lit. 'fix', hence also 'come to an agreement, engage, hire', fr. VLat. *fixāre, fr. fixus pple. of figere 'fix, fasten'. REW 3335.

Fr. engager, fr. gage(s) 'wages' (11.78).

Rum. tocmi, lit. 'bring to order, agree, stipulate', fr. Slavic, ChSl. tŭkŭmiti 'compare, liken'. Tiktin 1619.

3. Ir. gaibim ar faichill (quotable ?), lit. 'take on wages'; cf. ocus ni fuil ar cur na ar faichill 'and (if) he is not on placement or hire' (Laws 3.384 1.17), with foichell 'wages, pay' (11.78).

NIr. fostuighim, lit. 'fasten, hold, secure' (cf. fosta 'prop, buttress'), hence also 'engage, hire'.

W. hurio, fr. NE hire.

Br. gopra, fr. gopr 'wages, pay', (11.78).

4. OE (ā)hȳrian, ME, NE hire, MLG hüren (> Dan. hyre, Sw. hyra), Du. huren (MHG hüren 'hire' a horse and wagon, NHG heuren 'hire' esp. sailors), all primarily 'hire', but several also 'rent' (11.76) or even 'lease' (11.75), etym.? NED s.v. hire, vb. Falk-Torp 445. Weigand-H. 1.859.

OHG gileiten, lit. 'lead', but twice 'hire' in Tat. 109.1 after Lat. condūcere.

OHG, MHG dingen 'negotiate' (esp. in a court), settle by agreement' (fr. OHG dinc 'legal negotiation'), then esp. 'take into one's service on agreed terms, engage', in NHG 'hire' (formerly a horse, carriage, etc., now persons, esp. workmen; mieten still 'hire' of personal servants). Paul, Deutsches Wtb. 109, 349).

5. Lett. derēt, lit. 'come to an agreement' : Lith. derēti 'bargain', etc. Mühl.-Endz. 1.456.

6. Russ. rjadit' : rjad 'row, range, order', ChSl. redŭ 'order', etc.

11.78 WAGES, PAY

Grk.	μισθός	Goth.	mizdō, laun	Lith.	alga
NG	μισθός	ON	leiga, kaup, laun	Lett.	alga
Lat.	mercēs	Dan.	løn, betaling	ChSl.	mīzda
It.	paga, salario, soldo	Sw.	lön, betalning	SCr.	plaća
Fr.	salaire, gages, paye	OE	mēd, meord, lēan	Boh.	mzda, plat
Sp.	sueldo, paga, alquiler	ME	hire, wage(s), pay	Pol.	placa
Rum.	leafă, plată	NE	wages, pay	Russ.	plata, žalovan'e
Ir.	fochricc, foichell, tuarastal	Du.	loon, betaling	Skt.	vetana-, bhṛti-
NIr.	tuarastal, pādh	OHG	miata, lōn	Av.	zemanā-, dāθra-
W.	cyflog, hur	MHG	miete, lōn, solt		
Br.	gopr	NHG	lohn, sold, bezahlung		

Many of the words for 'wages, pay' (for work done), including an inherited group, rest on the more generic notion of 'reward'. Others are simply 'pay', derivatives of the verbs for 'pay'. Some are from notions like 'pledge, bargain, price', etc.

Besides the generic terms there are others of more restricted scope. Thus NG μερο-κάματο 'day's work' and 'day's wages', similarly Sp. jornal, SCr. nadnica (cf. It. mesata 'month's wages', etc.). For 'soldier's pay', Lat. stipendium, whence NE stipend formerly 'soldier's pay', but now applied to the pay of clergymen, professors, etc. (cf. NED) where salary would be U.S. usage, similarly It. stipendio, etc.; cf. also below, It. salario, etc. and It. soldo, etc.

The application to particular classes is highly idiomatic. For example the pay of a university professor is stipend in England (cf. NED) but salary in U.S., traitement in France, stipendio in Italy, gehalt in Germany, etc. Such special terms (for the great variety in French, cf. Vendryes, Le langage 263) are omitted in the following, except so far as they have become more generic.

1. IE *mizdho- in words for 'reward' and 'wages, pay', root connection? Walde-P. 2.301. Feist 364 f.

Grk. μισθός; Goth. mizdō, OE meord, and mēd (NE meed poet. 'reward'), OHG miata, MHG miete (NHG mostly

'rent'; OS mēda; ChSl. mīzda, Boh. mzda (Russ. mzda 'reward, profit', Pol. obs.); Skt. mīḍha- 'contest', Av. mīžda- 'reward' (always in religious sense), NPers. muzal 'reward, wages'.

2. Lat. mercēs, -ēdis, also 'price payed for merchandise' : merx, -cīs 'merchandise', mercārī 'trade', outside connections? Walde-P. 2.283. Ernout-M. 611. Walde-H. 2.78 f.

It., Sp. paga, Fr. paye, fr. It. pagare, etc. 'pay' (11.65).

Fr. gages ('wages' of a domestic), pl. of gage 'pledge' (11.67).

It., Sp. salario, Anglo-Fr. salaire (> ME salarie, NE salary), Fr. salaire (> Rum. salariu, re-formed after Lat.), all book words but used in part for 'wages' with varied application (Fr. salaire now 'wages' of a workman), fr. Lat. (post-Aug.) salārium 'stipend, allowance', orig. the soldier's 'salt-money', fr. sāl 'salt'. Ernout-M. 887. Gamillscheg 781.

It. soldo (> MHG solt, NHG sold), Sp. sueldo 'soldier's pay', but also more generic (esp. Sp.), fr. late Lat. sol(i)dus, name of a coin 'soldier's pay' (whence the Eur. words for 'soldier').

Sp. alquiler ('wages' and 'rent'), see vb. alquilar 'rent', 11.75.

Rum. leafă, fr. Turk. (Arab.) ulufe (pl.) 'wages'. Tiktin 897. Berneker 683. Lokotsch 2132.

Rum. plată, fr. Slavic, below, 6.

3. Ir. fochricc, Br. gopr (W. gobr 'recompense' arch.) : Ir. fochrinim 'buy, hire', cpd. of crenim 'buy', Br. prenna, etc. 'buy' (11.81). Pedersen 2.497.

Ir. foichell (cf. Laws, Gloss. 387), apparently : foichlim 'attend, wait upon, minister to', etc. (Pedersen 2.484).

Ir. tuarastal, cpd. of root *tal- in Ir. taile gl. salarium . W. tal 'payment, recompense', vb. talu 'pay' (11.65). Stokes 130.

NIr. pādh, pāgh, fr. NE pay.

W. cyflog, fr. cyflogi 'rent, hire' (11.76).

W. hur, fr. ME hur (below).

4. Goth. mizdō, etc., above, 1.

Goth. laun, ON laun, Dan. løn, Sw. lön, OE lēan, Du. loon, OHG, MHG lōn, NHG lohn, all in older periods mostly 'reward', prob. : Ir. lōg, lūag 'price, reward' (11.87), Lat. lucrum 'gain, profit' (11.73), Grk. λεία 'booty', etc. Walde-P. 2.379. Falk-Torp 681. Feist 325.

ON leiga : leiga 'rent, hire' (11.76).

ON kaup (also 'bargain'), fr. kaupa 'buy' (11.81).

Dan. betaling, Sw. betalning, Du. betaling, NHG bezahlung : Dan. betale, etc. 'pay' (11.65).

ME, NE hire (the labourer is worthy of

his hire in NT, but now obs. or dial.) : vb. hire (11.77).

ME wage(s), NE wages, fr. OFr. wage, guage 'pledge, wage' (Fr. gages, above, 2).

ME, NE pay : vb. pay (11.65).

MHG solt, NHG sold, fr. It. soldo (above, 2).

5. Lith., Lett. alga (OPruss. gen. sg. ālgas) : Grk. ἀλφή 'produce, gain', Skt. argha-, Av. arǝjah- 'value, price' (11.87), Skt. arh-, Av. arǝj- 'be worth'. Walde-P. 1.91.

6. ChSl. mīzda, Boh. mzda, above, 1. SCr. plaća, Boh. plat, Pol. placa, Russ. plata : SCr. platiti, etc. 'pay' (11.65).

Russ. žalovan'e : žalovat' 'grant, bestow'.

7. Skt. vetana-, etym.? Uhlenbeck 295.

Skt. bhṛti- (also 'support, maintenance, food'), fr. bhṛ- 'bear, carry'. Uhlenbeck 205.

Av. zemanā-, etym.? Barth. 1690 f.

Av. dāθra-, prob. as orig. 'fixed sum', fr. dā- = Skt. dhā- 'put, place' (cf. Skt. dhana- 'property, wealth, money' fr. same root). Barth. 733. Otherwise (: Skt. dātra- 'share, property', fr. dā- 'give') Walde-P. 1.715.

11.79 EARN

Grk.	κτάομαι, ἄρνυμαι	Goth.	....	Lith.	pelnyti, uždirbti
NG	κερδίζω, βγάζω	ON	vinna	Lett.	pelnit
Lat.	merēre	Dan.	fortjene	ChSl.	....
It.	guadagnare	Sw.	förtjäna	SCr.	zaraditi
Fr.	gagner	OE	(ge)earnian	Boh.	vydělati
Sp.	ganar	ME	erne, arne	Pol.	zapracować, zarobić
Rum.	cîstiga	NE	earn	Russ.	zarabotat'
Ir.	....	Du.	verdienen		
NIr.	saothruighim	OHG	ferdienōn, (g)arnēn		
W.	ennill	MHG	verdienen, arnen		
Br.	gounit	NHG	verdienen		

'Earn' in the sense of 'get by labor' (NE earn wages, earn one's bread, etc.) is in many languages merely covered by the more generic 'get' or 'gain'. This is

probably the case also where no words are entered in the list. Where there are more distinctive terms, they are mostly based on the notion of labor or service.

Even where there are such, the use of 'get' or the like may be the more colloquial, e.g. NE *how much do you get a day?*

1. Grk. μισθοφορέω and μισθαρνέω, cpds. of μισθός 'wages' with φορέω 'carry, bear' or ἄρνυμαι 'win, gain', are used for 'receive wages, work for wages', but not with other object of the amount earned.

Grk. κτάομαι 'get, obtain' (11.16) or ἄρνυμαι 'win, gain' would cover 'get by labor, earn'.

NG κερδίζω, or κερδαίνω, fr. κέρδος 'gain, profit' (11.73), is 'gain' by business or by labor.

NG βγάζω, aor. ἔβγαλα (fr. Grk. ἐκβάλλω) 'take out', etc., also 'earn', as βγάζω τὸ ψωμί μου 'I earn my bread'.

2. Lat. *merēre* 'deserve, gain, earn' : Grk. μέρος 'share', μείρομαι 'receive one's share', etc. Walde-P. 2.690. Ernout-M. 609 f. Walde-H. 2.75 f.

It. *guadagnare*, Fr. *gagner*, Sp. *ganar*, Rum. *cîstiga*, all 'gain' and 'earn', see sb. 'gain, profit' (11.73).

3. NIr. *saothruigim* 'labor' and 'earn', fr. *saoth-* beside *saothar* 'labor' (9.12) and *ruigim* = *rigim* 'reach, attain', Ir. *rigim* 'stretch out, extend' (: Lat. *regere* 'direct, rule', etc.; Pedersen 2.593 ff.).

W. *ennill* 'gain, earn', fr. sb. *ennill* 'gain' (11.73).

Br. *gounit* 'gain, earn', fr. sb. *gounid* 'gain' (11.73).

ON *vinna* 'work' (9.13), 'gain, win', also 'earn'.

OE *(ge)earnian*, ME *erne*, *arne*, NE *earn*, OHG *arnēn*, *garnēn*, MHG *arnen* ('earn' and 'reap') : Goth. *asans* 'harvest', Goth. *asneis*, OHG *asni* 'hireling' (μισθωτός, Jn. 10.12, 13), OE *esne* 'servant', root connection dub. Walde-P. 1.77, 161. Feist 59. NED s.v. *earn*, vb.[1].

OHG *ferdienōn* (Notker), *irthionōn* (Otfr.), MHG, NHG, Du. *verdienen*, and (prob. semantic borrowing), Dan. *fortjene*, Sw. *förtjäna*, cpds. of OHG *dienōn*, etc. 'serve', deriv. of words for 'slave', OHG *deo*, Goth. *þius*, etc. (19.42). Weigand-H. 2.1143, 1.355.

5. Lith. *pelnyti*, Lett. *pelnīt*, see Lith. *pelnas* 'gain, profit' (11.73).

Lith. *uždirbti*, lit. 'work out', cpd. of *dirbti* 'work' (9.13).

6. SCr. *zaraditi*, Boh. *vydělati*, Pol. *zapracować*, *zarobić*, Russ. *zarabotat'*, all cpds. of vbs. for 'work', SCr. *raditi*, etc. (9.13).

		11.81 BUY	11.82 SELL
Grk.		ὠνέομαι, aor. ἐπριάμην, ἀγοράζω	πωλέω, aor. ἀπεδόμην, perf. πέπραμαι
NG		ἀγοράζω	πουλῶ
Lat.		emere	vendere
It.		comprare	vendere
Fr.		acheter	vendre
Sp.		comprar	vender
Rum.		cumpăra	vinde
Ir.		crenim, cennaigim	renim, recaim
NIr.		ceannuighim	díolaim (reicim)
W.		prynu	gwerthu
Br.		prena	gwerza
Goth.		bugjan	frabugjan
ON		kaupa	selja
Dan.		kjøbe	sælge
Sw.		köpa	sälga
OE		bycgan	sellan
ME		bugge	selle
NE		buy, purchase	sell
Du.		koopen	verkoopen
OHG		koufen	firkoufen
MHG		koufen	verkoufen
NHG		koufen	verkaufen
Lith.		pirkti	parduoti
Lett.		pirkt	pārduot
ChSl.		kupiti	prodati
SCr.		kupiti	prodati
Boh.		kupiti	prodati
Pol.		kupić	przedać
Russ.		kupit'	prodat'
Skt.		krī- (paṇ-)	vi-krī-
Av.		....	....

There are two main lines of development in the history of words for 'buy' and 'sell'. Either they are derived from some notion common to both, as 'trade', 'price', 'tradesman', 'market place', with differentiation into 'buy' or 'sell', which are therefore often expressed by cognate forms. Or, conversely, words for 'take, obtain' and 'give', by absorbing the notion of trade from the situation, are specialized to 'take in trade, buy' and 'give in trade, sell'.

1. IE *kʷrei-*, *kʷrī-*. Walde-P. 1.523 f. Grk. aor. ἐπριάμην (reg. aor. for 'buy' Hom.+ and in dialects); Ir. *crenim*, W. *prynu*, Br. *prena* 'buy'; ORuss. *krīnuti*, *krenuti* 'buy' (Berneker 633); Skt. *krī-* 'buy', *vi-krī-* 'sell', NPers. *xarīdan* 'buy' (no Av. form quotable). Cf. OLith.

krieno (gen.) 'pretium pro sponsis', Lett. *kriens* 'bridal gift', Toch. B *käry-* 'trade' (vb.), sbs. A *kuryar*, B *karyor* 'trade', A *kuryart* 'trader' (SSS 6, 12).

2. IE *per-*, prob. the same ultimately as that in words for 'pass through, travel', as Grk. περάω, Goth. *faran*, etc. Walde-P. 2.40. Pedersen 2.339, 596.

Grk. πέρνημι, aor. ἐπέρασα, in Hom. always 'sell abroad' (esp. captives), as prose word for 'sell' most common in mid., as perf. πέπραμαι, Ion. πέπρημαι, hence new pres. πιπράσκομαι, later act. πιπράσκω; Ir. *renim* 'sell', also NIr. *reic*, whence *recaim*, NIr. *reicim* (now less common than *díolaim* for simple 'sell', but Gael. *reic* the usual word); Lith. *pirkti*, Lett. *pirkt* 'buy'.

3. Derivs. of nouns for 'price', etc.

Grk. ὠνέομαι the usual word for 'buy' in the present (aor. ἐπριάμην, above, 1), Cret. ὠνέω 'sell', fr. ὦνος 'price', ὠνή 'buying, purchase' : Skt. *vasna-m* 'price', Lat. *vēnum* (or *vēnus?*, nom. not quotable) 'sale' whence *vēnum dare*, *vēnum dare* (> the Romance words), IE *wes-no-*, etc., fr. a root *wes-* seen in Hitt. *was-* 'buy', *ussniya-* 'sell'. Walde-P. 1.311. Ernout-M. 1086. Sturtevant, Hitt. Gloss. 171, 178.

Grk. ἀγοράζω 'frequent the market place', then 'buy' (Aristoph.+, gradually replacing ὠνέομαι, fr. ἀγορά 'market-place' (11.85).

Ir. *cennaigim*, NIr. *ceannuighim* 'buy', fr. *cennach* 'purchase' or *cennaige* 'trader' (11.84).

W. *gwerthu*, Br. *gwerza* 'sell', fr. W. *gwerth* 'value, price, sale', Br. *gwerz* 'sale', prob. : Goth. *wairþ*, OHG *werd*, etc. 'value, price' (11.87), Lat. *vertere* 'turn', etc. Walde-P. 1.275. Pedersen 2.526.

ChSl. *věniti sę* 'be sold' (rendering πωλέομαι Mt. 10.29, Lk. 12.6) : *věno* 'dowry', Grk. ἕδνον 'wedding-gift'. Walde-P. 1.256, 312.

4. Lat. *caupō* 'petty tradesman, huckster, tavern-keeper (Plautus), itself of unknown origin, is the probable, though not undisputed, source of the widespread Gmc. group of words for 'trade, buy, sell, tradesman', etc., whence also the Slavic verb for 'buy'. Cf. the Gmc. loanwords based on Lat. *mangō* 'dealer, trader' (11.83, 11.84). Ernout-M. 465 f. Walde-H. 1.189. Falk-Torp 521. Feist 309. Berneker 647. Stender-Petersen 374 ff.

Goth. *kaupōn* 'carry on business' (πραγματεύεσθαι, Lk. 19.3), ON *kaupa* 'bargain, trade, buy', sb. *kaup* 'bargain, pay', Dan. *kjøbe*, Sw. *köpa* 'buy', OE *cēapan* 'trade, bargain, rarely 'buy', sb. *cēap* 'bargain, trade, market, price' (NE

adj. *cheap*), Du. *koopen* 'buy', *verkoopen* 'sell', OHG *koufen* (*koufōn*, *chaufan*, etc.) 'trade, buy, sell', Br. *gwerz* 'sale', *firkoufen* 'sell', etc. 'trade, buy, sell', *firkoufen* 'sell', sb. *kauf* 'bargain, trade', *koufo* 'tradesman', NHG *kaufen* 'buy', *verkaufen* 'sell', etc. Hence, prob. through a Goth. *kaupjan*, ChSl. *kupiti*, etc., general Slavic for 'buy'.

5. 'Buy' fr. 'take, obtain'.

Lat. *emere*, orig. 'take' (11.13).

It. *comprare*, OFr. *comperer*, Sp. *comprar*, Rum. *cumpăra*, fr. Lat. *com-parāre* 'prepare, provide, obtain'. Ernout-M. 735. REW 2094.

Fr. *acheter*, OProv. *acapter*, OIt. *accattare*, fr. VLat. *acaptāre*, a recomposition of *acceptāre* 'take, receive' after *captāre* 'strive to seize'. REW 65. Wartburg 1.12.

ME *purchase*, NE *purchase*, in ME mostly 'contrive, obtain', etc., fr. Anglo-Fr. *purchaser* = OFr. *purchasser* 'seek to obtain', cpd. of *chasser* 'chase', fr. VLat. *captiāre*. NED s.v.

6. 'Sell' fr. 'give'.

Grk. aor., ἀπεδόμην, fut. ἀποδώσομαι, the regular Attic and most widespread terms for 'sell' in these tenses, mid. of ἀποδίδωμι 'give back, pay' (11.65).

Lith. *parduoti*, Lett. *pārduot*, SCr., Boh. *prodati*, Pol. *przedać*, Russ. *prodat'*, all cpds. of verbs for 'give' (11.21).

ON *selja*, OE *sellan* 'hand over, give' and 'sell' (both senses also in ME), hence, with specialization to 'sell' complete, Dan. *sælge*, Sw. *sälga*, NE *sell* (also LG *sellen* esp. of the small tradesman) : OHG *sellen* 'hand over, give up', Goth. *saljan* 'offer' (sacrifice), caus. of *sel-* in Grk. ἑλεῖν 'take'. Walde-P. 2.504. Falk-Torp 1231. Feist 408.

7. Miscellaneous.

Goth. *bugjan* 'buy', *fra-bugjan* 'sell', OS *buggian*, OE *bycgan*, ME *bugge*, *bigge*, NE *buy*, all 'buy', ON *byggja* 'buy' (a

wife), 'lend' (money), 'let out' (land), root connection (as with Goth. *biugan* 'bend'?) dub. Falk-Torp 121. Feist 111.

Grk. πωλέω, the usual word for 'sell' in the present (Hdt.+), NG pop. πουλῶ, is according to the prevailing view fr. a root *pel-* seen in Lith. *pelnas* 'profit', OHG *fāli* (beside *feili*) 'for sale', Skt. *paṇ-* 'bet, bargain, buy', etc. (cf. below). Walde-P. 2.51. Boisacq 830. Falk-Torp 202. But in view of the internal relations and the frequent derivation of

'trade' fr. 'travel' (above, 2 and 11.83, 11.84), more prob. a new act. (cf. Cret. ὠνέω 'sell' beside ὠνέομαι 'buy') to πωλέομαι 'go and come, frequent' (Hom.+) : πέλομαι 'become', Lat. *colere* 'cultivate', Skt. *car-* 'move', etc. Schrader, Reallex. 1.437.

NIr. *díolaim* 'pay' and 'sell', see 11.65.

Skt. *paṇ-* 'bet' (cf. *paṇa-* 'gaming, a wager') sometimes also 'bargain, buy' (cf. *paṇyā* 'wares', etc.) and *vi-paṇ* 'sell' : Lith. *pelnas* 'profit', OHG *fāli* 'for sale'. Walde-P. 2.51.

	11.83 TRADE (vb.)				
Grk.	ἐμπορεύομαι	Goth.	kaupōn	Lith.	pirkliauti, prekiauti
NG	ἐμπορεύομαι	ON	kaupa, manga	Lett.	tirguot
Lat.	mercāri, negōtiāri	Dan.	handle	ChSl.	kupljǫ dějati
It.	negoziare, trafficare, commerciare	Sw.	handla	SCr.	trgovati
		OE	mangian, cēapian	Boh.	obchoditi, obchod vesti, kupčiti
Fr.	trafiquer, commercer, négocier	ME	mange, marchaunde		
		NE	trade	Pol.	handlować, kupczyć
Sp.	negociar, comerciar, traficar	Du.	handelen	Russ.	torgovat'
		OHG	koufen	Skt.	vāṇijyaṁ kṛ-
Rum.	negocia, negustori, trafica	MHG	koufen	Av.	....
		NHG	handeln		
NIr.	phrase with trācht				
W.	masnachu				
Br.	prena ha gwerza, kenwerza				

Verbs for 'trade' are in part derived from nouns for 'merchandise', 'merchant', 'commerce, business', or 'market-place'. But several are based on the notion of 'travel', specialized to 'travel for trade' (cf. also NE *traveler* = *commercial traveler*, NED s.v.), and one group is from 'handle'.

1. Grk. ἐμπορεύομαι, orig. 'travel (in or to)', then 'trade on business' whence 'trade, import', see ἔμπορος 'traveler, merchant' (11.84).

Grk. πραγματεύομαι 'transact business, trade' (cf. NT, Lk. 19.13), fr. πρᾶγμα 'affair'.

2. Lat. *mercāri*, cpd. *commercāri*, with sb. *commercium* (> It., Sp. *comercio*, Fr. *commerce*, whence the new vbs. It. *com-*

merciare, Fr. *commercer*, Sp. *comerciar*, all lit. loanwords), fr. *merx* 'merchandise'. Walde-P. 2.283. Ernout-M. 611.

Lat. *negōtiāri* (hence as lit. loanwords It. *negoziare*, Fr. *négocier*, Sp. *negociar*, Rum. *negocia*), fr. *negōtium* 'business, affair', deriv. of phrase like *mihi neg ōtium est* 'I have not leisure' where *neg* is a parallel form of *nec* (*ne-ge?* beside *ne-que*), as in *negāre*, etc. Ernout-M. 659, 664.

It. *trafficare* (> Fr. *trafiquer*, Sp. *traficar*, Rum. *trafica*, fr. *tra-* = Lat. *trāns* 'across' and *ficare* 'thrust in' (fr. VLat. *ficāre*, fr. *figere* 'fix', REW 3290), in the sense 'put across, transport' wares). Gamillscheg 856.

Rum. *negustori* deriv. of *negustor*

'merchant', fr. *neguța* 'traffic, haggle, bargain', fr. Lat. *negōtiārī* (above). Tiktin 1048.

3. Ir. (?), NIr. usually a phrase ('there is trade') with sbs. for 'trade', either *trācht* (also 'treatment, course', etc.; fr. Lat. *trāctus*) or *ceannaidheacht* (fr. *ceannuighim* 'buy'). Cf. also *dīol agus ceannacht* 'selling and buying' (Z. celt. Ph. 9.140.2).

W. *masnachu*, fr. *masnach* 'business, trade', orig.?

Br. *prena ha gwerza* 'buy and sell' = 'trade' (Vallée s.v. *trafiquer*).

Br. *kenwerza*, cpd. of *ken-* 'cum' (cf. Ernault s.v.) and *gwerza* 'sell'.

4. Goth. *kaupōn*, ON *kaupa*, OE *cēapian*, OHG *koufen*, etc., see 11.81, 11.82.

ON *manga*, OE *mangian*, ME *mange*, OS *mangōn*, fr. Lat. *mangō* 'dealer, monger' (who adorns his wares to give them an appearance of greater value), beside *mangōnium* 'displaying of wares', prob. loanword based on Grk. μάγγανον 'means of charming or bewitching'. Walde-P. 2.233. Ernout-M. 588. Walde-H. 2.28 f. NED s.v. *mong*, vb.[1].

ME *marchaunde*, fr. OFr. *marcheander* (Fr. *marchander* 'haggle, bargain'), fr. *marchand* 'merchant' (11.84). NED s.v.

NE *trade* orig. (early NE) 'tread (a path), traverse (the sea), lead (one's life)', etc., then (like Grk. ἐμπορεύομαι, above) 'resort to a place for the sake of business, carry on trade', fr. sb. *trade*, orig. 'course, way, path', fr. MLG *trade* 'track' = OHG *trata* 'track, trace, way', etc. : OE *tredan*, NE *tread*, etc. NED s.v.

Du. *handelen*, NHG *handeln* (> Dan. *handle*, Sw. *handla*), in this sense specialization of more general 'treat', orig. 'handle, touch with the hands', MHG *handeln*, OHG *hantalōn*, fr. *hant* 'hand'. Weigand-H. 1.806. Paul, Deutsches Wtb. 240. Falk-Torp 378.

5. Lith. *pirkliauti*, beside *pirklys* 'merchant', fr. *pirkti* 'buy' (11.81).

Lith. *prekiauti*, fr. *prekė* 'wares, merchandise' (formerly 'trade' and 'price'; see 11.87), this also : *pirkti* 'buy'.

Lett. *tirguot*, fr. *tirgus* 'market place' (11.85).

6. ChSl. *kupljǫ dějati* (renders πραγματεύεσθαι Lk. 19.13), also *kupljǫ sŭtvoriti* (διαπραγματεύεσθαι Lk. 19.15), lit. 'make trade', with *kuplja* fr. *kupiti* 'buy' (11.81).

SCr. *trgovati*, Russ. *torgovat'*, fr. SCr. *trg*, Russ. *torg* 'market place' (11.85).

Boh. *kupčiti*, Pol. *kupczyć*, fr. Boh. *kupec*, Pol. *kupiec* 'merchant' : ChSl. *kupiti* 'buy'.

Boh. *obchoditi* or *obchod vesti* (with *vesti* 'lead, carry on') fr. *obchod* 'commerce, business', cpd. of *ob* 'around, about' and *chod* 'passage, gait' (: *choditi* 'go, walk', etc.).

Pol. *handlować*, fr. NHG *handeln*. Brückner 168.

7. Skt. *vāṇijyaṁ kṛ-*, lit. 'make, do trade', with *vāṇijya-* 'trade, traffic', fr. *vaṇij-* 'merchant' (11.84).

11.84 MERCHANT, TRADESMAN

Grk.	ἔμπορος, κάπηλος	Goth.	. . . .	Lith.	*pirklys (kupčius)*
NG	ἔμπορος	ON	*kaupmaðr*	Lett.	*tirguotajs*
Lat.	*mercātor, negōtiātor*	Dan.	*købmand*	ChSl.	*kupĭcĭ*
It.	*mercante, commerciante*	Sw.	*köpman, handlare*	SCr.	*trgovac*
Fr.	*marchand, commerçant*	OE	*mangere, cēapman*	Boh.	*kupec, obchodník*
Sp.	*mercader, comerciante*	ME	*marchaund, chapman*	Pol.	*kupiec*
Rum.	*negustor, comerciante*	NE	*merchant, tradesman, trader*	Russ.	*kupec, torgovec*
Ir.	*cennaige*	Du.	*koopman*	Skt.	*vaṇij-*
NIr.	*ceannaidhe*	OHG	*koufman*	Av.	. . . .
W.	*masnachydd, marsiandwr*	MHG	*koufman*		
Br.	*marc'hadour*	NHG	*kaufmann, händler*		

Most of the words for 'merchant, tradesman' are connected with those for 'trade', 'buy', or 'market place', discussed elsewhere.

1. Grk. ἔμπορος 'traveler', then 'merchant', esp. one who trades on a large scale, usually but not necessarily by sea, with ἐμπορία and ἐμπορεύω, becoming the usual generic sb. and vb. for 'trade', all : πόρος 'passage, ford', πορεύω 'convey', περάω 'traverse', OE *faran* 'go, travel', etc. Cf. the use of the same root in words for 'sell' or 'buy', Grk. πέρνημι, Lith. *pirkti*, etc. (11.81). Walde-P. 2.39. Boisacq 248.

Grk. κάπηλος, the 'local retail dealer, shopkeeper' (also 'tavern-keeper'), etym.? Boisacq 408.

On the distinction between ἔμπορος and κάπηλος, see now M. I. Finkelstein, Cl. Ph. 30.320 ff.

Grk. πραγματευτής 'merchant' (Plut.+, Byz.), but NG 'small tradesman' or 'pedler', fr. πραγματεύομαι 'trade' (11.83).

2. Lat. *mercātor*, fr. *mercārī* 'trade' (11.83).

Lat. *negōtiātor*, fr. *negōtiārī* 'trade' (11.83), whence also Rum. *negustor* through vb. *neguța*. Tiktin 1048.

It. *mercante*, older *mercatante*, Fr. *marchant*, (Cat. >) Sp. *mercader*, derivs. of It. *mercato*, Fr. *marché*, Sp. *mercado*, etc. 'market' (11.85). REW 5516.

It. *commerciante*, Fr. *commerçant*, Sp., Rum. *comerciante*, fr. It. *commerciare*, etc. 'trade' (11.83).

3. Ir. *cennaige*, NIr. *ceannaidhe* beside Ir. *cennach* 'purchase' and 'redeeming' (K. Meyer, Contrib. 343), cf. also *cendaige*, *cendaithe* 'bequest', also 'head-money' (so translated by Atkinson, Laws 1.185), all apparently fr. Ir. *cend*, NIr. *ceann* 'head'. 'Purchase (price)' perh. as 'sum paid per capita'? On suffix cf. Pedersen 2.23.

W. *masnachydd*, fr. *masnachu* 'trade' (11.83).

W. *marsiandwr*, lit. 'merchant-man', *marsiand*, fr. ME *marcha(u)nd*.

Br. *marc'hadour*, fr. *marc'had* 'market' (11.85).

4. ON *kaupmaðr*, Dan. *købmand*, Sw. *köpman*, OE *cēapman*, ME *chapman*, Du. *koopman*, OHG, MHG *koufman*, NHG *kaufmann*, fr. ON *kaupa*, OE *cēapan*, OHG *koufen*, etc. 'trade' (11.83), with words for 'man'.

Sw. *handlare*, NHG *händler*, fr. Sw. *handla*, NHG *handeln* 'trade' (11.83).

ME *marcha(u)nd*, NE *merchant*, fr. Fr. *marchant* (above, 2).

NE *trader*, *tradesman*, fr. vb. *trade* (11.83).

5. Lith. *pirklys*, fr. *pirkti* 'buy' (11.81).

Lith. *prekiautojas*, fr. *prekiauti* 'trade'

(11.83), and *prekijas*, fr. *prekė* 'merchandise', both neologisms, given by NSB s.v. *kupčius*.

Lith. *kupčius* (formerly the usual word), fr. Pol. *kupiec* (below).

Lett. *tirguotajs*, also *tirguonis*, fr. *tirguot* 'trade' (11.83).

6. ChSl. *kupĭcĭ*, Boh., Russ. *kupec*, Pol. *kupiec*, fr. ChSl. *kupiti*, etc. 'buy' (11.81).

SCr. *trgovac*, Russ. *torgovec*, fr. SCr. *trgovati*, Russ. *torgovat'* 'trade' (11.83).

Boh. *obchodník*, fr. *obchoditi* 'trade' (11.83).

7. Skt. *vaṇij-* (also *vāṇij-*, *vaṇija-*, etc.), perh. fr. **vṛṇij-* : OE *waru* 'wares', *weorþ* 'worth, price', etc., but doubtful. Uhlenbeck 268. Wackernagel, Altind. Gram. 1.192.

11.85 MARKET (Place)

Grk.	ἀγορά	Goth.	*garuns, maþl*	Lith.	*turgus, rinka*
NG	παζάρι, ἀγορά	ON	*torg, mark(n)aðr*	Lett.	*tirgus*
Lat.	*forum, mercātus*	Dan.	*torv, marked*	ChSl.	*trŭgŭ, trŭžište, kuplja*
It.	*mercato*	Sw.	*torg, marknad*	SCr.	*trg, tržište*
Fr.	*marché*	OE	*cēapstōw, marcet*	Boh.	*trh, tržiště*
Sp.	*mercado*	ME	*market*	Pol.	*targ, rynek*
Rum.	*tîrg*	NE	*market*	Russ.	*bazar, rynok (torg)*
Ir.	*cēte, marcad*	Du.	*markt*	Skt.	*paṇyavīthī-, āpaṇa-, vipaṇa*
NIr.	*margadh*	OHG	*marc(h)at*	Av.	. . . .
W.	*marchnad*	MHG	*mark(e)t*		
Br.	*marc'had*	NHG	*markt*		

Words for 'market place' are partly connected with words for 'trade', and partly specialized from 'meeting place' or 'open place'. The spread of loanwords is extensive.

1. Grk. ἀγορά, orig. (and so only in Hom.) 'assembly, place of assembly' : ἀγείρω 'gather, assemble'.

NG παζάρι, fr. Turk. *pazar*, this fr. Pers. *bāzār* 'market' (etym.? Horn 166). The Persian word has been the source of a general Eur. borrowing, used more or less generally for 'market' as Russ. *bazar*, or with restricted use as NE *bazaar*, Fr., Sp. *bazar*, It. *baz(z)ar*. Lokotsch 278.

2. Lat. *forum*, orig. prob. 'inclosure about a house, court' (cf. its old use for 'forecourt before a tomb'), then in general 'public place, open market place' : ChSl. *dvorŭ* 'court' and the words for 'door', Lat. *forēs*, Grk. θύρᾱ, etc. (7.22). Ernout-M. 378, 383. Adversely Walde, IF 39.75 ff., Walde-H. 1.537 f.

Lat. *mercātus* 'trade' and 'market place' (> It. *mercato*, Fr. *marché*, Sp. *mercado*) : *mercārī* 'trade' (11.83). REW 5516.

Rum. *tîrg*, fr. Slavic, ChSl. *trŭgŭ*, etc. (below, 6).

3. Ir. *cēte* 'market, fair, gathering' (K. Meyer, Contrib. 356), NIr. *cēide* 'an assembly, a fair' (Dinneen 183), etym.?

MIr. *marcad*, *margad*, NIr. *margadh*, W. *marchnad*, Br. *marc'had*, fr. Lat. *mercātus*, mostly through Norse forms (below, 4). Pedersen 1.199. Loth, Mots lat. 185. Marstrander, Bidrag 61, 154.

4. Goth. *garuns* (also ῥύμη 'street', Mt. 6.2) : *garinnan* 'run together'.

Goth. *maþl* = OE *mæþel* 'assembly' (and 'speech'), etc., prob. : Goth. *gamōtjan* 'meet', OE *gemōt* 'meeting', etc. Walde-P. 2.304. Feist 349 f.

ON, Sw. *torg*, Dan. *torv*, fr. Russ. *torg* (below, 6). Falk-Torp 1275. Hellquist 1205.

ON *markaðr*, *marknaðr*, Dan. *marked*, ODan. *mark(n)ed*, Sw. *marknad*, late OE *marcet*, ME, NE *market*, Du., NHG *markt*, OHG *marc(h)at*, MHG *mark(e)t* (the Scand. forms prob. fr. OE and LG; their *n* after native words), fr. Lat. *mercātus*, in part OFr. (Picard) *market*. Falk-Torp 701. Weigand-H. 2.132 f. Hellquist 631.

OE *cēapstōw*, cpd. of *cēap* : *cēapian* 'trade' (11.83), and *stōw* 'place'.

5. Lith. *turgus*, Lett. *tirgus*, fr. Slavic (below, 7).

Lith. *rinka* (beside *rinkė* 'ring') fr. MHG *rinc* 'ring, circle', with sense of market place through Slavic influence (Pol. *rynek*, etc., below).

6. ChSl. *trŭgŭ*, SCr. *trg*, Boh. *trh*, Pol. *targ*, Russ. *torg* (now arch.), with their derivs. ChSl. *trŭžište* (in Gospels reg. renders ἀγορά), SCr. *tržište*, Boh. *tržiště* 'market place', either cognate with or loanword fr. the Illyrian word which is the source of the name *Tergeste* 'Triest'. Mühl.-Endz. 4.194 f. G. Meyer, IF 1.323 f. Schrader, Reallex. 2.40.

ChSl. *kuplja* (renders ἀγορά Mk. 7.4, otherwise ἐμπορία) : *kupiti* 'buy' (11.81).

Pol. *rynek*, Russ. *rynok* (Boh. *rynk* 'square, also market place'), fr. MHG *rinc*, OHG *ring* 'ring, circle'. Brückner 472. Schrader, Reallex. 2.40.

Russ. *bazar*, see above, NG παζάρι.

7. Skt. *paṇyavīthī-*, cpd. of *paṇya-* 'wares', and *vīthī-* 'street' : *paṇ-* 'buy, bargain', hence also *āpaṇa-* 'market, shop', *vipaṇa-* 'trading place, shop, market'.

11.86 STORE, SHOP

Grk.	-εῖον, -πώλιον	Goth.	. . . .	Lith.	*krautuvė*
NG	μαγαζί, κατάστημα	ON	*būð*	Lett.	*pārduotava*
Lat.	*taberna*	Dan.	*butik, forretning*	ChSl.	. . . .
It.	*bottega*	Sw.	*(handels)bod, butik*	SCr.	*dućan*
Fr.	*boutique, magasin*	OE	. . . .	Boh.	*krám*
Sp.	*tienda*	ME	*shoppe*	Pol.	*sklep*
Rum.	*prăvălie, magazin*	NE	*shop, store*	Russ.	*lavka, magazin*
Ir.	. . . .	Du.	*winkel*	Skt.	*vipaṇa-, āpaṇa-*
NIr.	*siopa*	OHG	. . . .	Av.	. . . .
W.	*maelfa, siop*	MHG	*lade(n)*		
Br.	*stal*	NHG	*laden*		

The place where goods are sold is *shop* in British, but *store* in native U.S. and colonial usage. The words are in only a few cases connected with words for 'sell' or 'trade'. Several are from the notion of 'storehouse', some of these still used preferably for the larger establishments (as Fr. *magasin*, NE *store* in British use). Others are from various terms appropriate to the antecedent crude form, as 'hut, tent, booth, stall, shed, corner'.

1. In Grk. there was no generic term in common use (πωλητήριον : πωλέω 'sell' being rare, and ἐργαστήριον mostly 'workshop'), but rather specific words. Thus with suffix -εῖον words for the place where particular articles were made (and sold), as ἀρτοκοπεῖον 'bakeshop', καπηλεῖον 'huckster's shop, tavern' (κάπηλος 'huckster, tavern keeper'), and cpds. in -πώλιον or -πωλεῖον, as κρεοπώλιον 'butcher's shop', ἀρτο-πώλιον 'baker's shop'.

NG pop. μαγαζί, fr. Turk. *magaza*, this fr. Arab. *maḫzan* 'storehouse, barn'. Cf. Fr. *magasin*, etc. below.

NG κατάστημα, class. Grk. 'state, condition', now esp. 'shop, store'. Cf. the occasional use of NE *establishment* for a 'business house'.

2. Lat. *taberna*, orig. 'hut (of boards)' then 'booth, shop, workshop' and esp. 'inn, tavern' (in this sense in Romance, It. *taverna*, Fr. *taverne*, etc.), prob. fr. **traberna* : *trabs* 'beam', Ir. *treb* 'dwelling', etc. Walde-P. 1.757. Ernout-M. 1011, 1050 (suggesting also possibility of Etruscan origin).

It. *bottega*, Fr. *boutique* (Sp. *bodega* 'wine shop, storehouse', *botica* 'drug store'), fr. Grk. ἀποθήκη 'storehouse' (ἀποτίθημι 'put away'). REW 531.

It. *negozio* 'trade, business', also 'place of business, shop', fr. Lat. *negōtium* 'business, affair' (cf. *negōtiārī* 'trade', 11.83).

It. *magazzino* (but chiefly 'storehouse, warehouse'), Fr. *magasin* (> Rum. *magazin*, Russ. *magazin*; also NE *magazine* in *powder-magazine*, but mostly through 'storehouse of information' to current use), Sp. *almacén*, all orig. 'storehouse', fr. Arab. *maḫzan* id. Lokotsch, 1362. REW 5240a. Berneker 2.3.

Sp. *tienda*, fr. VLat. **tenda* 'tent' (7.14). REW 8639.

Rum. *prăvălie*, fr. Slavic, cf. Bulg. *provalja* 'shop' (Bogorov, Fr.-Bulg. Dict. s.v. *boutique*), SCr. *pravlenije* 'manufacture' (: *praviti* 'make').

3. NIr. *siopa*, W. *siop*, fr. ME *shoppe*, NE *shop*.

W. *maelfa*, cpd. of *mael* 'gain, profit' and *ma* 'place'.

Br. *stal*, fr. OFr. *estal* (Fr. *étal*) 'table in a market place where goods are exposed' (now esp. of butchers, fishmongers), Gmc. loanword, cf. OE *steall*, OHG *stal*, etc. 'stall' (3.19).

4. ON *būð*, esp. 'temporary hut or booth of traders', Sw. *(handels)bod* (ODan. **bōð* > ME *bothe*, NE *booth*), Dan. *bod*, NHG *bude* 'booth, stall', locally 'shop' : ON *būa* 'dwell, prepare', OHG *būan* 'dwell', etc. Falk-Torp 89. Weigand-H. 1.303. NED s.v. *booth*.

Dan., Sw. *butik*, fr. Fr. *boutique*.

Dan. *forretning*, lit. 'business', also 'place of business, shop' (cf. Dahlerup s.v. 5), fr. *forrette* 'perform, discharge, execute'.

ME *shoppe*, NE *shop* (OE *sceoppa* 'treasury', Lk. 21.1) : OE *scypen* 'cattle-shed', OHG *scopf* 'porch, vestibule'. NED s.v. *shop*, sb.

NE *store* (U.S. and colonial = *shop*), lit. (so Brit. usually) 'supply, store of goods (of any sort)', fr. OFr. *estor* : *estorer* 'build, establish, furnish, store', Lat. *instaurāre*. NED s.v.

Although *store* definitely replaced *shop* in this sense (*shop* only as *workshop*, *blacksmith's shop*, etc.) and was the only term so used in my boyhood, the vb. *shop*, *go shopping* remained usual, and recently the sb. *shop* has been coming back, esp. for the more fashionable *shops* in the cities.

Du. *winkel*, orig. (MDu.) 'corner' = NHG *winkel*, etc. 'corner' (12.76).

NHG *laden*, MHG *lade*, *laden* rarely in this sense, mostly 'thick board, plank, window-shutter', etc., prob. : NHG *latte*, NE *lath*, etc. 'lath'. Weigand-H. 2.5. Kluge-G. 340.

Local equivalents of *laden* are *bude* 'booth', *gewölbe* 'vault', and more commonly *geschäft* 'business'. Kretschmer, Wortgeogr. 315.

5. Lith. *krautuvė*, also 'storehouse', fr. *krauju*, *krauti* 'heap up, hoard'.

Lett. *pārduotava*, fr. *pārduot* 'sell' (11.82).

6. SCr. *dućan*, Bulg. *djukjanĭ*, etc., fr. Turk. *dukjan*, Arab. *dukkan* id. Lokotsch 542. Berneker 237.

Boh. *krám*, fr. MHG *krām*, NHG *kram* 'retail (trade), small (retail) shop, stall, stand', orig. dub. Walde-P. 1.591. Weigand-H. 1.1135. Berneker 606.

Pol. *sklep*, also 'vault' = Boh. *sklep* 'vault, cellar', Russ. *sklep* '(burial) vault, crypt', etc. Brückner 493.

Russ. *lavka*, also 'bench', dim. of *lava* 'bench along the wall' = Boh. *lava*, *lavka* 'bench', Pol. *ława* 'bench, stand, stall in a market', etc. Berneker 695.

Russ. *magazin*, fr. Fr. *magasin* (above, 2).

7. Skt. *vipaṇa-*, *āpaṇā-*, see 11.85.

11.87 PRICE

Grk.	*τῑμή* (*ὦνος* Hom.)	Goth.	*wairþ*, *andawairþi*	Lith.	*kaina*
NG	*τιμή*	ON	*verð*	Lett.	*cena*
Lat.	*pretium*	Dan.	*pris*	ChSl.	*cěna*
It.	*prezzo*	Sw.	*pris*	SCr.	*cijena*
Fr.	*prix*	OE	*weorþ*	Boh.	*cena*
Sp.	*precio*	ME	*pris*, *worth*	Pol.	*cena*
Rum.	*preț*	NE	*price*	Russ.	*cena*
Ir.	*lōg*	Du.	*prijs*	Skt.	*vasna-* (Ved.), *mūlya-*, *argha-*
NIr.	*luach*	OHG	*werd*	Av.	*arəǰah-*, *pərəskā-*
W.	*pris*	MHG	*wert*, *prīs*		
Br.	*priz*	NHG	*preis*		

The 'price' of an article is at least assumed to be its 'value', and many of the words for 'price' are such as were used also for 'worth, value' in general. Several of these and some of the others involve the notion of 'return' or 'recompense'. The spread of Lat. *pretium* has furnished a more distinctive word to most of the western European languages.

1. Grk. ὦνος (reg. word for 'price' in Hom.) : Skt. *vasna-m* 'price' (RV, AV), Lat. *vēnum* 'sale', etc. (11.81, Grk. ὠνέομαι).

Grk. τῑμή, also 'worth, honor, reward, penalty' : τίω 'estimate, value, honor', τίνω 'pay', etc. (11.65).

Grk. ἀξία, mostly 'worth, value', also 'money-value, price' : ἄξιος 'of like value, worth(y)', lit. 'weighing as much', fr. *ἄγ-τιος : ἄγω 'lead', but also 'draw down the scales, weigh'. Walde-P. 1.36. Boisacq 65.

2. Lat. *pretium* (> It. *prezzo*, Fr. *prix*, Sp. *precio*, Rum. *preț*; OFr. *pris* > Br. *priz*, ME *pris* [> W. *pris*], NE *price*, MLG *prīs* [> Dan., Sw. *pris*], Du. *prijs*, MHG *prīs*, NHG *preis*), prob. as orig. 'return, recompense' neut. of an adj. **pretios* fr. the IE prep. **preti*, **proti* in Skt. *prati* 'against, back', ChSl. *protivŭ* 'towards', etc. (these fr. IE **per*, *pro*, etc. and so ultimately connected with Grk. πέρνημι 'sell', Lith. *pirkti* 'buy', etc., 11.81; but this remote formal connection is without bearing upon the semantic development). Walde-P. 2.38. Ernout-M. 808. REW 6746. Falk-Torp 850.

3. Ir. *lōg*, *lūag* (also 'value'), NIr. *luach* (also 'value, cost') : W. *golud* 'riches' (11.42), Goth. *laun*, etc. 'wages' (11.78), etc. Walde-P. 2.380. Pedersen 1.54.

4. Goth. *wairþ* (and *andawairþi* [*andwairþi* cod. Arg.], cpd. of *and* [*a*]- 'against, in return') = ON *verð*, OE *weorþ*, ME *worth*, OHG *werd*, MHG *wert* 'worth, value, price' (NE *worth*, NHG *wert*, etc.), beside adjs. Goth. *wairþs*, ON *verðr* 'worth, worthy', etc., perh. : Ir. *frith-*, MW *gwrth*, W. *wrth* 'against', fr. the root in Lat. *vertere* 'turn', Goth. *wairþan*, etc. 'become'. Walde-P. 1.275. Falk-Torp 1403.

Dan., Sw., ME *pris*, NE *price*, etc., above, 2.

5. Lith. *kaina*, ChSl. *cěna*, etc., general Slavic (Russ. *cena* > Lett. *cena*) : Av. *kaēnā-* 'revenge, punishment', Grk. ποινή 'retribution, penalty', IE **kʷoinā-*, fr. the root in Grk. τίω 'estimate, honor', τῑμή, etc. (above, 1). Walde-P. 1.509. Berneker 124.

Lith. *kaina* is now the accepted word for 'price', whence vb. *kainoti* 'cost' in *kiek kainoja* 'how much does it cost?', etc. Cf. NSB and Hermann, Lit.-deutsches Gesprächsb. 144. Lalis and Kurschat have *prekė* or *prekia* for 'price', but this is now 'wares' like Lett. *prece* (: Lith. *pirkti* 'buy', etc.). Fraenkel, Z. sl. Ph. 6.87.

6. Skt. *vasna-* : Grk. ὦνος, etc., above, 1.

Skt. *mūlya-* prob. : *mūla-* 'root, foundation'.

Skt. *argha-*, Av. *arəǰah-* (NPers. *arz* 'price') : Skt. *arh-*, Av. *arəǰ-* 'be worth', Lith., Lett. *alga* 'wages' (11.78). Walde-P. 1.91. Barth. 192.

Av. *pərəskā-*, prob. (**prt-skā-*) : Skt. *a-prata-* 'without recompense', and Lat. *pretium*, etc. (above, 2). Walde-P. 2.38. Barth. 896.

11.88 DEAR (= Costly, Expensive)

Grk.	*πολυτελής*, *τῑ́μιος*	Goth.	*galaufs*	Lith.	*brangus*
NG	*ἀκριβός*	ON	*dȳrr*	Lett.	*dārgs*
Lat.	*cārus*	Dan.	*dyr*	ChSl.	*dragŭ*
It.	*caro*	Sw.	*dyr*	SCr.	*skup*
Fr.	*cher*	OE	*dēore*	Boh.	*drahý*
Sp.	*caro*	ME	*dere*	Pol.	*drogi*
Rum.	*scump*	NE	*dear*	Russ.	*dorogoj*
Ir.	*lōgmar*	Du.	*duur*	Skt.	*mahārgha-*, *bahumūlya-*, etc.
NIr.	*daor*	OHG	*tiuri*	Av.	....
W.	*drud*	MHG	*tiur(e)*		
Br.	*ker*	NHG	*teuer*		

A few of the words listed are derivatives of those for 'price', 'cost, expense', or the like; and a few come through the notion of 'stingy'. But the most widespread development is from 'dear, beloved' or 'esteemed, worthy' through 'highly valued' to 'dear, expensive'. This may rest in part, but not wholly, on semantic borrowing from Lat. *cārus*. There is no trace of such use of Grk. φίλος.

Omitted are the words which, while meaning literally 'costly', are not the common words for 'dear' as applied to an article for sale, but are used mostly in in a figurative sense, more nearly 'costly', 'precious' or 'extravagant'. Thus Lat. *pretiōsus* fr. *pretium* 'price' and sometimes 'dear, expensive', but mostly 'valuable, precious'; and the numerous derivatives of It. *costo*, etc. 'cost' (11.72), as It., Sp. *costoso*, OFr. *costeus* (> ME *costouse* > W. *costus*), Fr. *coûteux*, NE *costly*, NHG *kostbar*, etc.

1. Grk. πολυτελής, cpd. of πολύ 'much' and last member fr. τέλος 'tax, toll, duty' (11.69).

Grk. τῑ́μιος, fr. τῑμή 'price' (11.87).

NG ἀκριβός, fr. class. Grk. ἀκριβής 'exact, precise, accurate' then (fr. 'exact in money matters') 'parsimonious, stingy' and hence 'dear' (as SCr. *skup*, below).

2. Lat. *cārus* (> It., Sp. *caro*, Fr. *cher*) 'dear' = 'beloved' (16.28) and 'expensive' (Plaut. in both senses).

Rum. *scump*, fr. Slavic, cf. Bulg. *skąpŭ*, etc. below, 6.

3. Ir. *lōgmar*, cpd. of *lōg* 'price' and *mār*, *mōr* 'great'.

NIr. *daor*, fr. ME *dere*. Macbain 123 (quoting Stokes). But undoubtedly confused with *daor* 'enslaved' and hence *saor* 'free' acquires the sense 'cheap' as antonym of *daor*.

W. *drud*, 'dear' fr. earlier sense 'mad, bold, daring, reckless, grievous' (Spurrell); MIr. *drūth* 'mad, foolish', orig. dub. Loth, RC 38.174 f.

Br. *ker* 'dear' in both senses, MBr. *quer*, fr. Norm. Fr. *quer* = Fr. *cher* (above). Henry 63.

4. Goth. *galaufs* = πολυτελής 'expensive', also *filu-galaufs* = πολύτιμος 'very precious' : *liufs*, ON *ljūfr*, etc. 'dear, beloved' (16.28).

ON *dȳrr*, Dan., Sw. *dyr*, OE *dēore*, OHG *tiuri*, etc. in early periods 'esteemed, valued, worthy' (later 'dear, beloved') and 'dear, expensive', etym. dub. Falk-Torp 172. Weigand-H. 2.1040 f.

In parts of the U.S. *dear* is not the colloquial word, but rather *high* = 'high-priced'.

NE *expensive* (in U.S. less restricted than in England), fr. a Lat. type **expensīvus*, fr. *expendere* 'spend', but associated with *expense* (11.72). NED s.v.

5. Lith. *brangus*, etym.? (: Du. *pronk* 'ostentation, show'?). Uhlenbeck 205. Franck-v. W. 524.

Lett. *dārgs*, either cognate with, or borrowed from, the Slavic (below). Mühl.-Endz. 1.448.

6. ChSl. *dragŭ*, etc., general Slavic (in the modern languages also 'dear, beloved'), etym. dub. Berneker 213.

SCr. *skup*, also 'stingy', Bulg. *skąpŭ* 'dear, expensive, stingy', in the other Slavic languages only 'stingy', Russ. *skupoj*, Boh. *skoupý*, Pol. *skąpy* (11.54).

7. Skt. *mahārgha-*, cpd. of *mahā-* 'large, great' and *argha-* 'price' (11.87).

Skt. *bahumūlya-*, cpd. of *bahu-* 'much, many' and *mūlya-* 'price' (11.87).

11.89 CHEAP

Grk.	*εὐτελής*, *εὔωνος*	Goth.	....	Lith.	*pigus*
NG	*φτηνός*	ON	*ūdȳrr*	Lett.	*lēts*
Lat.	*vīlis*	Dan.	*billig*	ChSl.	....
It.	*a buon mercato* (*vile*)	Sw.	*billig*	SCr.	*jeftin*
Fr.	(*à*) *bon marché*	OE	*undēor*	Boh.	*laciný*
Sp.	*barato*	ME	*good chepe*, *undere*	Pol.	*tani*
Rum.	*ieftin*	NE	*cheap*	Russ.	*deševyj*
Ir.	....	Du.	*goedkoop*, *billijk*	Skt.	*alpakrīta-*
NIr.	*saor*	OHG	*untiuri*	Av.	....
W.	*rhad*	MHG	*untiure*, *wolveil(e)*		
Br.	*marc'had-mat*	NHG	*billig*, *wohlfeil*		

Some of the words for 'cheap' are formed as opposites (negative compounds or otherwise) to those for 'dear', but most of them are unrelated to the latter. They rest on notions like 'good trade, bargain', 'abundant', 'fair, reasonable', or 'easy, light'.

Some of the words for 'cheap' are used also as derogatory terms, as Lat. *vīlis* (hence mostly 'vile' in its derivs.), NE *cheap*, but this is by no means general (and quite the opposite in NHG *billig*, in accordance with its origin).

1. Grk. εὐτελής, cpd. of εὐ- 'well' and τέλος 'tax, toll, duty' (11.68), hence 'easy to pay for', opp. to πολυτελής 'dear'.

Grk. εὔωνος, cpd. of εὐ- and ὦνος 'price' (11.87).

NG pop. φτηνός, lit. εὐθηνός, through 'abundant' fr. post-class. εὐθηνός 'thriving, flourishing', beside class. Grk. εὐθηνία 'prosperity, plenty', εὐθηνέω, εὐθενέω 'thrive', etc., prob. : Skt. *ghana-* 'compact, firm', Lith. *gana* 'enough', etc. (13.18).

2. Lat. *vīlis* (> It. *vile*, sometimes 'cheap' but mostly 'mean, vile'), etym. dub. Walde-P. 1.214, 312. Ernout-M. 1108.

It. *a buon mercato*, Fr. *(à) bon marché*, lit. 'at good trade', with *mercato*, *marché* 'trade (= sale, purchase), market' (11.85).

Sp. *barato*, fr. *baratar* 'buy a thing at less than its value' : It. *barattare* 'exchange', OFr. *barate* 'strife, trade, deceit', etc., a widespread group, including NE *barrat* (obs.) and *barter*, but of uncertain orig. REW 943 a (giving as source ON *baratta* 'strife' but this rather fr. OFr.). Gamillscheg 78. NED s.v. *barrat*. Diez 41.

Rum. *ieftin*, fr. Byz., NG εὐθηνός (ἐφτηνός), above, 1. Tiktin 592.

3. Ir. word for 'cheap'?

NIr. *saor*, orig. 'free' (19.44). The sense 'cheap' is prob. acquired by contrast with *daor* 'enslaved, captive' and 'dear, expensive' (11.88). The sense 'free' lent itself readily to 'cheap' (cf. W. *rhad*).

W. *rhad*, orig. 'gratuitous, free' = sb. *rhad* 'grace, gift' (fr. adv. and predicate noun constructions as *yn rhad* 'gratis') : Ir. *rath* 'grace, reward, success, result', etym. dub. Stokes 225. Pedersen 1.144. Thurneysen, Gram. 131.

Br. *marc'had-mat*, lit. 'good market', semantic borrowing fr. Fr. *bon marché*.

4. ON *ūdȳrr*, OE *undēor*, ME *undere*, OHG *untiuri*, MHG *untiure*, neg. cpds. of ON *dȳrr*, etc., 'dear, expensive' (11.88).

ME *good chepe*, NE *cheap* (shortened fr. *good cheap*), Du. *goedkoop*, lit. 'good

bargain, trade, or market', with OE *cēap*, ME *chepe*, Du. *koop* 'trade (= sale or purchase), market, bargain, etc.' : OE *cēapian*, etc., 'trade' (11.83). NED s.v. *cheap* sb. Cf. the It. and Fr. locution, above, 2.

NHG *billig*, MLG *billīk* (> Dan., Sw. *billig*), orig. 'fair, just', like OHG *billīch*, MHG *billich*, fr. **bili-* in OE *bile-wit* 'simple, innocent', MHG *un-bil(e)-de* 'injustice, monstrosity', etc. : Ir. *bil* 'good', Grk. φίλος 'dear, worthy'. Development of sense 'cheap' fr. phrases like *billiger preis*, orig. 'fair price'. Walde-P. 2.185. Falk-Torp 74. Weigand-H. 1.239. Paul, Deutsches Wtb. 82.

NHG *wohlfeil*, MHG *wolveil(e)* or two words *wol veil(e)*, lit. 'easy to buy', cpd. of *wohl*, MHG *wol* 'well' and *feil*, MHG *veil(e)* 'to be sold, for sale'. Weigand-H. 2.1281.

5. Lith. *pigus*, beside *pingu*, *pigti* 'become cheap', etym.?

Lett. *lēts*, also 'easy, light' : Lith. *lėtas*, *lėnas*, Lett. *lēns* 'slow, lazy, gentle', ChSl. *lěnŭ* 'lazy', Lat. *lēnis* 'soft', etc. Walde-P. 2.395. Mühl.-Endz. 2.460, 463.

6. SCr. *jeftin*, fr. Byz., NG εὐθηνός (ἐφτηνός), above, 1. Berneker 455.

Boh. *laciný*, in earlier use 'easy' : Pol. *łatwy*, *lacny* 'easy' (9.96).

Pol. *tani*, etym.? Brückner 565.

Russ. *deševyj*, fr. adv. *deševo* 'cheaply', etym. dub., perh. (as 'right, suitable, fitting' > 'moderate, cheap', cf. NHG *billig*, etc., above) : SCr. *u-desiti* 'set right, make right', ChSl. *desiti* 'find', etc. Or loanword? Berneker 188.

7. Skt. *alpakṛta-*, lit. 'bought for little', cpd. of *alpa-* 'little, small' and *kṛīta-* fr. *krī-* 'buy' (11.81).

CHAPTER 12

SPATIAL RELATIONS: PLACE, FORM, SIZE

12.11	PLACE (sb.)	12.51	FORM, SHAPE
12.12	PUT (Place, Set, Lay)	12.52	SIZE
12.13	SIT	12.53	GROW
12.14	LIE	12.54	MEASURE (vb.)
12.15	STAND (vb. intr.)	12.55	LARGE, BIG (GREAT)
12.16	REMAIN, STAY, WAIT	12.56	SMALL, LITTLE
12.17	REMAIN (= Be Left Over)	12.57	LONG
12.18	LEAVE	12.58	TALL
12.19	QUIET (adj.)	12.59	SHORT
12.21	COLLECT, GATHER	12.61	WIDE, BROAD
12.22	JOIN, UNITE	12.62	NARROW
12.23	SEPARATE (vb.)	12.63	THICK[1] (in Dimension)
12.232	DIVIDE	12.64	THICK[2] (in Density)
12.24	OPEN (vb.)	12.65	THIN[1] (in Dimension)
12.25	SHUT, CLOSE (vb.)	12.66	THIN[2] (in Density)
12.26	COVER (vb.)	12.67	DEEP
12.27	HIDE, CONCEAL	12.68	SHALLOW
12.31	HIGH	12.71	FLAT
12.32	LOW	12.72	HOLLOW (= Concave)
12.33	TOP	12.73	STRAIGHT
12.34	BOTTOM	12.74	CROOKED
12.35	END	12.75	HOOK
12.352	POINT	12.76	CORNER
12.353	EDGE	12.77	CROSS
12.36	SIDE	12.78	SQUARE (sb.)
12.37	MIDDLE (adj.)	12.81	ROUND (adj.)
12.38	CENTER	12.82	CIRCLE
12.41	RIGHT (adj.; vs. Left)	12.83	SPHERE
12.42	LEFT (adj.; vs. Right)	12.84	LINE (sb.)
12.43	NEAR (adv.)	12.85	HOLE
12.44	FAR (adv.)	12.91	EQUAL
12.45	EAST	12.92	LIKE, SIMILAR
12.46	WEST	12.93	CHANGE (vb.)
12.47	NORTH	12.94	SIGN (sb.)
12.48	SOUTH		

12.11 PLACE (sb.)

Grk.	τόπος	Goth.	staþs	Lith.	vieta
NG	τόπος	ON	staðr	Lett.	vieta
Lat.	locus	Dan.	plads, sted	ChSl.	město
It.	luogo, posto	Sw.	plats	SCr.	mjesto
Fr.	lieu, place	OE	stōw, stede	Boh.	místo
Sp.	lugar, sitio	ME	stede, place	Pol.	miejsce
Rum.	loc	NE	place	Russ.	mesto
Ir.	dū, ined, áitt, airm, maigen	Du.	plaats	Skt.	sthāna-, sthala-
		OHG	stat	Av.	gātu-, asah-, stāna-
NIr.	áit, ionad	MHG	stat (ort)		
W.	lle	NHG	stelle, ort, platz		
Br.	lec'h				

'Place' is understood here in the wide sense of NE *place* (sb.). Besides the words listed as the most important, there are many others which are used for 'place' mainly in the geographical sense, 'region' or 'town', as NG μέρος (properly 'part', 13.23), Sp. *paraje* (: *parar* 'stop'), etc.

1. Grk. τόπος, etym. dub., perh. : Lith. *tapti* 'become', Lett. *tapt* 'become, attain', OE *þafian* 'consent to' (as orig. 'give place to', like NE *allow* through Fr. *alouer* fr. Lat. *adlocāre*). Walde-P. 1.743. Boisacq 975.

2. Lat. *locus*, early *stlocus* (Festus), etym. disputed, but prob. (**stl-o-ko-*) fr. the root **stel-* in OHG *stellan* 'set up', etc. (12.12). Walde-H. 1.818. Hence It. *luogo*, Fr. *lieu*, OSp. *luego*, Rum. *loc*; Sp. *luego* now only as adv., as sb. replaced by deriv. *lugar* fr. Lat. *locālis*. REW 5097, 5093.

It. *posto*, Sp. *puesto*, fr. Lat. *positum*, pple. of *pōnere* 'put' (12.12).

Fr. *place* (> ME, NE *place*), also MHG, NHG *platz*, Du. *plaats* (MLG *plātse* > Dan. *plads*, Sw. *plats*), fr. Lat. *platea* 'street, open area, courtyard' (> It. *piazza*, etc.), this fr. Grk. πλατεῖα (ὁδός), fem. of πλατύς 'wide'. REW 6583. Falk-Torp 833. Franck-v.W. 504. NED s.v. *place*, sb.

Sp. *sitio*, deriv. of vb. borrowed fr. Gmc. **sitjan* in ON *sitja*, OHG *sizzan*, etc. 'sit' (12.13). REW 7961b.

3. Ir. *dū* (gen., acc. *don*), orig. 'earth' : Grk. χθών 'earth', etc. (1.21). Walde-P. 1.663. Pedersen 1.89. Vendryes, RC 40.437 ff. Cf. Toch. A *tkam* 'earth' and 'place' (JAOS 67.43).

Ir. *ined*, *inad*, NIr. *ionad*, cpd. **eni-pado-*, cf. Ir. *ed* 'space of time', Gall. *candetum* (**cant-edum*) 'spatium centum pedum' : Grk. πέδον 'ground', ChSl. *podŭ* 'ground, foundation', Hitt. *pedan* 'place' (Sturtevant, Hitt. Gloss. 123 with refs.). Walde-P. 2.24. Pedersen 1.91.

Ir. *áitt*, NIr. *áit* perh. (fr. **pōth-ni-*) : Skt. *pāthas-* 'spot, place' also *path-* 'path, way', ChSl. *pątĭ* 'way', etc. (10.71). Walde-P. 2.26. Pedersen 1.161.

Ir. *airm*, etym.?

Ir. *baile* 'place', but esp. 'dwelling place' (NIr. 'town, village, homestead, home'), etym.? Walde-P. 2.141.

Ir. *maigen*, fr. *mag* 'plain' (1.23). Pedersen 1.96.

W. *lle*, Br. *lec'h* : Ir. *lige* 'bed, grave', Grk. λέχος 'bed', fr. root in Ir. *laigim*, Goth. *ligan*, etc. 'lie' (12.14). Walde-P. 2.424. Pedersen 1.98.

4. Goth. *staþs*, ON *staðr*, Dan. *sted*, OE, ME *stede* (NE *stead* in *instead*, etc.), OHG *stat* (NHG *statt* 'place' mostly in phrases and cpds., also *stadt* 'city'), orig. 'standing place' : Lat. *statiō*, *status*, etc., fr. IE **stā-* 'stand'. Walde-P. 2.605. Falk-Torp 1154.

OE *stōw* (NE in place names) : Lith. *stovéti* 'stand', ChSl. *staviti* 'put', etc., fr. a parallel form of the same root as the preceding. Walde-P. 2.607 ff.

NHG *ort*, fr. OHG *ort* 'point, edge, shore' = ON *oddr*, OE *ord* 'point' (12.352). All stages of transition in MHG from 'point' through 'beginning or end, edge, boundary, region' to 'place'. Weigand-H. 2.347. Paul, Deutsches Wtb. s.v.

NHG *stelle*, back-formation fr. *stellen* 'put, place' (12.12). Weigand-H. 2.693. Paul, Deutsches Wtb. 515.

NE *place*, NHG *platz*, etc., see under Fr. *place*, above, 2.

5. Lith., Lett. *vieta* : ChSl. *vitati*, *obitati* (**obŭ-vitati*) 'rest, dwell', etc. (7.11), outside connection? Trautmann 345.

6. ChSl. *město*, etc., general Slavic (but Boh. *město* 'town', *místo* 'place',

Pol. *miasto* 'town', *miejsce* 'place') prob. : Lith. *mieta* 'stake', Skt. *methi-* 'pillar, post', Lat. *mēta* 'turning post in the circus', etc. For semantic parallel, cf. NHG *ort*, above, 4. Walde-P. 2.240. Berneker 2.52. Otherwise Trautmann 185 (Brückner 330 cites both views).

7. Skt. *sthāna-*, Av. *stāna-* (in cpds.), OPers. *stāna-*, fr. IE **stā-* 'stand', like Goth. *staþs*, etc., above, 4. Walde-P. 2.606.

Skt. *sthala-* : OHG *stellan* 'set up', etc. (12.12), IE **stel-* beside **stā-* 'stand'. Walde-P. 2.643 ff.

Av. *asah-* : Skt. *āça-* 'space, region', this prob. fr. *aç-* 'arrive at, reach'. Barth. 209.

Av. *gātu-*, OPers. *gāθu-* 'place' and 'throne' (NPers. *gāh* 'place') : Skt. *gātu-* 'going, way' also 'space, place, fr. *gā-* 'go'. Walde-P. 1.677.

12.12 PUT (Place, Set, Lay)

Grk.	τίθημι	Goth.	(ga)satjan, (ga)lagjan	Lith.	(pa)déti, statyti
NG	θέτω, βάζω, aor. ἔβαλα	ON	setja, leggja	Lett.	likt, dēt
Lat.	pōnere, collocāre	Dan.	sætte, stille, lægge	ChSl.	položiti, postaviti
It.	porre, mettere, collocare	Sw.	sätte, ställa, lägga	SCr.	metnuti, postaviti, klasti
Fr.	mettre, poser, placer	OE	settan, lecgan		
Sp.	poner, colocar	ME	sette, leye, pute	Boh.	postaviti, položiti, klasti
Rum.	pune, băga	NE	put, place, set, lay		
Ir.	cuirim (fo-cerd-), fuirmim	Du.	zetten, plaatsen, leggen	Pol.	postawić, położyć, klaść
		OHG	sezzen, leggan, stellan		
NIr.	cuirim	MHG	setzen, stellen, legen	Russ.	položit', postavit', klast'
W.	gosod, dodi	NHG	setzen, stellen, legen		
Br.	lakaat			Skt.	dhā-
				Av.	dā-

In most of the languages cited there is no single word of such general application as NE *put*, but rather a variety of expressions the choice of which depends on the nature of the object and the position it is placed in, but with variable idiomatic usage and much overlapping.

In derivs. of IE **dhē-* the meaning 'put, place' is inherited, and nothing further can be said of its origin. Of the other words, some are derived from

nouns meaning 'place' (12.11). But most of them come by generalization of more specific notions, esp. 'cause to sit, lie, or stand' or 'throw' or 'thrust'. Such sources are illustrated in NE *set*, *lay*, *stand* (trans.), of which the transitive use of *stand* (recent and colloq., NED s.v. 65) is restricted to 'put in an upright position' and 'lay' is mostly 'put in a lying position' (one may *lay* a book down or *stand* it on edge), while in *set* the original notion of 'make sit' is only rarely present. In general, words of the 'set' and 'lay' group were commonly or frequently used without reference to the original sense, and to a less extent those of the 'stand' group. In the Gospels Goth. *lagjan*, OE *lecgan*, OHG *leggan* were commonly used (beside Goth. *satjan*, etc.) to render Grk. τίθημι or Lat. *pōnere*. So also regularly ChSl. *položiti* (vs. *postaviti* for ἵστημι, Jagic, Entstehungsgesch. 381).

1. IE *dhē-. Walde-P. 1 826 ff. Walde-H. 1.440 ff. Here as 'put', Grk. τίθημι, NG θέτω (new pres. to late aor. ἔθεσα, Hatzidakis, Μεσ. 1.315 ff.; also τοποθετῶ, cpd. with τόπος 'place'); Lith. *(pa)dėti*, Lett. *dēt* (but mostly in special phrases, Mühl.-Endz. 1.464); ChSl. *děti*, etc., general Slavic, but not usual for 'put', mostly in some secondary senses, 'do, make' or 'say' (Berneker 192); Skt. *dhā-*, Av. *dā-*; Hitt. *dāi-*; Toch. A *tā-*, *tā̆s-*, B *tes*, etc. (SSS 438). Here also Lat. *condere* 'found', etc., *facere* 'do, make', OE *dōn* 'do' etc. (9.11).

2. NG βάζω, aor. ἔβαλα, the pop. equivalent of NE *put*, fr. Gr. βάλλω 'throw', which is also occasionally 'put' (LS s.v. A II 6). The same semantic development in Fr. *mettre*, etc. (below, 3) and NE *put* (below, 5). The present βάζω (more usual than βάλλω, for which also βάνω, βαίνω) is explained by Hatzidakis, Einleitung 410 and 'Αθηνᾶ 22.232 ff., as a blend with βιβάζω 'lift up'.

3. Lat. *pōnere*, fr. *po-s(i)nere (cf. pple. *positus*), cpd. of *po- (= Lith. *pa-*, ChSl. *po-*) and *sinere* in old sense of 'place' as in pple. *situs* 'placed', hence orig. 'put down, put aside'. Outside connections of *sinere* doubtful. Walde-P. 2.461. Ernout-M. 787, 945 f.

Hence It. *porre*, Sp. *poner*, Rum. *pune*, all in general sense, but Fr. *pondre* only in specialized sense of 'lay eggs', which also occurs elsewhere. REW 6647.

Lat. *conlocāre*, *collocāre* (> It. *collocare*, Sp. *colocar*; VLat. development in Fr. *coucher*, Rum. *culca* 'put to bed', Sp. *colgar* 'hang', REW 2052), cpd. of *locāre*, deriv. of *locus* 'place' (12.11).

It. *mettere*, Fr. *mettre*, fr. Lat. *mittere* 'let go' (whence the usual but secondary 'send'), 'throw' (*hastam*, *lapides*, etc.), 'put forth' (*radices*, *florem*, etc.), in late Lat. 'put forth, put in, put'. Cf. *manum autem nemo mittit ad tangendum* (Peregrinatio), [*ova*] *ut in tepida acqua mittantur* (Anthimi de observatione ciborum epistula), *mittis et modicum sale* (Oribasius), etc. Ernout-M. 621. REW 5616.

Fr. *poser*, fr. Lat. *pausāre* 'pause, rest', whence in late Lat. also 'cause to rest, put down' (cf. It. *posare* 'lie' and 'lay'), in this sense possibly, though not necessarily, influenced by forms of Lat. *pōnere* like *positus*. REW 6308. Gamillscheg 710.

Fr. *placer*, deriv. of *place* 'place' (12.11).

Rum. *băga*, esp. 'put in, thrust in', with numerous idiomatic uses similar to those of NG βάζω (above, 2), or its cpd. μπάζω (bazo) 'put in'. Some connection with the latter seems likely, though no explanation of the Rum. *g* is apparent. Tiktin 143 mentions βάζω, but not μπάζω.

4. Ir. *cuirim* (suppl. vb. *fo-cerd-*) 'throw' and 'put', NIr. *cuirim* 'put', perh. : Grk. σκαίρω 'skip, frisk', Skt. *kūrd-* 'jump', in any case with Irish development of 'put' from 'throw'. Walde-P. 2.567. Pedersen 2.498 ff.

Ir. *fo-rimim*, *fuirmim* : Goth. *rimis* 'rest', Lith. *rimti* 'become quiet', Grk. ἠρέμα 'gently', Skt. *ram-* 'stand still, rest', IE *rem-. Walde-P. 2.372. Pedersen 2.602. Laws, Gloss. 432.

W. *dodi*, etym.? (Morris Jones 332, fr. IE *dō- 'give' or *dhē- 'place'; not in-

cluded by Walde-P. or Stokes with either).

W. *gosod*, MW *gossot*, prob. a deriv. (through an abstract in *-otā*, for which cf. Pedersen 2.36 ff.; change to masc. gender as in all verbal nouns, Morris Jones 395 ff.) of an adj. *goss, this fr. *upo-sto-, parallel to Ir. *ross*, W. *rhos*, fr. *pro-sto-, and other like derivs. of IE *stā- 'stand' (Walde-P. 2.604). G. S. Lane, Language 13.24 f.

Br. *lakaat*, fr. Lat. *locāre* (above, 3). Loth, Mots lat. 180.

5. Goth. *(ga)satjan*, ON *setja*, Dan. *sætte*, Sw. *sätte*, OE *settan*, ME *sette*, NE *set*, Du. *zetten*, OHG *sezzen*, NHG *setzen*, caus. of Goth. *sitan* 'sit', etc. (12.13).

Goth. *(ga)lagjan*, ON *leggja*, Dan. *lægge*, Sw. *lägga*, OE *lecgan*, ME *leye*, NE *lay*, Du. *leggen*, OHG *leggan*, NHG *legen*, caus. of Goth. *ligan* 'lie', etc. (12.14).

Dan. *stille*, Sw. *ställa*, OHG *stellan*, MHG, NHG *stellen* (OE *stellan* mostly 'stand'), fr. *stalljan : Grk. στέλλω 'make ready, fit out' and 'send', Skt. *sthal-* 'stand' (Dhātup.), etc., IE *stel- beside *stā- 'stand'. Walde-P. 2.643 ff. Falk-Torp 1167. Weigand-H. 1.963.

ME *pute*, NE *put* (same word as *put* in golf with differentiated pronunciation), fr. OE *pūtian, *potian*, *pyten* 'thrust, push' : Sw. dial. *putta* 'strike, knock', Norw. dial. *pota* 'prick, poke', etc., perh. of imitative origin. Walde-P. 2.119. Falk-Torp 841. For the full phonetic and semantic history in English, cf. NED s.v. *put*, vb.[1].

NE *place*, prob. fr. sb. *place* (12.11), rather than direct from Fr. *placer*.

Du. *plaatsen*, fr. *platts* 'place' (12.11).

6. Lith. *(pa)dėti*, Lett. *dēt*, above, 1.

Lith. *(pa)statyti*, ChSl. *(po)staviti*, etc., caus. of words for 'stand' (12.15).

Lett. *likt* (also *nuolikt*, etc.), orig. and still also 'leave, let' : Lith. *likti* 'be left', Grk. λείπω 'leave', etc. (12.18). Walde-P. 2.396 ff. Mühl.-Endz. 2.467 ff.

7. ChSl. *(po)ložiti*, etc., caus. of words for 'lie' (12.14).

ChSl. *klasti*, *kladą*, etc., esp. 'lay', also 'put' : Lith. *kloti* 'spread out', OE, OHG *hladan* 'load', etc. Walde-P. 2.489. Berneker 507.

SCr. *metnuti*, orig. and still dial. 'throw' : ChSl. *mesti*, *metati* 'throw', etc. (10.25). Berneker 2.40.

8. Skt. *dhā-*, Av. *dā-*, above, 1.

12.13 SIT

Grk.	ἧμαι, κάθημαι (ἕζομαι)	Goth.	sitan	Lith.	sėdėti
NG	κάθομαι	ON	sitja	Lett.	sēdēt
Lat.	sedēre	Dan.	sidde	ChSl.	sěděti
It.	sedere	Sw.	sitta	SCr.	sjediti
Fr.	être assis	OE	sittan	Boh.	seděti
Sp.	sentarse, estar sentado	ME	sitte	Pol.	siedzieć
Rum.	sedea	NE	sit	Russ.	sidet'
Ir.	saidim	Du.	zitten	Skt.	ās-, sad-
NIr.	suidhim	OHG	sizzan	Av.	āh-, had-
W.	eistedd	MHG	sitzen		
Br.	azeza	NHG	sitzen		

The words for 'sit' belong to inherited groups representing IE *sed- and *ēs-.

1. IE *sed-. Walde-P. 2.483 ff. Ernout-M. 917 ff.

Grk. (beside sbs. ἕδος, ἕδρα 'seat') ἕζομαι 'sit', ἵζω (fr. redupl. *si-sdō) mostly caus. 'seat, place', but also 'sit', καθίζω mostly caus. 'seat' or 'take a seat' (so in NG); Lat. *sedēre* (> It. *sedere*, OFr. *seoir* now 'suit', Sp. *sentar* 'seat,

place', *sentarse* or *estar sentado* 'sit', Rum. *sedea*; Lat. *ad-sidēre* > Fr. *asseoir* 'seat, place', *s'asseoir* 'take a seat', *être assis* 'be seated, sit'; REW 7780); Ir. *saidim*, vbl. n. *suide*, whence NIr. *suidhim*; W. *eistedd* fr. sb. = OBr. *estid* gl. *sedile* fr. cpd. (*eks-di-sedo- Pedersen 1.20; otherwise Morris Jones 78), Br. *azeza* fr. cpd. *ad-sed- (Pedersen 2.605; Loth, Mots lat. 134); Goth. *sitan*, OE *sittan*, OHG *sizzan*, etc., general Gmc; Lith. *sėdėti*, Lett. *sēdēt*; ChSl. *sěděti*, etc. general Slavic, beside perfect. *sěsti* 'take a seat'; Skt. *sad-*, Av. *had-*.

2. IE *ēs-, perh. ultimately derived fr. a cpd. of preceding, 3sg. mid. *ē-sd-tai. Walde-P. 2.484.

Grk. ἧμαι, 3sg. ἧσται (= Skt. *āste*), more commonly κάθημαι, whence NG pop. κάθομαι; Skt. *ās-*, Av. *āh-*.

12.14 LIE

Grk.	κεῖμαι	Goth.	ligan	Lith.	gulėti
NG	κεῖμαι, κείτομαι	ON	liggja	Lett.	gulēt
Lat.	iacēre, cubāre	Dan.	ligge	ChSl.	ležati
It.	giacere	Sw.	ligga	SCr.	ležati
Fr.	être couché	OE	licgan	Boh.	ležeti
Sp.	yacer, estar acostado	ME	liggen, lie	Pol.	leżeć
Rum.	fi culcat (zace)	NE	lie	Russ.	ležat'
Ir.	laigim	Du.	liggen	Skt.	çī-, 3sg. çete
NIr.	luighim	OHG	li(g)gan	Av.	3sg. saēte
W.	gorwedd	MHG	ligen		
Br.	gourveza	NHG	liegen		

1. IE *legh-. Walde-P. 2.424. Walde-H. 1.778; Feist 331. Berneker 704 f. Grk. λέχομαι (Hesych.), Hom. aor. λέκτο, etc., and in derivs. λέχος, λέκτρον 'bed, couch', etc.; Lat. only in *lectus* 'bed, couch'; Ir. *laigim*, NIr. *luighim*; Goth. *ligan*, OE *licgan*, OHG *lig(g)an*, etc., general Gmc.; ChSl. *ležati*, etc., general Slavic, beside perfect. *lešti*, *legą* 'lie down'; Hitt. 3sg. *laki* 'causes to fall', mid. *lagāri* 'falls, lies' (Sturtevant, Hitt. Gram. 118, Gloss. 90); Toch. A *lake*, B *leke* 'lair' (SSS 464).

2. IE *k̑ei-. Walde-P. 1.358 ff. Grk. κεῖμαι, 3sg. κεῖται = Skt. *çete*, Av. *saēte*. Byz., NG κείτομαι (so, not κοίτομαι as if fr. sb. κοιτη) with shift to thematic type and κειτ- fr. old 3sg. κεῖται (?). Hatzidakis, Μεσ. 1.316 f.

3. Lat. *iacēre* (> It. *giacere*, Fr. *gésir*, Sp. *yacer*, Rum. *zace*), orig. 'throw oneself, be thrown down' : *iacere* 'throw', Grk. ἵημι 'throw'. Cf. Sp. *echarse* 'throw oneself down, lie down'. Walde-P. 1.199. Ernout-M. 466. Walde-H. 1.666 f. REW 4562.

Of the Romance derivs. of *iacēre*, Fr. *gésir* is obs. except in certain forms, Rum. *zace* is now in restricted use (esp. 'lie dead, lie ill' etc.), and in general 'lie' denoting the situation 'be lying' (in bed) is often expressed by phrases. Fr. *être couché* : *coucher* 'put to bed', *se coucher* 'lie down', fr. Lat. *collocāre* 'put, place' (12.12). Similarly Rum. *fi* (or *sta*) *culcat* : *culca* of same origin. Sp. *estar acostado* : *acostar* 'put to bed, lie down', deriv. of Lat. *costa* 'side, rib'.

Lat. *cubāre* : Goth. *hups*, OE *hype* 'hip' and with different root extensions Grk. κύπτω 'bend forward, stoop' and many other words denoting a bent position. Walde-P. 1.370 ff. Ernout-M. 237. Walde-H. 1.298.

4. Ir. *laigim*, NIr. *luighim*, above, 1. W. *gorwedd*, Corn. *gorwedha*, Br. *gourveza*, prob. cpd. of W. *gor*, Br. *gour* 'over' (*upor, Pedersen 1.246), but root?

5. Goth. *ligan*, etc., general Gmc., above, 1.

6. Lith. *gulėti*, Lett. *gulēt* : Lith. *guolis* 'resting place, lair', Lett. *guola* 'nest', OSw. *kolder* 'litter, brood', perh. Grk. γωλεός 'hole'. Walde-P. 1.639. Mühl.-Endz. 1.679.

7. ChSl. *ležati*, etc., above, 1.

8. Skt. *çī-*, 3sg. *çete*, Av. 3sg. *saēte*, above, 2.

12.15 STAND (vb. intr.)

Grk.	ἵσταμαι	Goth.	standan	Lith.	stovėti
NG	στέκω	ON	standa	Lett.	stāvēt
Lat.	stāre	Dan.	staa	ChSl.	stojati
It.	stare (essere) in piedi	Sw.	stå	SCr.	stojati
Fr.	être debout	OE	standan, stondan	Boh.	stati
Sp.	estar de pie	ME	stande, stonde	Pol.	stać
Rum.	sta in picioare	NE	stand	Russ.	stojat'
Ir.	duairsiur	Du.	staan	Skt.	sthā-
NIr.	seasuighim	OHG	stantan, stān	Av.	stā-
W.	sefyll	MHG	stēn		
Br.	beza(chom) enn he zao	NHG	stehen		

1. IE *stā-[1] in different formations variously distributed as regards usage between 1) 'stand' = 'be standing', 2) 'take a stand, stand up', and 3) 'cause to stand, set up'. Walde-P. 2.603 ff. Ernout-M. 979 ff.

Grk. ἵσταμαι, beside trans. ἵστημι; new pres., formed to perf. ἕστηκα in στήκω (NT), NG στέκω (Hatzidakis Μεσ. 1.279); Lat. *stāre* (> It. *stare*, OFr. *ester*, Sp. *estar*, Rum. *sta*, mostly in secondary sense 'be', etc.; for 'stand' in phrases); Ir. *duairsiur* fr. cpd. of reduplicated form (Pedersen 2.628 ff.), NIr. *seasuighim* : *seas*, MIr. *sessam* 'standing' (sb.) fr. reduplicated form (Pedersen l.c.); here also with *m-* suffix (Walde-P. 2.606. Pedersen 1.79) W. *saf* 'stamina', *sefyll* 'stand', Br. *sevel* 'rise, raise, build', Br. *sao* 'standing, elevation', whence the phrase for 'stand' *beza (chom) enn he zao*, lit. 'be (remain) in one's standing position', after Fr. *être (rester) debout*; Goth., OE *standan*, OHG *stantan*, *stān*, etc., general Gmc. with or without nasal present; Lith. *stovėti*, Lett. *stāvēt* (cf. ChSl. *staviti* 'cause to stand, put'), beside Lith. *stoti*, Lett. *stāt* 'take a stand, stand up'; ChSl., SCr. *stojati*, Russ. *stojat'*, beside perfect. ChSl. *stati*, *stanq* 'take a stand' (rendering Grk. aor.), but Boh. *stati*, Pol. *stać* simply 'stand'; Skt. *sthā-*, Av. *stā-*.

2. In the Romance languages where the derivatives of Lat. *stāre* have so expanded their use, 'stand' in the literal sense of 'be standing' is generally expressed by phrases with words for 'feet' or 'upright'. Thus It. *stare (essere) in piedi*, Fr. *être (rester) debout*, Sp. *estar de pie*, *tenerse derecho*, Rum. *sta in picioare*.

[1] The root is given in this form *stā-, here and elsewhere, to avoid repeating the clumsy *st(h)ā-. Furthermore, the Skt. *th* is due to some special cause—according to current theory, the former presence of a voiceless laryngeal. Similarly *stel-, not *st(h)el-.

12.16 REMAIN, STAY, WAIT

Grk.	*μένω*	Goth.	*saljan, wisan, beidan*	Lith.	*likti, laukti*
NG	*μένω*	ON	*dveljask, bīða*	Lett.	*palikt, gaidīt*
Lat.	*manēre*	Dan.	*blive, vente*	ChSl.	*prěbyti, ostati*
It.	*restare, rimanere, aspettare*	Sw.	*förbliva, stanna, vänta*	SCr.	*ostati, čekati*
Fr.	*rester, demeurer, attendre*	OE	*belīfan, dwellan, (a)bīdan*	Boh.	*zůstati, čekati*
Sp.	*quedar*	ME	*(a)bide, remayne, waite*	Pol.	*zostać, czekać*
Rum.	*rămînea, aștepta*	NE	*remain, stay, wait*	Russ.	*ostat'sja, ždat'*
Ir.	*anaim, mairim*	Du.	*blijven, wachten*	Skt.	*(ava-)sthā-*
NIr.	*fanaim, fuirighim*	OHG	*bilīban, bītan*	Av.	*man-*
W.	*aros*	MHG	*b(e)līben, bīten*		
Br.	*chom, gortozi*	NHG	*bleiben, warten*		

Words for 'remain, stay' (in one place as opposed to 'move, go') coincide in part with those for 'remain' = 'be left over' (12.17), the development being mostly from the first to the second, but sometimes the opposite. Furthermore, just as words for 'remain' may be used for 'await, wait for' (as Grk. *μένω* Hom. Il. 16.620, etc., Lat. *manēre hostem*, OPers. *mām amānaya* 'awaited me'), so conversely there is a group of words which, from such notions as 'watch, look for, hope for', have come to mean 'wait for' and may then be used also intransitively for 'wait' closely approaching 'remain, stay'. Hence such words are added in the list, even though most of them are still distinguished in feeling and range of use from those given in the first place.

1. IE **men-* 'remain', to be distinguished from **men-* 'think', even though they may be ultimately the same. Walde-P. 2.267. Ernout-M. 587. Walde-H. 2.26.

Grk. *μένω*, also *μίμνω* poet.; Lat. *manēre;* Av. *man-* in *upa-manaya-* 'wait for', *mānaya-* 'cause to remain', OPers. *mānaya-* 'wait for', NPers. *māndan* 'remain', Skt. *man-* in Ved. imperat. *mamandhi* 'delay'; Arm. *mnam* 'remain, wait for'; here prob. Ir. *ainmne*, W. *anmynedd* 'patience' (cf. Grk. *ὑπο-μονή* 'patience').

2. It. *restare*, Fr. *rester* (latter with *-s-* from the It. or Lat. form), fr. Lat. *restāre* 'stand firm, remain = be left', cpd. of *stāre* 'stand'. REW 7248. Gamillscheg 759 f.

It. *rimanere*, Rum. *rămînea*, OFr. *remaindre* (> ME *remayne*, NE *remain*), fr. Lat. *remanēre* 'be left' (cpd. of *manēre*, above, 1).

It. *aspettare* 'await, wait', fr. Lat. *aspectāre* 'look at attentively, desire', whence also by assimilation **astectare* > Rum. *aștepta*. REW 3039. Pușcariu 150.

Fr. *demeurer*, It. *dimorāre* (both also esp. 'dwell', Sp. *demorar* mostly 'delay'), fr. act. form of Lat. *dēmorārī*, cpd. of *morārī* 'delay' (14.24). REW 2552. Wartburg 3.38.

Fr. *attendre* 'await, wait', fr. Lat. *attendere* 'attend, heed', cpd. of *tendere* 'stretch'.

Sp. *quedar*, fr. Lat. *quiētāre* 'to calm, quiet', deriv. of *quiēs, -ētis* 'repose, quiet' (12.19). REW 6956.

3. Ir. *mairim* : Lat. *mora* 'delay' (14.24). Walde-P. 2.689 f. Pedersen 1.44.

Ir. *anaim*, NIr. *fanaim* : Skt. *aniti* 'breathes', etc., IE **an-* in words for 'breathe, breath' (4.51), with semantic development through 'breathe hard, pant'(?) to 'rest', or possibly a blend with forms of IE **men-* (above, 1). Walde-P. 1.57. Pedersen 2.456. Thurneysen, Gram. 337. Ernout-M. 587.

NIr. *fuirighim*, fr. Ir. *fuirech* 'a delay', vbl. n. of *forigim* 'delay, hold back' (cpd. of *reg-* in *con-riug* 'feud'). Pedersen 2.592 f.

W. *aros* orig.? Morris Jones 343 (but?).

Br. *chom*, also the regular word for 'dwell, live' (7.11).

Br. *gortozi*, Corn. *gortos* 'await, wait', prob. fr. the same Gmc. source as Fr. *garder* 'watch, keep' (11.24). Cf. also NHG *warten*, below, 4. Henry 138.

4. Goth. *saljan*, orig. and in most occurrences 'remain, abide' = 'have an abode' : *saliþwōs* 'inn, dwelling', OHG *selida*, OE *sælþ* 'dwelling', ON *salr*, OHG *sal* etc. 'room'. Walde-P. 2.503. Feist 408.

Goth. *wisan*, which, like the preceding, renders Grk. *μένω* and cpds., is the same word as *wisan* 'be', orig. 'dwell' : Skt. *vas-* 'dwell', etc. (7.11).

ON *dveljask* (refl. of *dvelja* 'delay', trans.), OE *dwellan* (also 'hinder, delay, mislead', trans.) see under 'dwell' (7.11).

Goth. *beidan* (*beidan*, *us-beidan* 'await', *ga-beidan* 'endure'), ON *bīða*, OE *(a)bīdan*, ME *(a)bide* (NE lit., dial., or in certain phrases), OHG *bītan*, MHG *bīten*, old Gmc. group for 'wait, await', agreeing formally with Grk. *πείθω* 'persuade', Lat. *fīdere* 'trust', and perh. connected through a common notion of 'patient waiting, steadfastness', but much disputed. Walde-P. 2.140. Feist 86 f.

OE *belīfan*, Du. *blijven*, MLG *blīven* (> Dan. *blive*, Sw. *bliva*, but in this sense now mostly *förbliva*), OHG *bilīban*, MHG *b(e)līben*, NHG *bleiben* = Goth. **bileiban* (assumed fr. *belaif*, Goth. cal.), beside caus. Goth. *bilaibjan* 'leave behind', OE (simplex) *lǣfan*, NE *leave*, etc. : Skt. *lipta-* 'sticky', *lip-* 'smear', Grk. (*λίπος* 'fat', *λιπαρός* 'oily', but also) *λῑπαρής* 'persisting', etc. The Gmc. development through 'remain stuck'. Walde-P. 2.403. Falk-Torp. 83, 638. Feist 91.

Dan. *vente*, Sw. *vänta* 'await, wait' : ON *vǣnta*, *vǣtta* 'expect, hope for', fr. an extended form of the root in Goth. *wēnjan* 'hope, expect', OE *wēnan* 'hope, think', Goth. *wēns*, OE *wēn*, OHG *wān* 'hope, expectation', Lat. *Venus*, Skt. *van-* 'desire, gain', etc. Walde-P. 1.260. Falk-Torp 1367 f. Hellquist 1392.

Sw. *stanna*, also 'stop' = ODan. *stadne*, ON *staðna* 'stop, pause' from *staðinn* past pple. of *standa* 'stand'. Falk-Torp 1151. Hellquist 1066.

Du. *wachten*, 'wait' in MDu. 'watch' = OHG *wahtēn*, MLG *wachten* 'watch'; whence also, through ONorth. Fr. *waitier*, ME *waite* 'watch' and 'await, wait', NE *wait*. NED s.v. *wait*. Franck-v. W. 770.

ME *remayne*, NE *remain*, see above, 2.

NE *stay*, earlier and ME 'stop, pause, stand', fr. OFr. *ester* (pres. ind. sg. Anglo-Fr. *estais*, *estait*), fr. Lat. *stāre* 'stand'. NED s.v. *stay*, vb.[1].

NHG *warten* 'wait', *erwarten* 'await', fr. MHG *warten*, OHG *wartēn* 'look out, watch for' : OE *weardian* 'watch, guard', NE *ward*, Goth. *wars*, ON *varr* 'heedful', Grk. *ὁράω* 'see', etc. Walde-P. 1.284. Weigand-H. 2.1213.

MHG, NHG *harren* (lit.), etym. dub. Walde-P. 1.411. Weigand-H. 1.814 Kluge-G. 233.

5. Lith. *likti*, *pasilikti*, Lett. *palikt* : Grk. *λείπω*, Lat. *linquere* 'leave', etc. (12.18).

Lith. *laukti* 'await, wait' : Lett. *lukāt* 'see, try', ChSl. *lučiti* 'find, meet', Grk. *λεύσσω* 'see', Skt. *lok-* 'look', etc. Walde-P. 2.411.

Lett. *gaidīt* 'await, wait' : Lith. *geisti* 'desire', ChSl. *žīdati* 'await', Russ. *ždat'* 'wait, await', MHG *gīten* 'be greedy', OE *gītsian* 'desire' etc., IE **gheidh-*. Walde-P. 1.553. Mühl.-Endz. 1.583.

6. ChSl. *prěbyti*, *prěbyvati* (commonest translation of *μένω*; in modern Slavic 'sojourn, reside, dwell'), cpd. of *byti*, 'be'.

ChSl. *žīdati*, Russ. *ždat'*, see under Lett. *gaidīt;* above, 5.

ChSl., SCr. *ostati*, Boh. *zůstati*, Pol. *zostać*, Russ. *ostat'sja* (refl.), cpds. of *stati*, etc. 'stand'. Brückner 656.

SCr. *čekati* (SCr.-ChSl. *čakati*), Boh. *čekati*, Pol. *czekać* 'wait', orig. disputed, perh. : ChSl. *čayati* 'hope, expect, await'. Berneker 134. Brückner 75.

7. Skt. *sthā-* 'stand', often 'remain' (esp. in a certain position, etc.), also cpd. *ava-sthā-*.

Av. *man-*, above, 1.

12.17 REMAIN (= Be Left Over)

Grk.	*λείπομαι*	Goth.	*aflifnan*	Lith.	*išlikti, pasilikti*
NG	*μένω*	ON	*lifa, lifna*	Lett.	*atlikt*
Lat.	*relinquī (remanēre, restāre)*	Dan.	*blive tilovers (tilbage)*	ChSl.	*ostati*
It.	*rimanere, restare*	Sw.	*bliva övrig (kvar)*	SCr.	*ostati*
Fr.	*rester*	OE	*belīfan, lǣfan*	Boh.	*zůstati*
Sp.	*restar, quedar*	ME	*leve, remayne*	Pol.	*zostać*
Rum.	*rămînea*	NE	*be left, remain*	Russ.	*ostat'sja*
Ir.	*do-fuarat, fedligedar* (3sg.)	Du.	*blijven*	Skt.	*çiṣ-* in pass.
NIr.	*fanaim*	OHG	*bilīban*		
W.	*bod yn weddill*	MHG	*belīben*		
Br.	*chom*	NHG	*bleiben*		

Most of the words for 'remain' = 'be left over' are the same as, or connected with, those for 'remain, stay' (12.16). But some belong with those for 'leave' (12.18).

1. Grk. *λείπομαι*, mid. of *λείπω* 'leave' (12.18) used for 'be left behind' and 'be left over, remain'.

Grk. *μένω* 'remain, stay' (12.16), in NG also 'remain, be left over'.

2. Lat. *relinquī*, pass. of *relinquere* 'leave' (12.18).

It. *rimanere*, Rum. *rămînea*, It. *restare*, Fr. *rester*, Sp. *restar*, *quedar*, see 12.16.

3. Ir. *do-fuarat*, cpd. of *di-od-* and *rethim* 'run' (10.46). Pedersen 2.600. Lit. 'run out from'; semantic development prob. through 'escape, survive' to 'be left'.

Ir. *fedligedar* (3sg.), fr. *fedil* 'enduring' (= W. *gweddill* 'remainder'), perh. : MIr. *feidm* 'exertion', Grk. *ἄεθλος* 'contest, battle'. Walde-P. 1.223. Pedersen 1.110.

NIr. *fanaim*, see 12.16.

W. *bod yn weddill*, lit. 'be as a remainder' (*gweddill*, above).

Br. *chom*, see 12.16.

4. Goth. *aflifnan*, ON *lifna*, *lifa* : OE *belīfan*, OHG *bilīban*, etc. (12.16) 'remain' in both senses.

ME *remayne*, NE *remain*, see 12.16.

5. Lith. *likti*, or esp. cpds. *išlikti*, *pasilikti*, Lett. *atlikt* : Grk. *λείπω*, etc. 'leave' (12.18).

6. ChSl. *ostati*, etc., see 12.16.

7. Skt. *çiṣ-* 'leave' (12.18) in pass. 'be left', cf. pple. *çiṣṭa-* 'residual'.

12.18 LEAVE

Grk.	*λείπω*	Goth.	*lētan*	Lith.	*palikti*
NG	*ἀφίνω*	ON	*leifa, lāta, skilja eptir*	Lett.	*atstāt*
Lat.	*relinquere*	Dan.	*efterlade, lade blive (levne)*	ChSl.	*ostaviti*
It.	*lasciare*	Sw.	*lämna*	SCr.	*ostaviti*
Fr.	*laisser*	OE	*lǣtan, lǣfan*	Boh.	*zůstaviti*
Sp.	*dejar*	ME	*lete, leve*	Pol.	*zostawić*
Rum.	*lăsa*	NE	*leave*	Russ.	*ostavit'*
Ir.	*fācbaim, lēicim*	Du.	*laten*	Skt.	*çiṣ-, ric-, hā-*
NIr.	*fāgaim*	OHG	*lāzan (leiben)*	Av.	*(paiti-)rič-*
W.	*gadael*	MHG	*lāzen*		
Br.	*lezel*	NHG	*lassen*		

1. IE **leikʷ-*. Walde-P. 2.396 f. Ernout-M. 554. Walde-H. 1.808 f.

Grk. *λείπω*; Lat. *linquere*, but more usually *relinquere;* Ir. *lēicim;* Lith. *likti* mostly intr. 'remain', *palikti* 'leave', Lett. *likt* mostly 'put, place'; Skt. *ric-*, Av. *(paiti-)rič-*; Arm. *lk'anem;* Goth. *leihwan*, ON *ljā*, etc. 'lend' (11.61).

2. Grk. *λείπω* is also intr. 'be absent, wanting, lacking', and it is this sense that prevails in NT and in NG (*λείπει* 'is missing, lacking'). In the sense of 'leave', its place was taken by *ἀφίημι* 'send forth, let go' (cpd. of *ἵημι* 'let go, throw' 10.25), in NT often 'leave', whence NG *ἀφίνω* (rightly *ἀφήνω*, since), new present formed to aor. *ἄφησα* (Hatzidakis, Μεσ. 1.288).

3. It. *lasciare*, Fr. *laisser*, OSp. *lexar*, Rum. *lăsa*, and with unexplained *d-* (fr. *dare* 'give'?), Sp. *dejar*, Cat. *dexar*, fr. Lat. *laxāre* 'loosen, slacken, relax', deriv. of *laxus* 'slack, loose'. REW 4955.

4. Ir. *foācbat* (3pl.), *fācbaim*, NIr. *fāgaim*, cpd. of *fo-ad-* and *gaibim* 'take, seize' (11.13). Pedersen 2.527 f. Thurneysen, Gram. 512.

W. *gadael*, *gadu*, Corn. *gase* etym.? Loth, RC 37.45.

Br. *lezel*, fr. Fr. *laisser*. Henry 185.

5. Goth. *lētan*, ON *lāta*, Dan. *lade* (*efterlade*, *lade blive*) OE *lǣtan*, ME *lete*, Du. *laten*, OHG *lāzan*, MHG *lāzen*, NHG *lassen* (all also 'let' = 'permit, allow', as Sw. *låta*, NE *let*) : Alb. *lë* 'leave, let', and with secondary meaning *lodh* (trans.) 'tire out', Grk. *ληδεῖν* 'be tired, lazy', cf. Goth. *lats*, ON *latr* 'lazy', IE **lēd-*. Walde-P. 2.395. Falk-Torp. 616 f. Feist 329 f.

ON *leifa*, OE *lǣfan* (also in ON and mostly in OE 'leave as an inheritance after death'), ME *leve*, NE *leave*, OHG *leiben* (but mostly 'leave over', MHG *leiben* 'let remain, spare'), Goth. *bilaibjan* (once *bilaibidans* 'left over'), caus. to root in OE *belīfan*, OHG *bilīban*, etc. 'remain' (12.16).

ON *skilja eptir* (and so reg. in NIcel.) with *eptir* 'after, behind' and *skilja* 'divide, separate' (12.23).

Sw. *lämna* (= Dan. *levne* 'leave over'), with change to trans. sense : ON *lifna*, Goth. *af-lifnan* 'be left' (12.17). Hellquist 607.

6. Lith. *palikti*, above, 1.

Lett. *atstāt*, also intr. 'separate from, give way, yield' (cf. Lith. *atstoti* 'step back, go away'), cpd. of *at-* 'back, again' and *stāt* 'stand up' (12.15).

7. ChSl., SCr. *ostaviti*, Russ. *ostavit'*, Boh. *zůstaviti*, Pol. *zostawić*, caus. formations to ChSl. *ostati*, etc. 'remain, be left' (12.16).

8. Skt. *çiṣ-*, etym. dub. Uhlenbeck 310.

Skt. *ric-*, Av. *(paiti-)rič-*, above, 1.

Skt. *hā-* : Av. *zā-* 'release', Grk. *χῆρος* 'bereft', *χήρα* 'widow', *χῶρος* '(empty) space, place', etc. Walde-P. 1.543.

12.19 QUIET (adj.)

Grk.	*ἥσυχος, ἠρεμαῖος*	Goth.	*rimis* (sb.)	Lith.	*ramus*
NG	*ἥσυχος*	ON	*rōr*	Lett.	*kluss*
Lat.	*quiētus, tranquillus*	Dan.	*rolig* (*stille*)	ChSl.	*tichŭ*
It.	*tranquillo, quieto, cheto*	Sw.	*stilla*	SCr.	*miran, tih*
Fr.	*tranquille*	OE	*rōw, stille*	Boh.	*klidný, tichý, pokojný*
Sp.	*quieto, quedo, tranquilo*	ME	*quyet(e), stille*	Pol.	*spokojny, cichy*
Rum.	*liniştit*	NE	*quiet* (*still*)	Russ.	*spokojnyj, tichij*
Ir.	*sāim*	Du.	*rustig* (*stil*)	Skt.	*çānta-*
NIr.	*suaimhneach, sāmh*	OHG	*ruowa, rāwa* (sbs.), *stilli*	Av.	*rāman-* (sb.)
W.	*llonydd, tawel*	MHG	*ruowic, stille*		
Br.	*sioul*	NHG	*ruhig* (*still*)		

The words listed under 'quiet' may refer to the absence of rapid motion, exertion, noise, or any physical or mental disturbance. They differ somewhat in range and in dominant application. Thus in what is perhaps the most popular use of NE *quiet* (e.g., *be quiet! keep quiet!*) reference to absence of noise is the dominant feeling, though not unmixed. But other uses are common enough, and the basic notion in the large group to which the word belongs, and in several of the others, is a 'state of rest'. Occasional semantic sources are 'even' (through 'calm'), 'peaceful', 'silent', 'orderly', 'obedient', 'weary'.

For one or another of the applications other words may be used in much the same sense, as NE *calm, still, peaceful*, etc.

1. Grk. ἥσυχος, ἡσύχιος, with sb. ἡσυχία, etym. dub., perh. based on a **sē-tu-* (> ἡσυ-), fr. the root **sē-* in Goth. *seiþus*, Lat. *sērus* 'late', Skt. *sāti-* 'conclusion, end', etc. Walde-P. 2.461. Boisacq 330.

Grk. ἠρεμαῖος, ἤρεμος : Goth. *rimis*, etc. (below, 4).

2. Lat. *quiētus* (> It. *quieto, cheto*, Sp. *quieto, quedo*, OFr. *quiete*, ME, NE *quiet*), pple. of *quiēscere*, this fr. sb. *quiēs, -ētis* 'quiet' : OPers. *šiyāti-*, Av. *šāiti-* 'well being', Av. *šyāta-, šāta-* 'happy', ON *hvīla* 'bed', Goth. *hweila*, OE *hwīl*, etc. 'time' (NE *while*), ChSl. vb. *po-čiti*, sb. *po-kojĭ* 'rest', all based on a notion of 'rest'. Here also Lat. *tranquillus* (> It. *tranquillo*, etc.), cpd. with *trāns*, here in its intensive force (cf. the resulting Fr. *très*, also NE *thorough* beside *through*, NHG *durchaus*), and *lo-* suffix. Walde-P. 1.510. Ernout-M. 840 f., 1052 (otherwise on the semantics of *tranquillus*).

Rum. *liniştit*, pple. of *linişti* 'make quiet', with sb. *linişte* 'quiet', fr. *lin* 'still, quiet', this fr. Lat. *lēnis* 'mild'. Tiktin 914.

3. Ir. *sāim*, NIr. *sāmh, sāimhe*, also NIr., Gael. *sāmhach* 'quiet, calm, pleasant', with sb. Ir. *sām*, NIr. *sāmh* 'quiet, rest', perh. through notion of 'evenness' : Skt. *sama-*, Av. *hama-, hāma-* 'equal, same', OE *sōm* 'agreement', etc. Walde-P. 2.492. Stokes 290.

NIr. *suaimhneach*, with sb. *suaimhneas*, etym.? Macbain 350.

W. *llonydd*, through vb. *lloni* 'gladden' fr. *llon* 'glad, cheerful', with development of 'quiet' through 'contented-' (?).

W. *tawel*, fr. *taw* 'silence' (18.23).

Br. *sioul*, etym. dub. Henry 247. Ernault, Glossaire 381.

4. Goth. *rimis* (sb.; adj. not quotable) : Lith. *ramas* 'quiet' (sb. obs.; now *ramumas*), adj. *ramus* 'quiet', *rōmus* 'gentle, mild', *rimti* 'be quiet'. Lett. *rāms* 'mild, calm', Skt. *ram-* 'rest, stay, delight in', Av. *ram-* 'rest, stay', sb. *rāman-* 'quiet'; here also (with prefix *ē-*) Grk. ἠρέμα 'gently, quietly', adj. ἠρεμαῖος, later ἤρεμος 'quiet, gentle'. Walde-P. 2.371 ff. Feist 398.

ON *rō* sb., *rōr* adj., Dan., Sw. *rō* sb., Dan. *rolig* adj. (but Sw. *rolig* 'amusing'), OE *rōw*, sb. and adj., ME *ro* sb., OHG *ruowa, rāwa* sb. (adj. not quotable), MHG *ruo(we)*, NHG *ruhe* sbs., with adjs. MHG *ruowic*, NHG *ruhig* : Grk. ἐρωή 'rest from, cessation', fr. IE **rē-, rō-*, perh. ultimately related to **rem-* in preceding group and **res-* in the following. Walde-P. 1.144 f. Falk-Torp 906.

Du. *rust* sb. ('rest', but esp. 'quiet'), *rustig* adj. : OE *ræst*, OHG *resta* 'rest', Goth. *rasta* 'mile' (as orig. 'resting place'), etc. Walde-P. 1.144. Franck-v. W. 565.

OE, ME *stille*, NE *still*, OHG *stilli*, MHG *stille*, NHG *still*, MLG *stille* (> Dan. *stille*, Sw. *stilla*), Du. *stil*, all orig. 'motionless', but used also for 'quiet, calm, silent', fr. **stel-* in words for 'make stand, put, place' (12.12) beside **stā-* 'stand'. Walde-P. 2.645. Falk-Torp 1167. NED s.v. *still*, adj.

5. Lith. *ramus* : Goth. *rimis*, etc., above, 4.

Lett. *kluss* : *klausīt* 'obey', Lith. *klausyti* 'listen, obey', etc. Mühl.-Endz. 2.216. Leskien, Ablaut 299. Trautmann 308.

6. ChSl. *tichŭ* (Supr. 'mild, calm, quiet'; sb. *tišina* in Gospels for 'calm' of the sea), SCr. *tih*, Boh. *tichý*, Pol. *cichy*, Russ. *tichij*, with primary sense 'calm' fr. 'even' : Lith. *tiesus* 'straight' (12.73). Cf. It. *piano* 'flat' and 'gentle, soft' (of sound, etc.). Pedersen, IF 5.41. Grünenthal, Arch. sl. Ph. 38.138 f. Brückner 61.

SCr. *miran*, orig. 'peaceful', fr. *mir* 'peace, quiet', ChSl. *mirŭ* 'peace', etc. (20.14). Berneker 2.61.

Boh. *klidný*, fr. sb. *klid*, old *kl'ud* 'quiet', beside *klouditi* 'make neat, tidy up', *kloudný* 'neat', Russ. (obs.) *kljud'* 'order, decency', etc., outside root connection dub., but 'quiet' apparently fr. 'orderly, neat'. Berneker 527.

Boh. *pokojný*, Pol. *spokojny*, Russ. *spokojnyj*, fr. sb. seen in ChSl. *pokojĭ* 'rest', beside vb. *po-čiti* 'rest', fr. the same root as Lat. *quiēs*, etc. (above, 2). Berneker 166, 538 f.

7. Skt. *çānta-*, pple. of *çam-* 'be quiet', ultimately the same as *çam-* 'labor, toil' (9.13), with development of 'quiet' fr. 'weary'. Walde-P. 1.387.

Av. *rāman-* (sb.) : Goth. *rimis* (above, 4).

12.21 COLLECT, GATHER

Grk.	*συλλέγω, συνάγω*	Goth.	*(ga)lisan*	Lith.	*rinkti*
NG	*μαζεύω, μαζώνω*	ON	*samna, lesa*	Lett.	*krāt, pulcēt*
Lat.	*colligere*	Dan.	*samle*	ChSl.	*sŭbĭrati*
It.	*radunare, raccogliere*	Sw.	*samla*	SCr.	*sabirati, sakupljati*
Fr.	*(r)assembler, recueillir*	OE	*gaderian, samnian, lesan*	Boh.	*sbírati, shromážditi*
Sp.	*juntar, recoger*	ME	*gader(e), samne*	Pol.	*zbierać, zgromadzić*
Rum.	*aduna, culege*	NE	*collect, gather*	Russ.	*sobirat'*
Ir.	*tinōlaim, tecmallaim*	Du.	*verzamelen*	Skt.	*sam-ci-*
NIr.	*bailighim, cruinnighim*	OHG	*samanōn, lesan*	Av.	*(han-či-)*
W.	*casglu, cynnull*	MHG	*samenen, lesen*		
Br.	*dastumi, kuntuilh*	NHG	*sammeln (lesen)*		

Several of the words for 'collect' belong to inherited groups from roots with prevailing sense of 'collect' or 'select'. Others are from such notions as 'bring (together)', 'join, unite', 'pile up', with a number of derivatives of words for 'together' or 'heap', 'mass', 'crowd', etc.

1. Grk. συλλέγω, Lat. *colligere*, cpds. of συν-, *con-* 'with, together' and λέγω, *legere* 'pick out, choose, select' (both also 'collect' but more usually the cpds. in this sense) : Alb. *mbleth* (i.e. *mb-leth*) 'collect, harvest', IE **leĝ-*. Walde-P. 2.422. Ernout-M. 535 f. Walde-H. 1.780.

Grk. συνάγω, cpd. of ἄγω 'lead, bring'.

NG μαζεύω, μαζώνω, fr. μαζί 'together', this orig. μαζίον dim. of Grk. μᾶζα 'barley-cake' in its late sense of 'lump, mass' (hence Lat. *massa*, NE *mass*, etc.). Hatzidakis, Μεσ. 1.117 ff.

2. Lat. *colligere* (above, 1) > Rum. *culege* (It. *cogliere*, Fr. *cueillir*, Sp. *coger* mostly in more specialized uses); Lat. *re-colligere* > It. *raccogliere* (blend with *accogliere* fr. **ad-colligere*), Fr. *recueillir*, Sp. *recoger*. REW 2048, 7127.

It. *radunare*, cpd. of *adunare* 'assemble' = Rum. *aduna* 'collect', fr. Lat. *adūnare* 'unite'. REW 209.

Fr. *rassembler*, fr. *assembler* 'assemble', MLat. *adsimulāre* fr. Lat. *simul* 'together'. REW 731. Gamillscheg 53. Wartburg 1.159 f.

Sp. *juntar*, also and orig. 'join' (12.22).

3. MIr. *tinōlaim* (OIr. 3sg. *do-in-ola* Ml. 25b3 but gl. *adplicat*), fr. **to-in-od-el-*, beside MIr. *tecmallaim* (OIr. 3sg. *do-ec-malla* Wb. 9d5), fr. **to-in-com-el-*, cpds. of the root *el-* seen in supplementary forms of the vb. 'go', as W. 3sg. subj. *el*, etc. (see 10.47). Pedersen 2.510, 511.

NIr. *bailighim*, fr. Ir. *bailighim* 'I husband' (K. Meyer, Contrib. 167), cf. NIr. *bailech* 'thrifty', Ir. *bailech* 'prosperous, successful' (op. cit.), prob. fr. Ir. *bail* 'excellence, prosperity, success'.

NIr. *cruinnighim*, fr. *cruinn* 'round', also used in sense 'assembled, gathered up'. Cf. NE *round up* (e.g. cattle) = 'collect'.

W. *casglu*, also *clasgu* : Br. *klaskout* 'seek' (11.31).

W. *cynnull*, Br. *kuntuilh*, Corn. *cuntell*, with sbs. OCorn. *cuntellet*, Ir. *comthinōl* 'assembly', cpd. of the same root as in Ir. *tinōlaim*, etc. (above). Pedersen 2.511 (without the Britannic words). Ernault, Glossaire 138.

Br. *dastumi*, cpd. of *das-* (iter. prefix), second part perh. : Ir. *tomm* 'little hill', W. *tom* 'mound, dung heap', Grk. τύμβος 'mound', etc. Stokes 135. Henry 90. Ernault, Glossaire 146 f.

4. Goth. *(ga)lisan*, ON *lesa*, OE *lesan*, OHG *lesan*, MHG, NHG *lesen* : Lith. *lesti* 'pick up (grains with the beak)', *aplasyti* 'pick out, separate'. Walde-P. 2.440. Falk-Torp 677.

ON *samna*, OE *samnian*, ME *samne*, OHG *samanōn*, MHG *samenen*, hence by dissimilatory change of suffix, Dan. *samle*, Sw. *samla* (also cpds. *indsamle, insamla*), Du. *verzamelen* (*zamelen* rare), MHG *samelen*, NHG *(ver)sammeln* : ON *saman*, OE *samen*, OHG *saman* 'together', Grk. ἅμα, Lat. *simul* id., etc. Falk-Torp 949.

OE *gaderian, gædrian*, ME *gader(e)*, NE *gather* : OFris. *gadia* 'unite', OHG *begatōn*, MHG *gaten* 'come together', OE *(ge)gada* 'companion, spouse' (NHG *gatte*), ChSl. *godŭ* '(fitting) time', etc. Walde-P. 1.531 f. Falk-Torp. 312.

NE *collect*, fr. pass. pple. of Lat. *colligere*. NED s.v.

5. Lith. *rinkti*, fr. the root which appears also in the Balto-Slavic word for 'hand', Lith. *ranka*, ChSl. *rąka*, etc. (4.33), perh. also Ir. *comrac* 'meeting, battle', W. *cyfranc* 'meeting'. Walde-P. 2.373.

Lett. *krāt* : Lith. *krauti*, Lett. *kraustīt* 'heap up', Lith. *kropti*, Lett. *krāpt*, ChSl. *krasti* 'steal', all fr. **krāu-* and **krā-* with extensions. Walde-P. 1.477.

Lett. *pulcēt, pulcināt* (also cpds. *sapulcēt, -pulcināt*), deriv. of *pulks* 'host, crowd' (13.19). Mühl.-Endz. 3.407.

6. ChSl. *sŭbĭrati*, SCr. *sabirati*, etc., general Slavic : Grk. φέρω, etc. 'carry' (10.61). Berneker 51, 57.

SCr. *sakupljati, skupljati*, also simply *kupiti, skupiti* (these usually 'pile up') : ChSl. *sŭ-kupiti* 'bring together' Russ. *skupit'*, Pol. *(s)kupić* 'heap up', derivs. of ChSl. *kupŭ* 'heap', etc. (: OE *hēap*, OHG *huof*, 'heap', etc.). Berneker 646.

Boh. *shromážditi*, Pol. *zgromadzić*, cpds. of Boh. *hromažditi*, Pol. *gromadzić* 'heap up' = Russ. *gromozdit'* 'pile up', etc. beside Russ.-ChSl. *gromada* 'a heap' : Skt. *grāma-* 'heap, crowd, community', etc., IE **grem-*, extension of **ger-* in Grk. ἀγείρω 'assemble'. Walde-P. 1.590 f. Berneker 345.

7. Skt. *sam-ci-* and other cpds. of *ci-* 'pile up, arrange' (sometimes also 'collect') : Av. *či-* 'select', *vī-či-* 'separate, distinguish', *han-či-* once 'take together' (paces in walking; Barth. 441), NPers. *čīdan* 'collect', ChSl. *činiti* 'arrange', Grk. ποι(ϝ)έω (fr. *ποι-ϝο-ς) 'construct, make', IE **kʷei-*. Walde-P. 1.509 f.

12.22 JOIN, UNITE

Grk.	*ζεύγνῡμι, συνάπτω*	Goth.	*gawidan*	Lith.	*sujungti, suvienyti*
NG	*ἑνώνω (συνάπτω)*	ON	*samtengja, samlaga*	Lett.	*salikt, savienuōt*
Lat.	*iungere*	Dan.	*forbinde, forene, føie*	ChSl.	*sŭčetati*
It.	*congiungere, unire*	Sw.	*förbinda, förena, foga*	SCr.	*sastaviti, spojiti*
Fr.	*joindre, unir*	OE	*(ge)fēgan, gesamnian*	Boh.	*spojiti, sloučiti*
Sp.	*juntar, unir*	ME	*ioigne, feien, unyte*	Pol.	*złączyć, spoić, kojarzyć*
Rum.	*împreuna, uni*	NE	*join, unite*	Russ.	*soedinit', sovokupit'*
Ir.	*adcomla* (3sg)	Du.	*voegen, vereenigen, verbinden*	Skt.	*yuj-*
NIr.	*ceanglaim*	OHG	*fuogen, giwetan*	Av.	*yuǰ-*
W.	*cysylltu, cydio*	MHG	*vuegen, verbinden, vereinigen*		
Br.	*staga kevret, unani*	NHG	*verbinden, fügen, vereinigen*		

Apart from the inherited group, words for 'join, unite' are most frequently connected with those for 'bind' or 'fasten', or with those for 'one'.

1. IE **yeug-* 'join', already in the IE period applied esp. to the yoking-together of beasts of burden or hitching them to a vehicle. This use is reflected in all the older derivs. beside the more general sense of 'join'. IE **yeug-* is probably an extension of the simple root **yeu-* in Skt. *yuvati, yāuti* 'harnesses, yokes, binds', Av. *yu-* 'attend to, be occupied with', etc. Walde-P. 1.201f. Ernout-M. 501 ff. Walde-H. 1.730.

Grk. ζεύγνῡμι; Lat. *iungere* (> Fr. *joindre*, but It. *giungere* 'arrive', Sp. *uñcir* 'yoke together', deriv. Sp. *junta* 'union' whence *juntar* 'join', REW 4620), Lat. *coniungere* (> It. *congiungere*); Lith. *sujungti* (simple *jungti* mostly 'yoke, harness'); Skt. *yuj-*, Av. *yuǰ-*.

2. Grk. συνάπτω, cpd. of ἅπτω, ἅπτομαι 'fasten, grasp, touch', beside ἁφή 'touch' (15.71).

Grk. ἑνόω, NG ἑνώνω 'unite', fr. stem of εἷς, ἑνός 'one'.

3. It. *unire*, Fr., Sp. *unir*, Rum. *uni*, fr. late (and rare) Lat. *ūnīre*, fr. *ūnus* 'one'. REW 9073a.

Rum. *împreuna*, fr. adv. *împreuna* 'together', this fr. Lat. phrase *in-per-ūnam*. Tiktin 769.

4. Ir. *adcomla* (3sg.), cpd. of *ad-com-* and the same root *el-* as in *tinōlaim* 'collect' (see 12.21). Pedersen 2.509.

NIr. *ceanglaim*, also and orig. 'bind', see 9.16.

W. *cydio*, fr. *cyd* adj. 'common, united' (sb. 'junction, joint') : Br. *ket-* 'con-', etym.? Pedersen 2.213. Morris Jones 264.

W. *cysylltu*, fr. *cyswllt* 'junction, joint', fr. Lat. *consolidāre* 'make solid, confirm'. Loth, Mots. Lat. 158.

Br. *staga kevret*, lit. 'bind together' (*staga* 'bind', 9.16), apparently the only popular term.

Br. *unani* 'unite' fr. *unan* 'one'.

5. Goth. *gawidan* (συζεύγνυμι Mk. 10.9), OHG *giwetan* 'bind, yoke', cf. Goth. *gawiss* 'bond', *diswiss* 'ἀνάλυσις, departure', OHG *wadal*, OE *wǣlla* 'bandage' : Ir. *fedan* 'yoke (of animals), harness', W. *gwedd* 'yoke, team', Skt. *vīvadha-* 'shoulder-yoke for carrying burdens'. Walde-P. 1.256. Feist 211 f.

ON *samtengja*, cpd. of *tengja* 'bind, tie together'.

ON *samlaga*, fr. *samlag* 'partnership, union', lit. 'a lying together'.

OE *(ge)fēgan*, early ME *feȝen*, *feien*, Du. *voegen*, OHG *fuogen*, MHG *vüegen*, NHG *fügen* (esp. cpd. *zusammenfügen*), MLG *vōgen* (> Dan. *føie*, Sw. *foga*): Grk. πήγνῡμι 'make fast, solid, fix', Lat. *pangere* 'fix in, fix, settle', Skt. *pāçaya-* 'bind', Av. *pas-* 'fasten, fetter together', IE **pāk-*, **pāg-*. Walde-P. 2.2 f. Falk-Torp 290.

OE *gesamnian*, also 'collect, gather' like the simple *samnian* (12.21).

MLG *vorbinden* (> Dan. *forbinde*, Sw. *förbinda*), Du., MHG, NHG *verbinden*, cpds. of *binden* 'bind, tie'. Falk-Torp 253.

MLG *vorēnigen* (hence by semantic borrowing Dan. *forene*, Sw. *förena*), Du. *vereenigen*, MHG, NHG *vereinigen* 'unite', fr. word for 'one'.

ME *ioigne*, *ioyne*, etc., NE *join* fr. OFr. *joign-* in old forms of *joindre* (above, 1). NED s.v. *join*, vb.[1].

NE *unite*, late ME *unyte*, fr. Lat. pass. pple. of *ūnīre* (above, 3).

6. Lith. *sujungti*, above 1.

Lith. *suvienyti*, Lett. *savienuōt*, fr. Lith. *vienas*, Lett. *viens* 'one'.

Lett. *salikt*, cpd. of *likt* 'set by, leave' (cf. *kuopā likt* 'join together' with loc. sg. of *kuopa* 'heap' in sense 'together') : Lith. *likti* 'leave', etc. Mühl.-Endz. 2.468, 3.671.

7. ChSl. *sŭčetati* : SCr.-ChSl. *četa* 'procession, crowd', Russ. *četa* 'pair, couple', Lat. *caterva* 'crowd, troop', Umbr. *kateramu* 'congregamini'. Walde-P. 1.383. Berneker 152 f.

SCr. *sastaviti*, lit. 'put together', cpd. of *staviti* 'place, put' (12.12).

SCr., Boh. *spojiti*, Pol. *spoić*, *spajać*, cpds. of simple vb. seen in Boh. *pojiti* 'bind', Russ. *pajat'* 'solder', etc., outside connections? Brückner 426.

Boh. *sloučiti*, Pol. *złączyć*, cpds. of Boh. *loučiti* 'join' and 'separate', Pol. *łączyć* 'join', ChSl. *lǫčiti* 'separate', see 12.23.

Pol. *kojarzyć*, cpd. with prefix *ko-* (of uncertain orig.) and last member : *jarzmo* 'yoke', ChSl. *jarĭmŭ* id. Berneker 31,532. Brückner 199.

Russ. *soedinit'*, fr. *edinyj* 'one, sole, only'.

Russ. *sovokupit'*, borrowed fr. ChSl. *sŭvŭkupiti* beside *sŭkupiti* 'bring together', fr. *kupŭ* 'heap'. Berneker 646.

8. Skt. *yuj-*, Av. *yuǰ-*, above 1.

12.23 SEPARATE (vb.)

Grk.	χωρίζω, σχίζω	Goth.	*(af)skaidan*	Lith.	*skirti (skiesti)*
NG	(ξε)χωρίζω	ON	*skilja*	Lett.	*šk'irt*
Lat.	*sēparāre, dīvidere, sēiungere*	Dan.	*(ad)skille*	ChSl.	*(raz)lǫčiti*
It.	*separare*	Sw.	*skilja*	SCr.	*rastaviti, razdvojiti, (raz)lučiti*
Fr.	*séparer*	OE	*sc(e)ādan, scylian*	Boh.	*odděliti, odloučiti*
Sp.	*separar*	ME	*schede, schille, separate*	Pol.	*rozłączyć, rozdzielić*
Rum.	*despărţi, separa*	NE	*separate*	Russ.	*otdelit', razlučit'*
Ir.	*scaraim*	Du.	*scheiden*	Skt.	*vi-yuj-*
NIr.	*scaraim*	OHG	*(ar)sceidan, -trennen*	Av.	. . . .
W.	*gwahanu*	MHG	*scheiden, trennen*		
Br.	*dispartia*	NHG	*scheiden, trennen*		

Verbs for 'separate' are mostly from various inherited roots with the notion of 'cut', 'split', etc., but several are formed with disjunctive prefixes from words for 'join' or 'put, place'.

1. Grk. χωρίζω, NG ξεχωρίζω (ξε- fr. ἐξ-ε- in augmented forms), fr. χωρίς 'separately, apart' : χῶρος (empty) space, place, country', χῆρος 'bereft', Skt. *hā-* 'leave, abandon', etc. Walde-P. 1.543. Boisacq 1059.

Grk. σχίζω 'split' (9.27), also 'separate' : Goth. *skaidan*, etc. 'separate' (below, 4), Lith. *skiesti* 'separate', Lat. *scindere* 'split, rend, tear', Skt. *chid-* 'cut (off), tear, bite, divide', etc., all fr. parallel *-t-* and *-d-* extensions of the root **skei-* seen in Skt. *chyati* 'cuts off', Ir. *scian* 'knife', etc. Walde-P. 2.54 ff. Ernout-M. 906. Feist 427.

2. Lat. *sēparāre* (> lit. loanwords It. *separare*, Fr. *séparer*, Sp. *separar*, Rum. *separa;* VLat. **sēperāre* > OFr. *sevrer* > ME, NE *sever*), cpd. of *sē-* 'apart' and *parāre* 'prepare, get' (11.16). Ernout-M. 785. REW 7826.

Lat. *dīvidere*, cpd. *dis-* and **videre* (not found as simplex) : Umbr. *vetu* 'dividito', *vef* 'partis', Skt. *vidh-* 'pierce, perforate'. Walde-P. 1.239. Ernout-M. 274.

Lat. *sēiungere*, *disiungere* (> OFr. *desjoindre*, Fr. *dé-* or *dis-joindre*, NE *disjoin*, etc.), neg. cpds. of *iungere* 'join' (12.16).

Rum. *despărţi* fr. VLat. **dispartīre* (> Fr. *départir* 'leave' etc.), for Lat. *dispertīre* 'distribute, divide', cpd. of *partīre* 'share, divide', fr. *pars* 'part'. REW 2679. Puşcariu 523.

3. Ir. *scaraim* : W. *ysgar* 'to part', sb. 'divorce', ON *skera*, OE *sceran*, etc. 'cut, shear', Lith. *skirti*, Lett. *šk'irt* 'separate', Grk. κείρω 'cut off, shear', etc., IE **(s)ker-* 'cut'. Walde-P. 2.575.

W. *gwahanu*, fr. *gwahan* 'separation, separate', cpd. of *gwa-* 'sub-' (= Ir. *fo* : Grk. ὑπό, etc.) and OW *han* gl. 'alium' (W. *han-* as prefix) : Ir. *sain* 'different, special', Lat. *sine* 'without', OE *sundor* 'apart, special', etc. Walde-P. 2.495. Pedersen 1.138, 2.661.

Br. *dispartia*, prob. through OFr., fr. VLat. **dispartīre* (above, 2).

4. Goth. *(af)skaidan*, OE *sc(e)ādan*, ME *schede*, *schode* (NE *shed*), OHG *(ar)-sceidan*, Du., MHG, NHG *scheiden* : Grk. σχίζω, etc. (above, 1).

ON, Sw. *skilja*, Dan. *(ad)skille;* OE *scylian*, ME *skilen*, *schille* (more probably Norse loanwords than cognates) : Lith. *skelti*, NIr. *scoiltim* 'split' (9.27). Walde-P. 2.592. Falk-Torp 994. NED s.vv. *shill*, vb.[2], and *skill*, vb.

ME, NE *separate*, deriv. of pass. pple. of Lat. *sēparāre* (above, 2).

MHG, NHG *trennen*, OHG *-trennen* only in cpds., prob. caus. to MHG *trinnen* (NHG *entrinnen* = *ent-trinnen*) 'separate oneself from, run away' : Goth.

dis-tairan 'tear to pieces', Grk. δέρω 'flay', etc. Walde-P. 1.798. Weigand-H. 2.1067.

5. Lith. *skirti*, Lett. *šk'irt* : Ir. *scaraim*, etc. (above, 3).

Lith. *skiesti* : Grk. σχίζω (above, 1).

6. ChSl. *lǫčiti*, *razlǫčiti* (in Gospels cpd.), SCr. *(raz)lučiti*, Boh. *od-*, *rozloučiti*, Pol. *roz-*, *od-łączyć*, Russ. *razlučit'*, beside Boh. *loučiti* 'join' and 'separate', Pol. *łączyć* 'join' : Lith. *lenkti*, ChSl. *-lęšti*, *-lęką* 'bend', with divergent development in Slavic to 'join' or 'separate', mostly distinguished by prefixes. Walde-P. 2.435. Berneker 738, 707.

SCr. *rastaviti* (**raz-staviti*), lit. 'set apart', cpd. of *staviti* 'put, set, place' (12.12).

SCr. *razdvojiti*, cpd. of *dvojiti* 'divide in two', fr. *dvoj*, collective form of *dva* 'two'. Berneker 247.

Boh. *od-*, *roz-děliti*, Pol. *roz-*, *od-dzielić*, Russ. *ot-delit'*, cpds. of ChSl. *děliti*, etc. 'divide', fr. *dělu* 'part, portion' etc. Berneker 195.

7. Skt. *vi-yuj-*, cpd. of *vi-* 'apart' and *yuj-* 'join' (12.16).

12.232. 'Divide' is simply 'separate into parts', and so may be covered, in part, by forms in 12.23. So notably Lat. *dīvidere*, whence It. *dividere*, Sp. *dividir*, ME *devide*, NE *divide;* Fr. *diviser* (> Rum. *diviza*), formed fr. the pple. *dīvīsus*.

But this notion is more distinctively expressed by derivs. of words for 'part' (13.23). Thus Grk., NG (δια)μερίζω; Lat. *partīre* (or *-īrī*), It. *(s)partire*, OFr. *partir* (whence sb. *partage* and new vb. *partager; partir* now 'depart'), Sp. *partir*, Rum. *împarţi;* Ir. *rannaim*, NIr. *roinnim*, W. *rhannu*, Br. *ranna*, *kevrenni;* Goth. *dailjan* (or cpds.), OE *dǣlan* (NE *deal* now mostly of cards), OHG *teilan*, etc., general Gmc.; Lith. *dalinti*, Lett. *dalīt;* ChSl. *(raz)děliti*, etc., general Slavic.

Dividing into parts is often for the purpose of giving away the parts, distributing them; and this notion is strong or sometimes dominant in such verbs. Conversely, the notion of separation may become dominant as in the history of Fr. *partir* and NE *part* (NED s.v. *part*, vb. 4 vs. 1).

12.24 OPEN (vb.)

Grk.	ἀνοίγω, ἀνοιγνῦμι	Goth.	*uslūkan*	Lith.	*atidaryti, atverti*
NG	ἀνοίγω	ON	*opna, lūka up*	Lett.	*atvērt, atdarit*
Lat.	*aperīre*	Dan.	*aabne, lukke op*	ChSl.	*otŭvrěsti, otvoriti*
It.	*aprire*	Sw.	*öppna*	SCr.	*otvoriti*
Fr.	*ouvrir*	OE	*openian*	Boh.	*otevříti*
Sp.	*abrir*	ME	*opene*	Pol.	*otworzyć*
Rum.	*deschide*	NE	*open*	Russ.	*otkryt', otvorit'*
Ir.	*asoilci* (3sg.), *oslaicim*	Du.	*openen*	Skt.	*apa-vṛ*
NIr.	*(f)osclaim*	OHG	*offanōn, antlūhhan*	Av.	. . . .
W.	*agor(i)*	MHG	*offenen, entlūchen*		
Br.	*digeri*	NHG	*öffnen, aufmachen*		

Apart from other sources, many of the verbs for 'open' are formed as opposites from those for 'shut, close' (11.25).

1. Derivs. of IE **wer-* 'cover, shut'. Walde-P. 1.280 ff. Ernout-M. 59 f. (with some doubt, and mention of other possibilities in the analysis of the Latin and Slavic forms). Walde-H. 1.56 ff. Brückner 633 f.

Lat. *aperīre* (> It. *aprire*, Fr. *ouvrir*, Sp. *abrir*), fr. **ap-verīre* (beside *operīre* 'shut' fr. **op-verīre*); Lith. *atverti* (beside *užverti* 'shut', *verti* 'open or shut'), Lett. *atvērt;* ChSl. (*vrěti* 'shut'), *otvoriti*, SCr. *otvoriti*, Boh. *otevříti*, Pol. *otworzyć*, Russ. *otvorit';* Skt. *apa-* (or *apā-*) *vṛ-*, *vi-vṛ-*, etc. (simple *vṛ-* mostly 'cover').

2. Grk. οἴγω, οἴγνῡμι, but more usually cpds. ἀνοίγω, ἀνοίγνῡμι, also διοίγω, διοίγνῡμι, perh. as 'cause to give way', from **ὀϝειγ-* : Skt. *vij-* 'recoil, flee from', ON *vīkja* 'turn, move, recede', OE *wīcan* 'yield, give way', etc., fr. IE **weig-* beside **weik-* in Grk. εἴκω 'yield'. Walde-P. 1.234. Boisacq 688. Falk-Torp 1376 f.

3. Rum. *deschide*, fr. Lat. *disclūdere* 'keep apart, separate', cpd. of *claudere* 'shut' (12.25). Tiktin 525 f. Puşcariu 509.

4. Ir. *asoilci* (3sg.), MIr. *oslaicim*, NIr. *(f)osclaim*, fr. **od-ess-lēic-;* Ir. *arosailcim*, fr. **air-od-ess-lēic-*, cpds. of Ir. *lēicim* 'leave, let, permit' (12.18). Pedersen 2.563 f.

W. *agor(i)*, Br. *digeri* (with substitution of neg. pref. *di-*), fr. the same root as Ir. *eochair*, W. *agoriad* 'key', outside connections? See 7.24.

5. Goth. *uslūkan*, ON *lūka up*, Dan. *lukke op*, OHG *antlūhhan*, MHG *entlūchen* : Goth. *ga-lūkan*, ON *lūka* 'shut, etc.' (12.25).

ON *opna*, OE *openian*, OHG *offanōn*, etc., general Gmc. (except Goth.) fr. the adjs., ON *opinn*, etc. 'open', Gmc. **upena*, **upana*, prob. : ON *upp*, etc. 'up', hence 'open' fr. 'turned up' (cf. ON *opinn* 'lying on one's back', i.e. 'face up'). Falk-Torp 2.

NHG *aufmachen*, lit. 'put up', hence through 'raise' (the window, the cover, etc.) to 'open', opp. to *zumachen* 'shut'. Paul, Deutsches Wtb. 37, col. 2 (on *auf* = *offen*).

6. Lith. *atidaryti*, Lett. *atdarit*, cpd. of *ati*, *at* 'from, back' and *daryti*, *darit* 'do, make'.

Lith. *atverti*, Lett. *atvērt*, above, 1.

7. ChSl. *otŭvrěsti*, cpd. of *otŭ* (: Lith. *ati*, above) and *-vrěsti* in *povrěsti* 'bind', cf. SCr. *otvrsti se* 'free oneself from', Slov. *vrzeti* 'stand open', etc., fr. *werĝh-*, extension of IE **wer-* 'turn, bind'. Walde-P. 1.273. Trautmann 355.

ChSl. *otvoriti*, etc., above, 1.

Russ. *otkryt'* (= SCr. *otkryti* 'uncover', etc.), cpd. of *kryt'* 'cover' (12.26).

8. Skt. *apā-vṛ-*, *vi-vṛ-*, above, 1.

12.25 SHUT, CLOSE (vb.)

Grk.	κλείω	Goth.	*galūkan*	Lith.	*uždaryti, užverti*
NG	κλείνω	ON	*lūka, lykja*	Lett.	*slēgt, aizdarit, aizvērt*
Lat.	*claudere, operīre*	Dan.	*(til)lukke*	ChSl.	*zatvoriti, zaklenąti, (za)vrěti, (za)kljųčiti*
It.	*chiudere, serrare*	Sw.	*stänga*		
Fr.	*fermer*	OE	*(be)lūcan, (be)clȳsan*		
Sp.	*cerrar*	ME	*shutte, shette, close*		
Rum.	*închide*	NE	*shut, close*	SCr.	*zatvoriti*
Ir.	*iadaim, dūnaim*	Du.	*sluiten, dichtmaken*	Boh.	*zavříti*
NIr.	*dūnaim, druidim*	OHG	*sliozan, bilūhhan*	Pol.	*zamknąć, zawrzeć*
W.	*cau*	MHG	*sliezen, (be)lūchen*	Russ.	*zakryt', zatvorit'*
Br.	*serra, prenna*	NHG	*schliessen, zumachen*	Skt.	*(a)pidhā-*
				Av.	. . . .

Some of the common verbs for 'shut, close' meant orig. 'lock', that is 'fasten shut' (by means of bar, bolt, lock and key, etc.), so especially the inherited group (below, 1).

1. Derivs. of IE **klāu-*, **klāwi-*, denoting the (wooden) 'peg' or primitive 'key', as Grk. κλῄς, κλείς, Lat. *clāvis*, ChSl. *ključĭ* 'key', Lat. *clāvus*, Ir. *clō* 'nail', etc. (cf. 'key' 7.24). Walde-P.

1.492 f. Ernout-M. 194 f. Walde-H. 1.229 f. Berneker 526, 528 f.

Grk. κλείω, NG κλείνω; Lat. claudere (> It. chiudere, arch. Fr. clore; Lat. includere 'shut in' > Rum. închide); ChSl. (za)ključiti; with initial s- (sl- fr. *skl-), OHG sliozan, MHG sliezen, NHG schliessen, Du. sluiten (beside OHG sluzzil, etc. 'key'); cf. Lith. kliuti 'hook, grapple, hinder'.

2. Lat. operīre, but chiefly 'cover': aperīre 'open' (12.24).

It. serrare, Sp. cerrar (Fr. serrer 'keep shut, hold tight, squeeze'), fr. VLat. serrāre for late Lat. serāre, fr. sera 'bar, bolt, lock' (7.23). Ernout-M. 927. REW 7867.

Fr. fermer, fr. Lat. firmāre 'make firm, fast' (firmus 'strong, firm'). REW 3318.

3. Ir. iadaim, perh. fr. a cpd. *epi-dhē-, with IE *dhē- 'place, put', cf. Grk. ἐπι-τίθημι 'lay, put on'. Pedersen 2.551, 653. Stokes 328.

MIr., NIr. dúnaim, fr. dún 'fortress, castle', either through the sense 'enclosure' (cf. W. cau, below) or through 'fortify, barricade'.

NIr. druidim, fr. Ir. druit 'close, firm, trustworthy', etym. disputed. Walde-P. 1.806. Osthoff, Parerga 132 f.

W. cau, MW caeu, fr. cae 'enclosure, field, fence, hedge' (: OE hecg, NE hedge, etc., Walde-P. 1.337).

Br. serra, fr. OFr. serrer : It. serrare, etc. (above, 2).

Br. prenna, orig. 'bar, bolt (a door)', fr. prenn 'wood', esp. 'wooden bar'.

4. Goth. galūkan, ON lūka, OE (be)lūcan, ME luke, OHG bilūhhan, MHG (be)lūchen; Dan. lukke, ODan. lykke (= ON lykja mostly with prep. 'shut in, enclose, etc.'); beside sbs. for 'lock' ON loka, OE loc, etc. (7.23), all possibly (with semantic development 'bend' > 'shut') : ON lykna 'bend the knees', Grk. λυγίζω 'bend, turn, wind', etc.

Walde-P. 2.414. Falk-Torp 661. Feist 189 f.

Sw. stänga = Dan. stænge, ON stengja 'bar (a door), lock with a bar', fr. ON stong, etc. 'pole, bar'. Falk-Torp 1196. Hellquist 1106.

OE (be)clŷsan, fr. clūs(e), fr. Lat. clūsa, clausa 'an enclosed place' : claudere 'shut'. Hence early ME cluse(n), but replaced by ME, NE close, fr. OFr. clos- stem of clore fr. Lat. claudere (above, 1). NED s.v. close, vb.

ME shette, shutte, NE shut, earlier and OE (scyttan) 'shoot a bolt into place' (so as to lock a door) : OE scēotan, ON skjōta, etc. 'shoot, move quickly'. NED s.v. shut, vb.

OHG sliozan, etc., above, 1.

Du. dichtmaken, dichtdoen, lit. 'make tight'.

NHG zumachen, lit. 'make to', cf. aufmachen 'open' (12.24).

5. Lith. uždaryti, Lett. aizdarīt, cpd. of Lith. už-, Lett. aiz- 'behind, back' and daryti, darīt 'do, make'.

Lith. užverti, Lett. aizvērt, cpds. of už-, aiz- (above), opposed to Lith. ativerti, Lett. at-vērt 'open' (12.24).

Lett. slēgt = Lith. slėgti 'press' : Lith. sloga 'pressure, weight', Lett. sluogs 'weight (used for pressing down)', sloudzīt 'press, weigh down', etc., outside connections dub. Walde-P. 2.714. Mühl.-Endz. 3.928.

6. ChSl. zatvoriti (= κλείω Mt. 6.6 etc., reg. opp. to otŭvrěsti 'open', cf. Jagić, Entstehungsgesch. 375), SCr. zatvoriti, Russ. zatvorit', cpds. of Slavic za- 'back, behind' and tvoriti 'make' (9.11). Cf. NHG zumachen. Perh. also influenced by otvoriti 'open', felt as o-tvoriti instead of ot-voriti.

ChSl. zaklenąti, aor. zaklepe (mostly κατακλείω, but zaklepe sę = ἐκλείσθη Lk. 4.25, cf. Jagić, op. cit. 346), orig. for the sound of closing (a door, etc.) : klepati

---

'signify' (by making a sound), Russ. klepat' 'pound, clap, sound', etc., all of imitative origin. Berneker 512.

ChSl. (za)vrěti, Boh. zavříti, Pol. zawrzeć : ChSl., SCr. otvoriti, Boh. otevříti 'open', etc. (12.24).

ChSl. (za)ključiti, above, 1.

Pol. zamknąć (= Boh. zamknouti, Russ. zamknut' 'lock up' cpd. of Pol.

mknąć 'shove' (esp. in pomknąc) : ChSl. mŭknąti sę 'transire', etc., Skt. muc- 'let go, release, free', Lith. mukti 'run away, escape', etc. Brückner 339. Miklosich 206 f.

Russ. zakryt', cpd. of kryt' 'cover' (12.21). Cf. otkryt' 'open' (12.17).

7. Skt. apidhā-, usually pi-dhā-, cpd. of api- 'at, in' and dhā- 'put, place'.

12.26 COVER (vb.)

Grk.	καλύπτω, σκεπάζω, στέγω	Goth.	(ga)huljan	Lith.	dengti, (už)kloti
NG	σκεπάζω	ON	þekja, hylja	Lett.	segt, (ap)klāt
Lat.	tegere, operire	Dan.	dække	ChSl.	pokryti
It.	coprire	Sw.	täcke	SCr.	pokriti
Fr.	couvrir	OE	þeccan, wrēon	Boh.	(po)krýti
Sp.	cubrir	ME	couere	Pol.	pokryć
Rum.	acoperi	NE	cover	Russ.	(po)kryt'
Ir.	tuigiur, fortugim	Du.	dekken	Skt.	vṛ-, chad-, sthag-
NIr.	clúduighim	OHG	decchen, (be)hullan	Av.	var-
W.	gorchuddio, toi	MHG	decken, (be)hüllen		
Br.	golei	NHG	decken		

1. IE *(s)teg- most widespread in sense of 'cover with a roof, roof, thatch' and in nouns for roof (7.28). Walde-P. 2.620 f. Ernout-M. 1020. Falk-Torp 1241. Pedersen 2.654 f.

Grk. στέγω 'cover' (but mostly in special senses, as 'shelter, protect' and esp. 'keep out water', whence 'hold water'); Lat. tegere (and esp. cpd. contegere); Ir. tuigiur (and esp. cpd. fortugim), Ir. toi (but chiefly 'roof, thatch'); ON þekja, Sw. täcke, OE þeccan (NE thatch), MLG decken (> Dan. dække), Du. dekken, OHG decchen, decken, MHG, NHG decken; Skt. sthag- (Dhātup.), caus. sthagaya- 'cover', but also 'conceal, hide'; Lith. stėgti 'roof (a house, etc.)'.

2. Grk. καλύπτω : Goth. huljan 'cover' (below, 5), Lat. occulere, cēlāre, OE helan, etc. 'hide' (12.27). Walde-P. 1.432. Boisacq 400.

Grk. σκεπάω, σκεπάζω, beside σκέπας, σκεπή 'shelter, cover', prob. : Lith. kepurė, Lett. cepure 'cap', Russ., Boh. čepec

'hood'. Walde-P. 2.559. Boisacq 873. Berneker 143 f.

3. Lat. tegere, above, 1.

Lat. operīre 'shut' (12.23) and 'cover', cpd. cooperīre, cōperīre (> It. coprire, OFr. covrir Fr. couvrir, Sp. cubrir, Rum. coperi, usually deriv. acoperi. REW 2205.

4. Ir. tuigiur, fortugim, W. toi, above, 1.

NIr. clúduighim 'cover, clothe', prob. fr. NE clothe. Macbain 90.

W. gorchuddio, cpd. of gor- 'over' and cuddio 'hide' (12.27).

Br. golei, older goloi, beside golo 'covering', W. (arch.) golo 'burial', vb. golo 'cover, bury' : Ir. fo-lug- in fullugaimm 'hide' (12.27), caus. to Ir. laigim 'lie'. Pedersen 1.97, 2.573.

5. Goth. (ga)huljan = ON hylja 'cover, hide', OHG (be)hullan, MHG (be)hüllen 'cover over, wrap' (NHG hüllen) : OE, OHG helan, Lat. cēlāre 'hide', etc. (12.27). Walde-P. 1.433. Feist 274.

ON þekja, etc., above, 1.

OE wrēon, wrīon (*wrīhan), cf. OHG intrīhhan 'uncover', MHG rigel 'head covering wound about the head', fr. *wreiḱ- in Av. urvisyeiti 'turns, twists', Grk. ῥοικός 'bent, twisted', extension of IE *wer- 'turn, bend'. Walde-P. 1.279.

ME couere, NE cover, fr. OFr. covrir (above, 3).

6. Lith. dengti, beside sbs. danga, dangelas 'cover', dangtis 'lid', dangus 'sky' : OE dung, etc. as orig. 'covering'. See 4.66.

Lett. segt (= Lith. segti 'stitch, button'), cf. sagts 'buckle', OPruss. sagis 'belt-buckle', etc. : Skt. saj- 'attach, adhere', Ir. sēn- (*segno-) 'net', etc. Lett. sense fr. 'fasten on, around', perh. first in cpd. apsegt (cf. Lith. apsegti 'fasten around, button up, pin up'). Mühl.-Endz. 3.812.

12.27 HIDE, CONCEAL

Grk.	κρύπτω	Goth.	filhan	Lith.	slėpti
NG	κρύβω	ON	leyna, fela, hylja	Lett.	slèpt
Lat.	abdere, abscondere, cēlāre, occulere	Dan.	skjule, gemme	ChSl.	sŭkryti
It.	nascondere, celare, occultare	Sw.	gömma, dölja	SCr.	sakriti
		OE	hŷdan, helan, (be)-diglian	Boh.	skrýti, schovati
Fr.	cacher, celer	ME	hide, hele	Pol.	(s)kryć, schować
Sp.	esconder, ocultar	NE	hide, conceal	Russ.	skryt', prjatat'
Rum.	ascunde	Du.	verbergen, versteken	Skt.	guh-
Ir.	celim, fullugaimm	OHG	(gi)bergan, helan	Av.	guz-, OPers. gud-
NIr.	foluighim	MHG	(ver)bergen, verheln		
W.	cuddio, celu	NHG	verbergen, verstecken, verhehlen		
Br.	kuzat				

The majority of words for 'hide' are connected with others for 'cover' or 'put away' or 'keep, preserve', the notion of concealment being secondary, though dominant in an inherited group (below, 1). But this latter notion is inherent in a few that are connected with words for 'steal', 'lie, deny', or 'secret'.

1. IE *ḱel-; Walde-P. 1.432 f. Ernout-M. 171 f. Walde-H. 1.196 f.

Lat. cēlāre (> It. celare, Fr. celer), oc-

culere, frequent. occultāre (> It. occultare, Sp. ocultar); Ir. celim, W. celu; OE, OHG helan, OE helian, OHG hellen, MHG verheln, NHG verhehlen, ON hylja, etc. (cf. Goth. huljan 'cover', 12.26) : Grk. καλύπτω, Skt. çarman- 'shelter, cover', etc.

2. Grk. κρύπτω, NG κρύβω; ChSl. kryti 'hide, cover', sŭkryti 'hide', pokryti 'cover', etc., see 12.26.

3. Lat. abdere 'put away, remove' and

esp. 'hide', condere usually 'put together, build, found', but also 'put away, hide', as reg. its cpd. abscondere (> It. ascondere, nascondere with n- fr. in, Sp. esconder, Rum. ascunde), all cpds. of the root *dhē- 'put, place', in Grk. τίθημι, etc. (12.12). Walde-P. 1.827. Ernout-M. 276. REW 41.

Fr. cacher, orig. 'press, squeeze' (cf. cachet 'a stamp, seal', écacher 'squeeze, crush'), fr. VLat. *coācticāre frequent. to Lat. coāctāre 'constrain, force', fr. coāctus, pple. of cōgere 'drive together'. Semantic development through 'press into a small space' through 'cover' to 'hide'. REW 2001. Gamillscheg 166. Wartburg 3.807 ff., esp. 811.

4. Ir. celim, W. celu, above, 1.

Ir. fullugaimm (gl. abdo, Sg. 22b4), NIr. foluighim, see under Br. golei 'cover' (12.26).

W. cuddio, Br. kuzat : OE hŷdan, ME hide, hude, NE hide, Grk. κεύθω 'cover, hide' (poet. Hom.+, esp. of the grave's 'hiding'), fr. *(s)keudh-, extension of *(s)keu-. Walde-P. 2.546 ff., 550.

5. Goth. filhan (also 'bury'), ON fela : OE befeolan 'commit, grant', OHG (bi)felahan 'bury', etc., perh. fr. an extension of a *pel- 'cover' inferred fr. Lat. pellis, OE fell, ON fjall, etc. 'hide, skin'. See under 'bury' (4.78).

ON leyna = Goth. laugnjan 'deny' (cf. galaugnjan 'be hidden', refl. 'hide oneself'), OE liegnan, OHG lougenen 'deny', etc., beside ON ljuga, Goth. liugan, etc. 'lie'. Walde-P. 2.415. Falk-Torp 681.

ON hylja, OE helan, helian, ME hele, heal, etc., above, 1.

Dan. skjule (ON skŷla 'shelter, screen') : MLG schülen 'be hidden', Du. schuilen 'take shelter, hide', all fr. sbs. Dan. skjul, ON skjōl : MHG schūl 'hiding place, shelter, etc.' fr. the root

*(s)keu- occurring with various extensions, as in W. cuddio, above, 4. Walde-P. 2.548. Falk-Torp 1007 f.

Dan. gemme (also 'keep'), Sw. gömma = ON geyma 'watch, heed, keep' : Goth. gaumjan 'notice, heed', OE gīeman 'take care, heed, observe', etc. Walde-P. 1.635 f. Falk-Torp 314. Hellquist 323.

Sw. dölja (Dan. dølge, ON dylja 'keep secret, dissemble', beside ON dul 'concealment, disguise', fr. the root in ON dvol 'delay', OE dwala 'error, doubt', Goth. dwals 'simple', OE dol 'silly', etc. Semantic development of 'conceal' fr. 'confuse, lead astray'. Falk Torp 177. Hellquist 171.

OE be-(ge-)dīglian, OHG tougalen (Tat.) : OE dēagol, dīgol, OHG tougol 'secret' (17.36).

NE conceal (ME concele only 'keep secret') fr. OFr. conceler, Lat. concēlāre 'hide carefully or completely', cpd. of cēlāre (above, 1).

Du. verbergen, OHG (gi)bergan, MHG (ver)bergen, NHG verbergen : Goth. bairgan 'save, keep', ON bjarga 'help', OE beorgan 'save, preserve' (11.24). Falk-Torp 77. Walde-P. 2.172.

Du. versteken, NHG verstecken (MHG verstecken only 'cause to choke'), lit. 'stick away'.

6. Lith. slėpti, Lett. slēpt : Grk. κλέπτω, Goth. hlifan 'steal', etc. (11.56). Walde-P. 1.497. Mühl.-Endz. 3.930.

7. ChSl. sŭkryti, etc., general Slavic : Grk. κρύπτω, etc. (above, 2).

Boh. schovati, Pol. schować 'preserve' and 'hide', cpds. of Boh. chovati, Pol. chować 'keep, preserve' (11.24).

Russ. prjatat' : ChSl. o-pretati 'adorn, cover' (with clothing), vŭz-pretati 'deprive' (Supr.), SCr. pretati 'cover with ashes', Pol. sprzataċ 'clear away', etc., etym. and primary sense dub., but Russ. 'hide' obviously fr. 'cover'. Miklosich 262 f. Brückner 436 f.

8. Skt. *guh-* (3sg. pres. *gūhati*, Av.

guz-, OPers. *gud-* (in *mā apagaudaya* 'do not hide') perh. : Lith. *gūžti* 'cover with something warm' (cf. NSB s.v.). Walde-P. 1.566 f.

12.31 HIGH

Grk.	ὑψηλός	Goth.	hauhs	Lith.	aukštas
NG	ψηλός	ON	hār	Lett.	augsts
Lat.	altus, (ex)celsus	Dan.	høj	ChSl.	vysokŭ
It.	alto	Sw.	hög	SCr.	visok
Fr.	haut	OE	hēah	Boh.	vysoký
Sp.	alto	ME	heigh	Pol.	wysoki
Rum.	înalt	NE	high	Russ.	vysokij
Ir.	ard, uasal	Du.	hoog	Skt.	ucca-, unnata-
NIr.	árd	OHG	hōh	Av.	barəz-, barəzant-
W.	uchel	MHG	hōch		
Br.	uhel	NHG	hoch		

Words for 'high' are partly from adverbs for 'above, over, up', partly from notions like 'grown up', 'heaped up', etc.

1. Grk. ὑψηλός, NG pop. ψηλός; Ir. *uasal*, W. *uchel*, Br. *uhel*, Corn. *huhel*, Gall. *Uxello-(dūnum)*; ChSl. *vysokŭ*, etc., general Slavic group : Grk. ὕψι adv. 'high', Ir. *ōs*, *ūas*, W. *uch*, Corn. *ugh* 'above, over', fr. IE *ŭp(e)s-*, etc., beside *upo-* in Grk. ὑπό 'under', Skt. *upa* 'unto', Ir. *fo*, Goth. *uf* 'under', etc. (for the contrast between 'over' and 'under' in this group, cf. Brugmann, Grd. 2.2.912). Walde-P. 1.193. Boisacq 1009.

2. Lat. *altus* (> It., Sp. *alto*; Fr. *haut* with *h-* fr. Frank. *hōh*; Rum. *înalt* fr. *in alto*), orig. pass. pple. of *alere* 'nourish, rear', but from earliest times used only as adj. in transferred sense 'high' (and 'deep'). Ernout-M. 36. Walde-H. 1.32.

Lat. *celsus*, and more usually *excelsus*, pass. pple. of *-cellere* in *antecellere* 'project, surpass', *excellere* 'surpass, excel', etc. : Lat. *collis* 'hill', Lith. *kelti* 'lift', etc. Walde-P. 1.435. Ernout-M. 170 f. Walde-H. 1.197.

3. Ir. *ard*, NIr. *árd* : Lat. *arduus* 'steep, elevated', also (in part fr. parallel *-dh-* forms) Av. *ərədwa-* 'lifted up, elevated', ON *ǫrðugr* 'steep', ChSl. *rasti*

'grow'. Walde-P. 1.148 f. Ernout-M. 69 f. Walde-H. 1.64. Pedersen 1.51.

Ir. *uasal*, W. *uchel*, etc., above, 1.

4. Goth. *hauhs*, OE *hēah*, etc., general Gmc., prob. as 'arched up' : Goth. *hiuhma* 'heap, multitude', *huhjan* 'heap up, collect', ON *haugr* 'grave-mound', MHG *houc* 'hill', Lith. *kaukas* 'swelling, boil', *kaukaras* 'hill', etc., fr. an extension of *keu-* in words for rounded, bent objects. Walde-P. 1.371. Falk-Torp 451. Feist 249. Here prob. (with *c* fr. a dental extension) Toch. A *koc*, B *kauc* 'high'. G. S. Lane, Language 14.26.

5. Lith. *aukštas*, Lett. *augsts* : Lith. *augti*, Lett. *augt* 'grow', Lat. *augēre* 'increase', etc. Walde-P. 1.23. Mühl.-Endz. 1.218.

6. ChSl. *vysokŭ*, etc., above, 1.

7. Skt. *ucca-*, beside advs. *ucca*, Av. *usča* 'above, up', derivs of Skt. *ud-*, Av. *us-*, *uz-* 'upward, out', etc. Uhlenbeck 27. Walde-P. 1.190.

Skt. *unnata-*, pple. of *ud-nam-* 'rise up, raise', cpd. of *nam-* 'bend' and *ud-* 'up, out'.

Av. *bərəzant-* (also *bərəz-*, *barəziman-*) : Skt. *bṛhant-* 'high, tall', but mostly 'great, strong', Ir. *brī*, W. *bre* 'hill', ON *bjarg*, OHG *berg* 'mountain', etc. Walde-P. 2.172 f.

12.32 LOW

Grk.	χθαμαλός, χαμηλός	Goth.	....	Lith.	žemas
NG	χαμηλός	ON	lāgr	Lett.	zems
Lat.	humilis	Dan.	lav	ChSl.	nizŭkŭ
It.	basso	Sw.	låg	SCr.	nizak
Fr.	bas	OE	niþerlic	Boh.	nízký
Sp.	bajo	ME	low	Pol.	nizki
Rum.	jos	NE	low	Russ.	nizkij
Ir.	ísel	Du.	laag	Skt.	níca-
NIr.	íseal	OHG	nidari	Av.	nitəma- (superl.)
W.	isel	MHG	nider(e), lǣge		
Br.	izel	NHG	niedrig		

Words for 'low' are mostly from adverbs for 'down' or 'under', but some are from the notion of 'on the ground' or 'lying'.

1. Grk. χθαμαλός, χαμηλός, Lat. *humilis*, Lith. *žemas*, Lett. *zems* : Grk. χθών 'earth', χαμαί 'on the ground', Lat. *humus*, Lith. *žemė*, Lett. *zeme* 'earth', etc. (1.21). Walde-P. 1.662 f.

2. It. *basso*, Fr. *bas*, fr. VLat. *bassus* 'low', (hence also *bassiare* > Sp. *bajar* 'lower', whence back-formation *bajo* prob. dial. word (cf. Osc. *Bassus*), perh. orig. 'thickset, short', but etym.? Ernout-M. 105. Walde-P. 1.98.

Rum. *jos*, fr. Lat. *deōrsum* 'downwards'. REW 2567.

3. Ir. *ísel*, W. *isel*, etc., general Celtic, fr. Ir. *ís(s)*, W. *is*, etc. 'below, under', this perh. fr. IE *pēdsu* 'at the feet', loc. pl. of IE *pēd-* 'foot'. Walde-P. 2.23. Pedersen 1.50.

4. ON *lāgr* (> ME *lah*, NE *low*), Dan. *lav*, Sw. *låg*, Du. *laag*, MHG

lǣge, prob. as orig. 'lying' : Goth. *ligan*, etc. 'lie' (12.14). Falk-Torp 626. Franck-v. W. 365. Otherwise (: Lett. *lēzns* 'flat' and the dubious Hom. λάχεια 'low'?) Walde-P. 2.425 f.

OE *niþerlic*, fr. *niþer* adv. 'down, beneath, below' = OHG *nidar*, NHG *nieder* adv. 'down', whence adj. OHG *nidari*, MHG *nider(e)*, NHG (*nieder*) *niedrig* (Du. *nederig* 'lowly, humble') : Skt. *nitarām* 'downwards', comparative formation to IE *ni-*, *nei-* in Skt. *ni-*, Av. *nī-* 'down', Av. *nitəma-* 'lowest', ChSl. *nizŭ* 'down' etc. Walde-P. 2.335. Weigand-H. 2.297 f.

5. Lith. *žemas*, Lett. *zems*, above, 1.

6. ChSl. *nizŭkŭ*, etc., general Slavic : ChSl. *nizŭ* 'down' (above, 4). Miklosich 216. Meillet, Études 326.

7. Skt. *nīca-*, deriv. of *ni-* 'down' (above, 4), either directly or fr. cpd. *ny-añc-* 'directed downwards'. Walde-P. 2.335. Uhlenbeck 149.

Av. *nitəma-* (superl.), above, 4.

12.33 TOP

Grk.	ἄκρος adj., ἄκρον, κορυφή	Goth.	....	Lith.	viršus, čiukuras
NG	κορ(υ)φή	ON	toppr	Lett.	virsus, gals
Lat.	summus adj., cacūmen, columen	Dan.	top, spids	ChSl.	vrŭchŭ
		Sw.	topp, spets	SCr.	vrh
It.	cima, il di sopra	OE	top	Boh.	vrch
Fr.	cime, le haut	ME	top	Pol.	wierzch
Sp.	cima, cumbre	NE	top	Russ.	verch, verchuška
Rum.	vîrf, culme	Du.	spids, top	Skt.	agra-, çikhara-, çṛñga-
Ir.	mullach, barr	OHG	spizzi, spizza	Av.	saēni-
NIr.	barr	MHG	spitze, gupfe		
W.	brig	NHG	spitze, gipfel, das obere		
Br.	lein, barr				

Few of the words listed are so generic as NE *top*, which may denote the upper part or surface of any object, regardless of shape. Most of them are used primarily with reference to something high, as a mountain, hill, or tree. With certain objects words for 'point' or 'end' or 'head' are often used. The top of a flat surface (top of a table, of the water), may be expressed quite differently, as NHG *oberfläche* 'upper surface', etc. Or more generic expressions may be supplied by phrases like It. *il di sopra*, Fr. *le haut*, NHG *das obere*, etc.

1. Grk. ἄκρος, adj. 'highest, topmost, extreme', used with sb. to express 'top', e.g. ἐπ' ἄκρου ὀρέων 'on mountain tops', etc. : Lat. *ācer* 'sharp', etc. Walde-P. 1.28. Boisacq 32 f. Hence also sb. ἄκρον 'highest or farthest' point.

Grk. κορυφή, esp. (Hom.+) 'crown on the head, mountain-top, peak', also general 'top' : Grk. κόρυς 'helmet', κόρυμβος 'top of a hill', pl. Hom. 'sterns of ships', prob. fr. an extension of the root *ker-* in words for 'head, horn, etc.', in Grk. κάρ, κάρα 'head', κέρας 'horn', Skt. *çiras-* 'head, point', etc. Walde-P. 1.406.

2. Lat. *summus* 'highest, topmost', used like Grk. ἄκρος, e.g. *in monte summo* 'on the top of the mountain', *in aqua summa* 'on the top of the water'; hence also sb. *summum* (> OFr. *som*, whence dim. OFr. *sommette* > ME *somette*, NE

summit) and late *summitās* (> It. *summità*, etc.). Ernout-M. 1002. REW 8454.

Lat. *cacūmen*, esp. 'top of tree or mountain' : Skt. *kakubh-*, *kakud-* 'peak, summit', perh. fr. reduplicated extensions of *keu-* in words for 'bend'. Walde-P. 1.371. Ernout-M. 125. Walde-H. 1.127.

Lat. *columen*, esp. 'ridge of house, gable', later *culmen* (> It. *colmo*, Sp. *cumbre*, Rum. *culme*) : *collis* 'hill', *celsus* 'high', etc. Ernout-M. 207 f. Walde-H. 1.249 f. REW 3276.

It., Sp. *cima*, Fr. *cime*, fr. Lat. *cyma* 'young sprout' of cabbage, etc., fr. Grk. κῦμα in this sense and others. Ernout-M. 250. REW 2438.

Rum. *vîrf*, fr. Slavic, SCr. *vrh*, etc. (below, 6). Tiktin 1752.

Fr. *haut* 'high' (12.31), used also as sb. for 'top'.

It. *il di sopra*, lit. 'the above', used for 'top'.

3. Ir. *mullach* : NIr. *mul*, *mol* 'heap, collection, eminence', also 'top or protuberant part of anything' (Dinneen), Ir. *mul-lethan* 'broad-headed', Br. *mellez* 'suture de la tête', outside connections dub. (Skt. *mūrdhan-* 'head'?). Walde-P. 2.295. Stokes 219.

Ir., Br. *barr* (also W. *bar* arch.) : Skt. *bhṛṣṭi-* 'point, edge', Lat. *fastīgium* 'gable, summit', OHG *parrēn* 'stand up

stiff', etc. Walde-P. 2.131. Pedersen 1.44.

W. *brig*, etym.? For that in Morris Jones 157 f., see Loth, RC 36.177.

Br. *lein*, OBr. *blein*, Corn. *blyn* : W. *blaen* 'point, top', etym.? Pedersen 1.125. Henry 37,182. Loth, RC 37.56 (vs. Morris Jones 418).

4. ON *toppr* (in *siglutoppr* 'masthead', but mostly 'tuft, lock of hair, forelock', Dan. *top*, Sw. *topp*, OE, ME, NE, Du. *top* = OHG-NHG *zopf* 'plait, tress (of hair)', cf. Norw. *tuppa*, NHG *zupfen* 'pluck, tug', outside connections dub., but evidently 'top' from 'topknot, crest' or the like. Falk-Torp 1272.

OHG *spizza*, *spizzī*, MHG, NHG *spitze* (> Dan. *spids*, Sw. *spets*), Du. *spits*, all also and orig. 'point' (12.352), but common for the 'top' (of a mountain, etc.).

MHG *gupfe*, with dim. late MHG *güpfel*, *gipfel*, NHG *gipfel*, prob., like the *k*-forms, MHG *kupfe*, *kuppe*, OHG *chuppa*, *chuppha* 'head-covering under helmet', fr. MLat. *cuppa* 'cup'. Weigand-H. 1.729, 1174 f. Kluge-G. 207, 337.

NHG *oberfläche* 'upper surface', used for the 'top' of a table, of water, etc.

5. Lith. *viršus*, Lett. *virsus*, ChSl. *vrŭchŭ*, etc., general Balto-Slavic (with derivs. as Lith. *viršunė*, SCr. *vršak*, Russ. *verchuška*) : Skt. *varṣman-* 'height, top, surface', *varšīyas-* 'higher', Lat. *verrūca*, OE *wearte* 'wart', etc. Walde-P. 1.267. Ernout-M. 1091.

Lith. *čiukuras*, esp. 'top (of a mountain), point (of a house-gable)', Lett. *čukurs* 'bundle, cluster' also 'mound, ridge, gable', etym.? Mühl.-Endz. 1.419.

Lett. *gals* 'end' (12.35), also 'point, top'.

6. ChSl. *vrŭchŭ*, etc., above, 5.

7. Skt. *agra-* ('point, top, front, beginning') : Av. *aɣra-* 'first, earliest', Lett. *agrs* 'early', root connection? Walde-P. 1.38 f.

Skt. *çikhara-*, also as adj. 'pointed', beside *çikhaṇḍa-*, *çikhā-* 'tuft of hair, lock', perh. fr. a root *kŏi-* in *çiçāti* 'whets, sharpens', Av. *saēni-* 'point, top', Lat. *cōs*, ON *hein*, NE *hone*, etc. Walde-P. 1.455. Uhlenbeck 309.

Skt. *çṛñga-* 'horn' (4.17), also 'mountain-top, peak, turret, etc.' (cf. Grk. κορυφή). Walde-P. 1.

Av. *saēni-*, cf. above, Skt. *çikhara-*.

12.34 BOTTOM

Grk.	πυθμήν	Goth.	....	Lith.	dugnas
NG	πάτος	ON	botn, grunnr	Lett.	dibens
Lat.	fundus	Dan.	bund	ChSl.	dŭno
It.	fondo	Sw.	botten	SCr.	dno
Fr.	fond	OE	botm, grund	Boh.	dno
Sp.	fondo	ME	botum, grounde	Pol.	dno
Rum.	fund	NE	bottom	Russ.	dno
Ir.	bun	Du.	bodem	Skt.	budhna-
NIr.	bun	OHG	bodam, grunt	Av.	būna-
W.	gwaelod (bon)	MHG	bodem, boden		
Br.	goueled	NHG	boden		

Most of the words for 'bottom' belong to an inherited group common to Grk., Lat., Gmc. and Indo-Iranian, or to another group common to Balto-Slavic.

1. IE *bhu(n)d(h)- with various suffixes, Walde-P. 2.190. Ernout-M. 401 f. Walde-H. 1.564 f.

Grk. πυθμήν; Lat. fundus (> Romance words); ON botn, OE botm, etc., general Gmc.; Skt. budhna-, Av. būna-; Ir. bond 'sole of the foot'.

2. NG pop. πάτος, fr. class. Grk. πάτος 'path' (10.72), through the Byz. meaning 'floor' (7.26).

3. Ir. bun, W. bon (both also 'trunk' or 'stump' of a tree), perh. orig. 'blow' (cf. W. bonclust 'box on the ear'), fr. root *bhen- in Goth. banja 'blow, wound' (Walde-P. 2.149), with semantic development 'blow' > 'club' > 'stock, trunk of a tree' > 'bottom'. Cf. Fr. bout 'end', orig. 'blow' (12.35). G. S. Lane, Language 13.22 f.

W. gwaelod, Br. goueled : W. gwael 'low, base', Ir. fáel 'evil', further connections dub. Stokes 259 (: Lat. vīlis; but cf. Walde-P. 1.214).

4. ON grunnr (only 'bottom' of the sea), OE grund, ME grounde 'bottom' and 'surface of earth, ground' (NE ground), OHG grunt (gl. Lat. fundus), MHG grunt 'bottom, abyss', etc. (NHG grund), cf. Goth. grundu-waddjus 'foundation wall', root connection dub. Walde-P. 1.656. Falk-Torp 352 ff. Feist 222.

5. Lith. dugnas (*dubnas), Lett. (*dubens >) dibens, ChSl. dŭno (*dŭbno), etc., general Slavic = Gall. dubno-, dumno- 'world' (in Dubno-rīx) : Lith. dubus 'deep, hollow', Goth. diups, etc. 'deep', W. dwfn, Ir. domain 'deep', etc. Walde-P. 1.848. Mühl.-Endz. 1.465. Berneker 245 f.

12.35 END

Grk.	ἄκρος adj., ἄκρον, ἄκρα, πέρας	Goth.	andeis
NG	ἄκρα, ἄκρη	ON	endi
Lat.	extrēmus adj., extrēmum	Dan.	ende
It.	capo, estremo, etc.	Sw.	ända
Fr.	bout	OE	ende
Sp.	cabo, estremo, etc.	ME	ende
Rum.	capăt	NE	end
Ir.	(for)cenn	Du.	einde
NIr.	deireadh	OHG	enti
W.	pen	MHG	ende
Br.	penn	NHG	ende

Lith.	galas
Lett.	gals
ChSl.	konĭcĭ
SCr.	kona, kraj
Boh.	konec, kraj
Pol.	koniec
Russ.	konec, kraj
Skt.	anta-, prānta-
Av.	karana-

'End' is understood here, of course, in the spatial sense, not in the temporal, though the latter is to a large extent expressed by the same words (14.26), nor in the frequent secondary sense of 'purpose'. In Greek and Latin 'end' is often expressed by adjectives in agreement with nouns denoting the object referred to.

1. Grk. ἄκρος 'at the farthest point, uttermost' (also 'highest', whence its use for 'top', 12.33), e.g. ἄκρη χείρ 'end of the arm' = 'hand' (Hom.), ἀπ' ἄκρων οὐρανῶν ἕως ἄκρων αὐτῶν 'from one end of heaven to the other' (NT). Hence also as sbs. ἄκρον and ἄκρα, NG pop. ἄκρη.

Grk. πέρας, Hom. πεῖραρ, fr. *πέρϝαρ : πέρᾱν 'on the other side', Skt. para- 'far,

opposite, last', Goth. fairra 'far', etc. Walde-P. 1.31 ff.

Grk. τέρμα, τέρμων, Lat. terminus 'boundary, limit', only rarely for more generic 'end', fr. the root of Lat. trāns 'across', Skt. tṛ- 'pass over, cross', etc. Walde-P. 1.733. Ernout-M. 1032.

2. Lat. extrēmus 'outermost', e.g. in extrēmō ponte 'at the end of the bridge', in extrēmō librō 'at the end of the book'. Hence also sb. extrēmum (> It. estremo, Sp. extremo, etc.).

For Lat. fīnis, which though orig. a spatial notion is in actual use 'border, limit', and 'end' only as 'purpose' or temporal, see 14.26.

It. capo, Sp. cabo, fr. Lat. caput 'head'; pl. capita > Rum. capete, hence new sg. capăt.

In Italian and Spanish various other words are used for 'end' in particular connections, as fondo 'bottom' (12.34) for 'lower end' or simply 'end' of a room, garden, etc., punta 'point, tip' for the end of a stick, etc., It. coda 'tail' for the end of a rope, a train, etc.

Fr. bout (OFr. also 'blow', hence 'end' as 'striking end'?), back-formation fr. OFr. bouter 'strike, thrust', this fr. Frank. *bōtan, cf. OHG bōzan, OE bēatan 'strike, beat'. REW 1228c. Wartburg 1.459 f.

3. Ir. cend, cenn, W. pen, Br. penn all lit. 'head' (4.20), esp. as 'end' also Ir. cpd. for-cenn, with for 'on, upon'.

NIr. deireadh (used in most of the senses of NE end), Ir. dered 'remains, remnant' also 'end' (temporal, as 'end

of the world', Wb. 10b3), fr. di-rethim 'run out, off', cpd. of rethim 'run'. Pedersen 2.598.

4. Goth. andeis, OE ende, etc., general Gmc. : Skt. anta- 'end', cpd. prānta- (pra-anta-), and prob. related ultimately to Skt. anti adv. 'opposite, before, near', Goth. and 'on, over, along', Lat. ante 'before', Grk. ἀντί 'opposite, for', etc. Walde-P. 1.67. Falk-Torp 193. Feist 49.

5. Lith. galas, Lett. gals, prob. through 'point, prick' : Lith. gelti 'sting', gelia 'it hurts', ChSl. žalĭ 'pain', OE cwelan, Ir. at-baill 'die'. Walde-P. 1.690. Mühl.-Endz. 1.595.

6. ChSl. konĭcĭ, etc., general Slavic, also and orig. 'end' temporal, deriv. of Slavic *konŭ in Russ. kon 'beginning', SCr. od kona do kona 'from beginning to end', Boh. do-kona 'to the end, completely' : ChSl. na-čęti, Russ. načat', etc. 'begin', Ir. cinim 'spring from, be born', Skt. kanīna- 'young', etc. Peculiar development fr. 'beginning' as one of the ends. Berneker 560 f. (otherwise on semantic relation).

SCr. kraj, etc., used more or less in certain connections for 'end', but the regular Slavic word for 'border, edge' (12.353), ChSl. krajĭ 'border, shore' (1.27).

7. Skt. anta-, prānta- : Goth. andeis, above, 4.

Av. karana- (also in special senses 'border, shore', etc.; NPers. karān 'shore, side'), etym.? Barth. 451.

12.352 POINT

Grk.	ἀκμή, ἀκίς, etc.	Goth.	....
NG	(ἀκίς, etc.), pop. μύτη	ON	oddr
Lat.	cuspis, mucrō	Dan.	spids, od
It.	punta	Sw.	spets, udd
Fr.	pointe	OE	ord
Sp.	punta	ME	point
Rum.	vîrf	NE	point
Ir.	rind	Du.	spits, punt
NIr.	rinn	OHG	spizza, spizzi, ort
W.	pwynt, blaen	MHG	spitze
Br.	beg	NHG	spitze

Lith.	galas
Lett.	gals
ChSl.	
SCr.	šiljak
Boh.	hrot, špička
Pol.	koniec
Russ.	konec
Skt.	agra-
Av.	....

Words for 'point' (here intended as 'sharp end') are in several cases, as might be expected, cognate with words for 'sharp' or names of particular sharp-pointed objects. Some are the usual words for 'end', used also for 'point', with or without a distinguishing adj. for 'sharp'. Or, since the 'top' of an upright object may also be a 'point', a word for 'top' may also cover 'point' (Rum. vîrf), as conversely NHG spitze is used for the 'top' (of a mountain, etc.).

But in the group of which NE point is representative the sense here intended is secondary in its historical development to that of 'point' as a small spot or mark (orig. a 'puncture'), whence any sharply defined 'point' in space, time, or thought (in this sense Lat. pūnctum also > NHG punkt, etc.).

These two notions, expressed by quite unrelated words in most languages and somewhat differentiated in Romance (Fr. point vs. pointe, etc.) are merged in NE point with the addition of a great variety of idiomatic uses. Cf. NED s.v. point, sb.¹.

1. Grk. ἀκμή ('point' or 'edge', more common in secondary senses), ἀκίς, ἀκωκή (usual word in Hom.) : ἄκρος 'topmost', Skt. açri- 'edge', Lat. acūtus 'sharp', Lith. aštrus, etc. 'sharp' (15.78).

NG (beside lit. ἀκίς, etc.) pop. μύτη 'snout, nose' (4.23), also 'point' (hence μυτερός 'pointed, sharp').

2. Lat. cuspis, etym.? Ernout-M. 248. Walde-H. 1.318.

Lat. mucrō : Grk. ἀμύσσω 'scratch, prick, sting', ἀμυκάλαι· αἱ ἀκίδες τῶν βελῶν (Hesych.). Walde-P. 2.255. Ernout-M. 635.

It., Sp. punta, Fr. pointe (> ME, NE point) fr. MLat. puncta, new formation beside Lat. pūnctum 'puncture, point' as small spot (> It., Sp. punto, Fr. point > ME, NE point in this sense), fr. pungere 'prick, puncture'. Ernout-M. 824. REW 6847.

Rum. vîrf, also and orig. 'top' (12.33).

3. Ir. rind, NIr. rinn, etym.? Walde-P. 1.139. Pedersen 1.87.

Ir. benn 'point, peak, tip', etc. (K. Meyer, Contrib. 198), NIr. beann id., W. ban 'peak, horn', Br. bann 'sprout, wing', etc., perh. : OE pintel, MLG pint 'penis'. Walde-P. 2.109 f.

Ir., NIr. corr 'point, peak' also 'edge, corner' (K. Meyer, Contrib. 491 f., Dinneen s.v.), Gael. curr 'corner', W. cwrr 'edge, corner', etym.? Loth, RC 34.148 f. Walde-P. 2.581.

W. blaen 'top, end') = Corn. blyn, Bret. blein 'top' (12.33).

W. pwynt, fr. ME point. Parry-Williams 197.

Br. beg, fr. Fr. bec 'beak', this of Gallic origin (cf. Beccus, Beccō), possibly (Thurneysen) : Ir. baccán, etc. 'hook' (12.75). NED s.v. beak, sb.

4. ON oddr, Dan. od, odde, Sw. udd, OE ord, OHG ort ('point, edge, shore', NHG ort 'place'), fr. Gmc. *uzda- prob. IE *ud-dho-, deriv. of *dhē- in Skt. dhā-, etc. 'put, place' with prefix *ud- as in Skt. ud- 'up, out'; or : Lith. usnis 'thistle', etc.? Walde-P. 1.308 f., 827. Falk-Torp 787, 1524. Hellquist 1271 f.

OHG spizza, spizzi, MHG, NHG spitze (> Dan. spids, Sw. spets), Du. spits : OHG spiz, OE spitu 'spit' (for roasting), fr. a root *spei- seen in numerous other words for sharp objects, as Lat. spīna 'thorn', spīca 'ear of grain', etc. Walde-P. 2.655. Falk-Torp 1118.

ME, NE point, Du. punt (> Dan., Sw. pynt 'point of land', etc.), fr. Fr. pointe (above, 2). NED s.v. point, sb.¹. Franck-v. W. 527.

5. Lith. galas, Lett. gals 'end' (12.35), also usual for 'point', though this may be expressed more specifically as 'sharp end', Lith. aštrus (or smailusis) galas.

6. SCr. šiljak, orig. a 'wooden awl' : šilo 'awl' (6.38).

Boh. hrot = Pol., ORuss. grot 'point of a spear, javelin' : MHG grāt 'fishbone, vertebra, tip'. Walde-P. 1.606. Berneker 354.

Boh. špic, dim. špička, fr. NHG spitze.

Pol. koniec, Russ. konec 'end' (12.35), also 'point' or more specifically with ostry, ostryj 'sharp'.

7. Skt. agra- (also 'top, front, beginning') : Av. aγra- 'first, earliest', Lett. agrs 'early', root connection? Walde-P. 1.38 f.

12.353 EDGE
(Of a Knife, Sword, etc.; of a Table, Forest, etc.)

Grk.	ἀκμή; κράσπεδον, χεῖλος	Goth.	....; (skaut)
NG	ἀθέρας, κόψη; χεῖλι	ON	egg; rǫnd
Lat.	aciēs; ōra, margō	Dan.	æg; kant, rand
It.	filo, taglio; orlo, margine	Sw.	egg; kant, rand
		OE	ecg; rand, ōra (snæd)
Fr.	fil, tranchant; bord	ME	egge
Sp.	filo; canto, orilla, borde	NE	edge
		Du.	scherp(e); kant, rand
Rum.	tais; margine	OHG	ekka (sarfi); (trādo)
Ir.	faebar; brū, brūach, cimas, ochar, bil	MHG	scher(p)fe, snide, ecke
		NHG	schneide, schärfe; kante, rand
NIr.	faobhar, bēal; bruach, ciumhais, eochair		
W.	min, awch; ymyll, ochr		
Br.	dremm, lemm, neudenn, barvenn; ribl, etc.		

Lith.	ašmens; kraštas, briauna
Lett.	asmens; mala
ChSl.	ostrĭje; krajĭ (vŭskrilĭje)
SCr.	oštrac; brid, ivica
Boh.	ostří; hrana, (o)kraj
Pol.	ostrze; brzeg, krawędź
Russ.	ostrie; kraj
Skt.	açri-, dhārā-; prānta-
Av.	dārā-; karana-

Words for the 'edge' of a knife, sword, etc. are mostly connected with adjectives for 'sharp' or verbs for 'cut'. In one group the words for 'thread' are used (through its fine line) for 'edge'. Some words for 'mouth' (through 'front') or 'lip' are also used for 'edge'.

But for the common secondary sense

which developed in ME egge, NE edge, as in edge of the table, forest, etc. (NED s.v. III), other languages have quite different words and sometimes in great variety according to the subject referred to. A few words are included in the list (but in parentheses) which are quotable only for the 'edge, fringe' of a garment, this being the only occurring sense of Grk. κράσπεδον in the NT.

1. Derivs. of IE *ak̂- in words for 'sharp' (15.78). Walde-P. 1.28 ff. Ernout-M. 7 ff. Falk-Torp 182. Pedersen 1.123, 412.

Grk. ἀκμή, Lat. *aciēs;* ON *egg,* Dan. *æg,* OE *ecg,* ME *egge,* NE *edge,* OHG *ekka* ('edge' of a sword in Notker; also 'point'), MHG *ecke* ('edge, point, corner'; NHG 'corner'); Lith. *ašmens,* Lett. *asmens;* ChSl. *ostrĭje,* SCr. *oštrac,* Boh. *ostři,* Pol. *ostrze,* Russ. *ostrie;* Skt. *açri-*; here also Ir. *ochar,* NIr. *eochair,* W. *ochr* 'edge, side', W. *hogi* 'sharpen, whet'; and prob. W. *awch* 'edge, sharpness' beside old *awg* 'sharpness, eagerness' (so Evans, Dict. s.v.; not mentioned in this group in Walde-P., Pedersen, or Stokes 5 f.) fr. the *ā*-grade of Lat. *ācer,* with *aw* reg. in monosyllables as *brawd* 'brother'.

2. Grk. κράσπεδον, cpd. of κράς = κάρā 'head' and πέδον 'ground'. Walde-P. 1.405. Boisacq 509.

Grk. χεῖλος, NG χείλι 'lip' (4.25), also 'edge' as 'rim, border'.

NG ἀθέρας 'spike of grain', 'edge' of a knife, etc. (also the 'choice, best part'), fr. Grk. ἀθήρ 'spike of grain', 'barb' of a weapon, perh. : Lat. *ador* 'a kind of grain'. Walde-P. 1.45. Boisacq 18. Walde-H. 1.14.

NG κόψη, fr. κόπτω 'cut'.

Grk. στόμα 'mouth' (4.24) was sometimes used (through 'front'), for the 'point' (Hom.) or for the 'edge' (Aesch.), of a weapon, e.g. στόμα μαχαίρας 'edge of a sword' in LXX and NT, rendered literally *ōs gladii* in the Vulgate, this again (Lk. 21.24) by OE *mūþ suordes* in Lindisf. vs. *swurdes ecg* in WSax. versions, likewise OHG *mund suertes* in Tat. (in Goth. the passage is lacking).

3. Lat. *ōra* (derivs. > It. *orlo,* Sp. *orilla*) : Lat. *ōs,* Skt. *ās* 'mouth', OE *ōr* 'beginning', *ōra* 'border, edge', etc. (see also under 'coast', 1.27). Ernout-M. 709, 714. REW 6080.

Lat. *margō* (> It., Rum. *margine,* etc.) : Goth. *marka,* OE *mearc,* etc. 'boundary'. Ernout-M. 593. Walde-H. 2.39 f.

It. *filo,* Fr. *fil* 'thread' and 'edge', Sp. *filo* 'edge' vs. *hilo* 'thread', fr. Lat. *fīlum* 'thread' (6.38), with development through the fine line of the edge. Wartburg 3.532.

It. *taglio,* Rum. *tais,* fr. It. *tagliare,* Rum. *tăia* 'cut' (9.22).

Fr. *tranchant,* fr. *trancher* 'cut' (9.22).

Fr. *bord* (Cat. > Sp. *borde*) fr. Gmc. *bord* (below, 5). REW 1215. Wartburg 1.436 ff.

It. *canto,* mostly 'corner, side', Sp. *canto* 'edge, border, side', OFr. *cant, chant* 'side', MLat. *cantus* 'corner, side', fr. Lat. *canthus* 'tire of a wheel' : Grk. κανθός 'corner of the eye' (later 'tire of a wheel' after Lat.?), ultimately of Celt. orig.? Ernout-M. 146. Walde-H. 1.155 f. REW 1616. Wartburg 2.232 f.

4. Ir. *faibur, faebar,* NIr. *faobhar,* loanword fr. Brit., cf. W. *gwaew* 'spear', pl. *gwaewawr.* Pedersen 1.23.

NIr. *bēal,* 'lip, mouth' (4.25), also 'edge'.

Ir. *brū, brūach* (also 'bank', 1.27) : ON *brūn* 'edge' (of ice, mountain, etc.), Lith. *briauna* 'edge, border'. Walde-P. 1.196. Pedersen 1.62.

Ir. *cimas* (K. Meyer, Contrib. 369), NIr. *ciumhais,* perh. : OE *hem* 'edge of cloth, border'. Walde-P. 1.388. Stokes, KZ 41.382.

Ir., W., Br. *or* (in part obs.), fr. Lat. or OE *ōra* (above, 3), Walde-P. 1.168. Pedersen 1.207. Vendryes, De hib. voc. 162. Otherwise Loth, Mots lat. 191.

Ir. *bil,* W. *byl,* cpds. Ir. *imbel,* W. *ymyll,* etym.? Pedersen 1.147, 302.

W. Lehmann, Z. celt. Ph. 6.438 (: OHG *bilar* 'gums').

Ir. *ochar,* W. *ochr, awch,* above, 1.

W. *min,* orig. 'lip', beside Ir. *mēn* 'open mouth', Br. *min* 'snout', perh. : OHG *mago* 'stomach', etc. Walde-P. 2.225. Pedersen 1.127. Stokes 197.

Br. *lemm,* fr. adj. *lemm* 'sharp' (15.78).

Br. *dremm,* also and orig. 'face, look' (like W. *drem*), fr. the root in Grk. δέρκομαι 'look', Skt. *dṛç-* 'see', etc. Walde-P. 1.807. Pedersen 1.42.

Br. *neud* 'thread' (6.38), used also for 'edge', like (semantic borrowing) Fr. *fil.*

Br. *barvenn,* fr. *barv* 'barb'.

Br. *ribl* (esp. 'shore, bank', but also 'edge, side'), fr. Lat. *rīpula,* dim. of *rīpa* 'bank' (1.27). Numerous other Br. words given by Vallée s.v. *bord.*

5. ON *egg,* OE *ecg,* etc., above, 1.

OHG *sarfī* (but mostly abstract 'roughness, sharpness', quotable as 'edge'?), MHG *scher(p)fe,* NHG *schärfe,* Du. *scherp,* fr. adjs. for 'sharp', OHG *s(c)arf,* etc. (15.78).

MHG *snīde,* NHG *schneide,* fr. *snīden* 'cut' (9.22).

ON *borð,* OE *bord,* OHG *bort,* etc., general Gmc. word, in part 'edge, border', but esp. 'ship's side', root connection dub. Walde-P. 2.163. Falk-Torp 94. Franck-v. W. 83. NED s.v. *board,* sb. Hence Fr. *bord* 'edge, border', etc. and, through a Fr. deriv., ME *bordure,* NE *border.*

MLG *kant, kante,* Du. *kant* (MLG > Dan., Sw. *kant,* NHG *kante*), used esp. for an angular 'edge' (as of a table, etc.), also ME, NE *cant* (formerly 'edge' or 'corner'), all fr. a form of the group It., Sp. *canto,* etc., prob. the OFr. *cant* (above, 3). Falk-Torp 492. NED s.v. *cant,* sb.[1].

ON *rǫnd,* OE *rand, rond,* OHG *rant,* used most commonly for the 'boss of a shield' or 'shield', but Dan., Sw., Du., NHG *rand* the most comprehensive word for 'edge' as 'border', etc., prob. fr. an extension of **rem-* in ON *rimi* 'strip of land, ridge', OE *rima* (mostly in cpds.), NE *rim,* OHG *rama* 'support, frame' (NHG *rahmen*), etc. Walde-P. 2.372. Falk-Torp 876.

Goth. *skaut* (reg. for κράσπεδον, but always 'edge' of a garment) : ON *skaut* 'corner of cloth, skirt, bosom', OE *scēat* 'corner, region, lap, cloth', fr. the root in OE *scēotan,* OHG *scīozan* 'rush, throw, shoot, hit', etc. Walde-P. 2.554. Feist 431.

OE *snǣd* 'bit, slice' and in Gospels reg. for Vulgate *fimbria* = κράσπεδον, fr. *snǣdan* 'cut off'.

OHG *trādo* (Otfr., Tat. for NT *fimbria,* κράσπεδον), prob. fr. the root in OE *teran* 'tear', etc. Walde-P. 1.798. Falk-Torp 1281.

6. Lith. *ašmens,* Lett. *asmens,* above, 1.

Lith. *kraštas* (also 'shore, bank', as Lett. *krasts*), etym.? Mühl.-Endz. 2.260.

Lith. *briauna* : Ir. *brū* (above, 4).

Lett. *mala* : Lith. *lyg-malas* 'full to the brim', perh. Alb. *mal* 'mountain', etc. Mühl.-Endz. 2.556.

7. ChSl. *ostrĭje,* etc., above, 1.

ChSl. *krajĭ,* Russ. *kraj,* Boh. *(o)kraj* (SCr., Pol. *kraj* mostly in other senses) : ChSl. *-krojiti,* etc. 'cut' (9.22). Berneker 605 f. Here also Pol. *krawędź,* fr. *krawać* iter. form of *kroić* 'cut'. Brückner 265, 268.

ChSl. *vŭskrilĭje* (reg. for κράσπεδον in Gospels), cpd. of *krilo* 'wing'. Berneker 615.

SCr. *brid,* fr. the root in SCr. *brijati,* Boh. *břiti,* etc. 'shave' (cf. ChSl. *britva,* etc. 'razor', 6.93).

SCr. *ivica,* etym.? Berneker 439.

Boh. *hrana* : late ChSl. *granĭ* 'chapter', Russ. *gran'* 'facet, side', SCr., Pol.,

Russ. *granica* 'boundary', etc., these prob. : Ir. *grend* 'beard', ON *grǫn,* OE *granu,* OHG *grana,* MHG *granne* 'mustache' (MHG also, as NHG, 'beard of grains', etc.), all with common notion of something projecting. Walde-P. 1.606. Berneker 346. Brückner 155.

Pol. *brzeg,* also 'shore', like ChSl. *brěgŭ,* etc. See 1.27.

8. Skt. *açri-,* above, 1.

Skt. *dhārā-,* Av. *dārā-* (also *tiži-dāra-* 'with sharp edge') : Skt. *dhāv-* 'rinse, polish'?? BR s.v. [2]*dhāra-.* Uhlenbeck 136 f.

Skt. *anta-, prānta-* 'end' (12.35), also 'edge'.

Av. *karana-* 'end' (12.35), also 'edge, shore'. Barth. 451.

12.36 SIDE

Grk.	πλευραί	Goth.	*fēra*	Lith.	*šonas, pusė*
NG	μεριά	ON	*sīða*	Lett.	*sāns, puse*
Lat.	*latus, costa*	Dan.	*side*	ChSl.	*(rebra, strana)*
It.	*lato, canto*	Sw.	*sida*	SCr.	*strana, bok*
Fr.	*côté*	OE	*sīde*	Boh.	*strana, bok*
Sp.	*lado, costado*	ME	*side*	Pol.	*strona, bok*
Rum.	*parte*	NE	*side*	Russ.	*storona, bok*
Ir.	*tōib, sliss, leth*	Du.	*zijde*	Skt.	*pārçva-, pakṣa-, ardha-*
NIr.	*taobh, slios, leath*	OHG	*sīt(t)a, fiara*		
W.	*ystlys, tu*	MHG	*sīte*	Av.	*arəδa-*
Br.	*kostez, tu*	NHG	*seite*		

Several of the words for 'side' were first used only for the 'side' of the body and are connected with words for 'rib'. Others are from such notions as 'half' or 'part, region'; and, in general, words for 'part' (besides those included in the list here) are often used in the sense of 'side'.

1. Grk. πλευραί, pl. of πλευρά 'rib', used for 'side' of the body (Hom.+), then for 'side' in general (πλευρά sg. for 'side' of the body in NT and NG); similarly πλευρά, pl. of πλευρόν 'rib', in narrow sense (Hom.) and later generic, etym.? Boisacq 794.

Grk. μέρος 'part, portion' (13.23), late 'region', NG μέρος, pop. μεριά usual word for 'side'.

2. Lat. *latus* (> It. *lato,* Sp. *lado,* OFr. *lez,* Rum. arch. *laturi*), prob. fr. another grade of the root in Lat. *lātus* 'wide' (12.61). Walde-P. 2.427. Walde-H. 1.772. Otherwise Ernout-M. 528.

Lat. *costa* 'rib' (4.162), also 'side'. Hence, through sb. form of Lat. *costātus* 'ribbed', Fr. *côté,* Sp. *costado* (It. *costato* 'region of the ribs'). REW 2280.

It. *canto* 'edge, corner' (12.76), also freq. 'side' (cf. *accanto* 'beside').

Rum. *parte* (replaces older *laturi,* above), fr. Lat. *pars, -tis* 'part'. Puşcariu 1274.

3. Ir. *tōib,* NIr. *taobh,* W., Br. *tu,* etym. dub., but perh. (as **toigʷes*) : Arm. *t'ēkn* 'shoulder', ChSl. *stĭgno* 'femur'. Walde-P. 2.614. Otherwise Pedersen 1.116 (: Lat. *tībia,* Lith. *staibiai* 'shin-bone', etc.).

Ir. *sliss,* NIr. *slios,* W. *ystlys,* cf. Ir. *sliosat* 'thigh', etym. dub., perh. : Grk. πλιχάς 'inside of the thighs', πλίσσομαι ('cross the legs' and so) 'trot'? Walde-P. 2.684. Pedersen 1.84. Otherwise (fr. **stel-* in ChSl. *stĭlati* 'spread out', Lat. *lātus* 'wide') Foy, IF. 6.319 (adversely Walde-H. 1.772).

Ir. *leth,* NIr. *leath* (both 'side', esp. as 'direction', and 'half', W. adv. *lled* 'in part'), prob. : Ir. *lethan,* Grk. πλατύς, etc.

'wide' (12.61). Walde-P. 2.99. Walde-H. 1.772.

Br. *kostez,* fr. OFr. **costed* > Fr. *côté* (above). Henry 77.

4. Goth. *fēra* 'part, region' and prob. 'side' (renders μέρος, κλίματα 'region' also μέρος 'part of body', Eph. 4.16, and cf. esp. *þaim af hleidumein fērai* 'unto them on the left hand', Mt. 25.41), OHG *fēra, fiara* 'side, part', etym.? Walde-P. 2.40. Feist 148.

ON *sīða,* OE *sīde,* etc., general Gmc. (except Goth.), prob. (through the notion 'broad, long') : ON *sīðr* 'hanging down, long', OE *sīd* 'wide, broad, long', etc., these : W. *hyd* 'length', Ir. *sīr* 'long, eternal', Lat. *sērus* 'late', etc. Walde-P. 2.462. Falk-Torp 961.

5. Lith. *šonas,* Lett. *sāns* ('side' of body, but extended in sense), perh. (as orig. 'rib'?) : Russ., Slov. *sani* (pl.) 'sled'. Mühl.-Endz. 3.804 f. Trautmann 298.

Lith. *pusė,* Lett. *puse,* lit. 'half' (13.24), but used commonly for 'side' of objects.

6. ChSl. *strana* (but mostly 'country, region'), SCr., Boh. *strana,* Pol. *strona,* Russ. *storona* 'side' : ChSl. *pro-stĭrą, -strěti,* Lat. *sternere,* Grk. στόρνῡμι, etc. 'spread out'. Walde-P. 2.639. Brückner 519.

Russ.-ChSl. *bokŭ,* etc., general Slavic, orig. dub. Walde-P. 2.105. Berneker 68 f.

ChSl. *rebra* 'side of the body' (Gospels, Jn. 14.34, etc.), pl. of *rebro* 'rib' (4.162).

7. Skt. *pārçva-,* fr. *parçu-* 'rib' (4.162).

Skt. *pakṣa-,* also 'wing, shoulder, half' : Lett. *paksis* 'corner of the house', *aiz pakša iet* 'do one's need' (lit. 'go aside'), Russ. *pach* 'groin', etc. Walde-P. 2.3 f. Mühl.-Endz. 3.50.

Skt. *ardha-,* Av. *arəδa-,* also 'half' (Av. 'half' adj. only in cpds.), perh. : Lith. *ardyti* 'split, divide', etc. Walde-P. 1.143. Uhlenbeck 14. Barth. 193.

12.37 MIDDLE (adj.)

Grk.	μέσος	Goth.	*midjis*	Lith.	*vidurinis*
NG	μέσος, μεσαῖος	ON	*miðr, mið-*	Lett.	*vidējs, vidus-*
Lat.	*medius*	Dan.	*midterst, mellemst, midt-*	ChSl.	*(srěda* sb.)
It.	*nel mezzo, medio*	Sw.	*mellerst, mid-*	SCr.	*srednij*
Fr.	*au milieu, mi-, moyen*	OE	*midlest, middel, midd*	Boh.	*střední*
Sp.	*medio*	ME	*middel, mid*	Pol.	*średni*
Rum.	*mijlociu*	NE	*middle, mid-*	Russ.	*srednij*
Ir.	*mid-, medōnach*	Du.	*middelste, midden-*	Skt.	*madhya-*
NIr.	*meadhōnach, meadhōn-*	OHG	*mitti, mittil*	Av.	*maiδya-, maδəma-*
W.	*canol, perfedd*	MHG	*mitte, mittel*		
Br.	*ekreiz, kreiz-*	NHG	*mittler, mittel-*		

Most of the words for 'middle' are derivatives of a single IE form. The others are from 'inner part', 'heart', and 'channel'. A recurring secondary sense of sb. 'middle' is 'means' (the medium by which one attains results), as in Fr. *moyen,* NHG *mittel,* etc. This notion is otherwise expressed by a case-construction (the old instrumental), a preposition ('through'), or by words for 'way, manner'.

1. IE **medhyo-* Walde-P. 2.261. Ernout-M. 601. Walde-H. 2.57 f. Falk-Torp 719 f.

Hence, either directly or in derivs., all the words listed, except in Britannic and

Balto-Slavic, where the word survives in W. *mewn* 'within', ChSl. *meždu* 'in the middle, between' and *mežda* 'street', etc., but as the adjective for 'middle' is displaced by other terms.

The original form is represented by Grk. μέσος, dial. μέσσος, μέττος (all fr. *μέθιος); Lat. *medius* (> It. *mezzo*, *medio*, Fr. *mi-*, Sp. *medio*, etc.), Osc. loc. sg. fem. *mefiaí;* Ir. *mid-*; Goth. *midjis*, ON *miðr*, OE *midd*, OHG *mitti*, etc.; Skt. *madhya-*, Av. *maiδya-*.

But many of these came to be partly replaced as adjectives for 'middle' by derivs., e.g. NG μεσαῖος, late Lat. *medi-ānus* (> It. *mezzano*, Fr. *moyen*), Ir. *medōnach*, fr. sb. *medōn* 'middle' (this also a deriv. form), OE *middel*, and the comp. and superl. forms like NHG *mittler*, OE *midlest* (more common than the positive), *midmost*, Sw. *mellerst*, Av. *maδəma-;* or by phrases, as Fr. *au* (or *du*) *milieu*, It. *nel mezzo;* or by derivs. of cpds., as Rum. *mijlociu* fr. sb. *mijloc*, this like Fr. *milieu*, fr. cpd. with forms of Lat. *locus* 'place'.

2. W. *canol* (sb. and adj.), fr. Lat. *canālis* 'channel, groove'. Loth, Mots lat. 143.

W. *perfedd* (cf. Corn. *a berwedh* 'within'), fr. Lat. *per medium*. Loth, Mots lat. 195.

Br. *ekreiz* cpd. of *e*, *en* 'in' and *kreiz* 'center = Ir. *cride* 'heart', etc. The simple *kreiz* is used as prefix 'mid-', e.g. *kreizdeiz* 'midi', *kreiznoz* 'minuit', etc.

3. Lith. *vidurinis*, Lett. *vidējs* fr. Lith., Lett. *vidus* 'middle, inner part', this prob. : Skt. *vidhu-* 'solitary, isolated', Lat. *dī-videre* 'separate, divide'. Walde-P. 1.239.

4. SCr. *srednij*, Boh. *střední*, Pol. *średni*, Russ. *srednij*, fr. the sbs. ChSl. *srěda*, etc. 'middle' : ChSl. *srŭdĭce* 'heart', etc. (4.44). Brückner 534.

12.38. 'Center'. Substantive forms of the adjectives for 'middle' were used for 'the middle', or in some cases the adjectives were derived from the nouns (cf. 12.37). These words originally covered 'middle' and 'center' without distinction. For the latter arose also cpds. like NHG *mittelpunkt* and Russ. *sredotočie* (*-točie* : *toc'* 'exactly'). But the widespread Eur. word for 'center' as applying especially to a circle or sphere, goes back to a development in Greek.

Grk. κέντρον 'sharp point, goad, sting' (: κεντέω 'prick, stab') was used also for the 'point' of a pair of compasses and for the 'center' of a circle or sphere. Hence in this sense Lat. *centrum* and the almost universal Eur. word.

12.41 RIGHT

(Adj.; vs. Left)

Grk.	δεξιός	Goth.	*taihswa*	Lith.	*dešinas*
NG	δεξιός	ON	*hægri*	Lett.	*labs*
Lat.	*dexter*	Dan.	*højre*	ChSl.	*desnŭ*
It.	*destro*	Sw.	*höger*	SCr.	*desni*
Fr.	*droit*	OE	*swīþra*	Boh.	*pravý*
Sp.	*diestro, derecho*	ME	*riht, swither*	Pol.	*prawy*
Rum.	*drept*	NE	*right*	Russ.	*pravyj (desnoj)*
Ir.	*dess*	Du.	*recht*	Skt.	*dakṣiṇa-*
NIr.	*deas*	OHG	*zeso*	Av.	*dašina-*
W.	*de, deheu*	MHG	*zese, reht*		
Br.	*dehou*	NHG	*recht*		

The history of words for 'right' and 'left' shows that they were used primarily with reference to the hands.

Many of those for 'right' belong to an inherited group pointing to an IE word for 'right' with reference to the hand, but without clear antecedent root meaning. Others are from notions like 'straight, correct, right (vs. wrong)', 'good', 'stronger' or 'easier', all with obvious reference to the right hand.

1. IE **dek̑s*(*i*)-, with various suffixes, ultimate root connection (: Grk. δέκομαι 'receive', Skt. *dāç-* 'make offering, honor'?) dub. Walde-P. 1.784. Ernout-M. 264. Walde-H. 1.346 f. Feist 471.

Grk. δεξιός (prob. *δεξιϝός, cf. Goth. *taihswa*), Hom. and poet. δεξιτερός; Lat. *dexter* (> It. *destro*, OFr. *destre*, Sp. *diestro*), Osc. *destrst* 'dextra est', Umbr. *destram-e* 'in dextram'; Ir. *dess*, NIr. *deas*, W. *de*, *deheu*, Br. *dehou;* Goth. *taihswa*, OHG *zeso*, MHG *zese;* Lith. *dešinas*, ChSl. *desnŭ*, SCr. *desni* (Russ. *desnoj* 'right', *desnica* 'right hand' fr. ChSl.); Skt. *dakṣiṇa-*, Av. *dašina-*.

2. Fr. *droit*, Sp. *derecho*, Rum. *drept*, fr. Lat. *dīrēctus*, VLat. **dērēctus* 'straight' (12.73). REW 2648. Wartburg 2.87 ff.

3. ON *hægri*, Dan. *højre*, Sw. *höger*, orig. comp. of ON *hægr* 'easy, convenient'. Falk-Torp 452. Hellquist 394.

OE *swīþra*, early ME *swither*, OS *suīthra* (*hand*), orig. comp. of OE *swīþ*, OS *swīði*, Goth. *swinþs* 'strong' (4.81).

ME *riht*, NE *right*, Du. *recht*, MHG *reht* (but rarely in this sense), NHG *recht*, but OE *riht*, OHG *reht*, etc. only 'straight, just, etc.' : Lat. *rēctus*, etc. Walde-P. 2.364. Weigand-H. 2.547. NED s.v. *right*, adj.

4. Lett. *labs*, also and orig. 'good' : Lith. *labas* 'good' (16.71), cf. MHG *diu bezzer hant* 'the better (= right) hand'.

5. Boh. *pravý*, Pol. *prawy*, Russ. *pravyj*, lit. 'just, right' : ChSl. *pravŭ* 'straight', etc. (12.73).

12.42 LEFT

(Adj., vs. Right)

Grk.	ἀριστερός, εὐώνυμος, σκαιός, λαιός	Goth.	*hleiduma*	Lith.	*kairias*
NG	ἀριστερός, ζερβός	ON	*vinstri*	Lett.	*kreiss*
Lat.	*sinister, laevus, scaevus*	Dan.	*venstre*	ChSl.	*šujĭ, lěvŭ*
It.	*sinistro*	Sw.	*vänster*	SCr.	*lijevi*
Fr.	*gauche*	OE	*winestra*	Boh.	*levý*
Sp.	*izquierdo, siniestro*	ME	*lift, luft*	Pol.	*lewy*
Rum.	*stîng*	NE	*left*	Russ.	*levyj*
Ir.	*clē, tūath*	Du.	*linker*	Skt.	*savya-, vāma-*
NIr.	*clē (tuath)*	OHG	*winistar, slinc*	Av.	*haoya-, vairyastāra-*
W.	*aswy, chwith*	MHG	*winster, linc*		
Br.	*kleiz*	NHG	*link*		

There is no such single widespread inherited group for 'left' as for 'right'. But there are some cases of correspondence between Greek, Latin, Celtic, and Baltic or Slavic, and between Slavic and Indic, all words without certain root connections.

Of the others, several are from notions applicable to the inferior left hand, as 'weak, useless', 'limp', 'bent, crooked', this last relation prob. in part through an intermediate 'awkward' (cf. NE *awkward* orig. 'turned the wrong way'), but also as opposite of 'straight' = 'right'.

Several are in origin terms applied to the normally inauspicious left side in taking omens, either 'inauspicious' or more frequently euphemistic 'good, better, friendly, pleasant, auspicious'.

1. Grk. ἀριστερός, orig. euphemistic 'better' : ἄριστος 'best', etc. Walde-P. 1.69. Boisacq 77 f. (with other views).

Grk. εὐώνυμος, likewise euphemistic, 'of good name' (ὄνομα 'name'), 'auspicious'.

Grk. σκαιός, Lat. *scaevus*, perh. : Lith. *kairias* 'left', *kairė* 'left hand', NIr. *ciotach* 'left-handed', *ciotān*, *cotōg* 'left hand', W. *chwith* 'left', but ultimate root connection? Walde-P. 2.537. Pedersen 1.77. Ernout-M. 899 f.

Grk. λαιός, Lat. *laevus*, ChSl. *lěvŭ*, etc., general Slavic, prob. as orig. 'bent' (cf. Serv. Gram. *laevi* [sc. *boues*], *quorum cornua ad terram spectant*) : Lith. *išlaivoti* 'make bends'. Walde-P. 2.378 f. Ernout-M. 518 f. Walde-H. 1.751. Berneker 714 f.

NG ζερβός 'left-handed' and simply 'left', Byz. ζαρβός, with metathesis fr. ζαβρός (extant dial.), this prob. with -ρός after ἀριστερός, fr. ζαβός 'crooked, inept', though this itself is of unknown age and origin. Hatzidakis, Glotta 1.127.

2. Lat. *sinister*, prob. euphemism, perh. : Skt. *sanīyān-* 'more useful, more advantageous'. Hence It. *sinistro*, but OIt. *sinestro*, OFr. *senestre*, Sp. *siniestro*, fr. VLat. **sinester* (cf. *senexter*, *senester* in late inscr.) after *dexter* 'right'. Ernout-M. 945. REW 7947.

Osc.-Umbr. *nertro-* (Osc. *nertrak* 'sinistra', Umbr. *nertru* 'sinistro' : Grk. (ἐ)νέρτερος 'lower', etc., with development 'lower' > 'inferior' > 'left'. Walde-P. 2.333 f.

Fr. *gauche*, back-formation to *gauchir* 'turn aside, dodge' (fr. OFr. *guenchir* 'turn' fr. Frank. **wankjan* = OHG *wankōn* 'stagger', crossed with OFr. *gauchier* 'full cloth', fr. Frank. **walkan* : OHG *walchan* 'full cloth', etc.), with sense of 'left', prob. through 'uneven, awkward'. Gamillscheg 462. Bloch 1.329. Otherwise REW 9492.

Sp. *izquierdo*, fr. Basque *ezker* 'left'. REW 3116.

Rum. *stîng*, fr. VLat. **stancus* 'weak' (cf. It. *stanco* 'tired', but OIt. *mano stanca* 'left hand', OFr., Prov. *estanc* 'weak'), ultimate orig. dub. REW 8225. Pușcariu 1647.

3. Ir. *clē*, Br. *kleiz*, Corn. *cledh*, W. (arch.) *cledd* : Goth. *hleiduma* 'left', Lat. *clīvius* 'inauspicious' (of omens), as orig. 'oblique', fr. the root **klei-* in Lat. *clīvus* 'hill' (orig. 'slope'), *clīnāre*, Grk. κλΐνω 'incline, lean'. Walde-P. 1.490. Ernout-M. 198. Feist 262.

Ir. *tūath* (esp. adv. *tūaith;* NIr. *tuath* mostly in secondary sense), euphemistic term : Goth. *þiuþ* sb. 'good', ON *þȳðr* 'friendly', Lat. *tūtus* 'safe', etc. Walde-P. 1.706. Vendryes, RC 33.255. Pedersen, Don. Nat. Schrijnen 422.

W. *aswy*, perh. fr. **ad-seuyo* : ChSl. *šujĭ*, Skt. *savya-* 'left' (below). Pedersen 2.16.

W. *chwith* : Grk. σκαιός, above, 1.

4. Goth. *hleiduma* : Ir. *clē*, etc., above, 3.

ON *vinstri*, Dan. *venstre*, Sw. *vänster*, OE *winestra*, OHG *winistar*, MHG *winster*, orig. as euphemistic 'more desirable, friendlier' : ON *vinr*, OHG *wini*, OE *wine* 'friend', OHG *wunnia*, OE *wynn* 'joy', Skt. *van-* 'desire, seek, gain', etc. Walde-P. 1.260. Falk-Torp 1367.

ME *luft*, *lyft*, *lift*, *left*, NE *left*, fr. OE *left* 'weak' (this, if a separate word from *lyft*, perh. : Grk. λεπτός 'peeled, fine, delicate, weak') and OE *lyft* 'weak' : MDu. *lucht*, *luft* 'left', fr. a root **leup-*). Walde-P. 2.430. Falk-Torp 658. NED s.v. *left*, adj.

Du. *linker*, MHG *linc*, *lenc*, NHG *link* (OHG *lenka* 'the left hand') : Dan. *linke*, Sw. *linka*, 'limp', etc., beside Sw. *slinka* 'dangle, slip', OE *slincan* 'crawl', OHG *slinc*, MDu. *slink* 'left', Lat. *languēre* 'be weak, faint, weary', Ir. *lacc* 'loose, weak', etc. Walde-P. 2.713. Falk-Torp 664.

For other MHG words for 'left', *tenc*, *lerc*, *lerz*, see G. S. Lane, JEGPh. 32.483 f.

5. Lith. *kairias*, perh. : Grk. σκαιός (above, 1).

Lett. *kreiss*, cf. Lith. *kreisa* 'vice, defect' : Lett. *kreilis* 'left hand', *krievs* 'crooked', Slavic *krivŭ* 'crooked'. Mühl.-Endz. 2.271. Berneker 618. Walde-P. 2.570.

6. ChSl. *šujĭ* : Skt. *savya-*, Av. *haoya-* 'left', prob. through 'bent', fr. the root **seu-* in Ir. *sōim* 'turn', etc. G. S. Lane, Language 11.195.

ChSl. *lěvŭ* : Grk. λαιός (above, 1).

7. Skt. *savya-*, Av. *haoya-*, above, 6.

Skt. *vāma-*, prob. = *vāma-* 'dear, pleasant, desirous of', fr. the root in *van-* 'desire, gain', etc. (cf. ON *vinstri*, etc., above, 4). Walde-P. 1.259. Uhlenbeck 282.

Av. *vairyastāra-* : *vairya-* 'the best', fr. *var-* 'choose'. Cf. Grk. ἀριστερός 'left' : ἄριστος 'best' (above, 1). Barth. 1373 f.

12.43 NEAR (adv.)

Grk.	ἐγγύς, πλησίον, πέλας	Goth.	*nēhw(a)*	Lith.	*arti*
NG	πλησίον, κοντά, σιμά	ON	*nær(i)*	Lett.	*tuvu*
Lat.	*prope, juxtā*	Dan.	*nær*	ChSl.	*blizĭ, blizŭ*
It.	*presso*	Sw.	*nära*	SCr.	*blizu*
Fr.	*près*	OE	*nēah*	Boh.	*blízko*
Sp.	*cerca*	ME	*ne(i)h, ner*	Pol.	*blizko*
Rum.	*aproape*	NE	*near (nigh)*	Russ.	*blizko*
Ir.	*i n-ocus*	Du.	*nabij*	Skt.	*samīpam, antikam, nikaṭam*
NIr.	*i n-aice, i bhfogus*	OHG	*nāh(o)*	Av.	*asne*
W.	*yn agos*	MHG	*nāhe, nā*		
Br.	*tost, nes*	NHG	*nah(e)*		

1. Grk. ἐγγύς, beside ἐγγύη 'pledge, surety', etc., prob. to be analyzed as ἐν-, γύ-ς, second part : γυῖον 'limb, hand', Av. *du.gava* 'the two hands'. Cf. Lat. *comminus* 'hand to hand (in combat), near to, close' : *manus* 'hand'. Walde-P. 1.637. Boisacq 212.

Grk. πλησίον, fr. adj. πλησίος 'near, close to', also πέλας, beside πελάζω 'approach', etc., outside connections dub. but possibly 'near' fr. 'striking upon' : Lat. *pellere* 'push, thrust, drive out'. Walde-P. 2.57 f. Boisacq 760 f.

NG κοντά, fr. adj. κοντός 'short' (12.59).

NG σιμά, through 'short' (like κοντά), fr. σῖμός 'snub-nosed'.

2. Lat. *prope*, prob. fr. **pro-que* (cf. *proximus*), with opposite assimilation to that seen in *quīnque* fr. **penque*. Semantic development through 'in front of' or 'forwards to'? Walde-P. 2.47. Ernout-M. 815.

Lat. *iuxtā* : *iungere* 'join' (12.22). Ernout-M. 504. Walde-H. 1.737.

It. *presso*, Fr. *près*, fr. Lat. *pressē* 'with pressure, closely, tightly' (: *premere* 'press'). REW 6742.

Sp. *cerca*, fr. Lat. *circā* 'around'. REW 6742.

Rum. *aproape*, fr. adv. phrase *ad prope* (cf. *ad pressum* > It. *appresso*, Fr. *après; ad ubi* > It. *dove*, etc.) with *prope* (above). REW 197.

3. Ir. *i n-ocus*, NIr. *i bhfogus*, W. *yn agos*, adv. phrases of adjs. *ocus*, NIr. *fogus*, W. *agos* 'near', perh. the same word as Ir. *ocus* conj. 'and', and to be connected with Ir. *oc* 'by, at'. Thurneysen, Gram. 549. Pedersen 1.161.

NIr. *i n-aice*, phrase 'in proximity'. Dinneen s.v. *aice*.

Br. *tost*, fr. OFr. *tost* 'soon' (Fr. *tôt*), with change of application from time to place. Henry 267.

Br. *nes* (but mostly adj.) = W. *nes* 'nearer' : Ir. *nessa* 'nearer', *nessam* 'nearest', Osc. *nessimas* 'proximae', formed fr. IE **ned-* in Lat. *nōdus* 'knot', etc. Walde-P. 2.328.

4. Goth. *nēhw*, *nēhwa*, ON *nær* (> ME *ner*, NE *near*), *næri*, Dan. *nær*, Sw. *nära* (comp. forms in Scand.), OE *nēah*, *nēh*, ME *ne(i)h*, NE arch. *nigh*, Du. *na* (usually cpd. *nabij*), OHG *nāh(o)*, MHG *nāhe*, *nā*, NHG *nah(e)*, outside connections dub., perh. : Lith. *pra-nokti* 'overtake', Lett. *nākt* 'come'. Walde-P. 1.129. Falk-Torp 778. Feist 373. Weigand-H. 2.267.

5. Lith. *arti* (old loc. **artēi*) : Grk. ἄρτι 'even, just', Arm. *ard* 'now, just', Skt. *ṛta-* 'fitting, right', etc., fr. the root in Grk. ἀραρίσκω 'fit, join together', etc. Walde-P. 1.72.

Lett. *tuvu*, fr. adj. *tuvs* 'near' : Lith. *tuvi* 'at once', OPruss. *tawischan* (acc. sg.) 'the nearest', etym. dub. Mühl.-Endz. 4.276 f.

6. ChSl. *blizĭ*, *blizŭ*, SCr. *blizu*, Boh. *blízko*, Pol., Russ. *blizko*, beside adj. ChSl. *blizĭnĭ*, etc. : Lett. *blaizit* 'press together, crush, beat', Lat. *flīgere* 'beat, strike down', Grk. φλίβω 'press, crush'. Walde-P. 2.217. Berneker 61 f.

7. Skt. *samīpam*, beside adj. *samīpa-*, prob. : *sam-āp-* 'obtain', cpd. of *āp-* 'reach'. Uhlenbeck 329.

Skt. *antikam*, beside *antika-* 'vicinity, presence', fr. *anti* 'opposite, before' (: Grk. ἀντί 'opposite', etc.).

Skt. *nikaṭam*, beside *nikaṭa-* adj. 'near, at one side', apparently cpd. with *ni-* 'down(wards)', but last member obscure. Uhlenbeck 147.

Av. *asne*, loc. sg. of adj. **asna-* (fr. **a-zd-na-* pple.) fr. root **sed-* 'sit' (Skt. *sad-*, Av. *had-*, etc.). Walde-P. 2.485. Barth. 220.

12.44 FAR (adv.)

Grk.	μακράν, πόρρω, τῆλε	Goth.	*fairra*	Lith.	*toli*
NG	μακριά, ἀλλάργα	ON	*fjarri, langt*	Lett.	*tālu*
Lat.	*procul, longē*	Dan.	*langt, fjernt*	ChSl.	*daleče*
It.	*lontano, lunge*	Sw.	*långt, fjärran*	SCr.	*daleko*
Fr.	*loin*	OE	*feor*	Boh.	*daleko*
Sp.	*lejos*	ME	*fer*	Pol.	*daleko*
Rum.	*departe*	NE	*far*	Russ.	*daleko*
Ir.	*in chēin*	Du.	*ver*	Skt.	*dūram, dūre*
NIr.	*i bhfad*	OHG	*fer(ro)*	Av.	*dūraē*
W.	*ymhell*	MHG	*ver(re)*		
Br.	*pell*	NHG	*fern, weit*		

Most of the adverbs for 'far' are connected with adjectives for 'long' or 'wide' or with the large group of adverbs meaning 'before, forth, beyond', etc.

1. Grk. μακράν, NG μακριά, fr. adjs. μακρός, NG μακρύς 'long' (12.52).

Grk. πρόσω and πόρσω, Att. πόρρω, also with notion of motion 'forewards, ahead' : Lat. *porrō* 'foreward, onward', Grk. πρό, Lat. *pro* 'before', Goth. *fairri*, etc. 'far' (below). Walde-P. 2.38. Ernout-M. 791.

Grk. (poet.) τῆλε, τηλοῦ, Aeol. πήλυι : Lat. *-cul* in *procul* (below), W., Br. *pell* 'far', Skt. *carama-* 'the last, extreme', *cira-* 'long' (of time), fr. the root **kʷel-*, orig. 'turn', in Grk. πόλος 'pivot', τέλος 'end', Lat. *colere* 'cultivate', etc. Walde-P. 1.517. Boisacq 966. Walde-H. 1.246.

NG ἀλλάργα, fr. It. *alla larga* : *largo* 'wide' (12.61). Ἰστ. Λεξ. 1.456.

2. Lat. *procul*, cpd. of *pro-* 'before' and an old adv. related to Grk. τῆλε, etc. (above). Ernout-M. 813.

Lat. *longē* (> It. *lungi*, *lunge*, Fr. *loin*), fr. adj. *longus* 'long' (12.52); VLat. **longitānus* > It. *lontano* (adj. and adv.), Fr. *lointain* (adj.). Ernout-M. 561. REW 5116, 5118.

Sp. *lejos*, fr. Lat. *laxus* 'loose, spacious, wide'. REW 4956.

Rum. *departe*, fr. Lat. *dē parte* 'from the side'. REW 6254. Tiktin 521.

3. Ir. *in chēin*, adv. fr. *cīan* adj. 'far' and 'long' (12.52), also alone as adv. *cid dīan ocus cīan notheisinn* 'though I went fast and far' (Ml.41d.9).

NIr. *i bhfad* (or *a bhfad*), lit. 'in length', cf. *fada* 'long' (12.52).

W. *ymhell*, adv. fr. *pell* adj., Br. *pell* (adj. and adv.) : Grk. τῆλε, etc. (above, 1). Pedersen 1.128.

4. Goth. *fairra*, ON *fjarri*, OE *feor* etc., general Gmc. : Grk. πέρā 'beyond, further', Skt. *para-* adj. 'far, distant', *paras* 'beyond', etc. (all ultimately connected with Grk. πρό, Lat. *prō*, Skt. *pra* 'before', etc.). Walde-P. 2.31 ff. Falk-Torp 225. Feist 141.

ON, Dan. *langt*, Sw. *långt*, neut. forms as advs. fr. ON *langr*, etc. 'long' (12.52).

NHG *weit*, fr. adj. *weit* 'spacious, far', OHG *wīt* 'spacious, wide, broad', general Gmc. in latter sense (12.61). Development fr. 'it is a wide distance to B' to 'it is far to B', and then also 'B is far', only NHG and still partially distinguished fr. *fern*. Paul, Deutsches Wtb. 639.

5. Lith. *toli*, Lett. *tālu*, fr. adj. Lith. *tolus*, Lett. *tāls* 'far' (OPruss. *tāls*, *tālis* adv. 'farther') : Boh. *otáleti* 'delay, linger', further connection dub. Trautmann, Altpreuss. 445. Zubatý, Arch. sl. Ph. 16.388.

6. ChSl. *daleče*, SCr. *daleko*, etc., general Slavic, fr. adj. forms ChSl. *dalekŭ*, SCr. *dalek*, etc., beside ChSl. *dalja* in *vŭ dalję* 'far', prob. : ChSl. *dlŭgŭ*, Skt. *dīrgha-* 'long' (12.57). Berneker 177. Otherwise Zubatý, l.c., and Brückner 84.

7. Skt. *dūram*, *dūre*, Av. *dūraē*, OPers. *duraiy*, acc. and loc. sg. neut. of adj. *dūra-* 'far, distant' : Vedic *duvas-* 'pressing foreward', *du-* 'go away(?)', MHG *zowen* 'hasten, progress, succeed', etc. Walde-P. 1.778 f.

	12.45 EAST	12.46 WEST	12.47 NORTH	12.48 SOUTH
Grk.	ἀνατολή, ἕως	ἑσπέρα, δυσμαί, δύσις	βορέᾱς, βορρᾶς	νότος, μεσημβρία
NG	ἀνατολή	δύσις	βοριάς, βορρᾶς	νότος, μεσημβρία
Lat.	*oriēns*	*occidēns, occāsus*	*septentriō*	*merīdiēs, auster*
It.	*est, levante*	*ovest, ponente*	*nord*	*sud, mezzogiorno, mezzodì*
Fr.	*est*	*ouest*	*nord*	*sud, midi*
Sp.	*este*	*oeste, poniente*	*norte*	*sur, mediodia*
Rum.	*est, răsărit*	*vest, apus*	*nord*	*sud*
Ir.	*airther*	*iarthar*	*tūascert*	*descert*
NIr.	*oirthear*	*īarthar*	*tuaisceart*	*deisceart*
W.	*dwyrain*	*gorllewin*	*gogledd*	*deheu, de*
Br.	*reter, savheol*	*kuzheol, kornaoueg*	*hanternoz*	*kreisteiz*
Goth.	*urruns*	*saggqs*	....	....
ON	*austr*	*vestr*	*norðr*	*suðr*
Dan.	*øst*	*vest*	*nord*	*syd*
Sw.	*öster*	*väster*	*nord, norr*	*söder*
OE	*ēast*	*west*	*norþ*	*sūþ*
ME	*est*	*west*	*north*	*south*
NE	*east*	*west*	*north*	*south*
Du.	*oosten*	*westen*	*noorden*	*zuiden*
OHG	*ōstan*	*westan*	*nord, nordan*	*sundan*
MHG	*ōsten*	*west(en)*	*nort, norden*	*sūden, sunden*
NHG	*osten*	*westen*	*norden*	*süden*
Lith.	*rytai*	*vakarai*	*šiaurė, žiemiai*	*pietūs*
Lett.	*austrums, rīti*	*rietums, vakari*	*ziemel'i*	*dienvidus*
ChSl.	*vŭstokŭ*	*zapadŭ*	*sěverŭ*	*jugŭ*
SCr.	*istok*	*zapad*	*sjever*	*jug*
Boh.	*východ*	*západ*	*sever, půlnoc*	*jih*
Pol.	*wschód*	*zachód*	*północ*	*południe*
Russ.	*vostok*	*zapad*	*sever*	*jug*
Skt.	*pūrvā-(diç-), prācī-(diç-)*	*pratīcī-(diç-), paçcimā-(diç-)*	*uttarā-(diç-), udīcī(diç-)*	*dakṣiṇā-(diç-)*
Av.	*upaošaŋhva-, ušastara-* (adjs.)	*daošatara-* (adj.)	*apāxtara-* (adj.)	*paurva-, rapiθwitara-* (adjs.)

The majority of words for the main points of the compass are based either on the position of the sun at a given time of day ('sunrise, dawn, morning' = 'east'; 'sunset, evening' = 'west'; 'midday' = 'south') or on one's orientation, which among the IE-speaking peoples was usually facing the sunrise ('in front' = 'east'; 'behind' = 'west'; 'right' = 'south'; 'left' = 'north'), though there are also traces of orientations toward the north or south (the latter in the Avesta, where 'in front' = 'south'; 'behind' = 'north'). Cf. Schrader Reallex. 1.500 f.

A few are from names of characteristic winds, and among those for 'north' some are connected with the name of a constellation in the north, with 'winter', or with 'midnight' as opposite of 'midday' = 'south'.

Notable is the spread of the English words, first as nautical terms, to the Romance languages.

The attested Goth. words for 'east' and 'west' (Mt. 8.11; those for 'north' and 'south' are not quotable) are not general Gmc. terms, but literal translations of the Grk. Cf. G. S. Lane, Phil. Quarterly 12.323 f.

But it may be noted that Luther used the Gmc. terms only for the winds, otherwise those for 'morning', 'evening', etc., and that these or others had almost replaced the old terms for a while. Paul, Deutsches Wtb. 379.

The words are listed in the sb. forms so far as possible. But some of the early Gmc. forms are quotable only as advs. or in cpds., as OE *ēast*, etc. (see NED s.v.). The Av. forms are adjs., and the Skt. are fem. adjs. with *diç-* 'direction', esp. 'cardinal point of the sky' (: *diç-* 'point out') either expressed or understood.

12.45. Words for 'east' are connected with words for 'dawn' or 'morning', with verbs for 'rise', or with words for 'before' or 'in front', all referring to the direction of the rising sun.

1. IE **āus-*, **āusos-*, **usos-*, etc., in words for 'dawn' and 'east', beside verb forms as Skt. *ucchati*, Av. *usati* 'lights up' (esp. of the dawn), Lith. *aušti*, Lett. *aust* 'to dawn'. Walde-P. 1.26 f. Ernout-M. 93. Walde-H. 1.86.

Grk. Aeol. αὔως, Dor. ἅως, Hom. ἠώς, Att. ἕως 'dawn' and 'east'; Lat. *aurōra* (**ausōs-ā*) 'dawn' and (mostly poet.) 'east' (prob. also *auster* 'south wind', 12.48); ON *austr*, OE *ēast*, OHG *ōstan*, etc., general Gmc., with various suffixes; Lith. *aušra* 'dawn', Lett. *austrums* 'east'; ChSl. *za ustra* 'in the morning'; Skt. *uṣās*, Av. *ušā* 'dawn', whence Av. *ušastara-*, *upaošaŋhva-* (fr. **upa-ušah-*) adjs. for 'east'.

2. Grk. ἀνατολή 'a rising', esp. pl. ἀνατολαί ἡλίου 'sunrise', hence 'east' : ἀνατέλλω 'rise' (esp. of the sun).

3. Lat. *oriēns*, pres. pple. of *orīrī* 'rise'. Hence as literary terms, It., Sp. *oriente*, Fr. *orient*.

It. *levante* (> Sp. *levante*, Fr. *levant*), fr. *levāre* 'raise, lift', refl. 'rise'. REW 5000.

Fr. *est* (> It., Rum. *est*), Sp. *este* fr. ME *est*. REW 2917a. Wartburg 3.247.

Rum. *răsărit*, lit. '(sun)rise', fr. *răsări*, 'go up, climb, rise' (of sun), cpd. of *raz-* (Slavic) and *sari* 'spring' fr. Lat. *salīre*. Tiktin 1300, 1367.

4. Ir. *airther*, NIr. *oirthear*, Br. *reter*, fr. Ir. *air-*, Br. *ar-* 'before' (: Skt. *pari* 'against, toward', Grk. περί 'around', etc.), but also 'east' in advs. *t-air* 'in the east', *s-air* 'to the east', *an-air* 'from the east'. Walde-P. 2.33. Pedersen 2.187. Ernault, Glossaire 572.

W. *dwyrain*, orig. 'sunrise', perh. fr. a cpd. of the root in Ir. *rigim* 'stretch out', Lat. *regere* 'direct, rule', etc. Pedersen 1.237, 2.56, 596 note 3.

Br. *savheol*, cpd. of *sav* 'upright, raised' and *heol* 'sun'.

5. Goth. *urruns* (lit. translation of Grk. ἀνατολή) : *urrinnan* 'run out, go up, rise (of sun)', ON *renna*, OE *rinnan* 'run', etc. Feist 528.

6. Lith. *rytai*, Lett. *rīti*, pl. of Lith. *rytas*, Lett. *rīts* 'morning' (14.34).

7. ChSl. *vŭstokŭ*, SCr. *istok*, Russ. *vostok*, orig. 'sunrise', lit. 'a running up, out' : ChSl. *tešti*, *teką* 'run', etc. (10.46).

Boh. *východ*, Pol. *wschód*, orig. 'sunrise', lit. 'a going out, up' : Boh. *choditi*, Pol. *chodzić* 'go' (10.47).

8. Skt. *pūrvā-(diç-)* fr. adj. *pūrva-* 'in front, former, eastern' = Av. *paorva-* 'in front, former', but 'southern' (see 12.48). OPers. *paruva-* 'eastern' (Barth. 871) is to be deleted. The correct reading is *paradraya* 'beyond the sea'. Cf. Cameron, J. Near East. Stud. 2.307 f.

Skt. *prācī-(diç-)*, fr. *prāñc-* 'directed forward, in front, facing, eastern'.

12.46. Words for 'west' are derived from those for the 'setting, going down' (of the sun), or 'evening' or 'behind' (as opposed to 'in front' = 'east', cf. 12.45).

1. Grk. ἑσπέρα 'evening' (14.36) and 'west'.

Grk. δυσμή (esp. pl. δυσμαί), and δύσις, both lit. 'the setting of the sun' (sc. ἡλίου) : δύω 'sink, go down, set' (of the sun). Walde-P. 1.777 f.

2. Lat. *occidēns*, pres. pple. of *occidere* 'fall down, perish, set (of the sun)', cpd.

of *cadere* 'fall'. Hence the lit. Romance words It., Sp. *occidente*, Fr. *occident* 'occident'.

Lat. *occāsus* (sc. *solis*), lit. 'sunset' : *occidere* (above).

It. *ponente*, Sp. *poniente*, fr. It. *porre*, Sp. *poner* 'put, place' (12.12). REW 6647.

Fr. *ouest*, Sp. *oeste* (> It. *ovest*), fr. OE *west* (below, 4). REW 9526.

Rum. *vest*, fr. NHG *west*.

Rum. *apus*, lit. '(sun)set', pple. of *apune* 'sink, go down, set (of the sun)', fr. Lat. *ad-pōnere* 'place near'. Tiktin 86.

3. Ir. *īarthar*, fr. *īar* 'behind', and 'west' in advs. *t-īar* 'in the west', *s-īar* 'toward the west', *an-īar* 'from the west' (: Skt. *api*, Grk. ἐπί). Pedersen 1.93. Walde-P. 1.123.

W. *gorllewin*, older *gollewin*, OW *gullengin*, etym.? Pedersen 1.107.

Br. *kuzheol*, lit. 'sunset', cpd. of *kuz* 'hiding' and *heol* 'sun'.

Br. *kornaoueg*, *kornog*, orig. only 'west wind', lit. 'trumpeter' fr. *korn* 'horn, trumpet'. Henry 76.

4. Goth. *saggqs* (only dat. sg. *saggqa* Mt. 8.11, rendering δυσμῶν) : *siggan* 'sink, go down'. Feist 403.

ON *vestr*, OE *west*, OHG *westan*, etc., general Gmc., prob. deriv. of a Gmc. *wes- : Skt. *avas* 'down' beside *ava* 'down from', and Grk. ἑσπερος, etc. 'evening' (14.46). Walde-P. 1.15. Falk-Torp 1371 f.

5. Lith. *vakarai*, Lett. *vakari*, pl. of Lith. *vakaras*, Lett. *vakars* 'evening' (14.36).

Lett. *rietums*, esp. pl. *rietumi*, fr. *riets* 'sunset' : *riest* 'roll, fall'. Mühl.-Endz. 3.550.

6. ChSl. *zapadŭ*, SCr., Russ. *zapad*, Boh. *západ*, fr. *za-* 'behind', and *padą*, *pasti* 'fall' (with reference to the disappearance of the sun behind the horizon).

Pol. *zachód* fr. *zachodzić* 'go behind, go down (of sun)'.

7. Skt. *pratīcī-(diç-)*, fr. *pratyañc-* 'turned toward, facing, behind, western' ('west' from 'behind').

Skt. *paçcimā-(diç-)*, lit. 'hinder(most), last', fr. *paçca-* 'behind, after' and 'in the west'.

Av. *daošatara-*, *daošastara-*, adj. (*-s-* fr. *ušastara-* 'eastern'), fr. *daoša- 'evening, west' = Skt. *doṣā-* 'evening, darkness' (prob. : δύσις, etc., above, 1). Barth. 674. Walde-P. 1.777 f.

12.47. Words for 'north' are from the name of a north wind, a northern constellation, 'midnight', 'winter', 'upper region', and from 'left', or under a southern orientation 'behind'.

1. Grk. βορέας, Att. βορρᾶς, NG pop. βοριάς (βοριάς, two syll.), orig. 'north wind' (personified), source uncertain, perh. a northern loanword related to Slav. *burja* 'storm'. Walde-P. 1.682.

2. Lat. *septentriō*, orig. pl. *septentriōnes* 'the seven plow-oxen' (*triō* 'plow-ox'), name of a constellation in the north (the great or little bear). Ernout-M. 925 f.

Fr. *nord* (> It., Rum. *nord*, Sp. *norte*), fr. OE *norþ*. REW 5957.

3. Ir. *tūascert*, NIr. *tuaisceart*, cpd. of *tūas : *tūath* 'left' (12.42) and *cert* (as in *des-cert* 'south') 'part, region', perh. orig. 'quarter' : Lat. *quartus*, etc. Loth, RC 43.160 ff. Pedersen, Don. Nat. Schrijnen 423 ff.

W. *gogledd*, cf. Ir. *fochla* 'the North' (as a section of Ireland), cpd. W. *go-*, Ir. *fo-* 'sub-' and last member : W. *cledd*, Ir. *clē* 'left' (12.42). Pedersen 1.68.

Br. *hanternoz*, 'midnight' (lit. 'half-night', fr. *hanter* 'half', 13.24) and 'north', as opposed to *kreisteiz* 'noon' and 'south'.

4. ON *norðr*, OE *norþ* (adv.), etc.,

general Gmc., prob. : Osc.-Umbr. *nertro-* 'left' (12.42), Grk. νέρτερος 'lower', with development 'lower' > 'inferior' > 'left', and fr. 'left' to 'north' as one faces the rising sun. Walde-P. 2.333 f. Falk-Torp 770 f.

5. Lith. *šiaurė*, ChSl. *sěverŭ*, etc., the latter also 'north wind', beside Lith. *šiaurys* 'north wind' : Lat. *caurus* 'northwest wind', Goth. *skūra windis* 'whirlwind', OHG *scūr* 'storm', etc. Walde-P. 1.377.

Lith. *žiemiai*, Lett. *ziemeľi* fr. Lith. *žiema*, Lett. *ziema* 'winter'.

6. ChSl. *sěverŭ* : Lith. *šiaurė*, above.

Boh. *půlnoc*, Pol. *północ* 'midnight' and 'north', cpds. of *půl*, *pol* 'half' and *noc* 'night'.

7. Skt. *uttarā-(diç-)*, fr. *uttara-* 'upper, higher' also 'left, northern', deriv. of *ud-* 'up, out'.

Skt. *udīcī-(diç-)*, fr. *udañc-* 'upward, northward', fr. *ud-* 'up, out'.

Av. *apāxtara-*, *apāxəδra-*, deriv. of *apānk-* 'turned backwards', adv. 'back', in accordance with the southern orientation in the Avesta. Barth. 79 f., 82.

12.48. Words for 'south' are often the same as those for 'midday, noon'. Other sources are '(rainy) south wind', 'sunny region'(?), and 'right', or with a different orientation 'in front'.

1. Grk. νότος, properly 'south wind', as 'rainwind' : νότιος, νοτερός 'damp, rainy', νοτία 'moisture, rain', etc., prob. fr. the root in Grk. νάω 'flow', Lat. *nāre* 'swim', etc. Walde-P. 2.692 f. Boisacq 673.

Grk. μεσημβρία, also and orig. 'midday' (14.45).

2. Lat. *merīdiēs*, also and orig. 'midday' (14.45). Similarly in the Romance languages It. *mezzogiorno*, *mezzodì*, Fr. *midi*, Sp. *mediodia*, all lit. 'noon, midday'.

Lat. *auster* 'south wind', also 'south', prob. orig. 'east wind' : ON *austr*, etc., 'east' (12.45), with shift through 'southeast' explained by the diagonal position of the axis of Italy. Walde-H. 1.87. Ernout-M. 94 (with some doubt).

Fr. *sud* (> It., Rum. *sud*), Sp. *sud*, *sur*, fr. OE *sūþ* (below, 4). REW 8424.

3. Ir. *descert*, NIr. *deisceart*, cpd. of *dess* 'right, southern' (12.41), with *cert* as in *tūascert* 'north' (12.47).

Ir. *tūas*, NIr. *thuas*, adv. 'above' and 'in the South', that is, *t-ūas*, fr. *ūas* 'above' : Grk. ὕψι 'on high'. Pedersen, Don. Nat. Schrijnen 424.

W. *deheu*, *de*, lit. 'right (hand, side)', as adj. 'right, southern' (12.41).

Br. *kreisteiz*, also and orig. 'midday' (14.45).

4. ON *suðr*, OE *sūþ*, etc., general Gmc. (the MHG and NHG form without *-n-* fr. LG), Gmc. *sunþa-, orig. perh. 'toward the sun, the sunny region' : Goth. *sunnō*, etc., 'sun', like the words for 'east' fr. 'dawn'. Walde-P. 2.447. Falk-Torp 1224 f.

5. Lith. *pietūs* (pl.) also and orig. 'midday meal, midday' (14.45).

Lett. *dienvidus*, also and orig. (beside *dienasvidus*) 'midday' (14.45).

6. ChSl. *jugŭ*, SCr., Russ. *jug*, Boh. *jih*, etym. dub. Walde-P. 1.25. Berneker 458.

Pol. *południe*, also and orig. 'midday' (14.45), similarly Boh. *podoní* adj. 'midday-, southern', *k podeni* 'to the south'.

7. Skt. *dakṣiṇā-(diç-)*, fr. *dakṣiṇa-* adj. 'right, southern' (12.41).

Av. *paurva-* 'in front, former' and 'southern' in contrast to Skt. *pūrva-* 'in front, eastern', owing to the southern orientation in the Avesta. Barth. 870 ff.

Av. *rapiθwitara-*, *rapiθwənatara-* 'southerly', derivs. of unattested simple adj. forms fr. *rapiθwā-* 'midday' (14.45). Barth. 1509.

12.51 FORM, SHAPE

Grk.	μορφή, σχῆμα, εἶδος	Goth.	*laudi, hiwi*	Lith.	*pavidalas*
NG	μορφή, σχῆμα	ON	*mynd, skapan*	Lett.	*stāvs, augums, veids*
Lat.	*fōrma, figūra*	Dan.	*skikkelse, dannelse*	ChSl.	*obrazŭ*
It.	*forma*	Sw.	*skapnad, gestalt*	SCr.	*oblik, lik*
Fr.	*forme*	OE	*hīw, gesceap*	Boh.	*podoba, tvar*
Sp.	*forma*	ME	*hiewe, forme, shap*	Pol.	*kształt, postać*
Rum.	*formă*	NE	*form, shape*	Russ.	*obraz, vid*
Ir.	*cruth, delb*	Du.	*gestalte, gedaante*	Skt.	*rūpa-, ākāra-*
NIr.	*cuma, cruth, dealbh*	OHG	*bilidi*	Av.	*vaēδi-, kəhrp-*
W.	*ffurf*	MHG	*gestalt, getǣne (bilde)*		
Br.	*furm, neuz, aoz*	NHG	*gestalt*		

Some of the words for 'shape, form' have also the more generic sense of 'appearance' and are connected with the IE root for 'see' and 'know'. Others are from verbs for 'fashion, mold, create, make' or from such diverse notions as 'hold', 'strike', 'grow', etc.

1. Grk. μορφή, etym.? Walde-P. 2.274. Boisacq 645.

Grk. σχῆμα, deriv. of ἔχω 'hold, have', fut. σχήσω, hence orig. 'manner of holding oneself', then 'form, shape, bearing, manner', etc., like Lat. *habitus* : *habēre*. Walde-P. 2.482.

Grk. εἶδος, orig. 'appearance, aspect', hence 'form, shape, kind' (NG 'kind'), fr. the root of εἶδον 'saw', οἶδα 'know', like Lith. *veidas* 'face, appearance', Lett. *veids* 'form, appearance', ChSl. *vidŭ* 'look, appearance', etc. Walde-P. 1.239. Boisacq 220.

2. Lat. *fōrma* (> It. *forma*, OFr. *fourme* > ME *forme*, NE *form*; Fr. *forme*, Sp. *forma*, Rum. *formă* are lit. borrowings), etym. dub. Connection with Grk. μορφή, either by borrowing and transposition of consonants (through Etruscan?) or otherwise is possible. Ernout-M. 378 f. Walde-H. 1.530 f.

Lat. *fōrma* has given a more or less literary or technical word in most of the Eur. languages, as Dan., Sw., NHG *form*, in Slavic languages *forma*.

Lat. *figūra*, properly 'shape given to an object' : *fingere* 'shape, mold', *figulus* 'potter', Skt. *dih-* 'smear', etc. Walde-P. 1.833. Ernout-M. 361 f. Walde-H. 1.502.

3. Ir. *cruth* : W. *pryd* 'appearance', Skt. *kṛ-* 'do, make'. Walde-P. 1.517. Stokes 60.

Ir. *delb*, NIr. *dealbh* : *dolbaim* 'form, mold', *doilbthid* 'figulus', W. *delw* 'image', Lat. *dolāre* 'hew, construct', Skt. *dal-* 'split, rend', etc. Walde-P. 1.810. Stokes 150.

NIr. *cuma*, fr. MIr. *cumma* 'a breaking, cutting, shaping, fashioning, manner', fr. *com-benim*, cpd. of *benim* 'strike, hew'. Pedersen 2.461. K. Meyer, Contrib. 563.

W. *ffurf*, fr. Lat. *fōrma*. Loth, Mots lat. 171.

Br. *furm*, fr. OFr. *fourme* (for this and the other Br. words, see Vallée s.v. *forme*).

Br. *neuz*, also *aoz* : Ir. *gnās* 'habit', W. *gnaws* 'nature', Lat. *nōtus*, Skt. *jñāta-* 'known', etc. Pedersen 1.49. Loth, RC 42.371.

4. Goth. *laudi* : *liudan*, OE *leodan*, OS *liodan* 'spring up, grow', Skt. *rudh-*, Av. *raod-* 'grow' (12.53). Walde-P. 2.416. Feist 323.

Goth. *hiwi*, OE *hīw*, *hēow* also 'color, appearance', ME *hiewe* (in all senses; NE *hue* restricted to 'color') : ON *hȳ* 'down', Sw. *hy* 'color of the skin', root connection disputed, perh. fr. that in OE *hǣwen* 'blue', Ir. *cīar* 'dark', ON *hārr*

'gray', etc.; or fr. *skeu- in words for 'covering'? Walde-P. 1.360 f. Falk-Torp 442. Feist 259. NED s.v. *hue*, sb.[1].

ON *mynd* = Norw. *mynd* 'manner, character, nature' : OE *gemynd* 'memory, mind', Goth. *gamunds* 'remembrance, memory', etc., Lat. *mēns*, *-tis* 'mind', etc. Semantic change fr. 'remembrance' to 'appearance' (as remembered) and 'form'. Torp, Nynorsk 443 f.

ON *skapan*, Sw. *skapnad*, OE *gesceap*, ME *shap*, NE *shape* : ON, Sw. *skapa*, OE *scieppan*, Goth. *gaskapjan*, OHG *scaphen* 'form, create', etc., perh. orig. 'chip, hew out', fr., a parallel form of the roots in Goth. *skaban*, OE *scafan* 'shave,' Lat. *scabere* 'scrape', Grk. σκάπτω 'dig', etc. Walde-P. 2.562. Falk-Torp 976, 977. Feist 200 f. NED s.v. *shape*, sb.

Dan. *skikkelse*, fr. *skik* '(good) custom, habit, usage', fr. MLG *schik* 'form, (correct) condition' : MLG *schicken* 'bring into order, direct, send', MHG *schicken* 'cause to happen, perform, bring to order' (NHG *schicken* 'send'), etc. Falk-Torp 993. Walde-P. 2.557.

Dan. *dannelse*, fr. *danne* 'form, mold', fr. adj. *dan* (Norw. and Dan. dial.) loanword fr. MLG pple. *dān* 'done, made' fr. *dōn* 'do'. Falk-Torp 136.

MHG, NHG *gestalt* (> Sw. *gestalt*, Du. *gestalte*), fr. *gestalt* 'arranged, constituted', pple. of *stellen* 'place, put'. Weigand-H. 1.707 f. Franck-v. W. 191 f.

ME *forme*, NE *form* fr. OFr. *fourme* (above, 2).

Du. *gedaante*, MDu. *ghedaente* 'form, appearance, quality', fr. *ghedane* id. = MHG *getǣne*, derivs. of the past pples. MDu. *ghedaen*, MHG *getān* 'done, made' (cf. Dan. *dannelse*, above). Franck-v. W. 178.

OHG *bilidi*, *biladi*, MHG *bilde* (but mostly 'image, figure', etc., NHG *bild*), prob. deriv. of an adj. *bil- 'fitting, becoming', seen also in *billig* 'cheap', OHG *billīch* 'fitting, according to', etc. Weigand-H. 1.237 f. Kluge-G. 57.

5. Lith. *pavidalas* : *veidas* 'face, appearance', Lett. *veids* 'form, appearance', ChSl. *vidŭ* 'look, appearance', Russ. *vid* 'face, look, form', Grk. εἶδος 'aspect, form', etc. (above, 1). Trautmann 358.

Lett. *stāvs*, also 'growth, stature' : *stāvēt* 'stand'. Mühl.-Endz. 3.1055.

Lett. *augums*, lit. 'growth' : *augt* 'grow'. Mühl.-Endz. 1.220 f.

6. ChSl. *obrazŭ*, Russ. *obraz* (Boh. *obraz* 'picture, image'), cpds. of simplex in Russ. *raz*, Boh. *ráz*, etc. 'blow' : ChSl. *uraziti* 'percutere', *rězati* 'cut', etc. Meillet, Études 221. Miklosich 273.

SCr. *oblik*, *lik* : ChSl. *lice* 'face, cheek', etc. (4.204). Berneker 719 f.

Boh. *tvar* : ChSl. *tvorŭ* 'condition, appearance', *tvoriti* 'make', etc. (9.11). Miklosich 366.

Boh. *podoba* : Slov. *podoba* 'picture, appearance', Pol. *podoba* 'similarity', ChSl. *po-doba jestŭ*, *po-dobajetŭ* 'it is fitting', etc. Berneker 203 f.

Pol. *kształt*, fr. NHG *gestalt* (above). Brückner 278.

Pol. *postać* : *stać* 'stand'. Brückner 432.

Russ. *vid*, see above, 5.

7. Skt. *rūpa-* : *varpas-* 'image, form'? Uhlenbeck 252, 275. Walde-P. 1.276 (without *rūpa-*).

Skt. *ākāra-*, *ākṛti-* fr. *kṛ-* 'do, make'.

Av. *vaēδi-* : *vid-* 'recognize, know', Grk. εἶδος 'form', etc. (above, 1). Barth. 1321.

Av. *kəhrp-*, also esp. 'body (of men and gods)' : Skt. *kṛp-* 'form, appearance, beauty' (only inst. sg. *kṛpā*), Lat. *corpus* 'body', etc. Walde-P. 1.486. Barth. 467 ff.

12.52 SIZE

Grk.	*μέγεθος*	Goth.	*mikilei*	Lith.	*didumas, didybė*
NG	*μέγεθος*	ON	*stōrleikr*	Lett.	*lielums*
Lat.	*magnitūdō*	Dan.	*størrelse*	ChSl.	*veličije, veličĭstvĭje*
It.	*grandezza*	Sw.	*störlek*	SCr.	*veličina*
Fr.	*grandeur*	OE	*micelness*	Boh.	*velikost'*
Sp.	*tamaño*	ME	*mikelnes, syse*	Pol.	*wielkość*
Rum.	*mărime*	NE	*size*	Russ.	*veličina*
Ir.	*mēit*	Du.	*grootte*	Skt.	*māna-, mahas-*
NIr.	*mēid*	OHG	*mihhelī, grōzī*	Av.	*mazah-, masah-*
W.	*maint*	MHG	*grœze, michel*		
Br.	*ment*	NHG	*grösse*		

Most of the words for 'size' are obvious derivs. of the adjectives for 'large, big' (12.55), that is, 'bigness' is used for 'the degree of bigness', as Grk. *μέγεθος* : *μέγας*, Lat. *magnitūdō* : *magnus*, Goth. *mikilei* : *mikils*, etc.—all the words listed, with the following exceptions:

1. Sp. *tamaño*, sb. of adj. *tamaño* 'so large' (Lat. *tam magnus* 'so large'). REW 8552.

2. Ir. *mēit*, NIr. *mēid*, W. *maint*, Br. *ment*, perh. **manti*, old abstract formation fr. root in Ir. *mār* 'large' (12.55). Pedersen 1.242 f., 2.48. Walde-P. 2.238.

3. ME *syse*, NE *size*, fr. OFr. *sise*, *cise* for *assise* lit. 'act of settling or fixing something' (esp. assessments, levies, etc.), pple. of OFr. *asseir* 'sit at, set down, settle' (Lat. *adsidēre*). The modern sense is late in ME, earlier 'assize' then esp. 'regulation of amount, quantity (of a tax, etc.)' and 'fixed quantity or size'. NED s.v. *size*, sb.[1].

4. Skt. *māna-*, esp. cpds. *parimāṇa-*, *pramāṇa-*, lit. 'measure' : *mā-* 'measure' (12.54).

12.53 GROW
(= Increase in Size)

Grk.	*αὐξάνομαι*	Goth.	*wahsjan*	Lith.	*augti*
NG	*μεγαλώνω, αὐξάνω*	ON	*vaxa*	Lett.	*augt*
Lat.	*crēscere, augēscere*	Dan.	*vokse*	ChSl.	*rasti*
It.	*crescere*	Sw.	*växa*	SCr.	*rasti*
Fr.	*croître*	OE	*weaxan*	Boh.	*růsti*
Sp.	*crecer*	ME	*waxe, growe*	Pol.	*rosnąć*
Rum.	*creşte*	NE	*grow*	Russ.	*rasti*
Ir.	*āsaim, forbiur*	Du.	*groeien, wassen*	Skt.	*vṛdh-, rudh-, ukṣ-*
NIr.	*fāsaim*	OHG	*wahsan*	Av.	*varəd-, rud-, uxš-*
W.	*tyfu*	MHG	*wahsen*		
Br.	*kreski*	NHG	*wachsen*		

Most of the words for 'grow' were probably used primarily with reference to plant life, as is demonstrably the case for NE *grow*.

1. IE **aweg-* (**aug-*, **ug-*, and with *-s-* extension **aweks-*, etc., orig. desid. formation). Walde-P. 1.22 f. Ernout-M. 88 ff. Walde-H. 1.82 f., 850. Falk-Torp 1390. Feist 67, 541.

Grk. *αὐξάνω*, also *αὔξω*, *ἀέξω* (**ἀϝέξω*) 'increase' (trans.) with mid. *αὐξάνομαι* etc. 'grow' (intr., but NG *αὐξάνω* trans. and intr.); Lat. *augēre* 'increase' trans., rarely also intr. 'grow', inchoat. *augēscere* intr.; Goth. *wahsjan*, OE *weaxan* etc., general Gmc. (NE *wax* of the moon, but mostly arch.); Lith. *augti*, Lett. *augt*; Skt. *ukṣ-*, Av. *uxš-* (3sg. pres. *uxšyeiti*);

Toch. A *oks-* 'grow', *okṣu*, B *aukṣu* 'old' (SSS 426).

2. NGr. *μεγαλώνω*, fr. *μεγάλος* 'large' (12.54).

3. Lat. *crēscere* (> It. *crescere*, Fr. *croître*, Sp. *crecer*, Rum. *creşte*) : *creāre* 'produce, create', Arm. *sernem* 'beget', Lith. *šerti* 'nourish, feed', Grk. *κορέσκω*, *κορέννυμι* 'satiate'. Walde-P. 1.408. Ernout-M. 232. Walde-H. 1.288.

4. Ir. *āsaim*, NIr. *fāsaim*, cf. Ir. *ās* 'growth', perh. (with loss of init. *w* in sandhi) fr. **wōks-* : Goth. *wahsjan*, etc. (above, 1). G. S. Lane, Language 13.21. Otherwise Strachan, IF 2.370.

Ir. *forbiur*, cpd. of *biru* 'carry' and *for* 'on', hence lit. 'carry on'. Pedersen 2.467 f.

W. *tyfu* : Lat. *tumēre* 'swell, be swollen', fr. an extension of the root **tēu-* in Skt. *tāuti* 'is strong', ChSl. *tyti* 'become fat', etc. Walde-P. 1.708. Ernout-M. 1064.

Br. *kreski*, prob. fr. Lat. *crēscere*. Henry 81. Loth, Mots lat. 154 (with some question on account of the short vowel).

5. ME *growe*, NE *grow*, Du. *groeien*, but OE *grōwan*, ON *grōa*, OHG *gruoan* only 'grow' (of plants), 'spring up, become green, etc.' : MHG *gruose* 'shoot of a plant, sap', Goth., ON, OHG *gras* OE *graes* 'grass', ON *grænn*, OE *grēne*, OHG *gruoni* 'green', Lat. *grāmen* 'grass'. Walde-P. 1.645 f. NED s.v. *grow*, vb.

6. ChSl. *rasti*, etc., general Slavic (Pol. *róść* replaced in present by *rosnąć*), fr. **ord(h)-t-*, prob. : Lat. *arduus* 'steep, high', Ir. *ard*, Av. *ərəδwa-* 'high'. Walde-P. 1.149. Brückner 463.

7. Skt. *vṛdh-* act. and caus. 'make grow or thrive, elevate', mid. 'grow, thrive', Av. *varəd-* act. (and mid.) 'make grow or thrive, increase', mid. and pass. 'grow, thrive' : *ūrdhva-* 'upward, upright, raised, elevated', Grk. *ὀρθός* 'upright, straight', Slavic *roditi* 'bear'. Walde-P. 1.289.

Skt. *rudh-*, *ruh-*, Av. *rud-* (pres. 3pl. Skt. *rodhanti*, Av. *raoδənti*) : Goth. *liudan* 'grow up' (of seed, Mk. 4.27), OE *lēodan*, OHG *ar-liotan* 'spring, grow' (of plants), ON *loδinn* 'grown over, hairy'. Walde-P. 2.416.

12.54 MEASURE (vb.)

Grk.	*μετρέω*	Goth.	*mitan*	Lith.	*matuoti, mieruoti*
NG	*μετρῶ*	ON	*mǣla*	Lett.	*mērīt*
Lat.	*mētīrī*	Dan.	*maale*	ChSl.	*měriti*
It.	*misurare*	Sw.	*mäta*	SCr.	*mjeriti*
Fr.	*mesurer*	OE	*metan*	Boh.	*měřiti*
Sp.	*medir*	ME	*mete, mesure*	Pol.	*mierzyć*
Rum.	*măsura*	NE	*measure*	Russ.	*merit'*
Ir.	*domidiur*	Du.	*meten*	Skt.	*mā-*
NIr.	*tōmhaisim*	OHG	*mezzan*	Av.	*mā-*
W.	*mesur(o)*	MHG	*mezzen*		
Br.	*muzula*	NHG	*messen*		

All the words for 'measure' are from one of two IE roots, themselves probably related ultimately.

1. IE **mē-* in nouns and verbs, the latter mostly through the nouns, except in Indo-Iranian. Walde-P. 2.237. Ernout-M. 612 f. REW 5503, 5552. Falk-Torp 685. Berneker 2.50.

Skt., Av. *mā-*; Grk. sb. *μέτρον* (: Skt. *mā-tra-m* as Skt. *da-tra-m* : Av. *dā-θrə-m*) whence vb. *μετρέω*; Lat. *mētīrī* through a sb. **mēti-* (cf. OE *mǣd* 'measure', Grk. *μῆτις* 'plan, wisdom'), VLat. **mētīre* (> Sp., Port. *medir*), pple. *mēnsus* (hence *mēnsura* sb. and late denom. *mēnsūrāre* > It. *misurare*, Fr.

mesurer, Rum. *măsura*); ON *mǣla*, Dan. *maale* (ON *māl*, Dan. *maal*, Sw. *mål* 'measure, point of time, meal, etc.'); Lith. *matuoti*; ChSl. sb. *měra*, whence vb. *měriti*, etc., general Slavic (hence Lith. *mieruoti*, Lett. *mērīt*); here (?) Toch. A *me-* (SSS 456, but B form lacking).

W. *mesur*, *mesuro*, Br. *muzula*, fr. sbs. W. *mesur*, Br. *muzul*, MBr. *mesur*, fr. Lat. *mēnsura*. Loth, Mots lat. 187.

ME *mesure*, NE *measure* fr. Fr. *mesurer*.

2. IE **med-* in words for 'measure' and esp. 'measure, estimate with the mind, reflect.' Walde-P. 2.259. Ernout-M. 599. Walde-H. 2.55 f. Feist 363.

Ir. *domidiur* (vbl. noun *tomus*, NIr. *tōmhas*, hence *tōmhaisim*), cpd. of *midiur* 'judge'; Goth. *mitan*, OE *metan*, OHG *mezzan*, etc., general Gmc. (but ON *meta* 'value, estimate') : Grk. *μέδομαι* 'be mindful of', Lat. *medērī* 'care for', esp. 'heal', *meditārī* 'reflect upon'.

12.55 LARGE, BIG (GREAT)

Grk.	*μέγας*	Goth.	*mikils*	Lith.	*didis, didelis*
NG	*μεγάλος*	ON	*stōrr, mikill*	Lett.	*liels*
Lat.	*magnus, grandis*	Dan.	*stor*	ChSl.	*velijĭ, velikŭ*
It.	*grande, grosso*	Sw.	*stor*	SCr.	*velik*
Fr.	*grand, gros*	OE	*micel*	Boh.	*vel(i)ký*
Sp.	*grande*	ME	*mikel, grete (bigg)*	Pol.	*wielki*
Rum.	*mare*	NE	*large, big (great)*	Russ.	*bol'šoj (velikij)*
Ir.	*mār, bras(s), oll*	Du.	*groot*	Skt.	*mahant-, mah-*
NIr.	*mōr*	OHG	*mihhil, grōz*	Av.	*mazant-, maz-, masan-*; OPers. *vazarka-*
W.	*mawr*	MHG	*grōz, michel*		
Br.	*bras*	NHG	*gross*		

Many of the words for 'large, big' belong to inherited groups, one of them so widespread as to leave no doubt that it reflects the chief IE expression for 'great, large' with the familiar extensions beyond the notion of size.

Yet this group is represented in the present European languages only by NG *μεγάλος* or by dialect forms like NE *mickle* and *muckle* (also NE *much* but no longer used of size). As Lat. *magnus* was replaced by *grandis*, so Goth. *mikils*, OE *micel*, etc., were replaced in Scandinavian by ON *stōrr*, Dan., Sw. *stor*, in West Gmc. by the group represented by NE *great*, which in turn is now used mostly in secondary senses or with emotional value, and with reference to size, except in certain phrases, compounds, and place names, is replaced by *large* or its more colloquial and expressive equivalent *big*.

The words not of the inherited groups reflect such diverse notions as 'thick, coarse', 'abundant, spacious', 'swollen', 'strong', etc.

'Large' and 'small' (12.56) are, of course, understood here in reference to size. For the corresponding notions of quantity, amount, or number, which are partly expressed by the same terms but partly differentiated, see 13.15, 13.17.

1. IE **meĝ-*, **meĝh-*. Walde-P. 2.257 f. Ernout-M. 580 f. Walde-H. 2.10 ff. Feist 358 f.

Grk. *μέγας*, gen. *μεγάλου*, NG *μεγάλος* (nom. normalized fr. stem of other cases); Lat. *magnus*; Ir. *maige*, *maignech* (not common), Gall. *magio-* (in *Magiorīx*, etc.); Goth. *mikils*, ON *mikill*, OE *micel*, *mycel*, ME *mikel*, etc. (NE dial. *mickle* and *muckle*), OHG *mihhil*, MHG *michel*; Skt. *mah-*, *mahant-*, Av. *maz-*, *mazant-*; Arm. *mec*; Alb. *madh*; Hitt.

mekkis 'great', esp. in number; Toch. A *māk*, B *māka* 'great in number'.

2. Derivs. of an IE **mē-*, **mō-*. Walde-P. 2.238. Falk-Torp 714.

Ir. *mār*, *mōr*, NIr. *mōr*, W. *mawr* (Br. *meur* 'majestic, grand, etc.') : Grk. *-μωρος* in *ἐγχεσί-μωρος* 'great in spear-throwing', OE *mǣre*, OHG *māri*, etc. 'famous', Slavic *-měrŭ* in *Vladi-měrŭ*, etc.; Ir. comp. *māu*, *mō(u)*, W. *mwy*; Goth. *mais* adv. 'more', *maists* 'greatest', OE *mā* 'more', *māra*, *mǣst* 'greater, greatest' (in size, quantity, or number; NE *more*, *most* not used of size).

3. Lat. *grandis* (> It., Sp. *grande*, Fr. *grand*), esp. 'great (morally and physically)' and often also 'full-grown', etym. dub., but perh. (as 'swollen'?) : Grk. *βρένθος* 'pride', ChSl. *grądĭ* 'breast', etc. Walde-P. 1.699. Ernout-M. 431 f. Walde-H. 1.617 f.

It. *grosso*, Fr. *gros* 'thick, coarse' (12.63), but also 'stout' and 'big'.

Rum. *mare*, fr. Lat. *mās*, *maris* 'male' (in designating the male animal of a species and consequently the larger). Puşcariu 1027. Tiktin 952.

4. Ir. *mār*, *mōr*, W. *mawr*, above, 2.

Ir. *brass*, Br. Corn. *bras* (W. *bras* 'stout, coarse'), prob. : Lat. *grossus* 'thick, coarse' (12.63). Walde-P. 1.698. Walde-H. 1.623. Stokes 183.

Ir. *oll*, also freq. as prefix *oll-* (cf. also Gall. *Ollo-gnatus*, etc.), prob. : Lat. *pollēre* 'be able', *pollēns* 'powerful', perh. Skt. *phala-* 'fruit' etc., with primary notion of 'swollen'. Walde-P. 2.102. Ernout-M. 785. Stokes 52 f.

5. ON *stōrr*, Dan., Sw. *stor* (late OE *stōr* is loanword), cf. OFris. *stōr* id., OS *stōri* 'famous' : ChSl. *starŭ* 'old', Lith. *storas* 'thick', fr. the root. **stā-* 'stand', with semantic development fr. 'standing (fast)' to 'big, thick, old'. Walde-P. 2.607. Falk-Torp 1174.

OE *grēat* (mostly 'coarse, stout, thick'), ME *grete*, NE *great* (but with strict reference to size, now mostly replaced by *large* or *big*), Du. *groot*, OHG, MHG *grōz*, NHG *gross*, prob. with primary meaning 'coarse' as in OE (freq. also in MHG) : ON *grautr* 'porridge', OE *grēot*, OHG *grioz* 'sand', fr. a root **ghrēu-* in words for 'rub, pound'. Walde-P. 1.648 f. Kluge-G. 219. NED s.v. *great*.

ME *bygge*, *bigg(e)*, *big* (earliest sense 'strong, stout, mighty'), NE *big*, prob. of Norse origin, fr. a form like Norw. *bugge* 'strong man'. NED s.v. *big*. Austin, Language 15.249.

ME, NE *large*, in ME 'ample, spacious, broad', etc., fr. OFr. *large* (Fr. *large* 'broad'), fr. Lat. *larga* fem. of *largus* 'abundant, copious', etym.? Ernout-M. 524. Walde-H. 1.764. REW 4912. NED s.v.

6. Lith. *didis*, *didelis*, etym. dub.; possibly through 'conspicuous' : Skt. *dīdi-* 'shining', *dī-* 'shine', etc. Walde-P. 1.772.

Lett. *liels* (Lith. *lielas* obs., not in NSB), prob. through 'tall' fr. 'slender' : Lith. *leilas* 'slender, thin', *leinas* 'thin, flexible', etc. Walde-P. 2.388. Mühl.-Endz. 2.501 f.

7. ChSl. *velijĭ*, *velikŭ*, SCr. *velik*, Boh. *vel(i)ký*, Pol. *wielki* (but Russ. *velikij* now used like NE *great* and replaced by *bol'šoj* with reference to size) beside **veli-* in ChSl. *velĭmi* 'very', *velĭ-lěpŭ* '*μεγαλοπρεπής*', and **valŭ-*, Russ. *valom* 'in abundance', *valovoj* 'wholesale', prob. : Grk. *ἅλις* 'in crowds, sufficiently', *εἴλω*, Att. *εἴλλω* 'pack close', etc. Walde-P. 1.296. Otherwise Brückner 616 f.(: ChSl. *velěti* 'order', Lat. *velle* 'wish', etc.).

Russ. *bol'šoj*, new positive to old comp. *bol'šij*, ChSl. *bolĭjĭ*, fem. *bolĭšī* 'greater' (positive *velijĭ*, *velikŭ*, above) : Skt. *balīyas-* 'stronger', *bala-* 'strength',

Grk. βελτίων, βέλτερος 'better', Lat. *dēbilis* 'weak'. Walde-P. 2.110. Walde-H. 1.327. Berneker 72.

8. Skt. *mahant-*, *mah-*, Av. *mazant-*, *maz-*, above, 1.

Av. *masan-* 'great, significant', *masit-*, *masita-* 'great, large', *masyah-* 'greater', *masišta-*, OPers. *maϑišta-* 'greatest', beside *masan-* 'greatness, importance', *masah-* 'length, size', and *mas-* 'long' : Grk. μακρός 'long' (12.57). Walde-P. 2.223. Barth. 1154 ff.

OPers. *vazarka-* ('great' king and 'great' = 'large' earth) : Skt. *vāja-* 'speed, vigor, contest', *vajra-* 'thunderbolt', Av. *vazra-* 'club', Lat. *vegēre* 'set in motion, excite'. Walde-P. 1.246 f. Barth. 1390.

12.56 SMALL, LITTLE

Grk.	*μῑκρός*	Goth.	*leitils (smals)*	Lith.	*mažas*
NG	*μικρός*	ON	*lītill, smār (smalr)*	Lett.	*mazs*
Lat.	*parvus*	Dan.	*lille*, pl. *smaa*	ChSl.	*malŭ (chudŭ)*
It.	*piccolo*	Sw.	*liten*, pl. *små*	SCr.	*mali, malen*
Fr.	*petit*	OE	*lȳtel, smæl*	Boh.	*malý*
Sp.	*pequeño, chico*	ME	*litel, smal*	Pol.	*mały*
Rum.	*mic*	NE	*small, little*	Russ.	*malyj*
Ir.	*becc*	Du.	*klein*	Skt.	*alpa-, kṣudra-*
NIr.	*beag*	OHG	*luzzil, smāh(i), smal*	Av.	*kasu-*
W.	*bach, bychan*	MHG	*lützel, smal, smæhe, klein*		
Br.	*bihan*				
		NHG	*klein*		

There is no widespread inherited group for 'small' parallel to that for 'large', and the majority of the words are of uncertain origin. Several seem to be based upon expressive (symbolic) syllables. 'Crushed, ground (fine)' is the certain source for one word and a possible one for some others. A peculiar development from 'bright, shining' through 'clean, delicate, fine, thin', etc., is seen in NHG *klein* vs. NE *clean*.

Words for 'small' naturally develop secondary opprobrious senses, 'petty, trivial, mean', etc. Conversely, for certain groups (Goth. *leitils*, etc., and OE *lȳtel*, etc.) in which the majority of the cognates have the notion of 'deceit, abuse' or the like, one must reckon with the possibility that this is the more original and 'small' in the literal sense secondary (cf. the history of 'right' and 'left', 12.41, 12.42).

1. Grk. μῑκρός, Ion., early Att. σμῑκρός, also hypocoristic μικκός (attested as Dor., Boeot. and prob. widespread pop. form, as in proper names Μίκκος etc.) : Lat. *mīca* 'crumb, little bit', ON *smār* 'little', OHG *smāhi* 'little, insignificant', perh. fr. an extension of a root **smē-*, **smēi-* in words for 'smear, rub'. Walde-P. 2.685 f. Boisacq 885. Falk-Torp 1075.

2. Lat. *parvus* (also 'little' in quantity) : Grk. παῦρος 'little', pl. 'few', Lat. *paucī*, Goth. *fawai*, etc. 'few' (13.17). Walde-P. 2.75. Ernout-M. 737, 742.

Replaced in pop. Lat. and the Romance languages as 'small' by a variety of obscure forms apparently based on expressive syllables like **pikk*, **pitt*, **pits*, etc. REW 6494, 6544a, 6550. Goldberger, Glotta 18.52.

Late Lat. *pisinnus* (first in Att. Labeo for 'child', in Peregrinatio *a pisinno = a puero; ecclesia pisinna* 'small church', also in Marc. Emp., Isid., etc., cf. App. Prob. *pusillus non pisinnus*), *pitinnus*

(CIL 6.35915), *pitulus* (Anton. Itin.). Löfstedt, Peregrinatio 197.

It. *piccolo*, *piccino*, cf. Rum. *pic* 'drop', *picĭu* 'little child', Calabr. *pikka* 'little (in quantity)', etc.

Fr. (also Prov., Cat.) *petit*, cf. Rum. *piti* 'make oneself small, hide', It. dial. *pitu* 'small', *pitin* 'little' (in amount), etc.

Sp. *pequeño*, Port. *pequeno*.

Sp. *chico* (beside other Romance forms), prob. fr. an expressive *čikk*, parallel to *pikk*, etc. REW 2451b, 9653 (p. 806). Or fr. Lat. *ciccum* in its use for something small or worthless (as Plaut. Rud. 580)? So Diez 98, Gamillscheg 218 ("vielleicht"), M. Pidal, Manual 120 (on *ch*), 125.

Rum. *mic*, prob. (not for Lat. *mīca* 'crumb', but) fr. Grk. μικκός (above, 1). Densusianu 1.201. Puşcariu 1067. REW 5559.

3. Ir. *becc*, *bec*, NIr. *beag*, W. *bach*, *bychan*, Br. *bihan*, etym. dub. Walde-P. 2.150. Pedersen 1.385. Stokes 166.

4. Goth. *leitils*, ON *lītill*, Dan. *lille* (for *liden*, older *lidel*), Sw. *liten*, cf. ON *lītt* adv. 'little, badly', prob. : Goth. *lita* 'hypocrisy', OHG *līz* 'pretext', *lizzōn*, *lizitōn* 'simulate', MHG *liz*, *litze* 'humor', outside connections dub., perh. Grk. λοιδορέω 'abuse, revile'. IE **leid-* beside a parallel **leud-* with similar semantic relations in the following. Walde-P. 2.402. Falk-Torp 640 f. Feist 328.

OE *lȳtel*, ME *litel*, NE *little*, OHG *luzzil*, *luzzig*, MHG *lützel*, *lütze*, prob. : Goth. *liuts* 'hypocritical', *liutai* 'conjurers', OE *lot* 'deceit', ON *lȳta* 'dishonor, blame'; and further Russ. *ludit'* 'deceive', ChSl. *ludŭ*, SCr. *lud* 'foolish', etc.; cf. also Ir. *lūta* 'little finger'. Walde-P. 2.416. Falk-Torp 641.

Goth. *smals* (only superl. *smalista*), late ON *smalr* 'little', OE *smæl*, ME *smal*, NE *small*, OHG, MHG *smal* 'slender, narrow, small' (NHG *schmal* 'narrow'), etym. dub., perh. best as orig. 'ground fine' : Norw. dial. *smola* 'grind to pieces', Sw. *smula* 'break into crumbs', etc., fr. **smel-* beside **mel-* in Goth. *malan*, Lat. *molere*, etc. 'grind'. Cf. ChSl. *malŭ*, below, 6. Walde-P. 2.296. Falk-Torp 1076.

ON *smār*, Dan. *smaa*, Sw. *små* (in Dan. and Sw. only as pl. to *lille*, *liten*), OHG *smāhi*, *smōh*, MHG *smæhe* (in OHG often and in MHG mostly 'insignificant, despised, shameful', cf. NHG *schmach* sb. 'dishonor') : Grk. μῑκρός 'small' (above, 1).

Du., MHG, NHG *klein*, in MHG mostly 'pure, neat, fine, pretty' (cf. NHG *kleinod* 'jewel, gem'), OHG *kleini* 'shining, slender, fine', etc., OE *clǣne* 'pure, clean' (NE *clean*), prob. : Grk. γλαινοί· λαμπρύσματα Hesych., γλήνεα 'bright things, trinkets, stars', γλήνη 'pupil of the eye', γελεῖν· λάμπειν, ἀνθεῖν Hesych., and other words with common notion of 'bright, shining'. 'Bright' > 'clean, neat', as in Lat. *nitidus* > Fr. *net*, etc. (15.87), hence through 'fine, delicate' to 'small'. Walde-P. 1.623.

5. Lith. *mažas*, Lett. *mazs*, cf. OPruss. *massais* 'less', Lith. *možis* 'smallness, trifle', etym.? Walde-P. 2.228. Mühl.-Endz. 2.574.

6. ChSl. *malŭ*, etc., etym. dub., but perh. as orig. 'ground fine' : ChSl. *mlěti*, Lat. *molere*, etc. 'grind'. Walde-P. 2.296. Berneker 2.14.

ChSl. *chudŭ*, rarely 'small' in lit. sense, mostly opprobrious term 'insignificant, cheap', etc., as in general Slavic (Russ. *chudoj* 'bad, evil, lean', Boh. *chudý* 'poor', etc.), perh. : Skt. *kṣudra-* 'small' (below, 7). Berneker 405. Walde-P. 1.502.

7. Skt. *alpa-* : Lith. *alpnas* 'weak', *alpti* 'faint'. Walde-P. 1.92.

Skt. *kṣudra-* : *kṣud-* 'pound, crush', perh. here ChSl. *chudŭ*, etc. (above, 6). Walde-P. 1.502.

Av. *kasu-*, perh. : Lith. *kašeti* 'lose weight', NHG *hager* 'lean, thin', ME *hagger*, NE *haggard*. Walde-P. 1.334.

8. For a group which, though not containing the usual words for 'small' as discussed here, seem to have some such central notion, see under Grk. μανός 'thin, sparse' (12.66).

12.57 LONG

Grk.	*μακρός, δολιχός*	Goth.	*laggs*	Lith.	*ilgas*
NG	*μακρός, μακρύς*	ON	*langr*	Lett.	*gar'š*
Lat.	*longus*	Dan.	*lang*	ChSl.	*dlŭgŭ*
It.	*lungo*	Sw.	*lång*	SCr.	*dug*
Fr.	*long*	OE	*long*	Boh.	*dlouhý*
Sp.	*largo*	ME	*long*	Pol.	*długi*
Rum.	*lung*	NE	*long*	Russ.	*dolgij, dlinnyj*
Ir.	*cīan, long, fota*	Du.	*lang*	Skt.	*dīrgha-*
NIr.	*fada*	OHG	*lang*	Av.	*darəga-, mas-*
W.	*hir, maith*	MHG	*lanc*		
Br.	*hir*	NHG	*lang*		

Most of the words for 'long' belong to one of two inherited groups, these probably related ultimately.

1. IE **deləgho-*(?), **dl̥gho-*. Walde-P. 1.813. Berneker 251 f.

Grk. δολιχός, poet. except in sb. δόλιχος 'the long course', cf. also ἐνδελεχής 'perpetual'; ChSl. *dlŭgŭ*, SCr. *dug*, etc., general Slavic; Skt. *dīrgha-*, Av. *darəga-*, OPers. *darga-*; Baltic with loss of *d-*, Lith. *ilgas* (OPruss. *ilgi*, *ilga* adv., Lett. *ilgs* adj. of time only); Hitt. *dalugaēs* (pl.), with sb. *dalugasti* 'length'.

2. IE **longho-*, prob. fr. **dlongho-* and ultimately related to preceding on the basis of a simple root **del-*. Walde-P. 1.812 f. Ernout-M. 561. Walde-H. 1.820 f. Falk-Torp 622.

Lat. *longus* (> It. *lungo*, Fr. *long*, Rum. *lung*); Goth. *laggs* (attested of time only), ON *langr*, OE *long*, etc., general Gmc.

3. Grk. μακρός, NG pop. μακρύς (after old υ-stem adjs. like πλατύς, παχύς etc. Hatzidakis, Μεσ. 2.12 f.), beside μῆκος, Dor. μᾶκος 'length' : Lat. *macer*, ON *magr*, OE *maegr*, etc. 'lean', Av. *mas-* 'long' (etc., below, 9). Walde-P. 2.223. Walde-H. 2.2.

4. Sp. *largo*, fr. Lat. *largus* 'abundant' (cf. Fr. *large*, etc. 'broad', 12.61).

5. Ir. *cīan* 'long, far, distant', as sb. 'long time', etym.? Deriv. fr. pron. stem in Ir. *cē* 'this', Grk. ἐκεῖ 'there', Lat. *-ce*, etc. (Stokes 75, Rozwadowski, Quaest. gram. 10) not convincing.

Ir. *long*, *lang*, loanword fr. Lat. *longus* or cognate? Vendryes, De hib. voc. 152.

Ir. *fota*, NIr. *fada*, cf. Ir. *fot* 'length', perh. : Lat. *vastus* 'vast, immense'. Walde-P. 1.220. Pedersen 1.32. Thurneysen, Gram. 50.

W., Br. *hir* = Ir. *sīr* 'long' (of time) : Lat. *sērus* 'late', Goth. *seiþus* 'late', etc. Walde-P. 2.462. Ernout-M. 933.

W. *maith*, MW *meith* fr. **mag-tio* : Ir. *mag-* in *mag-lorg* = *mor-lorg* 'big club', *magh-slaibh* 'big mountain', OW *digourmechis* 'added' (?), Ir. *do-for-maig* 'increases', etc., prob. fr. the root in Lat. *magnus* 'large', Grk. μέγας, etc. Loth, RC 40.342 f. Walde-P. 2.258 (without W. *maith*).

6. Goth. *laggs*, etc., above, 2.

7. Lett. *gar'š*, cf. Lith. *gargaras* 'lean, long-legged, long-necked horse', *gingaras* 'long-legged man', outside connections? Mühl.-Endz. 1.608.

8. Russ. *dlinnyj*, with sb. *dlina* 'length', vb. *dlit'* 'prolong' : ChSl. *prodŭliti* 'prolong', Boh. *(pro)dlíti* 'delay', etc., fr. the root seen in the general Slavic word, ChSl. *dlŭgŭ*, etc. (above, 1). Berneker 252 f.

9. Skt. *dīrgha-*, Av. *darəga-*, above, 1.

Av. *mas-* 'long', but superl. *masišta-*, OPers. *maϑišta-* 'greatest' (12.55) : Grk. μακρός, above, 3.

12.58. 'Tall'. The sense of NE *tall* (used of persons, animals, trees, buildings, etc.), that is, 'of considerable height', 'vertically long', is most commonly covered by the usual words for 'high' (12.31), but in part, esp. with reference to persons, by those for 'large' (12.55), as Grk. μέγας, NG μεγάλος (but NG ψηλός more common even of persons), Fr. *grand*, NHG *gross*, or by those for 'long', as OE, ME *long* (cf. NED s.v.), Du. *lang*, Sw. *lång*.

Other words are:

1. Lat. (besides *celsus*, *altus*, *grandis*, *magnus*, *longus*) esp. *prōcērus*, cpd. of *prō* and the root of *crēscere* 'grow'. Ernout-M. 813.

2. NE *tall*, fr. ME *tal*, *talle*, mostly 'stout in combat, brave, bold', OE *getæl* 'quick, prompt' : OHG *gizal* 'quick', Goth. *untals* 'disobedient', prob. fr. same root as Gmc. **taljan* 'count, tell'. Walde-P. 1.808. NED s.v.

12.59 SHORT

Grk.	*βραχύς*	Goth.	....	Lith.	*trumpas*
NG	*κοντός*	ON	*skammr*	Lett.	*īss*
Lat.	*brevis*	Dan.	*kort*	ChSl.	*kratŭkŭ*
It.	*corto, breve*	Sw.	*kort*	SCr.	*kratak*
Fr.	*court*	OE	*sceort*	Boh.	*krátký*
Sp.	*corto*	ME	*schort*	Pol.	*krótki*
Rum.	*scurt*	NE	*short*	Russ.	*korotkij*
Ir.	*gerr, cumbair, berr*	Du.	*kort*	Skt.	*hrasva-*
NIr.	*gearr*	OHG	*churz, scurz, skammēr*	Av.	*mərəzu-*
W.	*byr*				
Br.	*berr*	MHG	*kurz*		
		NHG	*kurz*		

Words for 'short' (opposite of both 'long' and 'tall') are mostly from the notion of 'cut off' or 'broken off'. In one case the notion is abstracted from a noun denoting a (short) 'pole, goad', etc.

1. IE **mreĝhu-*, **mr̥ĝhu-*, root connection? Walde-P. 2.314. Ernout-M. 117. Walde-H. 1.115.

Grk. βραχύς; Lat. *brevis*; Av. *mərəzu-* in *mərəzu-jīti-* 'short-lived' : OHG *murgfāri* 'transitory, fragile', Goth. *gamaurgjan* 'shorten', OE *myrge* 'pleasant' (NE *merry*) through notion of 'shortening, entertaining'.

2. Byz., NG κοντός (also attested in late Grk. κοντός or κονδός 'short'; cf. LS s.v. and κοντο-πορεία prob. 'short way', Polyb.), adj. use abstracted (prob. first in cpds.) fr. κοντός (Hom. +) 'pole, pike, goad' : κεντέω 'prick, goad'. Hatzidakis, Festschrift Kretschmer 35 ff.

3. Lat. *brevis* : Grk. βραχύς (above, 1). Hence It. *breve*, Fr. *bref* (> ME *bref*, NE *brief*), now mostly of time and generally replaced by the following (but It. *breve* also spatial beside *corto*).

It., Sp. *corto*, Fr. *court*, Rum. *scurt* (*s-* fr. MLat. derivs. in *ex-*) fr. Lat. *curtus* 'cut off, broken, mutilated, shortened' : Grk. κείρω 'cut off, shear', etc. Ernout-M. 248. Walde-H. 1.316 f. REW 2421.

4. Ir. *gerr*, NIr. *gearr* : Skt. *hrasva-*

'short, little', Grk. χερείων 'poorer, worse', Ir. *gair, garait* 'short (of time)', etc. Walde-P. 1.604 f. Pedersen 1.83.

Ir. *cumbair, cummair, berr* (K. Meyer, Contrib. 206), W. *byr*, Br. *berr*, OCorn. *ber* (gl. *brevis*) cf. Ir. *cuimre* 'shortness', Ir. *berraim* 'shear, clip', root connections? Walde-P. 2.160. Walde-H. 1.107 (Lat. *birrus*, loanword).

5. ON *skam(m)r*, OHG *skammēr*, beside OHG *hammēr* 'mutilated, feeble', perh. fr. **(s)kap-mó-* : Grk. σκάπτω 'dig', κόπτω 'strike, cut off', etc. Walde-P. 2.560. Or fr. **skambh-no-* : Av., OPers. *kamna-* 'small' in quantity or number? Walde-P. 2.601. Falk-Torp 1003.

Dan., Sw. *kort*, Icel. *kortr*, Du. *kort*, OHG *churz, kurt, churt*, MHG, NHG *kurz*, prob. fr. Lat. *curtus* (cf. It. *corto*, above, 3). Falk-Torp 568. Weigand-H. 1.1179.

OE *sceort*, ME *schort, short*, NE *short*, OHG *scurz* : ON *skort, skortr* 'lack', *skorta* 'be lacking', OE *sceortian* 'become shorter, be lacking', MHG *scherze, scherzel* 'cut off piece', etc., fr. an extension of the IE root **(s)ker-* in Lat. *curtus*, etc. (above, 3). Falk-Torp 1019. NED s.v. *short*.

6. Lith. *trumpas* : *trupiti* 'crumble, break in fragments', *trupus* 'brittle', OPruss. *trupis* 'block of wood', Grk. τρυπάω 'perforate, bore', etc. Bezzenberger, BB 27.142. (Walde-P. 1.732).

Lith. *įsas, ysas* (NSB, but prob. obs.), Lett. *īss*, OPruss. (acc. sg.) *īnsan*, etym.? Mühl.-Endz. 1.837. Trautmann, Altpreuss. 346.

7. ChSl. *kratŭkŭ*, etc., general Slavic : ChSl. *sŭ-kratiti* 'shorten', Russ.-ChSl. *črĭtu, črěsti* 'cut', fr. the root in Lat. *curtus*, OE *sceort*, etc. (above, 3, 5). Berneker 576 f. Walde-P. 2.579.

8. Skt. *hrasva-* : Ir. *gerr* (above, 4).

Av. *mərəzu-* : Grk. βραχύς (above, 1).

12.61 WIDE, BROAD

Grk.	πλατύς, εὐρύς	Goth.	*braiþs*	Lith.	*platus*
NG	πλατύς, φαρδύς	ON	*breiðr, víðr*	Lett.	*plats*
Lat.	*lātus*	Dan.	*bred, vid*	ChSl.	*širokŭ*
It.	*largo*	Sw.	*bred, vid*	SCr.	*širok*
Fr.	*large*	OE	*brād, wīd*	Boh.	*široký*
Sp.	*ancho*	ME	*brood, wid*	Pol.	*szeroki*
Rum.	*lat (larg)*	NE	*wide, broad*	Russ.	*širokij*
Ir.	*lethan, fairsiung*	Du.	*breed, wijd*	Skt.	*pr̥thu-, uru-*
NIr.	*leathan*	OHG	*breit, wīt*	Av.	*pərəθu-, paθana-*
W.	*llydan, eang*	MHG	*breit, wīt*		
Br.	*ledan*	NHG	*breit*		

Words for 'wide, broad' rest on the more general notion of 'spread out, spacious, extensive', and the specialization to extent in a given direction, that is 'wide' in distinction from 'long' and the opposite of 'narrow', is only partial. For all of them may also be used in the more general sense. In the two Gmc. groups represented by NE *broad* and *wide* the wider sense is generally stronger in the second group, and dominant in NHG *weit*, which is no longer used as the opposite of *eng* 'narrow', while, conversely, NE *wide* is the technical term in actual measurement (e.g. *six inches wide by three feet long*).

1. IE **pl̥tu-, *pl̥tho-*, etc., fr. an extension of **pel-* (**pelə-, *plā-*, etc.) in words for 'spread out, flat' as Lat. *plānus* 'flat', ChSl. *polje* 'field', OE *feld* 'field', etc. Walde-P. 2.99 f., 61 f. Thurneysen, Gram. 129, 131.

Grk. πλατύς; Ir. *lethan*, NIr. *leathan*, W. *llydan*, Br. *ledan* (beside W. *lled*, Br. *led* 'breadth'); Lith. *platus*, Lett. *plats*; Skt. *pr̥thu-*, Av. *pərəθu-*; Arm. *lian*.

2. IE **weru-, *uru-*, etc., root connection? Walde-P. 1.285.

Grk. εὐρύς; Skt. *uru-* beside *varas-* 'breadth', Av. *vouru-* (in cpds. as *vouru-kaša-* 'having broad bays', *vouru-gaoyaoti-* 'possessing broad meadows', etc.).

3. Byz., NG φαρδύς, orig. dub. G. Meyer, Neugr. Stud. 4.94, connects with NG dial. φάρδος 'large (meal-)bag', loanword fr. Ital. *fardo* or its source Arab. *farda* 'bundle of goods'. Hatzidakis, Μεσ. 2.29, suggests deriv. fr. εὐφραδής with semantic extension through 'copious in speech' > 'wide' in general. But the actual use of the rare εὐφραδής connotes skill, rather than copiousness, of speech.

4. Lat. *lātus* (> Rum. *lat*), prob. fr. **stlātos* (cf. *stlatta*, Festus) : ChSl. *stĭlati* 'spread out', *stelĭ, postelja* 'bed'. Walde-P. 2.643. Ernout-M. 527 f. Walde-H. 1.172.

It. *largo*, Fr. *large* (Rum. *larg* 'extensive, spacious', but under influence of Fr. *large* sometimes used for *lat* 'wide', cf. Tiktin s.v.), fr. Lat. *largus* 'abundant, copious', etym.? Ernout-M. 524. Walde-H. 1.764. REW 4912.

Sp. *ancho*, fr. Lat. *amplus* 'large, spacious, abundant', etym.? Ernout-M. 47. Walde-H. 1.42. REW 430.

5. Ir. *lethan*, etc., above, 1.

Ir. *fairsiung*, W. *eang* 'broad, ample', cpds. (Ir. *for-ess-*, W. *ess-*) of **enghi-*, etc. : OE *enge* 'narrow', etc. (12.62). Walde-P. 1.62. Pedersen 2.10.

6. Goth. *braiþs*, ON *breiðr*, OE *brād*, etc., general Gmc.; cf. Goth. *us-braidjan* 'spread out', etc., OHG *breta* 'the flat hand', etym. dub. Walde-P. 2.194. Falk-Torp 100. Feist 104.

ON *víðr*, OE *wīd*, etc., general Gmc., except Goth., perh. fr. **wi-ito-*, cpd. of **wi-* 'apart, away' (Skt. *vi-*, etc.) and pple. of IE **ei-* 'go' (Skt. *i-*, Grk. εἶμι), in form = Skt. *vīta-* (*vi-ita-*) 'gone, lacking, without', but with development of 'gone apart' to 'extensive, wide'. Walde-P. 1.103. Falk-Torp 1373.

7. Lith. *platus*, Lett. *plats*, above, 1.

8. ChSl. *širokŭ* (reg. for πλατύς in Supr., Ps.; in Gospels Mt. 7.13 for εὐρύχωρος, while πλατύς is rendered by *prostranŭ*, lit. 'spread out' = SCr. *prostran* 'extensive, spacious') etc., general Slavic, etym.? (Brückner 547 : Goth. *skeirs* 'clear', etc. improbable.)

9. Skt. *pr̥thu-*, Av. *pərəθu-*, above, 1. Skt. *uru-*, above, 2.

Av. *paθana-* (with θ for *t* fr. *pərəθu-*), NPers. *pahn* : Grk. πετάννῡμι 'spread out', Lat. *patēre* 'stand open', *pandere* 'spread out, open'. Walde-P. 2.18.

12.62 NARROW

Grk.	στενός	Goth.	*aggwus*	Lith.	*siauras, ankštas*
NG	στενός	ON	*þrǫngr, ǫngr*	Lett.	*šaurs*
Lat.	*angustus*	Dan.	*snæver, trang, smal*	ChSl.	*ązŭkŭ, těsnŭ*
It.	*stretto, angusto*	Sw.	*smal, trång*	SCr.	*uzak, tjesan*
Fr.	*étroit*	OE	*nearu, enge, smæl*	Boh.	*úzký, těsný*
Sp.	*estrecho, angosto*	ME	*narowe, streit, smal*	Pol.	*wązki, ciasny*
Rum.	*strîmt, îngust*	NE	*narrow*	Russ.	*uzkij, tesnyj*
Ir.	*cōil, cumung*	Du.	*nauw, smal, eng*	Skt.	*aṅhu-, avistīrṇa-*
NIr.	*cumhang, caol*	OHG	*engi, angi, smal*	Av.	. . . .
W.	*cul, cyfyng*	MHG	*enge, smal*		
Br.	*enk, striz*	NHG	*schmal, eng*		

Most of the words for 'narrow' rest on the notion of 'tight' or 'pressed', while some are from 'slender' or 'small'.

1. Derivs. of IE **anĝh-* in Av. *ąz-* 'tie, oppress', Grk. ἄγχω 'throttle', Lat. *angere* 'throttle, distress, torment', ChSl. *ąziti* 'crowd, straiten'. Walde-P. 1.62 f. Ernout-M. 51. Walde-H. 1.47.

Lat. *angustus* (> It. *angusto*, Sp. *angosto*, Rum. *îngust*); Br. *enk*, cpds. Ir. *cum-ung*, NIr. *cumhang*, W. *cyf-yng;* Goth. *aggwus*, ON *ǫngr*, OE *enge, ange*, OHG *angi, engi*, MHG *enge*, Du., NHG *eng;* Lith. *ankštas;* ChSl. *ązŭkŭ*, SCr. *uzak*, Boh. *úzký*, Pol. *wązki*, Russ. *uzkij;* Skt. *aṅhu-* (only in comp. *aṅhīyas-* and in cpd.) beside *aṅhas-* 'fear, oppression', Av. *ązah-* 'need, oppression'; Arm. *anjuk*.

2. Grk. στενός, Ion. στεινός (fr. *στενϝός), beside στενυγρός 'narrow', etc., prob. : ON *stinnr* 'stiff, firm, strong', OE *stīþ* id. and 'hard, severe', with secondary sense in Gmc. development (cf. Grk. στενοχωρία, Lat. *angustiae*, NHG *enge*, etc. 'narrowness' and 'difficulty, distress'). Walde-P. 2.627. Boisacq 909. Falk-Torp 1168.

3. It. *stretto*, Fr. *étroit*, Sp. *estrecho*, Rum. *strîmt* fr. Lat. *strictus* (**strinctus* for Rum.) 'drawn together, bound tight', pple. of *stringere* 'bind together'. REW 8305.

4. Ir. *cōil*, NIr. *caol*, W. *cul*, also 'slender, lean', cf. OBr. *culed* 'macies', perh. : Lett. *kails* 'naked, bald', *kaili l'audis* 'childless couple', in any case with Celtic extension of 'slender' to 'narrow'. Walde-P. 1.455. Stokes 88.

Br. *striz*, fr. Lat. *strictus* (above, 3). Loth, Mots lat. 208.

5. ON *þrǫngr*, Dan. *trang*, Sw. *trång*, cf. MLG *drange*, MHG *gedrenge* 'stuffed full, tight' : ON *þryngva*, Dan. *trænge*, Sw. *tränga*, OE *þringan*, NHG *drängen*, etc., 'press, crowd', Lith. *trankus* 'jolting, rough', Av. *θraxta-* 'close-packed' (ranks), etc. Walde-P. 1.758 f. Falk-Torp 1279. 1293 f.

OE *smæl*, ME *smal*, OHG, MHG, Du. *smal*, NHG *schmal* (largely also 'slender'), Dan., Sw. *smal* (meaning 'narrow' fr. German), Gmc. group in early period also or only 'small' (12.56).

Dan. *snæver* : ON *snæfr, snæfr* 'tight, narrow, quick, swift', *snæfugr* 'swift', without *s-* ON *næfr*, OSw. *næver* 'quick', perh. Arm. *nurb* 'narrow, slender, thin'. Walde-P. 2.698. Falk-Torp 1095.

OE *nearu*, ME *narowe*, NE *narrow*, OS *naru* : ON *Nǫrva-sund* 'Straits of Gibraltar', OHG *narwa* 'scar' (i.e. 'closed wound'), prob. fr. a root meaning 'draw together, tie'(?) in OHG *snuor* 'band, string', Lat. *nervus* 'tendon', 'nerve', etc. Walde-P. 2.699 f. (with 2.696). Falk-Torp 755.

ME *streit*, NE *strait* (still adj. for 'narrow' or 'difficult' in Bible, but now rare except in sb. *Straits*), fr. OFr. *estreit* (Fr. *étroit*, above, 3). NED s.v. *strait*.

Du. *nauw* : MLG *nouwe* 'narrow, close, exact', MHG adv. *nouwe, genouwe* 'close, scarcely' (NHG *genau* 'exactly'), OE *hnēaw* 'stingy', etc., all prob. as 'little' fr. 'crushed' : OHG *hniuwan*, MHG *niuwan* 'pound to pieces', etc. Walde-P. 1.396. Franck-v. W. 542. Falk-Torp 785.

6. Lith. *siauras*, Lett. *šaurs*, etym.? Mühl.-Endz. 4.7.

7. ChSl. *ązŭkŭ*, etc., above, 1.

ChSl. *těsnŭ* (renders στενός Lk. 13.24, τεθλιμμένος Mt. 7.14), SCr. *tjesan*, Boh. *těsný*, Pol. *ciasny*, Russ. *tesnyj* : ChSl. *tiskati* 'press'. Meillet, Études 435. Brückner 60.

8. Skt. *aṅhu-*, above, 1.

Skt. *avistīrṇa-, avistr̥ta-*, neg. of *vistīrṇa-, vistr̥ta-* 'spread out, extensive, wide', pples. of *vi-str̥-* 'spread out'.

12.63 THICK[1]

(In Dimension)

Grk.	παχύς	Goth.	. . . .	Lith.	*storas*
NG	χοντρός, παχύς	ON	*þykkr*	Lett.	*biezs, resns*
Lat.	*crassus*, (late) *grossus*	Dan.	*tyk*	ChSl.	*debelŭ*
It.	*grosso, spesso*	Sw.	*tjock*	SCr.	*debeo*
Fr.	*épais*	OE	*þicce*	Boh.	*tlustý*
Sp.	*grueso, espeso*	ME	*thikke*	Pol.	*gruby*
Rum.	*gros*	NE	*thick*	Russ.	*tolstyj*
Ir.	*tiug, remor*	Du.	*dick*	Skt.	*sthūla-, bahula-*
NIr.	*reamhar*	OHG	*dicchi*	Av.	. . . .
W.	*tew*	MHG	*dicke*		
Br.	*teo*	NHG	*dick*		

Words for 'thick' as applied to the dimension through, as in *a thick board*, are also or were once used in the less specific sense of 'coarse' or 'big, bulky', or of persons 'stout, fat'.

1. IE **bhenĝh-*, esp. **bhn̥ĝhu-*. Walde-P. 2.151.

Here as 'thick' Grk. παχύς, Lett. *biezs*, Skt. *bahula-* (also 'abundant, much' like *bahu-* = Grk. παχύς) : Av. *bązah-, bąšnu-* 'height, depth', ON *bingr* 'heap', etc.

2. NG χοντρός, fr. class. Grk. χονδρός 'granular, coarse (esp. of salt)' beside χόνδρος 'grain or lump (of salt), groats' : Lat. *frendere* 'rub to pieces', OE *grindan*, NE *grind*, etc. Walde-P. 1.656. Boisacq 1066.

3. Lat. *crassus*, perh. 'thick' as 'firm, solid' fr. 'firmly twisted together' : *crātis* 'wicker-work', Grk. κάρταλος 'basket', Skt. *kr̥t-* 'spin'. Walde-P. 1.421. Ernout-M. 227 f. Walde-H. 1.285 f.

Late Lat. *grossus* (> It. *grosso*, Sp. *grueso*, Rum. *gros;* Fr. *gros* mostly 'big, coarse'), prob. : Ir. *bras(s)* 'large, big', etc. (12.55). Walde-P. 1.698. Walde-H. 1.623.

It. *spesso*, Fr. *épais*, Sp. *espeso*, also 'thick' = 'dense', fr. Lat. *spissus* 'dense' (12.64).

4. Ir. *tiug* (NIr. *tiugh* only 'dense'), W. *tew*, Br. *teo* : ON *þykkr*, OE *þicce*, etc. (below, 5).

Ir. *remor* 'thick, fat', NIr. *reamhar* 'thick (of dimension)', W. (arch.) *rhef* 'big, thick', etym. dub. Pedersen 1.167. Walde-P. 2.371.

5. ON *þykkr*, OE *þicce*, OHG *dicchi*, etc., general Gmc. : Ir. *tiug*, etc., but root connection dub. Walde-P. 1.718. Falk-Torp 1308.

6. Lith. *storas* : ChSl. *starŭ* 'old', ON *stōrr* 'large', prob. fr. the root **stā-* 'stand', with semantic development to 'thick, big, old', fr. the notion of 'firm-standing'. Walde-P. 2.607.

Lett. *biezs* : Grk. παχύς (above, 1).

Lett. *resns* : Lith. *resnas* 'stout, vigorous, solid', perh. ChSl. *redŭ* 'food', Slov. *rediti* 'nourish', Skt. *vr̥dh-* 'increase, cause to grow'. Walde-P. 1.290. Mühl.-Endz. 3.513.

7. ChSl. *debelŭ*, SCr. *debeo*, Bulg. *debel* : OPruss. *debīkan* 'great', OHG *tapfar* 'heavy, weighty' (NHG *tapfer* 'brave' = 'firm, weighty in combat'). Walde-P. 1.850. Berneker 182.

Boh. *tlustý*, Russ. *tolstyj* (Pol. *tłusty* 'fat'), ChSl. **tlŭstŭ*, cf. *otlŭstě* 'ἐπαχύνθη' : Lith. *patulžęs* 'swollen', Lett. *tulzums* 'swelling', Lith. *tulžti* 'swell up, become soft, rotten', prob. fr. an extension of IE **tēu-* (in Lat. *tumēre* 'swell', etc.). Walde-P. 1.710. Trautmann 331.

Pol. *gruby* : SCr. *grub* 'coarse, ugly', Russ. *grubyj* 'rough, coarse', ChSl. *grąbŭ* 'rude, ignorant', all perh. 'rough, coarse' fr. 'wrinkled', fr. a nasalized form of the root in Slov. *grbati* 'hunch up, crook, wrinkle', Russ. *gorbit'* 'crook', etc. Walde-P. 1.596. Berneker 355, 368.

8. Skt. *sthūla-*, *sthavira-*, RV *sthūra-* : OHG *stūri* 'strong', OSw. *stūr* 'big', OHG *stiuri* 'strong, proud', Av. *stavah-* 'thickness, strength', Arm. *stvar-* 'thick'. Walde-P. 2.609. Uhlenbeck 346, 348.

Skt. *bahula-* : Grk. παχύς (above, 1).

12.64 THICK²

(In Density)

Grk.	*πυκνός*	Goth.	. . . .	Lith.	*tankus, tirštas*
NG	*πυκνός, πηχτός*	ON	*þykkr*	Lett.	*biezs*
Lat.	*dēnsus, spissus, crassus*	Dan.	*tæt, tyk*	ChSl.	(*čęstŭ*)
		Sw.	*tät, tjock*	SCr.	*gust*
It.	*spesso, denso, fitto*	OE	*þicce*	Boh.	*hustý*
Fr.	*épais (dense)*	ME	*thikke, thycht*	Pol.	*gęsty*
Sp.	*espeso, denso*	NE	*thick*	Russ.	*gustoj*
Rum.	*des*	Du.	*dicht*	Skt.	*ghana-, sāndra-, bahula-*
Ir.	*dlūith*	OHG	*dicchi*		
NIr.	*tiugh*	MHG	*dicke, dīhte*	Av.	. . . .
W.	*tew*	NHG	*dicht, dick*		
Br.	*teo, stank*				

'Thick' in density may be expressed by the same word as that for 'thick' in dimension, as in NE *thick* (soup, hair, woods, etc.) beside which *dense* is in more restricted use (*dense* or *thick* woods, forest, etc., only *dense* crowd, but never *dense* soup or hair). But more commonly it is expressed by quite different words, with primary notion of compactness.

1. Grk. πυκνός, Hom. πυκινός, beside adv. πύκα 'thickly', πυκάζω 'cover up tight', perh. : Alb. *puthë* 'kiss' (as orig. 'embrace'). Walde-P. 2.82. Boisacq 826.

NG πηχτός, fr. class. Grk. πηκτός 'fixed, jointed' (: πήγνυμι 'fix'), also of milk 'curdled'.

2. Lat. *dēnsus* (> Rum. *des*; lit. words It., Sp. *denso*, Fr. *dense*) : Grk. δασύς 'shaggy, rough, thick with leaves, trees, etc.' Walde-P. 1.793 f. Ernout-M. 261. Walde-H. 1.341.

Lat. *spissus* (> It. *spesso*, Fr. *épais*, Sp. *espeso*) : Grk. σπιδνόν· πυκνόν, συνεχές, πεπηγός Hesych., ἀσπιδής 'extended', Lett. *spiest* 'press', etc., dental formations fr. the root in Skt. *sphāyati* 'increases, thrives, grows fat'. Walde-P. 2.658. Ernout-M. 966.

Lat. *crassus*, usual for 'thick' of dimension (12.63) but also used of density, esp. of clouds, darkness, dust, etc.

It. *fitto*, fr. Lat. *fīctus* 'fixed'. REW 3280.

3. Ir. *dlūith* : *dluimm* 'mass, multitude', W. *dylwf* 'bundle', outside connections? Pedersen 1.169 f.

NIr. *tiugh*, W. *tew*, Br. *teo* also 'thick' of dimension (12.63).

Br. *stank*, adj. fr. *stank* 'pool' (fr. OFr. *estanc* 'pool'), with sense 'thick' fr. phrase for stagnant water? Henry 252. Ernault, Glossaire 651.

4. ON *þykkr*, OE *þicce*, OHG *dicchi*, etc. (12.63) are also used with reference to density, but in this sense partly replaced by forms of the following group. Thus NHG still *dicke suppe*, *dicker* or *dichter wald*, but *dicht* the more distinctive word in this sense. Similarly in Dan. and Sw.

ME *thycht*, fr. an ON **þēhtr* (cf. *þéttr* 'water-tight'), this with Dan. *tæt*, Sw. *tät*, MLG, MHG *dīhte*, Du., NHG *dicht* : Lith. *tankus* 'thick, standing close together', fr. the root in Goth. *þeihan* 'thrive' (= 'become solid'), Ir. *contēcim* 'coagulate', Skt. *tañc-* 'contract', etc. NED s.v. *thight*, adj. Falk-Torp 1313. Walde-P. 1.725 f. Weigand-H. 1.352.

5. Lith. *tankus*, see just above.

Lith. *tirštas* 'thick' of liquids (this perh. fr. 'turbid'), beside *tiršti* 'become thick' : *teršti* 'soil, pollute', East Lith. *tresti* 'manure', Lat. *stercus* 'dung, excrement', W. *trwnc* 'urin, lye', etc. Walde-P. 2.641.

Lett. *biezs*, also 'thick' of dimension (12.63).

6. ChSl. *čęstŭ* (renders πυκνός, but mostly in temporal sense 'frequent' as in modern Slavic; cf. esp. adv. *čęsto* 'often') : Lith. *kimšti* 'stuff full'. Berneker 154 f.

SCr. *gust*, Boh. *hustý*, Pol. *gęsty*, Russ. *gustoj* (Russ.-ChSl. *gustŭ*), Slavic **gąstŭ* fr. **gonĝ-to-* : Lith. *gunga* 'ball (of thread, of the foot, etc.)', *gungti* 'bend, crook', Grk. γόγγρος 'growth on tree-trunks', γογγύλος 'rounded', etc., all prob. fr. a root meaning 'to swell, become thick', or the like. Berneker 341, 343. Walde-P. 1.638.

7. Skt. *ghana-*, beside sb. *ghana-* 'solid mass, lump, club', fr. *han-* 'strike, slay'. Uhlenbeck 84.

Skt. *sāndra-*, etym.? Uhlenbeck 333.

Skt. *bahula-*, also 'thick' of density (12.63).

12.65 THIN¹

(In Dimension)

Grk.	*λεπτός*	Goth.	. . . .	Lith.	*plonas*
NG	*λεπτός, φτενός*	ON	*þunnr*	Lett.	*tievs, plāns*
Lat.	*tenuis*	Dan.	*tynd*	ChSl.	*tĭnŭkŭ*
It.	*sottile (tenue)*	Sw.	*tunn*	SCr.	*tanak*
Fr.	*mince*	OE	*þynne*	Boh.	*tenký*
Sp.	*delgado (tenue)*	ME	*thinne*	Pol.	*cienki*
Rum.	*subțire*	NE	*thin*	Russ.	*tonkij*
Ir.	*tana, sēim*	Du.	*dun*	Skt.	*tanu-*
NIr.	*tana*	OHG	*dunni*	Av.	. . . .
W.	*teneu*	MHG	*dünne*		
Br.	*tano*	NHG	*dünn*		

'Thin' comes from the notion of 'stretched out' in the large inherited group, and similarly from 'spread out' in the Baltic words. Otherwise it is from various sources through the notion of 'fine, delicate'.

1. IE **tenu-*, **tn̥u-* with meaning 'thin' fr. 'stretched', deriv. of **ten-* in Skt. *tan-*, Grk. τείνω, Lat. *tendere*, etc. 'stretch' (9.32). Walde-P. 1.724. Ernout-M. 1029.

Lat. *tenuis* (> lit. words It., Sp. *tenue*, Fr. *ténu*); Ir. *tana*, W. *teneu* (*e* fr. Lat. *tenuis*), Br. *tano*; ON *þunnr*, OE *þynne*, OHG *dunni*, etc., general Gmc.; Lett. *tievs*; (Lith. dial. *tenvas*, Leskien, Bildung d. Nom. 344; Mühl.-Endz. 4.215 f); ChSl. *tĭnŭkŭ*, etc., general Slavic; Skt. *tanu-*; but Grk. ταναός 'slender, long', τανυ- in cpds. 'long'.

2. Grk. λεπτός, lit. 'peeled' (of grains) hence 'fine, thin' : λέπω 'peel, husk', λέπος 'rind, husk', etc. Walde-P. 2.424. Boisacq 569.

Byz. πτενός (Const. Porph.), NG pop. φτενός, perh. fr. πτηνός 'flying, winged' (Eust. 855.42, Koraes, Ἄτακτα 1.123), despite the difficulty in form (ε fr. πτερόν?) and sense ('thin' as what easily flies?).

3. It. *sottile*, Rum. *subțire* fr. Lat. *subtīlis* 'fine, delicate' (of thread, Lucr.), prob. orig. a weavers' term 'finely woven' with the last part related to *tēla* 'web, loom', *texere* 'weave'. Ernout-M. 995. REW 8399.

Fr. *mince*, deriv. of OFr. *mincier* 'make small' fr. VLat. **minūtiāre*, fr. *minūtia* 'particle, trifle'. REW 5598.

Sp. *delgado*, fr. Lat. *delicātus* 'charming, tender, delicate'. REW 2538.

4. Ir. *sēim* 'thin, slender', of liquor 'mild, thin', perh. fr. **spei-mi-* : Grk. σπι-νός 'lean', fr. the root **spēi-* in Grk. σπάω 'draw out, pull, pluck out', OHG *spannan* 'stretch, span', etc. Walde-P. 2.656. Stokes 295.

5. Lith. *plonas*, Lett. *plāns*, the latter also 'flat' and 'weak' : Lat. *plānus* 'flat', etc. (12.71), with meanings 'flat' and 'thin' fr. 'spread out', common to the large group of cognates. Walde-P. 2.61. Mühl.-Endz. 3.330.

12.66 THIN²

(In Density)

Grk.	*μανός, ἀραιός*	Goth.	. . . .	Lith.	*retas, skystas*
NG	*ἀραιός, ἀνάριος*	ON	*þunnr*	Lett.	*rets, šk'idrs*
Lat.	*rārus*	Dan.	*tynd*	ChSl.	*rědŭkŭ*
It.	*rado, non fitto*	Sw.	*tunn, gles*	SCr.	*rijedak*
Fr.	*rare, clair, clairsemé*	OE	*þynne*	Boh.	*řídký*
Sp.	*ralo, claro*	ME	*thinne*	Pol.	*rzadki*
Rum.	*rar*	NE	*thin*	Russ.	*redkij, židkij*
Ir.	*tana*	Du.	*dun*	Skt.	*virala-*
NIr.	*tana*	OHG	*dunni*	Av.	. . . .
W.	*teneu*	MHG	*dünne*		
Br.	*tano*	NHG	*dünn*		

'Thin' in density is expressed by the old words for 'thin' in dimension in Celtic and Germanic, but elsewhere mostly by different words based on such notions as 'clear, bright' (what one can see through, hence 'thin') or 'loose, separated'. Many of these come to be used also or mostly for 'rare, scarce'.

But even where there are different words, there is some overlapping in idiomatic usage.

1. IE **erə-*, **rē-*, etc. in various derivs. meaning 'loose, thin (not dense), separated' etc.; vb. forms in Lith. *irti* 'dissolve, separate', ChSl. *oriti* 'dissolve, destroy', etc. Walde-P. 1.142 f. Ernout-M. 852.

Lat. *rārus* (> It. *rado*, Sp. *ralo*, Rum. *rar*; lit. words It., Sp. *raro*, Fr. *rare*); Lith. *retas*, Lett. *rets*; (with *-dh-* extension) ChSl. *rědŭkŭ*, etc., general Slavic; Skt. *vi-rala-*.

2. Grk. μανός, μᾱνός (*μανϝός) 'thin, sparse' (opp. to πυκνός in Emped., etc.) : Arm. *manr* 'small', Ir. *menb* 'small', Lith. *menkas* 'small, petty', Skt. *manāk* 'a little' (adv.), Toch. A *maṅk*, B *meṅki* 'fault, lack', Hitt. *maninkwess-* 'become short' (Sturtevant, Language 6.217 f., Hitt. Gloss. 97). Walde-P. 2.266 f. Ernout-M. 618.

Grk. ἀραιός (ἀ- Hdn.), in earliest use 'slender, narrow', later 'thin' vs. πυκνός, etym.? Sommer, Gr. Lautstud. 114.

Byz., NG also (cpd. with ἀνα-) ἀνάριος.

3. Fr. *clair*, Sp. *claro*, lit. 'clear', hence 'letting the light through, not dense', fr. Lat. *clārus* 'clear, bright'. Hence cpd. Fr. *clairsemé* (with *semé* 'sown'), used esp. of grass, grain, trees.

4. Ir. *tana* (cf. Thes. 2. xxii *is tana an dub* 'the ink is thin'), W. *teneu*, Br. *tano*, also 'thin' of dimension (12.65).

5. ON *þunnr*, etc., general Gmc. for 'thin' in both senses (12.65).

Sw. *gles*, older and dial. *glis* : older and dial. Sw., Norw. *glīsa* 'peep through', OE *glisian* 'shine, glisten', etc. Hellquist 286.

6. Lith. *skystas*, Lett. *šk'idrs* 'thin', of liquids, beside Lith. *skiesti* 'dilute' (milk with water), Lett. *skaidīt* 'thin (a drink)', prob. (as 'make clear') : Lith. *skaidrus*, Lett. *skaidrs* 'clear, bright', ChSl. *čistŭ* 'pure', etc. Walde-P. 2.537 f. Berneker 22 f.

7. Russ. *židkij* 'thin' of liquids, but also *židkaja boroda* 'thin beard', *židkije volosy* 'thin hair' = SCr. *židak* 'thin, diluted', etc., late ChSl. *židŭkŭ* 'watery', perh. : Grk. δεῖσα 'mud, filth'. Walde-P. 1.671. Solmsen, Beiträge 237.

8. ChSl. *rědŭkŭ*, etc., Skt. *virala-*, above, 1.

12.67 DEEP

Grk.	*βαθύς*	Goth.	*diups*	Lith.	*gilus (dubus)*
NG	*βαθύς*	ON	*djūpr*	Lett.	*dzil'š*
Lat.	*altus, profundus*	Dan.	*dyb*	ChSl.	*gląbokŭ*
It.	*profondo, fondo*	Sw.	*djup*	SCr.	*dubok*
Fr.	*profond*	OE	*dēop*	Boh.	*hluboký*
Sp.	*profundo, hondo*	ME	*deep*	Pol.	*głęboki*
Rum.	*adînc*	NE	*deep*	Russ.	*glubokij*
Ir.	*domain, fudumain*	Du.	*diep*	Skt.	*gabhīra-, gahana-, etc.*
NIr.	*doimhin*	OHG	*tiof*		
W.	*dwfn*	MHG	*tief*	Av.	*jafra-, gufra-*
Br.	*doun*	NHG	*tief*		

Many of the words for 'deep' are connected with others for 'hollow' or 'bent' and must have first been used of 'deep' holes, dishes, etc. Some, belonging with words for 'dip, plunge' were probably first used of the 'deep' sea, etc. Lat. *altus* is unique as a word for 'high' applied also to distance downward.

1. IE **dheub-* in words for 'deep', 'bottom', and 'hollow'. Walde-P. 1.847 f.

Here as 'deep' : Ir. *domain*, NIr. *doimhin*, W. *dwfn*, Br. *doun*, cpd. Ir. *fu-dumain;* Goth. *diups*, OE *dēop*, etc., general Gmc.; Lith. *dubus* 'deep' (of dishes), mostly 'hollow'; cf. Lith. *duobė* 'a hollow, hole', Lett. *duobs* 'hollow'.

2. Grk. βαθύς, beside βένθος, βάθος 'depth', etym. dub. Boisacq 112. Cuny, Mélanges linguistiques offerts à H. Pedersen, 208 ff.

3. Lat. *altus* 'high' (12.31) also 'deep'.

Lat. *profundus* (> It. *profondo*, Fr. *profond*, Sp. *profundo*), fr. *fundus* 'bottom' (12.34), whence It. *fondo*, Sp. *hondo* 'bottom' and as adjs. 'deep'. Ernout-M. 401 f. Walde-H. 1.565. REW 3585, 6772.

Rum. *adînc*, fr. Lat. *ad-uncus* (or VLat. **ad-ancus*) 'bent' : Lat. *ancus*, *uncus* 'hook', etc. (12.75), hence first 'bent, deep' (dish, etc.) in contrast to 'flat'. REW 144. Pușcariu 25. Tiktin 21 f.

4. Lith. *gilus*, Lett. *dzil'š* (OPruss. acc. sg. fem. *gillin*) beside Lith. *gelme*, Lett. *dzelme* 'depth', etym.? Berneker 321.

5. ChSl. *gląbokŭ*, Boh. *hluboký*, Pol. *głęboki*, Russ. *glubokij*, beside ChSl. *gląbina*, etc. 'depth', prob. fr. **glumbh-*, a nasalized form of the root in Grk. γλύφω 'carve out', etc. Berneker 307.

SCr. *dubok*, Bulg. *dŭlbokŭ*, beside sbs. SCr. *dubina*, Bulg. *dŭlbina* : SCr. *dubem*, *dupsti* 'hollow out', Russ. *dolbit'* 'chisel, hollow out', these : OE *delfan* 'dig' (8.22). Walde-P. 1.866 f. Berneker 251.

6. Skt. *gabhīra-*, *gambhīra-*, Av. *jafra-* (and *jaiwa-* in *jaiwa-vafra-* 'with deep snow'), beside Skt. *gambhan-* 'depth', Av. *jąfnu-* 'depression', perh. : Grk. βάπτω 'dip, dye', βαφή 'dipping, dye', ON *kvefja* 'submerge, overwhelm', intr. 'be swamped, sink', OSw. *kvaf* 'depth of the sea', etc. Walde-P. 1.674. Falk-Torp 504.

Skt. *gahana-*, *gaḍha-*, prob. : *gāh-* 'plunge, dive into', Grk. βῆσσα 'glen', Ir. *bāidim* 'sink, drown', W. *boddi* 'immerse', etc. Walde-P. 1.665.

Av. *gufra-* 'deep' and 'secret, wonderful', prob. : Grk. γύπη· κοίλωμα γῆς· θαλάμη, γωνία. (Hesych.), ON *kofi* 'hut, cell', etc., fr. an extension of **geu-* in numerous words with common notion of 'bent, hollow'. Walde-P. 1.562. Barth. 524.

12.68 SHALLOW

Grk.	*ἀβαθής*	Goth.	. . . .	Lith.	*seklus, lėkštas*
NG	*ρηχός*	ON	*grunnr*	Lett.	*sekls*
Lat.	*nōn altus, brevis*	Dan.	*grund*	ChSl.	*mělŭkŭ*
It.	*poco profondo, basso*	Sw.	*grund*	SCr.	*plitak*
Fr.	*peu profond, bas*	OE	*sceald*	Boh.	*mělký*
Sp.	*poco profundo, bajo*	ME	*schold, schalowe*	Pol.	*płytki, miałki*
Rum.	*puţin adînc*	NE	*shallow* (*shoal*)	Russ.	*melkij*
Ir.	*ēdomain*(?)	Du.	*ondiep*	Skt.	*gādha-*
NIr.	*ēadoimhin*	OHG	. . . .	Av.	. . . .
W.	*bas*	MHG	*sīhte*		
Br.	*bas*	NHG	*seicht, nicht tief, flach*		

In several languages 'shallow' is expressed simply as 'not deep' or 'little deep'. So Grk. ἀβαθής, Lat. *nōn altus*, It. *poco profondo*, Fr. *peu profond*, etc., NIr. *ēadoimhin* (Ir. *ēdomain* quotable?), Du. *ondiep*, NHG (*untief* rare, but sb. *untiefe* common) *nicht tief*.

Most of the other words for 'shallow' were first used only with reference to water, some still so restricted, but more of them extended to 'shallow' dishes, etc. Words for 'low, short' and 'flat' are sometimes used for 'shallow'.

1. NG ρηχός, back-formation to Grk. ῥᾱχία, Ion. ῥηχίη 'roar of the breakers, rocky shore' (: ῥάσσω, Ion. ῥήσσω 'strike, dash') through 'shoals, shallows' (cf. βράχεα καὶ ῥηχίαι καὶ τενάγεα Arr. Ind. 38.8), and with η in the κοινή (as also in the vb. ἐήσσω), perh. through pop. association with ῥήγνῡμι 'break'. Now used not only of 'shallow' water, but of 'shallow' dishes, etc.

2. Lat. *brevis* 'short' (11.59) sometimes 'shallow', as with *puteus* 'well', *vada* 'fords'; so *brevia* 'shoals', like Grk. βράχεα 'shoals' : βραχύς 'short'.

It. *basso*, Fr. *bas*, Sp. *bajo* 'low' (12.32), also for 'low' = 'shallow' water.

3. W., Corn., Br. *bas* (Br. *bas* Vallée, not in Ernault), fr. VLat. *bassus* 'low' (12.32), hence of 'low' = 'shallow' water. Loth, Mots lat. 137.

4. ON *grunnr*, Dan., Sw. *grund* : sbs. ON *grunnr* 'bottom', OE *grund* 'bottom, ground', etc. (12.34). Falk-Torp 352.

OE *sceald*, ME *schold(e)*, NE *shoal*, used only with reference to water, beside ME *schalowe*, NE *shallow* used also of dishes, etc., also LG *schol* 'shallow', etym. dub. Possibly through the notion of 'thin layer' : OE *scealu* 'shell, dish', etc. NED s.v. *shoal.*

MHG *sīhte*, NHG *seicht* 'shallow', but only of water or figurative : OHG *sīhan* 'flow slowly, drip', Skt. *sic-* 'pour out', etc., or (as fr. **senktis-*) : Lith. *senku*, *sekti* 'fall, sink' (of water), *seklus* 'shallow'. Walde-P. 2.473. Falk-Torp 1228. Weigand-H. 2.835.

NHG *flach* 'flat' (12.71), used also of what is approximately flat in contrast to high or deep, as of 'shallow' dishes, etc. Paul, Deutsches Wtb. s.v.

5. Lith. *seklus* (of 'shallow' water), Lett. *sekls* (also of dishes, etc.) : Lith. *senku*, *sekti* 'fall, sink' (of water), ChSl. *sęknąti* id., etc. Walde-P. 2.473. Mühl.-Endz. 3.814.

Lith. *lėkštas* 'flat' (12.71) used esp. of 'shallow' dishes.

6. Late ChSl. *mělŭkŭ*, OSCr. *mioki*, Boh. *mělký*, Pol. *miałki* (also 'finely ground'), Russ. *melkij* (also 'small, fine'), prob. through 'finely ground, fine' : ChSl. *mlěti*, Lat. *molere*, etc. 'grind'. Berneker 2.48.

SCr. *plitak*, Pol. *płytki* : SCr. *plivati*, Pol. *pływać*, ChSl. *plavati* 'swim, float' (11.34), hence of fordable water (cf. Pol. *plyt* 'a raft, float'), that is, 'shallow', then also of dishes. Brückner 422.

7. Skt. *gādha-* 'fordable, shallow', etym.? Walde-P. 1.665. Uhlenbeck 79.

12.71 FLAT

Grk.	*πλατύς, πεδινός*	Goth.	*ibns*	Lith.	*lėkštas*
NG	*πεδινός, πλακωτός*	ON	*flatr*	Lett.	*lēzns, plāns*
Lat.	*plānus*	Dan.	*flad*	ChSl.	*ploskŭ*
It.	*piano, piatto*	Sw.	*flat, platt*	SCr.	*plosnat*
Fr.	*plat*	OE	*efen*	Boh.	*plochý, ploský*
Sp.	*plano*	ME	*flat(t), playne*	Pol.	*płaski*
Rum.	*şes, lat*	NE	*flat*	Russ.	*ploskij*
Ir.	*rēid*	Du.	*vlak, plat*	Skt.	*sama-*
NIr.	*rēidh*	OHG	*flah*	Av.	. . . .
W.	*fflat, gwastad*	MHG	*vlach*		
Br.	*kompes, plat*	NHG	*flach, platt*		

The majority of the common words for 'flat' belong to an inherited group with basic notion of 'spread out'.

1. But many words for 'equal' (12.91) or 'even' are also used for 'level, flat'. With a few exceptions (where there seem to be no more common words for 'flat') these are not included in the list. Thus Grk. ὁμαλός 'even, level' : Lat. *similis* 'similar', Grk. ὁμός 'the same', Goth. *sama* 'the same', Skt. *sama-* 'equal, same', also 'even, level, flat' (cf. *sama-bhūmi-* 'plain' sb.); Grk. ἴσος 'equal' also 'level, flat', NG ἴσιος 'even', 'straight', and 'level, flat'; Lat. *aequus* 'equal' and 'level, flat'; Fr. *uni* 'united, uniform' and 'level, flat'; Goth. *ibns*, OE *efen*, etc. (see below); Lith. *lygus*, Lett. *līdzens* 'equal' (: Goth. *ga-leiks* 'like', etc.) and 'level, flat'; ChSl. *ravinŭ* (renders πεδινός Lk. 6.17, elsewhere in Gospels ἴσος), etc., general Slavic for 'equal, even' and so sometimes 'level, flat', whence words for 'plain' sb. (1.23) : Goth. *rūms* 'roomy, spacious', Av. *ravah-* 'open space', Lat. *rūs* 'country', etc.

2. Derivs. of IE **pelə-*, **plā-* with notion of 'spread out flat', seen in Lith. *ploti* 'flatten' etc., also in several words for 'wide, broad' (12.61). Walde-P. 2.61, 90 f., 99 f. Ernout-M. 776. REW 6581, 6586. Falk-Torp 230.

With *no*-formation, Lat. *plānus* (> It. *piano*, OFr. *plain*, Sp. *plano*, *llano*), Lett. *plāns* (mostly 'thin', like Lith. *plonas*); with guttural extension (cf.

Grk. πλάξ 'flat surface'), OHG *flah*, MHG *vlach*, NHG *flach*, Du. *vlak;* with dental extension, Grk. πλατύς 'broad, flat' (> VLat. **plattus* > It. *piatto*, Fr. *plat* > Br. *plat*, Du. *plat;* LG *plat* > NHG *platt* > Sw. *platt*), ON *flatr* (> ME *flatt*, NE *flat* > W. *fflat*), Dan. *flad*, Sw. *flat* : ChSl. *ploskŭ* (**plat-sko-* or **plak-sko-*?), SCr. *plosnat*, Boh. *ploský* (Boh. *plochý* prob. fr. OHG *flah*, Gebauer 1.441, Vondrak 1.436; otherwise Brückner 419), Pol. *płaski*, Russ. *ploskij*.

3. Grk. πεδιεινός, later πεδινός, only of 'flat' country, deriv. of πεδίον 'plain' : πέδον 'ground'.

NG πλακωτός 'compressed, flat', fr. πλακώνω 'compress', deriv. of πλάξ 'flat stone'.

4. Rum. *şes*, only of 'flat' country, fr. Lat. *sessus* 'seated, settled'. Tiktin 1411. Puşcariu 1586.

Rum. *lat* 'broad' (11.61), used also for 'flat' dishes. Tiktin 892.

5. Ir. *rēid*, NIr. *rēidh*, also 'clear, open, ready, smooth' prob. orig. 'passable' (of a road, etc.) : *rīadaim* 'ride', ON *rīða* id., etc. Walde-P. 2.349. Pedersen 1.58.

W. *gwastad* 'level, flat', also and orig. 'steady, constant' : Ir. *fossad* 'firm', fr. **upo-stato-*, IE **stā-* 'stand'. Walde-P. 2.605. Pedersen 1.34.

Br. *kompes*, also 'smooth, polished', MBr. *compoes* 'equal', beside W. *cymhwys-iad* 'adjustment, quality', prob. cpd. of *kom-*, *cym-* 'co-' and *poez* 'weight' (fr. Lat. *pēnsum*). Loth, Mots lat. 156. Henry 75.

6. Goth. *ibns* (only dat. sg. *ana stada ibnamma* = ἐπὶ τόπου πεδινοῦ Lk. 6.17), OE *efen* (ME, NE *even*), etc., general Gmc. word for 'even, level' and so sometimes of 'flat' land, etc., etym. dub. Walde-P. 1.102. Feist 287.

ME *playne* (NE *plain* only sb. in this sense), fr. OFr. *plain* (above, 2).

7. Lith. *lėkštas*, Lett. *lēzns*, prob. : MHG *læge* 'low, flat', ON *lāgr* 'low', etc. Walde-P. 2.462. Mühl.-Endz. 2.465.

8. Skt. *sama-*, see above, 1.

12.72 HOLLOW (= Concave)

Grk.	*κοῖλος*	Goth.	. . . .	Lith.	*dubus*
NG	*βαθουλός, κοῖλος*	ON	*holr*	Lett.	*duobs*
Lat.	*cavus*	Dan.	*hul*	ChSl.	. . . .
It.	*cavo*	Sw.	*ihålig*	SCr.	*izduben*
Fr.	*creux*	OE	*hol*	Boh.	*dutý*
Sp.	*hueco*	ME	*hol(we)*	Pol.	*wydrążony*
Rum.	*găunos*	NE	*hollow*	Russ.	*vognutyj*
Ir.	*cūa, cūassach*	Du.	*hol*	Skt.	*uttāna-*
NIr.	*cuasach*	OHG	*hol*	Av.	. . . .
W.	*cau*	MHG	*hol*		
Br.	*kleus*	NHG	*hohl*		

'Hollow' is understood here primarily in the less common sense of NE *hollow* as 'having a depression in the surface, concave' (NED s.v. *hollow*, adj. 2) rather than in its more usual sense of 'having an empty space inside', as opposite of *solid*. The latter sense is, to be sure, common also to many of the other words listed and indeed dominant in several. But words that are used for 'hollow' only in this latter sense as NG κούφιος (: Grk. κοῦφος 'light, unsubstantial', late also 'empty'), and others listed under 'empty' (13.22), Pol. *próżny*, Russ. *pustoj*, Skt. *çūnya-*, are not included in this list.

1. Derivs. of IE **k̑eu-* seen in numerous words with common notion of curved, whether convex (as Skt. *çvā-*

'swell', Grk. κυέω 'be pregnant', κῦμα 'wave', etc.) or concave, as here. Walde-P. 1.365 ff. Ernout-M. 167, 203. Walde-H. 1.191.

Grk. κοῖλος (*κοϝιλος); Lat. **covus* (> Port. *covo*), *cavus* (> It. *cavo*); Ir. *cūa*, W. *cau* (this with Br. *keo* 'cave', fr. **kowio-*, cf. Loth, Mots lat. 145).

2. NG βαθουλός, dim. of βαθύς 'deep' (12.67).

3. Fr. *creux*, OFr. *crues*, Prov. *cros*, orig. dub., but prob. Celtic. REW 2257. Gamillscheg 277. Bloch 1.190.

Sp. *hueco*, Port. *ouco*, *oco*, prob. (despite phonetic difficulties) fr. VLat. **voccus* = Lat. *vacuus* 'empty'. REW 9155.

Rum. *găunos*, deriv. of ORum. *găun* fr. VLat. **cavō* (*-ōnis*) 'cavity', fr. *cavus* (above, 1). REW 1794. Puşcariu 700.

4. Ir. *cūassach*, NIr. *cuasach*, fr. *cūas* 'hole' : *cūa* (above, 1).

Br. *kleus*, fr. Fr. *creux* with *l* fr. *kleuz* 'ditch'. Henry 70.

5. ON *holr*, OE, OHG *hol*, etc., general Gmc. (Sw. *ihålig*, *hålig* fr. *hål* 'hole', sb. fr. OSw. *hul* adj.), perh. : Grk. καυλός 'stalk of a plant, shaft of a spear, quill', Lat. *caulis* 'stalk of a plant', etc., Skt. *kulya-* 'bone', all fr. the notion 'hollow (shaft)'. Walde-P. 1.332. Walde-H. 1.189. Otherwise (: OE *helan* 'hide', etc.) Falk-Torp 427.

6. Lith. *dubus*, Lett. *duobs* : Goth. *diups* 'deep', etc. (12.67).

7. SCr. *izduben*, lit. 'hollowed out' fr. *iz-dupsti* (1sg.-*dubem*) 'hollow out' : Russ. *dolbat'* 'chisel, mortise', etc. Berneker 251.

Boh. *dutý*, through 'blown up, swollen', fr. the root of OBoh. *dunuti* 'blow' (ChSl. *dunąti*, etc. Berneker 236), Boh. *duoti* 'blow', refl. 'swell'.

Pol. *(wy)drążony*, lit. 'hollowed out', fr. *(wy)drążić* 'hollow out, dig out', older *drożony*, *drożić*, etc. : Boh. *drážiti* 'groove', Russ. *dorožit'* 'flute', etc. Berneker 212. Brückner 97.

Russ. *vognutyj* 'bent, concave', fr. *vognut'* 'bend, fold in' (9.15).

Russ. *glubokij* 'deep' (12.67), also 'hollow' (of dishes, etc.).

8. Skt. *uttāna-* 'stretched out' (fr. *tan-* 'stretch'), also 'hollow'.

12.73 STRAIGHT

Grk.	*εὐθύς* (*ὀρθός*)	Goth.	*raihts*	Lith.	*tiesus*
NG	*ἴσιος, εὐθύς*	ON	*rēttr, beinn, rakr*	Lett.	*taisns, tiešs* (*līdzens*)
Lat.	*rēctus, dīrēctus*	Dan.	*lige, ret*	ChSl.	*pravŭ*
It.	*dritto*	Sw.	*rak, rät*	SCr.	*ravan, prav*
Fr.	*droit*	OE	*riht*	Boh.	*rovný, přímý*
Sp.	*recto, derecho*	ME	*streiȝt, riȝt*	Pol.	*prosty*
Rum.	*drept*	NE	*straight*	Russ.	*prjamoj*
Ir.	*dīriuch*	Du.	*recht*	Skt.	*ṛju-*
NIr.	*dīreach*	OHG	*reht, gereht*	Av.	*ərəzu-*
W.	*union*	MHG	*reht, gereht*		
Br.	*eeun*	NHG	*gerade*		

Many of the words for 'straight' are the same as those for 'right, upright'. Some words for 'equal, even' are used also for 'straight', as well as 'level, flat'. Others are of various sources.

1. Derivs. of IE **reĝ-* in Skt. *ṛj-* 'straighten out, make straight', Grk. ὀρέγω 'reach, stretch', Lat. *regere* 'direct, lead', Ir. *rigim* 'stretch out', Goth. *ufrahjan* 'stretch out', etc. Walde-P. 2.362 ff. Ernout-M. 855, 856 ff. Falk-Torp 891. REW 2648.

Lat. *rēctus* (> Sp. *recto*), *dīrēctus*, VLat. **dērēctus* (> It. *diritto*, *dritto*, Fr.

droit, Sp. *derecho*, Rum. *drept*), verbal adjs. of *regere*, *dīrigere* (above); OIr. *dīriuch*, *dīriug*, MIr. *dīrech*, NIr. *dīreach* (loanwords? cf. Pedersen 1.229, 2.116); Goth. *raihts*, ON *rēttr*, etc. general Gmc. (the orig. meaning preserved in NHG *senkrecht* 'plumb', *aufrecht*, NE *upright*, and NHG *rechter winkel*, NE *right angle*, etc.); also ON *rakr*, Sw. *rak* (= East Frank. *rak* 'right', MLG *ṛak* 'straight, in order'); Skt. *ṛju-*, Av. *ərəzu-*.

2. Grk. εὐθύς, Ion. ἰθύς, relation and orig. obscure. Walde-P. 2.450. Boisacq 294, 370.

Grk. ὀρθός (ϝορθο-, *ϝορθϝο-), orig. and in actual use mostly 'upright, vertically straight' : Skt. *ūrdhva-* 'upright, raised', *vṛdh-* 'increase', mid. 'grow', Av. *varəd-* 'increase', etc. Walde-P. 1.289. Boisacq 711.

NG ἴσιος 'straight, even, flat', fr. ἴσος 'equal' (12.91).

3. W. *union*, cpd. of *un-* 'one' and *iawn* 'right, just' = Br. *eeun* 'straight, right, just', etym. dub. (see 16.73).

4. ON *beinn*, Norw. *bein*, Sw. dial. *ben*, beside ON *beinka* 'straighten', etym.? Falk-Torp 70. Torp, Nynorsk 20.

Dan. *lige*, also 'equal, alike', weak form of *lig* 'like, similar, equal to' (: ON *līkr*, Goth. *galeiks* 'like', etc.). Falk-Torp 642.

ME *streiȝt*, NE *straight*, orig. 'stretched out, extended', pple. of ME *strecche*, NE *stretch*. NED s.v. *straight*.

NHG *gerade*, fr. MHG *gerat*, *gerade* 'quick (with the hand), agile, capable', OHG *giradi* 'velocissimus' : OE *gerǣde* 'swift', related to OHG *(h)rato*, OE *hrǣde* id. Semantic development through attested 'quickly grown, shooting up long and slim', Weigand-H. 1.685. Paul, Deutsches Wtb. 201.

5. Lith. *tiesus*, Lett. *tiešs* and *taisns* (the latter also 'even, like, just, true') beside Lith. *tiesti* 'make straight', *taisyti* 'prepare', Lett. *taisīt* 'make, prepare' : Lith. *teisus* 'just, true', OPruss. *teisi* 'honor' (fr. 'uprightness'), Slav. *těšiti* 'comfort' (fr. 'set right'), ChSl. *tichŭ* 'calm, quiet' (fr. 'even'), root connection? The sense 'straight, even' seems the more original in the group. Mühl.-Endz. 4.124, 125, 215.

Lett. *līdzens* 'equal, even' (12.91) used reg. for 'straight' in NT, Mk. 1.3, Lk. 3.4, 5, etc. (this use not given by Mühl.-Endz. s.v.).

6. ChSl. *pravŭ* (the regular word for εὐθύς in Gospels), SCr. *prav* (also 'right, upright, just' as Boh. *prav*, Pol. *prawy*, Russ. *pravyj*), prob. as orig. 'straight, forward' : Skt. *pravaṇa-* 'inclined forward, steep', Lat. *prōnus*, Grk. πρανής 'inclined forward', derivs. of IE **pro*, **prō*, etc., 'forward, in front' in Skt. *pra*, Grk. πρό, etc. Walde-P. 2.38.

SCr. *ravan*, Boh. *rovný*, also 'equal, even, level', the prevailing Slavic meaning (see 12.91).

Boh. *přímý*, Russ. *prjamoj* : ChSl. *prěmŭ*, esp. adv. *prěmo* 'over against', orig. obscure. Meillet, Études 2.427. Vondrák 1.553. Gebauer 1.41.

Pol. *prosty*, also 'simple' the usual Slavic sense, as in ChSl. *prostŭ* (for ἁπλοῦς in Gospels, but also for ὀρθός in Supr., etc.), Boh. *prostý*, Russ. *prostoj*, prob. orig. 'straightforward' (hence 'upright, straight' and 'simple'), fr. **prosto-* (in form like Skt. *prastha-* 'plateau'), cpd. of **pro* 'forwards' and a vbl. adj. fr. **stā-* 'stand'. Walde-P. 2.604. Meillet, Études 1.611. Brückner 439.

7. Skt. *ṛju-*, Av. *ərəzu-*, above, 1.

12.74 CROOKED

Grk.	σκολιός, καμπύλος, ἀγκύλος	Goth.	*wraiqs*	Lith.	*kreivas, kumpas*
		ON	*krōkōttr*	Lett.	*līks (nelīdzens)*
NG	στραβός, καμπύλος	Dan.	*krum, kroget*	ChSl.	*strŭpĭtĭnŭ*
Lat.	*curvus, prāvus*	Sw.	*krokig, krum*	SCr.	*kriv*
It.	*torto*	OE	*þweorh, wōh (crumb)*	Boh.	*křivý*
Fr.	*tortueux*	ME	*croked, woȝe*	Pol.	*krzywy*
Sp.	*torcido, corvo*	NE	*crooked*	Russ.	*krivoj*
Rum.	*strîmb*	Du.	*krom*	Skt.	*vakra-, kuṭila-*
Ir.	*camm, cromm, cūar*	OHG	*crumb*	Av.	. . . .
NIr.	*cam, crom, cuar*	MHG	*krump*		
W.	*cam, crwm*	NHG	*krumm*		
Br.	*kamm, kromm, gwar*				

NE *crooked* is clearly the most distinctive opposite of *straight*. But many of the words listed as such opposites are terms that answer to both *crooked* and *curved*, that is, they are used without differentiation (except in technical language) as to whether the deflection is in the form of a curve or one or more sharp angles. They are derived from a variety of roots for 'bend' or 'turn'.

1. Grk. σκολιός : OHG *scelah* 'oblique, squinting', OE *sceolh* 'oblique, wry', Skt. *kuṭila-* 'crooked', NPers. *kul* id., etc., fr. IE **(s)kel-* in words for 'bent, crooked' (esp. in the name of crooked parts of the body, Grk. σκέλος 'leg', etc.) Walde-P. 2.598. Boisacq 873.

Grk. καμπύλος, beside καμπή 'a bend, crook', κάμπτω 'bend' : Lith. *kumpas* 'crooked', *kumpti* 'bend', Lett. *kumpt* 'become crooked, hunched', Goth. *hamfs*, OHG *hamf* 'mutilated', etc. Walde-P. 1.350. Boisacq 404.

Grk. ἀγκύλος : ἄγκιστρον, Lat. *uncus* 'hook', etc. (12.75).

Grk. στρεβλός, στραβός (latter 'squinting', but NG 'crooked' in general), fr. a by-form of root in στρέφω 'turn' (10.12). Boisacq 918.

2. Lat. *curvus* 'crooked, curved' (> Sp. *corvo*, *curvo*; It. *curvo*, Fr. *courbe*, mostly 'curved') : Grk. κυρτός 'humped, convex', Ir. *cor* 'circle', Av. *skarəna-* 'round', etc., fr. a root **(s)ker-* with numerous extensions. Walde-P. 2.568. Ernout-M. 248. Walde-H. 1.317 f.

Lat. *prāvus* (partly 'crooked' in lit. sense, but mostly fig. 'perverse, wrong'), etym. dub. Walde-P. 2.86. Ernout-M. 806 f.

It. *torto* (*storto*, *distorto*), Sp. *torcido*, lit. 'twisted', pples. of It. *torcere*, Sp. *torcer* 'twist' (10.13); Fr. *tortueux*, fr. Lat. *tortuōsus*; Fr. *tortu* (so in NT, Lk. 3.5, but now obs. or arch.), re-formed fr. *tort* : Gamillscheg 851.

Rum. *strîmb* (cf. It. *strambo* 'squinting, bandy-legged, distorted, queer'), fr. VLat. *strambus* for Lat. *strabus* 'squinting', this fr. Grk. στραβός (above, 1). Ernout-M. 985. REW 8281. Pușcariu 1658.

3. Ir. *camm*, NIr., W. *cam*, Br. *kamm* : Gall. *cambio-* (in *Cambiodūnum*), Gallo-Lat. *cambiāre* 'exchange' (orig. 'turn') Grk. σκαμβός 'crooked, bowed (of the legs)', Sw. *skumpa* 'limp', etc. Walde-P. 2.539 f. Pedersen 1.118 f.

Ir. *cūar* (K. Meyer, Contrib. 544), prob. fr. **kom-waro-* : Br. *gwar* 'crooked, curved', this : Lat. *vārus* 'bowlegged'. Loth, RC 42.83.

Ir. *cromm*, NIr. *crom*, W. *crwm*, Br. *kromm*, prob. fr. **krombos* : OE *gehrumpen* 'wrinkled', OHG *hrimfan* 'to wrinkle', Grk. κράμβη 'cabbage' (as orig. 'curly'), etc. (Walde-P. 2.589 ff., without the Celtic words). G. S. Lane, Language 8.296.

4. Goth. *wraiqs* (= OFris. *wrāk* 'crooked'), prob. fr. a by-form of **wreiḱ-* in OE *wrīgian* 'turn, move, tend', ME *wrien* 'swerve, turn obliquely' (whence adj. ME *wrye*, NE *wry*), Grk. ῥοικός 'crooked' (esp. of legs), Av. *urvis-* 'turn around'. Relationship of Grk. ῥαιβός (esp. of legs, like ῥοικός) obscure. Walde-P. 1.279. Feist 573. Falk-Torp 1397.

ON *krōkōttr*, Dan. *kroget*, Sw. *krokig*, ME *croked*, NE *crooked*, fr. ON *krōkr*, Dan. *krog*, Sw. *krok*, ME *crok* 'hook' (12.75).

OE *crumb* (rarely in general sense, mostly of persons or parts of body), OHG *crumb*, MHG *krump*, NHG *krumm*, MLG *krum* (> Dan., Sw. *krum*), beside OE *crump*, Du. *krom*, OHG *krumpf* id. : OHG *krimpfan* 'draw together, shrink', ON *kreppa* 'clinch, clasp', Russ. *gorb* 'hump, bump', *gorbit'* 'bend, bow', Ir. *gerbach* 'wrinkled', etc. Walde-P. 1.596.

OE *þweorh* : ON *þverr* 'crosswise', OHG *dwerah* 'slanting, oblique, across' (NHG *zwerch* 'across'), Goth. *þwairhs* 'angry', root connection dub., but possibly as orig. 'cut (crosswise)' : Av. *θwarəs-* 'cut', Grk. σάρξ 'flesh', root **twerḱ-*; or as 'twisted' fr. the root in OHG *dweran* 'turn rapidly', OE *þweran* 'twirl, stir', Skt. *tvṛ-* 'hasten', etc. Walde-P. 1.736. Weigand-H. 2.1353. Feist 507. NED s.v. *thwart*, adv.

OE *wōh*, ME *woȝe*, both also sb. 'evil', beside OS *wāh* sb. 'evil', Goth. *un-wāhs* 'blameless' (Gmc. **wanha-*) : W. *gwaeth* 'worse', Skt. *vañc-* 'totter, stagger', *vakra-* 'crooked' etc. Walde-P. 1.218. Feist 525.

5. Lith. *kreivas* : SCr. *kriv*, etc. (below, 6).

Lith. *kumpas* : Grk. καμπύλος (above, 1).

Lett. *līks* : Lith. *linkti*, *lenkti* 'bend' (9.14). Mühl.-Endz. 2.486.

Lett. *nelīdzens* in NT, Lk. 3.5, neg. of *līdzens* 'straight' in same passage (not in Mühl.-Endz.).

6. ChSl., *strŭpĭtĭnŭ* (Lk. 3.5 for σκολιός, not τραχύς as by error Jagić, index to Marianus, Meillet, Études 299, Walde-P. 2.635; correctly Jagić, Entstehungsgesch. 430, 474, with other references), also *strĭpĭtivŭ* (Jagić 430, Meillet loc. cit.), beside late ChSl. *strŭpĭtŭ* 'variety', Russ. *stropota* 'bend, curve' (here also ChSl. *strupŭ* 'wound', Pol., Russ. *strup* 'scurf'?), etym. dub. Walde-P. 2.635, 703.

SCr. *kriv*, etc., general Slavic (only ChSl. *krĭvŭ* in this sense not quotable), with Lith. *kreivas*, fr. **kreiwo-* with extension of the root in Lat. *curvus*, etc. (above, 2). Walde-P. 2.570. Berneker 618.

7. Skt. *vakra-* : OE *wōh* (above, 4).

Skt. *kuṭila-* : Grk. σκολιός (above, 1).

12.75 HOOK

Grk.	ἄγκιστρον	Goth.	. . . .	Lith.	*kablys*
NG	ἀγκίστρι	ON	*krōkr*	Lett.	*kāsis, āk'is*
Lat.	*uncus, hāmus*	Dan.	*krog, hage*	ChSl.	*ąkotĭ*
It.	*gancio, uncino*	Sw.	*krok, hake*	SCr.	*kuka*
Fr.	*croc, crochet*	OE	*hōc*	Boh.	*hák*
Sp.	*gancho, garabato*	ME	*hok, crok*	Pol.	*hak, kruk*
Rum.	*cîrlig*	NE	*hook*	Russ.	*krjuk*
Ir.	*baccān*	Du.	*haak*	Skt.	*añkuça-, añka-*
NIr.	*crūca, cromōg*	OHG	*hāko*	Av.	*anku-, aka-*
W.	*bach*	MHG	*hāke(n)*		
Br.	*krog, bac'h*	NHG	*haken*		

Words for 'hook' belong to an inherited group based on the notion of 'bent', or are cognate with others for various bent or crooked objects. Besides the words listed, there are, of course, many others in less common or more specialized use.

1. Derivs. of IE **ank-* in Skt. *añc-* 'bend', etc. (9.14). Walde-P. 1.60 f. Ernout-M. 1124. Walde-H. 1.46.

Grk. ἄγκιστρον, NG ἀγκίστρι (both mostly 'fishhook', but also general); Lat. *uncus*, late *uncīnus* (> It. *uncino*); ChSl. *ąkotĭ*; Skt. *añka-* (also 'bend', esp. 'side between breast and hip'), *añkuça-*, Av. *aka-* ('hook' or 'peg', part of the equipment for harnessing horses to wagon), *anku-* (in *anku-pəsəmna-* 'adorned with hooks or clasps'); also derivs. in special sense 'fishhook', as MIr. *ēcath*, OHG *ango*, *angul*, ON *ǫngoll*, OE *angel*, etc.

2. Lat. *uncus*, above, 1.

Lat. *hāmus*, esp. 'fishhook' (> It. *amo*, Fr. *hain* arch., dim. *hameçon* id.), etym. dub., perh. : Grk. χαμός· καμπύλος Hesych.; or (fr. **hāb-mos*) : χαβόν· καμπύλον, στενόν Hesych. Ernout-M. 444. Walde-H. 1.633. REW 4025.

It. *gancio* (> Sp. *gancho*) fr. Turk. *kanca* 'hook, barb, grapnel' (hence also Rum. *cange* 'claw, grapnel'). REW 4673.

Fr. *croc* (dim. *crochet*), fr. ON *krōkr*, etc. (below, 4). REW 4780.

Sp. *garabato*, deriv. of Lat. *carabus* 'crab' (fr. Grk. κάραβος 'crayfish, beetle'). REW 1671.

Rum. *cîrlig*, orig.? Tiktin 296.

3. Ir. *baccān*, fr. *bacc* 'turn, crook, bend, angle, hollow' (K. Meyer, Contrib. 160), W. *bach*, Br. *bac'h* 'hook', perh. : (or back-formation fr.?) Lat. *baculum* 'staff'. Walde-P. 2.105. Walde-H. 1.92.

NIr. *cromōg*, fr. *crom* 'crooked' (12.74).

NIr. *crūca*, prob. fr. NE *crook*.

Br. *krog* fr. Fr. *croc*. Henry 82.

4. ON *krōkr* (> ME *crok*, NE *crook*), Dan. *krog*, Sw. *krok* : OHG *crācho* 'hooked tool', ON *kraki* 'boathook, sort of anchor, stake', OE *crycc*, OHG *krucha*, NHG *krücke* 'crutch, crook', fr. guttural extensions of the root **ger-* 'turn', cf. Lith. *grežti* 'bore', Lett. *griezt* 'turn, wind', etc. Walde-P. 1.593 f. Falk-Torp 581.

OE *hōc*, ME *hok*, NE *hook*, OHG *hāko*, MHG *hāke(n)*, NHG *haken*, Du. *haak*, also with different vowel, Dan. *hage*, Sw. *hake* (= OE *haca* 'bolt, lock') fr. a root **keg-*, **keng-*, cf. Lith. *kengė* 'clamp, iron piece on door-jamb for catching bolt', Ir. *alchaing* 'rack for hanging up arms', Russ. *kogot'* 'claw, talon', etc. Walde-P. 1.382. Falk-Torp 371.

5. Lith. *kablys* (also *kablelis*, *kabliukas*, *kabė*, etc.) : *kabėti* 'hang' (intr.), *kabinti* 'hang' (trans.), prob. ChSl. *skoba* 'fibula', Russ. *skoba* 'cramp, clamp', fr. **(s)kab-*, by-form of **(s)kamb-* in

Grk. σκαμβός 'bow-legged', Ir. *camm* 'crooked'? Walde-P. 2.540.

Lett. *kāsis*, earlier 'forked limb' (for hanging kettle), also dial. *kārsis*, perh. : *kārt* 'hang' (trans.); or : Skt. *kāçi-* 'closed hand, fist'. Mühl.-Endz. 2.204.

Lett. *āk'is* (Lith. *okas*), fr. MLG *hake* (cf. above, 4). Mühl.-Endz. 1.237.

6. ChSl. *ąkotĭ*, above, 1.

SCr. *kuka*, cf. Bulg. *kuka* 'hook, crutch', Russ.-ChSl. *kuko-nosŭ* 'crooked-nosed' : Skt. *kuñc-* 'contract, bend', etc. Walde-P. 1.371. Berneker 639.

Boh. *hák*, Pol. *hak*, fr. Gmc., OHG *hāko*, etc. (above, 4). Brückner 167.

Pol. *kruk* fr. NHG *krücke*, dial. *krucke* 'crutch', and Russ. *krjuk*, fr. ON *krōkr* 'hook' (above, 4). Berneker 629. Brückner 272.

7. Skt. *añkuça-*, Av. *anku-*, etc., above, 1.

12.76 CORNER

Grk.	γωνία	Goth.	*waihsta*	Lith.	*kampas, kertė*
NG	γωνιά	ON	*horn, hyrning*	Lett.	*stūris, kakts*
Lat.	*angulus*	Dan.	*hjørne*	ChSl.	*ągŭlŭ (kutŭ)*
It.	*canto, cantone*	Sw.	*hörn*	SCr.	*kut, ugao*
Fr.	*coin*	OE	*hyrne, hwamm*	Boh.	*roh, kout, úhel*
Sp.	*esquina, rincón*	ME	*corner, hirne*	Pol.	*róg, kąt, węgieł*
Rum.	*colț*	NE	*corner*	Russ.	*ugol*
Ir.	*uilen, uillind, cern*	Du.	*hoek*	Skt.	*koṇa-*
NIr.	*cūinne (cearna)*	OHG	*winkil, ekka*	Av.	. . . .
W.	*congl, cornel*	MHG	*ecke, winkel*		
Br.	*korn, kogn*	NHG	*ecke, winkel*		

Words for 'corner' are connected with roots for 'bend' or with words which, whatever their root connections, suggest the notion of a sharp bend or angle, as those for 'knee', 'elbow', 'wedge', 'hook'. From such a common notion arises the interchange, observed in several groups, between 'corner' and 'edge' or 'point'. Noteworthy is the relation to words for 'horn', which may involve in part semantic borrowing. This relation might also rest on the general notion of 'bent, crooked' (so Schuchardt, Z. rom. Ph. 41.254), but probably comes more specifically through the use of words for 'horn' for projecting parts, as Lat. *cornua* for the tops of a mountain, ends of a sailyard, wings of an army, and (most relevant to 'corner') the tips of a bow or the crescent moon and the corners of the eye (cf. Thes. 4.470).

It is the notion of 'corner' viewed from the outside that is mainly dominant in the origin of the words. But they came to be used equally for the 'corner' viewed from the inside (e.g. 'corner' of the room vs. 'corner' of the house), and a few became more or less specialized in this direction, as Sp. *rincón*, ME *hirne* (see quotations in NED), NHG *winkel*.

1. Grk. γωνία, NG pop. γωνιά (γωνιά, two syll.), prob. : γόνυ, Lat. *genu*, Goth. *kniu*, Skt. *jānu-* 'knee'. Walde-P. 1.586. Boisacq 153 f.

2. Lat. *angulus* (hence the technical words for 'angle', It. *angolo*, Fr. *angle* > NE *angle*, etc.) : ChSl. *ągŭlŭ* (see below, 6), Arm. *ankiwn* 'corner', fr. IE **ang-* beside **ank-* in Skt. *añc-* 'bend', Grk. ἀγκών 'elbow', ἀγκύλος 'crooked, curved', ἄγκιστρον, Lat. *uncus* 'hook', etc. Walde-P. 1.61 f. Ernout-M. 52. Walde-H. 1.48 f.

It. *canto, cantone*, also 'edge, side', see 12.353.

Fr. *coin*, also 'wedge', fr. Lat. *cuneus* 'wedge'. REW 2396.

Sp. *esquina*, prob. through 'edge' (cf. It. *canto* and OHG *ecka* 'corner' and 'edge') : Prov. *esquina*, Fr. *échine* 'spine'. REW 7994 ("begrifflich schwierig", but why?).

Sp. *rincón*, old *rancon* : *ancón* 'bay' fr. Grk. ἀγκών 'elbow, bend, bay'. REW 443a. Schuchardt, Z. rom. Ph. 41.256 f.

Rum. *colț*, neut., as masc. 'fang, tusk, shoot (of a plant), bud', prob. Slavic, cf. Ukr. *kol*, Pol. *kiel* 'fang, tusk', Slov. *kal* 'bud', SCr. *kaloc* 'young grass, fang', etc. Tiktin 393.

3. Ir. *uilen* and (MIr.) *uillind*, latter also and both orig. 'elbow', like W. *elin*, etc. (4.32).

Ir. *cern, cerna* (NIr. *cearna* 'corner', esp. 'quarter, direction'; cf. also Corn. *Kernow* 'Cornwall') = W. *cern* 'cheek, jaw', Br. *cern* 'top of the head or a hill', prob. : Lat. *cornu* 'horn', ON *horn* 'horn, corner', etc. Pedersen 1.156. Loth, RC 42.354. Otherwise Walde-P. 1.427.

NIr. *cūinne*, early NIr. *cuinne* (cf. K. Meyer, Contrib. 552), apparently fr. ME, early NE *coyne* 'wedge, corner, angle', fr. OFr. *cuigne, coing*, Fr. *coin* (above, 2).

W. *congl* fr. MLat. **conculus*, dim. of *concus* 'angulus' (DuCange), whence OBr. *conc* 'corner, angle'. Loth, Mots lat. 152. This MLat. *concus* is fr. Lat. *conchus* (Gloss., cf. Thes., s.v.), beside *concha*, these fr. Grk. κόγχος, κόγχη 'mussel-shell', with numerous secondary uses some of which ('kneepan', 'niche', 'apse' in Grk.) must have suggested the notion of 'corner'.

W. *cornel*, fr. ME *corner* (with dissim. in W.; so Parry-Williams 249), or fr. ME, NE dial. *cornel* (NED s.v.), fr. OFr. *cornal* 'corner', deriv. of OFr. *cor(n)* 'horn' and 'corner' fr. Lat. *cornu* 'horn'.

Br. *korn* 'horn' and 'corner' (latter sense prob. fr. OFr. *corn*, above) fr. Lat. *cornu* 'horn'. Loth, Mots lat. 152.

Br. *kogn*, fr. OFr. *coing* (= Fr. *coin*, above). Henry 75.

4. Goth. *waihsta*, prob. : MHG *weigen* 'vacillate, waver', Lat. *vincīre* 'wind around, bind', etc., with semantic development fr. 'bent, crooked' to 'corner'. Walde-P. 1.234. Otherwise (: OHG *winkel*, below) Feist 543.

ON *hyrning*, late ON *hyrni*, Dan. *hjørne*, Sw. *hörn*, OE *hyrne*, ME *hirne* (cf. ON *hyrna* 'point of an axe-head'), fr. ON *horn* 'horn' and also 'corner', Dan. *horn*, etc. 'horn' : Lat. *cornu* 'horn', etc. Walde-P. 1.407. Falk-Torp 413.

OE *hwamm, hwemm*, beside *hwemman* 'bend, crook', cf. ON *hvammr*, OSw. *hwamber* 'slope, valley', etym. dub. Walde-P. 1.376, 398.

ME, NE *corner*, fr. Anglo-Fr. *corner* = OFr. *cornier*, deriv. of OFr. *cor(n)* 'horn, corner'. NED s.v.

Du. *hoek* = OE *hōc*, NE *hook* (12.75). Franck-v. W. 222.

OHG *winkil*, MHG, NHG *winkel* (cf. OE *wincel* in place names; (Du. *winkel* 'shop' fr. 'corner', 11.87) : OHG *winchan* 'move sideways, stagger, nod', OE *wincian* 'close the eyes, wink, nod', *wince* 'a winch', Lith. *vengti* 'shun, avoid', *vingis* 'bend, crook', etc., all fr. common notion of 'bend, turn'. Walde-P. 1.260. Weigand-H. 2.1269.

OHG *ekka*, MHG, NHG *ecke* (OHG, MHG also 'edge' of a weapon) : OE *ecg*, ON *egg*, Lat. *aciēs*, etc. 'edge' (12.353).

5. Lith. *kampas* : *kumpas* 'crooked', etc. (12.74).

Lith. *kertė*, etym.? Leskien, Bildung d. Nom. 265. Perh. as orig. 'edge' (cf. It. *canto*, NHG *ecke*) : Lith. *kirsti, kertu* 'cut down', Russ. *čerta* 'line', etc.

Lett. *stūris*, prob. with semantic development fr. 'point' to 'corner' : Grk. σταυρός, ON *staurr* 'stake', Skt. *sthūṇa-*, Av. *stŭna-* 'column', etc. (Walde-P. 2.608). Mühl.-Endz. 3.1110.

Lett. *kakts* : Lith. *kaktas* 'projecting room', further obscure. Mühl.-Endz. 2.139.

6. ChSl. *ągŭlŭ*, etc., general Slavic (SCr. *ugao*, Boh. *úhel*, Pol. *węgieł*, Russ. *ugol*) either loanword fr. or, more prob. cognate with, Lat. *angulus* (above, 2). Meillet, Études 183.

ChSl. *kutŭ* for **kątŭ*, SCr., Russ. *kut*, Boh. *kout*, Pol. *kąt*, prob. connected, as cognate or loanword, with the group Lat. *canthus*, It. *canto*, etc. (12.353). Walde-P. 1.351. Meillet, Études 226. Otherwise (: Grk. κοντός 'pole, pike') Berneker 602 f.

Boh. *roh*, Pol. *róg*, 'horn' and 'corner' (Gmc. influence? cf. above, 4) = ChSl. *rogŭ*, etc. 'horn'.

7. Skt. *koṇa-*, etym.? Uhlenbeck 66

12.77 CROSS

Grk.	σταυρός	Goth.	*galga*	Lith.	*kryžius*
NG	σταυρός	ON	*kross*	Lett.	*krusts*
Lat.	*crūx*	Dan.	*kors*	ChSl.	*krĭstŭ, križĭ*
It.	*croce*	Sw.	*kors*	SCr.	*krst, križ*
Fr.	*croix*	OE	*rōd (cros)*	Boh.	*kříž*
Sp.	*cruz*	ME	*cros(se), crois*	Pol.	*krzyż*
Rum.	*cruce*	NE	*cross*	Russ.	*krest*
Ir.	*croch*	Du.	*kruis*		
NIr.	*cros*	OHG	*krūzi*		
W.	*croes, crog*	MHG	*kriuz*		
Br.	*kroaz*	NHG	*kreuz*		

Most of the words for 'cross' are derived from Lat. *crūx*, which spread as the 'cross' of Christian terminology, with secondary development of generic use for an object or mark of similar shape.

1. Grk. σταυρός 'an upright stake' (Hom.+), later used regularly to render the Latin *crūx* : ON *staurr* 'stake', Skt. *sthavira-*, *sthūra-* 'thick, solid, strong', OHG *stūri* 'strong', etc. fr. a by-form of **stā-* 'stand'. Walde-P. 2.608 f.

2. Lat. *crūx*, the Roman instrument of punishment upon which criminals were impaled, prob. at first a stake, then a wooden frame in various forms (cf. illustrations in Daremberg et Saglio) but most commonly in the form of a cross, prob. : Goth. *hrugga* 'staff', ON *hryggr*, OE *hrycg*, OHG *(h)rucki* 'back, ridge', etc., fr. an extension of the root in Lat. *curvus* 'crooked', etc. Walde-P. 2.573. Walde-H. 1.296 f. Otherwise Ernout-M. 236, assuming a loanword from some Mediterranean language, perh. Punic. But, while the form of punishment prob. came from the Orient through Punic influence, there is no definite support for the view that the word itself was borrowed.

Hence the Romance words (REW 2348); the Celtic, Ir. *croch* (NIr. 'gallows, bar with hooks', etc.), W. *crog*, fr. acc. *crūcem*, but MIr. *cross*, NIr. *cros*, W. *croes*, Br. *kroaz* fr. nom. *crūx* (Pedersen 1.1926, 217. Vendryes, De hib. voc. 132. Loth, Mots lat. 154); most of the Gmc., with great variety of form and partly through Ir. and Fr. (Falk-Torp 567. NED s.v. *cross*); Lith. *kryžius* (through Pol.), late ChSl. *križĭ, kryži* (vs. *krĭstŭ* in Gospels, etc.; see below, 4), SCr. *križ*, Boh. *kříž*, Pol. *krzyż*, in general, West Slavic and Catholic, through Gmc. or Romance? (Berneker 619).

3. Goth. *galga* (reg. for σταυρός) = OE *galga*, OHG *galgo*, etc. 'gallows' (these also sometimes for the cross), prob. (as orig. simply the bent limb of a tree) : Lith. *žalga* 'rod, pole', Arm. *jałk* 'branch, twig'. Walde-P. 1.540. Falk-Torp 296. Feist 189.

OE *rōd*, orig. 'rod' as in cpd. *seglrōd* 'sailyard', but reg. for Lat. *crūx* (ME *rood* 'crucifix', NE in this sense archaic; OE *rood*, NE *rod* fr. a different form; ON *rōða* 'crucifix' fr. OE) : OHG *ruota* 'rod' (NHG *rute*), etc., outside connections dub. Walde-P. 2.368. Falk-Torp 908. NED s.v. *rood*.

4. ChSl. *krĭstŭ* (often written *krŭstŭ*), the reg. word for Grk. σταυρός in Gospels, Supr., etc. (cf. Jagić, Entstehungsgesch. 203, 356), SCr. *krst*, Russ. *krest* (White Russ. *krist*, East Lett. *krists;* Lett. *krusts* with *u* by influence of Lat. *crūx*? Mühl.-Endz. 2.290), in orig. the same word as ChSl. *Chrĭstŭ* 'Christ' (fr. Grk. χριστός through Goth. *Xristus*), but fr. an unattested Goth. *Kristus* (cf. OHG *Krist*), and differentiated in use through 'Christ on the cross, crucifix' to 'cross'. Berneker 634. Stender-Petersen 419 ff.

12.78 SQUARE (sb.)

Grk.	τετράγωνον	Goth.	. . . .	Lith.	*keturkampis, ketvirtainis*
NG	τετράγωνο	ON	*ferskeyttr, ferhyrndr* (adjs.)	Lett.	*četrstūris*
Lat.	*quadrātum, quadrum*	Dan.	*firkant*	ChSl.	. . . .
It.	*quadrato, quadro*	Sw.	*fyrkant*	SCr.	*četverokut*
Fr.	*carré*	OE	*fēowerscȳte* (adj.)	Boh.	*čtverec, čtverhran*
Sp.	*cuadrado, cuadro*	ME	*square, fourhuyrned* (adj.)	Pol.	*czworokąt, czworobok*
Rum.	*pătrat*	NE	*square*	Russ.	*četyreugol'nik*
Ir.	*cetharchoir, cetharuillech* (adjs.)	Du.	*vierhoek*	Skt.	*caturaçra-*
NIr.	*cearnach, cearnōg*	OHG	*fiorscōz* (adj.)	Av.	*čaθru.karana-* (adj.)
W.	*ysgwar, pedrongl*	MHG	*vierecke* (adj.)		
Br.	*karrezenn, pevarc'horneg*	NHG	*viereck*		

Nearly all the words for 'square' are derivatives or compounds of words for 'four'. The last member of the compounds is usually a word (or deriv. of a word) for 'corner' (12.76), 'edge' (12.353), or 'side' (12.36). Only the NIr. forms are simply from 'corner', without the four.

1. Grk. τετράγωνον, neut. of adj. τετράγωνος, cpd. of τετρα- 'four' and γωνία 'corner'.

2. Lat. *quadrātum*, neut. of *quadrātus* (> It. *quadrato*, Fr. *carré*, Sp. *cuadrado* adj. and sb.), pple. of *quadrāre* 'make square', fr. *quadrus* (> It. *quadro*, Sp. *cuadro*), rare and late in adj. use (mostly in sb. forms, *quadra* 'square, base of a pedestal, table', *quadrum* 'square'), all fr. *quattuor* 'four', in form *quadru-* as in *quadru-plex*, etc. Ernout-M. 836.

Rum. *pătrat*, fr. *patru* 'four' (with influence of Lat. *quadrātus*). Tiktin 1134.

3. Ir. *cethar-choir, cethr-ochair, cethar-ochair*, cpd. of *cethir* 'four' and *eochair* (NIr. *ochar*) 'border, edge'.

Ir. *cethar-uillech*, cpd. of *cethir* 'four' and *uillind* 'corner'.

MIr. *cernach*, NIr. *cearnach, cearnōg*, deriv. of Ir. *cern* 'corner'.

W. *ysgwar* fr. NE *square*.

W. *pedrongl*, cpd. of *pedwar* 'four' and *ongl* 'angle'.

Br. *karrezenn*, fr. *karre, karrezek*, adj., loanword fr. Fr. *carré*.

Br. *pevar-c'horneg* (sb. vs. adj. *-ek;* cf. Vallée), cpd. of *pevar* 'four' and *korn* 'corner'.

4. ON *ferskeyttr* (pple. of *ferskeyta* 'make square'), OE *fēower-scȳte, -scīte*, OHG *fior-scōz*, cpd. of ON *fjōrir* (in cpds. *fer-, fjōr-*), OE *fēower*, OHG *fior* 'four' and ON *skaut* 'corner (of a piece of cloth), quarter (of the heavens), skirt, sheet', OE *scēat* 'corner, quarter (of heavens, country), region, lap, etc.', OHG *scōz* 'skirt, lappet, lap' (: Goth. *skaut* 'hem of a garment').

ON *ferhyrndr*, ME *fourhuyrned* (one quot. in NED), cpd. of ON *fer-*, ME *four* 'four', and ON *horn*, ME *hirne* 'corner'.

Dan. *firkant*, Sw. *fyrkant*, cpd. of *fir, fyr* 'four' and *kant* 'edge'.

ME, NE *square*, fr. OFr. *esquare, esquire, esquerre*, etc., VLat. **exquadra*, fr. **exquadrāre* 'make square' (for *quadrāre*, cf. above, 2). REW 3060. NED s.v.

Du. *vierhoek*, MHG *vierecke* (adj.), NHG *viereck*, cpds. of *vier* 'four' and Du. *hoek*, MHG, NHG *ecke* 'corner'.

5. Lith. *keturkampis*, Lett. *četrstūris*, cpds. of Lith. *keturi*, Lett. *četri* 'four' and Lith. *kampas*, Lett. *stūris* 'corner'.

Lith. *ketvirtainis*, deriv. of *keturi* 'four'.

6. SCr. *četverokut*, Pol. *czworokąt*, Russ. *četyreugol'nik*, cpds. of SCr. *četiri*, etc. 'four', and SCr. *kut*, Pol. *kąt*, Russ. *ugol* 'corner'.

Boh. *čtverec*, deriv. of *čtyři* 'four'.

Boh. *čtverhran*, Pol. *czworobok*, cpds. of Boh. *čtyři*, Pol. *cztery* 'four' and Boh. *hrana* 'edge', Pol. *bok* 'side'.

7. Skt. *caturaçra-*, cpd. of *catur-* 'four' and *açri-* 'edge'.

Av. *čaθru.karana-*, adj., cpd. of *čaθwar-* 'four' and *karana-* 'end, border, wing (of an army).' Barth. 578.

12.81 ROUND (adj.)

Grk.	*στρογγύλος*	Goth.	....	Lith.	*apvalus, apskritas*
NG	*στρογγυλός*	ON	*sīvalr, kringlōttr*	Lett.	*apal'š*
Lat.	*rotundus*	Dan.	*rund*	ChSl.	*(o)kruglŭ*
It.	*tondo, rotondo*	Sw.	*rund*	SCr.	*okrugao*
Fr.	*rond*	OE	*sin-wealt, -trendel, -hwerfel*	Boh.	*okrouhlý, kulatý*
Sp.	*redondo*			Pol.	*okrągły*
Rum.	*rotund*	ME	*round*	Russ.	*kruglyj*
Ir.	*cruind*	NE	*round*	Skt.	*vartula-*
NIr.	*cruinn*	Du.	*rond*	Av.	*skarəna-*
W.	*crwn*	OHG	*sinwel, sinhwerbal*		
Br.	*krenn*	MHG	*sinwel, runt*		
		NHG	*rund*		

The common words for 'round', as listed here, are used of both circular and spherical shapes, though several of them were in origin 'circular'. More specific words distinguishing 'circular' and 'spherical' are derived from the words for 'circle' (12.82) or 'sphere' (12.83), e.g. Grk. κυκλοτερής 'circular', lit. 'circle-turned', cpd. of κύκλος 'circle' and the root in τείρω 'rub', τόρνος 'carpenter's tool for drawing a circle'; 'spherical' fr. 'sphere', Grk. σφαιρικός fr. σφαῖρα, Lat. *globōsus* fr. *globus*, ON *bǫllōttr* fr. *bǫllr*, Pol. *kulistý* fr. *kula*, etc.

1. Grk. στρογγύλος, NG στρογγυλός, prob. 'round' fr. 'twisted' : στραγγός 'twisted, squeezed', στράγξ 'something squeezed out, a drop', στραγγαλίζω 'strangle', Lat. *stringere* 'draw tight', etc. Walde P. 2.650. Boisacq 917.

2. Lat. *rotundus*, lit. 'wheel-shaped', then 'round' in general (VLat. *retundus*

> OIt. *ritondo*, It. *tondo*, Fr. *rond*, Sp. *redondo*, Rum. obs. or dial. *rătund;* reformed It. *rotondo*, Rum. *rotund*), deriv. (prob. through a vb. form) of *rota* 'wheel' (10.76). Walde-P. 2.368. Ernout-M. 871. REW 7400.

3. Ir. *cruind*, NIr. *cruinn*, W. *crwn*, OBr. *cron*, Br. *krenn*, fr. **krund-i-*, fr. IE **(s)kreu-*, extension of **(s)ker-* 'turn, bend', in ChSl. *krągŭ* 'circle', *(o)kruglŭ* 'round' (below, 6), Av. *skarəna-* 'round', Lat. *curvus* 'crooked', etc. Walde-P. 2.572 f.

4. ON *kringlōttr*, fr. *kringla* 'circle'.

ON *sīvalr* (also simple *valr*), OE *sin(e)wealt* (*seonuwalt*, etc.), OHG *sin(a)wel*, MHG *sinwel*, OS *sinuwel*, MLG *sinewolt*, cpds. of ON *sī-*, OE, OHG *sin-* 'always' (= 'entirely'), and last member : ON *velta*, OE *wealtan*, OHG *walzen* 'roll, turn', ChSl. *valiti* 'roll', Lith. *apvalus* 'round' (below, 5), etc. Walde-P. 1.302. Falk-Torp 789. Franck-v. W. 607.

OE *sin-trendel*, cpd. of *sin-* (cf. above, ON *sīvalr*) and *trendel* 'circle, ring' (12.82).

OE *sin-hwerfel*, OHG *sin(h)werbal*, cpd. of *sin-* (above) and last member : OE *hweorfan*, OHG *hwerban* 'turn, roll'.

Dan., Sw. *rund*, ME, NE *round*, Du. *rond*, MHG *runt*, NHG *rund*, fr. Fr. *rond* (above, 2). Falk-Torp 920.

5. Lith. *apvalus*, Lett. *apal'š* : Lith. *velti* 'to full', orig. 'roll', Lett. *velt* 'roll, full', ChSl. *valiti* 'roll', etc.; similarly Russ.-ChSl. *obĭlŭ* 'round' (SCr. *obal* 'cylindrical', Boh. *oblý*, Pol. *obły* 'oblong'). Walde-P. 1.303. Mühl.-Endz. 1.74. Trautmann 349.

Lith. *apskritas* : *apskritis* 'circle', etc. (12.82).

6. ChSl. *kruglŭ, okruglŭ* (for **kręglŭ*, **okrąglŭ*), SCr. *okrugao*, etc., general Slavic, fr. *krągŭ*, SCr. *krug*, etc. 'circle' (12.82). Berneker 626.

Boh. *kulatý*, fr. *kule, koule* 'ball, sphere' (12.83) and so orig. 'spherical', like Pol. *kulistý*, but now also for 'round, circular'.

7. Skt. *vartula-* : *vṛt-*, Lat. *vertere* 'turn', etc. Walde-P. 1.274. Uhlenbeck 275.

Av. *skarəna-* : Ir. *cruind*, etc. (above, 3). Barth. 1587.

12.82 CIRCLE

Grk.	*κύκλος*	Goth.	....	Lith.	*apskritis, ratas*
NG	*κύκλος*	ON	*hringr, kringla*	Lett.	*rin'k'is*
Lat.	*circulus*	Dan.	*kreds*	ChSl.	*krągŭ*
It.	*circolo, cerchio*	Sw.	*krets*	SCr.	*krug*
Fr.	*cercle*	OE	*trendel, hring*	Boh.	*kruh*
Sp.	*círculo*	ME	*cercle*	Pol.	*koło, krąg*
Rum.	*cerc*	NE	*circle*	Russ.	*krug*
Ir.	*cūairt, circul*	Du.	*cirkel, kring*	Skt.	*maṇḍala-, cakra-*
NIr.	*ciorcal*	OHG	*(h)ring, creiz*	Av.	....
W.	*cylch, cant*	MHG	*kreiz, rinc*		
Br.	*kelc'h, kant*	NHG	*kreis*		

Words for 'circle' are from various roots with the notion of 'turn'. But in several groups the most widespread and probably the earliest use was to designate a specific object of circular shape, especially 'wheel' or 'ring'.

1. Grk. κύκλος, also, esp. in neut. pl. κύκλα, 'wheel' : Skt. *cakra-* 'wheel, circle', Av. *čakra-*, ON *hjōl*, OE *hwēol*, etc. 'wheel' (10.76), fr. reduplicated forms of the root **kʷel-* in Grk. πέλομαι 'be in motion, be', Skt. *car-* 'move about', etc. Walde-P. 1.575.

2. Lat. *circulus* (> It. *cerchio*, Fr.

cercle; lit. loanwords It. *circolo*, Sp. *círculo*), dim. of *circus* (> Rum. *cerc* 'circle', but It. *cerco* obs., Sp. *cerco* in secondary uses), which it replaced in the sense 'circle', the latter coming to be the 'circus' (esp. *Circus Maximus*, and then others) : Grk. κίρκος, κρίκος 'ring', fr. the root **(s)ker-* in Lat. *curvus* 'crooked', etc. (12.74). Walde-P. 2.569. Ernout-M. 188 ff. Walde-H. 1.220 f. REW 1947, 1948.

3. Ir. *cūairt*, perh. loanword fr. Lat. *cohors, -tis* (> *cōrs, -tis*) 'court, enclosure'. Pedersen 1.205.

Ir. *circul*, NIr. *ciorcal*, fr. Lat. *circulus*. Vendryes, De hib. voc. 124 f.

W. *cylch*, Br. *kelc'h*, fr. Lat. *circ'lus* = *circulus*. Loth, Mots lat. 156.

W. *cant*, Br. *kant*, prob. : Gallo-Lat. *cant(h)us* 'iron rim of a wheel', etc. (see 12.353). Walde-P. 1.351 f.

4. ON *hringr*, OHG *(h)ring*, MHG *rinc*, OE *hring* (but the latter mostly 'ring'; this meaning also in ON, OHG, and MHG, and in the modern languages the usual one) : Umbr. *cringatro* 'cinctum, band about the shoulder as a sign of office', ChSl. *krągŭ* 'circle', etc. (below, 6), fr. extensions of the root **(s)ker-* as in Lat. *circus*, etc. (above, 2). Falk-Torp 901.

ON *kringla, kringr*, Du. *kring*, MLG *krink*, MHG *krinc, kranc* (NHG *kringen, kringel*) : Norw. *krenkja* 'wrench', Lith. *gręžti* 'bore', Lett. *griezt* 'turn', nasalized forms of the root in ON *krōkr* 'hook' (12.75). Walde-P. 1.594. Falk-Torp 580 f. Weigand-H. 1.1153.

Late OHG *creiz*, MHG *kreiz* (> Dan. *kreds*, Sw. *krets*), NHG *kreis* : MLG *krēt(e), kreit*, MDu. *krīt* id., MHG *krīzen* 'make a circular line', perh. further related to OHG *krizzōn*, MHG *kritzen* 'scratch, engrave', root connection? Weigand-H. 1.1145, 1155. Falk-Torp 578.

OE *trendel*, cf. MLG *trendel* 'round disk', MHG *trendel* 'ball, circle', OHG *trennila* 'ball, sphere', MLG *trint, trent* 'circular' : OE *trenden* (rare), ME *trende* 'turn round, rotate' (NE *trend*), but further root connections (as with NHG *trennen* 'separate') dub. Walde-P. 1.798. Falk-Torp 1283. NED s.v. *trend*.

ME *cercle*, NE *circle*, fr. Fr. *cercle* (above, 2). NED s.v.

5. Lith. *apskritis* : Lith. *skriesti* 'make a circle', *skrieti* 'run or fly in a circle', *skristi* 'fly', fr. an extension of the root in Lat. *circulus* (above, 2) and ON *hringr*, ChSl. *krągŭ*, etc. (above, 4). Walde-P. 2.571. Trautmann 267.

Lith. *ratas* 'wheel', also 'circle' : Lat. *rota*, OHG *rad*, etc. 'wheel' (10.76; cf. Lat. *rotundus* 'round', 12.81). Walde-P. 2.368.

Lett. *rin'k'is*, also 'ring', fr. MLG *rink* 'ring, circle' (above, 4). Mühl.-Endz. 3.529.

6. ChSl. *krągŭ*, etc., general Slavic : ON *hringr*, etc. 'ring, circle' (above, 4). Berneker 626.

Pol. *koło* 'wheel' (10.76), also 'circle', mostly replacing the older *krąg* in this sense.

7. Skt. *maṇḍala-*, etym. dub., perh. : Ir. *mell* 'globus'. Walde-P. 2.295. Uhlenbeck 211.

Skt. *cakra-* : Grk. κύκλος (above, 1).

12.83 SPHERE

Grk.	*σφαῖρα*	Goth.	....	Lith.	*kamuolys*
NG	*σφαῖρα*	ON	*bǫllr*	Lett.	*bamba*
Lat.	*globus, sphaera*	Dan.	*klode, kugle*	ChSl.	....
It.	*palla, globo, sfera*	Sw.	*klot*	SCr.	*kugla*
Fr.	*boule, globe, sphère*	OE	*cliwen*	Boh.	*koule*
Sp.	*bola, globo, esfera*	ME	*bal, spere, clewe*	Pol.	*kula*
Rum.	*glob, sferă*	NE	*sphere, globe*	Russ.	*šar*
Ir.	*mell*	Du.	*bol*	Skt.	*guḍa-, gola-, bimba-*
NIr.	*meall, cruinne*	OHG	*cliuwa, ballo*	Av.	....
W.	*cronnell*	MHG	*kugel(e), kliuwe, klōz*		
Br.	*boull*	NHG	*kugel*		

Words for 'sphere' as the generic and more or less technical terms are such as were popularly applied to particular objects of spherical shape, esp. 'ball' (several of the words listed are also or commonly 'ball') or 'clod, lump', these again based on various notions including 'blown up, swollen' or 'pressed together'.

1. Grk. σφαῖρα, etym. dub., perh. : σφυράς, σπυράς 'fall of dung (from sheep, goats, etc.), pill', Lith., Lett. *spira* 'sheep-dung', NIcel. *sparð* 'sheep-dung', *sperðill* 'goat-dung'; or : Grk. σπαίρω 'quiver', Skt. *sphur-* 'spring, quiver, trouble', etc. Walde-P. 2.672, 668. Boisacq 926, 900.

2. Lat. *globus* (hence the lit. words, It., Sp. *globo*, etc.) : *glēba* 'lump, clod', fr. **gleb-* in Lith. *glėbti, globti* 'take in the arms, embrace', Pol. *głobić* 'press, join together', etc., beside **glem-* in Lat. *glomus* 'ball (of yarn)', Lith. *glomoti* 'embrace', fr. extensions of **gel-* in words for 'press together', 'lump, ball', etc. Walde-P. 1.615. Ernout-M. 425. Walde-H. 1.608.

Lat. *sphaera* (hence the lit. words It. *sfera*, Fr. *sphère*, etc.) fr. Grk. σφαῖρα (above).

It. *palla*, also 'ball', fr. Langob. *palla* = OHG *balla, ballo* 'ball' (> It. *balla* 'bale', Fr. *balle* 'ball, bale', etc.), ON *bǫllr* 'ball, globe, sphere' (below, 4). REW 908.

Fr. *bǫule*, Sp. *bola*, fr. Lat. *bulla* 'bubble, knob' : Lett. *bulis* 'buttocks', MLG *poll* 'knob, point', East Fris. *pol* 'round', etc. Walde-P. 2.111, 115. REW 1385.

3. Ir. *mell* (cf. Gall. *Mello-dūnum*), NIr. *meall*, also 'lump, mass, knoll', etym. dub., perh. : Skt. *maṇḍala-* 'circle'. Walde-P. 2.295. Stokes 214 f.

NIr. *cruinne* (mostly 'the globe', also abstract 'roundness'), W. *cronnell*, fr. Ir. *cruinn*, W. *crwn* 'round' (12.81).

Br. *boull*, fr. Fr. *boule* (above). Henry 40.

4. ON *bǫllr* (> ME *bal*, NE *ball*), OHG *ballo, balla*, MHG *balle* (but mostly 'ball'), here also Du. *bol* 'sphere' beside OHG *bolla* 'bud', OE *bolla* 'round dish, bowl', etc. : Lat. *follis* 'bellows, money-bag, ball, or cushion inflated with air', Grk. φαλλός 'penis (as emblem)', fr. a root **bhel-* seen in Lat. *flāre* 'blow' and many others based on the notion of 'blow up' or 'swell'. Walde-P. 2.179. Ernout-M. 374. Walde-H. 1.524 f. Franck-v. W. 79 f. NED s.v. *ball*, sb.[1].

Dan. *klode*, Sw. *klot*, fr. MLG *klōt* = MHG *klōz* 'lump, clod, ball, sphere' : MHG *kloz*, NHG *klotz* 'block', OE *clott* 'lump' (NE *clot*), Russ. *gluda* 'lump', fr. **gleu-d-*, an extension of **gel-* in Lat. *globus*, etc. (above, 2). Walde-P. 1.618. Falk-Torp 535.

MHG *kugele*, NHG *kugel* (> Dan. *kugle*, older *kugel*), MLG *kogel* (Du. *kogel* 'bullet, ball, shot') : Lith. *guga* 'pommel, hill', Russ. *guglja*, Pol. *guga* 'bump', etc., guttural extensions of **geu-* seen also in Skt. *gola-* 'ball, sphere' (below), MHG *kiule* 'ball or knob on the end of a stick, club with a knob on the end' (NHG *keule*), etc. Walde-P. 1.558. Falk-Torp 590.

OE *cliwen*, ME *clewe*, OHG *cliuwa*, MHG *kliuwe* (all esp. 'ball of thread or yarn'; hence with further peculiar semantic development NE *clew*, cf. NED) : Skt. *glāu-* 'round lump', NPers. *gulūle* 'ball', fr. **gleu-* (cf. **gleu-d-* in Dan. *klode*, etc.). Walde-P. 1.617.

ME *spere*, NE *sphere*, fr. OFr. *espere*, Fr. *sphère* (above, 2).

5. Lith. *kamuolys* : *kamuoti* 'press together, stuff', Lett. *kams*, Russ. *kom* 'lump', Russ. *komit'* 'press into a ball', MHG *hemmen* 'restrain', etc. Walde-P. 1.388. Berneker 557.

Lett. *bamba*, also *bumba* (but the latter rather 'ball, bomb', etc.?), cf. Lith. *bamba* 'navel', *bumbulis* 'bubble', *bumburas* 'bud', Pol. *babel* 'bubble, blister', Boh. *boubel* 'bubble', Skt. *bimba-* 'sphere, orb, disc, rounded part of the body', etc., all prob. based on a syllable imitative of the sound made with puffed-up cheeks. Walde-P. 2.107 f. Mühl.-Endz. 1.261.

6. SCr. *kugla*, fr. MHG *kugele*, NHG *kugel* (above, 4). Berneker 641.

Boh. *koule*, Pol. *kula* fr. MHG or MLG *kūle* = MHG *kiule* (above, 4). Berneker 641. Brückner 281.

Russ. *šar*, orig.?

7. Skt. *guḍa-*, perh. for **gulda-*, fr. the root **gel-* in Lat. *globus*, OE *cliwen*, MHG *klōz*, etc. (above, 2, 4). Walde-P. 1.614.

Skt. *gola-* : MHG *kiule*, NHG *keule*, etc. (above, 4). Walde-P. 1.555.

Skt. *bimba-* : Lett. *bamba* (above, 5).

12.84. 'Line' (straight or curved 'line'). A list is omitted, since with few exceptions the Eur. words are obvious derivs. of the Latin. For a line of writing or printing there are often different words (18.63).

1. Grk. γραμμή, fr. γράφω 'write', hence orig. a stroke or line of the writing implement.

2. Lat. *līnea*, orig. 'linen thread, line', secondarily 'line' in sense here intended, sb. form of *līneus* 'made of flax, linen', fr. *līnum* 'flax, linen' (6.23). Hence the usual words for 'line' in most of the Eur. languages (Romance, Celtic, Gmc., Balto-Slavic).

3. Boh. *čara*, etym.? Berneker 136.

Skt. *reknā-*, fr. *rikh-* 'scratch' (with development like that in Grk. γραμμή) : Grk. ἐρείκω 'bend, bruise', OHG *rīga* 'line' (NHG *reihe* 'row, order'), OE *rǣw*, *rāw* 'row', etc. Walde-P. 2.344.

12.85 HOLE

Grk.	*ὀπή, τρῦπημα*	Goth.	*þairkō*	Lith.	*skylė*
NG	*τρῦπα*	ON	*rauf*	Lett.	*caurums*
Lat.	*forāmen*	Dan.	*hul*	ChSl.	*dupina*
It.	*buco*	Sw.	*hål*	SCr.	*rupa*
Fr.	*trou*	OE	*þyrel, hol*	Boh.	*díra*
Sp.	*agujero, hoyo*	ME	*hole, thirl*	Pol.	*dziura*
Rum.	*gaură*	NE	*hole*	Russ.	*dyra*
Ir.	*toll*	Du.	*gat*	Skt.	*bila-, chidra-*
NIr.	*poll*	OHG	*loh*	Av.	. . . .
W.	*twll*	MHG	*loch*		
Br.	*toull*	NHG	*loch*		

Several of the words for 'hole' denoted primarily a hollow place (NE *hole* in the ground, foxes' *holes*, etc.) and are cognate with adjectives for 'hollow' or with words for 'pit' or the like. Others, with the primary notion of perforation or opening, are derived from verbs for 'bore, pierce', 'tear' or 'split'. One of the Greek words is cognate with those for 'eye', and the use of 'eye' for the hole in a needle is widespread.

1. Grk. ὀπή, fr. the same root as words for 'eye', Skt. *akṣi-*, Grk. ὄσσε (dual), Lat. *oculus*, etc. (4.21). Cf. Arm. *akn* 'eye' and 'opening, hole'. Walde-P. 1.170. Boisacq 707.

Grk. τρῦπημα, fr. τρυπάω 'bore' (9.46), whence also the back-formation Byz., NG τρῦπα.

2. Lat. *forāmen*, fr. *forāre* 'bore' (9.46).

Lat. *cavum* 'hollow, hole', sb. fr. adj. *cavus* 'hollow' (12.72).

It. *buco*, prob. fr. VLat. *voc(u)us* = *vacuus* 'empty' (13.22). Cf. Sp. *hueco* 'hollow' (12.72). REW 9115.

Fr. *trou* (= Prov. *trauc*, Cat. *trau*, Lex Ripuaria *traugum*), orig. dub., perh. Gallic. REW 8864. Gamillscheg 870.

Sp. *agujero*, fr. *aguja* 'needle' (6.37) and must have referred first to the eye of a needle, or possibly to the hole pierced by a needle.

Sp. *hoyo* ('hole' as a hollow place, like one made by a bomb), beside *hoya*, fr. Lat. *fovea* 'pit'. REW 3463.

Rum. *gaură*, fr. **cavula*, dim. sb. fr. Lat. *cavus* 'hollow'. REW 1795. Pușcariu 701.

3. Ir. *toll* (also adj. 'hollow'), W. *twll*, Br. *toull*, perh. (**tukslo-*) : Grk. τύκος 'mason's hammer', ChSl. *tŭknąti* 'pierce, prick'. Walde-P. 2.615. Stokes 134.

NIr. *poll* = Gael. *poll* 'hole, pit, pond', W. *pwll*, Br. *poull* 'pool', prob. loanwords fr. OE *pōl* 'pool'. In any case the Ir. use is clearly a secondary extension of 'pool', through 'pit' or the like.

4. Goth. *þairkō* (quotable only in phrase for 'eye of a needle'), OE *þyrel*, ME and NE dial. *thirl*, fr. the root seen in Goth. *þairh*, OE *þurh*, etc. 'through'. Feist 489. NED s.v. *thirl*, sb.

OE *hol*, ME, NE *hole*, Dan. *hul*, Sw. *hål*, in earliest use mostly 'hollow place' (ON, OHG *hol* rarely otherwise), sb. of adj. for 'hollow' (12.72). NED s.v. *hole* sb.

ON *rauf* : ON *rjūfa*, OE *rēofan* 'break' (9.26). Falk-Torp 938.

ON (rare), OS, LG, Du. *gat* = OE *geat* 'gate' (specialization of 'hole, opening'), etym.? Connection with Skt. *had-*, Grk. χέζω 'void excrement' (Walde-P. 1.571 f., Falk-Torp 302) improbable. Franck-v. W. 176.

OHG *loh*, MHG, NHG *loch* = ON *lok* 'cover, lid', OE *loc* 'lock', etc. : Goth. *galūkan*, OE *lūcan* 'shut, fasten', etc. Semantic development through 'enclosed place' ('prison' and 'hiding place' attested in MHG) > 'hollow, hole'. Weigand-H. 2.75. Kluge-G. 362.

5. Lith. *skylė* : *skelti* 'split' (9.27). Leskien, Ablaut 341.

Lett. *caurums* : *caurs*, Lith. *kiauras* 'full of holes', *kiurti* 'become full of holes', outside root connections? Mühl.-Endz. 1.366.

6. ChSl. *dupina* (Supr. = ὀπή) : Russ. *duplo* 'hollow' (of a tree, etc.), Lith. *dubus* 'hollow, deep', Goth. *diups* 'deep', etc. (12.67). Berneker 237 f.

In the Gospels τρῦπημα, τρυμαλιά, in the phrase 'eye of a needle' are rendered by *ucho* 'ear'.

SCr. *rupa* (also Slov., Ukr. for 'hole in the ground, ditch'), fr. an extension of the root in ChSl. *rŭvati* 'tear', *ryti* 'dig', like that in Lat. *rumpere*, OE *rēofan* 'break', etc. (9.26). Cf. ON *rauf* 'hole' (above, 4). Walde-P. 2.355.

Boh. *díra*, Pol. *dziura*, Russ. *dyra* : ChSl. *dĭrati* 'tear' (9.28). Berneker 201. Brückner 113.

7. Skt. *bila-*, etym.? Walde-P. 2.110.

Skt. *chidra-* ('hole, opening, flaw, fault') : *chid-* 'cut, split' (9.22, 9.27).

12.91 EQUAL

Grk.	*ἴσος*	Goth.	*ibna, samaleiks*	Lith.	*lygus*
NG	*ἴσος*	ON	*(g)līkr*	Lett.	*līdz* (adv.), *līdzens*
Lat.	*aequus, aequālis, pār*	Dan.	*lige*	ChSl.	*ravinŭ*
It.	*uguale, pari*	Sw.	*lika*	SCr.	*jednak, ravan*
Fr.	*égal*	OE	*gelīc*	Boh.	*stejny, rovný*
Sp.	*igual*	ME	*ilike, egall*	Pol.	*równy*
Rum.	*egal*	NE	*equal, alike*	Russ.	*ravnyj*
Ir.	*i(n)no(n)n*	Du.	*gelijk*	Skt.	*sama-, tulya-*
NIr.	*ionann*	OHG	*gilīh, ebanlīh, samalīh*	Av.	*hama-*
W.	*cyfartal*				
Br.	*ingal, par*	MHG	*gelīch*		
		NHG	*gleich*		

The notion 'equal' and the following 'like, similar', and 'change' (vb.) are of course by no means confined to spatial relations (NE *equal* more often of quantity, number, strength, etc.), and least of all 'sign' (sb.). But they are conveniently added here.

The distinction between the absolute 'equal' and the approximate 'like, similar' (12.92) is not always sharply marked. Both notions are sometimes covered by the same word (at the same or different periods) or more often by members of the same cognate groups. This is notably true in the two groups represented by NE *same* and *like*.

Words for 'equal' are cognate with others for 'body, form', 'same, together', 'one', 'balance', etc. Several are used also of 'even, level' ground; and in some of these this is probably the earlier sense.

The notion of identity is also expressed by words for 'same' (in addition to those included in the list), like Lat. *idem* (whence NE *identity*, etc.), NE *same*, etc.

1. Grk. ἴσος, Hom. ἶσος, dial. ϝισϝος, prob., with secondary σϝ, fr. *ϝιτσϝος : εἶδος 'form' (12.51). Bechtel, Phil. Anz. 1886.15. Brugmann, Ber. Sächs. Ges. 1897.29, Grd. 2.205. Otherwise (: Skt. *viṣu* 'on both sides', but conflicting with the development of orig. σϝ in ἰός 'arrow', 20.25 and νᾱός 'temple', 22.13). Prellwitz s.v. Walde P. 1.312.

2. Lat. *aequus* (also 'level, even'), *aequālis* (> OIt. *iguale*, It. *uguale*, OFr. *ivel*, *egal*, etc., Fr. *égal*, Sp. *igual*; Rum. *egal* fr. Fr.), etym. dub. Walde-P. 1.7, 102. Ernout-M. 16 f. Walde-H. 1.13. REW 238.

Lat. *pār*, acc. *parem* (> It. *pari*; deriv. VLat. **pariculus* > Sp. *parejo* in phrase *por parejo* 'on equal terms', Fr. *pareil* 'like, similar'), etym.? Walde-P. 2.40. Ernout-M. 731. REW 6219, 6241.

3. Ir. *i(n)non(n)*, NIr. *ionann* 'the same, equal', orig. 'the one', cpd. of *in(d)* 'the' and *oin* 'one'. Pedersen 2.126, 177.

W. *cyfartal*, deriv. of *cyfar* 'co-tillage' (= Ir. *comar* id., cpd. of *ar-* 'plow').

W. *cystadl* (obs.), *cystal* (in NT, but esp. 'equal in goodness'), cpd. of *cy-* 'with' and **stadlo-*, fr. IE **stā-* 'stand'. Morris Jones, 139. Many other cpds. of *cy-* 'with' in common use, denoting more specifically 'of equal breadth, height, weight', etc.

Br. *ingal*, fr. a dialect form of OFr. *ivel*, Fr. *égal* (above, 2), like OProv. *engual*, *e(n)gal*, Anglo-Norm. *ingal* (Wartburg 1.44).

Br. *par*, fr. Lat. *pār*, acc. *parem* (above, 2). Loth, Mots lat. 192.

4. Goth. *ibna* : *ibns*, OE *efen* 'level, flat', etc. (12.71).

Goth. *samaleiks* (ἴσος) beside *galeiks* (ὅμοιος) and adv. *analeikō* (ὁμοίως), ON *glīkr*, *līkr*, Dan. *lige*, Sw. *lika* ('equal' and 'like'), OE *gelīc* (in Gospels renders Lat. *aequālis* and *similis*), ME *ilike*, NE *alike* (now used only predicatively, but stronger than *like*, e.g. *just alike*, *almost alike*), OHG *gilīh* (both 'gleich' and 'ähnlich', e.g. Otfr.), MHG *gelīch*, NHG *gleich*, also OHG *ebanlīh*, *samalīh* 'equal', and OHG *analīh*, MHG *anelīch*, NHG *ähnlich* 'similar', Du. *gelijk* (also 'like'), all cpds. or derivs. of Goth. *leik*, OE *līc*, etc. 'body, form'. Walde-P. 2.398. Falk-Torp 642. Weigand-H. 1.735. NED s.vv. *like*, *alike*, *ylike*.

ME *egall*, fr. OFr. *egal* (above, 2). NED s.v.

NE *equal* (ME rare), fr. Lat. *aequālis* (above, 2). NED s.v.

5. Lith. *lygus*, Lett. adv. *līdz*, *līdzi*, adj. *līdzens*, *līdzīgs* (also 'like, similar'), OPruss. adv. *polīgu* 'likewise' : Goth. *leik* 'body', *samaleiks* 'equal', etc. (above, 4). Walde-P. 2.398. Mühl.-Endz. 2.477, 480, 481.

6. ChSl. *ravinŭ* (reg. for ἴσος, but also for πεδινός 'level'), SCr. *ravan*, Boh. *rovný*, Pol. *równy*, Russ. *ravnyj*, also 'even, level, flat' (but Russ. *ravnyj* 'equal' vs. *rovnyj* mostly 'level, flat') : Av. *ravah-* 'open space', Lat. *rūs* 'country' vs. 'town', Goth. *rūms* 'roomy, spacious', OE *rūm* 'space' (NE *room*), etc. Walde-P. 2.356 f. Brückner 464.

SCr. *jednak*, lit. 'at one with', fr. *jedno* 'one'.

Boh. *stejny*, apparently (no discussion found) based on **stajĭnŭ* (*aj* > *ej*, cf. Gebauer 1.133 ff.; suffix as in Pol. *dostojny* 'worthy, dignified') : *státi* 'stand, stand still, remain', with development through 'stable, fixed, unchanging'. Cf. NE *standing epithet*, NHG *stehender ausdruck*.

7. Skt. *sama-* (also 'level, flat'), Av. *hama-* = Grk. ὁμός, Goth. *sama*, etc. 'same'. Walde-P. 2.490.

Skt. *tulya-*, fr. *tulā-* 'balance' (itself also used with notion of equality or similarity, cf. BR s.v.) : Grk. τάλαντον 'balance', Lat. *tollere* 'raise', etc. Walde-P. 1.738 f.

12.92 LIKE, SIMILAR

Grk.	*ὅμοιος*	Goth.	*galeiks*	Lith.	*panašus*
NG	*ὅμοιος*	ON	*līkr*	Lett.	*līdzīgs*
Lat.	*similis*	Dan.	*lignende, lige*	ChSl.	*podobĭnŭ*
It.	*simile, somigliante*	Sw.	*lika*	SCr.	*sličan, nalik*
Fr.	*semblable, pareil*	OE	*gelīc*	Boh.	*podobný*
Sp.	*semejante, parecido*	ME	*like*	Pol.	*podobny*
Rum.	*asemenea*	NE	*like, similar*	Russ.	*pochožij, podobnyj*
Ir.	*cosmail*	Du.	*gelijk*	Skt.	*upama-, pratima-*
NIr.	*cosmhail*	OHG	*gilīh, analīh*	Av.	. . . .
W.	*tebig, hafal*	MHG	*anelīch*		
Br.	*hevel, heñvel*	NHG	*ähnlich*		

As already observed in 12.91, the words for 'equal' and those for 'like, similar' are partly overlapping in use. The majority of those for 'like, similar' belong to groups discussed in 12.91, or are from similar sources, as 'same' or 'body, form'. Other semantic sources are 'suitable', 'going (or carrying) after', 'measuring up to'.

1. Derivs. of IE **somo-* 'same' (itself

related to others for 'together'). Walde-P. 2.488 ff. Boisacq 702. Ernout-M. 942. REW 7925–28. Pedersen 1.47, 165.

Grk. ὅμοιος; Lat. *similis* (in form : Grk. ὁμαλός 'even, level', hence It. *simile* (loanword), OFr. *semble*, and, through Lat. vb. *similāre*, Fr. *sembler*, etc., Fr. *semblable, ressemblant*, or, through VLat. **similiāre*, It. *somigliare*, Sp. *semejar*, the pple.-adj. It. *somigliante*, Sp. *semejante*; Rum. *asemenea* (also 'equal', esp. before introduction of *egal* fr. Fr.), fr. vb. *asemena*, Lat. *adsimilāre*; Fr. *similaire*, NE *similar*, re-formed as if Lat. **similāris*; Ir. *samail* 'likeness', whence (cpd. with *com-*) *cosmail*, NIr. *cosmhail, cosamhail* 'like'; W. *hafal*, Br. *hevel, heñvel*.

2. Fr. *pareil*, fr. VLat. **pariculus*, deriv. of *pār, paris* 'equal' (12.91). Ernout-M. 731. REW 6241.

Sp. *parecido*, fr. *parecer* 'appear' = Fr. *paraître* id., fr. VLat. **pārēscere* (= Lat. *pārēre, appārēscere*). Ernout-M. 733. REW 6237.

3. W. *tebig* (also adv. 'likely'), perh. : Ir. *doich* 'probable, likely' of uncertain origin. Pedersen 1.129 (but cf. 2.667).

4. Goth. *galeiks*, etc., general Gmc. for either 'equal' or 'like' or both, also

OHG *analīh*, NHG *ähnlich* 'like', see 12.91.

5. Lith. *panašus* (Lalis, Senn, etc.; not in Kurschat, and prob. neolog.) : *našus* 'comfortable, fertile' (cf. NSB s.v.), *nešti, panešti* 'carry, bear'.

Lett. *līdzīgs* : Lith. *lygus* 'equal', etc. (12.91).

6. ChSl. *po-dobinŭ* (reg. for ὅμοιος), Boh. *podobný*, Pol. *podobny*, Russ. *podobnyj* (but SCr. *podoban* 'suitable, capable', beside ChSl. *po-dobiti sę* 'be like' and 'vie with', *po-doba jestŭ, po-dobajetŭ* 'ought, must' (9.94), *u-dobĭ* 'easily', SCr. *dob, doba*, Boh. *doba*, etc. 'point of time', all with common notion of 'suitable' : Goth. *ga-daban* 'happen', *gadōb ist* 'is suitable, proper', etc. Walde-P. 1.824 f. Berneker 203 f.

SCr. *sličan* and *nalik*, both cpds. of *lik* 'countenance, appearance, form'. Berneker 719 f.

Russ. *pochožij* : *pochoditi* 'be like, resemble', lit. 'go after', cpd. of *choditi* 'go'. Berneker 392.

7. Skt. *upama-* and *pratima-*, both frequent at end of cpds. meaning 'similar to—', representing the sbs. *upamā-, pratimā-* 'comparison, similarity', these fr. vbs. *upa-mā-* 'compare', *prati-mā-* 'imitate', cpds. of *mā-* 'measure'.

12.93 CHANGE (vb.)

Grk.	ἀλλάσσω, ἀμείβω	Goth.	ismaidjan	Lith.	mainyti	
NG	ἀλλάζω	ON	skipta (byta)	Lett.	mainīt, mīt	
Lat.	mūtāre	Dan.	forandre, bytte, skifte,	ChSl.	měniti	
It.	cambiare, mutare		veksle	SCr.	mijeniti	
Fr.	changer	Sw.	ändra, byta, skifta,	Boh.	měniti	
Sp.	cambiar, mudar		vexla	Pol.	odmienić, mienać	
Rum.	schimba	OE	wrīxl(i)an	Russ.	menjat'	
Ir.	coimclōim	ME	cha(u)nge	Skt.	vi-kṛ-, vi-kḷp-	
NIr.	aistrighim, athruigh-	NE	change	Av.	. . . .	
	im	Du.	veranderen, wisselen			
W.	newid (troi)	OHG	wehslōn			
Br.	kemma, trei	MHG	wehslen, (ver)endern			
		NHG	verändern, wechseln,			
			tauschen			

The majority of the words listed cover 'change' in the sense of 'make different, substitute another', and also 'exchange' involving a reciprocal give and take (for which NE *exchange* is now usual). But cf. NHG *verändern* 'change' in the former sense vs. *wechseln* mostly 'exchange' (but *meinung* or *kleider wechseln* on the border line) and *tauschen* 'exchange'. Either notion readily extends to the other. Thus Grk. ἀλλάσσω, of similar semantic origin to NHG *verändern* and NE *alter*, came to cover also 'exchange'.

There is a widespread cognate group in which the primary notion seems to be that of mutual exchange. Other words are derived from those for 'other', 'apart, differently', 'divide', and 'turn' (cf. NE *turn* in this sense, NED s.v. *turn*, vb. 35–39).

1. IE **mei-, *meigʷ-, *meit-* in words for 'change, exchange', 'paired', 'common', etc. Walde-P. 2.240 f., 245, 247 f. Boisacq 51. Ernout-M. 648 f. REW 5785. Berneker 2.48 f., 62 f.

Grk. ἀμείβω (reg. word in Hom., 'change' and esp. 'exchange'; but later less common than ἀλλάσσω for 'change'); Lat. *mūtāre* (> It. *mutare*, Sp. *mudar*; Rum. *muta* 'remove, change one's place of residence') ; Goth. *is-maidjan* (*maidjan* = καπηλεύω 'hawk about, peddle' and so 'cheapen, corrupt') ; Lith. *mainyti*, Lett. *mainīt, mīt*; ChSl. *měniti* (mostly in cpds.), SCr. *mijeniti*, Boh. *měniti*, Pol. *mienać* or esp. *odmienić*, Russ. *menjat'* (Balto-Slavic forms, except Lett. *mīt*, through a deriv. **moi-no-* as in Lith. *mainas* 'exchange', Goth. *ga-mains*, Lat. *com-mūnis* 'common'); Skt. *mi-* 'exchange' (*mā-* in BR, Whitney Roots), pres. 3sg. *mayate, mimayati* (not common), *mith-* 'altercate' (cf. *mithuna-* 'a pair', etc.).

2. Grk. ἀλλάσσω, Att. ἀλλάττω (**ἀλλάγ-ιω, cf. sb. ἀλλαγή), NG ἀλλάζω, fr.

ἄλλος 'other'. Walde-P. 1.85. Boisacq 46.

3. Late Lat. *cambīre* and *cambiāre* (> It. *cambiare*, Fr. *changer*, Sp. *cambiar*; **excambiāre* > It. *scambiare*, Fr. *échanger*, Rum. *schimba*), prob. of Celtic origin, fr. a form = Ir. *camm* 'crooked, bent' (12.74). Walde-P. 2.539. Pedersen 1.118 f. Ernout-M. 138 f. Walde-H. 1.145 f. REW 1540, 2949.

4. Ir. *coimclāim* (OIr. gl. *cambio*), *coimclōim* (MIr.), cpd. of *com-imb* with *clōim* 'conquer', orig. 'turn' ('turn back, repulse'), perh. fr. IE **kʷel-* in Grk. πέλομαι 'become', πόλος 'axis, pole', κύκλος 'wheel, circle', etc. (Walde-P. 1.514 ff. without Ir. *clōim*); in any case 'change' fr. 'turn'. Pedersen 2.494.

NIr. *athruighim*, fr. *atharrach* 'change, alteration', Ir. *aitherrach* 'change' and 'repetition' (OIr. *aitherrech* gl. *repetitio*), vbl. n. of *aitherraigim* 'repeat, emend', cpd. (*aith-air-*) of *rigim* 'stretch out'. Pedersen 2.593 f. K. Meyer, Contrib. 72.

NIr. *aistrighim* (also 'travel, journey', the earlier sense) : Ir. *aistrech* 'roving, unsettled', *aister* 'toil, pains' and 'travel, journey' (K. Meyer, Contrib. 70; NIr. *aistear*).

W. *newid*, fr. sb. *newid(iau)* 'exchange, wares' : OBr. *nouitiu* gl. *nundinae*, prob. : W. *newydd*, Br. *nevez* 'new' (deriv. fr. words for 'nine' in imitation of Lat. *nūndinae* unlikely, since this source of the Lat. word long forgotten), in any case 'change' based on 'exchange of goods'. Pedersen 1.14. Loth, Voc. vieux-breton 196.

Br. *kemma* (beside sbs. *kemm, eskemm* 'exchange') fr. late Lat. *cambiāre* (above, 3). Loth, Mots lat. 148.

W. *troi*, Br. *trei* 'turn' (10.12) are also used for 'change', esp. Br. *trei*.

5. Goth. *ismaidjan*, above, 1.

ON *skipta* 'share, divide' and 'change', Dan. *skifte*, Sw. *skifta* 'change, shift' = OE *sciftan* 'arrange, divide', ME *shifte* id. and (prob. Norse influence) 'change' (NE *shift*), MLG, Du. *shiften* 'divide, sort out', etc., fr. extension of root in ON *skipa* 'put in order, arrange', etc. Walde-P. 2.545. Falk-Torp 993.

ON *byta* 'divide, exchange', Dan. *bytte*, Sw. *byta*, fr. MLG *būten* 'divide, exchange' beside sb. *būte* 'booty', root connection dub. Walde-P. 2.186. Falk-Torp 122.

OE *wrīxl(i)an*, with sb. *wrīxl* 'change, exchange' : *wrīgian* 'turn, move, go'. Walde-P. 1.278.

OHG *wehslōn*, MHG *wehslen*, NHG *wechseln* (> Dan. *veksle*, Sw. *vexla*), Du. *wisselen*, fr. sb. OHG *wehsal* 'exchange', etc. (all used esp., though not exclusively, with reference to exchange of money)

: Lat. *vicis* (gen.), *vicem*, etc. 'change'. Walde-P. 1.235. Falk-Torp 1364 f.

ME *cha(u)nge*, NE *change*, fr. Fr. *changer* (above, 3).

MHG *andern, endern*, NHG *ändern* (> Dan. *ændre*, Sw. *ändra*) and MHG *verändern, -endern*, NHG *verändern*, MLG *veranderen* (> Dan. *forandre*), Du. *veranderen*, fr. MHG, MLG *ander* (OHG *andar*) 'other'. Weigand-H. 1.58, 2.1139. Falk-Torp 253, 1412.

NHG *tauschen*, beside sb. *tausch*, of same orig. as *täuschen* 'deceive', cf. MLG *tūsch* 'joke, trick', so evidently first used of barter involving sharp practice. Weigand-H. 2.1031. Kluge-G. 615.

6. Balto-Slavic words, above, 1.

7. Skt. *vi-kṛ-* and *vi-kḷp-*, cpds. of *kṛ-* 'do, make' and *klp-* 'be adapted' with *vi-* 'apart, differently'.

Skt. *mi-*, above, 1.

12.94 SIGN (sb.)

Grk.	σῆμα, σημεῖον	Goth.	taikns	Lith.	ženklas, žymė	
NG	σημάδι	ON	tākn, teikn	Lett.	zīme	
Lat.	signum	Dan.	tegn	ChSl.	znamenije	
It.	segno	Sw.	tecken	SCr.	znak, znamen, zna-	
Fr.	signe	OE	tācn		menje	
Sp.	signo, seña	ME	token, signe	Boh.	znak, znameni	
Rum.	semn	NE	sign (token)	Pol.	znak, znamię, cecha	
Ir.	arde, comarde	Du.	teeken	Russ.	znak, znamenie	
NIr.	comhartha	OHG	zeihhan	Skt.	lakṣaṇa-, liñga-	
W.	arwydd	MHG	zeichen	Av.	daxšta-, daxšāra-	
Br.	arouez	NHG	zeichen			

Words for 'sign' (sb.), denoting something which 'points out, indicates', are from verbs for 'point out, observe, see, know, teach'.

1. Grk. σῆμα, Dor. σᾶμα, fr. **dyā-men-* : Skt. *dyā-na-* (the oft quoted *dyā-man-* seems to be a ghost word) 'thought, reflection', but orig. 'observation', fr. *dhī-, dhyā-* 'think', orig. 'observe' : Av. *dī-* 'look at, observe' (15.51). Walde-P. 1.832. Boisacq 861.

Hence σημεῖον (in prose more common than σῆμα, which came to mean esp.

'tomb, grave') and late σημάδιον, NG σημάδι.

2. Lat. *signum* (> Romance words), generally taken as orig. 'cut mark' fr. the root of *secāre* 'cut' (so Walde-P. 2.478, Ernout-M. 939), but much more probably fr. the root of *in-seque* 'say' in its earlier sense of 'point out' (18.22).

3. Ir. *arde*, cpd. *comarde*, NIr. *comhartha*, W. *arwydd*, Br. *arouez*, fr. **ar-wid-* cpd. of *ar* 'before, for' and the root of Lat. *vidēre* 'see', etc. Pedersen 2.6. Henry 18.

znak, and the less common, or partly specialized in use (e.g. to 'omen' or 'token, badge', SCr. *znamen, znamenje*, Boh. *znameni*, Pol. *znamię*, Russ. *znamenie*, all fr. the root of Lith. *žinoti*, ChSl. *znati*, etc. 'know' (17.17).

Pol. *cecha*, fr. NHG *zeichen*.

6. Skt. *lakṣaṇa-*, less commonly *lakṣa-*, etym.? Uhlenbeck 257.

Skt. *liñga-* (cf. Av. *haptō.iringa-* 'with seven signs'), etym. dub. Walde-P. 2.399. Uhlenbeck 261.

Av. *daxšta-, daxšāra-*, fr. *daxš-* 'teach' (17.25). Barth. 676.

CHAPTER 13

QUANTITY AND NUMBER

13.11 QUANTITY

Grk.	ποσότης	Goth.	(managei)	Lith.	kiekybė
NG	ποσότης	ON	(fjǫldi, mergð, mengi)	Lett.	kvantitate (daudzums)
Lat.	quantitās	Dan.	kvantitet	ChSl.	(mŭnogistvo)
It.	quantità	Sw.	kvantitet	SCr.	kolikost
Fr.	quantité	OE	(menigu)	Boh.	kolikost
Sp.	cantidad	ME	quantite(e)	Pol.	ilość
Rum.	cantitate	NE	quantity	Russ.	količestvo
Ir.	mēit	Du.	hoeveelheid	Skt.	pra-māṇa-, pari-
NIr.	mēid	OHG	(managi)		māṇa-, māna-, etc.
W.	maint	MHG	(menige)	Av.	. . . .
Br.	ment	NHG	quantität		

'Quantity' in the abstract is a sophisticated notion. It was expressed in Greek by ποσότης, perhaps a coinage of Aristotle, meaning literally the 'how-much-ness', which the Romans rendered by the equivalent quantitās, whence, directly or by further semantic borrowing, most of the European terms.

The nearest equivalent, preceding the adoption of these terms, would be the words for 'great quantity or number', which might come to be used for 'quantity' in general, just as words for 'great size' furnished most of the words for 'size' (12.52). Some of them are quotable for 'quantity, amount' or 'number' in the abstract, as Grk. πλῆθος ('amount' of the penalty, 'number' of the ships, etc.), Lat. magnitūdō or multitūdō, Russ. množestvo, etc. Accordingly, such words are entered in the list (but in parentheses) where abstract forms are lacking or

916

doubtful. But they are omitted from the discussion, since they are obvious derivatives or cognates of the words for 'much, many' (13.15) or 'great, large' (12.55).

Among other near equivalents to 'quantity' are NE amount, fr. vb. amount, orig. 'mount' (fr. OFr. amonter, Lat. ad montem), hence 'rise in quantity or number' (similarly Fr. montant, etc.); Lat. summa 'sum, amount' (> Fr. somme, NE sum, NHG summe, etc.), fem. of summus 'highest'.

1. Grk. ποσότης (Aristot.), fr. πόσος 'how much?' which served as a model for Lat. quantitās fr. quantus. Hence the Romance and Germanic words, It. quantità, Fr. quantité (> ME quantite(e), NE quantity), Sp. cantidad, Rum. cantitate; Dan., Sw. kvantitet, NHG quantität (> Lett. kvantitate; so Drawneek, not in Mühl.-Endz.); further, by semantic borrowing, Du. hoeveelheid (hoeveel 'how much?'), Lith. kieka, kiekybė (kiek 'how much?'), SCr. količina, Boh. kolikost, Russ. količestvo (ChSl. koliko 'how much?', etc.), Pol. ilość (ile 'how much?').

2. Ir. mēit, NIr. mēid, W. maint, Br. ment, also 'size' (12.52).

Skt. māna- and cpds., pra-māṇa-, pari-māṇa-, all also 'size, measurement' (of any sort) : mā- 'measure' (12.54).

13.12 NUMBER

Grk.	ἀριθμός	Goth.	raþjō	Lith.	skaičius, skaitlius
NG	ἀριθμός	ON	tala	Lett.	skaits, skaitlis
Lat.	numerus	Dan.	(an)tal	ChSl.	čislo, čismę
It.	numero	Sw.	antal	SCr.	broj
Fr.	nombre	OE	getæl, rīm	Boh.	počet, čislo
Sp.	número	ME	no(u)mbre, tale, rime	Pol.	liczba
Rum.	numǎr	NE	number	Russ.	čislo
Ir.	līn, rīm, (n)umir	Du.	getal	Skt.	saṃkhyā-
NIr.	uimhir	OHG	zala, rīm	Av.	. . . .
W.	rhif, nifer	MHG	zal(e)		
Br.	niver	NHG	zahl		

Many of the words for 'number' are connected with the words for 'reckon, count', these of various sources. Some rest on the notion of 'arrangement, order', or 'distribution'.

1. Grk. ἀριθμός, beside νήριτος 'uncounted', Arc. Ἐπάριτοι 'picked soldiers', fr. the root of ἀραρίσκω 'fit together' and its cognates in other languages, which often reflect such secondary uses as 'arrange, reckon, count'; hence 'number', prob. through 'arrangement, order'. Cf. Skt. r̥ta- 'suitable, proper', r̥tu- 'fixed time, season', Lat. rērī 'reckon, judge', ratiō 'reckoning', and esp. Ir. rīm, OE rīm 'number' (below, 3, 4). Walde-P. 1.75. Persson, Beiträge 742.

2. Lat. numerus (> Fr. nombre, Rum. numǎr, It. novero, and as literary words It., Sp. numero; also MIr. numir and umir, NIr. uimhir with loss of n- by sentence phonetics; W. nifer, Br. niver) prob. : Grk. νέμω 'distribute, share'. Walde-P. 2.331, Ernout-M. 686. REW 5994. Pedersen 1.196. Vendryes, De hib. voc. 159 f.

3. Ir. līn (also 'part') : līnaim 'fill', lān 'full', Lat. plēnus id., etc. Walde-P. 2.64, Pedersen 1.50. Semantic development through 'number fulfilled, reached' (cf. NE amount)?

Ir. rīm, W. rhif : OE rīm 'number', OHG rīm 'number, series', ON rīm 'computation, calculation', fr. the root seen

---

in Grk. ἀριθμός, etc. (above, 1). Walde-P. 1.75. Pedersen 1.51.

4. Goth. raþjō : garaþjan 'count', Gmc. *raþa 'number' in ON hund-raþ 'hundred', etc., fr. the root in Grk. ἀριθμός, etc. (above, 1). Walde-P. 1.74. Feist 394.

ON tala, Dan. tal, antal, Sw. antal, OE getæl, ME tale (OE talu only 'account, tale'), Du. getal, OHG zala, MHG zal(e), NHG zahl : ON tala 'speak, talk', OE talian 'consider, reckon, account', OHG zalōn 'count, relate, pay', etc., (perh. Grk. δόλος, Lat. dolus 'guile, deceit', but see 16.68). Walde-P. 1.808. Falk-Torp 1243. Walde-H. 1.366.

OE rīm, ME rime, OHG rīm : Ir. rīm, etc. (above, 3).

ME no(u)mbre, NE number, fr. Fr. nombre (above, 2).

5. Lith. skaičius, skaitlius, Lett. skaits, skaitlis : Lith. skaityti, Lett. skai-tīt 'count', Lett. šk'ist 'think, suppose', ChSl. čisti 'count, reckon', etc. (cf. below). Mühl.-Endz. 3.867, 4.47.

6. ChSl. čislo, čismę, Boh. čislo, Russ. čislo : ChSl. čisti 'count, reckon, read, honor', etc., Lett. šk'ist 'think, suppose', Skt. cit- 'perceive, observe'. Walde-P. 1.509. Berneker 157, 174 f.

Boh. počet : počitati 'count', ChSl. počitati 'read', iter. of čisti (above). Berneker 174 f.

SCr., Bulg. broj, prob. orig. 'notch' (as tally in counting) : Russ.-ChSl. briti 'shear', brič 'razor'. Berneker 87, 94.

Pol. liczba, beside liczyć 'count' : Boh. ličba 'computation, figure', ličiti 'relate, depict', ChSl. ličiti 'announce, divulge', these : ChSl. lice 'face, cheek', etc. (4.204). Berneker 720 f.

7. Skt. saṃkhyā-, fr. vb. sam-khyā- 'add up, calculate', cpd. of khyā- in caus. 'make known, tell'.

13.13 WHOLE

Grk.	ὅλος, πᾶς	Goth.	alls	Lith.	visas (čielas)
NG	ὅλος, ὁλόκληρος, ὁλάκερος	ON	allr	Lett.	viss
		Dan.	hel, al	ChSl.	vĭsĭ
Lat.	tōtus, omnis, integer	Sw.	hel, all	SCr.	cio, sav
It.	intero, tutto	OE	eal(l)	Boh.	celý, všechen
Fr.	entier, tout	ME	hole, al	Pol.	cały, wszystek
Sp.	entero, todo	NE	whole all	Russ.	celý, ves
Rum.	întreg, tot	Du.	geheel, gansch, al	Skt.	sarva-, kr̥tsna-, sakala-, viçva-
Ir.	(h)uile	OHG	al, ganz		
NIr.	iomlán, go lēir, ar fad	MHG	al, ganz	Av.	haurva-, vispa-
W.	holl, cwbl, cyfan	NHG	ganz, all		
Br.	holl				

On the various notions involving totality, and their expressions, cf. Brugmann, Ausdrücke für den Begriff der Totalität, and Sapir, Totality (Language Monograph 1930). The broad distinction between the collective 'whole' and the individualizing 'every', pl. 'all', is the most important, and even this is only partially observed in linguistic expression (cf. NE all in all day and all men).

In several cases 'whole' comes from an earlier attested 'whole in body, sound, well' (so NE whole and its cognates; NHG ganz, etc.; Lat. integer 'intact, whole' most commonly in body), and in these, and a few of the other words listed, there is no confusion with 'every, all'. In some others, 'whole' is clearly the more original and mainly the dominant sense, but with secondary develop-

---

ment of pl. 'all' and, through that, in part also sg. 'every' (Grk. ὅλος only 'whole', but NG pl. ὅλοι 'all', and the cognate Skt. sarva- 'whole' and 'every', pl. 'all'; Lat. tōtus 'whole', but later extended to cover 'every', pl. 'all'). In still other groups, of uncertain origin but probably with similar development from 'whole', the singular is used for 'whole' or 'every', the plural for 'all' (so Grk. πᾶς. Lat. omnis, the Gmc. all-group, and the group Lith. visas, ChSl. vĭsĭ, Skt. viçva-, etc.). All these words though appearing also and more conspicuously in the list for 'every', pl. 'all', are discussed here.

1. IE *sol-wo, *sol-no-, etc. Walde-P. 2.510 f. Ernout-M. 891. Pedersen 1.413.

Grk. ὅλος, Hom. οὖλος (*ὅλϝος) 'whole', NG ὅλος (also οὖλος) 'whole', but pl. ὅλοι 'all'; Lat. salvus early 'whole', usually 'safe, well, sound', Osc. sullus, pl. 'all'; Ir. (h)uile, W., Br. holl, Corn. ol 'whole', pl. 'all'; but NIr. mostly gach uile 'every' (gach 'each'), with pl. na h-uile 'all'; Skt. sarva- 'whole' and 'every', pl. 'all', Av. haurva-, OPers. haruva- 'whole'; Alb. gjallë 'strong, lively, gay'; Arm. olj 'sound, well, whole'; Toch. A salu, B solme, advs. 'entirely' (SSS 278 f.).

2. Grk. πᾶς 'whole' and 'every', pl. 'all' (rarely also 'whole'), prob. through 'comprehensive' or the like fr. a participial form of the root seen in Dor. πέπᾱμαι 'possess', Skt. çvā- 'swell', Grk. κνέω 'be pregnant', κῦρος 'power', etc. Walde-P. 1.366 f. Brugmann, Totalität 60 ff.

Grk. ὅλος (above, 1) has been partly displaced by other, orig. more emphatic, terms for 'whole', as follows: Grk. ὁλόκληρος 'complete, perfect, sound', compound of κλῆρος 'lot' is simply 'whole' in late times (cf. quotations in LS) and lit. NG. Grk. ἀκέραιος 'un-

mixed' (: κεράννῡμι 'mix') is also 'intact, perfect', hence (blend with ὅλος) NG pop. ὁλάκερος, ὁλάκερος 'whole'.

3. Lat. tōtus 'whole' (> Sp. todo; VLat. tōttus > It. tutto, Fr. tout, Rum. tot; sg. 'all' = 'whole' and, except It., 'every'; pl. 'all'), prob. fr. *toweto- 'packed full'(?), fr. the root *teu- in Skt. tu- 'be strong', Lat. tumēre 'swell', etc. Walde-P. 1.707. Brugmann, Totalität 55. Ernout-M. 1049 f. (without above etym.).

Lat. omnis 'every' (> It. ogni 'every') and also 'whole', pl. 'all', etym. dub. Ernout-M. 702 f. Brugmann, Totalität 64 ff.

Lat. integer 'intact, whole' (> It. intero, Fr. entier, Sp. entero, Rum. întreg), neg. cpd. of the root of tangere 'touch'. Walde-P. 1.703. Ernout-M. 1016. Walde-H. 1.708.

4. Ir. (h)uile, W., Br. holl, above, 1.

NIr. iomlán 'whole' = MIr. immlán 'full, complete', cpd. of lán 'full' (13.21).

NIr. lēir, usually as adv. go lēir with sg. 'whole', with pl. 'all' (ē go lēir 'it entirely, all of it', iad go lēir 'they entirely, all of them'), Ir. collēir 'wholly' : W. llwyr 'entirely, entire'. Stokes 242, Macbain 227 without further connection. Atkinson, Pass. and Hom. Gloss. 781 f. equates with lēir 'visible' as 'visibly' > 'wholly'.

NIr. ar fad, lit. 'in length', but commonly 'altogether, whole' (an sceal ar fad 'the whole story'). Evans, s.v.

W. cyfan, cpd. of cy (= cyf-, Ir. com-, Lat. com-) and mutated form of man 'place'. Evans, s.v.

W. cwbl, Corn. cowal, etym. dub. Loth, RC 37.37 f. (vs. Morris Jones 310).

5. Goth. alls, ON allr, OE eall, etc., general Gmc. forms, outside connections dub., perh. : Lith. aliai adv. 'all, completely' in aliai vienas 'every one', aliai metai 'every year' (NSB), if these are not fr.

Gmc. Mikkola, BB 25.73 ff. Walde-P. 1.90 (but Osc. *allo* almost certainly not 'tota'). Feist 40.

The general usage of this group is sg. 'all' = 'whole', pl. 'all'. The use of the sg. for 'every' is not properly Gothic (where Grk. πᾶς in this sense is expressed by pl. forms or by the neut. sg. with part. gen., cf. Streitberg, Got. Bibel, s.v.) nor OE (sometimes in ME, obs. in NE, cf. NED s.v. *all* 3), and in general is uncommon or restricted to certain phrases. Cf. Paul, Deutsches Wtb. for NHG *all* and the larger dictionaries for Du. *al*, Dan. *al*, Sw. *all*.

Dan., Sw. *hel*, ME *hole*, NE *whole*, Du. *geheel* (*heel* less usual), in the older languages Goth. *hails*, ON *heill*, OE *hāl*, OHG *heil* 'sound, well, uninjured' (4.83) : ChSl. *cělŭ* 'well, sound, unharmed', SCr. *cio*, etc., 'whole' (below, 7), W. *coel* '(good) omen', OW *coilou* 'auspiciis'; cf. ON *heil* 'good sign, happiness', OE *hǣl* id. Walde-P. 1.329. Falk-Torp 393 f.

OHG, MHG, NHG *ganz*, MLG *gans*, Du. *gansch* 'whole' and in older languages 'sound, uninjured', etym. dub. Kluge-G. 185. Weigand-H. 1.620.

6. Lith. *visas*, Lett. *viss*, ChSl. *vĭsĭ*, SCr. *sav* (pl. *svi*, deriv. *svaki*, all with transposition of *vs*-; Leskien, SCr. Gram. p. 53), Russ. *ves'* sg. 'whole', pl. 'all' (Boh. *vše* pl. rare), hence derivs. ChSl. *vĭsěkŭ* (renders πᾶς 'every' and in Gospels also ἕκαστος), SCr. *svaki*, Russ. *vsjakij* 'every', Boh. *všechen*, Pol. *wszystek* sg. 'whole, every', pl. 'all (also Boh. *všecek* id.) fr. **wi-so*-, beside **wi-k̑wo*- in Skt. *viçva*-, Av. *vispa*-, OPers. *vispa*- and *visa*- 'whole, every', pl. 'all', perh. all derivs. of the adverbial **wi*- 'apart', but semantic relation far from obvious. Walde-P. 1.312. Brugmann, Grd. 2.1. 200.

Lith. *čielas* (cf. NSB s.v.), fr. Slavic (below, 7).

7. SCr. *cio*, Boh. *celý*, Pol. *cały*, Russ. *celyj* 'whole', in part also in the older sense of 'well, sound', like ChSl. *cělŭ* : Goth. *hails*, etc. (above, 5).

8. Skt. *sarva*-, Av. *haurva*-, OPers. *haruva*-, above, 1.

Skt. *kṛtsna*- 'whole', perh. (as 'solid', fr. 'twisted tight'?) : *kṛt*- 'spin, twist' (thread). Walde-P. 1.421. Otherwise Uhlenbeck, p. 63.

Skt. *sakala*- 'whole', lit. 'having (all its) parts', cpd. of *sa*- cop. and *kalā*- 'part'.

Skt. *viçva*-, Av. *vispa*-, above, 6.

9. Hitt. *pankus* 'whole, all' : Skt. *bahu*- 'much', etc. (13.15). Sturtevant, Hitt. Gram. 118, Glossary 115.

13.14 EVERY; ALL (pl.)

Grk.	*πᾶς; πάντες*	Goth.	*hwazuh* (*hwarjizuh, alls*); *allai*	Lith.	*kiekvienas; visi*
NG	*κάθε; ὅλοι*	ON	*hverr, allr; allir*	Lett.	*ikviens, ikkatrs, ikkur's; visi*
Lat.	*omnis, quisque; omnēs*	Dan.	*(en)hver (al); alle*	ChSl.	*vĭsěkŭ, kŭžĭdo; vĭsi*
It.	*ogni; tutti*	Sw.	*var, varje (all); alle*	SCr.	*svaki; svi*
Fr.	*chaque, tout; tous*	OE	*ǣlc, gehwilc; ealle*	Boh.	*každý, všechen; všichni*
Sp.	*cada, todo; todos*	ME	*everi(ch), elch, al; alle*	Pol.	*każdy, wszystek; wszyscy*
Rum.	*fiecare, tot; toţi*	NE	*every; all*	Russ.	*každyj, vsjakij; vse*
Ir.	*cach; uili*	Du.	*ieder, elk (al); alle*	Skt.	*sarva-, viçva-; sarva-, viçva* (in pl.)
NIr.	*gach, gach uile; na h-uile, go lēir*	OHG	*iogilīh, (eo)giwelīh, al; alle*	Av.	*vispa-; vispa-* (in pl.)
W.	*pob; holl*	MHG	*iegelīch, ietwelīch, ietweder, al; alle*		
Br.	*pep; holl*	NHG	*jeder (all); alle*		

Words that were used in the singular for 'whole' or 'every' and in the plural for 'all' have already been discussed (13.13), and these cover all the words listed here for 'all' pl. But the use of these words in the singular for 'every' has been more or less displaced by other words, mostly of pronominal origin. Only these remain to be discussed here. Most of them are used without the distinction which is now felt between NE *every* and *each* (as, in fact, the OE form of *each*). Their primary sense was 'every, each' taken separately (that is more nearly = NE *each*); but, with weakening of the distributive feeling, they encroached upon or displaced those expressions for 'every' in which the notion of totality was original. However, certain words in which the distributive sense remained more distinctively dominant, like Grk. ἕκαστος, are not included here.

1. NG κάθε (indecl. adj.), fr. καθεὶς, καθένας 'every one', fr. Grk. καθ' ἕνα, καθ' ἕν 'one by one'. Hatzidakis, Μεσ. 2.152.

2. Lat. *quisque*, sb. and adj. pron. 'each (one)', 'every (one)', in early use also rel. 'whoever', fr. interrog. indef. *quis* with generalizing -*que*. Ernout-M. 844 f.

Fr. *chaque*, OFr. *chasque*, back-formation fr. *chacun*, OFr. *chascun*, like It. *ciascuno*, fr. a blend of VLat. *cisque* (Lat. *quisque*) *unus* and *cata unum* (cf. Sp. *cada*, below). REW 6968. Gamillscheg 200, 207. Wartburg 3.483.

Sp. *cada* (indecl. adj.), fr. VLat. *cata* (fr. Grk. κατά, cf. above, NG κάθε), which appears frequently in church writings in distributive phrases modeled on the Greek, e.g. *cata mane mane* in the Vulgate, *cata mansiones*, *cata singulos ymnos*, etc. in the Peregrinatio.

Rum. *fiecare*, cpd. of *fie* 3sg. and pl. subj. of *fi* 'be' and *care* 'who, which' (Lat. *quālis*), hence orig. 'whoever it may be'.

3. Ir. *cach* (and *cech*), NIr. *gach*, W. *pob*, Br. *pep* : Lith. *koks*, ChSl. *kakŭ* 'what sort?', fr. **kʷā-kʷos*, deriv. of pron. stem **kʷā*- (cf. Lat. *quā-lis*). Thurneysen, Gram. 310 f.

4. Goth. *hwazuh* (reg. for πᾶς 'everyone'), *hwarjizuh* (but mostly for ἕκαστος), fr. the interrog. indef. *hwas*, *hwarjis* with the particle -*uh* : Lat. -*que*. Feist 283 f.

ON *hverr* (also the interrog. indef. pron.), Dan. *hver*, Sw. *var* = Goth. *hwarjis* (cf. above), also ON *sērhverr* (*sēr* dat. of refl. pron.), Dan. *enhver* (*en* indef. article), Sw. *varje* (old oblique case of *var*).

In West Gmc. the earlier forms were various compounds of Gmc. **līk*- 'form, appearance, body' (Goth. *leik*, OE *līc*, etc.), in contrast to the use of the indef. pron. (or cpds.) in East and North Gmc.

OE *ǣlc*, ME *elch*, NE *each*, Du. *elk*, fr. **aiwa-līka*-, beside OHG *iogilīh*, MHG *iegelīch* (NHG *jeglich*), fr. **aiwa-galīka*-, cpds. of **aiwa*-, OE *ā*, *ǣ*-, OHG *eo*, Goth. *aiw* adv. 'ever', and **(ga)līka*-, Goth. *galeiks* adj. 'alike', *leik* 'body', etc. NED s.v. *each* (but precise equation of Eng.-Du. form with High German certainly wrong). Weigand-H. 1.946. Franck-v. W. 154 (but takes Eng. and Du. form fr. **aina-līka*-), 271.

ME *everi(ch)*, NE *every*, fr. OE *ǣfre ǣlc*, with *ǣfre* 'ever' related to the obscured first member of *ǣlc* (above). NED s.v. *every*.

OE *gehwilc*, early ME *iwilch*, *iwulch*, OHG *gi(h)welīh*, and, strengthened with OE *ǣ*-, OHG *eo* 'ever' (cf. above), OE *ǣghwilc*, ME *ewilc euych*, OHG *eogiwelīh*, MHG *iewelīch*, cpd. of interrog. OE *hwilc*, OHG *(h)welih* 'which?' (Gmc. **hwa-līka*- 'what sort?', with **līka*-, cf.

above); similarly MHG *iet-welīch*, *ietes-welīch*, cpd. of *ie*- (= OHG *eo*, above) and OHG *et(t)es*-, *et(t)e-(h)welīh* (adj.) 'aliquis'.

OHG *eo(h)wedar* 'each' (of two), MHG *ieweder* (and *iet-weder*, for *iet*-, see above) also 'each, every' (of several), NHG *jeder* (replacing *jeglich*, MHG *iegelīch*, etc., in late MHG). Paul, Deutsches Wtb. 272 f. Weigand-H. 1.946.

5. Lith. *kiekvienas*, fr. *kiek* 'how much?' and *vienas* 'one'.

Lett. *ikviens*, cpd. of *ik* 'ever' (: Lith. **jiek* in obs. *jiekas* 'something', and parallel to *kiek*, above) and *viens* 'one'; for use of *ik* alone with gen. in locutions expressing 'each, every', cf. Mühl.-Endz. 1.703.

Lett. *ikkatrs*, cpd. of *ik* and *katrs* interrog. 'who, which (of two)?', used also as indef. 'each' (of two'), and generally now also 'every' (of several). Mühl.-Endz. 2.172.

Lett. *ikkur's*, cpd. of *ik* and *kur'š* 'who' (interrog. and rel.), also used alone as indef. 'each, every'. Mühl.-Endz. 2.327.

6. ChSl. *kŭž(i)do* (Supr., etc. for ἕκαστος, which in Gospels is rendered by *vĭsěkŭ*), Boh. *každý*, Pol. *każdy*, Russ. *každyj*, all derivs. of the interrog.-indef. stem in ChSl. *kŭ-to* 'who, what?', etc. Berneker 675.

13.15 MUCH; MANY

(Where only one form is entered, this is also used, either in pl. or with pl., for 'Many')

Grk.	*πολύς*	Goth.	*manags, mikils, filu*	Lith.	*daug, daugel*
NG	*πολύς*	ON	*mikill; margir, mangir*	Lett.	*daudz*
Lat.	*multus*	Dan.	*megen; mange*	ChSl.	*mŭnogŭ*
It.	*molto*	Sw.	*mychen; många*	SCr.	*mnogo*
Fr.	*beaucoup de*	OE	*micel, fela; monige, micele, fela*	Boh.	*mnoho*
Sp.	*mucho*	ME	*muchel, mickel; monie, fele*	Pol.	*wiele, dużo*
Rum.	*mult*	NE	*much; many*	Russ.	*mnogo*
Ir.	*mōr, il; ili, imde, mōr*	Du.	*veel; vele, menige*	Skt.	*bahu-, puru-, bhūri-*
NIr.	*mōrān, a lān; iomdha, a lān*	OHG	*manag, mihhil, filu*	Av.	*paru-*
W.	*llawer*	MHG	*vil(e); manege, vil(e)*		
Br.	*kalz*	NHG	*viel*		

'Much' in quantity and 'many' in number are generally expressed by sg. and pl. forms of the same word or by adv. phrases applied equally to both (Fr. *beaucoup de*, NIr. *a lān*, Lith. *daug* with gen., etc.). Occasionally the sg. is used also with reference to number, 'many a', as Latin *multus* in poetry and late prose, OE *monig*, NHG *mancher*, etc.

The connections are mostly with words for 'full' or 'great, large'.

1. Derivs. of IE **pel(ə)*-, **plē*- in words for 'fill' and 'full' (Grk. πίμπλημι, πλήρης, Lat. *plēre*, *plēnus*, etc.; cf. 13.21), esp. **pelu*, **pḷu*, etc., neut. sg. sb. and adv. (Goth. *filu*, Grk. πολύ, Skt. *puru*), whence also adj. forms (Grk. πολύς, Skt. fem. *pūrvī*). Walde-P. 2.64 f. Ernout-M. 783. Falk-Torp 235. Feist 152 f.

Grk. πολύς, sg. 'much', pl. 'many', comp. πλείων, πλέων; Lat. *plūs* 'more'; Ir. *il* 'much' (rare in this sense, but cf. *cosintaidbse il* 'cum multa ostensione' Ml. 30b11), mostly pl. *ili*, *ile* 'many', NIr. *il*-, *iol*- (only as prefix), now usually *a lān* with gen. (: *lān* adj. 'full'), comp. *lia* 'more' (pl.), Br. *lies* 'several'; Goth., OHG *filu*, MHG *vil(e)*, neut. sb. with

gen. sg. or pl., NHG *viel*, Du. *veel* adj., OE *fela*, with gen. or as indecl. adj., ME *fele* pl. adj., ON *fiǫl*- only as prefix, comp. ON *fleiri*, Dan., Sw. *flere* 'more' (pl.); Skt. *puru*- (not fully declined; mostly nom.-acc. neut. sg. or pl., with fem. *pūrvī*, etc.), Av. *paru*- 'much', pl. 'many', comp. Av. *frāyah*- 'more' (Skt. *prāyas* adv. 'mostly').

2. Lat. *multus* 'much', pl. 'many' (> It. *molto*, OFr. *mout*, Sp. *mucho*, Rum. *mult*), prob. : Grk. μάλα 'very', Lett. *milns* (rare) 'very much', Lat. *melior* 'better'. Walde-P. 2.272. Ernout-M. 639. Walde-H. 2.63.

Fr. *beaucoup*, cpd. of *beau* 'beautiful, fine' and *coup* 'blow', replaces OFr. *mout* in 13/14th century. Gamillscheg 92. Wartburg 2,868.

3. Ir. *mōr*, NIr. mostly *a mhōr* or usually deriv. *mōrān*, sb. with gen. or partitive prep. *de*, fr. adj. *mōr* 'great, large' (12.55).

Ir. *imde*, NIr. *iomdha*, sg. 'many a', pl. 'many', fr. **imbde* : Ir. *imbed* 'copia, multitudo' (this of dub. etym., Walde-P. 1.125).

Ir. *il*, NIr. *lān*, above, 1.

W. *llawer* (with and without *o* 'of') : Ir. *lour*, *lōr* 'enough', perh. (with dissim.) fr. **rowero*- : Ir. *ro-fera* 'suffices' (: OHG *werēn* 'preserve', Pedersen 2.518). Thurneysen, Gram. 119.

Br. *kalz*, also and orig. sb. 'a heap' : Corn. *cals* 'heap', W. *cargl* 'heap, collection', outside connections? Thurneysen, IF 42.148.

4. Goth. *manags* 'much', pl. 'many', comp. *managiza* 'more' (sg. and pl.), ON (late) *mangir*, Dan. *mange*, Sw. *många*, OE *monige*, ME *monie* (pl.; sg. ON *mangr*, OE *monig*, etc. 'many a'); OHG *manag* 'much', pl. 'many', comp. *manigiron* 'more' (pl.), MHG *manige*, NHG *manche* (distrib. 'several'), Du. *menige* pl. 'many' (sg. MHG *manec*, etc. 'many a') : ChSl. *mŭnogŭ* 'much', etc. (below, 6), Ir. *menicc* 'often', W. *mynych* 'frequent, often', root connection dub. Walde-P. 2.268 f. Feist 343 f.

Goth. *mikils*, OE *micel* (*mycel*), OHG *mihhil* 'great, much', pl. 'many', ON *mikill* 'great, much' (pl. only 'great'), Dan. *megen*, Sw. *mychen* 'much', ME *muchel*, *mickel*, NE *much* 'much' (use as 'many' obs.; for ME forms and uses, cf. NED *mickle* and *much*) : Grk. μέγας, Lat. *magnus* 'great' (12.55). Walde-P. 2.257 f. Falk-Torp 708.

Goth. *filu*, etc., above, 1.

ON *margir* (pl., sg. 'many a'), etym. dub., perh. : ON *morð* 'multitude', etc. Falk-Torp 695, 730 (Walde-P. 2.277).

5. Lith. *daug*, *daugel*, Lett. *daudz*, adv. (used as indecl. sb.) with gen. sg. or pl. (Lett. also with nom., and nom. pl. *daudzi*), Pol. *dużo*, prob. : Pol. *duży* 'strong', Goth. *daug*, OE *dēag*, OHG *toug* 'is useful, avails', Grk. τυγχάνω 'meet, reach', etc. Walde-P. 1.847. Berneker 217 f. Mühl.-Endz. 1.443.

6. ChSl. *mŭnogŭ* 'much', pl. 'many', comp. *mŭnožějĭ*, SCr., Russ. *mnogo*, Boh. *mnoho*, adv. and sb. with gen., pl. adj. SCr. *mnogi*, etc., 'many' : Goth. *manags*, etc., above, 4.

Pol. *wiele*, adv. and sb. with gen. 'much, many' : ChSl. *velĭ*- (as prefix) 'very', *velijĭ*, *velikŭ*, Pol. *wielki* 'great, large', etc. (12.55). Brückner 616.

Pol. *dużo* : Lith. *daug*, above, 5.

7. Skt. *bahu*- 'much', pl. 'many', comp. *bahutara*- : Av. *bązah*- 'height, depth', Baluch. *bāz* 'much', *baz* 'thick', Grk. παχύς 'thick' (12.63), Hitt. *pankus* 'all, whole'. Walde-P. 2.151.

Skt. *bhūri*- 'much, strong', pl. 'many', comp. *bhūyas*- (i.e. *bhū-yas*- : *bhū-ri*) : Av. *būiri*- 'abundant, complete', Lith. *būrys* 'group, flock, shower', Lett. *bũra* 'crowd', perh. fr. **bhu*- in words for 'blow up, swell'. Walde-P. 2.114.

Skt. *puru*-, Av. *paru*-, *pouru*-, above, 1.

13.16 MORE

Grk.	πλείων, πλέων	Goth.	*managiza* (*maizo, mais* adv.)	Lith.	*daugiaus*
NG	περισσότερος	ON	*meiri; fleiri* (pl.)	Lett.	*vairāk*
Lat.	*plūs*	Dan.	*mer; flere* (pl.)	ChSl.	*bolijĭ, mŭnožějĭ, vęšte*
It.	*più*	Sw.	*mer; flere* (pl.)	SCr.	*više*
Fr.	*plus de*	OE	*mā*	Boh.	*víc(e)*
Sp.	*mas*	ME	*mo; more* (sg.)	Pol.	*więcej*
Rum.	*mai mult*	NE	*more*	Russ.	*bol'še*
Ir.	*mō; lia* (pl.)	Du.	*meer*	Skt.	*bhūyas-, bahutara-*
NIr.	*tuilleadh; lia* (pl.)	OHG	*mēr, mēro; manigiron* (pl.)	Av.	*frāyah-*
W.	*mwy*	MHG	*mē, mēre*		
Br.	*mui, muioc'h*	NHG	*mehr*		

For the most part, forms of the same word (or the same indeclinable form) are used with the singular for 'more' in quantity and with the plural for 'more' in number. But some words are mainly, if not absolutely, restricted to one or the other of these uses and are marked in the list as (sg.) or (pl.).

Many of the words for 'more' are comparatives, in form as well as in meaning, of words for 'much, many', though not always of those in use in the same languages (e.g. Lat. *multus* but *plūs*). Most of these have been included in the discussion of the latter (13.15), leaving only the following for notice here.

1. Grk. περισσότερος, comp. of περισσός 'beyond the usual quantity or number, superfluous' (deriv. of περί), is in NT sometimes 'more' (mostly in adv.) and the reg. word for 'more' in NG (πλείων archaic even in lit.; adv. πλέον pop. but 'more' in sense of 'in addition, any longer', etc.).

2. Sp. *mas*, fr. Lat. *magis* adv. 'more' : *magnus* 'great', etc.

Rum. *mai mult* (pl. *mai mulți*), comp. of *mult* 'much'; *mai* fr. Lat. *magis* (above).

3. Ir. *mō*, W. *mwy*, Br. *mui, muioc'h*, comp. of Ir. *mōr*, W. *mawr*, Br. *meur* 'great' (12.55).

Ir. *lia* (pl.) : Grk. πλείων, Lat. *plūs*, etc. (13.15).

NIr. *tuilleadh* (followed by nom. or gen. or by *de* or *is*, freq. also with proleptic *a* 'its', cf. Dinneen), lit. 'addition', Ir. *tuilled* id., fr. a verbal stem *to-līn-*, cpd. of *līnaim* 'fill' : Lat. *plēnus* 'full', etc. (13.21). Pedersen 2.567.

4. Goth. *maiza*, usually 'greater' (μείζων), as 'more' only neut. *maizo* (πλεῖον), *mais* adv. (μᾶλλον, πλεῖον), ON *meiri* adj. 'more, greater', *meirr* adv., Dan., Sw. *mer* adv. and adj., OE *mā*, ME *mo* adv., and as sb. with gen. 'more', ME also adj. (OE *mara* adj. 'greater in size'), ME *more* 'greater (in size), more (in quantity)', NE *more* also with pl. of number (1584+; NED s.v. 3), Du. *meer* adv. and adj.; OHG *mēr* adv. and as sb. with gen., *mēro* (*mērīro, mērōro*) adj. 'more', MHG *mē, mēre* adv., and as sb. with gen. 'more', NHG *mehr* adv. and adj. : Ir. *mō*, etc. 'greater, more' (above, 3), Ir. *mōr*, W. *mawr*, etc. 'great' (12.55). Walde-P. 2.238.

5. Lith. *daugiaus*, Lett. dial. *daudzāk*, comp. to *daug, daudz* adv. 'much' (13.15).

Lett. *vairāk*, comp. adv. with gen. 'more', fr. archaic *vairs* adj. 'more', perh. as orig. 'greater, stronger' (cf. below, 6) : Lith. *vyresnis* 'older', Skt.

vayas 'strength', etc. Mühl.-Endz. 4.442.

6. ChSl. *bolijĭ* 'greater' and 'more' (renders μείζων and πλείων), Russ. *bol'še* comp. adv. with gen., beside *bol'šij* adj. 'greater', etc. : Skt. *balīyas-* 'stronger', *bala-* 'strength', etc. Walde-P. 2.110. Berneker 72.

ChSl. *vęšte*, neut. only (but renders πλείονα Mt. 20.10, πλείους Mt. 26.53), Boh. *více, víc*, Pol. *więcej* (SCr. *veći* 'greater') adv., and as sb. with gen. 'more', etym.? Miklosich 381. Brückner 620 f.

SCr. *više*, comp. of *visok* 'high' (12.31).

13.162. Words for the superlative 'most' generally go with those for 'more', as Grk. πλεῖστος beside πλείων, Lat. *plūrimus* beside *plūs*, Goth. *managists* beside *managiza*, ON *flestr* beside *fleiri*, OE *mǣst* beside *mā*, etc.

13.17 LITTLE (Quantity); FEW (Number)

(Where only one form is entered, this is also used, either in pl. or with pl., for 'Few')

Grk.	ὀλίγος (παῦρος)	Goth.	*leitil; fawai*	Lith.	*maž*
NG	ὀλίγος	ON	*lītill; fāir*	Lett.	*maz*
Lat.	*parvus; paucē*	Dan.	*lidt* (sb.); *faa*	ChSl.	*malo*
It.	*poco*	Sw.	*litet* (sb.); *få*	SCr.	*malo*
Fr.	*peu de*	OE	*lȳtel; fēawe*	Boh.	*málo*
Sp.	*poco*	ME	*litel; fewe*	Pol.	*mało*
Rum.	*puțin*	NE	*little; few*	Russ.	*malo*
Ir.	*becc, terc; uath, uathad, terc*	Du.	*weinig*	Skt.	*alpa-*
NIr.	*beagān, beag; beag, tearc*	OHG	*luzzil; luzzil, fōhe*	Av., OPers.	*kamna-*
W.	*ychydig*	MHG	*lützel, wēnec*		
Br.	*nebeud*	NHG	*wenig*		

Several of the words for 'small, little' in size (12.56) are used also for 'little' in quantity, either in the same declined form (as Lat. *parvus*) or more commonly in a neut. sg. or adv. form with following gen. sg. for 'small quantity of, little' or gen. pl. for 'small number of, few' (as Goth. *leitil* with gen. sg., Lith. *mažž*, ChSl. *malo*, etc., with gen. sg. or pl.).

But there are others of which the prevailing use is in the sg. 'little' in quantity, in the pl. 'few'. Such words are also occasionally used with reference to number even in the sg., that is, with a sg. coll. in sense of 'not numerous'.

1. IE *pau- with various suffixes. Walde-P. 2.75 f., Ernout-M. 742. Feist 147. NED s.v. *few*.

Grk. παῦρος, poet. word for usual ὀλίγος, in sg. 'little' in quantity, time, or number (παῦρος λαός), pl. 'few'; Lat. *parvus* (fr. **pauros*, like *nervus* : Grk. νεῦρον, and Gall. *tarvos*, Ir. *tarb* : Lat. *taurus*, Grk. ταῦρος) 'little' in size, quantity, or time; Lat. *paucī* 'few', sg. *paucus* rare in class. Lat. but reg. in VLat. for *parvus* with reference to quantity (in late Lat. texts sometimes *parvī* for *paucī* by overcorrection), hence It., Sp. *poco*, Fr. *peu;* Goth. *fawai*, ON *fāir*, Dan. *faa*, Sw. *få*, OE *fēawe, fēawa*, ME *fewe*, NE *few*, OHG *fōhe* (sg. ON *fār* 'scarce, not numerous' with collectives; sg. forms in Goth., OHG rare); cf. also Lat. *paul(l)us* 'little', *pauper* 'poor'.

2. Grk. ὀλίγος 'little' (also 'small' of size, esp. in Hom.), pl. 'few' (not Hom. in this sense), perh. : λοιγός 'ruin, de-

struction', Lith. *liga* 'sickness', etc. Walde-P. 2.398. Boisacq 697.

Grk. βραχύς 'short' (12.59) is also sometimes used for 'little' in size or quantity, and 'few' esp. 'few words', like NE *in short* (LS s.v.).

3. Rum. *puțin* 'little', pl. 'few', fr. some variety of the VLat. forms *pisinnus, pitinnus, pusillus*, etc., 'small' (12.56). REW 6550, 6890.

4. Ir. *becc* 'little' of size or quantity (cf. 12.56), NIr. *beag* with gen. sg. or *de'n* with dat. sg. 'little' in quantity, as *beag airgid, beag de'n airgead* 'little money', with nom. sg. 'few' as *beag capall (padir)* 'little horse (prayer)' = 'few horses (prayers)'; hence sb. MIr. *becān*, NIr. *beagān* 'small quantity' with gen. sg. 'little' in quantity *beagān airgid (arāin)* 'little money (bread)'.

Ir. *terc*, NIr. *tearc* 'scarce', used often in the sense of 'little' and 'few' (e.g. *terca* gl. 'exigua' Ml. 48c30; *ba terc for bith mnai* 'few women in the world', Passions and Homilies 1.830, p. 64, etc., NIr. sometimes used for 'few' like *beag* above, perh. : Lat. *tesca, tesqua* 'waste, uncultivated regions'. Pedersen 1.81. Ernout-M. 1035.

Ir. *uath* 'few' (e.g. *is-na huathib laithib-se* 'in paucis istis diebus', Passions and Homilies 1.4992, p. 180), more usually sb. *uathad* 'fewness' (with gen.), etym. dub., perh. : ON *auðr*, OHG *ōdi* 'desert, waste', etc. Walde-P. 1.14.

W. *ychydig*, for *fychydig*, mutated form of MW *bychydic* : *bychod* 'small quantity', *bach, bychan* 'small' (12.56). Morris Jones 129, 312.

Br. *nebeud* : W. *nebawd* 'somebody, anybody', derivs. of Br. *nep* 'none', W. *neb* 'any, none' = Ir. *nech* 'any(one)', fr. **ne-kʷos* (neg. and pron. stem **kʷo-*, cf. Ir. *cach* 'every', 13.14). Pedersen 2.212.

5. Goth. *leitil* (neut. sg. of adj. *leitils* 'small' with gen., e.g. *weinis leitil* = οἴνῳ ὀλίγῳ 1 Tim. 5.23); ON *lītill* (adj.), Dan. *lidt*, Sw. *litet* (neut. sbs. with noun in apposition), OE *lȳtel*, ME *litel*, NE *little* (adj. and sb. with gen. or *of*, ME also rarely with coll. or pl. sb. 'few'), OHG *luzzil*, MHG *lützel* (adj. and sb. with gen., OHG also with pl. 'few', e.g. *uuirdit bifillit luzilen fillungon* = *plagis vapulabit paucis* Tat. 108.6), cf. Goth. *leitils*, ON *lītill*, OE *lȳtel*, etc. 'small' (12.56).

Du. *weinig*, NHG *wenig* (adjs.), MHG *wēnec* (both adj. and sb. with gen.), lit. 'weeping, unhappy, weak', hence 'little' (also of size) : OHG *wēnag* 'pitiable, unhappy, needy', Goth. *wainahs* 'wretched', OHG *weinōn*, etc. 'weep'. Weigand-H. 2.1241. Franck-v. W. 784.

6. Lith. *maž(a)*, Lett. *maz* (adv. with gen.) : Lith. *mažas*, Lett. *mazs* 'small' (12.56).

7. ChSl. *malo*, etc. (advs. with gen.; Boh. *málo* indecl. but used like *mnoho* 'much', 13.15) : ChSl. *malŭ*, etc. 'small' (12.56).

8. Skt. *alpa-* 'small' (12.56), also 'little' in quantity, pl. 'few'.

Av., OPers. *kamna-* 'little' in amount (Av.) or number (OPers. of an army), OPers. pl. 'few' (*hadā kamnaibiš martiyaibiš* 'with few men'; cf. also Av. cpd. *kamnā-nar-* 'having few men'), NPers. *kam* 'little, few', fr. **kambna-* (cf. Av. *kambištəm* superl. adv. 'least'), prob. : OHG *hammer* 'mutilated', ON *skammr* 'short', etc. Walde-P. 2.601.

13.18 ENOUGH (adj. or adv.)

Grk.	ἱκανός, ἀρκῶν	Goth.	*ganōhs*	Lith.	*gana*
NG	ἀρκετός	ON	*(g)nōgr*	Lett.	*gana*
Lat.	*satis*	Dan.	*nok*	ChSl.	*dovolĭnŭ*
It.	*abbastanza*	Sw.	*nog*	SCr.	*dosta*
Fr.	*assez*	OE	*genōg*	Boh.	*dost(i)*
Sp.	*bastante*	ME	*inoh*	Pol.	*dość*
Rum.	*destul*	NE	*enough*	Russ.	*dovol'no*
Ir.	*lour*	Du.	*genoeg*	Skt.	*alam*
NIr.	*dōthain, sāith, leor*	OHG	*ginuog(i)*	Av.	. . . .
W.	*digon*	MHG	*genuoc*		
Br.	*a-walc'h*	NHG	*genug*		

'Enough' is in part expressed by a declinable adj., but more commonly by an adv. form which is used also in the function of an adj. or sb. Such forms are given preference in the list even where there are also adj. forms in less common use.

Besides the words listed, there are others that answer more nearly to NE *sufficient* (fr. pres. pple. of Lat. *sufficere* 'put into, make take the place of', and so also 'suffice'), which with reference to quantity or number is only a less colloquial equivalent of *enough* but which carries the notion of 'adequate' and is used in many phrases where *enough* could not be substituted.

Semantic sources are notions of 'reaching, attaining', 'satiety' (orig. with reference to food), 'fulness, plenty', what is 'fitting', 'desirable, preferable', hence 'suitable', what will 'do' (cf. NE *that will do*) or 'hold out, last'(?).

1. Grk. ἱκανός : ἵκω, ἱκάνω, ἱκνέομαι 'come, reach, attain to', Lith. *at-siekti* 'reach, attain'. Walde-P. 2.465, Boisacq 372. Cf. NHG *aus-reichend, hinreichend, hin-länglich* 'sufficient'. In the NT ἱκανός is mostly an emphatic 'enough', that is, 'much, many', 'long' (time), etc., and so in NG or 'capable, adequate'.

Grk. ἀρκέω 'ward off, assist' and 'suffice, be enough' : Lat. *arcēre* 'inclose, contain', then esp. 'ward off'. Walde-P. 1.80. Ernout-M. 67 f. Hence ἀρκῶν· διαρκής, ἐξαρκής 'enough', and late ἀρκετός 'enough' in NT, etc., and the reg. word in NG.

NG also very commonly the vbl. φτάνει 'is enough', 3sg. of φτάνω 'arrive' (10.55).

Grk. ἅλις, adv. 'in plenty' and often 'enough' (cf. also γάλι· ἱκανόν Hesych.) : ἀλής 'crowded', εἴλω 'press', etc. Walde-P. 1.295, Boisacq 45, 223 ff.

2. Lat. *satis*, adv. (phrase cpd. *ad satis* > Fr. *assez*) : *satur* 'sated, full of food', Ir. *sāith* 'satiety, sufficiency', Goth. *saþs*, ON *saðr*, OHG *sat*, Lith. *sotus* 'sated' (ChSl. *sytŭ* 'sated' apparently here, but difficult), Grk. ἄω 'satiate', Skt. *a-sinva-* 'insatiable'. Walde-P. 2.444. Ernout-M. 897 f.

It. *abbastanza*, used as adv., adj., and sb. (also *bastante* adj. and *basta* 'enough, stop!'), Sp. *bastante*, adj. and adv., fr. It. *bastare*, Sp. *bastar* 'suffice' (cf. also Sp. *basto* 'supplied with provisions, coarse, rude', Port. *basto* 'pressed'), orig. disputed but best through It. fr. Grk. βαστάζω, late βαστῶ 'lift, carry, endure', then also 'hold out, last'. (Cf. NG δὲν βαστᾷ 'it won't hold out, last, be enough'.) Schuchardt, Z. rom. Ph. 33.339 ff. Wartburg 1.277. REW 984.

Rum. *destul*, adj. and adv., fr. cpd. of *de* and *satul* 'satiated', fr. Lat. *satullus* id. : *satur, satis*, etc. (above, 2). Pușcariu 1531. REW 7620.

3. Ir. *lour, lōr*, NIr. *leor* : W. *llawer* 'much, many' (13.15).

NIr. *dōthain* (South Ir.) sb. 'sufficiency, plenty', used with gen. to express 'enough', e.g. *ata mo dhōthain ārain agam*, lit. 'is my sufficiency of bread with me' = 'I have enough bread'; MIr. *doethain* (Windisch 495), orig. 'what comes to one', hence 'suffices' : *do-ethaim* 'go to, approach' (Zimmer, KZ 30.72. Pedersen 2.514).

NIr. *sāith* (North Ir.) 'sufficiency, satiety' (used exactly as *dōthain*, above) : Lat. *satis*, etc. (above, 2).

W. *digon*, MW *digawn*, orig. vbl. form fr. a phrase like *digawn hynny* 'that will do' : OW *digoni* 'make, do' (etym.?). Morris Jones 375. Loth, RC 37.43.

Br. *a-walc'h*, adv., lit. 'in sufficiency', fr. *gwalc'h* 'sufficiency', MBr. *gwalch* 'superfluity', W. *gwala* 'fulness' : Lat. *vulgus* 'the common people', Skt. *varga-* 'group'. Walde-P. 1.296. Pedersen 1.34.

4. Goth. *ganōhs* adj. (renders ἱκανός only in sense 'much, many', e.g. Lk. 7.11, 12, etc.; also once *ganōh* = πολλά Jn. 16.12, but in sense 'enough' *ni ganōhai sind þaim* = οὐκ ἀρκοῦσιν αὐτοῖς Jn. 6.7), ON *nōgr, gnōgr* adj., OE *genōg* adj. and adv., etc., general Gmc. (Dan. *nok* fr. MLG *nōch*) : Goth. *ganah*, OE *geneah*, OHG *ginah* 'it suffices' (fr. 'reaches'), Lat. *nanciscī* 'reach, obtain', Skt. *naç-* 'reach, attain', etc. Walde-P. 1.129. Falk-Torp 769. Feist 92,196.

5. Lith., Lett. *gana* (or shortened *gan*) : ChSl. *goněti* 'suffice', Skt. *ghana-* 'compact, tight, thick', *ā-hanas-* 'swelling, exuberant', Grk. εὐ-θενέω 'thrive, bloom', etc. Walde-P. 1.679.

6. ChSl. *dovolĭnŭ*, adj. beside *dovlěti* 'suffice', SCr. *dovoljno*, Russ. *dovol'no* advs., cpds. of *do-* 'to' and second member : ChSl. *volja* 'will', *voliti* 'wish, prefer' (: Lat. *velle*, etc.). Miklosich 377. Semantic development through 'desirable, preferable, suitable'.

SCr. *dosta, dosti*, Boh. *dost, dosti*, Pol. *dość, dosyć*, fr. a phrase like ChSl. *do syti* 'εἰς κόρον, to satiety' (Supr., etc.) : ChSl. *sytŭ*, etc., 'sated' (cf. Lat. *satis*, above, 2). Brückner 94. Gebauer 1.286, 392.

Boh. *dostatečný*, Pol. *dostateczny*, Russ. *dostatočnyj*, adjs. (with corresponding adverbial forms), fr. *dostati* in sense of 'suffice' (as ChSl.), orig. 'reach, attain' (whence 'obtain, get' in Boh., Pol., Russ.), cpd. of *do-* 'to' and *stati* 'stand'. Brückner 514.

7. Skt. *alam*, adv. used also as adj., prob. = *aram* 'suitable, right, sufficient', Av. *arəm* 'suitable, corresponding' : Grk. ἀραρίσκω 'join together, fit', Skt. *ṛta-* 'fitting', etc. Walde-P. 1.69 (without *alam*). Uhlenbeck 14, 12.

13.19 MULTITUDE, CROWD

Grk.	πλῆθος, ὄχλος	Goth.	*managei*	Lith.	*daugybė, minia*
NG	πλῆθος, ὄχλος	ON	*margr, mengi, þrǫng*	Lett.	*pulks (daudzums)*
Lat.	*multitūdō, turba*	Dan.	*mængde, hob*	ChSl.	*mŭnožĭstvo, narodŭ*
It.	*multitudine, folla*	Sw.	*mängd, hop*	SCr.	*mnoštvo, naloga, tišma*
Fr.	*multitude, foule*	OE	*menigeo, geþrang*		
Sp.	*multitud, muchedumbre, gentío*	ME	*multitude, press, thrang*	Boh.	*množství, dav, zástup, tlum*
Rum.	*mulțime, gloată*	NE	*multitude, crowd, throng*	Pol.	*mnóstwo, tłum, ciżba*
Ir.	*slūag*			Russ.	*množestvo, tolpa*
NIr.	*sluagh*	Du.	*menigte, gedrang*	Skt.	*bāhulya-, samūha-*
W.	*lliaws, torf*	OHG	*menigī, githrengi*	Av.	*frəni-*
Br.	*niver bras, engroez*	MHG	*menige, gedrenge*		
		NHG	*menge, gedränge*		

The majority of the words for 'multitude' are derivs. of, or cognate with, those for 'much, many' (13.15). Some of these are formally of learned origin and not frequent in common speech, e.g. Sp. *multitud* vs. *muchedumbre*, or Fr., NE *multitude* vs. *foule, crowd*.

Of the popular words for 'crowd', some are based on the notion of 'turmoil, disorder', these (and some of the others, too) often used in a derogatory sense. More frequently, as in NE *crowd, throng*, etc., they are derived from verbs for 'press' and properly denote a closely packed number of persons, but with this notion sometimes fading into that of large number. Many of the words for 'people' (19.21) are also used for 'crowd', e.g. very frequently in biblical renderings of Grk. ὄχλος, Lat. *turba*. Words for 'heap' are also often used for a large number or quantity, and in colloquial speech many others, not entered in the list, as NE *lot(s), pile, mass, sight, power*, etc. Furthermore, many of the collective words commonly applied to certain animals, like NE *drove, flock, herd, school, swarm* (13.192), are also quotable with reference to a large number of persons.

1. Grk. πλῆθος, fr. the same root as πολύς 'much', pl. 'many'.

Grk. ὄχλος, often, but not necessarily, with derogatory sense, perh. : Goth. *agls* 'shameful', *aglus* 'difficult', etc. Walde-P. 1.174. Feist 15.

2. Lat. *multitūdō* (> It., Fr., Sp. learned forms, also ME, NE; Sp. *muchedumbre* with pop. form of suffix as in *dulcedumbre*, etc.), fr. *multus* 'much', pl. 'many'. Rum. *mulțime*, new deriv. of *mult* (suffix *-ime* fr. Lat. *-īmen*).

Lat. *turba* 'turmoil, disorder', and 'crowd', generally with pejorative force, either loanword from or cognate with Grk. τύρβη 'turmoil, disorder', prob. fr. the root in OE *þweran* 'stir, shake', ON *þorp* 'hamlet, village', *þyrpask* 'crowd' (vb.), etc. Walde-P. 1.750. Ernout-M. 1065.

It. *folla*, Fr. *foule*, back-formation fr. vbs. *follare, fouler* orig. 'full cloth', hence 'press, crowd', fr. VLat. *fullāre* (pple. *fullātum* in gloss), deriv. of Lat. *fullō* 'fuller'. REW 3560.

Sp. *gentío*, fr. *gente* 'people'.

Rum. *gloată*, fr. Slavic, late ChSl., Bulg. *glota* 'crowd', etc. Tiktin 687 f. Berneker 306.

3. Ir. *slūag*, NIr. *sluag* 'crowd, host, army', see under 'army' (20.15).

W. *lliaws* : Br. *liez* 'several', Ir. *lia*, Grk. πλέων, etc. 'more' (13.15). Walde-P. 2.65. Pedersen 1.68, 2.120.

W. *torf*, fr. Lat. *turma* 'troop, throng' (: *turba*, above, 2). Loth, Mots lat. 211.

Br. *niver bras* 'large number' (12.55, 13.12).

Br. *engroez*, deriv. of *enk* 'narrow' (12.62), with semantic development as in NE *throng, crowd*. Henry 114.

4. Goth. *managei*, ON *mengi*, OE *menigeo*, OHG *menigī*, etc., general Gmc. (but lost in ME, NE), fr. Goth. *managš* 'much, many', etc.

ON *margr*, sb. use of adj. *margr*, pl. *margir* 'many'.

ON *þrǫng*, OE *geþrang*, ME *thrang*, NE *throng*, Du. *gedrang*, OHG *githrengi* (Otfr.), NHG *gedränge*, all orig. involving the notion of pressure : ON *þrǫngr* 'narrow', etc. (12.62).

Dan. *hob*, Sw. *hop*, fr. LG *hōp* 'heap' (= OE *hēap*, etc.). Cf. the colloq. use of NE *heap* for a large number (NED s.v. 4, but rarely of persons), NHG *haufe*. Falk-Torp 413.

ME, NE *press* (in this sense now mostly replaced by *crowd*), fr. Fr. *presse*, back-formation fr. *presser*, Lat. *pressāre*, frequent. of *premere* 'press'. NED s.v.

NE *crowd*, fr. vb. *crowd*, this fr. OE *crūdan* 'press' = MDu. *crūdan* 'press, push', MHG *kroten* 'oppress', etc. NED s.v.

5. Lith. *daugybė*, Lett. *daudzums*, fr. *daug, daudz* 'much, many'.

Lith. *minia*, fr. *minti* 'tread, trample on'. Leskien, Ablaut 336.

Lett. *pulks* (= Lith. *pulkas* 'regiment', 'flock, herd' of animals, etc.), fr. Slavic, esp. Pol. *pułk* 'regiment' (late ChSl. *plŭkŭ* 'crowd, band', etc.), the Slavic words fr. Gmc., OHG *folc*, etc. 'people, army'. Stender-Petersen 194 ff. Mühl.-Endz. 3.407.

6. ChSl. *mŭnožĭstvo* (in Gospels for πλῆθος), etc., general Slavic, fr. ChSl. *mŭnogŭ*, etc. 'much, many'.

ChSl. *narodŭ* (in Gospels for ὄχλος), reg. Slavic word for 'people' (19.21).

ChSl. *tlŭpa* (Supr.), Russ. *tolpa*, Boh. *tlum*, Pol. *tłum* (**tŭlp-m-*), perh. : Lith. *tilpti* 'have room for'. Brückner 572.

SCr. *naloga*, fr. the root of ChSl. *ležati* 'lie' (12.13) with *na-* 'upon', hence the notion of 'pressure' and 'crowd'. Berneker 728.

SCr. *tišma*, Pol. *ciżba*, fr. the root of ChSl., SCr. *tiskati* 'press' (Pol. *ciskać* 'throw'). Miklosich 357. Brückner 64.

Boh. *zástup*, fr. *zastoupiti* 'step behind, obstruct' (ChSl. *stąpiti* 'tread').

Boh. *dav*, fr. *dáviti* 'press (obs.), strangle'. Berneker 181.

7. Skt. *bāhulya-*, fr. *bahu-* 'much, many'.

Skt. *samūha-*, orig. 'heaping up, heap', fr. *sam-ūh-* 'sweep together'.

Av. *frəni-* (fr. **fr-ani-*, **pr-ani-*), fr. the same root as *paru-* 'much, many'. Barth. 1022.

13.192. Note on other words for a collective body (of persons, animals, or things). NE *group* (fr. Fr. *groupe*, fr. Ital. *gruppo* : *groppo* 'knot'), in earliest use an art term (group of sculptured or painted figures), has become the most nearly generic term; but even this is not applied to animals. For the most part, instead of any generic term, there is a wealth of individualistic terms, differentiated according to the object referred to. Thus, to illustrate from one language only, though a parallel variety may be seen elsewhere, note the following NE words (excluding military terms like *battalion, brigade, squadron*, etc., and otherwise far from exhaustive), with their most familiar applications (these are not exclusive; in fact, most of those commonly used of certain animals are sometimes used also of others and of persons). For the etymology and range of use, cf. NED.

Band (armed men, robbers, musicians); *bevy* (girls, roes, some birds); *body* (people, soldiers); *bunch* (grapes, flowers, keys, etc.; also people in U.S. slang); *cluster* (flowers, stars, also people); *covey* (partridges); *crew* (workmen, sailors); *drove* (cattle, sheep, etc.); *flock* (sheep, goats, geese, formerly also of people); *gang* (esp. workmen or criminals); *herd* (domestic animals, also bison, elephants, etc.); *horde* (nomadic tribes); *lot* (persons and things); *pack* (dogs, wolves); *school* (esp. fish); *shoal* (esp. fish); *squad* (soldiers, police); *stud* (esp. horses); *swarm* (esp. bees); *troop* (esp. soldiers, actors).

13.21 FULL

Grk.	πλήρης, μεστός	Goth.	*fulls*	Lith.	*pilnas*
NG	γεμᾶτος (πλήρης)	ON	*fullr*	Lett.	*pilns*
Lat.	*plēnus*	Dan.	*fuld*	ChSl.	*isplŭnŭ*
It.	*pieno*	Sw.	*full*	SCr.	*pun*
Fr.	*plein*	OE	*full*	Boh.	*plný*
Sp.	*lleno*	ME	*ful*	Pol.	*pełny*
Rum.	*plin*	NE	*full*	Russ.	*polnyj*
Ir.	*lān*	Du.	*vol*	Skt.	*pūrṇa-*
NIr.	*lān*	OHG	*fol*	Av.	*pərəna-*
W.	*llawn*	MHG	*vol*		
Br.	*leun*	NHG	*voll*		

Nearly all the words for 'full' belong to an inherited group reflecting IE words for 'fill' and 'full'.

1. Derivs. of IE **plē-*, etc., seen in verbs for 'fill', as Grk. πίμπλημι, Lat. *plēre* (mostly in cpds.), Ir. *līnaim*, Skt. *pṛ-, pūr-, prā-*, etc. All but the Greek are formed with the *-no-*suffix, and the majority of these from the weak grade of the dissyllabic stem, that is IE **pḹ-no-*. Walde-P. 2.63 ff. Ernout-M. 779 f.

Grk. πλήρης (cf. Lat. *plērus* 'very many'); Lat. *plēnus* (> Romance words); Ir. *lān*, W. *llawn*, Br. *leun;* Goth. *fulls*, etc., general Gmc.; Lith. *pilnas*, Lett. *pilns;* ChSl. *plŭnŭ* (renders μεστός and in phrases γέμω; cpd. *isplŭnŭ* = πλήρης), etc., general Slavic; Skt. *pūrṇa-*, Av. *pərəna-*; Arm. *lī*, Alb. *pl'otë*.

2. Grk. μεστός, etym. dub., perh. : μέζεα, Hom. μήδεα 'genitals', Ir. *mess* 'mast', W. *mes* 'acorns', fr. an unattested root **med-* in sense of 'swell'(?). Walde-P. 2.231. Walde-H. 2.7.

NG γεμᾶτος (already in late Byz.) formed with suffix fr. Latin *-ātus* (Hatzidakis, Μεσ. 1.422), fr. γέμω 'be full', beside γεμίζω 'fill' : Lat. *gemere* 'groan' (fr. 'be pressed, oppressed'), Umbr. *gomia* 'gravidas', ChSl. *žimą, žęti* 'press', all prob. fr. a common notion of 'press'. Walde-P. 1.572 f. Walde-H. 1.588 f.

The usual verbs for 'fill' are cognate with the adjectives for 'full', either their source (cf. above, 1) or derived fr. them, as Grk. (beside πίμπλημι) πληρόω (also 'fulfil' and 'pay', as NG πληρώνω), μεστόω (fr. μεστός, above, 2), Sp. *llenar*, Goth. *fulljan*, OE *fyllan*, etc. (general Gmc., all fr. adj.), ChSl. *(is)plŭniti*, SCr. *puniti*, etc., Lith. *pildyti*, Lett. *pildit*, with dental extension of the root (cf. Grk. πλήθω 'be full'). There is often a preference for cpd. forms, as Lat. *im-, re-* (also *com-*, etc.) *plēre* (simplex only in Festus), It. *empire, riempire*, Fr. *emplir, remplir*, Rum. *umplea* (also Sp. *henchir* beside *llenar*), ChSl. *isplŭniti*, Russ. *napolnit'*, etc.

But there are some alternative terms for 'fill' in certain connections, e.g. Fr. *combler*, fr. Lat. *cumulāre* 'heap up', hence 'fill up, fill' (esp. a void); Russ. *nabit'*, cpd. of *bit'* 'strike, beat', hence 'drive in, cram in' and so 'fill' (a pipe, etc.).

13.22 EMPTY

Grk.	*κενός*	Goth.	*laus*	Lith.	*tuščias*
NG	*ἄδειος, ἀδειανός*	ON	*tōmr (lauss)*	Lett.	*tukšs*
Lat.	*vacuus, inānis, vānus*	Dan.	*tom*	ChSl.	*tŭštĭ*
It.	*vuoto*	Sw.	*tom*	SCr.	*prazan*
Fr.	*vide*	OE	*īdel, ǣmtig, tōm, (ge)lǣre*	Boh.	*prázdný*
Sp.	*vacío*			Pol.	*próżny*
Rum.	*gol, deşert*	ME	*em(p)ti, toom, idel, lere*	Russ.	*pustoj*
Ir.	*fāss, folam*	NE	*empty*	Skt.	*çūnya-, rikta-, tuccha-*
NIr.	*folamh*	Du.	*ledig*	Av.	. . . .
W.	*gwag*	OHG	*ītal, lāri, zuomīg*		
Br.	*goullo*	MHG	*ītel, lǣr(e)*		
		NHG	*leer*		

Several of the words for 'empty' are cognate with words for 'loose, free', some of them more specifically derivs. of words for 'freedom from duties' or 'leisure', being first applied to persons who were unoccupied and then extended to things. Some others must have been first applied to land that was 'waste, wild' or 'stripped of crops'. Several are obscure. Specialization of 'empty' to 'vain' or 'idle' is frequent, as in NE *vain, idle*, NHG *eitel*.

1. Grk. *κενός*, Ion. *κεινός* (**κενϝός*) beside Hom. *κενεός*, Cypr. *κενευϝός* (**κενεϝός*) : Arm. *sin* 'empty, vain', root connection? Walde-P. 1.390.

NG *ἄδειος* (hence vb. *ἀδειάζω* 'empty'), *ἀδειανός*, derivs. of Grk. *ἄδεια*, orig. 'freedom from fear' (: *δέος* 'fear'), then as technical term 'amnesty, immunity, license', NG 'permission' and 'leisure'. The adj. *ἄδειος* must have been applied first to persons who enjoyed freedom from duties, leisure, and so were unoccupied, whence it was extended to objects that were unoccupied 'empty'. Buck, Cl. Ph. 15.198.

2. Lat. *vacuus* : *vacāre* 'be empty, be free', prob. fr. an extension of the root in Lat. *vānus* 'empty, idle, vain', Goth. *wans*, ON *vanr* 'lacking', Skt. *ūna-* 'insufficient', NPers. *vang*, Arm. *unayn* 'empty'. Walde-P. 1.108. Ernout-M. 1068 f.

Lat. *inānis*, plainly neg. cpd. with *in-*, but last member obscure. Walde-P. 1.57. Ernout-M. 482. Walde-H. 1.688.

It. *vuoto*, Fr. *vide*, OFr. *vuide* (also OFr. *voide* > ME *voide*, NE *void*), fr. VLat. **vocitus*, deriv. of VLat. *vocuus*, for Lat. *vacuus* (above). Cf. Lat. *vocīvus* Plaut. and inscr. *vocātiō* = *vacātiō*. Ernout-M. 1069. REW 9429.

Sp. *vacío* fr. Lat. *vacīvus* (Plaut., Ter.) beside *vacuus* (above). REW 9113.

Rum. *gol*, also 'naked, bald', fr. Slavic, cf. ChSl. *golŭ*, etc. 'naked, bare' (4.99). Tiktin 691.

Rum. *deşert* (= Fr. *désert* 'desert', etc.), fr. Lat. *desertus* 'deserted, abandoned'. REW 2592.

3. Ir. *fāss* : Lat. *vāstus* 'waste, desert', OHG *wuosti*, etc. 'waste', prob. fr. an extension of the root in Lat. *vacuus*, etc., above, 2. Walde-P. 1.219. Ernout-M. 1075 f.

Ir. *folam*, NIr. *folamh*, Br. *goullo* (cf. OW *gwallau* 'pour out', W. *gollwng* 'let go, loose'), fr. a cpd. of, Ir. *fo-*, etc. (**upo-*), but second part dub. Pedersen 1.34 (: Ir. *lām* 'hand'; semantic development?). Ernault, Dict. étym. s.v. *gollo* (: Lat. *languēre* 'be weary', *laxus* 'slack', etc.).

W. *gwag* fr. Lat. *vac(u)us* (above, 2). Loth, Mots lat. 174 f.

4. Goth. *laus* = ON *lauss* 'loose, free', also 'empty', cf. *sigla lausu skipi (lausum kili)* 'sail with empty ship (keel)', cf. also NIcel. *laust embætti* 'vacancy in an office'; similarly Du. *een loze noot* 'a hollow nut' (cf. van Wijk, IF 35.265), OE *lēas* 'loose, free from, without', etc. : Skt. *lu-* 'cut off', Grk. *λύω* 'loose, free', etc. Walde-P. 2.408. Feist 325.

ON *tōmr*, Dan., Sw. *tom*, OE *tōm*, ME *toom*, with suffix OS *tōmig*, OHG *zuomīg*, cf. ON *tōm* 'leisure', etym.? Falk-Torp 1269 f. NED s.v. *toom*, adj.

OE *īdel*, ME *idel* (NE *idle*), OS *īdal*, OHG *ītal*, MHG *ītel* (NHG *eitel*), etym. dub., but perh. as orig. 'going freely' (> 'loose' > 'empty'), fr. the root **ei-* 'go' (Grk. *εἶμι*, Lat. *īre*, etc.); better than orig. 'merely appearing' : Grk. *αἴθω* 'burn', etc. Walde-P. 1.5, 103 (but favoring the latter connection). Van Wijk, IF 35.266. Wood, MLN 17.6.

OE *ǣmetig, ǣmtig* (also 'at leisure' and 'unmarried'), ME *amti, em(p)ti*, NE *empty*, deriv. of OE *ǣmta, ǣmetta* 'leisure', etym. dub., but perh. a cpd. of *ǣ-* (neg. pref. as in *ǣ-wǣde* 'unclothed', etc., OHG *ā-*) and deriv. of root in *metan* 'measure, mete out' (12.54) hence orig. 'lack of assignment', then 'leisure'. Buck Cl. Ph. 15.198.

OE *lǣre, gelǣre*, ME *lere*, OHG *lāri*, MHG *lǣr(e)*, NHG *leer*, perh. : OE, OHG *lesan* 'collect, gather, glean' and first used of a field whose crop had been harvested and hence was 'empty'. Kluge-G. 350.

Du. *ledig, leeg* : NHG *ledig*, MHG *ledec* 'free (from difficulty), unmarried', ON *liðugr* 'free, unhindered, easily moved', prob. as more orig. in the latter sense fr. OHG *lid*, ON *liðr*, etc. 'limb, joint'. Walde-P. 1.158 f. Falk-Torp 630. Van Wijk, IF 35.265.

5. Lith. *tuščias*, Lett. *tukšs*, disputed, but prob. : ChSl. *tŭštĭ* (renders *κενός*), Skt. *tuccha-, tucchya* 'empty, vain', Av. *tuš-* in caus. *taošaya-* 'let loose, free', etc. Mühl.-Endz. 4.256 ff. Trautmann 333. Walde-P. 1.714.

6. ChSl. *tŭštĭ* : Skt. *tuccha-*, etc. (above, 5).

ChSl. *prazdĭnŭ* (in Gospels renders *ἀργός* 'idle', but 'empty' in neg. cpd. *neprazdĭna* 'pregnant'), SCr. *prazan*, Boh. *prázdný*, Pol. *próżny*, etym.? Miklosich 259 f. Brückner 439.

Russ. *pustoj* : ChSl. *pustŭ* 'desert, waste' (and so in most modern Slavic languages), OPruss. *pausto* 'wild', ChSl. *pustiti*, Russ. *pustit'* 'let, let go', Grk. *παύω* 'cause to cease'. Walde-P. 2.1. Trautmann 208 f.

7. Skt. *çūnya-* (the source, through Arab. *ṣifr*, of NE *cipher* and *zero*, with the other similar Eur. forms) : *çvā-* 'swell' (pple. *çūna-*), but line of semantic development not clear. Walde-P. 1.365. Günther, KZ 68.139 ff.

Skt. *rikta-*, pple. of *ric-* 'empty, leave, release' : Grk. *λείπω*, Lat. *linquere* 'leave, let', etc. Walde-P. 2.396.

Skt. *tuccha-*, *tucchya-* : ChSl. *tŭštĭ*, etc. (above, 5).

13.23 PART (sb.)

Grk.	*μέρος*	Goth.	*dails*	Lith.	*dalis*
NG	*μέρος, κομμάτι*	ON	*hlutr, deild*	Lett.	*dal'a*
Lat.	*pars*	Dan.	*del*	ChSl.	*čęstĭ (dělŭ)*
It.	*parte*	Sw.	*del*	SCr.	*dio, čest*
Fr.	*partie*	OE	*dǣl*	Boh.	*díl, část*
Sp.	*parte*	ME	*deel, part*	Pol.	*część, dział*
Rum.	*parte*	NE	*part*	Russ.	*čast'*
Ir.	*rann, cuit, pairt*	Du.	*deel*	Skt.	*bhāga-, aṅça-*
NIr.	*cuid*	OHG	*teil*	Av.	*baga-, baγā-*
W.	*rhan*	MHG	*teil*		
Br.	*rann*	NHG	*teil*		

Words for 'a part' as opposite of 'the whole' are such as are also used in general for 'portion, share', often also 'locality, region', and are derived from various roots for 'share, divide', etc.

1. Grk. *μέρος* (also 'share, portion' beside *μερίς* 'portion') : Hom. *μείρομαι* 'receive as one's portion', *μερίζω* 'divide', *μόρος* 'lot, fate', etc., Lat. *merēre* 'receive as portion or price', 'earn, merit', fr. a root *(*s*)*mer-*, perh. the same as *(*s*)*mer-* in Lat. *memor* 'mindful of', Skt. *smṛ-* 'remember'. Walde-P. 2.690. Ernout-M. 609 f. Walde-H. 1.75 f.

NG *μέρος* in pop. speech mostly 'locality, region' and in sense of 'part' often replaced by *κομμάτι* 'piece', fr. a dim. form of class. Grk. *κόμμα* 'piece cut off' (also 'stamp', etc.), fr. *κόπτω* 'strike, cut'.

2. Lat. *pars, -tis* (> It., Sp., Rum. *parte;* Fr. *part* now mostly 'portion, share'), prob. fr. the root of Ir. *ro-ir* '(he) granted', Grk. *ἔπορον* 'gave, brought', *πέπρωται* 'it is fated', and also Lat. *parere* 'bear, give birth to' (fr. 'obtain, get'). Walde-P. 2.41. Ernout-M. 735.

Fr. *partie* (now usual for 'part' of a whole, for older *part*), fr. *partir* in arch. sense 'divide' (now 'part, leave'), fr. VLat. *partīre* (for Lat. *partīrī*) 'divide', fr. *pars* (above). REW 6259.

3. Ir., Br. *rann*, W. *rhan*, generally taken as (**pr̥snā-*?) : Lat. *pars* (above, 2). Pedersen 1.52. Stokes 227. Or as orig. 'border' : OE *rand* 'border', etc.? Loth, RC 41.400 f. (but see also 43.411 f.).

Ir. *cuit*, NIr. *cuid* (in the older language chiefly 'portion, share') : W. *peth* 'thing', Br. *pez* 'piece', further connection doubtful. Pedersen 1.160 (: ChSl. *čęstĭ* 'part', etc.; rejected by Walde-P. 1.393). Henry 222.

Ir. *pairt* (NIr. *pāirt* now 'regard, sympathy', etc.), fr. Lat. *pars*. Vendryes, De hib. voc. 164.

4. Goth. *dails*, OE *dǣl*, OS *dēl* (MLG > Sw. *del*, and Dan. *del* as old masc.), ME *deel* (NE *deal*), etc., general WGmc., ON *deild* (> Dan. *del* as old fem.), beside vb. forms, Goth. *dailjan*, ON *deila*, OE *dǣlan*, etc. 'divide', etym. dub. (cf. ChSl. *dělŭ*, etc., below, 6). Falk-Torp 139. Feist 114.

ON *hlutr, hluti*, 'share, lot' and also 'part' : OE *hlot*, Goth. *hlauts* 'lot', etc., root connection dub. Walde-P. 1.493. Falk-Torp 651. Feist 262.

ME, NE *part*, fr. Fr. *part* (above, 2).

5. Lith. *dalis*, Lett. *dal'a*, OPruss. *dellīks*, with vbs. Lith. *dalyti*, Lett. *dalīt* 'divide' : Russ. *dolja* 'lot, share', Skt. *dala-* 'fragment, piece', fr. the root in Skt. *dal-* 'burst', Lat. *dolāre* 'hew', etc. Walde-P. 1.811. Mühl.-Endz. 1.435. Berneker 209.

6. ChSl. *čęstĭ*, SCr. *čest*, etc., general Slavic, as orig. 'bite, bit' : Lith. *kasti*, Lett. *kuost*, SCr. *kusati*, etc., 'bite'. Walde-P. 1.393. Berneker 155.

ChSl. *dělŭ* (late, but *raz-dĕliti* reg. in Gospels for 'divide'), SCr. *dio*, Boh. *díl*, Pol. *dział* (Russ. *djal* obs., but *delit'*, *razdelit'* 'divide'), prob. (as **dai-lo*), fr. the root **dā(i)-* in Skt. *dā-* 'cut off, divide, separate', Grk. *δαίομαι* 'divide, distribute', etc.; relationship to Goth. *dails*, etc. dub. (both as **dhai-l-* fr. a parallel root **dhā(i)-*??). Walde-P. 1.764, 811. Berneker 195.

7. Skt. *bhāga-*, also 'portion, share, allotment', Av. *baga-*, *baγa-* 'share, lot', *baγā-* 'part, piece' (of the holy word) : Skt. *bhaj-* 'deal out, divide, distribute', Av. *bag-* 'allot (as one's share)'. Walde-P. 2.127 f. Barth. 921 f.

Skt. *aṅça-* (Av. *ąsa-* 'party', i.e. one of the two religious divisions), prob. (as orig. 'share') : Skt. *naç-*, Av. *nas-* 'reach, attain'. Walde-P. 1.128. Uhlenbeck 1. Barth. 361.

13.24 HALF

(Adj. Except as Noted)

Grk.	*ἥμισυς; ἡμι-*	Goth.	*halbs*	Lith.	*pusė* (sb.), *pus-*
NG	*μισός*	ON	*halfr*	Lett.	*puse* (sb.), *pus-*
Lat.	*dīmidius; sēmi-*	Dan.	*halv*	ChSl.	*polŭ* (sb.)
It.	*mezzo; metà* (sb.)	Sw.	*halv*	SCr.	*po* (sb.)
Fr.	*demi; moitié* (sb.)	OE	*healf; sām-*	Boh.	*poloviční; půl* (sb.)
Sp.	*medio; mitad* (sb.)	ME	*half*	Pol.	*połowiczny; poł* (sb.)
Rum.	*jumătate* (sb.)	NE	*half*	Russ.	*pol-(polu-)*
Ir.	*leth* (sb.), *leth-*	Du.	*half*	Skt.	*ardha-; sāmi-*
NIr.	*leath* (sb.), *leath-*	OHG	*halp; sāmi-*	Av.	*naēma-*
W.	*hanner*	MHG	*halp*		
Br.	*hanter*	NHG	*halb*		

In contrast to the words for 'a third', 'a fourth', and other fractions, which are all numeral derivs., those for 'half' (adj.) or 'a half' have no connection with a numeral. There is an inherited group which probably rests on the notion of a single or even division, and in Latin 'divided in the middle' was 'half'. Other words, some of them used also for 'side' and some cognate with verbs for 'cut, divide', etc., must have gained the meaning 'half' through specialization of 'part, division'.

1. IE **sēmi-* in cpds., prob. with reference to a single or even division : IE **sem-*, **somo-*, etc., in Grk. *ὁμός*, Skt. *sama-*, Goth. *sama* 'same', Lat. *semel* 'once', Grk. *εἷς* 'one', etc. Walde-P. 2.493 (with doubt of the connection with **sem-*, etc.). Ernout-M. 921 f.

Grk. *ἡμι-* in cpds., hence *ἥμι-τυς*, orig. sb. 'a half', then as adj. (cf. Cret. *ἡμιτύεκτον*), Att. *ἥμισυς* (adj., with neut. *ἥμισυ* as sb.), many dial. also *ἥμισσος* (**ἡμιτϝος*), Cret. *ἡμίνα* sb. 'half'; *ἥμισυς* > NG pop. *μισός* adj., *τὸ μισό* sb.; Lat. *sēmi-*, OE, OS *sām-*, OHG *sāmi-*, Skt. *sāmi-* in cpds.

Of similar ultimate orig. prob. W. *hanner*, adj. and sb. (in cpds. *haner-*), Br. *hanter* adj. and sb. (fr. **sṃ-tero-*) : Grk. *ἅτερος*, Att. *ἕτερος* 'one or the other of two'. Walde-P. l.c. Pedersen 1.138 (with different root connection).

2. Lat. *dīmidius* (VLat. *dīmedius* > Fr. *demi*), orig. (with *pars*) 'divided in the middle', cpd. of *dis-* 'apart' and *medius* 'middle' (12.37). From the latter, It. *mezzo*, Sp. *medio*, and through sb. Lat. *medietās* 'middle, center' and 'half', It. *metà*, Fr. *moitié*, Sp. *mitad*. Ernout-M. 601. REW 2644, 5461.

Rum. *jumătate* (sb.), fr. Lat. *medietās* or *dimidietās*, with peculiar phonetic development. Tiktin 879, Elementarbuch 208. Densusianu 295 f. (assuming blend with a loanword fr. Alb. *gjysmë* 'half', this fr. Grk. *ἥμισυς*).

3. Ir. *leth* ('side' and 'half'), NIr. *leath* (fem. 'side', masc. 'half'), orig. 'side' : Lat. *latus* 'side' (12.36). Hence for adj. mostly cpds. with *leth-*, *leath-*.

W. *hanner*, Br. *hanter*, see above, 1.

4. Goth. *halbs*, etc., general Gmc., perh. (as orig. 'divided') : Lat. *scalpere* 'cut, carve, scrape, scratch', Lith. *sklempti* 'hew off smooth, polish', Grk. *σκόλοψ* 'pointed stake', etc. Walde-P. 2.595. Falk-Torp 375. Feist 239.

5. Lith. *pusė*, Lett. *puse* sb. (with gen.), also freq. Lith., Lett. *pus-* in cpds. : OPruss. *possisawaite* 'mittwoch', *esse ... pausan* 'on the part of', Toch. A *poṣi* 'side, wall'. Mühl.-Endz. 3.426. Fraenkel, IF 50.229.

6. ChSl. *polŭ*, SCr. *po* (dial. *pol*), Pol. *poł*, Boh. *půl* sbs., Russ. *pol-* (in cpds.

only in nom. and acc. with gen. of second member, in other cases *polu-* with second member regularly inflected), also adjs. Boh. *polovičnі*, Pol. *połowiczny;* Slavic *polŭ* 'half' = *polŭ* 'side, shore' (cf. above Ir. *leth* 'side, half') : ChSl. *rasplatiti*, OHG *spaltan* 'split', Skt. *spāṭaya-* 'split', etc. Walde-P. 2.678. Miklosich 256 f. Brückner 429.

7. Skt. *ardhá-*, beside sb. *árdha-* 'side, part, half' : Lith. *ardyti* 'divide, split', etc. Walde-P. 1.143. Uhlenbeck 14.

Av. *naēma-* (NPers. *nēm*) : Skt. *nema-* 'the one, the other', also 'half', orig. dub. Barth. 1036. Uhlenbeck 151.

13.31. NOTE ON THE NUMERALS

No class of words, not even those denoting family relationship, has been so persistent as the numerals in retaining the inherited words.

Except for some suffix-variation and actual substitution in the case of 'one' (13.32), the IE words for 'one' to 'ten' have persisted everywhere with only slight changes other than phonetic; likewise the IE word for 'hundred', while for 'thousand' there are several different groups.

The '-teens' are expressed by cop. cpds. of the digits with 'ten', with the exception of the Gmc. words for 'eleven' and 'twelve' (Goth. *ain-lif*, *twa-lif*) and the whole Lith. series (*vienio-lika*, *dvylika*, *try-lika*, *keturio-lika*, etc. for 11–19), which are cpds. with a form of IE **leikʷ-* 'leave, remain' (Grk. λείπω, etc., Walde-P. 2.396 f.), hence orig. 'one over' (the ten), etc.

For 20–90 certain IE cpds., the second part of which seems to be obscurely related to the numeral for 'ten', have been partly retained (for 20 Grk. εἴκοσι, Dor. ϝίκατι, Lat. *vīginti*, Skt. *viṅçati-*, etc.; for the others Grk. -κοντα, Lat. *-ginta*, Skt. *-çat-*, etc.), and partly replaced by more transparent phrases or cpds. (as for 20 Goth. *twai tigjus*, OE *twen-tig*, Lith. *dvi-dešimt*, Rum. *două-zeci*).

The decimal system, based on counting the fingers, prevails. But the influence of a duodecimal or sexagesimal system is indicated by certain breaks in the type of formation as that between 12 and 13 in Gmc., between 60 and 70 in Grk., Goth., etc.

The ordinals are formed from the cardinals, mostly with a *-to-* or *-mo-* suffix. Exceptions are those for 'first' (13.33), and many of those for 'second', which are literally 'the other' (Goth. *anþar*, OE *ōþer*, ChSl. *vŭtorŭ*, etc.) or 'the following' (Lat. *secundus* : *sequī* 'follow'; similarly Grk. δεύτερος prob. orig. 'the one after', cf. Hom. δεύτατος 'last').

For detailed discussion of the IE numerals, cf. Brugmann, Grd. 2.2.1 ff.

In the following we list and discuss only those for 'one' and 'first', and for 'three' with derivs., choosing these last as convenient illustrations of the various types.

13.32 ONE

Grk.	εἷς	Goth.	*ains*	Lith.	*vienas*
NG	ἕνας	ON	*einn*	Lett.	*viens*
Lat.	*ūnus*	Dan.	*en*	ChSl.	*jedinŭ*
It.	*uno*	Sw.	*en*	SCr.	*jedan*
Fr.	*un*	OE	*ān*	Boh.	*jeden*
Sp.	*uno*	ME	*oon*	Pol.	*jeden*
Rum.	*un*	NE	*one*	Russ.	*odin*
Ir.	*ōen*	Du.	*een*	Skt.	*eka-*
NIr.	*aon*	OHG	*ein*	Av.	*aēva-*, OPers. *aiva*
W.	*un*	MHG	*ein*		
Br.	*unan*	NHG	*ein*		

1. IE **oi-no-*, etc., derivs. of a pronominal *oi-* beside *i-* in Lat. *is*, etc. Walde-P. 1.101. Ernout-M. 1127 f.

**oi-no-*. Grk. οἰνός, οἰνή 'one on the dice, ace', but as numeral replaced by εἷς; OLat. *oinos*, *oenus*, Lat. *ūnus* (> It., Sp. *uno*, Fr., Rum. *un*); Ir. *ōin*, *ōen*, NIr. *aon*, W. *un*, Br. *unan*, *eun;* Goth. *ains*, OE *ān*, etc., general Gmc.; OPruss. *ains*, Lith. *vienas*, Lett. *viens* (init. *v* obscure); ChSl. *ino-* in cpds., otherwise *jedinŭ* (*jed-*, *ed-* prefixed pronominal element), SCr. *jedan*, Boh., Pol. *jeden*, Russ. *odin;* cf. Skt. pron. *ena-*.

**oi-wo-*. Av. *aēva-*, OPers. *aiva-*; cf. Grk. οἶος, Cypr. οἶϝος 'alone', and Skt. *eva* 'thus'.

**oi-ko-*. Skt. *eka-*, cf. *aika-* in Indic text in Hittite records.

2. Grk. εἷς, gen. ἑνός, fr. ἕνς (Cret.), *ἕμς, fem. μία fr. *σμία; Toch. A *sas* masc., *säm̥* fem., B *se* : Grk. ὁμός, Skt. *sama-*, Goth. *sama* 'same', Grk. ἅμα 'together', Lat. *semel*, Skt. *sa-kṛt* 'once', etc. Walde-P. 2.488 ff. NG pop. ἕνας with new nom. to acc. ἕνα.

13.33 ALONE, ONLY (adj.; adv.)

Grk.	μόνος; μόνον	Goth.	*ains, ainaha; þatainei*	Lith.	*vienas (sau), vienatinis; tik(tai)*
NG	μοναχός, μόνος; μόνον	ON	*einn, einga-*	Lett.	*viens pats, vienīgs; vien, tik(ai)*
Lat.	*sōlus, ūnus, ūnicus; sōlum, tantum, modo*	Dan.	*alene, eneste; alene, kun, blot*	ChSl.	*jedinŭ; jedino*
It.	*solo, unico; solo, solamente, soltanto*	Sw.	*allena, ende; allenast, blott*	SCr.	*sam, jedini; samo*
				Boh.	*sám, jediný; jen, toliko*
Fr.	*seul, unique; seulement*	OE	*āna, ānga, ānlīc; ān*		
		ME	*alone, onely; onely, but*	Pol.	*sam, jedyny; jeno, tylko*
Sp.	*solo, único; solo, solamente*	NE	*alone, only; only, but*	Russ.	*odin, jedinstvennyj; tol'ko*
Rum.	*singur, unic; numai*	Du.	*alleen, eenig; alleen, slechts*		
Ir.	*ōenur; nammā*			Skt.	*eka-, ekaka-*
NIr.	*aonar, aon; amhāin*	OHG	*eino, einac; ekkorodo*	Av.	*aēva-*
W.	*unig; yn unig*	MHG	*aleine, einec; ni wære, niwer*		
Br.	*e-unan, unan-penn; nemet, hep-ken*	NHG	*allein, einzig; nur, bloss*		

Where the adjectives 'alone' and 'only' are distinguished as in NE *alone* vs. *only*, NHG *allein* vs. *einzig*, etc., the differentiation is idiomatic and mainly one of position, predicative vs. attributive. In many languages the same word is used in both ways, e.g. Grk. μόνος, Lat. *sōlus*, Fr. *seul*, Goth. *ains*, etc. The underlying notion is an emphatic 'one', and it is most commonly expressed by

the numeral, either by itself or in derivs. or phrases.

1. 'One' used by itself for 'alone'. So Lat. *ūnus* (beside the more distinctive *sōlus*), Goth. *ains* (reg. for μόνος), ON *einn*, OE *ān*, etc., but esp. with weak inflection OE *āna*, OHG *eino;* Lith. *vienas;* ChSl. *jedinŭ*, Russ. *odin*, and for attrib. 'only' with def. adj. inflection, SCr. *jedini*, etc. (but Russ. *jedinyj* now arch., usually *jedinstvennyj*); Skt. *eka-*, Av. *aēva-*.

Derivs. of 'one'. Grk. μόνος (? see below, 2); Lat. *ūnicus* (> It. *unico*, etc.); Ir. *ōenur*, NIr. *aonar*, W. *unig;* Goth. *ainaha* (for μονογενής), ON *einga-*, OE *ānga*, OHG *einac*, *einig*, MHG *einec*, Du. *eenig*, NHG (*einig* obs. in this sense, replaced by) *einzig;* OE *ānlīc*, ME *onely*, NE *only;* Sw. *ende*, Dan. *eneste;* Lith. *vienatinis*, Lett. *vienīgs;* Skt. *ekaka-;* cf. also, fr. stem **sem-* in words for 'same', Rum. *singur* 'alone', fr. Lat. *singulus* 'single' (Ernout-M. 944 f. REW 1945) and SCr., Boh., Pol. *sam* 'alone' (ChSl. *samŭ* 'self').

Phrases with 'one'. Br. *e-unan* (*e* poss. pron.), *unan-penn* (*penn* 'head'), etc. (Vallée s.v. *seul*); ME *al(l) on(e)*, *alone*, NE *alone* (hence *lone*, *lonely*, *lonesome*, now mostly in emotional sense, as also NHG *einsam*), LG *alēne* (> Dan. *alene*, Sw. *allena*), MHG *aleine*, NHG *allein*, fr. *all* as adv. 'wholly' and word for 'one'; Lith. *vienas sau* (*sau* 'for oneself'), Lett. *viens pats* (*pats* 'self').

2. Grk. μόνος, Ion. μοῦνος (*μονϝος), generally taken (after Brugmann) as cognate with μανός, μᾱνός (*μανϝος) 'thin (in density), rare', etc. (12.66). Walde-P. 2.266 f. Ernout-M. 618. Miss Hahn, Language 18.88 f., reviving and improving an older suggestion, derives fr. *σμονϝος, formed fr. **sem-* in Grk. εἷς, μία (*σμία), ἕν 'one', Grk. ὁμός, Goth. *sama*, Skt. *sama-* 'same', etc. This is better on the semantic side, as in line with the most common source of 'alone' (above, 1), and quite possible, though complicated, on the formal side. Hence μοναχός 'unique', NG = μόνος.

3. Lat. *sōlus* (> It., Sp. *solo*, Fr. *seul*), etym. dub., perh. deriv. of refl., stem seen in *sē*, *sibi* and so orig. 'by oneself'. Walde-P. 2.458. Ernout-M. 954. Brugmann, Totalität 48 f.

4. Many of the adverbs for 'only' are simply adv. forms of (or phrases with) the adjectives, e.g. Grk. μόνον, Lat. *sōlum*, Fr. *seulement*, Goth. *þatainei* (fr. *þatain* 'that one'), OE *ān* (so reg. in Gospels for 'only'), ME *onliche*, *onely*, NE *only*, Lett. *vien*, ChSl. *jedino*, SCr. *samo*, Boh. *jen*, Pol. *jeno*, etc. But many others are of quite different origin.

Lat. *tantum*, fr. *tantus* 'so great, so much', hence as 'just so much and no more' to 'only'.

Lat. *modo*, fr. *modus* 'measure'. Hence also, with the preceding, *tantummodo*.

Rum. *numai*, fr. Lat. *nōn magis* 'not more'. Cf. OFr. *ne mais—que*, Fr. *ne—que*. REW 5228.

Ir. *nammā*, NIr. *amhāin*, fr. *na* 'not' and *mā*, *mō* 'more' (13.16). Br. *nemet* also fr. negative, but formation obscure. Pedersen 1.165, 2.261.

Br. *hepken*, fr. *hep* 'without' and *ken* 'more'.

Dan. *blot*, Sw. *blott*, NHG *bloss*, fr. the corresponding adjs. meaning 'naked, bare' (4.99). Cf. NE *barely*.

Dan. *kun*, fr. older *ikkun*, this fr. *ikke uden* 'not without' (cf. following). Falk-Torp 460.

ME, NE *but*, in this sense orig. with neg., fr. OE *ne būtan* 'not without'. NED s.v.

Du. *slechts*, fr. adj. *slecht*, now 'bad', but orig. 'level, smooth' (Goth. *slaihts*, ME, NE *slight*, etc.), with adj. development through 'evenly, directly, wholly' > 'only'. Franck-v. W. 614.

OHG *ekkorodo*, *ekrodo* : ON *ekla* 'dearth, want', adv. 'scarcely', Lat. *egēre* 'be in need'. Walde-P. 1.114.

MHG *ni wære*, *ni wer*, NHG *nur*, orig. phrase 'were it not, unless'. Weigand-H. 2.319. Kluge-G. 421.

On the distribution of *nur* and *bloss*, cf. Kretschmer, Wortgeogr. 130 f.

Lith. *tik*, earlier *tikt*, *tiktai*, Lett. *tik(ai)* : Lith. *tiek* 'so much', *tikti* 'fit, suit', with development through 'exactly, just' to 'only'.

Boh. *toliko*, Pol. *tylko*, Russ. *tol'ko*, fr. adj. ChSl. *tolikŭ*, etc. 'so much', with same development as in Lat. *tantum*.

13.34 FIRST

Grk.	πρῶτος	Goth.	*frumist, fruma*	Lith.	*pirmas*
NG	πρῶτος	ON	*fyrstr*	Lett.	*pirmais*
Lat.	*prīmus*	Dan.	*første*	ChSl.	*prŭvŭ*
It.	*primo*	Sw.	*förstr*	SCr.	*prvi*
Fr.	*premier*	OE	*fyrst, forma, fyrmest, ǣrest*	Boh.	*první*
Sp.	*primero*			Pol.	*pierwszy*
Rum.	*prim (întîiŭ)*	ME	*first(e)*	Russ.	*pervyj*
Ir.	*cētne, cēt-*	NE	*first*	Skt.	*prathama-*
NIr.	*cēad*	Du.	*eerste*	Av.	*fratəma-*
W.	*cyntaf*	OHG	*ēristo, furisto*		
Br.	*kenta*	MHG	*ēr(e)st*		
		NHG	*erst*		

The words for 'first' have no connection with the cardinal for 'one'. Most of them belong to a group in which the original sense was 'foremost'.

1. Derivs., with various suffixes, of IE **pro* 'before, in front' (Grk. πρό, Lat. *pro*, Goth. *fra*, Skt. *pra*, etc.) or allied forms. Walde-P. 2.29 ff., esp. 33, 37.

Grk. πρῶτος, Dor. πρᾶτος (these two not fr. the same form; πρᾶτος fr. **pṝ-to-*, a blend with **pṝ-mo-* seen in Lith. *pirmas;* **pṝ-* also in Skt. *pūrva-* 'former'; Schwyzer, Gr. Gram. 595); Lat. *prīmus* (fr. **prīs-mo-*, cf. Pael. *prismu* 'prima' and Lat. *prīscus;* Umbr. *promo* 'primum' adv., like Grk. πρόμος 'foremost man'), whence It. *primo*, Rum. *prim*, but Fr. *premier*, Sp. *primero* fr. Lat. *prīmārius* 'of the first rank' (of persons); ON *fyrstr*, Dan. *først*, Sw. *först*, OE *fyrst*, ME, NE *first*, OHG *furisto* (NHG *fürst* 'prince'), Goth. *fruma*, *frumist*, OE *forma*, *fyrmest;* Lith. *pirmas*, Lett. *pirmais;* ChSl. *prŭvŭ*, etc., general Slavic (cf. Skt. *pūrva-* 'former'); Skt. *prathama-*, Av. *fratəma-*.

2. Rum. *întîiŭ*, once the usual ordinal (*prim* a Latinism), fr. **antāneus*, deriv. of Lat. *ante* 'before'. Pușcariu 883, 1384.

3. Ir. *cētne*, *cēt-* in cpds., NIr. *cēad*, W. *cyntaf*, Br. *kenta* (cf. Gall. *Cintugnātus* 'first born'), prob. : ChSl. *načęti* 'begin', *konŭ* 'beginning', Lat. *recēns* (*re-cēns*) 'fresh, young', Goth. *hindumists* 'outermost'. Walde-P. 1.398. Pedersen 1.120. Brugmann, Grd. 2.2.52.

4. OE *ǣrest* (NE *erst* 'in former time'), OHG *ēristo*, MHG *ēr(e)st*, NHG *erst;* superl. of Goth. *air* 'early', OE *ǣr* (NE *ere*), OHG *ēr* (NHG *ehe*) 'early, formerly', hence orig. 'first' in time. Walde-P. 1.3. NED s.v. *erst*, Weigand-H. 1.405, 469.

13.35 LAST (adj.)

Grk.	*τελευταῖος, ὕστατος, ἔσχατος*	Goth.	*aftumists, spēdists*	Lith.	*paskutinis*
NG	*τελευταῖος, στερνός*	ON	*sīðastr*	Lett.	*pēdīgs*
Lat.	*ultimus, postrēmus, extrēmus, novissimus*	Dan.	*sidst*	ChSl.	*poslědĭnĭjĭ*
It.	*ultimo*	Sw.	*sist*	SCr.	*posljednji, zadnji*
Fr.	*dernier*	OE	*læt(e)mest, lætest, æftemest*	Boh.	*poslední*
Sp.	*ultimo*	ME	*last*	Pol.	*ostatni*
Rum.	*ultim*	NE	*last*	Russ.	*poslednij*
Ir.	*dedenach, derednach*	Du.	*laatst*	Skt.	*uttama-, antima-*
NIr.	*deireannach*	OHG	*lazzōst, lezzest*	Av.	*ustəma-*
W.	*olaf, diweddaf*	MHG	*lezzist, lest*		
Br.	*diweza*	NHG	*letzt*		

Many of the adjectives for 'last' are derivs. (most of them in superl. form) of words for 'up, out, after, behind' or 'late'. Several are formed from nouns for 'end', and a few from verbs for 'follow' (or through this sense from a noun for 'footstep, trace') or 'be left, remain'.

1. Grk. ὕστατος : Skt. *uttama-* ('highest' and 'last'), Av. *ustəma-*, superl. (beside comp. Grk. ὕστερος, Skt. *uttara-*) of an adv. seen in Skt. *ud-* 'up, out', Goth., OE *ut* 'out', etc. Walde-P. 1.189 f.

Grk. τελευταῖος (the most common prose word), deriv. of τελευτή 'end' (14.26).

Grk. ἔσχατος, 'uttermost, farthest' and 'last' in time (in this sense Pind.+, the only word in NT, and freq. in pap.), deriv. of ἐξ 'out'. Walde-P. 1.116 (with refs.).

NG ὑστερινός, pop. στερνός, in earliest use 'latter, next', deriv. of ὕστερος (cf. above, 1).

2. Lat. *ultimus* (> It., Sp. *ultimo*, Rum. *ultim*, all learned forms), superl. (beside comp. in *ultrā* 'beyond', etc.) based on the pron. stem seen in *uls* 'beyond', OLat. *ollus* = *ille*, etc. Walde-P. 1.84. Ernout-M. 475, 1121.

Lat. *extrēmus, postrēmus*, superl. formations (beside comp. in *extrā, posterus*, etc.) based on *ex* 'out' (cf. Grk. ἔσχατος) and *post* 'after'. Ernout-M. 313, 797.

Lat. *novissimus*, superl. of *novus* 'new', hence lit. 'newest, latest' but frequently 'last', even in position (in the Vulgate the reg. rendering of Grk. ἔσχατος).

Fr. *dernier*, fr. OFr. *deerrain, derrain*, deriv. of *derrière* 'backwards, behind', fr. Lat. *dē retrō* id. (*retrō* fr. *re-* like *intrō* fr. *in*). Ernout-M. 854. REW 2582.

3. Ir. *dedenach*, W. *diweddaf*, Br. *diweza*, derivs. of Ir. *deod*, W. *diwedd*, Br. *diwes* 'end' (14.26). Pedersen 1.309.

Ir. *derednach* (K. Meyer, Contrib. 619), NIr. *deireannach*, deriv. of Ir. *dered*, NIr. *deireadh* 'end' (12.35).

W. *olaf*, superl. form based on *ol* 'trace' and adj. 'behind'. Pedersen 2.123.

4. Goth. *aftumists* (once also *aftuma*), OE *æftemest*, superls. based on Goth. *afta* beside *aftra* 'behind, backwards', OE *æft* 'afterwards' beside *æfter* 'after', etc. Feist 12.

Goth. *spēdists* (also *spēdumists, spēdiza* once each), superl. of a form = OHG *spāti* 'late', etc. (14.17).

ON *sīðastr, sīðarstr*, Dan. *sidst*, Sw. *sist*, superl. based on ON *sīð* adv. 'late' (14.17). Falk-Torp 962.

OE *lætest, læt(e)mest* (quotable only in Northumbrian), ME, NE *last*, Du. *laatst*, OHG *lazzōst, lezzest*, MHG *lezzist, lest*, NHG *letzt* (this fr. LG), general W. Gmc., superl. of OE *læt*, OHG *laz*,

etc. 'slow, late' (14.22). NED s.v. *last* adj. Weigand-H. 2.57. Kluge-G. 356.

5. Lith. *paskutinis*, deriv. of *paskui* 'after, behind' (: Skt. *paçcā*, Lat. *post*, etc.; Walde-P. 1.79). Leskien, Bildung d. Nom. 407.

Lett. *pēdīgs*, deriv. of *pēds* 'footstep, trace' : Skt. *pād-*, Lat. *pēs, pedis*, etc. 'foot'. (Suffix = Lith. *-ingas*, Leskien, Bildung d. Nom. 528).

6. ChSl. *poslědĭnĭjĭ*, etc., general Slavic for 'last' except Pol. (where *pośledni* is 'inferior, mediocre'), fr. ChSl. *poslěditi*, etc. 'follow' (10.52).

SCr. *zadnji*, deriv. of *zad* beside *za* 'behind, after' (cf. adv. *nazad* 'back', ChSl. *za-dŭ, na-dŭ*, etc.).

Pol. *ostatni*, fr. the vb. seen in ChSl. *ostati* 'be left, remain', Pol. *ostać* 'hold out, remain', etc., cpd. of ChSl. *stati* 'take a stand', Pol. *stać* 'stand', etc. (12.15). Brückner 385.

7. Skt. *uttama-*, Av. *ustəma-*, above, 1. Skt. *antima-*, fr. *anta-* 'end' (12.35).

	13.41 THREE	13.42 THIRD (Ordinal)	13.43 A THIRD (Fraction)	13.44 THREE TIMES	13.46 THREEFOLD, TRIPLE
Grk.	*τρεῖς*	*τρίτος*	*τριτημόριον, τρίτον*	*τρίς*	*τριπλοῦς, τριπλάσιος*
NG	*τρεῖς*	*τρίτος*	*τριτημόριον, τρίτον*	*τρεῖς φορές*	*τριπλός, τρίδιπλος*
Lat.	*trēs*	*tertius*	*tertia(pars), triēns*	*ter*	*triplex, triplus*
It.	*tre*	*terzo*	*terzo*	*tre volte*	*triplo*
Fr.	*trois*	*troisième*	*tiers*	*trois fois*	*triple*
Sp.	*tres*	*tercero*	*tercio*	*tres veces*	*triplo*
Rum.	*trei*	*al treilea*	*a treia parte, treime*	*de trei orĭ*	*triplu, întreit*
Ir.	*trī*	*tris(s)*	*trīan*	*fo thrī*	*trēode, fo thrī*
NIr.	*trī*	*triomhadh*	*trian*	*trī h-uaire, fā thrī*	*trīfhillte, trī oiread*
W.	*tri*	*tryddydd*	*traean*	*teirgwaith*	*triphlyg, tridyblyg*
Br.	*tri*	*trivet, trede*	*tre derann (trederenn, tredearn)*	*teir gwech*	*tric'hement*
Goth.	*þreis*	*þridja*		*þrim sinþam*	**þrifalþs*
ON	*þrīr*	*þriði*	*þriðjungr*	*þrysvar, þrim sinnum*	*þrīfaldr, þrennr*
Dan.	*tre*	*tredje*	*tredjedel*	*tre gange*	*tredobbelt, trefold(ig)*
Sw.	*tre*	*tredje*	*tredjedel*	*tre gånger*	*tredubbel, trefaldig*
OE	*þrī*	*þridda*	*þridda dǣl*	*þriwa, þrim sīðum*	*þrīfeald*
ME	*thre*	*thride, thirde*	*thridde part, thrid*	*thryes, thre sithes (tiden, times)*	*threfold, trәble*
NE	*three*	*third*	*third*	*three times, thrice*	*threefold, triple*
Du.	*drie*	*derde*	*derde*	*driemaal*	*drievoudig, driedubbel*
OHG	*drī*	*dritto*	*dritto teil*	*drīostunt, ze drin mālen, etc.*	*drīfalt*
MHG	*drī*	*dritte*	*dritteil*	*drīestunt, drīmal, drīes*	*drīvalt(ec)*
NHG	*drei*	*dritte*	*drittel*	*dreimal*	*dreifach, dreifaltig*
Lith.	*trys*	*trečias*	*trečdalis*	*tris kartus, tris sykius*	*trigubas, trilinkas, trejopas*
Lett.	*trīs*	*trešais*	*trešdal'a*	*trīsreiz, trīskārt*	*trīskārtīgs*
ChSl.	*trĭje*	*tretĭjĭ*	(cf. *desętina* 'tithe')	*tri kraty, trišdy*	*trigubŭ*
SCr.	*tri*	*treći*	*trećina*	*tri puta*	*trostruk*
Boh.	*tři*	*třetí*	*třetina*	*třikrat*	*trojnásobný*
Pol.	*trzy*	*trzeci*	*trzecia część*	*trzy razy, trzykroć*	*potrójny, trójnasobny*
Russ.	*tri*	*tretij*	*tret'ja čast', tret'*	*triždy, tri raza*	*trojnoj*
Skt.	*trayas*	*tṛtīya-*	*tṛ́tīya-*	*tris, trikṛtvas*	*triguṇa-*
Av.	*θrāyō*	*θritya-*	*θrišva-*	*θriš, θrisarəm, āθritīm*	(cf. *haptaiθya-, vīsaitivant-*)

	13.47 CONSISTING OF THREE KINDS (Besides Words in 13.46)	13.48 CONSISTING OF THREE TOGETHER (Coll. Adj.)	13.49 GROUP OF THREE (Coll. Sb.)	13.51 BY THREES	13.52 THREE APIECE
Grk.	*τριφάσιος*	*τρισσός, τριξός*	*τριάς*	*ἀνὰ* (or *κατὰ*) *τρεῖς*	*τρεῖς καθ' ἕκαστον (καθ' ἕνα), ἀνὰ τρεῖς*
NG			*τριάδα*	*τρεῖς τρεῖς*	*ἀπὸ τρεῖς*
Lat.	(late) *trifārius*	*trīnī (ternī)*	*trias, trīnitās*	*trēs et trēs*	*ternī*
It.			*triade*	*tre a tre*	*tre a ciascuno (a uno)*
Fr.			*triade*	*trois à trois*	*chacun trois*
Sp.			*terno*	*tres a tres*	*cada uno tres*
Rum.			*treime*	*trei cîte trei*	*cîte trei*
Ir.			*trēde, triar*	*trēdaib*	*cach trī*
NIr.		*triūrach*	*triūr*	*'na dtriūr is 'na dtriūr*	*trī an ceann*
W.			*tri*	*bob yn dri*	*bob yn dri*
Br.			*trioz*	*tri ha tri*	*pep tri*
Goth.		(cf. *tweihnai*)		(*twans hwanzuh, bi twans*)	(*tweihnai*)
ON		*þrennir*	*þrenning*	*þrīr ok þrīr*	*hverjum þrīr, þrennir*
Dan.			*trehed*	*tre og tre*	*hver tre*
Sw.			*trehet*	*tre och tre*	*var tre*
OE		*þrinna*	*þrines*	*þrīm and þrīm*	*ǣlc þrī*
ME			*þrinness, thresum*	*by thres*	*ech thre*
NE			*triad, trio, threesome*	*by threes, three by three*	*three each, three apiece*
Du.			*drieheid*	*bij drieën, drie aan drie*	*elk drie*
OHG			*drinissa*	*io drī*	*io drī*
MHG			*drīheit*	*ie drī*	*ie drī*
NHG	*dreierlei*		*dreiheit*	*zu dreien, je drei, drei und drei*	*je drei*
Lith.	*trejopas (trejokas)*	*treji*	*trejetas*	*po tris*	*po tris*
Lett.	*trijāds*	*treji*	*trijādība*	*pa trim*	*pa trim*
ChSl.	*trojakŭ*	*trojĭ*, neut. sg. *troje*	*trojĭca*	*po trŭmŭ*	*po trŭmŭ*
SCr.	*trojak*	*troji, troje*	*trojstvo*	*po tri*	*po tri*
Boh.	*troji*	*trojí, troje*	*trojice*	*po třech*	*po třech*
Pol.	*trojaki*	*troje*	*trojca*	*po* (or *w*) *trzech*	*po trzech*
Russ.	*trojakij*	*troje*	*troica*	*po tri*	*po tri*
Skt.	*trividha-*	*traya-, trika-*	*trayam*	*triçās* (cf. *dvā́-dvā-*)	*trayas prati-*(?)
Av.					

13.41. IE stem *tri-, nom. pl. *treyes. Walde-P. 1.753. Brugmann, Grd. 2.2.11 f.

Here belong all the words listed, likewise Alb. *tre*, Toch. B *trai*, A *tre*, fem. *trī-*, Hitt. *tri-*.

A peculiar fem. form **tis(o)res* is attested by Skt. *tisras* (cf. also *catasras*, fem. of *catvāras* 'four'), Av. *tišrō*, Ir. *teoir, teora*, MW, Br. *teir*, W. *tair*. This is prob. fr. **tri-sores* (with dissimilatory loss of *r*), a cpd. with a word for 'woman' seen in IE **swe-sor-* 'sister' and perh. Lat. *uxor* 'wife'.

13.42. The ordinals for 'third' are derived from the cardinal, most of them

in an inherited type but some in new formations.

1. Inherited type, with suffix *-to-* or *-tio-*. Walde-P. 1.753. Brugmann, Grd. 2.2.53 ff.

Suffix *-to-*. Grk. τρίτος, Toch. A *trit*.

Suffix *-tio-*. Lat. *tertius* (> It. *terzo*, OFr. *tierz*, etc.); W. *tryddydd*, Br. *trede;* Goth. *þridja*, etc., general Gmc.; Lith. *trečias*, Lett. *trešais* (OPruss. *tirtis*, but also *tīrts*); ChSl. *tretĭjĭ*, etc., general Slavic; Skt. *tṛtīya-*, Av. *θritya-*, OPers. *θritiya-*.

2. Fr. *tiers*, Sp. *tercio* (fr. Lat. *tertius*) were specialized to 'a third' (fraction), the former replaced by *troisième*, with the same new formation as the other ordinals (orig.? Meyer-Lübke, Frz. Gram. 2.177); the latter by *tercero*, like OFr. *tercier*, fr. Lat. *tertiārius* (cf. Sp. *primero*, Fr. *premier* fr. Lat. *prīmārius*).

Rum. *al treilea*, fem. *a treia*, formed fr. the cardinal with preceding article and nom.-acc. sg. of the postpositive article. Tiktin, Rum. Elementarbuch 97.

3. Ir. *tris(s), tres*, fr. **tristo-* or **tristi-*, in form like Lat. *testis* 'witness' fr. **terstis*, **tristis*. Walde-P. 1.753. Pedersen 2.135. Thurneysen, Gram. 249 f.

NIr. *triomhadh*, formed after Ir. *cethramad* 'fourth', etc., with suffix *-meto-* starting in the ordinals for 7, 9, 10. Similarly, Br. *trivet* with suffix *-eto-* after *pemp(v)et* 'fifth', etc. Pedersen 2.135.

13.43. 'A third' (fraction) is often expressed by a cpd. or phrase containing the ordinal for 'third' and the word for 'part'. Such terms are so transparent, taken in connection with 13.23 and 13.42, as to require no further comment.

Or the ordinal is used alone, either in a form agreeing with the word for part understood (as Lat. *tertia* beside *tertia pars*) or in the neuter (or later indeclinable) form. Among such forms, Fr. *tiers*, Sp. *tercio* are now specialized to the fractional sense since their replacement as ordinals by *troisième, tercero* (13.42); and Skt. *tṛ́tīya-* neut. is distinguished by the accent from the ordinal *tṛtī́ya-*.

There are also some derivs. formed with various suffixes from the ordinal or cardinal, as follows:

1. Lat. *triēns, -ntis* 'a third' in general, but esp. 'a third of an *as*', a participial deriv. like *quadrāns, sextāns*, etc. Thurneysen, IF 39.201.

2. Rum. *treime* 'trinity' and 'a third', deriv. of the cardinal with suffix *-ime* fr. Lat. *-īmen*. Meyer-Lübke, Rom. Gram. 2.486.

3. Ir. *trīan*, NIr. *trian*, W. *traean*, derivs. of the cardinal. Thurneysen, Gram. 250.

4. ON *þriðjungr*, deriv. of the ordinal with suffix *-ungr*.

OE *þrimen* (rare), OFris. *thrimin*, deriv. of the cardinal.

5. SCr. *trećina*, Boh. *třetina*, formed fr. the ordinal with suffix *-ina*, like ChSl. *desętina* 'tithe'.

6. Av. *θrišva-*, like *čaθrušva-* 'a fourth', *haptahva-* 'a seventh', formed fr. the cardinals (*paṅtahva-* 'a fifth' fr. an ordinal?) with suffix *-sva-*, IE **swo-*, and perh. : Grk. θρῖον 'fig-leaf' (*θρί-σϝον). Barth. 812. Brugmann, Grd. 2.1.200.

13.44. For 'three times' there was an IE simple adv., reflected by forms in several of the IE languages. But, just as NE *thrice* is now obsolete in common speech and replaced by *three times* (in contrast to the living *twice*), such forms were sooner or later replaced by phrases with the numeral and words for 'time', 'turn', 'going, course', 'stroke', etc.

Forms of the cardinal meaning properly 'for a third time' also came to be used for 'three times'.

1. IE **tris*, that is, **tri-s* with the stem of the cardinal and adv. *-s*, analogous to **dwi-s* 'twice'. Walde-P. 1.753.

Grk. τρίς; Lat. *ter* (fr. **tris*); Skt. *tris*, Av. *θriš*; with added suffix Av. *θrižvaṯ*; with added suffix and influenced by forms of the cardinal (cf. Loewe, KZ 47.98 ff.) ON *þrysvar*, (ODan. *thryssæ*, *trysse*, OSw. *þryswar*, *þriswa*), OE *þriwa* (*þrywa*, *þreowe*, etc.), OS *thriwo*, *thrio*, OHG *driror* (rare).

2. Grk., besides usual τρίς (above, 1), also (rarely) τριάκις, and regularly, from 'four times' on, τετράκις, πεντάκις, etc., Lac. τετράκιν, ἑπτάκιν, etc., with adv. -κις (-κιν).

Grk. τρίτον 'for a third time' was used in late times also for 'three times'. Dieterich, Untersuch. 188 f. Jannaris, Hist. Grk. Gram. § 652.

Hellenistic τρεῖς καιρούς (e.g. LXX, Ex. 34.23), phrase with καιρός 'time'.

Byz., NG τρεῖς φορὰς (φορές), phrase with φορά 'rapid motion, rush'. Cf. Grk. πίνειν κατὰ φοράν (Hippocr.) 'drink at a gulp'.

NG dial. also τρεῖς βολές, with βολή 'blow, stroke'.

3. Lat. *ter* (above, 1), and likewise *quater* 'four times', fr. **quatrus* : Av. *čaθruš* 'four times'. But from 'five times' on, *quīnquiēns*, etc., like *quotiēns* : Skt. *kiyat* 'how much', with suffix *-yent-*, *-yn̥t-*.

Umbr. *trio-per*, nom.-acc. pl. neut. of the cardinal with postpositive *-per*, as in Lat. *sem-per* 'once' (less prob. : Skt. *-kr̥t* in *sa-kr̥t* 'once', etc., below, 8), and, by analogy of such a form, Osc. *petiro-pert* 'quater' fr. **petriā-pert*.

In late Latin *tertium* and *tertiō* 'for a third time' are also used for 'three times' (like τρίτον in late Grk.). Cf. Schulze, Graeca Latina. 13 ff.

Late Lat. *tribus vicibus* (e.g. Palladius) with abl. pl. of *vicis* 'change, turn', hence Fr. *trois fois*, Sp. *tres veces*.

It. *tre volte*, with *volta* 'turn', deriv. of Lat. *volvere* 'turn around'.

Rum. *de trei ori*, with *oara* fr. Lat. *hōra* 'hour, time'. Cf. Alb. *herë* (e.g. *tricherë* 'three times'), OIt. (and dial.) *ora*, OFr. *heure* in similar phrases. But 'once' is *odată*, fr. *o* fem. of *un* 'one' and Lat. *data* 'given'. Tiktin 507 f.

For other words formerly used in such phrases, as Fr. *voie*, *coup*, *bout*, etc., cf. Meyer-Lübke, Rom. Gram. 3.65. Tobler, Verm. Beitr. 183 ff.

4. Ir. *fo thrī*, NIr. *fā thrī*, phrase with prep. *fo* 'under, by' and the cardinal. Thurneysen, Gram. 250.

NIr. *trī h-uaire* : *uair* 'hour, time' (fr. Lat. *hōra*).

W. *teirgwaith*, Br. *teir gwech*, with W. *gwaith* 'act, turn', Br. *gwech* : Ir. *fecht* 'journey' (cf. also *ōen-fecht* 'once'), Lat. *vehere* 'carry', etc. Cf. Dan. *tre gange*, etc. Walde-P. 1.250. Pedersen 1.123 f.

5. Goth. *þrim sinþam*, ON *þrim sinnum* (also pleonastic *þrysvar-sinnum*), OE *þrim sīðum*, ME *thre sithes*, phrase with dat. pl. of words for 'going, journey', OE *sīþ*, etc. : Goth. *gasinþa* 'fellow-traveler', ON *sinna*, OHG *sinnan* 'travel'. Walde-P. 2.496. NED s.v. *sithe* sb.

Dan. *tre gange*, Sw. *tre gånger*, with Dan. *gang*, Sw. *gång* 'going, course'.

ME *thre tiden* or *thre times*, with *tide* or *time* 'time' (14.11), NE *three times*.

ME *þries*, *thryes*, etc., NE *thrice*, MHG *drīes*, *drīs*, formed fr. the cardinal with adv. *-s*, after the analogy of ME *ānes*, *ōnes*, MHG *eines* 'once'.

OHG *thrīa stunta*, *drīostunt*, MHG *drīestunt*, with forms of *stunta*, *stunt* 'point of time' (NHG *stunde* 'hour').

OHG *ze drin mālen*, MHG *drīmal*, NHG *dreimal*, Du. *driemaal*, with *māl* 'point of time' : Goth. *mēl* 'time' (14.11).

For the above Gmc. expressions, and others less common, cf. R. Loewe, KZ 47.95 ff.

6. Lith. *tris kartus*, Lett. *trīskārt*, ChSl. *tri kraty*, SCr. *trikrat* (obs.), Boh. *třikrat*, Pol. *trzykroć*, Skt. *trikr̥tvas* (cf. below, 8), with a word meaning orig. 'blow', fr. the root of Lith. *kertu*, *kirsti*, Russ.-ChSl. *čritu*, *črěsti*, Skt. *kr̥t-* 'cut'. Walde-P. 2.577 ff. Berneker 576.

Lith. also *tris sykius*, with *sykis* orig. 'blow', prob. : ChSl. *sęką*, *sešti*, Lat. *secāre* 'cut'. Walde-P. 2.475.

Lett. *trīsreiz* (cf. OPruss. *ainan reisan* 'once'; Lith. dial. *tris reizus*, cf. Kurschat s.v. *reizas*), with a loanword fr. MLG *reise* 'journey', which was also used in such phrases. Mühl.-Endz. 3.507. Endzelin, BB 27.179.

7. ChSl. *tri kraty* (so reg. in Gospels), etc., above, 6.

ChSl. *triš(t)dy*, *trišdi* (Supr.), Russ. *triždy*, with forms belonging to ChSl. *chodŭ* 'going, course' (cf. *šĭdŭ* pret. pple. of *iti* 'go') : Grk. ὁδός 'way', etc.

SCr. *tri puta*, with *put* 'road, way, journey' : ChSl. *pątĭ* 'road, way'.

Pol. *trzy razy*, Russ. *tri raza*, with *raz* 'blow, stroke'.

8. Skt. (besides *tris*, above, 1) *triṣ kr̥tvas* and *tri-kr̥tvas*, a combination of either the adv. (and so pleonastic, like ON *þrysvar-sinnum*) or the stem of the cardinal with *kr̥tvas* (cf. *sakr̥t* 'once' and *bhūri kr̥tvas* 'many times' already in RV) : Lith. *tris kartus*, ChSl. *tri kraty*, above, 6. Wackernagel, Altind. Gram. 3.425 f.

Skt. also later *tri-vāram*, cpd. with *vāra-* 'appointed time, turn'. Wackernagel, op. cit. 3.427.

Av. (besides *θriš*, *θrišvaṯ*, above, 1) *θri-sarəm*, cpd. with second part prob. : *sar-* 'unite'. Barth. 810. Wackernagel, op. cit. 3.427.

Av. *ā-θritīm*, cpd. of the ordinal and so properly 'for a third time', but used mostly as 'three times'. Cf. Grk. τρίτον and late Lat. *tertium* so used. Barth. 324.

13.45. Adjectives co-ordinate with the advs. for 'three times', etc., and meaning 'occurring three times' occur only in NHG and in some of the Balto-Slavic languages most subject to German influence. NHG *dreimalig* was formed from *dreimal* in the 17th century, and probably by semantic borrowing the analogous Lett. *trīsreizējs* and *trīskārtējs* (Mühl.-Endz. 4.241), Boh. *třikrátný*, Pol. *trzykrotny*. But also Russ. *trojekratnyj*.

13.46. The multiplicative adjs., like Lat. *triplex*, etc., are mostly cpds. of words for 'fold' or the like. Their earliest extension from the literal sense must have been to 'consisting of three parts', as in Lat. *triplex mundus* 'the threefold world' (of sky, sea, and land). This sense shades off to that 'of three kinds', as in Lat. *triplex ratiō* 'a triple system, three kinds of reasoning', a notion for which there may be also other more distinctive terms (13.47). Or the notion of subordination of parts to a whole may be lost, so that 'a whole consisting of three parts' becomes 'three making up a whole, three in a group or series', as in Lat. *triplex mūrus* 'a triple wall' or *triplex aciēs* 'a triple line of battle'. In such use the multiplicatives approach the collectives (13.51). Again, a group of three may be felt as one taken three times, a given unit raised to the third power, as in Lat. *triplex equitī* 'triple pay for the horseman'. This proportional use, though occasionally marked off from the others by a distinctive formal type (as Att. τριπλάσιος) becomes in general the commonest use, and the only one which leads to a full series running up

into the high numerals ('a hundred fold', etc.).

In many of the modern languages this proportional sense, though included in the uses of the adjs. listed, is more commonly expressed by a substantive phrase 'three times as much', as Fr. *trois fois autant*, etc. (below, 4), Lith. *tris karts tiek*, Russ. *tri raza bol'še*, etc.

1. From IE **pel-*, **pelt-*, **plek-* in words for 'fold' or 'plait'. Walde-P. 1.55 f., 97.

Grk. τριπλόος, Att. τριπλοῦς, the usual type of multiplicative in all dialects and in all uses, most commonly proportional and so used even in Attic (beside τριπλάσιος). Precise origin of formation uncertain, but separation from the main group and connection with πλέω 'sail', πλόος 'voyage' improbable. Forms like ἁπλός, διπλός are analogical fr. forms like fem. sg. ἁπλῆ, neut. pl. ἁπλᾶ, and not independent formations corresponding to Lat. *triplus*, etc. Cf. also Locr. διπλεῖος, Cret. διπλεία.

Att. τριπλάσιος, proportional, fr. -πλατιος formed to -πλατος, like τριφάσιος to -φατος. Later τριπλασίων with comp. suffix. Ion. διπλήσιος, etc. (in Hdt., but not found in Ion. inscr.) with η fr. fem. διπλῆ(?).

Lat. *triplex* : *plicāre* 'fold', *plectere* 'plait', etc.; or, on account of Umbr. *tuplak* ('furca'?), more directly : Grk. δίπλαξ, τρίπλαξ 'twofold, threefold' (mostly in literal sense, as of a cloak in Homer).

Lat. *triplus* (cf. Umbr. *tripler* 'trinis'), proportional, and eventually replacing *triplex*. Hence OFr. *treble* (> ME, NE *treble*) and as bookwords It. *triplo*, Fr. *triple* (> NE *triple*), Sp. *triplo* or *triple*, Rum. *triplu*.

Goth. **þrifalþs* (cf. *fidurfalþs* 'fourfold', etc.), ON *þrīfaldr*, Dan. *trefold(ig)*, Sw. *trefaldig*, OE *þrīfeald*, ME *threfold*, NE *threefold*, OHG *drīfalt*, MHG *drīvalt(ec)*, NHG *dreifaltig*, Du. *drievoudig*.

2. A recurring phenomenon is the use of words for 'twofold, double' to indicate any degree of multiplication, that is, simply '-fold'. Thus NG pop. τρί-διπλος 'threefold', τετρά-διπλος 'fourfold', etc. Lat. *duplus* must have come to be used the same way in VLat., as indicated by phrases like It. *a tre doppj* 'threefold', etc. (numerous quots. in Voc. degli Accad. della Crusca 863), OFr. *a cent doubles* 'hundred fold', Sp. *al tres doble* 'threefold', etc. Cf. Meyer-Lübke, Rom. Gram. 3.65, Tobler, Verm. Beitr. 1.148 ff. The idiom, as well as the word passed into the Celtic and Gmc. languages. Ir. *cōic-dīabuil* 'fivefold' (K. Meyer, Contrib. 412), W. *tridyblyg* 'three-fold' (*dyblyg* fr. Lat. *duplicem*; Loth, Mots lat. 162), Du. *driedubbel*, Dan. *tredobbelt*, Sw. *tredubbel*, NHG *drei(ge)doppelt* (poet. or dial.), NE *three-double* (NED quots. fr. 16th, 17th cent.; said to be still in use locally in U.S.).

3. Other Grk. types besides τριπλοῦς.

Grk. δί-πτυχος, τρί-πτυχος (: πτύξ, πτυχή 'fold') mostly in lit. sense, as Hom. δίπτυχος λώπη 'robe with two folds', sometimes as '-fold' as δίπτυχον δῶρον.

Grk. τριφάσιος, see 13.47.

Grk. τριφυής or -φυιος, see 13.47.

Grk. τρισσός, τριξός, see 13.48.

4. In the Romance languages (beside forms cited above, 1 and 2) the proportional sense is commonly expressed by phrases like It. *tre volte tanto*, Fr. *trois fois autant*, formerly also It. *tre tante*, Fr. *trois tanz*, as still Sp. *tres tanto*. Meyer-Lübke, Rom. Gram. 3.65.

Rum. *întreit*, pple. of *întrei* 'make threefold', formed fr. the cardinal like *îndoi* 'to double'.

5. Ir. *trēode* (cf. sb. *trēde*, 13.49), deriv. of the cardinal with suffix *-de* (*-odyo-*). Pokorny KZ 47.161. Thurneysen, Gram. 222, 243.

NIr. *trifhillte* (Lane, McKenna, O'Reilly; not in Dinneen), fr. *fillim* 'fold' (9.15).

But proportional sense expressed by Ir. *fo thrī* 'three times' (13.44) or NIr. *tri oiread* (*oiread* 'amount, quantity, number').

W. *triphlyg*, deriv. of *plyg* 'fold', vb. *plygu*, fr. Lat. *plica*, *plicāre*.

W. *tridyblyg*, above, 2.

Br. *tric'hement* in proportional sense, cpd. of *kement* 'as much', and doubtless modeled on OFr. *trois tans*, etc. (above, 4).

6. Most Gmc. words, above, 1 and 2.

ON *þrennr* sg. 'threefold', pl. coll. : Lat. *trīnī* (13.51).

NHG *dreifach* (late MHG *zwīvach*, etc.), cpd. of *fach* 'compartment, part', etc. (MHG *vach* also 'fold' of a garment, hence use in place of *-valt*), OHG *fah* 'wall' = OE *fæc* 'interval of space or time' : Grk. πήγνυμι 'fix' (cf. ἅ-παξ 'once'), etc. Walde-P. 2.3. Weigand-H. 1.487. Paul, Deutsches Wtb. 152. Kluge-G. 142.

7. Lith. *trigubas* (also *dvigubas*, OPruss. *dwigubbus*, but series not carried above 'threefold'), ChSl. *trigubŭ* (with numerals 1–4, not beyond; SCr. *dvogub*, *trogub*, Russ. *sugubyj* 'double', arch.) : Lett. *gubt*, ChSl. *gŭnati* 'bend'. Berneker 360, 366.

Lith. *trilinkas* (etc., with numerals 1–9) : *lenkti* 'bend'.

Lith. *trejopas* is used in proportional sense, and this is the type that runs up to the high numbers (cf. *vaisų šimteriopą* = καρπὸν ἑκατονταπλασίονα Lk. 8.8, Trowitsch NT). It is based on an adv. phrase, a case form of the coll. *treji* (13.51) with some postpositive form of *po*, hence orig. 'by threes', etc. The use in the sense of 'of three kinds' is secondary, *-opas* taking the place of older *-okas* (13.47). Leskien, Bildung d. Nom. 515, 589. Brugmann, Distrib. 52.

Lett. *trīskārtīgs*, formed fr. *trīskārt* 'three times' (13.44).

8. ChSl. *trigubŭ*, above, 7.

The proportional sense is also expressed by the instr. sg. of *-ica* derivs. of the coll. numerals (Leskien, Gram. 120), e.g. *četvericeją* = τετραπλοῦν Lk. 19.8, *sŭtoriceją* (so Zogr., etc.; *sŭtokraticeją* Mar.) = ἑκατονταπλασίονα Lk. 8.8.

ChSl. *trojinŭ*, Boh. *trojný*, Pol. *potrójny*, Russ. *trojnoj*, deriv. of the coll. adj., ChSl. *trojĭ*, etc. (13.48).

SCr. *trostruk*, cpd. of *struk* 'stalk, form, figure' (cf. *struka* used like NHG *fach*).

Boh. *trojnásobný*, Pol. *trójnasobny*, esp. in adv. *-násob*, *-nasób*, in proportional sense, cpd. of a word for 'folding, multiplying' (Boh. *nasoba*, not separately in Pol.; orig. *na* with reflexive pron. 'on itself').

9. Skt. *triguṇa-*, etc. (full series in proportional sense), cpd. of *guṇa-* 'thread, strand'.

Less common and only with the low numerals are cpds. with *vr̥t-* 'turn', *bhuj-* 'bend', *dhātu-* 'layer', and *vayā-* 'branch' (*catur-vaya-* 'fourfold' RV).

Av. *haptaiθya-* 'of seven parts' (the earth), deriv. of *haptaθa-* 'seventh'.

Av. *vīsaitivant-* 'twenty fold', deriv. of *vīsaiti* 'twenty' with suffix *-vant-* (so *čaθwarəsaθwant-* 'forty fold', *pañčasaθwant* 'fifty fold', etc., long series in Yt. 10.116). Cf. Ved. *çatavant*, *sahasravant-* in similar use.

13.47. The notion 'consisting of three kinds' is included among the various uses of the multiplicative adjs. for 'threefold, triple' (13.46), and of some of the coll. adjs. (13.48). In some languages there are also more distinctive types for this notion, though few of them are in such common use as NHG *dreierlei*.

1. Grk. (Ion.) δι-φάσιος, τρι-φάσιος, e.g. Hdt. διφασίοισι δὲ γράμμασι χρέωνται 'they [the Egyptians] use two kinds of writing', μουνομαχία τριφασία 'a duel of three kinds' (man vs. man, horse vs. horse, dog vs. dog), fr. -φατος (cf. δίφατος Hesych.), this : φαίνομαι 'appear'. So Brugmann, Grd. 2.2.71 (vs. 2.1.186, followed by Walde-P. 1.680, Boisacq 191).

τρι-(δι-)φυής and -φυιος (: φύσις 'nature'), e.g. Hdt. ἔχιδνα διφυής 'viper of double form' (woman and snake), Theophr. διφυεῖς καὶ τριφυεῖς '(date-palms) of double and triple form'. But Elean ζίφυιος is used in proportional sense = Att. διπλάσιος.

2. Late Lat. *trifārius*. Both adj. form and the sense 'of three kinds' are some three centuries later than the adv. form in *-fāriam*. The latter (prob. : *fās* and *fā-ri* 'speak') occur from Plautus on, e.g. Plaut. *edixit mihi ut dispartirem obsonium hic bifariam* 'told me to distribute the food in two parts', Liv. *castra bifariam facta, trifariam adortus castra* 'the camp in two, three sections'. Adjectives formed from these appear in the second century A.D. in the sense 'of three kinds, in three ways' and are common in late and medieval Latin, including *multi-fārius* whence NE *multifarious*. Skutsch IF 14.488 ff. Walde-H. 1.105.

3. NHG *dreierlei*, indeclin. adj. and sb., based upon MHG phrase with *lei* 'manner, condition', e.g. *nach irer ley, deiner lei, einer lei*, etc., the word being borrowed fr. OFr. *lei* (Fr. *loi*), which is often used in the same way, e.g. *a la lei de sa tere*. Kluge-G. 352. Weigand-H. 2.42. Paul, Deutsches Wtb. 319 (with strange denial of the obvious Fr. origin).

4. Lith. *trejokas*, formed on the analogy of *toks* 'talis', *koks* 'qualis', is used in 16th- and 17th-cent. writings, but is now replaced by *trejopas*, formerly only proportional (13.46). Thus in Jeremiah 15.3 Luther's *mit viererlei Plagen* was rendered by Bretkun *keturokais vargais*, where a modern version has *keturopomis slogomis*. Leskien, Bildung d. Nom. 515, 589.

Lett. *trijāds*, formed after *tāds* 'talis', *kāds* 'qualis'.

5. ChSl. *trojakŭ* (late), SCr. *trojak*, Pol. *trojaki*, Russ. *trojakij*, formed fr. the coll. adjs. *trojĭ*, etc. (13.48) after the analogy of ChSl. *takŭ* 'talis', *kakŭ* 'qualis', exactly like Lith. *trejokas* (above).

But Boh. *trojaky* has been in this sense mostly replaced by *troji* belonging to the coll. type (13.48).

6. Skt. *trividha-*, cpd. of *vidhā-* (*vidhā-* 'set apart') 'manner, kind', forming thus a distinctive series used mostly in sense of NHG *dreierlei*, etc.

13.48. The notion 'consisting of three together, three in a group' is included among the various uses of the multiplicative adjs. for 'threefold, triple' (13.46), e.g. Grk. τριπλαῖ ἀμαξιτοί 'the meeting of three roads', Lat. *triplex murus* 'a triple wall' = 'a set of three walls'. But in several of the IE languages there are also types with more distinctive coll. force. Thus Lat. *trīnī*, etc. were orig. coll., as in Lat. *bovēs bīnī* 'a pair of oxen', *trīnī annī* 'a period of three years', and (beside their secondary distrib. use, 13.52) are preferred to the cardinal with *pluralia tantum* or plurals that differ in sense from the singular, as Lat. *bīna castra* 'two camps', *bīnae litterae* 'two letters' (epistles) in contrast to *duae litterae* 'two letters' (of the alphabet). Hence they may become merely variant forms of the cardinals and tend to disappear. Cf. Brugmann, Die distributiven und die kollektiven Numeralia der idg. Sprachen 30 ff.

1. IE **treyo-*, **troyo-*.

Lith., Lett. *treji;* ChSl. *trojĭ*, neut. sg. *troje*, the latter esp. general Slavic; Skt. *traya-*, as in Ved. *trayī vidyā* 'the triple science', the group of three holy actions. This type is represented in Greek only by δοιός 'double', esp. in pl. δοιοί 'both', mostly poetical.

2. With suffix *-no-*. Lat. *trīnī* (also in part *ternī*, though mostly distrib.); ON *þrennir* (for use cf. Sievers ap. Brugmann op. cit. 71 ff.), OE *þrinna* (prob. fr. ON), Goth. *tweihnai*. Cf. Lith. *dvynai* 'twins' (formerly dual *dvynu*), *trynučiei* 'triplets'.

3. Grk. τρισσός, Att. τριττός fr. *τριχιος, also τριξός (Ion., but τετραξός, πενταξός also in Aristotle), fr. *τριχθιος, formed fr. the advs. τρίχα and τριχθά 'in three parts'. In use often not distinguishable from τριπλοῦς in its various uses (which include the coll.) or in pl. from the simple cardinal. But the coll. sense seems dominant. Cf. Hdt. διξὸς λόγος 'twofold account' = 'two accounts', Aristot. Metaph. ἐπίπεδα τριττά, γραμμαὶ τετραξαί, στιγμαὶ πενταξαί 'three (four, five) classes of planes (lines, points)', and esp. the frequent use in the papyri for triplicate (etc.) copies, as πρᾶσις τρισσὴ γραφεῖσα 'triplicate bill of sale' (POxy. 1698.23), γράμματα τετρασσὰ (ὀκτασσὰ) γραφέντα 'contract in four (eight) copies' (POxy. 1638.30, 171.4), etc.

Grk. συνδύο, συντρεῖς (both Hom.), cpds. with σύν 'together'.

4. NIr. *triūrach*, deriv. of sb. *triūr* 'group of three persons' (13.52).

5. Skt. *trika-* (*dvika-*, etc.), in part coll., deriv. of the cardinal with suffix *-ka-*.

Ved. *çatin-*, *sahasrin-* 'in hundreds, thousands', with common suffix *-in-*, also *daçagva-*, *daçagvin-*, *çatagvin-*, for which see M. Bloomfield, AJPh. 17.42 ff.

13.49. Nouns for a 'group of three', etc., are formed either from the cardinals with a coll. suffix or from the coll. adjs. (13.48).

Such terms tend to become specialized according to the nature of the things grouped, as the general Eur. ecclesiastical 'trinity' or musical 'trio'; the political Grk. τριττύς; the mathematical *ternion, quaternion;* the It., Sp. *terno* in dice-playing, lottery, etc.; NE *quartette* in music, *quatrain* in verse, *foursome* in golf, *decade* of years; Russ. *trojka* 'three-horse team'.

It is only in such specialized uses that these words belong to popular speech. A truly generic coll. sb. may be only a rare sophisticated term or may even be lacking in some of the IE languages. We have listed those that are generic or come nearest to this in that they cover a variety of specialized uses (like Sp. *terno*). Words for the 'trinity' are omitted, except as they are also sometimes used in a wider sense or are the only ones available.

1. Grk. τριάς, gen. -άδος, etc., full series, prob. starting from forms like δεκάδ- parallel to Skt. *daçát-* 'decade'. Used for a triad, the number three, and in Christian times for the 'trinity', as in NG pop. τριάδα. Hence in its wider sense (as 'trinity' it was rendered by *trīnitās*) late Lat. *trias*, It., Fr. *triade*, NE *triad*.

Att. τριττύς, used for a sacrifice of three animals and for a division of the tribe, fr. *τρικτύς (with ττ after τριττός), like τετρακτύς, formed fr. the adverbs τρίχα, τέτραχα (or fr. *τρικο-, like Skt. *trika-* 13.48) with suffix -τυ-, as also in πεντηκοστύς 'group of 50', etc.

NG δεκαριά, εἰκοσαρια, etc. formed fr. the cardinals with suffix -αριά, Byz. -αρέα, fem. of -άρις (fr. Lat. *-ārius*, 13.53). These are coll. equivalents of the numerals, like Fr. *dizaine*, etc. or NE *dozen* (fr. Fr. *douzaine*) and *score*, e.g. καμιὰ πενηνταριά 'some fifty' = 'about fifty'. Cf. also δεκάρα 'ten-centime piece' and δεκάρι 'ten-spot' in cards.

2. In classical Latin the only numeral coll. sbs. are *decuria* and *centuria* for groups of 10 or 100. This type prob. started in a **quetur-ia* or the like (with second syllable of *quattuor* in weak grade, as in Skt. *catur-*). Another type is seen in Umbr. *puntes* 'pentads', formed like Skt. *pañk-ti-* 'group of five'.

Late Lat. *terniō* and *trīniō* 'the number three', deriv. of *ternī*, *trīnī* (13.48). Similarly, *quaterniō*, *quīniō*, etc. Hence NE *ternion*, *quaternion*, mostly math., but also of persons (cf. NED).

From forms of Lat. *ternī* also It., Sp. *terno* (in a variety of highly specialized uses), Fr. *terne*, NE *tern*.

Late Lat. *trīnitās*, deriv. of *trīnī* and used for 'triad', but esp. the 'trinity'. Hence, mostly in latter sense, It. *trinità*, Fr. *trinité*, NE *trinity*, etc.

Still another type derived fr. the coll. adjs. is seen in Fr. *centaine* 'group of 100' (by analogy *dizaine*, etc.), fr. VLat. *centēna*, orig. neut. pl. of *centēnī*.

It. *trio*, a musical term formed after the analogy of *duo* 'duet'. As a musical term it spread to many of the modern Eur. languages (Fr., NE *trio*, etc.) but has also developed a wider use, e.g. It. *trio sorelle*, NE *trio of cousins*, etc. (cf. NED).

Rum. *treime* (and so *cincime*, *optime*, etc.), formed fr. the cardinal with the abstract suffix *-ime*. Meyer-Lübke, Rom. Gram. 2.486.

3. Ir. *trēde*, neut. sg. of adj. *trēode* 'threefold' (13.46). Thurneysen, Gram. 243.

Ir. *triar*, NIr. *triūr* 'group of three persons', cpd. of the cardinal with *fer* 'man'. Thurneysen, Gram. 243 f. Otherwise Pedersen 2.51, 136 (suffix *-aro-*).

W. *tri* 'three' is also used as sb., pl. *trioedd* 'threes'.

Br. *trioz*, pl. *trioed*, the latter = W. *trioedd*.

4. ON *þrenning*, used for the 'trinity' but also in wider sense, deriv. of *þrennr* 'threefold' (13.46).

OE *þrines*, OHG *drinissa*, mostly the 'trinity', fr. the cardinal with suffix = NE *-ness*. Later OE *þrinnis* with *nn* fr. *þrinna*, ME *þrinness* (cf. NED).

MHG *drīheit*, NHG *dreiheit*, Dan. *trehed*, Sw. *trehet*, fr. the cardinal with coll. suffix.

NE *triad*, *trio*, above, 1, 2.

ME *thresum* (*twasum*, *hundredsome*, etc.), NE *threesome*, etc., now chiefly Sc., whence the familiar *foursome* in golf, cpds. with *-sum* = OE indef. pron. *sum* as used after numerals. NED s.v. *-some*.

5. Lith. *trejetas* (so *dvejetas*, *penketas*, etc.), deriv. of the coll. adj. *treji*. Leskien, Bildung d. Nom. 571. Cf. Lett. *trijats* 'three-leafed clover' (also generic?), adv. *trijatā* 'by threes'. Mühl.-Endz. 4.233.

6. ChSl. *trojĭca*, Boh. *trojice*, Pol. *trojca*, Russ. *troica*, but SCr. *trojstvo*, all mostly but not exclusively the 'trinity', derivs. of the coll. adj. *trojĭ*.

7. Skt. *trayam*, neut. sb. of the coll. adj. *traya-*.

Other types in *pañkti-* 'group of five', with abstract suffix *-ti-* (cf. Umbr. *puntes*, above, 2), and *daçad-* 'group of ten' (cf. Grk. δεκάς, above, 1).

13.51. 'By threes'. The coll. notion is expressed more commonly by adv. phrases than by the adjs. (13.51). These may consist (1) of a preposition with the cardinal (or coll.), (2) of a repetition of the cardinal, (3) a combination of the two preceding ('three by three').

Several of these phrases are also used, and more originally, for the distrib. 'three apiece' (13.52). In fact, they are all commonly called "distributive phrases." It is remarkable that Brugmann, Die distributiven und die kollektiven Numeralia, while clearing up the relations of the distrib. and coll. uses of Lat. *bīnī*, etc., failed to make a similar distinction in the adv. phrases and lumped together phrases so distinct as NE *by threes, three by three*, and *three each, three apiece*. They are all distrib. in a loose sense (distributed in groups of three), but only the latter type in a technical sense. The former type 'by threes' is obviously co-ordinate with the coll. adjs. and sbs.

1. With preposition. Grk. ἀνὰ τρεῖς or κατὰ τρεῖς; It. *a tre*, Fr. *à trois*, etc. (but more commonly with repetition, below, 3); Goth. *bi twans* 'by twos' (1 Cor. 14.27; but Mk. 6.7, Lk. 10.1 *twans hwanzuh*, as if distrib.), ME *by thres*, NE *by threes, in threes*, NHG *zu (je) dreien*, Du. *bij drieën;* Lith. *po tris*, Lett. *pa trim;* ChSl. *po trŭmŭ*, SCr. *po tri*, Boh. *po třech*, Pol. *po trzech, w trzech*, Russ. *po tri*.

2. Repetition, with or without 'and'. Grk. μία μία 'one by one' (Soph.), but common only in late times, e.g. in NT δύο δύο Mk. 6.7 (= ἀνὰ δύο Lk. 10.1, κατὰ δύο 1 Cor. 14.27), τρία τρία POxy. 121, NG τρεῖς τρεῖς; late Lat. *duo et duo*, also *duo duo* (cf. Arch. f. lat. Lex. 2.323); Br. *tri ha tri;* OE *þrīm and þrīm* (so Aelfric, Gram. for Lat. *ternī*), NE *three and three*, NHG *drei und drei*, ON *þrīr ok þrīr*, Dan. *tre og tre*, Sw. *tre och tre*, Du. *drie en drie* (obs.); Skt. *dvā́-dvā* (Ved.).

3. Preposition and repetition. Late Grk. ἀνὰ δύο δύο (Ev. Petr. 35); It. *tre a tre*, Fr. *trois à trois*, Sp. *tres a tres*, Rum. *trei câte trei* or *câte trei trei;* NIr. *'na dtriūr is 'na dtriūr* (with *triūr* 'trio' 13.52); NE *three by three*, Du. *drie aan drie*.

4. Miscellaneous. Ir. *trēdaib*, dat. pl. of the coll. sb. *trēde* (13.49).

W. *bob yn dri*, or simply *bob dri*, with *pob* 'every', also and orig. distrib. (13.52). Morris Jones 260.

OHG *io drī*, NHG *je drei*, orig. and still mainly distrib., cf. 13.52.

Skt. *triças* (so *ekaças* 'one by one', *çataçás* 'by hundreds', etc.), with adv. suffix *-ças* : Grk. -κας in ἀνδρακάς 'man by man'.

13.52. Three each, three apiece. In general, the distrib. notion is not expressed by any distinctive deriv. of the numeral itself, but independently in the context.

1. Numeral with words for 'each one, every one'. Thus in Grk. with forms of ἕκαστος according to construction, and esp. καθ' ἕκαστον or καθ' ἕνα. Similarly in the Romance languages except Rum. (Fr. *chacun*, etc.), Celtic (Ir. *cach*, W. *pob*, etc.), and most of the Gmc. (OE *ǣlc*, NE *each*, Dan. *hver*, etc.). And even where other expressions are usual (as listed) this form is always a possible alternative, e.g. NHG *jedem gab er drei* beside *ihnen gab er je drei*.

NE *apiece* is virtually the same thing, orig. *a pece* 'a piece'; likewise NIr. *an ceann* 'the head' (cf. McKenna p. 371, col. 1, bottom).

2. In a sentence like NE *the pails held ten quarts each*, the *ten quarts* might be felt as coll. (cf. *ten-quart pail, gallon jug, bushel basket*) and so expressed. This is

conspicuously the case in Latin, where the orig. colls. *bīnī*, etc. (13.48), were regularly so used (with usual but not complete differentiation of *ternī* and *trīnī*) and thus came to be called 'distributives'. [In Umbrian the multiplicatives like Lat. *duplus, triplus* are used with a following distrib. phrase, as *numer tupler (tripler) pusti kastruwa* 'nummis binis (ternis) in singulos fundos'.] Similarly, ON *twennir, þrennir* are used in distrib. phrases but usually in connection with a form of *hverr* 'each, every one' (cf. Sievers ap. Brugmann, Distrib. 71). So Goth. *tweihnōs paidōs haban* = ἀνὰ δύο χιτῶνας 'have two coats apiece' Lk. 9.3.

3. Many of the adv. phrases that have been listed under the coll. 'by threes' are also used in distrib. sense, and in some the latter is probably the more original. Thus OHG *io drī* (*io siben* quotable), MHG *ie drī*, NHG *je drei*, with *io, je* 'always, in each case'. Lith. *po tris*, etc., general Balto-Slavic, with the same distrib. use of *po* as in Lith. *ten raste kožnas po lovą* 'there you will find each a bed, a bed apiece' (Leskien, Lit. Lesebuch, p. 4), or ChSl. *po* often = Grk. κατά.

Byz., NG ἀπὸ τρεῖς, quotable from 7th. century, is unequivocally distrib. (not coll.), e.g. τοὺς ἔδωσα ἀπὸ τρία μῆλα 'I gave them three apples apiece'.

4. Skt. *trayas prati-* (quotable?) with distrib. use of *prati* as in *pratyekam* 'one by one', *yajñam prati* 'at each sacrifice', etc.

13.53. Miscellaneous. Various types of numeral derivs. are used with specialized application, e.g. to the sequence of days or years.

Grk. τριταῖος 'on the third day', and so a whole series, πεμπταῖος (Hom.), ἑκταῖος, δεκαταῖος, etc., derivs. of the ordinal with suffix -αῖος.

Grk. τριτεύς 'third part of a μέδιμνος', and so also as a measure τεταρτεύς and ἑκτεύς (but δυωδεκατεύς 'twelfth month').

Grk. τριτεῖα, τά 'third place, third prize', and so δευτερεῖα, πρωτεῖα.

Grk. τρεῖος, τετρῷος 'three (four) on the dice' (μοῦνος 'ace' Ion. form of μόνος 'alone').

Lat. with suffix -*ārius*; fr. the cardinal, *triāriī* 'soldiers in the third rank'; fr. the ordinal, *tertiārius* 'of the third part', hence NE *tertiary* in geology, mathematics, etc.; fr. the coll., *ternārius* 'consisting of sets of three', hence NE *ternary* (*binary*, etc.) in mathematics and other sciences; the same formation with different specialization, late *octōgenārius, nōnāgenārius* 'eighty (ninety) years old', hence NE *octogenarian, nonagenarian* (both also -*ary*); with suffix -*ānus* fr. ordinal, *tertiānī* 'soldiers of the third legion' and *tertiānae febrēs* 'tertian fever', whence NE *tertian*.

Lat. *triēns* 'third part' mostly as a measure, and similarly *quadrāns, sextāns, dōdrāns*, participial formations. Thurneysen, IF 39.201.

For years of age (aside, of course, from epds. with words for year), cf. (beside Lat. *octōgenārius*, above) Ir. *nōichtech* 'ninety years old' (Pedersen 2.130, 136); Lith. *treigys* 'three years old' (so *dveigys, ketvergis, penkergis*, etc.; Leskien, Bildung d. Nom. 524); Skt. *ṣāṣṭika-, sāptatika* 'sixty (seventy) years old', with the same suffix as the multiplicative *trika-*, etc., but with vṛddhi in the forms of the cardinal (Wackernagel, Altind. Gram. 3.421).

CHAPTER 14

TIME[1]

14.11 TIME

Grk.	χρόνος	Goth.	þeihs, mēl, hweila	Lith.	laikas (čēsas)
NG	καιρός	ON	tīð, timi, stund	Lett.	laiks
Lat.	tempus	Dan.	tid	ChSl.	vrēme, časŭ, godŭ
It.	tempo	Sw.	tid	SCr.	vrijeme (doba)
Fr.	temps	OE	tid, tima, hwil, stund	Boh.	čas (doba)
Sp.	tiempo	ME	time, tide, while,	Pol.	czas (doba)
Rum.	timp, vreme		stounde	Russ.	vremja
Ir.	amm, aimser, tan	NE	time (while)	Skt.	kāla-
NIr.	am, aimsir	Du.	tijd	Av.	zrvan-
W.	amser, pryd	OHG	zīt, (h)wīla, stunta		
Br.	amser, pred	MHG	zīt, stunde, wile		
		NHG	zeit (weile)		

[1] Words for several of the notions classified under "Spatial Relations" or "Quantity and Number", like 'long', 'short', 'first', 'last', are applied equally to time, or in some cases specialized in this direction, e.g. Lett. *ilgs* 'long' only of time, NE *brief* 'short' mostly of time.

Some of the words for 'time' are from roots for 'stretch' or 'measure', with established temporal, rather than spatial, application. Others are of diverse and partly obscure orig.

Besides the most generic terms, there are others which are used mostly for a point or period of time (not time in its duration). These may become more generic (as Grk. καιρός) but, more frequently, are further specialized (e.g. to 'year', 'day', or esp. 'hour') or restricted to certain phrases (e.g. NE *while*).

1. Grk. χρόνος, etym. dub. Possibly, with analysis χρ-όνο-ς (cf. θρ-όνο-ς) and as orig. 'the comprehensive', fr. the root seen in Skt. *hṛ-* 'bring', Osc. *heriiad* 'capiat', etc. Boisacq 1071 f.

Grk. καιρός 'fitness, opportunity' and esp. 'fitting time, season', used of special times, not duration of time, but in NG the pop. word for 'time' (χρόνος pop. 'year', root connection dub., perh. best as orig. 'section of time' fr. *καρ-ιός : κείρω 'cut off, shear', etc. Walde-P. 1.419, 2.584. Boisacq 538 ftn. Walde-H. 1.206.

Grk. ὥρα 'period of time', in Hom. esp. 'time of year, season' or 'fitting time', later esp. 'time of day, hour', but wider use continued in part (so even NG κάμ-ποση ὥρα 'considerable time, quite a while') : Av. *yarə*, Goth. *jēr*, etc. 'year' (14.73), Slavic *jaro* 'spring' (14.75), all prob. fr. *yē-, yō-* beside *yā-* (cf. Skt. *yā-* 'go', Lith. *joti* 'ride', etc.), extensions of *ei-, i-* 'go'. Walde-P. 1.105. Boisacq 1083.

2. Lat. *tempus* (> Romance words), etym. much disputed, but prob. as 'stretch of time' : Lith. *tempti* 'stretch', etc., fr. *tem-p-*, beside *ten-d-* in Lat. *tendere* 'stretch', extension of *ten-* in Skt. *tan-*, Grk. τείνω 'stretch' (cf. Ir. *tan*, below, 3). Walde-P. 1.721. Ernout-M. 1025 f. (without etym.).

Rum. *vreme* (mostly replaced now in lit. language by *timp*), fr. Slavic (cf. below, 6). Tiktin 1780 f.

3. Ir. *aimser*, etc., general Celtic, deriv. of simple form in Ir. *amm* 'time, occasion, point of time', NIr. *am* (general term now; *aimsir* esp. 'weather', cf. McKenna), etym.? Pedersen 1.80.

Ir. *tan*, rare in later period in lit. sense, mostly used as conjunction *in tan, in tain* 'when' : Skt. *tan-*, Grk. τείνω, Lat. *tendere* 'stretch'. Walde-P. 1.723. Stokes 128. Otherwise Pedersen 2.14.

Ir. *trāth* 'time, period', esp. 'canonical hour' = W. *trawd* 'course, journey', prob. : Skt. *tṛ-* 'pass', Lat. *trāns* 'across', etc. Pedersen 1.52.

W. *pryd*, Br. *pred*, OCorn. *prit* (gl. *hora*) : Skt. *sa-kṛt* 'once', *tri-kṛtvas* 'thrice', Lith. *kartas*, ChSl. *kratŭ* in numeral advs. (13.44). Pedersen 1.43. Henry 227.

4. Goth. *þeihs* : OE *þing-gemearc* 'measured time', ON, OE *þing* 'judicial assembly', prob. fr. IE *ten-k-*, extension of *ten-* 'stretch'. Walde-P. 1.724. Falk-Torp 1263. Feist 494.

Goth. *mēl* (usually χρόνος, once ὥρα) : ON *māl*, OE *mæl*, OHG *māl* 'fixed time, mealtime, etc.', fr. the root in ON *mæla*, Lat. *mētīrī*, Skt. *mā-*, etc. 'measure'. Walde-P. 2.237. Falk-Torp 685. Feist 353.

Goth. *hweila*, mostly 'period of time, hour' (renders both χρόνος and καιρός, but chiefly ὥρα), OE *hwīl*, OHG (*h*)*wīla*, etc. = ON *hvīla* 'resting place, bed' : Skt. *cira-* 'delay', adj. 'long (of time)', Lat. *quiēs* 'rest', ChSl. *po-čiti* 'to rest', etc. Walde-P. 1.510. Falk-Torp 440. Feist 284. NED s.v. *while*, sb.

ON *tīð*, OE *tīd*, OHG *zīt*, etc., general Gmc. except ON (NE *tide*), fr. Gmc. *tī-d-*, beside *tī-m-* in ON *tīmi* (often 'period of time, appointed time', mod. Scand. 'hour'), OE *tīma*, ME, NE *time*

(NHG dial. *zīme* 'opportunity, time'), prob. as 'period of time' : Grk. δαίομαι, Skt. *day-, dā-* 'divide, share' (cf. fr. the same root Arm. *ti* 'age, year, time'). Walde-P. 1.764. Falk-Torp 1256. Kluge-G. 706.

ON, OE *stund*, ME *stounde*, OHG *stunta*, MHG *stunde*, mostly 'period of time' (whence 'hour' in NHG), as orig. 'fixed time' : Goth. *standan*, etc. 'stand'. Walde-P. 2.603. Falk-Torp 1190 f.

5. Lith. *laikas*, Lett. *laiks* : Lith. *palaikis* 'remainder', *laikyti* 'hold, keep (over)', *likti* 'remain', Grk. λείπω 'leave', etc. (12.16-18), semantic development through 'time left over'(?). Walde-P. 2.397. Mühl.-Endz. 2.407.

Lith. *metas* 'time' but mostly pl. *metai* 'year', see 14.73.

Lith. *čēsas* (fr. Pol. *czas*, below, 6), formerly the usual word (so in versions of the NT, in Kurschat, etc.) but now rejected in favor of the native *laikas*.

6. ChSl. *vrēmę*, SCr. *vrijeme*, OPol. *wrzemię*, Russ. *vremja*, Slavic *vermen*-, perh. fr. *vert-men*-, fr. the root in ChSl. *vratiti*, Lat. *vertere*, etc., 'turn'; for form cf. Skt. *vartman-* 'course'. Semantic development from the notion of time as a '(turning) cycle' of seasons, etc. Cf. Lat. *annus (mēnsis) vertēns* 'the course of a

year (month)'. Pokrowsky, Symbol. Gram. Rozwadowski 1.225. Brückner 634.

ChSl. *časŭ*, Boh. *čas*, Pol. *czas* (Russ. *čas* 'hour') : OPruss. *kisman* 'time', Alb. *kóhë* 'time, weather', perh. (as 'observation, calculation'?) fr. the root in ChSl. *čajati* 'expect, wait, hope', Skt. *cāy-* 'perceive'. Walde-P. 1.508. Berneker 137. Brückner 73.

ChSl. *godŭ*, in Gospels for ὥρα as a 'period of time' (hence Russ. *god* 'year' and derivs. for 'hour', 14.51) : ChSl. *u-goditi* 'be pleasing', OHG *gigat* 'fitting', etc. Walde-P. 1.531 f. Berneker 316 ff.

SCr., Boh., Pol. *doba*, used for 'time' in special senses or phrases, orig. 'fitting time' : ChSl. *po-doba jestŭ* 'is fitting', *u-dobĭ* 'easily', *po-dobĭnŭ* 'similar', Goth. *ga-daban* 'be suitable', etc. Walde-P. 1.824 f. Berneker 203 f.

7. Skt. *kāla-*, etym. dub. Uhlenbeck 52. Wüst, Z. Ind. Iran. 5.164 ff. (: *kālaya-* 'drive', as orig. 'morning' = 'time for driving cattle to pasture').

Av. *zrvan-*, cf. MPers. *zarman* 'age, time', prob. : Av. *zaurvan-* 'old age, weakness of age', Skt. *jarant-* 'old, frail', Grk. γέρων 'old man', etc. Walde-P. 1.599.

14.12 AGE

Grk.	ἡλικία	Goth.	(alds)	Lith.	amžius
NG	ἡλικία	ON	aldr	Lett.	vecums
Lat.	aetās	Dan.	alder	ChSl.	vŭzdrastŭ, vrŭsta
It.	età	Sw.	ålder	SCr.	dob, vijek
Fr.	âge	OE	ield	Boh.	vĕk
Sp.	edad	ME	age, eld(e)	Pol.	wiek
Rum.	virstă, etate	NE	age	Russ.	vozrast
Ir.	áis	Du.	leeftijd, ouderdom	Skt.	vayas-
NIr.	aois	OHG	altar	Av.	āyu-
W.	oed(ran), oes	MHG	alter		
Br.	oad	NHG	alter		

'Age' is understood here primarily as 'period of existence, time of life' (*how old?*). Many of the words are also used for a (long) period of time in general,

esp. 'eternity' or 'lifetime', this being the more orig. sense in some groups. Others reflect the notion of 'oldness' ('old age' > any 'age'; cf. 'greatness' > 'size', 12.52), 'strength, vigor' (through 'prime of life'), or 'grown stature' (due to the double use of Grk. ἡλικία).

1. Grk. ἡλικία 'age' and secondarily 'bodily growth, stature', fr. ἧλιξ 'of the same age, comrade', Dor. ἆλιξ, fr. *swā-lik-, formed fr. the refl. stem in Grk. ὅς, Cret. ϝός, Skt. sva-, etc. For the ā-stem and suffix, cf. ἡλίκος, τηλίκος, Lat. quālis, tālis. Boisacq 320 f. Brugmann, Grd. 2.1.382. Walde-P. 2.455.

2. Lat. aetās, -tātis (> It. età, OFr. aé, Sp. edad, lit. loanword Rum. etate; VLat. *aetāticum > Fr. âge), early Lat. aevitās, fr. aevum 'eternity, lifetime, age (in wide sense), generation' : Grk. αἰών with similar uses (cf. also αἰϝεί, Att. ἀεί 'always'), Goth. aiws 'αἰών', Skt. āyu- 'life, lifetime, living being', Av. āyu- 'duration, age', etc. Walde-P. 1.6 f. Ernout-M. 21. REW 251.

Rum. virstă, fr. Slavic, cf. ChSl. vrŭsta, etc. (below, 6). Tiktin 1754.

3. Ir. āis, NIr. aois, W. oes, and W. oed, cpd. oedran, Br. oad, etym. dub. Pedersen 1.56, 176 : Lat. aetās, etc. Adversely, Thurneysen, Idg. Anz. 6.196, Walde-P. 1.7, Walde-H. 1.21.

4. Goth. alds (renders αἰών, γενεά, βίος; wahstus 'growth' renders ἡλικία, but in the sense 'stature'), ON ǫld ('age' in wider sense), aldr, Dan. alder, Sw. ålder, OE ealdor (mostly 'life'), ield, yld, ME elde, OHG altar, MHG, NHG alter, Du. ouderdom (like NHG altertum in form but used of a person's age), all fr. the Gmc. adj. for 'old' (14.15).

ME, NE age, fr. Fr. âge (above, 2).

Du. leeftijd ('time of life', not 'lifetime'), cpd. of leven 'live' and tijd 'time'.

5. Lith. amžius : amžiauti 'last forever', amžinas 'eternal', etym.?

Lett. vecums, fr. vecs 'old' (14.15).

6. ChSl. vŭzdrastŭ, (cf. vŭzdrastŭ imatŭ, lit. 'has his growth' = 'is of age', ἡλικίαν ἔχει Jn. 9.21, 23), fr. vŭzdrasti 'grow up' (cpd. of rasti 'grow'). So Russ. vozrast, usual word for a person's age.

ChSl. vrŭsta (Supr. freq. for ἡλικία; SCr. vrsta 'sort, class', Pol. warsta 'layer'), beside vrŭstĭ 'situation, condition', Bulg. vrŭstĭ 'age and stature', fr. the root of ChSl. vrŭtěti 'turn', Lat. vertere, etc. Cf. fr. the same root Skt. vṛtta-m 'occurrence, behavior, appearance'. Walde-P. 1.275. Brückner 603.

SCr. dob : doba 'period of time, season' (see 14.11).

Boh. věk, Pol. wiek, SCr. vijek, also 'age' as 'period of time', 'lifetime', as ChSl. věkŭ (renders αἰών), all : Lith. viekas 'strength, life', vykis 'life', fr. the root in Lith. veikti 'make, work', Goth. weihan 'fight', Lat. vincere 'conquer' (semantic development 'strength', 'life' to 'lifetime, age'). Walde-P. 1.233. Brückner 615.

7. Skt. vayas-, also 'vigor, strength, prime of life' : Grk. ἶς, Lat. vīs 'strength', etc. Walde-P. 1.230. Uhlenbeck 272.

Av. āyu- 'duration, age', cf. Lat. aetās (above, 2).

14.13 NEW

Grk.	καινός, νέος	Goth.	niujis	Lith.	naujas
NG	καινούργιος	ON	nȳr	Lett.	jauns
Lat.	novus	Dan.	ny	ChSl.	novŭ
It.	nuovo	Sw.	ny	SCr.	nov
Fr.	neuf, nouveau	OE	nīwe	Boh.	nový
Sp.	nuevo	ME	newe	Pol.	nowy
Rum.	nou	NE	new	Russ.	novyj
Ir.	núe, núide	Du.	nieuw	Skt.	nava-, navya-
NIr.	nua, nuadh	OHG	niuwi	Av.	nava-
W.	newydd	MHG	niu(we)		
Br.	nevez	NHG	neu		

With but few exceptions the words for 'new' and those for 'young' (14.14) belong to inherited groups pointing to IE words for 'new' and 'young' respectively. But the Grk. word of the 'new' group was used chiefly, from the earliest times, for 'young', and the Lett. 'young' word serves also for 'new'. Furthermore, 'young', though primarily used of living things, is freq. applied by analogy to such objects as moon, month, and other periods of time, wine, etc. So NE young (NED s.v. 5), and similarly in other languages.

1. IE *newo- (a), *newyo- (b). Walde-P. 2.324. Ernout-M. 681.

a) Grk. νέος (chiefly 'young', but also in part 'new'; NG 'new' only in phrases like τί νέα; 'what news?'); Lat. novus (hence the Romance words; dim. Lat. novellus > Fr. nouveau); ChSl. novŭ, etc., general Slavic; Skt., Av. nava-; Toch. A ñu (SSS 47); b) Ir. núe (older nōe, nāue), W. newydd, Br. nevez, and with d-suffix Ir. núide, NIr. nuadh; Goth. niujis, etc., general Gmc.; Lith. naujas; Skt. navya-.

2. Grk. καινός : Skt. kanīna- 'young', Lat. recēns 'fresh, recent', Ir. cinim 'spring from, descend', ChSl. na-četi 'begin', etc. Walde-P. 1.397 f. Boisacq 391 f.

Hence, through cpd. καινουργής (: ἔργον 'work') 'newly made', καινούργιος (5th. cent. A.D.+), in NG the pop. word for 'new'.

3. Lett. jauns 'young' (14.14) also 'new'.

14.14 YOUNG

Grk.	νέος	Goth.	juggs	Lith.	jaunas
NG	νέος	ON	ungr	Lett.	jauns
Lat.	iuvenis	Dan.	ung	ChSl.	junŭ
It.	giovane	Sw.	ung	SCr.	mlad
Fr.	jeune	OE	geong	Boh.	mladý
Sp.	joven	ME	yong	Pol.	młody
Rum.	tînăr, june	NE	young	Russ.	molodoj, junyj
Ir.	ōac	Du.	jong	Skt.	yuvan-, kanīna-
NIr.	ōg	OHG	junc	Av.	yuvan-
W.	ieuanc	MHG	junc		
Br.	yaouank				

Most of the words for 'young' belong to an inherited group. The others come by extension from 'new' (Grk. νέος) or from the notion of 'tender'.

1. IE *yuwen- (a), *yuwṇko- (b), comp. *yeu-yes- fr. simple *yeu-. Walde-P. 1.200. Ernout-M. 509. Walde-H. 1.735 f. Falk-Torp 1334.

a) Lat. iuvenis (> Romance words; but Rum. june sb. 'young man', as adj.

due to Fr. influence); Lith. jaunas, Lett. jauns, ChSl. junŭ (positive not in Gospels, but junějĭ = ὁ νεώτερος, Lk. 15.12), Russ. junyj, Bulg., Slov. jun; Skt., Av. yuvan-, yūn- (Av. quotable only as sb. 'young man'); b) Ir. ōac, ōc, NIr. ōg, W. ieuanc, Br. yaouank; Goth. juggs, ON ungr, etc., general Gmc.; cf. Lat. iuvencus, -a 'steer, heifer', Umbr. iuenga 'iuvencas', Skt. yuvaça- 'youthful'.

2. Grk. νέος, orig. 'new' (cf. 14.13), but chiefly 'young' from Hom. to the present day.

14.15 OLD

Grk.	παλαιός, ἀρχαῖος, γέρων	Goth.	fairneis, alþeis, sineigs	Lith.	senas
NG	παλιός, ἀρχαῖος	ON	forn, gamall	Lett.	vecs
Lat.	vetus, senex	Dan.	gammel	ChSl.	vetŭchŭ, starŭ
It.	vecchio	Sw.	gammal	SCr.	star
Fr.	vieux (ancien)	OE	eald, gamol	Boh.	starý
Sp.	viejo	ME	old	Pol.	stary
Rum.	vechiu, bătrîn	NE	old (ancient)	Russ.	staryj
Ir.	sen	Du.	oud	Skt.	jīrṇa-, sana-, vṛddha-
NIr.	aosta, crionna, sean	OHG	alt, firni	Av.	hana-
W.	hen	MHG	alt, virne		
Br.	koz, hen	NHG	alt		

Most of the words for 'old' are used alike for 'old' vs. 'new' and 'old' vs. 'young', and this is to be understood in the following, except as otherwise noted. But a few are used wholly or chiefly in the latter sense, esp. of old persons; and this was the orig. application of many of the others, as indicated by their etym.

1. IE *sen-. Walde-P. 2.494. Ernout-M. 922 f.

Lat. senex (of living things, mostly persons); Ir. sen, NIr. sean, W. hen (Br. hen- as prefix, as often Ir. sen- and mostly NIr. sean-); Goth. sineigs, superl. sinista (only of persons, 'πρεσβύτης, πρεσβύτερος'); Lith. senas, Skt. (Ved.) sana- (opp. to nava- and yuvan-), sanaya-, Av. hana- (quotable only for old persons); Arm. hin; cf. Grk. ἕνος 'of last year'

3. Rum. tînăr, fr. Lat. tener 'delicate, tender', and also often 'of tender age' (cf. tenerī 'the young, boys', but this use strengthened by the similar development in Bulg., SCr. mlad (below). Ernout-M. 1029. REW 8645.

4. Bulg., SCr. mlad, Boh. mladý, Pol. młody, Russ. molodoj (also OPruss. malda- 'young') = ChSl. mladŭ 'tender' (of the branch of the fig tree) : Lat. mollis, Skt. mṛdu- 'soft, tender', etc. Walde-P. 288 f. Berneker 2.70.

5. Skt. kanīna- : Grk. καινός 'new', etc. (14.13).

ἕνη καὶ νέα (sc. ἡμέρα) 'the old and new day' = 'last day of the month', ON sina 'dry standing grass from the previous year'.

2. IE *wetus- (*wetos-?), prob. : Grk. ϝέτος 'year', etc. (14.73), as orig. 'full of years' or even 'one year old' (which would be 'old' vs. 'new' for wine, grains, fruits, etc.). Walde-P. 1.251. Ernout-M. 1100 (with doubt).

Lat. vetus, vetustus, dim. vetulus (> VLat. veclus > It. vecchio, Fr. vieux, Sp. viejo, Rum. vechiu), Lat. veterānus 'veteran' (> vetrānus > Rum. bătrîn), OLith. vetušas, Lett. vecs; ChSl. vetŭchŭ in the Gospels 'παλαιός'.

3. Derivs. of IE *ĝer- perh. orig. 'become old, ripe, frail, etc.', vb. forms in Skt. jarati 'makes frail, causes to age',

jīryati 'becomes frail, decays, grows old', ChSl. zĭrěti 'ripen', etc. Walde-P. 1.599 f.

Grk. γεραιός (mostly of men, 'old, revered'), γέρων (mostly sb. 'old man', pl. 'elders', but also adj. of things as shield, bronze, etc.; NG γέρων, γέροντας, γέρος sb. 'old man'), γραῦς and γραῖα 'old woman'; Skt. jīrṇa- (pple. of jīryati, above), jarant- (= Grk. γέρων); cf. Av. azaraśant- 'not growing old', zaurura- 'weakened by age', etc.

4. Grk. παλαιός (NG pop. παλιός, mostly of things; of persons only in derogatory sense as παλιάνθρωπος 'worthless fellow, rascal'), fr. adv. πάλαι 'of old, long ago' : τῆλε, Lesb. πήλυι 'far away', W. pell 'far distant', Skt. carama- 'the last', etc. Walde-P. 1.517.

Grk. ἀρχαῖος, lit. 'belonging to the beginning', hence 'ancient, old', fr. ἀρχή 'beginning' (14.25).

5. Fr. ancien (> NE ancient), both mostly with reference to things 'of former times', but also in Fr. and formerly in NE 'old' of persons, fr. deriv. of Lat. ante 'before'. REW 494. NED s.v. ancient.

6. NIr. aosta, lit. 'aged' (: aois 'age', 14.12), but now most general word for 'old'.

NIr. crionna, properly 'wise, experienced', but commonly 'old' of persons (Munster), MIr. crínda 'prudent, wise' (K. Meyer, Contrib. 518), orig.? Connection with crín 'withered, shrunk, worn out, old', as sb. 'dry wood fagots'? For the latter cf. Pedersen 2.498.

Br. koz, Corn. coth, cf. Gall. Cottos, etym.? Henry 78.

7. Goth. fairneis ('παλαιός'), ON forn ('old' and of old, of former times'), OE fyrn 'ancient', OHG firni, MHG virne ('old' and of persons 'experienced, wise') : Goth. af fairnin jēra 'of the previous year', Lith. pernai 'in the previous year', etc., all fr. *per- in Skt. para-, OE feor 'far, distant', Grk. πέρα 'beyond', etc. Walde-P. 2.31. Feist 140.

Goth. alþeis ('γέρων' and neut. pl. 'τὰ ἀρχεῖα'), OE eald, ME, NE old, Du. oud, OHG-NHG alt, all lit. 'nourished, grown' fr. the root of Goth. alan 'grow up', ON ala, Lat. alere 'nourish'. Walde-P. 1.86.

ON gamall (of persons), Dan. gammel, Sw. gammal, OE gamol mostly of persons (but also of sword in Beowulf), etym. dub., but prob. as orig. 'of many winters' : Lat. hiems, Ir. gemred 'winter', etc. (14.64). Walde-P. 1.547. Falk-Torp 298 f. Hellquist 269.

8. ChSl. starŭ (in Gospels 'πρεσβύτης, γέρων'), etc., general Slavic : Lith. storas 'thick, bulky', ON stórr 'large, big', fr. the root *stā- 'stand', semantic development from 'standing (firm)' to 'solid', whence 'large' and 'old'. Walde-P. 2.607.

9. Skt. sana-, Av. hana-, above, 1.

Skt. jīrṇa-, above, 3.

Skt. vṛddha- 'grown', pple. of vṛdh- 'grow', often used of 'old' persons.

14.16 EARLY (adv.)

Grk.	πρωΐ	Goth.	air	Lith.	anksti
NG	ἐνωρίς (πρωΐ)	ON	ār, ārla, snemma	Lett.	agri
Lat.	mātūrē (māne, mā-	Dan.	tidlig	ChSl.	rano (za utra)
	tūtīnē)	Sw.	tidigt (arla)	SCr.	rano
It.	per tempo, di buon'ora	OE	ǣr, ǣrlice	Boh.	časně (ranně)
Fr.	de bonne heure	ME	er(e), erliche, erli	Pol.	rano, wcześnie
Sp.	temprano	NE	early	Russ.	rano
Rum.	de vreme, de dimi-	Du.	vroeg	Skt.	(prātar)
	neaţă	OHG	fruo	Av.	....
Ir.	moch	MHG	vruo, vrūe		
NIr.	go luath, moch	NHG	früh		
W.	cynnar				
Br.	abret				

The majority of the words for 'early' denoted primarily 'early in the day, in the morning', and a few that are used only in this more specific sense are included in the list (in parentheses). Most of the other expressions are connected with words for 'time', that is, 'in time, in good time', etc.

1. Grk. πρωΐ, mostly 'early in the day, in the morning', but also generic 'early' (but NG only 'in the morning' or sb. 'morning'; in generic sense replaced by ἐνωρίς; cf. even ἐνωρίς τὸ πρωΐ 'early in the morning') : OHG fruo, MHG vruo, vrūe, NHG früh, MDu. vroech, Du. vroeg 'early', Skt. prā-tar 'early in the morning', fr. the adv. and prep. stem in Skt. pra- 'before, forward, away', Grk. πρό 'before', Lat. prō 'before, for', etc. Walde-P. 2.36. Weigand-H. 1.592. Franck-v. W. 763.

NG ἐνωρίς, formed fr. the phrase ἐν ὥρᾳ 'in season, in time' (cf. τώρα 'now' fr. τῇ ὥρᾳ), with -ις fr. other advs. in -ις (Koraes, Hatzidakis, Μεσ. 1.584).

2. Lat. mātūrē adv., mātūrus, adj., orig. 'taking place at the proper time, seasonable' (of fruits, etc. 'ripe, mature'), and mātūtīnus adj. (adv. mātūtīne) 'early in the morning, pertaining to the morning' (deriv. of Mātūta 'Goddess of the morning'), all derivs. of a stem *mā-tu-, fr. the same root as the following.

Lat. māne, adv. 'early in the morning' and sb. 'morning' : OLat. mānus, mānis 'good'. Walde-P. 2.220. Ernout-M. 588, 597 f. Walde-H. 2.25.

It. per tempo, Rum. de vreme, lit. 'through, of time', that is, 'in time'.

It. di buon', ora, Fr. de bonne heure, lit. 'of good hour'.

Sp. temprano : tiempo 'time', etc.

Rum. de dimineaţă, lit. 'of morning' (14.44).

3. Ir. moch, loanword (?) fr. MW moch 'early, soon' : Ir. mos-, Lat. mox 'soon', etc. (14.19). Walde-P. 2.303 f.

NIr. go luath, lit. 'quickly', adv. fr. adj. luath 'swift', but usual for 'early' (moch mostly 'early in the morning').

W. cynnar, fr. cyn 'before'.

Br. abret (abred), lit. 'at the proper time', fr. pred 'proper time, hour'.

4. Goth. air, ON ār, cpds. ON ārla, ārlega, Sw. arla (poet.), OE ār-līce, ME erliche, erli, NE early, beside comp. in OE ǣr, ME er(e) (often with positive force) : Goth. airis, OHG ēr 'before, earlier', all perh. as 'early in the morning' : Grk. ἤέριος 'of the morning', ἤρι 'in the morning', Av. ayarə 'day', root connection dub. Walde-P. 1.3. Falk-Torp 8. Feist 24 f.

ON snemma, snimma, in cpds. snemm-, etym. dub. Falk-Torp 1097, 1550. Walde-P. 2.696.

Dan. tidlig, Sw. tidigt (adj. tidig) fr. tid 'time'.

5. Lith. anksti : OPruss. angstainai, angsteina 'early in the morning', possibly fr. *onkt-st-, fr. *onkt- beside *nokt- in Lith. naktis, Goth. nahts, Lat. noctis, etc. 'night'. Walde-P. 2.339. Otherwise (Trautmann 9, etc.) : Skt. añjas 'quickly, suddenly', Goth. anaks 'at once', etc. (Walde-P. 1.59).

Lett. agri (adj. agrs), prob. : Skt. agra- 'beginning, point', agre 'at the beginning', Av. αγra- 'the first', as sb. 'beginning, point', etc. Walde-P. 1.38 f.

6. ChSl. rano (in Gospels, Supr., adv. 'early in the morning'), etc., general Slavic (but Boh. ráno sb. 'morning', hence adj. ranný 'early', adv. ranně, prob. as '(sun)rise' fr. *wrōdh-no- : Grk. ὄρθρος 'dawn', adj. ὄρθριος 'at dawn, early in the morning', etc., fr. the root in Skt. vṛdh- 'rise, grow'; cf. Bulg. ražda se '(the sun) rises'. Walde-P. 1.290. Vondrák 1.528.

ChSl. za utra (renders Grk. πρωΐ), lit. 'in the morning' (utro, 14.44).

Boh. časně, Pol. wcześnie (adjs. časný, wczesny), fr. Boh. čas, Pol. czas 'time' (14.11). Brückner 73.

7. Beside Skt. prātar 'early in the morning' (above, 1), there seem to be no generic words for 'early'. The nearest approach would be expressions for 'at the beginning, before, formerly', like agre (cf. above, 5), pūrvam, prāk.

14.17 LATE (adv.)

Grk.	ὀψέ	Goth.	seiþus (adj.)	Lith.	vélai
NG	ἀργά	ON	sīð, seint	Lett.	vēlu
Lat.	sērō	Dan.	sent	ChSl.	pozdě
It.	tardi	Sw.	sent	SCr.	kasno, pozno, dockan
Fr.	tard	OE	sīþ, late	Boh.	pozdě
Sp.	tarde	ME	late	Pol.	późno
Rum.	tîrziu	NE	late	Russ.	pozdno
Ir.	mall (adj.)	Du.	laat	Skt.	vilambena, vilambāt
NIr.	dēidheannach, deire-	OHG	spāto	Av.	....
	annach (adj.)	MHG	spāte		
W.	hwyr, diweddar (adj.)	NHG	spät		
Br.	diwezat				

Words for 'late' rest on such notions as 'slow', 'behind, after', or 'end'.

Except for a few adj. forms marked as such, they are listed in the adv. forms.

1. Grk. ὀψέ (NG only in ἀπόψε 'this evening' and ψές 'last evening' and 'yesterday'), prob., as orig. 'afterward', based on an *ὀψ, that is *ὀπ-ς (cf. ἄψ 'backward' beside ἀπό 'away from') beside ὀπισθεν 'behind', ὀπίσω 'backward' : Lat. obs-, ops- in o(p)s-tendere, etc., beside ob (cf. abs, ab), Osc. op 'apud', Grk. ἐπί 'on, to', Skt. api- 'to, by', etc. Walde-P. 1.122 f. Boisacq 736.

NG ἀργά, adv. to adj. ἀργός, 'slow' (14.22) and 'late'. Cf. It. tardi, etc., below, and Grk. βραδύς 'slow', whence NG βραδύνω 'be late' and βράδυ 'evening'.

2. Lat. sērō (sērus adj. > W. hwyr also 'evening') : Ir. sīr 'long (of time)', W. hir 'long', a root *sē(i)- (cf. comp. Ir. sia, W. hwy fr. *sē-is) seen also in Lat. sētius 'less', early 'later', Goth. seiþus, etc. (below, 4), Skt. sāya- 'evening', but orig. meaning of root dub. Walde-P. 2.462. Ernout-M. 933. Falk-Torp 962. Feist 415 f.

It. tardi, Fr. tard, Sp. tarde, fr. Lat. tardē 'slowly', adv. to tardus 'slow' (14.22). Hence VLat. *tardīvus > Rum.

tîrziu (adv. and adj.), adjs. It. tardivo, Sp. tardio, Fr. tardif > NE tardy. REW 8573–76.

3. Ir. mall, adj. 'slow, late' (NIr. mall 'slow', sometimes 'late', so esp. adv. go mall), see 'slow' (14.22).

NIr. dēidheannach, adj. (Ir. dedenach, didenach 'the last, final'), W. diweddar, Br. diwezat, fr. Ir. deod, W. diwedd, Br. diwez 'end' (14.26). Pedersen 1.309.

NIr. deireannach (MIr. dered,nach 'last', K. Meyer, Contrib. 619), fr. Ir. dered 'end' (14.26).

4. Goth. seiþus (adj. but only nom. sg. neut. seiþu 'ὀψία, evening'), ON sīð (OHG sīþ 'after, since', NHG seit) : Lat. sērus, etc. (above, 2).

ON seint, Dan., Sw. sent, advs. to the adjs. ON seinn, Dan., Sw. sen 'late' and 'slow' (14.22).

OE late, also 'slowly', ME, NE late, Du. laat (MLG late) : OE lǣt adj. 'late, slow', etc. (14.22).

OHG spāto, MHG spāt(e), NHG early spat, now spät (orig. only adj. OHG spāti, etc.). Goth. only comp. spēdiza, and superl. spēdists 'last'), perh. as orig. 'long-drawn-out' fr. the root *spē(i)- in Grk. σπάω 'draw', Skt. sphāy- 'grow fat, grow', OHG spuot, OE spēd 'suc-cess' (NE speed, see 14.21), ChSl. spěti 'have success', etc. Walde-P. 2.655, 657. Feist 444. Weigand-H. 2.903.

5. Lith. vélai, Lett. vēlu, with adjs. Lith. vēlus, Lett. vēls, prob. through 'delay' (cf. Lith. valanda 'a while', now 'hour') fr. 'turning, winding', fr. the root in Lett. velt, ChSl. valiti, Lat. vol-vere 'roll', Skt. val- 'turn (round)', etc. Walde-P. 1.303.

6. ChSl. pozdě (= ὀψέ Gospels, Mk. 11.19, but mostly indeclinable sb. = ὀψία), SCr. pozno, etc., general Slavic (whence adj. ChSl. pozdinъ, etc.), extended form fr. a prep. *pos- : Lith. pas 'at, by', pas-taras 'last, final', Lat. pos-t, OLat. pos-te 'after', Skt. paç-ca, Av. pas-ča- 'behind, later', etc. Walde-P. 2.78 f. Meillet, Études 161.

SCr. kasno, and adj. kasan : ChSl. kŭsinŭ 'slow' (14.22).

SCr. dockan (also dockna, docne, etc., comp. adj. docniji) : *do-kŭsna, etc. : do-cniti (*do-kŭsniti) 'tarry, delay', this : kasno, etc. (above). Berneker 672.

7. Skt. vilambena, vilambāt, instr. and abl. of vilamba- 'tardiness, delay', lit. 'a hanging down', fr. vi-lamb- 'hang down, delay, loiter' (14.24).

14.18 NOW

Grk.	νῦν	Goth.	nu	Lith.	dabar
NG	τώρα	ON	nū	Lett.	tagad
Lat.	nunc	Dan.	nu	ChSl.	nyně
It.	adesso, ora	Sw.	nu	SCr.	sada
Fr.	maintenant	OE	nū	Boh.	nyní, ted'
Sp.	ahora	ME	nou, now	Pol.	teraz
Rum.	acum	NE	now	Russ.	teper'
Ir.	indorsa	Du.	nu	Skt.	nū, nūnam
NIr.	anois	OHG	nū	Av.	nū, nūrəm
W.	yn awr	MHG	nū, nŭn, iezuo, etc.		
Br.	brema	NHG	jetzt, nun		

Among the words for 'now' there is a large inherited group connected with the IE adj. for 'new'. The others are mostly from phrases with words for 'time' or from pronominal stems with adv. endings of time.

1. IE *nū, etc., related to the adj. *newo- 'new' (14.13). Walde-P. 2.340.

Ernout-M. 685. Widespread in its orig. temporal sense and also, with loss of temporal force, in numerous idiomatic uses introducing a phrase or sentence.

Grk. νῦν (in pop. NG replaced by τώρα, below 2); Lat. nunc (fr. *num-ce); Goth. nu (nū?), ON, OE nū, OHG nŭ, etc., general Gmc.; Lith., Lett. nu, Lith. nūnai (all obs.); ChSl. nyně, Boh. nyní (Pol. ninie obs., Russ. nyne lit.); Skt. nū, nūnam, Av. nū, nūrəm; Toch. A nŭ, B no 'but' (SSS 308).

2. NG τώρα, quotable from the 12th cent., fr. τῇ ὥρᾳ, quotable from the 7th cent. in the sense of 'at this time, just now'. Hatzidakis, Glotta 3.77 ff.

3. It. adesso = OFr. ades, OSp. adieso 'at once', Rum. ades 'often', fr. a base of Lat. dēnsus 'thick' and ad pressum in It. appresso 'near', Fr. après 'after'. REW 2558. Otherwise (fr. ad id ipsum) Wartburg 1.30.

It. ora 'hour, time' used also as adv. 'now'. Similarly, Sp. ahora, OSp. agora, fr. hāc hōrā. REW 4176. Hanssen, Sp. Gram. 198.

Fr. maintenant, pple. of maintenir 'hold in the hand, maintain', with development through 'at hand, handy' to 'at once, soon' (12th cent.), then 'now'. REW 5339. Gamillscheg 581.

Rum. acum (also acuma and acu), fr. VLat. eccum modo 'just now'. Puşcariu 18. Tiktin 17.

4. Ir. indorsa, indossa, innossa, etc., NIr. anois, perh. fr. *ind ōr-sa 'this hour' : ōr, ūar 'hour, time' (14.51). Pedersen 1.207, O'Connell, Ir. Gram. 137. Otherwise Bergin (ap. Strachan, Stories from the Tain[2], 74) as ind fhoss-sa 'this staying' : foss 'staying, rest'.

W. yn awr, phrase with awr 'hour' (14.51).

Br. brema, MBr. breman, fr. *pred-man, this fr. pred 'time', with man 'here'. Henry 43. Ernault, Dict. étym. s.v. breman.

5. Goth. nu, etc., above, 1.

MHG ietso, iezuo, ieze, etc., NHG jetzt, fr. a combination of ie (NHG je) and zuo (NHG zu). Weigand-H. 1.948. Kluge-G. 268.

6. Lith. dabar, etym.?

Lett. tagad, fr. a form of the pron. stem to- and gad : ChSl. godŭ 'time' (14.11), hence similar to ChSl. tŭgda 'then'. Mühl.-Endz. 4.122.

7. ChSl. nyně, above, 1.

SCr. sada, fr. stem of the pron. seen in ChSl. sĭ 'this' and -da as in tada 'then', kada 'when', etc. Leskien, Serbo-kroat. Gram. 405.

Boh. ted', fr. pron. to- with adv. ending.

Pol. teraz, fr. pron. to- and raz 'time' in trzy razy 'three times', etc. (13.44).

Russ. teper', fr. to pervo : pervyj 'first'. Vondrák 2.271.

8. Skt., Av. nū, etc., above, 1.

14.19 SOON; IMMEDIATELY

Grk.	*τάχα, αὐτίκα, εὐθέως*	Goth.	*sprautō; suns*	Lith.	*greit; tuojau*
NG	*σὲ λίγο, γρήγορα, γλήγορα; ἀμέσως*	ON	*brātt, fljōtt*	Lett.	*drīz; tūlin*
Lat.	*mox; statim*	Dan.	*snart; straks*	ChSl.	*abĭje* *skoro;*
It.	*presto; subito*	Sw.	*snart; strax*	SCr.	*skoro; odmah*
Fr.	*bientôt; aussitôt, tout de suite*	OE	*sōna, hrædlīce*	Boh.	*brzo; hned*
Sp.	*luego, presto, pronto*	ME	*sone*	Pol.	*rychło; zaraz*
Rum.	*îndată*	NE	*soon; immediately, etc.*	Russ.	*skoro; totčas*
Ir.	*mos-*	Du.	*weldra, spoedig; dadelijk, onmiddellijk*	Skt.	*makṣū; sadyas*
NIr.	*go gairid; lāithreach*	OHG	*sār, baldō*	Av.	*mošu*
W.	*yn fuan; yn y fan*	MHG	*sā, balde*		
Br.	*hebdale, bremaik, kerkent*	NHG	*bald; sofort, sogleich*		

Words for 'soon' (in a short time) and 'immediately, at once' (without any delay) are separated in the list by a semicolon. But in some cases there is no sufficiently clear differentiation to justify this, the same word being used to cover the mild 'soon' and the emphatic 'immediately'. A positive transition from the latter to the former is seen in the history of OE *sōna*, NE *soon*.

The majority of the words for 'soon' are, or were once, simply 'quickly', advs. to adjs. for 'swift, quick'. There are generally alternative expressions, mostly not included in the list, parallel to NE *in a little while, in a short time, shortly*, e.g. Lat. *brevī tempore* or simply *brevī*, It. *poco tempo* or *poco* (*poco dopo* 'soon after'), Pol. *wkrótce* (: *krótko* 'shortly, briefly'), and formerly NHG *kürzlich* (now obs. in this sense and only 'shortly before').

Expressions for 'immediately' are too numerous to be listed in full (cf. NE *immediately, at once, directly*, the now archaic *straightway, forthwith*, etc.), and of the most diverse orig. They may come from words for 'straight', 'immediate', 'actually, exactly', 'place', with specialization to temporal sense, or from words for 'time' ('this time' or 'in time'), or again from the pronoun for 'this' with 'time' understood.

1. IE **mok̑s*. Walde-P. 2.303 f., Ernout-M. 635. Pedersen 1.78.

Lat. *mox;* Ir. vbl. particle *mos-* (*mo-, mu-*), MW *moch;* Skt. *makṣū*, Av. *mošu*.

2. Grk. *τάχα, ταχύ, ταχέως* : *ταχύς* 'swift, quick'.

Grk. *αὐτίκα* : *αὐτός* in intensive sense.

Grk. *εὐθέως* : *εὐθύς* 'straight'.

NG *γρήγορα, γλήγορα* 'quickly' : *γρήγορος* 'quick' (14.21) may serve for 'soon'; or, more exactly, *σὲ λίγο* (lit. *ἐντὸς ὀλίγου*) 'in a little while'.

NG *ἀμέσως* : *ἄμεσος* 'immediate', neg. cpd. of *μέσος* 'middle'. Used reg. of time, like NE *immediately*.

3. Lat. *mox*, above, 1.

Lat. *statim* : *status* 'standing', hence in early use 'steadfastly', then 'immediately', like NE *on the spot* in temporal sense (NED s.v. *spot* 9), Fr. *sur le champ*. Ernout-M. 980.

It., Sp. *presto* (mostly stronger than 'soon'), fr. Lat. *praestō* 'at hand, ready' (14.29). REW 6726.

It. *subito*, fr. Lat. *subitō* 'suddenly', adv. to *subitus* 'sudden', pple. of *sub-īre* 'come upon'. REW 8366.

OFr. *tost*, Fr. *tôt*, now mostly in *bientôt* 'soon', *aussitôt* 'immediately', *plutôt* 'sooner, rather', It. *tostō* ('soon' in some phrases) fr. Lat. *tostus* 'roasted, baked', semantic development uncertain, but prob. through 'hard, firm' (attested in

It. dialects), hence somewhat as in Lat. *statim* (above) and NE *fast* in sense of 'swift' (14.21). REW 8814. Gamillscheg 851.

Fr. *tout de suite*, lit. 'all in succession', fr. *suite* 'succession, sequence', etc. fr. VLat. **sequita* : Lat. *sequī* 'follow'.

Sp. *luego* 'presently, soon, immediately', fr. Lat. *locō* 'at the right place or time', abl. of *locus* 'place'.

Sp. *pronto* 'ready' (14.29), also 'quickly, soon'.

Rum. *îndată*, cpd. of *în* 'in' and *dată* in phrases *odată* 'once', etc., fr. Lat. *data* neut. pl. of *datus* 'given'. Tiktin 507 f.

4. Ir. *mos-*, above, 1.

NIr. *go gairid*, lit. 'shortly' : *gairid* 'short'.

NIr. *lāithreach*, adv. use of *lāithreach* 'spot, site'.

NIr. also for 'immediately' *ar an mball* 'on the spot', *ar āit na mbonn* 'on the spot of the sole', etc.

W. *yn fuan* : *buan* 'swift, quick' (14.21).

W. *yn y fan*, lit. 'on the spot' : *man* 'spot, place'.

Br. *hebdale*, lit. 'without delay', fr. *hep* 'without' and *dale* 'delay'.

Br. *bremaik* ('bientôt' Ernault; 'tout de suite' Vallée p. 66) : *brema* 'now' (14.18).

Br. *kerkent*, fr. *ken, ker* 'so', and *kent* 'before'. Henry 63.

5. Goth. *sprautō* 'quickly, soon' (cf. 1 Tim. 3.14 'soon'), see 14.21.

Goth. *suns* 'immediately, at once' ('*εὐθέως*' Mk. 1.21, etc.), as also OE *sōna* (ME *sone*, NE *soon* with gradual weakening to 'soon'), OS, OFris. *sān*, OHG *sār* (also *sān*), MHG *sār, sā*, outside connections? Feist 460. NED s.v. *soon*.

ON *brātt* (*brāðum, brāðan*), advs. fr. *brāðr* adj. 'sudden, hasty, hot (of temper)', Dan. *brad*, Sw. *bråd* 'sudden' : OE *brǣþ* 'vapor, breath', OHG *brādam* 'steam, breath, heat', etc. Semantic development prob. through 'hot'. Cf. NE *a hot race*. Falk-Torp 96.

ON *fljōtt*, esp. comp. and superl. *fljōtara, fljōtast*, advs. : adj. *fljōtr* 'swift' (14.21).

Dan., Sw. *snart*, adv. to *snar* 'swift, quick' (14.21).

Dan. *straks*, Sw. *strax*, fr. MLG *strakes* (Du. *straks*) = MHG *strackes*, adv. gen. of *strack* 'straight'. Falk-Torp 1176.

OE (beside *sōna*, above) *hrædlīce*, adv. to *hrædlīc* beside *hræd* 'swift, quick' (14.21).

NE *immediately*, formed with adv. *-ly* fr. MLat. *immediātē*, adv. of MLat. *immediātus* : Lat. *medius* 'middle'. NED s.v.

NE *at once, directly, straightway*, all of obvious derivation, with temporal sense secondary.

Du. *weldra*, fr. MDu. *wel drāde*, with *wel* 'well' and *drāde* = MLG *drade* (MHG *drāte*, OHG *drāto*) 'quickly'. Franck-v. W. 129, 785.

Du. *spoedig*, adv. use of *spoedig* 'speedy' (14.21).

Du. *dadelijk*, fr. *daad* 'deed, act', and in earlier use 'actually'. Franck-v. W. 104.

Du. *onmiddellijk*, fr. neg. cpd. of *middel* 'middle', and so parallel to NE *immediately*.

OHG *baldō*, MHG *balde* 'impetuously, boldly' and 'quickly, immediately', NHG *bald* 'soon' : adj. MHG *bald* 'bold' and 'swift, quick', OE *beald, bald* 'daring, bold', NE *bold*, Goth. *balþei* 'boldness', etc., outside connections dub. Walde-P. 2.179. Falk-Torp 91. Weigand-H. 1.141. Kluge-G. 34.

NHG *sofort*, lit. 'so forth' (without delay).

NHG *gleich* 'alike, exactly', hence also 'immediately' (*gleich kommen*), and in this sense esp. *sogleich*.

6. Lith. *greit* : *greitas* 'swift, quick' (14.21).

Lith. *tuojau*, fr. *tuo*, old instr. sg. of *tas* 'this'; hence lit. 'with this' (moment).

Lett. *drīz* : *drīzs* 'swift, quick' (14.21).

Lett. *tūlin*, prob. through a **tū-le* (like *nū-le* beside *nū* 'now'), fr. **tū* : *tas* 'this' (cf. Lith. *tuojau*, above). Mühl.-Endz. 4.280.

7. ChSl., SCr., Russ. *skoro* : ChSl. *skorŭ* 'swift, quick' (14.21).

ChSl. *abĭje*, perh. with init. vowel lengthening fr. **obĭ je* (*obŭ* 'at' and *je* acc. sg. neut. of sem *jo-* 'this'), hence 'at this' (time), like Lith. *tuojau*, etc. Walde-P. 1.52. Berneker 23.

SCr. *odmah*, fr. *od* 'from' and *mah* 'blow, stroke', also 'time' in phrases *jedan mah* 'once', etc. Berneker 2.4.

Boh. *brzo* : *brzý* 'swift', ChSl. *brŭzo*, SCr. *brzo* 'quickly', etc. (14.21).

Boh. *hned* (also OPol. *hnet*, Pol. *wnet*), fr. *nhed, inhed*, fr. *in-* : ChSl. *inŭ-* 'one', and second part : ChSl. *-gda* in *tŭ-gda* 'then'. Gebauer 1.230, 545. Brückner 627.

Pol. *rychło* : *rychły* 'early', Boh. *rychlý* 'swift, quick' (14.21).

Pol. *zaraz*, fr. *za* 'in, on' and *raz* 'time', as in *teraz* 'now' (14.18), etc.

Russ. *totčas*, fr. *tot* 'this' and *čas* 'time, hour' (14.11).

8. Skt. *makṣū*, Av. *mošu*, above, 1.

Skt. *sadyas*, lit. 'on the same day', fr. cop. *sa-* and second part : *div-, dyu-* 'sky, day'.

14.21 SWIFT, FAST, QUICK

Grk.	*ταχύς, ὠκύς, θοός, ὀξύς*	Goth.	*sprautō* (adv.)	Lith.	*greitas, skubus*
NG	*γρήγορος, γλήγορος*	ON	*fljōtr, skjōtr, hraðr, snarr*	Lett.	*ātrs, žigls*
Lat.	*celer, vēlōx, citus, rapidus*	Dan.	*rask, hurtig, snar*	ChSl.	*skorŭ; jędro, brĭzo* (advs.)
It.	*rapido, presto, veloce*	Sw.	*snabb, snar, rask*	SCr.	*brz, hitar*
Fr.	*rapide, vite* (adv.)	OE	*hræd, swift, snel(l)*	Boh.	*rychlý*
Sp.	*rápido, presto, veloz*	ME	*swift, rad, snel, spede*	Pol.	*prędki, szybki*
Rum.	*repede, iute*	NE	*fast, swift, quick, speedy*	Russ.	*bystryj, skoryj, šibkij*
Ir.	*dīan, lūath, crib*	Du.	*vlug, snel, gauw, ras(ch), spoedig*	Skt.	*āçu-, tvarita-, çīghra-, java(na)-*
NIr.	*luath, tapaidh*	OHG	*sniumi, (h)rad, snel, rasc*	Av.	*āsu-, aurvant-, θwaša-, xšviwra-*
W.	*buan, cyflym, chwyrn, clau*	MHG	*snel, rasch, sliume, geswinde*		
Br.	*buan, herrus*	NHG	*schnell, rasch, geschwind*		

There is a wealth of words denoting rapid motion (besides those listed, e.g. NE *rapid*, NHG *schleunig*) from which it is not always easy to select the most generic and usual and between which the choice is too idiomatic, according to the context, to permit any generalization. NE *swift* or the now more common *fast* may apply to rapid motion of any duration, while in *quick* (in accordance with its original sense of 'live, lively') there is a notion of 'sudden' or 'soon over'. We speak of a *fast* horse or runner in a race, a *quick* starter but not a *quick* horse. A somewhat similar feeling may distinguish NHG *schnell* and *rasch*, or it may be more a matter of local preference (for which cf. Kretschmer,

Wortgeogr. 385). And so in the other languages one could show the differentiation only by quoting phrases in great number.

The semantic sources are too diverse to summarize.

1. IE **ōku-*. Walde-P. 1.172. Ernout-M. 696.

Grk. *ὠκύς* (poet.); Skt. *āçu-*, Av. *āsu-*; Lat. *ōcior, ōcissimus* 'swifter, swiftest'; OW *di-auc*, W. *diog*, Br. *diek* 'lazy' (lit. 'not swift').

2. Grk. *ταχύς*, beside *τάχος* 'speed', *τάχα* 'quickly, soon, at once', etym. dub. Boisacq 946. G. S. Lane, Language 11.191.

Grk. *θοός* (poet.) : *θέω* 'run', etc. (10.46). Boisacq 342 f.

Grk. *ὀξύς* 'sharp' (15.78), but also (post- Hom., Hdt., etc.) 'swift'.

Byz., NG *γρήγορος*, pop. *γλήγορος*, through 'prompt, ready' (and perh. first in adv. *γρήγορα*), fr. Grk. *ἐγρήγορα* 'am awake', perf. of *ἐγείρω* 'awaken'.

3. Lat. *celer* : Grk. *κέλης* 'courser (horse), fast sailing ship', *κέλομαι* 'drive on, incite', Skt. *kal-* 'drive', etc. Walde-P. 1.443 f. Ernout-M. 170. Walde-H. 1.194 f.

Lat. *vēlōx* (> It. *veloce*, Sp. *veloz*), cf. *vēles* 'light-armed infantryman', etym. dub., perh. (**weg-slo-*) fr. the root of *vegēre* 'move, excite', *vegetus* 'live, animate' (cf. the semantic development of NE *quick*, below, 5); or (**wegh-slo-*) : *vehere* 'drive, transport'?). Ernout-M. 1082.

Lat. *citus*, pple. of *ciēre* 'set in motion, excite' : Grk. *κίω* 'go', *κῑνέω* 'move'. Ernout-M. 185 f. Walde-H. 1.213 f.

Lat. *rapidus* (> It. *rapido*, Sp. *rápido*, Rum. *repede;* Fr. *rapide* > NE *rapid*), orig. 'violent, tearing away' (esp. of swift-flowing currents), fr. *rapere* 'snatch, carry off, plunder'. Ernout-M. 854. REW 7054.

It., Sp. *presto* (Fr. *prêt* 'ready'), fr. late Lat. *praestus* fr. adv. *praestō* 'at hand, ready' (14.29). REW 6726.

Fr. *vite* (adv., but until 17th cent. also adj.), OFr. *viste* : It. *visto, vispo* 'quick, brisk, smart', prob. of imitative orig. REW 9379a. Otherwise Gamillscheg 894.

Rum. *iute*, also 'violent, impetuous', fr. the Slavic, cf. ChSl. *ljutŭ* 'cruel, fierce', etc. Tiktin 862.

4. Ir. *dīan*, beside *dēne* 'swiftness', prob. : Grk. *δίω* 'flee', Skt. *dī-* 'fly', etc. Walde-P. 1.775.

Ir. *lūath*, NIr. *luath*, also Ir. *luam* id., beside *luas* 'speed', fr. *lu-* 'move' (10.11).

Ir. *crib* (*cribb, crip*), etym. dub. Pedersen 1.161. Walde-P. 1.472, 2.568.

NIr. *tapaidh* = Gael. *tapaidh* 'clever, active' : NIr. *tap* 'a start or fight, an accident' (Dinneen), orig. dub. Possibly fr. a vbl. cpd. **to-ad-ben-* : *benim* 'strike' (cf. OIr. *taipe* 'epitome', Pedersen 2.461).

W., Br. *buan*, etym. dub. Pedersen 2.56. Henry 47. Loth, RC 36.143.

W. *cyflym*, cpd. of *llym* 'sharp, keen' (arch. also 'quick', cf.; Spurrell, s.v.) = Br. *lemm* 'sharp', etym. dub. Walde-P. 2.391, 435.

W. *chwyrn*, often with implication of a whirring sound (Evans, s.v.; cf. *chwyrnu* 'whiz, whir, snore'), prob. based on an imitative syllable, like that in Skt. *svar-* 'make a sound', Lat. *susurrus* 'humming', NE *swearm* 'swarm', Walde-P. 2.528 (adversely). Loth, RC 23.117. Morris Jones 146 (: Skt. *sphur-* 'jerk, dart'; improbable).

W. *clau* : Ir. *clō* 'whirlwind', root connection? Loth, RC 38.159.

Br. *herrus*, fr. *herr* 'speed, impulse', older *err*, fr. OFr. *erre* 'journey, way, course' in phrases like *de grant erre, de bonne erre*, etc. (cf. Godefroy, s.v.). Henry 116.

5. Goth. *sprautō*, adv. (renders ταχύ, ταχέως, etc.) : OE *ā-sprūtan*, *spryttan* 'sprout', MHG *spriezen* id., W. *ffrwst* 'haste', Lett. *sprausties pruojam* 'clear out'. Walde-P. 2.671. Feist 446.

ON *fljōtr* : *fljōta* 'float', etc., Grk. πλέω 'sail, swim' (cf. Ir. *lūath*, above, 4). Falk-Torp 242.

ON *skjōtr* (OE *scēot* 'quick, ready' not common) : *skjōta*, OE *scēotan*, etc. 'set in motion, shoot', Skt. *cud-* 'drive, press'. Walde-P. 2.554. Falk-Torp 1045.

ON *hraðr*, OE *hræd*, *hræþ*, ME *rad*, OHG (*h*)*rat*, (*h*)*rad* : Lith. *api-kratai* 'quickly', *krėsti* 'shake, shake out', *kretėti* 'move back and forth, waver', Ir. *crothaim* 'shake'. Walde-P. 1.484. Falk-Torp 870.

ON *snarr* 'swift, keen' (of eye, etc.), Dan., Sw. *snar*, lit. 'twisted tight, hard-pun' (of a cord), so rarely ON *snarr* (cf. Vigfusson, s.v.) : ON *snara* 'twist, wring, turn quickly'. Walde-P. 2.701. Falk-Torp 1090. Hellquist 1011.

Dan. *hurtig* (Sw. *hurtig* 'cheerful, brisk, agile'), fr. NHG *hurtig* 'brisk, quick (at work), alert', deriv. of MHG *hurt* 'shove, drive' fr. OFr. *hurt* 'shove'. Falk-Torp 433.

Sw. *snabb*, prob. : MHG *snaben* 'hurry' = *snaben* 'snap, hop, jump, shove, etc.', beside *snappen* 'snap', NE *snap*, etc., all fr. a Gmc. **snab-*, **snap-* indicating various types of quick motion, but root connection dub. Hellquist 1009 f. Falk-Torp 1089 f.

OE-NE *swift* : OE *swīfan* 'move, sweep', ON *svīfa* 'swing, turn, drift', OHG *sweibōn* 'sway, swing', etc. Walde-P. 2.520. NED s.v.

OE *snel*(*l*), ME *snel*, Du., OHG, MHG *snel*, NHG *schnell* : Sw. *snäll* 'good, nice', older 'quick, capable', Dan. *snild* 'shrewd', root connection dub. Falk-Torp 1096. Weigand-H. 2.764.

NE *quick*, in this sense rarely also ME but mostly 'vigorous, lively, alive, etc.', OE *cwicu* 'alive' : ON *kvikr*, OHG *quec*, Lat. *vīvus*, etc. 'alive'. NED s.v.

NE *fast*, orig. as still also 'firm', fr. OE *fæst* 'firm' : ON *fastr*, OHG *festi*, NHG *fest*, etc. 'firm'. The sense of 'swift' (for which it is now the pop. word) seems to have developed first in the adv. (quoted in NED from 1205) in phrases like *run fast* (cf. *run hard*). NED s.v.

NE *speedy*, Du. *spoedig*, fr. sbs. NE *speed*, Du. *spoed* 'speed', orig. 'success', as OE *spēd*, OHG *spuot*, beside vbs. OE *spōwan*, OHG *spuon* 'succeed' : ChSl. *spěti* 'succeed' (also *spěšiti*, etc. 'hasten' (14.23). Walde-P. 2.657. Franck-v. W. 648. NED s.v. *speed*, sb.

Du. *vlug*, fr. MDu. *vlugghe* 'able to fly' : Du. *vliegen*, NHG *fliegen*, etc. 'fly'. Franck-v. W. 752.

Du. *gauw*, MDu. *gā* : OHG *gāhi* 'sudden, hasty, quick' (NHG *jäh* 'abrupt'), etym. dub. (ablaut form with prefix *ga-* to Grk. ὠκύς, etc., above, 1?). Walde-P. 1.172. Franck-v. W. 176 f.

OHG *rasc*, MHG, NHG, Du. *rasch* (MLG > Dan., Sw. *rask*), with ME *rasch* (rare), NE *rash* 'hasty, impetuous, reckless' (loanword?, cf. NED), fr. Gmc. **raska-*, perh. **rad-ska-* : Ir. *rethim* 'run', Skt. *ratha-* 'wagon', etc. Walde-P. 2.368. Falk-Torp 882.

OHG *sniumi* (*sniumo*, *sliumo*, adv.), MHG *sliume*, *sniume* (OE *snēome* adv.) : Goth. *sniumjan*, *sniwan*, OE *snēowan* 'hasten' (14.23).

MHG *geswinde* (also 'bold, violent'), NHG *geschwind*, cpd. of MHG *swinde*, *swint* 'strong, mighty, vehement' : OE *swīþ*, OS *swīð* 'strong, vehement', Goth. *swinþs* 'strong, sound'. Walde-P. 2.525. Weigand-H. 1.702.

6. Lith. *greitas* : Lett. *greits* 'lively, angry, grim', etym.? Mühl.-Endz. 1.647.

Lith. *skubus*, beside *skubintis* 'hasten' : Goth. *af-skiuban* 'reject' (lit. 'shove off'), OE *scēofan*, etc. 'shove'. Walde-P. 2.556.

Lett. *ātrs*, Lith. dial. *otu* 'swift', perh. : OHG *ātar* 'acer, sagax, celer', OE *ǣdre* 'quickly, at once', OS *ādro* 'hastily, at once, early'. Walde-P. 1.118. Zupitza, KZ 37.406.

Lett. *žigls*, perh. loanword fr. Lith. *žiglus* 'lively' (old or dial.), beside *žygis* 'a turn, journey'. Mühl.-Endz. 4.809.

Lett. *drīzs*, etym.? Mühl.-Endz. 1.501.

7. ChSl. *skorŭ*, Russ. *skoryj*, prob. : Grk. σκαίρω 'jump, hop, dance', MHG *scher*(*e*)*n* 'hasten', NHG *sich scheren* 'clear out', etc. Walde-P. 2.567.

Russ.-ChSl. *jadrŭ* (ChSl. only adv. *jędro* 'ταχύ, ταχέως'), 'swift' fr. 'strong', cf. Bulg. (*j*)*édŭr* 'strong, capable, pithy', SCr. *jedar* 'full, strong', prob. also Russ.-ChSl. *jadro* 'kernel, testicle', etc., all fr. an orig. sense 'swollen' : Grk. οἰδάω 'swell', etc. Walde-P. 1.166. Berneker 455 f.

ChSl. *brĭzo* (adv., Russ.-ChSl. *bŭrzyjĭ* 'swift, brave'), SCr., Slov. *brz*, Bulg. *bŭrz*, etc. (general Slavic, but the usual word only in South Slavic; as adv. Boh. *brzo* 'quickly, soon'), perh. as orig. 'in short time' : Grk. βραχύς, Lat. *brevis*, etc. 'short'. Machek, KZ 64.264 f. (vs. Berneker 110).

SCr. *hitar*, also 'dexterous' : ChSl. *chytrŭ* 'dexterous', etc. fr. the root in ChSl. *chytati* 'snatch, tear', SCr. *hitati* 'seize, throw, hasten', *hitjeti* 'hasten', etc. Berneker 414.

Boh. *rychlý* (Pol. *rychły* 'early', adv. *rychło* 'soon', Russ. *rychlyj* 'porous, light') : Boh. *ruch* 'stir, commotion', Pol. *ruch* 'motion', Russ. *ruch* 'unrest, motion', etc. Walde-P. 1.142, 2.356.

Pol. *prędki* : *prąd* 'swift stream', Russ. *prjadat'*, ChSl. *prędati* 'jump'. Brückner 436. Walde-P. 2.676.

Pol. *szybki*, Russ. *šibkij* : Russ. *šibat'* 'throw', Skt. *kṣip-* 'throw, hurl', *kṣipra-* 'elastic (of a bow), quick'. Walde-P. 1.501. Brückner 559.

Russ. *bystryj* (ChSl. *bystrŭ* Supr. = εὐτρεχής 'skilful, ready', Russ.-ChSl. 'swift'; SCr. *bistar*, Boh. *bystrý*, Pol. *bystry*, mostly 'clear, quick-witted, etc.') perh. : ON *bysja* 'gush forth', Norw. *buse* 'pitch, fall head first', etc., Russ. *buchnut'* 'swell', etc. (cf. ChSl. *jędro* : Grk. οἰδάω, above). Walde-P. 2.118 f. Berneker 113.

8. Skt. *tvarita-*, Av. *θwaša-* (**twarta-*) : Skt. *tvar-* 'hasten' (14.23). Walde-P. 1.749.

Skt. *çīghra-* : Russ. *sigat'*, *signut'* 'jump'. Walde-P. 1.363 (but for OE *hīgian*, NE *hie*, see 14.23).

Skt. *java-*, *javana-* : *jū-* 'drive on, incite, etc.', mid. 'hasten', Av. *jav-* 'hasten', etc. Walde-P. 1.555. Barth. 504. Wackernagel, Altind. Gram. 1.161.

Skt. *āçu*, Av. *āsu*, above, 1.

Av. *aurvant-*, *aurva-* : Skt. *arvat-* 'racing', OE *earu* 'quick, active, ready', ON *ǫrr* 'ready, swift, liberal', prob. fr. the root in Skt. *ṛṇoti* 'rises, moves', Grk. ὄρνυμι 'stir, urge, rouse', etc. Walde-P. 1.141.

Av. *xšviwra-*, cf. *xšviwi-vāza-* 'going swiftly', *xšvaēwayaṭ-aštrā-* 'swinging the whip swiftly', prob. : ON *svipa* 'swoop, move quickly, whip', etc. Cf. OE *swift* fr. a parallel root (above, 5). Barth. 561, IF 9.274 f. Walde-P. 1.241.

14.22 SLOW (adj.)

Grk.	βραδύς	Goth.	(*lats*)	Lith.	*lėtas*, *palengva* (adv.)
NG	ἀργός, βραδύς; ἀγάλια, σιγά (advs.)	ON	*seinn*, *latr*	Lett.	*lēns*
Lat.	*tardus*, *lentus*	Dan.	*langsom*, *sen*	ChSl.	*mądĭnŭ*, *kŭsĭnŭ*
It.	*lento*	Sw.	*sakta*, *långsam*, *trög*	SCr.	*spor*
Fr.	*lent*	OE	*læt*, *sǣne*	Boh.	*zdlouhavý*
Sp.	*lento*	ME	*slow*, *lat*	Pol.	*powolny*
Rum.	*încet*	NE	*slow*	Russ.	*medlennyj*
Ir.	*mall*	Du.	*langzaam*	Skt.	*manda-*
NIr.	*mall*	OHG	*laz*, *trāgi*, *langseimi*	Av.	. . . .
W.	*araf*	MHG	*træge*, *seine*, *lanc-seime*, *laz*		
Br.	*gorrek*	NHG	*langsam*		

Words for 'slow' are cognate with others for 'late', 'dull, sluggish, lazy', 'soft, mild', 'long', 'rest', etc.

1. Grk. βραδύς, etym. dub. Walde-P. 1.641. Ernout-M. 438. Walde-H. 1.627.

NG ἀργός (also 'late', cf. adv. ἀργά 'late', 14.17), fr. Grk. ἀργός, Hom. ἀεργός (*ἀ-ϝεργός) 'idle, lazy' (4.92).

NG adv. ἀγάλια, esp. repeated ἀγάλια (ἀ)γάλια 'slowly', dial. (ἀ)γαληνά, fr. γαληνός 'calm'. Xanthoudidis, Ἀθηνᾶ 26, παράρτ. 126 f. Ἱστ. Λεξ. 1.49.

NG adv. σιγά, esp. repeated σιγὰ σιγά, fr. class. Grk. σῖγα 'silently' or σῖγα imperat. of σιγάω 'be silent'.

2. Lat. *tardus*, etym. dub. Walde-P. 1.728. Ernout-M. 1017 f.

Lat. *lentus*, orig. 'supple, pliant', hence 'soft, indolent' and 'slow' (> It., Sp. *lento*, Fr. *lent*), prob. : OHG *lind*(*i*) 'soft, tender', OE *līþe* 'gentle, mild', etc. Walde-P. 2.437. Ernout-M. 539 f. Walde-H. 1.784.

Rum. *încet*, cpd. of *în-* and *-cet* (= It. *cheto* 'quiet') fr. VLat. *quētus* for *quiētus* 'at rest, quiet'. REW 6958. Pușcariu 813.

3. Ir. *mall* = W. *mall* in early use 'slow', also 'soft' and in cpds. 'bad', with vb. *mallu* 'make soft, rotten', root connection dub. Stokes 214. Loth, RC 40, 345 f.

W. *araf*, perh. : Grk. ἐρωή 'rest' (from battle), ON *rō*, OE *rōw*, OHG *rouwa* 'rest', Av. *airime* adv. 'quietly'. Walde-P. 1.44.

Br. *gorrek*, fr. *goar* 'leisure, slowness', this : *gwar* 'crooked'. Henry 135, 137. Ernault, Dict. étym. 297.

4. Goth. *lats* 'idle, lazy' (not quotable as 'slow'; passages with βραδύς lacking), ON *latr* 'slow, lazy', OE *læt*, ME *lat* 'slow, late', OHG *laz* ('tardus' Tat. 227.1, 'piger' 149.7), MHG *laz* 'slow, lazy' : Lat. *lassus* (**lәd-to-*) 'tired, weary', Grk. ληδεῖν 'be tired', Goth. *lētan*, ON *lāta* 'leave, let', IE **lē*(*i*)*d-*, fr. a simpler **lē*(*i*)- in Lith. *lėtas* 'slow, quiet, calm', Lett. *lēns* 'slow, gentle, mild' (or **lēd-no-*?), etc. (cf. below, 5). Walde-P. 2.395. Falk-Torp 616. Feist 323.

ON *seinn*, Dan. *sen* 'late, slow' (advs. ON *seint* 'late, slowly', Dan., Sw. *sent* 'late', 14.17), OE *sǣne*, MHG *seine* 'slow' : Goth. *sainjan* 'delay, tarry', Lith. *at-sainus* 'negligent', prob. fr. the root **sēi-* in Goth. *seiþus*, Lat. *sērus* 'late', etc. (14.17). Walde-P. 2.462. Falk-Torp 957.

Sw. *sakta* 'gentle, slow' (in the latter sense esp. as adv.) = Dan. *sagte* 'soft, gentle', fr. MLG *sāchte*, altered form of *sāfte* : NE *soft*, NHG *sanft*, etc. Falk-Torp 944. Hellquist 880.

Sw. *trög* : Dan. *trøg* 'reluctant, sluggish', ON *trauðr* 'unwilling, reluctant', etc. Falk-Torp 1294 f. Hellquist 1236.

ME, NE *slow*, fr. OE *slāw* 'dull (of persons), sluggish, lazy' : ON *sljōr*, *slǣr*, OHG *sleo*, etc., 'dull, blunt' (15.79). NED s.v. *slow*, adj.

OHG *trāgi*, MHG *træge* 'slow, lazy' (NHG *träge* 'lazy') = OE *trāg* 'evil, bad' : Goth. *trigō* 'reluctance', ON *tregi* 'reluctance, grief', OE *trega* 'pain, grief', prob. fr. the root in Skt. *drāgh-* 'be tired', etc. Walde-P. 1.821. Falk-Torp 1291 f.

OHG *langseimi*, MHG *lancseime* (also *lanceine*, influence of *seine*, above), cpd. of *lang* 'long' and a deriv. of the root in ON, OHG *seinn* (above). NHG *langsam* (> Dan. *langsom*, Sw. *långsam*), in form fr. OHG *langsam* 'of long duration', but with absorption of the sense of the preceding. Walde-P. 2.463. Falk-Torp 623, 957. Weigand-H. 2.16.

5. Lith. *lėtas*, Lett. *lēns* : Goth. *lats*, etc. (above, 4). Mühl.-Endz. 2.460.

Lith. *palengva* (adv.), fr. *lengvas* 'light' (15.82).

6. ChSl. *mądĭnŭ* and *mudĭnŭ*, beside *mąditi* and *muditi* 'delay' (quotations of each form and vb. *kŭsněti*, Jagić, Entstehungsgesch. 365), also *mĭdĭlĭnŭ* (Ostr.), Russ. *medlennyj*, phonetic relations not clear but doubtless related forms (cf. Meillet, MSL 14.372, Études 164), prob. : Skt. *manda-* 'slow'. Walde-P. 2.305.

ChSl. *kŭsĭnŭ* (late, but vb. *kŭsněti* 'be slow', earlier) = SCr. *kasan* 'late', adv. *kasno*, Russ. *kosnyj* 'inert, slow to change' : Lett. *kust* 'tire' and 'melt, thaw', further connections dub. Walde-P. 1.468. Berneker 672.

SCr. *spor*, lit. 'long lasting', Russ. *sporyj* 'profitable, advantageous', ChSl. *sporŭ* 'abundant' : Skt. *sphira-* 'fat, plump', fr. the root in Skt. *sphāy-* 'grow fat, swell'. Walde-P. 2.657.

Boh. *zdlouhavý*, fr. *dlouhavý* 'longish, dull', fr. *dlouhý* 'long' (12.57).

Pol. *powolny*, fr. *wolny* 'free'. Brückner 630.

7. Skt. *manda-*, prob. : ChSl. *mądĭnŭ*, above, 6.

14.23 HASTEN, HURRY (vb. intr.)

Grk.	σπεύδω	Goth.	*sniumjan*, *sniwan*	Lith.	*skubintis*
NG	βιάζομαι (σπεύδω)	ON	*skynda* (*sēr*), *skunda* (*sēr*)	Lett.	*steigties*, *traukt*(*ies*)
Lat.	*festīnāre*, *properāre*	Dan.	*skynde sig*, *haste*, *ile*	ChSl.	*potŭštati sę*, *podvignąti sę*, *spěšiti*
It.	*affrettarsi*	Sw.	*skynda sig*, *hasta*, *ila*	SCr.	*hitjeti*, *brzati*, *žuriti se*
Fr.	*se dépêcher*, *se presser*, *se hâter*	OE	*ef*(*e*)*stan*, *scyndan*, *snēowan*	Boh.	*chvátati*, *spěchati*, *kvapiti*
Sp.	*apresurarse*, *darse prisa*	ME	*hye*, *haste*	Pol.	*spieszyć*, *kwapić się*
Rum.	*se grăbi*	NE	*hurry*, *hasten*	Russ.	*toropit'sja*, *spěšit'*
Ir.	*dīanaigur*	Du.	*zich haasten*, *zich spoeden*	Skt.	*tvar-*, *jū-*
NIr.	*brostuighim*	OHG	*īlen*, *sih gispuotōn*	Av.	*jav-*
W.	*brysio*, *hastu*	MHG	*īlen*, *scher*(*e*)*n*		
Br.	*hasta*, *buanaat*	NHG	*eilen*, *sich beeilen*		

In 'hasten' (and the generally parallel nouns for 'haste') there is involved, beside rapid movement, a notion of urgency or impetuosity. Only a few of the words are derived from those for 'swift'. The majority are connected with words denoting some kind of violent action.

1. Grk. σπεύδω, beside σπουδή 'haste' (also 'zeal, exertion, earnestness', etc.) : Lith. *spausti* 'press', *spudinti* 'hurry off, clear out', Alb. *punë* 'work, business', IE **speud-*, with development of 'press' to 'hasten' (cf. Fr. *se presser*). Walde-P. 2.659.

NG βιάζομαι (beside lit. σπεύδω), lit. 'be forced', mid. of βιάζω 'force, compel' : βία 'force'.

2. Lat. *festīnāre*, beside *festīnus* 'hasty', *confestim* 'hastily, at once', perh. fr. **fers-ti-* : W. *brys* 'haste', *brysio* 'hasten', MIr. *bras* 'quick, active', etc. Walde-P. 2.175. Ernout-M. 353 f. Walde-H. 1.488.

Lat. *properāre*, fr. *properus* 'hastening, speedy', fr. *pro-* 'before' and (prob.) deriv. of **per-* in Grk. πέρāν 'beyond', Lat. *portāre* 'carry', etc. Ernout-M. 815 f.

It. *affrettarsi*, refl. of *affrettare* 'dispatch, speed up', fr. *fretta* 'haste', deriv. of VLat. **frictāre* 'rub', frequent. of *fricāre*. REW 3505.

Fr. *se hâter*, refl. of *hâter* 'hasten', OFr. *haster* 'press on, pursue', fr. *hâte* 'haste', OFr. *haste* fr. the Gmc., cf. Goth. *haifsts* 'quarrel', OE *hǣst* 'enmity', OFris. *hāst* 'haste', etc. OFr. *haste* is the source of the sbs. ME *haste*, MLG *hast*, etc., whence (or in part fr. OFr. *haster*) the vbs. ME *haste*, NE *hasten*, MLG *hasten* (> NHG *hasten*), Du. *haasten* (Dan. *haste*, Sw. *hasta* through sb. fr. MLG), W. *hastu*, Br. *hasta*. REW 3990. Falk-Torp 384. Franck-v. W. 224. NED s.vv. *haste*, *hasten*.

Fr. *se dépêcher*, refl. of *dépêcher* 'expedite, dispatch', for **desempêcher* fr. *empêcher* 'hinder' (Lat. *impedicāre*). REW 4296. Gamillscheg 306.

Fr. *se presser*, refl. of *presser* 'press, squeeze', Sp. *darse prisa* 'make haste', with *prisa* 'haste, urgency', Sp. *apresurarse*, refl. of *apresurar* 'hasten, speed up', fr. *presura* 'anxiety, haste' (Lat. *pressura* 'pressure'), all fr. Lat. *pressāre* 'press'. REW 6741.

Rum. *se grăbi*, refl. of *grăbi* 'drive on, press, dispatch', fr. the Slavic, cf. ChSl. *grabiti* 'seize, plunder'. Tiktin 694 f.

3. Ir. *dīanaigur* (e.g. imperat. *dianaigthe* 'celera', Ml. 49d.9), fr. *dīan* 'swift' (14.21).

NIr. *brostuighim*, as trans. 'excite, goad', MIr. *brostaim*, and *brostaigim* 'incite, stir up' (K. Meyer, Contrib. 270 f.), prob. : Ir. *brot* 'goad' (sb.), but relation complicated. Stokes ap. Macbain 52.

W. *brysio*, see under Lat. *festīnāre*, above, 2.

W. *hastu*, Br. *hasta*, see under Fr. *se hâter*, above, 2.

Br. *buanaat*, fr. *buan* 'swift' (14.21).

4. Goth. *sniumjan* (fr. **sniu-m-* in OHG *sniumi* 'swift', etc., 14.21), *sniwan*, OE *snēowan*, ON *snyðja* (rare) : ON *snūa* 'turn', *snūðr* 'noose' and 'swiftness', OE *snūd* 'haste', ON *snūðigr* 'turning, swift', prob. Skt. *snāvan-* 'band', etc. Notion of swiftness fr. 'turning'. Walde-P. 2.696. Falk-Torp 1097. Feist 440 f.

ON *skynda* (> ME *skinde*, rare), *skunda*, Dan. *skynde*, Sw. *skynda*, OE *scyndan* (OS *farskundian* 'incite, urge', OHG *scuntan* 'incite, stimulate') : OE *scūdan* 'shake, tremble', OS *scuddian*, OHG *scutten* 'shake, swing', ChSl. *skytati sę* 'wander about', etc. Walde-P. 2.601 f. Falk-Torp 1046.

OE *efestan*, *efstan*, fr. *ofost*, *ofst*, *efest* 'haste, speed' (cf. OS *oðastlīco* 'swiftly'), prob. a cpd. **of-aist-* : ON *eisa* 'dash along, tear through', Lat. *īra* 'wrath', Skt. *iṣ-* 'set in motion, incite'. Walde-P. 1.107. Holthausen, IF 20.320.

OE *higian* (mostly 'strive, exert oneself'), ME *hye*, NE *hie* (arch. and poet.) : MLG *hīgen*, etc. 'pant', outside connection (as with Skt. *çīghra-* 'swift') dub. Walde-P. 1.363. Franck-v. W. 252. NED s.v. *hie* vb.

ME *haste*, etc., see under Fr. *se hâter*, above, 2.

NE *hurry*, only NE in this sense but now the common word vs. *hasten*, earlier 'carry or cause to go with haste', so ME *horye* (dub. quotation in NED), cf. MHG, NHG *hurren* 'whir', etc., all of imitative origin. NED s.v. Falk-Torp 432.

Du. *zich spoeden* (NHG *sich sputen* fr. LG) = OS *spōdian* 'grant success', OHG *gispuotōn* 'cause to succeed', refl. *sih gispuotōn* 'hasten', fr. Du. *spoed* 'speed', etc. (see 14.21).

OHG, MHG *īlen* (MLG *īlen* > Dan. *ile*, Sw. *ila*), NHG *eilen*, *sich beeilen*, OS *īlian*, perh. fr. a form with *l*-suffix of IE **ei-* 'go'. Walde-P. 1.104. Falk-Torp 461. Weigand-H. 1.414.

MHG *schern*, *scheren* (NHG refl. *sich scheren*) : Grk. σκαίρω 'jump, hop, dance', Skt. *kirati* 'strews, scatters', etc. Walde-P. 2.566.

5. Lith. *skubintis* (refl.) : *skubus* 'swift' (14.21).

Lett. *steigties*, refl. of *steigt* 'hasten, expedite' : Grk. στείχω 'walk, stride, march', Goth. *steigan* 'ascend', etc. Walde-P. 2.614. Mühl.-Endz. 3.1058 f.

Lett. *traukt*, also refl. *traukties*, lit. 'strike down', also 'fall upon (suddenly), frighten' : *trūkt* 'come in two, break', Lith. *trukti* 'tear, break, burst', ON *þrūga* 'threaten', OE *þryccan*, OHG *drucken* 'press'. Walde-P. 1.731. Mühl.-Endz. 4.224 f.

6. ChSl. *potŭštati sę* (for σπεύδω Lk. 19.5, 6) : Skt. *tuj-* 'press, shove, drive', Du. *stuken* 'pound', etc., fr. **(s)teu-g-*, beside **(s)teu-k-* in ChSl. *tŭknąti* 'prick, beat', Grk. τύκος 'hammer, chisel', etc. Walde-P. 2.616.

ChSl. *podvignąti sę* (*podvigŭšę sę* = σπεύσαντες Lk. 2.16, elsewhere for σαλεύομαι), refl. of perfect. of *dvignąti* 'move' (10.11). Walde-P. 1.235. Berneker 240 f.

ChSl. *spěšiti*, Boh. *spěchati*, Pol. *spieszyć*, Russ. *spěšit'*, fr. ChSl. *spěchŭ*, Boh. *spěch*, etc. 'haste' : ChSl. *spěti* 'be successful' (in modern Slavic also 'hasten'), Du. *spoeden*, etc. 'hasten' (above, 4). Walde-P. 2.657. Brückner 509.

SCr. *hitjeti* : *hitati* 'seize, throw' also 'hasten', ChSl. *chytati* 'tear', *chvatiti* 'seize', Boh. *chvátiti* 'seize' (11.14), *chvátati* 'hasten', etc. Berneker 407, 414. For the development of 'hasten' from 'seize', cf. Rum. *se grăbi* (above, 2) and NHG *sich packen*.

SCr. *brzati*, fr. *brz* 'swift' (14.21).

SCr. *žuriti se*, prob. : *gurati* 'thrust, press', ON *keyra* 'drive, thrust'. Peterson, IF 24.253 f.

Boh. *kvapiti*, Pol. *kwapić się*, prob. (through notion of hasty, unsteady motion) : ChSl. *kypěti* 'boil up, run over', Boh. *kypěti* 'boil up', etc. (general Slavic in this sense), Skt. *kup-* 'be excited, heave, boil (with rage), etc.'. Walde-P. 1.380. Berneker 655, 677 f.

Russ. *toropit'sja*, refl. of *toropit'* 'hasten' (trans.), beside *torop* 'haste' : Ukr. *torópyty* 'incite, frighten, torment', Boh. *trápiti* 'torment', Slavic **torpiti*, perh. caus. to ChSl. *trŭpěti* 'suffer', Lat. *torpēre* 'be stiff, numb'. Walde-P. 2.631.

7. Skt. *tvar-* (in mid.) : OHG *dweran* 'turn swiftly, stir', OE *þweran* 'twirl, stir', Grk. (Hom., poet.) ὀ-τρύνω 'rouse, stir up, egg on', mid. 'hasten'. Walde-P. 1.749.

Skt. *jū-* (in mid.; act. 'drive on, incite, etc.'), Av. *jav-* (Barth. 504), cf. Skt. *java-* 'swift' (14.21).

14.24 DELAY (vb. intr.)

Grk.	*μέλλω, χρονίζω, βραδύνω*	Goth.	*latjan, sainjan*	Lith.	*gaišti, užtrukti*
NG	*βραδύνω*	ON	*dwelja(sk), seina*	Lett.	*vilcināties, kavēties*
Lat.	*cunctārī, morārī*	Dan.	*nøle, tøve*	ChSl.	*mąditi, kŭsněti*
It.	*tardare, indugiare*	Sw.	*dröja*	SCr.	*oklijevati*
Fr.	*tarder*	OE	*ildan*	Boh.	*prodlévati, meškati, odkladati*
Sp.	*tardar, demorarse*	ME	*tarie*	Pol.	*ociągać się, odkładać*
Rum.	*întîrzia, zăbovi*	NE	*delay*	Russ.	*medlit', meškat'*
Ir.	*foregar, arfuiregar*	Du.	*dralen, toeven, talmen*	Skt.	*vi-lamb-*
NIr.	*moillighim, doghnīm moille*	OHG	*twellen, twālōn, lazōn*	Av.	. . . .
W.	*oedi*	MHG	*twellen, twālen, sich sūmen*		
Br.	*dalea*	NHG	*zögern, säumen*		

Several of the vbs. for 'delay' are from those for 'slow'. But there are many other semantic sources, such as 'take time', 'grow old', 'drag out', 'be long, prolong', 'be behind', 'put off', etc.

1. Grk. μέλλω, mostly 'be destined to, be likely to, be about to', but also 'delay', perh. : Lat. *promellere* 'postpone' (only in *promellere = litem promovere*, Paul. ex. Fest.), Ir. *mall* 'slow'. Walde-P. 2.291. Boisacq 625.

Grk. χρονίζω, fr. χρόνος 'time' (14.11). Cf. NE *take one's time*.

Grk. βραδύνω, fr. βραδύς 'slow' (14.22).

2. Lat. *cunctārī*, prob. : Skt. *çañk-* 'be anxious, fear', etc. (only of mental hesitation), Goth. *hāhan*, OE *hōn*, *hangian*, etc. 'hang'. Walde-P. 1.461. Ernout-M. 242. Walde-H. 1.307.

Lat. *morārī*, fr. *mora* 'delay' : Ir. *maraim* 'remain', and prob. ultimately (as orig. of mental hesitation) Lat. *memor* 'mindful', Grk. μέριμνα 'care', Skt. *smṛ-* 'remember', etc. Walde-P. 2.689 f. Ernout-M. 629 f. Walde-H. 2.67. Hence *demorārī* in same sense, VLat. *demorāre* in Romance languages mostly 'remain, dwell' (Fr. *demeurer*, etc.), but Sp. *demorarse* 'delay'.

It. *tardare*, Fr. *tarder*, Sp. *tardar*, fr. Lat. *tardāre*, deriv. of *tardus* 'slow' (14.22). Rum. *întîrzia*, through VLat. **tardīvus* (Rum. *tîrziu* 'late'). REW 8572–77. Puşcariu 887.

It. *indugiare*, fr. sb. *indugia* 'delay', fr. Lat. *indūtiae* 'truce', sometimes also 'cessation, delay'. REW 4388.

Rum. *zăbovi*, fr. Slavic, cf. SCr. *se za-baviti* 'delay' (e.g. NT, Lk. 1.21), lit. 'be behind' (*baviti* : *biti*, ChSl. *byti* 'be'). Tiktin 1785 f.

3. Ir. *foregar*, *arfuiregar* (assumed fr. the few quotable pass. forms.), pass. to *fo-reg-*, *air-fo-reg-* 'detain, delay' (trans.), cpds. of *reg-* 'bind'. Pedersen 2.592 f.

NIr. *moillighim*, fr. sb. *moille* 'delay' : Ir. *mall* 'slow' (14.22). Also phrase NIr. *doghnīm moille* 'I make delay'.

W. *oedi*, also trans. 'delay, postpone', fr. *oed* 'age' (14.12). Cf. Grk. χρονίζω (above, 1).

Br. *dalea*, fr. OFr. *délaier* 'delay' (cf. NE *delay*, below, 4). Henry 86.

4. Goth. *latjan* (χρονίζω Lk. 1.21), OHG *lazōn*, *lazēn* = ON *letja*, OE *lettan* 'hinder' (ME *lette* also rarely 'delay, tarry, wait'), derivs. of Goth. *lats*, OHG *laz* 'lazy' (4.22), OE *læt* 'slow, late' (14.22), etc.

Goth. *sainjan* (βραδύνω, 1 Tim. 3.15), ON *seina* : ON *seinn*, OE *sǣne* 'slow' (14.22).

ON *dveljask*, refl. of *dvelja* 'delay' (mostly trans.), OHG *twellen*, *twālōn* (sb. *twāla*), MHG *twellen*, *twālen* (OE *dwellan* 'mislead, delay, remain', NE *dwell*) : Goth. *dwals*, OE *dol*, OHG *tol* 'foolish', Ir. *dall* 'blind', Grk. θολός 'mud, dirt', all with a common notion of physical or mental confusion, more precise orig. use of root uncertain. Walde-P. 1.843. Falk-Torp 169.

Dan. *nøle*, fr. LG *nölen* 'be slow, delay, growl', prob. orig. 'growl, mutter' and of imitative origin. Falk-Torp 785.

Dan. *tøve* (also Sw. *töva* impers.) = MLG *tōven*, Du. *toeven* : ON *tefja* 'hinder, delay' (trans.), outside root connection dub. Falk-Torp 1319 f. (1237, 1240). Franck-v. W. 700.

Sw. *dröja* : *dryg* 'lengthy' (also 'large, stout', etc.), ON *drjūgr* 'substantial, ample', etc. Hellquist 159. Falk-Torp 161.

OE *ildan*, *yldan* = OHG *altēn*, *eltēn* 'grow old' and 'delay' (Otfr.), derivs. of OE *eald*, OHG *alt* 'old'. Holthausen 186.

ME *tarie*, NE *tarry* (now virtually obs. in spoken use, except locally in U.S. or 'remain, stay'), etym. disputed, but prob. another form of OE *tergan* 'vex, provoke', ME *targe* fr. OFr. *targier*, VLat. **tardicāre*, deriv. of *tardus* 'slow'. NED s.v. *tarry*, vb.

NE *delay*, fr. ME *delaye* only trans. 'delay, hinder', fr. OFr. *delaier* 'put off, retard' (whence Fr. sb. *délai* 'delay'), cpd. of OFr. *laier* 'leave'(?). NED s.v. Gamillscheg 302. REW 2542, 4955.

Du. *dralen* : LG dial. *drālen* 'drawl, be slow', further history obscure. Franck-v. W. 130.

Du. *talmen* = MLG *talmen* 'talk stupidly, drawl, babble', ME *talme* 'become exhausted, faint', ON *tālma* 'hinder', root connection dub. Franck-v. W. 686 f. Falk-Torp 1320. Walde-P. 1.812.

Du. *toeven*, *vertoeven* : Dan. *tøve*, etc., above.

MHG *sich sūmen* (*sūmen* trans. 'delay'), NHG *sich säumen*, now simply *säumen* (OHG *sūman* in *farsūman* = NHG *versäumen* 'miss, neglect'), root connection dub. Walde-P. 2.472. Weigand-H. 2.659. Kluge-G. 501.

NHG *zögern*, fr. MHG *zogen* 'draw, go', also 'postpone, delay' : NHG *ziehen* 'draw', etc. (9.33). Weigand-H. 2.1335 f. Kluge-G. 714.

5. Lith. *gaišti* (also 'disappear, perish'), *gaišuoti* (*gaišinti* trans.) : Lat. *haerēre* 'stick to' also 'hesitate'. Walde-P. 1.528. Ernout-M. 443. Walde-H. 1.632.

Lith. *užtrukti* (so for 'delay' in NT, both Trowitsch ed. and Kurschat), cpd. of old *trukti*, also 'delay', beside *trūkti* 'break, be wanting', Lith. *traukti* 'draw' (9.33), etc. Leskien, Ablaut 312 f.

Lett. *vilcināties*, refl. of *vilcināt* frequent. to *vilkt* 'draw'. Mühl.-Endz. 4.585.

Lett. *kavēties* (so for 'delay' in NT), refl. of *kavēt* 'pass the time', etym.? Mühl.-Endz. 2.181 f.

6. ChSl. *mąditi*, *muditi* (on interchange with *kŭsněti*, cf. Jagić, Entstehungsgesch. 365) : *mądĭnŭ*, *mudĭnŭ* 'slow' (14.22).

ChSl. *kŭsněti* : *kŭsĭnŭ* 'slow' (14.22).

SCr. *o-klijevati*, perh. : Lett. *klīt* 'wander about', etc. Berneker 518.

Boh. *prodlévati* (*prodliti*, *dliti*) : ChSl. *prodŭliti* 'prolong', Russ. *dlit'*, *prodlit'* 'prolong', etc. : ChSl. *dlŭgŭ*, etc. 'long' (12.57). Berneker 252 f.

Boh. *meškati*, Russ. *meškat'* (Pol. *mieszkać* formerly 'delay', now 'dwell'), fr. *meška*, old pop. form of word for 'bear' (ChSl. *medvědĭ*, etc., 3.73), with reference to the slow, clumsy movement of the bear. Berneker 2.30 f. Brückner 335.

Boh. *odkladati*, Pol. *odkładać* (with sbs. *odklad*, *odkład* 'delay'), cpds. of the root in ChSl. *klasti*, *kladą* 'put, lay' (12.12), hence lit. 'put off', then 'delay' trans. or intr.

Pol. *ociągać się* : *ciąg* 'draught, course of time', *ciągnąć* 'draw, pull' (9.33).

Pol. *odwlekać*, *zwloczyć*, cpds. of the root in *wlec* 'drag', ChSl. *vlesti* 'draw, pull' (9.33), are used also for 'delay'.

Russ. *medlit'* : *medlennyj* 'slow' (14.22).

7. Skt. *vi-lamb-*, cpd. of *lamb-* 'hang down', also sometimes 'remain behind, delay'.

14.25 BEGIN; BEGINNING

Grk.	*ἄρχομαι; ἀρχή*	Goth.	*duginnan, ana-, du-stōdjan; anastō-deins, frumisti*	Lith.	*pradėti; pradžia*
NG	*ἀρχίζω, ἀρχινῶ; ἀρχή*	ON	*hefja (upp), byrja; upphaf*	Lett.	*(ie)sākt; (ie)sākums*
Lat.	*incipere, coepere; initium, principium*	Dan.	*begynde; begyndelse*	ChSl.	*načęti; načęlo, načętŭkŭ*
It.	*incominciare, principiare; principio*	Sw.	*börja, begynna; början, begynnelse*	SCr.	*početi; početak*
Fr.	*commencer; commencement, début*	OE	*onginnan; angin, fruma, frymþ*	Boh.	*začíti, počíti; začátek, počátek*
Sp.	*empezar, comenzar; principio*	ME	*(a-, be-)ginne, commence; beginnunge, commencement*	Pol.	*zacząć, wszcząć; początek*
Rum.	*începe; început*	NE	*begin, commence; beginning commencement*	Russ.	*načat'; načalo*
Ir.	*doinscanna; tossach, tuus*	Du.	*beginnen, aanvangen; aanvang, begin*	Skt.	*ārabh-; ārambha-*
NIr.	*tosnuighim; tosach (tūs)*	OHG	*biginnan, anafāhan; anagin, anafang*	Av.	*aiwigarəd-; frataurun-na-, aiwigati-*
W.	*dechreu; dechreuad*	MHG	*beginnen, anvāhen; anvanc, begin, anegin*		
Br.	*deraoui, derou*	NHG	*anfangen, beginnen; anfang*		

Words for 'begin, beginning' are most commonly based upon notions like 'seize upon' or 'enter upon', but there are also other and diverse sources.

1. Grk. *ἄρχομαι* (act. *ἄρχω* in this sense more freq. in Hom., but in Att. prose mostly 'be first, rule'), NG *ἀρχίζω* and also (pop.) *ἀρχινῶ*, beside sb. *ἀρχή* ('beginning' Hom.+; 'rule' later), perh. through an old aor. form : *ἔρχομαι* 'come' ('came to > started, began'). McKenzie, Cl.Q. 15.44 f. Fraenkel, IF 49.203.

2. Lat. *incipere* (> Rum. *începe* with sb. *început*), cpd. of *capere* 'take, seize' (11.13). Ernout-M. 148. REW 4353.

Lat. *coepere*, orig. only perf. *coēpī* with pres. sense 'I begin' but which early acquired perf. sense 'I have begun', hence the formation of a new pres.; cpd. of **ēpi*, perf. of *apere* 'fasten, attach', hence *coēpī* orig. 'have fastened together' > 'begin'. Ernout-M. 202. Walde-H. 1.57 f.

Lat. *initium*, fr. *inīre* 'go into', whence 'enter upon', 'begin', cpd. of *īre* 'go'; hence late Lat. *initiāre* 'begin, initiate', VLat. cpd. **cominitiāre* > It. *(in)cominciare*, Fr. *commencer* (sb. *commencement*), Sp. *comenzar*. Ernout-M. 304 f. REW 2079.

Lat. *prīncipium* (> It., Sp. *principio*, with deriv. vb. It. *principiare*), fr. *prīnceps* lit. 'taking the first (place, rank, etc.)' whence 'chief, first person, etc.', cpd. of *prīmus* 'first' and *capere* 'take'. Ernout-M. 809 f.

Fr. *début*, back-formation fr. *débuter* 'make first move at a game', fr. *but* 'goal', but prob. in sense of 'point from which the play is made', cf. *de but en blanc* (artillery), where *blanc* indicates the center of target aimed at. Bloch, s.v. *but*. Wartburg 1.652.

Sp. *empezar*, prob. fr. *pieza* 'piece' (= It. *pezza*, Fr. *pièce*, etc.), perh. through notion of 'break open', cf. It. *spezzare* 'break in pieces'. REW 6450.

3. Ir. *doinscanna* 3sg. (**to-ind-scann-*), and *intinscanna* 3sg. (**ind-to-ind-scann-*), cf. *f-a-scannat* (*fo-scann-*) 'they toss it', NIr. *foscnaim* 'toss, winnow, purge, cleanse', etym. dub. Walde-P. 2.564. Pedersen 2.613.

Ir. sb. *tossach*, NIr. *tosach*, fr. the shorter form Ir. *tuus*, NIr. *tūs*, lit. 'a leading forth' : W. *tywys* 'lead' (10.64). Hence NIr. *tosnuighim* (also *tosuigim*, etc.). Pedersen 1.308.

W. *dechreu*, Br. *deraoui*, with sbs. W. *dechreuad*, Br. *derou*, etym. dub. Pedersen 1.484 (as perh. orig. 'draw blood' = 'begin battle' : Lat. *cruor*, etc.).

4. Goth. *duginnan;* OE *onginnan*, *aginnan*, rarely *beginnan*, ME *aginne*, *beginne* (and with dropping of prefix simply *ginne*), NE *begin*, with sbs. OE *angin*, *ongin*, ME *beginnunge*, *-ynge*, NE *beginning;* Du. *beginnen* (MLG *beginnen* > Dan. *begynde*, Sw. *begynna*, with sbs. *begyndelse*, *begynnelse*), OHG *biginnan*, *inginnan*, MHG, NHG *beginnen*, sbs. Du., MHG *begin*, OHG *anagin*, MHG *anegin*, etym. dub. Walde-P. 1.589. Falk-Torp 58. Feist 128.

Goth. *anastōdjan*, *dustōdjan*, with sb. *anastōdeins*, cpds. of *-stōdjan* (ON *stǣða* 'cause to stand, establish'), caus. of *standan* (pret. *stōþ*) 'stand', etc. Feist 44 f.

Goth. *frumisti*, fr. *frumists* superl. of *fruma* 'first', OE *frum* id. (mostly in cpds. *frum-*), whence *fruma*, *frymþ* 'beginning' : Lith. *pirmas*, Grk. *πρόμος* 'first', etc. Feist 170. Walde-P. 2.37.

ON *hefja* 'lift' (10.22), also 'begin', in the latter sense esp. *hefja upp* (hence *upphaf* 'beginning').

ON *byrja* (not so freq. in older language in this sense as *hefja*, but reg. in NIcel., also 'be fitting' and 'beget'), Sw. *börja* = MLG *boren* 'lift, carry' and 'be due', OHG *burien* 'lift up', *giburien* 'happen, be fitting', etc. : ON *bera*, Goth. *bairan*, etc. 'bear, carry'. Walde-P. 2.156. Falk-Torp 118. Hellquist 125.

ME, NE *commence*, *commencement*, fr. OFr. *commencer*, *commencement* (above, 2).

Du. *aanvangen*, OHG *anafāhan*, MHG *anvāhen*, NHG *anfangen*, beside sbs. Du. *aanvang*, OHG *anafang*, MHG *anvanc*, NHG *anfang*, cpd. of Du. *vangen*, OHG *fāhan*, NHG *fangen* 'seize, grasp, take' (like Lat. *incipere* fr. *capere*, cf. above, 2).

5. Lith. *pradėti*, also refl. *prasidėti*, sb. *pradžia*, cpd. of *dėti* 'put, place, lay'.

Lett. *sākt*, and cpd. *iesākt* with sbs. *sākums*, *iesākums*, prob. = Lith. *šokti* 'jump' (10.43), rarely also 'begin'; semantic development through 'jump' = 'hasten (eagerly to do something)', hence 'begin', Mühl.-Endz. 3.801. Fraenkel, IF 49.203 f.

6. ChSl. *načęti* (*začęti* 'conceive'), SCr. *početi*, Boh. *začíti*, *počíti*, etc., general Slavic in cpds. only, with sbs. ChSl. *načęlo*, *načętŭkŭ*, etc.; Ir. *cinim* 'spring from, be born', Grk. *καινός* 'new', etc. (14.13). Walde-P. 1.398. Berneker 168.

7. Skt. *ā-rabh-*, and *pra-ā-rabh-*, with sbs. *ārambha-*, *prārambha-*, cpds. of *rabh-* 'take, grasp, seize'.

Av. *aiwigarəd-*, lit. 'go toward', esp. 'begin' a hymn or some part of the ritual, cpd. of *garəd-* : Lat. *gradī* 'step, go', etc. Cf. Lat. *ingredī* 'enter upon' and freq. 'begin', esp. a speech. Barth. 514 f. Walde-P. 1.651 f.

Av. sb. *frataurunа-*, prob. as 'entrance', fr. *tar-* 'cross over'. Barth. 980. (Walde-P. 1.733).

Av. sb. *aiwigati-*, lit. 'entrance, coming forward', fr. *aiwi-gam-* 'come forward'. Barth. 88.

14.252 LAST (vb.)

Grk.	*διαρκέω*	Goth.	....	Lith.	*tęstis, trukti*
NG	*διαρκῶ, βαστῶ, κρατῶ*	ON	*haldask*	Lett.	*ilgt, būt ilgi*
Lat.	*dūrāre*	Dan.	*vare*	ChSl.	*trajati*
It.	*durare*	Sw.	*vara*	SCr.	*trajati*
Fr.	*durer*	OE	*lǣstan*	Boh.	*trvati*
Sp.	*durar*	ME	*laste, (en)dure*	Pol.	*trwać*
Rum.	*dura*	NE	*last (endure)*	Russ.	*dlit'sja*
Ir.	*maraim*	Du.	*duren*	Skt.	*(sthā-)*
NIr.	*mairim*	OHG	*werēn*	Av.	....
W.	*parhau*	MHG	*dūren, wern*		
Br.	*padout*	NHG	*dauern (währen)*		

The verbal notion of 'last', that is, 'continue', with special reference to the lapse of time, is mostly either included in the scope of, or specialized from, vbs. for 'continue, follow, remain, hold out, prolong', the last derived from adjs. for 'long'.

1. Grk. *διαρκέω*, cpd. of *ἀρκέω* 'ward off, assist' (poet.), mostly 'suffice', also sometimes 'hold out, last' : Lat. *arcēre* 'inclose' (old sense, but rare), 'keep off'. Walde-P. 1.80. Ernout-M. 67 f.

NG *βαστῶ* 'support, carry' (10.61), also 'bear' = 'endure', and intr. 'hold out, last'.

NG *κρατῶ* 'hold, keep' (11.85), also 'last'.

2. Lat. *dūrāre* (> Romance words, etc.), orig. 'make hard', then 'make ready, inure' and intr. 'endure, hold out, last', fr. *dūrus* 'hard' (15.74), also 'hardy'. Ernout-M. 291 (but with needless assumption of two orig. different vbs.). Walde-H. 1.386. REW 2805.

3. Ir. *maraim* 'remain' (12.16), also 'live, survive' and 'hold out, last', likewise NIr. *mairim*.

W. *parhau* 'continue' and 'last', prob., like *paru* 'suit, match', deriv. of *par*, fr. Lat. *par* 'equal'. Morris Jones 384 (but with dub. reconstruction).

Br. *padout*, fr. Lat. *patī* 'suffer, endure'. Loth, Mots lat. 194.

4. ON *haldask* (*-ast*), refl. of *halda* 'hold' (11.15), is used for 'continue, last'. Fritzner 1.694. Vigfusson 234.

OE *lǣstan*, ME *laste*, NE *last*, earliest sense 'follow, perform' (only in OE, where also already 'continue, last') : Goth. *laistjan* 'follow', etc. (10.52). NED s.v. *last*, vb.[1].

OHG *werēn*, MHG *wern*, NHG *währen* (mostly replaced by *dauern* except in pple. *während* 'during'), MLG *waren* (> Dan. *vare*, Sw. *vara*), fr. the same root as Goth. *wisan* 'be, remain', etc. (9.91). Weigand-H. 2.1202. Falk-Torp 1353.

ME, NE *dure* (now arch. or dial.), ME, NE *endure*, Du. *duren*, MHG *dūren*, NHG *dauern*, fr. Fr. *durer* or in part directly fr. Lat. *dūrāre* (above, 2). NED s.v. *dure*, vb. Franck-v. W. 143. Weigand-H. 1.334. Kluge-G. 97.

5. Lith. *tęstis*, refl. of *tęsti* 'extend, continue', fr. IE **tens-* (Skt. *taṅs-* 'shake', etc.), extension of **ten-* in Skt. *tan-*, Grk. *τείνω*, etc. 'stretch' (9.32). Walde-P. 1.727.

Lith. *trukti* (pres. *trunku*) : *trūkti* (pres. *trūkstu*) 'tear, break' intr., *traukti* 'draw, pull' (9.33). Walde-P. 1.731. Leskien, Ablaut 312. Semantic development through some such use as that of NHG *sich hinziehen* 'drag on, be prolonged'.

Lett. *ilgt* (Mühl.-Endz. 1.706), fr. *ilgs* 'long' (12.51). Or commonly phrases with adv. *ilgi* 'long' and *būt* 'be' (*ilgi nebija* 'it was not long'), *palikt* 'remain', etc.

6. ChSl., SCr. *trajati*, Boh. *trvati* (OBoh. *tráti*), Pol. *trwać*, prob. : Ir. *trāth* 'time, hour', Skt. *tṛ-* 'cross over', *trā-* 'rescue' (secondary sense, 11.25), Lat. *trāns* 'across', etc. Trautmann 325 f. Brückner 578. Pedersen 1.52.

Russ. *dlit'sja*, refl. of *dlit'* 'prolong' : ChSl. *pro-dĭliti* 'prolong', fr. the root seen in ChSl. *dlŭgŭ* 'long', etc. Walde-P. 1.812. Berneker 252.

7. Skt. *sthā-* 'stand', also 'remain, hold out', and prob. the nearest approach to a verb for 'last'.

14.26 END (sb., temporal)

Grk.	*τέλος, τελευτή*	Goth.	*andeis*	Lith.	*galas, (pa)baiga*
NG	*τέλος*	ON	*endi, lok*	Lett.	*gals, beigas*
Lat.	*fīnis*	Dan.	*ende, slutning*	ChSl.	*konĭčina, konĭcĭ*
It.	*fine*	Sw.	*ände, slut*	SCr.	*konac, svršetak*
Fr.	*fin, bout*	OE	*ende*	Boh.	*konec*
Sp.	*fin*	ME	*ende*	Pol.	*koniec*
Rum.	*sfîrşit*	NE	*end*	Russ.	*konec*
Ir.	*cend, dered, deod*	Du.	*einde, slot*	Skt.	*anta-, prānta-*
NIr.	*deireadh, crīoch*	OHG	*enti*	Av.	*θraošti-, θwarəsah-, karana-*
W.	*diwedd*	MHG	*ende*		
Br.	*diwez*	NHG	*ende, schluss*		

Nouns for 'end' in the temporal sense, the opposite of 'beginning', are in large measure the same as those used for 'end' in a spatial sense, for which see 12.35.

But some are different, though also connected with words for spatial application. Only those are discussed here.

1. Grk. *τέλος* with central notion of 'fulfilment, completion', hence 'end' and in latter sense esp. *τελευτή*, prob. as orig. 'turning-point' : *πέλομαι* 'be in motion' (Aeol. *π*), *πόλος* 'pivot, axis', Lat. *colere* 'cultivate', Skt. *car-* 'move, wander, go', etc., IE **k^{w}el-*. Walde-P. 1.514. Boisacq 952. Walde-H. 1.246.

2. Lat. *fīnis* (> It. *fine*, Fr., Sp. *fin*), in earliest and most common use 'limit, boundary' (of field, territory, etc.), prob. as 'fixed mark' : *fīgere* 'fix, fasten'. Walde-P. 1.832. Ernout-M. 363. Walde-H. 1.503.

Rum. *sfîrşit* : vb. *sfîrşi* 'finish' (14.27).

3. NIr. *crīoch*, also and orig. 'limit, boundary, furrow', as Ir. *crīch*, fr. the root in Grk. *κρίνω* 'decide, distinguish', etc. Walde-P. 2.584.

Ir. *deod*, W. *diwedd*, Br. *diwez*, perh. cpd. of **di-* 'from' and root **wedh-* 'lead' in Ir. *fedim*, W. *ar-weddu*, *cy-weddu*, Lith. *vesti* 'lead', etc. Morris Jones 251.

4. ON *lok* (pl. or sg., also cpd. *endalok*, *endilok*), also 'lid, cover' : ON *lūka* 'shut, finish' (14.27).

Dan. *slutning*, fr. *slutti* 'close, conclude' (Sw. *sluta*) fr. MLG *slūten* 'close, finish', beside sb. *slut* 'end, close' (> Dan. *slut* in cpds., Sw. *slut*), Du. *slot* = NHG *schluss* (MHG *sluz*, rare) :

OHG *sliozan*, NHG *schliessen*, etc. 'close, shut' (12.25). Cf. NE *close* in *close of the day*, etc. Falk-Torp 1070.

5. Lith. *baiga* (more usually *pabaiga*), Lett. *beigas*, beside vbs. Lith. *baigti*, Lett. *beigt* 'finish', etym.? Walde-P. 2.150. Mühl.-Endz. 1.277.

6. ChSl. *konĭcĭ*, etc. (12.35), also temporal, but deriv. ChSl. *konĭčina* more common for τέλος in the Gospels.

SCr. *svršetak* : *svršiti* 'finish' (14.27).

7. Av. *θraošti-* : *θraoš-* 'come or bring to maturity or completion', *θru-* 'rear, support', OHG *trowwen* 'grow, mature', etc. Walde-P. 1.754. Barth. 801.

Av. *θwarəsah-*, lit. 'the point at which something is cut off', fr. *θwarəs-* 'cut off'. Barth. 796.

Temporal use of Av. *karana-* (12.35) attested only in cpds. Barth. 451.

14.27 FINISH (vb.)

Grk.	*τελέω, τελευτάω*	Goth.	*ustiuhan, usfulljan*	Lith.	*(pa-)baigti*
NG	*τελειώνω*	ON	*enda, lūka(við)*	Lett.	*(pa-)beigt*
Lat.	*per-(con-)ficere, fīnīre*	Dan.	*ende, (af)slutte*	ChSl.	*(sŭ-)konĭčati*
It.	*finire*	Sw.	*(af)sluta, ända*	SCr.	*s-, do-vršiti*
Fr.	*finir*	OE	*ge-(full-)endian, full-fremman*	Boh.	*(do-, s-, u-) končiti*
Sp.	*acabar*	ME	*(full)ende, fenys, full-freme*	Pol.	*(do-, s-, wy-) kon'czyć*
Rum.	*isprăvi, sfîrşi*	NE	*finish, end*	Russ.	*(o-)končit', doveršit'*
Ir.	*forcennim*	Du.	*(vol)eindigen*	Skt.	*samāpaya-, avasā-*
NIr.	*criochnuighim, cuirim deireadh le*	OHG	*(gi)entōn, gi-(duruh-)fremen*	Av.	. . . .
W.	*diweddu, gorffen*	MHG	*vol-(ge-)enden, gevremen*		
Br.	*peurober*	NHG	*vollenden, beend(ig)en*		

The majority of the vbs. for 'finish' are derived from the sbs. for 'end' (14.26), hence lit. 'make an end of, bring to an end', and so also 'complete, accomplish, etc.'. But in some the latter is the primary notion and the temporal secondary. Cf. NE *complete, fulfil*, etc.

1. Grk. *τελέω, τελευτάω*, NG *τελειώνω*, fr. *τέλος, τελευτή* 'end' (14.26).

2. Lat. *perficere, conficere*, perfect. cpds. of *facere* 'do, make'.

Lat. *fīnīre* (> It. *finire*, Fr. *finir*), fr. *finis* 'end' (14.26).

Sp. *acabar*, fr. *cabo* 'end' (12.35).

Rum. *isprăvi*, fr. Slavic, cf. ChSl. *ispraviti* 'make straight', etc. Tiktin 857 f.

Rum. *sfîrşi*, fr. Slavic, cf. SCr. *svršiti*, etc. (below, 6). Tiktin 1418.

3. Ir. *forcennim*, W. *gorffen*, Corn. *gorfenne*, fr. Ir. *forcend*, W. (old) *gorffen*, Corn. *gorfen* 'end', cpd. of Ir. *cend*, W. *pen* 'head, end' (12.35).

Ir. *crīchnaigim* (K. Meyer, Contrib. 516), NIr. *crīochnuighim* fr. Ir. *crīch*, NIr. *crīoch* 'limit, boundary, furrow, end' (14.26).

NIr. usually phrase *cuirim deireadh le* 'put an end to' (*deireadh* 'end' 14.26).

W. *diweddu*, fr. *diwedd* 'end' (14.26).

Br. *peurober*, cpd. of perfect. prefix *peur-* and *ober* 'do' (cf. Lat. *perficere*, above).

4. Goth. *ustiuhan* (the usual rendering of *τελέω* and cpds., but also of *ἐξάγω, ἐκβάλλω*, etc.), lit. 'draw out, lead away', cpd. of *tiuhan* 'draw, lead' (9.33).

Goth. *usfulljan* (renders *τελέω* Mt. 11.1, *τελειόω* Nehm. 6.16, otherwise *πληρόω*, etc.), lit. 'fill out', cpd. of *fulljan* 'fill'.

ON *enda*, Dan. *ende*, Sw. *ända*, etc., in West Gmc. chiefly in cpds. with 'full-' or other perfect. prefix (NHG *(be)endigen* fr. late MHG *endec* 'coming to an end'), fr. the words for 'end', ON *endi*, etc. (12.35).

ON *lūka* (often also with prep. *við*), lit. 'shut, close' (12.25).

Dan. *(af)slutte*, Sw. *(af)sluta*, fr. MLG *slūten* 'close, finish', cf. Dan., Sw. *slut* 'end' (14.26).

OE *fullfremman, gefremman*, ME *full-freme*, OHG *gifremen, duruhfremen*, MHG *gevremen*, perfect. cpds. of OE *fremman*, OHG *fremen*, etc. 'perform, effect' (fr. OE *fram* 'stout, firm', etc.)

ME *fenys, finisch*, NE *finish*, fr. OFr. *fenir*, stem *feniss-* (Fr. *finir*, above, 2).

5. Lith. *baigti*, Lett. *beigt* (and perfect. cpds. with *pa-*) : Lith. *(pa)baiga*, Lett. *beigas* 'end'.

6. ChSl. *konĭčati, sŭkonĭčati*, etc., general Slavic except SCr. (esp. perfect. forms with *u-, do-*, etc.), fr. *konĭcĭ* 'end' (12.35).

SCr. *svršiti, dovršiti*, Russ. *doveršit'*, etc. perfect. cpds. of SCr. *vršiti*, Russ. *veršit'* 'accomplish, carry out, achieve', fr. SCr. *vrh*, Russ. *verch*, ChSl. *vrŭchŭ* 'top'. Miklosich 384.

7. Skt. *samāpaya-*, caus. of *samāp-* 'obtain', cpd. of *āp-* 'reach, obtain'.

Skt. *ava-sā-* (3sg. *-syati*), also intr. 'cease', prob. fr. the root in Goth. *seiþus*, Lat. *sērus* 'late', etc. (14.17). Walde-P. 2.461. Persson, Beiträge 365.

14.28 CEASE

Grk.	*παύομαι*	Goth.	*ga-andjan*(?), *sweiban*	Lith.	*liauti(s), nustoti*
NG	*παύω*	ON	*hætta, lētta*	Lett.	*beigties, l'auties*
Lat.	*dēsinere, dēsistere*	Dan.	*ophøre*	ChSl.	*prěstati*
It.	*cessare*	Sw.	*upphöra*	SCr.	*prestati*
Fr.	*cesser*	OE	*geswīcan, blinnan*	Boh.	*přestati*
Sp.	*cesar*	ME	*cesse*	Pol.	*przestać*
Rum.	*înceta*	NE	*cease, stop*	Russ.	*perestat'*
Ir.	*anaim, con-osna* (3sg.)	Du.	*ophouden*	Skt.	*upa-ram-, ni-vṛt-*
NIr.	*stadaim de*	OHG	*bilinnan*	Av.	. . . .
W.	*peidio*	MHG	*hœren, ūfhoeren*		
Br.	*ehana, paouez*	NHG	*aufhören*		

Words for 'cease' are based on such notions as 'stop', 'leave off', 'make an end', 'rest', etc., most of which appear also in NE substitutes for *cease*, which, though the distinctive word, is now little used in common speech. Of these the most common is *stop*. For *rest*, now esp. in law *the defense rests*, see NED s.v. *rest*, vb. 2.d, e.

1. Grk. *παύω* 'check, cause to cease', mid. *παύομαι* 'cease', NG *παύω* in both senses, etym. dub., perh. : OPruss. *pausto* 'wild', ChSl. *pustŭ* 'desert', *pustiti* 'let go', etc. Walde-P. 2.1. Boisacq 752 f.

Grk. *διαλείπω* 'leave an interval', only late 'cease', as in NT, Lk. 7.45, and pap.

2. Lat. *dēsinere*, cpd. of *dē* 'from, down' and *sinere* 'let, permit', earlier 'place, put'. Ernout-M. 945.

Lat. *dēsistere* (> OFr. *desister* > NE *desist*), cpd. of *dē* 'from, down' and *sistere* 'make stand, stop'.

Lat. *cessāre* 'be slow, inactive, remiss', hence also 'cease' (> It. *cessare*, Fr. *cesser*, Sp. *cesar*), frequent. of *cēdere* 'go, go away, withdraw, yield'. Ernout-M. 169. Walde-H. 1.193.

Rum. *înceta* 'be still, quiet', and

'cease', deriv. of *încet* 'gentle, slow' (14.22). Puşcariu 814.

3. Ir. *anaim* 'remain, rest', but also 'cease' (with prep. *o* or *di* 'cease from'), and cpd. **com-od-ess-an-* 'end, rest, cease' (e.g. 3sg. *con-osna*, etc.) : Skt. *an-* 'breathe', etc. (4.51). Here also Br. *ehana* = W. *ech-ain* 'to rest'. Pedersen 2.295, 455 f.

NIr. *stadaim* 'stop' with *de* 'cease (from)' : *stad* 'stop, pause', fr. Lat. *status* 'state, condition'. Pedersen 1.218.

W. *peidio*, through an earlier sense of 'suffer, endure' fr. VLat. **patīre*, Lat. *patī* id. with development through 'submit to, acquiesce in' (attested in Lat.), 'cease resistance'. Loth, Mots lat. 194.

Br. *paouez* (cf. Ernault s.v.), fr. sb. *paouez*, OBr. *poues* 'rest' = Corn. *powes* id., fr. Lat. *pausa* 'pause'? Pedersen 1.211. Henry 217. Not discussed in Loth, Mots lat.

4. Goth. *ga-nanþjan* in *gananþida* = *ἐπαύσατο* Lk. 5.4, but perh. to be read *ga-andida*, lit. 'ended'. Feist 174.

Goth. *sweiban* (in *swaif* = *διέλειπεν* Lk. 7.45) : ON *svīfa* 'turn, drift', refl. 'turn away from, shrink from', and perh. ultimately Grk. *σιγάω, σιωπάω* 'be silent'. Walde-P. 2.534. Falk-Torp 1216 f. Feist 465.

ON *hætta*, prob. same word as *hætta* 'risk, stake', fr. **hanhatjan* : Skt. *çank-* 'be in doubt', Lat. *cunctārī* 'delay'. Walde-P. 1.461. Falk-Torp 448.

ON *lētta* (with dat. or *af* with dat.) also and orig. 'lighten, lift' fr. adj. *lēttr* 'light' = Goth. *leihts*, etc. id. (15.82). Falk-Torp 637.

Dan. *ophøre*, Sw. *upphöra*, fr. NHG *aufhören*, MLG *uphōren* (below). Falk-Torp 796.

OE *geswīcan* : *swīcan* 'wander, depart', also sometimes 'cease', OHG *swīhhan* 'be weary, desert', ON *svīkja* 'betray', Lith. *svaigti* 'grow dizzy', etc. Walde-P. 2.519, 534. Falk-Torp 1215.

OE *linnan*, mostly *blinnan*, OHG *bilinnan* : Goth. *af-linnan* 'depart', ON *linna* 'stop', perh. ON *linr* 'soft, gentle', Grk. *λίναμαι· τρέπομαι* Hesych., *λιάζομαι* 'shrink, sink', etc. Walde-P. 2.387 f. Falk-Torp 645 f.

ME *cesse*, NE *cease*, fr. Fr. *cesser* (above, 2).

NE *stop* (*stopped speaking*, etc.), in this sense only a special variety of its common meaning 'come to a stand' (also and earlier 'bring to a stand'). NED s.v.

Du. *ophouden*, cpd. of *houden* 'hold', hence 'hold up' = 'support' and = 'cease'. Cf. NE *hold up* in many senses including 'stop, cease'.

MHG *hœren* 'hear, obey' and also (from a situation in which a command 'obey' was implicitly equivalent to 'stop, cease') 'cease', hence in this sense esp. MHG *ūfhœren*, NHG *aufhören*. Weigand-H. 1.103, 890.

5. Lith. *liauti*, esp. refl. *liautis* and perfect. *paliauti*, Lett. *l'aut* 'permit, allow', refl. *l'auties* 'cease, end' : OPruss. *aulāut* 'die', Lith. *lavonas* 'corpse', Goth. *lēwjan* 'betray', etc., all from a common notion of 'leave, let'(?). Cf. NE *leave* in sense of 'cease' (cf. Lk. 5.4 *when he had left speaking*, now obs., but *leave off* common; NED s.v. 10b, 14c). Walde-P. 2.405. Mühl.-Endz. 2.533.

Lith. *nustoti*, cpd. of *nuo-* 'from' and *stoti* 'take a stand'. Cf. Lat. *dēsistere* (above, 2), NHG *abstehen von* 'desist from, give up', etc.

Lett. *beigties*, refl. of *beigt* 'bring to an end' : *beigas* 'end' (14.26). Mühl.-Endz. 1.277. (Lith. *baigtis* 'come to an end', but not 'cease' with vbs. of action.)

6. ChSl. *prěstati*, etc., general Slavic (Lith. *perstoti* also used for 'cease' but prob. semantic borrowing), or less commonly ChSl., Boh. *ustati*, Pol. *ustać*, perfect. cpds. of *stati*, etc. 'take a stand', hence 'come to a standstill'. Cf. NE *stop* in sense of 'cease'.

7. Skt. *upa-ram-* and *ni-ram-* lit. 'come to rest', cpds. of *ram-* 'rest'.

Skt. *ni-vṛt-*, cpd. of *ni-* 'down, back' and *vṛt-* 'turn', hence 'turn back, abstain from, cease'.

14.29 READY

Grk.	*ἑτοῖμος*	Goth.	*manwus*	Lith.	*gatavas*
NG	*ἕτοιμος*	ON	*būinn*	Lett.	*gatavs*
Lat.	*parātus, praestō* (adv.)	Dan.	*færdig*	ChSl.	*gotovŭ*
It.	*pronto*	Sw.	*färdig*	SCr.	*gotov, spreman*
Fr.	*prêt*	OE	*gearo*	Boh.	*hotový*
Sp.	*pronto*	ME	*rædi(g), yare*	Pol.	*gotowy*
Rum.	*gata*	NE	*ready*	Russ.	*gotovyj*
Ir.	*airlam*	Du.	*bereid, gereed*	Skt.	*(upa-)kḷpta-*
NIr.	*ullamh*	OHG	*garo*	Av.	. . . .
W.	*parod*	MHG	*gare, bereite, gereite*		
Br.	*dare*	NHG	*bereit, fertig*		

Words for 'ready' are mostly based on notions like 'prepared, arranged', or 'at hand'.

1. Grk. *ἑτοῖμος, ἕτοιμος*, (cf. Hdn. 2.938), etym.? Boisacq 292.

2. Lat. *parātus* 'prepared' and hence 'ready', pple. of *parāre* 'prepare'.

Lat. *praestō* (adv.) 'at hand, ready', whence late adj. *praestus* (> Fr. *prêt* 'ready', It., Sp. *presto* 'quick, soon, at once'), fr. *prae* 'in front of, before', second part prob. : *stāre* 'stand' or *sinere* 'place, put' (i.e. **prae-sitō*, cf. *po-situs*). Ernout-M. 805 f.

Lat. *prōmptus* 'at hand, ready, prompt' (> It., Sp. *pronto*), pple. of *prōmere* 'produce'.

Rum. *gata*, fr. Slavic, ChSl. *gotovŭ*, etc. (below, 6).

3. Ir. *airlam* (*aurlam, irlam, erlam*), NIr. *urlamh, ullamh*, fr. **ar-ro-lām*, lit. 'at hand' : *lām* 'hand'.

W. *parod*, fr. Lat. *parātus* (above, 2). Loth, Mots lat. 193.

Br. *dare*, older *darev* (also 'done' = 'cooked', as now), orig. 3sg. (= MW *deryw* 'happens') of *darbout* 'be on the point of (doing something)', now *darv(ez)out* 'happen', cpd. of *bout* 'be'. Henry 89. Pedersen 2.442.

4. Goth. *manwus*, etym. disputed but prob. as orig. 'at hand' : Lat. *manus* 'hand'. Walde-P. 2.272. Feist 345.

ON *būinn*, pple. of *būa* 'prepare', hence 'prepared, ready', like Lat. *parātus*.

Dan. *færdig*, Sw. *färdig*, fr. MLG *verdich* = NHG *fertig* (below). Falk-Torp 289.

OE *gearo*, ME *yare* (NE *yare* now obs. or dial.), OHG *garo*, MHG *gare*, NHG *gar* (now mostly of finished products, as cooked food, dressed skins, etc.), prob. cpd. of Gmc. *ga-, ge-*, with forms like OE *earu*, OS *aru*, ON *ǫrr* 'swift, ready' : Skt. *aram* 'suitably', Grk. *ἀραρίσκω* 'join, fit', etc. Walde-P. 1.69 ff., 688. Weigand-H. 1.620. NED s.v. *yare*, adj.

OE *gerǣde* ('arranged, skilled'), ME *rædi(g)*, NE *ready*, OHG *bireiti*, MHG *bereite, gereite*, NHG *bereit*, Du. *bereid*, *gereed* : Goth. *garaiþs* 'arranged, appointed', *garaidjan* 'order', ON *greiðr* 'straight, clear, free' (> ME *graith* 'ready'), *greiða* 'arrange', OE *(ge)rǣdan* 'arrange, advise', etc. Walde-P. 1.75, 2.348. The development is clearly fr. 'arranged', like 'prepared', to 'ready'. There is no direct formal or semantic connection with OE *rīdan*, OHG *rītan* 'ride' (as Falk-Torp, Weigand-H., Kluge-G.), even if the two groups are ultimately related.

NHG *fertig*, fr. MHG *vertic*, *vertec* 'ready', esp. 'mobile, skilful, dexterous' (as still in part NHG *fertig* and Du. *vaardig*), OHG *fartig*, deriv. of *fart*, MHG *vart* 'journey', but prob. in the freq. special sense of 'military expedition'. Weigand-H. 1.522. Sperber, Einleitung 41. The present dominant sense of 'ready' = 'finished with preparations', whence even 'finished' in phrases like *er ist mit seinem gelde fertig*, is here, in contrast to the case of Lat. *parātus*, the end rather than the beginning of the evolution.

5. Lith. *gatavas*, Lett. *gatavs*, fr. Slavic (below, 6).

6. ChSl. *gotovŭ*, etc., general Slavic, etym.? Berneker 337 f. (but Alb. *gat* prob. loanword fr. Slavic, like Rum. *gata*).

SCr. *spreman* : *spremiti* 'prepare, make ready', cpd. of *-premiti* (i.e. *s-premiti*, like *o-premiti*, etc.) = late ChSl. *prěmiti*, deriv. of *prěmŭ* 'straight'. Miklosich 263.

7. Skt. *kḷpta-*, *upa-kḷpta*, pass. pple. of *kḷp-* 'be suitable, adapted to', hence 'arranged, prepared, ready'.

14.31 ALWAYS

Grk.	*ἀεί, πάντοτε*	Goth.	*sinteinō*	Lith.	*visada, visados, vis*
NG	*πάντοτε, πάντα*	ON	*alla tīð*	Lett.	*visad*
Lat.	*semper*	Dan.	*altid*	ChSl.	*vĭsegda*
It.	*sempre*	Sw.	*alltid*	SCr.	*uvijek*
Fr.	*toujours*	OE	*sym(b)le, ā, ǣfre, ealne weg*	Boh.	*vždy, vždycky, stále*
Sp.	*siempre*			Pol.	*zawsze*
Rum.	*totdeauna*	ME	*ever(e), alweye*	Russ.	*vsegda, vse*
Ir.	*do grēs, caidche*	NE	*always*	Skt.	*sarvadā*
NIr.	*choidhche, riamh*	Du.	*altijd*	Av.	. . . .
W.	*bob amser*	OHG	*simbolon, iomēr*		
Br.	*bepred*	MHG	*i(m)mer*		
		NHG	*immer, stets*		

Words for 'always' are most commonly connected with those for 'all', either derivs. with adv. suffixes of time or cpds. with words for 'time' or the like. Several are derived from a form appearing in a numeral for 'one' and in words for 'together', the development here being probably through 'once for all'. Some are cognate with words for 'age, lifetime'. More isolated semantic sources are 'until night' ('all day' > 'always'), 'steadily'.

1. Derivs. or cpds. of words for 'all' (13.14).

Grk. πάντοτε, formed fr. stem of πᾶς, παντός after temporal advs. like ὅτε, τότε; NG pop. πάντα; Fr. *toujours*, fr. OFr. *toz jorz*, also *tozdis*, lit. 'all days'; Rum. *totdeauna* fr. *tot* 'all', and *de-a-una* 'at once', phrase based on fem. of Lat. *ūnus* 'one', like Rhaet. *adūna* 'always' (Tiktin 1628, REW 211); NIr. phrases with *cach*, *gach*, *gach uile* 'every' (Dinneen s.v. *gach;* McKenna s.v. *always*); W. *bob amser* (*pob* 'every', *amser* 'time', 14.11), Br. *bepred* (*pep* 'every', *pred* 'time', 14.11); ON *alla tīð*, Dan. *altid*, Sw. *alltid*, Du. *altijd*, fr. words for 'all' and 'time' (14.11); OE *ealne weg*, phrase with *weg* 'way' (10.71) and presumably

at first spatial 'all the way' but in actual use temporal, hence ME *alweye*, *alwaye*, NE *alway* now displaced by *always* fr. ME *alleweyes*, *alles weis* a gen. phrase (NED s.v.); Lith. *visada*, *visados*, ChSl. *vĭsegda*, Boh. *vždy*, Russ. *vsegda*, derivs. with suffixes of temporal advs. (also Lith. *vis*, Russ. *vse*); Pol. *zawsze*, phrase with *za* 'in'; Skt. *sarvadā*, deriv. with suffix of temporal advs. like *tadā* 'then'.

2. Derivs. of *sem- in Grk. εἷς, μία, ἕν 'one', Lat. *semel* 'once', etc. Walde-P. 488 f. Ernout-M. 922. Feist 423.

Lat. *semper* (> It., OFr. *sempre*, Sp. *siempre*); Goth. *sinteinō*, adv. fr. *sinteins* 'daily', cpd. with second part : ChSl. *dĭnĭ*, Skt. *dina-*, etc. 'day' (14.31); OE *sym(b)le* (reg. for 'always' in Gospels), OHG *simbolon* (Goth. *simlē* 'once').

3. Grk. ἀεί, fr. αἰϝεί (attested in dial.) : Grk. αἰών, Lat. *aevum*, Goth. *aiws* 'lifetime, eternity, age', Skt. *āyu-* 'life', etc. Walde-P. 1.6.

4. Ir. *do grēs* ('always' in pres., past, or fut.), phrase with *grēss* 'attack, onset' : *in-grenn-* 'pursue', Lat. *gradī* 'step, go'. Pedersen 1.136.

Ir. *caidche*, NIr. *choidhche* (of future time), orig. *c-aidhche* 'until night' (*aidche* 'night' 14.42), Zimmer, KZ 30.55 ff. K. Meyer, Contrib. 299.

NIr. *riamh* 'always' or 'at any time' (used of past or pres. time, rarely of fut.; cf. Dineen s.v.), fr. Ir. *riam* 'formerly' : Lat. *prior* 'former', *prīmus* 'first', etc. (details of formation disputed). Walde-P. 2.34. Thurneysen, Gram. 528.

5. OE *ā*, OHG *eo*, *io* 'always' and 'at any time' (NHG *je*) : Goth. *aiws* (acc. *aiw* adv.), Lat. *aevum*, Grk. αἰών, etc., like Grk. ἀεί, αἰϝεί (above, 3).

OE *ǣfre*, ME *ever(e)*, NE *ever* 'always' (in Chaucer *ever* and *alwey* both common, but NE in this sense now arch.; cf. *it was ever thus* = *it was always so*), also 'at any time' (e.g. *did you ever see him? Never*), deriv. of *ā* (above), and prob. *feor* 'life'. Cf. *ā to feore* 'forever more'. NED s.v. *ever*, adv. Holthausen 9.

OHG *iomēr* (*iamēr*, *iemēr*), MHG, NHG *immer*, fr. *eo*, *io* (= OE *ā*, above) and *mēr* 'more' (13.16), hence at first only with reference to fut. time, but actually not so restricted. Weigand-H. 1.918. Kluge-G. 262.

NHG *stets*, adv. fr. *stet* 'fixed, steady' : *stehen* 'stand'. Weigand-H. 2.967.

6. SCr. *uvijek*, fr. *u* 'in' and *vijek* 'lifetime' = ChSl. *věkŭ* (reg. in Gospels for αἰών).

Boh. *stále*, fr. *stály* 'fixed, constant' : *státi* 'stand' (cf. NHG *stets*).

14.32 OFTEN

Grk.	*πολλάκις (συχνά, πυκνά)*	Goth.	*ufta*	Lith.	*dažnai, tankiai*
NG	*συχνά, πολλὲς φορές*	ON	*opt*	Lett.	*bieži*
Lat.	*saepe (frequenter)*	Dan.	*ofte*	ChSl.	*čęsto*
It.	*spesso (sovente)*	Sw.	*ofta*	SCr.	*često*
Fr.	*souvent (frequemment)*	OE	*oft*	Boh.	*často*
Sp.	*à menudo (frecuentamente)*	ME	*oft, ofte, often*	Pol.	*często*
Rum.	*adesea*	NE	*often (oft), frequently*	Russ.	*často*
Ir.	*in menice*	Du.	*dikwijls*	Skt.	*punaḥ punar, asakṛt*
NIr.	*minic*	OHG	*ofto*	Av.	. . . .
W.	*yn fynych*	MHG	*oft(e)*		
Br.	*alies*	NHG	*oft, häufig*		

'Often' is equivalent to 'many times' and may be so expressed, at least alternatively, beside other terms. Otherwise the most striking semantic source is 'thick, dense, crowded together' or 'heap, mass', with shift from spatial to temporal notion.

1. From words for 'many' (13.15), either adv. derivs. or phrases for 'many times' parallel to those for 'three times' (13.44). Grk. πολλάκις, with same suffix as in τριάκις 'three times', NG πολλὲς φορές, Fr. *bien de fois*, Sp. *muchas veces*, W. *llawer gwaith*, Br. *alies* (i.e. *a lies*) and *lies gwech* (*lies* 'several' : Ir. *lia* 'more', etc. 13.16), NE *many times*, etc. Most of these and other similar phrases are omitted from the list. Cf. also Ir. *menic* (below, 4).

2. Grk. συχνά, sometimes 'often' and so reg. in NG (beside freq. πολλὲς φορές), fr. συχνός 'abundant, long (in time), numerous, populous, many together', etc., prob. based on a common notion of 'compact' and perh. fr. a form of the same root as in σάττω 'stuff full'. Boisacq 926.

Grk. πυκνά, sometimes 'often' (e.g. NT, Lk. 5.33) fr. πυκνός 'thick, compact' (12.64) and 'frequent'; cf. NG συχνὰ πυκνά 'very frequently'.

3. Lat. *saepe*, neut. of an adj. **saepis*, prob. as orig. 'crowded together' : *saepēs* 'hedge, fence'. Walde-P. 2.445 f. Ernout-M. 885.

Lat. *subinde* 'immediately after', hence 'now and then, repeatedly, often' (> Fr. *souvent* > It. *sovente*). Ernout-M. 993. REW 8363.

Lat. *frequenter*, adv. fr. *frequēns*, *-entis* 'crowded, numerous' and 'frequent', prob. : *farcīre* 'stuff, fill full'. Similarly Fr. *frequemment*, Sp. *frecuentamente*, NE *frequently*. Walde-P. 2.134. Ernout-M. 388 f. Walde-H. 1.456 f.

It. *spesso*, fr. adj. *spesso*, Lat. *spissus* 'thick, dense' (12.64). REW 8160.

Sp. *à menudo*, phrase with *menudo* 'small' (fr. Lat. *minūtus*), with development through 'at short intervals, closely following'.

Rum. *adeseaorĭ*, *adesea*, *ades*, phrases with *des* 'thick', also adv. 'often', fr. Lat. *dēnsus* 'thick' (12.64). Tiktin 19, 524.

4. Ir. *menic* (adj. 'frequent', *in menice* adv. 'often'), NIr. *minic* (adj. and adv.), W. *mynych* (adj., *yn fynych* adv.) : Goth. *manags*, etc. 'much, many' (13.15). Pedersen 1.159.

5. Goth. *ufta*, ON *opt*, OE *oft*, OHG *ofto*, etc., general Gmc., but with no certain etym. Falk-Torp 788. Feist 513. Weigand-H. 2.333.

Du. *dikwijls*, fr. MDu. *dicke wīle(n)*, fr. *dick* 'thick' (12.63) here 'abundant' and *wīle* 'time' (: Goth. *hweila*, etc. 14.11). Cf. MLG, MHG, and NHG dial. *dicke* 'often'. Franck-v. W. 117.

NHG *häufig* (adj. and adv.), first 'in heaps, crowds' (fr. *haufe* 'heap'), hence 'abundant(ly)', and later 'frequent(ly)'. Weigand-H. 1.822. Paul, Deutsches Wtb. s.v. *haufe*.

6. Lith. *dažnai*, fr. *dažnas* 'many a, frequent' : Lett. *dažs* 'many a', OPruss. *ko-desnimma* 'so often as', root connection? Leskien, Bildung d. Nom. 355.

Lith. *tankiai*, fr. *tankus* 'thick, dense' (12.64).

Lett. *bieži*, fr. *biezs* 'thick, dense' (12.64). Mühl.-Endz. 1.307.

7. ChSl. *čęsto*, etc., general Slavic, fr. adj. ChSl. *čęstŭ*, etc. orig. 'thick, dense' (12.64) but mostly 'frequent'. Berneker 154 f.

8. Skt. *punaḥ punar* 'again and again' = 'often'.

Skt. *asakṛt*, cpd. of neg. *a-* and *sakṛt* 'once'.

14.33 SOMETIMES

Grk.	*ἐνίοτε*	Goth.	*hwan*	Lith.	*kartais, kada nekada*
NG	*κάποτε, ἐνίοτε*	ON	*stundum*	Lett.	*reizu reizem*
Lat.	*aliquandō*	Dan.	*undertiden, stundom*	ChSl.	*někŭgda*
It.	*alle volte, qualche volta*	Sw.	*ibland, emellanåt, stundom*	SCr.	*katkada*
Fr.	*quelquefois, parfois*			Boh.	*někdy*
Sp.	*algunas veces, a veces*	OE	*hwīlum, hwīle, stundum*	Pol.	*czasem, niekiedy*
Rum.	*cîteodată, uneori*			Russ.	*inogda*
Ir.	*īar n-ūairib, i n-ūairib*	ME	*while*	Skt.	*kadācit*
		NE	*sometimes*	Av.	. . . .
NIr.	*ar uaribh, amanna*	Du.	*soms, somtijds,*		
W.	*weithiau, ambell waith*	OHG	*sumes, sumenes, wanne*		
Br.	*a-wechou, gwechennou*	MHG	*bīwīlen, under wīlen*		
		NHG	*zuweilen, bisweilen*		

'Sometimes' is generally expressed either by temporal advs. formed from prons., esp. the indef. 'some', or by forms of, or phrases with, words for 'time', esp. 'at times, sometimes'.

Omitted here are those words which are used for the indef. 'at any time' mainly in neg., interrog., and subordinate clauses, rarely affirmative, such as Grk. ποτε, Lat. *umquam*, NE *ever*, NHG *je*, etc. But most such words are mentioned in the discussion, either here or in 14.31 or 14.34.

1. Pronominal advs. : Grk. ἐνίοτε, fr. phrase *ἔνι ὅτε = attested ἔσθ' ὅτε, lit. 'there are (times) when'. NG κάποτε fr. κά- (fr. κἄν, καὶ ἄν as in κάποιος 'some, somebody') and ποτέ indef. beside πότε 'when?'; Lat. *aliquandō*, fr. *aliquī* 'some' (Lat. also *nōnnumquam* 'not never'); Goth. *hwan*, OHG *wanne* ('when' and indef.); OHG *sumes*, *sumenes*, Du. *soms* : Goth. *sums*, etc. 'some'; Lith. *kada nekada* (NSB 2.143; *kada* 'when' and indef.); ChSl. *někŭgda* (cf. *ně-kŭto* 'someone', positive fr. neg.; Brugmann, Grd. 2.2.351 f.), Boh. *někdy*, Pol. *niekiedy*, SCr. *kad kad*, *katkada* (cf. *kada* 'when' or indef.), Russ. *inogda* (= ChSl. *inogda* 'at one time', fr. *inŭ* indef. 'one, some'; Berneker 430); Skt. *kadācit* (*kadā* 'when'? with indef. *cit*).

2. Forms of, or phrases with, the usual words for 'time' (14.11) or those used in phrases like 'three times' (13.44).

It. *alle volte* (*qualche volta*, *talvolta*, etc.), Fr. *quelquefois*, *parfois*, Sp. *a veces*, *algunas veces*, Rum. *cîteodată* (distributive *cîte* and *odată* 'once', Tiktin 507 f.), *uneori* (Tiktin 1067, 1682); Ir. *īar n-ūairib*, *i n-ūairib* (Thes. 2.332.21, 23; *ūar* 'hour, time', 14.51), NIr. *ar uaribh*, *amanna*, W. *weithiau*, *ambell waith*, Br. *a-wechou*, *gwechennou;* ON, OE *stundum*, Dan., Sw., *stundom*, OE *hwīlum*, *hwīle*, ME *while* (cf. NED s.vv. *whilom* and *while*, adv. 1), MHG *bīwīlen*, *under wīlen*, NHG *bisweilen*, *zuweilen*, Dan. *undertiden*, Du. *somtijds*, NE *sometimes;* Lith. *kartais*, Lett. *reizu reizem* (Mühl.-Endz. 3.507); Pol. *czasem*.

3. Sw. *ibland* 'among', also with time notion understood 'sometimes'. Similarly Sw. *emellanåt* fr. *emellan* 'between' and *åt* 'at'.

14.34 NEVER

Grk.	*οὔποτε, οὐδέποτε*	Goth.	*ni hwanhun, ni aiw*	Lith.	*niekad (-a, -os)*
NG	*ποτέ*	ON	*aldri(gi)*	Lett.	*nekad*
Lat.	*numquam*	Dan.	*aldrig*	ChSl.	*nikoliže, nikŭgdaže, nikŭdaže*
It.	*giammái*	Sw.	*aldrig*		
Fr.	*jamais*	OE	*nǣfre*	SCr.	*nikada*
Sp.	*nunca, jamás*	ME	*neuer(e)*	Boh.	*nikdy*
Rum.	*nicĭ-odată*	NE	*never*	Pol.	*nigdy*
Ir.	*nī riam, nī caedche*	Du.	*nooit, nimmer*	Russ.	*nikogda*
NIr.	*nī riamh, nī choidhche*	OHG	*nio, niomēr*	Skt.	*(na) kadā cana, na kadācit*
W.	*ni, (ni) byth*	MHG	*nie, nimmer*		
Br.	*nepred, biskoaz, birviken (birken)*	NHG	*nie, niemals, nimmer*	Av.	....

'Never' is expressed by combinations of the neg. with advs. for 'at any time, ever', many of these of pronominal origin, others cognate with words for 'time', 'age, lifetime', 'more', etc.

But in many cases the neg. sense has been absorbed and the formal neg. omitted—the familiar phenomenon observed in Fr. *pas* 'not', *rien* 'nothing', NG *τίποτε* 'nothing', *κανένας* 'no one', etc.

1. Grk. *οὔποτε, οὐδέποτε*, neg. of *ποτέ* 'at some time', indef. beside *πότε* 'when?'

NG *ποτέ* with neg. notion absorbed.

2. Lat. *numquam* (> Sp. *nunca*), fr. neg. *ne* and *umquam* 'at any time, ever'. Ernout-M. 1123.

It. *giammái*, Fr. *jamais*, Sp. *jamás*, fr. Lat. *iam* 'already' and *magis* 'more'. Used orig. and still in part for 'at any time, ever', but mostly after neg. and with neg. notion absorbed.

Rum. *nicĭ-odată*, fr. *nicĭ* 'not' (fr. Lat. *neque*) and *odată* 'once'. Tiktin 507 f.

3. Ir. *nī caedche*, NIr. *nī choidhche* ('never' in future), neg. of *caedche* 'always' (14.31).

Ir. *nī riam*, NIr. *nī riamh* ('never' in past time) neg. of Ir. *riam* 'formerly', NIr. *riamh* 'always, at any time' in past (14.31).

W. *ni byth*, neg. with *byth* 'ever' = Ir. *bith* 'world' used also in cpds. for 'ever' (K. Meyer, Contrib. 220. Pedersen 1.24). Also either *ni* alone or *byth* alone used for 'never'.

Br. *nepred* ('never' in pres.), neg. with *pred* 'time' (14.11).

Br. *biskoaz* ('never' in past), fr. *bis* = W., Corn. *byth* (above) and *choaz* 'still' = Corn. *whath, wheth* id., with neg. notion absorbed. Cf. MCorn. *ny bythqueth* 'never'. Pedersen 1.379. Henry 36.

Br. *birviken, birken* ('never' in future), fr. MBr. *bizhuyquen* = Corn. *bys vycken* 'forever', with *biz* as in *biskoaz* (above) + *huy*, Corn. *vy* (form of the vb. 'be'?) + *quen* 'as much, so', the whole with neg. notion absorbed. Henry 36. Ernault, Glossaire 61, Dict. étym. s.v. *bizhuyquen*.

4. Goth. *ni hwanhun*, neg. with deriv. of *hwan* 'when' and 'at any time', like *ni hwashun* 'no one', etc. Feist 281.

Goth. *ni aiw*, neg. with *aiw* adv., orig. acc. of *aiws* 'age, eternity'. Cf. OE *ā*, OHG *eo* 'always, at any time' (14.31), and OHG *nio* 'never'.

ON *aldri, aldrigi*, Dan., Sw. *aldrig*, fr. dat. sg. of *aldr* 'age, lifetime' (14.12) + indef. particle *-gi*, and with neg. notion absorbed, so orig. '(not) in a lifetime'. Falk-Torp 20. Hellquist 10.

OE *nǣfre*, ME *neuer(e)*, NE *never*, fr. neg. with OE *ǣfre*, etc., 'always' and 'at any time' (14.31).

Du. *nooit*, neg. with *ooit* 'at any time, ever', this fr. forms corresponding to OE *ā*, Goth. *aiw* and OE *giet* 'yet', and so like OE *nǣfre giet* (NED s.v. *yet*, 4.a). Franck-v. W. 475.

OHG *nio*, MHG, NHG *nie* (NHG *niemal*, now *niemals*, with *mal* as in *dreimal* 'three times', etc.), fr. neg. with OHG *io*, etc., 'always, at any time' (14.31). Weigand-H. 2.297, 299.

OHG *niomēr*, MHG, NHG *nimmer*, fr. neg. with OHG *iomēr*, etc. 'always' (14.31). Similarly Du. *nimmer*. Weigand-H. 2.303.

5. Lith. *niekad* (or *-a, -os*, NSB 2.185), Lett. *nekad*, neg. with Lith. *kada*, Lett. *kad* 'when?' and indef. : Skt. *kadā* 'when?', fr. interrog.-indef. stem *ka-*, IE **kʷo-*. Walde-P. 1.521, 571.

6. ChSl. *nikoli*, more commonly *nikoli-že* with indef. particle *-že*, neg. with *koli* 'at some time', deriv. of interrog.-indef. stem *ko-*. Berneker 673.

ChSl. *nikŭgda-že* (Supr.), Russ. *nikogda*, neg. with *kogda, kŭgda* 'when, at any time', fr. stem *ko-* (as above) with *-gda* as in *togda, tŭgda* 'then', etc. Berneker 673.

ChSl. *nikŭda-že*, SCr. *nikada*, neg. with ChSl. **kŭda*, SCr. *kada* 'when, at any time' : Lith. *kada*, Skt. *kadā* id. (above, 5).

Boh. *nikdy*, Pol. *nigdy*, may belong in either of the two preceding groups. Berneker 675. Brückner 138, 363.

7. Skt. *na kadā cana*, neg. with *kadā* 'when?' (like Lith. *kada*, above, 6) and the indef. *cana*. Also with *na* omitted in same sense, as RV 1.150.2. Also *na kadācit* (cf. 14.33).

14.35 AGAIN

Grk.	*πάλιν*	Goth.	*aftra*	Lith.	*vėl*
NG	*πάλι, ξανά*	ON	*aptr*	Lett.	*atkal*
Lat.	*iterum, dēnuo, rūrsus*	Dan.	*igen, atter*	ChSl.	*paky*
It.	*ancora*	Sw.	*igen, åter*	SCr.	*opet*
Fr.	*encore*	OE	*eft*	Boh.	*opět, zase*
Sp.	*otra vez*	ME	*aȝen*	Pol.	*znowu*
Rum.	*iar*	NE	*again*	Russ.	*opjat'*
Ir.	*arithissi, arīs*	Du.	*weer*	Skt.	*punar*
NIr.	*arīs*	OHG	*widar*	Av.	....
W.	*eilwaith, drachefn*	MHG	*wider*		
Br.	*c'hoaz*	NHG	*wieder(um), nochmal(s), abermal(s)*		

Several of the words for 'again' have such obvious semantic sources as 'another time, a second time', or 'anew'. But the most striking development is from the notion of 'back' or 'against', through 'back again, returning'.

1. Grk. *πάλιν*, in early use 'backwards', orig. acc. sg. of a **πάλις* 'turn' : *πόλος* 'pivot', etc. Walde-P. 1.515. Boisacq 743.

NG *ξανά*, fr. the freq. prefix *ξανα-*, orig. *ἐξ-ανα-* denoting repetition.

2. Lat. *iterum*, fr. **i-tero-*, pron. stem *i-* of *is* and suffix *-tero-* of contrasting relation (*dexter*, etc.). Walde-P. 1.100. Ernout-M. 499. Walde-H. 1.723 f.

Lat. *dēnuo* 'anew' and so freq. 'again', fr. *dē novō* (*novus* 'new'). Cf. Fr. *de nouveau*, and similar phrases elsewhere (not entered in the list except where the usual term, as Pol. *znowu*).

Lat. *rūrsus, rūrsum* 'backwards, in return' and often (Plautus+) 'again', fr. pass. pple. of *revertere* 'turn back'.

OFr. *oncore*, Fr. *encore* (> It. *ancora*), fr. *umquam hōra*. REW 4176, 9051.

Sp. *otra vez*, lit. 'another time', like Fr. *autrefois* 'formerly'.

Rum. *iar, iară*, etym.? REW 2886. Tiktin 748. Puşcariu 756.

3. Ir. *arithissi, arīs*, etym.? Macbain 292.

W. *eilwaith*, lit. 'a second time', fr. *eil-* 'second' and *gwaith* in cpds. like *teirgwaith* 'three times', etc. (13.44).

W. *drachefn*, 'backwards' and 'again', fr. *tra* 'beyond' and *cefn* 'back' (4.19). Morris Jones 410.

Br. *c'hoaz*, MBr. *hoaz* = Corn. *hweth* 'yet, again', etym. dub. Pedersen 1.379. Henry 170. Ernault, Dict. étym. 312.

4. Goth. *aftra* (reg. for *πάλιν*, but also 'backwards'), ON *aptr* ('backwards', late 'again'), Dan. *atter*, Sw. *åter*, OE *eft* (beside *aefter* 'after') : Goth. *aftarō* 'behind', Skt. *apataram* 'farther away', etc., derivs. of IE **apo* in Grk. *ἀπό*, Skt. *apa*, Lat. *ab*, etc. Walde-P. 1.49. Falk-Torp 36. Feist 12.

Dan., Sw. *igen* = ON *ī gegn* beside *gegn* 'against' = OHG *gegin* 'against', etc. Similarly OE *ongegn, ongeān* 'back, against', whence ME *aȝen*, NE *again* 'again', but locally also 'back' or 'against' (cf. U.S. rural *I'm agin it*). Falk-Torp 314. NED s.v. *again*.

Du. *weer*, OHG *widar*, MHG *wider*, also and orig. 'against', like OE *wiþer* : Goth. *wiþra* 'opposite, in the presence of', Skt. *vitaram* 'further', fr. **vi-* 'apart', in Skt. *vi-*, etc., with suffix *-tero-* in words of contrasting relations. NHG *wieder, wiederum*, with differentiated spelling for sense 'again' vs. *wider* 'against'. Walde-P. 1.312 f. Feist 570. Weigand-H. 1255.

NHG *nochmal(s)*, fr. *noch* 'still' and *mal* as in *dreimal* 'three times', etc. (13.44). Similarly *abermal(s)*, fr. *aber* in its sense of 'again'. Weigand-H. 1.6.

5. Lith. *vėl, vėlei* (Lett. *vēl* 'still') : *velti* 'to full' (orig. 'turn'), Lat. *volvere* 'turn around', etc. (10.13). 'Again' fr. 'turn' as Grk. *πάλιν* (above, 1). Walde-P. 1.303. Mühl.-Endz. 4.556.

Lett. *atkal* : Lith. *atkalas* 'turned around', this : *atsikalti* 'lean on'. Mühl.-Endz. 1.163. Trautmann 114.

6. ChSl. *paky* : *opako, opaky* 'backwards, behind', Pol. *opak* 'turned around, wrong way', Skt. *apāka-* 'far off', derivs. of **apo-* in Grk. *ἀπό*, Skt. *apa*, etc. Walde-P. 1.50. Brückner 380.

SCr. *opet*, Boh. *opět*, Pol. (obs.) *opięć*, Russ. *opjat'* = ChSl. *opętĭ* 'backwards' : Lith. *atpent, atpenč* 'back, in return, on the contrary' (cf. NSB), cpds. of words for 'heel', ChSl. *pęta*, Pol. *pięta*, Russ. *pjata*, OPruss. *pentis* (Lith. *pentis* now 'butt end of an ax'), and so orig. 'on the heels of'. Trautmann 214. Brückner 380, 412.

Boh. *zase* 'backwards' and 'again', fr. *za* 'behind' and refl. *se*, like Pol. *zaś* 'but', earlier *zasię*. Gebauer 1.206. Linde 6.887.

Pol. *znowu*, fr. *z* with old gen. sg. of *nowy* 'new', hence orig. 'anew', like Lat. *denuō*, etc., but now the reg. Pol. word for 'again'.

7. Skt. *punar* 'again' and 'back' : Grk. *πύματος* 'last', fr. **pu-* beside **po-* and **apo*. Walde-P. 1.48.

14.41 DAY

Grk.	*ἡμέρα*	Goth.	*dags*	Lith.	*diena*
NG	*ἡμέρα*	ON	*dagr*	Lett.	*diena*
Lat.	*diēs*	Dan.	*dag*	ChSl.	*dĭnĭ*
It.	*giorno (dì)*	Sw.	*dag*	SCr.	*dan*
Fr.	*jour*	OE	*dæg, dōgor*	Boh.	*den*
Sp.	*día*	ME	*day*	Pol.	*dzień*
Rum.	*zi*	NE	*day*	Russ.	*den'*
Ir.	*lāa, laithe, dia*	Du.	*dag*	Skt.	*ahan-, dina-, diva(sa)-*
NIr.	*lā*	OHG	*tag*		
W.	*dydd*	MHG	*tac*	Av.	*ayan-, azan-*, OPers. *rauča*
Br.	*deiz*	NHG	*tag*		

The majority of the words for 'day', certainly those of the large inherited group, denoted the bright 'day' vs. 'night', and only secondarily (like 'summers' or 'winters' for 'years') the comprehensive 24-hour 'day' (for which Dan., Sw. have distinctive forms).

1. Derivs. of IE **dei-* 'shine', rare in verbal forms (Skt. 3sg. imperf. *adīdet*, etc.), but widespread in words for 'sky, heaven' as Skt. nom. sg. *dyāus* and the personified Grk. *Ζεύς*, Lat. *Iūpiter, Iovis*; 'god' as Skt. *deva-*, Lat. *deus*, etc.; and 'day'. Walde-P. 1.772 ff. Ernout-M. 268 ff. Walde-H. 1.350. Here as 'day'.

a) IE **dyeu-*, **diw-*, etc.

Lat. *diēs* (> It. *dì*, OFr. *di*, Sp. *dia*, Rum. *zi*); Ir. *dia, die*, W. *dydd*, Br. *deiz*; Skt. *diva-* (in *dive dive* 'day by day', otherwise *divasa-*); Arm. *tiw*. Lat. deriv. adj. *diurnus* 'of the day', late sb. *diurnum* > Fr. *jour*, Prov., Cat. *jorn*; It. *giorno* vs. *dì* perh. due to lit. influence of Prov. or Fr. REW 2632, 2700. Wartburg 3.71 f., 105 f. Bonfante, PMLA 59.877 ff. (with refs.).

b) With nasal suffix.

Lith., Lett. *diena*; ChSl. *dĭnĭ*, etc., general Slavic; Skt. *dina-* (esp. in cpds.); cf. Ir. *tre-denus* 'triduum', Goth. *sinteins* 'daily'.

2. Grk. *ἡμέρα*, Dor. *ἁμέρα*, poet. *ἦμαρ*, Dor. *ἆμαρ* : Arm. *awr* (**āmōr*) 'day', root connection? Walde-P. 1.53. Boisacq 322.

3. Ir. *laithe*, beside *lae, lāa*, NIr. *lā*, Gall. *lat.* (Calendar of Coligny) : ChSl. *lěto* 'year, summer' (14.73). Walde-P. 2.427. Pedersen 1.133. Thurneysen, Gram. 35, 180. Pokorny KZ 50.43 f. (taking *lae* as of different orig., but cf. Vendryes, RC 42.234 f.).

4. Goth. *dags*, ON *dagr*, OE *dæg*, OHG *tag*, etc. general Gmc. (also derivs. Goth. *fidur-dōgs* 'of four days', OE *dōgor* 'day', ON *dœgr* '12-hour period, day or night', Dan. *døgn*, Sw. *dygn* (the last two denoting the 24-hour day), etym. dub., but perh. (despite phonetic difficulties with the gutturals) : Lith. *dagas* '(summer-) heat', OPruss. *dagis* 'summer', Skt. *nidāgha-* 'heat, summer', fr. the root **dhegʷh-* in Skt. *dah-*, Lith. *degti*, etc., 'burn', and also (with init. doublets, as Skt. *aççru-*, Lith. *ašara* : Grk. *δάκρυ* Goth. *tagr* 'tear', etc.). Skt. *ahan-*, Av. *azan* 'day'. Walde-P. 1.849 f. Walde-H. 1.467. Falk-Torp 133, 176. Feist 113.

5. Skt. *ahan-* (nom.-acc. sg. *ahar*, instr. sg. *ahnā*, etc.), Av. *azan-* (loc. sg. *asni*, etc.), see above, 4, with refs.

Av. *ayan-* (nom. sg. *ayarə*, gen. sg. *ayąn*, etc., neut. *r/n* stem like Skt. *ahan-*, above), prob. : Grk. *ἦρι* 'in the morning', Goth. *air*, ON *ār*, etc., 'early', Goth. *jēr*, Av. *yārə* 'year', etc. Walde-P. 1.3.

OPers. *rauča* (*xšapavā raučapativā* 'either by night or by day', 1 *rauča* 'one day', etc.) : Av. *raočah-* 'light', Skt. *ruc-* 'shine', Grk. *λευκός* 'bright', Lat. *lūx* 'light', etc. Walde-P. 2.308 ff.

14.42 NIGHT

Grk.	νύξ	Goth.	nahts	Lith.	naktis
NG	νύχτα	ON	nōtt	Lett.	nakts
Lat.	nox	Dan.	nat	ChSl.	noštĭ
It.	notte	Sw.	natt	SCr.	noć
Fr.	nuit	OE	niht	Boh.	noc
Sp.	noche	ME	night	Pol.	noc
Rum.	noapte	NE	night	Russ.	noč'
Ir.	adaig (nocht)	Du.	nacht	Skt.	rātrī-, kṣap-, nakt-
NIr.	oidhche	OHG	naht	Av. OPers.	xšap-
W.	nos	MHG	naht		
Br.	noz	NHG	nacht		

Most of the words for 'night' belong to an inherited group, pointing clearly to an IE word for 'night'. In Irish, except for an adv. relic, and in Indo-Iranian, except in Vedic and a classical Skt. adv. relic, the old word was displaced by others, but elsewhere has persisted as the usual word to the present day.

1. IE *nokt(i)-. Walde-P. 2.337 ff. Ernout-M. 682. Sturtevant (connecting this group and that for 'naked', 4.99) JAOS 52.10, Hitt. Gram. 122 f.

Grk. νύξ, νυκτός, NG νύχτα (υ prob. fr. a reduced grade); Lat. nox, noctis (> Romance words); Ir. nocht (in innocht 'tonight'), W. nos, Br. noz; Goth. nahts, ON nōtt, etc., general Gmc.; Lith. naktis, Lett. nakts; ChSl. noštĭ, etc.,

general Slavic; Ved. nakt- (nom. sg. nak, acc. sg. naktam), nakti- (class. Skt. only adv. naktam 'by night', cf. Wackernagel, Altind. Gram. 3.233 ff.); Alb. natë;— with e-grade Hitt. nekuz 'evening', nekuzi 'goes to bed' (Sturtevant, Hitt. Gloss. 108).

2. Ir. adaig, aidche, NIr. oidhche, etym. dub. Walde-P. 1.34. Walde-H. 1.61. Stokes 326.

3. Skt. rātrī- : Grk. Λητώ, Dor. Λᾱτώ 'Leto, mother of Apollo and Artemis', orig. personification of the night, perh. fr. the root in Grk. λήθω 'be hidden', etc. Walde-P. 2.377. Boisacq 555. Uhlenbeck 248.

Skt. kṣap-, Av.xšap-, xšapan-, xšapar-, OPers. xšap- (Barth. 548 f.) : Grk. ψέφας, ψέφος 'darkness'. Walde-P. 1.524 f

14.43 DAWN

Grk.	ἕως, ὄρθρος	Goth.		Lith.	auśra, brėkšta
NG	αὐγή, χαράματα, χαραυγή	ON	dagan, dagsbrūn	Lett.	rīta blāzma, rīta krēsla, ausma
		Dan.	dagning, daggry	ChSl.	rano(adv.), -brēzgŭ, zorę (pl.)
Lat.	aurōra, prima lūx	Sw.	dagning, gryning		
It.	alba, aurora	OE	dægrēd, dægrima, dagung	SCr.	zora, svanuće
Fr.	aube, aurore			Boh.	svítáni, úsvit
Sp.	alba, aurora	ME	dawing, dawning, dayrawe, etc.	Pol.	świt, brzask, zorza
Rum.	zori, aurorằ			Russ.	zarja, razsvet
Ir.	dedōl	NE	dawn, daybreak	Skt.	uṣas-, aruṇa-, prabhāta-
NIr.	fáinne an lae	Du.	dageraad	Av.	uṣah-, asūr-
W.	gwawr	OHG	morgenrōt, -rōta, tagarōt		
Br.	goulou-deiz, tarz an deiz	MHG	morgenrōt, -rœte, tagerāt		
		NHG	morgenrot, -röte, tagesanbruch, morgendämmerung		

Words for 'dawn' denote strictly the period just before sunrise, but some of them may be extended to cover 'sunrise' or even 'morning'. They are mostly, including the inherited group, connected with words meaning 'grow bright, shine, light', or 'white, gray, red', or in a few cases with the word for 'day'.

1. IE *ausos-, etc., fr. a root seen in the vbl. forms Skt. ucchati, Av. usaiti 'it grows bright, shines (of the dawn)', Lith. aušta, Lett. aust 'it dawns', etc. Cf. also *aus-tero- in words for 'east' (12.45). Walde-P. 1.26 f. Ernout-M. 93. Walde-H. 1.86. Pedersen 1.82.

Grk. Hom. ἠώς, Aeol. αὔως, Att. ἕως; Lat. aurōra (mostly poet., as also the lit. It., Sp. aurora, Fr. aurore, Rum. aurorằ); Ir. fáir ('sunrise'), W. gwawr (Br. gwere-laouen 'morning star'); Lith. aušra, Lett. ausma (new formation fr. aust, above); Skt. uṣas-, Av. ušah- (also Skt. uṣ-, uṣas-, Av. uš-, but secondary).

2. Grk. ὄρθρος, prob. 'dawn' fr. 'sunrise' : ὀρθός 'upright, straight', Skt. vṛdh- 'grow', ChSl. rano 'early in the morning', etc. (14.16). Walde-P. 1.289 f.

Grk. αὐγή 'light', esp. 'daylight', hence late (NT, pap.), NG 'dawn' : Alb. agon 'it dawns', agim 'dawn', ChSl. jugŭ 'south'. Walde-P. 1.25.

NG χαράματα, for χαράγματα pl. of χάραγμα 'incision, cut' : χαράζω 'cut, carve, engrave' (χαράζει 'it dawns'), prob. with reference to the sharp streaks of light on horizon. NG χαραυγή, a blend with αὐγή.

3. Lat. (beside poet. aurōra) often prīma lūx, lit. 'first light', esp. in abl. prīmā lūce 'at dawn'. Also dīlūculum : dīlūcēscere 'grow light, dawn', likewise fr. lūx 'light'.

It., Sp. alba, Fr. aube (Rum. albằ rare in this sense), fr. fem. of Lat. albus 'white'. REW 331.

Rum. zorĭ, esp. pl. zori, fr. Slavic, cf. below, 7. Tiktin 1829.

4. Ir. dedōl 'dawn' and 'twilight' (cf. K. Meyer, Contrib. 600), etym.? Stokes, RC 27.88, as *dwi-dhogʷhlo-, fr. *dhegʷh-'burn'. Marstrander, Ir. Acad. Dict. 1.213 f. as ded-ōl 'last-drinking'.

NIr. fáinne an lae, lit. 'ring of the day' (with ref. to the semicircle of light on the horizon).

W. gwawr, above, 1.

Br. goulou-deiz, lit. 'daylight'.

Br. tarz an deiz, lit. 'break of day'.

5. Goth.? (relevant passages lacking), ON dagan, Dan., Sw. dagning, OE dagung, ME dawing and (prob. fr. Norse, cf. NED) dawning, NE dawn, MHG tagunge, fr. ON daga, OE dagian, MHG tagen (OHG tagēn), etc. 'to dawn', fr. ON dagr, etc. 'day' (14.31). Falk-Torp 134.

ON dagsbrūn, lit. 'brow of day'.

Dan. daggry (lit., older also daggryning), Sw. gryning, ON grȳjandi (ἅπ. λεγ.), fr. an ON *grȳja 'become gray, dawn' (Dan., Sw. gry) : ON grār 'gray', etc. Falk-Torp 354.

OE dægrēd, ME daired, Du. dageraad, OHG tagarōt, MHG tagerāt (-rōt), fr. the words for 'day', but the orig. of the second part (impossible to combine with the words for 'red', OE rēad, Du. rood, etc.; OHG -rōt, secondary association) dub. Franck-v. W. 104. Holthausen 69. Graff 2.486 ff. Bremer, PBB 13.33.

OE dægrima, ME dairime, lit. 'dayrim'.

ME dayrawe, lit. 'day-row', where row, ME raw(e) has the arch. sense 'beam, ray'. NED s.v.

ME day-spring now obs., but still freq. in early NE.

NE daybreak (see NED s.v.), similarly Dan. daybrækning, NHG tagesanbruch.

OHG morgenrōt, morgenrōta, MHG morgenrōt, morgenrœte, NHG morgenrot,

morgenrōte, lit. 'morning-red(ness)'. Weigand-H. 2.219. Kluge-G. 399.

NHG morgendämmerung, lit. 'morning-twilight', (dämmerung, OHG demar 'twilight' : Skt. tamas- 'darkness', etc., 1.62).

6. Lith. brėkšta (with vb. brėkšti), ChSl. brėzgŭ in probrězgŭ ('time before dawn', Mk. 1.35), Pol. brzask (Boh. břesk 'twilight', Russ. obs. bresk 'dawn'), with vbs. Russ. brezžit 'dawns', Boh. brīská se 'becomes dark', etc. : Skt. bhrāj-, Av. brāz- 'shine, beam', Goth. bairhts, etc. 'bright'. Walde-P. 2.170. Berneker 85.

Lett. rīta blāzma, lit. 'morning shine'. Mühl.-Endz. 1.312.

Lett. rīta krēsla, lit. 'morning twilight' (like NHG morgendämmerung). Mühl.-Endz. 2.276.

7. ChSl. brēzgŭ, etc., above, 6.

ChSl. rano, adv. rendering ὄρθρος, ὄρθριος, see 14.16.

SCr. zora, Pol. zorza, Russ. zarja, lit.

'shine, splendor, redness of the sky' (sometimes with adjs. 'of the morning' to designate the dawn in particular), ChSl. zorja 'ray of light', pl. 'dawn' (e.g. vŭ zorę Supr. 205.21) : ChSl. zĭrěti 'see, glance', Lith. žėrėti 'shine, sparkle' etc. Walde-P. 1.602. Trautmann 366.

SCr. svanuće, Boh. svítáni, úsvit, Pol. świt, Russ. razsvet : vbs. SCr. svanuti, Boh. svítáti (se), Pol. świtać, Russ. svetat' 'grow light, dawn', ChSl. svĭtěti, svĭnǫti, svŭtáti, etc. 'shine', světŭ 'light' (1.61).

8. Skt. aruṇa-, lit. 'reddish', as 'dawn' chiefly personified as the charioteer of the sun, hence aruṇī- 'dawn' (RV) : aruṣa- 'red, fire-colored', Av. aruša- 'white'. Walde-P. 1.159.

Skt. prabhāta-, lit. 'having shown forth, become light', fr. pra-bhā- 'shine forth', bhā- 'shine'.

Av. asūr-, lit. (period of day) 'until morning', cpd. of a- 'to, until', and sūr- 'morning'. Barth. 221. Or with neg. a- as 'not (yet quite) morning'?

'Morning' fr. '(sun)rise'. Walde-P. 1.141. Mühl.-Endz. 3.541.

6. ChSl. utro, jutro, SCr. jutro, Boh. jitro, Russ. utro (Pol. jutro now adv. 'tomorrow'), prob. (despite the phonetic difficulty of tr fr. str, perhaps due to a blend) fr. *ustro (cf. ChSl. za ustra = za utra), *ausro- : Skt. uṣas, Lith. aušra, etc. 'dawn' (14.43). Berneker 462 f. Meillet, Études 406. Brückner, KZ 46.212 ff.

Boh. ráno, Pol. rano, (po)ranek : ChSl. adv. rano 'early in the morning' (14.16).

7. Skt. prātar, adv. 'early', and 'in the morning' (14.16), more usual than sb. forms (prātaḥ prātaḥ 'every morning', prātaḥkāla- 'morning time', etc.).

Skt. vastu- (RV) 'early morning', lit. 'time of dawn', fr. vas- (3sg. ucchati) 'grow bright, shine (of dawn)', the same root as in the old word for 'dawn' (14.43). Cf. Zimmer, Altind. Leben 361.

Skt. apiçarvara- (RV) 'early morning', lit. '(bordering) on the (starry) night', fr. çarvara- 'gay, speckled', fem. 'starry night'. Cf. Zimmer, Altind. Leben 361 f. (with other terms used for various times of morning, as saṃgava- 'time for gathering the cattle for milking', prapitva- lit. 'pressing forward' (of the day), fr. pĭ'swell, become fat').

Av. sūr-, only in acc. sg. sūrəm as adv. : Skt. çvas 'tomorrow', Av. savahī- 'the east', with n-suffix Skt. çona- 'red', etc. Walde-P. 1.368. Barth. 1631.

14.44 MORNING

Grk.	(ἕως), πρωΐα (late)	Goth.	maurgins	Lith.	rytas
NG	πρωΐ	ON	morginn	Lett.	rīts
Lat.	māne, mātūtīnum	Dan.	morgen	ChSl.	utro, jutro
It.	mattino (-a)	Sw.	morgon	SCr.	jutro
Fr.	matin	OE	morgen, mergen	Boh.	jitro, ráno
Sp.	mañana	ME	morwen, morwening	Pol.	rano, (po)ranek
Rum.	dimineațằ	NE	morning (morn)	Russ.	utro
Ir.	maten	Du.	morgen	Skt.	prātar (adv.), vastu-, apiçarvara-
NIr.	maidin	OHG	morgan		
W.	bore	MHG	morgen	Av.	sūr-
Br.	beure	NHG	morgen		

Words for 'morning', though many of them orig. denoted the time of dawn or sunrise, are used more comprehensively to include all the early part of the day (up to noon, and even in this scope not ousted by new terms like NE forenoon, etc.). Several are connected with the advs. for 'early' (14.16), others with the old word for 'dawn' (14.43) or from notions applicable to the dawn or sunrise.

1. Grk. ἕως 'dawn' (14.43) sometimes extended to 'morning', for which there is no distinctive word in classical Greek.

Late Grk. πρωΐα (LXX, NT+), for πρωΐα ὥρα 'early time of day', fr. adj. πρώϊος, fr. adv. πρωΐ 'early' (14.16), NG 'in the morning' and sb. τὸ πρωΐ 'morning'.

2. Lat. māne, indecl. sb. 'morning'

and adv. 'in the morning, early' (14.16). Hence (through *maneana) Sp. mañana. REW 5295.

Lat. mātūtīnum (Plin.) and mātūtīna dies, tempora, fr. adj. mātūtīnus 'of the morning, early' (cf. mātūtīnē adv., 14.16). Hence It. mattino, mattina, Fr. matin, Ir. maten, NIr. maidin. Ernout-M. 598. REW 5434. Vendryes, De hib. voc. 154.

Rum. dimineațằ, deriv. of late Lat. dē-māne (> Fr. demain 'tomorrow', etc.), fr. māne (above). REW 2348. Pușcariu 1083.

3. Ir. maten, NIr. maidin, above, 2.

W. bore, Br. beure : Ir. imbárach 'tomorrow', but etym.? Pedersen 1.99. Zimmer, KZ 30.17 f. Loth, RC 36.179 (vs. Morris Jones 163).

4. Goth. maurgins, ON morginn, OE morgen, etc., general Gmc. (ME morwening, NE morning, with addition of suffix -ing) prob. (as orig. denoting the morning twilight) : ChSl. mrŭknǫti, mrŭcati 'become dark', Lith. merkti 'shut the eyes, wink', ChSl. mrakŭ 'darkness', beside Lith. mirgéti 'glimmer, twinkle', fr. a guttural extension of the root in Grk. μαρμαίρω 'flash, gleam', Skt. marīci- 'beam of light'. Walde-P. 2.274. Falk-Torp 731. Feist 350.

5. Lith. rytas, Lett. rīts : Lett. rielēt 'come out, break forth' (sun, light, etc.), Goth. urreisan, ON rīsa, etc. 'rise'.

14.45 NOON

Grk.	μεσημβρία	Goth.	....	Lith.	pietūs
NG	μεσημέρι	ON	miðr dagr, miðdegi,	Lett.	pusdiena, dienasvidus
Lat.	merīdiēs		hādegi	ChSl.	poludĭne
It.	mezzogiorno, mezzodì	Dan.	middag	SCr.	podne
Fr.	midi	Sw.	middag	Boh.	poledne
Sp.	mediodìa	OE	middæg	Pol.	poludnie
Rum.	amiazi, miezul zilei	ME	midday, none	Russ.	polden'
Ir.	medon lái	NE	noon, midday	Skt.	madhyāhan-, madhy-
NIr.	meadhon lae, eadradh	Du.	midday, noen		aṁdina-
W.	canol (hanner) dydd,	OHG	mittilag	Av.	arəm-piθwā-, ra-
	navn	MHG	mit(te)tac		piθwā-
Br.	kreisteiz	NHG	mittag		

Most of the words for 'noon' are such as mean lit. 'mid-day', or in some cases 'half-day', rarely 'high-day'. A few orig. denoted the (principal, i.e. midday) 'meal'. Quite otherwise NE noon (see below, 5).

1. Combinations of words for 'middle' (12.37) and 'day' (14.41). Grk. μεσημβρία (: ἡμέρα with reg. μρ > μβρ), NG τὸ μεσημέρι (formed anew, with dim. type); Lat. merīdiēs (for medīdiēs by dissim.), It. mezzogiorno, mezzodì, Fr. midi (OFr. di 'day'), Sp. mediodìa, Rum. amiazi, amiaḑi (Lat. ad mediam diem), miezul zilei; Ir. medon lái (laithe), NIr. meadhon lae; W. canol dydd, Br. kreisteiz; ON miðr dagr (also cpd. miðdagr), miðdegi, OE middæg (also cpd. miðdagr), OHG mittilag, etc. (also two words as in ON, OE midd dæg, OHG mitti, mitter tag, MHG mitter tac); Lett. dienasvidus (lit. 'day's middle'); Skt. madhyāhan-, madhyaṁdina-.

2. Combinations of words for 'half' (13.24) and 'day'. W. hanner dydd; Lett. pusdiena; ChSl. poludĭne, etc., general Slavic.

3. ON hādegi (usual word in NIcel.), lit. 'high-day' (cf. also early NE high-day in this sense, NED s.v. 2).

4. NIr. eadradh, gen. eadartha (Dinneen, McKenna), fr. eadar 'between', but perh. blended with a form like Ir. anteirt, W. anterth 'forenoon', fr. Lat. ante (or inter, intrā) tertiam (hōram). Loth, Mots lat. 133.

5. ME none, NE noon, fr. Lat. nōna (sc. hōra) 'ninth hour' (about 3:00 P.M.), but since 14th cent. usually 'noon', owing to a change in the time of the eccl. office or a mealtime (cf. the shifts of time among terms for 'breakfast', 'lunch', and 'dinner', 5.42–5.44). NED s.v. Similarly, OFr. none (still dial. for 'mid-day meal'), Du. noen (now mostly obs.), and W. nawn (as 'noon' prob. semantic borrowing fr. English).

6. Lith. pietūs, also and orig. 'the mid-day meal, dinner' (5.44). Cf. Av. pitu- 'food', whence arəm-piθwā-, rapiθwā- 'noon', lit. 'suitable for food'. Barth. 189.

14.46 EVENING

Grk.	ἑσπέρα, ὀψία	Goth.	andanahti	Lith.	vakaras
NG	ἑσπέρα, βράδυ	ON	kveld, aptann	Lett.	vakars
Lat.	vesper, vespera	Dan.	aften (kvæld)	ChSl.	večerŭ
It.	sera	Sw.	afton, kväll	SCr.	večer
Fr.	soir	OE	æfen	Boh.	večer
Sp.	tarde	ME	even, evening	Pol.	wieczór
Rum.	seară	NE	evening	Russ.	večer
Ir.	fescor	Du.	avond	Skt.	doṣā-, sāya-
NIr.	tráthnóna	OHG	ābant	Av.	arəzah-
W.	min nos, hwyr	MHG	ābent		
Br.	abardaez	NHG	abend		

Apart from an inherited group, of obscure relations, words for 'evening' are most commonly connected with words for 'late', these in part orig. 'slow'.

1. IE *wespero- and *wekero-, parallel forms with first part prob. *wes- and *we- : Skt. avas, ava 'down' and OE west, etc. 'west' (12.46). Walde-P. 1.15, 311. Falk-Torp 1371 f.

Grk. ἑσπέρα (sc. ὥρα) fr. ἕσπερος 'of the evening', also as sb. 'evening' (Hom., etc.); Lat. vesper (> Ir. fescor, NIr. feascar now 'twilight'), and vespera; Lith. vakaras, Lett. vakars, ChSl. večerŭ, etc., general Slavic.

2. Grk. ὀψία (sc. ὥρα), fr. ὄψιος adj., ὀψέ 'late' adv. (14.17), cf. NG ἀπόψε 'this evening, tonight'.

NG pop. τὸ βράδυ, fr. Grk. βραδύς 'slow' (14.22), through 'late'.

3. It. sera, Rum. seară, fr. late Lat. sēra (sc. hōra) 'evening' (freq. in Peregrinatio); Fr. soir, fr. Lat. sēro (adv.); both fr. Lat. sērus 'late' (14.17). Ernout-M. 933. REW 7841.

Sp. tarde, fr. Lat. tardē 'slowly', fr. tardus 'slow'. REW 8573.

4. NIr. tráthnóna, properly the early evening (from three o'clock on, Dinneen), lit. 'time of the nones' (nóin 'nones, evening prayer'; tráth, 14.11).

W. min nos, lit. 'brink of night'.

W. hwyr, fr. Lat. sērus 'late' (cf. It.

sera, above). Pedersen 1.208. Loth, Mots lat. 178.

W. ucher (obs.), Corn. gurth-uher, etym. dub. Pokorny Z. celt. Ph. 15.377 (vs. Pedersen 1.75, etc.).

Br. abardaez, etym.? Henry 2. Ernault, Dict. étym. 193.

5. Goth. andanahti, lit. 'the period extending toward the night' (and, anda- 'on, to' and nahts 'night'). Feist 47.

ON kveld (Dan. kvæld poet. and arch.), Sw. kväll, NIcel. kvöld, OE cwield in cwield-tīþ (cwild-, cwyld-) 'evening-time', cwield-seten 'evening sitting, first part of night', OHG quilti-werc 'evening work', prob. identical with OE cwield 'destruction, death' : OE cwelan 'die, cwellan 'kill', OHG quelan 'suffer torment', Lith. galas 'end', etc. Walde-P. 1.690. Falk-Torp 604. Hellquist 538.

ON aptann (distinguished from kveld as longer, lasting from mid-afternoon on, cf. einn aptann at kveldi; NIcel. aftan, poet.), Dan. aften, Sw. afton; with different formation and grade of root syllable OE æfen, ME even, Du. avond, OHG ābant, etc. (OE æfning 'approach of evening' > ME, NE evening), prob. fr. the root in Goth. iftuma 'following, later', afar 'after', Skt. apara- 'later, western', Grk. ἐπί 'to, on', ὀψέ 'late', etc. Walde-P. 1.123. Falk-Torp 15. NED s.vv. even, sb.¹, evening, sb.¹.

6. Skt. doṣā- (RV etc., AV also

---

doṣas-), pradoṣa- (cf. Av. daoštara-, daošastara- 'western') : Grk. δύομαι, δύνω 'sink, go down', δυσμαί 'setting (of the sun), west'. Walde-P. 1.777 f. Uhlenbeck 131.

Skt. sāya-, perh. : Lat. sērus 'late', Goth. seiþus 'late', etc. Walde-P. 2.461. Uhlenbeck 334.

Av. arəzah-, etym. dub. Barth. 202. Walde-P. 1.82.

14.47 TODAY

Grk.	σήμερον	Goth.	himma daga	Lith.	šiandien
NG	σήμερα, σήμερον	ON	í dag	Lett.	šuodien
Lat.	hodiē	Dan.	i dag	ChSl.	dĭnĭsĭ
It.	oggi	Sw.	i dag	SCr.	danas
Fr.	aujourd'hui	OE	tō dæg	Boh.	dnes
Sp.	hoy	ME	to day	Pol.	dziś
Rum.	astăzi, azi	NE	today	Russ.	segodnja
Ir.	indiu	Du.	heden, vandaag	Skt.	adyá
NIr.	indiu	OHG	hiutu	Av.	....
W.	heddyw	MHG	hiute		
Br.	hizio	NHG	heute		

For 14.47–14.49, cf. Brugmann, Zu den Wörtern für 'heute', 'gestern', 'morgen' in den idg. Sprachen, Ber. Sächs. Ges. 1917, No. 1.

The expressions for 'today' are all derived from the words for 'day' (14.41), but many of them are, unlike NE today, so disguised in form that there is no consciousness of the relationship. The combination with the pron. stem IE *ki-, seen in Lat. cis, citra 'on this side', Lith. šis, (and Du. vandaag with new 'from, of', Balto-Slavic, and a part of the Gmc. forms.

1. Grk. Ion. σήμερον, Dor. σάμερον (Att. τήμερον rare), NG pop. σήμερα, fr. *κιᾱμερον, fr. ἡμέρα 'day' and pron. stem *ki-, *ky-. Walde-P. 1.452 f. Boisacq 861.

2. Lat. hodiē (> It. oggi, Sp. hoy, OFr. hui, Fr. cpd. aujourd'hui, fr. *hodiē : Lat. a-dyā 'today', or with vowel shortening fr. abl.-loc. *hō diē? Ernout-M. 456. Walde-H. 1.653 f. REW 4163.

Rum. astăzi (shortened azi), fr. astă zi 'this day'. Tiktin 114.

3. Ir. indiu, W. heddyw, Br. hizio,

cpds. of Ir. article in(d) and Britannic pron. stem he- (IE *so-) with old dat. (orig. instr.) sg. of the word for 'day', Ir. dia, etc. Pedersen 2.92, 190. Thurneysen, Gram. 217.

4. Goth. himma daga dat. sg. (once also hina dag acc. sg.), lit. 'this day' (pron. stem hi- fr. IE *ki-).

ON í dag, Dan., Sw. i dag (also idag), phrase with prep. í 'in'; similarly OE tō dæg, ME to day, NE today with to, and Du. vandaag with new 'from, of'.

Du. heden, MDu. hēden, beside hūde(n), OS hiudu, OHG hiutu, MHG hiute, NHG heute, fr. *hiu-tagu 'on this day', cpd. with pron. stem in Goth. himma, etc. (above). Weigand-H. 1.860. Franck-v. W. 237.

5. Lith. šiandien, Lett. šuodien, fr. forms of šis 'this' and diena 'day'.

6. ChSl. dĭnĭsĭ, etc., general Slavic fr. dĭnĭ and pron. sĭ 'this' (reformed Russ. sego-dnja adv. gen.). Berneker 253. Brückner 113.

7. Skt. adya, adyā, cpd. of pron. stem a- (in a-sāu 'that') and dyā : dyāus, Lat. diēs, etc. 'day'. Walde-P. 1.98.

14.48 TOMORROW

Grk.	αὔριον	Goth.	du maurgina (gistra-	Lith.	ryto(j)
NG	αὔριο		dagis)	Lett.	rīt
Lat.	crās	ON	á morgin	ChSl.	utrě
It.	domani	Dan.	i morgen	SCr.	sjutra
Fr.	demain	Sw.	i morgon	Boh.	zejtra
Sp.	mañana	OE	tō morgen(e)	Pol.	jutro
Rum.	mîîne	ME	to morwe(n)	Russ.	zavtra
Ir.	imbárach	NE	tomorrow	Skt.	çvas
NIr.	i mbáireach,	Du.	morgen	Av.	....
W.	yfory	OHG	morgane, in morgan		
Br.	arc'hoaz	MHG	morgen(e)		
		NHG	morgen		

Most of the expressions for 'tomorrow' are derived from words for 'morning' (14.44), the semantic development being 'in the morning' = 'on the following morning', whence with extension to the entire day 'tomorrow'.

1. Grk. αὔριον, fr. *αὔσριον : Lith. aušra 'dawn', etc. (14.43). Walde-P. 1.27. Schwyzer, Gr. Gram. 1.282.

2. Lat. crās, etym.? Ernout-M. 227 Walde-H. 1.285.

It. domani, Fr. demain fr. VLat. dēmāne, phrase cpd. of māne 'morning' (> Rum. mîîne 'tomorrow'). REW 2548, 5294.

Sp. mañana = mañana 'morning'.

3. Ir. imbárach, NIr. i mbáireach, W. yfory : W. bore 'morning' (14.44). Pedersen 1.99.

Br. arc'hoaz (also warc'hoaz, cpd. with war 'on'), MBr. arhoaz (beside an hoaz), cpd. ar- 'on' and hoaz (Br. c'hoaz) 'again' (14.35). Henry 277. Ernault, Dict. étym. s.v. an hoaz.

4. Goth. du maurgina, ON á morgin, Dan. i morgen, Sw. i morgon (but ON i morgin 'this (last) morning'; change of

prep. in modern Scand. due to í dag 'today', í gær 'yesterday'?), OE tō morgen (also on morgen), ME to morwen, to morwe, NE tomorrow, OHG in morgan, phrases with prepositions 'to, in, on' and 'morning', beside adv. dat. in OHG morgane, MHG morgen(e), NHG, Du. morgen. Weigand-H. 2.219. Franck-v. W. 422 f. NED s.v. tomorrow.

Goth. gistradagis (adv. gen.) : OE geostra-dæg, etc. 'yesterday' (14.49), renders αὔριον Mt. 6.30, with puzzling shift of meaning if not merely a blunder in translating. Cf. Brugmann, op. cit. p. 15.

5. Lith. ryto(j), Lett. rīt, rītu, rītā, orig. 'in the morning' fr. Lith. rytas, Lett. rīts 'morning'.

6. ChSl. utrě loc. sing. (renders reg. αὔριον in Gospels), also phrase za utra (but in Gospels only 'early in the morning, πρωΐ'), similarly SCr. sjutra, Boh. zejtra, Russ. zavtra, but Pol. simply jutro (acc. as adv.), all fr. ChSl. utro, etc. 'morning'. Berneker 462.

7. Skt. çvas : Av. sūr- 'morning'. Walde-P. 1.368. Walde-H. 1.285. Brugmann, op. cit., p. 17.

14.49 YESTERDAY

Grk.	*χθές, ἐχθές*	Goth.	. . . .	Lith.	*vakar*
NG	*χτές, ἐχτές, ψές*	ON	*ī gær*	Lett.	*vakar*
Lat.	*heri*	Dan.	*i gaar*	ChSl.	*vĭčera*
It.	*ieri*	Sw.	*i går*	SCr.	*jučer*
Fr.	*hier*	OE	*geostran dæg*	Boh.	*včera*
Sp.	*ayer*	ME	*yister(n)day*	Pol.	*wczoraj*
Rum.	*ieri*	NE	*yesterday*	Russ.	*včera*
Ir.	*indhē*	Du.	*gisteren*	Skt.	*hyas*
NIr.	*indē, inē*	OHG	*gesteron*	Av.	. . . .
W.	*doe*	MHG	*gester(n)*		
Br.	*dec'h*	NHG	*gestern*		

Most of the words for 'yesterday' belong to an inherited group, pointing clearly to an IE adv. of this meaning. The others (the Balto-Slavic, and pop. NG) meant orig. 'in the evening' or 'late', whence 'in the past evening', and with extension to the entire day 'yesterday'. Cf. the parallel but forward shift in the history of words for 'tomorrow' (14.48).

1. IE **ĝhes*, etc. (variant init. combinations). Walde-P. 1.664. Ernout-M. 449. Walde-H. 1.642 f. Falk-Torp 292.

Grk. *χθές*, and *ἐχθές*, adj. *χθιζός*, *χθεσινός*; Lat. *herī*, later *heri* (> Romance words), adj. *hesternus;* Ir. *indhē*, NIr. *indē*, *inē*, W. *doe*, Br. *dec'h* (cf. Pedersen 1.67, 89, 2.25); (Goth. *gistradagis*, 11.48), OE *giestron*, usually *geostran*, *giostran dæg* (with *geostra* adj.), ME *yister(n)day*, NE *yesterday*, OHG *gesteron*, *gesteren*, *gestre*, MHG *gester(n)*, NHG *gestern*, Du. *gisteren;* without deriv. suffix and in ablaut ON *ī gær*, *ī gjār*, Dan. *i gaar*, Sw. *i går;* Skt. *hyas* and adj. *hyastana-*, NPers. *dī*, *dīg*, *dīne;* Alb. *dje*. On the supposed meaning 'tomorrow' of ON *ī gær*, and 'day after tomorrow' of OHG *ē-gestern*, *ē-gestra*, often quoted in connection with Goth. *gistra-dagis*, cf. Brugmann, op. cit. pp. 11 ff.

2. NG pop. *ψές* (not fr. *χθές*, but) fr. *ὀψέ* 'late' (14.17), first specialized to 'late yesterday, yesterday evening' (as still in some dial.), then extended to 'yesterday'. Hatzidakis, Μεσ. 1.122.

3. Lith., Lett. *vakar* (orig. loc. sg.), ChSl. *vĭčera*, *vŭčera*, SCr. *jučer*, etc., general Slavic (prob. old instr. sg.) fr. the Balto-Slavic word for 'evening' (14.46). Walde-P. 1.311. Vasmer, IF 42.179 ff. Mühl.-Endz. 4.446.

14.51 HOUR

Grk.	*ὥρα*	Goth.	*hweila*	Lith.	*valanda (adyna)*
NG	*ὥρα*	ON	*tīð, stund*	Lett.	*stunda*
Lat.	*hōra*	Dan.	*time*	ChSl.	*godina (časŭ)*
It.	*ora*	Sw.	*timme*	SCr.	*sāt, ura*
Fr.	*heure*	OE	*tīd*	Boh.	*hodina*
Sp.	*hora*	ME	*(h)oure, tide*	Pol.	*godzina*
Rum.	*ceas*	NE	*hour*	Russ.	*čas*
Ir.	*ōr, ūar*	Du.	*uur*		
NIr.	*uair*	OHG	*zīt*		
W.	*awr*	MHG	*zīt, ūr(e)*		
Br.	*eur*	NHG	*stunde*		

The Greeks borrowed the division of the day into hours from the Babylonians (cf. Hdt. 2.109). However, the hour of the Babylonians was actually a double hour, i.e., $\frac{1}{12}$ the entire day, whereas the Greeks divided only the period of light (day vs. night) into twelve parts. This system was adopted likewise by the Romans. Much later the night was divided in similar fashion. Consequently, the period of time covered by an hour was variable according to the length of the day, depending upon the seasons. This state of affairs lasted well up into the Middle Ages. Cf. Schrader, Reallex. s.v. *stunde;* Kubitschek, Grd. d. antik. Zeitrechnung 178.

The 'hour' was designated by words which were originally, and often continued to be, used as more general terms for 'time' or for various periods of time. But Grk. *ὥρα*, through Lat. *hōra*, in its specialized sense, eventually spread over western Europe, either as 'hour' or as 'clock' (14.53).

1. Grk. *ὥρα*, 'period of time, season', etc. (14.11), specialized to 'hour'. Hence Lat. *hōra*, whence It. *ora*, Sp. *hora*, (Rum. *oara* only dial. 'hour', or pl. *ori* in phrases for 'what time' or 'so many times'), Fr. *heure*, OFr. *(h)ure*, *(h)ore* > ME *(h)ure*, *(h)oure*, NE *hour;* also Ir. *ōr*, *ūar*, NIr. *uair*, W. *awr*, Br. *eur*, Du. *uur*, MDu., MLG *ūre* > MHG *ūr(e)*, NHG *uhr*. REW 4176. Loth, Mots lat. 135.

2. Rum. *ceas* fr. Slavic, cf. ChSl. *časŭ*, below 5.

3. Goth. *hweila* 'period of time' (14.11), but most commonly 'hour'.

ON *tīð*, OE *tīd*, ME *tide*, OHG, MHG *zīt*, general words for 'time' also (14.11).

ON *stund* (sometimes 'hour'), NHG *stunde* (as 'hour' since 15th cent.), orig. 'period of time' (14.11).

Dan. *time*, Sw. *timme* fr. ON *tīmi* 'time' (often also 'period of time, fixed time', but NIcel. also 'hour'), see 14.11.

4. Lith. *valanda*, formerly 'a period of time, a while' (Kurschat), but now the standard word for 'hour' (cf. NSB. sv. *adyna*) : Lat. *volvendus* 'rolling on' (of years, months), *volvere* 'turn, roll', ChSl. *valiti* 'roll', etc. Semantic development through the notion of 'time' as a turning cycle (cf. Slavic *vrěmę*, 14.11). Walde-P. 1.303.

Lith. *adyna* (formerly the usual word), beside *gadynė* 'age, epoch, period', fr. WhRuss. *hodzina* 'hour, time', cf. ChSl. *godina*, etc. (below). Brückner, Sl. Fremdwörter 83.

Lett. *stunda* (also Lith. *stundas*, Kurschat, etc.), fr. MLG *stunde* 'hour'. Mühl.-Endz. 3.1106 f.

5. ChSl. *godina* (reg. rendering of *ὥρα* in this sense in Gospels), Boh. *hodina*, Pol. *godzina*, fr. ChSl. *godŭ* period of 'time' (14.11). Berneker 316 ff.

ChSl. *časŭ* (renders *ὥρα*, but in Gospels only in sense 'period of time'), Russ. *čas* : Boh. *čas*, Pol. *czas* general 'time' (14.11).

SCr. *sāt* and *sahat* 'hour' and 'clock', fr. Turk. *sāāt* id.

SCr. *ura* likewise 'hour' and 'clock', fr. NHG *uhr*.

6. The Sanskrit division of the day does not, of course, agree with the European, and the systems of division mentioned by the Hindus themselves vary according to period and type of literature. The later division consists of the *ghaṭaka-* (*ghaṭikā-*, *ghaṭa-*, etc.), *pala-*, *vipala-*, *prativipala-*, the relation being 60 *ghaṭikas* to the day, 60 *palas* to the *ghaṭaka*, etc. (cf. Sewell-Diksit, Indian Calendar, p. 2). The first term is prob. identical with *ghaṭa-*, *ghaṭakā-* 'jar, pitcher' through use as a measure. The origin of *pala-*, used also of a certain weight (4 *karṣas*) and a liquid measure

(cf. BR), is doubtful (: *pālavī-* 'sort of dish', Lat. *pēlvis* 'basin', etc.? Walde-P. 2.56).

For other systems (e.g. 30 *muhūrtas* in the day; *muhūrta-* 'moment, instance' : *muhur-* 'suddenly', Uhlenbeck 228), cf. Macdonell-Keith 1.49 f.; Zimmer, Altind. Leben 363 f.; Thibaut, Grd. d. indo-ar. Phil. 3.926 f.

14.52. Words for 'minute' and 'second'. These are so largely common Eur. words with slight variation that the lists are omitted.

There was no definite division of time within the hour among the Greeks and Romans. The Eur. terms for 'minute' and 'second' arise from the (medieval) application of the sexagesimal system (ὁ τῆς ἑξηκοντάδος τρόπος Ptolemy, 2d cent. A.D.) to time division.

1. MLat. *pars minūta prīma* is the smallest part of the first order of a whole, according to the sexagesimal system, the next division being the *pars minūta secunda*. Hence, either fr. the abbreviated *minūta*, *secunda*, or fr. the neut. forms *minūtum*, *secundum* (so It., Sp., Port.), or by semantic borrowing, nearly all the Eur. terms. NED s.v. *minute*, *second*. Kluge-G. 392.

2. NG *λεπτό*, 'minute', fr. *λεπτός* 'fine, thin, minute', a modern translation of Fr. *minute;* hence *δευτερόλεπτο* 'second'.

3. NIr. *nōimeat*, *neomat* 'minute', also *noimeint*, prob. by dissim. fr. *mōimeint*, *mōimēid*, etc., loanword fr. Lat. *mōmentum* 'brief space of time, moment'. Vendryes, De hib. voc. 157. Pedersen 1.234 Anm. 3.

W. *eiliad*, 'second', fr. *ail* (ordinal) 'second' (as pref. *eil-*). Semantic borrowing fr. English (or Romance).

4. Boh. *vteřina* 'second' : Pol. *wtory* 'other, second', ChSl. *vŭtorŭ* 'second'. Semantic borrowing fr. the general Eur. term.

5. For Sanskrit division of time, see under 'hour' (14.51).

14.53 CLOCK, WATCH

Grk.	*ὡρολόγιον*	Goth.	. . . .	Lith.	*laikrodis (ziegorius)*
NG	*ρολόϊ (ὡρολόγιον)*	ON	. . . .	Lett.	*pulkstens*
Lat.	*horologium*	Dan.	*ur (klokke)*	ChSl.	. . . .
It.	*oriolo, orologio, pendolo*	Sw.	*klocka, ur*	SCr.	*sāt, ura*
		OE	*dægmǣl*	Boh.	*hodiny*
Fr.	*horloge, pendule; montre*	ME	*clocke, orloge*	Pol.	*zegar*
		NE	*clock; watch*	Russ.	*časy*
Sp.	*reloj*	Du.	*klok; horloge*	Skt.	*(chāyā-yantra-, ambu-yantra-)*
Rum.	*orologiu; ceasornic*	MHG	*ōr(o)lei, ūr(e), seigære*		
Ir.	*uairle(?)*	NHG	*uhr*	Av.	. . . .
NIr.	*clog; uaireadōir*				
W.	*awrlais, cloc*				
Br.	*horolaj*				

In early Greece there was no general term to designate the different devices for timekeeping. The earliest was, of course, the sundial, the *πόλος* and *γνώμων*, the concave dial and the pointer, also called later *σκιοθήρας*, *σκιόθηρον* 'shadow-catcher'. The usual name among the Romans was *sōlārium* (: *sōl* 'sun'). The next common device among the ancients for measuring time (but not for telling the time of day) was the water-clock, the Grk. *κλεψύδρα* (lit. 'water-stealer', orig. applied to a sort of 'pipette'), or *ὑδροσκοπεῖον* (*σκοπέω* 'look

at'). The first term was borrowed by the Romans (Lat. *clepsydra*), but the name of the sundial, *sōlārium*, was extended to cover this instrument as well (cf. *cum solarium aut descriptum aut ex aqua contemplere*, Cic. Nat. deor. 2.34, 87). Cf. Pauly-Wissowa s.v. *horologium*. Kubitschek, Grd. d. antik. Zeitrechnung 188 ff., 203 ff.

Most of the words listed cover alike the different types of clocks and the watch. But some are, and others were once, restricted to certain types, as the clock in a tower, the clock with a pendulum, and esp. the pocket 'watch'. Those that are only or mostly 'watch' are separated in the list by a semicolon, but no notice is taken of cases like NHG *taschenuhr*, little used except for purposes of definition.

The commonest relation is to words for 'hour' (14.51), but there are other diverse sources.

1. Grk. *ὡρολόγιον* (late; used both of the sundial *ὡρολόγιον σκιοθηρικόν* and of the water-clock *ὡρολόγιον ὑδραυλικόν*), NG pop. *ρολόϊ*, fr. *ὥρα* 'hour, time' and *-λόγιον* : *-λόγος* 'telling', *λέγω* 'tell'. Hence Lat. *hōrologium* (> It. *orologio*, Fr. *horloge;* Prov., Cat. *rel(l)otge* > Sp. *reloj;* Rum. *orologiu* modern lit. word). REW 4183.

2. It. *oriolo* fr. VLat. **hōrāriolum*, deriv. of the late *hōrārium* 'dial, clock' (: *hōra* 'hour'). REW 4177a.

It. *pendolo*, Fr. *pendule* (> Du. *pendule*), properly 'pendulum', but by extension esp. a clock of which the movement is regulated by means of the pendulum.

Fr. *montre*, back-formation fr. *montrer* 'show', used for 'a showing', hence also 'face of a clock' (obs.) and later 'watch'.

Rum. *ceas*, *ceasornic*, formerly the general word for 'timepiece', but now (since the introduction of *orologiu* for 'clock') 'watch', fr. Slavic, cf. ORuss. *časovĭnikŭ*, deriv. of *casŭ* 'time'. Tiktin 329. Dicț. enc. s.v.

3. Ir. *uairle* ('clock'? NIr. *uairleān* 'sun-dial', Dinneen), prob. fr. Lat. *horologium*, Loth, RC 32.305.

NIr. *clog*, fr. Ir. *cloc(c)* 'bell' = W. *cloch* 'bell' : Grk. *κλαγγή* 'noise, clamor', Lat. *clangere* 'sound, cry', etc. From the Celtic, through MLat. *cloc(c)a* 'bell', come MLG *klocke* 'bell, striking clock' (> Dan. *klokke* 'bell', dial. 'clock', Sw. *klocka* 'clock, bell'), Du. *klok* (> ME *clocke*, NE *clock* > W. *cloc*), but OE *clucge*, OHG *glocka*, NHG *glocke* 'bell'. Walde-P. 1.496. Falk-Torp 535. Walde-H. 1.227. NED s.v. *clock*, sb.[1].

NIr. *uaireadōir* 'watch', deriv. of *uair* 'hour'. Vendryes, De hib. voc. 184.

W. *awrlais*, older *orlais* and *orlayds*, fr. ME *orloge* (with pop. transformation as cpd. of *awr* 'hour' and *llais* 'voice, sound'?). Parry-Williams 212 f.

Br. *horolaj*, fr. Fr. *horloge*.

4. OE *dægmǣl* (reg. gl. to *horologium*), cpd. of *dæg* 'day' and *mǣl* 'measure, mark'.

ME *clocke*, etc., above, 3.

ME *orloge*, MDu. *orloghe*, *orloy*, Du. *horloge* (now mostly 'watch'), MHG *ōr(o)lei* fr. OFr. *orloge* (Du. *horloge* with *h* fr. Fr. *horloge*, cf. Franck-v. W. 263).

ME *wecche* 'alarm' of a clock, NE *watch*, used since 16th cent. for pocket timepiece, same word as *watch* 'vigil', etc., fr. OE *wæcce* : vb. *wæccan* 'watch'. NED s.v. *watch*, sb. 21.

MLG *ūr(e)* 'hour' and also 'clock', whence MHG *ūr(e)* in both senses, NHG *uhr*, Dan., Sw. *ur* 'clock'. Weigand-H. 2.1105. Falk-Torp 1335.

MHG *seigære* 'clock', esp. 'tower-clock' (NHG *seiger* 'hourglass', but still 'clock' in some regions), also 'weight', esp. the weight controlling the movement of a tower-clock, fr. MHG *sîgen*, OHG *sîgan* 'sink, drip down'. Weigand-H. 2.837 f. Grimm s.v.

5. Lith. *laikrodis*, cpd. of *laikas* 'time' (14.11) and *rodyti* 'show'. A new formation to replace older *ziegorius* fr. Pol. *zegar*, fr. MHG *seigære* (above, 4). Fraenkel, Z. sl. Ph. 6.88.

Lett. *pulksten(i)s*, also 'bell' and 'pulse', fr. LG *puls* 'stroke of bell, pulse' (+ a form of *sist* 'strike'?). Mühl.-Endz. 3.408.

6. SCr. *sât* (also 'hour'), fr. Turk. *sâat* 'hour, clock' (14.51).

SCr. *ura* (also 'hour'), prob. fr. NHG *uhr*.

Boh. *hodiny*, pl. of *hodina* 'hour'.

Pol. *zegar*, fr. MHG *seigære* (above, 4). Brückner 651.

Russ. *časy*, pl. of *čas* 'hour'.

7. Skt. *chāyā-yantra-* 'sun-dial' and *ambu-yantra* 'water-clock', cpds. of *chāyā-* 'shadow' and *ambu-* 'water' with *yantra-* 'instrument, machine'.

14.61 WEEK

Grk.	(late) ἑβδομάς	Goth.	sabbatō		Lith.	savaitē (nedélia)	
NG	ἐβδομάδα	ON	vika		Lett.	nedēl'a	
Lat.	(late) septimāna,	Dan.	uge		ChSl.	sobota, nedēlja, sed-	
	hebdomas	Sw.	vecka			mica	
It.	settimana	OE	wice, wicu		SCr.	sedmica, nedjelja,	
Fr.	semaine	ME	weke, wike			tjedan	
Sp.	semana	NE	week		Boh.	týden, nedēle	
Rum.	sǎptǎmînǎ	Du.	week		Pol.	tydzień	
Ir.	sechtman	OHG	wecha, wocha		Russ.	nedelja	
NIr.	seachtmhain	MHG	woche, wuche				
W.	wythnos	NHG	woche				
Br.	sizun						

On the much-discussed origin of the week and the names of the week days, cf. esp. the articles in Z. deutsch. Wortf. 1.150 ff.; F. H. Colson, The Week; Schrader, Reallex. 2.662 ff.; J. Melich, Die Namen der Wochentage im Slavischen, Jagić Festschrift 212 ff.

If any division of time intermediate between the month and the day was recognized in the IE period, it was no doubt the most obvious one according to the phases of the moon. The Hindus divided the month into two halves (*pakṣa-* 'wing'), that of the crescent moon (*pūrva-* 'earlier' or *çukla-* 'light') and the waning moon (*apara-* 'later' or *kṛṣṇa-* 'black'). Cf. Thibaut, Grd. d. indo-ar. Phil. 3.9.12. For the Celts the Calendar of Coligny attests an old division of the month into halves (Thurneysen, Z. deutsch. Wortf. 1.191). The times

of new moon and full moon were the occasion of folk-assemblies among the Germans (Tacitus, Germ. ch. 1) and of religious festivals among the Greeks.

The regular Greek division of the month was into three decades. The Romans had their market-day, *nūndinae* (cpd. of *novem* 'nine' and old word for 'day'), held every ninth day, the intervening period (really eight days if reckoned from a given point of the first to the ninth) being *nūndinum*.

The seven-day week was unknown in Europe until its importation from the East. Whatever its ultimate source and explanation, the seven-day week is definitely known as an ancient Jewish institution. Hence first the Jewish week and, somewhat later, with an admixture of oriental astrology, the planetary week became known to the Greeks and Ro-

mans. It spread to the rest of Europe, probably to some extent before but mostly with the spread of Christianity.

The adopted 'week' was expressed by coll. derivs. of the numeral for seven, by words for 'Saturday' (or later 'Sunday') extended to cover 'week' like the Hebrew Sabbath; as 'eight nights' or 'eight days'; in Gmc. by a native word denoting 'change, alternation' and perhaps previously employed for some other division of time.

1. Grk. ἑβδομάς, -άδος (NG ἐβδομάδα), coll. numeral used for a period of seven days, seven years, etc., hence also for the Jewish 'week' (LXX+; not in NT, where σάββατον).

Grk. σάββατον, like its Hebrew original, was used not only for the Sabbath but also for the week. So in NT δὶς τοῦ σαββάτου 'twice in the week' (Lk. 18.12), πρώτη σαββάτου or μία σαββάτων 'first day of the week', etc. Hence the partial coincidence of 'Sunday' and 'week' in Slavic (below, 7).

2. Lat. *hebdomas*, fr. Grk. ἑβδομάς and first used in the earlier sense of the latter, then for the fixed 'week'.

Lat. *septimāna*, fem. of adj. *septimānus* 'belonging to the number seven', translating the Grk. ἑβδομάς and much more common than *hebdomas* in eccl. writings (e.g. in the Peregrinatio about 27:3). Hence the Romance words (REW 7834), also (but influenced by the native word for 'seven'; Pedersen 1.236, Thurneysen, Z. deutsch. Wortf. 1.191) Ir. *sechtman*, NIr. *seachtmhain*, OCorn. *seithun*, Br. *sizun*.

3. W. *wythnos*, lit. 'eight nights', like *pymthegnos, pythefnos* lit. 'fifteen nights' = 'fortnight'. Cf. Fr. *d'aujourd'hui en huit*, NHG *über acht tagen* 'a week hence' (similar phrases for 'a week ago'), Fr. *quinze jours* 'a fortnight', etc. The week, of course, generally (e.g. from Sunday

noon to Sunday noon) covers parts of eight different days.

4. ON *vika*, OE *wice*, etc., general Gmc. (but Goth. *wikō* only in Lk. 1.8 *in wikōn* 'in the course of'; cf. also ON *vika* 'sea-mile' orig. 'change of oar', MLG *weke ses* 'sea-mile') : ON *vīkja, vīkva* 'move, turn, veer, give way', OE *wīcan*, OHG *wīhhan* 'yield, give way', etc. Walde-P. 1.235. Falk-Torp 1326. Meaning primarily 'change, alternation', the word may once have denoted some earlier time division, such as the 'change of moon, half-month' (cf. Schrader, Reallex. 2.665), but there is no positive evidence of this. Walde-P. 1.235. Falk-Torp 1326. NED s.v. *week*.

Goth. *sabbatō* fr. Grk. σάββατον and likewise 'Sabbath' and 'week'.

5. Lith. *savaitē* (neolog. to replace the loanword *nedélia*) based on OPruss. *sawayte* (cf. also *possi-sawaite* 'Wednesday' : *possi-* 'half'), this through Pol. *sobota*, fr. Grk. σάββατον 'Sabbath' and 'week' (above, 1). Trautmann, Altpreuss. 420. Fraenkel, Z. sl. Ph. 6.86.

Lith. *nedélia, nedélē*, Lett. *nedēl'a*, fr. Slavic (below). Mühl.-Endz. 2.710.

6. ChSl. *sobota, sqbota*, fr. Grk. σάββατον and likewise used in Gospels for 'Sabbath' and 'week' (latter e.g. Lk. 18.12).

ChSl. *nedélja*, SCr. *nedjelja*, Boh. *nedéle*, Russ. *nedelja*, cpd. of neg. *ne-* and *dēlo* 'work', orig. 'day of rest', 'Sabbath' then 'Sunday', but like Grk. σάββατον (above, 1) also 'week'. Russ. *nedelja* now only 'week', as likewise the Baltic loanwords (above). Berneker 194.

ChSl., SCr. *sedmica*, fr. ChSl. *sedmŭ* 'seven', lit. translation of Grk. ἑβδομάς.

SCr. *tjedan*, Boh. *týden*, Pol. *tydzień*, cpds. of pron. stem *to-* and word for 'day', lit. 'this day', with reference to the same day (cf. NE *this day week*). Berneker 253.

	14.62 SUNDAY	14.63 MONDAY	14.64 TUESDAY	14.65 WEDNESDAY		14.66 THURSDAY	14.67 FRIDAY	14.68 SATURDAY
Grk.	μία σαββάτων, κυριακή, ἡμέρα Ἡλίου	δευτέρα σαββάτου ἡμέρα Σελήνης	τρίτη σαββάτου ἡμέρα Ἄρεως	τετάρτη σαββάτου ἡμέρα Ἑρμοῦ		πέμπτη σαββάτου ἡμέρα Διός	παρασκευή ἡμέρα Ἀφροδίτης	σάββατον ἡμέρα Κρόνου
NG	κυριακή	δευτέρα	τρίτη	τετάρτη		πέμπτη	παρασκευή	σάββατον, σαββάτο
Lat.	dies Sōlis, dies dominica	dies Lūnae secunda fēria	dies Martis te rtia fēria	dies Mercurī quarta fēria		dies Iovis quinta fēria	dies Veneris sexta fēria	dies Saturni sabbatum
It.	domenica	lunedi	martedi	mercoledi		giouedi	venerdi	sabato
Fr.	dimanche	lundi	mardi	mercredi		jeudi	vendredi	samedi
Sp.	domingo	lunes	martes	miércoles		jueves	viernes	sábado
Rum.	duminicǎ	luni	marti	miercuri		joui	vineri	sîmbǎtǎ
Port.	domingo	segunda feira	terça feira	quarta feira		quinta feira	sexta feira	sabado
Ir.	domnach	luan	māirt	cētāin		dardāin	óin diden	satharn
NIr.	domhnach	luan	māirt	cēadaoin		dardaoin	aoine	satharn
W.	dydd sul	dydd llun	dydd mawrth	dydd mercher		dydd iau	dydd gwener	dydd sadwrn
Br.	disul	dilun	dimeurz	dimerc'her		diziou	digwener	disadorn
Goth.	afarsabbatē dags	. . . .	. . . .	. . . .		paraskaiwē, fruma sabbatō	frjādagr	sabbatō dags
ON	sunnudagr, drōttins- dagr	mānudagr	tỹsdagr	ōðinsdagr		þōrsdagr		laugardagr, þvāttdagr
NIcel.	sunnudagur	mānudagur	þriðjudagur	miðvikudagur		fimtudagur	fōstudagur	laugardagur
Dan.	sóndag	mandag	tirsdag	onsdag		torsdag	fredag	lórdag
Sw.	sóndag	mándag	tisdag	onsdag		torsdag	fredag	lördag
OE	sunnandæg	mōnandæg	tūvesdæg	wōdnesdæg		þunresdæg	frigedæg	sæter(n)dæg
ME	son(n)eday	mone(n)day	tewesday	wednesday		thursday	friday	saterday
NE	sunday	monday	tuesday	wednesday		thursday	friday	saturday
Du.	zondag	maandag	dinsdag	woensdag		dondersdag	vrijdag	zaterdag
OHG	sunnūntag	mānetag	ziostag	mittwocha (mittwecha)		donerstag	friatag	sambaztag, sunnūnāband
MHG	sun(nen)tac	māntac	zi(e)stac, erintac	mittwoch(e) (miteche)		donerstac, pfinztac	vri(e)tac	sameztac, sunnābent
NHG	sonntag	montag	dienstag	mittwoch		donnerstag	freitag	samstag, sonnabend
Lith.	sekmadienis (nedélia)	pirmadienis (pane- dėlis)	antradienis (utar- ninkas)	trečiadienis (sereda)		ketvirtadienis (četvergas)	penktadienis (pétnycia)	šeštadienis (subata)
Lett.	svētdiena	pirmdiena	uotrdiena	trešdiena		ceturdiena	piektdiena	sestdiena
ChSl.	nedélja	ponedélŭkŭ	vŭtorŭkŭ	tretĭjīnikŭ, srēda		četurtŭkŭ	pętŭkŭ, pętĭnica	sobota, sqbota
SCr.	nedjelja	ponedjeljak	utorak	srijeda		četurtak	petak	subota
Boh.	nedéle	pondéli	úterý	stfeda		čtvrtek	pátek	sobota
Pol.	medziela	poniédzielek	wtorek	środa		czwartek	piątek	sobota
Russ.	voskresen'e	ponedel'nik	vtornik	sreda		četverg	pjatnica	subbota

14.52–14.58. Two systems are represented in the Eur. names of the days of the week: (1) the ecclesiastical or, as it is also called, the Jewish-Christian, being based on the Jewish and adopted by the Christian church, and (2) the planetary, based on astrology, though its more precise origin and the explanation of the peculiar order of the planet names is uncertain. In general, the ecclesiastical system prevailed in eastern Europe, the planetary, in part with some substitutions, in western Europe, except in Portuguese (wholly ecclesiastical) and Irish (only three planetary names).

Thus the complete set of Roman planetary names, reduced to five in the

Romance languages, is preserved in Breton and Welsh and in its Germanic form in English. The greatest mixture is in Irish, where there are three planetary names and four ecclesiastical, one of these old, the others special Irish terms. Cf. the references in 14.51.

1. Ecclesiastical system. The Jews named only one day of the week, namely, the last, the Sabbath, Grk. σάββατον. The other days were merely numbered. Since the Sabbath was the distinctive sign of the week, it came to be used also in the sense 'week' (cf. 14.51). Hence in the New Testament μία σαββάτων (Mt. 28.1, etc.), ἡ μία τῶν σαββάτων (Mk. 16.2, etc.), also πρώτη σαββάτου (Mk. 16.9),

'first of the week' = 'Sunday'; likewise in later Christian writings δευτέρα σαββάτου 'Monday', τρίτη σαββάτου 'Tuesday', τετάρτη σαββάτου 'Wednesday', πέμπτη τοῦ σαββάτου 'Thursday'. The day before the Sabbath was called παρασκευή 'preparation' (Mt. 27.62, etc.). For πρώτη σαββάτου, was early substituted κυριακὴ (ἡμέρα) 'Lord's day' (Rev. 1.10). The others remained without change (except for dropping of σαββάτου) until the present time in Greek.

These served as a model for the Christian Lat. terms, *diēs dominica*, or *diēs dominicus* (earlier *ūna sabbatī* after μία σαββάτου, also *diēs prīma*), *secunda sabbatī*, *tertia sabbatī*, etc. Thereafter comes the Lat. *fēria* (late sg. to *fēriae* 'festival, holidays') in place of the Jewish word *sabbatum*, which was retained only for 'Saturday'. So in the Peregrinatio regularly *sabbatum* 'Saturday', *diēs dominica* 'Sunday', *secunda fēria* 'Monday', etc., the full series being represented. Cf. also Isidor, Etym. 5.30, 9 : *Secunda sabbati secunda feria quem saeculares diem Lunae vocant. Tertia sabbati*, etc.

Of the Romance languages, Port. preserves all the eccl. terms (*domingo*, *segunda feira*, etc., see list), while It., Fr., Sp., and Rum. retain only (*diēs*) *dominica* and *sabbatum*.

In Ir. (and Gaelic) four of the weekday names are eccl., only one of these, however, reflecting the Lat. name. Ir. *domnach*, NIr. *domhnach* (adv. *dia domhnaigh*) 'Sunday', fr. Lat. *dominicus;* Ir. *cēt-āin*, NIr. *cēadaoin* (adv. *dia cēadaoin*) 'first fast, Wednesday'; Ir. *dardāin* (for *etar da āin*), NIr. *dardaoin* (adv. *diardaoin*) 'between the two fasts, Thursday'; Ir. *ōin dīdin* 'last fast' (NIr. simply *aoine* 'fast', adv. *dia h-aoine*) 'Friday'. Cf. Thurneysen, Z. deutsch. Wortf. 1.190.

In Germanic the eccl. names prevailed in Goth., and there are a few in West and North Gmc. amid the usual planetary names. Goth. *sabbatō* (mostly uninflected but also with *u*- and *i*-stem forms) with and without *dags* = Grk. σάββατον or ἡμέρα σαββάτων (but independently of the Grk. variation), *þis dagis afarsabbatē* = τῆς μιᾶς σαββάτων (Mk. 16.2), *frumin sabbatō* = πρώτῃ σαββάτου (Mk. 16.9), *fruma sabbatō* = προσάββατον (Mk. 15.42), beside the borrowed *paraskaiwē* = παρασκευή (Mt. 27.62, Mk. 15.42).

ON *drōttinsdagr* 'Sunday' (beside *sunnudagr*) translates Lat. *diēs dominica.* OHG *sambaz-tag* comes from a variant form of Grk. σάββατον (cf. below). OHG *mittwocha* (*mittawecha*, etc.), NHG *mittwoch* may reflect a MLat. *media hebdomas*, cf. It. dial. *mezzedima.* MHG *pfinztac*, through a Goth. **paintēdags*, fr. Grk. πέμπτη ἡμέρα (Kluge-G. 110).

In Slavic the few names that occur in the ChSl. Gospels are directly after the Greek. Thus *sobota* (so reg. cod. Mar.), *sǫbota* (Zogr., Supr., etc.) = σάββατον, *prŭva sobota* or *jedina sobota* = πρώτη σαββάτου, μία (τῶν) σαββάτων, *paraskevĭg'i*, *kŭ sobatě* = παρασκευή, προσάββατον (Mk. 15.42). The usual Slavic names apart from *sobota*, which in one form or another is general Slavic, are represented by later ChSl. *nedělja* 'Sunday' (neg. cpd. of *dělo* 'work', hence as 'rest-day', translating the Hebrew-Grk. word for Saturday, with Christian shift to Sunday), *ponedělŭkŭ*, *ponedělĭnikŭ* 'Monday' (cpd. of *nedělja* with *po*- 'after'; cf. Goth. *afar-sabbatē*, but also Grk. προσάββατον as possible models), *vŭtornikŭ* (Supr.) 'Tuesday' (lit. 'second'), and the others in numeral series (see list), but *srěda* 'Wednesday' (lit. 'middle', 12.37; cf. OHG *mittwocha*, above). There is some probability that this system is based upon a Gothic medium. Cf. Stender-Petersen 435 ff.

The older Lith. names, *nedėlia*, *panedėlis*, etc. (entered in list in parentheses), which are still generally used among the immigrants in U.S. (Senn), are direct loanwords from Slavic. The new names were formed from native words according to the numeral system, as *pirmadienis* 'first day, Monday', etc. (see list) and were introduced in the standard language in imitation of the Lett. terms, which already followed the numeral system except for *svētdiena* 'holy day, Sunday'. Fraenkel, Z. sl. Ph. 6.86. Senn, The Lithuanian Language 43.

Beside Grk. σάββατον there must have been a colloq. form σάμβατον, with an intrusive nasal which is paralleled in some other words and in this case attested in deriv. forms like σαμβαθικός and Σαμβάτιος beside σαββατικός and Σαββάτιος. Cf. G. Meyer, IF 4.326 ff., W. Schulze, KZ 33.366 ff. Such a form is reflected in ChSl. *sǫbota* (beside *sobota*), SCr. *subota*, Russ. *subbota*, and, through Slavic, Rum. *sîmbătă*, Hung. *szombat;* OHG *sambaztag*, MHG *sameztac*, NHG *samstag;* Fr. *samedi*.

2. Planetary system. Greek planetary names, ἡμέρα Ἡλίου, etc. (see list), are attested for the early centuries of our era, but their use was apparently restricted to certain circles; at any rate they never became popular. In Rome, on the other hand, the planetary names became the established popular terms, too strongly intrenched to be displaced by the eccl. names, and spreading through most of western Europe. They remain in the Romance languages, except Port., with the substitution of the church name for Sunday and Saturday They are preserved intact by the British Celts, that is in W., Br., and Corn. (Corn. *de sil*, *de lun*, etc., Williams 88), but furnish only three of the Ir. names, namely *luan* 'Monday', *māirt* 'Tuesday', *satharn* 'Saturday'.

The Latin planetary names were also adopted by the Gmc. peoples (except the Goths in the East), only put into Gmc. form—a simple procedure in the case of *diēs Sōlis* and *diēs Lūnae*, but for the next four involving a somewhat less obvious identification of Roman and Germanic gods. For Saturday the Lat. *Saturnus* was retained, at least in Anglo-Frisian and Low German (OE *sæter(n)-dæg*, OFris. *saterdei*, Du. *zaterdag*). Scandinavian shows a native substitution, ON *laugardagr*, Dan. *lørdag*, Sw. *lördag*, lit. 'bathday' (: ON *laug* 'bath'), also ON *þvāttdagr* 'washday' (: ON *þvāttr* 'washing'), both referring to the same custom (Falk-Torp 682). High German has the eccl. name, OHG *sambaztag*, NHG *samstag* (cf. above), beside the new term OHG *sunnūnāband*, NHG *sonnabend*, which orig. applied only to the eve preceding Sunday. The planetary name for Wednesday is lacking in High German, where OHG *mittwocha*, NHG *mittwoch* is prob. of eccl. origin (cf. above). MHG *erintac*, *ertac* (Bavar. *ertag*) may represent a Goth. **areinsdags*, fr. Grk. Ἄρεως ἡμέρα (Kluge-G. 105).

NIcel. is peculiar among the Gmc. languages in retaining only two of the planetary names, *sunnudagur* and *mānudagur*, and in having two numeral names, *þriðjudagur* for Tuesday and *fimtudagur* for Thursday. Wednesday is *miðvikudagur* like NHG *mittwoch*, Saturday is *laugardagur* 'washday' as in the other Scandinavian languages, and Friday is *föstudagur* 'fastday'.

14.71 MONTH

Grk.	μήν	Goth.	*mēnōþs*	Lith.	*mėnesis*, *mėnuo*
NG	μῆνας	ON	*mānaðr*	Lett.	*mēnesis*
Lat.	*mēnsis*	Dan.	*maaned*	ChSl.	*měsęcĭ*
It.	*mese*	Sw.	*månad*	SCr.	*mjesec*
Fr.	*mois*	OE	*mōnað*	Boh.	*měsíc*
Sp.	*mes*	ME	*mon(e)th*	Pol.	*miesiąc*
Rum.	*lună*	NE	*month*	Russ.	*mesjac*
Ir.	*mī*	Du.	*maand*	Skt.	*mās-*, *māsa-*
NIr.	*mī*	OHG	*mānōt*	Av., OPers.	*māh-*
W.	*mis*	MHG	*mānōt*	Toch.	A *mañ*, B *meñe*
Br.	*miz*	NHG	*monat*		

IE **mēnes-*, **mē(n)s-* 'moon' and 'month', prob. fr. **mē-* 'measure'. Walde-P. 2.271 f. Ernout-M. 607 f. Walde-H. 2.71.

While the words of this group have in many languages been replaced by others in the sense of 'moon', they have persisted nearly everywhere as the words for 'month'. In Gmc. a separate set of related forms distinguishes 'month' fr. 'moon', as Goth. *mēnōþs* vs. *mēna* 'moon', OE *mōnað* vs. *mōna* 'moon', etc. There is a similar but incomplete differentiation in Lith., where *mėnulis* is only 'moon' and *mėnesis* mostly 'month', but *mėnuo* in both senses. See also 1.53.

The only word in the list which does not belong to the group above is Rum. *lună*, fr. Lat. *lūna* 'moon', in which the identification of 'moon' and 'month' is repeated, doubtless owing to the identity in Slavic (ChSl. *měsęcĭ*, etc.).

14.72. Names of the months. Previous to the widespread, though still incomplete, Eur. adoption of the Lat. names, there was the utmost diversity. In ancient Greece alone there were dozens of different local calendars (cf. Pauly-Wissowa 10.1575 ff.). There was no agreement between the old Gmc. names (even the OHG lists vary somewhat), nor between Indic and Iranian, not even between the Av. and OPers. names. Neither the modern Lith. literary names, a recent coinage (Senn, Sprachl. 168), nor the diverse older and dialectic forms (Hermann, Gött. Nachr. 1929.97) agree with the older, now obs., Lett. names. Among the native Slavic names, which are still current except in Russ., there are a few cases of agreement between Boh. and Pol., and a few others of common words applied to different months (e.g. *listopad*, lit. 'leaf-falling', in SCr. 'October', Boh., Pol. 'November'; Boh. *květen* 'May' = Pol. *kwiecień* 'April', orig. 'flower-month'), but, on the whole, great diversity.

In general, the month-names are based upon religious festivals (so most of the Grk. and some of the Celtic and Gmc.) or upon some characteristic feature of the weather, vegetation, harvest, etc.

The enumeration and discussion of these so diverse month-names (even if one chose for the Greek only the Attic or for OHG only those prescribed by Charlemagne) would require so much space that it seems best here to consider only the Lat. names and their spread.

The Lat. names were adj. forms with *mēnsis* 'month' understood. Since the Roman year orig. began with March, the numeral derivs. which served for July–December, were *Quinctīlis* 'fifth' for July, *Sextīlis* 'sixth' for August (these later replaced by *Iūlius* and *Augustus* in honor of Julius Caesar and Augustus),

September, *Octōber*, *November*, *December* (fr. **septemri-s*, *novem-ri-s*, **decem-ri-s*, with reg. change of medial *mr* to *mbr*, hence by analogy also **octō-bri-s*).

Of the names of the first six months (in the new order beginning with January), four are obviously derived from the names of gods or goddesses, namely *Ianus*, *Mars*, *Maia*, and *Iūnō*. *Februārius*, the last month of the old calendar, was the 'month of purification', fr. *februāre* 'cleanse, purify' (Ernout-M. 341. Walde-H. 1.472). *Aprīlis*, prob. fr. an Etruscan name based on a short form of Grk. Ἀφροδίτη. Benveniste BSL 32.70 ff. Cortsen, Glotta 27.270 ff.

The Roman names have persisted in all the Romance languages. But most of the Rum. forms go back, partly through Slavic, to the later Grk. borrowed forms. And elsewhere there are various formal peculiarities, e.g. for *iānuārius* VLat. *ienuārius* (> It. *gennaio*, Sp. *enero*); for *augustus* VLat. *agustus* (> It., Sp. *agosto*, Fr. *août*); OFr. *juignet* 'June' fr. dim. form, and, by analogy to this, Fr. *juillet* 'July' for OFr. *juil*, etc.

The Romance names appear in Greece in authors and papyri of the early Roman period and eventually prevailed. Hence the NG lit. ἰανουάριος, φεβρουάριος, etc., beside pop. γενάρης, φλεβάρης, etc.

In Celtic, all the Old Irish names were of Lat. origin. In modern Irish those for January, February, March, April, July, and in part June, persist, while the others have been replaced, in part already in Middle Irish, by native terms. In Welsh and Breton the Lat. names are retained for January, February, March, April, May, and August, the others having native names.

The whole Lat. series is used in all the living Gmc. languages, likewise in Lett. (the older native names being obs.; cf. Mühl.-Endz. 2.616) and Russ.

14.73 YEAR

Grk.	ἔτος, ἐνιαυτός	Goth.	*jēr*, *aþn*, *ataþni*	Lith.	*metai*
NG	χρόνος, ἔτος	ON	*ār*	Lett.	*gads*
Lat.	*annus*	Dan.	*aar*	ChSl.	*lěto*
It.	*anno*	Sw.	*år*	SCr.	*godina*
Fr.	*an*	OE	*gēar*	Boh.	*rok*
Sp.	*año*	ME	*yeer*	Pol.	*rok*
Rum.	*an*	NE	*year*	Russ.	*god*
Ir.	*bliadain*	Du.	*jaar*	Skt.	*vatsara-*, *varṣa-*, *hāyana-*
NIr.	*bliadhain*	OHG	*jār*	Av.	*yār-*, *sarəd-*, OPers. *θard-*
W.	*blwyddyn*	MHG	*jār*		
Br.	*bloaz*	NHG	*jahr*		

There are three groups of cognates, each of which is represented by words for 'year' in at least two widely separated branches of the IE family. It is the first of these (in the order below) that has the best claim to reflect a distinctive IE word for 'year'. The second is more widespread as a formal group, but with various uses suggesting that in the IE period it was more generic, 'passing time, period of time', whence later specialization to 'year', 'season', 'spring', or 'hour'.

Most of the other words for 'year' are also cognate with words for 'time' or 'fixed period of time', including terms for various seasons of the year and for 'day' or 'hour'.

1. IE **wet-*, **wetes-*. Walde-P. 1.251. Grk. ἔτος, fr. widely attested ϝέτος;

Skt. *vatsa-* (only *tri-vatsa-* 'three years old', otherwise 'calf' = 'yearling'), usually *vatsara-*; Alb. *vjet*. Here prob. Lat. *vetus* 'old', etc. (14.15).

2. IE **yē-ro-*, **yō-ro-*, prob. fr. **yē-*, **yō-* beside **yā-* in Skt. *yā-* 'go', Lith. *joti* 'ride', extension of **ei-* 'go'. Walde-P. 1.105. Falk-Torp 6 f.

Goth. *jēr*, ON *ār*, OE *gēar*, etc., general Gmc.; Av. *yār-* (nom. sg. *yārə*); Grk. ὥρα 'period of time' (14.11), 'hour'; Boh. *jaro*, etc. 'spring' (14.75).

3. IE **at-no-*, perh. fr. **at-* in Skt. *atati* 'goes, wanders' (cf. above, 2). Walde-P. 1.41 f. Ernout-M. 55. Walde-H. 1.51.

Lat. *annus* (> Romance words); Goth. *aþn* (? only dat. pl. *aþnam*) and *at-aþni* (only gen. sg. *ataþnjis*) both for ἐνιαυτός. Here also (with *tn* > *kn*) Osc. *akenei* 'in anno', Umbr. *acnu* 'annos'.

4. Grk. ἐνιαυτός, orig. 'anniversary' as in Hom. and early inscriptions (Cretan law-code, etc.), but also (Hom.+) simply 'year', etym. disputed. Either fr. phrase ἐνὶ αὐτῷ 'in the same (time)', for which cf. Boh. *týden*, etc. 'week', fr. 'this day' (14.61); or perh. as orig. 'solstice, resting place of the sun', deriv. of ἐνιαύω 'rest, sleep in', cpd. of ἰαύω 'rest, sleep, pass the night'. Walde-P. 1.20. Brugmann IF 15.87 ff., 17.319.

Grk. χρόνος 'time' (14.11) is in pop. NG 'year', with new pl. χρόνια and new fem. coll. χρονιά 'space of a year' (Fr. *année*). But lit. ἔτος is also generally familiar.

5. Ir. *bliadain*, NIr. *bliadhain*, W. *blwyddyn*, OCorn. *blidhenn*, Br. dial. *blizenn*, all fem., fr. the shorter form seen in Br. *bloaz* 'year', W. *blwydd* 'year of age', etym. dub.; perh. orig. mythological conception. Pedersen 1.113. Morris Jones 212 (fantastic; cf. Loth, RC 36.401). Stokes 188.

6. Lith. *metai*, pl. of *metas* 'time' (14.11).

Lett. *gads*, fr. Russ. *god* (below). Mühl.-Endz. 1.582.

7. ChSl. *lěto* (= ἔτος, ἐνιαυτός, χρόνος, καιρός, Gospels, Supr.; also θέρος Ps. Sin.), modern Slavic 'summer', rarely also 'year' : Sw. dial. *låding* 'spring', Ir. *laithe* 'day'. Walde-P. 2.427. Berneker 713 f.

SCr. *godina* (rarely also 'hour') = ChSl. *godina*, Boh. *hodina*, Pol. *godzina* 'hour' (14.51), fr. ChSl. *godŭ* 'period of time' (14.11), as elsewhere in Slavic with various special applications, but Russ. *god* 'year'. Berneker 316 ff.

Boh., Pol. *rok* = Russ. *rok* 'fate, destiny', SCr. *rok* 'term, period', ChSl. *rokŭ* 'appointed time, goal', fr. the root of *reką*, *rešti* 'say'. Walde-P. 2.362. Trautmann 243. Brückner 461.

8. Skt. *vatsara-*, above, 1.

Skt. *varṣa-* 'rain' (1.75), also (the rainy season extended to) 'year'.

Skt. *hāyana-* : Av. *zaēn-* 'winter', *zayana-* 'wintry', (14.74).

Av. *yār-*, above, 2.

Av. *sarəd-*, OPers. *θard-* (certainly 'year', not 'manner' as Barth. 1566), NPers. *sāl* 'year', Osset. *särd* 'summer' : Skt. *çarad-* 'autumn', also 'year' in RV, etc., perh. as orig. 'warm season' : Lith. *šilius* 'August', *šilti* 'grow warm', Lat. *calēre* 'be warm', etc. Wood, AJPh. 21.182. Walde-P. 1.429. Walde-H. 1.137.

	14.74 WINTER	14.75 SPRING	14.76 SUMMER	14.77 AUTUMN
Grk.	χειμών	ἔαρ	θέρος	φθινόπωρον
NG	χειμῶνας	ἄνοιξη	καλοκαίρι	φθινόπωρο
Lat.	*hiems*	*vēr*	*aestās*	*autumnus*
It.	*inverno*	*primavera*	*estate*	*autunno*
Fr.	*hiver*	*printemps*	*été*	*automne*
Sp.	*invierno*	*primavera*	*verano, estío*	*otoño*
Rum.	*iarnă*	*primăvară*	*vară*	*toamnă*
Ir.	*gam, gemred*	*errach*	*sam, samrad*	*fog(a)mar*
NIr.	*geimhreadh*	*earrach*	*samhradh*	*fōghmhar*
W.	*gaeaf*	*gwanwyn*	*haf*	*hydref (cynhaeaf)*
Br.	*goañv*	*nevez-amzer*	*hañv*	*diskar-amzer, dilost-hañv*
Goth.	*wintrus*	. . . .	*asans*	. . . .
ON	*vetr*	*vār*	*sumar*	*haust*
Dan.	*vinter*	*voraar, vaar*	*sommer*	*efteraar (høst)*
Sw.	*vinter*	*vår*	*sommar*	*höst*
OE	*winter*	*lencten*	*sumor*	*hærfest*
ME	*winter*	*lente(n)*	*sumer*	*hervest, autum(p)ne*
NE	*winter*	*spring*	*summer*	*autumn, fall*
Du.	*winter*	*voorjaar, lente*	*zomer*	*herfst*
OHG	*winter*	*lenzo*	*sumar*	*herbist*
MHG	*winter*	*lenze*	*sumer*	*herb(e)st*
NHG	*winter*	*frühling*	*sommer*	*herbst*
Lith.	*žiema*	*pavasaris*	*vasara*	*ruduo*
Lett.	*ziema*	*pavasaris*	*vasara*	*rudens*
ChSl.	*zima*	*vesna*	*žętva, lěto*	*jesenĭ*
SCr.	*zima*	*proljeće*	*ljeto*	*jesen*
Boh.	*zima*	*jaro (vesna)*	*leto*	*podzim, jeseň*
Pol.	*zima*	*wiosna*	*lato*	*jesień*
Russ.	*zima*	*vesna*	*leto*	*osen'*
Skt.	*hemanta-, himā-*	*vasanta-*	*grīṣma-, nidāgha-*	*çarad-*
Av.	*zyam-, zaēn-, aiwigāma-*	*vaŋhar-, zarəmaya-*	*ham-*	

14.74–14.77. Of the now recognized four seasons of the year, the 'winter' is the one for which there is the most impressive agreement in the words denoting it, which in all the main branches of the IE family except Gmc. belong to an inherited group, pointing unmistakably to an IE word for 'winter'. For 'spring' and 'summer' there are less widespread cognate groups pointing to IE words which were probably used without precise separation of the two. The earliest division was presumably one of two seasons, 'winter' and 'non-winter' (or in some regions 'dry' and 'wet'; but this has no bearing on IE relations). Cf. Schrader, Reallex. 1.529 f., and, for the seasons in India (3 in the Vedic period, later 5, 6, or even 7), BR s.v. *ṛtu-*, Zimmer, Altind. Leben 371 f., Macdonell-Keith 1.110 f.

14.74. 'Winter'.

1. IE **gheim-*, **ĝhyem-*, etc., prob. with *m*-suffixes fr. **ĝhei-*. Walde-P. 1.546 ff. Ernout-M. 451 f. Walde-H. 1.645 f. Pedersen 1.66.

Grk. χειμών, NG χειμῶνας; Lat. *hiems* (adj. *hībernus*, whence *hībernum (tempus)* > Romance words. REW 4126); Ir. *gem-red* (*red*: *rāithe* 'season'; Loth, RC 43.143 f.), NIr. *geimhreadh*, Ir. *gam* (for **gem*, after *sam* 'summer'), W. *gaeaf*, Br. *goañv;* Lith. *žiema*, Lett. *ziema;* ChSl. *zima*, etc., general Slavic; Ved. *himā-*, class. Skt. usually *hemanta-* (also once RV; Macdonell-Keith, 1.110, 2.504, 507), Av. *zyam-*. Here also (fr. **ĝhei-*) Av. *zaēn-* (NPers. *dai*) 'winter' and *zayana-* 'wintry', Skt. *hāyana-* 'year'.

2. Goth. *wintrus*, etc., general Gmc., etym. dub., but perh. as 'wet season' : Goth. *watō*, ON *vatn*, OE *wæter*, Grk. ὕδωρ, etc. 'water' (*r/n*-stem; for nasalization cf. Lith. *vanduo*). Walde-P. 1.253. Falk-Torp 1385. Feist 566.

3. Av. *aiwigāma-* (mostly 'winter', also 'year'), NPers. *hangām* 'time', etym.? Barth. 89. Horn 248.

14.75. 'Spring'. Apart from certain inherited groups, words for 'spring' are based on 'early, fore-, first' (time, year, summer), or 'opening, beginning'.

1. IE **wesṛ-*, **wesn-* (*r/n*-stem neut.), whence perh. in part also IE **wēr-*. Walde-P. 1.310 f. Ernout-M. 1087. Falk-Torp 1340.

Grk. ἔαρ, Lat. *vēr* (cpds. > It., Sp. *primavera*, Rum. *primăvară*, OFr. *primevoire;* REW 6754); Ir. *errach*, NIr. *earrach* (**wesr-āk-*, with loss of *w-* by sentence phonetics? Pedersen 1.82, 435), W. *gwanwyn* (Pedersen 1.74); ON *vār*, Sw. *vår* (Dan. *vaar*, poet.); Lith., Lett. *vasara* 'summer', hence *pa-vasaris* 'spring', lit. 'a kind of summer, quasi-summer' (cf. Lith. *pa-motė*, Lett. *pa-māte* 'stepmother', etc.; Mühl.-Endz. 3.3); ChSl., Boh., Russ. *vesna*, Pol. *wiosna;* Skt. *vasanta-*, Av. *vaŋhar-*; Arm. *garun*.

2. Grk. ἄνοιξις 'opening', hence (opening of the flowers, etc.), NG 'spring', pop. ἄνοιξη.

3. OFr. *tamps prim* (= Lat. *tempus prīmum* 'first season'), Fr. *printemps* (replaces Fr. *primevère* as 'spring' in 16th cent.), lit. 'first season'. REW 6754. Gamillscheg 719. Bloch 2.318.

4. Br. *nevez-amzer*, lit. 'new-time' (cf. 14.11, 14.13).

5. Dan. *voraar*, Du. *voorjaar*, lit. 'fore-year'.

OE *lencten*, ME *lenten*, *lente* (NE *lent*), Du. *lente*, OHG *lenzo*, MHG *lenze*, NHG *lenz* (poet.), also OHG *lenzin*, *langiz* (cf. *lentzinmānōth* 'March'), perh. orig. 'having long days' fr. Gmc. *langa-* 'long' and *-tin-* : Goth. *sin-teins* 'daily', Lith. *diena*, ChSl. *dĭnĭ* 'day', etc. (14.41). Walde-P. 1.774. Kluge-G. 355. NED s.vv. *lenten*, *lent*, sb. 1.

NE *spring*, earlier in *spring of the yere* = 'beginning, rising of the year' (cf. *day-spring* 'dawn'). NED s.v.

NHG *frühling*, late MHG *vrüelinc*, fr. *früh*, MHG *vrüeje* 'early' (cf. NHG dial. *spätling* 'autumn'). Paul, Deutsches Wtb. s.v. Kluge-G. 177.

6. SCr. *proljeće*, also Boh. *podletí* 'early summer, spring', lit. 'pre-summer' (SCr. *ljeto*, Boh. *leto* 'summer').

Boh. *jaro*, Pol. obs. *jar*, *jarz*, old *jaro*, Russ.-ChSl. *jara* : Goth. *jēr* 'year', etc. (14.73). Berneker 446 f. Brückner 199.

7. Av. *zarəmaya-*, etym.? Barth. 1683.

14.76. 'Summer'. Apart from the inherited group, several of the words are cognate with those for 'hot' or 'burn'; some were orig. 'spring'; one is 'good season, fine weather'.

1. IE **sem-*. Walde-P. 2.492 f. Falk-Torp 1107.

Ir. *sam*, W. *haf*, Br. *hañv*, Ir. *samrad*, NIr. *samhradh* (*sam-r-ad* Pedersen 2.53, but *-rad* : *rāithe* 'season', Loth, RC 43, 143 f.); ON *sumar*, OE *sumor*, etc., general Gmc., except Goth.; Av. *ham-* (Skt. *samā-* 'season, year' rarely also 'summer', cf. Macdonell-Keith 2.429 f.); Arm. *am* 'year'.

2. Grk. θέρος, orig. 'summer heat', whence 'summer' and also 'crop, harvest' : θέρομαι 'become hot', Skt. *haras-* 'energy, fire', Grk. θερμός 'warm', Skt. *gharma-* 'heat', etc. Walde-P. 1.687.

Byz. καλοκαίριον, NG καλοκαίρι, lit. 'good season' (καλός 'good' and καιρός 'time, season, weather').

3. Lat. *aestās* (> It. *estate*, Fr. *été*; adj. Lat. *aestīvus* > Sp., Port. *estío*) : *aestus* 'fire, glow, heat', fr. the root **aidh-* in Grk. αἴθω 'kindle, burn', etc. (1.85). Walde-P. 1.5. Ernout-M. 20. Walde-H. 1.20. REW 245, 248.

Rum. *vară*, fr. Lat. *vēr* 'spring' (14.75), and Sp. *verano*, fr. deriv. VLat. (gloss) *vērānum (tempus)*. REW 9213, 9215.

4. Goth. *asans* (renders θέρος 'summer' once Mk. 13.28, otherwise θερισμός 'harvest') : OHG *aran*, etc. 'harvest', SCr. *jesen*, etc., 'autumn' (14.77). Walde-P. 1.161. 'Summer' prob. semantic borrowing fr. Grk.

5. Lith., Lett. *vasara* : Grk. ἔαρ, Lat. *vēr*, etc., 'spring' (14.75).

6. ChSl. *žętva* (renders both θέρος as 'summer' and θερισμός 'harvest') : *žęti* 'reap, harvest', etc. (8.32). 'Summer' prob. semantic borrowing fr. Grk.

ChSl. *lěto* ('summer' in Ps. Sin.; 'year' in Gospels and Supr.), etc., general modern Slavic for 'summer', see under 'year', 14.73.

7. Skt. *grīṣma-*, etym.? Uhlenbeck 84.

Skt. *nidāgha-* (Ved. also *nāidāgha-*; Macdonell-Keith 1.449, 459), fr. *ni-dah-* 'burn down, consume'.

Av. *ham-*, above, 1.

14.77. Autumn. For 'autumn', unlike the names of the other seasons, there is no certain agreement between any of the branches of the IE family, but only within some of them, e.g. a common Gmc. and a common Slavic word. Besides the connection with 'harvest', words for 'autumn' may mean lit. 'before winter' or 'end of summer', or may refer to the fall or the redness of the leaves in autumn.

1. Grk. φθινόπωρον (rarely also μετόπωρον), cpd. of φθίνω 'wane' (or μετά 'after') and ὀπώρα 'late summer, fruit-season' (also sometimes used for 'summer' or 'autumn') and 'fruit' (see 5.71).

2. Lat. *autumnus* (> Romance words), etym. dub. Later spelling *auctumnus* by popular (false) connection with *augēre* 'increase'. Walde-P. 1.16. Ernout-M. 96. Walde-H. 1.87 f.

3. Ir. *fogamar*, *fogmar*, NIr. *fōghmhar*, cpd. of *fo-* 'under' (= 'before') and *gamar* : *gam*, *gem-red* 'winter' (14.74). Macbain 177.

W. *hydref* 'autumn' and 'October' (Br. *here* formerly 'autumn', now only 'October'), MBr. *hezreff*, apparently fr. W. *hydr*, MBr. *hezr* 'powerful', but semantically not clear (the suggested analogy of Lat. *autumnus* is based on its false etym.). Henry 161. Ernault, RC 16.190, ftn.

W. *cynhaeaf* 'autumn' (obs. in this sense, Spurrell), 'harvest', cpd. of *cyn* 'preceding' and *gaeaf* 'winter' (14.74). Morris Jones, 265.

Br. *diskar-amzer*, lit. 'fall-time' (*diskar* 'a fall'. Cf. NE *fall*, below, 4).

Br. *dilost-hañv* lit. 'end of summer' (*dilost* : *lost* 'tail', 4.18).

For a great variety of other Br. words for 'autumn', cf. Ernault, RC 15.392 f.

4. ON *haust*, Dan. *høst* (mostly 'harvest, crop', but still dial. and poet. in this sense), Sw. *höst*, OE *hærfest*, ME *hervest*, Du. *herfst*, OHG *herbist*, etc. (but NE *harvest* no longer as the season) : Lat. *carpere* 'pluck', Grk. καρπός 'fruit', Ir. *corrān* 'sickle', etc. Walde-P. 2.581. Falk-Torp 454 f.

Dan. *efteraar*, lit. 'after-year'.

ME *autum(p)ne*, NE *autumn* fr. OFr. *autompne*, Fr. *automne* (above, 2).

NE *fall* (esp. U.S., where it is the usual pop. word), earlier in phrase 'fall of the leaf'. NED s.v. *fall*, sb.¹ 2.

5. Lith. *ruduo*, Lett. *rudens*, fr. Lith. *rudas*, Lett. *ruds* 'reddish, red-brown' (with reference to leaves, etc.). Mühl.-Endz. 3.554.

6. ChSl. *jeseně*, etc., general Slavic, also OPruss. *assanis* : Goth. *asans* 'harvest, summer', OHG *ar(a)n* 'harvest', etc. Walde-P. 1.161 f. Berneker 265.

Boh. *podzim*, lit. 'pre-winter' (*zima* 'winter', 14.74).

7. Skt. *çarad-* (also 'year', RV, etc.) = Av. *sarəd-*, OPers. *θard-* 'year' (14.73).

14.78. The generic 'season' of the year (this sense most unambiguously in the pl. forms) is commonly expressed by words for 'time' (14.11) with, or sometimes without, those for 'year' (14.73). Thus Grk. ὥρα, Lat. *tempus* (*anni*), NHG *jahreszeit* (hence by semantic borrowing Rum. *anotimp*, neolog.), Dan. *aarstid*, Sw. *årstid*, Du. *jaargetijde*, Lith. *metų*

laikas, Lett. *gada laiks*, SCr. *godišnje doba*, Boh. *roční počasi*, Pol. *pora roku* (*pora* 'fitting time', like Russ. *pora*, etc. = late ChSl. *pora* 'force' : ChSl. *perją*, *pĭrati* 'h t, pound'; Brückner 431), Russ. *vremja goda*.

But the following are different:

Grk. ἐποχή 'cessation, stoppage' (: ἐπ-έχω), late 'position, fixed point of time' (source of NE *epoch*, etc.), in NG also 'season'.

It. *stagione*, Sp. *estación*, fr. Lat. *statiō* 'station'. REW 8234.

Fr. *saison* (> ME *seson*, NE *season*), in OFr. also 'favorable time', through 'sowing-time' fr. Lat. *satiō* 'sowing'. REW 7616. Gamillscheg 781.

Ir. *ráthe*, NIr. *ráithe* 'quarter of the year, season' (cf. also *gem-red* 'winter', *sam-rad* 'summer') : W. *rhawd* 'troop, course', fr. the root in Ir. *rethim* 'run', etc. Loth, RC 43.143 f.

Skt. *ŗtu-* 'definite or fitting time' and the reg. word for 'season' of the year (BR s.v.; Zimmer, Altind. Leben 373), beside *ŗta-* 'right, proper, etc.', fr. the root seen in Grk. ἀραρίσκω 'fit', etc. Walde-P. 1.70.

CHAPTER 15

SENSE PERCEPTION

15.11 Perceive by the Senses; Sense (sb.)	15.57 Bright
15.21 Smell (vb. subj.)	15.61 Color (sb.)
15.22 Smell (vb. obj.)	15.62 Light (in Color)
15.23 Smell (sb. subj.)	15.63 Dark (in Color)
15.24 Smell (sb. obj.)	15.64 White
15.25 Good Smelling, Fragrant	15.65 Black
15.26 Bad Smelling, Stinking	15.66 Red
15.31 Taste (vb. subj.)	15.67 Blue
15.32 Taste (vb. obj.)	15.68 Green
15.33 Taste (sb. subj.)	15.69 Yellow
15.34 Taste (sb. obj.)	15.71 Touch (vb.)
15.35 Sweet	15.72 Feel (vb.), Feel of
15.36 Salt (adj.)	15.73 Touch (sb. subj.)
15.37 Bitter	15.74 Hard
15.38 Acid, Sour	15.75 Soft
15.41 Hear	15.76 Rough
15.42 Listen	15.77 Smooth
15.43 Hearing (sb.)	15.78 Sharp
15.44 Sound (sb.)	15.79 Blunt, Dull
15.45 Loud	15.81 Heavy
15.51 See	15.82 Light (in Weight)
15.52 Look (vb.), Look at	15.83 Wet, Damp
15.53 Sight (subj.)	15.84 Dry
15.54 Sight (obj.), Look (obj.), Appearance	15.85 Hot, Warm
	15.86 Cold
15.55 Show (vb.)	15.87 Clean
15.56 Shine	15.88 Dirty, Soiled

For the purposes of our discussion it is sufficient to follow the time-honored classification of the senses as smell, taste, hearing, sight, and touch, ignoring the modern technical elaboration of the old 'touch'.

Within the spheres of the several senses there are certain logical distinctions which find linguistic expression in some languages and not in others and which, moreover, work out differently for the several senses as regards linguistic consciousness of the relations.

First, the difference between the subjective and the objective notions. These terms (hereafter subj., obj.) apply to both the noun and the verb, and so are preferable to transitive and intransitive, which are applicable only to the verb. NE *smell* and *taste*, as verbs or nouns, are used both subjectively, with reference to the person perceiving, and objectively, with reference to the object which stimulates the sense. *I smell the rose, taste the apple* and *it smells sweet, tastes good*, and similarly a person's sense of

smell, taste, or the *smell of a rose*, the *taste of an apple*. The situation is the same in many other languages, but in some the two aspects are distinguished by different forms of the same root or even unrelated forms, or again the obj. verbal notion is expressed only by a phrase 'have a smell (taste)' or the like. In general, for the senses of smell and taste the obj. notion is the earlier and the most important in the history of the words.

For hearing and sight the parallel relations between the subj. and obj. aspects are less obvious and less conspicuous in linguistic consciousness, though also of considerable importance in the history of the words. *I hear the bell*, and *it is heard, it sounds* (one cannot say *it hears*, but cf. the recent slang *it listens well*), and the *sound of a bell* is like the *smell of a rose*. *I see* something, and the object *is seen, appears, seems, looks* (cf. Lat. *vidētur*); the parallel to the *smell of a rose* is the *appearance* or *look* of the object, though *sight* was also once used in such phrases and is still used objectively in *pleasant sight*, etc.

For the sense of touch, NE *feel* may be used both subjectively and objectively, like *smell* and *taste*. *I feel* something and *it feels smooth*. But, while there are some parallels for this, in most languages the latter notion is expressed by a phrase meaning 'it is smooth, it seems smooth, is smooth to the touch' or the like. Hence the obj. use of the verb, and also of a noun, as in NE the *feel(ing) of an orange*, will be left out of account.

Besides the distinction between subj. and obj., there is a further distinction, within the subj. It is that between the actual perception and the antecedent action provoking it, the application of the appropriate sense organs. It is a safe assumption on general psychological

grounds that for all the senses the notion of the provoking action is ultimately earlier than that of perception. But linguistically the distinction is of varying importance for the different senses, and for some of them the two notions are so blended that it is unprofitable to keep them apart in the discussion.

For smell there is such a distinction between *I smell the rose* and *smell it!*—that is, 'take a smell of it'. The latter notion is sometimes expressed by special words, as ON *daunsna*, NHG *wittern* (Fr. *flairer* is used most commonly in this way), or by the usual vb. for 'smell' with a prefix or preposition, as NHG *an-riechen, be-riechen*, or NE *smell of* (so in U.S., like *taste of, feel of*) or *smell at* (older and still British). But it is generally covered also by the simple vbs. for 'smell', without consciousness of the distinction and will be ignored in the lists and discussion.

For taste there is the same distinction between *I taste the apple* and *taste it!* or *taste of it*, that is 'take a taste of it'. The two notions may be expressed by different words, as NHG *schmecken* and *kosten*, though the former was once used in both senses. In the inherited group of verbs for 'taste' and several of the others the second notion, 'taste of', is the earlier and dominant one. Sometimes the only distinctive vb. for 'taste' is used only in this way (so NG δοκιμάζω), and 'perceive by taste' is expressed only by the generic vb. for 'perceive by the senses' or by some periphrasis.

The vb. *touch* does not denote the sense perception, but we speak of the *sense of touch*, and, in general, the vbs. for 'touch' are the most important in this group. Or still closer to *smell of, taste of* is the notion in *feel it!* or the more colloquial *feel of it*, that is 'examine by touch'. In most languages there are

distinctive verbs for this notion or for the closely allied 'feel about, feel one's way, grope', and sometimes these, rather than those for 'touch', underlie the sbs. for 'sense of touch'. This was also the primary sense in NE *feel* and its Gmc. cognates, which only secondarily came to be used for 'perceive by touch'. Elsewhere, generally, there is no distinctive vb. for 'feel' as 'perceive by touch', which is expressed by the generic word for 'perceive by the senses'.

Although the NE phrases *smell of, taste of, feel of* are regarded as colloquial or even inelegant, they will be used ('smell of', etc.) in translating, when it is desired to avoid confusion with 'smell', 'taste', 'feel', as denoting the perceptions.

For hearing and sight the corresponding distinction is of much greater linguistic importance. 'Hear' and 'listen', and likewise 'see' and 'look', are usually expressed by different words, though these are often cognate forms and there may be overlapping or shift of use not only within cognate groups but even in the history of the same word.

From the foregoing it is apparent that, while from the logical point of view a certain parallelism may be set up between the different notions pertaining to

the senses, this is unequally reflected in language, and it would be unprofitable to adhere to it rigidly in the arrangement of the material.

This chapter furnishes numerous illustrations of linguistic synesthesia, the extension or shift of meaning from one sense sphere to another. Conspicuous is the interchange between 'smell' and 'taste', and to some extent 'feel'. Conversely, in several cases, the old generic words for 'perceive by the senses' have been partly specialized and furnish the common words for one particular sense-perception. Thus Lat. *sentire* 'perceive', but It. *sentire* also esp. 'hear' (more popular than *udire*) and 'smell' (more usual than *odorare* for actual perception by smell), Fr. *sentir* also the usual word for 'smell'; Slavic *čuti* 'perceive', but 'hear' in SCr., Bulg., etc., often 'smell' in Pol., Boh., etc.

The words for the sense perceptions have been the subject of some of the earliest studies of semantic groups, namely, for Gmc., J. Grimm, Die fünf Sinne (1848 = Kl. Schriften 7.193 ff.), and, for IE, F. Bechtel, Ueber die Bezeichnungen der sinnlichen Wahrnehmungen in den indogermanischen Sprachen (1879).

15.11 PERCEIVE BY THE SENSES; SENSE (sb.)

Grk.	αἰσθάνομαι; αἴσθησις	Goth.	. . . .	Lith.	*jausti; jausmas*
NG	αἰσθάνομαι; αἴσθησις	ON	*kenna; vit*	Lett.	*jaust; jūteklis*
Lat.	*sentire; sensus*	Dan.	*fornemme; sans*	ChSl.	*počuti; čuvstvo*
It.	*sentire; senso*	Sw.	*förnimma; sinne*	SCr.	*osjetiti (ćutjeti); osjet, ćuvstvo*
Fr.	*sentir; sens*	OE	*ongitan; andgit*		
Sp.	*sentir; sentido*	ME	*fele, perceive; wit*	Boh.	*čiti; smysl*
Rum.	*simţi; simţ*	NE	*perceive; sense*	Pol.	*czuć; zmysl*
Ir.	*cetabiu, airigim,*	Du.	*gevoelen; zin*	Russ.	*oščutiť', čuvstvovať'; čuvstvo*
	mothaigim; cétbuid,	OHG	*intfindan; sin*		
	mothugud	MHG	*entvinden; sin*	Skt.	*grah-, jñā-, budh-; indriya-*
NIr.	*mothuighim, airi-*	NHG	*empfinden; sinn*		
	ghim; céadfadh			Av.	*bud-*
W.	*clywed; synnwyr*				
Br.	*n erzout, klevout; skiant*				

Most of the verbs listed are not restricted to the sense-perceptions but may be used also in a still wider sense for 'perceive' mentally or 'feel' emotionally. Many other words for 'perceive' that are not included in the list are also freely used with reference to sense-perception, as Fr. *percevoir*, NHG *wahrnehmen* (cf. *die sinnlichen wahrnehmungen*), etc., and it is sometimes difficult to select the best terms belonging here, for one uses commonly the vb. for a particular sense, 'I see, smell', etc., rather than a generic term. A few of those listed are used of most, not all, of the senses. For the sb. the words chosen are those used in the phrase 'the five senses'.

1. Grk. αἰσθάνομαι (so in NG more commonly in this form, even among writers in the δημοτική, than αἰστάνομαι), αἴσθησις, fr. *ἀ-ϝισ-θ- : Skt. *āvis*, Av. *āviš* 'openly, manifestly', Skt. *āvir-bhū-* 'become manifest, appear', *āviṣ-kṛ-* 'make manifest, reveal', beside **aw-* in Grk. ἀΐω 'perceive, hear', ChSl. *(j)avě* 'openly', *(j)aviti* 'show', *umŭ* 'reason, understanding'; here also the IE word for 'ear', Grk. οὖς, Lat. *auris*, etc. (4.22). Walde-P. 1.17 f. Walde-H. 1.80.

NG νοιώθω 'understand, perceive' (17.16), also 'feel' (pain, etc.).

2. Lat. *sentīre* (> It. *sentire*, Fr., Sp. *sentir*, Rum. *simți*), *sensus* (> It. *senso*, Fr. *sens*; Sp. *sentido*, Rum. *simț*, fr. vb.), prob. as fig. use of 'find one's way' : Ir. *sēt*, W. *hynt* 'way', Goth. *ga-sinþa* 'traveling companion', OHG *sind* 'way, journey', *sinnan* 'travel' (also 'strive for'), OE *sīþ* 'journey', also OHG *sin*, NHG *sinn* 'sense, mind', etc. (below, 4), MHG, NHG *sinnen* 'think'. Walde-P. 2.496 f. Ernout-M. 923 f.

3. Ir. *cetabīu* (3sg. *cetabī*), with sb. *cētbuid*, NIr. *cēadfadh*, cpd. of vb. for 'be' and *cita-*, *cēt-* : OW *cant* 'with', Grk. κατά, etc. Cf. also W. *canfod* 'perceive, see'. Pedersen 2.292, 442. Thurneysen, Gram. 501.

Ir. *airigim*, NIr. *airighim*, orig. 'watch, give attention to', fr. *aire* 'heed, attention, notice', etym. dub. (Walde-P. 2.29).

Ir. *mothaigim*, vbl. n. *mothugud* (see RIA Contrib. s.vv.), NIr. *mothuighim*, vbl. n. *mothughadh*, etym. dub. Macbain 254 (: Lith. *matyti* 'see', Lett. *matīt* 'feel, perceive, notice').

W. *clywed*, Br. *klevout*, 'hear' (15.41), but used in Welsh of all sense-perceptions except sight (cf. Evans, s.v., Loth, RC 40.359), in Br. also 'learn, understand' and 'smell' (Ernault s.v.).

Br. *merzout*, : dial. *armerhein* 'manage', W. *armerthu*, 'provide, prepare', *darmerth* 'provision', Ir. *arbert* 'prepare', prob. fr. **smer-t-* (cf. Gall. *Rosmerta*) : Lat. *merēre* 'earn, gain, deserve', Grk. μέρος 'share', etc. Ernault, Glossaire 409. Vendryes, Études celt. 2.133 f.

W. *synnwyr*, sb. (*y pump synnwyr* 'the five senses') : *synio* 'feel, think, consider', fr. Lat. *sentīre* (above, 2). Pedersen 1.198. Loth, Mots lat. 209.

Br. *skiant*, sb., fr. Lat. *scientia* 'knowledge'. Loth, Mots lat. 205 f.

4. ON *kenna* (of sense-perception, esp. of smell, taste, and feeling), lit. 'know, recognize' : Goth. *kannjan* 'make known', OE *cennan* 'declare, relate', etc. Falk-Torp 516.

Dan. *fornemme*, Sw. *förnimma*, fr. MLG *vornemen* 'notice, learn, understand' (= NHG *vernehmen*), cpd. of *nemen* (Dan. *nemme*, Sw. *nimma* 'take', etc.), in orig. prob. a translation of Lat. *percipere*. Falk-Torp 260.

OE *ongitan*, rarely *andgitan*, with sb. *andgit* (*þā fīf andgitu* 'the five senses', cf. Bosworth-Toller s.v. III), cpds. of OE *-gi(e)tan* in *begi(e)tan* 'get' (11.16).

ME *fele* 'feel' by sense of touch (15.72) was used also of taste and smell, and so NE *feel* in dial. (NED s.v. 7), and Du. *(ge)voelen* sometimes of other senses. But for the most part the expansion of application in this Gmc. group has been not to the other senses but to the emotions, as in NE *feel happy, sad, angry*, or trans. *feel anger, hate*, etc.

ME, NE *perceive* 'apprehend' with the mind or the 'senses', esp. those of sight or hearing, but now technical for all the senses, cf. *sense-perception*, fr. OFr. (North) **perceivre* = *perçoivre*, Lat. *percipere* 'seize, get, perceive (by mind or senses of sight and hearing), feel (pain, joy, etc.)', cpd. of *capere* 'seize, take'. NED s.v.

OHG *intfindan*, MHG *entvinden*, *emphinden*, NHG *empfinden* : OE *onfindan* 'find out, discover, experience, be aware of', etc., cpd. of OHG, OE *findan* 'find'.

Du. *gewaar worden* 'become aware of', like NHG *wahrnehmen*.

ON *vit*, ME *wit* used in the expression 'five senses' = OE *witt*, OHG *wizzi* 'understanding, knowledge, wit, etc.' (NE *wit*), fr. the vb. ON *vita*, OE *witan*, etc. 'know' (17.17). NED s.v. *wit*, sb. 3b.

Dan. *sans* (older *sens*; replacing *sind* in this sense), NE *sense*, fr. Fr. *sens* (above). Falk-Torp 951, 967.

OHG, MHG *sin*, NHG *sinn*, Du. *zin*, MLG *sins* (> Dan. *sind*, Sw. *sinne*), all also 'mind, understanding, meaning, etc.' : Lat. *sentīre*, *sensus*, etc. (above, 2). Falk-Torp 967 f. Hellquist 911 f.

5. Lith. *jausti*, Lett. *jaust* (beside *justi*, *just* 'feel, notice'), with sbs. Lith. *jausmas*, Lett. *jūteklis*, prob. : Skt. *api-vat-*, Av. *aipi-vat-* 'understand'. Walde-P. 1.216. Meillet, BSL 23.77.

6. ChSl. *počuti*, perfect. of *čuti* 'recognize, notice', SCr. *čuti* 'hear', Boh. *čiti* 'perceive, notice, smell', Pol. *czuć* 'perceive, smell', with sbs. ChSl. *čuvĭstvo*, Russ. *čuvstvo* (SCr. *čuvstvo*, old in this sense), whence Russ. *čuvstvovat'* 'feel, perceive' : Grk. κοέω 'notice', Lat. *cavēre* 'be on one's guard, heed', Grk. ἀκούω, Goth. *hausjan* 'hear', etc. (15.41). Berneker 162 f. Walde-P. 1.369.

SCr. *osjetiti*, with sb. *osjet*, cf. *dosjecati* 'take notice of', cpds. of *sjetiti se*, late ChSl. *sětiti sę* 'remember' (17.31).

SCr. *ćutjeti* (as 'perceive' dial.), Russ. *o-ščutit'*, with sb. SCr. *ćut*, *ćutilo* : ChSl. *štutiti* 'feel', etym.? Walde-P. 1.369. Osten-Sacken, IF 33.197. Miklosich 357.

Boh. *smysl*, Pol. *zmysł* (*smysł*), also 'meaning, mind' = SCr. *smisao*, Russ. *smysl* 'meaning', cpd. of ChSl. *myslĭ* 'thought', etc. Miklosich 208. Brückner 350.

7. 'Perceive' in Skt. rendered usually by *grah-* 'seize' (with instr. of sense-organ, *cakṣuṣā*, etc.), or by *jñā-* 'know, be acquainted with' or *budh-* 'awake, become aware of'; also sometimes by *dṛç-* 'see', used for 'see with the (other) senses' (Kena Up. 1.6, Praçna Up. 4.8; with *indriya-* Tattvas. 48.3.74).

Skt. *indriya-* 'sense' or 'sense-organ', lit. 'vigor, energy', sb. fr. adj. *indriya-* 'belonging to Indra'.

Av. *bud-* (= Skt. *budh-*, above) 'become aware of', 'feel' (hunger and thirst), 'smell'. Barth. 918.

15.21–24 SMELL

	15.21 vb. subj.	15.22 vb.obj.	15.23 sb. subj.	15.24 sb. obj.
Grk.	ὀσφραίνομαι	ὄζω	ὄσφρησις (ὀδμή)	ὀσμή
NG	μυρίζω, -ομαι	μυρίζω	μυρωδιά	μυρωδιά
Lat.	*olfacere, odorārī*	*olēre, fragrāre*	*odorātus*	*odor*
It.	*sentire, odorare*	*odorare*	*odorato*	*odore*
Fr.	*sentir, flairer*	*sentir*	*odorat, flair*	*odeur*
Sp.	*oler*	*oler*	*olfato*	*olor*
Rum.	*mirosi*	*mirosi*	*miros*	*miros*
Ir.	*boltigur*	*bolad, boltunud* with vb.	*boltanugud*	*bolad, boltunud*
NIr.	*boltnuighim*	*boladh* with vb.	*boladh*	*boladh*
W.	*arogli*	*arogli*	*arogliad*	*arogl*
Br.	*c'houesa*	*c'houez* with vb.	*c'houesa*	*c'houez*
Goth.			*dauns*	*dauns*
ON	*þefja, þefa(ilma)*	*þefa, þefja(ilma)*	*ilming*	*þefr (ilmr, daunn)*
Dan.	*lugte*	*lugte*	*lugt*	*lugt*
Sw.	*lukta*	*lukta*	*lukt*	*lukt*
OE	*gestincan, gesweccan*	*stincan*	*stenc, swæcc*	*stenc, swæcc*
ME	*smelle*	*smelle*	*smelle*	*smelle*
NE	*smell*	*smell*	*smell*	*smell, odor*
Du.	*ruiken*	*ruiken*	*reuk*	*reuk*
OHG	*stincan*	*stincan, riohhan, swehhan*	*stanc*	*stanc, rouh, sweche*
MHG	*riechen, smecken*	*riechen, smecken*	*geruch (stanc, smac)*	*rouch, geruch (stanc, smac)*
NHG	*riechen*	*riechen*	*geruch*	*geruch*
Lith.	*uosti, uostyti*	*kvepėti*	*uoslė*	*kvapas*
Lett.	*uost, uostīt*	*uost, smakuot*	*uoža*	*smaka, uoža*
ChSl.	*obonjati, ąchati*	*vonjati*	*obonjanĭje, ąchanĭje*	*vonja*
SCr.	*mirisati*	*mirisati, vonjati*	*njuh, njušni osjet*	*miris, vonj*
Boh.	*čiti, čichati*	*páchnouti, voněti*	*čich*	*zápach, vůně*
Pol.	*wąchać*	*pachnąć*	*węch*	*zapach, woń*
Russ.	*njuchat'*	*pachnút'*	*obonjanie*	*zapach*
Skt.	*ghrā-*	*gandha-* with vb.	*ghrāṇa-*	*gandha-, ghrāṇa-*
Av.	*bud-*			*baoδi-, ganti-*

The distinction between the subj. and the obj. aspects (cf. above, pp. 1017 f.) is shown in the list and will generally not be noted again in the following. In the majority of cases the obj. use is the earlier. This most frequently rests on the notion of 'exhalation', the connections being with words for 'breath, steam, smoke', etc.; but in several cases apparently on the notion of something that 'hits one, strikes one forcibly'. Verbs in which the subj. use is earlier are in several cases specialized from 'perceive by the senses'.

Words for 'smell' are apt to carry a strong emotional value, which is felt to a less degree in words for 'taste' and hardly at all in those for the other senses. According to circumstances and often with a difference of tone and facial expression, they are used with reference to smells that are pleasant or unpleasant. Some become definitely specialized in one direction or the other, as NE *fragrance* and *stench* (cf. 15.25–26). A converse generalization of 'good smell' to 'smell' is seen in NG μυρίζω, μυρωδιά.

Some interchange between 'smell' and 'taste' is observed in cognate groups.

1. IE **od-*. Walde-P. 1.174, 697. Ernout-M. 698 f., 700 f.

Grk. ὄζω, perf. ὄδωδα, sb. ὀδμή, ὀσμή (regularly obj., but Democritus used ὀδμή and vb. ὀδμάομαι for sense-perception; cf. Diel, Fragmenta der Vorsokratiker 1. p. 387), ὀσφραίνομαι, fut. ὀσφρήσομαι, aor. ὠσφρόμην, sb. ὄσφρησις, fr. *ὀδσ-φρη-; second part : Skt. *ghrā-* 'smell'; Lat. *olēre* (> OIt. *olere*, OFr. *oloir*, Sp. *oler*), with cpd. *odefacere* (Festus), *ol(e)facere*, sbs. *olfactus* (> Sp. *olfato*), *odor* (> It. *odore*, Fr. *odeur*; Sp. *olor* with *l* fr. vb.), whence *odorārī* (> It. *odorare*), *odorātus* (> It. *odorato*, Fr. *odorat*); Lith. *uosti* (1sg. *uodžiu*), Lett. *uost*; Arm. *hot* (sb., obj.), *hotim* (vb., subj.).

2. Grk. μυρίζω 'rub with ointment' (deriv. of μύρον 'ointment, perfume'), late μυρίζομαι 'be fragrant with', whence NG μυρίζω (pop. 'smell' both subj. and obj.), μυρίζομαι (lit. 'smell' subj.). Hence also, fr. aor. form, Bulg. *miriš*, SCr. *mirisati*, and, fr. a parallel aor. ἐμύρωσα (: μυρόω), late ChSl. *mirosati*, Rum. *mirosi*, sb. *miros*. NG μυρωδιά formed to late Grk. μυρώδης, cpd. of μύρον and the root of ὄζω (above, 1), parallel to εὐώδης 'fragrant', etc.

3. Lat. *fragrāre*, VLat. *flagrāre* (> OFr. *flairier* obj., but Fr. *flairer* subj. 'take a smell of, try to recognize by the smell'), prob. : OHG *bracko* 'hunting dog', MHG *bræhen* 'smell'. Walde-P. 2.192. Ernout-M. 385. Walde-H. 1.540. REW 3476. Wartburg 3.746 f.

Fr. *sentir*, also and orig. 'perceive, feel' (15.11), with early specialized use for 'smell', whence ME *sent*, NE *scent*.

4. Ir. *bolad*, NIr. *boladh*, whence vbs. Ir. *boltigur*, *boltanaigim* (with vbl. n. *boltanud*, *boltanugud*; for latter as 'sense of smell', cf. Anc. Laws 3.348.11 ff., an important passage for words denoting the sense-perceptions), NIr. *boltnuighim*, etym. dub., perh. : Lett. *buls* 'heavy, steamy air'. Walde-P. 2.189. For 'smell' vb. obj. Ir. *bolad* or *boltunud* with *tic-cim* 'come', NIr. *boladh* with vb. 'be', as *tā boladh uaidh*, lit. 'there is a smell from it'.

W. *arogl*, new sg. to older *aroglau* taken as pl. (Morris Jones, 199), this fr. **are-wo-clou-* : *clywed* 'perceive by the senses' (15.11). Hence vb. *arogli*. Loth, RC 40.359.

Br. *c'houez*, whence *c'houesa* vb. and sb., and phrase *kaout c'houez*, lit. 'have a smell', same word as *c'houez* 'breath' : W. *chwyth* 'breath, blast', Ir. *sētim* 'blow', etc. Pedersen 2.627 f.

5. Goth. *dauns* (mostly = ὀσμή, but = ὀσφρησις 2 Cor. 12.17) : ON *daunn* mostly 'bad smell', *daunsna* 'smell of, sniff at', deriv. of IE **dheu-* in Skt. *dhū-* 'shake', Grk. θέω 'rush, storm', ChSl. *dunąti* 'blow', Skt. *dhūma-*, Lat. *fūmus* 'smoke, vapor', etc. Walde-P. 1.835 ff. Feist 116 f.

ON *þefr* 'smell' (also 'taste'), with vbs. *þefa*, *þefja* (cf. also Norw. *tev*, vb. *teva* 'smell') : OE *þefian* 'pant, be heated', Lat. *tepor* 'warmth', Skt. *tapas-* 'heat', etc. Development of 'smell' (and 'taste') through the steaming of cooking food. Walde-P. 1.719. Falk-Torp 1251.

ON *ilmr*, mostly 'good smell' (vs. *daunn* 'bad smell'), but also 'smell', *ilming* or *ilmingar vit* 'sense of smell', with vb. *ilma*, etym.?

Dan. *lugt*, Sw. *lukt*, whence vbs. *lugte*, *lukta*, fr. MHG *lucht* 'air, breath, smell' (as Du. *lucht* also sometimes 'smell') = NHG *luft* 'air', etc. (1.71). Falk-Torp 661. Hellquist 593.

OE *stincan* (obj.), *gestincan* (subj.), with sb. *stenc*, OHG *stincan*, sb. *stank*, all used for 'smell' in general (the restricted application to bad smells as in NE *stink*, *stench*, NHG *stinken*, *gestank*, being later), prob. : Goth. *stiggan* 'hit, collide with', ON *støkkua* 'spring, leap', through the notion of something that hits one, strikes one forcibly (cf. Icel. *hniss* 'unpleasant smell or taste' : ON *hnīta* 'to strike'). Some prefer to assume a more complicated development through 'break up into small particles, vaporize, exhale'. Walde-P. 2.617. Falk-Torp 1168. Franck-v. W. 667.

OE *swæcc, swec* (also 'taste'), vb. *gesweccan*, OS *swec*, OHG *sweche*, vb. *swehhan* 'smell, stink' : W. *chweg* 'sweet, pleasant', *cwaeth* 'taste', etc. Walde-P. 2.521.

ME *smelle*, NE *smell*, sb. and vb. : LG *smelan*, Du. *smeulen* 'smolder', Flem. *smoll* 'hot', NE *smoulder*, outside connections dub., but English development through 'steam, vapor', as in NHG *riechen*. Walde-P. 2.691. Franck-v. W. 626.

OHG *riohhan* 'give forth smoke, steam or smell', sb. *rouh*, then for 'smell' also subj. MHG, NHG *riechen*, sb. MHG *rouch, geruch*, NHG (*rauch* 'smoke') *geruch*, Du. *ruiken*, sb. *reuk* : OE *rēc* 'smoke', *rēocan* 'give forth smoke or steam', NE *reek*, outside connections dub. Weigand-H. 2.585. Franck-v. W. 562.

MHG *smecken, smacken*, sb. *smac* 'taste' (15.31–34) are also used for 'smell' (both subj. and obj.), and so formerly and still dial. NHG *schmecken, schmack*. Cf. Paul, Deutsches Wtb. s.v.

6. Lith. *uosti, uostyti*, Lett. *uost, uostīt*, see above, 1. Hence sbs. Lith. *uoslė* (also 'nostril'), Lett. *uoža, uožľa*.

Lith. *kvapas*, vb. *kvapéti* : Grk. καπνός 'smoke', Lat. *vapor* 'steam, vapor', etc. Walde-P. 1.379 f.

Lett. *smaka, smakuot*, fr. MLG *smak(e)* 'smell' and 'taste' (cf. 15.31). Mühl.-Endz. 3.950.

7. ChSl. *qchati*, sb. *qchanĭje* (both rare), *vonjati, obonjati*, sb. *vonja, obonjanĭje*, SCr. *vonjati, vonj, njuh*, Boh. *voněti, vůně*, Pol. *wąchać, węch, woń*,

Russ. *njuchat', obonjanie* (*vonjat'* 'stink', *von'* 'stench'), all fr. *on-, *on-s*, with or without the development of initial *v* (cf. Vondrák 1.214) : Skt. *an-* 'breathe', Grk. ἄνεμος 'wind', Lat. *animus* 'mind', *halāre* 'breathe', etc. Walde-P. 1.56 ff.

Boh. *páchnouti*, Pol. *pachnąć*, Russ. *pachnút'*, Boh., Pol., Russ. *zapach* : ChSl. *pachati* 'toss, fan', Russ. *páchnut'* 'blow', prob. fr. a root **pēr-* 'blow', perh. seen in some Gmc. words, as OE *fœs* 'fringe'. Walde-P. 2.67. Brückner 389.

Boh. *čichati*, sb. *čich* : *čiti* 'perceive, feel' (15.11), also with specialization to 'smell' (so freq. also Pol. *czuć*, as in Fr. *sentir*. Berneker 162.

8. Skt. *ghrā-*, with sb. *ghrāṇa-* (mostly obj., but also subj.; cf. Böhtlingk, Wtb. s.v.), see Grk. ὀσφραίνομαι, above, 1.

Skt. *gandha-* : Av. *ganti-* 'bad smell', OPers. *gasta-* 'offensive' (NPers. *gast* 'bad'), fr. a root seen in *gandh-* 'hit, injure', Lith. *gesti, gendu* 'spoil', etc. Walde-P. 1.672 f.

Av. *bud-* 'become aware of', 'feel' (hunger, etc.), and 'smell', sbs. *baoδa-baoδi-* 'good smell, fragrance' (cf. NPers. sb. *bū*, vb. *būidan* 'smell') : Skt. *budh-* 'be awake', 'become aware of'. Walde-P. 2.147. Barth. 917 f.

15.25, 26. Aristotle (De anim. 2.9) remarked on the lack of any independent classification of smells analogous to that of tastes (as 'sweet, bitter', etc.), and the situation is the same today. There is still neither an accepted scientific classification nor a popular classification reflected in common speech, that is truly distinctive of the sense of smell. The only widespread popular distinction is that of pleasant and unpleasant smells—good and bad smells, to use the briefest

terms—and this is linguistically more important than any similar distinction, that is of good and bad, in the case of the other senses. Otherwise, we have recourse to terms belonging primarily to other senses, especially taste (the actual confusion of smell and taste, the fact that certain 'tastes' really depend upon smell, is hardly a factor in this, it is too little known), as *sweet, acrid, pungent* (orig. of touch, 'pricking'), etc. Or else we describe the smell by naming the object which emits it, as the *smell of a rose*. Similar expressions are, of course, used of other senses, the *taste of an apple*, the *sound of a bell*, etc., but we are less dependent upon them, since there are at least some generic terms.

The Hindus enumerated nine kinds of smell, the Skt. terms (quoted in BR, s.v.)

gandha-) meaning 'desirable, undesirable, sweet, sharp, diffusive, compressed, smooth, rough, soft', none of them primarily distinctive of smell.

It has been argued by some that the lack of classification is due to the lack of distinctive linguistic terms. Quite the opposite is true. Such terms would have arisen had there been any obvious basis of grouping. The lack of them reflects the inherent difficulty of classification, which even modern science has not overcome. Cf. also Kretschmer, Glotta 19.209 f., in review of Weisgerber, Der Geruchsinn in unseren Sprachen, IF 46.121 ff.

To illustrate the words referring to good or bad smells the adjs. are chosen. The corresponding sbs. and vbs. are in most cases cognate with them.

15.25 GOOD SMELLING, FRAGRANT

Grk.	εὐώδης	Goth.	(*dauns wōpi*, sb.)	Lith.	*kvapus, kvapingas*
NG	μυρωδᾶτος	ON	*vel þefaðr, vel ilmaðr,*	Lett.	*smaršains, smardīgs*
Lat.	*fragrāns, odōrifer*		*þefgōðr*	ChSl.	*blagovonĭnŭ*
	(*suāvis*)	Dan.	*velluglende, duftende*	SCr.	*mirisav*
It.	*olezzante, fragrante,*	Sw.	*välluktande, doftende*	Boh.	*vonný*
	odorifero	OE	*wel-, swōtstincende*	Pol.	*wonny*
Fr.	*odoriférant*	ME	*wel, swote stinkinge*	Russ.	*dušistyj, blagovonnyj*
Sp.	*oloroso, fragante*	NE	*fragrant*	Skt.	*sugandhi-*
Rum.	*mirositor*	Du.	*welriekend, geurig*	Av.	*hubaoδi-*
Ir.	*boladmar, cumra*	OHG	*suozo stinkenti*		
NIr.	*cumhra*	MHG	*wol riechende*		
W.	*peraroglus*	NHG	*wohlriechend, duftend*		
Br.	*c'houez-vat*				

The majority of the words for 'fragrant' are derived from words for 'smell' (15.21–24), either with an adv. prefix 'well', 'sweet', or more often resting on a specialization of 'smell' to 'good smell'.

1. Grk. εὐώδης, cpd. of εὐ- 'well' and the root of ὄζω 'smell'.

NG μυρωδᾶτος, deriv. of μυρωδιά 'smell' and 'good smell'.

2. Lat. *fragrāns* (> It. *fragrante*, OFr., NE *fragrant*, Sp. *fragante*); pple. of *fragrāre* 'emit a (good) smell'.

Lat. *odōrifer* (> It. *odorifero*, Sp. *odorífero*, Fr. *odoriférant*), cpd. of *odor* 'smell' (15.21) and *ferre* 'bear', lit. 'smell-bearing', but mostly of good smells.

Sp. *oloroso*, fr. VLat. **odōrōsus* (It. *odoroso*, OFr. *odoreux*, NE *odorous*), reformed fr. *olor* (15.21).

It. *olezzante*, fr. *olezzare* 'be fragrant' (whence also *olezzo* 'fragrance'), as if VLat. **olidiāre* formed to *olēre* after the analogy of forms like *baptidiāre* for Grk. βαπτίζω. REW 6055.

Rum. *mirositor*, deriv. of *mirosi* 'smell'.

3. Ir. *boladmar*, fr. *bolad* 'a smell', with *mōr* 'great' used to form adjs. (cf. *nert-mor* 'strong', Gall. *Nertomarus*).

!r. *cumra*, NIr. *cumhra*, cf. Ir. *cumrad* 'sweet herbs', *cumraide* 'sweet' (K. Meyer, Contrib. 565), etym.? (Macbain 113 *com-rae*, but?).

W. *peraroglus*, fr. *perarogl* 'fragrance', cpd. of *per* 'sweet' and *arogl* 'smell'.

Br. *c'houez-vat*, cpd. of *c'houez* 'smell' and *mat* 'good'.

4. Goth. *dauns wōpi* (renders Grk. εὐωδία sb.), cf. *dauns* 'smell', and *wōpeis* (only in this phrase) : OE *wēpe*, OS *wōthi*, OHG *wuodi* 'pleasant', root connection? Feist 572.

ON *vel þefaðr, vel ilmaðr*, Dan. *vellugtende*, Sw. *välluktande*, OE *welstincende, swōtstencende*, ME *wel stinkinge, swote stinkinge* (both in Chaucer; or with older pple. *stinkende*, later *swete* instead of *swote*), Du. *welriekend*, OHG *suozo stinkenti* (quotable?, cf. vbl. *suazo stinkent*, Otfr.), MHG *wol riechende*, NHG *wohlriechend*, cpds. of adv. 'well' or 'sweetly' with pples. of vbs. for 'smell'.

ON *þefgōðr*, cpd. of *þefr* 'smell' and *gōðr* 'good'.

NE *fragrant*, above, 2.

Du. *geurig*, fr. *geur* 'smell' and esp. 'fragrance', MDu. *gōre, göre* id., MLG *gōre* 'fermentation, odor of fermentation', prob. fr. the root in OE *gist* 'yeast', OHG *jesan*, NHG *gären* 'ferment', Grk. ζέω 'boil', etc. Franck-v. W. 192, 201.

NHG *duftend* (> Dan. *duftende*, Sw.

doftande), pple. of *duften* 'emit fragrance', deriv. of *duft* 'fragrance' (in this sense > Dan. *duft*, Sw. *doft*), also 'fine mist', fr. MHG *tuft*, OHG *duft* 'mist', fr. ON *dupt* 'dust, pollen', Skt. *dhūpa-* 'vapor, incense', *dhūma-* 'smoke, vapor', Lat. *fūmus* 'smoke', Goth. *dauns* 'smell', etc. Falk-Torp 163. Weigand-H. 1.387. (Otherwise, fr. **dumft* : *dampf* 'steam', etc., Kluge-G. 116).

5. Lith. *kvapus, kvapingas*, orig. merely 'smelling', then esp. 'fragrant' : *kvapas* 'smell'.

Lett. *smaršains, smaršīgs*, fr. *smarša* '(good) smell' (OLith. *smarstas*); also *smardīgs*, fr. *smards* '(good) smell' (Lith. *smardas*, ChSl. *smradŭ*, etc. 'stench'), all : Lett. *smirdēt* 'stink', *smirdīgs* 'stinking', etc. (15.26). Mühl.-Endz. 3.954.

6. ChSl. *blagovonĭnŭ* (Supr.), Russ. *blagovonnyj*, cpds. of *blagŭ* 'good' and deriv. of ChSl. *vonja* 'smell', Boh. *vůně*, Pol. *woń* (15.23), whence Boh. *vonný*, Pol. *wonny*, orig. 'smelling', then 'fragrant'.

SCr. *mirisav* or *mirisan* (also *miomirisan*, with *mio* 'dear'), fr. *mirisati* 'smell'.

Russ. *dušistyj*, fr. *dušit'* 'choke, stifle', refl. 'perfume oneself' : *duch* 'breath, spirit', etc. (4.51).

7. Skt. *sugandhi-*, fr. *su-gandha-* 'fragrance', cpd. of *su-* 'good' and *gandha-* 'smell'.

Av. *hubaoδi-*, also sb. 'fragrance', cpd. of *hu-* (= Skt. *su-*) and *baoδi-* 'fragrance', : *bud-* 'smell'.

15.26 BAD SMELLING, STINKING

Grk.	δυσώδης	Goth.	*fūls*	Lith.	*smirdqs, dvokus*
NG	βρωμερός, βρώμικος	ON	*illa þefaðr, illa il-*	Lett.	*smirdīgs*
Lat.	*foetidus, pūtidus*		*maðr, fūll*	ChSl.	*smradĭtī* (vb.), *smra-*
It.	*puzzolente*	Dan.	*stinkende*		*dū* (sb.)
Fr.	*puant*	Sw.	*stinkande*	SCr.	*smrdljiv, smradan*
Sp.	*hediondo*	OE	(*fūl*)*stincende, fūl*	Boh.	*smrdutý, smradlavý*
Rum.	*puturos*	ME	*stinkinge*	Pol.	*śmierdzący, smrodlivy*
Ir.	*brēn*	NE	*stinking*	Russ.	*vonjučij, smradnyj*
NIr.	*brēan*	Du.	*stinkend*	Skt.	*durgandhi-, pūti-*
W.	*drewllyd*	OHG	(*ubilo*)*stinkenti, fūl*	Av.	*dužganti-, paošišta*
Br.	*flaerius*	MHG	*stinkende*		(superl.)
		NHG	*stinkend*		

Some of the words for 'bad smelling, stinking' are derived from words for 'smell' (15.21–24) with an adv. prefix 'ill', or from such as have been specialized to 'bad smell'. But there are more words of independent origin.

1. Grk. δυσώδης, cpd. of δυσ- 'ill', parallel to εὐώδης (15.25).

NG βρωμερός, βρώμικος, derivs. of βρῶμα 'stench' : late Grk. βρῶμος 'stench', βρωμώδης 'stinking', βρῶμα in medical writers 'decay' in the tooth, fr. the root of βιβρώσκω 'devour, eat' (5.11), but in the special (attested) sense of 'eat away, cause decay'.

2. Lat. *foetidus* (> It. *fetido*, Fr. *fétide*, NE *fetid*), vb. *foetere* 'stink' (> Sp. *heder*, whence, as if VLat. **foetibundus*, Sp. *hediondo*; REW 3408), prob. fr. same root as *fimus* 'dung', *suf-fīre* 'fumigate, scent'. Walde-P. 1.837. Walde-H. 1.499.

Lat. *pūtidus* : *pūtēre* 'be rotten, stink' (> It. *putire*, Fr. *puer*, Rum. *puţi*, whence adj. Fr. *puant*, Rum. *puturos*; VLat. **pūtum* > It. *puzzo* 'stink', whence *puzzare* 'stink', *puzzolente* 'stinking') : Lat. *pūs*, Grk. πύος 'pus', Grk. πύθομαι, Lith. *pūti* 'rot', Skt. *pū-* 'stink', Goth. *fūls* 'stinking', OE *fūl* 'stinking, foul', etc. Walde-P. 2.82. Ernout-M. 826. REW 6876, 6880.

3. Ir. *brēn*, NIr. *brēan* : W. *braen* 'rotten', prob. fr. the root in Lat. *marcēre* 'wither, shrink, be weak', Lith. *mirkti* 'be soaked', etc. Walde-P. 2.282. Pedersen 1.125. Stokes 220.

W. *drewllyd*, fr. *drew* (old) 'stench', *drewi* 'stink, rot', etym.?

Br. *flaerius*, fr. *flaeria* 'stink', *flaer* 'stench', with dissim. (as in Fr. *flairer*, etc.) fr. Lat. *fragrāre* 'emit a smell' (cf. *fragrāns* 'fragrant', 15.25). Loth, Mots lat. 168.

4. Goth. *fūls* (only *fūls ist* = ὄζει 'stinks', Jn. 11.39), ON *fūll*, OE, OHG *fūl*, orig. (and later mostly) 'rotten, foul', but often with reference to the odor rather than to the state of decay : Lat. *pūtidus*, etc. (above, 2).

ON *illa þefaðr, illa ilmaðr*, OE *fūl-stincende*, OHG *ubilo stinkenti* (quotable?, cf. sb. *ubile stank*, Notker), phrases and cpds. with 'bad', or 'foul' and pples. of the vbs. for 'smell'; but in line with the tendency which ultimately prevailed in the West Gmc. words ('smell' to 'stink') the pples. are early found alone with pejorative sense, so OE *stincende*, ME *stinkinge* (early *stinkende*), NE *stinking*, Du. *stinkend* (Dan. *stinkende*, Sw. *stinkande*, with vbs. *stinke, stinka* fr. LG), OHG *stinkenti*,

5. Lith. smirdȩs (pple. of smirdḗti 'stink'), Lett. smirdīgs (smirdēt 'stink'); ChSl. smr̆dȇti 'stink', with corresponding vbs. in modern Slavic, whence adj. forms, SCr. smrdljiv, Boh. smrdutý, Pol. śmierdzący; sb. ChSl. smradŭ, etc., with adjs. SCr. smradan, Boh. smradlavý, Pol. smrodliwy, Russ. smradnyj, perh. : Lat. merda 'excrement, dung'. Walde-P. 2.691. Walde-H. 2.74 f. Brückner 532.

Lith. dvokas, and vb. dvokti 'stink' : dvėkti 'breathe', dukti 'rage', Lett. dukt 'roar, rage', etc., fr. an extension of the root seen in Goth. dauns 'smell' (15.23). Walde-P. 1.838.

6. ChSl. smr̆dȇti, etc., above, 5.

Russ. vonjučij, fr. von 'stench' : ChSl. vonja, etc. 'smell' (15.24).

7. Skt. durgandhi-, Av. dužganti-, cpds. of duṣ- 'ill, bad' and Skt. gandha- 'smell', Av. ganti- 'stench' (parallel to Skt. su-gandhi- 'fragrant', 15.25).

Skt. pūti-, Av. paošišta- (superl. of an adj. *paoša-) : Skt. pū- 'rot, stink', Av. pu- 'rot', etc., cf. Lat. pūtidus (above, 2). Barth. 818.

15.31–34 TASTE

	15.31 vb. subj.	15.32 vb. obj.	15.33 sb. subj.	15.34 sb. obj.
Grk.	γεύομαι	phrase	γεῦσις	χῡμός
NG	γεύομαι (lit.), δοκιμάζω	phrase	γεῦσις	γεῦσις
Lat.	gustāre	sapere	gustātus, gustus	sapor
It.	gustare	sapere, aver gusto	gusto	gusto, sapore
Fr.	goûter	avoir du goût	goût	goût, saveur
Sp.	gustar	saber, tener gusto	gusto	sabor
Rum.	gusta	avea gust	gust	gust
Ir.	blaisim	phrase with blas	mlassacht	mlas, blas
NIr.	blaisim	phrase with blas	blas, blaiseacht	blas
W.	chwaethu, blasu	phrase with blas	chwaeth	chwaeth, blas
Br.	tañva, blaza	blazet	blas, tañva	blas
Goth.	kausjan		(kustus)	
ON	bergja			þefr, dãmr
Dan.	smage	smage	smag	smag
Sw.	smaka	smaka	smak	smak
OE	byrgan	smæccan	smæcc	smæcc
ME	smakke, taste	smakke, taste	taste	smak, taste
NE	taste	taste	taste	taste
Du.	smaken	smaken	smaak	smaak
OHG	smecchen	smecchen	smac	smac
MHG	smecken, entseben	smecken	smac	smac
NHG	schmecken, kosten	schmecken	geschmack	geschmack
Lith.	ragauti	turėti skoni, būti skonio	ragavimas	skonis
Lett.	baudit	garšuot	garša	garša
ChSl.	vŭkusiti		vŭkusŭ	vŭkusŭ
SCr.	okusiti, kušati	imati okus	okus	okus
Boh.	okusiti	chutnati, miti chut'	chut'	chut' (okus)
Pol.	kosztować	smakować	smak	smak
Russ.	vkusit', otvedat'	imet' vkus	vkus	vkus
Skt.	svad-, ras-	svad-, ras-	rasendriya- (?)	rasa-

15.31–34. The distinction between the subj. and the obj. aspects (cf. above, pp. 1017 f.) of taste is shown in the table. But some further explanations are required. Of the vbs. listed under 15.31 the majority may be used for both notions 'perceive by the sense of taste' and 'take a taste of', but several only in the latter sense, as NHG kosten, NG δοκιμάζω, etc. In some languages there is no distinctive vb. for 'taste' in the former sense, which must be expressed by a phrase with a vb. for 'perceive, notice' or the like. The words that mean 'take a taste of' are from, and most of them (but not NHG kosten, which is now definitely special-ized) still used also for, the notion of 'try, make trial of' (9.98). Besides those listed, other vbs. for 'try' may, of course, be used with reference to taste, as NE try (this wine), NHG probieren, etc.

Of all the five senses, 'taste' is the one most closely associated with fine discrimination, hence the familiar secondary uses of words for 'taste, good taste' with reference to aesthetic appreciation.

The obj. notion is the earlier and more important for the sb. use and also underlies many of the vbs. But in several languages there is no vb. for the obj. notion (NE it tastes of, tastes good), which is expressed by 'have a taste', or other

phrases like 'be sweet', 'seem sweet' = 'taste sweet', etc.

The secondary use of sbs. for 'taste' in the sense of fine appreciation, as in NE has good taste is widespread, as in NE taste (NED s.v. 8 with antecedents 6, 7), Fr. goût, and by semantic borrowing from Fr. goût, also NHG geschmack, Russ. vkus, etc.

1. IE *ĝeus-, in words for 'taste' in Grk. and Lat., mostly 'try' or 'choose' in Gmc. and Celtic, 'enjoy' in Indo-Iranian. Semantic development fr. 'taste' to 'try, choose' and 'enjoy' or the converse fr. 'try' to 'taste' and 'enjoy' is equally possible. Walde-P. 1.568 f. Ernout-M. 439. Walde-H. 1.628 f.

Grk. γεύομαι, sb. γεῦσις; Lat. (fr. pple. *gusto-) gustāre (> It. gustare, Fr. goûter, Sp. gustar, Rum. gusta) sb. gustus (> It., Sp. gusto, Fr. goût, Rum. gust) and gustātus; Goth. kiusan 'make trial of, prove' (renders δοκιμάζω) OE cēosan 'choose', Goth. kausjan 'taste of' (renders γεύομαι, in lit. sense Lk. 14.24, elsewhere as in 'taste of death'; sb. kustus quotable only as 'trial, proof'), OE costian 'try, prove, tempt', OHG kostōn 'try', MHG, NHG kosten 'taste of'; Skt. juṣ- 'enjoy, be pleased', Av. zaoša- 'pleasure'.

2. Grk. χῡμός, orig. 'juice' (: χέω 'pour'), hence 'taste' obj. in contrast to γεῦσις 'taste' subj. (cf. esp. Aristot., De anim. 2.10), which in NG has both values.

Grk. δοκιμάζω 'make trial of, approve' (9.98), in NG 'make trial of' and 'taste', but only in sense of NHG kosten. For 'taste' = 'perceive by taste' NG γεύομαι lit., with no pop. substitute.

3. Lat. sapere, 'taste' obj. and 'be wise, know' (VLat. *sapēre > It. sapere, Sp. saber still 'taste' obj. beside 'know', Fr. savoir 'know'), sb. sapor (> It. sapore, Fr. saveur, Sp. sabor; NE savor fr. OFr. savur) : OE sefa 'under-standing, mind, sense', OHG inseffan 'perceive', MHG entseben 'perceive' and esp. 'taste'. Walde-P. 2.450 f. Ernout-M. 894.

4. Ir. mlas, blas (whence blaisim), W. blas (whence blasu), Br. blaz (whence blaza) : Russ. molsat' 'suck, gnaw', Boh. mlsati 'nibble, eat dainties'. Walde-P. 2.300. Pedersen 1.163. Stokes 221. In general, the vbs. are subj. and the sbs. mostly obj., but occasionally quotable in the subj. sense (e.g. NIr. blas in Keating, Three Shafts 1556; ref. given by M. Dillon).

The obj. 'it tastes' is usually expressed by a phrase with blas, e.g. NIr. tá blas 'there is a taste', W. y mae blas arno 'there is a taste on it'; but Br. with pass. pple. of blaza, as blazet (mat, fall) eo 'it tastes (good, bad)', lit. 'it is (good, bad) tasted'.

Derivs. of Ir. blaisim, used for the 'act of tasting' and in part at least for the sense, Ir. mlassacht (RIA Contrib. s.v.), blaisecht, NIr. blaiseacht (used for the sense?), also Ir. mlaissiud (Thes. 2.255.17), NIr. blaiseadh.

W. chwaeth (whence chwaethu) : W. chweg, Br. c'houek 'sweet', OE swæcc 'smell, taste', etc. (15.23). Walde-P. 2.521.

Br. tañva, MBr. taffhaff : MW tafaw, tavaw, Corn. dava 'feel of', these (not : teod, W. tafod 'tongue', as Henry 260, Stokes 127) fr. *tam-, perh. : Lat. temptāre 'feel, try'. Loth, RC 32.18 ff.

5. Goth. kausjan, above, 1.

ON bergja (sb. -bragð as 'taste' in late cpds.), OE byrgan perh. (with different extensions of *bher-) : Grk. φορβή 'fodder, food', Skt. bharv- 'devour'. Walde-P. 2.164.

ON sb. þefr 'smell' (15.23) also 'taste'.

ON dãmr, (obj. 'taste'; Norw. daam 'taste, smell, appearance'), prob. orig.

'vapor', fr. root *dhem- in Skt. dham- 'blow', etc. Falk-Torp 131.

OE smæcc, smæccan (NE smack, smatch), OHG smac, -smahhēn, smecchen, MHG smecken, smacken, smac (also 'smell', cf. 15.21–24), NHG geschmack, schmecken, Du. smaken, smaak (Dan., Sw. forms fr. LG), all most commonly in the obj. sense : Lith. smaguriai 'dainties', smagus 'pleasing' and prob. (init. sm/m) Lith. mégti 'be pleasing', méginti 'try'. Walde-P. 2.689. Falk-Torp 1075 f. Weigand-H. 2.745.

ME tast, taste, vb. taste(n), used both of 'touch' and 'taste', NE taste, fr. OFr. tast, vb. taster (Fr. tâter) 'feel of' (15.72).

6. Lith. ragauti, sb. ragavimas (act of tasting and sense of taste), etym.? Walde-P. 2.366.

Lith. skonis, orig. 'good taste' (not in Kurschat, where only vb. skonéti 'have a good taste', and šmokas for 'taste') : skanus 'good tasting', outside connections? Leskien, Ablaut 373.

Lett. baudīt 'try, taste', prob. : Lith. budéti 'be awake', Skt. budh- 'be awake, be conscious of, perceive', Av. bud- 'perceive, smell', Grk. πεύθομαι 'learn of', etc. Leskien, Ablaut 294. Mühl.-Endz. 1.266 f.

Lett. garša (whence vb. garšuot) : gards, Lith. gardus 'good tasting', perh. Skt. gṛdh- 'be greedy', gardha- 'greed'. Mühl.-Endz. 1.602, 604. Adversely, Walde-P. 1.633.

7. ChSl. vŭkusiti, sb. vŭkusŭ, SCr. okusiti, okus, ukus, Boh. okusiti, okoušeti, okus, Russ. vkusit' (archaic), vkus, cpds. (SCr. also kušati) of kus- loanword fr. Goth. kausjan 'taste' (above, 1). Berneker 625 f. Stender-Petersen 372 f. Otherwise (as native Slavic : ChSl. kъsa-ti 'bite'), Brückner 284 f., KZ 42.351.

Boh. chutnati, sb. chut' (also 'desire') : Pol. chęc 'desire', etc., fr. a nasalized form of the root in ChSl. chotěti 'wish', etc. Berneker 399.

Pol. kosztować, fr. NHG kosten (above, 1). Brückner 260.

Pol. smak, vb. smakować, fr. MHG smac, smacken (above, 5). Brückner 503.

Russ. otvedat', cpd. of vedat' 'know'.

8. Skt. svad- 'make palatable', also 'taste well' and subj. 'taste, enjoy' : svādu- 'sweet', Grk. ἡδύς 'pleasant', etc. (15.35).

Skt. rasa- 'juice, sap, fluid' and esp. 'taste' (obj.), whence vb. ras- 'taste' : Lith. rasa, ChSl. rosa, Lat. rōs 'dew'. Walde-P. 1.149.

Skt. word for 'sense of taste', rasendriya-(?), cpd. of rasa- and indriya- 'sense' (15.11). So Monier-Williams, Eng.-Skt. Dict., but not in BR and perh. fictitious.

No Av. words for 'taste' quotable.

15.35–39. The Hindus recognized six principal varieties of taste with sixty-three possible mixtures (cf. BR s.v. rasa), the Greeks eight (Aristot., De anima 422^b11 f., Plut. 913 B, etc.). These included the four that are now regarded as fundamental, namely 'sweet', 'bitter', 'acid', 'salt', the words for which are discussed in the following. The others were 'pungent' (Grk. δριμύς, Skt. kaṭuka-), 'astringent' (Grk. στρυφνός, Skt. kaṣāya-), and, for the Greeks, 'rough, harsh' (αὐστηρός), 'oily, greasy' (λιπαρός), with the occasional addition of 'winy' (οἰνώδης).

There is considerable interchange of 'bitter' and 'acid' in cognate groups. More remarkable is a shift from 'salt' to 'sweet', evidently through 'seasoned'.

15.35 SWEET

Grk.	γλυκύς (ἡδύς)	Goth.	....	Lith.	saldus
NG	γλυκός	ON	sœtr	Lett.	salds
Lat.	dulcis (suāvis)	Dan.	søb	ChSl.	sladŭkŭ
It.	dolce	Sw.	söt	SCr.	sladak
Fr.	doux	OE	swēte, swōt	Boh.	sladký
Sp.	dulce	ME	swete, sote	Pol.	slodki
Rum.	dulce	NE	sweet	Russ.	sladkij
Ir.	milis	Du.	zoet	Skt.	madhura-, svādu
NIr.	milis	OHG	suozi		
W.	melys	MHG	suoze		
Br.	c'houek	NHG	süss		

Words for 'sweet' are freely used with reference to other senses than taste (as NE *sweet smell, sweet voice*), and for 'pleasing' in general. In some of the more generic use has become dominant (or is it the earlier?), and different words are more commonly used with especial reference to taste, as Grk. γλυκύς, Lat. *dulcis* vs. the old ἡδύς, *suāvis*.

1. IE *svādu-. Walde-P. 2.516 f. Ernout-M. 991 f.

Grk. ἡδύς, Dor. ἁδύς, in Hom. often of taste, but later mostly 'sweet' as 'pleasant', cf. ἥδομαι 'be pleased', ἀνδάνω 'be pleasing'; Lat. *suāvis* (*svādvi-s) 'sweet, pleasant', not esp. distinctive of taste, cf. *suādēre* 'advise, persuade' (fr. 'make please'); ON *sœtr*, OE *swēte, swōt*, OHG *suozi*, etc., general Gmc.; Skt. *svādu-* (mostly 'pleasant tasting'), with vb. forms of *svad-* 'make taste well, taste well', *svād-* 'be pleased', etc.

2. Grk. γλυκύς (cf. also γλεῦκος 'sweet new wine'), NG γλυκός, prob. by assim.

for *δλυκύς : Lat. *dulcis* (> Romance forms), but further relations of both obscure. Walde-P. 1.816. Ernout-M. 288. Walde-H. 1.380.

3. Ir. *milis*, loanword fr. W. *melys*, deriv. of W. *mel* 'honey' (5.84). Pedersen 1.23, 205; 2.22.

Br. *c'houek* (arch. W. *chweg*, Corn. *whek* id.) : W. *chwaeth* 'taste', OE *swæcc* 'taste, smell' (15.23). Walde-P. 2.521. Stokes 322.

4. Lith. *saldus*, Lett. *salds*, ChSl. *sladŭkŭ*, etc., general Balto-Slavic, 'sweet' fr. 'seasoned' : ON *saltr*, OE *sealt* 'salty', Goth., ON *salt* 'salt', etc. (15.36). Cf. the opposite change in Lith. *sudyti* 'to salt, pickle' : Skt. *svādu-* 'sweet', etc. Walde-P. 2.453. Trautmann 249.

5. Skt. *madhura-*, this (not *svādu-*, above, 1) the technical word in the list of tastes, deriv. of *madhu-* 'honey, mead' (5.84). Uhlenbeck 231. Walde-P. 2.261.

15.36 SALT (adj.)

Grk.	ἁλμυρός	Goth.	(salt, sb.)	Lith.	sūrus
NG	ἁρμυρός	ON	salt	Lett.	sāilts, sāligs, sūrs
Lat.	salsus	Dan.	salt	ChSl.	slanŭ
It.	salato	Sw.	salt	SCr.	slan
Fr.	salé	OE	sealt	Boh.	slaný
Sp.	salado	ME	salt	Pol.	slony
Rum.	sărat	NE	salt	Russ.	solenyj
Ir.	(goirt)	Du.	zout(ig)	Skt.	lavaṇa-
NIr.	sāillte, goirt	OHG	(salz, sb.)		
W.	hallt	MHG	(salz, sb.)		
Br.	sall	NHG	salzig		

Most of the adjs. for 'salt' are derivs. of the inherited sbs. for 'salt' (5.81). But in some cases words for 'bitter' are also used for 'salt'.

1. Derivs. of IE *sal-, *sal-d- 'salt', in Grk. ἅλς, Lat. *sāl*, Goth. *salt*, etc. (5.81). Walde-P. 2.452 f. Ernout-M. 888. REW 7521.

Grk. ἁλμυρός (cf. ἅλμη 'brine'), NG pop. ἁρμυρός; Lat. *salsus*, replaced in Romance by pples. of VLat. vb. *salāre* in It. *salare*, Fr. *saler*, etc., namely It. *salato*, Fr. *salé*, Sp. *salado*, Rum. *sărat*; NIr. *saillte* (pple.), W. *hallt* (fr. sb. *halen*), Br. *sall* (fr. vb. MBr. *sallaff*, fr. Fr. *saler*, Henry 238); ON *saltr*, Dan., Sw. *salt*, OE *sealt*, ME, NE *salt* (late ME *salti*, NE *salty*), Du. *zout* (*zoutig*).

2. An exception to the usual Gmc., to which Professor Wartburg called my attention, is the common Swiss use of *räss* 'sharp, biting' (OHG *rāzi*, MHG *ræze* 'wild, sharp, biting') instead of *salzig*. Cf. Schweizerisches Idiotikon 6.1271.

3. Ir. *goirt* 'bitter' (15.37), also 'salt'.

4. Lith. *sūrus* (*sūras* Kurschat) : Lett. *sūrs*, mostly 'bitter', but also 'salt', ChSl. *syrŭ* 'damp, raw', ON *sūrr*, etc. 'sour' (15.38). Walde-P. 2.513. Mühl.-Endz. 3.1134.

5. Skt. *lavaṇa-*, adj. fr. sb. *lavaṇa-* 'salt' (5.81).

15.37 BITTER

Grk.	πικρός	Goth.	baitrs	Lith.	kartus
NG	πικρός	ON	beiskr	Lett.	rūgts, sūrs
Lat.	amārus	Dan.	bitter	ChSl.	gorĭkŭ
It.	amaro	Sw.	bitter	SCr.	gorak
Fr.	amer	OE	biter	Boh.	hořký
Sp.	amargo	ME	biter	Pol.	gorzki
Rum.	amar	NE	bitter	Russ.	gor'kij
Ir.	serb, goirt	Du.	bitter	Skt.	tikta-
NIr.	searbh, goirt	OHG	bittar		
W.	chwerw	MHG	bitter		
Br.	c'houero	NHG	bitter		

Most of the words for 'bitter' are (through 'sharp, cutting, biting', etc.) from roots for 'cut, be sharp' or the like. Two groups are from 'burn' (cf. NE *hot mustard*, etc.). Others are connected with words meaning orig. 'sour, acid', etc.

1. Grk. πικρός, lit. 'pointed, sharp', hence of taste 'piquant, pungent, bitter, sour', hence πικραίνω 'make bitter' (fig. 'embitter') : Skt. *piç-* 'hew out, carve, adorn', etc. Walde-P. 2.9.

2. Lat. *amārus* (> It. *amaro*, Fr. *amer*, Rum. *amar*; Sp. *amargo* deriv. of *amargar* 'make bitter', fr. VLat. *amāri-*

cāre) : Du. *amper* 'sour, tart', Sw. *amper* 'pungent', OE *ompre*, OHG *ampfaro* 'sorrel, dock', Skt. *amla-, ambla-* 'sour', etc., perh. fr. an extension of the root in Skt. *āma-* 'raw', Grk. ὠμός 'raw, coarse', etc. Walde-P. 1.179. Ernout-M. 40. Walde-H. 1.35. REW 401, 406.

3. Ir. *serb*, NIr. *searbh*, W. *chwerw*, Br. *c'houero*, etym. dub., perh. (as *swerwo-*) : ON *sūrr*, etc. 'sour' (15.38). Walde-P. 2.513, and 1.503 (vs. Pedersen 1.78).

Ir. *goirt* 'bitter, sour, salt' (Dinneen), fr. *gor-ti* : ChSl. *gorĭkŭ*, etc. 'bitter', fr. the root in Ir. *gorim* 'heat, burn',

---

Slavic *gorěti* 'burn', etc., IE *gʷher-. Walde-P. 1.688. Pedersen 1.33. Berneker 332 f.

4. Goth. *baitrs*, ON *beiskr*, beside ON *bitr* 'sharp, biting, cutting' (NIcel. also 'bitter'), Dan., Sw. *bitter*, OE *biter*, etc., general Gmc., lit. 'biting' : Goth. *beitan* 'bite', ON *bíta* 'bite, cut', etc. Falk-Torp 76. Feist 77.

5. Lith. *kartus*, OPruss. (nom. pl.) *kārtai* : Skt. *kaṭu-* 'sharp, pungent', orig. 'cutting', fr. the root in Lith. *kirsti, ker-*

tu, 'cut, hew, chop', Skt. *kṛt-* 'cut', etc. Walde-P. 2.578.

Lett. *rūgts* : Lith. *rugštas* 'sour', Lett. *rugt*, Lith. *rugti* 'ferment', etc. (15.38). Mühl.-Endz. 3.568.

Lett. *sūrs* (also 'salt') : Lith. *sūrus* 'salt', etc. (15.36).

6. ChSl. *gorĭkŭ*, etc., general Slavic, see under Ir. *goirt*, above, 3.

7. Skt. *tikta*, lit. 'sharp', pple. of *tij-* 'be sharp, sharpen' : Av. *taēža-* 'sharp', Goth. *stiks* 'point', etc. Walde-P. 2.612 f.

15.38 ACID, SOUR

Grk.	ὀξύς	Goth.	....	Lith.	rugštas
NG	ὀξύς, ξινός	ON	sūrr	Lett.	skābs, skān'š
Lat.	acidus, acerbus	Dan.	sur	ChSl.	kyslŭ
It.	acido, agro	Sw.	sur	SCr.	kiseo
Fr.	acide, aigre, sur	OE	sūr	Boh.	kyselý
Sp.	ácido, agrio	ME	sour(e), egre	Pol.	kwaśny
Rum.	acru	NE	acid, sour	Russ.	kislyj
Ir.	(serb)	Du.	zuur	Skt.	amla-, çukta-
NIr.	searbh, gēar	OHG	sūr		
W.	sur, egr	MHG	sūr		
Br.	trenk, sur	NHG	sauer		

Several of the words for 'acid, sour' are like those for 'bitter', with which they are often cognate, from roots meaning 'point, sharp, cut' and the like. Some are 'acid' as 'soured, fermented'.

1. Grk. ὀξύς, lit. 'sharp, keen', hence of tastes 'sharp, acid, sour' (hence ὄξος 'vinegar', whence ὀξίνης, NG ξινός, pop. ξινός, cf. Hatzidakis, Μεσ. 2.116), Lat. *ācer* 'sharp', of tastes 'piquant', VLat. *acrus* (> Lat. *agro*, Fr. *aigre*, Rum. *acru*; deriv. Sp. *agrio*), Lat. *acidus* 'sour' (> It. *acido*, Fr. *acide*, NE *acid*, Sp. *ácido*), and *acerbus* 'sour', esp. in speaking of unripe fruits, etc. : Grk. ἄκρος 'topmost', ἄκρον 'point', ὄκρις 'point, edge', OLat. *ocris*, Umbr. *ocar* 'mountain', Skt. *açri-* 'point, edge', etc. Walde-P. 1.28 ff. Ernout-M. 7 ff. REW 92. Wartburg 1.18 f.

2. Fr. *sur*, fr. the Gmc., OHG *sūr*, etc. (below, 4).

3. NIr. *searbh* 'bitter' (15.37), also 'sour'. Ir. *serb* likewise?

NIr. *gēar* 'sharp' (15.78), also 'sour'.

W. *sur*, fr. OE *sūr*. Parry-Williams 30.

W. *egr*, prob. fr. ME *egre* (below, 4). Parry-Williams 116.

Br. *trenk* : W. *trwnc* 'urin, lye, stale' (Walde-P. 2.641). Henry 270. Ernault, Glossaire 715.

Br. *sur*, fr. Fr. *sur* (above).

4. ON *sūrr*, OE *sūr*, etc., general Gmc. (NE *sour* partly replaced by *acid* as generic term, but used esp. for what is very acid or fermented as in *sour milk*) : Lith. *sūrus* 'salt' (adj.), ChSl. *syrŭ* 'damp, raw', the latter perh. nearer the orig. meaning, cf. ON *sūreygr*, OE

sūrīege, etc. 'blear-eyed', and with ablaut ON *saurr* 'damp earth, dung'. Walde-P. 2.513. Falk-Torp 1206.

ME *egre* ('acid, pungent', hence also 'eager'), fr. OFr. *aigre* (above, 1). NED s.v. *eager*.

5. Lith. *rugštas* (Lett. *rugts* 'bitter') : *rugti, rukstu*, 'sour, ferment', *rugti, rugiu* 'belch', Lat. *ē-rūgere, rūctāre* 'belch', Grk. ἐρεύγομαι 'belch', etc. 'Sour, bitter' fr. 'fermented'. Walde-P. 2.357. Ernout-M. 874 f.

Lett. *skābs* (Lith. dial. *skobas* id.) : Lett. *skabrs*, Lith. *skabus* 'sharp', *skabēti* 'cut, hew, shoot forth (branches)', Lat. *scabere* 'scrape, scratch', etc. Walde-P. 2.563. Mühl.-Endz. 3.878 f.

Lett. *skān'š* : Lith. *skanus* 'good tasting', *skonis* 'taste' (15.34)? Mühl.-Endz. 3.879. Leskien, Ablaut 373.

6. ChSl. *kyslŭ*, etc., general Slavic, fr. the root of ChSl. *-kysnǫti*, Russ. *kisnut'*, etc. 'become sour', ChSl. *kvasŭ* 'leaven', *kvasiti* 'to sour' (hence Pol. *kwaśny* = Boh. *kvasný* 'fermented'), etc., prob. : Skt. *kvath-* 'boil', Goth. *hwaþō* 'foam'. Walde-P. 1.468. Berneker 678 f., 655 f.

7. Skt. *amla-* : Lat. *amārus* 'bitter' (15.37).

Skt. *çukta-*, fr. *çuc-* 'shine, glow, burn', suffer violent heat or pain, etc.', as 'burning (of taste)'. Walde-P. 1.378. Uhlenbeck 313.

	15.41	15.42	15.43	15.44
	HEAR	**LISTEN**	**'HEARING' (sb.)**	**SOUND (sb.)**
Grk.	ἀκούω (κλύω)	ἀκροάομαι	ἀκοή	ψόφος, ἠχή, ἦχος
NG	ἀκούω, γροικῶ	ἀφακράζομαι	ἀκοή	κρότος, ἦχος
Lat.	audīre	auscultāre	audītus	sonus
It.	se.ntire, udire	ascoltare	udito	suono
Fr.	en¦.endre	écouter	ouïe	son
Sp.	oír	escuchar	oído	sonido
Rum.	auzi	asculta	auz	sunet
Ir.	cluinim	con-(in-)tuasi (3sg.), éitsim	éitsecht	fogur, fūaim, glōr
NIr.	cluinim, cloisim	éistim	éisteacht	fuaim, glōr, foghar
W.	clywed	gwrando	clyw, clybod	sain
Br.	klevout	selaou	kleo	son
Goth.	hausjan		hliuma	
ON	hǫyra (heyra)	hlȳða	heyrn	hljōð
Dan.	høre	lytte	hørelse	lyd
Sw.	höra	lyssna	hörsel	ljud
OE	hȳran	hlystan, heorcnian	hlyst	swēg, hlēoþor, hlyn(n)
ME	here	lystne, herken	hering	soun
NE	hear	listen, harken, hark	hearing	sound
Du.	hooren	luisteren	gehoor	geluid
OHG	hō(r)ran	(h)losēn, hōrechen	gihōrida	(h)lūta
MHG	hoeren	hōrchen, losen	gehoerde	lūt
NHG	hören	horchen (lauschen)	gehör	laut
Lith.	girdēti	klausyti(s)	girdējimas	garsas
Lett.	dzirdēt	klausīt	dzirde	skan'a
ChSl.	slyšati	slušati	sluchŭ	zvękŭ, zvǫkŭ
SCr.	čuti	slušati	sluh	zvuk
Boh.	slyšeti	slouchati	hering	zvuk
Pol.	slyszeć	sluchać	sluch	dzvięk
Russ.	slyšat'	slušat'	sluch	zvuk
Skt.	çru-	ā-çru-, ā-ghuṣ-	çruti-, çrotra-	çabda-, svāna-, ghoṣa-
Av.	sru-		gūš-	

15.41–15.44. The verbs for 'hear', denoting the actual perception, may also be used for 'listen', especially in the imperative. But generally there are also distinctive words for 'listen'. Most of these are cognate with the words for 'hear', either those so used in the same language (NHG *horchen* : *hören*, NE *harken* : *hear*, Russ. *slušat'* : *slyšat'*) or in other languages (NE *listen*, etc. : Grk. κλύω, etc.). In a Celtic group 'listen' rests on the notion of 'be silent, be still', which elsewhere is a secondary association of 'listen' (cf. below, 4). Other secondary developments of 'listen' are 'listen for' > 'watch for, wait for' (OE *hlosnian*) and 'be attentive to', esp. 'obey' (Lat. *auscultāre*, NHG *gehorchen*, Dan. *lyde*, Sw. *lyda*, Lith. *klausyti*, ChSl. *poslušati*, etc.).

The nouns for 'hearing' are all cognate with the verbs for 'hear' or 'listen'.

The logical relation of 'sound' to 'hearing', parallel to that of obj. 'taste, smell' to subj. 'taste, smell', is partially reflected in speech, and some of the words for 'sound' are cognate with vbs. for 'hear'. But more often the sbs. derived from the latter reflect the use of 'hear' with reference to the hearing of speech and are restricted to articulate sound 'what is heard from speech', hence esp. 'report, news, fame' (Grk. κλέος, Skt. *çravas-*, ChSl. *slava*) or 'word' (ChSl. *slovo*, Av. *sravah-*). The majority of the words for 'sound' are independent of the 'hear' groups, many of them of imitative origin. Out of the great wealth of words for 'sound' or some special kind of sound (ringing, rattling, vocal, etc.), it is intended to list those that are generic, covering both inarticulate and articulate sounds, or those that are the most nearly generic (in a few cases the selection is doubtful). Words like NE *noise* (though its use has extended to cover most of the ground of *sound*, at least for inarticulate sound), Fr. *bruit*, NHG *geräusch*, *lärm*, etc., are not included.

Verbs for 'sound', parallel to those for the obj. 'smell' or 'taste', are not listed. Where they exist, they are obvious derivatives of the words for 'sound', as Grk. ψοφέω, Lat. *sonāre*, Fr. *sonner*, NE *sound*, NHG *lauten*, etc.

1. IE **k̑leu-*, **k̑leu-s-*. Widespread in vbs. for 'hear' or 'listen' (hence also 'obey', etc.), also 'be heard, be called, be famous', sbs. for 'hearing' and for what is heard, 'fame', 'word', etc. Walde-P. 1.494 f. Ernout-M. 192. Walde-H. 1.237 ff. Pedersen 2.494 f.

Grk. κλύω 'hear' (poet.), κλυτός 'heard, famous', κλέος 'report, fame, glory' (fr. κλέϝος = Skt. *çravas-* id., ChSl. *slovo* 'word'), κλέω 'make famous, celebrate', mid. 'be famous'.

Lat. *cluēre* (later also *cluere*) 'be called, be famous', *inclutus* 'famous'.

Ir. *ro-cluiniur*, *cluinim*, NIr. also *cloisim* (re-formed fr. vbl. n. *clos*, Ir. dat. *cluas*, etc.), W. *clywed*, Br. *klevout* 'hear', with sbs. W. *clyw*, *clybod*, Br. *kleo* 'hearing'.

Goth. *hliuma* 'hearing' (= ἀκοή 2 Cor. 12.17; pl. = ἀκοαί 'ears'), ON *hljōð* 'a hearing' (but not for sense of hearing) and 'sound', *hlȳða* 'listen', Dan. *lytte* 'listen' (for ODan. *lyde* now 'obey', as Sw. *lyda*; Falk-Torp 669, 672); for 'sound' Dan. *lyd*, Sw. *ljud*, OE *hlēoþor* (*gehlȳd* 'tumult'), OHG *(h)lūta*, *(h)liodar*, MHG *lūt*, NHG *laut*, Du. *geluid* (also OE *hlūd*, OHG *(h)lūt*, etc. 'loud', 15.45); OE *hlyst* 'hearing', and for 'listen' OE *hlystan* (*hlosnian* 'listen for, wait for'), ME *lystne*, NE *listen*, MLG *lūsteren* (> Dan. *lystre* 'obey', Sw. *lystra* 'attend to'), Du. *luisteren*, Sw. *lyssna* (cf. Hellquist 601), OHG *(h)losēn*, MHG *losen*, OHG *lustrēn* (NHG dial. *laustern*; NHG *lauschen* 'listen furtively' with sense influenced by another word; cf. Weigand-H. and Kluge-G. s.v.).

Lith. *klausyti(s)*, Lett. *klausīt* 'listen'.

ChSl. *slyšati* 'hear', *sluchŭ* 'hearing', whence *slušati* 'hear, listen', etc., general Slavic.

Skt. *çru-* (also *çruṣ-*), Av. *sru-* 'hear', with derivs. Skt. *çruti-*, *çrotra-*, 'hearing'.

Cf. also Toch. A *klots*, B *klotso* 'ear' (SSS 128 f.).

2. Grk. ἀκούω 'hear', sb. ἀκοή, Hom. ἀκουή 'hearing' and 'thing heard, report' (but not 'sound' in general), etym. much disputed. Prob. not ἀκ-ουσ- fr. ἀκ- 'sharp' and οὖς 'ear' (Kretschmer, KZ. 33.565, Falk-Torp 454, etc.), but *ἀ-κουσ- : Goth. *hausjan* 'hear', and both : Grk. κοέω 'perceive, notice', also 'hear', Lat. *cavēre* 'beware', ChSl. *čuti* 'recognize, notice', *po-čuti* 'perceive' (15.11), Skt. *kavi-* 'wise, a seer', etc. Walde-P. 1.369. Boisacq 37 f. Feist 252. Walde-H. 1.186.

Grk. ἀκροάομαι 'listen', fr. *ἀκρ-ουσ-, cpd. of ἄκρος orig. 'sharp' and οὖς 'ear'. Kretschmer, KZ 33.566. Hence also ἐπακροάομαι, whence (as if fr. ἀπο- and with φ by some analogy) NG ἀφακράζομαι with numerous local variants (cf. also Byz. ἀφκράζομαι in Chron. Mor.). 'Ιστ. Λεξ. 3.311 f.

Byz., NG γροικῶ in earliest use 'perceive, understand, recognize' (so ἐγροικῶ, γροικῶ in Chron. Mor.), now esp. 'hear', but also 'feel' (cold, etc.), fr. an adj. *ἀγροικός 'knowing, understanding' (so ἔγροικος Chron. Mor. 1341), this fr. class. Grk. ἄγροικος (fr. ἀγρός 'field') 'rustic, boorish', hence also 'ignorant', in this latter sense felt as a neg. cpd., whence *(ἀ)γροικός in the opposite sense. Hatzidakis, 'Επετηρίς 9(1912–13). 47 ff. 'Ιστ. Λεξ. 1.230 f.

Grk. ψόφος, the most generic class. word for 'sound' (ἀκοὴ ψόφου parallel to γεῦσις χυμοῦ, Aristot., De anim. 2.6), prob. of imitative origin.

Grk. ἠχή 'sound' (usual word in Hom.), later ἦχος as NG (lit.) : Lat. *vāgīre* 'cry, squall', with different extensions of an imitative **wā-*. Walde-P. 1.215. Ernout-M. 1070.

Grk. κρότος 'a rattling or clashing sound', in NG the usual word for any inarticulate sound, perh. : OE *hrindan* 'strike, hit', ChSl. *krotiti* 'tame', etc. Walde-P. 1.484.

3. Lat. *audīre* 'hear' (> It. *udire*, Sp. *oír*, Rum. *auzi;* Fr. *ouïr* now nearly obs.), sb. *audītus* 'hearing' (> It. *udito*, Fr. *ouïe*, Sp. *oído;* Rum. *auz*, back-formation fr. vb.), by itself most simply taken as fr. **aus-dh-* (cf. *auscultāre*) : Lat. *auris*, Grk. οὖς, Lith. *ausis*, etc. 'ear' (4.22), but perh. better (to help explain the difficult cpd. *oboedīre*) fr. **awis-dh-* : Grk. αἰσθάνομαι 'perceive', Skt. *āvis* 'openly', etc. (15.11), belonging ultimately to the same group. Walde-P. 1.17 f. Walde-H. 1.80. Ernout-M. 86.

Lat. *auscultāre* 'listen', VLat. *ascultāre* (> the Romance forms listed), cpd. of **aus-* : Lat. *auris* 'ear', etc., second part prob. fr. **cultos* by metath. fr. **clutos* : IE **k̑leu-* (above, 1). Walde-H. 1.86 f. REW 802.

Lat. *sonus* 'sound' (> It. *suono*, Fr. *son*, OSp. *sueno*, Rum. *sun;* Sp. *sonido* new deriv.; Rum. *sunet* fr. Lat. *sonitus*), with vb. *sonere*, *sonāre* (> It. *suonare*, Fr. *sonner*, Sp. *sonar*, Rum. *suna*) : Skt. *svan-* 'to sound, make a noise', sb. *svana-*, *svāna-* 'sound', etc. Walde-P. 2.524 f. Ernout-M. 956 f.

Fr. *entendre* 'hear', fr. Lat. *intendere* 'stretch out, direct one's attention to', whence 'understand' (as It. *intendere*, Sp. *entender*, and still in part Fr. *entendre*), then 'hear', replacing the old *ouïr*. REW 4483.

It. *sentire* 'perceive by the senses' (15.11) is used also esp. for 'hear', tending to replace *udire* in pop. speech.

4. Celtic words for 'hear' and W., Br. words for 'hearing', above, 1.

Ir. *con-tuasi*, *in-tuasi* (both 3sg.), MIr. *ēitsim*, NIr. *ēistim* 'listen', with vbl. n. MIr. *ēitsecht*, NIr. *ēisteacht* 'hearing', cpds. of *-tois-*, *-tuais-* (only in cpds.), fr. *tō* 'still, silent', as also W. *gwrando* 'listen' (*gwr-an-do*, cf. MW *an-daw* 'listen'), fr. *taw* 'silence' : Skt. *tuṣ-* 'be content', *tūṣṇīm* 'silently', etc. For the converse semantic relation, cf. ON *hljōð*, Dan. *lyd* 'sound' and 'silence', etc. (Falk-Torp 668). Walde-P. 1.714 f. Pedersen 2.651 f.

Br. *selaou* 'listen', MBr. *sezlou*, Corn. *golsowas*, *goslow*, etym.? Pedersen 1.489. Henry 245.

Ir. *fūaim*, NIr. *fuaim* 'sound', etym.? Walde-P. 1.215 (vs. Stokes 260).

Ir. *fogur*, NIr. *foghar* 'sound' (esp. of the voice), cpd. *fo-gur* : *gairim* 'cry out, call', *gāir*, W. *gawr* 'a cry', Grk. γῆρυς 'voice', etc. Walde-P. 1.537. Pedersen 2.536.

Ir., NIr. *glōr*, perh. same word as *glōir* 'glory' (fr. Lat. *glōria*), with development through 'noisy celebration' to 'noise, sound'. Macbain 198.

W. *sain* 'sound', back-formation to vb. *seinio*, deriv. of *son* (arch.) = Br. *son* fr. Lat. *sonus*. Pedersen 1.195, 375. Walde-P. 2.627.

5. Goth. *hausjan*, OE *hȳran*, etc., general Gmc. word for 'hear', prob. : Grk. ἀκούω 'hear', κοέω 'perceive', etc. See above, 2. Hence also for 'listen' OE *hercnian*, *hercnian*, ME *herken*, NE *harken*, *hark*, OHG *hōrechen*, MHG *hōrchen*, NHG *horchen*. Hence also for 'hearing' ON *heyrn*, Dan. *hørelse*, Sw. *hörsel*, ME *hering*, NE *hearing*, OHG *gihōrida* (also *gihōrnessī* Tat.), MHG *gehoerde*, NHG *gehör*, Du. *gehoor*.

Goth. *hliuma*, OE *hlyst* 'hearing', and Gmc. words for 'listen' and 'sound', above, 1.

OE *swēg* 'sound' : *swōgan* 'roar', Goth. *ga-swōgjan* 'groan', prob. Lith. *svagėti* 'resound, ring', Lett. *svadzēt* 'rattle', all of imitative orig. Walde-P. 1.215.

OE *hlyn(n)* 'sound, noise' : *hlimma* 'make a sound', Grk. καλέω, Lat. *clāmāre* 'call', etc. Walde-P. 1.444.

ME *soun*, NE *sound*, fr. Anglo-Fr. *soun* = OFr. *son*, fr. Lat. *sonus* (above, 3).

6. Lith. *girdėti*, Lett. *dzirdēt* 'hear', sbs. Lith. *girdėjimas*, Lett. *dzirde* 'hearing', Lith. *garsas* 'sound', prob. : Grk. γῆρυς (Dor. γᾶρυς) 'voice', Ir. *gāir* 'cry', etc., or to one of the similar imitative groups (Walde-P. 1.537, 591, 686). Mühl.-Endz. 1.552.

Lith. *klausyti(s)*, Lett. *klausīt* 'listen', above, 1.

Lett. *skan'a* 'sound', vb. *skanēt* : Lith. *skambėti* 'to sound, ring', further connections? Mühl.-Endz. 3.870.

7. ChSl. *slyšati* 'hear', *slušati* 'listen', *sluchŭ* 'hearing', etc., general Slavic, above, 1.

SCr. *čuti* 'hear' : ChSl. *čuti* 'feel, notice', etc. (15.11 and above, 2), with specialization to 'hear' also in Bulg., Ukr., etc. Berneker 162.

ChSl. *zvękŭ*, *zvąkŭ*, SCr., Boh., Russ. *zvuk*, Pol. *dźwięk* 'sound' (beside ChSl. *zvonŭ* 'sound', *zvĭněti* 'to sound', Russ. *zvon* 'ringing sound', Boh. *zvon*, Pol. *dzwon* 'bell') : Lith. *žvengti* 'neigh', *žvangėti* 'ring, rattle', etc., prob. of imitative orig. Walde-P. 1.642.

8. Skt. *çru-*, Av. *sru-*, above, 1.

Av. *gūš-* 'give ear, listen to' (Barth. *gaoš-* 485 f.) : Av. *gaoša-*, OPers. *gauša-* 'ear', Skt. *ghoṣa-* 'sound, noise', *ghuṣ-* 'to sound', but also *ā-ghuṣ-* 'listen to', *Hari-ghoṣa-* 'Yellow-ear'. No clear connections outside of Indo-Iranian, so uncertain whether the subj. 'hearing' or the obj. 'sound' is the earlier. Walde-P. 1.569.

Skt. *çabda-* (the generic and technical word for 'sound'), perh. as *çab-da-* : Skt. *çap-* 'curse', ChSl. *sopĭcĭ* 'flute-player', Russ. *sopet'* 'snuffle', etc., an imitative group. Walde-P. 1.457.

Skt. *svana-*, *svāna-* 'sound' : Lat. *sonus* (above, 3).

15.45 LOUD

Grk.	*μέγας*	Goth.	*(mikils)*	Lith.	*balsus, garsus, didis*
NG	*δυνατός*	ON	*hār*	Lett.	*skan'š, skal'š*
Lat.	*magnus, clārus*	Dan.	*høj*	ChSl.	*(velĭjĭ)*
It.	*forte, alto*	Sw.	*hög*	SCr.	*glasan*
Fr.	*fort, haut*	OE	*hlūd*	Boh.	*hlasitý*
Sp.	*fuerte, alto*	ME	*loud(e)*	Pol.	*głośny*
Rum.	*tare*	NE	*loud*	Russ.	*gromkij*
Ir.	*ardd*	Du.	*luid*	Skt.	*ucca-, mahant-, bṛhant-, tāra-*
NIr.	*ard*	OHG	*(h)lūt*	Av.	*bərəzant-*
W.	*uchel*	MHG	*lut, hel*		
Br.	*uhel*	NHG	*laut*		

Nearly all the adjs. that are used to describe sound are words which primarily apply to other senses or other notions in general and only secondarily to sound or voice. Thus NE *sharp, harsh, soft, piercing, sweet, high, low, deep, faint*, etc., and similarly in other languages.

An important exception is NE *loud*, with its Gmc. cognates, and some of the other words for 'loud', though many of these too are from notions applied only secondarily to sound, as 'great', 'strong', 'high'.

There are no strictly distinctive words for the opposite of 'loud', which is generally covered by words for 'low', 'faint', 'gentle' or the like. But NHG *leise* (OHG *līso* 'gently') has come to be used mainly in relation to sound, as the opposite of *laut*. Paul, Deutsches Wtb. s.v.

1. OE *hlūd*, OHG *hlūt*, *lūt*, etc., general WGmc., fr. **k̑lū-to-* orig. 'heard' or 'to be heard' beside **klu-to-* in Grk. κλυτός 'famous', Skt. *çru-ta-* 'heard', fr. **k̑leu-* 'hear' (15.41).

2. Lat. *clārus* ('clear, loud' of sound, hence also 'clear, bright' of vision) : *clāmāre* 'call, cry out', *calāre* 'proclaim, summon', Grk. καλέω 'call, name', OE *hlāwan*, OHG *(h)lōian* 'bellow', etc., also OHG *gi-hel* 'consonans', MHG *hel* 'loud, resounding', also of vision 'clear, bright', NHG *hell*, with vbs. OHG *hellan* 'resound, echo', etc. Walde-P. 1.443 f. Ernout-M. 193.

3. Lett. *skal'š* : Lith. *skalyti* 'bark, bay', ON *skjalla* 'clash, clatter', OE *scellan* 'sound, make a noise', etc. Walde-P. 1.445. Mühl.-Endz. 3.870.

4. Derivs. of sbs. for 'sound', 'voice' or some special sound.

Lith. *balsus*, fr. *balsas* 'voice' (18.11); Lith. *garsus*, fr. *garsas* 'sound' (15.44); Lett. *skan'š*, fr. *skan'a* 'sound' (15.44); SCr. *glasan*, Boh. *hlasitý*, Pol. *głośny*, fr. Slavic *glasŭ* 'voice' (18.11); Russ. *gromkij*, fr. *grom*, ChSl. *gromŭ* 'thunder' (1.56).

5. Words for 'great, large' (12.55). Grk. μέγας, Lat. *magnus* (rendered lit. in this sense in the Gospel translations, by Goth. *mikils*, ChSl. *velĭjĭ*, OE *micel*, OHG *mihhil*, perh. mere semantic borrowings); Lith. *didis*; Skt. *mahant-*.

6. Words for 'strong' (4.81). NG δυνατός, It. *forte*, Sp. *fuerte*, Fr. *fort*, Rum. *tare*.

7. Words for 'high' (12.31). It. *alto*,

Fr. *haut*, Sp. *alto* (esp. of the voice, speech, etc.); Ir. *ardd*, NIr. *ard*, W. *uchel*, Br. *uhel;* ON *hār*, Dan. *høj*, Sw. *hög;* Skt. *ucca-*, and *bṛhant-*, Av. *bərəzant-*.

8. Skt. *tāra-* 'loud, shrill', also sb. 'a loud, shrill tone', orig. 'piercing', fr. *tṛ-* 'pass, cross', like other derivs. of IE **ter-* applied to sound, as Grk. τορός 'piercing' (of sound and sight), Ir. *tairm* 'noise', OPruss. *tārin* 'voice', Lith. *tarti* 'say', etc. Walde-P. 1.744.

	15.51 SEE	15.52 LOOK (vb.), LOOK AT	15.53 SIGHT (subj.)	15.54 SIGHT (obj.), LOOK (obj.), APPEARANCE
Grk.	ὁράω, ὄψομαι, εἶδον, δέρκομαι	βλέπω, σκέπτομαι	ὄψις, ὅρᾶσις	ὄψις, θέα
NG	βλέπω, εἶδα	κοιτάζω	ὄψις, ὅρασις	ὄψις, θέα
Lat.	*vidēre*	*aspicere*	*vīsus*	*aspectus, speciēs*
It.	*vedere*	*guardare, mirare*	*vista*	*vista, aspetto*, etc.
Fr.	*voir*	*regarder* (*mirer*)	*vue*	*vue, aspect*, etc.
Sp.	*ver*	*mirar*	*vista*	*vista, aspecto*, etc.
Rum.	*vedea*	*se uita*	*vedere*	*vedere*
Ir.	*ad-cīu*	*dēccu, fēchaim, sellaim*	*rodarc, imcaissiu*	*ēcosc*
NIr.	*(do-)chim*	*fēachaim, dearcaim*	*radharc, amharc*	*fēacham, radharc*
W.	*gweled*	*edrych, syllu*	*golwg*	*golwg, drych*
Br.	*gwelet*	*sellet*	*gwel(et)*	*gwel(et)*
Goth.	*saihwan*	*saihwan(wlaitōn)*	*siuns*	*siuns*
ON	*sjā*	*līta*	*sjōn (sȳn)*	*sȳn*
Dan.	*se*	*se paa*	*syn*	*udseende, syn*
Sw.	*se*	*se på, blicka*	*syn*	*utseende, syn*
OE	*sēon*	*wlītan, lōcian, scēawian*	*gesiht, sȳn*	*wlite, gesiht*
ME	*seen*	*loke*	*sighte*	*sight, lok(es)*
NE	*see*	*look*	*sight, vision*	*appearance, look(s), sight*
Du.	*zien*	*aanzien, kijken*	*geziht*	*aanzien*
OHG	*sehan*	*scouwōn*	*gisiht*	*gisiht, gisiuni*
MHG	*sehen*	*schouwen*	*gesiht*	*gesiht*
NHG	*sehen*	*schauen, blicken, ansehen*	*gesicht*	*aussehen*
Lith.	*matyti, regėti*	*žiūrėti (veizdėti)*	*matymas, regėjimas*	*išvaizda*
Lett.	*redzēt*	*skatīt, lūkuot*	*redze*	*izskats, veids*
ChSl.	*viděti, zĭrěti*	*žĭrěti,ględati, sŭmotriti*	*zĭrěnĭje*	*zrakŭ, vidŭ*
SCr.	*viditi*	*gledati*	*vid*	*vid*
Boh.	*viděti*	*hleděti, patřiti, dívati se*	*zrak*	*vid*
Pol.	*widzieć*	*patrzeć, spojrzeć*	*wzrok*	*wygląd*
Russ.	*videt'*	*smotret', gljadet'*	*zrenie*	*vid*
Skt.	*dṛç-, paç-, īkṣ-*	*dṛç-, īkṣ-, ava-lok-*	*dṛṣṭi-*	*dṛç-*
Av.	*vaēn-, darəs-*	*dī-*		

15.51–15.54. The majority of the words for 'see' belong to certain inherited groups, pointing to a variety of IE roots used for 'see', but doubtless with some differentiation of application which is now beyond our ken.

The words for 'see', denoting the actual perception, may also be used for 'look, look at', especially in the imperative. But nearly always there are distinctive expressions for the latter notion, or at least such as are mainly so used. These are mostly different words, but in some cases only cpds. or phrases containing the words for 'see' (as NHG *ansehen*, Dan. *se paa*). However, the differentiation is not always so marked as in NE *see* and *look*. A gradual shift from 'look' to 'see' is observed in the history of Grk. βλέπω.

Several of the words for 'look' rest on the notion of 'watch, guard', and this has led further to 'see' in Grk. ὁράω. Some have come, through weakening of an intermediate 'stare at, gaze at', from 'wonder at' or 'forget oneself'.

The dependence of sight upon light is reflected in several words for 'see' or 'look' that are cognate with others for 'light, shine', etc.

Words for the subj. 'sight' are nearly all derivs. of the verbs for 'see', or in some cases 'look'. Many of these are also used for the obj. 'look, appearance' of something. But this latter may also be expressed by different derivs., including some (as NHG *aussehen*, Dan. *udseende*) that rest on the vbs. for the obj. 'look, have the appearance', or even by words that have no orig. connection with the notion of sight, as NE *appearance*. Some words that orig. denoted precisely this notion of 'look, appearance' have been widened to 'form, kind', as Grk. εἶδος, Lat. *speciēs*. Some of the words listed here appear also under 'form' (12.51), and conversely several of the words listed there may be used for 'appearance'. In fact, there is such a variety of expressions for 'look, appearance' that the selection is for some languages difficult, and a few of those listed under this head (15.54) are most commonly used with some more special application, as It. *vista*, etc., esp. to the 'view' of a landscape, It. *aspetto*, Fr. *aspect*, esp. to the 'looks, aspect' of a person. NE *sight* is used objectively (*a strange sight*, etc.) but is now obsolete for the characteristic 'look, appearance' of something (cf. NED s.v. I. 3).

The verbs for the obj. 'look, have the appearance, appear, seem' are not listed. This notion is logically related to the subj. 'see' or 'look' in the same way as the obj. to the subj. 'smell' or 'taste', and in part is expressed by forms of, or related to, the vbs. for 'see' or 'look'. Thus Lat. pass. *vidērī*, ON *sȳnask* (refl. of *sȳna* 'show', deriv. of *sȳnn* 'visible'), NHG *aussehen*, Lett. *izskatīt*, SCr. *izgledati*, etc. But the same notion may be arrived at from quite other points of view. Thus Grk. φαίνομαι, pass. of φαίνω 'make appear, show' : Skt. *bhā-* 'shine', etc.; NHG *scheinen*, also and orig. 'shine' (OHG *scīnan*, OE *scīnan* 'shine', etc.); It. *parere*, Fr. *paraître*, Sp. *parecer*, Rum. 3sg. *pare*, NE *appear*, fr. Lat. (*ad-*)*parēre* 'be present, appear, be manifest', etc.; It. *sembrare*, Fr. *sembler*, fr. Lat. *simulāre* 'make like, pretend'; ME *seme*, NE *seem*, fr. OE *sēman* 'be suitable' (cf. NE *beseem*), orig. 'be like' : NE *same*, Grk. ὁμός 'same', Lat. *similis* 'like', etc.

1. IE **weid-* in words for 'see' (Grk., Lat., Balto-Slavic) and 'know' (Grk., Celtic, Gmc., Balto-Slavic, Indo-Iranian). It is probable that the meaning 'know' is a secondary development starting in the perf. (Grk. οἶδα, Goth. *wait*, Skt. *veda*) as 'have seen' > 'know', but the view that 'see' is only a specialization of 'know', or that both notions are based on a common 'recognize', is also held. Walde-P. 1.236 ff. Ernout-M. 1104 ff. Here only the words for 'see, look, sight'.

Grk. aor. εἶδον, NG εἶδα, with derivs. εἶδος 'appearance, form, kind', etc.; Lat. *vidēre* (> It. *vedere*, Fr. *voir*, Sp. *ver*, Rum. *vedea*), deriv. *vīsus* 'sight' (subj.; in this sense replaced in Romance by new derivs., It., Sp. *vista*, Fr. *vue*, fr. pples., Rum. *vedere* old infin.); Lith. *veizdėti* 'look' (obs.), Lett. *viedēt* 'see' (but in rather special uses, cf. Mühl.-Endz. 4.652), *veids* 'appearance' (Lith. *veidas* 'face'); ChSl. *videti*, etc., general Slavic for 'see', with sbs. for 'sight' or 'appearance', ChSl. *vidŭ*, SCr., Boh.,

Russ. *vid* (Pol. *wid* obs. except in a phrase).

2. IE **derk̂-*. Walde-P. 1.806 f.

Grk. δέρκομαι, δέδορκα, ἔδρακον 'see, look, gaze', poet. only; Ir. *ad-con-darc*, used as perf. of *ad-cīu* 'see', NIr. *dearcaim*, W. *edrych* 'look, behold', Ir. *rodarc* 'sight' (subj.), NIr. *radharc* 'sight' (subj., obj.), W. *drych* 'sight (obj.), appearance', here also Ir. *derc* 'eye'; Skt. *dṛç-* reg. word for 'see' except in pres. (*paç-*), deriv. *dṛṣṭi-* 'sight' (subj.), *dṛç-* 'sight (obj.), look, appearance' (cf. *tādṛç-* 'such, like'), Av. *darəs-* 'see, gaze on' (much less common for 'see' than *vaēn-*).

3. IE **spek̂-*. Walde-P. 2.659 f. Ernout-M. 960 ff.

Lat. *specere*, *spicere*, mostly in cpds., of which for simple 'look' esp. *aspicere*, whence *aspectus* sometimes for subj. 'sight', usually obj. 'look, appearance', as also *speciēs;* Grk. σκέπτομαι (for *σπέκτομαι) 'look carefully', later 'consider'; OHG *spehōn* 'look at carefully', NHG *spähen*, etc. (NE *spy* through OFr. *espier*); Skt. *paç-* (*spaç-* in some forms), usual word for 'see' in present, Av. *spas-* 'look upon, observe, regard'.

4. IE **okʷ-*, much more widespread in words for 'eye' (Grk. ὄσσε, ὄμμα, etc., Lat. *oculus*, Skt. *akṣi*, etc., 4.21) than in vb. forms. Walde-P. 1.169 ff. Ernout-M. 697 f.

Grk. ὄψομαι, serving as reg. fut. to ὁράω, also perf. ὄπωπα (poet.), with deriv. ὄψις 'sight' (subj. and obj.); Skt. *īkṣ-* 'see, look, observe' (desid. form), Av. *aiwi-ākš-* 'watch over' (Barth. 311).

5. IE **leuk-*, ultimately the same as in words for 'light, bright', Lat. *lūx*, Grk. λευκός, etc. Walde-P. 2.411.

Grk. λεύσσω 'look at, behold'; W. *golwg* 'sight' (**upo-luc-*, cf. Pedersen 1.122); Lett. *lūkuot* 'look at, observe' (Lith. *laukti* 'wait for, expect', OPruss. *laukīt* 'seek'); Skt. *lok-* (esp. cpds.) 'look'.

6. Grk. ὁράω, 'see' and 'look', as orig. 'watch' : Hom. οὖρος 'watcher, guard', Att. φρουρός 'guard' (*προ-hopos), ἔφορος 'overseer, guardian, ruler', ὤρα 'care', θυρωρός 'doorkeeper', etc., these (either with secondary unexplained ', or fr. **swer-* beside **wer-*) : OE *waru* 'guarding, care', *wær* 'on guard, careful' (NE *ware, aware, beware*, etc. large Gmc. group), Lat. *verērī* 'feel awe of, revere', etc. Walde-P. 1.284. Boisacq 709 f. Ernout-M. 1089.

Grk. εἶδον, above, 1; ὄψομαι, ὄψις, above, 4; δέρκομαι, above, 2.

Grk. βλέπω (derivs. βλέμμα 'look, glance', βλέφαρον 'eyelid', etc., and dial. forms γλέπω, γλέφαρον), mostly 'look', sometimes intr. 'see, have power of sight', later also trans. 'look at' and 'see' (all these uses in NT), now the reg. pres. for 'see' in NG, etym.? Boisacq 122 f. For detailed discussion of the preceding Grk. words (also those for 'eye'), cf. A. Prévot, Rev. de phil. 61.133 ff., 233 ff.

NG κοιτάζω 'look, look at' (also spelled κυττάζω, based on a false etym.), in form = late κοιτάζω 'put to bed', 'fold' (cattle), etc., deriv. of κοίτη 'bed, lair', but in the meaning 'observe' (attested from 10th. cent. A.D.) reflecting Hellenistic κοιτῶ 'keep, guard', attested in Hellenistic cpds. used as military terms (ἐπικοιτῶ, παρακοιτῶ Polyb., προκοιτῶ Dio Cass., etc.), and the use of κοίτη as a military term for the quarters of the 'guard, watch' (κοίτη τῶν φυλακιτῶν in pap. of 3d. cent. B.C.; κοίτη alone in Aen. Tact., etc.). Semantic development as in Grk. ὁράω (above), It. *guardare*, Fr. *regarder* (below, 7), and Grk. τηρέω 'watch over, guard' and 'watch, observe', NG παρατηρῶ 'look at, observe,' pop. τήρα 'look!'. For history of the long discussion of κοιτάζω, cf. Χατζῆς, 'Αθηνᾶ

41.202 ff., Hatzidakis, 'Αθηνᾶ 46.3 ff., 178 ff.

Grk. θέα 'sight' (obj.), 'aspect' : θαῦμα 'wonder', etc. (16.15).

NG φῶς 'light', also 'sight' (subj.) in phrases, as ἔχασε τὸ φῶς του 'lost his sight'.

7. Lat. *vidēre*, etc., above, 1; *aspicere*, etc., above, 3.

It. *guardare*, Fr. *regarder* 'look', through 'watch', fr. Gmc. word for 'guard, watch', OHG *wartēn*, OE *weardian*, etc. REW 9502.

It. *mirare*, Sp. *mirar* (Fr. *mirer* arch. in this sense) 'look', through 'gaze with wonder', fr. Lat. *mīrārī*, *mīrāre* 'wonder at'. REW 5603.

Rum. *se uita* 'look', orig. 'forget oneself' (*uita* 'forget', 17.32), then 'forget oneself, be lost in gazing at something, stare, look'. Cf. Bulg. *zabravyam se* 'forget oneself, gape at', and Sp. *mirar* (above), NE *gape* orig. 'yawn' in *gape at* 'stare at', etc. REW 6015. Tiktin 1673. Sandfeld, Idg. Anz. 20.182, Ling. balk. 87.

8. Ir. *ad-cīu*, NIr. (*do-*)*chim* 'see', Ir. *dēccu*, 3sg. *do-ēcai* 'see' and esp. 'look' (cf. *nī dēccu darmmēsi* 'I look not behind me' Thes. 1.650, *dēcce lat corintiu* 'look at the Corinthians', Thes. 1.562), here also *imc(c)aisiu* 'sight' vbl. n. of *imm-accai* 'considerat', all fr. **kʷeis-*, prob. an extension of **kʷei-* in Skt. *ci-* 'notice, observe', Grk. τίω 'honor', etc. Pedersen 2.487 ff. Walde-P. 1.509.

Ir. *fēchaim*, NIr. *fēachaim* 'look', with vbl. n. *fēachain*, etym. dub. Pedersen 2.490.

NIr. *dearcaim*, W. *edrych* 'look', with sbs., above, 2.

W. *gweled*, Corn. *gweles*, Br. *gwelet* 'see', with sb. Br. *gwel(ed)* 'sight' (subj., obj.) : Ir. *fili* (gen. *filed*) 'poet' (orig. 'seer'), OE *wlītan*, ON *līta* 'look', etc. Walde-P. 1.293.

Ir. *sellaim*, *sillim*, W. *syllu*, Corn. *sylly*, Br. *sellet* 'look', with sbs. Ir. *sell* 'eye, pupil', Br. *sell* 'look' : Grk. στίλβω 'glitter'? Walde-P. 2.646. Pedersen 1.78 f. Stokes 313 f.

NIr. *amharc* 'sight' (subj.), perh. : Lith. *merkti* 'blink'. Zupitza KZ 36.235. Rejected by Walde-P. 2.274.

W. *golwg* 'sight' (subj., obj.), above, 5.

Ir. *ēcosc* 'sight' (obj.), abstract of **ind-com-sech-* (3sg. *inchosig*) 'point out' : Goth. *saihwan* 'see', etc. Walde-P. 2.477 ff. Pedersen 2.619 ff.

9. Goth. *saihwan*, ON *sjā*, OE *sēon*, etc., general Gmc. (with cpds. Du. *aanzien*, NHG *ansehen* 'look at'), with sbs. for 'sight', Goth. *siuns*, OE *gesiht*, *sȳn*, etc. : Ir. *sech-* in words for 'point out' and 'sight' (above, 8), IE **sekʷ-*, prob. the same ultimately as **sekʷ-* in words for 'say', Grk. ἐνέπω, Lat. *inseque*, *inquam*, etc., and also **sekʷ-* in words for 'follow', Grk. ἕπομαι, Lat. *sequor*, etc., though opinions differ in regard to the semantic starting-point and sequences. Walde-P. 2.476 ff., esp. 480. Feist 404 f. Buck, AJPh. 36.128 f.

ON *līta*, OE *wlītan* 'look' (Goth. *wlaitōn* 'look around', once; *wlits* 'face') : W. *gweled* 'see', etc. (above, 8), perh. also Goth. *wulþus* 'glory', Lat. *vultus* 'countenance'. Walde-P. 1.293. Feist 571, 577.

OE *lōcian*, ME *loke*, NE *look*, with sb. ME *lok*, NE *look* (obj., now more commonly pl. *looks*) : OHG *luogēn* 'spy on', outside connections dub. Walde-P. 2.381.

OE *scēawian* 'look at' (ME *shewe*, NE *show* with shift to caus. meaning, cf. NED s.v.), OHG *scouwōn*, MHG *scouwen*, NHG *schauen*, etc. : Grk. θυοσκόος 'one who inspects the sacrifices, priest', κοέω 'perceive', Lat. *cavēre* 'beware', etc. Walde-P. 1.370. Walde-H. 1.186 f.

NE *vision* 'sight' (subj.), in earliest ME use only for the obj. mystical 'vision' (cf. NED s.v.), fr. OFr. *vision*, Lat.

vīsiō 'sight' (subj.) and esp. obj. 'vision, apparition'.

ME *apparance*, NE *appearance*, fr. OFr. *aparance*, late Lat. *appārentia* 'becoming visible', deriv. of *appārēre* 'become visible, appear'. Cf. NED s.v., esp. 11.

Du. *kijken* 'peep, stare', but also commonly 'look' : ME *kike* 'peep', NE dial. *keek* (cf. NED s.v.), etc., doubtless fr. an exclamatory syllable, as are also the similar, but not identical, NE *peep*, Dan. *titte*, Sw. *titta*, NHG *gucken* 'peep' and colloquial for 'look' (*guck mal hin!*). Hellquist 1192.

NHG *blicken* (NHG or LG > Sw. *blicka;* Hellquist 78) 'look' (also 'gleam, shine'), fr. MHG *blicken*, OHG *blicchen* 'gleam, shine', beside sb. OHG *blicch*, MHG *blic* 'gleam, lightning', whence NHG *blick* 'glance, look', and through this the use of the vb. in sense of 'look'. Weigand-H. 1.253.

10. Lith. *matyti* 'see' : Lett. *matīt* 'feel, perceive, notice', ChSl. *sŭ-motriti*, Russ. *smotret'* 'look at, regard, consider', perh. Grk. ματεύω 'seek', etc. Walde-P. 2.239. Trautmann 171. Mühl.-Endz. 2.566.

Lith. *regėti*, Lett. *redzēt* 'see', with sbs. Lith. *regėjimas*, Lett. *redze* 'sight' (subj.), etym.? Walde-P. 2.366. Mühl.-Endz. 3.503.

Lith. *žiūrėti* 'look' : Lett. *zvērs* 'flashing', *zvēruot* 'gleam, glow', etc. Cf. on NHG *blicken*, above. Walde-P. 1.643.

Lith. *veizdėti* 'look' (common in the Trowitsch NT, where Kurschat has *žiūrėti*, but now obs.), Lett. *veids* 'appearance', above, 1. Hence (like NHG *aussehen*) *išvaizda* 'look, appearance' (NSB, etc.).

Lith. *išrodyti* 'point out', also 'have the appearance' (sb. *išroda* 'appearance' (in NSB; "unsuccessful neolog." Senn), cpd. of *rodyti* 'point out' = Lett. *rādīt* id., etym.? Mühl.-Endz. 3.495.

Lett. *lūkuot* 'look at, observe', refl. *lūkuoties* 'look', above, 5.

Lett. *skatīt* 'look, look at, observe', with sb. *izskats* 'appearance' : Lith. *skatytis* 'cast one's eyes around', etym.? Mühl.-Endz. 3.874 f.

11. ChSl. *viděti* 'see', etc., above, 1.

ChSl. *zĭrěti* 'look, see' (renders Grk. βλέπω in both senses; perfect. *uzĭrěti* usual for aor. and fut. of ὁράω; much interchange with *viděti*, Jagić, Entstehungsgesch. 329, 409), Boh. *zřiti*, Pol. *źrzeć*, Russ. *zret'* (all these now mostly obs., but cpd. Pol. *spojrzeć* 'look'), with numerous derivs. including some for 'sight', as ChSl. *zĭrěnĭje* (cf. *prozĭrěnĭje* 'recovery of sight', Lk. 4.19), Russ. *zrenie* (subj.), ChSl. *zrakŭ* (obj. 'appearance, form', in Gospels), Boh. *zrak* (subj.), Pol. *wzrok* (subj.), all : Lith. *žerėti* 'gleam, shine'. Walde-P. 1.602. Miklosich 401 f. Brückner 651, 656.

ChSl. *ględati*, SCr. *gledati*, Boh. *hleděti*, Russ. *gljadet'* 'look', Pol. *wyglądać* 'look (obj.), appear', sb. *wygląd* 'look, appearance' : OHG *glanz* 'gleaming', etc. Walde-P. 1.625. Berneker 302 f.

Boh. *dívati se* 'look' : *div*, ChSl. *divo* 'wonder', with development as in It. *mirare*, Sp. *mirar* 'look' (above, 7), much less probably with retention of an early relation to the notion 'shine', as assumed by Berneker 203 and Walde-P. 1.774.

Boh. *patřiti*, Pol. *patrzeć* 'look', also 'belong to' as SCr. *patriti*, etym.? Brückner 399.

ChSl. *sŭmotriti*, Russ. *smotret'* : Lith. *matyti* 'see' (above, 10).

12. Skt. *dṛç-*, etc., above, 2.

Skt. *paç-*, above, 3.

Av. *vaēn-*, OPers. *vain-* 'see' (most widespread Iran. word, represented in

Pahl., Sogd., NPers., Afgh., Osset., etc.), prob. : Skt. *ven-* 'long for' (fr. 'look for'?), further connections dub. Walde-P. 1.229.

Av. *dī-* 'look at, observe' (Barth. 724 f.), OPers. imperat. *dīdiy* 'look at', NPers. *dīdan* 'see' : Skt. *dhī-* 'perceive, notice' but mostly, with transfer to mental perception, 'think'. Walde-P. 1.831 f.

15.55 SHOW (vb.)

Grk.	δείκνῡμι, φαίνω	Goth.	*(at)augjan*	Lith.	*(pa)rodyti*
NG	δείχνω	ON	*vīsa, sȳna*	Lett.	*rādīt*
Lat.	*mōnstrāre, ostendere*	Dan.	*vise*	ChSl.	*pokazati, (j)aviti*
It.	*mostrare*	Sw.	*visa*	SCr.	*pokazati*
Fr.	*montrer*	OE	*ēawan, ætēowan*	Boh.	*ukazati*
Sp.	*mostrar*	ME	*shew*	Pol.	*okazać, pokazać*
Rum.	*arăta*	NE	*show*	Russ.	*pokazat', ukazat'*
Ir.	*taisfenim*	Du.	*toonen*	Skt.	*diç-, darçaya-*
NIr.	*taisbeanaim*	OHG	*zeigōn, ougen*	Av.	*dis-*
W.	*dangos*	MHG	*zeigen, zougen, zounen*		
Br.	*diskouez*	NHG	*zeigen*		

'Show' is virtually 'cause to be seen', and, in fact, the most common relationship of the terms is with words for 'see, look, eye, appear, shine'. A few are connected with words for 'wise' or 'know', hence orig. 'cause one to know'. In one case the development is 'stretch' > 'spread out' > 'display, show'. In the one inherited group (below, 1), if one takes into account all the derivs. (e.g. Skt. *diç-* 'direction, cardinal point, region', Lat. *digitus* 'finger', etc.), it seems likely that the primary notion was 'point (as with the finger), point out'.

1. IE *deiḱ-*. Walde-P. 1.776. Ernout-M. 265 ff. Walde-H. 1.348 f.

Here as 'show'. Grk. δείκνῡμι, NG pop. δείχνω; OHG *zeigōn*, MHG, NHG *zeigen;* Skt. *diç-*, Av. *dis-*; cf. in secondary senses Lat. *dīcere* 'say' (earlier sense in *index* 'pointer', *iūdex* 'judge', etc.), Goth. *ga-teihan* 'announce', OE *tīon*, OHG *zīhan* 'accuse'.

2. Grk. φαίνω 'bring to light, cause to appear, show', mid. 'appear' : Skt. *bhā-* 'shine', etc. (15.56). Walde-P. 2.123 f.

3. Lat. *mōnstrāre* (> It. *mostrare*, Fr. *montrer*, Sp. *mostrar*), fr. *mōnstrum* 'portent, monster', but through an earlier unrecorded sense like 'memorable object', fr. the root of *monēre* 'remind, advise', *meminī* 'remember', Skt. *man-* 'think', etc. Ernout-M. 629. REW 5665.

Lat. *ostendere*, fr. **obs-tendere*, cpd. of *tendere* 'stretch, spread out' (9.32).

Rum. *arăta*, etym. dub. REW 671. Tiktin 91. Puşcariu 108.

4. Ir. *taisfenim* (cf. *asfenim* 'testify'), NIr. *taisbeanaim*, cpd. of *fen-* : *fiad-* 'announce', *finn-* 'know', etc. Pedersen 2.517.

W. *dangos*, *dan-* as in *dan-fon* beside *an-fon* 'send' (Pedersen 2.302), but second part? Morris Jones 269 (very dub.).

Br. *diskouez*, fr. *dis-* and MBr. *goez* in *a-goez* 'publicly' : Grk. εἶδος 'appearance', etc. Henry 101. Pedersen 1.58.

5. Goth. *augjan*, *at-augjan*, OE *ēawan*, *æt-ēowan*, OHG *ougen*, OHG, MHG *z-ougen*, also MLG *t-ōnen*, Du. *toonen*, MHG *zounen*, all : Goth. *augō* 'eye', etc. Walde-P. 1.171. Feist 64. Franck–v. W. 702.

ON *vīsa*, Dan. *vise*, Sw. *visa* (OE *wīsian* 'show the way, guide, direct,'

OHG *wīsan*, MHG *wīsen*, NHG *weisen*, Du. *wijzen* 'show the way, direct, point', etc.), fr. adj. ON *vīss*, OE, OHG *wīs* 'wise' (17.21), hence orig. 'make one wise, knowing' (*put one wise* in U.S. slang). Falk-Torp 1387.

ON *sȳna* (but most common in refl. for 'show itself, appear, seem'), fr. *sȳnn* 'visible', *sȳn* 'sight, appearance' : Goth. *siuns* 'sight', etc., all derivs. of vb. for 'see', Goth. *saihvan*, etc. (15.51). Falk-Torp 1227.

ME *shew*, NE *show*, fr. OE *scēawian* 'look at' (15.52), with shift to caus. sense. NED s.v. *show*, vb.

6. Lith. *(pa)rodyti*, Lett. *rādīt*, perh. : ChSl. *raditi* 'care, be anxious', Goth. *garēdan* 'be mindful of', *rōdjan* 'speak', etc. (18.21). Mühl.-Endz. 3.495. Trautmann 235.

7. ChSl. *kazati*, mostly *pokazati*, etc., this or other cpds. of *kazati* general Slavic : Skt. *kāç-* 'appear, shine', Av. *kas-* 'look at, see' (Barth. 459), with variant finals (*ĝ*, *ḱ*) of root. Walde-P. 1.511. Berneker 497.

ChSl. *aviti*, *javiti* (freq. in Gospels, etc.) beside adv. *avě*, *javě* 'openly' : Skt. *āvis*, Av. *āviš* 'openly', Grk. αἰσθάνομαι 'perceive', Lat. *audīre* 'hear', etc. Walde-P. 1.17. Berneker 34.

8. Skt. *diç-*, Av. *dis-*, above, 1.

Skt. *darçaya-*, caus. of *dṛç-* 'see' (15.51).

15.56 SHINE

Grk.	λάμπω, φαείνω, στίλβω	Goth.	*skeinan, liuhtjan, glitmunjan*	Lith.	*šviesti, žibėti, spindėti*
NG	λάμπω, γυαλίζω	ON	*skīna, lȳsa, glīta*	Lett.	*spīdēt, spīst*
Lat.	*lūcēre, nitēre, splendēre, candēre*	Dan.	*skinne, lyse*	ChSl.	*světiti, blĭštati, sijati, lĭštati sę*
It.	*rilucere, (ri)splendere, brillare*	Sw.	*skina, lysa, glänsa*	SCr.	*svijetliti(se), blistati, sjati*
Fr.	*briller, luire*	OE	*scīnan, līhtan, līxan*	Boh.	*svítiti, blýskati*
Sp.	*lucir, brillar*	ME	*schine, lihte*	Pol.	*świecić, błyszczeć*
Rum.	*străluci, luci*	NE	*shine*	Russ.	*svetit'sja, blistat', sjat'*
Ir.	*as-toidi* (3 sg.) *taitnim*	Du.	*schijnen, glansen*	Skt.	*ruc-, bhā-, dyut-, bhrāj-, çuc-*
NIr.	*soillsighim*	OHG	*scīnan, liuhten, glīzan*	Av.	*ruč-, brāz-, bā-*
W.	*disgleirio, llewyrchu*	MHG	*schīnen, liuhten, glīzen*		
Br.	*lugerni, skedi*	NHG	*scheinen, leuchten, glänzen*		

The majority of the words listed under 'shine' are used primarily of luminous bodies (*the sun shines*, etc.), and then also of things with surfaces which 'shine, gleam, glisten' with reflected light. But some are used only or mainly with either the former or the latter application. The number of words that may be used for 'shine, gleam, glisten', etc. is appallingly large, and only those that seem the most important are considered.

1. IE **bhā-*. Walde-P. 2.123 f.

Grk. φαίνω (partly 'shine', but esp. 'bring to light, show', mid. 'appear'), with sb. φάος 'light', whence Hom. φαείνω 'shine', φαεινός 'bright', Att. φῶς (gen. φωτός) 'light' whence φωτεινός 'bright' (φωτίζω mostly trans. 'light up'); Skt. *bhā-*, *bhās-*, Av. *bā-*.

2. IE **leuk-*, as in sbs. for 'light' (1.61). Walde-P. 2.408 ff. Ernout-M. 570 ff. Walde-H. 1.823 f. REW 5136. Falk-Torp 670.

Lat. *lūcēre* (> OIt. *lucere*, It. *rilucere;* VLat. **lūcīre* > Fr. *luire*, Sp. *lucir*, Rum. *luci* and with strengthening prefix *străluci*); NIr. *soillsighim* (fr. *soillse* 'light', 1.61), Br. *lugerni* (fr. *lugern* 'radiance'); Goth. *liuhtjan*, OE *līhtan* (and

leohtan), ME *lihte*, OHG, MHG *liuhten*, NHG *leuchten* (fr. a Gmc. **leuh-ta-* 'light'), ON *lȳsa*, Dan. *lyse*, Sw. *lysa*, OE *līxan* (fr. **leuh-sa-*); ChSl. *lĭštati sę* (**lĭsk-* for **lŭsk-* fr. **luk-sk-*, Berneker 750); Skt. *ruc-*, Av. *ruč-*.

3. Grk. λάμπω : λαμπάς, Lett. *lāpa* 'torch', OPruss. *lopis* 'flame', Ir. *lassaim* 'blaze', *lassair* 'flame', etc. Walde-P. 2.383. Boisacq 554.

Grk. στίλβω (of surfaces) with στίλβη 'lamp', στιλπνός 'glittering', etym. dub. (Ir. *sellaim* 'look at', etc.?). Walde-P. 2.646.

NG γυαλίζω 'shine, gleam' (of surfaces), fr. ὕαλος 'glass' (9.74).

4. Lat. *nitēre* (of surfaces), perh., beside *re-nīdēre* 'glitter, glisten, beam with joy', fr. a root **nei-* in Ir. *niam* 'luster', W. *nwyf* 'vivacity, animation', etc. Walde-P. 2.321. Ernout-M. 672.

Lat. *splendēre* (> It. *(ri)splendere*) : OLith. *splendėti* 'shine' (but not certainly attested), MIr. *liann* 'bright', W. *llathru* 'polish', fr. **(s)plēnd-*, perh. extension of **sp(h)el-* in Skt. *sphuliñga-* 'spark', etc. Walde-P. 2.679. Ernout-M. 966.

Lat. *candēre* (cf. the more common *candēns, candidus*) : Skt. *(ç)cand-* 'shine', *(ç)candra-* 'bright', etc. Walde-P. 1.352. Ernout-M. 442. Walde-H. 1.151.

It. *brillare* (> Fr. *briller*, Sp. *brillar*), OIt. 'turn, whirl', from an imitative *birl* (cf. NE *birl*, NED). REW 6522b. Otherwise (fr. the word for 'beryl') Diez 67, Wartburg 1.339.

5. Ir. *as-toidi* (3sg.), etym. dub., perh. : W. *tywydd* 'weather', and formally possible as cpd. **to-wid-*, fr. IE **weid-* 'see'. Pedersen 2.651 f.

Ir. *taitnim* (NIr. mostly 'please'), perh. fr. **to-aith-ten-* : *tene* 'fire' (1.81). Windisch 806. Macbain 358.

NIr. *soillsighim*, Br. *lugerni*, above, 2.

W. *disgleirio*, fr. *disglair* 'bright' (15.57).

W. *llewyrchu*, fr. *llewyrch* 'light, brightness, luster', corrupted for *llewych*, fr. **lug-iks-* (*-isk-* ?) : *go-leu*, Br. *goulou* 'light' (1.61). Pedersen 2.26. Morris Jones 109.

Br. *skedi*, fr. *sked* 'luster, brilliance', etym. dub. Henry 240.

6. Goth. *skeinan*, ON *skīna*, etc., general Gmc. : ChSl. *sijati*, *sinąti* 'shine', also ChSl. *sěnĭ*, Grk. σκιά, Skt. *chāyā-* 'shade, shadow' (1.63). Walde-P. 2.536. Falk-Torp 996. Feist 431 f.

Goth. *liuhtjan*, ON *lȳsa*, OE *līhtan*, etc., above, 2.

Goth. *glitmunjan* (for στίλβειν, Mk. 9.3), ON *glīta*, *glitra*, OE *glitenian*, OHG *glizinōn*, *glīzan*, MHG *glīzen* (NHG *gleissen*), etc., numerous other words for 'glitter, sparkle', etc., fr. **ghleid-*, beside **ghleis-* in OE *glisnian* (NE *glisten;* OFris. *glisia*, MHG *glistren* mostly 'sparkle', etc.), **ghlei-* in OE *glǣm* 'bright light', vb. ME *gleme*, NE *gleam*, and **ghlend-* in OHG, MHG *glanz* 'shining', whence OHG *glanzen*, MHG *glenzen*, NHG *glänzen* (> Du. *glansen*, Sw. *glänsa*), all extensions of the root **ghel-* seen in Ir. *gel*, NIr. *geal* 'bright, white' (15.64), Skt. *hari-* 'tawny, yellow', OE *geolo*, OHG *gelo* 'yellow', etc. (15.69). Walde-P. 1.624 ff. Falk-Torp 328 f.

7. Lith. *šviesti*, ChSl. *světiti*, general Slavic (in part refl.) : ChSl. *světŭ* 'light', Skt. *çveta-*, Av. *spaēta-*, Goth. *hweits* 'white', etc. (15.64). Walde-P. 1.470.

Lith. *žibėti* (Lett. *zibēt* 'lighten, glimmer') : Lith. *žiebti* 'light a fire', *žaibas* 'lightning', Lett. *zibt* 'glimmer', outside connections dub. Mühl.-Endz. 4.718.

Lith. *spindėti*, Lett. *spīdēt*, *spīst* (Lith. *spįsti* 'begin to shine'), perh. (semantic development similar to that in It. *brillare*) : Skt. *spand-* 'throb, palpitate, quiver'. Walde-P. 2.664. Mühl.-Endz. 3.1001.

8. ChSl. *světiti*, above, 7.

ChSl. *blĭštati*, etc., general Slavic : Lith. *blizgėti* 'glitter, flash', *blykšti* 'turn pale', OE *blīcan* 'glitter, dazzle, sparkle', ON *blīkja, blika* 'gleam, twinkle', OHG *blīhhan* 'turn pale', etc. Walde-P. 2.212. Berneker 63.

ChSl. *sijati*, SCr. *sjati*, Russ. *sjat'* : Goth. *skeinan*, etc. (above, 6).

ChSl. *lĭštati sę* (for στίλβω, Mk. 9.3), above, 2.

9. Skt. *bhā-, bhās-*, Av. *bā-*, above, 1.

Skt. *ruc-*, Av. *ruč-*, above, 2.

Skt. *dī-, dīp-* (*dīv-* mostly 'play'), and esp. *dyut-*, fr. IE **dei-, *deiw-, *dyeu-*, etc. in Grk. δέατο 'seemed', δέελος, δῆλος 'visible, plain', Skt. *dyāus* 'sky', Lat. *diēs* 'day', etc. Walde-P. 1.772 ff.

Skt. *bhrāj-*, Av. *brāz-* : Lith. *brėkšti* 'to dawn', Pol. *o-brzasknąć* 'become light', *brzask* 'dawn', Goth. *bairhts* 'bright', etc. Walde-P. 2.170.

Skt. *çuc-* (esp. 'flame, glow, burn') : Av. *suč-* 'burn, flame', outside connections dub. Walde-P. 1.378.

15.57 BRIGHT

Grk.	*λαμπρός, φαεινός, φαιδρός*	Goth.	*bairhts*	Lith.	*šviesus*
NG	*φωτερός, λαμπερός, γυαλιστερός*	ON	*ljōss, skǣrr, bjartr*	Lett.	*gaišs, spuožs*
Lat.	*clārus, lūcidus nitidus, splendidus, candidus*	Dan.	*lys, blank*	ChSl.	*světĭlŭ*
It.	*chiaro, lucido, brillante, risplendente*	Sw.	*ljus, blank*	SCr.	*svijetao, sjajan, jasan*
Fr.	*clair, brillant, luisant*	OE	*beorht, lēoht, scīr*	Boh.	*jasný, světlý*
Sp.	*claro, luciente, brillante, lustroso*	ME	*bright, lighte*	Pol.	*świetny, jasny*
Rum.	*strălucitor, luminos*	NE	*bright*	Russ.	*svetlyj, jarkij*
Ir.	*solus, sorche*	Du.	*helder*	Skt.	*çuci-, çukra-, dyumant-*, etc.
NIr.	*soillseach, glēineach, geal*	OHG	*beraht, lioht*	Av.	*raoxšna-, xšaēta-, bānvant-*, etc.
W.	*goleu, disglair*	MHG	*hel, berht(el), lieht*		
Br.	*sklaer, skedus, lugernus*	NHG	*hell, glänzend*		

Many of the adjs. for 'bright', like the vbs. for 'shine', are used both of luminous bodies or of anything that is 'light, full of light' (as the *bright sun, sky*, etc.) and of things with surfaces reflecting light (as *bright silver*, etc.), not to speak of the varied secondary applications to intelligence or disposition. But some of those listed are used only with reference to actual light and some only with reference to 'bright' surfaces and with still further idiomatic preferences according to the object described.

The majority of the words are related to those for 'light' (1.61) or those for 'shine' (15.56). Some are simply pples. of the latter, and many other such words for 'shining' might have been included as virtually equivalent to 'bright'.

1. Grk. λαμπρός (NG pop. only in fig. sense 'splendid'; in lit. sense λαμπερός) : λάμπω 'shine' (15.56).

Grk., Ion. φαεινός, Lesb. φάεννος, Att. φᾱνός, also φωτεινός, derivs. of φάος, φῶς 'light' (1.61), like φαείνω 'shine' (15.56).

Grk. φαιδρός (also 'gay, cheerful' as in NG) : Lith. *giedras* 'fair, clear, serene', *gaisas, gaisa*, Lett. *gaiss* 'reflected light in the sky', Lett. *dzīdrums* 'clearness', *gaišs* 'bright, clear', etc. Walde-P. 1.665. Boisacq 1010.

NG, beside φωτεινός, λαμπερός, also φωτερός new deriv. of φῶς 'light'. For 'bright' surfaces γυαλιστερός : γυαλίζω 'shine, polish', fr. ὕαλος 'glass'.

2. Lat. *clārus* (> It. *chiaro*, etc.), also and orig. of sound 'clear, loud' (15.45).

Lat. *lūcidus* (> It. *lucido*, etc.), deriv. of *lūx* 'light'.

Lat. *nitidus* (of surfaces) : *nitēre* 'shine'.

Lat. *splendidus* : *splendēre* 'shine'.

Lat. *candidus* : *candēre* 'shine'.

It., Sp. *brillante*, Fr. *brillant* : It. *brillare*, etc. 'shine'.

It. *(ri)splendente* : *(ri)splendere* 'shine'.

Sp. *luciente* : *lucir* 'shine'.

Sp. *lustroso*, deriv. of *lustre* (= It. *lustro*, OFr., NE *lustre*), fr. **lustrum*, back-formation to Lat. *lustrāre* 'make bright, illuminate' : *lūx* 'light', etc.

Rum. *strălucitor, lucitor* : *(stră)luci* 'shine'.

Rum. *luminos*, fr. Lat. *lūminōsus*, deriv. of *lūmen* 'light', or formed anew fr. *lumină* 'light'. Tiktin 931.

3. Ir. *solus*, with *soil(l)se* 'light', whence NIr. *soillseach*, fr. a cpd. of *so-* 'well' and **luk-s-*, fr. root of Lat. *lūcēre* 'shine', etc. Pedersen 1.351, 364.

Ir. *sorche*, that is *so-rche*, parallel to *do-rche* 'dark', formed with prefixes for 'good' and 'bad' (16.71, 16.72), second part dub., perh. : Grk. ῥέζω 'dye', Skt. *raj-* 'color'. Macbain 131.

NIr. *geal* 'white' (15.64), also 'bright'.

NIr. *glēineach*, apparently : *glē* 'clear, bright, perfect, pure', OE *glǣm* 'bright light', etc. (Walde-P. 1.626).

W. *goleu*, also sb. 'light' (1.61).

W. *disglair*, cpd. of *claer* 'clear, bright', orig. same word as *claear* 'lukewarm'? So Morris Jones 100, 385.

Br. *sklaer*, fr. Fr. *clair*, with init. *s* prob. fr. OFr. *esclairier* (Fr. *éclairer*). Henry 242.

Br. *skedus*, fr. *skedi* 'shine'.

Br. *lugernus*, fr. *lugerni* 'shine'.

4. Goth. *bairhts*, ON *bjartr*, OE *beorht*, ME, NE *bright*, OHG *beraht*, MHG *berht*, more often *berhtel* : W. *berth* 'fair, fine', Skt. *bhrāj-*, Av. *brāz-* 'shine', Hitt. *parkwis* 'pure'. Walde-P. 2.170. Feist 76 f.

ON *skǣrr* (Dan. *skær* 'sheer, pure', Sw. *skär* 'transparent') : ON *skīrr* 'pure, clear, bright' (as of water, glass, etc.), Goth. *skeirs* 'clear, plain', OE *scīr* 'bright, glittering, clear', fr. the root in Goth. *skeinan* 'shine', etc. Walde-P. 2.536. Falk-Torp 1008 f.

ON *ljōss*, Dan. *lys*, Sw. *ljus*, OE *lēoht* (use of NE *light* for 'bright' now obs.; cf. NED), OHG *lioht*, etc., adjs. to sbs. for 'light' (1.61).

ON *heiðr*, OE *hādor*, OHG *heitar* 'clear, bright' (esp. of the sky) : Skt. *citra-* 'conspicuous, clear, bright', Lith. *skaidrus* 'clear, bright', etc. Walde-P. 2.537. Falk-Torp 446.

Dan., Sw. *blank* (of surfaces), fr. MLG *blank* 'shining white' = OHG *blanc* 'shining white' (NHG *blank*), ON *blakkr* 'pale' : Lat. *flagrāre* 'flame, burn', Grk. φλέγω 'burn, blaze', etc. Walde-P. 2.215. Falk-Torp 80. Franck-v. W. 69.

MHG *hel*, NHG *hell*, MDu. *hel*, whence Du. *helder* (LG *heller*), all orig., like OHG *hel* 'clear, loud' of sound : Lat. *clārus*, etc. (15.45). Franck-v. W. 243. Weigand-H. 1.844.

5. Lith. *šviesus*, ChSl. *světĭlŭ*, SCr. *svijetao*, Boh. *světlý*, Pol. *świetny*, Russ. *svetlyj* : Lith. *šviesti*, ChSl. *světiti*, etc. 'shine'.

Lett. *gaišs* : Grk. φαιδρός (above, 1).

Lett. *spuožs* (also *spuods, spuodrs*) : *spīdēt* 'shine'. Mühl.-Endz. 3.1036.

6. ChSl. *světĭlŭ*, etc., above, 5.

SCr. *sjajan* : *sjati* 'shine'.

SCr. *jasan*, Boh. *jasný*, Pol. *jasny*

'bright' and 'clear' (Russ. *jasnyj* now mostly 'clear'), ChSl. *jasĭnŭ* 'clear', adv. *jasno* 'clearly', prob. : Lith. *aiškus* 'clear, plain', OLith. *iškus* id., Russ. dial. *jaska* 'bright star', Pol. *jaskry* 'blinding, sparkling', root connections dub. Walde-P. 1.2 (**ai-* 'burn, shine' ?). Berneker 276.

Russ. *jarkij* : *jaryj* 'burning, flashing', Pol. dial. *jarzyć się* 'glitter, shine', prob. also ChSl. *jarŭ* 'harsh, stern', Russ. *jaryj* 'furious, violent', etc., root connection dub. Walde-P. 1.197. Berneker 447 f.

7. Skt. *çuci-, çukra-* : *çuc-* 'glow, flame, burn' (15.56).

Skt. *dyumant-*, also *dyutimant-* (fr. *dyuti-* 'brightness') : *dyu-, dyut-* 'shine'.

Av. *raoxšna-* : *ruč-* 'shine'.

Av. *xšaēta-*, cf. *a-xšaē-na* 'dark-colored', etym. dub. Walde-P. 1.501. Barth. 541.

Av. *bānvant-, bānumant-*, fr. *bānu-* 'ray of light' : *bā-* 'shine'. Barth. 954.

15.61 COLOR (sb.)

Grk.	*χρῶμα*	Goth.	. . . .	Lith.	*spalva*
NG	*χρῶμα*	ON	*litr*	Lett.	*krāsa*
Lat.	*color*	Dan.	*farve (lød)*	ChSl.	. . . .
It.	*colore*	Sw.	*färg*	SCr.	*boja*
Fr.	*couleur*	OE	*bleo(h), hiew*	Boh.	*barva*
Sp.	*color*	ME	*colour, ble, hew*	Pol.	*farba, kolor, barwa*
Rum.	*coloare, față*	NE	*color (hue)*	Russ.	*cvet*
Ir.	*dath, lī*	Du.	*kleur, verf*	Skt.	*varṇa-, rañga-, rāga-*
NIr.	*dath, lī*	OHG	*farawa*	Av.	*gaona-*
W.	*lliw*	MHG	*varwe*		
Br.	*liv*	NHG	*farbe*		

'Color' is treated by Aristot., De anim. 418ª 27 ff. as the obj. parallel to the subj. 'sight', like 'sound' to 'hearing', etc.; and while 'color' is only one aspect (beside 'form, shape') of an object's 'look, appearance' (the true obj. notion parallel to 'sight'), it is the most conspicuous and one depending wholly on sight. Hence it is appropriate to discuss color words here, while those for the countless other objects of sight are distributed elsewhere, e.g. 'form, shape' under spatial relations.

Most of the words for 'color' reflect such notions as 'covering', 'surface, skin', 'countenance, look', or the 'hair' of animals, indicating that they were used primarily with reference to the color, the complexion of human beings, or the color of animals, which is that of their hair. But there is also a use of 'flower' for 'color', and some are connected with words used elsewhere of some special color.

1. Grk. χρῶμα (also χρόα, χροιά) : χρώς 'skin, surface', rarely also 'complexion, color', χρώζω 'touch the surface', whence 'tinge, stain', χραύω 'scrape, graze, wound slightly', Lith. *grusti* 'bruise, crush', etc. Walde-P. 1.648 ff. Boisacq 1071.

2. Lat. *color* (> Romance words), as orig. 'covering' : *occulere, cēlāre* 'hide' (cf. Skt. *varṇa-*, below, 7). Walde-P. 1.432. Ernout-M. 206. Walde-H. 1.247.

Rum. *față* 'face, surface', also 'color', fr. VLat. *facia* = *faciēs* 'face'. REW 3130.

3. Ir. *dath*, perh. : Ir. *date* 'agreeable' (cf. NIr. *dathamhail* 'pleasant, comely, graceful'). Pedersen 1.418.

Ir. *lī, līg* (also 'splendor'), W. *lliw*, Br. *liv* or *liou*, OCorn. *liu* (cf. also OBr.

liou gl. *naevum, da-liu* gl. *fascus*), prob. : Lat. *līvēre* 'be bluish-black, livid', *līvor* 'blue-black color', etc. Walde-P. 2.715. Pedersen 1.51. Stokes 251. Walde-H. 1.816.

4. ON *litr* (NIcel. *litur* reg. word for 'color', Dan. *lød* mostly replaced by *farve*), also 'countenance, complexion' : *līta*, OE *wlītan* 'look' (15.52). Walde-P. 1.293. Falk-Torp 679.

OE *bleo* and *bleoh* (after *feoh*, etc.), ME *ble*, OS *blī*, OFris. *blī(e)n*, perh. : Goth. *bleiþs* 'merciful, gentle', OE *blīos* 'glad', etc., Lith. *blyvas* 'violet-colored', and also OHG *blīo*, etc. 'lead' ('blue' metal), all fr. a root **bhlei-* 'shine(?)'. Walde-P. 2.210. Feist 99.

OE *hiew*, ME *hew*, NE *hue*, orig. 'form, appearance', as Goth. *hiwi*, etc. (12.51). NED s.v. *hue*, sb.[1].

OHG *farawa*, MHG *varwe*, NHG *farbe*, Du. *verf* (MLG *varwe* > Dan. *farve*, Sw. *färg*), beside adj. OHG *faro* 'colored', etc., this prob. (**pork̂-wo-*) : Skt. *pṛçni-* 'speckled, dappled', Grk. περκνός 'dark-colored, livid', Ir. *erc* 'gay-colored, red', etc. Walde-P. 2.45. Falk-Torp 206. Franck-v. W. 731.

ME *colur, colo(u)r*, NE *color (colour)*, Du. *kleur* (older *coloor, caloor*), fr. OFr. *color, col(o)ur, coulour*, etc., Fr. *couleur* (above, 2). NED s.v. Franck-v. W. 315.

5. Lith. *spalva* = Lett. *spalva* 'feathers, hair on quadrupeds, color of the hair of animals', etym. dub., prob. : Lat. *spolium* 'skin of an animal stripped off, spoils of war', Grk. σπολάς 'skin garment', etc., fr. the root of OHG *spaltan*, etc. 'split'. Walde-P. 2.679. Mühl.-Endz. 3.983.

Lett. *krāsa*, esp. 'beautiful complexion, beauty', as 'color' also *krāss* (Lith. *krosa* 'color', in Kurschat *krosas*, is no longer used, neither form in Lalis or NSB), fr. the Slavic, ChSl., Russ. *krasa* 'beauty', cf. Russ. *kraska* 'paint' (9.88), *krasnyj* 'red' (15.66). Mühl.-Endz. 2.267. Berneker 607 f.

6. SCr. *boja* (also 'paint, dye'), fr. Turk. *boya* 'paint, dye'. Berneker 68.

Boh. *barva*, Pol. (old) *barwa*, now *farba*, fr. MHG *varwe*, NHG *farbe* (above, 4). Berneker 44.

Pol. *kolor*, fr. Lat. *color* (above, 2). Brückner 246.

Russ. *cvet* (pl. *cveta*) = *cvet* (pl. *cvety*) 'flower, bloom, blossom', ChSl. *cvětŭ* 'flower', general Slavic. Berneker 656.

7. Skt. *varṇa-*, also and orig. 'covering', fr. *vṛ-* 'cover'.

Skt. *rañga-, rāga-* : *raj-* 'be colored, grow red', Grk. ῥέζω 'dye', ῥεγεύς 'dyer', etc. Walde-P. 2.366.

Av. *gaona-* 'hair', also 'color' (Yt. 8.58; cf. Afgh. *γūna* 'hair, color', NPers. *gūn* 'color') : Lith. *gaurai* 'hair', etc. (4.14). Walde-P. 1.557. Barth. 482.

15.62 LIGHT (in Color)

Grk.	*λευκός*	Dan.	*lys*	Lith.	*šviesus*
NG	*ἀνοιχτός*	Sw.	*ljus*	Lett.	*gaišs*
It.	*chiaro*	ME	*(pale)*	SCr.	*svijetao*
Fr.	*claire*	NE	*light*	Boh.	*světlý, jasný*
Sp.	*claro*	Du.	*helder, licht*	Pol.	*jasny*
Rum.	*deschis*	MHG	*lieht*	Russ.	*svetlyj*
NIr.	*ēadtrom*	NHG	*hell(licht)*		
W.	*golen*				
Br.	*sklaer*				

Most of the words for 'light' in color are the same as those for the broader 'light' = 'bright' (15.57), and this special use is mostly modern. So NE *light* in this sense from 15th cent., MHG *lieht* rarely in cpds. as *liehtblā* 'light blue', NHG *licht* usual in Austria vs. *hell* with reference to color (Kretschmer, Wortgeogr. 234).

Other terms are:

1. Grk. λευκός, orig. 'bright', but mostly 'light in color', esp. 'white' : Lat. *lūx*, OE *leoht* 'light', etc. (1.61).

2. NG ἀνοιχτός, lit. 'open', fr. ἀνοίγω 'open'. Similarly, and prob. by semantic borrowing, Rum. *deschis*, fr. *deschide* 'open' (12.24).

3. NIr. *ēadtrom*, 'light' in weight (15.82), also 'light' in color (Dinneen, McKenna), doubtless after the double use of NE *light* in which two different words are merged.

ME *pale* (NE also sometimes in this sense, as *pale blue*, etc., cf. NED s.v.), fr. OFr. *pâle*, Lat. *pallidus* 'pallid, pale' : Grk. πελιός 'livid', πολιός 'gray', Skt. *palita-* 'gray, hoary', *paṇḍu-* 'whitish yellow, white', OE *fealo*, OHG *falo*, Lith. *palvas* 'fallow' ('light brownish or reddish yellow'), ChSl. *plavŭ* (renders λευκός Jn. 4.35, but with reference to fields of grain, hence here also 'yellowish'). Walde-P. 2.53 f. Ernout-M. 725.

15.63 DARK (in Color)

Grk.	*μέλας, κελαινός*	Goth.	....	Lith.	*tamsus*
NG	*βαθύς, σκοῦρος*	ON	*døkkr*	Lett.	*tumšs*
Lat.	*fuscus, pullus*	Dan.	*mørk, dunkel*	ChSl.	*tĭmĭnŭ*
It.	*scuro, cupo*	Sw.	*mörk, dunkel*	SCr.	*taman*
Fr.	*foncé, sombre*	OE	*wann (deorc)*	Boh.	*temný*
Sp.	*obscuro*	ME	*dark, wan, dosc*	Pol.	*ciemny*
Rum.	*închis*	NE	*dark*	Russ.	*temnyj*
Ir.	*dorche, temen*	Du.	*donker*	Skt.	*kṛṣṇa-, çyāma-, tamasa-*
NIr.	*dorcha*	OHG	*tunchal*		
W.	*tywyll*	MHG	*tunkel*	Av.	*axšaēna-*
Br.	*du*	NHG	*dunkel*		

Many of the words for 'dark' in color are the same as those for 'dark' = 'lacking light', these again mostly connected with the sbs. for 'darkness' already discussed in 1.62. Some are the same as, or derived from, those for 'black'; some rest on the notion of 'deep'; others are of various sources.

1. IE **tem-*, etc., as in sbs. for 'darkness' (1.62). Walde-P. 1.720 f.

Ir. *temen*, *temnide* (here also W. *tywyll*? cf. ref. in 1.62); Lith. *tamsus*, Lett. *tumšs;* ChSl. *tĭmĭnŭ*, SCr. *taman*, etc., general Slavic; Skt. *tamasa-* (AV 11.9.22).

2. Grk. μέλας, κελαινός 'black' (15.65), also 'dark' in color.

NG βαθύς 'deep' (12.67), also 'dark' in color. Cf. It. *cupo*, Fr. *foncé*, and NE *deep* in *deep red*, *deep dyed*, etc.

NG σκοῦρος, fr. It. *scuro* (below).

3. Lat. *fuscus* : ME *dosc*, *dusk* 'dark, dark-colored' (NE *dusk* sb., *dusky* adj.), Skt. *dhūsara-* 'dust-colored', etc., prob. fr. the root in Grk. θύω 'blow, storm, rage', Skt. *dhvaṅs-* 'go to pieces, fall in ruin', OHG *tunist*, *dunst* 'storm, vapor', OE *dūst* 'dust', etc. Semantic development from 'hazy, dusty, smoky' to 'dust-, smoke-colored', etc. Walde-P. 1.846. Ernout-M. 405. Walde-H. 1.572.

Lat. *pullus* : *pallēre* 'be pale', *pallidus*

'pale, pallid', etc. (see 15.62). Walde-P. 2.53. Ernout-M. 725, 823.

It. *scuro*, Sp. *o(b)scuro*, fr. Lat. *obscūrus* 'dark, lacking light', as orig. 'covered' : OHG *scūr* 'shelter', etc. fr. the root in Skt. *sku-* 'cover'. Walde-P. 2.547. Ernout-M. 694.

It. *cupo*, lit. 'deep, hollow' (fr. Lat. *cūpa* 'tub, cask').

Fr. *foncé*, pple. of *foncer* 'deepen (a color), make darker', orig. 'furnish with a bottom', fr. *fond*, OFr. *fons* 'bottom', fr. Lat. *fundus* 'bottom'. REW 3585. Wartburg 3.870, 874.

Fr. *sombre*, prob. postverbal to an OFr. **sombrer*, fr. VLat. *subumbrāre*, fr. *umbra* 'shade'. REW 8405. Gamillscheg 806 f.

Rum. *închis*, lit. 'closed', pple. of *închide* 'shut, close', and so used as opposite of *deschis* 'open' and 'light' (15.62).

4. Ir. *dorche*, see under *sorche* 'bright' (15.57).

Ir. *temen*, W. *tywyll*, above, 1.

Br. *du* 'black' (15.65), also 'dark', as *glas du* 'dark green'.

5. ON *døkkr*, OS *dunkar*, Du. *donker*, OHG *tunchal*, MHG *tunkel*, NHG *dunkel* (> Dan., Sw. *dunkel*), see under 'darkness' (1.62).

Dan. *mørk*, Sw. *mörk* : ON *myrkr*, OE *mirce* 'dark' and 'darkness', etc. (1.62).

OE *wann*, ME *wan* (NE *wan* now mostly 'pale, pallid'), etym.? NED s.v. *wan*.

OE *deorc* (but mostly of absence of light, not of color, except of clouds, water, etc.), ME, NE *dark*, see under 'darkness' (1.62).

ME *dosc* : Lat. *fuscus* (above, 3).

6. Skt. *kṛṣṇa-*, *çyāma* 'black' (15.65), also 'dark' in color.

Av. *axšaēna-*, neg. cpd. : *xšaēta-* 'bright' (15.57). Barth. 51.

15.64–15.69. Abstract color names are late in linguistic history. They are generally lacking in languages of primitive peoples, whose notion of color is closely bound up with that of a specific object, as, for example, 'white' with snow or milk, 'blue' with the sky, 'green' with plant life, etc. Many of the words discussed below, and others, like NE *orange*, *violet*, have just such an origin.

In the IE period the development had probably not advanced much beyond this stage, and even in historical times there is still much fluctuation and overlapping in the application of color words. There is only one group of cognates that is so widespread and consistent in meaning as to point clearly to an IE color name with definite application, namely the group for 'red'. There are some cases of agreement between two branches in words applied to the same color, and there are some extensive groups from a common root but applied to a variety of colors, so that the primary application is obscure. The most conspicuous interchange is in words for 'green' and 'yellow', perhaps because they were applied to vegetation like grass, cereals, etc., which changed from green to yellow.

For the Skt. terms, cf. Macdonell-Keith 2.246 f.

Wood's Color-Names (Halle, 1902) covers a vast range of material and deals with the remoter root connections.

15.64 WHITE

Grk.	*λευκός (ἀργός)*	Goth.	*hweits*	Lith.	*baltas*
NG	*ἄσπρος*	ON	*hvītr*	Lett.	*balts*
Lat.	*albus, candidus*	Dan.	*hvid*	ChSl.	*bělŭ*
It.	*bianco*	Sw.	*hvit*	SCr.	*bijel*
Fr.	*blanc*	OE	*hwīt*	Boh.	*bílý*
Sp.	*blanco*	ME	*whit*	Pol.	*biały*
Rum.	*alb*	NE	*white*	Russ.	*belyj*
Ir.	*find, gel, bān*	Du.	*wit*	Skt.	*çukra-, çveta-, arjuna-*
NIr.	*bān, geal, fionn*	OHG	*(h)wīz*	Av.	*spaēta-, auruša-*
W.	*gwyn, can*	MHG	*wīz*		
Br.	*gwenn, kann*	NHG	*weiss*		

Most of the words for 'white' come from the notion of 'bright'.

1. Grk. λευκός : Lat. *lūx*, OE *lēoht*, etc. 'light' (1.61), Lat. *lūcēre*, Skt. *ruc-*, etc. 'shine' (15.56), IE **leuk-*. Walde-P. 2.408 ff.

Grk. ἀργός 'glistening, white' (also ἀργής, ἀργηέις, ἀργεννός), Skt. *arjuna-* 'light, white', Toch. A *ārki*, Hitt. *narkis* 'white', fr. the root seen in words for 'silver', Grk. ἄργυρος, Lat. *argentum*, etc. (9.65). Walde-H. 1.66, 848.

Byz., NG ἄσπρος, fr. Lat. *asper* 'rough' as used of work in bas-relief, as *aspera pōcula*, esp. coins as *nummī asperī* (cf. Thes. 2.809), hence Byz. ἄσπρος or ἄσπρον name of a coin, esp. a silver coin, and from the latter the use as adj. for 'white'. Psichari, MSL 6.312 f. G. Meyer, Neugr. Stud. 3.12.

2. Lat. *albus* (> Rum. *alb*), Umbr. *alfu* 'alba' : Grk. ἀλφός 'dull-white leprosy', ἀλφούς· λευκούς (Hesych.), OHG *albiz*, ON *elptr* 'swan', etc., IE **albho-*. Walde-P. 1.93. Ernout-M. 31 f. Walde-H. 1.26 f.

Lat. *candidus* 'bright' (15.57), also 'white'.

It. *bianco*, Fr. *blanc*, Sp. *blanco*, fr. Gmc., cf. OHG *blanc* 'shining white', MLG *blanc*, etc. (15.57). REW 1152.

3. Ir. *find*, NIr. *fionn*, W. *gwyn*, Br. *gwenn*, Gall. *Vindo-magus*, *Vindo-bona*, prob. as 'white' fr. 'visible' : Grk. ἰνδάλλομαι 'appear, seem', Skt. *vindati* 'finds', Ir. *finnaim* 'find, find out', etc., fr. the root **weid-* 'see, know' (in Grk. εἶδον, οἶδα, Skt. *vid-*, etc.). Walde-P. 1.237. Pedersen 1.41. Stokes 265.

Ir. *gel*, NIr. *geal* : OE *geolo*, etc. 'yellow' (15.69).

Ir. *bān* : Skt. *bhā-*, Av. *bā-* 'shine', etc. (15.56).

W. *can*, Br. *kann* ('brilliant white') : (or loanword fr.) Lat. *candidus* 'bright' (15.57). Walde-P. 1.352. Pedersen 1.199.

4. Goth. *hweits*, OE *hwīt*, etc., general Gmc. : Skt. *çveta-*, Av. *spaēta-* 'white', ChSl. *světŭ* sb. 'light' (1.61), *světiti* 'shine', etc. (15.56). Walde-P. 1.470. Falk-Torp 439.

5. Lith. *baltas*, Lett. *balts* (and fr. different grade without suffix) ChSl. *bělŭ*, etc., general Slavic : Grk. φαλός· λευκός (Hesych.), ON *bāl*, OE *bǣl* 'flame, funeral pile', Skt. *bhāla-* 'forehead', fr. IE **bhel-* (perh. related to **bhā-* 'shine', cf. above, Ir. *bān*). Walde-P. 2.175 f. Berneker 55 f. Trautmann 25, 29 f.

6. Skt. *çukra-*, *çukla-* 'bright, clear, pure' (15.57), also 'white'.

Skt. *çveta-*, Av. *spaēta-*, above, 4.

Skt. *arjuna-* : Grk. ἀργός, above, 1.

Av. *auruša-* : Skt. *aruṣa-*, *aruṇa-* 'ruddy', perh. OHG *elo*, MHG *el* (*elwer*) 'tawny, yellow'. Walde-P. 1.159, 2.359. Barth. 190.

15.65 BLACK

Grk.	*μέλας, κελαινός*	Goth.	*swarts*	Lith.	*juodas*
NG	*μαῦρος*	ON	*svartr*	Lett.	*melns*
Lat.	*āter, niger*	Dan.	*sort*	ChSl.	*črŭnŭ*
It.	*nero*	Sw.	*svart*	SCr.	*crn*
Fr.	*noir*	OE	*blæc, sweart*	Boh.	*černý*
Sp.	*negro*	ME	*blak, swart*	Pol.	*czarny*
Rum.	*negru*	NE	*black*	Russ.	*černyj*
Ir.	*dub*	Du.	*zwart*	Skt.	*kṛṣṇa-, çyāma-*
NIr.	*dubh*	OHG	*suarz*	Av.	*sāma-, syāva-*
W.	*du*	MHG	*swarz*		
Br.	*du*	NHG	*schwarz*		

Words for 'black' in part reflect such notions as 'dirty', 'smoky', 'blackened by fire'(?). Some belong to inherited groups containing words applied to various colors, the primary sense of which is obscure. Some old words for 'black' that were replaced by others survived in the sense of 'ink' (18.58).

1. Grk. μέλας (NG μελάνι 'ink', μελανός 'blue-black, livid') : Lett. *melns* 'black, dirty', Skt. *mala-* 'dirt, filth', *malina-* 'dirty', etc. (15.88).

Grk. κελαινός : Skt. *kalañka-* 'spot, blemish', *kalana-* 'spot, dirt', Swiss *helm* 'white spot on the forehead of cattle', etc. Walde-P. 1.440 f. Boisacq 430.

Byz., NG μαῦρος, late Grk. μαυρός, for ἀμαυρός 'dim, faint, hardly seen' (: ON *meyrr* 'tender, soft', Russ. *smuryj* 'dark-grey', *chmuryj* 'overcast, cloudy, sullen', etc. Walde-P. 2.223).

2. Lat. *āter*, Umbr. *atru*, *adro* 'atra', perh. as 'blackened, burned by fire' : Av. *ātarš* 'fire', Arm. *airem* 'kindle, burn', SCr. *vatra* 'fire', etc. Walde-P. 1.42. Ernout-M. 83 f. Walde-H. 1.75 f., 849 f.

Lat. *niger* (> Romance words), etym.? Walde-P. 2.322. Ernout-M. 671.

3. Ir. *dub*, NIr. *dubh*, W., Br. *du* : Goth. *daufs*, ON *daufr*, etc. 'deaf', Grk. τυφλός 'blind, dark', τῦφος 'smoke, vapor, stupor', τύφω 'smoke, burn slowly', fr. **dheu-bh-* (extension of **dheu-* seen also in Lat. *fuscus* 'dark', etc., 15.63). 'Black, dark', here prob. fr. 'confused, dimmed by vapor' or the like. Walde-P. 1.840. Pedersen 1.116.

4. Goth. *swarts*, ON *svartr*, etc., general Gmc. (NE *swart* only rhet., poet., or dial.) : Lat. *sordēs* 'filth', *sordidus* 'dirty' (15.88), *suāsum*, a kind of dark color. Walde-P. 2.535. Falk-Torp 1109. Ernout-M. 958, 991.

OE *blæc*, ME *blak*, NE *black* (as sb. OE *blæc*, OHG *blach*, OS *blak* 'ink'), etym. disputed, prob. : OHG *blecchen*, MHG *blecken* 'be visible, let see', OHG *blanc* 'shining white', Du. *blaken* 'burn, glow', Lat. *flagrāre* 'flame, burn', Grk. φλέγω 'burn, blaze', etc., with development of 'black' fr. 'burnt' or 'shining black'(?). Walde-P. 2.215. Falk-Torp 87. NED s.v.

5. Lith. *juodas* : Lett. *juods* 'evil spirit, wood or field demon'; but further connection? Mühl.-Endz. 2.125.

Lett. *melns* : Grk. μέλας (above, 1).

6. ChSl. *črŭnŭ*, etc., general Slavic : OPruss. *kirsnan*, Skt. *kṛṣṇa-* 'black', further, Lith. *keršas* 'black and white', *keršė* 'spotted cow', etc., Sw., Norw. *harr* 'ashes'. Walde-P. 1.428. Berneker 169 f.

7. Skt. *çyāma-*, Av. *sāma-* (*s-* fr. *sy-*), beside *syāva* = Skt. *çyāva-* 'dark-brown' : Lith. *šėmas* 'blue-gray', *šyvas* 'gray (of horses)', OPruss. *sywan*, ChSl. *sivŭ*, Russ. *sivyj* 'gray', OE *hǣwen* 'blue', etc. (15.67).

Skt. *kṛṣṇa-*, above, 6.

15.66 RED

Grk.	*ἐρυθρός*	Goth.	*rauþs*	Lith.	*raudonas*
NG	*κόκκινος*	ON	*rauðr, rjōðr*	Lett.	*sarkans*
Lat.	*ruber (rufus, russus)*	Dan.	*rød*	ChSl.	*črŭmĭnŭ (črĭvenŭ, rŭdrŭ)*
It.	*rosso*	Sw.	*röd*	SCr.	*crven*
Fr.	*rouge*	OE	*rēad, rēod*	Boh.	*červený*
Sp.	*rojo*	ME	*reed*	Pol.	*czerwony*
Rum.	*roşiu*	NE	*red*	Russ.	*krasnyj*
Ir.	*derg, rūad*	Du.	*rood*	Skt.	*rakta-, lohita-*
NIr.	*dearg, ruadh*	OHG	*rōt*	Av.	*raoiδita-*
W.	*coch, rhudd*	MHG	*rōt*		
Br.	*ruz*	NHG	*rot*		

The majority of the words for 'red' belong to an inherited group pointing to an IE word for 'red'. Several of the others are derived from names of vegetable or animal sources of red dye; some from 'rosy' or 'glowing'.

1. IE **reudh-*. Walde-P. 2.358 f. Ernout-M.872. REW 7408, 7465, 7466. Falk-Torp 932.

Grk. *ἐρυθρός*; Lat. *ruber*, and (dial.) *rūfus* mostly 'light red' (esp. of hair), Umbr. *rufru* 'rubros', also Lat. *rubeus* 'reddish' (> Fr. *rouge*, etc.), and (**rudhtos*) *russus* (> It. *rosso;* Fr. *roux* of hair), whence *russeus* 'reddish' (> Sp. *rojo*, Port. *roxo*); Ir. *rūad*, NIr. *ruadh*, W. *rhudd*, Br. *ruz;* Goth. *rauþs*, ON *rauðr*, OE *rēad*, etc., general Gmc., also with different grade ON *rjōðr*, OE *rēod;* Lith. *raudas*, now usually *raudonas*, also *rudas* 'red-brown', Lett. *ruds* 'reddish'; late ChSl. *rŭdrŭ* (*rĭdrŭ, rodrŭ*), *ryždĭ, rumĕnŭ* (SCr. *rumen*, Boh. *ruměný*, Pol. *rumiany*, Russ. *rumjanyj* 'flushed, red' of complexion), etc. (cf. Trautmann, 238 f.); Skt. (Vedic) *rohita-*, later *lohita-*, Av. *raoiδita-* (Skt. *rudhira-* 'bloody', exp. sb. 'blood').

2. NG *κόκκινος*, in class. Grk. 'scarlet', but now the pop. word for 'red', deriv. of Grk. *κόκκος* 'grain, seed', and esp. 'gall of the kermes oak' yielding scarlet dye. Hence Lat. *coccinus* and *coccum* (late *coccus*) used also for 'scarlet (color)' and 'scarlet garments'.

3. Rum. *roş(u), roşiu*, fr. Lat. *roseus* 'rose-colored', deriv. of *rosa* 'rose'. REW 7379. Puşcariu 1475.

4. Ir. *derg*, NIr. *dearg* : OE *deorc* 'dark', etc. (15.63). Walde-P. 1.855.

W. *coch*, fr. Lat. *coccus* (above, 2). Loth, Mots lat. 150.

5. Lett. *sarkans*, deriv. of *sarks* 'slightly red', prob. fr. the same root as *sārts* 'red' (in the face) : Lith. *sartas* 'sorrel', Lat. *sorbum* 'service berry', Skt. *sāra-* 'heart-wood' of a tree, *sārañga-* 'variegated'. Walde-P. 2.499. Mühl.-Endz. 3.721, 807.

6. ChSl. *črŭmĭnŭ* (Russ. *čermnyj* 'purple-red', fr. the ChSl., SCr. old *črman*), fr. **čĭrmĭ* 'worm' (Slov. *črm* 'fingerworm, carbuncle', etc.) : Skt. *kṛmi-* 'worm', etc. (3.84). Semantic development through the red dye obtained from various worms (cf. Fr. *vermeil*, fr. Lat. *vermiculus* 'little worm' and late = *coccum*). Berneker 169.

ChSl. *črŭvĭjenĭ*, sb. 'red color', Russ.-ChSl. *črĭvenŭ* 'red', etc., general Slavic (Russ. *červonnyj* 'purple-red', fr. Pol.), fr. ChSl. *črŭvĭ*, etc. 'worm'. Walde-P. 1.523. Berneker 169, 172 f.

Russ. *krasnyj* : ChSl. *krasĭnŭ* 'beautiful', etc. (general Slavic in this sense, but freq. also with special sense of 'shining, ruddy' and the like), deriv. of ChSl. *krasa* 'beauty', Russ. *krasa* 'beauty, adornment', etc. (Pol. *kras* 'color', esp. 'red color' also 'beauty', etc.), prob. as 'glow, splendor' (whence both 'red' and 'beautiful') : Lith. *karštas* 'hot', *kurti* 'to heat', etc. Berneker 607 f. Walde-P. 1.418 f.

7. Skt. *rakta-*, lit. 'colored', pple. of *raj-* 'be colored' (esp. red), be excited', etc. : *rañga-, rāga-* 'color', etc. (15.61).

15.67 BLUE

Grk.	*κυάνεος*	Goth.	. . . .	Lith.	*mėlynas*
NG	*γαλανός, γαλάζιος, μαβύς*	ON	*blār*	Lett.	*zils*
Lat.	*caeruleus*	Dan.	*blaa*	ChSl.	*sinĭ*
It.	*blu, azzurro*	Sw.	*blå*	SCr.	*modar*
Fr.	*bleu*	OE	*blǣwen, hǣwen*	Boh.	*modrý*
Sp.	*azul*	ME	*blew*	Pol.	*niebieski*
Rum.	*albastru*	NE	*blue*	Russ.	*sinij, goluboj*
Ir.	*gorm, glass*	Du.	*blauw*	Skt.	*nīla-*
NIr.	*gorm*	OHG	*blāo*	Av.	. . . .
W.	*glas*	MHG	*blā*		
Br.	*glas*	NHG	*blau*		

Many of the words for 'blue' are from roots that appear in the names of other colors, as 'gray', 'black', 'yellow', 'green', the primary application of which is uncertain. Some are derived from names of the sky, lapis lazuli, etc.

1. Grk. *κυάνεος, κυανοῦς*, fr. *κύανος* 'dark-blue enamel' used in adorning armor, 'lapis lazuli' (Theophr.), 'blue copper carbonate', etc. Prob. non-IE word. Boisacq 527.

NG *γαλανός*, etym. disputed. The old deriv. fr. a Doric form of *γαληνός* 'calm' (esp. of the sea) is unconvincing. Perh. as orig. 'bluish-white' (on some of the islands *γαλανός* = *ἄσπρος* 'white') fr. *γάλα* 'milk', with suffix often the analogy of *μελανός* (really *μελαν-ός*) 'blue-black, livid'. From the same source (*γάλα* or otherwise) Byz., NG *γαλάζιος* with different suffix.

NG *μαβύς*, fr. Turk. *mavi* 'blue'.

2. Lat. *caeruleus*, and earlier *caerulus*, by dissim. for **caelo-los*, deriv. of *caelum* 'sky'. Walde-P. 1.420. Ernout-M. 131. Walde-H. 1.133.

Fr. *bleu* (> It. *blu*, NG *μπλέ*), fr. a Frank. form corresponding to OHG *blāo*, etc. (below, 3). REW 1153.

It. *azzurro*, Fr. *azur*, Sp. *azul*, through Arab. *lāzwardī*, fr. Pers. *lāžward* 'lapis lazuli, azure-colored'. REW 4959. Lokotsch 1311.

Rum. *albastru*, orig. and still dial. 'whitish', deriv. of Lat. *albus* 'white', as if VLat. **albaster*, with suffix as in It. *biancastro* 'whitish', etc. REW 319. Tiktin s.v.

3. Ir. *gorm* (W. arch. *gwrm* 'dusky, dim, dark blue'), etym. dub. (: Lat. *formus* 'warm', Skt. *gharma-* 'glow, heat', etc.?). Walde-P. 1.688.

Ir. *glass* 'blue-gray, green-gray' (e.g. 'blue' of the eye, Windisch, Tāin 1.5550; 'gray' of mist, id. 1.5042, 5058; 'green' of garlic, Anc. Laws 2.254, 1.9), NIr. *glas* 'green, gray, bluish-gray' (Dinneen), W. *glas* 'blue', but also 'gray, green' (Spurrell), Br. *glas* 'green, blue, gray' (cf. Gall. *glastum* 'name of a plant'), see under 'green' (15.68).

4. ON *blār*, Dan. *blaa*, Sw. *blå*, Du. *blauw*, OHG *blāo*, MHG *blā*, NHG *blau;* OE *blāw* once gl. *blata, pigmentum*, and in deriv. *blǣwen* gl. *perseus* (Wright-Wülcker 1.163, 29; ME *blew*, NE *blue*, fr. OFr. *bleu*, above, 2), prob. : Lat. *flāvus* 'yellow', and with different suffix MIr. *blā* 'yellow(?)', Ir. *blār*, W. *blawr* 'gray', Lat. *flōrus* 'blond' (of hair), prob. fr. the root **bhel-* 'shine', seen in Slavic *bělŭ*, Lith. *baltas* 'white' (15.64). The exact color to which the Gmc. term applies varies in the older dialects; MHG *blā* is also 'yellow', whereas the Scandinavian words may refer esp. to a deep, swarthy black, e.g. ON *blāmaðr*, NIcel. *blāmaður* 'Negro'. Walde-P. 2.212. Walde-H. 1.513 f. Falk-Torp 78. NED s.v. *blue.*

OE *hǣwen* (gl. *glaucus, caeruleus, hyacinthinus, viridis*, etc.), also *hǣwe* 'blue, gray' : Ir. *cīar* 'dark, brown', ON *hārr*, OE *hār* 'hoary'; ChSl. *sinĭ*, Russ. *sinij* '(dark)blue', SCr. *sinji* 'gray-blue, sea-green', etc.; Lith. *šyvas*, ChSl. *sivŭ*, Russ. *sivyj* 'gray', Skt. *çyāma-* 'black' (15.65). Walde-P. 1.360 f.

5. Lith. *mėlynas* : Lett. *melns*, Grk. *μέλας* 'black' (15.65). Walde-P. 2.294.

Lett. *zils* : *zal'š*, ChSl. *zelenŭ* 'green', etc. (15.68).

6. ChSl. *sinĭ*, Russ. *sinij* : OE *hǣwen*, etc. (above, 4). Walde-P. 1.361. Otherwise Brückner 491 (: ChSl. *sinąti* 'shine').

SCr.-ChSl. *modrĭ* 'livid, bloodshot', SCr. *modar*, Boh. *modrý* 'blue', Pol. *modry* esp. 'dark-blue', perh. : Icel. *maðra* 'madder, goose grass', OHG *matara*, OE *mædere, mæddre* 'dyer's madder (rubia tinctorum)'. Walde-P. 2.305. Berneker 2.66 f.

Pol. *niebieski*, deriv. of *niebo* 'sky'.

Russ. *goluboj* (Ukr. *hołubyj* 'sky-blue') : Russ. *golub'*, ChSl. *goląbĭ* 'dove', this prob. in origin à color-name, cf. OPruss. *golimban* 'blue', and perh. fr. a root **g(h)el-* (in ChSl. *žlŭtŭ*, etc., 'yellow', etc., 15.69), beside **ĝhel-* (in Lith. *žalias*, ChSl. *zelenŭ*, etc., 'green', 15.68). Berneker 322. Walde-P. 1.623.

7. Skt. *nīla-* ('dark-blue, bluish black', cf. *nīlī-* 'indigo plant'; Macdonell-Keith 2.246), etym. dub. (: Lat. *niger* 'black' ?). Walde-P. 2.322.

15.68 GREEN

Grk.	*χλωρός*	Goth.	. . . .	Lith.	*žalias*
NG	*πράσινος*	ON	*grœnn*	Lett.	*zal'š*
Lat.	*viridis*	Dan.	*grøn*	ChSl.	*zelenŭ*
It.	*verde*	Sw.	*grön*	SCr.	*zelen*
Fr.	*vert*	OE	*grēne*	Boh.	*zeleny*
Sp.	*verde*	ME	*green*	Pol.	*zielony*
Rum.	*verde*	NE	*green*	Russ.	*zelenyj*
Ir.	*glass, uaine*	Du.	*groen*	Skt.	*harita-*
NIr.	*glas, uaine*	OHG	*gruoni*	Av.	. . . .
W.	*gwyrdd, glas*	MHG	*grüene*		
Br.	*gwer, glas*	NHG	*grün*		

Several of the words for 'green' are from a root that appears in names of other colors, especially 'yellow'. The others reflect the conspicuous green of plant life.

1. Derivs. of IE **ĝhel-* in words for bright, shining colors, esp. 'yellow, green' also 'white' (15.64) and 'blue' (15.67), in vbs. 'shine, glimmer, sparkle' (15.56). Walde-P. 1.624 ff.

Grk. *χλωρός*; Ir. *glass*, NIr., W., Br. *glas* (also 'gray, blue', cf. 15.67); Lith. *žalias*, Lett. *zal'š*, OPruss. *saligan;* ChSl. *zelenŭ*, etc., general Slavic; Skt. *harita-* (also 'yellow').

2. Byz., NG *πράσινος*, also rare class. Grk. (Aristot., Meteor. passim), orig. 'leek-green', fr. *πράσον* 'leek'.

3. Lat. *viridis* (VLat. **virdis* > Romance words, also W. *gwyrdd*, Br. *gwer*), fr. *virēre* 'be green', prob. : Lith. *veisti* 'propagate', ON *vīsir* 'bud, sprout', OE *wīse* 'sprout, stalk', etc. Walde-P. 1.242. Ernout-M. 1113. Loth, Mots lat. 177.

4. Ir. *uaine* (*uaithne*), etym.? Macbain 384.

5. ON *grœnn*, OE *grēne*, etc., general Gmc. : ON *grōa*, OE *grōwan*, OHG *gruoan* 'grow, become green' (in the older period used esp. of plant life, in contrast to ON *vaxa* 'grow, increase', etc.), with *s-* suffix Goth., ON *gras*, etc. 'grass', Lat. *grāmen* (**ghras-men*) id. Walde-P. 1.646. Falk-Torp 357.

15.69 YELLOW

Grk.	*ξανθός*	Goth.	. . . .	Lith.	*geltonas*
NG	*κίτρινος*	ON	*gulr*	Lett.	*dzeltāns*
Lat.	*flāvus (helvus)*	Dan.	*gul*	ChSl.	*žlŭtŭ*
It.	*giallo*	Sw.	*gul*	SCr.	*žut*
Fr.	*jaune*	OE	*geolo*	Boh.	*žlutý*
Sp.	*amarillo*	ME	*yelwe*	Pol.	*żółty*
Rum.	*galben*	NE	*yellow*	Russ.	*želtyj*
Ir.	*buide*	Du.	*geel*	Skt.	*pīta-, gāura-, harita-, hari-*
NIr.	*buidhe*	OHG	*gelo*	Av.	*zari-, zairita-*
W.	*melyn*	MHG	*gel*		
Br.	*melen*	NHG	*gelb*		

A considerable group of the words for 'yellow' are cognate with others for 'green'. Some are from names of things yellow, as 'citron', 'honey', etc.

1. IE **ĝhel-* (in part also **g(h)el-*), the same as **ĝhel-* in words for 'green' (15.68), etc. Walde-P. 1.624 ff. Ernout-M. 448, 456. Walde-H. 1.639.

Lat. *helvus* (rare and mostly 'yellowish, bay'); ON *gulr*, OE *geolo*, etc., general Gmc.; Skt. *hari-, harita-* (also 'green'), Av. *zari-, zāri-, zairita-;* fr. **g(h)el-*, Lith. *geltonas* (and *geltas, gelsvas* 'pale yellow'), Lett. *dzeltāns* (and *dzeltens, dzeltāins*), OPruss. *gelatynan* (= **geltaynan*); ChSl. *žlŭtŭ* (quotable? SCr.-ChSl. *žlŭtŭ*, Trautmann 84), SCr. *žut*, etc., general Slavic. Possibly here also fr. a related root form **ĝel-* (Walde-P. 1.622 ff.; but cf. Walde-H. 1.578), Lat. *galbus* (in glosses '*χλωρός*'), whence *galbinus* 'pale green' or 'yellow' > OFr. *jalne* (> It. *giallo*), Fr. *jaune*, Rum. *galben* (REW 3646).

2. Grk. *ξανθός* (in Hom. esp. 'yellow-haired'), later of all things 'yellow', honey, etc.; NG 'blond'), etym. dub., perh. : Lat. *cānus* 'gray, hoary', OHG *hasan* 'shining gray', ON *hǫss*, OE *hasu* 'gray'. Walde-P. 1.358. Walde-H. 1.156.

NG *κίτρινος*, in class. Grk. 'citron-colored', fr. *κίτρον* 'citron'.

3. Lat. *flāvus*, prob. : ON *blār*, OHG *blāo*, etc. 'blue' (15.67). Walde-P. 2.212. Ernout-M. 367. Walde-H. 1.513 f.

Sp. *amarillo*, Port. *amarelo*, prob. deriv. of Lat. *amārus* 'bitter', through application to some bitter (yellow) substance such as gall. REW 4062.

4. Ir. *buide*, NIr. *buidhe* = Lat. *badius* 'chestnut-brown, bay' (> Fr. *bai* > NE *bay*), root connection? Walde-P. 2.105. Ernout-M. 100.

W., Corn. *melyn*, Br. *melen*, as 'honey-colored', fr. W., Br., Corn. *mel* 'honey.' Walde-P. 2.293, 296. Pedersen 2.57.

5. Skt. *pīta-*, etym ? Uhlenbeck 168.

Skt. *gāura-* (also 'whitish, reddish'), as sb. 'sort of buffalo', cf. NPers. *gōr* 'wild ass', etym.? Uhlenbeck 83.

	15.71 TOUCH (vb.)	15.72 FEEL (vb.), FEEL OF	15.73 TOUCH (sb Act or Sense of Touch)
Grk.	ἅπτομαι, ψαύω	ψηλαφάω	ἁφή
NG	ἀγγίζω	ψηλαφῶ, ψάχνω, πασπατεύω	ἁφή
Lat.	*tangere*	*temptāre* (*palpāre*)	*tāctus*
It.	*toccare*	*tastare, tentare, palpare*	*tatto*
Fr.	*toucher*	*tâter, palper*	*toucher* (*tact*)
Sp.	*tocar*	*tentar, palpar*	*tacto*
Rum.	*atinge*	*pipăi*	*atingere*
Ir.	*do-aidlea* (*3 sg.*)		
NIr.	*taidhlim*	*glacaim*	*tadhall*
W.	*cyffwrdd*	*teimlo*	*teimlad*
Br.	*touch, steki*	*merat, dournata*	*touch, stok*
Goth.	(*at*)*tēkan*		
ON	*snerta, koma við*	*þreifa*	*viðkvāma*
Dan.	*berøre, røre*(*ved*)	*føle* (*paa*),	*følesans, følelse*
Sw.	(*vid*)*röra, beröra*	*känna* (*på*), *treva*	*känsel*
OE	*hrīnan, hreppan*	*fēlan, grāpian*	*hrepung, gefrēdnes*
ME	*touche, rine, repe*	*fele, taste, grope*	*feling, touche*
NE	*touch*	*feel* (*of*)	*touch, feeling*
Du.	*aanraken*	*voelen, tasten*	*gevoel*
OHG	(*h*)*rīnan*, (*h*)*ruoren*	*fuolen, greifōn*	*gihrōrida*
MHG	(*be*)*rüeren*, (*be*)*rīnen*	*tasten, vüelen*	*gerüerde, berüerde*
NHG	*berühren*	*fühlen, tasten*	*gefühl*
Lith.	*liesti*	*čiupinėti*	*čiuopimas*
Lett.	*aiztikt, aizskart*	*taustīt*	*tauste*
ChSl.	*kosnąti, prikasati, prisęšti*	*osęgnąti, osęzati*	*osęzanĭje*
SCr.	*doticati, dirati*	*pipati*	*opip*
Boh.	*dotknouti se*	*hmatati, makati*	*hmat*
Pol.	*dotknać*	*macać*	*dotykanie*
Russ.	*trogat'*	*ščupat', osjazat'*	*osjazanie*
Skt.	*spṛç-*		*sparça-*

15.71–15.73. The arrangement here is different from that followed in the lists for the other senses. First place is given to the vbs. for touch, which, though the source of many of the sbs. for the 'sense of touch', are not themselves used for 'feel' = 'perceive by touch', but only for the antecedent action—and so are not co-ordinate with 'smell', 'taste', 'hear', 'see'. The vbs. listed in 15.72 are used for 'feel of' (as defined above, pp. 1018 f.) or 'feel about, feel one's way, grope', some mostly in the one or the other sense, some in both—but not for 'feel' = 'perceive by touch', except W. *teimlo*, and NE *feel* with its Gmc. cognates, which primarily belong to this group but came to be used also for 'perceive by touch'. Generally there is no distinctive verb for 'perceive by touch', which is expressed by the generic words for 'perceive by the senses', so that a list of words for this notion would be virtually a repetition of that in 15.11 and is therefore omitted here.

The nouns for 'sense of touch', listed in 15.73, are all connected with the verbs listed in 15.71 or 15.72. Although some of the verbs and nouns are also used objectively (cf. NE *it feels soft, the feel of it*), the obj. notion is more often expressed by periphrasis and is ignored here.

In contrast to the words for the other senses, there is no important inherited group of cognates for 'touch' or 'feel'. The words reflect a great variety of notions, such as 'grasp, seize, catch', 'strike', 'stroke', 'tear', 'adhere', 'approach', 'reach', involving contact or sudden motion, several of these of imitative orig., based on syllables symbolic of sudden motion.

1. Grk. ἅπτομαι 'fasten, grasp, touch' (act. ἅπτω less common), sb. ἁφή 'touch', perh. : Skt. *yabh-*, SCr. *jebati* 'have sexual intercourse', as orig. 'lay hands on, touch' (cf. the similar special use of ἅπτομαι, Lat. *tangere*, and NE *touch*). Walde-P. 1.198. Brugmann, IF 32.319 ff.

Grk. ψαύω 'touch', whence ψαῦσις 'sense of touch' (Democr., Diel, Fragm. 1.389), perh. fr. another extension of a root **bhes-*, parallel to that in ψῆν 'rub'. Boisacq 1076. Persson, Beiträge 655, 826.

Hence NG pop. ψάχνω 'feel around for, search' (re-formed fr. aor. ἔψαξα, this by dissim. fr. ἔψαψα, i.e. old ἔψαυσα). Hatzidakis, Einl. 403, 409.

Grk. ψηλαφάω 'feel', esp. 'feel around for, grope', NG ψηλαφῶ id., fr. a cpd. of ἁφή, and a form of ψάλλω, aor. ἔψηλα 'touch sharply, pluck' (the hair, a bowstring, etc., then esp. the strings of a harp, etc.), this perh. : Lat. *palpāre* 'stroke', OE *fēlan* 'feel', etc. Walde-P. 2.6 f. Ernout-M. 726.

NG ἀγγίζω 'touch', fr. class. Grk. ἐγγίζω 'approach', deriv. of ἐγγύς 'near'.

NG pop. πασπατεύω 'feel around, grope', perh. re-formed (after some vb. in -τεύω) fr. a locally attested πασπαλεύω of similar meaning (: πασπάλη 'fine meal'). Hatzidakis, 'Αθηνᾶ 29, παράρτ. 8.

2. Lat. *tangere* 'touch' (*attingere* > Rum. *atinge* 'touch'), sb. *tāctus* (> It. *tatto*, Fr. *tact*, Sp. *tacto;* Rum. *atingere* old inf. of *atinge*) : Grk. τεταγών 'having seized', OE *þaccian* 'stroke', further connections dub. Walde-P. 1.703. Ernout-M. 1017.

Lat. *temptāre* (*tentāre*) 'feel of', also 'make trial of, try' (> It. *tentare*, Sp. *tentar* 'feel of', but mainly 'try' or 'tempt', as Fr. *tenter*), see 9.97.

It. *toccare*, Fr. *toucher* (> ME *touche*, NE *touch*), Sp. *tocar* 'touch', fr. VLat. *toccāre* 'strike, hit, give a knock' (cf.Sp. *tocar* also 'knock' on a door, 'ring' a bell, Rum. *toca* 'hack' and 'ring' a bell, It. *tocco* 'stroke' of a bell or knocker, etc.), deriv. of an imitative *toc* as in Fr. *toc toc*, NE *tick-tock*, etc. REW 8767.

Fr. *touche* 'act of touching' (> ME *touche*, NE *touch* used also for the sense of touch), back-formation fr. *toucher*.

Fr. *toucher* sb. use of infin., now usual expression for sense of touch, rather than *tact*, which is now mostly 'sense of propriety'.

It. *tastare*, Fr. *tâter* 'feel of, feel about' (OFr. *taster* > MHG, NHG *tasten* id., ME *taste* 'feel of' and 'taste'), fr. VLat. *tastāre*, this prob. fr. **taxitāre*, new frequent. to *taxāre* 'feel, handle', frequent. of *tangere*. But some assume a blend of Lat. *tangere* and *gustāre*. REW 8595. Gamillscheg 836.

Lat. *palpāre* 'stroke, touch lightly', late 'feel one's way' and 'feel of' (e.g. Vulgate, Lk. 24.39; in this sense > It. *palpare*, Fr. *palper*, Sp. *palpar*) prob. : OE *fēlan*, etc. (see below, 4).

Rum. *pipăi* 'feel of, feel about', fr. Slavic SCr. *pipati*, etc. (below, 6). Tiktin s.v.

3. OIr. *do-aidlea* (3sg.), lit. 'visit, approach', but usual also (cf. NG ἀγγίζω, above, 1) for 'touch' (e.g. *d-an-aidlea Cū Chulainn iarum co fogaid in chlaideb* 'Cūchulainn touches him then with the edge of the sword', cf. LU 5678), vbl. n. *tadall* ('visit'), NIr. *tadhall* ('sense of touch'), whence MIr. *taidlim*, NIr. *taidhlim* 'go up to, approach, visit, reach, touch, handle', etc. (Dinneen), fr. **to-ad-ell-*, cf. *ad-ell-* (3sg. *ad-ella*) 'visit', cpd.

of *el-* in forms of vb. for 'go' (10.47). Pedersen 2.509.

NIr. *glacaim* 'grasp, take hold of', also 'feel of' (e.g. NT, Lk. 24.39), fr. *glac* 'the half-open fist, grasp'.

W. *cyffwrdd* 'touch', cpd. of *cyf* 'con-' and *hwrdd* 'push, thrust'.

W. *teimlo* 'feel' (hence *teimlad* 'feeling, touch'), etym. dub. (Morris Jones 160 : Lat. *tangere*, but??).

MW *tafaw, tavaw*, Corn. *dava* 'feel of', see under Br. *tañva* 'taste' (15.31).

Br. *touch* 'touch', sb. *touch*, fr. Fr. *toucher, touche* (above, 2).

Br. *steki*, sb. *stok*, 'shock, hit' and 'touch', fr. Fr. *toquer* 'touch, hit'. Henry 254. Ernault, Glossaire 659.

Br. *merat, mera* 'feel of' through 'handle = *mera* 'direct, administer', fr. *maer, mer* 'mayor'. Ernault, Glossaire 383 f. Loth, Mots lat. 183.

Br. *dournata* 'handle, feel of', fr. *dourn* 'hand' (4.33).

4. Goth. *tēkan, attēkan* 'touch' : ON *tāka* 'seize, take', etc. (11.13).

ON *snerta* 'touch' : Dan. *snerte*, Sw. *snärta* 'lash, jibe', Norw. *snerta* 'set in rapid motion, lash', all prob. fr. an imitative syllable seen in ME *snar*, NE *snarl*, etc. Falk-Torp 1094. Hellquist 1021.

ON *koma við* 'touch', lit. 'come against', hence *viðkvāma* 'contact, touch', also *viðkoma* (so NIcel.).

ON *þreifa* 'grasp', also 'feel of', Sw. *treva* 'feel, grope', *treva på* 'feel of', prob. : Lith. *trypti* 'trample'. Falk-Torp. 1284. Hellquist 1219.

OE *fēlan, gefēlan*, ME *fele*, NE *feel*, Du. *voelen*, OHG *fuolen*, MHG *vüelen*, MLG *volen* (> Dan. *føle*), NHG *fühlen* (lost in South German; Kretschmer, Wortgeogr. 210 f.), the general WGmc. word for 'feel of' and for 'feel' as 'perceive by touch', and hence also with wider application to perceptions and emotions, even in the earliest periods (ME *fele*, Du. *gevoelen* the most general words for 'perceive by the senses', cf. 15.11), prob. : Lat. *palpāre* 'stroke', late 'feel' (above, 2), and perh. Grk. ψάλλω 'pluck', ψηλαφάω 'feel, grope' (above, 1). Walde-P. 1.7. Ernout-M. 726. Falk-Torp 290. Franck-v. W. 753. Otherwise (: Lat. *palma*, OE *folm*, etc., 'palm of the hand', which are fr. the root of Lat. *plānus* 'flat', etc.) Weigand-H. 1.595, Kluge-G. 178, NED s.v. *feel* vb. Hence the derivs. for 'touch, sense of touch', Dan. *følelse*, more specifically *føle-sans*, ME *fele, feling*, NE *feeling* (still in part specific, of NED s.v. 2), NHG *gefühl*, Du. *gevoel*.

Sw. *känna*, both 'feel of' (esp. with *på*) and, more generally, 'perceive, feel' : ON *kenna* 'perceive (by taste, smell, touch), know, recognize, etc.' (15.11). Hence Sw. *känsel* '(sense of) touch'. Hellquist 546.

OE, OHG *hrīnan*, ME *rine*, MHG (*be*)*rīnen* 'touch' : ON *hrīna* 'adhere, take effect on', perh. fr. a root **krei-* in Lett. *kriet* 'skim' (cream from milk), *kriens*, Lith. *kriena* (*krena*, NSB) 'thin skin on boiled food or milk', and OE *hrīm*, etc. 'hoar-frost'(??). Walde-P. 1.478. Falk-Torp 899 f. Mühl.-Endz. 2.284.

OE *hreppan, hrepian*, ME *repe, repie* (rare) 'touch' : ON *hreppa* 'catch, obtain', OE *ā-ræpsan* 'carry off', OHG *raspōn* 'scrape together', and MHG, NHG *raffen* 'snatch up', etc. Walde-P. 2.589. Falk-Torp 880.

OE *grāpian* (e.g. Gospels, Lk. 24.39 for ψηλαφάω, Vulgate *palpāre*), ME *grope* 'feel of' and 'feel about' (NE *grope*), OHG *greifōn*, MHG *greifen* 'feel of', iter. to OE *grīpan*, ON *grīpa*, Goth. *greipan* 'seize, grasp', OHG *grīfan*, MHG *grīfen* 'seize', sometimes (esp. MHG) also 'touch', NHG *greifen* 'seize' (11.14). NED s.v. *grope*.

OE *gefrēdan* 'feel, perceive, be sensible of' (hence *gefrēdnes* 'sense of feeling', mentioned along with 'sight' and 'hearing', in quot. in Bosworth-Toller s.v.), ME *ivrede, frede* = OHG *fruoten* 'teach, make wise', fr. OE *frōd*, OHG *fruot* 'wise, sagacious'. NED s.v. *frede*.

ME *touche*, NE *touch*, fr. Fr. *toucher* (above, 2).

ME *taste* (also 'taste' as NE), Du., MHG, NHG *tasten*, fr. OFr. *taster* (above, 2).

Du. *aanraken* 'touch', in this sense less usually simple *raken* but this mostly 'hit' = MLG *rāken* 'hit, reach, fall upon', prob. : Du. *rekken*, OHG *recken* 'stretch out', OE *reccan* 'stretch, reach, direct', Goth. *ufrakjan* 'stretch up', etc. 'Touch' prob. fr. 'stretch out' (the arm) or 'reach'. Falk-Torp 870 f., 929. French-v. W. 532, 543.

OHG (*h*)*ruoren*, MHG (*be*)*rüeren* 'touch, move, stir', NHG *berühren* 'touch' (simple *rühren* now reserved for 'move, stir'), Dan. *røre*, Sw. *röra* (properly 'move'; 'touch' prob. in imitation of German, and in this sense more usually Dan. *berøre, røre ved*, Sw. *beröra, vidröra*), with derivs. for 'touch, sense of touch', OHG *gihrōrida* (also 'motion'), MHG *gerüerde, berüerde* : ON *hrœra* 'move, stir', OE *hrēran* 'move, stir, shake', prob. fr. the root in Grk. κεράννῦμι 'mix', Skt. *çrā-* 'cook, bake' (fr. 'mix'). Walde-P. 1.419 f. Falk-Torp 937.

5. Lith. *liesti*, intens. *lytėti* 'touch' (NSB; Kurschat has *pakrutinti* 'touch' in Wtb. and NT) : Lett. *laitīt* 'stroke', fr. **lei-t-* (perh. in Grk. λίτομαι, λίσσομαι 'beseech', as orig. 'seek by caresses'), an extension of **lei-* in Lat. *linere* 'smear', etc. Walde-P. 2.391.

Lith. *čiupinėti* 'feel of', frequent. of *čiupti* 'grasp', here also *čiuopti* 'feel about' (and 'grasp'), whence *čiuopimas* 'sense of touch' (all in NSB; only *čiopti* 'grasp' in Kurschat), deriv. of an imitative syllable like Lith. *čiupt* symbolic of quick motion and used esp. in phrases with 'seize, grasp' (cf. Kurschat s.v.).

Lett. *aiztikt*, 'arrive, attain', and 'touch', cpd. of *tikt* 'arrive, attain, reach'. Mühl.-Endz. 1.156, 3.184 f.

Lett. *aizskart* 'touch' (this word used in NT), fr. *aiz-si-kart*, cpd. of *kart*, replaced by *k'ert* 'grasp'. Mühl.-Endz. 1.50, 2.369 f.

Lett. *taustīt* 'feel of', with sb. *tauste* 'sense of touch', prob. through notion of being careful : Lith. *tausoti* 'be sparing', fr. same root as Lith. *taupyti*, Lett. *taupīt* id. Mühl.-Endz. 4.140.

6. ChSl. *kosnąti, pri-kasati* 'touch' (the reg. words in the Gospels) : *česati* 'comb, stroke', Lith. *kasyti* 'scratch', etc. Walde-P. 1.449. Berneker 151 f., 581 f.

ChSl. *prisęgnąti, prisęšti* 'touch' (Supr.), *osęgnąti, osęzati* 'feel of' (Supr.), with sb. *osęzanĭje* (late), Russ. *osjazat'* 'feel of', *osjazanie* 'sense of touch', cpds. of ChSl. *sęgnąti* 'stretch out' (the hand), this prob. : Lith. *segti* 'fasten', Skt. *saj-* 'hang', etc. Miklosich 291. Brückner 490. Trautmann 252. Otherwise Walde-P. 2.480 f., 482 f.

ChSl. (late), SCr. *pipati*, Bulg. *pipam*, etc. 'feel of' (> Rum. *pipăi*), with SCr. *opip* 'sense of touch', prob. fr. an imitative syllable. Cf. Lith. *čiupinėti*, etc., above, 5.

SCr. *doticati*, Boh. *dotknouti se*, Pol. *dotknąć* 'touch', with Pol. *dotykanie* or *zmysł dotykania* 'sense of touch', cpds. of root seen in ChSl. *tŭknąti, tykati* 'fix, stick, prick, strike' : Grk. τύκος 'mason's hammer', Skt. *tuj-* 'thrust', etc. Walde-P. 2.615 f. Brückner 571.

SCr. *dirati* 'touch, handle' : ChSl.

dĭrati, etc., general Slavic for 'tear', Goth. *tairan* 'tear', etc. (9.28). Berneker 201.

Boh. *hmatati* 'feel of', *hmat* 'sense of touch', prob. of imitative orig. Berneker 391.

Boh. *makati*, Pol. *macać* 'feel of', perh. : Boh. *mačkati* 'squeeze', both of imitative orig.? Berneker 2.1, 2. Brückner 316.

Russ. *trogat'* 'touch', given without any connections in Miklosich 362, but prob. fr. ChSl. *trŭgati* 'tear, snatch', with semantic development through 'grasp' (as often), and phonetic treatment after analogy of cases in which ChSl. *rŭ* = Slavic *rŭ*, Russ. *ro*.

Russ. *(o)ščupat'* 'feel of, feel about', doubtless of imitative orig., like Lith. *čiupinėti* (above, 5).

7. Skt. *spṛç-* 'touch', also 'feel' as 'perceive by touch' (equated with vbs. for 'smell', 'taste', etc.; cf. BR s.v., 3), *sparça-* 'sense of touch', etym.?

15.74 HARD

Grk.	σκληρός	Goth.	*hardus*	Lith.	*kietas*
NG	σκληρός	ON	*harðr*	Lett.	*ciets*
Lat.	*dūrus*	Dan.	*haard*	ChSl.	(*žestokŭ, tvrŭdŭ*)
It.	*duro*	Sw.	*hård*	SCr.	*tvrd*
Fr.	*dur*	OE	*heard*	Boh.	*tvrdý*
Sp.	*duro*	ME	*hard*	Pol.	*twardy*
Rum.	*tare*	NE	*hard*	Russ.	*tverdyj* (*žestkij*)
Ir.	*crūaid, calad*	Du.	*hard*	Skt.	*dṛḍha-*
NIr.	*cruaidh*	OHG	*harti, herti, hart*	Av.	*xraoždva-, xrūždra-*
W.	*caled*	MHG	*herte, hart*		
Br.	*kalet*	NHG	*hart*		

'Hard' is understood here, of course, as 'hard, unyielding to the touch', and 'soft' (15.75) as its opposite, 'yielding to the touch'.

For the frequent use of words for 'hard' in the sense of 'difficult', see 9.97.

1. Grk. σκληρός, orig. 'dry' : σκέλλω 'dry up, parch', etc. Walde-P. 2.597. Boisacq 872.

2. Lat. *dūrus* (> It., Sp. *duro*, Fr. *dur*; also the rare Ir. *dūr*, and W. *dur*, Br. *dir* 'steel'), prob. fr. **drūros* : Grk. δροόν· ἰσχυρόν (Hesych.), Ir. *dron* 'solid', Lith. *drūtas* 'strong, solid', Skt. *dāruṇa-* 'rough, strong, hard', etc., and in the names of the 'oak tree', Grk. δρῦς, Ir. *daur*, etc. The root perh. orig. designated the '(hard) oak wood', whence the general 'hard'. Walde-P. 1.805. Ernaut-M. 291. Walde-H. 1.384 f.

Rum. *tare* (also 'strong'), fr. Lat. *tālis* 'such a', with meliorative development = 'such an excellent'. REW 8431. Tiktin 1562 f.

3. Ir. *crūaid*, NIr. *cruaidh* : Lat. *crūdus* 'raw, crude, cruel', Av. *xraoždva-, xrūždra-* 'hard', Skt. *krūḍ-* 'thicken, make firm', fr. the root in Skt. *kravis-* 'raw flesh', Grk. κρέας 'flesh', Lat. *cruor*, Ir. *crō* 'blood, gore', etc. Walde-P. 1.479.

Ir. *calad*, W. *caled*, Br. *kalet*, cf. Gall. *Caletes, Caleti*, perh. : ChSl. *kaliti* 'become cold, harden' (of iron), Lett. *kalst* 'dry out', and also Lat. *callum, callus* 'hard, thick skin'. Walde-P. 1.357. Walde-H. 1.141.

4. Goth. *hardus*, ON *harðr*, OE *heard*, etc., general Gmc. : Grk. κρατύς 'strong', κράτος, κάρτος 'strength', etc., with *t*-suffix fr. the root **kar-* in Skt. *karkara-* 'rough, hard' (cf. κάρκαροι· τραχεῖς Hesych.), etc. Walde-P. 1.354. Falk-Torp 370. Feist 246.

5. Lith. *kietas*, Lett. *ciets* (OPruss.

prob. in *keytaro* 'hail'), perh. : Bulg., SCr. *čitav* 'whole, uninjured'; root connection? Mühl.-Endz. 1.396. Berneker 158.

6. ChSl. *žestokŭ* (renders σκληρός 'harsh', of a person Mt. 25. 24, of words Jn. 6.60), Russ. *žestkij* mostly 'harsh', SCr. *žestok* 'vehement, fiery' : ChSl. *žegą, žešti* 'burn'. Miklosich 410.

ChSl. *tvrŭdŭ* 'firm, steady, stable' (Supr.), SCr. *tvrd*, etc., general modern Slavic 'hard' : Lith. *tvirtas* 'firm', *tverti* 'seize, inclose', ChSl. *tvoriti* 'make, create', etc. 'Hard, firm' fr. 'held firmly'. Walde-P. 1.750. Trautmann 334. Brückner 586.

7. Skt. *dṛḍha-* 'hard, firm', fr. *dṛh-* 'fasten, make firm', Av. *darəz* 'bind, fetter', etc. Walde-P. 1.859. Uhlenbeck 159.

Av. *xraoždva-, xrūždra-* : Ir. *crūaid* (above, 3).

15.75 SOFT

Grk.	μαλακός	Goth.	*hnasqus*	Lith.	*minkštas*
NG	μαλακός	ON	*mjūkr, blautr*	Lett.	*mīksts*
Lat.	*mollis*	Dan.	*blød*	ChSl.	*mękŭkŭ*
It.	*morbido, molle*	Sw.	*mjuk*	SCr.	*mek(an)*
Fr.	*mou (mol)*	OE	*hnesce*	Boh.	*měkký*
Sp.	*blando, muelle*	ME	*softe, nesche*	Pol.	*miękki*
Rum.	*moale*	NE	*soft*	Russ.	*mjagkij*
Ir.	*boc, mōith*	Du.	*zacht, week*	Skt.	*mṛdu-*
NIr.	*bog*	OHG	*weich*	Av.	*varədva-*
W.	*meddal*	MHG	*weich*		
Br.	*bouk, gwak*	NHG	*weich*		

Several of the words for 'soft', as appears from their probable root connections, are based on what is 'crushed, rubbed, bent' or 'moistened'. Or 'soft' and 'weak' may rest on the common notion of 'yielding'. In a few, 'soft' is secondary to 'pleasant'.

1. Grk. μαλακός : βλάξ 'stolid, stupid', βληχρός 'faint, gentle', fr. a guttural extension of the root **mel-* in Lat. *molere*, etc. 'grind'. Cf. Lat. *mollis*, etc. (below). Walde-P. 2.290. Boisacq 604.

2. Lat. *mollis* (> It. *molle*, Fr. *mou*, Sp. *muelle*, Rum. *moale*), fr. **moldwis* : Skt. *mṛdu-* 'soft, tender', Grk. ἀμαλδύνω 'weaken, destroy', W. *blydd* 'sappy, soft, tender', ChSl. *mladŭ* 'young, tender', etc., fr. an extension of the root **mel-* in Lat. *molere*, etc. 'grind' (orig. 'crush'). Walde-P. 2.288. Ernout-M. 626.

It. *morbido*, fr. Lat. *morbidus* 'sickly, diseased' (: *morbus* 'sickness'). REW 5677.

Sp. *blando*, fr. Lat. *blandus* 'flattering, pleasant, agreeable' (cf. also Rum. *blînd* 'gentle, mild'). REW 1151.

3. Ir. *boc(c)*, NIr. *bog*, Br. *bouk* 'soft', fr. 'pliant, flexible' (cf. *fid-bocc* 'wooden bow') : Skt. *bhugna-* 'bent', fr. *bhuj-* 'bend'. Walde-P. 2.145 f. Pedersen 1.159. Stokes 180.

Ir. *mōith, mōeth*, perh. loanword fr. Britannic, cf. W. *mwydion* 'soft parts', *mwydo* 'soak, steep', etc. : Lat. *mītis* 'mild, gentle, mellow', etc. Walde-P. 2.244. Pedersen 1.181, 184 Anm.

W. *meddal*, etym.? Morris Jones 161 (with cons. transposition fr. **meladd* : Lat. *mollis*, etc.).

Br. *gwak*, also 'vain, useless' = W. *gwag* 'empty', fr. Lat. *vacuus*. Loth, Mots lat. 174.

4. Goth. *hnasqus* (? only dat. pl. fem. *hnasqjaim*), with ablaut OE *hnesce*, ME *nesche* (NE dial. *nesh*), beside OE *hnescian* 'make or become soft', OHG *nascōn*

'eat on the sly, pilfer' (= 'pick off'), prob. : Skt. *kiknasa-* 'particle of bruised grain', Lett. *knuosīt* 'pick, tear to pieces with the beak'. 'Soft' fr. 'torn', or 'rubbed to pieces'. Walde-P. 1.394. Feist 265.

ON *mjūkr*, Sw. *mjuk* : Du. *muik* 'mellow', Goth. *mūka-* in *mūkamōdei* 'gentleness', beside forms with Gmc. *-g-* (IE *-k-'*) in ON *mugga* 'fine rain', etc. : Lat. *mūcus* 'mucus, snot', etc. 'Soft' fr. 'wet'. Walde-P. 2.253. Falk-Torp 744.

ON *blautr*, Dan. *blød* (Sw. *blöt* now esp. 'soggy, watery') : Grk. φλυδάω 'become soft, flabby, overflow', φλυδαρός 'flabby', φλύω 'bubble up', etc. Walde-P. 2.213. Falk-Torp 85, 88. Hellquist 85.

ME *softe*, NE *soft*, Du. *zacht* : OE *sōft(e)*, beside more usual *sēfte* 'agreeable, pleasant', OHG *semfti*, MHG *senfte, sanft* 'agreeable, comfortable, easy', NHG *sanft* 'gentle, smooth, soft' (but hardly 'soft' to the touch), prob. fr. the root in ON *sama, samða* 'happen', Goth. *samjan* 'please', and eventually Grk. ὁμός 'common, like', Goth. *sama*, ON *samr* 'same'. Walde-P. 2.491. Weigand-H. 2.647. NED s.v. *soft*, adj.

OHG-NHG *weich*, Du. *week* : ON *veikr* (> NE *weak*), OE *wāc* 'weak, yielding', fr. the root of ON *víkja* 'turn, veer', OE *wīcan*, OHG *wīhhan* 'yield, give way', etc. Walde-P. 1.235. Falk-Torp 1360.

5. Lith. *minkštas*, Lett. *mīksts*, with different suffix, ChSl. *mękŭkŭ*, general Slavic : Lith. *minkyti*, Lett. *mīcīt* 'knead', ChSl. *o-męčiti* 'soften', etc., Grk. μάσσω 'press, knead, stroke', OE *mengan*, etc. 'mix'. Walde-P. 2.268. Berneker 2.42 f. Mühl.-Endz. 2.640, 643.

6. Skt. *mṛdu-* : Lat. *mollis* (above, 2).

Av. *varədva-*, cf. Skt. *avradanta* 'they became soft' (RV), perh. : OE *wrōtan*, ON *rōta* 'root up', ChSl. *vrědŭ*, etc. 'abcess, wound'. Walde-P. 1.287. Barth. 1370.

15.76 ROUGH

Grk.	τρᾱχύς	Goth.	(*usdrusts*)	Lith.	*grubluotas, šiurkštus*
NG	τραχύς	ON	*ūslēttr, hrjūfr*	Lett.	*nelīdzens, grubulains*
Lat.	*asper*	Dan.	*ujævn, ru*	ChSl.	(*srŭchŭkŭ*)
It.	*ruvido, aspro, rude*	Sw.	*ojämn, skrovlig*	SCr.	*hrapav*
Fr.	*rude, âpre, rugueux*	OE	*unsmēþe, rūh*	Boh.	*drsný*
Sp.	*áspero, tosco, rudo*	ME	*rughe, uneven*	Pol.	*szorstki, chropawy*
Rum.	*aspru*	NE	*rough, uneven*	Russ.	*šerochovatyj*
Ir.	*garb*	Du.	*ruw, oneffen*	Skt.	*viṣama-*
NIr.	*garbh*	OHG	*uneban*	Av.	. . . .
W.	*garw*	MHG	*rūch, uneben*		
Br.	*garo*	NHG	*rauh, uneben*		

Words for 'rough' were doubtless all orig. used with some more specific application, as to the sea, the hair, the skin, etc. In some cases this is apparent from the etymology.

'Rough' may always be expressed as 'uneven' or 'not smooth', and for some languages or periods such terms are more common than any others.

1. Grk. τρᾱχύς : θράσσω, ταράσσω 'stir, disturb, trouble', this prob. : ON *dreggjar* 'dregs', OLith. *dragis* 'dregs', etc. Walde-P. 1.854 f. Boisacq 981. 'Rough' prob. first of the sea that is 'stirred up, made rough'. Cf. ἐτάραξε δὲ πόντον (Hom.), κύμασιν ταράσσεται πόντος (Archil.), etc.

2. Lat. *asper* (> It. *aspro*, Fr. *âpre*, Sp. *áspero*, Rum. *aspru*), prob. fr. **ap(o)-spero-* : Skt. *apa-sphur-* 'bursting forth,

splashing out', fr. the root of Lat. *spernere* 'reject, despise', Skt. *sphur-* 'spurn, dart, spring', etc. Walde-P. 2.669. Walde-H. 1.73.

It. *ruvido*, fr. Lat. *rūgidus* (gl.) = *rūgōsus* 'wrinkled' (> Fr. *rugueux*), deriv. of Lat. *rūga* 'wrinkle'. REW 7427. Gamillscheg 776. Ernout-M. 874.

It., Fr. *rude*, Sp. *rudo*, fr. Lat. *rudis* 'raw, crude, coarse (of cloth), green (of fruit)'. REW 7420.

Sp., Port. *tosco*, Cat. *tosc*, beside Cat. *tosca* 'crust formed by a liquid in a vessel', orig.? REW 9013.

3. Ir. *garb*, NIr. *garbh*, W. *garw*, Br. *garo*, prob. deriv. of the root **ĝher-* beside *ĝhers-* in Lat. *horrēre* 'stand on end, bristle, be rough', Skt. *hṛṣ-* 'bristle, stand erect', etc. Walde-P. 1.610. Stokes 107.

4. Goth. *usdrusts*, only in nom. pl. *usdrusteis* = τραχεῖαι (sc. ὁδοί), Lk. 3.5, fr. *us-driusan* 'fall out', hence perh. 'fallen to pieces' of 'rough' roads, but no evidence whether the word was used for 'rough' in general. Feist 530.

ON *ūslēttr*, lit. 'unsmooth' (15.77).

ON *hrjūfr* 'rough', but esp. of the body 'scabby' (sometimes with *līkþrār* 'leprous'), Norw. *ry* 'rough', OE *hrēof* 'rough (of stone), scabby (of body), leprous', OHG *hriob* 'leprous' : ON *hrufa* 'crust, scab', *hrufla* 'scratch', OE *hrēofl* 'leprous', Lith. *kraupus* 'easily frightened, fearful, horrid', also 'rough', Lett. *k'raupa* 'scab, wart', etc. Walde-P. 1.481. Falk-Torp 925.

Dan. *ujævn*, Sw. *ojämn*, ME *uneven*, Du. *oneffen*, OHG *uneban*, etc., lit. 'uneven', cf. Dan. *jævn* 'smooth, even', etc. (15.77).

Sw. *skrovlig*, cf. older Dan. *skrub* 'roughness', prob. : Lat. *scrūpus* 'sharp, pointed stone', and also ON *hrjūfr*, etc. (above), fr. parallel extensions, with and without *s-*, of IE **sker-* 'cut'. Walde-P. 1.482, 2.587. Falk-Torp 1030. Hellquist 951.

OE *unsmēþe, unsmōþe*, lit. 'unsmooth' (15.77).

OE *rūh, rūg*, ME *rughe, rught*, etc., NE *rough*, Du. *ruw* (MLG *rūch, rū* > Dan. *ru*), MHG *rūch*, NHG *rauh*, in the older languages also largely 'hairy, bushy, etc.' and in this sense only OHG *rūh* (NHG *rauch*, now differentiated from *rauh*), orig. 'plucked out (of hair), shaggy, rough-haired' : Skt. *luñc-* 'pluck, pull out', Lat. *runcāre* 'root out, weed out', Grk. ὀρύσσω 'dig, scrape', etc. Walde-P. 2.353. Falk-Torp 915.

5. Lith. *grubluotas, grublus*, Lett. *grubulains* : Lith. *grubus* 'stiff' and 'rough', *grubti* 'grow stiff or rough', prob. (*grub-* for **grumb-*) : ChSl. *grąbŭ* 'simple, foolish, ignorant', Russ. *grubyj* 'coarse, rough, rude', etc. (general Slavic for some uses of NE *rough*); ChSl. *grŭbŭ* 'back; convulsion', Ir. *gerbach* 'wrinkly', OHG *krimpfan* 'draw together, wrinkle', etc. The earlier meaning of these Balto-Slavic words for 'rough', 'stiff', 'coarse' was prob. 'wrinkled' (cf. Lat. *rūgidus* > It. *ruvido*, etc., above, 2). Walde-P. 1.596. Berneker 355, 368.

Lith. *šiurkštus*, fr. Slavic (cf. Pol. *szorstki*, etc., below, 6).

Lett. *nelīdzens*, also Lith. *nelygus*, lit. 'not smooth' (15.77).

6. Russ.-ChSl. *srŭchŭkŭ*, Pol. *szorstki*, Russ. *šerochovatyj* fr. the same root as ChSl. *srŭstĭ*, Boh. *srst'* 'hair', Russ. *šerst'* 'wool', OHG *hursti* 'tuft', etc. Walde-P. 1.427. Trautmann 305. Brückner 552.

ChSl. *ostrŭ* 'sharp' used in pl. *ostriji* for 'rough roads' (Lk. 3.5; no other occurrence of 'rough' in Gospels).

SCr. *hrapav*, Pol. *chropawy* (Boh. *chrapavý* 'rattling, hoarse'), beside forms with *k-*, Ukr. *koropavyj* 'rough', etc., or with g-, Slov. grapast 'rough', Bulg. grapav 'pock-marked', etc., perh. : Lith. karpa 'wart', OE scurf 'scurf', etc. Berneker 674 f. Brückner 184.

Boh. drsný, drsnatý, old drstný, drstnatý : (old) drst 'rubbish', Slov. drstev

'gravel, sand', Pol. dziarstwo 'gravel', etc., prob. fr. the root in ChSl. derą, dĭrati 'tear, flay'. Berneker 256. 'Rough' perh. directly fr. 'gritty'.

7. Skt. viṣama-, lit. 'uneven' : sama- 'even, smooth, level' (15.77).

15.77 SMOOTH

Grk.	λεῖος	Goth.	slaihts	Lith.	lygus, gludus
NG	λεῖος	ON	slēttr	Lett.	lĩdzens, gluds
Lat.	lēvis	Dan.	glat, jævn	ChSl.	gladŭkŭ
It.	liscio	Sw.	slät, jämn, glatt	SCr.	gladak
Fr.	lisse, uni	OE	smēþe	Boh.	hladký
Sp.	liso	ME	smothe, smethe, sleghte	Pol.	gładki
Rum.	neted	NE	smooth	Russ.	gladkij
Ir.	rēid, mín	Du.	glad, effen	Skt.	sama-, çlakṣna-
NIr.	rēidh, mín	OHG	sleht, eban	Av.	....
W.	llyfn	MHG	sleht, sleht, eben		
Br.	kompez	NHG	glatt, eben		

Words for 'smooth' reflect such notions as 'slippery', 'even', 'level', or 'bright, shining', all of which are naturally associated with smooth surfaces.

1. IE *lei-, *slei- (with various formations) in words for 'slimy, slippery' substances, and in vbs. for 'slip, smear, stick, etc.', cf. Lat. līmus 'mud, mire', OE lām, OHG leim 'clay', ON, OE slīm 'slime', etc.; Grk. ἀλίνω 'smear, anoint', Lat. linere 'smear', etc. Walde-P. 2.389 ff. Ernout-M. 542. Walde-H. 1.782. Falk-Torp 1061 f.

Here as 'smooth', Grk. λεῖος, Lat. lēvis, W. llyfn (: Ir. slemun 'slick, slippery'); Goth. slaihts, ON slēttr, Sw. slät, ME sleghte, slighte (NE slight now 'slender, small in quantity', etc.), OHG sleht (NHG schlecht now 'plain, bad'); ON slíkr (rare).

2. It. liscio, Fr. lisse, Sp. liso, prob. fr. Gmc., cf. MHG lise, NHG lise 'low, soft, gentle'. REW 5081. Bloch 2.19.

Fr. uni, lit. 'joined', hence (as 'joined closely') also 'smooth' (so also sometimes It. unito of road, land, etc.), pple. of unir, It. unire, etc. 'join, unite'.

Rum. neted, fr. Lat. nitidus 'bright, shining' (15.57). REW 5929.

3. Ir. rēid, NIr. rēidh, also 'open, clear, level, flat', prob. orig. of a way 'passable' : Ir. rīadaim, OE rīdan 'ride', etc. (cf. with similar development W. rhwydd 'free, easy, fluent, ready'). Walde-P. 2.349. Pedersen 1.58.

Ir. mín, also 'gentle, tender, fine' : W. mwyn 'kind, gentle, dear', fr. an extension of the root *mei- in Lat. mītis 'mild', Ir. mõith 'soft, tender' (15.75). Walde-P. 2.244. Pedersen 1.51.

W. llyfn, above, 1.

Br. kompez, fr. MBr. compoes 'equal' : W. cymmwys 'of the same weight, proper, meet', prob. fr. VLat. *com-pēnsum, fr. com-pēnsāre 'weigh together, equalize', or else an independent Britannic cpd. of the same elements (Br. poez, W. pwys 'weight', fr. Lat. pēnsum). Loth, Mots lat. 156. Henry 75, 226.

4. Goth. slaihts, ON slēttr, etc., above, 1.

Dan. jævn, Sw. jämn, ME (NE) even, Du. effen, OHG eban, MHG, NHG eben, all also and orig. 'even, level, flat' (12.71).

OE smēþe, ME smethe (NE dial. smeeth), beside OE smōþ (rare), ME smothe, NE smooth, etym.? Walde-P. 2.491. NED s.vv. smeeth, smooth, adj.

Du. glad, MHG glat, NHG glatt (> Dan. glat, Sw. glatt), but OHG glat mostly 'shining' = ON glaðr, OE glæd 'shining, bright, joyous' (NE glad) : Lat. glaber 'hairless, bald', Lith. glodus, glodnas 'lying smoothly, rubbed smooth, etc.', ChSl. gladŭkŭ 'smooth', etc., fr. IE *ghlhd-, *ghlhdh-, prob. extension of *ghel- 'shine'. Walde-P. 1.625 f. Walde-H. 1.603. Falk-Torp 324.

5. Lith. lygus, Lett. lĩdzens, older lĩdzs, orig. 'like, equal', whence 'flat, level' and 'smooth' : Goth. galeiks 'like', ON (g)līkr, OE gelīc 'like', etc., Goth.

leik, etc. 'body, corpse'. Walde-P. 2.398 f. Mühl.-Endz. 2.479.

Lith. gludus, Lett. gluds, gludens : Lith. gludoti, gludēti 'lie close, snug', Lith. glausti 'press close', Lett. glaust 'stroke, caress', cf. Russ. dial. gludkij 'slippery, smooth', further connections dub. Mühl.-Endz. 1.623. Walde-P. 1.618 f. Berneker 308.

6. ChSl. gladŭkŭ, etc., general Slavic : Du. glad, etc. (above, 4).

7. Skt. sama- 'even, smooth, level' : Av. hama- 'like, same', Grk. ὁμός 'the same, common', ὁμαλός 'even, level', etc. Walde-P. 2.489.

Skt. çlakṣna- 'slippery, smooth, polished', etym.? Uhlenbeck 321.

15.78 SHARP
(In part differentiated; a, of a Point; b, of an Edge)

Grk.	ὀξύς	Goth.	*hwass (sb. hwassei)	Lith.	aštrus
NG	μυτερός (a); κοφτερός (b)	ON	hvass, skarpr	Lett.	ass
Lat.	acūtus	Dan.	skarp	ChSl.	ostrŭ
It.	acuto (a); tagliente (b)	Sw.	skarp, hvass	SCr.	oštar
Fr.	aigu (a); tranchant (b)	OE	scearp, hwæs	Boh.	ostrý
Sp.	agudo (a, b); cortante (b)	ME	scharp	Pol.	ostry
Rum.	ascuţit (a, b); tăios (b)	NE	sharp	Russ.	ostryj
		Du.	scherp	Skt.	tīkṣṇa-
		OHG	s(c)arf, (h)was	Av.	taēγa-, tiži-, tiγra-
Ir.	gēr, áith	MHG	scharf, was		
NIr.	gēar	NHG	scharf		
W.	llym, siarp				
Br.	lemm				

Most of the words listed are used both of a 'sharp' point and a 'sharp' edge, but some only in the former (a) or the latter (b) sense. Apart from the large inherited group, the usual connection is with words for 'cut' (so all those used only in sense b, and some of the others) or 'prick'.

1. IE *aḱ-, *oḱ- in words for 'sharp, pointed', 'edge, point', etc., cf. Skt. açri- 'edge', Grk. ἄκρος 'topmost', ἄκρον 'peak,

highest point', Lat. ācer 'sharp' in secondary senses, etc. Walde-P. 1.28 ff. Ernout-M. 7 ff. Walde-H. 1.7.

Here as 'sharp' : Grk. ὀξύς (NG mostly in secondary senses); Lat. acūtus (> It. acuto, Fr. aigu, Sp. agudo); Lith. aštrus, Lett. ass, ChSl. ostrŭ, etc., general Balto-Slavic.

2. NG μυτερός, fr. μύτη 'snout, nose' (4.23) also 'point, tip'.

NG κοφτερός, lit. 'cutting' : κόφτω 'cut'.

3. It. tagliente, Fr. tranchant, Sp. cortante, Rum. tăios, all lit. 'cutting', fr. the verbs for 'cut' It. tagliare, Fr. trancher, Sp. cortar, Rum. tăia (9.22).

Rum. ascuţit, fr. ascuţi 'sharpen, whet', Lat. *ex-cōtīre, fr. cōs 'whetstone'. Puşcariu 140. Tiktin 106 f.

4. Ir. gēr, NIr. gēar, etym.? Ir. áith, etym.?

W. llym, Br. lemm, perh. : MIr. slemun 'slippery'. W. llyfn 'smooth', etc. (15.77). Walde-P. 2.391, 435.

W. siarp, fr. NE sharp.

5. ON, Sw. hvass, OE hwæs, OHG (h)was(s), MHG was, Goth. *hwass (cf. hwassaba adv. 'sharply', hwassei 'sharpness'), beside ON hvatr, OE hwæt 'quick' : ON hvetja, OE hwettan, OHG (h)wezzen 'whet, sharpen, incite', out-

side connections dub. Walde-P. 1.513. Falk-Torp 437. Feist 184.

ON skarpr, OE scearp, etc., general Gmc., in ON also 'shriveled, lean, barren, rough', OE and OHG also rarely 'rough', prob. in sense 'sharp' : OE sceorpan 'scrape, irritate', OHG scurfen 'cut open, gut, strike fire', Ir. scerbaim 'cut', etc., an extension of IE *(s)ker- in ON skera, OE sceran, etc. 'cut'. Walde-P. 2.582. Falk-Torp 987. Franck-v. W. 583 f.

6. Skt. tīkṣṇa-, tigita-, tigma-, etc., Av. taēγa- (in bi-taēγa- 'sharp on two sides'), tiγra-, OPers. tigra- 'sharp-pointed', Av. tiži- (in cpds. tiži-dāra- 'with sharp edge', etc.) : Skt. tij- 'be sharp, sharpen', Grk. στίζω 'prick, tattoo', Lat. īn-stīgare 'incite, instigate', OE stician 'prick, stick' etc. Walde-P. 2.612 f. Walde-H. 1.707. Barth. 623, 651, 653 f.

émousser 'to dull', pple. émoussé, deriv. of Fr. mousse 'blunt, hornless' (not common), It. mozzo 'cut off, shortened', fr. a VLat. *mutios beside mutilus 'cut off, shortened, mutilated'. REW 5792. Ernout-M. 648.

Sp., Port. boto (Sp. embotar 'to dull', pple. embotado), Fr. bot in piedbot 'clubfoot', loanword fr. Gmc., cf. Du. bot, LG but 'blunt', NE butt 'thick end', belonging to the same group as OFr. bouter 'strike', etc. fr. Frank. *bōtan or *buttan : OE bēatan 'beat', etc. (9.21). REW 1228 c. Wartburg, 1.455 ff.

Rum. tocit, fr. toci 'make blunt, dull', this fr. Slavic, cf. SCr. točiti 'whet, grind off the edge'. Tiktin 1616.

3. Ir. mael, NIr. maol, also 'bald, hornless' : OW mail 'mutilum', W. moel 'bare, bald, hornless', fr. the root *mai- in Goth. maitan 'cut, hew', etc. Walde-P. 2.222.

W. pwl, origin?

Br. souc'h : Ir. socc 'snout'. Thurneysen Ernault, Dict. étym. 382.

Br. dall, lit. 'blind' (W., Ir. dall 'blind', cf. ME dul(l), below).

Br. tougn also 'shortened, snub-nosed', MBr. touign, Ir. touigna 'make blunt', fr. Lat. tundere (cf. above). Ernault, Glossaire 703. Henry 268.

4. ON sljör, slær, Dan. sløv, Sw. slö, OHG slēo (also 'weak, tepid'), MHG slē (-wes) = OE slāw 'dull (of persons), sluggish, lazy' (ME slaw 'dull' in one quot. in NED, NE slow in dial. also 'dull'), root connection dub. Walde-P. 2.378. Falk-Torp 1075. Hellquist 998.

OE āstynt (= (ā)styntan, for-styntan 'make blunt' (NE stint), ON stytta 'shorten', fr. OE stunt 'foolish', ON stuttr 'short', etc., prob. fr. the root of Goth. stautan 'shove', Lat. tundere 'beat'

(cf. Lot. obtūsus, above, 2), etc. Walde-P. 2.618. Falk-Torp 1191 f. NED s.v. stint, vb.

ME, NE blunt, etym.? NED s.v.

ME dul(l), mostly 'slow of understanding, stupid', NE dull, fr. an OE *dyl, beside dol 'foolish' = OHG tol, NHG toll 'crazy' : Goth. dwals 'foolish', Ir. dall, etc. 'blind', Grk. θολός, θολερός 'muddy, foul', etc. Walde-P. 1.843. NED s.v. dull, adj.

Du. stomp, MLG (> Dan.) stump, NHG stumpf, (OHG, MHG stumpf mostly 'mutilated, stumpy, cut off') : OHG-NHG stumpf, ME stumpe sb. 'stump', fr. the root in OHG stampfōn 'stamp, beat', etc. Walde-P. 2.624. Falk-Torp 1190.

5. Lith. atšipęs, pple. of at-šipti, cpd. of šipti 'become blunt', etym.?

Lith. bukas (NSB, etc.), formerly bukus (Kurschat, Leskien, Lalis), perh. : Lett. bukāt 'hit with the fist', Russ. bukat' 'beat, pound', of imitative origin. Walde-P. 2.113 (146).

Lett. neass, neg. cpd. of ass 'sharp' (15.78).

Lett. truls, perh. as 'rubbed down', fr. the root in trunēt 'crumble to dust, decay', Grk. τρύω 'rub down, wear out', etc. Mühl.-Endz. 4.245.

6. ChSl. tąpŭ, etc., general Slavic, prob. : ChSl. stąpati 'tread', etc., fr. *(s)temp- beside *(s)temb- in NHG stumpf, etc. (above, 4). 'Blunt' fr. 'battered', as also in Lat. obtūsus (above, 2). Walde-P. 2.625. (Better than as orig. 'bloated, tight', hence 'thick, blunt' : Lith. tempti 'stretch'. Walde-P. 1.721, Brückner 570).

7. Skt. atīkṣṇa-, neg. cpd. of tīkṣṇa- 'sharp' (15.78).

15.79 BLUNT, DULL

Grk.	ἀμβλύς	Goth.	....	Lith.	atšipęs, bukas
NG	ἀμβλύς	ON	sljör	Lett.	neass, truls
Lat.	hebes, obtūsus	Dan.	sløv, stump	ChSl.	tąpŭ
It.	ottuso, smussato	Sw.	slö	SCr.	tup
Fr.	émoussé	OE	āstynt	Boh.	tupý
Sp.	boto, embotado	ME	blunt, dul(l)	Pol.	tępy
Rum.	tocit	NE	blunt, dull	Russ.	tupoj
Ir.	mael	Du.	stomp	Skt.	atīkṣna-
NIr.	maol	OHG	slēo	Av.	....
W.	pwl	MHG	slē, stumpf		
Br.	souc'h, dall, tougn	NHG	stumpf		

The words listed are used both of a point and of an edge, but in several it is clear that the former application is the earlier. The most frequent connection is with words for 'cut', 'strike', 'beat', 'stamp', etc., here as 'cut off', etc. Sometimes the development is through 'shortened, mutilated', or from 'weak, inefficient'. In a few cases the application to mentality, usually secondary, is the earlier.

1. Grk. ἀμβλύς, fr. *ἄμλυς : ἀμαλός

'weak, tender', prob. fr. the root in Lat. mollis, Grk. μαλακός 'soft', etc. (15.75). Walde-P. 2.285, 292).

2. Lat. hebes, beside hebēre 'be blunt', etym. dub. Walde 1.349. Ernout-M. 447 (suggesting borrowing). Walde-H. 1.637 f.

Lat. obtūsus (> It. ottuso), fr. obtundere 'beat back the point, dull', cpd. of tundere 'beat, pound'. Ernout-M. 1064.

It. smussato, pple. of smussare, fr. Fr.

15.81 HEAVY

Grk.	βαρύς	Goth.	kaurus	Lith.	sunkus
NG	βαρύς	ON	þungr, hǫfugr (svárr)	Lett.	smags
Lat.	gravis	Dan.	tung, svær	ChSl.	tęžĭkŭ
It.	pesante (grave)	Sw.	tung	SCr.	težak
Fr.	lourd, pesant	OE	swær, hefig	Boh.	těžký
Sp.	pesado, grave	ME	hevi	Pol.	ciężki
Rum.	greu	NE	heavy	Russ.	tjaželyj
Ir.	tromm	Du.	zwaar	Skt.	guru-
NIr.	trom	OHG	suâri, hebîg	Av.	gouru-
W.	trwm	MHG	swære		
Br.	ponner	NHG	schwer		

Apart from the inherited group, words for 'heavy' are mostly connected with others for 'lift', 'weigh', 'pull', etc. In a few cases the application to mentality, usually secondary, appears to be the earlier.

1. IE *gʷṛu-, *gʷru-, etc. Walde-P. 1.684 ff. Ernout-M. 434. Walde-H. 1.620 f.

Grk. βαρύς; Lat. gravis (> It., Sp. grave, but mostly 'grave', etc.), VLat. (after levis 'light') *grevis (> Rum. greu); perh. the rare Ir. bair (Stokes, RC 27.85); Goth. kaurus; Skt. guru-, Av. gouru- (in gouru-zaoθra- 'having heavy libations'); here also Lett. grūts 'difficult, wretched, pregnant' and locally 'heavy' (cf. Mühl.-Endz. 1.669 f.); Lat. brūtus 'cumbersome, dull, stupid', arch. 'heavy' (Paul. Fest.), loanword fr. Osc.-Umbr. (Ernout-M. 119. Walde-H. 1.117).

2. It. pesante, Sp. pesado, Fr. pesant fr. It. pesare, Sp. pesar, Fr. peser 'weigh' (Lat. pēnsāre). REW 6391.

Fr. lourd, Prov. lord, fr. OFr., OProv. lort 'foolish, heavy of mind' (physical sense in Fr. from 17th. cent.), cf. Lyon. lord 'dizzy', prob. fr. Lat. lūridus 'pale yellow, ghastly'. Semantic development from 'pale' to 'dizzy', whence 'heavy' of mind, later in physical sense. REW 5176. Bloch 2.24. Otherwise Gamillscheg 571.

3. Ir. tromm, NIr. trom, W. trwm,

MBr. troum, prob. (*trud-smo-) fr. the root of Lat. trūdere 'push, shove', Goth. us-priutan 'trouble, vex', ChSl. trudŭ 'toil', etc. Walde-P. 1.755. Pedersen 1.362. Stokes 139.

Br. ponner, prob. fr. an oblique case of Lat. pondus, gen. ponderis 'weight'. Loth, Mots lat. 197.

4. Goth kaurus, above, 1.

ON þungr, Dan., Sw. tung : ChSl. tęžĭkŭ 'heavy', tęgostĭ 'burden', Lith. tingus 'lazy', fr. the root in ChSl. tęgnǫti 'pull'. Walde-P. 1.726 f. Falk-Torp 1299. Brückner 64.

ON svárr (poet. and here in fig. sense; cf. Sw. svår 'difficult'), OE swær (ME swere, but never in physical sense), Du. zwaar, OHG suâri, MHG swære, NHG schwer (> Dan. svær) = Goth. swērs only 'honored' : Lith. sverti 'weigh', svarus 'weighty, ponderous', svaras 'pound', etc., prob. fr. *swer-, beside *wer- in Grk. ἀείρω 'lift'. Walde-P. 1.265. Falk-Torp 1222 f.

ON hǫfugr, OHG hebîg, OE hefig, ME hevi, NE heavy : Goth. hafjan, OE hebban, OHG heffen, heben 'lift' (10.21). Walde-P. 1.343 (but not necessarily as orig. 'capax'. The natural association between 'lift' and 'heavy' is sufficient). NED s.v. heavy.

5. Lith. sunkus : sunkti 'grow heavy', older Lith. sunkinga 'pregnant', fr. *sunk- beside *swenk- in OE swangor 'heavy of movement, slow, sluggish',

NHG schwanger 'pregnant'. Walde-P. 2.525.

Lett. smags : Lith. dial. smagus 'heavy to carry or pull', Grk. μόγος 'toil', μογερός 'laborious', etc. Walde-P. 2.692. Mühl.-Endz. 3.928.

6. ChSl. tęžĭkŭ, general Slavic (but Russ. tjažkij in physical sense mostly replaced by new formation tjaželyj) : ChSl. tęgnǫti 'pull', ON þungr 'heavy', etc. (above, 4).

7. Skt. guru-, Av. gouru-, above, 1.

15.82 LIGHT (in Weight)

Grk.	ἐλαφρός (κοῦφος)	Goth.	leihts	Lith.	lengvas
NG	ἐλαφρός	ON	léttr	Lett.	viegls
Lat.	levis	Dan.	let	ChSl.	lĭgŭkŭ
It.	leggiero (lieve)	Sw.	lätt	SCr.	lak
Fr.	léger	OE	lēoht	Boh.	lehký
Sp.	legero (leve)	ME	lēoht	Pol.	lekki
Rum.	uşor	NE	light	Russ.	legkij
Ir.	étromm	Du.	licht	Skt.	laghu-
NIr.	éadtrom	OHG	lîhti	Av.	....
W.	ysgafn	MHG	liht(e)		
Br.	skañv	NHG	leicht		

Words for 'light' in weight are commonly used also for 'light, nimble' in movement, and in one case the latter sense is clearly the earlier. But the great majority belong to an inherited group used in both senses.

1. IE *legʷh- and *lengʷh- in words for 'light in weight' and 'light, quick in movement'. Walde-P. 2.426. Ernout-M. 542 (assuming two orig. different groups, but this not called for). Walde-H. 1.788 f. Falk-Torp 637.

Grk. ἐλαφρός, NG pop. also ἀλαφρός, ἀλαφρύς; Lat. levis (> It. lieve, Sp. leve; Rum. uşor, old ʻuşor with suffix -ʻor, cf. Puşcariu 1844; VLat. *leviārius > Fr. léger > It. leggiero, Sp. legero. REW 5003-4); Goth. leihts, OE lēoht, etc., general Gmc.; Lith. lengvas; ChSl.

lĭgŭkŭ, etc., general Slavic; Skt. raghu-, laghu- (Av. ragu- 'quick'); Alb. lehtë; here also with different meaning Grk. ἐλαχύς 'little, paltry', Ir. laigiu, MW llei 'less', OHG lungar 'quick', etc.

2. Grk. κοῦφος (rarely of weight, mostly 'light, nimble, vain, etc.'), etym.? Boisacq 504.

3. Ir. étromm, NIr. éadtrom, neg. of tromm 'heavy' (15.81).

W. ysgafn, Br. skañv, skañ : Ir. scaman 'lung' (cf. NE lights 'lungs' and the related lung), etym. dub. Walde-P. 2.601. Pedersen 1.76. Stokes 308.

4. Lett. viegls : Lith. viglas or vigrus 'quick, lively', Slov. vegati 'waver', Skt. vij- 'gush, heave, be agitated', etc. Mühl.-Endz. 4.654. Walde-P. 1.234.

15.83 WET, DAMP

Grk.	ὑγρός, νοτερός	Goth.	(natjan, vb.)	Lith.	šlapias, drėgnas
NG	ὑγρός, βρεγμένος (νοτερός)	ON	vátr, vǫkr	Lett.	slapjs, mikls, mitrs, drēgns
Lat.	ûmidus, madidus, ûvidus	Dan.	vaad, fugtig	ChSl.	mokrŭ
It.	bagnato, umido	Sw.	våt, fuktig	SCr.	mokar, vlažan
Fr.	mouillé, humide, moite	OE	wǣt, fûht	Boh.	mokrý, vlhký
Sp.	mojado, húmedo	ME	wet, moyste	Pol.	mokry, wilgotny
Rum.	ud, umed	NE	wet, damp, moist	Russ.	mokryj, syroj, vlaʻžnyj
Ir.	fliuch	Du.	nat, vochtig	Skt.	ârdra-
NIr.	fliuch	OHG	naz, fûhti	Av.	napta-
W.	gwlyb, llaith	MHG	naz, viuhte		
Br.	gleb, leiz	NHG	nass, feucht		

It is impossible to draw a sharp line between 'wet' and 'damp'. The distinction according to the degree of wetness, as in the current use of NE wet and damp, holds also in the main for the Gmc. and Balto-Slavic words. But elsewhere this is ignored, where several words are in use, as in Latin and the Romance languages, the choice depends on the kind of object described, the ground, a rag, etc., whether naturally wet or made wet, etc., all too diverse and complicated to be noted here.

Apart from the inherited group, the words are connected with others for 'water', 'bathe', 'leak', 'melt', 'vapor', 'soften', 'mire, filth'(?).

1. IE *weg-. Walde-P. 1.248. Ernout-M. 1123. REW 4233, 9030.

Grk. ὑγρός; Lat. ûmidus, and (by association with humus 'earth') hûmidus (> It. umido, Rum. umed, Fr. humide, Sp. húmedo), and ûvidus, whence ûdus (> Rum. ud); ON vǫkr.

2. Grk. (Hom.) νότιος, Att. νοτερός, beside νοτίς 'moisture', νότος 'south wind' (= 'damp'), prob. : Arm. nay 'wet, liquid', Lat. natāre 'swim', fr. an extension of the root *(s)nā- in Grk. νήχω, Lat. nāre (cf. Umbr. veskla snata 'vessels for liquids', Skt. snā- 'swim', etc. Walde-P. 2.692 f.

NG βρεγμένος, pple. of βρέχω 'wet, moisten', intr. 'rain', class. Grk. 'wet,

steep', pass. 'get wet, be rained on' : βροχή 'rain', Lett. mãrga 'gentle rain', etc. Walde P. 1.280.

3. Lat. madidus, fr. madēre 'be wet, drip with' : Grk. μαδάω 'be moist, fall off (of hair)', Ir. maidim 'break out, go to pieces', etc. Walde-P. 2.231. Ernout-M. 579. Walde-H. 2.6 f.

It. bagnato, pple. of bagnare 'bathe, wet, moisten' (VLat. balneâre fr. balnea, earlier balineum 'bath', fr. Grk. βαλανεῖον). Ernout-M. 101. REW 913.

Fr. mouillé, Sp. mojado, pple. of Fr. mouiller, Sp. mojar 'wet, moisten', fr. a VLat. *molliâre, fr. mollis 'soft'. REW 5646.

Fr. moite, OFr. moiste (> ME moyste, NE moist), prob. fr. *muscidus for Lat. mûcidus 'moldy' blended with musteus 'musty'. REW 5711. Gamillscheg 618. Bloch 2.71.

4. Ir. fliuch, W. gwlyb, MBr. gloeb, Br. gleb, perh. : Lat. liquidus 'liquid', etc., root *wleik-(-?). Walde-P. 2.397. Pedersen 1.60. Stokes 285. Walde-H. 1.812.

W. llaith, Br. leiz : W. dad-laith 'thaw', Ir. legaim 'dissolve, melt', ON leka 'leak', OE leccan 'moisten, wet', etc. Walde-P. 2.422 f. Pedersen 1.123.

5. ON vátr, Dan. vaad, Sw. våt, OE wǣt, ME, NE wet, OFris. wēt : ON vatn, OE wæter, Goth. watō etc. 'water' (1.31). Falk-Torp 1337.

ON vǫkr, above, 1.

OE fûht, Du. vocht, now usually vochtig (MLG vuchtich > Dan. fugtig, Sw. fuktig), OHG fûht, fûhti, MHG viuhte, NHG feucht, prob. (*pṇk-to-) : Skt. paṅka- 'mud, mire', fr. the root in Goth. fani 'mud', ON fen 'bog', etc. Walde-P. 2.5. Falk-Torp 281. Weigand-H. 1.525.

ME moyste, NE moist, fr. OFr. moiste (above, 3).

NE damp, earlier 'of the nature of a damp or noxious exhalation', fr. damp sb. : NHG dampf 'steam', etc. NED s.v.

Du. nat, OHG, MHG naz, NHG nass (hence OHG nezzen = Goth. natjan 'moisten'), etym. dub. Feist 371. Weigand-H. 2.276.

6. Lith. šlapias, Lett. slapjs, perh. : Grk. κλέπας : νοτερόν, πηλῶδες, ἢ δασύ, ἢ ὑγρόν (Hesych.), Ir. cluain 'meadow'. Walde-P. 1.497. Mühl.-Endz. 3.916. Trautmann 366.

Lith. drėgnas, Lett. drēgns, prob. : Lith. dergia 'the weather is bad', darga(na) 'nasty weather', dargas 'dirty, foul', ORuss. pa-doroga 'bad weather', etc. (Berneker 212 f.), these fr. the root in Grk. θράσσω 'trouble, disturb'. Walde-P. 1.855. (Wood, MLN 29.70 : Norw. dragen 'damp', but for this cf. Torp, Nynorsk 68).

Lett. mikls and mitrs, both of dub. orig. Mühl.-Endz. 2.625, 639.

7. ChSl. mokrŭ, etc., general Slavic, beside ChSl. močiti 'moisten', etc. : Lith. makonė 'puddle', Lett. mãkuona 'cloud', Arm. mōr (*makro-) 'mud, mire', further connections dub. Walde-P. 2.224. Berneker 2.70.

ChSl. syrŭ (= ὑγρός but only 'green, full of sap', Lk. 23.31), Russ. syroj (also 'raw', so SCr. sirov, Boh. syrový) : Lith. suras 'salty', Lett. surs 'bitter, salty', ON súrr 'sour', etc. (15.38). Trautmann 293. Walde-P. 2.513.

Russ.-ChSl. vŭlgŭkŭ, Boh. vlhký, Pol. wilgotny (wilgnǫć 'get damp') : ChSl. vlaga 'moisture' (SCr. vlaga, etc.) whence late ChSl. vlažĭnŭ, SCr. vlažan, Russ. vlažnyj : Lith. vilgyti 'moisten, wet', Lett. valgs 'damp', velgt 'wash, soak', OHG welc, NHG welk 'flabby, withered', *welg-, beside *welk- in Ir. folcaim 'wash', etc. Walde-P. 1.306. Trautmann 358 f. Brückner 621.

8. Skt. ârdra- : ṛd- 'disperse', in cpds. 'flow', ṛdū- 'moisture', further connections dub. Walde-P. 1.148.

Av. napta- (cf. NPers. naft 'naphtha', the source of the Eur. words), prob. fr. the root *nebh- in Skt. nabhas- 'mist, cloud, sky', Grk. νεφέλη 'cloud', etc. Walde-P. 1.131. Barth. 1039.

15.84 DRY

Grk.	ξηρός, αὖος	Goth.	þaursus	Lith.	sausas
NG	ξερός, στεγνός	ON	þurr	Lett.	sauss
Lat.	siccus, âridus	Dan.	tør	ChSl.	suchŭ
It.	secco, asciutto (arido)	Sw.	torr	SCr.	suh
Fr.	sec (aride)	OE	drýge, þyrre, sēar	Boh.	suchý
Sp.	seco, arido	ME	drie, sere	Pol.	suchy
Rum.	sæt, sec	NE	dry	Russ.	suchoj
Ir.	tirim	Du.	droog	Skt.	çuṣka-
NIr.	tirim	OHG	durri, trucchan	Av.	huška-, hiku-, hišku-
W.	sych	MHG	trucken, dürre		
Br.	sec'h, krin	NHG	trocken, dürr		

In the principal inherited groups and in most of the other words one cannot go behind the sense of 'dry'. A few are from the notion of 'extract the juice', and in a Gmc. group 'dry' is probably associated with 'firm', as sometimes 'wet' with 'soft'.

1. IE **saus-*, **sus-*. Walde-P. 2.447.

Grk. (Hom.) αὖος, Att. αὖος; OE *sēar*, ME (NE) *sere* (esp. 'withered'), MLG *sōr;* Lith. *sausas*, Lett. *sauss*, ChSl. *suchŭ*, etc., general Balto-Slavic; Skt. *çuṣka-* (for **suṣ-ka-*), Av. *huška-*, OPers. *uška-*.

2. IE **ters-* in words for 'dry', 'be dry', (dry) 'land' (1.21), 'thirst' (5.15), etc. Walde-P. 1.737 f. Ernout-M. 1048. Falk-Torp 1318.

Here as adj. 'dry'. Ir. *tīr* (rare), usually *tīrim*, NIr. *tirim, trim;* Goth. *þaursus*, ON *þurr*, Dan. *tør*, Sw. *torr*, OE *þyrre*, OHG *durri*, MHG *dürre*, NHG *dürr*.

3. Grk. ξηρός, NG pop. ξερός (ηρ > ερ reg., as in νερό 'water', etc.) prob. : Lat. *serēscere* 'become dry', *serēnus* 'fair' (of weather), OHG *serawēn* 'become dry, wither'. Walde-P. 1.503 Ernout-M. 928.

NG στεγνός, fr. class. Grk. στεγνός 'waterproof', this fr. στέγω 'cover'.

4. Lat. *siccus* (> It. *secco*, Fr. *sec*, Sp. *seco*, Rum. *sec*), etym. disputed; perh. : Av. *hiku-* 'dry', *haēčah-* 'dryness', these : Av. Skt. *sic-*, *hič-* 'pour out'. Ernout-M. 937. Barth. 1812. Otherwise, fr. **sit(i)-co-s* : *sitis* 'thirst', Walde-P. 1.506, etc.

Lat. *āridus* (> It., Sp. *arido*, OFr. *are*, Fr. *aride*), with *ārēre* 'be dry' : Skt. *āsa-* 'ashes, dust', Toch. A *āsar* 'dry', root **ās-*, with guttural extension in Goth. *azgō*, OHG *asca* 'ashes', Arm. *azazem* 'I dry', dental in Grk. ἄζω 'dry up', etc. Walde-H. 1.65. Ernout-M. 70.

It. *asciutto*, fr. Lat. *exsūctus*, pple. of *exsūgere* 'suck out', cpd. of *sūgere* 'suck'. REW 3074.

Rum. *uscat*, pple. of *usca* 'to dry' (= It. *asciugare*, Fr. *essuyer* 'dry, wipe dry'), fr. VLat. **ex-sūcāre* 'extract the juice' (*sūcus* 'juice'). REW 3073. Puşcariu 1841.

5. Ir. *tīrim*, etc., above, 2.

W. *sych*, Br. *sec'h*, also MIr. *secc.* (Cormac), fr. Lat. *siccus* (above, 4). Loth, Mots lat. 209. Vendryes, De hib. voc. 176.

Br. *krin* : W. *crin* 'withered, sere', Ir. *crīn*, NIr. *crīon* 'worn out, withered, old', Ir. *air-crinim* 'disappear, perish', root connection? Pedersen 2.498.

6. Goth. *þaursus*, OE *þyrre*, etc., above, 2.

OE *drȳge*, ME *drie*, NE *dry*, Du. *droog*, and with *n*-suffix OHG *trucchan*, MHG *trucken*, NHG *trocken;* cf. ON *draugr* 'dry log', prob : OPruss *drūktai* 'firmly', Lith. dial. *drūktas* 'thick, strong', ON *drjūgr* 'lasting, strong', etc., fr. an extension of the root in Skt. *dhṛ-* 'hold, bear', etc. Walde-P. 860. Weigand-H. 2.1074.

7. Balto-Slavic words, above, 1.

8. Skt. *çuṣka-*, Av. *huška-*, above, 1.

Av. *hiku-*, above, 4.

Av. *hišku-* : Ir. *sesc* 'dry, not giving milk', W. *hysb*, Br. *hesk* (*hesp*) 'dried up (of a stream), not giving milk', etc., fr. **si-sk-us*, reduplicated form fr. the root root **sek-* in Lith. *sekti* 'fall' (of water), *nusekti* 'flow off, dry up', ChSl. *i-sęknąti* 'decrease', etc. Walde-P. 2.473. Barth. 1816 f.

15.85 HOT, WARM

(Separated by; where distinction holds)

Grk.	θερμός	Goth.	**warms* (vb. *warmjan*)	Lith.	*karštas; šiltas*
NG	ζεστός	ON	*heitr; varmr*	Lett.	*karsts; silts*
Lat.	*calidus*	Dan.	*hed; varm*	ChSl.	*toplŭ*
It.	*caldo*	Sw.	*het; varm*	SCr.	*vruć; topao*
Fr.	*chaud*	OE	*hāt; wearm*	Boh.	*horký; teplý*
Sp.	*caliente, cálido*	ME	*hoot; warm*	Pol.	*gorący; ciepły*
Rum.	*cald*	NE	*hot; warm*	Russ.	*žarkij, gorjačij; teplyj*
Ir.	*tē*	Du.	*heet; warm*	Skt.	*uṣṇa-, tapta-*
NIr.	*te*	OHG	*heiz; warm*	Av.	*garəma-, tapta-*
W.	*poeth, twym, brwd; cynnes*	MHG	*heiz; warm*		
Br.	*tomm*	NHG	*heiss; warm*		

The distinction according to the degree of heat, as in NE *hot, warm,* holds for the Gmc. and Balto-Slavic words. Most of the other words listed are used without such distinction, though there may be special words for 'lukewarm, tepid', which are not included.

Apart from inherited groups, the words are connected with verbs for 'boil' (5.22, 10.31) or 'burn' (1.84).

It is well known that extreme heat and cold, as in touching a red-hot iron or a piece of ice, produce the same sensation, and there is every probability that a certain group of words for 'hot' (Lat. *calidus*, etc.) and another for 'cold' are, in fact, cognate. Cf. also Lat. *pruīna* 'hoar-frost' beside *prūna* 'live coal', *prurīre* 'itch', and OE *frēosan*, etc. 'freeze'.

1. IE **gʷher-*, adj. esp. with *mo*-suffix, **gʷhermo-*, **gʷhormo-*. Walde-P. 1.687 f. Ernout-M. 380. Walde-H. 1.532 f.

Grk. θερμός; OLat. *formus;* Av. *garəma-* (also sb. 'heat' = Skt. *gharma-* id.); Arm. *ǰerm*. Here prob. the Gmc. group, ON *varmr*, OE *wearm*, etc., but disputed and taken by some (cf. Falk-Torp 1354, 1575) fr. the root of ChSl. *varŭ* 'heat', *vĭrěti* 'well up, boil' (cf. below, 8). With different suffix ChSl. *gorĭkŭ* 'bitter', etc., the usual sense in modern Slavic (cf. 15.37), but Boh. *horký*, Slov. *gorək* 'hot', with vb. Slav. *gorěti* 'burn', pres. act. pple. often merely 'hot' in modern Slavic, Pol. *gorący*, Russ. *gorjačij* (cf. Berneker 333 f.); also Russ. *žarkij* (: *žar* 'heat', *žarit'* 'roast, scorch', ChSl. *žeravŭ* 'glowing', *po-žarŭ* 'burning').

2. IE **tep-*. Walde-P. 1.718 f. Ernout-M. 1030 f. Pedersen 1.87, 92 f., 2.19. Stokes 124 f.

Ir. *tē*, pl. *téit* (pple. **tepent-*), NIr. *te;* W. *twym*, Br. *tomm*, OCorn. *toim* (**tepes-mo-*); ChSl. *toplŭ*, SCr. *topao*, Boh. *teplý*, Pol. *ciepły*, Russ. *teplyj;* Skt., Av. *tapta-* (pple. of *tap-* 'be hot, warm'); Lat. *tepidus* 'lukewarm, tepid', *tepēre* 'be tepid', etc. Here also W. *cynnes* fr. **cyn-tes*, cpd. of *tes*, Ir. *tess* 'heat' (**teps-tu*). Morris Jones 63.

3. IE **k̂el-*, prob. the same ultimately as in words for 'cold', Lith. *šaltas*, etc. Walde-P. 1.429. Ernout-M. 134. Walde-H. 1137.

Lat. *calidus* (> borrowed Sp. *cálido*), *caldus* (> It. *caldo*, Fr. *chaud*, Rum. *cald*), with vb. *calēre* 'be warm' (> OSp. *caler*, deriv. *caliente* 'hot'); Lith. *šiltas*, Lett. *silts*, with vb. Lith. *šilti*, Lett. *silt* 'grow warm'; fr. an extended form of the root prob. ON *hlȳ* 'warmth', *hlær* 'warm, mild' (of weather), OE *hleowe* 'comfortable, sheltered', OHG *lāo*, NHG *lau* 'tepid', etc.

4. NG ζεστός, in class. Grk. 'boiled, boiling hot', fr. ζέω 'boil' (10.31).

5. Ir. *tē*, W. *twym*, Br. *tomm*, W. *cynnes*, above, 2.

W. *brwd* : *berwi*, Ir. *berbaim*, etc. 'boil'. Walde-P. 2.168.

W. *poeth* = Br. *poaz* 'cooked, burning', Lat. *coctus* 'cooked', pples. of W. *pobi*, Lat. *coquere* 'cook', etc. Walde-P. 2.17.

6. ON *heitr*, OE *hāt*, OHG *heiz*, etc., general Gmc., fr. **kai-d-*, beside **kai-t-* in Lith. *kaisti*, Lett. *kaist* 'become hot', etc., and **kai-* in OHG *hei*, *gehei* 'heat'. Walde-P. 1.326 f. Falk-Torp 388.

7. Lith. *karštas*, Lett. *karsts*, beside Lett. *karst* 'become hot', fr. the root of Lith. *kurti*, Lett. *kurt* 'heat', ChSl. *kuriti sę* 'smoke', Goth. *hauri* 'coals', ON *hyrr* 'fire'. Walde-P. 1.418.

8. SCr. *vruć*, and *vreo* : *vreti*, ChSl. *vĭrěti* 'boil', Lith. *virti* 'bubble up, boil', etc. Walde-P. 1.269. Miklosich 381.

9. Skt. *uṣṇa-*, fr. *uṣ-* 'burn' : Grk. εὕω 'singe', Lat. *ūrere* 'burn'. Walde-P. 1.111.

15.86 COLD

Grk.	ψῡχρός	Goth.	*kalds*	Lith.	*šaltas*
NG	κρύος	ON	*kaldr*	Lett.	*auksts, salts*
Lat.	*frīgidus, gelidus*	Dan.	*kold*	ChSl.	*studenŭ*
It.	*freddo*	Sw.	*kall*	SCr.	*hladan, studen*
Fr.	*froid*	OE	*ceald*	Boh.	*studený*
Sp.	*frío*	ME	*cold*	Pol.	*zimny*
Rum.	*rece, friguros*	NE	*cold*	Russ.	*cholodnyj* (*studenyj*)
Ir.	*ūar*	Du.	*koud*	Skt.	*çīta-, çiçira-, hima-*
NIr.	*fuar*	OHG	*calt*	Av.	*aota-, sarəta-*
W.	*oer*	MHG	*kalt*		
Br.	*yen*	NHG	*kalt*		

A distinction similar to that of 'hot' and 'warm' is partially observed, but here ignored in the list. That is, beside the generic words for 'cold', there are others for 'moderately cold', 'cool', usually with the feeling of pleasant contrast to excessive heat. These may be cognate with those for 'cold', as NE *cool*, NHG *kühl*, etc., or they may be words which mean literally 'fresh', as It. *fresco*, Fr. *frais*, etc., similarly NG δροσερός in class. Grk. 'dewy, fresh' : δρόσος, NG δροσιά 'dew'. Again, NE *chilly*, also cognate with *cold*, is 'moderately but disagreeably cold', and NG ψυχρός (in class. Grk. 'cold') is now used in just this sense, or else figuratively.

Apart from inherited groups, there are other words connected with those for 'ice, frost', 'stiffness' (?), 'blow'.

1. IE **k̂el-*, prob. the same root as in words for 'hot', Lat. *calidus*, etc. See 15.85.

Lith. *šaltas*, Lett. *salts* (with vbs. Lith. *šalti*, Lett. *salt* 'freeze'); Skt. (with reduplication) *çiçira-*, Av. *sarəta-*, NPers. *sard*, also in Av. *sarə-δā-* 'bringing cold'; Osset. *sald* sb. 'cold'.

2. IE **gel-*. Walde-P. 1.622. Ernout-M. 412. Walde-H. 1.585 f. Falk-Torp 560 f.

Lat. *gelidus* (with sb. *gelu* 'cold, frost', vb. *gelāre* 'freeze'); Goth. *kalds*, OE *ceald*, etc., general Gmc. (orig. pple. to ON *kala* 'freeze', OE *calan* 'become cold', whence also sbs. ON *kuldi*, OE *ceald*, OHG *caltī*, etc.), here also sb. OE *cele*, *ciele* (> NE *chill*, whence adj. *chilly*), with ablaut OE *cōl*, NE *cool*, OHG *kuoli*, NHG *kühl* 'cool'.

3. Grk. ψῡχρός (NG 'chilly' or fig.), with sb. ψῦχος 'cold, coolness' : ψῡ́χω

'breathe, blow, refresh, cool off', ψῡχή 'breath, spirit'. Boisacq 1079.

NG κρύος, fr. sb. κρύος 'cold' (κάνει κρύο 'it is cold'), in class. Grk. 'icy cold, frost' : OHG (*h*)*roso* 'ice, crust', OE *hrūse* 'earth, ground', Lett. *kruvesis* 'rough frozen dung in the road', etc. Walde-P. 1.479. Boisacq 522.

4. Lat. *frīgidus* (> Sp. *frío*), VLat. also *frigdus* (> It. *freddo*, Fr. *froid*), with sb. *frīgus* 'cold' (> Rum. *frig*), whence late *frīgorōsus* (> Rum. *friguros*, etc.), vb. *frīgēre* 'be cold, freeze' : Grk. ῥῖγος 'frost', ῥῑγέω 'shiver (with cold), shudder'. Walde-P. 2.705. Ernout-M. 390. Walde-H. 1.547. REW 3512, 3514.

Rum. *rece*, fr. Lat. *recēns* 'fresh, recent, young', with development fr. 'fresh' through 'cool'. REW 7109.

5. Ir. *ūar*, NIr. *fuar*, W. *oer*, OCorn. *oir*, cf. Gall. *Ogron* name of a month (**oug-ro-*), beside sb. Ir. *ūacht* (**oug-to-*) : Arm. *oic* 'cold', *ucanam* 'grow cold', all prob. fr. an extension of a root **eu-* seen also in Lett. *auksts* 'cold', Lith. *aušti* 'grow cool', and in Av. *aota-* 'cold', sb. *aoδar-*, Skt. *ūdhar-* 'cold', further root connections (as with Grk. ἄημι, Skt. *vā-* 'blow', etc.; cf. above, Grk. ψῦχος : ψῡ́χω) more doubtful. Walde-P. 1.222. Persson, Beiträge 10 f. Pedersen 1.103. Löwenthal, Wört. u. Sach. 11.54.

Br. *yen* : W. *iaen* 'sheet of ice, glacier', *ia*, Ir. *aig* 'ice', ON *jaki* 'piece of ice', etc. Walde-P. 1.206.

6. Gmc. words, above, 2.

7. Lith. *šaltas*, Lett. *salts*, above, 1.

Lett. *auksts*, above, 5.

8. ChSl. *studenŭ*, SCr. *studen*, Boh. *studený*, Russ. *studenyj*, with sb. *studŭ* 'cold', vb. *stynąti* 'become cooler', fr. **steu-d-*, beside **steu-g-* in Grk. στύγες 'chill, frost', στύγος 'abomination', στυγέω 'abhor', etc., fr. **steu-* in Skt. *ghṛta-stāvas* 'drops of melted butter'. The primary meaning of the root was perh. 'congeal, become stiff'. Walde-P. 2.620.

SCr. *hladan*, Russ. *cholodnyj* (Boh. *chladný*, Pol. *chłodny* 'cool'), with sbs. Russ. *cholod* 'cold', ChSl. *chladŭ* 'coolness', etc., etym. dub. Berneker 393.

Pol. *zimny* beside sb. *zimno*, fr. *zima* 'winter' (14.74). Cf. Boh. *zima*, used also as 'cold' sb., and so ChSl. *zima* in Gospels, Jn. 18.18; likewise Skt. *hima-* as 'cold' sb. and adj.

9. Skt. *çīta-*, *çītila-* : *çyā-* 'freeze, congeal', outside connections dub. Uhlenbeck 318.

Skt. *çiçira-*, Av. *sarəta-*, above, 1.

Skt. *hima-*, see under Pol. *zimny*, above, 8.

Av. *aota-*, see under Ir. *ūar*, above, 5.

15.87 CLEAN

Grk.	καθαρός	Goth.	*hrains*	Lith.	*švarus, čystas*
NG	καθαρός, παστρικός	ON	*hreinn*	Lett.	*tīrs, glīts*
Lat.	*mundus, pūrus*	Dan.	*ren*	ChSl.	*čistŭ*
It.	*pulito, netto*	Sw.	*ren*	SCr.	*čist*
Fr.	*propre, net*	OE	*clǣne*	Boh.	*čistý*
Sp.	*limpio*	ME	*clene*	Pol.	*czysty*
Rum.	*curat*	NE	*clean*	Russ.	*čistyj*
Ir.	*glan*	Du.	*rein, zuiver*	Skt.	*çuddha-*
NIr.	*glan*	OHG	*reini, sūbar*	Av.	....
W.	*glan*	MHG	*reine, sūber*		
Br.	*net*	NHG	*rein, sauber*		

Words for 'clean' and 'dirty', though these notions are by no means exclusively distinguished by the sense of touch (more often by smell or sight), are conveniently introduced here. Many of the words for 'clean' are the same that are used for 'pure, unmixed', and in several of these this is clearly the earlier notion. Others are of too diverse or doubtful origin for summary.

1. Grk. καθαρός, etym.? Walde-P. 1.368. Boisacq 389.

NG pop. παστρικός, with πάστρα 'cleanliness', παστρεύω 'cleanse', Byz. σπαστρικός, πάστρα, σπάστρα, σπαστρεύω, etym. dub., perh. first σπάστρα fr. σπάω 'draw, carry off'. Otherwise (fr. σπάρτον 'Spanish broom', the plant) Koraes, Άτακτα 1.288f., Hatzidakis, Μεσ. 1.327.

2. Lat. mundus (> It. mondo 'peeled, cleaned', Sp. mondo 'neat, pure'), perh. as orig. 'washed' fr. *mudnos : ChSl. myti 'wash', MLG müten 'wash the face', OHG muzzan 'clean, adorn', Grk. μύδος 'dampness', etc. Walde-P. 2.250 f.

Lat. pūrus : Skt. pu- 'cleanse, purify', OHG fowen 'sift, clean grain', etc., root *peu-. Walde-P. 2.13. Ernout-M. 826.

It. pulito, pple. of pulire 'cleanse', fr. Lat. polīre 'smooth, polish'.

It. netto, Fr. net (OFr. neit, net > ME neate, nete 'clean, pure, bright', NE neat), fr. Lat. nitidus 'bright, shining, polished' (15.57). REW 5929.

Fr. propre, in sense 'clean' from perh. 16th cent., earlier 'correctly arranged' fr. 'having necessary qualities, proper', fr. Lat. proprius 'own, special, proper'. Bloch 2.188.

Sp. limpio, fr. Lat. limpidus 'clear, transparent' also late 'pure, clean' (l. panis, Cael. Aur.). REW 5056.

Rum. curat, fr. Lat. cōlātus, pple. of cōlāre 'filter, purify'. REW 2035a. Puşcariu 454.

3. Ir., W. glan : Ir. gel 'white', etc. (15.64). Walde-P. 1.624.

Br. net, neat, fr. Fr. net.

4. Goth. hrains, ON hreinn, Dan., Sw. ren, OHG (h)reini, MHG reine, NHG, Du. rein; in Rhine Frank. and in Swiss 'finely ground or sifted'; hence perh. fr. the root of Grk. κρίνω 'choose, decide, judge', κρῖμον 'coarse barley meal', Lat. cernere 'separate, sift, distinguish', crībrum, OE hrīdder 'sieve', etc. Walde-P. 2.585. Falk-Torp 889. Kluge-G. 477.

OE clǣne, ME clene, NE clean (OHG kleini 'shining, fine', etc., NHG klein 'small' prob. : Grk. γλήνεα 'bright things, trinkets, stars', γλήνη 'pupil of the eye', etc. (cf. 12.56), with development of 'bright' to 'clean' as in Fr. net, etc. (above, 2). Walde-P. 1.623.

OHG sūbar, sūbiri, MHG sūber, sūver, NHG sauber, OS sūbar, Du. zuiver (OE sȳfre 'sober, temperate, pure'), fr. Lat. sōbrius 'sober, moderate, temperate'. Weigand-H. 2.655. Franck-v. W. 829.

5. Lith. švarus, and vb. švarinti 'cleanse', etym.? Walde 1.462.

Lith. čystas (formerly the usual word but now being discarded in favor of švarus; NSB s.v.), Lith. čystas (below, 6).

Lett. tīrs : Lith. tyrus, tyras 'pure, unmixed', further connection dub. (Mühl.-Endz. 4.204 : Lith. tyras, tyrė 'pap, pulp', Lett. tīrelis 'swamp', etc., but semantically difficult.)

Lett. glīts, perh. : glits 'slippery soft', Lith. glitus 'viscous', Lett. glīts 'slimy', etc. Walde-P. 1.620. Mühl.-Endz. 1.627.

6. ChSl. čistŭ, etc., general Slavic, with vb. čistiti 'cleanse' : OPruss. skīstan (acc.) 'clean', skīstint 'cleanse', Lith. skystas 'liquid, fluid', Lett. šk' īsts 'thin' (of liquids), also 'clean, chaste', fr. the root of ChSl. cěditi 'strain, filter' (etc.,

general Slavic), Lith. skiesti 'adulterate, thin down' (a liquid), OHG heitar 'bright, shining', OE hādor 'brightness (of the sky)', Skt. ketu- 'light, shape, form', etc. Walde-P. 2.537 f. Berneker 157 f.

7. Skt. çuddha-, pple. of çudh- 'purify, cleanse', fr. *ku-dh- beside *ku-bh- in çubh- 'adorn, beautify' (root *keu- 'shine'?). Walde-P. 1.368.

15.88 DIRTY, SOILED

Grk.	ῥυπαρός, ἀκάθαρτος	Goth.	unhrains	Lith.	purvinas, suterštas
NG	λερός, λερωμένος,	ON	saurigr, ūhreinn	Lett.	netīrs, melns
	βρώμικος, ἄπαστρος	Dan.	smudsig, snavset, uren	ChSl.	nečistŭ
Lat.	sordidus, squālidus,	Sw.	smutsig, oren	SCr.	prljav
	spurcus, immundus	OE	fūl, horig, unclǣne	Boh.	špinavý
It.	sporco, sudicio	ME	unclene, foul, hori,	Pol.	brudny
Fr.	sale, malpropre		filthi	Russ.	grjaznyj
Sp.	sucio	NE	dirty, soiled	Skt.	malina-, etc.
Rum.	murdar	Du.	vuil, smerig	Av.	āhita-
Ir.	salach	OHG	unreini, unsūbar		
NIr.	salach	MHG	unreine, unsūber, hor-		
W.	budr, brwnt		wec		
Br.	lous, loudour	NHG	schmutzig, schmierig		

Words for 'dirty, soiled' are mostly connected with sbs. for 'dirt, filth', 'mud', 'excrement', 'snot', 'stench', etc. Several are from 'dark-colored, black'. Some are neg. cpds. of those for 'clean'. The majority of these last are used mainly with reference to moral or ritualistic uncleanliness. This is the only use occurring in the Gospels, where ἀκάθαρτος is rendered by Lat. immundus, Goth. unhrains, OE unclǣne, OHG unreini (Otfr.), unsūbiri (Tat.), ChSl. nečistŭ. However, these words are entered in the list, and some of them are also used in a less restricted sense, as frequently Lat. immundus, sometimes ME unclene, NE unclean (NED s.v. 4), and esp. the Scand. words, including NIcel. ōhreinn.

1. Grk. ῥυπαρός, fr. ῥύπος 'filth, dirt' : ChSl. strupŭ 'wound' (in modern Slavic 'poison, pus, scab, crust, etc.'), root connection dub. (*sreu- 'flow'?). Walde-P. 2.703. Boisacq 846.

NG λερός, vb. λερώνω 'soil', pple. λερωμένος 'soiled', fr. class. Grk. ὀλερός 'turbid' (Galen), ὀλερόν· βορβορῶδες, τεταραγμένον (Hesych.), deriv. of : ὁλός 'ink of the cuttlefish', but formed after or

influenced by the more common θολερός 'muddy, turbid', esp. of water, etc. but also 'dirty' (cf. ὕδατι νίζειν θολερὰν πλίνθον, Theocr. 16.62), deriv. of θόλος 'mud, dirt'.

NG βρώμικος, properly 'stinking' (15.26), used also for 'dirty' (the laundress used to come for τὰ βρώμικα).

NG ἄπαστρος, neg. : παστρικός 'clean' (15.87).

2. Lat. sordidus, with sordēre 'be dirty', sordēs 'dirt, filth' : Goth. swarts 'black', (15.65). Walde-P. 2.535. Ernout-M. 958.

Lat. squālidus, and rare (Enn.) squālus, with sbs. squālēs, squālor 'filth', vb. squālēre 'be filthy', properly of dirt and filth consisting of stiff or rough incrustations, scales, etc., etym.? Walde-P. 1.441. Ernout-M. 970.

Lat. spurcus (> It. sporco), etym. dub. (cf. spurius 'bastard'?). Ernout-M. 969 f.

Lat. immundus, neg. cpd. of mundus 'clean' (15.87).

It. sudicio, Sp. sucio, fr. Lat. sūcidus 'sappy, juicy'. REW 8414.

Fr. sale, fr. OHG salo, MHG sal

'dark-colored, turbid, dirty' : OE salu 'dark-colored' (cf. Ir. salach 'dirty', etc., below). REW 7547.

Fr. malpropre (esp. of persons 'habitually dirty'), cpd. of mal 'bad' with neg. force and propre 'clean' (15.87).

Rum. murdar, fr. Turk. murdar 'dirty', this fr. Pers. murdār 'corpse' (: murdan 'die', Av. mar-, etc.). Titkin 1022. Lokotsch 1516. Horn 973.

3. Ir. salach, fr. sal 'dirt, filth' : OHG salo 'dark-colored, turbid, dirty', OE salu 'dark-colored' (NE sallow), etc. Walde-P. 2.453.

W. budr, with vb. budro 'soil', MIr. buaidrim 'roil up, confuse', prob. : OE cwēad, OHG quāt, NHG kot 'dung, filth', etc. (4.66). Walde-P. 1.696.

W. brwnt, etym.?

Br. lous, same word as louz, MBr. louçc 'badger', fr. (or conversely) Fr. dial. louse 'badger' and 'trickery', etc., hence orig. an opprobrious term. Ernault, RC 14.287, Glossaire 377.

Br. loudour, cf. W. lludedic 'muddy' : Ir. loth 'dirt', Lat. lutum 'mud', Grk. λῦμα 'washings, filth', etc. Walde-P. 2.406. Stokes 250.

4. Goth. unhrains, ON ūhreinn, Dan. uren, Sw. oren, OHG un(h)reini, MHG unreine (NHG unrein), likewise OE unclǣne, ME unclene (NE unclean), and OHG unsūbar, unsūbiri, MHG unsūber (NHG unsauber), neg. cpds. of words for 'clean' (on use see above), and common today in the physical sense only in Scandinavian.

ON saurigr, saurugr, also saurligr, fr. saurr 'mud, dirt, excrements', this prob. : ON sūrr, OE sūr, etc. 'sour' (15.38). Walde-P. 1.469, 513. Falk-Torp 1236.

Dan. snavset, and vb. snavse, fr. snavs 'dirt, muck', Sw. dial. snafs, with vb. snaffsa 'spill', perh. = snaffsa 'snap,

bite'. Orig. meaning of snavs 'refuse of food, waste'. Falk-Torp 1091.

OE fūl, ME foul (NE foul according to NED not now used in this sense without admixture of the notion 'putrid, stinking'), Du. vuil (the usual term for 'dirty'), orig. 'putrid, stinking' (15.26). Hence sb. OE fylþ 'rottenness, filth', with adj. ME filthi (NE filthy, in earlier use without the present strong connotation, cf. NED s.v.).

OE horig, ME hori (NE dial. howry), OHG horawig(?), MHG horwec, fr. horu, OHG horo 'dirt, filth' = ON horr 'snot', root connection dub. NED s.v. hory, horry. Falk-Torp 936. Walde-P. 1.409.

NE dirty, fr. dirt, older and ME drit 'filth, excrement' (4.66). Cf. ON skitinn, with Dan. skiden, and NIcel. skītugur pop. terms for 'dirty', fr. the well-known Gmc. word for 'excrement'.

NE soiled, but in ME (Ancr. R. suilede) mostly 'defiled', fr. vb. soil, ME suile(n) 'defile, pollute', OFr. suillier, NFr. souiller 'stain, befoul', fr. VLat. *suculāre, deriv. of suculus, dim. of sūs 'hog'. REW 8418. Bloch 2.287. NED s.v.

Du. smerig, NHG schmierig, properly 'greasy', fr. Du. smeer, NHG schmiere 'grease'. Franck-v. W. 625. Weigand-H. 751.

NHG schmutzig, sb. schmutz (> Dan. smudsig, Sw. smutsig, sbs. Dan. smuds, Sw. smuts), MHG smuz = NE smut, etc., prob. : Ir. smūid 'smoke, steam', root connection dub. Walde-P. 2.251. Falk-Torp 1083.

5. Lith. purvinas, fr. purvas 'mud, filth' (1.214).

Lith. suterštas, fr. (su)teršti 'soil, befoul', prob. : Lat. stercus 'dung, excrement', W. troeth 'lye, urine', troethi 'urinate', etc. Walde-P. 2.641.

Lith. juodas and Lett. melns 'black' (15.65), also 'dirty'. Cf. NSB and Mühl.-Endz. s.vv.

Lett. netīrs, neg. of tīrs 'clean' (15.87).

6. ChSl. nečistŭ, SCr. nečist, etc., neg. of čistŭ, čist 'clean' (on use see above).

SCr. prljav, with vb. prljati 'soil', orig.?

Boh. špinavý, with vb. špiniti 'soil, sully', sb. špina 'dirt, filth' (Miklosich 342), orig.?

Pol. brudny with vb. brudzić 'soil', sb.

brud (also Ukr., etc.) 'dirt, filth', etym. dub. Berneker 88. Brückner 42 (connecting with a root *bru- in Slav. brukati 'burst out, throw', in Russ. also 'soil', etc., Berneker 89).

Russ. grjaznyj, fr. grjaz' 'dirt, mud' (1.214).

7. Skt. malina-, malavant-, etc., sb. mala- 'dirt, filth, impurity' : Grk. μέλας, Lett. melns 'black', etc. (15.65). Walde 2.293 f.

Av. āhita-, with sb. āhiti- 'spot, stain, pollution', etym.? Barth. 345 f.

CHAPTER 16

EMOTION (WITH SOME PHYSICAL EXPRESSIONS OF EMOTION); TEMPERAMENTAL, MORAL, AND AESTHETIC NOTIONS

16.11 Soul, Spirit
16.12 Emotion, Feeling
16.13 Passion
16.14 Care (sb.)
16.15 Wonder, Astonishment
16.16 Surprise
16.17 Fortune (Good or Bad)
16.18 Good Fortune
16.19 Misfortune
16.21 Please
16.212 Please (in polite phrase)
16.22 Joy
16.23 Joyful, Glad
16.24 Happy, Happiness
16.25 Laugh (vb.); Smile (vb.)
16.26 Play (vb.)
16.27 Love (sb.; vb.)
16.28 Dear
16.29 Kiss (vb.)
16.31 Pain, Suffering
16.32 Grief, Sorrow
16.33 Anxiety
16.34 Regret (vb.), Repent
16.35 Pity (sb.)
16.36 Sad
16.37 Cry, Weep
16.38 Tear (sb.)
16.39 Groan (vb.)
16.41 Hate (sb.)
16.42 Anger
16.43 Rage, Fury
16.44 Envy, Jealousy
16.45 Shame (sb.)
16.46 Honor (sb.)
16.47 Glory
16.48 Proud
16.51 Dare
16.52 Brave
16.53 Fear, Fright
16.54 Danger
16.55 Timid, Cowardly
16.61 Will, Wish (vb.)
16.62 Desire (vb.)
16.63 Hope (sb.)
16.64 Thanks
16.65 Faithful
16.66 True
16.67 Lie (sb.)
16.68 Deceit
16.69 Forgive
16.71 Good
16.72 Bad
16.73 Right (adj.)
16.74 Wrong (adj.)
16.75 Sin
16.76 Fault, Guilt
16.77 Mistake, Error
16.78 Blame (sb.)
16.79 Praise (sb.)
16.81 Beautiful
16.82 Ugly

In this chapter we need not be concerned with such moot questions as the definition and precise character of emotions; the differentiation of emotions, passions, moods, etc.; the selection of certain emotions as primary; the division into pleasant and unpleasant or other types of classification. The relations are so complex that no rigid classification has proved acceptable to psychologists generally; and there is certainly none which it would be profitable to impose upon our study, in which we are dealing with unsophisticated and often overlapping notions.

While attempting to bring into con-

junction certain obviously related emotions, we lay no emphasis on the arrangement adopted. Some of the items, if taken by themselves, would seem to have no proper place in a chapter on emotions but are most conveniently brought into a series with others of distinctly emotional value. So especially are certain situations or objective notions which inspire emotional reactions. Thus 'danger' may lead to 'fear'; 'what is wonderful, a wonder' to the feeling of 'wonder, astonishment'; 'fame, renown' to the highly emotional 'glory'; a 'shameful act, disgrace' to the feeling of 'shame'; 'care' as 'attention' to 'anxiety, grief, sorrow', sometimes 'danger' or 'hate' and 'fondness, love'; 'distress, trouble' may lead to 'anger'; objects of repulsion provoke 'disgust' and then 'hate' and similarly in other cases, while the opposite shift from subjective to objective ('fear' to 'danger', etc.) is, of course, also attested.

Words for certain actions that are expressive of emotion, whether or not they lead to actual names of emotions, are included, as 'laugh, smile', 'weep', 'kiss'. In a few cases the emotion is antecedent to its expression ('love' > 'kiss' in Grk. *φιλέω*, 16.29). Or there may be a shift of meaning from one physical act to another, when both are expressive of the same emotion ('beat the breast' > 'weep').

Some moral and aesthetic notions are also included for convenience, as 'good', 'bad', 'sin' (with the overlapping 'fault', 'error', 'blame'); and 'beautiful', 'ugly'.

It must be assumed, of course, that all expressions of emotion, as well as those for sense-perceptions and thought processes, rest ultimately on physical actions or situations. In large measure this is shown in the history of the words, either in a shift of application observable within the historical period of a given language or by the cognates in other languages. But in some groups of cognates an emotional value is so widespread that no certain trace is left of the underlying physical value, so that its determination is highly speculative or hopeless.

Many parts of the body or bodily actions are associated with emotions. Notably the heart, the words for which are universally used to denote the seat of emotion or 'temperament, disposition', and in part (alone or in derivs. or cpds.) for special emotions such as 'courage', 'fondness, love', 'sympathy, pity', and (in Balto-Slavic) 'anger'. Bristling of the hair may indicate 'horror' (Lat. *horror;* cf. NE adj. *hair-raising*) or pleasurable excitement, 'joy' (Skt. *harṣa-*, 16.22). To lower or wrinkle the eyebrows, 'frown, scowl', usually shows displeasure, but also arrogance (cf. numerous Grk. phrases with *ὀφρύς*, LS s.v.; NE *supercilious*). Not only tears but also downcast eyes indicate 'grief, sadness' (NG *κατηφής* 'sad', 16.36). Laughter may show pleasure or ridicule. Puffing out the chest suggests 'pride' (cf. NG *καμαρώνω* etc., 16.48), as does also strutting or a stiff bearing. Words for 'breath' are the most common source of those for 'soul, spirit', and heavy breathing may indicate 'hate' (OE *anda*, 16.41) or 'anger' (Lett. *dusmas*, 16.42). The bile or gall is associated with bitter anger (Grk. *χόλος*, 16.42; NE *gall* in U.S. slang 'excessive assurance, impudence'; cf. also Grk. *μελαγχολία* 'black gall, melancholy'; the spleen with a variety of quite disparate emotions (NED s.v. *spleen*). A Greek word for the principal internal organs (*σπλάγχνα*) was felt as the seat of various emotions (cf. LS s.v.), and later, through its use in the LXX and NT to translate a certain Hebrew word and rendered in our

version by *bowels* (lit. 'intestines', fr. OFr. *boll*, Lat. *botellus*, dim. of *botulus* 'sausage'), connoted esp. 'pity, compassion' (NED s.v. *bowel*, sb.[1] 3).

Yet relatively few of the usual words for a given emotion, as included in our lists, are of such origin.

Words for a great variety of physical actions or conditions came to be used for emotions, sometimes with an obvious logical relation, as between 'trembling' and 'fear' or between 'bright' and 'joyful', but more often without any compelling ground for the specialization. Especially words that denote some form of physical agitation are used of mental agitation and then may be specialized in different directions, e.g. to 'fear', 'anger', or 'joy'.

Many of the words are connected with others for sense-perceptions or thought processes, so that members of the same group of cognates appear in all three chapters (15, 16, 17).

Among the IE roots that are conspicuous in words of emotion are, for example, the following:

IE **men-*, covering mental processes in the widest sense, both thought and emotion, the former dominant ('mind, think, remember', etc.) but the latter also in words for 'soul, spirit', 'desire', 'love', 'anger, wrath'. IE **dheu-*, primarily of physical agitation in words for 'shake', 'rage', 'smoke, vapor', etc., secondarily (esp. Grk. *θυμός*) 'soul, spirit', 'courage' and 'anger'. IE **wel-* in words for 'wish, will', 'pleasure', and 'hope'. IE **ĝher-* in words for 'wish, will', 'desire', 'joy', and 'thanks'. IE **wen-* in words for ('strive for, gain, win', and here) 'wish', 'love', 'hope', 'passion', 'suffering'.

But, despite such cognate groups with variously developed emotional sense, it is rare that the usual words for a particular emotion are common to two or more of the main branches of IE. For notions included in this chapter but only on the border line of emotion, we have widespread agreement in words for a 'tear' (but not for 'weep'), 'smile' (Grk., Gmc., Balto-Slavic, Skt.), 'dare' (Grk., Gmc., Baltic, Indo-Iranian), more limited groups for 'true' (one in Lat., Celt., Gmc., also 'faith, faithful' in Slavic; another in Gmc., Skt.), 'lie' (Gmc., Slavic, traces in Celtic), 'trust, faithful' (Grk., Lat.).

For more strictly emotional notions, the most notable cases of agreement are between two branches, as for 'will, wish' (Lat., Gmc.), 'love' (Gmc., Slavic; elsewhere in related senses but not the common word for 'love'), 'fear' (Balto-Slavic, Indo-Iranian), 'anger' (Grk., Ir.), 'hate' (Celtic, Gmc.).

All this, of course, does not prove that the primitive IE lacked expressions of emotional reaction or some terms for particular emotions like 'love', 'hate', or 'anger'. But it is probable that the IE vocabulary in this field was of an ill-defined character.

Cf. H. Kurath, The Semantic Sources of the Words for the Emotions in Sanskrit, Greek, Latin, and the Germanic Languages (Chicago dissertation, 1921). F. Warfelmann, Die althochdeutschen Bezeichnungen für die Gefühle der Lust und der Unlust (Greifswald dissertation, 1906).

16.11 SOUL, SPIRIT

Grk.	*ψῡχή, θῡμός, πνεῦμα*	Goth.	*saiwala, ahma*	Lith.	*dūšia, dvasia*
NG	*ψυχή, πνεῦμα*	ON	*ǫnd, sāl(a), andi*	Lett.	*dvēsele, gars*
Lat.	*anima, animus, spīritus*	Dan.	*sjæl, aand*	ChSl.	*duša, duchŭ*
It.	*anima, spirito, animo*	Sw.	*själ, ande*	SCr.	*duša, duh*
Fr.	*âme, esprit*	OE	*sāwel, gāst*	Boh.	*duše, duch*
Sp.	*alma, espiritu, animo*	ME	*soule, spirit, gost*	Pol.	*dusza, duch*
Rum.	*suflet, spirit*	NE	*soul, spirit (ghost)*	Russ.	*duša, duch*
Ir.	*anim, spirut*	Du.	*ziel, geest*	Skt.	*ātman-, prāṇa-*
NIr.	*anam, spiorad*	OHG	*sēla, geist*	Av.	*urvan-, mainyu-*
W.	*enaid, ysbryd*	MHG	*sēle, geist*		
Br.	*ene, spered*	NHG	*seele, geist*		

Under 'soul, spirit' it is intended to group the main words that are used for the seat of emotion, as contrasted with 'mind' for the seat of intelligence (17.11). But there is no hard-and-fast line between the two groups. Several of the words listed here carry over into the field of intelligence (so Lat. *animus* also 'mind', Fr. *esprit* in which the intellectual element is now dominant, and imitated in NHG *geist*), as, conversely, several of those listed under 'mind' are also used with reference to feelings.

The distinction between 'soul' and 'spirit' (or NE *ghost* in *Holy Ghost*), which became current in Christian terminology (Grk. *ψῡχή* vs. *πνεῦμα*, Lat. *anima* vs. *spīritus*), is without significance for earlier periods, but the Eur. words are listed in accordance with this order.

The most usual semantic source is 'breath', hence first 'breath of life, vital principle'. But some are from (physical > mental) 'agitation' or other sources.

Besides the words listed, those for 'heart' are often used fig. in a similar sense. Likewise not included are certain words that are more nearly 'mood, temperament', as NHM *gemüt*.

1. Grk. *ψῡχή*, also and orig. 'breath of life' (Hom., etc.) : *ψύχω* 'breath, blow' (Hom.), whence commonly 'make cool' (cf. *ψῡχος* 'cold'), further connection dub. (*ψῡ-* with early transposition fr. *φῡσ-* in *φῡσάω* 'blow'?). Boisacq 1079.

Grk. *θῡμός*, with a wide range of meanings ('soul, spirit, mood, anger, courage, breath of life'), through 'agitation' fr. the root of *θύω* 'rage', Skt. *dhu-* 'shake, agitate', etc., and in form esp. : Lat. *fūmus*, Lith. *dūmai* 'smoke', Skt. *dhūma-* 'smoke, vapor'. For the shift of physical to mental, cf. Lat. *animus, anima* (below, 2), Lett. *gars* (below, 5) and NE *fume* (fr. Lat. *fūmus*) in *in a fume* or as vb. in *fret and fume*. Walde-P. 1.835 f. Boisacq 356 f.

Grk. *πνεῦμα*, orig. 'breath' (: *πνέω* 'breathe', 4.51), hence 'breath of life', and in NT and other Christian writings the usual term for 'spirit' contrasted with *ψῡχή* 'soul'.

For Grk. *φρήν*, poet. word for both the seat of emotion and 'mind', with numerous derivs., partly of emotional but more commonly of intellectual character, see under 'mind' (17.11).

2. Lat. *anima* (> It. *anima*, Fr. *âme*, Sp. *alma*), orig. 'air, breath' (4.51), and the semantic equivalent of Grk. *ψῡχή*; *animus* (> It., Sp. *animo*), also etymologically 'air, breath' (in form = Grk. *ἄνεμος* 'wind'), but never used in this sense, corresponds semantically to Grk. *θῡμός*, but eventually yields place to *spīritus* (cf. below). Ernout-M. 53 f. Walde-H. 1.49 f.

Lat. *spīritus* (> It. *spirito*, Fr. *esprit*, Sp. *espiritu*, Rum. *spirit*), usually in class. Lat. 'breath' (4.51), replaces *animus* in the sense 'spirit' in the imperial period and is used in Christian writings as the usual equivalent of Grk. πνεῦμα. Ernout-M. 966.

Rum. *suflet*, orig. 'breath', but not used in this sense now except in certain locutions : *sufla* 'blow', *răsufla* 'breathe', etc. (4.51). Tiktin 1526 f.

3. Ir. *anim*, NIr. *anam*, Br. *anaon* (only 'souls of the dead') : Lat. *anima* (above); fr. the same root with different suffix (**anə-ti*) W. *enaid;* Br. *ene*, MBr. *eneff*, Corn. *enef* loanwords fr. Lat. *anima?* Walde-P. 1.57. Pedersen 1.170.

Ir. *spirut*, NIr. *spiorad*, W. *ysbryd*, Br. *spered*, fr. Lát. *spīritus*. Pedersen 1.211.

4. Goth. *saiwala*, OE *sāwel* (> ON *sāla*, *sāl*), ME *soule*, NE *soul*, OS *siala* (> Dan. *sjæl*, Sw. *själ*), Du. *ziel*, OHG *sēla*, *sēula*, MHG *sēle*, NHG *seele* (in Gospel translations the usual renderings of Grk. ψῡχή or Lat. *anima*), etym. dub. (: Grk. αἰόλος 'quick moving' or ChSl. *sila* 'power'?). Falk-Torp 974. Feist 406. Weigand-H. 2.832.

Goth. *ahma* (= πνεῦμα) : *aha* 'mind', etc. (17.11). Feist 16 f.

ON *ǫnd*, *andi*, both lit. 'breath' (4.51), whence 'breath of life, soul, spirit', as 'soul' more frequently in early eccl. writings *ǫnd* (replaced by *sāla* in this sense, and *sāl*, not *önd* is the usual NIcel. word), *andi* esp. 'spirit, spiritual being', and so in NIcel., as also Dan. *aand* (distinguished fr. *aande* 'breath'), Sw. *ande*. Falk-Torp 5. Hellquist 20.

OE *gāst*, ME *gost* (NE *ghost* in *Holy Ghost*), OS *gēst*, Du. *geest*, OHG–NHG *geist*, the usual rendering of Lat. *spīritus*, but also old and general for a 'supernatural being' : OE *gǣstan* 'frighten', Skt. *hēḍa-* 'anger, wrath', Av. *zōizdišta-* 'most frightful', fr. IE **ĝheizd-*, extension of **ĝheis-* in Goth. *us-gaisjan* 'frighten', Av. *zaēša-* 'horrible'. Walde-P. 1.554. Feist 531. NED s.v. *ghost*.

ME, NE *spirit*, fr. Anglo-Fr. *spirit* = OFr. *esp(e)rit*, Fr. *esprit* (above, 2).

5. Liṭh. *dūšia* 'soul', fr. Slavic *duša* (below). Brückner, Sl. Fremdwörter 82.

Lith. *dvasia* 'spirit', dial. still 'breath', Lett. *dvēsele* 'soul' also 'breath' : Lett. *dvaša* 'breath', *dvašuot*, *dvest* 'breathe' (4.51) and the Slavic group below.

Lett. *gars* 'steam' and 'spirit, soul, intellect' : Lith. *garas* 'steam', ChSl. *gorěti* 'burn', Grk. θερμός 'hot', etc. Walde-P. 1.688. Berneker 234. Mühl.-Endz 1.604.

6. ChSl. *duša*, etc., general Slavic for 'soul' : ChSl. *duchŭ* 'breath' and 'spirit' (πνεῦμα), but in modern Slavic usual only in the latter sense : ChSl. *dychati*, *duchati* 'breathe', etc. (4.51). Walde-P. 1.846. Berneker 234 f., 239.

7. Skt. *ātman-*, orig. 'breath' : OHG *ātum* 'breath', etc. (4.51).

Skt. *prāṇa-*, orig. 'breath', and esp. 'inhalation', fr. *pra-an-*, cpd. of *an-* 'breathe' (4.51).

Av. *urvan-*, the usual term for 'soul, spirit', etym.? Barth. 1537 ff.

Av. *mainyu-* 'spirit' in various applications, partly personified = Skt. *manyu-* 'spirit, mood, anger' : Skt., Av. *man-* 'think', etc. (17.13). Barth. 1136 ff.

16.12 EMOTION, FEELING

Grk.	*πάθος, πάθημα*	Dan.	*følelse*	Lith.	*jausmas*
NG	*αἴσθημα*	Sw.	*känsla*	Lett.	*jūtas, jūsma*
Lat.	*mōtus animī, sēnsus*	NE	*emotion, feeling*	ChSl.	*čuvĭstvo*
It.	*sentimento, emozione*	Du.	*gevoel, aandoening*	SCr.	*čuvstvo*
Fr.	*sentiment, émotion*	NHG	*gefühl*	Boh.	*cit*
Sp.	*sentimiento, emoción*			Pol.	*(u)czucie*
Rum.	*simţire, emoţiune*			Russ.	*čuvstvo*
Ir.	*cētbuid*(?), *mothugud*			Skt.	*bhāva-*
NIr.	*mothughadh*				
W.	*teimlad*				
Br.	(*trivliad*)				

The majority of words for 'emotion, feeling', that is, generic terms covering the emotions of 'love, joy, anger, hate', etc., are derived from verbs for 'feel', which are either 'perceive by the senses' (15.11), or else originally denoted 'feel' by the sense of touch (15.72). Some are based on the notion of 'movement' (of the mind) or 'experience'.

In technical language there are many other terms, not included in the list, either loanwords or semantic borrowings, as NHG *affekt* fr. Lat. *affectus*, or OE *mōdes styrung*, NHG *gemütsbewegung*, Dan. *sindsbevægelse*, Sw. *sinnesrörelse* in imitation of Lat. *mōtus animī*.

1. Grk. πάθος, πάθημα 'what befalls one, experience, suffering, misfortune', but also generic 'emotion' (πάθημα Plato +; πάθος more common in Aristot., e.g. EN 1105[b] 21 ff.; NG πάθος 'disease, misfortune, malice', also 'passion'), beside πένθος 'grief, sorrow', πάσχω 'suffer, experience', prob. : Ir. *cēssaim*, Lith. *kenčiu*, *kęsti* 'suffer', etc. Walde-P. 1.513. Boisacq 766. Otherwise (ultimately : Lat. *patī* 'suffer') Ernout-M. 741.

Grk. αἴσθημα 'object of sensation' (: αἰσθάνομαι 'perceive by the senses', 15.11), in NG 'feeling, emotion'.

2. Lat. *mōtus animī* (cf. *īra et metus et reliquī mōtūs animī*, Cic.), lit. 'movement of the spirit'.

Lat. *sēnsus*, orig. 'sense, power of feeling', fr. *sentīre* 'feel, perceive by the senses' (15.11), whence also the vbs. It. *sentire*, etc. and their new derivs. It. *sentimento*, Fr. *sentiment*, Sp. *sentimiento*, Rum. *simţire*.

Lat. *adfectus* (*affectus*), like *adfectiō*, orig. translation of διάθεσις '(bodily) state or condition, disposition', later in the sense of πάθος (*adfectiō* in that of στοργή), fr. *adficere* 'exert an influence on (body or mind), put in a certain disposition', cpd. of *facere* 'do, make'. Ernout-M. 323 f.

Fr. *émotion* (> It. *emozione*, Sp. *emoción*, Rum. *emoţiune*), deriv. of *émouvoir* 'stir, agitate, move' (orig. in physical sense); formation after *motion* 'movement'. Gamillscheg 352.

3. Ir. *cētbuid* (MIr. *cētfaid*), the usual word for 'sense' (15.11), but prob. also 'feeling', cf. Passions and Homilies l. 722 (*in genntilecht*) *formuchaid na cētfada* '(paganism) stifles the senses' (but trans. p. 301 'opinions'), l. 6868 *ho dunmait-ne ar cētfaide fria cech n-olc* 'sensibus nostris contra mala obduratis' (trans. p. 469), where the reference is certainly not to physical feelings.

Ir. *mothugud*, NIr. *mothughadh* 'perception, sense' and 'feeling', see 15.11.

W. *teimlad*, also of physical feeling, and 'sense of touch' : *teimlo* 'feel' (15.72).

Br. *trivliad* (but hardly generic, for which there is apparently no single word), fr. *trivlia* 'tremble, shake'.

4. In the older Gmc. languages there seem to be no good generic terms for 'emotion'. Perhaps the nearest approach would be the group OE *mōd*, OHG *muot* 'mind, mood', etc., covering various emotions, in Goth., ON 'anger' (16.42).

Dan. *følelse*, NE *feeling*, Du. *gevoel*, NHG *gefühl*, all also of physical feeling, derivs. of the respective vbs. for 'feel' (orig. by sense of touch), Dan. *føle*, OE *fēlan*, NE *feel*, etc. (15.72). Similarly Sw. *känsla*, fr. *känsa* 'feel', orig. 'recognize'.

NE *emotion*, in earliest use 'a moving out, migration', then 'agitation' (physical or mental), finally (since early 18th cent.) in current sense, prob. fr. Fr. *émotion* (above, 2). Otherwise (as independently coined) NED s.v.

Du. *aandoening*, deriv. of *aandoen* 'touch upon, cause, affect', semantic borrowing fr. Lat. *adfectus*, *adficere* (above, 2). Franck-v. W. 3.

5. Lith. *jausmas*, Lett. *jūtas*, *jūsma* : Lith. *jausti*, Lett. *jaust* 'perceive by the senses, feel' (15.11).

6. ChSl. *čuvĭstvo*, SCr., Russ. *čuvstvo*, Pol. *czucie*, *uczucie* : ChSl. *po-čuti*, etc. 'feel, perceive by the senses' (15.11). Berneker 162.

Boh. *cit* : SCr. *ćut* 'sense', *ćutjeti* 'perceive by the senses', etc. (15.11). Gebauer 1.273, 384.

7. Skt. *bhāva-*, lit. 'becoming, being', whence 'state' of anything, and 'state of mind or body', 'way of thinking, feeling, sentiment' : *bhū-* 'become, be'.

16.13 PASSION

Grk.	*πάθος, πάθημα*	Goth.	*gairuni, winnō*	Lith.	*aistra*
NG	*πάθος*	ON	. . . .	Lett.	*kaislība*
Lat.	*perturbātiō*	Dan.	*lidenskab*	ChSl.	*strastĭ*
It.	*passione*	Sw.	*passion, lidelse*	SCr.	*strast*
Fr.	*passion*	OE	*þolung*	Boh.	*vášeň*
Sp.	*pasión*	ME	*passion*	Pol.	*namiętność*
Rum.	*patimă*	NE	*passion*	Russ.	*strast'*
Ir.	*cēssad, pāis*	Du.	*hartstocht*	Skt.	*bhāva-*
NIr.	*pāis*	OHG	*dolunga*		
W.	*nwyd*	MHG	*līdunge*		
Br.	*c'hoantidigez*	NHG	*leidenschaft*		

'Passion' is understood here as a generic word for violent emotion. But the distinction from 'emotion' in general is lacking in some languages (Grk. πάθος) and incomplete in others (e.g. NE *passions*, sometimes = *emotions;* cf. NED s.v., 6). Most of the words meant originally 'suffering', with generalization in imitation of Grk. πάθος : πάσχω 'suffer'.

A few are from other sources, as 'disturbance', 'inflammation', enmity'.

1. Grk. πάθος, πάθημα, see 16.12.

2. Lat. *perturbātiō* 'disturbance', used by Cicero to render Grk. πάθος, deriv. of *perturbāre* 'throw into confusion, disorder', cpd. of *turbāre* 'disturb, agitate'.

Late Lat. *passiō*, deriv. of *patī* 'suffer' (like Grk. πάθος : πάσχω). Used in eccl. Lat. esp. to render the 'passion' of Christ. Borrowed in It. *passione*, Fr. *passion*, Sp. *pasión*. Ernout-M. 741.

Rum. *patimă*, fr. Grk. πάθημα 'emotion' (16.12). Tiktin 1133.

3. Ir. *cēssad* 'suffering' (16.31) used also for 'passion' (NIr. *ceasadh* 'the crucifixion'), semantic borrowing fr. Lat. *passiō*. Pederson 2.486.

NIr. *pāis*, in early Ir. mostly 'passio Christi', fr. Lat. *passiō*. Vendryes, De hib. voc. 163.

W. *nwyd* (beside *nwy* 'spirit, vivacity', Pughe; now 'gas', Spurrell), etym.?

Br. *c'hoantidigez*, deriv. of *c'hoant* 'desire' (16.62).

4. Goth. *gairuni* (*gairunja lustaus* = πάθει ἐπιθυμίας, 1 Thess. 4. 5) : *gairnei* 'desire', vb. *gairnjan*, OE *giernan* 'desire', etc. (16.62).

Goth. *winnō*, *winna* (Col. 3.5 = πάθος 'passion' in bad sense) : *winnan* 'suffer' = OE *winnan* 'toil, suffer', etc. Semantic borrowing fr. Grk. Feist 566.

OE *þolung*, OHG *dolunga* (render Lat. *passiō*, cf. Bosworth-Toller, Suppl. s.v., Graff 5.135; clearly semantic borrowings), lit. 'suffering', derivs. of OE *þolian*, OHG *dolēn* 'suffer' : Goth. *þulan* 'endure', Lat. *tollere* 'raise, carry', Grk. τλᾱ- (aor. ἔτλη, etc.) 'bear, endure, suffer'. Walde-P. 1.739.

MHG *līdunge*, NHG *leidenschaft* (> Dan. *lidenskab*), Sw. *lidelse* fr. the vbs. MHG *liden*, NHG *leiden*, etc. 'suffer' (see under NHG *leiden*, etc. 'suffering' 16.31). Translations of Lat. *passiō* and Fr. *passion* (above, 2). Falk-Torp 641. Weigand-H. 2.47.

ME, NE *passion*, fr. OFr. *passion*, Lat. *passiō* (above, 2).

Du. *hartstocht*, cpd. of *hart* 'heart' and *trocht* 'pull, tug'. Franck-v. W. 234.

5. Lith. *aistra*, beside *aistrus* 'passionate' : Grk. οἶστρος 'vehement desire, madness, sting, gadfly', Lat. *īra* 'anger', etc. Walde-P. 1.107.

Lett. *kaislība*, lit. 'inflammation', fr. *kaisls* 'heated, hot' : *kaist* 'grow hot, burn, glow'. Mühl.-Endz. 2.135.

6. ChSl. *strastĭ*, SCr. *strast*, Russ. *strast'* : ChSl. *stradati* 'suffer'. Semantic borrowing fr. Grk. πάθος.

Boh. *vášeň* : Pol. *waśń* 'quarrel', ChSl. *vaditi* 'accuse'. Brückner 598, 603.

Pol. *namiętność*, deriv. of *namiętny* 'passionate', prob. fr. the root in ChSl. *mętą*, *męsti* 'disturb, trouble' (Berneker 2.45 without mention of these Pol. words). Otherwise Brückner 392 f. (: *pamięć*, ChSl. *pa-mętĭ* 'memory', but semantically unlikely).

7. Skt. *bhāva-*, see 16.12.

16.14 CARE (sb.)

Grk.	*μελέτη, φροντίς, μέριμνα*	Goth.	*kara, saurga*	Lith.	*rūpestis*
NG	*φροντίδα, προσοχή*	ON	*umhyggja*	Lett.	*rūpes* (pl.)
Lat.	*cūra*	Dan.	*omsorg, omhu*	ChSl.	(*roditi, raditi*, vbs.)
It.	*cura*	Sw.	*omsorg*	SCr.	*briga*
Fr.	*soin, souci*	OE	*caru*	Boh.	*peče, starost*
Sp.	*cuidado*	ME	*care*	Pol.	*piecza, staranie*
Rum.	*grijă*	NE	*care*	Russ.	*zabota*
Ir.	*uān menman, ōid, aire*	Du.	*zorg*	Skt.	(*yatna-*)
NIr.	*aire*	OHG	*sorga*		
W.	*gofal, pryder*	MHG	*sorge, vürsorge*		
Br.	*preder*	NHG	*fürsorge, sorge*		

'Care' is intended here as 'serious mental attention' rather than as 'mental distress, anxiety, worry'. But the latter sense is also common to most of the words listed, and, while partly secondary (so in words meaning orig. 'thought'), is in many cases the earlier, as indicated by the etym.

1. Grk. μελέτη : μέλω (esp. 3sg. μέλει) 'be an object of care', root connection dub. (: μάλα 'very', Lat. *melior* 'better'?). Walde-P. 2.292 (top). NG μελέτη is 'study', but cf. τί με μέλει; 'what do I care?', etc.

Grk. φροντίς 'earnest thought' and so 'care' : φρονέω 'think' (17.14).

Grk. μέριμνα (in class. Grk. mostly poet., but freq. in NT) : Lat. *memor* 'mindful', Skt. *smar-* 'remember', etc. Walde-P. 2.689.

Late Grk. (LXX+), NG προσοχή 'attention, care' : προσέχω 'hold to, turn to, attend to', cpd. of ἔχω 'hold'.

2. Lat. *cūra* (> It. *cura;* Fr. *cure* in OFr. and modern dial. 'care', now 'medical care'; Sp. *cura* 'medical or religious care' or 'curing' = 'seasoning'), fr. **koi-sā-* (cf. Pael. *coisatens* 'curaverunt', OLat. *coiravit*, etc.), but root connection dub. Walde-P. 1.455. Ernout-M. 245 f. Walde-H. 1.314. H. Hendriksen, IF 56.21 (: Skt. *çesa-* 'remainder', but??).

Fr. *soin*, MLat. *sonium*, prob. fr. Gmc., cf. OS *sunnea* 'care', etc. (: MHG *senen* 'long for passionately', NHG *sehnen*). REW 8089a. Gamillscheg 804.

Fr. *souci*, back-formation fr. *soucier* 'be anxious', fr. Lat. *sollicitāre* 'disturb, distress'. REW 8076. Gamillscheg 810.

Sp. *cuidado*, fr. late Lat. *cōgitātus* 'thought' : *cōgitāre* 'ponder, think'. REW 2028.

Rum. *grijă*, fr. Slavic, cf. Bulg. *griža* 'care' = ChSl. *gryža* 'ache' : *gryzą, grysti* 'bite, gnaw'. Tiktin 701. Berneker 359.

3. OIr. *ūan menman* (gl. Lat. *animadversio*, Ml. 28d12), lit. 'lending of the mind', *ūan* vbl. n. of *od-* 'lend' (Pedersen 2.587, Thurneysen, Gram. 466) with gen. sg. of *menme* 'mind'.

MIr. *ōid* (cf. RIA Contrib. s.v.), imperat. form of *od-* 'lend' (cf. *ōid menmain*, gl. *intuere*) used substantively with ellipsis of *menmain* (cf. Lat. *advertere* = *animadvertere*). Cf. T. O'Maille, Lia Fáil 1.181 f. NIr. *ūidh* 'heed, attention'.

Ir. *dethiden, dethitiu* mostly in the sense of 'care, anxiety', see 16.33.

Ir. *aire* 'watching, heed, attention', in NIr. the usual word for 'care', etym.? Walde-P. 2.29.

W. *gofal*, cpd. of *-mal* as in *dyfal* 'careful, diligent', *diofal* 'careless', vb. *malio* 'care for' (also Corn. *mal* 'desire', Br. *mall* 'haste'), perh. : Grk. μέλω, etc. (above, 1). Loth, RC 41.211 f. Henry 194.

W. *pryder*, Br. *preder* : W. *pryd*, Br. *pred* 'time' (14.11), with development through 'what takes time' or 'timeliness'. Pedersen 2.50. Henry 227.

4. Goth. *saurga* (mostly 'care' = 'worry, grief', but 'care' = 'attention' in 2 Cor. 11.28), (ON, Dan., Sw. *sorg* 'sorrow'), Dan., Sw. *omsorg* 'care' (OE *sorh* 'anxiety, grief, sorrow', ME *soru*, etc., NE *sorrow*). Du. *zorg* ('care' in all senses), OHG *sorga* (reg. for Lat. *cūra* in all senses), MHG, NHG *sorge* mostly 'care' as 'anxious thought', etc., for 'care, attention', esp. MHG *vürsorge*, NHG *fürsorge*—a group in which the notion of 'anxiety, grief, sorrow' is dominant, prob. : Skt. *sūrkṣ-* 'trouble oneself about', Lith. *sirgti* 'be ill', Ir. *serg* 'illness', etc. Walde-P. 2.529. Falk-Torp 1109. Feist 413.

Goth. *kara* (*ni kar' ist* = οὐ μέλει, etc.), OE *caru, cearu* (also 'grief, sorrow'), ME, NE *care* (OHG *kara* 'lamentation', NHG *kar-freitag*), prob. through 'cry of grief' : Ir. *gāir* 'cry', Grk. γῆρυς, Dor. γᾶρυς 'voice', etc. Walde-P. 1.537. Falk-Torp 520. Feist 307 f.

ON *umhyggja* (so also NIcel.), cpd. of *hyggja* 'thought' : vb. *hyggja* 'think' (17.14). Here also Dan. *omhu*.

5. Lith. *rūpestis*, Lett. *rūpes* (pl.), with vbs. Lith. *rūpėti*, Lett. *rūpēt* 'be anxious about', prob. : Lat. *rumpere* 'break', etc. Walde-P. 2.355. Mühl.-Endz. 3.571.

6. ChSl. *roditi, raditi* most usual vb. for Grk. μέλω (Jagić, Entstehungsgesch. 370) : Skt. *rādh-* 'prepare, succeed', etc. (cf. ChSl. *radi* 'on account of' = OPers. *rādiy* id.). Walde-P. 1.74.

ChSl. *pečalĭ* (but = μέριμνα as 'care, anxiety' or λύπη 'grief'), Boh. *péče*, Pol. *piecza* (SCr. *pečal*, Russ. *pečal'* 'grief') : ChSl. *peką, pešti* 'bake, roast' used in refl. phrases for 'be troubled, care', e.g. *ne pečeši sę* = οὐ μέλει σοι, *pečaše* = ἔμελεν (Jagić, Entstehungsgesch. 370). Brückner 406. Meillet, Études 416.

SCr. *briga*, fr. It. *briga* 'burden, trouble'. Berneker 86.

Boh. *starost* (also 'old age'), Pol. *staranie* : Boh. *starati* 'be anxious, be concerned with', Pol. *starać się* 'try' (9.99), orig. 'be old', fr. word for 'old', ChSl. *starŭ*, etc. (14.15), with the notion of 'care' accompanying 'old age' becoming dominant.

Russ. *zabota*, prob. through 'alarm' : Russ. *botat'* 'shake, beat, stamp with the feet'. Cf. Pol. *kłopot* 'trouble, anxiety, care' : ChSl. *klopotŭ* 'noise'. Berneker 78. Otherwise Walde-P. 1.530.

7. Skt. *yatna-* 'effort, pains' (: *yat-* 'strive for', etc.) is perh. also the best word for 'care' as intended here (*cintā-* is 'thought', and 'care' = 'anxiety').

16.15 WONDER, ASTONISHMENT

Grk.	*θάμβος, θαῦμα, ἔκπληξις*	Goth.	*sildaleik, afslauþnan*	Lith.	*nusistebėjimas, nustebimas*
NG	*ἔκπληξις*	ON	(*undr*)	Lett.	*brīnums*
Lat.	*admīrātiō, stupor*	Dan.	*undren, forundring, forbavselse*	ChSl.	*užasŭ*
It.	*maraviglia, stupore*	Sw.	(*för*)*undran, förvåning*	SCr.	*čudenje, zaprepašćenje, diōlenje*
Fr.	*étonnement*	OE	*wundrung*	Boh.	*údiv, úžas*
Sp.	*pasmo*	ME	*wonder*	Pol.	*zadziwienie*
Rum.	*mirare*	NE	*wonder, astonishment*	Russ.	*udivlenie*
Ir.	*machdad, ingantas*	Du.	*verbazing*	Skt.	*vismaya-*
NIr.	*iongantas*	OHG	(*wuntar*)		
W.	*rhyfeddod, syndod*	MHG	*wunder*		
Br.	*souez*	NHG	*bewunderung* (*wunder*), (*er*)*staunen*		

Many of the words for 'wonder' denoted originally the obj. 'wonder' ('a wonder' = 'something wonderful'), and only secondarily, mostly through the medium of their deriv. vbs. meaning 'to wonder at', the subj. feeling of 'wonder'. These are based on such notions as 'something seen, perceived', (felt as 'a sight' = 'something worth seeing'), or 'something unknown or of unusual form', etc.

On the other hand, the more distinctive words for the feeling of 'wonder, astonishment' are connected with words for '(be) struck, stunned, rigid, displaced', etc., with extension from a physical condition to a mental attitude. In some of these there is interchange between 'astonishment' and 'fear, terror'. 'Wonder' may turn to 'admiration'.

1. Grk. θάμβος, τάφος, beside vb. aor. ἔταφον, perf. τέθηπα 'be astonished', etym. dub. Walde-P. 1.824. Boisacq 333.

Grk. θαῦμα (mostly obj. 'wonder', but also subj.) : θέᾱ 'sight, aspect', fr. *θᾱϝᾱ,

fr. a root **dhāu-* beside **dhāi-* (?), **dhī-* in words for 'see, look' (15.51). Walde-P. 1.832. Boisacq 335.

Grk. ἔκστασις 'displacement, change' (: ἐξίστημι 'displace'), hence mental 'distraction', in NT 'amazement'.

Grk. ἔκπληξις 'consternation, terror', in NG the usual word for 'astonishment, surprise', fr. ἐκπλήσσω (cpd. of πλήσσω 'strike') 'drive out' and ('drive out of one's senses') 'astound, frighten', in pass. 'be astonished'.

2. Lat. *admīrātiō* ('wonder, surprise' and esp. 'admiration'), fr. (*ad-*)*mīrārī* 'wonder at', beside *mīrus* 'wonderful', etc. : Skt. *smi-* 'smile', etc. (16.25). Cf. esp. Skt. *vi-smi-* 'be astonished', *vismita-* 'astonished', *vismaya-* 'astonishment', *smaya-* 'astonishment' and 'pride, arrogance'. The development of 'smile' to 'wonder at' is not too difficult, and the connection is not to be doubted (as by Ernout-M. 619, without notice of Skt. *vi-smi-*, etc.). Walde-P. 2.686 f.

Lat. *stupor* 'numbness' also 'astonishment' (> It. *stupore* 'astonishment', as sometimes Fr. *stupeur*), fr. *stupēre* 'be struck senseless, stunned, be astonished' : Grk. τύπτω 'strike', etc. Walde-P. 2.618 f. Ernout-M. 990.

It. *maraviglia* (orig. obj. 'wonder', like Fr. *merveille*, NE *marvel*, but also subj. 'wonder, astonishment'), fr. Lat. *mīrābilia* 'wonders' : *mīrus*, etc. (above). REW 5601.

Fr. *étonnement*, fr. vb. *étonner* 'astonish', fr. VLat. **extonāre*, cpd. of *tonāre* 'thunder'. Cf. Lat. *attonitus* (lit. 'thundered at') 'astonished', NE *thunderstruck*. REW 3092.

Fr. *ébahissement*, fr. *ébahir* 'astonish', OFr. *esbahir*, based on the expressive syllable *ba*. REW 851. Gamillscheg 330. Somewhat otherwise Wartburg 1.285 (: forms derived fr. VLat. *batāre* 'open the mouth', itself based on *ba;* REW 988).

Sp. *pasmo*, also and orig. 'spasm', fr. late Lat. *spasmus*, fr. Grk. σπασμός 'spasm' : σπάω 'tear, wrench', etc. REW 8127.

Rum. *mirare*, old infin. of vb. *mira* 'wonder', fr. VLat. *mīrāre*, Lat. *mīrārī* (above). REW 5603.

3. Ir. *machdad* (usual word, both obj. and subj.) : vb. *ad-machdur* 'wonder, marvel', this perh. fr. the same root as OIr. *do-for-maig* 'increases' (: Grk. μέγας 'great', etc. Walde-P. 2.258). Pedersen 1.421 (2.573).

Ir. *ingantas*, NIr. *iongantas* (now the usual word for subj. 'wonder, surprise') : *ingnāth* (pl. *inganta*), NIr. *iongnadh* 'wonderful' and, as sb., obj. 'wonder', orig. 'unknown', neg. cpd. of *gnāth* 'known' : Grk. γνωτός, Lat. *nōtus*, etc. 'known'. Pedersen 1.45, 48.

W. *rhyfeddod*, fr. *rhyfedd* 'wonderful', cpd. of *rhy-* 'beyond' and *-medd* 'measure' as in *dyrn-fedd* 'breadth of the hand', etc. : Ir. *med* 'scales', *air-med* 'measure', etc. (IE **med-*, Walde-P. 2.259). Loth, RC 40.348.

W. *syndod* : *syn* 'dazed, astonished, astonishing', *synnu* 'look, stare at', perh. fr. **stunno-*, **studno-*, fr. **stū-* in words for 'fixed, stiff' (cf. NHG *staunen*, below). Loth, RC 44.271 f.

Br. *souez*, prob. fr. some VLat. deriv. of *subitō* 'suddenly', like the source of Fr. *soudain* 'sudden'. Ernault, Dict. étym. 381, Glossaire 632.

4. Goth. *sildaleik* (= θάμβος Lk. 5.9), beside adj. *sildaleiks* 'wonderful' = OE *sel(d)līc, syllīc* id. cpds. of *leik, līc* 'body, form', first part : OE *seldan*, OHG *seltan*, etc. 'seldom', hence lit. 'of rare form'. Walde-P. 2.457 f. Feist 421.

Goth. *afslauþnan* (= θάμβος Lk. 4.36) = infin. *afslauþnan* 'be astonished' : *afslauþiþs* 'anxious, perplexed', root connection dub. Walde-P. 2.709. Feist 9 f.

ON *undr*, OE *wundor*, OHG *wuntar*, etc., gen. Gmc. except Goth., etym.? Falk-Torp 1332. Weigand-H. 2.1290. These words expressed orig. the obj. 'wonder', and only secondarily emotion. Thus OE *wundor* 'a wonder', ME, NE *wonder* also of the emotion (NED s.v. 7); OHG *wuntar* mostly 'a wonder' (rarely subj., as *sie thē wuntar gifiang*, Otfr. 3.16.5), MHG, NHG *wunder* also of the emotion (NHG still in phrases like *wunder nimmt mich*). But emotional value prevailed in the vbs., as OE *wundrian*, OHG *wuntarōn*, etc. 'wonder at', and so in their derivs., as OE *wundrung*, Dan. *undren, forundring*, NHG *verwunderung*, etc.

Dan. *forbavselse*, fr. vb. *forbavse* 'astonish', fr. MLG *forbasen* 'disturb' = Du. *verbazen* 'astonish', *verbazing* 'astonishment', cpds. of MLG *basen* 'rave, rage'. Falk-Torp 253. Franck-v. W. 37.

Sw. *förvåning*, fr. vb. *förvåna* 'surprise, astonish', through the notion of 'beyond expectation' : *vån*, ON *vān* 'hope, expectation' (16.63), Sw. *vänta* 'expect', etc. Hellquist 264.

NE *astonishment*, fr. vb. *astonish*, earlier *astony*, ME *astone*, fr. OFr. *estoner* (Fr. *étonner*, above, 2). NED s.vv. *astone, astony*, etc.

NE *amazement*, fr. vb. *amaze* beside *maze* 'stupefy, daze'. NED s.v.

NHG (*er*)*staunen*, sb. use of vb., this fr. a Swiss form *stūnen* 'stare' ('stare at' > 'wonder at'), this prob. fr. **stū-* in words based on the notion of 'fixed, stiff'. Walde-P. 2.608. Falk-Torp 1187 f. Kluge-G. 588.

5. Lith. *nusistebėjimas, nustebimas*, fr. *stebėtis* 'be astonished', as orig. 'be stiff, rigid' : Lith. *stiebas* 'stake, mast', Skt. *stabh-* 'support, prop', *stabdha-* 'stiff, rigid', etc. Walde-P. 2.625.

Lett. *brīnums*, etym.? Mühl.-Endz. 1.335.

6. ChSl. *užasŭ* (renders θάμβος and ἔκστασις), Boh. *úžas* 'astonishment' and 'terror' (SCr., Russ. *užas* 'terror') : ChSl. *u-žasnąti sę* 'be frightened', etym.? Walde-P. 1.554.

SCr. *čudenje*, fr. vb. *čuditi se* 'wonder' = ChSl. *čuditi sę* id., fr. ChSl. *čudo*, etc. general Slavic for the obj. 'wonder' (rare or dial. for the feeling), this : *čuti* 'perceive' (17.11). Berneker 161.

SCr. *zaprepašćenje* (or *zaprepašćenost*), fr. *zaprepastiti se* 'be astonished' : *prepasti se* 'be frightened' (Pol. *przepaść* 'be lost'), ChSl. *pasti* 'fall'. Brückner 390.

SCr. *diolenje*, Boh. *údiv*, Pol. *zadziwienie, podziwienie*, Russ. *udivlenie*, all through deriv. vbs. : ChSl. *divŭ, divo*, etc., general Slavic for the obj. 'wonder', this as orig. 'a sight' (cf. θαῦμα, above) : Skt. *dī-, dīv-* 'shine', etc. Walde-P. 1.774. Berneker 202.

7. Skt. *vi-smaya-*, above, 2.

16.16. 'Surprise'. The feeling evoked by the unexpected is in large measure included in the scope of words listed in 16.15. So far as there are more distinctive terms, they are modern and originally denoted the physical act of 'surprise, sudden overtaking'.

1. It. *sorpresa*, Fr. *surprise* (> NE *surprise*, Rum. *surpriză*), orig. denoting the physical 'surprise, taking unawares', fr. fem. pple. of It. *sorprendere*, Fr. *surprendre*, MLat. *superprendere*, cpd. of *prēndere* 'seize' (11.14). Gamillscheg 824. NED s.v. *surprise*.

2. NHG *überraschung* (hence by semantic borrowing Dan. *overraskelse*, Sw. *överraskning*), fr. vb. *überraschen*, orig.

'surprise' in a military sense, lit. 'be swift over one' (cf. *überrumpeln, überlaufen*, etc.), fr. *rasch* 'swift'. Kluge-G. 638. Similarly Du. *verrassing*.

3. Boh. *překvapení*, fr. vb. *překvapiti*, cpd. of *kvapiti* 'hasten', fr. *kvap* 'haste, hurry'. Evidently modeled on NHG *überraschen, überraschung*, and likewise used for both act and emotion. There are various other Slavic words for the physical 'surprise', but they seem not to be current for the resulting feeling.

16.17 FORTUNE (Good or Bad)

Grk.	*τύχη, συμφορά*	Goth.	....	Lith.	*laimė*
NG	*τύχη*	ON	*happ, lukka*	Lett.	*laime*
Lat.	*fortūna (fors, cāsus)*	Dan.	*skæbne, lykke*	ChSl.	(*kobĭ*)
It.	*fortuna, ventura*	Sw.	*lycka*	SCr.	*sreća*
Fr.	*fortune, chance*	OE	*wyrd*	Boh.	*štěstí*
Sp.	*fortuna, ventura*	ME	*fortune, hap*	Pol.	*szczęście*
Rum.	*soarte, noroc*	NE	*fortune, luck*	Russ.	*sčastie*
Ir.	*tocad*	Du.	*geluk*	Skt.	*bhāgya-*
NIr.	*ādh*	OHG	*wurt*		
W.	*ffawd, ffortun*	MHG	*gelücke*		
Br.	*chans*	NHG	*glück*		

Words for 'fortune' in the neutral sense (good or bad) are based on notions like 'what happens, befalls, becomes, arrives', 'part, share', 'augury', 'declaration'; but several are of doubtful origin.

Most of them are used also and most commonly for 'good fortune'. A few tend to specialization in the other direction, to 'misfortune'.

1. Grk. *τύχη* 'fortune' and esp. 'good fortune', beside *τυγχάνω* 'happen', aor. *ἔτυχον*, prob. : *τεύχω* 'make, prepare', Goth. *daug*, OE *dēag*, OHG *toug* 'is of use', etc. Hence also *εὐτυχία, εὐτύχημα* 'good fortune' and *δυστυχία, δυστύχημα* 'misfortune'. Walde-P. 1.847. LS[9] s.v. *τυγχάνω*, end.

Grk. *συμφορά* 'fortune, circumstance', sometimes 'good fortune', but mostly 'misfortune' (as NG), fr. *συμφέρω* 'bring together', 3.sg. impers. *συμφέρει* 'is of use', pple. *συμφέρων* 'useful', etc.

2. Lat. *fortūna* (> It., Sp. *fortuna*, Fr. *fortune* > ME, NE *fortune*), beside *fors, fortis* 'chance', fr. the root of *ferre* 'bear, carry'. Walde-P. 2.155. Ernout-M. 382 (with doubt). Walde-H. 1.534. REW 3458. The development has been mostly in the direction of 'good fortune', hence also 'wealth, riches' in Fr. and NE, but among sailors of the Mediterranean (through 'risk' of the sea) 'storm', as It. *fortuna* (> NG *φουρτούνα*), etc.

Lat. *cāsus* 'what happens, chance', fr. *cadere* 'fall' (10.23), also 'befall, happen', whence OFr. *cheoir* and the new sb. OFr. *cheance* (> ME *cheance, chaunce, chance*, NE *chance*), Fr. *chance*, now esp. *bonne chance* 'good luck'. Ernout-M. 126. REW 1451.

Lat. *sors, sortis* 'lot, fate' (> Romance words, of which Rum. *soarte* is also the one for 'fortune'), prob. (with reference to drawing lots) fr. the root of *serere* 'bind together, arrange', *seriēs* 'row, series'. Walde-P. 2.500. Ernout-M. 959. REW 8107.

It., Sp. *ventura* 'fortune' and 'good' fortune' = OFr. *aventure* 'event' (> ME *aventure*, NE *adventure*), fr. deriv. of Lat. *advenīre* 'come to, arrive', hence 'happen' as Fr. *avenir*, etc. REW 216.

Fr. *heur*, now obs. but source of *bonheur* 'good fortune' and *malheur* 'misfortune', fr. Lat. *augurium* 'augury'. REW 785. Wartburg 1.174 f.

Rum. *noroc* (partly neutral, but mostly 'good fortune'), fr. Slavic, SCr. *narok* 'fortune' (obs.), ChSl. *narokŭ* 'declaration, appellation', etc., fr. cpd. of *reką, rešti* 'say' (18.22). Cf. Lat. *fātum* 'fate', fr. *fārī* 'speak, say'. Tiktin 1061. Brückner 355.

3. Ir. *tocad* ('fortune' and 'good fortune, wealth') = W. *tynget*, Br. *tonket* 'fate' (not : Grk. *τύχη*, as Pedersen 1.151, but) : Lith. *tenku, tekti* 'fall to one's share', Goth. *þeihan* 'prosper', etc. Walde-P. 1.725. Thurneysen, Gram. 126. Pokorny KZ 47.165.

Ir. *ād, āg* (K. Meyer, Contrib. 13, Hessen s.v.), NIr. *ādh*, Gael. *āgh*, mostly 'good luck', etym.?

W. *ffawd* ('fortune, good fortune', also and orig. 'fate'), fr. Lat. *fāta*, pl. of *fātum* 'fate'. Loth, Mots lat. 167.

W. *ffortun*, fr. NE *fortune*.

Br. *chans*, fr. Fr. *chance*.

Br. *eur*, not used alone except in dials., but seen in cpds. *eurvad* 'good fortune' (*mad* 'good') and *droukeur* 'misfortune' (*drouk* 'bad'), fr. Fr. *heur* (above, 2).

4. ON *happ* (> ME *happe, hap*; cf. OE *gehæp* 'fit'; Chaucer has *hap and fortune*) : ChSl. *kobĭ* 'augury', Ir. *cob* 'victory'. Walde-P. 1.457. Falk-Torp 398 f.

OE *wyrd* 'what happens, fortune, fate' (gl. Lat. *eventus, fortūna, fors, cāsus, sors*), OHG *wurt* (rare), fr. the root of OE *weorþan*, OHG *werdan* 'become' (9.92). NED s.v. *weird* sb.

MHG *g(e)lücke*, NHG *glück*, MLG (*ge*)*lucke* (> late ON *lukka*, Dan. *lykke*, Sw. *lycka*), Du. *geluk*, MDu. also *luk* (> ME, NE *luck*), all used for the neutral 'luck, fortune', but esp. for 'good fortune', etym. dub. Walde-P. 2.414, 426. Falk-Torp 669. NED s.v. *luck*.

Dan. *skæbne* ('fortune' and 'fate') : *skabe* 'create, make'. Falk-Torp 977, 1008.

5. Lith. *laimė*, Lett. *laime* (both mostly 'good fortune', and personified in folklore; OPruss. *laeims* 'rich'), etym. dub., perh. : ChSl. *lĕtĭ jestŭ* 'licet', etc. Walde-P. 2.394. Berneker 714. Mühl.-Endz. 2.409 (otherwise).

6. ChSl. *kobĭ* mostly 'augury' (: ON *happ*, above, 4), in Supr. renders *τύχη* (but in its sense of 'station in life', LS s.v. *τύχη* IV. 3; not as Berneker 535).

Boh. *štěstí*, Pol. *szczęście*, Russ. *sčastie*, fr. **sŭ-čęstĭje* cpd. of *čęstĭ* 'part' (13.23). Berneker 155. Brückner 544.

SCr. *sreća*, as orig. 'meeting' fr. *sresti*, ChSl. *sŭrěsti* 'meet'. Miklosich 278. Brückner 534.

7. Skt. *bhāgya-* 'lot, fate' and esp. 'good fortune' (cf. adjs. *bhāgyavant-, subhāgya-* 'fortunate', *durbhāgya-* 'unfortunate'), through *bhāga-* 'part, share', also 'good fortune', fr. vb. *bhaj-* 'apportion, share'. Av. *baγa-* 'share' and also 'good fortune'. Barth. 921.

16.18 GOOD FORTUNE

Grk.	*τύχη, εὐτυχία*	Goth.	....	Lith.	*laimė*
NG	*εὐτύχημα, εὐτυχία*	ON	*happ*	Lett.	*laime*
Lat.	*fortūna (secunda)*	Dan.	*lykke*	ChSl.	....
It.	*(buona) fortuna*	Sw.	*lycka*	SCr.	*sreća*
Fr.	*bonheur*	OE	*wyrd gōd*(?)	Boh.	*štěstí*
Sp.	*(buena) fortuna*	ME	*fortune, hap*	Pol.	*szczęście*
Rum.	*noroc*	NE	*(good) fortune, luck*	Russ.	*sčastie*
Ir.	*ād, tocad*	Du.	*geluk*	Skt.	*bhāgya-*
NIr.	*ādh, sonas*	OHG	....		
W.	*ffortun*	MHG	*gelücke*		
Br.	*eurvad*	NHG	*glück*		

'Good fortune' is expressed by words listed or discussed in 16.17, either with words for 'good, well, favorable', or, commonly in most languages, alone. Ir. *sonas*, fr. adj. *sona* 'fortunate, happy' (16.24).

A good part of these words come to express the resulting state of 'happiness' (see 16.24), a few 'wealth, riches'.

16.19 MISFORTUNE

Grk.	*συμφορά, δυστύχημα, ἀτύχημα*	Goth.	....	Lith.	*nelaimė*
NG	*συμφορά, δυστυχία*	ON	*ūlykka*	Lett.	*nelaime*
Lat.	*fortūna adversa, infortūnium*	Dan.	*ulykke, vanskæbne*	ChSl.	....
It.	*sfortuna, disgrazia*	Sw.	*olycka*	SCr.	*nesreća*
Fr.	*malheur, infortune*	OE	*unwyrd*	Boh.	*neštěstí, nehoda*
Sp.	*desgracia, infortunio*	ME	*mishap, mischaunce, infortune*	Pol.	*nieszczęście*
Rum.	*nenorocire*	NE	*misfortune*	Russ.	*nesčastie*
Ir.	*dodcad*	Du.	*ongeluk*	Skt.	*dāurbhāgya-*
NIr.	*mīādh, donas*	OHG	*ungifuari, wēnagheit*		
W.	*anffawd*	MHG	*ungelücke*		
Br.	*reuz, droukeur, droukverz*	NHG	*unglück*		

'Misfortune' is most commonly expressed by words for 'fortune' (16.17) combined with words for 'ill, mis-, adverse', or a negative prefix, rarely alone with specialization in this direction (Grk. *συμφορά*).

Thus with words for 'ill-' (16.72), etc. Grk. *δυστύχημα* (or *-ία*), Lat. *fortūna adversa*, It. *sfortuna*, OFr. *meschaunce* (> ME *mischaunce*), Fr. *malheur*, Ir. *dodcad* (fr. *tocad* with *do-* 'ill'; Thurneysen Gram. 231), NIr. *mīādh* (*mī-*, Pedersen 2.10), Br. *droukeur*, Dan. *vanskæbne* (*van-* 'mis-, un-', Falk-Torp 1347), NE *misfortune*, Skt. *dāurbhāgya-* (fr. adj. *dur-bhaga-* 'unfortunate', with vṛddhi of both syllables); with neg. prefix, Grk. *ἀτύχημα* (or *-ία*), Lat. *infortūnium* (> Fr., ME *infortune*, Sp. *infortunio*), Rum. *nenorocire*, W. *anffawd*, ON *ūlykka* (late), Dan. *ulykke*, Sw. *olycka*, Du. *ongeluk*, NHG *unglück*, OE *unwyrd*, Lith. *nelaimė*, SCr. *nesreća*, Russ. *nesčastie*, etc.

But several other words, of quite different origin, are used in substantially the same sense, of which may be mentioned the following. Still others which cover 'misfortune' but are felt as much stronger, like NE *disaster, catastrophe, calamity, ruin*, etc. are not considered, except the interesting *disaster* group.

Grk. *πάθος, πάθημα* 'what happens, emotion' (16.12), often 'misfortune'.

Lat. *incommodum*, neut. of *incommodus* 'inconvenient', frequent for 'misfortune, disaster'.

It. *disgrazia*, Fr. *disgrâce* (> NE *disgrace*), Sp. *desgracia*, fr. MLat. *disgrātia* 'dis-favor', but all used also for 'misfortune'. NED s.v. *disgrace* sb. ('misfortune' obs.).

It. *disastro*, hence Fr. *désastre* (> NE *disaster*), Sp. *desastre*, somewhat stronger than 'misfortune', cpd. of *dis-* with *astro* 'star' (cf. NE *ill-starred*). Prov. also *malastre* 'misfortune', *benastre* 'good fortune'. NED s.v. *disaster*. Wartburg 1.165.

NIr. *donas*, fr. adj. *dona* 'wretched, unfortunate', deriv. of *do-* 'ill-', see under *sona* 'happy' (16.24).

MW *dyvyđ*, cpd. of *dy-* 'ill-' and a form of IE **bhwiy-* (Ir. *bīu*, Lat. *fīō*, etc.), as in Ir. *dube* 'grief'. Pokorny, Z. celt. Ph. 15.290.

Br. *reuz*, etym.? Henry 233.

Br. *droukverz*, cpd. of *drouk* 'bad' and *berz* 'prosperity'.

OHG *ungifuari*, neg. of *gifuari* 'what is advantageous, convenient' (cf. Lat. *incommodum*, above) : OHG *faran* 'go, fare', *fuoren* 'lead', etc. Walde-P. 2.39. Falk-Torp 291.

OHG *wēnagheit* (mostly 'misery'), fr. *wēnag* 'wretched, unfortunate' = Goth. *wainahs* 'wretched', perh. formed fr. the the interjection Goth. *wai*, etc. Walde-P. 1.212 f.

Boh. *nehoda* (beside *náhoda* 'chance'), fr. *hod* 'throw, time' (= ChSl. *godŭ* 'point of time', 14.11) with neg. prefix. Berneker 318.

16.21 PLEASE

Grk.	*ἀρέσκω, ἁνδάνω*	Goth.	*(ga)leikan*	Lith.	*(pa)tikti*
NG	*ἀρέσω*	ON	*līka, hugna*	Lett.	*(pa)tikt*
Lat.	*placēre*	Dan.	*behage*	ChSl.	*ugoditi*
It.	*piacere*	Sw.	*behaga*	SCr.	*dopasti se*
Fr.	*plaire*	OE	*(ge)līcian, (ge)cwēman*	Boh.	*líbiti se*
Sp.	*placer, agradar, gustar*	ME	*plaise, like, (i)queme*	Pol.	*podobać się*
Rum.	*plăcea*	NE	*please*	Russ.	*nravit'sja*
Ir.	*toltanaigur, tolnur*	Du.	*behagen*	Skt.	*prī-, tarpaya-*
NIr.	*taitnim*	OHG	*(gi)līhhēn*	Av.	*voī* (inf.)
W.	*boddhau, boddio*	MHG	*(be)hagen, gelīchen*		
Br.	*plijout*	NHG	*gefallen*		

Verbs for 'please', whence some nouns for 'pleasure', are mostly based on notions like 'suitable, becoming, conforming to, falling to one's lot', less frequently on what is one's 'will', or 'pleasure'. Emotional value is secondary and less strongly developed than in their deriv. nouns.

1. Grk. *ἀρέσκω*, NG *ἀρέσω* (new pres. fr. aor. *ἤρεσα*), as orig. 'be fitting' : *ἀραρίσκω* 'fit' (cf. *ἄρμενα* 'fitting, pleasing'). Walde-P. 1.69. Boisacq 73.

Grk. *ἁνδάνω* 'please' beside *ἥδομαι* 'be pleased, enjoy oneself' and *ἡδονή* 'pleasure' : Skt. *svad-* 'take pleasure in, enjoy' and the more widespread adj. for 'sweet, pleasant' Skt. *svādu-*, Grk. *ἡδύς*, Lat. *suāvis*, etc. (15.35). Walde-P. 1.601. Ernout-M. 991.

2. Lat. *placēre* (> It. *piacere*, OFr. *plaisir*, Fr. *plaire*, Sp. *placer*, Rum. *plăcea*) : *plācāre* 'reconcile, soothe', *placidus* 'gentle, quiet, calm', prob. as orig. 'make smooth, flatten out' : Grk. *πλάξ* 'flat surface', etc. Cf. also Toch. A

plākām 'agreement', etc. (SSS 454). Walde-P. 2.90. Ernout-M. 773 f.

Sp. *agradar* (Fr. *agréer*, etc. 'agree'), fr. Sp. *grado* 'will, pleasure' (Fr. *gré*, etc.), fr. Lat. *grātum*, neut. of *grātus* 'agreeable, dear'. REW 3848.

Sp. *gustar* 'taste' (15.31), hence, through obj. 'taste' (= 'have a pleasant taste'), 'please' in *me gusta* 'it pleases me, I like'.

3. Ir. *toltanaigur*, MIr. *toltanaigim*, cf. *toltanach* gl. 'beneplacitus', also Ir. *tolnur* (e.g. 3sg. rel. *tolnathar*), both fr. *tol* 'will' (cf. NIr. *toilighim* 'will, wish', 16.61). Pedersen 2.47, 652.

NIr. *taitnim* (*taitnighim, taithnighim*), orig. 'shine', as Ir. *taitnim* (15.56).

W. *boddhau, boddio*, fr. *bodd* 'will, pleasure' = Corn. *both* 'will' : Ir. *buide* 'thanks', ON *boð*, MHG *bot* 'command', etc., fr. the root of Goth. *ana-biudan* 'command', Grk. πείθομαι 'learn', Skt. *budh-* 'awake, perceive', etc. Walde-P. 2.147. Pedersen 1.35.

Br. *plijout*, formed fr. the stem of Fr. *plaisir* (above, 2). Henry 225.

4. Goth. *(ga)leikan*, ON *līka*, OE *(ge)-līcian*, ME *like* (NE *like*), OHG *gilīhhēn*, *līhhēn*, MHG *gelīchen*, fr. the stem of Goth. *ga-leiks*, ON *g-līkr*, OE *ge-līc*, etc. 'equal, like' (12.91). Development 'be like' > 'be suitable' > 'be pleasing'. Walde-P. 2.398. NED s.v. *like* adj. and vb.

ON *hugna*, fr. *hugr* 'mind, mood, desire' : Goth. *hugs* 'mind, understanding', etc. (17.11).

OE *(ge)cwēman*, ME *(i)queme*, fr. OE *(ge)cwēme* adj. 'pleasing, agreeable' (OHG *bi-quāmi* 'fitting, useful'), fr. the stem of OE *cuman*, Goth. *qiman* 'come', etc. (cf. Goth. *ga-qimiþ* 'it is fitting', NE *become*, Lat. *con-venīre*). NED s.v. *queme* adj. and vb.

ME *plaise, pleise*, etc., NE *please*, fr. OFr. *plaisir* (above, 2). NED s.v.

Du. *behagen* (MLG *behagen* > Dan. *behage*, Sw. *behaga*), OS *bihagōn*, MHG, NHG *behagen* (now mostly 'suit'), cf. OE *onhagian* 'suit, be convenient or possible', ON *haga* 'manage, arrange', prob. : Skt. *çak-* 'be powerful, be able', etc. Walde-P. 1.333. Falk-Torp 58, 371. Kluge-G. 46.

NHG *gefallen*, fr. MHG *gevallen*, OHG *gifallan* 'fall to one's lot', in MHG rarely 'please' and always with *wol, baz*, etc.; used orig. in military language when dividing the booty by casting lots. Kluge-G. 191. Weigand-H. 1.646 f.

5. Lith. *(pa)tikti*, Lett. *(pa)tikt* (the simple vb. in Lith. mostly 'suit, fit') : Lith. *teikti* 'join', *tiekti* 'prepare', OPruss. *teickut* 'make', outside connections dub. Walde-P. 1.725. Mühl.-Endz. 4.157, 183 f.

6. ChSl. *ugoditi*, perfect. cpd. of the simple vb. in Russ.-ChSl. *goditi* id., Russ. *godit'sja* 'suit, fit, be of use', SCr. *goditi* 'be desirable, of use', etc. : ChSl. *godŭ* '(proper) time', etc. (14.11). Berneker 317. Walde-P. 1.532.

SCr. *dopasti se, dopadati se*, refl. of *dopasti, dopadati*, 'fall upon, fall to one's lot', etc., cpd. of *pasti, padati* 'fall'. Sense 'please' after NHG *gefallen*. Rjecnik Akad. 2.645.

Boh. *líbiti se*, refl. of *líbiti* 'like' (: ChSl. *ljubiti* 'love', etc., 16.27).

Pol. *podobać się*, cf. *podoba* 'gratification, pleasure, resemblance', ChSl. *podobiti* 'make fitting, like', *podoba* 'adornment' (*podoba jestŭ* 'it is proper'), Russ. *podobit'sja* 'resemble', etc. : Goth. *gadaban* 'happen', OE pple. *gedafen* 'proper', etc. Berneker 203 f.

Russ. *nravit'sja*, fr. *nrav* 'character, temper, humor', fr. ChSl. *nravŭ* (genuine Russ. *norov* 'habit, custom, usage'), this prob. : Lith. *norėti* 'wish, will'. Walde-P. 2.333.

7. Skt. *prī-* : ChSl. *prijati* 'be favorable', Goth. *frijōn* 'love', etc. (16.27). Walde-P. 2.86 f.

Skt. *tarpaya-*, caus. of *tṛp-* 'be satisfied, satiated, partake of' : Grk. τέρπω 'satisfy, delight, cheer', mid. 'enjoy', τέρψις 'joy', Lith. *tarpti* 'thrive', etc. Walde-P. 1.737.

Av. *vōī* (inf.) : Skt. *deva-vī-* 'pleasing to the gods', *devavīti-* 'feast of the gods', *vīta-* 'desired, pleasant', fr. root *vī-* (3sg. *veti*) 'seek eagerly, pursue, attack' : Grk. ἵεμαι 'hasten, be eager'. Walde-P. 1.228. Barth. 1427 f.

16.212. Note on polite phrases for 'please'.

In several languages the verbs for 'please' furnish the stereotyped polite 'please' (take a seat, etc.), as NE *please*, shortened from (*may it*) *please you* (NED s.v. *please* 6 c), It. *per piacere*, Fr. *s'il vous plaît*. But more widespread is the use of the first singular of a verb for 'ask, request' (18.35), as NG παρακαλῶ, NHG *bitte*, Lith. *prašau*, SCr. *molim*, Boh. *prosim*, Pol. *proszę*, Rum. *rog*. Among other such phrases are Sp. *hace el favor* 'do the favor' (or simply *favor*), Dan. *vær saa god* 'be so good', Russ. *požaluista* : *požalovat'* 'do a favor', Sp. *sirvase* (more formal than *favor*), refl. of *servir* 'serve'.

16.22 JOY

Grk.	*χαρά*	Goth.	*fahēþs*	Lith.	*džiaugsmas, linksmybė*
NG	*χαρά*	ON	*gleði, fagnaðr*		
Lat.	*gaudium, laetitia*	Dan.	*glæde, fryd*	Lett.	*prieks, līksma*
It.	*gioia*	Sw.	*glädje, fröjd*	ChSl.	*radostĭ*
Fr.	*joie*	OE	*gefēa, bliþs, glædnes, wynn*	SCr.	*radost*
Sp.	*alegría, gozo*			Boh.	*radost*
Rum.	*veselie, bucurie*	ME	*blisse, ioie, gladnes, wunne*	Pol.	*radość*
Ir.	*fāilte, sube, āithes*			Russ.	*radost'*
NIr.	*āthas, lūthghāir*	NE	*joy*	Skt.	*ānanda-, harṣa-, mayas-*
W.	*llawenydd, dywenydd*	Du.	*vreugde*		
Br.	*levenez, joa*	OHG	*gifeho, frewī, frewida, mendī, wunna*	Av.	*mᾰ̄yā-, šāiti-, urvāza-*
		MHG	*vröude, mende*		
		NHG	*freude*		

It is impossible to draw any sharp lines between the pleasurable emotions expressed by NE *pleasure, joy, delight, gladness, happiness*, etc., or by adjectives like *joyful, glad, merry, gay, happy*, etc.; and their differentiation in usage corresponds only in small measure to that in similar groups elsewhere.

The words listed here are those that seem to be the best generic terms for 'joy', the choice in some cases being difficult. Omitted are many others, as Grk. τέρψις 'delight, enjoyment' (: τέρπω 'delight, gladden', mid. 'enjoy', Skt. *tṛp-* 'be satisfied, pleased', Lith. *tarpti* 'thrive'. Walde-P. 1.737); NE *delight* (ME *delit* fr. OFr. *delit* = It. *diletto*, etc., through the vb. fr. Lat. *dēlectāre* 'allure, charm, delight', frequent. of *dē-licere* 'entice away', cpd. of *lacere* id. Ernout-M. 532 f. REW 2532. NED s.v.).

The moderate 'pleasure' may be covered in part by some of the words listed here under 'joy', as NHG *freude*. But it is most commonly expressed by words having an underlying notion of 'satisfaction'. Thus derivs., or infins. used substantively, of vbs. for 'please' (16.21), as Grk. ἡδονή (: ἁνδάνω 'please', ἡδύς 'pleasant', etc.), It. *piacere*, Fr. *plaisir* (OFr. infin.; hence ME *plesir*, NE *pleasure* with spelling after *measure*, etc.), Sp. *placer*, Rum. *plăcere*, NHG *gefallen*, Skt. *prīti-*. Or other words meaning orig. satisfaction, as NHG *vergnügen*, Du. *genoegen* (: NHG *genug* 'enough', etc.), Russ. *udovol'stvie* (cf. *udovol'stovat'* 'satisfy', *dovol'stvie* 'sufficiency, abundance, ease' : *dovol'no*, ChSl. *dovolĭno* 'enough', this : *volja* 'will', etc.). So Goth. *gabaurjōþus* (renders ἡδονή, beside adv. *gabaurjaba* = ἡδέως, ἥδιστα) : OE *gebyrian* 'pertain to, happen', etc. (Feist 175; for formation, cf. F. Metzger, Language 21.971 f.). NHG *lust*, orig. 'strong desire' (: Goth. *lustus*, OE *lust*, etc.) now common for the simple 'pleasure'. Lat. *voluptās* the most distinctive word for 'pleasure', beside neut. adj. *volup* 'pleasant, agreeable' : Lat. *velle* 'wish', Grk. ἐλπίς 'hope', etc.

For 'happy', 'happiness' see 16.24.

1. Grk. χαρά : χαίρω 'rejoice' (pples. χαίρων, NG χαρούμενος 'joyful'), χάρις 'favor, grace', Osc. *herest*, Umbr. *heriest* 'volet', Lat. *horīrī, hortārī* 'urge, encourage', Goth. *gairnjan*, OE *giernan* (NE *yearn*) 'desire', Skt. *haryati* 'delights in', etc. Walde-P. 1.601. Ernout-M. 460. Walde-H. 1.658.

2. Lat. *gaudium* (> Sp. *gozo*, Fr. *joie* > It. *gioia*) : *gaudēre* 'rejoice', Grk. γηθέω, Dor. γαθέω 'rejoice', Hom. γαίων 'rejoicing', etc., root **gāu-*. Walde-P. 1.529. Ernout-M. 411 f. Walde-H. 1.584. REW 3705.

Lat. *laetitia*, fr. *laetus* 'joyful' (> It. *lieto*), also (more orig.?) 'rich, fertile', etym. dub. Walde-H. 1.750. Ernout-M. 518.

Sp. *alegría*, fr. *alegre* 'lively, merry, joyful' = It. *allegro* id., fr. Lat. *alacer* 'lively', also 'joyful, merry' (joined with *laetus* in Cic.), perh. : Goth. *aljan* 'zeal', OE *ellen* 'strength, valor', etc. Walde-P. 1.156. Walde-H. 1.25. Otherwise (: Lat. *amb-ulāre*) Ernout-M. 31.

Rum. *veselie*, fr. Slavic (below, 6).

Rum. *bucurie*, beside adj. *bucuros*, fr. Alb. *bukurí* 'beauty', *búkur* 'beautiful', orig.? Tiktin 233. G. Meyer, Alb. Etym. Wtb. 52.

3. Ir. *fāilte* (also 'welcome', and NIr. in this sense), fr. *fāilid* 'joyful, glad', etym.? Dub. connections in Pedersen 2.17, Stokes 262.

Ir. *sube*, cpd. of *su-* 'good' (cf. *du-be* 'grief') and *-be* fr. some form of the vb. for 'be', as **bhwī-, bhwiy-* in Ir. *bīu*, Lat. *fīō*, etc. Pokorny Z. celt. Ph. 15.290.

Ir. *āithes*, NIr. *āthas*, perh. : Ir. *āith* 'sharp, keen' (Dillon).

NIr. *lūthghāir*, MIr. *lūthgūir* (Windisch, p. 673), cf. Gael. *lūthghāir* 'a great shout of joy', apparently the orig. sense, cpd. of *lūth* 'strength, movement' and *gāir* 'shout', whence also NIr. *gāirdighim* 'rejoice'.

W. *llawenydd*, Br. *levenez*, fr. W. *llawen*, Br. *laouen* 'joyful', prob. : Grk. ἀπολαύω 'have the enjoyment, benefit of', Goth. *launs* 'reward', etc. Walde-P. 2.380.

W. *dywenydd*, fr. *dywenu* 'smile, be glad', *dywen* 'a smile, glad mien', intensive cpd. of *gwen* 'smile' (16.25). Evans, W. Dict. s.v.

Br. *joa*, fr. Fr. *joie* (above, 2).

4. Goth. *fahēþs*, ON *fagnaðr*, OE *gefēa* with adj. *fægen*, ME *fayn* (NE *fain*), OHG *gifeho* : Goth. *faginōn*, ON *fagna*, OE *gefēon*, OHG *gifehan* 'rejoice', outside root connections dub. Walde-P. 2.16. Falk-Torp 201. Feist 135.

ON *gleði*, Dan. *glæde*, Sw. *glädje*, OE *glædnes*, etc., fr. adjs. ON *glaðr*, OE *glæd* 'cheerful, joyful', also 'bright, shining' = OHG, MHG *glat* 'bright' and 'smooth', NHG *glatt*, Du. *glad* 'smooth' : ChSl. *gladŭkŭ* 'smooth', Lat. *glaber* 'smooth, bald'. Whether 'smooth' > 'bright' or conversely (cf. 15.77), the sense 'joyful' comes fr. 'bright'. Walde-P. 1.625 f. Falk-Torp 324. NED s.v. *glad*.

OE *blīþs, blis(s)*, ME *blisse* (but the more restricted sense, as in NE *bliss*, influenced by *bless*; cf. NED s.v.), fr. adj. *blīþe* 'kind' and 'joyful', ME, NE *blithe* = OHG *blīdi*, MHG *blīde*, Du. *blijde*, *blij* 'joyful', Goth. *bleiþs* 'merciful, loving goodness', ON *blīðr* 'gentle, pleasing', root connection dub., perh. through 'bright' : OE *blēo* 'color, appearance', etc. Walde-P. 2.210. Falk-Torp 81.

OE *wynn*, ME *wunne, winne* (cf. NE *winsome*), OHG *wunna* 'great joy, bliss' (NHG *wonne*) : Lat. *venus* 'charm' (and *Venus*), Skt. *van-* 'desire, seek, gain', Goth. *wēns* 'hope', OHG *wunscan*, OE *wyscan* 'wish', etc. Walde-P. 1.258.

OHG *frewī, frewida*, MHG *vröude*, NHG *freude*, Du. *vreugde* (Dan. *fryd*, Sw. *fröjd*, sense prob. influenced by German; ON *frygð* 'bloom, magnificence'), fr. adj. OHG *frō* (inflected *frawer*, etc.), MHG *vrō*, NHG *froh* 'joyful, glad', in OHG also 'swift' as ON *frār*, this prob. the earlier meaning, hence perh. : Skt. *pru-* 'spring up', *prava-* 'hovering', Russ. *pryt'* 'swift pace', etc. Walde-P. 2.88. Weigand-H. 1.588. Somewhat otherwise formally but much the same semantically (as orig. 'forward moving' Gmc. **frawa-* = IE **pro-wo-*) Falk-Torp 278.

OE *ioie*, NE *joy*, fr. Fr. *joie* (above, 2).

OHG *mendī*, MHG *mende*, with vb. *menden* 'rejoice' : OHG *muntar* 'eager, zealous' (NHG *munter*), Goth. *mundōn sis* 'take notice of', Lith. *mandras* 'lively, impudent', Grk. μανθάνω 'learn', etc. Walde-P. 2.271. Feist 367.

Words of the group OE *lust*, etc. 'desire' (16.62) are also used for 'pleasure, joy', e.g. sometimes in OE (cf. NED s.v.), and esp. in MHG, NHG (Dan. *lyst*, Sw. *lust* prob. fr. LG).

5. Lith. *džiaugsmas*, fr. *džiaugti-s* 'be glad, rejoice', prob. with cons. transposition fr. *gaudž-* : Lat. *gaudium* (above, 2). Walde-P. 1.529. Walde-H. 1.584.

Lith. *linksmybė*, Lett. *līksma* (also *līksme, līksmiba*), fr. Lith. *linksmas*, Lett. *līksms* 'joyful', prob. : Lith. *lenkti* 'bend, bow', *linkėti* 'incline to, wish', with semantic development through 'inclined to, agreeable, pleasant'. Mühl.-Endz. 2.486. Leskien, Ablaut 334.

Lett. *prieks*, with adj. *priecīgs* 'joyful', perh. fr. the root of ChSl. *prijati*, Goth. *frijōn* 'love', Skt. *priya-* 'dear', etc. (Walde-P. 2.86 f., without the Lett. forms). Mühl.-Endz. 3.393.

6. ChSl. *radostĭ* (reg. for χαρά in Gospels), etc., general Slavic, fr. adj. ChSl. *radŭ*, etc. general Slavic for 'joyful, glad' or in part 'willing, ready' (so mostly SCr., Pol. *rad*) : Lith. *rōds* 'willing', OE *rōt* 'cheerful' more often 'noble, excellent', vb. *ā-rētan* 'comfort, delight', etc. Walde-P. 2.369. Trautmann 235. Otherwise (*rad-* fr. *ard-* on account of *Ardogastes* = *Rodogost*) Brückner 452, Liewehr, Einführung in die hist. Gram. d. tschechischen Sprache 190 f.

ChSl. *veselĭje* = ἀγαλλίασις 'great joy, exultation' (cf. Lk. 1.24 *radostĭ i veselĭje* = χαρὰ καὶ ἀγαλλίασις), and in modern Slavic esp. 'boisterous joy, merrymaking' (Pol. *wesele* 'wedding feast, wedding'), deriv., through the vb., fr. adj. ChSl. *veselŭ*, etc., general Slavic (> Rum. *vesel*), mostly 'merry' but not always sharply distinguished from the previous group (ChSl. *radŭ*, etc.); prob. as orig. 'feasting' : Goth. *wisan* (esp. *waila wisan*) 'be merry', *wailawizns* 'food', OE *wist* 'food', Ir. *feis* 'meal, feast', etc. Walde-P. 1.308. Feist 569. Or/and (?) : Skt. *vasu-* 'good'. Fraenkel, Mélanges Pedersen 453.

7. Skt. *ānanda-, nanda-*, fr. *ā-nand-*, *nand-* 'rejoice', etym. dub., but perh. :

nad- 'sound, cry' (so Whitney, Roots). Cf. Ir. *lūthghāir* (above, 3).

Skt. *harṣa-* : *hṛṣ-* 'bristle, be excited, rejoice', Lat. *horrēre* 'bristle, shudder', Ir. *gerb* 'rough'. Walde-P. 1.610.

Skt. *prīti* : *prī-* 'please', *priya-* 'dear', etc. (16.21).

Skt. *mayas-*, Av. *mayā-*, *māyā-*, prob. : Lat. *mītis* 'mild, gentle', Lith. *mielas* 'dear', etc. Walde-P. 2.244. Barth. 1141.

Av. *šāiti-* (OPers. *šiyāti-* 'well being, happiness'), fr. *šyā-* 'rejoice' : Lat. *quiēs* 'rest', ON *hvīld* 'rest', Goth. *hweila* 'time', ChSl. *po-kojĭ* 'rest'. Walde-P. 1.510. Barth. 1716.

Av. *urvāza-* : *urvāz-* and *urvād-* 'rejoice', root connection? Barth. 1545.

16.23 JOYFUL, GLAD

Grk.	*χαίρων*	Goth.	*(hlas)*	Lith.	*linksmas*
NG	*χαρούμενος*	ON	*glaðr, feginn*	Lett.	*priecīgs, līksms*
Lat.	*laetus*	Dan.	*glad*	ChSl.	*radŭ, veselŭ*
It.	*gioioso, lieto, allegro, contento*	Sw.	*glad*	SCr.	*veseo*
		OE	*glæd, faegen*	Boh.	*radostný, rad, veselý*
Fr.	*joyeux, content*	ME	*glad, fayn, joyful*	Pol.	*radosny, wesoły*
Sp.	*alegre, gozoso, contento*	NE	*joyful (glad)*	Russ.	*radostnyj, rad, veselyj*
		Du.	*blij, blijde*	Skt.	*hṛṣṭa-*
Rum.	*vesel, voios, bucuros*	OHG	*frō, blīde*	Av.	*šyāta-*
Ir.	*fāilid, subach*	MHG	*vrō, blīde*		
NIr.	*lūthghāireach*	NHG	*froh*		
W.	*llawen*				
Br.	*laouen*				

Nearly all the words for 'joyful' (or 'glad'; but NE *glad* now weaker than formerly, and of persons only predicative, cf. NED), as listed here are connected, either as derivs. or conversely, with some of those for 'joy', though without complete correspondence between the commonest sbs. and adjs. in the same language. Whether or not these have been mentioned in the discussion of 'joy' (16.22), their relations are obvious.

We comment here only on the few others of those listed, and on some of those used in related senses, especially 'merry'.

1. It., Sp. *contento*, Fr. *content* 'satisfied, contented' (fr. Lat. *contentus* id., pple. of *continēre* 'hold together, contain') are also commonly used in the sense of 'pleased, glad'.

2. Rum. *voios* (beside *vesel* fr. Slavic, cf. 16.22), orig. 'willing' (fr. *voie* 'will', this fr. Slavic *volja* id.), hence 'well-disposed' and 'glad, joyful'.

3. Goth. *hlas* (renders *ἱλαρός* 'cheerful', in eccl. writers a common word for 'joyful'), etym. dub. Feist 262. Walde-H. 1.228 (s.v. *clārus*).

4. Words for 'merry, gay' (including some of the words listed, in which this notion is more or less dominant) are of various sources, e.g. It. *allegro*, Sp. *alegre*, orig. 'lively' (16.22); NHG *munter* fr. OHG *muntar* 'eager' : OHG *mendī* 'joy' (16.22); NHG *lustig* fr. *lust* 'desire' and 'joy' (16.22); ChSl. *veselŭ*, etc. prob. orig. 'feasting' (16.22); OE *myrge*, ME *meri*, NE *merry* (with sb. OE *myrgþ*, NE *mirth*), as orig. 'time-shortening', hence 'amusing' (cf. NHG *kurzweilen* 'amuse') : OHG *murg* 'short', Goth. *gamaurgjan* 'shorten', etc. (Walde-P. 2.314, NED s.v.); ME, NE *gay*. fr.OFr. *gai* 'lively, gay', orig. disputed (REW 9477a; Gamillscheg 451).

16.24 HAPPY; HAPPINESS

Grk.	*εὐδαίμων, μακάριος; εὐδαιμονία*	Goth.	*audags; audagei*	Lith.	*laimingas; laimė, palaima*
		ON	*sǣll; sǣla*		
NG	*εὐτυχής; εὐτυχία*	Dan.	*lykkelig; lykke*	Lett.	*laimīgs; laimība*
Lat.	*beātus, fēlīx; beātum, fēlīcitās*	Sw.	*lyeklig; lycka*	ChSl.	*blaženŭ*
		OE	*gesǣlig, ēadig; gesǣlignes, ēad*	SCr.	*srećan; sreća*
It.	*felice; felicita*			Boh.	*šť'astny; štěstí*
Fr.	*heureux; bonheur*	ME	*seli; selinesse*	Pol.	*szczęśliwy; szczęście*
Sp.	*feliz; felicidad*	NE	*happy; happiness*	Russ.	*sčastlivyj; sčastie*
Rum.	*fericit; fericire*	Du.	*gelukkig; geluk*	Skt.	*bhagavant-; sāubhāgya-*
Ir.	*sona; sonas*	OHG	*sālig; sālida*		
NIr.	*sona; sonas*	MHG	*sælic; sælde*		
W.	*dedwydd; dedwyddwch*	NHG	*glücklig; glück*		
Br.	*eurus; eurvad*				

The great majority of the words for 'happy' and 'happiness' are based on the obj. 'good fortune', which leads to the feeling of happiness, as illustrated by ME *happy*, fr. *happe*, *hap* 'fortune, good fortune', hence 'fortunate' (as still in *happy choice*, etc.), but in NE commonly 'happy' in feeling, whence NE *happiness*. For words of early periods it is sometimes doubtful how far they refer to the actual emotion or merely to the external circumstances.

1. Words which are the same as (so often for the sb.), or connected with, those for 'good fortune', discussed in 16.17.

Grk. *εὐτυχής*, *εὐτυχία* 'fortunate, good fortune' (Aristot. EN 1153b21 ff. distinguishes *εὐτυχία* from *εὐδαιμονία*), but in NG also the usual words for 'happy, happiness'; Fr. *heureux* (> Br. *eurus*), *bonheur* (rendered lit. by Br. *eurvad*), Skt. *bhagavant-*, *sāubhāgya-*, and all the modern Gmc. (NHG *glücklig*, *glück*, etc.) and Balto-Slavic words.

2. Grk. *εὐδαίμων*, cpd. of *εὐ-* 'good' and *δαίμων* 'spirit, one's personal fortune', hence 'happy' with sb. *εὐδαιμονία* (the regular technical words in Aristot. etc.).

Grk. *μακάριος* (poet. *μάκαρ*; sb. *μακαρία* not common) 'blessed, happy' (with subtle distinction fr. *εὐδαίμων* in Aristot. EN 1101a7, 19), etym.? Boisacq 602. NG *μακάριος* 'blessed', esp. 'the deceased'.

3. Lat. *fēlīx*, in earliest use 'fruitful' (of trees), then 'fortunate' and 'happy', with sb. *fēlīcitās*, fr. IE **dhē(i)-* in Skt. *dhayati* 'sucks', Grk. *θῆσθαι* 'suck', *θηλή* 'teat', etc. Hence It. *felice*, *felicita*, Sp. *feliz*, *felicidad*, and Rum. (through the vb. *ferici*) *fericit*, *fericire*. Ernout-M. 341, 342 f. Walde-H. 1.474 f. Walde-H. 1.474 f.

Lat. *beātus*, sb. *beātum*, pass. pple. of *beāre* 'make happy, bless' : OLat. *duenos*, Lat. *bonus* 'good'. Walde-P. 1.778. Ernout-M. 107. Walde-H. 1.101.

4. Ir. *son*, *sona*, sb. *sonas*, parallel to *dona* 'wretched', NIr. *donas* 'misfortune', derivs. of *so-* 'well' (16.71) and *do-* 'ill-' (16.72), prob. formed directly with *n*-suffix (cf. Lat. *prōnus*, fr. *prō*, Umbr. *kumne* 'in comitio' fr. *com-*, etc., Brugmann, Grd. 2.1.270), not cpds. (as Macbain s.vv.).

W. *dedwydd* (hence sb. *dedwyddwch*), primary sense 'wise', cpd. of *det-* (*do-ate-*) with a form of IE **weid-* 'know', as W. *gwydd* 'knowledge'. Loth, RC 36.174 f.

5. Goth. *audags* (renders *μακάριος*; sb. *audagei*) : OE *ēadig* 'fortunate, happy, rich', deriv. of *ēad* 'wealth, riches' (11.42), also 'happiness'. Walde-P. 1.16. Feist 63.

ON *sǣll*, OE *gesǣlig*, ME *seli*, OHG *sālig*, MHG *sælic*, with sbs. ON *sǣla*, OE *gesǣlignes*, ME *selinesse*, OHG *sālida*, MHG *sælde* : Goth. *sēls* 'good', outside connections dub., but perh. (through 'whole, wholesome') : Grk. *ὅλος*, Skt. *sarva-* 'whole', Lat. *salvus* 'safe, well, sound'. Walde-P. 2.506 f. Falk-Torp 945. Feist 416.

6. ChSl. *blaženŭ* (reg. for *μακάριος*), pple. of *blažiti* 'bless', fr. *blagŭ* 'good'. Berneker 69.

16.25 LAUGH (vb.); SMILE (vb.)

Grk.	*γελάω; μειδιάω*	Goth.	*hlahjan*	Lith.	*juoktis; šypsotis*
NG	*γελῶ; χαμογελῶ*	ON	*hlǣja; brosa*	Lett.	*smieties; smaidīt*
Lat.	*rīdēre; (sub)rīdēre*	Dan.	*le; smile*	ChSl.	*smějati sę*
It.	*ridere; sorridere*	Sw.	*skratta; le*	SCr.	*smijati se; smiješiti se*
Fr.	*rire; sourire*	OE	*hliehhan*	Boh.	*smáti se; usmívati se*
Sp.	*reír; soureír*	ME	*laughe; smile*	Pol.	*śmiać się; usmiechać się*
Rum.	*rîde; surîde, zîmbi*	NE	*laugh; smile*		
Ir.	*tibiu; gen* (sb.)	Du.	*lachen; glimlachen*	Russ.	*smejat'sja; ulybat'sja*
NIr.	*gāirim; mionghāirim*	OHG	*(h)lahhan, lachēn*	Skt.	*has-; smi-*
W.	*chwerthin; gwenu*	MHG	*lachen; smielen, smieren*		
Br.	*c'hoarzin; mous-c'hoarzin*	NHG	*lachen; lächeln*		

Both 'laugh' and 'smile' are expressions, the one vocal, the other facial, of pleasure, amusement, and also derision, ridicule. They are so closely associated that they may be expressed by the same word in the same language (Lat. *rīdēre*) or in different languages (Dan. *le* 'laugh', Sw. *le* 'smile'), or more frequently by different forms of the same root. 'Smile' is often expressed as a little (or low, or veiled) 'laugh'. In the one inherited group the meaning is 'smile' in Grk., Gmc., and Skt., while in Lett. and Slavic the simple vb. is 'laugh' with secondary derivs. for 'smile'. The same root expresses astonishment in Lat. and in part in Skt.

Several of the words for 'laugh' are cognate with others for 'noise, sound, cry', and are partly of imitative orig.

The use of 'laugh' as 'laugh at, deride' is frequent and has gone so far in the case of NG *γελῶ* that this is a common expression for 'cheat'.

In a few cases 'smile' comes through 'grin' from 'bare the teeth'.

1. IE **smei-*. Walde-P. 2.686 f. Falk-Torp 1082. Hellquist 1002.

Grk. *μειδιάω* 'smile'; Dan., Norw., ME, NE *smile* 'smile' (Sw. *smila* obs. or dial., but sb. *smil*); Lett. *smiet* 'laugh at', refl. *smieties* 'laugh', *smaidīt* 'smile'; ChSl. *smějati sę* 'laugh' (sb. *směchŭ* 'a laugh, laughter'), SCr. *smijati se*, etc. general Slavic, with refl. of deriv. vbs. SCr. *smiješiti se*, Boh. *usmívati se*, Pol. *usmiechać się* for 'smile'; Skt. *smi-* 'smile'; cf. Skt. *smaya-*, esp. *vi-smaya* 'astonishment', and Lat. *mīrus* 'wonderful', *mīrārī* 'wonder at' (16.15); Toch. *smi-* 'smile' (SSS 481). A parallel **smeu-* in NHG *smielen*, *smieren*, old Du. *smuylen* 'smile', Russ. *u-chmyljat'sja* 'smirk, smile', etc.

2. Grk. *γελάω* 'laugh', *γέλως* 'laughter', perh., through a notion of 'bright, gay', fr. **ĝel-* in words for 'shine', 'bright', and names of bright objects, as Grk. *γελεῖν· λάμπειν, ἀνθεῖν* (Hesych.), *γαληνός* 'serene, calm', *γλήνη* 'pupil of the eye', OHG *kleini* 'shining, fine', OE *clǣne* 'clean'. Walde-P. 1.622 f. Boisacq 143. Cf. Lat. *renīdēre* 'shine, gleam, be radiant with joy', whence also 'smile'. But another connection, in line with the more usual semantic source of 'laugh', would be with the orig. imitative root in words like W. *galw* 'call', ChSl. *glagolati* 'speak', OE *callian*, NE *call*, etc. (Walde-P. 1.538).

NG likewise *γελῶ* 'laugh', and hence *χαμογελῶ* 'smile', with sb. *χαμόγελο* 'a smile', lit. 'a low laugh', cpd. with *χαμο-* = *χάμω* in form after *κάτω* 'down', *ἐπάνω* 'up' (Hatzidakis, Μεσ. 2.119) : *χαμαί* 'on the ground'.

A peculiarity of Boeotian speech, noted by a comic poet (Strattis 47) was the use of *κρίδδω* (= *κρίζω* 'creak, screech', plainly imitative) for *γελάω*.

3. Lat. *rīdēre*, both 'laugh' and 'smile' (VLat. **rīdere* > the Romance words for 'laugh'), but for 'smile' esp. *sub-rīdēre* (VLat. **surridere* > the Romance words for 'smile'), etym. dub. Walde-P. 1.277 (**wriz-d-* : Skt. *vrīḍ-* 'be embarrassed, ashamed', etc.). Ernout-M. 865 (: Skt. *krīḍ-* 'play, jest').

Rum. *zîmbi* 'smile', fr. a Slavic form corresponding to Bulg. *ząbja se* 'show the teeth', Boh. *zubiti se* 'show the teeth, smirk', deriv. of Slavic *ząbŭ* 'tooth'. Tiktin 1820 f.

4. Ir. *tibiu* 'laugh', also 'strike, hit', with development of 'laugh' through 'make a noise' (cf. Grk. *κροτέω* 'strike, hit' and 'make a noise', sb. *κρότος* 'noise'), but root connection dub. Vendryes, Étud. celt. 3.43 f.

Ir. *gen*, NIr. *gean*, W. *gwen* 'a smile', whence W. vb. *gwenu* 'smile', etym. dub. Vendryes, Étud. celt. 3.41, 42 f. Pedersen 1.96.

NIr. *gāirim* 'laugh' fr. *gāire* 'laughter' (cf. MIr. *gen gāire* 'loud laughter') : Ir. *gāir*, W. *gawr* 'cry', etc. (18.13). NIr. *mionghāire*, lit. 'a little laugh' (cpd. with *mion* 'small'), hence a 'smile', with vb. *mionghāirim*.

W. *chwerthin*, Br. *c'hoarzin* 'laugh' (OCorn. *hwerthim* 'laughter'), etym. dub., perh. fr. the root seen in Skt. *svar-* 'make a sound'. Vendryes, Étud. celt. 3.49, 43 (vs. Walde-P. 2.517, etc.).

Hence Br. *mousc'hoarzin* 'smile', lit. 'dissimulate a laugh', cpd. with *mous-* fr. *moucha* 'mask, veil', cf. *mous-kana* 'hum a tune', *mous-komz* 'mutter', etc. Henry 207.

5. Goth. *hlahjan*, ON *hlæja*, Dan. *le* (Sw. *le* now 'smile'), OE *hliehhan*, *hlæhhan*, ME *laughe*, NE *laugh*, OHG *(h)lahhan*, also weak vb. OHG *lachēn*, MHG, NHG, Du. *lachen* : Grk. *κλώσσω* 'cluck', *κλαγγή* 'noise', Lat. *clangere* 'sound, resound', etc., all of imitative orig. Walde-P. 1.496. Feist 259. Falk-Torp 627. Hellquist 564.

ON (rare), NIcel. *brosa* 'smile', etym.?

Du. *glimlachen* 'smile', for earlier *grimlachen* (influence of *glimmen* 'twinkle, glimmer'), fr. *grimlach* '(scornful) smile', cpd. of *grim-* : *grimmig* 'fierce, grim' and *lach* 'laughter'. Frank-v. W. 203.

NHG *lächeln* 'smile', MHG (rare) *lecheln* also 'feign friendliness', dim. of *lachen* 'laugh'.

ME, NE *smile*, etc., above, 1.

Sw. *skratta* 'laugh' (Dan. *skratte* 'give a cracked sound', Norw. 'laugh loudly') : Sw. dial. *skrata* 'resound', older Dan. *skrade* 'rattle', Ir. *scret*, NIr. *scread* 'cry', fr. an extension of an imitative **(s)ker-*, cf. Skt. *kārava-* 'crow', Grk. *κόραξ* Lat. *corvus* 'raven', etc. Walde-P. 1.415. Falk-Torp 1025. Hellquist 946.

6. Lith. *juoktis* 'laugh', beside *juokauti* 'laugh, joke', fr. *juokas* 'laughter, joke' = Lett. *iuoks* 'joke', these (not cognate with, but) loanwords fr. Lat. *jocus* through NHG students' slang (*jo-*

kus, iux, etc.). Mühl.-Endz. 2.126. Walde-H. 1.715.

Lith. *šypsotis* 'smile', beside *šieptis, šaipytis* 'grin', etym.? Walde-P. 1.364 (but Skt. *çiprā-* rarely 'nose', mostly dual, 'cheeks' or 'lips').

Lett. *smieties* 'laugh', *smaidīt* 'smile', above, 1.

7. ChSl. *smějati sę* 'laugh', etc., general Slavic, and SCr. *smiješiti se,* etc. 'smile', above, 1.

Russ. *u-lybat'sja* 'smile', precise source dub., but prob. fr. a form parallel to Ukr. *lupiti* 'peel, bare the teeth, grin' (cf. Rum. *zîmbi*, above, 3). Berneker 751.

16.26 PLAY (vb.)

Grk.	*παίζω* (*ἀθύρω* poet.)	Goth.	. . . .	Lith.	*žaisti, lošti*
NG	*παίζω*	ON	*leika*	Lett.	*spēlēt, ruotalāt*
Lat.	*lūdere*	Dan.	*lege, spille*	ChSl.	(*igrati*)
It.	*giocare*	Sw.	*leka, spela*	SCr.	*igrati se*
Fr.	*jouer*	OE	*plegian, spilian*	Boh.	*hráti se*
Sp.	*jugar*	ME	*pleie, spile, leyke*	Pol.	*grać*
Rum.	*se juca*	NE	*play*	Russ.	*igrat'*
Ir.	*imberim, cluchigur*	Du.	*spelen*	Skt.	*krīḍ-*
NIr.	*imrim, sūgruighim*	OHG	*spilōn*		
W.	*chware*	MHG	*spil(e)n*		
Br.	*c'hoari*	NHG	*spielen*		

Of the verbs for 'play', one is derived from the word for 'child', one group from a noun for 'jest', some from nouns for 'play, game' of obscure origin. But the most frequent relation is with words denoting quick action, as 'jump, dance', etc.

1. Grk. *παίζω*, fr. *παῖς, παιδός* 'child'.

Grk. *ἀθύρω* (poet., Hom.+), beside *ἄθυρμα* 'plaything, amusement', perh. cpd. *ἀ-* fr. **ŋ-* 'in' and **θυρίω* orig. 'jump about' or the like : *θοῦρος* 'rushing, impetuous', Russ. *durit'* 'play the fool', Av. *dvar-* 'walk (of daevic beings), hurry', etc. Walde-P. 1.842.

2. Lat. *lūdere*, beside *lūdus* 'game, play', old *loidos, loedos* : Grk. *λίζει· παίζει* (Hesych.), *λοίδορος* 'abusive'. Walde-P. 2.402. Ernout-M. 565 f. Walde-H. 1.829.

It. *giocare*, Fr. *jouer*, Sp. *jugar*, Rum. *juca* (Rum. 'play a game or instrument', 'dance'; refl. 'play' as a child), fr. VLat. **iocāre*, Lat. *iocārī* 'to jest, joke', fr. sb. *iocus* 'a jest', this through 'play on words' fr. 'saying', with different development in Umbr. *iuka* 'prayers', fr. a root **yek-*, seen in OHG *jehan* 'say, confess', etc. Walde-P. 1.204 f. Ernout-M. 495. Walde-H. 1.715. REW 4585.

3. Ir. *imberim*, NIr. *imrim* ('be busy with, practise', etc. hence also 'play'), cpd. of *berim* 'carry'. Pedersen 2.468. Laws, Gloss. 474.

Ir. *cluchigur* (K. Meyer, Contrib. 395), fr. *cluche* 'game, sport, play', prob. : *cless* 'feat, trick', *clechtaim* 'practise', this : Skt. *krīḍ-* 'play' (?). Pedersen 1.362, 2.493. Walde-P. 2.572.

NIr. *sūgruighim*, beside sb. *sūgradh* 'play, sport, fun', cf. also *sūgach*, MIr. *sucach* 'merry, cheerful', etym.?

W. *chware*, Br. *c'hoari*, with *chw-* fr. *gw-* (Corn. *gware* 'a play', MW *gware* beside *chware*), perh. as 'loiter, delay' : Ir. *fo-d-rig* 'delays', cpd. of the root in Ir. *con-rigim* 'bind', Lat. *corrigia* 'thong', etc. Pedersen 1.433 f., 2.593.

4. ON *leika* (> ME *leyke, layke*), Dan. *lege*, Sw. *leka* = Goth. *laikan* 'spring, hop', OE *lācan* 'move quickly, jump, play (a musical instrument),

fight', MHG *leichen* 'hop, deceive', etc. : Grk. *ἐλελίζω* 'cause to tremble', Skt. *rej-* 'make tremble, quiver', etc. Walde-P. 2.399. Falk-Torp 630 f.

OE *plegian, plegan*, ME *pleie*, NE *play*, in the older language also, and doubtless more orig., 'move about swiftly, spring, dance', etc., now generally separated from OHG *pflegan* 'care for, attend to, be wont', but in any case outside connections dub. Falk-Torp 836 f. NED s.v. *play*, vb.

OE *spilian*, ME *spile*, OHG *spilōn*, MHG *spil(e)n*, NHG *spielen*, Du. *spelen*, in the older languages esp. 'be in quick motion, move about', etym.? Hence the loanwords (fr. MLG) Dan. *spille*, Sw. *spela*, which have mostly replaced the native ones with reference to games, cards, music, etc. Falk-Torp 1120 f. Weigand-H. 2.915.

5. Lith. *žaisti*, perh. as orig. 'jump' : Lat. *haedus* 'young goat', Goth. *gaits*, etc. 'goat', ChSl. *zajęcĭ* 'hare', and Skt. *jihīte* 'bounds up, leaps up, runs off'. Walde-P. 1.527, 544.

Lith. *lošti* (esp. 'play' cards; cf. NSB and Hermann, Lit.-Deutsches Gesprächsb. pp. 76 ff.), orig. 'turn up' (the cards). Cf. *-lošti* in *at-si-lošti* 'lean, incline', etym.? Skardžius, Lietuvių kalbos žodžių daryba 483 f.

Lett. *spēlēt*, fr. MLG *spelen*.

Lett. *ruotalāt* : *ruotāt* 'be dexterous, turn, hop', also 'loaf about', refl. 'tumble about, play' : *rats* 'wheel', etc. Mühl.-Endz. 583, 584.

6. ChSl. *igrati* 'spring, dance', later also play and so general modern Slavic (in part refl. in sense 'play' as a child), cf. ChSl. *igrĭ* sb. 'play' (Supr.) : Skt. *ej-* 'stir, move, quake, tremble', *ing-* 'stir, move', ON *eikenn* 'wild, raging'. Walde-P. 1.11. Berneker 422. Brückner 154.

7. Skt. *krīḍ-*, prob. as **kriz-d-* : Goth. *-hrisjan*, OE *hrissan* 'shake', Ir. *cressaim* 'shake, swing', fr. an extension of the root **(s)ker-* in Grk. *σκαίρω* 'dance, hop, spring', etc. Or as **kliz-d* : Ir. *cless* 'feat, trick' ?. Walde-P. 2.572.

16.27 LOVE (sb.; vb.)

Grk.	*ἔρως, φιλία, στοργή; ἐράω, ἀγαπάω, φιλέω, στέργω*	Goth.	*frijaþwa; frijōn*	Lith.	*meilė; mylėti*
NG	*ἀγάπη, ἔρωτας; ἀγαπῶ*	ON	*āst, elska; elska, unna, frjā*	Lett.	*mīlestība, mīlība; mīlēt, mīl'uot*
Lat.	*amor, cāritās; amāre, dīligere*	Dan.	*kærlighed, elskov; elske*	ChSl.	*ljuby; ljubiti*
It.	*amore; amare*	Sw.	*kärlek, älskog; älska*	SCr.	*ljubav; ljubiti*
Fr.	*amour; aimer*	OE	*lufu, frēod; lufian, frēon*	Boh.	*láska; milovati*
Sp.	*amor; amar, quedar*	ME	*love; lovie*	Pol.	*miłość; kochać*
Rum.	*iubire, dragoste, amor; iubi*	NE	*love; love*	Russ.	*ljubov'; ljubit'*
Ir.	*grād, serc, cais; caraim*	Du.	*liefde; beminnen*	Skt.	*kāma-, preman-, sneha-; prī-, kam-, snih-*
NIr.	*grādh, searc; grādhaim*	OHG	*minna, liubī; minnōn, liubōn*	Av.	. . . . ; *kan-, zaoš-*
W.	*cariad, serch; caru*	MHG	*liebe, minne; lieben, minnen*		
Br.	*karantez; karout*	NHG	*liebe; lieben*		

The sbs. and vbs. for 'love' are generally parallel forms of the same root, but in some languages there is disparity; hence both are listed. Many of the adjs. for 'dear' are also cognate with the words for 'love' and so are included in the discussion here, though listed separately (16.28).

Although there are sometimes distinctive words for various aspects of love, especially sexual love vs. that of parents, children, friends, etc. (so most clearly in ancient Greek), it is more generally true that the same word is used, any distinction depending upon the context.

1. IE **leubh-* in words for 'love, yearn for', 'dear' (also 'approve, praise, believe'), etc.). Walde-P. 2.419. Walde-H. 1.793.

Here as the usual words for 'love' or 'dear'. Gmc. sbs. OE *lufu*, ME, NE *love*, OHG *liubī*, MHG, NHG *liebe*, Du. *liefde;* vbs. OE *lufian*, ME *lovie*, NE *love*, OHG *liubōn*, MHG, NHG *lieben;* adjs. 'dear' Goth. *liufs*, ON *ljūfr*, OE *leof*, ME *leve* (NE *lief*), OHG *liob, liub*, MHG *liep*, NHG *lieb*, Du. *lief;* ChSl. *ljuby* sb., *ljubiti* vb., *ljubŭ* adj. 'dear', etc. (below, 7); cf. Skt. *lubh-* 'long for' (mostly of violent desire), Lat. *lubet, libet* 'is pleasing' (Osc. *loufir* 'vel'), *lubīdō, libīdō* 'strong desire', Grk. *λυπτά· ἑταίρα, πόρνη* (Hesych.), etc. (Ir. *cobla* 'love' is a ghost-word; cf. Z. celt. Ph. 20.299).

2. Grk. *ἔρως*, Hom. *ἔρος*, with vb. Hom. *ἔραμαι*, Att. *ἐράω*, all usually of sexual love, as likewise NG *ἔρωτας*, with vb. *ἐρωτεύομαι* 'fall in love', *ἐρωμένη* 'sweetheart, mistress', outside root connections dub. Walde-P. 1.144. Boisacq 270 f.

Grk. *φιλέω* 'love' (have affection for), *φιλία* 'friendly love, friendship', fr. *φίλος* 'dear', sb. 'friend', in Hom. also 'one's own', this perh. the earliest sense and so fr. an Anatolian word represented by Lyd. *bilis* 'one's own'. Kretschmer, IF 45.267 ff.

Grk. *ἀγαπάω*, 'love' as 'have regard or affection for', 'be fond or contented with', etc., rarely of sexual love. Hence the late back-formation *ἀγάπη* (first in LXX), in NG the common word for 'love' as also the vb. *ἀγαπῶ*, adj. *ἀγαπητός* 'beloved, dear' (Hom.+). Etym. dub. Walde-P. 2.257. Boisacq 6.

Grk. *στέργω*, esp. of the love of parents and children, of a ruler and his subjects, etc., rarely of sexual love (another sense 'be contented with', hence NG 'consent, agree with') with sb. *στοργή*, 'affection', perh. : ChSl. *strěgą, strěšti* 'guard, keep', *stražĭ*, Russ. *storož'* 'watchman, guard', etc., general Slavic. Walde-P. 2.642. Boisacq 910.

3. Lat. *amor* (> It. *amore*, Fr. *amour*, Sp., Rum. *amor*, mostly of learned orig.), vb. *amāre* (> It. *amare*, Fr. *aimer*, Sp. *amar*), prob. fr. an infantile syllable seen in pet names like Grk. *ἀμμά*, OHG *amma* 'mother, nurse', Lat. *amita* 'aunt', etc. (above, p. 94). Walde-P. 1.53. Ernout-M. 45 f. Walde-H. 1.40 f. REW 399. Wartburg 1.46, 82.

Instead of the vbs. of this group the Romance languages or dials. show other more popular expressions for 'love', as Fr. *avoir cher* lit. 'hold dear' (cf. Swiss *gern haben*), It. *bene voler*, lit. 'wish well', (Lat. *bene velle alicui* Plaut., etc. already colloq. 'be fond of', but hardly yet quite = *amare;* Bonfante Riv.IGI 19.), Sp. *quedar* 'wish' (16.61), Cat. *estimar* orig. 'value, esteem' (Lat. *aestimāre*). See refs. above (REW, Wartburg) and Spitzer, Liebessprache 5.

Lat. *dīligere* (weaker than *amāre*, according to Cicero, and rarely of sexual love), fr. **dis-legere*, cpd. of *legere* 'pick up, choose'. Ernout-M. 536. Walde-H. 1.351 f.

Lat. *venus* 'love, charm' (but common only in the personified *Venus*) : Skt. *van-* 'seek, desire, gain', Goth. *wēns* 'hope', OE *wyn*, OHG *wunna* 'great joy, bliss', OHG *wunscan*, OE *wyscan*, etc. 'wish' (16.61). Walde-P. 1.258 ff. Ernout-M. 1037.

Lat. *cāritās* 'love, affection', fr. *cārus* 'dear' (> It., Sp. *caro*, Fr. *cher*) : Ir. *caraim*, W. *caru*, Br. *karout* 'love', OE *hōre*, OHG *huora*, etc. 'whore', Lett. *kārs* 'lewd, greedy'; prob. also Skt. *kāma-* sb. 'love' with vb. root *kam-*, etc. (below, 8). Walde-P. 1.325. Walde-H. 1.175. Ernout-M. 158 (rejecting the Indo-Iranian connection).

Rum. *iubire*, old infin. as sb., fr. the vb. *iubi*, fr. the Slavic, cf. ChSl. *ljubiti*, etc. (above, 1).

Rum. *dragoste* 'love' with *drag* 'dear', fr. the Slavic, cf. late ChSl. *dragostĭ* 'preciousness', ChSl. *dragŭ* 'precious', modern Slavic also 'dear' (16.28). Tiktin 569 f., 571.

4. Ir. *grād*, NIr. *grādh*, whence the vb. *grādhaim*, orig. dub., perh. loanword fr. Lat. *grātum* 'favor' (*grātus* 'acceptable, agreeable') in phrases like *grātum facere alicui*. Walde-P. 1.601. Walde-H. 1.620. Otherwise (as cognate) Pedersen 1.133.

Ir. *serc*, NIr. *searc* (now mostly poet.), W. *serch* (Br. *serc'h* 'concubine, whore'), etym. dub., perh. (**ser-k-* beside **ser-t-*) : W. *serth* 'obscene', ON *serða* 'stuprare'. Or : Grk. *στέργω*? Walde-P. 2.500, 642. Pedersen 1.78. Stokes 301.

Ir. *cais*, prob. same word as *cais* 'hate' (16.41), both senses fr. orig. 'care' developing as 'loving care' or 'anxiety, trouble, hate'. Pedersen 2.10. Walde-P. 1.340.

Ir. *caraim*, W. *caru*, sb. *cariad*, Br. *karout*, sb. *karantez* : Lat. *cārus* 'dear' (above, 3).

Ir. *cin*, NIr. *cion* (esp. 'fondness, esteem') : Skt. *canas-* 'delight', Av. *činman-* 'desire'. Walde-P. 1.325. Stokes KZ 40.246 f. Marstrander, Z. celt. Ph. 7.412.

5. Goth. *frijaþwa*, OE *frēod*, with vbs. Goth. *frijōn*, ON *frjā*, OE *frēon* (NHG *freien* 'woo') : Skt. *priya-* 'dear', *prīyate* 'is satisfied with, loves', ChSl. *prijati* 'be favorable, care for', etc. Walde-P. 2.86. Feist 168.

Goth. *liufs* 'dear', OE *lufu* 'love', etc., above, 1.

ON *āst* = Goth. *ansts*, OHG *anst*, OE *ēst* 'favor, grace', with vbs. ON *unna* 'love, grant' = OE, OS, OHG *unnan* 'grant, wish' (OHG *gi-unnan*, NHG *gönnen*), perh. : Grk. *προσ-ηνής* 'friendly', *ἀπ-ηνής* 'unfriendly, harsh'. Walde-P. 1.68. Feist 53.

ON *elska*, and *elsk-hugi*, Dan. *elskov*, Sw. *älskog* (with last member : ON *hugr* 'mind'), vbs. ON *elska*, Dan. *elske*, Sw. *älska*, fr. ON *elskr* adj. 'fond of, attached to', Gmc. **aliska-* : ON *ala* 'nourish, bear', Lat. *alere* 'nourish, rear', etc. Cf. Dan. *op-elske* 'raise, nurse', and similar use of the simple vb. in ODan. Falk-Torp 188. Hellquist 1433.

ON *kærr*, Dan. *kær*, Sw. *kär* 'dear', early borrowing fr. an old form of Fr. *cher* (above, 3). Hence ON (late) *kærleikr*, Sw. *kærlek*, ODan. *kærleg;* Dan. *kærlighed* (fr. *kærlig* 'kind', old 'dear'). Falk-Torp 519. Hellquist 547. For 'dear' as an affectionate term of address the more usual word is Dan. *elsket*, Sw. *älskad*, and similarly NIcel. *elskaður*.

OHG *minna*, MHG *minne*, esp. of sexual love, and by 1500 no longer decent and hence taboo, but revived again in poetic language in the late 18th century, NHG *minne*, Du. *minne* (only poet.), hence OHG *minnōn, minneōn*, MHG, NHG *minnen*, Du. *beminnen;* orig. 'thought, remembrance' : ON *minni*, Goth. *ga-minþi* 'memory', Goth. *munan* 'think, mean', Lat. *meminī* 'remember', etc. Walde-P. 2.265. Weigand-H. 2.188.

6. Lith. *meilė*, Lett. *mīlestība, mīlība*, vbs. Lith. *mylėti*, Lett. *mīlēt, mīl'uot*, with adjs. Lith. *mielas*, Lett. *mīl'š* 'dear' : ChSl. *milŭ* 'pitiful', in modern Slavic

also 'dear', SCr. *mio*, Boh. *milý*, Pol. *miły*, Russ. *mil*, whence vb. Boh. *milovati*, sb. Pol. *miłość*, etc., prob. fr. the root **mei-* in Skt. *mayas-* 'delight, joy', Lat. *mītis* 'mild, gentle', Ir. *mōith* 'tender', etc. Walde-P. 2.244. Berneker 2.57 f.

7. ChSl. *ljuby*, vb. *ljubiti*, adj. *ljubŭ* 'dear' (the last not in Gospels; instead *vŭzljublenŭ* pret. pass. pple. 'ἀγαπητός'), above, 1. Once general Slavic, but partly replaced. Boh. *libiti se* impers. 'be pleasing', Pol. *lubić* 'be fond of, like'. Berneker 756 f.

Boh. *láska*, with vb. *laskati* 'caress' : Russ. *laska* 'caress, kindness', *laskat'* 'caress, wheedle', ChSl. *laskati* 'flatter', etc., general Slavic in related senses, perh. fr. the root in Russ. *lasit'* 'flatter', *lasyj* 'fond of dainties', Pol. *łasy* 'hankering, greedy', etc., and Goth. *lustus* 'desire, lust', OE *lust*, etc. 'lust, joy'. Walde-P. 2.387. Otherwise Berneker 692.

Pol. *kochać* = Boh. *kochati* 'fondle', refl. 'delight in' : ChSl. *kosnąti*, Russ. *kosnut'sja* 'touch', etc. (15.71). Semantic development fr. 'touch' through 'caress' to 'love'. Berneker 538, 581 f.

8. Skt. *prī-* in *prīyate* (Av. *frī-* 'satisfy'), sb. *preman-*, adjs. *priya-*, Av. *frya-*, *friϑa-* 'dear' : Goth. *frijōn* 'love', etc. (above, 5).

Skt. *kāma-* sb. 'desire, wish' (as Av., OPers. *kāma-*) and 'love', *kam-* 'desire, love', beside *kan-* 'be pleased with, enjoy', Av. *kā-*, *kan-* 'desire', prob. (with secondary *kam-*, etc.) : Lat. *cārus* 'dear', etc. (cf. above, 3).

Skt. *sneha-*, lit. 'stickiness', whence 'attachment, love' : *snih-* 'be sticky', whence 'become attached to, feel affection for'.

Av. *zaoš-* 'find pleasure in, love' (cf. OPerz. *daušta* 'friend') : Skt. *juṣ-* 'taste, enjoy' (caus. mid. also 'love, caress'), Grk. γεύομαι 'taste, enjoy', etc. (15.31). Walde-P. 1.568 f.

16.28 DEAR

Grk.	*φίλος*	Goth.	*liufs*	Lith.	*mielas*
NG	*ἀγαπητός (φίλος)*	ON	*ljūfr, kærr*	Lett.	*mīl'š*
Lat.	*cārus*	Dan.	*kær, elsket*	ChSl.	*vŭzljublenŭ, ljubŭ*
It.	*caro*	Sw.	*kär, älskad*	SCr.	*mio, drag*
Fr.	*cher*	OE	*lēof, dēore*	Boh.	*drahý, milý*
Sp.	*caro*	ME	*leve, dēre*	Pol.	*luby, miły*
Rum.	*drag*	NE	*dear*	Russ.	*mil, dorog*
Ir.	*dil, cōim, inmain*	Du.	*lief*	Skt.	*priya-*
NIr.	*dīlis, ionmhain*	OHG	*liob*	Av.	*frya-, friϑa-*
W.	*annwyl, cu, hoff*	MHG	*liep*		
Br.	*ker, kaez*	NHG	*lieb, tener*		

The majority of words for 'dear' (= 'beloved') are connected with words for 'love' and have been included in the discussion of the latter (16.26). The others, including some in which the earlier sense was 'dear' = 'valuable, expensive' (11.88), are:

Ir. *dil*, etym. dub., perh. **dwe-li-* : **dwe-no-* in Lat. *bonus*, OLat. *duenos* 'good'. Vendryes, Miscell. K. Meyer, p. 289.

Ir. *cōim* (also 'handsome, fine'), W. *cu*, MBr. *cuff* (NBr. *kuñv* 'gentle, affable') : Lett. *saime* 'family', OE *hām*, OHG *heim*, 'home', etc. Walde-P. 1.259. Pedersen 1.58.

Ir. *inmain*, NIr. *ionmhain*, perh. as **eni-moni-* fr. the root of *menme* 'mind', etc. Macbain 218.

NIr. *dīlis*, also 'faithful', orig. 'one's own', in this sense OIr. *dīless* (cf. W. *dilys* 'certain'), cpd. of neg. *dī-* and *-less* as in *less-macc*, W. *llys-fab* 'stepson' : Ir. *leth*, 'side'. Pedersen 2.8.

W. *hoff* 'dear, desirable', etym.?

W. *annwyl*, etym.? Morris Jones 160 (but??).

Br. *ker*, MBr. *quer*, fr. a Norman form of Fr. *cher*. Henry 63.

Br. *kaez* (MBr. *quaez* 'captive, unfortunate') 'unfortunate, miserable', whence by affectionate commiseration 'dear' : W. *caeth*, Ir. *cacht* 'slave', Lat. *captus* 'captive', etc. Henry 57.

OE *dēore*, ME *dēre*, NE *dear*, also 'precious, expensive' (cf. 11.88) in OE and ME often 'glorious, noble' : ON *dyrr* 'precious, noble', OHG *tiure* 'glorious, excellent, valuable', NHG *teuer* 'dear' (in both senses), outside connection dub. Falk-Torp 172. Weigand-H. 2.1040 ff.

SCr., Bulg. *drag* (> Rum. *drag*), Boh. *drahý*, Russ. *dorog*, also 'precious, valuable', Pol. *drogi*, ChSl. *dragŭ* only in the latter sense (cf. also Lett. *dārgs* id., prob. loanword), etym.? Berneker 213.

16.29 KISS (vb.)

Grk.	*φιλέω, κυνέω*	Goth.	*kukjan*	Lith.	*bučiuoti*
NG	*φιλῶ*	ON	*kyssa*	Lett.	*bučuot, skūpstīt*
Lat.	*ōsculārī, sāviārī, bāsiāre*	Dan.	*kysse*	ChSl.	*lobŭzati, cělovati*
It.	*baciare*	Sw.	*kyssa*	SCr.	*ljubiti, cjelivati*
Fr.	*embrasser, baiser*	OE	*cyssan*	Boh.	*líbati (celovati)*
Sp.	*besar*	ME	*kisse*	Pol.	*całować*
Rum.	*săruta*	NE	*kiss*	Russ.	*celovat'*
Ir.	*pōcaim*	Du.	*kussen*	Skt.	*(cumb-)*
NIr.	*pōgaim*	OHG	*kussen*	Av.	. . . .
W.	*cusanu*	MHG	*küssen*		
Br.	*pokat*	NHG	*küssen*		

Kissing, as an expression of affection or love, is unknown among many races, and in the history of mankind seems to be a later substitute for the more primitive rubbing of noses, sniffing, and licking. The partial agreement among words for 'kiss' in some of the IE languages rests only on some common expressive syllables, and is no conclusive evidence that kissing was known in IE times. It was late in India, and a Slavic group probably reflects the 'lick' kiss. Schrader, Reallex. s.v. Kuss. Hopkins, The Sniff-Kiss in Ancient India, JAOS 28.120 ff. Meissner, Der Kuss im alten Orient, Ber. Preuss. Akad. 1934. 914 ff.

A distinction between the kiss of affection and that of erotic love is sometimes made as in Latin (cf. *Sciendum osculum religionis, savium voluptatis; quamvis quidam osculum filiis dari, uxori basium, scorto savium dicant*, Serv. ad Verg.), but even here is not maintained and in general is ignored.

Several of the words for 'kiss', as already stated, are of imitative origin. One is from a 'little mouth'. Some come, through church influence, from the kiss of 'peace' or 'greeting'. In some the feeling of 'love' is the antecedent of its expression as 'kiss'.

1. Derivs. of an expressive syllable *ku* or *kus* (cf. the more obviously imitative *bu*, *bus*, below, 2). Gmc. forms resisting the consonant shift by reason of the expressive character, or influenced by the group Goth. *kiusan*, Grk. γεύω etc. 'try, taste', or fr. a parallel *gu*, *gus?* Walde-P. 1.465. Feist 315.

Grk. κυνέω (aor. Hom. ἔκυσσα, mostly poet., in prose replaced early by φιλέω); Goth. *kukjan*, OFris. *kükken;* ON *kyssa*, OE *cyssan* (> W. sb. *cusan*, vb. *cusanu*), OHG *kussen*, etc. with sbs. ON *koss*, OE *coss*, OHG *kus*, etc.; Skt. *cumb-* (late, cf. below, 9); Hitt. *kuwass-* (Benveniste, MSL 33.139).

2. Derivs. of an imitative *bu*, *bus*, in words for 'kiss' and 'lip' or 'mouth'. Widespread group not confined to IE languages, but mostly dial. or colloq. words not included in the list. Walde-P. 2.113 f. Berneker 104. Mühl.-Endz. 1.344 f.

NE *buss* (sb. and vb.), NHG sb. *buss*, vb. *bussen*, Sp. *buz* ('kiss of respect', fr. Arab.), Pol. *buzia*, *buziak;* cf. Ir. *bus*, Alb. *buzë*, Rum. *buză* 'lip'. Here as regular verbs for 'kiss' Lith. *bučiuoti*, Lett. *bučuot*, beside Lith. *buč* an imitative exclamation inviting a kiss (NSB s.v.), perh. fr. NHG dial. forms like *butschen* and (Swiss) *butsch* 'a kiss'.

Other colloq. words of imitative orig., e.g. NE *smack* (with its Gmc. parallels); Rum. *pupa* (childish or derogatory) : It. *poppa* 'breast', *poppare* 'suck', etc. (Puşcariu 1403); Lett. *skūpstīt*, beside *čūpstīt* 'suck' (Mühl.-Endz. 3.908).

3. Grk. φιλέω 'love' (16.27), hence also 'show signs of love, kiss' (Hdt.+), with sb. φίλημα 'a kiss' (Aesch.+), NG pop. φιλῶ only 'kiss', sbs. φιλί (fr. infin. φιλεῖν), φίλημα. Cf. Corn. *a(m)me*, MBr. *affet* 'kiss', prob. fr. Lat. *amāre* 'love' (Henry 5; not in Loth, Mots lat.).

4. Lat. *ōsculārī*, fr. *ōsculum* 'a kiss', lit. 'little mouth', fr. *ōs* 'mouth'. Ernout-M. 715.

Lat. *sāviārī*, chiefly anteclass., fr. *sāvium* 'a kiss' (esp. in the erotic sense as contrasted with *ōsculum*), prob. by dissim. fr. **suāvium* : *suāvis* 'sweet'. Ernout-M. 898. Kretschmer, Glotta 9.208.

Lat. *bāsiāre* (> It. *baciare*, Fr. *baiser*, Sp. *besar*), fr. *bāsium* (Catull.+) orig. used like *sāvium*, but eventually displacing it and *ōsculum*, source dub. (loanword fr. Celtic?). Ernout-M. 105. Walde-H. 1.97 f. REW 971. Wartburg 2.268 ff.

Fr. *embrasser*, fr. *bras* 'arm', orig. 'take in the arms, embrace', but also 'kiss' since 17th cent., and now replacing *baiser* in this sense (except with added *lèvres* or the like, or as a noun; *donner un baiser*, etc.) owing to the obscene connotation which *baiser* has taken. REW 1256. Wartburg 2.268 ff. Bloch 1.61, 99.

Rum. *săruta*, fr. Lat. *salūtāre* 'greet'. Perh. semantic borrowing fr. Slavic (cf. ChSl. *cělovati*, etc., below, 8), but not necessarily. Cf. OSp. *saludar* also 'kiss', and so formerly sometimes NE *salute* (NED s.v. 2, e). REW 7556. Tiktin 1369.

5. Ir. *pōcaim*, NIr. *pōgaim*, Br. *pokat*, fr. Ir. *pōc*, Br. *pok* 'a kiss', fr. Lat. *pāx* 'peace' in church uses like *pācis ōsculum dāre*, etc. Vendryes, De hib. voc. 167. Loth, Mots lat. 197. Pedersen 1.24, 202.

W. *cusanu*, above, 1.

6. Gmc. words, above, 1.

7. Lith. *bučiuoti*, Lett. *bučuot*, above, 2.

8. ChSl. *lobŭzati* (reg. for 'kiss' in Gospels), Russ. *lobzat'* (obs. or archaic), SCr. dial. *lobzat*, *lozbat*, prob. : Lat. *lambere*, OHG *laffan* 'lick', OE *lapian* 'lap up' etc. Walde-P. 2.384. Berneker 726 f.

ChSl. *cělovati* 'greet' (cf. *cělŭ* 'sound, well', like Lat. *salūtāre* fr. *salūs* 'health'), hence also 'kiss' (Supr. once, and later) as SCr. *cjelivati*, Boh. *celovati*, Pol. *całować*, Russ. *celovat'*. Berneker 123 f.

SCr. *ljubiti* 'love' and 'kiss' (like Grk. φιλέω), Boh. *líbati* 'kiss' (*polibek* 'a kiss') : ChSl. *ljubiti* 'love' (16.27). Berneker 756 ff.

9. Skt. *cumb-* (above, 1) is of relatively late occurrence.

In Vedic, affection is expressed by *ghrā-* 'smell, sniff' (15.21), *lih-* 'lick' (4.59), and *niṅs-* 'approach, touch, embrace, greet' (*ni-ns-*, redupl. form of *nas-* 'approach, join', esp. in love : Grk. νέομαι 'come back, return', Goth. *ganisan* 'be saved', etc.; Walde-P. 2.334 f.). These are often translated 'kiss', but only loosely. The true 'kiss' is sometimes expressed, earlier than by *cumb-*, as 'set mouth to mouth'. Cf. Hopkins, l.c.

16.31 PAIN, SUFFERING

Grk.	*ἄλγος, ὀδύνη, πάθημα,* etc.	Goth.	*sair, winnō, balweins*	Lith.	*skausmas, kentėjimas, kančia*
NG	*πόνος, βάσανα*	ON	*verkr, sārsauki*	Lett.	*sāpes, ciešana*
Lat.	*dolor*	Dan.	*smerte, lidelse*	ChSl.	*bolěznĭ, strastĭ*
It.	*dolore, sofferenza*	Sw.	*smärta, lidande*	SCr.	*bol, patnja*
Fr.	*douleur, souffrance*	OE	*sār, æce, wærc, þrōwung*	Boh.	*bolest, utrpení*
Sp.	*dolor, padecimiento*	ME	*sor, peine, suffrynge, smerte*	Pol.	*ból, boleść, cierpienie*
Rum.	*durere, suferinţă*	NE	*pain, suffering*	Russ.	*bol', stradanie*
Ir.	*imned, cēssad*	Du.	*pijn, smart, lijden*	Skt.	*duḥkha-, pīḍā-, vedanā-*
NIr.	*pian, fulang*	OHG	*smerza, sēr, pīna*	Av.	*axti-, sādra; inti-, āri-*
W.	*poen, dioddef*	MHG	*smerze, sēr, līden, pīn(e)*		
Br.	*poan, gloaz*	NHG	*schmerz, leiden, pein, qual*		

'Pain, suffering' is understood here as primarily physical, though most of the words may be used also for mental suffering, for which see also 'grief, sorrow' (16.32). NE *pain* is mostly, though not exclusively, physical, while conversely Fr. *peine* is mostly mental.

Some of the words for 'emotion' or 'passion' are also used more specifically for 'suffering' as Grk. πάθος, πάθημα (not repeated here), or had the latter sense more originally (cf. 16.12, 16.13).

Several of the words belong with the verbs for 'suffer' but may show more specialization than the latter. Thus NE *suffer* 'suffer pain' and also 'endure, allow' (though now archaic), but *suffering* only in the specialized sense. The verbs for 'suffer' are included in the discussion, either here or in 16.12, 16.13. Several of these (but not all, by any means) cover also 'bear, endure', which in some is the primary sense. Some are connected with words for 'hard work, toil'.

1. Grk. ἄλγος, etym. dub. Walde-P. 2.423 (rejected in Walde-H. 1.352).

Grk. ὀδύνη, most frequently in pl. 'pains', etym. dub. Walde-P. 1.768. Boisacq 685.

NG πόνος (with vb. πονῶ 'suffer'), in class. Grk. 'hard work, toil' (9.12).

NG βάσανο 'torment, torture', but pop. also 'pain' (esp. pl. τὰ βάσανα), fr. Grk. βάσανος 'touchstone', whence 'test, trial', and 'inquiry by torture' of slaves, etc., and (NT) 'torment, torture', prob. loanword. Boisacq 115.

2. Lat. *dolor* (> It. *dolore*, Fr. *douleur*,

Sp. *dolor*, ORum. *duroare*) 'grief' and 'pain', *dolēre* 'suffer, feel pain' (> Rum. *durea*, whence sb. *durere*), prob. through notion of a 'throbbing' or 'splitting' pain (cf. NE *splitting headache*) : *dolāre* 'hew', Lith. *dalyti* 'divide', Skt. *dal-* 'burst'. Walde-P. 1.810. Ernout-M. 279. Walde-H. 1.364.

It. *sofferenza*, Fr. *souffrance*, Sp. *sufrimiento*, Rum. *suferință*, fr. It. *soffrire*, Fr. *souffrir*, Sp. *sufrir*, Rum. *suferi* 'suffer', Lat. *sub-ferre* 'hold up, bear, endure, suffer', cpd. of *sub* 'under' and *ferre* 'carry'. REW 8428.

Sp. *padecimiento*, fr. *padecer* 'suffer', fr. OSp. *padir*, Lat. *patīre*, class. *patī* 'suffer, endure, bear' : Grk. πῆμα 'evil, injury, harm', ταλαί-πωρος 'miserable', etc. Walde-P. 2.8. Ernout-M. 741 (placing here also Grk. πάθος, ἔπαθον, etc., 16.12). REW 6294.

Lat. *poena* 'penalty, punishment' (fr. Grk. ποινή 'penalty'), late Lat. also 'hardship, torment, suffering', has furnished many words for pain, physical or mental, namely It. *pena*, Fr. *peine* (OFr. > ME *peine* mostly 'penalty, punishment', NE *pain*), Sp. *pena* (the Romance words now mostly of mental affliction 'grief'); NIr. *pian* (MIr. mostly 'penalty'), W. *poen*, Br. *poan*; Du. *pijn* (MDu. *pine* also 'penalty'), OHG *pīna*, MHG *pīn*, *pīne*, NHG *pein*. Ernout-M. 784. REW 6628. Pedersen 1.213. Franck-v. W. 500. Weigand-H. 2.391.

3. Ir. *imned*, perh. a cpd. of *imb-* and root *neth-* in *air-neth-* (1sg. *ar-neut-sa*) gl. *expectare*, *sustinere*, etc. Pedersen 2.584 f. (but further connection with Goth. *niþan* 'support', etc., rejected by Walde-P. 2.327).

Ir. *cēssad*, vbl. n. of *cēssaim* 'suffer' : Lith. *kęsti*, *kenčiu* 'suffer', prob. Grk. πάσχω 'suffer'. Walde-P. 1.513. Pedersen 2.486.

NIr. *pian*, W. *poen*, Br. *poan*, above, 2.

NIr. *fulang* 'suffering, endurance, patience' (vbl. n. of *fulaingim* 'suffer') = Ir. *fulang* vbl. n. of *fo-long-* 'support, endure' (nasal pres. of *legh- 'lie'). Pedersen 2.568 ff. Thurneysen, Gram. 447.

W. *dioddef*, also vbl. n. 'to suffer', cpd. of *di-* (intensive) and *goddef* 'bear, suffer, permit' : Br. *gousañv* 'suffer, endure, bear', Ir. *fo-daimim* 'suffer', cpd. of root in Ir. *-daim* 'submit, endure, allow', Skt. *dam-*, Grk. δαμάζω, δάμνημι 'tame, subdue', etc. Walde-P. 1.789. Pedersen 2.504. Thurneysen, Gram. 118.

Br. *gloaz* (W. *gloes* 'pang, ache, pain'), etym.? Henry 135.

4. Goth. *sair*, OE *sār*, ME *sor* (NE *sore*), OHG, MHG *sēr* (NHG *sehr* 'very'), all used of both physical and mental pain, ON *sār* 'wound' (whence *sārs-auki* and *sārs-leikr* 'pain, soreness') : Ir. *sāeth* 'affliction, sickness', *saethar* 'affliction, toil', perh. Lat. *saevus* 'fierce'. Walde-P. 2.445. Feist 405.

Goth. *winnō* (renders πάθημα, πάθος), and *wunns* (πάθημα), beside *winnan* 'suffer' = ON *vinna* 'work', OE *winnan* 'work, labor, suffer', OHG *winnan* 'fight' : Skt. *van-* 'desire, gain', etc. Walde-P. 1.260. Feist 566.

Goth. *balweins* (renders βάσανος 'torment', Lk. 16.23, also κόλασις 'punishment', Mt. 25.46), beside *balwjan* 'torture' : OE *bealu* 'evil, harm', ON *bǫl* 'misfortune', OHG *balo* 'ruin', prob. also, with different suffix, ChSl. *bolĭ* 'sick person', SCr. *bol* 'pain', etc. (below, 6). Walde-P. 2.189. Feist 79.

ON *verkr* (Dan. *værk*, Sw. *värk* 'ache, rheumatic pain'), OE *wærc*, ME *warche*, *warke*, prob. fr. the same root as OE *weorc* 'work, toil', OHG *werah*, ON *verk* 'work', etc. Walde-P. 1.291. Falk-Torp 1369.

OE *æce*, ME *ache* (NE *ache* 'continuous pain'), beside the vb. OE *acan* 'ache' : LG *äken* 'pain, fester', MDu. *akel* 'in-

jury, wrong', NFris. *akelig*, *aekelig* 'horrid, miserable', perh. fr. the same root as Skt. *āgas-* 'offense, crime', Grk. ἄγος 'curse, guilt, pollution'. Walde-P. 1.38. Falk-Torp 459 f. NED sv. *ache*, vb.

OE *þrōwung*, fr. *þrōwan* 'suffer' : OHG *druoen* 'suffer', ON *þrā* 'long, yearn', ChSl. *truti* 'consume', Lith. *trunėti* 'rot', beside ChSl. *tryti* 'rub', Grk. τρύω 'rub down, wear out', fr. an extended form of the root in Grk. τείρω 'rub', etc. Walde-P. 1.731. Falk-Torp 1276 f., 1288 f.

ME *peine*, NE *pain*, Du. *pijn*, NHG *pein*, above, 2.

ME *suffrynge* (but mostly 'bearing of pain, tribulation'), NE *suffering*, fr. ME *soffre*, *suffre* 'undergo (pain, grief, penalty, etc.), bear, endure', etc., NE *suffer*, fr. Fr. *souffrir* (above, 2).

OHG *smerza*, MHG *smerze*, NHG *schmerz*, Du. *smart* (MLG *smerte* > Dan. *smerte*, Sw. *smärta*), also ME *sm(i)erte* 'sharp pain, grief, sorrow' (NE *smart*), perh. : Grk. σμερδνός, σμερδαλέος 'frightful, fearful', and fr. a root *smerd- beside *merd- in Lat. *mordēre* 'bite', Skt. *mṛd-* 'squeeze, crush, bruise', etc. Walde-P. 2.279. Falk-Torp 1080 f.

Du. *lijden*, MHG *līden*, NHG *leiden*, sbs. fr. infins. Du. *lijden*, 'to suffer' (MLG *līden* > Dan. *lide*, Sw. *lida*, whence sbs. Dan. *lidelse*, Sw. *lidande*), NHG *leiden*, but OHG *ir-līdan* 'endure, pass through', then 'experience (go through) pain' (cf. phrases like NE *what she went through!*), the simple *līdan* orig. 'go' = Goth. *-leiþan* 'go', OE *līþan* 'go, voyage', ON *līða* 'go, pass away, die' (cf. pple. *liðinn* 'dead'). Walde-P. 2.401 f. Kluge-G. 352 f. Weigand-H. 2.47.

OHG *quāla*, MHG *quāl(e)*, NHG *qual*, mostly 'violent pain, torment' (OHG also 'violent death') : OE *cwalu* 'violent death, torment', *cwelan* 'die' (4.75), etc. Walde-P. 1.680, Weigand-H. 2.498.

5. Lith. *skausmas*, *skaudėjimas*, with *skausti*, *skaudėti* 'be painful', adj. *skaudus* 'painful' : Lett. *skaust*, *skaudēt* 'envy', Grk. σκυδμαίνω, σκύζομαι 'be angry'. Walde-P. 2.554. Mühl.-Endz. 3.876.

Lith. *kentėjimas*, Lett. *ciešana*, fr. vbs. *kęsti*, *ciest* 'suffer' : Ir. *cēssaim* (above, 3).

Lith. *kančia*, *kanka* : *kenkia* 'it hurts, aches', Grk. κέγκει· ἐπιδάκνει (Hesych.), OE *hungor*, etc. 'hunger' (5.14). Walde-P. 1.401.

Lett. *sāpe*, usually pl. *sāpes*, cf. Lith. *sopėti* 'ache, ail', etym.? Mühl.-Endz. 3.805.

6. ChSl. *bolěznĭ*, also 'sickness', beside *bolěti* 'be sick, feel pain', *bolĭ* 'sick person', SCr. *bol*, Pol. *ból*, Russ. *bol'*, Boh. *bolest*, Pol. *boleść*, perh. : Goth. *balweins*, etc. (above, 4). Berneker 71.

ChSl. *strastĭ* (βάσανος Mt. 4.24, πάθος, πάθημα, Supr.), Russ. *stradanie* : ChSl. *stradati*, Russ. *stradat'* 'suffer', general Slavic, ChSl. *strada* 'labor, toil', perh. fr. the root of Grk. στερεός 'firm, stiff, hard', NHG *starr*, etc. 'stiff'. Walde-P. 2.628. Miklosich 324.

SCr. *patnja*, fr. *patiti* 'suffer, endure', loanword fr. It. *patire* 'suffer'. Miklosich 233.

Boh. *u-trpení*, Pol. *cierpienie*, fr. Boh. *trpěti*, Pol. *cierpieć* 'suffer' = ChSl. *trŭpěti* 'suffer, endure' (*trŭpěnie* 'patience'), etc., perh. : ChSl. *u-trŭpěti*, Russ. *terpnut'* 'grow stiff', Lat. *torpēre* 'be stiff, torpid', etc., with semantic development 'be stiff, hard' > 'last, endure' > suffer', cf. above ChSl. *strastĭ*, etc. Walde-P. 2.631.

7. Skt. *duḥ-kha-* 'pain, suffering', also adj. 'unpleasant' deriv. of *dus-* 'ill', opp. to *su-kha-* 'pleasant'.

Skt. *pīḍā-* : *pīḍ-* 'press, squeeze, pain, distress', Grk. πιέζω 'press', etc., fr. *pi-

sed-, cpd. of *pi- beside *epi (in Grk. ἐπί) and the root *sed- 'sit'. Walde-P. 2.486.

Skt. *vedanā-*, orig. 'sensation, perception', beside *vedana-* 'knowledge' : *vid-* 'know, become acquainted with'.

Av. *axti-*, etym.? Barth. 51.

Av. *sādra-* (mostly 'torment') : Grk. κῆδος, Dor. κᾶδος 'care, trouble, funeral rites', etc., Ir. *caiss*, Goth. *hatis* 'hate', etc. (16.41). Walde-P. 1.340.

Av. *inti-* ('violence, torment') : *aēn-* 'violate, injure', Skt. *in-* 'press, oppress, force', Grk. αἴνυμαι 'take, seize', etc. Walde-P. 1.1.

Av. *āri-* ('hurt, injury'), perh. : Skt. *ārti-* 'trouble, misfortune, pain' (Walde-P. 1.136). Barth. 334.

16.32 GRIEF, SORROW

Grk.	λύπη, ἄλγος, ὀδύνη	Goth.	*saurga, gaurei, gauriþa*	Lith.	*tužba, rūpestis*
NG	λύπη	ON	*harmr, hrygð, sorg, tregi*	Lett.	*bēda, raizes, skumjas, rūpes*
Lat.	*dolor, aegritūdo*	Dan.	*kummer, sorg*	ChSl.	*pečalĭ, skrŭbĭ*
It.	*dolore, pena, affanno*	Sw.	*sorg, grämelse*	SCr.	*briga, tuga, žalost, pečal*
Fr.	*chagrin, peine, douleur*	OE	*sār, sorh, hearm, gyrn*	Boh.	*zármutek, smutek, žal(ost)*
Sp.	*pesar, dolor, pena*	ME	*sorwe, gref, sor, harm*	Pol.	*boleść, żal, żałość, smutek*
Rum.	*mîhnire, supărare*	NE	*grief, sorrow*	Russ.	*gore, pečal', skorb'*
Ir.	*brōn, cuma, dube*	Du.	*kommer, verdriet*	Skt.	*çoka-, çuc-, duḥkha-*
NIr.	*brōn, cumha, doilgheas*	OHG	*sēr, sorga, harm*	Av.	. . . .
W.	*gofid, galar*	MHG	*sēr, sorge, harm*		
Br.	*doan, glac'har, anken, rec'h*	NHG	*kummer, betrübnis, sorge*		

Several of the words for 'grief, sorrow' are the same as those for physical 'pain, suffering' (16.31), and some belong to groups discussed under 'care' (16.14). The others are from a great variety of notions, mostly physical.

1. Grk. λύπη (rarely also of 'physical pain'), with λυπέω 'grieve, vex' (trans.), mid. 'grieve' (intr.; NG λυποῦμαι also 'be sorry, regret') : Skt. *lup-* 'break, injure, spoil', Lith. *lupti* 'flay, peel', Russ. *lupit'* 'peel, shell', etc. Walde-P. 2.417 f. Boisacq 591 f.

Grk. πένθος ('grief', but esp. 'mourning') : πάθος 'emotion', πάσχω 'suffer', etc. (16.12).

Grk. ἄλγος and ὀδύνη, see 16.31.

2. Lat. *dolor*, It. *dolore*, etc., see 16.31.

Lat. *aegritūdō*, also of physical 'illness', and *aegrimōnia* less frequent but only of mental 'sorrow, grief', fr. *aeger* 'sick, ill', etym. dub. (4.84).

It., Sp. *pena*, Fr. *peine*, fr. Lat. *poena* 'penalty', see 16.31.

It. *affanno*, also 'heavy breathing, severe exertion, exhaustion', with the vb. *affannarsi* 'grieve, tire oneself, overwork', fr. Prov. *afanar* = OFr. *ahaner* 'work in the field' (Fr. dial. 'work hard, suffer', etc.), etym. dub. REW 252. Gamillscheg 19. Wartburg 1.48.

Fr. *chagrin*, back-formation to Fr. dial. *chagraigner* 'sadden', deriv. of OFr. *graignier* 'sadden', fr. OFr. *graim* 'sad', this prob. fr. OHG *gram* 'angry, fierce' (16.42). Gamillscheg 201. REW 7513.

Sp. *pesar*, fr. *pesar* 'weigh, weigh upon, cause sorrow', fr. Lat. *pēnsāre* 'weigh, pay'. REW 6391.

Rum. *mîhnire*, fr. *mîhni* 'grieve' (trans.), perh. fr. the Slavic, cf. ChSl. *mŭknąti*, SCr. *maknuti* 'move' (10.11). Semantic development through 'move' emotionally. Tiktin 977 f.

Rum. *supărare*, fr. *supăra* 'oppress, afflict', fr. Lat. *superāre* 'overcome, conquer'. REW 8458. Tiktin 1534.

3. Ir. *brōn*, W. (arch.) *brwyn*, perh. (*n* fr. *gn*) : Grk. βρύχω 'grind the teeth, bite', Lith. *graužti*, ChSl. *grysti* 'gnaw'. Walde-P. 1.698. Pedersen 1.103.

Ir. *cuma*, NIr. *cumha*, Corn. *cavow*, MBr. *caffou* (NBr. *kañv* 'mourning') : Grk. κάμνω 'tire', Skt. *çam-* 'toil, labor', etc. Walde-P. 1.387. Pedersen 1.47. Henry 53.

Ir. *dube*, opp. to *sube* 'joy', see 16.22.

NIr. *doilgheas*, also *doilghe*, fr. Ir. *doilge* 'difficulty', deriv. of *dolig* 'difficult' (9.92).

W. *gofid*, MW *govut*, Corn. *govid*, apparently based on an interjectional phrase like Corn. *govy*, W. *gwae vy* 'woe is me'. Stokes 259 (but without *gofid*).

W. *galar*, Br. *glac'har*, cf. Ir. *galar* 'sickness', perh. : Grk. χολέρα 'cholera', χόλος 'gall', etc. Pedersen 2.25. Walde-P. 1.540.

Br. *doan*, perh. as 'what one has to bear' : MBr. *doen* 'carry, bear'. Ernault, Dict. étym. 275.

Br. *rec'h*, etym. dub. Henry 232.

Br. *anken* : W. *angen*, Ir. *ēcen* 'necessity' (9.93). Henry 11.

4. Goth. *sair*, OE *sār*, OHG *sēr*, etc., see 16.31.

Goth. *saurga* (renders μέριμνα 'care' and λύπη 'grief'), ON *sorg*, OE *sorh*, NE *sorrow*, etc., see under 'care' (16.14).

Goth. *gauriþa*, *gaurei* (each once for λύπη), OE *gyrn*, beside Goth. *gaurs* 'sad', *gaurjan* 'grieve' (act. = λυπεῖν, pass. = λυπεῖσθαι), OHG *gōrag* 'pitiful, miserable', etc., etym. dub., perh. : Skt. *ghora-* 'awful, dreadful'. Walde-P. 1.636. Feist 208.

Goth. *trigō* (once for λύπη, but rather 'reluctance', in phrase ἐκ λύπης 'grudgingly'), ON *tregi* 'reluctance' and 'grief', OE *trega*, ME *treie* 'pain, grief, trouble' : OHG *trāgi* 'slow, lazy' (14.22).

ON *harmr* 'grief', rarely 'hurt, harm', OE *hearm* 'hurt, injury', rarely and ME 'grief', OHG *harm* 'disgrace, calumny', rarely and MHG 'grief' (NHG *harm* taken up again in poet. language, cf. Paul, Deutsches Wtb. s.v.) : ChSl. *sramŭ* 'shame'. Walde-P. 1.463. Falk-Torp 381.

ON *hrygð*, fr. *hryggr* 'grieved, sad' (16.36).

Sw. *grämelse*, fr. *gräma* 'grieve' : Dan. *græmme sig* 'become angry', ON *gremja* 'make angry', *gremi* 'anger' (16.42). Falk-Torp 340.

ME *gref*, *grief*, NE *grief*, in ME also 'hardship, hurt, harm', fr. OFr. *grief*, *gref*, back-formation to *grever* (> ME *greve*, NE *grieve*), VLat. *grevāre, for *gravāre* 'weigh down, burden, oppress', fr. *gravis* 'heavy' (VLat. *grevis after opp. *levis* 'light'). NED s.v.

ME *destresse*, NE *distress*, fr. OFr. *destresse*, VLat. *districtia*, deriv. of Lat. *districtus*, pple. of *di-stringere* 'detain, hinder'. NED s.v. *distress*, sb.

Du. *kommer*, NHG (> Dan.) *kummer*, fr. MLG *kummer*, MHG *kumber* 'rubbish, heap of ruins', also 'hindrance', whence 'harm, injury, distress' and finally 'grief'. Cf. also MLat. (Merov.) *cumbrus* 'barrier of felled trees', OFr. *combre* id. Etym. disputed, but prob. a Gmc. word fr. the root seen in Grk. γέμω 'be full', etc. Falk-Torp 593 f. Franck-v. W. 334. Otherwise (as a Gallo-Lat. *com-boros 'brought together') Kluge-G. 336, REW 2075.

NHG *betrübnis*, late MHG *betrüebnisse*, fr. *betrüben*, MHG *betrüeben* 'grieve, afflict', orig. 'make turbid', fr. *trüb(e)* 'turbid, troubled, muddy'. Weigand-H. 1.223.

5. Lith. *tužba*, with vb. *tužytis* (refl.) 'be afflicted, grieved', fr. the Slavic, cf.

WhRuss. *tužba, tužić*, Russ. *tužit'* 'be afflicted' : ChSl. *tąga* 'distress, anxiety', SCr. *tuga* 'sorrow, affliction', etc. (below, 6). Walde-P. 2.616. Brückner, Sl. Fremdwörter 148.

Lith. *rūpestis*, Lett. pl. *rūpes*, see under 'care' (16.14).

Lett. *bēda* (Lith. *bėda* 'misfortune, misery'), fr. Slavic, cf. ChSl. *běda* 'necessity, distress' (9.93). Brückner, Sl. Fremdwörter 71. Walde-P. 2.185 (without the Baltic words). Mühl.-Endz. 1.288 (as cognate, not loanwords).

Lett. *raize*, usually pl. *raizes* : Lith. *rėzti* 'cut, scratch, tear', iter. *raižyti*, etc. Mühl.-Endz. 3.472. Walde-P. 2.344.

Lett. *skumjas* (pl.), cf. *skumjš* 'sad, distressed', *skumt* 'be sad, distressed', perh. as 'become dark' : ON *skūmi* 'shade, dusk', etc., fr. the root in Skt. *sku-* 'cover'. Walde-P. 2.548. Mühl.-Endz. 3.904.

6. ChSl. *pečalĭ*, SCr. *pečal*, Russ. *pečal'*, see under 'care' (16.14).

ChSl. *skrŭbĭ* (usually θλῖψις 'affliction', but also λύπη Jn. 16.6), Russ. *skorb'* (SCr. *skrb* mostly 'care'), beside ChSl. *skruběti* 'grieve', etc., perh. : Russ. *skorblyj* 'shrunk, shriveled', Lett. *skurbt* 'become dizzy', *skurbināt* 'make dizzy by whirling', ON *skorpna* 'shrivel up', etc. (Walde-P. 2.588 f.). Miklosich 306. Mühl.-Endz. 3.906.

SCr. *briga*, fr. It. *briga* 'burden, care' (orig. dub., REW 1299). Berneker 86.

SCr. *tuga* = ChSl. *tąga* 'distress, anxiety', etc. : *tęžŭkŭ* 'heavy', *ęgostĭ* 'burden', etc., fr. the root of *tęgnąti* 'pull, draw'. Walde-P. 1.726. Miklosich 359.

SCr. *žalost*, Boh. *žal, žalost*, Pol. *żal, żałość* (ChSl. *žalĭ* in Gospels only = μνημεῖον Mt. 8.28, Mar. vs. usual *grebŭ, grobŭ; žalostĭ* = ζῆλος) : Lith. *gėla* '(violent) pain', ON *kvǫl* 'torment', OHG *quāla* 'torment, violent death', Ir. *at-baill* 'dies', etc. Walde-P. 1.690. Meillet, Études 265, 284.

Boh. *žármutek* and *zámutek* (cf. Gebauer 1.47), Boh. Pol. *smutek* : ChSl. *mątŭ* 'trouble, confusion', *mętą, męsti*, iter. *mątiti* 'stir up, trouble', etc. Semantic development as in NHG *betrübnis*, above, 4. Walde-P. 2.269. Brückner 329.

Pol. *boleść* 'pain' (16.31) and 'grief'.

Pol. *strapienie*, fr. *strapić* 'afflict, torment', fr. the same root as *cierpieć* 'suffer, endure' = ChSl. *trŭpěti* id., etc. See 16.31 under Boh. *u-trpení*, etc.

Pol. *frasunek*, fr. *frasować*, old *fresować* 'disturb, grieve' (trans.), fr. NHG *fressen* 'eat, devour', older NHG *sich fressen* 'torment oneself'. Berneker 285. Brückner 127.

Russ. *gore* (ChSl. *gore* 'woe!', Boh. *hoře* 'misery', etc.) : Slav. *gorěti* 'burn'. Berneker 333.

7. Skt. *çoka-, çuc-*, both lit. 'flame, heat' : *çuc-* 'flame, glow, gleam', by extension 'suffer pain, grieve'.

Skt. *duḥ-kha-*, see 16.31.

16.33 ANXIETY

Grk.	(φροντίς, μέριμνα)	Goth.	*sorga*	Lith.	*rūpestis, bailė*
NG	ἀνησυχία	ON	*kvīða*	Lett.	*rūpes, baile*
Lat.	*anxietās*	Dan.	*ængstelse*	ChSl.	(*pečalĭ*)
It.	*ansietà, inquietudine*	Sw.	*ängslan*	SCr.	*tjeskoba*
Fr.	*anxiété, inquiétude*	OE	*angnes, angsumnes, sorh*	Boh.	*úzkost*
Sp.	*ansia, ansiedad, inquietud*			Pol.	*obawa, troska*
		ME	*anxumness, sorwe*	Russ.	*zabota*
Rum.	*îngrijorare, neliniște*	NE	*anxiety, worry*	Skt.	(*cintā-*)
Ir.	*dethiden, (imm)snīm*	Du.	*angst*	Av.	....
NIr.	*imshnīomh, imnidhe*	OHG	*angust, sorga*		
W.	*pryder*	MHG	*angest, bange, sorge*		
B.	*nec'h*	NHG	*angst, bangigkeit, sorge*		

Many of the words for 'care' = 'mental attention' (16.14) are also used for 'anxiety, worry', as still in part NE *care* (*my cares are many*), and in some, in fact, this is the earlier sense.

Of the more distinctive words, several are connected with adjs. for 'narrow' (12.62), whence also others for the stronger 'anguish', and some are simply 'disquietude'.

In general, there is much overlapping in use between words for 'care', 'sorrow', and 'anxiety'.

1. Grk. φροντίς and μέριμνα, see under 'care' (16.14).

NG ἀνησυχία, lit. 'uneasiness', fr. ἀνήσυχος 'uneasy, not quiet', neg. of ἥσυχος 'quiet, still' (12.19).

2. Lat. *anxietās* (> It. *ansietà*, Fr. *anxiété*, Sp. *ansiedad*), fr. *anxius* 'anxious' and 'causing anxiety' (late sb. *anxia* > Sp. *ansia*) : *angere* 'press tight, throttle' and of the mind 'distress, torment, vex', *angustus*, etc. 'narrow' (12.62). Ernout-M. 51. Walde-H. 1.47, 55.

It. *inquietudine*, Fr. *inquiétude*, Sp. *inquietud*, fr. Lat. *inquiētūdo* (*-inis*) 'restlessness, disquietude', fr. *inquiētus* 'restless, not quiet', neg. of *quiētus* 'quiet' (12.19).

Rum. *îngrijorare, îngrijare*, fr. *îngriji* 'care for, attend', refl. 'be grieved, anxious', fr. *grija* 'care' (16.14).

Rum. *neliniște*, lit. 'unrest', neg. of *liniște* 'quiet, rest', fr. *lin* 'still, quiet', this fr. Lat. *lēnis* 'smooth, mild'. Tiktin 912, 915.

3. Ir. *dethiden* 'care, anxiety', neg. to *dīdnad* 'comfort', vbl. n. of *dodonaim* 'comfort' : W. *diddanu* 'amuse', *diddan* 'pleasant, a joke', outside root connection? Pedersen 2.56 f., 508.

Ir. *snīm*, and cpd. *immsnīm* (also 'sorrow'), NIr. *imshnīomh* = *snīm* 'spinning', NIr. *sniomh* 'act of twisting, winding, spinning', etc., also 'wrench, struggle, anxiety, affliction' (cf. Dinneen s.v.) : W. *nyddu*, Br. *neza*, Grk. νήθω, Lat. *nēre* 'spin', etc. Pedersen 2.633. Walde-P. 2.694.

NIr. *imnidhe, imneadh*, fr. Ir. *imned* 'pain, suffering' (16.31).

W. *pryder*, see under 'care' (16.14).

Br. *nec'h* = W. *nych* 'languishing, pining, consumption', cf. W. *nychtod* 'phthisis', etym. dub. Stokes 190. Walde-P. 2.85.

4. ON *kvīða* (Dan. *kvide* 'agony') : ON *kvīða* 'feel apprehension', OE *cwīþan* 'mourn, lament', OS *quīthian* 'lament', and, with different suffix, Goth. *qainōn* 'weep, mourn', ON *kveina* 'wail, lament', outside connections dub. Walde-P. 1.665 f. Falk-Torp 606. Feist 385 f.

OE *angnes, angsumnes*, ME *anxumness*, Du. *angst* (MLG *angest* > Dan. *angest* 'fear, dread', Sw. *ångest* 'agony,

anguish', whence Dan. *ængstelse*, Sw. *ängslan*), OHG *angust*, MHG *angest*, NHG *angst* : OE *ange*, OHG *angi, engi*, NHG *eng* 'narrow'. Cf. Lat. *anxietās*, etc. (above, 2). Falk-Torp 29. Weigand-H. 1.61.

Goth. *sorga*, OE *sorh, sorg* (usual gl. for *anxietas*), ME *sorwe* also 'sorrow, grief', OHG *sorga*, etc., see under 'care' (16.14).

NE *anxiety*, fr. Lat. *anxietās* (above, 2).

NE *worry*, fr. vb. *worry*, fr. OE *wyrgan* 'strangle'. NED s.v.

MHG *bange*, and *benge* (adv. and sb.), NHG *bange* (usually adj. or adv., also sb.), fr. a cpd. *be-ange* : OHG *angi, engi*, etc. 'narrow' (cf. above). Hence NHG *bangigkeit*. Weigand-H. 1.149.

5. Lith. *rūpestis*, Lett. *rūpe*, also 'sorrow', see under 'care' (16.14).

Lith. *bailė, baimė*, Lett. *baile*, also and orig. 'fear' (16.53).

6. ChSl. *pečalĭ*, see under 'care' (16.14).

SCr. *tjeskoba*, lit. 'tightness, narrowness' : *tijesan* 'narrow, tight', etc. Miklosich 357.

Boh. *úzkost*, lit. 'narrowness', fr. *úzký* 'narrow, tight'.

Pol. *obawa* (also 'fear') : *bać się, bojać się* 'be afraid' (= ChSl. *bojati sę*, 16.53). Brückner 369.

Pol. *troska* : *trzaskać* 'crack, crash', ChSl. *trěskati*, Lith. *treškėti* id., late ChSl. *trěskŭ, troska* 'stroke of lightning', Boh. *trosky* (pl.) 'ruins'. Brückner 577, 579.

Russ. *zabota*, see under 'care' (16.14).

7. Skt. *cintā-*, properly 'thought, reflection', fr. *cint-* 'think, reflect' (17.13).

16.34 REGRET (vb.), REPENT

Grk.	μεταμέλει, μετανοέω	Goth.	*idreigōn(sik)*	Lith.	*apgailauti, gailėtis*
NG	λυποῦμαι, μετανοῶ, μετανοιώνω	ON	*iðra(sk)*	Lett.	*nuožēluot*
		Dan.	*beklage, angre*	ChSl.	*(ras)kajati sę*
Lat.	*paenitēre*	Sw.	*beklaga, ångra*	SCr.	*žaliti, kajati se*
It.	*rincrescere, pentirsi*	OE	*hrēowan, hrēowsian, ofþyncan*	Boh.	*litovati, želeti, káti se*
Fr.	*regretter, se repentir*			Pol.	*żałować, rozkajać się*
Sp.	*sentir, arrepentirse*	ME	*rewe, repent, ofthinke*	Russ.	*žalet', (ras)kajat'sja*
Rum.	*regreta, se căi*	NE	*regret, be sorry, repent, rue*	Skt.	*anu-tap-, anu-çuc-,* etc.
Ir.	*ad-errig* (3sg.)				
NIr.	*aithreachas* (with vb.)	Du.	*betreuren, berouwen*	Av.	....
W.	*edifarhau*	OHG	*hriuwan, hriuwōn*		
Br.	*kaout keuz, keuzedikaat*	MHG	*riuwen*		
		NHG	*bedauern, bereuen*		

'Regret' (with 'repentance' and the still deeper 'remorse') is a special kind of 'sorrow', mainly for something done or left undone. Some of the words are also, or were once, used for 'sorrow' in general, and many more are related to others for 'grief, sorrow', 'pity', etc. The notion of 'regret' is dominant in NE adj. 'sorry' (in contrast to the sb. *sorrow*), especially in *be sorry*, which is the popular equivalent of the vb. *regret* (*I am sorry that I came*). Cf. also NHG *es tut mir leid*, lit. 'it gives me pain' = 'I am sorry, I regret'.

On the other hand, a few (the Grk. words) denoted simply a 'change of mind', whence the resulting feeling of 'regret'.

Since the sbs. are mostly derived from vbs., the latter have been chosen for the list and the discussion.

NE *repent* is used especially with reference to regret for sins, crimes, faults, etc., and so most of the modern words

entered in second place in the list; and since Grk. μετανοέω has this application in the NT, so the Goth. and ChSl. words which render it. But, in general, such differentiation between 'regret' and 'repent' is secondary and does not hold for the older periods.

1. Grk. μεταμέλει (impers. with dat. of person; also pers. μεταμέλομαι), cpd. of μετά, in cpds. denoting esp. change, and μέλει 'is a care' (cf. 16.14).

Grk. μετανοέω 'perceive afterward', 'change one's mind', and esp. 'repent' (in LXX and NT), NG μετανοῶ (also μετανοιώνω, fr. μετάνοια 'repentance'), cpd. of μετά (cf. above) and νοέω 'perceive'.

NG pop. λυποῦμαι 'grieve' (16.32), also 'be sorry, regret'.

2. Lat. *paenitet*, impers., later spelled *poenitet* under influence of *poena* 'punishment' and used also personally (VLat. **poenitēre* > OFr. *peneir, pentir*, It. *pentirsi;* cpds. Fr. *se repentir*, Sp. *arrepentirse*), orig. (Plautus) 'is not enough, is unsatisfactory', prob. : *paene* 'nearly, almost'. Ernout-M. 722. REW 6630, 7224.

It. *rincrescere* (impers. *mi rincresce* 'I regret'), fr. *increscere* 'be wearisome, pity', VLat. **in-crēscere* lit. 'grow in', whence 'vex, grieve, etc.'. REW 4363.

Fr. *regretter* (> Rum. *regreta*), in this sense 16th cent., earlier only 'lament someone's death', OFr. also *regrater*, prob. fr. the Gmc., cf. ON *grāta*, Goth. *grētan* 'weep' (16.37). Gamillscheg 751. Bloch 2.219. Otherwise (fr. VLat. **regrevitāre*) REW 7176a.

Sp. *sentir*, lit. 'feel, perceive by senses' (15.11), whence in pregnant sense 'feel grief, regret'.

Rum. *se căi*, fr. Slavic, cf. SCr. *kayati se*, etc. (below, 6).

3. Ir. *ad-e(i)rrig* (3sg.), lit. 'repeat, better', and 'bring to repentance', but also Wb. 30b30 *dūus in-d-aithirset* 'if perchance they repent it', vbl.n. *aithrige* 'repentance' and 'penance' (MIr. also with *dognim* 'do, make', 'do penance' and 'repent', cf. *aithrige n-dīchra do dēnam iar-sin* 'to repent earnestly thereafter', Passions and Homilies l. 6457); also Ir. *aithrech* 'repentant' (in phrase 'regret, repent', e.g. *ni-pa aidrech lib a fulang* 'ye will not regret supporting them', Wb. 25d9), hence NIr. *aithreachas* 'repentance, regret' (phrase *tā sē i n-aithreachas orm* 'I regret it'). The finite verb forms at least are from *aith-air-rig-* : *rigim* 'stretch out', Lat. *regere* 'lead, direct, govern', etc. (Walde-P. 2.362 ff.). The adj. *aithrech* and perh. also the vbl. n. *aithrige* may be of independent origin, cf. MBr. *azrec*, Corn. *eddrek* 'regret, repentance', etym. dub.; possibly : Goth. *idreigōn* 'repent', etc. (below, 4). Pedersen 1.177, 2.594, Anm.

W. *edifarhau*, with adj. *edifar* 'penitent, sorry', etym.? Morris Jones 132.

Br. *keuz* 'regret' sb. = Corn. *cueth* 'sorrow', etym.? Pedersen 1.121 groups with Ir. *cais*, W. *cas*, Br. *kas* 'hate' (16.41), but phonetic relation? Hence for vb. 'regret', *kavout keuz* or *keuzedikaat*.

4. Goth. *idreigōn* (*sik*), ON *iðrask* (refl. with gen. of thing, later also impers. *mik iðrar*), sbs. Goth. *idreiga*, ON *iðran* 'rue, repentance', etym. dub. Feist 289. Falk-Torp 458.

Dan. *beklage*, Sw. *beklaga* 'lament, deplore, complain' (fr. NHG *beklagen* id.), but esp. 'regret'.

Dan. *angre* (pers. and impers.), Sw. *ångra* (pers., impers. and refl.) : ON *angra* 'anger, vex', impers. 'be grieved', fr. *angr* 'trouble, affliction' (hence NE *anger*, cf. 16.42).

OE *hrēowan* (impers. strong vb., pret. *hrēaw*), ME *reowe, rewe*, etc. (pers. and impers.), NE *rue*, OHG *hriuwan* (pers. and impers., strong vb. pret. *hrau*),

MHG *riuwen* (impers. and refl.), OHG *hriuwōn, -en,* MHG *riuwen* (pers. and refl., weak vb.), NHG *(be)reuen,* Du. *berouwen,* also OE *hrēowsian,* OHG *riuwisōn* (pers.) : ON *hryggja* 'grieve', *hryggr* 'grieved, sad', root connection dub. Walde-P. 1.180. Falk-Torp 917.

OE *ofþyncan* (impers. *mē ofþincþ* 'penetet', Aelfric), ME *ofthinke,* cpd. of *of-* orig. 'off, away', but often as here denoting opposition, and OE *þyncan* 'seem, seem fit' (NE *methinks*). NED s.v.

ME, NE *repent* (ME and older NE also refl. and impers.), fr. Fr. *repentir* (above, 2).

NE *regret* (this sense since middle of 15th cent.), ME *regrete, regrate* 'lament, feel sorrow' (at loss, death, etc.), fr. OFr. *regreter, regrater* 'lament someone's death', Fr. *regretter* (above, 2).

Du. *betreuren,* also 'mourn', cpd. of *treuren* 'mourn for, grieve over' : *treurig,* NHG *traurig* 'sad', etc. (16.36).

NHG *bedauern,* fr. MHG *(be)tūren, tiuren* (impers.) 'be expensive, cost too much' (: *tiure* 'dear, expensive', 11.91), whence *mich bedauert* 'it pains me', later pers. *ich bedauere* 'lament, deplore, am sorry'. Kluge-G. 97. Weigand-H. 1.174.

5. Lith. *apgailauti, gailėti-s (gailauti, gailėti* mostly 'mourn, pity') : adv. *gaila* '(it is) a pity', adj. *gailus* 'pitiful, doleful' also 'biting, sharp', these perh. : OHG *geil,* OE *gāl* 'wanton'. Walde-P. 1.634.

Lett. *nuožēluot,* cpd. of *žēluot* 'pity' (16.35).

6. ChSl. *(ras)kajati sę,* SCr. *kaja'i se,* Boh. *káti se,* Pol. *(roz)kajać się,* Russ. *(ras)kajat'sja,* with nonrefl. forms ChSl. *o-kajati* 'lament', SCr. *kajati* 'avenge', Russ. *kajat'* 'admonish' : Skt. *ci-* 'avenge, punish', Av. *či-* 'repay, atone', Grk. τίνω 'pay, atone', ποινή 'punishment', etc. Berneker 469. Walde-P. 1.508 f.

SCr. *žaliti,* Boh. *želeti* (Gebauer 1.197), Pol. *żałować,* Russ. *žalet',* but ChSl. *žaliti* 'mourn, lament' : SCr. *žalost,* etc. 'grief, sorrow' (16.32).

Boh. *litovati,* fr. *lítý* 'furious, fierce, cruel' (*je mi líto* 'I am sorry'), see under *lítost* 'pity' (16.35).

7. Skt. *anu-tap-,* cpd. of *tap-,* lit. 'be hot, burn', but also in fig. sense 'suffer pain'. Similarly *anu-çuc-,* cpd. of *çuc-* 'flame, glow', fig. 'suffer violent pain, feel sorrow', etc.

16.35 PITY (sb.)

Grk.	ἔλεος, οἶκτος	Goth.	*armaiō, armahairtei*	Lith.	*pasigailėjimas, susimilimas*
NG	ἔλεος, οἶκτος (both lit.)	ON	*miskunn*	Lett.	*žēlastība*
Lat.	*misericordia*	Dan.	*medlidenhed, medynk*	ChSl.	*milostĭ, milosrŭdĭje*
It.	*pietà*	Sw.	*medlidande, medömkan*	SCr.	*smilovanje, sažaljenje, milosrđe*
Fr.	*pitié*	OE	*mildheortnyss*	Boh.	*útrpnost, lítost*
Sp.	*piedad*	ME	*pite(e), mildhertness*	Pol.	*litość, miłosierdzie*
Rum.	*milă*	NE	*pity*	Russ.	*žalost', sožalenie*
Ir.	*airchissecht*	Du.	*medelijden, meedoogen*	Skt.	*dayā-, karuṇā-, kṛpā-,* etc.
NIr.	*truagh*	OHG	*irbarmida, miltida, miltnissa*	Av.	*mərəždika-*
W.	*tosturi, trugaredd*	MHG	*erbermede, barmunge, milde*		
Br.	*truez, trugarez*	NHG	*erbarmen, mitleid, barmherzigheit*		

Some of the words for 'pity' are specializations of 'affection, kindness, kindheartedness, love' or the like, and some, like the closely allied 'sympathy' and 'compassion', are from the notion of 'suffer with'.

Others are connected with words for 'wretched, poor' or 'harsh, cruel', which through 'miserable', etc. became 'pitiable', 'exciting pity', whence secondarily the subj. 'pity'.

Many of the words listed cover also 'mercy'.

1. Grk. ἔλεος, etym. dub. Boisacq 241.

Grk. οἶκτος, beside οἰκτρός 'pitiable', οἰκτῑρω 'pity' (whence new sb. οἰκτιρμός) : Goth. *aihtrōn* 'beg', and prob. Ir. *ar-ēgi* 'cries, out, complains'. Walde-P. 1.105. Boisacq 690.

In NG both the preceding words are lit. but familiar through use in the church. In common speech 'pity' would be most nearly expressed by the vb. λυποῦμαι 'be sorry' (cf. 16.32, 16.34), in phrases like τὸν λυποῦμαι 'I am sorry for him'. NG κρίμα (class. Grk. 'decision') is used for the obj. 'pity', as κρίμα εἶναι 'it's a pity', but not for the emotion.

2. Lat. *misericordia,* fr. *misericors, -dis* 'compassionate, pitiful', cpd. of *miser* 'wretched, miserable' and *cor* 'heart'. Hence the learned words in Romance, It., Sp. *misericordia,* Fr. *miséricorde* 'mercy, compassion'.

It. *pietà,* Fr. *pitié,* Sp. *piedad,* fr. Lat. *pietās, -tātis* 'piety, affection, duty', late 'gentleness, kindness, pity', fr. *pīus* 'pious, affectionate, loyal, etc.', outside connections dub. Walde-P. 2.69 f. Ernout-M. 773.

Rum. *milă,* fr. the Slavic, cf. ChSl. *milŭ* 'pitiable' (below, 6). Tiktin 980.

3. Ir. *airchissecht,* fr. *ar-cessi* 'pities' : W. *arbed(u)* 'spare, save', Br. *erbed(i)* 'spare, manage', etym. dub. Walde-P. 1.513. Pedersen 2.486.

NIr. *truagh,* W. *trugaredd,* Br. *truez, trugarez,* fr. Ir. *trōg, truag,* W., MBr. *tru* 'miserable', perh. : Grk. τρῡ́χω 'wear out, waste, distress', τρῦχος 'shred'. Pedersen 1.101. Walde-P. 1.732. Or : Grk. στρεύγομαι 'be exhausted, worn out, suffer pain'. Thurneysen, Gram. 40. Here also Ir. NIr. *trōcaire* 'mercy', cpd. with root of *carim* 'love'. Pedersen 1.418. Thurneysen, Gram. 87.

W. *tosturi,* fr. *tostur* 'pitiable', fr. *tost* 'hard, severe, cruel', fr. Lat. *tostus* 'roasted, burned', but deriv. influenced by Lat. *tortūra* 'torment'. Loth, Mots lat. 211 f.

4. Goth. *armaiō,* fr. *arms* 'pitiable' = OHG *arm,* OE *earm* 'miserable, poor, etc.' (cf. 11.52). Hence adj. cpds. Goth. *armahairts,* OHG *armherzi, barmherzi (bi-arm-),* MHG *barmherze(c),* NHG *barmherzig* 'compassionate', whence sbs. Goth. *armahairtei,* MHG *barmherze, barmherze(c)heit,* NHG *barmherzigkeit* 'pity, compassion' (Christian imitations of the Lat. *misericors, misericordia,* above, 2), and vbs. Goth. *arman sik,* OHG *irbarmēn (ir-bi-armēn),* MHG *(er)barmen,* NHG *(sich) erbarmen* 'have pity', whence OHG *irbarmida,* MHG *erbermede, (er)barmung,* etc., NHG *erbarmen* (infin. as sb.). Weigand-H. 1.158 f., 455 f. Kluge-G., 40, 135.

ON *miskunn* (Dan., Sw. *miskund,* biblical), cpd. of the Gmc. neg. and pejorative prefix *mis(s)-* and **kunþi* : ON *kenna* 'know, feel', but also 'lay to one's charge, impute', hence lit. 'non-accusation'. Falk-Torp 724.

Dan. *medynk,* Sw. *medömkan,* cpd. of *med* 'with' and Dan. *ynk* 'distress', Sw. *ömkan* 'compassion' : Dan. *ynke* 'regret', refl. 'complain', Sw. *ömka* 'commiserate, pity', ON *aumka* 'bewail, complain', refl. 'pity', fr. ON *aumr* 'miserable, unhappy', etc. Falk-Torp 1409, 1420.

OE *mildheortnyss,* ME *mildhertness,* fr. OE *mildheort* 'kindhearted, gentle, merciful' (OHG *milt-herzi* 'misericors'), cpd. of *milde* 'gentle, mild, merciful', and *heort* 'heart'.

ME *pite(e),* NE *pity,* fr. OFr. *pitet, pité,* Fr. *pitié* (above, 2).

Du. *medelijden* (MLG *medeliden, medelidinge* > Dan. *medlid(n)ing, medlidelse,* now *medlidenhed,* Sw. *medlidande*), MHG *mitelīdunge, mitelīden,* NHG *mitleiden* (Luther), now *mitleid,* cpd. of *mit* 'with' and Du. *lijden,* MHG *līden,* NHG *leiden* 'suffer' (cf. 16.32), orig. 'sympathy', whence 'compassion, pity'. Translation of Lat. *compassiō,* this of Grk. συμπάθεια. Falk-Torp 707. Kluge-G. 394. Weigand-H. 2.196 f.

Du. *meedoogen,* cpd. of *mede* 'with', and *doogen* (now only dial.), MDu. *dogen* 'endure, bear, suffer' : OS *adōgian* 'endure, suffer', OE *gedīegan* 'bear, overcome', caus. to OS *dōg,* OE *dēag,* Goth. *daug* 'is good, avails', etc. Falk-Torp 177, 163.

OHG *miltida, miltnissa,* MHG *milde,* etc., fr. OHG *milti,* etc. 'friendly, gracious, generous', etc. = OE *milde,* etc. (cf. above), ON *mildr* 'mild, gentle, graceful', etc. Walde-P. 2.289.

5. Lith. *pasigailėjimas,* fr. *pasigailėti* 'take pity on', perfect. of *gailėti(-s)* 'pity, regret' (16.34).

Lith. *susimilimas, susimylėjimas,* fr. *susimilti, susimylėti* 'have pity' : Lith. *mylėti* 'love', *mielas* 'dear', etc. (16.27).

Lett. *žēlastība* (adj. *žēlīgs,* vb. *žēluot*), fr. *žēlas* 'grief, sorrow', adv. *žēl* '(it's) a pity', this fr. Russ. *žal'* id. : Russ. *žalost',* etc. (below, 6). Mühl.-Endz. 4.805.

6. ChSl. *milostĭ,* SCr. *smilovanje,* fr. *milŭ* 'piteous', in modern Slavic also 'dear' (16.27). Berneker 2.57 f.

ChSl. *milosrŭdĭje,* SCr. *milosrđe,* Pol. *miłosierdzie,* fr. the adj. ChSl. *milosrŭdŭ* 'piteous', fr. *milŭ* 'piteous' and words for 'heart' (4.44), semantic borrowing fr. Goth. *armahairts,* Lat. *misericors* (above, 2, 4). Meillet, Études 385.

SCr. *sažaljenje,* Russ. *sožalenie, žalost'* : SCr., Boh. *žalost* 'grief, sorrow', etc. (16.32).

Boh. *útrpnost,* fr. *(u)trpěti* 'suffer, endure', cf. *u-trpení* 'pain, suffering', etc. (16.31).

Boh. *lítost,* Pol. *litość,* old *ljutość* = ChSl. *lju'ostĭ* 'harshness' (Supr.), Russ. *ljutost'* 'cruelty', etc., fr. ChSl. *ljutŭ* 'harsh, cruel, frightful, pitiable' (Boh. *lítý,* Pol. *luty,* etc.), with development through the obj. 'pity'. Cf. Boh. *je mi líto,* Pol. *lito mi,* like NHG *es tut mir leid* 'I am sorry'. Berneker 759 f. Brückner 300.

7. Skt. *dayā-,* fr. *day-* 'divide, allot', fig. 'have compassion on, sympathize'.

Skt. *karuṇā-,* fr. *karuṇa-* 'doleful, pitiable', perh. : OE *hrēowan,* OHG *hriuwan* 'grieve, vex', impers. 'regret', etc. (16. 34). Walde-P. 1.480.

Skt. *kṛpā-* : *kṛp-* 'lament, implore', Lat. *crepere* 'rattle, creak', ON *hrafn,* OE *hræfn* 'raven', etc. Uhlenbeck 64. Walde-P. 1.415 f. Walde-H. 1.290.

Av. *mərəždika-, marždika-,* also adj. 'compassionate' (Skt. *mṛḍīka-* 'favor') : *mərəžda* 'pardon', Skt. *mṛḍ-* 'be gracious, pardon'. Walde-P. 2.298. Barth. 1175.

16.36 SAD

Grk.	λυπούμενος, δύσθῡμος, etc.	Goth.	*gaurs*	Lith.	*liudnas, nuliudęs*
NG	λυπημένος, κατηφής	ON	*hryggr, dapr*	Lett.	*bēdīgs, skumīgs*
Lat.	*trīstis*	Dan.	*sørgmodig, bedrøvet*	ChSl.	*pečalĭnŭ, skrŭbę, priskrŭbĭnŭ*
It.	*triste*	Sw.	*sorgsen, bedrövad*	SCr.	*žalostan, tužan*
Fr.	*triste*	OE	*unrōt, drēorig*	Boh.	*smutný*
Sp.	*triste*	ME	*sad, drery*	Pol.	*smutny*
Rum.	*trist, mîhnit*	NE	*sad*	Russ.	*pečal'nyj*
Ir.	*bronach, dubach*	Du.	*treurig, droevig*	Skt.	*viṣaṇṇa-, mlāna-*
NIr.	*bronach, doilgheasach*	OHG	*gitruobit, trūrag*	Av.	*ašāta-*
W.	*trist, athrist*	MHG	*trūrec, trüebe, betruobt*		
Br.	*trist, teñval*	NHG	*traurig, betrübt, trübe*		

In many languages the words for 'sad' are simply derivs. of those for 'grief, sorrow' (16.32) and so mean lit. 'grieving' or 'sorrowful'. But in others the common words for 'sad' are of quite different origin, based on such diverse notions as 'downcast', 'sated', 'troubled', 'dark', 'heavy', 'faded', 'sitting apart'.

1. Grk. λῡπούμενος, pple. of λῡπέομαι 'grieve', act. λῡπέω 'cause grief' : λῡ́πη 'grief' (16.32). NG λυπημένος, fr. perf. mid. pple. λελῡπημένος, also περί-λυπος 'very sad'.

Grk. δύσ-θῡμος, cpd. of δυσ- 'ill' and θῡμός 'soul, spirit' (16.11).

Grk. δύσ-φρων, cpd. of δυσ- 'ill' and -φρων as in σώ-φρων 'wise', etc. (: φρήν as seat of thought and feeling, 17.11), hence 'ill-disposed' and also 'sad'.

Grk. κατηφής 'with downcast eyes', also fig. 'downcast, dejected, sad' and so in NG, cpd. of κατά 'down' and the root of ἅπτω 'fasten, touch', sb. ἁφή 'touch', etc. Walde-P. 1.198. Boisacq 421 f.

2. Lat. *trīstis* (> It. Fr., Sp. *triste;* late *trīstus* > Rum. *trist;* REW 8918), etym. dub. Walde-P. 1.754 (as orig. 'grim' or the like : OE *þrīste,* OHG *drīsti* 'bold' in both good and bad sense). Ernout-M. 1058 ("sans étymologie").

Rum. *mîhnit,* fr. *mîhni* 'grieve', cf. *mîhnire* 'grief' (16.32).

3. Ir. *bronach,* fr. *bron* 'grief'.

Ir. *dubach,* fr. *dube* 'grief'.

NIr. *doilgheasach,* fr. *doilgheas* 'grief'.

W., Br. *trist* (W. also *athrist* with intensive *a-*), fr. Lat. *trīstis.* Loth, Mots lat. 213.

Br. *teñval,* orig. 'dark' (: Ir. *temel* 'darkness', 1.62), hence 'somber, sad'. Cf. the use of Fr., NE *sombre,* orig. 'under a shadow'.

4. Goth. *gaurs* : *gauriþa, gaurei* 'grief', etc.

ON *hryggr* : OE *hrēow* 'regret, sorrow', etc. (16.34).

ON *dapr* ('heavy, slow', and 'sad') : OHG *tapfer* 'firm, weighty, durable' (NHG *tapfer* 'brave'), and prob. ChSl. *debelŭ* 'stout', Russ. dial. *dobolyj* 'strong', OPruss. *debīkan* 'big', etc. Walde-P. 1.850. Falk-Torp 1248. Berneker 182.

Dan. *sørgmodig,* cpd. of *sørge* 'grieve' (fr. *sorg* 'grief') and *modig,* fr. *mod* 'heart, courage'.

Sw. *sorgsen,* fr *sorg* 'grief'.

OE *unrōt,* neg. of *rōt* 'cheerful, glad', more often 'noble, excellent' : ChSl. *radŭ* 'glad, willing', *radostĭ* 'joy', etc. (16.22).

OE *drēorig* (also 'gory, bloody', and 'cruel'), ME *drery* (NE *dreary* 'dismal, gloomy'), OHG *trūrag,* MHG *trūrec,* NHG *traurig,* Du. *treurig* (Du. *t* fr. HG, or WGmc. init. variants?), with vbs. OHG *trūrēn, drūrēn,* MHG *trūren,* NHG *trauern* 'grieve, mourn' : OE *drēosan,*

Goth. *driusan* 'fall', OHG *trōren* 'drip', OE *drēor* 'blood, gore', MHG *trōr* 'dew, rain, blood', outside connections dub., but semantic development clear—'sad' fr. 'downcast, drooping', and 'gore, gory', fr. 'drip'. Walde-P. 1.873. Weigand-H. 2.1064. Franck-v. W. 708.

ME, NE *sad*, fr. OE *sæd* 'sated' : Goth. *saþs*, OHG *sat* 'full, sated', Lat. *satis* 'enough', etc. Semantic development through ME 'steadfast, firm, serious, grave'. NED s.v.

MHG *trüebe*, NHG *trübe*, Du. *droef*, *droevig*, orig. 'troubled, turbid', as OHG *truobi*, OE *drōf*, etc., beside vbs. Goth. *drōbjan*, OE *drēfan*, OHG *truoban* 'trouble' : ME *draf* 'dregs, refuse' (NE *draff*, cf. NED), MHG, NHG *treber* 'grains, huskş', all prob. fr. a parallel extension of the root in ON *dreggjar* 'dregs', Grk. ταράσσω 'trouble', etc.; hence the vbs. Du. *bedroeven*, MLG *bedroven* (> Dan. *bedrøve*, Sw. *bedröva*, with pples. *bedrøvet*, *bedrövad* 'sad'), OHG *gitruoben*, MHG *be-*, *ge-trüeben*, NHG *betrüben* 'trouble, sadden', with pples. OHG *gitruobit*, MHG *betruobt*, NHG *betrübt* 'sad'. Walde-P. 1.856. Falk-Torp 57. Feist 126. Weigand-H. 2.1079.

5. Lith. *liudnas*, with vb. *liusti* 'be sad, grieve', perfect. *nuliusti*, pple. *nuliudęs* 'sad' : ChSl. *ludŭ*, SCr. *lud* 'foolish', Russ. *ludit'* 'deceive', Goth. *liutei* 'deceit, hypocrisy', *lutōn* 'deceive', ON *luta*, OE *lūtan* 'bow, fall'. 'Sad' prob. as 'downcast, dejected'. Walde-P. 2.416.

Lett. *bēdīgs*, fr. *bēda* 'grief'.

Lett. *skumīgs* : *skumjas* 'grief'.

6. ChSl. *pečalĭnŭ* (with *byti* for λῡπέομαι), Russ. *pečal'nyj*, fr. ChSl. *pečalĭ*, Russ. *pečal'* 'grief'.

ChSl. *skrŭbę* (renders λυπούμενος), pple. of *skrŭběti* (λυπέομαι), also *priskrŭbĭnŭ* (περίλυπος) : *skrŭbĭ* 'grief'.

SCr. *žalostan*, fr. *žalost* 'grief'.

SCr. *tužan*, fr. *tuga* 'grief'.

Boh. *smutný*, Pol. *smutny* : Boh. *zármutek*, *smutek* 'grief'.

7. Skt. *viṣaṇṇa-*, pple. of *vi-ṣad-* 'be dejected, despond', lit. 'sit apart', cpd. of *sad-* 'sit'.

Skt. *mlāna-*, lit. 'faded, withered', pple. of *mlā-* 'fade, wither'.

Av. *ašāta-*, neg. of *šāta-* 'glad' (16.23).

16.37 CRY, WEEP

Grk.	*κλαίω*	Goth.	*grētan*	Lith.	*verkti*
NG	*κλαίω*	ON	*grāta*	Lett.	*raudāt*
Lat.	*flēre, plōrāre*	Dan.	*græde*	ChSl.	*plakati (sę)*
It.	*piangere*	Sw.	*gråta*	SCr.	*plakati*
Fr.	*pleurer*	OE	*wēpan, grētan, grēotan*	Boh.	*plakati*
Sp.	*llorar*	ME	*wepe, grete, crie*	Pol.	*płakać*
Rum.	*plînge*	NE	*cry, weep*	Russ.	*plakat'*
Ir.	*cīim*	Du.	*weenen*	Skt.	*rud-*
NIr.	*goilim*	OHG	*wuofan, riozan, weinōn*	Av.	*(rud-, garəz-)*
W.	*wylo*	MHG	*weinen, riezen, wüefen*		
Br.	*gouela*	NHG	*weinen*		

Most of the words for 'cry, weep', as expressive of pain or grief, are like NE *cry* (the usual spoken word) from words meaning 'cry' in wider sense, 'cry out, shout, scream, wail, groan'. Some show a shift from a different expression of the same emotion, namely 'beat' (the breast, etc.), as in Romance and Slavic, prob.

Lat. *plōrare*. Cf. also Grk. κόπτομαι sometimes 'bewail', mid. of κόπτω 'strike' (cf. LS s.v. II. 2).

Some derivatives of words for 'tear' (16.38) are used for 'shed tears, weep', as Grk. δακρύω, Lat. *lacrimāre* (> It. *lacrimare*, etc.), Lith. *ašaroti*; but these are not the common words.

1. IE **reud-*, an extension of a simpler **reu-* in verbs meaning 'make a loud noise', like 'roar, bellow, howl', etc., prob. of imitative origin. Walde-P. 2.349 ff.

OHG *riozan*, MHG *riezen* (OE *rēotan* rarely 'weep', mostly 'lament'), Lett. *raudāt* (Lith. *raudoti* 'wail, lament'); Skt., Av. *rud-* : Lat. *rūdere* 'roar, bellow, bray', ON *rauta* 'roar'.

2. Grk. κλαίω (*κλάϝ-ιω, cf. aor. ἔκλαυσα), etym. dub., possibly *κλαυ- fr. **klə-u-*, as extension of the root in καλέω 'call', κέλαδος 'noise', etc. Alb. *kl'an'*, *k'an'* 'weep' (in current spelling *qaj*), taken by G. Meyer as cognate (cf. Walde-P. 1.490, Boisacq 465) is more prob. a loanword (cf. NG 3sg. κλαίει, 3pl. κλαίνε).

3. Lat. *flēre*, prob. fr. **bhlē-* beside **bhel-* in OE *bellan* 'bellow, bark, roar', OHG *bellan* 'bark, bay', ON *belja* 'bellow', etc. Ernout-M. 368. Walde-H. 1.516.

Lat. *plōrāre* (> Fr. *pleurer*, Sp. *llorar*), more common than *flēre* in late Lat. (e.g. Peregrinatio), in earliest use 'cry aloud' (cf. *implōrare* 'implore'), perh. : *plōdere* (*plaudere*) 'beat, clap the hands' (**plō-ro-*, **plō-d-*) : Lith. *plōti* 'clap the hands'. Cf. the development in Lat. *plangere*, etc. (below). Specht, KZ 66.241 ff.

It. *piangere*, Rum. *plînge* (= Fr. *plaindre* 'lament, pity'), fr. Lat. *plangere*, orig. 'beat', whence esp. 'beat the breast', etc. as sign of grief, and then 'lament, bewail', fr. a root **plāg-*, **plāk-* in Grk. πλήσσω 'beat, strike', πληγή 'blow', Lith. *plakti* 'beat, punish', OE *flōcan* 'clap in applause' (OHG *fluohhōn* 'curse'), and, with the same semantic development as in Italic, Goth. *flōkan* 'bewail' (Lk. 8.52 *faiflōkun þō* = ἐκόπτοντο αὐτήν), ChSl. *plakati* (*sę*) 'lament, weep', etc. (below, 7). Walde-P. 2.91 f. Ernout-M. 775.

4. Ir. *cīim*, etym. dub., perh. as orig. 'wrinkle the nose' : Lith. *šieptis* 'grin', *šypsotis* 'smile' (12.25). Walde-P. 1.364. Stokes 75.

NIr. *goilim*, cf. MIr. *gol* 'weeping', prob. as orig. 'cry out' : OE *galan* 'sing', *giellan* 'cry out' (NE *yell*), etc. (Walde-P. 1.628, without these Ir. forms). Not : Lith. *gėla*, OHG *qual* 'pain', etc. (Walde-P. 1.690) with init. *gʷ*, which would give Ir. *b*.

W. *wylo* (*gwylo*), Br. *gouela*, prob. with unetym. *g-* (cf. Pedersen 1.321, 435), fr. Lat. *ēiulāre* 'wail, lament'. Lloyd-Jones, BBCS 2.298.

5. Goth. *grētan*, ON *grāta*, Dan. *græde*, Sw. *gråta*, OE *grētan* (Angl. = **grǣtan*), ME *grete* (NE dial. *greet*) : (caus.) ON *grœta* 'make weep', OE *grētan* 'speak to, call upon, hail, approach', OHG *gruozzen* 'address, approach', perh. fr. the root in Skt. *hrād-* 'sound' (or the latter : Ir. *ad-glādur* 'address', etc. with IE *l*?). Walde-P. 1.659. Falk-Torp 339. Feist 221.

OE *grēotan* (and in part ME *grete*, etc., entered above), OS *griotan*, etym. dub., possibly : W. *griddfan*, *gruddfan* 'groan', but root connection? Walde-P. 1.650. Zupitza, Gutt. 176. NED s.v. *greet*, vb.[2].

OE *wēpan*, ME *wepe*, NE *weep*, OHG *wuofan*, MHG *wüefen* = Goth. *wōpjan* 'cry out, call', ON *œpa* 'cry out, scream' (NIcel. sometimes also 'cry' of children) : ChSl. *vabiti* 'call, summon'. Walde-P. 1.217. Falk-Torp 1408.

ME *crie*, NE *cry* 'cry out, shout', fr.

Fr. *crier* (18.13), also 'cry' = 'weep'. NED s.v. *cry*, vb. 9, 10.

OHG *weinōn*, MHG, NHG *weinen*, Du. *weenen* : OE *wānian* 'lament', ON *veina* 'wail', derivs. of the interj. OHG, MHG *wē*, OE *wā*, ON *vei*, Goth. *wai* 'woe', as expressive of pain, sorrow, etc. A parallel deriv. is ON *vœla*, *veila* 'wail' (> ME *weile*, NE *wail*). Walde-P. 1.213.

6. Lith. *verkti* : *urkti* 'growl, snarl', Boh. *vrčeti* id., *vrkati* 'purr, coo', Russ. *vorčat'* 'growl, snarl', etc., prob. of imitative origin. Walde-P. 1.284 (top). Trautmann 353.

Lett. *raudāt*, above, 1.

7. ChSl. *plakati* (refl. in Gospels), etc., general Slavic, see under It. *piangere*, etc. (above, 3).

8. Skt., Av. *rud-* (but Av. *rud-* 'moan' of cattle and daevic beings, Barth. 1492), above, 1.

Av. *garəz-* ('moan, bemoan', Osset. *γärzun* 'groan'; Barth. 516) : Skt. *garh-* 'blame, reproach', OHG *klagōn*, NHG *klagen* 'complain', etc., fr. a guttural extension of the root in W. *galw* 'cry out, call', etc. Walde-P. 1.539.

16.38 TEAR (sb.)

Grk.	*δάκρυ*	Goth.	*tagr*	Lith.	*ašara*
NG	*δάκρυ*	ON	*tār*	Lett.	*asara*
Lat.	*lacrima*	Dan.	*taare*	ChSl.	*slĭza*
It.	*lacrima*	Sw.	*tår*	SCr.	*suza*
Fr.	*larme*	OE	*tēar, teagor*	Boh.	*slza*
Sp.	*lágrima*	ME	*tere*	Pol.	*łza*
Rum.	*lacrimă*	NE	*tear*	Russ.	*sleza*
Ir.	*dēr*	Du.	*traan*	Skt.	*açru-, bāṣpa-*
NIr.	*deor*	OHG	*zahar, trahan*	Av.	*asru-*
W.	*deigryn*	MHG	*zaher, trahen*		
Br.	*dåeraouenn*	NHG	*träne (zähre)*		

The usual words for 'tear', except the Slavic, belong to a group which, while showing some peculiar variations, points clearly to the existence of a distinctive IE word for 'tear'.

1. IE **dakru-*, also **draku-* and **akru-*, relations variously explained. Walde-P. 1.769. Walde-H. 1.746. Ernout-M. 516. Pedersen 1.124. Falk-Torp 1239.

Grk. δάκρυ, pl. δάκρυα, whence new sg. δάκρυον; OLat. *dacruma*, Lat. *lacruma*, *lacrima* (> Romance words); Ir. *dēr*, NIr. *deor*, *dēar*, W. (old) *deigr*, pl. *dagrau*, OBr. *dacr*, Br. *daer*, pl. *daerou*, new sgs. W. *deigryn*, Br. *daeraouenn*; ON *tār*, OE *tēar*, OHG *zahar*, etc. (NHG *zähre*, poet.), with gramm. change Goth. *tagr*, OE *teagor*, also OHG *trahan*, *drahan*, MHG *trahen* (and *traher* by confusion with *zaher*), NHG *träne*, OS pl. *trahni*, Du. *traan*; Lith. *ašara*, Lett. *asara*, Skt. *açru-*, Av. *asru-* (in *asrū-azan-* 'shedding tears'), Toch. *ākär*.

2. ChSl. *slĭza*, etc., general Slavic, etym.? Brückner 316 compares Grk. λύζω 'hiccough, sob', Ir. *slucim* 'swallow', MHG *slucken* 'swallow', etc. (Walde-P. 2.711).

3. Skt. *bāṣpa-* (also 'steam'), prob. a MIndic form of **varṣman-* : *vrṣ-* 'rain', sb. *varṣa-* (1.75). Tedesco, Language 22.184 ff.

16.39 GROAN (vb.)

Grk.	*στένω, στενάζω*	Goth.	*swōgatjan*	Lith.	*stenėti*
NG	*στενάζω*	ON	*stynja*	Lett.	*stenēt*
Lat.	*gemere*	Dan.	*stønne*	ChSl.	*stenati*
It.	*gemere*	Sw.	*stöna*	SCr.	*stenjati*
Fr.	*gémir*	OE	*grānian, stenan*	Boh.	*stenati*
Sp.	*gemir*	ME	*grone*	Pol.	*jęczeć, stękać*
Rum.	*geme*	NE	*groan*	Russ.	*stonat'*
Ir.	*cnetim*	Du.	*steunen, stenen*	Skt.	*kūj-*
NIr.	*osnuighim*	OHG	*sūftōn*	Av.	. . . .
W.	*griddfan, ochain, ocheneidio*	MHG	*siufzen, siuften*		
Br.	*hirvoudi*	NHG	*stöhnen, ächzen*		

The majority of the vbs. for 'groan', as expressive of pain or grief, are related to others used for various loud sounds, as 'roar, yell, thunder', etc., from which they have become specialized. A few are derived from characteristic interjections. But in the case of Lat. *gemere* the feeling of distress must have been antecedent to its vocal expression.

Some of the words for 'groan' cover also the milder 'sigh', as Grk. στένω, στενάζω (so still in NG), Lat. *gemere*; and in a few 'sigh' is the earlier sense. In such cases the similarity of the emotion has overcome the difference in its expression, with resulting extension of 'groan' to 'sigh' or conversely.

For to 'sigh', expressive of grief (in part also longing) is actually to 'breathe heavily', and most of the specific words for this notion are in fact derived from those for 'breathe' (4.51). Thus Lat. *su-spīrāre* (> Fr. *soupirer*, etc.); NIr. *osnuighim*, W. *ocheneidio*, etc. (below, 3); Lith. *dūsauti*; ChSl. *vŭz-dychati*, Russ. *vzdychat'*, etc., general Slavic; Skt. *çvas-* and cpds. Cf. also NHG *seufzen*, Du. *zuchten*, Dan. *sukke*, etc. (below, 4). OE *sīcan* (ME *sighen*, NE *sigh* re-formed fr. pple.; NED s.v.), is of unknown root connection.

1. IE **sten-* in words for loud noises, esp. 'roar, thunder', or 'groan'. Walde-P. 2.626. Falk-Torp 1199. Franck-v. W. 664.

Grk. στένω, στενάζω; ON *stynja*, Dan. *stønne*, Sw. *stöna*, OE *stenan*, MLG *stenen*, Du. *stenen*, MLG *stonen*, Du. *steunen*, NHG (fr. LG) *stöhnen*; Lith. *stenėti*, Lett. *stenēt*; ChSl. *stenati*, etc., general Slavic; cf. Skt. *stan-* 'roar, thunder', and without *s-* Lat. *tonāre* 'thunder', OE *þunor*, etc. 'thunder'.

2. Lat. *gemere* (> Romance words), prob. through 'be full, oppressed' or 'heavy-hearted' (cf. Umbr. *gomia* 'gravidas') : Grk. γέμω 'be full', ChSl. *žĭmą*, *žęti* 'press', etc. Walde-P. 1.572. Ernout-M. 414 (dubious of this etym.). Walde-H. 1.589.

3. Ir. *cnetim*, etym.?

NIr. *osnuighim* (cf. MIr. *osnad*, MW *ucheneit*, Br. *huanad* 'a sigh'), W. *ocheneidio* (*o* by popular connection with *ochain*, below; cf. Lloyd-Jones, BBCS 1.6), all orig. 'sigh', fr. **ud-eks-an-* : Goth. *us-anan* 'breathe out', Skt. *an-* 'breathe', etc. Walde-P. 1.57. Pedersen 2.295, 455 f.

W. *ochain*, fr. the interjection *och*. Cf. NHG *ächzen*, below, 4.

W. *griddfan* (*gruddfan*), etym. dub., possibly : OE *grēotan*, OS *griotan* 'weep' (16.37). Zupitza, Gutt. 176. Walde-P. 1.650.

Br. *hirvoudi*, with sb. *hirvoud*, cpd. of *hir* 'long' and *boud* 'humming (sound)'.

4. Goth. *swōgatjan, gaswōgjan*, both for στενάζω, also *ufswōgjan* for ἀναστενάζω : OE *swōgan, swēgan*, OS *swōgan* 'make a noise, rush, roar', *swēg* 'sound', etc. (15.44).

ON *stynja*, OE *stenan*, etc., above, 1.

OE *grānian*, ME *grone*, NE *groan* : OHG *grīnan*, MHG *grīnen* 'snarl, mutter, spread the mouth' (in laughing or weeping, NHG *greinen*), NIcel. *grīna* 'open the mouth, stare', further NHG *grinzen* 'grin', fr. a root **ghrei-* 'stand open'(?), whence through 'open the mouth' both 'grin' and 'groan'. Falk-Torp 348. Kluge-G. 216. Weigand-H. 1.764.

OHG *sūftōn*, MHG *siuften, siufzen*, the usual renderings for Lat. *gemere*, NHG *seufzen* mostly 'sigh', as MLG *suchten* (Dan. *sukke*, Sw. *sucka*), Du. *zuchten* : OE *sēofian* 'lament, complain of', prob. as 'suck, draw in the breath', fr. the root of OHG *sūfan*, OE *sūpan* 'sip (a fluid)', and OHG *sūf* 'soup, broth', etc. Walde-P. 2.469. Falk-Torp 1203. Weigand-H. 2.856.

NHG *ächzen*, MHG *achzen, echzen*, intens. to MHG *achen* 'say *ach*'. Weigand-H. 1.21.

5. Lith. *stenėti*, ChSl. *stenati* (Supr.; in the Gospels στενάζω is rendered by *vydychati* 'sigh'), etc., general Balto-Slavic, above, 1.

Pol. *jęczeć* (beside sb. *jęk* 'groan, moan') = Boh. *ječeti* 'roar' (sb. *jek* 'roar'), SCr. *ječati* 'sound, yell' (sb. *jek* 'sound, echo'), etc., these prob. : Grk. ὀγκάομαι 'bray' (> Lat. *oncāre, uncāre* 'bray, roar'), Ir. *ong* 'tribulation, moan', MLG *anken* 'groan, sigh', etc. Berneker 267 f. Brückner 208.

6. Skt. *kūj-* 'hum', etc., also 'groan' (cf. BR s.v.), beside *kū-* 'cry out, moan', etc. : Grk. κωκύω 'shriek, wail', Lith. *kaukti* 'howl', etc., all of imitative origin. Walde-P. 1.331.

16.41 HATE (sb.)

Grk.	μῖσος, ἔχθρα	Goth.	*fijaþwa*	Lith.	*neapykanta*
NG	μῖσος, ἔχθρα	ON	*hatr*	Lett.	*(ie)naids*
Lat.	*odium*	Dan.	*had*	ChSl.	*nenavistĭ*
It.	*odio*	Sw.	*hat*	SCr.	*mržnja*
Fr.	*haine*	OE	*hete, hatung*	Boh.	*nenávist*
Sp.	*odio*	ME	*hete, hate, hatrede*	Pol.	*nienawiść*
Rum.	*ură*	NE	*hate, hatred*	Russ.	*nenavist'*
Ir.	*(mis)cais*	Du.	*haat*	Skt.	*dviṣ-, dveṣa-*
NIr.	*fuath*	OHG	*haz*	Av.	*dvaēšah-*
W.	*cas, casineb*	MHG	*haz*		
Br.	*kas, kasoni*	NHG	*hass*		

Words for 'hate', expressing intense dislike, and the strongest opposite of 'love', show a variety of connections, as with words for 'shudder', 'smell'(?), 'loathe, revile, blame', etc., in large measure through the obj. notion 'object of repulsion'. Some are from verbs for 'hate' which mean literally 'not endure' (cf. NE colloq. *I can't bear him* or *I can't stand him = I dislike him intensely*), or 'not look upon' (with favor).

While only the nouns are given in the list, they all have corresponding verbs.

1. Grk. μῖσος (not in Hom.), with vb. μισέω (once in Hom. as 'hate the thought of' with infin. clause), etym.? Boisacq 640.

Grk. ἔχθος, with vb. ἐχθαίρω (usual words for 'hate' in Hom.), prose sb. ἔχθρα 'hatred, enmity', beside ἐχθρός 'hated, hateful, enemy' (19.52), derivs. of ἐξ 'out' through notion of 'alien' or 'exile'. Walde-P. 1.116 (with references).

2. Lat. *odium* (> It., Sp. *odio*), beside vb. *ōdī* : Arm. *ateam* 'hate', *ateli* 'hated, hostile', OE *atol* 'terrible, horrible', ON *atall* 'fierce', fr. a root **od-*, perh. ultimately the same as **od-* 'smell' in Grk. ὄζω, Lat. *odor*, etc. (15.21) through notion of 'disgust' (Lat. *odium* is also and in Plautus most frequently obj., an object of disgust, repulsion; cf. esp. Skutsch, Glotta 2.230 ff.; cf. also SCr. *mržnja*, below, 6). Walde-P. 1.174. Ernout-M. 698 (not accepting connection with *odor*, etc.).

Fr. *haine*, for *haïne*, fr. vb. *haïr*, loanword, fr. Gmc., cf. Goth. *hatjan* 'hate', etc. (below, 4). REW 4075.

Rum. *ură*, back-formation fr. vb. *urî* 'hate', this fr. Lat. *horrēre, horrēscere* 'shudder'. Cf. Alb. *urretje* 'hate' fr. the same source. REW 4185. Tiktin 1688, 1692. G. Meyer, Alb. Etym. Wtb. 459.

3. Ir. *cais* and *miscais* (cpd. with pejorative *mis-*), W. *cas*, Br. *kas*, derivs. W. *casineb*, Br. *kasoni* : Goth. *hatis*, etc. (the Gmc. group, below, 4), Grk. κῆδος 'care, anxiety, grief, mourning', Av. *sādra-* 'hurt, harm'. The orig. meaning was perh. 'care', whence both 'hate' and 'love' in Ir. *cais* (cf. 16. 27). Walde-P. 1.340. Pedersen 1.121, 2.10. Falk-Torp 370 f.

NIr. *fuath*, same word as *fuath* 'form, figure' and 'specter', with development of 'hate' through 'horror' (cf. Rum. *ură*, above, 2).

4. Goth. *hatis* (only for θυμός, ὀργή 'anger', but vbs. *hatan, hatjan* for μισέω), ON *hatr*, OE *hete*, OHG *haz*, etc., general Gmc., with corresponding vbs. Goth. *hatjan*, OE *hatian*, etc. (influence of vowel of vb. on sb. in ME, NE *hate;* OE *hatung*, fr. vb.; ME *hatereden, hatrede*, etc., NE *hatred*, cpd. with OE *rǣden* 'condition') : Ir. *cais* 'hate', etc. (above, 3).

Goth. *fijaþwa* (reg. for ἔχθρα), with vb. *fijan* (more common than *hatan, hatjan* for μισέω) = ON *fjā*, OE *fēon, fēogan*, OHG *fīēn* 'hate' (hence pples. Goth. *fijands*, OHG *fīant* 'enemy', ON *fjāndi*, OE *fēond* 'enemy, devil', NE *fiend*) : Skt. *pīy-* 'abuse, revile' and Goth. *faian* 'blame'. Walde-P. 2.9. Falk-Torp 214 f. Feist 150.

5. Lith. *neapykanta*, fr. vb. *neapkęsti* 'hate', neg. of *apkęsti* 'endure, tolerate', cpd. of *kęsti* 'suffer, bear' (cf. *kentėjimas* 'suffering' 16.31).

Lett. *(ie)naids* : Lith. *pa-niedėtas* 'despised', Goth. *ga-naitjan* 'treat shamefully', Skt. *nind-* 'blame, abuse, despise', etc. Walde-P. 2.322 f. Mühl.-Endz. 2.689.

6. ChSl. *nenavistĭ* (Supr.), fr. vb. *nenaviděti* 'hate' (reg. in Gospels for μισέω), both with corresponding Boh., Pol., Russ. forms, neg. of **na-viděti* 'look upon', cpd. of *viděti* 'see'. 'Hate' fr. 'not look upon' (with favor). Miklosich 390. Brückner 361.

SCr. *mržnja* (also SCr., Slov., Bulg. *o-mraza*), fr. vb. *mrziti* 'hate' : *mrzak* 'disgusting', ChSl. *mrŭznąti* 'loathe', and perh. ON *morkna* 'rot', W. *merydd* 'moist, damp, sluggish, lazy', etc., IE **merĝ-* beside **merk-* in Lat. *marcēre* 'wither', etc. Walde-P. 2.282. Berneker 2.80.

7. Skt. *dviṣ-, dveṣa-*, Av. *dvaēšah-, ṭbaēšah-*, with vbs. Skt. *dviṣ-*, Av. *dviš-, ṭbiš-*, fr. **dweis-* beside **dwei-* in Av. *dvaēθā-* 'threat', Grk. δέος 'fear', etc. (16.53), either with 'fear' resulting in 'hate', or both groups through a common notion of 'discord' fr. IE **dvi-*, **dwis-* 'apart, asunder' in Goth. *twisstandan* 'separate', NHG *zwist* 'discord, quarrel', etc. Walde-P. 1.817, 821. Uhlenbeck 134.

16.42 ANGER

Grk.	θυμός, ὀργή (μῆνις, χόλος)	Goth.	*þwairhei, mōþs, hatis*	Lith.	*piktumas*
NG	θυμός, ὀργή	ON	*reiði, gremi, mōðr*	Lett.	*dusmas* (pl.)
Lat.	*īra*	Dan.	*vrede*	ChSl.	*gněvŭ, jarostĭ*
It.	*collera, rabbia (ira)*	Sw.	*vrede*	SCr.	*gnjev, ljutina, srdžba*
Fr.	*colère, courroux*	OE	*wrǣþþu, irre, torn, grama*	Boh.	*hněv, zlost*
Sp.	*cólera (ira)*	ME	*angre, wrathe, ire*	Pol.	*gniew, złość*
Rum.	*mînie*	NE	*anger (wrath)*	Russ.	*gnev, serdce*
Ir.	*ferg, baran*	Du.	*toorn*	Skt.	*krodha-, kopa-, heḍa-*
NIr.	*fearg*	OHG	*zorn, gibuluht, ābulgī*	Av.	*aēšma-*, adj. *granta-*
W.	*dig, llid*	MHG	*zorn, ābulge*		
Br.	*buanegez, droug*	NHG	*zorn*		

Words for 'anger' show the most diverse connections, as with words for 'bile, gall', 'heart', 'vapor, smoke' ('ebulliation'), 'swell', 'twist', 'tear', 'crosswise', 'astray', 'rot', 'hasty', 'bad, evil', etc., the primary sense in some of the groups being doubtful. In several cases the emotion is clearly secondary to some outward expression of it, as 'make a thundering noise', 'breathe heavily, pant'.

Some of the words listed have the force of NE *wrath*, which, though once simply 'anger' (so OE, ON, etc.), is now used more specifically of 'lasting anger'.

Most of the adjectives for 'angry' are related to the nouns, but sometimes different forms are popular, as NE *mad* (orig. 'insane' 17.23; colloq. 'angry'; cf. NED s.v. 5), NHG *böse* 'bad, wicked' (16.72) and 'angry'.

1. Grk. θυμός 'soul, spirit', etc. (16.11), also 'anger' (Hom.+) and in NG reg. 'anger' with vb. θυμώνω 'make angry' and 'be angry', θυμωμένος 'angry'.

Grk. ὀργή 'mood, temperament', but esp. 'anger' (not in Hom.) : Ir. *ferg*, NIr. *fearg* 'anger', Skt. *ūrj-, ūrjā-* 'sap, juice, rich food or drink', also 'strength, vigor' (of men), primary sense of the root 'swell, ripen' as in Grk. ὀργάω 'swell, ripen' (of fruit, trees, etc.), hence also 'swell with lust', 'be excited', etc., ὀργάς 'fertile land'. Walde-P. 1.289. Boisacq 710. Cf. OHG *gibuluht* (below, 4), and Lat. *turgēre* 'swell' and colloq. 'be angry', as (*uxor*) *turget mihi* 'is angry with me', Plaut.

Grk. χόλος and χολή, orig. 'bile, gall', but also 'bitter anger' (mostly poet.) : Lat. *fel*, ON *gall*, OE *gealla*, etc. 'gall'. Walde-P. 1.624. Boisacq 1065.

Grk. μῆνις (poet.), Dor. μᾶνις 'wrath' (cf. Cret. ἔμμανις 'wroth') : μαίνομαι 'rage, be mad', μανία 'madness, rage', which, though starting fr. μαν- weak grade of IE **men-*, follows in this semantic group (cf. perh. μέμηνα vs. μέμονα 'be eager') the α/ā series of forms like φαίνω, perf. πέφηνα, Dor. πέφᾱνα. Cf. Skt. *manyu-* 'spirit, anger, rage', Av. *mainyu-* 'spirit' (of good or evil). Otherwise Walde-P. 2.233, with separation from μαίνομαι and attachment to Lat. *Mānēs, immānis*, and Schwyzer, Rh. M. 80.216 (*μᾱ-νις), both views rejected by Walde-H. 2.27.

2. Lat. *īra* (> It., Sp. *ira*, OFr. *ire* > ME, NE *ire*, all now only lit. words), Plaut. *eira*, prob. : Skt. *iṣira-* 'vigorous, strong', Skt. *iṣ-*, Av. *iš-* 'set in rapid motion', Av. *aēšma-* 'anger, rage', Lith. *aistra* 'passion' (16.13), Grk. οἶστρος 'gadfly, sting, madness', etc. Walde-P. 1.107. Ernout-M. 496. Walde-H. 1.718.

It. *collera*, Fr. *colère*, Sp. *cólera* (OFr. > ME *coler*, NE *choler*), fr. Lat. *cholera* 'a bilious disorder' (fr. Grk. χολέρα id., prob. : χολή, above), but in late Lat. also (like Grk. χολή) 'bile' and 'anger'. REW 1879. Gamillscheg 236.

It. *rabbia* 'rage' (16.43) is now, I am told, also the pop. word for 'anger'.

Fr. *courroux*, OFr. *corroz*, prob. back-formation to *courroucer* 'make angry', fr. VLat. **corruptiāre*, this fr. *corruptum*, pple. of *corrumpere* 'destroy, ruin'. REW 2261 f. Bloch 1.185. Gamillscheg 266. Wartburg 2.1235 f.

Sp. adj. *enfadado* 'angry' (in common use in contrast to sb. *cólera*), pple. of *enfadar* 'vex', deriv. of Fr. *fade* fr. VLat. **fatidus* beside *fatuus* 'stupid'. REW 3223. Ernout-M. 337.

Rum. *mînie*, fr. Grk. μανία 'rage' (above, 1). Tiktin 987 f.

3. Ir. *ferg*, NIr. *fearg* : Grk. ὀργή, etc. (above, 1).

Ir. *bare, baran*, MW *bar, baran* : Lat. *ferīre* 'strike', Lith. *barti* 'scold', ChSl. *brati* 'fight', etc. Walde-P. 2.160. Stokes 161. Loth, RC 38.152.

W. *dig* (also adj. 'angry'), cf. *ystig*. (**ex-dic*) 'assiduous', MBr. *dig* 'zealous, diligent' (Loth, RC 42.85), perh. : Russ. *dikij*, Pol. *dziki*, etc. 'wild' (Berneker 199 f.), used also of 'savage' temper. So briefly E. Lewy, Z. sl. Ph. 1.415 (quoted with approval by Pokorny, Z. celt. Ph. 20.513) and independently by G. S. Lane, Language 8.297, 9.268 ff. Adversely A. Senn, Language 9.206 ff., Mélanges Pedersen 456 ff.

W. *llid* perh. = Ir. *lith*, Br. *lid* 'festival', with development of 'anger' through the characteristic brawls of a celebration. Zimmer, Z. deutsch. Alt. 32.284. Pedersen 1.133. Walde-P. 2.394. Otherwise (: Ir. *lūth* 'vigor, impetuosity') Loth, RC 40.358.

Br. *buanegez*, fr. *buanek* 'angry, irritable', this apparently fr. *buan* 'swift', as orig. 'quick to anger' (cf. NE *hasty*, NED s.v. 4).

Br. *droug*, properly 'an evil, harm', etc. : W. *drwg* id. and adj. 'bad' (16.72).

4. Goth. *þwairhei*, fr. *þwairhs* 'angry' : OE *þweorh* 'crooked' (12.74), esp. 'perverse' (cf. NE *thwart*, adj., adv., vb. and NE *cross* colloq. for 'ill-tempered'). Walde-P. 1.736. Feist 507.

Goth. *mōþs* (hence *mōdags* 'angry'; both rare vs. preceding), ON *mōðr* = OE *mōd* 'spirit, mind, mood, courage', ME *moode* also 'anger' (NED s.v. *mood* 2b), OHG *muot* 'mind, spirit, courage', etc., also 'anger' (NHG *mut* 'mood', but mostly 'courage'), outside connections (as : Grk. μαίομαι 'seek', ChSl. *sŭ-měti* 'dare', etc.) dub. Walde-P. 2.239. Falk-Torp 726. Feist 365 f.

Goth. *hatis* (freq. for ὀργή), see under 'hate' (16.41).

ON *reiði*, Dan., Sw. *vrede*, OE *wrǣþþu*, ME *wrathe*, NE *wrath*, beside adjs. ON *reiðr*, Dan., Sw. *vred*, OE *wrāþ*, NE *wroth*, orig. 'twisted' : ON *rīða*, OE *wrīþan* 'twist, bind', etc. Walde-P. 1.279. Falk-Torp 1396.

ON *gremi*, OE *grama*, etc., fr. adjs. ON *gramr*, OE, OHG *gram* (also OE, NE *grim*, etc.) 'angry, fierce' (whence also the vbs. Goth. *gramjan*, OE *gremian* 'make angry') : Grk. χρεμίζω, χρεμετίζω 'whinny', Lith. *gramėti* 'fall with a crash', *grumėti* 'thunder', ChSl. *gromŭ* 'thunder', etc., Av. *gram-* 'be angry', pple. *granta-* 'angry'. In this group the notion of 'anger' (in Gmc. and Av.) has developed from its outward expression. Walde-P. 1.655. Falk-Torp 340.

OE *irre*, fr. adj. *irre* = OS *irri* 'angry' : OHG *irri* 'wandering, deranged', also 'angry' (NHG *irre*), Goth. *airzeis* 'astray', Lat. *errāre* 'wander, go astray, err', and perh. ultimately also Skt. *irasya-* 'be angry' and the group discussed under NHG *raserei* 'rage' (16.43). Walde-P. 1.150. Feist 27.

OE *torn* 'violent emotion, anger, grief', OHG, MHG *zorn* 'anger, offense, strife', NHG *zorn*, Du. *toorn* 'anger', through 'cleavage, strife', or sb. fr. adj. like OE *torn*, fr. the root of OE *teran*, OHG *zeran*, etc. 'tear'. Walde-P. 1.798. Kluge-G. 715.

OE *anda*, etc. sometimes 'anger', see 16.44.

ME *angre*, NE *anger*, fr. ON *angr* 'trouble, affliction' (so also ME *angre*) : Lat. *angor* 'constriction of the throat, anguish, trouble', Skt. *aṅhas-* 'distress, need', ON *ǫngr*, OE *enge*, OHG *angi*, *engi* 'narrow', etc. Falk-Torp 29. Walde-P. 1.62.

ME, NE *ire*, fr. OFr. *ire* (above, 2).

OHG *gi-buluht*, *ā-bulgī*, MHG *ābulge* : OHG *belgan* 'swell', refl. 'be angry', OE, OS *belgan* 'be angry', Ir. *bolgaim* 'swell'. Walde-P. 2.183.

5. Lith. *piktumas*, fr. *piktas* 'angry', beside *pykti* 'become angry', *paikas* 'stupid, silly', *peikti* 'blame', OPruss. *paikemmai* 'we deceive', *pickuls* 'devil' : Goth. *bi-faih* 'covetousness', OE *fāh*, OHG *gifēh* 'hostile', Skt. *piçuna-* 'betrayer, slanderer, malignant', etc. Walde-P. 2.10 f. Feist 89 f.

Lett. *dusmas* (pl.) : *dusēt* 'pant, breathe', Lith. *dusėti* 'cough slightly', *dūsėti* 'breathe heavily', ChSl. *dychati* 'breathe', etc. Orig. 'heavy breathing' indicating 'anger'. Cf. OE *anda* 'anger, hate, envy' (16.44) = ON *andi* 'breath', etc. Mühl.-Endz. 1.521. Walde-P. 1.846.

6. ChSl. *gněvŭ* (reg. for ὀργή), SCr. *gnjev*, Boh. *hněv*, Pol. *gniew*, Russ. *gnev*, Russ.-ChSl. *gněvŭ* once 'σαπρία, rottenness', prob. : ChSl. *gnĭją*, *gniti*, Russ. *gnit'* 'rot', ChSl. *gnojĭ* 'dung', Russ. *gnoj* 'pus', etc., with development of 'anger' through notion of disgust. Cf. NHG *gift* 'poison' and 'hate, anger'. Berneker 312 f. Brückner 147.

ChSl. *jarostĭ* (reg. for θυμός; cf. Jagić, Entstehungsgesch. 419), Russ. *jarost'* 'rage', SCr. *jarost* old and dial. 'heat, rage', etc., beside ChSl. *jariti sę* 'become angry', *jarŭ* 'severe, harsh', Russ. *jaryj* 'furious', etc., prob. : Grk. ζωρός used of unmixed wine, etc., orig. 'harsh' (cf. Hesych. ζωρός· ἐνεργής, ταχύς leg. τραχύς?). Berneker 447 f. Walde-P. 1.197. Boisacq 312.

SCr. *ljutina*, *ljutost*, etc., fr. *ljut* 'harsh, angry' = ChSl. *ljutŭ* 'violent, frightful', etc., outside connections? Walde-P. 2.415. Berneker 759 f.

Boh. *zlost*, Pol. *złość* ('anger, spite, malice'; Russ. *zlost'* 'ill-nature, wrath'), orig. 'badness', fr. Boh. *zly*, Pol. *zły* (ChSl. *zŭlŭ*) 'bad, evil' (16.72). Cf. NHG *böse* 'evil' and now esp. 'angry'.

Russ. *serdce* 'heart' (4.44) is also used for 'anger' (now only in certain phrases), and the deriv. vb. *serdit'sja* is more common than *gnevit'sja* for 'be angry'. Cf. also Lith. *širdytis* 'be angry' (prob. with semantic borrowing), SCr. *srditi se* 'be angry', *srdit* 'angry', *srdžba*, etc. 'anger'.

7. Skt. *krodha-*, with vb. *krudh-* 'be angry', etym.? Walde-P. 1.481. Uhlenbeck 68.

Skt. *kopa-*, fr. *kup-* 'become agitated, grow angry' : ChSl. *kypěti* 'boil, run over', Lith. *kvapas* 'breath, odor', Grk. καπνός 'smoke', etc. Walde-P. 1.379. Uhlenbeck 58.

Skt. *heḍa-*, *heḍas-* (RV, AV) : Av. *zōiždišta-* 'most hateful', *zōišnu-* 'shivering, frightful' (Barth. 1692 f.), Goth. *usgaisjan* 'frighten', OE *gāst*, OHG *geist* 'spirit', etc. Walde-P. 1.553 f. Feist 531.

Av. *aēšma-* : Lat. *īra*, etc. (above, 2).

Cf. vbs. Skt. *hṛ-* in mid. (*hṛṇīte*, etc). 'be angry', Av. *zar-* 'make angry', mid. 'be angry', outside connections? Walde-P. 1.601, 603. Barth. 1669 f.

Av. *gram-* 'be angry', pple. *granta-* 'angry' : ON *gremi*, etc, (above, 4).

16.43 RAGE, FURY

Grk.	*λύσσα, μανία*	Goth.	(cf. adj. *wōds*)	Lith.	*(pa)dūkimas*
NG	*λύσσα, μανία*	ON	*œði*	Lett.	*trakums*(?)
Lat.	*rabiēs, furor*	Dan.	*raseri*	ChSl.	*jarostĭ*
It.	*furore, furia, rabbia*	Sw.	*raseri*	SCr.	*bijes*
Fr.	*fureur, rage*	OE	*wōdness*	Boh.	*vztek*
Sp.	*furor, furia, rabia*	ME	*wodnes, rage, furie*	Pol.	*wściekłość*
Rum.	*furie*	NE	*rage, fury*	Russ.	*bešenstvo, jarost'*
Ir.	*dāsacht, baile*	Du.	*woede*	Skt.	*kopa-*
NIr.	*buile*	OHG	*wuot(i)*	Av.	*aēšma-*
W.	*cynddaredd*	MHG	*wuot*		
Br.	*kounnar*	NHG	*wut, raserei*		

Some of the words for 'anger' cover also the more violent 'rage, fury', especially Greek θυμός (with its Goth. and ChSl. translations; λύσσα, μανία do not occur in NT), Skt. *kopa-*, Av. *aēšma-*. But there are usually distinctive words for 'rage, fury'. Several of these mean also or even principally 'madness', and the still more specific 'hydrophobia' is the orig. sense of the W. and Br. words, which are derived from the word for 'dog'.

In general, they are specialized from 'mental excitement' based in part upon notions of violent physical action.

1. Grk. λύσσα, Att. λύττα, etym. disputed, prob. : ChSl. *ljutŭ* 'fierce'. Walde-P. 2.415. Boisacq 592.

Grk. μανία, see 16.42 under Grk. μῆνις.

2. Lat. *rabiēs* (> Fr. *rage*; It. *rabbia*, Sp. *rabia* in part, as also Lat. *rabiēs*, spec. 'hydrophobia, rabies'), beside vb. *rabere* 'be enraged', prob. : Skt. *rabhas-* 'vehemence, violence', *rabhasa-* 'fierce, impetuous', etc. (IE *rabh- beside *labh- 'seize'?) Walde-P. 2.341. Ernout-M. 848.

Lat. *furor* (> It. *furore*, Fr. *fureur*, Sp. *furor*), and *furia* (> It., Sp. *furia*, Fr., Rum. *furie*), the latter esp. pl. *furiae* 'the Furies', with vb. *furere* 'rage, rave, be out of one's mind', etym. dub. (fr. *dhus- : Grk. θύω 'rage', etc.?). Walde-P. 1.844. Ernout-M. 404. Walde-H. 1.571.

3. Ir. *dāsacht* (gl. *amentia* Ml. 20b7, *furor* Ml. 34a21), cf. vb. *dāsaid immum* (impers.) 'I rage' (K. Meyer, Contrib. 591) : OE *dwǣs* 'foolish, stupid', OHG *getwās* 'ghost', Lith. *dvasia* 'spirit', Lett. *dusmas* 'anger', Grk. θύω 'rage', fr. an extension of the same root as in Grk. θυμός 'spirit, anger, rage'. Walde-P. 1.845. Pedersen 2.32.

Ir. *baile* 'madness, frenzy' (K. Meyer, Contrib. 166 f.), NIr. *buile*, Gael. *boile*, etym.?

W. *cynddaredd* (cf. old *cynddar* 'raging'), Br. *kounnar* (cf. OBr. *cunnaret* gl. *rabies*), orig. only 'hydrophobia', cpd. of W. *ci* (pl. *cwn*), Br. *ki* 'dog' (second part?). Pedersen 1.422. Morris Jones 261.

4. Goth., see under 'anger'.

ON *œði*, OE *wōd* (rare except in cpds.), *wōdness*, ME *wodnes*, Du. *woede*, OHG *wuot*, *wuoti*, MHG *wuot*, NHG *wut*, with adjs. ON *ōðr* 'furious, mad', OE

wōd 'mad, raving' (NE *wood*), Goth. *wōds* 'raging, possessed' : Ir. *fāith* 'poet', W. *gwawd* 'satire, sneer' (arch. 'song'), Gall. οὐάτεις 'seers', Lat. *vātes* 'seer, poet' (cf. Grk. μάντις 'seer' : μαίνομαι 'be mad'), perh. (with a common element of mental excitement) fr. the root in Skt. *api-vat-* 'understand'. Walde-P. 1.216. Weigand-H. 2.1296 f. Ernout-M. 1076.

ME, NE *rage*, fr. Fr. *rage* (above, 2).

ME, *furie*, NE *fury*, fr. Fr. *furie* (above, 2).

NHG *raserei* (> Dan., Sw. *raseri*), fr. *rasen*, MHG *rāsen* 'rage, rave' : OE *rǣsen* 'rush, assault', ON *rās*, OE *rǣs* 'running, race', etc., perh. fr. a form of the same root as in Lat. *errāre* 'go astray', OE *irre* 'anger', etc. (16.42). Walde-P. 1.150. Weigand-H. 2.530 f.

5. Lith. *(pa)dūkimas* : *dūkti* 'rage', Lett. *dūkt* 'rage, storm, roar', Skt. *dhukṣ-* 'kindle, influence, animate', etc., fr. the same root as Grk. θυμός 'spirit, anger, rage'. Walde-P. 1.838.

Lett. *trakums* (Drawneek, Ulmann-Brasche, not given by Mühl.-Endz.) : *trakuot* 'romp, rush, rage', *traks* 'unruly, foolish, mad', Lith. *trakas* 'mad', perh. as 'twisted' : Lat. *torquēre* 'twist, wind', etc. Mühl.-Endz. 4.219.

6. ChSl. *jarostĭ* (= θυμός 'anger, rage'), Russ. *jarost'* 'rage', see under 'anger' (16.42).

SCr. *bijes* = ChSl. *běsŭ* 'δαίμων', Boh. *běs*, Pol. *bies*, Russ. *bes* 'devil', cf. SCr. *bijesan* 'raging', ChSl. *běsĭnŭ* 'possessed', etc. : Lith. *baisa* 'fright', *baisus* 'monstrous, terrible', fr. the root of ChSl. *bojati sę*, Skt. *bhī-* 'fear', etc. Walde-P. 2.125. Berneker 56.

Boh. *vztek*, *vzteklost*, Pol. *wściekłość*, beside Boh. *vzteklý*, Pol. *wściekły* 'raging, mad', Boh. *vztekati se*, Pol. *wściekać się* 'rage', cpd. of Slavic *tek-* in ChSl. *teką*, *tešti* 'run, flow' with *vŭz-* 'up', with specialization of 'surge up' or the like to the emotion. Brückner 635. Miklosich 348.

Russ. *bešenstvo*, fr. *besit'sja* 'rage' : *bes* 'devil', cf. SCr. *bijes* (above).

7. Skt. *kopa-*, Av. *aēšma-* 'anger, rage', see under 'anger' (16.42).

16.44 ENVY (sb.), JEALOUSY

Grk.	*φθόνος, ζηλοτυπία*	Goth.	*neiþ, aljan*	Lith.	*pavydas, skaugė*
NG	*φθόνος, ζήλεια*	ON	*ǫfund, ǫfundsýki*	Lett.	*skaudība, greizsirdība*
Lat.	*invidia, līvor, aemulātiō*	Dan.	*misundelse, jalousi, skinsyge*	ChSl.	*zavistĭ, rĭvĭnĭje*
It.	*invidia, gelosia*	Sw.	*avund, svartsjuka*	SCr.	*zavist, ljubomornost*
Fr.	*envie, jalousie*	OE	*nīþ, æfest, anda*	Boh.	*závist, žárlívost*
Sp.	*envidia, celos*	ME	*envie, jalousie, nith(e), evest, onde*	Pol.	*zazdrość, zawiść*
Rum.	*învidie, gelozie*	NE	*envy, jealousy*	Russ.	*zavist', revnost'*
Ir.	*format, ēt, tnūth*	Du.	*nijd, afgunst, jaloerschheid*	Skt.	*īrṣyā-*
NIr.	*tnūth, formad, ēad*	OHG	*nīd, abunst, anto*	Av.	*ərəši-, araska-*
W.	*cenfigen, eiddigedd*	MHG	*nīd, abegünste*		
Br.	*gwarizi, gourvenn, oaz*	NHG	*neid, missgunst, eifersucht*		

Words for 'envy' and 'jealousy' are taken together, since often the same word covers both notions and the distinction is a subtle one. Most of the words for 'envy' (or 'envy' and 'jealousy') had from the outset a hostile force, based on 'look at' (with malice), 'not love', etc. Conversely, most of

those which became distinctive terms for 'jealousy' were originally used also in a good sense, 'zeal, emulation'.

1. Grk. φθόνος, orig. 'diminution' (cf. ἄφθονος 'abundant', ἀφθονία 'abundance', φθονέω often 'begrudge, be reluctant') : Av. *a-γžōnvamna-* 'not diminishing'. Cf. NE *belittling*, NHG *verkleinerung* in the sense of 'disparagement'. Walde-P. 1.699. Boisacq 1026 f. Barth. 50 f.

Grk. ζηλοτυπία, with ζηλοτυπέω 'be jealous', fr. ζῆλος (Dor. ζᾶλος) sometimes 'jealousy', but more often in a good sense, 'emulation, rivalry, zeal' (-τυπία : τύπος 'form'), whence NG ζήλεια; etym. dub. Walde-P. 1.775. Boisacq 309.

2. Lat. *invidia* (> It. *invidia*, Fr. *envie*, Sp. *envidia*, Rum. *învidie*), with *invidus* 'envious', fr. *invidēre* 'envy', earlier 'look at with malice, cast an evil eye upon', cpd. of *vidēre* 'see'. Ernout-M. 493 f. Walde-H. 1.713.

Lat. *līvor*, properly 'lead-color, blue-black spot' like the vb. *līvēre* 'be lead-colored, blue-black' and 'be envious' : Ir. *lī*, W. *lliw* 'color', etc. (15.61). Cf. NE *be green with envy*. Ernout-M. 558. Walde-H. 1.816.

Lat. *aemulātiō*, also in good sense 'emulation', beside vb. *aemulārī* 'emulate, rival, be envious of', fr. *aemulus* 'striving after, emulating, envious', perh. : *imitārī* 'represent, copy, imitate', *imāgō* 'copy, image, likeness', etc., but root connection dub. Walde-P. 1.102. Ernout-M. 16, 476. Walde-H. 1.17.

It. *gelosia*, Fr. *jalousie*, Rum. *gelozie*, fr. the adjs. It. *geloso*, Fr. *jaloux*, Rum. *gelos*, fr. VLat. *zēlōsus deriv. of late Lat. *zēlus* 'zeal' (fr. Grk. ζῆλος, above, 1), whence Sp. *celo* 'zeal', pl. 'jealousy, suspicion'. Important in the history was the biblical 'jealous god' in the Vulgate *zēlōtēs*, fr. Grk. ζηλωτής. REW 9613, 9614. M. Grzywacz, "Eifersucht" in den rom. Sprachen.

3. Ir. *format*, NIr. *formad*, Br. *gourvenn*, arch. W. *gorfyn*, fr. a cpd. of Ir. *for-*, W. *gor-*, etc. 'over' and *mento-* (with influence of W. *mynnu*, etc. 'wish') fr. the root *men- 'think'. Cf. Hom. ὑπερ-μενέων 'arrogant'. Pedersen 1.168.

Ir. *tnūth* (NIr. also 'longing for, desiring'), perh. (as 'tension' with complete transfer fr. physical to mental) : Skt. *tan-*, Lat. *tendere* 'stretch', IE *ten-. Pedersen 1.132.

Ir. *ēt*, NIr. *ēad*, W. *-iant* in arch. *addiant* 'longing', Gall. *Iantu-mārus* (= Ir. *ētmar*) : Skt. *yat-* 'seek, strive', Av. *yat-* 'move (oneself), be active, zealous'. Walde-P. 1.197. Pedersen 1.64 f.

W. *cenfigen*, older *cynfigen*, orig. ? Cf. Evans s.v.

W. *eiddigedd*, fr. *eiddig* 'jealous', this fr. *aidd* 'zeal, ardor', Br. *oaz* 'zeal' and 'jealousy' in love : Ir. *aed* 'fire', Lat. *aestus* 'heat', Grk. αἴθω 'kindle, burn', etc. Walde-P. 1.5.

Br. *gwarizi*, etym.? Henry 147.

4. Goth. *neiþ*, OE *nīþ*, ME *nith(e)*, Du. *nijd*, OHG, MHG *nīd*, NHG *neid*, but ON *nīð* 'contumely, libel' : Ir. *nīth* 'battle, distress', root connection dub. Walde-P. 2.336. Falk-Torp 765. Feist 374. Perh. fr. *neit- beside *neid- in Goth. *ga-naitjan* 'to dishonor', Grk. ὄνειδος 'reproach, blame', etc. (16.78).

Goth. *aljan* (renders ζῆλος as 'jealousy', Rom. 13.13, otherwise 'zeal') = ON *eljan* 'energy, endurance', OE *ellen* 'strength, vigor, courage', OHG *ellen* 'zeal, strength', etc., etym. dub., perh. : Lat. *alacer* 'lively, eager, glad'. Walde-P. 1.156. Falk-Torp 188. Feist 38. Walde-H. 1.25.

ON *ǫfund*, Dan. *avind* (replaced by new formation *mis-undelse*), Sw. *avund*, OE *æfest*, ME *evest*, OHG *abunst*, MHG *abegünste* (*-gunst*), Du. *afgunst*, NHG *abgunst* (now mostly replaced by *missgunst*), cpds. of neg. pref. *aba- (*miss-*)

and derivs. of root in ON *unna* 'to love', *āst* 'love', etc. (16.27). Falk-Torp 37. Hence cpds. with adjs. for 'sick' ON *ǫfundsjūkr*, Sw. *avundsjuk* 'envious', whence sbs. ON *ǫfundsȳki*, Sw. *avundsjuka* 'envy'.

Dan. *jalousi*, ME *jalousie*, NE *jealousy*, fr. Fr. *jalousie* (above, 2).

Dan. *skinsyge*, fr. *skinsyg* 'jealous', fr. earlier *skind-syg*, cpd. of *skind* 'hide, skin' and *syg* 'sick'. Explained by the Sw. dial. expression *få skinn* 'receive a refusal in courtship.' Falk-Torp 998.

Sw. *svartsjuka*, fr. adj. *svartsjuk* 'jealous', cpd. of *svart* 'black' and *sjuk* 'sick', fr. the phrase *bära svarta strumpor* lit. 'wear black stockings' = 'be jealous'. Hellquist 914.

OE *anda* 'zeal, hate, anger' and esp. 'envy' with vb. *andi(g)an* 'envy' and 'be zealous', ME *onde* 'envy', OHG *anto* 'zeal, envy', OS *ando* 'anger' : ON *andi* 'breath, spirit', Goth. *uz-anan* 'breathe out', etc., with application to various emotions. Falk-Torp 5. Weigand-H. 1.29 f. NED s.v. *onde*, sb.

ME *envie*, NE *envy*, fr. Fr. *envie* (above, 2).

Du. *jaloerschheid*, fr. *jaloersch* 'jealous', MDu. *jaloes*, fr. Fr. *jaloux* (above, 2). Franck-v. W. 278.

MHG (late) *yfer* 'jealousy', NHG *eifer* in Luther mostly 'passion, anger', now 'zeal' in good sense, and for 'jealousy' *eifersucht*, cpd. with *sucht* 'illness'; perh. : OHG *eivar*, *eibar* 'harsh, severe', OE *āfor* 'vehement, dire'. Kluge-G. 124. Weigand-H. 1.412. Walde-P. 1.6.

5. Lith. *pavydas*, beside *pavydus* 'envious', *pavydėti* 'envy', cpd. with perfect. *pa-* : *veizdėti* 'see, look', ChSl. *viděti*, Lat. *vidēre* 'see', etc. (cf. Lat. *invidēre*, above, 2). Walde-P. 1.238.

Lith. *skaugė* : Lett. *skaug'is* 'an envious person, enemy', perh. Ukr. *skuhnij* 'miserable', Boh. *skuhrati* 'whine', root connection? (From a parallel extension of the root seen in Lett. *skaudība*, etc., below?) Mühl.-Endz. 3.876. Zubatý, Arch. sl. Ph. 16.413.

Lett. *skaudība*, with *skaudīgs* 'envious, fr. *skaudu*, *skaust*, *skaudēt* 'envy' : Lith. *skaudėti* 'hurt, ache', Grk. σκύζομαι 'be angry', etc. Walde-P. 2.554. Mühl.-Endz. 3.875, 876.

Lett. *greizsirdība*, with *greizsirdīgs* 'jealous', cpds. of *greizs* 'slanting, oblique' and *sirdība* 'zeal, courage', *sirdīgs* 'zealous, courageous', fr. *sirds* 'heart, courage'. Mühl.-Endz. 1.648, 3.843.

6. ChSl. *zavistĭ* (in Gospels reg. = φθόνος, later also = ζῆλος; also *zavida*; cf. Jagić, Entstehungsgesch. 287, 343 f.), SCr. *zavist*, etc., general Slavic, fr. *zaviděti* 'to envy', cpd. of *za-* 'after' and *viděti* 'see' (cf. Lith. *pavydas*, above, 5, Lat. *invidia*, above, 2).

ChSl. *rĭvĭnĭje* (= ζῆλος, cf. Jagić, Entstehungsgesch. 343 f.), and *rĭvĭnostĭ* (Supr.), Russ. *revnost'*, fr. ChSl. *rĭvĭnŭ* 'emulating, zealous', *rĭvĭnovati* 'emulate', etc., prob. : Russ. *erit'* 'be busy, zealous', and ChSl. *reją*, *rijati* 'flow', modern Slavic also 'press, shove', etc., Grk. ὀρίνω 'stir, raise, rouse', etc. Walde-P. 1.141. Meillet, Études 283, 386.

SCr. *ljubomornost*, fr. *ljubomoran* 'jealous', cpd. of derivs. of the stems of *ljubiti* 'love' and *mor* 'death'.

Boh. *žárlivost*, fr. *žárlivý* 'envious' = Pol. *żarliwy* 'fiery, zealous', etc., fr. Boh. *žár* 'heat, glow, ardor, passion', Pol. *żar* 'glow, embers', etc. Miklosich 409 f.

Pol. *zazdrość*, earlier *zazrość* : *zajrzeć*, *zaźrzeć* 'look at', and 'envy' (*zajrzeć komu czego*), cpd. of *źrzeć* 'see, look' (15.52). New formation parallel to and replacing the older *zawiść*. Brückner 646, 656.

7. Skt. *īrṣyā-*, Av. *ərəši-*, *araska-* : Skt. *īrṣ-* 'be jealous, envy', Av. *arəšyant-* 'envious', OS *irri*, OE *irre* 'angry', etc. (16.42). Walde-P. 1.150.

16.45 SHAME (sb.)

Grk.	*αἰδώς, αἰσχύνη (ἐντροπή)*	Goth.	*gariudei (aiwiski, skanda)*	Lith.	*gėda*
NG	*ἐντροπή*	ON	*kinnroði*	Lett.	*kauns*
Lat.	*pudor, verēcundia*	Dan.	*skam*	ChSl.	*studŭ, sramŭ*
It.	*vergogna*	Sw.	*skam*	SCr.	*stid, sram*
Fr.	*honte*	OE	*sceamu*	Boh.	*stud*
Sp.	*verguenza*	ME	*shame*	Pol.	*wstyd, wstydliwość*
Rum.	*ruşine*	NE	*shame*	Russ.	*styd, stydlivost'*
Ir.	*mebul, rucce, nāire*	Du.	*schaamte*	Skt.	*lajjā-, hrī-, vrīḍā-*
NIr.	*nāire*	OHG	*scama*	Av.	*fšarəma-*
W.	*cywilydd, gwaradwydd*	MHG	*scham(e), scham(e)de*		
Br.	*mez*	NHG	*scham*		

Most of the words listed are used not only for the subj. sense of 'shame', but also or even more commonly for the obj. 'shame, dishonor, disgrace' (note the secondary differentiation in NHG *scham* vs. *schande*).

In some an earlier sense of 'respect, reverence or modesty' led to 'shame' in a good sense. In others, as shown by usage or etymology or both, 'shame' in a bad sense was the primary notion. Thus, for example, Grk. αἰδώς and αἰσχύνη are contrasted in origin and in their prevailing usage. Several are connected with words for 'red' through 'blushing' as a sign of shame.

1. Grk. αἰδώς, mostly 'shame' in good sense, 'respect, reverence, modesty', with αἴδομαι, αἰδέομαι 'be ashamed, stand in awe, respect', prob. : Goth. *aistan* 'revere', Skt. *īḍ-* 'praise, supplicate', fr. **ais-d-*, extension of **ais-* in OHG *ēra*, NHG *ehre* 'honor', etc. Walde-P. 1.13. Boisacq 22. Feist 27 f.

Grk. αἰσχύνη, beside αἰσχύνω 'dishonor', pass. 'be dishonored, feel shame', αἶσχος 'a shame, disgrace', prob. fr. **aigʷh-s-* : Goth. *aiwiski* 'a shame, disgrace', OE *ǣwisc* 'dishonor, offense', MHG *eisch* 'ugly, repulsive', etc. Walde-P. 1.7. Boisacq 30. Feist 30.

Grk. ἐντροπή, in class. Grk. 'respect, modesty', in LXX 'humiliation', NT and NG reg. 'shame' : ἐντρέπω 'turn about', also 'put to shame' (NT, etc.), used mostly in mid. 'hesitate' and 'give heed to, respect, reverence' (Hom.+), later 'feel shame' (Polyb., NT), as reg. in NG.

2. Lat. *pudor* (also 'modesty' as mostly the borrowed Romance words, It. *pudore*, Fr. *pudeur*, etc.), with vb. impers. *pudet* 'feels ashamed', prob. as orig. 'feel repulsed or cast down' : *repudium* 'divorce, repudiation', *tri-pudium* 'a certain dance', etc., those fr. the root of *pavīre* 'beat, stamp' (or : *pēs, pedis* 'foot'?). Walde-P. 2.12. Ernout-M. 761, 820.

Lat. *verēcundia*, also 'bashfulness, modesty' (> It. *vergogna*, Sp. *verguenza;* Fr. *vergogne* obs.), beside *verēcundus* 'ashamed, bashful, modest', fr. *verērī* 'feel awe of, be afraid (religious sense)' : OE *wær* 'careful', *warian* 'preserve, protect', etc. Walde-P. 1.284. Ernout-M. 1089.

Fr. *honte*, fr. the Gmc., Frank. **haunipa* fr. vb. **haunjan* (> Fr. *honnir*) : OHG *hōnen* 'despise, dishonor', Goth. *haunjan* 'debase', *hauns* 'humble', etc. REW 4080. Feist 249. Weigand-H. 1.881.

Rum. *ruşine*, fr. *ruşi*, *roşi* (now *in-roşi*) 'redden, make red', refl. 'blush'. Tiktin 1348.

3. Ir. *mebul*, also obj. 'a shame', but reg. subj. in phrase *is mebul lemm* 'I am ashamed', NIr. *meobhal*, W. *mefl* obj. 'a shame, disgrace', etym. dub. (: Grk.

μέμφομαι 'blame, find fault with'?). Walde-P. 2.261. Pedersen 1.117, 119. Stokes 208.

Ir. *rucce*, subj. and obj. (cf. RIA Contrib. s.v.), prob. (**rud-k-*) : *ruad* 'red'. Pedersen 1.126.

Ir. *nāire*, subj. and obj. (cf. RIA Contrib. s.v.), NIr. now reg. for subj. 'shame', cf. Ir. *nār* 'modest, noble' and 'shameful', etym. dub. Walde-P. 2.317. Pedersen 1.109.

W. *cywilydd*, cpd. *cy-gwilydd*, fr. *gwyl* 'modest, bashful' : Ir. *fīal* 'generous, modest', etym. dub. Walde-P. 1.214. Pedersen 1.181.

W. *gwaradwydd*, cpd. *gwar* = *gor-* intensive, *ad-* = Ir. *ad* giving reverse sense, and *-wydd* : Ir. *fīad* 'honor' (16.46). Loth, RC 47.171.

Br. *mez* (Vann. *meh*) : W. *methu* 'fail, miss, perish', Ir. *metacht* 'cowardice', outside connections dub. Stokes 206. Henry 201 (Grk. μάτην 'in vain', in different but also dub. grouping Walde-P. 2.220).

4. Goth. *gariudei* (αἰδώς I Tim. 2.9) beside *gariuþs* 'reverend' : *rauþs* 'red', etc. Feist 199.

ON *kinnroði*, orig. 'blush (of shame)', cpd. of *kinn* 'cheek' and *roði* 'redness' : *rauðr* 'red'.

Goth. *skanda* (αἰσχύνη Phil. 3.19), OE *sceamu*, ME, NE *shame*, Dan., Sw. *skam*, OHG *scama*, MHG *scham(e)*, NHG *scham*, all (NHG now only dial., cf. Grimm s.v. 2) also obj., and only so ON *skǫmm* 'dishonor', with vbs. OE *sceamian* 'be ashamed', OHG *scamēn* (*-ōn*), Goth. *skaman*, refl. 'be ashamed', etc., with deriv. sbs. OE *sconde*, ME *shonde* (mostly obj. 'disgrace'), Du. *schaamte*, MLG *schēmede*, MHG *scham(e)de* (NHG *schande* now only obj.), outside connections dub. Falk-Torp 983. Feist 428 f. Weigand-H. 2.672 f.

ME *vergoyne* (not common) fr. Fr. *vergogne* (above, 2).

5. Lith. *gėda*, with *gėdinti* 'to shame', *su-si-gesti* 'be ashamed', OPruss. acc. *gīdan* 'shame' : ChSl. *gaditi* 'detest, blame', Boh. *haditi* 'abuse, blame', Pol. *żadzić się* 'abominate', OHG *quāt*, NHG *kot* 'dung, filth', etc. Walde-P. 1.695. Berneker 289.

Lett. *kauns* : Grk. καυνός· κακός Hesych., Goth. *hauns* 'humble', OE *hēan* 'low, mean, humble', etc. (cf. above, Fr. *honte*), cf. also Lith. *kūvėtis* 'be ashamed'. Walde-P. 1.330. Mühl.-Endz. 2.176 f.

6. ChSl. *studŭ* (αἰσχύνη, Lk. 14.9), Boh. *stud*, and Slavic **stydŭ* in SCr. *stid*, Pol. *wstyd*, Russ. *styd*, and deriv. Pol. *wstydliwość*, Russ. *stydlivost'*, beside ChSl. *styděti* 'be ashamed', etc., fr. **steu-d-* beside **steu-g-* in Grk. στύγος 'hatred, abomination', στυγέω 'hate, abhor'. Walde-P. 2.620. Brückner 635.

ChSl. *sramŭ*, SCr. *sram* (Pol. *srom* not the usual word; Russ. *sorom*, and *sram* fr. ChSl., mostly obj. 'disgrace') : ON *harmr* 'grief', etc. (16.32), and prob. also Av. *fšarəma-*, NPers. *šarm* 'shame'. Walde-P. 1.463. Meillet, Études 228.

7. Skt. *lajjā-*, beside vb. *lajj-* 'be ashamed', prob. in orig. a MInd. form, based on Skt. *rajyate* 'grows red'. Wackernagel, Altind. Gram. 1.163.

Skt. *hrī-*, beside vb. *hrī-* 'be ashamed', etym. dub. Uhlenbeck 101. Walde-P. 1.647.

Skt. *vriḍa-*, *vrīḍa-*, beside vb. *vrīḍ-* 'be ashamed', fr. **vriz-d-* perh. : Lat. *rīdēre* 'laugh' (16.25), etc. Walde-P. 1.277. Otherwise Uhlenbeck 300.

Av. *fšarəma-*, NPers. *šarm*, see under ChSl. *sramŭ*, etc. (above, 6).

16.46 HONOR (sb.)

Grk.	*τῑμή*	Goth.	*swēriþa*	Lith.	*garbė*
NG	*τιμή*	ON	*sōmi, sæmd, heiðr*	Lett.	*guods, ciens*
Lat.	*honor*	Dan.	*ære, hæder*	ChSl.	*čĭstĭ, cěna*
It.	*onore*	Sw.	*ära, heder*	SCr.	*čast*
Fr.	*honneur*	OE	*ār, weorþscipe*	Boh.	*čest*
Sp.	*honor, honra*	ME	*(h)onor, worshipe*	Pol.	*cześć, honor*
Rum.	*onoare*	NE	*honor*	Russ.	*čest', počet*
Ir.	*enech, mīad, fīad*	Du.	*eer*	Skt.	*māna-, pūjā-*
NIr.	*onōir*	OHG	*ēra*	Av.	. . . .
W.	*anrhydedd*	MHG	*ēre*		
Br.	*enor*	NHG	*ehre*		

Words for 'honor' are based on such notions as 'value, worth', 'what is seemly or pleasant', 'praise', 'thought' (through 'think highly of, esteem'), and in the case of some Celtic words 'face' (cf. some uses of NE *face* NED s.v. 7 and the Chinese idiom 'lose face, gain face, save face').

1. Grk. τῑμή, also 'value, price, penalty', with τῑμάω 'revere, honor, esteem, set a price or penalty', τίμιος 'of value, precious, honored', etc. : τίω 'honor, value', τίνω 'pay for, atone, requite', Skt. *ci-* 'punish, avenge', Av. *či-* (*kāy-* Barth. 464) 'atone, avenge', etc. Walde-P. 1.509.

2. Lat. *honor* (> It. *onore*, OFr. *enor*, *onor*, etc., Fr. *honneur*, Sp. *honor*, Rum. *onoare;* vb. *honōrāre* > It. *onorare*, Sp. *honrar* whence *honra*), early *honōs*, gen. *honōris*, etym. dub. Walde-P. 1.583 f. Ernout-M. 458. Walde-H. 1.656.

3. Ir. *enech*, same word as *enech* 'face' (4.204). Loth, RC 41.380.

Ir. *mīad* (also 'pride'; RIA Contrib. s.v.; OBr. *muold* 'pride') : *mōidim* 'boast of' (18.45), outside connections? Walde-P. 2.222. Pedersen 1.184.

Ir. *fīad* (esp. in *ar-moiniur fēid* 'revere, honor', vbl. n. *airmitiu fēid* simply 'honor, reverence') : *fīad* 'coram', MW *gwed* 'face' and 'honor', *yngwyd* 'in sight of', MBr. *a goez* 'openly' (: Lith. *veidas* 'countenance', Grk. εἶδος 'appearance', etc. Walde-P. 1.239). Loth, RC 41.380, 47.171 f.

MIr., NIr. *onōir*, fr. Lat. *honor* (above, 2). Vendryes, De hib. voc. 161.

W. *anrhydedd*, MW *enryded*, prob. through 'high rank' and the obj. 'honor' (cf. *cadair anrhydedd* 'seat of honor') : Ir. *ānsruth* (*ānruth*, *ānrad*) 'noble, champion' (Thurneysen, Abh. Preuss. Akad. 1928. phil.-hist. Kl. 2.14), *ānrata* 'warlike, heroic'.

Br. *enor*, fr. OFr. *enor* (above, 2).

4. Goth. *swēriþa*, fr. *swērs* 'respected, honored', *swēran* 'honor, respect' : ON *svārr*, OE *swǣr*, OHG *swār(i)* 'heavy', etc. Walde-P 1.265. Feist 466.

ON *sōmi*, *sæmd* : *sæmr* 'becoming, fit', *sōma* 'be becoming, fit', OE *sōm* 'agreement, concord', *gesōm* 'unanimous, peaceable', MHG *suome* 'pleasant', etc. (these further : Skt. *sama-*, Goth. *sama-*, etc. 'same'). Walde-P. 2.492. Falk-Torp 1234.

ON *heiðr*, Dan. *hæder*, Sw. *heder* : *heiðr* 'clear, bright', OE *hādor* 'clear, serene', OHG *heitar* 'clear, shining', etc., Skt. *kētu-* 'light, shape, form', etc. Walde-P. 2.537. Falk-Torp 446.

OE *ār*, Du. *eer* (MLG *ēre* > late ON *æra*, Dan. *ære*, Sw. *ära*), OHG *ēra*, MHG *ēre*, NHG *ehre* : Goth. *aistan* 'stand in awe of, esteem', Grk. αἰδώς 'shame'. Walde-P. 1.13. Falk-Torp 1413.

OE *weorþscipe*, ME *worshipe* (NE *worship*), deriv. of OE *weorþ* 'worth, worthy'. NED s.v. *worship*, sb.

ME (h)onor, NE honor, fr. OFr. onor (above, 2). NED s.v.

5. Lith. garbė, beside vb. gerbti : OPruss. gerbt 'speak', fr. an extension of the root in Lith. girti 'praise', Skt. gṛ- 'invoke, praise, sing, recite', etc. Walde-P. 1.686.

Lett. guods, Lith. dial. goda : ChSl. godĭnŭ 'pleasing', u-goditi 'please', Goth. gōþs, etc. 'good'. Mühl.-Endz. 1.690 f. Walde-P. 1.532.

Lett. ciens, either cognate with or more prob. borrowed fr. Russ. cena 'price, value, worth' = ChSl. cěna id., fr. the same root as Grk. τιμή (above, 1) and in form = Grk. ποινή 'penalty'. Mühl.-Endz. 1.394 f.

6. ChSl. čĭstĭ, etc., general Slavic, with vb. čisti, čĭtą 'honor', also 'count, reckon' : Skt. citti-, Av. čisti- 'thought', Skt. cit- 'perceive, observe, mark', etc. Walde-P. 1.509. Berneker 173 ff.

Pol. honor, fr. Lat. honor (above, 2). Brückner 172.

Russ. počet, fr. po-čest', počitat' 'honor, respect, esteem' : ChSl. čisti 'honor' (above). Berneker 174.

7. Skt. māna-, also 'opinion, notion, will' : man- 'think', manas- 'mind', etc. (17.1). Uhlenbeck 222. Walde-P. 2.264 ff.

Skt. pūjā-, etym. dub. Uhlenbeck 172.

16.47 GLORY

Grk.	κλέος, δόξα, κῦδος	Goth.	wulþus	Lith.	šlovė, garbė
NG	δόξα	ON	dȳrð, tīrr	Lett.	slava, guodība
Lat.	glōria	Dan.	ære, herlighed	ChSl.	slava
It.	gloria	Sw.	ära, härlighet	SCr.	slava
Fr.	gloire	OE	wuldor, tīr, mægenþrym	Boh.	sláva, chvala
Sp.	gloria			Pol.	sława, chwała
Rum.	slavă, mărire, glorie	ME	glorie	Russ.	slava
Ir.	glōir	NE	glory	Skt.	çravas-, yaças-
NIr.	glōir	Du.	roem, heerlijkheid	Av.	x^{v}arənah-
W.	gogoniant	OHG	tiurida, guollichī		
Br.	gloar, hano kaer	MHG	ruom		
		NHG	ruhm, herrlichkeit		

'Glory' is for the most part, in feeling and in origin, a highly emotionalized 'fame, renown' or 'honor'. But Grk. δόξα in biblical writings (LXX, NT) was used also, translating a Hebrew word, in the sense of 'brightness, splendor, magnificence, majesty'. This was followed in the translations (Lat. glōria, ChSl. slava, etc.; but Luther differentiated, ehre vs. klarheit or herrlichkeit) and so has affected the use of most of the Eur. words (e.g. NE glory, cf. NED s.v. 5–9). In fact the notion of 'splendor' or the like, rather than 'fame', is dominant, in use and etymology, in some of the Gmc. words, and, quite apart from biblical influence, probably in Skt. yaças- and certainly in Av. x^{v}arənah-. The inclusion of such words in the list is justified by their similar emotional value, rather than under any strict definition of 'glory'.

1. Derivs. of IE *k̂leu- in Grk. κλύω, Skt. çru- 'hear', Lat. cluēre 'be heard of, be famed', Grk. κλυτός, Lat. inclutus, Skt. çruta- 'renowned, famous', etc. Walde-P. 1.494 f. Ernout-M. 199 f. Walde-H. 1.237 ff.

Grk. κλέ(ϝ)ος; Lat. cluor (only in a gloss); Lith. šlovė, Lett. slava; ChSl. slava, etc. general Slavic (slovo 'word' in form = Grk. κλέος); Skt. çravas- (Av. sravah- 'word').

2. Grk. δόξα 'expectation' (Hom.), 'opinion', and 'fame, glory' and eventually the most usual word for 'glory' : δοκέω 'expect, think, seem', δέκομαι (Att. δέχομαι) 'receive, expect', ChSl. desiti 'find', etc. Walde-P. 1.783. Boisacq 172 f.

Grk. κῦδος (poet.), prob. : ChSl. čudo 'wonder' (obj.), both fr. the root of Grk. κοέω 'perceive', ChSl. čuti 'perceive, feel'. Walde-P. 1.369. Boisacq 529.

3. Lat. glōria (> It., Sp. gloria, OFr. glorie, Fr. gloire; Rum. glorie recent borrowing), etym.? Walde-P. 1.538. Ernout-M. 426. Walde-H. 1.609 f.

Rum. slavă, fr. Slavic (above, 1).

Rum. mărire, fr. mări 'enlarge, praise, glorify', fr. mare 'large'.

4. Ir. glōir, fr. Lat. glōria. Br. gloar, fr. Fr. gloire.

W. gogoniant and gogonedd (obs.), cpd. of go- and conedd 'pride, glory' (obs.), root connection?

Br. hano kaer, lit. 'good name, reputation' (hano 'name, reputation' : Lat. nōmen 'name', etc., and kaer 'good').

5. Goth. wulþus, OE wuldor (ON Ullr name of a god), prob., as first 'glory' in the sense of 'splendor' (as Lk. 2.9, 9.31, 32, etc.) : Lat. vultus 'facial expression, face', Goth. wlits 'face, form', OE wlite 'aspect, form, splendor, glory' (often used in connection with wuldor, as þines wuldres wlite 'gloria tua', tō wlite and wuldre, etc.), etc. Walde-P. 1.293. Feist 577.

ON dȳrð, OHG tiurida, diurida (reg. for Lat. glōria in Tat., Otfr., etc.), through 'value', fr. 'costliness, dearness' (so MHG tiurde, cf. ME derth, NE dearth now 'scarcity') : ON dȳrr, OHG tiuri, etc. 'dear, expensive' (11.88).

ON tīrr, OE tīr : OHG ziarī 'adornment' (NHG zier, zierde), fr. an extension of IE *dei- in words for 'shine' (Skt. dī-, etc. 15.56). Walde-P. 1.774. Falk-Torp 970.

Dan. ære, Sw. ära 'honor' (16.46) are used also with the stronger feeling of 'glory' (as NHG ehre by Luther for δόξα, glōria).

OE mægenþrym (mostly the 'glory, majesty' of god), cpd. of mægen 'might' and þrymm 'host, multitude, force, power, glory, majesty' (: ON þrymr 'alarm, noise', etc. Walde-P. 1.749. Falk-Torp 1174).

ME glorie, NE glory, fr. OFr. glorie (above, 3).

OHG guollichī, fr. adj. guollich 'glorious, boasting' : OHG ur-guol 'distinguished', Goth. gōljan 'greet', ON gala 'crow, sing', etc. Falk-Torp 296.

OHG (h)ruom (gl. clamor, gloria, etc., mostly 'fame, renown'), MHG ruom, NHG ruhm, Du. roem, prob. fr. the same root as Goth. hrōps 'cry', OHG ruof 'call' (NHG ruf), etc. (18.41). Walde-P. 1.353. Weigand-H. 2.621.

NHG herrlichkeit ('glory' as 'splendor, majesty', used by Luther for δόξα, glōria in this sense, e.g. Mt. 6.13), fr. herrlich 'magnificent, glorious', OHG hērlich deriv. of hēr 'exalted, august, sacred' (NHG hehr) : OE hār 'gray, hoary', etc. Similarly Du. heerlijkheid, Dan. herlighed, Sw. härlighet (Dan. herlig, Sw. härlig fr. NHG herrlich). Weigand-H. 1.854. Kluge-G. 247. Franck-v. W. 238. Falk-Torp 399.

6. Lith. šlovė, Lett. slava, above, 1.

Lith. garbė 'honor' (16.46), also 'glory'.

Lett. guodība : guods 'honor' (16.46). Mühl.-Endz. 1.689.

7. ChSl. slava, etc., general Slavic, above, 1.

Boh. chvala, Pol. chwała 'praise' (16.79) but also 'glory'.

8. Skt. çravas-, above, 1.

Skt. yaças- 'splendor, beauty' and 'glory, fame', etym.? Uhlenbeck 236.

Av. x^{v}arənah- (OPers. farnah- in proper names) 'glory' of divine beings, of the Iranian people, etc., sometimes a physical 'glory' or 'halo' (Barth. 1870 f.) orig. 'brightness, splendor' : Av. hvar- 'sun', Skt. svar- 'light, sun', Grk. ἥλιος 'sun', etc. Walde-P. 2.446 f.

16.48 PROUD

Grk.	ὑπερήφανος	Goth.	hauh-hairts, -þūhts, mikil-þūhts	Lith.	puikus, (iš)didus
NG	(ὑ)περήφανος (cf. sb. καμάρι)			Lett.	lepns
		ON	stōrlātr, dramblātr	ChSl.	grŭdŭ
Lat.	superbus	Dan.	stolt	SCr.	ponosit, ohol
It.	orgoglioso	Sw.	stolt	Boh.	pyšný, hrdý
Fr.	fier, orgueilleux	OE	ofer-mōd(ig), -mēde, -hygdig	Pol.	pyszny, dumny
Sp.	orgulloso			Russ.	gordyj, nadmennyj
Rum.	mîndru	ME	over-mod(i), prud	Skt.	garvita-, dṛpta-
Ir.	ūallach, dīummusach	NE	proud	Av.	. . . .
NIr.	mōrdha(ch), uaibhreach	Du.	trotsch		
		OHG	ubar-muoti, -huhtīg, hōhmuotig		
W.	balch				
Br.	balc'h	MHG	stolz, übermüete(c), hōchmüetec		
		NHG	stolz, hochmütig		

The nouns for 'pride' are derived from the adjs. for 'proud', or conversely. The adjs. are chosen here for discussion. Most of them are used for 'proud' in both the good and the bad sense. But a few of the words listed are used only in the latter sense, that is 'proud' = 'haughty, arrogant', and in many of the others this is the earlier, either in actual use or as indicated by the etymology.

Several are compounds of 'over' or 'high' with words for 'heart, mood, thought, appearance', thus connoting superiority of spirit or mind. Mental superiority is also basic in some that are cognate with words for 'wise' or 'judgment'. Other sources are 'high, great, fierce, pampered, stubborn'. Some reflect a physical expression of pride, being 'puffed up' or 'swollen'.

1. Grk. ὑπερήφανος, cpd. of ὑπέρ 'over' and -φανος 'appearing' : φαίνομαι 'appear', with η (Dor. ā) after the analogy of words with composition lengthening, esp. ὑπερ-ήνωρ 'arrogant'. Brugmann, Ber. Sächs. Ges. 1901.104 derives the second member fr. -φϝανος, comparing ὑπερφίαλος 'arrogant, proud' fr. -φϝιαλος and Lat. superbus 'proud'. But there is no good reason to separate ὑπερήφανος from the large group of cpds. in -φανος.

NG (beside adj. (ὑ)περήφανος, sb. lit. (ὑ)περηφάνεια) pop. sb. καμάρι 'pride', back-formation to καμαρώνω 'be proud', this fr. Grk. καμαρόω 'furnish with a vault', pass. 'be vaulted' (fr. καμάρα 'anything with an arched cover, vaulted chamber'), with development through 'make an arch, puff out the chest, be puffed up'. For semantic parallels, cf. ON dramblātr (below, 4), Boh. pyšný, etc. (below, 6), and NE puffed up, U.S. slang chesty. Koukoules, Ἀφιέρωμα Hatzidakis 39 ff., derives the use more specifically from Byzantine marriage customs, in which the bride makes a bow (and is proud of the event). But this seems hardly necessary.

2. Lat. superbus, fr. super 'over' with suffix as in probus 'upright', either *-bhwo- (: *bheu- 'become', cf. Grk.

ὑπερφυής 'marvelous', etc.) or *-bho-. Ernout-M. 813, 1004 f.

It. orgoglioso, Fr. orgueilleux, Sp. orgulloso, fr. sbs. It. orgoglio (fr. Prov. orgolh), Fr. orgueil, Sp. orgullo (fr. Cat. orgull), loanwords fr. Gmc., Frank. *urgōli : OHG urguol 'distinguished' (see under guollichī, 16.47). REW 9084.

Fr. fier, fr. Lat. ferus 'wild, fierce', with development through 'high-tempered'. REW 3264.

Rum. mîndru, orig. 'wise', fr. Slav. mądrŭ 'wise' (17.21). Tiktin 986. For semantic relation, cf. Ir. dīummusach (below, 3) and Pol. dumny (below, 6).

3. Ir. ūallach, fr. sb. ūall (*oup-slā-) : uasal, W. uchel 'high', Grk. ὑψηλός 'high', etc. Walde-P. 1.193.

Ir. dīummusach, fr. sb. dīummus (*dī-ud-mess) cpd. of midiur 'judge'. Pedersen 2.579. K. Meyer, Contrib. 665.

NIr. mōrdhach, cf. mōrdha id. also 'great, grand, stately', Ir. mōrda 'haughty', fr. mōr 'great, large'.

NIr. uaibhreach, fr. sb. uabhar, Ir. obar 'arrogance, boasting' : W. ofer 'vain', Br. euver 'vapid, spiritless', perh. also Goth. abrs 'strong, violent', abraba 'very'. Walde-P. 1.177. Pedersen 1.49.

W. balch, Br. balc'h : Ir. balc(c) 'strong, stout, mighty', prob. fr. the root *bhel- 'swell', in Grk. φαλλός 'penis', Lat. follis 'leather bag', Ir. ball 'limb', etc., in which case the W., Br. meaning 'proud' may be directly fr. 'swollen'. Walde-P. 2.178.

4. Goth. hauhhairts, OE hēahheort, cpds. of words for 'high' and 'heart'.

Goth. hauhþūhts (renders τετύφωται, I Tim. 6.4, Vulgate superbus est, King James is proud), and mikilþūhts (ὑπερήφανος, Lk. 1.51), cpds. of hauhs 'high' or mikils 'great' and -þūhts : þugkjan 'think, believe, intend', þūhtus 'conscience', etc. Feist 249, 359.

ON dramblātr, fr. dramba 'be haughty, pompous', dramb 'arrogance', also 'roll of fat on back of neck' (hnappa-dramb), NIcel. drambr 'knot (in wood, etc.)'; development of 'arrogance' fr. 'swelling'.

ON stōrlātr, fr. stōrr 'great, large'.

OE ofermōd, ofermōdig (also simple mōdig but mostly 'high-spirited, brave'), ofer-mēde, ME overmod, ofermodi, OHG ubarmuoti, MHG übermüete, übermüetec (NHG übermütig mostly 'wanton, insolent', etc.), cpds. of OE ofer, OHG ubar, etc. 'over, above' and derivs. of OE mōd, OHG muot 'mind, spirit, disposition' = Goth. mōþs, ON mōðr 'anger', etc. (16.42).

OE oferhygdig, OHG ubarhuhtīg (Tat.), cpds. of OE ofer, OHG ubar, as above, and derivs. of OE hyge, OHG hugi 'mind, heart'.

ME prud, NE proud, fr. late OE prūt, prud = ON prūðr 'brave, gallant, magnificent', etc., fr. OFr. prūd, prōd 'valiant, doughty', fr. VLat. prōde 'advantage, use', formed fr. Lat. prōd-esse 'be of use'. NED s.v. REW 6766.

OHG hōhmuotig, MHG hōchmüetec, NHG hochmütig (now 'proud' in bad sense, 'haughty, arrogant'), fr. sb. OHG hōhmuotī (cf. OE hēahmōd 'proud'), cpd. of words for 'high' and 'spirit, mood'.

Du. trotsch, fr. trots 'pride, arrogance' : NHG trotz 'defiance, stubbornness', MHG truz, traz, adj. traz 'stubborn', vb. tratzen 'defy', root connection dub. Walde-P. 1.798. Franck-v. W. 689.

MHG, NHG stolz (MLG stolt > late ON stoltr, Dan., Sw. stolt), late OHG stolz 'arrogant, presumptuous' (MHG also 'foolish', prob. infl. of Lat. stultus), through 'strutting, walking with a stiff bearing' : MHG, NHG stelze 'stilt', NE stilt, etc., fr. *stel-d-, beside *stel-g- in Norw. stjelk, etc. 'stalk', NE stalk, etc., all fr. the root in OHG stellen 'place, put, set up', etc. Walde-P. 2.646. Falk-Torp 1173. Kluge-G. 596.

5. Lith. *puikus* (also 'splendid, magnificent'), fr. OLith. *puyka* 'pride', this fr. Pol. *pycha* (below, 6). Senn, Language 14.149 f. Otherwise (: *piktas* 'bad') Fränkel, Rev. ét. indo-eur. 1.426 f.

Lith. *išdidus*, cpd. of *didus* 'lofty, majestic', also 'proud' : *didis* 'great, large' (12.55).

Lett. *lepns* (Lith. *lepnas* 'pampered, spoiled, sensual, dainty') : *lept* 'be proud, become proud', Lith. *lepti* 'be pampered, etc.', Lat. *lepidus* 'pleasant, fine, neat', Grk. λεπτός 'fine, thin, weak', etc. Walde-P. 2.430. Mühl.-Endz. 2.452 f.

6. ChSl. *grŭdŭ*, with sb. *grŭdyni* 'pride' (both in Gospels), Boh. *hrdý*, Russ. *gordyj*, prob. same word as in ChSl. *grŭdŭ* 'frightful' (Supr.), SCr. *grd* 'ugly', SCr. *grditi*, Pol. *gardzić* 'scorn, despise', etc. Outside connections dub., but uses best combined under some such notion as 'repelling', whence 'proud', first in bad sense (as always in NT) and 'repulsive'. Walde-P. 1.641 (and 649, 650, making two separate groups). Berneker 370. Brückner 135.

SCr. *ponosit*, *ponosan* : *ponijeti se* 'carry oneself, have a certain bearing, be proud', ChSl. *nesti* 'carry', etc. Rječnik Akad. 10.741, 755.

SCr. (also Slov., Bulg.) *ohol* : Bulg. *o-holen* 'satisfied', *o-halen* 'living in ease', Russ. *na-chal'nyj* 'impudent' (through 'pampered, spoiled', cf. Lett. *lepns*, above), Russ. *cholit'* 'clean, dress neatly, fondle, pamper', *cholja* 'neatness, caresses', but root connection dub. Berneker 395.

Boh. *pyšný*, Pol. *pyszny*, fr. sb. *pycha* : Boh. *pychati* 'be proud, puff up, blow up', Russ. *pychat'* 'pant, puff', ChSl. *pachati* 'blow', etc. Brückner 449. Walde-P. 2.81.

Pol. *dumny*, with *duma* 'conceit, pride' : Russ. *duma* 'thought, idea, council, assembly', etc., Bulg. *duma* 'word', etc., fr. Gmc., Goth. *dōms* 'judgment', *dōmjan* 'judge', etc. Berneker 237.

Russ. *nadmennyj*, fr. ChSl. *na-dŭmenŭ* 'blown up' : ChSl. *dŭmą*, *dąti* 'blow'. Berneker 244.

7. Skt. *garvita-*, with sb. *garva-* 'pride, conceit', perh. as 'pomposity, weighty manners' : *guru-* 'heavy'. Walde-P. 1.684.

Skt. *dṛpta-*, also 'wild, arrogant', fr. *dṛp-* 'become mad, go crazy', etym.? Uhlenbeck 129.

16.51 DARE

Grk.	*τολμάω, θαρρέω*	Goth.	*gadaursan*	Lith.	*drįsti*
NG	*τολμῶ*	ON	*þora, dirfask*	Lett.	*drīkstēt*
Lat.	*audēre*	Dan.	*vove, turde*	ChSl.	*sŭmĕti, drŭzati*
It.	*osare*	Sw.	*våga, töras*	SCr.	*smjeti, odvažiti se*
Fr.	*oser*	OE	*durran*	Boh.	*odvážiti se*
Sp.	*osar*	ME	*durre, dore*	Pol.	*(od)ważyć się, śmieć*
Rum.	*îndrăzni, cuteza*	NE	*dare*	Russ.	*smet', derzat'*
Ir.	*ro-lāmur*	Du.	*wagen*	Skt.	*dhṛṣ-*
NIr.	*lāmhaim, dānuighim*	OHG	*giturran*	OPers.	*darš-*
W.	*beiddio*	MHG	*turren*		
Br.	*kredi*	NHG	*wagen*		

Apart from an inherited group, verbs for 'dare' are based on such varied notions as 'endure, undertake, be firm, be strong, be eager, have spirit, believe (have confidence), have need'. A few come through 'risk' from words for 'play with dice' or 'wager'.

1. IE *dhers-. Walde-P. 1.864. Feist 177.

Grk. θαρσέω, Att. θαρρέω ('be of good courage, have confidence', not the common vb. for 'dare', but cf. θάρσος 'courage', θρασύς 'bold, daring'); Goth. *gadaursan*, OE *durran*, ME *durre*, *dore*, NE *dare*, OS *gidurran*, OHG *giturran*, MHG *turren*; nasalized Lith. *drįsti*, Lett. *drīkstēt*, *drīstēt* (on *k*, cf. Endz., Gramm. 172 ff.); Skt. *dhṛṣ-*, OPers. *darš-*.

2. Grk. τολμάω 'endure, submit, undertake' and esp. 'dare', beside τόλμα 'courage, boldness' : ταλάσσαι, τλῆναι, etc. 'bear, suffer, undergo', Lat. *tollere* 'lift', Goth. *þulan* 'bear, suffer', etc. Walde-P. 1.738 f. Ernout-M. 1044.

3. Lat. *audēre* (pple. *ausus*, whence VLat. **ausāre* > It. *osare*, Fr. *oser*, Sp. *osar*), deriv. of *avidus* 'eager' : *avēre* 'desire eagerly'. Earliest sense 'desire', preserved in *sī audēs*, *sōdēs* 'if you like, if you please'. Development of 'dare' prob. first in neg. phrases like *haud ausim dare*, *nōn ausit crēdere* (Plaut.) 'wouldn't like to' = 'wouldn't risk, dare'. Walde-P. 1.19. Ernout-M. 86, 87 f. Walde-H. 1.880, 1. REW 801.

Rum. *îndrăzni*, fr. Slavic, cf. ChSl. *drŭznąti*, Bulg. *drŭznŭ* (below, 7). Tiktin 802.

Rum. *cuteza*, fr. late Grk. κοττίζω 'play at dice' (fr. κόττος 'die'), through the metaphorical sense 'risk, venture' (like Grk. κυβεύω 'play dice, risk'). REW 2287.

4. Ir. *ro-lāmur* 'dare', *lāmaim* 'take in hand, undertake', NIr. *lāmhaim* 'dare' and 'handle', beside W. (old) *llafasu* 'venture, attempt', Corn. *lauasos* 'dare, be permitted', W. *llawio* 'take in hand, undertake', fr. Ir. *lām*, W. *llaw* 'hand'. Pedersen 2.560 f. K. Meyer, Zur kelt. Wortkunde 179.

NIr. *dānuighim*, *dānuim*, fr. *dāna* 'bold' (16.52).

W. *beiddio*, also 'challenge, defy' (cf. NE *dare* in this sense), perh. : Ir. *bidcais* 'sprang' (pret.), *bedc* 'start, leap', NIr. *bīodhgaim* 'start, rouse, startle', outside connections dub. Pedersen 1.88, 2.476.

Br. *kredi* 'believe' (17.15) is also 'dare', through 'have confidence'.

5. Goth. *gadaursan*, OE *durran*, OHG *giturran*, etc., above, 1.

ON *þora*, Dan. *turde* (secondary form; ODan. *thuræ*, *thoræ*), Sw. (refl.) *töras* (also in Dan. and Sw. as auxiliary 'may, will'), beside ON *þoran* 'daring, courage', root connection dub. Walde-P. 1.710, 728. Falk-Torp 1299. Hellquist 1269 f.

ON *dirfask* (refl.) : *djarfr* 'bold, brave' (16.52).

NHG, Du. *wagen*, fr. MHG, MLG *wāgen* 'wager, put up as a stake, risk' (MLG > Dan. *vove*, Sw. *våga*, late ON *vāga*), this fr. *wāge*, NHG *wage* 'balance, scales' (MHG also 'hazard, risk'), hence lit. 'put in the balance, weigh'. Falk-Torp 1394. Paul, Deutsches Wtb. 623.

Du. *durven*, NHG *dürfen* 'may' (9.95), used also for a mild 'dare' (much as in NE *I dare say*).

6. Lith. *drįsti*, Lett. *drīkstēt*, above, 1.

7. ChSl. *sŭ-mĕti* (usual for τολμάω in Gospels, Supr., etc.), SCr. *smjeti*, Boh. *smít* (now 'may', old 'dare'), Pol. *śmieć*, Russ. *smet'*, with adj. ChSl. *sŭmĕlŭ*, Russ. *smelyj* 'brave' (hence Russ. *osmelivat'sja* 'dare'), etc., prob. : Goth. *mōþs* 'anger', OE *mōd*, OHG *muot* 'spirit, courage', etc. (16.42). Walde-P. 2.239. Berneker 2.47.

ChSl. *drŭznąti* (mostly for θαρσέω, sometimes for τολμάω), Bulg. *drŭznŭ*, OBoh. *drzati*, Russ. *derzat'*, etc., with adj. ChSl. *drŭzŭ* 'bold', etc., prob. through adj. 'firm' > 'bold' : Skt. *dṛh-* 'make firm', Av. *dərəza-* 'firm', etc. Connection with IE **dhers-* (above, 1), leaving the Slavic *z* unexplained (except by a blend with **dherĝh-* in Skt. *dṛh-*, etc.), is less likely. Walde-P. 1.859, 864. Berneker 257 f.

SCr. *odvažiti*, Boh. *odvážiti*, Pol. *(od)ważyć* (all in refl. form), fr. NHG *wagen*. Brückner 598 f. Miklosich 374.

8. Skt. *dhṛṣ-*, OPers. *darš-*, above, 1.

16.52 BRAVE

Grk.	*θρασύς, τολμηρός, ἀγαθός*	Goth.	**balþs*	Lith.	*narsus, drąsus*
NG	*ἀντρεῖος, γενναῖος*	ON	*djarfr, hraustr*	Lett.	*dūšīgs, druošs*
Lat.	*fortis, animōsus, audāx*	Dan.	*tapper, modig*	ChSl.	*drŭzŭ, chrabŭrŭ*
It.	*bravo, coraggioso*	Sw.	*tapper, modig*	SCr.	*hrabar, odvažan*
Fr.	*brave, courageux*	OE	*beald, cēne, mōdig, dyrstig*	Boh.	*udatný, statečný*
Sp.	*bravo, valiente*	ME	*bold, keene, modi, corageus*	Pol.	*odważny, waleczny, mężny*
Rum.	*viteaz, brav, curagios*	NE	*brave, courageous*	Russ.	*chrabryj*
Ir.	*dāna, essamin (gal sb.)*	Du.	*dapper, moedig, koen*	Skt.	*çūra-, vīra-*
NIr.	*calma, crōdha*	OHG	*kuoni, bald*	Av.	*čirya-, darši-, daršyu-*
W.	*dewr, gwrol*	MHG	*küene, balt, türstic, muotec*		
Br.	*kalonek, kadarn*	NHG	*tapfer, mutig, kühn*		

Some of the words listed are used only in the good sense, as terms of approval, like NE *brave*, while others are used also, or some of them more usually, in the bad sense, with feeling of reproof, 'bold, rash'

Several are in origin 'daring', cognate with verbs for 'dare'. Others are derived from words for 'spirit, soul', 'mood', or 'heart' through the notion of 'courage'; or as originally 'manly' from words for 'man'; or as 'fearless' from 'fear'. Still others are words for 'strong, mighty', 'firm, steadfast', 'skilful', 'good' etc., either used also as common expressions for 'brave' or definitely specialized in this sense. A few are connected with words for 'war', 'anger', or 'blood' (through 'cruel').

1. Grk. θρασύς (most often in bad sense 'bold, rash', but also in good sense 'brave, bold' as of Hector and others in Hom.) : θαρσέω 'dare', θάρσος 'courage', etc. (16.51).

Grk. τολμηρός (poet. also τολμήεις), deriv. of τόλμα 'courage, daring' : τολμάω 'dare' (16.51).

Grk. ἀγαθός 'good' (16.71) used also for 'brave' (Hom.+), as conversely κακός 'bad' for 'cowardly' (16.55).

Grk. ἀνδρεῖος 'manly' (fr. ἀνήρ, ἀνδρός 'man') in NG reg. 'brave', with ἀνδρεία 'bravery, courage'.

Grk. γενναῖος 'high-born, noble, excellent' (fr. γέννα 'birth, descent'), in NG 'noble' but esp. 'brave'.

2. Lat. *fortis* 'strong' (4.81), and esp., as mentally strong, 'brave'.

Lat. *animōsus*, fr. *animus* 'soul, spirit, mind, etc.' (16.11), and hence 'spirit, courage'.

Lat. *audāx* (more often 'bold' in bad sense) : *audēre* 'dare' (16.51).

Sp. *bravo*, 'wild' in OSp., later 'brave' (and in this sense > It. *bravo* > Fr. *brave* > Rum. *brav*), fr. Lat. *barbarus* 'wild, savage', orig. 'foreign, a foreigner', fr. Grk. βάρβαρος id. REW 945. Gamillscheg 142. Wartburg 2.248 ff.

It. *coraggioso*, Fr. *courageux* (> Rum. *curagios*), fr. It. *coraggio* (fr. Prov. *coratge*), Fr. *courage* 'courage', derivs. of Fr. *cœur*, Prov. *cor*, etc. 'heart'. REW 2217.

Sp. *valiente* (and in this sense also It. *valente*, Fr. *vaillant* > ME *vailant*, NE *valiant*), pple. of *valer* (It. *valere*, Fr. *valoir*) 'be worth', fr. Lat. *valēre* 'be strong, be good for'. REW 9130.

Rum. *viteaz*, as sb. 'hero', fr. the Slavic, cf. late ChSl. *vitęzĭ* 'hero', Boh. *vítěz* 'victor', Russ. *vitjaz'* 'knight', etc., these prob. fr. ON *víkingr* 'viking'. Tiktin 1760. Stender-Petersen 67 (with refs. in ftn.). Otherwise on the Slavic words Brückner 658 f.

3. Ir. *dāna* (gl. *audax*, NIr. 'bold, impudent'), prob. through 'gifted' or 'cunning' (cf. OE *cēne*, etc., below, 4) fr. *dān* 'gift, art, skill'. Stokes 143 (but *dān* 'art', orig. 'gift' : Lat. *dōnum*, etc. 'gift'. Walde-P. 1.815. Pedersen 1.48, 177).

Ir. *essamin*, cf. MW *eh-ofyn* 'fearless', Gall. *Ex-obnus*, *Ex-omnus*, cpd. of **eks-* (neg. force) and last member : Ir. *ōmun* 'fear' (16.53). Pedersen 2.12.

Ir., NIr. *calma* : OBr. *celmed* 'efficax', W. *celfydd* 'skilled', etym. dub. Pedersen 1.168.

Ir. sb. *gal* 'bravery' (more common than any adj.) : W. *gallu*, Lith. *galėti* 'be able'. Walde-P. 1.539. Stokes 107 f. Pedersen 1.157 (another suggestion 2.25, but ?).

NIr. *crōdha*, fr. Ir. *crōda* 'bloody, cruel' (K. Meyer, Contrib. 525), fr. *crō* 'blood, gore'.

W. *dewr*, as sb. 'hero', cpd. of *de-* 'good' (prefix beside *da* id., 16.71) and *gwr* 'man'. Pedersen 1.39.

W. *gwrol*, lit. 'manly, virile', whence 'brave' (cf. Grk. ἀνδρεῖος, above, 1), fr. *gwr* 'man'.

Br. *kalonek*, fr. *kalon* 'heart' (imitation of Fr. *courageux*?).

Br. *kadarn* = W. *cadarn* 'strong' (4.81).

4. ON *djarfr* : OS *derbi* 'strong, bold, hostile', OFris., MLG *derve* 'sturdy, robust, stout' (NHG *derb* fr. LG), root connection dub. Walde-P. 1.863. Falk-Torp 144.

ON *hraustr*, also 'strong, hearty, doughty', etym. dub. Walde-P. 1.481. Falk-Torp 905.

Dan., Sw. *modig*, OE *mōdig* (also 'highspirited, noble, proud'), ME *modi* (also 'angry', NE *moody*), Du. *moedig*, MHG *muotec*, NHG *mutig* (OHG only in sb. *muotigī* 'excitement of spirit') : ON *mōðugr* 'fierce', Goth. *mōdags* 'angry', derivs. of OE *mōd*, OHG *muot* 'mind, spirit, disposition, courage', etc. = ON *mōþr*, Goth. *mōþs* 'anger' (16.42). Falk-Torp 726. Weigand-H. 2.245.

Goth. **balþs* (in *balþaba* 'openly, boldly', *balþei* 'boldness', *balþjan* 'be bold'; cf. ON *ballr* 'dangerous, frightful'), OE *beald*, ME *bold*, NE *bold* (in good sense now mostly replaced by *brave*), OHG *bald*, MHG *balt* (also 'quick', hence NHG adv. *bald* 'soon'), perh. orig. 'swollen', *-to-*pples. fr. the root **bhel-* 'swell'. Walde-P. 2.179. Falk-Torp 91. Feist 79.

OE *cēne*, ME *keene* (OE and ME also 'wise, clever' and 'fierce', first 'sharp' in ME), Du. *koen*, OHG *kuoni* (also 'warlike' and 'sharp, rough'), MHG *küene*, NHG *kühn* : ON *kœnn* 'wise, skilful, clever', prob. fr. the root of OE *cunnan* 'know, know how, be able', OHG *kunnan* id., ON *kunna*, Goth. *kunnan*, Lat. *nōscere*, Grk. γιγνώσκω, etc. 'know' (17.17). Cf. Lat. *ignāvus* 'cowardly', neg. cpd. of the same root. Walde-P. 1.580. Falk-Torp 523.

OE *dyrstig*, MHG *türstic*, beside OE *gedyrst*, OHG *giturst* 'boldness, bravery' : OE *durran*, OHG *turran* 'dare' (16.51).

ME *corageus*, NE *courageous*, fr. Anglo-Fr. *corageus*, Fr. *courageux* (above, 2).

NE *brave*, fr. Fr. *brave* (above, 2).

Du. *dapper* (Central German *tapper* > MLG *tapper* > Dan., Sw. *tapper*), NHG *tapfer*, fr. MLG *dapper* 'important, capable, industrious, brave', MHG *tapfer* 'firm, compact, weighty, important, enduring (in combat)', OHG *tapfar* 'firm, fast, weighty, lasting' : ON *dapr* 'heavy, slow, sad' and prob. ChSl. *debelŭ* 'stout', Russ. dial. *debelyj* 'strong, firm', OPruss. *debīkan* 'big', etc. Walde-P. 1.850. Berneker 182. Falk-Torp 1248.

5. Lith. *narsus*, *narsingas* 'angry' and 'brave', beside *narsas* 'violent anger' and 'courage', *nartinti*, *naršinti* 'make angry', etc. (cf. NSB 2.119), OPruss. *nerties* (gen. sg.) 'anger', *er-nertimae* 'we anger', etc. (cf. Trautmann, Altpreuss. 331, 384) : Ir. *nert* 'strength, might', Grk. ἀνήρ 'man', etc. Walde-P. 2.332 f. (but preferring to connect the Baltic words with Skt. *nṛt-* 'dance' with common notion of violence in motion or temperament). Trautmann, Altpreuss. 384. Endzelin, KZ 44.67.

Lith. *drąsus*, Lett. *druošs* : Lith. *drįsti*, Lett. *drīkstēt* 'dare' (16.51).

Lett. *dūšīgs*, fr. *dūša* 'courage, spirit, heart' : ChSl. *duša* 'soul', etc. (16.11). Mühl.-Endz. 1.530.

6. ChSl. *drŭzŭ* : *drŭzati* 'dare' (16.51).

ChSl. *chrabŭrŭ* (Supr. for ἀριστεύς, πολεμιστής, πολεμικός, etc.), SCr. *hrabar*, Russ. (old) *chorobrŭ*, now (fr. ChSl.) *chrabryj*, Bulg. *hrabŭr*, Slov. *hrabər*, etc., etym.? Berneker 396 f.

SCr. *odvažan*, Pol. *odważny* : SCr. *odvažiti se*, Pol. *odważyć się* 'dare' (16.51).

Boh. *statečný* = Pol. *stateczny* 'firm, fast, standing firmly', fr. Boh. (Pol.) *statek* 'strength, help', lit. 'stand' (now 'estate, landed property') : Boh. *státi*, Pol. *stac* 'stand', etc. Brückner 514.

Boh. *udatný*, fr. *udati* 'give', refl. *udati se* 'give oneself to, be at one's disposal', cpd. of *dati* 'give'. Development through 'devoted'.

Pol. *waleczny* : *walka*, Boh. *valka* 'war', Pol. *wι lczyć* 'fight', etc. Walde-P. 1.304 f. Brückner 599 (but with mistaken root connections).

Pol. *mężny*, orig. 'manly' (fr. *mąż* 'man'), now common for 'brave'.

7. Skt. *çūra-* (also 'heroic, warlike, mighty', as sb. 'hero') : Av. *sūra-* 'strong, powerful', Grk. κῦρος 'power', Skt. *çavas-* 'strength', W. *cawr* 'giant', etc. Walde-P. 1.365 ff.

Skt. *vīra-*, also 'heroic, powerful, excellent', lit. 'manly' : *vīra-* 'man, hero', Lat. *vir* 'man', etc. (2.21).

Av. *čirya-*, etym.? Barth. 598.

Av. *darši-*, *daršyu-*, *daršita-* : OPers. *darš-* 'dare', etc. (16.51).

16.53 FEAR, FRIGHT

Grk.	δέος, φόβος	Goth.	*agis, faurhtei*	Lith.	*baimė, bailė, išgąstis*
NG	φόβος, τρόμος	ON	*ōtti, ōgn, hrǣzla, skelkr*	Lett.	*bailes*
Lat.	*timor, metus, pavor, terror*	Dan.	*frygt, skræk*	ChSl.	*strachŭ, bojaznĭ*
It.	*paura, timore, spavento*	Sw.	*fruktan, skräck*	SCr.	*strah, bojazan*
Fr.	*peur, crainte, effroi*	OE	*ege, egesa, fyrhto*	Boh.	*strach, bázeň*
Sp.	*miedo, temor, pavura, susto*	ME	*fere, eye, friȝt*	Pol.	*bojaźń, strach, trwoga*
Rum.	*frică, teamă, spaimă*	NE	*fear, fright, terror*	Russ.	*strach, bojazn'*
Ir.	*ōmun, ecla*	Du.	*vrees, schrik*	Skt.	*bhaya-, bhīti-, bhī-, trāsa-*
NIr.	*eagla, faitcheas, uamhan*	OHG	*forhta, egi, egiso*	Av.	*θwaēšah-, byah-, taršti-*
W.	*ofn, dychryn*	MHG	*vorht(e), ege, eis, schreke*		
Br.	*aon, efreiz*	NHG	*furcht, schrecken*		

Words for 'fear' and the stronger (and in part more sudden) 'fright, terror' are mostly based upon those for physical actions expressive of fear, especially 'tremble, shake', also 'flee', 'be struck', etc. In some cases there has been a shift from the objective 'danger' to the subjective 'fear', as, conversely, words for 'fear' are often used objectively for what inspires fear, 'a horror, a terror, danger'. An important cognate group is common to Balto-Slavic and Indo-Iranian.

1. Derivs. of IE **bhəi-*(?), **bhī-* in Balto-Slavic and Indo-Iranian words for 'fear', prob. (though disputed) the same root as in OE *beofian*, OHG *bibēn*, etc. 'shake, tremble' (redupl. formation). Walde-P. 2.124 f. Falk-Torp 125. Weigand-H. 1.173. Berneker 68.

Lith. *baimė*, *bailė* (also *baisa* 'fright', *baisus* 'frightful', fr. **bai-d-s-*), Lett. *baile* (usually pl. *bailes*); ChSl. *bojaznĭ*, etc., general Slavic; Skt. *bhaya-*, *bhīti-*, *bhī-*, Av. *byah-* (*s*-extension); vb. forms Skt. *bhī-* 'fear', Av. 3pl. *bayente*, *byentē* 'frighten', OPruss. *biatwei*, Lith. *bijoti(s)*, Lett. *bītiēs*, *bijāt(iēs)*, ChSl. *bajati sę*, etc. 'fear, be afraid'.

2. Grk. δέος, δεῖμα (latter often obj. 'a terror'), with vb. δείδω (fr. **δε-δϝοια*; δϝ attested also in Hom. ἔδδεισε and Corinth. Δϝεινίας) : Av. *dvaēθā-* 'threat' and Skt. *dviṣ-* 'hate' (cf. 16.41).

Grk. φόβος, orig. 'flight' (still the only sense in Hom.), hence 'panic, fright' and eventually the most common word for 'fear' : φέβομαι 'flee', Lith. *bėgti* 'run, flee', etc. Walde-P. 2.148 f.

Grk. τρόμος 'a trembling', esp. with fear, whence NG 'terror, fright' : τρέμω, Lat. *tremere* 'tremble', Lith. *trimti* 'shake', IE **trem-* beside **tres-* in Skt. *tras-* 'tremble, be afraid', Grk. τρέω 'tremble, flee', Lat. *terrēre* 'terrify', *terror* 'terror'. Walde-P. 1.785. Ernout-M. 1054.

3. Lat. *timor* (> It. *timore*, Sp. *temor*, ORum. *temoare*), with vb. *timēre* (> It. *temere*, Sp. *temer*, Rum. *teme*, whence Rum. sb. *teamă*), etym. dub. Walde-P. 2.611. Ernout-M. 1040.

Lat. *metus* (> Sp. *miedo*), hence *metuere* 'fear', etym. dub., possibly : ChSl. *motati sę* 'be disturbed, moved', Grk. μόθος 'battle-din', etc. Walde-P. 2.269. Wood, Cl. Pl. 5.306.

Lat. *pavor*, orig. 'a shaking, quaking' with emotion, esp. with fear, hence 'alarm, dread, fear' (> OFr. *paor*, Fr. *peur*; with change of suffix It. *paura*, Sp. *pavura*), with vb. *pavēre* 'be struck with fear, tremble, quake with fear', prob.

orig. 'be struck' : *pavīre* 'beat, strike'. Ernout-M. 743. REW 6314.

Lat. *terror* (> It. *terrore*, Fr. *terreur*, etc., NE *terror*), see above under Grk. τρόμος.

It. *spavento*, Fr. *épouvante* ('terror'), fr. It. *spoventare* 'frighten', Fr. *épouvanter* 'terrify, horrify', fr. VLat. **expaventāre*, deriv. of *pavor*, etc. (above). REW 3035.

Fr. *crainte*, fr. vb. *craindre* 'fear', orig. *criembre*, representing a Gallo-Lat. **cremere*, fr. Lat. *tremere* 'tremble' blended with a Gallic **crit-* : Ir. *crith* 'a trembling, shaking'. Cf. OProv. *cremer* 'fear'. REW 8877. Bloch 1.187. Gamillscheg 271.

Fr. *effroi*, fr. *effrayer* 'frighten', orig. *esfreer*, fr. VLat. **exfridāre*, deriv. of a Frank. form corresponding to OHG *fridu*, NHG *friede* 'peace'; orig. 'rouse from a state of peace', whence 'frighten'. REW 3008. Wartburg 3.293. Gamillscheg 344.

Sp. *susto*, deriv. of Lat. *suscitāre* 'lift, raise, rouse, set in motion', also 'scare' (*suscitat vulturium a cano capiti*, Cat. 68.126), cpd. of *citāre* 'put in motion'. REW 8482.

Rum. *frică*, fr. Grk. φρίκη 'shivering, shuddering', esp. with 'fear' : φρίσσω 'be rough, bristle up, ripple, shiver'. Tiktin 646 f.

Rum. *spaimă*, fr. VLat. **expavīmen* : *pavor*, etc. (above). Tiktin 1463.

4. Ir. *ōmun*, *ōman*, NIr. *uamhan*, W. *ofn*, Br. *aon*, Gall. *obnus*, *omnus* (in proper names, *Ex-obnus*, *-omnus* 'fearless'), etym. dub. Walde-P. 1.177 f. (Pedersen 1.49, Stokes 50 : Ir. *ōbar* 'arrogance', W. *ofer* 'vain', Goth. *abrs* 'strong, violent').

Ir. *ecla*, NIr. *eagla*, deriv. of Ir. *ecal* 'afraid', fr. **ek-gal*, neg. cpd. of *gal* 'bravery'. Pedersen 1.477.

NIr. *faitcheas*, fr. Ir. *faitches* 'caution', deriv. of *faitech* 'cautious' (NIr. 'fearful, timid'), cpd., prob. : *techim* 'flee'. Pedersen 2.639.

W. *dychryn*, as vb. (also *dychrynu*) 'frighten, scare', orig. 'shiver, tremble', cpd. of *dy-* intensive and *cryn* 'a shake, quake'.

Br. *efreiz*, fr. OFr. *esfrei*, Fr. *effroi* (above, 3). Henry 110.

5. Goth. *agis* (ON *agi* 'terror'), OE *ege*, *egesa*, ME *eye* (NE *awe*), OHG *egi*, *egiso*, *egisa*, etc., MHG *ege*, *eis*, ON *ōtti*, *ōgn*, with vbs. Goth. *ōg* (pret. pres.) 'be afraid', *ōgjan* and *us-agjan* 'frighten', etc. : Grk. ἄχος 'pain, distress', Ir. *-āgur* 'I fear', vbl. n. *āighthiu* 'fear'. Walde-P. 1.40. Falk-Torp 37. Feist 14, 380.

Goth. *faurhtei*, OE *fyrhto*, ME *friȝt*, NE *fright*, MLG *vruchte* (> Dan. *frygt*, Sw. *fruktan*), OHG *forhta*, MHG *vorht(e)*, NHG *furcht*, beside adj. Goth. *faurhts*, OE *forht*, etc. 'afraid', etym. dub. Walde-P. 2.48 f. Feist 146.

ON *hrǣzla* (*hrǣðsla*), fr. *hrǣða* 'frighten', pple. *hræddr* 'afraid' : Lith. *kresti* 'shake, scatter', *kretėti* 'move to and fro, shake', Ir. *crothaim* 'shake', etc. Walde-P. 1.484. Falk-Torp 928. Hellquist 866.

ON *skelkr*, prob. fr. **sḱel-* 'spring' in MHG *schellec* 'springing up, timid', etc. Walde-P. 2.600. Falk-Torp 981, 1436.

ME *fere*, NE *fear*, in ME mostly 'alarm, dread, apprehension', fr. OE *fǣr* 'a sudden and terrible event, danger' (see 16.54).

ME *drede*, NE *dread* ('extreme fear or anxiety'), fr. vb. ME *dreden*, fr. OE *ondrǣdan* 'fear, dread' = OHG *intrātan* id., perh. : Grk. θρώσσει· φοβεῖται (Hesych.). NED s.v. *dread*, vb. Walde-P. 1.484 (after Wood). Otherwise Falk-Torp 928.

Du. *vrees*, MDu. *vrēse* also 'danger', see 16.54.

Du. *schrik*, MHG *schreke*, NHG *schreck* (> Dan. *skræk*, Sw. *skräck*), now usually *schrecken*, fr. the vbs. Du. *schrikken*, NHG *schrecken* 'take fright, be frightened', MHG *schrecken* 'start, spring up, be frightened', OHG *screcchan* 'jump', beside MHG *schricken*, *scricchan* 'jump', prob. fr. the root in Grk. σκαίρω 'jump, hop, dance', etc. Walde-P. 2.567. Falk-Torp 1033 f. Weigand-H. 2.787 f. Franck-v. W. 600.

6. Lith. *baimė*, *bailė*, Lett. *bailes*, above, 1.

Lith. *išgąstis*, beside *išgąsčiuoti*, *išgąstauti* 'be afraid', *gąsčioti* 'start with fright', *gąstas* 'apprehension, fright', caus. *gandinti* 'frighten', etym.?

7. ChSl. *strachŭ*, etc., general Slavic, perh. (**strōg-so-*) : Lith. *strėgti* 'grow stiff, congeal', OHG *strach*, etc. 'stiff, stretched tight, ready', with Slavic specialization of 'stiffness' to '(stiffness from) fright'. Walde-P. 2.629. Otherwise Brückner 517 f.

ChSl. *bojaznĭ*, etc., general Slavic, above, 1.

Pol. *trwoga* ('fright' and 'alarm'), apparently fr. *trwać* 'last, continue', but semantic relation? Brückner 578.

8. Skt. *bhaya-*, *bhīti*, *bhī-*, Av. *byah-*, etc., above, 1.

Skt. *trāsa-*, Av. *taršti-* (in cpds. as *haθra-taršti-* 'sudden fright'), cf. Av. *taršta-* 'afraid', Skt. *trasta-* 'trembling, frightened', fr. Skt. *tras-* 'tremble, be afraid', Av. *θrah-* 'fear' : Grk. τρέω 'tremble, flee', Lat. *terrēre* 'terrify', *terror* 'terror', Ir. *tarrach* 'fearful', Lith. *trišu* 'tremble'. Walde-P. 1.760.

Av. *θwaēšah-* : *θwi-* 'rouse fear', *upaθwi-* 'fear', *θwyā-* 'object of terror, danger', etc., Skt. *tviṣ-* 'be excited, shine, flame', Grk. σείω 'shake, swing'. Walde-P. 1.748.

16.54 DANGER

Grk.	κίνδῡνος	Goth.	*bireikei, sleiþei*	Lith.	*pavojus*
NG	κίνδυνος	ON	*hætta, hāski*	Lett.	*briesmas*
Lat.	*perīculum, discrīmen*	Dan.	*fare*	ChSl.	*běda*
It.	*pericolo*	Sw.	*fara*	SCr.	*opasnost*
Fr.	*danger, péril*	OE	*pleoh, pliht, frēcen, fǣr*, etc.	Boh.	*nebezpečí*
Sp.	*peligro*	ME	*peril, plyȝt*	Pol.	*niebezpieczeństwo*
Rum.	*pericol, primejdie*	NE	*danger, peril*	Russ.	*opasnost'*
Ir.	*gūas(acht), gābud, bāigul*	Du.	*gevaar*	Skt.	*bhaya-, saṁçaya-*
NIr.	*baoghal, contabhairt*	OHG	*freisa, pfligida, fāra*	Av.	*iθyajah-, θwayaŋha-*
W.	*perigl, enbydrwydd*	MHG	*vreise, vāre*		
Br.	*riskl, gwall*	NHG	*gefahr*		

In several words 'danger' is a specialization of 'experience' (good or bad), 'critical moment, crisis', 'care', etc. Some are connected with words for 'fear' with shift from subjective to objective or conversely. Others are based on miscellaneous notions, 'insecurity', 'doubt', 'power', 'punishment', 'pitfall', etc.

1. Grk. κίνδῡνος, plausibly explained as fr. **κύν-δυνος* : κύων, κυνός 'dog', with *dū-* : Skt. *dīv-* 'play with the dice' (form *du-* in aor. imperat. Ved. *daviṣāṇi*), with orig. reference to the risk in dice-playing, in which the 'dog' was the worst throw (attested for Grk. κύων, Lat. *canis*, and for Skt. *çva-ghnin-* 'the lucky player', lit. the 'dog-killer'). W. Schulze ap. Sittig, KZ 52.207. Kretschmer, KZ 55.90 f. Specht, KZ 66.5. Earlier views Walde-P. 1.361, Boisacq 461, 1115.

2. Lat. *perīculum* (> It. *pericolo*, Fr. *péril*, Sp. *peligro*, Rum. *pericol*), orig.

'trial, attempt' (cf. *perīculum facere*), whence 'risk' and (the usual class. sense) 'danger, peril' : *ex-perīrī* 'try, test, prove', *op-perīrī* 'wait, expect', *perītus* 'experienced', etc., Grk. πεῖρα 'trial, attempt', and the Gmc. groups OE *fǣr* and OHG *freisa*, etc. (below, 4), ultimately as 'experience' fr. the same root as Grk. περάω 'go through', OE *faran* 'go, fare', etc. Walde-P. 2.28 ff. Ernout-M. 756 f.

Lat. *discrīmen*, orig. 'that which separates' (with various applications, 'parting of the hair', 'diaphragm', etc.), whence 'act of deciding, decisive moment, crisis' and esp. 'moment of peril, danger' (often used in connection with *perīculum*) : *discernere* 'separate, distinguish', cpd. of *cernere* 'separate, sift, distinguish, perceive', etc. Walde-P. 2.584. Ernout-M. 178.

Fr. *danger*, OFr. *dongier, dangier* (*a* by influence of *dam*, Lat. *damnum*), orig. 'power, jurisdiction, domination', whence 'peril, danger' in phrases like *estre en dangier* 'be in the power, at the mercy' (of someone), fr. VLat. **dominiārium* 'power', deriv. of *dominus* 'lord, master'. REW 2736. Gamillscheg 290. Wartburg 3.128.

Rum. *primejdie*, fr. Slavic, cf. Bulg. *prě-mězdije* 'danger', lit. 'that which is beyond the boundary', fr. *mežda* 'border, boundary' (= ChSl. *mežda* 'street' : Skt. *madhya-*, Grk. μέσος 'middle', etc.). Tiktin 1255. Berneker 2.32.

3. Ir. *gūas, gūasacht*, perh. (**ĝhaud-to-*) : Lith. *žudyti* 'kill', OE (*ā*)*gētan* 'injure, kill'. Walde-P. 1.564.

Ir. *gāba, gābud* (NIr. *gābadh* mostly 'want, need', but also 'danger'; cf. Dinneen), etym.? G. S. Lane, Language 13.24.

Ir. *bāigul* (also 'chance, opportunity'), NIr. *baoghal*, perh. : ChSl. *bojati sę* 'be afraid', *bojaznĭ*, Lith. *baimė, bailė*, etc. 'fear' (16.53). Pedersen 1.56.

NIr. *contabhairt*, fr. Ir. *cundubart* 'dubium', fr. **con-di-fo-ber-*, cpd. of root of *berim* 'bear, carry'. Pedersen 2.467.

W. *perigl*, fr. Lat. *perīculum* (above, 2). Loth, Mots lat. 195.

W. *enbydrwydd*, fr. *enbyd* 'dangerous', cpd. of *pyd* (arch.) 'pit, pitfall, snare, danger' (this fr. OE *pytt*, ME *pyt, pit*, fr. Lat. *puteus* in spite of Morris Jones 269). For the suffix *-rwydd* '-ness' (orig. 'course' : Ir. *riadaim* 'ride') cf. Pedersen 2.14 f.

Br. *riskl*, also 'risk', cf. *riskla, riska* 'slip', *risklus* 'slippery, dangerous', and *ri(n)kl* 'slippery', *rikla* 'slip'. Evidently a blend of Fr. *risque* 'risk' with a native word for 'slip'. Henry 234.

Br. *gwall*, also 'evil, fault', as adj. 'bad' (16.72).

4. Goth. *bireikei*, etym. dub. Feist 9.94.

Goth. *sleiþei*, fr. *sleiþs* 'bad, dangerous' : ON *slīðr* 'fearful', OE *slīþe* 'dire, dangerous', OHG *slīdīc* 'angry, cruel', further connections dub. Walde-P. 2.401. Feist 437. Walde-H. 1.813.

ON *hætta* (fr. vb. *hætta* 'risk', fr. **hanhatjan*), *hāski* (**hankaskan-*) : Skt. *çañk-* 'be anxious, apprehensive, or distrustful', *çankā-* 'apprehension, alarm, fear, suspicion', Lat. *cunctārī* 'delay, hesitate, doubt', these perh. further : Goth. *hāhan*, ON *hanga*, etc. 'hang'. Walde-P. 1.461. Falk-Torp 448, 1480. Walde-H. 1.307.

OE *pleoh* : *plēon* 'dare, risk', prob. fr. the same root as the following, but exact relation obscure (Gmc. *h* beside *g*).

OE *pliht* (also 'damage'), ME *plyȝt* (NE *plight*), OHG *pfligida* : OHG *pflicht* 'care, service, duty', NHG *pflicht* 'duty', OHG *pflegon* 'care for, be accustomed', etc., outside connections dub. Walde-P.

1.869. Weigand-H. 2.412 f. Kluge-G. 442.

OE *frēcen*, also *frēcen(n)es, frēcednes* : *frēcne* 'horrible, savage, daring, dangerous', OS *frōkan* 'wild, bold, impudent', ON *frækn, frækinn* 'unafraid, courageous', OE *frec* 'greedy, bold', ON *frekr* 'greedy, severe', OHG *freh* 'greedy', etc., outside connections dub. Falk-Torp 279. Walde-P. 2.88.

ON *fǣr* (ME *fere*, NE *fear*, 16.53), OHG *fāra*, MHG *vāre* (also 'ambush', as OS *fār*; > Dan. *fare*, Sw. *fara*), NHG *gefahr*, Du. *gevaar* : Lat. *perīculum*, etc. (above, 2). Falk-Torp 205. Hellquist 200. Franck-v. W. 192.

NE *danger*, fr. ME *daunger*, mostly 'power of a lord or master, jurisdiction' (first quoted in modern sense 1489 in NED), fr. OFr. *dongier, dangier* id. (above, 2).

ME, NE *peril*, fr. Fr. *péril* (above, 2).

OHG *freisa*, MHG *vreise* (also 'trial, hurt', etc., Du. *vrees* 'fear') : Goth. *fraisan* 'try', etc. fr. an extension of the root in OE *fǣr* and Lat. *perīculum* (above, 2). Falk-Torp 275 f. Franck-v. W. 761 f.

5. Lith. *pavojus*, whence *pavojingas* 'dangerous' : *veju, vyti* 'hunt, pursue' (10.53).

Lett. *briesma*, usually pl. *briesmas*, etym. dub. Muhl.-Endz. 1.337 (Slavic *bridŭ* 'sharp, sour'?).

6. ChSl. *běda* (in Gospels once = ἀνάγκη 'distress'; in Supr. 'necessity, distress, force', and 'danger', also *bezbědĭnŭ* = ἀκίνδυνος), in modern Slavic 'distress, wretchedness' : *běditi* 'compel' (19.48).

SCr. *opasnost*, Russ. *opasnost'* ('danger' fr. 'care'), fr. Slavic *opasti sę* 'be on one's guard' (cf. Russ. *opasat'sja* 'guard against, take heed', ChSl. *opasŭmŭ, opasenĭje* 'exactness, care'), cpd. of Slavic *pasti* 'pasture, graze, watch cattle' : Lat. *pāscere* 'pasture, feed', etc. Walde-P. 2.72. Miklosich 232 f.

Boh. *nebezpečí*, Pol. *niebezpieczeństwo*, neg. cpds. of *bezpečí, bezpieczeństwo* 'security, safety', these cpds. of *bez* 'without' and derivs. of *peče, piecza* 'care' (16.14). Brückner 406 f.

7. Skt. *bhaya-* 'fear' (16.53), also freq. 'danger'.

Skt. *saṁçaya-* 'hesitation, doubt' (fr. *saṁ-çi-* 'be in doubt', lit. 'lie together'), also 'danger'.

Av. *iθyajah-, iθyejah-* : Skt. *tyāga-* 'abandonment, desertion, sacrifice', *tyaj-* 'forsake, leave'. Walde-P. 1.746. Barth. 799.

Av. *θwayaŋha-*, fr. *θwayah-* in adj. *θwayahvant-* 'frightful, dangerous' : *θwi-* 'rouse fear', *θwaēšah-* 'fear' (16.53). Barth. 794.

16.55 TIMID, COWARDLY

Grk.	δειλός, ἄτολμος, ἄνανδρος	Goth.	*faurhts*	Lith.	*bailus, bailingas*
NG	δειλός, ἄναντρος	ON	*hræddr, ragr*	Lett.	*bail'š, bailīgs*
Lat.	*timidus, ignāvus*	Dan.	*frygtsom, ræd, fejg*	ChSl.	*strasivŭ*
It.	*timido, vile, vigliacco, codardo*	Sw.	*rädd, feg*	SCr.	*strašljiv, bojazljiv, kukavički*
Fr.	*timide, craintif, peureux, lâche*	OE	*forht, earg*	Boh.	*bázlivý, zbabělý*
Sp.	*tímido, cobarde*	ME	*ferfull, argh, coward*	Pol.	*bojaźliwy, tchórzliwy*
Rum.	*timid, fricos, mișel*	NE	*timid, cowardly*	Russ.	*robkij, bojazlivyj, truslivyj*
Ir.	*ecal, midlachda*	Du.	*vreesachtig, lafhartig*	Skt.	*bhīru-, kātara-*
NIr.	*eaglach, faiteach, cladhardha*	OHG	*forhtal, zagi*	Av.	. . . .
W.	*ofnus, llwfr*	MHG	*vorhtec* (etc.), *zage, zaghaft*		
Br.	*aonik, laosk*	NHG	*furchtsam, zaghaft, feig*		

Most of the words for 'timid' are cognate with those for 'fear'. Some of these are 'fearful' in both the subj. ('feeling fear') and the obj. ('causing fear') senses, as ME *ferfull*, NE *fearful* (now mostly obj.; as subj. largely replaced by *timid*). Or these two senses may be differentiated by the endings, as NHG *furchtsam* (subj., but MHG also obj.) vs. *furchtbar* (obj.).

Several of these words cover in feeling both the mild 'timid' and the more opprobrious 'cowardly', e.g. Grk. δειλός, Lith. *bailus*, Skt. *bhīru-*. But there are also more distinctive terms for 'coward' and 'cowardly', most of them derived from a variety of abusive epithets (to which might be added others, not included in the list).

Most of the words for 'timid', since their relationship to those for 'fear' is obvious by comparison of the list of the latter (16.53), are omitted in the following discussion, which deals mainly with words for 'cowardly'.

1. Grk. δειλός (: δέος 'fear') covers also, in fact is most commonly, 'cowardly', for which also the following:

Grk. ἄτολμος, neg. cpd. of τόλμα 'daring' : τολμάω 'dare' (16.82).

Grk. ἄνανδρος, neg. cpd. of ἀνήρ, ἀνδρός 'man' (cf. ἀνδρεῖος, 16.52).

Grk. κακός 'bad' (16.72), sometimes (e.g. Hom.) of a warrior 'cowardly' (cf. ἀγαθός 'good' and 'brave').

2. Lat. *ignāvus*, also and more orig. 'lazy', neg. of (*g*)*nāvus* 'industrious, active' : W. *go-gnau* 'activity, active', prob. belonging with IE **gnō-* 'know', in Lat. (*g*)*nōscere*, etc. Walde-P. 1.580. Ernout-M. 657.

It. *codardo*, Sp. *cobarde*, fr. Fr. *couard* (no longer the usual world), deriv. of OFr. *coe*, Lat. *cauda* 'tail'. Semantic development perh. through 'having the tail between the legs' (like dogs, etc. when frightened), but there are other possibilities. REW 1774. Wartburg 3.523, 533. NED s.v. *coward*.

It. *vigliacco*, fr. Sp. *bellaco* 'sly, cunning, deceitful', deriv. of Lat. *villus* 'shaggy hair'. REW 9328, 9335.

It. *vile*, also 'vile, base, common', fr. Lat. *vilis* 'cheap, poor, worthless, mean'. REW 9328.

Fr. *lâche*, lit. 'slack, loose', fr. VLat. **lascus* for *laxus* 'open, wide, loose', etc. REW 4918. Gamillscheg 546.

It. *poltrone* 'coward' (> Fr. *poltron* > NE *poltroon*), deriv. of OIt. *poltro*, not in the sense 'bed' (as NED s.v. *poltroon*), but in its orig. sense of 'foal, colt' (3.45), with reference to the timidity of the young animal. Bloch 2.168 ("qui s'effraie comme un poulain"). Sperber, Wört. u. Sach. 2.193 (but through 'lazy' from 'ass').

Rum. *mișel*, properly 'miserable, poor', fr. Lat. *misellus* 'poor, wretched, unfortunate'. REW 5607.

3. Ir. *midlachda*, fr. *midlach* 'coward', prob. deriv. of *mid-* 'middle, half', orig. sense something like 'half-ling'. I. Williams, BBCS 1.37.

NIr. *cladhardha*, fr. *cladhaire* 'coward', orig. 'digger' (: *cladhaim* 'dig'), apparently used as an abusive epithet.

W. *llwfr* : MBr. *llofr* 'leprous', Ir. *lobur* 'weak, infirm', Lat. *labāre* 'totter, be ready to fall', etc. Walde-P. 2.432.

Br. *laosk*, orig. 'loose, slack', of the same origin (but *k* fr. vb.) and in the sense 'cowardly' prob. influenced by Fr. *lâche* (above, 2). Loth, Mots lat. 180 f.

4. ON *ragr, argr*, OE *earg* (also 'lazy, base, vile'), ME *argh, arwe* (still dial., cf. NED s.v.), OHG *arg* (mostly 'avaricious, base'), NHG *arg*, Du. *erg* 'bad, evil', a generally opprobrious term, outside connections dub.; perh. : Lith. *ragana* 'witch', Skt. *ṛghāya-* 'quiver, rage', Av. *ərəγant-* 'frightful, horrible', ultimate root meaning? Walde-P. 1.147. Kluge-G. 22. Franck-v. W. 158. Weisweiler, IF 41.16 ff.

Dan. *fejg*, Sw. *feg*, see under NHG *feig*, below.

ON *hræddr*, Dan. *ræd*, Sw. *rädd* 'afraid, timid' : ON *hræda* 'frighten', *hræzla* 'fright' (16.53).

Dan. *krysteragtig*, fr. *kryster* 'coward', prob. : *kryste* 'squeeze, press, hug', hence orig. 'squeezer, hugger' as an abusive epithet. Falk-Torp 587. Dahlerup s.v.

ME *coward*, NE *cowardly* (*coward* only sb.), fr. OFr. *coart*, Fr. *couard* (above, 2).

Du. *laf* 'cowardly, insipid' (MDu. 'slack, weak, faint') : ON *lafa* 'hang down', etc. Hence also *lafhartig*, cpd. of *hart* 'heart'. Franck-v. W. 367.

OHG *zagi*, MHG *zage, zag(e)haft*, NHG (*zag*), *zaghaft* (in older periods 'cowardly', now much milder 'faint-hearted, timid, hesitant'; replaced in older sense by *feig*) with vb. OHG *zagēn* 'lose courage, be undecided', NHG *verzagen* 'despair', perh. : Goth. *tahjan* 'tear', Norw. dial. *tæja, taa* 'shred', cf. also Norw. dial. *taag* 'slow, lasting', and for semantic development NHG *zögern* 'delay' : OHG *zogōn* 'pull, tear'. In any case semantic development prob. through 'hesitant, irresolute'. Walde-P. 1.785. Falk-Torp 261.

NHG *feig* (hence the sense 'cowardly' in Dan. *fejg*, Sw. *feg*), through 'fearful of death' fr. MHG *veige*, OHG *feigi* 'fated to die' = ON *feigr*, OE *fǣge* id. (NE, esp. Sc. *fey*), beside OE *fāh, fāg* 'hostile, foe', etc., prob. : Lith. *piktas* 'angry', etc. (16.42). Walde-P. 2.10. Falk-Torp 211. Kluge-G. 151. Weigand-H. 1.513.

5. SCr. *kukavički*, fr. *kukavica* 'coward', lit. 'cuckoo' used as a popular abusive epithet.

Boh. *zbabělý*, cf. *zbabělec* 'coward', fr. *baběti* 'grow cowardly', fr. *baba* 'old woman'.

Pol. *tchórzliwy*, fr. *tchórz* 'a coward', lit. 'polecat', as an abusive epithet 'stinker', like NE (U.S.) *skunk*.

Russ. *robkij*, through 'servile', fr. *rab*, ChSl. *rabŭ, robŭ* 'slave'. Brückner 459.

Russ. *truslivyj*, fr. *trus* 'coward' : *trusit'* 'fear, be afraid' also 'scatter, strew', ChSl. *trąsŭ* 'quake', *tręsti*, Russ. *trjasti* 'shake', refl. 'shiver', etc. (Walde-P. 1.758). Trautmann 330. Brückner 579.

6. Skt. *kātara-*, perh. as 'disgraceful' : *kātkṛta-* 'despised, derided', and ON *hāð* 'ridicule', Grk. κωτίλος 'chattering'. Walde-P. 1.384. Uhlenbeck 51.

16.61 WILL, WISH (vb.)

Grk.	*(ἐ)θέλω, βούλομαι*	Goth.	*wiljan*	Lith.	*norėti*
NG	*θέλω*	ON	*vilja, æskja*	Lett.	*gribēt (vēlēt)*
Lat.	*velle*	Dan.	*ville, ønske*	ChSl.	*chotěti, chŭtěti*
It.	*volere*	Sw.	*vilja, önska*	SCr.	*htjeti*
Fr.	*vouloir*	OE	*willan, wȳscan*	Boh.	*chtíti*
Sp.	*querer*	ME	*wille, wisshe*	Pol.	*chcieć*
Rum.	*voi, vrea*	NE	*will, wish, want*	Russ.	*chotet'*
Ir.	*dūthraccar*	Du.	*willen, wenschen*	Skt.	*vaç-, iṣ-*
NIr.	*toil* (in phrases)	OHG	*wellen, wunscen*	Av.	*vas-, iš-*
W.	*ewyllysio, mynnu*	MHG	*wellen, wollen, wünschen*		
Br.	*mennout, youli*				
		NHG	*wollen, wünschen*		

The words listed are the most common verbs for 'will, wish'. The majority of them cover 'will' and 'wish' without distinction between the notions of 'volition' in the modern technical sense and the simple 'wish'. But for 'wish', besides the Gmc. group which is included here, cf. also the verbs listed under 'desire' (16.62), many of which are often scarcely stronger than 'wish'.

1. IE *wel-. Walde-P. 1.294 f. Ernout-M. 1129 f. REW 9180. Falk-Torp 1379.

Lat. *velle*, 1sg. *volō*, perf. *voluī*, whence VLat. **volēre* (> It. *volere*, Fr. *vouloir*, Rum. *vrea*); Goth. *wiljan*, OE *willan*, etc., general Gmc.; elsewhere not the common verb for 'will, wish' but in more emphatic sense 'choose, command', etc., e.g. Umbr. *veltu* 'diligito', *ehueltu* 'iubeto', OLith. *(pa)velti* 'will, grant', Lett. *vēlēt* 'grant, wish' (in phrases like 'wish one joy'), ChSl. *velěti* 'will, command, permit' (but sb. *volja* 'will', vb. *voliti* 'will, choose'), Skt., Av. *var-* 'choose'. The 'wish' notion may be reinforced by the use of opt. instead of indic. forms, e.g. 1sg. Goth. *wiljau* reg., Lat. *velim* frequently.

2. Grk. *ἐθέλω* and *θέλω* (the most generic word) : ChSl. *želěti* 'desire' (16.62), further connections dub. Walde-P. 1.692.

Grk. *βούλομαι* (Att.-Ion.; dial. *βόλομαι*, *δείλομαι*, *δήλομαι*, *βέλλομαι*, etc., all pointing to IE **gʷel-*), usually implying a decisive choice, with sb. *βουλή* 'counsel, Council', etc., prob. : *βάλλω* 'throw, put' (Arc. *δέλλω*, cf. Skt. *gal-* 'drip', hence likewise fr. a root **gʷel-*), with development in mid. through 'cast about in the mind, ponder, resolve' (cf. *βάλλομαι* in phrases with *ἐνὶ θυμῷ*, *ἐνὶ φρεσί*, *εἰς νοῦν*, etc.). But details of the formal evolution (through aor. subj. **βόλσομαι*?) still uncertain. Kretschmer, Glotta 3.160 ff. Schwyzer, Gr. Gram. 284.

Grk. dial. *λείω*, *λῶ* (in several Dor. dialects and Elean) : *λῆμα* 'will', prob. *λελίημαι* 'desire eagerly', outside root connections dub. Walde-P. 2.392.

3. Lat. *velle*, etc. above, 1.

Osc.-Umbr. has rather *her-* (e.g. fut. Osc. *herest*, Umbr. *heriest* 'volet'; *vel-* in Umbr. *veltu* 'diligito', etc., above, 1) : Lat. *horī*, *hortārī* 'urge, encourage', Grk. *χαίρω* 'rejoice', Goth. *gairnjan* 'desire', etc. (16.22, 16.62).

Sp. *querer*, fr. Lat. *quaerere* 'seek'. REW 6923.

Rum. *voi* (beside *vrea*, above, 1), fr. *voe*, fr. Slavic, ChSl. *volja* 'will' (above, 1). Tiktin 1779.

4. Ir. *dūthraccar*, fr. **di-fo-tracc-*, etym. dub., perh. as 'be pressed' : OE *þringan* 'press, crowd', OHG *dringan* 'press, push, squeeze', etc. (cf. NHG *es drängt mich*

'I am eager'). Walde-P. 1.758 f. Pedersen 2.653 f. Thurneysen, Gram. 504.

Ir. *tol*, NIr. *toil* 'will' (sb.), perh. : Goth. *þulan*, ON *þola*, OE *þolian* 'bear, endure', Lat. *tollere* 'lift', etc., but semantic relation not clear. Walde-P. 1.739. Hence the NIr. usual expression by *toil* in phrases e.g. *is toil liom* 'it is my will' = 'I will, wish'.

W. *ewyllysio*, Br. *youli*, fr. sbs. W. *ewyllys* 'will, volition', Br. *youl* 'desire' : Lat. *avēre* 'desire eagerly', Skt. *av-* 'favor', etc. Walde-P. 1.19. Pedersen 1.314.

W. *mynnu*, Br. *mennout* (beside *menna* 'propose, think, intend'), also W. *dymuno* 'desire' : Ir. *do-muinur* 'believe', Lat. *meminī* 'remember', *monēre* 'warn', Skt. *man-* 'think', IE **men-*. Walde-P. 2.264 f. Pedersen 2.451, 581 f.

5. Goth. *wiljan*, etc., general Gmc., above, 1.

ON *æskja*, Dan. *ønske*, Sw. *önska*, OE *wȳscan*, ME *wisshe*, NE *wish*, Du. *wenschen*, OHG *wunscen*, MHG, NHG *wünschen*, fr. the sbs. ON *ōsk*, OE *wȳsc*, OHG *wunsc*, etc. : Skt. *vāñchā-* 'desire, wish', sb. *vāñchā-*, all fr. an extension of IE **wen-* in Skt. *van-* 'seek, desire, gain', Lat. *venus* 'charm' (and *Venus*), OHG *wunna* 'joy, bliss', Goth. *wēns* 'hope', etc. Walde-P. 1.260. Falk-Torp 1420.

NE *want*, orig. 'be lacking, lack', hence 'need' and now a common colloq. equivalent of *wish*. NED s.v. *want*, vb. 5.

6. Lith. *norėti* : ChSl. *nravŭ* 'virtue, custom', Russ. *norov* 'habit', Grk. *νωρεῖ· ἐνεργεῖ* (Hesych.). Walde-P. 2.333.

Lith. *linkėti* (mostly in phrases like 'wish you joy', cf. NSB s.v.) : *linkti* 'bow', *lenkti* 'bend', ChSl. *sŭ-lęką*, *-lęšti* 'bend together', etc. Walde-P. 2.435. 'Wish' fr. 'incline toward'.

Lett. *gribēt*, beside sb. *gribe* 'will, wish', orig. 'grasp after' : *greibt*, Lith. *griebti* 'grasp after, seize', Goth. *greipan*, OE *gripan*, etc. 'seize, grasp'. Walde-P. 1.647. Mühl.-Endz. 1.653 f.

7. ChSl. *chotěti*, Russ. *chotet'*, beside ChSl. *chŭtěti*, Russ. dial. *chtět'*, SCr. *htjeti*, Boh. *chtíti*, Pol. *chcieć*, etym. much disputed and still dub. Berneker 398 f. Brückner 177.

8. Skt. *vaç-*, Av. *vas-* : Grk. *ἑκών* 'willing', etc. Walde-P. 1.224 f. Barth. 1381 f.

Skt. *iṣ-* (3sg. *icchati*), Av. *iš-* 'seek, strive for, desire, wish' : OE *āscian*, *āxian* 'ask, ask for, demand', OHG *eiscōn* 'seek out, ask, demand', etc. (18.31, 18.35). Walde-P. 1.12.

16.62 DESIRE (vb.)

Grk.	*ἐπιθυμέω, ποθέω*	Goth.	*gairnjan*	Lith.	*geisti*
NG	*ἐπιθυμῶ, ποθῶ*	ON	*girna*	Lett.	*gribēt*
Lat.	*cupere, dēsīderāre*	Dan.	*begære*	ChSl.	*želěti*
It.	*desiderare, bramare*	Sw.	*åstunda, begära*	SCr.	*željeti, žudjeti*
Fr.	*désirer, souhaiter*	OE	*wilnian, giernan*	Boh.	*žádati*
Sp.	*desear*	ME	*wilnen, yerne, desire*	Pol.	*żądać*
Rum.	*dori*	NE	*desire, long for (yearn)*	Russ.	*želat', žaždat'*
Ir.	*adcobra* (3sg.)	Du.	*begeeren (verlangen)*	Skt.	*iṣ-, laṣ-, vāñch-*
NIr.	*mianuighim, dūilighim*	OHG	*gerōn*	Av.	*iš-*
		MHG	*(be)gern*		
W.	*dymuno, chwantu*	NHG	*begehren (verlangen)*		
Br.	*c'hoantaat*				

Words expressing some degree of 'desire' are so numerous that in the case of some languages the choice of the most important is difficult. Even among those listed (the vbs.; most of the sbs. for 'desire, longing', etc. are derived from them, or conversely) there is considerable difference in feeling. Some are stronger than others, 'desire eagerly, long for'. Most of them are used in both the good and the bad sense, but the latter may become dominant (as definitely in NE *covet*, *lust*). In some, 'desire' is used also for a polite 'request, demand' (the latter now dominant in NHG *verlangen*). Several are more or less literary, and nearly everywhere in common speech one would substitute for a mild 'desire' the words for 'wish' (NE *want*) or locutions like NE *I should like*, Fr. *je voudrais*, NHG *ich möchte*, etc.

The words for 'desire' are related to others denoting mental and physical agitation, also 'rejoice', 'seek', 'expect', and such physical notions as 'thirst', 'hunger' (as, in general, words for 'thirst' and 'hunger' may be used figuratively), 'cry for', etc. In several cases 'lack, need' is the source, or an intermediate stage in the development, of 'desire' (like NE colloq. *want* 'desire, wish').

1. Grk. *ἐπιθυμέω*, lit. 'set one's heart on', fr. *θυμός* 'spirit, etc.' (16.11).

Grk. *ποθέω*, *ἐπιποθέω*, fr. *πόθος* 'longing, yearning', also 'regret' (for something lost or absent) : *θέσσασθαι* 'beseech, pray for', Ir. *guidim* 'pray, ask', Lith. *gedauti* 'long for, desire', ChSl. *žędati* 'thirst, desire', etc. (below, 6), Av., OPers. *jad-* 'beseech, pray for or to'. Walde-P. 1.673.

2. Lat. *cupere* and *cupīre*, 1sg. *cupiō*, prob. through 'be agitated' : Skt. *kup-* 'become agitated, grow angry', ChSl. *kypěti* 'boil', Lett. *kūpēt* 'smoke, steam', etc. Walde-P. 1.379 f. Ernout-M. 244. Walde-H. 1.312.

Lat. *dē-sīderāre* (> It. *desiderare*, Fr. *désirer*) 'lack, miss, desire', beside *considerāre* 'observe closely, consider', both fr. *sīdus*, mostly pl. *sīdera* 'stars (in a constellation), heavenly bodies (including the sun and moon)'. The semantic development is obvious in *consīderāre* ('consult the stars'; cf. *contemplārī* 'observe, consider' fr. *templum* 'place of augury'), while for *dēsīderāre* the precise stages are uncertain, but certainly through 'lack, miss' (> 'desire', not conversely). Ernout-M. 938. Walde-H. 1.263.

It. *bramare* (= Sp. *bramar*, Fr. *bramer* 'bellow', OFr. also 'cry', Prov. also 'desire'), fr. a Gmc. **brammōn* 'bellow' (: MLG *brammen*), semantic development through 'cry for' (food, etc.). REW 1270. Wartburg 1.494 ff.

Fr. *souhaiter*, cpd. of OFr. *haitier* 'make well disposed', fr. sb. *hait* 'good disposition, joy', this fr. a Gmc. form belonging with OHG *heit* 'manner' *heitar* 'bright, clear', etc. Bloch 2.287. Gamillscheg 811 (somewhat otherwise).

Sp. *desear*, fr. sb. *deseo* = It. *desio*, *disio*, fr. Lat. *dēsidia*, deriv. of *dēsīdēre* 'sit idle', hence 'indolence' but also applied to other faults such as 'license, lust' (so prob. Plautus, Bacch. 1083, Trin. 650; cf. gl. *libido amor desidens*; see also Thes. s.v. p. 711, ll. 39 ff.); sense development 'indolence' > 'lust' > 'desire'. REW 2590. J. Corominas, Anales del instituto de Linguistica 2.128 ff.

Rum. *dori*, deriv. of *dor* '(mental) pain, suffering, longing', fr. VLat. **dolus*, for *dolor* (16.31). Tiktin 565.

3. Ir. 3sg. *adcobra* (with sb. *accobor* 'desire'), perh. (fr. **ad-com-bher-*) : *topur* (**to-od-bher-*) 'spring', Skt. *bhur-* 'move convulsively, quiver', Grk. *πορφύρω* 'swell, surge' (cf. Lat. *cupere*, above 2). Pedersen 2.478, 675.

NIr. *mianaim* or *mianuighim*, fr. *mian* 'desire' : W. *mwyn* 'enjoyment, use', prob. fr. the root in OHG *meinen*, OE *mǣnan* 'have in mind, intend', Ir. *do-moiniur* 'believe', etc. Walde-P. 2.302. Loth, RC 41.398.

Ir. *dūilighim*, fr. sb. *dūil* 'desire' (used also in phrases like 'it is my desire' = 'I desire'), through the notion of 'agitation' fr. the same root as Skt. *dhūli-* 'dust', Grk. *θυμός* 'spirit', etc. (16.11). Walde-P. 1.836. Stokes 153. Pedersen 1.111.

W. *dymuno* : *mynnu* 'will, wish', etc. (16.61).

W. *chwantu*, Br. *c'hoantaat*, fr. sbs. W. *chwant* 'desire, appetite, lust', Br. *c'hoant* 'desire', perh. : Arm. *xand* 'desire', Grk. *χατις* 'need', etc. Walde-P. 2.517. Pedersen 1.24, 139. But cf. also Loth, RC 45.182.

4. Goth. *gairnjan*, ON *girna* (mostly in refl. form), OE *giernan*, *gyrnan*, ME *yerne*, NE *yearn*, OHG *gerōn*, MHG *gern*, *begern*, NHG *begehren*, Du. *begeeren* (MLG > Dan. *begære*, Sw. *begära*), beside adjs. Goth. *-gairns*, OE *georn*, OHG *gern* (adv. *gerno*, NHG *gern*) 'eager' and sbs. Goth. *gairnei*, OHG *girida* (NHG *begehr*, *begierde*), etc., fr. the root of Grk. *χαίρω* 'rejoice', Osc. *herest* 'volet', Lat. *hortārī* 'urge, encourage', Skt. *haryati* 'delights in', etc. Walde-P. 1.601. Walde-H. 1.658. Feist 186.

Gmc. sb. Goth. *lustus* (usual word for *ἐπιθυμία*; vb. *lustōn* only once), OE, OHG *lust* 'desire' and 'joy, pleasure' (NE *lust* mostly of sexual desire), perh. fr. a weak grade of **las-* in Lat. *lascīvus* 'playful, licentious', Grk. *λάσται· πόρναι* (Hesych.), Skt. *laṣ-* (**la-ls-*) 'desire', etc. Walde-P. 2.386. Walde-H. 1.766 ff. Falk-Torp 761.

Sw. *åstunda*, cpd. of *stunda* 'expect' (cf. ON *stunda á* 'strive for', Dan. *stunde til*, Sw. *stunda til* 'aspire to, long for'), deriv. of ON *stund* 'period of time, hour' (14.41). Falk-Torp 1191. Hellquist 1096.

OE *wilnian*, ME *wilnen* : OE *willan* 'will, wish' (16.61).

ME, NE *desire*, fr. OFr. *désirer* (above, 2).

OE *langian* (impers.), ME *longe*, NE *long* (*long to*, *long for*, with sb. *longing*), OHG *langēn* (impers.), MHG *verlangen* (impers.), Du., NHG *verlangen* (now mostly 'request, demand', but sb. *verlangen* still 'longing'), similarly also Dan. *længes*, Sw. *längta*, all fr. adjs. for 'long' (spatial and temporal) through impers. 'it seems long' (to wait). NED s.v. *long*, vb. Weigand-H. 2.1153.

5. Lith. *geisti* (1sg. *geidžiu*) : Lett. *gaidīt* 'wait', OPruss. *gēide* 'they wait', ChSl. *žīdati* 'wait', OHG *gīt* 'greediness', etc. Walde-P. 1.553. Trautmann 82.

Lett. *gribēt*, see under 'will, wish' (16.61).

6. ChSl. *želěti* (for *ἐπιθυμέω*, *ἐπιποθέω*, and rarely *θέλω*; sb. *želěnĭje* = *ἐπιθυμία*), SCr. *željeti*, Russ. *želat'* : Grk. *θέλω* 'wish' (16.61).

ChSl. *žędati* (in Gospels for *διψάω* 'thirst' in both lit. and fig. sense, later also for *ποθέω*), Boh. *žádati*, Pol. *żądać*, Russ. *žaždat'* (SCr. *žednjeti* 'thirst' in lit. sense) : Grk. *θέσσασθαι* 'beseech, pray for', *πόθος* 'longing', etc. (above, 1).

SCr.-ChSl. *žlŭděti*, SCr. *žudjeti* : ChSl. *gladŭ* 'hunger', Skt. *gṛdh-* 'desire eagerly', etc. Walde-P. 1.633. Berneker 320.

Slavic sbs. mostly fr. the preceding vbs., but cf. also Boh. *touha* 'desire, longing' : ChSl. *tąga* 'distress, anxiety', SCr. *tuga* 'grief, sorrow', etc. (16.32).

7. Skt. *iṣ-*, Av. *iš-*, see under 'wish' (16.61).

Skt. *laṣ-* (**la-ls-*), see under Goth. *lustus*, above, 4.

Skt. *vāñch-* : OHG *wunscen* 'wish', etc. (16.61).

16.63 HOPE (sb.)

Grk.	*ἐλπίς*	Goth.	*wēns*	Lith.	*viltis*
NG	*ἐλπίδα*	ON	*vān*	Lett.	*cerība*
Lat.	*spēs*	Dan.	*haab*	ChSl.	*upŭvanĭje, nadežda*
It.	*speranza*	Sw.	*hopp*	SCr.	*nada*
Fr.	*espoir, espérance*	OE	*tōhopa, wēn*	Boh.	*naděje*
Sp.	*esperanza*	ME	*hope, won, wene*	Pol.	*nadzieja*
Rum.	*speranţa, nădejde*	NE	*hope*	Russ.	*nadežda*
Ir.	*frescissiu, dōchus*	Du.	*hoop*	Skt.	*āçā-*
NIr.	*dōchas, sūil*	OHG	*gedingi, wān*	Av.	*vyaθra-*
W.	*gobaith*	MHG	*gedinge, hoffe(nunge), wān*		
Br.	*spi, ged*	NHG	*hoffnung*		

'Hope' is 'wishful expectation', and in the majority of the words 'hope' comes from, or at least through the medium of, either 'expectation' or 'wish'. A few of these are also used for simple 'expectation' (even of evil), as, conversely, words for 'expectation' may in certain contexts have the feeling of 'hope', e.g. NHG *erwartung*, especially in *erwartungsvoll* 'full of hope'.

1. Grk. *ἐλπίς* (NG pop. *ἐλπίδα*), with vb. *ἐλπίζω* 'hope', Hom. *ἔλπω* 'make hope', *ἔλπομαι* 'hope' : Lat. *volup* 'gladly', *voluptās* 'pleasure', fr. an extension of the root **wel-* in Lat. *velle* 'wish, will', etc. (16.61). Walde-P. 1.295. Boisacq 246.

2. Lat. *spēs* (OLat. pl. *spērēs*) with vb. *spērāre* (> It. *sperare*, Fr. *espérer*, Sp. *esperar*, whence derivs. It. *speranza* > Rum. *speranţa*, Fr. *espoir*, *espérance*, Sp. *esperanza*), prob. through 'success, confidence' : ChSl. *spěti* 'prosper, succeed', Lith. *spėti* 'have leisure, be fast enough', OE *spōwan* 'prosper, succeed', Skt. *sphāy-* 'grow fat, grow'. Ernout-M. 964. Persson, Beiträge 400. Otherwise Walde-P. 2.680 (but??).

Rum. *nădejde*, fr. Slavic, cf. ChSl. *nadežda*, etc. (below, 6).

3. Ir. *frescissiu*, *frescsiu*, vbl. n. of *frisaiccim* 'hope, expect', fr. **frith-ad-ci-* : *ad-cīu* 'see', etc. (15.51). Pedersen 2.488. Thurneysen, Gram. 514.

Ir. *dōchus*, NIr. *dōchas*, also 'expectation, supposition', orig. 'likelihood', fr. *dōig*, *dōich* 'likely' (cf. locutions like *is dōig lemm* 'I ween'), etym.? Pedersen 2.666 f. Macbain 137.

NIr. *sūil*, the same word as *sūil* 'eye' (4.21), but with special semantic development through 'sight, view, prospect' (cf. W. *gobaith*). Gael. has *dūil* 'hope' = NIr. *dūil* 'desire' (16.62).

W. *gobaith*, cpd. of *go-* 'sub-' and *paith* 'glance, prospect, scene', orig. dub. (cf. Loth, Mots lat. 192).

Br. *spi*, fr. vb. *spia* 'spy on, watch, hope', fr. OFr. *espier* (Fr. *épier*) 'spy'. Henry 250.

Br. *ged*, properly 'watch, guard' and, with semantic development as in *spi* (above), fr. Fr. *guet* 'watch'. Henry 131.

4. Goth. *wēns*, ON *vān* (> ME *won*), OE *wēn*, ME *wene*, OHG, MHG *wān*, all, except Goth., also more general 'opinion, expectation', etc., MHG already 'supposition, fancy, false opinion, etc.' (NHG *wahn*), with vbs. Goth. *wēnjan*, ON *væna*, OE *wēnan* (NE *ween*), OHG *wānen*, prob. (with grade **wēn-* beside **wen-*) : OE *winnan* 'work, strive, fight', Goth. *winnan* 'suffer', ON *vinna* 'work', etc., Skt. *van-* 'seek, desire, gain', etc. Walde-P. 1.260. Feist 561. Weigand-H. 2.1200.

OE *tō-hopa*, late *hopa*, ME, NE *hope*, OLG *tō-hopa*, MLG *hope* (> Dan. *haab*,

Sw. *hopp*), Du. *hoop*, central MHG (fr. LG) *hoffe* and *hoffenunge*, NHG *hoffnung*, a group evidently starting fr. OE, OLG *tō-hopa*; etym. much disputed, but perh. as orig. 'refuge' fr. 'place one springs to' : OE *hoppian* 'spring, hop'. Jespersen, Nord. Tidsskrift 8 (1919), 151 f. Weigand-H. 1.877 f. Otherwise Falk-Torp 365 f.

OHG *gedingi*, MHG *gedinge* (both also 'agreement') with vbs. OHG *(ge)dingen*, MHG *(ge)dingen*, not to be separated (as Walde-P. 1.705) fr. OHG *dingōn* 'negotiate, come to terms', etc. (NHG *dingen* 'bargain') : OE *þingian* 'plead, make terms', etc. (Walde-P. 1.725). Development through 'agreement, promise' (attested for OHG, MHG forms) to 'expectation' and 'hope'.

5. Lith. *viltis*, beside vb. *vilti-s* : *pavelti* 'wish, permit', Lat. *velle* 'will', etc. (16.61). Walde-P. 1.294. Trautmann 348.

Lett. *cerība* fr. *cerēt* 'guess, suppose, hope, think about, love', prob. deriv. of *ceras* 'devotion, reverence, ardor', also coll. 'hopes', perh. : MHG, NHG *harren* 'wait, award, tarry'. Walde-P. 1.411. Otherwise Mühl.-Endz. 1.374.

6. ChSl. *upŭvanĭje* (with modern Slavic words for 'expectation, hope, trust', etc., as SCr. *ufanje*, Boh. *úfání*, *doufání*, Pol. *ufność*, etc., but not reg. for 'hope'), fr. vb. *upŭvati* 'hope', SCr. *ufati se*, etc., etym.? Miklosich 269. Brückner 403, 449. For this group vs. following in ChSl., cf. Jagić, Entstehungsgesch. 410.

ChSl., Russ. *nadežda*, SCr. *nada*, Boh. *naděje*, Pol. *nadzieja*, fr. ChSl. *na-dějati sę* 'rely, hope', Russ. *na-dejat'sja* 'hope', etc., lit. 'place oneself on', cpd. of *děją*, *děti* 'place, put'. Berneker 182, 193.

7. Skt. *āçā-*, *āçās-*, fr. *ā-çās-* 'ask, supplicate, wish, hope for, expect', cpd. of *çās-* 'correct, instruct, rule'. Uhlenbeck 22.

Av. *vyaθra-*, etym.? Barth. 1475 f.

16.64 THANKS

Grk.	*χάρις*	Goth.	*awiliuþ, þank*	Lith.	*padėka*
NG	*εὐχαριστῶ* (vb.)	ON	*þǫkk*	Lett.	*pateikšana*
Lat.	*grātiae*	Dan.	*tak*	ChSl.	*blagodětĭ, chvala*
It.	*grazie*	Sw.	*tack*	SCr.	*hvala*
Fr.	*remercîments, grâces*	OE	*þanc*	Boh.	*díky*
Sp.	*gracias*	ME	*thanke(s)*	Pol.	*dzięki*
Rum.	*mulţumire*	NE	*thanks*	Russ.	*blagodarnost'*
Ir.	*buide*	Du.	*dank*	Skt.	*kṛtajñatā-*
NIr.	*buidheachas*	OHG	*danc*		
W.	*diolch*	MHG	*danc*		
Br.	*trugarez*	NHG	*dank*		

Words that express the feeling of 'thankfulness, gratitude' are either the same as, or more often derived from, those for 'thanks' (e.g. through the adjs., NE *thank-ful-ness*, NHG *dank-bar-keit*, etc.), which are therefore preferred in the list and discussion. This heading is intended as = NE *thanks* in *give thanks*, etc. (sg. *thank* obs., and in several of the other languages the pl. obligatory or usual in this sense); not as = *thanks!* and similar polite expressions, which, though of the same group, with some exceptions (e.g. Lith. *ačiū*, fr. the sound of a sneeze = 'good luck, God bless you'; Russ. *spasibo* : *spasat'* 'save, spare'), are not always identical with the forms listed (e.g. Fr. *merci*).

The words are cognate with others for 'joy, pleasure, praise, favor, recognition',

with good-will greetings (Rum.); and the Gmc. group was orig. 'thought' (> 'thoughtfulness' > 'thanks'). Or a verb for 'say' or the like may be specialized to 'say thanks, give thanks' (cf. under Ir. and Lett., below).

1. Grk. *χάρις* 'favor, grace' and esp. 'thanks' (Hom.+) : *χαρά* 'joy', *χαίρω* 'rejoice', etc. (16.22). Hence *εὐχαριστέω* usual vb. for 'thank' in LXX, NT, etc. (earlier *χάρις* with vbs.), as reg. in NG (where the sb. is used mostly in other senses or in phrases 'thanks to, for the sake of'); also *εὐχαριστία* 'giving of thanks, thankfulness' (so NG, but *εὐχαρίστησις* is 'satisfaction, pleasure').

2. Lat. *grātia* 'favor, kindness' and (mostly pl.) *grātiae* 'thanks' (> It. *grazie*, Fr. *grâces*, Sp. *gracias*), beside adj. *grātus* 'pleasing' and 'thankful', prob. (cf. Osc. *brateis* 'gratiae') : Skt. *gūrta-* 'welcome, agreeable', *gr-* 'praise' (3sg. *gṛṇāti*), Lith. *girti* 'praise', etc. Walde-P. 1.686. Ernout-M. 432 f. Walde-H. 1.619 f.

Fr. *remercîments*, fr. vb. *remercier*, OFr. *mercier* 'thank', fr. *merci* 'favor, kindness' (> ME, NE *mercy*), now 'thanks!', fr. Lat. *mercēs* 'wages, price', whence in eccl. language 'reward, favor'. REW 5517. Gamillscheg 607, 753.

Rum. *mulţumire*, fr. vb. *mulţumi* 'thank', this fr. the greeting *mulţi anĭ* 'many years' (like NG *ἔτη πολλά*). Tiktin 1019.

3. Ir. *buide*, NIr. *buidhe* or *buidheachas* (fr. adj. *buidheach* 'thankful') : W. *bodd* 'will, good will, pleasure', *boddhau* 'please' (16.21), etc.

For vb. 'thank' Ir. *atluchur* (with or without *buide*), cpd. *ad-tluch-* : *do-tluchur* 'ask for', perh. ChSl. *tlŭkŭ*, Russ. *tolk* 'meaning, sense'. Walde-P. 1.744. Pedersen 1.43, 2.650.

W. *diolch*, older *diolwch*, cpd. of *golwch* 'worship, prayer', cf. also *adolwch* 'entreaty', root connection? Pedersen 2.650.

Br. *trugarez* 'pity' (16.35), used also for 'thanks' under influence of Fr. *merci*.

4. Goth. *þank* (once, acc. sg.), OE *þanc*, OHG *danc*, etc., general Gmc., orig. 'thought' (as, beside 'thanks', in OE, OHG) : Goth. *þagkjan*, OE *þencan*, OHG *denken*, etc. 'think' (17.14). Walde-P. 1.744. Falk-Torp 1242.

Goth. *awiliuþ* (for *χάρις* and *εὐχαριστία*), with vb. *awiliudōn* (reg. for 'thank', once also 'praise'), cpd. *awi-liud-*, first part : Skt. *av-* 'favor', Lat. *avēre* 'desire eagerly', etc., second part : OE *lēoþ*, OHG *liod* 'song'. Walde-P. 1.19, 2.406. Feist 51.

5. Lith. *padėka*, less commonly *dėka*, through Slavic fr. Gmc., cf. Boh. *dík*, below, 6.

Lett. *pateikšana*, fr. *pateikti* 'say, relate' and esp. 'thank', cpd. of *teikt* 'say' (18.22). Mühl.-Endz. 3.120, 4.156 f.

6. ChSl. *blagodětĭ*, *blagodatĭ* (reg. for *χάρις* in Gospels), SCr. *blagodjet*, *blagodat* (mostly biblical), cpd. of *blagŭ* 'good' (influence of Grk. *εὐ-* in *εὐχαριστέω*) and **dětĭ* : ChSl. *děti* 'place, put', Grk. *τίθημι*, etc. Berneker 178. Similarly Russ. *blagodarnost'* ('thankfulness' and 'thanks'; SCr. *blagodarnost* 'thankfulness'), *blagodarenie*, fr. vb. *blagodarit'*, late ChSl. *blagodariti*, cpd. of *dariti* 'give'.

ChSl. *chvala* (in Gospels freq. for *χάρις*, but also for *αἶνος* 'praise'), SCr. *hvala*, both also and general Slavic 'praise' (16.79), use as 'thanks' prob. secondary. K. Meyer, Donum nat. Schrijnen 408 ff.

Boh. *dík* (mostly in pl. *díky*), earlier *děk*, *diek* (> Pol. *dzieka* > Ukr. *djaka*, Lith. *dėka*; Pol. now usually *dzięki* pl.), fr. OHG, MHG *danc* (above, 4). Berneker 193 f. Brückner 112.

7. Skt. *kṛtajñatā-*, beside adj. *kṛtajña-* 'thankful', lit. 'recognizing the deed', cpd. of *kṛta-* 'done' and *jñā-* 'know'.

16.65 FAITHFUL

Grk.	*πιστός*	Goth.	*triggws*	Lith.	*ištikimas*
NG	*πιστός*	ON	*tryggr, trūr*	Lett.	*uzticīgs*
Lat.	*fīdus, fidēlis*	Dan.	*tro*	ChSl.	*věrĭnŭ*
It.	*fedele, leale*	Sw.	*trogen*	SCr.	*vjeran*
Fr.	*fidèle, loyal*	OE	*getriewe, trēowe*	Boh.	*věrný*
Sp.	*fiel, leal*	ME	*trewe, faithful*	Pol.	*wierny*
Rum.	*credincios, statornic*	NE	*faithful, loyal (true)*	Russ.	*vernyj*
Ir.	*iressach*	Du.	*trouw*	Skt.	*bhakta-*
NIr.	*dīlis*	OHG	*gitriuwi*	Av.	*arədra-*
W.	*ffyddlon*	MHG	*getriuwe, triuwe*		
Br.	*feal, leal*	NHG	*treu, getreu*		

Words for 'faithful' are most commonly connected with vbs. for 'trust' or 'believe', or with adjs. for 'true' (in the current sense of NE *true*, 16.66). The Gmc. group rests ultimately on the notion of 'sound, steadfast', or the like. Certain words for 'loyal', orig. 'conforming to the law', have come to be equivalent to 'faithful' in many phrases (cf. NE *loyal friend* = *faithful friend*).

1. Grk. *πιστός*, beside *πίστις* 'faith, belief' : *πείθω* 'persuade', mid. 'trust, obey, believe', Lat. *fīdere* 'trust', *fīdus*, *fidēlis* 'faithful', *fidēs* 'faith, belief', further connections dub. Walde-P. 2.139. Ernout-M. 356 ff. Walde-H. 1.493 ff.

2. Lat. *fīdus*, *fidēlis* (> It. *fedele*, OFr. *feoil*, and *feel*, *feal*, Fr. *fidèle*, Sp. *fiel*. REW 3283), above, 1.

Fr. *loyal* (OFr. *leel* > It. *leale*), Sp. *leal*, orig. 'according to law', fr. Lat. *lēgālis*, deriv. of *lēx* 'law'. REW 4968.

Rum. *credincios*, fr. *credinţă* 'faith, honor, uprightness', VLat. **credentia* (cf. It. *credenza*, Fr. *croyance*, etc.), fr. Lat. *crēdere* 'believe'. REW 2307. Tiktin 433 f.

Rum. *statornic*, lit. 'constant, firm, steady', late formation fr. *sta* 'stand, sit, lie', in imitation of Slavic *stalan* 'stable, firm'. Tiktin 1486 f.

3. Ir. *iressach* (mostly in religious sense), fr. *iress* 'faith, belief' (22.11).

NIr. *dīlis* (*dīleas*), also 'dear', orig. 'one's own' (16.28).

W. *ffyddlon*, cpd. of *ffydd* 'faith' (fr. Lat. *fidēs*) and *llawn* 'full', prob. semantic borrowing fr. NE *faithful*.

Br. *feal*, fr. OFr. *feal* (above, 2). Henry 120.

Br. *leal*, fr. OFr. *leel* (above, 2). Henry 181.

4. Goth. *triggws*, ON *tryggr* (Dan. *tryg*, Sw. *trygg* 'safe'), OE *getriewe*, *trēowe*, ME *trewe*, NE *true* (now mostly arch. in this sense), OS *triuwi*, Du. *trouw*, OHG *gitriuwi*, MHG *getriuwe*, late *triu(we)*, NHG *treu*, *getreu*, Gmc. **trewwi-* beside **trūwia-* in ON *trūr*, Dan., Sw. *tro* (Sw. now only religious 'believing'; for general sense *trogen*, deriv. of vb. *tro* 'believe', cf. Hellquist 1008) : OPruss. *druwis* 'belief, faith', *druwīt* 'believe', Lith. *driutas* 'strong, firm', ChSl. *sŭ-dravŭ* 'well, sound', Skt. *dhruva-*, Av. *drva-*, OPers. *duruva-* 'firm, sound, secure', Ir. *derb* 'certain', *dron* 'firm', all ultimately, with notion of 'firm', connected with words for 'oak' and 'tree'. Walde-P. 1.804 ff. Falk-Torp 1284 f., 1290.

ME, NE *faithful*, fr. sb. *faith*, fr. OFr. *feid*, *feit*, fr. Lat. *fidēs* (above, 1). NED s.v.

NE *loyal*, fr. Fr. *loyal* (above, 2). NED s.v.

5. Lith. *ištikimas*, Lett. *uzticīgs*, fr. Lith. *ištikėti*, Lett. *uzticēt* 'trust', perfect. forms of Lith. *tikėti*, Lett. *ticēt* 'believe' (17.15).

6. ChSl. *věrĭnŭ*, etc., general Slavic,

fr. *věra* 'belief, faith' : Lat. *vērus* 'true', etc. (16.66). Walde-P. 1.286.

7. Skt. *bhakta-*, also 'devoted to', lit. 'allotted to, granted' (cf. NHG *ergeben*), pple. of *bhaj-* 'deal out, distribute, divide'. Walde-P. 2.127 f.

Av. *arədra-*, perh. : *arəd-*, *ərəd-* 'promote, advance, make thrive', Skt. *ṛdh-* 'thrive, prosper', *rādh-* 'be successful, prosper, be happy'. Walde-P. 1.74. Barth. 195.

16.66 TRUE

(Or in part sb. Truth)

Grk.	ἀληθής	Goth.	*sunja* (sb.)	Lith.	*teisingas*
NG	ἀλήθεια (sb.), ἀληθής, ἀληθινός	ON	*sannr*	Lett.	*patiess*
Lat.	*vērus*	Dan.	*sand*	ChSl.	*istina* (sb.)
It.	*vero*	Sw.	*sann*	SCr.	*istina* (sb.)
Fr.	*vrai*	OE	*sōð, sōþ-līc, wǣr*	Boh.	*pravda* (sb.)
Sp.	*verdad* (sb.)	ME	*sooth, trewe*	Pol.	*prawda* (sb.)
Rum.	*adevăr* (sb.), *adevărat*	NE	*true*	Russ.	*pravda* (sb.)
Ir.	*fīr*	Du.	*waar*	Skt.	*satya-*
NIr.	*fīor*	OHG	*wār(i)*	Av.	*haiϑya-*, OPers. *hašiya-*
W.	*gwir*	MHG	*wār, wære*		
Br.	*gwir*	NHG	*wahr*		

'True' is intended here, not as 'faithful, trustworthy' or 'real, genuine', but as 'consistent with fact', that is, in that sense of NE *true* which prevails in the sb. *truth* as the opposite of *lie*. The sbs. for 'truth' are most commonly derived from the adjs. for 'true', hence the latter are generally preferred in the list. But in some cases the opposite relation holds. Furthermore, in several languages the substantival is preferred to the adj. expression, that is, 'it is true' is expressed as 'it is the truth', while the adj. derivs. are used more in the sense of 'truthful', or 'real, genuine'. So NG ἀλήθεια, Sp. *verdad*, Russ. *pravda*, and frequently elsewhere. Hence the sb. forms instead of adjs. are in part entered in the list.

It is worthy of note that there are no primary vbs. for 'speak the truth' (usually a phrase, sometimes a denom.) in contrast to those for 'lie'.

Apart from an inherited group, the words are based on such notions as 'not escaping notice', 'existing, actual', 'straight, upright, just', and 'faithful'.

For this and the following group, cf. H. Frisk, "Wahrheit" und "Lüge" in den indogermanischen Sprachen (Göteborgs Högskolas Årsskrift 1935.3).

1. IE **wēro-*, ultimate root connection dub. Walde-P. 1.285 f. Ernout-M. 1095.

Lat. *vērus*, with sb. *vēritas;* Ir. *fīr*, NIr. *fīor*, W., Br. *gwir;* OE *wǣr* (but rare and dub. in this sense), OS *wār*, OHG *wār, wāri*, MHG *wār, wære*, NHG *wahr*, Du. *waar;* cf. Goth. *tuz-wērjan* 'doubt', ChSl. *věra* 'belief, faith', *věrĭnŭ* 'faithful', *věrovati* 'believe'; further connections, as with the group Lat. *verērī* 'revere', OE *waru* 'care, heed', *wær* 'aware', OHG *bi-warōn* 'care for, guard', etc., or with the group preferred by Walde-P. l. c., wholly doubtful.

2. Grk. ἀληθής, Dor. ἀλᾱθής, with sb. ἀλήθεια (in pop. NG the usual expression, as ἀλήθεια εἶναι 'it is true'), neg. cpd. of *λῆθος, Dor. λᾶθος = λήθη 'forgetting' : λανθάνω (also λήθω) 'escape notice', mid. 'forget', Lat. *latēre* 'be concealed, be unknown', etc. Walde-P. 2.377 f. Boisacq 554 f. Ernout-M. 526. Walde-H. 1.768 f. Deriv. Grk. ἀληθινός 'trusty, genuine', NG also 'true'.

Grk. ἐτεός (poet.) : Skt. *satya-* 'true', Goth. *sunja* 'truth', etc. (below, 5).

3. Lat. *vērus* (> It. *vero*, OFr. *voir*, OSp. *vero*), above, 1.

Fr. *vrai*, prob. fr. *veratius* (Merov.), i.e. *vērācius* comp. of *vērāx* 'truthful'. REW 9216a. Otherwize (**vēraius* fr. *vērārius*, like *primārius* for *primus*) Gamillscheg 898.

Sp. *verdad* (sb., usual expression), fr. Lat. *vēritas* (above, 1).

Rum. *adevăr* (sb., formerly also adj., orig. adv.), fr. adv. phrase *ad-ad-vērum* (cf. It. *davvero* 'truly'). Hence, through vb., *adevărat* 'true'. REW 9262. Puşcariu 24.

4. Celtic words, above, 1.

5. Goth. *sunja* sb. (for ἀλήθεια, and prob. also sb. not fem. adj. when used for ἀληθής Jn. 8.14, 17, Jn. 10.41; also adj. *sunjeins*), adj. (in part also sb.) ON *sannr*, Dan. *sand*, Sw. *sann*, OE *sōð*, deriv. *sōðlic*, ME (NE arch.) *sooth* : Skt. *satya-*, Grk. ἐτεός 'true', all orig. 'existing, actual', fr. pple. forms of IE **es-* 'be, exist'. Walde-P. 1.160 f. Feist 459. Falk-Torp 950.

ME *trewe*, NE *true*, fr. OE *trēowe* 'faithful' (16.65).

OHG *wār*, etc., above, 1.

6. Lith. *teisingas* (also 'right, just'; with sbs. *teisa*, *teisybė* 'truth'), Lett. *patiess* : Lith. *teisus* 'right, just', *tiesus* 'straight', Lett. *taisns* 'straight, just' (12.73, 16.73).

Lith. *tikras* is 'true' rather in the sense of 'real, sure, certain' (17.37).

7. ChSl., SCr. sb. *istina* (Russ. less common than *pravda;* Boh. *jistina* through 'reality' to 'capital'), whence adjs. ChSl. *istinĭnŭ* (usual form in Gospels), *istovŭ*, SCr. *istinit* (Russ. *istinnyj* in NT, but in current use 'true' = 'real, genuine'), fr. ChSl. *istŭ*, Russ. *istyj*, etc. 'real, actual', prob. fr. **iz-sto-*, cpd. of *iz* (ChSl. *izŭ*) 'out' and *-sto-* : IE **stā-* 'stand', like *pro-stŭ* 'straight, simple', etc. (Walde-P. 2.604). Berneker 435 f. Otherwise (fr. **es-* 'be', Slav. *jes-*) Miklosich 185, Brückner 436.

ChSl. *rěsnota* sb. (later than *istina;* cf. Jagić, Entstehungsgesch. 352), with adj. *rěsnotivŭ* : Lith. *reikšti*, pres. *reiškiu* 'reveal, mean', *raiškus* 'evident'. Trautmann 242.

Boh., Russ. *pravda*, Pol. *prawda*, sbs. = ChSl. *pravĭda* 'right, justice', fr. *pravŭ* 'straight' (12.73). Hence adjs. Boh. *pravidivý*, Pol. *prawdziwy*, Russ. *pravdivyj*, but these esp. 'truthful' or 'real, genuine', while 'true' in sense here intended is expressed by a phrase with the sb.

8. Skt. *satya-* (adj. and neut. sb.), Av. *haiϑya-*, OPers. *hašiya-* : Goth. *sunja* 'truth', etc. (above, 5).

16.67 LIE (sb.)

Grk.	ψεῦδος	Goth.	*liugn*	Lith.	*melas*
NG	ψέμα	ON	*lygi, lygð*	Lett.	*meli*
Lat.	*mendācium*	Dan.	*løgn*	ChSl.	*lŭža*
It.	*menzogna, bugia*	Sw.	*lögn*	SCr.	*laž*
Fr.	*mensonge*	OE	*lyge*	Boh.	*lež*
Sp.	*mentira*	ME	*lie*	Pol.	*kłamstwo*
Rum.	*minciună*	NE	*lie*	Russ.	*lož'*
Ir.	*brēc, gāu*	Du.	*leugen, logen*	Skt.	*asatya-, mithyā-vākya-*, etc.
NIr.	*brēag*	OHG	*lugin(a), lug(i)*		
W.	*celwydd*	MHG	*lüge, lügen(e)*	Av.	*druj-*, OPers. *drauga-*
Br.	*gaou*	NHG	*lüge*		

The opposite of 'true' may be expressed by negative compounds, e.g. OE *un-sōþ*, NE *un-true*, NHG *un-wahr*, Ir. *neb-fīr*, Lith. *ne-teisingas*, Skt. *a-satya-;* by Lat. *falsus* (pple. of *fallere* 'deceive') and its Romance and Gmc. derivs. (also opp. to 'faithful'); by OE *lēas*, also and more orig. 'destitute of, void' (: Goth. *laus* 'empty, vain', *fraliusan* 'lose', etc., 11.33). Similarly, the opposite of 'truth' may be expressed as 'untruth' or 'falsehood'. But in nearly all the IE languages there are distinctive downright terms for a 'lie', with corresponding verbs.

There is a notable agreement between Gmc. and Slavic in the words for 'lie', an inherited group for which it is impossible to determine any remoter underlying notion. 'Lie' and 'deceit' are sometimes expressed by the same or cognate terms. 'Lie' may evolve from milder notions, such as 'defect, error', or 'harm'. Several of the words are of obscure origin.

1. Grk. ψεῦδος, also ψεῦσμα (rare), Byz., ψεῦμα, NG pop. ψέμα, beside ψεύδω 'deceive', mid. 'lie', ψεύστης 'liar', ψευδής 'false', etc., etym. dub. Walde-P. 1.502. Boisacq 1075 f.

2. Lat. *mendācium*, with *mendāx* 'lying, false, liar', fr. *mendum, menda* '(physical) defect, error (in writing)', perh. : Ir. *mennar* 'spot', *mind* 'sign, mark', W. *man* 'place, spot, mark'. Walde-P. 2.270, Ernout-M. 605. Walde-H. 2.68 f.

Lat. vb. *mentīrī* 'lie' : *mēns, mentis* 'mind, intelligence, thought' (17.11), with semantic development perh. through 'say something thought up, invented' (cf. also the cognate OPruss. *mēntimai* 'we lie'). Walde-P. 2.270. Ernout-M. 606. Hence the sbs., Sp. *mentira* (fr. vb. *mentir*) and, through VLat. derivs. (**mentionia*, **mentio*), It. *menzogna*, OFr. *mensogne*, Fr. *mensonge* (influence of *songe* 'dream'), Rum. *minciună*. Walde-P. 2.270. Ernout-M. 606. Walde-H. 2.68. REW 5508–10.

It. *bugia*, fr. Prov. *bauzia* 'knavery, deceit', fr. *bauza* 'deceit', beside OFr. *boise* id., fr. the Gmc., cf. OHG *bosi*, etc. 'bad, evil' (16.72). REW 1006.

3. Ir. *brēc*, NIr. *brēag*, etym. dub.; perh. : Skt. *braṅça-* 'fall, destruction'. Walde-P. 2.204. Stokes 183.

Ir. *gāu* (also prefix *gu-* 'false-', cf. Laws, Gloss. 456), Br. *gaou*, Corn. *gow* (both also adj. 'false', as W. *gau*), etym. dub. Walde-P. 1.530. Thurneysen IF 21.179. Stokes 108.

W. *celwydd*, cpd. of *cel* 'hidden' and *gwydd* (arch.) 'knowledge'.

4. Goth. *liugn*, ON *lygi, lygð*, OE *lyge*, etc., general Gmc., with vbs. Goth. *liugan*, ON *ljūga*, OE *lēogan*, etc. : ChSl. *lŭža* 'lie', vb. *lŭgati*, adj. *lŭžĭ* 'lying', etc., perh. also MIr. *logaisse* 'lie' (only *logaissi. i. brēgi*, gl.; cf. BB 16.244). Walde-P. 2.415. Here also OLith. vb. *luginti* 'lie'. Specht, KZ 68.36.

5. Lith. *melas*, Lett. *meli* (pl.), with vbs. Lith. *meluoti*, Lett. *meluot* : Lett. *melst* 'gossip, talk nonsense', *maldīt* 'err, make a mistake', *malds* 'mistake, error', etc. (16.77). Mühl-Endz. 2.595. Walde-P. 2.291.

6. ChSl. *lŭža*, etc., general Slavic (but Pol. *łga*, vb. *łgać* obs.) : Goth. *liugn*, etc. (above, 4).

Pol. *kłamstwo*, fr. *kłam* (obs.) : Boh. *klam* 'deceit' (16.68).

7. Skt. *asatya-*, neg. of *satya-* 'true, truth'.

Skt. *mithyā-vākya-*, *-vāda-* and *mṛṣā-vāda-*, etc., cpds. of advs. *mithyā* and *mṛṣā* 'wrongly' with words for 'speaking'.

Skt. *alīka-* 'untrue', also neut. sb., prob. orig. 'crooked' : Grk. ὠλένη, Lat. *ulna* 'elbow', etc. Walde-P. 1.157. Uhlenbeck 15.

Av. *druj-* (rarely *draoga-*), OPers. *drauga-* 'lie, deceit' : Skt. *drogha-, droha-* 'injury, harm', *druh-* 'harm, be hostile to', OHG (*bi-*)*triogan*, etc. 'deceive' (16.68). Walde-P. 1.874. Barth. 768, 778 f.

16.68 DECEIT

Grk.	ἀπάτη, δόλος	Goth.	*afmarzeins, liutei, lists*	Lith.	*apgaulė, apgavas*
NG	ἀπάτη, δόλος, γέλασμα			Lett.	*krāpšana, vilšana*
Lat.	*fraus, dolus*	ON	*svik, tāl*	ChSl.	*lĭstĭ, ląka*
It.	*inganno*	Dan.	*bedrageri, svig*	SCr.	*prijevara*
Fr.	*déception, tromperie*	Sw.	*bedrägeri, svek*	Boh.	*klam, šal*
Sp.	*engaño, dolo*	OE	*fācen, swicdōm, lot*	Pol.	*oszustwo, szalbierstwo*
Rum.	*înşelăciune, amăgire*	ME	*deseyte, swike(dom)*	Russ.	*obman*
Ir.	*togāis, celg, fell, meng*	NE	*deceit*	Skt.	*kapaṭa-, chala-, māyā-*
NIr.	*cealg, feall*	Du.	*bedrog, list*		
W.	*twyll*	OHG	*feichan, biswih*	Av.	*druj-, diwža-*
Br.	*touellerez*	MHG	*veichen, (be)swīch(e), betroc*		
		NHG	*betrug, list*		

The principal words for 'deceit' (many others not mentioned here include this notion), with the corresponding vbs. for 'deceive', are from the most diverse sources. 'Wisdom' may degenerate through 'cunning' to 'deceit'. In several cases 'deceive' comes from 'laugh at, mock, make fun of' or the like. Other connections are with vbs. for 'injure, harm, hinder', 'catch', 'anticipate' ('get the better of'), 'bend' ('deviate'), etc.

1. Grk. ἀπάτη, etym.? Walde-P. 2.27. Boisacq 67.

Grk. δόλος (in Hom. 'bait, lure, wile'), Lat. *dolus* (> Sp. *dolo*), also Osc. *dolom, dolud*, 'dolum, dolo', perh. (and generally so taken) : ON *tāl* 'deceit, device', etc. But there is some probability that the Italic word is borrowed from the Greek; and in the Gmc. group the sense of 'deceit' or 'slander, blame' seems to be secondary and explainable on an internal Gmc. basis (see below, 4). Ernout-M. 280 f. Walde-H. 1.366 f.

NG (beside ἀπάτη, δόλος, mostly lit.) γέλασμα, fr. γελῶ 'laugh' and 'deceive, cheat' (τὸν ἐγέλασε, etc.; cf. 16.25).

2. Lat. *fraus, fraudis* 'injury, harm, crime', then esp. 'deceit, fraud' (> It. *frode*, Fr., Sp. *fraude* 'fraud' mostly in legal sense; OFr. > ME *fraude*, NE *fraud* in less restricted use but also omitted in the list) : Skt. *dhvṛ-* 'injure', *dhruti-* 'deception', and ultimately (**dhreu-gh-*) Skt. *druh-* 'injure', Av. *druj-* 'lie, deceit', OHG *triogan* 'deceive', etc. (below, 4). Walde-P. 1.869 f., 874. Walde-H. 1.543.

It. *inganno*, Sp. *engaño*, fr. It. *ingannare*, Sp. *engañar* 'deceive' = Rum. *îngîna* 'imitate, mock', fr. VLat. **ingannāre*, *gannāre* attested in glosses in sense of 'laugh at, mock', fr. Lat. *gannīre* 'bark, growl' (of animals and persons), late 'chatter', etc. 'Deceive' fr. 'laugh at, mock' as in NG (above, 1). REW 4406. Densusianu 191 f.

Fr. *déception*, fr. late Lat. *dēceptiō*, deriv. of *dēcipere* 'catch, ensnare, beguile, deceive' (> Fr. *décevoir*), cpd. of *capere* 'take, seize'.

Fr. *tromperie*, fr. *tromper* 'deceive', OFr. and dial. 'blow in a horn', then refl. 'make merry over', deriv. of *trompe* 'trumpet, horn'. REW 8952. Gamillscheg 869.

Rum. *înşelăciune, înşelătorie*, fr. *înşela* 'deceive' = *înşela* 'saddle'. This use influenced by SCr. *nasamariti* 'play a joke on', deriv. of *samar* 'pack-saddle'. Skok, Arch. sl. Ph. 37.84.

Rum. *amăgire*, fr. *amăgi* 'deceive, delude', prob. (with prefix *a-* fr. *ad-*) fr. Grk. μαγεύω 'bewitch'. Tiktin 55.

3. Ir. *togāis*, vbl. n. of *do-gāithim* 'deceive' : *gāith* 'wise', *gāes* 'wisdom'. Cf. development in Lat. *mentīre* 'lie' (16.67). Pedersen 2.19, 412. Thurneysen, Gram. 446.

Ir. *celg*, NIr. *cealg* : Arm. *kełck'* 'hypocrisy', OE *hylc* 'bend, turn', Pol. *czołgać* 'creep, crawl'. Walde-P. 1.447. Pedersen 1.106.

Ir. *fell*, NIr. *feall*, prob. : Lith. *ap-*, *pri-vilti* 'deceive', Lett. *vilt* id., etc. (cf. Lett. *vilšana*, below, 5). Walde-P. 1.298.

Ir. *meng* 'guile, deceit' (RIA Contrib. s.v.), prob. : Grk. μαγγανεία 'trickery', etc., Osset. *mäng* 'deceit', Toch. A *maṅk* 'fault'. Walde-P. 2.223. K. Schneider, KZ 66.253.

W. *twyll*, Br. *touellerez*, *toellerez*, beside vbs. W. *twyllo*, Br. *touella*, Corn. *tulle* 'deceive', etym.? Henry 267. Loth, RC 36.393 (vs. Morris Jones 182).

4. Goth. *afmarzeins* (ἀπάτη), fr. *afmarzjan*, *marzjan* 'σκανδαλίζω, offend' : OE *mierran* 'hinder', OHG *merren* 'hinder, vex', MHG *marren* 'delay', outside connections dub. Feist 347. Walde-P. 2.279.

Goth. *liutei* (δόλος, also ὑπόκρισις 'hypocrisy'), OE *lot* : Goth. *liuts* 'hypocritical', OE *lytig* 'deceitful', ON *ljōtr* 'ugly', perh. fr. the root in OE *lūtan*, ON *lūta* 'bow, stoop, fall', etc.; cf. also ChSl. *ludŭ* 'foolish', Russ. *ludit'* 'deceive', Lith. *liusti* 'be sad', *liudnas* 'sad'. Feist 335. Walde-P. 2.416.

Goth. *lists* (μεθοδεία 'wile') = ON, OE OS, OHG *list* 'wisdom, art, artifice, cunning', whence with development of a bad connotation Du., NHG *list* 'cunning, craft, guile' and for 'deceit', esp. NHG *hinterlist* (cf. Paul, Deutsches Wtb. s.v.), fr. the root of Goth. *lais* (pret. pres.) 'know', *laisjan*, OHG *lēren*, OE *lǣran* 'teach', etc. Feist 331 f. Walde-P. 2.404 f.

ON *svik*, Dan. *svig*, Sw. *svek*, OE *swic* in *swicdōm*, ME *swike*, *swikedom*, OHG *bīswih*, also (with *ī* as in vb.) MHG *swīch(e)*, *beswīch*, MLG *swīk* : ON *svīkja* 'betray', OE *swīcan* 'depart, cease, desert, betray', OHG *swīchan* 'leave behind, desert', etc., prob. as 'bend, turn aside' fr. **sweig-* beside **sweik-* in ON *sveigr* 'pliant', *sveigja* 'bend', etc. Walde-P. 2.519. Falk-Torp 1215.

ON *tāl* = OE *tǣl* 'slander, blame' (16.78), OHG *zāla* 'ambush, peril', prob. fr. strong grade of the root in (Grk. δόλος, Lat. *dolus?*) ON *tal*, *tala*, OE *talu* 'talk, tale, reckoning, number', ON *telja*, OE *tellan* 'count, tell', etc. For semantic development cf. the use of ON *telja at* 'blame', OE *tellan an* 'charge, impute to', NE *tell on*. Walde-P. 1.808 f. Walde-H. 1.166 f. Falk-Torp 1243.

OE *fācen*, OS *fēcn*, OHG *feichan*, MHG *veichen* (ON *feikn* 'hurt, ruin') : Lat. *piget* 'vexes, disgusts', *piger* 'unwilling, lazy', fr. **peig-* beside **peik-* in Lith. *peikti* 'blame', etc. Walde-P. 2.11.

ME *deseyte* (*deceipte*, *deceit*, etc.), NE *deceit*, fr. OFr. *deceite*, *deceyte*, fr. past pple. of *deceveir*, Fr. *décevoir* (above, 2). NED s.v.

MHG *betroc*, NHG *betrug* (OHG *bitroc* 'phantom'), Du. *bedrog*, with vbs. OHG *bitriogan*, MHG, older NHG *betriegen* (NHG *betrügen*, after *betrug*), MLG *bedrēgen* (pple. *bedragen*, whence Dan. *bedrage*, Sw. *bedraga*, with derivs. *bedrageri*, *bedrägeri* 'deceit'), simple forms OHG *triogan*, MHG *triegen* (NHG

trügen), etc. : ON *draugr* 'ghost', Skt. *droha-* 'injury, harm', *druh-* 'harm, be hostile to', Av. *druj-*, OPers. *draoga-* 'lie, deceit'. Walde-P. 1.874. Falk-Torp 56, 153. Weigand-H. 1.233, 2.1080.

5. Lith. *apgaulė*, *apgavas*, etc. : *apgauti* 'deceive', perfect. cpd. of *gauti* 'get' (11.16).

Lett. *krāpšana*, fr. *krāpt* 'deceive' (Lith. *kropti* 'deceive, get the best of, defraud'), perh. : Lett. *kr'aut* 'heap', Lith. *krauti* 'lay up, heap, load', etc. 'Deceive' fr. 'lay on, cover'? Walde-P. 1.477. Berneker 605.

Lett. *vilšana*, *viltiba*, fr. *vilt* 'deceive' (Lith. *ap-*, *pri-vilti* id.) : Ir. *fell*, NIr. *feall* 'deceit' (above, 3). Mühl.-Endz. 4.596. Walde-P. 1.298.

6. ChSl. *lĭstĭ* (in Gospels for ἀπάτη, δόλος, also πλάνη 'error', πανουργία 'guile'), fr. Goth. *lists* (above, 4). Berneker 755. Stender-Petersen 336.

ChSl. *ląka* (for δόλος, Supr., etc., later 'gulf, meadow'; cf. *ląkavŭ* 'evil'), Russ. *luka* 'bend' (of a river, etc.) also 'deceit' (obs.), orig. 'bend' : ChSl. *sŭ-lęką*, *-lęšti* 'bend', Lith. *lenkti* 'bend', etc. Walde-P. 2.435. Berneker 707 f., 739.

SCr. *prijevara*, fr. vb. *prevariti* 'deceive, cheat' (also *varanje* fr. vb. *varati* id.), prob. : ChSl. *variti* 'go before, anticipate, forestall' (e.g. Mk. 6.33 *varisę ję* = προῆλθον αὐτούς 'outwent them' in K. James version, 'beat them to it' in U.S. slang; cf. NE *overreach* in sense of 'get the better of, outwit', NED s.v. 6), this : Lett. *vert* 'run' (Trautmann 353).

Boh. *klam*, vb. *klamati* 'cheat, deceive' = Pol. *kłam*, *kłamstwo* 'lie', vb. *kłamać* 'lie', SCr. dial. *klamati* 'reel, totter, nod', Slov. *klam* 'sleep', *klamati* 'walk as if dizzy, reel, stagger'. Semantic development prob. from 'ramble' (in speech) to 'lie, deceive'. Berneker 508 f. Brückner 236.

Boh. *šal*, *šáleni*, *šalba*, Pol. *szalbierstwo* : Boh. *šáliti* 'deceive, cheat', Pol. *szaleć*, *szalić* 'go mad, drive mad', *szalony* 'mad' (17.23), Russ. *šalit'*, SCr. *šaliti se* 'play jokes', etc. Semantic development as in NE vb. *fool (someone)*. Brückner 539 f. Miklosich 336 f.

Pol. *oszustwo*, *oszukanie*, etc. : *oszustać*, *oszukać* 'deceive', *oszust* 'deceiver', cf. Boh. *ošusta* 'knave', *ošustiti* 'cheat' : Pol. *szust* 'sudden start, whim', Boh. *šust* 'rustle, noise', dial. 'folly, fool', etc. (prob. of imitative orig.), with development of various opprobrious terms fr. 'noisy'. Brückner 385.

Russ. *obman* : *manit'* 'entice, lure', Russ.-ChSl. *maniti* 'deceive', etc., from the root in ChSl. *na-majati* 'beckon to', Russ. *na-majat'* 'let know by sign, deceive', Skt. *māyā-* 'artifice, trick, deceit, fraud'. Lith. *moti*, Lett. *mat* 'make a sign, beckon', etc. Walde-P. 2.218 f. Berneker 2.17 f.

7. Skt. *kapaṭa-*, perh. (**kmp-*) : *kamp-* 'tremble' (if orig. 'bend, stoop'), Grk. κάμπτω 'bend', Lith. *kumpti* 'bow'. Uhlenbeck 42. Walde-P. 1.350.

Skt. *chala-*, hence *chalaya-* 'deceive', etym. dub., perh. : *chada-* 'cover, covering', *chādaya-* 'cover, hide', *chadman-* 'disguise, pretext, fraud'. Wackernagel, Altind. Gram. 1.222. Otherwise (: *skhal-* 'stumble') Uhlenbeck 94 (cf. Wackernagel, Altind. Gram. 1.154).

Skt. *māyā-* : Russ. *obman*, etc. (above, 6).

Av. *druj-* 'lie, deceit', see 16.67.

Av. *diwža-* : *diwžadyāi* (infin.) 'deceive', fr. *diwž-* orig. desid. to *dab-* 'deceive', Skt. *dabh-* 'injure, hurt, deceive'. Walde-P. 1.850 f. Barth. 747.

16.69 FORGIVE

Grk.	συγγιγνώσκω (ἀφίημι, etc.)	Goth.	*aflētan, fragiban*	Lith.	*atleisti, dovanoti*
NG	συγχωρῶ, συμπαθῶ	ON	*fyrirgefa, miskunna*	Lett.	*pieduot*
Lat.	*ignōscere* (*remittere, perdōnāre*, etc.)	Dan.	*tilgive*	ChSl.	*otŭpustiti, prostiti*
It.	*perdonare*	Sw.	*tillgiva*	SCr.	*oprostiti*
Fr.	*pardonner*	OE	*forgiefan*	Boh.	*odpustiti*
Sp.	*perdonar*	ME	*forgive*	Pol.	*przebaczyć*
Rum.	*ierta*	NE	*forgive*	Russ.	*prostit'*
Ir.	*maithim*	Du.	*vergeven*	Skt.	*kṣam-, mṛḍ-*
NIr.	*maithim*	OHG	*bilāzen, furlāzen, fargeben*	Av.	*mərəždā-, apaharəz-*
W.	*maddeu*	MHG	*vergeben*		
Br.	*pardoni, trugarezi*	NHG	*verzeihen, vergeben*		

'Forgive' has an emotional value and in a few cases an emotional background of sympathy or the like. But the majority of the words are based on prosaic notions, many being derivatives of words for 'give' (hence 'remit' a debt, etc.) or words for 'let go, release'.

Words for 'free from blame, excuse', like It. *scusare*, Fr. *excuser*, NE *excuse*, NHG *entschuldigen*, are often virtually 'forgive'.

1. Grk. συγγιγνώσκω, cpd. of συν- 'with' and γιγνώσκω 'know', so orig. 'agree with', hence 'have sympathy with, excuse, forgive' (the usual class. word; not in NT; NG sb. συγγνώμη as polite term for 'pardon!').

Grk. ἀφίημι 'let go, release' (11.34), sometimes 'remit' a charge or debt, in NT also the usual word for 'forgive'.

Grk. χαρίζομαι 'do a favor, grant' (fr. χάρις 16.64), in NT also sometimes 'forgive'.

Grk. συγχωρέω (: χῶρος 'place' 12.11), sometimes 'come together, meet' but mostly 'give way, yield, assent to, agree', hence NG 'forgive'.

NG συμπαθῶ 'sympathize with', in polite phrases 'excuse, forgive'.

2. Lat. *ignōscere*, cpd. of *in-* prob. = prep. *in* and *(g)nōscere* 'know', with development through 'recognize one's attitude', hence 'have sympathy with, excuse, forgive', the last stage as in Grk. συγγιγνώσκω. Ernout-M. 474. Walde-H. 1.677. The old view neg. *in-*, with development through 'ignore, overlook', is still not impossible. Specht, KZ 69.124 ff.

Lat. *dīmittere* 'let go, release, renounce' and *remittere* 'return, release', both in late Lat. also 'forgive' (e.g. *dī-* in Itala, *re-* in Vulgate).

Late Lat. *perdōnāre* (> It. *perdonare*, Fr. *pardonner*, Sp. *perdonar*), cpd. of *dōnāre* 'give'. REW 6405. Gamillscheg 670.

Rum. *ierta*, fr. late Lat. *lībertāre* (cf. Arch. lat. Lex. 8.450) 'set free'. REW 5014.

3. Ir. *maithim*, fr. W. *maddeu* 'let go' and 'forgive', this prob. (through 'make or consider worthless, abolish'?) : Ir. *in made* 'in vain', *maidim* 'break in pieces', etc. Walde-P. 2.231 f. Pedersen 1.110.

Br. *pardoni*, fr. Fr. *pardonner*.

Br. *trugarezi*, deriv. of *trugarez* 'pity' (16.35).

4. Goth. *aflētan* (reg. for ἀφίημι in all senses, including 'forgive'; also *fralētan*), OHG *furlāzen* (Tat., etc.), *bilāzen* (Otfr., etc.), cpds. of Goth. *lētan*, etc. 'leave, let' (12.18).

Goth. *fragiban* (mostly 'give, grant', but also for χαρίζομαι as 'forgive'), ON *fyrirgefa*, OE *forgiefan*, ME, NE *forgive*, Du. *vergeven*, OHG *fargeben*, MHG, NHG *vergeben*, but Dan. *tilgive*, Sw. *tillgiva* (after MLG *togeven* = NHG *zugeben*; Falk-Torp 1260), cpds. of Goth. *giban*, etc. 'give'.

ON *miskunna*, cpd. of *mis-* and *kunna* 'know', with development through 'ignore, overlook'. Specht, KZ 69.124 f.

NHG *verzeihen*, formerly 'renounce' (whence *verzicht*), fr. OHG *farzīhan*, MHG *verzīhen* 'deny, renounce', cpd. of OHG *zīhan* 'accuse' : Grk. δείκνῡμι 'point out', etc. Weigand-H. 2.1171, 1310. Kluge-G. 655.

ME, NE *pardon* (more formal than *forgive*), fr. Fr. *pardonner* (above, 2).

5. Lith. *atleisti*, cpd. of *leisti* 'let go, let' (11.34, 19.47).

Lith. *dovanoti*, 'grant' and 'forgive', fr. *dovana* 'gift'.

Lett. *pieduot*, cpd. of *duot* 'give'.

6. ChSl. *otŭpustiti* (reg. for ἀφίημι and ἀπολύω as 'let go' and 'forgive', Jagić, Entstehungsgesch. 375 f.), Boh. *odpustiti* (Pol. *odpuścić* bibl. in this sense), cpds. of *pustiti* 'let go' (11.34).

ChSl. *prostiti* (Supr. 'set free, release' and 'forgive'), SCr. *oprostiti*, Russ. *prostit'* (Boh. *prostiti* 'set free'), deriv. of ChSl. *prostŭ* 'simple, upright', etc., for which see 12.73.

Pol. *przebaczyć*, cpd. of *baczyć* 'be attentive, take heed' with *prze-* 'over across', semantic development through 'overlook' (cf. *przemilczec* 'pass over in silence'). But also *wybaczyć*, with perfect. *wy-*. Brückner 10.

7. Skt. *kṣam-* 'have patience, endure', hence 'forgive', etym.?

Skt. *mṛḍ-*, Av. *mərəždā-* 'be gracious, forgive' (cf. NPers. *amurzīdan* 'forgive'), fr. an extension of Skt. *mṛj-*, Av. *marəz-* 'rub, stroke'. Walde 2.298. Barth. 1175.

Av. *apaharəz-* ('remit' a penalty, Vd. 5.26), cpd. of *harez-* 'let go, release' (11.34). Barth. 586 s.v. *čiθā-*, 1793.

16.71 GOOD (adj.)

Grk.	ἀγαθός, καλός (εὐ-)	Goth.	*gōds, þiuþeigs, sēls*	Lith.	*geras, labas*
NG	καλός, ἀγαθός	ON	*gōðr*	Lett.	*labs*
Lat.	*bonus*	Dan.	*god*	ChSl.	*dobrŭ, blagŭ*
It.	*buono*	Sw.	*god*	SCr.	*dobar*
Fr.	*bon*	OE	*gōd*	Boh.	*dobrý*
Sp.	*bueno*	ME	*gode*	Pol.	*dobry*
Rum.	*bun*	NE	*good*	Russ.	*chorošij*
Ir.	*maith* (*dag-, so-*)	Du.	*goed*	Skt.	*sādhu-, bhadra-, vasu-* (*su-*)
NIr.	*maith* (*deagh-, so-*)	OHG	*guot*	Av.	*vaṇhu-* (*hu-*), OPers. *naiba-*
W.	*da, mad* (*hy-*)	MHG	*guot*		
Br.	*mat*	NHG	*gut*		

'Good' is understood as the most generic adjective of approval, by no means restricted to moral qualities. All the words were doubtless more specific originally, and among those the etymology of which is clear we note as sources such as 'fitting', 'straight, right', 'beautiful', 'orderly', etc.

Certain important prefixes for 'good-, well-' are listed. A more comprehensive treatment would include also the advs., which may belong with the common adjs. (e.g. Lat. *bene* : *bonus*) or be quite unrelated (e.g. NE *well*, NHG *wohl*, etc., general Gmc.), and the comps. and superls. For the adjs. for 'good' and 'bad' are among those in which irregular (supplementary) comparison is most widespread (e.g. Lat. *bonus*, *melior*, *optimus*, NE *good*, *better*, *best*, etc. general Gmc.).

1. Prefix IE **su-*, Walde-P. 2.512. Pedersen 2.9.

Skt. *su-*, Av. *hu-*; Grk. ὑ- in ὑγιής 'in

good health'; Gall. *Su-* in proper names, Ir. *so-*, W. *hy-*. For traces in Balto-Slavic, cf. Fraenkel, Mélanges Pedersen 443 ff.

Grk. *εὐ-*, the semantic equivalent (*εὐ-* related to *δυσ-* precisely as Skt. *su-* to *dus-*), beside Hom. *ἐΰς*, *ἠΰς* 'good, brave', prob. : Hitt. *assus* 'good' fr. IE **es-* 'be'. Friedrich, IF 41.370 f.

2. Grk. *ἀγαθός*, etym. disputed, perh. : *ἀγα-* 'very', *ἄγαμαι* 'admire', etc. Boisacq 4 f.

Grk. *καλός*, mostly 'beautiful' (16.81), but often also 'good', and so reg. in NG, where *ἀγαθός* is less common.

3. Lat. *bonus* (> Romance words), OLat. *duenos*, *duonus*, etym. dub. Walde-P. 1.778. Ernout-M. 114. Walde-H. 1.111.

4. Ir. *maith*, W. *mad*, Br. *mat*, Corn. *mas* (cf. Gall. *Teutomatos*), prob. : Lat. *Mātūta* 'Goddess of morning', *mātūrus* 'seasonable, early', *māne* 'morning', OLat. *mānus* 'good'. Walde-P. 2.220 f. Ernout-M. 588. Walde-H. 2.54.

Ir. *dag-*, *deg-*, NIr. *deagh-*, W. *da* (Br. *da* in phrases *da eo d'in* 'je veux bien'), Gall. *Dago-vassus*, etym. dub. Walde-P. 1.784. Pedersen 1.39.

5. Goth. *gōþs*, ON *gōðr*, OE *gōd*, etc., general Gmc. : OHG *gigat* 'fitting', MLG *gaden* 'fit, please', OE *geador* 'together', etc., ChSl. *godŭ* '(proper) time', *u-goditi* 'please', etc. Walde-P. 1.532. Feist 218. Falk-Torp 336.

Goth. *þiuþ* neut. (renders *τὸ ἀγαθόν*), whence also *þiuþeigs* (freq. for *ἀγαθός*) : ON *þȳðr* 'kind', OE *geþīede* 'good, virtuous', perh. fr. the root in Lat. *tuērī* 'regard, protect', *tūtus* 'safe', etc. Walde-P. 1.705 f. Feist 498. Falk-Torp 1306.

Goth. *sēls* 'good, kind' (*ἀγαθός*, *χρηστός*), with sb. *sēlei* : OE *gesǣlig* 'blessed, happy', etc., outside connections disputed (16.24).

6. Lith. *geras* : *girti* 'praise', Skt. *gṛ-* 'sing, praise', etc. (16.79). Walde-P. 1.686. Buga, Kalba ir Senovė 168.

Lith. *labas* (usual only in greetings, as *labas rytas*, *laba diena* 'good morning, good day'), Lett. *labs*, OPruss. *labs* : Lith. *lobis* 'possessions, riches', *lobti* 'get rich', Skt. *labh-* 'seize, grasp'. Walde-P. 2.385.

7. ChSl. *dobrŭ*, etc., general Slavic (Russ. *dobryj* now in phrases like 'good day', but mostly 'kind') : *po-doba jestŭ* 'it is becoming', *po-dobiti* 'make fitting', Goth. *ga-daban* 'happen', OE *ge-dafen* 'becoming', etc. Berneker 203–5. Walde-P. 1.824 f.

ChSl. *blagŭ* (reg. for *ἀγαθός* and *χρηστός* 'good' in moral sense, cf. Jagić, Entstehungsgesch. 326), in modern Slavic mostly 'gentle, blessed, noble', etc., never general for 'good', etym. dub. Walde-P. 2.182. Berneker 69.

Russ. *chorošij* (has displaced *dobryj* as the common word for 'good'), orig. 'orderly, neat', hypocoristic formation fr. ORuss. *choronenŭ*, pple. of *choroniti* 'put in order' : ChSl. *chraniti* 'guard, keep'. Berneker 397. Jagić, Arch. sl. Ph. 6.282 ff.

8. Skt. *sādhu-*, orig. 'straight, right, ready', fr. *sādh-* 'reach one's goal, accomplish, guide aright, etc.'. Walde-P. 2.450.

Skt. *bhadra-*, also 'blessed, auspicious, fair', prob. : Goth. *batiza* 'better', *batists* 'best'. Walde-P. 2.151 f. Falk-Torp 67.

Skt. *vasu-* (Vedic in this sense; later mostly as neut. sb. 'goods, wealth'), Av. *vaŋhu-*, *vohu-* (OPers. only in proper names, as *Dāraya-vauš*, *Vau-misa*) : Gall. *-vesus* (in *Bello-*, *Sigo-vesus*, etc.), Gmc. *Wisu-rīh*, *-mār*, *Wisi-Gothae*, etc., Ir. *feib* 'excellence' (dat. sg.), W. *gwych* 'fine, splendid, gay', etc. Walde-P. 1.310.

OPers. *naiba* (clearly 'good' in the Daiva inscr. 43, and so, rather than 'beautiful', elsewhere) : Ir. *nōib* 'holy', prob. (**noi-bho-*) fr. the root seen in Ir. *niam* 'brilliance', Lat. *nitēre* 'shine, glitter'. Walde-P. 2.321.

For the numerous other Indo-Iranian words that may be used for 'good' (and 'bad'), cf. Schwyzer, Die altindischen und altiranischen Wörter für gut und böse, Festgabe Kaegi 12 ff.

16.72 BAD

Grk.	*κακός* (*δυσ-*)	Goth.	*ubils*	Lith.	*blogas, negeras, piktas*
NG	*κακός*	ON	*vāndr, īllr, dāligr*	Lett.	*slikts, nelabs, l'auns*
Lat.	*malus*	Dan.	*ond, slet, slem, daarlig*	ChSl.	*zŭlŭ*
It.	*cattivo, malo*	Sw.	*ond, elak, dålig*	SCr.	*nevaljan, zao*
Fr.	*mauvais*	OE	*yfel* (*earg*)	Boh.	*špatný, zlý*
Sp.	*mal(o)*	ME	*uvel, ill, badde*	Pol.	*zły*
Rum.	*rău*	NE	*bad* (*ill, evil*)	Russ.	*plochoj, chudoj, durnoj*
Ir.	*olc* (*droch-, do-*)	Du.	*slecht, kwaad, erg*		
NIr.	*olc* (*droch-, do-*)	OHG	*ubil*	Skt.	*pāpa-, asādhu-, abhadra-* (*dus-*)
W.	*drwg* (*dy-*)	MHG	*übel, bœse*		
Br.	*fall, gwall, drouk*	NHG	*schlecht, schlimm* (*böse, übel, arg*)	Av.	*aka-, aγa-, avaŋhu-* (*duš-*)

For 'bad' as the opposite of 'good' there are equally generic words in some of the IE languages, but in others a variety of terms partly differentiated in feeling and according to the object qualified, so that it may be difficult to say which is the more nearly generic. Some are mainly 'evil, wicked' in the moral sense.

An adj. denoting any undesirable quality, physical or mental, any opprobrious epithet, may easily be generalized to 'bad'. Thus, either in earlier attested meanings or in cognates, 'disgusting, ugly, defective, faulty, weak, timid, worthless', etc. In some languages neg. cpds. of words for 'good' are in fairly common use.

The only agreement between different branches of IE is in a prefix for 'ill-, mis-', most common in Greek and Indo-Iranian. Even in the same branch there is vastly greater diversity than in the words for 'good'.

1. IE prefix **dus-* 'ill-, mis-'. Walde-P. 1.816. Pedersen 2.9.

Grk. *δυσ-*, reg. opp. of *εὐ-*; Skt. *dus-* (*duṣ-*, *duḥ-*, *dur-*), Av. *duš-* (*duž-*), reg. opp. of *su-*, *hu-*; Gmc. *tuz-* in Goth. *tuz-wērjan*, ON *tor-tryggja* 'mistrust, doubt', etc.; Ir. *do-* in *do-cruth* 'ugly' (vs. *so-cruth*), W *dy-* in *dybryd* 'sad'.

2. Grk. *κακός*, prob. a nursery word expressing disgust and to be connected with the terms for 'void excrement', Grk. *κακκάω*, Lat. *cacāre*, etc. Walde-P. 1.336. Boisacq 395 f.

3. Lat. *malus* (> It. *malo*, Sp. *mal*, *malo*; Fr. *mal* mostly sb. or adv.), etym. dub., perh. fr. the root in Ir. *mellaim* 'deceive', *mell* 'sin, fault', Lith. *melas* 'lie', Av. *mairya-* 'deceitful', etc.; or : OE *smæl*, OHG *smal*, etc. 'small'? Ernout-M. 583. Walde-H. 2.19 f.

It. *cattivo*, fr. Lat. *captīvus* 'prisoner, captive' through its moral application (cf. *irae captivus*, Seneca) in eccl. language to one 'captive of evil'; similarly Prov. *caitiu* 'captive' and 'bad', Fr. *chétif* 'wretched', etc. REW 1663. Gamillscheg 216. Wartburg 2.330 ff.

Fr. *mauvais*, fr. VLat. *malefātius* 'ill fated', cpd. of *malus* 'bad' and deriv. of *ātum* 'fate'. REW 5265a. Gamillscheg 601.

Fr. *méchant* (esp. 'evil, wicked'), fr. OFr. *mescheant* 'unfortunate', pple. of

OFr. *mescheoir*, cpd. of *mes-* 'mis' (fr. Gmc.) and *cheoir* fr. Lat. *cadere* 'fall' (cf. OFr. *cheance* 'chance'). REW 1451 Gamillscheg 602.

Rum. *rău*, fr. Lat. *reus* 'defendant, culprit'. REW 7274.

4. Ir. *olc*, etym. dub., perh. : Lith. *alkti*, Lett. *alkt*, ChSl. *alŭkati* 'be hungry', Lat. *ulcīscī* 'avenge', Grk. *ὄλλυμι*, *ὀλέκω* 'destroy', ON *illr* 'bad, evil'. Walde-P. 1.159. Pedersen 1.126.

Ir. *droch-* W. *drwg*, Br. *drouk*, etym. dub. Walde-P. 1.800, 860. Pedersen 1.96. Henry 108. Stokes 157.

Br. *fall*, prob. fr. OFr. *fel* 'faithless, cruel, bad', this prob. of Gmc. origin. Loth, Mots lat. 166. REW 3304. Wartburg 3.523 f.

Br. *gwall* : W. *gwall* 'defect, lack', Ir. *fāill* 'neglect', outside connections dub. Walde-P. 1.298. Pedersen 1.34.

5. Goth. *ubils*, OE *yfel*, ME *uvel*, *yvel*, NE *evil*, OHG *ubil*, MHG, NHG *übel*, the most widespread Gmc. (except Scand.) generic term (but now in NHG and NE in more restricted use; cf. NED and Paul, Deutsches Wtb. s.v.), prob. fr. **upelo-* deriv. of IE **upo-* in Goth. *uf*, Grk. *ὑπό* 'under', Skt. *upa* 'at, to', etc., through sense of 'extreme, excessive'. Walde-P. 1.193. Feist 508. Kluge-G. 637.

ON *vāndr*, Dan., Sw. *ond*, prob. (pples. of a vb. **wanhōn*) : ON *vā* 'harm, hurt', OE *wōh* 'wrong, perversity', Goth. *un-wahs* 'blameless', fr. the root in Skt. *vañc-* 'totter, stagger', Lat. *vacillāre* 'waver'. Here also prob., with the same semantic development, W. *gwaith* 'worse', *gwaethaf* 'worst' (comp. and superl. forms of *drwg* 'bad'). Walde-P. 1.218. Falk-Torp 793. Hellquist 731 f.

ON *īllr* (> ME *ill*, NE *ill* still in this sense in *ill fame*, etc.), with adv. *illa* (Dan. *ilde*, Sw. *illa*) 'badly', perh. fr. **ilhila* : Ir. *olc*, etc. (above, 4). Falk-Torp 461, 1490. Hellquist 402.

ON *dāligr* (esp. 'injurious'), Sw. *dålig*, ODan. *daalig*, Dan. *daarlig* : ON *dā* 'swoon, senseless state', *dā* 'marvel at', *dāinn* 'dead', etc. (Walde-P. 1.835). Falk-Torp 132. Hellquist 168.

Sw. *elak*, Norw. *ilak*, cpd. of *e-*, *i-* = ON *æ* 'ever'; second part : ON *lakr* 'deficient in quality or weight'. Hellquist 178. Torp, Nynorsk 242, 367.

OE *earg* 'cowardly, timid, lazy', also sometimes 'base, vile', Du. *erg*, NHG *arg* 'bad, evil', see 16.55.

ME *badde*, NE *bad*, prob. fr. OE *bæddel* 'hermaphrodite' through use as an opprobrious epithet. NED s.v.

MHG *bœse* (NHG *böse*, Du. *boos* now mainly in moral sense, or 'angry'), fr. OHG *bōsi* 'worthless, vain' : Norw. *baus* 'proud, impudent', ME *boste*, NE *boast*, perh. fr. a root **bhu-* in words for 'swell'. Walde-P. 2.118. Falk-Torp 54 f. Paul, Deutsches Wtb. 89 f. Weigand-H. 1.271 f.

NHG *schlecht*, Du. *slecht*, orig. 'level, straight, smooth', whence 'simple, ordinary' then 'bad'; OHG, MHG *sleht* = Goth. *slaihts*, ON *slēttr* 'smooth, plain' (whence Dan. *slet*, also 'bad' by influence of NHG), ME, NE *slight* etc. Falk-Torp 1061. Weigand-H. 2.724 f. Paul, Deutsches Wtb. 444.

NHG *schlimm*, fr. MHG *slim* 'crooked, wrong' (MLG > Dan. *slem* 'bad', Sw. *slem* 'vile', NE *slim* 'small, slender'), OHG **slimb* in *slimbi* 'crookedness', perh. : Lett. *slīps* 'crooked, steep'. Walde-P. 2.433. Falk-Torp 1059. Weigand-H. 733. Paul, Deutsches Wtb. 447.

Du. *kwaad* (adj. and sb.) = OHG *quat* 'filth' (NHG *kot*) : Lith. *gėda* 'shame, dishonor', etc. Walde-P. 1.695. Franck-v. W. 359.

6. Lith. *blogas* (now the correct word, cf. NSB, Lalis, Senn; formerly 'weak, sick', as in Kurschat, etc.), Lett. *blāgs* 'weak, bad, mean', both prob. fr. Slavic, WhRuss. *błahij* 'bad, ugly', Russ. *blagoj* 'stubborn, ugly', perh. : Lat. *flaccus* 'flabby', etc. Berneker 58. Mühl.-Endz. 1.311. Walde-H. 1.507.

Lith. *negeras*, neg. of *geras* 'good'.

Lith. *piktas* 'angry' (16.42), also 'bad'.

OPruss. *wargs* : Lith. *vargas*, Lett. *vargs* 'misery', Lith. *vargus* 'miserable, difficult', ChSl. *vragŭ* 'enemy', etc. Walde-P. 1.329. Trautmann 342.

Lett. *slikts*, fr. MLG *slicht* (: NHG *schlecht*, etc., above, 5). Mühl.-Endz. 3.931 f.

Lett. *nelabs*, neg. of *labs* 'good'.

Lett. *l'auns* (Lith. *liaunas* 'pliant, slender, lazy') : *l'aut* 'permit, allow', Lith. *liauti(s)* 'cease, quit', OPruss. *aulaut* 'die', etc.; 'bad', fr. 'pliant, yielding'. Walde-P. 2.405. Mühl.-Endz. 3.532.

7. ChSl. *zŭlŭ*, SCr. *zao*, Boh. *zlý*, Pol. *zły*, Russ. *zloj* (in SCr. and Russ. now mostly 'malicious' or 'angry'), prob. as 'bent, crooked' : Lith. *pa-žvilti* 'bow', *pa-žulnus* 'slanting, sloping', Lett. *zvelt* 'turn aside', Skt. *hvar-*, *hval-* 'go crookedly, bend, fall down', Av. *zūrah-* 'wrong' (sb.), OPers. *zūra-kara-* 'evil-doer'. Walde-P. 1.643. Trautmann 372 f. Brückner 654 f.

SCr. *nevaljan*, neg. of *valjan* 'honest, capable, good' : *valjati* 'be worth'.

Boh. *špatný* (also 'ugly, misshapen', etc. cf. Pol. *szpetny* 'ugly, nasty') fr. *špata* 'ugliness', this, with generalization through 'physical defect', fr. *špat* 'spavin', fr. NHG *spat* id. Brückner 553.

Russ. *plochoj* (now perh. the most common word) : Pol. *płochy* 'negligent, careless', ChSl. *plachŭ* 'wavering, timid', etc., perh. fr. the root in Grk. *πάλλω* 'sway, swing, shake'. Walde-P. 2.52.

Russ. *chudoj* (also 'lean, worn out') : ChSl. *chudŭ* 'little, needy, paltry' (12.56), Boh. *chudy* 'poor' (11.52), etc. Walde-P. 1.502. Berneker 405.

Russ. *durnoj* (also 'ugly') : *dur'* 'foolishness, caprice', Pol. *dur* 'swoon, senselessness', etc., Grk. *θοῦρος* 'rushing, raging, furious'. Walde-P. 1.842. Berneker 239.

8. Skt. *pāpa-*, prob. redupl. nursery word (like Grk. *παπαῖ*, *πόποι* 'alas') fr. the root in Grk. *πῆμα* 'evil, misfortune, hurt', etc. Walde-P. 2.8.

Skt. *asādhu-*, *abhadra-*, Av. *avaŋhu-*, neg. cpds. of the words for 'good' (16.71)

Av. *aka-* (NPers. *ak* 'insult, misfortune'), etym.? Barth. 44 f.

Av. *aγa-* : Skt. *agha-* 'mischief, guilt, wickedness', and perh. Goth. *agls* 'shameful', Ir. *āil* 'insult', etc. Walde-P. 1.41. Barth. 47 f.

Av. *aŋra-*, mostly in *aŋra- mainyu-* 'evil spirit, Ahriman' : Av. *ąsta-* 'hate, enmity', root connection? Walde 1.134. Barth, 103 f.

OPers. *gasta-* ('repugnant' or already 'bad', as NPers. *gast*), pple. of root in Skt. *gandha-* 'smell' (obj.), Av. *ganti-* NPers. *gand* 'stench' (15.23).

16.73 RIGHT (adj., in moral sense, vs. Wrong)

Grk.	δίκαιος	Goth.	*garaihts*	Lith.	*teisus*
NG	δίκαιος	ON	*rēttr*	Lett.	*taisns*
Lat.	*iūstus* (*rēctus*)	Dan.	*ret*	ChSl.	*pravĭdĭnŭ*
It.	*giusto* (*retto*)	Sw.	*rätt*	SCr.	*prav*
Fr.	*juste*	OE	*riht*	Boh.	*pravý*
Sp.	*justo*	ME	*riȝt, right*	Pol.	*prawy*
Rum.	*drept, just*	NE	*right*	Russ.	*pravyj*
Ir.	*cert, cōir*	Du.	*recht*	Skt.	*ṛta-, ṛju-*
NIr.	*ceart, cōir*	OHG	*reht*	Av.	*ərəšva-*, OPers. *rāsta-* (sb.)
W.	*iawn, cyfiawn, cywir*	MHG	*reht, gereht*		
Br.	*gwirion, eeun*	NHG	*recht, gerecht*		

'Right' is understood here in its moral sense and in the adj. form.

Many of the words are used alike of things and persons, but in the latter context different forms (mostly not included in the list) may be preferred, e.g. NE *upright* or *just* (NE *right* formerly of persons in moral sense, but now obs.), NHG *gerecht* vs. *recht*, and so generally in Slavic. Many mean also, some primarily, 'right' in the legal sense. Several are also the usual terms for 'right' = 'correct'; but this notion is often expressed by differentiated forms (e.g. NHG *richtig*) or quite unrelated words (e.g. Grk. ἀληθής 'true' or ὀρθός 'straight', NG σωστός 'certain, correct', orig. 'safe'). Again, several have come to be used for the directional 'right' ('right hand', etc.), but the older terms for this were quite different (12.41).

The most common semantic source is 'straight'. Some meant originally 'in accordance with custom or law', or 'certain, true'.

1. Grk. δίκαιος (Hom. 'observant of custom', later 'right, just' in both moral and legal sense), fr. δίκη 'custom, right', later esp. 'lawsuit' (21.13).

2. Lat. *iūstus* (> It. *giusto*, Fr. *juste*, Sp. *justo;* Rum. *just* recent borrowing) 'right, just' in moral as well as legal sense : *iūs* 'right', esp. 'legal right, law' (21.11).

Lat. *rēctus* (> It. *retto*) 'straight' (12.73) also 'right', esp. sb. *rēctum*.

Rum. *drept* ('right' in all senses including moral, cf. *drept om* 'just man', etc.) fr. Lat. *dērēctus* for *dīrēctus* 'straight' (12.73). Other Romance derivs. of this form (or the neut. sb.), as It. *d(i)ritto*, Fr. *droit*, Sp. *derecho*, are mostly 'straight', or 'right' in other senses, or sbs. for 'right' esp. legal.

3. Ir. *cert*, NIr. *ceart*, fr. Lat. *certus* 'fixed, true, faithful' (cf. *amīcus certus* 'true friend', etc.). Pedersen 1.227. Vendryes, De hib. voc. 125 (with?).

Ir. *cōir*, W. *cywir* (these also 'correct, true'), cpd. of Ir. *co-*, W. *cy-* 'com-' and Ir. *fīr*, W., Br. *gwir* 'true' (16.66); whence also Ir. *fīriān*, Br. *gwirion* 'just' (both mostly of persons; W. *gwirion* 'innocent, foolish'), second part to following(?). Pedersen 1.64, 92. Thurneysen, Gram. 123, 569.

W. *iawn* and *cyf-iawn*, Br. *eeun*, etym. dub. (: Goth. *ibus* 'level'?). Pedersen 1.92. Henry 110. Thurneysen, Idg. Anz. 26.26.

4. Goth. *garaihts* (reg. for δίκαιος; *raihts* only for εὐθύς 'straight'), ON *rēttr*, OE *riht*, OHG *reht*, etc. general Gmc. (with numerous derivs. partly differentiated in use, but not added in list) : Lat. *rēctus* 'straight', etc. (12.73).

ME *iust*, NE *just*, fr. Fr. *juste* (above, 2), but mostly of narrower scope.

5. Lith. *teisus*, *teisingas* (also 'true'), Lett. *taisns* (also 'straight') : Lith. *tiesus* 'straight', etc. (12.73).

6. ChSl. *pravŭ* 'straight' (12.73), but general Slavic 'right'. Hence sb. ChSl. *pravĭda* 'right' (SCr. id.; Boh., Pol., Russ. 'truth'), and fr. this ChSl. *pravĭdĭnŭ* (reg. for δίκαιος), SCr. *pravedan*, Boh. *spravedlivy*, Pol. *sprawiedliwy*, Russ. *spravedlivyj* (forms used esp. of 'just' persons).

7. Skt. *ṛta-* 'suitable, right', beside sb. *ṛta-m* = OPers. *arta-*, Av. *aša-* 'truth, right' in religious sense, whence Skt. *ṛtāvan-*, Av. *ašāvan-* 'just, righteous, holy', all fr. root in Grk. ἀραρίσκω 'fit', etc. Walde-P. 1.70.

Skt. *ṛju-* 'straight' (: Lat. *rēctus*, etc., 12.73), also 'right, just' = Av. *ərəzu-* 'straight, right', whence adv. *ərəš* 'rightly' (cf. also *arš-uxda-* 'rightly spoken'), and fr. this (at least in sense) *ərəšva-* 'just' and 'true' (perh. in form = Skt. *ṛṣva-* 'high'). Barth. 352, 355, 356.

Av. *rašnu-* 'just, righteous' but mostly sb. 'lord of justice', fr. *raz-* 'direct' : Lat. *regere* 'direct, rule' (same root as in preceding group). Barth. 1516 f.

OPers. *rāsta-* neut. sb. (NR a 59, b 7, 11), fr. the same root as the preceding and in form = Lat. *rēctum*.

16.74. Words for 'wrong' in moral sense as opposite of 'right' are not given in a formal list, since they are in large measure simply neg. cpds. of those for 'right' (or allied forms), e.g. Grk. ἄ-δικος, Lat. *in-iūstus*, OE *un-riht*, OHG *un-reht*, etc. Or else 'wrong' is expressed more colloquially by words for 'bad'.

But there are a few distinctive words in most of which 'wrong' comes from 'crooked' (12.74), just as 'right' often from 'straight'.

1. Lat. *prāvus* 'crooked', most commonly 'wrong, bad'.

2. It. *torto* (sb.; adj. *torto* only 'crooked'), Fr. *tort* (sb.), Sp. *tuerto* (sb., but now obs. in this sense), fr. Lat. *tortus* 'crooked'.

3. Late OE *wrang* (rare), ME *wrang*, *wrong* 'crooked' and 'wrong', NE *wrong*, fr. ON **wrangr*, *rangr* 'crooked, wrong' : OE *wringan* 'twist, press' (NE *wring*). NED s.v.

4. From Slavic *krivŭ* 'crooked' come as sbs. for 'wrong' SCr. *krivica* (also 'fault'), Boh. *křivda*, Pol. *krzywda*. Berneker 618.

5. OPers. *miθa-* (sb., NRb 7, 9) : Av. *miθō* 'falsely', *miθaoxta* 'falsely spoken', *maēθā-* change, vacillation', Skt. *mithu* 'falsely', *mith-* 'meet' (as friend or foe), Lat. *mūtāre* 'change', Goth. *maidjan* 'change, corrupt', all with basic notion of 'change', whence secondary moral notion. Cf. NHG *täuschen* 'deceive' beside *tauschen* 'exchange' Walde-P. 2.247 f.

16.75 SIN

Grk.	(μίασμα, etc.) ἁμαρτία	Goth.	*frawaurhts*	Lith.	*nuodėmė* (*griekas*)
NG	ἁμαρτία	ON	*synd*	Lett.	*grēks*
Lat.	*peccātum*	Dan.	*synd*	ChSl.	*grěchŭ*
It.	*peccato*	Sw.	*synd*	SCr.	*grijek*
Fr.	*péché*	OE	*syn(n)* (*forwyrht*)	Boh.	*hřích*
Sp.	*pecado*	ME	*sinne*	Pol.	*grzech*
Rum.	*păcat*	NE	*sin*	Russ.	*grech*
Ir.	*peccad, immarmus*	Du.	*zonde*	Skt.	*pāpa-, pātaka-, enas-*
NIr.	*peacadh*	OHG	*sunta*	Av.	*stara-, a-stara-, aēnah-*
W.	*pechod*	MHG	*sunde*		
Br.	*pec'hed*	NHG	*sünde*		

Words for 'sin', although they are felt now as belonging chiefly to the terminology of religion (and so to Chap. 22), cover also an offense against morals, and in earlier periods denoted also (some even primarily) the milder 'fault' or 'mistake, error'.

1. Grk. ἁμαρτία, ἁμάρτημα 'failure, fault, error', then esp. ἁμαρτία 'sin' (Plat., Arist., esp. LXX, NT+), fr. ἁμαρτάνω 'miss the mark, fail, err, do wrong' (all these uses in Hom.), etym. dub. Boisacq 50.

In earlier times 'sin' would be expressed as a 'wrong' (ἀδικία, ἀδίκημα : ἄ-δικος 'wrong') or in religious sense as 'pollution' (μίασμα : μιαίνω 'stain, pollute'), 'impiety' (ἀσέβεια, ἀσέβημα : σέβομαι 'revere, worship'), etc.

2. Lat. *peccātum* 'fault, error', then 'sin' (> Romance and Celtic words), fr. *peccāre* 'make a mistake, err', perh. fr. **ped(i)cāre* 'stumble' : *pēs*, *pedis* 'foot', cf. *pedica* 'fetter, snare'. Walde-P. 2.24. Ernout-M. 745.

3. Ir. *peccad*, NIr. *peacadh*, W. *pechod*, Br. *pec'hed*, fr. Lat. *peccātum* (above). Pedersen 1.105.

Ir. *immarmus* (also *im(m)ormus*, etc.; cf. also MW *amryvys* 'erroneous, wrong'), vbl. n. of *imb-ro-mid-*, 3sg. *-imruimdethar* 'sins', cpd. of root in *midiur* 'judge'. Pedersen 2.579. Loth, RC 40.348, 350. Thurneysen, Gram. 70, 528.

Ir. *col*, W. *cwl*, see under 'fault' (16.76).

4. Goth. *frawaurhts*, OE (rare) *forwyrht*, OS *farwurht*, with adjs. Goth. *frawaurhts*, OS *farwarht*, OHG *farworaht* 'sinful', fr. Goth. *frawaurkjan*, etc. 'sin', cpd. of *waurkjan* 'work, do', with pejorative prefix *fra*, etc. Feist 166 f.

ON *synð*, *synd*, OE *syn(n)*, OHG *sunta*, etc., general Gmc. (except Goth.), etym. disputed, but prob. : Goth. *sunjis*, ON *sannr* 'true', Skt. *satya-* 'real, true', with semantic development fr. 'true, real' to '(the really) guilty'. Cf. ON *verða sannr at* 'be found guilty of' or *bera sannan at* 'find guilty of', and Lat. *sons, sontis* 'guilty'. So (since Grimm) Falk-Torp 1226, Weigand-H. 2.110, Ernout-M. 957. Otherwise and variously Walde-P. 2.514, Kluge-G. 606 (after E. Schroeder, KZ 56.106 ff.).

5. Lith. *griekas* (formerly the reg. word and so in biblical texts), Lett. *grēks*, OPruss. *grīka*, fr. the Slavic, cf. below.

Lith. *nuodėmė* (now favored as a native word vs. the loanword *griekas*), fr. *nusidėti* 'commit a sin', lit. 'lower oneself', refl. of *nudėti* 'put down', cpd. of *dėti* 'put'.

6. ChSl. *grěchŭ*, etc., general Slavic, with vb. ChSl. *grěšiti* 'sin', etc., etym. dub. Berneker 350 f. Brückner 161.

7. Skt. *pāpa-*, also general 'evil, harm', fr. adj. *pāpa-* 'bad, evil (16.72).

Skt. *pātaka-* (with cpds. *ati-*, *mahā-*, etc. for different gradations of sin), fr. caus. of *pat-* 'fly, descend, fall', hence 'what causes one to fall' (either from right conduct, or perh. orig. from one's caste).

Skt. *enas-*, Av. *aēnah-* 'evil deed, sin', orig. 'deed of violence', fr. Skt., Av. *in-*, in Skt. 'send forth, force, overcome', in Av. 'overcome, give pain to'. Barth. 21.

For numerous other Skt. words, cf. Jolly, Recht und Sitte 115.

Av. *šyaoθna-* 'deed', also esp. 'evil deed, sin'. Barth. 1712.

Av. *stara-*, *astara-*, fr. *star-*, esp. *ā-star-* 'commit a sin', etym. dub. Walde-P. 2.636, 641. Barth. 1597 f. (but OPers. *mā starava* is a false reading).

16.76 FAULT, GUILT

Grk.	σφάλμα, αἰτία	Goth.	*fairina*	Lith.	*kaltė*
NG	σφάλμα, φταίσιμο, ἐνοχή	ON	(*sǫk*)	Lett.	*vaina*
Lat.	*culpa, noxa*	Dan.	*skyld*	ChSl.	*vina*
It.	*colpa*	Sw.	*skuld*	SCr.	*krivica, krivnja*
Fr.	*faute*	OE	*scyld, gylt*	Boh.	*vina*
Sp.	*falta, culpa*	ME	*faute, gilt*	Pol.	*wina*
Rum.	*vină*	NE	*fault, guilt*	Russ.	*vina*
Ir.	*cin, locht, col*	Du.	*schuld*	Skt.	*aparādha-, ṛṇa-, doṣa-*
NIr.	*locht, cion*	OHG	*sculd*	Av.	*pāra-*
W.	*bai*	MHG	*schult*		
Br.	*fazi*	NHG	*schuld*		

Several of the words listed, as Lat. *culpa*, Fr. *faute*, NE *fault*, cover 'fault' in two senses, namely: (*a*) a moral defect milder than 'sin' or 'vice' but more serious than a casual 'error', e.g. NE *he has many faults;* (*b*) moral responsibility for wrong doing, 'culpability, guilt', e.g. Lat. *mea culpa*, NE *my fault*. Others are used only or mainly in the one sense or the other, e.g. Grk. σφάλμα (*a*), αἰτία (*b*). The Gmc., Balto-Slavic, and Indo-Iranian words are properly 'fault' in sense *b*, though some of them are or were once used for the wrongdoing itself (e.g. OE *scyld* for Lat. *scelus*, *dēlictum* as well as *culpa;* NHG *eine schuld tun*, now obs.). In these languages 'fault' in sense *a* is covered by words listed under 'error' (e.g. NHG *fehler*) or others; and a few of those listed here belong equally under 'error'. In sense *b* there is generally no distinction between 'fault' and 'guilt', but NE *guilt* has a much stronger implication of wrongdoing than *fault*.

Furthermore, 'fault' (*a*) may be expressed by various other words meaning properly 'lack, defect', e.g. Grk. ἔλλειμμα (fr. ἐλ-λείπω 'leave undone'), Lat. *dēlictum* (fr. *dē-linquere* 'fail, transgress'), or 'spot, blemish', e.g. Lat. *macula* often 'fault', esp. in church Latin.

1. Grk. σφάλμα, lit. 'a fall, misstep' : σφάλλω 'cause to fall, overthrow', etym. dub. Walde-P. 2.599, 678. Boisacq 927.

Grk. αἰτία 'responsibility, guilt, cause', covering 'fault' in sense *b*, beside adj. αἴτιος 'responsible, culpable', etym. dub., perh. : αἶσα (*αἴτι̯α) 'lot, destiny', Osc. *aeteis* 'partis'. Walde-P. 1.2. Boisacq 30 f.

NG φταίξιμο, fr. the vb. φταίω 'be at fault' (e.g. φταίω ἐγώ 'it's my fault, I am to blame'), fr. class. Grk. πταίω 'stumble, make a mistake', etym. dub. Walde-P. 2.21. Boisacq 820.

NG ἐνοχή, in late Grk. (pop.) 'liability', cf. ἔνοχος 'guilty' (21.35).

2. Lat. *culpa* (> It. *colpa*, OFr. *coupe*, Sp. *culpa*), OLat. *colpa*, Osc. *kulupu* 'culpa', etym. dub. Walde-P. 1.440. Ernout-M. 240. Walde-H. 1.304.

Lat. *noxa*, *noxia* 'harm, injury', hence also 'fault, offense, guilt' (*noxa* also 'punishment') : *nocēre* 'harm, injure' (11.28). Ernout-M. 669.

For Lat. *dēlictum*, It. *delitto*, etc., see under 'crime' (21.41).

Fr. *faute*, Sp. *falta*, also and orig. 'lack', fr. VLat. **fallita*, fr. *fallere* 'deceive, fail'. REW 3169.

Rum. *vină*, fr. the Slavic (below, 6).

3. Ir. *cin*, NIr. *cion* (also *cionnta*) : Grk. τίνω 'pay, atone', mid. 'punish', ποινή 'penalty', Skt. *ci-* 'revenge, punish', Av. *či-* 'pay a penalty, atone', etc. Walde-P. 1.509. Pedersen 1.365.

Ir. *locht*, also (and in OIr. chiefly) 'a defect', perh. : ON *lǫstr* 'defect, fault, vice', OHG, OS *lastar* 'blame, reproach, insult', vbs. OHG *lahan*, OE *lēan* 'blame, reproach, scorn, etc.'. Walde-P. 2.436 f.

Ir. *col*, W. (obs., Spurrell) *cwl* 'fault, sin', fr. **kulo-* : OHG *sculd*, etc. (below, 4). Loth, Z. celt. Ph. 17.147 f. Walde-H. 1.304.

W. *bai* (cf. vb. *beio* 'blame, censure') : Ir. *bāg* 'battle', *bāgaim* 'fight', OHG *bāgan*, *bāgēn* 'quarrel, fight', etc. Walde-P. 2.130. Pedersen 1.101.

Br. *fazi*, fr. MBr. *faziaff* 'be mistaken', fr. Fr. *faillir* 'fail, err' (Lat. *fallere*, cf. above Fr. *faute*). Henry 120.

4. Goth. *fairina* (reg. for αἰτία, once for μομφή 'blame') : ON *firn* 'an abomination', OE *firen*, OHG *firina* 'wicked deed, crime', etc., prob., as orig. 'transgression', deriv. of IE **per-* in Skt. *paras*, Grk. πέρᾱν 'beyond', and the Gmc. prefix Goth. *fair-*, OE *fer-*, OHG *fir-*, etc. 'away, past, out', Walde-P. 2.31. Feist 139 f.

ON *sǫk*, properly 'charge, accusation' : OE *sacu* 'strife, contention, crime, guilt', OHG *sacha* 'strife, affair, cause', etc., vbs. Goth. *sakan* 'quarrel, contend', OE *sacan* 'fight, contend, charge, blame', etc. Falk-Torp 942 f. Walde-P. 2.449.

OE *scyld*, OHG *sculd*, MHG *schult*, also 'guilt, due, debt, crime, sin', Du., NHG *schuld* also 'guilt, debt', Dan. *skyld*, Sw. *skuld* id., prob. influenced in meaning by German, cf. ON *skyld* 'tax, due, sake', *skuld* 'debt, bondage' : OE *sculan*, etc. 'owe, be obliged' (11.63). Walde-P. 2.596. Falk-Torp 1045.

OE *gylt*, ME *gilt*, NE *guilt*, etym. dub., perh. as orig. 'debt' (cf. OE *scyld*, etc., above), in form Gmc. **gulti-*, IE **ghḷdi-* fr. **gheld-*, beside **ghelt-* in Goth. *fragildan* 'pay, compensate', etc. Doubted in NED s.v.

ME *faute*, NE *fault*, fr. Fr. *faute* (above, 2).

5. Lith. *kaltė* (*kalčia*), beside *kaltas* 'guilty, faulty', perh. fr. a form without initial *s-* of root in OE *scyld* etc. (above, 4). Walde-P. 2.596.

Lett. *vaina* : ChSl. *vina*, etc. (below). Mühl.-Endz. 4.437 f.

6. ChSl. *vina*, Boh., Russ. *vina*, Pol. *wina*, Lett. *vaina*, perh. as 'consequence' (of evil) : Lett. *vaijāt* 'pursue', Lith. *vyti* 'hunt, pursue', ChSl. *po-vinąti* 'subdue, overcome', etc. Walde-P. 1.230. Trautmann 344 f. Brückner 622.

SCr. *krivica*, *krivnja*, fr. *kriv* 'crooked' (12.74) also fig. 'false, wrong, guilty' (cf. also *nisam ja kriv* 'it's not my fault'). Berneker 618.

7. Skt. *aparādha-*, fr. *apa-rādh-* 'miss the mark, be guilty', cpd. of *rādh-* 'be successful, prosper' with *apa-* 'off, away'. Uhlenbeck 9.

Skt. *ṛṇa-* 'debt' (11.64), also 'fault, guilt'.

Skt. *doṣa-* 'fault, harm, guilt, sin', fr. *dus-* 'ill' (16.72).

Av. *pāra-* : *par-* 'condemn' (21.32). Barth. 849 f., 889. Here, perh. as loanword fr. Iran., Toch. A *pare*, B *pere* 'fault, guilt'. Meillet, MSL 19.159. Otherwise (: Goth. *fairina*, above, 4) K. Schneider, KZ 66.253.

16.77 MISTAKE, ERROR

Grk.	*ἁμαρτία, σφάλμα*	Goth.	*airziþa, airzei*	Lith.	*klaida, apsirikimas*
NG	*λάθος, σφάλμα*	ON	*villa*	Lett.	*kl'ūda, klaida, malds*
Lat.	*error, errātum*	Dan.	*fejl*	ChSl.	(*lĭstĭ*)
It.	*sbaglio, errore*	Sw.	*fel*	SCr.	*pogrješka, zabluda*
Fr.	*faute, erreur*	OE	*gedwyld, gedwola*	Boh.	*chyba, omyl, blud*
Sp.	*error*	ME	*errour, mistake*	Pol.	*błąd, omyłka*
Rum.	*greşală*	NE	*mistake, error*	Russ.	*ošibka, zabluždenie*
Ir.	*comrorcon*	Du.	*fout, dwaling*	Skt.	*bhrama-, bhrānti-*
NIr.	*dearmad*	OHG	*irrido, irrituom*	Av.	. . . .
W.	*camgymeriad*	MHG	*irre, irretuom*		
Br.	*fazi*	NHG	*fehler, irrtum*		

Words for 'error, mistake' are most commonly derived from vbs. meaning 'wander about' or the like. But there are various other connections. Several of the words are the same that have been listed under 'sin' or 'fault'.

1. Grk. ἁμαρτία, see under 'sin' (16.75).

Grk. σφάλμα, see under 'fault' (16.76).

Grk. πλάνη 'wandering about, going astray' is in the NT a fig. 'straying from the truth', namely 'false doctrine, deceit, delusion' (and so the early Gmc. and ChSl. forms which render it; partly *error* in the Vulgate), in NG 'error', esp. 'delusion'.

NG λάθος, fr. late Grk. λάθος 'escape from detection', fr. λανθάνω, aor. ἔλαθον 'escape notice' (see ἀχηθής, 19.66).

2. Lat. *error* (> It. *errore*, Fr. *erreur*, Sp. *error*), *errātum*, fr. *errāre* 'wander, go astray, err, mistake' : Goth. *airzeis* 'astray, erring', *airzei*, *airziþa* 'error', etc. (below, 4). Walde-P. 1.150. Ernout-M. 309.

It. *sbaglio*, with vb. *sbagliare* 'make a mistake, blunder, miss', doubtless *s-bagliare* : *abbagliare* 'dazzle, blind', but orig. unknown. Diez 355. REW 9157.

Fr. *faute*, see under 'fault' (16.76).

Rum. *greşală*, fr. *greşi* 'fail, miss, err', fr. Slavic, cf. SCr. *pogrješka* (below, 6).

3. Ir. *comrorcon*, vbl. n. of **com-air-org-* 'err', cpd. of *orgim* 'slay, lay waste' (1.76). Pedersen 2.588.

NIr. *dearmad*, *dearmhad*, fr. Ir. *dermat* 'a forgetting', vbl. n. of **di-ro-moin-* (*doroimnethar*, 3sg.) 'forget' (17.32).

W. *camgymeriad*, cpd. of *cam-* 'mis-' and *cymeriad* 'taking', fr. *cym(e)ryd* 'take', prob. semantic borrowing fr. NE *mistake*.

Br. *fazi*, see under 'fault' (16.76).

4. Goth. *airziþa*, *airzei*, OHG *irrido*, MHG *irre*, derivs. OHG *irrituom*, MHG *irretuom*, NHG *irrtum* : Goth. *airzjan* 'lead astray', OHG *irran* 'cause to err', *irrōn* 'err', Lat. *errāre*, etc. (above, 2). Feist 27. Weigand-H. 1.936 f.

ON *villa*, properly 'a straying', fr. *villr* 'bewildered, erring, astray' : Goth. *wilþeis* 'wild', OE *wilde*, OHG *wildi* 'wild, desert', etc. Falk-Torp 1377 f.

OE *gedwyld*, *gedwola*, Du. *dwaling* : OE *gedwellan*, *gedwelian* 'deceive, lead astray, err', *dwellan*, *dwelian* 'lead into error', OHG *twallen* 'delay, hinder', ON *dvelja* 'delay, tarry' (14.24), Du. *dwalen* 'err, wander'. Walde-P. 1.843.

ME *errour*, NE *error*, fr. Fr. *erreur* (above, 2).

ME, NE *mistake*, fr. vb. *mistake*, in ME and early NE mostly 'take wrongly, have a misconception, err', fr. ON *mistaka* 'take by mistake, take the wrong thing'. NED s.v.

Du. *fout*, fr. Fr. *faute* (above, 2). Franck-v. W. 169.

NHG *fehler*, orig. 'a shot which misses the mark', deriv. of *fehlen* 'miss' and re-

placing older *fehl* 'lack, defect, mistake, oversight, etc.', early also *feil*, fr. MHG *væl*, *væle* 'lack, missing', MLG *feil*, *fēl* (> Dan. *fejl*, Sw. *fel*), fr. OFr. *faille*, OIt. *faglia* 'lack' (fr. Lat. *fallere* 'deceive, etc.', cf. Fr. *faute* 'fault, mistake, lack' 16.76). Falk-Torp 211. Weigand-H. 1.511 f.

5. Lith., Lett. *klaida* : Lett. *klaidīt* 'wander about' (prob. = *klaidīt* 'scatter, waste'), *klīst* 'wander about, go to pieces', Lith. *klysti* 'err, be mistaken', etc. Walde-P. 2.596. Mühl.-Endz. 2.208, 231.

Lith. *apsirikimas*, fr. *apsirikti* 'err, mistake', refl. cpd. of *rikti* id. ('sich versprechen', Kurschat), same word as *rikti* 'cry out, shout', with development through 'misspeak' (cf. NHG *versehen* 'oversight, mistake').

Lett. *kl'ūda* (Lith. *kliuda* 'defect, lack, flaw') : *kl'ūt* 'come upon, reach', *kl'ūdīt* 'cause to come upon, wander, stray, etc.', Lith. *kliuti* 'remain hanging, catch on, run against, hinder, hold back'. Walde-P. 1.493. Mühl.-Endz. 2.240 f.

Lett. *malds*, *maldība*, fr. *maldīt* 'err, lead into error, deceive', perh. : *meli*, Lith. *melas* 'lie' (16.67), etc. Walde-P. 2.291. Mühl.-Endz. 2.557, 595.

6. ChSl. *lĭstĭ*, 'deceit' (16.68), once also for πλάνη (Mt. 27.64).

SCr. *zabluda*, Boh. *blud*, Pol. *błąd* (Russ. *blud* 'fornication', but *zablydit'sja* 'go astray, err', *zabluždenie* 'error, mistake') : ChSl. *blǫdŭ* 'fornication', *blędą*, *blęsti* 'err, talk nonsense' (cf. *blędŭ* 'idle talk, nonsense') and 'fornicate' (latter sense in this group widespread but secondary), prob. : Goth. *blinds* 'blind', NE *blunder*, etc. Walde-P. 2.216. Berneker 60, 62.

SCr. *pogrješka* : *pogriješiti* 'err', perfect. cpd. of *griješiti* 'sin, err', fr. *grijeh* 'sin' (16.75).

Boh. *chyba* (Pol. *chyba* 'failure, miscarriage, lack') : Boh. *chybati* 'doubt', Pol. *chybać* 'move to and fro, swing', etc., Skt. *kṣubh-* 'sway, tremble'. Walde-P. 1.502 f. Berneker 412 f.

Boh. *omyl*, Pol. *omyłka* : Boh. *omýliti* 'deceive', *mýliti* 'mislead, puzzle', Pol. *(o)mylić*, *mylić* 'cause to err', etc., outside connections? Brückner 350. Miklosich 207.

Russ. *ošibka*, fr. *ošibat'sja* 'mistake, err', prob. : *o-šibat'* 'beat down', *šibat'* 'throw', *šibkij* 'quick', Skt. *kṣip-* 'throw'. Walde-P. 1.501.

7. Skt. *bhrama-*, *bhrānti-* : *bhram-* 'wander about', also 'be confused, mistaken', *bhṛmi-* 'quick, active', further connections dub. Walde-P. 2.202.

16.78 BLAME (sb.)

Grk.	*μομφή, ὄνειδος, ψόγος, μῶμος*	Goth.	*fairina* (vb. *faian*)	Lith.	(*pa*)*peikimas*
NG	*κατηγορία* (*μομφή, ψόγος*)	ON	*last*	Lett.	*pal'a*
Lat.	*reprehēnsiō, vituperātiō*	Dan.	*dadel*	ChSl.	(*zazĭrěti*, vb.)
It.	*biasimo*	Sw.	*tadel*	SCr.	*prijekor*
Fr.	*blâme, reproche*	OE	*tǣl, tāl*	Boh.	*hana*
Sp.	*censura, reproche*	ME	*blame*	Pol.	*nagana*
Rum.	*blam*	NE	*blame, reproach*	Russ.	*chula, poricanie*
Ir.	*caire*	Du.	*blaam*	Skt.	*nindā-, garhā-, parivāda-*
NIr.	*milleān*	OHG	*lastar*	Av.	. . . .
W.	*bai*	MHG	*laster* (*tadel*)		
Br.	*tamall*	NHG	*tadel, vorwurf*		

'Blame' is properly 'censure of a fault, reproof of wrongdoing', the opposite of 'praise'. The use of NE *blame* in the sense of 'responsibility for a wrong' (*lay the blame on*, *the blame is mine*, etc.), although old, is secondary (cf. NED s.v.), this sense being expressed in other languages by words listed under 'fault', as Lat. *culpa*, NHG *schuld*, Russ. *vina*, etc. (16.76).

The majority of the words are connected with others meaning 'speak ill of, revile, abuse, shame, accuse', etc., that is, they are in origin abusive terms.

But conversely to the development in English, some words for 'fault' or 'defect' may come to be used for the resulting 'blame', mainly through the medium of verbal derivs. meaning 'lay the fault on, find fault with, blame' (cf. esp. the shift in NHG *tadel*).

1. Grk. μομφή, μέμφις, beside vb. μέμφομαι, perh. : Ir. *mebul* 'shame', W. *mefl* 'disgrace, reproach' (but see 16.45).

Grk. ὄνειδος : Goth. *ga-naitjan* 'dishonor', Skt. *nind-* 'deride, abuse, blame' (sb. *nindā-*), Av. *naēd-* 'deride, abuse', etc. Walde-P. 2.322 f.

Grk. ψόγος, beside vb. ψέγω, adj. ψεκτός 'blamable', etym. dub. Boisacq 1075.

Grk. μῶμος 'blame, disgrace', with vb. μωμάομαι 'blame' (both Hom.+, but less common than preceding), etym. dub. Walde-P. 2.249. Boisacq 655.

Grk. κατηγορία 'charge, accusation' (cf. κατηγορέω 'accuse', orig. 'speak against'), in NG used also for 'blame'. Cf. Fr. *accuser* 'accuse, blame'.

2. Lat. *reprehēnsiō*, fr. *reprehendere* 'hold back, restrain', in moral sense 'reprehend, rebuke, blame, censure', fr. *prehendere* 'take, seize'.

Lat. *vituperātiō* (a stronger term than *reprehēnsiō*, but not so abusive as NE *vituperation*), fr. *vituperāre* 'find fault with, disparage, blame', first part prob. : *vitium* 'defect, blemish, fault, vice', and last part : *parāre* 'prepare, provide, procure'. Ernout-M. 1118.

Fr. *blâme* (> Rum. *blam*), fr. *blâmer*, OFr. *blasmer* (> It. *biasimare*, whence sb. *biasimo*), fr. VLat. **blastēmāre* for Lat. *blasphēmāre* 'blaspheme, revile', fr. Grk. βλασφημέω 'speak ill of, blaspheme' (cons. dissim. already in colloq. Grk., cf. NG pop. βλαστημῶ). REW 1155. Wartburg 1.403.

Fr. *reproche* (> NE *reproach*), Sp. *reproche*, all covering verbal 'blame' (but in part mild), fr. VLat. **repropriāre*, deriv. of Lat. *prope* 'near' (cf. *approach* 10.56). REW 7229. NED s.v. *reproach*, sb. and vb.

Sp. *censura* 'criticism' and esp. 'blame', as commonly NE *censure* (NED s.v., 4), fr. Lat. *cēnsūra* 'judgment', deriv. of *cēnsēre* 'think'[2] (17.14).

Sp. *culpa* 'fault' (16.76) and so 'blame' in secondary sense of NE *blame* (cf. above), hence for verbal 'blame' *culpar*, or *echar la culpa*, lit. 'lay the fault (blame) on'.

3. Ir. *caire* = MBr. *carez* 'blame', OW *cared*, arch. W. *caredd* 'sin, crime, fault' : Lat. *carināre* 'abuse, revile', OE *hierwan* 'speak ill, blaspheme, despise', OHG *harawēn* 'mock', Lett. *karināt* 'tease', ChSl. *ukoriti* 'insult', etc. Walde-P. 1.353. Walde-H. 1.169.

NIr. *milleān*, prob., like *milleadh* 'spoiling, injury', fr. *millim* 'spoil, injure'.

W. *bai* 'fault' (16.76), also 'blame'.

Br. *tamall* : Ir. *tāmailt* 'infamy, shame', etym.? Walde-P. 2.624. Stokes 122. Henry 259.

4. Goth. *fairina*, mostly 'αἰτία' (see 16.76), but once for μομφή, with vb. *fairinōn* 'μωμᾶσθαι, blame', adj. *unfairina* 'ἄμεμπτος, blameless'.

Goth. faian, vb. 'blame' : Goth. fijan, etc. 'hate' (16.41), Skt. pīy- 'abuse, revile'. Walde-P. 2.9. Feist 135.

ON last, also cpds. lastorð, lastmæli (orð 'word', mæli 'speech'), OHG, OS lastar, MHG laster also 'reproach, insult, fault', etc., beside ON lǫstr 'defect, fault, vice', OE leahter 'moral defect, crime, fault', etc. : vbs. OHG lahan, OE lēan 'blame, reproach, scorn', etc., and perh. Ir. locht 'fault, defect' (16.76). Walde-P. 2.436 f. Falk-Torp 626. Torp, Nynorsk 365.

OE tæl, tāl (mostly 'slander' but also best word for 'blame', cf. e.g. Aelfric, Gram. p. 12, tāl as opp. of herunge 'praise'), ME (rare) tele, tole = ON tāl 'deceit', etc. (16.68).

ME, NE blame, Du. blaam, fr. Fr. blâme (above, 2).

NHG tadel (> Dan. dadel, Sw. tadel), fr. MHG tadel 'defect' (moral, or physical as 'spot on the skin'; cf. NHG tadellos 'faultless'; shift to 'blame' first in vb. tadeln 'find a defect in, find fault with', hence 'blame'), prob. orig. a LG form corresponding to MHG zadel, OHG zadal 'lack, suffering from hunger', etym. dub. Falk-Torp 133. Weigand-H. 2.1018.

NHG vorwurf, fr. vorwerfen 'throw before', hence, like NE throw in one's teeth, 'reproach, blame'.

5. Lith. (pa)peikimas, fr. (pa)peikti 'blame' : piktas 'angry' (16.42).

Lett. pal'a (also 'defect, fault') : pelt 'abuse, calumniate', this perh. : Grk. ἀπειλή 'threat' and (with s-) Goth. spill

'story, tale', etc. Walde-P. 2.677. Mühl.-Endz. 3.64, 198.

6. ChSl. vb. zaziřěti (renders μέμφεσθαι, Mk. 7.2), cpd. of za- 'after' and ziřěti 'look' (15.52).

SCr. prijekor (ukor, pokor) : ChSl. u-korŭ 'ύβρις, insult', u-koriti 'insult, scold', SCr. koriti 'reproach', etc., Ir. caire 'blame', etc. (above, 3). Berneker 578. Walde-P. 1.353.

Boh. hana, Pol. nagana, with vbs. Boh. haniti, Pol. ganić, etym. dub. Brückner 134 (: ChSl. goněti 'suffice', Lith. gana 'enough', as orig. 'have enough of' in deprecatory sense?). Miklosich 60.

Russ. chula = ChSl. chula 'blasphemy', with vbs. Russ. chulit' 'blame', ChSl. chuliti 'blaspheme', etc., perh. as 'lower, debase' (cf. Slov. huliti 'bend', Boh. chouleti se 'bend, stoop') : ChSl. po-chylŭ 'bent, crooked', Boh. chyliti 'incline, bend', Russ. dial. chilut'sja 'bow', etc. Berneker 406, 413.

Russ. poricanie, fr. poricat' 'blame, reprove', cf. otrekat', otricat' 'deny' : ChSl. rekǫ, rešti, ORuss. rku, reči 'say' (18.22), ChSl. rěči 'accusation', etc. Miklosich 274 f.

7. Skt. nindā- (nid-, nidā-) also 'defamation, abuse, etc.', with vb. nind- 'deride, abuse, blame', see above, 1, under Grk. ὄνειδος.

Skt. garhā-, with vb. garh- 'blame, reproach' : Av. garəz- 'moan, bemoan', etc. (16.37).

Skt. parivāda-, fr. parivad- 'talk about' and 'blame', cpd. of vad- 'speak' (18.21).

16.79 PRAISE (sb.)

Grk.	ἔπαινος, αἶνος	Goth.	hazeins	Lith.	garbė
NG	ἔπαινος	ON	lof	Lett.	slava, teikšana
Lat.	laus	Dan.	ros (pris, lov)	ChSl.	chvala
It.	lode	Sw.	berōm (pris, lov, ros)	SCr.	(po)hvala
Fr.	louange	OE	lof, herung	Boh.	chvála
Sp.	alabanza	ME	prayse, lofe, heriynge, laude	Pol.	(po)chwala
Rum.	laudă			Russ.	(po)chvala
Ir.	molad	NE	praise	Skt.	praçañsā-, stuti-, gir-, gūrti-
NIr.	moladh	Du.	lof		
W.	mawl	OHG	lob	Av.	gar-, garah-
Br.	meuleudi	MHG	lop, pris		
		NHG	lob, preis		

Some of the important words for 'praise' are of doubtful etymology. But the commonest source, mostly through the verbs, is the notion of 'recite formally, sing, shout' (in honor of the gods), the terms belonging primarily to religious terminology. Some of the verbs mean also, or are cognate with others meaning 'boast', owing to similar origin from 'cry, shout', etc. Some are derivs. of words for 'fame' or 'glory' (16.47), meaning first 'attribute fame, give glory to', then simply 'praise', this sense reacting sometimes on the sbs. Besides those included in the list there are many other such derivs. meaning 'glorify, praise highly, laud', e.g. Grk. δοξάζω in NT rendered by Goth. hauhjan (fr. hauhs 'high'), ChSl. slaviti (fr. slava 'glory'). Development from 'put a value on, appraise' is seen in NE praise, etc.

The sb. forms are given in the list, but the verbs are parallel and often the source, especially in the semantic development (e.g. in NE praise). There is sometimes, however, a difference in relative frequency, e.g. OE lof the usual sb., but herian the usual vb. (more common than lofian), or NHG vb. preisen more common than sb. preis in sense of 'praise'.

1. Grk. αἶνος (also 'tale, story' and dial. 'decree'), more commonly ἔπαινος, with vb. ἐπαινέω, cf. also αἴνιγμα 'riddle', all based on the notion of 'a saying', but root connection dub. Walde-P. 1.2. Boisacq 26.

2. Lat. laus, laudis (> It. lode), with vb. laudāre (> It. lodare, Fr. louer, etc., whence also sbs. Fr. louange, Rum. laudă; Sp. loar, sb. loa now arch.), earliest sense perh. 'mention', the use of laudāre as 'name, cite' being quoted as early; etym. dub., but perh. as *laud- beside *leu-t- (based on an imitative syllable) : Goth. liuþōn 'sing praises', OE lēoþian 'sing', etc. Walde-P. 2.406. Walde-H. 1.776.

Sp. alabanza, fr. vb. alabar 'praise', fr. VLat. alapārī 'boast' (cf. Lindsay, Cl. Q. 23.112), this in form as if fr. Lat. alapa 'blow, slap', but semantic relation difficult, and so perh. fr. or influenced by Grk. λαπίζω 'swagger' (used by Cicero). REW 311. Rönsch, Z. rom. Ph. 3.103 f. Walde-H. 1.26.

3. Ir. molad, NIr. moladh, W. mawl, Br. meuleudi, with vbs. Ir. molur, etc., general Celtic group, etym. dub., but perh. : Grk. μέλπω 'sing', μολπή 'song'. Walde-P. 2.292 (adversely). Stokes, IF 12.191.

4. Goth. hazeins, OE herung, hering, ME heriynge, fr. vbs. Goth. hazjan, OE herian, ME herie 'praise' : OHG harēn, OS harōn 'cry, shout', outside connections dub. Walde-P. 1.338. Feist 252 f. NED s.v. hery.

ON, OE, Du. lof, OHG lob, etc. (Dan., Sw. lov mostly biblical) with vbs. ON lofa, OE lofian, etc. : Goth. liufs, OE lēof, etc. 'dear' (16.28) and OE lufu, etc. 'love' (16.27), with development of 'praise' (vb.) fr. 'find pleasing'. Walde-P. 2.419. Falk-Torp 657.

Dan., Sw. ros (usual word in Dan., not in Sw.) with vbs. Dan. rose, Sw. rosa, fr. ON vb. hrōsa 'praise, boast' (> ME rose, NE dial. roose) : ON hrōðr 'praise, fame', OE hrēþ 'fame', Goth. hrōþeigs 'famous', OHG hruom 'fame' (NHG ruhm), whence vbs. OHG hruomen, NHG rühmen 'praise' (MLG berōmen > Dan. berǫmme, Sw. berömma, whence Sw. sb. berōm, now the common word), all fr. the same root as Goth. hrōþs 'cry', Grk. κῆρυξ 'herald', etc. Walde-P. 1.353. Falk-Torp 61, 911.

ME preyse, prayse, NE praise, fr. vb. ME preise 'appraise' and 'praise', fr. OFr. preisier, fr. late Lat. preciāre, pretiāre, deriv. of Lat. pretium 'price'. From the same source likewise MHG prīsen, NHG preisen, Du. prijzen (MLG prīsen > Dan. prise, Sw. prise), all now vbs. for 'praise' (in part more formal, 'praise highly, laud'), whence sbs. NHG preis, Dan., Sw. pris 'praise', but more commonly 'price'. Only in English is the word in this sense differentiated in form. NED s.v. Falk-Torp 850. Weigand-H. 2.468.

ME laude, with vb. laude (NE laud) fr. Lat. laudāre (above, 2).

5. Lith. garbė (also 'honor, glory') : girti, OPruss. girtwei 'praise' (Lett. dzirties 'boast'), Skt. gr-, Av. gar- 'praise' (below, 7), Lat. grātus 'pleasing, thankful', etc. Walde-P. 1.686. Walde-H. 1.619 f.

Lett. slava (also 'fame, glory'), with vb. slavēt 'praise', orig. 'glorify' like ChSl. slaviti, etc. : Lith. šlovė, ChSl. slava, Grk. κλέος, etc. 'fame, glory' (16.47).

Lett. teikšana, fr. teikt 'say' (18.22) and 'praise'. Mühl.-Endz. 4.156 f.

6. ChSl. chvala, etc. with vb. chvaliti, etc., general Slavic, etc. Berneker 406. Brückner 186 f. K. Meyer, Donum nat. Schrijnen 413 (fr. *svala by metathesis fr. slava 'fame, glory').

7. Skt. stuti-, fr. stu- 'praise' (also Av.), beside stubh- 'shout, praise in exclamations', prob. : Grk. στεῦμαι 'promise, threaten, boast' (what one will do). Walde-P. 2.620.

Skt. gir-, gūrti-, Av. gar-, garah- 'praise', esp. 'song of praise', fr. Skt. gr-, Av. gar- 'praise' (Av. only in cpds.) : Lith. girti 'praise', etc. (above, 5).

Skt. çañsa-, pra-çañsā-, fr. çañs- 'recite (hymns or invocations), praise', also 'declare, tell' : Av. sqh-, OPers. θah- 'announce, declare, say', Lat. censēre 'declare solemnly, resolve, judge', etc. Walde-P. 1.403. Walde-H. 1.199.

16.81 BEAUTIFUL (also Pretty)

Grk.	καλός (εὐειδής, εὔμορφος, ὡραῖος)	Goth.	skauns	Lith.	gražus, dailus
NG	ὄμορφος, ὡραῖος	ON	fagr	Lett.	skaists, jauks, grezns
Lat.	pulcher, fōrmōsus, bellus	Dan.	skøn, køn, smuk	ChSl.	krasinŭ
It.	bello	Sw.	skön, fager, vacker	SCr.	lijep, krasan
Fr.	beau, joli	OE	wlitig, fæger, sciene	Boh.	krásný, hezký, pěkný
Sp.	hermoso, bello, bonita	ME	faire, shene	Pol.	piękny, śliczny, ladny
Rum.	frumos	NE	beautiful, pretty	Russ.	prekrasnyj, krasivyj
Ir.	sochrud, álind	Du.	schoon, mooi, fraai	Skt.	çrira-, sundara-, kalyāṇa-, çubha-, etc.
NIr.	áluinn, deas	OHG	scōni	Av.	srira-, huraoδa-, x*aini-
W.	glan, teg, tlws	MHG	schœn(e), fager, hübesch		
Br.	kaer, brao	NHG	schön, hübsch		

Besides the main words for 'beautiful', several are listed which answer more nearly to the inferior NE pretty. But it would be futile to include the vast number of expressions of admiration which may be used with specific reference to beauty (e.g. NE lovely in lovely face, etc.). Nor is it feasible here to state for the words of each language the differences both in feeling and in application (e.g. NE beautiful, handsome, pretty). Some are used of both persons and things, some mostly of persons, some only of women and children (or of men in derogatory sense); some with reference to both form, figure, and face, some (e.g. NE lit. fair) mainly with reference to the face.

Some of the words have such a logical semantic source as 'of good form, shape, appearance'. But in the majority of cases 'beautiful' is specialized from expressions of approval or admiration of the most diverse character, e.g. 'good, seasonable, pleasant, gay, courteous, fit, suitable, skilful, bright, neat'. Many of the words are again extended to apply to anything that gives pleasure (not merely to the visual sense), as NE beautiful in colloquial use (cf. NED s.v.) or NHG schön (cf. Paul, Deutsches Wtb. s.v.). Weinacht, Zur Geschichte des Begriffs "schön" im Altdeutschen, emphasizes the ethical rather than aesthetic value of Goth. skauns, OHG scōni in Otfr., etc. But this results from the character of the writings and has no necessary bearing on the primary sense and etymology.

1. Grk. καλός (also 'good', which became the prevailing sense), Hom. κᾱλός, fr. καλϝός, beside κάλλος (*καλϳος) 'beauty', etc. : Skt. kalya- 'healthy, vigorous', kalyāṇa- 'beautiful'. Walde-P. 1.356. Boisacq 399.

Grk. εὐειδής, lit. 'well-formed', and used esp. with reference to female beauty, cpd. of εὐ- 'well' and εἶδος 'form, shape, figure' (12.51). Boisacq 220.

Grk. ὡραῖος, fr. ὥρα 'proper time, season' and orig. 'seasonable' (esp. of crops, etc.), then of persons 'youthful, blooming' (not necessarily implying beauty according to Plato and Aristot., but evidently tending to), 'beautiful' (LXX, NT+).

Grk. εὔμορφος 'fair of form, beautiful', cpd. of εὐ- 'well' and μορφή 'form, shape' (12.51). Hence NG pop. ὄμορφος, the most usual word with reference to personal beauty (ὄμορφη γυναῖκα, etc.; ὡραῖος mostly used of more general approval, 'fine').

2. Lat. pulcher, properly pulcer (h favored by fanciful connection with Grk. πολύχρους), old polcer, etym. dub., perh. fr. *pelcros by dissim. fr. *perk-ros, orig. 'gay colored, variegated' (cf. interchange

of 'beautiful' and 'red' in group of ChSl. *krasĭnŭ*, etc., below, 6) : Skt. *pṛçni-* 'speckled, Grk. περκνός 'dark, bluish-black', MIr. *erc* 'gay colored, red', OHG *forhana* 'trout,' etc. Walde-P. 2.46. Ernout-M. 822.

Lat. *fōrmōsus* (> Rum. *frumos*, Sp. *hermoso*), orig. 'finely formed', whence 'shapely, beautiful', fr. *fōrma* 'form, shape' (12.51). Ernout-M. 379. REW 3450.

Lat. *bellus* (> It. > Sp. *bello;* Fr. *beau*), used esp. of women and children, or ironically of men in class. period, fr. **dwenelos* : *bonus* (*dwenos*) 'good' (16.71). Ernout-M. 114. Walde-H. 1.100. REW 1027.

Fr. *joli*, OFr. *jolif*, orig. 'gay, agreeable, pleasant', prob. deriv. of a loanword = ON *jōl* 'Yule-festival'. REW 4590. Bloch 1.389. Gamillscheg. 540.

Sp. *bonito* 'very good, fine' and esp. fem. *bonita* 'pretty', deriv. of *bueno* 'good'.

3. Ir. *sochrud*, lit. 'well formed', cpd. of *so-* 'well-' and *crud* 'shape, form' (12.51).

Ir. *ālind*, NIr. *āluinn*, prob. fr. *āil* 'pleasant' (: ON *fagr* 'beautiful', etc., below, 4; Walde-P. 2.3, Strachan, BB 20.24, both without *ālind*). Stokes ap. Macbain 13 (Macbain **ad-lainn* : *lainn* 'bright').

NIr. *deas* ('right', etc., also 'pretty'), fr. Ir. *dess* 'right, dexter' (12.41) and 'well arranged, suitable, neat, fair, becoming'.

W. *glan* 'clean' (15.87), also 'beautiful'.

W. *teg* (cf. Ir. *ē-tig* 'ugly') : ON *þægr* 'acceptable, agreeable, pleasant', fr. the root in ON *þiggja* 'receive, accept', Ir. *techtaim* 'possess'. Walde-P. 1.715. Stokes 126.

W. *tlws* (fem. *tlos*), prob. fr. *tlws* 'jewel' (: Ir. *tlus* 'cattle', with common notion of 'valuable possession, treasure'; cf. Loth, RC 34.150), felt as 'pretty thing'.

Br. *kaer*, OBr. *cadr* = W. *cadr* (arch.) 'handsome, mighty' : W. *cadarn* 'strong' (4.81), Ir. *cath*, W. *cad*, etc. 'battle'. Walde-P. 1.339, 340. Pedersen 1.323, 2.50, 53.

Br. *brao*, fr. Fr. *brave* 'brave' (16.52, formerly and dial. also 'beau' (cf. Wartburg 1.249). Henry 42.

4. Goth. *skauns* (or *skauneis;* only nom. pl. *skaunjai*), OE *sciene*, ME *shene* (NE *sheen*), Du. *schoon* (MLG *schōne* > Dan. *skøn*, Sw. *skön*), OHG *scōni*, MHG *schœn(e)*, NHG *schön*, in older WGmc. also 'bright, shining', prob. through 'visible, apparent' (cf. Goth. *ibna-skauns* 'of like form', *guda-skaunei* 'likeness of God') : OE *scēawan*, OHG *scouwōn* 'look at', etc. (15.52). Walde-P. 1.370. Falk-Torp 1014. Feist 431.

ON *fagr* (Dan. *fager* rhet. and poet.), Sw. *fager*, OE *fæger*, ME *faire* (NE *fair* in this sense now mostly lit., esp. poet.), OHG *fagar*, MHG *fager* = Goth. *fagrs* 'εὔθετος, fit' (the orig. sense) : OE *gefēgan*, OHG *fuogan* 'fit, join', etc. Walde-P. 2.3. Falk-Torp 201. NED s.v. *fair*.

Dan. *køn*, older sense 'capable, courageous' : ON *kœnn* 'wise, clever', OE *cēne*, OHG *kuoni* 'brave', etc. (16.52). Falk-Torp 523.

Dan. *smuk*, fr. LG *smuk* 'supple, tidy, trim, elegant' (hence also NHG *schmuck*) : MHG *smiegen*, NHG *schmiegen* 'press close, cringe, crawl', ON *smjūga* 'slip, step through', etc. Falk-Torp 1085. Walde-P. 2.254.

Sw. *vacker* (Norw. *vakker*), fr. MLG *wacker* 'watchful, gay, quick, good, honest', NHG *wacker* 'good, honest', OHG *wacker*, OE *wacor* 'watchful' : OHG *wachēn*, OE *wacian* 'watch, wake', etc. Falk-Torp 1343. Hellquist 1292 f.

OE *wlitig*, early ME *wliti*, OS *wlitig*,

fr. OE *wlite* 'beauty, appearance, shape, form', OS *wliti* 'splendor, appearance, form', etc. : OE *wlītan* 'look' (15.52). Walde-P. 1.293.

NE *beautiful*, fr. sb. *beauty*, ME *bealte, beaute*, etc. fr. OFr. *belte, beltet*, Lat. *bellitās* fr. *bellus* (above, 2).

NE *pretty* (since 1440 of personal appearance, but inferior to *beautiful*, cf. NED), OE *prættig* 'cunning, wily, etc.', ME 'clever, skilful', late ME and NE general epithet of admiration 'fine, etc.', fr. OE *prætt* 'trick, wile, craft' : Icel. *prettr* 'trick', Du. *pret* 'fun', etc. Falk-Torp 848 f. NED s.v.

NE *handsome* (implying dignified, stately beauty), deriv. of *hand* and orig. 'easy to handle, handy' with development through 'suitable, generous, admirable', etc. NED s.v.

Du. *mooi*, MDu. *mōy*, MLG *mōi(e)*, prob. through 'neat' fr. 'washed' (Gmc. **mauja-*) : ChSl. *myti* 'wash', MLG *muten* 'wash the face', Lith. *maudyti*, Lett. *maudāt* 'bathe'. Franck-v. W., KZ 48.156.

Du. *fraai* (also 'nice'), MDu. *fray, vray* 'true, upright, clever, strong', fr. Fr. *vrai* 'true' (16.66). Frank-v. W. 169.

NHG *hübsch*, fr. MHG *hübesch*, 'courteous, well-bred', also late 'beautiful', fr. MFrank. *höfesch, hüfesch* id. fr. *hof* 'court' (imitating and later replacing MHG *kurteis* fr. Fr. *courtois*). Kluge-G. 257. Paul, Deutsches Wtb. s.v.

5. Lith. *gražus*, also *gražnas* : Lett. *grazns, grezns* 'beautiful, magnificent, splendid, exuberant, proud', *grazuot* 'adorn oneself', outside connections? Mühl.-Endz. 1.615. Leskien, Ablaut 362.

Lith. *dailus* (cf. *dailinti* 'beautify'), prob. fr. the root of Skt. *di-deti* 'shines', Grk. δέαμαι 'seem', δῆλος 'clear, evident', etc. Walde-P. 1.772. (cf. also 1.764, Berneker 194 f.).

Lett. *skaists* : Lith. *skaistus* 'clear, lucid, bright, sublime', etc., OPruss. *skīstan* (acc.) 'pure', Skt. *ketu-* 'light, shape, form', ON *heiðr* 'clear, bright', etc. Walde-P. 2.537. Mühl.-Endz. 3.866, 4.53 (but with different root connection).

Lett. *jauks*, also 'tame, gay' = Lith. *jaukus* 'tame, gentle' : Lett. *jūkt*, Lith. *junkti* 'habituate, accustom', Goth. *bi-ūhts* 'accustomed', Skt. *uc-* 'like, be accustomed to'. Walde-P. 1.111. Mühl.-Endz. 2.98.

6. ChSl. *krasĭnŭ*, SCr. *krasan*, Boh. *krásný*, Russ. *pre-krasnyj* (*krasnyj* now 'red'), *krasivyj*, deriv. of *krasa* 'beauty' in ChSl., Russ., etc., in Pol. 'color', esp. 'red', Boh. *krása* also old 'light, splendor', prob. orig. 'glow, splendor' : Lith. *karštas* 'hot', *kurti* 'to heat', etc. Walde-P. 1.418 f. Berneker 607 f.

SCr. *lijep* (Boh. *lepý* 'fine, beautiful', Russ. *lepyj* 'beautiful, splendid', not in ordinary use) : ChSl. *lěpŭ* 'proper, fitting' ('beautiful' only late), ChSl. *prilěpiti* 'stick, cleave to', Russ. *lepit'* 'stick, stick together', etc., general Slavic, Skt. *lip-* 'anoint, besmear', Grk. λίπος 'fat', etc. Walde-P. 2.404. Berneker 711 f.

Boh. *hezký* ('pretty'), according to Gebauer 1.240, 454, Miklosich 61, with *e* fr. *o* : Russ. *gožij, pri-gožij* 'good, fitting, dainty', etc., Boh. *hodný* 'worthy', etc., derivs. of Slavic *godŭ* 'fitting time' (Berneker 316 ff. without mention of Boh. *hezký*).

Boh. *pěkný* ('pretty'), Pol. *piękny* (main word for 'beautiful'), prob. (despite Boh. *ě*, Pol. *ię*) through 'careful, neat' : Boh. *peče*, Pol. *piecza* 'care' (16.14). Brückner 412.

Pol. *śliczny* (Boh. *sličný* not common), cpd. of Pol. *-liczny* (in *roz-liczny* 'different', etc.), Boh. *ličný* 'clear, apparent', deriv. of Slavic *likŭ* in Russ.-

ChSl. *zŭlo-likŭ* 'evil-looking' (ChSl. *lice* 'face', etc.). Berneker 719 ff.

Pol. *ładny* ('pretty, nice'), Boh. *ladný* (not common; cf. *ladnost* 'neatness') = ChSl. *ladĭnŭ* 'equal', Russ. *ladnyj* 'on good terms, in accord', derivs. of Pol. *lad*, Boh. *lad* 'order', Russ. *lad* 'accord, tune', root connection dub. Berneker 682.

7. Skt. *çrīra-* only in neg. cpd. *a-çrīra-* 'ugly' (RV; *çrīla-* rare or in different sense), Av. *srīra-*, comp. Skt. *çreyas-*, Av. *srayas-*, superl. Skt. *çreṣṭha-*, Av. *sraēšta-*, with sb. Skt. *çrī-*, Av. *srī-* 'beauty' (for Vedic *çrī-* cf. esp. Oldenberg, Gött. Nachr. 1918. 35 ff.), prob. : Grk. κρείων 'lord, ruler', but ultimate root connection? Walde-P. 1.478. This is clearly the one important Indo-Iranian word-group, though not furnishing the common positive adj. for 'beautiful' in Skt.

Skt. *sundara-*, perh. dial. for *sūnara-* 'glad, joyous, delightful', cpd. of *sū-* = *su-* (cf. *vī-* = *vi-*, *anū-* = *anu-*, etc. Wackernagel, Altind. Gram. 2.130) 'well, good' and *nar-*, *nara-* 'man'. Walde-P. 2.332. Uhlenbeck 337, 339.

Skt. *kalyāṇa-* : Grk. καλός 'beautiful' (above, 1).

Skt. *çubha-* : *çubh-* 'adorn, deck, beautify', perh. fr. a root **k̂eu-bh-* beside **k̂eu-dh* in Skt. *çuddha-* 'clean', etc. (15.87). Walde-P. 1.368.

Skt. *rūpavant-*, fr. *rūpa* 'form, shape' (12.57) also 'beauty'.

Av. *huraoδa-*, cpd. of *hu-*(= Skt. *su-*) and *raoδa-* 'growth', pl. 'outward appearance' (: *rud-*, Skt. *rudh-* 'grow' 12.53).

Av. *xᵛaini-* (only in cpds., as *xᵛaini-starəta-* 'having a beautiful coverlet', etc.), prob. : *xᵛanvant-* 'bright, splendid', *xᵛan-* beside *xᵛar-* 'sun', etc. Otherwise (: Skt. *sundara-*) Barth. 1864, IF 11.136.

16.82 UGLY (in Appearance)

Grk.	*δυσειδής, αἰσχρός*	ON	*ljōtr, ūfagr*	Lith.	*negražus*
NG	*ἄσκημος*	Dan.	*styg, grim, hæslig*	Lett.	*nejauks, neskaists*
Lat.	*dēformis, turpis*	Sw.	*ful, stygg*	ChSl.	(*rąžĭnŭ*)
It.	*brutto, deforme*	OE	*unwlitig, unfæger, fūl*	SCr.	*ružan*
Fr.	*laid*	ME	*ugli, unfaire, foul*	Boh.	*ošklivý, nehezký*
Sp.	*feo*	NE	*ugly, plain, homely*	Pol.	*szpetny, brzydki*
Rum.	*urît*	Du.	*leelijk*	Russ.	*nekrasivyj, durnoj*
Ir.	*dochrud, ētig, grānna*	OHG	*unscōni, unsāni, missescōni*	Skt.	*ku-(vi-, apa-)rūpa-, açrīra-*
NIr.	*grānna*				
W.	*hagr, hyll*	MHG	*ungestalt, ungeschaffen, unschœne*	Av.	. . . .
Br.	*divalo*				
		NHG	*hässlich, unschön*		

Some of the words for 'ugly' are formally as well as semantically the opposites of those for 'beautiful'. That is, they are formed with prefixes for 'ill-' vs. 'well-' from words for 'form, shape', etc., or with neg. prefixes, e.g. Grk. δυσ-ειδής vs. εὐ-ειδής or Lith. *ne-gražus* vs. *gražus*. Words of the latter kind, lit. 'not beautiful', may in part be felt as merely mild, euphemistic terms (as perh. NHG *unschön* where it is in use), but need not be so felt and may be the usual words with all the feeling of 'ugly' (cf. e.g.Lith. *Onytė buvo negrazi, pikta ir tingi mergaitė* 'Anna war ein hässliches, böses und faules Mädchen', NSB s.v.).

The others, analogous to many of those for 'beautiful', are based upon more general expressive terms, in this case opprobrious, denoting various disagreeable qualities, e.g. 'shameful, base, foul, repulsive, dreadful'. Many of

them are used also in such earlier senses, being by no means restricted to 'ugly' in appearance.

Besides the words listed there are, of course, other still stronger terms (e.g. NE *hideous* when applied to looks, as a *hideous face*) and many euphemistic terms besides those mentioned.

1. Grk. δυσ-ειδής, δύσ-μορφος, cpds. of δυσ- 'ill-' and so opp. of εὐ-ειδής, εὔ-μορφος (16.81).

Grk. αἰσχρός, mostly 'shameful' but also (Hom.+) 'ugly' in appearance : αἶσχος 'a shame, disgrace' also 'ugliness', αἰσχύνη 'shame', etc. (16.45).

NG ἄσκημος, fr. ἄσχημος, late form for class. Grk. ἀσχήμων 'misshapen, ugly, unseemly, shameful', cpd. of ἀ- privative and σχῆμα 'form, shape, figure'.

2. Lat. *dēfōrmis* (> It. *deforme*), cpd. of *dē-* with privative force and *fōrma* 'form, mold' (cf. *fōrmōsus* 'beautiful', 16.81).

Lat. *turpis* 'ugly, base, shameful', used in both a moral and a physical sense, perh. as orig. describing what one turns away from: Grk. τρέπω 'turn'; cf. Skt. *trap-* 'be embarrassed, ashamed', *trapā-* 'embarrassment, shame', also (but with different historical development) NG ἐντροπή 'shame' (16.45). Walde-P. 1.757.

It. *brutto*, fr. Lat. *brūtus* 'dumb, stupid, irrational', orig. 'heavy' (*brutum antiqui gravem dicebant*, Festus), Osc.-Umbr. loanword : Lat. *gravis* 'heavy', etc. (15.81). Ernout-M. 119. Walde-H. 1.117. REW 1348.

Fr. *laid*, fr. a Frank. form = OHG *leid* 'hateful, sorrowful', OE *lāð* 'hateful, repulsive', etc. (cf. Du. *leelijk*, below, 4). REW 4858a.

Sp. *feo*, fr. Lat. *foedus* 'foul, filthy, loathsome' (in part, of appearance), etym. dub. Walde-P. 1.837 f., 186. Ernout-M. 373. Walde-H. 1.522 f. REW 3406.

Rum. *urît*, orig. 'hateful', pple. of *uri* 'hate' (16.41).

3. Ir. *dochrud*, cpd. of *do-* 'ill-' (16.72) and *crud* 'shape, form, manner' (cf. *sochrud* 'beautiful', 16.81).

Ir. *ētig*, neg. of *-tig*, not found as simplex, but = W. *teg* 'beautiful' (16.81).

Ir. *grānna, grande*, NIr. *grānna*, deriv. of *grāin* 'disgusting, loathsome' : W. (obs.) *graen* 'sorrow, grief', perh. fr. **gragnis* : Ir. *garg* 'rough, wild', Grk. γοργός 'grim, fierce, terrible'. Walde-P. 1.537. Pedersen 1.103, 538.

W. *hagr* : Corn. *hager*, Br. *hakr* 'horrible, hideous', etym. dub. Pedersen 1.125. Loth, RC 36.142.

W. *hyll*, etym.?

Br. *divalo*, cpd. of *di-* neg. and **malavo-* 'soft' : Grk. μαλακός 'soft', etc. Henry 102. Ernault, Glossaire 188 f.

4. ON *ljōtr* : Goth. *liuts* 'hypocrite', *liutei* 'deceit', etc. (16.68). Walde-P. 2.416. Falk-Torp 659.

ON *ūfagr*, OE *unfæger*, ME *unfaire*, neg. of ON *fagr*, OE *fægr* 'beautiful' (16.81).

Dan. *styg*, Sw. *stygg* : ON *styggr* 'repellent, unfriendly', Du. *stug* 'surly, sullen', perh. orig. 'repellent', fr. **steuk-*, beside **steug-* in Norw. *stauka* 'pound, stamp', Grk. στύγος 'hatred'(?), etc., extensions of **steu-*. Walde-P. 2.616. Falk-Torp 1193 (assuming development through 'stiff'). Hellquist 1099. Franck-v. W. 680.

Dan. *grim*, ODan., Norw. dial. *grem* also 'nasty' : ON *grimmr* 'fierce, savage, grim', OE *grimm* 'sharp, severe, fierce', OE, OS *grimman* 'to rage', ON *gramr* 'angry', etc. (cf. *gremi* 'anger', 16.42). Falk-Torp 347. Walde-P. 1.655.

Sw. *ful*, OE *fūl*, ME *foul*, all properly 'foul, stinking' (so mostly OE *fūl* = ON *fūll*, etc., cf. 15.26), in Sw. the usual word for 'ugly', frequent in this sense in ME (cf. NED s.v. 11, where first quotation is from Chaucer), and incipiently even in OE (cf. the contrast with *fæger* 'beautiful' in *byrgen ūtan fæger and innan fūl* quoted in Bosworth-Toller s.v.; and also gl. *fedus, deformis, turpis uel ful, uel pudor*, Wright-Wülcker 1.238.13).

OE *unwlitig*, neg. of *wlitig* 'beautiful' (16.81).

ME *ugli*, NE *ugly*, early ME *uglike*, *iglic* 'horrible', fr. ON *uggligr* 'fearful', deriv. of *uggr* 'apprehension, dread', vb. *ugga* 'fear, suspect, apprehend' : Sw. *agg* 'grudge, spite', etc. Walde-P. 1.32. Falk-Torp 16. NED s.v.

NE *plain*, orig. 'flat, level' (12.71), then 'simple, ordinary', now a freq. euphemistic term for 'ugly'. NED s.v.

NE *homely*, orig. 'belonging to the home', then 'simple' (in good or bad sense), 'commonplace' and esp. as mild term for 'ugly'. NED s.v. In U.S. (at least in New England) *homely* is or was the usual word, *ugly* being mostly 'ill-tempered' (*an ugly horse* had no reference to appearance).

Du. *leelijk*, MDu. *lelijc, leedlijk*, fr. *leed* = OHG *leid* 'hateful, sorrowful' (NHG *leid*), OE *lāð* 'hateful, repulsive' (also *lāðlik* id., like the Du.), ON *leiðr* 'disliked, loathed' (: Grk. ἀλείτης 'sinner'?). Walde-P. 2.401. Franck-v. W. 374.

OHG *unscōni*, MHG *unschæne*, NHG *unschön*, also OHG *missescōni* (cf. *informis missesconer* Ahd. Gloss. 3.425), all neg. of OHG *scōni*, etc. 'beautiful' (16.81).

OHG *unsāni* (*deformis unsconer unsani*, Ahd. Gloss. 3.425), neg. cpd. of the last member in OHG *selt-sāni* 'wonderful, strange, valuable' (NHG *seltsam*) :

OHG *sehan*, Goth. *saihwan*, etc. 'see'. Walde-P. 2.479. Weigand-H. 2.846.

MHG *ungestalt* (OHG *ungistalt* 'lacerus', Graff 6.667), neg. of *gestalt* (pple. of *stellen* 'place, put'), as sb. 'form, appearance'. Weigand-H. 2.1116.

MHG *ungeschaffen*, neg. of *schaffen*, pple. of *schaffen* 'make, create, shape'.

NHG *hässlich* (> Dan. *hæslig*), first late MHG in this sense, MHG *hazzelīch, hezlīch*, OHG *hazlīh* 'full of hate, hostile', MHG also 'hated', fr. OHG *haz*, etc. 'hate' (16.41). Weigand-H. 2.818.

5. Lith. *negražus*, Lett. *nejauks, neskaists*, all neg. cpds. of words for 'beautiful' (16.81).

6. ChSl. *rǫžĭnŭ*, orig. 'ridiculous' (καταγέλαστος Supr.; ἀσχήμων SCr.-ChSl.), SCr. *ružan*, deriv. of ChSl. *rǫgŭ* 'mockery', SCr. *rug* 'scorn, ridicule' : *ręgnǫti* 'gape', Lat. *ringī* 'show the teeth, snarl'. Walde-P. 1.272. Meillet, Études 221.

Boh. *ošklivý*, orig.? cf. *šklivě* 'dwarf'.

Boh. *nehezký*, neg. of *hezký* 'pretty' (16.81).

Pol. *szpetny*, old *szpatny* = Boh. *špatný* 'bad' (16.72). Brückner 553.

Pol. *brzydki* = Ukr. *brydkyj* id., Russ. dial. *bridkyj* 'sharp, cold', ChSl. *bridŭkŭ* 'piercing, sharp, pungent' : Russ.-ChSl. *briti* 'sheer', ChSl. *britva* 'razor', etc. 'Ugly' through 'unpleasant' fr. 'sharp'. Berneker 86.

Russ. *nekrasivyj*, neg. of *krasivyj* 'beautiful' (16.81).

Russ. *durnoj* 'bad' (16.72), also used for 'ugly'.

7. Skt. *ku-rūpa-, vi-rūpa-, apa-rūpa-*, all cpds. of pejorative or neg. prefixes with *rūpa-* 'form, shape, figure' (12.51). Skt. *a-çrīra-* (RV), cf. 16.81.

CHAPTER 17

MIND, THOUGHT

17.11 MIND

Grk.	νοῦς	Goth.	*aha, fraþi, hugs*	Lith.	*protas*
NG	νοῦς	ON	*hugr, munr*	Lett.	*gars, prāts*
Lat.	*mēns, animus*	Dan.	*aand, sind*	ChSl.	*umŭ*
It.	*mente*	Sw.	*sinne*	SCr.	*um*
Fr.	*esprit*	OE	*mōd, hyge, gewit(t)*	Boh.	*mysl*
Sp.	*mente*	ME	*mode, mynde, (i)wit*	Pol.	*umysł*
Rum.	*minte*	NE	*mind*	Russ.	*um*
Ir.	*menme, intinn*	Du.	*geest, zin*	Skt.	*manas-, citta-*
NIr.	*aigne, intinn*	OHG	*muot, sin, hugu*	Av.	*manah-*
W.	*meddwl*	MHG	*muot, sin, huge*		
Br.	*spered*	NHG	*sinn, geist*		

'Mind' is intended here as the seat of intelligence, parallel to 'soul, spirit' (16.11) as the seat of emotions. But, as already remarked in 16.11, the two groups overlap. Several of the words there listed may cover also the 'mind', and conversely many of those in this list cover mental states in the widest sense, that is, may be used with reference to feelings as well as thoughts, as Lat. *mēns*, Skt. *manas-*, Grk. νοῦς (rarely), OE *mōd*, *hyge*, NE *mind*, etc.

Apart from those discussed under 'soul, spirit', most of the words for 'mind' are connected with verbs for 'think, understand, know', or the like, and many of them are used also for the mind's activity, 'intelligence, reason, thought', etc.

The actual physical seat of the mind in the brain, though recognized by some of the Greek philosophers (Plato, but not Aristotle, who favored the heart), was not generally enough known to have any effect on linguistic usage, except in modern phrases like NE *has brains, has a good head* = *has a good mind*, NG ἔχει μυαλό 'has good sense', ἔχασε τὰ μυαλά του 'lost his head'. It was rather the vague νοῦς-φρένες (cf. below) that affected the terminology.

1. Derivs. of IE **men-* in Skt. *man-* 'think', Lat. *meminī* 'remember', etc. Walde-P. 2.264 ff. Ernout-M. 606. Walde-H. 2.69 f.

Lat. *mēns, mentis* (> It., Sp. *mente*; Rum. *minte*); Ir. *menme* (NIr. *meanma*, but not the usual word for 'mind'); ON *munr* (also 'longing, love', OE *myne* 'desire, love', rarely 'mind', Goth. *muns* 'thought, intention', etc.), ME *mynde*, NE *mind* (OE *gemynd* 'memory'); Skt. *manas-*, Av. *manah-*.

2. Grk. νόος, Att. νοῦς, whence νοέω 'perceive, notice, think', etc., νόημα 'thought, purpose, understanding', etym. dub. Walde-P. 2.324. Boisacq 672. Schwyzer, Festschrift Kretschmer 247 ff. For the technical uses, Schottlaender, Hermes 64.228 ff.

Grk. φρήν, esp. pl. φρένες, in Homer when used in lit. sense (with reference to wounds) hardly 'diaphragm' in the strict sense, but rather as if membranes inclosing the vital organs (heart, liver, etc.); hence a vague general term for the vital organs and most frequently in fig. sense 'heart, mind' as the seat of both emotion and thought—in this sense mostly poetic, but important for the large group of derivs., in some of which the thought element is dominant, as φρονέω 'think', φροντίς 'thought, care', σώ-φρων 'of sound mind, wise, prudent' (but also 'of restrained senses'), in others the emotional, as εὔ-φρων 'cheerful, merry', εὐφραίνω 'cheer, gladden'. Etym. dub. Walde-P. 1.699. Boisacq 1037 f.

3. Lat. *animus* 'spirit' (16.11) also

'mind'. Fr. *esprit* 'spirit' (16.11) also 'mind'.

4. Ir. *menme*, above, 1.

NIr. *aigne* (also 'spirit, desire, intention', etc.) fr. *aigneadh*, Ir. *aicned* 'nature', fr. a cpd. of *ad-* and the root in *gnīu* 'do, make', Lat. *gignere* 'beget', Grk. γίγνομαι 'be born, become'. Walde-P. 1.576. Pedersen 2.34, 534.

Ir. *intinn* 'intention, purpose', but also in certain phrases 'mind', fr. Lat. *intentiō*. Pedersen 1.234. Vendryes, De hib. voc. 147.

W. *meddwl*, orig. 'thought', vbl. n. to *meddwl* 'think' (17.13).

Br. *spered* 'spirit' (16.11), also 'mind'.

5. Goth. *aha* (reg. for νοῦς, beside *ahjan* 'think' : *ahma* 'spirit', OHG *ahta* 'intention, consideration, notice', OE *eaht* 'deliberation, council', OHG, OS *ahtōn* 'consider, take notice of, estimate', ON *ætla* 'think, intend', outside connections dub. Walde-P. 1.169. Feist 15.

Goth. *fraþi* (sometimes for νοῦς, but mostly 'thought, understanding') : *fraþjan* 'understand, think' (17.16).

Goth. *hugs* (νοῦς Eph. 4.17), ON *hugr* (Dan. *hu*, Sw. *håg* more nearly 'mood', except in certain phrases), OE *hyge*, OHG *hugu*, beside Goth. *hugjan*, etc. 'think' (17.13), deriv. Goth. *gahugds* (reg. for διάνοια, also νοῦς Rom. 7.25, and συνείδησις 1 Cor. 8.12, etc. : OE *gehygd* 'thought', OHG *gihugt* 'memory, joy', etc.), etym. dub. Walde-P. 1.378. Falk-Torp 424 f. Feist 272 f.

OE *mōd*, ME *mode*, OHG, MHG *muot*, partly 'mind' in intellectual sense, but more often with emotional value (cf.

NE *mood* 'state of feeling', NHG *mut* 'courage') : Goth. *mōþs*, ON *mōðr* 'anger' (16.42).

OE *gewit(t)*, ME *(i)wit*, also 'intelligence' (NE *wit*), and in the latter sense ON *vit*, OHG *wizzi*, MHG *witze* (NHG *witz*) : OE *witan*, OHG *wizzan*, Goth. *witan* 'know' (17.17).

OHG, MHG *sin*, NHG *sinn*, Du. *zin*, MLG *sin* (> Dan. *sind*, Sw. *sinne*), also and more orig. 'sense' (15.11).

Dan. *aand* 'spirit' (16.11), also 'mind'. Du. *geest*, NHG *geist*, orig. 'spirit' (16.11).

6. Lith. *protas*, usual word for 'mind' and 'reason', Lett. *prāts* mostly 'intelligence, understanding, reason' (OPruss. *prātin* acc. sg. 'counsel') : Lith. *su-prasti*, Lett. *sa-prast*, Goth. *fraþjan* 'understand', etc. (17.16).

Lett. *gars*, orig. 'spirit' (16.11).

7. ChSl. *umŭ* (renders νοῦς Lk. 24.45; also *bez uma* = εἰκῆ 'without reason', SCr., Russ. *um* 'mind, intelligence', cpd. ChSl., SCr., Russ. *razum*, Boh., Pol. *rozum* 'intelligence, reason' : ChSl. (*j)a-vě* 'manifestly', (*j)aviti* 'show', Skt. *āvis* 'manifestly', *pra-av-* 'notice, heed', Grk. αἰσθάνομαι 'perceive (by the senses)', etc. (15.11). Walde-P. 1.17. Berneker 34. Brückner 201.594.

Boh. *mysl*, Pol. *u-myst* : ChSl. *myslĭ* 'thought', *mysliti* 'think', etc., general Slavic (17.13).

8. Skt. *manas-*, Av. *manah-*, above, 1. Skt. *citta-*, properly 'thought, observation', pple. of *cit-* 'perceive, observe, understand', mid. 'reflect, meditate', etc. (17.13).

17.12 INTELLIGENCE, REASON

Grk.	νοῦς, διάνοια, σύνεσις	Goth.	gahugds, frōdei	Lith.	protas
NG	νοῦς, διάνοια	ON	vit, skilning	Lett.	prāts, jēga
Lat.	ratiō, intelligentia,	Dan.	forstand, fornuft	ChSl.	umŭ, razumŭ
	intellēctus	Sw.	förstånd, förnuft	SCr.	um, razum
It.	intelligenza, intelletto,	OE	andgit, gescēad	Boh.	rozum
	ragione	ME	(i)wit, intellect, resun	Pol.	rozum
Fr.	intelligence, raison	NE	intelligence, reason	Russ.	um, razum, razsudok
Sp.	inteligencia, razón	Du.	verstand, rede	Skt.	mati-, buddhi-
Rum.	deşteptăciune, inteli-	OHG	furstannessi, fernu-	Av.	xratu-
	genţa		mest, wizzī		
Ir.	cíall, intliucht, cond	MHG	verstantnisse, ver-		
NIr.	tuigsint, cíall		nunst, witze		
W.	deall, rheswm	NHG	verstand, vernunft		
Br.	skiant				

Many of the words listed under 'mind' (17.11) are used also of the mind's activity, 'intelligence, reason', and some of them are repeated here as the best words for the latter notion. But this is also expressed by a variety of words, which are mostly derived from verbs for 'understand, think, perceive, distinguish, know', etc., but in actual usage are broader than 'understanding, thought, knowledge', etc. in the literal sense. Thus NHG verstand is more comprehensive than verständnis or das verstehen. Their varying sources may have some effect on their usage and feeling, but in general not permanently. Artificial technical distinctions like Kant's verstand vs. vernunft are ignored here.

For an exhaustive treatment of the usages, as regards words of this kind, of the OHG and MHG writers, cf. Jost Trier, Der deutsche Wortschatz im Sinnbezirk des Verstandes.

1. Grk. νοῦς 'mind' (17.11) also the main word for 'intelligence' and so in NG. But πνεῦμα 'spirit' (16.11) is used in NG for 'keen intelligence', much like Fr. esprit and NHG geist.

Grk. διάνοια, also 'thought, intention, purpose', fr. διανοέω 'have in mind, intend, propose', cpd. of νοέω 'think' : νοῦς 'mind' (17.11).

Grk. σύνεσις : συνίημι 'understand' (17.16).

2. Lat. ratiō (> It. ragione, Fr. raison, Sp. razón), orig. 'account', whence 'faculty or method of computation' > 'judgment, reason', etc. : rērī (ratus sum) 'count, calculate', then 'think, estimate, judge', Goth. *garaþjan (in pple. garaþana) 'count', raþjō 'number, account', OHG reda 'account, speech, answer', OS redia 'account', etc. Walde-P. 1.73 f. Ernout-M. 860 f. (but taking the Gmc. group as borrowed fr. Lat.). Feist 394.

Lat. intelligentia (> It. intelligenza, Fr. intelligence, Sp. intelligencia, Rum. inteligenţa, all lit. words), Lat. intellēctus (> It. intelletto), both orig. 'perception, discernment', fr. intellegere 'perceive, comprehend, understand' (17.16). Ernout-M. 537.

Rum. deşteptăciune, lit. 'wakefulness', fr. deştepta 'waken' (4.63).

3. Ir. cíall, NIr. ciall : W. pwyll 'wisdom, prudence, sense', Br. poell 'discretion, prudence, wisdom', prob. fr. the root in Ir. ad-cíu 'see'. Walde-P. 1.509. Pedersen 2.490. Thurneysen, Gram. 132.

Ir. intliucht, fr. Lat. intellēctus (above). Vendryes, De hib. voc. 147.

Ir. cond : Goth. handugs 'wise'

(17.21), Lat. condere 'put together, establish'. Walde-P. 1.458. Pedersen 2.502.

NIr. tuigsint, fr. tuigim 'understand' (17.16).

W. deall : vb. dealt 'understand' (17.16). Also W. deallgarwch, deriv. of deallgar 'intelligent', cpd. of deall and -car 'loving, disposed to' (suffix form of car 'friend').

W. rheswm, fr. ME resun (below, 4). Parry-Williams 124.

Br. skiant, fr. Lat. scientia 'knowledge' (17.17). Henry 241.

4. Goth. gahugds (reg. for διάνοια) : hugs 'mind', hugjan 'think', etc. (17.11, 13).

Goth. frōdei (reg. for σύνεσις; also σοφία Lk. 2.52, and φρόνησις, Lk. 1.17, etc.), fr. frōþs 'wise' (17.21).

ON vit, ME (i)wit, OHG wizzī (Otfrid's favorite word, 'knowledge, recognition', hence the intelligence gained thereby; Trier, op. cit. 38 f.), MHG witze (but OE gewit chiefly 'mind', cf. 17.11) : ON vita, OHG wizzan, OE, Goth. witan 'know' (17.17).

ON skilning : skilja 'understand' (17.16).

OE andgit, also 'sense' : ongietan 'perceive, understand' (see 17.16, and 15.11).

OE gescēad (cf. ratio gescead, Aelfric Gram., Zupitza p. 35), lit. 'distinction, difference' : gescēadan 'separate, distinguish, decide', Goth. ga-skaidan 'separate', etc. (12.17).

ME, NE intellect, fr. Lat. intellēctus (above, 2).

NE intelligence, fr. Fr. intelligence (above, 2).

ME reisun, resun, NE reason, fr. OFr. reison, Fr. raison (above, 2).

OHG furstannessi ('intellectus', Tat., Trier, op. cit. 32, 66), MHG verstantnisse (NHG verständnis now only 'understanding'), NHG, Du. verstand (MLG vorstant > Dan. forstand, Sw. förstånd) : OHG farstantan (fir-, fur-), Du. verstaan, etc. 'understand' (17.16). Falk-Torp 263. Weigand-H. 2.1165. Kluge-G. 654.

OHG fernumest (esp. Notker for intellectus, partly as 'perception, sense'; Trier, op. cit. 51), MHG vernu(n)st, vernu(n)ft, NHG vernunft (MLG vornunft > Dan. fornuft, Sw. förnuft) : OHG farneman, MHG vernemen 'take, grasp, comprehend, perceive, hear', NHG vernehmen (semantic development prob. influenced by Lat. percipere, perceptio). Falk-Torp 260. Weigand-H. 2.1157 f.

Du. rede, also 'speech', MDu. rede, reden(e) also 'propriety, account', etc. : OHG reda 'account, speech' (sometimes also 'intelligence', esp. Notker; Trier, op. cit. 48 f.), Goth. raþjō 'account, number' (cf. Lat. ratio, above, 2). Franck-v. W. 538 f.

5. Lith. protas, Lett. prāts, also 'mind' (17.11).

Lett. jēga, orig. physical 'power, strength', now mostly mental 'intelligence' = Lith. jéga 'power, strength' : Grk. ἥβη 'youthful strength, youth'. Walde-P. 1.206 f. Mühl.-Endz. 2.111.

6. ChSl. umŭ, razumŭ, etc., general Slavic, see 'mind' (17.11).

Russ. razsudok, orig. 'judgment' : razsudit' 'judge', cpd. of sudit' 'judge, try', deriv. of sud 'court'. Cf. Pol. rozsądek 'judgment, understanding', etc.

7. Skt. mati-, also 'thought, worship, intention, piety' : manas- 'mind', man- 'think', etc. (17.11).

Skt. buddhi- (cf. Av. baodah- 'consciousness, perception') : budh- 'be awake, perceive, understand', Grk. πυνθάνομαι 'learn', etc. Walde-P. 2.147.

Av. xratu- = Skt. kratu- 'plan, will,

---

intelligence' but in RV also 'power, might' (of body or mind) : Grk. κράτος 'strength, might, power', Goth. hardus 'hard', with shift from physical to mental

17.13 THINK¹ (= REFLECT, etc.)

Grk.	ἐννοέω, φρονέω	Goth.	hugjan, þrafjan	Lith.	galvoti (mislyti, dū-
NG	σκέπτομαι, στοχάζομαι	ON	hugsa, hyggja		moti)
Lat.	cōgitāre	Dan.	tænke	Lett.	duomāt
It.	pensare	Sw.	tänka	ChSl.	mysliti
Fr.	penser, songer	OE	(ge)þencan, hycgan	SCr.	misliti
Sp.	pensar	ME	thenke	Boh.	mysliti
Rum.	cugeta, gîndi	NE	think	Pol.	myśleć
Ir.	imrādim, smuainim	Du.	denken	Russ.	dumat'
NIr.	smaoinim	OHG	denken, huggen	Skt.	cint-, cit-, man-, dhī-
W.	meddwl	MHG	denken, hügen	Av.	man-, čit-
Br.	soñjal	NHG	denken		

'Think' is intended here to cover the most generic verbs expressing mental activity, whence are derived the common nouns for 'thought'. But most of them are used also in one or another narrower sense, as 'understand', 'intend', or esp. (cf. 17.14) 'be of the opinion'.

1. Grk. ἐννοέω (also 'understand' and so N.) cpd. of νοέω (less common for 'think', mostly 'perceive, intend') : νοῦς 'mind' (17.11).

Grk. φρονέω (but esp. 'be so and so minded' or 'be prudent') : φρήν used as seat of thought or emotion (17.11).

Grk. σκέπτομαι, orig. 'look' (15.52), then of the mind 'examine, consider' (Soph.+), in NG (also σκέφτομαι) the usual verb for 'think'.

Grk. στοχάζομαι 'shoot at, aim at' (in lit. sense), 'seek for' and esp. 'try to understand, guess at', NG pop. 'think about' with στοχασμός 'thought, reflection'.

2. Lat. cōgitāre (> Rum. cugeta, OIt. coitare, OFr. coidier, etc.), fr. *co-agitāre, cpd. of agitāre 'put in motion, drive, impel, shake', etc., also of mental activity 'turn, revolve in the mind, ponder', frequent. of agere 'drive'. Ernout-M. 25 f. Walde-H. 1.242. REW 2027.

It. pensare, Fr. penser, Sp. pensar, fr. Lat. pēnsāre 'weigh, pay, requite', and of mental activity 'ponder, examine, consider', frequent. of pendere (pple. pēnsus) 'weigh, pay, ponder, consider' : pendēre 'hang', etc. Ernout-M. 750 ff. REW 6391.

Fr. songer, orig. 'dream', fr. Lat. somniāre 'dream' also 'think or talk idly', deriv. of somnium 'dream' : somnus 'sleep', etc. (4.61). REW 8086.

Rum. gîndi, deriv. of gînd 'thought, intention, wish', fr. Hung. gond 'care, worry'. Tiktin 680. Densusianu 1.378.

3. Ir. imrādim, also 'consider, deliberate', cpd. of im(m)- 'about' and rādim 'speak' : Goth. rōdjan 'speak', Lat. ratio 'reason', etc. (17.12). Walde-P. 1.74. Pedersen 2.591 f.

Ir. smuainim, NIr. smaoinim, etym.? Connection with ChSl. myslĭ 'thought', etc. (Pedersen 1.113) dub. Walde-P. 2.256.

W. meddwl : Ir. midiur 'judge', Lat. meditāre 'study, reflect, meditate', Grk. μέδομαι 'be mindful of', Goth. mitan 'measure'. Walde-P. 2.259 f.

power in Indo-Iranian. Cf. Lett. jēga. above, 5. Walde-P. 1.354 f. (rejecting the connection on semantic grounds!). Barth. 533 f.

Br. soñjal, fr. Fr. songer (above, 2).

4. Goth. hugjan (renders both φρονέω and νομίζω), ON hyggja, OE hycgan, OHG huggen, MHG hügen, with different suffix ON hugsa : Goth. hugs, ON hugr, etc. 'mind' (17.11).

Goth. þrafjan mostly 'perceive, understand' (17.16), but also for φρονέω 'think' and 'be minded', e.g. Rom. 12.3, 16.

(Goth. þagkjan 'ponder, reason, take counsel, be perplexed', rendering βουλεύομαι, λογίζομαι, etc.), Dan. tænke, Sw. tänka (meaning fr. LG, cf. ON þekkja 'perceive, know, be acquainted with'), OE (ge)þencan, OHG denken, etc., usual WGmc. words for 'think' : Lat. tongēre 'know' (old, rare), Osc. tanginud 'sententia', Praenest. tongitio 'notio'. Walde-P. 1.744. Falk-Torp 1312.

5. Lith. galvoti (now the accepted term, vs. the following loanwords; cf. NSB), fr. galva 'head'.

Lith. mislyti, fr. the Slavic, cf. ChSl. mysliti (below). Brückner, Sl. Fremdwörter 109.

Lith. dūmoti, Lett. duomāt, fr. the Slavic, cf. Russ. dumat' (below). Mühl.-Endz. 1.533.

6. ChSl. mysliti, etc., general Slavic (but mostly replaced by dumat' in Russ.), fr. sb. ChSl. myslĭ, etc. 'thought', prob. (*mūdsljo-) : Lith. maudžiu, mausti 'long for', Goth. (ga-)maudjan 'remind'. Walde-P. 2.255 f.

Russ. dumat', usual for 'think' in both senses but orig. only 'think' as 'be of the opinion', fr. the Gmc., cf. Goth. dōmjan 'judge', OE dēman 'judge, deem, think' (cf. 17.15). Berneker 237.

7. Skt. cint- (3sg. cintayati, denom. of cintā- 'thought, reflection, apprehension'), beside cit- (3sg. cetati, perf. ciketa, etc.) in act. 'perceive, observe, intend', etc., mid. 'reflect, meditate', Av. čit- (Barth. 427 f.), prob. fr. *kweit- extension of *kwei- in Skt. ci- 'notice, perceive', ChSl. čajati 'expect, hope', Grk. τίω 'honor, esteem', τίνω 'atone, pay', etc. Walde-P. 1.509.

Skt., Av., OPers. man- (Skt. mostly 'think' = 'be of the opinion', OPers. only so) : Lat. meminisse 'remember', mēns 'mind', Grk. μιμνήσκω 'remember', Lith. minéti 'think about, remember, mention', at-si-minti 'remember', Goth. munan 'think' ('be of the opinion'), gamunan 'remember', muns 'thought, opinion', etc. Walde-P. 2.264 ff.

Skt. dhī-, dhyā- 'think', fr. 'observe' : Av. dī- 'look at, observe' (15.51).

17.14 THINK² (= BE OF THE OPINION)

Grk.	*νομίζω, ἡγέομαι*	Goth.	*hugjan, munan, ahjan*	Lith.	*manyti*
NG	*νομίζω, θαρρῶ*	ON	*hyggja, halda*	Lett.	*duomāt, šk'ist*
Lat.	*arbitrārī, opīnārī, cēnsēre, putāre*	Dan.	*mene, tænke, tro*	ChSl.	*mĭnēti, mēniti*
It.	*pensare, credere*	Sw.	*tycka, mena, tänka, tro*	SCr.	*misliti, mniti*
Fr.	*penser, croire*	OE	*wēnan, dēman, munan*	Boh.	*mysliti, míniti*
Sp.	*pensar, creer*	ME	*wene, thenke, deme, beleve*	Pol.	*myśleć, mniemać*
Rum.	*socoti, crede*	NE	*think, believe*	Russ.	*dumat'*
Ir.	*do-moiniur*	Du.	*meenen, denken, gelooven*	Skt.	*man-*
NIr.	*sīlim, ceapaim*	OHG	*wānen, meinen*	Av.	*man-*
W.	*tybio*	MHG	*wænen, meinen, denken*		
Br.	*kredi*	NHG	*meinen, denken, glauben*		

'Think' in the sense of 'be of the opinion' is most widely expressed by verbs for 'think' = 'reflect' discussed in 17.13 or by cognates of these, or by verbs for 'believe' (17.15). But this is not true of all the IE languages, in some of which the usual terms are of quite different and diverse sources. Besides the words listed there are, of course, many other expressions, e.g. verbs for 'judge' used also for simple 'think' as here understood, as NE *judge*, NIr. *measaim*, etc.; or for 'suppose, guess', as NHG *vermuten;* ChSl. *gadati*, Russ. *gadat'*, Boh. *hádati* (: Lat. *pre-hendere* 'seize', etc.; Berneker 289 f.), NE *guess*, etc.

1. Words for 'think' = 'reflect' discussed in 17.13. It. *pensare*, Fr. *penser*, Sp. *pensar;* Goth. *hugjan*, ON *hyggja;* OE *þencan*, OHG *denken*, etc. (in earlier periods this sense rare, but quotable in OE; cf. NED s.v. *think* 9); Lett. *duomāt;* SCr. *misliti*, etc., Russ. *dumat';* Skt., Av. *man-*.

2. Derivs. of IE **men-* in Skt. *man-* 'think', etc. (17.13), but in sense belonging here. Ir. *do-moiniur;* Goth., OE *munan* (Goth. *ga-munan*, OE *ge-munan* 'remember'); Lith. *manyti* (also 'have in mind, intend'; cf. NSB s.v.); ChSl. *mĭnēti*, SCr. *mniti*, Boh. *míniti*.

3. Words for 'believe' (17.15), in this sense most commonly in Romance and Gmc. So Lat. *crēdere* with its Romance derivs.; Br. *kredi* (this sense prob. fr. Fr. *croire*, since not common to the other Celtic forms); Dan., *tro* (cf. NE *trow* arch.), NE *believe*, NHG *glauben*.

4. Grk. *νομίζω*, orig. 'use, practice', whence 'take for, consider, think', deriv. of *νόμος* 'usage, custom, law' (21.11).

Grk. *ἡγέομαι*, orig. and in Hom. only 'lead, conduct' (10.64), hence also 'hold, consider, think' (cf. Lat. *dūcere* 'lead' and 'reckon, consider').

Grk. *θαρρέω* 'be of courage, have confidence' (16.51), NG *θαρρῶ* freq. pop. term for 'think'. Cf. NE *dare say* expressing a mild opinion.

5. Lat. *arbitrārī* (partly legal term, but also common, esp. in Cic., for 'think, be of the opinion'), deriv. of *arbiter* 'witness, judge', etym. dub. Walde-P. 1.678. Ernout-M. 66. Walde-H. 1.62.

Lat. *opīnārī*, etym. dub. Walde-P. 1.177 (fr. *op-* in *optāre* 'choose, wish', Umbr. *upetu* 'eligito, optato'). Ernout-M. 704.

Lat. *putāre*, history difficult. Disputed whether of a single source or several. As 'cut' whence esp. 'trim, prune' (trees) : Lith. *piauti* 'cut, mow'. As 'purify, cleanse' (wool) perh. : Skt. *pu-* 'purify', Lat. *pūrus* 'clean'. As 'reckon, count', whence 'suppose, think', it could come from either source (cf. *ratiōnem putāre* 'clear the account'); or, with ChSl. *pytati* 'examine, study', belong to what might possibly be still a third group. But on the whole the development 'cut, prune' > 'count, reckon' > 'suppose, think' is the most probable. Walde-P. 2.12, 13. Ernout-M. 828 f. Kretchmer, Glotta 10.164 f.

Lat. *cēnsēre*, orig. used with reference to a formally expressed opinion, resolve : Skt. *çaṅs-* 'recite, announce, praise', Av. *sąh-* 'recite, announce', OPers. *θah-* 'announce, say', etc. Walde-P. 1.403. Ernout-M. 173 f. Walde-H. 1.199 (with other views).

Rum. *socoti*, orig. only 'regard, esteem', prob. fr. Slavic, cf. Bulg. dial. *sokoti*, Ukr. *sokotyty* 'watch, take care of'. Tiktin 1452 f.

6. NIr. *sīlim (saoilim)*, also 'expect,' Ir. *sāilim* 'expect, wait for', perh. : ON *seilask* (refl.) 'stretch out the hand, seek for', OPruss. *seilins* (pl.) 'mind', ChSl. *sila* 'strength', etc. (Walde-P. 2.460 f.) G. S. Lane, Language 7.282 f.

NIr. *ceapaim* 'think', fr. 'stop, catch, seize', prob. denom. of *ceap* 'block' (Ir. *cepp* fr. Lat. *cippus*). Pedersen 1.200.

W. *tybio*, fr. *tyb* 'opinion', etym.?

7. Goth. (beside *hugjan, munan*) once *ahjan* (for *νομίζω*) : *aha* 'mind' (17.11).

ON *halda*, lit. 'hold', but frequent in this sense (cf. Fritzner s.v. 25), as similarly NE *hold*, NHG *halten*.

Sw. *tycka*, also refl. *tyckas* 'seem' : ON *þykkja*, OE *þyncan*, etc. 'seem' (17.18), beside OE *þencan*, etc. 'think' (17.13). Falk-Torp 1308. Hellquist 1255.

OE *wēnan*, ME *wene* (NE *ween*), OHG *wānen*, MHG *wænen* (NHG *wähnen*), also 'hope' = ON *væna*, Goth. *wēnjan* 'hope' : Goth. *wēns*, ON *vān*, OE *wēn*, OHG *wān* 'hope' (16.63), NED s.v.

OE *dēman*, ME *deme* (NE *deem*), orig. 'judge' = Goth. *dōmjan*, OHG *tuomen* 'judge', fr. OE *dōm*, Goth. *dōms* 'judgment', etc. NED s.v. *deem*.

NE *guess* 'estimate', also familiar U.S. colloq. for 'think' (*I guess so*), ME *gessen*, of Norse orig. and deriv. of the root in NE *get*. NED s.v. Falk-Torp 311.

OHG–NHG *meinen*, Du. *meenen* (MLG *meinen, mēnen* > Dan. *mene*, Sw. *mena*) = OE *mǣnan* 'have in mind, purpose, intend, mean', NE *mean* : ChSl. *mēniti* 'call to mind, mention, mean, think', perh. Ir. *mian* 'wish, desire', W. *mwyn* 'enjoyment'. Walde-P. 2.302 f. Berneker 2.49.

8. Lett. *šk'ist* : *skaitīt* 'count, reckon', Lith. *skaityti* 'count, read', prob. from **sk^{w}eit-*, beside **k^{w}eit-* in Skt. *cit-, cint-* 'think' (17.13). Walde-P. 1.509. Mühl.-Endz. 4.47.

9. ChSl. *mēniti* : OHG *meinen*, etc. (above, 7). Berneker 2.49.

Pol. *mniemać*, old *mnimać*, prob. fr. old *wnimać* in same sense = Russ. *vnimat'* 'hear, heed' (cpd. of ChSl. *imati* 'take'), crossed with *-mnieć* (in *po-mnieć* 'keep in the mind', etc.) : ChSl. *mĭnēti*, etc. (cf. above, 2). Brückner 342. Berneker 264.

17.15 BELIEVE

Grk.	*πείθομαι, πιστεύω*	Goth.	*galaubjan*	Lith.	*tikėti*
NG	*πιστεύω*	ON	*trūa*	Lett.	*ticēt*
Lat.	*crēdere*	Dan.	*tro*	ChSl.	*věrą jęti, věrovati*
It.	*credere*	Sw.	*tro*	SCr.	*vjerovati*
Fr.	*croire*	OE	*gelīefan*	Boh.	*věřiti*
Sp.	*creer*	ME	*beleve, (i)leve, trowen*	Pol.	*wierzyć*
Rum.	*crede*	NE	*believe*	Russ.	*verit'*
Ir.	*crētim*	Du.	*gelooven*	Skt.	*çraddhā-*
NIr.	*creidim*	OHG	*gilouban*	Av.	*zrazdā-, var-*
W.	*credu*	MHG	*gelouben*		
Br.	*kredi*	NHG	*glauben*		

Words for 'believe' (a person as speaking the truth or a statement as true) had first the sense now surviving in NE *believe in*, NHG *glauben an*, etc., based on 'have confidence, faith in, trust'.

There is an inherited group common to Latin, Celtic, and Indo-Iranian, probably an old cult word.

1. IE **k̂red-dhē-*, cpd. of **dhē-* 'put, place' and *k̂red-* seen in Skt. *çrad-* (isolated in Ved. *çrad asmāi dhatta* 'believe in him!', etc.), this prob. not, as formerly assumed, the same words as IE **k̂red-*, **k̂r̥d-* in words for 'heart' (Lat. *cor, cordis*, Grk. *καρδία*, Ir. *cride*, etc., 4.44), but perh. : Ir. *cretair*, W. *crair* 'relic, reliquary'. Ernout-M. 229. Walde-H. 1.287. Vendryes, RC. 44.90 ff.

Lat. *crēdere* (> Romance words); Ir. *cretim*, etc., general Celtic; Skt. *çraddhā-*, Av. *zrazdā-* (init. *z* by assimilation).

2. Grk. *πείθομαι*, mid. of *πείθω* 'persuade', hence 'be persuaded, obey, trust' and finally (already in Hom.) simply 'believe' : Lat. *fīdere* 'trust' (this not used for 'believe', but *fidēs* 'faith, belief' serves as sb. also for *crēdere*). Walde-P. 1.139. Ernout-M. 358. Walde-H. 1.493 ff.

From the same root *πιστός* 'faithful' and *πίστις* 'faith, belief', whence *πιστεύω* 'trust' and 'believe', eventually displacing *πείθομαι*.

3. Goth. *galaubjan*, OE *gelīefan* (Anglian *gelēfan*, ME *ileve*, shortened *leve*, whence *beleve*, NE *believe*), Du. *gelooven*, OHG *gilouban*, MHG *gelouben*, NHG *glauben*, early also *gleuben* : Goth. *liufs*, OE *lēof*, etc. 'dear' (16.27), OE *lufu*, etc. 'love' (16.26), and OE *lof*, etc. 'praise' (16.79), with development of 'trust, believe' through 'be pleased, satisfied with'? Walde-P. 2.419. Feist 188. NED s.v. *believe*.

ON *trūa*, Dan., Sw. *tro*, ME *trowen*, NE *trow* (arch.), all orig. 'trust' (as Goth. *trauan*, OE *trūwian*, OHG *trūan*, etc.) : ON *trūr*, OE *trēowe*, etc., 'faithful' (16.65).

4. Lith. *tikėti*, Lett. *ticēt* : Lith. *tikti* 'fit, suit', *tiekti* 'prepare', *teiktis* 'be pleased', *tikras* 'real, correct, certain', outside connections dub. Leskien, Ablaut 287. Buga, Kalba ir Senovė 100 f. Mühl.-Endz. 3.179, 157. Otherwise Walde-P. 1.286 (: OHG *dingan* 'hope', for which see 16.63).

5. ChSl. *věrą jęti* (lit. 'take faith', reg. for *πιστεύω*), *věrovati*, SCr. *vjerovati*, Boh. *věřiti*, Pol. *wierzyć*, Russ. *verit'*, fr. *věra* 'faith' : Lat. *vērus* 'true', etc. (16.66).

6. Skt. *çrad-dhā-*, Av. *zrazdā-*, above, 1.

Av. *var-*, act. 'choose', whence (esp. mid.) 'choose for oneself, profess, believe (a religion)', also 'persuade, convert', cf. OPers. *θuvām varnavatām* 'let it convince you, be believed by you' : Skt. *vr̥-* 'choose', Lat. *velle* 'will, wish', etc. (16.61). Barth. 1360 ff. Walde-P. 1.294.

17.16 UNDERSTAND

Grk.	*συνίημι, συν-, ἐν-νοέω, καταλαμβάνω*	Goth.	*fraþjan*	Lith.	*suprasti*
NG	*καταλαβαίνω, ἐννοῶ, νοιώθω*	ON	*skilja*	Lett.	*saprast, jēgt*
Lat.	*intellegere, comprehendere*	Dan.	*forstaa*	ChSl.	*razumēti*
It.	*capire, comprendere, intendere*	Sw.	*förstå*	SCr.	*razumijeti*
Fr.	*comprendre*	OE	*understandan, ongietan*	Boh.	*rozuměti*
Sp.	*entender, comprender*	ME	*understande, angete*	Pol.	*rozumieć*
Rum.	*înțelege*	NE	*understand*	Russ.	*ponjat'*
Ir.	*tucu*	Du.	*verstaan*	Skt.	*-jñā-, api-vat-, ava-gam-*
NIr.	*tuigim*	OHG	*farstantan*	Av.	*aipi-aot-*
W.	*deall*	MHG	*verstān*		
Br.	*klevout, meiza*	NHG	*verstehen, begreifen*		

Some of the words for 'understand' are connected with others of intellectual content discussed under 'mind', 'intelligence', or 'think'. Others represent fig. uses of 'put together', 'pick out', 'separate', 'stand' (WGmc.), and esp. 'take, seize, grasp'. This last named fig. use repeats itself in many other words besides those listed, e.g. NHG *fassen*, NE *grasp*, and the recent U.S. slang *I get you*.

1. Grk. *συνίημι*, lit. 'bring together' (as sometimes in Hom.) but mostly fig. 'perceive' and esp. 'understand', cpd. of *ἵημι* 'let go, throw, send' (10.25).

Grk. *συννοέω, ἐννοέω*, NG *ἐννοῶ*, cpds. of *νοέω* 'perceive, think' : *νοῦς* 'mind' (17.11).

Grk. *καταλαμβάνω* (as 'understand' Plato+), cpd. of *λαμβάνω* 'seize, take'. Hence NG pop. *καταλαβαίνω* (new present, as simple *λαβαίνω* formed to aor. *ἔλαβα*), often aor. *κατάλαβα* 'I understood' = 'I understand'.

NG *νοιώθω* (also 'perceive, feel'), new present for **ἐννοιόω*, fr. *ἔννοια* in its older sense 'thought, notion' (: *ἐννοέω*, above). Hatzidakis, Byz. Z.30.219 f.

2. Lat. *intellegere* (> Rum. *înțelege*), cpd. of *inter* 'between', and *legere* 'collect, choose'. Ernout-M. 537. Walde-H. 1.352. REW 4482.

Lat. *comprehendere* (> It. *comprendere*, Fr. *comprendre*, Sp. *comprender*), cpd. of *prehendere* 'take, seize' (11.14), also mentally 'grasp'. Ernout-M. 803. Meyer-Lübke 2106.

It. *intendere*, Sp. *entender* (Fr. *entendre* now esp. 'hear'), fr. Lat. *intendere* 'stretch (toward)', whence 'direct' and mentally 'direct the mind toward, intend', etc. Ernout-M. 1027. REW 2106.

It. *capire* (the usual spoken word), fr. Lat. *capere* 'seize, grasp, take'. REW 1625.

3. Ir. *tucu*, NIr. *tuigim* fr. **to-ucc-*, orig. same as in perfect. forms of *do-biur* 'bring' (see 10.62). Pedersen 2.471.

W. *deall*, etym.? Morris Jones 101 (: Skt. *dhī-* 'think').

Br. *klevout*, also and orig. 'hear' (15.41).

Br. *meiza*, fr. *meiz* 'comprehension, intelligence', MBr. *meis* : W. *meddwl* 'think', etc. Ernault, Glossaire 400.

4. Goth. *fraþjan* : Lith. *su-prasti* 'understand', etc. (below, 5).

ON *skilja*, properly 'separate, divide' (12.23), but reg. (as also NIcel.) for 'understand'. Hence ME *skille*, NE dial. *skill* 'understand' (NED s.v.).

OE *understandan*, ME *understande*, NE *understand;* OE *forstandan* (mostly 'oppose, withstand', but also 'understand', cf. NED s.v. *forstand*), Du. *verstaan* (MLG *vorstān* > Dan. *forstaa*, Sw. *förstå*), OHG *farstantan* (*fir-*, *fur-*), MHG *verstān*, NHG *verstehen*, cpds. of the verbs for 'stand', with development of 'stand under' and 'stand before' through the notion of 'be close to' (?). Cf. Grk. ἐπίσταμαι 'know how, know' (17.17).

OE *ongietan*, ME *angete*, also general 'perceive' ('see, hear, feel', etc.), cpd. of *-gietan*, in *begietan*, etc. 'get, obtain' (11.16).

NHG *begreifen*, also in other senses but now most commonly 'understand', cpd. of *greifen* 'seize, take hold of' (11.14) with same development as in Lat. *comprehendere*. Paul, Deutsches Wtb. 66.

5. Lith. *suprasti*, Lett. *saprast*, cpds. of Lith. *-prasti* (only in cpds. *at-prasti* 'break a habit', *įprasti* 'get used to', etc.), Lett. *prāst* 'understand, notice', with sbs. Lith. *protas* 'mind, reason', Lett. *prāts* 'reason' : Goth. *fraþjan* 'understand, think', *frōþs* 'wise', etc. Walde-P. 2.86. Mühl.-Endz. 3.378. Feist 165.

Lett. *jēgt* and cpds. (*nuo-*, *sa-*) fr. *jēga* 'understanding, good sense', orig. 'power, might', like Lith. *jėga* (4.81). Mühl.-Endz. 2.112.

6. ChSl. *razuměti*, also 'know' (cf. 17.17) but usual word for 'understand' (συνίημι, etc.) and so in modern Slavic, SCr. *razumijeti*, Boh. *rozuměti*, Pol. *rozumieć*, deriv. of ChSl. *razumŭ*, etc. 'intelligence, reason' (17.12).

Russ. *ponjat'*, cpd. of *-jat'* (only in cpds. *uzjat'* 'take', etc.), ChSl. *jęti* 'take', etc. Berneker 427.

7. Skt. several cpds. of *jñā-* 'know' (17.17), as *ā-*, *pra-*, *vi-*, are used, among other senses, for 'understand'.

Skt. *api-vat-*, Av. *aipi-vat-*, *aipi-aot-* prob. : Lith. *justi*, *jausti* 'feel, perceive' (also Lat. *vātēs*, Ir. *fāith* 'seer, poet'?). Walde-P. 1.216. Meillet, BSL 23.77. Barth. 41, 1343.

Skt. *ava-gam-*, lit. 'come down to' (cpd. of *gam-* 'go, come', 10.47) is used also for 'understand' (cf. BR. s.v.).

17.17 KNOW

Grk.	*οἶδα, ἐπίσταμαι, γιγνώσκω*	Goth.	*witan, kunnan*	Lith.	*žinoti, pažinti*
		ON	*vita, kunna, kenna*	Lett.	*zināt, pazīt*
NG	*ἠξεύρω (ξέρω), γνωρίζω*	Dan.	*vide, kende*	ChSl.	*věděti, razuměti, znati*
Lat.	*scīre, nōscere, cognōscere*	Sw.	*veta, känna*	SCr.	*znati, poznavati*
		OE	*witan, gecnāwan, cunnan*	Boh.	*věděti, znáti*
It.	*sapere, conoscere*			Pol.	*wiedzieć, znać*
Fr.	*savoir, connaître*	ME	*wite, (i)knowe, kunne, kenne*	Russ.	*znat'*
Sp.	*saber, conocer*			Skt.	*vid-, jñā-*
Rum.	*ști, cunoaște*	NE	*know*	Av.	*vid-, zan-*
Ir.	*rofetar, adgēn, asagninaim*	Du.	*weten, kennen*		
		OHG	*wizzan, cunnan, bi-, ir-cnāan, -chennan*		
NIr.	*tā a fhios agam, aithnigim*				
		MHG	*wissen, künnen, be-, er-kennen*		
W.	*gwybod, adnabod*				
Br.	*gouzout, anaout*	NHG	*wissen, kennen*		

The two main notions which are covered by NE *know*, namely a) 'know as a fact' (*I know it is so* vs. *believe*) and b) 'be acquainted with' (a person or thing), were originally expressed by different words and still are in many of the IE languages. But even where there are two words, the distinction is not always

rigorously observed. Thus in NT οὐκ οἶδα τὸν ἄνθρωπον 'I know not the man' (Mt. 26.72, 74, Mk. 14.71, etc.), which in ChSl. is rendered once by *věmi* and three times by *znają* in the parallel passages. Grk. γιγνώσκω is rendered in Gothic by both *kunnan* and *witan*. OHG *wizzan* is sometimes used where NHG would require *kennen*, e.g. Tat. 186.4 *ni weiz ih inan noh ih ni weis was thu quidis* 'non novi illum neque scio quid dicas'. Fr. *savoir* is used for 'know of', sometimes in phrases where the sense is hardly distinguishable, if at all, from that of *connaître*. Hence the words are given here together, instead of in separate lists, but in the order of senses a and b according to their prevailing usage.

Most of the words belong to one or the other of two inherited groups, which had originally senses a or b respectively. Those of the second group are the most widespread, and in several languages have absorbed the uses belonging orig. to the first. But for sense a there are several others, based on notions like 'find out, distinguish, be wise', etc.

Differences of aspect (e.g. Grk. γιγνώσκω, Lat. *nōscere* in present 'come to know, recognize') are ignored.

Words for 'know' may cover 'know how' (to do something), and this sense became dominant in those which finally resulted in NE *can*, NHG *können*. The opposite development is seen in Grk. ἐπίσταμαι. Lith. *mokėti* (not included in the list) is 'know how, can' (write, read, etc.), also used of knowing a lesson, a language, etc.

Virtually all the nouns for 'knowledge' are derived from the prevailing verbs, so that a separate list and discussion are superfluous.

1. IE **weid-* 'see' (15.51), perf. **woida* 'have seen' > 'know', whence the latter sense may be transferred to the other tenses or a distinct conjugation may be established for this sense. Walde-P. 1.236 ff. Ernout-M. 1105. Pedersen 2.522 ff.

Grk. οἶδα, pl. ἴδμεν; Ir. *fetar* (after neg.), *ro-fetar*, with sb. *fiuss* 'knowledge', fr. **wid-tu-*; hence the usual NIr. expressions like *tā a fhios agam*, lit. 'its knowledge is with me'; W. *gwn* 'I know', MBr. *gounn*, etc. (partly cpds. with vb. 'to be', as W. *gybyddaf* 'I shall see', W. *gwy-bod*, Br. *gou-zout* 'know'; cf. Pedersen 2.446 f.); Goth. *witan*, OE *witan*, OHG *wizzan*, etc., general Gmc. (NE *wit* arch. or legal), with pret.-presents, 1sg. Goth. *wait*, 1pl. *witum*, OE *wāt*, *witon*, etc. (NE *wot*); ChSl., Boh. *věděti*, Pol. *wiedzieć*, Russ. *vedat'* (now distinctly arch.); Skt., Av. *vid-* (esp. perfect).

2. IE **ĝenə-*, etc., esp. **ĝnō-*. Walde-P. 1.578 ff. Ernout-M. 678 f. Pedersen 2.546 f. Feist 317. Grk. γιγνώσκω, later γινώσκω, also (less common in class. Grk., but reg. NG form) γνωρίζω (deriv. of a form with *r*-suffix; cf. γνώριμος, Lat. *gnārus*, etc.); Lat. *nōscere* (early *gnōscere*), *cognōscere* (> Romance words); Ir. *ad-gēn* (*adgēn sa* gl. *cognosco* Wb. 12c13), vbl. n. *aithgne*, NIr. *aithne*, whence *aithnighim*, also Ir. *asa-gninaim*, *itar-gninim* (both gl. *sapio*, but also freq. 'recognize, understand'), W. *adnabod*, Br. *anaout*, MBr. *aznaout* (**ati-gna-* + vbl. n. W. *bod*, etc. 'being', cf. Pedersen 1.104, 2.447); Goth. *kunnan*, ON *kunna*, OE *cunnan*, ME *kunne* (NE *can*), OHG *cunnan*, MHG *künnen* (NHG *können*); ON *kenna* (also 'teach'), Dan. *kende*, Sw. *känna*, (OE *cennan* 'make known'), ME *kenne*, NE dial. *ken*, OHG *bi-*, *ir-chennan*, MHG *be-*, *er-kennen*, NHG *kennen;* OE *gecnāwan*, ME *(i)knowe*, NE *know*, OHG *bi-*, *ir-cnāan;* Lith. *žinoti*, Lett. *zināt*, Lith. *pa-žinti*, Lett. *pa-zīt;* ChSl. *znati*, etc. general Slavic (Russ. in both senses, SCr. in sense a, with *poznavati* in sense b); Skt. *jñā-*, Av. *zan-*, OPers. *dan-* (3sg. imperf. *adānā* = Skt. *ajānāt*) and *xšnā-* (Barth. 1659, 559); Toch. *knān-* (both senses).

3. Grk. ἐπίσταμαι, in Hom. 'know how, be able, be versed in', later simply 'know' (mostly in sense a), cpd. of ἵσταμαι 'stand', but detached in form (prob. starting fr. aor. forms like ἐπιστάμενος, etc.) and use fr. ἐφ-ίσταμαι 'stand upon, be set over, be master of' (cf. ἐπιστάτης 'chief, overseer, etc.). Walde-P. 2.603.

NG ἠξεύρω, pop. ξέρω, new present formed fr. ἠξεῦρον, class. ἐξεῦρον aor. of ἐξ-ευρίσκω 'find out'. Koraes, Ἄτακτα 4.164. Hatzidakis, πρακτικά 1926.64 ff. Τραχίλης, Ἀθηνᾶ 45.220.

4. Lat. *scīre* (> Rum. *ști;* otherwise in Romance mostly replaced by derivs. of Lat. *sapere;* REW 7722), prob. : Skt. *chyati* 'cuts off', Ir. *scian* 'knife', etc., with development through 'separate, distinguish'. Walde-P. 2.542. Ernout-M. 908.

It. *sapere*, Fr. *savoir*, Sp. *saber* fr. VLat. **sapēre*, Lat. *sapere* 'taste' (15.32) and 'have sense, be wise'. REW 7586.

5. ChSl. *razuměti* 'understand' (17.16), also freq. for γιγνώσκω (e.g. *po česomu razuměją se* = κατὰ τί γνώσομαι τοῦτο Lk. 1.18), deriv. of *razumŭ* 'intelligence' (17.12).

17.18 SEEM

Grk.	*φαίνομαι, δοκέω*	Goth.	*þugkjan*	Lith.	*rodytis*
NG	*φαίνομαι*	ON	*þykkja, sȳnast*	Lett.	*likties*
Lat.	*vidērī*	Dan.	*synes, tyckes*	ChSl.	*(j)aviti sę*
It.	*parere, sembrare*	Sw.	*synas, tyckas*	SCr.	*činiti se*
Fr.	*paraître, sembler*	OE	*þyncan, bēon gesewen*	Boh.	*zdati se*
Sp.	*parecer*	ME	*thinke, sēme*	Pol.	*zdać się*
Rum.	*parea*	NE	*seem*	Russ.	*kazat'sja*
Ir.	*da, dar, indar, anadchiter*, (all 3sg.)	Du.	*schijnen*	Skt.	*dṛçya-*
		OHG	*dunken, wesan gisehan*	Av.	. . . .
NIr.	*dar* (3sg.), *dochitear* (3sg.), *samhluighim*	MHG	*dunken*		
		NHG	*scheinen (dünken)*		
W.	*ymddangos*				
Br.	*he(ñ)velout, kaout doare*				

Verbs for 'seem' are now used most commonly with reference to something which we rather think, but do not know positively, is so. Such relation to thought, opinion is original in a few (Grk. δοκέω, Goth. *þugkjan*, etc.), but most of them are based in origin on the notion of visual appearance. These are mostly cognate with verbs for 'see', 'show', or 'shine', or with adjectives for 'similar'. Some are refl. forms of verbs for 'put', 'do, make', or 'give', with development through an intermediate 'represent'.

In these verbs the impersonal use, 'it seems' (to me, etc.) is the most widespread, but with some exceptions the personal use is also not uncommon, e.g. Lat. *videor*, *vidēmur*, like NE *I seem*, *we seem*.

1. Grk. φαίνομαι, 'appear' in lit. sense and 'seem', mid. of φαίνω 'give light, cause to appear' : Skt. *bhā-* 'shine', etc. (15.56).

Grk. δοκέω 'think' and 'seem' : δέκομαι 'receive', Lat. *decet* 'is seemly', *docēre* 'teach', etc. Walde-H. 1.330 f. Ernout-M. 278 f.

Grk. δοκέω by orig. and use refers to thought, opinion, while φαίνομαι referred primarily to visual appearance, but was not so restricted, and eventually prevailed. Cf. ἐμοὶ φαίνεται, NG μοῦ φαίνεται 'it seems to me'.

Grk. δέαμαι (rare; δέατο Hom., δέαται Hesych., δέατοι Arc. inscr.) : δέελος, δῆλος 'visible, plain', Skt. *dī-* 'shine'. Walde-P. 1.82. Boisacq 855.

2. Lat. *vidērī*, pass. of *vidēre* 'see' (15.51).

It. *parere*, OFr. *paroir*, Fr. *paraître*, Sp. *parecer*, Rum. *parea*, fr. Lat. *pārēre* 'appear' (commonly 'obey', but this sense secondary), with 3sg. impers. *pāret* 'it is evident', etym. dub., perh. : Grk. πεπαρεῖν 'show'. Also cpd. Lat. *appārēre* > OFr. *apareir* > ME *apere*, NE *appear*. Walde-P. 2.6. Ernout-M. 733. REW 6235, 6237.

It. *sembrare*, Fr. *sembler*, fr. Lat. *simulāre* 'make like' with shift to 'be like, seem', deriv. of *similis* 'like' (12.92). Ernout-M. 942. REW 7925.

3. Ir. 3sg. *da*, *dar*, *indar*, as *da lim* (Thes. 2.291.5), *dar limm*, *indar limm*, NIr. *dar liom* 'it seems to me', prob. based on the *tā-* in supplementary forms of the verb 'be'. Pedersen 2.432 f.

Ir. *an-adchiter* 'videtur' (Wb. 12c), NIr. *dochitear* (*dochitear dam* 'it seems to me', Dinneen) pass. of *adcīu*, NIr. *dochim* 'see' (15.51).

NIr. *samhluighim* 'appear, be like', sometimes 'seem', as *samhluigheadh dam* 'it seemed to me' (Dinneen), fr. *samhail* 'likeness' (12.92).

W. *ymddangos*, cpd. of *dangos* 'show' (15.55).

Br. *he(ñ)velout*, fr. *he(ñ)vel* 'like' (12.92).

Br. *kaout doare* 'have the appearance', *doare* 'appearance' : W. *dwyre* 'rise', *dwyrain* 'the east', root connection? Pedersen 1.526. Henry 103.

Many other Br. phrases in Vallée s.vv. *paraître*, *sembler*.

4. Goth. *þugkjan* (reg. for φαίνομαι and δοκέω), ON *þykkja*, Dan. *tyckes*, Sw. *tyckas* (refl. : Sw. *tycka* 'think'), OE *þyncan*, ME *thinke* (NE *methinks*), OHG, MHG *dunken*, NHG *dünken*, all fr. another grade of the root in the vb. for 'think', OE *þencan*, etc. (17.13). In this group the impersonal use is the orig., and in large measure the dominant or even the only one. Falk-Torp 1308. NED s.v. *think*, vb.[1].

ON *sȳnast* (esp. impers., as *sȳnist mer* 'it seems to me'), Dan. *synes*, Sw. *synas*, refl. of ON *sȳna*, etc. 'show' (15.55). Falk-Torp 1227.

OE, OHG pass. of *sēon*, *sehan* 'see' (15.51), e.g. OE *byþ gesewen* beside *ys geþuht* = Lat. *vidētur* in Aelfric's Colloquy, *gesene woeron* Lk. 24.11 Lindisf. = *wæron geþukte* in WSax. versions, OHG *gisehan warun* in Tat. 223.5.

ME *sēme*, NE *seem*, in ME mostly 'beseem', fr. ON *sœma* 'conform to, honor', but with the sense of the parallel ON *sōma* 'beseem' : Goth., ON, OHG *sama-* 'same'. Falk-Torp 1234. NED s.v. *seem*, vb.[2].

NHG *scheinen*, Du. *schijnen*, also and orig. 'shine' (15.56), with development through 'be clear, appear' to 'seem', as in the sb. *schein* 'brightness', now 'appearance, pretense'. Paul, Deutsches Wtb. s.v.

5. Lith. *rodytis* (esp. *rodos* 'it seems'), refl. of *rodyti* 'show' (15.55). In older Lith. also *regėtis* (so Trowitsch NT vs. *rodytis* Kurschat), refl. of *regėti* 'see' (15.51).

Lett. *likties* (esp. *liekas* 'it seems', etc.), refl. of *likt*, *lieku* 'put' (12.12), with development through 'put oneself, represent'. Mühl.-Endz. 2.469.

Lett. *šk'ist*, *šk'ietu* 'think' (17.14) is also used impers. for 'seem', as *šk'iet*, or refl. *šk'ietas* 'seems'. Mühl.-Endz. 4.47.

6. ChSl. *(j)aviti sę* (reg. in Gospels for φαίνομαι), refl. of *(j)aviti* 'show' (15.55).

SCr. *činiti se*, refl. of *činiti* 'do, make' (9.11), with development through 'make oneself, give oneself the appearance, represent'.

Boh. *zdati se*, Pol. *zdać się*, cpd. refl. of *dati*, *dać* 'give' (11.21), with development prob. through 'give oneself out as, represent' (this sense formerly in Pol. cf. Linde s.v.).

Russ. *kazat'sja*, refl. of *kazat'* 'show' (15.55).

7. Skt. *dṛçya-* or cpds., pass. of *dṛç-* 'see' (15.51).

17.19. 'Idea, notion', understood here as the 'mental image', is a kind of thought, only less complex than 'thought' or 'a thought' in general may be, and evoked by an actual object or act or commonly by a word. As is natural, it is generally expressed by words derived from verbs for 'think', 'know' or 'understand'—occasionally as 'representation'. A full list is not attempted, owing to the numerous gaps in our knowledge of the technical word, if any. Only the accepted classical and modern European words are noted.

1. Grk. ἔννοια, orig. 'act of thinking' (: ἐννοέω 'have in mind, think, understand', νοῦς 'mind'; 17.11, etc.), is the reg. term (Plato, Aristot., etc.) for 'idea, notion'.

Grk. ἰδέα, mostly 'appearance, form, kind' (: ἰδεῖν 'see'), then in Plato a sort of 'ideal type, pattern', but almost never 'idea' in the sense here intended. Hence the widespread Eur. words, It. *idea*, Fr. *idée*, NE *idea*, etc., at first in some of the Grk. senses, later also in the one here intended. NED s.v. *idea*.

2. Lat. *nōtiō* (> Romance words and NE *notion*), reg. term in Cic. = Grk. ἔννοια, fr. the root in *nōscere* 'know'.

Lat. *conceptum*, fr. pple. of *concipere* 'take hold of, conceive, perceive', not used for 'idea, notion', but source of modern learned words so used, as It. *concetto*, Fr. NE *concept*, etc.

3. NHG *begriff* (Du. *begrip*, MLG *begrep* > Dan. *begreb*, Sw. *begrepp;* Hellquist 60), fr. *begreifen* 'understand' (17.16). Paul, Deutsches Wtb. 66.

Cf. also as 'mental image' NHG *denkbild*, Du. *denkbeeld*, and NHG *vorstellung*, Dan. *forestillung*, Sw. *forestallning*, fr. vbs. NHG *vorstellen*, etc. 'represent'.

4. Lith. *supratimas*, fr. *suprasti* 'understand' (17.16).

Lett. *sajēga*, *sajēgums*, fr. *sajēgt* 'understand' (17.16).

5. SCr. *pojam*, Boh. *pojem*, Pol. *pojęcie*, Russ. *ponjatie*, fr. cpds. of vb. for 'take' (ChSl. *jęti*, etc. 11.13), through sense of 'understand' as in Russ. *ponjat'* (17.16).

17.21 WISE

Grk.	*σοφός, φρόνιμος, σώφρων*	Goth.	*snutrs, frōþs, handugs*	Lith.	*išmintingas*
NG	*φρόνιμος, σοφός*	ON	*horskr, snotr, vitr, vīss, frōðr*	Lett.	*gudrs*
Lat.	*sapiēns, prūdēns*	Dan.	*vis, klog*	ChSl.	*mądrŭ, prěmądrŭ*
It.	*savio, saggio*	Sw.	*vis, klok*	SCr.	*mudar*
Fr.	*sage*	OE	*wīs, glēaw, frōd, snotor*	Boh.	*moudry*
Sp.	*sabio*	ME	*wise*	Pol.	*mądry*
Rum.	*înțelept*	NE	*wise*	Russ.	*mudryj*
Ir.	*gāith, ecne, glicc*	Du.	*wijs*	Skt.	*vidvāṅs-, jñānin-, prājña-*, etc.
NIr.	*eagnuidhe*	OHG	*spāhi, wīs(i), frōt, snottar*	Av.	*mązdra-, dāθa-*
W.	*doeth*	MHG	*wīs(e), spæhe, vruot, kluoc*		
Br.	*fur*	NHG	*weise, klug*		

The adjs. for 'wise', whence are derived the sbs. for 'wisdom', are in the majority of cases connected with words of intellectual force, as 'know, think, understand, mind', yet have come to mean something more than mere 'knowing', etc., that is, they usually imply also good sense, sound judgment, etc. Some are based on physical notions like 'quick, sharp, clear-sighted', etc., with special application to the mind. Several are used also for 'skilful' (in handicraft, etc.), and in some this sense is probably the earlier. Some include the notion of 'cunning, crafty' even in the derogatory sense, and in one case (Br. *fur* fr. Lat *fūr* 'thief') this is clearly the earlier stage.

As already implied by the preceding remarks, the words listed differ widely in their range of uses and many of them correspond only in part to NE *wise*. The sense of 'knowing, learned' beside 'having good judgment', etc. is stronger in some than in others.

1. Grk. σοφός (also 'skilful' in art or craft), etym. dub. Boisacq 888. Brugmann, IF 16.499 ff.

Grk. φρόνιμος : φρήν as 'seat of intelligence' (17.11), φρονέω 'think, be wise' (17.13). In NT and later this is more common than σοφός, which tends to be mainly 'wise' = 'learned'.

Grk. σώφρων, cpd. of σάος, σῶς 'safe, sound' (11.26) and φρήν (17.11).

2. Lat. *sapiēns*, pres. pple. of *sapere* 'taste' (15.32) and 'have sense, be wise' (whence in Romance 'know', 17.17). Hence also late Lat. *sapidus* 'savory' and 'wise', and **sapius* (*ne-sapius* 'foolish' Petr., modeled on *ne-scius*), the latter prob. the source of the Romance forms, It. *sapio* (old), *savio*, Fr. *sage* (> It. *saggio*), Sp. *sabio*. Ernout-M. 894. REW 7587.2 (preferring *sapidus*). Gamillscheg 780.

Lat. *prūdēns*, lit. 'foreseeing' (fr. *prōvidēns*), hence 'knowing, wise, prudent', etc.

Rum. *înțelept*, fr. Lat. *intellēctus*, pple. of *intellegere* 'understand' (17.16). Pușcariu 880.

3. Ir. *gāith*, beside *gāes* 'wisdom', etym. dub., perh. as orig. a poet-sage (like Lat. *vātēs*, Skt. *ṛṣi-*, etc.) : Skt. *gāi-* 'sing, chant, celebrate', *gīta-* 'sung', etc. (Walde-P. 1.526 f.). Pedersen 2.19.

Ir. *ecne* (also sb. 'wisdom', NIr. *eagna*), also *ecnaid*, NIr. *eagnuidhe*,

eagnaidhe : Ir. *asa-gninaim* 'know' (17.17). Pedersen 1.350, 2.546.

Ir. *glicc*, perh. : NHG *klug* (below).

W. *doeth*, fr. Lat. *doctus* 'learned', pple. of *docēre* 'teach, instruct'. Pedersen 1.228. Loth, Mots lat. 162.

Br. *fur* (W. *ffur* 'wise, learned, wary', arch.), fr. Lat. *fūr* 'thief', with semantic development through 'sly, cunning'. Loth, Mots lat. 171.

4. Goth. *snutrs*, ON *snotr*, OE *snotor*, OHG *snottar*, prob. as orig. 'scenting well' (of animals) : Norw. *snotra* 'scent, snort', OE *snȳtan*, OHG *snūzen*, ON *snȳta* 'blow the nose', etc. (cf. semantic development in Lat. *sapiēns*, above, 2). Walde-P. 1.397. Falk-Torp 1102. Feist 441 f.

Goth. *frōþs*, ON *frōðr* (mostly 'learned'), OE *frōd*, OHG *frōt*, *fruot*, MHG *vruot* : Goth. *fraþjan* 'understand', etc. (17.16).

Goth. *handugs* (with *handugei* most common word for σοφία) = ON *hǫndugr* 'capable, dexterous', OE *-hendig*, ME *hendy* (NE *handy* re-formed), MHG *handec*, *hendec* 'skilful, dexterous', etc., all prob. (but much disputed) derivs. of Goth. *handus*, etc. 'hand', with semantic development 'handy, skilful, etc.', whence Goth. 'wise'. Walde-P. 1.458 f. Falk-Torp 447 f. Feist 244.

ON *horskr* = OE, OHG *horsc* 'quick, lively' (OE esp. of mental action, 'quick-witted', so in part OHG), prob. : Lat. *currere* 'run', *cursus* 'running, course, way', etc. Walde-P. 1.428. Falk-Torp 421.

ON *vīss* (but this usually 'certain'), Dan., Sw. *vis*, OE *wīs*, ME, NE *wise*, Du. *wijs*, OHG *wīs(i)*, MHG *wīs(e)*, NHG *weise* (Goth. *-weis* in *un-weis* 'unlearned', etc.), fr. **weid-to-* : Goth., OE *witan*, etc. 'know' (17.17); ON *vitr* (more common than *vīss* in this sense), fr. weak grade of same root and *r*-suffix (cf. Grk. ἴδρις 'knowing, skilful'). Walde-P. 1.239. Falk-Torp 1387.

OE *glēaw* = OHG *glau* 'perspicacious, shrewd, ingenious', etc. ON *glǫggr* 'clear-sighted, sharp, stingy', Goth. *glaggwō* 'exactly', etc., fr. the root in OE *glōwan* 'glow', ON *glōa* 'shine, glitter', etc. Walde-P. 1.627. Feist 216.

OHG *spāhi*, MHG *spæhe* : ON *spār* 'prophetic', *spā* 'prophesy', OHG *spehōn* 'look at, spy', Lat. *specere* 'look at, behold'. Walde-P. 2.660.

NHG *klug* (often more nearly 'shrewd, clever'), fr. MHG *kluoc* 'fine, tender, neat, courteous', also 'cunning, clever, wise' (MLG *klok* > Dan. *klog*, Sw. *klok*), perh. : Ir. *glicc* 'wise', but root connection dub. Walde-P. 1.613. Falk-Torp 535. Weigand-H. 1.1065.

5. Lith. *išmintingas*, beside *išmintis* 'wisdom' : *mintis* 'thought, idea, meaning', *minėti* 'think about, remember', Lat. *mēns* 'mind', Skt. *man-* 'think', etc. (17.14).

Lett. *gudrs* (Lith. *gudras*, *gudrus* 'clever, crafty, cunning'), prob. as orig. 'experienced, practiced' : Lith. *gundu*, *gusti* 'become habituated, get practice in', this fr. an extension of the root in Lith. *gauti* 'get, obtain'. Mühl.-Endz. 1.675. Osten-Sacken, IF 33.264.

6. ChSl. *mądrŭ*, *prěmądrŭ*, SCr. *mudar*, etc., general Slavic : Lith. *mundrus*, *mandrus* 'lively, reckless', OHG *muntar* 'zealous, dexterous, lively', fr. the root in Grk. μανθάνω 'learn', Skt. *medhā-* 'mental power, wisdom, thought', Av. *mązdā-* 'memory, remembrance', etc. Walde-P. 2.271.

7. Skt. *vidvāṅs-*, *viduṣ-*, perf. act. pple. of *vid-* 'know' (17.17).

Skt. *jñānin-*, *prajña-*, etc., fr. *jñā-* 'know' (17.17).

Av. *mązdra-*, deriv. of *mązdā-* 'fix in the memory, have in mind', cf. Skt. *mandhātar-* 'thoughtful or pious man', prob. fr. IE **men-* 'think' and **dhē-* 'put, place'. Walde-P. 2.271. Uhlenbeck 215. Barth. 1181.

Av. *dāθa-*, as orig. 'having insight' : Av. *dī-*, *dā-* 'see', Skt. *dhī-*, *dhyā-* 'contemplate, meditate, think', etc. Walde-P. 1.831 f. Barth. 731.

17.22 FOOLISH, STUPID

Grk.	*ἄφρων, μωρός, βλάξ, ἀνόητος, ἠλίθιος*	Goth.	*unfrōþs, dwals*	Lith.	*kvailas, paikas, durnas*
NG	*τρελλός, κουτός, βλάκας*	ON	*heimskr*	Lett.	*g'ek'īgs, mul'k'isks, dumjš*
Lat.	*stultus, fatuus, stolidus*, etc.	Dan.	*taabelig, dum*	ChSl.	*bezumĭnŭ, bujĭ*
It.	*sciocco, stupido, stolto*	Sw.	*tokig, dum*	SCr.	*budalast, glup*
Fr.	*sot, bête, stupide, niais*	OE	*dysig, stunt, dol, dwæs, sot*	Boh.	*bláznivý, pošetilý, hloupý*
Sp.	*tonto, necio, estúpido*	ME	*fol, folish, dull, dysi, sott*	Pol.	*nierozsądny, głupi*
Rum.	*prost, neghiob, dobitoc, stupid*	NE	*foolish, silly, stupid, dull*	Russ.	*durackij, glupyj*
Ir.	*bāith*	Du.	*dwaas, zot, dom*	Skt.	*mūrkha-, mūḍha-, jaḍa-, mūra-*
NIr.	*baoth, dallaigeanta*	OHG	*tumb, tol, tulisc, tusīc, gimeit*	Av.	*adāθa-*
W.	*ffol, ynfyd, hurt*	MHG	*tump, tōreht, tœrisch, tol, sot*		
Br.	*diod, sot*	NHG	*töricht, närrisch, dumm, albern*		

The difference that is felt between NE *foolish* (milder than the sb. *fool*) and the more opprobrious *stupid* is approximately matched in some of the other words listed, e.g. NHG *töricht* vs. *dumm*. But in general such a distinction will not hold.

Some of the words are merely etymological opposites (neg. cpds., etc.) of words for 'wise', without necessarily being so mild as NE *unwise*. The majority are based upon diverse notions, e.g. 'soft, weak, stricken, stunned, dumb, wandering, confused', with specialized application to the mind. A few are from (having the mind of a) 'beast, animal' (Fr. *bête*, etc.) or 'chicken'(?). Several come from or through the notion of 'simple', which tends to develop a pejorative sense in many words besides those included in the list, e.g. NE *simple* now dial. in this sense, but preserved in *simpleton;* Fr. *simple*, NHG *einfältig*, etc.; NE *daft* beside *deft* (NED s.v. *daft*), etc.

Some words for 'foolish' have come to be used also or mainly for 'mad, crazy', as Grk. τρελλός, Fr. *fou*, NHG *toll* (17.23).

1. Grk. ἄφρων, neg. cpd. with -φρων and so opposite of σώ-φρων 'wise' (17.21).

Grk. μωρός (> Lat. *mōrus* Plaut.), prob. : Skt. (Ved.) *mūra-* 'dull, stupid, foolish', IE **mō(u)ro-*, root connection? Walde-P. 2.303. Boisacq 655. NG lit. in this sense, but pop. μωρό 'baby', and voc. μωρέ > βρέ in familiar address.

Grk. βλάξ, NG pop. βλάκας, prob. as orig. 'weak, soft' fr. *μλāκ- : μαλακός 'soft', etc. (15.75). Walde-P. 2.290. Boisacq 121.

Grk. ἀνόητος (also 'not thought of, unthinkable'), neg. cpd. of νοητός 'mental', fr. νοέω 'perceive, think' : νοῦς 'mind' (17.11).

Grk. ἠλίθιος : ἠλεός 'distraught, crazed', ἄλη 'wandering', ἀλάομαι 'wander, roam', etc. Walde-P. 1.87 f. Boisacq 319.

NG τρελλός (esp. 'mad, insane', but

also 'foolish') prob., despite some difficulties, fr. τραυλός 'lisping' with shift from oral to mental defect. Cf. Byz. τραλίζομαι 'be stunned, dizzy', perh. influenced in form and sense by the synonymous ζαλίζομαι. For the NG ε cf. dial. τραυλός, etc. (Hatzidakis, Μεσ. 1.238). Koraes, Ἄτακτα 1.186. Pernot, Recueil 96, note 59.

NG κουτός, orig. dub., perh. as orig. 'having the brain of a chicken' : κόττος 'cock' (Hesych.), NG κόττα 'hen' (3.54). Kukules quoted in Glotta 5.285.

2. Lat. stultus (> It. stolto), stolidus, prob. as orig. 'stiff, standing stock-still' : stolō 'shoot, branch, twig', Grk. στελεά 'shaft', OE steall 'standing place, stall', etc. Walde-P. 2.644. Ernout-M. 985.

Lat. fatuus, etym. dub., perh. as orig. 'stricken' (in the head) fr. *bhăt- in Gallo-Lat. battuere 'beat, strike'. Walde-P. 2.126. Walde-H. 1.464.

Lat. stupidus 'confounded, amazed', also 'senseless, stupid' (> It. stupido, Fr. stupide, etc.), fr. stupēre 'be struck senseless, be stunned, amazed, etc.' : Grk. τύπτω 'strike', Skt. tup- 'harm, hurt'. Walde-P. 2.619. Ernout-M. 990.

It. sciocco, etym. dub. Since the word has also the sense of 'tasteless, insipid', the deriv. fr. Lat. ex-sūcus (Diez 388) is the most attractive semantically, but the vowel development is unexplained. Spitzer, Arch. rom. 7.393, suggests connection with the cry to which (characteristically stupid animals), as scio used like NE shoo. REW 3075.

Lat. follis 'bag, bellows', in VLat. through 'windbag' > 'fool', glossing Lat. fatuus, stultus, and morio (CGL 5.568.58; 621.24). Hence (It. folle not in common use, Sp. fol in Prov.) OFr. fol 'fool, foolish' (or more general abusive term; Fr.

fou 'mad') > ME fol 'fool, foolish'. REW 3422.

Fr. sot, orig. obscure. REW 2454. Bloch 2.286. Gamillscheg 809.

Fr. bête, adj. use of bête 'beast, animal' (3.11) and, of persons, 'stupid person, idiot'.

Fr. niais, orig. 'nestling', fr. VLat. *nīdax, deriv. of Lat. nīdus 'nest', hence through 'helpless, simple' to 'foolish, silly' (cf. Lat. silly, below, 4).

Sp. tonto (also It. tonto, Rum. tînt, tont), orig. nursery word, imitative of sound. Cf. also NHG tunte 'an affected or prudish person'. REW 8988.

Sp. necio, fr. Lat. nescius 'ignorant, not knowing how, unable' (: scīre 'know', 17.17). REW 5900.

Rum. neghiob, apparently cpd. of neg. ne- (cf. nebun 'crazy', 17.23), but last member? Densusianu 1.38. Tiktin 1047.

Rum. dobitoc, adj. use of dobitoc 'animal, beast' (Slavic dobytŭkŭ) and of persons 'stupid person, idiot' (imitation of Fr. bête?). Tiktin 556.

3. Ir. báith, baeth (beside báes 'folly'), NIr. baoth, etym. dub., perh. orig. 'timid' : Skt. bhī- 'fear', Lith. baimė 'fear', etc. (16.53). Pedersen 1.56.

Ir. drúth sb. 'fool', also 'unchaste' : (or fr.) W. drud 'senseless, brave, expensive', etym.? Loth, RC 38.174 ff. Thurneysen, Keltorom. 56 ff.

NIr. dallaigeanta, deriv. of dall-aigne 'dull-mind', cpd. of dall 'blind, dull', and aigne 'mind' (17.11).

W. ffol, fr. ME fol (below). Parry-Williams 185 (Loth, Mots lat. 169 takes it fr. Fr.).

W. ynfyd, also 'furious, mad' (cf. ynfydu 'rave'), like MIr. ônmit 'fool', fr. OE unwita 'fool, stupid person' (: witan 'know'). Pedersen 1.21.

W. hurt, orig. 'hurt', whence 'stunned' > 'stupid', fr. the English. Parry-Williams 172.

Br. diod, fr. pop. Fr. diot for idiot 'idiot, fool'. Henry 99.

Br. sot, fr. Fr. sot.

4. Goth. unfrōþs (reg. for ἄφρων, also ἀνόητος), neg. cpd. of frōþs 'wise' (17.21).

Cf. other similar Gmc. cpds. for 'unwise', or in part 'foolish', not included in the list: Goth. unweis, ON ūvitr, OE unwīs, OHG unwīs; ON ūfrōðr, OHG unfruot (OE unfrōdness 'ignorance', but unfrōd 'not old'); ON ūsnotr, OE unsnotor; OE ungléaw; MHG unspœhe, etc.

Goth. dwals (for μωρός), OE dol, ME dull, NE dull, OHG, NHG toll (NHG toll 'mad'), OHG tulisc : Goth. dwalmōn 'rage', OE ge-dwolen 'perverse, wrong', dwelian 'lead astray', OHG twallen 'halt, stop', etc. — fr. the same root as Grk. θολός 'dirt', θολερός 'muddy, turbid', etc. Walde-P. 1.843. Feist 130.

ON heimskr, through 'inexperienced' fr. 'home-bred' (cf. heimskt er heimalit barn), fr. heimr 'abode, land', in the older sense 'home' (cf. heima adv. 'home, at home'). Torp, Nynorsk 206. Vigfusson 251.

Dan. taabelig, fr. taabe 'fool', Sw. dial. tåp, tåpa, etc., prob. as 'fumbler' : Sw. dial. tåpa 'touch lightly', MLG tāpen, tappen 'grope, fumble, pluck', ME tappe, NE tap, etc. Falk-Torp 1237.

Sw. tokig, fr. tok 'fool', cf. Dan. dial. tok(k)et 'crazy', tokke 'act crazy', etc., orig. dub., perh. fr. MLG token 'play, joke'. Falk-Torp 1238. Torp, Nynorsk 793. Hellquist 1200.

OE dysig, ME dysi, dusi (NE dizzy now only dial. in this sense, and not in common use since 13th cent.; NED s.v.), OHG tusic, MHG tōreht, toereht, toerisch, etc., NHG töricht; OE dwǣs, dwǣslīc, Du. dwaas, MLG dwās, (MHG twās, dwās 'a fool') : OFris. dusia 'be dizzy',

MLG dusen, dosen 'pass by without thought', etc., fr. a parallel extension of the root in OE dēaf 'deaf' and dumb 'dumb' (4.95, 4.96). Walde-P. 1.845. Weigand-H. 1.398, 2.1053 f. Franck-v. W. 144.

OE sot, ME sott (but mostly sb. 'fool', NE sot), Du. zot, MLG, MHG sot (also sb. 'fool'), apparently early loan-words fr. OFr. sot (above, 2). NED s.v. Frank-v. W. 827.

ME fol (adj. and sb.), whence folish, NE foolish, fr. OFr. fol (cf. above, 2).

NE silly, early also 'feeble-minded' and 'pitiful, weak, helpless', ME sily, seli 'innocent, harmless, blessed, happy', OE gesǣlig 'happy, prosperous, fortunate', etc. = OHG sālig id. (NHG selig) : Goth. sēls 'good', OE sǣl 'happiness', etc. Semantic development through 'harmless, helpless, weak, simple'. NED s.v.

OHG tumb, MHG tump, NHG dumm (hence this sense in Dan., Sw. dumm), Du. dom, in OHG also 'deaf, mute' = OE dumb, ON dumbr, Goth. dumbs 'dumb', (see 4.95, 4.96). The popular use of NE dumb in this sense in U.S. is doubtless due to German (and Dutch?) influence (cf. Mencken, American Language 109,112), but cf. also the quotations in NED s.v. 7, fr. 16–17 cent.

NHG närrisch, fr. sb. narr, OHG narro 'fool', etym. dub. Weigand-H. 2.273. Kluge-G. 410. Falk-Torp 754 f.

NHG albern, fr. MHG alwære 'simple', OHG alawāri 'kind'. Weigand-H. 1.36.

5. Lith. kvailas, cf. kvailti 'become foolish', kvailinti 'make stupid', etc., etym.? Cf. Berneker 657.

Lith. paikas : piktas 'angry, bad', etc. (16.42).

Lith. durnas, fr. the Slavic, cf. Pol. durny 'foolish, proud', Russ. durnoj 'bad,

---

ugly' (16.72), dur' 'folly', durak 'fool', etc. (below, 6).

Lett. ģ'ek'īgs, deriv. of ģ'ek'is 'a fool', fr. MLG geck, cf. Du. gek 'crazy' (17.23). Mühl.-Endz. 1.695.

Lett. mul'k'isks, mul'k'īgs, derivs. of mul'k'is = Lith. mulkis 'fool, idiot', prob. : Grk. βλάξ, etc. (above, 1), rather than : Skt. mūrkha- (below, 7). Walde-P. 2.290. Mühl.-Endz. 2.666.

Lett. dumjš, fr. MLG dum (above, 4). Mühl.-Endz. 1.514.

6. ChSl. bezumĭnŭ (ἄφρων, Lk. 14.40, 12.20), Russ. bezumnyj (also 'mad, crazy'), deriv. of bezŭ 'without' and umŭ 'mind, reason' (17.11).

ChSl. bujĭ (μωρός, Mt. 23.17, 19, etc.), also 'wild, fierce' (Russ. bujnyj 'turbulent, wild, violent', etc.), prob. : Skt. bhūyas- 'more, more numerous, greater, stronger', bhūri- 'abundant, much, vast, great', etc., fr. an imitative *bhu- in words for 'blown up'(?). Walde-P. 2.115. Berneker 98. Trautmann 40.

SCr. budalast, fr. budala 'fool', fr. Turk. budala 'silly, foolish'. Berneker 96.

SCr. glup, Boh. hloupý, Pol. głupi, Russ. glupyj, perh. old Gmc. loanword, cf. ON glópr 'idiot, baboon' : glœpr 'crime, wickedness', glœpask 'transgress,

do foolishly' (modern 'be fooled'), etc. (cf. Walde-P. 1.626, Falk-Torp 325). So Berneker 308 f., but not mentioned by Stender-Petersen. Brückner 145 takes as fr. same root as ChSl. gluchŭ, etc. 'dumb'.

Boh. bláznivý, bláznavský, fr. blázen 'fool' (Pol. blazen, etc. id.) : ChSl. blazna 'error, offense', blazniti 'cause to stumble', etc., root connection dub. Berneker 58 f.

Boh. pošetilý, deriv. of (po)šetiti se 'become foolish', cf. šetek 'goblin, sprite', etym.? Miklosich 338.

Pol. nierozsądny, neg. of rozsądny 'intelligent' : rozsądek 'judgment, understanding'; cf. Russ. razsudok 'reason, intelligence' (17.12).

Russ. durackij, fr. durak 'fool' : dur' 'folly', durnoj 'bad, ugly', etc. Berneker 239.

7. Skt. mūrkha- : mūrch- 'congeal, become solid, faint'. Walde-P. 2.280.

Skt. mūḍha-, lit. 'bewildered, gone astray', fr. muh- 'go astray, err, be bewildered', etc. Uhlenbeck 228.

Skt. jaḍa-, lit. 'cold, rigid, numb', etym. dub. Uhlenbeck 96.

Skt. mūra-, cf. Grk. μωρός (above, 1).

Av. adāθa-, neg. cpd. of daθa- 'wise' (17.21).

17.23 INSANE, MAD, CRAZY

Grk.	μαινόμενος, λυσσώδης, etc.	Goth.	(dwalmōn vb.) wōþs	Lith.	pasiutęs, beprotiškas
NG	τρελλός	ON	vitlauss, ōðr	Lett.	traks, ārprātīgs
Lat.	insānus, āmēns, dēmēns, etc.	Dan.	forrykt, gal, vanvittig	ChSl.	neistovŭ
		Sw.	förryckt, galen, vansinnig	SCr.	lud, mahnit
It.	pazzo			Boh.	šilený
Fr.	fou	OE	gewitlēas, wōd, gemǣd(e)d	Pol.	szalony
Sp.	loco			Russ.	bezumnyj, sumasšedšij
Rum.	nebun, smintit	ME	wode, madde	Skt.	vātūla-, unmatta
Ir.	dásachtach, mer	NE	crazy, mad, insane	Av.	....
NIr.	ar mire, ar buile	Du.	gek, dol, krankzinnig		
W.	gorffwyll, gwallgof	OHG	ur-, un-sinnig, wuotag		
Br.	foll, diskiant	MHG	unsinnec, wüetec		
		NHG	verrückt, toll, wahnsinnig		

Some of the words for 'insane' meant originally 'unsound', specialized to 'unsound of mind', or 'without mind, without wits'. But popular terms, analogous to NE mad, crazy, that are commonly used for 'insane' but are not confined to the strictly medical sense, are of diverse origin, related to words for 'foolish, crippled, twisted, raging, distracted', etc. A few are related to words for 'poet, seer, song', hence orig. 'inspired, enchanted, bewitched'.

Many of the more technical terms of Latin origin are omitted from the list, as It. insano, etc., It. demente, Fr. insensé (lit. 'senseless'), Fr. aliéné, etc. (Lat. aliēnus 'strange').

1. Grk. μαίνομαι 'be furious, rage, be mad', whence pple. μαινόμενος or adj. μανικός 'mad', sb. μανία 'madness', all used most commonly in wider sense but covering also the notion of 'mad' = 'insane', see under Grk. μῆνις 'wrath', 16.42.

Grk. λύσσα 'rage, fury' (16.43), later also 'madness', whence adjs. λυσσαλέος, λυσσώδης (with νόσος) and, combined with form of preceding group, λυσσομανής.

NG τρελλός, also 'foolish', see 17.22.

2. Lat. insānus, lit. 'unsound' but in actual use 'unsound in mind', neg. cpd.

of sānus 'sound, well' (4.83), this also esp. 'sound in mind, sane'. Similarly poet. vē-sānus.

Lat. āmēns, dēmēns (less technical than insānus), cpds. of ā- and dē- 'away from' (in cpds. often 'without') with mēns 'mind'.

It. pazzo, orig. a euphemistic term fr. Lat. patiēns 'suffering', in medicine 'the patient'. REW 6292.

Fr. fou, see under 'foolish' (17.22, Lat. follis).

Sp. loco (Port. louco), orig. dub. REW 9038a.

Rum. nebun, lit. 'not good', neg. of bun 'good'.

Rum. smintit, pple. of sminti 'confuse, put in disorder, displace', fr. Slavic, cf. ChSl. sŭmęsti, -mętǫ 'confuse'. Tiktin 1446 f.

3. Ir. dásachtach (gl. amens Ml. 18a13, freq. in older language; also sb. 'madman'), deriv. of dásacht 'madness, fury' (16.43).

Ir. mer (cf. fear fris-a-r-heterscarad a chiall, in duine mear 'a man from whom his sense has parted, the insane person', Anc. Laws 5.234 bottom), NIr. mear 'swift, sudden, lively, valiant, joyous, giddy, raging, mad, wild' (Dinneen), hence mire 'madness', and for 'mad, insane' usually NIr. ar mire lit. 'on madness'; cf. Ir. *meraige* 'idiot', OBr. *mergidhaam* 'je suis fou, stupide', etym.? Loth, Voc. vieux-bret. 184 f. (: Grk. poet. μάργος 'mad').

NIr. (beside *ar mire*) also *ar buile* with *buile* 'frenzy, madness' (also gen. as adj. *fear buile* 'madman', cf. Dinneen, s.v.), etym.?

W. *gorffwyll*, adj. and sb. 'madness', cpd. of *gor*- 'super' and *pwyll* 'wisdom, discretion, prudence, sense' (: Ir. *ciall* 'reason, sense', 17.12).

W. *gwallgof*, old also sb. 'madness', cpd. of *gwall* 'defect, want' and *cof* 'memory, right mind, senses' (17.31).

Br. *foll*, fr. Fr. *fol*. Loth, Mots lat. 169.

Br. *diskiant*, neg. cpd. of *skiant* 'sense' (fr. Lat. *scientia* 'knowledge').

4. Goth. *dwalmōn* 'be mad' (renders μαίνομαι) : *dwals* 'foolish, stupid' (17.22).

Goth. *wōþs* (renders δαιμονιζόμενος, δαιμονισθείς), ON *ōðr*, OE *wōd*, ME *wode* (NE *wood*, obs. or dial.), OHG *wuotag*, *wuotīg*, MHG *wüetec* (OHG *wuot*, adj. only in cpds.), orig. prob. 'inspired' (cf. ON *ōðr* 'poetry', OE *wōþ* 'song, sound') : Lat. *vātēs*, Ir. *fāith* 'poet, seer'. Walde-P. 1.216. Falk-Torp 793. Feist 572 f.

ON *vitlauss*, OE *gewitlēas*, lit. 'witless', cf. ON *vit* 'intelligence, reason', OE *gewit* 'mind' (17.11).

Dan. *forrykt*, Sw. *förryckt*, see NHG *verrückt* (below).

Dan. *gal*, older *galen*, Sw. *galen* = ON *galinn*, lit. 'enchanted' also 'frantic, mad, sensual', pple. of *gala* 'crow, chant, sing' = OHG *galan* 'sing, bewitch', etc. Falk-Torp 294 f.

Dan. *vanvittig*, Sw. *vansinnig*, see under NHG *wahnsinnig*, below.

OE *gemǣd(e)d*, ME *madde*, NE *mad*, orig. pple. of an OE **gemǣdan* deriv. of *gemād* (*vecors gemaad*, gl.) = OS *gimēd* 'foolish', OHG *gimeit* 'foolish, boastful, vain', Goth. *gamaiþs* 'crippled, hurt', fr. the root of ON *meiða* 'injure, cripple', etc. Walde-P. 2.222. Feist 191. NED s.v. *mad*.

NE *crazy* (this sense since 17th cent.), older 'unsound, impaired', also 'ailing, diseased' (of body), orig. 'full of cracks or flaws' (so still *a crazy house, ship*), fr. *craze* 'a crack, breach, flaw', vb. *craze*, ME *crase* 'break violently, shatter', this, either through OFr. *acraser* 'crush', or directly, fr. an ON form like Sw. *krasa* 'crackle', NE *crash*, etc. of imitative origin. NED s.v. REW, 4762. Gamillscheg 341.

NE *insane*, fr. Lat. *insānus*.

ME *lunatyk*, NE *lunatic* (now mostly as sb.), fr. late Lat. *lūnāticus* 'moonstruck, epileptic', deriv. of *lūna* 'moon'. Cf. Grk. σεληνιάζομαι 'be epileptic' in NT, fr. σελήνη 'moon'. NED s.v.

Du. *gek*, MLG *geck* : NHG *geck* 'idiot', prob. = MLG *geck* 'something which may be turned' (a cover of a vessel, etc.), hence orig. a 'vacillating, changeable person'. Falk-Torp 318. Weigand-H. 1.641. Franck-v. W. 181.

Du. *dol*, NHG *toll* = OHG, MHG *tol* 'foolish' (17.22).

Du. *krankzinnig*, fr. *krank* 'sick' and *zin* 'sense'.

OHG *ursinnig*, *unsinnig*, MHG *unsinnec* (NHG *unsinnig* 'nonsensical, irrational', etc.), fr. OHG *ur*- 'out' or neg. prefix *un*-, and *sin*, NHG *sinn* 'sense'.

NHG *wahnsinnig* (> Sw. *vansinnig*), replaces older *wahnwitzig* by association with *wahn* (sb.) for MHG *wanwitzec* (MLG *wanwittich* > Dan. *vanvittig*, Sw. *vanvettig*), later form for MHG *wanwitze*, OHG *wanwizzi* 'lacking in intelligence', cpd. of *wan* 'lacking, empty', and OHG *wizzi* 'intelligence, wit' (17.12). Falk-Torp 1348. Weigand-H. 2.1200.

NHG *verrückt*, pple. of *verrücken* 'displace', applied to the brain as to a clock that is 'out of order'. Similarly (prob. semantic borrowing) Dan. *forrykt*, Sw. *förryckt*, fr. the corresponding vbs. Falk-Torp 261.

NHG *irre*, as 'insane' esp. in *irrenhaus* 'hospital for the insane', orig. 'astray', fr. *irren* 'go astray'.

5. Lith. *pasiutęs*, pret. act. pple. of perfect. of *siuntu*, *siusti* 'go mad' : *siaučiu*, *siausti* 'winnow (grain), play, rage', Russ. *šutit'* 'joke', *šut* 'buffoon', Slov. *šutec* 'fool', root connection dub. Walde-P. 2.472. Trautmann 260.

Lith. *beprotiškas*, cpd. of *be* 'without, un-' and *protiškas* 'intellectual, mental' fr. *protas* 'mind, intelligence' (17.11). Cf. *beprotis* 'madman'.

Lett. *traks* (also Lith. *trakas*, KZ 52.285), perh. as orig. 'twisted' : Lat. *torquēre* 'turn, wind', etc. (10.13). Mühl.-Endz. 4.219.

Lett. *ārprātīgs*, cpd. of *ār* 'outside of' and *prātīgs* 'intelligent' fr. *prāts* 'mind, intelligence' (17.11).

6. ChSl. *neistovŭ* (*neistovŭ jestŭ* Mk. 3.21, Jn. 10.20), cpd. of neg. *ne*- and *istovŭ* 'true, genuine' (16.66). Cf. Russ. *neistovyj* 'furious, raging'.

SCr. *lud* = late ChSl. *ludŭ* 'foolish', Boh., Russ. *lud* 'fool' (both obs.), with obs. Russ. *ludit'* 'deceive', etc. : Goth. *liutei* 'deceit', etc. (16.68). Walde-P. 2.416. Berneker 743 f.

SCr. *mahnit* : *mahati* 'swing, brandish', ChSl. *mahati* 'swing', etc., with development through 'making wild gestures'. Berneker 2.4.

Boh. *šílený*, fr. *šíleti* 'be mad', this fr. MHG *schilhen*, NHG *schielen* 'squint', perh. also influenced by the group MHG *schel* 'loud sounding' (fr. *schal* 'sound'), also 'excited, wild', *schellec*, NHG *schellig* also 'mad' (Weigand-H. 2.694).

Pol. *szalony*, beside vbs. *szaleć*, *szalić* 'be mad, drive mad' : late ChSl. *bogomĭ šalenŭ* = θεόπληκτος, Boh. *šal* 'deceit' (16.68), *šaliti* 'deceive, cheat', SCr. *šaliti se*, Russ. *šalit'* 'play jokes', Russ. *šalet'* 'go mad', etc., without outside connections. Brückner 539 f. Miklosich 336 f.

Russ. *bezumnyj*, also 'foolish', as ChSl. *bezumĭnŭ*. See 17.22.

Russ. *sumasšedšij*, lit. 'gone out of reason', fr. *soiti* (pple. *sošedšij*) *s uma* 'go mad', lit. 'go off one's mind'.

7. Skt. *vātula*-, *vātūla*-, lit. 'windy, inflated with wind' (: *vāta*- 'wind', *vā*- 'blow', etc. 1.72). Cf. the derivation of Fr. *fou*. (17.22).

Skt. *unmatta*-, pple. of *unmad*- (*ud-mad*-) 'become disordered (in intellect), be distracted, frantic, mad', cpd. of *mad*- 'rejoice, be glad, be drunk', etc.

17.24 LEARN

Grk.	*μανθάνω*	Goth.	*laisjan sik*	Lith.	*mokintis, mokytis*
NG	*μαθαίνω*	ON	*nema*	Lett.	*mācīties*
Lat.	*discere*	Dan.	*lære*	ChSl.	*učiti sę*
It.	*imparare, apprendere*	Sw.	*lära (sig)*	SCr.	*učiti*
Fr.	*apprendre*	OE	*leornian*	Boh.	*učiti se*
Sp.	*aprender*	ME	*lerne*	Pol.	*uczyć się*
Rum.	*învăța*	NE	*learn*	Russ.	*učit'sja*
Ir.	*fogliunn*	Du.	*leeren*	Skt.	*çikṣ-, adhi-i-*
NIr.	*foghlumaim*	OHG	*lernēn*	Av.	*sikš-*
W.	*dysgu*	MHG	*lernen*		
Br.	*deski*	NHG	*lernen*		

The complementary 'learn' and 'teach' are often expressed by related words. Thus 'learn' by refl. forms of words for 'teach' (Goth., ON, Balto-Slavic); or conversely 'teach' by caus. forms of words for 'learn' (Lat., Skt.). The two Gmc. groups represented by Goth. *laisjan*, OE *lǣran*, etc. 'teach' and OE *leornian*, OHG *lernēn*, etc. 'learn' are formally connected and in actual use much confused (see below). Other words also are used in both senses (mostly 'learn' extended to 'teach'), as NG pop. μαθαίνω, Fr. *apprendre*, W. *dysgu*, Br. *deski*. Such words or groups which belong in part under both headings are discussed here.

In general, words for 'learn' are based upon notions like 'take, receive, get' specialized to mental acquisition, 'come upon', 'become accustomed to', or in part are connected with other words of mental application.

1. Grk. μανθάνω, NG μαθαίνω (new pres. to aor. ἔμαθον; pop. also 'teach') : Goth. *mundōn sis* 'observe', ON *munda* 'aim', Av. *mazdāh*- 'memory', Skt. *medhā*- 'wisdom', fr. IE **mendh*-, ultimately IE **men*- 'think' with weak grade of **dhē*- 'put'. Walde-P. 2.270 f. Boisacq 607.

Grk. aor. ἐδάην, δαῆναι, etc. (poet.) 'learn' (also Hom. δέδαε 'taught'), fr. *δασ- : δήνεα 'counsels, plans', Skt. *daṅsas*- 'wonderful deed or power', Av. *dahišta*- 'most wise', etc. Walde-P. 1.793. Boisacq 168. Here also (rather than : Lat. *discere*, as commonly taken) Grk. διδάσκω 'teach'. Debrunner, Mélanges Boisacq 1.251 ff.

2. Lat. *discere* 'learn' (**di-dc-scere*) with *docēre* 'teach', prob. fr. the same root **deḱ*- as in Grk. δέκομαι 'receive' (Att. δέχομαι), ChSl. *desiti* 'find', also Grk. δοκέω 'seem' and Lat. *decet* 'is fitting', but semantic relations open to various interpretations. Most simply 'receive' > 'learn' (as in Fr. *apprendre*, ON *nema*, etc., below); Grk. δοκέω, Lat. *decet* based on notion of 'be acceptable'. Walde-P. 1.782 ff. Ernout-M. 272, 278 f. Walde-H. 1.331.

It. *imparare*, fr. VLat. **imparāre*, cpd. of *parāre* 'acquire, get' (11.16). REW 4293.

It. *apprendere*, Fr. *apprendre* (also 'teach'), Sp. *aprender*, fr. Lat. *appre(he)ndere* 'seize, lay hold of', cpd. of *pre(he)ndere* id. (11.14). REW 554.

Rum. *învăța* 'learn' and 'teach', also 'accustom', fr. VLat. **invitiāre*, deriv. of Lat. *vitium* 'fault, defect, vice', prob. with a local shift fr. 'bad habit' > 'habit, custom', hence 'habituate, accustom' > 'teach' > 'learn' (cf. Slavic group, below, 6).

3. Ir. *fo-gliunn*, vbl. n. *foglaim*, hence NIr. *foghlumaim* (*foghlumuighim*, etc.), cpd. of *fo*- 'under' and the root *glenn*- found only in cpds., e.g. *do-glinn* 'collects', *as-glinn* 'investigates', etc. : Russ. *gljadět'*, ChSl. *ględati* 'look at', OHG, MHG *glanz* 'shining', etc. Walde-P. 1.625. Pedersen 2.540.

W. *dysgu*, Br. *deski*, *diski* (both also 'teach'), fr. Lat. *discere* (above). Pedersen 1.200.

4. Goth. *laisjan* 'teach', *laisjan sik* 'learn', OE *lǣran* 'teach' (> ON *læra* 'teach'), ME *lere* 'teach' and 'learn' (cf. NED s.v.), NE *lere* obs. (but cf. sb. *lore*), MLG *lēren* (> Dan. *lære*, Sw. *lära* 'teach' and 'learn'; Sw. also refl. for 'learn' in phrases like 'learn English'), Du. *leeren* in both senses, OHG, MHG *lēren*, NHG *lehren* 'teach' but widespread dial. also 'learn', all orig. caus. of the root in Goth. pret.-pres. *lais* 'have learned, know how', Goth., OE, OHG *list* 'cunning, craft, wile', prob. the same as in Goth. *laists*, OE *lāst* 'footstep, track', Lat. *līra* 'furrow'. Walde-P. 2.404 f. Feist 320. Falk-Torp 676.

OE *leornian*, ME *lerne*, NE *learn* (ME and NE locally also 'teach'), OHG *lernēn*, *lirnēn*, MHG, NHG *lernen* (dial. and formerly even lit. also 'teach', cf. Paul, Deutsches Wtb. s.v., Kretschmer, Wortgeogr. 36), Gmc. **liznan* 'become knowing', fr. the pple. of the same root as the preceding group.

ON *nema*, also and orig. 'take, seize' (: Goth., OE *niman*, etc., 11.13) but the usual word for 'learn' (largely replaced by *læra* in NIcel.).

5. Lith. *mokyti*, *mokinti*, Lett. *mācīt*, OPruss. *mukint* 'teach', refl. Lith. *mokytis*, *mokintis*, Lett. *mācīties* 'learn' : Lith. *mokėti*, Lett. *mācēt* 'know how, be able' (Lith. also 'pay, cost'), outside connections? Walde-P. 2.223.

6. ChSl. *učiti* 'teach', refl. *učiti sę* 'learn' (both often with *na*-), general Slavic (but SCr. *učiti* in both senses; Russ. *učit' urok* 'learn a lesson', but otherwise refl. for 'learn') : ChSl. *vyknąti* 'get accustomed to', Lith. *junkti* id. (hence of animals 'become tame'), Goth. *bi-ūhts* 'accustomed', Skt. *uc*- 'be accustomed, delight in'. Walde-P. 1.111.

7. Skt. *çikṣ*- 'learn', caus. *çikṣaya*- 'teach', Av. *sikš*- 'learn', desid. of Skt. *çak*- 'be strong, be able', Av. *sak*- 'understand thoroughly, have in mind', caus. *sāčaya*- 'teach'. Walde-P. 1.333. Barth. 1552 f.

Skt. *adhi-i* 'notice, understand' and esp. mid. 'learn', caus. *adhyāpaya*- 'teach', lit. 'come upon', cpd. of *i*- 'go, come'.

17.242. 'Study' (in school, in books, etc.) is sometimes covered by words for 'learn', as generally in Slavic (SCr. *učiti*, Boh. *učiti se*, etc.; otherwise Lat. loanwords). The special terms have arisen by specialization of 'pay attention to, be eager, zealous'. Thus Grk. μελετάω (: μελέτη 'care, attention' 16.14) 'care for, attend to, practice', whence also 'study', as reg. NG μελετῶ. Grk. σπουδάζω 'be eager' (: σπεύδω 'hasten'), late 'study', as reg. in NG. Lat. *studēre* (prob. fr. the root in Lat. *tundere*, Goth. *stautan* 'strike'. Walde-P. 2.618. Ernout-M. 990) 'be eager, strive for, apply oneself to', hence (first with *litteris*, etc., later alone) 'study', beside sb. *studium* 'zeal, study', whence, partly through VLat. **studiāre*, the widespread Eur. words, Fr. *étudier*, NE *study*, etc. (Romance, Gmc., Lett., Boh., Pol.).

17.25 TEACH

Grk.	*διδάσκω*	Goth.	*laisjan*	Lith.	*mokyti, mokinti*
NG	*διδάσκω, μαθαίνω*	ON	*kenna, læra*	Lett.	*mācīt*
Lat.	*docēre*	Dan.	*lære, undervise*	ChSl.	*učiti*
It.	*insegnare*	Sw.	*lära, undervisa*	SCr.	*uciti*
Fr.	*enseigner, apprendre*	OE	*lǣran, (ge)tǣcan*	Boh.	*učiti*
Sp.	*enseñar*	ME	*teche, lere, lerne*	Pol.	*uczyć*
Rum.	*învăța*	NE	*teach*	Russ.	*učit'*
Ir.	*for-canim, mūn-*	Du.	*leeren, onderwijzen*	Skt.	*çās-, çikṣ-, adhy-*
NIr.	*mūinim*	OHG	*lēren*		*āpaya-, upadiç-*
W.	*dysgu*	MHG	*lēren*	Av.	*daxš-, sāh-, čaš-, xsā-,*
Br.	*deski, kelenn*	NHG	*lehren, unterrichten*		*sāčaya-*

The majority of the words for 'teach' are connected with others meaning 'learn' and have been discussed with the latter (17.24).

The others are mostly from 'point out, make known', but also from 'command, direct' and in one case from 'sing over'.

1. It. *insegnare*, Fr. *enseigner*, Sp. *enseñar*, fr. VLat. **insignāre*, for *insignīre* 'distinguish, mark', deriv. of *insignis* 're-

markable, notable, distinguished' : *signum* 'mark, sign' (12.94). REW 4462.

2. Ir. *for-canim*, cpd. of *for-* 'on, over' and *canim* 'sing', referring orig. to instruction by song (simply?) or magical incantations(?). Pedersen 2.480.

Ir. *mūn-* (in pret. *ro-m-mūnus* with infixed refl. pron. 'I have learned', vbl. n. *munud*), NIr. *mūinim*, etym.? Pedersen 2.582.

Br. *kelenn*, orig. only sb. *kelenn* 'lesson', cpd. of prefix *ke-* 'com-' and *lenn* 'reading' (fr. Lat. *legendum*). Henry 59, 183.

3. ON *kenna* 'know' and in caus. sense 'teach' = Goth. *kannjan*, OE *cennan* 'make known', etc. (17.17).

OE *tǣcan*, *getǣcan*, mostly 'show, point out', ME *teche*, NE *teach* : OE *tācn*, OHG *zeihhan*, Goth. *taikns* 'sign', Goth. *taiknjan* 'show', etc. Walde-P. 1.777. NED s.v. *teach*.

NHG *unterrichten* 'inform' and 'teach' (hence back-formation *unterricht* 'teaching'), in MHG 'arrange, inform, dispute', cpd. of *richten* 'arrange, direct'. Weigand-H. 2.1124.

MLG *underwīsen* (> Dan. *undervise*, Sw. *undervisa*), Du. *onderwijzen* (NHG *unterweisen* less common than *unterrichten*), cpd. of *wīsen* 'make known' : OE *wīs* 'wise', etc. Falk-Torp 1334.

4. Skt. *çās-* 'reprove, punish, give orders, rule', also 'instruct, teach' (whence *çāstra-* 'rule, teaching, doctrine'), Av. *sāh-*, *fra-sāh-* 'teach' (*sāsnā-* 'teaching, doctrine') : Arm. *sastem* 'scold, threaten, command', further connections dub. Walde-P. 1.358. Barth. 1574 f.

Skt. *upa-diç-* 'point out' and 'teach' (hence *upadeça-* 'instruction, teaching'), cpd. of *diç-* 'point out, show' : Grk. δείκνυμι id., etc. Walde-P. 1.776.

Skt. *çikṣ-*, desid. of *çak-* 'be able' (9.95).

Skt. *adhyāpaya-*, caus. of *adhi-i-* 'understand, learn', lit. 'come upon', cpd. of *i-* 'go'.

Av. *daxš-*, esp. cpd. *fra-daxš-*, etym. dub. Walde-P. 1.784. Barth. 676.

Av. *xsā-* and *čaš-* (3sg. *čašte*), *ā-* and *s*-extensions of *kas-* 'notice, catch sight of' : Skt. *kāç-* 'be visible, appear, shine'. Walde-P. 1.510 f. Barth. 461, 541.

17.26 PUPIL

Grk.	μαθητής, φοιτητής	Goth.	*sipōneis*	Lith.	*mokinys, mokintinis*
NG	μαθητής	ON	*lærisveinn*	Lett.	*māceklis*
Lat.	*discipulus, alumnus*	Dan.	*elev*	ChSl.	*učenikŭ*
It.	*allievo, alunno*	Sw.	*lärjunge*	SCr.	*učenik*
Fr.	*élève*	OE	*leornungcniht, þegn*	Boh.	*žák (učenik)*
Sp.	*discípulo, alumno*	ME	*scoler(e)*	Pol.	*uczeń*
Rum.	*elev*	NE	*pupil*	Russ.	*učenik*
Ir.	*dalte, felmac*	Du.	*leerling*	Skt.	*çiṣya-, chāttra-*
NIr.	*scolāire*	OHG	*jungiro, degan*	Av.	*aēθrya-*
W.	*disgybl*	MHG	*junger*		
Br.	*skoliad*	NHG	*schüler*		

Many of the words for 'pupil' are, as one might expect, derivs. of those for 'learn' (17.24), that is, lit. 'learner'. Some are specialized from 'one who is brought up', a 'young person' or 'attendant', or in one case generalized from 'theological student'. Derivs. of words for 'school' (17.28) more often denote a member of a school or a learned person (like NE *scholar* in its current use), but also in some cases 'pupil' (as reg. NHG *schüler*).

From the nature of the records, the Goth., OE, OHG, and ChSl. words are mainly renderings of Grk. μαθητής, Lat. *discipulus* in its eccl. sense 'disciple' (of Christ), but cf. e.g. Mt. 10.24 ('the disciple is not above his teacher'), where the same words are used. But the modern words which are mainly 'disciple' and not common words for 'pupil' are omitted. Likewise omitted are those for 'student' in a college or university.

1. Grk. μαθητής : μανθάνω 'learn' (17.24).

Grk. φοιτητής (NG 'university student') : φοιτάω 'go to and fro, wander, frequent, resort to (a teacher or school)', etym. dub. Walde-P. 1.103. Boisacq 1033, 1122.

2. Lat. *discipulus*, doubtless felt as deriv. of *discere* 'learn', but as such the formation is unexplained, so perh. rather fr. an unattested **dis-cipere*, lit. 'take apart' (cf. *disceptāre* 'decide, judge, debate'). Walde-H. 1.355. Adversely Ernout-M. 272.

From its use in the church language as 'disciple' (of Christ) the word passed into the western Eur. languages, mainly in this restricted sense, though again extended somewhat ('disciple of Socrates', etc.; cf. NED s.v. *disciple*). Only Sp. *discípulo* and W. *disgybl* are in common use for 'pupil'. For the Celtic forms, cf. Loth, Mots lat. 161, Vendryes, De hib. voc. 135.

Lat. *alumnus* (> It. *alunno*, Sp. *alumno*) 'nursling, foster-child', whence (Cic.) 'pupil', fr. *alere* 'nourish, rear'. Ernout-M. 36. Walde-H. 1.34.

It. *allievo* (> Fr. *élève* > Rum. *elev*), deriv. of *allevare* 'rear' fr. Lat. *allevāre* 'lift, raise up, alleviate'. REW 359.

3. Ir. *dalte*, orig. 'foster-child', but usual also for 'pupil', perh. a cpd. *d-alte*, with *d-* zero grade of *ad-* 'to' and root of *alim* 'nourish'. Pedersen 2.292 (top).

Ir. *felmac*, cpd. of *mac* 'boy' with *fel* 'instruction'(?), prob. : *fili* 'poet', W. *gweled* 'see'. Stokes, Gloss. O'Dav. 880. Laws, Gloss. 346. The *felmac* according to Joyce's compilation (Social Hist. of Ireland 1.430 ff.) was actually the lowest grade in the monastic or eccl. system. For the various other grades of students in this and in the Bardic system cf. op. cit., and also on the value of various terms, cf. Anc. Laws 4.355 ff.

NIr. *scolāire*, also a 'scholar, student', fr. Lat. *scholāris* or more probably new deriv. of *scoil* 'school'. Vendryes, De hib. voc. 175.

W. *disgybl*, fr. Lat. *discipulus*, cf. above, 2.

Br. *skoliad* (Ernault 'écolier, élève, disciple'), deriv. of *skol* 'school'.

4. Goth. *sipōneis* (with vb. *sipōnjan* 'be a disciple'), prob. a loanword, but source uncertain. Feist 424.

ON *lærisveinn*, also *lærisunr*, Sw. *lärjunge*, cpds. of ON *læra*, Sw. *lära* 'teach, learn' and words for 'boy, son' or 'youth'.

Dan. *elev*, fr. Fr. *élève*.

OE *leornungcniht*, also *leornungcild*, cpd. of *leornung* 'learning' and *cniht* 'boy' or *cild* 'child'.

OE *þegn*, OHG *degan* 'servant, attendant' (19.43), also freq. 'disciple'. NED s.v. *thane*. Graff 5.119 ff.

ME *scoler(e)*, NE *scholar*, arch. or locally 'pupil' (NED s.v. *scholar*, 1 *b*), fr. OE *scolere* 'a scholar, learner', fr. late Lat. *scholāris* 'pertaining to school' (*schola*).

NE *pupil*, orig. 'young person in charge of a guardian', hence 'one receiving instruction', fr. Fr. *pupille*, Lat. *pūpillus* 'orphan, ward'. NED s.v.

Du. *leerling* (NHG *lehrling* 'apprentice'), deriv. of *leeren* 'learn'.

OHG *jungiro*, MHG *junger* (NHG *jünger* 'disciple' of Christ, but recently revived to designate a pupil in relation to

his master, cf. Paul, Deutsches Wtb. s.v.), comp. of *jung* 'young' in sb. use, orig. reflection of Lat. *iunior* 'younger', in MLat. esp. 'subject, apprentice, pupil'. Cf. OE *geongra* 'vassal, attendant, subject' also rendered 'discipulus' (Bosworth-Toller s.v.). Kluge-G. 271. Weigand-H. 1.955.

NHG *schüler* (rarely now for 'student, scholar'), fr. MHG *schuolære*, OHG *scuolāri* 'student, scholar', fr. late Lat. *scholāris* (cf. ME *scolere*, above). Weigand-H. 2.799.

5. Lith. *mokinys* and *mokintinis* (cf. NSB), Lett. *māceklis* ('Lehrling, Jünger', Mühl.-Endz. s.v.), derivs. of Lith. *mokyti*, *mokinti*, Lett. *mācīt* 'teach', refl. 'learn' (17.24).

6. ChSl. *učenikŭ*, SCr., Russ. *učenik*, Pol. *uczeń* (Boh. *učenik* esp. 'apprentice'), deriv. through pass. pple. *učenŭ* 'taught' of *učiti* 'teach'. Cf. ChSl. *učitelĭ*, etc. 'teacher' formed with suffix of agency.

Boh. *žák* (SCr. *đak* 'student', *đace* 'school-boy', Pol. *żak* 'school-boy') = ChSl. *dijakŭ* (Supr.), fr. Byz. διάκος, pop. form of Grk. διάκονος, orig. 'servant, attendant', but here 'deacon' in its early eccl. sense. Referring to a subordinate rank in the church, it was extended to include those studying for service in the church and then to students in general. Berneker 198 f. Brückner 661.

7. Skt. *çiṣya-*, lit. 'to be taught' : *çās-* 'teach' (17.25).

Skt. *chāttra-*, fr. *chattra-* 'parasol'. Orig. 'one who carries the parasol for the teacher'. Uhlenbeck 94.

Av. *aēθrya-*, fr. *aēθra-*, in *aēθrapati* 'teacher' (17.27). Barth. 20 f.

17.27 TEACHER

Grk.	διδάσκαλος	Goth.	*laisareis*	Lith.	*mokytojas, mokintojas*
NG	δάσκαλος	ON	*kennimaðr, kennandi, kennari*	Lett.	*skuoluotājs*
Lat.	*doctor, magister*	Dan.	*lærer*	ChSl.	*učitelĭ*
It.	*maestro*	Sw.	*lärare*	SCr.	*učitelj*
Fr.	*maître*	OE	*lārēow, mægister*	Boh.	*učitel*
Sp.	*maestro*	ME	*techer(e), lorthew, maister*	Pol.	*nauczyciel*
Rum.	*învăţător*	NE	*teacher*	Russ.	*učitel'*
Ir.	*forcitlaid*	Du.	*leeraar*	Skt.	*adhyāpaka-, upadeçaka-, çikṣaka-*
NIr.	*māighistir*	OHG	*lērāri, meistar*	Av.	*aēθrapati-, fradaxštar-, čašan-*
W.	*athro*	MHG	*lērære, meister*		
Br.	*mestr, skolaer*	NHG	*lehrer*		

The majority of the words for 'teacher' are derivs. of the verbs for 'teach' (17.25), a few from words for 'school' (17.28). The others are words for 'master' used in specialized sense. Only the most generic terms are listed, with omission of others used mainly for 'tutor', 'instructor', 'professor', etc.

1. Grk. διδάσκαλος, NG pop. δάσκαλος, fr. διδάσκω 'teach'.

2. Lat. *doctor*, fr. *docēre* 'teach'.

Lat. *magister* (> It., Sp. *maestro*, Fr. *maître*) 'master, chief, head, director, leader' (19.41), as 'teacher' abbr. for *magister lūdī* (*lūdus* as 'school', cf. 17.28). Ernout-M. 580.

Rum. *învăţător* (but now esp. 'teacher of a rural school', with other terms for teachers in city schools, *institutor*, *profesor*), fr. *învăţa* 'teach'. Tiktin 845 f. Formerly and still dial. *dascal*, fr. NG δάσκαλος. Tiktin 506.

3. Ir. *forcitlaid*, fr. *forcital* 'teaching' : *for-canim* 'teach' (17.25).

NIr. *māighistir*, Br. *mestr*, fr. Lat. *magister* (above, 2). Pedersen 1.222.

W. *athro* = Br. *aotrou* 'master, lord', Ir. *altru* 'fosterer', fr. the root of Ir. *alim*, Lat. *alere* 'nourish', etc. Pedersen 1.137. Walde-P. 1.87.

Br. *skolaer*, fr. *skol* 'school'.

4. Goth. *laisareis*, Dan. *lærer*, Sw. *lärare*, Du. *leeraar*, OHG *lērāri*, MHG *lērære*, NHG *lehrer*, fr. Goth. *laisjan*, etc. 'teach'.

ON *kennimaðr* (*maðr* 'man'), *kennandi*, *kennari*, fr. ON *kenna* 'teach'.

OE *lārēow*, ME *larew*, more usually *larthew*, *lorthew* implying an orig. OE **lār-þēow*, cpd. of *lār* 'teaching, learning doctrine' (: *lǣran* 'teach') and *þēow* 'slave' (19.42). NED s.v. *lorthew*.

OE *mægister*, ME *maister*, *meister* (in part fr. OFr. *maistre*; NE *master* still in this sense in 'schoolmaster', also in British usage as *head-master*, etc.), OHG *meistar*, MHG *meister* (NHG *meister* in this sense in Luther's Bible translation, but usual only in cpds., as *schulmeister*, etc.), fr. Lat. *magister* (above, 2). NED s.v. *master*. Weigand-H. 2.163. Kluge-G. 385 f.

ME *techer(e)*, NE *teacher*, fr. ME *teche*, NE *teach*.

5. Lith. *mokytojas*, *mokintojas*, fr. Lith. *mokyti*, *mokinti* 'teach'. Cf. Lett. *mācītājs* 'one who teaches', but chiefly 'preacher, pastor'. Mühl.-Endz. 2.576.

Lett. *skuoluotājs*, fr. *skuoluot* 'teach school', fr. *skuola* 'school'. Mühl.-Endz. 3.910.

6. ChSl. *učitelĭ*, etc., general Slavic, fr. ChSl. *učiti*, etc. 'teach' (Pol. *nauczyciel*, fr. the perfect. *nauczyć*).

7. Skt. *adhyāpaka-*, fr. *adhy-āpaya-* 'teach'.

Skt. *upadeçaka-*, fr. *upa-diç-* 'teach'.

Skt. *çikṣaka-*, fr. *çikṣ-* 'learn', caus. 'teach'.

Av. *aēθra-pati-*, cpd. of *aēθra-* (etym.?, cf. *aēθrya-* 'pupil') and *pati-* 'lord, master'. Barth. 20.

Av. *fradaxštar-*, fr. *fra-daxš-* 'teach'. Barth. 982.

Av. *čašan-*, fr. *čaš-* 'teach'. Barth. 583.

17.28 SCHOOL

Grk.	διδασκαλεῖον (σχολή)	Goth.	....	Lith.	*mokykla*
NG	σχολεῖον, σχολειό, σκολειό	ON	*skōli*	Lett.	*skuola*
Lat.	*lūdus, schola*	Dan.	*skole*	ChSl.	....
It.	*scuola*	Sw.	*skola*	SCr.	*škola*
Fr.	*école*	OE	*scōl*	Boh.	*škola*
Sp.	*escuela*	ME	*scol*	Pol.	*szkoła*
Rum.	*şcoală*	NE	*school*	Russ.	*škola, učilišče*
Ir.	*scol*	Du.	*school*	Skt.	*(vidyālaya-, pāṭhaçālā-)*
NIr.	*scoil*	OHG	*scuola*		
W.	*ysgol*	MHG	*schuole*		
Br.	*skol*	NHG	*schule*		

1. The majority of the Eur. words for 'school' are borrowed directly or indirectly fr. the Lat. *schola*, fr. Grk. σχολή 'leisure', hence also 'employment of leisure, learned discussion, lecture' and eventually 'school' (first as group, then as place), with late Grk. (Epict.), NG σχολεῖον (pop. σχολειό, σκολειό). Here belong all the Romance, Celtic, Germanic, the usual modern Slavic words, and Lett. *skuola* (fr. MLG *scole*).

2. Grk. διδασκαλεῖον, deriv. of διδάσκαλος 'teacher' (17.27).

3. Lat. *lūdus* 'play' (16.25) is also

used for 'school' (cf. Grk. σχολή). Ernout-M. 565.

4. Lith. *mokykla* : *mokyti* 'teach' (17.25).

5. Russ. *učilišče* : *učit'* 'teach' (17.25).

6. Skt. *vidyālaya-* (rare), lit. 'abode of knowledge' (*vidyā-* 'knowledge' : *vid-* 'know', 17.17).

Skt. *pāṭhaçālā-* (rare), cpd. of *pāṭha-* 'recitation, study' (: *paṭh-* 'recite, study') and *çālā-* 'house, building'.

17.31 REMEMBER

Grk.	*μέμνημαι, μιμνήσκομαι*	Goth.	*gamunan, andþagkjan sik*	Lith.	*at(si)minti*
NG	*(ἐν)θυμοῦμαι, θυμᾶμαι*	ON	*muna, minna, minnask*	Lett.	*atminēt(ies)*
Lat.	*meminisse, reminiscī, recordārī*	Dan.	*huske, mindes, erindre*	ChSl.	*poměnąti, pomęnąti, pomĭněti*
It.	*ricordarsi*	Sw.	*ihågkomma, minnas*	SCr.	*sjetiti se, pamtiti*
Fr.	*se souvenir, se rappeler*	OE	*gemunan, gemynan, (ge)myndgian*	Boh.	*pamatovati se*
Sp.	*acordarse, recordarse*	ME	*mone, mynde, remembre*	Pol.	*pamiętać*
Rum.	*şi aduce aminte*	NE	*remember, recall, recollect*	Russ.	*pomnit'*
Ir.	*cumnigur, foraithminedar* (3sg.)	Du.	*zich herinneren, gedenken, heugen*	Skt.	*smṛ-*
NIr.	*cuimhnighim*	OHG	*gihugen*	Av.	*mar-, mązdā-, mand-*
W.	*cofio*	MHG	*gehügen, (sich) innern*		
Br.	*kouna*	NHG	*sich erinnern, gedenken*		

Many of the words for 'remember' belong to an inherited group, from an IE root that is also widespread in words for 'mind' and for 'think', and several outside this group are connected with other words for 'mind' or 'think'. In another inherited group 'remember' or 'memory' (Indo-Iranian, Lat.) alternates with 'be anxious, care' (Grk., Gmc.). Some are connected with words for 'heart' (as = 'mind'), and some are from phrases 'come to', 'bring to', 'call to' with 'mind' expressed or understood. In several of the words the notion 'remind, call to mind in words, mention' is prominent.

The nouns for 'memory' are generally parallel to the verbs for 'remember', but note Lat. *memoria* vs. *meminisse*, representing two different inherited groups. Most of them cover both the abstract (faculty of) 'memory' and the concrete 'memory, remembrance', but some are used only in the latter sense, e.g. Fr. *souvenir* vs. *mémoire*, NHG *erinnerung* vs. *gedächtnis*.

1. IE **men-*, the same root as in words for 'mind', as Lat. *mēns*, etc. (17.11) and for 'think' as in Skt. *man-*, etc. (17.13). Walde-P. 2.264 ff. Ernout-M. 604. Boisacq 625 f., 638. Pedersen 1.171, 2.581. Berneker 2.45.

Grk. (*μνā-*, Att.-Ion. *μνη-* in all words with this sense) *μέμνημαι* perf. used as pres., pres. (Hom. *μνάομαι*) *μιμνήσκομαι*; Lat. *meminī* perf. used as pres. (cf. Grk. *μέμονα* 'be eager, purpose, intend'), *reminiscī*; Ir. *cumnigur*, NIr. *cuimhnighim*, W. *cofio*, Br. *kouna* (derivs. of the respective sbs. for 'memory', Ir. *cuman*, *cumne*, W. *cof*, MBr. *couff*, Br. *koun*, cpds. of prefix **kom-* with **men-*), Ir. *for-aithminedar*, and *do-aithminedar* (3sg.; 1sg. not quotable); Goth. *gamunan* (*munan* 'think'), ON *muna*, OE *gemunan*, ME *mone*, ON *minna* ('remind', impers. refl. with gen. 'remember', as *minnir mik eins hvers* 'I remember someone'), also refl. *minnask*, Dan. *mindes*, Sw. *minnas* (derivs. of ON *minni*, etc. 'memory'), OE *gemynan*, OE *(ge)myndgian* (*gmyndig* 'mindful', fr. *gemynd* 'memory', ME *mynd*, NE *mind* 'memory, mind', whence vb.), ME *mynde* (NE *mind* as 'remember' arch. and dial., still common in certain sections of U.S.; cf. *remind* 'make remember'); Lith. *atminti*, Lett. *atminēt*, and refl. *atsiminti*, *atminēties*; ChSl. *pomĭněti* (*mĭněti* 'think'), Russ. *pomnit'*; SCr. *pamtiti*, Boh. *pamatovati*, Pol. *pamiętać* (derivs. of ChSl. *pamętĭ*, etc. 'memory'); also by crossing with *poměnąti* (cf. below), ChSl. *pomęnąti* (Berneker 2.49).

2. IE *(*s*)*mer-* in words for 'remember, memory' and 'be anxious, care'. Walde-P. 2.689. Ernout-M. 604 f.

Skt. *smṛ-* 'remember' with sb. *smṛ-ti-* 'memory', Av. *mar-* (also redupl. *hišmar-*) 'remember, be mindful of'; Lat. *memor* 'mindful', *memoria* 'memory'; Grk. *μέρμηρα*, *μέριμνα* 'care, anxiety'; OE *gemimor* 'in memory, known', Goth. *maurnan* 'take thought for, be anxious', OE *murnan* 'be anxious, feel sorrow' (NE *mourn*), etc.

3. NG (*ἐν*)*θυμοῦμαι*, pop. *θυμᾶμαι*, fr. class. Grk. *ἐνθυμέομαι* 'take to heart, ponder, form a plan, etc.', fr. *θῡμός* 'soul, spirit', etc. (16.11).

4. Lat. *recordārī* (> It. *ricordarsi*, Sp. *recordarse*), deriv. of *cor*, *cordis* 'heart' (used also for 'mind'). Ernout-M. 219. REW 7129.

Fr. *se souvenir*, fr. Lat. *subvenīre* 'come up to one, aid, assist', also rarely 'come to the mind'. Ernout-M. 1085. REW 8408.

Fr. *se rappeler*, refl. of *rappeler* 'call back, recall', cpd. of *re-* and *appeler* 'call', fr. Lat. *appellāre* 'call upon, appeal'.

Sp. *acordarse*, refl. of *acordar* 'resolve, agree, remind, tune' (= Fr. *accorder*, It. *accordare* 'harmonize, accord'), fr. Lat. **acchordāre*, deriv. of *chorda* 'chord, string of a musical instrument.' REW 71a. Wartburg 1.13.

Rum. *şi aduce aminte*, lit. 'bring to the mind', *şi* dat. refl. pron., and *aminte* adv. fr. Lat. *ad mentem*. Tiktin 62.

5. Celtic forms, above, 1.

6. Goth. *andþagkjan sik* (in this sense Skeir. 7.1 f., otherwise 'bethink oneself' Lk. 16.4), Du., NHG *gedenken*, MHG (*sich*) *gedenken* (the non-refl. form chiefly 'think on, consider, decide, etc.', so OHG *gidenken*), cpds. of Goth. *þagkjan* 'ponder, consult, doubt, etc.', OHG *denken*, etc. 'think' (17.13).

Dan. *huske*, ODan. *hugse* = ON *hugsa* 'think' (17.13).

Sw. *ihågkomma*, also *komma ihåg*, Dan. *komme ihu*, lit. 'come into the mind', with *håg*, Dan. *hu* 'mind, heart, mood' = ON *hugr* 'mind' (17.11).

ME *remembre*, NE *remember*, fr. OFr. *remembrer*, late Lat. *rememorārī*, deriv. of *memor* 'mindful, remembering'. NED s.v. REW 7195.

NE *recall*, *recollect*, deriv. (*re-call*, etc.) obvious.

OHG *gihugen*, MHG *gehügen*, Du. *heugen* : OHG *huggen*, Goth. *hugjan*, etc. 'think' (17.13). Franck-v. W. 250.

NHG *sich errinern* (hence Du. *zich herinneren*, Dan. *erindre*, Sw. *erinra sig*), refl. of *erinnern* 'remind', MHG *sich innern*, refl. of *innern* 'remind, acquaint with, teach, persuade', OHG *innarōn*, deriv. of OHG *innaro* 'the inner part', orig. 'cause to be within'. Kluge-G. 136. Weigand-H. 1.462. Falk-Torp 196.

7. Lith. *at*(*si*)*minti*, ChSl. *pomĭněti*, etc. (most of the Balto-Slavic forms), above, 1.

ChSl. *poměnąti*, beside *měniti* 'remember' and 'think, believe' : OHG

meinen, etc. 'think, believe' (17.14). Berneker 2.49.

SCr. *sjetiti se*, late ChSl. *sětiti sę* (beside *sětovanĭje* 'grief', Supr.), etym.?

8. Skt. *smṛ-*, Av. *mar-*, above, 2.

Av. *mand-* and *mazdā-*, *mązdā-* 'put in mind' and 'hold in mind, remember' : Grk. *μανθάνω* 'learn' (17.24) and ultimately fr. IE **men-* (above, 1). Barth. 1136, 1181.

17.32 FORGET

Grk.	*(ἐπι)λανθάνομαι*	Goth.	*ufarmunnōn*	Lith.	*užmiršti*
NG	*ξεχάνω, λησμονῶ*	ON	*gleyma*	Lett.	*aizmirst, piemirst*
Lat.	*oblīvīscī*	Dan.	*glemme*	ChSl.	*zabyti*
It.	*dimenticare*	Sw.	*glömma*	SCr.	*zaboraviti*
Fr.	*oublier*	OE	*forgietan*	Boh.	*zapomenouti*
Sp.	*olvidar*	ME	*forgete*	Pol.	*zapomnieć*
Rum.	*uita*	NE	*forget*	Russ.	*zabyt'*
Ir.	*doroimnethar* (3sg.)	Du.	*vergeten*	Skt.	*vi-smṛ-, mṛṣ-*
NIr.	*dearm(h)adaim*	OHG	*argezan, fargezan*	Av.	. . . .
W.	*anghofio, ebargofi*	MHG	*vergezzen, ergezzen*		
Br.	*ankounac'haat*	NHG	*vergessen*		

'Forget' as the opposite of 'remember' is not infrequently so expressed, that is, by words for 'remember' (or in some cases related words for 'mind' or 'think') with prefixes of negative force, just as in the now only dial. or illiterate NE *disremember*.

Other sources are 'lose' (with specialization to 'lose from the mind'), 'rub out', or transfer from impersonal 'escape notice, lie hidden, be left behind' to personal use—in one group 'make merry with' (> 'be careless, neglect, forget').

1. IE **mers-*, perh. the same as in Goth. *marzjan* 'vex', OE *mierran*, OHG *merren* 'vex, bother, hinder', etc., and fr. an extension of **mer-* 'rub' (Skt. *mṛ-* 'crush', etc.). Walde-P. 2.279.

Lith. *už-miršti*, Lett. *mirst*, mostly cpds. *aiz-mirst*, *pie-mirst*; Skt. *mṛṣ-*, NPers. *farā-mūšīdan* (Horn 812), Arm. *moṙanam*.

2. Grk. *λανθάνομαι* (also *λήθομαι*), esp. cpd. *ἐπι-*, mid. of *λανθάνω*(*λήθω*) 'escape one's notice', also caus. 'make forget', Byz., NG *λησμονῶ* (deriv. of Grk. *λήσμων* 'unmindful') : Lat. *latēre* 'be hidden', etc. Walde-P. 2.377 f. Ernout-M. 526. Walde-H. 1.768 f.

NG pop. *ξεχάνω*, also *ξεχνῶ*, new pres. to aor. *ἐξ-έχασα*, cpd. of *χάνω* 'lose', aor. *ἔχασα* (11.33). Hatzidakis, Einl. 410. Buck, Cl. Ph. 15.39.

3. Lat. *oblīvīscī* (pple. *oblītus*, whence VLat. **oblītāre* > Fr. *oublier*, Sp. *olvidar*, Rum. *uita*) : *ob-linere* 'rub out, smear over', hence 'rub out, efface' (writing) > 'efface from memory'. Ernout-M. 693. Walde-H. 1.807 f. REW 6015.

It. *dimenticare*, neg. deriv. of *mente* 'mind'. REW 5496.

4. Ir. *doroimnethar* (3sg.), vbl. n. *dermat*, whence MIr. *dermatim*, NIr. *dearm(h)adaim*, fr. a cpd. **di-ro-moin-* (with neg. prefix *di-*) : *for-aithminedar* 'remembers' (17.31), etc. Pedersen 2.581. Thurneysen, Gram. 528.

W. *anghofio*, neg. of *cofio* 'remember' (17.31).

W. *ebargofi*, cpd. of *eb* for *heb* 'without' and *argofio* (arch.) 'call to mind, remember', cpd. of *cofio* 'remember'.

Br. *ankounac'haat*, deriv. of *ankounac'h* 'forgetfulness', neg. deriv. of *kouna* 'remember' (17.31).

5. Goth. *ufarmunnōn*, cpd. of *ufar* 'over' (neg. force as in *ufar-swaran* 'swear falsely', NE *overlook*, etc.) and cognate of *munan* 'think', *ga-munan* 'remember'. Feist 512.

ON *gleyma*, orig. 'be gay, make merry', with dat. 'forget' (still in this construction in NIcel.), Dan. *glemme*, Sw. *glömma*, deriv. of ON *glaumr* 'merriment, cheer, noisy joy', with development fr. 'make merry with' > 'be careless with, neglect' > 'forget'. Falk-Torp 326. Hellquist 291.

OE *forgietan*, ME *forgete*, NE *forget*, Du. *vergeten*, OHG *fargezan*, MHG *vergezzen*, NHG *vergessen*, OHG *argezan* (more usual than *far-*), MHG *ergezzen*, cpds. of prefixes having neg. force and the root seen in OE *begietan*, OHG *bigezzan*, 'get' (11.16), hence 'lose' > 'forget'.

6. ChSl. *zabyti*, Russ. *zabyt'*, cpd. of *za-* 'behind' and *byti* 'be', semantic development prob. 'be left behind' > 'be forgotten' (cf. ChSl. pple. *zabvenŭ* 'forgotten') > 'forget' (cf. Grk. *λανθάνομαι*, above, 2). Berneker 114.

SCr. *zaboraviti* (similar form in Bulg. for 'forget'), cpd. of *za-* 'behind' and *boraviti* 'stay, tarry', semantic development as in preceding. Berneker 72.

Boh. *zapomenouti*, Pol. *zapomnieć*, cpds. of *za-* (cf. above, but here mere neg. force) and Boh. *pomenouti*, Pol. *pomnieć* 'remember' (neither now the usual word) : ChSl. *pomĭněti* 'remember' (17.31).

7. Skt. *vi-smṛ-*, neg. cpd. of *smṛ-* 'remember' (17.31).

17.33 MEANING

Grk.	*σημασία, νοῦς, δύναμις*	Goth.	. . . .	Lith.	*reikšmė*
NG	*σημασία, ἔννοια*	ON	*þýðing*	Lett.	*nuozīme*
Lat.	*significātiō, sententia, sēnsus*	Dan.	*betydning, mening*	ChSl.	. . . .
It.	*significato, senso*	Sw.	*betydelse, mening*	SCr.	*značenje, smisao*
Fr.	*sens, signification*	OE	*tācnung, andgit*	Boh.	*smysl, význam*
Sp.	*significado* (or *-ación*), *sentido*	ME	*mening, tokening*	Pol.	*znaczenie*
Rum.	*înţeles, însemnare, sens*	NE	*meaning, sense*	Russ.	*značenie, smysl,*
Ir.	*cīall, inne*	Du.	*beteeknis, zin*	Skt.	*artha-*
NIr.	*brīgh, ciall*	OHG	*zeichnunga*	Av.	. . . .
W.	*ystyr, meddwl*	MHG	*bezeichenunge, sin*		
Br.	*talvoudegez, ster*	NHG	*bedeutung, sinn*		

The 'meaning' (of a word, sentence, etc., in part also of an action) is expressed by derivs. of words for 'sign, point out, explain', and by words meaning primarily 'reason, thought, sense, understanding, intention, power, force, value, inwardness', etc., all of obvious application.

1. Grk. *σημασία*, the word finally adopted in grammar, fr. *σημαίνω* 'point out, signify', also 'mean' (hence mid. pple. *τὸ σημαινόμενον* 'meaning', Aristot. etc.), deriv. of *σῆμα* 'sign, mark' (12.94). Hence also the modern Eur. terms for the science of meaning, like NE *semasiology* and (fr. adj. *σημαντικός*) adj. *semantic*, sb. *semantics*.

Grk. *νοῦς* 'mind, reason' (17.11), also 'meaning' (Hdt.+).

Grk. *ἔννοια* 'notion, idea' (cf. *ἐννοέω* 17.13), also late and frequently in NG 'meaning'.

Grk. *δύναμις* 'power' (4.81), also sometimes 'meaning', like NE *force* (of a word).

For the verbal 'mean' NG has (beside σημαίνω) a pop. phrase τί θὰ πῇ; lit. 'what will it say?', like Fr. *que veut dire?*

2. Lat. *significātiō* (> Fr., NE *signification*, Sp. *-ación*), fr. *significāre* 'point out, signify' and 'mean' (whence It. *significato*, Sp. *significado*), cpd. of Lat. *signum* 'sign' (12.94).

Lat. *sententia* 'way of thinking, opinion', also 'meaning' (Lucr., Cic., etc.), also *sēnsus* (> It. *senso*, Fr. *sens*) 'sense, feeling', as 'meaning' mostly poet. and post-Aug. (freq. in Quint.) : *sentīre* 'feel' (15.11), whence also Sp. *sentido* 'sense, feeling' and 'meaning'. Rum. *sens* 'meaning' (vs. native *simț*), fr. Fr. *sens*.

Lat. *vīs* 'strength, force', also sometimes 'meaning', like Grk. δύναμις, NE *force*.

Rum. *înțeles* 'understanding', also 'meaning', fr. *înțelege* 'understand' (17.16).

Rum. *însemnare*, old infin. of *însemna* 'note, denote, signify, mean', deriv. of *semn* 'sign' (Lat. *signum*, above).

3. Ir. *cīall* 'intelligence, reason' (17.12), also 'meaning' (cf. Sg. 140b.3,4, also K. Meyer, Contrib. 364).

Ir. *inne* (cf. Sg. 4b.4, gl. *significatio*) = *inne* 'intestine', orig. 'inner part', as **end-yo-* : Lat. *endo*, *indu*, *ind-* 'in', etc. Vendryes, MSL 15.358 f., but without mention of *inne* as 'meaning'.

NIr. *brīgh* 'power, force', also 'meaning'.

W. *ystyr*, Br. *ster*, fr. Lat. *historia* 'narrative, history', prob. as 'explanation', fr. the sense of 'subject of a discourse' and esp. the eccl. usage for biblical passages read and the responses to the readings (cf. Du Cange s.v. *historia*). Loth, Mots lat. 218 (without comment on semantic development).

W. *meddwl* 'mind, thought' (17.11), also 'meaning'.

Br. *talvoudegez* 'value' and 'meaning', fr. *talvout* 'be worth, cost, deserve'.

4. ON *þȳðing*, Dan. *betydning*, Sw. *betydelse*, NHG *bedeutung*, all orig. 'explanation, interpretation', fr. the vbs. ON *þȳða* 'interpret, mean', Dan. *betyde*, Sw. *betyda* (for *tyde*, *tyda* by influence of MLG form), NHG *bedeuten* 'mean, signify', MHG *(be)diuten* id., orig. 'put into the language of the people' (cf. OE *geþēode* 'language'), derivs. of ON *þjōð*, OHG *diot(a)*, Goth. *þiuda*, etc., 'people, folk'. Walde-P. 1.712. Weigand-H. 1.349. Falk-Torp 65, 1306 f.

Dan., Sw., ME *mening*, NE *meaning*, orig. 'opinion, intention', etc. (so still in Scand.), fr. Dan. *mene*, Sw. *mena* 'have an opinion, mean, think', OE *mǣnan* 'intend, have an opinion', etc. : OHG, NHG *meinen*, etc. 'think' (17.14).

OE *tācnung*, ME *tokening* (also 'token, emblem, mark, portent, etc.'), Du. *beteeknis*, OHG *zeichnunga* (also 'description', Graff), MHG *(be)zeichenunge*, *bezeichenheit*, *bezeichenisse* (NHG *bezeichnung* 'mark, description', etc.), fr. OE *tācnian* 'be a sign of, signify, mean', OHG *zeihhenen*, *zeihhonōn* 'show, signify', etc., these fr. OE *tācn*, etc. 'sign' (12.94). NED s.v. *tokening*. Weigand-H. 2.1309.

OE *andgit* 'understanding, sense' (15.11), also 'meaning'. Cf. Bosworth-Toller Suppl. s.v. *andgit*, IV.

NE *sense* (in this meaning since 1530, NED), fr. Fr. *sens* (above).

Du. *zin*, MHG *sin*, NHG *sinn*, orig. 'sense' (15.11, also 'mind' 17.11), as 'meaning' perh. by semantic borrowing fr. Lat. *sēnsus*, or Fr. *sens* (cf. above).

5. Lith. *reikšmė*, fr. *reikšiu*, *reikšti* 'reveal, mean' : *raiškus* 'apparent', Russ.-ChSl. *rěsnyj* 'true', ChSl. *rěsnota* 'truth'. Trautmann 242.

Lett. *nuozīme*, lit. 'mark', cpd. of *zīme* 'sign' (12.94).

6. SCr. *značenje*, Pol. *znaczenie*, Russ. *značenie* (cf. SCr., Pol., Russ. *znak* 'mark, sign'), Boh. *význam* : ChSl. *znati*, etc. 'know' (17.17).

SCr. *smisao*, Boh., Russ. *smysl* (Pol. *zmysł* also in this sense, cf. Linde s.v., but apparently not usual) = ChSl. *sŭmyslŭ* 'thought' (Supr.) : ChSl. *myslĭ* 'thought', *mysliti* 'think', etc. (17.13).

7. Skt. *artha-* 'aim, purpose' (17.41), 'object, thing', etc., also 'meaning'. Walde-P. 1.136. Uhlenbeck 13.

17.34 CLEAR, PLAIN

(To the Mind)

Grk.	δῆλος, σαφής, ἐναργής	Goth.	*skeirs, bairhts, swikunþs*	Lith.	*aiškus*
NG	φανερός, σαφής	ON	*skȳrr*	Lett.	*skaidrs*
Lat.	*clārus, plānus, apertus, ēvidēns*, etc.	Dan.	*klar, tydelig*	ChSl.	*(j)avě* (adv.), *jasno* (adv.)
It.	*chiaro*	Sw.	*klar, tydlig*	SCr.	*jasan*
Fr.	*clair*	OE	*swutol*	Boh.	*jasný*
Sp.	*claro*	ME	*cler, pleyn, sutel*	Pol.	*jasny*
Rum.	*clar*	NE	*clear, plain*	Russ.	*jasnyj, javnyj*
Ir.	*follus, rēil*	Du.	*klaar, duidelijk*	Skt.	*spaṣṭa-, vyakta-*
NIr.	*soilēir, lēir*	OHG	*zoraht*	Av.	*čiϑra-*
W.	*goleu, eglur*	MHG	*klār*		
Br.	*sklaer*	NHG	*klar, deutlich*		

'Clear, plain' (to the mind, opposite of 'obscure'; as in NE *a clear statement*, *the meaning is plain*) is generally expressed by words for visually 'clear, bright' (15.57), most of them still used in the latter sense. Less common relations are with words for 'level, plain', 'open', and 'point out, explain'.

Several of the words listed cover also 'evident, manifest, obvious', but others in which this related but somewhat different sense is dominant, like NE *evident*, NHG *offenbar*, are not included.

1. Grk. δῆλος, Hom. δέελος, orig. 'visible, conspicuous', as once in Hom. and reg. in ἀρί-δηλος, ἀρί-ζηλος : δέαμαι 'seem', Skt. *dī-* 'shine'. Walde-P. 1.772. Boisacq 168.

Grk. σαφής (in Hom. only adv. σάφα 'clearly'), etym. dub. Boisacq 855.

Grk. ἐναργής, in Hom. 'visible, palpable', later also 'clear', with sb. ἐνάργεια 'clearness' : ἀργής, ἀργός 'shining, bright', Skt. *arjuna-* 'light, white', etc. Walde-P. 1.82. Boisacq 74.

Grk. φανερός 'visible, manifest', in NG the usual word for 'evident, clear' (to the mind) : φαίνω 'bring to light, show', etc., φαίνομαι 'appear, seem', Skt. *bhā-* 'shine', etc. (15.56, 17.18).

2. Lat. *clārus* (> It. *chiaro*, Fr. *clair*, Sp. *claro*, Rum. *clar*), also 'bright' (15.57), orig. 'loud' (15.45).

Lat. *plānus* 'level, flat' (12.71), freq. 'plain, clear' (Plaut.+), with adv. *plānē* 'plainly, clearly'.

Lat. *apertus*, lit. 'open', pple. of *aperīre* 'open' (12.24), cf. NHG *offenbar* 'evident, obvious'.

Lat. *ēvidēns* (> It., Sp. *evidente*, Fr. *évident*, ME, NE *evident*, but these mostly 'obvious, not requiring proof'), orig. of things 'visible, apparent', used from Cic. on for Grk. ἐναργής, cpd. of *ē* 'from' and *vidēns*, pple. of *vidēre* 'see' (cf. NHG *aus-sehen* 'appear'). Ernout-M. 312.

Lat. *perspicuus*, orig. 'transparent', fr. *perspicere* 'see through'.

3. Ir. *follus* (fr. **upo-luksu-*) : *so-lus* 'bright' (15.57).

Ir. *rēil*, prob. back-formation to vb.

rēlaim 'reveal', this fr. Lat. *re-vēlāre* 'uncover, reveal'. Walde-P. 2.366. Pokorny, KZ 46.152 f.

NIr. *lēir*, more usually, cpd. *soilēir* (with ameliorative prefix *so-*), fr. Ir. *lēir* 'visible', etym. dub. Walde-P. 2.381.

W. *goleu*, orig. 'bright' (15.57).

W. *eglur*, etym.?

Br. *sklaer*, orig. 'bright' (15.57).

4. Goth. *skeirs* = ON *skīrr* 'clear, bright, pure', OE *scīr* 'bright, glittering, clear' : ON *skǣrr* 'bright' (15.57).

ON *skȳrr*, beside *skȳra* 'explain', *skȳring* 'explanation', fr. a root **skeu-*, **skū-* beside **skəi-*, **skī-* in preceding group, but otherwise appearing mostly in words for 'cover', 'grow dusk', etc. For similar peculiar semantic relations in the other formal group, cf. Grk. σκιά 'shade'. Falk-Torp 1008, 1040.

Goth. *bairhts* 'bright' (15.57), also 'clear, manifest' (*bairht þatei* = δῆλον ὅτι 1 Cor. 15.27).

Goth. *swikunþs*, cpd. of *swi-* : *swes* 'own' (cf. OE *swutol*, below) and *-kunþs* 'known' (: *kunnan* 'know'), lit. 'self-known'. Feist 468.

OE *swutol* (Anglian *sweotol*), ME *sutel*, etym. dub., perh. cpd., first part : Goth. *swi-* in *swikunþs* (above) and last part fr. **tāl* : Grk. δῆλος (above, 1). Walde-P. 1.772. Holthausen, IF 20.321.

ME *cler*, NE *clear*, fr. OFr. *clair* (above, 2).

ME *pleyn*, NE *plain*, fr. OFr. *plain*, Lat. *plānus* (above, 2).

Du. *klaar* (MLG *klār* > Dan., Sw. *klar*), MHG *klār*, NHG *klar*, fr. Lat. *clārus* (above, 2).

OHG *zoraht*, *zorft* = OE *torht* 'splendid, bright, beautiful' : Ir. *an-drocht* (*an-* neg.) 'offensive, dark', fr. the root of Grk. δέρκομαι 'see', etc. Walde-P. 1.807.

NHG *deutlich* (MHG *diutlīche* adv.), Du. *duidelijk*, Dan. *tydelig*, Sw. *tydlig*, derivs. of NHG *deuten* (MHG *diuten*), Du. *duiden*, Dan. *tyde* 'explain, interpret' (cf. NHG *bedeutung*, etc. 'meaning', 17.33).

5. Lith. *aiškus*, beside OLith. *iškus*, prob. : ChSl. *jasno*, etc. (below). Walde-P. 1.2. Berneker 276.

Lett. *skaidrs* (Lith. *skaidrus* 'fair, clear' of weather, etc.) : ChSl. *čistŭ* 'clean', ON *heiðr*, OHG *heitar* 'clear, bright' (sky, weather, etc.), Skt. *ketu-* 'splendor, brightness, sign, mark', Av. *čiϑra-* 'apparent, clear' (below). Walde-P. 2.537.

6. ChSl. *avě*, *javě* (adv.), Russ. *javnyj*, beside ChSl. *aviti*, *javiti* 'make known, show' : Skt. *āviṣ* 'visible, manifest', Grk. αἰσθάνομαι (*ἀϝισ-θ-) 'perceive'. Walde-P. 1.17. Berneker 34.

ChSl. *jasno* (adv.), SCr. *jasan*, etc., general Slavic, orig. 'bright' (15.57).

7. Skt. *spaṣṭa-*, orig. 'visible, seen (clearly)', pple. of *spaç-*, doublet of *paç-* 'see'.

Skt. *vyakta-*, pple. of *vi-añj-* 'make appear, reveal', orig. 'beautify, adorn', cpd. of *añj-* 'anoint'. Cf. BR 1.77.

Av. *čiϑra-* : Lett. *skaidrs*, etc. (above, 5).

17.35 OBSCURE

Grk.	ἀσαφής, ἄδηλος, σκοτεινός	Goth.	....	Lith.	*neaiškus*
NG	ἀσαφής, σκοτεινός	ON	*myrkr*	Lett.	*neskaidrs*
Lat.	*obscūrus*	Dan.	*dunkel*	ChSl.	....
It.	*oscuro*	Sw.	*dunkel*	SCr.	*nejasan*
Fr.	*obscur*	OE	*forsworcen, deorc*(?)	Boh.	*nejasný*
Sp.	*obscuro*	ME	*derk, merke, obscur*	Pol.	*niejasny*
Rum.	*obscur*	NE	*obscure*	Russ.	*nejasnyj*
Ir.	*dorche, dorchaide*	Du.	*duister*	Skt.	(*gūḍha-*)
NIr.	*doilēir, dorcha*	OHG	*tunchal*	Av.	....
W.	*aneglur*	MHG	*tunkel*		
Br.	*disklaer*	NHG	*dunkel, unklar*		

'Obscure' (to the mind) is expressed by words for visually 'dark, devoid of light' (cf. 'darkness' 1.62 and 'dark' in color 15.63), or by neg. cpds. of words for 'clear, plain' (17.34).

1. Grk., NG lit. ἀσαφής, and Grk. ἄδηλος, neg. cpds. of σαφής and δῆλος 'clear, plain'.

Grk. σκοτεινός, lit. 'dark'.

2. Lat. *obscūrus* (whence Romance forms), lit. 'dark'.

3. Ir. *dorche*, whence *dorchaide*, lit. 'dark'.

NIr. *doilēir*, neg. (*do-*) of *lēir* 'clear'.

W. *aneglur*, neg. of *eglur* 'clear'.

Br. *disklaer*, neg. of *sklaer* 'clear'.

4. ON *myrkr*, ME *merke*, lit. 'dark' (OE *mirce* 'dark, wicked').

OE *forsworcen* (the usual gloss for Lat. *obscūrus*, but quotable in fig. sense?), pple. of *forsweorcen* 'darken, make obscure', intensive cpd. of *sweorcan* 'become dark, troubled' = OS *swerkan* 'grow dark, cloudy', OHG *giswerc*, *gisworc* 'darkening (by clouds)', etym. dub. Walde-P. 2.535.

OE *deorc* 'dark', apparently not quotable in fig. sense, ME *derk*, NE *dark* (*a dark saying*, but not common in this sense). NED s.v. *dark*, 6.

ME *obscur*, NE *obscure*, fr. OFr. *obscur* (Lat. *obscūrus*, above, 2).

Du. *duister*, lit. 'dark'.

OHG *tunchal*, MHG *tunkel*, NHG *dunkel* (> Dan., Sw. *dunkel*), lit. 'dark'.

NHG *unklar*, neg. of *klar* 'clear'.

5. Lith. *neaiškus*, Lett. *neskaidrs*, negs. of Lith. *aiškus*, Lett. *skaidrs* 'clear'.

6. SCr. *nejasan*, etc., general Slavic, negs. of the corresponding words for 'clear', SCr. *jasan*, etc.

7. Skt. *gūḍha-*, lit. 'hidden, secret' (17.36).

17.36 SECRET (adj.)

Grk.	κρυπτός, λαθραῖος	Goth.	*fulgins*	Lith.	*slaptas, paslėptas*
NG	κρυφός	ON	*leyndr, leyniligr*	Lett.	*slepens, sleps*
Lat.	*occultus, secrētus, clandestīnus*	Dan.	*hemmelig* (*lønlig*)	ChSl.	*tajĭnŭ*
It.	*segreto*	Sw.	*hemlig* (*lönnlig*)	SCr.	*tajan*
Fr.	*secret*	OE	*dīegel* (*dēagol*), *dierne*	Boh.	*tajný*
Sp.	*secreto*	ME	*secre(t), derne, diȝel*	Pol.	*tajny*
Rum.	*tainic, ascuns, secret*	NE	*secret*	Russ.	*tajnyj*
Ir.	*inchlide, diam(a)ir*	Du.	*geheim, heimelijk*	Skt.	*gupta-, gūḍha-*
NIr.	*rūnach, rūnda*	OHG	*tougan, tougal*	Av.	*gūzra-, taya-*
W.	*dirgel*	MHG	*tougen, heimelich*		
Br.	*kuzet*	NHG	*geheim, heimlich*		

Most of the words for 'secret' mean lit. 'hidden' and so are connected with the verbs for 'hide' discussed in 12.22.

1. Grk. κρυπτός, NG κρυφός : κρύπτω 'hide' (12.22).

Grk. λαθραῖος (in NG 'smuggled') : λανθάνω 'escape notice, lie hidden', mid. 'forget' (17.32). Boisacq 554 f.

2. Lat. occultus, pple. of occulere 'hide' : cēlāre id., etc. (12.22). Here also Lat. clandestīnus, deriv. through *clam-de of clam 'secretly, in private'. Ernout-M. 171 f. Walde-H. 1.196 f., 226 f.

Lat. secrētus, pple. of sēcernere 'put apart, separate, set aside', cpd. of disjunctive particle sē- and cernere 'separate, distinguish, decide'. Ernout-M. 178.

Hence It. segreto, Fr. secret, Sp. secreto; Rum. secret in the senses 'deserted, lonesome, cursed', but as 'secret' prob. fr. French. REW 7765. Tiktin 1405.

Rum. tainic, fr. the Slavic (tajĭnikŭ), cf. ChSl. tajĭnŭ, etc. (below, 6).

Rum. ascuns, lit. 'hidden' : ascunde 'hide' (12.22).

3. Ir. inchlide, pple. of ind-cel- (but no finite forms found) : celim 'hide'. Pedersen 2.485.

Ir. diam(a)ir (K. Meyer, Contrib. 630), etym.?

NIr. rūnach, rūnda, derivs. of Ir. rūn 'a secret' : OE, ON rūn 'secret, rune', Goth. rūna 'secret, mystery' (Walde-P. 2.350).

W. dirgel, cpd. of dir 'sure, certain' (often mere intensive prefix) and cel 'hidden' : celu 'hide'.

Br. kuzet, lit. 'hidden', pple. of kuzat 'hide'.

4. Goth. fulgins, beside sb. fulhsni : filhan 'hide'.

ON leyndr, leyniligr (Dan. lǿnlig, Sw. lǿnnlig, esp. poet. and arch., in Dan. freq. used by purists for hemmelig), derivs. of leyna 'hide'.

OE dīegel, ME diȝel (*daugilo-), beside OE dēagol, OHG tougal (*daugulo-), and OHG tougan, MHG tougen, prob. : OE dēag 'dye, color', dēagian 'to dye, color', but outside connections dub., possibly fr. the root in Lith. dvēkti 'breathe, pant', Lett. dukt 'roar, rage, storm', cf. dukans 'dark-colored', with semantic development from 'dusty, hazy, misty' or the like to 'dark', whence 'secret'? Walde-P. 1.838.

OE dierne, ME derne : OS derni, OHG tarni 'hidden', OHG tarnen 'cover, hide', OE darian 'lurk, lie hidden', perh. fr. the root in Skt. dhr̥- 'hold, support', etc. But semantic development ('hold' > 'lie quietly' > 'hide')? Walde-P. 1.858.

ME secre, secret, NE secret, fr. OFr. secrē, Fr. secret (above, 2).

Du., NHG geheim, Du. heimelijk (MLG heimelīk > Dan. hemmelig, Sw. hemlig), NHG heimlich, in MLG, MHG chiefly 'intimate, familiar' whence 'private, secret', orig. 'domestic', fr. heim 'home, house'. Fali-Torp 397. Weigand-H. 1.653, 837.

5. Lith. slaptas, pasléptas, Lett. sleps, slepens : Lith. slépti, Lett. slēpt 'hide'.

6. ChSl. tajĭnŭ, etc., general Slavic, beside taj adv. : tati 'thief', Skt. (s)tāyu-, Av. tāyu- 'thief', Av. taya- 'secret, furtive', sb. 'thief', etc. Walde-P. 2.610.

7. Skt. gupta-, lit. 'guarded, hidden', pple. of gup- 'guard, hide', cf. Av. gufra- 'deep, mysterious, wonderful', root connection dub. Walde-P. 1.562.

Skt. gūḍha-, Av. gūzra- : Skt. guh-, Av. guz- 'hide'.

17.37 SURE, CERTAIN

Grk.	βέβαιος, ἀσφαλής	Goth.	-wiss (astaþ, þwasti-	Lith.	tikras
NG	βέβαιος, σίγουρος		þa, sbs.)	Lett.	druošs
Lat.	certus	ON	viss	ChSl.	. . . .
It.	sicuro, certo	Dan.	sikker, vis	SCr.	siguran
Fr.	sûr, certain	Sw.	säker, viss	Boh.	jistý
Sp.	seguro, cierto	OE	gewiss	Pol.	pewny
Rum.	sigur, cert	ME	siker, certeyn	Russ.	vernyj
Ir.	derb, demin	NE	sure, certain	Skt.	a-sañçayam (adv.),
NIr.	cinnte, deimhin,	Du.	zeker, gewis		sthira-, dhruva-
	dearbh	OHG	giwis	Av.	. . . .
W.	siwr, sicr	MHG	sicher, gewis		
Br.	sur	NHG	sicher, gewiss		

Words for 'sure, certain' are based upon such notions as 'firm, steady', 'decided', 'actual', 'trustworthy', and especially 'safe' ('free from danger' > 'free from doubt').

1. Grk. βέβαιος, orig. 'firm, steady' (: βαίνω 'walk, step, go'), hence also 'sure, certain', as reg. in NG.

Grk. ἀσφαλής 'safe' (11.26), sometimes also 'sure, certain', esp. in adv. ἀσφαλῶς.

NG σίγουρος, fr. a Ven. form of It. sicuro (below, 2). G. Meyer, Neugr. Stud. 4.81.

2. Lat. certus (> It. certo, OFr., Rum. cert, Sp. cierto; Fr. certain, fr. deriv. in -ānus), orig. 'determined, decided', pple. of cernere 'separate, distinguish, decide'. Ernout-M. 178. Walde-H. 1.205.

It. sicuro, Fr. sûr, Sp. seguro, Rum. sigur, fr. Lat. sēcūrus, orig. 'free from care' (cūra), hence 'free from harm or danger, safe' (11.26), hence also 'free from doubt, sure'.

3. Ir. derb, NIr. dearbh, as orig. 'firm' : Ir. dair 'oak', dron 'firm', OE trēowe 'faithful' (NE true), etc. Walde-P. 1.805. Pedersen 1.175.

Ir. demin, NIr. deimhin, etym. dub. Pedersen 1.174 (de-min as orig. 'without change' : Lith. mainas 'exchange', etc.). Walde-P. 2.241.

NIr. cinnte, lit. 'fixed', pple. of cinnim 'fix, determine'.

W. sicr, fr. ME siker (below, 4).

W. siwr, fr. ME, NE sure.

Br. sur, fr. Fr. sûr. 'Sure' also expressed by gwir 'true' (16.66) or anat 'known, clear, evident', fr. MBr. haznat, fr. *ati-gnatos (cf. Gall. Ategnatos) : Grk. γνωτός 'known', etc. Henry 11. Ernault, Dict. étym. 309.

4. Goth. astaþ 'certainty', perh. as 'firmness', deriv. of IE *stā- 'stand'. Feist 60.

Goth. þwastiþa 'certainty' : ga-þwast-jan 'make firm, establish', ON þvest 'firm parts of the flesh'. Walde-P. 1.708. Feist 507.

Goth. -wiss (un-wiss 'uncertain'), ON viss (in form = OE wis 'wise', but in sense of 'certain' for viss), Dan. vis, Sw. viss, OE gewiss (ME ywis adv.), Du. gewis, OHG giwis, MHG gewis, NHG gewiss, fr. *wid-to-, pple. of Goth. witan, etc. 'know' (17.17). Walde-P. 1.238. Falk-Torp 1388.

ME siker (OE sicor 'safe', as 'sure' 1200+, NE dial. sicker, cf. NED s.v.), MHG, NHG sicher (OHG sihhur 'safe'), MLG seker (> Dan. sikker, Sw. säker), Du. zeker, all orig. 'safe' and, like the Romance words, fr. Lat. sēcūrus 'safe'. Falk-Torp 965. Weigand-H. 2.857.

ME certeyn, NE certain, fr. OFr. certain (above, 2).

5. Lith. tikras (also 'real, correct', etc.) : tikéti 'believe' (17.15), etc.

Lett. druošs 'safe' (11.26), also 'sure, certain'.

6. SCr. siguran 'safe' (11.26) also 'sure, certain'.

Boh. jistý : ChSl. istŭ, istovŭ 'real, actual', istina 'truth', etc., general Slavic group mostly 'actual, true', etc. Berneker 435 f. Brückner 193 f.

Pol. pewny (Boh. pevný 'firm'), as orig. 'trustworthy' : ufać (f fr. pw),

ChSl. upŭvati, Russ. upovat' 'trust'. Brückner 403.

Russ. vernyj 'faithful, trustworthy' (16.65), also the usual word for 'sure, certain'.

7. Skt. asañçaya-, sb. 'absence of doubt, certainty', adv. asañçayam 'without doubt, certainly', neg. of sañçaya- 'doubt' (17.43).

Skt. sthira- and dhruva- 'firm', both sometimes 'sure, certain'.

17.38 EXPLAIN

Grk.	ἐξηγέομαι, σαφηνίζω	Goth.	gaskeirjan	Lith.	išaiškinti
NG	ἐξηγῶ	ON	skýra	Lett.	izskaidruot
Lat.	explānāre, explicāre,	Dan.	forklare	ChSl.	sŭkazati
	expōnere	Sw.	förklara	SCr.	objasniti
It.	spiegare	OE	(ā)reccan	Boh.	vysvětliti, objasniti
Fr.	expliquer	ME	reche	Pol.	objaśnić
Sp.	explicar	NE	explain	Russ.	ob-, po-jasnit'
Rum.	explica	Du.	verklaren	Skt.	vy-ā-khyā-, vy-ā-kr̥-,
Ir.	etar-certaim	OHG	(ar)recchen		etc.
NIr.	mīnighim	MHG	(er)recken	Av.	āzan-(?)
W.	egluro	NHG	erklären		
Br.	diskleria				

Many of the words for 'explain' are derivs. of those for 'clear, plain' (17.34). Others represent figurative uses of 'show the way, point out, set forth, unfold, spread out, make smooth', etc.

Words that are used mainly with reference to the interpretation of foreign languages or learned exposition, like Grk. ἑρμηνεύω, NE interpret, expound, Russ. istolkovat', etc., are not included. But the Goth. and ChSl. renderings of ἑρμηνεύω are given as the only available words and probably used for 'explain' in general. For the group ON þýða partly 'explain, interpret', MHG (be)diuten 'explain, point out', see under 'meaning' (17.33).

1. Grk. ἐξηγέομαι 'lead, show the way', hence also 'narrate, explain', this sense becoming dominant (cf. ἐξήγησις 'narration, explanation'), cpd. of ἡγέομαι

'lead' (10.64). Hence NG ἐξηγῶ (cf. ἡγέω Hdn. = ἡγέομαι).

Grk. σαφηνίζω, deriv. of σαφής 'clear, plain'.

2. Lat. explānāre, deriv. of plānus 'level, flat' and 'plain, clear' and, unlike the latter, used almost entirely in the fig. sense.

Lat. explicāre (> It. spiegare and as lit. borrowings Fr. expliquer, Sp. explicar, Rum. explica), lit. 'unfold, spread out', cpd. of plicāre 'fold'.

Lat. expōnere (> OFr. espondre, ME expoune, expounde, NE expound), lit. 'put out, set forth', but more freq. in fig. sense 'expose, expound, explain', etc., cpd. of pōnere 'put, place'. Cf. the similar fig. use (prob. semantic borrowing) of NHG aus-legen, Boh. vy-ložiti, vy-kladati, Pol. wy-kładać, etc.

3. Ir. etar-certaim, cpd. of etar 'between' and deriv. of cert 'right' (fr. Lat. certus). Cf. con-certaim 'correct, adjust'. Pedersen 2.485 f.

NIr. mīnighim, lit. 'make smooth, polish', deriv. of mīn 'smooth, fine, gentle'.

W. egluro, deriv. of eglur 'clear, plain' (17.34).

Br. diskleria, also 'declare', fr. OFr. desclairier 'make clear, declare', deriv. of clair, fr. Lat. clārus 'clear' (17.34).

4. Goth. gaskeirjan (renders ἑρμηνεύω 'interpret', but prob. reg. word for 'explain', and ON skýra, derivs. of Goth. skeirs, and ON skýrr 'clear, plain' respectively.

OE reccan, āreccan, ME reche, recche, OHG recken, arrecchen, MHG recken, errecken, lit. 'stretch out, extend', but also the usual old WGmc. word for 'explain' = ON rekja 'spread out, unwind', Goth. uf-rakjan 'stretch out, up' : Ir. rigim 'stretch out (the hand)', Skt. r̥j- 'make straight, arrange', Lat. regere 'direct, rule', etc. Walde-P. 2.364.

NE explain, also early 'make even,

smooth', fr. Lat. explānāre (above, 2). NED s.v.

Du. verklaren (MLG vorklaren > Dan. forklare, Sw. förklara), NHG erklären (MHG erklæren only lit. 'make clear'), derivs. of Du. klaar, NHG klar, etc. 'clear'.

5. Lith. aiškinti, more usually išaiš-kinti, deriv. of aiškus 'clear, plain'.

Lett. skaidruot, more usually izskai-druot, deriv. of skaidrs 'clear, plain'.

6. ChSl. sŭkazati (mostly 'point out, show' but also for ἑρμηνεύω 'interpret'), cpd. of kazati 'point out, show' (15.55).

SCr., Boh. objasniti, Pol. objaśnić, Russ. objasnit', pojasnit', derivs. of SCr. jasan, etc. 'clear'.

Boh. vysvětliti, cpd. of světliti 'lighten', deriv. of světlý 'light, bright' (15.56).

7. Skt. vy-ā-khyā-, cpd. of khyā- 'make known', ā-khyā- 'tell, narrate', etym.? Uhlenbeck 75.

Skt. vy-ā-kr̥-, lit. 'separate, undo', cpd. of kr̥- 'do, make'.

Av. ā-zan-? (cf. maṯ-āzanti- 'along with the interpretation'), cpd. of zan- 'know' (17.17).

17.39 SOLVE

Grk.	λύω, διαλύω	Goth.	. . . .	Lith.	išrišti
NG	λύνω	ON	leysa, rāða	Lett.	atrisināt
Lat.	solvere	Dan.	lǿse	ChSl.	. . . .
It.	risolvere	Sw.	(upp)lösa	SCr.	riješiti
Fr.	résoudre	OE	rǣdan	Boh.	rozřešiti, rozluštiti
Sp.	resolver	ME	rede	Pol.	rozwiązać
Rum.	rezolva, deslega	NE	solve	Russ.	rešit'
Ir.	do-fuasailcim, iccaim	Du.	oplossen		
NIr.	rēidhtighim	OHG	. . . .		
W.	dadrys, datod	MHG	zerlæsen		
Br.	diskoulma	NHG	(auf)lösen, erraten		

'Solve' (problems, riddles, etc.) is generally expressed by words which mean literally 'loose' or the like, most of these either negative compounds of those for 'bind' (9.16) or related to words discussed under 'lose' (11.33) or

'release' (11.34). But there are some other sources.

1. Words meaning literally 'loose' or the like.

Grk. λύω, διαλύω; Lat. solvere (> NE solve; resolvere > It. risolvere, Fr. ré-

soudre, Sp. *resolver*, Rum. *rezolva*), Rum. *deslega* (neg. of *lega* 'bind'); Ir. *dofuasailcim* (cf. *dofuasailcet animmchomarc* 'they solve the question' Sg. 27a2, lit. sense in *dofuasalcat greic oe in -u-* 'the Greeks resolve oe into u' Sg. 19a1), cpd. (**to-od-ess-*) of *lēicim* 'let, let go' (Pedersen 2.564); W. *datod*, cpd. of neg. *dad-* and *dodi* 'put, place, lay'; W. *dadrys*, lit. 'disentangle', cpd. of neg. *dad-* and *-rys* as in *dyrys* 'intricate' with intensive prefix *dy-*; Br. *diskoulma*, neg. of *koulma* 'tie', fr. *koulm* 'knot'; ON *leysa*, Dan. *løse*, Sw. (*upp*)*lösa*, Du. *oplossen*, MHG *zerlæsen*, NHG (*auf*)*lösen* (so also NE *loose* in Spenser, cf. NED s.v. 9); Lith. *išrišti*, Lett. *atrisināt* (: Lith. *rišti*, Lett. *rist* 'bind'); SCr. *riješiti*, Boh. *rozřešiti*, Russ. *rešit'* (: ChSl. *rěšiti* 'loose, release', 11.34); Pol. *rozwiązać* (: *wiązać* 'bind').

2. Ir. *iccaim* (cf. *īcaid som didiu anisin anasmbeir*, etc. 'he solves that when he says . . .', Ml. 55d11), lit. 'heal' (4.86).

NIr. *rēidhtighim*, lit. 'adjust, arrange, clear, make smooth' : *rēidh* 'smooth, level' (15.77).

3. ON *rāða*, OE *rǣdan*, ME *rede* (still NE *read a riddle*), fr. more general sense 'advise, counsel, plan', etc. NED s.v. *read*. Similarly NHG *erraten*.

4. Boh. *rozluštiti*, lit. 'crack open', cpd. of *luštiti* 'shell' (nuts, etc.).

17.41 INTENTION, PURPOSE

Grk.	*πρόνοια, γνώμη, πρόθεσις*	Goth.	*muns*	Lith.	*ketinimas, tikslas*
		ON	*ætlan*	Lett.	*nuoduoms*
NG	*σκοπός*	Dan.	*hensigt, forsæt*	ChSl.	(*pomyšlenĭje*)
Lat.	*cōnsilium, prōpositum*	Sw.	*afsigt, föresats, uppsåt, syfte*	SCr.	*namjera, svrha*
				Boh.	*úmysl, záměr, účel*
It.	*intenzione, scopo*	OE	*ingehygd*	Pol.	*zamiar, zamysł*
Fr.	*intention, dessein*	ME	*entencion, porpos, mening*	Russ.	*namerenie*
Sp.	*intención, propósito*			Skt.	*artha-, abhiprāya-,* etc.
Rum.	*intenţiune, gînd, scop*	NE	*intention, purpose*		
Ir.	*airbert, airmert*	Du.	*voornemen, doel, bedoeling*	Av.	*xratu-, zaoša-*
NIr.	*aigne, intinn*				
W.	*bwriad, amcan*	OHG	*meinunga*		
Br.	*rat, ratoz*	MHG	*meinunge*		
		NHG	*absicht, zweck*		

'Intention, purpose' is frequently expressed by words for 'mind' or 'thought'. Besides those listed, cf. also phrases like Lat. *mihi in animō est*, NE *I have in mind to, it is my thought to*, etc. Other semantic sources are 'resolution, counsel, plan', 'effort', 'what is set before one', 'what is aimed at'. Besides the words listed, many others for 'end' or 'aim, goal, object' are freely used to express 'purpose', as Fr. *fin, but* NE *end, aim, object* (cf. also the vb. *aim*, pop. in rural U.S. for 'intend', as *I aim to*), NHG *ziel*, with the loanwords SCr. *cilj*, Pol. *cel*, Russ. *cel'*.

'Purpose' is, of course, often expressed simply by prepositional phrases, like Grk. *ἐπὶ τοῦτο*, Lat. *in hoc* 'for this purpose', etc. Here the frequent NIr. *chuige*, lit. 'toward it' = 'for the purpose', fr. *chum* 'toward' with 3d pers. pron. Dinneen s.vv. *chum* and *chuige*.

1. Grk. *διάνοια, ἔννοια, ἐπίνοια* 'thought, notion' and *πρόνοια* 'forethought', cpds. fr. *νοέω* 'think' (17.13), are also used for 'intention, purpose'.

Grk. *γνώμη* 'thought, judgment' and 'intention, purpose', deriv. of *γνω-* in *γιγνώσκω* 'know' (17.17).

Grk. *πρόθεσις* 'a setting forth, statement', also 'purpose' (the usual Hellenistic word, Polyb., NT, etc.) : *προτίθημι* 'set forth, display', also 'purpose'.

Grk. *βούλευμα* 'resolution' and 'purpose' : *βουλεύω* 'deliberate, resolve', *βούλομαι* 'will, wish' (16.61).

Grk. *σκοπός* 'watchman' and 'mark', hence 'objective, aim' and in NG reg. word for 'intention, purpose' : *σκέπτομαι* 'look, look at' (15.52).

2. Lat. *cōnsilium* 'counsel, plan' and 'intention, purpose' : *cōnsulere* 'deliberate, take counsel'. Ernout-M. 214 f. Walde-H. 1.264 f.

Lat. *prōpositum* (> Sp. *propósito*), lit. 'what is set forth' : *prōpōnere* 'put forth, display, propose'. Cf. Grk. *πρόθεσις*.

Lat. *intentiō*, lit. 'a stretching out, tension', whence 'exertion, effort, attention', also (Pliny) 'design, intention' (> It. *intenzione*, Fr. *intention*, Sp. *intención*, Rum. *intenţiune*) : *intendere* 'stretch out', also mental 'exert the attention, intend' (*intendere animō*), cpd. of *tendere* 'stretch' (9.32).

Fr. *dessein*, beside *dessin* 'design, drawing', fr. It. *disegno* (both senses), deriv. of *disignare* (> Fr. *dessiner*), fr. Lat. *dēsignāre* 'mark, design, designate' (: *signum* 'sign'). REW 2596. Gamillscheg 310.

Rum. *gînd* 'thought' and 'plan, purpose' : *gîndi* 'think' (17.13).

It. *scopo*, Rum. *scop*, fr. Grk. *σκοπός* 'aim' (above, 1).

3. Ir. *airbert, airmert* (K. Meyer, Contrib. 45), vbl. n. of *ar-bertaim* (*-mertaim*) 'prepare, determine', cf. W. (*d*)*armerthu* 'prepare', MBr. *armerhein* 'manage', etym.? Pedersen 2.475 f.

NIr. *aigne* 'mind' (17.11), esp. 'intention'.

NIr. *intinn*, fr. Lat. *intentiō* (above, 2). Pedersen 1.234.

W. *bwriad*, orig. 'aim' : *bwrw* 'throw, cast, hit'.

W. *amcan*, orig.? Morris-Jones 264 (but??).

Br. *rat, ratoz*, also 'thought', prob. = OBr. *rad* 'stipulation', fr. Lat. *ratum* 'what is agreed upon'. Ernault, Dict. étym. 367. Otherwise Henry 230.

4. Goth. *muns* (*πρόθεσις* 'purpose', also *νόημα* 'thought', *βουλή* 'decision', etc.) : *munan* 'think' (17.14).

ON *ætlan*, fr. *ætla* 'intend' = Norw. *æsle*, Sw. dial. *ättla* : OHG *ahtōn*, NHG *achten* 'heed, observe', etc., Goth. *aha* 'mind', etc. (17.11). Walde-P. 1.169. Falk-Torp 17, 1415.

Dan. *forsæt*, fr. MLG *vorsat*, and Sw. *föresats*, fr. NHG *vorsatz*, cpds. of vbs. for 'set', and translations of Lat. *prōpositum*. Falk-Torp 264. Hellquist 1285.

Sw. *uppsåt*, fr. MLG *upsat* : *upsetten* 'set up, have as a purpose'. Hellquist 1285.

Sw. *syfte* 'aim, purpose', fr. *sikte*, this fr. MLG *sigte* 'sight' (cf. NHG *absicht*, etc.). Falk-Torp 964. Hellquist 1135, 907.

OE *ingehygd*, also 'thought, understanding', etc., cpd. of *gehygd* 'thought, meditation' : *hycgan* 'think' (17.13).

ME *entencion*, NE *intention*, fr. OFr. *entencion, intencion*, Fr. *intention*, (above, 2).

ME *porpos*, NE *purpose*, fr. OFr. *po(u)rpos*, deriv. of *porposer* 'propose, purpose', cpd. of *por-, pour-* 'for' and *poser* 'put, place', so virtually a repetition of Lat. *prōpositum* (above, 2). NED s.v.

ME *mening*, OHG *meinunga*, MHG *meinunge* : OE *mǣnan* 'have in mind, purpose, intend', OHG *meinen* 'think, mean, intend' (17.14).

Du. *voornemen*, orig. 'undertaking' (cf. NHG *vornehmen* 'undertake', vb.), cpd. of *nemen* 'take'.

Du. *doel* (hence, through cpd. vb., also *bedoeling*), lit. 'aim, goal', orig. 'a sand heap' used as a target in shooting, 'mound of earth' : MLG *doel* 'ditch' as boundary mark, OHG *tuolla*, MHG *tüele* 'small valley, depression'. Franck-v. W. 120 f.

NHG *absicht* (> Sw. *afsigt;* Dan. *hensigt* by confusion with NHG *hinsicht*), deriv. of *absehen* 'reach by the eye, foresee, aim at', etc., cpd. of *sehen* 'see'. Falk-Torp 398. Weigand-H. 1.15.

NHG *zweck*, also and orig. 'peg', fr. OHG *zwek* gl. *clavus*. Used esp. for the peg in the center of the target, hence the 'object of one's aim' and 'purpose' in general. Weigand-H. 2.1350. Kluge-G. 720.

5. Lith. *ketinimas*, fr. *ketinti* 'intend' beside *ketėti* id., this perh. fr. Slavic, ChSl. *chotěti*, etc. 'wish' (16.61). Brückner, Sl. Fremdwörter 92 (with ? Not in Skardžius).

Lith. *tikslas*, fr. the root of *tikti* 'fit, suit', hence the desired 'object, aim, purpose'. Leskien, Bildung d. Nom. 453.

Lett. *nuoduoms* : *nuoduomāt* 'intend, have in mind', cpd. of *duomāt* 'think' (17.13). Mühl.-Endz. 2.778.

6. ChSl. *pomyšlenĭje* (renders *διάνοια, διαλογισμός*, etc., but no examples where the meaning is 'purpose'), fr. *pomyšljati* 'reflect, ponder' : *mysliti* 'think' (17.13).

SCr. *namjera*, Boh. *záměr*, Pol. *zamiar*, Russ. *namerenie* : ChSl. *měriti*, etc. 'measure', general Slavic (12.54), with development in cpds. 'take the measure' > 'aim' > 'intend'. Berneker 2.50.

SCr. *svrha* 'end, goal, purpose', cpd. : *vrh* 'top' (12.33).

Boh. *úmysl*, Pol. *zamysł* : Boh. *mysl*, etc. 'mind' (17.11).

Boh. *účel* 'aim, purpose' : *čelo* 'forehead' (4.205), *čeliti* 'aim at, strive for'. Berneker 140.

7. Skt. *artha-* (also 'object, thing, affair') = Av. *arəθa-* 'affair, concern', fr. Skt., Av. *ar-* 'move, reach, attain'. Walde-P. 1.136.

Skt. *abhiprāya-*, fr. *abhipre-* 'approach', also 'approach mentally, think of, intend', cpd. (*abhi-pra-i-*) of *i-* 'go'.

Av. *xratu-* 'intelligence, reason' (17.12), also 'will, intention'. Barth. 535.

Av. *zaoša-*, lit. 'inclination, pleasure' : *zuš-* 'be pleased with, like', Skt. *juṣ-* 'taste, enjoy, love', etc. Barth. 1656 f.

17.42 CAUSE

Grk.	*αἰτία*	Goth.	*fairina*	Lith.	*priežastis*
NG	*αἰτία*	ON	*efni, vǫld*	Lett.	*vaina*
Lat.	*causa*	Dan.	*aarsag*	ChSl.	*vina*
It.	*causa, cagione*	Sw.	*orsak*	SCr.	*uzrok*
Fr.	*cause*	OE	*intinga*	Boh.	*příčina*
Sp.	*causa*	ME	*cause*	Pol.	*przyczyna*
Rum.	*cauză*	NE	*cause*	Russ.	*pričina*
Ir.	*accuiss, cōis, adbar*	Du.	*oorzaak*	Skt.	*kāraṇa-*
NIr.	*cuis, adhbhar*	OHG	*sacha*	Av.	. . . .
W.	*achos*	MHG	*ursache*		
Br.	*abeg*	NHG	*ursache*		

The Grk. and Lat. words for 'cause', both of doubtful etymology, have affected directly or indirectly much of the Eur. vocabulary for this notion. Grk. *αἰτία* denoted also esp. 'guilt, fault, charge', and the Goth. and ChSl. words are translations of it primarily in this sense. Lat. *causa* is the source of the Romance words (with ME, NE *cause*) and most of the Celtic; and some of the older Gmc. words were primarily translations of it in some of its other senses, as 'legal strife, charge', or later 'matter, subject'.

Besides the words listed, cf. the similar (though not quite identical) use of NE *reason* (cf. 17.12), NE *ground*, NHG *grund* (orig. 'foundation') or words meaning properly 'motive'.

1. Grk. *αἰτία*, see under 'fault' (16.76).

2. Lat. *causa* (> It., Sp. *causa*, Fr. *cause*, Rum. *cauză*, learned words in contrast to pop. development in It. *cosa*, Fr. *chose*, etc. 'thing'), etym. unknown. Ernout-M. 166 f. Walde-H. 1.190.

It. *cagione*, fr. Lat. *occāsiō, -ōnis* 'occasion, opportunity', sometimes also 'reason, cause'. REW 6029.

3. Ir. *accuiss*, W. *achos*, fr. Lat. *occāsiō* (above, 2). Pedersen 1.195. Vendryes, De hib. voc. 110.

Ir. *cōis*, NIr. *cuis*, fr. Lat. *causa* (above, 2). Vendryes, De hib. voc. 128.

Ir. *adbar* ('material' and 'cause'), NIr. *adhbhar*, Gael. *aobhar*, prob. cpd. fr. the root of Ir. *berim* 'carry, bring' (10.61). Macbain 18. Otherwise Pedersen 2.518.

Br. *abeg*, MBr. *abec*, orig. the 'A B C'. Cf. the OFr. and ME spelling *abece* and the uses quoted in NED s.v. (*ABC* 3). Henry 2.

4. Goth. *fairina*, the reg. word for *αἰτία* in the sense of 'guilt, fault' (16.76), is sometimes used also for *αἰτία* as simple 'cause', as 2 Tim. 1.12 *in þizei fairinōs* = *δι' ἣν αἰτίαν* 'for which cause', but this is more commonly rendered by a phrase, as Lk. 8.47 *in þizei* 'on account of what', 2 Tim. 1.6 *in þizei waihtais* 'on account of which thing'.

ON *efni* 'stuff, material, subject', also 'cause' : ON *efna*, OE *æfnan* 'perform', ON *afl*, OE *afol* 'power', Lat. *opus* 'work', etc. Walde-P. 1.176. Falk-Torp 38, 198.

ON *vǫld*, pl. of *vald* 'power'. Fritzner, s.v. *vald*, 6.

OE *intinga* (also 'matter, affair, business') : *tengan* 'hasten', *ge-tengan* 'hasten, devote oneself to', *ge-tenge* 'close to'. Walde-P. 1.790.

ME, NE *cause*, fr. Fr. *cause* (above, 2).

OHG *sacha* (reg. word for Lat. *causa*, orig. in its sense of 'legal strife, fault', etc.), hence cpd. with *ur-* 'original', MHG, NHG *ursache*, MLG *orsake* (hence the similar use of Dan. *aarsag*, Sw. *orsak*), Du. *oorzaak* : Goth. *sakjō* 'strife', OE *sacu* 'strife, lawsuit, guilt, fault', etc. Weigand-H. 2.633, 1130 f. Falk-Torp 8, 942.

5. Lith. *priežastis*, cpd. of *prie* 'near' and second part fr. **žad-ti-s* : *žadėti* 'promise', *žadas* 'voice', *prie-žada* 'vow', *žodis* 'word'. Leskien, Ablaut 374.

Lett. *vaina*, mostly 'guilt, fault' (16.76), but also simple 'cause'.

6. ChSl. *vina* (reg. word for *αἰτία*, but mostly as 'guilt, fault'), see under 'fault' (16.76).

SCr. *uzrok*, orig. 'declaration' or the like, cpd. of *uz-* 'up' and deriv. of *reći* = ChSl. *rešti* 'say' (cf. ChSl. *pro-rokŭ* 'prophet', etc.).

Boh. *příčina*, Pol. *przyczyna*, Russ. *pričina*, cpds. of Slavic *pri-* 'near, at' and deriv. of Boh. *činiti*, etc. 'do', with development of 'cause' perh. first in verb 'do, effect, cause'. Berneker 156 f.

7. Skt. *kāraṇa-*, fr. caus. stem of *kṛ-* 'do'.

17.43 DOUBT (sb.)

Grk.	ἀπιστία, διστἁγμός	Goth.	tweifl (acc. sg.)	Lith.	abejojimas, abejoné
NG	ἀμφιβολία (διστἁγμός,	ON	ef, tȳja	Lett.	šaubas
	ἀπορία)	Dan.	tvivl	ChSl.	sąmnenĭje
Lat.	dubitātiō, dubium	Sw.	tvivel	SCr.	dvojba, sumnja
It.	dubbio	OE	twēo, twēonung	Boh.	pochybnost
Fr.	doute	ME	doute	Pol.	wątpienie, wątpliwość
Sp.	duda	NE	doubt	Russ.	somnenie
Rum.	îndoială	Du.	twijfel	Skt.	saṁçaya-, saṁdeha-
Ir.	condubart, amaires	OHG	zweho, zwîfal	Av.	....
NIr.	dabht, amhras	MHG	zwîvel		
W.	ameu, petruster	NHG	zweifel		
Br.	mar, arvar				

The most common relation of words for 'doubt' is with words for 'two' or 'both', through the notion 'of two minds'. A few mean strictly 'disbelief, distrust'. Others come from various sources through the medium of notions like 'difficulty, perplexity, confusion', and especially 'hesitation'.

1. Grk. ἀπιστία, lit. 'disbelief, distrust' : ἀπιστέω 'distrust, doubt', fr. ἄπιστος 'untrustworthy, incredible', neg. of πιστός 'faithful, trustworthy' (16.65) beside πιστεύω 'believe' (17.15), etc.

Grk. διστἁγμός, δίσταγμα (neither common), fr. διστάζω 'doubt, hesitate', prob. fr. a *δίστος = Skt. dviṣṭha- 'ambiguous', etc., fr. *dwi- or *dwis- in words for 'in two, apart', related to the numeral for 'two'. Cf. Goth. tweifl, etc. (below, 4). Walde-P. 1.820. Boisacq 191.

Grk. ἀμφιβολία 'state of being attacked on both sides' (Hdt.), 'ambiguity', late also 'doubt' as reg. in NG : ἀμφίβολος 'attacked on both sides', 'ambiguous, doubtful', ἀμφιβάλλω 'put about, beset (on all sides), doubt', cpd. of ἀμφί 'about, on both sides' and βάλλω 'throw'.

Grk. ἀπορία 'difficulty, perplexity', NG 'perplexity', fr. ἄπορος orig. 'impassable' (: πέράω 'pass across', etc.), hence 'difficult'.

2. Lat. dubitātiō, deriv. of dubitāre (> Fr. douter, Sp. dudar, whence back-formations Fr. doute, Sp. duda), frequent. of dubāre (gl.) beside adj. dubius,

neut. dubium used as adv. and sb. (> It. dubbio), deriv. of a *dubus, fr. *du-bhos (cf. du-plex and pro-bus) : duo 'two'. Walde-P. 1.818. Ernout-M. 285. Walde-H. 1.375 f.

Rum. îndoială, deriv. of vb. îndoi 'doubt', lit. 'double', fr. doi 'two'. Tiktin 801.

3. Ir. condubart (contubart), fr. *com-di-fo-ber- (but no finite vb. forms quotable), cpd. of ber- in berim 'carry', etc. Pedersen 2.467.

Ir. amaires, NIr. amhras, lit. 'disbelief', neg. to Ir. ires(s) 'belief, faith' (22.11). Cf. Grk. ἀπιστία, above, 1.

Ir. dabht, fr. NE doubt.

W. ameu, etym.? Morris Jones, 264 (but??).

W. petruster, also 'hesitation', deriv. of petruso 'hesitate, doubt', petrus 'doubtful' (MW also sb. 'doubt'), apparently cpd. of intens. adj. pet (Spurrell 309) and rhus 'a start, recoil, hesitation, fear', etc.

Br. mar, cpd. arvar (ar- 'before, toward', Corn. mar, orig. 'hesitation' : Ir. maraim 'remain', Lat. mora 'delay'. Walde-P. 2.690.

4. Goth. tweifl (acc. sg., Skeir. 2.14), Du. twijfel (MLG twîvel > Dan. tvivl, Sw. tvivel), OHG zwîfal (also zwîfo, blend with zweho), MHG zwîvel, NHG zweifel; ON tȳja, OE twēo, OHG zweho; OE twēon, rare, usually twēonung; all derivs. of *dwi-, *dwei- related to the

numeral for 'two'. Walde-P. 1.818 ff. Falk-Torp 1303 f.

ON ef (NIcel. efi, Norw. eve, OSw. jæf) : OHG iba in āne iba 'without fail', prob. sb. fr. conj. ON ef, OHG ibu, OE gif 'if', Goth. interrog. particle ibai, iba, etc. Falk-Torp 1524. Torp, Nynorsk 91. Feist 286 f.

5. Lith. abejojimas, abejoné, derivs. of vb. abejoti, beside sb. abejas (only in locution be abejo 'without doubt') : abu, abeji 'both', ChSl. oba, Skt. ubhāu, Goth. bai, etc. id.

Lett. šaubas : šaubīt 'shake, waver', refl. 'doubt', Lith. siaubti 'rage', siaubytis 'waver, stagger', siūbuoti 'shake, rock', perh. also Boh. chybati 'waver, doubt', etc. (below, 6). Mühl.-Endz. 4.5. Walde-P. 1.502 f. Berneker 412 f.

6. ChSl. sąmnenĭje (in Gospels for παρατήρησις 'observation', in Supr. for εὐλάβεια 'caution' and τὸ διστάζειν 'doubt'), SCr. sumnja, Russ. somnenie :

ChSl. sąmněti sę (Supr. 'suspect, doubt', etc.; in Gospels usąmněti sę 'doubt'), cpd. of měněti 'think' (17.14).

SCr. dvojba : dvoji, dva 'two'. Berneker 247.

Boh. pochybnost, pochyba (bez pochyby 'without doubt') : chybati 'doubt, waver', Pol. chybać 'shake, move to and fro', etc. (general Slavic in related senses), Skt. kṣubh- 'shake, tremble', etc. Walde-P. 1.502 f. Berneker 188 (: Lith. skubus 'swift').

Pol. wątpienie, wątpliwość, fr. vb. wątpić : Ukr. vomp (sb.), vompyty (vb.) id., Boh. vtip 'wit', root connection? Brückner 605 (fr. *tĭp- : tep- in ChSl. tepǫ, teti 'strike'). Miklosich 352.

7. Skt. saṁçaya- : saṁ-çī- 'hesitate, doubt', cpd. of çī- 'lie' with sam- 'together'.

Skt. saṁdeha- : sam-dih- lit. 'smear, besmear, cover', in mid. 'be doubtful, uncertain', pass. 'be smeared over, be confused', cpd. of dih- 'smear'.

17.44 SUSPICION

Grk.	ὑποψία, ὑπόνοια	Goth.	anaminds	Lith.	nužiurêjimas
NG	ὑποψία, ὑπόνοια	ON	grunr	Lett.	aizduomas
Lat.	suspīciō	Dan.	mistanke	ChSl.	....
It.	sospetto	Sw.	misstanke	SCr.	sumnja
Fr.	soupçon	OE	....	Boh.	podeřreni
Sp.	sospecha	ME	suspecio(u)n, suspect	Pol.	podejrzenie
Rum.	bănueală	NE	suspicion	Russ.	podozrenie
Ir.	amaires	Du.	verdenking, achter-	Skt.	çañkā-
NIr.	(droch-)amhras		docht, argwaan	Av.	....
W.	drwgdybiaeth	OHG	argwān, zurwân		
Br.	diskred	MHG	arcwān		
		NHG	verdacht, argwohn		

Words for 'suspicion' are most commonly derived, through the verbs, from words for 'look' or 'think' with prefixes meaning 'under' or 'behind' or with pejorative force. A few are the same words that are used for 'doubt' (17.42).

1. Grk. ὑποψία, deriv. of ὑπόψομαι, fut. of ὑφοράω 'suspect', cpd. of ὑπό 'under' and ὁράω, fut. ὄψομαι 'see'.

Grk. ὑπόνοια (also 'inner sense, conjecture', etc.), deriv. of ὑπονοέω 'suspect' (and 'conjecture'), cpd. of ὑπό 'under' and νοέω 'think' (17.13).

2. Lat. suspīciō : suspicārī 'suspect', suspicere 'look up toward, admire, suspect' (hence, through pple. suspectus, It. sospetto, Sp. sospecha; VLat. *suspectiō or *suspiciō > Fr. soupçon),

cpd. of su(b)s- 'under' and specere 'see, look at'. Ernout-M. 961, 1008. REW 8484, 8488. Gamillscheg 812. Bloch 2.288.

Rum. bănueală, deriv. of banui 'suspect, imagine, presume', fr. Hung. bánni, bán 'regret, be sorry, care, be concerned' (cf. Rum. îmĭ bănuesc 'I am sorry'). Tiktin 156.

3. Ir. amaires, NIr. amhras, lit. 'disbelief', also 'doubt' (17.43), hence NIr. drochamhras, cpd. with pejorative prefix droch- 'ill-' (16.72).

W. drwgdybiaeth, cpd. of drwg = Ir. droch (above) and tybiaeth 'supposition, conjecture', deriv. of tybio 'think, suppose' (17.14).

Br. diskred, lit. 'disbelief' : diskredi 'doubt, not believe', neg. of kredi 'believe' (17.15).

4. Goth. anaminds, cpd. of ana- 'to, on' and *minds : Lat. mēns 'mind' (17.11), Goth. munan 'think' (17.13), etc., evidently a close translation of Grk. ὑπόνοια.

ON grunr, beside gruna 'suspect' (impers. grunar mik), etym. (e.g. relation to Grk. φρήν) dub. Walde-P. 1.699. Falk-Torp 353, 1474.

Dan. mistanke, Sw. misstanke, cpd. of mis-, miss- (= NE mis-, NHG miss-, etc.) and tanke 'thought'. Falk-Torp 724.

ME suspecio(u)n, NE suspicion, fr. Anglo-Fr. suspecioun = OFr. souspeçon, Fr. soupçon (above, 2). NED s.v. NE suspect, fr. Lat. suspectus (above, 2).

Du. verdenking, NHG verdacht, derivs. of Du. verdenken 'suspect', NHG ver-

denken 'find fault, take amiss', older also 'suspect', MHG verdenken 'think, remember, ponder', cpd. of denken 'think' (17.13). Weigand-H. 2.1142.

Du. achterdocht, lit. and in ODu. often 'afterthought', cpd. of achter 'behind, after' and -docht dial. for -dacht : denken 'think'. Franck-v. W. 8 f.

Du. argwaan, OHG argwān, MHG arcwān (Luther still argwahn), NHG argwohn, cpds. of arg, OHG ar(a)g 'worthless, bad', etc. (: ON argr, OE earh 'fearful, cowardly', etc.) and OHG wān, etc. 'hope, expectation' (16.56). Weigand-H. 1.83.

OHG zurwān, cpd. of pejorative prefix zur- (= ON, OE tor-, Goth. tuz-, Grk. δυσ-, etc.) and wān (cf. above).

5. Lith. nužiurêjimas, fr. nužiurêti 'suspect' (also 'observe, notice'), cpd. of nu- 'down' and žiurêti 'look, gaze' (17.13).

Lett. aizduomas, fr. aizduomāt 'suspect', cpd. of aiz 'behind' and duomāt 'think' (17.13).

6. SCr. sumnja 'doubt' (17.43), also 'suspicion'.

Boh. podezřeni, Pol. podejrzenie, Russ. podozrenie, derivs. of Boh. podezříti, Pol. podejrzeć, Russ. podozrevat' 'suspect', lit. 'look under, look from beneath', etc., cpd. of Slavic podŭ 'under', and forms related to ChSl. zĭrjǫ, zĭrĕti 'see, look'.

7. Skt. çañkā-, also 'anxiety, fear', etc. : çank- 'hesitate, be anxious, fear, distrust', etc., prob. : Lat. cunctārī 'delay', Goth. hāhan, OE hōn, hangian 'hang'. Walde-P. 1.383. Uhlenbeck 301. Ernout-M. 242. Walde-H. 1.307.

CHAPTER 18

VOCAL UTTERANCE, SPEECH; READING AND WRITING

18.11 VOICE (sb.)

Grk.	φωνή	Goth.	stibna	Lith.	balsas
NG	φωνή	ON	rǫdd, raust	Lett.	balss
Lat.	vōx	Dan.	stemme, røst	ChSl.	glasŭ
It.	voce	Sw.	röst, stämma	SCr.	glas
Fr.	voix	OE	stefn, reord	Boh.	hlas
Sp.	voz	ME	vois, steven	Pol.	głos
Rum.	voce, glas	NE	voice	Russ.	golos
Ir.	guth	Du.	stem	Skt.	vāc-
NIr.	guth, glór	OHG	stimma, stimna, rarta	Av.	vāč-
W.	llais	MHG	stimme		
Br.	mouez	NHG	stimme		

Words for 'voice' are mostly connected with verbs for 'speak, say' (18.21, 22) or are words for the more generic 'sound' (15.44), several of which (besides those repeated here) are, as including vocal sound, also frequently 'voice'.

1. Derivs. of IE *wekʷ- 'speak, say' (18.21). Walde-P. 1.245 f. Ernout-M. 1135 f.

Grk. ὄψ (poet.); Lat. vōx (> It. voce, Fr. voix, Sp. voz, Rum. lit. voce); Skt. vāc-, Av. vāč- (nom. sg. Skt. vāk, Av. vāxš); Toch. A wak, B wek.

2. Grk. φωνή : φημί 'say, speak' (18.21).

Grk. φθόγγος, see 'sound' (15.44).

3. Rum. glas, fr. Slavic (below, 7), but largely replaced in modern lit. language by voce (above). Tiktin 686.

4. Ir. guth, etym. dub., perh. : Skt. havate, Av. zavaiti 'calls', etc. (18.41). Walde-P. 1.529 (vs. Pedersen 1.108).

NIr. glór, see 'sound' (15.44).

W. llais, etym.?

Br. mouez, moez for *vouez, *voez, fr. OFr. vois. The initial v was considered a mutated consonant, e.g. da vouez 'thy voice'; hence also with the other possible reconstruction Van. boeh. Henry 207.

5. Goth. stibna, OE stefn, stemn, ME steven, Du. stem, MLG stemme (> Dan. stemme, Sw. stämma), OHG stimma, stimna, MHG stimme, etym. dub., relation to Grk. στόμα 'mouth' (as Weigand-H. 2.973, Kluge-G. 595) improbable. Walde-P. 2.648. Falk-Torp 1156 f. Feist 452.

ON rǫdd, OE reord (mostly 'speech, language'), OHG rarta (also 'melody, rhythm') : Goth. razda 'speech, language', Skt. rās- 'roar, yell, cry, sound', rasita- 'noise, roar, cry, etc.'. Walde-P. 2.342. Falk-Torp 873.

ON raust, Dan. røst (rhet.), Sw. röst : ON raus 'loud talk', rausa 'talk loudly and rapidly', ODan. ruse 'roar, hurry', MHG rūschen, NHG rauschen 'rush, roar', outside connections dub., prob. of imitative origin. Walde-P. 1.142, 2.351. Falk-Torp 938. Hellquist 876.

ME voix, vois, etc., NE voice, fr. OFr. voix, vois, etc. (above, 1). NED s.v. voice, sb.

6. Lith. balsas, Lett. balss : Lith. biliti, byloti, Lett. bilst, formerly common words for 'speak, say' (18.21).

7. ChSl. glasŭ, etc., general Slavic : Lith. galsas 'echo', ChSl. glagolŭ 'word', glagolati 'speak', etc. (18.21). Walde-P. 1.538. Berneker 323.

8. Skt. vāc-, Av. vāč-, above, 1.

18.12 SING

Grk.	ἀείδω	Goth.	siggwan	Lith.	dainuoti, giedoti
NG	τραγουδῶ	ON	syngva, gala	Lett.	dziedāt
Lat.	canere	Dan.	synge	ChSl.	pěti
It.	cantare	Sw.	sjunga	SCr.	pjevati
Fr.	chanter	OE	singan, galan	Boh.	zpívati
Sp.	cantar	ME	singe, gale	Pol.	śpiewać
Rum.	cînta	NE	sing	Russ.	pet'
Ir.	canim, gaibim	Du.	zingen	Skt.	gā-
NIr.	canaim	OHG	singan, galan	Av.	....
W.	canu	MHG	singen		
Br.	kana	NHG	singen		

Several of the words for 'sing' belong to inherited groups. In others 'sing' is specialized from 'sound, cry, utter', etc.

1. IE *kan-. Walde-P. 1.351. Ernout-M. 144 f. Walde-H. 1.154 f.

Lat. canere, frequent. cantāre (> Romance words), Umbr. kanetu 'canito'; Ir. canim, NIr. canaim, W. canu, Br. kana : Goth. hana, ON hani, etc. 'cock' (orig. 'singer'), Grk. καναχή 'noise', etc.

2. IE *gā(y)-, *gī-. Walde-P. 1.526 f.

Lith. giedoti (now esp. 'sing religious hymns' or 'sing' of birds), Lett. dziedāt; Skt. gā- (3sg. gāyati, gāti, cf. gāthā- 'song' = Av. gāθā- 'hymn') ORuss. gajati 'crow', etc.

3. Grk. ἀείδω, Att. ᾄδω, with ἀοιδός 'singer, bard', ἀοιδή, Att. ᾠδή 'song', fr. ἀϝειδ- (ϝ attested in derivs.), this prob. ἀ-ϝειδ- with prothetic a- and ϝειδ- by dissim. fr. *ϝε-ϝδ- redupl. stem with weak grade of IE *wed- (in Skt. vad- 'speak', etc.) as in ὑδέω 'praise, sing of', αὐδή 'sound, voice'. Walde-P. 1.252. Boisacq 15.

NG τραγουδῶ, fr. class. Grk. τραγῳδέω 'act, chant a tragedy', late 'chant, recite', fr. τραγῳδία 'tragedy', cpd. belonging to preceding group.

4. Ir. gaibim 'take, seize' (11.13), also 'sing' (so still NIr. gabhaim amhrān

'sing a song'). Semantic development through 'take up' the song = 'begin to sing'. Cf. the parallel development of 'bring forth' to 'say' in Ir. asbiur (18.22), NE utter, and Skt. cpds. of hr̥- 'bring' (ud-ā-, vy-ā-).

5. Goth. siggwan, OE, OHG singan, etc., general Gmc., beside sbs. Goth. saggws 'song, music, recitation', OE sang, song, etc. 'song' prob. : Grk. ὀμφή 'voice' (esp. of a god, oracle), W. dehongli 'explain, interpret'. Walde-P. 2.496. Falk-Torp 1227 f. Feist 419.

ON gala (also 'crow'), OE galan, ME gale, OHG galan (esp. 'enchant, sing incantations') : ON gjalla 'scream, shriek, shout', OHG giellan 'yell, cry out', OHG gellan 'sound, cry', Goth. göljan 'greet', Russ. galit'sja 'mock', etc. Walde-P. 1.628. Falk-Torp 296.

6. Lith. dainuoti (Lett. dial. dainuot 'sing', refl. 'dance') : Lith. daina, Lett. dain'a 'folksong', outside connections? Mühl.-Endz. 1.432.

Lith. giedoti, Lett. dziedāt, above, 2.

7. ChSl. poją, pěti, SCr. pjevati, etc., general Slavic, in part cpds., outside connections? Miklosich 245. Brückner 404.

8. Skt. gā-, above, 2.

18.13 SHOUT, CRY OUT

Grk.	βοάω, κράζω, κραυγάζω	Goth.	hrōpjan, wōpjan	Lith.	rēkti, šaukti
NG	φωνάζω	ON	œpa, kalla, hrōpa	Lett.	kliegt, saukt
Lat.	clāmāre	Dan.	raabe	ChSl.	vŭpiti, vŭzŭpiti, kričati
It.	gridare	Sw.	ropa		
Fr.	crier	OE	hrȳman, clipian, hrōpan	SCr.	kričati, vikati
Sp.	gritar			Boh.	křičeti
Rum.	striga, țipa	ME	shoute, reme, clepe, rope	Pol.	krzyczeć
Ir.	gairim			Russ.	kričat'
NIr.	gáirim, glaodhaim, screadaim	NE	shout, cry	Skt.	kruç-
		Du.	schreeuwen, roepen	Av.	xraos-
W.	bloeddio	OHG	(h)ruofan, harēn, scrīan		
Br.	krial	MHG	ruofen, schrīen		
		NHG	schreien, rufen		

Most of the words for 'shout, cry out' are of imitative origin, as are numerous others covering 'scream, screech, shriek, yell', etc. (cf. also 18.14). Several of those listed here are also used for 'call' = 'summon' (18.41).

1. Grk. βοάω, with sb. βοή 'shout, cry', prob. of imitative origin. Walde-P. 2.112. Other views in Boisacq 125.

Grk. κράζω, also and perh. orig. 'croak' (of frogs), 'caw' (of ravens), cf. κρώζω 'caw', prob. : ON hrókr, OE hrōc, etc. 'rook, raven', Skt. kharj- 'creak', khargala- 'a certain night-bird', all of imitative origin. Walde-P. 1.415. Boisacq 505.

Grk. κραυγάζω, with sb. κραυγή 'cry, shout', perh. : ON hraukr 'cormorant' (but cf. Falk-Torp 866), Goth. hruk 'crowing', hrukjan 'crow', fr. *krau-g- beside *krau-k- in ChSl. krukŭ 'raven', etc., *krau-k̑- in Skt. kruç-, Av. xraos- 'cry, shout', etc. (below, 7), all from parallel extensions of the root in κράζω (above). Walde-P. 1.417. Boisacq 511 f.

NG φωνάζω, fr. φωνή 'voice' (18.11).

2. Lat. clāmāre : calāre 'call, out, proclaim, summon', Grk. καλέω 'call, name', κέλαδος 'noise', Lett. kal'uot 'chatter', Lith. kalba 'language', etc. Walde-P. 1.443 f. Ernout-M. 136, 192. Walde-H. 1.141 f.

It. gridare, Fr. crier, Sp. gritar, fr. Lat. quirītāre 'cry plaintively, wail, scream', this prob. of imitative orig. like quirrītāre 'grunt'. Ernout-M. 844. REW 6967. Gamillscheg 278.

Rum. striga, deriv. of Lat. strix, -gis 'screech-owl'. Pușcariu 1656. Tiktin 1514 f.

Rum. țipa, doubtless based on some imitative syllable.

3. Ir. gairim, NIr. gáirim (ā fr. gāir; gairim, goirim 'call' = 'summon, name'), beside sbs. gairm and gāir 'a cry' : W. gawr 'a cry', gair 'word', Lat. garrīre 'chatter, prate', Grk. γῆρυς, Dor. γᾶρυς 'voice, speech', etc. Walde-P. 1.537. Walde-H. 1.533. Pedersen 1.144, 2.533 f.

NIr. glaodhaim, with glaodh, MIr. glóed 'a shout, cry', OIr. glaidim, gloidim 'bellow, roar', root connection? Pedersen 2.538 Anm.

NIr. screadaim, fr. sb. scread, Ir. scret : Dan. scratte 'give a cracked sound', etc. Walde-P. 1.415. Falk-Torp 1025. Loth, RC 43.151 f.

W. bloeddio, fr. bloedd 'cry, shout' = Ir. blaed 'cry, clamor', etym. dub. Walde-P. 2.211, 218.

Br. krial, fr. Fr. crier. Henry 81.

4. Goth. hrōpjan, ON hrōpa (but older sense 'slander, defame'; that of 'cry out' fr. LG rōpen > Dan. raabe, Sw.

ropa), OE hrōpan, ME rope, Du. roepen, OHG (h)ruofan, MHG ruofen, NHG rufen (now esp. 'call', 18.41) with sbs. Goth. hrōps, OHG ruof 'cry', etc., root connection dub., perh. of imitative origin. Walde-P. 1.353. Falk-Torp 865. Feist 270.

Goth. wōpjan, ON œpa : OHG wuofan, OE wēpen 'weep' (16.37). Walde-P. 1.217. Feist 572.

ON kalla, also 'call, summon' = OE callian (once; ME calle, NE call, prob. fr. ON), OHG callōn 'talk much or loud, chatter' : ChSl. glasŭ 'voice', etc. (18.11). Walde-P. 1.538. Falk-Torp 485 f. NED s.v. call.

OE hrȳman, ME reme, deriv. of OE hrēam, ME ream 'cry, outcry, tumult', cf. ON hraumi 'noisy fellow', perh. : Skt. kārava-, Lat. corvus 'raven', from an extension of the root seen in Grk. κράζω, κραυγάζω, etc. (above, 1). Walde-P. 1.417. Walde-H. 1.275.

OE clipian, ME clepe, cf. OFris. klippe 'ring', LG klippen 'sound, resound', NHG dial. kliffen 'yelp, yap', all prob. fr. an imitative syllable parallel to that in clappan 'clap', OHG claphōn 'clap, resound', etc. Cf. NHG klipp beside klapp! NED s.v. clepe, vb. Weigand-H. 1.1046.

ME shoute, NE shout : ON skúta, skúti 'taunt, jibe', prob. fr. *skeud- beside *keud- in Grk. κυδάζω, Skt. kuts- 'revile, abuse'. Walde-P. 1.378.

ME crie, NE cry, fr. Fr. crier (above, 2).

OHG scrīan, MHG schrīen, NHG schreien, Du. schreeuwen : Dan. skrige, Sw. skrika, ME shriken 'shriek, scream', etc., Grk. κρίζω 'creak, screech', ChSl. krikŭ 'a cry', vb. kričati, etc. (below, 6), all prob. fr. *(s)krei-, extension of the root seen in Grk. κράζω, etc. (above, 1). Walde-P. 1.416. Falk-Torp 1027 f. Franck-v. W. 598.

OHG harēn : Goth. hazjan, OE herian 'praise' (16.79). Walde-P. 1.358. Feist 252.

5. Lith. rēkti, also 'howl' = Lett. rēkt 'bellow, howl, bawl' : MHG ruohen 'bellow, grunt', Lat. raccāre 'roar' (of the tiger), all of imitative origin. Walde-P. 2.343. Mühl.-Endz. 3.519.

6. ChSl. vŭpiti, vŭzŭpiti, prob. of imitative origin. Iljinskij, KZ 43.177 ff. Walde-P. 1.187.

ChSl. kričati, etc. (in Gospels ἀλαλάζω 'wail', Mk. 5.38, but general modern Slavic for 'shout') : NHG schreien, etc. (above, 4). Berneker 616.

SCr. vikati : late ChSl. vyti, Boh. výti, Pol. wyć, Russ. vyt' 'howl'. Miklosich 397. Brückner 637.

7. Skt. kruç-, Av. xraos- : Grk. κραυγάζω, etc. (above, 1).

18.14. Words denoting various cries, especially of animals. These are very numerous and are nearly all of imitative origin. In general there is a high degree of differentiation between expressions for the cries of different animals. On the other hand, a single word may be used for a great variety of cries. Thus Grk. φθέγγομαι 'make a sound' is applied to the human voice and the cries of the eagle ('scream'), raven ('croak'), and birds in general, also the horse ('neigh'), fawn, and even sounds made by worms and fish. The verbs for 'sing' frequently cover the cock's 'crow' and several different bird cries.

To trace the many words of this type through many of the IE languages would require an altogether disproportionate space. But it is feasible here to quote the verbs for some of the distinctive cries in a few languages, omitting discussion (which is superfluous in view of the obvious imitative origin) and references. To illustrate still further the great variety, many other NE words are added.

1. 'Bark' (esp. dog). Grk. ὑλακτέω, NG γαβγίζω, Lat. *latrāre* (> Sp. *ladrar*, Rum. *latra*), It. *abbaiare*, Fr. *aboyer* (OFr. *bayer*, ME *baye*, NE *bay*, used of large dogs), NE *bark* (OE *beorcan*), NHG *bellen*, Lith. *loti*, Russ. *lajat'*.

2. 'Bellow' (cattle). Grk. μυκάομαι, Lat. *mugīre* (> It. *muggire*, Fr. *mugir*, etc.; Fr. also *beugler*), Ir. *burim* (cf. Loth, RC 41.372 f.), NE *bellow* (NE *low* and *moo*, now of cows), NHG *brüllen*, Russ. *myčat'*, *revet'*.

3. 'Bleat' (sheep, goat, calf). Grk. βληχάομαι, Lat. *balāre*, late *bēlāre* (> Fr. *bêler*, etc.), NE *bleat*, NHG *blöcken*, Russ. *blejat'*.

4. 'Croak' (a of frog, b of raven or crow, the latter NE *caw*). Grk. κράζω (a, b), κρώζω (b), late Lat. *coaxāre* (a; > Fr. *coasser*), *crōcire* (b; > Fr. *croasser* b, rarely a; form influenced by *coasser*), NE *croak* (a, b), NHG *quaken* (a; also 'quack' of ducks), *krächsen* (b), Russ. *kvakat'* (a), *karkat'* (b).

5. 'Crow' (cock). Commonly covered by the words for 'sing' (18.12), as Grk. ἀείδω, Lat. *canere*, Fr. *chanter*, Russ. *pet'*, but also special words as NE *crow*, NHG *krähen*.

6. 'Growl'. Lat. *fremere*, Fr. *grogner*, NE *growl*, NHG *knurren*, Russ. *vorcat'*.

7. 'Grunt' (swine). Grk. γρυλίζω, Lat. *grunnīre* (> Fr. *grogner*, also 'growl'), NE *grunt*, NHG *grunzen*, Russ. *chrjokat'*.

8. 'Hiss' (serpent). Grk. συρίζω, Lat. *sībilāre*, *sīfilāre* (> Fr. *siffler*), NE *hiss*, NHG *zischen*, Russ. *šipet'*.

9. 'Howl' (dog, wolf, etc.). (Grk. ὀλολύζω not used of animals), Lat. *ululāre* (> Fr. *hurler*), NE *howl*, NHG *heulen*, Russ. *vyt'*.

10. 'Mew' (cat). NG νιαουρίζω, Fr. *miauler*, NE *mew*, NHG *miauen*, Russ. *mjaukat'*.

11. 'Neigh' (horse). Grk. χρεμετίζω, Lat. *hinnīre* (> Fr. *hennir*), NE *neigh* (dial. *nicher*, *nicker*), *whinny*, NHG *wiehern*, Russ. *ržat'*.

12. 'Roar' (lion, etc.). Grk. βρυχάομαι, Lat. *fremere*, *rugīre* (> Fr. *rugir*), NHG *brüllen*, Russ. *revet'*.

Cf. also NE *baa* (sheep), *buzz*, *hum*, *drone* (insects), *bray* (donkey), *bugle* (moose), *cackle* (hen), *caw* (crow), *cheep* (young birds, mice, etc.), *chirp* (small birds), *cluck* (hen), *gobble* (turkey), *hoot* (owl), *low* (cattle), *moo* (cattle), *peep* (young birds, etc.), *purr* (cat, etc.), *quack* (duck), *scream*, *screech*, *snarl*, *snort*, *squeak*, *squeal*, *squawk*, *trumpet* (elephant), *twitter*, *warble*, *whine*, *whistle*, *yap*, *yelp*, *yowl*.

18.21 SPEAK, TALK

Grk.	λέγω (aor. εἶπον, fut. ἐρῶ, etc.), ἀγορεύω, λαλῶ	Goth.	*rōdjan*, *maþljan*	Lith.	*kalbėti*
NG	μιλῶ	ON	*mæla*, *rœða*, *tala*	Lett.	*runāt*
Lat.	*loquī*, *fārī*	Dan.	*tale*, *snakke*	ChSl.	*glagolati*, *věštati*
It.	*parlare*	Sw.	*tala*, *språka*	SCr.	*govoriti*
Fr.	*parler*	OE	*sprecan*, *mǣlan*, *mæþlan*	Boh.	*mluviti*
Sp.	*hablar*	ME	*speke*, *mele*, *talk(i)e*, *tal(i)e*	Pol.	*mówić*
Rum.	*vorbi*, *grăi*, *cuvînta*	NE	*speak*, *talk*	Russ.	*govorit'*
Ir.	*labrur*, *rādim*	Du.	*spreken*, *praten*	Skt.	*vac-*, *brū-*, *vad-*, *bhāṣ-*
NIr.	*labhraim*	OHG	*sprehhan*, *redōn*, *mahelen*	Av.	*vač-*, *mrū-*, *aoj-*
W.	*llefaru*, *siarad*	MHG	*sprechen*, *reden*		
Br.	*komz*	NHG	*sprechen*, *reden*		

In the majority of the IE languages there are distinctive verbs for 'speak', denoting the actual speech activity, and for 'say' with emphasis on the result rather than the action. But the commonest classical Greek and Indo-Iranian words cover both uses, and some words belonging to the same cognate group may mean 'speak' in one language and 'say' in another. In several cases a transition from 'speak' to 'say' is attested or indicated by the etymology. Even where the distinction holds in the main, there is some overlapping (e.g. NHG *sprechen* in Luther's time often used with direct and indirect quotations).

Verbs for 'speak' are often cognate with words denoting various sounds, partly of imitative origin. Some were used first in a depreciatory sense, 'babble, chatter, prattle', etc., then as colloquial and finally standard words for 'speak'. Cf. the loss of depreciatory sense in NE *chat* vs. *chatter*, the increasing encroachment of NE *talk* upon *speak*, and the history of Grk. λαλῶ and others (below). Some are derived from nouns for 'assembly', used first for 'speak in the assembly, harangue' and then more generally; others from nouns for 'speech, saying, word'. Some are cognate with words for 'reason, plan, reckon, count' or 'pick out, select', or 'consort with' (cf. the specialization in NE *converse*, *conversation*), with secondary specialization to vocal expression.

Words for 'say' (apart from those which mean also, or are from, 'speak') are based on notions like 'point out, make clear, make known', 'bring forth', 'arrange, order, make', etc.

Cf. Buck, Words of Speaking and Saying, AJP 36.1 ff., 125 ff., where many words not included here (obsolete, colloquial, dialectal, etc.) are discussed. For exhaustive details of the usage of the Grk. words, cf. H. Fournier, Les verbes "dire" en grec ancien.

Groups that belong in part under both headings are discussed here.

1. IE *wek^w- in words for 'speak' or 'say', also 'word', 'voice', etc.—primary sense 'give vocal utterance', hence properly 'speak', secondary 'say'. Walde-P. 1.245. Ernout-M. 1135 f.

Skt. *vac-*, Av. *vač-* 'speak, say'; Grk. aor. εἶπον, εἶπα 'spoke, said' (NG εἶπα mostly 'said') by dissim. fr. *ἐ-ϝε-υπον = Skt. aor. *avocam*. Cf. Skt. *vacas-*, Av. *vačah-*, Grk. ἔπος (ϝέπος) 'word', Skt. *vāc-*, Lat. *vōx*, etc., 'voice' (18.11), Lat. *vocāre* 'call', OPruss. *wackis* 'cry', etc.

2. Grk. λέγω, in Hom. 'pick out, select', also 'collect, enumerate, recount', later the usual word for both 'speak' and 'say' (NG 'say') : Lat. *legere* 'pick out, select' (whence 'read'), etc. Walde-P. 1.422. Walde-H. 1.780.

Grk. aor. εἶπον, above, 1.

Grk. fut. ἐρῶ, perf. εἴρηκα, aor. pass. ἐρρήθην (pres. εἴρω Hom., but not common), common in Hom. and later supplementing λέγω in both senses, beside derivs. ῥήτωρ 'public speaker', ῥῆμα 'word, saying', ῥήτρα 'agreement, covenant', fr. ϝερ-, ϝρη- (cf. Arg. ϝεϝρημένος, El. ϝράτρα, etc.), IE **wer-* seen elsewhere in derivs. as Lat. *verbum*, OE *word*, etc. 'word', Av. *urvāta-* 'command', Skt. *vrata-* 'command, vow', etc. Walde-P. 1.283 f. Ernout-M. 1088 f. Here also Hitt. *weriya-* 'call, summon' (Pedersen-Goetze, Muršilis Sprachlähmung 74).

Grk. ἀγορεύω, orig. 'speak in the assembly, harangue' (fr. ἀγορά 'assembly') but already in Hom. one of the most general terms for 'speak', though in Attic largely replaced by λέγω.

Grk. λαλέω, in the class. period 'babble, chatter', but the usual Hellenistic vb. for 'speak', reg. in NT and down through the medieval period. Of imitative orig., cf. Lat. *lallāre* 'lull to sleep', NHG *lallen* 'stutter, mumble', etc. Walde-P. 2.376.

NG pop. μιλῶ (lit. ὁμιλῶ), fr. Grk. ὁμιλέω 'consort with, join battle with, be familiar with, etc.', also (Xen.+) 'converse with', and common in this sense in Hellenistic Grk., now the usual word for 'speak' (replacing λαλῶ).

3. Lat. *loquī*, etym. dub., perh. of imitative orig. fr. a syllable similar to, though not identical with, that in Grk. λάσκω, ἔλακον 'ring, crash, shriek, howl' and (esp. Att. poet.) 'utter, tell'. Walde-P. 2.377. Ernout-M. 561 f. Walde-H. 1.821.

Lat. *fārī* (poet. and arch.) : Grk. φημί, Dor. φᾱμί 'say', OE *bōian* 'boast', Russ.-ChSl. *bajati* 'tell, heal', Russ. dial. *bajat'* 'speak', etc. (Berneker 39), OE *bannan* 'summon', etc., prob. ultimately the same root as in Skt. *bhā-* 'shine', Grk. φαίνω 'make clear, show'. Walde-P. 2.123 f. Ernout-M. 375 f. Walde-H. 1.437 f. Buck, op. cit. 127. Hence *fābula* 'conversation, dialogue, story', with derivs. *fābulārī* and *fābulāre*, colloq. word for 'speak, talk' since Plautus, whence the Romance derivs. of which Sp. *hablar* is the standard word. REW 3125.

It. *parlare*, Fr. *parler*, derivs. of VLat. *parabola* 'word' (> Fr. *parole*, etc. 18.26).

Rum. *vorbi*, with sb. *vorbă* 'saying, talk', prob. a loanword but of uncertain source. Densusianu 1.74 (not fr. Lat. *verbum*). Tiktin 1771 (fr. Slavic). Diculescu, Z. rom. Ph. 41.427 (fr. Gmc.).

Rum. *grăi* (with *graiu* 'speech, language'), fr. Slavic, cf. SCr. *grājati* 'crow', *grájati* 'talk loud, talk'. Tiktin 695. Berneker 344.

Rum. *cuvînta*, deriv. of *cuvînt* 'word, talk' (18.26).

4. Ir. *labrur*, NIr. *labhraim*, W. *llefaru* 'speak' (MW also 'say'), Corn. *leverel*, 1sg. *lavaraf*, Br. *lavarout* 'say', beside Ir. *labar* 'loquacious', *amlobar* 'dumb', W. *llafar* 'speech, sound', Br. *lavar* 'word, idiom, language', W. *aflafar* 'speechless', etc., perh. : LG *flappen* 'strike, clap, chatter', NE *flap*, etc., all of imitative origin. Walde-P. 2.93. Stokes 239.

Ir. *rādim* 'speak' and 'say', cf. MW *ad-rawdd* 'relate', etc. : Goth. *rōdjan* 'speak' (below, 5).

W. *siarad*, also and orig. sb. 'talk', a loanword certainly to be connected with NE, Fr. *charade*, but in meaning much closer to the orig. Prov. *charrada* 'conversation' (fr. the vb. *charra* 'chat, talk', of imitative origin, REW 2451). Parry-Williams 79.

Br. *komz*, MBr. *comps*, Corn. *cows*, also and orig. sb. 'talk', prob. a cpd. of **kom-* and **med-tu-*, fr. the root of Ir. *midiur* 'judge', W. *meddwl* 'think', etc. (17.13). Cf., fr. the same root, Br. *eme*, W. *medd*, Corn. *meth* 'inquit'; also the semantically parallel NG dial. κρένω 'speak' = κρίνω 'judge' and Pol. *gadać* 'speak, talk' = ChSl. *gadati* 'think, suppose' (Berneker 288). Pedersen 1.170, 2.580. Ernault, Dict. étym. s.v. *comps*.

5. Goth. *rōdjan*, ON *rœða* : Goth. *garēdan* 'be mindful of', ON *rāða*, OE *rǣdan* 'advise, plan, rule, explain, read', OHG *rātan* 'advise, consider, interpret', ChSl. *raditi* 'care, be anxious', Skt. *rādh-* 'perform, achieve, carry out, prepare', Ir. *rādim* 'speak', *imm-rādim* 'think about, consider', all fr. **rē-dh-*, beside **rē-t-* in OHG *red(i)ōn*, *redinōn*, MHG, NHG *reden* 'speak', Goth. *garaþjan* 'count', Lat. *ratio* 'account, consideration, reason', etc., extensions of the root in Lat. *rērī* 'believe, think, reckon, calculate', etc. Walde-P. 1.73 ff. Feist 400.

Goth. *maþljan*, ON *mæla*, OE *maþelian*, *mæþlan*, *mǣlan*, ME *mele*, OHG *mahelen* (but the last mostly 'promise'), MHG *maheln*, *mālen* 'summon before court, promise, give in marriage', NHG *ver-māhlen*), derivs. of Goth. *maþl* 'assembly, market', ON *māl* 'speech, suit, action, cause', OE *mæþel* 'assembly, council, speech', OHG *mahal* 'court, compact', etc., all orig. 'meeting (place), assembly', fr. the root of Goth. *gamōtjan*, ON *mœta*, OE *mētan* 'meet'. Semantic development as in Grk. ἀγορεύω (above, 2). Walde-P. 2.304. Falk-Torp 285 f. Feist 349 f.

ON *tala*, Dan. *tale*, Sw. *tala*, ME *talie*, *tale* (cf. NED s.v. *tale*, vb. 5, 6, but OE *talian* only 'account, reckon', etc.), and deriv. forms ME *talkie*, *talke*, NE *talk* (cf. NED s.v.), also OE *tellan*, ME *telle*, NE *tell* 'count, tell' (rarely 'speak'; NED s.v. 13, 15), OHG *zalōn* 'count' (NHG *zahlen*), and *zellan* 'count, reckon, relate, tell' (NHG *zählen*, *erzählen*), with sbs. ON *tal* 'talk, series, number', OE *talu* 'tale, talk, charge, case' (NE *tale*), Du. *taal* 'language', OHG *zala* 'inheritance, order, series, account', etc. (NHG *zahl*), outside root connections (as with Grk. δόλος, Lat. *dolus* 'deceit'; see 16.68) dub. Walde-P. 1.808. Falk-Torp 1243.

Dan. *snakke*, lit. 'chatter, chat', but also pop. 'talk, speak' (*snakke dansk*, *engelsk*, etc.), with sb. *snak*, like Sw. *snacka*, *snak* 'chatter', fr. MLG *snacken*, *snack* 'talk, chatter, prattle' (NHG *schnacken* 'prattle'), belonging with NE *snack* 'snap, bite, seize', Dan. *snage* 'snuff about', etc., prob. of imitative origin. Falk-Torp 1089. Walde-P. 1.397.

OE *sprecan* and (later) *specan*, ME *speke*, NE *speak*, Du. *spreken*, OHG *sprehhan* (rarely also *spehhan*), MHG, NHG *sprechen*, with sbs. OE *sprǣc*, NE *speech*, OS *sprāka*, MLG *sprāke* (> Dan. *sprog*, Sw. *språk*, whence vb. *språka* 'talk'), OHG *sprācha*, NHG *sprache*, etc. (the history of the *r*-less forms is obscure, but they are undoubtedly of secondary origin) : ON *spraka*, Dan. *sprage* 'crackle', Grk. σφαραγέω 'crackle, sputter, hiss', Lith. *spragėti* 'crackle', Skt. *sphūrj-* 'crackle, rustle, rumble'. Cf. NE *crack*, dial. 'chat, talk' (NED s.v. 7). Walde-P. 2.673. Falk-Torp 1134.

Du. *praten*, cf. MLG *praten*, *proten*, Icel., Sw. *prata* 'chatter, prate', NE *prate*, etc., prob. of imitative origin. Falk-Torp 847. NED s.v. *prate*. Franck-v. W. 520 (: Pol. *bredzić* 'chatter, prattle', but cf. Berneker 83).

6. Lith. *kalbėti*, with *kalba* 'speech, language' : Lett. *kaluot* 'chatter', OPruss. *kelsāi* 'they sound', Grk. κέλαδος 'noise, din', καλέω 'call, name', Lat.

calāre 'call together', *clāmāre* 'call', etc. Walde-P. 1.445.

OPruss. *billit* (renders NHG *sprechen* and *sagen*, but *waitiatun* for *reden*), OLith. *bilti*, *byloti*, common word for 'speak, say' (*byloti* now 'litigate'), Lett. *bilst* 'speak, say' (not common) : Lith. *balsas* 'voice', OE *bellan* 'roar', Skt. *bhāṣ-* (**bhel-s-*) 'speak', etc. Walde-P. 2.182.

Lett. *runāt*, with sb. *runa*, prob. loanword fr. some form of the Gmc. group seen in OE *rūnian*, OHG *rūnēn* 'whisper', ON *rȳna* 'speak confidentially' (with Goth. *rūna* 'secret', ON, OE *rūn* 'secret, rune', Ir. *rūn*, W. *rhin* 'secret', etc.; Walde-P. 2.350). Mühl.-Endz. 3.560 (but regarding Lett. form as cognate, not loanword).

7. ChSl. *glagolati* (cf. Russ. dial *gologolit'* 'babble, joke'), beside *glagolŭ* 'word', etc., fr. redupl. form of root in *glasŭ* 'voice', etc. (18.11). Walde-P. 1.538. Berneker 321.

ChSl. *věštati*, with *otŭ-věštati* 'answer', *vŭz-věštiti*, *-věštati* 'announce', *vě* = εἶπε : OPruss. *waitiatun* 'speak', further connections dub. Walde-P. 1.246. Trautmann, Altpreuss. 455 f.

SCr. *govoriti*, Russ. *govorit'* (but Boh. *hovořiti* 'chat, converse') = ChSl. *govoriti* 'make a noise', fr. the sb. *govorŭ* 'noise' (in modern Slavic freq. 'speech, language, dialect') : Lith. *gausti* 'howl', OE *cīegan* 'call', OHG *gikewen* 'call, name', Grk. γοάω 'lament', Skt. *gu-* 'sound', etc. Walde-P. 1.635. Berneker 339.

Boh. *mluviti*, Pol. *mówić* = Russ. *molvit'* 'utter', ChSl. *mlŭviti* 'make a disturbance', beside sbs. Boh. *mluva* 'speech', etc., ChSl. *mlŭva* 'tumult', prob. : Skt. *brū-*, Av. *mrū-* 'speak, say', but disputed (see below, 8).

8. Skt. *vac-*, Av. *vač-*, above, 1.

Skt. *brū-*, Av. *mrū-*, disputed whether fr. IE **mreu-* with dub. connections or fr. **mleu-* and connected with ChSl. *mlŭva* 'tumult', Boh. *mluviti* 'speak', etc. (above, 7). Walde-P. 2.313.

Skt. *bhāṣ-* (**bhel-s-*) and *bhaṇ-* (**bhel-n-*) : Lith. *balsas* 'voice', OPruss. *billit*, OLith. *byloti* 'speak, say', etc. (above, 7).

Skt. *vad-* : ChSl. *vaditi* 'accuse', Lith. *vadinti* 'call, name', Grk. αὐδάω 'speak, say' (Hom. and poet.), etc. Walde-P. 1.251 f.

Av. *aoj-*, esp. 3sg. pret. mid. *aoxta* (Gath. *aogədā*) 'spoke, said' (esp. in a formal, solemn sense) : Skt. *ūh-* 'observe, regard, consider', Grk. εὔχομαι 'pray, vow, boast', Lat. *vovēre* 'vow', etc. Walde-P. 1.110. Barth. 37 f. Ernout-M. 1135.

18.22 SAY

Grk.	*λέγω, φημί,* aor. *εἶπον,* fut. *ἐρῶ*	Goth.	*qiþan*	Lith.	*sakyti, tarti*
NG	*λέγω,* aor. *εἶπα*	ON	*segja, kveða*	Lett.	*teikt, sacīt*
Lat.	*dīcere*	Dan.	*sige*	ChSl.	*rešti, pověděti*
It.	*dire*	Sw.	*säga*	SCr.	*kazati, reći*
Fr.	*dire*	OE	*cweþan, secgan*	Boh.	*říci, praviti, pověděti*
Sp.	*decir*	ME	*saye, quethe*	Pol.	*rzec, powiedzieć*
Rum.	*zice*	NE	*say*	Russ.	*skazat'*
Ir.	*asbiur*	Du.	*zeggen*	Skt.	*vac-, brū-,* etc.
NIr.	*(a)deirim*	OHG	*quedan, sagēn*	Av.	*vač-, mrū-, aoj-,* OPers. *θah-*
W.	*dywedyd*	MHG	*sagen, queden*		
Br.	*lavarout*	NHG	*sagen*		

For verbs for 'speak' and 'say' in general, and those that cover both senses, see 18.21.

Besides the usual verbs for 'say', there are often more isolated forms which are common in the parenthetical use, before or after direct quotations, like Lat. *inquit*. These are not included in the list, but several are noticed in the discussion, where this use is conveniently shown by the rendering 'inquit' (some are restricted to the third person, others not). Cf. also such use of verbs for 'do, make' or 'put' (through 'make a response', etc.) as forms of It. *fare*, Fr. *faire*, NG κάνω, Boh. *diti*, etc. Buck, op. cit. 134. Spitzer, "Romanisch *facit* 'er sagt'", Stilstudien 1.223. Berneker 192. Here also Hitt. *tezzi* 'says', fr. *dāi-*, *te-* 'put' (IE **dhē-*, 12.12). Goetze-Pedersen, Muršilis Sprachlähmung 68. Cf. Toch. A *plāc wāwim* 'might speak (lit. lead) a word'.

1. IE **sek^w-* in words for 'say, tell', prob. orig. 'point out' (as in ChSl. *sočiti*) and ultimately the same as **sek^w-* in words for 'follow' (10.52) and 'see' (15.51), though the semantic relations may be variously interpreted. Walde-P. 2.477 ff. Ernout-M. 489. Falk-Torp 963. Buck, op. cit. 128 f.

Grk. ἔννεπε; Lat. *inseque*, *insece* 'relate, tell', Umbr. *pru-sikurent* 'pronuntiaverint', Lat. *inquam* (*-quis*, *-quit*) 'say'; OW *hepp*, W. *eb* 'inquit'; ON *segja*, OE *secgan*, OHG *sagēn*, general Gmc. (except Goth.) for 'say' (but connection rejected by Collitz, Praet. 78 ff.); Lith. *sakyti*, Lett. *sacīt*; Arm. *ogem* 'say'.

2. Grk. λέγω, aor. εἶπον, fut. ἐρῶ, etc., see 18.21.

Grk. φημί 'say, affirm' : Lat. *fārī* 'speak', etc. (18.21).

3. Lat. *dīcere* (> Romance words), Osc. *deicum* 'dicere', orig. 'point out' (preserved in *index*, *indicāre*) : OHG *zeigōn*, Grk. δείκνῡμι, Skt. *diç-* 'point out, show' (15.55). A late parallel development of Skt. *diç-* as 'say' is attested in Buddhistic Hybrid Sanskrit and in Apabhraṅça, as Professor F. Edgerton informs me. Walde-P. 1.766. Ernout-M. 265 ff. Walde-H. 1.348.

Lat. *aiō* (*ais*, *ait*, etc., infin. rare), early 'say yes, affirm', whence weakened 'say', fr. **agyō*, cf. *ad-agiō* 'proverb', *prōdigium* 'portent' : Grk. ἦ 'spoke', ἄν-ωγα (perf.) 'command', Arm. *asem* 'say'. Walde-P. 1.114. Ernout-M. 29 f. Walde-H. 1.24 f.

4. Ir. *asbiur*, lit. 'bring forth', cpd. of *as-*, pretonic for *ess-* = Lat. *ex*, and *berim* 'carry'. Hence NIr. *adeirim* (usually spoken *deirim*), fr. forms with infixed pronoun, Ir. *at-beir* 'he says it'. Pedersen 2.466, 1.469.

Ir. *ol*, NIr. *ar* 'inquit', orig. an adv. of pronominal origin. Pedersen 1.273, 2.141. Havers, KZ 44.26 ff.

W. *dywedyd*, beside OW *guetid* 'says' prob. fr. the same root as W. *gwadu* 'deny', Lat. *vetāre* 'forbid'. Stokes 268. Loth, RC 42.362 f., 367 f.

Br. *lavarout* : Ir. *labrur* 'speak' (18.21).

W. *medd*, Br. *eme* 'inquit', see under Br. *komz* 'speak' (18.21).

5. Goth. *qiþan*, ON *kveða* (Dan. *kvæde*, Sw. *kväda* 'sing, chant'), OE *cweþan*, ME *quethe* (past tense in NE *quoth* now arch.), OHG *quedan*, MHG *queden*, cf. ON *kveðja* 'call on, address, request, summon, welcome', OS *queddian*, OHG *chetten* 'greet', outside connections dub. Walde-P. 1.672. Feist 289 f.

ON *segja*, OE *secgan*, etc., above, 1.

6. Lith. *sakyti*, Lett. *sacīt*, above, 1.

Lith. *tarti* : OPruss. *tarīn* 'voice', Russ. *torotorit'* 'chatter, prattle', ChSl. *trŭtorŭ* 'noise', Ir. *torann*, W. *taran* 'thunder', Grk. τορός, Skt. *tāra-* 'piercing' (esp. of sound). Walde-P. 1.744.

Lett. *teikt* : Lith. *-teikti* (in cpds. *įteikti*, *suteikti*, etc.) 'put at one's disposal, bestow, impart', OPruss. *teickut* 'make', Lith. *tikti* 'fit, suit', *tikras* 'correct, real' (root connection dub.; cf. Walde-P. 1.725). Semantic development prob. 'bestow, impart' > 'inform, tell' > 'say'. Mühl.-Endz. 4.157. Buck op. cit. 133.

7. ChSl. *reką*, *rešti*, SCr. *reći*, Boh. *říci*, Pol. *rzec* (once the general Slavic for 'say', but obs. in Russ., and elsewhere much encroached upon by other words) : Toch. A *rake*, B *reki* 'word', and prob. ChSl. *rokŭ* 'fixed time, goal', Russ. *rok* 'fate, destiny, lot', Skt. *rac-* 'produce, fashion, form', Goth. *rahnjan* 'reckon', etc. Walde-P. 2.362.

ChSl. *pověděti* in Gospels mostly 'tell' (renders ἀπαγγέλλω, διηγέομαι, etc., but also frequently εἶπε, λέγω; cf. Jagić, Entstehungsgesch. 287, 335, etc.), Boh. *pověděti*, Pol. *powiedzieć*, orig. 'let know' : *věděti* 'know', Grk. οἶδα, Skt. *vid-* 'know', etc. (17.17). Cf. Skt. *vedaya-* (caus.) 'tell', Ir. *ad-fiadat* 'they tell'.

SCr. *kazati*, Russ. *s-kazat'* = ChSl. *kazati* 'show' (15.55), Boh. *kázati*, Pol. *kazać* 'preach'. Berneker 497.

Boh. *praviti* (Pol. *prawić* 'talk, prate') = ChSl. *praviti* 'set right, direct, guide', deriv. of *pravŭ* 'straight' (12.73). Specialization to speech West-Slavic.

8. Skt. and Av. words, see 18.21.

OPers. *θah-* regular verb for 'say' (e.g. *θātiy Dārayavauš* 'saith Darius', *čiščiy θastanaiy pariy Gaumātam* 'say anything about Gaumāta', cf. Buck, op. cit. 130 ftn.), like Alb. *thom* 'say', ChSl. *sętŭ* 'inquit' : Skt. *çaṅs-* 'recite, announce, praise', Av. *sąh-* 'recite, announce', prob. Lat. *cēnsēre* 'be of the opinion, resolve, assess', etc. Walde-P. 1.403. Ernout-M. 174. Walde-H. 1.199.

18.23 BE SILENT

Grk.	*σιωπάω, σῑγάω*	Goth.	*þahan, slawan*	Lith.	*tylėti*
NG	*σιωπῶ, σωπαίνω*	ON	*þegja*	Lett.	*klusēt*
Lat.	*tacēre, silēre*	Dan.	*tie*	ChSl.	*mlŭčati*
It.	*tacere*	Sw.	*tiga*	SCr.	*ćutjeti, mučati*
Fr.	*se taire*	OE	*swīgan*	Boh.	*mlčeti*
Sp.	*callar*	ME	*swi(ȝ)e*	Pol.	*milczeć*
Rum.	*tăcea*	NE	*be silent*	Russ.	*molčat'*
Ir.	*ar-tuaissi, tōaim*	Du.	*zwijgen*	Skt.	*tūṣṇīṁ bhū-*
NIr.	*taim im'thost*	OHG	*swīgēn, dagēn*	Av.	(*tušni-* 'silently')
W.	*tewi*	MHG	*swīgen*		
Br.	*tevel*	NHG	*schweigen*		

The majority of the words for 'be silent' belong to one of three inherited groups, covering respectively Lat.-Gmc., Celtic-Baltic-Indo-Iranian, and Grk.-Gmc. Some are related to words for 'cease' (cf. NE *stop!* or *be still!* addressed to a speaker), or 'listen' (as conversely 'be silent, be still!' may suggest 'listen'), or through 'be quiet' with words for 'weak, slack, sleep', etc.

1. IE **takē-*. Walde-P. 1.703. Ernout-M. 1011 f. Feist 487 f. REW 8517. Gamillscheg 829.

Lat. *tacēre* (> It. *tacere*, OFr. *taisir*, Fr. *se taire*, Rum. *tăcea*); Goth. *þahan*, ON *þegja* (beside *þegna* 'become silent', *þagga* 'silence'), Dan. *tie*, Sw. *tiga*, OHG *dagēn*, OS *thagian*, *thagōn*.

2. IE **teus-*. Walde-P. 1.714 f. Pedersen 1.55, 2.651 f.

Ir. *ar-tuaissi* (3sg., with *ar-*, 'listen', beside *contuasi* id.), with adj. *tō* 'silent', whence MIr. *tōaim* 'be silent', sb. *tost* 'silence' (in phrase NIr. *tāim im thost*, lit. 'I am in my silence', cf. MIr. *boi Cuchulaind ina thost* 'C. was silent', Windisch 842), W. *tewi*, Br. *tevel* (derivs. of sbs. W. *taw*, Br. *tao* 'silence'); Skt. *tūṣṇīm* adv. 'silently, in silence', with *bhū-* 'be or become silent' (vb. *tuṣ-* 'become calm, be satisfied, etc.'), Av. *tušni-* in *tušni-šad* 'sitting silently', etc.; OPruss. *tuīsse* 'er schweige', *tusnan* 'quiet', Lith. *tausytis* 'subside' (of the wind).

3. IE **swī-g-*, **swī-k-*, perh. as 'cease speaking' extensions of a simple root **swī-* in ON *svīa* 'abate', OHG *swīnan* 'abate, disappear', cf. also **swī-p-* in Goth. *sweiban* 'cease, abate', ON *svīfask* 'shrink, hesitate'. Walde-P. 2.534.

Grk. σῑγάω, sb. σῑγή; OE *swīgan*, *swigian*, ME *swiȝe*, *swie*, Du *zwijgen*, OHG *swīgēn*, *swīgōn*, MHG *swīgen*, NHG *schweigen*.

Here prob. also Grk. σιωπάω, NG σιωπῶ, σωπαίνω, fr. **swiyō-p-*. Boisacq 867. Walde-P. l.c.

4. Lat. *silēre*, prob. : Goth. *ana-silan* 'abate' (of the wind), and as orig. 'cease speaking' (cf. above, 3), fr. the root of Lat. *sinere* 'let, permit', *dēsinere* 'leave off, cease', etc.? Walde-P. 2.462. Feist 44.

Sp. *callar*, fr. VLat. **calāre* (It. *calare* 'let down the anchor'), fr. Grk. χαλάω 'slacken, let down'. REW 1487.

5. Goth. *slawan*, etym.? Walde-P. 2.708. Feist 437.

NE *silent* in phrase *be silent*, fr. pres. pple. of Lat. *silēre* (above, 4).

6. Lith. *tylėti*, with *tylus* 'silent', *tilti* 'become silent' : ChSl. (*u*)*toliti* trans. 'quiet, still' (hunger, thirst), Ir. *tuilim* 'sleep'. Walde-P. 1.740 f.

Lett. *klusēt*, with *kluss* 'still, quiet', *klust* 'become silent' : *klausīt*, Lith. *klausyti* 'listen, heed' (15.42). Mühl.-Endz. 2.237 (216).

7. ChSl. *mlŭčati*, SCr. *mučati*, Boh. *mlčeti*, Pol. *milczeć*, Russ. *molčat'*, beside ChSl. *umlŭčiti* 'restrain, subdue', *umlŭknąti* 'become silent', etym. dub., perh. : SCr., Bulg. *mlak* 'tepid', SCr. *mlahav*, *mlohav* 'weak', Ir. *malcaim* 'rot', Grk. μαλακός 'soft'. Walde-P. 2.290.

SCr. *ćutjeti* in this sense since 17th. cent. (Rječnik Akad. s.v. *ćutjeti* 2) = *ćutjeti* 'perceive' (ChSl. *štutiti*, etc., 15.11), also *šutjeti* with dial. interchange of *ć*/*š*. Leskien, Serbo-kroat. Gram. § 64. Semantic development through 'listen, be still!'

8. Skt. *tūṣṇīṁ bhū-*, see above, 2.

18.24 LANGUAGE

Grk.	*γλῶσσα, φωνή*	Goth.	*razda*	Lith.	*kalba* (*liežuvis*)
NG	*γλῶσσα*	ON	*māl, tunga*	Lett.	*valuoda* (*mēle*)
Lat.	*lingua; ōrātiō, sermō*	Dan.	*sprog* (*maal, tungemaal*)	ChSl.	*językŭ*
It.	*lingua; linguaggio*			SCr.	*jezik*
Fr.	*langue; langage*	Sw.	*språk* (*mål, tungomål*)	Boh.	*jazyk*
Sp.	*lengua; lenguaje*	OE	*spræc, reord, tunge*	Pol.	*język*
Rum.	*limbă; graiu*	ME	*speche, tunge, langage*	Russ.	*jazyk*
Ir.	*bēlre; urlabra*	NE	*language* (*tongue*); *speech*	Skt.	*bhāṣā-*
NIr.	*teanga; urlabhra*				
W.	*iaith*	Du.	*taal; spraak*		
Br.	*yez*	OHG	*sprāhha, zunga*		
		MHG	*sprāche, zunge*		
		NHG	*sprache* (*zunge*)		

'Language' is most commonly expressed by words for the tongue as the most important organ of speech. So regularly in Grk., Lat., Romance, NIr., Slavic; and, beside other words, in Gmc. and Baltic, though here the use, as in NE *tongue*, is now mostly poetical or archaic. Others are from verbs for 'speak' (18.21), a few from words for 'lip' or 'voice'.

The majority of these words are used both for a specific 'language' (*English language*, etc.) and for the more generic 'language, speech' as a faculty and institution (whence phrases or derivs. for history of language, etc.). But for the wider notion there may be other expressions, alternative like NE *speech*, or now preferred like Fr. *langage*. The more important of these are entered in the list (after;), but many other derivatives of verbs for 'speak' or 'say' which may sometimes be so used but are mostly 'act or manner of speaking, a speech, talk' or the like, e.g. Grk. λόγος, Fr. *parler*, NHG *rede*, SCr. *govor*, Boh. *řeč*, *mluva*, etc., are not entered.

1. Words for 'tongue' (4.26). Grk. γλῶσσα; Lat. *lingua* (> Romance words); NIr. *teanga*, ON *tunga*, Dan. *tunge*, Sw. *tunga* (but more commonly cpds. with old words for 'speech,' Dan. *tungemaal*, Sw. *tungomål*), OE, ME *tunge*, NE *tongue*, OHG *zunga*, MHG, NHG *zunge*; Lith. *liežuvis*, Lett. *mēle*; ChSl. *językŭ*, etc., general Slavic; Toch. A *käntu*.

2. Grk. φωνή 'voice' (18.11) is used for a language or dialect and for the generic 'language'.

3. Lat. *ōrātiō*, generic 'language, speech', deriv. of *ōrāre* 'plead, beseech' but in a more original sense of 'speak formally', prob. : Grk. ἀρά 'prayer, curse', etc. Walde-P. 1.183. Ernout-M. 714.

Lat. *sermō*, mostly 'speaking, discourse, talk' but also sometimes 'language' even in the specific sense, either deriv. of *serere* 'bind together, join, compose' (so the Romans and still Ernout-M. 929), or fr. **swer-* in Osc. dat. sg. *sverrunei* 'spokesman', OE *swerian* 'swear', *andswerian* 'answer', etc. (so Walde-P. 2.527).

Fr. *langage* (Prov. *lenguatge* > It. *linguaggio*, Sp. *lenguaje*), deriv. of *langue* 'language', from which it is now (but not orig.) distinguished as the generic 'language'. REW 5067.

Rum. *graiu*, generic 'language', fr. *grăi* 'speak' (18.21).

4. Ir. *bēlre*, NIr. *bēarla*, now esp. 'the English language' (i.e. 'the language' par excellence as contrasted with the native), deriv. of *bēl* 'lip' (4.25). Pedersen 1.489, 2.51.

Ir. *urlabra*, NIr *urlabhra*, generic 'language, speech' : *labrar* 'speak'.

W. *iaith*, Br. *yez* : OHG *jehan*, MHG *jehen* 'assert, say, admit, confess', OS *gehan* 'confess', OHG *jiht*, *bijiht* 'assertion, confession' (NHG *beichte*), Lat. *iocus* 'joke' (orig. 'saying', cf. Umbr. *iuka* 'preces'; Lith. *iuokas* 'laughter, joke' is not cognate, but a loanword fr. Lat. *iocus*, Walde-H. 1.715), etc. Walde-P. 1.204 f. Pedersen 1.65.

5. Goth. *razda*, OE *reord*, the latter also 'voice' : ON *rǫdd* 'voice' (18.11).

ON *māl*, Dan. *maal*, Sw. *mål* : ON *mæla* 'speak', etc.

OE *spræc*, ME *speche* (NE *speech*), Du. *spraak* (mostly 'speech'; MLG *sprāke* > Dan. *sprog*, Sw. *språk*), OHG *sprāhha*, MHG *sprāche*, NHG *sprache* : OE *sprecan*, etc. 'speak'.

ME *langage*, NE *language*, fr. Fr. *langage* (above, 3).

Du. *taal* : ON *tala*, etc. 'speak'.

6. Lith. *kalba* : *kalbėti* 'speak'.

Lett. *valuoda*, perh. like *vãluodze* 'oriole', fr. the root seen in Pol. *wołać* 'call'. Mühl.-Endz. 4.462, 498. Endzelin, KZ 52.123.

7. Skt. *bhāṣā-* : *bhāṣ-* 'speak'.

18.25. Dialect. The distinction between a 'language' and a subordinate 'dialect' was not observed in early times, when the words for 'language' (18.24) covered also what we now call a 'dialect'. Thus Grk. Ἀττικὴ γλῶσσα, Ἀττικὴ φωνή, Lat. *lingua* with reference to Greek dialects (*Crassus quinque Graeci sermonis differentias sic tenuit ut, qua quisque apud eum lingua postulasset*, etc. Quint.), and Skt. *bhāṣā-* used esp. of the Prakrit dialects.

1. But Grk. διάλεκτος 'discourse, conversation' (: διαλέγομαι 'converse, discuss', etc.), also sometimes 'language', finally became the technical word for 'dialect', and through Lat. *dialectus* furnished the most widespread Eur. terms.

Of native words, some of popular origin and some prob. artificial substitutes for the loanword, the following may be mentioned.

2. Fr. *patois*, orig. 'coarse, vulgar speech' : *pataud* 'clumsy fellow', *patauger* 'flounder', etc. REW 6301. Gamillscheg 677.

3. NIr. *canamhain*, also 'pronunciation, accent', fr. *canaim* 'sing' (18.12), also 'recite, pronounce'.

W. *tafodiaith*, *cangheniaith*, cpds. of *tafod* 'tongue' and *cangen* 'branch' with *iaith* 'language'.

Br. *rannyez*, cpd. of *rann* 'part' and *yez* 'language' (but *yez* alone commonly used).

4. NHG *mundart* (whence by semantic borrowing Dan. *mundart*, Sw. *mu-nart*), cpd. of *mund* 'mouth' and *art* 'manner'.

Du. *tongval*, cpd. of *tong* 'tongue' and *val* 'fall' (here with notion of error, 'slip of the tongue').

5. Lith. *tarmė* : *tarti* 'say' (18.22).

Lett. *izluoksne*, as lit. 'divergence' : *izluocīt* 'bend away, turn aside'.

6. SCr. *narječje*, Boh. *nářečí*, Pol. *narzecze*, Russ. *narečie*, fr. cpd. of verb for 'say', ChSl. *reką*, *rešti*, SCr. *reći*, etc. (18.22). Cf. ChSl. *narešti* 'define', *narokŭ* 'determination, vote', Boh. *narok* 'claim', etc.

18.26 WORD

Grk.	ῥῆμα, λέξις, ἔπος	Goth.	*waurd*	Lith.	*žodis*
NG	λέξις	ON	*orð*	Lett.	*vãrds*
Lat.	*verbum*, *vōx*	Dan.	*ord*	ChSl.	*glagolŭ*, *slovo*
It.	*parola*	Sw.	*ord*	SCr.	*riječ*
Fr.	*mot*, *parole*	OE	*word*	Boh.	*slovo*
Sp.	*palabra*	ME	*word*	Pol.	*słowo*
Rum.	*cuvînt*	NE	*word*	Russ.	*slovo*
Ir.	*brīathar*, *focal*	Du.	*woord*	Skt.	*çabda-*, *pada-*, *vacas-*, etc.
NIr.	*focal*, *briathar*	OHG	*wort*	Av.	*vǎč-*, *vačah-*, *uxδa-*, *sravah-*, *mąθra-*
W.	*gair*	MHG	*wort*		
Br.	*ger*, *komz*	NHG	*wort*		

Words for 'word' originally denoted something said, 'saying, utterance' (and several of the words listed are quotable mostly in this general sense), and only secondarily the individual 'word'. Many are connected with verbs for 'speak, say', though in some cases not the one current in the same language.

1. Derivs. of IE **wekʷ-* 'speak, say' (18.21). Walde-P. 1.245 f.

Grk. ἔπος; Lat. *vōx* (also 'voice'), Skt. *vacas-*, Av. *vačah-*, Av. *vǎč-* (also 'voice, speech'), *uxδa-* (also 'saying', pl. 'speech').

Here also Lat. *vocābulum* (more directly fr. *vocāre* 'call') 'appellation, name', later also 'substantive' and in MLat. 'word'.

2. Derivs. of IE **wer-* in Grk. fut. ἐρῶ, etc. 'speak, say' (18.21), esp. IE **wer-dh-* (**wr̥-dh-*, **wor-dh-*) 'word'. Walde-P. 1.2833. Ernout-M. 1088 f.

Grk. ῥῆμα (orig. 'word, saying', later gram. term. for 'verb'); Lat. *verbum*, Goth. *waurd*, OE *word*, etc., general Gmc.; OPruss. *wirds*, Lett. *vãrds* (latter also 'name', as Lith. *vardas*).

3. Grk. λέξις, orig. 'speech, diction, style', whence 'single word or phrase' (Aristot., etc.), then usual gram. term for 'word' and so in NG : λέγω 'speak, say' (18.21). Hence also Grk. λόγος, used of a verbal expression or utterance, but rarely of a single word and never a gram. term in this sense.

4. It. *parola*, Fr. *parole* (now mostly 'saying, utterance'; for the individual 'word' replaced by *mot*), Sp. *palabra*, fr. VLat. *parabola*, fr. Grk. παραβολή (orig. 'juxtaposition, comparison' : παραβάλλω 'set beside') in its biblical sense of 'parable, saying'. Wackernagel, IF 31.262 f. REW 6221. Ernout-M. 731.

Fr. (Prov., Cat.) *mot*, fr. VLat. *muttum* 'a grunt', back-formation to *muttīre*, *mutīre* 'mutter, grunt'. REW 5795. Gamillscheg 625.

Rum. *cuvînt*, also '(one's) word, promise, agreement', fr. Lat. *conventum* 'agreement, compact, accord'. Cf. NG κουβέντα 'conversation', κουβεντιάζω 'converse'. REW 2194.

5. Ir. *briathar*, formally = W. *brwydr* 'battle' (orig. 'word-battle'?), but root connection and orig. meaning uncertain. Walde-P. 1.687, 2.194. Pedersen 2.45.

Ir. *focal*, fr. Lat. *vocābulum* (above, 1). Pedersen 1.206, 228. Vendryes, De hib. voc. 143.

W. *gair*, Br. *ger* : Ir. *gairim* 'shout' (18.13).

Br. *komz*, also vb. 'speak' (18.21).

6. Goth. *waurd*, etc., above, 2.

7. Lith. *žodis* : *žodas* 'speech-sound', *žadėti* 'promise', *žadinti* 'cause to speak, talk to', Lett. *zadināt* 'speak to, make laugh, ridicule, blame', etc., Lett. *pražastis* 'epithet', etc., root connection dub. Mühl.-Endz. 4.679.

8. ChSl. *glagolŭ* (reg. for ῥῆμα) : *glagolati* 'speak' (18.21).

ChSl. *slovo* (reg. for λόγος), Boh., Russ. *slovo*, Pol. *słowo* : *slava* 'fame', Av. *sravah-* 'word, teaching, saying', Skt. *çravas-* 'praise, fame', Grk. κλέος, Ir. *clū* 'fame', etc., fr. the root of ChSl. *slyšati*, Skt. *çru-*, etc. 'hear' (15.41). Walde-P. 1.494 f. Trautmann 308.

SCr. *riječ* = Boh. *řeč*, Russ. *reč* 'speech, language' : ChSl. *reką*, *rešti* 'say', etc. (18.22).

9. Skt. *çabda-*, lit. 'sound, noise' (15.44), but also the common term for 'word' (so reg. Pāṇini).

Skt. *pada-*, lit. 'pace, step' and 'foot' (as measure), whence 'part, portion', esp. as 'portion of a verse', whence 'word' (: *pad-* 'foot', etc.).

Skt. *vacas-*, Av. *vǎč-*, *vačah-*, *uxδa-*, above, 1.

Av. *sravah-* : Slavic *slovo* (above, 8).

Av. *mąθra-*, also 'saying, promise', esp. 'holy word' : Skt. *mantra-* 'sacred text, hymn', fr. Av., Skt. *man-* 'think' (17.13). Barth. 1177 ff.

18.27 DICTIONARY

Grk.	(λέξεις, γλῶσσαι) late λεξικόν	Dan.	*ordbog*	Lith.	*žodynas*
NG	λεξικόν	Sw.	*ordbok*	Lett.	*vardnīca*
Lat.	(*glossārium*), MLat. *dictiōnārium*	NE	*dictionary*	SCr.	*rječnik*
It.	*dizionario*	Du.	*woordenboek*	Boh.	*slovník*
Fr.	*dictionnaire*	NHG	*wörterbuch*	Pol.	*słownik*
Sp.	*diccionario*			Russ.	*slovar'*
Rum.	*dicţionar*			Skt.	*koça-*, *nighaṇṭu-*
NIr.	*foclōir*				
W.	*geiriadur*, *geirlyfr*				
Br.	*geriadur*				

The antecedents of the modern comprehensive dictionaries of a language were the glossaries or vocabularies, as we should now call them, of rare words or dialect words or words of a given author or group of writings. The early Greek terms for such were λέξεις or γλῶσσαι (whence Lat. *glossārium* > NE *glossary*, etc.), later λεξικόν (sc. βιβλίον), whence MLat. *lexicon* and the similar forms familiar in the modern Eur. languages, though less common than those listed.

Grk. ὀνομαστικόν, the title of the well-known work of Pollux (more properly pl. τὰ ὀνομαστικά for the whole work, -κόν for each book), with its classification by subjects, neut. (sc. βιβλίον) of adj. ὀνομαστικός, deriv., through vb. ὀνομάζω, of ὄνομα 'name'. Hence also ὀνομασία or pl. ὀνομασίαι applied to similar classified lists.

MLat. *dictiōnārium* (or *dictiōnārius* sc. *liber*), deriv. of Lat. *dictiō* 'saying', in MLat. also 'word'. Hence the Romance and English words.

Skt. *koça-* 'container, box, chest, treasury', etc., prob. fr. **(s)keu-* in words for 'cover' (Walde-P. 2.548), was also the usual word for 'treasury of words' (cf. the *Amara-koça-*, etc.).

Skt. *nighaṇṭu-*, a term applied to the old Vedic glossaries, a Mid. Ind. form of **nir-grantha-* : Skt. *grantha-* 'text', *granth-* 'tie'. Uhlenbeck 148. Wackernagel, Altind. Gram. 1.167. For the two Skt. words, see also Zachariae, Grd. indo-ar. Phil. 1.3B.1 f.

The other words are obvious derivatives or compounds ('wordbook' in Gmc. and W. *geirlyfr*) of the usual words for a 'word' as listed in 18.26, e.g. NIr. *foclōir* (W. *geiriadur*), Lith. *žodynas*, SCr. *rječnik*, Russ. *slovar'*.

18.28 NAME

Grk.	ὄνομα	Goth.	*namo*	Lith.	*vardas*
NG	ὄνομα	ON	*nafn*	Lett.	*vãrds*
Lat.	*nōmen*	Dan.	*navn*	ChSl.	*imę*
It.	*nome*	Sw.	*namn*	SCr.	*ime*
Fr.	*nom*	OE	*nama*	Boh.	*jméno*
Sp.	*nombre*	ME	*name*	Pol.	*imię*
Rum.	*nume*	NE	*name*	Russ.	*imja*
Ir.	*ainm*	Du.	*naam*	Skt.	*nāman-*
NIr.	*ainm*	OHG	*namo*	Av.	*nāman-*, *nąman-*
W.	*enw*	MHG	*name*		
Br.	*hano*	NHG	*name*		

Nearly all the common words for 'name' belong to an inherited group of unknown root connection.

1. IE *enmen-, *n̥men-, *n̥̄men-, etc. with manifold gradation. Walde-P. 1.132. Ernout-M. 675 f. Falk-Torp 758. Berneker 426.

Here belong all the words listed except the Lith. and Lett.; also OPruss. emmens (cf. Grk. dial. ἔνυμα in Lac. Ἐνυμακρατίδας, etc.), Arm. anun, Alb. émën, Hitt. lāman (with dissim.), and Toch. A ñom, B ñem (SSS 50).

2. Lith. vardas, Lett. vārds (the latter also 'word') : Lat. verbum 'word' (18.26).

18.31 ASK¹ (Question, Inquire)

Grk.	ἐρωτάω	Goth.	fraihnan	Lith.	klausti
NG	ρωτῶ	ON	spyrja, fregna, frētta	Lett.	jautāt, vaicāt, klaust
Lat.	rogāre, quaerere	Dan.	spørge	ChSl.	vŭprositi
It.	domandare	Sw.	fråga	SCr.	pitati
Fr.	demander	OE	fregnan, āscian, spyrian	Boh.	ptáti se
Sp.	preguntar			Pol.	pytać
Rum.	intreba	ME	aske, frayne	Russ.	sprosit'
Ir.	iarmi-foig, imm-comairc	NE	ask	Skt.	pracch-
		Du.	vragen	Av.	fras-
NIr.	fiafruighim	OHG	frāgēn, eiscōn		
W.	gofyn	MHG	vrāgen, eischen		
Br.	goulenn	NHG	fragen		

There is considerable interchange, in the same word or among cognates, between the two notions covered by NE ask, namely 1) ask 'question, inquire' and 2) ask 'request' (ask a person to do something, and with the thing requested as object, ask aid, but for the latter now most commonly ask for, like NHG bitte um). In such groups the development may be in either direction or from a common 'seek' (an answer or a thing). In the following, for the sake of brevity, the two senses are distinguished as 'ask'¹ and 'ask'². But except in words or groups in which both senses are involved 'ask'¹ is understood here, and expressions for 'ask'² are combined in 18.35.

1. IE *preḱ- and *pr̥(ḱ)-sḱ-, etc. in words for 'ask' in one or both senses. Walde-P. 2.44. Ernout-M. 794. f.

Lat. poscere 'ask'²; Ir. arcu 'beg, beseech', cpds. com-aircim 'inquire', imm-comairc (3sg.) 'ask'¹, W. arch 'request', MBr. archas 'il commanda'; Goth. fraihnan, ON fregna (sb. frētt 'question, in-

vestigation', whence vb. frētta), OE fregnan, frignan, ME frayne, MLG vrāgen (> Sw. fråga), Du. vragen, OHG frāgēn, MHG vrāgen, NHG fragen all 'ask'¹; Lith. prašyti 'ask'², Lett. prasīt id. and rarely also 'ask'¹ (cf. Mühl.-Endz. s.v.); ChSl. prositi, etc. 'ask'², for 'ask'¹ ChSl. vŭ-prositi, Russ. sprosit'; Skt. pracch-, praç-, Av. fras- 'ask'¹, Arm. harçanem id., Toch. A pärk-, prak-, B prek- act. 'ask'², mid. 'ask'¹ (SSS 449).

2. Grk. Hom. εἰρωτάω, Att. ἐρωτάω, NG ρωτῶ, orig. deriv. of an *ἔρϝος : Grk. (epic) ἐρέω, ἐρέομαι 'ask, inquire about, search, explore', ON reyna 'try', raun 'trial, attempt'. Walde-P. 2.356. Boisacq 278.

3. Lat. rogāre ('ask' in both senses), prob. orig. 'direct (oneself) to, address' : regere 'direct, guide, rule', Ir. rigim 'stretch out (the hand)', etc. Walde-P. 2.363. Ernout-M. 868 f.

Lat. quaerere 'seek' (11.31) also common for 'ask'¹. Hence sb. quaestiō 'questioning, investigation' (rarely for

the concrete 'question'), whence Fr., ME, NE question, etc. Cf. also cpd. inquīrere 'inquire into', NE inquire, etc.

It. domandare, Fr. demander ('ask' in both senses; Sp. demandar mostly 'ask'²), fr. Lat. dēmandāre 'give in charge, intrust, commit', cpd. of mandāre 'intrust, command, charge with', orig. 'put in the hand' : manus 'hand', etc. Ernout-M. 586. Walde-H. 2.25. REW 2547.

Sp. preguntar, Port. perguntar, fr. Lat. percontārī 'investigate, inquire', fig. use of 'sound' (the depth), deriv. of contus 'pole, pike' (fr. Grk. κοντός id.). Ernout-M. 217. REW 6400.

Rum. intreba, fr. Lat. interrogāre, cpd. of rogāre (above). REW 4496.

4. OIr. iarmi-foig (3sg.), MIr. iar-mafaigim, iarfaigim, hence NIr. fia-fruighim, cpd. (*iarm-fo-saig-) of saigim 'go after, seek' : Goth. sōkian 'seek', etc. (11.31). Pedersen 2.608, 610.

W. gofyn 'ask' in both senses, perh. fr. *upo-men- : mynnu 'wish', fr. the root *men- in Skt. man- 'think', etc. Pedersen 2.451. Walde-P. 2.265.

Br. goulenn 'ask' in both senses, etym. dub., perh. as orig. 'seek, search' = Ir. fo-gliunn 'learn', fr. the root of ChSl. ględati 'see', etc. (Walde-P. 1.625). Loth, RC 45.185. Otherwise Henry 138.

5. Goth. fraihnan, OE fregnan, etc., above, 1.

ON spyrja, Dan. spørge (Sw. spörja less common), OE spyrian, ME spyre

(NE dial. speer), lit. (and so often in ON and OE) 'track, trace' = OHG spurian 'trace, search, notice' (NHG spüren 'trace, feel'), fr. ON, OE, OHG spor 'track'. Falk-Torp 1141. NED s.v. Walde-P. 2.669.

OE āscian, ācsian, ME aske, axe, NE ask, OHG eiscōn, MHG eischen 'ask' in both senses (NHG heischen 'request, demand', with h- fr. heissen) : Lith. ieškoti, ChSl. iskati 'seek', Skt. iṣ- 'seek, wish', etc. Walde-P. 1.12. Weigand-H. 1.840. NED s.v. ask, vb.

6. Lith. klausti, Lett. klaust, prob. as 'will hear' (orig. fut. formation) : klau-syti, Lett. klausīt 'listen', etc. (15.41). Walde-P. 1.495. Mühl.-Endz. 2.216 f.

Lett. jautāt, cf. Lith. jautotis (refl.) 'inquire, inform oneself' : Lett. jaust 'perceive, notice, feel', Lith. jausti 'feel, notice', etc. (15.11). Cf. for semantic development Grk. πυνθάνομαι 'find out, inquire' : Skt. budh- 'be awake, notice', and NE feel someone out. Mühl.-Endz. 2.104.

Lett. vaicāt, fr. the interrog. particle vai, fr. Liv. voi. Mühl.-Endz. 4.433 f.

7. ChSl. vŭprositi, Russ. sprosit', above, 1.

SCr. pitati, Boh. (old) pytati, now ptáti se (refl.), Pol. pytać = ChSl. pytati 'examine, study', Russ. pytat' 'attempt, strive' : Lat. putāre 'prune, reckon, suppose, think' (17.14). Walde-P. 2.13. Brückner 450.

8. Skt. pracch-, Av. fras-, above, 1.

18.32 ANSWER (vb.)

Grk.	ἀποκρίνομαι	Goth.	andhafjan, usbairan	Lith.	atsakyti
NG	ἀπαντῶ, ἀποκρίνομαι	ON	svara, andsvara	Lett.	atbildēt
Lat.	respondēre	Dan.	svare	ChSl.	otŭvěštati
It.	rispondere	Sw.	svara	SCr.	odgovoriti
Fr.	répondre	OE	andswarian, andwyrdan	Boh.	odpovĕdĕti
Sp.	responder			Pol.	odpowiedzieć
Rum.	răspunde	ME	answere, andwurde (replye)	Russ.	otvetit'
Ir.	fris-gairim			Skt.	prati-vac-, prati-bhāṣ-, etc.
NIr.	freagraim	NE	answer (reply, respond)	Av.	paiti-mrū-
W.	ateb	Du.	antwoorden		
Br.	respont	OHG	antwurten, antlingen		
		MHG	antwurten		
		NHG	antworten		

'Answer' (vb.) is generally expressed by compounds, especially of prefixes having the force (among others) of 'back, against, in return', with verbs for 'say' (also 'shout, call, pledge', etc.) or (through sb. 'answer') from nouns for 'word'.

1. Grk. ἀποκρίνομαι, mid. of ἀποκρίνω 'separate, set apart, choose, reject', cpd. of ἀπό 'from, away, apart' and κρίνω 'separate, decide'.

NG ἀπαντῶ, also 'meet' fr. class. Grk. ἀπαντάω 'meet' (19.65).

2. Lat. respondēre (VLat. respondere > Romance words), orig. 'pledge in return', cpd. of spondēre 'engage, pledge, promise' (: Grk. σπένδω 'pour a libation'). Ernout-M. 967 f. REW 7247.

3. Ir. fris-gairim, lit. 'shout or call against', cpd. of gairim 'shout, call' (18.13). Hence (fr. vbl. n. frecre) NIr. freagraim. Pedersen 2.535.

W. ateb, cpd. of at- 're-' (= prep. at 'to, toward') and heb 'inquit' (18.22).

Br. respont (vb. and sb.), fr. OFr. respont, beside respon(d)s (Fr. réponse : répondre, above 2).

4. Goth. andhafjan, cpd. of and(a)- 'along, against, toward' and hafjan 'lift' (10.22).

Goth. usbairan, lit. 'carry out, bring forth' (renders ἐκ-, προ-φέρω), whence

'bring forth' (an answer) = ἀποκρίνομαι (Mk. 11.14), cpd. of bairan 'carry'.

ON svara, Dan. svare, Sw. svara, and in cpds. with ON, OE and- (= Goth. and-, above), ON andsvara (rare and usually 'be responsible for'), OE and-swarian, ME answere, NE answer : ON sverja, OE swerian, Goth. swaran, etc. 'swear' (21.24). Falk-Torp 1211, 1215.

OE andwyrdan, ME (early) andwurde, andwerde, Du. antwoorden, OHG, MHG antwurten, NHG antworten (Goth. and-waurdjan = ἀνταποκρίνομαι 'answer back, argue against', Rom. 9.20), derivs. of sbs. OE andwyrde, OHG antwurti, Goth. andawaurdi 'answer' (ON and-yrði 'objection'), cpds. of OE, ON and-, etc. (above) and coll. deriv. of OE word, etc. 'word' (18.26). Weigand-H. 1.74.

OHG antlingen, antlingōn, deriv. of an adj. *antlang = OS andlang 'directed against', etc. (Walde-P. 2.435). Cf. Braune, Ahd. Lesebuch⁹ 215.

ME replye, NE reply, fr. OFr. replier 'fold again, turn back, reply', cpd. of plier 'fold' (9.15). NED s.v. reply, vb.

ME respond, respoundre, NE respond (now often in fig. sense), fr. OFr. re-spoundre, respundre, Lat. respondēre (above, 2). NED s.vv. respond, re-poun(d).

5. Lith. atsakyti, cpd. of at- 'off, away, back' and sakyti 'say' (18.22).

Lett. atbildēt, cpd. of at- (= Lith. at-, above) and bildēt 'speak, say' (not used except in cpds.) : OPruss. billīt 'say, speak', etc. (18.21).

6. ChSl. otŭvěštati (sb. otŭvětŭ), Russ. otvetit', otvečat', cpds. of otŭ 'from, away' and věštati 'speak', etc. (18.21).

SCr. odgovoriti, cpd. of od- (= ChSl. otŭ, above) and govoriti 'speak' (18.21).

Boh. odpovĕdĕti, Pol. odpowiedzieć, cpds. of od- (= ChSl. otŭ, above) and Boh. povĕdĕti, Pol. powiedzieć 'tell, say' (18.22).

7. Skt. prati-vac-, prati-bhāṣ-, cpds. of prati 'back, toward' and roots for 'speak, say', vac-, bhāṣ-, etc. (other roots listed 18.21, 18.22 may be likewise used).

Av. paiti-mrū-, cpd. of paiti- 'again, against' and mrū- 'speak, say' (18.21).

18.33 ADMIT, CONFESS

Grk.	ὁμολογέω	Goth.	andhaitan	Lith.	pripažinti
NG	παραδέχομαι, ὁμολογῶ	ON	jāta	Lett.	atzīt
Lat.	fatērī, cōnfitērī	Dan.	tilstaa, bekende	ChSl.	ispovĕdati
It.	ammettere, confessare	Sw.	medgiva, tillstå, be-känna	SCr.	priznati
Fr.	admettre, avouer, con-fesser			Boh.	připustiti, uznati
		OE	andettan, oncnāwan	Pol.	przyznać
Sp.	admitir, confesar	ME	confesse, aknowe	Russ.	priznat', soznat'
Rum.	mărturisi	NE	admit, acknowledge, confess	Skt.	svī-kr-, anu-bhāṣ-
Ir.	almu				
NIr.	admhuighim	Du.	toegeven, bekennen		
W.	addef	OHG	jehan		
Br.	anzao	MHG	jehen, gestān		
		NHG	zugeben, gestehen, be-kennen		

'Admit' (as true, 'acknowledge, confess') is expressed by words meaning literally 'agree with, accept, let into (permit), say, (say) yes', etc., and especially by compounds of words for 'know, recognize'.

Some words for 'confess' that are mainly restricted to eccl. use are omitted.

1. Grk. ὁμολογέω 'agree with, admit, confess' (NG chiefly in eccl. usage), deriv. of ὁμόλογος 'agreeing, corresponding', cpd. of ὁμός 'same' and λόγος 'reckoning, reason, etc.').

NG παραδέχομαι, in class. Grk. usually in the lit. sense 'receive, receive into' (cpd. of δέχομαι 'receive'), but freq. in papyri 'recognize as correct, agree to' (cf. LS s.v.).

2. Lat. fatērī, and esp. cpd. cōn-fitērī (pple. confessus, whence VLat. *confessāre > It. confessare, Fr. con-fesser, Sp. confesar, all esp. in eccl. usage), cf. Osc. fatíum 'speak' : fārī 'speak' (18.21). Ernout-M. 335. Walde-H. 1.462 f.

It. ammettere, Fr. admettre, Sp. ad-mitir, all also 'admit' in the lit. sense 'let into' : fr. Lat. admittere id., cpd. of mittere 'let go, send' (10.63).

Fr. avouer (> NE avow), in OFr. 'recognize', prob. as orig. 'take oath to', cpd. of vouer 'vow' (fr. VLat. *vō-tāre, deriv. of vōtum 'promise, vow'), but perh. merged with deriv. of Lat. advocāre 'call to'. Gamillscheg 63. Wartburg 1.42.

Rum. *mărturisi*, orig. 'bear witness', through Slavic (cf. Serb.-ChSl. *marturisati* 'testari'), fr. aor. of Grk. μαρτυρέω 'bear witness'. Tiktin 956 f.

3. Ir. *atmu*, 3 pl., *ataimet*, NIr. *admhuighim*, W. *addef*, Br. *anzao*, cpds. of *ad-* 'to' and Ir. *daimim* 'permit, grant', etc. : Lat. *domāre*, Grk. δαμάζω 'tame, subdue', etc. Walde-P. 1.789. Pedersen 1.388, 2.503–4.

4. Goth. *andhaitan*, OE *andettan*, cpd. of *and-* 'along, against' (cf. Goth. *and-hafjan* 'answer', etc.) and *haitan* 'call, name', pass. 'be called', etc. (18.42).

ON *jāta*, orig. 'say yes' = OHG *gi-jāzen*, MHG *jāzen* 'say yes, agree', deriv. of ON *jā*, OHG *jā*, etc. 'yes'. Falk-Torp 472.

OE *oncnāwan*, ME *aknawe*, Du., NHG *bekennen* (> Dan. *bekende*, Sw. *bekänna*), all orig. 'recognize, admit knowledge of', whence 'recognize as true', cpds. of OE *cnāwan*, NHG *kennen*, etc. 'know, recognize' (17.17). Hence early NE *acknowledge* sb., whence NE *acknowledge* vb. NED s.vv.

ME *confesse*, NE *confess*, fr. OFr. *confesser* (above, 2).

NE *admit*, fr. Lat. *admittere* (cf. It. *amittere*, etc., above, 2).

Du. *toegeven*, NHG *zugeben* (hence the use in this sense of Sw. *medgiva*, and less commonly Dan. *medgive*; cf. Falk-Torp 707), cpd. of *toe-*, NHG *zu* 'to' and *geven*, *geben* 'give'.

OHG *jehan*, also *bi-*, *gi-jehen*, MHG *jehen*, *bijehen* : W. *iaith*, Br. *yez* 'language' (18.24). Deriv. OHG *bijiht*, MHG *begiht* > *bīht*, NHG *beichte* 'confession', whence NHG *beichten* in eccl. usage. Weigand-H. 1.188.

MHG *gestān*, NHG *gestehen*, *zugestehen*, MLG *tōstān* (Dan. *tilstaa*, Sw. *tillstå* by semantic borrowing), orig. (and so mostly in MHG) 'stand, remain standing', whence 'stand beside, stand by, assist', and finally 'admit'. Falk-Torp 1261. Weigand-H. 1.708.

5. Lith. *pripažinti*, Lett. *atzīt*, orig. 'recognize' : Lith. *žinoti*, Lett. *zināt* 'know' (17.17).

6. ChSl. *ispovědati* (quotable only as 'confess' in eccl. sense, and so in modern Slavic), cpd. of *izŭ* 'out' and *povědati* 'tell, relate, say' (18.22).

SCr. *priznati*, Boh. *uznati*, Pol. *przyznać*, Russ. *priznat'*, *soznat'*, all orig. 'recognize', cpds. of SCr. *znati* 'know', etc. (17.17).

Boh. *připustiti*, cpd. of *pustiti* 'let go, release' (11.34).

7. Skt. *svī-kṛ-*, lit. 'make one's own', cpd. of *svī-* in cpds. for *sva-* 'own' and *kṛ-* 'make, do'. Cf. English *own*, *own up* in same sense.

Skt. *anu-bhāṣ-*, also 'speak to, address', cpd. of *anu-* 'along, to, toward', and *bhāṣ-* 'speak' (18.21).

18.34 DENY

Grk.	ἀρνέομαι	Goth.	*laugnjan, afaikan*	Lith.	*ginčyti, išsiginti*
NG	ἀρνοῦμαι, ἀρνειέμαι	ON	*synja, neita*	Lett.	*liegt(ies)*
Lat.	*negāre*	Dan.	*nægte*	ChSl.	*otŭvrěšti sę, otŭmetati sę*
It.	*negare*	Sw.	*neka*	SCr.	*od-, po-ricati*
Fr.	*nier*	OE	*wiþ-, æt-sacan, līgnian*	Boh.	*popříti*
Sp.	*negar*	ME	*denye, withsaye, withsake*	Pol.	*przeczyć, zaprzeć się*
Rum.	*nega, tăgădui*	NE	*deny*	Russ.	*otricat', otperet'*
Ir.	*dosluindim*	Du.	*loochenen*	Skt.	*ni-hnu, apa-hnu-, apa-lap-*
NIr.	*dīultaim, sēanaim*	OHG	*loug(a)nen, farsahhan*		
W.	*gwadu*	MHG	*lougen(en), versachen*		
Br.	*nac'h*	NHG	*leugnen*		

Several of the words for 'deny' are derivs. of neg. adverbs, that is, '(say) no'. Others are connected with words for 'refuse, reject, lie', etc.

1. Grk. ἀρνέομαι (cf. ἄπ-αρνος, ἔξ-αρνος 'denying'), perh. : Alb. *rrem* 'false', *rremë*, *rrenë* 'lie'. Walde-P. 1.78.

2. Lat. *negāre* (> It. *negare*, Fr. *nier*, Sp. *negar*; Rum. *nega* recent borrowing), deriv. of a neg. **neg(i)* strengthened form of *ne* (cf. Skt. *nahi*, Grk. οὐχί, μήχι, Lith. *negi*, etc.). Walde-P. 542, 2.319. Ernout-M. 659, 664.

Rum. *tăgădui*, fr. Hung. *tagad* 'deny'. Tiktin 1548.

3. Ir. *dosluindim*, cpd. of *di-* 'from, off' and *sluindim* 'designate' (: OW *istlinnit* gl. *profatur*, *loquitur*, etc., outside connections dub., cf. Pedersen 1.83 f.); vbl. n. *dīltud* 'denial', whence NIr. *dīultaim*.

NIr. *sēanaim* (= *sēanaim* 'bless, sanctify'), deriv. of *sēan* 'omen, lucky sign, charm' (fr. Lat. *signum*). Orig. 'make the sign' (of the cross), whence 'deny' (or 'bless'). Cf. NE colloq. *cross my heart and hope to die.*

W. *gwadu* : Lat. *vetāre*, early Lat. *votāre* 'forbid', OW *guetid* 'says'. Loth, RC 42.367 f. (vs. Morris Jones 370).

Br. *nac'h* : W. *nacau* 'refuse', derivs. of W. *nac*, Br. *nag*, prevocalic forms of neg. *na*. Henry 208.

4. Goth. *laugnjan*, OE *līgnian*, Du. *loochenen*, OHG *loug(a)nen*, MHG *lougen(en)*, NHG *leugnen* : Goth. *liugan*, ON *ljūga*, etc. 'lie' (16.67).

Goth. *afaikan*, cpd. of *af-* 'from, away' and *aikan* : OHG *eihhōn* 'award, adjudge', root connection dub. Walde-P. 1.11. Feist 3.

ON *synja*, with *syn* 'denial' : Goth. *sunjōn* 'justify, excuse', OHG *sunna* 'legal hindrance from appearing in court', fr. the root of Goth. *sunjis*, ON *sannr*, etc. 'true' (16.66), through notion of 'true statement' (in denial). Falk-Torp 1227.

ON *neita*, Dan. *nægte* (ODan. *nege*), Sw. *neka*, derivs. of ON, Dan., Sw. *nei* 'no'. Falk-Torp 761. Hellquist 695.

OE *wiþsacan*, ME (early) *withsake*, also OE *ætsacan*, ME (early) *atsake*, ME *forsake*, OHG *farsahhan*, MHG *versachen*, cpds. of prefixes expressing separation, and OE *sacan* 'fight, strive, contend', OHG *sahhan* 'quarrel, contend' : Goth. *sakan* 'strive, rebuke', etc.

ME *withsaye*, cpd. of *with-* (cf. above) and *saye* 'say' (18.22).

ME *denye*, NE *deny*, fr. OFr. *deneier*, Fr. *dénier* 'refuse, disown', fr. Lat. *dēnegāre* 'reject, refuse', cpd. of *negāre* (above, 2). NED s.v.

5. Lith. *ginčyti*, *išsiginti* (also *už-*) : *ginti* (*ginu*, *gyniau*) 'defend, protect, forbid', also refl. 'deny', and *ginti* (*genu*, *giniau*) 'drive', ChSl. *ženą*, *gŭnati* 'drive', etc. (10.65). NSB s.vv. Walde-P. 1.680 f.

Lett. *liegt* (also 'forbid, refuse'), refl. *liegties*, etym. dub.; perh. as 'restrain' : Ukr. *za-lyhaty* 'tie up, bind, pledge', Lat. *ligāre* 'tie', etc. (Walde-P. 2.400). Mühl.-Endz. 2.494.

6. ChSl. *otŭvrěšti sę* (1sg. *otŭvrŭgą sę*; the usual rendering of ἀρνέομαι in the Gospels), refl. of *otŭvrěšti* 'throw away, reject', cpd. of *vrěšti* 'throw' (10.25).

ChSl. *otŭmetati sę*, and *otŭmětati sę*, refl. of *otŭmetati*, *otŭmětati* 'throw away' iter. to *mesti* 'throw' (10.25). Berneker 2.40, 53.

SCr. *odricati*, *poricati*, Russ. *otricat'*, cpd. of *od-*, *po-*, *ot-* with sense 'away, back' and iter. forms to SCr. *reći*, ChSl. *rešti*, etc. 'say' (18.22). Cf. ChSl. *prěrěkati* 'contradict' (Supr.).

Boh. *popříti*, Pol. *zaprzeć się*, *zapierać się*, Russ., *otperet'*, cpds. (in part refl.) of Boh. *příti* 'contest, dispute', Pol. *przeć*, Russ. *peret'* 'press, push, jostle', ChSl. *pĭrěti* 'beat, wash (by beating)', refl. 'contend, strive' : Skt. *pṛt-* 'fight, quarrel', Arm. *hari* 'strike', etc. Walde-P. 2.42. Brückner 442.

Pol. *przeczyć*, fr. the adv. *przeko* 'across, diagonally through'. Brückner 443.

7. Skt. *ni-hnu-*, *apa-hnu-*, cpds. of *ni-* 'down, back', or *apa-* 'away, back', and *hnu-* 'hide from, drive or take away' (etym. dub., Uhlenbeck 362).

Skt. *apa-lap-*, cpd. *apa-* (cf. above) and *lap-* 'prate, chatter, talk'.

18.35 ASK[2], REQUEST

Grk.	αἰτέω (ἐρωτάω)	Goth.	*bidjan*	Lith.	*prašyti, reikalauti*
NG	ζητῶ, παρακαλῶ	ON	*biðja*	Lett.	*prasīt*
Lat.	*poscere, petere, rogāre*	Dan.	*bede, forlange, fordre*	ChSl.	*prositi, moliti*
It.	*domandare, (ri)chiedere*	Sw.	*bedja, begära, fordra*	SCr.	*moliti, iskati, tražiti*
Fr.	*demander*	OE	*biddan, āscian, giwian*	Boh.	*prositi, žádati*
Sp.	*pedir, rogar*	ME	*bidde, aske, demaund*	Pol.	*prosić, żądać*
Rum.	*cere*	NE	*ask, request*	Russ.	*prosit', trebovat'*
Ir.	*condaigim, cuingim*	Du.	*verzoeken, verlangen*	Skt.	*yāc-, (pra-)arthaya-*
NIr.	*iarraim*	OHG	*bitten, eiscōn*	Av., OPers.	*jad-*
W.	*gofyn*	MHG	*bitten, eischen, vordern*		
Br.	*goulenn*	NHG	*bitten, verlangen, fordern*		

Several of the words for 'ask, request', briefly 'ask'[2], are the same as, or related to, those for 'ask, inquire', briefly 'ask'[1]. See 18.31. Others are cognate with words for 'seek, desire', etc. Besides the words listed, those for 'wish, will' are often used with the implication of a mild, or even firm, request.

Cf. also words for 'pray' (22.17), of which several are the same as those listed here, and some of the others are also used in a nonreligious sense as NE *pray*.

1. IE **preḱ-* in words for 'ask' in both senses. See 18.31.

Here as 'ask'[2] Lat. *poscere*, Lith. *prašyti*, Lett. *prasīt*, ChSl. *prositi*, etc., general Slavic (but SCr. *prositi* now 'beg, woo').

2. Grk. αἰτέω, prob. as 'demand one's share' : αἶσα (*αἰτ̯α) 'share, fate', αἴσιος 'auspicious', αἴσιμος 'fated, destined', etc., Osc. *aeteis* 'partis', Av. *aeta-* punishment, guilt' (i.e. 'one's lot'). Walde-P. 1.2.

NG ζητῶ, fr. class. Grk. ζητέω 'seek' (11.31). Also rarely 'demand, require'.

Grk. ἐρωτάω 'ask'[1] (18.31) is frequently used for 'ask'[2] in Hellenistic times (LXX, NT, pap.).

NG παρακαλῶ (milder than ζητῶ, used like NE *I beg you, I pray you, please*), fr. class. Grk. παρακαλέω (cpd. of καλέω 'call', 18.41) 'summon, invite, exhort', etc., late also 'beseech' (Polyb., NT, etc.).

3. Lat. *petere* (> Sp., Port. *pedir*), orig. ('fly at') 'assail, attack', hence 'seek' and 'ask, request' : Grk. πέτομαι 'fly', Skt. *pat-* 'fly, fall', etc. Walde-P. 1.20. Ernout-M. 763 f.

Lat. *rogāre* 'ask' in both senses (18.31), as 'ask'[2] > Sp. *rogar;* Rum. *ruga* in polite phrase *te rog*, *vă rog* 'please', or refl. 'pray'.

Ir. *domandare*, Fr. *demander* 'ask' in both senses (18.31).

It. *(ri)chiedere*, Rum. *cere*, fr. Lat. *quaerere* 'seek' (11.31). REW 6923, 7235.

4. Ir. *condaigim*, *cuingim*, fr. **com-di-saigim*, cpd. of *saigim* 'go toward, seek' (11.31). Pedersen 2.607. Thurneysen, Gram. 116,450.

Ir. *guidim*, mostly 'pray', see 22.17.

NIr. *iarraim*, also (and in OIr. mostly) 'seek' (11.31).

W. *gofyn*, 'ask' in both senses (18.31).

Br. *goulenn*, 'ask' in both senses (18.31).

5. Goth. *bidjan* (*baþ*, *bēdum*, *bidans*), ON *biðja*, Dan. *bede*, Sw. *bedja*, OE *biddan*, ME *bidde*, (NE *bid* 'command, invite', etc. by crossing with OE *bēodan*; Du. *bidden* mostly 'pray'), OHG, MHG, NHG *bitten*, etym. disputed, perh. (with secondary ablaut) : Grk. πείθω 'persuade', Lat. *fīdere* 'believe, trust', etc. Walde-P. 2.139. Kluge-G. 60. Falk-Torp 66. Feist 89. NED s.v. *bid.*, vb.

Sw. *begära*, orig. only 'desire' (16.62).

OE *āsciān*, ME *aske*, NE ask, OHG *eiscōn*, MHG *eischen*, 'ask' in both senses (18.31).

OE *giwian* (freq. in Lindisf. Gospels) : *gīnam*, OHG *ginēn*, *giwēn*, etc. 'yawn' (4.52). Sievers, Anglia 16.98 f. Cf. NE *gape after*, hence *gape* 'desire eagerly' (NED s.v. *gape*, vb. 4 b) and Lat. *hiāre ac poscere* (Cic. Verr. 2, 3.4).

NE *request*, fr. OFr. *requester*, deriv. of sb. *requeste*, fr. OFr. *requerre* : It. *richiedere*, etc. (above, 3).

ME *demaund*, NE *demand* (now stronger than *ask*, *request*), fr. OFr. *demander* (above, 3).

NE *beg*, primarily 'ask alms', but also a humble or polite expression for 'ask, request', orig. dub. NED s.v.

Du. *verzoeken*, NHG *ersuchen*, cpds. of Du. *zoeken*, NHG *suchen* 'seek'.

Du., NHG *verlangen* (> Dan. *forlange*), orig. 'desire, long for' (16.62).

Du. *vorderen*, MHG *vordern*, NHG *fordern*, fr. MLG *vorderen* (> Dan. *fordre*, Sw. *fordra*), OHG *fordarōn*, lit. 'cause (command) that something go forward', deriv. of OHG *fordar*, etc. 'fore, forward'. Weigand-H. 1.568. Falk-Torp 266.

6. Lith. *reikalauti* (mostly 'demand'), fr. *reikalas* 'necessity' : *reikėti* 'be necessary' (9.93).

7. ChSl. *prositi*, etc., above, 1.

ChSl., SCr. *moliti* 'ask, beg', refl. 'pray', see under 'pray' (22.17).

SCr. *iskati*, also 'seek' (the general Slavic meaning, ChSl. *iskati*, etc., 11.31).

SCr. *tražiti*, also 'seek' (11.31).

Boh. *žádati*, Pol. *żądać*, orig. 'desire' (16.62).

Russ. *trebovat'*, orig. 'need' : ChSl. *trěbě* 'opus ut', *trěbŭ* 'necessary', etc. (9.93, 9.94).

8. Skt. *yāc-*, perh. : OHG *jehan* 'confess, acknowledge, say', W. *iaith* 'language', etc. Walde-P. 1.205.

Skt. *arthaya-*, esp. *prārthaya-* (*pra-arthaya-*), lit. 'strive to obtain, desire' : *artha-* 'aim, purpose' (17.41).

Av., OPers. *jad-* 'beseech, pray for', see under 'pray' (22.17).

18.36 PROMISE (vb.)

Grk.	*ὑπισχνέομαι, ἐπαγγέλλω*	Goth.	*gahaitan*	Lith.	*(pri)žadėti*
NG	*ὑπόσχομαι, τάζω*	ON	*heitan*	Lett.	*(ap)suolīt*
Lat.	*prōmittere*	Dan.	*love*	ChSl.	*oběštati*
It.	*promettere*	Sw.	*lova*	SCr.	*obećati*
Fr.	*promettre*	OE	*(be)hātan*	Boh.	*slíbiti*
Sp.	*prometer*	ME	*(be)hote*	Pol.	*obiecać, przyrzec*
Rum.	*promite, făgădui*	NE	*promise*	Russ.	*obeščat', sulit'*
Ir.	*duairngir, gellaim*	Du.	*beloven*	Skt.	*pratijñā-, pratiçru-*
NIr.	*geallaim*	OHG	*giheizan*		
W.	*addaw*	MHG	*ge-, ver-heizen, versprechen*		
Br.	*gouestla*	NHG	*versprechen, verheissen*		

Words for 'promise' include some meaning literally 'undertake' or 'put forth', several cpds. of verbs for 'speak, say, call, know, hear', derivs. of nouns for 'vow, pledge', and some cognates of words for 'dear' and 'love' ('find agreeable, acceptable' > 'promise').

1. Grk. ὑπισχνέομαι and (Ion., Delph., etc.) ὑπίσχομαι, late Byz., NG ὑπόσχομαι (cf. Grk. fut. ὑπο-σχήσομαι, 2d aor. ὑπεσχόμην), orig. 'undertake', cpd. of ὑπό 'under' with forms of ἴσχω 'hold, hold back' (**si-zĝh-*) and ἔχω 'hold, have'.

Grk. ἐπαγγέλλω 'proclaim, announce', but freq. also 'promise', cpd. of Grk. ἀγγέλλω 'announce'.

NG pop. τάζω, fr. class. Grk. τάσσω 'array, assign', etc., in mid. also 'agree upon', whence 'promise' (cf. NE *agree to* = 'promise') in Byz. (Chron. Mor. ἔταξε, etc., also ἐτάχτη κ'ὑπησχήθμ) and NG.

2. Lat. *prōmittere* (> Romance words), lit. 'put forth', cpd. of *mittere* 'let go, send' (10.63). Ernout-M. 622.

Rum. *făgădui*, also 'entertain' (a guest), fr. Hung. *fogad* 'receive, welcome, vow, promise'. Tiktin 605.

3. Ir. *duairngir* (3sg.), cpd. of *gairim* 'shout, call' (18.41). Pedersen 2.534.

Ir. *gellaim*, NIr. *geallaim*, in the older language largely 'pledge', deriv. of *gell* 'pledge' : *gīall*, W. *gwystl*, ON *gīsl*, etc. 'hostage'. Walde-P. 1.554. Pedersen 2.537.

W. *addaw, addo*, fr. *ad* + *do* 'yes', hence orig. 'say yes to'.

Br. *gouestla*, deriv. of *gouestl* 'vow, promise, pledge, hostage' (= W. *gwystl*, etc.; cf. Ir. *gellaim*, above).

4. Goth. *gahaitan* ('call together' and 'promise'), ON *heita*, OE *(be)hātan*, ME *(be)hote, (be)hete, (be)highte*, NE arch. *hight*, OHG *giheizan*, MHG *geheizen, verheizen*, NHG *verheissen*, cpds. (or the simple form) of Goth. *haitan*, etc. 'call' (18.41) and 'command' (19.45). Feist 236. NED s.v. *hight*, vb., B2.

Dan. *love*, Sw. *lova* (ON *lofa* 'allow, permit', but NIcel. 'promise'), Du. *beloven* (MLG *loven*, OFris. *lovia* id.) : OHG *gelobōn* 'agree, permit' (NHG *geloben* 'vow, pledge'), Goth. *us-laubjan*, OE *ā-līefan*, OHG *ir-louben* 'permit', Goth. *liufs*, etc. 'dear' (16.26; cf. also words for 'praise' and 'believe' belonging to same group of cognates). Walde-P. 2.419. Falk-Torp 656 f. Franck-v. W. 48.

NE *promise*, fr. the sb. *promise*, fr. Lat. *prōmissum* (: *prōmittere*, above, 2).

MHG, NHG *versprechen*, fr. OHG *firsprehhan* 'refuse, forbid, hinder', also 'speak for someone, defend' (these senses also in MHG), cpd. of OHG *sprehhan* 'speak' (18.21). Paul, Deutsches Wtb. 602.

5. Lith. *žadėti, prižadėti* : *žodis* 'word' (18.26).

Lett. *suolīt, apsuolīt*, fr. Russ. *sulit'* id. (below). Mühl.-Endz. 3.1137 f.

6. ChSl. *oběštati*, SCr. *obećati*, Pol. *obiecać*, Russ. *obeščat'*, beside sb. ChSl. *obětŭ*, etc., fr. **ob-věštati*, **ob-větŭ* : ChSl. *věštati* 'speak' (18.21). Brückner 370, 614.

Boh. *slíbiti* (with sb. *slib*), cpd. of *sŭ-* and *líbiti* 'like, love' : ChSl. *ljubiti* 'love, kiss', *ljubŭ* 'dear' (Goth. *liufs* 'dear', etc., cf. above, Dan. *love*, etc.). Miklosich 171.

Pol. *przyrzec, -rzekać*, cpd. of *przy-* 'to' and *rzec* 'say' (18.22).

Russ. *sulit'*, prob. (through use as 'promise well') : ChSl. *sulějĭ* 'better'. (Brückner 525, also : ChSl. *sŭlati* 'send', very dub.).

7. Skt. *prati-jñā-*, lit. 'recognize', cpd. of *prati-* 'toward' and *jñā-* 'know'.

Skt. *prati-çru-*, lit. 'listen to', cpd. of *prati-* (cf. above) and *çru-* 'hear'.

18.37 REFUSE

Grk.	*ἀρνέομαι*	Goth.	. . . .	Lith.	*atsakyti*
NG	*ἀρνοῦμαι, ἀρνειέμαι*	ON	*neita*	Lett.	*liegt*
Lat.	*recūsāre*	Dan.	*afslaa, vægre sig (ved)*	ChSl.	*otŭrešti*
It.	*rifiutare*	Sw.	*(för)vägra, avslå*	SCr.	*odbiti, uskratiti*
Fr.	*refuser*	OE	*wiþsacan*	Boh.	*odmítnouti*
Sp.	*rehusar*	ME	*refuse, withsaye, denye*	Pol.	*odmówić*
Rum.	*refuza*	NE	*refuse (deny)*	Russ.	*otkazat'*
Ir.	*astoing* (3sg.), *ēmdim*	Du.	*weigeren, afslaan*	Skt.	*pratyākhyā-*
NIr.	*eitighim*	OHG	*widarsahhan, weigarōn*		
W.	*nacau, gomedd*	MHG	*weigern, abeslahen*		
Br.	*dinac'h*	NHG	*verweigern, abschlagen*		

Several of the words for 'refuse' (a request, an offer, etc.) are the same as, or from the same source as, those for 'deny' (18.34). Others are from 'say off, swear off, strike off', etc.

1. Grk. ἀρνέομαι, NG ἀρνοῦμαι 'deny' (18.34), also 'refuse'.

2. Lat. *recūsāre*, prob. orig. as law term 'challenge, object to', deriv. of *causa* 'cause, lawsuit'. Ernout-M. 166.

It. *rifiutare*, for OIt. *rifutare* (influenced by *fiutare* 'sniff'), fr. Lat. *refūtāre* 'drive back, repel, disprove, refute', cpd. like *confūtāre* 'repress, confute', perh. (**bhaut-* beside **bhaud-*) : ON *bauta*, OE *bēatan* 'strike, beat'. Walde-H. 1.258. REW 7165.

Fr. *refuser* (> Rum. *refuza*), Sp. *rehusar*, fr. VLat. **refūsāre*, prob. blend of *recūsāre* and *refūtāre* (above). REW 7164. Gamillscheg 750. Diez 270.

3. Ir. *astoing* (3sg.), lit. 'swears off', cpd. of *ess-* 'off, from' and *tongu* 'swear' (21.24); vbl. n. *eitech*, whence MIr. *eitchim*, NIr. *eitighim*. Pedersen 2.652. Thurneysen, Gram. 509.

Ir. *ēmdim* (*forēmdim* 'be unable'), W. *gomedd*, cpds. of vb. seen in Ir. *midiur* 'judge', W. *meddu* 'possess.' Pedersen 2.578 ff. Loth, RC 38.296.

W. *nacau*, Br. *dinac'h* (with *di-* 'from'), cf. Br. *nac'h* 'deny' (18.34).

4. ON *neita* 'deny' (18.34), also 'refuse'.

OE *wiþsacan* 'deny' (18.34), also 'refuse'; similarly OHG *farsahhan* both 'deny' and 'refuse', but more esp. in the latter sense OHG *widarsahhan*.

ME, NE *refuse*, fr. Fr. *refuser* (above, 2).

ME *withsaye* 'deny' (18.34), also 'refuse'.

ME *denye*, NE *deny* (18.34), also 'refuse' (NED s.v. III).

Du. *weigeren* (MLG *wēgeren* > Dan. *vægre* only refl. with prep. *ved*, Sw. *vägra*), OHG *weigarōn*, MHG *weigern*, NHG *weigern*, mostly *verweigern* : OHG *weigar*, MDu. *weiger, wēger* 'resisting, stubborn', fr. the root of Goth. *weihan*, OHG *wīgan* 'fight', etc. Walde-P. 1.232. Falk-Torp 1401. Weigand-H. 2.1229.

MHG *abeslahen, abeslān* (MLG *afslān* > Dan. *afslaa*, Sw. *avslå*), NHG *abschlagen*, lit. 'strike off, down'. Falk-Torp 14.

5. Lith. *atsakyti*, also 'answer' (18.32), lit. 'say back'.

Lett. *liegt* 'deny' (18.34), also 'refuse'.

6. ChSl. *otŭrešti* 'renounce, refuse', also 'forbid', cpd. of *otŭ* 'from, away' and *rešti* 'say' (18.22). Cf. Lith. *atsakyti*, Pol. *odmówić*.

SCr. *odbiti*, lit. 'strike off, back', cpd. of *od* (= ChSl. *otŭ*, above) and *biti* 'strike' (9.21).

SCr. *uskratiti*, cpd. of *uz-* (*us-*, Leskien, Serbo-kroat. Gram. 69) 'off, back' and *kratiti* 'shorten' (also simply 'refuse') : ChSl. *sŭkratiti* 'shorten, end', *kratŭkŭ* 'short' (12.59), etc.

Boh. *odmítnouti*, lit. 'throw, reject', cpd. of *od-* (= ChSl. *otŭ*, above) and *-mítnouti*, iter. to *mésti*, ChSl. *mesti* 'throw'. Cf. ChSl. *otŭ-mětati, -metati* 'deny' (18.34). Berneker 2.53 f.

Pol. *odmówić*, cpd. of *od-* (= ChSl. *otŭ*, above) and *mówić* 'speak' (18.21).

Russ. *otkazat'*, cpd. of *ot-* (= ChSl. *otŭ*, above) and *kazat'* 'show' (cf. *s-kazat'* 'say', 18.22). Cf. NHG *abweisen* 'decline, reject'.

7. Skt. *prati-ā-khyā-*, cpd. of *prati-* 'back' and *ā-khyā-* 'tell, inform, announce', *khyā-* in pass. 'be named, be known', caus. 'make known, relate'.

18.38 FORBID

Grk.	*ἀπαγορεύω*, fut. *ἀπερῶ*, aor. *ἀπεῖπον*	Goth.	*faurbiudan*	Lith.	*(už)drausti*
NG	*ἀπαγορεύω*	ON	*banna, fyrirbjōđa*	Lett.	*(aiz)liegt*
Lat.	*vetāre, prohibēre, interdīcere*	Dan.	*forbyde*	ChSl.	*(vŭz)braniti*
It.	*proibire, vietare, interdire*	Sw.	*förbjuda*	SCr.	*zabraniti*
Fr.	*défendre, interdire, prohiber*	OE	*forbēodan*	Boh.	*zapověděti, zakázati*
Sp.	*prohibir, interdecir*	ME	*forbede*	Pol.	*zakazać, zabronić*
Rum.	*opri, interzice*	NE	*forbid, prohibit*	Russ.	*zapretit'*
Ir.	*argàirim, arcuillim*	Du.	*verbieden*	Skt.	*niṣidh-, pratiṣidh-*
NIr.	*coiscim, toirmeascaim*	OHG	*farbiutan*	Av.	*antarə-ā-mrū-*
W.	*gwahardd*	MHG	*verbieten, undersagen*		
Br.	*difenn, berza*	NHG	*verbieten, untersagen*		

'Forbid' is often expressed by compounds of verbs for 'command' or 'say' with various prefixes which have come to connote exclusion, interference, negation, etc. (Grk. ἀπο-, Lat. *pro-*, *inter-*, NE *for-*, NHG *ver-*, Slavic *za-*). Or words for 'hinder, prevent' (19.59), 'repel', etc. come to be used also as the verbal 'forbid'.

1. Grk. ἀπαγορεύω, cpd. of ἀπό 'away from', in its use indicating exclusion, negation, and ἀγορεύω 'speak'. Outside of present system, supplemented by fut.

ἀπ-ερῶ, aor. ἀπ-εῖπον, cpds. of other verbs for 'speak, say' (18.21).

Grk. οὐκ ἐάω 'not permit' (19.47) serves for the positive 'forbid' in Hom. (where ἀπαγορεύω does not occur).

Grk. κωλύω 'hinder, prevent' (19.59), late also sometimes 'forbid'. In NT (ἀπαγορεύω does not occur; 'forbid' in strict sense is expressed as 'command not', e.g. Mk. 6.8, 8.30, etc.) κωλύω is generally rendered by OE *forbēodan*, NE *forbid* (e.g. Mt. 19.14 = Lk. 18.16, etc.), but these words are also used, like Lat. *prohibēre*, for 'hinder, prevent'.

2. Lat. *vetāre* (> It. *vietare*, OFr. *veer*, OSp. *vedar*), OLat. *votāre*, prob. : W. *gwadu* 'deny', OW *guetid* 'says'. Ernout-M. 1099. Loth, RC 42.367 f.

Lat. *interdīcere* (> It., Fr. *interdire*, Sp. *interdecir*, Rum. *interzice*, all with legal or formal nuance), orig. a legal term, cpd. of *dīcere* 'say' and *inter* 'between' in its use indicating interference, destruction, etc. (*inter-īre, -ficere, -imere*, etc.). Ernout-M. 491 f. Walde-H. 1.709.

Lat. *prohibēre* 'hinder, prevent' (19.59) and 'forbid', whence in latter sense It. *proibire*, Sp. *prohibir*, Fr. *prohiber*.

Fr. *défendre*, 'defend' and now the common word for 'forbid', fr. Lat. *dēfendere* 'repel, defend', orig. 'strike down' : Grk. θείνω 'strike', etc. Walde-P. 1.680. Ernout-M. 344. Walde-H. 1.332 f. REW 2517.

Rum. *opri* 'hinder' (19.59) also 'forbid'.

3. Ir. *argairim*, cpd. of *gairim* 'call' (18.41), cf. *forcongur* 'command' (19.45). Pedersen 2.534.

Ir. *arcuillim*, fr. earlier *arcelim* 'take away', cpd. of *celim* 'hide' (12.27). Pedersen 2.482. Laws, Gloss. 72.

NIr. *coiscim* and *toirmeascaim* 'hinder, prevent' (19.59), also 'forbid'.

W. *gwahardd*, MW *guahrt*, etym.?

Br. *difenn*, fr. Fr. *défendre*.

Br. *berza*, fr. sb. *berz* 'prohibition', orig. dub. Loth, Mots lat. 138.

4. Goth. *faurbiudan* ('command', with neg. phrase = 'forbid'), OE *forbēodan*, etc., general Gmc., cpds. of Goth. *-biudan*, OE *bēodan*, etc. 'command, announce' (19.45) with the Gmc. prefix in its excluding, negating sense (as in NE *for-get*, NHG *ver-kennen*, etc.).

ON *banna* = OE, OHG *bannan* 'summon', fr. the root of Grk. φημί 'say', Lat. *fārī* 'speak', etc. (18.21). The secondary notion of prohibition is more widespread in the noun (NE *ban*, etc.). Falk-Torp 46. NED s.v. *ban*.

Late ME, NE *prohibit*, through pple. *prohibit* 'prohibited' fr. Lat. *prohibitus*, pple. of *prohibēre* (above, 2). NED s.v.

MHG *undersagen*, NHG *untersagen*, semantic borrowing of Lat. *interdīcere* (above, 2). Weigand-H. 2.1124.

5. Lith. *drausti* (also 'threaten'), esp. *už-drausti* : Lett. *draudēt* 'threaten' (18.44).

Lett. *liegt, aizliegt*, both also 'deny, refuse', see 18.34.

6. ChSl. *braniti, vŭz-braniti* (both in Gospels for κωλύω, for which see above, 1), SCr. *zabraniti*, Pol. *zabronić*, beside SCr., Boh. *braniti* 'defend, hinder', ChSl. *branĭ* 'strife', Boh. *brań*, Pol. *broń* 'weapon, armor', all : ChSl. *brati* 'fight', Lat. *ferīre* 'strike', etc. Walde-P. 2.161. Berneker 74, 76. Brückner 41 f.

Boh. *zapověděti*, cpd. of *pověděti* 'say, tell' (18.22) with *za-* in its use like that of NHG *ver-* in *verbieten*, etc. (Leskien, Gram. 164).

Boh. *zakázati*, Pol. *zakazać*, cpds. of *kázati*, *kazać* 'order, preach' (= ChSl. *kazati* 'show, admonish', SCr. *kazati* 'say', etc.; cf. 18.22), with *za-* (as in preceding).

Russ. *zapretit'* : ChSl. *(za-)prětiti* 'rebuke, threaten', SCr. *prijetiti* 'threaten' (18.44).

7. Skt. *niṣidh-*, *pratiṣidh-* 'drive off, prevent' and 'forbid', cpds. of *sidh-* 'drive off, repel', etym.?

Av. *antarə-ā-mrū-* 'renounce' or 'forbid', with sb. *antarə-ukti-* 'interdict' (Y. 19.15), cpds. of *antarə* (= Lat. *inter*) with *mrū-* and *vač-* 'speak, say' (18.22). Cf. Lat. *interdīcere*, above, 2.

18.41 CALL (vb. = Summon)

Grk.	*καλέω*	Goth.	*haitan*	Lith.	*šaukti*
NG	*φωνάζω, κράζω, καλῶ*	ON	*kalla*	Lett.	*saukt*
Lat.	*vocāre*	Dan.	*kalde*	ChSl.	*(pri)zŭvati*
It.	*chiamare*	Sw.	*kalla*	SCr.	*zvati*
Fr.	*appeler*	OE	*clipian, cīegan*	Boh.	*volati*
Sp.	*llamar*	ME	*clepe, calle*	Pol.	*wołać*
Rum.	*chema*	NE	*call*	Russ.	*zvat'*
Ir.	*(do-)gairim*	Du.	*roepen*	Skt.	*hvā-*
NIr.	*gairim, gairmim*	OHG	*(h)ruofan, halōn*	Av.	*zav-*
W.	*galw*	MHG	*ruofen*		
Br.	*gervel*	NHG	*rufen*		

Several of the words for 'call' (summon or attract attention) are the same as, or are derived from, those meaning 'shout, cry out' (18.13). This is especially true in the popular language. Some of them, but by no means all, are used also for 'call' = 'name' (18.42).

1. Grk. *καλέω* (NG *καλῶ* lit. and esp. 'invite') : Lat. *calāre* 'call out, proclaim, convoke', Lat. *clāmāre* 'shout, cry out' (18.13).

Grk. *κράζω* 'shout', freq. 'call' in pop. Byz. (e.g. Chron. Mor.; sometimes also 'call' = 'name') and NG.

NG pop. *φωνάζω* 'shout' and 'call'.

2. Lat. *vocāre* : *vōx* 'voice' (18.11).

It. *chiamare*, Sp. *llamar*, Rum. *chema*, fr. Lat. *clāmāre* 'shout' (18.13). REW 1961.

Fr. *appeler*, fr. Lat. *appellāre* 'address, call upon, invoke', cpd. (*ad-p-*) like *com-pellāre* 'accost, reproach', *interpellāre* 'interrupt', fr. the root of *pellere* 'drive, drive out, strike' (10.65). Walde-P. 2.677. Ernout-M. 749 f. Walde-H. 1.59. REW 542.

3. Ir. *gairim* 'shout' and (esp. in OIr. cpd. *do-gairim*, with prefix *to-*) 'call'; here also NIr. *gairmim*, fr. *gairm* 'a call, summons'.

W. *galw*, MBr. *galu*, Br. *gervel* (pple. *galvet*, cf. *galv* sb. 'call, summons'; Pedersen 1.491) : ON *kalla* 'shout, call, claim', Dan. *kalde*, Sw. *kalla*, OE (rare) *callian*, ME *calle*, NE *call* 'call', OHG *kallōn* 'speak loudly or much, gossip', ChSl. *glagolati* 'speak', *glasŭ* 'voice'. Walde-P. 1.538. Falk-Torp 485.

4. Goth. *haitan*, also 'call' = 'name' and pass. 'be called (named)' : ON *heita* 'call (name), be called, promise, vow', OE *hātan* 'command, promise, call (name)', 'be called (named)', OHG *heizan* 'command, call (name), be called', etc. (18.42), perh. orig. 'incite' (whence 'command, call by name') : Ir. *cid-* in pple. *cisse* gl. *invecta*, **to-di-cid-* in *di-an-dichdet* gl. *deducunt*, fr. the root in Lat. *ciēre* 'set in motion, arouse', Grk. *κινέω* 'set in motion, drive', etc. Walde-P. 1.362. Walde-H. 1.214. Pedersen 2.490 f. Falk-Torp 388. Feist 236.

ON *kalla*, etc. : W. *galw*, etc. (above, 3).

OE *clipian*, ME *clepe* 'shout' (18.13) and 'call'.

OE *cīegan*, OHG *(gi)kewen* (chiefly 'name') : Grk. *γοάω* 'lament', ChSl. *govoriti* 'make a noise' (Russ. *govorit'* 'speak', etc., 18.21). Walde-P. 1.635.

OHG *(h)ruofan*, MHG *ruofen*, NHG *rufen*, Du. *roepen*, orig. 'shout', whence increasingly also 'call'.

OHG *halōn*, *holōn*, *holēn* 'bring' and freq. 'call' (Otfr., Tat., etc.), see 10.62.

5. Lith. *šaukti*, Lett. *saukt* 'shout' and 'call'.

6. ChSl. *zŭvati* (and esp. in Gospels *pri-zŭvati*), SCr. *zvati*, Russ. *zvat'* : Lith. *žavėti*, Lett. *zavēt* 'bewitch', Skt. *hvā-*, *hū-*, Av. *zbā-*, *zav-* 'call', Grk. *καυχάομαι* 'boast', perh. Ir. *guth* 'voice'. Cf. esp. the 3sg. ChSl. *zovetŭ* = Av. *zavaiti*, Skt. (but mid.) *havate*. Walde-P. 1.529.

Boh. *volati*, Pol. *wołać*, perh. deriv. of the exclamation attested in OBoh. *vele*, ChSl. *o vele*, *vole* '*ἄγε, ἄρα*' (Supr., etc.). Brückner 630.

7. Skt. *hvā-*, *hū-*, Av. *zbā-*, *zav-* : ChSl. *zŭvati*, etc. (above, 6).

18.42 CALL (vb. = Name; b) Be Called, Named)

Grk.	*καλέω, ὀνομάζω*	Goth.	*haitan, namnjan*	Lith.	*vadinti*
NG	*λέγω, ὀνομάζω*	ON	*heita* (also b), *kalla*	Lett.	*saukt*
Lat.	*vōcāre*	Dan.	*kalde, hede* (b)	ChSl.	*narešti*
It.	*chiamare*	Sw.	*kalla, heta* (b)	SCr.	*nazvati*
Fr.	*appeler*	OE	*hātan* (also b), *clipian, nemnan*	Boh.	*nazvati*
Sp.	*llamar*			Pol.	*nazwać*
Rum.	*chema*	ME	*hote, hight* (esp. b), *clepe, calle nemne*	Russ.	*nazvat'*
Ir.	*gairim* (?)			Skt.	*abhi-dhā-*
NIr.	*gairim*	NE	*call, name*		
W.	*galw*	Du.	*noemen, heeten* (b)		
Br.	*gervel* (or phrase with *hano* 'name')	OHG	*heizan* (also b)		
		MHG	*heizen* (also b)		
		NHG	*nennen, heissen* (b)		

The majority of the common words for 'call' = 'name' are the same as those for 'call' = 'summon' (18.41) or belong to groups which once had this sense (as SCr., Boh. *nazvati*, etc. : ChSl. *zŭvati* 18.41). In general, pass. or refl. forms are used for 'be called, bear a certain name', as Grk. *καλοῦμαι*, Lat. *vōcārī*, Fr. *s'appeler*, Dan. *kaldes*, Russ. *nazvat'sja*, etc. But forms of the Gmc. group, Goth. *haitan*, ON *heita*, OE *hātan*, OHG *heizan* were used for both 'call' and 'be named' (but pass. in Goth. *haitada* and OE *hātte*; cf. NED s.v. *hight*, vb.[1]), and the latter use prevails in the modern forms (Dan. *hede*, Sw. *heta*, Du. *heeten*, NHG *heissen*, NE arch. *hight* pple.).

Other terms are derivs. of nouns for 'name' (18.28), as Grk. *ὀνομάζω*, the Gmc. group Goth. *namnjan*, OE *nemnan*, etc., and the Slavic group (not included in the list; some of them mostly 'name' = 'appoint' or the like) ChSl. *imenovati*, Boh. *jmenovati*, etc.

A few are words for 'say'. So Grk. *λέγω* as 'call, name' rarely in class. Grk., freq. in NT, and the usual expression in NG (*πῶς τὸν λένε, πῶς λέγεται*; 'what is his name?'); ChSl. *narešti* (in Gospels reg. for *καλέω*, also *ὀνομάζω*), cpd. of *rešti* 'say' (18.22). Cf. also Lith. *vadinti* : Skt. *vad-* 'speak, say' (18.21).

Skt. *abhi-dhā-*, lit. 'put on', but esp. 'put a name upon, call', with sbs. *abhidhā-*, *abhidhāna-* 'appellation, name'.

18.43 ANNOUNCE

Grk.	*ἀγγέλλω, ἀναγγέλλω*	Goth.	*gateihan, mērjan, spillōn*	Lith.	*skelbti, garsinti*
NG	*ἀναγγέλλω*			Lett.	*pazin'uot, sludināt*
Lat.	*nūntiāre*	ON	*boða, tjā, kynna*	ChSl.	*vŭzvěstiti, pověděti*
It.	*annunziare*	Dan.	*kundgøre, forkynde*	SCr.	*navijestiti, obznaniti, oglasiti*
Fr.	*annoncer*	Sw.	*kungöra, förkunna*		
Sp.	*anunciar*	OE	*cȳþan, mǣran, bodian, bēodan*	Boh.	*ohlásiti, zvěstiti, oznamiti*
Rum.	*anunţa, vesti*				
Ir.	*foōcair*	ME	*kythe, bode, bede*	Pol.	*ogłosić, obwieścić, oznajmić*
NIr.	*fōgraim*	NE	*announce*		
W.	*cyhoeddi, datgan*	Du.	*aankondigen*	Russ.	*ob'javil', vozvestit'*
Br.	*kemenn, embann*	OHG	*cundan, mār(r)en*	Skt.	*ākhyā-, çaṅs-*, etc.
		MHG	*kunden, kundigen*	Av.	*sąh-, aoǰ-*
		NHG	*ankündigen, verkündigen*		

'Announce' is expressed by words meaning literally 'bring a message, bring news, make known, make public', etc. But besides the words listed, common verbs for 'say' or 'speak' may be used in a formal way so as to be virtually equivalent to 'announce' or 'declare' (*thus saith the king*, bibl. *I say unto you*, etc.).

1. Grk. *ἀγγέλλω*, cpd. *ἀναγγέλλω*, fr. *ἄγγελος* 'messenger', of dub. orig. (: Pers. *ἄγγαρος* 'messenger' or early loanword fr. the same source?). Walde-H. 1.46.

2. Lat. *nūntiāre* (later and esp. eccl.), *adnūntiāre* (> Romance words), fr. *nūntium* 'message', *nūntius* 'messenger', generally derived fr. *novus* 'new' (e.g. as cpd. **novi-ventio-*, Brugmann, IF 17.366 f.) but perh. as an orig. augural term (cf. Ernout-M. 687) : Ir. *nūall* 'noise, cry', Skt. *nu-* 'sound, exult, praise'. Cf. Chruška, reported by Niedermann, Idg. Anz. 19.33 f.

Rum. *vesti* fr. sb. *vesti* 'announcement, news', fr. ChSl. *věstĭ* id. (below, 6), Tiktin 1733.

3. Ir. *foōcair, fouacair* (3sg.), NIr. *fōgraim*, fr. **fo-od-gair-*, cpd. of *gairim* 'shout, call' (18.13). Pedersen 2.535.

W. *cyhoeddi*, also 'publish', fr. *cyhoedd* 'public', cpd. of *cy-* 'with, common', but second part dub. Morris Jones 98 (but?).

W. *datgan*, cpd. of *dad-* with intensive force and *canu* 'sing'. Morris Jones 266.

Br. *kemenn*, also 'command' (and so always the cpd. *gourc'hemenn*), fr. Lat. *commendāre* (cf. 19.45).

Br. *embann*, also 'proclaim, publish', as sb. 'proclamation, bans', fr. French phrase (*proclamer*) *en ban*. Henry 112.

4. Goth. *gateihan*, ON *tjā*, also 'show' (OE *tēon*, OHG *zīhan* 'accuse') : Grk. *δείκνῡμι*, Skt. *diç-* 'show', etc. (15.55). Feist 204.

Goth. *mērjan*, OE *mǣran*, OHG *mār(r)en* (ON *mǣra* 'praise') : ON *mǣrr*, OE *mǣre*, OHG *māri* 'famous', Ir. *mār*, *mōr* 'great', *māraim* 'make great, magnify', etc. Walde-P. 2.238. Feist 355.

Goth. *spillōn* : *spill* 'story', ON *spjall*, OE *spell*, OHG *spell* 'story, account', ON *spjalla*, OE *spellian* 'talk, converse', outside connections dub. Walde-P. 2.676 f. Feist 445.

ON *boða*, OE *bodian*, ME (NE) *bode*, fr. ON *boð* 'offer, message, command', OE *bod* 'command, message' : ON *bjōða* 'offer, command', OE *bēodan* 'offer, command, announce', ME *bede*, etc. (19.45).

ON *kynna* (rare in this sense, usually refl. with dat. or pass. 'learn, study', cf. Fritzner s.v.), OE *cȳþan*, ME *kythe*, MLG (*vor*)*kunden* (> Dan. *forkynde*, Sw. *förkunna*), OHG *cundan*, MHG *kunden*, *künden*, NHG (*ver*)*künden*, fr.

ON *kunnr*, OE *cūþ*, OHG *cund*, Goth. *kunþs* 'known' (orig. pple. to Goth. *kunnan*, etc. 'know'); hence adj. OHG, NHG *kundig*, with deriv. vb. MHG *kündigen*, NHG more usually in cpds. *ankündigen*, *verkündigen*, Du. *aankondigen*, *verkondigen*. Weigand-H. 1.1171. Falk-Torp 258.

Dan. *kundgøre*, Sw. *kungöra*, prob. translations of NHG *kundmachen*, *kundtun* 'notify, make known', cpds. of Dan. *kund*, etc. 'known' (= ON *kunnr*, cf. above) and words for 'make, do'. Falk-Torp 594.

NE *announce*, early *anounce*, fr. OFr. *anonc(i)er* (above, 2).

5. Lith. *skelbti* (freq. also with prefixes *ap-*, *pa-*) : *skalyti* 'bark, bay' (of dogs), Pol. *skolić* 'whine (as a dog)', OHG *scellan* 'sound, resound, make a noise, ring', ON *skjalla* 'clash, clatter', etc. Walde-P. 1.445.

Lith. *garsinti* (also *ap-*), fr. *garsas* 'sound, tone' (15.44).

Lett. *pazin'uot*, caus. to (*pa*)*zīt* 'know' (17.17).

Lett. *sludināt* : *sludēt* 'be rumored about', fr. the root of *slava* 'fame, glory', etc. (16.47). Mühl.-Endz. 3.940 f.

6. ChSl. *vŭz-věstiti* (the usual word in the Gospels for *ἀπαγγέλλω*), SCr. *navijestiti*, Boh. *zvěstiti*, Pol. *obwieścić*, Russ. *vozvestit'* : ChSl. *věstĭ* 'news', *věštati* 'speak', etc. (18.21).

ChSl. *pověděti*, freq. in Gospels for *ἀπαγγέλλω*, but also for *εἶπε, λέγω* 'say' (18.21).

SCr. *obznaniti*, Boh. *oznamiti*, Pol. *oznajmić*, cpds. with caus. force to Slavic *znati* 'know' (17.17).

SCr. *oglasiti*, Boh. *ohlásiti*, Pol. *ogłosić*, fr. Slavic *glasŭ* 'voice' (18.11); cf. ChSl. *glasiti* 'make a sound'. Berneker 323.

Russ. *ob'javil'*, SCr. *objaviti* = ChSl. *ob-aviti* 'show' (15.55).

7. Skt. *ā-khyā-*, cpd. of *khyā-* in pass. 'be named, be known', and caus. 'make known, proclaim, relate, tell', etym.? Uhlenbeck 75.

Skt. *çaṅs-*, Av. *sąh-* : OPers. *θah-* 'say', etc. (18.22).

Av. *aoǰ-*, see 18.21.

18.44 THREATEN

Grk.	*ἀπειλέω*	Goth.	*(ga)hwōtjan*	Lith.	*grasinti, grumoti*, etc.
NG	*φοβερίζω, ἀπειλῶ*	ON	*ōgna, hōta*	Lett.	*draudēt, grasīties*
Lat.	*minārī*	Dan.	*true*	ChSl.	*(za-)prětiti (groziti)*
It.	*minacciare*	Sw.	*hota*	SCr.	*prijetiti*
Fr.	*menacer*	OE	*hwōpan, bēotian, þrēatian*	Boh.	*hroziti*
Sp.	*amenaza-*			Pol.	*grozić*
Rum.	*ameninţa*	ME	*threte, boste, menasse*	Russ.	*grozit'*
Ir.	*domaithim, bacraim*	NE	*threaten, menace*	Skt.	*tarj-, bharts-*
NIr.	*bagraim*	Du.	*dreigen*	Av.	*avi-spas-*
W.	*bygwth*	OHG	*drewen, drowen*		
Br.	*gourdrouz*	MHG	*drouwen, drōn*		
		NHG	*drohen*		

Several of the words for 'threaten' were used also for 'urge, press' (as OE *þrēatian*) or are cognate with others of such meaning, that is, 'threaten' was to 'exert pressure'. Several others meant originally 'frighten'. There are also connections with words for 'keep away, prevent' (through 'warn'), 'project, hang over' (a threat hangs over one), 'disgusting' ('make oneself disagreeable' > 'threaten'), and 'loud noise, cry, call'.

1. Grk. *ἀπειλέω*, beside sb. *ἀπειλή*

mostly in pl. 'threats', etym. much disputed; various outside connections suggested (Boisacq 67 f. Walde-H. 1.59), but prob. the same word as ἀπειλέω 'force' (Hdt.), Elean ἀποϝηλέω 'keep away, exclude' (from the altar, etc.), cpd. of εἴλω (*ϝέλνω) 'force, press, shut in or out, prevent'. Cf. also Heracl. ἐγ-(= ἐκ-)ϝηλέω 'keep away'. Semantic development 'keep away' through 'warn off, warn' to 'threaten'?

NG φοβερίζω, orig. 'frighten' (so LXX, Byz.), fr. φοβερός 'terrible, fearful' : φόβος 'fear' (16.53).

2. Lat. *minārī*, lit. but only poet. 'jut out, project', whence usually 'threaten', beside *minax* 'projecting, threatening', whence VLat. *minacia* sb. 'threat' (> It. *minaccia*, Fr. *menace*, Sp. *(a)menaza*, with deriv. vbs. for 'threaten', It. *minacciare*, Fr. *menacer*, Sp. *amenazar*, Rum. *amenința*. REW 5584), fr. *minae* (pl.) 'projection', whence '(something hanging above >) threats' : *ē-*, *prominēre* 'project, hang over', etc. Ernout-M. 615 f.

3. Ir. *do-maithim*, perh. : Alb. *matem* 'lift the hand to strike, throw', but root connection dub. Walde-P. 2.237. Pedersen 2.575.

MIr. *bacraim*, NIr. *bagraim*, fr. *bacar* 'threat, threatening', orig.? Macbain 26.

W. *bygwth*, orig. 'frighten', deriv. of *bwg* 'goblin, ghost' (22.45).

Br. *gourdrouz*, also sb. 'a threat', cpd. of *gour-* 'super' and *trouz* 'noise', in sense 'violent noise' > 'threat'. Henry 139.

4. Goth. *hwōtjan*, *gahwōtjan* (quotable only for ἐπιτιμάω, ἐμβριμάομαι 'rebuke, admonish sternly', but *hwōta* = ἀπειλή Eph. 6.9), ON *hōta*, *hǣta*, Sw. *hota* : ON *hvetja*, OE *hwettan* 'whet, urge, encourage', etc. Walde-P. 1.513. Falk-Torp 446. Feist 286.

ON *ōgna*, fr. *ōgn* 'dread, terror', pl. 'threats' : Goth. *agis* 'fright', *ōgan* 'be afraid', etc. (16.53).

Dan. *true* : ON *þrūga* 'urge, compel, threaten', OE *þryccan*, OHG *drucken* 'press', etc. (9.342). Falk-Torp 1288 f.

OE *hwōpan* = Goth. *hwōpan* 'boast', etym. dub., perh. reconstruction fr. Goth. *wōpjan* 'cry, shout', etc. (18.13). L. Bloomfield, PBB 37.251. Feist 286.

OE *bēotian* (also 'boast, vow, promise'), fr. *(ge)bēot* 'a threat, boast' for **bi-hāt* = OHG *bi-heiz* 'promise', Goth. *bi-hait* 'evil talk', etc. : OE *behātan* 'promise, boast, threaten', OHG *beheizan* 'promise', cpds. of OE *hātan*, OHG *heizan*, etc. 'call, name' (18.42) and 'command' (19.45). NED s.v. *beot*. Feist 90.

OE *þrēatian* (also 'urge, press, rebuke'), and *þrēatnian* (rare), ME *threte*, *thret(e)ne*, NE *threaten* : OE *(ā)þrēotan* 'make weary', Goth. *usþriutan* 'make trouble for, annoy', OHG *driozan* 'press, oppress', Lat. *trūdere* 'thrust, push, crowd', ChSl. *trudŭ* 'trouble', etc. (fr. the same root as OHG *drewen*, etc., below). Walde-P. 1.755. NED s.v. *threat*, sb.

ME *boste* (also 'boast'), orig. dub., perh. as 'puff oneself up' : MHG *būs* 'swelling, fullness, conceit', *būsen* 'revel', etc. Walde-P. 2.118.

ME *menasse*, NE *menace*, fr. Fr. *menacer* (above, 2).

Du. *dreigen*, OS *thrēgian*, perh. fr. an extension of **trei-* beside **treu-* in OHG *drewen*, etc. (below), OE *þrēatian*, etc. (above). Franck-v. W. 131 f.

OHG *drewen*, *drowen*, MHG *drouwen*, *dröuwen* (NHG *dräuen*), and (fr. sb. *drō*) also *drōn*, NHG *drohen* : OE *þrēan* 'reprove, reproach, punish, torture', ChSl. *trovą*, *truti* 'consume, devour', *tryją*, *tryti* 'rub', etc. (fr. the root seen in Dan. *true*, OE *þrēatian*, etc. (above). Walde-P. 1.731. Weigand-H. 1.380 f.

5. Lith. *grasinti*, *grasyti*, and *grėsti*, Lett. *grasīties* : Lith. *grasus* 'disgusting', *gristi* 'become satiated, disgusted', NHG *garstig* 'nasty'. Trautmann 95. Mühl.-Endz. 1.638.

Lith. *grumoti*, beside *grumenti*, also 'thunder slightly, mumble', *grumsti* also 'grate, creak' : Lett. *gremt* 'mumble, speak in passion, threaten, grumble', ChSl. *-grimiti*, Russ. *gremet'*, etc. 'thunder', Goth. *gramjan*, etc. 'become angry', Grk. χρεμίζω 'neigh', Walde-P. 1.655 f. Trautmann 97.

Lett. *draudēt* : Lith. *draudžiu*, *drausti* 'forbid, prohibit, threaten', *drausmė* 'discipline', etc., root connection dub. Mühl.-Endz. 1.491. Walde-P. 1.870.

6. ChSl. *(za-)prětiti* (*zaprětiti* in Gospels mostly 'rebuke', also 'command'), SCr. *prijetiti* (Russ. *zapretit'* 'forbid'), perh. fr. a deriv. of **per-* parallel to that in ChSl. *prěko* 'against', *prěkosloviti* and *vŭ prěko glagolati* 'speak against'.

ChSl. *groziti* (late), Boh. *hroziti*, Pol. *grozić*, Russ. *grozit'*, with sb. ChSl. *groza* 'fright, horror', Russ. *groza* 'threat, severity, storm', etc. : Grk. γοργός 'grim, terrible', Ir. *garg* 'rough, wild', etc. Walde-P. 1.537. Trautmann 95. Otherwise (with *z* fr. *s* : Lith. *grasyti*, etc. above, 5) Berneker 355, Brückner 159.

7. Skt. *tarj-* : Lat. *torvus* 'keen, wild, fierce', Grk. τάρβος 'fright, alarm, terror'. Walde-P. 1.736. Uhlenbeck 110.

Skt. *bharts-*, possibly deriv. of an *s*-stem **bhardhas-* : *bardhaka-* 'cutting off, shearing', Lat. *forfex* 'scissors', etc. Walde-P. 2.174. Uhlenbeck 196.

Av. *avi-spas-*, lit. 'aim at', cpd. of *spas-* 'look, watch, observe'. Barth. 1614.

18.45 BOAST (vb.)

Grk.	*εὔχομαι, κομπέω, καυχάομαι*	Goth.	*hwōpan*	Lith.	*girtis, didžiuotis*
		ON	*hrōsa, gambra*	Lett.	*lielīties, dzirties*
NG	*καυχῶμαι*	Dan.	*prale, skryde*	ChSl.	*chvaliti sę*
Lat.	*glōriārī, iactāre se*	Sw.	*skryta*	SCr.	*hvaliti se, hvastati se*
It.	*vantarsi*	OE	*gielpan*	Boh.	*chlubiti se, chvastati se*
Fr.	*se vanter*	ME	*yelpe, boste, bragge*	Pol.	*chwalić się, chełpić się*
Sp.	*jactarse*	NE	*boast, brag*	Russ.	*chvalit'sja, chvastat'sja*
Rum.	*se lăuda, se făli*	Du.	*zich beroemen, pochen, pralen*		
Ir.	*(ar-)bāgim, mōidim*			Skt.	*çlāgh-, katth-*
NIr.	*maoidhim*	OHG	*sih ruomen*		
W.	*ymffrostio, brolio*	MHG	*sich rüemen, gelfen*		
Br.	*fougeal*	NHG	*sich rühmen, prahlen*		

Several of the words for 'boast' are refl. (or med. pass.) forms of verbs derived from nouns for 'praise' or 'glory', hence orig. 'praise oneself, glorify oneself'. Others are mostly cognate with words for 'shout, cry out' or 'make a noise', partly of imitative origin. Occasional connections are with words for 'empty, vain', 'big' ('make oneself big' > 'boast').

1. Grk. εὔχομαι, mostly 'pray, vow' but also 'boast' (both senses in Hom.) : Lat. *vovēre* 'vow', Skt. *vāghat-* 'sacrificer', Av. *aoǰ-* 'say solemnly' (18.43). Walde-P. 1.110. Boisacq 300. Ernout-M. 1135.

Grk. κομπέω (also 'ring, clash'), κομπάζω, with sb. κόμπος 'din, clash, boast', etym.? Boisacq 489 f.

Grk. καυχάομαι, prob. of imitative orig. (cf. Lith. *šaukti* 'shout, cry out', 18.13). Boisacq 423. Otherwise (as **ĝhau-ĝhau* : Skt. *hvā-*, Av. *zav-* 'call') Walde-P. 1.529.

2. Lat. *glōriārī*, deriv. of *glōria* 'fame, glory' (16.47), also 'vainglory, boasting'.

Lat. *iactāre se* (> Sp. *jactarse*), lit. 'throw oneself about', frequent. of *iacere* 'throw'. Ernout-M. 466 f.

It. *vantarsi*, Fr. *se vanter* refl. (non-refl. 'vaunt, boast of'), fr. VLat. *vānitāre*, deriv. of *vānitās* 'emptiness, vanity' (: *vānus* 'empty, vain'). REW 9138.

Rum. *se lăuda*, refl. of *lăuda* 'praise' (16.79).

Rum. *se făli*, deriv. of *fală* 'praise, fame', fr. ChSl. *chvala* 'praise' (cf. below, 7). Tiktin 606 f.

3. Ir. *bāgim* and cpd. *ar-bāgim*, 'fight' and 'boast' or 'threaten' (OHG *bāga* 'strife', OS *bāg* 'boasting', etc., perh. fr. Celtic), prob. used orig. with reference to a war of words, but root connection? Walde-P. 2.130. Zimmer KZ 36.447 ff.

Ir. *mōidim* (orig. trans., 'boast of'; RIA Contrib. s.v.) NIr. *maoidhim* (also 'praise, celebrate') : *mīad* 'honor' (16.46), outside connections? Walde-P. 2.222. Pedersen 1.184.

W. *ymffrostio*, also simple *ffrostio*, deriv. of *ffrost* sb. 'boast, pomp', orig.?

Br. *fougeal*, deriv. of *fouge* 'vanity', fr. Fr. *fougue* 'fury'. Henry 124.

4. Goth. *hwōpan* = OE *hwōpan* 'threaten' (18.44).

ON *hrōsa* 'praise' (16.79), also (partly with dat. refl.) 'boast'.

ON *gambra*, prob. fr. *gambr* 'a mythical bird, vulture' (for which cf. Falk-Torp 298). Cf. NE *crow over*.

Dan. *skryde*, Sw. *skryta* : MLG *schrūten* 'snort, puff', OE *hrūtan* 'make a noise, snore', etc., fr. a dental extension of the root seen in Skt. *kruç-*, and Grk. κραυγάζω 'shout, cry' (18.13). Walde-P. 1.417. Falk-Torp 1033. Hellquist 954.

OE *gielpan*, ME *yelpe* (NE *yelp*), MHG *gelfen*, beside sbs. OE *gielp*, ON *gjalpr* 'boasting' : OS *galpōn* 'cry aloud, boast', *gelp* 'defiance', Sw. dial. *galpa* 'cry' (of birds), etc., fr. an extension of the root seen in ON *gala*, OE *galan*, etc. 'sing' (18.12). Walde-P. 1.628. NED s.v. *yelp*, vb.

ME *boste*, NE *boast*, earlier also 'threaten' (18.44).

ME *bragge*, NE *brag*, early 'sound loudly' of a trumpet, deriv. of *brag*, ME *bragg(u)e* 'loud noise, bray (of a trumpet)', orig. dub. Cf. 16th. cent. Fr. *braguer* 'flaunt, brave, brag', etc. (all later than the English words). NED s.v.

Du. *zich beroemen*, OHG *sih ruomen*, MHG *sich rüemen*, NHG *sich rühmen*, refl. of verbs for 'praise' (16.79).

Du. *pochen*, orig. 'strike (with noise), pound', cf. NHG *pochen* 'knock, rap, thump', etc., of imitative origin. Franck-v. W. 512. Weigand-H. 2.443 f.

Du. *pralen* (MLG *prālen* > Dan. *prale*), *brallen*, NHG *prahlen*, cf. NHG dial. *prālen* 'cry', *bral* 'noise', NE *brawl* 'noisy quarrel', Icel. *bralla* 'trick, cheat', etc., orig. dub. Weigand-H. 2.461 f. Franck-v. W. 520. Falk-Torp 846 f. NED s.v. *brawl*, vb.[1].

5. Lith. *girtis*, Lett. *dzirties*, refl. of Lith. *girti* (Lett. *dzirt* not used) 'praise' (16.79).

Lith. *didžiuotis* (refl.), deriv. of *didis* 'great, large'.

Lett. *lielīties*, refl. of *lielīt* 'praise', deriv. of *liels* 'great'.

6. ChSl. *chvaliti sę* (not in Gospels or Berneker, but renders καυχάομαι Ps. 48.7, ἐγ-κ- Ps. 96.7, etc., ed. Geitler 103, 215), SCr. *hvaliti se*, Pol. *chwalić się*, Russ. *chvalit'sja*, refl. of ChSl. *chvaliti* 'praise' etc. (16.79).

SCr. *hvastati se*, Boh. *chvastati se*, Russ. *chvastat'sja*, prob. of imitative origin. Berneker 407.

Boh. *chlubiti se*, Pol. *chełpić się*, beside Boh. *chlouba* 'boasting', Pol. *chłuba* 'fame, pride', prob. of imitative orig. (**chŭlb-*, **chŭlp-*), cf. Pol. *chełbać* 'shake, rattle', *chłupać* 'splash', etc. Berneker 410. Brückner 178.

7. Skt. *çlāgh-*, etym.? Uhlenbeck 321.

Skt. *katth-*, etym.? Uhlenbeck 41. Walde-P. 1.384.

18.51 WRITE

Grk.	*γράφω*	Goth.	*mēljan*	Lith.	*rašyti*
NG	*γράφω*	ON	*skrifa, rīta*	Lett.	*rakstīt*
Lat.	*scrībere*	Dan.	*skrive*	ChSl.	*pīsati*
It.	*scrivere*	Sw.	*skriva*	SCr.	*pisati*
Fr.	*écrire*	OE	*wrītan*	Boh.	*psáti*
Sp.	*escribir*	ME	*write*	Pol.	*pisać*
Rum.	*scrie*	NE	*write*	Russ.	*pisat'*
Ir.	*scrībaim*	Du.	*schrijven*	Skt.	*likh-*
NIr.	*scrīobhaim*	OHG	*scrīban, rīzan*	OPers.	*ni-pis-*
W.	*ysgrifennu*	MHG	*schrīben*		
Br.	*skriva*	NHG	*schreiben*		

Writing as a record of speech had developed in Egypt and western Asia as early as 4000 B.C., but was unknown in the place and time of IE unity. It spread from non-IE sources to the historical IE-speaking peoples. The terminology, however, is native IE, and in western Europe to a considerable extent of Latin origin.

The majority of the words for 'write', including Lat. *scrībere*, which is the source of the western European words except the English, meant originally 'scratch, cut, carve', applicable to writing on stone or wood or the later wax tablet. The Goth. *mēljan* and the verb common to Slavic, Old Persian, and Tocharian (a notable and probably not accidental agreement) belong to groups which include verbs for 'paint' (NHG *malen* and Lat. *pingere*), and one is tempted to assume the development 'color, paint' > 'write' as appropriate to writing on papyrus or parchment. This might apply to the Gothic and Slavic—and even to the Old Persian word if we assume that it was first used, not of the cuneiform (as in actual occurrence) but with reference to the contemporaneous Aramaic script. Yet this is an unsafe inference, since the groups in question cover other senses (as 'mark, adorn') from which 'paint' and 'write' may be derived independently.

1. Grk. γράφω, orig. 'scratch, graze' : OE *ceorfan* 'cut, carve', OHG *kerban*, NHG *kerben* 'notch, indent', etc. Walde-P. 1.606 f.

2. Lat. *scrībere* (> Romance words, also Ir. *scrībaim*, NIr. *scrīobhaim*, W. *ysgrifennu*, Br. *skriva*, ON *skrifa*, Dan. *skrive*, Sw. *skriva*, Du. *schrijven*, OHG *scrīban*, MHG *schrīben*, NHG *schreiben*, all 'write'; but OE *scrīfan* 'decree, pass judgment, shrive'), Umbr. *screhto* 'scriptum', Osc. *scriftas* 'scriptae', etc. : Grk. σκαριφάομαι 'scratch an outline, sketch', ON *hrīfa* 'scratch', Lett. *scrīpāt* 'notch, scratch', fr. extensions of the root **sker-* in OE, OHG *sceran*, Grk. κείρω, etc. 'cut off, shear'. Walde-P. 2.586. Ernout-M. 91 f.

3. Goth. *mēljan* (with sb. *mēla* pl. 'writing') : OE *mǣlan* 'mark, stain', OHG *mālōn* 'sketch, paint' (NHG *malen*, etc.), ON *māl* 'engraving (on a weapon)', OE *mǣl* 'mark, sign', OHG *māl* 'sign, mark', etc., fr. the same root as Grk. μέλας 'black', Skt. *malina-* 'dirty, black', etc. Walde-P. 2.293. Feist 353 f.

ON *rīta*, also 'scratch, outline', OE *wrītan* also 'cut, engrave', OHG *rīzan* also 'scratch, tear' (NHG *reissen*), Goth. only *writs*, = κεραία, 'apex of a letter', outside connections remote or dub., but semantic development fr. 'scratch, cut' clear. Walde-P. 1.287, 2.344. Falk-Torp 897. Feist 574.

4. Lith. *rašyti*, etym.? (Wiedemann, BB 28.59 : Lith. *rėžti*, ChSl. *rězati* 'cut', but formal relation difficult).

Lett. *rakstīt*, deriv. of *raksts* 'writing' (also 'embroidery, pattern'); this prob. : Lith. *rakštas* 'tomb' (orig. 'grave'), *rakštis* 'splinter', fr. the root of Lett. *rakt* 'dig', Lith. *rakti* 'dig, rake'. Mühl.-Endz. 3.475.

5. ChSl. *pĭsati*, *pišą*, etc., general Slavic : OPruss. *peisai* 'writes', Lith. *piešti* 'sketch, draw', ON *fā* 'color, adorn' (*fā rūnar* 'write runes'), OE *fāg* 'colored, stained', etc., Grk. ποικίλος 'gay-colored', Skt. *piç-* 'carve, prepare, adorn', Av. *pis-* 'color, adorn', OPers. *ni-pis-* 'write', Lat. *pingere* (*peig- beside *peiḱ-) 'embroider, paint', Toch. *pik-* 'write, paint' (SSS 451).

6. Skt. *likh-*, older *rikh-*, lit. 'scratch, scrape' : Grk. ἐρείκω 'rend, tear', Lith. *riekti* 'slice (bread)'. Walde-P. 2.344.

OPers. *ni-pis-* : ChSl. *pĭsati* (above, 5).

18.52 READ

Grk.	ἀναγιγνώσκω	Goth.	*ussiggwan, anakunnan*	Lith.	*skaityti*
NG	διαβάζω (ἀναγινώσκω)	ON	*rāða, lesa*	Lett.	*lasīt (skaitīt)*
Lat.	*legere*	Dan.	*læse*	ChSl.	*čisti*
It.	*leggere*	Sw.	*läsa*	SCr.	*čitati*
Fr.	*lire*	OE	*rǣdan*	Boh.	*čísti*
Sp.	*leer*	ME	*rede*	Pol.	*czytać*
Rum.	*citi*	NE	*read*	Russ.	*čitat'*
Ir.	*lēgaim*	Du.	*lezen*	Skt.	*paṭh-*
NIr.	*lēighim*	OHG	*lesan*	Av.	*aiwi-ah-*
W.	*darllen*	MHG	*lesen*	OPers.	*pati-pars-*
Br.	*lenn*	NHG	*lesen*		

Words for 'read' are based on notions like 'recognize, pick out, gather, observe, interpret, go through', etc., secondarily applied to written characters.

Just as in the case of 'write' Lat. *scrībere* is the source of the western European words except English, so Lat. *legere* is the source of the Romance (except Rum.), the Celtic, and, at least in part by semantic borrowing, of the most widespread Gmc. group.

1. Grk. ἀναγιγνώσκω, lit. (Hom., etc.) 'know, recognize', whence 'recognize written characters', 'read' (Pindar+), cpd. of γιγνώσκω 'know, recognize' (17.17).

NG διαβάζω (the pop. word for 'read'; ἀναγινώσκω lit.), fr. Grk. διαβιβάζω 'carry across', Byz. διαβάζω also 'pass the time, converse' (Chron. Mor.). Cf. NE *run through*, Fr. *parcourir* in sense 'read rapidly'. Koraes, Ἄτακτα 1.268.

2. Lat. *legere* (> It. *leggere*, Fr. *lire*, Sp. *leer*), orig. 'pick up, gather, collect', whence 'read', prob. through 'pick up, put together the individual written characters', or merely 'gather' as 'comprehend the meaning of something written. (cf. NE *gather* in this sense. NED s.v. I, 10) : Grk. λέγω 'gather, collect' and also 'speak, say' (18.21). Walde-P. 2.422. Ernout-M. 535 ff. Walde-H. 1.780.

Rum. *citi*, fr. the Slavic (below, 6).

3. Ir. *lēgaim*, NIr. *lēighim*, fr. Lat. *legere* (above).

W. *dar-llen* (with intensive prefix), Br. *lenn*, orig. only sb. 'reading', fr. Lat. *legendum* 'what is to be read' (: *legere*, above). Pedersen 1.222, 225.

4. Goth. *ussiggwan* or simply *siggwan* reg. render Grk. ἀναγιγνώσκω; *siggwan* also 'sing' (18.12). Prob. orig. applied to reading aloud, reciting (as in Lk. 4.16, etc., the usual sense in NT; but also simply 'read' as in Lk. 6.3).

Goth. *anakunnan*, cpd. of *ana* 'on' and *kunnan* 'know' (renders ἀναγιγνώσκω 'read'" Cor. 1.13, 3.2), lit. translation of the Greek.

ON *rāða*, OE *rǣdan* (also 'advise, plan, rule, explain', etc.), ME *rede*, NE *read* = OHG *rātan* 'advise, consider, interpret', etc. : ON *rœða*, Goth. *rōdjan* 'speak, talk' (18.21). ON *rāða* is the older word and is always used where reference is to reading of runes, whereas *lesa* (below) is used only of reading writing in Latin characters (cf. B. M. Olsen, Runerne i den oldislandske literatur, 35 f.). The earliest citation of OE *rǣdan* in NED refers to reading a book (Aelfred, Boeth., ca. 888).

ON *lesa*, Dan. *læse*, Sw. *läsa*, Du. *lezen*, OHG *lesan*, MHG, NHG *lesen*, all lit. 'gather, pick up' (= Goth. *lisan*, OE *lesan* in the lit. sense only). The use for 'read', which spread fr. OHG, etc. to Norse, may be in part a native development, but was doubtless affected by the double use of Lat. *legere* (above). Falk-Torp 677. Weigand-H. 2.56. Kluge-G. 355.

5. Lith. *skaityti*, Lett. *skaitīt*, both also 'count', and 'read' only dial. in Lettic : Lett. *šk'ist* 'think, intend, suppose, heed', fr. *sk^{w}eit-, beside *k^{w}eit- in ChSl. *čisti*, etc. (below). Mühl.-Endz. 3.866 f., 4.47.

Lett. *lasīt*, 'gather, select', and 'read' : Lith. *lesti*, Lett. *lest* 'pick up with the beak' (Lett. also 'court', etc.), OHG *lesan*, etc. (above, 4). Mühl.-Endz. 2.423, 454.

6. ChSl. *čisti* (*čĭtą*) 'read, count, calculate, honor', Boh. *čisti* 'read, count', as 'read' mostly replaced by iter. form *čitati* (ChSl. *po-čitati* 'read') in modern Slavic : Skt. *cit-* 'observe, notice', etc. Walde-P. 1.509. Berneker 174 f.

7. Skt. *paṭh-*, properly 'read or speak aloud' (also 'study, teach'), MInd. for *prath-* 'spread'. Wackernagel, Altind. Gram. 1.167. Walde-P. 2.677.

Skt. *adhi-i-*, lit. 'come upon' (cpd. of *i-* 'go, come'), hence 'remember, understand', and in mid. (*adhīte*) 'learn, study, read'.

Av. *aiwi-ah-*, also 'study, occupy the mind with' (esp. applied to studying the holy writ), cpd. of *aiwi-* 'to, at' and *ah-* 'be'. Barth. 278.

OPers. *pati-pars-* 'read' (an inscription) = Av. *paiti-fras-* 'ask', cpd. of *fras-* 'ask' (18.31). Cf. Pahl. *patpurs-*, Sogd. *ptβs-* 'read'. Barth. 999. Benveniste, BSL 31.2.71.

18.53 LETTER (of the Alphabet)

Grk.	γράμμα	Goth.	*bōka*	Lith.	*raidė, litara*
NG	γράμμα	ON	*(bōk)stafr*	Lett.	*burts*
Lat.	*littera*	Dan.	*bogstav*	ChSl.	*(kŭniga)*
It.	*lettera*	Sw.	*bokstaf*	SCr.	*slovo*
Fr.	*lettre*	OE	*(bōc)stæf*	Boh.	*písmeno*
Sp.	*letra*	ME	*lettre, bocstaf*	Pol.	*litera*
Rum.	*literă*	NE	*letter*	Russ.	*bukva*
Ir.	*liter*	Du.	*letter*	Skt.	*akṣara-, varṇa-*
NIr.	*litir*	OHG	*buohstab*		
W.	*llythyren*	MHG	*buochstap*		
Br.	*lizerenn*	NHG	*buchstabe*		

Words for 'letter' (of the alphabet) are of diverse origin, but here again the Latin word has been widely borrowed.

1. Grk. γράμμα : γράφω 'write' (18.51).

2. Lat. *littera* (> Romance words), early *leitera*, orig. dub. Ernout-M. 557 f. Walde-H. 1.814 f.

3. Ir. *liter*, NIr. *litir*, W. *llythyren*,

Br. *lizerenn* (W., Br. with singulative suffix, the simple form is 'epistle'), fr. Lat. *littera*.

4. Goth. *bōka*, in pl. 'writing, book' : ON *bōk*, OE *bōc*, etc. 'book' (18.61).

ON *stafr*, OE *stæf*, lit. 'staff, stick', prob. orig. applied to the perpendicular line which forms the basis of most runes (cf. ON *rūnastafr*, OE *rūnstæf*), whence transferred to the Latin letter, esp. in cpd. with 'book', ON *bōkstafr*, Dan. *bogstav*, Sw. *bokstaf*, OE *bōcstæf*, early ME *bocstaf*, OHG *buohstab*, etc. Falk-Torp 89 f. Kluge-G. 83.

ME *lettre*, NE, Du. *letter*, fr. Fr. *lettre* (above, 2).

5. Lith. *raidė* (now the preferred word, cf. NSB s.v. *litara*) beside *raida* 'development', both neologisms and apparently based on *riedėti* 'roll' (cf. NSB *išraida* 'development', *išriedėti* 'roll out').

Lith. *litara*, *litera*, through Pol. *litera*, fr. Lat. *littera*.

Lett. *burts*, orig. 'magic sign' = Lith. *burtas* 'lot', pl. 'sorcery' : Lett. *burt*, Lith. *burti* 'enchant, bewitch', etc. (22.42). Mühl.-Endz. 1.355.

6. ChSl. *kŭniga* in pl. as 'letters' (Lk. 23.38, but could be simply 'writing' as elsewhere), usually 'writing, book' (18.61).

SCr. *slovo* = ChSl., etc. *slovo* 'word' (18.26).

Boh. *písmeno* : *psati* 'write' (18.51).

Pol. *litera*, fr. Lat. *littera* (above, 2).

Russ. *bukva*, new sg. based on Russ.-ChSl. dat. pl. *bukvamŭ* (gen. *bukovŭ*) : ChSl. *buky, pl. *bukŭvi* 'writing, letter' (18.54).

7. Skt. *akṣara-*, lit. 'imperishable, unalterable' (*kṣṛ-* 'flow, melt away, wane, perish'), hence, as an unalterable element of speech, 'speech-sound, letter, syllable, vowel, word'.

Skt. *varṇa-*, lit. 'covering, exterior, form' (: *vṛ-* 'cover'), whence 'sort, category' and gram. 'speech-sound, letter, vowel, word'.

18.54 LETTER (= Epistle)

Grk.	ἐπιστολή, γράμματα	Goth.	*aipistaulē*	Lith.	*laiškas (gromata)*
NG	γράμμα	ON	*brēf, rit*	Lett.	*vēstule (grāmata)*
Lat.	*litterae, epistula*	Dan.	*brev*	ChSl.	*epistolĭja, bukŭvi, kŭnigy, posŭlanĭje*
It.	*lettera*	Sw.	*bref*		
Fr.	*lettre*	OE	*(ǣrend)gewrit, stafas*	SCr.	*pismo, list*
Sp.	*carta*	ME	*lettre(s), writ*	Boh.	*dopis, psaní, list*
Rum.	*scrisoare (carte)*	NE	*letter*	Pol.	*list*
Ir.	*scrībend, epistil*	Du.	*brief*	Russ.	*pis'mo*
NIr.	*litir*	OHG	*briaf*	Skt.	*lekha-, pattra-*
W.	*llythyr*	MHG	*brief*		
Br.	*lizer*	NHG	*brief*		

A 'letter' (= epistle) was expressed in Greek and Latin by the plural of the word for 'letter' (of the alphabet) used collectively, and later (e.g. NG, It., Fr., NE, etc.) by the singular. Other terms are words for 'message, writing, short (writing), leaf'.

1. Grk. ἐπιστολή, orig. 'message, commission' : ἐπιστέλλω 'send to, send a message, command'. Hence Lat. *epistula*.

Grk. γράμματα, pl. of γράμμα 'letter' (18.53), but NG sg. γράμμα 'letter' in both senses (γράμματα 'letters' and 'literature').

2. Lat. *litterae*, pl. of *littera* 'letter' (18.53). Hence It. dial. *littere*, OFr. *lettres* in this sense. But sg. It. *lettera*,

Fr. *lettre* now 'letter' in both senses. REW 5087.

Sp. *carta*, Rum. *carte* (Rum. also 'book') = It. *carta* 'paper', etc. (18.56).

Rum. *scrisoare* (modern for the now arch. or pop. *carte*), deriv. of *scris* pple. of *scrie* 'write' (18.51). Tiktin 1394.

3. Ir. *scrībend*, lit. 'writing', fr. Lat. *scrībendum*, gerundive of *scrībere* 'write' (18.51). Pedersen 1.225.

Ir. *epistil*, fr. Lat. *epistula*.

NIr. *litir* (also, and earlier only, 'letter' of the alphabet), W. *llythyr*, Br. *lizer* (whence new singulative forms for 'letter' of the alphabet, 18.53), fr. Lat. *littera*. Pedersen 1.234.

4. Goth. *aipistaulē*, fr. Grk. ἐπιστολή. Similarly, through Lat. *epistula*, ON *pistill*, OE (*e*)*pistol*, OHG *epistula*, MHG *epistole*, etc. 'epistle', but generally only in the biblical sense.

ON *brēf*, Dan. *brev*, Sw. *bref*, OHG *briaf*, *brief*, MHG, NHG, Du. *brief*, fr. late Lat. *breve* (*scriptum*), lit. 'short writing', whence 'document, record, etc.'. Falk-Torp 101. Weigand-H. 1.287.

ON *rit*, OE *gewrit*, ME *writ*, lit. 'writing' : ON *rīta*, OE *wrītan*, etc. 'write', esp. (for Lat. *epistula*) OE *ǣrendgewrit* with *ǣrend* 'message, errand' (cf. Wright-Wülcker 163.46, 541.4).

OE *stafas*, pl. of *stæf* 'letter' (18.53), prob. so used by the influence of Lat. *litterae*. Cf. also OHG *buohstaba* 'litterae, i.e. 'writings' (Tat. 88.13, 104.4, etc., used also for 'litterae' = 'epistula'?).

ME *lettre*, and pl. *lettres*, NE *letter*, fr. OFr. *lettre* (above, 2).

5. Lith. *laiškas*, orig. 'leaf (of a plant)', now 'letter', semantic borrowing fr. Pol. *list* (below, 6).

Lith. *gromata* (discarded in the new lit. lang., cf. NSB s.v.), Lett. *grāmata* (mostly 'book', as 'letter' replaced by *vēstule*), fr. ORuss. *gramota* 'writing, document', fr. Grk. γράμματα (above, 1). Mühl.-Endz. 1.644. Berneker 345 f.

Lett. *vēstule* (recent), deriv. of *vēsts* 'news, message, messenger', fr. Russ. *vest'* 'news' (: *vedat'* 'know', etc.). Mühl.-Endz. 4.571.

6. ChSl. *epistolĭja*, fr. Grk. ἐπιστολή, for which also the following. Cf. Jagić, Entstehungsgesch. 307.

ChSl. *bukŭvi*, also 'writing, document', pl. of *buky, fr. the Gmc. word, Goth. *bōka* 'letter', pl. 'writing, book', etc. (18.53, 18.61). Berneker 99. Stender-Petersen 450 ff.

ChSl. *kŭnigy*, but mostly 'writing, book' (18.61).

Late ChSl. *posŭlanĭje* : (*po*)*sŭlati* 'send' (10.63), lit. translation of Grk. ἐπιστολή.

SCr. *pismo*, Boh. *dopis*, *psaní*, Russ. *pis'mo*, lit. 'writing' : ChSl. *pĭsati*, etc. 'write' (18.51).

SCr., Boh., Pol. *list*, lit. 'leaf' : ChSl. *listŭ*, Russ. *list*, etc. 'leaf' (8.56).

7. Skt. *lekha-*, lit. 'writing' : *likh-* 'write' (18.51).

Skt. *pattra-*, lit. 'leaf', whence 'leaf for writing on, paper, letter' (cf. 18.56).

18.55 TABLET

Grk.	στήλη, πίναξ	Goth.	spilda	Lith.	lentelé, lentuté
NG	πινακίδα	ON	spjald, speld	Lett.	galdin'š
Lat.	tabula, tabella, pugil-lāris	Sw.	tafla	ChSl.	dŭstica
It.	tavoletta	OE	bred, writbred, wex-bred	SCr.	tablica
Fr.	tablette			Boh.	tabulka
Sp.	tablilla	ME	table, tablette	Pol.	tabliczka, tablica
Rum.	tablă	NE	tablet	Russ.	tablica
Ir.	clār, pōlaire, taball	Du.	tablet	Skt.	paṭṭa-, phalaka-
NIr.	tabhall	OHG	tavala		
W.	llech	MHG	tavel(e)		
Br.	taolenn	NHG	tafel		

Tablets of stone, metal, wood, or wax were in common use for writing purposes in ancient times (besides parchment or papyrus), in contrast to their restricted role in modern times.

Most of the European terms are words for 'board', 'plank', or 'slab', or diminutive forms of these, and in large part go back to the Lat. tabula.

1. Grk. στήλη, Dor. στάλα, Aeol. στάλλα, the most widespread term for an inscribed monument of stone or bronze, orig. a block or slab of stone (in Hom. as part of a wall or a gravestone), fr. the root of στέλλω 'make ready', orig. 'put in place', OE stellan 'set, establish', OHG stollo 'support, post', etc., IE *stel- beside *stā- 'stand'. Walde-P. 2.644.

Grk. πίναξ, orig. 'board, plank', hence 'platter' (5.32) and 'tablet'. Hence for 'tablet' also πινάκιον, πινακίς, πινακίδιον.

Grk. πλάξ, used of various objects with flat surface (: NHG flach 'flat', etc., 12.71), including 'tablet'.

Grk. δέλτος, Cypr. δάλτος : δαιδάλλω 'adorn', Lat. dolāre 'hew', Skt. dal- 'split, burst'. Walde-P. 1.810. Boisacq 174.

Grk. πέτευρον, πετεύριον, in several regions 'tablet', in literature (also πέταυρον) 'perch for fowls' and 'springboard', prob. fr. *πετήορον, *πετάορον = πεδάορον = μετέωρον 'in mid-air'. Schwyzer, Gr. Gram. 198.

2. Lat. tabula 'board, plank' (9.52), 'table, tablet' for writing (e.g. the XII tabulae), in latter sense esp. dim. tabella. Hence (fr. tabula) new dim. forms It. tavoletta, Fr. tablette, Sp. tablilla. Rum. tablă fr. tabula through Slavic. Ernout-M. 1011. REW 8514. Tiktin 1544.

Lat. pugillāris, orig. adj. 'to be held in the hand', fr. pugillus 'handful' : pugnus 'fist'. Ernout-M. 821.

3. Ir. clār, lit. 'board, plank' (9.52).

Ir. pōlaire, fr. Lat. pugillāris (above). Pedersen 1.222. Vendryes, De hib. voc. 167.

Ir. taball, NIr. tabhall, fr. Lat. tabula. Vendryes, De hib. voc. 181.

W. llech, lit. 'flat stone, slat' : Ir. lecc 'stone, flagstone', etc.

Br. taolenn, dim. of taol 'table', fr. Lat. tabula. Loth, Mots lat. 210.

4. Goth. spilda, ON spjald, speld : OE speld 'splinter, thin piece of wood', MHG spelte 'split piece of wood, handtool used in weaving', etc., fr. the root of OHG spaltan, MLG spalden 'split'. Walde-P. 2.678. Feist 445.

OE bred, lit. 'board, plank' (9.52), also cpds. writbred with writ 'writing', and wex-bred (for pugillāris Lk. 1.63) with wæx, wex 'wax'.

ME, early NE table, ME tablette (rare in this sense), NE, Du. tablet, fr. Fr. table, tablette (above, 2).

OHG tavala, MHG tavel(e), NHG tafel (specifically schreibtafel), MLG tavele

---

(> Dan. tavle, Sw. tafla), fr. Lat. tabula (above, 2). Falk-Torp 1250. Weigand-H. 2.1018.

5. Lith. lentelé, lentuté, dims. of lenta 'board' (9.52).

Lett. galdin'š, dim. of galds, orig. 'piece of hewn timber, plank', now 'table' (7.44). Mühl.-Endz. 1.590.

6. ChSl. dŭstica (= πινακίδιον Lk. 1.63), dim. of dŭska 'board' (9.52).

SCr., Pol., Russ. tablica, Boh. tabulka, Pol. tabliczka, dim. forms more usual in this sense than SCr. tabla, Boh. tabule, Pol. tabla, late ChSl. tabla, fr. Lat. tabula. Brückner 562 f.

7. Skt. paṭṭa-, etym.? Uhlenbeck 153.

Skt. phalaka-, lit. 'board' (9.52).

18.56 PAPER

Grk.	χάρτης	Dan.	papir	Lith.	popieris
NG	χαρτί	Sw.	papper	Lett.	papīrs
Lat.	charta, papȳrus	ME	papir	ChSl.	chartija
It.	carta	NE	paper	SCr.	papir, hartija
Fr.	papier	Du.	papier	Boh.	papir
Sp.	papel	MHG	pappīr, karte	Pol.	papier
Rum.	hîrtie	NHG	papier	Russ.	bumaga
NIr.	pāipēar			Skt.	pattra-
W.	papur				
Br.	paper				

The words for 'paper' (like those for 'pen') furnish a conspicuous example of the transfer in dominant sense from a material to its function. Of the various materials used, as skins (and the later refined parchment), bark, papyrus, rags, and the modern wood pulp, it was the papyrus plant, from the pith of which was produced the writing material of Egypt and that most commonly employed by the Greeks and Romans, which furnished the majority of the Eur. words for 'paper'. Skt. pattra- is properly 'leaf', especially applied to the strips of palm leaves upon which Skt. MSS were most commonly written. Only the Russ. bumaga, from an oriental word for 'cotton', reflects a later process.

The words for 'parchment', Grk. διφθέρα 'prepared hide', as writing material Hdt.+; Lat. membrāna 'membrane, thin skin'; late Lat. Pergamēna (sc. charta) from the name of Pergamum in Asia Minor, hence the modern Eur. words; and vellum (orig. 'calfskin', deriv. of Lat.

vitulus 'calf'), retained their specific application without any such extension as those for the papyrus.

1. Grk. πάπῡρος, the usual name of the papyrus plant (but not of its product 'paper'), a loanword but source unknown. Hence Lat. papyrus, also mostly as plant name, but also 'paper', and as such the source of the main group of Eur. words (see list). Schrader, Reallex. 2.153. REW 6218. Falk-Torp 815.

2. Grk. βύβλος (also βίβλος, dim. βυβλίον, βιβλίον), another and earlier attested name of the papyrus plant (Hdt. 2.92; cf. also βυβλίνα μασχάλα 'papyrus marsh' Tab. Heracl. 1.92), fr. the name of the Phoenician city Βύβλος (its Grk. form; Phoen. Gᵉbal), which was an early center of the exportation of papyrus to Greece. Schrader, Reallex 2.153. Sometimes used for the strips of papyri, but mainly for the collective roll, hence the words for 'book' (18.61).

3. Grk. χάρτης, the usual word for the

---

sheet of papyrus (cf. πάπυρος γνώριμος πᾶσιν, ἀφ' ἧς ὁ χάρτης κατασκευάζεται Diosc. 1.86), prob. a loanword, but source unknown. Hence Lat. charta (> It. carta; many other derivs. for paper as 'document, chart, card', etc., but not usual words for paper as writing material). Dim. χαρτίον, pl. χαρτία (> ChSl. chartija, SCr. hartija, Rum. hîrtie), NG χαρτί, pl. χαρτιά. Boisacq 1052. Ernout-M. 182. REW 1866. Berneker 385.

4. Russ. bumaga, Ukr. bumaha, of the same orig. as SCr. pamuk, etc. 'cotton' (6.24). Berneker 100 f.

5. Skt. pattra- 'leaf' (8.54, 62).

18.57 PEN

Grk.	κάλαμος	Goth.	....	Lith.	plunksna
NG	πέννα	ON	penni	Lett.	spalva
Lat.	calamus (penna)	Dan.	pen	ChSl.	trŭstĭ
It.	penna	Sw.	penna	SCr.	pero
Fr.	plume	OE	feþer	Boh.	péro
Sp.	pluma	ME	penne	Pol.	pióro
Rum.	pană, condeiu	NE	pen	Russ.	pero
Ir.	penn	Du.	pen	Skt.	lekhanī-, kalama-
NIr.	peann	OHG	fedara		
W.	pin	MHG	veder(e)		
Br.	pluenn	NHG	feder		

The instrument for writing on tablets in ancient Greece and Rome was the 'style', Grk. γραφίς (: γράφω 'write'), Lat. stilus (orig. any pointed instrument). The 'pen', for writing on parchment, papyrus, and the later paper, was a 'reed' (reed-pen) or later a 'feather' (quill-pen). The latter is the source of nearly all the Eur. words, which are either from the Latin or are native words for 'feather', and which have come to be felt as distinct words even when formally the same (as NHG feder in contrast to NE pen vs. feather) and so applied without any sense of incongruity to metal pens.

1. Grk. κάλαμος (> Lat. calamus), lit. 'reed'. Hence ChSl. trŭstĭ renders κάλαμος as 'reed' (Jagic, Entstehungsgesch. 398), and also as 'pen' (Psalt. p. 96 Geitler = Psalms 45.1).

Late Byz. κονδύλι (NG κοντύλι now esp. 'slate pencil'; cf. μολυβοκόντυλο

'lead pencil'), dim. of κόνδυλος 'knuckle, joint, knob', here with reference to the joints of the reed. Hence Rum. condeiu the old word for 'pen' or 'pencil' (in mod. lit. mostly replaced by pană) in Koraes, Ἄτακτα 4.241. Tiktin 400.

2. Lat. penna 'feather', late (Isid.) 'pen'. Hence It. penna, OFr. penne (> ME penne, NE pen > W. pin), Rum. pană, NG πέννα, Ir. penn, NIr. peann, late ON penni, Dan. pen, Sw. penna, Du. pen. REW 6514. Vendryes, De hib. voc. 165. Falk-Torp 821.

Similarly Fr. plume, Sp. pluma, Br. pluenn, OE feþer, OHG fedara, etc., Lith. plunksna, Lett. spalva, SCr. pero, etc., gen. Slavic, all lit. 'feather' (4.393).

3. Skt. lekhanī- : likh- 'write' (18.11).

Skt. late kalama- fr. Grk. κάλαμος. For this and melā- 'ink', fr. Grk. μέλαν, cf. Weber, Ber. Preuss. Akad. 1890. 912 ff.

18.58 INK

Grk.	μέλαν	Goth.	swartiz(l)a (dat. sg.)	Lith.	rašalas
NG	μελάνι	ON	blek	Lett.	tinte
Lat.	ātrāmentum	Dan.	blæk	ChSl.	črŭnilo
It.	inchiostro	Sw.	bläck	SCr.	tinta, mastilo
Fr.	encre	OE	blæc	Boh.	inkoust
Sp.	tinta	ME	enke	Pol.	atrament
Rum.	cerneală	NE	ink	Russ.	černila
Ir.	dub	Du.	ink	Skt.	maṣi-, melā-
NIr.	dubh	OHG	atraminza, blach, tincta		
W.	inc (du)				
Br.	liou	MHG	tin(c)te		
		NHG	tinte		

Most of the words for 'ink' are derived from words for 'color' or a color, especially 'black' (15.65). The Latin words were widely borrowed.

1. Grk. μέλαν, neut. of μέλας 'black', used for 'ink' as also dim. μελάνιον in papyri, whence NG μελάνι.

2. Lat. ātrāmentum (> OFr. arrement, etc., REW 758; also OHG atraminza, MDu. atrament, Pol. atrament), deriv. of āter 'black'.

It. inchiostro, Fr. encre (OIt. incostro, OFr. enque), fr. late Lat. encaustum, encautum 'red-purple ink' used by emperors in their signature, neut. of encaustus 'painted in encaustic', fr. Grk. ἔγκαυστος 'burned in, painted in encaustic'. Ernout-M. 301. Walde-H. 1.404. REW 2869. Wartburg 3.224 f.

Sp. tinta, fr. MLat. tincta, fem. of Lat. tinctus, pple. of tingere 'dye, color'. REW 8744. Wartburg 3.225.

Rum. cerneală, fr. the Slavic, cf. ChSl. črŭnilo (below, 6). Tiktin 327.

3. Ir. dub, NIr. dubh, W. (arch.) du, sb. fr. adj. dub, du 'black'.

W. inc, fr. NE ink (below).

Br. liou, also adj. orig. 'color' (15.61).

4. Goth. dat. sg. swartiza (Cod. A), swartizla (B), deriv. of swarts 'black', and so lit. translation of Grk. μέλαν. Feist 464.

OE blæc (> ON blek, Dan. blæk, Sw. bläck), OS blak, OHG blach : OE blæc 'black', etc. Falk-Torp 87.

ME enke, NE ink, fr. OFr. enque (above, 2).

Du. inkt (MDu. also ink, inket, MLG inket, etc.), fr. OFr. enque or its source (above, 2). Franck-v. W. 276.

OHG tincta, MHG tincte, tinte, NHG tinte, fr. MLat. tincta (above, 2).

On the distribution of the Gmc. words, cf. Th. Frings, Germania Romania 171 ff.

5. Lith. rašalas : rašyti 'write'.

Lett. tinte, fr. NHG tinte (above).

6. ChSl. črŭnilo (Boh. černidlo now obs. for 'ink'), Russ. černila (pl.), deriv. of ChSl. črŭnŭ, etc. 'black'. Berneker 169 f.

SCr. mastilo (beside tinta fr. NHG tinte), deriv. of mast 'lard, ointment, color' : ChSl. mastĭ 'ointment, fat' : ChSl. mazati 'anoint', etc. Berneker 2.24.

Boh. inkoust (Pol. inkaust now replaced by atrament), fr. Lat. encaustum (above, 2). Berneker 430.

Pol. atrament, fr. Lat. ātrāmentum (above, 2).

7. Skt. maṣi-, maṣī- 'black powder, lamp-black' and 'ink', prob. fr. *mers- in MHG mursch, NHG morsch 'rotten, decayed, frail' extension of *mer- in Skt. mṛ- 'crush, smash, break', etc. Walde-P. 2.279.

Skt. late melā- fr. Grk. μέλαν (above, 1). See under 'pen'.

18.59 PENCIL

NG	μολύβι, μολυβοκόντυλο	Dan.	blyant	Lith.	paišelis, pieštukas
It.	lapis	Sw.	blyertspenna	Lett.	zīmulis
Fr.	crayon	NE	pencil	SCr.	olovka
Sp.	lápiz	Du.	potlood	Boh.	tužka, olůvko
Rum.	creion	NHG	bleistift	Pol.	ołówek
NIr.	penna luaidhe			Russ.	karandaš
W.	pensel				
Br.	pluenn-bloum				

Many of the words for the modern 'pencil' are based on those for the material 'lead' (9.68), here to be understood as 'black lead', an old term for 'graphite' before its true composition was known (cf. NED s.v. black lead) and still so used of the lead(s) of a pencil. When I was a boy in school we spoke of lead pencils in distinction from the slate pencils still in common use. A few are based on terms for other mineral materials. Some words for a chalk crayon or for a small brush have been extended to cover 'pencil'. Some others are not connected with the material used, but are simply from the notion of 'mark, draw'.

1. Derivs., cpds., or phrases with words for 'lead' (9.68). NG μολυβοκόντυλο (cf. κοντύλι, 18.57), but pop. simply μολύβι; NIr. penna luaidhe, Br. pluenn-bloum; Dan. blyant, Sw. blyertspenna, Du. potlood (pot 'pot', hence orig. 'pot lead', parallel to NE potash, etc.; Franck-v. W. 519), NHG bleistift (stift 'peg, pen, crayon', etc.); SCr. olovka, Pol. ołówek, Boh. olůvko (less common than tužka).

2. It. lapis, Sp. lápiz, orig. the material 'hematite', fr. Lat. lapis 'stone'. Cf. It. matita 'drawing pencil', fr. Grk. αἱμα-τίτης 'hematite' (deriv. of αἷμα 'blood').

3. Fr. crayon (> Rum. creion), also and orig. 'crayon', fr. craie, Lat. creta 'chalk'. REW 2319.

4. W. pensel, fr. ME pensel = pencil. Parry-Williams 110.

5. NE pencil, in ME pensel 'paintbrush', fr. OFr. pincel (Fr. pinceau), VLat. *pēnicellum = Lat. pēnicillum, dim. of pēniculus 'brush', dim. of pēnis 'tail'. NED s.v.

6. Lith. paišelis and pieštukas, fr. the root in piešti, paišyti 'mark, draw' : ChSl. pīsati 'write', etc. (18.51). Trautmann 210 f.

7. Lett. zīmulis, fr. zīme (Lith. zymė) 'sign' : Lith. žinoti, Lett. zināt 'know'.

8. Boh. tužka, fr. tužiti 'stiffen, fasten', influenced by the stift of NHG bleistift (?).

9. Russ. karandaš, fr. Turk. karadaş 'slate' (cpd. of kara 'black' and taş, daş 'stone'), hence doubtless first used of the slate pencil. Lokotsch 1076.

18.61 BOOK

Grk.	βίβλος, βιβλίον	Goth.	bōkōs	Lith.	knyga
NG	βιβλίον	ON	bōk	Lett.	grāmata
Lat.	liber	Dan.	bog	ChSl.	kŭnigy
It.	libro	Sw.	bok	SCr.	knjiga
Fr.	libro	OE	bōc	Boh.	kniha
Sp.	libro	ME	book	Pol.	książka
Rum.	carte	NE	book	Russ.	kniga
Ir.	lebor	Du.	boek	Skt.	pustaka-, grantha-
NIr.	leabhar	OHG	buoh	Av.	....
W.	llyfr	MHG	buoch		
Br.	levr	NHG	buch		

Most of the words for 'book' are based on names of various materials used for writing.

1. Grk. βίβλος, βιβλίος, orig. 'papyrus' (18.56), hence also 'roll of papyrus, book' (in Christian times The Book, the Bible). Hence dim. βυβλίον, βιβλίον eventually the common word for 'book'.

2. Lat. liber (> It., Sp. libro, Fr. livre), orig. 'thin inner bark of a tree', used for writing material before the introduction of papyrus : Russ. lub 'bark, bast', Lith. luba 'board', etc. Walde-P. 2.418. Ernout-M. 544. Walde-H. 1.790.

While liber was the generic term, others were used for the book form, as volūmen for the usual 'roll' (fr. volvere 'turn'), and cōdex, orig. 'block of wood', then a set of wooden tablets fastened together on the edge, finally the similar arrangement of papyrus or parchment leaves and so the ancestor of the modern book form.

Rum. carte (old also 'letter'), fr. Lat. charta 'paper' (18.56). REW 1866.

3. Ir. lebor, NIr. leabhar, W. llyfr, Br. levr, fr. Lat. liber. Pedersen 1.226.

4. Goth. bōkōs (pl. 'writing, document, book', sg. 'letter of the alphabet'),

ON bōk, OE bōc, etc., general Gmc., orig. (pl. as in Goth.) 'tablets of beechwood' : ON bōk, OE bōc, OHG buocha, etc. 'beech' (8.62). Walde-P. 2.128. Falk-Thorp 89. Kluge-G. 82.

5. Lith. knyga, fr. the Slavic (below, 6).

Lett. grāmata, old also 'letter' (Lith. gromata id.), fr. ORuss. gramota 'writing, document', ChSl. gramata 'scriptures', fr. Grk. γράμματα 'writing, letter' (18.54). Mühl.-Endz. 1.644. Berneker 345 f.

6. ChSl. kŭnigy (pl. tantum) 'writing, letter, book', SCr. knjiga, Boh. kniha, etc. (but orig. in pl.), general Slavic for 'book', etym. disputed, but prob. as orig. 'wooden tablets' (like Goth. bōkōs), deriv. of a *kŭnŭ in Pol. kien 'stump', etc. Brückner 277 f. (and esp. KZ 45.313 ff.). Otherwise (as loanword) Berneker 664.

7. Skt. pustaka- (less usually pusta-), also 'manuscript', etym. dub. Uhlenbeck 171.

Skt. grantha-, lit. 'tying, binding, knot', whence 'a joining together, composition' and 'treatise, book' : granth- 'fasten, arrange, compose'. Walde-P. 1.595.

18.62 PAGE

Grk.	σελίς	Dan.	side	Lith.	puslapis, šalis
NG	σελίδα	Sw.	sida	Lett.	lapas puse
Lat.	pāgina	NE	page	SCr.	strana
It.	pagina	Du.	bladzijde	Boh.	stránka
Fr.	page	NHG	seite	Pol.	stronnica
Sp.	página			Russ.	stranica
Rum.	pagina			Skt.	pattra-
NIr.	leathanach				
W.	tudalen				
Br.	pajenn				

The Greek and Latin words denoted the column of a papyrus roll, and, this being usually written only on one side, the column was in fact the 'page'. After the advent of the codex, with writing on both sides of the leaf and each side numbered, the same words were kept for this 'page' in the modern sense.

But in many of the Eur. languages 'page' is expressed, logically enough from its relation to the leaf, as 'side of a leaf' or more commonly simply as 'side'.

1. Grk. σελίς, -ίδος, used as an architectural term for 'cross-piece', also 'block of seats', 'rowing-bench', etc. (beside σέλμα 'deck, rowing-bench, scaffold', etc.), was applied to the column of a papyrus roll (not necessarily identical with the sheet of papyrus, the writing in column sometimes crossing the juncture of the sheets; cf. also κολλήματα ϛε, σελί-δες ρλζ '95 sheets, 137 columns', Riv. fil. 37.361), and later to the 'page' of codices. Hence NG σελίδα 'page'.

2. Lat. pāgina (> It., Sp., Rum. pagina directly adopted; Fr. page > NE page, Br. pajenn), fr. the root of pangere 'fix, fasten' (cf. the use of pāginae for rows of vines fastened together in Pliny), usually denoted the column (= Grk. σελίς), and after the introduction of the codex, the 'page'. Ernout-M. 722.

3. Words meaning literally 'side of the leaf' (cf. 'leaf' 8.56 and 'side' 12.36). W. tu-dalen, Du. bladzijde, Lith. pus-lapis, Lett. lapas puse.

4. Words for 'side' (12.36) or derivs. of these.

NIr. leathanach (deriv.); NHG seite, Dan. side, Sw. sida; (NE side in this sense obs. or arch.; NED s.v., 9a); Lith. šalis (orig. 'side', but now mostly 'region', 19.14); SCr. strana, derivs. Boh. stránka, Pol. stronnica, Russ. stranica.

5. OW let-einepp, OCorn. eneb (both gl. pagina) : MW enep 'face' (4.204). Pedersen 1.38.

6. Skt. pattra- 'leaf' (8.56), also the 'leaf' of a manuscript, would be, as written only on one side, also the 'page'. But in modern printed texts 'page' is expressed by pṛṣṭha- 'back' (of an animal), 'upper side', cpd. of sthā- 'stand' (Walde-P. 2.604).

18.63 LINE (of Writing or Printing)

Grk.	στίχος	ON	līna	Lith.	eilute
NG	στίχος	Dan.	linie	Lett.	rinda
Lat.	versus	Sw.	rad	SCr.	redak
It.	riga	OE	līne	Boh.	řadek
Fr.	ligne	ME	lyne	Pol.	wiersz
Sp.	linea, renglón	NE	line	Russ.	stroka, stročka
Rum.	rînd	Du.	regel	Skt.	rekhā- (?)
NIr.	line	OHG	zīla		
W.	llin	MHG	zīle		
Br.	linenn	NHG	zeile		

The 'line' of writing or printing is expressed in part by the usual words for 'line', mostly from Lat. līnea (12.84), in part by words for 'row, series, order' or 'rule'.

1. Grk. στίχος 'row' (: στείχω 'march, go', 10.47), hence 'verse' of poetry and 'line' of prose.

2. Lat. versus, orig. 'furrow' (fr. ver-tere turn), hence 'row, line' and esp. 'verse, line' of writing (esp. poetry, but not so restricted). Hence the widespread Eur. words, Fr. vers, OE fers, NE verse, NHG vers, etc., all most commonly applied to poetry (or 'verses' in the Bible), but Pol. wiersz reg. word for 'line' of prose or poetry.

It. riga, fr. OHG (Langob.) rīga 'line' (MHG rīhe, NHG reihe 'line, row, order') : OE rāw, rāw 'row'.

Sp. renglón, deriv. of ringla (Cat. rengla), colloq. form of regla 'rule' (Lat. rēgula). Diez 483.

Rum. rînd 'row, order' and 'line', fr. Slavic, ChSl. rędŭ 'order', etc. (below, 5).

3. Sw. rad 'row, series' and 'line' : ON rǫð 'row, series', outside connections dub. Walde-P. 1.74. Falk-Torp 869. Hellquist 809.

Du. regel 'rule' and 'line', fr. Lat. rēgula 'rule'.

NHG zeile, fr. OHG zīla, MHG zīle 'row, line', perh. fr. the same root as ziel 'object', zeit 'time', etc. Falk-Torp 1259. Kluge-G. 706.

4. Lith. eilutė, fr. eilė 'row, series', root-connection? Walde-P. 1.104.

Lett. rinda 'row' and 'line' = (or fr.) Lith. rinda 'row' : ChSl. rędŭ 'order'. Mühl.-Endz. 3.527.

5. SCr. redak, Boh. řadek, řadka, fr. SCr. red, Boh. řad, řada, 'order, row, series' = ChSl. rędŭ 'order'.

Pol. wiersz, fr. Lat. versus (above, 2), prob. through HG vers.

Russ. stroka (or more commonly dim. stročka) = ChSl. stroka 'center, point' : ChSl. strŭknqti, Russ. streknuti 'goad, prick'. Brückner 519.

6. Skt. rekhā- (12.84), quotable also for line of writing?

18.64 PRINT (vb.)

NG	τυπώνω	Dan.	trykke	Lith.	spaudinti
It.	imprimere	Sw.	trycka	Lett.	iespiest, drukāt
Fr.	imprimer	NE	print	SCr.	štampati
Sp.	impremir	Du.	drukken	Boh.	tisknouti
Rum.	imprima	NHG	drucken	Pol.	drukować
NIr.	clōdhaim			Russ.	pečatat'
W.	argraffu, printiu				
Br.	moula				

Verbs for 'print' are most commonly derived from those for 'press' (9.342). Some are from nouns meaning 'stamp, impression, seal'.

1. NG τυπώνω, fr. τύπος 'stamp, print' (cf. also ὁ τύπος 'the press'), in class. Grk. 'impression', fr. τύπτω 'strike, beat'.

2. It. imprimere, Fr. imprimer, Sp. impremir, Rum. imprima, fr. Lat. imprimere 'impress, stamp', cpd. of premere 'press'.

3. NIr. clōdhaim, fr. sb. clō 'stamp, print, form', etym.?

W. argraffu (sb. argraff 'impression, print'), fr. ar- 'upon' and obs. grafio 'engrave', fr. ME grave id. Parry-Williams 83.

W. printiu, fr. NE print.

Br. moula, fr. moul 'mold, impression', fr. Fr. moule id.

4. Dan. trykke, Sw. trycka, Du. drukken, NHG drucken, orig. 'press', like OE þryccan, etc. On the NHG distinction,

drucken 'print' vs. drücken 'press', cf. Kluge-G. 115, Paul, Deutsches Wtb. 113.

NE print, fr. sb. print, early prient, fr. OFr. priente, deriv. of Lat. premere 'press'.

5. Lith. spaudinti, also and orig. 'press', beside spausti 'press', whence also spausdinti 'print' with sb. spaustuvė 'printing house'.

Lett. iespiest, cpd. of spiest 'press'.

Lett. drukāt, fr. sb. druka, fr. LG druk.

6. SCr. štampati, fr. sb. štampa 'print', fr. It. stampa 'stamp, press, print'.

Boh. tisknouti, also 'press', with sb. tisk 'pressure, press'.

Pol. drukować, fr. sb. druk 'print, press', fr. NHG druck.

Russ. pečatat', fr. pečat' 'seal, stamp, the press' = ChSl. pečatĭ, Boh. pečet, etc. 'seal', fr. the root of ChSl. pekǫ, pešti 'bake', hence something 'baked in'. Cf. SCr. opeka 'brick' fr. the same root. Brückner 407.

18.65 LITERATURE

Grk.	γράμματα	Goth.	(mēla)	Lith.	literatūra
NG	λογοτεχνία	ON	(script, ritning)	Lett.	literatura
Lat.	litterae	Dan.	literatur	ChSl.	(kŭnigy, bukŭvĭ, pisanĭje)
It.	letteratura	Sw.	literatur		
Fr.	littérature	OE	(writ)	SCr.	književnost
Sp.	literatura	ME	litterature	Boh.	literatura, pisemnictvi
Rum.	literatură	NE	literature	Pol.	literatura
Ir.	(scriptur)	Du.	letterkunde	Russ.	literatura, slovesnost'
NIr.	litridheacht	OHG	(giscrip, script)	Skt.	grantha-, çāstra-
W.	llenyddiaeth	MHG	(schrift)		
Br.	lennegez	NHG	literatur		

Most words for 'literature' are based on the notion of 'letters', and a Lat. deriv. has furnished what is virtually an international Eur. term.

For the earlier periods of the Eur. languages, before the adoption of Lat. litterātūra, the entries in the list (namely, the Ir., Goth., OE, OHG, ChSl.) are words for 'writing(s)' which are mostly quotable only with reference to the holy 'scripture'. But it may be assumed that they might cover also 'writings, literature' in general.

1. Grk. γράμματα, pl. of γράμμα 'letter' (18.54), covers 'letter' = 'epistle', 'documents', and 'writings' of an author, also the science of literature and grammar. Though apparently not quotable in class. times in a phrase like 'Greek literature', it was eventually so used, e.g. NG Ἑλληνικὰ γράμματα.

NG λογοτεχνία, lit. the 'art of words', a modern creation, now the technical literary term.

2. Lat. litterae, pl. of littera 'letter' (18.54), used like Grk. γράμματα for 'letter' = 'epistle', 'writings', and literature. This last use is preserved in Fr. lettres (cultiver les lettres, un homme de lettres, belles-lettres, etc.), NE letters (man of letters, etc.), also in derivs., Ir. litrid 'man of letters', whence NIr. litridheacht (or liteardhacht) 'literature', and Du. letter-kunde. Otherwise replaced by the following.

Lat. litterātūra, a rendering of Grk.

γραμματική 'writing', esp. 'science of language, grammar', only later (not class.) 'literature', but source of the most widespread Eur. term.

3. Ir. scriptur 'scripture', fr. Lat. scriptūra. Vendryes, De hib. voc. 175.

W. llenyddiaeth, Br. lennegez, derivs. (W. through vb. llenydda) of W. llen 'lore, learning', Br. lenn 'reading', fr. Lat. legendum 'what is to be read' (cf. 18.52).

4. Goth. mēla, ON script, ritning, OE writ, OHG giscrip, scrift (also buochscrift = literatura, Notker), all fr. verbs for 'write' (18.51), and the reg. words for holy 'scripture'.

5. In ChSl. the Grk. γράμματα is rendered by kŭnigy (whence words for 'book', cf. 18.61), bukŭvĭ (orig. 'letters', cf. 18.54) and pisanĭje (: pĭsati 'write', 18.51). Cf. Jagić, Entstehungsgesch. 357.

SCr. književnost, deriv. (through adj. književni 'literary') of knjiga 'book' (18.61).

Boh. pisemnictvi, deriv. (through adj. pisemný) of pisati 'write' (18.51).

Russ. slovesnost' (now rather archaic), deriv. (through adj. slovesnyj) of slovo 'word' (18.26).

6. Skt. grantha- 'composition, literary production, book' (18.61).

Skt. çāstra- 'instruction' (: çās- 'teach', 17.25), 'instructive work' and applied to various forms of literature.

18.66 AUTHOR, WRITER

Grk.	συγγραφεύς	Dan.	forfatter, skribent	Lith.	rašytojas
NG	συγγραφεύς, λογογράφης	Sw.	skriftställare, författare	Lett.	rakstnieks
				SCr.	spisatelj, književnik
Lat.	scriptor, auctor	OE	writere	Boh.	původce, spisovatel
It.	autore, scriptore	ME	autor, writer	Pol.	autor, pisarz
Fr.	auteur, écrivain	NE	author, writer	Russ.	avtor, pisatel'
Sp.	autor, escritor	Du.	schrijver	Skt.	grantha-kāra-, -kṛt-
Rum.	scriitor, autor	OHG	scriptor		
Ir.	augtor, scribnid	MHG	tihtære		
NIr.	ughdar, scríobnóir	NHG	verfasser, schriftsteller		
W.	awdur				
Br.	skrivagner				

The majority of words for the literary 'author, writer' are words for 'writer', derived from the usual verbs for 'write'. But Lat. auctor 'author' has a large progeny, and in some languages the 'author'-words have a superior rank to the 'writer'-words, since the latter are so comprehensive, covering the veriest scribbler (so e.g. Fr. auteur vs. écrivain, Sp. autor vs. escritor; but NE writer, though comprehensive, is used, no less than author, of the greatest).

A few of the words listed are used for the author of particular works, but not in phrases like 'the Greek authors'. So NHG verfasser, while the corresponding Dan. forfatter, Sw. författare may be used also in such phrases.

1. Derivs. of verbs for 'write'. Obvious by comparison with the list 18.51, But NHG schriftsteller for 'literary writ-

er vs. schreiber 'writer' in general, 'scribe', etc.

2. Lat. auctor 'author' as 'originator, founder, proposer', etc., hence also literary 'author', fr. augēre 'increase, augment'. Ernout-M. 89. Hence the widespread Eur. words.

3. MHG tihtære 'composer, writer' and 'poet', see 18.67.

NHG verfasser, fr. verfassen 'put together, compose', cpd. of fassen 'hold, seize' (11.14). Similarly Dan. forfatter, Sw. författare, fr. vbs. borrowed fr. MLG vorvaten. Falk-Torp 255.

4. SCr. književnik, fr. književni 'literary', fr. knjiga 'book' (18.61). Cf. ChSl. kŭnižĭnikŭ 'scribe'.

Boh. původce, 'author' in wider and narrower sense, fr. původ 'origin'.

5. Skt. grantha-kāra-, grantha-kṛt-, cpds. of grantha- 'literary production, book' (18.61) and forms of kṛ- 'make'.

18.67 POET

Grk.	ποιητής	ON	skáld	Lith.	poētas
NG	ποιητής	Dan.	digter	Lett.	dzejnieks
Lat.	poēta	Sw.	skald, diktare (poet)	SCr.	pjesnik
It.	poeta	OE	scop	Boh.	básnik
Fr.	poète	ME	poet	Pol.	poeta
Sp.	poeta	NE	poet	Russ.	poet, stichotvorec
Rum.	poet	Du.	dichter	Skt.	kavi-
Ir.	fáith, fili	OHG	scof		
NIr.	file	MHG	tihtære, poëte		
W.	prydydd, bardd	NHG	dichter (poet)		
Br.	barz				

The largest group of words for 'poet' goes back to the Grk. word, in which 'maker' was specialized to 'poet'. But such a borrowed word may fall to an inferior rank by virtue of the revival and glorification of an old native word. So notably Sw. poet vs. skald (Hellquist 774, 923), and NHG poet vs. dichter, the former of which after being in part an inferior or derogatory term 'poetaster, versifier' (cf. Maas, Z. deutsch. Wortf. 6.234 f.), is now little used.

A few others reflect a similar specialization, being derived from other verbs meaning 'create' or 'compose'.

The predecessor of the literary 'poet' was the 'singer' or 'seer', or 'story-teller' (in verse), and some words which originally had such senses have become the usual words for 'poet'.

1. Grk. ποιητής, orig. 'maker, constructor' (: ποιέω 'make'), specialized to 'author' and esp. 'poet' (Hdt.+). Hence Lat. poēta and the widespread Eur. words.

Before ποιητής became the common word for 'poet', this was expressed by ἀοιδός 'singer, bard' (: ἀείδω 'sing' 18.12).

2. Lat. vātēs 'seer' and 'poet' (the old word for 'poet' before the introduction poēta, and later revived in this sense): Ir. fáith 'seer, poet', W. gwawd 'song, poetry' (now 'satire, ridicule'), OE wōd 'possessed, mad', wōþ 'sound, song', etc, Walde-P. 1.212. Ernout-M. 1076.

3. Ir. 'seer, poet' : Lat. vātēs, etc., above, 2.

Ir. fili, NIr. file, orig. 'seer' : W. gweled 'see', etc. (15.51). Walde-P. 1.293. Pedersen 1.249.

Gael. bard (also MIr., NIr., but not the usual word), W. bardd, Br. barz (cf. Gall. Bardo-magnus, etc.), Celtic word borrowed in late Grk. βάρδος, late Lat. bardus and NE bard (now not restricted to Celtic bards, cf. NED s.v. 4), etym.

dub., perh. (IE *gʷ > Celt. b reg.) : Skt. gṛ- 'invoke, praise', Lith. gìrti 'praise', OPruss. gerdat 'say', etc. (Walde-P. 1.686 f., without Celt. bard). Stokes 162.

W. prydydd, fr. vb. prydu 'compose verse' : Ir. creth 'poetry', fr. root in W. peri 'cause, create', Skt. kṛ- 'make', etc. Walde-P. 1.517 f. Pedersen 1.128.

4. ON skáld, whence Sw. skald, revived at the expense of poet and now the usual word (but Dan. skjald 'bard, minstrel'), etym. dub. Falk-Torp 980. Hellquist 923 f.

OE scop, OHG scof (masc. 'poet', neut. 'poetry' and 'mockery') : ON skop, skaup 'mockery', MLG schoven 'deceive', etc. (ME, NE scoff), hence apparently first a poet of satire. Walde-P. 2.556. Falk-Torp 1037. NED s.v. scop.

MHG tihtære ('composer, writer' and 'poet'), NHG, Du. dichter (Dan. digter), Sw. diktare, fr. vbs., with sense influenced by HG), fr. vb. seen in OHG tihtōn, dihtōn 'write, compose' (cf. OE dihtan 'order, compose', etc., NE dight), later esp. 'compose poetry' (NHG dichten), fr. Lat. dictāre 'dictate, order' and 'compose' (e.g. dictāre carmina Hor.). Deriv. fr. a Gmc. root (: Lat. fingere 'fashion'), preferred by Falk-Torp 141 f., Kluge-G. 104, is superfluous and improbable. Weigand-H. 1.353. NED s.v. dight. Hellquist 923.

5. Lett. dzejnieks, with vb. dzejuōt, fr. dzeja 'poetry', prob. an artificial creation abstracted from dziesma 'poetry' (given by Ulmann, s.v. Dichtung) = Lith. giesmė 'song' : giedoti 'sing' (18.12).

6. SCr. pjesnik, deriv. of pjesna, pjesma 'song', or more exactly of a form = ChSl. pěsnŭ 'song, hymn, psalm' (freq. in Supr.), fr. the root of ChSl. pěti 'sing' (18.12).

Boh. básnik, fr. báseň 'tale, poem',

this fr. OBoh. *báti* 'speak, relate, tell stories' (Berneker 39). Gebauer 2.366. Russ. (beside usual *poet*) *stichotvorec*, lit. 'verse-maker', cpd. of *stich*, ChSl. *stichŭ*, fr Grk. στίχος 'verse'.

7. Skt. *kavi-* 'wise, wise one, sage, seer', later 'poet', fr. the root seen in *ā-kūti-* 'intention', Grk. κοέω 'perceive', Lat. *cavēre* 'beware', ChSl. *čuti* 'feel, perceive', etc. Walde-P. 1.368 ff.

CHAPTER 19

TERRITORIAL, SOCIAL, AND POLITICAL DIVISIONS; SOCIAL RELATIONS

19.11	COUNTRY ("European Countries")	19.44	FREE (adj.)
19.12	ONE'S NATIVE COUNTRY	19.45	COMMAND, ORDER (vbs.)
19.13	COUNTRY vs. TOWN	19.46	OBEY
19.14	REGION, TERRITORY	19.47	LET, PERMIT
19.15	CITY, TOWN	19.48	COMPEL
19.16	VILLAGE	19.51	FRIEND
19.17	BOUNDARY	19.52	ENEMY
19.21	PEOPLE (Populace)	19.53	COMPANION
19.22	A PEOPLE, NATION	19.54	NEIGHBOR
19.23	TRIBE, CLAN, FAMILY (in Wide Sense)	19.55	STRANGER
19.31	RULE (vb.), GOVERN	19.56	GUEST
19.32	KING	19.57	HOST
19.33	QUEEN	19.58	HELP, AID (vbs.)
19.34	EMPEROR	19.59	HINDER, PREVENT
19.35	PRINCE	19.61	CUSTOM
19.352	Note on Other Titles of Nobility	19.62	STRIFE, QUARREL
19.36	NOBLE (sb.), NOBLEMAN	19.63	PLOT, CONSPIRACY
19.37	CITIZEN	19.64	COMMON (adj.)
19.38	SUBJECT (sb.)	19.65	MEET (vb.)
19.41	MASTER	19.71	Note on Terms for Members of a Trade or Profession
19.42	SLAVE		
19.43	SERVANT	19.72	WHORE, PROSTITUTE

19.11 COUNTRY ("European Countries")

Grk.	χώρα, γῆ, χθών	Goth.	*land*	Lith.	*kraštas, žemė*
NG	χώρα, τόπος	ON	*land*	Lett.	*zeme*
Lat.	*fīnēs, terra*	Dan.	*land*	ChSl.	*strana, zemlja*
It.	*paese*	Sw.	*land*	SCr.	*zemlja*
Fr.	*pays*	OE	*land*	Boh.	*země*
Sp.	*pais*	ME	*land, contree*	Pol.	*ziemia*
Rum.	*ţară*	NE	*country, land*	Russ.	*strana*
Ir.	*tír, crích*	Du.	*land*	Skt.	*deça-, viṣaya-, jana-*
NIr.	*tír*	OHG	*lant*		*pada-*
W.	*gwlad*	MHG	*lant*	Av.	*daiŋhu-*, OPers. *dah-*
Br.	*bro*	NHG	*land*		*yu-*

'Country' is intended here as the territory of a whole people or nation ("European countries"), though the words are used also in a more general sense for areas of indeterminate extent.

The majority are the same as words for 'land', but a few are from 'boundaries' or other sources.

1. Words for 'land' already discussed in 1.21.

Grk. γῆ, χθών (poet.); Lat. *terra*, Rum. *ţară*; Ir. *tír*; Goth. *land*, etc., general Gmc. (in NE now replaced in common use by *country*); Lith. *žemė* (formerly so used), Lett. *zeme*; ChSl. *zemlja* (reg. for γῆ including 'country', but *strana* for χώρα, SCr. *zemlja*, Boh. *země*, Pol. *ziemia* (Russ. *zemlja* formerly so used, but mostly *strana*).

2. Grk. χώρα, also 'space, place' like χῶρος, both orig. 'empty space' : χῆρος 'bereft', Skt. *hā-* 'leave', etc. Walde-P. 1.543. NG χώρα, lit. 'country', pop. 'town' (19.15).

Grk. τόπος 'place' (12.11), 'region', NG pop. also 'country'.

3. Lat. *fīnēs*, lit. 'boundaries, limits', pl. of *fīnis* 'limit, border' and temporal 'end' (14.26).

It. *paese*, Fr. *pays* (> Sp. *pais*), fr. VLat. *pāgēnsis*, deriv. of *pāgus* 'country district' (19.14). REW 6145. Gamillscheg 679.

4. Ir. *crích* (beside more usual *tír*), see under 'region' (19.14).

W. *gwlad* : Br. *glad* 'wealth, fortune', Ir. *flaith* 'ruler', etc., fr. the root in Ir. *foln-* 'rule', Lat. *valēre* 'be strong', OE *wealdan*, etc. 'rule' (19.31). Walde-P. 1.219. Pedersen 1.157.

Br. *bro*, also 'region' as W. *bro*, see 19.14.

5. ME *contree*, NE *country*, fr. OFr. *cuntrée, contrée* (now mostly 'country' in

more general sense), fr. VLat. *contrāta* (*regiō*), lit. '(region) opposite', deriv. of *contra* 'against, opposite'. REW 2187 NED s.v. *country*.

6. Lith. *kraštas* (now more usual than *žemė* for 'country'; cf. Hermann, Lit.-Deutsches Gesprächsb. 22, 36), also 'region' and (more orig.) 'side, edge, shore' = Lett. *krasts* 'shore', etym. dub. Mühl.-Endz. 2.260.

7. ChSl. *strana* (reg. for χώρα), Russ. *strana* (ChSl. form) = SCr., Boh. *strana*, Pol. *strona*, Russ. *storona* 'side' (12.36).

8. Skt. *deça*, also 'region', lit. 'direction' : *diç-* 'show, point out'. Uhlenbeck 130.

Skt. *viṣaya*, also 'territory, realm, kingdom', as orig. 'sphere of influence' : *viṣ-* 'be active', outside root connections dub. Uhlenbeck 289. Whitney, Roots 161.

Skt. *janapada*-, cpd. of *jana-* 'race' and *pada-* 'station, abode' (lit. 'step' : *pad-* 'foot').

Av. *daiŋhu-, dah'yu-*, OPers. *dahyu-* (in OPers. used of the great provinces and also of regions within them; MPers. *deh* 'country', NPers. *dih* 'village', prob. = Skt. *dasyu-*, the designation of the pre-Aryan inhabitants of India (orig. 'inhabitants of the country'?), root connections dub. Barth. 706 ff. Uhlenbeck 123.

19.12 ONE'S NATIVE COUNTRY

Grk.	πατρίς	Goth.	*gabaurþs, land*	Lith.	*tėvynė*
NG	πατρίδα	ON	*fōstrjǫrð (-land)*	Lett.	*tēvija, tēvzeme*
Lat.	*patria*	Dan.	*fædreland (fosterland)*	ChSl.	*otĭčĭstvije*
It.	*patria*	Sw.	*fädernesland, fosterland*	SCr.	*domovina, otačastvo*
Fr.	*patrie*	OE	*ēþel (ēþelland, fæ-*	Boh.	*vlast, otčina*
Sp.	*patria*		*derēþel), eard*	Pol.	*ojczyzna*
Rum.	*patrie*	ME	*contree*	Russ.	*rodina, otečestvo*
Ir.	*atharde, atharthīr*	NE	*country, fatherland*	Skt.	*svadeça*
NIr.	*tír dhúthchais*	Du.	*vaderland*		
W.	*gwlad*	OHG	*fateruodil*		
Br.	*mamvro*	MHG	*vaterheim, vaterland*		
		NHG	*vaterland*		

The notion of 'one's native country' may be expressed by the regular words for 'country' with appropriate context, as in NE *my country, die for one's country*, which (rather than *fatherland, native country*, etc.) carry the emotional value of Fr. *patrie*, NHG *vaterland*, etc. Where words for 'country' are repeated in this list, a similar context is, of course, to be understood.

But in most of the IE languages there are special terms. These are most commonly derivs. or cpds. of the words for 'father', possibly but not necessarily, reflecting semantic borrowing from the Greek πατρίς. Much less commonly from words for 'mother'. Terms like NE *mother country* or *motherland*, though quotable in this sense, are used mainly to denote the relation of a country to its colonies or the home of certain products, etc.

Others are derived from words for 'home', 'birth', 'race', 'family', and (through 'possession') 'power'.

1. Derivs. or cpds. of words for 'father' (2.35).

Grk. πατρίς (also πάτρα, Hom. πάτρη), NG πατρίδα; Lat. *patria* (> Romance words); Ir. *atharde, atharthīr* (K. Meyer, Contrib. 144); OE *fæderēþel*, OHG *fateruodil*, NE *fatherland*, NHG *vaterland*, Dan. *fædreland*, etc. (see list); Lith. *tėvynė*, Lett. *tēvija, tēvzeme*; ChSl. *otĭčĭstvije* (reg. for πατρίς), SCr. *otačastvo*, *otadžbina*, Boh. *otčina*, Pol. *ojczyzna*, Russ. *otečestvo*.

2. NIr. *tír dhúthchais*, i.e. *tír* 'country' with gen. sg. of MIr., NIr. *dúthchas*

'inheritance, one's homeland or country' (cf. MIr. *firduchus* 'true native country', deriv. of MIr. *dúthaig* 'belonging to, fitting', NIr. *duthaigh* 'estate, land, region' (19.14).

W. *gwlad* 'country' (19.11) and 'native country' (cf. *gwladgar* 'patriotic').

Br. *mamvro*, cpd. of *mamm* 'mother' and *bro* 'country'.

3. Goth. *gabaurþs* 'birth', hence as 'birthplace' for πατρίς (Mk. 6.4, Lk. 4.23, 24; but *in landa seinamma* = εἰς τὴν πατρίδα αὐτοῦ Mk. 6.1).

ON *fōstrjǫrð* and *fōstrland*, Dan. (arch. or poet.), Sw. *fosterland*, cpds. of *fōstr* 'fostering' and words for 'land'.

OE *æþel, ēþel* (freq. for *patria* in Gospels), also *ēþelland* and *fæderēþel* (= OHG *fateruodil* so used by Tat.) = ON *ōðal*, OHG *uodal, uodil* inherited 'estate, patrimony' (as OE *ēþel* also), with strong grade of root in ON *aðal* 'nature', OE *æþele* 'noble', OHG *adal* 'noble descent, nobility' (NHG *adel*), etc., prob. : Goth. *atta* 'father', etc. Walde-P. 1.44. Falk-Torp 787, 1430, 1524.

OE *eard* (for *patria* in Mt. 13.54, 57, Aelfric, etc.), but mostly more general 'region' (19.14).

4. SCr. *domovina*, fr. *dom* 'house, home' (7.12).

Boh. *vlast* = ChSl. *vlastĭ* 'power', Pol. *vlość* 'landed property', Russ. *volost'* 'district', fr. the root of ChSl. *vladǫ, vlasti* 'rule' (19.31). Brückner 625 f.

Russ. *rodina*, fr. *rod* 'descent, race, family' (19.23).

5. Skt. *svadeça*-, cpd. of *sva-* 'own' and *deça-* 'country'.

19.13 COUNTRY
(vs. Town)

Grk.	*ἀγροί, χώρα*	Goth.	*weihsa, haimōs*	Lith.	*sodžius, kaimas*
NG	*ἐξοχή*	ON	*land*	Lett.	*lauki*
Lat.	*rūs, agrī*	Dan.	*land*	ChSl.	*sela*
It.	*campagna*	Sw.	*land*	SCr.	*selo*
Fr.	*campagne*	OE	*land*	Boh.	*venkov*
Sp.	*campo*	ME	*land, feeld*	Pol.	*wieś*
Rum.	*ţară*	NE	*country*	Russ.	*derevnja*
Ir.	. . . .	Du.	*land*		
NIr.	*tuath*	OHG	*lant*		
W.	*gwlad*	MHG	*lant*		
Br.	*maez, ploue*	NHG	*land*		

Many of the words for 'country' as listed in 19.11 are used also for 'country' vs. 'city, town', as NE *in the country*, NHG *auf dem lande*, etc. Otherwise this is expressed by words for 'field' (often in plural) or derivs. of these, words cognate with others for 'space', some for 'village', and in a few cases by terms reflecting the notion of 'outside'.

1. Grk. *ἀγρός* 'field' (8.12), also 'country' in this sense, esp. pl. *ἀγροί* (but also sg. Hom.).

Grk. *χώρα* 'country' (19.11), sometimes also in this sense.

NG *ἐξοχή*, in class. Grk. 'prominence, protuberance' (so in lit. NG, also *κατ' ἐξοχήν* 'par excellence, especially'), late also 'extremity', whence 'remote place' and so 'country' vs. 'town' (*εἰς τὴν ἐξοχήν* 'in the country'). Koraes, "Ατακτα 4.2.630.

2. Lat. *rūs* : Av. *ravah-* 'space, freedom', Goth., OE *rūm*, etc. 'space, room', ChSl. *ravĭnŭ, rovĭnŭ* 'level'. Walde-P. 2.356 f. Ernout-M. 879.

Lat. *ager* 'field' (8.12), also 'country' in this sense, esp. pl. *agrī*. Cf. Lat. *pāgus* 'country district' and the derivs. for 'country' (19.11), these also often 'country' vs. town, hence words for 'peasant'.

It. *campagna* (> Fr. *campagne*), OFr. *champaigne*, etc., fr. MLat. *campānia* (cf. Lat. *Campānia*), fem. of MLat. *campānius, -eus*, deriv. adj. fr. Lat. *campus* 'plain, field' (1.23), whence Sp. *campo* also 'country' vs. 'town'. REW 1557, Ernout-M. 140.

Rum. *ţară* 'country' (19.11), also in this sense.

3. NIr. *tuath* 'territory, region' and 'country' vs. 'town' (Dinneen), fr. Ir. *tūath* 'people, notion' (19.22).

W. *gwlad* 'country' (19.11), also in this sense.

Br. *maez* 'plain, field' (1.23), also 'country' vs. 'town'.

Br. *ploue*, formerly 'parish, community' (= W. *plwyf*), fr. Lat. *plēbēs* 'the common people' (cf. 19.21). Loth, Mots lat. 196.

4. Goth. *weihsa* and once *haimōs* render *ἀγροί* 'country' as contrasted to *baurgs* '*πόλις*' (Lk. 8.34, etc. *weihsa;* Mk. 5.14 *haimōs*), pls. of *weihs, haims* '*κώμη*, village' (19.16).

ON, OE *land*, etc. 'country' (19.11), also in this sense general Gmc., except Goth. and NE.

ME *feeld* 'field' (8.12), also 'country' vs. 'town' (NE *field* obs. or arch. in this sense; NED s.v. 2).

5. Lith. *sodžius* and *kaimas* 'village' (19.16), both used also for 'country' vs. 'town' (cf. Senn, Lit. Sprachl.).

Lett. *lauki*, pl. of *lauks* 'open country, field' : Lith. *laukas* 'field' (8.12).

6. ChSl. *sela* (renders *ἀγροί* Mk. 5.14, Lk. 8.34), pl. of *selo* 'field' (8.12), SCr. *selo* 'village' (19.16) and 'country'.

Boh. *venkov* (cf. *venek* 'the outside, country place'), fr. *ven* 'out' = Russ. *von*, SCr. *van*, ChSl. *vŭnŭ* id.

Pol. *wieś* 'village' (19.16), also 'country' vs. 'town'.

Russ. *derevnja* 'small village, hamlet' (19.16), also 'country' vs. 'town'.

19.14 REGION, TERRITORY

Grk.	*χώρα, τόπος*	Goth.	*gawi*	Lith.	*šalis, kraštas*
NG	*χώρα, τόπος, μέρος*	ON	*herað, sveit*	Lett.	*vidus, mala, puse*
Lat.	*regiō, tractus, territōrium*	Dan.	*egn, omraade, gebed*	ChSl.	*strana*
It.	*regione, territorio*	Sw.	*trakt, område, gebit*	SCr.	*kraj, predjel, oblast*
Fr.	*région, territoire, endroit*	OE	*eard, land(scipe)*	Boh.	*kraj(ina), obvod, oblast*
Sp.	*región, territorio*	ME	*contree, regioun, erd*	Pol.	*kraina, obwód*
Rum.	*regiune, ţinut*	NE	*region, territory*	Russ.	*kraj, strana, oblast'*
Ir.	*crīch, mruig*	Du.	*streek, gebied*	Skt.	*deça-, viṣaya-*, etc.
NIr.	*dūthaigh, ceanntar*	OHG	*lant(scaf), gawi*	Av.	*daiŋhu-, zantu-*
W.	*ardal, bro, tiriogaeth*	MHG	*gegende, lantschaft, göu(we)*		
Br.	*bro*	NHG	*gegend, gebiet, landschaft*		

It is intended to group together here the most important of the words that denote an area of indeterminate extent and may serve for various areas intermediate between the whole 'country' and the 'city, town'. Most of the words for 'country' (19.11) are used also in a more general sense, and some of them are repeated in this list. Many of the words listed may have a more special technical application in certain periods or contexts, but no strict classification according to larger or smaller scope is feasible. A great number of others that are mainly technical terms for administrative divisions, 'province, district, canton, parish', etc., are omitted.

The words are based mainly on various spatial notions, as 'place, side, part, extent, line' and especially 'boundary', but several on the notion of possession or rule ('domain'), as NHG *gebiet*, etc.

1. Grk. *χώρα* 'space, place, country' (19.11), also 'region'.

Grk. *τόπος* 'place' (12.11), also 'region'.

NG *μέρος* 'part' (13.23), pop. 'region'.

2. Lat. *regiō*, lit. 'a direction, a (straight) line', whence 'boundary line', and so 'region, territory' (hence It. *regione*, etc.) : *regere* 'direct, rule', etc. Ernout-M. 857.

Lat. *tractus*, lit. 'a drawing out, extent', whence 'extent or stretch of land, tract, region' : *trahere* 'draw'. Ernout-M. 1051.

Lat. *territōrium* (> It. *territorio*, etc.), deriv. of *terra* 'land, country' (1.21, 19.11). Ernout-M. 1034.

Lat. *pāgus* 'country district, rural canton', orig. 'boundary fixed in the ground' : *pangere* 'fix'. Walde-P. 2.2. Ernout-M. 722 f.

Fr. *endroit* 'place' and 'region', orig. 'right side', fr. *en droit*. Gamillscheg 359.

Rum. *ţinut*, orig. 'possession', fr. pple. of *ţinea* 'possess'. Tiktin 1601.

3. Ir. *crīch* 'furrow, border, boundary', whence also 'territory, region' (cf. K. Meyer, Contrib. s.v.) : Lat. *cernere* 'separate, distinguish', Grk. *κρῑ́νω* 'separate, decide', etc. Walde-P. 2.584.

Ir. *mruig, bruig*, W., Br., Corn. *bro*

(Gall. *brogae* 'ager', *Allo-brogēs*) : Lat. *margō* 'border', Goth. *marka* 'boundary', etc. (19.17). Walde-P. 2.283 f. Pedersen 1.97.

NIr. *dūthaigh* (also 'estate, land', orig. 'inherited land'), fr. MIr. *dūthaig* 'belonging to, fitting', cf. *dūthaig na fine* 'belonging to the family, inheritance' (Laws, Gloss. 283), perh. cpd. of *toich* 'natural, belonging to by nature'. Pedersen 2.667.

NIr. *ceanntar*, orig. 'pars citerior' (as opposed to *altar* 'pars ulterior'), fr. MIr. *centar* 'this side', deriv. of OIr. *cen-* 'this side of' (as in *cenalpande* 'cisalpinus'). Pedersen 2.44, 197.

W. *ardal*, orig. 'border, marches', cpd. of *ar* 'on' and *tal* 'forehead, front, end' = Ir. *tel, tul* 'forehead' : Ir. *talam* 'earth', Skt. *tala-* 'flat surface', etc. Walde-P. 1.740. Pedersen 1.132.

W. *tiriogaeth*, deriv. of *tir* 'land' (prob. after Lat. *territōrium*).

4. Goth. *gawi*, OHG *gawi, gewi*, MHG *göu, göuwe*, etc. (NHG *gau* 'district, canton'), etym. dub. Walde-P. 1.565. Feist 210 f. Kluge-G. 188. Weigand-H. 1.629.

ON *herað* (also as a more definite political division, cf. Dan. *herred*, Sw. *härad* 'jurisdictional district'), fr. **her-rað* cpd. of *herr* 'host, people, army' and *rāð* 'counsel, plan, management' (: *rāða* 'advise, plan, rule'). Hence orig. the district over which the *hersir* 'chief' ruled. Falk-Torp 400 f. Torp, Nynorsk 210. Hellquist 387.

ON *sveit* (also often a more definite political 'district'), orig. 'body of men' as a military term, cf. OE *swēot* 'troop, band', perh. : Av. *xᵛaētu-* 'belonging to', and other derivs. of the refl. pronoun like ON *sveinn* 'boy, lad' (orig. 'dependent, one of the same family'), Lith. *svainis* 'wife's sister's husband', etc. Walde-P. 2.457. Falk-Torp 1214.

Dan. *egn*, fr. ODan. *egn* 'possession, estate' = ON *eign* 'property', etc. : *eiga* 'own', Dan. *eie* (11.12). The modern meaning is due to the influence of LG *jegen, jegnode* 'region' = MHG *gegen*, etc. (below). Falk-Torp 183.

Sw. *omrâde* (> Dan. *omraade*), deriv. of phrase *råda om* 'be master of, possess'. Falk-Torp 792. Hellquist 730.

Sw. *trakt*, fr. Lat. *tractus* (above, 2). Hellquist 1213.

OE *eard*, ME *erd* : OS *ard* 'dwelling', ON *ǫrð* 'harvest', OHG *art* 'plowing', fr. the root of OE *erian*, Goth. *arjan*, Lat. *arāre*, etc. 'plow'. Walde-P. 1.72, 78. NED s.v. *erd*.

OE *land*, etc., the general Gmc. word for 'land, country' (19.11), may often be used for 'region', or esp. with the deriv. suffixes OE *-scipe*, and OHG *-scaf*, later *-scaft*, MHG, NHG *-schaft*, denoting orig. 'condition, state' (of being so and so) and also (as here) with collective sense. Cf. NED s.v. *-ship*.

ME *contree*, see 'country' (19.11).

ME *regioun* (also 'kingdom, realm'), NE *region*, fr. Anglo-Fr. *regiun* = Fr. *région* (above, 2). NED s.v.

ME, NE *territory* (in ME chiefly rendering Lat. *territōrium* in the sense of 'land about a city', later esp. 'land belonging to the dominion of a certain ruler', etc.), fr. Lat. *territōrium* (above, 2). NED s.v.

Du. *streek* (similarly ODan. *streg*, Dan. *strøg*; cf. NHG *landstrich*), orig. 'line, stroke' (= OHG *strih*, NHG *strich* 'stroke, line', Goth. *striks* 'stroke', etc.). Franck-v. W. 674 f. Falk-Torp 1177 f., 1185.

Du. *gebied* (LG *gebēd* > Dan. *gebed*), NHG *gebiet* (> Sw. *gebit*), but MHG *gebiet(e)*, chiefly 'command' : *gebieten* 'command' (18.36). Orig. 'territory under one's command'. Weigand-H. 1.636. Falk-Torp 303. Hellquist 273.

MHG *gegen, gegende, gegenōte*, NHG *gegend*, deriv. of *gegen* 'against, opposite', in imitation of VLat. *contrāta* (> OFr. *contrée*, etc., 19.11), fr. *contra*. Weigand-H. 1.650 f. Kluge-G. 192.

5. Lith. *šalis*, orig. 'side' (cf. *į šalį*, *šalin* 'aside, away') : OE *heald*, OHG *hald* 'inclined', OHG *halda* 'slope, bank', etc., fr. **k̂el-* beside **k̂lei-* in Grk. *κλῑ́νω*, Lat. *in-clīnāre*, etc. 'incline'. Walde-P. 1.430.

Lith. *kraštas*, see 'country' (19.11).

Lett. *vidus*, lit. 'middle, interior' = Lith. *vidus* 'middle, inside', etc. (12.37).

Lett. *mala*, lit. 'border, margin, bank', prob. orig. in the latter sense : Alb. *mal* 'mountain', *majë* 'point, peak', Ir. *mell* 'elevation, hill', etc. Walde-P. 2.295. Mühl.-Endz. 2.555 f.

Lett. *puse*, lit. 'half, side' (12.36, 13.24).

6. ChSl., Russ. *strana* (SCr., Boh. *strana*, Pol. *strona* 'side', also sometimes 'region, quarter'), see 'country' (19.11).

SCr. *kraj*, etc., general modern Slavic (or esp. derivs. as Boh. *krajina*, Pol. *kraina*), lit. 'edge, margin' = ChSl. *krajĭ* 'edge, shore' : ChSl. *krajati* 'cut, separate', Grk. *κρῑ́νω* 'separate, decide', etc. Walde-P. 2.585. Berneker 605 f.

SCr. *predjel* (= Russ. *predel* 'boundary, limit'), lit. 'forepart', cpd. of ChSl. *dělŭ*, etc. 'part' (13.23).

SCr., Boh. *oblast*, Russ. *oblast'* = ChSl. *oblastĭ* 'power' (also rarely for *περίχωρος* 'country round about') : *obladati* 'rule over', fr. **ob-vlad-*, cpd. of *vladą, vlasti* 'rule'.

Boh. *obvod*, Pol. *obwód* (= Russ. *obvod* 'surroundings', etc.) : Boh. *voditi*, Pol. *wodzić*, iter. to *vesti, wieść* 'lead'. Brückner 629. Miklosich 376 f.

7. Skt. *deça-, viṣaya-*, and Av. *daiŋhu-*, see 'country' (19.11).

Av. *zantu-* (a political division between the *daiŋhu-* and the *vīs-* 'village'; but in orig. a social rather than geographical division, cf. Sp. *pueblo* 'people' and 'village') = Skt. *jantu-* 'offspring, living being, etc.', derivs. of Skt. *jan-*, Av. *zan-* 'beget, bear'. Walde-P. 1.577. Barth. 1660 f.

19.15 CITY, TOWN

Grk.	*πόλις, ἄστυ*	Goth.	*baurgs*	Lith.	*miestas*
NG	*πόλις, πολιτεία*	ON	*borg*	Lett.	*pilsēta*
Lat.	*urbs, oppidum*	Dan.	*by, stad*	ChSl.	*gradŭ*
It.	*città*	Sw.	*stad*	SCr.	*grad, varoš*
Fr.	*ville*	OE	*burg, ceaster*	Boh.	*město*
Sp.	*ciudad*	ME	*citee, toun, burgh*	Pol.	*miasto*
Rum.	*oraş*	NE	*city, town*	Russ.	*gorod*
Ir.	*cathir*	Du.	*stad*	Skt.	*nagara-, pura-*
NIr.	*cathair, baile mōr*	OHG	*burg*	OPers.	*vardana-*
W.	*dinas*	MHG	*burc, stat*		
Br.	*kêr*	NHG	*stadt*		

In the heading 'city, town' it is intended to ignore the difference between NE *city* and *town*, the latter being partly generic and including city, and partly subordinate to city, the technical distinction showing wide local variation (in U.S., especially New England, according to the form of local government). Cf. NED s.vv. *city* and *town*. The nearest parallel is in Latin, where *oppidum* is occasionally applied, like *urbs*, to cities like Rome or Athens, but mostly to other towns.

In general, terms for 'town' as intermediate between 'city' and 'village' are not included in the list, e.g. Fr. *bourg*,

NHG *kleinstadt*, Grk. κώρη, κωμόπολις, etc. Here belongs NG pop. χώρα (used for the chief town of a district or island; as 'town' in Const. Porph.) with peculiar development of χώρα 'country, place' or perhaps re-formed (or reinterpreted) as augmentative of χωρίον, NG χωριό 'village' (Kretschmer, KZ 39.554 ff.).

Many of the words denoted first an 'inclosed and fortified place'. Several are specializations of 'place' or 'dwelling-place', and one group is narrowed from 'state'.

1. Grk. πόλις (in early use partly = ἀκρόπολις 'citadel') : Skt. *pur-* (nom. *pūr*) 'stronghold, fortified place' ('town'? Cf. Macdonell-Keith 1.539), also *pura-*, sometimes simply 'town', Lith. *pilis*, Lett. *pils* 'castle', root connection dub., but 'citadel' prob. the earliest sense. Walde-P. 2.51. Boisacq 802.

NG πόλις, though now restored to generic use, was for a long time in pop. speech 'the city, Constantinople', its place in generic sense being taken by πολιτεία, orig. 'citizenship, government, state', whence (like *cīvitās* in late Lat.) pop. 'city, town'.

Grk. ἄστυ (partly the town proper vs. the acropolis, the suburbs or other parts of the city-state), Arc., Boeot. ϝάστυ, doubtless (despite the ϝασ- for expected ϝεσ-) : Skt. *vastu* 'place, thing', *vāstu* 'site, dwelling place, house', fr. the root of Skt. *vas-* 'dwell', OE *wesan* 'be, remain', etc.; here prob. also Toch. A *waşt*, B *ost* 'house'. Walde-P. 1.307. Boisacq 92.

2. Lat. *urbs*, etym. dub., possibly as orig. 'wicker-work (inclosure)' : *verbera* 'rod, whip, scourage', Lith. *virbas* 'stem, stalk, vine', ChSl. *vrŭba* 'willow'. Walde-P. 1.275. (Ernout-M. 1136 say borrowed, without suggestion of any source.)

Lat. *oppidum*, in form doubtless fr. **op-pedom* and belonging to the group of words for 'foot', also Grk. πέδη, Lat. *pedica* 'fetter', Grk. πέδον 'ground', πεδίον 'plain', etc., but line of semantic development uncertain. Perh. best (cf. *oppidum* quoted as once used for the barriers of the circus) as orig. 'place fortified with barriers'. Walde-P. 2.22 f. Ernout-M. 705.

Lat. *cīvitās*, 'citizenship', whence 'the citizenry, state', late 'city' (> It. *città*, Sp. *ciudad;* Fr. *cité* no longer used in general sense; Rum. *cetate* 'castle'), deriv. of *cīvis* 'citizen' (19.37). Ernout-M. 191. REW 1959. Wartburg 2.725 (esp. the history of Fr. *cité* vs. *ville*).

Fr. *ville*, fr. Lat. *villa* 'country house, farm', late 'village' : *vīcus* 'village', etc. (19.16). Walde-P. 1.231. Ernout-M. 1103. REW 9330. Gamillscheg 891.

Rum. *oraş*, fr. Hung. *város* 'town, city'. Tiktin 1092.

3. Ir. *cathir*, NIr. *cathair*, with W. *cader, caer* 'fortress', Br. *kêr, kear* 'city', prob. not fr. Lat. *castra*, as Thurneysen, Hdb. 517 (not repeated in Gram.), Walde-H. 1.180, but etym. dub. Loth, Mots lat. 95, Walde-P. 1.338, Pedersen 1.31, G. S. Lane, Language 8.295 f.

NIr. *baile mōr*, lit. 'large place', see under 'village'.

W. *dinas*, deriv. of MW *din* 'fortress' = Ir. *dūn* id., OE *tūn*, NE *town*, etc. (below, 4).

4. Goth. *baurgs*, ON *borg* (also 'fortress, castle'), OE *burg*, ME *burgh* (NE *borough*), OHG *burg*, MHG *burc* (also 'fortress, castle', as NHG *burg*), all, except Goth., in earliest use 'fortified place', either as 'place of refuge' : OE *beorgan*, OHG *bergan* 'shelter'; or else as 'height' : OE *beorg*, OHG *berg*, etc. 'mountain', Skt. *bṛhant-*, Av. *bərəzant-* 'high', etc. Walde-P. 2.173. Feist 85 f. Falk-Torp 94. Weigand-H. 1.308 f. Kluge-G. 87. NED s.v. *borough*.

Dan. *by* = ON *byr* 'town, village, farm', Sw. *by* 'village', etc. (19.16) : Dan., Sw. *bo*, ON *būa*, Goth. *bauan* 'dwell' (7.11). Walde-P. 2.142. Falk-Torp 120.

Dan., Sw. *stad*, orig. 'place', meaning 'city' fr. NHG *stadt* (below). Falk-Torp 1144.

OE *ceaster*, fr. Lat. *castra* 'military camp', pl. of *castrum* 'fortified place'. NED s.v. *chester*.

ME *toun*, NE *town*, fr. OE *tūn* 'inclosed land, field, farm' and 'village' = ON *tūn* 'inclosed land, homestead', OHG *zūn*, NHG *zaun* 'hedge, fence', Ir. *dūn*, W. *din* 'fortress', all fr. notion of 'inclosed place', but root connections dub. Walde-P. 1.778. NED s.v. *town*.

ME *cite(e)*, NE *city*, fr. OFr. *cité* (above, 2).

Du. *stad*, NHG *stadt* (hence the similar use of Dan., Sw. *stad*), fr. MLG, MHG, OHG *stat* 'place' (MHG also sometimes 'town, city') = Goth. *staþs* 'place', etc. (12.11). Weigand-H. 2.842.

5. Lith. *miestas*, fr. Slavic, cf. Pol. *miasto*, etc. (below, 6). Brückner, Sl. Fremdwörter 108.

Lett. *pilsēta*, cpd. of *pils* 'castle' (: Grk. πόλις, above, 1) and *sēta* 'fence, hedge, farmyard, farmhouse'. Mühl.-Endz. 3.217, 833.

6. ChSl. *gradŭ*, SCr. *grad*, Russ. *gorod* (ChSl. also 'castle, garden', Boh. *hrad*, Pol. *gród* 'castle, fortress'), disputed whether native word : Goth *gards* 'house, court', ON *garðr*, OE *geard* 'yard, court', etc. (7.15) or loanword fr. Gmc. Walde-P. 1.608. Walde-H. 1.243. Berneker 330 f. Stender-Pedersen 255 ff. Feist 198.

SCr. *varoš*, fr. Hung. *város* id. (cf. Rum. *oraş*, above, 2).

Boh. *město*, Pol. *miasto* = ChSl. *město*, Russ. *mesto* 'place' (12.11). Berneker 2.51.

7. Skt. *nagara-*, etym. dub., perh. : *agāra-* 'house', both as cpds. of the root in Grk. ἀγορά 'market place, assembly', Grk. ἀγείρω 'gather, assemble', etc. Walde-P. 1.590. Uhlenbeck 141.

Skt. *pura-*, above, 1.

OPers. *vardana-* prob. : Av. *vərəzə̄na-* 'community, state, common people', Skt. *vṛjana-* 'inclosure, settlement', etc., fr. the root in Av. *varəz-* 'shut off', Grk. εἴργω 'shut in (out)', etc. Walde-P. 1.290. Barth. 1424 f. But the OPers. word could also correspond to Skt. *vardhana-* in town-names like *Puṇḍra-vardhana-*. R. A. Hall, Jr., Language 12.297 ff. (suggesting deriv. fr. the root of OE *wardōn* 'watch over, protect'). Still otherwise on Skt. *vardhana-* (as loanword fr. OPers.) Wackernagel-Debrunner) KZ 67.168 f.

Av. *vīs-*, used of the Mazdayasnian villages or towns (no actual cities), see under 'village' (19.16).

19.16 VILLAGE

Grk.	κώμη	Goth.	*haims, weihs*	Lith.	*kaimas, sodžius*
NG	χωριό	ON	*þorp, bȳr*	Lett.	*sādža, ciems*
Lat.	*vīcus*	Dan.	*landsby*	ChSl.	*vĭsĭ*
It.	*villaggio*	Sw.	*by*	SCr.	*selo*
Fr.	*village*	OE	*wīc, tūn, þorp*	Boh.	*ves*
Sp.	*pueblo, aldea*	ME	*village, toun, thorp, wike*	Pol.	*wieś*
Rum.	*sat*			Russ.	*selo, derevnja*
Ir.	*baile (fīch)*	NE	*village*	Skt.	*grāma-*
NIr.	*baile*	Du.	*dorp*	Av.	*vīs-*
W.	*pentref*	OHG	*dorf, wīch*		
Br.	*keriadenn*	MHG	*dorf*		
		NHG	*dorf*		

Words for 'village' are based on the notions of 'dwelling place' (whence the modest 'village', only rarely the 'town, city') or 'field, piece of land', 'settlement', etc. A few are connected with words for 'people' or 'multitude', that is, denoted first the group of inhabitants. Only rarely are they derivatives of words for 'city, town' (Fr. *village*, etc.).

1. Grk. κώμη, etym. dub. Walde-P. 1.360, 389. Boisacq 544.

Grk. χωρίον 'place', also 'landed property, estate', Byz. and NG (χωριό) 'village', dim. of χώρα 'place, country' (19.11).

2. Lat. *vīcus* (> Ir. *fīch*, OE *wīc*, OHG *wīch*), Goth. *weihs*, ChSl. *vĭsĭ*, Boh. *ves*, Pol. *wieś* : Grk. οἶκος (ϝοῖκος) 'house', Skt. *viç-* 'dwelling place, house', Av. *vīs-* 'dwelling place, house, family', also 'village' (Barth. 1456). Lat. *vīcus* is also in part 'quarter, street'. Walde-P. 1.213. Ernout-M. 1103.

Lat. *castellum* 'fortress' was often used in the Vulgate to render κώμη, hence OE *castel* in the Gospels and later. Cf. NED s.v. *castle*.

Fr. *village*, Prov. *villatge* (> It. *villaggio*, Sp. *villaje*), derivs. of Fr. *ville*, Prov. *villa* 'city' (19.15). REW 9330.

Sp. *pueblo* 'people' (19.21) and 'village'.

Sp. *aldea*, fr. Arab. *daiᶜa* 'piece of land'. REW 2460.

Rum. *sat*, fr. Alb. *fshat* id., fr. late Lat. *fossātum* 'place surrounded by a moat' (cf. Byz. φοσσᾶτον 'camp, army'), deriv. of *fossa* 'ditch'. REW 3461. Tiktin 1370. Densusianu 353, 355.

3. Ir. *fīch* (gl. *municipium*), fr. Lat. *vīcus* (above, 2).

Ir. *baile* 'place, town, village' (K. Meyer, Contrib. 166), NIr. 'town, village, home', and esp. *baile beag*, lit. 'little town', or *sraidbhaile*, lit. 'street-town' ('village of one street') vs. *baile mōr* 'large town', etym.? Walde-P. 2.141.

W. *tref* (also 'homestead'; in NT reg. for 'village' vs. *dinas* 'city'), now esp. *pentref* (cpd. with *pen* 'head'), fr. OW *treb* 'dwelling' : Ir. *atreba* 'habitat', Umbr. *trebeit* 'versatur', OE *þorp*, OHG *dorf* 'village', etc. Walde-P. 1.757.

Br. *keriadenn*, dim. of *ker* 'city, town' (19.15), prob. in imitation of Fr. *village* vs. *ville*.

4. Goth. *haims* = ON *heimr* 'home, world', OE *hām*, OHG *heim* 'home', etc. (7.122), orig. 'dwelling, resting place', fr. the root in Grk. κεῖμαι, Skt. *çī-* 'lie'. Walde-P. 1.259 f. Feist 233 f. Cf. OE *hamel, hamelet* (> NE *hamlet*), dim. of *ham*, fr. MLG *hamm* of this group.

Goth. *weihs*, OE *wīc*, ME *wike*, OHG *wich*, see Lat. *vīcus* (above, 2).

ON *þorp*, OE *þorp*, *þrop*, ME *thorp*, *throp*, Du. *dorp*, OHG-NHG *dorf* = Goth. *þaurp* 'cultivated land, field' : W. *tref*, etc. (above, 3). Falk-Torp 1274. Feist 492.

ON *bȳr* (*bœr*) 'town, village, farm' (> OE *by*, retained in place names *Derby*, *Whitby*, etc.; cf. NED s.v. *by* sb.), Sw. *by*, Dan. *landsby* (cpd. with *land* 'country'; Dan. *by* 'city'), orig. 'dwelling place' : Goth. *bauan*, ON *būa*, etc. 'dwell' (7.11). Falk-Torp 120. Hellquist 115.

OE *tūn* (often renders Lat. *vīcus*), ME *toun*, and NE *town* (still locally for what is no more than a village), see under 'city, town' (19.15).

ME, NE *village*, fr. OFr. *village, vilage* (above, 2).

5. Lith. *sodžius*, Lett. *sādža*, orig. 'settlement' : *sodinti* 'set, plant', ChSl. *saditi* 'plant', Goth. *satjan* 'set', etc. Mühl.-Endz. 3.801.

Lith. *kaimas* (beside *kiemas* 'court, farmyard'), OPruss. *caymis*, Lett. *ciems*, either cognate with (but with West IE guttural) or loanwords fr. the Gmc. group, Goth. *haims*, etc. (above, 4). Walde-P. 1.360. Mühl.-Endz. 1.394.

6. ChSl. *vĭsĭ*, Boh. *ves*, Pol. *wieś*, see Lat. *vīcus* (above, 2).

SCr., Russ. *selo* (Pol. *sioło* obs.) = ChSl. *selo* 'field' (8.12).

Russ. *derevnja* ('small village, hamlet', also 'landed property', dial. 'piece of cultivated land') : Lith. *dirva*, Lett. *druva* 'field' (8.12). Berneker 186.

7. Skt. *grāma-*, also 'community, multitude, troop' : Slavic *gramada* 'heap, mass, multitude', Lat. *gremium* 'lap, bosom', fr. the root in Grk. ἀγείρω 'collect, assemble'. Walde-P. 1.591. Uhlenbeck 83. Berneker 345.

Av. *vīs-*, see Lat. *vīcus* (above, 2).

19.17 BOUNDARY

Grk.	ὅρος, ὅριον	Goth.	*marka*	Lith.	*siena (rubežius, rība)*
NG	σύνορον, ὅριον	ON	*landamǣri*	Lett.	*ruobeža*
Lat.	*fīnis, līmes*	Dan.	*grænse*	ChSl.	*prĕdĕlŭ*
It.	*frontiera, confine*	Sw.	*gräns*	SCr.	*granica*
Fr.	*frontière, limite*	OE	*(ge)mǣre, mearc*	Boh.	*hranice*
Sp.	*frontera, límite, lindero*	ME	*mere, mark, bonde, frounter*	Pol.	*granica*
Rum.	*hotar, frontiera, margine*	NE	*boundary, frontier (border)*	Russ.	*granica (rubež)*
Ir.	*crīch*	Du.	*grens*	Skt.	*sīmā-, sīman-*
NIr.	*teora, crīch*	OHG	*marcha*	Av.	*karana-*
W.	*terfyn, ffin*	MHG	*marke, grenice*		
Br.	*harzou* (pl.)	NHG	*grenze*		

Most of the words listed are generic for 'boundary', covering that between countries and that between lands. But some are used only or mainly for the former, as Lat. *fīnis* (hence pl. *fīnēs* 'country') and the group represented by NE *frontier;* some for the latter, as Lat. *līmes*. There are connections with words for 'end, edge, front, wall'. Several denoted originally some particular physical form of boundary, such as a stake, a furrow, a blazed trail, etc. There are some loanwords, introduced through contact with adjacent countries.

1. Grk. ὅρος (Ion. οὖρος, Arg., Cret. ὦρος, Corcyr. ὅρϝος), ὅριον, perh. (Att.ᶜ not orig.) as orig. 'furrow' : Lat. *urvum* 'curved part of a plow', *urvāre* 'mark the boundary with a plow'. Walde-P. 2.352. Boisacq 716. Hence adj. σύνορος 'neighboring', NG sb. σύνορον 'boundary' (σύνορα usual word for the

'frontiers', ὅρια for boundaries between pieces of land).

2. Lat. *fīnis*, prob. as orig. 'fixed mark' : *fīgere* 'fix'. Walde-P. 1.832. Ernout-M. 363. Walde-H. 1.503. Hence adj. *confīnis* 'neighboring', sb. *confīne* (> It. *confine*, Sp. *confín*, etc.).

Lat. *līmes*, *-itis*, orig. a path between fields, hence 'boundary' (but still mostly between lands, not countries) : *līmen* 'threshold', *līmus* 'sidelong', etc. Walde-P. 1.158. Ernout-M. 551. Hence It., Fr., Sp. *limite* (Rum. *limită* neolog. fr. Fr.), mostly in secondary uses but also in pl. for 'boundaries' of countries; hence also the vb. *līmitāre* 'fix the boundaries' > Sp. *lindar* id. with sb. *lindero* 'boundary' (between lands).

It. *frontiera*, Fr. *frontière* (> ME *frounter*, NE *frontier*, now mostly of the border region; Rum. *frontiera*, neolog., Sp. *frontera*), all used only of the boundary or boundary region between countries (not between farms, etc.), deriv. of It. *fronte*, Fr. *front*, etc., orig. 'forehead' (4.205), but here through the secondary 'front'. REW 3533. NED s.v. *frontier*.

Rum. *hotar*, fr. Hung. *határ* id. Densusianu 1.374 f.

Rum. *margine* 'edge' (12.353), used also for 'boundary'. Tiktin 953.

Rum. *graniţă*, fr. Slavic, SCr. *granica*, etc. (below, 6).

3. Ir. *crīch* : Lat. *cernere* 'separate, distinguish', *crībrum* 'sieve', Grk. κρίνω 'separate, distinguish, decide', etc. Walde-P. 2.584. Pedersen 2.33.

NIr. *teora*, W. *terfyn*, fr. Lat. *terminus* 'bound, end'. Pedersen 1.241. Loth, Mots lat. 211.

W. *ffin*, fr. Lat. *fīnis*. Loth. Mots lat. 168.

Br. *harzou*, pl. of *harz* 'obstacle' and 'boundary stone' (cf. Ernault s.v.), etym.? Henry 158.

4. Goth. *marka*, OE *mearc*, ME *mark*, OHG *marcha*, MHG *marke* : Lat. *margō* 'edge', Ir. *mruig*, *bruig* 'cultivated land, district', Av. *marəza-* 'borderland' (Barth. 1153; NPers. *marz* 'borderland, district').

The sense of the Gmc. words passed into that of the 'borderland' (hence ON *mǫrk* 'forest'), as in the borrowed OFr. *marches* (> ME, NE *marches*), also 'district', etc. Walde-P. 2.283 f. Feist 347. NED s.v. *mark*, sb.[1].

ON *landa-mǣri*, OE (*ge*)*mǣre*, ME (and NE dial.) *mere*, MDu. *mēre*, orig. the (boundary) 'stake', fr. Gmc. **mairia-* : Lat. *mūrus*, old *moiros* 'wall', *moenia* 'walls', Skt. *mi-* 'fix, build', etc. Walde-P. 2.239 f. Franck, KZ 37.120 ff. NED s.v. *mere*, sb.[2].

ME *bordure*, NE *border*, fr. OFr. *bordure*, deriv., through vb., of *bord* 'edge' (12.353). NED s.v.

ME *bonde*, NE *bound*, whence *boundary* (now the most distinctive word), fr. OFr. *bodne*, *bonde*, etc. (source also of Fr. *borne* > NE *bourne*), MLat. *butina*, *bodina*, etc., orig. perh. Celtic(?). NED s.v. *bound*, sb.[1]. REW 1235. Wartburg 1.465 f.

MHG *grenice*, NHG *grenze* (> Du. *grens*, Dan. *grænse*, Sw. *gräns*), fr. Pol., Russ. *granica* (below, 6), and first appearing in the adjacent land of the German Order. Weigand-H. 1.765. Kluge-G. 216.

5. Lith. *siena* 'wall' (7.27) and 'boundary' (now the preferred word, Senn).

Lith. *rubežius* (the usual old word, NT, Kurschat, etc.), Lett. *ruobeža*, fr. Russ. *rubež* 'boundary' (below, 5). Mühl.-Endz. 3.575. Skardžius 192.

Lith. *riba*, prob. orig. a clearing or track in the woods where the light shines through : *ribėti* 'shine', *raibas* 'spotted'. Buga, Kalba ir Senovė 20 f.

6. ChSl. *prědělŭ* (reg. for ὅριον, in Gospels, Supr., etc.) cpd. of *dělŭ* 'part' with *prě-* 'through, out, over', hence lit. 'the outer parts'. Berneker 195.

SCr., Pol., Russ. *granica*, Boh. *hranica*, deriv. of word seen in ChSl. *granĭ* 'chapter', Russ. *gran'* 'facet, side', Boh. *hrana* 'edge' (12.353), etc. Berneker 346. Brückner 155.

Russ. *rubež* (still in use, but much less common than *granica*), orig. a blazed trail in the forest : *rubiti* 'cut, hew' (9.22). Dal' s.v.

7. Skt. *sīmā-*, *sīman-* (latter also 'parting of the hair'), fr. the root in Skt. *sā-*, *si-* 'bind', Lith. *sieti* 'bind' (9.16), Grk. ἱμάς, 'strap', Lith. *siena* (above, 5), etc. Walde-P. 2.463.

Av. *karana-* 'end' (12.35), also 'edge, shore, boundary'. Barth. 451.

19.21 PEOPLE (POPULACE)

Grk.	*λᾱός, δῆμος, πλῆθος*	Goth.	*managei*	Lith.	*žmonės, liaudis*
NG	*λαός, κόσμος*	ON	*folk, lȳðr*	Lett.	*l'audis*
Lat.	*populus, plēbs, vulgus*	Dan.	*folk*	ChSl.	*ljudĭje, narodŭ*
It.	*popolo*	Sw.	*folk*	SCr.	*narod*
Fr.	*peuple*	OE	*folc, lēode*	Boh.	*lid, narod*
Sp.	*pueblo*	ME	*folk, lede, poeple*	Pol.	*lud, naród*
Rum.	*popor, norod*	NE	*people*	Russ.	*narod*
Ir.	*tūath, lucht*	Du.	*volk, lieden*	Skt.	*jana-, prajā-, loka-*
NIr.	*daoine*	OHG	*folc, liuti*	OPers.	*kāra-*
W.	*pobl, gwerin*	MHG	*volc, liute*		
Br.	*pobl*	NHG	*volk*		

'People' is understood here as the populace of a country, region, town; in part the 'common people' in contrast to the ruling class, and some of the words, as Latin *plēbs*, *vulgus*, Lith. *liaudis*, definitely so. Many of the words are used likewise for 'a people' as a national group (19.22), but the two lists are not identical. Some are used also like NE colloq. *people* 'persons' (*people say*, *poor people*, etc.). But others that correspond to people only or mainly in this sense are not included (e.g. Fr. *gens* or *monde* with Romance cognates, NHG *leute*, Russ. *ljudi*).

Several of the words (some certainly, others probably) are derived from a root for 'fill' and must have meant originally 'multitude', and some of the others are connected with words for 'crowd, fullness, many', etc. Some belong with words for 'birth, race, growth' or 'world' or 'men'.

1. Derivs. of IE **pel*(*ə*)-, **plē-*, etc. 'fill'. Walde-P. 2.64 ff. Ernout-M. 777, 789 f. Falk-Torp 250.

Grk. πλῆθος 'multitude' and 'people, common people'; Lat. *populus* (prob., but disputed) and *plēbs* 'common people'; ON *folk*, OE, OHG *folc*, etc., general Gmc. except Goth.

2. Grk. λᾱός (dial. λᾱϝός, Ion. ληός, Att. λεώς, but λαός in the κοινή and so NG λαός), etym.? Boisacq 556.

Grk. δῆμος 'district, land' (Hom.), hence in Att. the local 'deme', but also 'people' (Hom.) : δαίομαι 'divide, share', Skt. *dāti*, *dyati* 'cuts off, divides', etc. Walde-P. 2.764. Boisacq 182.

NG κόσμος 'world' (1.11), also 'people' (more important in this use than Fr. *monde*, etc.).

3. Lat. *populus* (> Romance words, but Rom. *popor* in earliest use 'parish', now replacing *norod* as 'people'; Tiktin 1213) and *plēbs*, above, 1.

Lat. *vulgus* (*volgus*), esp. 'common people', perh. : Skt. *varga-* 'division,

group', W. *gwala* 'fullness, enough', ChSl. *velijĭ* 'large', Russ. *valom* 'in abundance', etc. Walde-P. 1.296. Ernout-M. 1128 (without etym.).

Rum. *norod* (formerly reg. word for 'people', esp. 'a people, nation', now chiefly 'common people, crowd'), fr. Slavic, cf. ChSl. *narodŭ*, etc. (below, 7).

4. Ir. *tūath*, esp. 'a people, nation' (19.22), but also 'people' vs. king or clergy (Laws, Gloss. s.v.).

Ir. *lucht* 'load, part, division' and 'group of persons, people' : W. *llwyth* 'load, burden, tribe', prob. Lith. *lužti*, Skt. *ruj-* 'break'. Walde-P. 2.412. Pedersen 1.123.

NIr. *daoine* ('people' = 'persons', but also 'the public, people'), pl. of *duine* 'man, person' (2.11).

W., Br. *pobl* (NIr. *pobal* mostly bibl. or 'parish'), fr. Lat. *populus* (above, 1). Loth, Mots lat. 196.

W. *gwerin* (esp. 'common people) in OW gl. *factio* : Ir. *foirenn* 'company, party', NIr. *foireann* 'crowd, body of troops', OE *wearn* 'great number, crowd', Skt. *vṛnda-* 'crowd, herd, swarm', etc. Walde-P. 1.265 f. Pedersen 1.375.

5. Goth. *managei* (the reg. rendering of λαός and πλῆθος, also of ὄχλος 'throng, crowd'), lit. 'multitude, crowd', fr. *managș* 'many' (13.15).

ON *folk*, OE *folc*, etc., above, 1.

ON *lȳðr*, and esp. pl. *lȳðir*, OE *lēode*, ME *lede*, Du. *lieden*, OHG *liuti*, MHG *liute*, NHG *leute*, all pl. of OE *lēod*, OHG *liut*, etc. (see list 19.22 'a people, nation'; OE, OHG also 'a man') : Lat. *līber*, Grk. ἐλεύθερος 'free', and all prob. fr. the root of Goth. *liudan*, OE *lēodan*, OHG *liotan* 'grow', Skt. *rudh-* 'grow', etc. Walde-P. 2.416. Weigand-H. 2.58. Kluge-G. 356. NED s.v. *lede*.

ME *poeple*, NE *people*, fr. Anglo-Fr. *poeple* = Fr. *peuple* (above, 3).

6. Lith. *liaudis* (esp. 'common people'), Lett. *l'audis*, see below, 7.

Lith. *žmonės*, pl. of *žmogus* 'man, person' (12.11), is used not only for 'people' = 'persons' but also in the sense intended here, and formerly (by Kurschat) even for 'a people, nation' (19.22).

7. ChSl. *ljudĭje* pl. (in Gospels reg. for λαός; SCr., Russ. *ljudi*, Boh. *lidé*, Pol. *ludzie* 'people' = 'persons'), sg. coll. ORuss. *ljud*, Boh. *lid*, Pol. *lud* 'people' and 'a people', all, with Lith. *liaudis*, Lett. *l'audis*, either cognate with or (more prob., on account of the close agreement in use) early loanwords fr. the Gmc. group OE *lēod*, pl. *lēode*, etc. (above, 5). Berneker 758. Stender-Petersen 190 ff.

ChSl. *narodŭ* (in Gospels reg. for ὄχλος 'multitude, throng, people'; in Supr. also for λαός, δῆμος, etc.), modern Slavic *narod* most widespread word for 'people' in both senses, cpd. of ChSl. *rodŭ*, etc. 'birth, generation, race, family' (19.23).

8. Skt. *jana-* 'person, family' and 'people', and *prajā-* 'offspring' and 'people' : *jan-* 'beget, bear', etc.

Skt. *loka-* 'world' (12.11), also 'people'.

OPers. *kāra-* 'army' and 'people' : Lith. *karias*, Goth. *harjis* 'army' (20.15).

19.22 A PEOPLE, NATION

Grk.	*ἔθνος, λᾱός*	Goth.	*þiuda*	Lith.	*tauta*
NG	*ἔθνος*	ON	*þjōð*	Lett.	*tauta*
Lat.	*gēns, nātiō, populus*	Dan.	*folk, nation*	ChSl.	*językŭ*
It.	*popolo, nazione, gente*	Sw.	*folk, nation*	SCr.	*narod*
Fr.	*peuple, nation*	OE	*þēod, lēod, folc*	Boh.	*národ*
Sp.	*pueblo, nación*	ME	*nacioun, poeple, folk, thede, lede*	Pol.	*naród*
Rum.	*popor, naţiune*			Russ.	*narod*
Ir.	*tūath*	NE	*nation, people*	Skt.	*janapada-*
NIr.	*nāisiūn, muinntir*	Du.	*volk, natie*	Av.	*daiŋhu-*
W.	*cenedl, pobl*	OHG	*diot, liut, folc*		
Br.	*pobl, broad*	MHG	*liut, diet, volc*		
		NHG	*volk, nation*		

'People' is understood here as 'a people' (*the English people*, *das deutsche volk*, etc.) = *nation* (but without necessary implication of political unity or independence) or *nationality* (sometimes used as distinguished from nation in political sense), or *race* (in its popular, not anthropological, use). This is most widely expressed by the same words (or sg. vs. pl. in OE *lēod*, etc.) as those for 'people' listed and discussed in 19.21. In some languages where other terms are usual, these may also be so used, e.g. Grk. (beside ἔθνος) λᾱός (Λυδῶν λαός Aesch., freq. in NT esp. λαός Ἰσραήλ vs. other ἔθνη), Lat. (beside *gēns*, *natiō*) *populus Rōmānus*, *Latīnus*, etc. Goth. (beside *þiuda* for ἔθνος) *managei* for λᾱός also in this sense, OE (beside *þēod*) *folc*, etc.

For all these, see 19.21. Only the other words are discussed here. They are based on such notions as 'strength, power'(?), common 'birth', 'customs', or 'language', or are words for 'country' used also for its 'people'.

1. IE **teutā-*, prob. fr. the root in Skt. *tu-* 'be strong' (3sg. pres. *tāuti*, *tavīti*), Lat. *tumēre* 'swell', *tōtus* 'whole', etc. Walde-P. 1.706 ff., 712. Feist 496. NED s.v. *thede*.

Osc. *touto* 'populus' (*Bansae touto*, τοϝτο Μαμερτινο; cf. *toutico* 'publica', etc.), Umbr. *tota-* 'people' (in this special sense) or 'state' or 'city' (cf. e.g. *seritu poplom totar Iiouinar* 'servato populum civitatis Iguvinae'); Ir. *tūath* (W. *tud* 'country', older 'people', Br. *tud* 'people' = 'persons'); Goth. *þiuda*, ON *þjōð*, OE *þēod*, ME *thede*, OHG *diot*, MHG *diet;* Lith., Lett. *tauta*.

2. Grk. ἔθνος (ϝέθνος attested by Hom. prosody), prob. : ἔθος 'custom, usage', Skt. *svadhā-* 'one's own nature, custom, home', derivs. of refl. stem **swo-*. Cf. also Goth. *sibja*, OE *sib*(*b*), OHG *sippa*, etc. 'relationship'. Walde-P. 2.456. Boisacq 218.

3. Lat. *gēns* (in narrow sense 'clan, family', but freq. for 'people, nation'; so also It. *gente*, but mostly as Fr. *gens*, etc. 'people, persons'), fr. the root of *gignere* 'beget, bear', etc. (cf. Grk. γένος 'race, kin, clan', etc.). Walde-P. 1.576 ff. Ernout-M. 416.

Lat. *nātiō*, orig. 'birth' : *nāscī* 'be born', *nātus* 'born', fr. the same root as *gēns*. Hence It. *nazione*, Fr. *nation* (> ME *nacioun*, NE *nation* > NIr. *nāisiūn*), Sp. *nación*, Rum. *naţiune*, Dan., Sw., NHG *nation*, Du. *natie*, all with tendency to be used esp. as 'nation' in political sense.

4. Ir. *tūath*, above, 1.

NIr. *muinntir*, mostly 'household, family, clan' (19.23), now used also for a national group.

W. *cenedl* (reg. word for a 'people, nation') : Ir. *cenēl* 'race, family' : Ir. *cinim* 'spring from', ChSl. *-čīnq*, *-čęti* 'begin', etc. Walde-P. 1.398.

Br. *broad* (now reg. = Fr. *nation*, for which *pobl* in NT), deriv. of *bro* 'country' (19.11).

5. Goth. *þiuda*, OE *þēod*, etc., above, 1. For other Gmc. words see 19.21.

6. Lith., Lett. *tauta*, above, 1. Lith *tauta*, now the accepted word, was known to Kurschat only as *Tauta* 'Oberland'; in his NT he used *žmonės* (cf. 19.21), as also Deutsch.-lit. Wtb. s.v. *Volk;* the Trowitz NT had *giminė* 'family, race'.

7. ChSl. *językŭ* 'tongue, language' (18.24), reg. in Gospels for ἔθνος.

8. Skt. *janapada-* 'country' (19.11) and its 'people'.

Av. *daiŋhu-* 'country' (19.11) and its 'people'. Barth. 706 ff.

19.23 TRIBE, CLAN, FAMILY (in Wide Sense)

Grk.	φῦλή, γένος	Goth.	*kuni*	Lith.	*gentis, kiltis, giminė*
NG	φυλή	ON	*kind, kyn, ætt*	Lett.	*cilts, dzimta*
Lat.	*tribus, gēns*	Dan.	*stamme, slægt, æt*	ChSl.	*kolěno, rodŭ, plemę*
It.	*tribù*	Sw.	*stam, slägt, ätt*	SCr.	*pleme, rod, zadruga*
Fr.	*tribu*	OE	*cyn(n), mǣgþ, strȳnd*	Boh.	*kmen, rod*
Sp.	*tribu*	ME	*kin, kinrede, tribu*	Pol.	*plemię, ród*
Rum.	*trib, seminţie*	NE	*tribe, clan, sept*	Russ.	*plemja, rod*
Ir.	*tūath, fine, muinter*	Du.	*stam, geslacht*	Skt.	*jana-, jāti-, kula-, vaṅça-*
NIr.	*treabh, fine, muinntir*	OHG	*cunni, gislahti*		
W.	*cenedl, llwyth, gwely*	MHG	*künne, geslehte, stam*	OPers.	*taumā-*
Br.	*meuriad*	NHG	*stamm, geschlecht. sippe*		

The 'tribe' and the 'clan' or 'family' in a wide sense, based on varying degrees of kinship, real or fictitious, have their chief importance in primitive society, though in some cases they continued to play a role in a more advanced organization. Thus the Grk. φῦλή, applied for example to the old Doric and the old Ionic tribes, became in the Athenian state a highly important, but artificially constructed, political organization. Lat. *tribus*, besides rendering Grk. φῦλή, in native use denoted in the historical period a local district. The Grk. γένος and Lat. *gēns* 'clan' continued important because of the noble families rather than as definite social and political organizations. Midway between the φῦλή and the γένος was the φρᾱτρία 'brotherhood' (fr. φράτηρ, orig. 'brother' = Lat. *frāter*, etc.), which in the developed Athenian state survived as a large family organization for cult purposes, without political significance. But in Homer φρήτρη, not γένος, is the technical term best rendered 'clan', as in κατὰ φῦλα, κατὰ φρήτρας 'by tribes, by clans', Il. 2.362. Likewise the Roman *cūria* (perh. fr. **co-uiriā* : *vir* 'man') was originally a division of the people more comprehensive than the *gēns*.

Classifications of this kind, so far as they are found among other IE-speaking peoples (as the early Irish), correspond only approximately, and for modern society are without significance. Several of the words listed denote 'kin' without distinction of degree. The modern words are merely those commonly used to render terms applicable to other times or places (e.g. the Hebrew *tribes* of the Bible, *savage tribes*, etc.). For these reasons it is impossible to carry through a separation of 'tribe' and 'clan', though the words are entered in this order where such a gradation is observed (e.g. NHG *stamm*, reg. used for 'tribe' vs. *geschlecht* for 'clan, family'). In many of the modern languages there is no special term for 'clan' (apart from the widely borrowed *clan*), but only words for 'family' (2.82) used also for 'family' in a wide sense.

1. Derivs. of IE **ĝen-* in Grk. γίγνομαι 'be born', Lat. *gignere*, Skt. *jan-* 'beget, bear', etc. Walde-P. 1.576 ff. Ernout-M. 415 ff. All orig. 'kin, race' in wide sense, but also used in narrower sense.

Grk. γένος; Lat. *gēns;* Goth. *kuni*, ON *kyn*, *kind*, OE *cyn(n)*, ME *kin*, also deriv. *kinrede* (Wyclif for φῦλή Mt. 21.30; NE *kindred*), OHG *cunni*, MHG *künne;* Skt. *jāti-*, *jana-*.

2. Grk. φῦλή (Hom. φῦλον) : φύω 'bring forth, produce, grow, be born', etc. (IE **bheu-* 'become, be'). Walde-P. 2.141.

3. Lat. *tribus* (here in its use = Grk. φῦλή, not in its technical Roman sense, which was more local), Umbr. *trifu*, fr. **tribhu-*, prob. deriv. of *tri-* 'three' and denoting orig. a tri-partite division. But substantial historical evidence of this is lacking, and the precise history of the Roman *tribus* is difficult. Ernout-M. 1056 f. Pauly-Wissowa s.v. Hence (but in its biblical use as 'tribe') the Romance words (all lit.), etc.

Rum. *seminţie*, deriv. of *sămînţă* 'seed' (VLat. **sēmentia* = *sēmentis*). Puşcariu 1508.

4. Ir. *tūath* 'a people' (19.22), also applied to a large division, a 'tribe'. Thurneysen, Heldensage 76.

Ir. *fine* (group of kin within the tribe, cf. Thurneysen l.c. and RC 25.1 ff.) : OBr. *co-guenou* 'indigena', ON *vinr*, OE *wine* 'friend', etc. Walde-P. 1.259. Pedersen 1.156.

Ir. *treb*, NIr. *treab*, orig. 'dwelling place' (: Ir. *atreba* 'habitat', OE *þorp* 'village', etc.; Pedersen 1.132), but as 'tribe' (esp. in translations) fr. (or influenced by) Lat. *tribus*.

Ir. *muinter*, NIr. *muinntir* 'people, household', also 'family' in wide sense, disputed whether fr. Lat. *monastērium* (cf. esp. Pokorny, Z. celt. Ph. 10.202 f.), or : Lat. *manus* 'hand', OE *mund*, OHG *munt* 'hand, protection, guardianship'. Vendryes, De hib. voc. 157. D'Arbois de Jubainville, RC 25.2 ff. Vendryes, RC 43.210.

NIr. *clann* 'offspring, children' and 'clan, party, sect', etc. (Gael. *clann* > NE *clan*) = Ir. *cland*, *clann* 'plant' and 'offspring, children' = W. *plant* 'offspring, children', fr. Lat. *planta* 'shoot, sprout'. Pedersen 1.234, 235.

W. *cenedl*, listed under 'people, nation' (19.22) but in early Welsh history more properly 'tribe' or 'clan'. Cf. Ellis, Welsh Tribal Law and Customs in the Middle Ages 1.46 ff.

W. *gwely* 'bed, couch' (7.42) was in early times the technical term (now obs. in this sense) for a subdivision of the *cenedl*. Cf. Ellis l.c.

W. *llwyth* : Ir. *lucht* 'load, part, division, people', etc. (19.21).

Br. *meuriad* ('tribe, clan' Ernault; Vallée s.v. *tribu*), deriv. of *meur* 'great'.

5. Goth. *kuni* (used for φυλή), ON *kyn*, *kind*, OE *cyn*, etc., above, 1.

ON *ætt*, Dan. *æt*, Sw. *ätt* ('family' in wide sense), orig. 'what is one's own' : Goth. *aihts*, OE *ǣht* 'property', Goth. *aigan*, OE *āgan* 'own', etc. Walde-P. 1.105. Falk-Torp 1415. Hellquist 1449 f.

OE *mǣgþ* ('kin, family'; for *tribus* in Gospels, Aelfric, etc.), fr. *mǣg* 'relative, kinsman', pl. *māgas* (2.81).

OE *strȳnd* (in Lindisf. Gospels for *tribus*), fr. *gestrȳnan* 'beget' (4.71).

ME *tribu*, NE *tribe*, fr. OFr. *tribu*, or in part later directly fr. Lat. *tribus*. NED s.v.

NE *clan*, fr. Gael. *clann* = Ir. *clann* (above, 4). First used only of the Scottish clans, later as convenient rendering of Lat. *gēns*, etc. NED s.v. Hence (esp. through W. Scott's novels) widely borrowed in the modern Eur. languages, mostly for the Scottish clans, but also (at least by French writers) used to render Lat. *gēns*, etc.

NE *sept*, prob. variant of *sect* influenced by *sept* 'inclosure'. NED s.v.

MHG *stam*, NHG *stamm*, Du. *stam* (MLG *stam*, *stamme* > Dan. *stamme*, Sw. *stam*), orig. 'stem, stalk, trunk', OHG *stam* only in the lit. sense (but 'tribe, race' in cpd. *liut-stam*) : OS *stamn* 'stem, race', OE *stefn*, *stemn* 'trunk, prow' (in cpds. *lēodstefn*, etc. 'race'), all fr. IE **stā-* 'stand'. Falk-Torp 1148. Weigand-H. 2.945 f.

OHG *gislahti*, MHG *geslehte*, NHG *geschlecht*, Du. *geslacht*, MLG *geslecht*, orig. coll. forms to MLG *slechte* (> Dan. *slægt*, Sw. *slägt*), OHG *slahta* 'species, sort, kind', fr. OHG *slahan* 'strike' in a specialized sense of 'take a certain direction' (cf. NHG *nach diesem schlag* 'after this manner'). Walde-P. 2.706. Falk-Torp 1059. Weigand-H. 2.698.

NHG *sippe* (revived and now a favorite term in anthropology), fr. MHG *sippe*, OHG *sibba* 'kinship' = Goth. *sibja*, OE *sib(b)* id. (cf. 2.81).

6. Lith. *gentis* 'relative by marriage', now also, influenced by Lat. *gēns*, *gentis*, 'tribe' (cf. NSB s.v.) : *žentas* 'son-in-law', etc., but with *g-* fr. *gimti* 'be born'. Walde-P. 1.578.

Lith. *kiltis* (cf. NSB s.v.), Lett. *cilts*, orig. 'origin', fr. Lith. *kelti*, Lett. *celt* 'raise, lift' and intr. 'arise' : Lat. *excellere* 'raise up', *collis* 'hill', etc. Walde-P. 1.434. Mühl.-Endz. 1.382.

Lith. *giminė* (in NT 'tribe', but mostly 'family' in wide sense; hence Lett. *g'imene*), Lett. *dzimta*, fr. Lith. *gimti*, Lett. *dzimt* 'be born'. Walde-P. 1.676.

7. ChSl. *kolěno* (reg. for φυλή in the Gospels; SCr. *koljeno*, Russ. *koleno*, Boh. *pokolení*, Pol. *pokolenie* in this sense mostly biblical or archaic) = *kolěno* 'knee' (4.36), with semantic development through 'joint' or 'limb'. Berneker 545 f. Walde-P. 2.599.

ChSl. *plemę* (for φυλή in Supr.), SCr. *pleme*, Pol. *plemię*, Russ. *plemja*, fr. **pled-men-* : *plodŭ* 'harvest, fruit' (8.41). Walde-P. 2.103. Brückner 421.

SCr. *zadruga* (the much studied patriarchal family composing a single household) : ChSl. *drugŭ*, etc. 'companion' (19.53).

Boh. *kmen*, lit. 'stem, stock' (cf. NHG *stamm*) : LSorb. *kmjeń* 'bud, stem', Pol. *kien*, *kień* 'block, stump, stem', etc. Berneker 663.

ChSl. *rodŭ*, modern Slavic *rod* 'birth, generation, race' and 'family' in wide sense, prob. : Skt. *vṛdh-* 'grow', etc. Walde-P. 1.289 f. Vondrák 1.375.

8. Skt. *jana-*, *jāti-*, above, 1.

Skt. *vaṅça-* 'bamboo cane', hence also, on the analogy of the series of joints, 'lineage, race, family'.

Skt. *kula-* 'family' in wide and narrow sense (also 'herd, crowd'), see 2.82.

OPers. *taumā-* ('family' in wide sense) : Av. *taoxman-* 'seed', Skt. *tokman-* 'young blade of grain', *toka-* 'offspring', etc. Walde-P. 1.713. Barth. 624. Meillet-Benveniste, Grammaire du vieux-perse 81.

19.31 RULE (vb.), GOVERN

Grk.	ἄρχω, κρατέω, ἡγέομαι	Goth.	*reikinōn*	Lith.	*valdyti, viešpatauti*
NG	κυβερνῶ	ON	*stȳra*	Lett.	*valdit*
Lat.	*regere, imperāre, gubernāre*	Dan.	*styre, herske*	ChSl.	*vlasti*
		Sw.	*styra, herska*	SCr.	*vladati*
It.	*gobernare, reggere*	OE	*wealdan, rīcsian, reccan*	Boh.	*vládnouti*
Fr.	*gouverner*			Pol.	*rządzić, wladać*
Sp.	*gobernar*	ME	*welde, reule, gouern(e)*	Russ.	*pravit'*
Rum.	*guberna, cîrmui*	NE	*rule, govern*	Skt.	*çās-, kṣi-, īç-*
Ir.	*foln-*	Du.	*regeeren, besturen*	Av.	*xši-*
NIr.	*riaghluighim*	OHG	*waltan, rīhhisōn, hērisōn*		
W.	*rheoli, llywio, llywodraethu*				
		MHG	*walten, hersen, regieren*		
Br.	*sturia, gouarn*				
		NHG	*herrschen, regieren*		

Verbs for 'rule, govern' in the political sense are based upon such notions as 'be first, have power, be master of, command, put in order, direct, guide, steer'. The development from 'steer' (a ship) is common to Grk. κυβερνάω with its numerous offspring (the group to which NE *govern* belongs) and also (semantic borrowing?) the usual Scandinavian words and some others.

Many derivs. of words for 'master' (19.41), besides those included in the list, are used mostly like NE *dominate* and not commonly for 'rule' in the political sense. So, for example, Grk. κυριεύω, Lat. *dominārī* (VLat. *-āre* > Fr. *dominer*, etc.), Goth. *fraujinōn*, Lith. *ponavoti*, Boh. *panovati*, Pol. *panować*, Russ. *gospodstvovat'*.

Most of the usual words for 'ruler', as a generic term covering more special titles like 'king', etc., are derived from some of the verbs listed here. Otherwise It. *sovrano*, Sp. *soberano*, Fr. *souverain* (OFr. *soverain* > ME *soverain*, NE *sovereign* with spelling influenced by popular association with *reign*), fr. VLat. **superānus*, fr. *super* 'above' (REW 8457, NED s.v. *sovereign*).

Likewise most of the usual words for 'government' are derived from some of the verbs listed here. Otherwise Grk. πολῑτεία, orig. 'citizenship', fr. πολίτης 'citizen', or Fr. *état*, NE *state*, NHG *staat*, etc. 'state' in political sense, fr. Lat. *status* 'situation, condition, state'.

1. Grk. ἄρχω, also 'begin' (14.25), with ἄρχων 'ruler', ἀρχή 'beginning' and 'rule, office', primary sense prob. 'be first', but etym. dub. Walde-P. 2.367. Boisacq 85 f. R. McKenzie, Cl. Q. 15.44 f.

Grk. κρατέω, deriv. of κράτος 'strength, might, power' (4.81).

Grk. ἡγέομαι 'lead' (10.64), also 'rule', with ἡγεμών 'leader, chief, ruler'.

Grk. κυβερνάω, orig. 'steer' (a ship), hence also 'guide, govern', with κυβέρνησις 'steering' and 'government', eventually the usual words as in NG. Possibly deriv. of a word for 'rudder', and : Lith. *kumbras* 'curved handle of the rudder', etc. Walde-P. 1.467. Osthoff, IF 6.14. But more prob. fr. a pre-Greek source. Cuny, Rev. ét. anc. 12.156. Fohalle, Mélanges Vendryes 164 f. Walde-H. 1.625.

2. Lat. *regere* 'direct, guide' and 'rule' (> It. *reggere* with many uses, but partly 'rule' in political sense; Fr. *régir* 'administer, manage') : Grk. ὀρέγω, Ir. *rigim* 'stretch out', Skt. *ṛj-* 'direct, attain', etc., IE **reĝ-*, whence also the

widespread group for 'straight' (12.73). Walde-P. 2.362 ff. Ernout-M. 858.

Lat. *imperāre* 'command' (19.45), also 'rule'.

Lat. *gubernāre* 'steer' and (freq. in Cic.) 'govern' (> It. *gobernare*, Fr. *gouverner*, Sp. *gobernar*; Rum. *guberna* neolog. fr. Fr.), fr. Grk. κυβερνάω (above, 1). Ernout-M. 437. Walde-H. 1.625. REW 3903.

Rum. *cîrmui* 'steer' and 'rule' (the old word), deriv. of *cîrma* 'rudder', fr. Slavic, ChSl. *krŭma*, etc. 'rudder' (10.86). Tiktin 297.

3. Ir. *foln-* in deponent forms, beside sb. *flaith* 'rule' and 'ruler' : Lat. *valēre* 'be strong', Toch. A. nom. *wäl*, obl. *lānt* 'king' (SSS 44), OE *wealdan* 'rule', etc. (below, 4). Walde-P. 1.219. Pedersen 1.157, 2.525.

NIr. *riaghluighim*, W. *rheoli*, fr. sbs. NIr. *riaghail*, Ir. *riagol*, W. *rheol* 'rule', fr. Lat. *rēgula* 'rule'. Pedersen 1.210. Vendryes, De hib. voc. 171. Loth, Mots lat. 202.

W. *llywio*, also and orig. 'steer', fr. *llyw* 'rudder' (10.86) and 'ruler'. Hence also *llywodraeth* 'government', with vb. *llywodraethu* 'govern'.

Br. *sturia*, also 'steer', fr. *stur* 'rudder' (10.86).

Br. *gouarn*, fr. Fr. *gouverner*.

4. Goth. *reikinōn*, fr. sb. *reiki* 'rule', fr. *reiks* 'ruler', early loanword fr. Celtic, cf. Gall. *-rīx* in *Dumno-rīx*, etc., Ir. *rī*, gen. *rīg* 'king'. Similarly OE *rīcsian*, OHG *rīhhisōn*. Walde-P. 2.365. Feist 396.

Goth. *waldan* (but not quotable for 'rule' in political sense), ON *valda* (but mostly in other senses), OE *wealdan*, ME *welde* (NE *wield* in specialized sense), OHG *waltan*, MHG, NHG *walten* (NHG poet. or rhet.) : Lith. *valdyti*, ChSl. *vlasti*, *vladą*, etc. (below, 5), both groups fr. a dental extension of **wel-* in Lat. *valēre* 'be strong', Ir. *foln-* 'rule', etc. (above, 2). Walde-P. 1.219. Falk-Torp 1391. Feist 548.

ON *stȳra*, Dan. *styre*, Sw. *styra*, Du. *besturen*, all also and orig. 'steer' = OE *stīeran* 'steer' (OE, ME also sometimes 'rule', cf. NED s.v. *steer*, 7), etc., fr. ON *stȳri*, OE *stēor*, etc. 'rudder' (10.86). Falk-Torp 1194.

OE *reccan* mostly 'tell, narrate', but also 'rule' (Bosworth-Toller s.v. vii) : Lat. *regere* 'direct, rule', etc. (above, 2).

ME *reule*, NE *rule*, fr. OFr. *reuler*, fr. Lat. *rēgulāre* 'regulate', fr. *rēgula* 'rule' : *regere* (above, 2).

ME, NE *govern*, fr. Fr. *gouverner* (above, 2).

OHG *hērisōn*, *hērresōn*, MHG *hersen*, *herschen*, NHG *herrschen* (MLG *herschen* > Dan. *herske*, Sw. *herska*), fr. OHG *hēro*, *hērro*, NHG *herr* 'master' (19.41). Falk-Torp 401. Weigand-H. 1.855. Kluge-G. 247.

MHG, NHG *regieren*, Du. *regeeren*, fr. Fr. *régir*, Lat. *regere* (above, 2).

5. Lith. *valdyti*, Lett. *valdīt*, ChSl. *vlasti*, *vladą*, SCr. *vladati*, Boh. *vládnouti*, Pol. *władać* (Russ. *vladet'* mostly 'possess, own') : Goth. *waldan*, etc. (above, 4). As loanwords fr. Gmc. Stender-Petersen 213 ff.

Lith. *viešpatauti*, fr. *viešpatis* 'ruler, Lord' (19.41). For current use, cf. Fraenkel, Z. sl. Ph. 6.90.

Pol. *rządzić*, fr. sb. *rząd* 'order, row' and 'rule' = ChSl. *rędŭ*, Boh. *řad* 'order, arrangement, regulation' : Lith. *rinda* 'row, rank', prob. Lat. *ordō* 'row, order', etc. Brückner 474. Walde-P. 1.75, 2.368.

Russ. *pravit'* = ChSl. *praviti* 'guide', fr. *pravŭ* 'straight' (12.73).

6. Skt. *çās-* 'command' (18.45) and 'rule'.

Skt. *kṣi-* 'possess, rule', Av. *xšī-* 'have power, rule' (with sbs. Skt. *kṣatra-*, Av. *xšaθra-*, OPers. *xšaθ*[r]*a-* 'rule, realm', Av. *xšaya-* 'ruler, king', OPers. *xšāyaθiya-* 'king') : Grk. κτάομαι 'possess'. Walde-P. 1.405. Barth. 550, 551, 553.

Skt. *īç-* 'own' (11.12), also 'rule'.

19.32 KING

Grk.	βασιλεύς (ἄναξ poet.), Byz. ῥήξ	Goth.	*þiudans*	Lith.	*karalius*
NG	βασιλεύς, pop. βασιλιάς	ON	*konungr*, *þjōðann*	Lett.	*karalis*, *k'ēnin'š*
Lat.	*rēx*	Dan.	*konge*	ChSl.	*cěsar'ĭ*, *kral'ĭ*
It.	*re*	Sw.	*konung*	SCr.	*kralj*
Fr.	*roi*	OE	*cyning*, *þēoden*	Boh.	*král*
Sp.	*rey*	ME	*kyng*	Pol.	*król*
Rum.	*rege*	NE	*king*	Russ.	*korol'*
Ir.	*rī*	Du.	*koning*	Skt.	*rājan-*, *rāj-*
NIr.	*rī*	OHG	*kuni(n)g*	Av.	*xšaya-*, OPers. *xšāyaθiya-*
W.	*brenin*, *teyrn*	MHG	*kunec*		
Br.	*roue*	NHG	*könig*		

The title of 'king' has been, in the course of history, applied not only to the rulers of independent states, even great empires (before the rise of a superior title 'emperor', 19.34), but also to the petty chiefs of tribes or clans. Cf. NED s.v. *king*.

1. IE **rēĝ-*, fr. the root **reĝ-* in Lat. *regere* 'direct, guide, rule', etc. (19.31) Walde-P. 2.362 ff. Ernout-M. 864.

Lat. *rēx*, gen. *rēgis* (> the Romance words; but Rum. *rege* modern; older *craĭŭ*, fr. Slavic *kral'ĭ*); Gall. *-rīx* in *Dumno-rīx*, etc., Ir. *rī*, gen. *rīg* (W. *rhi* arch. 'lord, nobleman'), OCorn. *ruy*, Br. *roue*, MBr. *roe* (Pedersen 1.51; or Br. forms fr. Fr. *roi* ?); Skt. (Vedic) *rāj-*, but commonly *n*-stem *rājan-*; cf. Goth. *reiks* 'ruler', loanword fr. Celtic.

2. Grk. βασιλεύς, NG pop. βασιλιάς, without etym. (connection with λᾱός 'people' impossible) and prob. of pre-Greek origin. Boisacq 115 f. Wackernagel, Sprachl. Untersuch. zu Homer 212. Kretschmer, Glotta 10.222. Wienewiez, Eos 31.526 ff.

Grk. ἄναξ, dial. ϝάναξ, poet. word often applied to kings but also to gods and heroes, 'lord, master' (for Hom. use of ἄναξ vs. βασιλεύς, cf. Wackernagel, op. cit. 209 ff.), possibly : Skt. *van-* 'win, gain', etc. (Schwyzer, Glotta 6.86), but more prob. of pre-Greek origin. Cuny, Rev. ét. anc. 16.297. Debrunner in Ebert, Reallex. 4.2.527. Śmieszek, Eos 31.547 ff.

In Byzantine times βασιλεύς was 'emperor', the regular title of the Roman emperor and the Persian 'king of kings' (19.34). For 'king' Lat. *rēx* was adopted, e.g. ῥὴξ Γότθων, ῥὴξ φράγκων, etc. Theophanes (1.472 f. De Boor) notes the crowning of Charlemagne, ῥὴξ τῶν φράγκων, as βασιλεὺς Ῥωμαίων. But generally the German emperors were not according the emperor title by the Byzantine court. NG ῥῆγας 'king' in cards.

3. W. *brenin* : W. *bry* 'high', Ir. *bri*, W. *bre* 'hill', Skt. *bṛhant-* 'great, high' (cf. fem. *bṛhatī-*, Ir. *Brigit* 'the exalted one'), Av. *bərəzant-* 'high', etc. Walde-P. 2.173. Pedersen 1.100.

W. *teyrn* 'ruler, king. : Ir. *tigerne* 'master, lord' (19.41). Here also W. *mechdeyrn*, OBr. *machtiern* ('tributary prince'), OCorn. *mychtern* (reg. word for 'king', Williams Lex. 260), cpd. with word seen in Ir. *mac*, W. *mach* 'bond, surety'. Loth, L'Émigration bretonne en Armorique 218 ff., Voc. vieux-bret. 182. Thurneysen Z. celt Ph. 19.130. Otherwise (but to be rejected) Pedersen 1.137 and Ifor Williams, BBCS 10.39 ff.

4. Goth. *þiudans*, ON *þjōðann*, OE *þēoden*, derivs. of Goth. *þiuda*, ON *þjōð*, OE *þēod* 'people, nation' (19.22).

ON *konungr*, OE *cyning*, etc. (with short forms OE *cyng*, etc.), general Gmc. except Goth. : Goth. *kuni*, OE *cyn*, etc. 'family, race' (NE *kin*), but prob. more directly as patronymic of ON *konr* 'man of noble birth', OE *cyne-*, OHG *kuni-* in cpds., hence orig. 'descendant of one of noble birth'. Falk-Torp 563. Weigand-H. 1.1108. NED s.v. *king*.

5. Lith. *karalius* (> Lett. *karalis*), fr. the Slavic (below, 6). Brückner, Sl. Fremdwörter 90. Mühl.-Endz. 2.160.

Lett. (pop.) *k'ēnin'š*, fr. MLG *konink* (Du. *koning*, etc., above). Mühl.-Endz. 2.374.

6. ChSl. *cěsar'ĭ* (reg. for βασιλεύς, whether 'king' as in the Gospels or the Roman 'emperor'), see under 'emperor' (19.34).

Late ChSl. *kral'ĭ*, etc., general modern Slavic, fr. OHG *Karl*, the name of Charlemagne, who came into conflict with various Slavic peoples and was known to them all as the great 'king' of the time. An adverse, but improbable, view is that the source is not the personal name but the antecedent appellative seen in OHG *karl* 'man, freeman'. Berneker 572 f. (with lit., to which add, for the adverse view, Stender-Petersen 206 ff.)

7. Skt. *rāj-*, *rājan-*, above, 1.

Av. *xšaya-*, OPers. *xšāyaθiya-* : Av. *xšī-* 'have power, rule', Skt. *kṣi-* 'possess, rule' (19.31).

19.33 QUEEN

Grk.	βασίλεια, βασίλισσα	Goth.	. . . .	Lith.	*karalienė*
NG	βασίλισσα	ON	*drōttning*	Lett.	*karaliene*, *k'eniniene*
Lat.	*rēgīna*	Dan.	*dronning*	ChSl.	*cěsarica*
It.	*regina*	Sw.	*drottning*	SCr.	*kraljica*
Fr.	*reine*	OE	*cwēn*	Boh.	*kralovna*
Sp.	*reina*	ME	*quene*	Pol.	*królowa*
Rum.	*regina*	NE	*queen*	Russ.	*koroleva*
Ir.	*rīgan*	Du.	*koningin*	Skt.	*rājñī-*
NIr.	*bainrīoghan*	OHG	*kunninginna*, *kunningīn*		
W.	*brenhines*	MHG	*küninginne*, *künigin*		
Br.	*rouanez*	NHG	*königin*		

Nearly all the words for 'queen' are obvious fem. derivs. of those for 'king' (NIr. *bainrīoghan*, with common prefix *ban-*, *bain-* : *bean* 'woman'). Exceptions are the following:

OE *cwēn*, ME *quene*, NE *queen* : Goth. *qēns* 'wife', *qinō* 'woman', Grk. γυνή 'woman, wife', etc. (2.22, 2.32). In OE sometimes simply 'wife', but mostly specialized to 'king's wife'. NED s.v. *queen*.

ON *drōttning*, Dan. *dronning*, Sw. *drottning*, in ON also 'mistress', fem. of ON *drōttinn* 'master' (19.41).

19.34 EMPEROR

Grk.	(Byz.) βασιλεύς, αὐτοκράτωρ	Goth.	*kaisar*	Lith.	*ciesorius*, *imperatorius*
NG	αὐτοκράτορας	ON	*keisari*	Lett.	*k'eizars*
Lat.	*Caesar*, *imperātor*	Dan.	*kejser*	ChSl.	*cěsarĭ* (*kesarĭ*)
It.	*imperatore*	Sw.	*kejsare*	SCr.	*car*
Fr.	*empereur*	OE	*cāsere*	Boh.	*císař*
Sp.	*emperador*	ME	*emperere*	Pol.	*cesarz*
Rum.	*împărat*	NE	*emperor*	Russ.	*imperator*, *car'*
Ir.	*imper*	Du.	*keizer*	OPers.	*xsāyaθiya xsāyaθiyānām*
NIr.	*impire*	OHG	*keisar*		
W.	*ymerawdwr*	MHG	*keiser*		
Br.	*impalaer*	NHG	*kaiser*		

The ancient oriental 'empires' (of Egypt, Assyria, Persia, etc.), as we now rightly call them, were expanded 'kingdoms', and their rulers retained the old title of 'king', in part amplified to 'great king', 'mighty king', or especially 'king of kings', the last adopted in the OPers. *xšāyaθiya xšāyaθiyānām*. In India, Açoka was still a *rājā*, and the Mogul rulers used the Persian title *šāh*. Skt. *samrāj-* 'supreme ruler' (freq. epithet of Indra) was not a political title.

The European notion of an 'empire' and a superior title 'emperor' is based on the Roman Empire and all the Eur. words, except the Greek, are derived from Latin, *imperātor* prevailing in the Romance and Celtic languages, *Caesar* in the Germanic and Balto-Slavic.

1. Lat. *imperātor*, fr. *imperāre* 'command' (18.36), hence lit. 'commander', in early use mostly a military term 'commander-in-chief, general', used by Augustus as part of his title (*imp. Caesar*), and eventually superseding *Caesar* as the main title. Cf. Pauly-Wissowa s.v. *imperator*. Hence the Romance words (OFr. *emperere* > ME *emperere*, NE *emperor;* Rum. *împărat*, pop. also 'king' and so Alb. *mbret*), W. *ymerawdwr*, Br. (with dissim.) *impalaer*, Lith. *imperatorius*, Russ. *imperator;* but MIr. *imper*, NIr. *impir(e)*, fr. Lat. *imperium* 'empire' (Pedersen 1.237. Vendryes, De. hib. voc. 147).

2. Lat. *Caesar*, cognomen and, from Augustus on, the imperial title. Hence (besides Grk. καῖσαρ) the Gmc. words, Goth. *kaisar*, OE *cāsere*, Du. *keizer* (MLG *keiser* > ON *keisari*, Dan. *kejser*, Sw. *kejsare*, Lett. *k'eizars*), OHG *keisar*, MHG *keiser*, NHG *kaiser*. Hence again, prob. through Goth. *kaisar*, the Slavic words, ChSl. *cěsarĭ* (but 'king' in the Gospels, where for the Roman emperor *kesarĭ*, transcription of καῖσαρ of the Grk. text, with ending of *cěsarĭ;* elsewhere *cěsarĭ* usual also for 'emperor'), Boh. *císař*, Pol. *cesarz* (> Lith. *ciesorius*), and (with shortening characteristic of titles), Bulg., SCr. *car*, Russ. *car'*. Falk-Torp 506. Feist 305. Berneker 126 f. Stender-Petersen 351 f.

Among the Slavs the *car* title was assumed by the Bulgarian Simeon ca. 923 A.D. (the earlier rulers bore the native Bulgarian, non-Slavic, title *khan*), by the Serbian Dušan in 1346 (in place of *kralj* 'king') and by the Russian Ivan IV in 1547 (the title of his predecessors was first *knjaz'* 'prince', then *velikij knjaz'*, generally rendered as 'grand duke'). Peter the Great substituted the western *imperator*, which remained the official title; while *car'* persisted as the popular term.

3. Grk. *βασιλεύς* 'king' was used also of the Roman 'emperor' (both uses in NT), and only as 'emperor' in Byzantine times. See 19.32.

Grk. *καῖσαρ*, fr. Lat. *Caesar*, is used of the Roman emperor (NT, inscriptions), but later, in accordance with later Roman use (Hadrian named his designated successor *Caesar*), of the appointed successor to the throne or a viceroy. In Byzantine times it is a common official title (cf. DuCange s.v.), but always subordinate to the *βασιλεύς*.

Grk. *αὐτοκράτωρ*, cpd. of *αὐτός* 'self' and *-κράτωρ* : *κρατέω* 'rule'; in class. times mostly adj. 'independent, absolute' (of rulers, etc.), then used to render Lat. *dictātor* and later *imperator* (often *αὐτοκράτωρ καῖσαρ* = Lat. *imperātor Caesar*). In Byz. writers frequent enough beside usual *βασιλεύς*, and the reg. NG word, since *βασιλεύς* is again 'king'.

Lat. *Augustus* as title appears also in Grk. *Αὔγουστος* or translated *Σεβαστός*, and *Αὐγοῦστα* was the usual Byz. title of the empress.

19.35 PRINCE

Grk.	*ἄρχων*	Goth.	*reiks*	Lith.	*kunigaikštis*
NG	*πρίγκιπας, βασιλόπουλο*	ON	....	Lett.	*kn'azs*
Lat.	*prīnceps*	Dan.	*fyrste, prins*	ChSl.	*kŭnęzĭ*
It.	*principe*	Sw.	*furste, prins*	SCr.	*knez*
Fr.	*prince*	OE	*ealdor*	Boh.	*kníže*
Sp.	*principe*	ME	*prince*	Pol.	*książę*
Rum.	*prinț*	NE	*prince*	Russ.	*knjaz'*
Ir.	*flaith, triath*	Du.	*vorste, prins*		
NIr.	*flaith*	OHG	*furisto, hēristo*		
W.	*tywysog*	MHG	*vürste, prinze*		
Br.	*priñs*	NHG	*fürst, prinz*		

The title of 'prince' is mainly medieval and modern, and one of varied application, a generic term for 'ruler' (covering 'king', etc.), but especially the ruler of a small or vassal state, or member of royal family, or title of nobility ranking first below 'king' or in several countries below 'duke'. The title is also sometimes used with special reference to the heir to the throne, as Lat. *prīnceps* (after *Augustus*), NE *Prince of Wales* (which has a particular historical background), NHG *kronprinz*, etc., but this notion is more commonly expressed otherwise, as NG *διάδοχος* 'successor', Fr. *dauphin* (based on a personal name), or phrases with 'heir'. Cf. NED and Encycl. Brit. s.v. *prince*.

In earlier times the nearest equivalents would be words for 'king', which were often used where we should render 'prince' (so Grk. *βασιλεύς*, Lat. *rēx* with dim. *rēgulus*, Skt. *rājan-*, etc.), or words for 'ruler, leader' (so Grk. *ἄρχων* in the Bible commonly rendered 'prince'), or words for 'a noble' (as ON *ǫðlingr*, OE *æþeling*, etc.).

Lat. *prīnceps* is the source of the majority of the Eur. words, either directly or in translation (OHG *furisto*, NHG *fürst*, etc.). But the Slavic group (also Lith.) represents an early borrowing from the Gmc. word for 'king'.

1. Grk. *ἄρχων* 'ruler' (pple. of *ἄρχω* 'rule', 19.31), in various technical applications and freq. in the Bible, where it is rendered as 'prince' in modern versions (NE *prince*, NHG *fürst*, etc.). In Byz. writers it is the usual equivalent of the Slavic terms (below, 6).

NG (beside *πρίγκιπας*, below) *βασιλόπουλο* 'king's son', the pop. 'prince' of fairy tales.

2. Lat. *prīnceps*, fr. **prīmo-caps* cpd. of *prīmus* 'first' and *capere* 'take', hence as adj. 'taking first place, first, most distinguished' and as sb. 'principal person, chief', later 'ruler' (applied to the emperor, sometimes to the heir to the throne).

Hence NG *πρίγκιψ*, pop. *πρίγκιπας*; It., Sp. *principe*, Fr. *prince* (> Rum. *prinț*, Br. *priñs*, ME, NE *prince*, etc., common to all modern Gmc. languages).

3. Ir., NIr. *flaith* 'ruler, prince' : Ir. *foln-* 'rule', etc. (19.31).

Ir. *triath*, one of the highest titles (cf. Laws, Gloss. s.b.), etym.? Macbain 376.

W. *tywysog* (title of the Welsh rulers, formerly 'kings', after they became vassals of the English king), lit. 'leader' (= Ir. *tōisech* 'leader') : W. *tywys* 'lead, guide' (10.64). Walde-P. 1.255. Pedersen 1.308.

W. *gweledig* (obs.), MBr. *gloedic*, a kind of 'prince' or 'duke', deriv. of W. *gwlad*, etc. 'country'. Loth, RC 33.352 f.

4. OHG *furisto*, MHG *vürste*, NHG *fürst*, Du. *vorste* (MLG *vurste* > Dan. *fyrste*, Sw. *furste*), sb. fr. superl. adj. OHG *furist* 'first', etc. (13.33). Weigand-H. 1.603. Falk-Torp 286.

OHG *hēristo*, *hērōsto*, superl. of *hēr* 'excellent, distinguished, venerable' (NHG *hehr*) = OE *hār* 'gray, gray-haired, venerable' (NE *hoar*). Cf. OHG *hē(r)ro*, NHG *herr* 'master' (19.41).

Grk. *ἄρχων* in NT (see above, 1) is rendered in Goth. by *reiks* (loanword fr. Celtic, see 19.32); in OE by *ealdor* (lit. 'elder') and *ealdorman*.

5. Lith. *kunigaikštis* : *kunigas* 'priest, pastor' (secondary sense, as in Pol. *ksiądz*, formerly 'prince' and 'priest'), loanword fr. Gmc., OHG *kuni(n)g* 'king', etc. See below, 6.

6. ChSl. *kŭnęzĭ*, SCr. *knez*, Boh. *kníže*, Pol. *książę* (Boh. *kněz*, Pol. *ksiądz*, now only 'priest'), Russ. *knjaz'* (> Lett. *kn'azs*), early loanword fr. Gmc., OHG *kuni(n)g*, etc. 'king', but prob. reflecting an earlier less specific use of the latter (19.32). Berneker 663. Brückner 277. Stender-Petersen 200 ff.

19.352. Note on some other titles of nobility.

1. Duke. Lat. *dux* 'leader', esp. 'military leader, general'. Hence as title OFr. *ducs*, Fr. *duc* (> ME *duc*, NE *duke*), etc. In the Gmc. languages rendered in its old sense as 'army-leader' (cf. words for 'army' and 'lead', 20.15, 10.64), OE *heretoga*, OHG *her(i)zogo* (these not yet titles), NHG *herzog* (> Russ. *gercog*), Du. *hertog*, Dan. *hertug*, Sw. *hertig;* and so in Slavic, ChSl. *vojevoda* (fr. *vojĭ* 'army' and the root of *vedą*, *vesti* 'lead'), etc., of which SCr. *vojvoda* and Boh. *vévoda* are used for 'duke'. But Pol. *książę* 'prince' (19.35) is also used for 'duke', and not only Pol. *wielki książę*, but also Russ. *velikij knjaz'* for 'grand duke', (though Russ. *gercog* is the reg. word for a foreign duke).

2. Count. Lat. *comes*, gen. *-itis* 'companion' (*com-* and the root of *īre* 'go'), in late Lat. a title of various state officials. Hence OFr. *cunte*, *conte*, Anglo-Fr. *counte* (> NE *count*), etc.

The corresponding native English title is ME *eorl*, *erl*, NE *earl* (but the earl's wife is a *countess*), fr. OE *eorl* 'man of noble rank', later esp. governor of one of the large divisions like Wessex, Mercia, etc. = ON *jarl* 'nobleman, chief' OS *erl* 'man', root connection dub. Falk-Torp 471, 1491. NED s.v. *earl*, sb.

OHG *grāfo*, *grāvo* ('judge', Tat., etc.), MHG *grāve*, NHG *graf* (> SCr. *grof*, Boh. *hrabě*, Pol. *hrabia*, Russ. *graf*) : OE

gerēfa 'prefect, judge' (> NE *reeve*), *scīr-gerēfa* (> NE *sheriff*), root connection dub. Weigand-H. 1.755. Kluge-G. 214. NED s.v. *reeve*, sb.

3. Marquis. OFr. *marchis*, later *marquis* (> ME *markys*, NE *marquis*), It. *marchese*, etc., fr. a deriv. of *marca*, Fr. *marche*, etc. 'borderland, marches', orig. Gmc. word for 'boundary', Goth. *marka*, etc. (19.17), whence, with word for 'count', the corresponding OHG *marcgrāvo*, MHG *marcgrave*, NHG *markgraf*. REW 5364. NED s.v. *marquis*. Weigand-H. 2.130.

4. Viscount. OFr. *vescuens*, *visconte*, Anglo-Fr. *viscounte* (> ME *viscounte*, NE *viscount*), Fr. *vicomte*, lit. 'vice-count', MLat. *vicecomes* (cf. Du Cange). Gamillscheg 889. NED s.v. *viscount*.

5. Baron. OFr. *baron*, *barun* (>ME *barun*, *baron*, NE *baron*), It. *barone*, etc., It. *barone*, etc., fr. late Lat. *barō*, *-ōnis* 'man' in Lex Salica, orig. Gmc. word. See Sp. *varón* 'man', 2.21 with refs.

19.36 NOBLE (sb.), NOBLEMAN

Grk.	*γενναῖος, εὐγενής*	Goth.	*manna gōdakunds*	Lith.	*bajoras*
NG	*εὐγενής*	ON	*ǫðlingr*	Lett.	*muižnieks*
Lat.	*nōbilis, patricius*	Dan.	*adelig, adelsmand*	ChSl.	*boljarinŭ*
It.	*nobile*	Sw.	*ädling, adelsman*	SCr.	*plemić*
Fr.	*noble*	OE	*æþeling*	Boh.	*šlechtic*
Sp.	*noble*	ME	*noble*	Pol.	*szlachcic*
Rum.	*nobil*	NE	*noble, nobleman*	Russ.	*dvorjanin*
Ir.	*aire, māl, flaith*	Du.	*edelman*	Skt.	*kulīna-* (adj.)
NIr.	*flaith, triath*	OHG	*edeling*		
W.	*pendefig*	MHG	*edelman, edelinc*		
Br.	*nobl*	NHG	*adlige(r), edelmann*		

A few of the forms listed are adjs., used with 'man' to express the sb., or without this especially in the plural (Grk. *οἱ γενναῖοι, οἱ εὐγενεῖς*, Lat. *nōbilēs*, *patriciī*).

The majority are derived from words for 'birth, family, estate', that is, they mean literally 'of (good) birth', etc. But in some this notion comes secondarily from 'famous, chief', etc.

1. Grk. *γενναῖος*, fr. *γέννα* 'descent, birth, origin' : *γένος* 'race, family' (19.23), whence *εὐγενής* lit. 'well-born'.

2. Lat. *nōbilis* (> the Romance words), fr. **gnōbilis* (cf. *ignōbilis*), lit. 'known', whence 'famous' and then esp. 'noble (of birth)' : *nōscere* 'know, recognize'. Ernout-M. 677.

Lat. *patricius*, fr. *pater* 'father', esp. pl. *patrēs* as honorary title, itself also sometimes 'nobles'.

3. Ir. *aire* ('noble, chief', cf. Hessen) : Skt. *arya-* 'master, lord', *ārya-* 'Aryan'. Walde-P. 1.80. Pedersen 2.32, 100.

Ir. *māl* 'prince, chief, noble' (RIA Contrib. s.v.), beside proper names *Maglo-* in Lat. inscriptions of Britain, W. *Mael* : Lat. *magnus* 'great', etc. Walde-P. 2.258. Pedersen 1.103.

Ir. *flaith*, see 19.35.

NIr. *triath*, see 19.35.

W. *pendefig* (cf. Br. *pinvidik* 'rich' with metathesis), deriv. of a superl. fr. *pen* 'head, chief'. Pedersen 1.381.

Br. *nobl*, fr. Fr. *noble*.

4. Goth. *manna gōda-kunds* (= *ἄνθρωπος εὐγενής* Lk. 19.12), cpd. of *gōþs* 'good' and *-kunds* (as in *himina-kunds* 'heaven-born, heavenly') : *kuni* 'race, tribe, family' (NE *kin*, etc.; 19.23).

ON *ǫðlingr*, OE *æþeling* (both esp. 'prince'), OHG *edeling*, MHG *edelinc*

(esp. 'son of a nobleman'), MLG *edelinc* (> Sw. *ädling*), fr. OE *æþele*, OHG *edili*, NHG *edel*, adjs. 'noble' (whence again Du., MHG *edelman*, etc.), beside ON *aðal* 'nature', OE *æþelu* 'noble extraction', OHG *adal* '(noble) race', etc., with adjs. NHG *adlig* and Dan. *adelig* (but with influence of NHG meaning) : ON *óðal*, OE *ēþel*, OHG *uodal* 'estate, (inherited) land, patrimony', and all prob. : Goth. *atta* 'father', etc. Walde-P. 1.44. Falk-Torp 11, 1430, 1524. Weigand-H. 1.22 f., 403. NED s.v. *athel*.

ME, NE *noble*, fr. Fr. *noble* (above, 2); also cpd. *nobleman*.

5. Lith. *bajoras* (Lett. *bajārs* 'rich person'), fr. Slavic, cf. ChSl. *boljarinŭ* (below). Mühl.-Endz. 1.252.

Lett. *muižnieks*, deriv. of *muiža* 'estate (of a noble)', this fr. Liv. or Esth. *moiz* (perh. through Russ. *myža* 'farm, country house'?). Mühl.-Endz. 2.662. Thomsen, Beröringer 270.

6. ChSl. (in Gospels only *člověkŭ dobra roda* 'man of good family', but Supr.) *boljarinŭ* (pl. *boljare*) = Russ. *bojarin* 'grandee', *barin* 'gentleman, sir', etc., widespread Slavic term, prob. early loanword fr. Turk. *bayar* 'magnate' (or fr. Turk. *boylu* 'tall'; cf. Byz. *βοϊλάδες*, *βολιάδες*). Berneker 72. Brückner 34 f. NED s.v. *boyard*.

SCr. *plemić*, deriv. of *pleme* 'tribe' (19.23).

Boh. *šlechtic*, Pol. *szlachcic*, beside Boh. *šlechta*, Pol. *szlachta* 'nobility', fr. MHG *slechte*, OHG *slahta* 'species, sort, kind', cf. NHG *geschlecht* (19.23). Brückner 550.

Russ. *dvorjanin*, deriv. of *dvor* 'court, yard' (7.15). Berneker 241.

7. Skt. *kulīna-* (mostly adj.), deriv. of *kula-* 'tribe, family' (19.23).

19.37 CITIZEN

Grk.	*πολῑ́της, ἀστός*	Goth.	*baurgja*	Lith.	*pilietis*
NG	*πολίτης*	ON	*borgarmaðr*	Lett.	*pilsuonis*
Lat.	*cīvis*	Dan.	*borger*	ChSl.	*graždaninŭ, žiteljĭ*
It.	*cittadino*	Sw.	*borgare*	SCr.	*građanin*
Fr.	*citoyen*	OE	*ceasterware, burhsittend*	Boh.	*občan*
Sp.	*ciudadano*			Pol.	*obywatel*
Rum.	*cetățean*	ME	*burgeis, citesein*	Russ.	*graždanin*
Ir.	*cathrar*	NE	*citizen*	Skt.	*pāura-, nāgara-*
NIr.	*cathruightheoir, saorānach*	Du.	*burger*		
		OHG	*burgāri*		
W.	*dinesydd*	MHG	*burgære*		
Br.	*keodedour*	NHG	*bürger*		

The majority of the words for 'citizen' are derived from those for 'city' (19.15) and meant orig. 'city dweller', the political sense of 'citizen' (vs. 'alien, subject', etc.) being secondary. This use of Grk. *πολῖτης* beside *πόλις* 'city' but also the 'city-state', and of Lat. *cīvis* beside *cīvitās* (though here the *cīvis* is the earlier) doubtless influenced the formation and use of the other Eur. words.

A few of the words are derived from verbs for 'dwell' and so meant orig. 'inhabitant'. One is derived from a word for 'community'.

1. Grk. *πολῖτης*, and *ἀστός* (latter less common, and at Athens 'city dweller' with only civil rights in contrast to *πολῖτης*), fr. *πόλις* and *ἄστυ* 'city' (19.15).

2. Lat. *cīvis*, whence *cīvitās* 'citizenry, state', late 'city' and Romance words for 'city' (in part obs., 19.15), whence again derivs. for 'citizen', It. *cittadino*, Fr.

citoyen, Sp. *ciudadano*, Rum. *cetățean* : Goth. *heiwa-frauja* 'master of the house', OE *hīw-rǣden*, Lith *šaima*, etc. 'household, family' (2.82). Extension fr. 'member of the household' to 'member of the city or state'. Cf. *hostis* 'stranger' > 'enemy'. Walde-P. 1.359. Ernout-M. 191 b. Walde-H. 1.224.

3. Ir. *cathrar* (Sg 28a8, 33a10), NIr. *cathruightheoir*, fr. Ir. *cathir*, NIr. *cathair* 'city'.

NIr. *saorānach*, lit. 'freeman', fr. *saor* 'free' (19.44).

W. *dinesydd*, fr. *dinas* 'city'.

Br. *keodedour*, *keodedad*, derivs. of *keoded* 'cité', MBr. *queudet*, fr. Lat. *cīvitātem*. Loth, Mots lat. 149.

4. Goth. *baurgja* (= πολίτης Lk. 15.15, 19.14), ON *borgarmaðr* (with *maðr* 'man'), OE *burhsittend* (with pple. of *sittan* 'sit, dwell'), less usually *burhware* = Du. *burger* (MLG *borgere* > Dan. *borger*, Sw. *borgare*), OHG *burgāri*, MHG *burgære*, NHG *bürger*, formed with the suffix *-wari* (as in Germano-Lat. *Chasuarii*, etc.), fr. the older Gmc. word for 'city', Goth. *baurgs*, etc. (19.15). Falk-Torp 94. Kluge-G. 87. From the same source also ME *burgeis*, fr. OFr. *burgeis*, late Lat. *burgēnsis*. NED s.v. *burgess*.

OE *ceasterware*, *ceastergeware*, fr. *ceaster* 'city'. For the suffix, cf. above.

ME *citesein*, NE *citizen*, fr. Anglo-Fr. *citeseyn* beside OFr. *citean* (Fr. *citoyen*, above, 2). NED s.v. *citizen*.

5. Lith. *pilietis* (neolog.), Lett. *pilsuonis*, derivs. of Lith. *pilis* 'castle, fort', old 'city', Lett. *pils* 'castle, stronghold' (cf. Lett. *pilsēta* 'city' 19.15).

6. ChSl. *žiteljĭ* (= πολίτης Lk. 15.15), lit. 'inhabitant' : *žiti* 'live, dwell' (7.11).

ChSl. *graždaninŭ* (> Russ. *graždanin*), SCr. *građanin*, fr. ChSl *gradŭ*, etc. 'city' (19.15). Berneker 330.

Boh. *občan*, fr. *obec* 'community' = Pol. *obec* 'totality' (: ChSl. *obĭštĭ* 'common', etc., Meillet, Études 381).

Pol. *obywatel*, lit. 'inhabitant', fr. *obywać* 'live, inhabit' (7.11).

7. Skt. *pāura-* and *nāgara-* (both 'city dweller' without political sense), fr. *pura-* and *nagara-* 'city'.

19.38 SUBJECT (sb.)

Grk.	*ὑπήκοος*	Goth.	*(ufhausjands)*	Lith.	*pavaldinis, valdinys*
NG	*ὑπήκοος*	ON	*undirmaðr*	Lett.	*pavalstnieks*
Lat.	*subiectus, subditus*	Dan.	*undersaat*	ChSl.	. . . .
It.	*suddito*	Sw.	*undersåte*	SCr.	*podanik*
Fr.	*sujet*	OE	*underþēod(ed)*	Boh.	*poddaný*
Sp.	*súbdito*	ME	*suget*	Pol.	*poddany*
Rum.	*supus*	NE	*subject*	Russ.	*poddannyj*
Ir.	*aithech*	Du.	*onderdaan*	Skt.	*prajā-*
NIr.	*ōmōsaidhe*	OHG	*untartān, untarthiutit*	OPers.	*ba(n)daka-*
W.	*deiliad*	MHG	*undertān(e), undersāze*		
Br.	*sujed*	NHG	*untertan*		

Words for 'subject' (here, of course, in the political sense) are mostly adjectives, used also as nouns, meaning orig. 'put under' or (in Grk., followed in Goth.) 'obedient'. A few are from other sources, as through 'tenant' from 'hold' or 'repay', or through 'servant' from 'bind'.

1. Grk. ὑπήκοος, orig. 'obedient', but reg. word for 'subject' (adj. and sb.) : ἀκοή 'hearing', ἀκούω 'hear, listen to' (15.41). Boisacq 37.

2. Lat. *subiectus* (> Fr. *sujet*), pple. of *subicere* 'throw under', 'when 'subject, subdue', cpd. of *iacere* 'throw'.

Lat. (late) *subditus* (> It. *suddito*, Sp. *súbdito*), pple. of *subdere* 'put under', late 'subject'.

Rum. *supus*, pple. of *supune* 'put under' (Lat. *subpōnere*).

3. Ir. *aithech* (strictly 'tenant-farmer, one of the rent-paying classes', cf. Laws, Gloss. s.v., Thurneysen, Heldensage 77; but no better word for 'subject' in political sense), deriv. of *aithe* 'a return, retribution, rent', vbl. n. of *aith-fen-* 'repay'. Pedersen 2.517. Thurneysen, Gram. 449.

NIr. *ōmōsaidhe*, deriv. of *ōmōs* 'obedience, respect', fr. NE *homage*. Pedersen 2.22.

W. *deiliad*, older 'tenant, vassal', fr. *dal* 'hold'.

Br. *sujed*, fr. Fr. *sujet*.

4. Goth. *ufhausjands* (quotable only as 'obedient', but), pres. pple. of *ufhausjan*, both 'obey' and 'be subject to' (Lk. 10.17, 20), cpd. of *hausjan* 'hear' (15.41).

ON *undirmaðr* (pl. *undirmenn* or *undirfolk*), lit. 'under-man'.

OE *underþēoded*, *underþēod*, OHG *untarthiutit* (Tat.), pples. of *underþēodan*, *untarthiuten* 'subdue, subjugate', fr. the adjs. OE *underþēod* (also sb.), etc. : OE *þēodan*, ON *þȳða* 'join, attach', etc. Holthausen 364.

ME *suget*, NE *subject* (with approximation to Latin), fr. the French.

OHG *untartān*, MHG *undertān(e)*, NHG *untertan*, Du. *onderdaan*, orig. pple. of OHG *untartuon* (NHG *untertun*) 'put under', whence 'subjugate'. Weigand-H. 2.1125.

MHG *undersāze*, *undersæze*, etc., MLG *undersāte* (> Dan. *undersaat*, Sw. *undersåte*) : OHG *untarsizzan* 'be subject to', lit. 'sit under'. Falk-Torp 1333. Hellquist 1279.

5. Lith. *valdinys*, *pavaldinis*, Lett. *pavalstnieks*, cf. Lett. *pavalste* 'province' : Lith. *valdyti*, Lett. *valdīt* 'rule' (19.31).

6. SCr. *podanik*, Boh. *poddaný*, etc., general Slavic (but not quotable in ChSl.) fr. cpds. of *podŭ* 'under' and *dati* 'put, place', and modeled after MHG *undertān*. Brückner 84.

7. Skt. *prajā-*, lit. 'offspring', whence 'people' and (19.21) 'subjects' of a ruler.

OPers. *ba(n)daka-*, cf. NPers. *band* 'slave' : Av., OPers. *band-*, 'bind, fetter', etc. Barth. 924 f.

19.41 MASTER

Grk.	*δεσπότης, κύριος*	Goth.	*frauja*	Lith.	*ponas*
NG	*κύριος, ἀφέντης*	ON	*drōttinn*	Lett.	*kungs*
Lat.	*dominus, erus*	Dan.	*herre*	ChSl.	*gospodĭ*
It.	*padrone (signore)*	Sw.	*herre*	SCr.	*gospodar, gazda*
Fr.	*maître (seigneur)*	OE	*hlāford, drihten*	Boh.	*pán*
Sp.	*amo (señor)*	ME	*louerd, drichte, maister*	Pol.	*pan*
Rum.	*stăpîn*			Russ.	*chozjain (gospodin)*
Ir.	*coimdiu, tigerne, fēda*	NE	*master (lord)*	Skt.	*svāmin-, īçvara-, pati-*
NIr.	*maighistir (tighearna)*	Du.	*heer, baas*	Av.	*paiti-*
W.	*meistr (arglwydd)*	OHG	*hērro, truhtin*		
Br.	*mestr (aotrou)*	MHG	*herre (trehtin)*		
		NHG	*herr*		

Under 'master' we have in mind especially 'master' vs. 'slave, servant', and in several of the words this was in fact the primary sense, as shown by the etymology (connection with words for 'house') or the actual use. But most of them have a wider scope, and it is not intended to restrict the group wholly to that special sense.

The semantic sources are diverse, as (besides the connection with 'house') 'powerful, chief, first, protector', etc.

Included in the list are several words which (like NE *lord*) were once in common use for 'master, lord' (cf. e.g. translations of NT, Lk. 12.43 ff., etc.), but are now mostly 'Lord' or titles like 'Sir' or 'Mr.'.

The eccl. use of words of this group, as 'Lord', goes back ultimately to the Jewish substitution of Hebr. *adōnāi* for the 'ineffable name *Yahweh*'. This substitute name was faithfully rendered in the LXX by κύριος, followed by Lat. *dominus* (> Rum. *Domn*, or *Dumnezeu*, fr. voc. *domine deus*; but It. *Signore*, Fr. *Seigneur*, Sp. *Señor*), Goth. *frauja*, OE *drihten* (not *hlāford*), OHG *truhtin* (not *hērro*, but NHG *Herr*), ChSl. *gospodĭ*, etc. Some became restricted to this use, as Rum. *Domn*, Lith. *Viešpats* (but also 'ruler'), SCr. *Gospod*, Russ. *Gospod'*, Boh. *Hospodin*.

Words of this group furnish also most of the modern Eur. terms corresponding to NE *Mr.* (*mister*, orig. *master*), as NG κύριος, It. *Signor*, Fr. *Monsieur*, Sp. *Señor*, Rum. *Domn*, NHG *Herr*, Du. *Heer*, Dan., Sw. *Hr.*, Lith. *Ponas*, Boh. *Pán*, Pol. *Pan*, Russ. *Gospodin*, etc.

1. IE *poti- and cpds. Walde-P. 2.77 f. See also 2.31.

Skt. *pati-*, Av. *paiti-* 'master, husband', with fem. Skt. *patnī-* 'mistress, wife' : Grk. πόσις 'husband', πότνια 'mistress', Lat. *potis* 'able', Lith. *pats* 'husband, self', *pati* 'wife', Goth. *brūþ-faþs* 'bridegroom', etc.

Grk. δεσπότης 'master' (with fem. δέσποινα 'mistress', cf. πότνια), fr. *δεμσ-ποτ- : Skt. *patir dan* (Ved.), *dam-pati-* 'master of the house', Av. *dəng.pati-* 'master', cpds. with forms related to Grk. δόμος, Lat. *domus*, Skt. *dama-* 'house'. Walde-P. 1.787. Boisacq 179. Wackernagel, Altind. Gram. 3.243 f.

Lith. *viešpatis* (now 'ruler' and 'Lord'; cf. OPruss. fem. acc. *waispattin* 'wife', orig. 'mistress') : Skt. *viç-pati-*, Av. *vīs-paiti-* 'master' (of the house, people, etc.), cpds. with forms related to Skt. *viç-* 'dwelling, house, tribe', Av. *vīs-* 'dwelling, village', Grk. οἶκος 'house', etc. Walde-P. 1.231.

ChSl. *gospodĭ* (renders κύριος and οἰκοδεσπότης; but modern Slavic forms now the 'Lord', with new derivs. for 'master', as SCr. *gospodar*, Russ. *gospodin*, the latter again obs. except as 'Mr.'), prob. *gos-podĭ* fr. *gosti-pot- (change of dental variously explained), cpd. of *gostĭ* 'guest' (19.56), like Lat. *hospes* 'guest, host' fr. *hosti-pot-. Berneker 336. Brückner 152. Cf. also Skt. *jās-pati-* 'head of the family', first part : *jana-* 'person, people', etc.

2. Grk. κύριος, sb. use of adj. κύριος 'having power, supreme' : κῦρος 'power', Skt. *çūra-* 'strong, brave', etc. Walde-P. 1.365 ff. Boisacq 538.

NG ἀφέντης, fr. αὐθέντης in earliest use 'murderer, suicide', later 'doer, author', but once (Eur.) 'master', prob. fr. αὐτο-θέντης : θείνω 'strike, slay', φόνος 'murder'. Psichari, Mélanges Havet 387 ff. Kretschmer, Glotta 3.289 ff.

3. Lat. *dominus*, orig. 'master of the house', fr. *domus* 'house'. Hence Romance words used as 'Lord' or in titles (Sp. *Don*, etc.). Ernout-M. 282. Walde-H. 1.367.

Lat. *erus* (old pop. word for 'master of the house' vs. 'slave', but displaced by *dominus*), etym.? Ernout-M. 309 f. Walde-H. 1.419.

Lat. *magister* 'chief, master' (with various special applications, esp. 'teacher', but not used for 'master' vs. 'slave'), fr. *mag-is-tero- : *magnus* 'great', *magis* 'more'. Ernout-M. 580. Walde-H. 2.10. Hence Fr. *maître*, ME *maister*, NE *master*, OHG-NHG *meister*, and similar words in nearly all the modern Eur. languages, but the majority of them in special senses as 'teacher', 'master of a craft, art or science', 'master-workman', 'steward', etc., and so not included in the list (yet NHG *meister* locally, e.g. in Switzerland, usual word for 'master' vs. 'servant').

It. *signore*, Fr. *seigneur*, Sp. *señor* (formerly 'master, lord', now titles or 'Lord'), fr. Lat. *senior* 'elder', through its use as term of respectful address.

It. *padrone*, fr. Lat. *patrōnus* 'protector' : *pater* 'father'.

Sp. *amo*, new masc. to *ama* 'mistress', orig. 'wet nurse', fr. Lat. (Isid.) *amma* 'mamma, nurse' (nursery word). REW 425. Ernout-M. 44.

Rum. *stăpîn*, fr. Slavic, cf. late ChSl. *stopanŭ* 'dominus', Bulg. *stopan* 'master, proprietor, husband', SCr. dial. *stopanin* 'master of the house', orig.? Tiktin 1483 f. G. Meyer, Alb. Etym. Wtb. 393.

4. Ir. *coimdiu* (in later eccl. Ir. specialized to 'Lord') : *con-midiur* 'rule, be able, determine'. Pedersen 2.578.

Ir. *tigerne*, NIr. *tighearna* (cf. W. *teyrn* 'ruler', Gall. *Thigernum castrum*, etc.), fr. *tech*, gen. *tige* 'house', hence orig. 'master of the house'. Pedersen 1.99.

Ir. *fēda*, *fiadu* ('master, owner, Lord'), fr. *weidont-, with same root as in *ro-fetar* 'know', etc. Pedersen 2.103. Thurneysen, Gram. 208 f.

NIr. *maighistir*, W. *meistr*, Br. *mestr*, fr. Lat. *magister*. Vendryes, De hib. voc. 152 f. Loth, Mots lat. 185.

W. *arglwydd*, cpd. of *ar* 'over' and a form related to arch. *glyw* 'ruler, lord', this perh. : Lat. *valēre* 'be strong', OE *wealdan* 'rule', etc. (19.31). Morris Jones 186.

W. *por* (obs.) : *peri* 'cause', Skt. *kṛ-* 'do, make', etc. Loth RC 38.165.

W. *ner* (obs.) : Skt. *nar-*, etc. 'man'. Loth, RC 41.207.

Br. *aotrou* : W. *alltraw* 'sponsor, godfather', Ir. *altram* 'nourishing', etc., fr. the root of Ir. *alaim*, Lat. *alere*, etc. 'nourish'. Pedersen 1.137.

5. Goth. *frauja* (cf. ON *Freyr*, name of a god, OE *frēa* 'a lord, the Lord', OHG *frō mīn* 'my Lord', applied to Christ or an angel), deriv. of IE *pro, Goth. *fra*, etc. 'before, in front', cf. Skt. *pūrva-*, *pūrvya-* 'former', ChSl. *prŭvŭ* 'first', etc. (13.33). Walde-P. 2.37. Feist 166. Falk-Torp 278.

ON *drōttinn* (Dan. *drot*, Sw. *drott*, poet. 'king'), OE *drihten*, ME *drichte*, OHG *truhtin*, MHG *trehtin*, etc. (chiefly 'the Lord'), deriv. of ON *drott*, OE *dryht*, OHG *truht* 'multitude, people, army' : Goth. *drauhti-witōþ* 'στρατεία', *gadrauhts* 'soldier', etc. (20.17), Lith. *draugas* 'companion, friend', ChSl. *drugŭ* 'friend, other', etc. (19.51). Walde-P. 1.860. Falk-Torp 158. Feist 179. NED s.v. *drightin*.

OE *hlāford*, once *hlāfweard*, ME *louerd* (NE *lord*), cpd. of OE *hlāf* 'bread, loaf' and *weard* 'guard, protector, keeper'. NED s.v. *lord*.

ME *maister*, *meister*, NE *master*, partly fr. OE *mægester* 'leader, chief', etc. (fr. Lat. *magister*), and partly fr. OFr. *maistre* (> Fr. *maître*, above, 3). NED s.v. *master*.

OHG *hērro* (reg. word for 'master, lord' vs. *truhtin* 'Lord', cf. Z. deutsch. Wortf. 7.173 ff.), MHG *herre*, NHG *herr*, Du. *heer* (OS *hērro* > late ON *herra, herri*, Dan., Sw. *herre*), contracted fr. OHG *hēriro*, comp. to *hēr* 'excellent, distinguished, venerable', etc. (NHG *hehr*) = OE *hār* 'gray, gray-haired, venerable'. Falk-Torp 400. Weigand-H. 1.854.

Du. *baas* (> NE esp. U.S. *boss*), orig.? Franck-v. W. s.v.

6. Lith. *ponas*, fr. Ukr., Pol. *pan* (below, 7). Brückner, Sl. Fremdwörter 120.

Lett. *kungs* (cf. Lith. *kunigas* 'priest, pastor'), fr. the Gmc. word for 'king', ON *konungr*, OHG *kuni(n)g* (19.32). Mühl.-Endz. 2.314 f.

7. ChSl. *gospodĭ*, SCr. *gospodar*, etc., above, 1.

SCr. *gazda* (pop.), fr. Hung. *gozda* 'master'.

Boh. *pán*, Pol. *pan*, prob. abbr. (first as term of address) of the title seen in ChSl. *županŭ* (Supr.), SCr. *župan* 'head of a district' (orig.?). Brückner 393.

Russ. *chozjain*, fr. Turk. (orig. Pers.) *hoca* 'teacher, master, priest'. Berneker 400. Lokotsch 850.

8. Skt. *pati-*, Av. *paiti-*, above, 1.

Skt. *svāmin-*, deriv. (or cpd.) of pron. *sva-* 'own'. BR s.v. Uhlenbeck 356.

Skt. *īçvara-* : *īç-* 'own (11.12), rule'.

19.42 SLAVE

Grk.	*δοῦλος, οἰκέτης*	Goth.	*skalks, þius*	Lith.	*vergas*
NG	*δοῦλος, σκλάβος*	ON	*þræll, þȳ* (fem.)	Lett.	*vergs*
Lat.	*servus, mancipium*	Dan.	*slave, træl*	ChSl.	*rabŭ*
It.	*schiavo*	Sw.	*slaf, träl*	SCr.	*rob*
Fr.	*esclave*	OE	*þēow, þrǣl, scealc, wealh*	Boh.	*otrok*
Sp.	*esclavo*			Pol.	*niewolnik*
Rum.	*sclav, rob*	ME	*sclave, thral(l)*	Russ.	*rab, nevol'nik*
Ir.	*mug, dōir, daer*	NE	*slave*	Skt.	*dāsa-*
NIr.	*sclābhuidhe*	Du.	*slaaf*		
W.	*caethwas, slaf*	OHG	*scalc, deo*		
Br.	*sklav*	MHG	*schalc, slave, diu*		
		NHG	*sklave*		

There is some overlapping between 'slave' and 'servant' (19.43). A word for 'slave' may cover also or eventually denote simply 'servant' (cf. Lat. *servus* and its derivs.). Conversely some of the words listed under 'servant' applied to servants who were in fact slaves (as Lat. *famulus, ancilla*). For older periods there is no such sharp distinction as later, and the assignment of certain words (esp. some of the old Gmc.) to one or the other group is bound to be somewhat arbitrary.

Words for 'slave' are cognate with words for 'house, oppress, work, trouble, distress, quick', etc., while some are of wholly doubtful origin. The widespread modern Eur. word, NE *slave*, etc., was originally a 'Slav', the use of which for 'slave' goes back to Byzantine times when so many Slavs were taken captive and enslaved. Analogous is the use of OE *Wealh* 'Briton' for 'slave'. In general on words for 'slave' and 'servant', cf. Brugmann, IF 19.377 ff.

1. Grk. *δοῦλος* (Cret. *δῶλος*, but early Att. *δοῦλος* with genuine diphthong), etym.? Boisacq 198. Brugmann, op. cit. 386 ff. Lambertz, Glotta 6.1 ff. (loanword).

Grk. *οἰκέτης* (Hom., Cret. *οἰκεύς*, dial. also *οἰκιάτᾱς*), prop. a 'household slave' (freq. contrasted with *δοῦλος*, but also as synonym of; cf. LS s.v.), deriv. of *οἶκος* 'house'.

Grk. *δμώς* (poet.), uncertain whether

as orig. 'captive' : *δαμάω* 'conquer', or as orig. 'house-slave' : *δόμος* 'house'. Walde-P. 1.788. Boisacq 193.

Grk. *ἀνδράποδα* (pl.), formed fr. *ἀνήρ, ἀνδρός* 'man' on the analogy of *τετράποδα* 'quadrupeds' in phrases referring to captured 'men and beasts'. Boisacq 61.

Byz., NG *σκλάβος* = Byz. *Σκλάβος* 'a Slav, Slavic', shortened form of *Σκλαβηνός* id., fr. Slavic *Slověninŭ*. Hence MLat. *sclavus* (> It. *schiavo* > Fr. *esclave*, Sp. *esclavo;* Fr. > Rum. *sclav* recent), and, through a Romance, esp. Fr. medium, the Gmc. words ME *sclave*, NE *slave*, late MHG *slave, sclave*, NHG *sklave*, etc. REW 8003a. Falk-Torp 1059. Weigand-H. 2.877. Kluge-G. 566.

2. Lat. *servus*, often explained as orig., though unattested, 'watcher, guardian' : *servāre* 'save, preserve, keep', Av. *pasuš-haurva-* 'guarding the flocks', etc. (see under Lat. *servāre*, 11.24). Walde-P. 2.498. Ernout-M. 933. Otherwise Benveniste, Rev. ét. lat. 10.429 ff. (as Etruscan loanword), Vendryes, BSL 36.126 ff. (: Ir. *serbh* 'pillage', W. *herw* 'outlawry'). Brugmann, op. cit. 383 (as 'running' : Skt. *sr-* 'run, flow').

Lat. *mancipium* 'possession, property' (: *manceps*, cpd. of *man-* = *manus* 'hand' and *capere* 'take'), also esp. 'slave'. Ernout-M. 585. Walde-H. 2.23.

Lat. *famulus* and *ancilla*, see under 'servant' (19.43).

Rum. *rob*, fr. Slavic (below, 6).

3. Ir. *mug* (Ogam *magu*) = Corn. *maw*, MBr. *mao* 'boy, servant', W. *meudwy* 'hermit' = 'servant of God', Gall. *Magu-rīx* : Goth. *magus* 'boy', ON *mǫgr* 'boy, son', etc. (2.25). Walde-P. 2.228.

Ir. *dōir, daer* 'unfree, serf, slave', opp. of *sōir, saer* 'free', see 19.44.

Ir. *cumal* 'bondmaid', orig. dub., perh. : *cuma* 'grief' (16.32). Walde-P. 1.387 f. Stokes 70. Laws, Gloss. 211.

NIr. *sclābhuidhe*, lengthened form of older *sclābha, sclābh*, prob. fr. ME *sclave*.

W. *caethwas*, cpd. of *caeth* 'captive' (= Lat. *captus*, etc.) and *gwas* 'servant' (19.43).

W. *slaf*, fr. NE *slave*.

Br. *sklav*, fr. Fr. *esclave*.

4. Goth. *skalks*, OE *scealc*, OHG *scalc*, MHG *schalc* = ON *skalkr* 'weapon-bearer, rogue', etym. dub. Walde-P. 2.594. Falk-Torp 980 f. Feist 428.

Goth. *þius* (ON *þewaʀ* runic; *-þēr* in names), OE *þēow* (ME forms rare), OHG *deo* (with fem. Goth. *þiwi*, ON *þȳ*, OE *þēow*, OHG, MHG *diu*), prob. : Skt. *takva-, taku-* 'hasty, quick, active', fr. the root in Skt. *tak-* 'rush along', Av. *tač-* 'run, flow', Lith. *tekėti* 'run, flow'. Walde-P. 1.716. Feist 497 f. Falk-Torp 1307. NED s.v. *theow*.

ON *þræll* (> OE *þrǣl*, ME *thral*), Dan. *træl*, Sw. *träl*, etym. disputed; either as orig. 'one oppressed' : Goth. *þreihan*, OHG *dringan*, etc. 'press, oppress, afflict', or as orig. 'runner, messenger' : Goth. *þragjan* 'run', etc. (10.46). Walde-P. 1.753. Falk-Torp 1293, 1568. Hellquist 1234.

OE *Wealh* 'Briton', used also for 'slave'.

5. Lith. *vergas*, Lett. *vergs* : Lith. *vargas* 'misery, distress', Lett. *vārgs* 'miserable', sb. 'misery', OPruss. *wargs* 'evil', ChSl. *vragŭ* 'enemy', etc. (19.52). Walde-P. 1.320. Trautmann 352. Mühl.-Endz. 4.539.

6. ChSl. *rabŭ*, SCr. *rob*, Russ. *rab* : Goth. *arbaiþs* 'trouble, work', Lat. *orbus* 'bereft', Grk. *ὀρφανός* 'orphan', etc. Walde-P. 1.184.

Boh. *otrok* = Pol. *otrok* 'male person, youth, boy', ChSl. *otrokŭ* 'boy' (2.25).

Pol. *niewolnik*, Russ. *nevol'nik* (Boh. *nevolník* less common), deriv. of Pol.

niewola, Russ. *nevolja* 'slavery' = ChSl. *nevolja* 'necessity', neg. cpd. of *volja* 'will'.

7. Skt. *dāsa-*, in Veda 'fiend, demon, non-Aryan' and 'slave' (cf. NPers. *dāh* 'slave'), prob. : Skt. *dasyu-*, designation of the pre-Aryan inhabitants of India. Uhlenbeck 125.

19.43 SERVANT

Grk.	*ὑπηρέτης, διάκονος, θεράπων*	Goth.	*andbahts*	Lith.	*tarnas, bernas*
		ON	*þjōnn, þjōnustumaðr*	Lett.	*sulainis, kalps*
NG	*ὑπηρέτης, ὑπερέτης*	Dan.	*tjener*	ChSl.	*sluga*
Lat.	*famulus, minister, ancilla* (fem.)	Sw.	*tjänare*	SCr.	*sluga*
		OE	*þegn, ambeht, cniht*	Boh.	*sluha*
It.	*servo, servitore*	ME	*servaunt, thain*	Pol.	*sługa*
Fr.	*domestique, serviteur*	NE	*servant*	Russ.	*sluga*
Sp.	*criado, sirviente*	Du.	*dienaar, knecht*	Skt.	*bhṛtya-, sevaka-, ceṭaka-*, etc.
Rum.	*servitor, slugă, slujnic*	OHG	*ambaht, kneht*		
Ir.	*timthirthid, foss*	MHG	*dienestman, dienære, kneht*	Av.	*vaēsa-*
NIr.	*seirbhīseach*				
W.	*gwas, gweinidog*	NHG	*diener, knecht*		
Br.	*mevel, matez* (fem.)				

Most of the words for 'servant' have parallel forms for 'female servant', of which no notice is taken here. But a few distinctive terms for the latter are included (marked fem.), to which might be added NHG *magd*, Du. *meid*, etc. = NE *maid* also in part so used.

The words are often cognate with those for 'slave, serve, boy', but are also from diverse other sources. Besides those included in the list, the words for 'boy' and 'girl' (2.25, 2.26) are widely used, and often the most popular terms, for the male or female servant. So sometimes those for 'man' (2.1), as Lat. *homō* (*homō Quintī*, Cic., etc.; cf. deriv. OFr. *homage* > ME, NE *homage*), ON *maðr*, NE *man* (NED s.v., 10), etc.

1. Grk. *ὑπηρέτης*, orig. 'under-rower', cpd. of *ἐρέτης* 'rower, oarsman' : *ἐρέσσω, ἐρέττω* 'row', Skt. *aritra-* 'oar', etc. Boisacq 275.

Grk. *διάκονος* ('servant, messenger, temple-attendant', late 'deacon'), cpd. *διά-κονος* (ᾱ variously explained) : *ἐγ-κονέω* 'be active, make haste', *ἐγ-κονίς* 'maid-servant' (Suid.), *ἀγ-κόνους· διακόνους, δούλους* (Hesych.), *κονέω* 'hasten' (Hesych.), 'serve' (EM). Walde-P. 1.398 f. Boisacq 184, 213.

Grk. *θεράπων* (in Hom. 'attendant'), etym. dub., perh. fr. the same root as *θρησκεία* 'religious worship', etc. : Skt. *dhṛ-* 'hold, support, carry'. Walde-P. 1.857. Boisacq 340 f.

2. Lat. *famulus*, etym. dub. Walde-P. 1.828. Ernout-M. 329 f. Walde-H. 1.452 f.

Lat. *minister*, deriv. of *minor, minus* 'less, smaller' (on the model of *magister* : *magis*). Ernout-M. 617 f.

Lat. *ancilla* (usual fem. to both *servus* and *famulus*, instead of the less common *serva, famula*), deriv. of an obs. *anculus*, this : Grk. *ἀμφίπολος* mostly fem. 'handmaid', both orig. 'one who goes about, is busy with', cpds. of Lat. *am-*, Grk. *ἀμφί* 'about' and the root of Lat. *colere* 'cultivate, dwell' (secondary meanings fr. 'go about, be busy with'), Grk. *πέλομαι* 'become, be', Skt. *car-* 'move, wander, be engaged in', etc. Cf. Osc. *ampu[l]ulum* 'servant', Skt. *abhi-cara-* (rare) and *pari-cara-* 'attendant, servant'. Walde-P. 1.514 f. Ernout-M. 49 f. Walde-H. 1.45.

It. *servo*, fr. Lat. *servus* 'slave' (19.42), whence *servīre* 'be a slave, serve', It. *servire*, Fr., Sp. *servir* with derivs. for 'servant' It. *servitore*, Fr. *serviteur*, Sp. *servidor*, Rum. *servitor*, also (fr. act. pple.) OFr. *servant* (only fem. *servante* now in use), Sp. *sirviente*.

Fr. *domestique*, sb. fr. the adj. *domestique* 'domestic', fr. Lat. *domesticus*, deriv. of *domus* 'house'.

Sp. *criado*, orig. 'one reared' (in the house), fr. *criar* 'raise, rear' (Lat. *creāre* 'create, beget'). REW 2305.

Rum. *slugă* and *slujnic*, fr. Slavic, cf. ChSl. *sluga*, dim. *služĭnikŭ*. Tiktin 1443–44.

3. Ir. *timthirthid*, fr. **to-imb-di-reth-* 'serve' (e.g. perf. *do-d-r-imthirid* 'has served it'), cpd. of *rethim* 'run' (cf. Grk. *ἀμφί-πολος* 'handmaid', Lat. *ancilla*, above, 2). Pedersen 2.598 f.

Ir. *foss*, W. *gwas*, OBr. *guas*, MBr. *goas* (Br. *gwaz* now esp. 'man', 2.21), cf. Gall. *Dago-vassus*, lit. 'Good Servant', MLat. *vasus* 'vassal' (fr. Gall.), prob. fr. **upo-sto-* 'standing under' (: IE **stā-* 'stand'; cf. Skt. *upa-sthāna-* 'standing near, attendance, worship'). Pedersen 1.35. Walde-P. 1.307.

NIr. *seirbhīseach*, orig. adj. 'serviceable, useful', fr. *seirbhīs* 'service, work' (fr. NE *service*).

W. *gweinidog*, fr. *gweini* 'serve' (: Ir. *fo-gnīu* id., cpd. of *gnīu* 'do, perform'). Pedersen 2.545.

Br. *mevel*, prob. fr. **magw-illo-* and so with fem. *matez* (cf. OCorn. *mahtheid* 'virgo', Ir. *ingen maccdaht* 'young full-grown girl', etc.) : Ir. *mug* 'slave' (19.42), etc. Walde-P. 2.228 (without *mevel*). Henry 201. Ernault, Dict. étym. 336.

4. Goth. *andbahts*, OE *ambeht*, OHG *ambaht* (ON only fem. *ambātt*), fr. Celt. **ambaktos* (cf. Gallo-Lat. *ambactus* 'slave, vassal', W. *amaeth* 'farmer, plowman'), fr. a cpd. of *ambi-* 'about' (Ir. *imb-*, etc.) and the root **aĝ-* 'drive'. Walde-P. 1.35. Feist 48 f.

ON *þjōnn*, with vbs. ON *þjōna*, Dan. *tjene*, Sw. *tjäna*, OHG *dionōn*, NHG *dienen*, whence for 'servant' Dan. *tjener*, Sw. *tjänare*, MHG *dienære*, NHG *diener*, or, through sbs. for 'service' (ON *þjōnusta*, OHG *dionost*, etc.), ON *þjōnustumaðr*, MHG *dienestman*, etc., all : Goth. *þius*, etc. 'slave' (19.42). Walde-P. 1.716. Falk-Torp 1266.

OE *þegn*, ME *thain*, also esp. 'military servant, follower, retainer' (NE *thane*) = OHG *degan* 'boy, warrior, hero', ON *þegn* 'freeman' : Grk. *τέκνον* 'child' (2.43). NED s.v. *thane*.

OE *cniht*, OHG, MHG *kneht*, NHG, Du. *knecht*, in the older languages also 'boy', and esp. 'military servant, follower' (NE *knight*), see under 'boy' (2.25).

ME *servaunt*, NE *servant*, fr. OFr. *servant* (above, 2).

5. Lith. *tarnas*, prob. orig. 'young boy' : Skt. *taruṇa-* 'young, tender', as sb. 'boy, girl', Grk. *τέρην* 'tender'. Walde-P. 1.728.

Lith. *bernas* ('young man', esp. 'farm-servant') : Goth. etc. *barn* 'child' (2.27).

Lett. *sulainis*, fr. Esth. *sulane* 'servant'. Mühl.-Endz. 3.1119.

Lett. *kalps*, fr. **cholpŭ*, older form of Russ. *cholop* 'serf, servant' = ChSl. *chlapŭ*, etc. (below, 6). Mühl.-Endz. 2.144.

6. ChSl. *sluga*, etc., general Slavic, as orig. coll. 'household, retainers' : Ir. *sluag* 'host', W. *llu* 'army', Ir. *teglach*, W. *teulu* 'family'. Walde-P. 2.716. Brugmann, IF 19.377 (with refs.).

ChSl. *chlapŭ* (Supr.; SCr. *hlap*, Boh. *chlap*, Pol. *chłop*, Russ. *cholop*, mostly 'peasant, serf'), etym. dub. Berneker 394. Brückner 180 (: Goth. *skalks* 'slave').

7. Skt. *bhṛtya-*, lit. 'one to be supported, maintained' : *bhṛ-* 'carry, support'.

Skt. *sevaka-*, fr. *sev-* 'serve, attend, honor, dwell by', etym.? Uhlenbeck 341.

Skt. *ceṭa*, *ceṭaka-*, prob. MInd. form : *ceṣṭ-* 'be busy with'. Uhlenbeck 93.

Av. *vaēsa-* = Skt. *veça-* 'tenant, dependent, vassal', fr. Av. *vīs-* 'court, (ruler's) dwelling', etc., Skt. *viç-* 'settlement, dwelling', etc. Barth. 1328.

19.44 FREE (adj.)

Grk.	*ἐλεύθερος*	Goth.	*freis*	Lith.	*laisvas, liuosas*
NG	*ἐλεύθερος, λεύτερος*	ON	*frjāls*	Lett.	*brīvs, svabads*
Lat.	*līber*	Dan.	*fri*	ChSl.	*svobodĭ*
It.	*libero*	Sw.	*fri*	SCr.	*slobodan*
Fr.	*libre*	OE	*frēo*	Boh.	*svobodný*
Sp.	*libre*	ME	*fre(e)*	Pol.	*wolny*
Rum.	*liber, slobod*	NE	*free*	Russ.	*svobodnyj, vol'nyj*
Ir.	*sōir, saer*	Du.	*vrij*	Skt.	*svādhīna-*
NIr.	*saor*	OHG	*frī*		
W.	*rhydd*	MHG	*vrī*		
Br.	*frank*	NHG	*frei*		

'Free' is understood here in its primary social and political application to one who is not a slave and enjoys civil liberty. But most of the words have also many of the secondary uses characteristic of NE *free* (NED s.v. 1–32).

These adjectives are the sources of the nouns for 'freedom, liberty' (or conversely in Slavic) and the verbs for 'free, liberate'.

1. Grk. *ἐλεύθερος*, Lat. *līber* (> It. *libero*, Fr., Sp. *libre*; Rum. *liber* neolog.), Pael. *loufir* (cf. Fal. *loferta* 'liberta'), fr. **leudhero-*, prob. deriv. of the stem in OE *lēod*, OHG *liut* 'people, nation' (19.22), hence orig. 'belonging to the nation, native' (vs. 'captive' or 'slave'). Walde-P. 2.417. Ernout-M. 544 f. Walde-H. 1.791 f.

2. Rum. *slobod* (in modern lit. replaced by *liber*), fr. Slavic (below, 6).

MLat. *francus* (It., Sp. *franco*, Fr. *franc*, formerly used for 'free' vs. 'slave', now mostly 'free' in other senses), same word as the name MLat. *Francus*, etc. 'Frank'.

3. Ir. *sōir*, *saer*, NIr. *saor*, beside *dōir*, *daer* 'unfree' (cf. *sōir* et *dōir* Wb. 27c15), cpds. of *so-* 'good' (Skt. *su-*) and *do-* 'bad' (Skt. *dus-*), second part perh. **wiro-* 'man' (Ir. *fer*, etc.). Stokes 280.

W. *rhydd* : Goth. *freis*, etc. (below, 4).

Br. *frank* ('vast, open' and 'free', cf. *frankiz* 'freedom'), fr. Fr. *franc* (above, 2).

4. Goth. *freis*, OE *frēo*, etc., general Gmc. (but only cpd. in ON *frjāls* = *frī-hals* 'free-necked', cf. Goth. *freihals*, OE *frēols* 'freedom', etc.; NIcel. *frī*, Dan., Sw. *fri*, fr. MLG *vrī*, Falk-Torp 273) : Goth. *frijōn* 'love', Skt. *prī-* 'please', *priya-* 'dear', etc., also W. *rhydd* 'free'. Walde-P. 2.86 f. Feist 167 f. Kluge-G. 173. NED s.v. *free*.

5. Lith. *laisvas* : *leisti* 'let, permit' (19.47). Leskien, Ablaut 276, Bildung d. Nom. 344 f.

Lith. *liuosas*, fr. NHG (or LG) *los* 'loose, free'. Alminauskis 81.

Lett. *brīvs*, fr. LG *vrī* (above). Mühl.-Endz. 1.336.

Lett. *svabads* (mostly 'loose, slack, tired', but also = *brīvs*), fr. Slavic, ChSl. *svobodĭ*, etc. (below, 6). Mühl.-Endz. 3.1139.

6. ChSl. *svobodĭ* (indecl.), SCr. *slobodan*, Boh. *svobodný* (Pol. *swobodny* now mostly 'free' = 'at leisure', etc.), Russ. *svobodnyj*, fr. sb. ChSl. *svoboda* 'freedom', etc. : OPruss. *sups*, acc. *subban* 'self, own', Goth. *sibja*, OE *sib(b)* 'kinship, kin', etc., all fr. the pron. stem **s(w)o-*. Walde-P. 2.456. Trautmann 291. Brückner 528.

Pol. *wolny*, Russ. *vol'nyj* : ChSl. *volja* 'will' (cf. Pol. *niewolnik*, Russ. *nevol'nik* 'slave', 19.42).

7. Skt. *svādhīna-* : *svadhā-* 'peculiarity, custom', Grk. *ἔθος* 'custom', etc., fr. the pron. stem **s(w)o-* (cf. ChSl. *svobodĭ*, above, 6).

19.45 COMMAND, ORDER (vbs.)

Grk.	*κελεύω, προστάσσω,* etc.	Goth.	*haitan, anabiudan*	Lith.	*liepti, įsakyti*
		ON	*bjōða*	Lett.	*pavēlēt*
NG	*προστάζω, διατάζω*	Dan.	*befale, byde*	ChSl.	*(po)velěti, zapověděti*
Lat.	*iubēre, imperāre*	Sw.	*befalla, bjuda*	SCr.	*zapovijedati, narediti*
It.	*comandare, ordinare*	OE	*hātan, (ge)bēodan*	Boh.	*nařiditi, rozkázati*
Fr.	*commander, ordonner*	ME	*coma(u)nde, bede, hote, charge*	Pol.	*rozkazać*
Sp.	*mandar, ordenar*			Russ.	*prikazat'*
Rum.	*comanda, ordona, porunci*	NE	*command, order (bid, charge)*	Skt.	*ājñāpaya-, ādiç-, çās-*
				Av., OPers.	*ništā-*
Ir.	*forcongur*	Du.	*bevelen, gebieden*		
NIr.	*ōrdūighim*	OHG	*gibiotan, heizan*		
W.	*gorchymyn*	MHG	*heizen, gebieten*		
Br.	*gourc'hemenn*	NHG	*befehlen, gebieten, heissen*		

Verbs for 'command, order' are based on such diverse semantic sources as 'drive, urge, incite, intrust, arrange, put in order, point out, make known, announce, will', etc., all with acquired imperative force.

1. Grk. *κελεύω*, orig. 'urge, drive on' : *κέλλω* 'drive (a ship to land), put to shore', *κέλης* 'courser', Lat. *celer* 'swift', Skt. *kal-* 'drive', etc. Walde-P. 1.442. Boisacq 431.

Grk. *προστάσσω*, *ἐπιτάσσω*, cpds. of *τάσσω* 'arrange, appoint', esp. 'draw up (an army in battle order)'; similarly *διατάσσω* in class. Grk. chiefly in sense of simple verb 'appoint, draw up', but NG *διατάζω* and *προστάζω* the usual words for 'command'.

2. Lat. *iubēre*, prob. orig. 'set in motion, incite' (cf. Grk. *κελεύω*) : Lith. *judėti* 'move (tremblingly), be in motion', *judinti* 'move' (trans.), Pol. *judzić* 'excite, seduce', Skt. *yudh-* 'fight' (but *ud-yudh-* 'boil up, go off in anger'). Walde-P. 1.204. Ernout-M. 500. Walde-H. 1.725.

Lat. *imperāre*, cpd. of *parāre* 'prepare, procure'; semantic development 'prepare, arrange', whence 'put in order' and thence 'command' (cf. Grk. *προστάσσω*, etc., above, and It. *ordinare*, below). Ernout-M. 478. Walde-H. 1.683.

It. *comandare*, Fr. *commander*, Rum. *comanda* (neolog.), fr. MLat. *commandāre*, for *commendāre* 'intrust, commend to, recommend', cpd. of *mandāre* 'commit to one's charge, enjoin, command' (> Sp. *mandar*), fr. **mandhā-* (cf. Osc. *aamanaffed* 'mandavit'), a cpd. of *man-* = *manus* 'hand' (cf. *man-ceps*, etc.) and a deriv. form of IE **dhē-* 'put'. Ernout-M. 586. Walde-H. 2.24. REW 2084

It. *ordinare*, Fr. *ordonner*, Sp. *ordenar* (Rum. *ordona*, fr. Fr.; native *urdina* in different sense), fr. Lat. *ōrdināre* 'set in order, arrange, appoint', deriv. of *ōrdō* (*-inis*) 'order, rank, class'. Ernout-M. 712. REW 6090.

Rum. *porunci*, fr. the Slavic, cf. ChSl. *porǫčiti* 'trust, charge with' (deriv. of *rǫka* 'hand'. Miklosich 276. Cf. Lat. *mandāre*, above). Tiktin 1218.

3. Ir. *forcongur* (also *forcongrimm*), cpd. (**for-com-gair-*) of *gairim* 'shout, call' (18.13). Pedersen 2.534 f.

NIr. *ōrdūighim*, deriv. of *ōrd* 'order', fr. Lat. *ōrdō* (above). Vendryes, De hib. voc. 162.

W. *gorchymyn*, Br. *gourc'hemenn*, cpds. of Br. *kemenn* 'inform, announce, command' (W. *cymyn* only sb. 'bequest, legacy', orig. 'command'), fr. Lat. *commendāre* (above, 2). Loth, Mots lat. 156 f.

4. Goth. *haitan*, OE *hātan*, ME *hote*, OHG *heizan*, MHG *heizen*, NHG *heissen* = Goth. *haitan* 'call', etc. (18.41).

Goth. *ana-biudan*, ON *bjōða*, Dan. *byde*, Sw. *bjuda*, OE *(ge-) bēodan*, ME *bede* (and by confusion with OE *biddan* 'ask, request', also *bidde*, NE *bid* in this sense, cf. 18.35), Du. *gebieden*, OHG *gibiotan*, MHG, NHG *gebieten*, in North and West Gmc. also 'offer' (so usually the simple verb OHG *biotan*, NHG *bieten*), in OE also 'announce' : Grk. *πυνθάνομαι* 'find out, hear', Lith. *budėti* 'wake', ChSl. *buditi* 'awaken', Skt. *budh-* 'wake, be awake, notice, be aware', etc. Walde-P. 2.147. Falk-Torp 120 f. Feist 41.

ME *coma(u)nde*, NE *command*, fr. OFr. *comander* (Fr. *commander*, above, 2).

ME, NE *charge*, orig. 'load' (fr. OFr. *charger*, late Lat. *carricāre*, deriv. of *carrus* 'car'), formerly very freq. for 'command', esp. in our version of the Bible. NED s.v. *charge*, vb., 14.

NE *order*, fr. ME *ordre* 'arrange, put in order', deriv. of sb. *ordre*, fr. OFr. *ordre*, for earlier *ordene*, fr. Lat. *ōrdō* (*-inis*). NED s.v. REW 6094. Gamillscheg 651.

Du. *bevelen*, NHG *befehlen*, fr. MDu. *bevelen* (MLG also *befalen* > Dan. *befale*, Sw. *befalla*), MHG *bevelhen* 'intrust, commend, charge with', OHG *befelahan* 'give over to, grant, commend', also 'hide, bury' (cf. OE *befēolan* in various senses, including 'be urgent with'; Bosworth-Toller, Suppl. s.v.), simple verb in Goth. *filhan* 'bury, hide', etc. (4.78). Falk-Torp 57. Kluge-G. 45. Weigand-H. 1.178.

5. Lith. *liepti*, *paliepti* : OPruss. *pallaipsitwei* 'desire', *pallaips* 'command', Grk. *λίπτομαι* 'be eager, long for'. Walde-P. 2.404.

Lith. *įsakyti*, cpd. of *į-* 'to' and *sakyti* 'say' (18.22).

Lett. *pavēlēt*, also 'permit, grant', cpd. of *vēlēt* 'wish'.

6. ChSl. *(po)velěti* : *voliti* 'will, prefer', Lat. *velle* 'will, wish', etc. Walde-P. 1.294.

ChSl. *zapověděti*, SCr. *zapovijedati*, cpds. of ChSl. *pověděti*, SCr. *povijedati* 'say, tell' (18.22).

SCr. *narediti*, Boh. *nařiditi*, orig. 'put in order' : SCr. *red*, Boh. *řad*, ChSl. *rędŭ* 'order, arrangement'. Miklosich 276.

Boh. *rozkázati*, Pol. *rozkazać*, Russ. *prikazat'*, cpds. of Boh. *kázati*, Pol. *kazać* 'order, preach', Russ. *kazat'* 'show' (cf. Russ. *skazat'* 'say', 18.22). Berneker 497.

7. Skt. *ājñāpaya-*, lit. 'cause to notice', caus. of *ā-jñā-* 'perceive, notice', cpd. of *jñā-* 'know'.

Skt. *ā-diç-*, lit. 'point out, indicate', cpd. of *diç-* 'point out, show'.

Skt. *çās-*, also general 'rule, govern, punish, correct' = Av. *sāh-* 'command' (cf. *sāstar-* 'ruler'), esp. 'teach' : Arm. *sastem* 'scold, threaten, command'. Walde-P. 1.358.

Av., OPers. *ni-štā-*, lit. 'establish, arrange', cpd. of *ni-* 'down', and *stā-* 'stand, place'. Barth. 1604.

19.46 OBEY

Grk.	*πείθομαι, ἀκούω, ὑπακούω*	Goth.	*ufhausjan*	Lith.	*klausyti*
		ON	*hlȳða, hlȳðnask*	Lett.	*klausīt*
NG	*ὑπακούω, ἀκούω*	Dan.	*lystre, lyde*	ChSl.	*poslušati*
Lat.	*oboedīre, pārēre*	Sw.	*lyda, hörsamma*	SCr.	*slušati*
It.	*obedire*	OE	*hyrsumian*	Boh.	*poslouchati*
Fr.	*obéir*	ME	*obeie, hersumie*	Pol.	*słuchać*
Sp.	*obedecer*	NE	*obey*	Russ.	*slušat'sja*
Rum.	*asculta*	Du.	*gehoorsamen*	Skt.	*anu-vṛt-, anu-ṣṭhā-*
Ir.	*irladigur, gīallaim*	OHG	*hōren, hōrsamōn*		
NIr.	*gēillim*	MHG	*(ge)hōrchen, gehōrsamen*		
W.	*ufuddhau*				
Br.	*senti*	NHG	*gehorchen*		

The majority of the words for 'obey' are the same as, or connected with, words for 'hear' or 'listen'. Other semantic sources are 'be persuaded', 'follow', 'stand by'.

1. Grk. *πείθομαι*, also 'believe', lit. 'persuade oneself, be persuaded', mid. of *πείθω* 'persuade' : Lat. *fīdere* 'trust', *fīdus* 'faithful', etc. (16.65, 17.15).

Grk. *ἀκούω* 'hear' (15.41), but also 'listen to, obey', so already in Hom., and common in pop. NG; cpd. *ὑπακούω* 'listen to, give ear', class. also freq. 'obey' and reg. lit. NG in the latter sense.

2. Lat. *oboedīre* (> It. *obedire*, Fr. *obéir*, Sp. *obedecer*), cpd. of *audīre* 'hear' in an earlier form (15.41), but phonology still difficult. Ernout-M. 86, 693 f. Walde-H. 1.80. REW 6016.

Lat. *pārēre* 'appear, be present', whence 'be present at one's command, obey', perh. : Grk. (rare) *πεπαρεῖν* 'show'. Walde-P. 2.6. Ernout-M. 733.

Rum. *asculta*, fr. Lat. *auscultāre* 'listen' (15.42).

3. Ir. *irladigur* (cf. *no-erladaigtis*, gl. *parebant*, Ml. 16b14, *do aurlatu*, gl. *ad oboediendum* Wb. 3b14, etc.), beside sb. *irlatu* 'obedience', adj. *irlithe* 'obedient', root connection? Thurneysen, Gram. 166. Walde-P. 2.393 (bottom).

MIr. *gīallaim*, *ar-gīallaim*, NIr. *gēillim*, orig. 'serve, be the *gīall* of' (OIr. *giallaid* 'becomes a vassal', Ml. 115d12, etc.), deriv. of *gīall* 'hostage'. Pedersen 2.537 Anm.

W. *ufuddhau*, deriv. of *ufudd*, *ufydd* 'humble, obedient', this fr. Lat. *oboediens* or a blend with *ufyll*, fr. Lat. *humilis*? Cf. Ir. *oibid. i. umal.* Pedersen 1.195, Anm. Loth, Mots lat. 214.

Br. *senti*, fr. Lat. *sentīre* 'feel', with semantic development through 'hear, listen to', cf. It. *sentire* (15.41). Pedersen 1.198.

4. Goth. *ufhausjan*, cpd. of *uf* 'under' (influence of Grk. *ὑπακούω*?) and *hausjan* 'hear', OHG *hōren*, *hōrran* 'hear' and also 'obey' (reg. for *oboedire* in Tat.) = ON *heyra*, OE *hyran*, etc. 'hear' (15.41). Here also OE *hyrsumian*, ME (early) *hersumie*, Du. *gehoorsamen*, OHG *(gi)-hōrsamōn*, MHG *gehōrsamen*, derivs. of OE *(ge)hyrsum*, OHG *(gi)hōrsam* 'obedient'; and MHG *hōrchen*, *gehōrchen*, NHG *gehorchen* < OHG *hōrechen*, OE *heorcian* 'listen' (15.42).

ON *hlȳða*, Dan. *lyde*, Sw. *lyda*, in ON mostly 'listen' (15.42). Here also ON, NIcel. *hlȳðnask* (refl.).

Dan. *lystre* (now more pop. than *lyde*, cf. Dahlerup s.v.), fr. MLG *lūsteren* 'listen, hear' = Du. *luisteren* 'listen', etc. (15.42).

Sw. *hörsamma*, fr. *hörsam* 'obedient', fr. *höra* 'hear'.

ME *obeie*, NE *obey*, fr. Fr. *obéir* (above, 2).

5. Lith. klausyti, Lett. klausīt, lit. 'listen' (15.42).

6. ChSl. poslušati (reg. for ὑπακούω in Gospels), Boh. poslouchati, cpds. of ChSl. slušati, Boh. slouchati 'listen', SCr. slušati, Pol. słuchać 'listen, obey' (SCr. freq. also po-slušati), Russ. slušat' 'listen', refl. slušat'sja 'obey', all orig. 'listen' (15.42).

7. Skt. anu-vṛt-, lit. 'go after, follow', hence 'attend, obey', cpd. of anu- 'after, with', and vṛt- 'turn, move, proceed'.

Skt. anu-ṣṭhā-, lit. 'stand by', hence 'perform, obey', cpd. of anu- (cf. above) and sthā- 'stand'.

19.47 LET, PERMIT

Grk.	ἐάω, ἐφίημι, ἐπιτρέπω	Goth.	lētan, uslaubjan	Lith.	leisti, pavelyti
NG	ἀφίνω, ἐπιτρέπω	ON	lāta, leyfa	Lett.	(at)ḷaut, atvēlēt
Lat.	sinere, patī, permittere	Dan.	tillade	ChSl.	poveḷēti, ostaviti
		Sw.	tillāta	SCr.	dozvoliti
It.	lasciare, permettere	OE	lǣtan, lȳfan, þafian	Boh.	dovoliti, nechati
Fr.	laisser, permettre	ME	leve, lete	Pol.	pozwolić
Sp.	dejar, permitir	NE	let, permit	Russ.	pozvolit', razrešit'
Rum.	lăsa, permite	Du.	toelaten, veroorloven	Skt.	anu-jñā-
Ir.	lēicim, cetaigim	OHG	lāzan, irlouben		
NIr.	leigim, ceaduighim	MHG	lazan, erlouben		
W.	gadael, caniatau	NHG	zulassen, erlauben, gestatten		
Br.	lezel				

Many of the words for 'let, permit' coincide, or are cognate, with those for 'leave' (12.18) or 'let go, release' (11.34), that is, meant originally 'leave free to do'. Other sources are such notions as 'give a place to', 'suffer, endure', 'be well disposed to, trust'. For some special forms meaning 'is permitted, may', like Lat. impers. licet, see 9.96.

1. Grk. ἐάω, fr. *ἐϝάω (cf. ἔβασον ἔασον and εὐα- ἔα Hesych.), etym. dub. Walde-P. 2.472. Boisacq 211.

Grk. ἐφίημι, cpd. of ἵημι 'send, throw' (10.25), hence 'send to, let go, give up' and also 'permit'.

Grk. ἐπιτρέπω, cpd. of τρέπω 'turn' (10.12), hence 'turn over to, intrust', and also 'permit' as reg. in NG.

NG ἀφίνω 'leave' (12.18), also pop. word for 'let, permit'.

2. Lat. sinere, earlier sense 'place', seen in situs 'placed' and the cpd. pōnere 'place' (12.12), but root connections dub. Walde-P. 2.461. Ernout-M. 945 f.

Lat. permittere (> It. permettere, Fr. permettre, Sp. permitir, Rum. permite; NE permit), cpd. of mittere 'send', orig. 'throw, let loose' (10.63), hence 'let go, intrust' and 'let, permit'.

Lat. patī 'suffer, endure' (cf. 16.31), also 'permit', as likewise Fr. souffrir, NE suffer (now arch. or dial. in this use, cf. NED).

It. lasciare, Fr. laisser, Sp. dejar, Rum. lăsa, all 'leave' (12.18) and 'let, permit'.

3. Ir. lēicim, NIr. leigim : Grk. λείπω 'leave', etc. (12.18).

Ir. cetaigim, NIr. ceaduighim, fr. cet 'permission', abbr. of lecet (e.g. Ml. 69a23), this fr. Lat. licet or licitum. K. Meyer, Ber. Preuss. Akad. 1914. 939. Pokorny, Z. celt. Ph. 18.159.

W. caniatau : caniad 'permission, leave', loanword fr. Lat. commeātus 'leave of absence, furlough'. Thurneysen, IF 14.131 f. Pedersen 1.205.

W. gadael, also 'leave' (12.18).

Br. lezel, also 'leave', fr. Fr. laisser (12.18).

4. Goth. lētan, OE lǣtan, NE let, OHG lāzan, etc., general Gmc. 'leave' (12.18), and 'let, permit', with partial dominance of latter sense as in NE let, and esp. cpds. Dan. tillade, Sw. tillāta, Du. toelaten, NHG zulassen.

Goth. uslaubjan, ON leyfa, OE lȳfan, ME leve (cf. NE sb. leave 'permission' and vb. leave in U.S. locally = 'let, permit'), Du. veroorloven, OHG irlouben, MHG erlouben, NHG erlauben : Goth. liufs 'dear', OE lufian 'love', Skt. lubh- 'desire', etc. Sense 'permit', prob. through 'be well disposed to, trust'. Cf. the development of the same root in Goth. galaubjan 'trust, believe', NHG glauben, NE believe, etc. Walde-P. 2.419. Falk-Torp 656 f.

OE þafian (also 'submit to, endure'), perh. : Grk. τόπος 'place' (but no trace of a Gmc. cognate of this), with development as in NHG gestatten (below). Walde-P. 1.743.

NE allow, in some of its uses = permit, ME allowe, fr. OFr. aloer, fr. late Lat. ad-locāre 'allocate, lease', blended with a deriv. of Lat. ad-laudāre 'praise'. NED s.v. Gamillscheg 29.

Du. toestaan, cpd. of staan 'stand', cf. NHG zugestehen 'grant, concede'.

NHG gestatten, fr. MHG gestaten, OHG gistatōn 'fix, establish', deriv. of OHG stata 'standpoint, opportunity', with semantic development through 'give a place, opportunity to'. Weigand-H. 1.708.

5. Lith. leisti, pres. leidžiu 'let go, let loose' and 'let, permit' : Lett. laist 'let loose, let', Goth. lētan 'leave, let', etc. (*lēid- beside *lēd-). Walde-P. 2.395.

Lett. ḷaut, at-ḷaut : Lith. liautis 'cease', Goth. lēwjan 'give over, betray', all fr. a common notion of 'leave, give up'. Walde-P. 2.405. Mühl.-Endz. 2.533.

Lith. duoti 'give' (11.21) is also used for 'permit', likewise ChSl. dati (e.g. Gospels, Mk. 5.19, Lk. 4.41).

6. Lith. pavelyti, Lett. atvēlēt, ChSl. poveḷēti, SCr. dozvoliti, Boh. dovoliti (also po-), Pol. pozwolić (also doz-), Russ. pozvolit', cpds. of Lith. velyti 'wish', ChSl. velěti 'order', etc. : Lat. velle 'wish', etc. Cf. NHG bewilligen 'grant, permit'.

ChSl. ostaviti 'leave' (12.18), also 'permit' (e.g. Mk. 24.43).

Boh. nechati, lit. 'not care, not mind', neg. cpd. of *chati : SCr. hayati 'care, mind'. Berneker 382.

Russ. razrešit' 'resolve, solve' and 'permit', cpd. of rešit' 'resolve, solve, decide' (17.39).

7. Skt. anu-jñā-, cpd. of jñā- 'know, recognize', hence 'give recognition to, assent, permit'.

There seems to be no special Av. vb. for 'permit', but it may be expressed by the use of a modal form of the vb. denoting the action permitted, e.g. kaṭ tā vastra hamyūta (infin.), lit. 'are the clothes to be used?' = 'is it permitted to use the clothes?' Barth. 1810.

19.48 COMPEL

Grk.	ἀναγκάζω, βιάζω	Goth.	nauþjan, baidjan	Lith.	priversti
NG	ἀναγκάζω, βιάζω	ON	nauða, neyða	Lett.	
Lat.	cōgere, compellere	Dan.	twinge, nøde	ChSl.	uvěditi, prinuditi, běditi
It.	forzare, costringere, obligare	Sw.	tvinga, nödga		
Fr.	forcer, contraindre, obliger	OE	nīdan, nēadian, bēdan	SCr.	prisiliti, prinuditi, primorati
		ME	nede, compelle, constreyne, force	Boh.	prinutiti, přimusiti
Sp.	forzar, obligar	NE	compel, force, oblige, make	Pol.	zmusić, znaglić
Rum.	sili, constringe, forța	Du.	dwingen	Russ.	prinudit', zastavit'
Ir.	comēicnigim	OHG	nōtien, beiten	Skt.	causatives
NIr.	cuirim (d'fhiachaibh), cōimhēiginighim	MHG	nōten, dwingen		
W.	gorfod	NHG	zwingen, nōtigen		
Br.	derc'hel, redia				

Words for 'compel' are cognate with words for 'necessity, force, drive, press, bind'. But the notion may also be expressed by verbs for 'put, place' or 'make' in causative use, the latter being in fact the most common expression in NE colloquial speech (make him stop). In Indo-Iranian there is no distinctive verb for 'compel', which is rather expressed by the causative forms. In several modern Eur. languages there is a wealth of terms, with some differences of nuance (ranging from the strong 'force, compel' to the milder 'urge') or style, which are ignored here.

1. Grk. ἀναγκάζω, fr. ἀνάγκη 'necessity' (9.93).

Grk. βιάζω 'force', sometimes = 'compel', as freq. in NG, fr. βία 'force'.

2. Lat. cōgere 'drive together, collect, compress' and 'compel', cpd. of agere 'drive'. Ernout-M. 27.

Lat. compellere 'drive together, collect' hence also 'impel, compel' (> OFr. compeller, Sp. compeler, lit.), cpd. of pellere 'drive'. Ernout-M. 749.

Lat. constringere 'bind together, compress, restrain', sometimes 'compel' (> It. costringere, OFr. constraindre, Fr. contraindre, Sp. constreñir; Rum. constrînge, neolog. after Fr., It.), cpd. of stringere 'bind'. Ernout-M. 988. REW 2173.

It. obligare, Fr. obliger, Sp. obligar, fr. Lat. obligāre 'bind, oblige', cpd. of ligāre 'bind'. Ernout-M. 6012a.

It. forzare, Fr. forcer, Sp. forzar (Rum. forța, neolog. fr. Fr., It.), fr. VLat. *fortiāre fr. *fortia 'strength, force' (It. forza, Fr. force, Sp. fuerza), fr. Lat. fortis 'strong'. REW 3456.

Rum. sili, fr. Slavic, cf. ChSl. siliti, fr. sila 'power' (> Rum. sila 'power, compulsion'). Tiktin 1424.

3. Ir. comēicnigim, NIr. cōimhēiginighim, fr. Ir. ēcen 'necessity, compulsion' (9.93).

NIr. cuirim 'put, place' (12.12), also 'cause' and (esp. cuirim d'fhiachaibh, cf. fiach 'duty, debt') 'compel'.

W. gorfod, orig. 'overcome', cpd. of gor- 'over' and bod 'be'. Morris Jones 268, 352.

Br. derc'hel 'hold' (11.15), also 'compel'.

Br. redia, fr. red 'necessity' (9.93).

4. Goth. nauþjan, ON neyða, Dan. nøde, OE nīdan, nēadian, ME nede, OHG (ga)nōtien, MHG næten, nōten (NHG dial. nōten), fr. Goth. nauþs, etc. 'necessity' (9.93). Also ON nauðga, Sw. nödga, OHG nōtegōn, MHG nōtigen, NHG nötigen (now used esp. in mild sense 'urge, invite'), fr. adj. ON nauðigr, OHG nōteg (NHG nötig). Falk-Torp

782 f. Hellquist 720. Weigand-H. 2.312 f.

Goth. baidjan (ON beiða 'ask, request'), OE bēdan, OHG beiten, etym. disputed, but best : Goth. bidjan, etc. 'ask, request', if latter group orig. of i-series (18.35). Falk-Torp 66. Adversely Feist 74.

NHG zwingen, Du. dwingen, Dan. twinge, Sw. tvinga, fr. OHG dwingan 'press, oppress', late ON þvinga 'oppress', cf. OE twengan, ME twenge 'pinch' (NE twinge), outside connections dub., perh. : Av. θwaz- 'oppress'. Walde-P. 1.748. Falk-Torp 1305. Kluge-G. 723.

NE compel, force, oblige, constrain (now mostly legal or arch. except in be, feel constrained), all, with the ME forms, fr. Fr. (above, 2). NED s.v. But the most common colloquial expression is make, NED s.v. 54.

5. Lith. priversti, cpd. of versti 'turn' (10.12).

Lett. spiest (and prispiest), also and orig. 'press' (9.342).

6. ChSl. uvěditi (reg. for ἀναγκάζω in Gospels), orig. 'make known, command, bid', caus. of věděti 'know'.

ChSl. prinuditi, ponuditi (Supr., etc.), SCr. prinuditi, Boh. (pri)nutiti, Russ. prinudit' : ChSl. nąžda, nužda 'necessity' (9.93). Walde-P. 2.316.

ChSl. běditi, etym. disputed, either (ě = IE ē) : Skt. bādh- 'oppress', or (ě fr. IE oi) : Goth. baidjan (above, 4). Berneker 54. Walde-P. 2.185.

SCr. (pri)siliti : ChSl. sila 'strength, power'.

SCr. primorati : morati 'must' (9.94).

Boh. přimusiti, Pol. zmusić (also musić, przymusić) : Boh. musiti, Pol. musieć 'must' (9.94).

Pol. znaglić (also 'make hurry') : znagła 'suddenly'.

Russ. zastavit', cpd. of stavit' 'put, place'.

7. In Indo-Iranian 'compel' is expressed by the caus. forms.

19.51 FRIEND

Grk.	φίλος	Goth.	frijōnds	Lith.	draugas, bičiulis
NG	φίλος	ON	vinr	Lett.	draugs
Lat.	amīcus	Dan.	ven	ChSl.	drugŭ, prijateljĭ
It.	amico	Sw.	vän	SCr.	prijatelj
Fr.	ami	OE	frēond, wine	Boh.	přítel
Sp.	amigo	ME	frend	Pol.	przyjaciel
Rum.	amic, prieten	NE	friend	Russ.	drug, prijatel'
Ir.	care	Du.	vriend	Skt.	sakhi-, suhṛd-, mitra-
NIr.	cara	OHG	friunt, wini	Av.	urvaθa-, haxi-, frya-
W.	cyfaill	MHG	vriunt, win(e)	OPers.	dauštar-
Br.	mignon	NHG	freund		

Words for 'friend' are most commonly cognate with words for 'love' or 'dear'. Some mean also and more originally 'companion'. A curious Lith. popular term for 'friend' means properly 'beekeeper'.

1. Grk. φίλος, orig. adj. 'dear' (16.28).

2. Lat. amīcus (> Romance words, but Rum. amic neolog.) : amāre 'love' (16.26).

Rum. prieten, fr. Slavic, cf. ChSl. prijateljĭ (below, 6). Tiktin 1252.

3. Ir. care, NIr. cara, orig. pres. pple. (*karant-) of caraim 'love' (16.27). Pedersen 1.244. Thurneysen, Gram. 110, 209.

W. *cyfaill*, old *cyfaillt* = Ir. *com-alta* 'foster-brother', orig. pres. pple. of **com-alim*, cpd. of *alim* 'nourish, rear'. Pedersen 2.35.

Br. *mignon*, fr. Fr. *mignon* 'darling, pet' (REW 5581.2). Henry 203.

4. Goth. *frijōnds*, OE *frēond*, etc., general East and West Gmc., but ON *frœndi* 'relative', orig. pres. pples. of Goth. *frijōn*, OE *frēon*, etc. 'love' (16.27). Feist 168. Weigand-H. 1.583.

ON *vinr*, Dan. *ven*, Sw. *vän*, OE *wine*, OS, OHG *wini*, MHG *win(e)* : Ir. *fine* 'clan', Skt. *van-* 'desire, love, wish, acquire', etc. Walde-P. 1.259. Falk-Torp 1366.

5. Lith. *draugas* (also 'companion'), Lett. *draugs* = ChSl. *drugŭ* (also 'companion', pron. and adj. 'other'), Russ. *drug* (SCr. *drug*; Boh. *drug* 'companion', SCr. *drugi*, etc. 'other') : Goth. *driugan* 'do military service', *ga-drauhts* 'soldier', ON *drōtt*, OE *dryht*, OHG *truht* 'multitude, people, army', etc. Whatever the root and primary sense in this group, 'friend' comes fr. 'companion'. Mühl.-Endz. 1.492. Berneker 230 f.

Lith. *bičiulis* (pop. word for 'bosom-friend'), lit. 'bee-keeper', deriv. of *bitė* 'bee'. The bee-keepers of a neighborhood are bound together in close friendship and form a kind of 'bee-fraternity'. Cf. Žemaitės Raštai 1.231 ff., and Tauta ir Žodis 4.459.

6. ChSl. *drugŭ*, Russ. *drug*, cf. Lith. *draugas* (above).

ChSl. (late) *prijateljĭ*, etc., general modern Slavic, fr. *prijati* 'favor, be well-disposed to' : Goth. *frijōn* 'love', *frijōnds* 'friend', etc., and esp. OHG *friudil*, ON *friðill* 'lover'. Walde-P. 2.87. Meillet, Études 312 f.

7. Skt. *sakhi-*, *sakhā-*, Av. *haxi-*, both also 'companion', etym. dub. (: Skt. *sac-* 'follow', but *kh?*; cpd. of *sa-* 'with'?). Walde-P. 2.476. Uhlenbeck 324. Ernout-M 949.

Skt. *suhṛd-*, lit. 'having a good heart', cpd. of *su-* 'good' and *hṛd-* 'heart'.

Skt. *mitra-* (Vedic 'friend, companion', later mostly 'Mitra') = Av. *miθra-* 'agreement, compact', *Miθra-*, OPers. *Mitra-*, etym. dub., perh. : Skt. *mith-* 'exchange', *mithuna* 'a pair', etc. Walde-P. 2.241. Uhlenbeck 223.

Av. *urvaθa-*, etym. dub., perh. : *var-* 'choose'. Barth 1537.

Av. *frya-*, as adj. 'dear' (16.28).

OPers. *dauštar-* (NPers. *dost*) : Av. *zuš-*, Skt. *juṣ-* 'take pleasure in, enjoy', Av. *zaoša-* 'pleasure', Grk. γεύομαι 'taste, enjoy', etc. (15.31). Barth. 674 f.

19.52 ENEMY

Grk.	*ἐχθρός, πολέμιος*	Goth.	*fijands*	Lith.	*priešas*
NG	*ἐχθρός, πολέμιος*	ON	*fjāndi, ūvinr*	Lett.	*ienaidnieks*
Lat.	*inimīcus, hostis*	Dan.	*fjende, uven*	ChSl.	*vragŭ, neprijateljĭ*
It.	*nimico*	Sw.	*fiende*	SCr.	*neprijatelj, dušmanin*
Fr.	*ennemi*	OE	*fēond, gefā*	Boh.	*nepřítel*
Sp.	*enemigo*	ME	*enemi, fend, fo*	Pol.	*nieprzyjaciel*
Rum.	*duşman*	NE	*enemy (foe)*	Russ.	*vrag (neprijatel', nedrug)*
Ir.	*nāme, escara, ecra*	Du.	*vijand*		
NIr.	*namhaid*	OHG	*fīant*	Skt.	*çatru-, ari-*
W.	*gelyn*	MHG	*vī(e)nt*	Av.	*dušmainyu-, hamərəθa-*
Br.	*enebour*	NHG	*feind*		

Words for 'enemy', as the opposite of 'friend', are in several cases neg. cpds. of those for 'friend'; or are cognate with words for 'hate', parallel to 'friend' from 'loving'. Some are derived from words for 'against' and so had originally the milder sense of 'opponent, adversary'. Another semantic source is 'alien' or

'exile, outcast'. In a Balto-Slavic group of cognates 'enemy' interchanges with 'misery, miserable, slave, devil, murderer', all from a common pejorative 'wretch' or the like.

1. Grk. ἐχθρός, sb. use of adj. ἐχθρός 'hated, hateful' (so Hom.) and 'hating, hostile' (cf. also ἔχθρα, ἔχθος 'hate'), fr. *ἐξ-τρός, deriv. of ἐξ 'out, forth, from', and so orig. 'alien' or 'exile, outcast'. For suffix *-tro-* beside *-tero-*, cf. Skt. advs. like *tatra* 'there', *anyatra* 'elsewhere', etc., and Grk. ἀλλότριος 'belonging to another, foreign', sometimes 'hostile'. Schwyzer, Gr. Gram. 226. E. Hermann, Gött. Nachr. 1918 ff. (otherwise as to suffix). Walde-P. 1.116.

Grk. πολέμιος 'hostile' (fr. πόλεμος 'war') is also used as sb., esp. pl. οἱ πολέμιοι (also ἀντιπολέμιοι, ἀντιπόλεμοι) for 'enemy in war'. Similarly in lit. NG, where sg. πολέμιος is not restricted to 'enemy' in war.

2. Lat. *inimīcus* (> It. *nimico*, Fr. *ennemi*, Sp. *enemigo*), neg. cpd. of *amīcus* 'friend' (19.51).

Lat. *hostis*, orig. 'stranger' (19.55), then the reg. word for 'enemy' in war.

Rum. *duşman* (like Bulg., SCr. *dušman*), fr. Turk. *düşman*, this fr. NPers. *dušman* (cf. Av. *dušmainyu-*, below, 7). Lokotsch 554. Berneker 239.

3. Ir. *nāme*, NIr. *namhaid*, prob. : Alb. *nëmë* 'curse', Grk. νέμεσις 'retribution, righteous anger', fr. the root in Grk. νέμω 'deal out, distribute', Goth. *niman* 'take', etc. Walde-P. 2.331. Stokes 192.

Ir. *escara*, *ecra*, cpd. of **eks-* and *care* 'friend' (19.51). K. Meyer, Ber. Preuss. Akad. 1912. 792.

W. *gelyn*, new sg. to older *gal* (pl. *galon*) : Ir. *gall* 'foreigner', outside connections dub. Walde-P. 1.641. Stokes 108.

Br. *enebour*, deriv. of *enep* 'against' (MBr. *enep* 'face', *a enep* 'against', Ir. *enech* 'face').

4. Goth. *fijands*, OE *fēond*, etc., general Gmc. (but NE *fiend* no longer used in this sense), orig. pples. of Goth. *fijan*, OE *fēon*, etc. 'hate' (16.41).

ON *ūvinr*, Dan. *uven*, neg. cpds. of ON *vinr*, Dan. *ven* 'friend' (19.51).

OE *gefā*, ME *ifo*, *fo*, NE *foe* (now poet. or rhet.), fr. the adj. OE *fāh* 'hostile' : OHG *gifēh* 'hostile', Goth. *bi-faih* 'covetousness', Lith. *piktas* 'angry', Skt. *piçuna-* 'slanderous, wicked', etc. Walde-P. 2.10. NED s.v. *foe*.

ME *enemi*, NE *enemy*, fr. OFr. *enemi* (above, 2).

5. Lith. *priešas*, lit. 'opponent, adversary', but now the preferred word for 'enemy', deriv. of *prieš* 'against'. Cf. OPruss. *prēisiks* 'enemy'.

Lett. *ienaidnieks*, fr. *ienaids* 'enmity, hate', cpd. of *naids* 'hate' (16.41).

6. ChSl. *vragŭ* (reg. for ἐχθρός in Gospels), Russ. *vrag* (fr. ChSl.; genuine Russ. *vorog* not in common use, SCr. *vrag* 'devil', Boh. *vrah* 'murderer', Pol. *wróg* arch. 'foe') : Lith. *vargas*, Lett *vārgs* 'distress, misery', OPruss *wargs* 'evil', Lith. *vergas*, Lett. *vergs* 'slave', prob. also the Gmc. group Goth. *wrikan* 'persecute', OE *wrecan* 'drive, punish', *wrœc*, *wracu* 'suffering, misery', etc. (NE *wreak*, *wretch*, etc.). Walde-P. 1.320. Trautmann 342.

ChSl. *neprijateljĭ*, etc., general Slavic (Russ. *neprijatel'* mostly 'enemy' in war), neg. cpds of ChSl. *prijateljĭ*, etc. 'friend' (19.51).

SCr. *dušman*, now *dušmanin*, fr. Turk. *düşman* (cf. Rum. *duşman*, above, 2).

Russ. *nedrug* (now rather arch.), neg. cpd. of *drug* 'friend' (19.51).

7. Skt. *çatru-*, etym. dub. (perh. : Ir. *cath* 'battle', OHG *Hadu-*, etc., but ChSl. *kotora* with *k*). Walde-P. 1.339. Uhlenbeck 302.

Skt. *ari-* in part 'enemy', but also in other senses ('stranger' in RV according to P. Thieme, Abh. DMG 23.2), etym. dub. Walde-P. 1.136. Uhlenbeck 13.

Av. *dušmainyu-*, as adj. 'hostile', deriv. of *dušmanah-* 'thinking evil, hostile' (cf. Skt. *durmanas-* 'low-spirited, sad', Grk. δυσμενής 'hostile', pl. sb. 'enemies'), cpd. of pejorative prefix **dus-* and **menes-* 'mind'. Walde-P. 2.264. Barth. 754.

Av. *hamərəθa-*, lit. 'meeting', fr. *ham-* 'together' and *ar-* 'reach, come to'. Cf. OPers. *hamarana-* 'battle'. Barth. 1776.

19.53 COMPANION

Grk.	*ἑταῖρος, ἧλιξ, κοινωνός*	Goth.	*gadaila, gahlaiba, gaman*	Lith.	*draugas, bendras*
NG	*σύντροφος*			Lett.	*biedrs*
Lat.	*socius, comes, sodālis*	ON	*fēlagi, nautr*	ChSl.	*drugŭ, obĭštĭnikŭ*
It.	*compagno*	Dan.	*kammerat, ledsager*	SCr.	*drug*
Fr.	*compagnon, camarade*	Sw.	*kamrat*	Boh.	*(sou)druh, společnik*
Sp.	*compañero, camarada*	OE	*gefēra, gesīþ, genēat*	Pol.	*towarzysz*
Rum.	*tovarăş*	ME	*felawe, (y)fere, compainoun, partener*	Russ.	*tovarišč*
Ir.	*cēle*			Skt.	*sahāya-, sahacara-, sakhi-*
NIr.	*compānach*	NE	*companion, comrade*		
W.	*cydymaith*	Du.	*metgezel, makker, kameraad*	Av.	*asti-, haxi-*
Br.	*keneil*				
		OHG	*ginōz, gesello, gasint*		
		MHG	*genōz(e), geselle, gesinde*		
		NHG	*genosse, gefährte*		

Words for 'companion' include derivs. of a pron. stem meaning 'one's own', of verbs for 'follow, attend', of adjs. for 'common', and various cpds. of a prefix for 'with'. Most of the last, and some others, originally denoted, as shown by the earliest use or the cognates, a more specific kind of companionship, as in travel, in military service ('having common rations'), in lodging (lit. 'room-mate'), in business, in bringing up, etc. Thus NE *fellow* is from a compound of a word for 'property, money' and must have first denoted a 'business partner', while conversely a specialization is seen in the current use of NE *partner* in origin simple 'sharer'.

Certain words or groups covering both 'companion' and 'friend' have been discussed under the latter head (19.51), though the development was 'companion' > 'friend'.

1. Grk ἑταῖρος, for ἕταρος (rare), reformed after fem. ἑταίρα, orig. *ἕταιρα fr. *ἕταρια, prob. fr. refl. pron. stem **s(w)o-*, like Grk. ἔτης 'clansman, citizen', Lat *sodālis* 'companion', ChSl. *svatŭ* 'relative', *svobodĭ* 'free', Skt. *svaka-* 'relative', etc. Walde-P. 2.457. Boisacq 291.

Grk. ἧλιξ, Dor. ἇλιξ, esp. 'companion of the same age', fr. *σϝᾶλιξ, prob. fr. refl. pron. stem **swo-* in form **swā-* (cf. Lat. *tālis*, *quālis*). Walde-P. 2.455. Boisacq 320.

Grk. κοινωνός (also κοινών, Dor. κοινᾶν), fr. κοινός 'common' (19.64). Walde-P. 1.458. Boisacq 482.

Grk. σύντροφος, orig. 'one brought up together with' (: συντρέφω 'feed together', mid. 'be brought up together'), then esp. 'foster-brother', in NG 'companion'.

2. Lat. *socius*, fr. **sokʷ-yo-s* : Lat. *sequī*, etc. 'follow'. Walde-P. 2.476 f. Ernout-M. 949.

Lat. *comes* (*-itis*), fr. **com-it-*, cpd. of

com- 'with' and *-i-t-* : *īre* 'go'. Ernout-M. 209.

Lat. *sodālis*, perh. : Grk. ἔθος 'custom, usage', Skt. *svadhā-* 'peculiarity, custom', etc., fr. **swe-dh-*, fr. the refl. pron. stem **s(w)o-*. Walde-P. 2.456. Ernout-M. 950.

It. *compagno*, Fr. *compagnon* (OFr. > ME *compainoun*, *compaignioun*, etc., NE *companion*), Sp. *compaño*, now deriv. *compañero*, fr. MLat. *compānio*, *-ōnis*, cpd. of *com-* 'together', and *pānis* 'bread', orig. a military term modeled on the Gmc., cf. Goth. *gahlaiba* (below). REW 2093. Gamillscheg 240. NED s.v. *companion*.

Sp. *camarada* (> Fr. *camarade* > NE *comrade*, Du. *kameraad*, NHG *kamerad* > Dan. *kammerat*, Sw. *kamrat*), orig. 'chamber-mate', fr. *camara* 'chamber'. REW 1545. NED s.v. *comrade*. Some of the words of this group have an emotional nuance of familiarity, like NE *comrade* vs. the prosaic *companion*, but some are the normal terms for 'companion', as Sw. *kamrat*.

Rum. *tovarăş*, fr. the Slavic, cf. Russ. *tovarišč*, etc. (below, 6). Tiktin 1629.

3. Ir. *cēle*, also 'other' = W. (old) *cilydd* 'fellow' (now *gilydd* 'one another'), etym. disputed. Walde-P. 1.359, 446. Pedersen 1.51.

NIr. *compānach*, with change of suffix fr. NE *companion*.

W. *cydymaith*, fr. MW *cydymdeith*, cpd. of *cyd-* 'co-' and *ymdeith* 'travel'. Cf. NHG *gefährte* (below).

Br. *keneil*, cpd. of *ken-* 'co-' and *eil* 'other, second'.

4. Goth. *gadaila* (renders κοινωνός, etc.), fr. *daila* 'fellowship, partnership' : *dailjan* 'share', etc.

Goth. *gahlaiba* (renders συστρατιώτης 'fellow-soldier', and συμμαθητής 'fellow-disciple'), also *gahlaifs* in dat. pl. (Naples Doc.), lit. 'bread-sharer', cpd. of *hlaifs* 'bread'.

Goth. *gaman* (renders κοινωνός, μέτοχος), lit. 'co-man', cpd. of **man* (in cpds. *mana-* as *manasēþs* 'world') : *manna* 'man'. Feist 192.

ON *fēlagi* (> late OE *fēolaga*, ME *felawe*; NE *fellow* in this sense esp. in cpds. *fellow-student*, etc.), Dan. *fælle* (esp. in cpds.) deriv. of ON *fēlag* 'partnership', cpd. of *fē* 'property, money' and *lag* 'laying'. Falk-Torp 288. NED s.v. *fellow*, sb.

ON *nautr*, in West Gmc. only cpds. OE *genēat*, OHG *ginōz* MHG *genōz*, *genōze*, NHG *genosse* : ON *njōta*, OE *nēotan*, OHG *(gi)niuzan* 'use, enjoy' (9.423) and the cognate ON *naut*, OE *nēat*, OHG *nōz* 'cattle', orig. 'useful property' (3.20); hence prob. 'one who has property in common'. Otherwise semantically, but less prob., Meringer, IF. 234.

Dan. *ledsager* (also and orig. 'guide, attendant'), fr. *ledsage* 'direct, guide, accompany', built on ON *leiðsaga* 'guidance', cpd. of *leið* 'way' (Dan. *led*) and *saga* : *seggja* 'say' (Dan. *sige*). Falk-Torp 628.

Dan. *stalbroder*, Sw. *stallbroder* (latter now 'chum, crony'), fr. MLG *stalbrōder* = MHG *stalbruoder* 'room-mate', cpd. of *stal* 'place, stall' and 'brother', prob. rendering MLat. *constabulārius*. Falk-Torp 1147. Hellquist 1064.

OE *gefēra*, *foera*, ME *yfere*, *fere*, orig. 'traveling companion' : *faran* 'go, fare'. NED s.vv. *yfere*, sb. and *fere*, sb.[1].

OE *gesīþ*, OHG *gasint*, *gisindo*, MHG *gesint*, *gesinde* (NHG *gesinde* coll.), orig. 'traveling companion', as is Goth. *gasinþa* (συνέκδημος) : ON *sinni* 'fellowship, company' : OE *sīþ*, OHG *sint* 'way, journey', Goth. *sinþs* in advs. for 'so many times'. Weigand-H. 1.704 f. Feist 423.

ME *partener*, NE *partner* (now mostly with reference to business or games, but formerly of wider application, as often in the Bible), variant form (influenced by *part*) of *parcener*, fr. OFr. *parcener*, fr. MLat. *partiōnarius*, variant form of deriv. of *pars* 'part'. NED s.v. *partner*.

OHG *gesello*, *gesellio*, MHG *geselle* (NHG *geselle* now esp. 'journeyman'), Du. *gezel*, usually *metgezel* (with *met* 'with'), orig. 'house-companion' : OHG *sal* 'large room, hall, building', NHG *saal*, etc. Weigand-H. 1.703. Paul, Deutsches Wtb. s.v.

Du. *makker*, prob. (with substitution of suffix) : OE *gemæcca* 'mate, consort, husband or wife', (*ge*)*maca* 'mate, equal', OHG *gimahho* id., OE *gemæc* 'equal, well matched', OHG *gimah* 'fit, matched', etc., fr. the root of OE *macian*, OHG *mahhōn*, etc. 'make'. Franck-v. W. 409 f. NED s.v. *make* sb. 1.

NHG *gefährte*, orig. 'traveling companion' (so OHG *giferto*, *gafarto*, MHG *geverte*) : *fahrt*, OHG *fart* 'journey'. Weigand-H. 1.646. Paul, Deutsches Wtb. s.v.

5. Lith. *draugas*, also 'friend', see 19.51.

Lith. *bendras* (also 'partner', as adj. 'common, general'), Lett. *biedrs* : Grk. πενθερός 'father-in-law, relative by marriage', Skt. *bandhu-* 'relative', fr. the root in Skt. *bandh-*, Goth. *bindan*, etc. 'bind'. Walde-P. 2.152. Mühl.-Endz. 1.305 f.

6. ChSl. *drugŭ* (ἑταῖρος Mt. 35.12, etc.), SCr. *drug*, Boh. *druh*, *soudruh*, in ChSl. also 'friend' as Russ. *drug*, see 19.51.

ChSl. *obĭštĭnikŭ* (κοινωνός Mt. 23.30, etc.; Jagić, Entstehungsgesch. 367), deriv. of *obĭštĭnŭ* 'sharing' : *obĭštĭ* 'common' (19.64).

Boh. *společnik* : *spolčiti*, *spojiti* 'bind together, unite' (12.22).

Boh. *tovaryš* (also 'journeyman, assistant'), Pol. *towarzysz*, Russ. *tovarišč*, deriv. of Boh., Russ. *tovar*, Pol. *towar* 'goods, wares' = SCr. *tovar* 'load, burden' (itself of unknown source), with development through 'porter' or 'peddler' (?). Brückner 574.

7. Skt. *sahāya-*, cpd. of *saha-* 'together with' and *aya-* 'going' (: *i-* 'go').

Skt. *sahacara-*, cpd. of *saha-* 'together with' and *cara-* 'moving, going' (*car-* 'move, go').

Skt. *sakhi-* Av. *haxi-* also 'friend', see 19.51.

Av. *asti-*, prob. : Skt. *atithi* 'guest' (fr. *at-* 'go, wander'). Barth. 213. Uhlenbeck 5.

19.54 NEIGHBOR

Grk.	*γείτων*	Goth.	*garazna*	Lith.	*kaimynas*
NG	*γείτονας*	ON	(*nā*)*būi*, (*nā*)*granni*	Lett.	*kaimin'š*
Lat.	*vīcīnus*	Dan.	*nabo*	ChSl.	*sąsědŭ*
It.	*vicino*	Sw.	*granne*	SCr.	*susjed*
Fr.	*voisin*	OE	*nēahgebūr*	Boh.	*soused*
Sp.	*vecino*	ME	*neighebour*	Pol.	*sąsiad*
Rum.	*vecin*	NE	*neighbor*	Russ.	*sosed*
Ir.	*comnessam*, *comarsa*	Du.	*buurman*	Skt.	*prativeçin-*, *prativāsin-*
NIr.	*comharsa*	OHG	(*nāh*)*gibūr*(*o*)		
W.	*cymydog*	MHG	(*nāch*)*gebūr*(*e*)		
Br.	*amezeg*	NHG	*nachbar*		

Words for 'neighbor' are based on such notions as 'dwelling together or near', sometimes simply 'dwelling' or 'next, nearest', and 'of the (same) village or house'.

1. Grk. γείτων, NG pop. γείτονας, beside γείτνιος 'neighboring, adjacent', γειτονία, γειτνία, Ion. γειτνίη 'neighborhood', etc., etym.?

2. Lat. *vīcīnus* (VLat. **vecīnus* > Romance forms), deriv. of *vīcus* 'quarter, street' and 'village' (19.16). Ernout-M. 1103. REW 9312.

3. Ir. *comnessam* 'next, nearest' and 'neighbor', cpd. of *com-* 'with' and *nessam* 'next, nearest'. Thurneysen, Gram. 233.

Ir. *comarsa* (K. Meyer, Contrib. 433), NIr. *comharsa*, perh. cpd. of *ursa* 'doorpost' (cf. NE *next-door neighbor*). Zimmer ap. Macbain 94.

W. *cymydog*, fr. a cpd. of *cy-* 'co-' and *bydio* 'live'.

Br. *amezeg*, adj. *amezek*, MBr. *amnesec*, fr. cpd. of *am*, **ambi* 'about' and *nes* 'near' (cf. Ir. *comnessam*, above). Henry 9. Ernault, Dict. étym. 203.

4. Goth. *garazna*, ON *granni* (and cpd. *nāgranni* with *nā* 'near'), Sw. *granne*, fr. Goth. *razn*, ON *rann* 'house' (7.12). Feist 197.

ON *būi*, lit. 'a dweller' (in cpds.), but commonly 'neighbor' (esp. 'a neighbor acting as a juror'), also cpd. *nā-būi* (with *nā* 'near'), Dan. *nabo*; in West Gmc., OE *gebūr*, OHG *gibūr*(*o*), MHG *gebūr*(*e*) 'dweller, husbandman', but in OHG and MHG also 'neighbor', beside the cpds. (with *nēah*, etc. 'near') OE *nēahgebūr*, ME *neighebour*, NE *neighbor*, OHG *nāhgibūr*(*o*), MHG *nāchgebūr*(*e*), NHG *nachbar;* Du. *buur* but more commonly cpd. *buurman* (fem. *buurvrouw*) : Goth. *bauan*, ON *būa*, OE, OHG *būan* 'dwell' (7.11). Falk-Torp 752. Weigand-H. 2.253 f. Franck-v. W. 100 f.

5. Lith. *kaimynas*, Lett. *kaimin'š* : Lith. *kaimas* 'village, country', *kiemas* 'court, farmyard', Lett. *ciems* 'village', etc. (19.16). Mühl.-Endz. 2.133.

6. ChSl. *sąsědŭ*, etc., general Slavic, cpd. of *są-* 'with' and *sědŭ* pple. of *sędą*, *sěsti* 'sit'. Cf. Skt. *saṁsad-* 'assembly'. Walde-P. 2.490.

7. Skt. *prativeçin-*, *prativeça-*, cpds. of *prati-* 'toward, near, against' and *veçin-*, *veça-*, lit. 'settler' : *viç-* 'settle down on, enter, resort to', etc.

Skt. *prativāsin-* : *prati-vas-* 'live, dwell', cpd. of *prati-* and *vas-* 'dwell, remain'.

19.55 STRANGER

Grk.	*ξένος*	Goth.	*gasts*	Lith.	*svetimas*
NG	*ξένος*	ON	*gestr*	Lett.	*svešinieks*
Lat.	*peregrīnus*, *hospes*, *advena*	Dan.	*fremmed*	ChSl.	*stranĭnŭ*
		Sw.	*främling*	SCr.	*stranac*, *tuđinac*
It.	*forestiere*, *straniero*	OE	*cuma*, *giest*	Boh.	*cizinec*
Fr.	*étranger*	ME	*strangere*, *gest*	Pol.	*cudzoziemiec*
Sp.	*extranjero*	NE	*stranger*	Russ.	*čužoj*
Rum.	*străin*	Du.	*vreemdeling*	Skt.	*vaideçika-*, *videçin-*
Ir.	*echtrann*	OHG	*gast*		
NIr.	*duine iasachta*	MHG	*gast*, *vremdelinc*		
W.	*dieithr*, *estron*	NHG	*fremde*(*r*), *fremdling*		
Br.	*estren*, *diavesiad*, *divroad*				

Owing to their mutual relations, there is much interchange between 'stranger', 'guest', and 'host', especially in the large inherited group, the ultimate root connection of which is quite uncertain. But in such cases it is safe to say that the development was 'stranger' > 'guest' > 'host'.

Outside the inherited group, words for 'stranger' are mostly derived from words for 'from away, outside' or from words for 'country, region' or 'people, nation' with 'other' expressed or understood.

1. IE **ghosti-*. Walde-P. 1.640 f. Ernout-M. 462, 463. Walde-H. 1.660 f., 662 f.

Lat. *hostis*, arch. 'stranger', class. 'enemy', hence *hospes* gen. *hospitis* (**hosti-potis*, last member : Skt. *pati-* 'master', etc. 19.41), orig. 'host', by extension 'guest, stranger' (> It. *ospite*, OFr. *oste*, Fr. *hôte*, Sp. *huesped* 'host' and 'guest', Rum. *oaspe* 'guest'); Goth. *gasts* (renders ξένος but only as 'stranger'), ON *gestr*, OE *giest*, *gist*, ME *gest*, OHG, MHG *gast* 'stranger, guest' (NE *guest*, NHG *gast* 'guest'); ChSl. *gostĭ*, etc. general Slavic, only 'guest'.

Here possibly also Grk. ξένος, Ion. ξεῖνος, Corcyr. ξένϝος as **ghs-enwo-s*. Boisacq 677 f. Walde-H. 1.662 f.

2. Lat. *peregrīnus*, deriv. of *peregrī* 'abroad, away from home', cpd. of *per* 'through' and *ager* 'field, district'. Ernout-M. 22 f.

Lat. *advena* : *advenīre* 'come to, arrive'.

It. *forestiere*, fr. Prov. *forestier* id., deriv. of VLat. **forasticus* 'from the outside', fr. Lat. *foras* 'out of doors, forth, out'. REW 3432.

It. *straniero*, Fr. *étranger* (> Sp. *extranjero*), derivs. of It. *strano*, Fr. *étrange* 'strange', fr. Lat. *extrāneus* (mostly post-Aug.) 'external, strange, foreign', also sb. 'stranger' : *extrā* 'on the outside, without', *exter* 'from without, foreign, strange', etc. Ernout-M. 313. REW 3098.

Rum. *străin*, prob. (not : group above, but) fr. ChSl. *stranĭnŭ* (below, 6). Puşcariu 1651. REW 3098.

3. Ir. *echtrann*, either native deriv. of *echtar* 'outside' (: Lat. *extrā*, etc.) influenced by Lat. *extrāneus*, or directly fr. the latter. Pedersen 2.257. Vendryes, De hib. voc. 137.

NIr. *duine iasachta*, lit. 'strange man'; *iasachta* 'strange, foreign', lit. 'loaned', fr. *iasacht* 'loan' (cf. Laws, Gloss. 468).

W. *dieithr*, fr. MW *dieithyr* 'outside', cpd. of OW *di* 'from' and *eithr* 'beyond' (now 'except, without') : Ir. *echtar*, etc. (cf. above).

W. *estron*, Br. *estren*, fr. Lat. *extrāneus* (above, 2). Loth, Mots lat. 165.

Br. *estranjour*, fr. OFr. *estrange*, Fr. *étranger* (above, 2).

Br. *diavesiad*, deriv. of *diavaez* 'outside', cpd. of *di-* (= OW *di*, cf. above), *a-* 'from, to' and *maez* 'field, plain' esp. in sense of 'country' vs. 'town' (19.13). Henry 95. Ernault, Glossaire 162.

Br. *divroad*, cpd. of *di-* (cf. above) and deriv. of *bro* 'country' (19.11) Cf. *broad* 'countryman'.

4. Goth. *gasts*, ON *gestr*, etc., general Gmc., above, 1.

Goth. *framaþeis*, OE *frem*(*e*)*de*, ME *fremde*, OHG *framadi*, MHG *vrem*(*e*)*de*, NHG *fremd*, Du. *vreemd*, MLG *vremede* (> Dan. *fremmed*), all adjs. 'strange, foreign', fr. Goth., OHG *fram*, OE *from* 'from, away'. Hence sbs. MHG *vremdelinc*, NHG *fremdling* (> Sw. *främling*), Du. *vreemdeling*, and NHG *fremde*, Dan. *fremmed*. Falk-Torp 273. Weigand-H. 1.528. NED s.v. *fremd*.

OE *cuma*, lit. 'a comer' : *cuman* 'come' (cf. Lat. *advena*, above, 2).

ME *strangere*, NE *stranger*, fr. OFr. *estrangier* (Fr. *étranger*, above, 2).

5. Lith. *svetimas* (adj. and sb.), Lett. *svešinieks*, beside Lith. *svečias* 'guest' (earlier also 'stranger'), Lett. *svešs* 'strange, foreign', prob. as orig. 'by oneself, apart', fr. the pron. stem **swo-* 'one's own' (cf. Grk. ἑκάς 'afar', fr. the same stem). Walde-P. 2.457. Mühl.-Endz. 3.1151, 1152.

6. ChSl. *stranĭnŭ*, SCr. *stranac* : ChSl. *strana* 'region' (19.41).

SCr. *tuđinac*, Boh. *cizinec*, Pol. *cudzoziemiec*, Russ. *čužoj*, fr. the adjs. SCr. *tuđ*, Boh. *cizí*, Pol. *cudzy*, Russ. *čužoj*, ChSl. *tuždĭ*, *štuždĭ* 'foreign, strange', fr. a Slavic **tjudjĭ* (by dissim. **tudjĭ*), fr. the Gmc., Goth. *þiuda* 'people, nation', etc. (19.22), with development 'Germanic' > 'foreign, strange'. Meillet, Études 175. Walde-P. 1.712. Stender-Petersen 187 f.

Pol. *obcy* (mostly adj.), prob. fr. *obec* in *w obec* 'in one's presence' = Boh. *obec* 'community' (fr. *ob* 'about'), but semantic development not clear. Brückner 369.

7. Skt. *vaideçika-*, *videçin-*, derivs. of *videça-* 'another country, foreign country', cpd. of *deça-* 'country' (19.11).

19.56 GUEST

Grk.	*ξένος*	Goth.	. . . .	Lith.	*svečias*
NG	*ξένος*, *μουσαφίρης*	ON	*gestr*	Lett.	*viesis*, *ciemin'š*
Lat.	*hospes*	Dan.	*gæst*	ChSl.	*gostĭ*
It.	*ospite*	Sw.	*gäst*	SCr.	*gost*
Fr.	*hôte*	OE	*giest*	Boh.	*host*
Sp.	*huésped*	ME	*gest*	Pol.	*gość*
Rum.	*oaspe*(*te*), *mosafir*	NE	*guest*	Russ.	*gost'*
Ir.	*ōegi*	Du.	*gast*	Skt.	*atithi-*
NIr.	*aoighe*	OHG	*gast*		
W.	*gwestai*	MHG	*gast*		
Br.	*ostiziad*	NHG	*gast*		

Most of the words for 'guest' are the same as, or cognate with, those once meaning also and more originally 'stranger', and included in the discussion of the latter. They have persisted more widely in the sense of 'guest'. The few others are (like NE *visitor* freq. = *guest*) based on expressions for 'visit, go visiting', these partly from 'go' or 'village'.

1. Words discussed under 'stranger' (19.55).

Grk. ξένος, Lat. *hospes* (> Romance words), OE *giest*, etc., general Gmc., ChSl. *gostĭ*, etc., general Slavic, Lith. *svečias*.

2. NG μουσαφίρης, Rum. *mosafir*, fr. Turk. *müsafir*, fr. Arab. *musāfir* 'voyager, guest'. Lokotsch 1510a.

3. Ir. *ōegi*, NIr. *aoighe*, perh. : Grk. οἴχομαι 'go away', Arm. *ej* 'descent', *ijamen* 'descend', cf. esp. *ijavor* 'guest'. Walde-P. 1.104. Pedersen 1.101.

W. *gwestai*, fr. *gwesta* 'visit' : *gwest* 'inn, lodging, feast', Ir. *feis* 'feast', etc. Walde-P. 1.308. Pedersen 1.80, 2.23.

Br. *ostiziad*, deriv. of *ostiz* 'host' (19.51).

4. Lett. *viesis*, fem. *viešn'a* = Lith. *viešnė* 'female guest'; cf. also vbs. Lith. *viešėti*, Lett. *viešuot* 'be on a visit, be a guest' : Lith. *vieš-pats* 'Lord, sovereign', Goth. *weihs*, Lat. *vīcus* 'village', etc. (19.16). Mühl.-Endz. 4.669 f. Walde-P. 1.231.

Lett. *ciemin'š*, fr. *ciems* 'village' (19.16). Cf. *ciema iet* 'go on a visit', like NHG dial. *ze dorfe gehen* (Grimm 2.1277). Mühl.-Endz. 1.393, 394.

5. Skt. *atithi-* lit. 'wanderer' : *at-* 'go, walk, wander'. Uhlenbeck 5.

19.57 HOST

Grk.	*ξενοδόκος, ξένος*	Goth.	*wairdus*	Lith.	*šeimininkas*
NG	*οἰκοδεσπότης (ξενοδόχος)*	ON	*hūsbōndi, gestgjafi*	Lett.	*saimnieks*
		Dan.	*vært*	ChSl.	*gostinĭnikŭ*
Lat.	*hospes*	Sw.	*värd*	SCr.	*domaćin*
It.	*ospite*	OE	. . . .	Boh.	*hostitel*
Fr.	*hôte*	ME	*hoste*	Pol.	*gospodarz*
Sp.	*huésped*	NE	*host*	Russ.	*chozjain*
Rum.	*gazdă*	Du.	*gastheer (waard)*	Skt.	*gṛhastha-, atithipati-*
Ir.	*biatach*	OHG	*wirt*		
NIr.	*fear tighe (ōstōir)*	MHG	*wirt, gastgebe(r)*		
W.	*(lletywr)*	NHG	*wirt, gastgeber*		
Br.	*ostiz*				

'Host', as the correlative of 'guest', is sometimes expressed by the same word, but more often by a cpd. or deriv. as 'one who receives guests'. Other terms are from 'master of the house' used with a reference to his position as 'host', or (the Gmc. group) of doubtful source.

'Host' covered the public host 'innkeeper', and in some cases this has become the most familiar or even the only current use (shown in the list by parenthesis).

1. Grk. ξένος 'stranger' (19.55), 'guest', and sometimes 'host' (as Hom. Il. 15.532, NT Rom. 16.23), but for 'host' usually ξενοδόκος, later -δόχος, 'one who receives guests', cpd. with the root of δέκομαι, Att. δέχομαι 'receive'.

NG ξενοδόχος, now only 'innkeeper' (cf. ξενοδοχεῖον 'hotel'). For 'host' in social sense οἰκοδεσπότης, lit. 'master of the house'.

2. Lat. *hospes, -itis*, It. *ospite*, etc. 'host' and 'guest', see 19.55.

Rum. *gazdă*, fr. Hung. *gazda* 'master, landlord, innkeeper'. Tiktin 667.

3. Ir. (perh. nearest approach to 'host') *biatach*, lit. 'a victualer' ('a sort of public victualer . . . who was bound to entertain travellers and the chief's soldiers whenever they came that way', Joyce, Soc. Hist. 2.174) : *biathaim* 'feed, nourish'.

NIr. *ōstōir* 'innkeeper', fr. *ōsta* 'lodging, inn', this fr. ME *ooste, oste* id. (NED s.v. *host* sb.³). Otherwise 'host' expressed by *fear tighe* 'man of the home', or by some other phrase.

W. *lletywr* 'lodger, innkeeper' (also 'host' in wider sense in NT Rom. 16.23; but now?), cpd. of *llety* 'inn, lodging' and *gwr* 'man'. Other current W. word for social 'host'?

Br. *ostiz*, prob. fr. OFr. *ostisse, hostise* 'habitation, tenure d'hôtes'. Loth, Mots lat. 191.

4. Goth. *wairdus*, OHG, MHG, NHG *wirt*, OS *wert*, Du. *waard* (MLG *wert* > Dan. *wært*, Sw. *värd*), perh. : ON *verðr* 'meal', MHG *urte, ürte* 'bill, account', but root connection (as : OHG *bewarōn* 'keep', etc., or : OHG *(gi)werēn* 'grant, perform', etc.) wholly doubtful. Walde-P. 1.285. Falk-Torp 1371. Feist 545. Weigand-H. 2.1274. Kluge-G. 694.

ON *hūsbōndi* 'master of the house, husband', but freq. of the master of the house where a guest stays (cf. Fritzner s.v. 2).

ON *gestgjafi* (late and rare), cpd. of *gestr* 'guest' and last member : *gjǫf* 'gift'. Probably reflection of the custom of giving presents to departing guests (cf. Vigfusson, s.v.).

OE word for 'host'? In the Gospels Lk. 10.35 *lǣc* 'physician' substituted for 'host' (as Lk. 10.34 *lǣcehūs* 'hospital' instead of 'inn').

ME *oste, hoste* (rarely also 'guest'), NE *host*, fr. OFr. *(h)oste* (above, 2).

Du. *gastheer*, lit. 'guest lord'.

MHG, NHG *gastgeber*, orig. 'one who gives a banquet' (*gastmahl*).

5. Lith. *šeimininkas*, Lett. *saimnieks*, lit. 'master of the house' : Lith. *šeimyna, šeima*, Lett. *saimė* 'family' (2.82).

6. ChSl. *gostinĭnikŭ* (πανδοχεύς 'host' = 'innkeeper', Lk. 10.35), Boh. *hostitel* : ChSl. *gostĭ*, etc. 'guest' (19.56).

SCr. *domaćin*, lit. 'master of the house', fr. *dom* 'house'. Berneker 210.

Pol. *gospodarz* = SCr. *gospodar*, etc. 'master' (19.41). Berneker 335.

Russ. *chozjain* 'master' (19.41) and 'host'.

7. Skt. *gṛhastha-* 'householder, married Brahman conducting his own household', often used (Gṛhyasutras) with especial reference to his duties as 'host', similarly sometimes also *gṛhin-*, both fr. *gṛha-* 'house'.

Skt. *atithipati-*, lit. 'lord of guests' (but only AV 9.6 on the entertainment of guests).

19.58 HELP, AID (vbs.)

Grk.	*βοηθέω, ὠφελέω, ἐπικουρέω, ἀρήγω*	Goth.	*hilpan*	Lith.	*gelbėti, padėti*
		ON	*duga, hjalpa*	Lett.	*palīdzēt*
NG	*βοηθῶ*	Dan.	*hjælpe*	ChSl.	*pomošti*
Lat.	*(ad)iuvāre, adiūtare, succurrere, auxilium ferre*, etc.	Sw.	*hjälpa*	SCr.	*pomoći*
		OE	*helpan*	Boh.	*pomoci*
		ME	*helpe, socoure, ayde*	Pol.	*pomodz*
It.	*aiutare, soccorrere, giovare*	NE	*help, aid, assist (succor)*	Russ.	*pomoč'*
				Skt.	*av-*
Fr.	*aider, secourir*	Du.	*helpen*	Av.	*av-*
Sp.	*ayudar*	OHG	*helfan*		
Rum.	*ajuta*	MHG	*helfen*		
Ir.	*fortiag, foreith, cobraim*	NHG	*helfen*		
NIr.	*cabhruighim, fōirim, cuidighim*				
W.	*cymorth, cynnorthwyo*				
Br.	*skoazia*				

Verbs for 'help' are based on such varied notions as 'go, come, or run to', 'stand by', 'bring with, support', 'take part', 'be able, avail', etc. Some were used first with reference to military aid. But for some of the most important words there is no helpful etymology.

Sometimes there is a differentiation between 'help' to gain something and 'help' out of difficulty (It. *aiutare*, Fr. *aider* vs. *soccorrere, secourir*), those with the latter nuance verging on 'save, rescue'.

Apart from the words listed, 'help' in a particular action may be expressed by cpds. with 'with' (Grk. συλ-λαμβάνω, συμ-πράσσω, συμ-μαχέω, etc.), and such words are sometimes used also for the more generic 'help'.

The use of NE *help* in the sense of 'prevent, avoid' (*I can't help laughing*) is a peculiar development (cf. NED s.v. 11) with which we are not concerned here.

1. Grk. βοηθέω, fr. βοᾱθοέω (attested in Dor.), deriv. of βοηθόος, cpd. of βοή 'cry, shout' in Hom. esp. 'battle-cry' and θοός 'quick, swift', hence in Hom. 'quick to the cry, hastening to battle', later 'helping' and 'helper'. Cf. βοη-δρόμος 'helping'. Walde-P. 1.834. Boisacq 125.

Grk. ὠφελέω 'help', esp. as 'be of serv-

ice', deriv. of ὄφελος 'advantage, help' : Skt. *phala-* 'fruit, result, advantage', etc. Walde-P. 2.102. Boisacq 732.

Grk. ἐπικουρέω, deriv. of ἐπίκουρος 'helper, ally', cpd. with second part fr. *-κορσος : Lat. *currere* 'run', *cursus* 'course', OE *hors* 'horse', etc. Walde-P. 1.428. Boisacq 266. Walde-H. 1.315.

Grk. ἀρήγω, with ἀρωγός 'helping, helper' (both mostly poet., Hom.+), perh. : ON *rækja*, OE *reccan*, etc. 'take care of, heed', fr. strong grade of the root in Lat. *regere* 'direct', etc. Walde-P. 2.365. Boisacq 76 f.

2. Lat. *iuvāre* (> It. *giovare* 'help' in special uses, 'be of service, be suitable', etc.), *adiuvāre, adiūtāre* (> It. *aiutare*, Fr. *aider*, Sp. *ayudar*, Rum. *ajuta*), root connection dub. (*iuvāre* also 'please', cf. *iūcundus* 'pleasant'). Walde-P. 1.201. Ernout-M. 509 f. Walde-H. 1.736 f. Specht, KZ 65.207 f., 68.52 ff. (: Skt. *av-* 'favor'). REW 172, 4638.

Lat. *succurrere* (> It. *soccorrere*, Fr. *secourir;* Sp. *socorrer* not in common use), lit. 'run to' (one's help), cpd. of *currere* 'run', cf. *subvenīre* 'come to' and esp. 'help'. Ernout-M. 247. REW 8412.

Lat. *auxilium*, the main sb. for 'help, aid' (whence phrases *auxilio esse, auxilium ferre* for 'help' vb.), orig. military 'reinforcement' : *augēre* 'increase'. Ernout-M. 90. Walde-H. 1.89.

3. Ir. *fortiag*, cpd. of *tiagu* 'go'. Pedersen 2.643.

Ir. *foreith*, cpd. of *rethim* 'run'. Hence NIr. *fōirim*. Pedersen 2.599.

Ir. *cobraim*, NIr. *cabhruighim*, deriv. of sb. *cobair*, NIr. *cabhair* 'help', cpd. of *co-* 'with' and the root of *berim* 'bear'. Pedersen 1.119.

NIr. *cuidighim*, deriv. of *cuid*, Ir. *cuit* 'share, part' (13.23).

W. *cymorth*, cpd. of *cyn-* 'co-' and (arch.) *porthi* 'support, help', fr. Lat. *portāre* 'carry'. Loth, Mots lat. 198.

W. *cy(n)northwyo*, fr. sb. *cynhorthwy*, MW *canhorthwy*, perh. as **canh-or-thwy*, cpd. of OW *cant* 'with', *or* = Ir. *for*, and the root of Ir. *tiagu* 'go' (cf. Ir. *fortiag*, above). J. Lloyd Jones, Z. celt. Ph. 8.242 ff. Pedersen 2.648.

Br. *skoazia*, fr. *skoaz* 'shoulder' (4.30), with semantic development through 'lend a shoulder, support'. Like and prob. influenced by the similar fig. use of Fr. *épauler*.

4. Goth. *hilpan*, ON *hjalpa* (but mostly 'help' in sense of 'save, rescue'), OE *helpan*, OHG *helfan*, etc., general Gmc., without outside connections except Lith. *šelpti* 'help, support', OLith. refl. *šelbinos*. Walde-P. 1.447. Falk-Torp 413. Feist 255 f.

ON *duga* 'do one's best, be of service', but most commonly 'help' : OE *dugan* 'avail, be of use, be strong' (NE dial. *dow*), Goth. *dugan* 'be of use', etc. (NHG *taugen*). Walde-P. 1.847. Falk-Torp 163. NED s.v. *dow*.

ME *socoure*, NE *succor* (now only lit.), fr. OFr. *socorre* = Fr. *secourir* (above, 2). NED s.v.

ME *ayde*, NE *aid*, fr. Fr. *aider* (above, 2).

NE *assist*, formerly also 'stand by, be present', fr. Fr. *assister*, fr. Lat. *adsistere* 'take a stand' and sometimes 'stand by, defend, aid'. NED s.v.

5. Lith. *gelbėti*, OPruss. *galbimai* (1pl. subj.), beside Lith. *gilbti* 'be in good health, get well', outside connections dub. Walde-P. 1.116.

Lith. *padėti* 'put in place' and 'help', cpd. of *dėti* 'place'.

Lett. *palīdzēt*, also less commonly *līdzēt*, fr. adv. *līdz* 'like' : Lith. *lygus* 'like', etc. Semantic development through 'be equal to, avail' (cf. ChSl. *pomošti*, etc.)? Mühl.-Endz. 2.480.

6. ChSl. *pomošti*, SCr. *pomoći*, etc., general Slavic, cpd. of ChSl. *mošti*, etc. 'be able' (9.95). Development through 'avail, be of service'. Berneker 2.67 f.

7. Skt. *av-* 'enjoy, be kind, favor' and 'help', Av. *av-* 'care for, help' (Barth. 162), with sbs. Skt. *avas-* 'enjoyment, favor, help', Av. *avah-* (Barth. 178) : Lat. *avēre* 'long for', etc. Walde-P. 1.19. Walde-H. 1.81.

19.59 HINDER, PREVENT

Grk.	*κωλύω, ἐμποδίζω*	Goth.	*warjan, ga-, ana-latjan*	Lith.	*kliudyti, trukdyti*
NG	*ἐμποδίζω, κωλύω* (lit.)			Lett.	*kavēt*
Lat.	*impedīre, obstāre, prohibēre*	ON	*hindra, letja*	ChSl.	*(vŭz)braniti*
		Dan.	*(for)hindre, hemme, forbygge*	SCr.	*prijećiti, smetati*
It.	*impedire*			Boh.	*překažeti, předejiti*
Fr.	*empêcher*	Sw.	*(för)hindra, hämme, förekomma*	Pol.	*przeszkodzić, zapobiedz*
Sp.	*impedir*				
Rum.	*împiedeca, opri*	OE	*lettan, hindrian*	Russ.	*mešat', prepjatstvovat'*
Ir.	*derban* (3sg.), *coscaim, baccaim*	ME	*lette, hindre*	Skt.	*rudh-, vṛ-*
		NE	*hinder, prevent*	Av.	*rud-*
NIr.	*bacaim, coiscim, toirmeascaim*	Du.	*(ver)hinderen, beletten, voorkomen*		
W.	*rhwystro, atal*	OHG	*hinderen*		
Br.	*herzel, mirout*	MHG	*(ver)hindern*		
		NHG	*(ver)hindern, hemmen, vorbeugen*		

Although 'hinder' and the conclusive or perfective 'prevent' are clearly differentiated in NE *hinder* vs. *prevent* (which are hardly associated in linguistic consciousness), they are more commonly expressed by the same word.

Most of the words originally denoted some more specific impeding or preventive action, e.g. 'fetter, lame, bind, confine, stand in the way, hold back, ward off, delay, mix' (hence 'disturb'), etc. Some mean literally 'come before' or 'be before', hence 'anticipate, forestall' and 'prevent'. The variety of expressions is so great that it is sometimes difficult to judge which are the most generic.

1. Grk. κωλύω, etym. dub., perh. fr. a *κῶλος = σκῶλος 'stake' (cf. Lith. *kuolas* 'stake'), and orig. 'fasten' a domestic animal (but there is no trace of such literal meaning). Walde-P. 2.591. Boisacq 543.

Grk. ἐμποδίζω, orig. 'catch by the foot, fetter', with adj. ἐμπόδιος, adv. ἐμποδών, orig. 'under foot, in the way', cpds. of πούς, ποδός 'foot'.

Grk. ἐγκόπτω (cpd. of κόπτω 'cut, smite') is in late use 'interrupt, hinder' (NT, etc.).

2. Lat. *impedīre* (> It. *impedire*, Sp. *impedir;* latter restored form; OSp. *empecer* 'injure'), orig. 'fetter' (by the foot, then also 'entangle' by the horns, 'ensnare' by nets, etc.), deriv. of *pēs, pedis* 'foot'. Mostly replaced in VLat. by *impedicāre* (> OIt. *impedicare*, Fr. *empêcher*, Rum. *împiedeca*), fr. *pedica* 'fetter'. Ernout-M. 760. REW 4296, -98.

Lat. *obstāre* (> Fr. *ôter* 'remove, deprive'; deriv. *obstāculum* > It. *ostacolo*, OFr. *ostacle, obstacle* > ME, NE *obstacle*), lit. 'stand in the way of', cpd. of *stāre* 'stand' and *ob* as in adv. *obviam*, adj. *obvius* 'in the way'. Ernout-M. 982.

Lat. *prohibēre* 'hold back, hinder, prevent', also 'forbid', cpd. of *habēre* 'hold, have'. Ernout-M. 441.

Rum. *opri*, 'withhold, hinder, forbid', fr. Slavic, late ChSl. *oprěti*, SCr. *oprijeti* 'oppose' (cf. Boh., Pol. *odpor* 'resistance'), cpd. of ChSl. *p(ĭ)rěti sę* 'contend, dispute' (cf. *pĭrja* 'strife', 19.62). Tiktin 1091.

3. Ir. *derban* (3sg.), fr. **di-ro-ben-*, opposite of *torban* 'is of service, promotes', OIr. *dororban* 'proficit', fr. **to-ro-ben-*, cpd. of *ben-* 'be', used like Lat. *prō-sum, prōd-esse*. Pedersen 2.445. Somewhat otherwise Thurneysen, Gram. 529.

Ir. *baccaim*, NIr. *bacaim*, also and orig. 'hack, lame', fr. Ir. *bacc*, NIr. *bac* 'crook, hook, shackle', etc. = W. *bach* 'angle, corner', Br. *bac'h* 'crook, hook'. Walde-P. 2.105.

Ir. *coscaim* 'blame' and 'hinder', NIr. *coiscim* 'hinder, prevent, forbid', fr. *con-sech-*, cpd. of *sech-* = IE **sekʷ-* in words for 'point out' and 'say', Lat. *insece*, etc. (18.22). Pedersen 2.618.

NIr. *toirmeascaim* 'hinder, prevent, forbid', fr. Ir. *tairmesc-* in *tarmasca* 'disturb', *tairmescc* 'disturbance', cpd. of *mesc-* 'mix' (: Lat. *miscēre* 'mix', etc.). Pedersen 2.577, 612 ftn. Thurneysen, Gram. 531.

W. *rhwystro*, fr. *rhwystr* 'hindrance, obstacle' : Ir. *riastraim* 'distort', and prob. fr. **reigstro* : W. *rhym* 'bond, bound', fr. the root in Ir. *conriug* 'bind', Lat. *corrigia* 'strap', etc. Walde-P. 2.347 (without W. *rhwystro*, etc.). Pedersen 2.45 (1.87). Morris Jones 140.

W. *atal*, also and orig. 'withhold, stop, check', cpd. of *at-* 'back' and *dal-* 'hold' (11.15). Morris Jones, 186.

Br. *herzel, harzel*, fr. *harz* 'obstacle, limit', etym.? Henry 158.

Br. *mirout* 'guard, preserve' (11.24) and 'prevent'.

4. Goth. *warjan* (reg. for κωλύω) = ON *verja*, OE *werian*, OHG *werjan* 'defend, ward off, avoid' (NHG *wehren*) : Skt. *vṛ-* 'cover, ward off, hinder, prevent', etc. Walde-P. 1.280 ff. Feist 551 f. Falk-Torp 1369.

Goth. *ga-latjan, ana-latjan* (both for ἐγκόπτω; *latjan* 'delay, loiter'), ON *letja* (but esp. 'dissuade'), OE *lettan*, ME *lette*, NE *let* (obs.), OHG *lezzan* (rare), MHG *letzen* (mostly 'injure', as NHG *verletzen*), Du. *beletten*, etc. : Goth. *lats* 'lazy', OE *læt*, OHG *lass* 'slow, lazy, late', etc. Walde-P. 2.395. Feist 322 f. NED s.v. *let* v.[2].

ON *hindra* (but mostly 'keep back, delay'), Dan. *(for)hindre*, Sw. *(för)hindra*, OE *hindrian* (also 'injure'), ME *hindre*, NE *hinder*, Du. *(ver)hinderen*, OHG *hinderen*, MHG, NHG *(ver)hindern*, all orig. 'keep back', fr. the adv. seen in Goth. *hindar*, OE *hinder*, OHG *hintar* 'behind'. Falk-Torp 406. NED s.v. *hinder*.

Dan. *hemme*, Sw. *hämme*, MHG, NHG *hemmen* 'obstruct, restrain, hinder' = ON *hemja* 'restrain', Salic Frank. *chamian* 'press', ME *hemme*, NE *hem* 'confine' (now mostly *hem in*; NED s.v. *hem* v.[1] 3) : OE *hem* 'border', OE, OFris. *ham*, LG *hamm* 'inclosed land, pasture, meadow', Lith. *kamuoti* 'press, oppress', etc. Walde-P. 1.388. Falk-Torp 396.

Dan. *forbygge*, Sw. *förebygga*, cpds. of *bygge, bygga* in their earlier sense of 'dwell' or 'be', hence 'forestall, prevent'.

Sw. *förekomma*, Du. *voorkomen*, lit. 'come before', hence 'forestall, prevent'.

NE *prevent*, in earlier use 'act beforehand, anticipate, forestall', fr. pple. of Lat. *praevenīre* 'come before, anticipate' and also 'prevent'. NED s.v.

NHG *vorbeugen*, lit. 'bend forward', hence 'avert, prevent'.

5. Lith. *kliudyti*, beside (but for 'hinder' now more usual than) *kliūti* 'catch on, hit on, befall', also 'hinder' (NSB s.v.) : Lett. *kl'ūt* 'reach, befall', sb. *kl'ūme* 'hindrance, defeat', prob. with

development of 'hinder' from 'get caught' on something and so 'be in the way' : Lat. *claudere* 'shut', *claudēre* 'limp' and ultimately the group of words for 'hook, peg, key', Grk. κλείς, Lat. *clāvis*, etc. Walde-P. 1.492 ff. Mühl.-Endz. 2.241.

Lith. *trukdyti* 'hinder, obstruct, delay', caus. of *trùkti* 'delay' beside *trúkti* 'tear' and 'be wanting'. Walde-P. 1.731. Leskien, Ablaut 312. Mühl.-Endz. 4.251.

Lett. *kavēt* 'pass the time, delay' and 'hinder', with sb. *kautra* 'delay, indecision', perh. : Lat. *cavēre* 'beware', etc. Walde-P. 1.370. Mühl.-Endz. 2.181 f.

6. ChSl. *(vŭz)braniti*, see under 'forbid' (18.38).

SCr. *priječiti* : *prijeći* 'go over, cross', cpd. of vb. for 'go', with development through 'make crooked' (cf. *prijek* 'crooked') or 'interfere'.

SCr. *smetati* 'disturb' and 'hinder', cpd. of *metati* 'throw', with development through 'throw down, disturb'.

Boh. *překažeti* 'hinder' beside *překaziti* 'hinder, spoil', cpd. of *kaziti* 'spoil' = ChSl. *kaziti* 'destroy', caus. of *česnąti* 'disappear'. Berneker 498.

Boh. *předejiti* 'come before, forestall, prevent', cpd. of vb. for 'go, come'.

Pol. *przeszkodzić*, cpd. of *szkodzić* 'harm, injure' (11.28).

Pol. *zapobiedz*, cpd. of *biedz* 'run' (10.46), cf. *zabiedz* 'run to' and in phrases 'get in the way of, prevent'. Semantic development as in Lat. *obstāre* (above, 2) and late Lat. *obviāre*, NE *obviate*.

Russ. *mešat'* (*pomešat'*) 'mix, stir' and 'disturb, hinder, prevent' : ChSl. *měsiti* 'mix', Lat. *miscēre* 'mix', etc. Berneker 2.52 f.

Russ. *prepjatstvovat'*, fr. sb. *prepjatstvie* 'obstacle, hindrance', fr. *prepjat'* 'hinder' (obs.; hence also *prepona* 'obstacle', now obs.), cpd. of the verb seen in ChSl. *pęti* 'stretch' (cf. *pątŭ* 'fetter'), Russ. *pjat', pnut', pinat'* 'strike with the foot, kick', etc. Walde-P. 2.661.

7. Skt. *rudh-*, Av. *rud-* 'obstruct, avert, exclude, hinder, prevent', outside connections dub. Walde-P. 1.283.

Skt. *vṛ-* 'cover, ward off, hinder, prevent' : Goth. *warjan*, etc. (above, 4).

19.61 CUSTOM

Grk.	*ἔθος, ἦθος* (*νόμος, δίκη*)	Goth.	*sidus, biuhti*	Lith.	*paprotys, papratimas*
NG	*ἔθιμο*	ON	*siðr, vani*	Lett.	*ieradums, ieraša*
Lat.	*mōs, cōnsuētūdō*	Dan.	*skik, sæd, sædvane*	ChSl.	*obyčaj, nravŭ*
It.	*costume, usanza*	Sw.	*sedvänja, sed, vana*	SCr.	*običaj, navada*
Fr.	*mœurs* (pl.), *coutume, usage*	OE	*þēaw, sidu, gewuna*	Boh.	*obycej, zvyk, mrav*
		ME	*custume, usage, thew*	Pol.	*obyczaj, zwyczaj*
Sp.	*costumbre, usanza*	NE	*custom, usage*	Russ.	*obyčaj, nravy* (pl.)
Rum.	*obiceiŭ, moravurĭ* (pl.)	Du.	*zede, gebruik*	Skt.	*ācāra-, vyavahāra-, svadhā-*
Ir.	*bēs, gnās*	OHG	*situ, giwona*		
NIr.	*nōs, bēas, gnās*	MHG	*site, gewon(e), gewonheit*		
W.	*defod, arfer*				
Br.	*boaz, giz*	NHG	*sitte, (ge)brauch*		

Words for 'custom' ('customs' of a people, etc.) are most commonly derived from words for 'one's own' or 'be accustomed to, use, usual' ('usual' in one case from 'known'). A few seem to be connected with words of emotional value (ChSl. *nravŭ*, perh. Lat. *mōs*), in which case they must have first denoted mental habits. Words for 'way, manner' (9.992), most of them not included in

this list, may also be used in the sense of 'custom', like NE *manners and customs* of a people, *folk-ways*.

1. IE **s(w)ĕdh-*, deriv. of the refl. pron. stem **s(w)o-* in Skt. *sva-* 'own', Grk. ὅς 'his, her', etc. Walde-P. 2.456. Falk-Torp 1230.

Grk. ἔθος (whence late adj. ἔθιμος 'customary' and sb. ἔθιμον, the usual NG word) and ἦθος (in pl. also 'accustomed places, haunts'; only so in Hom.); Goth. *sidus*, ON *siðr*, Dan. *sæd*, Sw. *sed*, OE *sidu*, Du. *zede*, OHG *situ*, MHG *site*, NHG *sitte*; Skt. *svadhā-* (Vedic, also 'one's own power, pleasure, share', etc.).

2. Grk. νόμος, in early use often 'custom', hence 'law' (21.11) : νέμω 'deal out, allot', Goth., etc. *niman* 'take'. Walde-P. 2.330. Boisacq 662 f.

Grk. δίκη, in Hom. 'way, custom, right', hence later 'lawsuit' (21.13) : δείκνυμι 'point out', Skt. *diç-* 'point out', sb. *diç-* 'direction', etc. Walde-P. 1.776. Boisacq 170.

3. Lat. *mōs* (pl. *mōrēs* > Fr. *mœurs*), etym. dub.; possibly (with extension from mental habits) : Goth. *mōþs* 'anger', OE *mōd* 'mood', etc. Walde-P. 2.239. Ernout-M. 633 f.

Lat. *cōnsuētūdō* (> It. *costume*, Fr. *coutume*, Sp. *costumbre*), fr. *cōnsuēscere*, cpd. of *suēscere* 'become accustomed, be used to', prob. fr. the same root as Grk. ἔθος, etc. (above, 1). Walde-P. 2.456. Ernout-M. 997.

It., Sp. *usanza*, OFr. *usance*, fr. *usant-*, pple. stem of VLat. **ūsāre* (It. *usare*, Fr. *user*, etc.) for *ūtī* (past pple. *ūsus*) 'use' (9.243). REW 9093. Gamillscheg 875.

Fr. *usage*, deriv. of *us* (rare, only *les us et les coutumes*), Lat. *ūsus* 'use, exercise', also 'habit, custom' : *ūtī* 'use'. REW 9099. Gamillscheg 875.

Rum. *obiceiŭ*, fr. the Slavic, cf. ChSl. *obyčaj*, etc. (below, 7).

Rum. *năravi* (arch. or pop.; in modern lit. instead *moravurĭ* pl., re-formation after Lat. *mōrēs*), fr. Slavic, cf. ChSl. *nravŭ*, etc. (below, 7). Tiktin 1035.

4. Ir. *bēs*, NIr. *bēas*, perh. loanword fr. W. *moes* '(good) manners' (for **boes*) = Br. *boaz*, perh. orig. 'peculiarity, eccentricity' : Ir. *baes* 'foolishness', *baeth* 'simple', Gall. *bessu* 'more feritatis', but root connection dub. Pedersen 1.56, 540.

Ir. *gnās* = W. *(g)naws* 'nature, disposition' (> MIr., NIr. *nōs* 'custom') : Ir. *gnāth* 'usual, known' (in NIr. also sb. = *gnās*), W. *gnawd* 'customary' : Lat. *nōtus*, Grk. γνωτός 'known', etc. Pedersen 1.23, 48 f. Walde-P. 1.579.

W. *arfer*, also vb. 'to use, accustom', cpd. of the root **ber-* (IE **bher-*) 'carry' (only in cpds. in Britannic, W. *cymeryd* 'take', etc.). Walde-P. 2.472.

W. *defod*, MW *defawd*, orig.? Cf. *def* 'right, one's own' (in Evans and earlier editions of Spurrell).

Br. *giz*, fr. Fr. *guise* 'manner, way, fashion' (Gmc., OHG *wisa*, NHG *weise*, etc.). Henry 132.

5. Goth. *biuhti*, deriv. of *biuhts* 'accustomed', cpd. **bi-uhta-* : Lith. *j-unkti* 'become accustomed to', ChSl. *učiti* 'teach', Skt. *okas-* 'pleasure, dwelling-place', etc. Walde-P. 1.111. Feist 97.

ON *vani*, Sw. *vana* (Dan. *vane*, mostly 'habit'), in cpds. Dan. *sædvane*, Sw. *sedvänja* (for *sæd, sed*, cf. above, 1), with ablaut OE *gewuna*, OHG *giwona*, MHG *gewone, gewonheit* (Du. *gewoonte*, NHG *gewohnheit*, mostly 'habit'), fr. the adjs. ON *vanr*, OE *gewun*, OHG *giwon* 'accustomed, usual' : ON *una* 'be satisfied with', OHG *wonēn, wonōn* 'be used to, dwell, remain', etc., Skt. *van-* 'wish, desire, get, win', etc. Walde-P. 1.260. Falk-Torp 1350.

Dan. *skik* = Sw. *skick* '(good) condition, (good) form', fr. MLG *schik* 'form,

proper condition' = MHG *schic* 'manner, opportunity' : MLG *schicken* 'bring into order, set up, send', MHG *schicken* 'cause, perform, equip, send', etc. (NHG *schicken*). Falk-Torp 993.

OE *þēaw*, ME *thew*, cf. OS *thau* 'custom', OHG *thau* 'discipline', perh. as 'observation' : Lat. *tuērī* 'observe, heed, protect', *tūtus* 'safe', Goth. *þiuþ* 'the good', ON *þȳðr* 'mild, friendly', etc. Walde-P. 1.706. NED s.v. *thew*, sb.[1].

ME *custume*, NE *custom*, fr. OFr. *custume* (Fr. *coutume*, above, 3).

ME, NE *usage*, fr. OFr. *usage* (above, 3).

ME *usance*, fr. OFr. *usance* (above, 3).

Du. *gebruik*, NHG *(ge)brauch* (MHG *gebrūch* 'use', OHG *prūh*), fr. Du. *bruiken*, NHG *brauchen*, OHG *brūhhan*, etc. 'use, enjoy' (9.423).

6. Lith. *paprotys, papratimas* : *paprantu, -prasti* 'accustom oneself', *paprastas* 'customary', *protas* 'mind, reason', Goth. *fraþjan* 'understand', *frōþs* 'wise', etc. Walde-P. 2.86. Trautmann 230.

Lett. *ieradums, ieraša* (also *paradums, paraša*) : *ie-rast* (*pa-rast*) 'become accustomed' (*parast* also 'find'), cpds. of *rast* = Lith. *rasti* 'find' (11.32). Mühl.-Endz. 2.55, 56, 3.86, 87.

7. ChSl. *obyčaj*, etc., general Slavic (fr. **ob-vyk-*), also Boh. *zvyk*, Pol. *zwyczaj* (**z-vyk-*) : ChSl. *vyknąti*, SCr. *naviknuti se*, Pol. *nawyknąć*, etc. 'become accustomed, accustom oneself', Goth. *bi-uhts*, etc. (above, 5). Walde-P. 1.111. Brückner 638. Trautmann 335.

ChSl. *nravŭ* (rare beside *obyčaj*; Jagić, Entstehungsgesch. 372), Boh. *mrav*, Russ. *nravy* (pl.), in modern Slavic esp. 'manners, habit' : Lith. *noras* 'desire, will', *norėti* 'wish', etc. (16.61). Walde-P. 2.333. Trautmann 197 f.

SCr. *navada* : *navaditi* 'make accustomed to', Slov. *vaditi* id. also 'lure', Russ. *vadit'* 'lure, attract', *povadnyj* 'customary, habitual', all perh. : ChSl. *vaditi* 'accuse', Lith. *vadinti* 'call, name', Skt. *vad-* 'speak', with complicated semantic development, such as 'speak' to 'speak against, accuse', and also through 'call' to 'lure, attract' and 'make accustomed to'? Miklosich 373 (with separation). Trautmann 337 (without mention of the SCr. words). Rječnik Akad. 7.725 f.

8. Skt. *ācāra-* : *ā-car-* 'approach, manage, behave, exercise', cpd. of *car-* 'go, move, proceed'.

Skt. *vyavahāra-*, lit. 'action, practice, behavior' (later esp. 'legal procedure') : *vi-ava-hṛ-* 'have intercourse with, act, behave, deal with', cpd. of *hṛ-* 'take, carry'.

19.62 STRIFE, QUARREL

Grk.	*ἔρις, νεῖκος*	Goth.	*haifsts, sakjō, þwairhei*	Lith.	*ginčas, barnis, vaidas*
NG	*μάλωμα, καβγᾶς*	ON	*strīð, deila, þræta*	Lett.	*k'ilda, strīde*
Lat.	*līs, iūrgium, rixa*	Dan.	*strid, trætte, tvist*	ChSl.	*pĭrja (sŭvada)*
It.	*contesa, disputa, alterco*	Sw.	*strid, tvist, gräl, träta*	SCr.	*razdor, svađa, kavga*
Fr.	*dispute, querelle*	OE	*geflīt, sacu, cēas(t)*	Boh.	*hadka, spor, svár*
Sp.	*contienda, reyerta*	ME	*strif, chest, flit, sake*	Pol.	*sprzeczka, spór, kłótnia*
Rum.	*ceartă, gîlceava*	NE	*strife, quarrel*	Russ.	*ssora, razdor, rasprja, spor*
Ir.	*imbresan, debuith, essōintu, cointinn*	Du.	*strijd, twist*	Skt.	*kalaha-, vivāda-, dvandva-*
NIr.	*imreas, bruighean, achrann*	OHG	*strīt, sechia, flīz*	Av.	*mrvī-, stəmba-*
W.	*cynnen, ymryson, ymrafael*	MHG	*strīt, hader, zwist*		
Br.	*dael, tabut*	NHG	*streit, hader, zwist, zank*		

Words for 'strife' may in part cover also 'armed strife', e.g. Grk. ἔρις in Homer, OHG *strīt* commonly and still NHG *streitaxt* 'battle-ax'. But for words in which the notion of violence is dominant, see under 'fight' and 'battle' (20.11, 20.12). Several of the words denoted primarily 'legal strife, litigation', for which see also 21.13.

Besides the words listed, themselves differing in nuance, there are many others, like NE *row* (now the common colloq. term), *brawl, wrangle, squabble,* Fr. *rire,* Rum. *sfordă* (fr. Slavic), NG τσάκωμα, etc.

1. Grk. ἔρις : ὄρνῡμι, ὀρῑ́νω 'rouse, stir up, incite', Lat. *orīrī* 'rise', Skt. *ṛ-* 'move', *sam-araṇa-* 'strife, battle' (20.12). Walde-P. 1.136 ff. Boisacq 280.

Grk. νεῖκος (mostly poet., but common prose word φιλονεικία 'love of strife, rivalry'; freq. v.l. -νῑκία as if fr. νῑ́κη 'victory'), perh. : Lith. *apnikti* 'fall upon, befall', Lett. *apnikt* 'become bored'. Walde-P. 2.321. Boisacq 660.

NG μάλωμα, also 'scolding, reproof', fr. μαλώνω 'scold, reprove, quarrel', fr. *ὁμαλόω = ὁμαλίζω 'smooth out, make level', deriv. of ὁμαλός 'smooth, level'. Semantic development through 'correct, reprove' to 'scold, quarrel'. Hatzidakis, Einl. 155, Μεσ. 1.140 f.

NG καβγᾶς, SCr. *kavga*, fr. Turk. *kavga* id. Lokotsch 696. Berneker 495.

2. Lat. *līs*, gen. *lītis*, esp. 'a legal quarrel, lawsuit' (21.13) old form *stlīs*, etym. dub. Walde-P. 2.401. Ernout-M. 557. Walde-H. 1.813 f.

Lat. *iūrgium*, fr. *iūrgāre*, old *iūrigāre* 'quarrel, dispute', deriv. of *iūs* 'right, justice, law' (21.11), perh. through phrase *iūre agere*. Ernout-M. 506. Walde-H. 1.732 f.

Lat. *rixa* (> It. *rissa*, Fr. *rixe* 'brawl'), perh. as orig. 'a tear, break' : Grk. ἐρείκω 'break, tear', Skt. *rikh-* 'scratch', etc. Walde-P. 2.344. Ernout-M. 867.

It. *contesa*, Sp. *contienda* : *contendere, contender* 'contend, dispute', fr. Lat. *contendere* 'stretch, strain, strive, contend', cpd. of *tendere* 'stretch' (9.32).

It. *disputa*, Fr. *dispute*, back-formation fr. *disputare, disputer* 'quarrel, dispute', fr. Lat. *disputāre* 'estimate, examine, discuss, maintain' (Vulgate 'dispute'), cpd. of *putāre* 'reckon, ponder, think' (17.14).

It. *alterco* : *altercare* 'quarrel', fr. Lat. *altercārī* 'differ with, dispute, wrangle' (orig. legal term indicating the propositions of the lawyers given turn by turn), deriv. of *alter* 'other'. Ernout-M. 35. Walde-H. 1.33.

Fr. *querelle*, fr. Lat. *querēla, querella*

'complaint', deriv. of *querī* 'complain, lament, bewail'. Development prob. through legal usage 'a plaint'. So freq. in ME (cf. NED s.v. *quarrel*, sb.³, 1).

Sp. *reyerta*, back-formation fr. *reyertar* = Port. *refertar* 'quarrel' orig. 'press together', deriv. of Lat. *refertus* 'stuffed, crammed full' (pple. of *refercīre*). REW 7152.

Rum. *ceartă*, back-formation fr. *cearta* 'scold, quarrel', fr. Lat. *certāre* 'debate, struggle, contend' (: *cernere* 'distinguish, decide'). Ernout-M. 178 f. REW 1840.

Rum. *gîlceava* (also 'noise'), fr. Slavic, Bulg. *gŭlč* 'noise', etc. (Berneker 367). Tiktin 678.

3. Ir. *imbresan*, NIr. *imreas(ān)*, MW *amrysson*, W. *ymryson*, with vb. Ir. (3sg.) *imfresna* 'quarrels', prob. fr. **imbfrith-senn-* : Ir. *sennim* 'sound, play', etc. Pedersen 2.296, 625.

Ir. *debuith*, lit. 'cut in two' : *bīthe*, pple. of *benim* 'strike'. Thurneysen, Gram. 246. Otherwise Pedersen 2.442.

Ir. *essōintu*, lit. 'disunion', neg. to *ōintu* 'union', fr. *ōin, ōen* 'one'.

NIr. *bruighean*, prob. = Gael. *bruidheann* 'talk, conversation', perh. fr. the root in Ir. *frith-bruith* 'negatio', *frisbruidi* 'negat'. Stokes 221. Macbain 54.

NIr. *achrann*, orig. (MIr.) 'entanglement, perplexity', etym.?

Ir. *cointinn* (NIr. mild 'controversy, discussion'), W. *cynnen*, fr. a deriv. of Lat. *contendere* (cf. It. *contesa*, above, 2). Pedersen 1.234. Loth, Mots lat. 157.

W. *ymrafael*, also 'variance, difference', orig.?

Br. *dael* : Ir. *dāl*, NIr. *dāil* 'assembly' (fr. the root **dhē-* 'put, place'). Walde-P. 1.828. Henry 85.

Br. *tabut*, also and orig. 'noise', fr. Norm. Fr. *tabut* 'noise', cf. Prov. *tabus, tabut*, OFr. *tabust* id. Henry 257. Cf. NE *brawl*, fr. vb. *brawl*, orig. 'make a noise, shout' (NED s.v.).

4. Goth. *haifsts* (renders ἔρις and ἀγών) : ON *heipt* 'feud, bane, hate', OE *hǣst* 'violence, fury', *hǣst* adj., OHG *heist* 'violent, vehement', etc., perh. : Skt. *çībham* 'quickly'. Walde-P. 1.364. Feist 231.

Goth. *sakjō* (renders μάχη, but in sense of 'strife'), OE *sacu*, ME *sake*, OHG *sahha, sechia* (several of these also 'lawsuit' 21.13 and 'thing' 9.90), with vbs. Goth. *sacan* 'quarrel, rebuke', OE *sacan* 'quarrel, contend', OHG *sachan* 'quarrel, rebuke, litigate', these prob. : Goth. *sōkjan* 'seek' (cf. *miþ-sōkjan* 'strive with someone'), OE *sēcan* 'seek, attack', OHG *suohhan* 'seek', etc. (11.31). Walde-P. 2.449. Weigand-H. 2.633. Feist 407.

Goth. *þwairhei*, renders ἔρις 2 Cor. 12.20, otherwise θυμός, ὀργή 'anger' (see 16.46).

ON *strīð* (but earlier mostly 'woe, grief', later mostly of armed strife, 'war'), Dan., Sw. *strid*, Du. *strijd*, OS *strid*, OHG, MHG *strīt*, NHG *streit* (OHG > OFr. *estrif* > ME *strif*, NE *strife;* REW 8316, NED s.v.), cf. ON *strīðr* 'stiff, stubborn, severe', OHG *ein-strīti* 'stubborn', with vbs. ON *strīða* 'torment, punish, fight', OHG *strītan* 'quarrel, strive' (OE *strīdan* 'stride'), perh. fr. an extension of the root in Grk. στερεός 'stiff, firm', ON *starr* 'stiff, hard', etc. Walde-P. 2.633. Falk-Torp 1180.

ON *deila*, fr. vb. *deila* 'deal, divide', fig. 'divide on a point, quarrel' = Goth. *dailjan*, etc. 'divide', beside Goth. *dails* 'part' etc. (13.23). Falk-Torp 139.

ON *þræta*, Dan. *trætte*, Sw. *träta*, also vb. ON *þræt(t)a*, etc., perh. : ON *þryngva*, OE *þringan*, etc. 'press, crowd'. Walde-P. 1.759. Falk-Torp 1294.

Sw. *gräl*, vb. *gräla*, prob. of imitative origin. Hellquist 306.

OE *geflīt*, ME *flit*, OHG *flīz* (also 'zeal, industry', NHG *fleiss*), OS *flīt* 'fight, zeal in combat', with vbs. OE *flītan* 'quarrel, strive', OHG *flīzan* 'be zealous', etc., etym. dub., perh. fr. the root seen in Lett. *plīties* 'press, obtrude, demand'. Petersson, PBB 38.316. Walde-P. 2.684 (adversely).

OE *cēas*, later *cēast* (with additional suffix), ME *chest*, fr. Lat. *causa* 'lawsuit'. Holthausen 45. NED s.v. *chest*, sb.².

ME *strif*, NE *strife*, see above under ON *strīð*.

NE *quarrel* (ME 'complaint, ground of complaint', etc.), fr. OFr. *querelle* (above, 2). NED s.v.

Du. *twist* (MLG *twist* > Dan., Sw. *tvist*), late MHG, NHG *zwist*, lit. 'division, split' (cf. ON *tvistra* 'divide, scatter'), from Gmc. **twis-* 'apart' (cf. Goth. *twis-standan* 'separate'), orig. 'in two' : Goth. *twai* 'two', etc. Walde-P. 1.820. Falk-Torp 1305 f. Weigand-H. 2.1357 f.

MHG, NHG *hader* : OHG *hadu-*, OE *heaðа-*, Ir. *cath*, etc. 'battle' (20.12). Weigand-H. 1.788.

NHG *zank*, fr. vb. *zanken*, late MHG *zanken, zenken*, perh. deriv. of *zanke* 'prong, point'. Weigand-H. 2.1302. Paul, Deutsches Wtb. 662. Kluge-G. 703.

5. Lith. *ginčas* : *ginti* 'drive away, scare', ChSl. *gŭnati* 'drive', Grk. θείνω 'strike', Skt. *han-* 'strike, slay', etc. Walde-P. 1.681.

Lith. *barnis* (= ChSl. *branĭ* 'fight') : *barti* 'scold', refl. 'quarrel', ChSl. *brati* 'fight', etc. (20.11). Walde-P. 2.160 f.

Lith. *vaidas* (esp. pl. *vaidai*) = Lett. *vaids* 'war' (20.13).

Lett. *k'ilda*, prob. fr. Liv. *kildo nust* 'begin a brawl', lit. 'pick up splinters' (cf. Germ. *spāne heben*). Mühl.-Endz. 2.380.

Lett. *strīde* (*strīds, strīdus*), fr. MLG *strīt* (above, 4). Mühl.-Endz. 3.1091.

6. ChSl. *pĭrja* (φιλονεικία Lk. 22.24; also *ras-pĭrja, są-pĭrja, sŭ-porŭ*), Russ. *rasprja*, Boh., Russ. *spor*, Pol. *spór* : ChSl. *pĭrěti sę* 'strive, contend', *pĭrati* 'beat, trample', Lith. *perti* 'beat, flog', Skt. *pṛt-*, Av. *pərət-* 'battle' (20.12), etc. Walde-P. 2.42. Miklosich 239. Brückner 441 f.

ChSl. *sŭvada*, lit. 'accusation, contest', SCr. *svađa* : ChSl. *vaditi* 'accuse', Skt. *vad-* 'speak', etc. Meillet, Études 256.

SCr., Russ. *razdor* = ChSl. *razdorŭ* 'tear, split' : ChSl. *derą, dĭrati* 'tear, flay' (*razdĭrati* 'tear to pieces'). Berneker 214 f.

SCr. *kavga*, fr. Turk. (cf. NG καβγᾶς, above, 1).

Boh. *hadka* : *hádati* 'guess', refl. 'quarrel', ChSl. *gadati* 'guess, think', etc., with semantic development through 'dispute'. Berneker 288 f.

Boh. *svár* = ChSl. *svarŭ* 'battle, fight' (late also *svara* 'quarrel'), with vb. *svariti* 'scold' : ON *svǫr* (sb.), *svara* (vb.) 'answer', OE *and-swaru*, etc. 'answer', Goth. *swaran*, etc. 'swear'. Walde-P. 2.527. Meillet, Études 239.

Pol. *sprzeczka*, cpd. of *przeczka* 'contradiction' : *przek(o)* 'crosswise'. Brückner 445.

Pol. *kłótnia* : *kłócić* 'stir, shake, disturb', refl. 'quarrel', ChSl. *klatiti* 'move, shake, shove', etc. Berneker 550. Brückner 237.

Russ. *ssora*, etym. dub. (: Boh. *svár*, etc. above?). Walde-P. 2.527.

7. Skt. *kalaha-*, etym. dub.; perh. with *kali-* 'discord, strife' : Arm. *čelk'em* 'split', ChSl. *kolją, klati* 'prick, split', etc. Walde-P. 2.591.

Skt. *vivāda-*, fr. *vi-vad-* 'contradict, dispute, quarrel', cpd. of *vad-* 'speak' (cf. ChSl. *sŭvada*, above, 6).

Skt. *dvandva-*, lit. 'pair, couple' (: *dvā*, etc. 'two'), hence 'pair of opposites', 'strife, etc.'.

Av. *mrvī-*, etym. dub. Barth. 1197.

Av. *stəmba-* (Barth. 1606, IF 11.139), cf. NPers. *sitamba* 'violent, quarrelsome' : Skt. *stambha-* 'inflation, arrogance', lit. 'post, pillar, support'. Cf. Horn 718.

19.63 PLOT, CONSPIRACY

Grk.	*συνωμοσία*	Goth.	. . . .	Lith.	*sąmokslas, suokalbis*
NG	*συνωμοσία*	ON	*samblāstr, samsvarning*	Lett.	*sazvērestība*
Lat.	*coniūrātiō, cōnspīrātiō*	Dan.	*sammensværgelse*	ChSl.	. . . .
It.	*congiura, cospiracione*	Sw.	*sammansvärjning*	SCr.	*urota*
Fr.	*complot, conspiration*	OE	*gecwidrǣden, gecwis*	Boh.	*spiknutí*
Sp.	*conjuración, conspiración*	ME	*coniuracion, conspiracioun*	Pol.	*spisek, spiknienie*
Rum.	*complot, conspirațiune*	NE	*plot, conspiracy*	Russ.	*zagovor*
Ir.	*comlugae, cocur*	Du.	*samenzwering*	Skt.	*kapaṭaprabandha-*
NIr.	*cealg, coimhchealg, cogar*	OHG	*eidswartī*		
W.	*cydfwriad*	MHG	*beswerunge*		
Br.	*irienn, kavailh*	NHG	*verschwörung*		

Words for 'conspiracy' are most commonly connected with those for 'swear' or 'oath', especially 'swear together', whence 'form a pact or confederacy by oath' and in a bad sense 'conspire against'. There is much semantic borrowing, especially in the case of the Gmc. group. Others are from 'breathe together' (here also both formal and semantic borrowing), 'talk together', 'deceit', with some isolated and partly doubtful sources.

1. From words for 'swear' (21.24) or 'oath' (21.25). Grk. συνωμοσία (: συνόμνυμι); Lat. *coniūrātiō* (: *coniūrāre*), with the Romance words It. *congiura*, Fr. *conjuration* (> ME *conjuracion*), Sp. *conjuración;* Ir. *comlugae* (lit. 'joint oath', gl. *coniuratione* Ml. 44b5); ON *samsvarning*, Dan. *sammensværgelse*, Sw. *sammansvärjning*, Du. *samenzwering*, OHG *eidswartī* (lit. 'oath-swearing', gl. *coniuratio*), MHG *beswerunge*, NHG *verschwörung;* Lett. *sazvērestība* (: *sazvērēties* 'conspire', cpd. refl. of *zvērēt*, fr. MLG *sweren*); SCr. *urota* (: ChSl. *rota* 'oath').

2. Lat. *cōnspīrātiō* (> It. *cospiracione*, Fr. *conspiration* > ME *conspiracioun;* Sp. *conspiración*, Rum. *conspirațiune;* ME *conspiracie*, NE *conspiracy*), lit. 'a blowing or breathing together', whence 'unity of feeling, harmony' (cf. Grk. σύμπνοια 'agreement', συμπνοή, gl. *conspiratio*), and in bad sense 'conspiracy', fr. *conspīrāre* 'blow, breathe together, agree' and 'conspire', cpd. of *spīrāre* 'blow, breathe' (4.51).

Fr. *complot* (> Rum. *complot*, also It. *complotto*, Sp. *complot*, and more or less usual forms in Gmc., Dan. *komplot*, Sw. *komplott*, Du. *complot*, NHG *komplott*, NE *complot* freq. in 16th.-17th. cent.), earliest sense 'packed crowd', orig. dub., perh. back-formation fr. a **comp(e)loter* 'make into a ball', deriv. of *pelote* 'ball'. Gamillscheg 241 f. Bloch 1.164.

3. Ir. *cocur* 'whisper, secret talk, council' and 'conspiracy' (K. Meyer, Contrib. 408), NIr. in this sense also *cogar* or *cogar ceilge* with gen. of *cealg;* Dinneen, McKenna), vbl. n. of *concuiriur*, cpd. of *cuiriur* 'put, place,

throw'. Cf. W. *cynghor* 'council'. Pedersen 2.500, 501 Anm.

NIr. *cealg*, lit. 'deceit' (Ir. *celg*, 16.68), but also 'plot, conspiracy', also cpd. *coimh-chealg* with *comh-* 'con-'.

W. *cydfwriad*, cpd. of *cyd-* 'con-' and *bwriad* 'design, purpose, intention' (17.41).

Br. *irienn*, also and orig. 'woof' (in weaving), cpd. of *lien* 'linen'. Cf. Fr. *trame* in similar use. Ernault, Dict. étym. 317.

Br. *kavailh*, prob. fr. Fr. *cabale* 'cabal'.

4. ON *samblāstr*, deriv. of *samblāsa* 'conspire', lit. 'blow together' (translations of Lat. *cōnspīrātiō*, *cōnspīrāre*).

OE *gecwidrǣden* (gl. *conspiratio*, also 'agreement'), and *gecwis* (gl. *conspiratio*), both : *gecweðan* 'say, speak, arrange, agree'; *rǣden* 'condition, stipulation'. Cf. Goth. *gaqiss* 'agreement'.

NE *plot*, same word as *plot* 'small surface' (*plot of land*) used also for 'plan, scheme', but as 'conspiracy' doubtless influenced by *complot* used only in this sense, and prob. itself also fr. Fr. *pelote* (above, 2). NED s.v. Weekly, Words Ancient and Modern 93 ff.

5. Lith. *sąmokslas*, cpd. of *są-* (*sam-*, *san-*) 'together, with' and *mokslas* 'knowledge, teaching'.

Lith. *suokalbis* : *su-si-kalbėti* 'discuss, confer', refl. cpd. of *kalbėti* 'speak'.

6. Boh. *spiknutí*, Pol. *spiknienie*, with vbs. Boh. *spiknouti se*, Pol. *spiknać się*, etc. (cf. also Boh. *pikel* 'intrigue'), root connection? Brückner 509 takes from **pik-* in the imitative group Boh. *pikati*, Pol. *pikać*, Russ. *pikat'* 'peep', etc. (Walde-P. 2.70), but without comment on the semantic development (through notion of a secret cabal? Russ. *pikat'* is used also like NE colloq. *don't peep* 'don't utter a sound').

Pol. *spisek*, fr. *spis* 'list, inventory, census' : *spisać* 'write up, make a list, register', etc., cpd. of *pisać* 'write'. Orig. 'list (of conspirators)'. Brückner 509.

Russ. *zagovor*, cpd. of *govor* 'rumor, jargon' = ChSl. *govorŭ* 'noise' (cf. Russ. *govorit'* 'speak', 18.21).

7. Skt. *kapaṭaprabandha-*, cpd. of *kapaṭa-* 'fraud, deceit, cheating' and *prabandha-* 'connection, band, tie'.

19.64 COMMON (adj.)

Grk.	*κοινός*	Goth.	*gamains*	Lith.	*bendras*
NG	*κοινός*	ON	*fēlags-*, *sameiginn*	Lett.	*kuopejs*, *kuopīgs*
Lat.	*commūnis*	Dan.	*fælles*	ChSl.	*obĭštĭ*
It.	*commune*	Sw.	*gemensam*	SCr.	*zajednički*
Fr.	*commun*	OE	*gemǣne*	Boh.	*obecný*, *společny*
Sp.	*común*	ME	*commun*, *imene*	Pol.	*(w)spólny*
Rum.	*comun*	NE	*common*	Russ.	*obščij*
Ir.	*coitchenn*	Du.	*gemeenschappelijk*	Skt.	*sāmānya-*, *sādhāraṇa-*
NIr.	*coitcheann*	OHG	*gimeini*		
W.	*cyffredin*	MHG	*gemein*		
Br.	*boutin*	NHG	*gemeinsam*, *gemeinschaftlich*		

'Common' is understood here as 'belonging to two or more', the primary sense, from which are derived words for notions of still more definitely social import, as 'community', 'companion, partner', 'commonwealth', etc.

But various secondary uses such as 'public', 'general', 'frequent' (esp. in NE *common*), and especially the derogatory 'common, vulgar, inferior', are 'common' (in sense here intended) to many of the words listed, and in some cases the old words have come to be used mainly or only in the derogatory sense (as NE *mean*, NHG *gemein*, Du. *gemeen*, Dan., Sw. *gemen*).

A cognate group, common to Italic and Germanic (strictly Goth. and West Gmc.), is derived from a root meaning 'change, exchange', mostly with a prefix for 'together'. Others are derived from expressions for 'together' (these in part from 'bind', 'heap', etc.) or various combinations with prefix for 'together'.

1. IE **moini-*, fr. the root **mei-* 'exchange' in Skt. *mayate*, Lett. *mit*, and with *t*-extension, Lat. *mūtāre*, etc. Walde-P. 2.240 f. Ernout-M. 642 f. Walde-H. 1.255. Feist 190 f.

Lat. *commūnis* (> Romance and ME, NE words), OLat. *comoinis*, Osc. *muiniku* (nom. sg. fem.), Goth *gamains*, OE *gemǣne*, ME *imene* (rare; ME *mene*, NE *mean* in secondary senses), OHG *gimeini*, MHG, NHG *gemein*, MLG *gemēn* (> Dan., Sw. *gemen*), Du. *gemeen* (all these now in derogatory sense; in older sense now NHG *gemeinsam* or *gemeinschaftlich*, Du. *gemeenschappelijk*, Sw. *gemensam*); cf. Lith. *mainas* 'exchange', Lat. *mūnus* 'service, office', etc.

2. Grk. κοινός, fr. *κομ-ιος : Lat. *cum*, early *com* 'with'. Walde-P. 1.258. Boisacq 482.

3. Ir. *coitchenn*, NIr. *coitcheann*, cpd. of *com-* 'with' (: Lat. *cum*) and (?) the root of *techtaim* 'own, possess' (11.12). Pedersen 1.327 (without comment on the verbal root).

W. *cyffredin*, earlier *cyffred* (also vb. 'comprise, embrace') : Br. *kevret* 'together', Ir. *combart*, *comfert* 'conception' (of a woman), fr. **com-od-ber-* cpd. of *berim* 'bear, carry'. Pedersen 1.476 f.

Br. *boutin*, fr. Fr. *butin* 'booty', through notion of 'common property'. Henry 41.

4. Goth. *gamains*, etc., above, 1.

ON *fēlags* in *til fēlags* 'in common' and cpds. like *fēlagsfē* 'common property', etc., gen. of *fēlag* 'partnership' (cf. *fēlagi* 'partner' late OE *fēolaga*, NE *fellow*), cpd. of *fē* 'property'. So Dan. *fælles*, fr. *fælligs*, gen. of *fællig* = ON *fēlag*. Falk-Torp 288.

ON *sameiginn*, *sameiginligr*, lit. 'having joint possession', fr. *sam-* 'together' and *eiga* 'own, possess'.

Sw. *gemensam*, see above, 1.

5. Lith. *bendras* (also as sb. 'partner, companion'), fr. IE **bhendh-* 'bind' in Goth. *bindan*, Skt. *bandh-*, etc. (9.16). Walde-P. 2.152.

Lett. *kuopejs*, *kuopīgs*, fr. *kuopa* 'heap', loc. adv. *kuopā* 'together, in common'. Mühl.-Endz. 2.344 f.

6. ChSl. *obĭštĭ* (SCr. *opći* obs. or dial.; Pol. *obcy* 'strange, foreign'), Russ. *obščij* (fr. ChSl.), fr. **obŭ-tjo-*, deriv. of *obŭ* 'about', formed like Skt. *apa-tya-*, *upa-tya*, etc. Hence also ChSl. *obĭštĭnŭ*, Boh. *obecný* (Pol. *obecny* 'present, at hand'). Brückner 369 f.

SCr. *zajednički*, fr. *zajedno* 'together, at the same place or time', lit. 'at one', fr. *jedan* 'one'.

Boh. *pospolný*, *společny* (through *spolek* 'union'), Pol. *spólny*, *wspólny*, fr. advs. Boh. *spol*, *pospol*, Pol. *społ*, *wspól* 'together', lit. 'on the same side', fr. *s-* = ChSl. *sŭ-* 'with' and a form = ChSl. *polŭ* 'side, shore' (mostly in phrases like *obŭ onŭ polŭ* 'on that side, beyond'). Brückner 429.

7. Skt. *samāna-* 'same, like, common', whence *sāmānya-*, deriv. of *sam-* 'together', *sama-* 'same, like'.

Skt. *sādhāraṇa-*, cpd. deriv. (with vṛddhi) of *sa-* 'together' and *dhṛ-* 'hold'.

19.65 MEET (vb.)

Grk.	*ἀπαντάω*, *συναντάω*	Goth.	*gamōtjan*	Lith.	*sutikti*
NG	*ἀνταμώνω*, *ἀπαντῶ* (*συναντῶ*)	ON	*mœta*	Lett.	*satikt*, *sastapt*
Lat.	*obviam* with vbs., *occurrere*	Dan.	*møde*, *træffe*	ChSl.	*sŭrěsti*
It.	*incontrare*	Sw.	*möta*, *träffa*	SCr.	*sresti*
Fr.	*rencontrer*	OE	*mētan*, *ongēn*, etc. with vbs.	Boh.	*potkati*
Sp.	*encontrar*	ME	*mete*	Pol.	*(s)potkać*
Rum.	*întîlni*	NE	*meet*	Russ.	*vstretit'*
Ir.	*conriccim*	Du.	*ontmoeten*	Skt.	*āsad-*
NIr.	*casadh* (impers.), etc.	OHG	*ingegin* with vbs., *begagenen*		
W.	*cyfarfod*	MHG	*begegenen*		
Br.	*en em gavout*	NHG	*begegnen*, *treffen*		

Many of the terms for 'meet' are derivatives of, or phrases with, adverbs for 'face to face', 'against', 'in the way', or 'together'. Some are based on notions like 'hit', 'happen on, find', or the like. The source of the Gmc. group (NE *meet*, etc.) is obscure.

1. Grk. ἀπαντάω, συναντάω, cpds. of ἀντάω, also 'meet' (Hom. etc., but not Att.), fr. adv. ἄντα 'face to face', belonging with ἀντί, Skt. *anti*, Lat. *ante*, etc. Walde-P. 1.66 f. Boisacq 64.

NG (beside ἀπαντῶ, now also 'answer', and συναντῶ) pop. ἀνταμώνω, fr. adv. ἀντάμα 'together', Byz. and dial. ἐντάμα, this fr. ἐν τῷ ἅμα = ἅμα 'together'. Koraes, Ἄτακτα 2.124.

2. Lat. adv. *obviam* 'in the way', used reg. with vbs. (*īre*, *venīre*, etc.) for 'meet'.

Lat. *occurrere*, cpd. of *currere* 'run', partly 'run against, attack', etc., but also simply 'meet'. Cf. the ambiguous NE *I ran into* (= *collided with* or simply *met*).

It. *incontrare*, OFr. *encontrer* (> ME *encountre*, NE *encounter*), Fr. *rencontrer*, Sp. *encontrar*, fr. Lat. (*in*) *contra* 'against'. REW 4361. Gamillscheg 755.

Rum. *întîlni*, fr. Hung. *talalni* 'hit, come across, meet'. Tiktin 834.

3. Ir. *conriccim* (also 'reach'), cpd. of *riccim* 'come, reach' (cf. *do-iccim* 'come', 11.48).

NIr. *casaim* 'turn, twist' (: Ir. *cass* 'wreathed, twisted', etym. dub.; Walde-P. 1.450. Stokes 57) is used impersonally for 'meet' as *casadh fear liom* 'I met a man', etc. (Dinneen, McKenna). Also similar impers. phrases with *buailim* 'strike', *teagmhaim* 'happen', etc.

W. *cyfarfod*, cpd. of *cyf-* 'together', *ar* 'on, upon', and *bod* 'be'.

Br. *en em gavout*, refl. of *kavout* 'find' (11.32).

4. Goth. *gamōtjan*, ON *mœta*, Dan. *møde*, Sw. *möta*, OE *mētan*, ME *mete*, NE *meet*, Du. *ontmoeten*, outside root connections dub. Walde-P. 2.304. Feist 193 f.

OE *tōgēa(g)nes*, *ongēn*, etc. 'against' with vbs., used like and prob. modeled on the Lat. phrases with *obviam* (so always, not *mētan*, in the Gospels). Similarly OHG *ingegin* 'against' with vbs. (Otfr., Tat., etc.), but also vbl. deriv. of *gagan* 'against', OHG *begagenen* (esp. Notker), MHG *begegenen*, NHG *begegnen*.

NHG *treffen*, also and orig. 'hit' (OHG *treffan* 'strike, hit', OE *drepan* 'strike', etc., 9.21), now a pop. term for 'meet'. Paul, Deutsches Wtb. Hence Dan. *træffe*, Sw. *träffa* with same uses.

5. Lith. *sutikti* (also refl.), Lett. *satikt*, cpds. of Lith. *tikti* 'fit, suit', Lett. *tikt* 'please' (16.21).

Lett. *sastapt*, cpd., with *sa-* and refl. *s*, of *tapt* 'attain' also 'become' = Lith. *tapti* 'become' (9.92). Mühl.-Endz. 3.745.

6. ChSl. *sŭrěsti*, SCr. *sresti*, Russ. *vstretit'*, cpds. of the same root as in ChSl. *obrěsti* 'find' (11.32).

Boh. *potkati*, Pol. *(s)potkać*, cpds. of the root seen in ChSl. *potŭknąti* 'hit, prick', Pol. *tkać* 'thrust, stick', etc. (: Grk. τύκος 'hammer'). Walde-P. 2.615. Miklosich 368. Trautmann 331. Brückner 571.

7. Skt. *āsad-* 'reach, approach, happen on, meet', cpd. of *sad-* 'sit'.

19.71. Note on terms for members of a trade or profession. Most of the more important of these, or words from which they are readily supplied (as 'miller', fr. 'mill'), are included in various other chapters. Thus 'hunter' (3.79); 'herdsman' (3.18); 'farmer' (8.11); 'craftsman, artisan' (9.42); 'carpenter' (9.43); 'smith' (9.60); 'wagonmaker, cartwright, wheelwright' (mostly fr. 'carriage, wagon, cart', 10.75, but also in part generalized from one who makes special parts, as 'wheel' 10.76 or 'frame'; cf. NHG *wagner*, *radmacher*, *stellmacher*, Kretschmer, Wortgeogr. 485 f.); 'mason' (9.53); 'potter' (9.71); 'miner' ('mine', p. 608); 'cook' (5.21); 'baker' (mostly fr. 'bake', 5.24; or fr. 'bread', 5.51, as Grk. ἀρτο-κόπος, -ποιός, -πώλης, NG ψωμᾶς, Sp. *panadero*, Russ. *chlebnik*, etc.; Fr. *boulanger*, OFr. *boulengier*, dial. *boulenc*, fr. MLG *bolle* 'round bread'; fr. 'oven' 5.25, as It. *fornaio*, Sp. *hornero*, NG φούρναρης; Lat. *pistor*, orig. 'one who pounds the grain, miller'); 'butcher, (5.612); 'miller' (5.57), 'weaver' (6.33); 'tailor' (6.13), 'shoemaker, cobbler' (6.54); 'sailor' (10.82); 'soldier' (20.17), 'author, writer' (18.62); 'poet' (18.63).

But there seems to be no more appropriate chapter than this in which to include reference to a conspicuous female profession, that of the 'prostitute' (19.72).

19.72 WHORE, PROSTITUTE

Grk.	*πόρνη*	Goth.	*kalkjō*	Lith.	*kekšė*, *kurva*
NG	*πόρνη*, *πουτάνα*	ON	*hōra*, *pūta*, *skœkja*	Lett.	*mauka*, *kurva*
Lat.	*meretrīx*, *scortum*, *lupa*, *prōstitūta*	Dan.	*hore*, *skøge*	ChSl.	*ljubodějica*, *blądĭnica*
It.	*puttana*, *meretrice*, *prostituta*	Sw.	*hora*, *sköka*	SCr.	*bludnica*, *kurva*
Fr.	*putain*, *prostituée*	OE	*miltestre*, *hōre*	Boh.	*kurva*, *nevěstka*
Sp.	*puta*, *ramera*, *prostituta*	ME	*hore*, *strumpet*, *putaine*	Pol.	*kurwa*, *nierządnica*, *wszetecznica*
Rum.	*curvă*, *prostituată*	NE	*whore*, *prostitute*, *harlot*	Russ.	*bljad'*, *bljudnica*
Ir.	*mertrech*, *stripach*	Du.	*hoer*, *deern*	Skt.	*veçyā-*, *gaṇikā-*, *puṁçcalī-*
NIr.	*mēirdreach*, *striopach*	OHG	*huora*	Av.	*jahi-*, *jahikā-*, *kūnāiri-*
W.	*putain*	MHG	*huore*		
Br.	*gast*, *vilgen*	NHG	*hure*, *dirne*, *metze*		

For the 'prostitute' there is a wealth of terms, some the more official and legal like NE *prostitute*, some euphemistic (or originally so) like Fr. *courtisane*, NE *courtesan*, Fr. *fille de joie*, and the greatest variety of popular words, of which only the most important are listed here. These latter include words for 'dear one' (so prob. the Gmc. group, NE *whore*, etc.), 'woman, girl, bride', which came to be used in derogatory sense, and opprobrious epithets of diverse sources.

1. Grk. πόρνη : πέρνημι 'sell' (11.83), hence the female slave sold for prostitution. Walde-P. 2.40. Boisacq 805.

NG πουτάνα, fr. It. puttana (below, 2).

2. Lat. meretrīx, lit. 'one who earns wages' : merēre 'earn, gain'. Hence It. meritrice (learned form), and by dissim. meletrix (Lex Salica), OE miltestre, etc. Ernout-M. 609. REW 5523.

Lat. scortum 'skin, hide' (4.12), also 'prostitute'; cf. vulg. Fr. peau, NHG balg. Ernout-M. 909. Hammarström, Eranos 23.104 ff., Glotta 20.203.

Lat. lupa, properly 'she-wolf' (fem. to lupus 'wolf'). The sense 'prostitute' is preserved in the Romance languages Sp. loba, It. lupa, and esp. Fr. louve (cf. Benveniste, Mélanges Vendryes 55 f.). Ernout-M. 567.

Lat. prōstitūta (Plin.+), fem. of pass. pple. of prōstituere cpd. of statuere 'place', hence lit. 'place in front', in actual use 'expose publicly to prostitution, prostitute'. Hence It., Sp. prostituta, Fr. prostituée, NE prostitute, etc., now virtually an international Eur. official term, together with forms for the institution 'prostitution', e.g. NHG prostituierte, prostitution, Russ. prostitutka, prostitucnja, and other similar Gmc. and Slavic forms omitted in the list.

OFr. pute, Fr. putain, Sp. Prov. puta, Prov. putana (> It. puttana), prob. fr. fem. of VLat. *pūttus (cf. OIt. putto 'boy', putta 'girl', Lat. pūtus, Ernout-M. 829), with derogatory use like that of NHG dirne, etc. Diez 259. REW 6890. Otherwise (fr. fem. of OFr. put, Lat. putidus 'stinking') Gamillscheg 726, Bloch 2.195.

Fr. courtesane (> NE courtesan), orig. 'woman of the court', in present sense since 16th cent. Wartburg 2.851. NED s.v. courtesan.

Sp. ramera, Port. ramiera, fem. to ramero, ramiero 'young bird of prey', lit. 'little branch', fr. ramo 'branch' (fr. Lat. ramus id.). REW 7035.

Rum. curvă, fr. Slavic (below, 6).

3. Lat. meretrix (above, 2). Vendryes, De hib. voc. 155.

Ir. stripach, NIr. striopach, fr. Lat. stuprum 'dishonor, disgrace, debauchery' (with metathesis, cf. NE strumpet, below). Vendryes, De. hib .voc. 180.

W. putain, prob. fr. ME putaine (rather than directly fr. Fr. putain). Parry-Williams 173.

Br. gast = W. gast 'bitch', etym.? Loth, RC 36.166 (vs. Morris Jones 139).

Br. vilgen, deriv. of vil 'bad, ugly' (fr. Fr. vil). Henry 276.

4. Goth. kalkjō (or kalki; only dat. pl. kalkjōm), prob. a loanword, but source dub. Feist 307.

ON hóra = OE hōre, ME hore, NE whore), Dan. hore, Sw. hora, Du. hoer, OHG huora, etc.; Goth. only masc. hōrs 'adulterer, fornicator', with vbs. Goth. hōrinōn 'commit adultery', etc. : Lat. cārus 'dear', Ir. caraim 'love', etc. (16.26). Walde-P. 1.325. Weigand-H. 1.907. Falk-Torp 418.

ON pūta, fr. OFr. pute (above, 2).

ON skœkja, Dan. skøge, Sw. sköka, prob. fr. MLG schöke id., this perh. deriv. of schöde 'foreskin on the horse's penis' : MHG schöte 'shell, husk', ON skauðir 'foreskin on the horse's penis'. Falk-Torp 1013. The sense 'prostitute' could be from 'skin' as in the case of Lat. scortum (above), or (so Falk-Torp) through an intermediary 'vagina'. But cf. Hellquist 977 f.

OE miltestre, fr. Lat. meretrīx (above, 2).

ME, NE strumpet prob. fr. OFr. strupe beside stupre fr. Lat. stuprum (cf. NIr. striopach, above, 3). Skeat, Etym. Dict. s.v. Wyld, Univ. Eng. Dict. s.v.

ME putaine, fr. Fr. putain (above, 2).

NE prostitute, fr. Lat. prostitūta (above, 2).

NE harlot, only late ME in this sense, chiefly 'vagabond, beggar, rogue, etc.', fr. OFr. herlot, (h)arlot 'lad, knave, etc.' (widespread Romance word of dub. orig.). NED s.v.

Du. deern, NHG dirne 'girl, lass, wench', but commonly 'prostitute' : MHG dierne, OHG diorna 'girl, maidservant', deriv. of OHG deo 'slave', etc. (19.42). Weigand-H. 1.360. Kluge-G. 106 f.

NHG metze, fr. MHG Metze, Mätze, orig. pet name for Mechthild, Mathilde, but in MHG (14th. cent.) already 'girl' and 15th-16th cent. in present sense. Weigand-H. 2.177. Kluge-G. 389 f.

5. Lith. kekšė, etym. dub. Berneker 538.

Lith., Lett. kurva, fr. Slavic (below). Mühl.-Endz. 2.326.

Lett. mauka : maukt 'pull off or on' (clothes, etc.), Lith. maukti 'strip'. Mühl.-Endz. 2.568.

6. ChSl. ljubodějica (reg. for πόρνη in Gospels), also ljubodějĭ, fr. ljuby dějati 'fornicate', phrase with ljuby 'love' and dějati 'put, perform'. Berneker 756.

ChSl. blądĭnica (Supr. for πόρνη), SCr. bludnica, Russ. bljudnica, deriv. of ChSl. blądŭ 'πορνεία, fornication', bląditi 'err, fornicate', beside ChSl. blędŭ 'gossip, trick', blędą, blęsti 'err, fornicate', Russ. bljad' 'whore', etc. : Goth. blinds, ON blindr, etc. 'blind', Goth. blandan, etc. 'mix', etc. Berneker 60, 62. Walde-P. 2.216.

SCr.-ChSl. kurĭva, SCr., Boh. kurva, Pol. kurwa, orig. dub.; borrowing fr. the Gmc. group (ON hóra, etc. above, 4), is difficult phonetically. Berneker 651. Stender-Petersen 27.

Boh. nevěstka, dim. of nevěsta 'bride'.

Pol. nierządnica, lit. 'disorderly woman', deriv. of nie-rząd 'disorder, confusion', also 'dissipation, debauchery' (neg. of rząd 'order, series, etc.'). Brückner 474.

Pol. wszetecznica (the word used in Pol. Bible), deriv. of adj. wszeteczny 'debauched, lewd, lecherous', cpd. of wsze- 'all, common, etc.' and second member root of ciec 'run'. Brückner 636.

7. Skt. veçyā-, deriv. of veça 'house, dwelling' and esp. 'house of ill fame, brothel' (: viç- 'dwelling, house', Lat. vīcus 'village', etc. 19.16).

Skt. gaṇikā- : gaṇ- 'count', gaṇa- 'number, class', etc., Semantic development through 'paid woman' (cf. gaṇaka- 'bought for a large sum' Pāṇini, but usually 'one who counts, arithmetician', etc.)?

Skt. puṃçcalī (AV+), lit. 'one who runs after men', fr puṃs- 'man' and cal 'move'.

Av. jahi-, jahikā-, both lit. 'woman' but only of evil creatures, hence 'prostitute'. Barth. 606 f.

Av. kūnāirī-, cpd. of kū- (Skt. ku-) pejorative prefix and nāirī- 'woman'. Barth. 474.

CHAPTER 20

WARFARE

20.11 FIGHT (vb.)

Grk.	μάχομαι, πολεμέω	Goth.	weihan	Lith.	kovoti, kautis, muštis
NG	πολεμῶ	ON	berjask, vega	Lett.	kauties
Lat.	pugnāre, proeliārī	Dan.	slaas, kæmpe	ChSl.	pĭrěti sę, brati
It.	combattere, pugnare	Sw.	kämpa, fäkta, slåss	SCr.	boriti se (biti se)
Fr.	combattre	OE	feohtan, wīgan, win-	Boh.	bojovati (biti se)
Sp.	pelear, combatir		nan	Pol.	walczyć, bić się
Rum.	combate, (se)lupta	ME	fehte, kempe	Russ.	sražat'sja, bit'sja,
Ir.	fichim, cathaigur	NE	fight		drat'sja
NIr.	cómhraicim, troidim	Du.	kampen, vechten	Skt.	yudh-
W.	ymladd	OHG	fehtan	Av.	parət-, yud-
Br.	en em ganna	MHG	vehten, wīgen		
		NHG	kämpfen (fechten)		

Verbs for 'fight' (understood here in the military sense, though the words are not so restricted) are most commonly based on the notion of striking, but a few on other forms of violent action including 'hair-pulling'.

1. Grk. μάχομαι, with μάχη 'battle', μάχαιρα 'knife', outside connections dub. Walde-P. 2.227. Boisacq 616, 1118.

Grk. πολεμέω, mostly 'make war', but also 'fight' and 'contend, quarrel', NG πολεμῶ 'fight, struggle', deriv. of πόλεμος 'war' (20.13), in early use also 'a fight, battle'.

2. Lat. pugnāre (> It. pugnare), orig. 'strike with the fist', but the most general term for 'fight', fr. pugnus 'fist'. Ernout-M. 821.

Lat. proeliārī, deriv. of proelium 'battle' (20.12).

WARFARE 1371

It. combattere, Fr. combattre, Sp. combatir, Rum. combate, cpds. of It. battere, Fr. battre, Sp. batir, Rum. bate 'strike' (9.21).

Sp. pelear, orig. 'pull hair', deriv. of pelo 'hair' (Lat. pilus). REW 6508.

Rum. (se) lupta (= It. lottare, Fr. lutter, Sp. luchar 'struggle, wrestle', etc., fr. Lat. luctāre, beside usual luctārī 'wrestle, contend' (orig. a gymnastic term) : Grk. λυγίζω 'bend, twist oneself'. Walde-P. 2.413. Ernout-M. 564. Walde-H. 1.826 f. REW 5148. Tiktin 934.

3. Ir. fichim : Goth. weihan, OE wīgan, etc. 'fight', Lat. vincere 'conquer, win', Lith. veikti 'act, work', etc. Walde-P. 1.232 f. Ernout-M. 1109. Feist 557.

Ir. cathaigur, deriv. of cath 'battle' (20.12).

NIr. cómhraicim, deriv. of cómhrac 'contest, fight', MIr. comrac 'encounter, meeting, combat', vbl. n. of conriccim 'meet' (19.65). Pedersen 2.556.

NIr. troidim, deriv. of troid, MIr. trot 'a fight, struggle', prob. : W. trythu 'swell', OE þrūtian 'swell' (with pride or anger), strūtian 'swell, struggle'. Walde-P. 2.634. Pedersen 1.160.

W. ymllad, cpd. of ym- with reciprocal or refl. force and llad 'kill, slay', earlier 'strike' (4.76).

Br. en em ganna, refl. of kanna 'strike' (9.21).

4. Goth. weihan, ON vega, OE wīgan (OHG pple. wīgant, wīkant), MHG wīgen : Ir. fichim, etc. (above, 3).

ON berjask, refl. of berja 'strike' (9.21).

Dan. slaas, Sw. slåss, refl. of slaa, slå 'strike' (9.21); similarly also NHG sich schlagen.

ME kempe, Du. kampen (MLG kempen > Dan. kæmpe, Sw. kämpa), NHG kämpfen (OE campian, OHG champfan, MHG kempfen, chiefly 'fight a duel'),

derivs. of OE camp 'battle', MHG kampf, OHG campf 'duel', NHG kampf 'battle' (20.12).

OE feohtan, ME fehte, fihte, NE fight, Du. vechten (MLG > Sw. fäkta; Dan. fægte poet. or arch.), OHG fehtan, MHG vehten, NHG fechten (now mostly 'fence'), prob. as orig. 'pull hair' : Lat. pectere 'comb', Grk. πεκτέω 'shear, clip', πέκω 'comb', Lith. pešti 'pluck, pull', refl. peštis 'scuffle' (cf. Leskien, Lit. Lesebuch p. 2, last 12 lines). Cf. Sp. pelear (above, 2) and NHG raufen 'pluck, pull', sich raufen 'scuffle'. Walde-P. 2.17. Franck-v. W. 724.

OE winnan 'labor, toil' (9.13), also 'strive, fight'.

5. Lith. kovoti : kova 'battle' (20.12) and following.

Lith. kautis, Lett. kauties, refl. of Lith. kauti, Lett. kaut 'strike' (Lett. kaut also 'fight' in NT, James 4.2) : ChSl. kovati, Russ. kovat', etc. 'forge' (9.61), ON hǫggva, OE hēawan, etc. 'strike, hew' (9.22), Lat. cūdere 'pound, beat'. Walde-P. 1.330. Walde-H. 1.300f.

Lith. muštis, refl. of mušti 'strike' (9.21).

6. ChSl. pĭrěti sę, refl. of pĭrěti 'contend, dispute' : pĭrati 'wash' (by beating), Lith. perti 'bathe (by striking with a besom), Arm. hari, aor. 'struck', Av. parət- 'fight', pərət-, Skt. prt- 'battle', OPers. partaram acc. sg. (NR a 47; 'foe' or 'battle'?). Walde-P. 2.42.

ChSl. borą, brati, SCr. boriti se : ON berja 'strike', refl. berjask 'fight' (above), Lat. ferīre 'strike', etc. (9.21). Berneker 76.

SCr. biti se, Boh. bíti se, Pol. bić się, Russ. bit'sja, all refl. of the Slavic word for 'strike', ChSl. biti, etc. (9.21).

Boh. bojovati, deriv. of boj = ChSl. bojĭ 'battle' (this : biti, above). Berneker 68.

Pol. *walczyć* : *walka* 'fight, combat, struggle', Boh. *valka* 'war' (20.13).

Russ. *srazať sja*, refl. of *srazať* 'throw down, fling down, smite', cpd. of *razit* 'beat, smite' beside *raz* 'blow', ChSl. *u-raziti* 'strike', etc. (9.21).

Russ. *drať sja*, refl. of *drať*, ChSl. *dirati* 'tear' (9.28).

20.12 BATTLE (sb.)

Grk.	μάχη	Goth.	waihjō	Lith.	kova, mušis
NG	μάχη	ON	orrosta, bardagi, víg,	Lett.	kauja
Lat.	proelium		hildr	ChSl.	kotora (ratĭ, bojĭ)
It.	battaglia	Dan.	slag	SCr.	bitka, boj
Fr.	bataille	Sw.	slag	Boh.	bitva, boj
Sp.	batalla	OE	gefeoht, wīg, camp,	Pol.	bitwa, bój
Rum.	bătăie, bătălia		beadu, hild	Russ.	boj, bitva, sraženie
Ir.	cath (gleo, irgal)	ME	fihte, bataille, camp	Skt.	yuddha-, yudh-, raṇa-,
NIr.	cath, āg (gleo, iorghail)	NE	battle		pṛtanā-
W.	brwydr, cad	Du.	slag	Av.	pəšana-, arəza-, rōna-,
Br.	kann, emgann	OHG	gifeht, wīg, hiltia, strīt		hamarəna-
		MHG	wīc, gevehte, strīt	OPers.	hamarana-
		NHG	schlacht, kampf, gefecht		

The majority of the words for 'battle' are connected with the verbs for 'fight' (20.11) or with others for 'strike, beat', etc. Some are words for 'strife', used also for 'armed strife', and one group shows the development 'field' > 'battle-field' > 'battle'.

1. Grk. μάχη : μάχομαι 'fight' (20.11). Grk. πόλεμος 'war' (20.13), in Hom. more freq. 'battle'.

2. Lat. *proelium*, perh. fr. **pro-voiliom*, fr. the root in Lith. *vyti, veju* 'pursue, chase', ChSl. *vojĭnŭ* 'soldier', Russ. *vojna* 'war', etc. Boisacq, Mélanges Pedersen 251 ff.

It. *battaglia* (> Rum. *bătălia*), Fr. *bataille*, Sp. *batalla* (Rum. *bătăie* in the older language only 'blow, beating', etc., but now used also like *bătălia* as 'battle'), fr. VLat. *battuālia*, deriv. of *battuere* 'beat' (9.21). REW 995.

Rum. *luptă* (fr. Lat. *lucta* 'wrestling, wrestling-match') is a general word for 'fight, struggle' or esp. 'wrestling-match', not usual for 'battle'. But cf. the corresponding Alb. *luftë* 'war'.

3. Ir. *cath*, W. *cad* (cf. Gall. *Catu-rīges*, etc.) : ON *Hǫðr*, and *Hǫð-* in cpd. names, OE *heaþu-* in *heaþubyrne* 'battle corslet', *heaþulind* 'war-linden' = 'shield', etc., OHG *Hadu-brand*, etc., MHG, NHG *hader* 'quarrel, strife', ChSl. *kotora* 'battle'. Walde-P. 1.339.

Ir. *āg* : Skt. *āji-* 'race, contest', *aj-* 'drive', etc. Pedersen 1.101. Walde-H. 1.24.

Ir. *gleo*, perh. fr. **gliwā-* : Skt. *jri-* 'spread out to, overpower'(?). Thurneysen, Z. celt. Ph. 20.364 ff.

Ir. *irgal*, NIr. *iorghail*, cpd. : *gal* 'bravery' (16.52). Pedersen 1.101, 358.

W. *brwydr* = Ir. *briathar* 'word', with W. development through 'battle of words'? But root connection and primary sense uncertain. Walde-P. 1.687, 2.194. Pedersen 2.45.

7. Skt. *yudh-*, Av. *yud-* : Grk. ὑσμῖνη 'fight, battle', Lith. *judéti* 'move, be in motion', *judinti* 'agitate, move, shake', Pol. *judzić* 'tempt, entice', and Lat. *iubēre* 'command' (as orig. 'stir, rouse'). Walde-P. 1.203 f.

Av. *parat-* : ChSl. *pĭrěti sę*, etc. (above, 6).

Br. *kann*, back-formation to *kanna* 'strike' (after Fr. *bataille* : *battrẽ*); similarly *emgann*, back-formation to *en em ganna* 'fight'.

4. Goth. *waihjō*, ON *víg*, OE, OHG *wīg*, MHG *wīc* : Goth. *weihan*, ON *vega*, etc. 'fight' (20.11).

ON *orrosta*, prob. as orig. 'unrest' cpd. of *or-* 'out' (Goth. *uz-*, etc.) and a form corresponding to OHG *rasta* 'rest, period of time', OE *ræst* 'rest, resting place', etc. Noreen, Altisland. Gram. 78.

ON *bardagi*, lit. 'battle-day', cpd. of *bar-* : *berjask* 'fight' (20.11) and *-dagi* : *dagr* 'day'. Vigfusson, s.v.

ON *hildr*, OE *hild*, OHG *hiltia* (all poet. or in proper names), prob. : Ir. *cellach* 'contention, strife', Ir., W. *coll* 'loss, injury', etc., fr. the root in Grk. κλάω 'break', Lith. *kalti* 'pound, hammer, forge', etc. Walde-P. 1.439. Falk-Torp 427 f.

Dan., Sw., Du. *slag*, also and orig. 'a blow' : Dan. *slaa*, Sw. *slå*, Du. *slaan* 'strike' (cf. Dan. *slaas*, Sw. *slåss* 'fight', 20.11).

OE *gefeoht*, ME *fihte*, NE *fight*, OHG *gifeht*, MHG *gevehte*, NHG *gefecht* : OE *feohtan*, OHG *fehtan* 'fight', etc. (20.11).

OE, ME *camp*, NHG *kampf* (but OHG *campf*, MHG *kampf*, chiefly 'duel'), fr. Lat. *campus* 'field' (whence 'battle-field' and finally 'battle'). NED s.v. *camp* sb. Weigand-H. 1.975.

ME *bataille*, NE *battle*, fr. Fr. *bataille* (above, 2).

OHG, MHG *strīt* (NHG *streit*), the most general word for any form of 'strife' (19.62), also including 'armed strife', as still in NHG *streitaxt* 'battle-ax'.

NHG *schlacht*, fr. MHG *slahte*, OHG *slahta* 'killing, slaughter' : OHG *slahan* 'strike', etc. (cf. Dan. *slag*, etc., above).

5. Lith. *kova*, Lett. *kauja*, fr. the root of Lith. *kauti*, Lett. *kaut* 'strike', refl. 'fight' (20.11).

Lith. *mušis* : *muštis* 'fight' (20.11).

6. ChSl. *kotora* (Supr., etc.) : Ir. *cath* (above, 3). Berneker 588.

ChSl. *ratĭ*, mostly 'war' (20.13), sometimes 'battle'.

ChSl. *bojĭ* (late), SCr., Boh. *boj*, etc. and SCr. *bitka*, Boh., Russ. *bitva*, Pol. *bitwa* : Slavic *biti* 'strike', refl. 'fight' (20.11). Berneker 68, 117.

Russ. *sraženie* : *srazať sja* 'fight' (20.11).

7. Skt. *yuddha-*, *yudh-* : *yudh-* 'fight' (20.11).

Skt. *raṇa-*, Av. *rōna-*, and cpds. Skt. *samara-*, *samaraṇa-*, Av. *hamarəna-*, OPers. *hamarana-* : Skt. *r̥-* 'rise, move', Grk. ὄρνῦμι 'stir up, rouse', etc. Walde-P. 1.136.

Skt. *pṛtanā-*, Av. *pəšana*, *pašanā-* : Av. *parət-*, ChSl. *pĭrěti sę* 'fight', etc. (20.11). Walde-P. 2.42. Barth. 896 f.

Av. *arəza* (*arəzah-*, *arəzya-*), etym.? Barth. 201 f.

20.13 WAR

Grk.	πόλεμος	Goth.	wigana (dat. sg.)	Lith.	karas
NG	πόλεμος	ON	styrjǫld, gunnr, strīð	Lett.	kar's
Lat.	bellum	Dan.	krig	ChSl.	branĭ, ratĭ
It.	guerra	Sw.	krig	SCr.	rat, vojna
Fr.	guerre	OE	gewin, gefeoht, wīg,	Boh.	válka
Sp.	guerra		orlege, gūþ	Pol.	wojna
Rum.	războiu	ME	werre	Russ.	vojna
Ir.	cocad	NE	war	Skt.	vigraha-
NIr.	cogadh	Du.	oorlog, krijg		
W.	rhyfel	OHG	gifeht, strīt, wīg, ur-liugi		
Br.	brezel	MHG	urliuge, strīt, wīc		
		NHG	krieg		

'War' is a prolonged state of organized fighting, and the distinction from the single 'battle' is secondary and far from universal. Several of the words listed here were also in part more commonly used for 'battle', some in the same period (e.g. OE, OHG *wīg*, OE *gefeoht*, OHG *gifeht*), some only earlier (e.g. Grk. πόλεμος). One is a compound of the word for 'battle'. Others are from semantic sources similar to those for 'battle', and logically might equally well have denoted 'battle' (cf. e.g. ChSl. *branĭ* : *brati*).

1. Grk. πόλεμος (also πτόλεμος in Hom. and various dial.), in Hom. freq. 'battle', prob. : πάλλω 'shake, brandish' and in form esp. πελεμίζω 'shake, cause to tremble', pass. 'tremble', Goth. *us-filma* 'amazed', ON *felmtr* 'fright', *felmta* 'be frightened, tremble'. Walde-P. 2.52. Boisacq 762.

2. Lat. *bellum*, old *duellum*, etym. dub. : *duo* 'two'; sense 'duel' only for MLat. *duellum*, the archaic form revived and consciously associated with *duo*), perh. : Hom. δαΐ 'in battle' (**daϝi), δαΐ-φρων 'tried in battle', δήϊος 'hostile', etc. Walde-P. 1.766. Walde-H. 1.100 f. Ernout-M. 107 ("origine inconnue").

It., Sp. *guerra*, Fr. *guerre*, fr. a Frank. form = OHG *werra* 'confusion, strife' : *werran* 'confuse, entangle'. REW 9524a.

Rum. *războiu*, older 'battle', fr. Slavic, cf. ChSl. *razbojĭ* 'murder, robbery', *bojĭ* 'battle', etc. (20.12). Tiktin 1313.

3. Ir. *cocad*, NIr. *cogadh*, cpd. of *con-*, *co-* 'together' and *cath* 'battle' (20.12).

W. *rhyfel*, cpd. of intensive *rhy-* (**pro-*) and *bel* (arch.) 'tumult, havoc, war', beside *belu* 'make war, bicker', orig. 'prick, sting', cf. *belydd* 'gadfly', all prob. : Lith. *gelti* 'sting', Grk. βελόνη 'needle, point', Ir. *at-baill* 'dies', etc. (Walde-P. 1.689). The meaning is prob. influenced by Lat. *bellum*. Loth, Mots lat. 137. G. S. Lane, Language 7.278 f.

Br. *brezel* = Corn. *bresel* 'strife' (Ir. *Bresal*, W. *Com-bresel*, etc.), prob. fr. the root of Ir. *brissim* 'break'. Walde-P. 2.206. Pedersen 2.54, 668.

4. Goth. *wigana* (dat. sg. Lk. 14.31, written *wigā na* Cod. Arg., cf. Feist 562f.) beside *waihjō*, OE, OHG *wīg*, MHG *wīc* both 'war' and 'battle' (20.12).

ON *styrr* (gen. *styrjar*), lit. 'tumult', but also 'battle, war', in prose chiefly cpd. *styrjǫld* (with *ǫld* 'time, age') : OE *styrian* 'set in motion, stir, rouse', *gestyr* 'motion', etc. Falk-Torp 1194. Vigfusson 601.

ON *gunnr*, OE *gūþ*, OS *gūðea*, in cpds. *gūð-*, OHG *gund-* : Grk. θείνω 'strike, kill', φόνος 'murder', Ir. *gonim* 'wound, kill', Skt. *han-* 'strike, kill', etc. Walde-P. 1.680.

ON *strīð* (late in this sense, earlier chiefly 'woe, grief'), OHG, MHG *strīt*, general terms for 'strife' (19.62), but also armed strife 'battle, war', as freq. also Dan., Sw. *strid*, NHG *streit*.

OE *gewin* 'toil, labor', also 'struggle, contest' and 'war' (e.g. *Troiāna gewin* 'Trojan war') : *winnan* 'toil, labor, strive, fight' (20.11).

OE *gefeoht*, OHG *gifeht* 'battle' (20.12), also 'war'.

OE *orlege*, OS *orlag, orlogi*, MLG *orloge, orloch*, Du. *oorlog*, OHG *urliugi*, MHG *urliuge*, perh. as 'situation lacking oaths' (of peace) : Goth. *liuga* 'marriage', Ir. *luige*, W. *llu* 'oath', but in part confused with the Gmc. group for 'fate', OE *orlæg*, OS *orlag*, OHG *orlac*, etc. (fr. **legh-* 'lie'). Walde-P. 2.415, 425. Franck-v. W. 477. Falk-Torp 801.

Late OE *wyrre, werre*, ME *werre*, NE *war*, fr. Northeastern OFr. *werre* = Central OFr., NFr. *guerre* (above, 2). NED s.v.

Du. *krijg*, NHG *krieg*, but MLG *krich* (> Dan., Sw. *krig*) mostly 'strife', MHG *kriec* mostly 'exertion, opposition, enmity', etc., less often 'war', OHG *krīg* 'stubbornness, defiance' (cf. vb. NHG *kriegen* 'get', orig. 'strive', 11.16), prob. : Ir. *brīg* 'strength, worth', Grk. ὕβρις 'violence', βριαρός 'firm, strong'. Walde-P. 1.686. Franck-v. W. 349 f.

5. Lith. *karas, karē*, Lett. *kar's* : Lith. *karias*, OPruss. *kragis* (= *kargis*) 'army', Goth. *harjis* 'army', etc. (20.15).

6. ChSl. *branĭ* (reg. for πόλεμος in Gospels) : *brati* 'fight' (20.11). Berneker 74.

ChSl. *ratĭ* (Supr. freq., sometimes 'battle' but mostly = πόλεμος), SCr. *rat* (Russ. *rat'* formerly used for 'army' and 'war') : ChSl. *retĭ* 'strife, emulation', *retiti* 'contend' : Skt. *r̥-* 'rise, move', Grk. ὄρνῦμι 'stir up, rouse', etc. Cf. Skt. *raṇa-*, etc. battle (20.13), fr. the same root. Walde-P. 1.139.

SCr. Russ. *vojna*, Pol. *wojna* (Boh. *vojna* now mostly in phrases like 'call to war', i.e. to military service), beside ChSl. *vojĭnŭ* (pl. *voji*) 'soldier, warrior' : Lith. *veju, vyti* 'pursue, chase', Skt. *veti* 'pursues, strives after, drives, etc.', Av. *vayeiti* 'pursues', etc. Walde-P. 1.230. Brückner 629.

Boh. *válka* (Pol. *walka* 'fight, combat, struggle', WhRuss. *valka* 'battle, woodcutting') : Boh. *váleti* 'make war', OPruss. *ūlint* 'fight', OE *wæl* 'battle-field, corpses of the slain', ON *valr* 'bodies of the slain', OHG *wuol* 'defeat, ruin, plague', etc. Walde-P. 1.304 f. Otherwise Brückner 599 (: ChSl. *valiti*, Lat. *volvere* 'turn', etc.).

7. Skt. *vigraha-* 'strife', sometimes 'war', fr. *vi-grabh-* 'stretch apart, separate, divide', and also 'fight, wage war'.

But in general for Indo-Iran., see words listed under 'battle'.

20.132. 'Enemy' in war. As noted in 19.52, most of the words for personal 'enemy' (vs. 'friend') cover the 'enemy' in war, but in some languages separate words are preferred in the latter sense. Thus Grk. πολέμιοι vs. ἐχθροί, Lat. *hostis* (orig. 'stranger', 19.55) vs. *inimīcus*, Russ. *neprijatel'* vs. *vrag*.

20.14 PEACE

Grk.	*εἰρήνη*	Goth.	*gawairþi*	Lith.	*taika*
NG	*εἰρήνη*	ON	*friðr*	Lett.	*miers*
Lat.	*pāx*	Dan.	*fred*	ChSl.	*mirŭ*
It.	*pace*	Sw.	*fred*	SCr.	*mir*
Fr.	*paix*	OE	*sib(b), friþ*	Boh.	*mír*
Sp.	*paz*	ME	*pais, frith*	Pol.	*pokój*
Rum.	*pace*	NE	*peace*	Russ.	*mir*
Ir.	*sīd*	Du.	*vrede*	Skt.	*saṁdhi-*
NIr.	*sīothchāin*	OHG	*fridu, sibba*	Av.	*āxšti-*
W.	*heddwch*	MHG	*vride*		
Br.	*peoc'h*	NHG	*friede*		

Words for 'peace' are based on such notions as 'stable condition, quiet', 'friendship', 'kinship' and 'agreement'. Brugmann, Ber. Sächs. Ges. 1916. no. 3.

1. Grk. *εἰρήνη* (dial. *ἰράνα*, etc.), etym.? Brugmann, op. cit. (fr. the root of *ἀραρίσκω* 'fit, join'). Kretschmer, Glotta 10.238. Debrunner, Gött. Gel. Anz. 1916.741 (pre-Greek origin).

2. Lat. *pāx* (> Romance words), fr. **pāk̑-* beside **pāĝ-* in *pangere* 'fasten, fix, join together', Grk. *πήγνυμι* 'fix, drive in', etc. Walde-P. 2.2. Ernout-M. 720.

3. Ir. *sīd*, *sīth*, NIr. *sīothchāin* (cpd. with *cāin* 'law, rule'), fr. **sēdo-*, beside W. *hedd* (poet.), deriv. *heddwch*, Corn. *hedh*, fr. **sedo-*, both prob. as orig. 'stable condition' fr. **sed-* 'sit'. Stokes 297 f. Loth, RC 36.162. Otherwise Walde-P. 2.462 (with refs.).

W. (obs.) *tanc*, *tangnef*, *tangnefedd* (cf. *Tancorix*, etc.), prob. : OE *þanc* 'satisfaction, pleasure', etc. Loth, RC 41.225.

Br. *peoc'h*, fr. Lat. *pāx*. Loth, Mots lat. 194.

4. Goth. *gawairþi*, cf. OHG *giwurt* 'liking', prob. fr. the root of Goth. *wairþan* 'become', with development through 'coming together, agreement'. Brugmann, op. cit. 13. Feist 209. Otherwise (: *wairþ* 'value, worth') Schrader, Reallex. 1.650 and others (refs. in Feist).

ON *friðr*, OE *friþ*, OHG *fridu*, etc., general Gmc. (Goth. only in the name *Friþa-reiks*) : Goth. *frijōn*, OE *frēon* 'love', Goth. *frijōnds*, OE *frēond* 'friend', Skt. *prī-* 'please', *priya-* 'dear', etc. Walde-P. 2.87. Falk-Torp 271 f.

OE *sib(b)*, OHG *sibba* (reg. for *pāx* in Tat.), properly 'kinship, kin' (2.81, 19.23), whence 'peace' as the normal condition among kin.

5. Lith. *taika* (neolog. in place of *pakajus*, formerly the usual word, fr. Pol. *pokój*) : *tikt* 'fit, suit, agree', *taikyti* 'mediate', *taikus* 'suitable, peaceful', *pataika* 'idleness' (Walde-P. 1.725, Leskien, Ablaut 287, etc.).

OLith. *mieras*, Lett. *miers* = ChSl. *mirŭ* (below, 6).

6. ChSl. *mirŭ* (also secondarily 'world', 1.1), SCr., Russ. *mir*, Boh. *mír* (Pol. *mir*, mostly replaced by *pokój*), *r*-formation fr. the same root as ChSl. *milŭ* 'pitiful', Russ. *mil* 'dear', Lith. *mielas* 'dear', *mylėti* 'love', Lat. *mītis* 'mild, gentle', etc. Walde-P. 2.244 Berneker 2.60 f.

Pol. *pokój* = Boh. *pokoj* 'quiet, rest, room', Russ. *pokoj* 'rest' : ChSl. *pokojĭ* 'rest', *po-kojiti* 'calm, put at rest', *po-čiti* 'rest', etc. Berneker 538 f.

7. Skt. *saṁdhi-*, lit. 'putting together, union, conjunction', whence 'accord compact, peace' : *saṁ-dhā-* 'put together'.

Av. *āxšti-*, NPers. *āšti*, prob. : *ā-(x)štā-* in caus. 'put in place, appoint', cpd. of *stā-* (*xštā-*) 'stand'. Brugmann, op. cit. 11. Barth. 311, 1602.

20.15 ARMY

Grk.	*στρατός, στράτευμα*	Goth.	*harjis*	Lith.	*kariuomenė* (*karias, armija*)
NG	*στρατός* (Byz. *φοσσᾶτον*)	ON	*herr*	Lett.	*kar'š* (*kar'a spēks*)
Lat.	*exercitus*	Dan.	*hær, armé*	ChSl.	*vojĭ*
It.	*esercito, armata*	Sw.	*här, armé*	SCr.	*vojska, armija*
Fr.	*armée*	OE	*here, fierd*	Boh.	*vojsko, armáda*
Sp.	*ejército*	ME	*(h)oste, here, ferd*	Pol.	*wojsko, armia*
Rum.	*armată, oştire* (*oaste*)	NE	*army*	Russ.	*armija* (*vojsko*)
Ir.	*slūag*	Du.	*heer, leger*	Skt.	*senā-*
NIr.	*arm, sluagh*	OHG	*heri*	Av.	*haēnā-, spāda-*
W.	*byddin* (*llu*)	MHG	*her(e)*	OPers.	*kāra-, hainā-*
Br.	*arme(ad)*	NHG	*heer, armee*		

Words for 'army' are based upon such notions as 'armed' (force), 'training' (> 'military training, trained force'), 'enemy' ('hostile army' > 'army'), 'expedition' (> 'military expedition' > 'army'), 'camp' (through 'military camp'), and 'missile' (?). Several of the words, including a considerable cognate group, are used also in part for 'people, crowd', which may well be secondary (as in NE *host*), but the development 'people' > 'people in arms, army' is also possible. The French *armée* has been extensively borrowed all over Europe.

1. IE **kor-* in words for 'war', 'army', and 'people, crowd'. Walde-P. 1.462 f. Feist 247.

Here as 'army' Goth. *harjis*, ON *herr*, etc., general Gmc.; Lith. (*karias*, *karauna*) *kariuomenė* (now the preferred form; cf. NSB s.v. *armija*), Lett. *kar'š* (also 'war', hence for 'army' esp. *kar'a spēks*, with *spēks* 'strength, might' also sometimes alone 'army'), OPruss. *kragis* (= *kargis*); OPers. *kāra-* (also 'people, nation'), NPers. *kār-zār* 'battle-field' (Barth. 465); cf. Ir. *cuire* 'crowd, band', Grk. *κοίρανος* (**κόρμανος*) 'ruler, leader'.

2. Grk. *στρατός*, in form = Skt. *stṛta-* 'spread out, extended', vbl. adj. fr. the root **ster-* 'spread out' in Grk. *στόρνυμι*, Skt. *stṛ-*, Lat. *sternere*, etc. Development through 'crowd, people' (attested in Pind., Aesch., etc., and cf. Cret. *σταρτός* a division of the people); or through 'camp, encamped army' (cf. *στρατόπεδον*, Byz. *φοσσᾶτον*, Du. *leger*)? Hence also *στρατία* 'army' and vb. *στρατεύω* 'serve as soldier, campaign', *στράτευμα* 'army', *στρατιώτης* 'soldier', *στρατόπεδον* 'camp', sometimes 'army'. Walde-P. 2.638 f. Boisacq 918.

Byz. *φοσσᾶτον* 'camp' and pop. word for 'army', fr. late Lat. *fossātum* 'ditch' (: *fossāre*, *fodere* 'dig'). Hence also OSp. *fousado*, OPort. *fossado*, Prov. *fosat* 'army' (REW 3461). Development through 'moat' > 'camp' (provided with a moat) > 'army'.

3. Lat. *exercitus* (> It. *esercito*, Sp. *ejército*, both lit. words in orig.), orig. 'training', abstract of *exercēre* 'pursue, practice, exercise' (cpd. of *arcēre* 'inclose, confine, hold off'), hence esp. 'military training' and in concrete sense 'body of trained men, army'. Ernout-M. 67 f.

Lat. *hostis* 'enemy' (orig. 'stranger' 19.55) was used in MLat. for 'military service, army' (whence Rum. *oaste*, and the older Romance terms OIt. *oste*, OFr. *ost*, Sp. *huesta*, Port. *hoste*, all obs. except Rum. *oaste*, and for this now pop. *oştire*, prop. 'campaign', fr. the deriv. vb. *oşti* 'go to war', and in lit. *armată*; cf. Tiktin 1068, 1098). Although the direct transition 'hostile army' to 'army' in general is, of course, possible, the more likely development was through use in such phrases as *convenire in hostem*, *exire in hostem*, etc., where *in hostem* meant orig. 'against the enemy' but was easily construed 'into military service' and consequently 'into the army'. Buck, Cl. Ph. 14.12 f. Diez 229. REW 4201.

MLat. *armata* 'armed force', either land force or more commonly naval force (cf. Du Cange), fr. fem. sg. of Lat. *armātus* (pple. of *armāre* 'provide with arms', fr. *arma* 'arms, weapons', 20.21), and prob. abstracted fr. *armāta classis* (cf. *classis*, 20.16). Hence It. *armata* used of either 'army' or 'fleet', Sp., Port. *armada* 'fleet', Fr. *armée* 'army' (> Dan., Sw. *armé*, NHG *armee*, SCr., Russ. *armija*, etc.; Russ. > Lith. *armija*); Rum. *armată* (neolog.). Also OFr. > ME *armie*, NE *army*, but the early use was 'armed expedition' or 'armed force', either of sea or of land, sometimes 'fleet', and only later restricted to a land force (NED s.v. *army*).

4. Ir. *slūag* 'host, troop, army', NIr. *sluagh* (now as 'army' mostly replaced by *arm*, fr. NE *army*), W. *llu* (mostly 'host'), OCorn. *luu* : ChSl. *sluga* 'servant' (orig. coll. 'body of servants, household', as in Ir. *teglach*, W. *teulu* 'family', cpds. with Ir. *tech*, W. *ty* 'house'). Walde-P. 2.716. Pedersen 1.84.

W. *byddin*, in MW 'troop' : Ir. *buden* 'troop, band, quantity', etym. dub. Pedersen 1.363, 2.59. Thurneysen, Keltorom. 91.

Br. *arme*, fr. Fr. *armée* (above, 3).

5. Goth. *harjis*, etc., above, 1.

Dan., Sw. *armé*, NE *army*, NHG *armee*, fr. Fr. *armée* (above, 3).

OE *fierd* (*ferd*, *fyrd*), ME *ferd*, orig 'expedition' : OHG *fart*, ON *ferð* 'journey', etc., OE, OHG *faran*, ON *fara* 'travel', etc. NED s.v. *ferd*.

ME *(h)oste*, fr. OFr. *ost* (above, 3).

Du. *leger* : NHG *lager* 'lying place, lair, (military) camp', OHG *legar*, OE *leger* 'couch, bed, lair' (NE *lair*), fr. the root of OE *licgan*, OHG *liggen* 'lie', etc. 'Army' fr. 'camp'. Franck-v. W. 376.

6. ChSl. *vojĭ* (Gospels, Supr., etc.), late *vojsko*, *vojska*, SCr. *vojska*, Boh., Russ. *vojsko*, Pol. *wojsko* : ChSl. *vojinŭ* 'soldier', SCr., Russ. *vojna* 'war', etc. (20.13).

But Russ. *vojsko* is now arch., or used in pl. for 'troops'; for the modern 'army' now replaced by *armija* (also familiar in other Slavic languages and in part perh. also more common as a technical term than the native words), fr. Fr. *armée*. Cf. also Boh. *armáda*, fr. Sp. *armada*, but in sense of 'army'.

7. Skt. *senā-*, Av. *haēnā-* (esp. 'daevic army, enemy'), OPers. *hainā-* ('hostile army'), prob. the same word as Skt. *senā-*, Av. *haēnā-* 'missile', beside Skt. *sāyaka-* 'intended for hurling', sb. 'missile, arrow', fr. a root meaning 'throw', ultimately the same as in the Eur. words for 'sow', Lat. *serere*, etc. (8.31). Walde-P. 2.459 ff. (with refs.).

Av. *spāda-*, *spāδa-*, OPers. *spāθmaidaya* loc. sg. 'in the army, on campaign' (NR b 30), NPers. *sipāh*, etym.? Barth. 1617.

OPers. *kāra-*, above, 1.

20.16 FLEET

Grk.	*στόλος*	Goth.	....	Lith.	*laivynas*
NG	*στόλος*	ON	*skipastōll, skipaherr, floti*	Lett.	*flote*
Lat.	*classis*	Dan.	*flaade*	SCr.	*flota*
It.	*flotta, armata*	Sw.	*flotta*	Boh.	*lod'stvo*
Fr.	*flotte*	OE	*flota, scipfyrd, sciphere*	Pol.	*flota*
Sp.	*armada, flota*	ME	*flete, navie*	Russ.	*flot*
Rum.	*flotă*	NE	*fleet*		
Ir.	*coblach*	Du.	*vloot*		
NIr.	*cabhlach*	OHG	*scefmenigī*		
W.	*llynges, fflyd*	MHG	*schifmenige*		
Br.	*listri*	NHG	*flotte*		

The most widespread group of words for 'fleet' is one of Gmc. origin, derived from a verb meaning 'float'. The OE word passed into French and hence to the other Romance languages and by various paths to Lettic and Slavic.

Other words are from 'expedition' or 'class', or are derived from words for 'ship'.

Some of the words may cover also 'navy', that is, the whole naval force of a nation (as contrasted with 'fleet' as a naval unit corresponding to an 'army' as a land force), and NE *navy* was in its earlier use only 'fleet'. But generally there are other terms for 'navy', as Grk. simply *νῆες* 'ships' or the deriv. *τὸ ναυτικόν* (so also NG), It. *marina*, Fr. *marine* (> NHG *marine*, etc.) fr. the fem. of Lat. *marīnus*, deriv. of *mare* 'sea'.

1. Grk. *στόλος*, the most common word, but also general 'an expedition' (by land or sea) : *στέλλω* 'set in order, arrange, equip'.

2. Lat. *classis* 'summons to arms' (old and rare), 'class' (of citizens), sometimes 'land force, army' (early), but mostly 'navy', etym. dub. (: *calāre* 'call, summon'?). Walde-P. 1.444. Ernout-M. 193 f. Walde-H. 1.228.

Fr. *flotte* (> It. *flotta*, *frotta*, Sp., Port. *flota*, Rum. *flotă*) fr. OE *flota* (below, 4). REW 3383 a. Gamillscheg 426.

Sp. *armada*, It. *armata*, see 20.15.

3. Ir. *coblach*, NIr. *cabhlach*, perh. cpd. (**com-luga-* or **com-logo-*) : Ir. *long*, W. *llong* 'ship' (if not Lat. loanword, see 10.87). Loth, RC 43.135.

W. *llynges*, coll. of *llong* 'ship' (10.81).

W. *fflyd*, fr. NE *fleet*. Parry-Williams 126.

Br. *listri*, pl. of *lestr* 'ship'.

4. ON *floti*, Dan. *flaade*, Sw. *flotta*, OE *flota* (also 'ship, vessel'), Du. *vloot* (NHG *flotte*, fr. Fr. *flotte*), with ablaut also OE *flēot* 'raft, ship, vessel, bay' (once 'fleet', cf. NED), ME *flete*, NE *fleet* : OE *flēotan* 'float', ON *fljōta* 'float, flow' (10.34). Falk-Torp 224.

ON *skipastōll*, cpd. of *skip* 'ship' and *-stōll* based on MLat. *stolus*, Grk. *στόλος* (above, 1), cf. *stōlaherr* 'equipped army'. Falk-Torp 1556.

ON *skipaherr*, OE *sciphere*, cpd. of *skip*, *scip* 'ship' and *herr*, *here* 'army'.

OE *scipfyrd*, cpd. of *scip* 'ship' and *fierd*, *fyrd* 'expedition, army'.

OHG *scefmenigī*, also *scefo managī*, MHG *schifmenige*, lit. 'a multitude of ships, a ship-horde'.

ME *navie* (NE *navy*), fr. OFr. *navie* 'fleet', VLat. **navia* deriv. of Lat. *nāvis* 'ship'. NED s.v.

5. Lith. *laivynas*, fr. *laivas* 'ship' (10.81).

Lett. *flote*, fr. NHG *flotte*.

6. SCr. *flota*, prob. fr. It. *flotta* (or

NHG *flotte*), Pol. *flota*, fr. NHG *flotte*, Russ. *flot*, prob. (in view of Peter the Great's study of shipbuilding in Holland) fr. Du. *vloot*.

Boh. *lod'stvo*, fr. *lod'* 'ship' (10.81).

7. The interpretation of OPers. *nāviyā* (Bh. 1.86) as nom. sg. meaning 'flotilla' is disputed and indeed in the context improbable. Cf. Kent, JAOS 62.270 f. But the form is just the one to be expected as an Indo-Iranian word for 'fleet', if there were one, that is, deriv. of the word for 'ship', Skt. *nāus*, etc.

20.17 SOLDIER

Grk.	*στρατιώτης*	Goth.	*gadrauhts*	Lith.	*kareivis, žalnierius*
NG	*στρατιώτης*	ON	*hermaðr*	Lett.	*zaldāts, karenieks*
Lat.	*mīles*	Dan.	*soldat*	ChSl.	*vojinŭ*
It.	*soldato*	Sw.	*soldat*	SCr.	*vojnik, soldat*
Fr.	*soldat*	OE	*wīgend, cempa*	Boh.	*voják, vojín*
Sp.	*soldado*	ME	*soudiour, kempe*	Pol.	*żołnierz*
Rum.	*soldat (ostaș)*	NE	*soldier*	Russ.	*soldat*
Ir.	*mīl, ōc, lāech*	Du.	*soldaat*	Skt.	*sainika-, sainya-*
NIr.	*saighdiūir*	OHG	*wīgant, cempho*	Av.	*raθaēštar-*
W.	*milwr*	MHG	*wīgant, kempfe, soldenære*		
Br.	*soudard*	NHG	*soldat*		

The widespread group of Eur. words for 'soldier' comes from late Lat. derivs. of a word for 'soldiers' pay'. Others are derived from words for 'war' (NE *warrior*, NHG *krieger*, which are more comprehensive than 'soldier', are not included in the list; but some of the older words included are also more nearly 'warrior'), 'army', or 'fight'. A few were in origin 'young man', 'layman', or 'member of a crowd, band'.

1. Derivs. of Lat. *solidus*, the name of the gold coin which was the standard unit from the time of Constantine the Great. Hence *solidum* or *solidāta* 'soldier's pay', *solidāre* 'pay the soldiers' wages', and derivs. with various suffixes for 'soldier'.

1) *Sol(i)dārius*, *sol(i)dātārius* > OFr. *soldoier*, *soudoier*, etc. ME *soudiour*, *souldier*, etc., NE *soldier*, NIr. *saighdiūir* (perh. influenced by MIr. *saigdeoir* 'sagittarius'). Fr. *soudard* (16th cent. re-formation of *soudoier*; Bloch 2.280) > Br. *soudard*.

2) *Sol(i)denārius* > OIt. *soldaniere*, OFr. *saudenier*, MHG *soldenære* (NHG *söldner* only 'mercenary' after the introduction of *soldat*) > Pol. *żołnierz* > Lith. *žalnierius*.

3) *Sol(i)dātus* > It. *soldato* > Sp., Port. *soldado*, Fr. *soldat* > Rum. *soldat*, Du. *soldaat*, NHG *soldat* > Dan., Sw. *soldat*, Lett. *zaldāts*, SCr., Russ. *soldat*. The wider prevalence of this type is due to the influence of It. military terms in the 16th cent. wars. REW 8069. Du Cange 7.516 ff. NED s.v. *soldier*. Buck, Cl. Ph. 14.17 f.

2. Grk. *στρατιώτης*, deriv. of *στρατός*, *στρατιά* 'army' (20.15).

3. Lat. *mīles*, etym. dub., but perh. orig. 'member of a crowd, band' (cf. Goth. *gadrauhts*, below, 5) : Grk. *ὅμῑλος* 'crowd, throng' (occasionally in military application). Walde-P. 2.491. Ernout-M. 614.

Rum. *ostaș* (now poet.), deriv. of *oaste* 'army' (20.15).

4. Ir. *ōc*, lit. 'young man', hence 'warrior' (cf. RIA contrib. s.v.) sb. fr. the adj. *ōc* 'young' (14.14).

Ir. *lāech*, fr. Lat. *lāicus* 'layman'.

Hence freq. also *ōclach*, cpd. with *ōc* (above). Vendryes, De hib. voc. 148.

Ir. *mīl*, W. *milwr* (cpd. with *gwr* 'man'), fr. Lat. *mīles*.

5. Goth. *gadrauhts* : ON *drōtt*, OE *dryht* 'people, followers', OHG *truht* 'multitude', etc., Goth. *driugan* 'do military service', ON *drȳgja* 'commit', OE *drēogan* 'perform, endure', Lith. *draugas* 'companion', ChSl. *drugŭ* 'friend', etc. Military application peculiar to Gothic. Walde-P. 1.860. Feist 185 f., 179.

ON *hermaðr* (less usually also OE, MHG *hereman*), lit. 'war-man'.

OE *wīgend*, OHG, MHG *wīgant* (NHG *Weigand* as name), orig. pres. pple. of OE *wīgan*, etc. 'fight' (20.11).

OE *cempa* (reg. for *mīles* in OE Gospels, etc., also 'champion, athlete'), ME *kempe*, OHG *cempho*, MHG *kempfe* (both esp. 'one who fights in single combat', but also general; reg. for *mīles* in Tat.), ON *kappi* mostly 'champion', fr. VLat. *campio* 'champion, fighter' (fr. *campus* 'field' and 'battle-field', cf. NHG *kämpfen*, etc., 20.11). Weigand-H. 1.975. Falk-Torp 519.

6. Lith. *kareivis* (neolog. replacing the loanword *žalnierius*), also Lett. *kareivis* (but prob. fr. Lith., Mühl.-Endz. 2.161), genuine Lett. *karenieks*, fr. Lith. *karias*, Lett. *kar'š* 'army, war' (20.15).

7. ChSl. *vojinŭ* (pl. *voji*), Boh. *vojín*, *voják* (Pol. *wojak*, Russ. *vojin* arch. or 'warrior') : *vojna* 'war', etc. (20.13).

8. Skt. *sainika-*, *sainya-*, derivs. of *senā-* 'army' (20.15).

Av. *raθaēštar-*, *raθaēštā-*, *raθōištā-*, lit. 'standing in the chariot', cpd. of loc. sg. of *raθa-* 'wagon, chariot' and derivs. of *stā-* 'stand'. Cf. Skt. *ratheṣṭhā-* 'chariot-fighter'. Barth. 1506.

20.18 GENERAL

Grk.	*στρατηγός*	Goth.	*(kindins)*	Lith.	*generolas*
NG	*στρατηγός*	ON	*(hers) hǫfðingi, hertogi*	Lett.	*g'eneralis*
Lat.	*dux, imperātor*			ChSl.	*(vojevoda)*
It.	*generale*	Dan.	*general*	SCr.	*general*
Fr.	*général*	Sw.	*general*	Boh.	*generál*
Sp.	*general*	OE	*heretoga, lādþēow*	Pol.	*generał, jenerał*
Rum.	*general*	ME	*marscal, heretoge*	Russ.	*general*
Ir.	*tōisech (catha)*	NE	*general*	Skt.	*senāpati-*
NIr.	*taoiseach*	Du.	*generaal*	OPers.	*maθišta-*
W.	*cadfridog*	OHG	*herizogo, leitid(o)*		
Br.	*jeneral*	MHG	*houbetman, herzoge*		
		NHG	*general*		

'General' is understood here as the commander of an army, without regard to the more technical applications in modern military terminology. The modern international term comes from the adjective 'general', of Lat. orig., used substantively and finally specialized to military use.

The older terms are words meaning literally 'leader of an army' or simply 'leader', or 'head-man, chief'.

1. Lat. *generālis*, orig. 'related or belonging to a *genus* (sort)', later 'common, general', was borrowed in most of the Eur. languages in this sense. Fr. *général* as sb. came to mean esp. 'chief of a religious community (cf. MLat. *abbas generalis*, *magister generalis*), or of a group of military units' (*capitaine général*, 14th cent.), whence (in part through NHG) the common Eur. word.

2. Grk. *στρατηγός*, fr. *στρατός* 'army' and *ἄγω* 'lead'. The regular term (Archil.+), but not found in Homer,

who has only the less technical *ἡγεμών* 'leader', applied to Agamemnon, Hector, etc., but also to many minor chiefs.

3. Lat. *dux* 'leader' in wide sense, but also esp. military, fr. *dūcere* 'lead'.

Lat. *imperātor* 'commander', esp. 'commander-in-chief, general', fr. *imperāre* 'command'.

4. Ir. *tōisech (catha)*, lit. 'leader (of battle)', NIr. *taoiseach* = W. *tywysog* 'leader, prince', beside Ir. *tūus* 'beginning', W. *tywys* 'direction', prob. fr. **to-wid-t-*, deriv. of IE *weid-* 'see, know'. Walde-P. 1.255. Pedersen 1.308.

W. *cadfridog*, lit. 'battle-inciter', cpd. of *cad* 'battle' and *bridog*, deriv. of *brido* 'break out, erupt' also 'stir, incite' (Evans, s v.).

5. Goth. *kindins* (quotable only for *ἡγεμών* as 'governor'; also military term?), orig. 'head of a people or tribe' : ON *kind*, OE *cyn(n)* 'kin, people', Lat. *gēns*, *gentis* 'people, clan', etc. Cf. Goth. *þiudans* 'king' : *þiuda* 'nation'. Feist 311.

ON *hǫfðingi* 'chief' both political and military, for the latter esp. *hershǫfðingi* (*herr* 'army') : *hǫfuð* 'head'.

ON *hertogi*, OE *heretoga*, ME *heretoge*, OHG *her(i)zogo*, MHG *herzoge* (NHG *herzog* 'duke' as title), cpd. of ON *herr*, etc. 'army' and agent noun to Goth. *tiuhan* 'lead, draw', OE *tēon*, OHG *ziohan* 'draw' (cf. Lat. *dux* : *dūcere*, above, 3).

OE *lādþēow* (*lātteow*, etc.), the reg. rendering of *dux* in the Gospels, early ME *lattow*, cpd. of *lād* 'way, course, leading' and *þēow* 'servant'.

ME *marscal* (NE *marshal*), fr. OFr. *marescal*, fr. the Gmc., cf. OHG *marahscalh*, lit. 'horse-servant', whence in OFr. and Frankish-Latin usage (through 'master of horse') used as a title of dignity, and in a military sense loosely for 'commander, general' (in early ME possibly the best word for 'highest military officer'; cf. NED s.v. 3a).

OHG *leitid*, *leitido*, lit. 'leader', fr. *leiten* 'lead'. Regular for *dux* in Tat., but prob. mere semantic borrowing.

MHG *houbetman*, lit. 'head-man', used also for the 'chief military officer' (NHG *hauptmann* 'captain').

6. ChSl. *vojevoda* in Gospels renders *ἡγεμών* and *στρατηγός* (once simply transcribed *stratigŭ*), both only 'governor' in NT, and in general Slavic the word is an official title 'governor' or 'duke' (anglicized as *voivode*, *vaivode*, *waywode*, cf. NED s.v.). But in origin it was a military term, like NHG *herzog* 'duke' (above, 5), and a literal translation of Grk. *στρατηγός*—namely a cpd. of *vojĭ* 'army' (20.15, also pl. *voji* 'soldiers, troops' 20.17) and the root of *vedą*, *vesti*, *voditi* 'lead'.

7. Skt. *senāpati-*, cpd. of *senā-* 'army' and *pati-* 'lord, master'.

OPers. *maθišta-*, lit. 'greatest' (= Av. *masišta-*, superl. of *mas-*), but used as 'chief military officer', e.g. *Vidarna nāma Pārsa manā bandaka avamšām maθištam akunavam* "Vidarna, a Persian, my servant, him I made their chief".

20.19. Admiral. What is the all but universal modern Eur. title (the old Greek term has not yielded) is of Arabic origin. Arab. *amir-al-*, that is *amir* 'commander' (anglicized as *emir*) followed by the article, in phrases like *amir-al-mā* 'commander of the water', *amir-al-bahr* 'commander of the sea', was interpreted as an independent noun and was so adopted. There arose a great variety of forms, partly by association with words of Lat. origin (so MLat. *admiralis*, *admirabilis*, as if fr. Lat. *ad-mīrārī* 'wonder at, admire'; hence the *d* in the most common current

form), partly by adoption of native suffixes (It. *ammiraglio*, OIt. also *almiraglio*, Sp. *almirante*, OFr. *amirand*, Lith. *admirolas*, etc.). NED s.v. *admiral*.

The older words, so far as quotable, were derivs. or phrases with words for 'ship' or 'fleet'. Thus Grk. *ναύαρχος* (so still NG), cpd. of *ναῦς* 'ship' and the root of *ἄρχω* 'lead, rule'; late also *στολάρχης*, cpd. of *στόλος* 'fleet'; Lat. *praefectus classis* 'commander of the fleet'. So also W. *llyngesydd*, fr. *llynges* 'fleet' with suffix *-ydd* (Pedersen 2.17).

20.21 WEAPONS, ARMS

(pl. or coll.)

Grk.	*ὅπλα*	Goth.	*wēpna*	Lith.	*ginklai*
NG	*ὅπλα, ἅρματα*	ON	*vāpn*	Lett.	*ieruoci*
Lat.	*arma, tēla*	Dan.	*vaaben*	ChSl.	*orąžĭja*
It.	*armi*	Sw.	*vapen*	SCr.	*oružje*
Fr.	*armes*	OE	*wǣpnu*	Boh.	*zbraně*
Sp.	*armas*	ME	*wepens, armes*	Pol.	*broń, oręż*
Rum.	*arme*	NE	*weapons, arms*	Russ.	*oružie*
Ir.	*airm*	Du.	*wapens*	Skt.	*āyudha-, astra-, çastra-*
NIr.	*airm*	OHG	*wāfan, giwāfani*		
W.	*arfau*	MHG	*wāfen, gewǣfen*	Av.	*zaēna-, zaya-, snaiθiš-, sōiδiš-*
Br.	*armou*	NHG	*waffen*		

Generic words for 'weapons, arms' come by specialization of 'implements' to 'implements of warfare', or of 'fittings' through 'defensive armor', or by generalization from missile or cutting weapons derived from verbs for 'throw' or 'cut'. Some are from verbs for 'strike' or 'fight'.

1. Grk. *ὅπλον* 'instrument, implement, weapon', pl. *ὅπλα* 'arms, weapons' : *ἕπω* (in cpds. *ἀμφι-*, *δι-*, *ἐφ-*, etc.) 'be busy about, look after, etc.' : Skt. *sap-* 'care for, attend to', Av. *hap-* 'hold, support'. Walde-P. 2.487. Boisacq 270, 707 f.

NG *ἅρματα* (pl.; sg. *ἅρμα* not used), fr. Lat. *arma* (below). G. Meyer, Neugr. Stud. 3.11.

2. Lat. *arma* (pl.; VLat. fem. sg. *arma* > Romance forms, all in pl. 'arms, weapons'. REW 650), sometimes defensive armor (vs. *tēla*), but mostly generic : Lat. *armus* 'upper arm, shoulder', Goth. *arms*, etc. 'arm' (orig. 'joint'), Lat. *artus*, *articulus* 'joint', Grk. *ἁρμός* 'joint', *ἀραρίσκω* 'join, fit'. Walde-P. 1.72. Ernout-M. 72 f. Walde-H. 1.67 f.

Lat. *tēla* 'missile weapons' (spear, etc.) and more generically 'offensive weapons' (sword, etc.), etym. dub. Walde-P. 1.717. Ernout-M. 1021.

3. Ir. *arm*, W. *arf* 'weapon', pl. *airm*, *arfau*, (arch. *eirf*) 'weapons', fr. Lat. *arma* (above). Vendryes, De hib. voc. 114. Loth, Mots lat. 134.

Br. *arm* 'arm, kitchen utensil', pl. *armou* 'weapons', fr. Fr. *arme*.

4. Goth. *wēpna* (pl., renders *ὅπλα*), ON *vāpn*, OHG *wāfan*, MHG *wāfen* (sg. and pl.), Dan. *vaaben* (pl.), Sw. *vapen* (sg. and pl.). OE *wǣpen*, ME *wepen* (sg. and coll., pl. OE *wǣpnu*, ME *wepens*), NE *weapon*, Du. *wapen* (sg., pl. *wepens* and *wepenen*), NHG *waffe* (sg., pl. *waffen*; NHG *wappen* 'coat-of-arms', fr. LG), OHG *giwāfani*, MHG *gewǣfen* (coll.), etym.? Walde-P. 1.257. Feist 561.

5. Lith. *ginklas* (sg.; pl. *ginklai*) : *ginu*, *ginti* 'defend', *genu*, *ginti* 'drive', Grk. *θείνω* 'strike', etc. Walde-P. 1.681.

Lett. *ieruocis* (sg. also 'tool, implement', pl. *ieruoci*) : *ruocis* 'handle', *ruoka*, Lith. *ranka* 'hand'. Cf. Lith. *įrankis* 'tool, means'. Trautmann 237. Mühl.-Endz. 2.60.

6. ChSl. *orążĭje* (sg. 'sword', pl. *orążija* = ὅπλα), SCr. *oružje*, (Boh. *oruži* arch.), Pol. *oręż*, Russ. *oružie* (sg. and coll.; cf. also *ruž'e* 'gun'), apparently fr. an otherwise unattested Slavic root *ręg-*, meaning? Miklosich 281. Brückner 381.

Boh. *zbraň* (sg.; pl. *zbraně*), Pol. *broń* (sg. and coll.) : ChSl. *branĭ* 'war', *brati* 'fight', etc. (20.11). Berneker 74.

7. Indo-Iranian words given in stem-form.

Skt. *āyudha-* (most generic word, cf. Macdonell-Keith 1.60), deriv. of *ā-yudh-* 'make war on, attack', cpd. of *yudh-* 'fight' (20.11).

Skt. *astra-*, perh. (as orig. 'missile') : *as-* 'throw'. Uhlenbeck 19. Walde-P. 1.134.

Skt. *çastra-*, mostly a cutting weapon 'knife, sword, dagger', fr. *ças-* 'cut'.

Av. *zaēna-*, and *zaya-*, with *zayan-* 'armed' : Skt. *heti-* 'missile', *hi-* 'urge, hurl', prob. also Ir. *gae*, OE *gār*, etc. 'spear' (20.26). Walde-P. 1.546. Barth. 1650, 1666. Walde-H. 1.576.

Av. *snaiϑiš-* : *snaϑ-* 'strike', Skt. *çnath-* 'pierce'. Walde-P. 1.402. Barth. 1628.

Av. *sōiδiš-* : *sid-*, Skt. *chid-* 'split'. Barth. 1577.

20.22 ff. For fuller description of weapons and their names, cf. the following. Schrader, Reallex. passim (Keule, Schwert, etc.). Couissin, Les armes romaines. M. L. Keller, Anglo-Saxon Weapon Names. Falk, Altnordische Waffenkunde, Vidensk. Skr. 1914, no. 6. H. Bauersfeld, Die Kriegsaltertümer im Lebor na Huidre, Z. celt. Ph. 19.294 ff. Niederle, Manuel de l'antiquité slave 2.274 ff. Zimmer, Altindisches Leben 298 ff. Macdonell-Keith, 2.591 f. with refs. Geiger, Ostiranische Kultur 441 ff.

20.22 CLUB

Grk.	*ῥόπαλον, κορύνη, ξύλον*	Goth.	*(triu)*	Lith.	*kuoka, kūlė*
NG	*ρόπαλο, ματσούκα*	ON	*klumba, klubba, kylfa,*	Lett.	*vāle*
Lat.	*clāva, fūstis*		*rudda*	ChSl.	*drŭkolĭ*
It.	*mazza*	Dan.	*kølle*	SCr.	*buzdovan*
Fr.	*massue*	Sw.	*klubba*	Boh.	*palice, obušek*
Sp.	*porra*	OE	*sāgol, cycgel*	Pol.	*pałka*
Rum.	*măciucă*	ME	*clubbe (kuggel)*	Russ.	*bulava, dubyna*
Ir.	*lorg*	NE	*club (cudgel)*	Skt.	*vadha-, vadhar, gadā-*
NIr.	*lorg, lorgaid*	Du.	*knots*	Av.	*vazra-, vadar, gaδā-*
W.	*clwb*	OHG	*kolbo*		
Br.	*bataraz*	MHG	*kolbe, kiule*		
		NHG	*keule*		

The 'club' was man's earliest weapon and continued to be one of the recognized weapons down into the historical period, or even to the present day among backward tribes or in rural feuds. It was mainly a striking, but in part also a hurling, weapon.

The words for 'club' are connected with 1) verbs for 'strike' (function), 2) words for 'wood' (material), and 3) words for rounded objects ('knob, knot, ball, lump, wart', etc.) with reference to the characteristic bulging head of a club.

1. Grk. ῥόπαλον, beside ῥαπίς 'rod', ῥάβδος 'rod, wand, staff', perh. : ῥέπω 'incline, bend down', Lith. *virpti* 'quiv-

er', *varpa* 'ear of corn, spike', etc. Walde-P. 1.276 f. Boisacq 835 f.

Grk. κορύνη (Hom., Hdt.; cf. also the κορυνη-φόροι 'club-bearers' of Peisistratus), prob. : κόρυμβος, κορυφή 'top, head', etc. Boisacq 498.

Grk. ξύλον 'wood, piece of wood' (1.43), also 'club' (Hdt., so freq. ξύλα in NT, rendered 'staves'; cf. NG pop. ἔφαγε ξύλο 'got a beating'.

NG ματσούκα, loanword fr. some form of the Romance group, Rum. *măciucă*, Fr. *massue*, etc. (below, 2). G. Meyer, Neugr. Stud. 4.50 f.

2. Lat. *clāva* : *clāvus* usually 'nail' (9.50) but also 'excrescence' on the body or trees. Ernout-M. 194. Walde-H. 1.229.

Lat. *fūstis*, etym. dub., perh. : MHG, NHG *būsch* 'club, swelling', etc. Walde-P. 1.118, 127. Ernout-M. 405. Walde-H. 1.573.

It. *mazza* (Fr. *masse* 'mace, maul'; OFr. also *mace* > ME, NE *mace*), fr. VLat. **mattea;* Fr. *massue*, Rum. *măciucă* (cf. OE *mattuc, mattoc* 'mattock'), fr. VLat. **matteūca*, beside attested Lat. *mateola* a kind of 'mallet, maul' : ChSl. *motyka* 'hoe', Skt. *matya-* 'harrow'. Walde-P. 2.229. Walde-H. 2.49. REW 5425, 5426.

Port., Sp. *porra*, formed to Port. *porro* (cf. Lat. *clāva* : *clāvus*) = Sp. *puerro*, It. *porro* 'leek', fr. Lat. *porrum* id., with reference to the shape of the stalk with its thick base (cf. It. *porro*, Fr. *poireau* also 'wart'). REW 6670.

3. Ir. *lorg* (cf. Z. celt. Ph. 19.309 f.), NIr. *lorg, lorgaid* = OCorn. *lorch* 'staff' : ON *lurkr* 'club, cudgel' (or this fr. Celtic?), root connection? Walde-P. 2.443.

W. *clwb*, fr. NE *club.*

Br. *bataraz*, fr. Fr. *matras* (this fr. Gall. *matara, mataris* 'javelin, pike' in Caesar, etc.), with *b* fr. *baz* 'stick'. Henry 28. REW 5402.

4. Goth. *triu* (= OE *trēow* 'tree, wood', etc., 1.42) in pl. renders ξύλα 'clubs, staves' (above, 1).

ON *klumba, klubba* (> ME *clubbe*, NE *club*), ODan. and still Norw. *klubbe*, Sw. *klubba* : OE *clympre* 'lump of metal', LG *klump*, NE *clump*, and a widespread group of words applied to round objects, as Lat. *globus* 'ball, sphere', *glēba* 'lump of earth', etc. Walde-P. 1.616. Falk-Torp 537.

ON *kylfa*, Dan. *kølle*, OHG *kolbo*, MHG and early NHG *kolbe* (NHG *kolben* 'club, butt-end', etc.), fr. the same root as the preceding group. Walde-P. l.c. Weigand-H. 1.1093. Falk-Torp 560.

ON *rudda* (Norw. dial. *rudda* 'a pliant stick for whipping'; cf. also OE *rodd*, NE *rod*), etym. dub. Hellquist quoted by Falk, Altnordische Waffenkunde 126 (: ON *rydja* 'root out, get rid of'). Torp, Nynorsk 546 (perh. : ON *rōda*, OE *rōd* 'cross', OHG *ruota* 'rod', etc.).

OE *sāgol* (NE dial. *sowel*, cf. NED) : MHG *siegel* 'rung of a ladder', root connection dub. Walde-P. 2.475.

OE *cycgel*, ME *kuggel*, NE *cudgel* : MHG, NHG *kugel* 'ball', etc. Walde-P. 1.558. Falk-Torp 850.

Du. *knots* : OE *cnotta* 'knot', NE *knot*, also NE *knop, knob*, etc. Cf. NHG *knüttel* 'cudgel', deriv. of *knoten* 'knot'. Franck-v. W. 328.

MHG *kiule*, NHG *keule* : ON *kūla* 'swelling, boil', MHG *kūle* 'ball', NHG *kugel* 'ball', Skt. *gola-* 'ball', and many other words for round objects. Walde-P. 1.556. Falk-Torp 590, 591. Weigand-H. 1.1027.

5. Lith. *kuoka* ("apparently best word", Senn; see also NSB s.v.) = Lett. *kuoks* 'tree, piece of wood, stick'. Mühl.-Endz. 2.342.

Lith. *kūlė* ("Keule, Streitkolben", NSB s.v.), fr. MHS *kūle* 'ball' and 'club'. Alminauskis 74.

Lett. *vāle* = Lith. *volė* 'cock' (of a keg, etc.) : Lith. *velti*, Lett. *velt* 'full' (cloth), Lat. *volvere* 'turn around', etc. Walde-P. 1.303. Mühl.-Endz. 4.497.

6. ChSl. *drŭkolĭ*, *drĭkolĭ* (despite the variant spelling *drĭ-* and OBoh. *dřkolna*) a cpd. or deriv. of *drŭ-* in *drŭva* 'wood', etc. Berneker 232 (adversely).

ChSl. *palica* (Supr. = ῥάβδος 'rod for punishment'), Boh. *palice*, Pol. *pałka* 'club' (but Russ. *palka*, SCr. *palica* 'stick, cane'; Pol., Russ. *palica* arch), root connection dub. Walde-P. 2.102. Brückner 391.

SCr. *buzdovan* (*buzdohan* obs.; Bulg. *buzdogan*, Pol. *buzdygan*, etc.), fr. Turk. *bozdogan* 'club'. Berneker 105. Lokotsch 333.

Boh. *obušek*, fr. cpd. of *bušiti* 'hammer, pound', beside *bouchati* 'bang, knock' = Russ. *buchat'* 'throw with a crash, strike', etc., of imitative origin. Berneker 97.

Russ. *bulava* (the pop. word; Pol. *buława* esp. 'hetman's staff'), prob. : OE *bȳl*, NHG *beule*, etc. 'swelling, boil'. Berneker 100. Brückner 48.

Russ. *dubyna*, fr. *dub* 'oak' = ChSl. *dąbŭ* 'tree'. Berneker 216.

7. A prob. Indo-Iranian word for 'club' (cf. Geiger, Ostiran. Kultur 444) is Skt. *vadha-, vadhar* (weapon of striking and hurling, esp. Indra's weapon), Av. *vadar-* (striking weapon) : Skt. *vadh-* 'smite, slay', Av. *vādaya-* 'repulse', Grk. ὠθέω 'thrust, push'. Walde-P. 1.254 f.

Skt. *gadā-*, Av. *gaδā-* (Barth. 488), etym.? Osthoff, Parerga 143.

Av. *vazra-* (Barth. 1392) = Skt. *vajra-* 'Indra's thunderbolt' : Skt. *vāja-* 'strength', OPers. *vazarka-* 'great', etc. Walde-P. 1.246 f.

Av. *dāru* 'piece of wood, trunk of a tree' (= Skt. *dāru* 'piece of wood', etc., cf. 1.43), also once 'club'. Barth. 738.

20.222. The nearest successor of the 'club' as a weapon is the 'battle-ax'. It was not a usual weapon of the Greeks (a few times in Homer) or the Romans, but an important one among the Celtic and Germanic tribes. Most of the terms are the same as those used for 'ax' as a tool (9.25), or in modern times made more specific by a compound or phrase with words for 'battle', 'war', or 'arms', as NE *battle-ax*, NHG *streit-axt*, NIr. *tuagh cogaidh*, W. *cad-fywall*, Fr. *hache d'armes*, Boh. *sekera válečná*, etc. Thus Grk. πέλεκυς and ἀξίνη (both as weapons in Hom., later esp. πέλεκυς), Lat. *secūris* and esp. *bipennis*, Ir. *biail* (Bauersfeld, op. cit. 343 f.), ON *øx* (Falk, op. cit. 104 ff.), OE *æx* (Keller, op. cit. 56 ff.), OHG *acchus* and *bīhal*, Slavic *sěkyra* (Niederle, op. cit. 2.286 ff.), Skt. *paraçu-*.

Occasionally an old word has survived only in the sense of 'battle-ax', as Russ. *sekira* (as tool replaced by *topor*), It. *azza* (prob. a by-form of *accia*, fr. Fr. *hache*).

A further development of the 'battle-ax' was the 'halberd', both in fact (a combination of a long-handled, double-headed ax, of the ax-adze type, and spearhead) and in name, orig. MHG *helmbarte* (LG, NHG *hellebarde*, It. *alabarde*, Fr. *hallebarde* > NE *haubert, halbert, halberd*), a cpd. of *barte* 'ax' (orig. 'beard', 9.25) with *helm* 'handle' (better than *helm* 'helmet'). Kluge-G. 244. REW 4101a. NED s.v. *halberd*. Cf. also Pol. *berdysz*, Russ. *berdyš*, likewise fr. MLG *barde* through a MLat. **bardūcium* (cf. **matteūca* > Fr. *massue* 'club'). Brückner 21.

20.23 SLING

Grk.	*σφενδόνη*	Goth.	. . . .	Lith.	*vilksnė*
NG	*σφενδόνη, σφεντόνα*	ON	*sløngva*	Lett.	*linga*
Lat.	*funda*	Dan.	*slynge*	ChSl.	*prašta*
It.	*fionda*	Sw.	*slunga*	SCr.	*praća*
Fr.	*fronde*	OE	*liþere*	Boh.	*prak*
Sp.	*honda*	ME	*slinge*	Pol.	*proca*
Rum.	*praștie*	NE	*sling*	Russ.	*prašča*
Ir.	*tailm, taball*	Du.	*slinger*	Skt.	. . . .
NIr.	*crann tabhaill*	OHG	*slinga, slengira*	Av.	*fradaxšanā-*
W.	*ffon dafl*	MHG	*slinge, slenger*		
Br.	*batalm, talm*	NHG	*schleuder*		

Some of the words for 'sling' are connected with verbs for 'jerk' or 'wind, twist', some with nouns for 'leather' or 'strap'. An Irish-Welsh word denoted orig. the 'staff-sling'. Several are of obscure origin.

1. Grk. σφενδόνη, prob. : σφαδάζω 'jerk, struggle', σφεδανός 'violent, impetuous', Skt. *spand-* 'quiver, tremble, throb'. Walde-P. 2.664. Boisacq 926. But combined by others with Lat. *funda*, either as both loanwords fr. a common source (Ernout-M. 400), or as cognate fr. *(*s*-)*bhend*(*h*)- : Goth. *bindan* 'bind', etc., and orig. 'bandage' (Cuny, BSL 37.1 ff.).

2. Lat. *funda* (> It. *fionda*, OFr. *fonde*, Sp. *honda;* Prov. *fronda*, Fr. *fronde* with unexplained -*r*-; REW 3577), etym. dub. Walde-H. 1.562 f. and above, 1.

Rum. *praștie*, fr. the Slavic, cf. ChSl. *prašta* (below, 6).

3. Ir. *tailm*, MBr, NBr. *talm* (now usually *batalm* with *baz* 'stick'), but W. *telm* 'snare, trap', perh. : Grk. τελαμών 'strap (for carrying arms), buckler', fr. the root in Grk. ταλάσσαι 'bear, endure', Lat. *tollere* 'raise, lift', etc. Walde-P. 1.739. Pedersen 1.169.

Ir. *taball*, NIr. *crann tabhaill* (*crann* 'tree, staff'), W. *ffon dafl* (*ffon* 'stick'), the same word as Ir. *taball* 'tablet', W. *taf(a)l* 'scales, balance', fr. Lat. *tabula* 'tablet'. It must have denoted orig. the 'staff-sling' (OE *stæf-liþere*, ON *staf-sløngva*, Lat. *fustibalus*, described by Veget. 3.14). Vendryes, De hib. voc. 181. Bauersfeld, op. cit. 306 f.

4. ON *sløngva* (*staf-, hand-sløngva*), Dan. *slynge*, Sw. *slunga*, ME *slinge* (loanword fr. the Continent), NE *sling* (same word as *sling* for holding up objects), OHG *slinga*, MHG *slinge* (NHG *schlinge* 'noose, snare'), beside OHG *slengira*, MHG *slenger*, OS *slingira*, Du. *slinger* : ON *slyngva*, *slyngja* 'swing, twist, sling', OE *slingan* 'creep', OHG *slingan* 'swing, plait, wind', Lith. *slinkti* 'crawl, creep'. Walde-P. 2.714 f. Falk-Torp 1071. NED s.v. *sling*, sb.[1].

OE *liþere*, deriv. of *leþer* 'leather'. NED s.v. *lither*, sb.

NHG *schleuder*, fr. MLG *slūder*, *slūter*, orig.? Kluge-G. 524. Weigand-H. 2.730.

5. Lith. *vilksnė, vilkstynė* (also *vilpšnė*, *vilpštynė*), fr. *vilkti* 'draw'. Leskien, Ablaut 354.

Lett. *linga* (also 'snare'), through Liv. *lĩṅga*, fr. MLG *slinge* (above, 4). Mühl.-Endz. 2.471. Sehwers, Z. sl. Ph. 5.309.

6. ChSl. *prašta* (*praštĭnikŭ* 'slinger' Supr.), SCr. *praća*, Boh. *prak*, Pol. *proca*, Russ. *prašča* (ChSl. form; ORuss. *porokŭ* 'battering-ram'), fr. root of ChSl.

prati, porją 'split'. Meillet, Études 398. Brückner 437. Niederle, Antiquité slave 2.287 f.

7. Skt. *açan-* 'stone' (1.44) and likewise *adri-* 'stone' occur in RV as weapons of Indra (Zimmer, Altind. Leben 301, Macdonell-Keith), but there is no quotable word or evidence for a special instrument for throwing stones.

Av. *fradaxšanā-*, evidently fr. a *fradaxš-*, but no apparent relation to the known *daxš-* 'teach'. Barth. 981.

20.24 BOW

Grk.	*τόξον*	Goth.	. . . .	Lith.	*lankas*
NG	*τόξο*, pop. *δοξάρι*	ON	*bogi*	Lett.	*stuops*
Lat.	*arcus*	Dan.	*bue*	ChSl.	*ląkŭ*
It.	*arco*	Sw.	*båge*	SCr.	*luk*
Fr.	*arc*	OE	*boga*	Boh.	*luk*
Sp.	*arco*	ME	*bowe*	Pol.	*łuk*
Rum.	*arc*	NE	*bow*	Russ.	*luk*
Ir.	*fidbocc, boga*	Du.	*boog*	Skt.	*dhanvan-*
NIr.	*bogha*	OHG	*bogo*	Av.	*θanvan-*
W.	*bwa*	MHG	*boge*		
Br.	*gwareg*	NHG	*bogen*		

The derivation of words for 'bow' from verbs for 'bend' is, as to be expected, widespread. Other connections are with verbs for 'stretch, draw' or names of kinds of wood furnishing the material.

1. Grk. *τόξον* (dim. *τοξάριον*, NG pop. *δοξάρι*), in pl. also 'bow and arrows, arrows', etym. dub. The two possibilities, both involving some difficulty, are 1) connection with Lat. *taxus* 'yew', or 2) as orig. 'hewn, fashioned', deriv. fr. the root of *τέκτων* 'carpenter', Skt. *takṣ-* 'hew', etc. Walde-P. 1.717. Boisacq 975.

2. Lat. *arcus* (> Romance words) : Goth. *arhwazna*, ON *ǫr*, OE *earh*, NE *arrow* 'arrow', derivs. of a corresponding word for 'bow', all possibly connected with certain names of trees, woods, but uncertain. Walde-P. 1.81. Ernout-M. 69. Walde-H. 1.64.

3. Ir. *fidbocc*, cpd. of *fid* 'wood' and *-bocc* : ON *bogi*, etc. 'bow' (below). Walde-P. 2.145 f. Pedersen 1.159.

Ir. *boga*, NIr. *bogha*, fr. ON *bogi* (below). Marstrander, Bidrag 59, 127.

W. *bwa*, prob. fr. ME *bowe*. Parry-Williams 35.

Br. *gwareg*, deriv. of *gwar* 'bent' (: W. *gwyr*, Ir. *fīar* id.).

4. ON *bogi*, OE *boga*, OHG *bogo*, etc., general Gmc. : Goth. *biugan*, etc. 'bend' (9.14). Walde-P. 2.146.

5. Lith. *lankas*, lit. 'bend, arch, bow', also for shooting (*šaujamas lankas*) = Lett. *luoks* 'anything bent, felloe', etc. : Lith. *lenkti*, Lett. *liekt*, ChSl. *sŭ-lęšti* 'bend' (9.14), *ląkŭ*, etc. 'bow'. Berneker 739 f.

Lett. *stuops, stuopa*, fr. *stiept* 'stretch' (9.32). Sehwers, Z. sl. Ph. 5.308.

6. ChSl. *ląkŭ*, etc., general Slavic : Lith. *lankas*, etc. (above, 5).

7. Skt. *dhanvan-, dhanuṣ-* (Macdonell-Keith 1.388 f.), perh. : *dhanvana-* 'a certain fruit-tree', OHG *tanna* 'fir', etc. Walde-P. 1.825. Uhlenbeck 134.

Av. *θanvan-, θanvar-* (OPers. *θanuvaniya-* 'bowman' NRb 42) : *θanǰ-* 'draw' (9.33)? Walde-P. 1.726. Barth. 785. Or better = Skt. *dhanvan-* with Iran. *θ* for *d* by association with *θanǰ-*?

20.25 ARROW

Grk.	*τόξευμα, βέλος* (poet. *ἰός, οἰστός*)	Goth.	*arhwazna*	Lith.	*vilyčia, strėla*
NG	*βέλος*	ON	*ǫr, fleinn*	Lett.	*bulta, šautra*
Lat.	*sagitta*	Dan.	*pil*	ChSl.	*strěla*
It.	*freccia, saetta*	Sw.	*pil*	SCr.	*strijela*
Fr.	*flèche*	OE	*strǣl, flān, earh*	Boh.	*šíp, střela*
Sp.	*flecha, saeta*	ME	*ar(e)we, flone, strale*	Pol.	*strzała*
Rum.	*săgeată*	NE	*arrow*	Russ.	*strela*
Ir.	*saiget*	Du.	*pijl*	Skt.	*iṣu-, çaru-, bāṇa-*
NIr.	*saighead*	OHG	*strāla, pfīl*	Av.	*išu-, tiγri-, ašti-*
W.	*saeth*	MHG	*pfīl, strāle*		
Br.	*bir, saez*	NHG	*pfeil*		

A few of the words for 'arrow' are derivs. of those for 'bow', either through the medium of a verb 'shoot with the bow, shoot arrows', or directly as 'belonging with the bow'. For the association, cf. also the use of Grk. *τόξον* 'bow' in the plural for 'bow and arrows' or even 'arrows'.

But the majority are from the more generic notion of 'missile', from verbs for 'throw' or the like, or are connected with names of various sharp-pointed objects.

There is one small group common to Grk. and Indo-Iranian, besides the one for 'bow' or 'arrow' common to Lat. and Gmc. Loanwords are frequent.

1. Grk. *ἰός* (the oldest word, but only poet.) fr. *ἰσϝο-ς : Skt. *iṣu-*, Av. *išu-* 'arrow', fr. the root seen in Skt. *iṣ-* 'set in quick motion, swing, hit', etc. Walde-P. 1.107. Boisacq 378.

Grk. *οἰστός*, Hom. *ὀϊστός* (mostly poet.), etym. dub., perh. as *ὀ-ισ-τό-ς* fr. the same root as the preceding. Walde-P. 1.107. Brugmann, IF 29.231.

Grk. *τόξευμα* (the usual prose word), fr. *τοξεύω* 'shoot the bow', fr. *τόξον* 'bow'.

Grk. *βέλος*, a 'missile' of any sort but esp. an 'arrow' (so freq. in Hom., and the NG word) : *βάλλω* 'throw'. Walde-P. 1.689, 691. Boisacq 118.

2. Lat. *sagitta* (> It. *saetta*, OFr. *saete*, Sp. *saeta*, Rum. *săgeată*), prob. loanword (Etruscan?). Ernout-M. 886. REW 7508.

Fr. *flèche* (> It. *freccia*, Sp., Port. *flecha*), fr. a Frank. form corresponding to MDu. *vleke, vlieke* 'arrow', orig. 'pinion' of a bird (cf. also OHG *flukhe* 'sagitta', Graff 3.763), orig. **flugika* : OHG *fliugan* 'fly'. REW 9424a. Gamillscheg 423. Wartburg 3.622 f.

3. Ir. *saiget*, NIr. *saighead*, W. *saeth*, Br. *saez*, fr. Lat. *sagitta*. Vendryes, De hib. voc. 173. Loth, Mots lat. 204.

Br. *bir*, etym.? Henry 35.

4. Goth. *arhwazna*, ON *ǫr*, OE *earh*, ME *ar(e)we*, NE *arrow*, derivs. of a word for 'bow' : Lat. *arcus* 'bow' (20.24).

ON *fleinn* (also a 'dart, short spear'; Dan. *flen* 'tine'), OE *flā, flān*, ME *flone, flo* (Sc. *flane*, NED), etym. dub., perh. as orig. 'something split off' : ON *flīs* 'splinter', MLG *vlīse* 'four-cornered flat stone', and (with *sp-* beside *p-*) MHG *splīzen* 'split'. Walde-P. 2.684. Falk-Torp 235.

Late ON *pīla*, Dan., Sw. *pil*, Du. *pijl*, OHG, MHG *pfīl*, NHG *pfeil* (OE *pīl* 'dart', NE *pile*), fr. Lat. *pīlum* 'heavy javelin' (20.26). Falk-Torp 825. Weigand-H. 2.407.

OE *strǣl, strǣle*, ME *strale*, OHG *strāl, strāla*, MHG *strāle* (NHG *strahl*, in OHG also 'flash of lightning'), ChSl. *strěla*, etc., general Slavic : Lett. *stars* 'beam' (of light), MHG *strām* 'streak of

light, beam, stream', Norw. dial. *strīl(a)* 'streak, vein, ray', etc. Walde-P. 2.637. Weigand-H. 2.982. Kluge-G. 598.

5. Lith. *vilyčia*, Lett. dial. *vīliča*, fr. WhRuss. *vilica*, dim. of Russ. *vilka, vilij* 'fork'. Mühl.-Endz. 4.639 (with refs.).

Lith. *strėla*, fr. the Slavic, cf. ChSl. *strěla*, etc. (below).

Lett. *bulta* (also 'bolt'), fr. MLG *bolte* 'arrow, fetter' = OHG *bolz*, MHG *bolz(e)*, NHG *bolzen*, OE, NE *bolt*, etc., all used for a 'short heavy arrow or dart' and various other objects of iron. Mühl.-Endz. 1.349.

Lett. *šautra* : *šaut* 'shove quickly, give a blow, shoot', Lith. *šauti* 'shoot', etc. Mühl.-Endz. 4.10.

6. ChSl. *strěla*, etc., general Slavic : OE *strǣl* etc. (above, 4).

Boh. *šíp*, orig. prob. 'thorn', cf. deriv. *šipek* 'dog-rose, hawthorn', Russ. *šip* 'thorn', etc. Miklosich 340.

7. Skt. *iṣu-*, Av. *išu-* : Grk. *ἰός* (above, 1).

Skt. *çaru-* (in RV, AV a missile weapon, often 'arrow', sometimes perh. 'spear'), *çarya-, çara-* (also 'reed'; for group, cf. Macdonell-Keith 2.357, 363), outside connections (as Goth. *hairus* 'sword', etc.) dub. Walde-P. 1.410. Uhlenbeck 304, 305.

Skt. *bāṇa-* = *vāṇa* 'reed', perh. (*ṇ* fr. *ln*) : Goth. *walus* 'staff', ON *valr* 'round', etc. Walde-P. 1.298, 301. Uhlenbeck 281.

Av. *tiγri-* (NPers. *tīr*) : *tiγra-*, OPers. *tigra-* 'sharp-pointed', etc. (15.78). Walde-P. 2.612.

Av. *ašti-*, etym.? Barth. 261.

20.26 SPEAR

Grk.	*δόρυ, λόγχη, αἰχμή*	ON	*spjōt, geirr, spjǫr*	Lith.	*ietis, iešmas* (*ragotinė*)
NG	*δόρυ, κοντάρι*	Dan.	*spyd, lanse*		
Lat.	*hasta, lancea*	Sw.	*spjut, lans*	Lett.	*šk'ēps*
It.	*lancia, asta*	OE	*spere, gār*	ChSl.	*kopĭje, sulica*
Fr.	*lance, épieu*	ME	*spere, launce*	SCr.	*koplje, sulica*
Sp.	*lanza, asta*	NE	*spear, lance*	Boh.	*oštěp, kopí, sudlice*
Rum.	*lance, suliţă*	Du.	*speer, spie(t)s, lans*	Pol.	*włócznia, kopja*
Ir.	*gae, sleg*	OHG	*sper, spioz*	Russ.	*kop'e*
NIr.	*sleagh*	MHG	*sper, spiez, lanze*	Skt.	*ṛṣṭi-*
W.	*gwayw, gwaywffon*	NHG	*speer, spiess, lanze*	Av., OPers.	*aršti-*
Br.	*goaf*				

Besides the most generic words for 'spear', as a weapon of thrusting or throwing, there are numerous terms for special types (NE *lance, pike, javelin*, etc.), most of which are left unnoticed.

The words are partly based upon such notions as 'throw, thrust' or the like, 'sharp, pointed', and (orig. denoting the shaft) 'wood, spar'. But several are of obscure origin.

1. Grk. *δόρυ* 'tree-trunk, beam', etc., whence 'spear-shaft' and eventually 'spear' (the most common word in Hom.) : Skt. *dāru-* 'piece of wood, stake', Av. *dāru-* 'tree-trunk, piece of wood, club', Grk. *δρῦς* 'tree, oak', ChSl. *drŭva* 'wood', Goth. *triu* 'tree, wood', etc. (1.42). Walde-P. 1.804. Boisacq 197.

Grk. *λόγχη* (Hdt., not in Hom.), prob. fr. the same (Celtic) source as Lat. *lancea*. Boisacq 586. Walde-H. 1.757 f. Ernout-M. 521.

Grk. *αἰχμή*, prob. fr. *αἰκ-σμᾱ- : Lat. *īcere* 'strike', Cypr. *ἰκμαμένος* 'wounded'. Walde-P. 1.7 f. Walde-H. 1.670. Boisacq 31.

Grk. *ἔγχος* (freq. in Hom. as 'spear';

later for other weapons), etym.? Walde-P. 1.608, 2.327. Boisacq 214.

Grk. *ἄκων* 'javelin' (Hom.+) : *ἄκαινα* 'spike, goad', *ἀκίς* 'pointed object', *ἄκρος* 'topmost', Lat. *ācer* 'sharp', etc. Walde-P. 1.20. Boisacq 32.

NG *κοντάρι*, fr. late Grk. *κοντάριον*, dim. of *κοντός* '(boat-)pole, pike, crutch, goad' (> Lat. *contus* 'pole' and 'pike' as weapon) : *κεντέω* 'sting, prick', W. *cethr* 'nail', Br. *kentr* 'spur', etc. Walde-P. 1.402. Boisacq 434.

2. Lat. *hasta* (> It., Sp. *asta*), Umbr. *hostatu* 'hastatos' : Ir. *gat* 'withe', Goth. *gazds* 'prick, sting', ON *gaddr* 'prick, point', OHG *gart* 'stimulus'. Walde-P. 1.541. Ernout-M. 445. Walde-H. 1.636.

Lat. *lancea* (> It. *lancia* [> Hung. *lancsa* > Rum. *lance*], Fr. *lance*, Sp. *lanza*), see under Grk. *λόγχη*, above, 1.

Lat. *pīlum*, the heavy javelin of the Roman infantry, orig. and earliest form much disputed. Thought by some to be the same word as *pīlum* 'pestle' and first applied to a more primitive club-like weapon. Kropatchek, Jahrb. d. deutsch. arch. Inst. 1908 86 f. Couissin, op. cit. 22 f.

OFr. *espieu*, Fr. *épieu* (now heavy spear for hunting boars, etc.), fr. a Frank. **speut* = OHG *spioz* (below, 4).

Rum. *suliţă*, fr. Slavic, cf. ChSl. *sulica* (below, 6).

3. Ir. *gae* (*gāi*), W. *gwaew, gwayw* and (cpd. with *ffon* 'stick') *gwaywffon*, Br. *goaf*, Gall.-Lat. *gaesum*, Gallo-Grk. *γαῖσον* : ON *geirr*, OE *gār* 'spear', Grk. *χαῖος* 'shepherd's staff', prob. fr. the same root as Skt. *heti-* 'missile', Av. *zaēna-* 'weapon', Skt. *hi-* 'urge, hurl'. Walde-P. 1.528, 546. Pedersen 1.96. Walde-H. 1.575 f.

Ir. *sleg*, NIr. *sleagh*, perh. : Skt. *sṛj-* 'release, shoot, pour', MHG *selken* 'drip, sink' Ir. *selg* 'hunt' (fr. the releasing of the hunting dogs). Walde-P. 2.508. Pederson 1.100.

Other Ir. 'spear'-names (Bauersfeld, op. cit.) *crōisech* (etym.?), *laigen* (= W. *llain* 'blade, sword', Pedersen 1.97, Walde-P. 2.381), *mānais* (etym.?).

4. ON *spjōt*, Dan. *spyd*, Sw. *spjut*, MLG *spēt*, OHG *spioz*, MHG *spiez*, NHG *spiess* (> Du. *spies, spiets*), etym. dub., perh. : Lith. *spaudžiu, spausti* 'press', Grk. *σπεύδω* 'hasten, urge'. Persson, Beitr. 415. Falk-Torp 1553 (with refs.; vs. 1138 and Walde-P. 2.119).

ON *geirr*, OE *gār* (OHG *gēr* rare except in proper names like *Gērhart*, etc.) : Ir. *gae*, etc. (above, 3).

ON *spjǫr* (poet.), OE, ME *spere*, NE *spear*, OHG, MHG *sper*, NHG, Du. *speer* : ON *sparri* 'spar, timber', *sperra* 'rafter', OHG *sparro* 'beam, rafter, pole', Lat. *sparus, sparum* 'hunting spear'. Walde-P. 2.665. Falk-Torp 1140.

ME *launce*, NE *lance*, Du. *lans*, MHG, NHG *lanze* (> Dan. *lanse*, Sw. *lans*), fr. Fr. *lance* (above, 2).

5. Lith. *ietis* (quotable from 16th cent.; Buga, Kalba ir Senovė 166; still usual word, Senn) : *eiti* 'go'.

Lith. *iešmas*, also 'spit' (for roasting) : OPruss. *aysmis*, Lett. *iesms* 'spit', Grk. *αἰχμή* 'spear-point', *αἴκλοι· αἱ γωνίαι τοῦ βέλους* (Hesych.), Lat. *icere* 'hit, wound', etc. Walde-P. 1.8. Trautmann 4.

Lith. *ragotinė* (bibl., e.g. NT Jn. 19.34) : *ragas*, ChSl. *rogŭ* 'horn'.

Lett. *šk'ēps* : *šk'ēpele* 'splinter, piece', SCr.-ChSl. *stapŭ*, SCr. *štap* 'staff', Boh. *štěp* 'scion', *oštěp* 'spear', fr. the root in Pol. *szczepać*, Russ. *ščepat'* 'split', ChSl. *skopiti* 'castrate'. Walde-P. 2.560 f. Mühl.-Endz. 4.33. Trautmann 265.

6. ChSl. *kopĭje*, SCr. *koplje*, Boh. *kopí*, Pol. *kopja*, Russ. *kop'e* : Lith. *kaplys*, Lett. *kaplis* 'hoe', fr. the root of ChSl. *kopati* 'dig', etc., Lith. *kapoti*

'hew, hack', Grk. κόπτω 'strike, hew'. Walde-P. 2.561. Berneker 566. Trautmann 116.

ChSl., SCr. (Pol., Russ. obs.) sulica, Boh. sudlice : ChSl. sujǫ, sovati 'thrust, shove', Lith. šauti 'shoot', etc. Walde-P. 2.553. Brückner 525.

Boh. oštěp, cf. Lett. šk'ēps (above, 5).

Pol. włócznia, prob. (as 'trail', fr. the position of the spear when carried) : włóczyć, ChSl. vlěsti 'drag'. Brückner 627. Miklosich 379.

Pol. spisa, lanza, fr. NHG.

7. Skt. ṛṣṭi, Av., OPers. aršti- : Skt. ṛṣ- 'push, thrust, stab, kill'. Uhlenbeck 35.

20.27 SWORD

Grk.	ξίφος, μάχαιρα	Goth.	hairus, mēki (acc. sg.)	Lith.	kalavijas, kardas
NG	σπαθί, ξίφος (lit.)	ON	sverð, mækir, hjǫrr	Lett.	zuobens
Lat.	gladius, ēnsis (poet.),	OS	sverd	ChSl.	mečĭ, kor(ŭ)da
	spatha (late)	Sw.	svärd	SCr.	mač
It.	spada	OE	sweord, mēce, heoru	Boh.	meč
Fr.	épée (glaive)	ME	swerd	Pol.	miecz
Sp.	espada	NE	sword	Russ.	meč
Rum.	sabie, spadă	Du.	zwaard	Skt.	asi-, khaḍga-
Ir.	claideb, colg	OHG	swert	Av.	karəta-
NIr.	claidheamh	MHG	swert		
W.	cleddyf	NHG	schwert		
Br.	kleze				

Some of the words for 'sword' are connected with verbs for 'cut, strike' or the like, and in one group the basic characteristic is the flat blade. But many are of obscure root connection, and loanwords are frequent.

1. Grk. ξίφος, prob. a loanword fr. the same source as Egypt. sft 'knife, sword'. Boisacq 679 with references. Myres, Who were the Greeks? 590.

Grk. ἄορ (poet., freq. in Hom.), the sword as hung on the belt : ἀείρω 'raise', pass. 'be suspended'. Solmsen, Untersuchungen 292.

Grk. μάχαιρα 'knife' (9.23), also used for a kind of sword, 'dagger', and 'saber', in NT reg. word for 'sword'.

NG σπαθί (the reg. pop. word; ξίφος lit., but official term in the army), fr. Grk. σπαθίον, dim. of σπάθη 'flat wooden blade, spattle, blade' (of an oar or sword, etc.) : OE spadu 'spade' etc. Walde-P. 2.653.

2. Lat. gladius (> OIt. ghiado; Fr. glaive, now arch., by blend with a Gallic form; REW 3773), early loanword fr. Celtic (Ir. claideb, etc., below, 3). Ernout-M. 423. Walde-H. 1.603 f.

Lat. ēnsis (old word, but only poet., in prose replaced by gladius) : Skt. asi- 'sword', root connection? Ernout-M. 302. Walde-H. 1.406.

Lat. spatha 'spattle', also 'sword' of the auxiliaries (Tac.), later reg. word for 'sword', displacing gladius, loanword fr. Grk. σπάθη (above, 1). Hence It. spada (> Rum. spadă), Fr. épée, Sp. espada. Couissin, op. cit. 489. REW 8128.

Rum. sabie, fr. the Slavic, cf. Bulg. sab(i)ja, SCr. sablja, Pol. szabla, etc. 'saber' (whence also NHG sabel, säbel, It. sciabla, Fr. sabre > NE sabre), prob. orig. fr. Hung. száblya (: szab 'cut'). Tiktin 1350. Kluge-G. 493.

3. Ir. claideb, NIr., Gael. claidheamh (hence with mōr 'great', NE claymore), W. cleddyf, Br. kleze, Corn. clethe, beside Lat. gladius (fr. Celtic) : Ir. claidim, W. claddu 'dig', Lat. clādēs 'damage, injury', Skt. khaḍga- 'sword', Lith. kalti

'strike', Grk. κλάω 'break', etc. Walde-P. 1.439. Walde-H. 1.603 f. (with refs. for Celtic).

Ir. colg (less common than claideb and denoting some special type of sword, Bauersfeld, op. cit. 339 ff.; also 'beard on grain, prickle') : W. cola 'beard (on grain)', col 'sting', cala, Br. kalc'h 'penis' perh. fr. a root *kel- 'prick, stick' (or ultimately identical with *kel- 'strike' in above group?). Walde-P. 1.435.

4. Goth. hairus, ON hjǫrr, OE heoru, OS heru, prob. fr. IE *(s)ker- in Grk. κείρω 'shear', OE sceran 'cut, shear', etc. (9.22). Walde-P. 2.576. Feist 235.

Goth. mēki (acc. sg.), ON mækir, OE mēce (loanword fr. ON?), OS māki, Crim.Goth. mycha 'ensis', orig. dub., perh. a loanword, but source unknown (cf. ChSl. mečĭ, below, 6). Feist 352 f.

ON sverð, OE sweord, etc., general Gmc. (except Goth.), etym. dub., perh. : OHG sweran 'cause or suffer pain', swero, swer(a)do 'pain', Ir. serb 'bitter', Av. xᵛara- 'wound' (Walde-P. 2.529), with orig. sense of root 'sting, cut'(?). W. Krogmann, KZ 59.204. Kluge-G. 552. Otherwise Falk-Torp 1214 (cf. also 1560).

ON brandr, OE brand, OHG brant 'burning, brand' were used (mostly poet.) for the 'blade of a sword' and 'sword'. Hence as 'sword' It. brando,

OFr. brant. NED s.v. brand, sb. 8. REW 1273.

5. Lith. kalavijas : OPruss. kalabian id., Lat. clāva 'club', fr. the root in Lith. kalti 'strike', etc. (cf. Ir. claideb, above 3). Trautmann, Altpreuss. 351. (Walde-P. 1.437).

Lith. kardas (cf. NSB; formerly the usual word), fr. Pol. kord, cf. ChSl. kor(ŭ)da (below, 6).

Lett. zuobens : zuobs 'tooth', as 'cutting', or orig. actual sword with teeth. Mühl.-Endz. 4.756.

6. ChSl. mečĭ, etc., general Slavic, belongs in some way with Goth. mēki, etc. (above, 4), but not directly fr. the attested Gmc. form (for which one would expect ChSl. mĕčĭ, etc.), perh. fr. the same unknown source. Berneker 2.29 f. Stender-Petersen 221 f., 507, Brückner 331.

Late ChSl. kor(ŭ)da, etc. (general Slavic, but no longer the usual word anywhere), fr. Pers. kārd = Av. karəta- (below, 7). Berneker 569. Brückner 256.

7. Skt. asi- (Av. aṇhū- 'sword' Barth. 110, but dub.) : Lat. ēnsis (above, 2). Skt. khaḍga-, cf. W. cleddyf (above 3).

Av. karəta- 'knife', as weapon 'dagger' or 'sword' (Darmesteter 'épée') : karət-, Skt. kṛt- 'cut'. Barth. 454.

20.28 GUN; CANNON

Grk.	Byz. τηλεβολίσκος,	Dan.	gevær, bøsse; kanon	Lith.	šaudyklė; patranka,
	μολυβδοβόλος,	Sw.	gevär, bössa; kanon		kanuolė
	τηλεβόλος, χωνεία,	ME	gonne, gunne; (gret)-	Lett.	bise, flinte; lielgabals
	etc.		gonne, cannon	SCr.	puška; top
NG	ὅπλο, τουφέκι; πυρο-	NE	gun, rifle; gun, can-	Boh.	puška; dělo
	βόλον, κανόνι		non	Pol.	strzelba; działo
MLat.	—; bombarda	Du.	geweer; kanon	Russ.	ruž'e; puška
It.	fucile, schioppo; can-	MHG	bühse		
	none	NHG	gewehr (flinte,		
Fr.	fusil; canon		büchse); geschütz,		
Sp.	fusil, escopeta; cañon		kanone		
Rum.	puşcă; tun				
NIr.	gunna; gunna mōr				
W.	gwn; gwn mawr,				
	cyflegr, magnel				
Br.	fusil; kanol				

NE gun covers firearms from the heaviest naval or siege guns (but in technical use excluding mortars and howitzers) to the soldier's rifle or the sportsman's shotgun, and in current U.S. use even the gangster's revolver. In the other Eur. languages there is no such comprehensive word, but different terms for the small or hand gun of the soldier or sportsman (even these, sometimes differentiated) and the heavy naval guns or artillery pieces, for which also NE cannon was until recently the usual term, and will be used in the following for purposes of definition.

Although guns are attested for more than a century earlier, their use on a large scale is conspicuous in the siege of Constantinople (A.D. 1453), and the most detailed description of their construction, especially the famous monster cannon, is found in the historians of that siege, notably (as quoted in the following), Ducas, Phrantzes, Chalcondylas, Critobulus (the first three quoted from the Bonn edition, the last from Müller, Fragmenta historicorum Graecorum, Vol. V).

A primitive type of hand gun was probably the earliest gun made, but it was for some centuries relatively unimportant in contrast to the siege gun. Of the old names, some have remained the common terms, unaffected by the change of type (e.g. Fr. fusil), some are now used only or mainly for the shotgun (It. schioppo, Sp. escopeta, NHG büchse), and others have disappeared from use except with reference to earlier history, e.g. NE hackbut, (h)arquebus (= MLG hakebusse, MHG hakenbühse, lit. 'hook-gun'), flintlock, musket (orig. name of a bird), carbine (weapon of the carabin, for which see now Gamillscheg 184).

The words for 'gun' reflect their tubular form (from words for 'tube' or 'cylindrical box'), their action ('fire, throwing, shooting'), some special feature of the mechanism ('flint-lock', etc.), the sound of the explosion (MLat. bombarda, etc.), or they may be words for 'weapon, machine, piece, piece of work' used in specialized sense.

1. Byz. τηλεβόλος, in class. Grk. adj. 'shooting from afar', is the regular term for 'cannon' in Chalcond., e.g. 1.231 passim.

Byz. ἐλεβόλις, usual for 'cannon' in Phrantzes (e.g. p. 239), is apparently due to a confusion of the preceding (so regularly in cod. Par.) with the old ἑλέπολις (lit. 'city-taking') which was

a siegetower (in this form so used and minutely described by Phrantzes, p. 244 f.).

Byz. χωνεία, orig. 'a casting' of metal is used by Critob. in this sense and for the barrel of the cannon, by Ducas for the 'cannon' itself (e.g. pp. 247, 248, 271, 273).

Byz. μηχανή 'machine' and σκευή 'apparatus' were both often used with especial reference to cannon. Critob. (1.30.8) remarks that there is no old name for this 'machine', unless one should call it ἑλέπολις or ἀφετήριον, but "all now living call it by the common name σκευή". Ducas also has σκευή and σκευαὶ πετροβόλοι (p. 266.3).

Reference to hand guns is to be seen in the dim. τηλεβολίσκος, ἐλεβολίσκος, τοὺς τουφάκας (Critob. 1.51.1, 4; fr. Turk., cf. NG τουφέκι, below), and μολυβδοβόλος (Ducas 266.18, 284.15, cf. βολίδας μολιβδίνας, Ducas p. 211.10).

NG πυροβόλον (the official army term for 'cannon'), neut. of πυροβόλος, orig. 'fire-throwing'.

NG pop. κανόνι, fr. It. cannone (below, 2).

NG ὅπλον 'weapon' (20.21) and official term for the soldier's rifle.

NG pop. τουφέκι (the common word for the old musket in klephtic songs, and now for the soldier's rifle or the shotgun), fr. Turk. tüfek 'gun' (cf. τοὺς τουφάκας in Critob., above).

2. MLat. bombarda (cf. Du Cange), It. bombarda (> Sp. lombarda, Fr. bombarde > ME bombard), all in early use for 'cannon', deriv. of Lat. bombus 'booming, humming', early loanword fr. Grk. βόμβος id. REW 1199.

It. cannone (> Sp. cañon, Fr. canon > NE canon, cannon), deriv., with augmentative suffix of Lat. canna 'reed, tube', loanword fr. Grk. κάννα 'reed'.

It. fucile (> Fr., Sp. fusil), fr. OIt.

focile 'flint', deriv. of Lat. focus 'fire'. REW 3399.

It. schioppo (dim. schioppetto > Sp. escopeta), formerly any 'handgun', now 'shotgun', fr. Lat. stloppus 'sound made by snapping the cheek', imitative. REW 8270.

Rum. puşcă, fr. Slavic (below, 6).

Rum. tun, formerly 'thunder', hence 'cannon', fr. Lat. tonus 'sound'. Tiktin 1661 f. Puşcariu 1772.

3. NIr. gunna, W. gwn (also gunna mōr, gwn mawr 'great gun, cannon'), fr. ME gonne, gunne (below, 4). Parry-Williams 158.

W. cyflegr 'cannon' (cf. Evans s.v.), etym.?

W. magnel 'cannon', fr. ME magnel, fr. OFr. mangonel, dim. of MLat. manganum, fr. Grk. μάγγανον πολεμικόν 'ballista'. Parry-Williams 75. NED s.v. mangonel. REW 5297.

Br. fusil and kanol, fr. Fr. fusil and canon.

4. ME gonne, gunne (Latinized as gunna, cf. magister gunnarum, 1414), NE gun, etym. disputed, but prob. orig. a nickname (like Brown Bess, Big Bertha, etc.), shortened fr. a name like ON Gunnhilda. Cf. una magna ballista de cornu quae vocatur Domina Gunilda, 1330. NED s.v. For another possible main or contributory source, namely OFr. dial. engon = engin (source of NE engine), cf. Weekly s.v. and Jenkins, Language 4.235 ff.

ME, NE cannon (canones, seu instrumenta Anglice gunnes vocata 1407, gret gonnes of brasse called cannons 1525), NHG kanone, Du., Dan., Sw. kanon, fr. Fr. canon, It. cannone (above, 2).

NE rifle in earliest use the 'groove' in the gun barrel, fr. vb. rifle 'form the grooves', fr. LG rifeln id. : OE gerifled 'wrinkled' (NE obs. rivel 'wrinkle' sb. and vb.), etc. NED s.v. Falk-Torp 898.

MHG *bühse*, NHG *büchse* (as a kind of gun since 14th cent., still in local use), MLG *busse* (> Dan. *bøsse*, Sw. *bössa*), all also and orig. 'box' (as OHG *buhsa*, OE-NE *box*), esp. one of cylindrical shape (hence 'gun'), fr. MLat. *buxis*, Grk. πυξίς 'box'. Weigand-H. 1.300. Falk-Torp 129.

NHG *gewehr* (> Dan. *gevær*, Sw. *gevär*, Du. *geweer*), orig. 'defense' (: NHG *wehren* 'prevent, defend', etc.), hence 'defense weapon, weapon', finally specialized to 'gun'. Weigand-H. 1.717. Falk-Torp 305.

NHG *flinte* (17th cent.+, still in local use), fr. NE *flint*, borrowed at the time when the *flint-lock* was introduced. Weigand-H. 1.544.

NHG *geschütz*, formerly only coll. 'artillery', now also of the single cannon, coll. formation to *schütz* 'shot'. Weigand-H. 1.701.

5. Lith. *šaudyklė* (formerly only 'shuttle', neolog. for 'gun'), fr. *šaudyti* 'shoot'.

Lith. *kanuolė* (NSB; not in Kurschat or Lalis), fr. NHG dial. *kanol* = *kanone*. Alminauskis 62.

Lith. *patranka* (neolog. for 'cannon', given as preferred form by NSB s.v. *kanuolė*) : *patrankyti* 'strike, hit', *trenkti* 'strike, clash', etc. (Leskien, Ablaut 352).

Lett. *bise*, fr. MLG *büsse* = NHG *büchse*, etc. (above, 4). Mühl.-Endz. 1.300. Sehwers, Z. sl. Ph. 5.310.

Lett. *flinte*, fr. NHG *flinte* (above, 4).

Lett. *lielgabals* 'cannon', lit. 'big piece', cpd. of *liels* 'large' and *gabals* 'piece'. Cf. NE *field-piece*, NHG *stück* in *stückgiesser*, *stückkugel*, etc. (Paul, Deutsches Wtb. 527). Mühl.-Endz. 2.498.

6. SCr., Boh. *puška* 'gun' (rifle, shotgun), Pol. *puszka*, formerly 'gun' esp. 'cannon', Russ. *puška* 'cannon', loanword fr. OHG *buhsa* (above, 4). Brückner 448 f.

SCr. *top* 'cannon', fr. Turk. *top* 'ball' and 'cannon'. Lokotsch 2089.

Boh. *dělo*, Pol. *działo* 'cannon', orig. 'work' (concrete, 'piece of work'), as ChSl. *dělo*, etc. (9.12). Berneker 194. Brückner 109.

Pol. *strzelba* 'gun', fr. *strzelić* 'shoot', fr. *strzała* 'arrow' (20.25). Brückner 522.

Russ. *ruž'e* 'gun' : *oružie* 'weapons' (20.21). Brückner 381.

20.29 GUNPOWDER

Grk.	Byz. βοτάνη	Dan.	*krudt*	Lith.	*parakas*
NG	μπαρούτι (πυρῖτις)	Sw.	*krut*	Lett.	*bi(s)zāles*
MLat.	*pulvis*	ME	*poudre*	SCr.	*barut, prah*
It.	*polvere*	NE	*powder*	Boh.	*prach*
Fr.	*poudre*	Du.	*kruit*	Pol.	*proch*
Sp.	*pólvora*	MHG	*krūt*	Russ.	*poroch*
Rum.	*praf, iarbă*	NHG	*pulver*		
NIr.	*pūdar*				
W.	*pylor, powdr*				
Br.	*poultr*				

Most of the words for 'gunpowder' are the same as those for 'powder' in general, which are the same as, or derived from, those for 'dust' (1.213). While they may be made more specific by compounds or phrases, like NE *gunpowder*, NHG *schiesspulver*, Fr. *poudre à fusil*, *à canon*, they are ordinarily used alone, their special application being clear from the context or the situation. But sometimes there is a choice between parallel forms for 'powder', e.g. for 'gunpowder' always Sp. *pólvora* vs. *polvo*, Du. *kruit* vs. *kruid*; or definite specialization to 'gunpowder', as Russ. *poroch*.

A few are words for 'plant, herb' (8.53), which included medicinal herbs and spices and were applied to gunpowder from its resemblance to ground spices or medicaments.

1. Grk. βοτάνη 'herb, plant', Byz. 'gunpowder', e.g. Ducas pp. 211, 249, 266, Critob. 1.29, 30. Chalcond., p. 231.21 f. uses κόνις 'dust'.

NG lit. πυρῖτις, fr. πῦρ 'fire'.

NG μπαρούτι, fr. Turk. *barut*.

2. Lat. *pulvis*, gen. *pulveris* 'dust, powder' (1.213), in late MLat. 'gunpowder'. Hence It. *polvere*, OFr. *poldre*, *pouldre* (> Br. *poultr*), Fr. *poudre* (> ME *poudre*, NE *powder* > NIr. *pūdar*, W. *powdr*), Sp. *pólvora*, Rum. *pulbere* (not in common use), W. *pylor* (Loth, Mots lat. 196), NHG *pulver*. REW 6842.

Rum. *praf* 'dust, powder' and (*praf de pușcă*) 'gunpowder', fr. Slavic, SCr. *prah*, etc. (below, 5). Tiktin 1231.

Rum. *iarbă* 'herb, plant' (fr. Lat. *herba* id.), also (*iarbă de pușca*) 'gunpowder'. Tiktin 748 f.

3. MHG, MLG *krūt* 'plant, herb, spice' and 'gunpowder' (> Dan. *krudt*, Sw. *krut*), NHG *kraut* formerly used also for 'gunpowder', Du. *kruit* 'gunpowder' vs. *kruid* 'herb'. Falk-Torp 583. Hellquist 515. Weigand-H. 1142. Franck-v. W. 353.

4. Lith. *parakas*, fr. Russ. *poroch* (below, 5).

Lett. *bi(s)zāles* (pl.), cpd. of *bise* 'gun' and *zāle* 'plant, grass', semantic borrowing of MLG *büssenkrūt* (cf. 20.28 and above, 3). Mühl.-Endz. 1.300, 4.696.

5. SCr. *prah*, Boh. *prach*, Pol. *proch*, Russ. *poroch*, general Slavic for 'dust', as ChSl. *prachŭ* (1.213).

SCr. *barut*, like NG μπαρούτι, fr. Turk. *barut*.

20.31 ARMOR (Defensive)

Grk.	ὅπλα, τεύχεα, πανοπλία	Goth.	*sarwa*	Lith.	*šarvai, apsiginklavimas*
NG	ὁπλισμός, πανοπλία, ἀρματωσιά	ON	*herklæði, herneskja*	Lett.	*brun'as*
Lat.	*arma, armatūra*	Dan.	*rustning, harnisk*	ChSl.	*orǫžĭja*
It.	*armatura, arnese*	Sw.	*(vapen)rustning, harnesk*	SCr.	*oklop*
Fr.	*armure (harnois)*	OE	*searu, herewǣd*	Boh.	*brněni*
Sp.	*armadura, arnés*	ME	*armure, harneis*	Pol.	*zbroja*
Rum.	*armură*	NE	*armor*	Russ.	*bronja*
Ir.	*gaisced*	Du.	*uitrusting, harnas*	Skt.	*āyudha-*
NIr.	*ēide (catha)*	OHG	*saro, gisarawi*	Av.	*varəθa-*
W.	*arfogaeth*	MHG	*harnas(ch), sar, geserwe*		
Br.	*harnez*				
		NHG	*rüstung, harnisch*		

Many of the words for 'weapons, arms' (20.21) cover both offensive and defensive arms. The latter may, of course, be expressed more specifically by the addition of 'defensive', 'of (or for) defense', e.g. Grk. ὅπλα ἀμυντικά, Fr. *armes défensives*, NHG *schutzwaffen*, Lett. *aissardzības ieroci*, SCr. *oružje za obranu*, Boh. *zbraně ochranně*, Pol. *broń odporna*. Such obvious phrases are not entered in the list. Apart from a few repeated from 20.21, those entered are such as correspond most nearly to NE *armor* in its historical uses.

Some of them may cover the whole military equipment but are used mostly of defensive armor. Some may cover all defensive arms including the shield,

others only the body-armor in the widest sense, 'breastplate, coat of mail, helmet', etc. These latter may result from a specialization of 'clothing' or an extension of 'breastplate' or the like (20.31).

In recent times, when the old defensive armor of the individual fighter has become obsolete, 'armor' is used for armored equipment, as of ships and vehicles.

In this sense NHG *panzer* (orig. 'breastplate', 20.32), e.g. *panzerwagen* 'tanks', *panzertruppen*, etc.

1. Grk. ὅπλα 'weapons, arms' (20.21) includes defensive arms. Hence, through vb. ὁπλίζω, ὁπλισμός, etc.

Grk. τεῦχος, but chiefly pl. τεύχεα ('arms', esp. defensive), prob. orig. 'implement' (like ὅπλον) : τεύχω 'make, prepare, produce, cause', etc. Boisacq 963.

Grk. πανοπλία 'full armor' (including offensive and defensive arms), deriv. of adj. πάνοπλος 'in full armor', cpd. of πᾶς 'all' and ὅπλα 'arms' (above).

Byz., NG ἀρματωσία (also 'armament, equipment'), deriv., through vb. ἀρματώνω of ἅρματα 'arms' (20.21).

2. Lat. *arma* 'weapons, arms' (20.21) includes and was prob. first 'defensive armor'. Hence, through vb. *armāre*, *armatūra* > It. *armatura*, Fr. *armure* (> Rum. *armură*), Sp. *armadura*. REW 653.

OFr. *herneis*, Fr. *harnais* (> It. *arnese*, Sp. *arnés*), now Fr. *harnois* arch. or lit. and distinguished from *harnais* 'harness'), fr. ON **her-nest* 'provisions for the army', cpd. of *herr* 'army', and *nest* 'provisions, viands'. REW 4119. Gamillscheg 509. Formerly taken as fr. Celtic cpd. of word for 'iron', Ir. *iarn*, etc. (so Falk-Torp 381, NED s.v. *harness*; still otherwise for second part Jenkins, Mod. Ph. 10.439).

Hence (directly or partly through MLG) ON *herneskja*, Dan. *harnisk*, Sw. *harnesk*, ME *harneis* (NE *harness*, now familiar only in the specialized sense, with reference to horses, etc.), Du. *harnas*, MHG *harnas(ch)*, NHG *harnisch*. Although these words are most commonly used of 'coat-of-mail, body-armor', they also have a wider scope, as originally.

3. Ir. *gaisced*, possibly late borrowing fr. W. *gwisgad* 'clothing' (6.12). Pedersen 2.4.

NIr. *ēide* (*catha*), lit. 'clothing (of war)', cf. Ir. *ētach*, NIr. *ēadach* 'clothes' (6.12).

W. *arfogaeth*, deriv. of *arfog* 'armed', fr. *arf* 'weapon' (20.21).

Br. *harnez*, prob. fr. Fr. *harnais*, *harnois*, but with change of suffix. Henry 157. Otherwise Thurneysen, Keltorom. 37 f.

4. Goth. *sarwa* (pl.; renders ὅπλα, πανοπλία), OE *searu* (also 'cunning'), OHG *saro*, *gisarawi*, MHG *sar*, *geserwe*, cf. ON *sørvi* 'necklace' (of pearls or precious stones), prob. : Lat. *serere* 'join, compose, contrive', Ir. *sreth* 'row, series', Grk. ὅρμος 'necklace', εἴρω 'fasten together in rows, string', etc. Walde-P. 2.500. Falk-Torp 960. Feist 411.

ON *herklæði*, OE *herewǣd*, both lit. 'army-clothes' (cf. 20.15, 6.12).

ON *herneskja*, ME *harneis*, NHG *harnisch*, etc., see under OFr. *herneis* (above, 2).

ME *armure*, NE *armor*, fr. OFr. *armure* (above, 2).

NHG *rüstung* ('equipment', esp. military; OHG *rustunga* 'tool'), Du. *uitrusting*, derivs. of NHG *rüsten*, Du. *rusten* 'arm, equip' (MLG *rusten* > Dan. *ruste*, Sw. *rusta*, whence *rustning*, in Sw. usually cpd. *vapenrustning*), OHG *rusten* 'prepare, adorn' = OE *hyrstan* 'decorate, ornament', cf. (pples.) ON *hroðinn* 'adorned', OE *gehroden* 'laden, adorned', prob. fr. the root in Lith. *krauti* 'pile up, pack, load', ChSl. *kryti* 'cover, hide', etc. Walde-P. 1.477. Falk-Torp 924.

5. Lith. *šarvai* (pl.) : OPruss. *sarwis* 'weapon', fr. Goth. *sarwa* (above, 4). Feist 411. Stender-Petersen 132.

Lith. *apsiginklavimas*, deriv. of *apsiginkluoti* 'arm oneself', refl. of *apginkluoti*, this fr. *ginklas* 'weapon' (20.21).

Lett. *brun'as* (orig. 'breastplate' as OPruss. *brunyos*, pl.), fr. (through Slavic?) Gmc., Goth. *brunjō*, OHG *brunia*, etc. (20.32). Mühl.-Endz. 1.340.

6. ChSl. *orǫžĭja* 'weapons' (20.21), also renders πανοπλία Lk. 11.22.

SCr. *oklop*, mostly 'breastplate' (20.32).

Boh. *brněni*, Russ. *bronja* 'coat-of-mail', also and orig. 'breastplate', fr. Gmc. (20.32).

Pol. *zbroja* (Boh. *zbroj* 'arms, armor'), etym.? Miklosich 390. Brückner 648.

7. Skt. *āyudha-* 'arms' (20.21) includes defensive armor. Macdonell-Keith, 1.60.

Av. *varəθa-* (Yt. 13.26, 71 clearly 'defensive armor' vs. *snaiθiš-*), like *vārəθman-*, Skt. *varman-* 'body-armor, corslet' (20.32), fr. *var-* 'cover'.

20.32 BREASTPLATE, CORSLET

Grk.	θώρᾱξ	Goth.	*brunjō*	Lith.	*antkrūtis*
NG	θώραξ	ON	*brynja*	Lett.	*krūšu brun'as*
Lat.	*lōrīca*	Dan.	*kyras, panser*	ChSl.	*(brŭnja)*
It.	*corazza*	Sw.	*kyras, pansar*	SCr.	*oklop, pancijer*
Fr.	*cuirasse, haubert*	OE	*byrne*	Boh.	*pancéř, kyrys, krunýř*
Sp.	*coraza*	ME	*brinie, hauberc, brist-plate, curas*	Pol.	*pancerz, kirys*
Rum.	*cuirasă, platoşă*			Russ.	*pancyr'*
Ir.	*lūrech*	NE	*breastplate, cuirass, corslet*	Skt.	*varman-, kavaca-*
NIr.	*lūireach, uchtphlata*			Av.	*vārəθman-*
W.	*dwyfronneg, llurig*	Du.	*borstharnas, kuras*		
Br.	*hobregon*	OHG	*brunja*		
		MHG	*brünne, küriss, panzier*		
		NHG	*panzer, kürass*		

Here are included the main words for armor protecting the trunk of the body, regardless of the changing material or form, ranging from the single front plate (as orig. NE *breastplate*) to the full corslet or coat-of-mail. A few of the words reflect simply the notion of 'covering, protection' and so would be equally applicable to all forms. But more are based upon either the material used or the part of the body protected, especially the breast, but in some cases originally the belly or the neck—such names being unaffected by subsequent changes of material or form.

1. Grk. θώρᾱξ ('corslet' Hom.; only secondarily the part covered 'trunk, chest'), perh. : Skt. *dhāraka-* 'receptacle' fr. IE **dher-* 'hold'. Walde-P. 1.858. Boisacq 361.

2. Lat. *lōrīca*, prob. deriv. of *lōrum* 'thong, strap'. Walde-H. 1.822. Otherwise, as loanword fr. unknown source, Ernout-M. 562.

OFr. *halberz*, *hausberc* (> It. *usbergo*), *hauberc*, Fr. *haubert* (> ME *hauberc*, *haubert*), orig. protecting the neck and shoulders, then lengthened to a full coat-of-mail, fr. OHG *halsberg*, cpd. of *hals* 'neck' and *berg* : *bergan* 'cover, protect'. REW 4009. Gamillscheg 510. NED s.v. *hauberk*.

It. *corazza* (> Sp. *coraza*, Fr. *cuirasse* > Rum. *cuirasă*), deriv. of Lat. *corium* 'leather'. REW 2233. Gamillscheg 284.

Rum. *platoşă*, formed fr. a loanword

like MHG *platte* 'plate-armor'. Tiktin 1184.

3. Ir. *lūrech*, NIr. *lūireach*, W. *llurig*, fr. Lat. *lōrīca*. Vendryes, De hib. voc. 152. Loth, Mots lat. 183.

NIr. *uchtphlata*, transl. of NE *breastplate* (*ucht* 'breast', 4.40).

W. *dwyfronneg*, deriv. of *dwyfron* 'breast' (4.40), after NE *breastplate*. Also direct loanword *brestblad*. Parry-Williams 82.

Br. *hobregon*, fr. Fr. *haubergeon*, dim. of OFr. *hauberc* (above, 2).

4. Goth. *brunjō*, ON *brynja* (Dan. *brynje*, Sw. *brynja* revived), OE *byrne*, ME *brunie*, *brinie*, OHG *brunna*, MHG *brünne* (NHG revived), early Gmc. loanword fr. Celtic word for 'breast', Ir. *bruinne*, etc. (4.40). Feist 107 f. Falk-Torp 110. NED s.v. *brinie*.

ME *bristplate*, NE *breastplate*, orig. single plate for the breast, but actually not so restricted in use.

ME *hauberc*, fr. OFr. *hauberc* (above, 2).

ME *curas*, NE *cuirass*, Dan., Sw. *kyras*, Du. *kuras*, MHG *küriss*, NHG *kürass*, fr. Fr. *cuirasse* (above, 2).

NE *corslet*, fr. Fr. *corselet*, dim. of *cors* 'body'. NED s.v.

MHG *panzier*, NHG *panzer* (now esp. 'armored equipment', as also Du. *pantser*), MLG *panser* (> Dan. *panser*, Sw. *pansar*), fr. It. *panciera* 'belly-armor', deriv. of *pancia*, Lat. *pantex* 'paunch'. REW 6207. Falk-Torp 813. Weigand-H. 2.366.

Du. *borstharnas*, lit. 'breast-armor' (*harnas*, 20.32).

5. Lith. *antkrūtis* (neolog. in place of *pancerius*, fr. NHG *panzer*), cpd. of *ant* 'on' and *krūtis* 'breast' (4.40).

Lett. *krūšu brun'as*, gen. pl. of *krūts* 'breast' and *brun'as* 'armor' (20.31). Mühl.-Endz. 2.293.

6. Russ.-ChSl. *brŭnja* (Russ. *bronja*, Boh. *brnění* now mostly in the wider sense of 'body-armor'), fr. Gmc., Goth. *brunjō*, OHG *brunna*, etc. (above, 4). Berneker 90. Stender-Petersen 225.

SCr. *oklop*, cpd. of *o* 'about' and the root of *za-klopiti* 'cover, lock up', etc. Berneker 523.

SCr. *pancijer*, Boh. *pancéř*, Pol. *pancerz*, Russ. *pancyr'*, fr. MHG *panzier*, NHG *panzer*. Brückner 393.

Boh. *kyrys*, Pol. *kirys*, fr. MHG *küriss*, fr. Fr. *cuirasse* (above). Brückner 231.

Boh. *krunýř*, the oldest word for 'breastplate', etc., but also 'neck-piece' of armor, and so perh. deriv. of *kruh* 'circle, ring' (ChSl. *krągŭ*), with *hn* > *n* (cf. Gebauer-Trávníček 46). No discussion found.

In chronological order the Boh. words are *krunýř*, *kyrys*, *pancéř*.

7. Skt. *varman-* (cf. Zimmer, Altind. Leben 298, Macdonell-Keith 2.271 f.), Av. *vārəθman-* (Yt. 11.2 and in *zaranyō-vārəθman-*, adj. 'with golden breastplate' Yt. 10.112), prob. also *vərəθra-* (in *ayō-vərəθra-* Yt. 13.45 'à la cuirasse de fer' Darmesteter; 'mit metallenem Schild' Barth.), all fr. Skt., Av. *var-* 'cover'.

Skt. *kavaca-* (Macdonell-Keith 1.143), prob. fr. a **ku-* beside **sku-* 'cover'. Walde-P. 2.546 (without *kavaca-*).

20.33 HELMET

Grk.	*κόρυς, κράνος, περικεφαλαία*	Goth.	*hilms*	Lith.	*šalmas*
NG	*περικεφαλαία, κράνος*	ON	*hjalmr*	Lett.	*k'ivere, brunu cepure*
Lat.	*cassis, galea*	Dan.	*hjelm*	ChSl.	*šlěmŭ*
It.	*elmo, casco*	Sw.	*hjelm*	SCr.	*kaciga*
Fr.	*casque*	OE	*helm*	Boh.	*přilba*
Sp.	*yelmo, casco*	ME	*helm, helmet*	Pol.	*helm*
Rum.	*coif*	NE	*helmet*	Russ.	*šlem*
Ir.	*cathbarr*	Du.	*helm*	Skt.	*çiprās* (pl.)
NIr.	*cathbharr*	OHG	*helm*	Av.	*xaoda-, sāravāra-*
W.	*helm*	MHG	*helm*		
Br.	*tok-houarn*	NHG	*helm*		

Words for 'helmet' are mostly derived from nouns for 'head', 'top', 'cap', or verbs for 'cover'.

1. Grk. κόρυς, gen. κόρυθος : κάρᾱ 'head', κέρας 'horn', κορυφή 'summit', Skt. *çiras-*, Av. *sarah-* 'head', etc. Walde-P. 1.406. Boisacq 499.

Grk. κράνος, prob. : preceding group. Walde-P. 1.405.

Grk. (late and NG) περικεφαλαία, lit. 'what is around the head' : κεφαλή 'head'.

2. Lat. *cassis*, gen. *-idis* ('metal helmet'), could be fr. **kadh-ti-s* : OE *hætt* 'hat', OHG *huot* 'hat, helmet', etc., but perh. is a loanword (Etruscan?). Walde-P. 1.341 f. Ernout-M. 159 f. Walde-H. 1.177.

Lat. *galea* ('leather helmet'), prob. loanword fr. Grk. γαλέη 'weasel, marten', through generalization of 'weasel skin' to 'skin, leather'. Cf. Grk. κυνέη, lit. 'dog's skin', but usually 'helmet'. Walde-P. 1.630. Ernout-M. 409 (adversely). Walde-H. 1.579.

It. *elmo*, OFr. *helme*, *heaume*, Sp. *yelmo*, fr. Gmc., Goth. *hilms*, OE, OHG *helm*, etc. (below, 4). REW 4130.

Sp. *casco* 'potsherd, skull, cask', etc., also 'helmet' (> It. *casco*, Fr. *casque*), fr. *cascar* 'break in pieces'. REW 6941. Gamillscheg 191.

Rum. *coif* (= Fr. *coiffe* 'headdress', It. *scuffia*, Sp. *escofia*, MLat. *cuphia*, *cofea*), loanword of disputed source, but prob. fr. Grk. σκυφίον 'skull' (dim. of σκύφος 'cup', with development as in NHG *kopf* 'head', 4.20). REW 2024. Gamillscheg 235. Wartburg 2.838.

3. Ir. *cathbarr*, NIr. *cathbharr*, lit. 'battle-top', cpd. of *cath* 'battle' (20.12), and *barr* 'top, extremity, tip' (12.33).

W. *helm*, fr. ME, OE *helm* 'helmet'.

Br. *tok-houarn*, lit. 'iron-hat', cpd. of *tok* 'hat, cap' (6.55), and *houarn* 'iron' (9.67).

4. Goth. *hilms*, ON *hjalmr*, OE, OHG *helm*, etc., general Gmc., dim. ME, NE *helmet*, fr. root of OE, OHG *helan*, Ir. *celim*, Lat. *oc-culere*, etc. 'cover, hide'. Walde-P. 1.433. Falk-Torp 408. Feist 255.

5. Lith. *šalmas*, OPruss. *salmis*, fr. OPol. *szłom* (below, 6). Brückner, Arch. sl. Ph. 20.449.

Lett. *k'ivere*, fr. Russ. *kiver* 'soldier's cap, shako'. Mühl.-Endz. 2.387.

Lett. *brunu cepure* (so in Lett. NT Eph. 6.17), lit. 'cap of armor' (6.55, 20.31).

6. ChSl. *šlěmŭ*, etc., once general Slavic (SCr. *šljem*, Boh. *šlem*, Pol. *szłom* obs.; ORuss. *šelm* now replaced by *šlem* fr. ChSl.), early loanword fr. Gmc., OHG *helm*, etc. (above, 4) with regular change of **chelmŭ* > **šelmŭ*. Miklosich 338. Brückner 170. Stender-Petersen 227.

SCr. *kaciga*, *kacida*, prob. (through an unknown intermediate source) fr. Lat. *cassis*, *-idis* (above, 2). Berneker 465.

Boh. *přilba*, cpd. of *při* 'at, on' and *leb*, gen. *lbi* 'skull'. Berneker 748.

Pol. *helm* (replacing the old *szłom*), fr. MHG, NHG *helm*.

7. Skt. *çiprās*, pl. of *çiprā-* 'cheek', in RV the 'cheek-pieces of the helmet' apparently used for 'helmet'. Cf. *ayaḥ-çipra-*, *hiranya-çipra-* 'having bronze (golden) helmets'. Zimmer, Altind. Leben 298. Macdonell-Keith 2.379 f.

Av. *xaoda-* in *ayō-xaoda-* adj. 'with bronze (or iron) helmet' (Yt. 13.45, 15.57), cf. OPers. *tigra-xauda-* 'with pointed cap', NPers. *xūd* 'helmet', perh. fr. the root in Grk. κεύθω 'hide', etc. Walde-P. 2.550. Barth. 162, 531.

Av. *sāravāra-*, cpd. of *sāra-* 'head' and *var-* 'cover, protect'. Barth. 1572.

20.34 SHIELD

Grk.	*ἀσπίς, σάκος, θυρεός*	Goth.	*skildus*	Lith.	*skydas*
NG	*ἀσπίδα (ἀσπίς)*	ON	*skjǫldr*	Lett.	*vairuogs*
Lat.	*scūtum, clipeus*	Dan.	*skjoldr*	ChSl.	*štitŭ*
Ir.	*scudo*	Sw.	*sköld*	SCr.	*štit*
Fr.	*bouclier*	OE	*scild*	Boh.	*štít*
Sp.	*escudo*	ME	*scheld*	Pol.	*tarcza*
Rum.	*scut*	NE	*shield*	Russ.	*ščit*
Ir.	*sciath, fern, boccōit*	Du.	*schild*		
NIr.	*sciath*	OHG	*scilt*		
W.	*tarian*	MHG	*schilt*		
Br.	*skoed*	NHG	*schild*		

Besides the commonest and most generic words for 'shield', some of the most important of those used less commonly or for special types are mentioned.

A recurring connection is that with words for 'board', properly applied to the wooden shield. Some of the terms orig. denoted some part of the shield as the boss or rim. The function of 'protection' is a rare source.

1. Grk. ἀσπίς, etym.? Walde-P. 1.50, 2.658. Boisacq 90.

Grk. σάκος : Skt. *tvac-*, *-tvacas-* 'skin, hide'. Walde-P. 1.747. Boisacq 849.

Grk. θυρεός, in Hom. 'stone placed against the door' (: θύρα 'door'), in late writers freq. 'oblong shield' and esp. for Lat. *scūtum*, vs. ἀσπίς = Lat. *clipeus*.

2. Lat. *scūtum* (> It. *scudo*, OFr. *escut*, Fr. *écu* now obs., Sp. *escudo*, Rum. *scut*), either fr. **skouto-m*, fr. the root **skeu-* 'cover' in Skt. *skāuti* 'covers', Grk. σκῦτος 'skin, hide', Lat. *obscūrus* 'dark, obscure', etc.; or fr. **skoito-m* : Ir. *sciath*, etc. 'shield' (below, 3). Walde-P. 2.543, 548. Ernout-M. 913.

Lat. *clipeus* (*clupeus*, *clipeum*), the round bronze shield, etym. dub., perh. loanword. Walde-P. 1.432. Ernout-M. 198. Walde-H. 1.235 f.

Fr. *bouclier*, OFr. *bocler* (> ME *bocler*, NE *buckler*; also It., Sp., MHG, Boh., Pol. forms, but mostly special 'small shield'; only in Fr. reg. for 'shield', replacing *écu*), orig. adj. with *escut* (above) 'shield having a boss', deriv. of *boucle* 'boss', fr. Lat. *buccula* 'cheek'. REW 1364. Gamillscheg 125. NED s.v. *buckler*.

3. Ir. *sciath*, W. *ysgwyd* (obs.), Br. *skoed* : ChSl. *štitŭ*, etc. 'shield' (below, 6), OE *scīd*, OHG *scīt* 'board, plank', fr. the root of Goth. *skaidan* 'cut', etc. Walde-P. 2.543. Pedersen 1.58.

Ir. *fern*, fr. IE **wer-* in Goth. *warjan*, OE *werian* 'ward off, hinder, defend', Skt. *vr-* 'cover', etc. Walde-P. 1.282.

Ir. *boccōit* ('boss of a shield' and 'small shield'), fr. Lat. *bucca* 'cheek' (cf. Fr. *bouclier*, etc., above, 2). Pedersen 1.196.

W. *tarian*, fr. ME *targe* (below, 4). Parry-Williams 33.

4. Goth. *skildus*, ON *skjǫldr*, OE *scild*, etc., general Gmc., prob. as orig. a 'flat piece, board' (cf. *tenues tabulae* of the German shields, Tac. Ann. 2.14. and OE *bord* 'board', often 'shield') : Lith. *skiltis* 'slice', fr. the root in Lith. *skelti* 'split', ON *skilja* 'separate', Goth. *skilja* 'butcher', etc. Walde-P. 2.592. Falk-Torp 1006 f. Feist 432.

Other, less common or more special, Gmc. words.

ON *targa*, OE *targa*, *targe* (> OFr. *targe* > ME, NE *targe*, whence dim. *target*) = OHG *zarga* 'border'. Fr. *targe* also > NHG *tartsche* > Slavic forms, of which Pol. *tarcza* has become the reg. word for 'shield'. Walde-P. 1.807. NED s.v. *targe*. Brückner 565.

ON *rǫnd*, OE *rand*, *rond*, OHG *rant*, orig. 'border, edge', hence 'shield-rim' or 'shield-boss' and 'shield'. Walde-P. 2.372. Falk-Torp 876. NED s.v. *rand*.

5. Lith. *skydas* (Lett. obs. *sckyde*, Z. sl. Ph. 5.315), fr. a Gmc. form, cf. OHG *scīt* 'board' (above, 3). Alminauskis 116.

Lett. *vairuogs*, deriv. of *vairīt* 'ward off, protect'. Mühl.-Endz. 4.443.

6. ChSl. *štitŭ*, etc., general Slavic (but Pol. *szczyt* now obs. in this sense) : Ir. *sciath*, etc. (above, 3). Brückner 546.

Pol. *tarcza*, see under ON *targa*, etc. (above, 4).

7. There is no reference to shields in Skt. or Av., only 'shield' in fig. sense 'protection', or 'corslet' (20.33).

20.35 FORTRESS

Grk.	*τεῖχος, φρούριον*	Goth.	. . . .	Lith.	*tvirtovė*
NG	*φρούριο(ν), κάστρο*	ON	*borg*	Lett.	*cietuoksnis*
Lat.	*castellum*	Dan.	*fæstning*	ChSl.	(*gradište*)
It.	*fortezza*	Sw.	*fästning*	SCr.	*tvrđava*
Fr.	*forteresse*	OE	*castel, burg*	Boh.	*pevnost', tvrz*
Sp.	*fuerte, fortaleza*	ME	*fort(e)ress, castel*	Pol.	*twierdza, forteca*
Rum.	*fortăreaţă*	NE	*fortress, fort*	Russ.	*krepost'*
Ir.	*dūn*	Du.	*vesting*	Skt.	(*pur-*)
NIr.	*dūn*	OHG	*burg*	OPers.	*didā-*
W.	*caer, castell*	MHG	*vestenunge, vestunge*		
Br.	*kreñvlec'h*	NHG	*festung*		

'Fortress' may be expressed by words that denoted also or originally the all-important 'wall', or an 'inclosed place', 'guard, shelter' or 'stronghold'. Most of the modern words are derived from those for 'strong' or 'firm', some of these involving borrowing either formal or semantic, the latter probable in the Balto-Slavic words, which seem to be modeled on NHG *festung* or the corresponding LG form.

1. Grk. τεῖχος 'wall' (7.27) is also the usual means of expressing 'fortress'. The city-walls, the κλυτὰ τείχεα of Troy, the μακρὰ τείχεα of Athens, were the fortress, and τεῖχος is frequently used where the sense is not strictly 'wall', but 'fortress' e.g. Hdt. 7.59, Thuc. 3.51, 3.85, etc. To fortify a place was to 'build walls, wall it in', τειχίζω (τὴν πόλιν ἐτείχισαν, ἐτειχίσθη 'Αταλάντη, Thuc. 1.93, 2.32), whence also ἐπιτειχίζω 'build fortifications against' and ἐπιτείχισμα 'frontier fortress'.

Grk. φρούριον (also 'garrison') : φρου-ρός 'guard' (fr. *προ-hορος : ὁράω 'watch, see', 15.51), vb. φρουρέω 'keep guard', etc.

Byz. κάστρον, NG κάστρο, fr. Lat. castrum (below, 2).

2. Lat. castellum, deriv. of castrum, rarely 'fortress', mostly in place-names or esp. pl. castra 'fortified camp', beside Umbr. castruo 'fundos', prob. as orig. a piece of land cut off, that is, laid out, fr. the same root as castrāre 'castrate', orig. 'cut' (3.14). Walde-P. 1.448. Ernout-M. 1.180. Walde-H. 1.180.

Hence the widespread Eur. words which in earlier periods denoted a fortress, as OFr. castel, ME castel, Ir. caisel, W. castell, but later a 'castle' even without fortifications, as Fr. château, NE castle. NED s.v. castle, sb. 3.

It. fortezza, Fr. forteresse (> ME, NE fortress, Rum. fortăreață), OFr. also forte-lece (> Sp. fortaleza), in earliest use 'might', derivs. of Lat. fortis 'strong, mighty' (4.81), whence also in sb. use for 'fortress' Fr. (> NE) fort, Sp. fuerte. REW 3457.

3. Ir. dūn (Gall. -dūnum in place names, MW din) : OE tūn 'inclosed place' (NE town), OHG zūn 'hedge, fence', etc. (19.15). Walde-P. 1.778. Pedersen 1.50.

W. cader (cf. Evans s.v., not in Spur-rell, now obs.?) and caer, prob. : Ir. cathir 'city' (see 19.15).

Br. krenvlec'h, fr. krenv 'strong' (4.81).

4. ON borg, OE, OHG burg 'fortified

place', hence 'city' (Goth. baurgs reg. = πόλις), see under 'city' (19.15).

MHG vestenunge, MLG vesteninge (> Dan. fæstning, Sw. fästning), Du. ves-ting, MHG vestunge, NHG festung, fr. MHG vesten 'make fast', veste 'firm, fast'. Weigand-H. 1.524. Falk-Torp 289.

5. Lith. tvirtovė : tvirtas 'firm', ChSl. tvrŭdŭ 'firm, stable', etc., see under 'hard' (15.74).

Lett. cietuoksnis, fr. ciets 'hard, firm' (15.74). For suffix, cf. Leskien, Bildung d. Nom. 319.

6. ChSl. (late), Bulg. gradište, Boh. hradište, Russ. gorodišče, old Slavic word for 'fortified place' (Niederle, op. cit. 2.299 ff.; but now used mostly of a ruined city or fortress), deriv., through vb., of ChSl. gradŭ, etc. 'city' (19.15).

SCr. tvrđava, Boh. tvrz, Pol. twierdza, fr. SCr. tvrd, etc. 'hard', orig. 'firm' (15.74).

Boh. pevnost', fr. pevný 'firm' = Pol. pewny 'sure', both as orig. 'trustworthy' : ChSl. upŭvati 'trust', etc. Brückner 403.

Pol. forteca, fr. It. fortezza (above 2). Brückner 126.

Russ. krepost', fr. krepkij 'firm, solid, strong' : ChSl. krěpŭkŭ 'strong' (4.81).

7. Skt. pur- (nom. sg. pūr) 'fortified place, stronghold' (cf. Macdonell-Keith 1.538 f.) : Grk. πόλις 'city', in early use also 'citadel', Lith. pilis, Lett. pils 'castle', see 19.15.

OPers. didā- : Skt. dehī-, Grk. τεῖχος 'wall', etc. (7.27).

20.36 TOWER

Grk.	πύργος, τύρσις	Goth.	kēlikn	Lith.	bokštas
NG	πύργος	ON	turn	Lett.	turnis
Lat.	turris	Dan.	taarn	ChSl.	stlŭpŭ, synŭ
It.	torre	Sw.	torn	SCr.	toranj
Fr.	tour	OE	stēpel, stýpel, torr	Boh.	věž
Sp.	torre	ME	toure	Pol.	wieža
Rum.	turn	NE	tower	Russ.	bašnja
Ir.	tor, tur	Du.	toren		
NIr.	tor, túr	OHG	turri		
W.	twr	MHG	turm		
Br.	tour	NHG	turm		

The 'tower', which was primarily military, may conveniently be considered here. The majority of Eur. words go back, directly or indirectly, to Lat. turris.

1. Grk. πύργος, orig. dub., perh. fr. some Anatolian source. Boisacq 829. Feist 85 (with refs.).

Grk. πύρσις, τύρσις, prob. of Anatolian orig., perh. the word upon which Τυρση-νός, Τυρρηνός 'Etruscan' is based.

2. Lat. turris (Osc. tiurri 'turrim', fr. Grk. τύρρις or the same source. Ernout-M. 1066.

Lat. turris > It., Sp. torre, OFr. tor, Fr. tour (> ME toure, NE tower, Ir. tor, tur, W. twr, Br. tour; so for Celtic Peder-sen 1.238, but W. twr prob. through ME toure), OE torr, OHG turri.

MHG, MLG torn, turn, Du. toren, fr. an OFr. torn (cf. Fr. tournelle 'small tower'), a by-form or tor, tour by con-fusion with torn, tour 'turning lathe'. MLG (or in part MHG) torn, turn > ON (late) turn, Dan. taarn, Sw. torn, Lett. tuornis, turnis, Rum. turn, SCr. toranj. MHG turm (beside turn), NHG turm, with m for n, as in MHG harm be-side harn 'urine', etc. Hence Lith. tur-mas ('tower' Kurschat; now dial. 'jail'), Pol. turma 'dungeon', Russ. tjur'ma 'prison, jail' (21.39). Franck-v. W. 703. Falk-Torp 1239. Weigand-H. 2.1089. Kluge-G. 635 (but OFr. torn, not fr. Lat. acc. turrim).

3. Goth. kēlikn (renders πύργος, also ἀνώγεον 'upper room', fr. Gall celicnon 'tower', orig. and course of transmission dub. Feist 310 f. (full refs.).

OE stēpel, stýpel (freq. for turris, as in Gospels, WSax. versions vs. torr Lin-disf.; NE steeple now only of a church) : stēap 'high, lofty' (NE steep), stūpian 'bow', etc. Walde-P. 2.619. NED s.v. steeple.

4. Lith. bokštas (NSB, etc.), fr. Wh-Russ., Ukr. bakšta (Brückner, Sl. Fremd-wörter 73), this: Boh. bašta, etc. 'bas-tion', Russ. bašnja 'tower', fr. It. bastia 'bastion'. Berneker 45.

Lith. kuoras (NSB, and the word used in the NT versions), prob. fr. NHG chor 'choir' in its special application to the 'choir-loft' (Paul, Deutsches Wtb. s.v.), Kurschat s.v. koras.

5. ChSl. stlŭpŭ (= πύργος Gospels, etc.; also 'column, pillar', as SCr. stup, Boh. sloup, Russ. stolp, stolb) : ON stolpi, etc. 'post', fr. p- and b- extensions of stel- 'set, place'. Walde-P. 2.646. Falk-Torp 1173.

ChSl. synŭ (freq. for πύργος in Supr.; also late sunŭ), fr. the root of sŭpa, suti, iter. sypati 'strew, pour', whence such derivs. as ChSl. sŭpŭ 'heap', Russ. nasyp 'heaped up earth, mound, dam', Pol. wysyp 'mound, terrace, etc.' Mi-klosich 334, 335. Brückner 524.

Boh. věž, Pol. wieža : ORuss. veža 'tower, hut, tent', late ChSl. veža 'cell, tent'(?), Slov. veza 'hall', fr. the root of ChSl. vezq, vesti 'carry'(?). 'Tower' fr. resemblance in shape to the (peaked) tent or hut. Brückner 619 f.

Russ. bašnja, see under Lith. bokštas (above, 4).

20.41 VICTORY

Grk.	νίκη	Goth.	sigis	Lith.	laimėjimas
NG	νίκη	ON	sigr	Lett.	uzvara
Lat.	victōria	Dan.	sejr	ChSl.	pobĕda
It.	vittoria	Sw.	seger	SCr.	pobjeda
Fr.	victoire	OE	sige, sigor	Boh.	vítězstvi
Sp.	victoria	ME	victorie	Pol.	zwycięstwo
Rum.	victorie, biruință, iz-bîndă	NE	victory	Russ.	pobeda
		Du.	zege	Skt.	jaya-
Ir.	búaid	OHG	sigi, sigu	Av.	vərəθraγna-, vanati-, nivāti-
NIr.	buaith	MHG	sige, sic		
W.	buddugoliaeth	NHG	sieg		
Br.	gounid, trec'h				

The majority of the words for 'vic-tory' are derived from verbs for 'con-quer, win', and these are cognate with others for 'strive, gain', 'compel', 'have power, be able', 'put down' (prob.). In some cases the nouns are earlier (so in Gmc., where verbs like NHG siegen are secondary), and these may be based on notions like 'power' or 'profit'.

Most of the common verbs for 'con-quer' belong with nouns for 'victory' and are mentioned in the following. Among others may be noted ME conquere, NE conquer, fr. OFr. conquerre, fr. VLat. *conquaerere, recomposition of Lat. con-quīrere 'seek for', hence 'gain, acquire' (NED s.v.).

1. Grk. νίκη, vb. νῑκάω, prob. through notion of 'put down' : Skt. nīca- 'low', ChSl. nicĭ 'prone', Skt. ni 'down', etc. Walde-P. 2.335.

2. Lat. victōria (> Romance words), through victor, fr. vincere 'conquer, win' : Ir. fichim, Goth. weihan, OE wīgan, etc. 'fight' (20.11).

Rum. biruință (usual word before the introduction of victorie, e.g. in NT), fr. birui 'conquer, master', this fr. Hung. bir 'be able, can'. Tiktin 193.

Rum. izbîndă, fr. vb. izbîndi 'fulfil, succeed, win', fr. Slav., cf. ChSl. iz-byti, pres. iz-bqndq 'be free of, be saved, dis-pose of', cpd. of byti 'be'. Tiktin 864.

3. Ir. búaid, NIr. buaidh, W. buddu-goliaeth (deriv. of buddug-ol 'victorious'; budd 'profit' = Ir. búaid), perh. : MLG būte 'booty' (> NHG beute), but dis-puted and root connection? Walde-P. 2.186. Pedersen 1.111.

Br. gounid, also and orig. 'profit, wage' : W. gweini 'serve', Ir. fogniu id., cpd. of *upo- and the root in Ir. gníu 'do'. Pedersen 1.104. Henry 139.

Br. trec'h ('victory' and adj. 'victori-ous', with vb. trec'hi 'conquer') also and orig. 'stronger' = W. trech, Ir. tressa 'stronger' (cf. Ir. trēn, 4.81). Pedersen 1.296.

4. Goth. sigis, ON sigr (sig poet.), OE sige, sigor, OHG sigi, sigu, etc., gen-eral Gmc. : Skt. sahas- 'strength, power, might, victory', cpd. 'prevail, conquer, win', Grk. ἔχω 'hold', etc. Walde-P. 2.481 f. Falk-Torp 954. Feist 419.

ME victorie, NE victory, fr. OFr. vic-torie beside victoire (above, 2).

5. Lith. laimėjimas, fr. laimėti 'have

luck, win', fr. laimė 'luck, good fortune, success' (16.17).

Lett. uzvara, cpd. of vara 'power, might' (4.81).

6. ChSl. pobĕda, SCr. pobjeda, Russ. pobeda, with vb. ChSl. pobĕditi, etc. 'con-quer', perfect. cpd. of bĕditi 'compel' (19.48). Berneker 54.

Boh. vítězstvi, Pol. zwycięstwo, derivs., through vbs., of word seen in late ChSl. vitęzŭ 'hero', Boh. vítěz 'victor', SCr. vitez, Russ. vitjaz' 'knight', old loanword fr. a Gmc. *wiþing or the like (cf. Vith-ungi), beside ON vikingr, etc. Miklo-sich 393. Brückner 658 f.

7. Skt. jaya- : ji- 'conquer', Grk. βία 'power', etc. Walde-P. 1.666.

Av. vərəθraγna-, cpd. of vərəθra- 'at-tack' and a form of Jan- 'smite, slay' (4.76). Barth. 1421.

Av. vanati-, ni-vāti- (also vanya- in cpds.), fr. van- 'overcome, conquer' : Skt. van- 'gain, acquire', OE winnan 'strive, conquer, win', etc. Walde-P. 1.258 ff. Barth. 1085, 1350, etc.

Curiously, there is no quotable OPers. word for 'victory', though victories are constantly described, "Auramazda bore me aid, by the grace of Auramazda I smote the army of . . .".

20.42 DEFEAT (sb.)

Grk.	ἧσσα, ἧττα	Goth.	. . . .	Lith.	pralaimėjimas
NG	ἧττα	ON	ūsigr	Lett.	kaviens
Lat.	clādēs	Dan.	nederlag	ChSl.	. . . .
It.	sconfitta	Sw.	nederlag	SCr.	poraz
Fr.	défaite	OE	cwild(?)	Boh.	porážka
Sp.	derrota	ME	losse	Pol.	porážka
Rum.	înfringere	NE	defeat	Russ.	poraženie
Ir.	maidm	Du.	nederlaag	Skt.	parājaya-, parā-bhāva-
NIr.	diombuaidh, briseadh	OHG	vuol(?)		
W.	gorchfygiad	MHG	(unsige)		
Br.	faezidigez	NHG	niederlage		

The verbal notion 'to defeat' is virtu-ally equivalent to 'be victorious over, conquer', and is generally expressed by the verbs mentioned in 20.41 (e.g. Grk. νῑκάω, Lat. vincere, in pass. regularly 'be defeated'), the nouns corresponding to which mean 'victory'. Such verbal ex-pressions of defeat are more common than the use of a noun for 'defeat' vs. 'victory', and in some cases such a dis-tinctive noun seems to be lacking or at least has not been found quotable.

Most of the nouns for 'defeat' are based on such notions as 'inferiority, de-struction, disaster, loss, breaking, blow'.

1. Grk. ἧσσα, Att. ἧττα (also NG lit.), back-formation to ἡσσάομαι 'be inferior, be defeated', fr. ἥσσων 'inferior, weaker', comp. to adv. ἧκα 'slightly, gently',

perh. : Lat. sēgnis 'slow, inactive'. Walde-P. 2.474. Boisacq 317. Wacker-nagel, KZ 30.299.

Grk. σφάλμα 'fault, error' (16.76), and σύμπτωμα 'mishap', are also used for a military defeat.

2. Lat. clādēs 'destruction, disaster' and in military use 'defeat': -cellere 'strike' in per-cellere, and -cellere 'strike', Grk. κλάω 'break', Lith. kalti 'strike, beat', etc. Walde-P. 1.436 ff. Ernout-M. 171, 192. Walde-H. 1.225.

It. sconfitta, fr. sconfiggere 'defeat', fr. ex- + Lat. conficere 'weaken, destroy'. Cf. OFr. desconfit, NE discomfit, simi-larly fr. *dis-conficere. REW 2984.

Fr. défaite, substantivized fem. pple. of défaire 'undo, destroy, defeat', fr.

VLat. *dis-facere, cpd. of dis- 'apart' and facere 'do, make'. Gamillscheg 298.

Sp. derrota, substantivized fem. pple. of OSp. derromper, fr. Lat. dis-rumpere 'break to pieces'.

Rum. înfrîngere, substantivized old infin. of înfrînge 'defeat' = It. infrangere 'break, crush', fr. VLat. *in-frangere (= Lat. in-fringere), cpd. of frangere 'break'. REW 4412. Tiktin 809.

3. Ir. maidm, lit. 'a breaking', vbl. n. of maidim 'break', intr. (9.26), and reg. for 'defeat' (cf. RIA Contrib. s.v.). Pedersen 2.574.

NIr. diombuaidh, cpd. of neg. diom- and buaidh 'victory'.

NIr. briseadh 'breaking', also 'defeat' (Dinneen) : brisim 'break' (9.26).

W. gorchfygiad, fr. gorchfygu 'conquer, defeat', cpd. (*upor-ko-) of mygu in dir-mygu 'despise', ed-mygu 'admire', orig. sense 'look' (Pedersen 2.576, without inclusion of gorchfygu). J. Lloyd-Jones, BBCS 2.104 f.

Br. faezidigez, cpd. of faez 'conquered, beaten' (faeza 'conquer' = Corn. fethe id., outside root connection?) and digouez 'happening, encounter'.

4. ON ūsigr, neg. cpd. of sigr 'victory'. So rarely MHG unsige.

OE cwild (: cwellan 'kill') glosses Lat. clādēs, but is quotable only as 'disaster, disease', etc.

ME losse 'loss' (11.74), sometimes 'loss of a battle, defeat'. NED s.v. loss.

NE defeat, fr. vb. defeat after Fr. défaite (above, 2).

OHG wuol glosses Lat. clādēs but is mostly 'destruction', beside wal : OE wōl 'pestilence', wæl 'the dead in battle', also 'slaughter, destruction', Ir. fuil 'blood', etc. Walde-P. 1.304 f. Falk-Torp 1344.

NHG niederlage, quotable as 'defeat' in 15th cent. (> Dan., Sw. nederlag), Du. nederlaag (sense 'defeat' prob. fr. NHG), in earlier use (MHG niderlāge, etc.) 'laying down, place of rest'. Development of 'defeat' fr. the 'laying-down of arms'. Weigand-H. 2.298.

5. Lith. pralaimėjimas, fr. pra- in its sense of 'away, failing' and laimėjimas 'victory'.

Lett. kaviens 'a blow' and (Drawneek) 'defeat' : kaut 'strike'. But generally expressed verbally by sakaut 'beat' (the enemy), sakauts 'beaten, defeated'.

6. SCr. poraz, Boh. porážka, Pol. porażka, Russ. poraženie, fr. vb. ChSl. (SCr., etc.) poraziti 'strike, smite, beat', deriv. of SCr., Boh., Pol., Russ. raz 'blow'. Miklosich 273. Brückner 454.

7. Skt. parājaya-, fr. parā-ji- 'conquer, overcome', in pass. 'lose, be defeated', cpd. of ji- 'conquer'. Cf. jaya- 'victory' (20.41).

Skt. parābhāva- 'disappearance, humiliation' and 'defeat' (quotable in military sense?), fr. parā-bhū- 'disappear, perish', cf. parābhūta- 'defeated'.

20.43 ATTACK (sb.)

Grk.	προσβολή, ἔφοδος, ἐπίθεσις	Goth.	....	Lith.	užpuolimas
NG	ἐπίθεσι(ς)	ON	atsōkn	Lett.	uzbrukums
Lat.	impetus	Dan.	angreb	ChSl.	napadenĭje
It.	attacco	Sw.	anfall	SCr.	navala
Fr.	attaque	OE	rǣs	Boh.	útok
Sp.	ataque	ME	rese, asaut, saut	Pol.	atak
Rum.	atac	NE	attack	Russ.	ataka
Ir.	fóbart	Du.	aanval	Skt.	(abhiyoga-)
NIr.	ionnsaighe, fóbairt	OHG	anaging	Av.	draoman-
W.	ymosodiad	MHG	anval		
Br.	stourm	NHG	angriff		

Words for 'attack' are based on such notions as 'go after, fall upon, rush upon strike against, seize upon, apply oneself to'.

1. Grk. προσβολή : προσβάλλω 'strike against'.

Grk. ἔφοδος 'approach, access' and often military 'advance, attack', cpd. of ἐπί 'upon' and ὁδός 'way, road'.

Grk. ἐπίθεσις (in NG the usual term), fr. ἐπιτίθεμαι 'apply oneself to' and 'attack'.

2. Lat. impetus, fr. vb. impetere 'attack' (less common than sb.), cpd. of petere 'fall upon, attack' (also commonly 'seek', 11.31). Ernout-M. 763 f. Walde-H. 1.684.

It. attacco (> Fr. attaque, Sp. ataque, Rum. atac), fr. vb. attaccare 'make fast, attach' (= Fr. attacher), hence, first in phrases 'join battle' or 'apply oneself to', 'attack' (in this sense > Fr. attaquer, etc.), cpd. deriv. of word seen in OFr. estache 'stake', orig. Gmc. (OE staca, MLG stake, etc.). REW 8218. Gamillscheg 56, 828. NED s.v. attack and attach.

3. Ir. fóbart, NIr. fóbairt, vbl. n. of fuabar 'attacks', fr. *fo-od-ber-, cpd. of berim 'carry'. Pedersen 2.469. Windisch 554 f.

NIr. ionnsaighe, fr. ionnsaighim, Ir. insaigim, cpd. of saigim 'go after'. Pedersen 2.608.

W. ymosodiad, fr. vb. ymosod 'set upon, attack', cpd. of refl. prefix ym- and gosod 'put, place' (12.12), hence orig. 'set oneself to'.

Br. stourm, loanword fr. Gmc. (OE-NE storm, etc.). Henry 254.

4. ON atsōkn, fr. sœkja 'seek' (11.31), esp. 'go after, pursue, attack'.

OE rǣs, on-rǣs (also 'rush, onrush'), ME rese = ON rás 'running, race' (> NE race) : Grk. ἐρωή 'quick motion, rush', prob. also Skt. rasa- 'sap, juice', etc. Walde-P. 1.149 f. Falk-Torp 881. NED s.v. rese, sb.

ME asaut, saut (NE assault), fr. OFr. asaut, VLat. *ad-saltus, recomposition of Lat. ad-sultus, like vb. *ad-salīre (> OFr. asalir, ME, NE assail) for ad-silīre 'leap upon', cpd. of salīre 'leap'.

NE attack, fr. Fr. attaque, fr. vb. attack, this fr. Fr. attaquer (above, 2).

OHG anaging (Otfr.; other more common words?), lit. 'a seeking after' : gingēn 'long for', etc.

MHG anval, NHG anfall (> Sw. anfall), Du. aanval, fr. vb. MHG anvallen, etc. 'fall upon, attack'.

NHG angriff, fr. MHG angrif, OHG anagrif 'handling, seizure, undertaking', fr. vb. OHG ana-grīfan 'lay hands on', NHG angreifen 'handle, seize' and 'attack'. Hence semantically Dan. angreb, with vb. angribe 'attack'.

5. Lith. užpuolimas, fr. užpulti 'fall upon, attack', cpd. of pulti 'fall' (10.23).

Lett. uzbrukums, fr. uzbrukti 'fall upon, attack', cpd. of brukti 'break off' (intr.) = Lith. brukti 'slip into, force into', etc. Mühl.-Endz. 4.319, 1.339.

6. ChSl. napadenĭje, SCr., Boh., Pol. napad, Boh. napadenĭ, Russ. napadenie, etc., fr. vb. ChSl. na-pasti, etc. 'fall upon', cpd. of pasti 'fall' (10.23). These words are used mostly for a sudden attack, onset (like NHG überfall).

SCr. navala : na-valiti 'attack', orig. 'roll upon', cpd. of ChSl. valiti, etc. 'roll' (10.15).

Boh. útok, Pol. atak, Russ. ataka, loanwords fr. Fr. attaque (above, 2).

7. Skt. abhiyoga- (but more common in other senses), fr. abhi-yuj- 'attack', cpd. of abhi- 'against' and yuj- 'join'.

Av. draoman- : dru- 'run'. Barth. 770.

20.44 DEFENSE

Grk.	ἀμῦνα	Goth.	....	Lith.	ginimas
NG	ἄμυνα, ὑπεράσπισις	ON	verja	Lett.	aizstāviba
Lat.	dēfēnsiō	Dan.	forsvar	ChSl.	
It.	difesa	Sw.	försvar	SCr.	obrana
Fr.	défense	OE	waru	Boh.	obrana
Sp.	defensa	ME	were, defens(e), defence	Pol.	obrona
Rum.	apărare			Russ.	oborona, zaščita
Ir.	dītiu	NE	defense	Skt.	(rakṣaṇa-)
NIr.	cosnamh	Du.	verdediging		
W.	amddiffyn	OHG	werī		
Br.	difenn	MHG	were		
		NHG	verteidigung		

Many of the verbs for 'defend', from which the nouns listed here are derived, meant first 'ward off, avert' something from or for the object defended (construed accordingly), later 'defend' with person or place defended as the direct object. Some are from such notions as 'fight about, contend, stand behind', and 'protect' from 'shield'. A few are based upon 'answer for, represent or argue in court', that is, were first used with reference to legal defense.

1. Grk. ἀμῦνα (not in Hom., and condemned by the Atticists, the verbal expression being preferred; the usual NG term) beside the vb. ἀμύνω 'ward off, defend, aid' (object defended in gen. or dat.), etym. dub., perh. : ἀμεύσασθαι 'pass over, surpass', Lat. movēre 'move', etc. (10.11). Walde-P. 2.252. Boisacq 57.

NG ὑπεράσπισις, fr. ὑπερασπίζω 'cover with a shield', hence 'shield, protect' (Polyb., LXX, etc.), fr. ἀσπίς 'shield' (20.34).

2. Lat. dēfēnsiō (also late dēfēnsa > It. difesa, Fr. défense, Sp. defensa), fr. dē-fendere 'ward off, defend' : Grk. θείνω, Skt. han-, etc. 'strike' (9.21). Walde-P. 1.680. Ernout-M. 344. Walde-H. 1.332 f. Wartburg 3.28.

Rum. apărare, fr. apăra, fr. Lat. apparāre, cpd. of parāre 'prepare', with development ('be prepared for' and so 'avert') as in It. parare 'ward off' (>Fr. parer > NE parry), etc. Tiktin 76. REW 6229. Gamillscheg 670.

3. Ir. dītiu 'protection' (quotable for military 'defense'?), vbl. n. of do-eim 'protect', cpd. of em- (simplex not in use) : Lat. emere, Lith. imti, etc. 'take'

(11.13). Walde-P. 1.124 f. Pedersen 2.512.

NIr. cosnamh, fr. Ir. cosnam 'contest', fr. vb. cosnaim 'contend (against), defend', NIr. 'defend', cpd. of snīim 'spin' (6.31) and 'exert oneself'. Walde-P. 2.694. Pedersen 2.633.

W. amddiffyn, sb. and vb., cpd. of am- 'about' and diffyn, likewise Br. difenn, with vb. difenni, fr. Lat. dē-fendere. Loth, Mots lat. 236. Henry 96.

4. ON verja (but sb. rare, vb. common), OE waru, ME were, OHG warī, werī, MHG were, NHG wehr : vbs. Goth. warjan 'hinder, prevent', ON verja, OE werian, OHG werien, weren, NHG wehren, all 'hinder, prevent' and 'protect, defend' : Skt. vṛ- 'cover, hinder, prevent' (cf. varūtha- 'protection'), Grk. ἐρύομαι 'protect, rescue', etc. Walde-P. 1.282. Falk-Torp 1369. Feist 551 f.

Dan. forsvar, Sw. försvar, fr. vbs. forsvare, försvara 'defend', cpds. of svare, svara 'answer' (18.32). Perh. translation of MLG vorantworden 'answer for, defend in court', at any rate obviously first applied to legal defense.

ME, NE defence, defense (both spellings freq.), fr. Fr. défense (above, 2). NED s.v.

Du. verdediging, NHG verteidigung, fr. vbs. verdedigen, verteidigen 'defend',

these fr. MDu. verdēdinghen, MHG verteidingen, vertädingen 'argue or defend in court' : OHG tagading 'discussion, argument', MDu. dā(ghe)dinc 'term of court, discussion', cpds. of dag, tag 'day' and ding 'legal procedure'. Weigand-H. 2.1166. Kluge-G. 654. Franck-v. W. 730.

5. Lith. ginimas, fr. ginti 'defend' : Lat. dēfendere. etc. (above, 2).

Lett. aizstāviba, fr. aizstāvēt 'defend', also 'represent', cpd. of aiz and stāvēt 'stand' and so lit. 'stand behind'. Mühl.-Endz. 1.16, 52, 53.

SCr., Boh. obrana, Pol. obrona, Russ. oborona, cpd. of o 'about' and second part : ChSl. braniti 'ward off', SCr., Boh. braniti, Pol. bronić 'defend', ChSl. branĭ 'war', brati 'fight', etc. (20.11, 20.13). Berneker 74. Brückner 41.

Russ. zaščita 'protection, defense' in widest sense, including military (SCr., Boh. zaštita 'protection, shelter', Pol. zaszcyt 'honor, glory'), cpd. of za- 'behind' and second part : ChSl. štitŭ, Russ. ščit, etc. 'shield' (20.34), late ChSl. zaštititi rendering Grk. ὑπερασπίζω (cf. above, 1). Brückner 546.

6. Skt. rakṣaṇa- ('protection', quotable for military defense?), fr. rakṣ- 'protect' : Grk. ἀλέξω 'ward off, defend, aid'. Walde-P. 1.89.

20.45 RETREAT (sb.)

Grk.	*ἀνα-(ὑπο-)χώρησις*	Goth.	(*þlauhs*)	Lith.	*atsitraukimas*
NG	*ὑποχώρησι(ς)*	ON	(*flótti*)	Lett.	*atkāpšanas*
Lat.	*receptus*	Dan.	*retræte*	ChSl.	(*běstvo*)
It.	*ritirata*	Sw.	*reträtt*	SCr.	*uzmak*
Fr.	*retraite*	OE	(*flēam*)	Boh.	*ústup*
Sp.	*retirada*	ME	(*fliht*) *retret*	Pol.	*rejterada, odwrót*
Rum.	*retragere*	NE	*retreat*	Russ.	*otstuplenie*
It.	(*teched*)	Du.	*terugtocht*	Skt.	(*palāyana-*)
NIr.	*cūl*	OHG	(*flucht*)		
W.	*cil, encil*	MHG	(*vlucht*)		
Br.	*kizadenn, kizadeg*	NHG	*rückzug*		

The nouns for 'retreat' are from verbs denoting 'draw back, step back, turn aside'. In the widespread Eur. group to which NE *retreat* belongs, the orig. literal sense 'withdrawal' is forgotten, and NE *withdrawal* is now a euphemistic substitute.

Prior to the rise of distinctive military terms for 'retreat' the notion was covered by words for 'flight', parallel with the verbs for 'flee' (10.51). So Hom. φύγαδε 'in flight', and in the older Gmc. languages and some others, there seem to have been no more distinctive terms.

1. Grk. ἀναχώρησις and ὑποχώρησις, fr. ἀνα-, ὑπο-χωρέω 'go back, draw back', cpds. of χωρέω 'make room for, draw back', deriv. of χῶρος 'place'.

2. Lat. *receptus*, fr. *se recipere* 'draw back, retreat', refl. of *recipere* 'take back', cpd. of *capere* 'take'.

Fr. *retraite* (OFr. also *retret*), Rum. *retragere*, fr. vbs. OFr. *retraire*, Rum. *retrage* (Rum. cpd. forms after Fr.), fr. Lat. *retrahere* 'draw back', cpd. of *trahere* 'draw' (9.33).

It. *retirata*, Sp. *retirada*, fr. vbs. *retirare, retirar* 'withdraw, retire' (Fr. *retirer*), cpds. of *tirare, tirar* 'draw' (9.33).

3. Ir. *teched* 'flight' (: *techim* 'flee') is virtually 'retreat', e.g. in M1.44a, 18, 19 ('in flight before their enemies').

NIr. *cūl*, W. *cil* 'back' (4.19), and 'retreat' through phrases like 'turn one's back'. So cpd. W. *encil*.

Br. *kizadenn, kizadeg*, derivs. of *kiz* 'backward movement'.

4. Goth. *þlauhs*, ON *flótti*, OE *flēam*, OHG *flucht* 'flight' (: vbs. for 'flee', 10.51) would cover military 'retreat'.

ME *retret*, NE *retreat*, fr. OFr. *retret*; Dan. *retræte*, Sw. *reträtt*, fr. Fr. *retraite* (above, 2).

Du. *terugtocht*, NHG *rückzug*, cpds. of words for 'back' (Du. *terug* = NHG *zurück*), and 'march'.

5. Lith. *atsitraukimas*, fr. *at-si-traukti* 'draw back, withdraw', refl. cpd. of *traukti* 'draw' (9.33).

Lett. *atkāpšanas* (Drawneek; not in Mühl.-Endz.), fr. *at-kāpt* 'draw back', cpd. of *kāpt* 'mount'.

6. ChSl. *běstvo* (quotable only as 'flight'), fr. the root of *běžati, běgati* 'flee'.

SCr. *uzmak* : *uzmaći* 'draw back', cpd. of *uz-* 'back' and *maći* 'touch, move' (: Boh. *macati* 'touch, handle', etc., Berneker 2.1).

Boh. *ústup*, Russ. *otstuplenie* : vbs. Boh. *ustoupiti*, Russ. *otstupit'* 'step back, withdraw', cpds. of *stoupiti, stupit'* 'step .

Pol. *rejterada* (Russ. *retirada* formerly in use), fr. It. *retirata* (above, 2).

Pol. *odwrót* 'turn', also used for 'retreat' : *odwrócić* 'turn aside', cpd. of *wrócić* 'return' (: Lat. *vertere* 'turn', etc.).

7. Skt. *palāyana-* 'flight', fr. cpd. of *palā* = *parā* 'away' and *i-* 'go'.

20.46 SURRENDER (vb.)

Grk.	*παραδίδωμι*	Goth.	*atgiban*	Lith.	*paduoti*
NG	*παραδίδω*	ON	*gefa upp*	Lett.	*paduot*
Lat.	*dēdere, trādere*	Dan.	*overgive*	ChSl.	*prědati*
It.	*arrendere*	Sw.	*överlämna* (*uppgiva*)	SCr.	*predati*
Fr.	*rendre, livrer*	OE	*āgifan*	Boh.	*vzdati*
Sp.	*rendir*	ME	*yelde*	Pol.	*poddać*
Rum.	*preda*	NE	*surrender*	Russ.	*sdat'*
Ir.	*giallaim*	Du.	*overgeven*	Skt.	*parādā-*
NIr.	*gēillim*	OHG	*irgeban*		
W.	*rhoddi i fyny*	MHG	*ergeben*		
Br.	*daskori*	NHG	*übergeben*		

Under 'surrender' preference is given here to the verbal expressions as more generally quotable than nouns. Most of these verbs are compounds of verbs for 'give' (11.21), meaning lit. 'give up, give over', etc., and of which the military use is only one of many and in fact for some of the languages (e.g. Goth., ChSl.) is not strictly quotable. A few are from 'yield' or through 'deliver' from 'set free'.

The nouns are mostly corresponding forms, but in some cases the usual verbs and nouns, though of the same semantic source, are not parallel, e.g. It. vb. *arrendere* (intr. *arrendersi*) but sbs. *dedizione* or *resa*, Fr. vbs. (*se*) *rendre* or (*se*) *livrer*, but sb. only *reddition*, not *livraison*.

1. Grk. παραδίδωμι, NG παραδίδω 'give over, transmit', also 'surrender', cpd. of δίδωμι 'give'. So sb. παράδοσις 'transmission, tradition', also 'surrender' (παράδοσις πόλεως, Thuc.).

2. Lat. *dēdere* (sb. *dēditiō* > It. *dedizione*), and less commonly in military sense *trādere, reddere* (VLat. **rendere* > It. *rendere*, now mostly *arrendere*, Fr. *rendre*, Sp. *rendir*; sbs. It. *resa*, Sp. *rendicion*; Fr. *reddition* re-formed fr. Lat. *redditiō*), cpds. of *dare* 'give'. Ernout-M. 277.

Rum. *preda* (sb. *predare*, old infin.), fr. Slavic, ChSl. *prědati*, SCr. *predati* 'give over' (below, 6). Tiktin 1240.

3. Ir. *giallaim*, NIr. *gēillim* 'obey' (19.46), also 'yield, surrender'.

W. *rhoddi i fyny*, vb. for 'give' (11.21) with *i fyny* 'up'.

Br. *daskori* (sb. *daskor*), cpd. of prefix *das-* and vb. cognate with Ir. *cuirim* 'put, place', etc. Pedersen 2.501. Henry 89.

4. Goth. *atgiban*, ON *gefa upp*, OE *āgifan*, OHG *irgeban*, MHG *ergeben*, NHG *übergeben*, Du. *overgeven*, Dan. *overgive* (semantic borrowing fr. NHG or LG), Sw. *uppgiva*, all cpds. of Gmc. word for 'give', but older forms not quotable in military sense.

Sw. *överlämna*, cpd. of *lämna* 'leave, deliver' : ON *lifna*, Goth. *aflifnan* 'be left over', ON *leifa*, OE *lǣfan*, etc. 'leave' (12.18).

ME *yelde* (NE *yield*), fr. OE *gieldan* 'pay, give back', etc. (11.65). NED s.v. *yield* vb. 14–16.

NE *surrender* (vb. and sb.), fr. OFr. *surrendre* (Anglo-Fr. *surrender*), cpd. of *rendre* (above, 2).

5. Lith. *paduoti*, refl. *pasiduoti* (NSB s.v.), Lett. *paduot*, refl. *paduoties*, cpd. of vb. for 'give'.

6. ChSl. *prědati* (reg. for παραδίδωμι, though not quotable in strictly military sense), SCr. *predati*, Boh. *vzdati*, Pol. *poddać*, Russ. *sdat'* (all with corresponding sbs.), cpds. of vb. for 'give'.

7. Skt. *parādā-* 'give up' (quotable in military sense?), cpd. of *dā-* 'give'.

20.47 CAPTIVE, PRISONER

Grk.	*αἰχμάλωτος*	Goth.	*frahunþans*	Lith.	*kalinys*
NG	*αἰχμάλωτος*	ON	*haptr, fangi*	Lett.	*gūsteknis*
Lat.	*captīvus*	Dan.	*fange*	ChSl.	*plěnĭnikŭ*
It.	*prigioniero*	Sw.	*fånge*	SCr.	*zarobljenik, sužanj*
Fr.	*captif, prisonnier*	OE	*hæft, hæftling*	Boh.	*zajatec*
Sp.	*cautivo, prisionero*	ME	*captive, prisoner*	Pol.	*jeniec*
Rum.	*captiv, prizonier*	NE	*captive, prisoner*	Russ.	*plennyj* (*plennik*)
Ir.	*cimbid, brage*	Du.	*gevangene*	Skt.	*baddhaka-*
NIr.	*brāighe* (*geimhleach, cime*)	OHG	*haft*	Av., OPers.	*basta-*
		MHG	*haft*		
W.	*carcharor*	NHG	*gefangener*		
Br.	*prizoniad*				

Most of the words for 'captive, prisoner' (of war) are either from verbs for 'take, seize' (in Greek 'taken by the spear'), or are derivs. of nouns for 'prison' (21.39), in which the sense 'prisoner' as inmate of a prison has been extended to 'prisoner' as one captured in war.

In the case of NE *captive, prisoner*, the former, though given in first place, is now used with reference to earlier times or to those taken by brigands or savages, while in present-day warfare so many *prisoners* are taken. Similarly in the Fr., Sp., Rum. groups listed.

1. Grk. αἰχμάλωτος, lit. 'taken by the spear', cpd. of αἰχμή 'spear' (20.26) and vbl. adj. of ἁλίσκομαι, aor. ἧλων 'be taken, seized'.

2. Lat. *captīvus* (> OFr. *chetif*, now only in secondary sense and as 'captive' replaced by *captif* > Rum. *captiv*; Sp. *cautivo*), deriv. of *captus*, pple. of *capere* 'take' (11.13).

It. *prigioniero* (or *-e*), Fr. *prisonnier* (> Rum. *prizonier*), Sp. *prisionero*, deriv. of It. *prigione*, Fr. *prison*, Sp. *prisión* 'prison' (21.39).

3. Ir. *cimbid*, NIr. *cime* : Ir. *cimb* 'tribute', Gallo-Lat. *cambiāre* 'exchange' (12.93). Pedersen 1.45.

Ir. *brage* (K. Meyer, Contrib. 243 f.), NIr. *braighe* (also *brāighe*, as if fr. *brāgha* 'neck'), beside Ir. *braig* 'chain', prob. : Grk. βρόχος 'noose', etc. Walde-P. 2.272 f. Stokes 181.

NIr. *geimhleach*, fr. *geimheal* 'chain, bond' = MIr. *gemel* 'fetter' : Grk. γέντο 'fastened', etc. Walde-P. 1.572 f. Pedersen 1.95.

W. *carcharor*, fr. *carchar* 'prison, fetters', fr. Lat. **carcarem* for *carcerem*. Loth, Mots lat. 144.

Br. *prizoniad* (so Vallée and Ernault), deriv. of *prizon* 'prison' (fr. Fr.).

4. Goth. *frahunþans*, pple. of *frahinþan* 'take captive', beside *hunþs* 'captivity' : OE (*here-*)*hūþ*, OHG *heri-hunda* 'booty', Sw. *hinna* 'reach', prob. fr. a parallel form of the root in OE *hentan* 'pursue', *huntian* 'hunt', outside connections? Feist 161.

ON *haptr*, OE *hæft, hæftling*, OHG, MHG *haft* (also adj. 'taken, seized', NHG *-haft*), beside Goth. *hafts* 'taken, joined', pple. of root seen in Goth. *hafjan* 'raise', Lat. *capere* 'take', etc.

ON *fangi* (late), Dan. *fange*, Sw. *fånge* (these formed after MLG *vangene*), Du. *gevangene*, NHG *gefangener*, fr. vb. seen in Goth. *fahan*, NHG *fangen*, etc. 'seize, capture' (11.14). Walde-P. 2.2. Falk-Torp 204 f.

ME, NE *captive, prisoner*, fr. Fr.

5. Lith. *kalinys*, beside *kalėti* 'be in prison', *kalinti* 'put in prison', *kalėjimas* 'prison', etym. dub. Connection with the remote Skt. *kārā-* 'prison' (Walde-P. 1.356 after Zupitza) hardly convincing. Or through the medium of

'fetter(ed)' : Lith. *kalti, kalinėti* 'beat, hammer, forge'?

Lett. *gūsteknis*, fr. *gūstīt* 'seize, bind'. Mühl.-Endz. 1.686.

Lett. *cietumnieks* (only 'prisoner' as inmate of prison?), fr. *cietums* 'prison' (21.39).

6. ChSl. *plěnĭnikŭ* (> Russ. *plennik*, now more commonly *plennyj*), through *plěniti* 'take captive', fr. *plěnŭ* 'booty' (20.48).

SCr. *zarobljenik*, fr. *zarobiti* 'take captive', cpd. of *robiti* 'enslave, plunder', fr. *rob* 'slave' (19.42).

SCr. *sužanj*, etym.?

Boh. *zajatec*, Pol. *jeniec*, fr. vb. seen in ChSl. *jęti* 'take, seize' (11.13). Berneker 429. Brückner 206.

7. Skt. derivs. of *bandh-* 'bind, capture' (9.16), pple. *baddha-* 'captured', as *baddhaka-* (AV), *bandhana-stha-*, also (with *d*, as if Iran.) *bandin-*, *bandīkṛta-*. So Av., OPers. *basta-* (in form= Skt. *baddha-*) is prob. 'prisoner' rather than lit. 'bound'. So OPers. *basta* in Bh. 2, 13, 14 "I cut off his ears, nose, and tongue, and put out his eyes; he was held prisoner in my court". Av. *bastō-* Yt. 15.52 is translated 'prissonier' by Darmesteter.

20.48 BOOTY, SPOILS

Grk.	*λεία, λάφῡρα, σκῦλα*	Goth.	. . . .	Lith.	*grobis*
NG	*λάφυρα, πλιάτσικα*	ON	*herfang*	Lett.	*laupījums*
Lat.	*praeda, spolia*	Dan.	*bytte, rov*	ChSl.	*koristĭ, plěnŭ*
It.	*preda, bottino, spoglie*	Sw.	*byte, rov*	SCr.	*plijen*
Fr.	*butin*	OE	*rēaf, fang,* (*here-*)*hūþ*	Boh.	*kořist* (*plen*)
Sp.	*botin*	ME	*botye, spoyle(s), preye*	Pol.	*łup* (*zdobycz*)
Rum.	*pradă*	NE	*booty, spoil(s)*	Russ.	*dobyča*
Ir.	*brat*	Du.	*buit*	Skt.	*loptra-*
NIr.	*creach*	OHG	*roub, herehunda*		
W.	*ysglyfaeth, ysbail*	MHG	*roup, biute*		
Br.	*preiz*	NHG	*beute*		

Many of the words for 'booty' are from verbs for 'seize' or 'obtain', or are cognate with words for 'advantage, profit'. Several, denoting originally the arms (or clothing) stripped from the slain foe, are cognate with nouns for 'skin, hide' (or 'cloak') or verbs for 'strip off, tear off, flay, peel'.

1. Grk. λεία (Ion. ληΐη, Dor. λάϊα, Hom. ληΐς), fr. root of ἀπολαύω 'enjoy, take advantage of', Lat. *lucrum* 'gain, profit', Goth. *laun* 'reward, pay', ChSl. *loviti* 'hunt'. Walde-P. 2.379. Walde-H. 1.826.

Grk. λάφῡρα (pl.; sg. rare), fr. a by-form of root of λαμβάνω 'take' (11.13; cf. Skt. *labh-* 'seize, take'). Walde-P. 2.385. Boisacq 561.

Grk. σκῦλα (pl.; sg. less frequent), esp. 'arms stripped off the slain foe' : σκύλος, σκῦτος 'hide', OE *hȳd* 'skin, hide', etc. (4.12). Walde-P. 2.547. Boisacq 880.

NG pop. πλιάτσικα (pl.), fr. a Balkan word seen in Bulg., SCr. *pljačka*, Alb. *plaçkë*, Turk. *plaçka*, Rum. *pleaşcă* 'booty', this group itself of Grk. origin, derivs. of NG πλακώνω 'flatten out, crush, overwhelm'. G. Meyer, Alb. Etym. Wtb. 344. P. Skok, Revue intern. des études balkaniques 2.31 ff.

2. Lat. *praeda* (> It. *preda*, Rum. *pradă*; OFr. *preie*, Fr. *proie* now only 'prey'), fr. **prai-heda* : *prae-hendere* 'seize, take'. Walde-P. 1.589. Ernout-M. 802. REW 6714.

Lat. *spolia* (pl., but VLat. sg. > It. *spoglia*, pl. *spoglie*, OFr. *espoille*, etc.), orig. 'arms stripped off the slain foe' (like Grk. σκῦλα) : Grk. σπόλια 'pieces of wool stripped from the legs of sheep' (Hesych.), fr. the root of OHG *spaltan* 'split', etc. Walde-P. 2.678. Ernout-M. 966 f. REW 8168.

OFr. *esch(i)ec* (reg. for 'booty' in Chanson de Roland, etc.), fr. a Frank. form of OHG *scāh*, MHG *schāch* 'robbery, booty'. REW 7969. Weigand-H. 2.663.

Fr. *butin* (> It. *bottino*, Sp. *botin*), fr. Gmc., cf. MLG *būte*, etc. (below, 4). REW 1422b. Gamillscheg 162. Wartburg 1.654 f.

3. Ir. *brat* (K. Meyer, Contrib. 246), prob. same word as *brat* 'cloak', with similar interchange of sense (but shift in opposite direction) to that in OE *rēaf* 'booty, garment' and Fr. *robe*, fr. OHG *rouba* (below, 4, and 6.12, 6.42).

NIr. *creach*, fr. Ir. *crech* 'plundering, raid', etym.? Macbain 105.

W. *ysglyfaeth*, fr. *ysglyf* (arch.), etym.? Morris Jones 159.

W. *ysbail*, fr. Lat. *spolia*. Pedersen 1.194, 219. Loth, Mots lat. 216.

Br. *preiz*, fr. Lat. *praeda*. Loth, Mots lat. 198.

4. Goth. ? (Lk. 11.22 missing).

OE *fang*, ON *herfang* (with *herr* 'army') : Goth. *fahan*, ON *fā*, OE *fōn* (pple. *fangen*), etc. 'seize, grasp' (11.14).

OE *rēaf* (also 'clothing'), OHG *roub, rouba*, MHG *roup* (NHG *raub* 'robbery'), MLG *rōf* (> Dan., Sw. *rov*) : OE *rēofan* 'break, tear up', Lat. *rumpere* 'break', etc. Walde-P. 2.354 f. Falk-Torp 913 f.

OE *hūþ* and (with words for 'army') OE *here-hūþ*, OHG *here-hunda* : Goth. *fra-hinþan* 'take captive', *hunþs* 'captivity', etc. (20.47).

MLG *būte* (> Dan. *bytte*, Sw. *byte*, MHG *biute*, NHG *beute*), Du. *buit*, ME *botye, boty, buty* (immediate source uncertain), NE *booty* : MLG *būten* 'di-

vide, exchange' (12.93), root connection dub. Walde-P. 2.186. Falk-Torp 122. Weigand-H. 1.226. NED s.v. *booty*.

ME *spoyle*, NE *spoil* (now most commonly in pl.), fr. OFr. *espoille*, Lat. *spolia* (above, 2).

ME *preye* (often 'booty', also like NE *prey*), fr. OFr. *preie* (above, 2). NED s.v. *prey*, sb.

5. Lith. *grobis* (NSB, Lalis, etc.; now best word, Senn) : *grobti* 'seize', *grēbti* 'rake', etc. Leskien, Ablaut 362 (where *grobė*).

Lith. *išplėša* (NSB, Lalis) : *išplėsti* 'tear out, rob', cpd. of *plėsti* 'tear' (9.28), whence also *plėsimas* used for 'spoils' in NT, Lk. 11.22 (pl. Trowitsch, sg. Kurschat).

Lith. *išvarža* (NSB, Lalis), fr. *isverżti* 'unwind, snatch away', cpd. of *verżti* 'draw tight, squeeze' (: ChSl. *po-vrěti, -vrŭzą* 'bind', 9.16).

Lett. *laupijums*, fr. *laupīt* 'flay, peel, rob, plunder' : *lupt*, Lith. *lupti* 'flay, peel', Russ. *lupit'* 'peel', etc. (cf. Pol. *łup*, below, 6). Mühl.-Endz. 2.429.

6. ChSl. *koristĭ*, Boh. *kořist* = SCr. *korist*, Pol. *korzyść*, Russ. *koryst'* 'advantage, gain', root connection dub. Berneker 571. Brückner 258.

ChSl. *plěnŭ* (Supr.), SCr. *plijen* (Boh. *plen* less common, Pol. *plon* now mostly 'profit, harvest') : Lith. *pelnas* 'profit, gain', etc. (11.73). Walde-P. 2.51. Brückner 418.

Pol. *łup* (Boh. *lup* now obs. in this sense) : *łupić* 'flay, peel, rob' = Russ. *lupit'* 'peel', etc. : Lith. *lupti*, Lett. *lupt* 'flay, peel, rob', Skt. *lup-* 'break, rob', etc. Walde-P. 2.417. Berneker 315.

Russ. *dobyča*, fr. *dobyt'* 'get, obtain' (11.16). Pol. (less common) *zdobycz*, fr. *zdobyć* 'conquer', cpd. of *dobyć* = Russ. *dobyt'*. Berneker 114 f.

7. Skt. *loptra-*, fr. *lup-* 'break, rob' (cf. Pol. *łup*, above, 6).

20.49 AMBUSH (sb.)

Grk.	ἐνέδρα	Goth.	....	Lith.	slaptynė, slėpykla
NG	ἐνέδρα, καρτέρι	ON	launsāt	Lett.	slėptuve, glūnētuve
Lat.	īnsidiae	Dan.	baghold	ChSl.	zasada
It.	imboscata, agguato	Sw.	bakhåll	SCr.	zasjeda
Fr.	embuscade, guet-apens	OE	searu	Boh.	záloha
Sp.	emboscada	ME	embusshe	Pol.	zasada
Rum.	pîndă	NE	ambush, ambuscade	Russ.	zasada
Ir.	intled	Du.	hinderlaag	Skt.	sattra-
NIr.	luigheachān	OHG	lāga		
W.	cynllwyn	MHG	lāge		
Br.	spi-brezel	NHG	hinterhalt		

Most of the nouns for 'ambush' are from verbs for 'sit' or 'lie' or 'watch', all through the notion of 'lying in wait for'. The group represented by NE *ambush* is derived from a word for 'woods', through a verb 'be in the woods', hence 'lie in wait for'.

1. Grk. ἐνέδρα (late also ἔνεδρον) : ἕδρα 'seat'.

NG pop. καρτέρι, back-formation fr. καρτερῶ 'wait for', fr. class. Grk. καρτερέω 'be steadfast, endure'.

2. Lat. *īnsidiae* : *sedēre* 'sit'. Ernout-M. 918. Walde-H. 1.703.

It. *imboscata*, Fr. *embuscade* (as milit. term now preferred to older *embûche*), Sp. *emboscada*, fr. vbs. It. *imboscare*, etc., derivs. of It. *bosco*, etc. 'woods' (1.41). REW 1419b. Gamillscheg 350. Wartburg 1.452.

OFr. *aguait* 'watch' (> It. *agguato*, Fr. *aguet* obs.; now *guet-apens* with *apens* fr. *apenser* 'think over, plan'), fr. vb. OFr. *aguaitier*, cpd. fr. OHG *wahten* 'watch'. REW 9479. Gamillscheg 19, 496.

Rum. *pîndă*, back-formation fr. *pîndi* 'watch for, spy', fr. Slavic, cf. late ChSl. *pąditi* 'drive', *pądarĭ* 'custos' (> Rum. *pîndar* 'guardian' of a field, etc.), with prob. development of 'watch' through 'drive, tend' cattle. Tiktin 1164.

3. Ir. *intled* (Thes. 1.63; NIr. *intle* 'snare'), etym.? Macbain 214.

NIr. *luigheachān*, fr. *luighe* 'act of lying', vbl. n. of *luighim* 'lie, lay'.

W. *cynllwyn*, cpd. of *cyn-* 'com-, con-' and *llwyn* 'grove, bush', prob. influenced by NE *ambush*.

Br. *spi-brezel* (so Vallée s.v. *embuscade*), cpd. of *spi* 'watch, trap' (fr. *spia* 'watch, spy', fr. Fr. *espier* 'spy') and *brezel* 'war' (20.13).

4. ON *launsāt*, cpd. of *laun-* 'secret' and *sāt* 'seat'.

Dan. *baghold*, Sw. *bakhåll*, semantic borrowing of NHG *hinterhalt*, MLG *achterholt*. Falk-Torp 42.

OE *searu* 'wile, deceit' and often for Lat. *insidiae*, also 'armor, arms', like the cognate Goth. *sarwa*, etc. (20.31).

ME (late) *embusshe*, NE *ambush, ambuscade*, fr. Fr. *embûche, embuscade* (above, 2).

OHG *lāga*, MHG *lāge*, fr. OHG *ligan* 'lie'. Weigand-H. 2.7. Paul, Deutsches Wtb. s.v. *lage*.

NHG *hinterhalt*, in early use also 're-serve of troops', fr. *hinter* 'behind' and *halten* 'hold'. Weigand-H. 1.868.

Du. *hinderlaag*, formed with *laag* 'bed, layer, snare' after NHG *hinterhalt*. Franck-v. W. 253.

5. Lith. *slaptynė, slėpykla* (both in Lalis; *paslapta*, Leskien, Ablaut 344), Lett. *slėptuve*, fr. Lith. *slėpti*, Lett. *slėpt* 'hide' (12.27), Lith. *slaptās* 'secret'.

Lett. *glūnētuve*, fr. *glūnēt* 'watch, lurk', fr. Sw. dial. *gluna* 'squint at'. Mühl.-Endz. 1.631.

6. ChSl. (late), Russ. *zasada*, SCr.

---

zasjeda, Pol. *zasadska*, fr. *za* 'behind' and derivs. of verb for 'sit', ChSl. *sěděti*, etc. (12.13).

Boh. *záloha*, fr. *za* 'behind' and deriv. of *ležeti* 'lie' (12.14).

7. Skt. *sattra-* (lit. a 'seating, session', fr. *sad-* 'sit') most commonly used for the 'soma-festival', also 'house, asylum', and 'assumed form, disguise', and now attested for 'ambush' in Kaut. Arth. 7.17, 10.2–4 (cf. translation of J. J. Meyer, p. 14, note 6).

CHAPTER 21

LAW

21.11 LAW (General = Lat. *iūs*)

Grk.	νόμος	Goth.	witōþ	Lith.	teisė
NG	νομική, νομικά	ON	rēttr	Lett.	likumi
Lat.	iūs	Dan.	ret	ChSl.	....
It.	diritto	Sw.	rätt	SCr.	pravo
Fr.	droit	OE	riht, lagu	Boh.	právo
Sp.	derecho	ME	right, lawe	Pol.	prawo
Rum.	drept	NE	law	Russ.	pravo
Ir.	dliged, cert	Du.	recht	Skt.	dharma-, smṛti-
NIr.	dlighe(adh), reacht	OHG	reht	Av.	aša-, OPers. arta-
W.	cyfraith	MHG	reht		
Br.	gwir (reiz)	NHG	recht		

The 'law' in its general sense, the institution or body of laws (Lat. *iūs*), is in part expressed by the same words as those denoting a specific law (Lat. *lēx*), or by the plural or derivs. of the latter. More commonly, however, the two notions are expressed by different terms, though even then the distinction is not always rigidly maintained. Especially the plural of words for 'lēx' may be used collectively = 'iūs'.

The words for 'iūs' are mostly based on the notion of 'what is right', connected with adjectives for 'right' (these

in part from 'straight, upright', 'true', or 'fitting'), or on 'usage, custom'. One is from 'memory' through 'tradition'. The Lat. *iūs* was in origin a term of religious cult, as indicated by its cognates, and the Indo-Iranian words covered primarily religious law. Other examples of the religious source of legal terms will be noted occasionally in this chapter.

1. Grk. νόμος, in earliest use 'usage, custom', hence 'law' in both senses : νέμω 'dispense, distribute, apportion'. Walde-P. 2.330. Boisacq 663.

NG νόμος mostly 'lēx'; for 'iūs' either

sg. νομική or neut. pl. νομικά (σπουδάζει νομικά 'studies law'), fr. adj. νομικός 'pertaining to the law, legal'.

2. Lat. *iūs* (OLat. *ious*), orig. a term of religious cult, perh. 'sacred formula' (cf. *iūrāre* 'swear') : Ved. *yōs* 'health!', Av. *yaož-dā-* 'make ritually pure', Ir. *huisse* (**ius-tios*) 'just'. Walde-P. 1.203. Ernout-M. 506 ff. Walde-H. 1.733.

As a legal term this is peculiar to Latin, not general Italic. The Oscan-Umbrian term is **medos*, seen in Umbr. *meřs*, *mers* 'ius', Osc. *meddíss*, an official title (formed like Lat. *iūdex*), *medicim* 'magistracy' (in form like Lat. *iūdicium*), etc. : Lat. *meditārī* 'think, reflect', Grk. μέδομαι 'give heed to', Ir. *midiur* 'judge', etc. Walde-P. 2.259. Ernout-M. 599. Walde-H. 2.56.

It. *diritto*, Fr. *droit*, Sp. *derecho*, Rum. *drept*, fr. Lat. *dīrēctus*, VLat. **dērēctus* 'straight' (12.73), whence through 'right' as sb. 'right way, law'. REW 2648. Wartburg 2.87 ff.

3. Ir. *dliged*, NIr. *dlighe(adh)*, also 'right, duty' : *dligim* 'have a right to, claim upon', Br. *dle*, W. *dyled* 'debt', etc. (11.64).

Ir. *cert*, sb. use of *cert* 'right' (16.73).

Ir. *recht*, NIr. *reacht* (in the older language chiefly, if not exclusively, in the sense of 'lēx', but now limited largely to 'iūs'), W. *rhaith* now arch. or obs., replaced by cpd. *cyf-raith* usual for both 'iūs' and 'lēx', Br. *reiz* ('law' in both senses, but less common than *gwir* and *lezenn*, respectively), ON *rēttr*, OE *riht*, etc., general Gmc. for 'iūs'; all : Lat. *rēctus* 'straight, right' (12.73, 16.73). Walde-P. 2.362 ff. Pedersen 1.123. Falk-Torp 892.

Br. *gwir*, sb. use of *gwir* 'true' (16.66; cf. *gwirion* 'right, just' 16.73).

4. ON *rēttr*, OE *riht*, OHG *reht*, etc., general Gmc., above, 3.

OE *lagu* ('iūs' in earliest use), ME *lawe*, NE *law*, see 21.12.

Goth. *witōþ*, see 21.12.

5. Lith. *teisė* (revival of a rare *teisė* 'truth'; Leskien, Bildung d. Nom. 283; *teisybė* 'truth, justice' formerly used in this sense) : *teisus* 'right' (16.73).

Lett. *likumi*, pl. of *likums* 'lēx' (21.12).

6. SCr. *pravo*, etc., general Slavic, neut. sb. fr. adj. ChSl. *pravŭ* 'straight', but general Slavic 'right' (16.73).

7. Skt. *dharma-*, the most common word in both senses, lit. 'right, justice, usage, established order' : *dhṛ-* 'hold, support' (11.15).

Skt. *smṛti-*, esp. '(traditional) lawbook, code', orig. 'memory' : *smṛ-* 'remember' (17.31).

Av. *aša-*, esp. 'divine law', OPers. *arta-* (now attested as personified in Daiva-inscr. 41 ff., formerly only in proper names like *Arta-xšaθ^ra-* 'Artaxerxes') : Skt. *ṛta-* 'fitting, right', etc. (16.73). Walde-P. 1.70. Barth. 229 ff.

21.12 LAW (Special = Lat. *lēx*)

Grk.	*νόμος (θεσμός, ῥήτρα)*	Goth.	*witōþ*	Lith.	*įstatymas, įstatai*
NG	*νόμος*	ON	*lǫg* (pl.)	Lett.	*likums*
Lat.	*lēx*	Dan.	*lov*	ChSl.	*zakonŭ*
It.	*legge*	Sw.	*lag*	SCr.	*zakon*
Fr.	*loi*	OE	*ǣ(w), lagu, dōm*	Boh.	*zákon*
Sp.	*ley*	ME	*lawe, dome*	Pol.	*ustawa*
Rum.	*lege*	NE	*law*	Russ.	*zakon*
Ir.	*recht, dliged, cāin*	Du.	*wet*	Skt.	*dharma-, vidhi-*
NIr.	*dlighe(adh), reacht*	OHG	*ēwa, wizzōd, gisatzida*	Av., OPers.	*dāta-*
W.	*cyfraith, deddf*	MHG	*ēwe, gesetze(de), wizzōt*		
Br.	*lezenn*	NHG	*gesetz*		

Words for a 'law' (Lat. *lēx*), so far as they are not the same as those discussed in 21.11, are most commonly derived from verbs for 'put, place, set, lay' (12.12), hence orig. what is 'laid down, established'. Other semantic sources are 'knowledge', 'collection'(?), and 'beginning, foundation'.

1. Grk. νόμος, see 12.11.

Grk. θεσμός, Dor. τεθμός (dial. also θεθμός, τέθμιον, etc.), an old word, applied to the laws of Draco and Solon and usual in archaic inscriptions of several dialects, fr. τίθημι 'put, place' (12.12) and esp. 'lay down (a law), establish'.

Grk. ῥήτρα (dial. ῥήτρη, ϝράτρα, ϝρήτρα) 'covenant, treaty', also sometimes simply 'law', orig. a 'declaration', fr. the root of ἐρῶ 'will speak, say', etc. (18.21).

2. Lat. *lēx* (> Romance forms), general Italic term (cf. Osc. *ligud* 'lege', etc.), prob. : *legere* 'collect', but precise semantic development ('collection' or 'selection'?) uncertain. Ernout-M. 542 f. Walde-H. 1.789 f.

3. Ir. *recht*, *dliged*, W. *cyfraith*, see 12.11.

Ir. *cāin*, etym. dub. Pedersen 1.333 (after Zimmer, fr. Lat. *canōn* 'rule'). Stokes, KZ 37.255 (: Skt. *çās-* 'command, rule', 19.45). Vendryes, De hib. voc. 119.

W. *deddf*, fr. MW *deðyf* 'custom, usage' : Grk. θεσμός, Dor. τεθμός (above, 1). Pedersen 1.333. Thurneysen, IF 51.57.

Br. *lezenn*, fr. OFr. *leis* (Lat. *lēx*, above, 2). Henry 185.

4. Goth. *witōþ* (reg. for νόμος, mostly 'lēx', but also 'iūs'), OHG *wizzōd*, MHG *wizzōt*, Du. *wet* : Goth. *witan*, OHG *wizzan*, etc. 'know' (17.17). Feist 570. Franck-v. W. 790.

ON *lǫg*, pl. of *lag* 'laying, good order', etc. (with many special senses, but not 'law' in sg.) : *leggja* 'lay, put, place'. Here also Dan. *lov*, Sw. *lag*. ON **lagu* pl. (ancestor of *lǫg*) > late OE *lagu* fem. sg., in earliest use coll. 'iūs' (and so in Aelfric's Gram.), then (at first only in pl.) 'lēx', ME *lawe*, NE *law*. Falk-Torp 655 f. Hellquist 555. NED s.v. *law*, sb.[1].

OE *ǣ*, *ǣw*, OHG *ēwa*, MHG *ēwe*, *ē*, OS *ēo*, OFris. *ēwa* (all also 'marriage', as NHG *ehe*), prob. : Skt. *eva-* 'course, way, manner, custom', fr. IE **ei-* 'go', with semantic development 'custom' > 'law'. Walde-P. 1.104. Kluge-G. 121, 141. Weigand-H. 1.405 f.

OE *dōm*, ME *dome* 'judgment' (21.17), also freq. 'law'.

OHG *gisatzida*, MHG *gesetzede*, *gesetze*, NHG *gesetz* : OHG *sezzen*, NHG *setzen* 'put, place, set' (12.12).

5. Lith. *įstatymas*, *įstatai* : *įstatyti* 'set up, establish', cpd. of *statyti* 'cause to stand, set'.

Lett. *likums* 'what is laid down, command, law' : *likt* 'leave, let, put, place' (: Lith. *likti* 'be left, remain', Grk. λείπω 'leave', etc. 12.28), but also 'determine, command'. Mühl.-Endz. 2.467 ff., 470.

6. ChSl. *zakonŭ*, etc. general Slavic (but Pol. *zakon* now arch. or eccl., or 'order' of monks, knights), cpd. of Slavic *konŭ* (in Russ. *kon* 'beginning, series, order', Boh. *do-kona* 'to the end', etc.; cf. ChSl. *konĭcĭ* 'end' 12.35, 14.26, *načęti* 'begin' 14.25, etc.), hence orig. 'starting-point, original determination' or the like. Berneker 560. Brückner 643 f.

Pol. *ustawa* : *ustawić* 'set in order, arrange', *ustać* 'stop, stand', cpd. of *stać* 'stand'.

7. Skt. *dharma-*, see 12.11.

Skt. *vidhi-* properly 'injunction, command', fr. *vi-dhā-* 'determine, ordain, bestow, distribute', cpd. of *dhā-* 'put, place' (12.12).

Av., OPers. *dāta-* fr. *dā-* 'put, place' (= Skt. *dhā-*, above). Barth. 726 f.

21.13 LAWSUIT

Grk.	*δίκη*	Goth.	*staua*	Lith.	*byla, prova*
NG	*δίκη*	ON	*māl, sǫk, deild*	Lett.	*prāva*
Lat.	*līs, causa, actiō, rēs*	Dan.	*proces, retssag (søgsmaal)*	ChSl.	*(sądŭ)*
It.	*processo, causa, lite*	Sw.	*process, rättegång*	SCr.	*parnica, parba, proces*
Fr.	*procès*	OE	*sacu*	Boh.	*pře, soud, proces*
Sp.	*proceso, pleito*	ME	*seute, process*	Pol.	*proces*
Rum.	*proces*	NE	*(law)suit*	Russ.	*process (tjažba)*
Ir.	*acraidecht, toiched, caingen*	Du.	*proces, rechtsgeding*	Skt.	*vyavahāra-, vivāda-*
NIr.	*cūis*	OHG	*sahha, strīt*	Av.	*araθya-*
W.	*cyngaws*	MHG	*sache, kriec, strīt*		
Br.	*prosez, breud*	NHG	*prozess, rechtshandel,* etc.		

Terms for 'lawsuit' are mostly legal specializations of notions like 'strife', 'cause, case', 'affair', 'pursuit', 'procedure', sometimes made more specific by compounding with words for 'law' (as in NE *lawsuit*). Some of the words for 'law, iūs' or 'judgment' or 'court' come also, through phrases like 'bring to judgment or court', to be used for 'lawsuit'.

1. Grk. δίκη, in Hom. 'way, custom, usage' (: δείκνῡμι, Skt. *diç-*, etc. 'point out, show', Skt. sb. *diç-* 'direction, region'), also 'order, right, judgment', hence in Attic and likewise in the other dialects the regular technical word for 'lawsuit'. Walde-P. 1.776. Boisacq 170.

Grk. γραφή 'writing', hence as law-term 'written indictment', in Attic law applied (as distinct from δίκη) to certain kinds of public suits.

Grk. κρίσις, κρῖμα 'judgment' (21.17) are sometimes used for its subject, the 'lawsuit' (e.g. κρίσις in Thuc., Plato, etc., κρῖμα in LXX, NT).

2. Lat. *līs*, *lītis* 'strife, quarrel' (19.62), esp. 'legal strife, lawsuit' (> lit. It., Sp. *lite*; Sp. *lid* 'contest, fight').

Lat. *causa* 'cause' (17.42), hence esp. 'cause for legal action, lawsuit'. Ernout-M. 166 f. Walde-H. 1.190.

Lat. *actiō*, lit. 'action', fr. *agere* 'drive, act, perform', etc., and in particular 'bring' a suit, 'plead' a case, and the like.

Lat. *rēs* 'thing, affair' (9.90), but also 'legal matter, suit'.

It. *processo*, Fr. *procès* (> Rum. *proces*), Sp. *proceso*, fr. Lat. *prōcessus* 'advance, progress' (fr. *prō-cēdere* 'go forward, advance'), MLat. 'lis, causa' (Du Cange), with specialization to 'legal procedure'.

OFr. *plaid* (> ME *plaid*, *plai*, NE *plea*), Sp. *pleito*, fr. Lat. *placitum* 'opinion, decision, decree', orig. 'what is pleasing' : *placēre* 'please'. REW 6561.

3. Ir. *acraidecht*, beside *acre* 'a suing' vbl. n. to *ad-gairim* 'proclaim, summon, cite', cpd. of *gairim* 'call' (18.41). Pedersen 2.533.

Ir. *toiched* (cf. Laws, Gloss. 733), vbl. n. to *do-saigim*, cpd. of *saigim* 'go after, claim'. Pedersen 2.610.

Ir. *caingen* ('business, affair', sometimes legal 'dispute'), etym. dub. Zupitza, KZ 36.71. Osthoff, IF 27.179 f.

NIr. *cūis* or esp. *cūis dlighidh*, W. *cyngaws* (cpd. *cyn-caws*), fr. Lat. *causa*. Loth, Mots lat. 157.

Br. *prosez*, fr. the Fr. *procès*.

Br. *breud* (esp. 'plea') : *barn*, Ir. *breth* 'judgment', etc. (21.17).

4. Goth. *staua* 'judgment' (21.17), also sometimes 'lawsuit' (Mt. 5.40, 1 Cor. 6.1). Cf. Grk. κρίσις, κρῖμα (above, 1).

ON *māl* (the usual word) = *māl* 'speech', OE *mæþel*, OHG *mahal* 'discourse, assembly' and esp. 'court' (21.15).

ON *sǫk* (also and esp. the 'charge, accusation'), Dan. *sag*, esp. *retssag* (with *ret* 'law'), OE *sacu*, OHG *sahha*, MHG *sache*, all belonging to the group meaning 'strife' (Goth. *sakjō*, etc. 19.62), with widespread special application to 'legal strife' and also, through 'subject of the dispute', to 'thing' (9.90).

ON *deild* 'share, part' (: Goth. *dails*, etc. 13.23), hence 'dealings' and esp. 'legal dealings, lawsuit'.

ME *seute*, *suite*, NE *suit* or more specifically *lawsuit*, fr. Anglo-Fr. *siwte*, *seute*, etc. (= OFr. *sieute*, *suitte*, Fr. *suite*), fr. **sequita*, fem. sg. of pple. of VLat. *sequere* = Lat. *sequī* 'follow' (10.52), whence also, through OFr., the vb. ME *sewen*, NE *sue*, with gradual specialization of 'pursuit' through legal 'prosecution'. NED s.v. *suit*, sb.

OHG, MHG *strīt* 'strife, quarrel' (19.62), and MHG *kriec* 'battle, war' (20.12, 20.13), both used also for 'legal strife'.

Sw. *rättegång*, Dan. *rettergang* 'legal procedure', also esp. Sw. 'lawsuit', formed after MLG *rechtgank* = NHG *rechtsgang*, lit. 'the course of law'. Hellquist 870.

Dan. *søgsmaal* (not in common use now), fr. *søge* 'seek, sue' and *maal* 'speech'.

Du. *rechtsgeding*, cpd. of *recht* 'law' and *-geding*, coll. to *ding* 'thing, affair' = OHG *ding*, etc. 'assembly, court' (21.15).

NHG *rechtshandel*, *gerichtshandel*, cpds. of *handel* 'business, affair' with *recht* 'law' (21.11) and *gericht* 'court' (21.15).

Dan., Du. *proces*, Sw. *process*, NHG *prozess* (now more common than native terms), also ME *process* (NED s.v., 7), fr. Fr. *procès* (above, 2).

5. Lith. *byla* 'talk, conversation' and 'lawsuit' (cf. NSB s.v.) : *byloti* 'litigate, sue', OLith. 'speak' (18.21).

Lith. *prova*, Lett. *prāva*, fr. Slavic *pravo* 'law' (21.11). Mühl.-Endz. 3.383.

6. ChSl. *sądŭ* 'judgment' (21.17) in Mt. 5.40 *sądŭ prijęti*, lit. 'take judgment' for κριθῆναι 'be judged', here 'take legal action, bring suit'. So Boh. *soud* 'judgment, court' and also 'lawsuit'.

SCr. *parnica*, *parba*, Boh. *pře* : ChSl. *sŭ-pĭrěti sę* 'strive, contend', *pĭrja* 'strife', etc. (19.62).

Russ. *tjažba* (formerly common, now unusual) = late ChSl. *tęžiba* 'strife' : ChSl. *tęžiti*, *tęgnąti*, Russ. *tjanut'* 'draw' (9.33). Miklosich 351.

SCr., Boh., Pol. *proces*, Russ. *process* (in part more common than the native terms), fr. Fr. *procès* (above, 2).

7. Skt. *vyavahāra-* 'conduct, action, business', also used for 'legal action', fr. *vi-ava-hṛ-* 'have intercourse with, behave, fight, etc.', cpd. of *hṛ-* 'carry, bring' (10.61).

Skt. *vivāda-* 'strife' (19.62), also 'legal strife'.

Av. *araθya-*, *arəθra-* : *arəθa-* 'matter, affair', Skt. *artha-* 'business, cause, aim, thing, etc.'. Barth. 196.

21.14 LAWYER

Grk.	(*ῥήτωρ, συνήγορος,* etc.)	Goth.	(*witōdafasteis*)	Lith.	*advocatas*
NG	*δικηγόρος* (*συνήγορος*)	ON	*lǫgmaðr*, etc.	Lett.	*advocats*
Lat.	*iūriscōnsultus*	Dan.	*sagfører, advocat*	ChSl.	(*zakonĭnikŭ*)
It.	*avvocato*	Sw.	*advocat, jurist*	SCr.	*advokat, odvjetnik*
Fr.	*avocat*	OE	*ǣglēaw, lageglēaw, rihtscrīfend*	Boh.	*advokát, právník*
Sp.	*abogado*	ME	*lawyere, legist(er), avocat*	Pol.	*adwokat, prawnik*
Rum.	*advocat, avocat*	NE	*lawyer, attorney*	Russ.	*advocat, prisjažnyj poverennyj*
Ir.	*aigne, fechem*	Du.	*advocaat, rechtsgeleerde*		
NIr.	*dligheadōir, fear dlighe*	OHG	*ēwa gilērter, furisprehho*		
W.	*cyfreithiwr, twrnai*	MHG	*vürspreche(r), rehtwīser*		
Br.	*breutaer, advocad*	NHG	*rechtsanwalt, advokat*		

Words for 'lawyer' are commonly derivs. or cpds. of those for 'law'. But the most widespread modern Eur. term was in origin 'one summoned' (to assist). A few are based on 'answerer' (denoting at first the defending lawyer), 'one who speaks for', 'one who is sworn' (as agent), 'one who cares for, attends to'.

Some of the terms included in the list from older periods were applied to persons learned in the law, but only distantly corresponding to the modern lawyers.

1. Grk. *ῥήτωρ* 'speaker, orator' (: *ἐρῶ*, *ἐρρήθην*, etc. 'speak', 18.21) was the term always used of the great pleaders like Lysias and Demosthenes, who were, if also politicians, the nearest thing to professional lawyers in fact, though not in name.

Grk. *νομικός*, adj. 'pertaining to the law' (deriv. of *νόμος* 11.11), is also used as sb., often rendered 'lawyer', but mostly denoting one learned in the law (in NT 'one learned in the Mosaic law') rather than a practicing 'lawyer'.

Grk. *νομοθέτης* 'establisher of laws, lawgiver' was the term applied to the early founders of legal codes, like Zaleucus, Charondas, Lycurgus, Draco, etc.

Grk. *συνήγορος* (*-ήγορος* : *ἀγορεύω* 'speak in the assembly', 18.21) and *σύνδικος* (: *δίκη* 'lawsuit'), both orig. adjs. and with *συν-* denoting assistance, were terms for public advocates and also those who assisted a private individual in litigation. Cf. Bonner and Smith, Administration of Justice 2.8.

Late Grk. *δικηγόρος*, quotable fr. 6th cent. and the regular NG term, cpd. of *δίκη* 'lawsuit' (18.13), second part as in *συνήγορος* (above), but accent as in *δημηγόρος*.

2. Lat. *iūriscōnsultus*, phrase cpd. with gen. sg. of *iūs* 'law' (21.11) and *cōnsultus* 'experienced, skilled' (also used alone in legal sense), pple. of *cōnsulere* 'reflect, take counsel'.

Lat. *advocātus*, pple. of *advocāre* 'call, summon', hence 'one called' (to assist), esp. in legal matters, and in imperial times 'lawyer'. Hence the Romance words (in learned or semi-learned form, e.g. Fr. *avocat* vs. *avoué*; Rum. *advocat*, or *avocat* fr. Fr.) and similar words in Gmc. and Balto-Slavic (see list). NE *advocate* is the usual term in Scotland (NED s.v.).

Lat. *causidicus*, cpd. of *causa* 'lawsuit' (21.13) and root of *dīcere* 'say'.

3. Ir. *aigne* (nom. pl. *aigneda*, *aichneda*), beside *aignes* (*aidnes*, *aines*) 'pleading, arguing, questioning', etym.?

Ir. *fechem* 'litigant', either 'plaintiff' or 'defendant' (21.21), also sometimes his 'lawyer'. Laws, Gloss. 336 ff.

NIr. *dligheadōir* or *fear dlighe* 'man of law', fr. *dlighe(ad)* 'law' (21.11).

W. *cyfreithiwr*, fr. *cyfreithio* 'litigate', this fr. *cyfraith* 'law' (21.11).

W. *twrnai*, fr. ME *aturne* (NE *attorney*). Parry-Williams 154.

Br. *breutaer*, fr. *breutaat* 'plead' : *breud* 'plea, lawsuit' (21.13).

4. Goth. *witōdafasteis* (renders *νομικός*, for which see above, 1), cpd. of *witōþ* 'law' (21.12) and *-fasteis*, fr. **fasts* = OE *fæst*, OHG *festi* 'firm, fast', semantic development prob. through 'one who is fast (= well grounded) in the law'. Feist 570.

ON *lǫgmaðr*, commonest term in Iceland for one learned in law, lit. 'lawman', but also in Norway a particular official at the *thing*, the 'law speaker' (for which NIcel. *lögsögumaðr*). Cf. Vigfusson 405.

ON *málafylgjumaðr*, *málafylgismaðr*, used for one who takes up a case for another, lit. 'case-follower, prosecutor of the case', cpd. of *mál* 'lawsuit' (21.13) with *fylgja* 'follow' and *maðr* 'man'.

Dan. *sagfører*, cpd. of *sag* 'lawsuit' and *føre* 'bring, carry'.

Sw. *jurist* (like NE *jurist*, etc., but a more popular term), fr. MLat. *jurista* : *iūs*, *iūris* 'law' (21.11).

OE *ǣglēaw* and *lageglēaw* (e.g. in parallel versions of Lk. 7.30, 11.45), cpds. of *ǣ* and *lagu* 'law' (21.12) with *glēaw* 'wise' (17.21).

OE *rihtscrīfend* (gl. Lat. *iūriscōnsultus*, *iūrisperītus*), cpd. of *riht* 'law' and *scrīfend* pres. pple. of *scrīfan* 'prescribe, ordain, impose (punishment), shrive'.

ME *lawyere*, NE *lawyer*, fr. *law* (21.12).

ME *legist*, fr. Fr. *légiste*, MLat. *legista* : Lat. *lēx* 'law' (21.12).

NE *attorney*, short for *attorney-at-law* (technically = British *solicitor*, but in U.S. the general term preferred by lawyers themselves to the pop. *lawyer*), earlier 'deputy, agent', fr. ME *aturneye*, fr. *attorn* 'direct, dispose', this fr. OFr. *atorner*, cpd. of *a-* 'to' and *torner* 'turn'. NED s.v.

OHG *ēwa gilērter* and *fon theru ēwa gilērter* both render Lat. *lēgisperītus* in Tat. Similarly MHG *rehtlērer*, *rehtmeister*, *rehtwīser* for Lat. *lēgisdoctor*, *jūrista* (cf. Lexer, svv.), NHG *rechtsgelehrter*, Du. *rechtsgeleerde*.

OHG *furisprehho*, MHG *vürspreche*, *vürsprecher* (Swiss *fürsprech*), lit. 'one who speaks for, in behalf of someone'. Kluge-G. 474.

NHG *rechtsanwalt* and (like U.S. *attorney*) also simply *anwalt* = MHG *anwalte* 'deputy, agent' : *walten* 'have power, rule'.

5. Lith. *advocatas*, Lett. *advocats*, see above, 2.

6. ChSl. *zakonĭnikŭ* (renders *νομικός*, for which see above, 1), fr. *zakonŭ* 'law' (21.12).

SCr. *pravnik*, Boh. *právník*, Pol. *prawnik* (SCr. mostly 'one learned in the law, jurist'), fr. *pravo* 'law' (21.11).

SCr. *pravni zastupnik*, Boh. *právní zástupce*, lit. 'law-agent', phrases with *zastupnik*, *zástupce* 'agent, deputy' (: SCr. *zastupiti* 'represent', Boh. *zastupovati* 'take one's place, act as a substitute').

SCr. *odvjetnik*, fr. *odvjet* = ChSl. *otŭvětŭ* 'answer' (18.32).

Russ. *prisjažnyj poverennyj*, lit. 'sworn agent or trustee', fr. past pples. of *prisjagat'* 'swear, take oath' (21.24) and *poverit'* 'believe, trust'.

Russ. *strjapciy* (now obs. or arch.) : *strjapat'* 'look out for, arrange, prepare' (now esp. 'prepare food, cook'). Miklosich 326.

7. Skt. *dharmajña-* 'knowing the law', would be an appropriate term for a 'lawyer', but there is no evidence for such a class (only advisers of the king as judge, etc.) in the judicial procedure of ancient India.

21.15 COURT (The Body of Judicial Magistrates)

Grk.	*δικαστήριον*	Goth.	. . . .	Lith.	*teismas, sudas*
NG	*δικαστήριο*	ON	*þing, dōmr, lǫgrētta*	Lett.	*tiesa*
Lat.	*iūdicium, iūdicēs*	Dan.	*ret*	ChSl.	(*sądŭ*)
It.	*tribunale, corte*	Sw.	*rätt*	SCr.	*sud*
Fr.	*tribunal, cour*	OE	*gemōt, þing, riht, mæþel*	Boh.	*soud*
Sp.	*tribunal*	ME	*court*	Pol.	*sąd*
Rum.	*tribunal, curte*	NE	*court*	Russ.	*sud*
Ir.	*airecht*	Du.	*rechtbank, gerechtshof*	Skt.	*dharmādhikaraṇa-*
NIr.	*cūirt*	OHG	*ding, mahal, girihti*		
W.	*llys*	MHG	*(ge)rihte, dinc, reht*		
Br.	*lez*	NHG	*gericht*		

Many of the words for a 'court' of law are connected with words for 'law', 'judge', and 'judgment', and in some cases the same forms are used for 'law' and 'court' or for 'judgment' and 'court', doubtless through the medium of phrases like 'go to law', 'summon to judgment'. Several are words for 'meeting, assembly', including or specialized to the judicial 'court'. The group represented by NE *court* is based on 'court' = 'yard', in which the development to 'royal court' and 'judicial court' took place first in France.

Many of the words listed are used also for the place where justice is administered (e.g. Grk. *δικαστήριον*, NE *court*, etc.), and in case of Fr. *tribunal*, etc., this sense is the earlier. Or the place is expressed more specifically by compounds, like NHG *gerichtshof*.

1. Grk. *δικαστήριον*, fr. *δικαστής* 'judge' (21.18).

2. Lat. *iūdicium*, also 'judgment', fr. *iūdex* 'judge' (21.18) of which the pl. *iūdicēs* is also equivalent to the 'court' (as the body).

It. *corte*, OFr. *cort*, *curt*, *court* (> ME, NE *court*), Fr. *cour*, Rum. *curte*, fr. Lat. *cohors*, *cohortis* 'court' = 'yard' (7.15). The application to a judicial 'court' developed earliest in France (later in It., quite modern in Rum.), through the 'royal court' where justice was dispensed (influence of Lat. *cūria*, in MLat. often used of eccl. and judicial courts, not necessary). It was the most general word for 'court' (as still in English) until the introduction of *tribunal*, after which it was used mainly of special higher courts. REW 2032. Wartburg 3.851 f. NED s.v. *court*.

It. *tribunale*, etc., fr. Lat. *tribūnal* 'the raised platform on which seats of magistrates were placed' (: *tribūnus* 'tribune', orig. 'magistrate of the tribe, *tribus*').

3. Ir. *airecht*, orig. 'assembly of nobles', fr. *aire* 'noble' (19.36).

NIr. *cūirt*, fr. ME, NE *court*.

W. *llys*, Br. *lez*, orig. 'castle, court' (of a noble) : Ir. *liss*, *less* 'fortified place' (further etym. dub.; Stokes 247, Walde-P. 2.99), judicial sense doubtless after French and English.

4. ON, OE *þing*, OHG *ding*, etc., in the older period the most general word for the popular assembly both for legislative and judicial purposes (cf. Norges Gamle Love 5.737 ff.; Liebermann, Gesetze der Angelsachsen 2.222, 449 f.) : Goth. *þeihs* 'time' (14.11), with development through 'appointed time'. Walde-P. 1.724 f. Falk-Torp 1263. Feist 494.

ON *dōmr* 'judgment' (21.17), also 'court'. So rarely OE *dōm*. Liebermann, op. cit. 2, 2.54. Bosworth-Toller Suppl. s.v.

ON *lǫgrētta* ('legislature' and 'court'), cpd. of *lǫg* 'law' and *-rētta* : *rētta* 'straighten, adjust, raise', *rēttr* 'law', etc. (21.11). On history of its uses, cf. Vigfusson 405, and Heusler, Das Strafrecht der Isländersagas, p. 24.

OE *riht*, MHG *reht*, Dan. *ret*, Sw. *rätt* 'law' (21.11), used also for 'court of law'. Hence collectives OHG *girihti*, MHG *(ge)rihte*, NHG *gericht*, and cpds. Du. *rechtbank*, *gerechtshof* (both orig. the place, like NHG *gerichtshof*, but extended to the body).

OE *gemōt*, ME *imōt*, *mōt*, *mote*, NE (obs.) *moot*, the most general word for assembly (: ON *mōt* 'meeting, assembly', Goth. *gamōtan* 'have room', etc.) and for the judicial assembly more usual than the general Gmc. *þing* (cf. Liebermann, op. cit. 2.94, 449), also OE *mōt* in cpds., *folc-mōt*, etc. NED s.v. *moot*, sb.[1].

OE *mæþel*, OHG *mahal*, also general 'assembly' and 'discourse' : Goth. *maþl* 'meeting place, market', ON *māl* 'speech, lawsuit, case', Gmc. **maþla-*, prob. fr. the same root as OE *gemōt*, etc. (above). From the Gmc., MLat. *mallum*, *mallus* 'court'. Walde-P. 2.304. Falk-Torp 685 f. Feist 349 f.

5. Lith. *teismas* (neolog. for *sudas*), Lett. *tiesa* 'truth' (as Lith. *tiesa*), 'right', but esp. 'court' (Mühl.-Endz. 4.212) : Lith. *teisė* 'law' (21.11), *teisus* 'right' (16.73), *tiesus* 'straight' (12.73), etc.

Lith. *sudas*, loanword fr. Slavic (below, 6). Brückner, Sl. Fremdwörter 139.

6. SCr., Russ. *sud*, Boh. *soud*, Pol. *sąd* = ChSl. *sądŭ* 'judgment' (21.18).

7. Skt. *adhikaraṇa-* (in many senses, but including 'court', for which also esp. *dharmādhikaraṇa*, cpd. with *dharma-* 'law'), fr. *adhi-kṛ-* 'place at the head, appoint'.

21.16 JUDGE (vb.)

Grk.	δικάζω, κρῑνω	Goth.	dōmjan, stōjan	Lith.	teisti, spręsti
NG	δικάζω, κρίνω	ON	dœma	Lett.	tiesât, spriest
Lat.	iūdicāre	Dan.	dømme	ChSl.	sąditi
It.	giudicare	Sw.	dōma	SCr.	suditi
Fr.	juger	OE	dēman	Boh.	souditi
Sp.	juzgar	ME	deme, iuge	Pol.	sądzić
Rum.	judeca	NE	judge	Russ.	sudit′
Ir.	midiur, berim brith ar	Du.	oordeelen	Skt.	nirṇayam vad-, etc.
NIr.	beirim (tugaim) breith ar	OHG	rihten, irteilen, suonen	Av.	(vī-či-)
W.	barnu	MHG	rihten, erteilen, ur-teilen		
Br.	barn	NHG	urteilen, richten		

The words for 'judge' (vb.), 'judge' (sb.), and 'judgment' are in large measure parallel forms in a given language, but not always so. Thus, beside Grk. δικάζω and κρῑνω, the former more exclusively legal, only δικαστής (not κριτής) is the legal term for the 'judge', and only κρίσις for 'judgment'. Cf. also NHG urteilen, urteil, but still richter (not urteiler) for the 'judge'.

Most of the verbs for 'judge' are derived from words for 'judge' (sb.), 'judgment', 'law', or 'lawsuit'. Some come through 'decide' from 'separate', divide', 'reflect', 'draw out', or the like.

Besides Grk. κρῑνω, others of the usual verbs for 'decide' (cf. 21.162), like Lat. dēcernere, NHG entscheiden, though less distinctively legal terms, may, beside their more general applications, refer to the decision of a magistrate or official body.

Instead of 'judge', the judge may 'declare', 'pronounce', 'rule', etc.

1. Grk. δικάζω, fr. δίκη 'right, justice, lawsuit' (21.13).

Both δικάζω and κρῑνω 'decide' (21.162) are common legal terms, with a distinction not always maintained but especially clear in the Gortyn law-code, the former being used where the judge pronounces formal judgment according to the law and the evidence, the latter where he acts directly as arbiter in case of conflicting evidence.

2. Lat. iūdicāre (> Romance words), fr. iūdex 'judge' (21.18).

3. Ir. midiur : W. meddu 'possess, be able', Lat. meditārī 'think, reflect', Grk. μέδομαι 'give heed to', Umbr. mers 'ius' (21.11), etc. Walde-P. 2.259. Pedersen 2.580.

Ir. breth, brith, NIr. breith 'judgment' (21.17), in phrases Ir. berim brith ar, NIr. beirim (or tugaim) breith ar 'put judgment on'; also NIr. denom. breath-nuighim.

W. barnu, Br. barn : W. barn, Br. barn 'judgment' (21.17).

4. Goth. dōmjan, ON dœma, OE dē-man, etc., the older Gmc. words (OHG tuomen not the common term), fr. Goth. dōms 'judgment', etc. (21.17).

Goth. stōjan : staua 'judgment, lawsuit' (21.17).

ME iuge, NE judge, fr. Fr. juger, above, 2.

OHG irteilen (also ubarteilen), MHG erteilen, with sbs. OHG urteil(i), OS urdēli, MDu. ordeel, Du. oordeel, whence vbs. MHG, NHG urteilen, Du. oordeelen, cpds. of teilen, etc. 'divide' : teil, etc. 'part' (13.23). Kluge-G. 646. Franck-v. W. 477.

OHG-NHG rihten, richten, fr. reht, recht, 'law' (21.11).

OHG suonen (NHG sühnen 'expiate, atone'), fr. suona 'judgment, court, atonement' (21.17).

5. Lith. teisti (neolog. for sudyti) : teisus 'right' (16.73), teisė 'law' (21.11).

Lett. tiesāt : tiesa 'truth, right, judgment, court' (21.15). Mühl.-Endz. 4.214.

Lith. spręsti, Lett. spriest, both orig. 'span, stretch, measure' : Lith. sprindys, Lett. sprīdis 'span', with development through 'draw' (a conclusion). Mühl.-Endz. 3.1022 f.

Lith. sudyti (old; now replaced by the native words), Lett. suodīt, fr. Russ. sudit′ (below, 6). Mühl.-Endz. 3.1135.

6. ChSl. sąditi, etc., general Slavic, fr. sądŭ, etc. 'judgment' (21.17), 'court' (21.15).

7. Skt. nirṇī- 'lead out, take away' (cpd. of nī- 'lead', 10.64), hence 'find out, decide'. Hence sb. nirṇaya- 'judgment', and nirṇaya- with vad- 'speak, say' or the like, prob. more common legal expression for vb. 'judge' than nirṇī-.

Av. vī-či- 'distinguish, decide' (but not quotable in strictly legal sense) = Skt. vi-ci- 'distinguish, investigate', cpd. of ci- 'notice, observe'. Barth. 441.

21.162. 'Decide'. Some of the verbs listed under 'judge' are used also for 'decide' in general. Conversely, the usual verbs for 'decide', while generally not legal terms, may, more or less frequently, refer to a legal decision. Hence some of these (not a full list) are noted here.

1. The most common development is through 'distinguish', fr. 'separate', this in part fr. 'cut' or 'split'.

Grk. κρῑνω, διακρῑνω, Lat. dēcernere : Grk. κείρω, OE sceran 'cut off, shear', Ir. scaraim, Lith. skirti 'separate', etc. Walde-P. 2.584. Ernout-M. 178 f. Walde-H. 1.205.

Lat. dēcīdere (> Romance words and, through Fr., NE decide), cpd. of caedere 'cut' (9.22).

NHG entscheiden, in MHG 'separate, distinguish', cpd. of scheiden 'separate' (12.23).

SCr. odlučiti, cpd. of lučiti 'separate' (12.23).

2. NG ἀποφασίζω, fr. ἀπόφασις 'decision', this fr. ἀποφαίνω 'make known, declare', cpd. of φαίνω 'show'.

3. NHG bestimmen, MLG bestemmen (> Dan. bestemme, Sw. bestämme), in earliest use 'vocally designate', hence best : stimme 'voice'. Weigand-H. 1.219. Paul, Deutsches Wtb. 77. Franck-v. W. 55. Otherwise (: OE stefnan 'regulate, fix') Falk-Torp 1157.

4. NHG beschliessen, entschliessen, Du. beslissen, Dan. beslutte, Sw. besluta, cpds. of vbs. for 'shut' (12.25), hence 'bring to a conclusion, decision'.

5. SCr. riješiti, Russ. rešit′ 'solve' (17.39), also 'decide'. Cf. NE resolve beside solve.

6. Cpds. of vbs. for 'do, make' (9.11) may be used for 'decide' through the notion 'dispose of', as Dan. afgøre, Sw. af-göra, Du. uitmachen, NHG ausmachen.

21.17 JUDGMENT

Grk.	κρίσις	Goth.	staua (dōms)	Lith.	sprendimas
NG	κρίσις	ON	dōmr	Lett.	spriedums
Lat.	iūdicium	Dan.	dom, kendelse	ChSl.	sądŭ
It.	giudizio	Sw.	dom	SCr.	presuda, osuda
Fr.	jugement	OE	dōm	Boh.	rozsudek
Sp.	juicio	ME	dom, iugement	Pol.	wyrok
Rum.	judecată	NE	judgment	Russ.	prigovor
Ir.	breth, mess	Du.	oordeel	Skt.	nirṇaya-
NIr.	breith	OHG	urteil, reht, suona, tuom	Av.	ratu-
W.	barn, brawd	MHG	urteil(e), reht, gerihte		
Br.	barn, barnedigez	NHG	urteil		

Several of the words for 'judgment' are derived from the verbs for 'judge', while in others the converse relation holds. For those not derived from the verbs for 'judge', the sources are such as 'what is brought', 'what is set down, established', 'agreement', 'pronouncement', and 'law'.

1. Grk. κρίσις : κρῑνω 'decide, judge' (21.162).

2. Lat. iūdicium, fr. iūdex 'judge' (21.18). Hence It. giudizio, Sp. juicio; Fr. jugement, Rum. judecată, fr. the vbs. Fr. juger, Rum. judeca (21.16).

3. Ir. breth (also brāth 'doom'), NIr. breith, W. barn, brawd, Br. barn, barne-digez, all derivs. of the root of Ir. berim, Grk. φέρω, etc. 'bear, carry, bring', with specialization of 'bringing, what is brought'. Walde-P. 2.155. Pedersen 1.42, 51, 52.

Ir. mess (less common), vbl. n. to midiur 'judge' (21.16).

4. Goth. staua (reg. word for κρίσις; cf. also OHG stūa-tago 'day of judgment') : OE stōw 'place', etc. (12.11), with development through specialized 'place of judgment, court' > 'judgment'. Cf. MHG stuol 'seat, chair' in specialized uses including 'seat of the judge'. Walde-P. 2.608. Feist 451.

Goth. dōms (but only in Skeireins and here prob. with secondary sense 'fame, glory'), ON dōmr, Dan., Sw. dom, OE dōm, ME dom (NE doom), OHG tuom (usual word in Tat.), fr. the root of OE dōn, OHG tuon 'do', Grk. τίθημι, Skt. dhā- 'put, place', with semantic development through 'what is set down, established'. Walde-P. 1.828. Feist 122 f.

Dan. kendelse, fr. kende 'know' (17.17), in its use = dømme 'judge' (this use fr. that of MLG kennen). Falk-Torp 516.

ME iugement, NE judgment, fr. OFr. jugement.

ME verdit, NE verdict (as legal term properly the 'decision of a jury', but in U.S. sometimes used also of the judge's decision), fr. OFr. verdit, MLat. veredic-tum (whence later English spelling), lit. 'what is truly said' (Lat. vērē dictum). The legal use above in England, hence Fr. verdict, It. verdetto, Russ. verdict. NED s.v. verdict. Gamillscheg 884.

OHG urteil(i), MHG urteil(e), NHG urteil, Du. oordeel : OHG irteilen, etc. 'judge'. See 21.16. Here OE ordāl in special sense, revived in NE ordeal (NED s.v.).

OHG, MHG reht 'law' (21.11), also 'judgment'.

MHG gerihte 'court' (21.15), also 'judgment'. So NHG gericht in das jüngste gericht, but generally obs. in this sense.

OHG suona, also 'atonement' (MHG suone, süene, NHG sühne in this sense only) : ON sōn 'atonement' (in cpds.), MLG swōne, sōn, etc., outside connec-

tions dub. Walde-P. 2.452. Kluge-G. 606. Franck-v. W. 824.

5. Lith. sprendimas, Lett. spriedums : spręsti, spriest 'judge' (21.16).

6. ChSl. sądŭ, i.e. sq-dŭ, cpd. of sq- 'together', second part fr. weak grade of root in dēti, Grk. τίθημι, Skt. dhā-, etc. 'put, place' (12.12). Cf. Skt. sam-dhā-, sam-dhi- 'union, agreement, compact', etc. The corresponding modern Slavic words (still used in phrases like 'day of judgment') are terms for the 'court' (21.15), but 'judgment' is expressed by the cpds. SCr. presuda, osuda, Boh. rozsudek. Walde-P. 1.827. Berneker 123. Brückner 483.

Pol. wyrok = Boh. vyrok 'declaration' (also sometimes 'judgment'), cpds. (like prorok 'prophet', etc.) of root in ChSl. rešti, rekq, etc. 'say' (18.22).

Russ. prigovor : govorit′ 'speak' (18.21).

7. Skt. nirṇaya-, fr. nir-ṇī- 'decide'. See 21.16.

Av. ratu- 'judge' (21.18), also sometimes 'judgment'. Barth. 1502.

21.18 JUDGE (sb.)

Grk.	δικαστής	Goth.	staua	Lith.	teisėjas
NG	δικαστής	ON	dōmāri, dōmandi	Lett.	tiesnesis
Lat.	iūdex	Dan.	dommer	ChSl.	sądĭji
It.	giudice	Sw.	domare	SCr.	sudija, sudac
Fr.	juge	OE	dēma, dōmere	Boh.	soudce
Sp.	juez	ME	demere, iuge	Pol.	sędzia
Rum.	judecātor	NE	judge	Russ.	sud′ja
Ir.	brithem	Du.	rechter	Skt.	sabhya-, prāḍvivāka-
NIr.	breitheamh	OHG	rihtāri, irteilāri, suonari	Av.	ratu-
W.	barnwr, brawdwr	MHG	rihtære, urteilære		
Br.	barner	NHG	richter		

Most of the nouns for 'judge' are derived from the verbs for 'judge' (21.16) or the nouns for 'judgment' (21.17). But conversely the Lat. noun for 'judge', a cpd. of the word for 'law', is the source of the others in the group. The numerous Skt. terms are of diverse origin.

1. Grk. δικαστής (at Athens mostly pl. δικασταί 'jurors', but sg. as 'judge' frequent in Gortynian law-code, etc.), fr. vb. δικάζω 'judge' (21.16).

2. Lat. iūdex (> It. giudice, Fr. juge, Sp. juez), cpd. of iūs 'law' (21.11) and -dic-, weak grade of the root in dīcere 'say', perh. in its earlier sense of 'point out' (cf. 18.22), as in index (nom. -dex for -dix after cpds. in -fex, -ficis : facio). Rum. judecātor new deriv. of vb. judeca 'judge'.

3. Ir. brithem, NIr. breitheamh, W. barnwr, brawdwr, Br. barner, fr. verbs for 'judge'.

4. Goth. staua (masc. n-stem), fr. staua (fem. ō-stem) 'judgment'. Feist 451.

ON dōmāri, dōmandi, Dan. dommer, Sw. domare, OE dēma, dōmere, ME demere : ON dōmr 'judgment', dœma 'judge', etc.

ME iuge, NE judge, fr. Fr. juge (above, 2).

OHG rihtāri, MHG rihtære, NHG richter, fr. OHG rihten, etc. 'judge'.

OHG irteilāri, MHG urteilære, fr. OHG irteilen 'judge', etc.

5. Lith. teisėjas, Lett. tiesnesis : Lith. teisti, Lett. tiesāt 'judge'.

Lith. sūdža, Lett. suog′is (but now replaced by native words), fr. Russ. sud′ja (below, 6). Brückner, Sl. Fremdwörter 139. Mühl.-Endz. 3.1136.

6. ChSl. *sądĭji*, SCr. *sudija*, *sudac*, etc., general Slavic, fr. ChSl. *sądŭ*, etc. 'judgment, court'.

7. In ancient India the king exercised judicial functions, and the following terms denoted in the first instance the king's advisers in judicial matters. But they are generally rendered 'judge'. Cf. Jolly, Recht und Sitte 132 ff., where still other terms besides those noted here are mentioned.

Skt. *sabhya-* and *sabhā-sad-* (both common in Manu, Yajñ., etc.) deriv. and cpd. (with *sad-* 'sitting') of *sabhā-* 'assembly, court'.

Skt. *prāḍvivāka-* (Manu, etc.; cf. Jolly, op. cit. 133), cpd. of *prāç-* 'asking' (: *praç-*, *pracch-* 'ask', 18.31) and *vivāka-* 'one who gives judgment' (fr. *vi-vac-* 'announce, explain', cpd. of *vac-* 'speak, say', 18.21), thus combining the notions of investigation and judgment. Jolly, op. cit. 133.

Skt. *dharmādhikārin-*, *dharmādhikāraṇika-*, etc. (BR 3.894, but less common than the preceding), cpds. of *dharma-* 'law' and derivs. of *adhi-kṛ-* 'place at the head, appoint'.

Skt. *draṣṭar-* 'one who sees', also 'judge', fr. *dṛç-* 'see'.

Av. *ratu-* : Av. *aša-*, OPers. *arta-* 'law' (21.11).

21.21 PLAINTIFF

Grk.	*ὁ διώκων, ὁ ἐνάγων*	Goth.	. . . .	Lith.	*ieškovas*
NG	*ὁ ἐνάγων*	ON	*sōknari*, etc.	Lett.	*apsūdzētājs*
Lat.	*petītor, accusātor, actor*	Dan.	*sagsøger, klager*	ChSl.	. . . .
		Sw.	*kärande*	SCr.	*tužitelj*
It.	*attore, querelante*	OE	*tēond*	Boh.	*žalobce*
Fr.	*demandeur, plaignant*	ME	*askere, pleintif*	Pol.	*skarżący, powód*
Sp.	*demandante*	NE	*plaintiff*	Russ.	*istec*
Rum.	*acuzator*	Du.	*(aan)klager, eischer*	Skt.	*arthin-, vādin-, abhiyoktar-*
Ir.	*līth, fechem*	OHG	*sahhu*(?)		
NIr.	*ēilightheoir, agarthōir*	MHG	*klager*	Av.	. . . .
W.	*hawlblaid, achwynwr*	NHG	*(an)kläger*		
Br.	*klemmer*				

Most of the terms for 'plaintiff' are derivs. (act. pples. used as sbs., or agent nouns) of the usual verbs for 'accuse' (21.31) or others meaning 'seek, demand, pursue, summon, complain, bring in', most of these also used as legal terms.

Some Irish terms for 'plaintiff' and 'defendant' involve the notion of 'debt'. In certain civil suits the 'debtor' and 'creditor' would be the 'defendant' and 'plaintiff' respectively. Cf. Lat. *reus* 'defendant', also 'debtor'.

1. Grk. *ὁ διώκων*, pres. act. pple. of *διώκω* 'pursue' (10.53), as legal term 'prosecute, bring suit against'.

Grk. *ὁ ἐνάγων* (late and NG), pres. act. pple. of *ἐνάγω* 'bring in' in its late legal use for 'bring into court, accuse'.

Grk. *ἀντίδικος* 'opponent in a suit', cpd. of *ἀντί* 'against' and *-δικος* : *δίκη* 'lawsuit' (21.13), occurs with special reference to the plaintiff and also to the defendant.

In the Gortyn law-code the plaintiff is called *μεμφόμενος* (pple. of *μέμφομαι* 'blame, censure') or *ἄρχων τᾶς δίκας* 'initiator of the suit'.

2. Lat. *petītor*, lit. 'seeker', fr. *petere* 'seek'.

Lat. *accusātor* 'accuser', fr. *accusāre* 'accuse'.

Lat. *actor* (> It. *attore* also legal term), fr. *agere* 'bring suit', cf. *actiō* 'lawsuit' (21.13).

It. *querelante*, pres. act. pple. of *querelare* 'bring suit against', fr. *querela* 'complaint, charge'.

Fr. *plaignant*, pres. act. pple. of *plaindre* 'pity', but in refl. *se plaindre* 'complain', esp. 'make a (legal) complaint'.

Fr. *demandeur*, Sp. *demandante*, fr. Fr. *demander*, Sp. *demandar* 'request, demand' (18.35).

Rum. *acuzator*, fr. *acuza* 'accuse'.

3. Ir. *līth*, fr. *līim* 'accuse'.

Ir. *fechem* 'litigant', both 'defendant' and 'plaintiff' (for the latter esp. *fechem toicheda* or *tobaig*, lit. 'litigant of the suing' or 'of the collection'), orig. 'debtor' : *fiach* 'debt' (11.64). Laws, Gloss. 336 f.

NIr. *ēilightheoir*, fr. *ēilighim* 'demand, sue for', cf. Ir. *eiliugud* 'claim, accusation', *inlongat*, *eillgit* 'they claim', cpd. of *long-* 'lay, put' (only in cpds.) : Grk. *λέχος* 'couch', etc. Pedersen 2.570.

NIr. *agarthōir*, *agrathōir*, fr. *agraim*, Ir. *adgairim* 'claim, sue', cpd. of *gairim* 'call'. Pedersen 2.533.

W. *hawlblaid*, cpd. cf *hawl* 'demand, claim' and *plaid* 'side, party, faction'.

W. *achwynwr*, fr. *achwyn* 'complain, accuse'.

Br. *klemmer*, fr. *klemma* 'complain'.

4. ON *sōknari*, fr. *sōkn* 'prosecution' (= Goth. *sōkns*, OE *sōcn* 'investigation', fr. the same root as *sǫk*, OE *sacu*, etc. 'lawsuit'). Also *sakarāberi* (cf. OHG *sacebaro* in Lex Salica), cpd. of *sǫk* and form of *bera* 'bring'. Also *sōknaraðili*, *sakaraðili* with *aðili* 'chief' like *aðal-* in cpds. (Vigfusson 3).

Dan. *sagsøger*, cpd. of *sag* 'suit' and *søger*, fr. *søge* 'seek, resort to', as legal term 'sue'.

Dan. *klager*, fr. MLG (below).

Sw. *kärande*, fr. *kära* 'bring suit, prosecute' = ON *kæra* 'accuse' (21.31).

OE *tēond*, pres. pple. of *tēon* 'accuse'. Less commonly *wrēgend* and *onspreca*, *onsprecend*, fr. *wrēgan* and *onsprecan* 'accuse'.

ME *askere*, fr. *aske* 'ask, seek' (18.35).

ME *pleintif*, NE *plaintiff*, the same word as adj. *plaintive* fr. OFr. *plaintif* 'complaining, plaintive' (: *plaindre*, cf. above, Fr. *plaignant*). NED s.v. *plaintiff*.

OHG *sahhu* ('der ankläger' Grimm, Deutsche Rechtsaltertümer 2.488; where quotable? Graff has *sahhari* 'litigator') : *sahha* 'lawsuit' (21.13).

MHG, MLG *klager* (> Dan. *klager*), NHG *(an)kläger*, fr. MHG, NHG *klagen* 'complain, charge' (OHG *klagōn* 'complain'), NHG *anklagen* 'accuse'. Similarly Du. *(aan)klager*.

Du. *eischer*, fr. *eischen* 'demand, claim' (18.35).

5. Lith. *ieškovas*, fr. *ieškoti* 'seek' (11.31).

Lett. *apsūdzētājs*, fr. *apsūdzēt* 'accuse, sue'.

6. SCr. *tužitelj*, fr. *tužiti* 'complain, sue, accuse'.

Boh. *žalobce*, fr. *žaloba* 'complaint, charge', cf. *(ob)žalovati* 'sue, accuse'.

Pol. *skarżący*, fr. *(o)skarżyć* 'accuse'.

Pol. *powód* 'cause, occasion' (like Russ. *povod*), also 'plaintiff', orig. 'leading' : ChSl. *vedą*, *vesti* 'lead' (10.64). Brückner 433, 628.

Russ. *istec*, also 'creditor' : *istyj* 'true, genuine', ChSl. *istŭ* id. (16.66), with development 'real owner' > 'creditor' > 'plaintiff'.

7. Skt. *arthin-*, fr. *artha-* 'object, matter, thing' (9.90), hence lit. 'having to do with a certain matter', as 'plaintiff', with *praty-arthin*, 'defendant', e.g. Manu 8.79, Yājñ. 2.6, 7.

Skt. *vādin-* 'speaking' (fr. *vad-* 'speak', 18.21), hence 'one who speaks for, represents', as 'plaintiff', with *prativādin-* 'defendant', e.g. Yājñ. 2.73.

Skt. *abhiyoktar-*, agent noun fr. *abhi-yuj-* 'attack', as legal term 'charge, accuse' (21.31), hence 'plaintiff', e.g. Manu 8.58, Yājñ. 2.95.

21.22 DEFENDANT

Grk.	*ὁ φεύγων*	Goth.	. . . .	Lith.	*atsakytojas, atsakovas*
NG	*ἐναγόμενος, κατηγορούμενος*	ON	*varnarmaðr*	Lett.	*apsūdzētais*
		Dan.	*indstævnte*	ChSl.	. . . .
Lat.	*reus*	Sw.	*svarande*	SCr.	*(op)tuženik*
It.	*imputato, accusato*	OE	*betigen*	Boh.	*(ob)žalovaný*
Fr.	*défendeur*	ME	*defendaunt*	Pol.	*oskarżony*
Sp.	*demandado*	NE	*defendant*	Russ.	*otvetčik*
Rum.	*akuzat*	Du.	*beschuldigde*	Skt.	*pratyarthin-, prativādin-, abhiyukta-*
Ir.	*bibdu, cintach, fechem*	OHG	*inzihtigo, gasachio*		
NIr.	*cosantōir, cosnamhach*	MHG	*antwürter, inzihtec*	Av.	. . . .
W.	*diffynnydd*	NHG	*beklagter, angeklagter*		
Br.	*difenner*				

Most of the terms for 'defendant' are from either 1) act. pples. or agent-nouns fr. verbs for 'defend', 'answer', in one case 'flee' = 'be prosecuted', or 2) pass. pples. of verbs for 'accuse' (21.31), 'summon', 'demand' and in such cases often parallel to the active forms as 'plaintiff', as Sp. *demandado* vs. *demandante*, NHG *beklagter* vs. *kläger*, etc.

In a few cases the word for a 'criminal, culprit', that is, the guilty defendant, came to be used also for 'defendant' in general. Conversely Lat. *reus* 'defendant' came to be used mostly of the one guilty, 'criminal, culprit', as in It., Sp. *reo* (cf. also Rum. *rău* 'bad').

For Grk. *ἀντίδικος* and Ir. *fechem* used of either 'defendant' or 'plaintiff', see under latter (21.21).

1. Grk. *ὁ φεύγων*, pres. act. pple. of *φεύγω* 'flee' (10.51), as law term 'be prosecuted'.

NG *ἐναγόμενος*, pres. pass. pple. vs. pres. act. pple. *ἐνάγων* 'plaintiff' (21.21).

NG *κατηγορούμενος*, pres. pass. pple. of *κατηγορῶ* 'accuse'.

2. Lat. *reus* (> It., Sp. *reo* 'culprit'), prob. fr. **rēyos*, old gen. to *rēs* (Skt. *rās*, gen. *rāyas*) 'legal matter, lawsuit' (21.13); *reus est* lit. 'he is of the lawsuit'. Thurneysen, IF 14.131. Sturtevant, TAPA 71.573 ff.

It. *imputato*, pass. pple. of *imputare* 'ascribe, impute, charge' (fr. Lat. *imputāre* id.).

It. *accusato*, Rum. *akuzat*, pass. pple. of It. *accusare*, Rum. *acuza* 'accuse'.

It. *convenuto*, pass. pple. of *convenire* 'summon'.

Fr. *défendeur*, fr. *défendre* 'defend'.

Sp. *demandado*, pass. pple. of *demandar* 'demand, bring suit', vs. act. pple. *demandante* 'plaintiff'.

3. OIr. *bibdu* 'reus', MIr. *bidba* 'defendant', also 'criminal, culprit, enemy' (Laws, Gloss. 98), OW *bibid*, gl. 'rei', perh. (as redupl. perf. act. pple. fr. **bhebhudwōts*) : ON *bauta*, OE *bēatan* 'beat, strike', etc. Pokorny, KZ 47.163 (vs. Sommer, Festschrift Stokes 24 f.).

Ir. *cintach*, mostly 'criminal, offender, debtor', fr. *cin* 'crime' (21.41), but also 'defendant' who is not guilty (K. Meyer, Contrib. 373).

NIr. *cosantōir*, *cosantach*, *cosnamhach* : *cosnaim* 'defend' (cf. *cosnamh* 'defense', 20.44).

W. *diffynnydd*, Br. *difenner*, fr. W. *diffyn*, Br. *difenn* 'defend'.

4. ON *varnarmaðr* ('defendant' or 'representative of defendant'; Norges Gamle Love 5.691), cpd. of *varnar*, gen. of *vǫrn* 'defense' and *maðr* 'man'. Also *varnaraðili*, cpd. with *aðili* as in *sōknaraðili* 'plaintiff' (21.21).

Dan. *indstævnte* (older spelling *indstævnede*), past pple. of *indstævne* 'summon, cite'.

Sw. *svarande*, lit. 'answering' : *svara* 'answer' (18.32).

OE *betigen*, *betogen*, pass. pple. of *tēon* 'accuse'.

ME *defendaunt*, NE *defendant*, fr. Fr. *défendant* pres. pple. of *défendre* 'defend'.

OHG *(der) inzihtigo*, MHG *inzihtec* (adj.), fr. OHG *inziht* 'accusation' : *zīhan* 'accuse'.

OHG *gasachio* in Lex Salica 'opponent' = 'defendant, debtor' = OE *gesaca* 'opponent' : OHG *sahha*, OE *sacu* 'lawsuit' (21.13).

MHG *antwürter*, lit. 'answerer' : *antwürten* 'answer' (18.32).

NHG *beklagter* and *angeklagter*, fr. pass. pples. of *beklagen* 'lament', formerly also 'accuse', *anklagen* 'accuse'.

Du. *beschuldigde*, fr. *beschuldigen* 'accuse'.

5. Lith. *atsakytojas*, *atsakovas* : *atsakyti* 'answer' (18.32).

Lett. *apsūdzētais* (beside *apsūdzētājs* 'plaintiff') : *(ap)sūdzēt* 'accuse, sue'. Mühl.-Endz. 1.127.

6. SCr. *(op)tuženik* : *(op)tužiti* 'complain, accuse'.

Boh. *(ob)žalovaný* : *(ob)žalovati* 'accuse'.

Pol. *oskarżony* : *oskarżać*, *(o)skarżyć* 'accuse'.

Russ. *otvetčik* : *otvečat'*, *otvetit'* 'answer' (18.32).

7. Skt. *pratyarthin-*, cpd. of *prati-* 'against' and *arthin-* 'plaintiff' (21.21).

Skt. *prati-vādin-*, cpd. of *prati-* 'against' and *vādin-* 'plaintiff' (21.21).

Skt. *abhiyukta-*, pass. pple. of *abhi-yuj-* 'charge, accuse', and so opp. of *abhiyoktar-* 'plaintiff' (21.21).

21.23 WITNESS (sb.)

Grk.	*μάρτυς*	Goth.	*weitwōþs*	Lith.	*liudininkas*
NG	*μάρτυρας*	ON	*vāttr, vitni*	Lett.	*liecinieks*
Lat.	*testis*	Dan.	*vidne*	ChSl.	*sŭvědětelĭ*
It.	*testimonio*	Sw.	*vittne*	SCr.	*svjedok*
Fr.	*témoin*	OE	*gewita, gewitnes*	Boh.	*svědek*
Sp.	*testigo*	ME	*witnesse*	Pol.	*świadek*
Rum.	*martor*	NE	*witness*	Russ.	*svidetel'*
Ir.	*fiadu*	Du.	*getuige*	Skt.	*sākṣin-*
NIr.	*fiadhnēidh*	OHG	*giwizzo, urcundo*	Av.	*vīkaya-*
W.	*tyst*	MHG	*geziuc, urkunde*		
Br.	*test*	NHG	*zeuge*		

Words for 'witness' are derived from verbs for 'know, recognize, see, remember, or declare'. A few are based on 'third person', or 'outsider', or just 'people', through the common inference of 'not party to the suit'.

Words for 'testify' and 'testimony' are generally parallel forms, mostly derived from those for 'witness', as Grk. *μαρτυρέω*, *μαρτυρία*, Lat. *testificārī*, *testimōnium*, Goth. *weitwōdjan*, *weitwodei*, ChSl. *sŭvědětelĭstovati*, *sŭvědětelĭstvo*. The Lith. current nouns are derived from the verb, but the latter is ultimately based on a noun for 'witness'.

In several cases the words for 'testimony' came to be used also, and then mainly, for the personal 'witness', as Fr. *témoin*, NE *witness*.

1. Derivatives of IE **weid-* 'see' (15.51) and 'know' (17.17). Walde-P. 1.236 ff. Feist 560.

Ir. *fiadu*, acc. *fiadna* (Laws, Gloss. 356), NIr. *fiadhnēidh;* Goth. *weitwōþs* (perf. act. pple.), ON *vitni*, Dan. *vidne*, Sw. *vittne*, OE *gewita*, *(ge)witnes*, ME *witnesse*, NE *witness* (ON, OE also and orig. 'testimony' and so still NE, esp. *bear witness*), OHG *giwizzo;* ChSl. *sŭvědětelĭ* (prefix *sŭ-*), Russ. *svidetel'*, SCr. *svjedok*, Boh. *svědek*, Pol. *świadek*.

2. Grk. μάρτυς, gen. -υρος (nom. also μάρτυρ, Hom. μάρτυρος), NG μάρτυρας : μέριμνα 'care', Lat. *memor* 'mindful of', Skt. *smṛ-* 'remember', etc. Prob. based on *μαρ-τυ- (IE *-tu-* suffix in abstracts, etc.) orig. 'testimony'. Walde-P. 2.689. Boisacq 612.

3. Lat. *testis*, lit. 'the third' (= Ir. *triss* 'third'), fr. **tristi-* : *trēs* 'three'. Cf. Osc. *trstus* 'testēs' (fr. **tris-to-*), *tristaamentud* 'testāmentō'. Hence *testimōnium* 'testimony' > It. (learned) *testimonio*, Fr. *témoin* (both with shift fr. 'testimony' > 'witness'), and vb. *testificārī* 'testify', VLat. *-āre* > OSp. *testiguar* with deriv. Sp. *testigo* 'witness'. Walde-P. 1.755. Ernout-M. 1036 f. REW 8684-85.

Rum. *martor*, loanword fr. Grk. (above, 2). Tiktin 956.

4. W. *tyst*, Br. *test*, fr. Lat. *testis* (above, 3). Loth, Mots lat. 214.

5. ON *váttr*, prob. (Gmc. **wahtaz*) : OHG *giwahanen* 'mention, remember', *giwaht* 'mention, fame', Lat. *vōx* 'voice', Grk. ἔπος 'word', etc. Walde-P. 1.245. Falk-Torp 1376.

MHG *geziuc*, *geziuge*, late *ziuc*, NHG *zeuge* (in MHG also 'testimony', for which NHG *zeugnis*), Du. *getuige* (MDu. *getūgh* 'testimony') : OHG *geziugōn* 'explain, declare' (orig. 'bring out'), OHG *ziohan* 'pull, draw, bring' (9.33). Formation and early usage indicate the development 'testimony' > 'witness'. Weigand-H. 2.1321. Kluge-G. 709. Franck-v. W. 192.

OHG *urcundo* (reg. for *testis* in Tat.), beside *urcundī* 'testimonium' (NHG *urkunde* 'document' and in some phrases 'evidence') : OHG *ircennen*, NHG *erkennen* 'recognize, perceive', etc. Kluge-G. 645 (without *urcundo*).

6. Lith. *liudininkas* (also *liuditojas*), beside *liudyti* 'bear witness, testify', based on a loanword fr. Russ. *ljudi* 'people' quotable in ORuss. as 'witnesses'. Brückner, KZ 46.223.

Lett. *liecinieks*, lit. 'one who is superfluous, an outsider, a hireling' : *lieks* 'superfluous, extra' and 'false'. Mühl.-Endz. 2.492, 496.

7. Skt. *sākṣin-* : *sākṣāt* 'with the eye, clearly', fr. *sa-* 'with' and *akṣa-*, reg. at end of cpds. for *akṣi-* 'eye'.

Av. *vīkaya-*, fr. *vī-či-* 'distinguish, decide' (21.16). Barth. 1436.

21.24 SWEAR

Grk.	ὄμνῡμι	Goth.	*swaran*	Lith.	*prisiekti*
NG	ὁρκίζομαι (ὀμνύω)	ON	*sverja*	Lett.	*zvērēt*
Lat.	*iūrāre*	Dan.	*sverge*	ChSl.	*klęti sę*
It.	*giurare*	Sw.	*svärja*	SCr.	*zakleti se, priseći*
Fr.	*jurer*	OE	*swerian*	Boh.	*přísahati*
Sp.	*jurar*	ME	*swere*	Pol.	*przysięgać, kląć się*
Rum.	*jura*	NE	*swear*	Russ.	*prisjagat', kljast'sja*
Ir.	*tongu*	Du.	*zweren*	Skt.	*çap-*
NIr.	*beirim mionna*	OHG	*sweren*		
W.	*tyngu*	MHG	*swern*		
Br.	*toui*	NHG	*schwören*		

Verbs for 'swear' include a deriv. of the word for 'law', words for 'speak' which have been specialized in legal sense, 'touch' (through practice of touching an object in taking the oath), and 'curse' (through 'curse oneself' if the statement be not true; cf. NE colloq. *I'll be damned if it isn't so*). Some are of obscure origin.

'Swear' may also be expressed by phrases with words for 'oath' (21.25), like NE *take oath*, Fr. *prêter serment*, NHG *eid ablegen (leisten)*, NG παίρνω ὅρκο.

1. Grk. ὄμνῡμι, NG lit. ὀμνύω : Skt. *am-* 'swear' in imperat. *amīṣva*, etc. (Aufrecht, Rh. Mus. 40.160), but further identity of this *am-* with *am-* 'injure', etc. dub. Walde-P. 1.178. Boisacq 701.

Grk. ὁρκίζω 'administer an oath', whence rare ὁρκιζόμενος 'the one sworn', but NG ὁρκίζομαι usual word for 'swear'.

2. Lat. *iūrāre* (> Romance forms), fr. *iūs* 'law' (21.11). Ernout-M. 506 f. Walde-H. 1.733. REW 4630.

3. Ir. *tongu*, W. *tyngu*, Br. *toui*, Corn. *toy*, outside connections dub. Pedersen 1.106, 2.652 f.

NIr. *beirim* (or *tugaim*) *mionna* 'bring oath', cf. *mionna* 'oath' (21.25).

4. Goth. *swaran*, OE *swerian*, etc., general Gmc. : Lat. *sermō* 'talk, conversation', Osc. *sverrunei* (dat.) 'spokesman', etc. Walde-P. 2.527. Feist 463. Falk-Torp 1214 f. Kluge-G. 553.

5. Lith. *prisiekti*, cpd. of *siekti* 'reach with the hand, swear' (Leskien, Ablaut 282), with the same semantic development as in, and perh. influenced by, Slavic (Pol. *przysięgać*, etc., below). Trautmann 252.

Lett. *zvērēt*, fr. MLG *sweren*. Mühl.-Endz. 4.772.

6. ChSl. *klęti sę*, SCr. *zakleti se*, Pol. *kląć się*, Russ. *kljast'sja*, refl. forms of ChSl. *klęti*, etc. 'curse' (22.24), with development through 'curse oneself' (if the statement be not true). Berneker 525 f. Otherwise Brückner 232.

SCr. *priseći*, Boh. *přísahati*, Pol. *przysięgać*, Russ. *prisjagat'* : ChSl. *prisęgą*, *prisęšti* 'touch' (15.71). 'Swear' from touching the object on which the oath was taken. Miklosich 291. Brückner 490. Trautmann 252.

7. Skt. *çap-* 'curse' (22.24), usually mid. 'swear', with development as in ChSl. *klęti sę*, etc. (above, 6).

21.25 OATH

Grk.	ὅρκος	Goth.	*aiþs*	Lith.	*priesaika*
NG	ὅρκος	ON	*eiðr*	Lett.	*zvēri, zvērējums*
Lat.	*iūs iūrandum*	Dan.	*ed*	ChSl.	*klętva (prisęga)*
It.	*giuramento*	Sw.	*ed*	SCr.	*prisega, zakletva*
Fr.	*serment*	OE	*āþ*	Boh.	*přísaha*
Sp.	*juramento*	ME	*oth*	Pol.	*przysięga*
Rum.	*jurămînt*	NE	*oath*	Russ.	*kljatva, prisjaga*
Ir.	*luge, ōeth*	Du.	*eed*	Skt.	*çapatha-*
NIr.	*mionn*	OHG	*eid*		
W.	*llw*	MHG	*eit*		
Br.	*le*	NHG	*eid (schwur)*		

Many of the words for 'oath' are derivs. of the verbs for 'swear' (21.24). But the Grk., Celtic, and Gmc. groups are quite unrelated to the verbs. These words are mostly of uncertain semantic origin, but the case of NIr. *mionn* in which 'oath' is based on the 'relics' upon which the oath is taken shows that some special place or object in connection with taking the oath must be taken into account as a source (cf. also 'touch' > 'swear' in the Slavic verbs).

1. Grk. ὅρκος (sometimes also the object by which one swears) : ἕρκος 'inclosure, wall, fence', etc., with development through 'what constrains one' (to the truth) or perh. orig. a sacred 'inclosure' in which the oath was taken. Walde-P. 2.502. Boisacq 713.

2. Lat. *iūs iūrandum*, lit. 'right, law to be sworn', i.e. the formula used in taking oath, phrase cpd. of *iūs* 'right, law' and fut. pass. pple. of *iūrāre* 'swear'. From *iūrāre* also late Lat. *iūrāmentum* > It. *giuramento*, Sp. *juramento*, Rum. *jurămînt*. Ernout-M. 506. Walde-H. 1.733. REW 4629.

Fr. *serment*, fr. Lat. *sacrāmentum* 'pledge, oath of allegiance, military oath', fr. *sacrāre* 'make holy, consecrate' (: *sacer* 'holy'). REW 7492.

3. Ir. *luge*, W. *llw*, Br. *le* : Goth. *liuga* 'marriage', *liugan* 'marry', OHG *urliugi* 'war' (i.e. 'condition without oaths'). Gmc.-Celtic group for 'solemn promise' or 'oath', without further known connections. Walde-P. 2.415. Pedersen 1.69.

Ir. *ōeth*, cf. below, Goth. *aiþs*, etc.

NIr. *mionn*, orig. 'a sign, diadem' (so OIr. *mind*), whence 'relic, reliquary', then the 'oath' (taken upon the holy relics of saints, etc.). Cf. phrase *beirim mionna*, lit. 'bring relics' = 'take an oath, swear'.

4. Goth. *aiþs*, OE *āþ*, OHG *eid*, etc., general Gmc., Ir. *ōeth* (rare), W. *anudon* 'false oath', Gmc.-Celtic word of dub. etym. Walde-P. 1.103. Falk-Torp 179. Feist 29.

NHG *schwur*, as simplex only early NHG, OHG only *eidswuor* and MHG *meinswuor* 'false oath' : *schwören*, etc. 'swear' (21.24). Kluge-G. 554.

5. Lith. *priesaika* (neolog. in place of loanword *prisiega*), formed fr. *prisiekti* 'swear' (21.24).

Lett. *zvērs*, usually pl. *zvēri*, and *zvērējums* : *zvērēt* 'swear' (21.24). Mühl.-Endz. 4.772.

6. ChSl. *klętva* (also 'curse'), SCr. *zakletva* (*kletva* 'curse'), Russ. *kljatva* : ChSl. *klęti* 'curse', refl. 'swear' (21.24). Berneker 525.

ChSl. *prisęga* (late), SCr. *prisega*, Boh. *přísaha*, Pol. *przysięga*, Russ. *prisjaga* : SCr. *priseći*, etc. 'swear' (21.24).

7. Skt. *çapatha-*, also 'curse' : *çap-* 'curse', mid. 'swear' (21.24).

21.31 ACCUSE

Grk.	κατηγορέω (ἐγκαλέω αἰτιάομαι)	Goth.	*wrōhjan*	Lith.	*(ap)kaltinti, (ap)-skųsti*
NG	κατηγορῶ	ON	*kæra (ā)*	Lett.	*(ap)sūdzēt*
Lat.	*accūsāre*	Dan.	*anklage, beskylde*	ChSl.	*(vŭz)glagolati (na), vaditi (na)*
It.	*accusare*	Sw.	*anklaga, beskylla*	SCr.	*(op)tužiti*
Fr.	*accuser*	OE	*(be)tēon, wrēgan, onsprecan*	Boh.	*obžalovati, obviniti*
Sp.	*acusar*	ME	*a(c)cuse*	Pol.	*oskarżyć, obwinić*
Rum.	*acuza*	NE	*accuse*	Russ.	*obvinit'*
Ir.	*līim, (to-)ad-ness-, eiligim*	Du.	*aanklagen, beschuldigen*	Skt.	*abhiçaṅs-, abhiyuj-*
NIr.	*ēilighim*	OHG	*ruogen, zīhan, sculdigōn*		
W.	*cyhuddo*	MHG	*zīhen, ruegen, (be)-schuldigen*		
Br.	*tamall*	NHG	*anklagen, beschuldigen*		

Words for 'accuse' are partly derived from nouns for 'cause' or 'fault, guilt', partly from verbs meaning primarily 'speak against', 'summon', or 'complain'.

1. Grk. κατηγορέω (the usual term; also κατήγορος 'accuser', κατηγορία 'accusation'; so still NG), cpd. of κατά 'against' and a form parallel to ἀγορεύω 'speak in the assembly, harangue' and simply 'speak' (18.21).

Grk. ἐγκαλέω 'bring a charge, charge something (acc.) against (dat.)', cpd. of καλέω 'call' (18.41) also a legal term for 'summon'.

Grk. αἰτιάομαι 'accuse, censure, allege' (but not a usual legal term), fr. αἰτία 'cause, guilt' (16.76, 17.42).

In the archaic inscriptions of Elis 'accuse' is expressed by καταιραίω in form = Att. καθιερεύω 'consecrate' but here prob. with the adversative force of κατά and so orig. 'make impious, charge with impiety', in any case illustrating the religious background of legal procedure.

2. Lat. *accūsāre* (> Romance words; Rum. *acuza* neolog.), fr. **ad-causāre* : *causa* 'cause' (17.42), also 'lawsuit' (21.13).

3. Ir. *līim* : Goth. *laian* (pret. *lailō*) 'abuse, revile', Lith. *loti* 'bark', etc. Walde-P. 2.376. Pedersen 1.147.

Ir. *ad-ness-* and *to-ad-ness-*, cpds. of *ness-* seen in other cpds. meaning 'trample on, bruise' and 'disdain, condemn', with 'trample on' primary sense, and so perh. fr. **ni-stā-*, cpd. of IE **stā-* 'stand'. Walde-P. 2.603. Pedersen 2.583 f. Thurneysen, Gram. 523.

Ir. *eiligim*, with sb. *eiliugud* 'accusation' (Laws, Gloss. 293). NIr. *ēilighim* : Ir. 3sg. *in-loing* 'claims', orig. 'puts in' : Grk. λέχος 'couch', etc. Pedersen 2.570.

W. *cyhuddo* (MW *kuhud* 'accusation, complaint') : Ir. *consāidim* 'stir up strife', *cossāitim* 'complain, accuse', *cossāit*, NIr. *casaoid* 'accusation, complaint' (Ir. forms in Pedersen 2.605 f., K. Meyer, Contrib. 480, 498; no mention of W. forms). Evans, Welsh Dict. s.v. Lewis, Gloss. of Med. Welsh Law s.v. *kuhud* (p. 95).

Br. *tamall*, also sb. 'blame, accusation' (16.78), root connection?

4. Goth. *wrōhjan*, OE *wrēgan* (ME *bewreye* 'expose, reveal', as NE arch. *bewray*), OHG *ruogen*, MHG *ruegen* (NHG *rügen* 'reprove, denounce'), OS *wrōgian* (ON *rægja* 'slander, defame'), fr. sb. Goth. *wrōhs* 'accusation', beside OE, OS *wrōht* 'accusation, quarrel', MHG *ruoge*, *ruege* 'accusation, plaint', ON *rōg* 'slander, strife', root connection dub. Walde-P. 1.318. Feist 575.

ON kœra (with or without ā and acc., also with acc. 'plead a case', kœra māl), with sb. kœra 'plaint, dispute' : ON kǫr 'sick-bed', Goth. kara, OE cearu 'care, sorrow', OHG kara 'lamentation', etc. (16.14). Falk-Torp 520. Hellquist 547.

OE tēon, betēon (reg. words in the Laws, not wrēgan), OHG zīhan, MHG zīhen (NHG zeihen) = Goth. gateihan 'announce, make known' : Grk. δείκνυμι 'point out', Lat. dīcere 'say', etc. (18.22).

OE onsprecan, cpd. of sprecan 'speak' (18.21).

ME, NE accuse, fr. Fr. accuser (OFr. acuser, ME earliest spelling acuse), Lat. accūsāre (above, 2).

Du. aanklagen, NHG anklagen (> Dan. anklage, Sw. anklaga), cpds. of Du., NHG klagen 'complain, lament'.

OHG sculdigōn, MHG (be)schuldigen, NHG beschuldigen, Du. beschuldigen (hence semantically Dan. beskylde, Sw. beskylla), derivs., through OHG sculdig, NHG schuldig, etc. 'guilty, culpable', of OHG sculd, etc. 'fault, guilt' (16.76).

5. Lith. (ap)kaltinti : kalté 'guilt, blame' (16.76).

Lith. (ap)skųsti (so in the NT versions, and still in use; NSB), with skundas 'complaint, accusation' : skauda 'it hurts', skaudus 'painful', Grk. σκυδμαίνω, σκύζομαι 'be angry'. Walde-P. 2.554. Leskien, Ablaut 308.

Lett. (ap)sūdzēt, perh. : Lith. sugti 'howl, whine', saugti 'sound'. Mühl.-Endz. 3.1130 f.

6. ChSl. (vůz)glagolati (na), less commonly rešti (na), both vbs. for 'speak, say' (18.21, 18.22) with prep. na 'on, at, against', and so literal translations of κατηγορέω (Jagić, Entstehungsgesch. 325).

ChSl. vaditi (na) : Skt. vad- 'speak', Lith. vadinti 'call, name', etc. (18.21).

SCr. (op)tužiti, also and orig. 'complain' : tuga 'complaint, sorrow', ChSl. tǫga 'distress', tǫžiti 'be in distress', etc. (16.32). Miklosich 350.

Boh. obžalovati (Russ. obžalovat' 'complain', in legal use 'complain of, protest' a judgment) : ChSl. žalovati 'grieve, mourn', Boh. žal 'grief', etc. (16.32).

Boh. obviniti, Pol. obwinić, Russ. obvinit' : ChSl., Boh., Russ. vina, Pol. wina 'fault, guilt' (16.76).

Pol. oskarżyć, fr. skarga 'complaint, accusation' : ChSl. skrŭgati 'gnash' (the teeth), skrŭžetŭ 'gnashing' (Walde-P. 1.416). Brückner 493, 652. Miklosich 298, 303.

7. Skt. abhiçaṅs- cpd. of çaṅs- 'recite, announce' (= OPers. θah- 'say', 18.22; also 'praise' 16.79) and abhi- 'toward, against'.

Skt. abhiyuj- 'attack' and sometimes 'accuse', cpd. of yuj- 'yoke, join' (12.22).

21.32 CONDEMN

Grk. καταδικάζω, κατακρίνω	Goth. afdōmjan, gawargjan	Lith. nuteisti, nusmerkti
NG καταδικάζω	ON dœma	Lett. nuotiesāt, nuosuodīt
Lat. damnāre, condemnāre	Dan. dǿmme	ChSl. osǫditi
It. condannare	Sw. dōma	SCr. osuditi
Fr. condamner	OE fordēman	Boh. odsuditi
Sp. condenar	ME condem(p)ne	Pol. skazać, osǫdzić
Rum. condamna	NE condemn, dam(p)ne	Russ. osudit'
Ir. com-ness	Du. veroordeelen	Skt. nind-
NIr. beirim breith ar	OHG firtuomen	Av. par-
W. condemnio	MHG vertüemen, verteilen	
Br. barn	NHG verurteilen	

'Condemn' is most commonly expressed by compounds of the verbs for 'judge' with an adversative or perfective prefix, or by the simple verbs, the context ('against' or mention of the penalty) showing that the judgment is adverse. The Lat. word, which is the source of the Romance terms and our condemn, is derived from a noun for 'damage', with development through 'make pay damages'.

Other semantic sources are 'blame', 'trample on', 'submerge', and simply 'point out, declare'.

1. Grk. καταδικάζω, κατακρίνω, cpds. of κατά 'against' and δικάζω and κρίνω 'judge' (21.16).

2. Lat. damnāre and cpd. condemnāre (hence, or fr. re-formed *con-damnāre, the Romance words), deriv. of damnum 'damage, loss' (11.74) and in legal language 'damages', hence the vb. orig. 'inflict loss upon, make one pay damages'. Ernout-M. 252. Walde-H. 1.322.

3. Ir. com-ness- 'trample on', and 'condemn', cpd. of ness- as in ad-ness-, to-ad-ness- 'accuse', etc. (21.31).

NIr. usually simply beirim breith ar 'judge' (21.16), e.g. beirim breith chum bāis air 'I condemn him to death'.

W. condemnio, fr. NE condemn.

Br. barn 'judge' (21.16) used also for 'condemn', e.g. barn d'ar maro 'condemn to death' (cf. Vallée s.v. condamner).

4. Goth. afdōmjan, OE fordēman, OHG firtuomen, MHG vertüemen, cpds. of Goth. dōmjan, OE dēman, OHG tuomen 'judge' (21.16) and partly also (esp. OE) 'condemn'; ON dœma, Dan. dǿmme,

Sw. dōma both 'judge' and 'condemn' (ON fyrirdœma mostly 'curse, damn').

Goth. ga-wargjan (with sb. wargiþa 'condemnation') : OE wiergan 'curse', etc. (22.24).

ME condempne, condemne, NE condemn, ME damne, dampne (NE damn), fr. OFr. condem(p)ner (beside condam(p)ner), dam(p)ner, Lat. condemnāre, damnāre (above, 2). NED s.vv.

MHG verteilen (with dat. of pers. and acc. of penalty, or absolute with acc. of person), lit. 'distribute, share', cpd. of teilen 'divide'.

MHG (late), NHG verurteilen, Du. veroordeelen, cpds. of urteilen, oordeelen 'judge' (21.16).

5. Lith. nuteisti, Lett. nuotiesāt, Lith. nusudyti (Kurschat, Lalis; not in NSB), Lett. nuosuodīt, perfect. cpds. of verbs for 'judge' (21.16).

Lith. nusmerkti (NSB), pasmerkti, cpds. of smerkti 'submerge, plunge'.

6. ChSl. osǫditi, etc., general Slavic (but Pol. osǫdzić less usual than skazać), perfect. cpds. of ChSl. sǫditi, etc. 'judge' (21.16).

Pol. skazać = Russ. skazat' 'say', etc., orig. 'point out' (18.22).

7. Skt. nind- 'blame' (16.18), used also as legal term 'condemn' (e.g. Manu 8.19).

Av. par- (cf. also parəta-, pəša- in cpds. 'condemned, forfeit', pāra- 'fault, guilt', prob. the same root as in par-, aipi-par- 'pay off' (a penalty), this : Lat. pār, paris 'equal', or : par-, IE *pel- 'fill'?. Walde-P. 2.40. Barth. 849, 850.

21.33 CONVICT (vb.)

Grk. αἱρέω (ἐλέγχω)	Goth. gasakan	Lith. apreikšti kaltu
NG ἀποδεικνύω ἔνοχον	ON dœma sekan	Lett. atzīt par vainigu
Lat. convincere	Dan. overbevise	ChSl. obličiti
It. convincere, condannare	Sw. överbevisa	SCr. dokazati
Fr. convaincre, condamner	OE oferstælan	Boh. usvědčiti
Sp. convencer, condenar	ME convict(e)	Pol. przekonač
Rum. găsi vinovat	NE convict	Russ. priznat' vinovnym
Ir. cintach + vb. (?)	Du. schuldig verklaren	Skt. vibhāvaya-
NIr. daoraim	OHG giwinnan, thwingan	
W. euogfarnu, euogbrofi	MHG gewinnen	
Br. kavout kablus	NHG überführen	

Verbs for 'convict' are based on such notions as 'take, catch' (a natural and frequent nontechnical expression, but only in Greek the reg. legal term), 'conquer, prevail, overcome', 'prove', 'bear witness', 'confront', etc. Some words for 'condemn' or 'accuse' are also used for 'convict'. The use of the Lat. convincere, mainly 'convict' but also 'prove' and later 'convince', has fostered some interchange of 'convince' and 'convict' elsewhere.

'Convict' is also frequently expressed by phrases made up of words for 'prove', 'declare, pronounce', 'judge', or 'find' with those for 'guilty' (21.35), e.g. Fr. déclarer coupable, Rum. găsi vinovat (găsi 'find', both words fr. Slavic), Br. kavout kablus, ON dœma sekan, NE find guilty, NHG für schuldig erklären, Lith. apreikšti kaltu, Russ. priznat' vinovnym, etc. W. euogfarnu and euogbrofi are similar phrase cpds. of euog 'guilty' with barnu 'judge' and profi 'prove'.

Such phrases are the usual expressions in several languages, and in some others may perhaps be more common than the simple verbs entered in the list. They require no further comment.

1. Grk. αἱρέω 'seize, take, catch' (11.13) is the reg. legal term for 'convict', not only in Attic, but elsewhere, e.g. in the Gortyn law-code αἴ κα αἱλεθῇ 'if one is caught', i.e. 'convicted'.

Grk. ἐλέγχω, in Hom. 'treat with contempt', later 'examine', 'prove', also 'convict' (Hdt.+ and so in part in the NT), perh. : Lett. langāt 'treat with contempt, call names', further connections? Walde-P. 2.436. Boisacq 240. Mühl.-Endz. 2.420.

2. Lat. convincere, cpd. of vincere 'conquer, prevail' (20.41). Cf. Osc. eizeic (loc. sg.) vincter = Lat. eius (or in eo) convincitur. The Romance derivs. mean 'convince' in common use, but are also used for 'convict', esp. in the pples. It. convinto, Fr. convaincu, Sp. convicto 'convicted, guilty'.

Lat. arguere 'declare, assert', but esp. 'censure, accuse', late also 'convict', orig. 'make clear' : Grk. ἀργός, Skt. arjuna- 'shining, white', Grk. ἄργυρος, Lat. argentum 'silver', etc. Walde-P. 1.82 f. Ernout-M. 71 f. Walde-H. 1.66 f. This verb is the Vulgate rendering of ἐλέγχω including the passages where the meaning is 'convict', and this has affected other versions, e.g. in Jn. 8.46 OE āscūnian (mostly 'shun, detest'), NE argue in a version of 1582 (cf. NED s.v.).

It. condannare, Fr. condamner, Sp. condenar 'condemn' (21.32) are also sometimes used where the sense is 'convict'.

3. Ir. cintach 'guilty' with vb., used for 'convict' (quotable?).

NIr. daoraim, fr. daor 'enslaved,

guilty', opp. of saor 'free' and prob. formed directly as a pendant to saoraim 'acquit' (21.34).

4. Goth. gasakan (rendering ἐλέγχω, including the sense 'convict', as Jn. 8.46), cpd. of sakan 'contend, reproach' (cf. sakjō 'strife', 19.62).

Dan. overbevise, Sw. överbevisa 'convince' and 'convict', cpds. of Dan. bevise, Sw. bewisa 'prove', fr. MLG bewisen = NHG beweisen 'prove'. Falk-Torp 66.

OE oferstælan 'confute' and 'convict', cpd. of stælan 'impute (a crime to), charge' : on-stāl 'charge, accusation', stellan 'set, place', etc.

ME, NE convict, fr. pple. of Lat. convincere (above, 2).

NE convince was formerly also used not only as 'convince', but also as 'convict' (NED s.v. 4).

OHG giwinnan, MHG gewinnen 'gain, acquire, overcome' (: NE win, etc.) were also used for 'convict', like and prob. influenced by Lat. convincere.

OHG dwingan 'press, oppress' (NHG zwingen 'compel', 19.48), also 'convict' (thwingan Tat. for Vulgate arguere).

NHG überführen, since late 16th cent. 'convict' and for a time also 'convince' (now überzeugen), fr. überführen 'lead across, transport' (cf. führen 'lead', 10.64). Semantic development through 'bring over' to one's side by arguments, or through 'bring in' witnesses, or still more specifically through 'lead by' the corpse of the slain (with allusion to a popular belief that the corpse bleeds in the presence of the murderer)? Paul, Deutsches Wtb. 559. Weigand-H. 2.1096.

5. Lith. and Lett. now apparently have only the phrases 'declare guilty'. In the Lith. NT versions kaltinti 'accuse' (21.31) is used for 'convict', e.g. Jn. 8.46, following Luther's zeihen. The Lett. version has pierādīt 'prove'.

6. ChSl. obličiti (in Gospels renders ἐλέγχω, including Jn. 8.46), fr. lice 'face', hence orig. 'bring face to face, confront'. Cf. Russ. obličit' 'convince, denounce', also 'convict' (of a lie, etc.) but not a legal term (for which priznat' vinovnym 'recognize as guilty').

SCr. dokazati 'prove', sometimes 'convince' and 'convict', cpd. of kazati 'say', orig. 'point out, show' (18.22). More commonly (?) the phrase proglasiti krivim 'pronounce guilty'.

Boh. usvědčiti 'bear witness, prove', also 'convince' and 'convict', fr. svědek 'witness' (21.23).

Pol. przekonać 'convince' and 'convict', in early use 'finish, dispose of' (cf. Linde s.v.), cpd. of konać : koniec 'end' (14.26).

7. Skt. vibhāvaya- (caus. of vi-bhū- 'come into existence, appear', cpd. of bhū- 'become, be') 'make appear, prove' is also sometimes 'convict' (Yajñ. 2.20, Minor Nārāda 1.9.5).

Cf. Skt. dṛṣṭa-doṣa-, lit. 'having one's sin seen', hence 'detected' or 'convicted' (e.g. Manu 8.64).

21.34 ACQUIT

Grk.	ἀπολύω	Goth.	(fralētan)	Lith.	išteisinti
NG	ἀθῳώνω, ἀπαλλάσσω	ON	dœma syknan	Lett.	attaisnuot
Lat.	absolvere	Dan.	frikende, frifinde	ChSl.	(pustiti)
It.	assolvere	Sw.	frikänna	SCr.	riješiti
Fr.	acquitter, absoudre	OE	(forlætan)	Boh.	osvoboditi
Sp.	absolver	ME	acwite, assoille	Pol.	uznać niewinnym
Rum.	achita	NE	acquit	Russ.	opravdat', priznat'
Ir.	lēicim(?)	Du.	vrijspreken		nevinovnym
NIr.	saoraim	OHG	(ar-lōsen)	Skt.	(muc-)
W.	dieuogi	MHG	(læsen)		
Br.	didamall	NHG	freisprechen		

Most of the words for 'acquit' in a legal sense are the same as, or cpds. of, those for 'release' (11.34). Some are based on words for 'free', or 'justify', or the notion may be expressed by phrases 'pronounce innocent'. In several cases words for 'release' have been put in the list, inclosed in parentheses, by which is meant that quotable examples for the legal 'acquit' have not been found.

1. Grk. ἀπολύω 'release' (11.34) and 'acquit'.

NG ἀθῳώνω, fr. ἀθῷος 'innocent' (21.36).

NG ἀπαλλάσσω 'release' (as in class. Grk., 11.34) and 'acquit'.

2. Lat. absolvere (> It. assolvere, Fr. absoudre, Sp. absolver), cpd. of solvere 'untie, release, set free' (11.34).

Fr. acquitter (> Rum. achita), fr. quitter, OFr. quitier 'free of a debt or obligation, leave', deriv. of quitte 'free from debt or obligation', fr. Lat. quiētus 'at rest, quiet'. REW 6958. Gamillscheg 10,732.

3. Ir. lēicim 'leave, let, let go, release' (11.34), prob. used also for 'acquit'.

NIr. saoraim, lit. 'free, deliver', fr. saor 'free' (19.44).

W. dieuogi, fr. dieuog 'innocent' (21.36).

Br. didamall (Vallée), cpd. of neg. di- and tamall 'blame', as vb. 'accuse' (21.31).

4. Goth. fra-lētan, af-lētan, usual for ἀπολύω 'release, dismiss, set free' (11.34)

and presumably 'acquit', though not quotable in this sense.

ON dœma syknan, lit. 'judge innocent' (sykn 'innocent', 21.36).

Dan. frikende, Sw. frikänna, cpds. of fri 'free' and kende, känna 'know, feel, deem'.

Dan. frifinde, cpd. of fri 'free' and finde 'find'.

OE forlætan 'release' (11.34), 'forgive' (crimes, sins, etc.), also 'acquit'(?).

ME acwite, acwyte, NE acquit, fr. OFr. aquiter (above, 2). For history of uses, cf. NED s.v.

ME assoille, NE assoil (now arch.), fr. OFr. assoill-, pres. stem of assoldre (Fr. absoudre, above, 2). NED s.v. assoil.

NE absolve, fr. Lat. absolvere. Now unusual as legal term. NED s.v. absolve 4.

OHG lōsen esp. with ar-, zi- (common for Lat. solvere, absolvere), MHG læsen 'release' (11.34), used for 'acquit'?

NHG freisprechen, Du. vrijspreken, cpds. of frei, frij 'free' and sprechen, spreken 'speak'.

5. Lith. išteisinti, cpd. of teisinti 'justify' : teisė 'right, law' (21.11).

Lett. attaisnuot, cpd. of taisnuot 'make straight, justify', fr. taisns 'straight, right' (12.73).

6. ChSl. pustiti, otŭpustiti 'release' (11.34), also 'acquit'(?).

SCr. riješiti 'solve, dispose of' and

'acquit' = ChSl. rěšiti 'loose, release' (11.34), Russ. rešat' 'solve, decide'.

Pol. uznać niewinnym, Russ. priznat' nevinovnym 'pronounce not guilty, innocent' (21.36).

Russ. opravdat' 'justify' and 'acquit', fr. pravda 'truth' (16.66).

7. Skt. muc-, the general word for 'release, set free' (11.34).

21.35 GUILTY

Grk.	αἴτιος, ἔνοχος	Goth.	skula	Lith.	kaltas
NG	ἔνοχος	ON	sekr, sannr	Lett.	vainīgs
Lat.	sōns, noxius	Dan.	skyldig	ChSl.	(po)vinĭnŭ
It.	colpevole, reo	Sw.	skyldig	SCr.	kriv
Fr.	coupable	OE	scyldig, gyltig	Boh.	vinný
Sp.	culpable, reo	ME	gylti	Pol.	winny
Rum.	vinovat	NE	guilty	Russ.	vinovnyj
Ir.	cintach	Du.	schuldig	Skt.	aparādhin-, aparā-
NIr.	cionntach	OHG	sculdig		dha-, ṛṇa-
W.	euog	MHG	schuldic		
Br.	kablus	NHG	schuldig		

Most of the words for 'guilty' are obvious derivs. of those for 'guilt', which are among those discussed with 'fault' (16.76). Only the few others require further comment.

1. Grk. ἔνοχος, orig. 'held in, bound by' (: ἐνέχω 'hold in'), hence as legal term 'liable to' the laws, etc., whence also 'liable to' a certain penalty or to the penalty for a certain crime, and so 'guilty', becoming the usual word (rather than αἴτιος) from Hellenistic times (e.g. NT) to the present.

2. Lat. sōns, sontis (most commonly sb. 'guilty person', but also adj.), orig. pres. pple. of esse 'be', hence 'actual', like Skt. satya- 'true', etc. (16.66). Cf. esp. the cognate ON sannr 'true' and sometimes 'guilty'. Walde-P. 1.160 f. Ernout-M. 957.

Lat. reus 'defendant' (21.22) was used more often than not of the guilty party and eventually restricted to this sense. Hence It., Sp. reo sb. and adj.

3. W. euog, fr. MW geuawc 'false', this fr. geu, gau 'false' : Ir. gáu, etc. 'lie' (16.67). Lewis-Pedersen 130. Morris Jones 188.

Br. kablus, fr. a late Lat. cavillōsus, deriv. of cavilla 'jeering, railery'. For sense cf. Corn. cably 'calumniate, incriminate'. Loth, Mots lat. 141.

4. Goth. skula (also 'debtor'), though not fr. the noun, like OE scyldig, etc., is fr. the same underlying verb, Goth. skulan 'owe'.

ON sannr 'true' and 'guilty' : Lat. sōns (above, 2).

21.36 INNOCENT

Grk.	ἀθῷος	Goth.	swikns	Lith.	nekaltas
NG	ἀθῷος	ON	úsekr, úsannr, sykn	Lett.	nevainīgs
Lat.	innocēns	Dan.	uskyldig	ChSl.	ne povinĭnŭ
It.	innocente	Sw.	oskyldig	SCr.	nekriv
Fr.	innocent	OE	unscyldig	Boh.	nevinný
Sp.	inocente	ME	innocent	Pol.	niewinny
Rum.	inocent, nevinovat	NE	innocent	Russ.	nevinnyj
Ir.	na cintach (?)	Du.	onschuldig	Skt.	anṛṇa-, niraparā-
NIr.	neamhchionntach	OHG	unsculdig		dhavat-
W.	dieuog, diniwed	MHG	unschuldic		
Br.	dikablus	NHG	unschuldig		

Most of the words for 'innocent' are simply neg. cpds. of those for 'guilty' (21.35). Only the few others need comment. It is a widespread phenomenon that the words for 'innocent', apart from their legal use, develop, through 'harmless, guileless', a disparaging sense 'credulous, naïve, simple, foolish'.

1. Grk. ἀθῷος, neg. cpd., second part : θωά, Ion. θω(ι)ή 'penalty', fine (21.38).

2. Lat. innocēns, -entis (> Romance words and ME, NE forms), lit. 'not injuring, harmless', neg. cpd. of pres. pple. of nocēre 'harm, injure' (11.28).

3. Goth. swikns (mostly for ἁγνός 'pure, chaste', once for ὅσιος 'holy'; for ἀθῷος in Mt. 27.4, the passage Mt. 27.24 being lacking), ON sykn : OE (ge)swicn 'cleansing, clearance from a charge', root connection? Feist 467. Falk-Torp 1233, 1562.

21.37 PENALTY, PUNISHMENT

Grk.	ζημία, τιμωρία (ποινή, τίμη)	Goth.	(balweins)	Lith.	bauda, bausmė
		ON	refsing, víti	Lett.	suods
NG	ποινή, τιμωρία	Dan.	straf	ChSl.	(po)kaznĭ
Lat.	poena (damnum, noxa)	Sw.	straff	SCr.	kazan
		OE	wíte	Boh.	trest, pokuta
It.	pena	ME	peine, punisshement	Pol.	kara
Fr.	peine	NE	penalty, punishment	Russ.	nakazanie, kara
Sp.	pena	Du.	straf	Skt.	daṇḍa-
Rum.	pedeapsă	OHG	wīzi	Av.	čiϑā-, kaēnā- (OPers.
Ir.	pían, dīgal	MHG	strâfe, pīn(e)		pars-, vb.)
NIr.	pionōs, smachtbhann	NHG	strafe		
W.	cosb, poen				
Br.	poan				

Among the words for 'penalty' or legal 'punishment' an important group is based on a root the primary sense of which was probably 'repay, requite' (either good or evil), whence the derivs. denoted, on the one hand, the 'penalty', and on the other 'reward, price, honor'. Cf. the double force, according to the context, of words like NE requital and retribution (the latter now felt as return

for evil, but formerly also return for good, 'reward'; NED s.v.).

Just as Lat. animadvertere 'turn the mind to, observe, notice' came to be used in a pregnant sense 'censure, punish', so several of the words for 'penalty' come from verbs meaning 'point out, show'.

A recurring relationship between 'education' and 'punishment' is illustrated,

with all the stages quotable, by Grk. παιδεύω 'rear a child' (: παῖς, παιδός 'child'), 'educate', 'correct, discipline', and finally 'chastise, punish', whence, through the noun παίδευσις, the reg. Rum. word for 'penalty'. Cf. also NHG zucht 'rearing, breeding' (of cattle, plants, etc.), 'education', 'discipline', and esp. züchtigen 'censure' and 'chastise, punish'; Skt. çās- 'teach' (17.23) and 'censure, punish' (cf. NE colloq. threatening I'll teach you).

A shift from 'ask, question' through 'examine, investigate' to a resulting 'punish' is seen in the OPers. verb for 'punish' (below, 8).

A word for the 'rod' may, as the symbol, be used for 'punishment', not merely parental but covering any legal 'penalty' (Boh. trest, Skt. daṇḍa-, below, 7, 8). In the Avesta the most common penalty is so many 'blows with the horse-goad', etc.

In words reflecting the 'rod', the primary application was obviously to corporal punishment. In some others the verbal 'censure, blame' seems to be earlier. Still others (ON refsing, NHG strafe) may, on the basis of their cognates, have developed in either of these two ways or both together.

In one case the development has been from 'judgment' through 'legal condemnation'.

Verbs for 'punish' are mostly parallel with the nouns listed, either derived from them, as Lat. pūnire, fr. poena, or conversely. But there are also others unrelated, as Lat. animadvertere (cf. above), OPers. pars- (below, 8), Grk. κολάζω (orig. 'check' : κόλος 'docked', hence κόλασις late 'punishment, damnation, hell'), Lat. castīgāre (fr. castus 'pure' 'correct, blame, chastise, punish' (> Fr. châtier, Sp. castigar, with

back-formation castigo 'punishment' but not a legal term), Skt. çās- (cf. above).

1. Derivs. of *kʷei-, seen in Grk. τίνω (fut. τείσω, aor. ἔτεισα) 'pay (a debt, esp. a penalty), atone for', Skt. ci- (pres. mid. cayate) 'avenge, punish', Av. či- (redupl. pres. subj. čikayat; kāy- Barth.) 'pay, atone for' (perh. ultimately the same root as in Skt. ci- 'notice, observe, honor', ChSl. čayati 'expect, hope', with development like that in Lat. animadvertere). From the sense of 'pay for, requite' (in good or bad sense) was derived a group of nouns denoting either 'penalty' or 'reward, honor, price'. Walde-P. 1.508 f.

Grk. ποινή (> Lat. poena, etc., see below), τίμη (see below); Av. čiϑā- and kaēnā-; cf. Lith. kaina, ChSl. cěna 'price' (11.88).

2. Grk. ποινή (above, 1), occurring mainly in poetry, is sometimes simply 'return, recompense' including 'reward', but mostly 'penalty', esp. recompense for the slain, either 'wergeld' or 'vengeance'. The word plays no role in Attic legal writings or in the legal inscriptions of the dialects. Yet the Doric ποινά must have been current in Magna Graecia when the Lat. poena was borrowed. It has been revived in NG as the main legal term.

Grk. τίμή, mostly 'honor' or 'value, price', rarely 'penalty'. Hence (through cpd. adj. τίμά-opos) τιμωρία 'vengeance, punishment'.

Grk. ζημία 'loss, damage' (11.74) is also the usual Attic term for 'penalty, fine', whence ζημιόω 'penalize, fine', these being also the most widespread terms in the dialects (mostly with reference to fines).

3. Lat. poena, an early loanword fr. Grk. ποινά, was, in contrast to its Grk. source, the persistent legal term and also

a popular word for 'punishment' in general and in late use 'suffering, pain'. Hence the double sense, 'penalty' vs. 'pain' or 'grief', in its derivatives, It., Sp. *pena*, Fr. *peine*, Ir. *pian*, W. *poen*, Br. *poan*, ME *peine* (fr. Fr.; NE *pain* in older sense now only in phrases like *on pain of death*), MHG *pīn*, *pīne* (both senses, that of 'penalty' reintroduced; OHG *pīna* only 'affliction, distress'), Russ. *penja* 'fine'. From Lat. adj. *poenālis* 'penal' was formed MLat. *poenālitās*, whence NE *penalty*.

Hence also the vb. *pūnīre* 'punish' (> It. *punire*, Fr. *punir*, the latter through the *puniss-* forms > ME *punisse*, *punisshe*, etc., NE *punish*) and new derivs. like late Lat. *pūnītiō* (> It. *punizione*, Fr. *punition*), OFr. *puni(s)sement* (> ME *ponissement*, *punysshement*, NE *punishment*, this group being used mostly for 'punishment' in the broader, non-legal, sense).

Lat. *damnum* 'damage, loss' (11.74) is also used for 'penalty'.

Lat. *noxa* 'injury, guilt' (16.76) is also in late use 'penalty'.

Rum. *pedeapsă*, in earliest use also 'education', fr. Grk. παίδευσις (in late pronunciation = -εψις) 'education', NG παιδεψι 'punishment', which shared in the development attested for the vb. παιδεύω, namely 'educate' > 'correct, discipline' > 'chastise, punish' (LXX, NT, e.g. Lk. 23.16).

4. Ir. *smacht* 'authority, control', also a kind of 'penalty' or 'fine' (Laws, Gloss. 665 f.), etym.? Cf. NIr. *cuirim smacht ar* 'punish' (lit. 'put control on').

Ir. *dīgal* 'vengeance, retribution, punishment' (cf. e.g. Thes. 1.55.26, 29, 31), vbl.n. to *dofichim* 'avenge, punish' (cpd. of *fichim* 'fight'), but in form : Ir. *gal* 'bravery' (16.52). Pedersen 1.101, 2.25, 521.

NIr. *pionōs* (given by McKenna for 'penalty', and so Gael. *peanas;* in Dinneen 'penance, worry'), fr. *pian*, formerly 'penalty' (above, 3) now only 'pain'.

NIr. *smachtbhann* ('penalty' Dinneen), cpd. of *smacht* (above) with *bann* 'bond'.

W. *cosb* = Ir. *cosc* 'correcting, chastising', vbl. n. of *coscaim* 'check, correct', cpd. (*con-sech-*) of the root in Grk. ἔννεπε, Lat. *inseque* 'relate, tell', OE *secgan* 'say', etc., IE **sekʷ-* (18.22). Walde-P. 2.478. Pedersen 2.619 ff.

5. Goth. *balweins* 'punishment, torment' (but not legal 'penalty', for which nothing is quotable) : *balwa-wesei* 'wickedness', OE *bealo* 'evil, wickedness', etc. Feist 79.

ON *refsing*, fr. *refsa* 'punish' (Dan. *revse* 'chastise, punish') = OE *refsan*, *repsan*, OHG *refsen*, etc. 'reprove, blame' : Lat. *rapere* 'seize, carry off', Skt. *rapas-* 'bodily defect, injury', etc. Walde-P. 2.369 f. Falk-Torp 894 f.

ON *vīti*, OE *wīte* (ME, NE dial. *wite*, *wyte* 'blame, reproach', NED s.v.), OHG *wīzi*, fr. the root **weid-* in words for 'see' and 'know'. Cf. OE *wītan*, OHG (*far*)-*wīzan* 'impute the guilt, blame', Goth. *fra-weitan* 'avenge', and the parallel semantic development in Lat. *animadvertere*.

MHG *strāfe*, NHG *strafe*, MLG *straffe* (> Dan. *straf*, Sw. *straff*), Du. *straf*, beside vb. MHG *strāfen*, etc. 'blame, censure, punish', prob. as orig. 'treat severely' (physically, verbally, or both?) : MHG *straf*, NHG *straff* 'tense, severe'. Falk-Torp 1176. Franck-v. W. 673.

6. Lith. *bauda*, *bausmė*, fr. *bausti* 'punish' (but refl. *baustis* 'prepare oneself, intend') : *budėti* 'be awake', Skt. *budh-* 'be awake, notice', etc., with development as in Lat. *animadvertere*, etc.

Lett. *suods*, fr. ORuss. *sud* 'legal condemnation', orig. 'court' and 'judgment' (21.15, 21.17). Mühl.-Endz. 3.1136.

7. ChSl. (*po*)*kaznĭ*, SCr. *kazan*, Russ. *nakazanie*, fr. ChSl. *kazati*, etc. 'point out, show' (cf. SCr. *kazati*, Russ. *skazat'* 'say', 18.22). Cf. ChSl. *pokazati* rendering παιδεύω 'chastise' Lk. 23.16, 22, *nakazanĭje* 'admonition' (Supr.), etc. Berneker 496 f.

Boh. *trest* (masc.) : *trest'* (fem.) 'reed, cane' (whence also 'juice pressed out, extract, essence', etc.), Pol. *treść* 'pith, essence, contents', ChSl. *trŭstĭ* 'reed'. Cf. OPol. *tres(t)kać* 'chastise, torment, punish' (Linde s.v.). Development through the 'rod' of punishment, as in Skt. *daṇḍa-*. Prob. through vb. *trestiti* ('use the rod' >) 'punish', whence backformation *trest*. Brückner 576.

Boh. *pokuta* = Pol. *pokuta* 'penance', formerly 'guilt' and 'punishment' : ChSl. *sŭ-kątati* (Supr.) rendering κατα-στέλλω 'restrain, appease, quiet' (Russ. *kutat'* 'wrap up, envelop', etc.), with development through 'appeasement'. Berneker 601 f. Brückner 428.

Pol., Russ. *kara* = SCr. *kar* 'scolding', Boh. *kara* 'censure' : ChSl. *u-korŭ* 'insult', SCr. *u-kor*, *prije-kor*, *po-kor* 'blame', vbs. ChSl. (*u*)*koriti* 'insult, slander', SCr. *koriti* 'blame', etc. (16.78). Berneker 487 f., 578 f.

8. Skt. *daṇḍa-* 'rod, staff' (etym.? Walde-P. 1.810), hence in various symbolic uses (e.g. 'power'), but esp. as the reg. legal term for 'penalty' of any kind.

Av. *čiθā-*, *kaēnā-*, above, 1.

In OPers. the regular verb for 'punish' is *pars-*, *fras-* (e.g. *parsāmiy* 'I punish', *avam ufrasatam aparsam* 'him well punished I punished', i.e. 'punished severely') = Av. *pərəs-*, *fras-*, Skt. *pṛcch-*, *pracch-* 'ask' (18.31).

21.38 FINE

Grk.	*ζημία* (*θωά*, *πρόστīμον*)	Goth.	....	Lith.	(*piniginė*) *bausmė*
NG	*πρόστιμο*	ON	*vīti*, *bōt*	Lett.	(*naudas*) *suods*
Lat.	*multa*	Dan.	*mulkt*, *bøde*	ChSl.	....
It.	*ammenda*, *multa*	Sw.	*plikt*, *böter*	SCr.	*globa*
Fr.	*amende*	OE	*wīte*, *bōt*	Boh.	*pokuta*
Sp.	*multa*	ME	*fin*	Pol.	*kara pieniężna*
Rum.	*amendă*, *gloabă*	NE	*fine*	Russ.	*štraf*
Ir.	*dīre*, *ēric*	Du.	*boete*	Skt.	*daṇḍa-*
NIr.	*cāin*	OHG	*buoza*	Av.	*čiθā-*
W.	*ffin*, *dirwy*	MHG	*buoze*		
Br.	*tell-gastiz*	NHG	*busse* (*geldbusse*, *geldstrafe*, *strafgeld*)		

The words listed under 'penalty' (21.37) are comprehensive, covering the 'fine' in money or other property. Most of them are in fact, for the earlier periods, those commonly employed when the reference is to a 'fine', e.g. Grk. ζημία (Lat. *poena* in XII Tables, but not commonly), OE *wīte*, Skt. *daṇḍa-*, Av. *čiθā-*. Or they may be made more specific by the addition of words for 'money', like NHG *geldstrafe*, *strafgeld*, Lith. *piniginė bausmė*, Pol. *kara pieniężna*, etc. Such words are repeated in this list, but need no further comment.

But there are also special words for 'fine', as follows.

1. Grk. Att. θωά (IG 1^2.114.42; but unknown in Att. authors, where reg. ζημία), Hom. θωή, Ion. θωιή, θωυή, fr. the root of τίθημι 'place, put' (with the ō-grade as in θωμός 'heap', OE *dōms* 'judgment'), and so orig. the 'set' amount. Hence the more widely quotable vbs. for 'pay a fine', pass. 'be fined',

θωάω (early Att., Locr., Delph.), Cret. θωαίω, El. θωάδδω. Walde-P. 1.829. Boisacq 360.

Grk. πρόστīμον ('penalty' Hipp.), freq. as 'fine' from 3d cent. B.C. and the usual NG word : τιμή (21.37).

2. Lat. *multa* (early *molta*, Osc. acc. sg. *moltam*, Umbr. gen. sg. *motar*), etym. dub., perh. fr. **molktā* either as orig. 'appeasement' : *mulcēre* 'stroke, soothe, appease', or as orig. 'injury' : *mulcāre* 'beat, injure', Skt. *mṛc-* 'hurt, injure', pple. *mṛktá-* 'hurt', etc. Hence (learned words) It., Sp. *multa*, OFr. *multe* (> NE *mult*), and, through a medieval spelling *mulcta*, OFr. *mulcte*, NE *mulct*, Dan. *mulkt*. Walde-P. 2.297. Ernout-M. 638 f.

It. *ammenda*, Fr. *amende* (> Rum. *amendă*), back-formation fr. obs. OIt. *ammendare*, Fr. *amender*, these fr. Lat. *ēmendāre* 'free from fault (*mendum*), correct, emend'.

Rum. *gloabă*, fr. SCr., Bulg. *globa* (below, 6).

3. Ir. *dīre* and *ēric* (for their special applications cf. Laws, Gloss., and Thurneysen, Abh. Preuss. Akad. 1931, no. 2, pp. 1 ff.), vbl. ns. of *dī-renim* and *as-renim* 'pay' (11.65). Here also W. *dirwy*. Pedersen 2.596 f.

NIr. *cāin*, fr. Ir. *cāin* 'law, rule' (21.12).

W. *ffin*, fr. NE *fine*.

MW *galanas* 'fine for homicide, wergeld' (Lewis, Gloss. of Med. Welsh Law, s.v.), rarely also 'murder' : Ir. *fingal* 'murder of fellow-clansmen' (Laws, Gloss. 363; cpd. of *fine* 'clan, kindred' 19.23), *dīgal* 'punishment' (21.37), *irgal* 'battle' (20.12), *gal* 'bravery' (16.52).

Br. *tell-gastiz* (so Vallée s.v. *amende*), cpd. of *tell* 'tax' (11.69) and *kasti(z)* 'punishment', fr. OFr. *c(h)aste*, back-formation fr. vb. *c(h)astier* (Fr. *châtier*), Lat. *castigāre* (Loth, Mots lat. 145).

4. ON, OE *bōt* (ON mostly in pl. *bœtr*), Dan. *bøde*, Sw. *böter*, Du. *boete*, OHG *buoza*, MHG *buoze*, NHG *busse*, in earlier period 'betterment, profit, remedy' (Goth. *bōta* 'profit', cf. NE *to boot*), fr. the root of Goth. *batiza* 'better', NE *better*, etc. Hence also (even early) 'atonement, compensation' and esp. 'fine' (for which also more specifically e.g. NHG *geldbusse;* also *geldstrafe* or *strafgeld*). Walde-P. 2.152. Feist 103. NED s.v. *boot* sb.

ON *manngjǫld*, OE *wergeld*, OHG *wer(i)gelt*, etc. 'fine for homicide, wergeld', cpds. of words for 'man' (2.11) and 'payment' (later 'money' 11.43).

Sw. *plikt* 'duty' (fr. MLG *plicht* = NHG *pflicht* id.) is also a legal term for 'fine'.

ME *fin* (rarely in this sense), NE *fine*, through OFr. *fin*, fr. Lat. *fīnis* 'end', with development through 'ending of a dispute, final settlement' a sense known also in MLat. and OFr. NED s.v. *fine*, sb.[1] III.

5. Lith. (*piniginė*) *bausmė*, Lett. (*naudas*) *suods*, that is, the words for 'penalty' with or without words for 'money' (11.43).

6. SCr., Bulg. *globa* (> Rum. *gloabă*, Alb. *gjobë*) : SCr. *z-globiti* 'put together', *z-glob* 'joint' (OPol. *głobić* 'oppress', *globa* 'distress', etc.), with development prob. through 'fitted, fixed' (amount). Berneker 143.

Russ. *štraf*, fr. NHG *strafe* (21.37).

21.39 PRISON, JAIL

Grk.	*εἱρκτή*, *δεσμωτήριον*, *φυλακή*	Goth.	*karkara*	Lith.	*kalėjimas*
		ON	*myrkvastofa*, *fangelsi*	Lett.	*cietums*
NG	*φυλακή*	Dan.	*fængsel*	ChSl.	*temĭnica*
Lat.	*carcer*	Sw.	*fängelse*	SCr.	*zatvor*
It.	*prigione*, *carcere*	OE	*cweartern*, *carcern*	Boh.	*vězení*, *žalář*
Fr.	*prison*, *geôle*	ME	*prison*, *gay(h)ol(e)*	Pol.	*więzienie*
Sp.	*prisión*, *cárcel*	NE	*prison*, *jail*	Russ.	*tjur'ma* (*temnica*, *ostrog*)
Rum.	*închisoare*	Du.	*gevangenis*		
Ir.	*carcar*	OHG	*karkari*	Skt.	*kārā-*
NIr.	*prīosūn*	MHG	*karker*, *kerker*	Av.	(*grāfa-*)
W.	*carchar*	NHG	*gefängnis*, *kerker*		
Br.	*bac'h*, *prizon*				

Several of the words for 'prison' are derived from verbs for 'seize' or 'guard' and denoted at first the act or state of 'imprisonment', hence also its place, the 'prison'. Others are connected with words for 'bond', 'shut in', 'hook, corner', 'cage', 'tower', 'dark', 'hard' (through 'hard situation'), and 'grief' (through 'place of grief'). A few, including one of the most important, are of obscure origin.

1. Grk. εἱρκτή, fr. εἵργω 'shut in'.

Grk. δεσμωτήριον, beside δεσμώτης 'prisoner', fr. δεσμός 'bond' (9.17).

Grk. φυλακή 'guarding, keeping', hence 'custody, imprisonment' and 'prison' (usual word in NT and in NG), fr. φύλαξ 'watcher, guardian', φυλάσσω 'watch, guard, preserve' (11.24).

2. Lat. *carcer* (> It. *carcere*, OFr. *chartre*, Sp. *cárcel*), late *carcar* (> Ir. *carcar*, W. *carchar*, Goth. *karkara*, etc.), used also for the barrier or starting place in the race course and earliest sense prob. 'inclosure', plainly a redupl. form (**car-car-*), but root connection? Ernout-M. 153. Walde-H. 1.166. REW 1679. Wartburg 2.363. Vendryes, De hib. voc. 122. Loth, Mots lat. 144. Feist 388.

It. *prigione*, Fr. *prison* (> ME, NE *prison*), Sp. *prisión*, fr. Lat. *prēnsiō* 'seizure' (: *prehendere*, *prēndere* 'seize', 11.14), hence used first for 'imprisonment' then for the place. REW 6737. NED s.v. *prison*.

Fr. *geôle*, fr. OFr. *gaiole*, *jaiole*, etc. 'prison' and 'cage' = Sp. *gayola* 'cage, watch-house', fr. VLat. **gaviola*, late Lat. *caveola*, dim. of Lat. *cavea* 'hollow, cage'. REW 1790. Gamillscheg 466.

3. Ir. *carcar*, W. *carchar*, above, 2.

NIr. *prīosūn*, fr. NE *prison*.

Br. *bac'h*, same word as *bac'h* 'hook' (12.75). Cf. Ir. *baccaim* 'hinder, obstruct'. Henry 23. Ernault, Glossaire 49.

Br. *prizon*, fr. Fr. *prison*.

4. Goth. *karkara*, OHG *karkari*, etc. fr. Lat. *carcer*, *carcar* (above, 2).

ON *myrkvastofa*, cpd. of *myrkr* 'dark', *myrkva* 'grow dark' and *stofa* 'room'.

ON (late) *fangelsi*, Dan. *fængsel*, Sw. *fängelse*, re-formed fr. MLG *vangnisse* = NHG *gefängnis* (below). Falk-Torp 289.

OE *cweartern*, cpd. of *ern* 'place, house', first part : ON *kvarta* 'complain'. Cf. Boh. *žalář*, orig. 'place of grief'. Holthausen s.v.

OE *carcern*, blend of Lat. *carcer* with *ern* 'place, house'.

ME *gay(h)ol(e)*, *jaiole*, etc., NE *jail* (also spelling *gaol* in Britain), fr. ONorm. Fr. *gaiole*, *gaole*, OFr. *jaiole*, *jaile*, etc. (Fr. *geôle*, above, 2). NED s.v. *jail*, sb.

NHG *gefängnis*, Du. *gevangenis*, fr. *fangen*, *vangen* 'seize, catch' (11.14), hence orig., and still in part 'imprisonment'.

5. Lith. *kalėjimas*, see under *kalinys* 'prisoner' (20.47).

Lett. *cietums*, fr. *ciets* 'hard' (15.74). Cf. Lith. *kietimas* 'hardness' and 'hard situation' (NSB). Mühl.-Endz. 1.397.

6. ChSl. *temĭnica*, Russ. *temnica* : ChSl. *tĭma*, etc. 'darkness' (1.62).

SCr. *zatvor* : *zatvoriti* 'shut' (12.25).

Boh. *vězení*, Pol. *więzienie* : ChSl. *vęzati*, Boh. *vazati*, Pol. *wiązać*, etc. 'bind' (9.16).

Boh. *žalář*, fr. *žal* 'grief, sorrow' (16.32).

Russ. *tjur'ma*, fr. NHG *turm* 'tower' or more precisely in form fr. the verb *türmen* once used for 'put in prison' (cf. Paul, Deutsches Wtb. s.v.). The association between 'tower' and 'prison' was once widespread (cf. esp. the *Tower of London*), but this seems to be the only case in which it has yielded the regular word for 'prison'.

Russ. *ostrog* 'fortified place' and 'prison', fr. the root of ChSl. *strěšti*, *strěgą* 'guard'.

7. Skt. *kārā-* (also *kārāgṛha-*, *kārāgārā-*, cpds. with *gṛha-* and *agāra-* 'house'), etym.? See under Lith. *kalinys* 'prisoner' (20.47).

Av. *grāfa-* (*grāfě* Yt. 15.52, but text and sense dub.), fr. *grab-* 'seize'. Darmesteter, Zend-Avesta 1.591, note.

21.41 CRIME

Grk.	ἀδικία, ἀδίκημα	Goth.	(*inwindiþa*)	Lith.	*nusikaltimas*
NG	ἔγκλημα	ON	*glæpr*, *sǫk*, *afbrigð*	Lett.	*nuoziegums*
Lat.	*facinus*, *scelus*, *crīmen*	Dan.	*forbrydelse*	ChSl.	(*nepravĭda*)
It.	*delitto*, *crimine*	Sw.	*brott*, *förbrytelse*	SCr.	*zločin*(*stvo*)
Fr.	*délit*, *crime*	OE	*mān*(*dǣd*), *firen*	Boh.	*zločin*
Sp.	*crimen*, *delito*	ME	*crime*, *misdede*	Pol.	*zbrodnia*
Rum.	*crimă*, *vină*	NE	*crime*	Russ.	*prestuplenie*
Ir.	*cin*	Du.	*misdaad*	Skt.	see 16.75
NIr.	*cion*, *coir*	OHG	*firina*, *mein*, *missitāt*	Av.	see 16.75
W.	*trosedd*	MHG	*missetāt*, *meintāt*		
Br.	*torfed*	NHG	*verbrechen*		

'Crime' is intended to cover the usual generic words for a serious offense against the law, without regard to such technical legal distinctions as those in NE *felony* vs. *misdemeanor*, Fr. *délit* (or *crime*) vs. *contravention*, NHG *verbrechen* vs. *vergehen*, etc.

Most of the words are based on such notions as 'injustice, wrong', 'evil deed' (in part from simple 'deed'), 'crookedness', 'transgression', 'breaking, breach', 'fault, guilt, flaw'. These were originally, and in part remained, more comprehensive than 'crime', applying equally to offenses against religion and against morals. The Goth. and ChSl. words listed are not actually quotable in the legal sense, but render the Grk. word which does also include 'crime'. In Indo-Iranian, where the law was mainly one of religion, there is no real distinction between 'crime' and 'sin'.

In a few cases a legal word for 'accusation, charge' (in part from 'judgment') has come to denote the subject of the charge, the 'crime' itself.

1. Grk. ἀδικία, ἀδίκημα, both lit. 'injustice, wrong', fr. ἄδικος 'unjust, wrongdoing' : δίκη 'right, justice, lawsuit' (21.13).

Grk. ἔγκλημα 'accusation, charge' (fr. ἐγκαλέω 'bring a charge, accuse', 21.31), hence the subject of the charge, 'crime'

(this sense perh. in some pap. passages, but could still be 'charge'), so reg. in NG.

2. Lat. *facinus* 'deed' (good or bad)', but esp. 'evil deed, crime' : *facere* 'do, make'. Ernout-M. 323.

Lat. *scelus* 'evil deed, crime', prob. : Grk. σκολιός 'crooked' (12.74), also in moral sense 'unjust'. Walde-P. 2.598. Ernout-M. 904 ("sans correspondant").

Lat. *crīmen*, prob. orig. 'decision' (like Grk. κρῖμα), but in actual use 'charge, accusation', later (Cic.) 'crime' : *cernere* 'separate, distinguish, discern', *dēcernere* 'decide', Grk. κρῑνω 'judge, decide' (21.16). Ernout-M. 179. Otherwise (as orig. 'charge' : OHG *scrīan* 'cry', etc.) Walde-H. 1.291. Hence It. *crimine*, Fr. *crime* (> ME, NE *crime*), Sp. *crimen*, Rum. *crimă* (neolog. fr. Fr.).

Lat. *dēlictum* 'fault, offense, transgression', fr. *dēlinquere* 'commit a fault', orig. 'leave undone', cpd. of *linquere* 'leave' (12.18). Hence the much stronger It. *delitto*, Fr. *délit*, Sp. *delito*. These are, in fact, more commonly employed as the generic words for 'crime' than those of the preceding group (Fr. *crime*, etc., or both indiscriminately by some writers), e.g. in discussions of the history of law or Greek or Roman law. But in the technical language of the penal codes there may be a distinction. Thus It. *reato* (fr. *reo* 'culprit, criminal') is the comprehensive term for any breach of the law, the *reati* being classified, formerly as *crimini*, *delitti*, *contravenzioni*, now as *delitti* vs. *contravenzioni*. Fr. *délit* may also denote an offense intermediate between *crime* and *contravention*.

Rum. *vină* 'fault, guilt' (16.76), also 'crime'. Tiktin 1742.

3. Ir. *cin*, NIr. *cion* (also *cionnta*) 'fault, guilt' (16.76), also 'crime'.

W. *trosedd*, lit. 'transgression', fr. *tros* 'over, across' (= Lat. *trāns*). Cf. *traws* 'adverse, perverse, wicked'.

Br. *torfed*, fr. OFr. *tortfait*, *torfet* 'misdeed, forfeit' (Godefroy 7.754). Henry 266.

4. Goth. *inwindiþa*, reg. for ἀδικία, beside adj. *inwinds* 'unjust' : OE *inwid* 'guile, wickedness', ON *vindr* 'slanting, twisted', root connection disputed but prob. : Goth. *bi-windan* 'turn', NE *wind*, etc., with strengthening prefix *in-*. Walde-P. 1.261. Feist 296.

Goth. *missadēþs* (renders παράβασις, παράπτωμα), OE *misdǣd*, ME *misdede* (NE *misdeed*), Du. *misdaad*, OHG *missitāt*, MHG *missetāt* (NHG *missetat*), all except Du. *misdaad* now used chiefly for 'misdeed, transgression' in moral sense, a use common also from the earliest times, as shown by the Gothic.

ON *glæpr*, with *glōpr* 'fool' : *glap* 'hallucination, flaw', *glepja* 'confuse', root connection dub. Walde-P. 1.626. Falk-Torp 325.

ON *sǫk* 'accusation, charge' and 'lawsuit' (21.13), also the subject of the charge, 'crime'.

ON *afbrigð*, properly a 'deviation, transgression', fr. *bregða af* 'deviate from, disregard' (*bregða* 'move quickly, draw a sword, break off', etc.).

Dan. *forbrydelse*, Sw. *förbrytelse*, translations of NHG *verbrechen* (: Dan. *bryde*, Sw. *bryta* 'break'). Falk-Torp 254.

Sw. *brott*, lit. 'a break, breach', cf. NIcel. *afbrot* 'trespass, sin', ON *lǫgbrot* 'violation of the law' : Sw. *bryta*, etc. 'break' (cf. above).

OE *mān*, OHG *mein* (also 'wickedness, sinful deed, falsehood', in cpds. OE *māndǣd*, MHG *meintāt* 'evil deed, sin, crime') : ON *mein* 'harm, disease, sore', sb. use of adj. OE *mān* 'wicked', OHG *mein* 'false', these (through 'changed, deceptive') : Lith. *mainas* 'exchange', Goth. *gamains* 'common', etc. Walde-P. 2.241. Falk-Torp 713.

OE *firen*, OHG, OS *firina* : ON *firn*

pl. 'something shocking, abomination', Goth. *fairina* 'guilt, blame', all prob. orig. 'transgression'. See Goth. *fairina*, 16.76.

ME, NE *crime*, fr. Fr. *crime* (above, 2).

NHG *verbrechen*, substantivized infin. = MHG *verbrechen* 'break to pieces, destroy'. Kluge-G. 648.

5. Lith. *nusikaltimas* (NSB, etc.), fr. *nusikalsti* 'commit an offense or crime' : *kaltinti* 'accuse' (21.31), *kaltas* 'guilty' (21.35), *kaltė* 'guilt, blame' (16.76).

Lett. *nuoziegums* : *nuoziegties* 'commit a sin, crime', Lith. *nusižengti* 'make a mistake', cpd. of *žengti* 'step' (Lett. *ziegt* = *nuoziegties* but not now popular), with development through 'transgress'. Mühl.-Endz. 4.471.

6. ChSl. *nepravĭda* (Gospels, Supr. for ἀδικία, ἀδίκημα), neg. cpd. of *pravĭda* 'right, righteousness' : *pravŭ* 'straight', hence 'right', *pravo* 'law' (21.11).

SCr. *zločin*, *zločinstvo*, Boh. *zločin*, cpds. of Slavic *zŭlŭ* 'bad' (16.72) and SCr., Boh. *činiti* 'do, make' (9.11).

Pol. *zbrodnia*, fr. *z* 'from' and *bród* 'ford', orig. 'deviation from the ford', that is, 'from the right way', parallel to *zdrożny* 'culpable, criminal, wicked', fr. *z* and *droga* 'way, road'. Berneker 1.87. Brückner 648.

Russ. *prestuplenie* = ChSl. *prěstąplĭjenĭje* 'transgression', fr. *prěstąpiti* 'transgress', cpd. of *stąpiti* 'tread, step'.

7. Of the numerous Skt. words which might serve for 'crime' (or 'sin', which was the same thing) the most important in the lawbooks seems to be *pātaka-* (with cpds. *ati-*, *mahā-*, etc. for different gradations), for which see 16.75.

For other Skt. and Av. words see under 'sin' (16.75) and 'fault, guilt' (16.76), also Jolly, Recht und Sitte 115.

21.42 MURDER

Grk.	φόνος	Goth.	*maurþr*	Lith.	*žmogžudystė*
NG	φόνος, φονικό	ON	*morð* (*vīg*, *manndrāp*)	Lett.	*slepkavība*
Lat.	*caedēs*, *nex*, *homicīdium*	Dan.	*mord*	ChSl.	*ubijĭstvo*, *ubojĭ*
It.	*omicidio*	Sw.	*mord*	SCr.	*ubistvo*
Fr.	*meurtre*	OE	*morþor*, *morþ* (*mannsliht*)	Boh.	*vražda*
Sp.	*homicidio*	ME	*mordre*	Pol.	*zabójstwo*, *mord*
Rum.	*omor*	NE	*murder*	Russ.	*ubijstvo*
Ir.	*marbad*	Du.	*moord*	Skt.	*vadha-*
NIr.	*dūnmharbhadh*	OHG	*mord* (*manslaht*)	Av.	(*ǰənərā-*)
W.	*llofruddiaeth*	MHG	*mort* (*manslaht*)		
Br.	(*drouk-*)*laz*, *muntr*	NHG	*mord*		

'Murder' in primitive society was not a public 'crime' but an offense for which vengeance or blood-money was exacted by the victim's kinsmen. Such was still the situation in Homeric times and among all the peoples of IE speech in the earliest period. Only later did 'murder' come to be recognized as a public matter to be dealt with in the laws (even in the Gortyn code and the fragments of the Roman XII Tables there is nothing about murder), and it was still generally not distinguished verbally from justifiable 'killing'.

That is, with few exceptions, the words are derived from verbs for 'kill' and generally denoted simply 'killing', whether in battle or accident or criminal 'murder'. But the Gmc. group (NE *murder*, NHG *mord*, etc.), though etymologically 'death', denoted from the earliest times some sort of highly reprehensible (in ON often esp. secret) killing.

A few of the words are of quite different origin, namely, derived from those for 'murderer' and this from 'red-handed' (W.), 'secret' (Lett.), 'enemy' (Boh.), and, if one includes Fr. *assassin*, etc., 'hashish-eater'.

1. Grk. φόνος, fr. the root of ἔπεφνον, πέφαμαι 'kill', θείνω 'strike', Skt. *han-* 'strike, kill', etc. (4.76). The word covered any 'killing' (in battle, etc.) but was the regular term for 'murder', in Attic classified as φόνος ἑκούσιος vs. φόνος ἀκούσιος 'voluntary' vs. 'involuntary murder'. NG pop. also τὸ φονικό, neut. of φονικός 'murderous'.

2. Lat. *caedēs*, most frequently 'slaughter' in battle, but also 'murder', fr. *caedere* 'strike, beat, kill' (4.76).

Lat. *nex* 'violent death' (4.75), used also for 'murder'.

Lat. *parricīda* (early nom. *-as*), generally defined as 'murderer of a near relative' (and so *parricīdium* 'murder' defined in the same way), but without such restriction in an early law quoted by Festus (*si qui hominem liberum dolo sciens morti duit, parricidas esto*) and sometimes later (*parricida civium* Cic.), prob. the earliest distinctive term for 'murderer'; cpd. of *-cīda* : *caedere* 'kill', first part much disputed but perh. : Skt. *puruṣa-* 'man', so that the whole word would be parallel to Grk. ἀνδρο-φόνος. Ernout-M. 733 f. Wackernagel, Gnomon 6.449 f., 458. Believed by the Romans to be from **patr-cīda*, it gave rise to *mātricīda*, *frātricīda*, etc.

Lat. *homicīda* 'murderer' (Cic.), formed like and prob. directly to *parricīda*, with first part fr. *homō* 'man'. This and the parallel *homicīdium* (post-Cic.) became henceforth the usual words and the source of the similar It., Fr., Sp. and NE forms (but Fr., NE *homicide* only as more comprehensive than *meurtre*, *murder*).

It. *assassinio*, Fr. *assassinat* (> Rum. *asasinat*), Sp. *asesinato* (also usually somewhat more special than 'murder', like NE *assassination*), fr. Fr. *assassin* (> It. *assassino* > Sp. *asesino*) 'murderer', this fr. an Arab. word meaning lit. 'hashish-eaters' but applied to a certain sect. REW 4071. NED s.v. *assassin*.

Fr. *meurtre*, fr. Gmc. (below, 4). REW 5753.

Rum. *omor*, back-formation to *omorî* 'kill' (4.76).

3. Ir. *marbad*, lit. 'slaying', vbl. n. to *marbaim* 'kill' (4.76), NIr. *mharbhadh*, but esp. *dūnmharbhadh*, lit. 'man murder' (*duine* 'man').

W. *llofruddiaeth*, through vb. *llofruddio* 'murder', fr. *llofrudd* 'murderer', lit. 'red-handed', cpd. of *llof-* (in cpds. and derivs. = *llaw*) 'hand' and *rhudd* 'red'.

Br. *laz* (also *lazerez*, *lazidigez*), *droukl-az* (cpd. with *drouk-* 'bad, evil'), fr. *laza* 'kill' (4.76), *drouk-laza* vb. 'murder'.

Br. *muntr*, fr. Fr. *meurtre* (with dissim.).

4. Goth. *maurþr*, OE *morþor* and *morþ*, ME *mordre*, NE *murder*, ON *morð*, OHG *mord*, etc., general Gmc. : Lat. *mors*, *mortis* 'death', *mortuus* 'dead', *morī* 'die', etc., the widespread group for 'die, dead, death' (4.75), with general Gmc. specialization, prob. through 'violent death' (like Lat. *nex*).

ON *vīg* (legal term for 'manslaughter' vs. *morð* 'murder') : *vega* 'fight' (20.11) and 'kill'.

ON *manndrāp*, OE *mannsliht*, OHG, MHG *manslaht*, all lit. 'manslaughter' (ON *drepa*, OE *slēan*, OHG *slahan* 'strike, kill', 4.76) and frequent legal terms for 'homicide', more comprehensive than ON *morð*, etc.

5. Lith. *žmogžudystė* (NT and still

best word), deriv. cpd. of *žmogus* 'man' and *žudyti* 'kill' (4.76).

Lett. *slepkavība*, fr. *slepkava* 'murderer, bandit' : *sleps* 'secret, hidden', *slēpt*, Lith. *slėpti* 'hide', etc. Mühl.-Endz. 3.926, 930.

6. ChSl. *ubijĭstvo* (Gospels, Supr.), *ubojĭ* (Supr.), SCr. *ubistvo*, Pol. *zabójstwo*, Russ. *ubijstvo*, all fr. the root in ChSl. *biti* 'strike', *ubiti* 'kill' (4.76).

Boh. *vražda* = ChSl. *vražĭda*, Russ. *vražda* 'enmity, hate' : Boh. *vrah* 'murderer' = ChSl. *vragŭ* 'enemy' (19.52).

Pol. *mord*, fr. NHG *mord* (above).

7. Skt. *vadha-* 'killing' in general, often the 'death-penalty, capital punishment', but also 'murder' (e.g. Manu 11.127) : *vadh-* 'smite, kill' (4.76).

Av. *ǰənərā-* 'killing, murder'(?) : *ǰan-* 'kill' (4.76). Barth. 607 f.

21.43 ADULTERY

Grk.	*μοιχεία*	Goth.	*kalkinassus, hōrinassus*	Lith.	*svetmoterystė* (or *-ybė*)
NG	*μοιχεία*			Lett.	*laulības pārkāpšana*
Lat.	*adulterium*	ON	*hōr*	ChSl.	*prěljubodějanĭje*
It.	*adulterio*	Dan.	*ægteskabsbrud, hor*	SCr.	*preljub*
Fr.	*adultère*	Sw.	*äktensbrott, hor*	Boh.	*cizoložtví*
Sp.	*adulterio*	OE	*ǣwbryce*	Pol.	*cudzołostwo*
Rum.	*adulter(iŭ)*	ME	*avoutrie*	Russ.	*preljubodejanie*
Ir.	*adaltras*	NE	*adultery*	Skt.	*pāradārya-*, etc.
NIr.	*adhaltrannas*	Du.	*echtbreuk, overspel*		
W.	*godineb*	OHG	*huor* (*ubarhīwī*)		
Br.	*avoultriez*	MHG	*ēbruch, huor(e)*		
		NHG	*ehebruch*		

Several of the words listed are derived from verbs used for sexual intercourse (e.g. 'lie', 'play', 'love'), or from words for 'whore', and these denoted any kind of illicit sexual intercourse without distinction between 'adultery' and 'fornication'.

The more distinctive words are mostly based on such notions as 'breach of marriage', 'relations with strange women', or (Lat. *adulterium*, etc.) 'corruption'.

1. Grk. *μοιχεία*, with *μοιχός* 'adulterer', whence vbs. *μοιχάω*, *μοιχεύω*, prob. fr. the root of *ὀμείχω* (*ὀμῑχέω*), Lat. *mingere*, Skt. *mih-*, etc. 'make water' (4.65)—despite the semantic incongruity. One must assume that a sense 'debauch' started from such vulgar phrases as that in Catullus 67.30 (*qui ipse sui gnati minxerit in gremium*) and that *μοιχός* as orig. 'debaucher' was used esp. for the 'adulterer'. For this last cf. Goth. *hōrs* 'fornicator' (*πόρνος*) and 'adulterer' (*μοιχός*) and the double use of Goth. *hōrinassus*, ON *hōr*, etc. (below, 4).

2. Lat. *adulterium*, with *adulter* 'adulterer', etc., fr. *adulterāre* 'alter, falsify, corrupt' (: *alter* 'other'), then, through phrases like *adulterāre mātrōnās*, 'commit adultery'. Hence OIt. *avoltero*, OFr. *a(v)ulterie* (> Br. *avoultriez*), *avoutire*, *avoutrie* (> ME *avoutrie*), and the later (re-formed fr. the Lat.) It., Sp. *adulterio*, Fr. *adultère* (> Rum. *adulter*, hence also *adulteriŭ*), NE *adultery;* also, through *adaltair* 'adulterer', Ir. *adaltras*, *adaltrach*, NIr. *adhaltrannas*. Ernout-M. 35. Walde-H. 1.15. REW 207. Vendryes, De hib. voc. 110. NED s.v. *adultery*.

3. Ir. and Br. words, above, 2.

W. *godineb* ('adultery' and 'fornication'), fr. the root seen in Ir. *goithim* 'futuo' (4.67). Pedersen 2.34. Stokes 113.

4. Goth. *kalkinassus* (renders both *μοιχεία* and *πορνεία* 'fornication'), deriv.,

through vb. **kalkinōn*, of *kalkjō* 'whore' (19.72).

Goth. *hōrinassus* (likewise for both *μοιχεία* and *πορνεία*), deriv., through vb. *hōrinōn*, of word for 'whore' seen in ON *hōra*, etc. (19.72. Goth. only masc. *hōrs*). Here likewise ON *hōr*, Dan., Sw. *hor*, OHG *huor*, *huar*, *huora*, MHG *huor*, *huore*, all used for illicit intercourse, whether 'adultery' or 'fornication' (e.g. OHG *huar* Otfr. 'adultery', *huor* Tat. 'fornication').

OE *ǣwbryce*, MHG *ēbruch*, NHG *ehebruch*, Dan. *ægteskabsbrud*, Sw. *äktensbrott*, Du. *echtbreuk*, all lit. 'breach of marriage', cpds. of words for 'marriage' (orig. 'law' whence 'legal married state', 2.34) and derivs. of vbs. for 'break' (9.26).

OHG *ubarhīwī* (only Tat. 120.1, 2 = Jn. 8.3.4, where Otfr. has *huar*), cpd. of *ubar* 'over, beyond' and *hīwī* 'married state, matrimony' : *hīwan* 'marry', etc. (2.33).

OHG *uorligirī* (pl. Tat. 84.9 = *adulteria*), fr. *furligan* 'commit adultery' (so reg. in Tat.) = OE *forlicgan* 'commit fornication', cpds. of OHG *liggen*, OE *licgan* 'lie'.

ME *avoutrie*, NE *adultery*, see above, 2.

Du. *overspel*, cpd. of *over* 'over, beyond' and *spel* 'play' in its vulgar sense of 'coition'. Franck-v. W. 483 f.

5. Lith. *svetmoterystė* (or *-ybė*), with *svetmoterius* 'adulterer', lit. 'one who has to do with strange women', cpd. of *svet-* (cf. *svetimas* 'strange, stranger', *svečias* 'guest'; formerly also 'stranger', 19.55) and *moteris* 'woman' (2.22).

Lett. *laulības pārkāpšana*, phrase with gen. of *laulība* 'marriage' (2.34) and deriv. of *pārkāpt* 'overstep, transgress' (Mühl.-Endz. 3.160), hence lit. 'transgression of marriage'.

6. ChSl. *prěljubodějanĭje* (beside *ljubodějanĭje* 'fornication' and *ljubodějica* 'whore'; cf. Jagić, Entstehungsgesch. 360), SCr. *preljub*, Russ. *preljubodejanie*, fr. *liubiti* 'love' (16.26), here in its sexual sense.

Boh. *cizološtví*, Pol. *cudzołostwo*, fr. vbs. *cizoložiti*, *cudzołożyć* 'commit adultery', cpds. of *cizí*, *cudzy* 'strange' (see under 'stranger', 19.55) with *o*-grade forms of root in vbs. for 'lie' (12.14); hence orig. 'lie with strange (women)'.

7. Skt. *pāradārya-*, fr. *paradāra-* 'wife of another'.

Skt. *saṁgrahaṇa-* 'seizing' (fr. *grah-* 'seize'), also with or without preceding *strī-* 'woman', 'adultery' or 'fornication'. BR s.v. Jolly, Recht und Sitte 128 ("Ehebruch").

Skt. *vyabhicāra-* 'going astray, misdeed' and sometimes esp. 'unfaithfulness' to husband, fr. *vy-abhi-car-* 'commit a misdeed', cf. *abhi-car-* often esp. 'be unfaithful' to husband.

21.44 RAPE (sb.)

Grk.	*ὕβρις, βιασμός*	Goth.	....	Lith.	*išanavimas, iššaginimas*
NG	*βιασμός*	ON	*kvennanām*		
Lat.	*stuprum*	Dan.	*voldtægt*	Lett.	*varas darbs*
It.	*stupro*	Sw.	*våldtägt*	ChSl.	....
Fr.	*viol*	OE	*nīedhǣmed*	SCr.	*silovanje*
Sp.	*estupro*	ME	*rape*	Boh.	*násilné smilstvo*
Rum.	*viol*	NE	*rape*	Pol.	*zgwałcenie*
Ir.	*forcur, sleith*	Du.	*verkrachting*	Russ.	*iznasilovanie*
NIr.	*ēigean*	OHG	*nōtnumft*	Skt.	(*dūṣaṇa-*)
W.	*trais*	MHG	*nōtnumft, -twanc, -zoc*		
Br.	*gwalladur*	NHG	*notzucht*		

Most of the terms for 'rape' are words denoting 'force, violence' or 'compulsion', with the notion of sexual relations either expressed or, more commonly, left to be understood. Cf. the current use (at least in U.S.) of NE *assault* and *attack* = *rape*.

A few are more general terms for 'shameful act' or 'defilement', which include, but are not restricted to, 'rape'. In NE *rape* the criminal sense here intended is secondary to that of forcible abduction.

1. Grk. *ὕβρις* 'violence, insolence, outrage', as law term 'assault' in wide sense, but esp. 'rape', etym. dub., perh. *ὕ-βρις* cpd. of *ὑ-* (= Skt. *ud* 'up, out'), second part : *βαρύς* 'heavy', etc. (15.81) with development through the notion of 'putting forth one's whole weight'? Walde-P. 1.686. Boisacq 997.

Grk. *βιασμός* 'violence' and esp. 'rape' (Menander+) : *βιάω*, *βιάζω* 'constrain', *βία* 'violence, force', Skt. *jī-* 'conquer', etc. Walde-P. 1.666 f. Boisacq 119.

In the Gortyn code 'rape' is specifically expressed by verbal phrases consisting of *κάρτει* 'by force' with either *οἴφω* 'have sexual intercourse' (4.67) or mid. of *δαμάζω* 'overcome'.

2. Lat. *stuprum* 'disgrace' (only anteclass.), in class. period 'shameful act', always with reference to sexual relations, such as 'debauchery, adultery, incest, rape' (hence as 'rape' It. *stupro*, Sp. *estupro*) : *stupēre* 'be struck senseless, be stunned, astonished', Grk. *τύπτω* 'strike', etc., with prob. development through 'act which shocks one, shocking act'. Walde-P. 2.619 (with less prob. view of semantic development). Ernout-M. 991.

Lat. *raptus* (: *rapere* 'carry off') and likewise It. *ratto*, Fr. *rapt*, Sp. *rapto*, are used for 'rape' = 'abduction' ("rape of the Sabine women", etc.), but not (or only very rarely) for 'rape' as intended here.

Fr. *viol* (> Rum. *viol*, neolog.), backformation to *violer* 'violate', fr. Lat. *violāre* 'violate, outrage', deriv. of *vīs* 'force, strength'.

The Rum. vb. for 'rape' is *silui*, fr. Slavic (below, 6).

3. Ir. *forcur* (reg. word, cf. Thurneysen, Irisches Recht, p. 37), prob. vbl. n. to unattested **for-curiur* 'put upon' (cf. *curi-* and cpds. in Pedersen 2.498 ff.), cf. W. *guorcher* gl. *summitas inferni*. I. Williams, BBCS 3.259.

Ir. *sleith* (Laws, Gloss. 663), vbl. n. to *tle-n-* 'carry off, steal'. Pedersen 2.649.

Ir. also *lānamnas ēcne* 'cohabitation by force' (Laws, Gloss. 288, 522), and so commonly NIr. simply *ēigean* 'force', also 'rape' (cf. Ir. *ēcen* 'necessity', 9.93).

W. *trais* 'oppression, force, violence' and 'rape' (MW *treys* 'rape, abduction', etc.), etym. dub., perh. : Ir. *tress* 'battle, skirmish'. Loth, RC 36.168 (vs. Morris Jones 142).

Br. *gwalladur* (Vallée s.v. *viol*), through vb. *gwalla* 'harm, violate', fr. *gwall* 'bad, evil' (16.72).

4. ON *kvenna-nām* (*konu-nām*, *-tak*), lit. 'taking of women'. For vb. 'rape' reg. *taka konu nauðga* (with adj. *nauðigr* 'forced, unwilling'), hence late sb. *nauðgan* 'compulsion, rape'.

Dan. *voldtægt*, Sw. *våldtägt*, lit. 'taking by force', fr. Dan. *vold*, Sw. *våld* 'force, might' and *tage*, *taga* 'take'.

OE *nīedhǣmed*, cpd. of *nīed* (*nēad*, etc.) 'compulsion, necessity' (9.93) and *hǣmed* 'sexual intercourse' (: vb. *hǣman*, 4.67).

ME, NE *rape*, fr. Anglo-Fr. *raap*, *rap(e)*, back-formation to *raper*, Lat. *rapere* 'carry off by force'. NED s.v. *rape* sb. Also *ravishing*, *ravishment*, fr. vb. *ravish*, OFr. *ravir* (*raviss-*), VLat. **rapīre* = Lat. *rapere*. NED s.vv. In

this group the sense of 'rape' as here intended is secondary and rare in ME.

Du. *verkrachting*, lit. 'violation', with vb. *verkrachten* 'violate (a law, etc.), rape', fr. *kracht* 'force, power, strength' (4.81).

OHG, MHG *nōtnumft*, lit. 'compulsory taking' (*nōt* 'necessity' and *neman* 'take'); MHG *nōt-twanc* (: *twingen* 'compel').

MHG *nōtzoc* (with vb. *nōtzogen*, OHG *nōtzogōn*), NHG *nōtzucht* (back-formation fr. MHG vb. *nōt-zühten*), last member : OHG *ziohan*, NHG *ziehen* 'pull, draw' (9.33). Kluge-G. 420. Weigand-H. 2.314.

5. Lith. *išanavimas*, also 'botching, bungling, dishonoring', with vb. *išanuoti* 'botch, bungle, dishonor, rape' : *anuoti* 'do, act' (also vulg. 'have sexual intercourse', Lalis).

Lith. *iššaginimas*, with vb. *iššaginti* (= *išanuoti*) : *žaginti*, *žagti* 'pollute, defile, debauch'.

Lett. (apparently only) *varas darbs*, lit. 'deed of violence', cf. *varas darbu* (*pie sievietes*) *darīt* 'do a deed of violence (to a woman)' = 'rape'. Mühl.-Endz. 4.475 (col. 1).

6. SCr. *silovanje*, Russ. *iznasilovanie*, with vbs. SCr. *silovati*, Russ. *iznasilovat'* : ChSl., SCr., Russ. *sila* 'strength, force' (4.81).

Boh. *násilné smilstvo*, phrase consisting of *násilné* 'violent' (: *sila* 'force, strength') and *smilstvo* 'illicit intercourse, whoring', beside *smilný* 'lecherous' : Lith. *smilus* 'sweet-toothed, loving dainties'. Brückner 503. Cf. the shift from gluttony to sexual debauchery in NE *lecher*, *lecherous*, *lechery* (ME *lechur*, fr. OFr. *lecheur* : Fr. *lécher* 'lick', etc.; NED s.vv.).

Pol. *zgwałcenie*, with vb. *zgwałcić*, fr. *gwałt* 'violence, outrage', fr. NHG *gewalt* 'power, force'.

7. Skt. *dūṣaṇa-* 'corruption, defilement', also esp. 'defilement' of a woman (but without distinction between rape and seduction), fr. *duṣ-* 'be corrupted, defiled' (fr. prefix *duṣ-* 'bad').

21.45 THEFT

Grk.	*κλοπή*	Goth.	*þiubi*	Lith.	*vagystė*
NG	*κλοπή, κλεψιά, κλέψιμο*	ON	*þȳfð, þȳfi, stuldr*	Lett.	*zādzība*
Lat.	*furtum*	Dan.	*tyveri*	ChSl.	*tatĭva, kražda, kradĭba*
It.	*furto*	Sw.	*tjuvnad, stöld*		
Fr.	*vol*	OE	*þiefþ, stalu*	SCr.	*krađa*
Sp.	*hurto*	ME	*thefte, stale*	Boh.	*krádež, zlodějství*
Rum.	*furt(işag)*	NE	*theft*	Pol.	*kradzież*
Ir.	*mēirle*	Du.	*diefstal*	Russ.	*vorovstvo, kraža*
NIr.	*gadaidheacht, goid*	OHG	*diuba, stāla*	Skt.	*caurya- moṣa-, stainya-*
W.	*lladrad*	MHG	*diube, diupstāle*		
Br.	*laerez*	NHG	*diebstahl*		

All the words for 'theft' are cognate with those for 'steal' or 'thief', both combined in Du. *diefstal*, NHG *diebstahl*. The relation is so obvious, by reference to the lists for 'steal (11.56) and 'thief' (11.57), that no further comment on the etymology is needed.

NG *κλοπή* is still the legal term, beside pop. *κλεψιά* and *κλέψιμο*, new formations fr. the verb.

The NE legal term *larceny* comes, through Fr., fr. Lat. *lātrōcinium* 'robbery', for which, and in general for 'robbery' vs. 'larceny,' see words for 'robber' (11.58).

21.46 ARSON

Grk.	πυρκαϊά	Goth.	....	Lith.	padegimas
NG	ἐμπρησμός	ON	brenna	Lett.	uguns pielikšana
Lat.	incendium	Dan.	mordbrand	ChSl.	....
It.	incendio	Sw.	mordbrand	SCr.	zapaljenje
Fr.	incendie	OE	bærnet	Boh.	žhařstvi
Sp.	incendio	ME	(arsoun)	Pol.	podpalenie
Rum.	incendiu	NE	arson	Russ.	podžog
Ir.	loscad	Du.	brandstichting		
NIr.	dóghadh	OHG	brant		
W.	llosg, llosgiad	MHG	brant, mortbrand		
Br.	tan-gwall	NHG	brandstiftung, mordbrand		

Words for 'arson' are connected with those for 'burn' (11.84) or 'fire' (11.81), or both together (Grk. πυρ-καϊά). Many of them cover 'burning, conflagration' in general. The criminal application might be brought out by expressions for 'evil', 'caused', 'intentional' or the like, but this would not be necessary in legal language, where only 'arson' could be meant (e.g. Grk. γραφὴ πυρκαϊᾶς).

1. Grk. πυρκαϊά, in Hom. 'funeral pyre', in general 'conflagration', in law 'arson', cpd. of πῦρ 'fire' and sb. : καίω 'burn'.

Grk. ἐμπρησμός 'burning', in NG the reg. word for 'arson', fr. πίπρημι 'burn'.

2. Lat. incendium (> Romance words) 'burning', including 'arson' (cf. Cic. domus ardēbat nōn fortuitō, sed oblātō incendiō), fr. incendere 'set fire to, burn'.

3. Ir. loscad (or esp. loscad comraite 'intentional burning'; cf. Laws, Gloss. 541), W. llosg, llosgiad, fr. Ir. loscim, W. llosgi 'burn'.

NIr. dóghadh, fr. dóighim 'burn'.

Br. tan-gwall, cpd. of tan 'fire' and gwall 'evil' (16.62).

4. ON brenna 'burning, conflagration' and 'arson' (cf. Norges Gamle Love 5.114), fr. brenna 'burn'.

Dan., Sw. mordbrand, MHG mortbrand, NHG mordbrand, cpd. of brand 'burning' with mord 'murder', hence orig. 'murderous burning, burning for purpose of killing enemies', as frequently ON brenna.

OE bærnet 'burning', also 'arson', fr. bærnan 'burn'. Cf. also blæsere (fr. blæse 'flame, blaze') used for the 'incendiary' in Laws of Aethelstan.

NE arson (arsoun in ME period quotable only in laws written in French and there qualified, as arsoun feloniousement fait, fr. OFr. arson, arsun 'burning', fr. late Lat. arsiō, -ōnis id. : ardēre 'burn'). NED s.v.

OHG, MHG brant 'burning', including 'arson', fr. brennan 'burn'. Hence NHG brandstiftung (in first occurrence with muthwillige 'wanton', cpd. with deriv. of stiften 'cause, make'. Similarly Du. brandstichting.

5. Lith. padegimas, fr. padegti 'set on fire', cpd. of degti 'burn'.

Lett. uguns pielikšana (Drawneek; uguns likšana Ullmann; Mühl-Endz. only uguni pielikt 'brand stiften'), gen. of uguns 'fire' and deriv. of pielikt 'put on' (Mühl.-Endz. 3.267) and modeled on NHG brandstiftung.

6. SCr. zapaljenje, Pol. podpalenie, fr. SCr. zapaliti, Pol. podpalić 'set fire to', cpds. of SCr. paliti, Pol. palić 'burn'.

Boh. žhařstvi, fr. žhař 'incendiary', this fr. root of Boh. hořeti, ChSl. gorěti 'burn' (cf. žar 'heat, glow', požar 'conflagration').

Russ. podžog, fr. podžeč, podžigat' 'set fire to', cpd. of žeč' = ChSl. žesti, žegą 'burn'.

7. There seems to be no reference to 'arson' in the Indo-Iranian sources.

21.47 PERJURY

Grk.	ψευδομαρτυρία (or -ιον)	Goth.	*galiugaweitwōdiþa	Lith.	neteisi priesaika
NG	ψευδομαρτυρία, ψευδορκία	ON	meineiðr, ljúgeiðr, ljúgvitni	Lett.	nepatiesi zvēri
Lat.	periūrium	Dan.	mened	ChSl.	lŭžesŭvĕdĕnĭje
It.	spergiuro	Sw.	mened	Boh.	křivá přisaha
Fr.	parjure	OE	mānáþ, lēas gewitnes	Pol.	krzywoprzysięstwo
Sp.	perjurio	ME	false witness, perjury	Russ.	kljatvoprestuplenie
Rum.	sperjur	NE	perjury	Skt.	kūṭasākṣya-
Ir.	éithech	Du.	meineed		
NIr.	éitheach	OHG	meineid		
W.	anudon	MHG	meineit		
Br.	le faos	NHG	meineid		

Words for 'perjury' are derived from those for 'witness' (21.23), 'swear' (21.24), or 'oath' (21.25) combined with words for 'false' (cf. 'lie' 16.67), 'crooked, wrong', 'evil', 'breaking', 'crime', or with prefixes having pejorative force.

1. Grk. ψευδο-μαρτυρία and -μαρτύριον (both esp. in pl.), cpd. of ψευδής 'false' and deriv. of μάρτυς 'witness'.

Grk. ψευδορκία (late, but also NG), similar cpd. with second part : ὅρκος 'oath'.

2. Lat. periūrium (> Romance words, partly with ex-), deriv. of iūrāre 'swear' with per- in the sense seen in per-fidus 'contrary to faith, faithless'. Ernout-M. 506, 754.

3. Ir. éithech, NIr. éitheach, fr. cpd. of tongu 'swear', first part perh. *epi- as in Grk. ἐπι-ορκέω 'swear falsely'. Pedersen 2.653.

W. anudon, cpd. of neg. an-, second part : Ir. óeth 'oath'. Pedersen 1.58.

Br. le faos or faos le or gwall le, phrases with le 'oath' and faos 'false' or gwall 'evil' (16.62).

4. Goth. *galiugaweitwōdiþa (quotable only galiugaweitwōps 'perjurer' and galiug weitwōdjan 'bear false witness'), cpd. of galiug 'lie' and deriv. of weitwōps 'witness'.

ON meineiðr, Dan., Sw. mened, OE mānáþ, Du. meineed, OHG-NHG meineid, cpd. of ON meinn 'painful, harmful', OE mǣne, OHG mein 'false' (: Goth. gamains 'common', etc., 19.64) and words for 'oath'. Falk-Torp 713. Kluge-G. 385.

ON ljúgeiðr, ljúgvitni, cpds. of ljúg-'false' (: ljúga 'lie', vb., lygi 'a lie') with words for 'oath' and 'witness'.

OE lēas gewitness (also lēas gecýpnes, both in Gospels) 'false witness' (: lēas 'false', also 'destitute of' = Goth. laus 'empty, vain', etc.).

Late OE, ME, NE false witness (so, not perjury, in Wyclif, Tyndale, etc.).

ME, NE perjury, fr. OFr. perjurie, Lat. periūrium (above, 2). NED s.v.

5. Lith. neteisi priesaika (Gailius-Šlaža; cf. neteisiai prisiekti 'swear falsely' NSB s.v. neteisus), lit. 'false oath', with fem. of neteisus, neg. of teisus 'right, just' (16.73).

Lett. nepatiesi zvēri, lit. 'false oath', with neg. of patiess 'true' (16.66).

6. ChSl. lŭžesŭvĕdĕnĭje, cpd. of lŭži 'false' (: lŭža 'lie') and sŭvĕdĕnĭje 'testimony' (cf. sŭvĕdĕtelĭ 'witness').

SCr. kriva prisega, Boh. křivá přisaha, Pol. krzywoprzysięstwo, words for 'crooked, wrong' (12.70, 16.74) with those for 'oath'.

Russ. kljatvoprestuplenie, cpd. of words for 'oath' and 'crime' (21.25, 21.41).

7. Skt. kūṭasākṣya-, fr. kūṭasākṣin-'false witness', cpd. of kūṭa- 'deceitful, false' and sākṣin- 'witness'.

CHAPTER 22

RELIGION AND SUPERSTITION

22.11	Religion	22.25	Baptize
22.12	God	22.26	Fast (vb.)
22.13	Temple	22.31	Heaven
22.14	Altar	22.32	Hell
22.15	Sacrifice, Offering	22.33	Angel
22.16	Worship (vb.)	22.34	Devil
22.17	Pray	22.35	Demon (Evil Spirit)
22.18	Priest	22.36	Pagan, Heathen (sb.)
22.182	Clergyman, Minister, Parson, etc.	22.37	Idol
22.183	Monk	22.41	Superstition
22.184	Nun	22.42	Magic, Witchcraft, Sorcery
22.19	Holy, Sacred	22.43	Witch, Sorceress
22.21	Church	22.44	Fairy (or the Like)
22.22	Preach	22.45	Ghost, Specter, Phantom
22.23	Bless	22.46	Guardian Spirit
22.24	Curse (vb.)	22.47	Omen

22.11 RELIGION

Grk.	θρησκεία (εὐσέβεια, τὰ θεῖα)	Goth.	....	Lith.	tikyba, tikėjimas
NG	θρησκεία	ON	trúa	Lett.	ticība
Lat.	religiō	Dan.	religion	ChSl.	věra
It.	religione	Sw.	religion	SCr.	vjera
Fr.	religion	OE	geléafa	Boh.	náboženstvi, vira
Sp.	religion	ME	religion, feith	Pol.	religja
Rum.	religiune, religie	NE	religion	Russ.	religija, vera
Ir.	cretem, iress, crābud	Du.	godsdienst	Skt.	dharma-
NIr.	creideamh, iris, crábhadh	OHG	gilouba	Av.	daēnā-
W.	crefydd	MHG	g(e)loube		
Br.	kredenn	NHG	religion		

'Religion' involves a belief in supernatural powers, the desire to stand well with them, and practices devoted to this end. 'A religion' denotes a particular body of such beliefs and practices. In its early phases, as still among primitive peoples and with survivals among those of IE speech, it consisted of crude 'superstition' (22.41).

The most common semantic source of 'religion' is 'belief, faith', but a few are based on 'worship', 'service of god', or 'insight'.

1. There is no distinctive early Grk. word for 'religion'. One may note θεογονία 'genealogy of the gods, mythology'; εὐσέβεια 'piety' (toward gods or parents, also 'loyalty'), fr. εὐσεβής 'pious, religious, holy' : σέβομαι 'feel awe, revere, worship' (22.16); τὰ θεῖα 'acts of the gods' and sometimes 'divine

matters, religion', neut. pl. of θεῖος 'divine, holy', fr. θεός 'god' (22.12).

Grk. θρησκεία 'religious worship', in pl. 'religious rites' (Hdt.+), the reg. word for 'religion' in LXX, NT, and down to the present day (cf. θρήσκω, θράσκω 'understand, remember' Hesych.), etym. dub., perh. fr. the root *dher- in Skt. dhṛ- 'hold, support', dharma- 'usage, right, law', etc. (cf. below, 7). Walde-P. 1.857. Boisacq 340, 350.

2. Lat. religiō (> the widespread modern Eur. word), etym. disputed from ancient times to the present, whether : legere 'collect, select' or : ligāre 'bind'; both equally possible phonetically, but the former preferable on the semantic side. The presumably earlier, and certainly well attested, sense was 'scruple, doubt, hesitation', which may well come from a 'repeated (re-) mental collecting, selecting, consideration'. Hence 'awe of the supernatural' and eventually 'religion' in the current sense. Warde Fowler, Trans. Third International Congress for the History of Religions 2.169 ff. W. Otto, Archiv für Religionswissenschaft 12.533 ff., 14.406 ff. Ernout-M. 858 f. Walde-H. 1.352 f.

3. Ir. cretem, NIr. creideamh, Br. kredenn, all properly 'belief, faith', fr. Ir. cretim, Br. kredi 'believe' (17.15).

Ir. iress, NIr. iris, properly 'belief, faith', fr. cpd. of preverb air- (: Grk. περί) and *stā- 'stand'. Cf. Pahl. parast 'worshiper', of like origin. Pedersen 1.91. Pokorny, Z. celt. Ph. 9.444 ff. Thurneysen, KZ 48.72 ff. Vendryes, MSL 20.266 f.

Ir. crābud, NIr. crábhadh, W. crefydd,

creddyf, prob. : Skt. vi-çrambhate 'trusts'. Pedersen 1.492. Vendryes, MSL 20.266.

4. ON trúa 'belief, faith', also in religious sense, fr. trúa 'believe' (17.15).

OE geléafa, OHG gilouba, MHG g(e)loube 'belief, faith' also in religious sense, fr. the corresponding vbs. for 'believe' (17.15).

ME feith, NE faith 'belief, faith', also 'religion' (NED s.v. 4), fr. OFr. feid, Lat. fidēs 'faith'.

Du. godsdienst, lit. 'service of god' = NHG gottesdienst 'divine service', but now the usual term for religion.

5. Lith. tikyba, tikėjimas, Lett. ticība 'belief, faith, religion', fr. Lith. tikėti, Lett. ticēt 'believe' (17.15). Mühl.-Endz. 4.180 f.

6. ChSl. věra ('faith' and in Supr. sometimes for εὐσέβεια and θρησκεία), SCr. vjera, Boh. vira, Russ. vera, all orig. 'belief, faith' (cf. 17.15).

Boh. náboženstvi, fr. adjs. náboženský, nábožný 'religious, pious', orig. 'following after god', cpds. of na 'after' and derivs. of bǔh (ChSl. bogǔ) 'god'.

7. There is no distinctive Skt. word for 'religion'. It is best covered by dharma- (Ved. dharman-) 'what is established, law, usage, right conduct' (for such was religion in India), deriv. of dhṛ- 'hold, support'. Walde-P. 1.856 ff. Skt. mārga- 'way' (10.71) is used for the 'right way of life', the 'Buddhist way', etc.

Av. daēnā- (distinctive and frequent; NPers. dīn), prob., as orig. 'insight', fr. dī- 'see, look at, observe' (15.52). Walde-P. 1.832. Geldner, BB 15.261. Hübschmann, KZ 27.101. (Barth. 666 doubtful.)

22.12 GOD

Grk.	*θεός*	Goth.	*guþ*	Lith.	*dievas*
NG	*θεός*	ON	*goð, guð, tīvar* (pl.), *āss*	Lett.	*dievs*
Lat.	*deus*			ChSl.	*bogŭ*
It.	*dio*	Dan.	*gud*	SCr.	*bog*
Fr.	*dieu*	Sw.	*gud*	Boh.	*bůh*
Sp.	*dios*	OE	*god, ōs*	Pol.	*bóg*
Rum.	*dumnezeu, zeu*	ME	*god*	Russ.	*bog*
Ir.	*dia*	NE	*god*	Skt.	*deva-, sura-*
NIr.	*dia*	Du.	*god*	Av.	*baγa-*, OPers. *baga-*
W.	*duw*	OHG	*got*		
Br.	*doue*	MHG	*got*		
		NHG	*gott*		

For 'god' there is a group of cognates common to Italic, Celtic, Baltic, and Indo-Iranian (traces in Gmc., but not the usual word for 'god'), related to words for 'sky', 'day' and the widespread 'Sky-god', all from the notion of 'bright, shining'. A smaller group, common to Slavic and Iranian, is based on the notion of 'one who dispenses, gracious'. The other words are of disputed etymology.

The old words for a pagan 'god' were generally retained for the Christian 'God'. But a few forms are used only in the former sense.

For the biblical 'Lord', see 19.41.

1. IE **deiwo-s* in words for 'god', beside **dyew- *diw-* in words for 'sky' (1.51), 'day' (14.31), and the personified Grk. Ζεύς, gen. Διός, Lat. *Iuppiter* (earlier *Iūpiter*, fr. voc. = Grk. Ζεῦ πάτερ), gen. *Iovis*, early *Diovis*, Skt. *dyāus*, all with the common notion of 'bright, shining' and representing an extension of a simpler **dei-* seen in Skt. *dīdeti* 'shines', etc. Walde-P. 1.772 ff. Ernout-M. 263 f. Walde-H. 1.345 f. Grace Sturtevant Hopkins, IE **deiwos* and related words (exhaustive semantic study of the group, but with needless doubt of the underlying notion of 'bright').

OLat. *deiuos*, Lat. *deus* (> It. *dio*, Fr. *dieu*, Sp. *dios;* Rum. *zău* interj., *zeu* 'pagan god'; but for Christian God *dumnezeu*, fr. Lat. voc. *domine deus* 'Lord God'), Osc. fem. dat. sg. *deívaí;* Ir. *dia*, W. *duw*, Br. *doue;* ON *tīvar* (pl.; cf. ON *Tȳr*, OE *Tig*, gen. *Tīwes*, OHG *Zīo*); Lith. *dievas*, Lett. *dievs*, OPruss. *deiws;* Skt. *deva-* (Av. *daēva-*, OPers. *daiva-* 'demon', 22.35).

2. ChSl. *bogŭ*, etc., general Slavic (perh. early loanword fr. Iran. through the Scythians; cf. the Slavic word for 'dog', 3.61), Av. *baγa-*, OPers. *baga-* : Skt. *bhaga-* 'dispenser, gracious lord', *bhaj-* 'divide, distribute, share', Grk. aor. φαγεῖν ('partake of' >) 'eat'. Walde-P. 2.127 f. Berneker 66 f. Barth. 922.

3. Grk. θεός, fr. *θεσός (cf. θέσφατος 'spoken by god, ordained'), but root connection much disputed and still dub. Perh. best (but difficulties) : Lat. (*diēs*) *fēstus* 'holiday', *fēriae* 'holidays', Osc. *fíísnam*, Lat. *fānum* (**fas-no-*) 'shrine', fr. **dhēs-*, **dhəs-*, prob. an extension of **dhē-* 'put' in its frequently attested religious application. Walde-P. 1.867. Boisacq 339 f. Prellwitz, Festschrift Bezzenberger 121 ff. Walde-H. 1.454. Mrs. Hopkins, op. cit. 81 ff., rejects all the proposed IE etymologies and suggests that, like some of the names of the Greek gods, so θεός itself is a loanword from pre-Greek sources.

4. Goth. *guþ* (pl. *guda*), ON *goð, guð*, OE *god*, etc., general Gmc., orig. neut. and fr. **ghu-to-m*, neut. of pple. of **ĝheu-*

in Skt. *havate*, Av. *zavaiti*, ChSl. *zovetŭ* 'calls' (18.41), hence orig. 'what is invoked'; or, less probably, fr. **ĝheu-* in Skt. *hu-* 'pour an oblation, make an offering', Grk. χέω 'pour', etc. Walde-P. 1.530. Falk-Torp 359. Feist 228.

ON *āss* (runic inscr. *ansuR*), OE *ōs* (OHG *ans-* in proper names; Goth. Latinized acc. pl. *ansis*), used only of the old pagan gods, etym. dub.; taken by some as orig. 'spirit' fr. **ans-* an extension of **an-* 'breathe' (4.51); now more commonly as the same word as ON *āss* 'pole, beam' (Goth. *ans* 'mote'), with reference to the primitive worship of poles. Falk-Torp 9, 1429. Feist 52.

5. Skt. *sura-*, abstracted fr. *asura-* (as if *a-sura-*) after this had come to mean 'evil spirit' vs. earlier sense 'spiritual, beneficent spirit' (in RV freq. epithet of the gods, esp. Varuṇa; = Av. *ahura-* mostly in *Ahurō Mazdå*), prob. *asu-ra-*, fr. *asu-* 'breath of life, life'. Uhlenbeck 18, 338.

22.13 TEMPLE

Grk.	*νᾱός, ἱερόν*	Goth.	*alhs, gudhūs*	Lith.	*dievnamis*
NG	*ναός*	ON	*hof, vē*	Lett.	*dievnams*
Lat.	*templum, aedēs*	Dan.	*tempel*	ChSl.	*crŭky (chramŭ)*
It.	*tempio*	Sw.	*tempel*	SCr.	*hram*
Fr.	*temple*	OE	*temp(e)l, hearh, ealh*	Boh.	*chrám*
Sp.	*templo*	ME	*temple*	Pol.	*świątynia*
Rum.	*templu*	NE	*temple*	Russ.	*chram*
Ir.	*tempul*	Du.	*tempel*	Skt.	*cāitya-, stūpa-*, etc.
NIr.	*teampall*	OHG	*tempel*		
W.	*teml*	MHG	*tempel*		
Br.	*templ*	NHG	*tempel*		

'Temples' were unknown in the earliest times among most of the peoples of IE speech, who were still in the stage of more primitive worship, associated with hilltops, sacred stones, trees, or wooden pillars.

Many of the words for 'temple' are from 'dwelling, house' (with 'god' expressed or understood) or 'holy place', derived from adjs. for 'holy'. But the Latin *templum*, which furnished the most widespread Eur. word, was orig. a technical augural term.

1. Grk. νᾱός (Ion. νηός, Att. νεώς, but the νᾱός of most dialects common in the κοινή and reg. NG), Aeol. ναῦος, Lac. νᾱϝός, fr. *νασϝός : ναίω 'dwell' (*νασιω, cf. aor. ἔνασσα), hence orig. 'dwelling' (of the gods). Walde-P. 2.335. Boisacq 656. Otherwise, but improbably, Schrader, Reallex. 2.518 f.

Grk. ἱερόν 'holy place, shrine', and frequently 'temple', neut. of ἱερός 'holy' (22.19).

2. Lat. *templum* (hence the Romance, Celtic, and most of the Gmc. words), orig. 'the space in the heavens marked out by the augur', then 'consecrated place, sanctuary' and 'temple', fr. **tem-* in Grk. τέμνω 'cut' (9.22), τέμενος 'sacred precinct' (for Lat. *p*, cf. *exemplum*, fr. **exemlom : eximere*); or fr. *temp-* in Lith. *tempti* 'stretch' (9.32), Lat. *tempus* 'time'. Walde-P. 1.722. Ernout-M. 1023 f.

Lat. *aedēs* : Grk. αἴθω 'light up, kindle', mid. 'burn, blaze', Lat. *aestus* 'heat', etc. (1.85), hence orig. the 'sacred fire' and peculiarly applicable to the *aedēs Vestae*. Ernout-M. 15 f. Walde-H. 1.15.

3. Goth. *alhs*, OE *alh, ealh* (rare), OS *alah* (OHG *Alah-* in proper names), prob. : Lith. *alkas* 'sacred grove', and

further as orig. 'place of refuge' (cf. OE *ealh-stede* in this sense) : OE *ealgian* 'defend', Grk. ἀλέξω, aor. ἄλαλκα 'ward off'. Walde-P. 1.89 f. Feist 36 f.

Goth. *gudhūs* (once for ἱερόν) 'house of god'.

ON *hof* = OHG *hof* 'courtyard' (7.15).

ON *vē* 'shrine, temple' (also 'house, home') : Goth. *weihs*, OHG *wīh* 'holy' (22.19), OE *wēoh, wīh* 'idol' (22.37). Walde-P. 1.232. Falk-Torp 1376.

OE *hearh* 'shrine, temple' (mostly heathen) and 'idol' = OHG *haruc* 'sacred grove', ON *hǫrgr* 'pile of stones' as heathen shrine, outside connections dub. Walde-P. 1.31. Falk-Torp 418 f.

4. Lith. *dievnamis*, Lett. *dievnams* (or *dieva nams*), lit. 'house of god', cpd. of words for 'god' and 'house' (7.12).

5. ChSl. *crŭky* 'church' (22.21), also used for νᾱός and ἱερόν (so reg. in Gospels).

ChSl. *chramŭ* 'house' (7.12), only late 'temple', but in latter sense (also sometimes for 'church') SCr. *hram*, Boh. *chrám*, Russ. *chram* (fr. ChSl.). Berneker 397.

Pol. *świątynia*, fr. *święty* 'holy' (22.19). Brückner 537.

Pol. *kościół* 'church' (22.21) is used for 'temple' in the Bible.

6. There were no temples in Vedic times. Later names are the following.

Skt. *cāitya-* 'funeral monument', 'sacred tree', and 'shrine, temple', deriv. of *citā-* 'funeral pile', fem. of *cita-*, pple. of *ci-* 'arrange, pile up'.

Skt. *stūpa-*, in RV 'tuft of hair on top of head, top of head', later used for the dome-like structure over relics of Buddha, hence virtually Buddhist 'shrine, temple', etym.?

Skt. *devagṛha-* and *devālaya-*, cpds. of *deva-* 'god' with *gṛha-* 'house' and *ālaya-* 'dwelling' (*laya-* 'rest, dwelling', fr. *lī-* 'cling to').

There is no reference to temples in the Avesta, and, according to Herodotus, the Persians had no temples. OPers. *āyadana-* is 'place of worship', the nature of which is unknown, fr. *yad-* 'worship' (22.16). Barth. 332.

22.14 ALTAR

Grk.	*βωμός, θυσιαστήριον*	Goth.	*hunslastaþs*	Lith.	*altorius, aukuras*
NG	*βωμός*	ON	*altari (stallr)*	Lett.	*altars*
Lat.	*āra, altāre*	Dan.	*alter*	ChSl.	*ol(ŭ)tarĭ*
It.	*altare*	Sw.	*altare*	SCr.	*oltar*
Fr.	*autel*	OE	*wēobud (altar)*	Boh.	*oltář*
Sp.	*altar*	ME	*alter, auter, weved*	Pol.	*ołtarz*
Rum.	*altar*	NE	*altar*	Russ.	*altar'*
Ir.	*altōir*	Du.	*altaar*		
NIr.	*altōir*	OHG	*altari*		
W.	*allor*	MHG	*alter*		
Br.	*aoter*	NHG	*altar*		

Most of the Eur. words for 'altar' are derived from one of the two Lat. words, both of which seem to have first denoted an altar for burnt-offerings. In Greek a 'step' became 'platform' and 'altar'.

There are a few other words, meaning literally 'place of sacrifice' or 'holy table'.

1. Grk. βωμός (in Hom. also 'raised platform' and 'base of a statue'), orig. a 'step', like βῆμα, Dor. βᾶμα 'step, platform', fr. the root of ἔβην, Dor. ἔβᾱν,

aor. of βαίνω 'step, walk' (IE **g*ʷ*ā-* beside **g*ʷ*em-*, 10.47). Walde-P. 1.677. Boisacq 138.

Grk. θυσιαστήριον (usual word in LXX and NT), fr. θυσιάζω 'sacrifice', fr. sb. θυσία 'sacrifice' (22.15).

2. Lat. *āra*, OLat. *āsa* (Osc. loc. sg. *aasai*, Umbr. *asam-e* 'ad aram', etc.), fr. a root **ās-* 'burn, glow' (?) seen in Lat. *ārēre* 'be dry', *āridus* 'dry', *ardēre* 'burn, blaze', Skt. *āsa-* 'ashes, dust', Goth. *azgō*, OE *asce*, etc. 'ashes'. Ernout-M. 65, 70. Walde-H. 1.61, 65, 848.

Lat. *altāria*, pl. (later sg. *altāre* > Romance, Celtic, Gmc., and Balto-Slavic forms), sometimes 'burnt-offerings', but mostly 'high altar' (more splendid than *āra*), prob. : *adolēre* 'burn', but in popular feeling fr. *altus* 'high'. Walde-P. 1.88. Ernout-M. 38. Walde-H. 1.32, 845.

3. Goth. *hunslastaþs* (reg. for θυσιαστήριον), cpd. of *hunsl* 'sacrifice' (22.15) and *staþs* 'place'.

ON (beside *altari* for Christian altar) *stallr* 'block, pedestal of heathen statues' and so a sort of heathen 'altar' = OE *steall*, OHG *stal* 'standing place, stall', etc. Walde-P. 2.644. Falk-Torp 1147.

Cf. also ON *hǫrgr* 'pile of stones', a sort of 'stone altar' = OE *hearh* 'shrine, temple' (22.13).

OE (*altar* rare) *wēobud* (*-bud, -bod, -bed, wīgbed*, etc.), ME *weved*, cpd. of *wēoh-, wīh-* 'holy' (as sb. 'idol') : Goth. *weihs* 'holy', etc. (22.19) and *bēod* 'table' (7.44). NED s.v. *weved.*

4. Lith. *aukuras* (neolog. for 'heathen altar'), formed after *ugniakuras* 'fireplace' fr. *auka* 'offering, sacrifice' (22.15). Fraenkel, Z. sl. Ph. 6.89.

5. SCr. *žrtvenik*, Russ. *žertvennik*, used for a pagan 'altar' in distinction from the altar of the church (which in the Orthodox Church is really the whole chancel), fr. *žrtva, žertva* 'offering, sacrifice' (22.15).

22.15 SACRIFICE, OFFERING

Grk.	*θυσία*	Goth.	*hunsl, sauþs*	Lith.	*auka (apiera)*
NG	*θυσία*	ON	*blōt, tafn, fōrn*	Lett.	*upuris*
Lat.	*sacrificium*	Dan.	*offer*	ChSl.	*žrŭtva*
It.	*sacrificio*	Sw.	*offer*	SCr.	*žrtva*
Fr.	*sacrifice*	OE	*onsægedness, offrung, tiber, blōt*	Boh.	*obět*
Sp.	*sacrificio*			Pol.	*ofiara*
Rum.	*sacrificiu, jertfă*	ME	*offryng, sacrifise*	Russ.	*žertva*
Ir.	*idbart*	NE	*sacrifice, offering*	Skt.	*yajña-, medha-, hotrā-*
NIr.	*iodhbairt*	Du.	*offer*	Av.	*yasna-, zaoθrā-*
W.	*aberth, offrwm*	OHG	*bluostar, opfar, zebar*		
Br.	*aberz*	MHG	*opfer*		
		NHG	*opfer*		

Nouns for 'sacrifice', derived from the corresponding verbs (or in some cases conversely), are cognate with verbs for 'bring to' (hence 'offer'), 'worship', 'praise', or 'dedicate', with words for 'holy', and in some cases, as in origin 'burnt-offerings', with words for 'smoke, seethe, boil'.

Besides the most generic words, a few are noted which refer only to an 'animal sacrifice, victim'.

1. Grk. θυσία (also θῦμα less common) : θύω 'make a sacrifice' (in Hom. mostly a burnt-offering), this ultimately fr. the same root as θύω 'rage, seethe', θῡμός 'spirit, courage, anger', Lat. *fūmus*, Skt.

dhūma-, etc. 'smoke', all with basic notion of 'agitation'. Grk. θυσία orig. 'burnt-offering', though by no means so restricted in actual use. Walde-P. 1.837. Boisacq 360.

Grk. ἱερεῖον 'animal sacrifice', fr. ἱερός 'holy' (22.19).

2. Lat. *sacrificium* (> Romance words, etc.), with vb. *sacrificāre* 'make a sacrifice', cpd. of *sacer* 'holy, sacred' (22.19) and *facere* 'make'.

Lat. *victima* 'animal sacrifice', prob. : Umbr. *eveietu* 'voveto', Goth. *weihs* 'holy', etc. (22.19). Walde-P. 1.232. Ernout-M. 1102 f.

Lat. *hostia* 'animal sacrifice', etym. dub. Ernout-M. 462. Walde-H. 1.661 f.

Rum. *jertfă* (old word, before introduction of *sacrificiŭ*), fr. Slavic, SCr. *žrtva*, etc. (below, 6). Tiktin 870.

3. Ir. *idbart* (*edbart*), NIr. *iodhbairt*, vbl. n. of *adopuir* (3sg.) 'makes a sacrifice', cpd. of *berim* 'bear, carry'. Here also W. *aberth* and Br. *aberz* (Vallée s.v. *sacrifice;* not in Ernault; only *sakrifiz* in Le Gonidec, Ostervald NT, etc.). Pedersen 2.468, 472.

W. *offrwm*, fr. OE *offrung*, ME *offryng* (below, 4), with final *m* as in *botwm* 'button', fr. ME *boto(u)n* 'button'. Parry-Williams 42, 246.

4. Goth. *hunsl* = OE *hūsl* 'sacrifice' in Lindisf. Gosp. Mt. 12.7, but usually denoting the Christian 'housel, eucharist', as also ON *hūsl*, prob. : Lith. *šventas*, ChSl. *svętŭ*, etc. 'holy' (22.19). Feist 277. NED s.v. *housel*.

Goth. *saups* = ON *sauðr* 'sheep' (fr. the boiled mutton offered in pagan sacrifices, 3.25) : ON *sjōða*, OE *sēoþan* 'boil' (5.22). Walde-P. 2.471. Feist 413. Falk-Torp 952.

ON, OE *blōt*, OHG *bluostar* : Goth. *blōtan* 'worship', ON *blōta* 'worship, sacrifice', OE *blōtan*, OHG *bluozan* 'sacrifice'. See 22.16.

ON *tafn* : Arm. *taun* 'feast, festival', Lat. *daps* 'sacrificial feast, feast', Grk. δάπτω 'devour, rend', δαπάνη 'expense', etc. Walde-P. 1.764. Falk-Torp 1240.

ON *fōrn*, fr. *fœra* 'bring' (10.62). Falk-Torp 269.

OE *tiber, tifer(ī?)*, OHG *zebar* (Goth. *tibr*, dub. correction of *aibr*), etym. dub., perh. fr. a parallel form of the root in ON *tafn* (above). Walde-P. 1.765. Falk-Torp 1240. Feist 477. Walde-H. 1.323 f.

OE *onsægedness*, fr. vb. *onsecgan* 'sacrifice', cpd. of *secgan* 'say', with development through 'dedicate'.

OE *offrung*, ME *offryng*, NE *offering*, Dan., Sw., Du. *offer*, MLG *opper*, OHG *opfar, offar*, MHG *opfer, offer*, NHG *opfer*, fr. vbs. OE *offrian*, OHG *opfarōn, offaron*, these fr. Lat. *offerre* 'bring to, offer' in its eccl. sense of 'sacrifice'. But the *p, pf* forms require explanation and are perh. fr. (or by confusion with) Lat. *operārī* in its religious sense 'perform sacred rites'. NED s.v. *offering*. Falk-Torp 787 f. Weigand-H. 2.34 f. Kluge-G. 426. Franck-v. W. 467.

ME *sacrifise*, NE *sacrifice*, fr. Fr. *sacrifice*.

5. Lith. *auka*, neolog. based on a misunderstanding of *alko(s) kalnas*, in which *alka(s)* is gen. sg. of *alkas* or *alka* 'sacred grove'. Buga, quoted by Fraenkel, Z. sl. Ph. 6.88 f.

Lith. *apiera* (so Kurschat, Trowitsch NT, etc.; now replaced by *auka*), fr. Pol. *ofiara* (below, 6). Brückner, Sl. Fremdwörter 68.

Lett. *upuris*, fr. MLG *opper* (above, 4). Mühl.-Endz. 4.301.

6. ChSl. *žrŭtva*, SCr. *žrtva*, Russ. *žertva* (Boh. *žertva*, but not the usual word), fr. the vb. seen in ChSl. *žrŭti* (*žrěti, žirą*) 'sacrifice', this through 'worship' : Lith. *girti*, Skt. *gṛ-* 'praise' (17.79). Trautmann 88. Meillet, MSL 14.379 f.

Boh. *oběť* (Pol. *obiata, obieta* obs.) = ChSl. *obětŭ* 'vow, promise, covenant' : *oběštati* 'promise' (18.36). Brückner 370, 614.

Pol. *ofiara*, displacing *obiata* but owing to it the *ia* instead of *ie* in *ofiera*, this (through Boh. *oféra* or directly) fr. MHG *offer* (above, 4). Brückner 375.

7. Skt. *yajña-*, Av. *yasna-*, both 'worship' in widest sense (concretely with prayers, hymns, etc.), but also 'sacrifice' (so RV+; in Avesta Yt. 3.18, 5.89, etc.), fr. Skt. *yaj-*, Av. *yaz-* 'worship' (22.16).

Skt. *medha-* 'juice, sap', then also 'animal sacrifice, victim' (cf. *açva-medha-* 'horse sacrifice', etc.), etym.? Uhlenbeck 232.

Skt. *hotrā-*, Av. *zaoθrā-*, both mostly a 'liquid offering', fr. the root in Skt. *hu-* 'pour a libation, make an offering', Grk. χέω 'pour', etc. Barth. 1654 f.

22.16 WORSHIP (vb.)

Grk.	*σέβομαι, προσκυνέω*	Goth.	*inweitan, blōtan*	Lith.	*garbinti*
NG	*προσκυνῶ*	ON	*blōta*	Lett.	*pielūgt*
Lat.	*venerārī, adōrāre*	Dan.	*tilbede*	ChSl.	*klaněti sę, pokloniti sę (čisti)*
It.	*adorare*	Sw.	*tillbedja*		
Fr.	*adorer*	OE	*gebiddan, geēaþmēdan, weorþian*	SCr.	*(po)štovati*
Sp.	*adorar*			Boh.	*ctíti, klaněti se*
Rum.	*adora*	ME	*worschip*	Pol.	*czcić, wielbić*
Ir.	*adraim*	NE	*worship*	Russ.	*poklonjat'sja*
NIr.	*adhraim*	Du.	*aanbidden, vereeren*	Skt.	*yaj-*
W.	*addoli*	OHG	*betōn*	Av.	*yaz-*, OPers. *yad-*
Br.	*azeuli*	MHG	*anbeten*		
		NHG	*anbeten, verehren*		

Verbs for 'worship' are most commonly connected with verbs for 'pray', or based on some gesture of homage ('kiss' or 'bow'), or are verbs for 'honor', which when used with 'god' or the like are intensified to 'worship'. Other scattered sources are 'shrink from, feel awe of', 'love', 'cultivate', 'heed', 'humble oneself'. On the history of Grk. προσκυνέω and Lat. *adōrāre*, cf. B. M. Marti, Language 12.272 ff.

1. Grk. σέβομαι 'feel awe of', sometimes 'fear', commonly 'revere, worship', as orig. 'shrink from' : Skt. *tyaj-* 'leave, abandon, shun'. Walde-P. 1.746. Boisacq 857.

Grk. προσκυνέω, cpd. of κυνέω 'kiss' (16.28) and orig. denoting a gesture of homage, NG προσκυνῶ 'worship' and 'salute' (σέβομαι mostly 'revere, respect').

2. Lat. *venerārī*, deriv. of *venus* 'love, charm' (16.26). Walde-P. 1.259. Ernout-M. 1083.

Lat. *adōrāre* (stronger than *venerārī;* hence the Romance words, but Rum. *adora* neolog. fr. Fr.), orig. 'speak to', then 'pray to' and 'worship', cpd. of *ōrāre* 'plead', esp. 'pray' (22.17). Ernout-M. 714.

Lat. *colere* 'inhabit, frequent, cultivate' (cf. *incolere* 7.11), frequently with forms of *deus*, etc. 'honor, worship'. Ernout-M. 205.

Rum. *slavi* 'glorify' (fr. Slavic, ChSl. *slaviti* beside *slava* 'glory', 16.37), formerly also 'worship'. Tiktin 1438 ff.

3. Ir. *adraim*, NIr. *adhraim*, W. *addoli*, Br. *azeuli*, fr. Lat. *adōrāre* (above, 2). Pedersen 1.206, 207, 2.450. Vendryes, De hib. voc. 110. Loth, Mots lat. 130.

4. Goth. *inweitan* (reg. for προσκυνέω, once for ἀσπάζομαι 'salute'), cpd. of **weitan* = OE *wītan* 'see to, heed, guard, blame', OHG *wīzzan* 'notice, heed', fr. the same root as Goth., OE *witan* 'know'. Walde-P. 1.238. Feist 167.

Goth. *blōtan* (= σέβομαι Mk. 7.7, λατρεύω 'serve' Lk. 2.37; as sb. *guþ blōtan* θεοσέβεια; *guþblōstreis* θεοσεβής), ON *blōta* 'worship' and 'sacrifice' = OE *blōtan*, OHG *bluozan* 'sacrifice', outside connection dub., perh. : Lat. *flāmen* 'priest' (22.18). Walde-P. 1.209. Feist 101. Falk-Torp 86. Walde-H. 1.512.

OE *gebiddan*, OHG *betōn*, MHG, NHG *anbeten*, Du. *aanbidden*, Dan. *tilbede*, Sw. *tillbedja*, all words for 'pray' (22.17) used also, alone or in cpds., for 'worship'.

OE *ge-ēaþmēdan* 'humble' and 'worship' (latter freq. in Gospels), fr. *ēaþmēd* 'humility', *ēaþmōd* 'humble' (= OHG *ōdmuoti* 'humble'), cpd. of *ēaþe* 'easy' (9.96) and *mōd* 'mood, feeling' (= Goth. *mōþs* 'anger' 16.42).

OE *weorþian* 'value, honor' and 'worship' (*worþian* reg. for 'worship' in Lindisf. Gospels), fr. *weorþ* 'value, worth' (11.87).

ME *worschip* (etc., numerous spellings), NE *worship*, fr. sb. of like form, this fr. OE *weorþscipe* 'esteem, honor, high rank', cpd. of *weorþ* 'value, worth'. NED s.v. *worship*.

NHG *verehren*, intensive cpd. of *ehren* 'honor' (OHG *ērōn*, MHG *ēren*, fr. sb. OHG *ēra* 'honor', 16.46), hence 'greatly honor' and with 'god' or the like virtually 'worship'. Similarly Du. *vereeren*.

5. Lith. *garbinti* 'honor' and 'worship' : *garbė* 'honor' (16.46).

Lith. *melsti* 'pray' (22.17), also usual for 'worship' in NT versions.

Lith. *pasikluonoti* (often 'worship' in Trowitsch NT; now only in literal sense 'bow to' or 'salute'), cpd. of *kluonotis* 'bow', fr. Pol. *kłaniać się* id. Brückner, Sl. Fremdwörter 94.

Lett. *pielūgt*, cpd. of *lūgt* 'pray' (22.17). Mühl.-Endz. 269.

6. ChSl. *klaněti sę, pokloniti sę* (reg. in Gospels for προσκυνέω), Boh. *klaněti se*, Russ. *poklonjat'sja*, all lit. 'bow (to)' : ChSl. *kloniti* 'bow', etym. dub. Berneker 509, 522 f.

ChSl. *čisti* (reg. for τιμάω, but also σέβομαι), SCr. *(po)štovati*, Boh. *ctíti*, Pol. *czcić*, all also and orig. 'honor' : ChSl. *čĭstĭ*, etc. sb. 'honor' (16.46).

Pol. *wielbić*, orig. 'make much of, magnify', hence 'glorify, worship', fr. *wiele* 'much' (13.15).

7. Skt. *yaj-*, Av. *yaz-*, OPers. *yad-* (cf. e.g. Daiva inscr. 39 f. *yadāyā paruvam daivā ayadiy avadā adam auramazdām ayadaiy* 'where formerly the daivas were worshiped, there I worshiped Auramazda') : Grk. ἅγιος 'holy', ἅζομαι 'stand in awe of'. Walde-P. 1.195. Barth. 1274 ff.

22.17 PRAY

Grk.	*εὔχομαι, ἀράομαι*	Goth.	*bidjan*	Lith.	*melsti(s)*
NG	*προσεύχομαι*	ON	*biðja*	Lett.	*lūgt*
Lat.	*precārī, ōrāre*	Dan.	*bede*	ChSl.	*moliti sę*
It.	*pregare (orare)*	Sw.	*bedja*	SCr.	*moliti se*
Fr.	*prier*	OE	*biddan*	Boh.	*modliti se*
Sp.	*orar*	ME	*bidde, preye*	Pol.	*modlić się*
Rum.	*ruga*	NE	*pray*	Russ.	*molit'sja*
Ir.	*guidim*	Du.	*biddan*	Skt.	*yāc-, prārthaya-*
NIr.	*guidhim*	OHG	*betōn*	Av., OPers.	*ǰad-*, Av. *frī-*
W.	*gweddio*	MHG	*beten*		
Br.	*pedi*	NHG	*beten*		

Many of the words for 'pray' are the same as, or cognate with, those for 'ask, request', discussed in 18.35. Some are cognate with verbs for 'seek' or 'long for'. Some seem to rest on the notion of 'speak' in a formal manner. One considerable group comes (through 'propitiate') from 'soften'.

Words for 'call upon, invoke', mostly like those for 'call' (18.41), are often virtually 'pray to'.

1. Grk. εὔχομαι (sbs. εὐχή, εὐχωλή) and cpds. ἐπ-, κατ-, προσ-(προσ- reg. in NT and NG) : Av. *aoǰ-* in *aoxta, aogədā* (Gathas) 'spoke, said', Skt. *ohate* 'notices, listens for', and (**wegʷh-* beside **eugʷh-*) Skt. *vāghat-* 'one who makes offerings', Lat. *vovēre* 'vow', Umbr. *vufetes* 'votis'. Walde-P. 1.110. Ernout-M. 1135.

Grk. ἀράομαι, fr. ἀρά 'prayer' (*ἀϝϝά shown by Arc. κάταρϝος 'accursed'), prob. : Lat. *ōrāre* 'pray, plead' (see below, 2).

2. Lat. *precārī* (late *precāre* > It. *pregare*, OFr. *preier*, Fr. *prier*, OSp. *pregar*), with sb. *prex, precis*, mostly pl. *precēs*, fr. the same root as Lat. *poscere*, ChSl. *prositi* 'ask for', Goth. *fraihnan*, Skt. *pracch-, praç-* 'ask', etc., (18.31, 18.35). Walde-P. 2.49. Ernout-M. 795. REW 6733.

Lat. *ōrāre* 'plead' (Osc. *urust* 'oraverit' likewise a legal term), but mostly 'pray' (> It. *orare*, OFr. *orer*, Sp., Port. *orar*, of which only the last is the usual word for 'pray'; Rum. *ura* 'bless'), prob. (not fr. *ōs* 'mouth', in which case Osc. *urust* would be a loanword, not in itself difficult), with a common notion of 'speak formally' : Grk. ἀράομαι 'pray', ἀρύω 'say, shout' (only Hesych.), Russ. *orat'* 'cry out, bawl', Skt. *āryanti* 'they praise' (dub., cf. Oldenberg, Rigveda, Textkrit. und exeget. Noten p. 97), Arm. *uranam* 'deny'. Walde-P. 1.182. Ernout-M. 714.

Rum. *ruga* 'ask for', but mostly 'pray', with sb. *rugă* 'prayer', fr. Lat. *rogāre* 'ask' (18.31, 18.35).

3. Ir. *guidim* 'ask for', mostly 'pray', NIr. *guidhim*, W. *gweddio*, with sbs. Ir. *guide*, NIr. *guidhe*, W. *gweddi* 'prayer' : Grk. ποθέω 'long for, regret', θέσσασθαι, Av., OPers. *ǰad-* 'pray for, beseech', Lith. *gedauti* 'long for', *gedėti* 'mourn', etc. Walde-P. 1.673. Pedersen 1.108, 2.550 f.

Br. *pedi* (or *pidi*), fr. Lat. *petere* 'seek'. Loth, Mots lat. 194.

4. Goth. *bidjan*, ON *biðja*, Dan. *bede*, Sw. *bedja*, OE *biddan*, ME *bidde*, Du. *bidden*, the same words as those for 'ask, request' (18.35). But differentiated OHG *betōn*, MHG, NHG *beten* 'pray', fr. sb. OHG *beta* = Goth. *bida* 'prayer'. Weigand-H. 1.221 f.

ME *preye*, NE *pray*, fr. OFr. *preier* (above, 2).

5. Lith. *melsti, meldžiu* (also 'ask, request', but reg. word for 'pray', formerly trans. and intr., now refl. *melstis* for latter), with sb. *malda* 'prayer', ChSl. *moliti sę*, SCr. *moliti se*, Boh. *modliti se*, Pol. *modlić się*, Russ. *molit'sja*, with sbs. ChSl., SCr., Russ. *molitva*, Boh. *modlitba*, Pol. *modła, modlitwa* 'prayer' (Slavic *modl-* fr. **mold-l-*), fr. **meld-*, **mḷd-* in Lat. *mollis* 'soft', ChSl. *mladŭ* 'tender', Grk. μέλδω, ἀμαλδύνω 'soften', OE *meltan* 'melt', etc. Walde-P. 2.289 f. Berneker 2.65 f.

Lett. *lūgt*, etym. dub., perh. : ON *lokka*, OE *loccian*, etc. 'entice'. Mühl.-Endz. 2.518. Endzelin, KZ 52.114 ff.

6. Skt. *yāc-* and *prārthaya-*, see 18.35. Av., OPers. *ǰad-* 'beseech, pray for' : Ir. *guidim*, etc. (above, 3).

Av. *frī-* 'propitiate' and sometimes 'pray' (Y. 29.5) : Skt. *prī-* 'please', *priya-* 'dear'. Barth. 1016.

22.18 PRIEST

Grk.	*ἱερεύς*	Goth.	*gudja*	Lith.	*kunigas*
NG	*παπᾶς*	ON	*goði, prestr*	Lett.	*priesteris*
Lat.	*sacerdōs*	Dan.	*præst*	ChSl.	*ierejĭ, čistitelʹĭ, žĭrĭcĭ, svęštenikŭ, popŭ*
It.	*prete, sacerdote*	Sw.	*präst*		
Fr.	*prêtre*	OE	*sacerd, prēost*	SCr.	*svećenik, pop*
Sp.	*sacerdote (preste)*	ME	*preste*	Boh.	*kněz, pop*
Rum.	*preot, popă*	NE	*priest*	Pol.	*ksiądz*
Ir.	*drui, sacart, cruimther*	Du.	*priester*	Russ.	*svjaščennik, pop*
		OHG	*ēwart, priestar*	Skt.	*ṛtvij-, hotar-*
NIr.	*sagart*	MHG	*priester, ēwart*	Av.	*āϑravan-, zaotar-*
W.	*offeiriad*	NHG	*priester*		
Br.	*beleg*				

Of the words for 'priest', some are those used for the pagan priest, a few of which were retained in the Christian Church. More are terms arising in the Christian Church, which are used also when referring to a pagan priest.

Some are derived from words for 'holy', 'god', 'sacrifice', or 'invoke'. The most widespread Eur. group goes back to a Greek word for 'elder'; some others, likewise orig. terms of respect, to a child's word for 'father', or to a word denoting 'one of noble birth' which developed to 'king' or 'prince' and also, through 'master, lord', to 'priest'.

1. Grk. ἱερεύς, fr. ἱερός 'holy' (22.19). Also ἱεροθύτης, cpd. with deriv. of θύω 'sacrifice'.

NG παπᾶς, fr. Byz. παπᾶς title of a bishop (as eccl. Lat. *pāpa*), fr. Grk. πάππας (Hom.), later πάπας child's word for 'father'.

2. Lat. *sacerdōs, -ōtis* (> It., Sp. *sacerdote*), fr. **sakro-dō-t-*, cpd. of *sacer* 'holy' (22.19) and a form of the root **dhē-* in Lat. *facere* 'do, make', etc. Ernout-M. 883. Walde-H. 1.442.

OFr. *prestre*, Fr. *prêtre* (Sp. *preste* now only in a specialized application), fr. eccl. Lat. *presbyter*, eccl. Grk. πρεσβύτερος 'elder' of the church, orig. comp. of πρέσβυς 'old man'; It. *prete*, Rum. *preot*, fr. a late Lat. by-form *praebyter* (as if : *praebēre* 'grant'). REW 6740.

Rum. *popă*, fr. Grk. through Slavic (cf. below, 6).

3. Ir. *drui* (gen. *druad*) 'druid', name of the old pagan priest, cpd. of **dru-* seen in words for 'tree, firm, true', etc. and **wid-* 'know'. Walde-P. 2.805. Pedersen 1.61, 175. Thurneysen, Z. celt. Ph. 16.276 f.

Ir. *sacart*, NIr. *sagart*, fr. Lat. *sacerdōs*. Vendryes, De hib. voc. 172.

Ir. *cruimther*, OW *premter*, fr. late Lat. *praebyter* (above, 2). Pedersen 1.198, 235, 287. Vendryes, De hib. voc. 132.

W. *offeiriad*, fr. MW *offeren* 'mass', fr. MLat. *offerenda* 'offerings, oblation'. Loth, Mots lat. 191.

Br. *beleg*, MBr. *baelec*, fr. **baclācos* 'one carrying the pastoral staff', fr. Lat. *baculum, baculus* (> W. *bagl*) 'staff'. Henry 30. Loth, Mots lat. 136. Ernault, Dict. étym. s.v. *baelec*.

4. Goth. *gudja*, ON *goði* (the old pagan priest vs. the Christian *prestr*), fr. Goth. *guþ*, ON *goð* 'god', but perh. through an underlying root notion of 'invoke' (cf. 22.12) and so orig. 'invoker'. Feist 224.

OE *sacerd*, fr. Lat. *sacerdōs* (above, 2).

OE *prēost* (> ON *prestr*), ME *preste*, NE *priest*, Dan. *præst*, Sw. *präst*, OHG *priestar* (rare), MHG, NHG, MLG, Du. *priester*, all (partly through OFr. *prestre*) fr. Lat. *presbyter* (above, 2). Falk-Torp 848. NED s.v. *priest*.

OHG, MHG *ēwart*, lit. 'guardian of the law', cpd. of *ēwa* 'law' (21.12) and *wart* 'guardian'. Weigand-H. 2.472.

5. Lith. *kunigas* (used for either Catholic priest or Lutheran pastor) = Lett. *kungs* 'master, lord', ChSl. *kŭnędzĭ* 'prince', etc. (19.35), fr. a Gmc. **kuningas* = OHG *kuning*, etc. ('king', orig. 'one of noble birth' (19.32). Specialization of 'noble, master, lord' to 'priest', as in Boh. *kněz*, Pol. *ksiądz* (below, 6). Cf. also NE *Domine, Dominie* (fr. Lat. voc. *domine* 'lord') applied to the clergy, and NE *parson*, orig. 'person' of note. Berneker 663. Stender-Petersen 199 ff.

Lett. *priesteris*, fr. MLG *priester* (above, 4).

6. ChSl. *ierejĭ* (so reg. in Gospels), fr. Grk. ἱερεύς. For the following native words, cf. Jagić, Entstehungsgesch. 309.

ChSl. *čistitelʹĭ* (Supr.), fr. *čisti* 'honor, revere, worship' (22.16).

ChSl. *žĭrĭcĭ* (Supr. freq.), fr. *žrŭti* 'sacrifice' (22.15).

ChSl. *svęštenikŭ* (late), SCr. *svećenik*, Russ. *svjaščennik*, fr. ChSl. *svętŭ*, etc. 'holy' (22.19).

ChSl. *popŭ* (reg. in Euchol.), *pop* in all modern Slavic languages popular term, sometimes disrespectful, fr. Grk. πάπας (cf. Byz. παπᾶς, above, 1). Miklosich 258. Brückner 430. Stender-Petersen 428 f.

Boh. *kněz*, Pol. *ksiądz*, earlier 'prince' (19.35), Brückner 277.

7. Skt. *ṛtvij-* (most generic word), cpd. of *ṛtu-* 'right time' and weak form of *yaj-* 'worship' (22.16).

Skt. *hotar-*, Av. *zaotar-*, fr. the root seen in Skt. *hu-* 'pour an oblation, make an offering', Grk. χέω 'pour', etc., and that in Skt. *havate*, Av. *zavaiti*, ChSl. *zovetŭ* 'calls upon, invokes', both notions blended in the priest who worships with hymns and sacrifice. Barth. 1653. Oldenberg, Religion des Veda 386. Macdonell-Keith 1.112 ff.

Av. *āϑravan-, aϑaurun-* (main word) = Skt. *atharvan-* 'fire- and soma-priest', fr. the word attested in Av. *ātar-* (nom. *ātarš*, gen. *āϑrō*) 'fire', despite the difficulty of the Skt. *th* (Av. *ϑ* easily fr. forms like *āϑrō*). Walde-P. 1.42. Barth. 66. Uhlenbeck 6.

22.182. 'Clergyman, minister, parson', etc. The Eur. words listed in 22.18 are used for the 'priest' in the Roman Catholic and Greek Orthodox Churches. NE *priest* is also used in the Anglican Church (cf. NED s.v. 2b), Dan. *præst*, Sw. *präst* are generic 'clergyman', and Lith. *kunigas* is the usual term for the Lutheran 'parson' as well as the Catholic 'priest'.

But for the most part other terms are preferred in the Protestant Church, of which the following may be noted.

NE *clergyman*, deriv. of *clergy*, fr. OFr. *clergie* in use = *clergié* (Fr. *clergé*), fr. eccl. Lat. *clēricātus*, fr. *clēricus* 'cleric', fr. Grk. κληρικός, fr. κλῆρος 'lot, inheritance', in eccl. Grk. 'clerical office' and coll. 'clergy'. NED s.vv. *clergy* and *cleric*.

NHG *geistlicher*, Du. *geestelijke*, Dan. *gejstlig*, fr. NHG *geist*, etc. 'spirit' (16.11).

NE *minister*, orig. 'servant' (fr. Lat. *minister* id.), hence in specialized use *minister* of the church, etc. (now prob. the most usual term except in the Anglican Church, where also formerly common). NED s.v.

NE *parson* (now mostly in rural communities or even there old-fashioned, where *parsonage* may be still in common use), same word as *person* (fr. Lat. *persōna* 'mask, person'), from which it became differentiated in both sense and form (normal phonetic development as

in *heart*, old *sarvant*, etc. vs. spelling-pronunciation in *person*). NED s.v.

NHG *pfarrer*, fr. *pfarre*, OHG *pfarra* 'parish', this : OHG *pfarrik*, OE *pearroc* 'inclosure', but taken as the equivalent of late eccl. Lat. *parochia* (source of NE *parrish*, etc.), earlier *paroecia*, fr. Grk. παροικία 'diocese, parish' in eccl. use, earlier 'sojourning', fr. πάροικος 'dwelling near, neighboring'. Weigand-H. 2.404. Kluge-G. 439. NED s.v. *parrock*.

NE, NHG, Dan., Sw. *pastor*, Du. *pastoor*, orig. 'shepherd' (fr. Lat. *pāstor* id.). Similarly Du. *herder* 'shepherd' and 'pastor'.

NE *preacher*, NHG *prediger*, Du. *predikant*, fr. the vbs. for 'preach' (22.22).

Lett. *mācītājs* = Lith. *mokytojis* 'teacher' (17.27). Mühl.-Endz. 2.576.

22.183. 'Monk'. Grk. μοναχός 'alone, solitary' (: μόνος 'alone', 13.33) was used in early Christian times as a sb. for the solitary 'hermit' and then for 'monk' as now understood. Hence, mostly through Lat. *monachus* (or in part VLat. **monicus*), nearly all the Eur. words. NED s.v. *monk*. REW 5654. Kluge-G. 397. Berneker 2.75.

But Grk. γέρων 'old man' was a popular term, e.g. in Jo. Moschus regularly, rarely μοναχός. Hence also καλόγηρος (cpd. with καλός 'good'), now the pop. NG καλόγερος with fem. καλόγρηα 'nun', whence also Rum. *călugăr* with fem. *călugăriţa*, and SCr. *kaluđer* with fem. *kaluđerica*.

Lith. *vienuolis* (with fem. *vienuolė*), deriv. of *vienas* 'one', is a neolog. in place of *minykas* (latter in Kurschat, Lalis; not in NSB).

In Brahmanic India there were hermits, ascetics, sages, etc., but communities of monks and nuns are characteristic of Buddhism. The Pali name for 'monk' was *bhikku* = Skt. *bhikṣu-* 'beggar, religious mendicant', whence fem. *bhikkunī* 'nun'.

22.184. 'Nun'. There is much more variety in words for 'nun' than in those for 'monk'.

1. Several are feminine forms corresponding to the words for 'monk', as Grk. μονάστρια, μοναχή, Lat. *monacha*, It. *monaca*, Sp. *monja*, ChSl. *monachija*, etc.; NG καλόγρηα, Rum. *călugăriţa*, SCr. *kaluđerica*; Lith. *vienuolė*.

2. The principal other group is late Lat. *nonna* (*nonnus* 'monk' also occurs), whence Fr. *nonne* and the general Gmc. words. Used also for 'nurse', this was originally an infantile term of endearment like Grk. νέννος, νάννας 'uncle', νάννα 'aunt', It. *nonno, nonna* 'grandfather, grandmother', etc. Ernout-M. 676. NED s.v. *nun*.

3. It. *religiosa*, Fr. *religieuse*, fem. sb. of adj. for 'religious'.

4. NIr. *bean riaghalta*, lit. 'regulated woman', *bean* 'woman' and *riaghalta* : *riaghal* 'rule'. Cf. Ir. *manaig riagalta* 'monk' (Laws, Gloss. 613).

5. W. *llean*, Br. *leanez*, Corn. *laines*, derivs. of words for 'oath, vow', W. *llw*, Br. *le* (21.25).

6. SCr. *duvna*, fr. earlier *dumna*, fr. Lat. *domina* 'mistress'. Rječnik Akad. 2.886, 907.

7. Boh. *jeptiška*, fr. late Lat. *abbatissa* 'abbess'. Gebauer 1.97.

22.19 HOLY, SACRED

Grk.	*ἱερός, ἅγιος, ὅσιος*	Goth.	*weihs (hailags)*	Lith.	*šventas*
NG	*ἅγιος (ἱερός, ὅσιος)*	ON	*heilagr*	Lett.	*svēts*
Lat.	*sacer, sānctus*	Dan.	*hellig*	ChSl.	*svętŭ*
It.	*santo, sacro*	Sw.	*helig*	SCr.	*svet*
Fr.	*saint, sacré*	OE	*hālig*	Boh.	*svatý*
Sp.	*santo, sacro*	ME	*holy, sacrid*	Pol.	*święty*
Rum.	*sfînt, sacru*	NE	*holy, sacred*	Russ.	*svjatoj*
Ir.	*nōib*	Du.	*heilig*	Skt.	(*puṇya-*, etc.)
NIr.	*naomhtha*	OHG	*heilag, wīh*	Av.	*spənta-*
W.	*sanctaidd*	MHG	*heilec*		
Br.	*santel, sakr*	NHG	*heilig*		

Words for 'holy, sacred' are from diverse sources, and in the majority of them the ultimate root connection is doubtful.

1. Grk. ἱερός (dial. ἱαρός, ἰαρός, ἶρος), etym. much disputed; perh. fr. a pre-Greek form going with Etrusc. *aesar* 'god', Osc. *aisusis* 'sacrificiis', Umbr. *esono-* 'sacer', etc.; or (with rejection of the view that words of different origin are merged in ἱερός) : Skt. *iṣira-* 'vigorous, lively' with development in Greek through 'powerful, supernatural'. Boisacq 368. Schulze, Quaest. Epic. 210 ff. Kretschmer, Glotta 11.278 ff. Walde-H. 1.718. Duchesne-Guillemin, Mélanges Boisacq 1.333 ff.

Grk. ἅγιος, beside ἁγνός (only latter in Hom.) and vb. ἅζομαι 'stand in awe of' : Skt. *yaj-*, Av. *yaz-* 'worship' (22.16). Walde-P. 1.195. Boisacq 7.

Grk. ὅσιος (differentiated in use from the preceding, 'sanctioned by divine law' and even contrasted in phrases like ἱερὰ καὶ ὅσια 'things sacred and profane'), etym. dub., perh. : ἐτεός 'true', ἐτάζω 'examine', etc. Walde-P. 1.161. Boisacq 721.

In Christian terminology ἅγιος became the main word (like Lat. *sānctus* vs. *sacer*), hence also in names of Saints. NG ἱερός and ὅσιος are lit., current in certain phrases.

2. Lat. *sacer* (> It., Sp. *sacro*, Rum. *sacru*, learned forms), Osc. σακορο 'sacra', *sakrím* 'hostiam', Umbr. *sacra* 'sacras', *sacris* 'hostiis', etc. (Italic stems *sakro-* and *sakri-*, with numerous derivs.); hence vb. *sacrāre*, pple. *sacrātus* (> Fr. *sacré*), and fr. the same root *sancīre*, pple. *sānctus* (> It., Sp. *santo*, Fr. *saint*; Rum. *sînt* in names of holidays, Tiktin 1432), Osc. *saahtúm* 'sanctum', Umbr. *sahatam* 'sanctam', a distinctive Italic group, without any clear outside connections. Walde-P. 2.448. Ernout-M. 882 ff.

Rum. *sfînt*, fr. Slavic, cf. ChSl. *svętŭ*, etc. (below, 5).

3. Ir. *nōib, nōeb, noem*, NIr. *naomh* (sb. 'a saint'), whence *naomhtha* (lit. 'saint-ed') : OPers. *naiba-* 'good' (16.71).

W. *sanctaidd*, learned borrowing fr. Lat. *sanctus* with W. suffix *-aidd* added.

Br. *santel*, adj. deriv. of *sant* 'a saint', fr. Lat. *sānctus*. Loth, Mots lat. 205.

Br. *sakr*, learned borrowing fr. Lat. *sacer*.

4. Goth. *weihs* (reg. for ἅγιος), OHG *wīh* (Otfr., etc., but only *heilag* in Tat., Notker, etc.), MHG *wīch* (mostly in names of holidays; NHG *weih-* in *weihnacht* 'Christmas', etc.), OE *wēoh-* in *wēobud* 'altar' 22.14, beside sb. *wēoh* 'idol', ON *vē* 'temple' (22.13), prob. : Lat. *victima* 'animal sacrifice', Umbr. *eveietu* 'voveto', but further root connections dub. Walde-P. 1.232. Falk-Torp 1376. Feist 557 f.

Goth. *hailags* (but only in neut. *heilag* 'dedicated' in a runic inscription), ON *heilagr*, OE *hālig*, OHG *heilag*, etc., general Gmc., fr. Goth. *hails*, ON *heill*, OE *hāl*, OHG *heil* 'in good health, sound, uninjured' (4.83), with semantic development through 'inviolate' or possibly 'bringing well-being'. Falk-Torp 396. Feist 232. NED s.v. *holy*.

ME *sacrid*, NE *sacred*, orig. pple. of *sacre* 'consecrate', fr. OFr. *sacrer* id., Lat. *sacrāre*, with history parallel to that of Fr. *sacré* (above, 2). NED s.v.

5. Lith. *šventas*, OPruss. *swints*, Lett. *svēts* (Lett. and perh. OPruss. forms fr. Slavic), ChSl. *svętŭ*, etc. general Slavic, Av. *spənta-*, all fr. **k̂wento-*, deriv. of a *k̂wen-* attested in Lett. *svinēt* 'celebrate', Av. *spanyah-*, *spəništa-* 'holier, holiest', *spānah-* 'holiness', prob. Goth. *hunsl* 'sacrifice' (22.15), but further root connections dub. Walde-P. 1.471. Barth. 1619 ff.

6. There is no quite distinctive Skt. word for 'holy', but the following sometimes have this sense.

Skt. *puṇya-* (etym.?) 'fortunate, pleasant, good', also 'pure' and 'holy', esp. in cpds. as *puṇya-bhū-* 'holy land', *puṇya-sthāna-* 'holy place'.

Skt. *tīrthaka-*, fr. *tīrtha-* 'passage, ford' (: *tṛ-* 'pass over, cross') and 'place of pilgrimage'.

Much more common is the sb. *muni-* 'holy man, saint, seer, ascetic' (but in RV 'impulse'), etym.?

22.21 CHURCH

(Both as the Body, Community, and as the Building except as noted, a for former, b for latter)

Grk.	(late) ἐκκλησία; κῡριακόν (b)	Goth.	*aikklēsjō* (a)	Lith.	*bažnyčia*
		ON	*kirkja*	Lett.	*baznīca*
NG	ἐκκλησία	Dan.	*kirke*	ChSl.	*crŭky*
Lat.	(late) *ecclēsia; basilica* (b)	Sw.	*kyrka*	SCr.	*crkva*
		OE	*cirice, circe*	Boh.	*církev* (a); *kostel* (b)
It.	*chiesa*	ME	*cherch(e), church(e)*	Pol.	*kościoł*
Fr.	*église*	NE	*church*	Russ.	*cerkov'*
Sp.	*iglesia*	Du.	*kerk*		
Rum.	*biserică*	OHG	*chirihha, kirihha*		
Ir.	*eclais*	MHG	*kirche*		
NIr.	*eaglais*	NHG	*kirche*		
W.	*eglwys*				
Br.	*iliz*				

With a few exceptions the same words cover 'church' both as the body, community, and as the building. But in all such cases one of these applications was the earlier, with subsequent extension to the other.

There are two main groups. In one, the Grk. ἐκκλησία, the old term for a political assembly, came to be used for the Christian 'church' as a body, later as a building, and was adopted in Latin and through Latin in the Romance and Celtic languages of western Europe.

In the other group, Grk. κῡριακόν 'Lord's house', in general less common than ἐκκλησία but a familiar name of the church (as building) in various regions, was adopted, prob. through an unattested Gothic form, in the Gmc. and Slavic languages, and then used also for the church as a body, like and very likely influenced by Lat. *ecclesia* in both senses. This adoption of the less usual Grk. term has been much discussed and often brought into connection with the spread of Arianism. But this is disputed and

unnecessary. We need only conclude that the churches which first impressed the Goths (or other Gmc. peoples in the East) bore this name, as did, we know, many in Constantinople and Asia Minor. Kretschmer KZ 39.541 ff. (but against derivation through a pop. κυρικόν, cf. Streitberg, Gesch. d. idg. Sprachwissenschaft 2.2.95). NED s.v. *church*. Stender-Petersen 424 ff. A. Pompen, Donum nat. Schrijnen 516 ff.

The few other words denoted orig. the church as a building.

The old words for 'temple' (22.13) were not generally retained to designate the Christian 'church', but (unlike those for 'god') were rejected as pointing to pagan worship. None of them furnished the usual word for 'church', but some have come into use in this sense also (not included in the list). Thus NG ναός may be used as a generic term for 'place of worship' of any religion, and occurs in legal terminology (νόμος περὶ ἐνοριακῶν ναῶν) and many names of churches (ναὸς τοῦ ἁγίου Νικολάου, etc.); NIr. *teampall* is frequently 'church', formerly only Protestant; It. *tempio*, Sp. *templo*, Fr. *temple* sometimes 'church', esp. Protestant; NE *temple* sometimes 'church' (NED s.v. 2); so ChSl. *chramŭ*, SCr. *hram*, Boh. *chrám*, Russ. *chram*.

1. Grk. ἐκκλησία 'assembly' (: ἐκκαλέω 'call, summon', ἐκκλητός 'selected'), the common political term, then in LXX the Jewish 'congregation', in NT also and usually the community of Christians, the 'church' as a body; later (ca. 300 A.D.) the 'church' as a building (e.g. Eus. οἶκος τῆς ἐκκλησίας and simply ἐκκλησία). Hence Goth. *aikklēsjō* (in NT as body, in Calendar as building), Lat. *ecclēsia* (both senses), and therefrom the Romance (except Rum.) and Celtic words (for Br. *iliz*, cf. Loth, Mots lat. 163).

2. Grk. κῡριακόν (sc. δῶμα) quotable as 'Lord's house, church' 300 A.D.+, neut. of κῡριακός, fr. κύριος 'master, Lord' (19.41). Hence, prob. through an unattested Goth. form, OE *cir(i)ce* (> ON *kirkja*), OHG *chirihha*, *kirihha*, etc., and the Slavic words, ChSl. *crŭky*, SCr. *crkva*, Boh. *církev* (as body), Pol. *cerkiew* (now only 'Greek church'), Russ. *cerkov'*. Cf. references above.

The parallel late Lat. *dominicum*, though quotable as 'church', was short lived, in contrast to the persistent *dominica* or *dominicus* 'Lord's day, Sunday', like Grk. κυριακή (14.52).

3. Lat. *basilica*, fr. Grk. βασιλική, fem. of βασιλικός 'royal', but used (first with στοά, then alone) for a certain type of building, and later applied to the early Christian churches of this form. Hence Rum. *biserică*, also Alb., Vegliot and Rhaeto-Roman words for 'church' (Fr. *basoche* in a quite different sense), and according to the evidence of Christian inscriptions *basilica* was once current over a much wider area. REW 972. Wartburg 1.270. Bartoli, Le tre basilche di Ragusa e la coppia *basilica* ed *ecclesia* (Dubrovnik, Vol. II).

4. Lith. *bažnyčia*, Lett. *baznīca*, fr. Pol., Russ. *božnica* (Russ. 'chapel, small church', Pol. now 'synagogue') deriv., through adj. like ChSl. *božĭ*, of the word for 'god'. Brückner, Sl. Fremdwörter 71, 167. Mühl.-Endz. 1.369.

5. Boh. *kostel* 'church' as building (> Pol. *kościoł* 'church' in both senses; also Russ. *kostel* for Catholic church), fr. Lat. *castellum* 'fortress' and at first applied to a type of medieval fortified church, the existence of which is well attested. Cf. e.g. Sebastian, German Fortified Churches in Transylvania, Antiquity 6(1932).301 ff. Berneker 582. Brückner 260.

22.22 PREACH

Grk.	κηρύσσω (εὐαγγελίζομαι)	Goth.	*mērjan*	Lith.	*pamokslą sakyti*
		ON	*predika*	Lett.	*sludināt, spredik'uot*
NG	κηρύττω	Dan.	*praedike*	ChSl.	*propovědati*
Lat.	*praedicāre*	Sw.	*predika*	SCr.	*propovijedati*
It.	*predicare*	OE	*bodi(g)an* (*predician*)	Boh.	*kázati*
Fr.	*prêcher*	ME	*preche*	Pol.	*kazać*
Sp.	*predicar*	NE	*preach*	Russ.	*propovedat'*
Rum.	*predica, propovedui*	Du.	*prediken*		
Ir.	*pridchim*	OHG	*bredigōn*		
NIr.	*seanmōirim*	MHG	*bredigen*		
W.	*pregethu*	NHG	*predigen*		
Br.	*prezeg*				

'Preach' is expressed by verbs for 'proclaim, announce' (most of these connected with verbs for 'say', or through 'make known' with verbs for 'know'), which became partly or wholly specialized to religious terms.

Most of the nouns for 'sermon' are parallel forms, derived from the verbs, like Grk. κήρυγμα, NHG *predigt*, etc. But Lat. *sermō* 'discourse' was 'religious discourse' in eccl. writers, and so a rival of *praedicātiō*, persisting beside the latter in Romance languages and the usual term in NE *sermon* vs. vb. *preach*. A few of the verbs for 'preach' are, conversely, derived from nouns for 'sermon'.

1. Grk. κηρύσσω 'summon, proclaim, announce' (fr. κῆρυξ 'herald'), hence 'preach' NT+ (NG in ττ form).

Grk. εὐαγγελίζομαι 'bring good tidings' (fr. εὐ-ἄγγελος : ἀγγέλλω 'announce'), in NT 'preach the gospel, preach' (but much less common than κηρύσσω).

2. Lat. *praedicāre* 'proclaim' (cpd. of the root in *dīcere* 'say'), in eccl. Lat. 'preach'. Hence the Romance (but Rum. *predica* neolog.) and most of the Celtic and Gmc. words.

Rum. *propovedui*, fr. Slavic, cf. ChSl. *propovědati*, etc. (below, 6).

3. Ir. *pridchim*, Br. *prezeg*, fr. Lat. *praedicāre*. Vendryes, De hib. voc. 168. Loth, Mots lat. 199.

NIr. *seanmōirim*, fr. *seanmōin*, MIr. *senmōin*, *sermōin* 'sermon', fr. Lat. *sermō*, *-ōnis*, with *n* for *r* by assim. or pop. etym. Vendryes, De hib. voc. 177.

W. *pregethu*, fr. *pregeth* 'sermon', fr. Lat. *praeceptum* 'precept'. Loth, Mots lat. 198.

4. Goth. *mērjan* = OHG *māren* 'proclaim', fr. **mēri-* in Goth. *waila-mēreis* 'praiseworthy', ON *mærr*, OE *mǣre*, OHG *māri* 'famous', with development of verb through 'make known'. Walde-P. 2.238. Feist 355.

OE *bodian*, *bodig(e)an* 'announce' and reg. word for 'preach' (*predician* rare; NE *bode* 'portend') = ON *boða* 'announce, command', fr. OE *bod*, ON *boð* 'command, message', beside OE *boda*, ON *boði*, OHG *boto*, NHG *bote*, etc. 'messenger', all fr. the root of OE *bēodan* (pple. *boden*), ON *bjōða*, OHG *biotan*, etc. 'offer, announce, command' (19.45). Walde-P. 2.147. NED s.v. *bode*.

All the other Gmc. words are fr. Lat. *praedicāre*, most of them directly, but NE *preach* through Fr. (above, 2).

5. Lith. *apsakyti* 'relate, describe' and formerly 'preach' (reg. word in Trowitsch NT; Kurschat *apsakyti* and *kozoni sakyti*, with *kozonis* 'sermon' fr. Pol. *kazanie*), cpd. of *sakyti* 'say' (18.22).

Lith. *pamokslas*, now the reg. word for 'sermon', formerly 'teaching' : *mokyti*

'teach' (17.25). Hence now *pamokslą sakyti* 'preach'.

Lett. *sludināt* (reg. word in Lett. NT), orig. 'make known', caus. of *sludēt* 'spread as news, be heard of', fr. the root **k̂leu-* in words for 'hear, be heard' (15.41). Mühl.-Endz. 3.940 f.

Lett. *spredik'uot*, fr. *spredikis*, *predikis* 'sermon', fr. MLG *predikie* 'sermon'. Mühl.-Endz. 3.1016, 385.

6. ChSl. *propovědati* (with the SCr. and Russ. forms), cpd. of *povědati* 'announce, relate' (cf. *pověděti* also 'say', 18.22), orig. 'make known', cpd. of *věděti* 'know' (17.17).

Boh. *kázati*, Pol. *kazać* = ChSl. *kazati* 'show, admonish', SCr. *kazati*, Russ. *skazat'* 'say' (18.22), with specialization to 'preach'. Berneker 497.

22.23 BLESS

Grk.	εὐλογέω	Goth.	*þiuþjan*	Lith.	(*pa*)*laiminti* (*žegnoti*)
NG	εὐλογῶ, βλογῶ	ON	*bleza*	Lett.	*svetīt*
Lat.	*benedīcere*	Dan.	*velsigne*	ChSl.	*blagosloviti*
It.	*benedire*	Sw.	*välsigna*	SCr.	*blagosloviti*
Fr.	*bénir*	OE	*blētsian, segnian*	Boh.	*blahoslaviti, žehnati*
Sp.	*bendecir*	ME	*blesse*	Pol.	*błogosławić, żegnać*
Rum.	*binecuvînta, blagoslovi*	NE	*bless*	Russ.	*blagoslovit'*
		Du.	*zegenen*	Skt.	*svasti dhā-*, etc.
Ir.	*bendachaim*	OHG	*seganōn*	Av.	(*ā*)*frī-*
NIr.	*beannuighim*	MHG	*segen(en), sēnen*		
W.	*bendithio*	NHG	*segnen*		
Br.	*binniga*				

Most of the words for 'bless' are from either 'speak well of' or 'make the sign of the cross'. But the English *bless* comes through 'consecrate' from the word for 'blood'.

1. Grk. εὐλογέω 'speak well of, praise', in LXX, NT+ 'bless', fr. εὐ- 'well' and λόγος 'speech, word'.

2. Lat. eccl. *benedīcere* (in class. Lat. *bene dīcere* 'speak well, speak well of, praise'), fr. *bene* 'well' and *dīcere* 'say'. Hence It. *benedire*, Fr. *bénir*, Sp. *bendecir;* Rum. *binecuvînta* similar cpd. with *cuvînta* 'speak' (18.21), now more common than old *blagoslovi* fr. Slavic (below, 6). REW 1029. Tiktin 190, 197.

3. Ir. *bendachaim*, NIr. *beannuighim*, fr. Lat. *benedīcere* (but independent borrowings); hence also Br. *binniga*, W. (arch.) *bendigo;* but W. *bendithio* (usual word now), fr. *bendith* 'blessing, benediction', fr. Lat. *benedictiō*. Vendryes, De hib. voc. 116. Loth, Mots lat. 137 f.

4. Goth. *þiuþjan*, fr. *þiuþ* 'the good' (16.71). Feist 498.

OE *blōedsian*, *blētsian* (> ON *bleza*, NIcel. *blessa*), in earliest use also 'consecrate', deriv. of OE *blōd* 'blood'. Hence ME *blesse*, NE *bless*. NED s.v. *bless*, vb.[1].

OE *segnian*, *sēnian*, OHG *seganōn*, MHG *segen(en)*, *sēnen*, NHG *segnen*, Du. *zegenen* (Dan. *signe*, Sw. *signa*, but now as 'bless' mostly), Dan. *velsigne*, Sw. *välsigna* with *vel*, *väl* 'well', all orig. 'make the sign of the cross' (OE *segnian* mostly in this sense), fr. Lat. *signāre*, deriv. of *signum* 'sign', eccl. esp. 'sign of the cross'. Falk-Torp 963 f. Weigand-H. 2.834.

5. Lith. (*pa*)*laiminti*, fr. *laimė*, *palaima* 'good fortune' (16.17).

Lith. *žegnoti* (the old word), fr. Pol. *żegnać* (below, 6). Brückner, Sl. Fremdwörter 157.

Lett. *svetīt* (also 'celebrate'), fr. Russ.

svjatit' 'hallow, consecrate' (cf. *svjatoj* 'holy' 22.19). Mühl.-Endz. 3.1155.

6. ChSl. *blagosloviti*, etc., general Slavic, cpd. of *blagŭ* 'good' (16.71) with deriv. of *slovo* 'word' (18.26, reg. for λόγος), and so an exact translation of Grk. εὐλογέω. Berneker 69.

Boh. *žehnati*, Pol. *żegnać*, fr. NHG *segnen* (above, 4). Brückner 664.

7. Skt. *svasti-* 'well-being (*su-asti-*), good fortune', is used in phrases (with *dhā-* 'place', *kṛ-* 'make', etc.) which are virtually equivalent to 'bless', e.g. *svasti* .... *dadhātu naḥ* (RV), *svasti* .... *naḥ kṛṇotu* (AV) 'may .... bless us'.

Skt. *mañgala-* 'good fortune, happiness' and the wish for such, 'benediction, blessing' : *mañju-* 'beautiful, charming', Grk. μάγγανον 'means of charming'. Walde-P. 2.233.

Av. *frī-*, *ā-frī-* 'propitiate', sometimes virtually 'bless' (Yt. 13.50, V. 22.5, both rendered 'bénir' by Darmesteter) : Skt. *prī-* 'please', *priya-* 'dear'. So sb. *ā-fri-* (in cpds.) and *āfrīti-* 'blessing' or 'curse', cf. Skt. *āprī-* name of a special kind of invocation. Barth. 330, 1016 f.

22.24 CURSE (vb.)

Grk.	*καταράομαι*	Goth.	*fraqiþan, unþiuþjan*	Lith.	*(pra)keikti*
NG	*καταρῶμαι*	ON	*bǫlva, banna*	Lett.	*nuolādēt*
Lat.	*exsecrārī, maledīcere*	Dan.	*forbande*	ChSl.	*(pro)klęti*
It.	*maledire*	Sw.	*förbanna*	SCr.	*prokleti*
Fr.	*maudire*	OE	*wiergan (cursian)*	Boh.	*proklíti*
Sp.	*maldecir*	ME	*curse*	Pol.	*przekląć*
Rum.	*blestema*	NE	*curse*	Russ.	*(pro)kljast'*
Ir.	*maldachaim*	Du.	*vervloeken*	Skt.	*çap-*
NIr.	*malluighim*	OHG	*fluochōn*	Av.	*zav-*, sb. *āfrī-*
W.	*melltithio*	MHG	*vluochen*		
Br.	*milliga*	NHG	*verfluchen, verwünschen*		

One group of words for 'curse' is the exact pendant, in form as well as sense, of those for 'bless', namely the eccl. Lat. *maledīcere* with its descendants, orig. 'speak ill of' vs. *benedīcere*, orig. 'speak well of'. The Grk. word means literally 'pray against', and the class. Lat. word is an opposite of 'consecrate'. But some nouns for 'prayer' or 'blessing' may themselves be used also for a 'curse' (cf. Grk. ἀρά, εὐχωλή, Av. *āfrī-*, below).

Other verbs are based on 'say away, reject', or 'forbid', or are derivs. of words for 'misfortune, evil' with the notion of 'invoke' implicit in the verb. A few are connected with words for 'howl, bark' or 'sound, noise', with development through some such notion as 'howl at, shout at' > 'revile'.

1. Grk. καταράομαι, fr. deriv. of ἀρά 'prayer' (22.17) with κατά 'against'. But ἀρά itself is frequently used also for a 'curse'. Similarly εὐχωλή 'prayer, vow' is used as 'imprecation, curse' in an Arcadian inscription (Schwyzer, Dial. Gr. Exempla 661.24).

2. Lat. *exsecrārī*, *-āre* (> It. *esecrare*, Fr. *exécrer*, etc. 'abhor, detest', but not the words for 'curse'), cpd. of *sacrāre* 'consecrate' (fr. *sacer* 'holy', 22.19) with *ex-* in its negating force. Ernout-M. 883.

Lat. eccl. *maledīcere* (in class. Lat. *male dīcere* 'speak ill of, abuse'), fr. *male* 'ill' and *dīcere* 'say'. Hence It. *maledire*, Fr. *maudire*, Sp. *maldecir*. REW 5258.

Rum. *blestema*, fr. VLat. *blastēmāre (> OFr. *blasmer* 'reproach, blame', etc.)

= eccl. Lat. *blasphēmāre*, fr. Grk. βλασφημέω 'speak ill of, slander, blaspheme', with cons. dissim. already in colloquial Grk. (cf. NG pop. βλαστημῶ). REW 1155. Wartburg 1.403.

3. Ir. *maldachaim*, Br. *milliga*, W. (arch.) *melligo*, fr. Lat. *maledīcere*, but NIr. *malluighim* (older *mallachdaim*), W. *melltithio*, derivs. of Ir. *maldacht*, W. *melltith* (*melldith*), fr. Lat. *maledictiō* (whence also Br. *malloz* 'a curse'). Vendryes, De hib. voc. 153. Loth, Mots lat. 186.

4. Goth. *fraqiþan* (in one case 'reject', but reg. 'curse'), cpd. of *qiþan* 'say' and *fra-* 'forth, away'.

Goth. *unþiuþjan* (once), neg. cpd. of *þiuþjan* 'bless' (22.23).

ON *bǫlva*, fr. *bǫl* 'misfortune' = OE *bealu* 'evil, woe' (NE *bale*), etc. Falk-Torp 46.

ON *banna* 'forbid' (18.38), also 'curse' (cf. Fritzner, s.v.), and in latter sense now Dan. *forbande*, Sw. *förbanna*.

OE *wiergan* (*wirgan*), OHG *furwergit* 'maledictus' (Tat.) : Goth. *gawargjan* 'condemn', *wargiþa* 'condemnation' (= OE *wiergþu* 'curse'), OE *wearg*, OHG *warg* 'villain, criminal', ON *vargr* 'wolf, thief, robber', prob. fr. the same root as OE *wyrgan*, OHG *wurgan* 'strangle'. Walde-P. 1.273. Falk-Torp 1354. Feist 325, 551.

OE *cursian* (late), ME, NE *curse*, fr. sb. OE *curs* (also late, but earlier and more frequent than the vb.), generally regarded as of unknown origin (so NED s.v.), but plausibly explained by Weekley, Etym. Dict., as orig. 'wrath' (cf. earliest quotation *Goddes curs*), fr. an OFr. *curuz* = *corroz* 'anger, wrath' (Fr. *courroux* 16.42). Cf. the development of Grk. ὀργή 'wrath' (16.42), through 'wrath of god' in NG pop. phrase νὰ τὸν πάρῃ ἡ ὀργή, virtually = 'curse him!'

OHG *fluochōn*, MHG *vluochen*, NHG *verfluchen*, Du. *vervloeken* (NHG *fluchen*, Du. *vloeken* now 'curse, swear' = 'use bad language') : OE *flōcan* 'clap the hands', OS *for flōcan* 'curse', Goth. *flōkan* 'lament' : Lat. *plangere* 'strike, lament', Grk. πληγή 'blow', etc., with development of 'beat the breast' > 'lament' and 'curse'. Walde-P. 2.92. Falk-Torp 239. Weigand-H. 1.561.

NHG *verwünschen*, cpd. of *wünschen* 'wish', with *ver-* as in *ver-achten* 'despise', etc., but esp. influenced by the early pop. use of *wunsch* as denoting some magical power. Paul, Deutsches Wtb. s.v. *wunsch*.

5. Lith. *keikti*, *prakeikti*, etym.?

Lett. *lādēt*, esp. *nuolādēt*, fr. *lāt* 'howl, bark' and 'revile' : Lith. *lõti*, ChSl. *lajati*, Lat. *lātrāre* 'howl, bark', Goth. *lailōun* 'they reviled'. Walde-P. 2.376. Berneker 686 f. Mühl.-Endz. 2.435 f., 442, 808 f.

6. ChSl. *klęti*, *proklęti* (*klęti sę* also 'swear'), SCr. *prokleti*, Boh. *proklíti*, Pol. *przekląć*, Russ. *(pro)kljast'*, with iter. ChSl. *proklinati*, etc. and sbs. ChSl. *klętva*, etc., etym. dub. Berneker 525. Brückner 232 (: ChSl. *kloniti* 'incline, bow').

7. Skt. *çap-* (also 'swear'), with sb. *çāpa-* 'curse', prob. : *çabda-* 'sound, noise' (15.44).

Av. *zav-* 'call, invoke' (18.41) may be 'curse', and *āfrī-* (in cpds.), *āfrīti-* denote 'blessing' or 'curse' (cf. 22.23). Cf. Y. 11.1 *θrāyō haiθim ašavanō āfrivačanhō zavainti, . . . gāuš zaotārəm zavaiti* 'three truly righteous creatures with maledictions curse, . . . the ox curses the priest'. Barth. 1667.

22.25 BAPTIZE

Grk.	*βαπτίζω*	Goth.	*daupjan*	Lith.	*krikštyti*
NG	*βαπτίζω*	ON	*skīra, kristna*	Lett.	*kristīt*
Lat.	*baptizāre*	Dan.	*døbe*	ChSl.	*krŭstiti*
It.	*battezzare*	Sw.	*döpa*	SCr.	*krstiti*
Fr.	*baptiser*	OE	*fullian (dēpan, dyppan)*	Boh.	*křtiti*
Sp.	*bautizar*			Pol.	*chrzcić*
Rum.	*boteza*	ME	*baptise, cristen (fulle)*	Russ.	*krestit'*
Ir.	*baitsim*	NE	*baptize (christen)*		
NIr.	*baistim*	Du.	*doopen*		
W.	*bedyddio*	OHG	*toufen*		
Br.	*badezi*	MHG	*toufen*		
		NHG	*taufen*		

Most of the words for 'baptize' are such as meant originally 'dip'. But the Greek word in its specialized eccl. sense was adopted in eccl. Latin and hence in the Romance and Celtic languages, as well as later English, while in most of the Gmc. languages native words for 'dip' were used for 'baptize'.

Other semantic sources are 'cleanse, purify', 'consecrate', and 'christianize', of which baptism was the outward symbol.

1. Grk. βαπτίζω, orig. 'dip', like βάπτω (see under 'dye', 6.40). Hence eccl. Lat. *baptizāre* (often *baptidiāre*), the Romance words (OFr. *ba(p)toier* beside *ba(p)tisier*, Fr. *baptiser*; REW 939, Wartburg 1.241 f.), the Celtic (but Ir. *baitsim*, NIr. *baistim* through the sb. *baithis*, fr. Lat. *baptisma*; Pedersen 1.237, Vendryes, De hib. voc. 115), and (through OFr. *baptisier*) ME *baptise*, NE *baptize*.

2. Lat. *tingere* 'moisten, dye' was used by some eccl. writers for 'baptize', as translation of Grk. βαπτίζω.

3. Goth. *daupjan* (ON *deyfa*, *deypa* only 'dip'), Dan. *døbe*, Sw. *döpa*, OE *dīepan* ('dip', but Anglian *dēpan* also 'baptize'; so also *dyppan* from weak grade), OHG, MHG *toufen*, NHG *taufen*, Du. *doopen*, all orig. 'dip', caus. deriv. of Goth. *diups*, etc. 'deep' (12.67). Except in ON and OE, the orig. sense has been displaced by the secondary. Walde-P. 1.847 f. Falk-Torp 175 f. Feist 117. Kluge-G. 614. NED s.vv. *depe* and *dip*.

ON *skīra* 'cleanse, purify' and 'baptize' : ON *skīrr* 'clear, bright, pure' = OE *scīr* id. (NE *sheer*), Goth. *skeirs* 'plain', etc. Walde-P. 2.536. Falk-Torp 1008.

OE *fulwian*, *fullian*, ME *fulle*, *folle*, etc., cpd. of *full* 'full' and a verb = Goth. *weihan*, OHG *wīhen* 'consecrate' : Goth. *weihs* 'holy', etc. (22.19). NED s.v. *full*, vb.[1].

ON *kristna* 'christianize' and 'baptize', OE *cristnian* 'christianize', ME *christen* 'baptize', NE *christen* (now esp. in connection with naming a child), derivs. of the word for 'Christ', with development fr. 'christianize' to 'baptize' as the symbol of conversion. NED s.v. *christen*, vb.

4. Lith. *krikštyti*, Lett. *kristīt*, fr. Slavic (below, 5). Brückner, Sl. Fremdwörter 97, 175. Mühl.-Endz. 2.281.

5. ChSl. *krŭstiti*, etc., general Slavic, fr. ChSl. *krŭstŭ*, etc. 'cross', this fr. Gmc. form for 'Christ' (12.77). Semantically the verb does not necessarily come through 'make the sign of the cross', but may be from the earlier sense of *krŭstŭ* as 'Christ' and so have the same development, through 'christianize', as ME *cristen*, etc. (above, 3). Berneker 634. Brückner 185. Stender-Petersen 421 f.

22.26 FAST (vb.)

Grk.	*νηστεύω*	Goth.	*fastan*	Lith.	*gavėti, pasnikauti*
NG	*νηστεύω*	ON	*fasta*	Lett.	*gavēt*
Lat. (eccl.)	*iēiūnāre*	Dan.	*faste*	ChSl.	*postiti*
It.	*digiunare*	Sw.	*fasta*	SCr.	*postiti*
Fr.	*jeûner*	OE	*fæstan*	Boh.	*postiti se*
Sp.	*ayunar*	ME	*faste*	Pol.	*pościć*
Rum.	*posti (ajuna)*	NE	*fast*	Russ.	*postit'sja*
Ir.	*troscim*	Du.	*vasten*	Skt.	*upavas-*
NIr.	*troscaim*	OHG	*fastēn*		
W.	*ymprydio*	MHG	*vasten*		
Br.	*iun(i)*	NHG	*fasten*		

Among the verbs for 'fast' in the religious application here intended, only the Grk. word is clearly derived from a noun with the literal sense of 'not eating'. The Lat. word is from an adj. which, though of doubtful etymology, means 'fasting, hungry' without religious connotation, and the W. word is connected with one for a 'meal'. In the others there is no original relation to 'eat' or 'food'.

The largest group, to which NE *fast* belongs, comes from the notion 'hold fast, keep, observe', and the use for 'go without food' without reference to the religious observance, though quotable in English from the earliest times (cf. NED s.v. *fast*, vb.[2]) and common to the modern Gmc. and Slavic languages, is secondary.

1. Grk. νηστεύω, fr. νῆστις 'not eating, fasting', cpd. of neg. prefix νη- or *νε- and *ἔστις, fr. the root of ἔδω 'eat' (5.11). Schwyzer, Gr. Gram. 431.

2. Lat. (eccl.) *iēiūnāre* (> Fr. *jeûner*, Sp. *ayunar*, ORum. [and dial.] *ajuna*; with *dis-* > It. *digiunare*), fr. *iēiūnus* 'fasting' (*iāiūnus* Plaut.), etym. dub. Ernout-M. 472. Walde-H. 1.674 f. REW 4581.

Rum. *posti*, fr. Slavic (below, 6).

3. Ir. *troscim*, NIr. *troscaim* (or more commonly phrase with sb. *trosgadh* 'fast'), etym. dub., perh. : Ir. *tart* 'thirst', Lith. *troškus* 'thirsty', with development fr. 'go without drink' to 'go without food'? Cf. ME, NE *fast*, sometimes 'go without drink'. Pedersen 1.77, 174. Otherwise Stokes 139.

W. *ymprydio*, fr. sb. *ympryd*, cpd. of *pryd* 'a meal' (5.41) with *ym-* 'about, concerning, on the other side of', here in an adversative sense.

Br. *iun(i)*, fr. sb. *iun*, fr. Lat. *iēiūnium* 'fast' (: *iēiūnus*, above, 2). Loth, Mots lat. 179.

4. Goth. *fastan* (also 'keep, observe'), ON *fasta*, OE *fæstan*, OHG *fastēn*, etc., general Gmc., fr. adj. seen in OE *fæst*, OHG *fasti*, etc. 'firm', with development through 'hold fast, keep, observe', as attested in the Gothic uses, and parallel to the late use of Lat. *observāre* 'observe' as 'abstain from' (Vulgate) or 'fast' (Isid.). Falk-Torp 207. Feist 143. NED s.v. *fast*, vb.[2].

5. Lith. *gavėti*, Lett. *gavēt*, fr. Russ. *govet'* 'prepare for the sacraments by fasting' = ChSl. *gověti* 'revere', etc. Berneker 338 f. Brückner Sl. Fremdwörter 83, 171. Mühl.-Endz. 1.614.

Lith. *pasnikauti*, fr. sb. *pasnikas*, fr. Pol. *post* 'fast' (sb.), *postnik* 'one who keeps fast', fr. vb. *pościć* (below, 6). Brückner, Sl. Fremdwörter 116.

6. ChSl. *postiti*, etc., general Slavic, fr. Gmc., Goth. *fastan*, etc. (above, 4). Brückner 432. Stender-Petersen 431 f.

7. Skt. *upavas-* 'abide, wait for' and 'fast' (sb. *upavāsa-* 'fasting'), cpd. of *vas-* 'abide, dwell' (7.11).

22.31 HEAVEN

Grk.	οὐρανός	Goth.	himins	Lith.	dangus
NG	οὐρανός	ON	himinn	Lett.	debesis
Lat.	caelum	Dan.	himmel	ChSl.	nebo
It.	cielo	Sw.	himmel	SCr.	nebo
Fr.	ciel	OE	heofon	Boh.	nebe
Sp.	cielo	ME	heven	Pol.	niebo
Rum.	cer	NE	heaven	Russ.	nebo
Ir.	nem (ríched)	Du.	hemel	Skt.	yamasya bhavana-,
NIr.	neamh, flaitheass	OHG	himil		svarga-, devaloka-,
W.	nef	MHG	himel		etc.
Br.	neñv	NHG	himmel	Av.	garō dəmāna-, vaṅheuš
					dəmāna- manaṅhō,
					vahišta- aṅhu

Nearly all the Eur. words for 'heaven', as the abode of the gods and the blessed, are such as orig. denoted the 'sky', most of them still so used, though there is occasional differentiation. Most of the Indo-Iranian terms are of quite different origin, expressions meaning literally 'abode of Yama', 'world of the gods', 'house of praise', 'best world', etc.

1. Words for 'sky' used also for 'heaven', see. 1.51. A few of the old words are now used only or mainly in the latter sense, as NIr. neamh, W. nef. Or there may be differentiation of parallel forms, as MLG hemmel 'heaven' vs. heven 'sky', NE heaven vs. pl. heavens = sky, conversely Lett. debess 'sky' vs. pl. debesis 'heaven'. Furthermore, in the sense 'heaven' the pl. form is much more common than the sg. in the Grk. NT (Blass-Debrunner 141), and this is generally followed in the Vulgate, Goth., OE, OHG (Tat.), ChSl. and often in later versions (in English pl. Wyclif, sg. Tyndale).

2. Ir. ríched, fr. *rīgo-sedo- or *rīgi-sedo- lit. 'king's seat'. K. Meyer, Ber. Preuss. Akad. 1913.955. Pokorny, Z. celt. Ph. 10.199.

NIr. flaitheas, 'kingdom, realm' and (esp. in pl.) 'heaven', fr. flaith 'ruler, prince' (19.35).

3. Skt. yamasya (gen. sg.) with bhavana-, yoni- (RV), loka-, sādana-, gṛha-, rājya- (AV), the 'abode' ('world, seat, realm', etc.) of Yama, the Vedic ruler of the spirits of the departed in heaven (later of the dead in the underworld).

Similarly, later, indrasya loka- or indraloka- 'Indra's world' and devaloka- 'world of the gods' (loka- 'place, world', 1.11).

Skt. svar- 'sun' (1.52), 'sky' and 'heaven', in latter sense esp. svarga- (cpd. with the root of gam- 'go').

Av. garō dəmāna- (nmāna-) lit. 'house (7.12) of praise' (16.79), and vaṅheuš dəmāna- manaṅhō 'house of the good spirit'. Barth. 1092.

Av. vahišta- aṅhu-, lit. the 'best life, world' (1.11). Barth. 109.

22.32 HELL

Grk.	ᾅδης	Goth.	halja, gaiainna	Lith.	pekla
NG	κόλασις	ON	hel, helvíti	Lett.	elle (pekle)
Lat.	inferna (neut. pl.),	Dan.	helvede	ChSl.	adŭ, g'eona
	infernus, infernum	Sw.	helvete	SCr.	pakao
It.	inferno	OE	hel (hellewīte)	Boh.	peklo
Fr.	enfer	ME	helle	Pol.	pieklo
Sp.	infierno	NE	hell	Russ.	ad
Rum.	iad	Du.	hel	Skt.	naraka-, etc.
Ir.	ifern	OHG	hella (hellawīzi)	Av.	drūjō dəmāna-, etc.
NIr.	ifreann	MHG	helle		
W.	uffern	NHG	hölle		
Br.	ifern				

Words for 'hell' are based on such notions as 'place below', 'place of hiding', 'unseen' (?), 'punishment', 'house of the lie, worst world', etc. The burning 'pitch' of hell, so vividly portrayed by Christian writers, has furnished (through MHG) the regular words for 'hell' in several of the Balto-Slavic languages.

1. Grk. ᾅδης (Hom. Ἀΐδης, gen. Ἀΐδος, proper name and place of the departed spirits; in LXX reg. for the Hebr. še'ol), etym. much disputed, e.g. fr. *ṇ-ϝιδ- 'unseen' (ancients and Schulze, Quaest. Ep. 468, Schwyzer, Gr. Gram. 266), or fr. *aiϝιδ- : Lat. saevus 'fierce' (Wackernagel, Walde-P. 2.445, etc.).

Grk. γέεννα (LXX, NT, taken over as gehenna in Vulgate and elsewhere), fr. a Hebr. word, orig. name of a valley where children were thrown to Moloch. NED s.v. Gehenna.

Grk. κόλασις 'chastisement' (: κολάζω 'chastise, punish', 21.37), hence NG pop. 'damnation' and 'hell'.

2. Lat. inferna (neut. pl.), eccl. Lat. infernus, later infernum (> It. inferno, Fr. enfer, Sp. infierno), fr. adj. infernus 'belonging to the underworld' (epithet of Pluto), deriv. of inferus 'below, underground' (cf. inferī 'inhabitants of the lower world, the dead') : Goth. undar, etc. 'under'. Walde-P.

1.323. Ernout-M. 487. Walde-H. 1.698. REW 4397.

Rum. iad, fr. ChSl. jadŭ beside adŭ (below, 6). Tiktin 746.

3. Celtic words fr. Lat. infernum. Pedersen 1.201. Vendryes, De hib. voc. 146. Loth, Mots lat. 214.

4. Goth. gaiainna, reg. for Grk. γέεννα (above, 1).

Goth. halja (reg. for Grk. ᾅδης), ON hel 'abode of the dead, death'), OE hel(l), OHG hella, etc., general Gmc., fr. the root of OE, OHG helan, Ir. celim, Lat. occulere, cēlāre 'conceal, hide', etc. (12.27). Walde-P. 432 f. Falk-Torp 393. Feist 240. NED s.v. hell.

ON helvíti, Dan. helvede, Sw. helvete, OE hellewīte, OHG hellawīzi, cpd. of preceding with ON víti, OE wīte, etc. 'punishment' (21.37), and orig. 'hell-punishment', then its place and so equivalent to the simple hel (in ON Christian terminology usual vs. hel for the pagan hel, but only a less common variant in OE, OHG, MHG). Falk-Torp 393.

5. Lith. pekla (Lett. pekle 'abyss', sometimes 'hell', with final e, fr. elle), fr. WhRuss. or Ukr. peklo (below, 6). Brückner, Sl. Fremdwörter 117, 180. Mühl.-Endz. 3.193.

Lett. elle, fr. MLG helle (above, 4) Mühl.-Endz. 1.568.

6. ChSl. adŭ and g'eona, fr. Grk. ᾅδης

and γέεννα, reg. in Gospels, former more common in Supr., Russ. ad and geenna in church writings, only the former pop. word.

SCr. pakao, Boh. peklo, Pol. piekto (Russ. peklo dial.), fr. MHG pech 'pitch' in its use for the burning pitch of hell and also for 'hell' itself. Brückner 407. Grimm, Deutsches Wtb. s.v. Pech.

7. Skt. naraka- (adj. nāraka-, hence nārāka-loka- 'hell', AV 12.4.36) : Grk. (ἐ)νέρτερος 'of the nether world', Umbr. nertru 'sinistro', etc. (12.42). Walde-P. 2.333 f. Uhlenbeck 143.

Other expressions for 'hell' in AV, etc., asāu loka- 'yonder world', adharād gṛha-

'the house below', adhama- tamas- 'lowest darkness', etc. Cf. also Norman Brown, The Rigvedic equivalent of Hell, JAOS 61.76 ff.

Av. drūjō dəmāna- 'house of the lie' (16.67) vs. garō dəmāna 'house of praise' (22.31). Barth. 779, 1092.

Av. ačišta- aṅhu- 'worst world' (acišta-superl. of aka- 'bad', 16.72) vs. vahišta- aṅhu- 'best world' (22.31), also ačištahyā- dəmāna- manaṅhō 'house of the worst spirit' vs. vaṅheuš dəmāna manaṅhō 'house of the good spirit'. Barth. 53.

Av. dužaṅhu- and daozahva-, cpd. of duš- 'evil' and aṅhu- 'world'. Barth. 675, 755.

22.33 ANGEL

Grk.	ἄγγελος	Goth.	aggilus	Lith.	angelas, aniolas
NG	ἄγγελος	ON	engill	Lett.	eñg'elis
Lat. (eccl.)	angelus	Dan.	engel	ChSl.	ang'elŭ
It.	angelo	Sw.	ängel	SCr.	andeo
Fr.	ange	OE	engel	Boh.	andĕl
Sp.	ángel	ME	angle, aungel	Pol.	aniol
Rum.	înger	NE	angle	Russ.	angel
Ir.	aingel	Du.	engel	Skt.	(āditya-)
NIr.	aingeal	OHG	engil	Av.	yazata-
W.	angel	MHG	engel		
Br.	ael, eal	NHG	engel		

All the Eur. words for 'angel' come from the Grk. word meaning orig. 'messenger'. The Indo-Iranian words considered here are only such as may loosely (Skt.) or more closely (Av.) be rendered 'angel'.

1. Grk. ἄγγελος 'messenger' (orig. dub., Walde-P. 1.65. Boisacq 6), hence later (LXX) 'angel'. Hence all the Eur. words, mostly through Lat. angelus (Lett. fr. MLG; Lith. aniolas, fr. Pol.).

2. Skt. āditya-, fr. aditi- the personified 'infinity', is used in the plural of the

seven deities of the heavens, but including the highest, but only very loosely to be compared with 'angels'.

Av. yazata-, lit. 'to be worshiped, worshipful' (fr. yaz- 'worship', 22.16) is used in the plural for a large group of holy beings subordinate to Ahura Mazda, and so may well be rendered 'angels'. Highest of these are the aməšā spənta 'immortal holy ones' (aməša- = Skt. amṛta- 'immortal', spənta- 'holy', 22.19), approximately 'archangels'. Jackson, Grd. iran. Phil. 2.632 ff., 640 ff.

22.34 DEVIL

Grk.	διάβολος	Goth.	diab(a)ulus, unhulþa	Lith.	velnias
NG	διάβολος	ON	djofull	Lett.	velns
Lat. (eccl.)	diabolus	Dan.	djævel	ChSl.	dijavolŭ
It.	diavolo	Sw.	djävul	SCr.	davo, vrag
Fr.	diable	OE	dēoful	Boh.	d'ábel, d'as, čert
Sp.	diablo	ME	devell	Pol.	djabel, czart
Rum.	drac, diavol	NE	devil	Russ.	čort, djavol
Ir.	diabul	Du.	duivel	Skt.	....
NIr.	diabhal	OHG	tiufal, diufal	Av.	aṅra- mainyu-
W.	diafol (diawl arch.)	MHG	tiuvel		
Br.	diaoul	NHG	teufel		

Most of the usual Eur. words for 'devil' come from a Grk. word meaning orig. 'slanderous, a slanderer'.

Besides this group, the Hebr. šātān, orig. 'adversary', though rendered by διάβολος in the LXX, is adopted in the NT as Σατανᾶς, hence the familiar Satan or the like in most Eur. languages, but less generic than 'devil'.

Words for 'dragon' and 'enemy' are also used for 'devil'.

1. Grk. διάβολος 'slanderous, a slanderer' (: διαβάλλω 'slander', orig. 'throw across', cpd. of βάλλω 'throw'), later (LXX+) 'devil'. Hence the widespread Eur. forms, mostly through Lat. diabolus. The diphthong of OHG tiufal, etc. is possibly due to pop. association with tiuf 'deep' (Frings, Don. Nat. Schrijnen 486). There are some popular short forms, as Boh. d'as beside d'abel, d'as beside d'abel, Fr. dial. drac, and MDu. drake. Cf. NT, Rev. 12.9

Rum. drac, pop. vs. eccl. diavol, fr. Lat. dracō 'dragon'. Same development in Alb. dreq beside djall, Fr. dial. drac, and MDu. drake. Cf. NT, Rev. 12.9

ὁ δράκων ὁ μέγας, ὁ ὄφις ὁ ἀρχαῖος, ὁ καλούμενος Διάβολος καὶ ὁ Σατανᾶς (similarly Rev. 20.2); Av. ažim dahākəm .... yam drujim 'the dragon Dahaka, the lie'. REW 2759. Tiktin 567. Wartburg 1.150.

3. Goth. unhulþa, see Goth. unhulþō 'demon' (22.35).

ON fjāndi, OE fēond, OHG fīant 'enemy' (19.52) were often used for the 'arch-enemy', the devil.

4. Lith. velnias (older velinas, velnas), Lett. velns : Lith. vėlė, Lett. velis 'spirit of the dead, ghost' (22.45). Mühl.-Endz. 4.532 f.

5. SCr. vrag = ChSl. vragŭ 'enemy', etc. (19.52).

Boh. čert, Pol. czart, Russ. čort, etym. dub. Berneker 172. Brückner 73.

6. Of the Skt. words for 'evil spirit, demon' (22.35) there seems to be none which can be singled out as particularly appropriate for 'devil'.

Av. aṅra- mainyu-, the personified 'evil spirit' (aṅra- 16.72, mainyu- 16.11), the 'demon of demons' (daēvanqm daēvō, Vd. 19.1), clearly the Zoroastrian 'devil'.

22.35 DEMON (Evil Spirit)

Grk. (eccl.)	*δαίμων, δαιμόνιον*	Goth.	*unhulþō, skōhsl*	Lith.	*velnias, demonas*
NG	*δαίμονας, δαιμόνιον*	ON	*djǫfull (troll)*	Lett.	*velns*
Lat. (eccl.)	*daemon, daemonium*	Dan.	*ond aand, dæmon*	ChSl.	*běsŭ*
		Sw.	*ond ande, dämon*	SCr.	*zloduh*
It.	*demonio*	OE	*dēoful (unholda)*	Boh.	*zlý duch, démon*
Fr.	*démon*	ME	*devil, demon*	Pol.	*zly duch*
Sp.	*demonio*	NE	*demon*	Russ.	*bes*
Rum.	*demon*	Du.	*demon*	Skt.	*rakṣas-*
Ir.	*demon*	OHG	*tiufal, unholdo*	Av.	*daēva-*, OPers. *daiva-*
NIr.	*deamhan*	MHG	*tiufel, unholde*		
W.	*cythraul*	NHG	*dämon, unhold*		
Br.	*aerouant*				

Among the words for 'demon' a widespread Eur. group goes back to a Grk. word which in classical times denoted one's good or evil genius and only later had the definitely bad sense of 'evil spirit'.

Others are connected with words for 'hostile', 'adversary', 'frightful', 'injury', etc. In some cases 'evil spirit' is the common term. The Iranian words reflect the fall of the old Aryan gods to the role of demons under the Zoroastrian reform.

But frequently the words for 'devil' (22.34) are used also to cover the lesser devils or 'demons'. In the NT Grk. *διάβολος*, always sg. 'the devil, Satan', and *δαίμων* or *δαιμόνιον* 'demon' are kept apart, and this distinction was followed in the Vulgate. But in the English and German versions, from the earliest to the present, the words for 'devil' have been used also in the latter sense (e.g. Mt. 9.34 *devils* in King James and Revised, *teufel* in Luther), and similarly (through Luther) in the Lith. and Lett. versions. Cf. NED s.v. *demon*.

1. Grk. *δαίμων*, in Hom. 'divine power', hence power that controls one's fate, one's good or evil genius, but eccl. (NT+) 'evil spirit, demon', prob. : *δαίομαι* 'distribute, allot'. Walde-P. 1.763. Boisacq 162. Hence, or fr. *δαιμόνιον*, eccl. Lat. *daemon, daemonium*, and the widespread Eur. forms.

2. W. *cythraul*, orig. 'adversary' = *cythrawl* 'contrary', fr. Lat. *contrārius*. Pedersen 1.234. Loth, Mots lat. 158.

Br. *aerouant*, fr. *aer* 'serpent' (3.77).

3. Goth. *unhulþō* (usual for *δαιμόνιον*; also *unhulþa*, but this mostly for *διάβολος*), OE *unholda* (rare), OHG *unholdo*, also fem. *unholda* (both rare), MHG *unholde*, NHG *unhold* : adj. OE, OHG *unhold* 'hostile', neg. cpd. of Goth. *hulþs*, OE, OHG *hold* 'merciful, gracious', this prob. : OE *heald*, OHG *hald* 'leaning forward, inclined'. Walde-P. 1.430. Feist 274. Weigand-H. 2.1118.

Goth. *skōhsl*, prob. : Ir. *scāl* 'supernatural being, specter' (22.45), perh. (as 'wandering' spirit?) fr. the root of Goth. *skēwjan* 'wander', Ir. *scuchim* 'depart, disappear'. Walde-P. 2.557. Feist 434.

ON *troll*, a supernatural being, a sort of 'giant, monster' mostly evil, the nearest pagan predecessor of 'demon', etym. dub. Walde-P. 1.796. Falk-Torp 1286. Hellquist 1223.

Dan. *ond aand*, Sw. *ond ande* (latter reg. in NT version, where Dan. *djævel*) 'evil spirit' (*ond* 16.72; *aand, ande* 16.11).

ON *djǫfull*, OE *dēoful*, OHG *tiufal*, etc. 'devil' (22.34), used also for 'demon' (and so still in NE, NHG, Du., Dan. versions of NT).

4. Lith. *velnias*, Lett. *velns* 'devil' (22.34), also 'demon'.

5. ChSl. *běsŭ* (reg. for *δαιμόνιον*), SCr. *bijes* (but mostly 'rage'), Boh. *běs*, Pol. *bies*, Russ. *bes* (only ChSl. and Russ. the usual words) : Lith. *baisa* 'fright', *baisus* 'frightful' beside *baimė* 'fear', etc. (16.53). Berneker 56.

SCr. *zloduh*, Boh. *zlý duch*, Pol. *zly duch* 'evil spirit' (16.72, 16.11), now apparently the best words (but words for 'devil' in NT versions).

6. Skt. *rakṣas-* (most usual term for 'demon', but also 'injury') : Av. *rašah-* 'injury', *raš-* 'injure', prob. Grk. *ἐρέχθω* 'rend, break'. Walde-P. 2.362. Barth. 1516.

Skt. *asura-*, orig. 'spiritual, beneficent spirit' and epithet of the gods (see 22.12), then (already sometimes in RV, commonly in AV and the Brahmanas) 'evil spirit, demon'.

Skt. *piçāca-*, used of a special class of demons : *piçuna-* 'slanderous, wicked', Lith. *piktas* 'bad', etc. (16.72). Walde-P. 2.10. Uhlenbeck 167.

Av. *daēva-*, OPers. *daiva-* (the latter only recently quotable; cf. the Daiva-inscription of Xerxes, Herzfeld, Arch. Mitt. aus Iran 8.56 ff., Kent, Language 13.292 ff.) = Skt. *deva-* 'god', etc. After the Zoroastrian rejection of the old religion and the worship of Ahura Mazda as the supreme deity, the old Aryan gods came to be regarded as 'evil spirits, demons'. Barth. 669 f.

22.36 PAGAN, HEATHEN (sb.)

Grk. (eccl.)	*ἔθνη* (pl.), *ἐθνικός*	Goth.	*haiþnō* (nom. sg. fem.), *þiudōs* (pl.)	Lith.	*stabmeldys, pagonis*
NG	*εἰδωλολάτρης*			Lett.	*pagāns*
Lat. (eccl.)	*gentēs* (pl.), *gentīlis, ethnicus, pāgānus*	ON	*heiðingi*	ChSl.	*języci* (pl.), *językĭnikŭ*
		Dan.	*hedning*	SCr.	*poganin, neznabožac*
		Sw.	*hedning*	Boh.	*pohan*
It.	*pagano*	OE	*hǣþen, þeoda* (pl.)	Pol.	*poganin*
Fr.	*païen*	ME	*hethen, paygane*	Russ.	*jazyčnik*
Sp.	*pagano*	NE	*pagan, heathen*		
Rum.	*pagîn*	Du.	*heiden*		
Ir.	*genti* (pl.), *pāgān*	OHG	*heidan, diota* (pl.)		
NIr.	*pāgānach*	MHG	*heiden*		
W.	*pagan*	NHG	*heide*		
Br.	*pagan*				

Most of the words for 'pagan, heathen' are either formal or semantic borrowings from Grk. or Lat. eccl. terms.

A few words for 'idolater' (in general these are formal or semantic borrowings from Grk.; cf. NG below) which serve also for 'heathen' are included.

1. Grk. *ἔθνη*, pl. of *ἔθνος* 'people, nation' (19.22), was used by Jewish writers (LXX, NT) with special reference to the non-Jewish nations, 'heathen' from their point of view. Hence the similar use of words for 'nations' in the other versions, as Lat. *gentēs*, Goth. *þiudōs*, OE *þeoda*, OHG *diota*, ChSl. *języci*. Deriv. *ἐθνικός*, properly 'national', but in NT 'heathen'. Similarly Lat. *ethnicus* or *gentīlis*.

Grk. *Ἕλληνες* 'Greeks' was used in the NT (e.g. Jn. 7.35) in the same way as *ἔθνη* (and in other versions often rendered by the same words), and so in Christian writers often 'heathen'. (Hence its long disuse as a national name, revived in modern times.)

Grk. eccl. *εἰδωλολάτρης* (NT) 'idol-worshiper, idolater' (cpd. of *εἴδωλον* 'image' and agent noun : *λατρεύω* 'serve,

worship'), besides being the source of the widespread terms for 'idolater', may also serve for 'heathen' in NG, where *ἐθνικός* is restored to its original sense of 'national' (but still pl. *ἐθνικοί* 'heathen' eccl.).

2. Lat. eccl. *gentēs, gentīlis*, see above, 1.

Lat. eccl. *pāgānus* (Tertullian, Augustine, etc.), fr. *pāgus* 'country district' (19.14). But the familiar old explanation, namely that the old beliefs survived longer in the country, has been shown to be chronologically untenable. The term came to be used for 'civilian' vs. 'soldier' (*mīlitēs et pāgānī*), and the early Christians, who called themselves soldiers of Christ, accordingly applied it to those not so enrolled. NED vol. VII, add. (last p. of Preface). Weekley, Words ancient and modern 76 ff. This word became the most common one and is the source of the widespread group (Romance, Celtic, English, in part Balto-Slavic, and everywhere familiar).

3. Ir. *genti* (pl.), fr. Lat. *gentēs* (above, 2). Pedersen 1.223. Vendryes, De hib. voc. 163.

Ir. *pāgān* (whence NIr. *pāgānach*), W., Br. *pagan*, fr. Lat. *pāgānus* (above, 2).

4. Goth. *haiþnō* (nom. sg. fem. Mk. 7.26 = *Ἑλληνίς* = *mulier gentīlis* Vulgate; otherwise *þiudōs*, pl., see below), ON *heiðinn* (adj.; sb. expressed by added *maðr* 'man') or *heiðingi*, OE *hǣþen*, OHG *heidan*, etc., general Gmc., deriv. of word seen in Goth. *haiþi*, ON *heiðr*, OE *hǣþ* 'field, heath', and so orig. 'uncultivated person, barbarian' (cf. Goth. *haiþiwisks* 'wild'). Influence of Lat. *pāgānus?* A different view, held by several scholars (Goth. fr. Grk. *ἔθνη*) is more difficult. Feist 238 (with full refs.). NED s.v. *heathen*.

Goth. *þiudōs* (also *þai þiudō* 'those of the nations' = *ἐθνικοί* Mt. 6.7), OE *þeoda*, OHG *diota*, see above, 1.

ME *paygane* (rare), NE *pagan*, fr. Lat. *pāgānus* (above, 2).

5. Lith. *pagonis, pagonas*, Lett. *pagāns*, OPruss. *poganans* (acc. pl.), fr. Lat. *pāgānus* through Slavic (below, 6). Brückner, Sl. Fremdwörter 113, 178. Mühl.-Endz. 3.28 f.

Lith. *stabmeldys*, orig. 'idolater', used also for 'heathen', cpd. of *stabas* 'idol' (22.37) and agent noun of *melsti* 'pray' (22.17).

6. ChSl. *języci*, pl. of *językŭ* 'nation' (19.22), is used like Grk. *ἔθνη* in sense noted above. Hence deriv. *językĭnikŭ* = *ἐθνικός* (Gospels Mt. 6.7, 18.17), Russ. *jazyčnik*.

ChSl. *poganŭ, poganinŭ* (Supr.; in Gospels only nom. sg. fem. *poganyni* = *Ἑλληνίς* Mk. 7.26, same passage in which Goth. has *haiþnō*), SCr., Pol. *poganin*, Boh. *pohan*, fr. Lat. *pāgānus* (above, 2).

SCr. *neznabožac* (term used in NT, Mt. 6.7, etc.), lit. 'one who knoweth not god', cpd. of neg. *ne*, 3sg. of *znati* 'know', and *bog* 'god'. Rječnik Akad. s.v.

22.37 IDOL

Grk.	*εἴδωλον*	Goth.	....	Lith.	*stabas, balvonas*
NG	*εἴδωλον*	ON	*skur(ð)goð*	Lett.	*elks*
Lat.	*īdōlum*	Dan.	*afgud(sbillede)*	ChSl.	*kumirŭ*
It.	*idolo*	Sw.	*avgud(abild)*	SCr.	*idol, kumir*
Fr.	*idole*	OE	*afgod, wēoh, hearh*	Boh.	*modla, bůžek*
Sp.	*ídolo*	ME	*ydele, ydol, idol*	Pol.	*bałwan, bożek*
Rum.	*idol*	NE	*idol*	Russ.	*idol, kumir*
Ir.	*idol, idal*	Du.	*afgod*	Skt.	*(pratimā-)*
NIr.	*īodhal*	OHG	*abgot*		
W.	*eilun*	MHG	*abgot*		
Br.	*idol*	NHG	*götze*		

The most widespread group of words for 'idol' comes from a Greek word for 'image' which was used in Jewish and Christian writers specifically for 'image of a false god', hence also 'false god' without special notion of the image. Conversely, a considerable group (Gmc.) is derived from words for 'god', as 'false god', hence also 'image of a false god', the latter sense also expressed more specifically by cpds. with words for 'image' (as NHG *götzenbild* beside *götze*). Other terms reflect certain objects or places of pagan worship, as 'post, block' ('pillar cult', cf. Tylor, Primitive Culture 2.160 ff., 215 ff., Schrader, Reallex. 2.182 f., Meringer, IF 21.296 ff.) or 'grove'. One means literally 'carved god', probably in imitation of the biblical 'graven image'.

1. Grk. *εἴδωλον* (: *εἶδος* 'form, shape', *εἶδον* 'saw', Lat. *vidēre* 'see', etc.) 'phantom' (Hom.), 'image' (reflected in a mirror or water, or in the mind), hence in Jewish and Christian writings 'image of a false god'. Hence Lat. *īdōlum*, first in earlier Grk. sense, but eccl. 'idol', whence again the widespread Eur. forms. But OFr. *idle, idele* (> ME *ydele*), fr. late *īdolum* resulting from retention of the Grk. accent.

2. Celtic forms, except W., fr. Lat. *īdōlum*. Vendryes, De. hib. voc. 146.

W. *eilun* (also 'image', but reg. word for 'idol' in W. Bible), perh. cpd. of *eil* 'second' and *llun* 'shape'. Pedersen 2.59.

W. *delw* ('image', also 'idol') : Ir. *delb* 'form'. Pedersen 1.64.

3. OE, MLG, Du. *afgod* (MLG > Dan. *afgud*, Sw. *avgud*, whence for the image also Dan. *afgudsbillede*, Sw. *avgudabild*, cpds. with words for 'image'), OHG, MHG *abgot*, cpds. of *af, ab* 'away' and *god, got* 'god', hence orig. 'false god'. Cf. Goth. *afguþs* 'godless, impious', *afgudei* 'impiety' ('idol' does not occur in the texts surviving in Gothic). Falk-Torp 13. Weigand-H. 1.10.

ON *skur(ð)goð*, lit. 'carved god' (cf. the biblical 'graven image'), cpd. of *skurð* : *skurðr* 'carving', *skera* 'cut, carve', and *goð* 'god'.

OE *wēoh, wīh* : Goth. *weihs* 'holy', etc. (22.19). As orig. 'holy image' (like ON *vē* 'holy place, temple') in pagan times, it became eccl. 'idol'.

OE *hearh* 'shrine, temple' (22.13), also 'idol'.

ME *ydele*, ME, NE *idol*, above, 1.

NHG *götze*, dimin. of *gott* 'god', first applied to statues of the saints; as 'false god, idol' since Luther, who used it where *götzenbild* is now preferred (*die götzen ihrer götter*). Weigand-H. 1.753. Kluge-G. 213.

4. Lith. *stabas* (old for 'idol', and revived in place of the borrowed *balvonas*, with derivs., as *stabmeldys* 'idolater, heathen'), also and orig. 'post, stake' :

stabyti 'stop', Skt. *stabh-* 'support, prop', etc. Walde-P. 2.625.

Lith. *balvonas* (reg. word for 'idol' in Trowitsch and Kurschat NT versions), fr. Pol. *bałwan* 'idol' (below, 5).

Lett. *elks* with sense of 'idol' abstracted fr. phrase *elka dievs* (so reg. for 'idol' in Lett. NT), lit. 'god of the grove' (*elka* gen. sg. : Lith. *elkas, alkas* 'sacred grove'). Mühl.-Endz. 1.567.

5. ChSl. *kumirŭ* (> SCr., Russ. *kumir*), etym.? Berneker 644.

SCr., Russ. *idol*, fr. Lat. *īdōlum* (above, 1).

Boh. *modla* = Pol. *modła* 'prayer' (OPol. also 'idol') : ChSl. *moliti sę*, etc. 'pray' (22.17). 'Idol' through '(pagan) object of prayer'. Berneker 2.65. Brückner 343.

Pol. *bałwan*, also and orig. 'block, post' = Boh. *bolvan* 'block, clod, lump', ORuss. *bolvan* 'block, post, idol, altar', etc., loanword fr. some Asiatic form. Development of 'idol' through the sacred 'block, pillar' of pagan worship. Berneker 41. Brückner 13.

Boh. *bůzek*, Pol. *bożek*, derivs. of words for 'god' (22.12), prob. influenced by NHG *götze*.

6. Skt. *pratimā-* 'image, statue' (9.83), applied to images of the gods, hardly has any reference to false gods in ancient times, but is used for 'idol' in a modern Skt. translation of the NT.

22.41 SUPERSTITION

Grk.	δεισιδαιμονία	Goth.	. . . .	Lith.	*niektikystė*
NG	δεισιδαιμονία	ON	*hindrvitni*	Lett.	*mān'ticība*
Lat.	*superstitiō*	Dan.	*overtro*	ChSl.	. . . .
It.	*superstizione*	Sw.	*vidskepelse, vantro, övertro*	SCr.	*praznovjerje*
Fr.	*superstition*	OE	*æfgælþ*	Boh.	*pověra*
Sp.	*supersticione*	ME	*supersticion*	Pol.	*zabobon*
Rum.	*superstițiune, superstiție*	NE	*superstition*	Russ.	*sujeverie*
Ir.	. . . .	Du.	*bijgeloof*		
NIr.	*baoischreideamh*	OHG	*ubermezziki*		
W.	*coelgrefydd, ofergoel*	MHG	*abergloube*		
Br.	*treuskredenn, brizkredenn*	NHG	*aberglaube*		

Much of what we regard as superstition was once, and still is among many peoples, an integral part of religious cult; and at best the line between 'religion' and 'superstition' is a variable one according to time and place. But a distinction was made even in pagan times. Theophrastus (Charact. 28) expounds it, and Cicero (Nat. deorum 2.28.71) remarks that not only the philosophers but also *nostri maiores superstitionem a religione separaverunt.*

The Grk. word means 'fear of supernatural power' in good or bad sense, the latter becoming dominant. The semantic history of Lat. *superstitiō* is disputed (but see below). Most of the other terms are cpds. of words for 'belief' with words for 'perverse, vain, bad' or prefixes having pejorative force. A few are based on 'what is beyond (the normal), abnormal'. Development through 'survival (of older beliefs)' has been assumed in certain cases, but in all these it is doubtful.

1. Grk. δεισιδαιμονία lit. 'fear of supernatural power', used in good or bad sense (for latter cf. Theophr. Charact.

28 with Jebb's comment), fr. adj. δεισιδαίμων 'pious' and 'superstitious', cpd. of δεισι- : δείδω 'fear', sbs. δέος, δεῖμα (16.53), and δαίμων 'divine power', later 'demon' (22.35).

2. Lat. *superstitiō* (> Romance words), fr. *superstāre* 'stand over'. Semantic development disputed, prob. not 'survival' (this sense in *superstes*, only late in vb.), perh. best fr. 'standing over' through 'wonder, astonishment, awe'. Cf. Lith. *stebėtis* 'be astonished', orig. 'be stiff, rigid', and some other words for 'wonder' based on similar notions (16.15). NED s.v. *superstition.* Ernout-M. 983 (not clear as to semantic history). W. Otto, Archiv für Religionswissenschaft 12.548 ff.

3. Ir. word for 'superstition'?

NIr. *baoischreideamh* and *saobhchreideamh*, cpds. of *baois* 'folly, foolish' (Ir. *bāes* 'folly', 17.22) and *saobh* 'perverse' with *creideamh* 'belief'.

W. *coelgrefydd*, cpd. of *coel* 'omen' (22.47) and *crefydd* 'religion', orig. 'belief' (22.11).

W. *ofergoel*, cpd. of *ofer* 'waste, vain' and *coel* 'omen' and 'belief'.

Br. *treuskredenn* (Vallée, Ernault), *brizkredenn* (Vallée), *gwallgreden, gwallfeiz* (Le Gonidec), cpds. of *treus* 'across, contrary', *briz* 'spotted' (as prefix pejorative) or *gwall* 'bad' (16.72) with words for 'religion, belief' (22.11).

4. ON *hindrvitni*, cpd. of *hindri* 'hinder, latter' and *vitni* 'witness', orig. 'knowledge'. Semantically prob. not through 'survival of old beliefs' (as Falk-Torp 807), but through sense seen in vb. *hindra* 'hinder, be wrong'.

Dan. *overtro*, Sw. *övertro*, cpd. of *over, över* 'over' and *tro* 'belief', like ODu. *overgeloof*, prob. as 'what is beyond, contrary to true belief' (rather than 'surviving belief', as Falk-Torp). Falk-Torp 807. Franck-V. W. 65. Hellquist 1473.

Sw. *vantro* (Dan. *vantro* formerly also 'superstition', now 'disbelief'), cpd. of *van-* 'mis-' (= OE, OHG *wan-*, cf. NE *wanton*, NHG *wahnsinn*, etc.) and *tro* 'belief'. Falk-Torp 1348. Hellquist 1307.

Sw. *vidskepelse* (OSw. *vidhskipilse*), fr. a phrase *skipa vidh* 'practice' (magic)? Hellquist 1340.

OE *æfgælþ* (glosses Lat. *superstitio*, cf. Bosworth-Toller, Suppl. s.v.), cpd. of *æf-* (*af-*, *of-*), here with pejorative or negating force (cf. *ofunnan* 'begrudge, refuse', beside *unnan* 'grant', *ofþyncan* 'displease', beside *þyncan* 'seem', *afgod* 'idol', beside *god* 'god', etc.) and deriv. of *galan* 'sing, enchant'.

ME *supersticion*, NE *superstition* fr. Fr. *superstition* or its Lat. source. NED s.v.

Du. *bijgeloof*, cpd. of *bij-* 'by' and *geloof* 'belief'. Franck-v. W. 65.

OHG *ubermezziki, -chi* (gloss *supersticio*, Steinmeyer-Sievers 1.96), lit. 'immoderation', fem. abstract of adj. = NHG *übermässig.*

MHG *abergloube*, NHG *aberglaube*, cpd. of *gloube, glaube* 'belief' with *aber-* in its pejorative sense (as in *aberwitz* 'false wit, absurdity', etc.). Weigand-H. 1.6. Kluge-G. 2. Early NHG also *missglaube* (Luther; but MHG *missegloube* 'mistrust') and *afterglaube*, cpd. with *after* 'after' but here in its pejorative sense (cf. MHG *aftergloube* 'perfidia' and Weigand-H. 1.27).

5. Lith. *niektikystė* (NSB, Lalis), cpd. of neg. *niek-* (: *niekas* 'no one, nothing') and deriv. of *tikėti* 'believe'.

Lett. *mān'ticība*, cpd. first part : *mānīt* 'deceive', *mānis* 'phantom, ghost', etc., and *ticība* 'belief'.

6. SCr. *praznovjerje*, fr. cpd. of *prazan* 'empty, vain' (13.22) and *vjera* 'belief'.

Boh. *pověra*, cpd. of *po* 'after' and *věra*

'belief' (imitation of early NHG *afterglaube*?).

Pol. *zabobon* (OBoh. *bobona, bobonek*, Ukr. *bobona, zabobony* pl.; Russ. *zabobony* pl.; 'absurd, superstitious talk') : OPol. *bobo* 'bogey, scarecrow', OSCr. *boboniti* 'make a noise' ('hum, buzz', etc.), of imitative origin (cf. NE *boo!*). Berneker 36 f. Brückner 32, 643.

Russ. *sujeverie* (also SCr. *sujevjerje*, but less common than *praznovjerje*), fr. cpd. of *suje* in *vsuje*, ChSl. *vŭ suje* 'in vain', *sujeta* 'vanity', and forms = ChSl. *věra* 'belief'.

22.42 MAGIC, WITCHCRAFT, SORCERY

Grk.	μαγεία, μαγικὴ τέχνη, γοητεία, φαρμακεία, βασκανία	Goth.	*lubjaleisei*	Lith.	*magija, žynystė, burtai* (pl.), *kerai* (pl.)
NG	μαγεία, μάγεια (pl.), μαγικά (pl.)	ON	*seiðr, taufr*, etc.	Lett.	*burvība*
Lat.	*magica ars, magicē, magia*	Dan.	*trolddom, magi*	ChSl.	*čari* (pl.), *vlŭšiba*
It.	*magia, sortilegio, stregoneria*	Sw.	*trolldom, svartkonst*	SCr.	*čar, mađije* (pl.)
Fr.	*magie, sorcellerie*	OE	*wiccecræft, wīglung, drȳcræft*	Boh.	*kouzlo, čarodějství*
Sp.	*magia, brujeria, hechiceria*	ME	*magik, wichecraft, sorcerye*	Pol.	*magia, czary, czarodziestvo, gusła*
Rum.	*vrăjitorie, farmec, magie, fapt*	NE	*magic, witchcraft, sorcery*	Russ.	*magija, čary, čarodejstvo, volšebstvo*
Ir.	*druidecht, aimmitecht*	Du.	*tooverkunst*	Skt.	*yātu-, kṛtyā-, māyā-*
NIr.	*draoidheacht, piseog*	OHG	*zoubar*	Av.	*yātu-*
W.	*hud, swyngyfaredd*	MHG	*zouber, zouberie*		
Br.	*strobinell, breou (hud)*	NHG	*zauberei, zauber, hexerei*		

Under 'magic' it is intended to group the more generic terms covering magical art and practices, omitting those for more specific forms such as 'incantation, charm, spell', etc. (some of these noted in the discussion).

Most of the words for the male 'magician' belong to the same etymological groups (but NE *wizard*, orig. 'wise man'), likewise some of those for 'witch' (22.43).

A widespread Eur. group comes from Grk. derivs. of the name of the Persian priests, the Magi, who were regarded as magicians. Similarly, the Ir. words are from the name of the old Celtic priests, the druids. Specialization of 'act' to 'magical act, magic' is frequent. 'Singing' may be specialized, as in the large groups represented by NE *incantation, enchant* (: Lat. *canere* 'sing'), *charm* (of which the magical sense is the earlier; through Fr., fr. Lat. *carmen* 'song'), Grk. ἀοιδή 'song' sometimes, and cpd. ἐπαοιδή regularly, 'enchantment, spell'. A 'wailer' may become a 'wizard' (Grk. γόης, below). A 'saying' may become a 'spell' (cf. NED s.v. *spell* sb.). To 'call' may become 'bewitch' (Lith. *žavėti*, Lett. *zavēt* : Skt. *havate* 'calls', etc., 18.41). Some of the terms are connected with the use of 'drugs'. Many words for 'witch' have derivs. denoting 'witchcraft, sorcery'. Other occasional semantic sources are 'wisdom', 'black art', 'lots, oracles', 'sign' or 'document' (> 'magic formula'), 'whirlwind, whirlpool' (as if supernatural), etc. Cf. Osthoff, Allerhand Zauber etymologisch beleuchtet, BB 24.109 ff., 177 ff.

1. Grk. μαγεία, μαγευτική (sc. τέχνη), μαγικὴ τέχνη, derivs. of Μάγοι, orig. name

of a Median tribe, then the Persian 'priests' (Hdt.+; OPers. nom. sg. *maguš*), who in Greek popular belief were associated with magical practices (perh. only because of their, to the Greeks, strange rites; no factual warrant in native Iranian sources; cf. also Aristot. τὴν δὲ γοητικὴν μαγείαν οὐδ' ἔγνωσαν and E. Meyer, Geschichte des Altertums 4^2.1.117). NG μαγεία, and neut. pl. μάγεια and μαγικά.

Grk. φαρμακεία 'giving of drugs', also esp. 'poisoning' and 'witchcraft', fr. φάρμακον 'drug, poison, spell' (4.88). Cf. also Lith. *burti* 'bewitch' (below, 5).

Grk. γοητεία (in NG mostly in good sense, 'charm'), beside γόης 'sorcerer, wizard' : γοάω 'wail', outside connection dub. Boisacq 154.

Grk. βασκανία, beside vb. βασκαίνω 'bewitch', adj. βάσκανος 'malicious' (> Lat. *fascinum* 'witchcraft', with *f* from *fārī* 'speak'?), prob. loanword, fr. some Thracian or Illyrian form of the root in Grk. φάσκω, φημί, 'say', Lat. *fārī* 'speak', etc. (18.21). Walde-H. 1.459.

2. Lat. *magicus*, adj. (> It. *magico*, Fr. *magique*, etc.) fr. Grk. μαγικός, hence as sb. *magica ars*, also *magicē*, fr. Grk. μαγικὴ τέχνη, also late *magia* (> It., Sp. *magia*, Fr. *magie* > Rum. *magie*), fr. Grk. μαγεία.

It., Sp. *sortilegio*, Fr. *sortilège, sorcellerie*, OFr. *sorcerie*, derivs. of Lat. *sors, sortis* 'lot' and esp. pl. *sortēs* 'oracular responses, oracles'. REW 8107.

It. *stregoneria*, fr. *strega* 'witch' (22.43).

Sp. *brujeria*, fr. *bruja* 'witch' (22.43).

Sp. *hechizo*, whence *hechizar* 'bewitch', *hechicero* 'wizard', *hechicera* 'witch', *hechiceria* 'witchcraft' (cf. Port. *feitiço* 'charm, sorcery' > Fr. *fétiche*, NE *fetish*), fr. Lat. *facticius* 'artificial'. Cf. Rum. *fapt* 'deed' and 'witchcraft', and other old or dial. forms fr. derivs. of Lat. *facere* 'do, make'. REW 3132, 3135, 3136. Wartburg 3.359, 362 f.

Rum. *vrăjitorie*, fr. *vrăji* 'bewitch', fr. Slavic, late ChSl. *vražiti* 'take omens', Russ. *vorožit'* 'tell fortunes', etc. (Brückner 632). Tiktin 1775.

Rum. *farmec* (whence *fermeca* 'bewitch', *fermecător* 'magician, wizard', *fermecătoare* 'witch'), fr. Grk. φάρμακον 'drug, poison, spell'. REW 6462. Tiktin 611, 619.

3. Ir. *druịdecht*, NIr. *draoidheacht*, lit. 'druidism', fr. *drui* (gen. *druad*), name of the old pagan priest and magician (22.18).

Ir. *aimmitecht*, fr. *ammait* 'wizard, witch' (22.43).

Ir. *bricht*, NIr. *briocht* 'charm, spell', etym.? (: Skt. *brahmaṇ-* 'sacred text, prayer, spell', Osthoff l.c. 117, but very dub.).

NIr. *piseog*, = Ir. *pisoc* 'charm', orig.? Macbain 276.

W., Br. *hud* (Br. *hud* archaic, Vallée), Corn. *hus* : ON *seiðr* 'spell, charm, magic', prob. fr. the root seen in ChSl. *šětiti sę* 'remember'. Cf. Goth. *afhugjan* 'bewitch', cpd. of *hugjan* 'think'. Walde-P. 2.509. Pedersen 1.58. G. S. Lane, Language 11.194 f.

W. *swyngyfaredd*, cpd. of *swyn* 'charm, spell, love-potion', fr. Lat. *signum* 'sign' (Pedersen 1.223, Loth, Mots lat. 209) and *cyfaredd* 'charm, spell' (etym.?).

Br. *strobinell* 'whirlwind, whirlpool' (deriv. of Lat. *turbō, -inis*, Henry 256), regarded as supernatural, hence used for 'magic'. Le Gonidec s.v.

Br. *breou*, pl. of **brev*, fr. Fr. *bref* 'brief, document'. Cf. the use of Fr. *brevet* for 'magic formula, charm'. Henry 44. Ernault, Glossaire 83.

4. Goth. *lubjaleisei* (= φαρμακεία; also *lubjaleisai liutai* = γόητες 'magicians, sorcerers'), cpd. of *lubja-* : OE *lybb*

'drug', *lyblāc* 'sorcery, witchcraft', OHG *luppi* 'poison, magic', etc., second part : *lais* 'know', *laisjan* 'teach', etc. Feist 337.

ON *seiðr*, see under W., Br. *hud* (above, 3).

ON *taufr*, MLG *tōver*, Du. *tooverkunst* (or *-kraft*), OHG *zoubar*, MHG *zouber*, NHG *zauber, zauberei*, prob. : OE *tēafor*, 'pigment, red lead' (NE dial. *tiver*). The fact that the runes were colored red may furnish the connecting link, but root connection and primary sense are obscure. Weigand-H. 2.1304. Kluge-G. 704. Franck-v. W. 703.

ON *gørningar*, pl. of *gørning* 'act, deed' (: *gørva* 'do, make', 9.11) is used also for 'magical acts, witchcraft'.

ON *galdrar*, pl. of *galdr* 'song, chant, spell' (: *gala* 'sing, chant', 18.2), freq. 'magic, witchcraft'.

Dan. *trolddom*, Sw. *trolldom*, fr. ON *troll* 'giant, monster, demon' (22.35), Dan. *trold*, Sw. *troll* 'goblin, imp'.

Sw. *svartkonst*, lit. 'black art'.

OE *wiccecræft*, ME *wichecraft*, NE *witchcraft*, cpd. of *wicce* 'witch' (22.43) and *cræft* 'power, skill'.

OE *drȳcræft*, similar cpd. of *drȳ* 'magician', fr. Ir. *drui* 'priest, magician'.

OE *wīglung, wīgle*, beside vb. *wīglian* 'practice divination or sorcery' = MLG *wichelen* id. : OE *wicce* 'witch', etc. (22.43).

OE *scīnlāc* 'phantom' (22.45), also 'magic'. Hence *scīnlǣca* 'magician'.

ME *magik*, NE *magic*, through OFr. *magique*, fr. Lat. *magica ars* (above, 2). NED s.v.

ME *sorcerye*, NE *sorcery*, fr. OFr. *sorcerie* (above, 2).

NHG *hexerei*, fr. *hexe* 'witch' (22.43).

5. Lith. *magija*, through Pol. or Russ. fr. Lat. *magia* (above, 2).

Lith. *žynystė* (with *žynys* 'diviner, sorcerer', *žynė* 'witch') : *žinoti* 'know'. Leskien, Ablaut 358.

Lith. *burtai* (pl.) 'lot' and 'magic', Lett. *burvība* 'magic', with vbs. Lith. *burti*, Lett. *burt* 'practice magic, bewitch', prob. : Grk. φάρμακον 'drug, poison, spell' (see above, 1). Walde-P. 2.161. Mühl.-Endz. 1.354.

Lith. *kerai* (pl.), beside *kerėti* 'bewitch', fr. the same root as ChSl. *čari*, etc. (below, 6).

6. ChSl. *čari*, pl. (cf. *čaro-dějĭ* 'wizard'; general Slavic *čaro-* in cpds.), SCr. *čar* (*čarobia, čarolia*, etc.), Pol. *czary*, Russ. *čary* (both pl.), Boh. *čarodějství*, Pol. *czarodziestwo*, Russ. *čarodejstvo*, etc., prob. fr. the root seen in Skt. *kr-* 'make, do', with specialization of 'act' as in Skt. *krtyā-* (below, 7). Walde-P. 1.518. Berneker 136 f. Brückner 72.

ChSl. *vlŭšiba* (Supr. = μαγεία), Russ. *volšebstvo*, fr. ChSl. *vlŭchvŭ* (Supr.), obs. Russ. *volchvŭ* 'wizard, magician', orig. dub., perh. a loanword based on ON *vǫlva* 'prophetess, sibyl'. Pedersen, IF 5.66. Vondrák 1.442.

Boh. *kouzlo*, Pol. *gusła* (pl.), etym.? Berneker 654.

SCr. *mađije* (pl.), Pol. *magia*, Russ. *magija*, fr. Lat. *magia* (above, 2).

7. Skt., Av. *yātu-* (both more commonly personal 'sorcerer'), with derivs., e.g. Skt., Av. *yātumant-* 'practicing magic'), root connection? Walde-P. 1.197. Barth. 1283 f.

Skt. *krtyā-* 'deed, act', but esp. 'magic, witchcraft' (also 'witch'), fr. *kr-* 'make, do'. Walde-P. 1.517 f.

Skt. *māyā-* 'supernatural power, magic', etym. dub. Walde-P. 2.220. Uhlenbeck 222.

22.43 WITCH, SORCERESS

Grk.	φαρμακίς	Goth.	**lubjaleisa*	Lith.	*ragana, žynė*
NG	μάγισσα, στρίγλα	ON	*galdrakona, fordæða*	Lett.	*ragana, burve*
Lat.	*sāga, striga, maga*	Dan.	*heks, troldkvinde*	ChSl.	(*věštica, vědīma*)
It.	*strega, maliarda, fattuchiera*	Sw.	*häxa*	SCr.	*vještica*
Fr.	*sorcière, magicienne*	OE	*wicce, hægtesse*	Boh.	*čarodějnice*
Sp.	*bruja, hechicera*	ME	*wycche, hegge, sorceress*	Pol.	*czarownica, strzyga*
Rum.	*vrăjitoare, fermecătoare*	NE	*witch, sorceress*	Russ.	*ved'ma, koldun'ja, čarodejka*
Ir.	*ammait*	Du.	*heks, toovenares*	Skt.	*yātudhānī-*
NIr.	*bandraoi*	OHG	*hagazussa*	Av.	*jahī-* (or *jahikā-*) *yātumaitī-, pairikā-*
W.	*dewines, rheibes, swynwraig*	MHG	*hecse, zouberinne*		
Br.	*boudig, kevnidenn*	NHG	*hexe, zauberin*		

Most of the words for the male 'magician, sorcerer' are connected with those for 'magic, witchcraft' (22.42). Many of those for the female 'witch' are the corresponding feminine forms. But the 'witch', more persistent and often with more malevolent connotation in folklore, is also often expressed by words for which corresponding masculine forms are lacking (e.g. Lat. *striga*, NHG *hexe*, Lith., Lett. *ragana*) or have become obsolete (OE masc. *wicca*, fem. *wicce*; NE *witch* now only fem., except dial.; masc. supplied by *wizard*, orig. 'wise man').

Apart from those belonging to the groups discussed in 22.42, several of the words must have originally denoted the female 'diviner, seer, soothsayer', being connected with words for 'divine' or verbs for 'see', 'know', or 'foretell'. Scattered semantic sources are 'woman-druid', 'spell-woman', 'night-owl', 'spider's web', 'murmurer' (of spells), 'hedge-ghost' (?).

Words for 'witch' are also used as opprobrious terms without special reference to magical practice—more rarely of an enticing, bewitching young woman, as sometimes NG μάγισσα, NE *witch*, NHG *zauberin* (but not *hexe*).

1. Grk. φαρμακίς, fem. of φαρμακεύς 'sorcerer', also φαρμακός both masc. and fem. (in LXX 'witch'), fr. φάρμακον 'drug, poison, spell'. Cf. φαρμακεία, 22.42.

Byz., NG μάγισσα, fem. of μάγος 'wizard'. Cf. μαγεία, etc., 22.42.

NG στρίγλα (also as opprobrious term 'vixen, shrew'), fr. Lat. **strigula*, dim. of *striga* 'witch' (below, 2). G. Meyer Neugr. Stud. 3.64.

2. Lat. *sāga* : *sāgīre* 'perceive keenly', *praesāgīre* 'presage, foretell'. Ernout-M. 887.

Lat. *striga* (> It. *strega* 'witch', Rum. *strigă* 'owl'), fr. Grk. *στρίγα beside στρίγγα, acc. of στρίξ, στρίγξ (= Lat. *strix*), some kind of night bird that was believed to suck the blood of young children. Ernout-M. 987. Pauly-Wissowa s.v. Striges. REW 8308.

Lat. *maga*, fem. of *magus* 'magician', fr. Grk. μάγος id. (22.42).

For other less common Lat. words for 'witch' cf. E. E. Burriss, Cl. Ph. 31.138 ff.

It. *maliarda*, fr. *malia* 'charm, spell', fr. *malo* 'evil'. Cf. Lat. *malum carmen* 'incantation, spell'.

It. *fattuchiera*, fr. deriv. of Lat. *fātum* 'fate'. REW 3221. But cf. also *fattura* 'witchcraft', fr. Lat. *factūra* 'form', REW 3136.

Fr. *sorcière*, fem. of *sorcier* 'sorcerer',

deriv. of Lat. *sortēs* 'oracles' (cf. It. *sortilegio*, OFr. *sorcerie*, etc. 22.42).

Fr. *magicienne*, fem. of *magicien* 'magician, wizard', deriv. of Lat. *magicus* 'magic' (22.42).

Sp. *bruja*, etym.?

Sp. *hechicera* : *hechizo*, etc. (22.42).

Rum. *vrăjitoare*, fr. *vrăji* 'work magic' (22.42).

Rum. *fermecătoare*, fr. *fermeca* 'bewitch', fr. *farmec* 'magic, witchcraft' (22.42).

3. Ir. *ammait* (both masc. and fem., 'wizard, witch'; cf. K. Meyer, Contrib. 86), etym.?

NIr. *ban-draoi*, lit. 'female druid', cpd. of *ban-*, prefix for *bean* 'woman', and *draoi*, Ir. *drui* 'priest, magician' (22.18).

W. *dewines*, fem. of *dewin* 'diviner, wizard', fr. Lat. *dīvīnus* in its special sense of 'soothsayer, prophet'. Loth, Mots lat. 160.

W. *rheibes*, fem. deriv. of *rheibio* 'ravage', secondarily 'bewitch, enchant', fr. Lat. *rapere* 'seize, ravish'. Loth, Mots lat. 202.

W. *swynwraig*, cpd. of *swyn* 'charm, spell' (fr. Lat. *signum* 'sign') and *gwraig* 'woman'. Pedersen 1.223.

Br. *boudig* (also 'fairy'), apparently fr. *boud* 'murmur, buzzing' from the mumbling of formulae to enchant.

Br. *kevnidenn* 'spider's web', also used for 'old witch' (Ernault, Vallée).

4. Goth., no word for 'witch' quotable, but presumably **lubjaleisa*, fem. of *lubjaleis* in *lubjaleisai liutai* 'sorcerers'. Cf. *lubjaleisei* 'witchcraft' (22.42).

ON *galdrakona*, cpd. of *galdr* 'song, spell', pl. 'sorcery, witchcraft' (22.42) and *kona* 'woman'.

ON *fordæða*, lit. 'evil deed' (: *dāð* 'deed'), used for 'witchcraft' (cf. derivs. of words for 'do' in this sense, 22.42), and esp. 'witch'.

OE *wicce*, ME *wycche*, NE *witch* (beside masc. OE *wicca*, etc.) : OE *wiccian* 'practice witchcraft', MLG *wicken* id., also OE *wīglian*, MLG *wichelen* 'practice divination or sorcery', these : Goth. *weihs* 'holy' (22.19), *weihan* 'consecrate', etc. Walde-P. 1.232. Falk-Torp 1376. Frank-v. W. 791. NED s.v. *witch*.

OE *hægtesse* (whence shortened form ME *hegge, hagge*, NE *hag*, partly 'witch'; cf. NED s.v.), OHG *hagazussa* (*hagzissa, hāziz*, etc.), MHG *hecse, hexse*, NHG *hexe* (> Du. *heks*, Dan. *heks*, Sw. *häxa*), etym. dub., perh. a cpd. of word seen in ON *hagi* 'pasture land', OE *haga* 'inclosure', Du. *haag* 'hedge', etc. (cf. ON *tūnrīða*, OHG *zūnrīta*, lit. 'hedge-rider', used of witches and ghosts), second part : Norw. dial. *tysja* 'elf'. Falk-Torp 392. Kluge-G. 248. Otherwise J. Franck, Geschichte des Wortes Hexe (cf. IF Anz. 15.100).

ME, NE *sorceress*, fem. of *sorcer, sorcerer*, fr. OFr. *sorcier* 'sorcerer' (above, 2). NED s.v.

MHG *zouberinne*, NHG *zauberin*, fem. of *zouberer, zauberer* 'sorcerer' : OHG *zoubar*, etc. 'magic' (22.42). Similarly Du. *toovenares*, fem. of *toovenaar* 'sorcerer' : MLG *tover* 'magic'.

Dan. *troldkvinde*, fem. of *troldmand* 'sorcerer' : *trolddom* 'magic' (22.42). But Sw. *trollkarl* 'sorcerer' without corresponding fem.

5. Lith., Lett. *ragana*, as orig. 'seer' (so actually Lett. *paragana*) : Lith. *regėti*, Lett. *redzēt* 'see' (15.51). Leskien, Ablaut 365 (with?). Buga, Kalba ir Senovė 260. Mühl.-Endz. 3.464.

Lith. *žynė* (beside masc. *žynys* 'diviner, sorcerer' and *žynystė* 'magic') : *žinoti* 'know'. Leskien, Ablaut 358.

Lett. *burve* : Lith. *burti*, Lett. *burt* 'practice magic', Lith. *burtai*, Lett. *burvība* 'magic' (22.42).

6. ChSl. *věštica, vědīma* (both rare and

late), SCr. *vještica*, Russ. *ved'ma* : ChSl. *věděti* 'know'. Miklosich 390 f.

Boh. *čarodějnice*, Pol. *czarownica, czarodziejka* (SCr. *čarobnica*, Russ. *čarodejka* less common), cpds. or derivs. of *čaro-* in ChSl. *čari* (pl.) 'magic', etc. (22.42).

Pol. *strzyga*, fr. Lat. *striga* (above, 2). Brückner 523.

Russ. *koldun'ja*, prob. fr. some Finno-Ugrian form related to Hung. *koldulni* 'beg', *koldus* 'beggar'. Berneker 544.

7. Skt. *yātudhānī-*, fem. of *yātudhāna-* 'wizard, magician' (both in RV, AV), cpd. of *yātu-* 'witchcraft' (22.42) and *dhā-* 'put, do, make'.

Av. *jahī- yātumaitī-* and *jahikā- yātumaitī-*, phrase containing words for (daevic) 'woman', with fem. of adj. *yātumant-* (= Skt. id.), deriv. of *yātu-* 'witchcraft' (22.42). Barth. 606, 1284 f.

Av. *pairikā-* ('enchantress, witch', seducing men from the true belief, but later good 'fairy', as NPers. *pari* > NE *Peri*), prob. : Ir. *airech* 'concubine' (Thurneysen, IF 2.146 f.), Grk. παλλακίς, Lat. *paelex* id., with Hebr. *pilleges* id., an old loanword from some Anatolian source. Walde-P. 2.7. Boisacq 743 f. Nehring, Studien zur idg. Kultur und Urheimat 173 ff.

22.44 FAIRY (or the like)

Grk.	(νύμφη)	Goth.	. . . .	Lith.	*laumė*
NG	μοῖρα	ON	*ālfr*	Lett.	*lauma*
Lat.	(*nympha*)	Dan.	*fe* (*alf*)	ChSl.	. . . .
It.	*fata*	Sw.	*fe* (*älfa*)	SCr.	*vila, rusalka*
Fr.	*fée*	OE	*ælf*	Boh.	*vila*
Sp.	*hada*	ME	*elfe, fay, fairie*	Pol.	*boginka, rusałka*
Rum.	*zînă, ursitoare*	NE	*fairy* (*elf*)	Russ.	*feja*
Ir.	*ben sīde*	Du.	*fee*		
NIr.	*bean sīdhe, sīdhbhean*	OHG	. . . .		
W.	*tylwyth teg* (pl.)	MHG	*feie*		
Br.	*korrigez, boudig*	NHG	*fee*		

'Fairy' is introduced here as the opposite of 'witch', which is true of the most familiar current use of NE *fairy*, Fr. *fée*, etc. But actually the words listed denoted beings with magical powers for both good and evil, sometimes more impish or malevolent than otherwise. The typical good 'fairy' seems to have established herself in medieval Germanic folklore.

Many of the words are of obscure origin, but the principal known source is 'fate'.

1. Nearest to 'fairies' in ancient Greek folklore were the 'nymphs', with their various special classes, 'water-nymphs, tree-nymphs, mountain-nymphs'.

Grk. νύμφη 'bride' (: Lat. *nūbere* 'marry'), 'young maiden', and 'nymph'. Grk. μοῖρα 'fate' : μόρος 'fate', μέρος 'part, share', etc. (13.23). NG also 'fate', but in folklore esp. in pl. the good 'fairies' who appear at the birth of a child and assign its fate. (Cf. e.g. Pernot, Recueil de textes en grec usuel, p. 50).

2. Lat. *nympha* 'nymph' (fr. Grk. νύμφη id.), also the nearest approach to 'fairy'.

Lat. *fāta*, neut. pl. of *fātum* 'prophetic declaration, fate' (: *fārī* 'speak'), becoming VLat. sg. > It. *fata*, Fr. *fée*, Sp. *hada*, and through Fr. the widespread Eur. words. REW 279. Wartburg 3.432 f.

Rum. *zînă* (also spelled *zină*) = OIt. *jana*, OFr. *gene* 'witch', fr. Lat. *Diana*. The pagan goddess of the woodlands survived thus in later folklore. REW 2624. Tiktin 1822. Wartburg 3.66.

Rum. *ursitoare* (used like NG *μοῖρα*, above, 1), fr. vb. *ursi* 'determine one's fate', this fr. NG *ὁρίζω* 'determine' (orig. 'bound'). Tiktin 1698 f.

3. Ir. *sīde*, NIr. *sīdhe* (pl.) 'fairy creatures' : *sīd*, NIr. *sīodh* 'mound, knoll', esp. as 'abode of the fairies' (etym.?). Hence sg. fem. *ben sīde* (*ben* 'woman'), NIr. *bean sīdhe* (> NE *banshee*, cf. NED s.v.), NIr. also *sīdhbhean*, *sīobhra*, etc. (McKenna).

W. *tylwyth teg* (pl.), lit. 'beautiful family' (*tylwyth* 'household, family', *teg* 'beautiful'). Cf. Rhys, Celtic Folklore 82 ff.

Br. *korrigez*, fem. of *korrig*, dim. of *korr* 'dwarf' (**korso-* : Lat. *curtus* 'mutilated, short', etc.).

Br. *boudig* 'witch' or 'fairy', see 42.43.

4. Nearest to 'fairies' in early Gmc. folklore were the 'elves', dwarfed beings with magical powers, generally impish if not malevolent. They are, at least in part, the antecedents of the more beneficent medieval fairies. Cf. NED s.v. *elf*.

ON *ālfr*, OE *ælf*, ME *elfe*, NE *elf* (> NHG *elf*, fem. *elfe*), Dan. *alf*, Sw. *älfa* (OHG *alp* 'nightmare'), etym. dub., perh. : Skt. *ṛbhu-*, a name given to three semidivine craftsmen (or even less convincingly : Lat. *albus* 'white'). Walde-P. 1.93. Falk-Torp 22. Kluge-G. 12. Weigand-H. 1.43.

ME, NE *fay* (now arch. or poet.), Dan., Sw. *fe*, Du. *fee*, MHG *feie*, NHG *fee*, fr. OFr. *faie*, Fr. *fée* (above, 2).

ME *fairie*, NE *fairy*, in earliest use 'fairy-land' or 'fairy-folk' (fr. OFr. *fairie* id., deriv. of *faie*), then displacing the simple *fay*. NED s.v.

5. Lith. *laumė*, Lett. *lauma*, a kind of 'fairy', but more often impish or malevolent than beneficent, etym. dub., perh. : ChSl. *loviti* 'seize, catch'. Mühl.-Endz. 2.428 f. Solmsen, KZ 34.553 f.

6. In Slavic folklore the nearest approach to 'fairy' would be the *vila* or the *rusalka*, both used of a sort of nymph, but often malevolent. Cf. Niederle, Manuel de l'antiquité slave, 2.132 ff. (with refs.).

SCr., Bulg., Boh. *vila* (Pol. *wiła* 'buffoon') : Lith. *vilti*, Lett. *vilt* 'deceive' (outside connections dub.; Mühl.-Endz. 4.596), and/or Russ. *viljat'* 'run about', Boh. *viliti* 'fornicate', etc. Brückner 622. Niederle, op. cit. 133 f.

SCr., Bulg., Russ. *rusalka* (Russ. > Pol. *rusałka*, lit.), formed fr. the name of the festival, late ChSl. *rusalija*, etc., fr. MLat. *rōsālia*, Byz. *ρουσάλια*, lit. 'rose-festival'. Brückner 469. Niederle, loc. cit.

Pol. *boginka* (also *bogunka*), dim. of *bogini* 'goddess'. Brückner 34.

Russ. *feja*, fr. Fr. *fée* (above, 2).

7. There seem to be no fairies or anything like them in early Indo-Iranian mythology. But cf. AV *pairikā-* with its later development (22.43).

22.45 GHOST, SPECTER, PHANTOM

Grk.	*φάντασμα* (*σκιά* poet.)	Goth.	....	Lith.	*vėlė*, *šmėkla*, *monas*
NG	*στοιχειό*, *φάντασμα*	ON	*draugr*, *aptrganga*	Lett.	*velis*, *spuoks*, *māns*
Lat.	*mānēs* (pl.), *lārva*, *phantasma*	Dan.	*spøgelse*, *genfærd*	ChSl.	*prizrakŭ*
It.	*spettro*, *fantas(i)ma*	Sw.	*spöke*	SCr.	*avet*, *utvara*
Fr.	*spectre*, *fantôme*, *revenant*	OE	*scīn*, *scīnlāc*, *gāst*	Boh.	*strašidlo*, *přišera*
Sp.	*espectro*, *fantasma*	ME	*gost*, *fantome*	Pol.	*widmo*, *strach*
Rum.	*stafie*, *spectru*, *fantomă*	NE	*ghost*, *spook*, *specter*, *phantom*	Russ.	*prividenie*, *prizrak*
Ir.	*scāl*	Du.	*spook*	Skt.	*pitaras* (pl.), *preta-bhūta-*
NIr.	*taidhbhse*, *samhail*	OHG	*gitrog*, *bitrog*, *giskīn*		
W.	*bwgan*, *drychiolaeth*	MHG	*gespenste*, *getwās*		
Br.	*bugelnoz*, *teuz*	NHG	*gespenst*		

Most of the words for 'soul, spirit' (16.11) are also used with reference to the supernatural spirits, but these are not repeated here, with the exception of NE *ghost*, in which this sense has become the dominant one.

The most common development is through the notion of 'appearance' (cf. the specialization of NE *apparition* vs. *appearance*) in words derived from verbs for 'see, appear, shine'. Other sources are 'likeness', 'fright', 'darkness', 'enticement' and 'returning' (i.e. from the dead). The use of 'shade' in this sense, common in Homer, has been widely imitated in poetry.

1. Grk. *σκιά* 'shade, shadow' (1.63), poet. for 'ghost, phantom'. Imitated in the similar use of Lat. *umbra*, NE *shade*, etc.

Grk. *φάντασμα* (also *φάσμα*), lit. 'appearance, apparition' : *φαίνομαι* 'appear'.

NG pop. *στοιχειό*, fr. *στοιχεῖον* 'element' (: *στείχω* 'walk, march', *στίχος* 'row, line', etc.), in Byz. sometimes a kind of guardian spirit. The eccl. use of *στοιχεῖα τοῦ κόσμου* (NT Col. 2.8, 20, Gal. 4.3, 9) as 'cosmic powers' furnishes the connecting link. Sophocles s.v. *στοιχεῖον*. Moulton-Milligan 591.

2. Lat. *mānēs* (pl.) : *mānus* 'good'. Ernout-M. 587. Walde-H. 2.27.

Lat. *lārva* (early *lārua*) : *Lār*, pl. *Lārēs*, this of Etruscan orig.(?). Ernout-M. 524 f. Walde-H. 1.762 f., 766.

Lat. *phantasma*, fr. Grk. *φάντασμα* (above, 1). Hence It. *fantas(i)ma*. But Prov. *fantauma*, Fr. *fantôme* (> Rum. *fantomă*), apparently fr. a Grk. dial. by-form *φάνταγμα*, parallel to Dor. *ψάφιγμα* = *ψήφισμα* and indicated by modern Lesb. *φάδαμα* (cf. *πρᾶγμα* > *πρᾶμα*). The OFr. spelling *fantosme* (also found in ME) will then be due to *fantasme*, which also occurs. REW 6460. Kretschmer, Der heutige lesbische Dialekt 461.

It. *spettro*, Fr. *spectre* (> INE *specter*, Rum. *spectru*), Sp. *espectro*, fr. Lat. *spectrum* 'appearance, image' (: *specere* 'perceive, look').

Fr. *revenant*, sb. use of adj. *revenant* 'returning', as of one returning from the other world.

Rum. *stafie*, fr. NG *στοιχειό* (above, 1). Cf. Alb. *stihī*, fr. same source. Tiktin 1482. G. Meyer, Alb. Etym. Wtb. 393.

3. Ir. *scāl* 'supernatural being, specter' (also rendered as 'giant, hero'), NIr. *scāil* 'reflection, image', also 'ghost' (Dinneen), prob. : Goth. *skōhsl* 'demon' (22.35). M. A. O'Brien, Eriu 11.89 f. Otherwise Pedersen 1.76.

NIr. *taidhbhse* = Ir. *taidbse*, beside *taidbsiu* 'a showing, appearance', vbl.n.

of *doadbat* 'shows' (**to-ad-fiad-* : IE **weid-* 'see'). Pedersen 1.421, 2.519.

NIr. *samhail* 'likeness, image' (Ir. *samail* id. : Lat. *similis* 'like', etc.), also 'ghost, specter'. Similarly Br. *semeilh* (Van.).

W. *bwgan* (arch. *bwg*), beside *bwgwl* 'threat', arch. 'fear', also NE *bogle*, *bogy*, NHG *bögge*, *böggel-mann*, all terms for 'goblins', etc., ultimate source dub. Cf. NED s.v. *bogle*.

W. *drychiolaeth*, fr. *drych* 'sight, appearance, aspect' = Ir. *drech* 'face' : Grk. *δέρκομαι* 'see', etc. Cf. NE *apparition*, etc.

Br. *bugelnoz*, cpd. of *bugel* 'child' (2.25, 2.27) and *noz* 'night' (14.42).

Br. *teuz*, etym. dub. (: Ir. *tucht* 'form, appearance'?). Henry 263. Ernault, Glossaire 691.

4. ON *draugr*, Norw. *draug*, OHG *gitrog* ('deceit', like NHG *betrug*, and 'ghost'; also OHG *bitrog* in gl. *pitroch* = *fantasma*) : OHG *triugan* 'deceive', Skt. *droha-* 'harm, injury', Av. *druj-*, OPers. *drauga-* 'lie', etc. (16.67, 16.68). Walde-P. 1.874. Falk-Torp 153.

ON *aptr-ganga*, lit. 'back-comer' (cf. Fr. *revenant*, above, 2). Imitated in Dan. *gen-færd*, *gen-ganger*. Falk-Torp 315.

OE *scīn*, OHG *giskīn* (Tat. for *phantasma*, Mt. 14.26), orig. 'appearance, apparition' : OE *scīnan*, OHG *skinan*, etc. 'shine (15.55). Hence also OE *scīnlāc* 'phantom' and 'magic', cpd. of *lāc* 'offering, gift' : vb. *lācon* 'swing, play' = ON *leika* 'play', etc. (16.25).

OE *gāst* 'soul, spirit' (16.11), also 'ghost, specter' (e.g. *unfǣle gāst* for *phantasma* Mk. 6.49, where Lindisf. *yfel wiht*, lit. 'evil creature'), and, with increasing dominance of this sense, ME *gost*, NE *ghost*. NED s.v. Du. *geest* in both senses.

ME *fantome*, NE *phantom*, NE *specter*, fr. Fr. (above, 2).

MLG *spōk*, *spūk*, Du. *spook* (> NE *spook*, first used in U.S., NHG *spuk*, Sw. *spöke*, Dan. *spøgelse*), etym. dub. Falk-Torp 1140 f. Franck-v. W. 648 f.

MHG *gespenste*, NHG *gespenst*, fr. OHG *gispanst* 'enticement' : *(gi)spanan* 'entice'. In MHG used of a spirit inciting evil, and especially in association with *teufel*. Weigand-H. 1.706. Sperber, Einleitung 24.

MHG *getwās*, MDu. *ghedwas* : MHG *twās*, *dwās*, Du. *dwaas* 'fool' (17.22). Walde-P. 1.845. Franck-v. W. 144.

5. Lith. *vėlė*, Lett. *velis* (both mostly in pl.), etym. dub. Walde-P. 1.305. Mühl.-Endz. 4.530 f. Buga, Rev. Sl. 6.23 f.

Lith. *šmėkla* ('apparition, specter'), beside vb. *šmėkšoti* (also *šmykšoti*, *šmūkšoti*) 'appear in vague outlines', prob. with variant forms of the root syllable : Russ. *šmygnut'* 'flit by'. Senn (privately).

Lett. *spuoks*, fr. MLG *spōk* (above, 4). Mühl.-Endz. 3.1035.

Lett. *k'ēms*, fr. Livon. *kāms* (or conversely?). Mühl.-Endz. 2.373 f.

Lith. *monas*, Lett. *māns* (NSB, Mühl.-Endz. s.vv.), fr. WhRuss. *man'* 'deceiver', etc. Berneker 2.17 f. Brückner, Sl. Fremdwörter 109. Skardžius 134.

6. ChSl. *prizrakŭ* (in Gospels = *φάντασμα*, beside *zrakŭ* = *εἶδεα* 'appearance, aspect') : *priz(ĭ)rěti* 'look', cpd. of *z(ĭ)rěti* 'look, see' (15.51). Hence Russ. *prizrak*.

SCr. *avet*, fr. Turk. (= Arab.) *afet* 'misfortune'. Miklosich, Türk. Elem. 242.

SCr. *utvara* : *utvoriti se* 'appear' (cpd. of *tvoriti* 'form, create' = ChSl. *tvoriti* 'do, make', 9.11).

Boh. *strašidlo*, fr. *strašiti* 'frighten', fr. *strach* 'fright' (16.35) = Pol. *strach* 'fear' and 'ghost'.

Boh. *přišera* : *přišeři* 'twilight', *šerý*

'gray, dim, dark' (late ChSl. *sěrŭ*, Russ. *seryj*, etc. 'gray').

Pol. *widmo*, Russ. *prividenie* : ChSl. *viděti* 'see' (15.51).

7. Skt. *pitaras* 'fathers', also used for the spirits of one's ancestors.

Skt. *preta-* 'dead' (pple. *pra-ita-* 'gone forth, departed'), also 'spirit of the dead, ghost'.

Skt. *bhūta-* 'a being' (: *bhū-* 'become, be'), often a supernatural being, a kind of 'ghost' (cf. BR s.v.).

Av. *fravaši-*, in pl. in part like Lat. *mānēs*, see. 22.46.

22.46. Guardian spirit. Most of the words for 'soul, spirit' (16.11) are also used with reference to a mystical spirit of the living and dead, and, among many peoples, of inanimate things ('animism'). But there are also a few other words which are used specifically in this sense.

1. Grk. *δαίμων* in its usual class. use, later 'evil spirit, demon'. See 22.35.

2. Lat. *genius*, through the notion of 'creative' : *gignere* 'beget, bear', *genus* 'birth', etc. Ernout-M. 398 f. Walde-H. 1.591.

Av. *fravaši-*, mostly in pl., the Fravashis, guardian spirits of the faithful before birth, during life and after death, fr. **fra-varti-*, this prob. fr. root *var-*, IE **wer-* 'cover, guard, protect' (Walde-P. 1.280 ff.). Barth. 992 ff.

22.47 OMEN

Grk.	*οἰωνός*, *ὄρνις*	Goth.	*taikns*	Lith.	*ženklas*
NG	*οἰωνός*	ON	*heill*, *furða*	Lett.	*zīme*
Lat.	*ōmen*, *augurium*, *auspicium*	Dan.	*omen*, *varsel*	ChSl.	*znamenĭje*
It.	*augurio*, *presagio*	Sw.	*förebud*	SCr.	*znamenje*
Fr.	*augure*, *présage*	OE	*hǣl*, *tāc(e)n*	Boh.	*znamení*
Sp.	*agüero*, *presagio*	ME	*token*	Pol.	*wróżba*
Rum.	*augur*, *prevestire*	NE	*omen*	Russ.	*predznamenovanie*
Ir.	*cēl*	Du.	*voorteeken*	Skt.	*lakṣaṇa-*
NIr.	*tuar*	OHG	*zeihhan*		
W.	*argoel* (*coel*)	MHG	*zeichen*		
Br.	*diougan*	NHG	*omen*, *vorzeichen*		

A few of the words for 'omen' are based upon words for 'bird', and so must have first applied specifically to omens taken from the flight of birds. Several mean primarily 'foretelling, foreboding', or 'warning'. Some are connected with words for 'well, healthy, sound' or 'increase, further', and so must have originally denoted good omens.

Words for 'sign' (12.94) are often used for 'wonder sign, portent, omen', and in many languages these (in some cases one of the several parallel forms) are the usual terms for 'omen'.

1. Grk. *οἰωνός* 'bird of prey, bird of omen' and 'omen', etym. dub. Walde-P. 1.21, 107. Boisacq 694 f. Walde-H. 1.84.

Grk. *ὄρνις* 'bird' (3.64), also 'omen'.

Grk. *σημεῖον* 'sign' (12.94), also 'omen' (Soph.+).

2. Lat. *ōmen*, etym. dub. Ernout-M. 702. Stolz-Leumann, Lat. Gram. 113 ftn.

Lat. *augurium*, the 'taking of omens' and the 'omen' itself (> It. *augurio*, Fr. *augure*, Sp. *agüero*, Rum. neolog. *augur*), based on the personal *augur* 'augur, diviner', this prob. not a cpd. of *avis* 'bird', but fr. **augos* (cf. *augustus*) : *augēre* 'increase, further', with transfer fr.

the abstract and applied at first to the person observing favorable omens. Ernout-M. 89. Walde-H. 1.83. REW 785.

Lat. *auspicium* (> It., Sp. *auspicio*, Fr. *auspice*) 'divination from birds' and sometimes the 'omen', with the personal *auspex*, cpd. of *avis* 'bird' (3.64) and the root of *specere* 'look, observe' (15.51). Ernout-M. 91. Walde-H. 1.87.

It., Sp. *presagio*, Fr. *présage*, fr. Lat. *praesāgium* 'foreboding' (but not used for 'omen'), fr. *prae-sāgīre* 'perceive beforehand'. Ernout-M. 887.

Rum. *prevestire*, fr. *prevesti* 'prophecy', cpd. of *vesti* 'announce' (fr. Slavic, cf. 18.43).

3. Ir. *cēl*, loanword fr. Britannic, OW *coilou* (pl.) gl. *auspiciis*, W. *coel* 'omen, portent', but usually cpd. *ar-goel* (*ar-* 'on-, for-', but also merely intensive), as orig. a 'good omen' : Goth. *hails*, ON *heill*, OE *hāl*, ChSl. *cělŭ* 'well, in good health' (4.83). Cf. ON *heill* 'omen'. Walde-P. 1.329. Pedersen 1.57.

NIr. *tuar* = Ir. *tūar* 'creation, preparation, attainment', etc. (Gael. 'appearance, hue, merit'), vbl. n. of *do-ferim* (*duferthar*, gl. *conditur*) 'establish' (: OHG *gi-werēn* 'grant', Pedersen 2.518). K. Meyer, Ber. Preuss. Akad. 1918. 628.

Br. *diougan* ('prediction, sign, omen'), fr. cpd. of *kana* 'sing'. Pedersen 2.481. Henry 99.

4. Goth. *taikns*, OE *tāc(e)n*, ME, NE *token*, OHG *zeihhan*, MHG, NHG *zeichen*, all words for 'sign' (12.94), used also for 'wonder, miracle' and 'sign of the future, omen', in this last sense NE *token* now obs., and NHG *zeichen*, Du. *teeken* mostly replaced by *vorzeichen*, *voorteeken*. For such early Gmc. use, cf. the early loanword Finn. *taika* 'omen' and 'magic'. Karsten, Kluge Festschrift 65 ff. Kluge-G. 706.

ON *heill*, OE *hæl* 'health, good luck' and (orig. good) 'omen' : adj. *heill*, Goth. *hails*, etc. 'well, in good health' (4.83).

ON *furða* 'strange thing, wonder' and often 'omen', fr. **for-riða* lit. 'one who rides before'. Falk-Torp 268.

Dan. *varsel* 'warning' and 'omen', fr. *vare* 'guard', refl. 'beware of'. Falk-Torp 1353.

Sw. *förebud*, also and orig. 'foreboding', cpd. of *bud* 'command, message' (: vb. *bjuda* 'command', 19.45).

Dan., NE, NHG *omen*, fr. Lat. *ōmen* (above, 2).

5. Lith. *ženklas*, Lett. *zīme* 'sign' (12.94) and 'omen'.

6. ChSl. *znamenĭje*, SCr. *znamenje*, Boh. *znamení* 'sign' (12.94) and 'omen'.

Pol. *wróżba*, fr. *wróżyć* 'foretell' = late ChSl. *vražiti* 'tell fortunes', etc. Brückner 632.

Russ. *predznamenovanie*, fr. *predznamenovati* 'take omens, foretell', fr. *pred* 'before' and *znamenie* 'sign' (12.94).

7. Skt. *lakṣaṇa-* 'sign' (12.94), also 'favorable sign, omen'. Cf. *sulakṣaṇa-* adj. 'provided with a favorable sign'.

Concluding note.—I have said in the Preface: "The specialist in any given language will always find facts of pertinent interest to supply." How often, even for my own language, have alternative terms come to mind, too late for mention even if worth while. However, I shall not *start* (=*begin*, but not in 14.25) to make a list of "additions and corrections", which might have no end.

INDEX OF HEADINGS[1]

[1] Also some words which, although not in the headings, denote related notions and are incidentally or partially covered in the discussion. In such cases the references are in parentheses.

spoon 5.39
spread 9.34
spring (sb., of water) 1.37
spring (sb., season) 14.75
square (sb.) 12.78
stable 3.19
stall 3.19
stallion 3.42
stand (vb.) 12.15
star 1.54
statute 9.83
stay (vb. intr.) 12.16
steal 11.56
stepdaughter 2.74
stepfather 2,71
stepmother 2.72
stepson 2.73
stingy 11.54
stinking 15.26
stockings 6.49
stomach 4.46
stone 1.44
stop (= cease) 14.28
store (sb.) 11.86
stove 7.32
straight 12.73
strand (shore) 1.27
stranger 19.55
stream 1.36
street 10.73
strength (4.81)
stretch 9.32
strew 9.34
strife 19.62
strike 9.21
string (sb.) (9.19)
strong 4.81
student (17.242; 17.26)
study 17.242
stupid 17.22
subject (sb.) 19.38
suck (vb.) 5.16
suffer (vb.) (16.31)
suffering 16.31
sugar 5.85
suitable 9.943

sum (13.11)
summer 14.76
summit (12.33)
summon (18.41)
sun 1.52
Sunday 14.62
superstition 22.41
supper 5.45
sure 17.37
surety 11.67
surprise (sb.) 16.16
surrender (vb.) 20.46
suspicion 17.44
swear (take oath) 21.24
sweat (sb.) 4.55
sweep 9.37
sweet 15.35
swift 14.21
swim 10.35
swine 3.31
sword 20.27

table 7.44
tablet (for writing) 18.55
tail 4.18
tailor 6.13
take 11.13
take hold of 11.14
talk (vb.) 18.21
tall 12.58
taste (vb. and sb.) 15.31–15.34
tax (sb.) 11.69
teach 17.25
teacher 17.27
tear (sb.) 16.38
tear (vb.) 9.28
temple 22.13
tempt (9.98)
tent 7.14
territory 19.14
tertiary 13.54
test (9.98)
testicle 4.49
thanks 16.64
theft 21.45

thick (in dimension) 12.63
thick (in density) 12.64
thief 11.57
thin (in dimension) 12.65
thin (in density) 12.66
thing 9.90
think[1] (= reflect) 17.14
think[2] (= be of the opinion) 17.15
third (ordinal) 13.42
third (sb., fraction) 13.43
thirst (sb.) 5.15
thought (17.14)
thread 6.38
threaten 18.44
three 13.41
three apiece 13.52
three, group of 13.49
threefold 13.46
three kinds, consisting of 13.47
three times 13.44
three times, occurring (adj.) 13.45
three together (coll. adj.) 13.48
threes, by (coll. adv.) 13.51
thresh 8.34
threshing-floor 8.35
thrice 13.44
throat 4.29
throne (7.43)
throw 10.25
thumb 4.342
thunder 1.56
thunderbolt 1.57
Thursday 14.66
tie (vb.) (9.16)
till (vb.) 8.15
time 14.11
timid 16.55
tin, tin-plate 9.69
tired 4.91
tobacco 8.68
today 14.47
toe 4.38